International Directory of COMPANY HISTORIES

INTERNATIONAL DIRECTORY OF COMPANY HISTORIES

VOLUME I
ADVERTISING–DRUGS

VOLUME II
ELECTRICAL & ELECTRONICS–FOOD SERVICES & RETAILERS

VOLUME III
HEALTH & PERSONAL CARE PRODUCTS–MATERIALS

VOLUME IV
MINING & METALS–REAL ESTATE

VOLUME V
RETAIL–WASTE

International Directory of
COMPANY HISTORIES

VOLUME III

Editor
Adele Hast

Associate Editors
Diane B. Pascal (Chicago)
Kate Berney (London)

Assistant Editors
Philippe A. Barbour
Jessica Griffin

St J
St James Press
Chicago and London

For further information, write:

ST. JAMES PRESS
233 East Ontario Street
Chicago, Illinois 60611
U.S.A.

or

2-6 Boundary Row
London SE1 8HP
England

Library of Congress Catalog Number: 89-190943

British Library Cataloguing in Publication Data

International directory of company histories. Vol. 3
1. Large companies, to 1991
I. Hast, Adele
338.7´4´09

ISBN 1-55862-059-1

First published in the U.S.A. and U.K. 1991
Typeset by BookMasters, Inc., Ashland, Ohio, U.S.A.
Printed by BookCrafters, Chelsea, Michigan, U.S.A.

Cover photograph of The London Stock Exchange by Tom Hanley

INDUSTRIES COVERED IN THE DIRECTORY

VOLUME I

Advertising
Aerospace
Airlines
Automotive
Beverages
Chemicals
Conglomerates
Construction
Containers
Drugs

VOLUME II

Electrical & Electronics
Entertainment & Leisure
Financial Services
- –Bank
- –Non-Bank

Food Products
Food Services & Retailers

VOLUME III

Health & Personal Care Products
Health Care Services
Hotels
Information Technology
Insurance
Manufacturing
Materials

VOLUME IV

Mining & Metals
Paper & Forestry
Petroleum
Publishing & Printing
Real Estate

VOLUME V

Retail
Rubber & Tire
Telecommunications
Textiles & Apparel
Tobacco
Transport Services
Utilities
Waste

CONTENTS

EDITOR'S NOTE

The *International Directory of Company Histories* provides accurate and detailed information on the development of the world's largest and most influential companies. When completed, the *Directory's* five volumes will cover approximately 1,200 companies.

Most companies chosen for inclusion in the *Directory* have achieved a minimum of two billion U.S. dollars in annual sales. Insurance companies, listed in Volume III, are measured by assets rather than sales, with minimum assets of ten billion U.S. dollars. Some smaller companies are included if they are leading influences in their respective industries or geographical locations. State-owned companies that are major competitors in their industries and operate much like public or private companies also are included. Wholly owned subsidiaries of other companies are entries if they meet the requirements for inclusion, provided they were independent within the past five years or are still highly visible and important in their respective industries.

Each entry begins with a company's legal name, the address of its headquarters, its telephone number, and a statement of public or private ownership. A company with a legal name in both English and the language of its headquarters country is listed by the English name, with the native-language name in parentheses. In Volume III the fax number has been added because of its increasing importance in communication.

The company's earliest incorporation date, the number of employees, and the most recent sales or assets figures available, for fiscal year 1989 or 1990, are also provided. Sales figures are given in local currencies with equivalents in U.S. dollars at the exchange rate on December 29, 1989, the last trading day of the year. Finally, the entry lists the cities where a company's stock is traded. Throughout the *Directory* spelling is according to American style and the word "billion" is used in its American sense of a thousand million.

The histories were compiled from publicly accessible sources such as magazines, general and academic periodicals, books, and annual reports, as well as from material supplied by the companies themselves. The *Directory* is intended for reference use and research, for students, business people, librarians, historians, economists, investors, job candidates, and others who want to learn more about the historical development of the world's most important companies.

St. James Press does not endorse any of the companies or products mentioned in this book. Companies that appear in the *Directory* were selected without reference to their wishes and have in no way endorsed their entries. The companies were given the opportunity to read their entries for factual inaccuracies, and we are indebted to many of them for their comments and corrections. We thank them for allowing the use of their logos for identification purposes.

St. James Press would like to thank the staffs of the following institutions for their courteous assistance and invaluable guidance: in Chicago, The Chicago Public Library, the University of Chicago Library, the Paul V. Galvin Library at the Illinois Institute of Technology, The Newberry Library, and the Japan External Trade Organization; Northwestern University Library in Evanston, Illinois; and in London, The British Library, Business Archives Council, The City Business Library, The Financial Times Editorial Library, The London School of Economics and Political Science Business History Unit, and Westminster Reference Library.

The editors wish to thank the advisers, whose counsel assisted us in the organization of industries and the selection of companies. In addition, we thank Ginger G. Rodriguez and Naomi S. Suloway for their editorial assistance and meticulous attention to content and style.

Adele Hast

ADVISERS

T.C. Barker
Beate Brüninghaus
Alfred D. Chandler, Jr.
William Y. Rial
Stephanie Zarach

CONTRIBUTORS

Robert E. Ankli
George P. Antone
Claire Badaracco
Philippe A. Barbour
T.C. Barker
Joseph Bator
Elaine Belsito
John C. Bishop
Nils G. Björklund
Bernard A. Block
Peter Borscheid
A. Bowden
Jim Bowman
Juliette Bright
John Burton
Louis P. Cain
Robin Carre
John D. Cathcart
Tracy Chevalier
Alison Classe
Olive Classe
Hugh Cockerell
Peter A. Coclanis
Paula Cohen
Paul Conrad
Marc Cowling
Michael Doorley
Marc Du Ry
Vera A. Emmons
Sebastian Fries
Patrick J. Furlong
Sari Gilbert
Jessica Griffin
Daniel Gross
William R. Grossman
Lynn Hall
Leslie C. Halpern
Joan Harpham
R.M. Healey
Carole Healy
Thomas J. Heed
Patrick Heenan
Aileen C. Hefferren
Stephanie Jones
Lynn M. Kalanik
Carol I. Keeley
Serena Kelly
Peter Koch
Sonia Kronlund
Gwen M. LaCosse
Adam Lashinsky
Joseph A. LeMay
Scott M. Lewis
Andreas Loizou
Susan Mackervoy
Kim M. Magon
Jonathan Martin
Neal R. McCrillis
Diane C. Mermigas
Paul R. Merrion
Peter W. Miller
Mary Sue Mohnke
Betty T. Moore
Frances E. Norton
D.H. O'Leary
Lori Oleinick
Charles Pekow
Wolfgang Pfeiffer
Kathleen Poole
Karin Potisk
Jenny L. Presnell
Janie Pritchett
Karl F. Rahder
Trudy Ring
Ginger G. Rodriguez
Wallace Ross
Roger W. Rouland
Elizabeth Rourke
D.J. Rowe
Ann T. Russell
Martin Rüther
Wieland Sachse
Harm G. Schroter
Sandy Schusteff
Christopher A. Scott
Timothy J. Shannon
John Simley
Judy Slinn
Virginia L. Smiley
Donald R. Stabile
René Steinke
Timothy E. Sullivan
Douglas Sun
John Swan
Mary F. Sworsky
Thomas M. Tucker
Bob Vincent
Etan Vlessing
Lynn M. Voskuil
David M. Walden
Ray Walsh
Horst A. Wessel
Claus Wohlert
Gillian Wolf

ABBREVIATIONS FOR FORMS OF COMPANY INCORPORATION

A.B.	Aktiebolaget (Sweden)
A.G.	Aktiengesellschaft (Germany, Switzerland)
A.S.	Atieselskab (Denmark)
A/S	Aksjeselskap (Denmark, Norway)
A.Ş.	Anonim Şirket (Turkey)
B.V.	Besloten Vennootschap met beperkte, Aansprakelijkheid (The Netherlands)
Co.	Company (United Kingdom, United States)
Corp.	Corporation (United States)
G.I.E.	Groupement d'Intérêt Economique (France)
GmbH.	Gesellschaft mit beschränkter Haftung (Germany)
H.B.	Handelsbolaget (Sweden)
Inc.	Incorporated (United States)
KGaA	Kommanditgesellschaft auf Aktien (Germany)
K.K.	Kabushiki Kaisha (Japan)
Ltd.	Limited (Canada, Japan, United Kingdom, United States)
N.V.	Naamloze Vennootschap (The Netherlands)
PLC	Public Limited Company (United Kingdom)
PTY.	Proprietary (Australia, Hong Kong, South AFrica)
S.A.	Société Anonyme (Belgium, France, Switzerland)
SpA	Società per Azioni (Italy)

ABBREVIATIONS FOR CURRENCY

A$	Australian dollar
BFr	Belgian franc
Cz	Brazilian cruzado
C$	Canadian dollar
DKr	Danish krone
Fmk	Finnish markka
FFr	French franc
DM	German mark
HK$	Hong Kong dollar
L	Italian lira
¥	Japanese yen
W	Korean won
Dfl	Netherlands florin
R	South African rand
Pts	Spanish peseta
SKr	Swedish krone
SFr	Swiss franc
TL	Turkish lira
£	United Kingdom pound
$	United States dollar
B	Venezuelan bolivar

International Directory of

COMPANY HISTORIES

HEALTH & PERSONAL CARE PRODUCTS

Alco Health Services Corporation
Amway Corporation
Avon Products Inc.
Bristol-Myers Squibb Company
The Clorox Company
Colgate-Palmolive Company
The Gillette Company
Henkel KGaA
Johnson & Johnson
Kao Corporation
Kimberly-Clark Corporation
Kyowa Hakko Kogyo Co., Ltd.
Lion Corporation
L'Oréal
The Procter & Gamble Company
Revlon Group Inc.
S.C. Johnson & Son, Inc.
Shionogi & Co., Ltd.
Shiseido Company, Limited
SmithKline Beecham PLC
Wella Group

HEALTH CARE SERVICES

American Medical International, Inc.
Beverly Enterprises, Inc.
Hospital Corporation of America
Humana Inc.
Maxicare Health Plans, Inc.
National Medical Enterprises, Inc.

HOTELS

Hilton Hotels Corporation
Holiday Inns, Inc.
Hyatt Corporation
ITT Sheraton Corporation
Marriott Corporation
Trusthouse Forte PLC

INFORMATION TECHNOLOGY

Amdahl Corporation
Amstrad plc
Apple Computer, Inc.
Automatic Data Processing, Inc.
Canon Inc.
Compagnie des Machines Bull S.A.
Compaq Computer Corporation
Control Data Corporation
Cray Research, Inc.
Digital Equipment Corporation
Electronic Data Systems Corporation
Fujitsu Limited
Hewlett-Packard Company
Ing. C. Olivetti & C., S.p.a.
International Business Machines Corporation
NCR Corporation
Nixdorf Computer AG
Pitney Bowes Inc.
Ricoh Company, Ltd.
STC PLC
Unisys Corporation
Wang Laboratories, Inc.
Xerox Corporation

INSURANCE

AEGON N.V.
Aetna Life and Casualty Company
Allianz AG Holding
American Family Corporation
American Financial Corporation
American General Corporation
American International Group, Inc.
N.V. AMEV
Aon Corporation
Assicurazioni Generali SpA
Axa
Berkshire Hathaway Inc.
Capital Holding Corporation
The Chubb Corporation
CIGNA Corporation
CNA Financial Corporation
Commercial Union plc
Connecticut Mutual Life Insurance Company
The Continental Corporation
Empire Blue Cross and Blue Shield
The Equitable Life Assurance Society of the United States

Fireman's Fund Insurance Company
First Executive Corporation
General Accident plc
General Re Corporation
Great-West Lifeco Inc.
The Home Insurance Company
John Hancock Mutual Life Insurance Company
Kemper Corporation
Legal & General Group plc
Lincoln National Corporation
Lloyd's of London
Marsh & McLennan Companies, Inc.
Massachusetts Mutual Life Insurance Company
The Meiji Mutual Life Insurance Company
Metropolitan Life Insurance Company
Mitsui Marine and Fire Insurance Company, Limited
Mitsui Mutual Life Insurance Company
Munich Re (Münchener Rückversicherungs-Gesellschaft)
The Mutual Benefit Life Insurance Company
The Mutual Life Insurance Company of New York
Nationale-Nederlanden N.V.
New England Mutual Life Insurance Company
New York Life Insurance Company
Nippon Life Insurance Company
Northwestern Mutual Life Insurance Company
Pennsylvania Blue Shield
Principal Mutual Life Insurance Company
Provident Life and Accident Insurance Company of America
Prudential Corporation plc
The Prudential Insurance Company of America
Reliance Group Holdings, Inc.
Riunione Adriatica di Sicurtà SpA
Royal Insurance Holdings plc
SAFECO Corporaton
The St. Paul Companies, Inc.
The Standard Life Assurance Company
State Farm Mutual Automobile Insurance Company
Sumitomo Life Insurance Company
The Sumitomo Marine and Fire Insurance Company, Limited
Sun Alliance Group plc
Swiss Reinsurance Company (Schweizerische Rückversicherungs-Gesellschaft)
Teachers Insurance and Annuity Association
The Tokio Marine and Fire Insurance Co., Ltd.
The Travelers Corporation
Union des Assurances de Paris
USF&G Corporation
VICTORIA Holding AG
"Winterthur" Schweizerische Versicherungs-Gesellschaft
The Yasuda Fire and Marine Insurance Company, Limited
The Yasuda Mutual Life Insurance Company, Limited
"Zürich" Versicherungs-Gesellschaft

MANUFACTURING

Aisin Seiki Co., Ltd.
Alfa-Laval AB
Armstrong World Industries, Inc.
Atlas Copco AB
Baker Hughes Incorporated
Bally Manufacturing Corporation
BICC plc
The Black & Decker Corporation
Borg-Warner Corporation
Brunswick Corporation
Carl-Zeiss-Stiftung
Casio Computer Co., Ltd.
Caterpillar Inc.
Citizen Watch Co., Ltd.
Daewoo Group
Daikin Industries, Ltd.
Deere & Company
Deutsche Babcock AG
Dover Corporation
Dresser Industries, Inc.
Eastman Kodak Company
Electrolux Group
Fanuc Ltd.

Fleetwood Enterprises, Inc.
Fuji Photo Film Co., Ltd.
The Furukawa Electric Co., Ltd.
GKN plc
Halliburton Company
Hanson PLC
Hasbro, Inc.
Hawker Siddeley Group Public Limited Company
The Henley Group, Inc.
Hitachi Zosen Corporation
Hyundai Group
Illinois Tool Works Inc.
Inchcape PLC
Ingersoll-Rand Company
Interco Incorporated
Ishikawajima-Harima Heavy Industries Co., Ltd.
Johnson Controls, Inc.
Kawasaki Heavy Industries, Ltd.
KHD Konzern
Komatsu Ltd.
Konica Corporation
Kubota Corporation
Lucas Industries Plc
McDermott International, Inc.
MAN Aktiengesellschaft
Mannesmann AG
Masco Corporation
Maytag Corporation
Minolta Camera Co., Ltd.
Mitsubishi Heavy Industries, Ltd.
NHK Spring Co., Ltd.
Nikon Corporation
Nintendo Co., Ltd.
Nippon Seiko K.K.
Nippondenso Co., Ltd.
NTN Corporation
Outboard Marine Corporation
Parker Hannifin Corporation
Pioneer Electronic Corporation
Polaroid Corporation
Premark Interntional, Inc.
Rubbermaid Incorporated
Schlumberger Limited
Seiko Corporation
Aktiebolaget SKF
The Stanley Works
Sulzer Brothers Limited (Gebrüder Sulzer Aktiengesellschaft)
Sumitomo Heavy Industries, Ltd.
Toyoda Automatic Loom Works, Ltd.
TRINOVA Corporation
Tyco Laboratories, Inc.
Valmet Corporation (Valmet Oy)
Varity Corporation
Whirlpool Corporation
Yamaha Corporation

MATERIALS

American Standard Inc.
Asahi Glass Company, Limited
Blue Circle Industries PLC
Boral Limited
Compagnie de Saint-Gobain S.A.
Cookson Group plc
Corning Incorporated
CSR Limited
ECC Group plc
Feldmühle Nobel AG
Harrisons & Crosfield plc
"Holderbank" Financière Glaris Ltd.
Lafarge Coppée S.A.
Manville Corporation
Matsushita Electric Works, Ltd.
Mitsubishi Materials Corporation
Nippon Sheet Glass Company, Limited
Onoda Cement Co., Ltd.
Owens-Corning Fiberglas Corporation
Pilkington plc
Pioneer International Limited
PPG Industries, Inc.
Redland plc
RMC Group p.l.c.
Sekisui Chemical Co., Ltd.
The Sherwin-Williams Company
Ssangyong Cement Industrial Co., Ltd.
Tarmac PLC
Toto, Ltd.
Toyo Sash Co., Ltd.
Ube Industries, Ltd.
USG Corporation
Walter Industries, Inc.

HEALTH & PERSONAL CARE PRODUCTS

ALCO HEALTH SERVICES CORPORATION
AMWAY CORPORATION
AVON PRODUCTS INC.
BRISTOL-MYERS SQUIBB COMPANY
THE CLOROX COMPANY
COLGATE-PALMOLIVE COMPANY
THE GILLETTE COMPANY
HENKEL KGAA
JOHNSON & JOHNSON
KAO CORPORATION
KIMBERLY-CLARK CORPORATION
KYOWA HAKKO KOGYO CO., LTD.
LION CORPORATION
L'ORÉAL
THE PROCTER & GAMBLE COMPANY
REVLON GROUP INC.
S.C. JOHNSON & SON, INC.
SHIONOGI & CO., LTD.
SHISEIDO COMPANY, LIMITED
SMITHKLINE BEECHAM PLC
WELLA GROUP

ALCO HEALTH SERVICES CORPORATION

Post Office Box 959
Valley Forge, Pennsylvania 19482
U.S.A.
(215) 296-4480
Fax: (215) 647-0141

Wholly Owned Subsidiary of AHSC Holdings Corporation
Incorporated: 1985
Employees: 2,381
Sales: $2.30 billion

Alco Health Services Corporation is one of the largest wholesale pharmaceutical distributors in the United States. Made up of 12 major operating units, Alco serves more than 14,000 customers, including independent and chain drugstores, hospitals, mass merchandisers, nursing homes, clinics, and physicians, throughout the East, South, and Midwest. Alco Health generates about 80% of its revenue from pharmaceutical products, but it also provides a growing line of health and beauty products and a number of support services to its retailing customers.

Alco Health was incorporated in August 1985 with an initial public stock offering of 4.7 million shares. The company's origins date back to 1977, when a diversified conglomerate, the Alco Standard Corporation, entered the pharmaceutical-distribution business by purchasing The Drug House, a major wholesaler operating in Pennsylvania and Delaware.

Alco Standard was the brainchild of entrepreneur Tinkham Veale II, who had built a multimillion-dollar conglomerate on the principle of corporate partnership. Veale sought to acquire healthy, owner-managed companies in the $5 million to $10 million range. He allowed each company practically full autonomy, while providing support in legal and tax matters. When Alco Standard was incorporated in 1960, it was a modest $5 million chemical company. By 1968 sales were $140 million, coming from 52 subsidiaries with products ranging from stamped metal parts to wax paper.

Shortly after Alco Standard's acquisition of The Drug House, the company began to build a network of drug wholesalers. In early 1978 Duff Brothers of Chattanooga, Tennessee, was acquired, and later that year Marsin Medical Supply Company of Philadelphia, Pennsylvania, was purchased. Geer Drug, with annual sales of about $45 million, was acquired in 1979. Headquartered in Charleston, South Carolina, Geer foreshadowed an expansive drive southward. By the early 1980s, Alco Standard's pharmaceutical distribution network was the third largest in the nation.

Alco Standard soon made other acquisitions of pharmaceutical wholesalers, including Kauffman-Lattimer of Columbus, Ohio; Smith-Higgins of Johnson City, Tennessee; Strother Drug of Virginia; and Brown Drug, which operated in South Dakota, Iowa, and Minnesota. At the same time, the drug industry itself was undergoing intense change. Health-care expenditures in the United States were on the uptrend, amounting to about 10% of the gross national product by 1985. As the population grew older, the health-care industry promised continued growth.

In 1985 Alco Standard's drug-distribution operations were spun off into a separate company, Alco Health Services Corporation. Alco Standard retained approximately 60% of the new company's stock. The new company continued to use Alco Standard's administrative functions on a fee basis. Alco Health was led by John H. Kennedy as chairman and Joseph B. Churchman as president.

Shortly after Alco Health began to operate independently, it acquired the Valdosta Drug Company of Valdosta, Georgia, with $22 million in annual sales, and the $100-million-a-year Meyers and Company of Tiffin, Ohio. These two acquisitions helped push Alco's sales over the $1 billion mark.

In the early 1980s drug wholesalers found new ways to support the independent drug retailers who comprised nearly 60% of their business. Wholesalers offered more non-drug products, like hospital supplies and health and beauty aids. Alco Health sought to strengthen its independent customers by sharing its own primary strength—marketing. By offering services like in-store merchandising and group advertising, wholesalers could help their customers compete with the growing drugstore chains. Alco Health introduced its retail support program in 1982. Support like customized price stickers gave a boost to those independent druggists who participated. A year later, Alco introduced a complete line of medical equipment for home use, from wheelchairs to disposable syringes under the Total Home Health Care program, which provided independent retailers the marketing support they needed for such products, through direct-to-customer delivery and accounting assistance.

Computer services provided by the wholesaler included management-information reports, automated retail accounts-receivable systems, and shelf labels for automated inventory control. By 1985 Alco Health was marketing an in-pharmacy computer system based on an IBM personal computer that was capable of being used for total store automation.

At the same time, wholesalers including Alco Health began to develop the business of large drugstore chains and mass merchandisers. In 1981 25% of all wholesalers' business was to drugstore chains, up from 15% in 1971. The opportunity arose because of the reluctance of manufacturers to maintain the costly sales force needed for direct selling to chains. The trend continued throughout the 1980s. By 1985 chain drugstores and mass merchandisers made up 18% of Alco Health's annual revenues.

Sales to hospitals also increased in the early 1980s, as health-care facilities attempted to lower their costs by reducing their pharmaceutical inventories. Alco was able to provide rapid, often same-day, service to many facilities. By 1985, 24% of Alco Health's sales were to hospitals.

During the latter half of the 1980s, Alco Health continued to grow at a tremendous rate. In 1986 further acquisitions included L.S. DuBois Son and Company of Paducah, Kentucky; Pennington Drug of Joplin, Missouri; Mississippi Drug of Jackson, Mississippi; and MD Pharmaceuticals of Dothan, Alabama, adding $300 million in annual revenues. Archer Drug of Little Rock, Arkansas, and Michiana Merchandising of Mishiwaka, Indiana, were also purchased.

In 1987 Alco Health reorganized several of its operating units. Smith-Higgins, Valdosta Drug, MD Pharmaceuticals, Mississippi Drug, and Duff Brothers were combined to make up the southeastern region of Alco Health. Geer Drug and Strother Drug were combined to eliminate overlap. Management of the new units remained in the hands of regional managers, and their territories were enlarged considerably.

Alco Health's marketing strategy, which focused on three areas—independent druggists, hospitals, and chain drugstores and mass merchandisers—remained constant throughout the 1980s. A major boost to the third segment came in 1987, when Alco Health was selected as the primary wholesale supplier to 1,000 of the Revco chain's 2,000 drugstores. In 1988 revenues passed $2 billion.

John F. McNamara, formerly chief operating officer, became president of Alco Health in 1987. McNamara came to the company in 1981 when Kauffman-Lattimer was acquired. Kennedy remained chairman until August 1988, when previously retired Ray Mundt returned temporarily to oversee changes in Alco Health's ownership. Mundt previously had served as president of Alco Standard and on the Alco Health board of directors.

In early 1988 a management group attempted a leveraged buyout of Alco Health, offering $26 per share to take the company private. Shortly thereafter, in June, McKesson, formerly Foremost-McKesson, the largest drug wholesaler in the country with 28% of the national market, offered $30 per share, or $508 million, for Alco Health. The deal, however, fell through three months later when the Federal Trade Commission ruled against the acquisition on antitrust grounds. Alco Health was still 49% owned by its former parent, Alco Standard Corporation. Alco Health explored options with its investment banker, Drexel Burnham Lambert.

In November 1988 a group of investors, which included Citicorp Venture Capital Ltd. and a group of Alco management-level employees proposed a cash tender offer for Alco Health's shares at $31 per share. A holding company, AHSC Holdings Corporation (Holdings), was set up to handle the acquisition. The proposal was accepted and when the tender offer expired at the end of December 1988, Holdings owned 92% of Alco Health's stock. The merger allowed for the conversion of the remaining equity into debentures due in the year 2004. Alco Health continued its normal daily operations during the transition of ownership. John F. McNamara led the company as chairman, CEO, and president from 1989.

The 1990s will provide new challenges and opportunities to Alco Health Services, and pharmaceutical wholesalers in general. The drug market promises to continue its expansion, fueled by an aging population and its need for health care. The trend in pharmaceutical distribution has been toward fewer competitors handling a greater market share. From 1979 to 1990 the number of U.S. drug wholesalers decreased from 150 to 90, while the role of middlemen has increased. The top five companies, including Alco Health, handle about half of the business nationwide. As the field of suitable acquisitions thins out, and as the pharmaceutical-distribution field becomes a battle of the giants, Alco Health may have to place greater emphasis on internal expansion, but considering the company's tradition of efficiency Alco Health appears to be up to the task.

Principal Subsidiaries: Health Services Capital Corporation; Health Services Plus, Inc.

Further Reading: Werner, Thomas, " 'Without Negatives': That's How Alco Health Services' Chief Describes its Business," *Barron's*, April 13, 1987; "Alco Standard Corporation," in *International Directory of Company Histories*, Volume I, edited by Thomas Derdak, Chicago, St. James Press, 1988.

—Thomas M. Tucker

AMWAY CORPORATION

7575 Fulton Street East
Ada, Michigan 49355
U.S.A.
(616) 676-6000
Fax: (616) 676-8140

Private Company
Incorporated: 1959 as Amway Sales Corporation and Amway Services Corporation
Employees: 7,500
Sales: $2.20 billion

"Don't let anyone steal your dream" is a popular rallying cry for many Amway distributors, independent businessmen and women whose goals of financial independence have led to the success of the Amway Corporation. The slogan indicates that this company is more than just a business; it has some traits of a social movement. Amway is well-known as one of the largest network, or multilevel marketing (MLM), firms in the world. Its own products and services and brand-name goods from other companies are marketed by approximately one million self-employed distributors in the United States, Canada, Europe, United Kingdom, Asia, Latin America, and a number of Caribbean and Pacific islands. Unlike many other MLM firms, Amway offers a wide variety of items, ranging from cleaning products, cosmetics, and vitamins to prepaid legal services, discount car purchases, and catalog merchandise. Its rapid growth, zealous distributors, unusual corporate culture, and certain political and legal controversies have made Amway a well-recognized name since its founding in 1959.

Amway's independent distributors are different from sales forces for more traditional, retail companies. Credentials, such as education and work skills, are irrelevant to becoming a distributor. Sociologist Nicole W. Biggart, in her book *Charismatic Capitalism*, quoted an Amway distributor to illustrate this point:

> It still gives me goose bumps just to think about how a person could come in with no experience in business or sales [and succeed]. I've listened to chicken farmers—I mean *chicken farmers*—the guys don't have any teeth. They can't speak with any etiquette at all, and they get up on the stage and they're crown direct distributors. And they say, "Aw, hell, me and Mabel, we just decided we needed some money one day." And they're multimillionaires. Really, I mean *seriously.*

Relationships among distributors are based on cooperation, unlike the competition needed to climb the typical corporate ladder. Emotional rallies and close interpersonal relations in a family-like atmosphere contrast with the impersonal usual corporate world. Last but not least, charismatic leadership and few bureaucratic rules characterize Amway.

Amway's history is a recent chapter in the long history of direct selling, which began in America's colonial period with unorganized Yankee peddlers selling tools and other much-needed items door to door. By the 1800s, direct selling decreased with the advent of mass merchandising, such as department stores and mail order sales. In the later 19th century and early 20th century, however, some manufacturers found direct sales had advantages over the sales of their products in large stores. They preferred the personal touch, with salesmen making home demonstrations of only their products. By the 1920s door-to-door salesmen were marketing brushes, cooking utensils, and other products. Retail stores fought back with local laws on peddlers. The federal government's regulations of company-employee relations led to the independent contractor solution. As independent contractors, salesmen were no longer employees: they were independent businessmen who bought products for resale. The first network marketing began in 1941 when two men created a mechanism to distribute Nutrilite vitamins. Within this mechanism, in addition to making money in retail sales, distributors earned a bonus on the sales of those individuals whom they personally recruited.

Amway's story began with the friendship between two youths who would become the founders. Jay Van Andel, born in Grand Rapids, Michigan, in 1924, and Richard M. De Vos, born in the small nearby community of Ada in 1926, became friends when De Vos got rides from Van Andel to Christian High School in Grand Rapids. Their common Dutch heritage of hard work, thrift, and entrepreneurship drew them together.

Both served in the Army Air Corps during World War II. Back in Michigan after the war, they founded Wolverine Air Service to teach flying. After selling Wolverine and a couple of other small businesses, the two young men bought a schooner and sailed off to see Latin America. The vessel sank in the Caribbean, but the two spent the next six months in South America. Back in Michigan they started the Ja-Ri Corporation to import and sell Caribbean handicraft.

In 1949 they became distributors of vitamins for the Nutrilite Company of California. They enjoyed modest success from their own retail sales and from bonuses earned on the sales force they created in the Midwest.

Increasing government regulations and an internal conflict in Nutrilite, however, led Van Andel, De Vos, and several other leading Nutrilite distributors to start their own venture. In April 1959 they created The American Way Association, later renamed the Amway Distributors Association, to protect the independent distributors. They chose as their first product a biodegradable liquid organic cleaner made by a small Michigan firm, the kind of high-demand merchandise that easily could be sold by MLM. By September 1959 the Amway Sales Corporation and the Amway Services Corporation were begun to assist the distributors. Van Andel and De Vos, with the help of their wives and a handful of employees, began operations from offices in their basements. Van Andel created sales literature and supervised new product development. De Vos motivated and trained new distributors.

The company rapidly expanded. The first full year of operations in 1960 resulted in gross sales of $500,000. That figure doubled in each of the next two years, and in 1964 it reached $10 million. Thousands of distributors signed up each month. The expansion was so rapid that as soon as they moved into new facilities, they were already crowded. In the company history, *Commitment to Excellence; The Remarkable Amway Story,* De Vos said, "We were always scrambling, just trying to catch up on back orders, working to train people adequately."

In 1964 the business underwent a major reorganization. The three divisions, sales, services, and manufacturing, were merged to create the Amway Corporation, with Van Andel as chairman of the board and De Vos as president. Major business decisions were always made jointly by the two founders.

A laundry detergent, S-A-8, was introduced in 1960. Amway's reputation for selling soap is based primarily on its experience with this product. Other products included a dishwashing liquid, aerosol shoe spray, cookware, hair products, and cosmetics. In 1962 Amway started international growth, with its expansion into Canada. In 1968 the Personal Shoppers Catalog allowed distributors to sell merchandise made by other companies. Catalog sales increased thereafter.

The 1960s also brought some false starts and problems for the new firm. It began marketing underground fallout shelters, for example, in an era when civil defense against atomic warfare was a priority, but gradually consumers lost interest in the shelters. Other short-lived products included 110-volt automobile generators and water-conditioning units. It is not surprising that some items were not successful, for by 1968 the company was selling more than 150 products through its 80,000 distributors.

In July 1969 Amway's aerosol manufacturing plant burned completely to the ground. Losses were estimated at $700,000. The next day plans were made for a temporary substitute supplier and a new facility. Six months later the new facility was completed and the company moved in.

The 1970s began with a change in corporate structure. Van Andel and De Vos remained board chairman and president, respectively, but four vice presidents were added to handle the daily burden of a rapidly expanding firm. In addition, 30 regional warehouses were replaced by seven new regional distribution centers in Georgia, Michigan, Texas, California, New Jersey, Washington, and Colorado.

Overseas expansion in the 1970s began with Australia in 1971, a choice that was partly influenced by the common culture and economic system. Operations in the United Kingdom began in 1973. Other European operations began with West Germany in 1975, France in 1977, and the Netherlands and the Republic of Ireland in 1978. The Asian market was opened with ventures into Hong Kong in 1974, Malaysia in 1976, and Japan in 1979.

Diversification and acquisitions marked Amway's experience in the 1970s. In 1972 the company purchased Nutrilite Products, Inc., the firm that had introduced Van Andel and De Vos to direct selling.

To reward and train its key distributors, the company acquired a yacht, Enterprise II, to serve as a floating conference center. A luxury resort and hotel complex on Peter Island in the British Virgin Islands was purchased in 1978, another amenity used to motivate Amway distributors. To house distributors coming to corporate headquarters, the firm bought the dilapidated Pantlind Hotel in Grand Rapids. The hotel, renovated and renamed Amway Grand Plaza Hotel, along with the newly constructed adjoining Grand Plaza Tower, marked a significant addition to downtown Grand Rapids.

Amway's growth has been predicated on the success of its independent distributors. Lacking formal control over the distributors, Amway has relied on bonuses and incentives to motivate them. As the company grew, distributors built larger and larger sales organizations. Their status and income increased and were marked by achievement levels identified as "pin levels." The first major milestone of a successful distributor is reaching the level of Direct Distributor (DD), thus buying products and literature directly from the corporation instead of from a sponsor or other DD. Soon after Amway's origin, it began recognizing further sales milestones by using the names of jewels in achievement awards. The first Ruby DD was awarded in 1962, followed by Pearl, Emerald, and Diamond, in each instance the award including a decorative pin in which the specific stone was mounted. In 1966 the first Double Diamond level was reached, the Triple Diamond in 1969, Crown in 1970, and the highest level, Crown Ambassador DD, in 1977. By Amway's 25th anniversary in 1984, there were 24 Crown DDs and 15 Crown Ambassador DDs. Almost all of these 39 distributors were couples; 28 were in the United States.

The corporation keeps in touch with its distributors through a monthly magazine, the *Amagram,* and provides a wide variety of sales literature, audio cassettes, and videocassettes. Although much of the product promotion is done by distributors, since 1965 Amway has sponsored advertising in magazines, newspapers, radio, and TV. Its advertising costs are much less than other corporations, however, and this factor allows Amway inexpensively to introduce new products.

Amway's most important legal battle was its successful defense against the allegation that it was engaged in an illegal pyramid scheme, characterized in part by making money on recruiting new distributors. Pyramid sales are a variation of chain-letter frauds. The Federal Trade Commission (FTC) in 1969 began investigating several companies, including Amway and Nutrilite. In 1975 formal charges were filed against Amway. Three months of FTC hearings began in May 1977. A ruling by the full FTC in 1979 declared Amway's MLM plan legitimate. The decision was based on findings that distributors were not being paid to recruit new distributors, that products had to be sold for distributors to receive bonuses, and that the firm was willing to buy back excess distributor inventory. Lawyer Rodney K. Smith in his book *Multilevel Marketing,* after reviewing several cases, concluded, "Amway is not and never has been an illegal pyramid scheme."

In another legal controversy the Canadian government charged Amway with not paying millions of dollars in customs duties on goods imported from the United States. In 1983, after pleading guilty in the criminal case, Amway paid a C$25 million fine in an out-of-court settlement. *Maclean's,* Canada's weekly newsmagazine, reported in its November

21, 1983, issue that the fine was "the largest sum that a Canadian court has ever levied and one of the heaviest criminal penalties ever imposed against any corporation in the world." A separate civil case was continued by the Canadian government to collect the duties it should have been paid in the 1970s. Amway again settled out of court, this time in 1989 for C$45 million, 40% of the amount the Canadian government tried to collect.

Other serious problems occurred in the first half of the 1980s. For the first time Amway sales declined. Some of the major distributors sold their businesses, and a substantial number of top executives either quit or were demoted or fired. The pyramid allegations surfaced again, not against the corporation, but against certain distributors who advised their sales groups to downplay retail sales, buy Amway merchandise for their own use, and purchase many motivational items, such as tapes and books, from the distributor.

One new corporate executive, William W. Nicholson, formerly appointments secretary to former President Gerald R. Ford, has been a key player at Amway headquarters since 1984. Under this chief operating officer, Amway introduced many new goods and services. According to Nicholson, a turning point was reached in 1985 when MCI decided to market its long-distance telephone services through Amway. By 1990 Amway was gaining more than 40,000 new clients per month for MCI. This record proved Amway was primarily an alternative distribution system, not just a manufacturing company.

In the 1980s discount purchases of new cars was an Amway innovation. By 1988 this service competed with five other discount auto-buying services, including the American Automobile Association. Other new items in the Amway inventory included Visa cards, prepaid legal services, real estate, and Tandy computers. The increase in high-tech merchandise and services was a dramatic shift for Amway, but the bulk of its sales remained in traditional products such as home care items. Amway's transition to include more services reflected the generalized U.S. movement from a goods-and-manufacturing economy to a service economy.

Not all new ventures worked for Amway. The Mutual Broadcasting System (MBS), with its hundreds of affiliated radio stations, was purchased in 1977. De Vos explained that Amway's inexperience, unfulfilled goals, and lack of profitability led to the sale of MBS, except for its satellite division, in 1985. For a few years Amway manufactured and sold satellite dishes, but the last unit was sold in 1989.

Probably the most publicized Amway activity in the late 1980s was its failed bid to take over Avon Products, Inc. Amway and corporate raider Irwin L. Jacobs in 1989 jointly acquired 5.5 million Avon shares, 10.3% of the company's stock. A week later Amway, without Jacobs' cooperation, offered to buy Avon for $2.1 billion in cash. Although a billion dollars in debt, Avon rejected the bid, citing Amway's evasion of Canadian customs duties and an incompatible corporate culture. In May 1989 Amway withdrew its bid. *Business Week*, in its May 22, 1989, issue, said Amway was "flexing its muscles for the first time." Although the bid failed, it was a good indication of Amway's financial strength.

Since 1980 Amway had continued its international expansion. European efforts were extended to Switzerland and Belgium in 1980, and to Spain and Italy in 1986. Panama in 1985 was the first Latin American nation with Amway operations, followed by Guatemala in 1986. Amway de Mexico began in June 1990 with headquarters in Monterrey and distribution centers in Mexico City, Guadalajara, Tijuana, and Juarez.

Amway and its founders have influenced more than just their employees, distributors, and customers. Amway has been a major sponsor of the arts. In 1982 Jay Van Andel chaired the Netherlands-American Bicentennial Commission. Amway sponsored an art exhibit at Amsterdam's Stedelijk Museum. The corporation has also supported tours of the Hong Kong Children's Choir and the Malaysian Youth Symphony Orchestra. In Grand Rapids it has helped fund the Art Museum, Arts Council, and the Gerald R. Ford Presidential Museum. Amway received in 1983 the Business in the Arts Award.

Amway has promoted the cause of free enterprise even to those not associated with the firm. The founders have given many presentations to promote free enterprise. Amway's headquarters in Ada, Michigan, at one time called the Center of Free Enterprise, housed the Free Enterprise Institute with outreach programs for students and teachers throughout the nation. Van Andel was the first chairman of Citizen's Choice and the president of the U.S. Chamber of Commerce. Both he and De Vos have been associated with many business organizations and causes.

The vision of businessmen De Vos and Van Andel from the 1959-beginning of Amway has included concern for the environment. Several Amway products are biodegradable, and its S-A-8 detergent is available in a phosphate-free formula to limit pollution of waterways. Products are concentrated, reducing the amount of packaging that ends up in landfills. After chlorofluorocarbons were reported to damage the ozone layer, Amway modified its aerosol products to delete those compounds. In 1989 Amway was a main sponsor of the two-month-long Icewalk, an expedition to the North Pole, designed to focus attention on environmental issues. In cooperation with the American Forestry Association, Amway participated in the Global ReLeaf Program, to plant 100 million trees by 1992. On June 5, 1989, Amway received the United Nation's Environmental Programme's Achievement Award for Excellence, one of two corporations to gain that honor. The same day the firm announced it was ending all animal testing in its research programs and that it would not cooperate with the Cosmetics, Toiletry and Fragrance Association's campaign against the ban on animal testing.

What evidence is there that Amway has become a household word? Comedians, politicians, and reporters have made jokes about Amway. Gary Larson in a "Far Side" cartoon compared dividing amoebas to Amway distributors recruiting others. Jane dreams of become a Double Diamond DD in a recent version of the *Dick and Jane* readers. Millions saw the "60 Minutes" program on Amway in 1989.

Amway has been a leader in the rapidly expanding direct selling industry. According to the Direct Selling Association (DSA), total retail sales were approximately $9.7 billion in 1988, up 10.3% from 1987, and Amway accounted for about 16% of the total. A 1976 Harris poll of U.S. households found that 16% of the respondents had tried direct selling. One MLM salesman, after working with many firms, was quoted in the June 1987 issue of *Money* as saying that he hoped his current firm will be the "Amway of the future."

The boom in direct selling in the 1970s and 1980s was influenced by employment factors. First, more women had moved into the workplace, and were selling Amway products. The DSA reported that in 1988, 81.4% of all salespeople were women. Further, instability of corporate employment influenced more individuals to look at alternative vocations.

In other nations, Amway's success partially depended on its accommodation to local conditions. In Japan, for example, a small induction range made by Japan's Sharp Company, ideal for the small homes of Japan, sold well when demonstrated in the home by Amway distributors. Previously, it had not sold well in stores. Perseverance and high quality goods resulted in 1988 sales of $536 million for Amway (Japan) Ltd. It is Amway's largest overseas subsidiary.

Based on rapid international expansion, the position of Amway's founding families still at the helm with new blood in upper management, and Amway's good financial condition, the company should have a bright future in the 1990s. With the failure of socialist economies in Eastern Europe and in other nations, Amway's promotion of free enterprise may become increasingly noteworthy in the years ahead. It is significant that Van Andel and De Vos in 1977 began training their children to become corporate leaders. By 1984 seven of the eight children of the founders held administrative positions in the company. Only time will tell, however, if Amway will remain a firm owned by two close families.

Principal Subsidiaries: Nutrilite Products, Inc.; Amway Gesellschaft m.b.H. (Austria); Amway of Australia Pty. Ltd.; Amway Belgium Company; Amway (U.K.) Limited; Amway France; Amway (HK) Limited (Hong Kong); Amway Italia s.r.l. (Italy); Amway (Japan) Limited; Amway (Malaysia) Sdn. Bhd.; Amway Nederland Ltd. (Netherlands); Amway of New Zealand Ltd.; Amway de Panama, S.A.; Amway (Schweiz) AG (Switzerland); Amway De España S.A. (Spain); Amway (Taiwan) Limited; Amway (Thailand) Ltd.; Amway GmbH (Germany); Amway de Mexico; Amway Communications Corporation; Amway Hotel Corporation; Amway Global, Inc.; Amway International, Inc.

Further Reading: Conn, Charles Paul, *An Uncommon Freedom: The Amway Experience & Why It Grows,* New York, Berkley Publishing Group, 1983; Smith, Rodney K., *Multilevel Marketing: A Lawyer Looks at Amway, Shaklee, and Other Direct Sales Organizations,* Grand Rapids, Michigan, Baker Book House, 1984; Butterfield, Stephen, *Amway, the Cult of Free Enterprise,* Boston, South End Press, 1985; Conn, Charles Paul, *Promises to Keep: The Amway Phenomenon and How it Works,* New York, G. P. Putnam's Sons, 1985; Cross, Wilbur, and Gordon Olson, *Commitment to Excellence: The Remarkable Amway Story,* Elmsford, New York, The Benjamin Company, 1986; Biggart, Nicole Woolsey, *Charismatic Capitalism: Direct Selling Organizations in America,* Chicago, University of Chicago Press, 1989.

—David M. Walden

Avon

AVON PRODUCTS INC.

9 West 57th Street
New York, New York 10019
U.S.A.
(212) 546-6015
Fax: (212) 546-6136

Public Company
Incorporated: 1886 as the California Perfume Company
Employees: 28,400
Sales: $3.30 billion
Stock Exchanges: New York Tokyo

The oldest beauty company in the United States, Avon Products has grown from a modest line of perfumes sold door-to-door to the world's leading brand of cosmetics. The unique direct-selling method so responsible for Avon's success, however, also contributed to its dramatic slowdown in the mid-1970s, when women entered the workforce in record numbers. Unsuccessful efforts at diversification into the health-care service industry left the company with massive debts and a few moderately successful entries into the prestige fragrance industry. By mid-1990, Avon had reduced its debt by more than 40%. Fighting takeover bids, Avon has begun to refocus on its roots: beauty and direct selling. Its products are sold in more than 100 countries by nearly 1.5 million representatives.

In 1886, eager to leave the bookselling business, and finding his customers often preferred his promotional perfumes, David H. McConnell created a line of perfumes, brewed in a pantry-sized space in New York City, to be sold door-to-door. The first product line, called the Little Dot Perfume Set, consisted of five scents: white rose, violet, lily of the valley, heliotrope, and hyacinth. McConnell named his endeavor the California Perfume Company in an effort to invoke the beauty and excitement of that state. McConnell intended to build a business around quickly used products sold directly to the consumer, and to use the national network of sales agents he had organized during his years as a bookseller. The nation's first Avon Lady was Mrs. P. F. E. Albee of Winchester, New Hampshire, the wife of a U.S. senator. Within the first six months of operation, Albee had assembled a solid base of 100 salespeople and their customers; within 12 years, Albee had recruited and trained nearly 5,000 representatives.

In addition to new scents, other products were soon added to California Perfume Company's product line. Popular early items included spot remover, Witch Hazel Cream, machine oil, mending cement, Almond Cream Balm, food flavorings, Tooth Tablet, and carpet cleaner. In 1896, ten years after setting out, McConnell hired Adolf Goetting, a noted perfumer who had been in the business for 25 years. The following year, a new laboratory was built in Suffern, New York. That same year, the first illustrated catalogue was produced. The company's product line had expanded to more than 100 products by its 20th year. In 1914, its expansion into Canada was marked by the opening of an office in Montreal.

The first products in the California Perfume Company's line of Avon Products—a toothbrush, cleanser, and vanity set—appeared in 1920. The Avon name was inspired by the area around the Suffern lab, which McConnell thought resembled the countryside of William Shakespeare's home, Stratford-on-Avon, England. Never wavering from its strategy of door-to-door sales and catalogues filled with low-cost home and beauty products, the company passed the $2 million sales mark in 1926. By 1928, the company was doing business in 48 states.

During this time, the representatives, under Albee's supervision, were partaking in one of the first opportunities for American women to experience a degree of economic freedom without upsetting their culturally accepted role as homemakers. The three-week sales campaigns and "specials" strategy was launched in 1932. McConnell died in 1937 and was replaced by his son, David H. McConnell Jr., who was chairman for the next seven years; growth remained steady. In 1939 the California Perfume Company became Avon Products. During World War II, over 50% of the Suffern lab was devoted to wartime production of such things as insect repellent, pharmaceuticals, and paratrooper kits, and cosmetic production slowed.

Avon instituted several changes during the 1950s, not least of which was its entry into overseas markets. In the early 1950s, the sales representatives' territories were downsized by several hundred homes, a strategy which allowed more representatives to be added, quadrupling the sales force and increasing sales sixfold over the next 12 years. Avon advertisements appeared on television for the first time, including the famous slogan, "Ding Dong, Avon Calling," which was first televised in 1954. That same year, Avon opened bases in Venezuela and Puerto Rico—its first ventures in what would become the lucrative Latin American market. It also hit the European market in 1957 with Avon Cosmetics, Ltd., in the United Kingdom.

W. Van Alan Clark had taken the reins from McConnell in 1944 and remained chairman through 1966, overseeing such changes as the rapid expansion of foreign sales and Avon's listing on the New York Stock Exchange in 1964. Clark was replaced by J. A. Ewald, who was followed by W. Hicklin in 1967. Under Hicklin, the traditional three-week sales cycle was changed to two weeks to improve sales. The three-week campaign is still used overseas, including Asia, whose market Avon entered in 1969 by opening operations in Japan. Japan has remained one of Avon's key foreign markets, along with Brazil, Mexico, and the United Kingdom.

The 1970s presented Avon with its greatest upsets. Though sales topped $1 billion in 1972, and its profitable costume-jewelry line—begun in 1971—had made Avon the world's biggest jewelry manufacturer in just five years, Avon's growth stalled in 1973, hard hit by a recession and the mass entry of women into the workforce. The direct-selling system, Avon's innovation and strength, was nearly toppled by social changes management had not anticipated. The status of the U.S. dollar reduced the company's international profits; recession and inflation crippled its high-sales decanter products line; in 1975, about 25,000 Avon Ladies quit; Avon products were outpaced by retail cosmetic firms offering jazzier products to women with new attitudes. All these factors converged and led to troubled times—and eventual restructuring.

The most visible change Avon then made was to become more sensitive to its market. Sales representatives began to follow women into the workplace, where about 25% of Avon's sales are made today; new businesses were tested, including direct-mail women's apparel; changes were also made in product line and pricing as a result of market studies. Fred Fusee, who had advanced through the manufacturing side of Avon to become its chairman in 1972, was replaced in 1975 by David W. Mitchell, whose years with Avon had been spent in marketing. Mitchell worked to solidify Avon's presence in the beauty business via consumer and product research, product development, and promotion. The image of Avon products was overhauled to give it a more contemporary appeal, advertising time was more than tripled, and sales were revamped. And in 1979, Avon purchased Tiffany & Company, the upmarket jeweler, for $104 million.

The Tiffany purchase set the tone for the next decade: diversification through acquisition. This included an ill-fated billion-dollar plunge into the health-care industry and a later entry into the prestige-fragrance industry.

Hicks Waldron, who had helped turn around General Electric, left his post at R. J. Reynolds to become Avon's chairman in 1983. Shortly before Waldron's appointment, Avon had purchased Mallinckrodt, a chemical and hospital supply company. Waldron followed this purchase up, in 1984, with the acquisition of Foster Medical Corporation. Initially thriving in the home-health-care-equipment field, Foster became the fastest-growing division of Avon. Almost immediately, however, Foster was devastated by Medicare cost-containment efforts, coupled with lack of management foresight. At the same time, Tiffany's profits were steadily declining—in part because customers were alienated by the introduction of lower-priced merchandise—and the Tiffany subsidiary was sold in 1984.

Avon then tried to focus in on health care for the elderly with the 1985 purchases of the Retirement Inns of America and The Mediplex Group, a nursing home operation. In this same year, almost 15% of Avon's sales came from health care and its annual profits overall were about half of what they were in 1979. Given this, Waldron abandoned the diversification. Mallinckrodt was sold in early 1986 and Foster in 1988, both at great loss. Avon also announced plans to sell the remaining health-care divisions. The company sold Retirement Inns of America in 1989 and The Mediplex Group in 1990. Avon's brief health-care industry foray left it $1.1 billion in debt.

Diversification into prestige fragrances has proven more stable. Parfums Stern and Giorgio, Inc. were both acquired in 1987. Parfums Stern includes Oscar de la Renta, Perry Ellis, and other designer perfumes. Giorgio remains a top-selling national brand and has introduced additions to the Giorgio line under Avon. Strapped for cash, the company sold Parfums Stern in early 1990 and has entertained bids for Giorgio.

When Waldron retired in 1989, his successor, James E. Preston, immediately faced a number of potential raiders. Avon fought off a bid by Amway Corporation in partnership with Irwin L. Jacobs, a Minneapolis, Minnesota–based raider who then launched a takeover attempt himself. While these efforts receded in late 1989, a new suitor appeared in the form of the Chartwell Association, an investment group which includes the chief financial officer of Mary Kay Cosmetics. The Avon sales force has proven the greatest deterrent to takeovers. In massive letter-writing campaigns, the crucial sales representatives have told aggressors that they would be unwilling to work for them. While the company is instituting internal safeguards, the loyalty of Avon's sales representatives may well remain the greatest protection against takeover. Entering the 1990s trimmed of its unwieldy diversification into the health-care industry, Avon remains a leading beauty company.

Principal Subsidiaries: Cosmeticos Avon S.A.C.I. (Argentina); Avon Products Pty. Limited (Australia); Avon Cosmetics Vertriebsgesellschaft m.b.H. (Austria); Arlington Limited (Bermuda); Stratford Insurance Co., Ltd. (Bermuda); Avon Cosmeticos, Ltda. (Brazil); Avon Canada, Inc.; Cosmeticos Avon S.A. (Chile); Avon Capital Corp.; Avon Diversified Services, Inc.; Avon International Operations, Inc.; Avon-Lomalinda, Inc.; Avon-Mirabella, Inc.; Avon Pacific, Inc.; Giorgio Beverly Hills, Inc.; Manila Manufacturing Co.; Productos Avon del Paraguay, Ltd.; Productos Avon S.A. (Dominican Republic); Productos Avon, S.A. (El Salvador); Avon S.A. (France); Productos Avon de Guatemala, S.A.; Productos Avon, S.A. (Honduras); Avon Cosmetics (FEBO) Limited (Hong Kong); Avon Limited (Ireland); Avon Cosmetics S.p.A. (Italy); Avon Products Company Limited (Japan, 60%); Avon Cosmetics (Malaysia); Dendirian Berhad (Malaysia); Avon Cosmetics, S.A. de C.V. (Mexico); Avonova, S.A. de C.V. (Mexico); Avon International Finance N.V. (Netherlands Antilles); Avon Cosmetics Limited (New Zealand); Avon Cosmetics (Nigeria) Ltd. (40%); Cosmeticos Aliados S.A. (Peru); Productos Avon S.A. (Peru); Productos De Bellesa, S.A. (Peru); Avon Cosmetics, Inc. (Philippines); Avon Products Mfg., Inc. (Philippines); Avon Cosmeticos, Lda. (Portugal); Avon Cosmetics, S.A. (Spain, 75%); Avon Cosmetics (Taiwan) Ltd.; Avon Cosmetics (Thailand) Ltd.; California Manufacturing Co. Ltd. (Thailand); Avon Cosmetics Limited (U.K.); Avon Cosmetics de Venezuela, C.A.; Avon Cosmetics GmbH (Germany).

Further Reading: Hayes, Linda, "The Changes in Avon's Makeup Aren't Just Cosmetic," *Fortune,* August 13, 1979; Kleinfield, Sonny, *Staying at the Top,* New York, New American Library Books, 1986; *The Greatest Beauty Story Ever Told,* New York, Avon Products, 1986.

—Carol I. Keeley

BRISTOL-MYERS SQUIBB COMPANY

345 Park Avenue
New York, New York 10154
U.S.A.
(212) 546-4000
Fax: (212) 546-4020

Public Company
Incorporated: 1900 as Bristol-Myers Company
Employees: 54,100
Sales: $9.19 billion
Stock Exchange: New York

During the late 1980s, competitive pressure and the increasing cost of research led many pharmaceutical firms to seek business partners in order to survive. One such combination united Bristol-Myers Company and the Squibb Corporation, two large and successful firms with compatible operations. The merger created the second largest pharmaceutical company in the world. Bristol-Myers Squibb Company is also recognized worldwide as a major producer and distributor of consumer products like toothpaste and drain opener.

Bristol-Myers was founded in 1887 by two former fraternity brothers, William McLaren Bristol and John Ripley Myers. They each invested $5,000 in a failing Clinton, New York–based drug manufacturer, the Clinton Pharmaceutical Company, and their one-man sales force began selling medical preparations by horse and buggy to local doctors and dentists. For the first few years the company struggled due to insufficient capital and the new owners' lack of understanding of how drugs were made. The firm relocated from Clinton to Syracuse, New York, in 1889 to improve its shipping capability, and then moved again, ten years later, to Brooklyn in order to be more accessible to its expanding base of customers in Pennsylvania and New England.

In 1898 the company's name was changed to Bristol, Myers Company. One year later John Ripley Myers died. To help the company grow, the firm increased its sales force, referred to as "detail men," and began shifting its attention from physicians to wholesale and retail druggists who were now recognized as primary suppliers of medication.

In 1900 the firm incorporated and modified its name, replacing the comma with a hyphen. The same year, Bristol-Myers Company made its first profit and entered the market for specialty products. Sales of such Bristol-Myers items as Sal Hepatica, a laxative mineral salt, and Ipana toothpaste, the first such product to contain a disinfectant, grew rapidly between 1903 and 1905. Strong demand caused a number of changes in the company's operation, including the creation of an export department to handle international orders and the opening of new manufacturing facilities in Hillside, New Jersey.

In 1915 Henry Bristol, William Bristol's oldest son, became general manager. Henry Bristol was joined in 1928 by his brothers, William Jr. and Lee, who handled manufacturing and advertising, respectively. During the recession that followed World War I the company discontinued its line of "ethical," or prescription drugs to focus production on its two best-selling specialty products and other toiletries, antiseptics, and cough syrups. Bristol-Myers also moved to its present location in Manhattan at this time. The shift in product focus was accompanied by a new emphasis on advertising, but to consumers rather than to doctors and dentists. Bristol-Myers sponsored a radio show featuring a group called the Ipana Troubadours, and introduced the slogan "Ipana for the Smile of Beauty; Sal Hepatica for the Smile of Health."

The company became a part of Drug, Inc., a large, newly formed holding company, in 1928. Drug, Inc., produced proprietary drugs and other medications and also operated a large retail chain. Bristol-Myers continued to grow and advertised heavily during the Great Depression, launching a number of new and successful consumer products. Other operations affiliated with Drug, Inc., did not fare nearly as well, however, and the holding company disbanded in 1933.

Upon the outbreak of World War II, Bristol-Myers again became a manufacturer of ethical pharmaceuticals. It mass produced penicillin for the Allied armed forces through its Bristol Laboratories subsidiary, which had been previously acquired under the name of Cheplin Laboratories. Bristol Laboratories' experience in the process of fermentation—which was required to make its primary product, acidophilus milk—was easily converted to the manufacture of the antibiotics. This led to the firm's formal re-entry into the ethical drug area and enabled it to take advantage of the growing demand for antibiotics after the war

The company continued to grow over the next decade, assisted by television advertisements. In 1957 Henry Bristol became chairman of the board and was succeeded as president and chief executive officer by Fredric N. Schwartz, the former head of Bristol Laboratories. Assisted by Gavin K. MacBain, the company's treasurer who later assumed the position of chairman, Schwartz acquired a number of smaller, well-managed companies in growing industries. The new subsidiaries grew quickly with help from Bristol-Myers's research and marketing expertise. These acquisitions included Clairol, a maker of hair-coloring products, purchased in 1959; Drackett, a household-products manufacturer, acquired in 1965; and Mead Johnson, which produced infant formula and children's vitamins, purchased in 1967. Clairol had already made marketing history as a result of the popular "Does she or doesn't she? Hair color so natural only her hairdresser knows for sure!" advertising campaign.

Richard Gelb, the son of Clairol's founder, reluctantly joined Bristol-Myers after the acquisition to head the Clairol operation. Gelb was given a wide berth in managing Clairol and did so well that he was promoted to executive vice president and then to president under chairman Gavin MacBain. Gelb became president just as Bristol-Myers's growth flattened out. A string of new-product failures during the late 1960s drained finances and depressed stock value. In 1972 Gelb was appointed chairman and CEO. He initiated a comeback over the next decade by spending $400 million advertising the company's most popular brands and by expanding its line of health-care products. This growth was accomplished in part through the acquisitions of Zimmer Manufacturing Company, a producer of orthopedic and surgical products, in 1972, and of Unitek Corporation, a dental-equipment supplier, in 1978.

Under Gelb's leadership, Bristol-Myers was able to shift gears quickly in response to market changes. When concern over the use of fluorocarbons threatened the spray-deodorant market in the mid-1970s, the company increased advertising of its Ban roll-on deodorant. This strategy vaulted Ban into the top-selling spot and increased the sales of all other roll-on products by 75% in one year.

Soon afterward, however, the company suffered a major marketing setback with its Clairol products. In 1977 the National Cancer Institute reported a link between an ingredient used in hair colorants, 2-4 DAA, and cancer in laboratory rats. Bristol-Myers disputed these findings at first but later introduced a new line of hair-coloring products and reformulated the original line without the ingredient in question.

Bristol-Myers's continued attention to health-care research was also a major factor in its resurgence. Beginning in the late 1970s Bristol-Myers began to use cash generated by its consumer-products business to fund the research and development of additional drugs beyond its antibiotics and synthetic penicillins. A number of new areas were explored, including cardiovascular agents and anticancer drugs.

At the time, Bristol-Myers was the only pharmaceutical company to invest in anticancer drugs, because growth potential appeared small. The company obtained the marketing rights to several anticancer drugs developed by the National Institutes of Health and other research institutions, universities, and drug companies, and was well positioned when this market took off. Between 1974 and 1980 Bristol-Myers launched 11 new drugs for treatment of cancer and other diseases. Although none of these products was a breakthrough drug, they contributed over $200 million in sales to the company by 1980. This growth occurred despite the company's relatively small research budget.

The company was already an experienced marketer of over-the-counter (OTC) analgesics. Its Excedrin and Bufferin brands had accounted for one-quarter of the total market for nonprescription pain relievers until the early 1960s, when an OTC version of Johnson & Johnson's Tylenol—a nonaspirin product—took a significant percentage of Bristol-Myers's market share. In the mid-1970s Bristol-Myers challenged Johnson & Johnson with Datril, a nonaspirin product priced lower than Tylenol. Johnson & Johnson responded quickly, lowering the price of Tylenol.

In 1981 the company settled a series of ten-year-old antitrust suits alleging that Bristol-Myers and Beecham Group, a British pharmaceutical company, had improperly obtained a patent on the antibiotic ampicillin. The suits also accused the firms of engaging in restrictive licensing practices which had resulted in excessive charges to hospitals, wholesalers, and retailers.

The following year a series of product-tampering incidents occurred involving various over-the-counter analgesic products, including Bristol-Myers's Excedrin capsules. The company responded to new Food and Drug Administration (FDA) regulations in 1983 with tamper-resistant packaging for its capsule products.

In 1984 Bristol-Myers signed an agreement with Upjohn which enabled it to introduce Nuprin, a new nonprescription form of ibuprofen pain reliever. The agreement gave Bristol-Myers the means to take on Tylenol once again. It also pitted the firm against American Home Products, which already sold a pain reliever under the Anacin brand and was planning to launch a new ibuprofen-based product called Advil.

At this time, Bristol-Myers entered the market for drugs used to treat anxiety and depression. The company licensed the rights to products manufactured by foreign firms while continuing to invest heavily in its own pharmaceutical research and development. The firm had reorganized its internal research operations and, in 1984, built a multi-million dollar research facility in Wallingford, Connecticut. Two years later Bristol-Myers received FDA approval to market its own tranquilizer product, BuSpar, which did not produce many of the negative side effects of other antidepressant drugs already on the market.

In 1986 the firm became enmeshed in the complex acquisition of Genetic Systems Corporation (GSC), a Seattle, Washington–based biotechnology company. GSC was founded in 1980 by a group of entrepreneurial microbiologists who teamed up with Syntex Corporation, a drug company, to manufacture and market tests for sexually transmitted diseases. Three years later the partners formed another venture, Oncogen, to manufacture products for cancer treatment, and in 1985 they offered Bristol-Myers an opportunity to invest in the operation. Later that year, after a Bristol-Myers competitor, Eli Lilly & Company, acquired Hybridtech, a leading producer of monoclonal antibodies, Bristol-Myers negotiated an agreement with GSC management to buy GSC and Oncogen, unaware that GSC had negotiated a similar deal with Syntex two months before. After threatening a lawsuit, Syntex elected to withdraw its offer for GSC in exchange for a $15 million compensation package provided by Bristol-Myers and for marketing rights to selected GSC and Oncogen products. Bristol-Myers sold GSC to Sanofi, a French pharmaceutical firm, in 1990.

In June 1986 a second incident of tampering with capsule-type pain-relief products caused two deaths in the Seattle area. This incident led Bristol-Myers to recall its Excedrin capsules nationwide. It soon withdrew all of its nonprescription capsule products from the market, including Comtrex cold-relief medication. The capsules were replaced with the caplet, a specially coated, capsule-shaped pill. With this action, Bristol-Myers became the second company in its industry, after Johnson & Johnson, to end the sale of OTC medication in capsule form.

In an attempt to establish a stronger position in the field of coronary care, Bristol-Myers negotiated an agreement in March 1987 to acquire SciMed Life Systems, a manufacturer of coronary balloon angioplasty catheters and other disposable products for treating cardiovascular disease. Two months later Bristol-Myers withdrew its offer after SciMed was sued by Eli Lilly & Company for patent infringement.

Bristol-Myers continued to grow as a manufacturer of prescription pharmaceuticals and to lessen its dependence on consumer products by focusing on acquired immune deficiency syndrome (AIDS) research. Since both cancer and AIDS research are virology-based, this area was a natural fit for the company. In 1987 Bristol-Myers obtained an exclusive license to produce and test two new AIDS drugs, dideoxyadenosine (DDA) and dideoxyinosine (DDI). It also received FDA approval to test an experimental AIDS vaccine on humans.

In November 1989 Bristol-Myers merged with Squibb Corporation. Squibb had been established in 1858 and was among the oldest U.S. pharmaceutical companies. Over half of Squibb's sales were generated by pharmaceuticals, and the company also owned a profitable cosmetic business. The two firms had similar corporate cultures. The merger also brought together two chief executives, Gelb and Richard M. Furlaud of Squibb, who had been friends for 25 years and had discussed the idea of a merger occasionally over the previous three years.

As part of the merger agreement Richard Gelb became chairman and chief executive officer of the combined company, while Furlaud, his counterpart at Squibb, became president and headed up the company's pharmaceutical business. Squibb benefited from Bristol-Myers's biomedical research capabilities and established presence in consumer health products. This market was becoming increasingly important to Squibb, since several competitors were already negotiating agreements to market their prescription drugs in OTC forms to consumers. In Squibb, Bristol-Myers obtained a new source of prescription drugs with strong sales potential, particularly in the cardiovascular area, and a sizable budget to add to its own continuing-research operation.

Bristol-Myers Squibb Company is comprised of four major product areas with significant global growth potential: pharmaceuticals, consumer products, medical devices, and nutritionals. The company's pharmaceutical products include cardiovascular and anticancer drugs, anti-infective agents, drugs for treating the central nervous system, diagnostic imaging agents, and dermatological products which are marketed through the company's Westwood Pharmaceuticals subsidiary. As the population ages and health-care costs continue to increase, Bristol-Myers Squibb's goals is to develop new pharmaceutical products which will reduce hospitalization and keep health-care expenses down.

The company currently markets over 140 consumer brands, including nonprescription medicines, vitamins, skin-care preparations, toiletries, beauty aids, and household-care items. Its medical-devices division serves the orthopedics market with such products as artificial hip and knee replacements, and also supplies various items needed for ostomy procedures, wound and burn care, and other surgical specialties.

The second-largest maker of infant formula in the world, Bristol-Myers Squibb Company also manufactures products for people of all ages requiring nutritional support. In 1989 the company negotiated an agreement with Gerber Products Company to manufacture and market Gerber Baby Formula directly to U.S. consumers. Controversial advertising for this product touched off a boycott of the company's line of formula products by a group of pediatricians who felt that Bristol-Myers Squibb was attempting to discourage breast-feeding and to compromise the physician's influence in baby formula selection.

The future of Bristol-Myers Squibb Company is dependent upon continued product leadership on an international basis in each of its highly competitive core businesses, as well as a continuing commitment to research and development of new products. Several forces—including an aging population, an increasing percentage of women in the full-time workforce, and a growing number of nontraditional households—are expected to create needs which will have a strong influence on the company's consumer-products business.

Further Reading: Bristol-Myers Company Special Report: The Next Century, New York, Bristol-Myers Company, 1987; "Squibb Corporation," in *International Directory of Company Histories*, Volume I, edited by Thomas Derdak, Chicago, St. James Press, 1988.

—Sandy Schusteff

THE CLOROX COMPANY

1221 Broadway Street
Oakland, California 94612
U.S.A.
(415) 271-7000
Fax: (415) 832-1463

Public Company
Incorporated: 1913 as the Electro-Alkaline Company
Employees: 5,300
Sales: $1.36 billion
Stock Exchanges: New York Pacific

Although best known for the household bleach that bears the firm's name, The Clorox Company is a diversified international manufacturer and marketer of a variety of consumer products ranging from household cleaners to salad dressings. It also manufactures and markets equipment and products for the food-service industry and distributes bottled water in several areas of the United States.

Clorox was founded in 1913 as the Electro-Alkaline Company by five Oakland, California–area businessmen, only one of whom had any knowledge of chemistry. Their objective was to convert brine from ocean water into sodium hypochlorite bleach using an electrolytic process considered to be technologically advanced for its time. Each partner invested $100 in the new venture, and in August 1913 they purchased a plant site. The company's first product, Clorox liquid bleach, was packaged in five-gallon returnable containers and delivered by horse-drawn wagon to local breweries, dairies, and laundries for cleaning and disinfecting their facilities. Labels for the new product identified it as being "made by electricity."

An initial stock issue of 750 shares at $100 each provided $75,000 in start-up capital. The company struggled through its early years and often depended upon personal loans from its directors to pay expenses.

In 1916 a less concentrated liquid bleach product—5¼% sodium hypochlorite instead of 21%—for household use was developed and sold in amber glass pint bottles. William C.R. Murray, the company's general manager, came up with the idea of producing and promoting household bleach. Murray's wife, Annie, gave away samples of the formula to customers of the family's Oakland-based grocery store. Its value as a laundry aid, stain remover, deodorant, and disinfectant was also promoted by door-to-door salespeople who demonstrated how a solution of Clorox bleach and water could whiten an ink-stained piece of fabric. Orders were collected on the spot and then given to local grocers who purchased the necessary inventory from the company to fulfill them. Small and local at the time, Clorox was not affected by World War I.

In the 1920s Clorox's manufacturing plant could produce about 2,000 cases, or 48,000 bottles of bleach per day. Assembly line workers filled bottles by hand using hoses attached to overhead tanks. After being filled, the bottles were sealed with rubber stoppers and labeled, also by hand.

As demand for Clorox household bleach grew, the company expanded its manufacturing and distribution capabilities nationwide. By the early 1930s Clorox had become the best-selling liquid bleach in the country. The company was known by its amber glass bleach bottle, which continued to be used with minor adaptations in size and design until the early 1960s, when Clorox became the first bleach manufacturer to use plastic containers.

In 1929 Murray became president of Clorox Chemical Company, a name that had replaced the company's original name in 1922. He served in that capacity until his sudden death in 1941, just prior to the United States's entry into World War II and was succeeded by William J. Roth. In contrast to Murray's relatively uneventful tenure, Roth immediately had to deal with the impact of the country's wartime involvement on the company. Due to the decreased availability of chlorine, the U.S. government permitted bleach manufacturers to reduce the concentration of sodium hypochlorite in their products. Roth, however, opted to decrease production rather than change the quality of Clorox bleach and jeopardize customer satisfaction. He also terminated a number of contracts for chlorine that had been negotiated before the war because those agreements paid suppliers too little for a substance now in such short supply. Although these decisions were costly at the time, the company retained the respect of the industry and customer loyalty once the war was over.

By the mid-1950s Clorox, still a one-product company, held the largest share of the domestic market for household bleach. The Procter & Gamble Company, a successful manufacturer of consumer products, viewed Clorox bleach as a compatible addition to its existing line of laundry products, and acquired the company in 1957.

Procter & Gamble changed the firm's name to The Clorox Company. However, within three months of the purchase, the Federal Trade Commission challenged the Clorox acquisition on the grounds that it might lessen competition or tend to create a monopoly in household liquid bleaches, a violation of the Clayton Act. Even though Procter & Gamble allowed Clorox to handle its own affairs, in 1967 the U.S. Supreme Court upheld the commission's order that Procter & Gamble divest itself of the Clorox operation. By 1969 Clorox had been spun off as a public company and was once again independent.

Clorox's new president, former Procter & Gamble executive Robert B. Shetterly, and his top management team faced a more competitive marketing environment in which enzyme laundry products were rapidly encroaching on Clorox's core business. Realizing that diversification beyond bleach was essential to the company's survival, Clorox management implemented a three-pronged strategic plan aimed at the acquisition and internal development of a line of nonfood grocery products, the acquisition of a food specialty business, and the development of a line of institutional food and cleaning products. They drew up a list of potential targets for acquisition, many of which were purchased within the year, including Jiffee Chemical Corporation, the manufacturer of Liquid-plumr drain opener; Shelco, which manufactured Jifoam aerosol oven cleaner; and the 409 division of Harrell International, which produced Formula 409 spray cleaners. One year later the company introduced Clorox 2, its first entry in the dry, nonchlorine segment of the bleach market.

In 1971 Clorox purchased McFadden Industries, makers of Litter Green cat litter. Clorox had first tested McFadden's product in the market with an option to acquire the entire company if the product proved successful. Clorox also acquired Grocery Store Products Company, which manufactured such specialty food products as B&B mushrooms, Kitchen Bouquet gravy thickener, and Cream of Rice cereal. A year later Clorox added a line of salad dressings and party dips to this operation by buying Hidden Valley Ranch Food Products. Sales of the company's chlorine bleach rebounded in the first years of the decade as concerns arose over the health and environmental effects of enzyme and phosphate detergents.

In 1972 Clorox met the third objective of its strategic plan with the acquisitions of Martin-Brower Corporation, a manufacturer and supplier of disposable packaging and paper goods for the food-service industry, and Nesbitt Food Products, a manufacturer and distributor of soft drink concentrates. Joining the fold the following year was Kingsford Corporation, a leading manufacturer of charcoal briquettes.

The company soon encountered a series of setbacks, however. Just after the Kingsford acquisition, a cool and wet summer depressed sales of charcoal and the recreational products manufactured by other parts of the Kingsford operation. Clorox's introduction of a new product, Mr. Mushroom, coincided unexpectedly with a nationwide botulism scare, which adversely affected Mr. Mushroom and the company's B&B brand. Mushroom production at its newly acquired Country Kitchen Foods subsidiary in England decreased significantly due to a virus in the fertilizer used. Sales of Clorox's cleaning products also fell because of consumers' fears of recession.

Although these problems led to a temporary halt in further acquisitions, the company successfully negotiated an agreement in 1974 with Henkel, a German producer of consumer and industrial food and cleaning products. Clorox gained access to Henkel's research-and-development capabilities and acquired manufacturing and marketing rights to Henkel-developed products in the United States, Canada, and Puerto Rico. Henkel in turn became a minority shareholder in Clorox. In 1975 a civil antitrust suit brought against both Clorox and Procter & Gamble by Purex Corporation, a competitor in the bleach market, came to trial. The suit sought over $520 million in damages, which Purex claimed had resulted from Procter & Gamble's acquisition of Clorox in the late 1950s. Purex admitted defeat in 1982, when the Supreme Court refused to hear the case. Both a federal court and federal appeals court had ruled that Purex had failed to prove that either company had caused it to suffer any loss of business.

Shetterly retired as chief executive officer in 1980 and was succeeded by Calvin Hatch, another former Procter & Gamble executive. Under Shetterly's leadership, the company had diversified beyond bleach into a number of other areas; however, most of these new ventures never became profitable. Conceding that Shetterly's growth plan had failed, Clorox sold its Martin-Brower subsidiary at a loss in 1979 to Dalgety PLC—a U.K. company—and Country Kitchen Foods—its British mushroom canning operation—to H.J. Heinz Company, Ltd., the U.K. subsidiary of the U.S. company. These divestitures gave Clorox plenty of capital to use in its search for niches in the consumer packaged-goods market in which the company could develop its own products and capture a dominant share.

Clorox devoted a significant amount of money and corporate support to research and development. However, until the company was able to come up with a breakthrough product of its own, it continued to rely upon outside acquisitions to diversify its business and fill its new-product pipeline. Some of the acquisitions made under Hatch's leadership, such as the 1979 purchase of the Emil Villa chain of barbecue restaurants, paralleled Shetterly's mistakes in fueling growth but not profits, while other products gained through earlier acquisitions, such as Cream of Rice cereal, fell short of the company's goals and were eventually sold. Efforts to generate and rapidly build a base of international business were also stymied by solidly entrenched competition.

In 1981 the company acquired Comerco, a Tacoma, Washington–based producer of stains and wood preservatives marketed under the Olympic brand name to hardware and home-improvement stores. Two years later, the company purchased Lucite house paints from E.I. Du Pont de Nemours Company. Clorox attempted to model these acquisitions after its successful Kingsford charcoal operation, using marketing techniques and heavy advertising to produce premium-priced, brand-name products. The subsidiary formed to manage these businesses was never effectively able to integrate the operations of these two product lines nor to attain the company's sales expectations, however. It was sold to PPG Industries in 1989.

Over the years, Clorox had retained leadership of the laundry-bleach market despite numerous attempts by competitors to chip away at its share with other brand-name, private-label, and generic products. In 1982 Clorox faced its toughest challenge when Procter & Gamble decided to launch its own bleach product called Vibrant in a test market. Clorox quickly responded by introducing a new bleach with a similar formula called Wave. Although Vibrant never made it out of the test-market stage due to manufacturing problems, this competitive advance against Clorox set the stage for future attempts by each company to invade the markets for products long dominated by the other.

In 1986 Calvin Hatch retired as chairman, a post he had held since 1982, and was succeeded by president and chief executive officer, Charles R. Weaver. Jack W. Collins, the company's executive vice president and chief operating officer, was promoted to Weaver's former positions. Beginning in 1987, the company diversified into another new business area by purchasing a number of bottled-water companies, including the Deer Park Spring Water Company and Deep Rock Water Company, followed by the Aqua Pure Water Company and Emerald Coast Water Company in 1988.

After several years of uneasy coexistence after the Vibrant incident, the battle between Clorox and Procter & Gamble for dominance of the consumer marketplace erupted. In 1988 the company introduced its Clorox Super Detergent brand of laundry soap powder in four western states and was quickly attacked by Procter & Gamble's new Tide With Bleach brand. Procter & Gamble also began the market test of a new brand of liquid bleach targeted at Clorox customers, a move intended to warn Clorox against entering the laundry-detergent market. By mid-1989 Procter & Gamble had withdrawn its bleach product due to disappointing sales. Clorox kept its detergent on the market but continued to face an uphill battle against the entrenched brands. The fact that consumer preferences were slowly moving away from powders toward liquid detergents added to the company's marketing problems. In an attempt to inject new life into its consumer products business, the company acquired the Pine Sol cleaner and Combat insecticide lines of American Cyanamid Company in 1990.

Clorox products are sold in nearly 60 countries and are manufactured in more than 35 plants around the world. Led by Chairman Weaver and President Robert A. Bolingbroke, who succeeded Jack W. Collins upon his retirement in 1990, the company's future initiative will focus on continuing to develop the institutional segment of its business while strengthening consumer product lines with new brands and companion products to established brands. This approach, which has led to such product successes as Kingsford Charcoal Lighter and Lemon Fresh Clorox Liquid Bleach, is viewed as a key factor in the company's growth. While nurturing new products, the company will be challenged to find innovative ways to rejuvenate its mature brands, such as Clorox chlorine bleach, and broaden their appeal to both domestic and international consumers. In all cases, Clorox will rely heavily on its ability to identify emerging consumer needs and trends and then quickly apply its manufacturing and marketing expertise to preempt entry by larger competitors with greater resources. Clorox liquid bleach remains an ongoing source of marketing strength, and the company is well prepared to protect and solidify its position as a major force in the consumer products industry both at home and abroad.

Principal Subsidiaries: Brita (USA) Inc.; Deep Rock Water Company; Deer Park Spring Water, Inc.; Food Service Products Company; The HVR Company; The Household Products Company; The Kingsford Products Company; Prince Castle, Inc.; Clorox International Trading Limited; The Clorox Company of Canada, Ltd.; The Clorox Company of Puerto Rico; The Clorox International Company; Colgate-Clorox (Far East) Ltd. (50%); The Household Cleaning Products Company of Egypt, Ltd. (49%); Industrias Lesedo S.A. de C.V. (Mexico); National Cleaning Products Limited (Saudi Arabia, 40%); Progar S.A. (Argentina, 51%), Tecnoclor, S.A. (Colombia, 49%).

Further Reading: Shisgall, Oscar, Eyes on Tomorrow: The Evolution of Procter & Gamble, Chicago, J.G. Ferguson Publishing Company, 1981; *About the Company on its Diamond Anniversary,* Oakland, California, The Clorox Company, [1988].

—Sandy Schusteff

COLGATE-PALMOLIVE COMPANY

300 Park Avenue
New York, New York 10022
U.S.A.
(212) 310-2000
Fax: (212) 310-3284

Public Company
Incorporated: 1923 as the Eastern Operating Company
Employees: 24,100
Sales: $5.04 billion
Stock Exchanges: New York Amsterdam Frankfurt London Paris Zürich

Colgate-Palmolive Company's growth from a small candle and soap manufacturer to one of the most powerful consumer products giants in the world is the result of aggressive acquisition of other companies, persistent attempts to overtake its major U.S. competition, and an early emphasis on building a global presence overseas where little competition existed. Today the company markets a wide range of household and personal-care products, including such well-known brands as Colgate toothpaste, Irish Spring soap, Softsoap liquid soap, Fab laundry detergent, and Palmolive dishwashing liquid.

In 1806, when the company was founded by 23-year-old William Colgate, it concentrated exclusively on selling starch, soap, and candles from its New York City–based factory and shop. Upon entering his second year of business, Colgate became partners with Francis Smith, and the company became Smith and Colgate, a name it kept until 1812 when Colgate purchased Smith's share of the company and offered a partnership to his brother, Bowles Colgate. Now called William Colgate and Company, the firm expanded its manufacturing operations to a Jersey City, New Jersey factory in 1820, this factory produced Colgate's two major products, Windsor toilet soaps and Pearl starch.

Upon its founder's death in 1857, the firm changed its name to Colgate & Company and was run by President Samuel Colgate until his death 40 years later. During his tenure several new products were developed, including perfumes and essences and perfumed soap. The manufacture of starch was discontinued in 1866 after a fire destroyed the factory.

In 1873, Colgate began selling toothpaste in a jar, followed 23 years later by the introduction of Colgate Ribbon Dental Cream, in the now-familiar collapsible tube. By 1906, the company was also producing several varieties of laundry soap, toilet paper, and perfumes.

While the Colgate family managed its manufacturing operations in New York, soap factories were also opened in 1864 by B. J. Johnson in Milwaukee, Wisconsin, and in 1872 by the three Peet brothers in Kansas City, Kansas. In 1898, Johnson's company introduced Palmolive soap, which soon became the best-selling soap in the world and led the firm to change its name to the Palmolive Company in 1916.

The Peets, who sold laundry soap mainly in the midwest and western United States, merged their company with Palmolive in 1926. Two years later the company that resulted from that merger joined with Colgate & Company to form Colgate-Palmolive-Peet, with headquarters in Jersey City.

Although Palmolive's management initially assumed control of the combined organization, the Colgate family regained control of the company after the 1929 stock market crash and installed Bayard Colgate as president in 1933. The firm adopted its present name in 1953 and moved its offices for domestic and international operations to New York City in 1956.

Between 1914 and 1933, the company began establishing international operations, with subsidiaries in Canada, Australia, Europe, and Latin America. It also built upon its strategy of growth by acquisition by buying a number of smaller consumer product companies over the next two decades. These acquisitions did little to close the gap between Colgate and its archrival, Procter & Gamble, a company which had been formed in the 1830s and now assumed a commanding lead over Colgate in selling detergent products in the United States.

In 1960 George H. Lesch was appointed Colgate's president in the hopes that his international experience would produce similar success in the domestic market. Under his leadership, the company embarked upon an extensive new-product-development program which created such brands as Cold Power laundry detergent, Palmolive dishwashing liquid, and Ultra Brite toothpaste. In an attempt to expand beyond these traditional, highly competitive businesses into new growth areas, Colgate also successfully introduced a new food wrap called Baggies in 1963. As a result of these product launches, the company's sales grew between 8% and 9% every year throughout the 1960s.

Lesch assumed the chairmanship of Colgate, and David Foster became president in 1970 and CEO in 1971. Foster was the son of the founder of Colgate-Palmolive's United Kingdom operations. He joined the company in 1946 as a management trainee and rose through the sales and marketing ranks both in the United States and overseas.

During the 1970s, as environmental concerns about phosphate and enzyme detergent products grew, the company faced additional pressure to diversify beyond the detergent business. In response to this pressure, Foster instituted a strategy that emphasized internal development via a specialized new venture group; joint ventures for marketing other companies' products; and outright acquisitions of businesses in which Colgate could gain a marketing advantage over Procter & Gamble. In 1971, for example, the company began selling British Wilkinson Sword Company razors and blades in the United States and other countries. In 1972 Colgate-

Palmolive acquired Kendall & Company, a manufacturer of hospital and industrial supplies. It was originally hoped that the Kendall acquisition would bolster the pharmaceutical sales of Colgate's Lakeside Laboratories subsidiary, which had been acquired in 1960. The partnership never materialized, however, and Lakeside was sold in 1974. The Kendall business proved to be one of Foster's most successful acquisitions. Within two years, the subsidiary was producing sales, and earnings results well above the company's targeted goals.

In 1971 the Federal Trade Commission enacted restrictions on in-store product promotions, such as couponing. In response to these restrictions, Foster began to employ other tactics designed to enhance Colgate's visibility in the marketplace. Two such programs awarded money to schools and local civic groups whose young people collected the most labels and boxtops from selected Colgate products. Under Foster Colgate-Palmolive also began to sponsor a number of women's sporting events, including the Colgate–Dinah Shore Winner's Circle, a women's professional golf tournament. Foster chose women's sports in an effort to appeal to Colgate-Palmolive's primarily female customer base. He even went so far as to have Colgate buy the tournament's home course, the Mission Hills Country Club in Palm Springs, California, so that he could supervise the maintainence of the greens.

In 1973, Colgate acquired Helena Rubinstein, a major cosmetics manufacturer with strong foreign sales but a weak U.S. presence. Believing that its marketing expertise could solve Rubinstein's problems, Colgate reduced both the number of products in the company's line and the number of employees in its workforce, increased advertising expenditures, and moved the products out of drugstores and into department stores. The following year the company acquired Ram Golf Corporation and Bancroft Racket Company, and in 1976 it bought Charles A. Eaton Company, a golf and tennis shoe manufacturer.

Although total U.S. sales of consumer products appeared to be slowing by the end of 1974, particularly in soaps and detergents, Colgate's international sales continued to carry the company forward. It maintained its leadership position abroad through new-product development geared specifically to local tastes throughout Europe as well as through its involvement in the growing markets of less-developed countries in Latin America, Africa, and Asia.

Foster's diversification strategy initially improved earnings, but Colgate's domestic sales, market share, and profit margins were beginning to soften. This was due, in large part, to an economic recession and an advertising cutback the company had made in an attempt to boost earnings. Colgate was consistently losing the marketing battle in personal-care products to Procter & Gamble. It had no leading brands and few successful new-product introductions because of reduced spending for research and development. In an effort to remedy this problem and broaden its product mix, Colgate moved into food marketing in 1976 with the acquisition of Riviana Foods, a major producer of Texas long-grain rice, with its own subsidiaries in the pet food, kosher hot dog, and candies businesses.

The Riviana acquisition, however did not live up to the company's expectations. Along with purchasing a successful rice-milling business, Colgate found that it had also saddled itself with two unprofitable restaurant chains and a low-quality candy company. In 1977 declines in the price of rice seriously eroded Riviana's cash flow.

Helena Rubinstein created additional headaches. While other cosmetic manufacturers had moved their products from department store distribution to higher-volume drugstores, Colgate's management elected to keep Rubinstein products in department stores, even though stores' demands for marketing support eroded the company's margins so severely that it lost money on every cosmetic item sold. Colgate finally sold the business in 1980 to Albi Enterprises.

Foster had been made chairman in 1975. In 1979, embattled by a series of marketing failures and the pressures of an acquisition strategy that yielded more losers than winners, David Foster suddenly resigned, citing ill health. Colgate president and chief operating officer Keith Crane was appointed as Foster's successor. A 42-year Colgate employee, Crane quickly instituted a new management structure consisting of several group vice presidents, reunited all domestic operations under one group, and realigned division managers in an attempt to promote a more cohesive organization. Consumer advertising and product research were given renewed emphasis to support the company's basic detergent and toothpaste lines.

Over the next two years, Crane sold a number of Foster's acquisitions that no longer fit with the company's long-term strategic plan, including Hebrew National Kosher Foods, which had been part of the Riviana purchase; Ram Golf; and the Bancroft Racket Company. Crane also put the Mission Hills Country Club up for sale and withdrew Colgate's sponsorship of the sporting events his predecessor had nurtured.

Also during the late 1970s and the 1980s, Colgate found itself named as a defendant in two lawsuits. In 1981 the company lost a suit brought by United Roasters. United Roasters successfully argued that Colgate had violated the terms of a contract between the two firms for Colgate to market Bambeanos, a soybean snack produced by United Roasters, and was awarded $950,000. The following year, the company was sued by the federal government for alleged job discrimination. According to a complaint filed with the Equal Employment Opportunity Commission, Colgate had failed or refused to hire people between the ages of 40 and 70 since 1978 and had also deprived employees in that age group of opportunities for promotion.

By the end of 1982, Crane had also begun to have problems at Colgate. Several attempts at new-product development never made it out of the test market stage. Increased advertising expenditures for a limited number of major brands produced only temporary gains in market share, while slowly killing off other products receiving little or no media support. Even Fresh Start detergent, one of the most successful new products to come out of the Foster era, was having problems retaining market share. While Procter & Gamble's sales and margins were increasing, Colgate's were on the decline. To make matters worse, the strong dollar overseas hurt Colgate's international sales, while changes in Medicare policy weakened Kendall's business.

In 1983, Crane relinquished the title of president to Reuben Mark, one of the company's three executive vice presidents and a member of Crane's management advisory team. Mark also assumed the position of chief operating officer at that time, and one year later succeeded Crane as CEO. Mark built upon his predecessor's restructuring efforts in an attempt to increase profits and shareholder value. Between 1984 and 1986, several inefficient plants were closed, hundreds of employees were laid off, and non-core businesses were sold, including the remaining parts of the Riviana Foods acquisition, except for the Hills Pet Products subsidiary.

In an attempt to refocus the company's marketing and profitability, Mark developed a set of corporate initiatives intended to address business areas ranging from production cost reduction to new-product development, with a heavy emphasis on employee motivation and involvement in decision making. In response to the implementation of these ideas, the company's U.S. toothpaste business enjoyed a boost with first-to-the-market introductions of a gel toothpaste and a pump-type dispenser bearing the Colgate brand name. Similar U.S. market share gains were earned by new and improved versions of its Palmolive and Dynamo detergents and Ajax cleaner.

With a turnaround firmly underway, business units managed by key executives were formed to develop plans for the company's major product categories. The purpose of each plan was to identify how products under development could be best introduced in domestic and international markets. Two years into this strategic reorganization, coinciding with Mark's appointment as chairman in 1986, Colgate confronted an embarrassing controversy.

Since the early 1920s, Hawley & Hazel Chemical Company had marketed a product called Darkie Black and White Toothpaste in the Far East. Colgate had acquired a 50% interest in this company in 1985. The following year, the Interfaith Center on Corporate Responsibility, a coalition of Protestant and Roman Catholic groups, demanded that Colgate change what it deemed to be the product's racially offensive name and packaging, which depicted a likeness of Al Jolson in blackface. The company acknowledged the criticism and agreed to make the necessary changes.

Colgate also continued to seek out growth areas in its personal-care-product and detergent businesses. In 1987, it acquired a line of liquid soap products from Minnetonka Corporation, the first transaction the company had made in the personal-care area in several years. Building upon its success in launching an automatic dishwashing detergent in liquid form ahead of its competitors, the company also beat Procter & Gamble to the market with a laundry detergent packaged in a throw-in pouch called Fab 1 Shot, although this product failed to sustain consumer interest and reach sales expectations over the long term.

Buoyed by product-development breakthroughs and a renewed commitment to consumer products marketing, Colgate sold its Kendall subsidiary and related health-care businesses in 1988 to Clayton & Dubilier. The sale enabled Colgate to retire some debt, sharpen its focus on its global consumer products businesses, and invest in new product categories.

Mark's global approach has enabled the company to maintain its overall profitability despite its continuing lack of a leadership position in the United States. Although Colgate lags behind Procter & Gamble in the toothpaste category, for example, it holds a commanding 40% share of the toothpaste market worldwide.

Marks's strategy appeared to pay off handsomely. By the end of the third quarter of 1989, Colgate's international operations performed strongly while the profitability of its U.S. operations rose, due mostly to manufacturing-cost economies and greater control over promotional and sales expenses. Not yet ready to concede the U.S. market for personal-care products to Procter & Gamble, though, Colgate acquired Vipont Pharmaceutical, a manufacturer of oral-hygiene products, toward the end of that year. Vipont's products, several of which Colgate had already been marketing overseas, enabled Colgate to strengthen the market position it had recently established with the introduction of a new tartar-control formula toothpaste.

Colgate's global presence as a consumer products company extends to over 160 countries. Its manufacturing and marketing operations are organized into five core segments: toothpaste, soap, detergents, household cleaners, and pet foods. This latter category consists of veterinary food items produced by Hill's Pet Products, and other support services for the veterinary profession provided by its subsidiary, Veterinary Companies of America, which was acquired in 1987. A substantial amount of Colgate-Palmolive's U.S. profits come from the Hill's pet foods.

Colgate continues to seek out opportunities for long-term global growth through a combination of internal product development, strategic acquisitions, and joint ventures. Colgate's future depends upon its ability to accurately identify unmet consumer needs and swiftly launch products to satisfy the expectations of the world market.

Principal Subsidiaries: Colgate-Palmolive Development Corporation; Colgate-Palmolive International Inc.; Southampton-Hamilton Company; Purity Holding Company; Kendall do Brasil Industriale Commercia Ltda. (Brazil); Lournay Sales, Inc.; ELM Company Limited (Bermuda); Colgate-Palmolive Global Trading Company; Institutional Financing Services, Inc.; Princess House, Inc.; Colgate-Palmolive S.A. Industrial Y Commercial (Argentina); Softsoap Enterprises, Inc.; Veterinary Companies of America, Inc.; Colgate-Palmolive Pty. Limited (Australia); Colgate-Palmolive Gesellschaft mbh (Austria); CKR, Inc.; CKR, S.A. (Belgium); Colgate-Palmolive, Ltda. (Brazil); Colgate-Palmolive (Caribbean) Inc.; Colgate-Palmolive Cia.; Colgate-Palmolive (Dominican Republic) Inc.; Colgate-Palmolive (Central America) Inc.; Colgate-Palmolive A/S (Denmark); Colgate-Palmolive del Ecuador, S.A.; Colgate-Palmolive (Egypt) S.A.E.; Colgate-Palmmolive (Fiji) Limited; Colgate-Palmolive (France); Colgate-Palmolive Gmbh (Germany); Colgate-Palmolive (Hellas) S.A. (Greece); Colgate-Palmolive Limited (New Zealand); Colgate-Palmolive (Eastern) Pte. Ltd.; (Singapore); Hawley & Hazel Chemical Company (H.K.) Ltd. (Hong Kong); Hill's Colgate (Japan) Ltd.; Colgate-Palmolive (H.K.) Limited (Hong Kong); Colgate-Palmolive (India) Limited; P.T. Colgate-Palmolive Indonesia; Colgate-Palmolive S.p.a. (Italy); Colgate-Palmolive Co. (Jamaica) Ltd.; Colgate-Palmolive (East Africa) Limited (Kenya); Colgate-Palmolive (Malaysia) SDN. BHD.; Colgate-Palmolive, S.A. de C.V. (Mexico); CKR Nederland B.V. (Netherlands); Colgate-Palmolive Philippines Inc.; Colgate-Palmolive Portuguesa Lda. (Portugal); Colgate-Palmolive Limited (South Africa); Colgate-Palmolive, S.A.E. (Spain); Colgate-Palmolive A.G. (Switzerland); Colgate Holdings (U.K.) Ltd.; Colgate-Palmolive Compania Anonima (Venezuela); Colgate-Palmolive (Zambia) Ltd.; Colgate-Palmolive (Zimbabwe) (Private) Limited; Vipont Pharmaceutical Inc.

Further Reading: "The Marriage of Marketing and Technology to Improve Company Performance: How David Foster runs Colgate-Palmolive," *Nation's Business*, August 1975; Campanella, Frank W., "Soap to Nuts: Colgate-Palmolive Is Steadily Broadening Its Product Mix," *Barron's*, February 23, 1976; Bronson, Gail, "Colgate Works Hard to Become the Firm It Was a Decade Ago," *The Wall Street Journal*, November 23, 1981.

—Sandy Schusteff

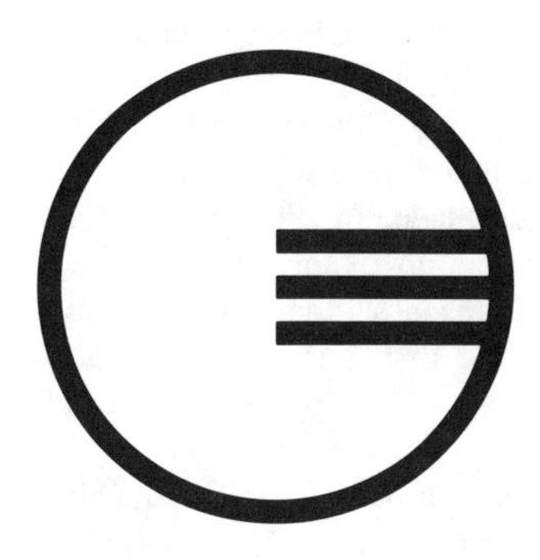

THE GILLETTE COMPANY

Prudential Tower Building
Boston, Massachusetts 02199
U.S.A.
(617) 421-7000
Fax: (617) 421-7123

Public Company
Incorporated: 1917 as Gillette Safety Razor Company
Employees: 30,400
Sales: $3.82 billion
Stock Exchanges: New York Boston Midwest Pacific London Frankfurt Zürich

The Gillette Company offers a wide range of personal-care products for men and women, including deodorants, shampoos, and hair spray. Acquisitions of other companies have added pens, stationery supplies, and small appliances to its product line. Shaving equipment, however, still accounts for slightly over 70% of Gillette's profits, and the company's ability to compete effectively in that area will determine if it will look sharp into its second century.

One summer morning in 1895, an ambitious traveling salesman found that the edge of his straight razor had dulled. King Gillette later said that the idea for an entirely new kind of razor, with a disposable blade, flashed into his mind as he looked in irritation at his dull blade.

King Gillette had been searching for the right product, one that had to be used—and replaced—regularly, around which to build a business. His innovation in shaving technology was just such a product. Another safety razor, the Star, was already on the market at the time but, like the straight razor it was meant to replace, its blade needed stropping before each use and eventually had to be professionally honed. Gillette envisioned an inexpensive, double-edged blade that could be clamped over a handle, used until it was dull, and then discarded.

Gillette spent the next six years trying to perfect his safety razor. Scientists and toolmakers he consulted were pessimistic, and thought the idea impractical. Gillette, 40 years old at the time and a successful salesman, inventor, and writer, did not give up. In 1901, he joined forces with William Nickerson, a Massachusetts Institute of Technology–educated machinist. Nickerson developed production processes to make Gillette's idea a reality, while Gillette formed the American Safety Razor Company to raise the estimated $5,000 they needed to begin manufacturing the razor. Gillette became president of the company and head of a three-man directorate. Production of the razor began early in 1903.

The renamed Gillette Safety Razor Company began advertising its product in October 1903. The company sold 51 razor sets at $5 each and an additional 168 blades—originally at 20 for $1— that first year.

In 1904, Gillette received a patent on the safety razor and bought a six-story building in Boston. By 1906 the company had paid its first cash dividend. During the years before World War I Gillette steadily increased earnings through print advertisements, emphasizing that with his razor men could shave themselves under any conditions without cutting or irritation.

At the same time, Gillette was expanding abroad. He opened his first foreign office, a London sales branch, in 1905. By 1909 he had established a small manufacturing plant in Paris and offices in Germany, Austria, Scandinavia, and Russia. By 1923, foreign business accounted for about 30% of Gillette's sales, and today the company earns about half its profit abroad.

In 1910 King Gillette decided to sell a substantial portion of his controlling share of the company to the company's major investor, John Joyce. Gillette had succeeded in fighting off challenges for control of the company from Joyce in the past, but this time he took approximately $900,000 and bowed out. Gillette retained the title of president and frequently visited foreign branches, but he no longer played an active role in company management. Joyce was made vice president, a position he used to manage day-to-day operations. When Joyce died in 1916, his longtime friend, Edward Aldred, a New York investment banker, bought out the Gillette shares left to Joyce's estate and took control of the company. Aldred kept on Joyce's management team.

During World War I the U.S. government ordered 3.5 million razors and 36 million blades to supply all its troops. In order to meet military supply schedules, shifts worked around the clock and Gillette hired over 500 new employees. Gillette thus introduced a huge pool of potential customers to the still-new idea of self-shaving with a safety razor. After the war, ex-servicemen needed blades to fit the razors they had been issued in the service.

In 1921, Gillette's patent on the safety razor expired, but the company was ready for the change. It introduced the "new improved" Gillette razor, which sold at the old price, and entered the low-priced end of the market with the old-style razor, renamed the Silver Brownie razor, priced at only $1. Gillette also gave away razor handles as premiums with other products, developing customers for the more profitable blades. Expansion and growth continued.

The company also continued to expand abroad. In 1922 Gillette became royal purveyor to the prince of Wales and in 1924 to King Gustav V of Sweden. More favorable publicity followed when the Paris office gave Charles Lindbergh a Gillette Gold Traveler set the day after he completed the first transatlantic flight.

By the end of the decade, Gillette faced its first major setback. Auto Strop Safety Razor Company, owned by Henry J. Gaisman, filed suit for patent infringement after Gillette produced a new blade using a continuous-strip process similar to one originally presented to Gillette by Gaisman.

Gillette resolved the suit by merging with Auto Strop, only to face another problem. When Gaisman checked the company's financial records, he found that Gillette had overreported its earnings for the past five years by about $3 million. Confidence in Gillette fell, as did its stock. From a high of $125 early in 1929, the stock bottomed out after the disclosure, at $18.

The crisis led to management reorganization. King Gillette resigned as nominal president, and died 14 months later at age 77. Gaisman from Auto Strop became the new chairman of Gillette and Gerard Lambert, son of the founder of the Lambert Pharmacal Company—makers of Listerine—and a former manager there, came out of retirement to become president of Gillette. Lambert agreed to work for no salary with the guarantee of company stock if he could bring earnings up $5 per share.

Under Lambert, The Gillette Company made a bold advertising move: it admitted that the new blade it had brought out in 1930 was of poor quality. The company then announced what became its most recognizable product, the Gillette Blue Blade. Made under Gaisman's strip-processing method, the Blue Blade promised uniformly high quality.

The Blue Blade kept Gillette the leader in the field, but profits remained disappointing throughout the Depression, as men increasingly turned to bargain blades. Lambert resigned in 1934 without meeting his goal of improving earnings and without receiving compensation from the company. He was replaced by a former Auto Strop executive, Samuel C. Stampleman, who had no more success. With profits at their lowest since 1915, the board of directors appointed Joseph P. Spang Jr. president in December 1938 in an effort to invigorate the company.

Spang immediately restored the company's advertising budget, which had been cut to save money. Under this policy, Gillette's trademark sports advertising developed. Spang purchased radio broadcast rights to the 1939 World Series for $100,000. Despite a short series, in which the Cincinnati Reds lost four straight games to the New York Yankees, sales of Gillette's World Series Special razor sets were more than four times company estimates.

This success encouraged more sports advertising. By 1942, the events Gillette sponsored were grouped together as the "Gillette Cavalcade of Sports." Although it eventually included the Orange Bowl, the Sugar Bowl, and the Kentucky Derby, in addition to the World Series and the All-Star game, the "Cavalcade of Sports" is perhaps best known for bringing boxing to U.S. men. Spang attributed Gillette's continuing success to the sports advertising program, and sports programs remain an important vehicle for Gillette advertising.

During World War II foreign production and sales declined, but domestic production more than made up for those losses. Almost the entire production of razors and blades went to the military. In addition, Gillette manufactured fuel-control units for military-plane carburetors. The backlog of civilian demand after the war led to consecutive record sales until 1957.

During the profitable postwar period Spang began to broaden Gillette's product line. The company had introduced Gillette Brushless shaving cream, its first, non-razor, non-blade product, in 1936. In 1948 Spang began to diversify by acquiring other companies when he bought The Toni Company, a firm that made home permanents. In 1955 Spang purchased Paper Mate Company, a manufacturer of ball-point pens.

When Spang retired in 1956, Carl Gilbert became CEO. During the 1960s Gillette faced a threat to its bread-and-butter product, the double-edged blade. In 1962, the English Wilkinson Sword Company began to export stainless-steel blades to the United States. Wilkinson had developed a polymer coating that made it possible to put an edge on stainless steel, which resists corrosion, increasing the number of shaves from a blade.

Two of Gillette's domestic competitors—Eversharp, which makes Schick blades, and American Safety Razor—rushed versions of the stainless-steel blade onto the market. Gillette, the market leader, was left behind without a stainless-steel blade of its own to compete, and profits slumped in 1963 and 1964. Gillette recovered much of its market share through a simple strategy: develop a better blade and initiate aggressive advertising campaign emphasizing quality. After its own blade hit the market, Gillette's market share stabilized at 60% to 65%, compared to 70% to 75% before the challenge.

Vincent C. Ziegler, head of the company's North American razor operation, had developed the razor-marketing strategy, and when Gillette reorganized in July 1964, Ziegler was named president. He took over as chairman of the board in 1965. The stainless-steel blade controversy taught Ziegler not to rely on one product. He saw Gillette as "a diversified consumer products company," and promoted both internal development of new product lines and acquisition of other companies.

During the later 1960s Gillette pursued this strategy actively, but with mixed results. A new line of Toni hair-coloring products failed, as did Earth Born shampoos, luxury perfumes, and a line of small electronic items such as digital watches, calculators, smoke alarms, and fire extinguishers. Many of the companies Gillette acquired, such as Eve of Roma high-fashion perfume, Buxton leather goods, Welcome Wagon, and Hydroponic Chemical Company—which produces Hyponex plant foods—never found the fit with Gillette comfortable. The acquisitions led to shrinking profit margins.

Gillette did have some successes. The Trac II twin-blade shaving system introduced in the 1970s was a success, and the 1970 acquisition of the French S.T. Dupont gave Gillette the disposable Cricket lighter, which Gillette introduced to the U.S. market.

By the mid-1970s Ziegler was ready to retire, and began to groom outsider Edward Gelsthorpe to succeed him, but Gelsthorpe left Gillette to join United Brands, now Chiquita Brands, 15 months after his appointment as president. Ziegler next tapped Colman M. Mockler Jr. to replace him when he retired in 1975. Mockler had been at Gillette since 1957 and had an entirely different background and style than Ziegler. He had come up from the financial end of the business rather than sales.

Mockler moderated Ziegler's diversification policy. He concentrated on a limited number of promising markets, particularly high-volume, repeat-purchase consumer items, selling Ziegler's least sucessful acquisitions and pumping money into promising companies compatible with already-existing manufacturing or distribution capabilities. Mockler stuck with the Cricket disposable lighter even though high introductory marketing costs and a costly price war with the Bic Pen Corporation, owned by the French Société Bic kept it from showing a profit.

Mockler also held on to the West German Braun company. Ziegler had bought the family-owned business in 1967 to gain entry to the European electric-shaver market and for the quality and style of its small-appliance designs. Mockler pared Braun's less profitable lines and rode out a Justice Department antitrust suit against the acquisition. The suit eventually prevented Gillette from introducing Braun shavers in the U.S. market before 1984. Mockler also increased Gillette's advertising budget and undertook companywide cost-cutting measures in all other divisions. Before the results of those policies could be seen, Mockler faced other problems. Growing fear of fluorocarbons, which deplete the earth's ozone layer, affected sales of products in aerosol cans during the 1970s.

Gillette eventually developed new product-delivery systems to replace aerosol cans, such as non-aerosol pumps and roll-ons, for Gillette's already-established product line, and he put advertising dollars behind the products, which included Right Guard and Soft & Dri deodorants and Adorn and White Rain hair sprays. He also started development of a new deodorant product, Dry Idea, which feels dry when applied. Dry Idea was launched in 1978 after two years of development at a cost of $118 million. It quickly recovered a quarter of the deodorant market for Gillette.

Gillette faced a more serious threat from Bic. In the 1960s Bic came to the United States with a 19¢ disposable pen, which made dramatic cuts into sales of Gillette's 98¢ Paper Mate pens. In the 1970s Bic attacked Gillette's Cricket disposable lighter with its own disposable lighter. Since the Cricket was more expensive to make—it had more moving parts than the Bic—Gillette was losing the price war. Lighters and pens, however, produced only 15% of Gillette's pretax profits; razor blades accounted for 71% of profits. When Bic began producing disposable razors and purchased American Safety Razor, with its 13% of the blade market, from Personna and Gem blades, Gillette had to respond. Gillette countered by competing with Bic on price while emphasizing the higher quality of its products. Gillette brought out the Eraser Mate pen despite marketing studies that questioned demand for an erasable pen, and sales soared. By 1980 Gillette had improved profitablity despite the attack by Bic.

Mockler's policies led to a higher profit margin and a surplus of cash. That in turn led to a new threat in the mid-1980s: the threat of takeover. In 1986 Ronald O. Perelman, head of Revlon, offered $4.1 billion for Gillette. He was attracted by Gillette's well-known personal-care brands, the possibility of combining the sales and distribution systems of the two companies, and Gillette's expertise in marketing abroad.

Gillette rejected Revlon's offer of $65 a share and bought back stock from Perelman at $59.50 a share and paid some expenses, for a total of $558 million. Revlon made two other unsolicited requests to buy the company in 1987, both of which were refused by the Gillette board of directors.

In response to the takeover threats, Gillette reorganized top management; thinned out its workforce through layoffs; modernized its plants while shifting some production capacity to lower-cost locations; and sold many smaller and less profitable divisions.

That was not the end of the takeover threats. In early 1988 Coniston Partners announced that it had acquired approximately 6% of the company and was determined to replace four members of Gillette's 12-member board so it could influence company policy. Members of the partnership said they would actively seek offers to sell or dismantle Gillette if they managed to get representation on the board. Coniston Partners's battle to get shareholders' proxy rights was intense, but in 1988 Gillette came out on top with 52% of the votes for directors to Coniston's 48%. The matter was finally resolved when Gillette instituted a stock repurchase for all shareholders, which included 16 million of Coniston's 112 million shares at $45 a share.

Finally, in August 1989, Warren Buffett's Berkshire Hathaway bought $600 million of Gillette convertible preferred shares. The deal potentially placed 11% of Gillette's stock with Buffett, who had agreed to give the company the right of first refusal on the block, should he wish to sell it. The friendly agreement decreased the threat of takeover, though it tightened up cash flow at the company. Buffett's dividend was $52.5 million a year.

With takeover threats behind it and restructuring completed, Gillette returned to emphasizing its powerful brand names and its bread and butter, shaving products. While toiletries and cosmetics are low-margin items and profitable stationery products account for only 9% of the company's total profits, razors and blades still account for a little over 70% of profits. Gillette has brought in a new head of shaving operations, John W. Symons, formerly head of European operations, and developed new ad campaigns to emphasize the more profitable shaving systems over disposable shavers such as its own Good News.

In October 1989, Gillette unveiled the Sensor shaving system, which features thinner blades mounted on springs by lasers so they can follow contours. The blades, to be used in a permanent shaving system, cost close to $200 million to develop and commanded about $100 million in advertising.

Gillette made another effort to expand its presence in shaving when it attempted to buy the U.S. and non-European operations of its old competitor, Wilkinson Sword, early in 1990. The Justice Department blocked the sale of Wilkinson's U.S. interests since Gillette controls about half the U.S. market and Wilkinson is number-four in the market with about 3%. The company is still investing about $150 million in an attempt to enhance its position in shaving products.

Gillette's reorganization indicates that the company is willing to take the necessary steps to remain highly profitable. The company is emphasizing traditional strengths in shaving equipment through technological development and acquisitions. The company is also returning to a heavy use of advertising in support of its shaving products. If these trends continue, Gillette should remain on the cutting edge of the personal-care business.

Principal Subsidiaries: Compañia Gillette de Argentina; Gillette (Australia) Pty. Ltd.; Braun Inc.; Gillette Beteiligungs—

GmbH (Germany); Gillette do Brasil, Inc.; Rio Manufacturing Co.; Gillette Canada Inc.; Gillette de Colombia S.A.; Colton Development, Inc.; Colton Gulf Coast, Inc.; Colton East, Inc.; Colton North Central, Inc.; Colton West, Inc.; Gillette Capital Corporation; Gillette Direct Response Group, Inc.; Gillette Española, S.A. (Spain); Gillette Foreign Sales Corporation Ltd. (Jamaica); Gillette France S.N.C. (99.9%); Compañia Giva, S.A.; Compania Interamericana Gillette, S.A. (Panama); Gillette Internile S.A.E. (Egypt, 80%); Inversiones Gilco (Chile) Limitada; Gillette Italy S.p.A.; Jafra Cosmetics, S.A. de C.V. (Mexico, 74%); Gillette (Japan) Inc.; Gillette de Mexico, Inc., Mexico Manufacturing Co.; Gillette del Peru, Inc.; Lima Manufacturing Co.; Gillette (Philippines), Inc.; Gillette South Africa Ltd.; Gillette (Switzerland) A.G.; Gillette Industries Ltd. (U.K.); The Gillette Company.

Further Reading: "The Gillette Company, 1901–1976," *Gillette News,* 1977; Adams, Russell B., Jr., *King C. Gillette: the Man and His Wonderful Shaving Device,* Boston, Little, Brown & Co., 1978; "Chronology," Gillette corporate typescript, 1989.

—Ginger G. Rodriguez

HENKEL KGAA

Henkelstrasse 67
4000 Düsseldorf 1
Federal Republic of Germany
(211) 7971
Fax: (211) 798 4008

Public Company
Incorporated: 1876 as Henkel & Cie
Employees: 38,145
Sales: DM11.64 billion (US$6.89 billion)
Stock Exchanges: Düsseldorf Frankfurt Zürich Vienna

In terms of technology, marketing, and staff management, Henkel's first century was characterized by adaptability and opportunism. This has led to the rise of a company which, though still recognizable as the Henkel family business, is one of Germany's largest chemical concern. The Henkel Group does more than two-thirds of its trade outside its home country, and operates not only throughout Europe but also in Africa, India, the Far East, Australasia, North America, and South America. Its best-known products, detergents and household cleansers, accounted for 31% of 1989 sales, but it also produces chemicals, which were 31% of sales; institutional hygiene and industrial cleaning products, which were 15% of sales; adhesives and related products, which were 15% of sales; and cosmetics and toiletries, which were 7% of sales.

Henkel's roots go back to September 26, 1876, when Fritz Henkel founded Henkel & Cie, a three-man company based in Aachen and making a ''Universal Detergent.'' Henkel was from the Hesse region, and was then aged 28. Two years later, the company launched one of the first German consumer products to bear a brand name. This was Henkel's Bleaching Soda. The packet bore the company's early trademark, a benevolent-looking lion in front of a halo of sunbeams. The same year, 1878, saw the young firm's move to a new factory in Düsseldorf, where the company still has its headquarters. The actual site changed in 1899, when Henkel transferred production to a much larger plant at Düsseldorf-Holthausen. Convenient for transporting goods either by railway or on the Rhine, this was to be Henkel's permanent home. Over the years, however, it has grown from 600,000 square feet to 14 million square feet. In 1877 and 1879 Fritz Henkel bought out his two co-founders, and from then on control was kept firmly in the family.

From the start Henkel appreciated the power that the control of raw materials confers. Not only does such control insulate the manufacturer from the vagaries of third-party suppliers; it also puts control of ingredient quality into its hands. Sodium silicate, or water glass, was one of the main ingredients of Henkel's detergents; accordingly in 1884 Henkel acquired the Rheinische Wasserglasfabrik and started to make its own water glass. Already the importance of research and development was appreciated; the process for making water glass was improved upon to the point where, in 1898, Henkel was to patent its own process. Today Henkel owns the largest water glass production operation in Europe.

The drive to control as much of the production process as possible continued to be apparent. In 1908 and 1909 Henkel opened soap factories for detergent production and a fat-splitting plant for fatty acid production, which in turn went into the soap. In 1910 came a plant to process glycerol, a by-product of the manufacture of fatty acids.

In 1893 Fritz Henkel had welcomed his elder son, 18-year-old Fritz Henkel Jr., into the firm as an apprentice. In due course, Fritz was to play a key role in developing the company's innovative policy of marketing under brand names. Fritz Henkel Jr.'s brother, Hugo Henkel—a trained chemist—joined the family firm 12 years later. While contributing to the company's technological side in particular, he helped Henkel to diversify into the well-rounded chemical business we know today.

At the turn of the century, Henkel was already demonstrating a forward-looking concern for the welfare of its 80 employees: it provided free staff lunches from 1900. A few years later Henkel became involved in a building cooperative providing rental housing for workers' families and low-cost mortgages for executives. Recreation facilities such as gyms were supplied by the firm, as were the washrooms, which factory workers needed in order to comply with the company stipulation that they bathe at least once a week. Some early staff benefits may strike the modern reader as overly paternalistic: for example, female workers who announced their intention of getting married were offered a trousseau and a cookery and domestic-science course to be taken at the firm's expense.

The year 1907 was exceptionally important for product development. It marked the launch of Henkel's arguably most famous brand, the revolutionary detergent Persil. The name came from two of its most important ingredients, a perborate and a silicate. The product, Henkel's own invention was almost simultaneously invented by two Stuttgart chemists. To be on the safe side, Henkel acquired the chemists' patent but never used it. Three years later, after further intensive research on Henkel's part, the product was registered as Persil. The product was a breakthrough in labor-saving since no rubbing or bleaching was required to clean clothes.

Since those early days, the brand name Persil has caused some confusion. In 1909, the English firm of Joseph Crosfield acquired the patent rights and trademarks of Persil for the United Kingdom and various British, Dutch, and Danish colonies. Crosfield was later absorbed by Lever Brothers, which in turn became part of Unilever. Today both Henkel and Unilever continue to market a product named Persil. In Western Europe, for example, Unilever owns the trademark

Persil in Britain and France, while Henkel has Germany, Belgium, Luxembourg, the Netherlands, Italy, and Denmark. Some brushes with the EEC authorities over the market-sharing aspects of this arrangement were resolved in 1978. Different logos are used and there are no restrictive practices. Henkel anticipates no problems over continuing the arrangement in the unified markets of 1992.

In the early 1900s, Henkel's use of brand names was innovative. Its products were easy to spot by their packaging and were widely distributed. Henkel felt that there was more to be gained by informative advertising than from what would now be called hype. The objectives were to make the Henkel name synonymous with quality and reliability, and to keep reminding the public of Henkel's presence by having its goods and name on display everywhere. As early as 1911, motorized delivery vans bearing the Henkel livery were to be seen in Düsseldorf. There was a famous slogan, "Persil bleibt Persil"—"Persil remains Persil." By 1914, Henkel had 120 salesmen out in the field.

Henkel had been quick to set up marketing operations in Germany's neighbor countries. In 1913 Henkel opened a subsidiary, the first of many, at Basel-Pratteln in Switzerland, a country whose appetite for Persil and bleaching soda had already proved particularly healthy. Four years later it was to acquire another subsidiary, this time German, when it bought Matthes & Weber of Duisburg.

Henkel played a patriotic part in World War I. Jobs of workers who went to the defence of their country were kept open for their return—though 71 never returned. A hospital was set up for the employees who were wounded. Henkel employees fighting in the German trenches continued to receive not only food parcels but also copies of the company newspaper, which had begun to be published in 1914.

Rationing of oils and fats made it necessary in 1916 to bring in a low-soap version of Persil. In general, the war had less effect on Henkel's business than did the Allied occupation of the Rhineland from 1919 onwards. Some of the effects of the occupation were positive. The danger that the Holthausen plant would be cut off from its customer base led to the construction of a new factory at Genthin in central Germany, which opened in 1921. The extra capacity would be valuable later on.

The war was followed in Germany by a period of hyperinflation. At its peak, in November 1923, a packet of Persil cost 1.25 billion marks. Once this situation was brought under control, Henkel's expansion continued apace, in line with a general western European trend towards higher standards of living, and in particular of personal and domestic hygiene. In Germany, soap products were becoming affordable, and thanks in part to Henkel's advertisements, their virtues were well known. For most of its first half-century the company had focused on the manufacture of detergent and cleaning products. A period of vigorous diversification began in the 1920s under the guidance of Hugo Henkel, now supported not only by his sons but by a board of eight directors. This activity continued throughout the interwar period, but the stimulus to diversify again came from the occupation of the Rhineland. In 1923, fearing that the occupying forces would restrict the supply of the adhesives it needed for detergent packaging, Henkel started to manufacture its own glues. With characteristic opportunism, it was soon putting the glue department's products on the market. Today, Henkel can claim the most comprehensive range of adhesives in the world.

Henkel's next move, in 1924, was to start marketing cleaning products aimed at institutional and industrial markets. In 1929 the P3 phosphate-based cleaning agents were added to Henkel's product lines for industrial machinery and food production. By buying Thompson-Werke in 1930 and Deutsche Hydrierwerke in 1932, it acquired an interest in the market for home-care products, such as polishes and scouring powders, and increased its capacity to manufacture the fatty alcohols needed for its detergents.

Henkel's acquisition of Böhme-Fettchemie, Chemnitz, in 1935, followed the latter's launch of a new type of detergent named Fewa. This synthetic product, designed to wash delicate fabrics, was the first of its kind. The same year saw the foundation by Henkel of a German whaling association which sent a fleet to the Antarctic Ocean three times in the prewar years. The fleet's catches were of relevance to oleochemical production. By 1939 Henkel could boast of 15 European plants in addition to the main factory in Düsseldorf.

Henkel's expansion of its product range between the wars meant more research and development. A laboratory had existed since the early 1900s, but in 1920 a test department for new products was set up. At first the focus was inorganic chemistry, but later on other branches of chemistry were included. Further new laboratories were built and equipped during the 1930s, culminating in a major laboratory which opened on the Deutsche Hydrierwerke site at Rodleben, shortly before the outbreak of World War II, designed to support all of Henkel's products. Cash-starved Germany could ill afford to import natural fats and so one important object of research was the development of soapless washing powders. By 1936 Henkel was producing powders using fatty acids derived from coal. Meanwhile, improvements had been made in the manufacturing process: packaging of detergents became fully automatic in 1926.

Always keen to take advantage of new technology in management as well as production, Henkel installed an automatic telephone exchange in 1928, and in 1935 became the first subscriber to the Düsseldorf teleprinter service.

Alongside its policy of expansion and diversification in the interwar period, Henkel maintained an imaginative approach to advertising. Skywriting planes emblazoned the name of Persil far above the heads of astonished German spectators, and in an interesting variation on the sandwich board, six men carried through the streets snow-white umbrellas bearing the name "Persil." Henkel continued to forge ahead in the field of staff management and welfare. First-aid facilities, the precursor of today's Henkel staff medical centers, had arrived in 1912. A pension scheme began three years later. In 1925 a training structure for specialist staff was established, and two years later Henkel became the first member of the German chemical industry to appoint a safety engineer to reduce the risk of accidents.

Jost Henkel, son of Hugo Henkel, had joined the company in 1933, and it was under his leadership that Henkel weathered World War II. The war itself had relatively little impact on the Düsseldorf works, although 259 employees were lost in action, prison camps, and air raids. Henkel had to abandon Persil in favor of basic, state-approved products during wartime. Once again the aftermath of war was more serious. The occupying British forces removed the Henkel family from the head of the firm, and did not allow it to return until 1947. In line with the German economy, which began to recover at that time, Henkel was able to get back on a level footing in time for its 75th anniversary in 1951.

After World War II, Henkel, under first Jost Henkel and then his brother Konrad Henkel, did not simply set about rebuilding what it had before, but entered one new market after another, diversifying its products through innovation and acquisition, and gaining representation in parts of the world not previously penetrated. In 1946, the Düsseldorf factory started to manufacture chemical products for use in the textile and leather industries, and the Poly hair-care brand was launched. A couple of years later, personal hygiene and cosmetic products were added to the range. During this period, Henkel's production facilities for oil-related chemicals were brought together at the Düsseldorf-Holthausen plant, giving a greatly increased capacity for the manufacture of ingredients for soaps, detergents, cosmetics, and pharmaceutical products. In 1951 Pril dishwashing liquid was introduced. During the 1950s, the company set up manufacturing plants in Japan and Brazil, gaining its first footholds in the East Asian and South American marketplaces.

The acquisition of a U.S. company, Standard Chemical Products, in 1960, heralded the two decades of Henkel's most dramatic expansion. To give a solid foundation to its growth program, the Henkel Group opened a state-of-the-art research center in 1962 at the main Düsseldorf plant. This laboratory complex had been in phased construction since 1959 and was not completed until 1967.

Pritt, the solid glue in a cylindrical tube, was launched in 1969, contributing to Henkel's current lead in the European adhesive market.

By the 1970s, there was mounting concern about the environmental impact of the chemical industry in general, and specifically about the use of phosphates in detergents. As early as 1973, Henkel was taking the first steps toward patenting a compound known as Sasil, which was to prove a good substitute for the offending phosphates. Now there could be a phosphate-free Persil. This discovery has helped Henkel to win its present position in the European detergent market. Henkel can also collect license fees from other users of Sasil or related products.

A biological institute was added to Henkel's group of laboratories in 1974. The scientists and technologists who work there concentrate on the protection of the consumer and the environment.

When the founder, Fritz Henkel, died in 1930, ownership of the company had been divided between the families of his three children. By 1985, control was held by 66 family members who in that year decided, together with president Helmut Sihler, that it was time to go public. So Henkel shares were issued at last to an eager market. At the same time steps were taken to guard against excessive outside interference: the issue was of non-voting preferred shares, and all ordinary shares were to belong to the family at least until the year 2000.

Expansion continued apace through the 1980s, most notably with the acquisition of Union Générale de Savonnerie in France, and of Parker, maker of metal surface treatment; Oxy Process Chemicals; and Emery Group, a base-materials and chemicals company, in the United States. An important new production plant opened in Malaysia in 1984.

Henkel has succeeded in maintaining a sound balance sheet throughout all its acquisition activities. Although outsiders sometimes regard the group as over-diversified, its management is satisfied with the mix. It has clear rules for acquisition: not to diversify through acquisition, to retain acquired companies' existing management, and to purchase companies that comply with their profit requirements. Unprofitable companies, or those which do not fit in, are rejected. Strategic relationships are formed, and minority shareholdings bought as the least risky and cheapest way of getting a foothold in a new market. *The Wall Street Journal,* November 25, 1988, has described Henkel's business approach as "a blend of America's short-term emphasis on profit and West Germany's long-term emphasis on the future." Certainly, Henkel's consistently healthy results give credibility to its strategies.

In its research and development, Henkel continues to target environmental and consumer protection issues. DM282 million was spent on this area in 1989 alone, while DM30 million was earmarked for related capital expenditure. In addition to measures to develop safer and more environmentally sound products in all ranges, there are programs to minimize the pollution generated by the manufacturing plants. Henkel claims that environmental damage caused by its parent plant has been decreased by between 50% and 75% between 1984 and 1990.

On the marketing and production front Henkel says it is preparing intensively for the single European market. It is designing its branding concepts with Europe in mind and is reviewing its distribution and production facilities. Management development programs too are being specifically targeted at international business. Language classes are offered to staff throughout the group.

Konrad Henkel, the grandson of founder Fritz Henkel, continues as chairman of the supervisory board and shareholders' committee until the end of 1990, working alongside Sihler to ensure that Henkel, though a global company operating in more than 150 locations, upholds its family traditions of technical advance, active marketing, and looking after its staff.

Principal Subsidiaries: Chemische Fabrik Grünau GmbH; Matthes & Weber GmbH; Henkel Austria Gesellschaft mbH; S.A. Henkel Belgium N.V.; Henkel France S.A.; Société des Produits Chimiques du Sidobre-Sinnova S.A. (France); Henkel Chemicals Limited (U.K.); Henkel Italiana S.p.A. (Italy); Henkel Sud S.p.A. (Italy); Henkel Chimica S.p.A. (Italy); Henkel Nederland BV (Netherlands); Henkel Ibérica S.A. (Spain); Henkel & Cie AG (Switzerland); Turyag A.S. (Turkey); Türk Henkel A.S. (Turkey); Henkel S.A. Industrias Quimicas (Brazil); Henkel Hakusui Corp. (Japan); Mexico Group (Mexico); Henkel of America, Inc. (U.S.A.); GFC Gesellschaft für Chemiewerte mbH (46%); The Clorox Company (U.S.A., 27.3%); Loctite Corporation (U.S.A., 26.7%).

Furthur Reading: 1876–1976 Hundert Jahre Henkel, Düsseldorf, Henkel, [1976]; Schöne, Manfred, *Stammwerk Henkel*

80 Jahre in Düsseldorf-Holthausen, Düsseldorf, Henkel, 1981; O'Boyle, Thomas F., "Henkel Makes Mark with Acquisitions," *The Wall Street Journal/Europe,* November 25, 1988; Marsh, Peter, "The Secret is in the Mix for Germany's Brightest," *Financial Times,* December 7, 1988; *Henkel—Specialist in Applied Chemistry,* Düsseldorf, Henkel, 1989; *Henkel Past and Present,* Düsseldorf, Henkel, [n.d.].

—Alison Classe and Olive Classe

Johnson & Johnson

JOHNSON & JOHNSON

One Johnson & Johnson Plaza
New Brunswick, New Jersey 08933
U.S.A.
(201) 524-0400
Fax: (201) 214-0332

Public Company
Incorporated: 1887
Employees: 83,100
Sales: $9.76 billion
Stock Exchange: New York

Johnson & Johnson is an international giant in the manufacture and sale of a wide range of consumer and professional pharmaceutical, health-care and medical products. The world's largest manufacturer of health-care products, it traces its beginnings to the late 1800s when Joseph Lister's discovery that airborne germs were a source of infection in operating rooms sparked the imagination of Robert Wood Johnson, a New England druggist. Johnson joined forces with his brothers, James Wood Johnson and Edward Mead Johnson, and the three began producing dressings in 1886 in New Brunswick, New Jersey, with 14 employees in a former wallpaper factory.

Because Lister's recommended method for sterilization—spraying the operating room with carbolic acid—was found to be impractical and cumbersome, Johnson & Johnson (J&J) found a ready market for its product. The percentage of deaths due to infections following surgery was quite high and hospitals were eager to find a solution.

J&J's first product was an improved medicinal plaster that used medical compounds mixed in an adhesive. Soon afterward, the company designed a soft, absorbant cotton-and-gauze dressing, and Robert Wood Johnson's dream was realized. Mass production began and the dressings were shipped in large quantities throughout the United States. By 1890 J&J was using dry heat to sterilize the bandages.

The establishment of a bacteriological laboratory in 1891 gave research a boost and by the following year the company had met accepted requirements for a sterile product. By introducing dry heat, steam, and pressure throughout the manufacturing process, Johnson & Johnson was able to guarantee the sterility of its bandages. The adhesive bandage was further improved in 1899 when, with the cooperation of surgeons, Johnson & Johnson introduced a zinc oxide–based adhesive plaster that was stronger and overcame much of the problem of the skin irritation that plagued many patients. J&J's fourth original design was an improved method for sterilizing catgut sutures.

From the beginning, J&J was an advocate of antiseptic surgical procedures. In 1888 the company published *Modern Methods of Antiseptic Wound Treatment,* a text used by physicians for many years. That same year, Fred B. Kilmer began his 45-year stint as scientific director at J&J. A well-known science and medicine writer, and father of poet Joyce Kilmer, Fred Kilmer wrote influential articles for J&J's publications, including *Red Cross Notes* and *The Red Cross Messenger.* Physicians, pharmacists, and the general public were encouraged to use antisepsic methods, and Johnson & Johnson products were promoted.

R.W. Johnson died in 1910 and was succeeded as chairman by his brother James. It was then that the company began to grow quickly. To guarantee a source for the company's increasing need for textile materials, J&J purchased Chicopee Manufacturing Corporation in 1916. The first international affiliate was founded in Canada in 1919. Several years later, Robert W. Johnson's sons, Robert Johnson, and J. Seward Johnson, returned from an around-the-world tour that had convinced them that Johnson & Johnson should expand overseas. Consequently, Johnson & Johnson Limited was established in Great Britain a year later. Diversification continued with the invention of Band-Aid brand adhesive bandages and Johnson's Baby Cream in the early 1920s.

The younger Robert Johnson, who came to be known as "the General," had joined the company as a mill hand while still in his teens. By the age of 25, he had become a vice president, and was ultimately elected president in 1932. Johnson was dynamic and restless and had a keen sense of duty. His moniker derived from the fact that he had attained the rank of brigadier general in World War II and served as vice chairman of the War Production Board.

The General subscribed to a decentralized form of business and was the driving force behind Johnson & Johnson's organizational structure, in which divisions and affiliates were given autonomy to direct their own operations. This policy coincided with a move into pharmaceuticals, hygiene products, and textiles. During Robert Johnson's tenure, the division for the manufacture of surgical packs and gowns became Surgikos, Inc.; the department for sanitary napkin production was initially called the Modess division and then became the Personal Products Company; birth control products were under the supervision of the Ortho Pharmaceutical Corporation; and the separate division for suture business became Ethicon, Inc. In 1959, Johnson & Johnson acquired McNeil Laboratories, a producer of prescription drugs, and Cilag-Chemie, a Swiss pharmaceutical firm. When the General took over as head of J&J, annual sales were $11 million. At the time of his death in 1968, sales had reached $700 million.

Following his father's lead as an advocate of public welfare, Johnson spoke out in favor of raising the minimum wage, improving conditions in factories, and emphasizing business' responsibility to society. Johnson called for management to restore workers' self-respect and to create programs that would improve workers' skills and better prepare them for success in a modern industrial society. As the head of J&J, Johnson wrote a credo outlining the company's four areas of social responsibility. This credo states that the company's responsibility is first to its customers; second its to its employees; third to the community and environment; and fourth to the stockholders.

In 1959 McNeil Pharmaceutical Company was purchased by Johnson & Johnson. In that same year Cilag-Chemie, a Swiss pharmaceutical firm was purchased, followed in two years by the purchase of Janssen Pharmaceutica.

In 1963 Johnson retired. Although he remained active in the business, chairmanship of the company went outside the family for the first time. Johnson's immediate successor was Philip Hofmann, who, much like the General, had started as a shipping clerk and worked his way up the ladder. During Hofmann's ten-year term as chairman, Johnson & Johnson's domestic and overseas affiliates flourished. Hofmann was a firm believer in decentralization and encouraged the training of local experts to supervise operations in their respective countries. Foreign management was organized along product lines rather than geographically, with plant managers reporting to a person with expertise in the field.

In the early 1960s federal regulation of the health-care industry was increasing. When James Burke, who had come to Johnson & Johnson from the marketing department of Procter & Gamble, became president of J&J's Domestic Operating Company in 1966, the company was looking for ways to increase profits from its consumer products to offset possible slowdowns in the professional-products divisions. By luring top marketing people from Procter & Gamble, Burke was able to put together several highly successful advertising campaigns. The first introduced Carefree and Stayfree sanitary napkins into a market that was dominated by the acknowledged feminine-products leader, Kimberly-Clark. Usually limited to women's magazines, advertisments for feminine hygiene products were low-key and discreet. Under Burke's direction, Johnson & Johnson took a more open approach and advertised Carefree and Stayfree on television. By 1978, J&J had captured half of the market.

One of Burke's biggest challenges was Tylenol, a non-aspirin pain reliever. Ever since J&J had acquired McNeil Laboratories, maker of Tylenol, the drug had been marketed as a high-priced product. Burke saw the opportunity to make Tylenol more than that. Johnson & Johnson's policy of decentralization and autonomy meant that each of the companies had its own boss with his own ideas about how to market his product. Therefore, the consumer products division developed its own non-aspirin product and called it Truce. It failed to attract consumers.

In 1975, Burke got the chance he was waiting for. Bristol-Myers Company introduced Datril and advertised that it had the same ingredients as Tylenol but was available at a significantly lower price. Burke convinced J&J Chairman Richard Sellars that they should meet this competition head on by dropping Tylenol's price to meet Datril's. With Sellar's approval, Burke took Tylenol into the mass-marketing arena, slashed its price, and ended up beating not only Datril, but number-one Anacin as well. This signaled the beginning of an ongoing battle between American Home Products, maker of Anacin, and McNeil Laboratories. Each new campaign brought a new round of lawsuits as the two products vied for the title of top pain reliever. Sellars, Hofmann's protege, had become chairman in 1973, but served for only three years. Burke succeeded Sellars in 1976 as CEO and chairman of the board, and David R. Clare was appointed president.

Johnson & Johnson had always maintained a balance between the many divisions in its operations; particularly between mass consumer products and specialized professional products. No single J&J product accounted for as much as 5% of the company's total sales. With Burke at the helm, consumer products began to be promoted aggressively, and Tylenol pain reliever became Johnson & Johnson's number-one seller.

Burke did not turn his back on the company's position as a leader in professional health-care products. In May, 1977 Extracorporeal Medical Specialties, a manufacturer of kidney dialysis and intravenous treatment products, became part of the corporation. Three years later, J&J acquired Iolab Corporation, maker of ocular lenses for cataract surgery, and effectively entered the field of eye care and ophthalmic pharmaceuticals. The increased in-house development of critical-care products resulted in the creation of Critikon, Inc., in 1979, and in 1983 Johnson & Johnson Hospital Services was created to develop and implement corporate marketing programs.

In September, 1982 several containers of Tylenol capsules were found to have been laced with cyanide in Chicago. Seven people died. Johnson & Johnson was suddenly faced with the greatest challenge of its corporate life, and the packaging of over-the-counter drugs was changed forever. Johnson & Johnson recalled all Tylenol products from store shelves. Advertising of the pain reliever had been canceled immediately. After the Food and Drug Administration (FDA) found that the tampering had been done at the retail level rather than during manufacturing, Johnson & Johnson was left with the problem of how to save its number-one product and its reputation. In the week after the cyanide deaths, Johnson & Johnson's stock dropped 18% and its prime competitors' products, Datril and Anacin-3, were in such demand that supplies were back-ordered.

Until the mass marketing of Tylenol, no one product had represented a large portion of the company's profits. In addition, J&J's policy of decentralization meant that the general public did not know how strong a hold the corporation had on the health-care market. After the tampering, public awareness that Johnson & Johnson owned McNeil Laboratories reached 47%.

Johnson & Johnson was able to recoup its losses through several marketing strategies. The company ran a one-time ad that explained how to exchange Tylenol capsules for tablets or refunds, worked closely with the press, responding directly to reporters' questions as a means for keeping the public up-to-date. The company also placed a coupon for $2.50 off any Tylenol product in newspapers across the country. In addition to reimbursing consumers for Tylenol capsules they may have discarded during the tampering incident, the coupon offered an incentive for purchasing Tylenol in other forms.

Within weeks of the poisoning incidents, the FDA issued guidelines for tamper-resistant packaging for the entire food and drug industry. To bolster public confidence in its product, J&J used three layers of protection, two more than recommended, when Tylenol was put back on store shelves. Within months of the cynanide poisoning, Johnson &

Johnson was gaining back its share of the pain-reliever market. By 1989, Tylenol sales were $500 million annually.

Johnson & Johnson's foray into the disposable-diaper market was less spectacular. A failed attempt to take an appreciable piece of the action from Proctor & Gamble's Pampers in the 1960s had left J&J executives wary of another try. However, in the 1970s, James Burke used his past successes to convince them to try again. J&J stopped selling disposable diapers in the United States in 1981, however.

Burke and Clare retired in 1989 and were succeeded by three men: CEO and Chairman Ralph S. Larsen, who came from the consumer section; Vice Chairman Robert E. Campbell, who had headed the professional sector; and President Robert N. Wilson, who had headed the pharmaceutical sector. The three men were responsible for overseeing the network of 175 companies in 54 countries.

Principal Subsidiaries: Advanced Care Products; Chicopee; Codman & Shurtleff, Inc.; Critikon, Inc.; Devro, Inc.; Ethicon, Inc.; Iolab Corporation; Janssen Pharmaceutica Inc.; Critikon Canada Inc.; Johnson & Johnson Consumer Products, Inc.; Johnson & Johnson Development Corporation; Johnson & Johnson Finance Corporation; Johnson & Johnson Health Management, Inc.; Johnson & Johnson Hospital Services, Inc.; Johnson & Johnson Interventional Systems; Johnson & Johnson Medical Inc.; Johnson & Johnson Othopaedics, Inc.; Johnson & Johnson Professional Diagnostics, Inc.; LifeScan, Inc.; McNeil Consumer Products Company; McNeil Pharmaceutical; Noramco, Inc.; Ortho Diagnostic Systems Inc.; Ortho Pharmaceutical Corporation; Personal Products Company; Therakos, Inc.; Vistakon, Inc.

Further Reading: Brief History of Johnson & Johnson, New Brunswick, New Jersey, Johnson & Johnson, 1989.

—Mary F. Sworsky

KAO CORPORATION

14-10, Nihonbashi Kayabacho 1-chome
Chuo-ku, Tokyo 103
Japan
(03) 3660-7111
Fax: (03) 3660-7044

Public Company
Incorporated: 1887 as Kao Soap Company, Ltd.
Employees: 6,768
Sales: ¥620.43 billion (US$4.32 billion)
Stock Exchanges: Tokyo Osaka

Kao Corporation, a highly diversified manufacturer of household and personal-care products, as well as industrial and specialty chemicals, has been called the Procter & Gamble of Japan. Founded in 1887 as Kao (face) Soap Company, by the Nagase family, the company introduced its first soap product in 1890. By the end of the 1920s, Kao had developed coconut alcohol–based synthetic detergents, and after World War II, began manufacturing heavy-duty detergents.

It is a company in which 25% of the employees are involved in research, particularly in the field of surface technology. Early research in the properties of oils and fats, the basic elements in soap, allowed Kao to expand its product line quickly to include finishing products, polishing agents, waxes, insecticides, antiseptics, fungicides, and deodorants.

The biggest advertiser in Japan, Kao's approach is unique. Most Japanese advertisments for detergents and personal-care products are image-oriented, but Kao focuses on the products themselves. Commercials for Sofina skin-care products, for example, show freshly cleaned skin through the lens of a microscope.

A major force behind this technical approach had been Yoshio Maruta, Kao's chairman in 1990 and the company's president from 1971 to 1990. Maruta, who holds a doctorate in chemical engineering and 16 patents, invented a process for producing aircraft lubricant from vegetable oil during World War II, when Japanese supplies of petroleum were low. An aggressive and charismatic leader, Maruta often is criticized for his domineering style that leaves little room for open discussion. He has a fierce respect for consumers, however. As one of his assistants told *Forbes*, July 25, 1988, "You can cheat housewives once, but not twice." Maruta's successor as president, Fumikatsu Tokiwa, joined the company in 1965 in the research-and-development library and is likely to continue the company's emphasis on in-depth research.

With a solid home base and a reputation for being one of Japan's best-managed companies, Kao's top products are Attack detergent and the Sofina line of cosmetics. In addition, Kao consistently is in the first or second position with its soap products, disposable diapers, sanitary napkins, and hair-care products.

Kao spent several decades preparing for its entrance into the European and U.S. markets. The company modifies its products to compete worldwide. In research laboratories in Berlin, Paris, Barcelona, Los Angeles, and Taipei, Kao employees adapt the company's toiletries, cosmetics, and other products to different hair- and skin-care and bathing habits and to the local water, climate, and consumer preferences.

Such intense research operations have proved to be successful for Kao. In 1983 the company's Merries brand of disposable diapers far outsold Procter & Gamble's in Japan, because Kao had developed a highly absorbant polymer that reduced diaper rash. Before introducing Attack laundry detergent, Kao researchers collected dirt samples from around the world for four years in order to discover the bacteria that produces alkaline cellulose, an enzyme that cleans cotton. The researchers then spent two years synthesizing the enzyme through genetic engineering. The resultant detergent was four times as concentrated as cleaners that were then being sold, and Attack's share of the detergent market has since fluctuated between 30% and 50%.

In 1988 Kao acquired the Andrew Jergens Company, headquartered in Cincinnati, Ohio. Jergens now operates within the U.S. subsidiary, Kao Company of America. High Point Chemical Corporation, a specialty chemical company based in North Carolina that was acquired in 1987, supplies the raw materials for the Jergens toiletry and skin-care products. The move into Germany was made in 1989 when Kao purchased a 75% interest in Goldwell, a company that sells hair-care and beauty products through professional hairdressers around the world.

Kao's research in surface technology has led the company into the electronics-software field as well. A research project on face powders resulted in the discovery of a dispersing system that was ideal for the management of magnetic particles spread over floppy discs. With the acquisition of West Coast Telecom in Portland, Oregon; Sentinel Technologies in Hyannis, Massachusetts; and the completion of a $60 million plant in Plymouth, Massachusetts, Kao Infosystems became in 1990 the largest North American maker of 3.5-inch floppy discs.

To support the company's belief in the need for continuing education, Kao opened the Kasumigaura Creativity Center in 1989. Here employees are trained to keep current in management trends and consumer issues. In the 1990s Kao planned to enter the food arena with the introduction of both a cooking oil and a salad oil. Kao also planned to continue the decentralization of its Tokyo management base by opening regional offices in New York, Düsseldorf, and Singapore.

Principal Subsidiaries: Kao Corporation of America (U.S.A.); Kao Infosystems Company (U.S.A.); Kao-Didak Ltd. (Canada); Quimi-Kao S.A. de C.V. (Mexico); Bitumex

S.A. de C.V. (Mexico); Kao Corporation S.A. (Spain); Kao Corporation (France) SARL; Kao Corporation GmbH (Germany); Buhl Ikebana GmbH (Germany); Goldwell AG (Germany); Taiwan Kao Company, Ltd.; Kao Industrial Company (Thailand), Ltd.; Kao (Hong Kong) Limited; Kao (Singapore) Private Limited; Kao (Malaysia) Sdn. Bhd.; Fatty Chemical (Malaysia) Sdn. Bhd.; P.T. Dino Indonesia Industrial Ltd.; P.T. Polekao Indonesia Chemicals; Pilipinas Kao Incorporated (Philippines); Kao Corporation (B) Sdn. Bhd. (Brunei); Ehime Sanitary Products Company, Limited; Nivea-Kao Company, Limited; Kao-Quaker Company, Limited; Kao Engineering Company, Limited; Kao Merchandising Information Service Company, Ltd.; Kao Media Sales Co., Ltd.; Kao Professional Beauty Sales Company, Limited; Kao Cosmetics Sales Co., Ltd.; Kao Shoji Company, Limited.

Further Reading: Gray, James, ''Turnarounds/United Appeal,'' *Canadian Business,* April 1988; Tanzer, Andrew, ''High noon in Cincinnati,'' *Forbes,* July 25, 1988; *An Inexhaustible Spring: Research and Development Activities at Kao,* Tokyo, Kao Corporation, 1988; van Raalte, John A., ''A Visit with Kao,'' *HAPPI,* July 1990.

—Mary F. Sworsky

Kimberly-Clark

KIMBERLY-CLARK CORPORATION

P.O. Box 619100
DFW Airport Station
Dallas, Texas 75261
U.S.A.
(214) 830-1200
Fax: (214) 830-1289

Public Company
Incorporated: 1880 as Kimberly & Clark Company
Employees: 39,664
Sales: $5.73 billion
Stock Exchange: New York

While probably best known as the maker of industry-leading Huggies diapers and Kleenex tissues, Kimberly-Clark Corporation's products and services range from cigarette papers to air transportation. Originally a small newsprint maker, Kimberly-Clark (K-C) is now a highly diversified, international company divided into three primary operations. The first and most profitable division includes consumer products, such as tissues and feminine-, child-, and incontinence-care products; the second division includes newsprint and printing papers as well as tobacco papers and technical and correspondence paper products. Aircraft services and air transportion is the third division—its best recognized asset is Midwest Express Airlines.

Kimberly, Clark & Company was founded in Neenah, Wisconsin, in 1872 as a partnership of four men—John A. Kimberly, Charles B. Clark, Frank C. Shattuck, and Kimberly's cousin, Havilah Babcock. The company began the first paper mill in Wisconsin. Its initial product was newsprint made from linen and cotton rags. Within six years the company expanded by acquiring a majority interest in the nearby Atlas paper mill, which converted ground pulpwood into manila wrapping paper. The business was incorporated in 1880 as Kimberly & Clark Company, with John Kimberly as president. In 1889 the company constructed a large pulp- and paper-making complex on the Fox River. The community that grew up around the factory was named Kimberly, in honor of John Kimberly.

Among the company's early innovations was the paper used for rotogravure, a procedure for printing photographs with a rotary press. In 1914 researchers working with bagasse, a pulp by-product of processed sugar cane, produced creped cellulose wadding, or tissue. During World I this product, called cellucotton, was used to treat wounds in place of scarce surgical cottons. At that time field nurses also discovered that cellucotton worked well as a disposable feminine napkin. The company later recognized the commercial potential of this application, and in 1920 introduced its Kotex feminine napkin.

In 1924 the company introduced another disposable tissue product, Kleenex, to replace the face towels then used for removing cold cream. A survey showed, however, that consumers preferred to use Kleenex as a disposable handkerchief, prompting the company to alter its marketing strategy entirely. Nationwide advertisments promoting Kleenex for its current use began in 1930, and sales doubled within a year. Uncomfortable marketing such personal-care items as feminine napkins, Kimberly & Clark had created a separate sales company—International Cellucotton Products—which it contracted to manufacture Kotex and Kleenex.

During the 1920s the company built a Canadian pulp mill and power plant called Spruce Falls Power and Paper Company in Kapuskasing, Ontario. In 1925 the company formed what would become Canadian Cellucotton Products Limited, for marketing cellucotton products internationally. The following year Kimberly & Clark, in partnership with The New York Times, added a newsprint mill to the Spruce Falls complex and expanded its pulping capacity.

The company was reorganized and reincorporated in 1928 as Kimberly-Clark Corporation. That same year, as shares of Kimberly-Clark were being traded on the New York and Chicago stock exchanges for the first time, John Kimberly died. He was 90 years old and still president at the time of his death.

During the 1930s Kimberly-Clark concentrated on marketing its new products. During World War II the company devoted many of its resources to the war effort. The company also contracted Margaret Buell, creator of the cartoon strip "Little Lulu," to promote Kleenex. Buell and Little Lulu continued to promote Kleenex for Kimberly-Clark into the 1960s.

After the war, Kimberly-Clark initiated a growth program to handle revived consumer product demand. Facilities were built or acquired in Balfour, North Carolina, and Memphis, Tennessee, in 1946; and in Fullerton, California, and New Milford, Connecticut, in the late 1950s. Pulp production at Terrace Bay, Ontario, was launched in 1948, and in 1949 the company, along with a group of investors and newspaper publishers, began the large Coosa River Newsprint Company in Coosa Pines, Alabama. Kimberly-Clark acquired the Michigan-based Munising Paper Company in 1952, Neenah Paper Company in 1956, Peter J. Schweitzer, Inc.—which had mills in France and the United States—in 1957, and the American Envelope Company in 1959. International Cellucotton Products Company formally merged with its parent company in 1955, as did Coosa River Newsprint Company in 1962.

Throughout the 1960s the tampon, first manufactured by Tampax, gained favor among women, and the tampon ate into Kotex's market share. Kimberly-Clark turned its attention to new products. In 1968 the company introduced Kimbies, a disposable diaper with tape closures. Initial sales were strong despite competition from Procter & Gamble's Pampers. While K-C tended to its diverse operations, however, it failed to keep up with early disposable diaper improvements and market innovations. As a result of continued poor sales and leakage problems, Kimbies were withdrawn from the market in the mid-1970s. Competition in the infant-care product industry caused Kimberly-Clark to re-evaluate the balance between its consumer products and lumber and paper products divisions.

Darwin E. Smith, who was elected president of Kimberly-Clark in 1971, took on Procter & Gamble's challenge. Smith decided that in order to compete properly in consumer product markets Kimberly-Clark had to prune its coated-paper business. Within one year of taking control of the company, Smith initiated changes that included the sale or closure of six paper mills and the sale of more than 300,000 acres of prime northern California land. With cash reserves of more than $250 million, primarily from the land sale, Smith then inaugurated an aggressive research campaign. He assembled a talented research-and-development team by hiring specialists away from competitors. The company's advertising budget was increased substantially, and plans were made for the construction of additional production facilities.

Marketing was central to Smith's strategy for growth, as Kimberly-Clark emphasized its commitment to consumer products. Research-and-development efforts enlarged the company's technological base from traditional cellulose fiber–forming technologies to lightweight non-wovens utilizing synthetic fabrics.

A new premium-priced diaper in an hourglass shape with refastenable tapes was introduced in 1978 under the name Huggies. By 1984, Huggies had captured 50% of the higher-quality disposable diaper market. The sudden popularity of the product caught Kimberly-Clark by surprise, and it was forced to expand production to meet consumer demand.

Facial tissue and feminine-care products were also part of Kimberly-Clark's growing consumer product operations. In 1984, it was estimated that the company's Kleenex brand held 50% of the tissue market. A chemically treated virucidal tissue called Avert was test marketed that same year, but the higher price and limited utility of the product prevented it from gaining widespread popularity. Aimed at health-care institutions and at companies as a product to reduce absenteeism, Avert never really got off the ground, and in 1987 Kimberly-Clark decided not to mass market the product.

The 1980 toxic shock syndrome scare caused a slump in tampon sales. Kimberly-Clark began an aggressive advertising campaign on television for Depend incontinence products in the early 1980s. At the time, incontinence products were as unmentionable as feminine-care products had been some 60 years earlier. The promotion resulted in Depend gaining a profitable share of the incontinence-products market, and it quickly became the best-selling retail incontinence brand in the United States. In an effort to broaden its position in therapeutic and health-care products, Kimberly-Clark acquired Spenco Medical Corporation in Waco, Texas, that same year.

While sales from primary growth operations—personal-care products—were increasing, approximately 25% of Kimberly-Clark's sales continued to come from the pulp, newsprint, and paper businesses. The company further diversified its operations in 1984 by converting its regularly scheduled executive air-shuttle service into a regional commercial airline.

The company's foray into aviation was initiated by the purchase of a six-seat plane in 1948 to shuttle executive's between company headquarters in Wisconsin and Kimberly-Clark factories around the country. With six planes in 1969, Smith, then an executive vice president for finance, suggested that company air travel be converted from a "cost center into a profit center" by offering corporate aircraft maintenance services. K-C Aviation, as the subsidiary was called, later remodeled three DC-9s and in June 1984 intitiated flight service between Appleton and Milwaukee, Wisconsin; Boston; and Dallas, Texas. The fledgling airline operated under the name Midwest Express. Despite a 1985 crash in Milwaukee, Midwest Express remains a modest but successful venture for Kimberly-Clark.

In 1985, stating that the state had a bad climate for business, Smith relocated Kimberly-Clark's headquarters from Wisconsin to Texas. Just before this move Kimberly-Clark was sued by Procter & Gamble, who claimed that Kimberly-Clark had unlawfully infringed on its patented disposable diaper waistband material. Huggies had increased its market share to 31%, upsetting Procter & Gamble's Pampers. After nearly two years of litigation, a federal grand jury ruled against Procter & Gamble.

During the 1980s Kimberly-Clark met the challenges of its competitors in the consumer products industry by relinquishing some of its paper interests. The "diaper wars" have proven profitable for Kimberly-Clark; the company has been forced to market aggressively and to concentrate on its own strengths—consumer markets in which its well-recognized trademarks reign. Since restructuring and focusing on marketing and investment in technological growth and innovation, Kimberly-Clark has enjoyed steady growth.

Principal Subsidiaries: Avent, Inc.; Avent, S.A. de C.V. (Mexico); K-C Advertising, Inc.; K-C Aviation Inc.; K-C do Brasil Ltda. (Brazil); Kimberly-Clark Benelux Operations B.V. (Netherlands); Kimberly-Clark Canada Inc.; Kimberly-Clark Computer Services, Inc.; Kimberly-Clark de Centro America, S.A. (El Salvador, 39.6%); Kimberly-Clark France S.A.R.L.; Kimberly-Clark GmbH (Germany); Kimberly-Clark Integrated Services Corporation; Kimberly-Clark International, S.A. (Panama); Kimberly-Clark International Services Corporation; Kimberly-Clark Limited (U.K.); Kimberly-Clark Philippines Inc. (87%); Kimberly-Clark Puerto Rico, Inc.; Kimberly-Clark Sales Corporation (Netherlands); Kimberly-Clark Technical Products, Inc.; Kimberly-Clark Thailand Limited (60%); Kimfibers Ltd.; LTR Industries S.A. (France, 72%); Ridgeway Insurance Company Limited (Bermuda); Spenco Medical Corporation; Spruce Falls Power and Paper Company, Limited (Canada, 50.5%); SYZYGY, Inc.; YuHan-Kimberly, Limited (South Korea, 60%).

Further Reading: "Kimberly, John Alfred," in *Biographical Dictionary of American Business Leaders*, Volume II, edited by John N. Ingham, Westport, Connecticut, Greenwood, 1983; Freeman, Laurie, "Kimberly holds its own against giants," *Advertising Age*, November 19, 1984.

—Carol I. Keeley

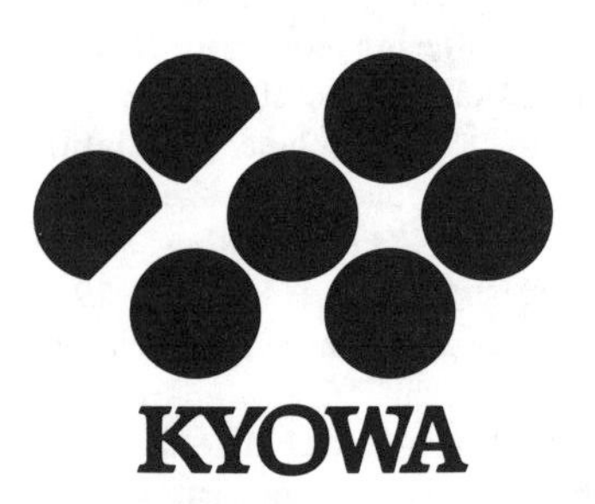

KYOWA HAKKO KOGYO CO., LTD.

6-1, Ohtemachi, 1-chome
Chiyoda-ku, Tokyo 100
Japan
(03) 3201-7211
Fax: (03) 3284-1839

Public Company
Incorporated: 1949
Employees: 5,326
Sales: ¥274.87 billion (US$1.91 billion)
Stock Exchanges: Tokyo Osaka Nagoya

Kyowa Hakko Kogyo Co., Ltd., a leader in biotechnology, is one of the world's largest producers of amino acids. The company also produces and markets pharmaceuticals, chemicals, foods, alcoholic beverages, fertilizers, veterinary medicines, and agricultural chemicals. Kyowa Hakko is active in the research and development of fermentation and chemical-synthesis technologies, as well as genetic engineering. The company employs nearly 20% of its staff in research and development, and holds 1,500 overseas patents and 270 Japanese patents.

In June 1936 Takaro Shuzo, Godo Shusei, and Dainippon Shurui, three alcohol distillers, created a consortium. In November 1937 they further formalized their relationship, forming the Kyowa Chemical Research Laboratory. Benzaburo Kato became the first director of the Kyowa Laboratory, and later chairman of Kyowa Hakko. Through extensive research, he discovered a fermentation process vital to the company's development. The company specialized in fermented products from the start. The company's first commercially marketed products were ethyl alcohol, used in sake and other beverages; acetone; and butane.

A turning point for the newly formed research laboratory occurred when the Japanese government, noting Kyowa Laboratory's early ventures in chemical research, commissioned it to develop technology for the production of the chemical isooctane—used to determine octane levels in fuel.

During World War II alcohols were much in demand. The extent of Kyowa's contribution to the war effort is difficult to gauge, but the company was forced by the occupation authorities to undergo some restructuring as a result of its wartime activities, as were many other Japanese businesses. Following restructuring Kyowa Laboratory emerged as Kyowa Sangyo. The company did very well at this time by shifting some of its resources from research to production. Establishing a plant in Hofu, Kyowa Sangyo manufactured food items in high demand, including salt; gin; and *shochu,* traditional grain-based liquor. In 1947 Kyowa Sangyo entered the pharmaceutical field for the first time, manufacturing penicillin.

Kyowa Sangyo was incorporated on July 1, 1949, as Kyowa Hakko Kogyo Co., Ltd. Kyowa Hakko means "harmony fermentation." The goals of the company were to develop its own fermentation biotechnology while attracting foreign technology to Japan.

In 1951 Kyowa Hakko negotiated an agreement with Merck & Company, a U.S. pharmaceutical company, to produce and market the antibiotic streptomycin. This project engendered a separate pharmaceutical division of Kyowa Hakko. The company had also created the Allospas distiller in 1950, which helped to improve alcohol and wine production methods.

Kyowa Hakko gained international recognition in 1955 with the development of an anticancer drug called Mitomycin-C. Shigetoshi Wakaki of Kyowa Hakko, in conjunction with the Kitasato Research Institute, shared responsibility for this treatment for stomach, lung, breast, and other solid cancers. The drug was developed using Kyowa Hakko's fermentation expertise. Mitomycin-C remains an effective cancer treatment.

The year 1956 was also significant for Kyowa Hakko in the food industry. Once again, the company's leadership in fermentation led to achievement: Kyowa Hakko became the first company to control the internal metabolism of a microorganism in order to produce an amino acid. Prior to Kyowa Hakko's work, amino acid production had been expensive, because it required the use of protein-rich substances such as decomposed wheat and soybeans. Kyowa Hakko substituted inexpensive and readily available molasses. The discovery resulted in cheaper production of monosodium glutamate, an amino acid–based seasoning.

In 1958 Kyowa Hakko produced another amino acid, the feed-grade L-Lysine, a base for livestock feed. Kyowa Hakko's cost-effective production system has since become standard and is used internationally to develop amino and nucleic acids for medical treatment and as post-surgery nutrition supplements.

Steadily continuing chemical research and production, Kyowa Hakko also manufactures acetone, butanol, and other solvents and plasticizers. In 1961, the company decided to replace its fermentation method of producing solvents with petrochemical technology. Low oil prices instigated the change. Noting that the fermentation process resulted in large amounts of waste water, Kyowa Hakko studied various methods of water treatment, and, in 1964 began to market an organic compound fertilizer, a product popular in Japan and other nations.

Throughout the 1970s Kyowa Hakko maintained its place as an innovator in antibiotic production. The company also moved into new arenas, including the production of cardiovascular agents, gastrointestinal drugs, hormones, dermatological medicines, vitamins, and advanced chemotherapeutics. Kyowa Hakko continued to apply biotechnology to create diagnostic reagents for cancer, the goal being to give accurate cancer diagnoses within minutes. In 1977 the company filed 45 drug-related patents in Japan, and in 1978 it formed the affiliate Janssen-Kyowa, dedicated to pharmaceutical research.

Recognizing that the pharmaceutical industry was growing increasingly international in scope, Kyowa Hakko stepped up collaborative efforts in the early 1980s. The company jointly funded development of a thrombolytic agent with Genentech, a U.S. pharmaceutical company. In 1982 Kyowa Hakko formed Biokyowa in the United States as fully owned subsidiary. In a project with the Mexican government and Sumitomo Corporation, Fermentaciones Mexicanas (Fermex) was formed in Orizaba, Mexico. Both new ventures were organized to produce and market feed-grade L-Lysine.

The Japan Chemical Industry Association granted Kyowa Hakko its 1983 technology award for Sagamicin, another advance in chemotherapy. The same year Kyowa Hakko developed a genetic-engineering technique, involving DNA recombination, expected to make amino acid production easier and less expensive.

By March 1984 Kyowa Hakko had launched another joint venture, with Native Plants, of the United States; Tata Enterprises, of Switzerland; and the Sumitomo Corporation. The consortium's goal was to develop new strains of coffee and tea in Southeast Asia.

Demand for feed-grade L-Lysine increased significantly in the late 1980s. Kyowa Hakko responded with plans for a plant in Hungary, to be operated by Agroferm Hungarian Japanese Fermentation Industry, and scheduled to open in fall 1990. Kyowa Hakko also agreed to several joint projects in Japan, including ventures to produce and market frozen foods with Kitchenbell, develop cosmetic biotechnology with Shu Uemura, and introduce the frozen-food wholesaler, Sun Kyowa.

In 1989 Kyowa Hakko agreed to import Kane Foods products from the United States. The same year the company became the sole agent for the U.S. wine producer Alexis Lichine.

Kyowa Hakko entered the 1990s with representative offices in the United States, Mexico, China, Hungary, and Germany, and with ventures in progress in Southeast Asia. The company operated seven plants in Japan and two overseas, and exported goods to over 80 countries. Projects underway are international in scope, as Kyowa Hakko studies cloning and gene-mapping to develop new plant strains, researches amino acid application, and studies the safety of pharmaceuticals.

Principal Subsidiaries: Kyowa Yuka Co., Ltd.; Ohland Foods Co., Ltd.; Sanko Pharmaceutical Industry Co., Ltd.; Kyowa Medex Co., Ltd.; Biokyowa Inc. (U.S.A.); Japan Oxocol Co., Ltd.

Further Reading: Formulating the Future, Tokyo, Kyowa Hakko Kogyo Co., Ltd., 1986; *Forty Years of Exciting Technological Development,* Tokyo, Kyowa Hakko Kogyo Co., Ltd., 1990.

—Frances E. Norton

LION CORPORATION

3-7, Honjo 1-chome
Sumida-ku, Tokyo 130
Japan
(03) 3621-6211
Fax: (03) 3621-6029

Public Company
Incorporated: 1919 as Lion Soap Co., Ltd. and T. Kobayashi & Co., Ltd.
Employees: 3,842
Sales: ¥314.43 billion (US$2.19 billion)
Stock Exchanges: Tokyo Osaka

Lion Corporation is Japan's biggest seller of toothpastes, and a major producer of other toiletries and soaps. Operated by the same family, the Kobayashis, throughout its entire history, the company has earned a prominent place in its domestic market, while maintaining successful overseas ventures.

Kobayashi Tomijiro Shoten was founded in 1891 by Tomijiro Kobayashi, to produce soap. In 1902 Japan concluded an alliance with Great Britain, and just three years later, in 1905, Kobayashi first exported its products to the United Kingdom and the United States. In 1919 Kobayashi split into two entities. Lion Soap Co., Ltd. was comprised of Kobayashi's soap division and T. Kobayashi & Co., Ltd. was comprised of the remainder of Kobayashi Tomijiro Shoten. The Kobayashi family retained control of both companies. In 1940 Lion Soap Company became Lion Fat & Oil Co., Ltd., reflecting a shift in its activities in conjunction with Japan's military buildup. T. Kobayashi became the Lion Dentifrice Co., Ltd. in 1949. During the first part of its history, both portions of the Kobayashi's enterprise flourished. Starting in the 1960s, however, substantial changes were made in the operations of the companies.

In the mid-1960s Lion Fat & Oil found itself in heated competition with the Kao Soap Company, which, in Japan, held the lead in sales of synthetic detergents. With the generous use of public relations and advertising, Lion challenged that lead, accomplishing a strong rise in sales in the first half of 1968. Later that year, the company aggressively confronted Kao in its area of greatest strength, western Japan, by building a new plant in Sakai, Osaka. This new factory, capable of producing both powder and liquid detergents, increased Lion's production capacity by about 30%, from 14,500 tons to 19,000 tons monthly. Lion benefited from its substitution of petrochemical products for agricultural oils. The use of alcohol-rich petrochemicals enabled the company to cut production costs.

Lion's growth during this period was based on the development of new technology and the expansion of its foreign connections. By 1972 sales reached US$27 million. In 1973 Lion Fat & Oil entered into a cooperative arrangement with Akzo, a Dutch chemical company, with the expectation of benefiting its chemical and household-products operations.

By the mid-1970s Lion Dentifrice was running second to Kao in the field of toiletries, but the forecast was for sinking profits for the next term as a consequence of rising costs for raw materials and stiff competition, from Japanese companies and from U.S. giant Procter & Gamble, which had recently entered the market in a joint venture with another Japanese firm. Lion Dentrifice sales began to grow, however, in the first half of 1976, increasing 12% over the same period a year earlier, as demand for its traditional dental products increased, and sales of new, products, such as products for the eye and for hair, grew as well. Throughout this period, both Lion companies enjoyed strong financial positions and relative lack of debt.

Given the intense competition the two Lion companies faced and the need to control costs for high-volume, low-price products, separate corporate structures for Lion Fat & Oil and Lion Dentrifice were inefficient. The similarity in the companies' names caused confusion among wholesalers and business partners. In late 1977 it was announced that the two companies would merge into one, on an equal basis, with the aim of creating one sales force to market all Lion products. Facing a stagnant market and subject to cut-throat competition, Lion leaders expected the reunited company, with a solidified corporate image, to expand in old areas, initiate new products, and enter into new markets.

In 1978 Lion Products Co., Ltd. was created, and in 1980 this sales organization joined with the two older Lion companies to form Lion Corporation. The newly unified company moved to increase the efficiency of its product distribution by implementing a retail-information system for its wholesalers, which in turn led to the 1985 creation of a management company for the entire toiletries industry.

Throughout the 1980s Lion continued its research-and-development activities, leading to new products that were keyed to new niches in a crowded market. Responding to environmental concerns, the company marketed Top, a non-phosphorous detergent, in 1980. In 1981 the company introduced Clinica, a plaque-fighting toothpaste that used enzymes to clean the teeth. Other new products, such as Look bathroom cleaner and Soft in 1, a combination shampoo and rinse, made strong contributions to the company's sales for the late 1980s.

In 1983 Lion laid out its goals for the next eight years, in a program designed to coincide with the arrival of the company's centennial. The campaign involved strengthening existing fields, improving global business, and exploiting new business sectors, In order to facilitate the plan, a company-wide restructuring was implemented. In an attempt to meet these goals, Lion developed new techniques in production and distribution. In conjunction with Akzo the company had finished construction of a plant for the refinement of raw materials in 1981 that used a new, low-pressure process to produce ingredients for household detergents. In 1983 in an effort to reduce production costs, essential in an industry where retail price-slashing is rampant and profit margins are low, Lion installed computer surveillance of the manufacturing process in its Kawasaki plant as a test, and ultimately scheduled controlled production to be implemented in all seven of the company's plants by 1989.

Throughout the 1980s the company continued to work with foreign partners. In conjunction with Henkel, of Düsseldorf, Lion operated joint ventures in Taiwan, Hong Kong, and Germany, as well as in Japan. In 1987 the company entered into a joint venture with the U.S. firm S.C. Johnson & Son to buy the previously unprofitable line of plaque-fighting dental products, Check-Up. S.C. Johnson already was marketing Lion's Zact toothpaste for smokers, in the United States. In June 1989 the company bought out S.C. Johnson's 50% interest in Rydelle-Lion to form a wholly owned subsidiary, Lion Corporation (America), in an effort to establish a base for further entries into the U.S. oral-care and hair-care markets. Lion subsequently turned over the marketing of its Zact and Check-Up products to Schering-Plough, another U.S. firm, under a licensing agreement.

In July 1989 Lion announced a joint venture with Akzo and two other entities to build a plant for the production of silica in Map Ta Phud, Thailand. Lion further expanded its Thai operations later that year, when it announced plans to build another plant in Rayong, Thailand, with five other partners for the production of a chemical used to make detergents. Construction of the plant, with economic incentives granted by the Thai government, was slated to begin in May 1990. This overseas expansion, though aggressive, was not enough to prevent a 1988 decline in Lion's sales and profits. Although 10% of the company's sales came from outside Japan, "we are a little bit behind our main competitors in Japan in globalizing our operations," a Lion representative admitted to *Advertising Age* on October 2, 1989.

Lion lagged behind its competitors in introducing a compact, highly concentrated detergent, a big market-winner in crowded Japan, where smaller is inevitably better. It was not until 1989 that Lion introduced Hi-Top, its compact product with fat-dissolving enzymes, in answer to Kao's Attack. Attack had enabled Kao to grab better than half the detergent market when it hit the stores in 1987. In 1990 compact detergents made up 70% of the Japanese detergent market, with Lion's overall share rising to around 25% after the introduction of its compact product.

Lion's development of new products was not without problems, however. In mid-1989 the Health and Welfare Ministry of Japan closed a Lion factory after discovering that the company in 1986 had misrepresented certain qualities of its Pentadecan hair-growth product while attempting to get it approved. As a penalty, the company was forced to withdraw Pentadecan, the market leader, from Japanese and Southeast Asian distribution, and to cease the manufacture for 20 days of all products made by the same division, a move that cost Lion $14 million. More importantly, the resulting negative publicity damaged the company's reputation, leading to fears about its overall image and sales.

Given these factors, it became clear by the end of 1989 that the company would not meet its goals until, perhaps, 1992. Shaken by its failure to beat Kao to market with an innovative compact detergent and facing a detergent price war and an overall lower market share, Lion set out to shore up profits by the end of 1989 by holding prices firm on its other products. In addition, the company planned to open a new fat-and-oil plant in Kagawa Prefecture, enabling it to launch a new product to vanquish Kao's lead.

It remains to be seen whether Lion's historical emphasis on innovative product development and foreign expansion will enable it to continue to thrive, or even take the lead, in an ever-changing market characterized by severe competition.

Principal Subsidiaries: Lion Fat & Oil (Taiwan) Co., Ltd.; Yu Kuo Chemical Co., Ltd. (Taiwan); Lionboy Trading Co., Ltd. (Taiwan); Taiwan Lion Chemistry Co., Ltd.; Taiwan Lion Trading Co., Ltd.; Lion Henkel (Taiwan) Ltd. (50%); Lion Corporation (T) Ltd. (Thailand); Lion Home Products (International) Ltd. (Hong Kong); Southern Lion Sdn. Bhd. (Malaysia); Lion Home Products (M) Sdn. Bhd. (Malaysia); Lion Home Products Pte., Ltd. (Singapore); Lion Corp. (America) (U.S.A.); Qingdao Lion Daily Necessities Chemicals Co., Ltd. (China, 50%).

—Elizabeth Rourke

L'ORÉAL

L'ORÉAL

41, rue Martre
92117 Clichy
France
(1) 47 56 83 68
Fax: (1) 47 56 86 42

Public Company
Incorporated: 1939
Employees: 27,600
Sales: FFr24.44 billion (US$4.23 billion)
Stock Exchange: Paris

L'Oréal, one of the largest companies in France, is the world's largest manufacturer of high-quality cosmetics and perfumes, producing such well-known brands as Lancôme, Ambre Solaire, and Cacharel. Its cosmetics sales are 1.5 times those of its closest competitior, Unilever, and more than double those of Revlon and Shiseido. It boasts a worldwide distribution network, as well as the industry's highest research-and-development budget and the largest cosmetological laboratories in the world.

L'Oréal's story begins in turn-of-the-century Paris, at a time when women of the demi-monde dyed their hair, their choice restricted to fiery red or coal black. In 1907, Eugène Schueller, a young chemist, began to concoct the first synthetic hair dyes by night in his kitchen and sell them to hair salons in the morning under the brand name of Auréole. His strategy was successful; within two years he established the Société Française des Teintures Inoffensives pour Cheveux, which soon afterward became L'Oréal.

In 1912, the company extended its sales to Austria, Holland, and Italy and by 1920 its products were available in a total of 17 countries, including the United States, Brazil, Chile, Peru, Equador, Bolivia, and the Soviet Union, and in the Far East. At this stage, L'Oréal consisted of three research chemists and ten sales representatives.

Schueller's timing had been singularly fortunate. The end of World War I was celebrated by the Jazz Age, when short hairstyles became fashionable, with a new emphasis on shape and color. By the end of the 1920s, there were 40,000 hair salons in France alone and L'Oréal's new products O'Cap, Imédia Liquide, and Coloral captured the growing market. In 1928 the company made its first move toward diversification, purchasing the soap company Monsavon.

In the 1930s and 1940s, platinum-haired screen idols such as Jean Harlow and Mae West made blond hair especially popular and bleaches such as L'Oréal Blanc sold well. L'Oréal was quick to make use of both old and new media to promote its products. In 1933, Schueller commissioned famous artists of the time to design posters and also launched his own women's magazine, *Votre Beauté*. Dop, the first mass-market shampoo, was promoted through children's hair-lathering competitions at the highly popular French circuses and by 1938 L'Oréal was advertising its hair products with radio jingles.

During this period L'Oréal demonstrated its ability to meet new consumer demands. When the Front Populaire won the 1936 elections and introduced the first paid holidays for French workers, L'Oréal's Ambre Solaire was ready to capture the new market for suntan lotions. Meanwhile the company's sales network was expanding on both a national and an international scale. Products began to be sold through pharmacies and perfumiers and new Italian, Belgian, and Danish subsidiaries were established between 1936 and 1937.

Even the outbreak of World War II in 1939 failed to curb the company's growth. At a time of strict rationing, women permed their hair and bought cosmetics to boost their morale. L'Oréal launched the first cold permanent wave product, Oréol, in 1945. At the same time the company continued to expand; by the end of the war there were 25 research chemists and distribution had been extended to the United Kingdom, Argentina, and Algeria.

During this period, François Dalle and Charles Zviak joined the group, both recruited by Monsavon at a time when the cosmetics industry held far less attraction for graduate chemical engineers than the atomic-energy or oil industries. Both men would play an important role in the company's future; by 1948, Dalle had already been appointed joint general manager of L'Oréal.

The consumer boom of the 1950s and the arrival of new blond screen idols Marilyn Monroe and Brigitte Bardot (originally a brunette) meant further expansion for L'Oréal. By 1950, a research-and-development team of 100 chemists had created further innovative products, including the first lightening tint, Imédia D, introduced in 1951, and the first coloring shampoo, Colorelle, introduced in 1955, which answered an increasing demand for subtlety. The company advanced further into the field of skin care, entering into technological agreements with the company Vichy, in 1954. Vichy was to become part of the L'Oréal group in 1980.

Eugène Schueller's promotional talents were recognized in 1953 when he was awarded an advertizing Oscar. Schueller died in 1957 and François Dalle took over as chairman and CEO at 39 years of age.

The 1960s were years of revolution, both cultural and commercial. As music and fashion became increasingly teen-oriented, there was a growing interest in conserving—or simulating—youthful looks. At the same time hundreds of new boutiques, supermarkets, and chain stores sprang up to supply this rapidly growing market. L'Oréal made a growing commitment to capital investment. In 1960 a new research-and-production center was established in Aulnay-sous-Bois, bringing the number of research staff up to 300. In 1963 and 1964 the company opened new cosmetological and bacteriological facilities, evidence of a highly scientific approach to skin care. Another production unit, Soprocos, opened in St. Quentin in 1965, and over the decade new distribution outlets were established in Uruguay, Algeria, Canada, Mexico, and Peru. L'Oréal was listed on the French stock exchange in 1963, during a period of restructuring within the group. In 1962, owing to the boom in hair-product sales, L'Oréal sold Monsavon in order to concentrate on its core business. At the same time it bought the hair-hygiene specialist Cadoricin. In 1964 L'Oreal bought Jacques Fath perfumes and a year later Lancôme, thereby gaining a significant entry into the high-quality skin-care, make-up, and perfume market and gaining increased access to perfumery outlets. Garnier, a hair-product company, and Laboratoires d'Anglas were also added to the group. In 1968 the company took major stakes in Golden in the United Kingdom and in Ruby, a personal hygiene and household products manufacturer. In the same year, L'Oréal bought the fashion and perfumes house, André Courrèges.

With increased resources and expertise, L'Oréal launched a number of successful products, many of which are market leaders to this day. These included the hairspray Elnett, Récital hair dyes, and the perfume Fidji. Fidji was launched under the Guy Laroche brand name.

In 1969, L'Oréal recruited a young Welshman, Lindsay Owen-Jones, from the prestigious Fontainebleau business school INSEAD. An Oxford languages graduate, he would go on to become the fourth chairman and managing director of L'Oréal. At the age of 25 he became general manager of L'Oréal's public-products division in Belgium and turned around unprofitable subsidiaries in France and Italy, before going to the United States to take charge of L'Oréal's distributor, Cosmair, in 1980.

L'Oréal benefited from the emphasis on health and fitness in the 1970s. From this time onwards, L'Oréal's earnings outstripped those of any other French blue chip and grew twice as fast as the cosmetics-industry average.

L'Oréal's success permitted further commitment to research and development; the number of research staff rose from 500 in 1970 to 750 in 1974. New production facilities were opened in France and in 1979 the International Centre for Dermatological Research was established at Sofia-Antipolis, in the South of France, for the treatment of skin disorders and aging.

Over the decade, structural and tactical changes were made within the group, based on the findings of the 1969 management study done by McKinsey & Co. The year 1970 saw the establishment of new operational divisions and management structure. A few years later, the company began to speed up the process of internationalization, with particular emphasis on New Zealand, Australia, Japan, and Hong Kong. In 1976 L'Oréal signed a technical-assistance contract with the Soviet Union.

Expansion into overseas markets—particularly Japan—was aided greatly by the company's new alliance with the Swiss foods giant Nestlé, to whom Eugène Schueller's daughter, Madame Liliane Bettencourt, sold nearly half of her L'Oréal stock in 1974. The two allies established a French holding company, Gesparal, which is 51%-owned by Bettencourt and 49%-owned by Nestlé. Gesparal controls 72% of L'Oréal's voting rights. Bettencourt is the largest individual shareholder of Nestlé, holding roughly 5%.

Throughout the 1970s, L'Oréal continued to make purchases within the cosmetics and hair-care industry: Biotherm in 1970; Gemey, Ricils, and Jeanne Piaubert in 1973; and Roja in 1975. The latter merged with Garnier in 1978. This was also a time for diversification for L'Oréal. In 1973 it took a controlling stake of 53.4% in the pharmaceutical company Synthélabo, a specialist in the production of cardiovascular drugs and hospital materials, followed in 1979 by the purchase of Metabio-Joullie, manufacturer of aspirins, over-the-counter drugs, veterinary, cosmetic, and dietary items. Metabio-Joullie and Synthélabo were merged in 1980 under the latter's name. In 1977 L'Oréal ventured into another complementary field, magazine publishing, taking stakes in Marie-Claire Album and Interedi-Cosmopolitan.

Meanwhile in the new division Parfums et Beauté International, several of L'Oréal's most successful products were launched—Vichy's moisturizer Equalia and the Cacharel perfume Anaïs Anaïs, now reckoned to be the world's best-selling perfume—while the well-known Kérastase hair products were redesigned.

The 1980s were particularly favorable for L'Oréal. François Dalle won the post of first vice president on Nestlé's administrative council, the title of Man of the Year in the chemicals and cosmetics sector from the Fragrance Foundation of the United States, and title of Manager of the Year from the *Nouvel Economiste*. In 1984, he gave up the leadership of L'Oréal, although he continued to act as chairman of the group's strategic committee. The position of chairman and CEO went to Charles Zviak. Lindsay Owen-Jones became vice president and Marc Ladreit de Lacharrière, joint vice president, soon to take control of the company's financial policy.

This event was followed by some restructuring within the group; in 1985 the Parfums et Beauté division was split into three departments—Lancôme/Piaubert, perfumes, and active cosmetics—and five geographical areas. At the same time the new management clearly felt it necessary to centralize control of the company's finances, and in 1987 a financial bulletin was issued announcing the creation of L'Oréal Finances, which would implement the financial strategy established approximately ten years before.

In 1986, L'Oréal's shares were distributed to investors outside France for the first time when the company raised FFr1.4 billion through a one-for-ten rights issue, offering new shares to stockholders. This was followed, in 1987, by a one-for-five stock split.

At this time L'Oréal began to play an increasingly active role in the management of Synthélabo, which, after merging with Metabio-Joullie, had become France's third-largest pharmaceutical company. Synthélabo's research-and-development budget was increased considerably, allowing the company in 1982 to become the first private laboratory to participate in the World Health Organization's project for research and education in neuroscience.

During the 1980s Synthélabo enhanced its international status, setting up joint marketing affiliates in the United States and Britain with the U.S. company G. D. Searle, and establishing joint ventures in Japan with Fujisawa and Mitsubishi Kasei. The company also took controlling stakes in Kramer of Switzerland, in 1982, and LIRCA of Italy in 1983. Nevertheless Synthélabo continued to report poor sales figures, owing to difficulty in updating its product line and unfavorable market conditions in France. L'Oréal subsequently reiterated its commitment to Synthélabo, keeping restructuring to a minimum and increasing its holding from 63% to 65% after October 1987's Black Monday when the shares fell considerably. L'Oréal saw that the solution to Synthélabo's problems lay in extending its overseas sales, thereby offsetting unfavorable domestic pricing and reimbursement policies. By the end of the decade, profitability had improved and some promising new drugs were ready to be approved for marketing in the 1990s.

Meanwhile, L'Oréal's research-and-development facilities continued their steady growth, with research staff reaching 1,000 by 1984. L'Oréal's enormous commitment to research resulted in the success of products such as Lancôme's Niosôme, launched in 1986, one of the few anti-aging creams found to be effective by independent dermatologists.

If this was the age of high-tech skin care, it was also the era of designer brands; in 1980 a new distribution company, Prestige et Collections, was created for Cacharel, whose perfume Loulou, launched in 1987, went on to become a best seller. In 1984, Nestlé took over Warner Cosmetics of the United States on behalf of L'Oréal's U.S. agent Cosmair, thereby acquiring for the group the prestigious names of Ralph Lauren, Paloma Picasso, and Gloria Vanderbilt. At this stage, however, L'Oréal was interested only in the perfumes and cosmetics divisions of the designer brands. In 1983, the company sold its 49.9% stake in the couture house Courrèges to Itokin of Japan, although it retained 100% of Courrèges Parfums.

A further addition to the L'Oréal group was the Helena Rubenstein skin-care and cosmetics range. In 1983, L'Oréal began by taking major stakes in Helena Rubenstein's Japanese and South American subsidiaries, the former integrated with Lancôme in the new Japanese affiliate, Parfums et Beauté, in 1984. In 1988, L'Oréal bought Helena Rubenstein Inc., a U.S. company that was in financial difficulties as a result of the sharp drop in sales following the founder's death. It would not be an easy matter to bring the company back into profit. Bought in the same year, Laboratoires Goupil, a dental-care-products manufacturer whose toothpastes held over 90% of the French market, was also unprofitable, but it was felt that L'Oréal's skillful marketing could remedy the situation. L'Oréal's last acquisition of the 1980s was the skin-care specialist Laboratoires Roche Posay.

While making acquisitions, L'Oréal also took the opportunity to sell off unwanted components of the group. These included the personal hygiene and comfort products of Laboratoires Ruby d'Anglas and Chiminter, which were felt to be too far outside the group's main area of interest and did not accord with L'Oréal's policy of internationalization

L'Oréal was keen to diversify into communications. In 1984 the company took a 10% stake in the French pay-TV company, Canal Plus, with the stake raised to 10.4% in 1986. In 1988, L'Oréal took a 75% stake in Paravision International, an organization charged with the creation, production, and distribution of audiovisual products for an international audience. The following year, L'Oréal entered by way of Paravision into a joint venture with the U.S. company Carolco Pictures Inc., to handle foreign television-distribution and programming rights.

In 1988, Lindsay Owen-Jones became the new chairman and chief executive of L'Oréal at the age of 42. Marc Ladreit de Lacharrière became director and executive vice president while Charles Zviak moved on to the chairmanship of Synthélabo. Zviak died the following year, having been one of the few chemists to attain leadership of a major French company. The end of the decade was marked further by rumors of L'Oréal's involvement in a proposed joint takeover bid for the French luxury-goods company Louis Vuitton Moët Hennessy, together with Vuitton's head, Monsieur Racamier, and Paribas/Parfinance. Although the existence of such a plan was denied by L'Oréal, the company joined with Orcofi, a Vuitton-controlled holding company, to buy 95% of the perfume and couture house Lanvin. L'Oréal explained that although Vuitton owned Dior and Givenchy, competitors in the perfume and cosmetics market, L'Oréal had no Vuitton shares and no intention of attacking the company. On the contrary, the Vuitton alliance would give L'Oréal an entrée into the field of luxury goods.

The cosmetics industry is still growing, but there is increasing rivalry. While L'Oréal's alliance with Nestlé should protect it from corporate marauders, it is still vulnerable to competition in Western markets from Japanese competitors Shiseido and Kao—although 90% of the turnover of both companies come from their home market—and from Unilever, following the latter's takeover of Elizabeth Arden and Fabergé.

L'Oréal has said that it sees opportunities for further profit growth in the United States, which represents one-third of the world market. Currently, despite having full control of strategy, management, and marketing in this region, L'Oréal reaps only 5.5% from the profits of its sole U.S. agent Cosmair Inc. The only advantage of this system for L'Oréal has been protection from the weakness of the U.S. dollar and from high marketing costs. Other markets targeted for expansion include Japan.

L'Oréal's structure remains unchanged, with the group consisting of a federation of competitive companies, including 147 production and distribution facilities worldwide, divided into five divisions. Only research-and-development facilities and overall management control are centralized.

There has been speculation as to the fate of L'Oréal when Bettencourt, in her mid-60s in 1990, relinquishes her corporate involvement. The French government is taking a strong interest in the issue. French government agree ments restrict foreigners from taking over French companies before 1994. After this date, Nestlé will have first option to purchase.

In future, L'Oréal may be forced to pay attention to a more discerning generation of customers. As consumers become more environmentally aware, L'Oréal is under increasing pressure to conform to new standards of product safety. The company has been forced to phase out the use of chlorofluorocarbons which are said to be harmful to the ozone layer. L'Oréal has also come under attack from the animal-rights lobby, which accuses the company of subjecting laboratory animals to inhumane tests, although L'Oréal claims that animal testing of new products is down to 5% from 50% in

1985. So far, L'Oréal's innovative abilities, emphasis on quality, marketing skills, and sound balance sheet have taken the group to the head of its category.

Principal Subsidiaries: Lancôme Parfums et Beauté; Helena Rubenstein Inc.; Parfums et Beauté International et Cie; Cie et Artoisienne de Gestion; Diparco; H.U.P. (Germany, 98.6%); Laboratoire Garnier Paris; L'Oréal UK.

Further Reading: Benjamin, Patricia, "Sitting Pretty," *Business,* January 1987; Fearnley, Helen, "L'Oréal—Not Just A Pretty Face," *Financial Weekly,* May 5, 1988; *L'Oréal,* Paris, L'Oréal, [n.d.].

—Jessica Griffin

THE PROCTER & GAMBLE COMPANY

One Procter & Gamble Plaza
Cincinnati, Ohio 45202
U.S.A.
(513) 983-1100
Fax: (513) 983-2060

Public Company
Incorporated: 1890
Employees: 79,000
Sales: $24.08 billion
Stock Exchanges: New York Cincinnati Amsterdam Paris Basel Geneva Lausanne Zürich Frankfurt Antwerp Brussels Tokyo

Few companies have influenced American lifestyles as has The Procter & Gamble Company (P & G). The company is recognized as one of the most aggressive marketers in the world. Committed to remaining the leader in almost all of the product markets in which it operates, P & G is among the larges advertisers in the world. Many customs of corporate America were first established at Procter & Gamble, including extensive market research, the brand-management system, and employee profit-sharing programs.

In 1837, William Procter and James Gamble formed Procter & Gamble, a partnership in Cincinnati, Ohio, to manufacture and sell candles and soap. Both men had emmigrated from the United Kingdom. William Procter emigrated from England in 1832 after his woolen shop in London had been destroyed by fire and burglary. Gamble came from Ireland as a young boy in 1819 when famine struck his native land. Both men settled in Cincinnati, then nicknamed "Porkopolis" for its booming hog-butchering trade. The suggestion for the partnership apparently came from their mutual father-in-law, Alexander Norris, who pointed out that Gamble's trade—soapmaking—and Procter's trade—candlemaking—both required use of lye, which was made from animal fat and wood ashes. The partnership began October 31, 1837, with paid-in capital of $7,192.24.

Procter & Gamble first operated out of a storeroom at Main and Sixth streets. Procter ran the store while Gamble ran the manufacturing operation, which at that time consisted of a wooden kettle with a cast-iron bottom set up behind the shop. Early each morning James Gamble visited houses, hotels, and steamboats collecting ash and meat scraps. Gamble bartered soap cakes for the raw materials. Candles were Procter & Gamble's most important product at that time.

Procter & Gamble was in competition with at least 14 other manufacturers in its early years, but the enterprising partners soon expanded their operations throughout neighboring Hamilton and Butler counties. James Gamble was assisted in his morning collection round by the company's first employee. Cincinnati's location on the Ohio River proved advantageous as the company began sending its goods downriver. In 1848 Cincinnati was also linked to the major cities of the East via rail, and Procter & Gamble grew.

About 1851, when P & G shipments were moving up and down the river and across the country by rail, the company's famous moon-and-stars symbol was created. Because most people were illiterate at this time, trademarks were frequently used to distinguish one company's products from another's. Company lore asserts that the symbol was first drawn as a simple cross on boxes of Procter & Gamble's Star brand candles by dock hands so that they would be easily identifiable when they arrived at their destinations. Another shipper later replaced the cross with an encircled star, and eventually William Procter added the familiar 13 stars, representing the original 13 U.S. colonies, and the man in the moon.

The moon-and-stars trademark became a symbol of the company's quality. While some other companies short-weighted their goods, Procter & Gamble never did so, even if it meant charging more. This philosophy built up a base of loyal customers, and in the days before advertising, Procter & Gamble's trademark was the only way of identifying the product. In 1875 when a Chicago soapmaker began using an almost-identical symbol, P & G sued and won. In 1882 it registered its trademark with the U.S. Patent Office to protect itself against future copycats. The emblem changed slightly over the years until 1930, when Cincinnati sculptor Ernest Bruce Haswell refined the emblem to its current form.

During the 1850s Procter & Gamble's business grew rapidly. In the early part of the decade the company moved its operations to a bigger factory. This location gave the company better access to shipping routes and stockyards where hogs were slaughtered. In 1854 the company leased an office building in downtown Cincinnati. Procter managed sales and bookkeeping and Gamble continued to run the manufacturing. By the end of the decade, the company's annual sales were more than $1 million, and Procter & Gamble employed about 80 people.

Procter & Gamble's operations were heavily dependent upon rosin—derived from pine sap—which was supplied from the South. In 1860 on the brink of the Civil War, two young cousins, James Norris Gamble and William Alexander Procter (both sons of the founders), traveled to New Orleans to buy as much rosin as they could. The two were successful in procuring a large supply at the bargain price of $1 a barrel. When wartime shortages forced competitors to cut production, Procter & Gamble prospered. The company supplied the Union Army with soap and candles, and the moon and stars became a familiar symbol with Union soldiers.

Although Procter & Gamble had foreseen the wartime scarcities, as time wore on, its stockpile of raw materials shrank. In order to keep up full production the company had to find new ways of manufacturing. Until 1863 lard stearin was used to produce the stearic acid for candlemaking. With lard in short supply and expensive, a new method was discovered to produce the stearic acid using tallow. What lard and lard stearin was available was instead developed into a cooking compound. The same process was later adapted to create Crisco, the first all-vegetable shortening. When P & G's supply of rosin ran out toward the end of the war, the company experimented with silicate of soda as a substitute, which later became a key ingredient in modern soaps and detergents.

After the war Procter & Gamble expanded and updated its facilities. In 1869 the transcontinental railroad linked the two coasts and opened still more markets to Procter & Gamble. In 1875 the company hired its first full-time chemist to work with James Gamble on new products. One of those products was a new soap equal in quality to expensive castile soaps, but which could be produced less expensively. In 1878 Procter & Gamble's White Soap hit the market with little more than the usual fanfare, but it was this product that catapulted P & G to the forefront of its industry.

The most distinctive characteristic of the product, soon renamed Ivory soap, was developed by accident. A worker accidently left a soap mixer on during his lunch break, causing more air than usual to be mixed in. Before long Procter & Gamble was receiving orders for "the floating soap." Although the office was at first perplexed, the confusion was soon cleared up, and P & G's formula for White Soap changed permanently.

Harley Procter, William Procter's son, developed the new soap's potential. Harley Procter was inspired to rename the soap by Psalm 45: "all thy garments smell of myrrh, and aloes, and cassia, out of the ivory palaces whereby they have made thee glad." Procter devoted himself to the success of the new product and convinced the board of directors to advertise Ivory. Advertising was risky at the time; most advertisements were placed by disreputable manufacturers. Nevertheless, in 1882 the company approved an $11,000 annual advertising budget. The slogan "99⁴⁴⁄₁₀₀% pure" was a welcome dose of sobriety amidst the generally outlandish advertising claims of the day, and endeared Ivory to the public. Procter, committed to the excellence of the company's products, had them analyzed and improved even before they went to market. This practice was the origin of P & G's superior product development. Procter believed that "advertising alone couldn't make a product successful—it was merely evidence of a manufacturer's faith in the merit of the article."

The success of Ivory and the ability of Procter & Gamble to spread its message further through the use of national advertising caused the company to grow rapidly in the 1880s. In 1886 P & G opened its new Ivorydale plant on the edge of Cincinnati to keep up with demand. In 1890 James N. Gamble hired a chemist, Harley James Morrison, to set up a laboratory at Ivorydale and improve the quality and consistency of Procter & Gamble's products. P & G soon introduced another successful brand: Lenox soap. Marketed as a heavier-duty product, the yellow soap helped P & G reach sales of more than $3 million by 1889.

The 1880s was a decade filled with labor unrest, and Procter & Gamble was not exempt from the struggle. It experienced a number of strikes and demonstrations, and although these were relatively mild, the company sought to avert labor problems before they became significant. Behind P & G's progressive labor policies was a founder's grandson, William Cooper Procter. William Cooper Procter had joined the company in 1883 after his father, William Alexander Procter, requested that he return from the College of New Jersey (now Princeton University) just one month before graduation to help with the company's affairs. The 24-year old learned the business from the ground up, starting in the soap factory. He quickly became acquainted with the circumstances and attitudes of the workers.

In 1885 the young Procter recommended that the workers be given Saturday afternoons off, and the company's management agreed. Nevertheless there were 14 strikes over the next two years. In 1887 the company implemented a profit-sharing plan in order to intertwine the employees' interests with those of the company. Although the semiannual dividends were met enthusiastically by employees, that enthusiasm rarely found its way back into the workplace. The next year William Cooper Procter recommended tying the bonuses to employee performance and received better results.

In 1890 Procter & Gamble incorporated, with William Alexander Procter as the first president. Two years later the company implemented an employee stock-purchase program, which in 1903 was tied to the profit-sharing plan. By 1915 about 61% of the company's employees were participating. The company introduced a revolutionary sickness-disability program for its workers in 1915, and implemented an eight-hour workday in 1918. Procter & Gamble has been recognized as a leader in employee-benefit programs ever since.

Meanwhile, new soaps, including P & G White Naphtha introduced in 1902, kept P & G at the the forefront of the cleaning-products industry. In 1904 the company opened its second plant, in Kansas City, Missouri, followed by Port Ivory on Staten Island, New York. Also in 1907 William Cooper Procter became president of the company after his father's suicide.

Procter & Gamble soon began experimenting with a hydrogenation process which combined liquid cottonseed oil with solid cottonseed oil. After several years of research, Procter & Gamble patented the procedure, and in 1911 Crisco was introduced to the public. Backed by strong advertising budget Crisco sales took off.

World War I brought shortages, but Procter & Gamble management had again foreseen the crisis and had stockpiled raw materials. William Cooper Procter was also active in the wartime fundraising effort.

During the 1920s the flurry of new products continued. Ivory Flakes came out in 1919. Chipso soap flakes for industrial laundry machines were introduced in 1921. In 1926 Camay was introduced and three years later Oxydol joined the P & G line of cleaning products. The company's market research became more sophisticated when F.W. Blair, P & G chemist, began a six-month tour of U.S. kitchens and laundry rooms to assess the effectiveness of Procter & Gamble's products in practical usage and to recommend improvements. After Blair returned, the economic-research department under, D. Paul Smelser, began the careful study of consumer behavior. Market research complemented Procter & Gamble's laboratories and home economics department in bringing new technology to market.

Soon after Richard R. Deupree became president of the company in 1930, synthetic soap products hit the market. In 1933 Dreft, the first synthetic detergent for home use, was introduced, followed by the first synthetic hair shampoo, Drene, in 1934. Further improvements in synthetics resulted in a host of new products years later.

In 1931 Neil McElroy, a former promotions manager who had spent time in England and had an up-close view of Procter & Gamble's rival Unilever, suggested a system of "one man—one brand." In effect, each brand would operate as a separate business, competing with the products of other firms as well as those of Procter & Gamble. The system would include a brand assistant who would execute the policies of the brand manager and would be primed for the top job. Brand management became a fixture at Procter & Gamble, and was widely copied by other companies.

The Depression caused hardship for many U.S. corporations as well as for individuals, but Procter & Gamble emerged virtually unscathed. Radio took Procter & Gamble's message into more homes than ever. In 1933 Procter & Gamble became a key sponsor of radio's daytime serials, soon known as "soap operas." In 1935 Procter & Gamble spent $2 million on national radio sponsorship, and by 1937 the amount was $4.5 million. In 1939 Procter & Gamble had 21 programs on the air and spent $9 million. That year P & G advertised on television for the first time, when Red Barber plugged Ivory soap during the first television broadcast of a major league baseball game—between the Brooklyn Dodgers and Cincinnati Reds.

In 1940 Procter & Gamble's packaging expertise was given military applications when the government asked the company to oversee the construction and operation of ordinance plants. Procter & Gamble Defense Corporation operated as a subsidiary and filled government contracts for 60-milimeter mortar shells. Glycerin also became key to the war effort for its uses in explosives and medicine, and Procter & Gamble was one of the largest manufacturers of that product.

After World War II the availability of raw materials and new consumer attitudes set the stage for unprecedented growth. Procter & Gamble's postwar miracle was Tide, a synthetic detergent that, together with home automatic washing machines, revolutionized the way people washed their clothes. The company was not ready for the consumer demand for heavy-duty detergent when it introduced the product in 1947; within two years Tide, backed by a $21 million advertising budget, was the number-one laundry detergent, outselling even the company's own Oxydol and Duz. In 1950 Cheer was introduced as bluing detergent, and over the years other laundry products were also marketed: Dash in 1954, Bold in 1965, Era in 1972, and Solo in 1979.

The 1950s were highly profitable for the company. In 1955, after five years of research, Procter & Gamble firmly established itself in the toiletries business with Crest toothpaste. Researchers at the company and at Indiana University developed the toothpaste using stannous fluoride—a compound of flourine and tin—which could substantially reduce cavities. In 1960 the American Dental Association endorsed Crest, and the product was on its way to becoming the country's number-one toothpaste, nudging past Colgate in 1962.

Procter & Gamble began acquiring smaller companies aggressively in the mid-1950s. In 1955 it bought the Lexington, Kentucky–based nut company W.T. Young Foods, and acquired Nebraska Consolidated Mills Company, owner of the Duncan Hines product line, a year later. In 1957 the Charmin Paper Company and the Clorox Chemical Company were also acquired.

In 1957, Neil McElroy, who had become Procter & Gamble president in 1948, left the company to serve as secretary of defense in President Dwight D. Eisenhower's cabinet. He was replaced by Howard Morgens who, like his predecessor, had climbed the corporate ladder from the advertising side. In 1959 McElroy returned to Procter & Gamble as chairman and remained in that position until 1971, when Morgens succeeded him. Morgens remained CEO until 1974.

Morgens oversaw Procter & Gamble's full-scale entry into the paper-goods markets. A new process developed in the late 1950s for drying wood pulp led to the introduction of White Cloud toilet paper in 1958, and Puffs tissues in 1960. Procter & Gamble's Charmin brand of toilet paper was also made softer.

Procter & Gamble's paper-products offensive culminated in the 1961 test marketing of Pampers disposable diapers. The idea for Pampers came from a Procter & Gamble researcher, Vic Mills, who was inspired while changing an infant grandchild's diapers in 1956. The product consisted of three parts: a leak-proof outer plastic shell, several absorbent layers, and a porous film that let moisture pass through into the absorbent layers, but kept it from coming back. Test market results showed that parents liked the diapers, but disliked the 10¢-per-Pamper price. Procter & Gamble reduced the price to 6¢ and implemented a sales strategy emphasizing the product's price. Pamper's three-layer design was a phenomenal success, and within 20 years disposable diapers had gone from less than 1% to more than 75% of all diapers changes in the United States. Procter & Gamble improved the technology over the years, and added a premium brand, Luvs, in 1976.

In the 1960s Procter & Gamble faced charges from the Federal Trade Commission that its Clorox and Folgers acquisitions violated antitrust statutes. In a case that found its way to the Supreme Court, Procter & Gamble was finally forced to divest Clorox in 1967. The Folgers action was dismissed after Procter & Gamble agreed not to make any more grocery acquisitions for seven years, and coffee acquisitions for ten years.

In the late 1960s public attention on water pollution focused on a key group of ingredients in products—phosphates. After an initial struggle Procter & Gamble, along with other soapmakers, drastically reduced the use of phosphates in its products.

In 1974 Edward G. Harness became chairman and CEO of Procter & Gamble and the company continued its strong growth. Many familiar products were improved during the 1970s, and new ones were added as well, including Bounce fabric softener for the dryer in 1972 and Sure antiperspirant and Coast soap in 1974.

In 1977, after three years of test marketing, Procter & Gamble introduced Rely tampons. The product's "superabsorbent" qualities contributed to its rapid acceptance. In 1980 the Centers for Disease Control (CDC) published a report showing a statistical link between the usage of Rely and a rare but often fatal disease known as toxic shock syndrome (TSS). The CDC reported that "35% of women were using

Rely at the onset of TSS.'' On September 22, 1980, the company suspended further sales of Rely tampons. The company took a $75 million write-off on the product.

In 1981 John G. Smale became CEO of Procter & Gamble. He had been president since 1974. Smale led the company further into the grocery business through a number of acquisitions. Procter & Gamble added the Ben Hill Griffin citrus products in 1981 to its Crush International soft drinks purchase of a year before. The company also entered the over-the-counter (OTC) drug market with the 1982 purchase of Norwich-Eaton Pharmaceuticals, makers of Pepto Bismol and Chloraseptic. The company completed its biggest purchase in 1985, with the acquisition of the Richardson-Vicks Company for $1.2 billion, and bought Dramamine and Metamucil from G.D. Searle & Company. These purchases made Procter & Gamble a leader in the over-the-counter drug sales.

In 1985, unable to squelch perennial rumors linking Procter & Gamble to Satanism, the company reluctantly removed the famous moon-and-stars logo from product packages. The logo began to reappear on some packages in the early 1990s, and the company continues to use the trademark on corporate stationary and on its building.

During fiscal 1985, Procter & Gamble experienced its first decline in earnings since 1953. Analysts said Procter & Gamble's corporate structure had failed to respond to important changes in consumer shopping patterns. The company's standard practice of extensive market research slowed its reaction to the rapidly changing market. The mass-marketing practices that had served Procter & Gamble so well in the past lost their punch as broadcast television viewership fell from 92% to 67% in the mid-1980s. Many large companies responded to the challenge of cable TV and increasingly market-specific media with appropriately targeted ''micro-marketing'' techniques. Procter & Gamble was forced to rethink its marketing strategy. In the latter years of the 1980s, Procter & Gamble diversified its advertising, reducing its reliance on network television. Computerized market research including point-of-sale scanning also provided the most up-to-date information on consumer buying trends.

In 1987, the company restructured its brand-management system into a ''matrix system.'' Category managers became responsible for several brands, making them sensitive to the profits of other Procter & Gamble products in their areas. Procter & Gamble brands continued to compete against one another, but far less actively. The restructuring also eliminated certain layers of management, quickening the decision-making process. The company became more aware of profitability than in the past. A company spokesperson summed it up for *Business Week*: ''before it had been share, share, share. We get the share and the profits will follow.'' In the later 1980s, Procter & Gamble did not settle just for market share.

Procter & Gamble initiated a major thrust overseas in the late 1980s as well, where its micro-marketing emphasis took cultural differences into account. Advertisments in Japan, for example, were less bold than those shown in U.S. markets.

In September 1988 Procter & Gamble made its first move into the cosmetics business with the purchase of Noxell Corporation, maker of Noxema products and Cover Girl cosmetics, in a $1.3 billion stock swap. Procter & Gamble also planned to further develop its international operations. In 1988, the company acquired Blendax, a European health- and beauty-care goods manufacturer. The Bain de Soleil sun care–product line was also purchased that year. By 1989, foreign markets accounted for nearly 40% of group sales, up from 14% in 1985.

In the late 1980s, health-care products were one of the fastest-growing markets as the U.S. population grew both older and more health conscious. To serve this market, Procter & Gamble's OTC drug group, which had been built up earlier in the decade, entered a number of joint ventures in pharmaceuticals. Procter & Gamble teamed up with the Syntex Corporation to formulate an OTC version of its best-selling antiarthritic, Naprosyn. Cooperative deals were also struck with the Dutch Gist-Brocades Company for its De-Nol ulcer medicine; UpJohn for its antibaldness drug, Minoxidil; and Triton Bioscience and Cetus for a synthetic interferon.

William Procter and James Gamble could never have imagined how their soap-and-candle company would blossom. After more than 150 years, the Procter & Gamble Company continues to maintain the same standards of quality that its founders introduced. The company continues to invest heavily in research and development, and remains committed to marketing products that are often superior to competitors'. Despite its recent stress on profitability, Procter & Gamble insists that it will continue to produce the best products. Former chairman John Smale and Edwin L. Artzt, who replaced Smale in early 1990, have been quite successful at adapting to new market conditions—container recycling has taken on new importance at P & G for the 1990s. Given the company's long tradition of excellence, it is certain to remain a leader.

Principal Subsidiaries: The Procter & Gamble Distributing Company; The Procter & Gamble Manufacturing Company; The Procter & Gamble Paper Products Company; The Procter & Gamble Cellulose Corporation; The Folger Coffee Company; Norwich Eaton Pharmaceuticals, Inc.; Richardson-Vicks Inc.; Procter & Gamble A.G. (Switzerland); Procter & Gamble Benelux (Belgium); Procter & Gamble Inc. (Canada); Procter & Gamble Espana, S.A. (Spain); Procter & Gamble France; Procter & Gamble GmbH (Germany); Procter & Gamble Italia, S.p.A. (Italy); Procter & Gamble Limited (U.K.); Procter & Gamble de Mexico, S.A. de C.V.; Procter & Gamble Philippines, Inc.; Procter & Gamble de Venezuela, C.A.

Further Reading: Lief, Alfred, *It Floats: The Story of Procter & Gamble,* New York, Rienhart & Company, 1958; Schisgall, Oscar, *Eyes on Tomorrow: Evolution of Procter & Gamble,* Chicago, J.G. Ferguson Publishing Co., 1981; *Memorable Years in P & G History,* Cincinnati, Ohio, The Procter & Gamble Company, [1987]; ''The house that Ivory built: 150 years of Procter & Gamble,'' *Advertising Age,* August 20, 1987.

—Thomas M. Tucker

REVLON

REVLON GROUP INC.

21 East 63rd Street
New York, New York 10021
U.S.A.
(212) 593-4300
Fax: (212) 527-5000

Private Company
Incorporated: 1933 as Revlon Products Corporation
Employees: 7,000
Sales: $2.60 billion

Revlon Group is a holding company for Revlon, Inc.; Almay, Inc.; Max Factor & Company; and several other manufacturers of beauty products, personal grooming aids, and wigs. All products are sold internationally. The company's first beauty item was nail enamel. Opaque and long-lasting, it was an improvement over the more transparent, dye-based products of other manufacturers. Revlon's nail polish owed its superiority to the use of pigments, which also allowed a wider color range than the light red, medium red, and dark red then available.

Initially, the revolutionary "cream enamel" came from the tiny Elka company, in Newark, New Jersey, a polish supplier to beauty salons for whom Charles Revson began to work as a sales representative in 1931. Charles Revson and his older brother, Joseph Revson, distributed Elka nail polish as Revson Brothers. Within a year, however, Charles Revson decided to open his own nail polish company, going into partnership with Joseph Revson and a nail polish supplier named Charles R. Lachman, who contributed the "l" to the Revlon name. Revlon was formed on March 1, 1932.

Revson had a keen fashion instinct, honed by seven earlier years of sales experience at the Pickwick Dress Company in New York. Coupling this with his experience at Elka, he noted that the permanent wave boom was making beauty salons more popular, and that demand for manicures was rising in tandem. He therefore targeted beauty salons as a market niche—a fortunate choice whose importance would grow.

Within its first nine months, the company boasted sales of $4,055. In 1933 there was a sharp rise to $11,246. Also in 1933, the company incorporated as Revlon Products Corporation. At the end of 1934, the company grossed $68,000. By 1937, sales had multiplied more than 40 times.

In 1937 Revson decided to enlarge his market by retailing his nail polish through department stores and selected drugstores. This gave him access to more affluent customers as well as those with a moderate amount of money to spend on beauty products. Formulating a maxim he followed for the rest of his life, Revson steered clear of cut-rate stores, selling his product only at premium prices.

Advertising helped Revson stick to this rule. Its use was a fateful step for the industry; never again would major cosmetics companies attempt to sell beauty items without it. Revson began by labeling his nail enamels with evocative names like Fatal Apple and Kissing Pink, that were descriptive while offering the promise of novelty. The company's first commercial advertisement appeared in *The New Yorker* in 1935. Aimed carefully at the upper-income clientele Revson was trying to attract, the advertisement came with a price tag of $335, constituting Revlon's entire advertising budget for the year.

By 1940 Revlon had a whole line of manicure products. Lipstick, Revlon's next major item, appeared in 1940. A perfectionist by nature, Revson made sure that its quality was the best he could produce. Its introduction was marked by a full-color advertising campaign stressing the importance of cosmetics as a fashion accessory, and featuring the novel idea of "matching lips and fingertips." The campaign's success showed in the 1940 sales figures; reaching $2.8 million, they more than doubled those of 1939.

World War II brought shortages of glass bottles and metal lipstick cases. Paper had to be substituted. Also in short supply were aromatic oils, fixatives, and packaging materials, which had previously been imported from Italy, Ethiopia, and France. Since the shortages affected the entire industry, secrecy was replaced by mutual cooperation; new synthetics and domestic sources of supply were shared, and a new U.S. aromatics industry was born.

During wartime, patriotic activities replaced expansion. In addition to cosmetics, Revlon turned out first-aid kits, dye markers for the navy, and hand grenades for the army. Characteristically, Revson's military products were the best his company could produce. His attention to detail was rewarded in 1944 with an army-navy production award for excellence.

By the end of the war, Revlon listed itself as one of America's top five cosmetic houses. Expanding its capabilities, the company bought Graef & Schmidt, a cutlery manufacturer seized by the government in 1943 because of German business ties. Costing $301,125, this acquisition made it possible for Revlon to produce its own manicure and pedicure instruments, instead of buying them from outside supply sources.

Postwar sales strategy, too, was influenced by rises in spending and department store credit sales. Returning interest in dress sparked the company's twice-yearly nail enamel and lipstick promotions, which were crafted in anticipation of the season's clothing fashions. Each promotion featured a descriptive color name to tempt the buyer, full-color spreads in fashion magazines, color cards showing the range of colors in the promotion, and display cards reproducing or enlarging consumer ads. Packaging was designed specifically for each line.

The Fire and Ice promotion for fall 1952 was one of the most successful. Its features included the cooperation of *Vogue*, which planned its November issue around the lipstick and nail enamel; "push" money given to demonstrators in stores without Revlon sales staff to insure full retail coverage;

and radio endorsements written into scripts for performers like Bob Hope and Red Skelton. These efforts produced excellent publicity and helped to raise 1952 net sales to almost $25.5 million.

The company received its next boost from its 1955 sole sponsorship of the CBS television show, "The $64,000 Question." Though initially reluctant to go ahead with this project, Revson was persuaded by the success of rival Hazel Bishop, whose sponsorship of "This is Your Life" was providing serious competition for Revlon's lipsticks. Attracting a weekly audience of 55 million people, "The $64,000 Question" topped the ratings within four weeks of its debut. Revlon's advertising budget for the year, $7.5 million, proved Charles Revson's adage that publicity had to be heavy to sell cosmetics; as a result of the television show, sales of some products increased 500%, and net sales for 1955 grew to $51.6 million, from $33.6 million one year previously.

In November 1955 an allegation of wiretapping was filed against Revlon by Hazel Bishop. In testimony given in a hearing before the New York State Legislative Committee to Study Illegal Interception of Communications, the charge was denied by Revlon controller William Heller, who nevertheless admitted "monitoring" employees' telephones for training purposes. Underscoring the denial of Hazel Bishop's charges, a Revlon attorney added a denunciation of wiretapping for industrial espionage, and promised cooperation in efforts to stop it.

Also in November 1955, Revlon reorganized as Revlon, Inc. A month later, in December 1955, the company went public. Initially offered at $12 per share, Revlon stock reached $30 within weeks, and the company was listed on the New York Stock Exchange at the end of 1956.

Meanwhile, the success of "The $64,000 Question" soon spurred a spinoff called "The $64,000 Challenge." The two shows helped to raise the company's net sales figures to $95 million in 1958, and to $110 million in 1959. The three-year bonanza came to an end, however, in 1959, amidst charges that both shows had been rigged. At the resulting congressional hearings, the shows' producers and the Revsons blamed each other. Nevertheless, the committee's verdict cleared Revlon of any blame in this matter.

As the 1960s began, Charles Revson became aware that his company was in danger of locking itself into a narrow, upper-middle-class image that could restrict sales. To avoid this, he borrowed a technique from General Motors, and segmented his product line into six principal cosmetics houses, each with its own price range, advertising program, and image. Princess Marcella Borghese aimed for international flair; Revlon was the popular-priced house; Etherea was the hypoallergenic line; Natural Wonder served youthful consumers; Moon Drops catered to dry skins; and Ultima II was the most expensive range. Top-priced lines were sold only in department stores, while others were available in other outlets. This strategy allowed the company to cover a wide market area without in-house conflict.

Early attempts to diversify into other fields were unsuccessful. For instance, Knomark, a shoe-polish company bought in 1957, sold its shoe-polish lines in 1969. Other poorly chosen acquisitions, such as Ty-D-Bol, the maker of toiler cleansers, and a 27% interest in the Schick electric shaver company were also soon discarded. Evan Picone, a women's sportswear manufacturer which came with a price tag of $12 million in 1962, was sold back to one of the original partners four years later for $1 million.

The company's first successful acquisition came in January 1966, when Revson bought U.S. Vitamin & Pharmaceutical Corporation in exchange for $67 million in Revlon stock. The buy-out brought Revlon a company with annual sales of $20 million, most of them coming from a drug used to treat diabetes. Within a year, U.S. Vitamin proved its worth with its acquisitions of Laboratorios Grossman, a Mexican pharmaceutical company; a comparable concern in Argentina; and another in Chile. In 1971 Revson traded U.S. Vitamin's diabetes drug and $20 million cash for a group of drugs Ciba-Geigy was required to divest for antitrust reasons. Another U.S. Vitamin acquisition was Nysco Laboratories, and its Nyscap process for timed-release medication. This, in turn, led to the introduction of vasodilation drugs. Fully disposable injectables, introduced in 1968, also came from U.S. Vitamin.

The company had begun to market its products overseas at the end of the 1950s. By 1962, when Revlon debuted in Japan, there were subsidiaries in France, Italy, Argentina, Mexico, and Asia. The Revlon debut in the Japanese market was typical of its international sales strategy. Instead of adapting its ads and using Japanese models, Revlon chose to use its basic U.S. advertising and models. Japanese women loved the American look, and the success of this bold approach was reflected in the 1962 sales figures, which were almost $164 million.

By 1967, expanding worldwide markets produced sales of $281 million, showing a 5.7% increase over the figure of almost $266 for 1966. Planning further expansion, Revlon spent $12.5 million on improvements to existing facilities plus a new cosmetics and fragrance manufacturing plant in Phoenix, Arizona.

During the 1960s the company consisted of four divisions: international, professional products, Princess Marcella Borghese, and U.S.V. Pharmaceutical. In 1968 Revson decided to add two more divisions: the cosmetics and fragrances division, headed by Joseph Anderer, and the Revlon Development Corporation, which was concerned chiefly with long-range planning concepts and strategies for marketing opportunities. Headed by Evan William Mandel, the Revlon Development Corporation brought the total number of divisions to six.

The 1970s began with annual sales of about $314 million. The cosmetics division, its six lines separately aimed, advertised, and marketed, was the industry leader in all franchised retail outlets. Revlon fragrances, such as Norell and Intimate for women and Braggi and Pub for men, had also become familiar to U.S. consumers. Revlon also had a new line of wig-maintenance products called Wig Wonder.

An important 1970 acquisition was the Mitchum Company of Tennessee, makers of antiperspirants and other toiletries. Mitchum joined the Thayer Laboratories subsidiary, formerly Knomark. Mitchum-Thayer division's widely publicized products required a 1971 advertising budget of $4 million.

In 1973 Revlon introduced Charlie, a fragrance designed for the working woman's budget. Geared to the under-30 market, Charlie models in Ralph Lauren clothes personified the independent woman of the 1970s. Charlie was an instant success, helping to raise Revlon's net sales figures to $506 million for 1973, and to almost $606 million the following year.

High profits apart, 1974 was a difficult year. Charles Revson began to suffer from pancreatic cancer. Determined to leave a worthy successor, he picked Michel Bergerac, a president of International Telephone and Telegraph's European operations. Terms of Bergerac's contract included a $1.5 million signing bonus, an annual salary of $325,000 for five years, bonuses, and options on 70,000 shares.

Company profitability was Bergerac's chief interest. Impressed with Revson's experienced management team, he induced them to stay by introducing the Performance Incentive Profit Sharing Plan, which allotted each executive points based on profit objectives achieved for the years 1974 to 1976. He also cut company spending with tighter inventory controls, and instituted an annual saving of $71.5 million by the elimination of 500 jobs. Bergerac installed a management-information system, requiring that all managers report monthly on problems, sales, and competition.

Bergerac tried to reduce Revlon's dependence on the increasingly crowded cosmetics market, by acquisition. His first major purchase came in 1975. Coburn Optical Industries was an Oklahoma-based manufacturer of ophthalmic and optical processing equipment and supplies, which cost 833,333 Revlon common shares. Barnes-Hind, the largest U.S. marketer of hard contact lens solutions, was bought in 1976, and strengthened Revlon's share of the eye-care market. Other acquisitions included the Lewis-Howe Company, makers of Tums antacid, acquired in 1978, and Armour Pharmaceutical Company, makers of thyroid medicines, acquired in 1977. These health-care operations helped sales figures to pass the $1 billion mark in 1977, bringing total sales to $1.7 billion in 1979.

By the late 1970s company pharmaceutical research and development had extended into plasma research and new drugs for the treatment of osteoporosis and hypertension. The markets for soft contact lenses and their rinsing solutions were also growing. Bergerac compounded a successful 1979 by buying Technicon Corporation, a leading maker of diagnostic and laboratory instruments for both domestic and international markets, in 1980.

During the mid-1970s Bergerac also organized the six cosmetics lines into three groups for easier administration. Revlon, Moon Drops, Natural Wonder, and Charlie now belonged to group one. Group two was comprised of Flex hair-care products and other toiletries, and group three included Princess Marcella Borghese and Ultima II, the prestige cosmetic brands sold in upscale department stores. The domestic cosmetics operations also included the government sales division, carrying almost all the beauty lines through military exchanges and commissaries in the United States and overseas. By the mid-1980s, Revlon's health-care companies, rather than Revlon's beauty concerns, were innovating and expanding. Reluctant to initiate beauty-product development or department store promotions, Revlon lost ground to Estée Lauder, a privately held company whose marketing strategy of high prices with accompanying gifts had earned it almost universal center-aisle department store space. This caused Revlon's share to drop from 20% to 10% of department store cosmetics sales.

Drugstore and supermarket sales were also suffering; Natural Wonder, a low-priced line, lost 24% of its supermarket volume in 1983 alone, and competitor Noxell's inexpensive Cover Girl line was claiming more drugstore sales. Comparisons of profits from total operations told the story: $358 million in 1980 sank to $337 million in 1981, which fell to $234 million by 1982.

By 1984, industry analysts believed that Revlon would be worth more if it were broken up and sold. Within a year, this opinion was borne out by a takeover bid from the much-smaller Pantry Pride, a subsidiary of Ronald Perelman's MacAndrews & Forbes Holdings. In defense, Bergerac accepted a $900 million offer for the cosmetics businesses from Adler and Shaykin, a New York investment company. The rest of Revlon was to go to Forstmann Little & Company, a management buyout corporation, for about $1.4 billion. These sales, however, were disallowed by a Delaware judge, who ruled that the deal was not in Revlon's shareholders' best interests. On November 5, 1985, at a price of $58 per share, totaling $2.7 billion, Revlon was sold to Pantry Pride, becoming a private company and giving the name of Revlon Group to the former Pantry Pride.

Perelman immediately began to divest the company of the health-care businesses. By the end of 1988, he had recovered $1.5 billion of his borrowed funds, partly by selling the eye-care businesses to the British firm of Pilkington for $574 million.

Divested companies were replaced with others geared to the Perelman objective—restoring the luster to the original beauty business. Costing about $500 million, Max Factor joined the Revlon lineup in 1987, along with its Halston perfume and its Almay toiletries. Other newcomers were Yves Saint Laurent fragrances and cosmetics; and Charles of the Ritz, Germaine Monteil, and Alexandre de Markoff followed soon after.

Other innovations of the 1980s meshed with national trends. The concern of a burgeoning older population with health and fitness led to wider company research on skin-care products as well as on make-up. International concerns for animal rights found a response in Perelman's Revlon, which abandoned the Draize test in 1989, after closing its animal testing center in 1986.

Revlon's last public sales figures, issued for 1986, were $1.6 billion. During the late 1980s fears of an approaching recession made bankers generally wary of highly leveraged transactions, and Revlon's junk bonds began to lose value.

Internal problems stemmed partly from the department store market, where an attempt by Revlon to economize by grouping its Ritz, Monteil, and Borghese prestige brands at one counter failed. Other problems included the introduction of No Sweat, a deodorant which was unable to garner market share and was introduced with a $12 million advertising budget; the reformulation of Flex, a popular shampoo which lost market share when Revlon introduced a new formula and new packaging and raised the price; and a 2% shrinkage in the fragrance market, affecting the entire industry. Nevertheless, by 1990's end, Revlon held 11% of the mass cosmetics market.

Principal Subsidiaries: Almay, Inc.; Charles of the Ritz Group Ltd.; Germaine Monteil Cosmetiques Corp.; Halston Enterprises, Inc.; Max Factor & Co.; National Health Laboratories Inc.; Norell Perfumes, Inc.; The Princess Marcella Borghese, Inc.; Revlon, Inc.; Revlon-Realistic Professional Products, Inc.; Roux Laboratories, Inc.

Further Reading: ''Revlon's Formula: Smart Words, Quality, and Freud,'' *Business Week,* August 12, 1950; Tobias, Andrew, *Fire and Ice: The Story of Charles Revson—The Man Who Built the Revlon Empire,* New York, William Morrow & Company, 1976; Berman, Phyllis, ''Revlon Without Revson,'' *Forbes,* June 26, 1978; Cole, Robert J., ''High-Stakes Drama at Revlon,'' *The New York Times,* November 11, 1985; Ramirez, Anthony, ''The Raider Who Runs Revlon,'' *Fortune,* September 14, 1987.

—Gillian Wolf

S.C. JOHNSON & SON, INC.

1525 Howe Street
Racine, Wisconsin 53403
U.S.A.
(414) 631-2000
Fax: (414) 631-2133

Private Company
Incorporated: 1932
Employees: 13,000
Sales: $2.50 billion

S.C. Johnson & Son is one of the largest family-owned companies in the United States and a leading manufacturer of home, personal-care, and insect-control products. Known internationally as S.C. Johnson Wax, its well-known products include Raid bug spray, Agree shampoo, Pledge furniture polish, and Edge shaving gel. Johnson was founded in 1886 as a parquet flooring company and became one of the first U.S. corporations to expand worldwide, entering Great Britain in 1914. It has operations in 47 countries. Still in family hands after more than a century, Johnson's strength is its ability to develop and market new products.

In 1882 Samuel Curtis Johnson began selling parquet flooring made by the Racine Hardware Company in Racine, Wisconsin. Four years later, Johnson purchased the flooring business from the hardware company. The new organization had four employees and showed a first-year profit of less than $300.

Johnson's parquet customers often asked him about caring for their new floors. At that time shellac had been used for that purpose, but it tended to build up and peel off. Johnson created a product called Johnson's Prepared Wax to sell along with his flooring. The concept was borrowed from the European use of wax to care for old wooden floors. It was very successful, and Johnson began selling it even to people who had not bought his flooring. It was nationally advertised by 1888.

Samuel's son, Herbert F. Johnson Sr., joined the firm in 1892, beginning a century-long tradition of family involvement in the business. By the following year the company was already experimenting with products such as wood dye, crack filler, and car wax. When the car wax proved to be popular, Johnson made a radiator cleaner. He was forced to buy back 900 Model T Ford radiators that were dissolved by the insufficiently tested product. This setback provided a valuable experience. Johnson Wax has given priority to top-rate research teams and chemists ever since.

As simple maple and oak flooring replaced the intricate parquet floors in the late 1800s, the company's diversification paid off. In 1898 sales of the floor wax and other woodcare products exceeded Johnson's flooring sales. Floor wax became Johnson's major product.

The company changed its formal name to S.C. Johnson & Son in 1906, when Herbert F. Johnson Sr. became a partner. While continuing to add to their product line—Floor Renewer, Under-Lac, and Flat Color Finish—the company expanded overseas in 1914, when the British Johnson company was established. The company opened in Australia in 1917. Johnson discontinued the manufacture of parquet flooring, and the last shipment of it was made in 1917. Johnson concentrated on wax products and preservation products for cars, such as Hastee Patch and Self-Vulcanizer. S.C. Johnson died in 1919, and his son succeeded him as president. The three keys to Johnson Wax's continued success had been already established: international operations, chemical technology, and the use of advertising.

During this time, the company's innovations as an employer were also notable: it was one of the first U.S. companies to give paid vacations, a policy begun in 1900. With its 200 employees in 1917, S.C. Johnson Wax began one of the first profit-sharing programs in the country; the program in 1990 was the fifth oldest. It started offering group life insurance for employees also in 1917. In 1920 the Canadian Johnson company was formed. Throughout this decade, product offerings expanded, including enamel paints, carbon remover, weighted brushes for painters, and Kleen Floor and Restorer. Herbert F. Johnson Jr. became president after his father's death in 1928. At that time, the company had 500 employees.

The French Johnson company opened in 1931, the same year in which sales began of one of Johnson Wax's longest-selling products, Glo-Coat Floor Finish. The product involved a colloid technology developed at Johnson Wax that freed it of the need for resins that caused yellowing. Glo-Coat became one of the most successful floor-care products of all time. In 1932 S.C. Johnson & Son was incorporated. The company's pension plan was initiated two years later, and product innovations continued. The most notable event of the decade, however, was the 1939 unveiling of the company's new office building, designed by Frank Lloyd Wright. An accomplishment in any era, it was particularly stirring at the close of the Great Depression, which Johnson weathered without laying off any employees. The Racine building continues to be headquarters for the company. In 1989 the company was still giving 5% of its pretax profits to charity, a tradition begun with the founder, who gave 10% of his annual income to civic improvements.

By 1942 the company was concentrating its output on products for the war effort, while many employees were called upon to serve. Its contribution during World War II was marked by army and navy production awards. A Research & Development Tower was opened in 1950. The Lighthouse Resort for employees and retirees was unveiled in northern Wisconsin the following year.

The West German Johnson company was established in 1953. Samuel C. Johnson, great-grandson of the founder, joined the company in 1954. He headed the new-products department that was created the following year. Not long after, he produced his first new product within that division, an aerosol insecticide. His father, Herbert F. Johnson Jr., sent him back to the lab, claiming the insecticide was no different from others on the market. In 1956 Johnson came forward with Raid House & Garden Bug Killer; water-based, it was the first product that could be used on plants and in the home without killing the plants. Raid would become one of Johnson Wax's most profitable lines. Along with this breakthrough came Glade Air Fresheners, introduced the same year; they featured advanced technology in aerosol manufacturing. Insecticide products continued with Off!, an insect repellent first sold in 1957. Another very successful product, Pledge, came out in 1958. Herbert F. Johnson Jr. became company chairman in 1958, and the presidency was assumed by the first non-family member, H. M. Packard.

In 1959 S.C. Johnson Wax established a presence in Italy, and this marked the start of a decade of international expansion: Chile, Switzerland, Sweden, and South Africa in 1961; Belgium, Japan, and the Netherlands in 1962; Norway, Austria, Spain, and Ghana in 1964; and Denmark, east Africa, Greece, Hong Kong, Singapore, and Thailand by 1968. Establishing an international base allowed Johnson Wax to manufacture its products from local materials for local markets; exporting the products would not have been profitable. In 1966 Packard became chairman and S.C. Johnson was named president.

Johnson Wax entered the personal-care-product market in 1970, with the introduction of Edge, a shaving gel, which also went on to become a company mainstay. Entering into eight more countries by 1972, Johnson Wax's innovations slowed as it dealt with its own growth. Johnson Diversified, Inc. (JDI), a wholly owned subsidiary was formed in 1970. JDI began acquiring highly diversified companies, many of them recreational-equipment manufacturers. In the early 1970s 15 companies—ranging from Eureka Tent & Awning Company to Under Sea Industries—were acquired. William K. Eastham was elected president of S.C. Johnson & Son in 1972.

Gas prices and related mid-1970s economic circumstances made the company's diversification into recreational equipment costly. Five of the weaker companies were sold. During this time, there was a notable slowdown in the introduction of new products while Johnson Wax adjusted to its size and variety. JDI changed its name to Johnson Wax Associates (JWA) in 1977. After H.F. Johnson Jr. died in 1978, S.C. Johnson took a sabbatical from his post as chairman and CEO in order to settle his father's estate; Eastham served as CEO in the interim. The company entered Egypt, Taiwan, and the Dominican Republic in 1979, but the decade was closing with lost momentum. Johnson Wax had introduced Agree conditioner and shampoo in 1977 and 1978. During that time, sales increased while profits declined. All consumer packaged goods saw slowed profits during this time, and Johnson Wax had acquisitions and overseas expansions sapping profits in addition. While foreign markets accounted for 60% of the company's sales for a period during the late 1970s, the recession-affected U.S. dollar undercut this portion of earnings, and the company was faced with a call to change in the early 1980s.

Raymond F. Farley became president in 1980, the same year S.C. Johnson resumed the CEO seat and began instituting needed reforms. In 1982 Johnson imposed a one-year wage freeze. It was the first time in 20 years that a wage freeze had been instituted without governmental exigency. He reduced the company's U.S. work force by 3% with early retirement programs, then increased the research and marketing staffs. The company was restructured into four enterprise units: personal care, insecticides, home care, and commercial products. Units were organized to speed up the time between product idea and introduction, and new products were pouring forth by the mid-1980s. The advertising budget was nearly 70% higher in 1984 than in 1979, the research-and-development budget increased by 40%, and product price increases were reduced.

One week before the October 1987 stock market plunge, JWA went public. Johnson called this move "going public to stay private," as the move created liquid assets needed for potential estate taxes, thus protecting the company's assets and its private status. Family owns 90% of Johnson Wax, with employees holding the other 10%. JWA was selling $250 million annually in the late 1980s, mostly fishing and other recreational gear, as well as ink-stamping equipment. JWA was the nation's largest producer of electric fishing-boat motors and a major seller of reels and lures.

In late 1988, Farley became the second non-family member in Johnson's history to become chief executive. S.C. Johnson remained chairman. All four of his children were then involved with the company, with his eldest son, S. Curtis Johnson III, heading a venture-capital unit he induced his father to bankroll in 1983.

In January 1990 Farley retired and was succeeded by Richard M. Carpenter, president and CEO. Johnson Wax started the 1990s with its strength reinforced—a very strong research-and-development emphasis, with labs around the world. Careful planning had insured that the company will stay private, if the great-great-grandchildren of the founder so choose.

Principal Subsidiaries: Johnson Venture Capital, Inc.; Micro-Gen Equipment Corporation; PRISM.

Further Reading: Johnson Wax Magazine, December 1986. Ellis, James, "Sam Johnson is 'Going Public to Stay Private,' " *Business Week*, December 5, 1988.

—Carol I. Keeley

SHIONOGI & CO., LTD.

1-8, Doshomachi 3-chome
Chuo-ku, Osaka 541
Japan
(06) 202-2161
Fax: (06) 229-9596

Public Company
Incorporated: 1919
Employees: 6,500
Sales: ¥216.8 billion (US$1.50 billion)
Stock Exchanges: Tokyo Osaka Nagoya Fukuoka Sapporo

Japan's leading developer, producer, and exporter of antibiotics is Shionogi & Co., Ltd. Antibiotics have been at the heart of the company's operations only since the post–World War II years, when Shionogi began to acquire the state-of-the-art technology necessary to compete with overseas suppliers of the then-new "wonder drugs." Prior to that time, the company had developed a reputation as an all-around manufacturer of pharmaceuticals—and company spokespersons continue to describe Shionogi in those terms.

The decision to devote a substantial portion of the company's resources to the development of one type of product represented a departure from Shionogi's many decades of fairly evenhanded expansion of its range of medicines, drugs, and other health-care-related products. Despite the sudden focus on antibiotics, however, the company did not stop developing and producing its broad lines of pharmaceutical products. While Shionogi has continued to invest in new technology and technical expertise in order to remain on the cutting edge of antibiotic development and production, the company has also continued to expand its facilities for the manufacture of other products and for laboratory research. Development of new products and services and improvement of production methods have been important parts of the company's operations since its early years. A new facility—the Institute for Medical Science—opened in 1988 and extended Shionogi's thrust into basic research. Its current emphasis is on exploring the causes of disease and linking those findings to the development of products to combat those causes.

Although much of Shionogi's business in the past has been based on licensing products from prominent manufacturers, such as Eli Lilly and Merck in the United States, new projects undertaken in Shionogi's laboratories indicate a growing emphasis on development and production of original product lines. The company's confidence in its existing and projected output may be judged by its plans to phase out its handling of other manufacturers' wares by 1996 and to replace them with original products. Shionogi's lines encompass medical drugs, agricultural and animal health products, diagnostic products, and chemicals for industrial and other uses. In addition, the company provides clinical testing facilities.

In 1878 Osaka was already a center of commercial activity, a logical place for a wholesaler of traditional Japanese and Chinese medicines and herbal remedies to open a business. Gisaburo Shiono began supplying local distributors with the herbal and folk remedies that had been in popular use in Japan for more than 1,000 years. Eventually he introduced something new: medicines and drugs manufactured in the United States and Europe. This development was a more radical step than simply importing pharmaceutical products for wholesale distribution. The decision required confidence on Shiono's part in his countrymen's willingness to accept a Western-style approach to the treatment of illness.

His confidence turned out to be well placed. In the quarter-century since their government's barriers to trade with those countries had been lifted, Japanese consumers' initial resistance to the infiltration of Western ways into their culture had waned. Some groups still tried to stem the tide of curiosity and interest in Occidental lifestyles and products, but consumers were ready for the Western nations' innovations, which also had the blessing of the newly restored imperial government.

The Shiono family business found a ready clientele in Osaka-area merchants. Within his first two decades of wholesaling both Oriental and Western-style medications, Gisaburo Shiono began to develop new products in-house. By the turn of the century, his reputation for quality and dependability had brought sufficient profits to the company to enable him to build his own research laboratory. Difficulties with transportation and supply lines cropped up as a result of the nation's brief wars with China and Russia, but Shionogi retained a hard-won reputation for quality and service. Early in the 20th century, the company added a new dimension to its wholesale medication business: drug manufacture.

The drug trade proved both profitable and brisk, and the company grew even faster than before. Not even Japan's entry into World War I slowed it down. On the contrary, the demand for pharmaceutical products increased as battlefields became impromptu testing grounds for improvised treatment of injuries under emergency conditions. That situation held true not only during both world wars, but also through far-ranging flu epidemics and disasters such as the Great Kanto Earthquake of 1923.

As Western-style medical practice spread throughout Japan, the company increasingly enhanced its reputation as a reliable supplier to hospitals and pharmacies. However, it was the discovery and development of antibiotics during World War II that was pivotal in Shionogi's business.

Like many other Japanese companies whose premises and personnel were devastated during the country's defeat in World War II, Shionogi began working immediately to reorganize and restore its product lines and rekindle the interest of a civilian market for its goods and services. Unlike some companies, Shionogi had the advantage of consistent management. Shiono had looked ahead to groom successors from within the family circle to take over responsibility as needed. At least three of his direct descendants held significant positions in the company's leadership in 1990, including Chairman of the board of directors Kotaro Shiono, Senior Managing Director Yoshihiko Shiono, and Managing Director Motozo Shiono.

After an unprecedented military defeat during World War II, Japan still had many businesses that had survived the war and were determined to survive under peacetime occupation by the invading forces. Those business and industrial leaders encountered no opposition from the occupation authorities or the new government based on the revised constitution that took effect in 1948. Instead, they received help, encouragement, and guidance—the latter in the form of principles of efficient, far-sighted business practices such as those recorded in the writings of W. Edwards Deming. Those principles had been all but ignored when offered to already-prosperous Western businesses.

Shionogi's management decided to specialize in antibiotics at a time when worldwide attention was drawn to the dramatic role they had played in combating diseases formerly considered incurable and in reducing the incidence of fatal infection from battlefield injuries. With the resumption of Japanese self-governance in the early 1950s, Shionogi already had plans underway for expansion into worldwide markets. The company's research laboratories took their first steps toward the successful synthesis of a sulfanilamide at that time. Launched in 1958 under the name of Sinomin, Shionogi's first sulfa drug was popular from the start, encouraging the company to increase its focus on development of original products.

In addition to originating products, Shionogi also formed relationships with overseas manufacturers to handle their products for other Far Eastern markets as well as Japan. A notable example was the line of cephalosporin antibiotics developed by Eli Lilly.

Astute management, especially financial management, has helped keep the company profitable overall despite recurrent problems. The antibiotics market softened late in the 1980s, posing a challenge for the company's marketing techniques. Because of the elaborate bureaucracy that new products, intended for public use in Japan must face, much time has been lost in introducing new products; this condition has been true since before the turn of the century. Changes in the system to shorten the waiting period were reportedly planned in 1990, but there were no plans to abolish the system altogether.

The Japanese national health system is the source of another problem; it periodically lowers drug-reimbursement prices, thus limiting the profits Shionogi can make on sales made within the country. This policy provides strong motivation to further build up the company's international business. However, other factors such as fluctuations in the value of the yen and the effectiveness of competitors marketing campaigns have also affected profits on overseas sales from time to time.

Licensure to market other manufacturers' products has continued to be profitable overall. Examples include dilevalol, an antihypertensive, a long-acting sulphate preparation, and an ultrasound contrast imaging agent from Molecular Biosystems. Shionogi also handles Molecular Genetics's drugs for veterinary practice. In 1988 Schering-Plough began marketing a new oral antibiotic developed by Shionogi.

However, Shionogi has emphasized expanding its internal operations in basic research as well as in development of new products and product applications rather than building up business by acquiring overseas companies or participating with them in joint ventures to any great extent. Shionogi has established wholly owned subsidiaries in several countries, including the United States, Germany, and Taiwan. This emphasis on company control enables Shionogi to keep a close rein on the policies and procedures associated with its products and to safeguard the reputation it has long held for top-quality production and service.

Achievement through basic research has long been a major goal for Shionogi, which has also used its findings to develop a number of innovative products. In 1986, for example, Shionogi became the first of Japan's pharmaceutical companies to place biotechnology-based drugs on the market. Two years later, in order to expand its activities in antibiotics research and to examine the nature and causation of certain diseases, the company established a new laboratory and technical resource center, the Institute for Medical Science, in Osaka near its other laboratories. An eminent virologist heads the research teams exploring three basic areas: immunology and the causes of diseases such as cancer and viral ailments; cells, proteins, and genes; and instrumentation. About one-fourth of the company's employees are engaged in some aspect of research and development.

From future findings, the company hopes to develop and market the new "wonder" products to follow the example of Flumarin, the Shionogi antibiotic that quickly soared to a top position internationally despite being introduced in the midst of a soft period early in 1990.

Principal Subsidiaries: Taiwan Shionogi & Co., Ltd.; Shionogi U.S.A., Inc.; Shionogi & Co. GmbH (Germany).

—Betty T. Moore

/HI/EIDO

SHISEIDO COMPANY, LIMITED

75-5, Ginza, 7-chome
Chuo-ku, Tokyo 104-10
Japan
(03) 3572-5111
Fax: (03) 3574-8380

Public Company
Incorporated: 1927
Employees: 20,000
Sales: ¥456.35 billion (US$3.17 billion)
Stock Exchanges: Tokyo Luxembourg

Shiseido Company is the world's third-largest distributor and retailer of cosmetics, surpassed only by Avon Products and L'Oréal. In the rapidly expanding Southeast Asian market, Shiseido is a front-runner. High-quality products and personalized service, skillful and sometimes innovative marketing techniques, and judicious profit investment have kept the company ahead of most of its competitors—domestic and overseas—over many decades. The company's 27% share of the Japanese market reflects some slippage, from 34% in 1970 and 30% in 1985. In order to continue growing, Shiseido is conducting a multilevel campaign to hold loyal customers and also attract a significant portion of new generations of consumers.

The product formulas and techniques that brought the company its greatest success and long-term status as a trendsetter are no longer sufficient to attract younger consumers. As a result, Shiseido has become more attentive to forecasts of demographic and taste changes, and is investing in research-and-development activities geared to improve cosmetic lines and diversify into other types of products. In the late 1980s, Shiseido shifted 10% of its business from cosmetics to foods, fashions, and other goods. Cosmetic products still constitute three-fourths of the company's sales, however, and are expected to continue doing so. The late 1980s were a period of intensified change for the company, with a new president and new corporate plan and increased sensitivity to trends in fashion and fitness.

In 1872 Yushin Fukuhara, former head pharmacist for the Japanese Admirality, opened the Shiseido Pharmacy on the Ginza in Tokyo—a bold stroke that created Japan's first Western-style pharmacy. The characters in the store's name and the store's philosophy were derived from classic Asian philosophy. Shiseido's name implies "richness of life," which, according to Confucian thought, can be reached only through harmony of mind, body, and soul. The small store, in a populous shopping area, attracted purchasers of traditional remedies as well as curiosity-seekers interested in the novelty of Western imports; personalized service and high-quality products won their loyalty. In the 1880s Shiseido began to manufacture medicines, and in 1888 introduced a new product to Japan: toothpaste. Shiseido began selling cosmetic products that were processed by the standards used for medicines in 1897. The first such product was Eudermine skin lotion.

During the late 19th century Japan was transformed by changes that had swept the country since the lowering of the two-centuries-old international trade barriers in the mid-1850s: some women still wore traditional white rice powder, hair lacquer, and stylized brows; others wore the lip salve, rouge, and skin-tone powder worn by Western women.

Traditional Japanese cosmetics and medicinal remedies came from herbs and other plants and minerals that were ground and processed according to recipes that had been part of the Japanese culture since being introduced from China in the sixth and seventh centuries. Similar ingredients and processes were used to produce both lip balm and lipstick. The pharmacist was the purveyor of both.

In Japan, cosmetics for men had had their heyday in the courtly and elegant latter part of the first millenium A.D. During the 19th century men still wore theatrical make-up—only males were permitted stage careers. But during the period, many kabuki performers were poisoned by the lead in their make-up. In order to prevent future tragedies, the Japanese government established strict product and marketing regulations—so elaborate, frustrating, and time-consuming that few foreign companies tackled the Japanese market. The regulations also hurt domestic companies, however. In the two years it takes to license a product, many products lose their timeliness, and thus their appeal. The Ministry of Health and Welfare eased some of these restrictions during the 1980s, but they still constitute a problem for Shiseido, and there is little hope that they will disappear in the near future.

Shipping was impeded just before and after the turn of the century—due first to the Sino-Japanese War of 1894 to 1895, then to the Russo-Japanese War of 1904 to 1905. Because of the difficulty of delivering imports, by 1915 the cosmetics Shiseido had begun to manufacture in 1897 replaced imports in popularity, to the point that the company began to concentrate almost exclusively on cosmetics, shifting its emphasis away from pharmaceuticals. In addition, in 1902 the company opened Japan's first soda fountain. The sale of foods has remained a modest but profitable venture.

Shinzo Fukuhara, the son of Yushin Fukuhara, led Shiseido during this period, and became Shiseido's first president in 1927. Shinzo Fukuhara had spent five years studying pharmacology at Columbia University, in New York City, and had visited France for one year. In France, he made important ties with artists whose ideas influenced the development of Shiseido's marketing, advertising, and packaging. Shiseido's marketing director, Noboru Matsumoto, had also studied in the United States, at New York University.

Tokyo's growth helped the family business grow and prosper, even through World War I, when production and delivery of the company's products were adversely affected by wartime restrictions. It was after the war, in 1923—remembered by so many in Japan as the year of the great Kanto Earthquake—that Shiseido took a daring step that eventually expanded its business far beyond the city and made it a national concern. At Matsumoto's urging, the company opened a series of retail outlets for Shiseido products—a franchise operation, in principle not unlike the franchise concept Ray Kroc of McDonald's introduced in the United States some 30 years later.

Shiseido had built its business as a mom-and-pop operation, paying special attention to the needs of its customers in Tokyo and the surrounding area. Repeat business resulted both from product excellence and personalized service. Special needs were recorded along with transactional details so that reminders could be tailored and timed to catch orders for replenishment. The franchised shops were to replicate the Tokyo store—with stock variations responding to local tastes and needs. The idea caught on because most franchisees, like the founding family, were willing to work long hours to earn customer loyalty.

In addition to over-the-counter retail sales, franchise owner-operators began conducting a mail-order business in 1937. They called it the Camellia Club, referring to the art nouveau–inspired flower logo Matsumoto designed and Shiseido began using in 1915. The 25,000 franchise stores still do a steady large-volume business, with members numbering about 9.6 million. The stores issue credit cards to members, and keep in touch through a monthly magazine featuring fashion and beauty pointers.

The company's size ballooned quickly, outgrowing its status as a limited partnership. Reorganized as a corporation in 1927, Shiseido was listed on the Tokyo Stock Exchange. Neither the Depression nor the following years of Japanese concentration on military buildup and action did much to flatten the company's growth curve.

By the 1940s Shiseido had become a trendsetter in the cosmetics industry. Even the bombing and devastation of many manufacturing sites during World War II did not result in the company's destruction. With the economic policies introduced by General Douglas MacArthur during the postwar years, Shiseido again reorganized, and, in 1949, again was listed on the Tokyo Stock Exchange.

Regaining its position as the cosmetics leader in the early 1950s—a position not successfully challenged until the 1970s, when foreign companies began to challenge Shiseido in earnest—Shiseido opened thousands of additional outlets, prospering with the franchisees as the economy's upsurge produced newly affluent customers. In 1952 the company set up a wholesale network for sales of soap, toothpaste, and sundries. The following year the Shiseido Institute of Beauty Technology was opened.

In 1957 Shiseido began international operations, when it initiated manufacturing and sales operations in Southeast Asia. In 1960 the company began marketing in Hawaii. International operations boomed in the 1960s, as subsidiaries were established in Hawaii, New York, and Milan. Others opened during the following two decades in Singapore, New Zealand, Bangkok, Australia, France, West Germany, and the United Kingdom. In 1965 Shiseido began marketing products that were formulated especially for export markets.

During the early 1970s Shiseido introduced its broad product line in the United States, but the expected sales volume failed to materialize. About ten years later, Yoshio Ohno—at that time director of overseas operations—took a different, more successful approach: Shiseido offered an exclusive product line to each of several top-flight fashion retailers—for example, Bloomingdale's in New York and Bullock's in Los Angeles. By the mid-1980s, these lines were earning $75 million annually, growing by 40% each year. This strategy succeeded not only in the United States, but in other countries as well.

During the 1970s, interest in the company's broad product line as a whole began to wane, and Shiseido began to consider new organizational and marketing directions. Many owner-operators who had worked diligently for decades to maintain a loyal customer following were nearing retirement and seemed out of touch with the interests and tastes of the new generation of consumers. To young consumers, the stores lacked the freshness and excitement that earlier generations had discovered in them. Shiseido refurbished the stores and new marketing analysis and techniques were applied.

Serge Lutens, a French "international image creator," joined Shiseido in 1980. The following year, the company began marketing cosmetics in China. In 1983 and 1987, respectively, Shiseido began to manufacture and sell Hua Zi brand hair-care products and then cosmetics in China.

Segmentation of the broad product line into five age groups for marketing purposes was instituted in 1982, with encouraging results. Other ideas that have succeeded as part of the new approach are product diversification and institution of diversity among the respective stores. Rather than making each store an outlet for all product lines, some have become convenience stores, carrying household products as well as cosmetics. Others carry youth-oriented fashions. High-end beauty consultation services and exclusive product lines similar to those in the high-fashion centers overseas are other specialties. Still other stores carry cosmetics and fitness aids for men and women. Shiseido has no intention of departing from its major role in the cosmetics industry, however; the stores handle other products to lure in customers who purchase the beauty aids.

Despite Shiseido's size, the company has not strayed far from its founder's practice of associating beauty aids with health concepts. For example products in the Elixir skin-care-product line contain an ingredient to protect sunbathers from ultraviolet rays. The company has carefully researched all market segments, targeting them with certain products. For the rapidly growing older group, Shiseido introduced Medicated Flowline Active, used to prevent hair loss, promote its regeneration, and aid in circulation of the blood. Cle de Peau Program Care is designed to prevent skin from aging and to help it recover a youthful look. A chain of sports clubs and restaurants and a line of health foods also promote physical fitness. In 1986 Shiseido acquired Carita, a French beauty salon and beautician school chain, and in 1987 Shiseido opened another beauty salon in Paris. The company acquired the U.S. hair-wave-product manufacturer Zotos International in 1988.

Some product lines have been discarded despite brisk sales. Environmental concerns have caused Shiseido to phase out products such as aerosol spray cans and nonbiodegradable diapers. New products and product lines continue to spur additional business. Research and development have been important to Shiseido's operations since its earliest days. Pharmaceuticals, as well as cosmetics, are being developed and tested in the company's domestic and overseas research centers. In 1990 Shiseido's first prescription drug, a cataract treatment, was on the verge of introduction. Shiseido also opened research facilities in France, in 1988, and the United States, in 1989. In 1990 the company announced plans to begin manufacturing cosmetics in France in 1992.

During the late 1980s Shiseido's three-year reorganization program strengthened its sales network and reaffirmed its long-held leadership position in the field, under the direction of president and CEO Yoshiharu Fukuhara, a grandson of Shiseido's founder and nephew of Shinzo Fukuhara. The company has enjoyed growth and longevity in a field where a product's appeal is often ephemeral.

Principal Subsidiaries: Osaka Shiseido Co., Ltd.; Shiseido Kako Co., Ltd.; Shiseido Shoji Co., Ltd.; Shiseido Higashikanto Sales Co., Ltd.; Shiseido Cosmetics (America) Ltd. (U.S.A.); Shiseido International Corporation (U.S.A.); Zotos International, Inc. (U.S.A.)

Further Reading: Tanner, Andrew, ''Is beauty more than skin-deep?,'' *Forbes,* December 16, 1985; *Shiseido: Company Press Kit,* Tokyo, Shiseido Company, Limited, 1990.

—Betty T. Moore

SB
SmithKline Beecham

SMITHKLINE BEECHAM PLC

SB House
Great West Road
Brentford, Middlesex TW8 9BD
United Kingdom
(081) 847-0830
Fax: (081) 560-5151

Public Company
Incorporated: 1989
Employees: 62,800
Sales: £4.28 billion (US$6.90 billion)
Stock Exchanges: London New York

In 1989 the Beecham Group merged with the U.S. company SmithKline Beckman to form one of the world's largest pharmaceutical companies. The merger was the latest response to changes in the pharmaceutical industry. Faced with growing competition, higher research costs, and the prospect of an economically unified Europe after 1992, both companies adapted as they had many times before.

One of the first British companies to undertake intensive advertising, Beecham grew from a small regional pill-peddling operation to a multinational patent medicine company at a time when very few companies branched beyond their own communities.

In 1847 Thomas Beecham began hawking his own brand of pills throughout the town of Wigan and the surrounding countryside. He soon set up shop as an herbalist and grocer in Wigan. Beecham, born the son of a farm worker in 1820, had spent his youth as a shepherd boy, and in that job he had learned a good deal about herbal remedies. Beecham was said to have had a special knack for healing sick animals and, on occasion, even humans. For several years Beecham sold his laxatives at local markets with a sales pitch that included showing off a jar of intestinal worms.

In 1859, after mixed results in Wigan, Beecham moved his operation to nearby St. Helens, where he focused on two products: a cough tablet and the famous laxative Beecham's Pills, advertised in the local newspaper as "worth a guinea a box." Both products were available through mail order and Beecham increased spending on advertising to take advantage of a rapidly growing demand for health products.

In 1881, when Thomas Beecham's son Joseph took effective control of the company, Beecham's sales were at £34,000, demonstrating average annual growth of about 18%, a rate it had sustained since 1865. The elder Beecham remained active in the operations of the company until his official retirement in 1895.

Joseph Beecham increased the company's advertising expenditures considerably. By 1891 annual advertising expenditures had increased to £120,000, from £22,000 in 1884, and Beecham introduced more creative ads. Advertising gimmicks included free distribution of sails printed with Beecham slogans to boat owners and inexpensive general information booklets bearing Beecham's messages.

During the 1880s Joseph Beecham spearheaded the company's expansion overseas. First, Beecham's Pills were exported to countries throughout the British Empire. In 1888 they were distributed in the United States and Canada, and two years later a manufacturing facility was set up in New York.

Extensive advertising had made Beecham's Pills practically a household word on several continents by the end of the 19th century. This success was not at first duplicated after the turn of the century, however. Although Beecham remained profitable, its rate of growth slowed considerably. Joseph Beecham spent more of his time on projects unrelated to the business, including numerous philanthropic endeavors and patronage of his music-minded son, Thomas, later to become a renowned conductor. In 1913 sales remained static at £290,000, although the firm's profitability had improved.

In 1916 Joseph Beecham died, leaving a complicated estate. Beecham had never incorporated the pill buisness and it remained entwined with his other affairs. Henry Beecham, Joseph's younger son, ran the business with three other executors until 1921, but had no active role after that time. Three years later the pill business was acquired by financier Philip Hill. Hill incorporated the company as Beecham's Pills in 1928 and launched a new period of growth.

For the next ten years Hill made acquisitions broadening the product line of the company. He purchased patent medicines like Yeast Vite, Iron Jelloids, Phosferine, and Phyllosan. In the later 1930s the company entered the toiletries business with the acquisition of Prichard and Constance, a shampoo manufacturer that distributed the brand name Amami. In 1938 Beecham acquired Macleans Ltd., well-known for toothpaste; County Perfumery, manufacturers of Brylcreem; and Eno Proprietaries, makers of a popular antacid. In 1938 Beecham acquired Lucozade, a popular glucose drink, from its inventor W. W. Hunter, to enter the health-drink field. The company changed its name to Beecham Group Ltd. in 1945 to reflect its diversified nature.

When Beecham acquired Maclean's in 1938 it unknowingly changed its direction. With the purchase came company secretary and director H. G. Leslie Lazell. Lazell became corporate secretary of Beecham's Pills, and during the war took over as managing director of the Maclean's unit. Leslie Lazell had always been a firm believer in research, and he developed a research department at the company, which soon entered the medicines field.

Beecham Research Laboratories Ltd. employed 115 people, 34 of them graduate-level scientists. In 1947 a 27-acre facility was opened at Surrey, with Alexander Fleming, the discoverer of penicillin, presiding over the opening ceremonies. Beecham Research Laboratories started out researching both pharmaceuticals and food products but before long concentrated solely on pharmaceutical research. In 1949 Beecham's acquisition of the C.L. Bencard company, a manufacturer of allergy vaccines, paved the way for entry into the prescription drug field.

During the 1950s Beecham expanded its consumer-products line and pumped the profits into drug research. It purchased new health drinks, including Ribena blackcurrant juice, Shloer apple and grape drinks, and PLJ. Horlicks beverages were acquired in 1969. The toiletries division also expanded, adding Vosene shampoo among others. A real breakthrough came in 1957 when company researchers isolated the penicillin nucleus 6-aminopenicillanic acid (6-APA). This discovery opened the door to the manufacture of a multitude of new antibiotics.

In 1959 Beecham marketed Broxil (phenethicillin), followed shortly by Celbenin (methicillin). The introduction of these products represented a medical breakthrough, as many bacterial strains had built up a resistance to the original penicillins—Penicillin G and Penicillin V. In 1961 Penbritin (ampicillin) hit the market, and soon Beecham's facilities were inadequte for the worldwide demand. A 35-acre complex at Worthing came on line in the early 1960s to produce 6-APA, the base for semisynthetic penicillins. Beecham's lead in antibiotics brought tremendous growth in the 1960s and 1970s.

Lazell's emphasis on marketing was also key to Beecham's growth. By 1960 the company was the second largest advertiser in the United Kingdom. Beecham was one of the first British firms to put the CEO directly in charge of the marketing team, long a standard practice in the United States.

In the mid-1960s, Beecham products penetrated the European continent. Within 20 years, this region comprised Beecham's largest single market. In the later 1960s Beecham Pharmaceutical marketers turned their attention to the United States, where an expanding business had been built on foundations provided by Brylcreem hair dressing. In 1967 the company opened an antibiotics factory in Piscataway, New Jersey. In 1971 Beecham bought the U.S. feminine hygiene company S. E. Massengill.

In 1972 the company planned to increase the size of its prescription drug business by merging with on one of its chief British competitors, the Glaxo Group. The British government blocked the merger, citing the possibility of reduced spending on research and development within the industry. Glaxo was particularly attractive because it had a large network overseas.

In the mid-1970s new non-antibiotic drugs such as the allergy vaccine Pollinex and the antidepressant Norval joined Beecham's growing antibiotic line, which included three widely used products: Amoxil (amoxicillin), Floxapen (flucloxacillin), and Ticar (ticarcillin).

Acquisitions of American drug and consumer products companies accelerated toward the end of the decade and into the 1980s. In 1977 Beecham bought Sucrets throat lozenges for $76 million and acquired the floundering Calgon bath products line. Beecham turned the businesses around, revamping old products and packaging, and using aggressive marketing strategies. In 1979 Beecham purchased Jovan, the U.S. perfume manufacturer, for $85 million. Other fragrance lines were later acquired, including Diane Von Furstenberg in 1983 and the cosmetics and fragrances of the BAT company in 1985. Other big acquisitions in the early 1980s included the J. B. Williams company, makers of Geritol, Sominex, Aqua Velva, and Lectric Shave among others for $100 million in 1982; DAP, Inc., manufacturer of caulk and other home improvement products for $68 million in 1983; and Norcliff Thayer, a major manufacturer of OTC drugs including the well-known antacid, Tums, in the United States for $369 million in 1985. Beecham also acquired a number of European pharmaceutical companies in France, West Germany, and Italy.

In 1984, Beecham's profits began to level off, due in part to decreased popularity of ampicillin, caused by increased antibiotic competition, and pressure from the British government to cap profits on drugs. Following Lazell's formula, Beecham's new chairman, Sir Ronald Halstead, hoped to pay for rising research-and-development costs through profits on consumer goods. A number of acquisitions of consumer products companies in 1984 and 1985 seemed to the company's directors too costly and out of line with Beecham's overall thrust. Halstead was let go in 1985. In 1986 Robert P. Bauman became chairman of Beecham. Bauman the company's first U.S. chairman, knew the North American market well, having worked at General Foods, Avco, and Textron. Bauman sold off some of Beecham's consumer products lines, primarily soft drinks lines, although he retained the successful Ribena, Horlicks, and Lucozade brands, and implemented cost-cutting measures worldwide. Between 1986 and mid-1989, Bauman disposed of £400 million of noncore businesses.

By the mid-1980s Beecham had made significant headway into the U.S. marketplace and continued to hold its place as the largest OTC drug producer in its home market. Beecham's pharmaceutical research focused on three general areas: cardiovascular therapy, diseases affecting the central nervous system, and anti-infectives. Demand for health care products increased substantially as the wealthy U.S. market grew older. Relifex, a nonsteroidal anti-inflammatory used by arthritis patients, began limited marketing in 1985 and by the late 1980s showed promise for the company. An anticlotting agent, Eminase, introduced in Europe in 1987, also appeared to be a significant breakthrough for cardiac patients. Two new antibiotics, Augmentin and Timentin, earned the Queen's Award for technological achievement in 1986. Both drugs received widespread acceptance throughout the medical community.

In July 1989, Beecham merged with an equally well established business, the U.S. SmithKline Beckman Corporation to form what was at the time the second-largest pharmaceutical company in the world, behind Merck and Company. The new SmithKline Beecham, based in London, tallied US$6.9 billion in sales annually. Beecham was widely considered the healthier half of the new company. With Eminase and Relifex about to hit the American market, Beecham looked solid enough to shore up its ailing U.S. partner for at least a short time. SmithKline had failed to come up with a blockbuster product since it introduced the ulcer remedy Tagamet in the mid-1970s despite substantial research and development expenditures. New competition from Glaxo's Zantac had eroded some of Tagamet's expected market share, and SmithKline was accused by stock analysts of lacking direction. A headline in *The Wall Street Journal*, July 7, 1989, called the merger "just what the doctor ordered" for SmithKline. SmithKline's chairman Henry Wendt became chairman of the merged company while Robert Bauman, who became the new company CEO, faced combining two distinct corporate cultures and had little time to spare: just one week after the Beecham SmithKline merger was finalized, two U.S. giants, Squibb and Bristol-Myers, announced their own merger plans. Beecham, with its new prescription drugs and strong presence in the over-the-counter drug market looks like a good partner for SmithKline, with its strong American sales staff. The SmithKline Beecham merger permitted both companies to compete on a global level neither could manage alone. In addition, the companies' research-and-development programs were complementary. Beecham had several new products ready for market while SmithKline was at the opposite end of the research-and-development cycle, promising results down the road. Geographically, Beecham's strength in Europe fit well with SmithKline's coverage in the United States and Japan. Bauman expressed his intentions to cut costs by eliminating administrative and production personnel, rather than by paring sales or research staffs. Although the company will face problems with its reorganization, its sheer size and its continued commitment to developing new products should insure it a place at the forefront of the pharmaceutical industry.

Principal Subsidiaries: Beecham Group p.l.c.; SmithKline Beecham Corporation (U.S.A.).

Further Reading: Francis, Anne, *A Guinea a Box: A Biography,* London, Hale, 1968; Hindley, Diana, and Geoffrey Hindley, *Advertising in Victorian England, 1837–1901,* London, Wayland, 1972; Corley, T.A.B., "Sir Joseph Beecham" and "Thomas Beecham," in *Dictionary of Business Biography: A Biographical Dictionary of Business Leaders Active in Britain in the Period, 1860–1980,* Volume I, edited by David Jeremy, London, Butterworth & Co. Ltd., 1985; Holland, Kenneth, "Pharmaceutical Industry Profiles: Beecham Group PLC," *The Pharmaceutical Journal,* Volume 238, 1987; "SmithKline Beckman Corporation," in *International Directory of Company Histories,* Volume I, edited by Thomas Derdak, Chicago, St. James Press, 1988; "Beecham Group PLC: A Brief History," Beecham corporate typescript, 1989.

—Thomas M. Tucker

WELLA GROUP

Berliner Allee 65
6100 Darmstadt
Federal Republic of Germany
(06151) 340
Fax: (06151) 342748

Public Company
Incorporated: 1880 as Franz Ströher–Rothenkirchen
Employees: 14,000
Sales: DM2.41 billion (US$1.43 billion)
Stock Exchanges: Frankfurt Zürich Basel Berlin Vienna Geneva

Wella is Germany's largest—and the world's second-largest—producer of hairdressing products for home and professional use. Wella AG operates in Darmstadt as the head company of the worldwide Wella Group. In the latter half of the 1980s, Wella took a significant step forward into the international hygiene-products market. This period was marked by a number of acquisitions and diversifications into new fields, by expansion into new markets, and by heavy investment in new production technology. Subsidiary companies of international importance include the French companies Parfums Rochas and René Garraud.

From its earliest days, Wella has preserved its character as an independent family business. Although, since 1983, a third of the company's shares have been traded as preference shares with no voting rights, the majority of shares belong to the third and fourth generations of the founding Ströher family and its branches. Since 1973, managing directors from outside the family have run the business, although there are family representatives on the supervising and advisory boards, in accordance with a family contract. Wella's fortunes have been linked strongly to the German economy for many years, as a long-standing supplier to the hairdressing in dustry as well as to the consumer. Wella's logo is one of the most familiar in Germany.

In examining the company's history, a strong sense of tradition emerges. This is particularly evident in its clearly defined production and sales strategies, cooperation with the hairdressing industry, and the image of the company as a family business. This strong sense of continuity has cushioned Wella in times of crisis.

In 1880, at the age of 26, the hairdresser Franz Ströher, the grand- and great-grandfather of today's generations of owners, founded a company for the production and distribution of artificial hair in the Saxon Vogtland. His company was registered on July 1 at the Auerbach district court. The region in which he chose to operate was a traditional stronghold of the textile industry, with a well-established local manufacturing base. Here, the people were skilled, diligent, and poor—an ideal workforce for the labor-intensive production of hairpieces and wigs, which were made out of natural and artificial hair. During his years spent traveling as an apprentice hairdresser in Germany, Holland, Switzerland, and, above all, France, Ströher learned about new hair fashions and acquired the necessary hairdressing techniques. In 1872 undulation waving was invented by the Frenchman François Marcel. This became a popular method for waving women's hair, and was supplemented with the addition of natural or artificial hairpieces. In 1880 Ströher set up his own private firm, Franz Ströher–Rothenkirchen, for the manufacture and distribution of artificial hair. After initial difficulties with the development of new production methods he eventually found a material in England that could, with the aid of a waterproof finish that he had developed himself, be used to make wigs. This product, "Tullemoid waterproof," became a considerable success at the turn of the century, and in 1904 a larger manufacturing plant was built in Rothenkirchen. This plant still exists, although it has been modified extensively.

In 1908 Ströher's two older sons, Karl Ströher, a merchant, and Georg Ströher, a hairdresser, joined the business. They were to shape the company's history over the following 60 years. As early as 1931 sales extended to the United States, and in Rothenkirchen a staff of 30 was employed in addition to family members. They manufactured many kinds of wigs and hairpieces. The permanent wave had not yet become widely popular. Promising experiments were carried out in the United Kingdom and their results impressed the Continent, but World War I broke out before the hot-wave technique for women could be offered at a reasonable price. The war had a significant impact in more than one respect upon the history of the family business. Franz Ströher's three younger sons were killed, and Franz Ströher himself, almost broken by the events, left the management increasingly to his sons Karl and Georg, and took the less active role of senior partner until he died in 1936. To compound the problems, international hair fashions suddenly changed; the popularity of bobbed hair caused a rapid decline in the demand for hairpieces. This change led to a difficult period of readjustment for the company. There was a brief episode of production of wigs for dolls, clothing for workers, mannequins for hairdressers, and sales of hairbrushes, washing brushes, toothbrushes, face towels, and shaving towels. The war also cut contacts abroad that were difficult to reestablish under new circumstances.

However, one new development after the mid-1920s led to a phase of relative prosperity for Franz Ströher OHG, as the company had been called since 1918. The permanent waving process was at last proving successful and gave a much wider scope to the hairdressing trade. François Marcel's waving technique was developed further in Germany by Karl Nessler and Josef Mayer. At this point the Ströher brothers took the opportunity to acquire a license for the manufacture of a new generation of permanent wave machines that used 16 to 24 volts and were easy to operate.

In the meantime the brand name "Wella" had been registered at the German patent office as a hairdressing trademark. Since 1927 the production and distribution of perm machines, hair driers, hairdressers' equipment, and salon furniture have been carried out under this name. Soon cosmetic hair products appeared as part of the production program alongside professional hairdressing equipment. These took into account the demands of hairdressers. A well-known product at this time was the hair treatment Kolestral, based on recent biological discoveries.

The year 1930 was the 50th anniversary of the company, and marked the beginning of a new phase of expansion. The business adopted the legal status of a public limited company, Franz Ströher AG, with an original capital of 250,000 marks, and employed 150 staff members. From this time the licensed Wella emblem, with a woman's head and stylized waves of hair, became an international symbol. The *Wella News*, a new trade magazine, was published by the company. This journal had a widespread distribution and, combined with the regular training courses offered to hairdressers, helped to establish a strong connection between the company and the hairdressing trade. The factory at Rothenkirchen was by this time manufacturing hair driers, hydraulic chairs, and electric hair-cutting equipment. The program also incorporated the production of furnishings for hairdressing salons and cosmetic products. These were partly produced by the company itself, and partly supplied by others.

In the years before 1938 the company established many subsidiaries, and a manufacturing plant was set up in Plauen, Vogtland. International branches and subsidiary companies all over the world promoted the growth of the family business. It no longer was restricted by the unfavorable location of the Saxon Vogtland. In the course of an allocation policy pursued in the Thüringen region, the head offices of the corporation, together with the manufacturing and export divisions, were transferred to the town of Apolda, although the production of hair cosmetics continued at the parent plant at Rothenkirchen. When the factory at Apolda was dismantled at the end of World War II, in 1945, the firm had well over 800 employees.

This period of expansion also brought about important welfare innovations within the company, such as subsidies for children of employees and allowances for marriage, childbirth, death, and accidents. Provision for the retirement of former staff and their dependents was secured by regular benefit payments, and advanced training within the establishment was extended. Typical of the family business was the strong, almost patriarchal relationship between management and staff. Documents from the Wella archive in Darmstadt demonstrate that employees at the end of the 1930s were on average fairly young. Many surnames occur several times, which points to the recruitment of employees' relatives, and a major proportion of staff moved with the management from Sachsen to Thüringen.

As early as the 1930s, Wella laboratories were developing and constantly improving numerous hair cosmetic products, which became best sellers, such as the bleaching compound Blondor, a non-alkaline washing agent concentrate called Wellapon, and the liquid foaming hair tint Wellaton, which came in an wide range of colors. Whereas bleaching and tinting agents were relatively well developed, it took longer to find an effective dyeing compound. Wella Percol Liquid was the best known product. Koleston, a gentle, conditioning cream dye available in a tube, had been developed but could not be produced during wartime, when the raw materials it required were unobtainable.

The economic policy of the National Socialists and wartime conditions were not favorable to Wella. The Ströher brothers were active Freemasons and were opposed to National Socialism. In the course of time, important products could no longer be manufactured due to restrictions on raw-material supplies. The factory in Apolda built new ventilation systems and equipment for submarines, and could no longer make permanent wave machines and hair driers. At the end of World War II the Ströhers had to face the dismantling of the plant in Apolda and expropriation by the government of the plant in Rothenkirchen, still intact with more than 300 working staff, as communal state property.

The Ströhers, supported by a few tireless colleagues, began to look for a new sphere of influence and orientation. In September 1945, at the Hotel Krone, the reconstruction of the business began on a very small scale in Huenfeld, Osthessen, under the new name of Ondal GmbH. The brothers stayed for the time being in Rothenkirchen. It was only in 1946 that the production of cosmetic products resumed there, followed by the production of hairdressing equipment in May of that year. At the same time, Wella Hairdressing Requirements GmbH was founded in Berlin. After the expropriation of Rothenkirchen, a large-scale manufacturing plant was set up in Huenfeld, which has since been extended several times and represents the center of the company's production. After the division of Germany, Wella's former plant in Rothenkirchen continued to operate. As VEB Londa it became part of a larger chemical concern, which had very limited development potential due to the strict principles of Eastern economic planning. Nevertheless, it came to hold a significant position in the market before the reunification of Germany and had established a considerable number of outlets for the export of goods, mainly to Eastern Europe. However, the profile of the enterprise and the quality of its products were not compatible with Western standards. In February 1990, political changes in East Germany brought about the reintegration of the Rothenkirchen plant into Wella in the form of a joint venture which was to produce and market hairdressing products and equipment in Germany and other European markets. Without the strong bond resulting from their shared origins in the family business the reintegration of the factory at Rothenkirchen with Wella would not have been possible.

From 1950 the business was registered as Wella AG. The central management of the company operated from Darmstadt, Hessen, where the head offices were based. The reintroduction of the successful Wella logo proved highly advantageous. Wella, having had a modest turnover of DM10 million in 1950, then attempted to retrieve international rights for trademarks which had been expropriated, and business connections which had been lost after 1945.

Wella owes its international reputation to its early and aggressive penetration of international markets. As early as the 1950s Wella had included Third World countries in its trading policies, and had met with strong opposition. Production started in 1952 in Chile, Italy, and the Netherlands, in 1953 in Africa, and in 1954 in Australia and Brazil. In the 1960s the Asian and Pacific territories were entered in stages. An international distribution network was set up and larger manufacturing plants all over the world helped protect the firm from world trade friction, and set the prototype for Germany's international business relations after World War II.

In 1950 Koleston, the first hair-conditioning cream tint, was introduced and initiated a new generation of hair products that conquered the markets. Koleston still is produced. Its high research-and-development costs are reflected in a high price for both hairdressers and consumers. Wella has a large range of successful products including such well-known brands as Wella Balsam, Shock Waves, Bellady, and System Professional. For some time now, a change in consumer attitudes and a stronger awareness of the environment have caused increasing recourse to natural ingredients, the abolition or reduction of propellant gas in sprays, and the increasing use of biodegradable packaging made of raw materials that break down naturally. In most cases it is costly to develop new environmentally friendly products, as well as to market them effectively, since there is often a discrepancy between ecological requirements and consumer demand.

The Wella Group still sees itself as an independent family business, in which the founder's influence can still be felt. Since the beginning of the 1950s, members of the third generation were additionally brought into the management of the company. However, Wella's considerable growth and diversification have resulted in its transcendence beyond the role of a middle-class family business. In 1973 the day-to-day running of the group was entrusted to directors, who were not members of the founding family. The family members concentrate their capacities on supervising and advisory activities. It was due to these changes that in 1978 Wella's worldwide sales passed DM1 billion for the first time, and have continued to rise ever since. In 1983 Wella turned to the stock market in a move to adjust its capital structure to cope with its rapid growth.

Principal Subsidiaries: Kadabell GmbH & Co. KG (99.8%); Emil Kiessling & Cie. GmbH & Co.; Dr. rer. nat. Peter Theiss Naturwaren OHG (75%); Wilhelm Oberle Verwaltungsgesellschaft mbH; Tondeo-Werk GmbH; Wella Friseurbedarf GmbH; Intercosmetic S.A. (Belgium); Ondal-France E.u.r.l. (France); Ets. Pelleray E.u.r.l. (France); René Garraud S.A. (France); Parfums Rochas S.A. (France); Ondawel (G.B.) Ltd. (U.K.); Intercosmetic (G.B.) Ltd. (U.K.); Soc. Labocos s.a.s. di Rolf Kissing & C. (Italy, 80%); N.V. Handelsmaatschappij van Ravensberg (Netherlands); Wella International Finance B.V. (Netherlands); Interkosmetik Ges.m.b.H. (Austria, 95%); Intercosmetic AB (Sweden); Wella Beteiligungen AG (Switzerland); Productos Cosméticos S.A. (Spain); Cosmetic Products Pty. Ltd. (Australia); Cosmetic Suppliers Pty. Ltd. (Australia); Belcosa Distribuidora de Cosméticos Ltda. (Brazil); Tianjin Liming Cosmetics Joint Industrial Co. Ltd. (China, 51%); Fine Care Co. Ltd. (Japan, 63.3%); Productora de Cosméticos S.A. (Mexico, 99.8%); Sonata Laboratories Ltd. (New Zealand); Chemo-Technische Manufacturing Inc. (Philippines, 62.2%); Myungmy Cosmetics Co. Ltd. (South Korea, 50%); The Wella Corporation (U.S.A., 99.8%).

—Wieland Sachse
Translated from the German by Karin Potisk

HEALTH CARE SERVICES

AMERICAN MEDICAL INTERNATIONAL, INC.
BEVERLY ENTERPRISES, INC.
HOSPITAL CORPORATION OF AMERICA
HUMANA INC.
MAXICARE HEALTH PLANS, INC.
NATIONAL MEDICAL ENTERPRISES, INC.

AMERICAN MEDICAL INTERNATIONAL, INC.

8201 Preston Road, Suite 300
Dallas, Texas 75225
U.S.A.
(214) 360-6300
Fax: (214) 987-0632

Wholly Owned Subsidiary of American Medical Holdings, Inc.
Incorporated: 1956 as Medlabs Inc.
Employees: 25,000
Sales: $2.75 billion

American Medical International was the first investor-owned hospital company in the world. It is currently among the largest hospital-management companies in the United States. American Medical International (AMI) experienced difficulties during the 1980s, largely due to over-expansion and over-diversification, as well as the industry's volatility. After suffering large losses in 1986 the company retreated in order to strengthen its position in an increasingly competitive hospital environment. At one time busily branching into other countries, AMI now pays closer attention to its domestic operations. AMI was bought out by IMA Holdings Corporation in late 1989 and has since undergone major restructuring, including continued down-sizing. Its focus has shifted from bouts of expansion to the management of solidly profitable ventures such as acute-care and psychiatric hospitals.

American Medical International was founded in 1956 by 39-year-old bacteriologist and bioanalyst Uranus "Bob" J. Appel. Originally called Medlabs, AMI began as an independent medical reference laboratory contracting with Los Angeles–area hospitals. In June 1960, when a 26-bed client hospital was about to close its doors, Medlabs bought it. With this acquisition, and another hospital purchase a year later, AMI initiated the investor-owned hospital industry.

In 1960 Appel also took Medlabs public and changed its name to American Laboratories. After a rash of acquisitions and a resultant financial squeeze, AMI diversified in 1963, forming its first subsidiary: American RX Pharmacy. The subsidiary and the 1964 sale of some valuable commercial real estate helped the young company strengthen its shaky finances. In January 1965, because of its diversification, the company's name was changed again—to American Medical Enterprises.

In the late 1960s the company acquired two wholly owned subsidiaries: Professional Research, which produced health-interest films and videos, and a cardio-pulminary management company called Inhalation Therapy Services. Two more hospital purchases in 1967 doubled the company's bed capacity. AMI then sought to expand beyond southern California with the 1969 purchase of three facilities in Texas.

The company made its first foreign acquisition with the purchase of the prestigious Harley Street Clinic in London during the late 1960s. Six months after the purchase, the Harley Street Clinic was performing more open-heart surgery than any other British hospital. The clinic was an excellent marketing tool because of its visibility. It also fulfilled a commitment to invest in Europe that AMI made to investors when the company issued its first Eurodollar note that year. Also, because AMI was the first hospital-management company to arrive in Europe, it held a strategic advantage over its competitors in the international health-care marketplace.

In 1970 the company, in the fastest growing industry in the United States, had most of its operations based in the most rapidly developing parts of the country. AMI acquired its first hospital in Florida and two more in Texas. AMI doubled its size in late 1971 with the purchase of Chanco Medical Industries. Chanco owned 24 hospitals in eight states. In 1972 the company adopted its current name, American Medical International, to reflect its growing activities overseas, including a recent acquisition in Switzerland. Experiencing a dip in earnings in 1974 due to rapid expansion, massive construction costs, and inflation, AMI instituted severe cost-containment policies and restructured.

During this time AMI put a three-year halt on growth while it assimilated these changes. The sacrifice of short-term profits for long-term growth began to bear fruit in 1976, when profits rose by 65%. In the meantime, Royce Diener, a former investment banker, had succeeded Appel as company president. Appel became chairman and CEO. Diener set out to build up AMI's international operations in Europe, South America, and Saudi Arabia: in 1976 AMI signed a management contract with Ecuador; the following year an AMI regional office and the Princess Grace Hospital were opened in London.

Throughout the late 1970s, AMI focused on broadening its reach, acquiring an international consulting firm called Gordon A. Freisen, International. The consulting subsidiary brought AMI's activities into ten countries; there were more construction projects in England and Australia, as well as new projects in Spain and Singapore. By the end of the decade, AMI's revenues were over $500 million. Founder Appel retired as chairman in 1979, and Diener succeeded him. Walter L. Weisman took over as president. Formerly a corporate lawyer, Weisman had joined the company after orchestrating its merger with Chanco seven years earlier. Diener and Weisman ran a company that had grown more than 500% in the previous decade.

Growth continued during the 1980s. In September 1980 AMI bought Hyatt Medical Enterprises, owner of eight hospitals. The purchase price was $66 million cash. AMI then acquired Brookwood Health Services in June 1981 and with it 11 more hospitals and 3 substance-abuse facilities for $156 million. The following month AMI's growth was challenged when the Federal Trade Commission charged, and later ruled, that the company's 1979 purchase of a Luis Obispo, California, hospital created a monopoly of the hospital market in that county. The purchase had given AMI control of three of the county's five hospitals, or 68% of the hospital beds, and American Medical was forced to divest French Hospital, for which it had paid twice the asking price.

American Medical's stated aim throughout the early 1980s was to acquire small hospitals and related medical facilities approximately every six weeks. To this end, AMI invested more than $750 million over a three-year period ending in fiscal 1983 to expand, modernize, and diversify its operations.

International growth boomed in 1982 and 1983, with management contracts signed in Saudi Arabia, Greece, and Canada and the opening of more hospitals in England, Switzerland, and Scotland. Domestically, AMI's outpatient surgical and industrial medical centers were the largest providers in their respective fields, as were AMI's physical-therapy and respiratory-therapy subsidiaries.

During this time, the industry was changing. In 1981 the health-care industry was the second-largest in the United States. By 1984, however, the hospital business was experiencing a decline. In 1983 the federal government had initiated major changes in the industry with a new Medicare and Medicaid reimbursement system. These cost-cutting measures sparked industrywide streamlining. In a short time, empty hospital beds began to plague hospital chains.

Nonetheless, AMI made one of the largest acquisitions in investor-owned hospital history in 1984. Lifemark Corporation was an oil belt–based chain of 25 hospitals and 3 substance-abuse facilities. The purchase was made just as the industry had begun to cut costs and slow down. The merger was expected to boost AMI's earnings by improving the company's economies of scale. Instead, AMI almost toppled under its own weight.

Between merger costs and dropping occupancy rates—along with other results of industry decline—AMI saw depressed earnings in 1984. By 1986, AMI was widely considered to be the poorest-performing of the big hospital chains. Steadily profitable until 1986, AMI lost more than $97 million that year. Those losses and the threat of takeover forced the company into an austerity program: the operating budget was slashed by one-third, corporate overhead was reduced by $30 million, and lay-offs were extensive. Ten underperforming hospitals were put up for sale, as well as most of the alcohol rehabilitation centers and the entire physical-therapy operation.

The remainder of the 1980s was spent dismantling the expansion that had taken place under Diener, whose earnings projections had been unrealistic to start, but became impossible when AMI's hospital occupancy rate fell below 50%. The Lifemark acquisition was failing to pay for itself; the industry was still slowing, and regulations were increasing; revenues from psychiatric and alcohol rehabilitation acquisitions that Diener calculated would generate 40% of AMI's profits brought in less than 10%.

In 1987 Diener resigned as chairman and was replaced by Weisman. Facing takeover rumors, Weisman stepped up the cost-cutting and streamlining of the company. Underproducing assets were sold, including the nation's first AIDS facility in Houston, Texas. Only open for one year, the hospital had lost $8 million.

These changes helped AMI see a slight increase in revenues for 1987; the same year the company fought off a $1.9 billion takeover bid by Chicago physician LeRoy Pesch. Selling money-losing hospitals in a troubled industry was a challenge, and AMI faced more takeover threats. In 1988, the company sold 104 hospitals and continued to cut back on corporate overhead and concentrate on dependable specialities such as obstetrics.

In March 1989, when the AMI board announced that it would entertain takeover bids, there were several offers. Shortly before the June 29 deadline for offers, AMI received a $3.3 billion bid from IMA Holdings Corporation. In October AMI agreed to be bought out by IMA, a group controlled by Corpus Christi, Texas–based merchant banker Harry Gray and Mel Klein and Partners. IMA was subsequently renamed American Medical Holdings. On April 3, 1990, AMI's shareholders approved the merger, and on April 12 AMI was merged into American Medical Holdings. Harry Gray, former United Technologies Corporation chairman, then became AMI's chairman and CEO. AMI's new owners launched a divestiture program, selling 12 acute-care and psychiatric hospitals, as well as 65% of AMI's stake in its British subsidiary. Corporate overhead was cut by the elimination of regional offices and the decision to relocate headquarters from its expensive Beverly Hills, California, location to Dallas, Texas.

With the help of these measures AMI reported an increase in revenues and cash flow for their first fiscal quarter in 1990. AMI must continue to trim its unwieldy assets. No longer threatened by takeover bids, the company can now concentrate on adjusting to the changing health-care industry.

Principal Subsidiaries: A.M.E. Leasing Corp; American Medical (Central), Inc.; American Medical Home Care, Inc.; AMI Ambulatory Centres, Inc.; AMI Diagnostic Services, Inc.; AMI Family Health Care Centers, Inc.; AMI Group Health Services, Inc.; AMI Healthcare Centers–Houston, Inc.; AMI Information Systems Group, Inc.; AMI Purchasing Services, Inc.; Amisub (American Hospital), Inc.; Amisub (Anclote), Inc.; Amisub (Comprecare), Inc.; Amisub (Culver Union Hospital), Inc.; Amisub (Del Amo), Inc.; Amisub (FPC), Inc.; Amisub (Irvine Medical Center), Inc.; Amisub (Lanham), Inc.; Amisub (McIntosh Trail Regional Medical Center), Inc.; Amisub (North Ridge Hospital), Inc.; Amisub of California; Amisub of Florida, Inc.; Amisub of North Carolina, Inc.; Amisub of Orlando, Inc.; Amisub of South Carolina, Inc.; Amisub (Prince George's), Inc.; Amisub (PSL), Inc.; Amisub (Saint Joseph Hospital), Inc.; Amisub (Sierra Vista), Inc.; Amisub (South Bay), Inc.; Amisub (The Retreat), Inc.; Amiwoodbroke, Inc.; Arroyo Grande Community Hospital; Atlanta Medical Ventures, Inc.; Brookwood Health Services, Inc.; Brookwood Primary Care Centers, Inc.; Central Arkansas General Hospital, Inc.; Circle City Hospital; Clairemont General Hospital, Inc.; Community Hospital of Santa Cruz, Inc.; Cumming Medical Ventures, Inc.; East Cooper Community Hospital, Inc.; Eastern Professional Properties, Inc.; Fayette Medical Venture, Inc.; Frye Regional Medical Center, Inc.; GCH, Inc.; Greenway Insurance Company (75%); Hamilton Credit Corporation, Inc.; Heartland Corporation; Inhalation Therapy

Services, Inc.; Lanham Medical Ventures, Inc.; LifeCare Management Systems, Inc.; Lifemark International Health Care, Ltd. (Cayman Islands); Lucy Lee Hospital, Inc.; Medical Center of Garden Grove; Mid-Continent Medical Practices, Inc.; North Fulton Medical Center, Inc; North Fulton MOB Ventures, Inc.; Orlando Medical Ventures, Inc.; Palm Beach Gardens Community Hospital, Inc.; Parkway Regional Medical Center, Inc.; Physicians Development, Inc.; Professional Medical Advisors, Inc.; Roswell Medical Ventures, Inc.; San Dimas Community Hospital; Sierra Vista Hospital, Inc.; St. Mary's Hospital, Inc.; Stewart Design Group, Inc.; Tampa Health Ventures, Inc.; Texas Professional Properties, Inc.; West Alabama General Hospital, Inc.

—Carol I. Keeley

BEVERLY ENTERPRISES, INC.

155 Central Shopping Center
Fort Smith, Arkansas 72903
U.S.A.
(501) 452-6712
Fax: (501) 452-3760

Public Company
Incorporated: 1964
Employees: 96,000
Sales: $2.10 billion
Stock Exchanges: New York Pacific

Beverly Enterprises is the largest nursing home chain in the United States. Formed in 1964, the company was clearly the industry leader by the mid-1980s after an aggressive acquisition campaign. As the majority of the patients in Beverly homes was covered by Medicare and Medicaid, the federal cost-containment legislation of 1983 that changed the reimbursement system hurt the company at the same time that labor costs were soaring. In the late 1980s, a rash of bad publicity slashed Beverly's occupancy, after numerous state health officials charged neglect on Beverly's part and put the company on probation. By 1989 the company was obliged to scale down considerably in order to pay debts and return to profitability.

At the time of its incorporation, the company consisted of three convalescent hospitals in the Pasadena region of southern California. The founder, Roy E. Christensen, was a Utah accountant. In its first decade, Beverly expanded into such things as plastics, printing, real estate development, and mirror-manufacturing. As a result, the company was heavily leveraged and in the red by 1973. In 1971 Robert Van Tuyle was recruited as a director from his 40-year career in the chemical industry, and he immediately began to streamline Beverly, divesting the company of its unrelated interests and focusing on long-term health care.

In the late 1960s and early 1970s, the nursing home industry was experiencing a glut. The onset of Medicare and Medicaid in the mid-1960s had sparked a rush of new entrepreneurs in what had previously been a largely nonprofitable industry. The too-rapid expansion stalled at about the time Van Tuyle joined Beverly, but he believed that the nursing home industry still had growth potential. Growth became Beverly's trademark beginning in 1977 when it purchased Leisure Lodges, from its parent company, Stephens, of Little Rock, Arkansas. Leisure Lodges was a chain of nursing homes. The purchase doubled Beverly's size, making it number-two in the industry. David R. Banks, who had been chairman of Leisure Lodges chain, joined Beverly as president and CEO in 1979.

Small chains and solo organizations were ripe for acquisition in the early 1980s because they were having trouble turning a profit on Medicaid reimbursements. Beverly's size and centralization, on the other hand, permitted economies of scale. Between 1976 and 1983, Beverly's revenues increased 12 times, primarily through acquisitions. The company grew from 47 homes in 1971 to 1,136 homes in 1985, when it had a presence in 45 states and Canada. By 1983 Beverly was the nation's largest operator of nursing homes. It had more than twice as many beds as the Hillhaven Corporation, its nearest competitor, and represented 7% of the industry.

A new "prospective payment plan," the result of federal legislation, promised to increase the flow of patients into convalescent centers by forcing hospitals to release them sooner. At the same time, the 1983 legislation changing Medicaid-Medicare reimbursement made the health care industry suddenly cost-conscious. These changes also meant that the industry was subjected to greater regulation by state and federal governments. Beverly posted record profits in 1985. The company was less concerned by its growth-fueled debts and Medicaid cost-capping than by the industrywide labor problem with potential for a union battle. Turnover was high in the low-wage, high-stress work force of nursing homes.

Problems began to surface by 1986, as allegations of neglect prompted investigations by various state health officials. Between 1985 and 1988, six Beverly facilities in Missouri were threatened with license revocation. In 1986, officials in Texas suspended Medicaid payments to 24 of Beverly's 134 nursing homes in that state, citing hazardous health-deficiencies; the state revoked the license of one home. That same year, Beverly settled a legal battle with the state of California's department of health services by paying a record $724,000 in fines. The company was accused of care so negligent that it contributed to or caused the death of nine patients in that state. Beverly agreed to pay the fines without admitting to the specific charges and was put on probation for two years. In 1987 health care officials in Maine and Washington, D.C., denied Beverly permission to open any new homes in their domains because of its poor patient-care record. In Michigan, the health department claimed that Beverly owned almost half of the facilities facing denial of Medicaid payments because of substandard care in 1987. Regulators in Minnesota said eight deaths in Beverly homes there were related to neglect.

The sensational details of some of the specific charges—including gangrene and amputation caused by infected bedsores, and rape—damaged Beverly's reputation and caused a drop in occupancy rates. The company lost $30.5 million on $2.1 billion in revenues in 1987. The same year, Beverly's top management tried an unsuccessful leveraged buyout of the company.

While occupancy rates were dropping and reimbursement problems worsened, labor expenses increased by between $90 and $120 million in 1987 when Beverly had to raise its wages. Nurse salaries were still less than competitive, and there was a shortage of nurses at this time. In addition, the expanding economy was offering other options to unskilled workers. About 70% of the nursing home work force consisted of poorly paid, low-skilled nurses' aides. With its image and occupancy problems, Beverly was obliged to remedy its employee troubles. Violations of statutory requirements for staffing, training, and patient care were not unusual in an industry whose biggest expense was labor. Labor costs accounted for 60% of Beverly's expenses. To combat the charges of chronic neglect, Beverly started a quality improvement program in 1988 and established a $5.7 million training center in Atlanta for nurses and administrators.

Beverly's $1.1. billion debt was beginning to pinch by 1988. The company considered filing for reorganization under bankruptcy-court protection in that year. Instead, it began selling off properties. Beverly was fined another $124,000 after a reinspection of its Oak Meadows Nursing Center in Los Gatos, California, where negligence had contributed to four patient deaths in 1985. Officials found evidence of medical record falsification, medication errors, and neglect. The facility's license was revoked and Beverly sold the home in February 1988.

About the same time that Beverly was taken off probation in California late in 1988, Minnesota moved to revoke the license of all 42 of the company's nursing homes in that state. The National Labor Relations Board brought a case against Beverly, charging it with more than 200 labor violations in 36 homes in six states, and accusing the company of engaging in a pattern of unfair labor practices. Management claimed that staff turnover, at 78%, not company policy, had precluded the formation of unions. At that time, about 11% of its staff was organized.

Troubles in California homes did not end with the probation. Beverly was fined more than $130,000 for patient neglect in its northern California Novato Convalescent Hospital, and the probational status of another home was extended for two more years. In the first nine months of 1988, Beverly lost $12.3 million.

The occupancy rate at Beverly's more than 1,000 homes stabilized at 88% by 1989. Staff turnover had also been cut. At that time, the $40 billion nursing home industry, which served 1.5 million people in the United States, was in crisis. Although 63% of patient-days were to be paid by Medicaid, money from Medicaid only accounted for 41% of payments. The squeeze between rising costs and inadequate government reimbursement meant many companies were losing money. The average daily payment by Medicaid for a nursing home patient had risen an average of 4% between 1985 and 1988, but labor costs had risen 11%. Two-thirds of Beverly's staff were aides whose wages were only 50¢ an hour more than workers at fast-food restaurants. High turnover contributed to the quality-of-care problems that plagued the industry.

Beverly underwent extensive reorganization in 1989, including the elimination of three layers of management and a substantial reduction in the number of its properties. Although there was an increase in revenues in 1989 over 1988, Beverly announced a $120 million charge in the second quarter of 1989, a charge associated with the planned sales of 35% of its homes. Proceeds of the sale of 370 homes would help the company reduce its debt, as well as trim it of homes that did not fit into a new long-term strategy. Some of these planned sales, however, were not completed by the end of 1989.

Beverly sold 11.5 million shares of common stock in March 1990, netting about $45.7 million, to be used in refinancing debt. With about $470 million in debt to be restructured, the company made a public offering of $40 million of convertible debentures in mid-1990 and had plans to complete its debt refinancing by year's end.

Robert Van Tuyle stepped down as chairman of the board in May 1990, after 19 years of leadership. He was succeeded by David Banks. In summer 1990, the company moved its headquarters from Pasadena to Fort Smith, Arkansas.

Principal Subsidiaries: Affiliated Medical Center, Inc.; BESC, Inc.; Bonterra, Inc.; Brandywood, Inc.; Columbia-Valley Nursing Home, Inc.; Community Nursing Home, Inc.; Gulf States Pharmacies, Inc.; Hospital Facilities Corp.; K-D Investment Co.; Liberty Nursing Homes, Inc.; Melrose Health Care Center, Inc.; Moderncare of Lumberton, Inc.; Northcrest Nursing Home, Inc.; Northgate Services, Inc.; Nursing Home Operators, Inc.; Oaks Nursing Home, Inc.; Progressive Medical Group, Inc.; Retirement Communities of America; Sheltered Care Homes, Inc.; Sherman Oaks Convalescent Hospital, Inc.; South Alabama Nursing Home, Inc.; Tampa Health Care Center, Inc.

Further Reading: More, Thomas, "Way Out Front," *Fortune,* June 13, 1983; Hurst, John, "For Nursing Homes, Big Isn't Best," *Los Angeles Times,* April 7, 1988; Miles, Gregory, "This Nursing Home Giant May Need Intensive Care," *Business Week,* November 7, 1988; Feder, Barnaby, "What Ails a Nursing Home Empire," *The New York Times,* December 11, 1988.

—Carol I. Keeley

HCA The Healthcare Company

HOSPITAL CORPORATION OF AMERICA

One Park Plaza
Nashville, Tennessee 37203
U.S.A.
(615) 327-9551
Fax: (615) 320-2685

Private Company
Incorporated: 1960 as Park View Hospital, Inc.
Employees: 68,000
Sales: $4.27 billion

Hospital Corporation of America is among the largest U.S. hospital-management companies. Although it offers traditional services, Hospital Corporation of America (HCA) has been a trailblazer in the rapidly growing for-profit medical-services and hospital-management industry, achieving a strong international presence. The company went private in March 1989 and faced the 1990s with more than 130 acute-care and psychiatric hospitals, mostly located in the South and Southwest. HCA is ahead on its considerable debt payments, incurred when the company went private, but still faces challenges.

During the late 1950s, Thomas F. Frist Sr., a practicing Nashville, Tennessee, internist and cardiologist, became disgruntled with what he regarded as a lack of efficiency and quality care in area hospitals. To provide better care for his own patients, Frist, together with ten investors, built Nashville-based Park View Hospital in 1960, which later became the company's flagship operation. At the time, Frist's goals were simple: he wanted a well-managed hospital whose capital could be used to expand and improve its health-service offerings. It was not his intent to launch a hospital business.

Frist's son, Thomas F. Frist Jr., then a 29-year-old surgeon, convinced his father to build the hospital into a wide-ranging, standard-setting business enterprise, arguing that a hospital could be run most efficiently if it were part of a chain. Thus, in 1968, Hospital Corporation of America was formed to own and manage hospitals with Thomas Frist Sr. at the helm as president and Jack C. Massey, a businessman with hospital-management experience, serving as the first chairman.

The Frists and Massey were convinced that the delivery of hospital services could be vastly improved through the application of sound business principles and management practices and, in turn, that hospitals that turned a profit would attract strong investors and superior medical personnel, improve the fiscal health of the community through tax payments, and provide excellent health care at a reasonable cost to patients. Such a concept, which Frist Sr. summed up as "quality attracts quality," was radical in the late 1960s, when many not-for-profit hospitals were floundering.

Jack Massey was largely responsible for propelling HCA to the forefront of hospital management. Before arriving at HCA, Massey had built Kentucky Fried Chicken into an internationally recognized chain. Together with Thomas Frist Jr., Massey recognized the value and importance of operating a chain of for-profit hospitals given the ailing state of the health-care industry. Frist Jr., who is also a pilot, began a barnstorming campaign, flying to small community hospitals throughout the South to coax them to sign up with HCA. By 1969, the Hospital Corporation of America had acquired or built 11 hospitals, and in March of that year, HCA went public, with stock rising from $18 to $40 a share in the first day of trading.

Hospital Corporation developed a novel, standardized design for the construction of community hospitals. By using a prototype and a small group of contractors, the company significantly cut time and costs. HCA's hospital construction and expansion program continued apace, concentrated in the sunbelt states. John A. Hill, former chairman and CEO of Aetna Life & Casualty, was appointed president and Thomas Frist Sr. became vice chairman and chief medical officer of HCA, in 1970.

During this time the hospital industry itself was changing, which further spurred the growth and acceptance of Hospital Corporation. The increased costs of maintaining, equipping, and replacing outdated hospitals made it impossible for many smaller communities to obtain adequate levels of financing. Consequently, the decade between 1970 and 1980 saw more than a 200% increase in the number of hospitals subsumed under multiple-hospital systems, both investor owned and not for profit.

Within three years of operation, HCA had 10,000 employees. Despite being in a capital- and labor-intensive business, subject to heavy government regulation, HCA continued to grow steadily throughout the 1970s. In 1972 Hospital Corporation put together its first board of governors, consisting of prominent physicians from throughout the HCA network of hospitals. The organization of the board of governors was one in a series of attempts HCA has made to shed its image of "franchised health care" and to attain respect within the medical establishment. By 1973, Hospital Corporation had become the world's largest publicly owned hospital-management company, representing 51 hospitals with a total of 7,900 beds. In 1973, HCA also entered the international marketplace, taking on management of the King Faisal Specialist Hospital and Research Centre in Riyadh, Saudi Arabia.

Much of HCA's rapid growth and success resulted from the company's ability to abide by a relatively safe plan for growth and from the broad-based approach it took to attracting investors, led by finance officer Sam A. Brooks. Brooks's main task was to locate new sources of capital to finance HCA's expansion. Because the company was young, as was the chain-hospital business, HCA could not command the financing it needed to maintain operations, much less expand. Moreover, loans to hospitals were considered bad investments at the time because of speculation that the federal government would institute a national health insurance program and thus put investor-owned hospital companies like HCA out of business.

Though all these factors posed problems, HCA still grew to 10,000 beds by 1975. In the previous year HCA had expanded its foreign operations to include Central America. Its reputation for hospital management flourished during this period and investors began to see the advantages investor-owned-and-operated hospitals had over nonprofit hospitals, not the least of which was an almost guaranteed return on investment. HCA's multi-facility operation permitted it to finance its hospitals as a group, rather than individually, with long-term mortgages, thus creating an attenuated risk—an innovative financing tool in the hospital industry. The speed and efficiency of building hospitals from a prototype, with established contractors, continued to be a precedent-setting cost-cutting device. Economies of scale, such as bulk purchasing also greatly lowered costs.

Throughout the 1970s, HCA had an annual growth rate of 35%, with revenues in 1968 totaling $29 million and increasing to more than $1 billion in 1980. Industry observers attributed Hospital Corporation's consistently strong performance to the predictability of the hospital-management business, as well as good strategic planning and the company's financial conservativism. HCA never took on a financial burden greater than it could handle, comfortably riding a 60:40 debt-to-equity ratio.

Another key to HCA's successful operation was its decentralized management. Each hospital's administrator developed the hospital's own budget, set up individual pricing systems, and determined services. Corporate headquarters, through a computerized monitoring system, then measured each hospital's efficiency in relation to that of other hospitals within the HCA network. Inefficiencies could thereby be redressed quickly while still allowing hospitals to function autonomously.

With the launching of its management contracts division, HCA Management Company, and Parthenon Insurance Company in 1977, HCA ushered in a period of heightened expansion and diversification. HCA Management Company was established to help coordinate activities and to serve as a support center for independently owned HCA-managed hospitals across the United States. The Parthenon Insurance Company was established as a wholly owned subsidiary of HCA, offering general and professional liability insurance coverage to company hospitals.

In 1978 the corporation celebrated its tenth anniversary with 100 hospitals and 28,000 employees. Thomas F. Frist Jr. became president and chief operating officer of HCA, and Donald S. MacNaughton—retired chairman and CEO of the Prudential Insurance Company of America—joined the company as chairman of the board and CEO. MacNaughton used his connections to open new doors to outside capital, and HCA acquired three Australian hospitals—the company's first foreign equity holding. Hospital Corporation also entered the Eurodollar market in 1978, and was favorably received. Jack Massey's move to the chairmanship of the executive committee that year allowed the company to establish a new pace and tone, which, with the help of MacNaughton's efforts to assemble a prestigious board of directors, eventually helped HCA establish a blue-chip image.

During the early 1980s, many hospitals turned to HCA because of its ability to raise capital. Some analysts predicted that $160 billion would be needed during the coming decade to revamp the nation's hospitals, money that for-profit multiple-hospital systems like HCA could more easily provide. HCA had another advantage in the millions of dollars it saved by building new hospitals in half the usual time. HCA was able to charge patients 25% less than the national average while still providing the latest in medical care and technology, and its reputation as a good employer attracted employees.

Changes in the federal government's reimbursement system for Medicare and Medicaid patients during this time hurt many poorly managed non-profit hospitals and altered the industry as a whole, but actually worked in HCA's favor by creating economic incentives. It was an opportunity for reinforcement of HCA's basic business tenets.

HCA was the first company on the New York Stock Exchange to pass the billion-dollar mark in sales in its first ten years of operation and it continued to grow by leaps and bounds. In April 1980, HCA acquired General Health Services, which owned 14 hospitals and various ancillary health-care services. Company operations began branching out of the South and into the northeastern United States, as well as further overseas.

In 1981, Hospital Corporation bought rival Hospital Affiliates International (HAI), a wholly owned subsidiary of INA Corporation. HAI operated 154 hospitals, giving HCA control of about one-fifth of all privately owned U.S. hospitals. HCA also purchased the Health Care Corporation, which spawned HCA's extensive psychiatric-hospital network. As a result of these acquisitions, HCA later faced a Federal Trade Commission antitrust challenge. It was determined in 1987 that HCA had a monopoly in a portion of the Tennessee market, which the company rectified by selling two hospitals and terminating the management contract with a third.

By 1983, multiple-hospital systems were booming. Of the four leading U.S. hospital-management firms—HCA, Humana Corporation, National Medical Enterprises, and American Medical International—HCA emerged as the leader. Revenues exceeded $4 billion; the company covered a broad geographical area, with HCA's hospitals being the only hospitals in more than a third of the cities it covered; and HCA profitability was virtually insured by government regulations limiting hospital construction—hence reducing competition—and the fact that Medicare and Medicaid payments produced almost 45% of HCA's revenues at that time.

HCA also diversified into other new markets. HCA Psychiatric Company, the new subsidiary stemming from the 1981 purchase of Health Care Corporation, grew into a network of 53 hospitals, becoming one of the nation's largest owners and managers of psychiatric facilities. By 1983, HCA ran 30 projects in seven foreign countries. The company continued, however, to concentrate an owning and managing hospitals in the United States, limiting the growth of its foreign operations to 25% annually.

With Thomas Frist Jr. then the company's CEO, HCA made attempts to diversify into the service sector of the health-care industry. Although in 1982 HCA sold the 18 nursing homes it had acquired via HAI, in exchange for an 18% interest in Beverly Enterprises, the nation's largest nursing home–management company. HCA later sold its Beverly investment for a pretax gain of $42.24 million. In 1985 HCA also purchased Kansas-based Wesley Medical Center, a non-profit teaching hospital affiliated with the University of Kansas School of Medicine. HCA's biggest gamble on diversification at this time came with its attempted merger with American Hospital Supply Corporation (AHSC). The deal fell through when a rival hospital supplier outbid HCA. The company realized a $64.4 million gain on the failed merger, however, when it terminated the merger agreement.

Despite diversification, HCA's profits had begun to wane during the early 1980s. In 1986 HCA's money-losing health insurance units were folded into a joint venture with the Equitable Life Assurance Society of America, called EQUICOR-Equitable HCA Corporation. The venture combined Equitable Group and Health Insurance with HCA Health Plans, a division of HCA. In 1987, Frist also began a reorganization plan to streamline HCA, then worth $4.9 billion, by selling 104 of the corporation's less-profitable, rural general hospitals to a new employee-owned company, HealthTrust, creating the largest employee stock-ownership plan (ESOP) in the nation. Also in 1987 a private investor group offering $3.85 billion made an unsuccessful takeover bid for HCA. The board refused to consider the offer, but it launched speculation which placed further pressure on the company.

After the thwarted takeover, Frist completed the sale of the primarily rural, less-profitable hospitals to the employee-owned HealthTrust. He then accelerated the restructuring of HCA, slashing both management ranks and general overhead by $75 million, until the company was left primarily with its most solid projects. By late 1988 Frist planned to concentrate on the profitable psychiatric and medical and surgical hospital businesses.

In March 1989 Frist Jr. and chief financial officer Roger Mick, along with other HCA managers, had taken the company private via a $4.9 billion leveraged buyout. This left HCA in a difficult fiscal condition by mid-1989. To meet its loans, HCA continued dismantling, and even considered selling, its most profitable units: the 53 psychiatric hospitals and the drug-treatment centers. Instead of the hospitals, HCA sold its interest in the Equitable joint venture, its management company, its clinical-laboratory division, and its international holdings.

The newly private company was ahead on debt repayment by $300 million in its first fiscal quarter. HCA's new owners—Frist Jr. and an equity group that includes Goldman, Sachs; Morgan Guaranty; the Rockefeller group; and Texas financier Richard Rainwater—will have to run a tight ship in the 1990s, keeping capital spending up to maintain their hospitals.

Principal Subsidiaries: Autauga Acquisition Corp.; Diamondhead Development Corp.; Montgomery Center for Psychiatry, Inc.; Prattville Aquisition Corp.; HCA Health Services of Arkansas, Inc.; HCA Allied Health Services of San Diego, Inc.; HCA Hospital Services of San Diego, Inc.; Hospital Corporation of California; Los Robles Regional Medical Center; HCA Psychiatric Company; Health Services Acquisition Corp.; Lakeland Manor, Inc.; University Hospital, Inc.; Bay Hospital, Inc.; Central Florida Regional Hospital, Inc.; HCA Development Corporation of Florida; HCA Family Care Center, Inc.; HCA Healthcare-Florida, Inc.; HCA of Florida, Inc.; Largo Medical Center, Inc.; Lawnwood Medical Center, Inc.; Marion Community Hospital, Inc.; New Port Richey Hospital, Inc.; Okaloosa Hospital, Inc.; Okeechobee Hospital, Inc.; Putnam Hospital, Inc.; Tallahassee Medical Center, Inc.; Tamarac Hospital Corporation, Inc.; West Florida Regional Medical Center, Inc.; Clayton Acquisition Corp.; Coliseum Park Hospital, Inc.; Dublin Community Hospital, Inc.; HCA Health Services of Georgia, Inc.; Med Corp., Inc.; Medical Center-West, Inc.; Palmyra Park Hospital, Inc.; Redmond Park Health Services, Inc.; Redmond Park Hospital, Inc.; West Paces Ferry Hospital, Inc.; West Paces Services, Inc.; HCA of Idaho, Inc.; HCA-Indiana, Inc.; HCA Health Services of Iowa, Inc.; HCA Health Services of Kansas, Inc.; Frankfort Hospital, Inc.; Greenview Hospital, Inc.; HCA Health Services of Massachusetts, Inc.; HCA Physician Services of Mississippi, Inc.; Forum Springfield, Inc.; HCA Health Services of Missouri, Inc.; HCA Health Services of New Hampshire, Inc.; HCA Health Services of New Jersey, Inc.; Guadalupe Medical Center, Inc.; Hobbs Community Hospital, Inc.; HCA-Raleigh Community Hospital, Inc.; HCA Health Services of Ohio, Inc.; HCA Affiliated Services of Oklahoma, Inc.; HCA Health Services of Oklahoma, Inc.; HCA of Oregon, Inc.; HCA Pennsylvania Health Services, Inc.; HCA Health Services of Rhode Island, Inc.; Aiken Community Hospital, Inc.; HCA South Carolina Health Services, Inc.; Myrtle Beach Hospital, Inc.; North Trident Regional Hospital, Inc.; Athens Community Hospital, Inc.; Bradley Community Hospital, Inc.; The Center for Health Studies, Inc.; Community and Occupational Health Services, Inc.; General Care Corp.; HCA Capital Corporation; HCA Development Company, Inc.; HCA Finance, Inc.; HCA Government Services, Inc.; HCA Home and Clinical Services, Inc.; HCA Information Services, Inc.; HCA Medical Services, Inc.; HCA Physician Services, Inc.; HCA Properties, Inc.; HCA Realty, Inc.; Health Enterprises, Inc.; Hospital Capital Corporation; Hospital Corporation of Tennessee; Hospital Realty Corporation; Indian Path Hospital, Inc.; Park Plaza Realty, Inc.; Parkridge Hospital, Inc.; Parthenon Financial Services, Inc.; TransMed Clinical Services Company; TransMed Medical Supply Company; WDC, Inc.; Fort Worth Medical Plaza, Inc.; HCA-Arlington, Inc.; HCA Plano Imaging, Inc.; HSP of Texas, Inc.; Lockhart Acquisition Corp.; Navarro Memorial Hospital, Inc.; Rio Grande Development Corp.; Woman's Hospital of Texas, Incorporated; HCA Health Services of Utah, Inc.; Ambulatory Services Management Corporation of Chesterfield County, Inc.; Brandermill Medical Ancillaries, Inc.; Chippenham Hospital, Inc.; Circle Terrace Hospital Corporation; HCA Health Services of Norfolk, Inc.; HCA Health Services of Portsmouth, Inc.; Johnston-Willis Limited; Lewis-Gale Hospital, Incorporated; HCA Health Services of West Virginia, Inc.; Raleigh General Hospital; Teays Valley Health Services, Inc.

Further Reading: "HCA: Champion In a New Growth Industry, *Dun's Business Month*, December 1982; "HCA History," Hospital Corporation of America Corporate typescript [n.d.].

—Carol I. Keeley

Humana®

HUMANA INC.

The Humana Building
500 West Main Street
Louisville, Kentucky 40202
U.S.A.
(502) 580-1000
Fax: (502) 580-1441

Public Company
Incorporated: 1961 as Heritage House of America Inc.
Employees: 55,100
Sales: $4.09 billion
Stock Exchange: New York

One of the largest health-care companies in the world, Humana commands attention in a fast-changing industry. The company is noted for its combination of conservative and innovative strategies: growing selectively while other hospital chains were exploding, championing artificial-heart research, buying the nation's second-largest health-care chain while Humana itself was third, and linking its hospitals with a health insurance plan in an effort to beat the low-occupancy rates plaguing the industry in the wake of government cost-containment measures. This last move, implemented in early 1984, threatened the company's stability through persistent losses. With higher premiums and a new marketing strategy, however, Humana's health was greatly improved by late 1989, and it embarked on the new decade with its strengths intact.

In 1961 two lawyers in Louisville, Kentucky, built a nursing home, pledging $1,000 apiece together with four friends. Wendell Cherry and David Jones—co-founders of that first home, Heritage House—were soon approached with other offers to buy and build nursing homes. Expansion was rapid in the first seven years, and the two men added facilities in Kentucky, Virginia, and Connecticut. With the establishment of Medicare and Medicaid in the mid-1960s, the industry grew quickly. Slightly ahead of the pack in what was to become the most rapidly expanding sector of the nation's economy, Jones and Cherry reincorporated their venture in 1961 and sold stock seven years to finance further growth. Extendicare, as the group was known, grew to more than 40 facilities, becoming the nation's largest nursing home company.

As Medicare spawned a nursing home glut and stocks suffered, Extendicare experimented with alternatives. There was a brief and unfortunate diversification into mobile home parks between 1969 and 1971, which the company quickly unloaded. Extendicare acquired its first hospital in late 1968, realizing it could apply the same business practices it had developed for operating nursing homes. Within two years, the company had acquired nine more hospitals. The hospitals proved so successful that Extendicare divested all of its nursing homes in 1972.

With a focus now entirely on hospitals, the company's name was changed to Humana. Some of the features that distinguished Humana from other hospital chains early on were its nonconforming management decisions, the refusal to overpay in buying hospitals, the refusal to manage hospitals it did not own, and rigid cost-control measures well-enforced through the company's centralized management. These methods have been much discussed: first because they seemed remarkable in the industry; later because of complaints by some physicians about overcontrol. For example, Humana's efforts to insure reimbursement include the insistence on a specific payment-plan agreement before patients are discharged.

The cost controls eventually became one of Humana's greatest assets. Between 1975 and 1980, Humana, grew quickly and achieved economies of scale, like other hospital chains, by making bulk purchases of supplies and equipment. Unlike some competitors, however, Humana remained very centralized, operating all patient-billing and data-collection out of its home office in Louisville. Freed from the distraction of managing hospitals it did not own—also unlike most competitors—Humana concentrated on strict productivity and profitability goals.

As the nation's third-largest hospital-management chain in 1978, Humana committed a bold act: it acquired the number-two chain, American Medicorp. This purchase doubled Humana's size and stretched its debt. Having used leveraged debt with confidence for some time during its expansion, Humana was now faced with a debt that one company official claimed was "nearly 90% of capital."

Co-founders Jones and Cherry, chairman and president, respectively, remained untroubled because 45% of hospital revenues were coming from government-guaranteed Medicare and Medicaid. The two men also saw the hospital business as recession resistant, even though Humana suffered from low-occupancy rates at some of its facilities during these years.

Meanwhile, Humana unloaded unprofitable hospitals. While the health-care industry was burgeoning into the second-largest industry in the United States, Humana alone was honing its cost controls: between its own growth and government-subsidized medical care, the industry in general had not yet felt the need for cost efficiency.

To build its medical reputation, Humana established a Centers for Excellence program in 1982 for the purpose of specialty care. This included centers for neuroscience, diabetes, spinal injuries, and artificial-heart research and surgery. The artificial-heart projects which were undertaken partly for the publicity they generated, helped push Humana's name into public view. In 1982, Humana had 90 hospitals, primarily in the sunbelt states. Humana also leases and operates the University of Louisville's teaching hospital, where Jefferson County, Kentucky, citizens without the ability to pay for hospital care receive inpatient treatment for no charge—state, city, and county governments pay.

During the following years the health-care industry's overexpansion and the government and private insurers' cost-containment efforts began to clash. Here, Humana's tradition of tight cost controls helped, but the industry reeled from severe changes: industry wide hospital occupancy rates dropped below 50% from a high of 80% just three years earlier. From the onset of federal policies in 1983, with private insurers following suit, the industry changed drastically.

Early in 1984, Humana launched Humana Health Care plans, to offer insurance plans with attractively low premiums and punitive deductibles for patients who used rival hospitals. Competitors soon imitated this vertical integration. Humana banked on a 70% referral rate from its insurance business, thus insuring a healthy occupancy rate for its hospitals. Two years into the venture, however, Humana discovered its plan was seriously flawed.

The premiums had been underpriced, missing costs by at least 20%. It was assumed policyholders would use Humana hospitals, but in 1986, as losses began to mount, it was found that only 46% of Humana's Care Plus group-plan members were using its facilities. The deductibles offered to lure users to their hospitals were not sufficient; independent physicians could recommend any hospital to their patients, and did. Since policyholders were not restricted in their choice of physician, there was no guarantee that they would be referred to Humana facilities by independents. In fact, by this time, a rancor had developed between medical professionals and the business forces behind the cost wars. Humana had incurred further animosity because of its strict business policies. Jones himself contended that in 1986 doctor resentment had resulted not only in patients being steered to other hospitals, but also in strategies to bypass Humana's deductibles for use of other facilities. Doctors would, for instance, claim that a standard admission was an emergency.

Humana addressed these problems by campaigning to change doctors' perceptions of the company, and preventing the use of outside hospitals by enforcing stricter procedures. These procedures included requiring doctors to speak with a health-plan nurse and to accept the Humana hospital recommended for use. Refusal to follow this process would prevent reimbursement. Humana also trimmed back the number of policies it offered and avoided cities where the company was not a dominant presence.

In 1987, with founders Jones and Cherry still at the helm, Humana worked to right its insurance plans. Net income had plunged nearly 75% between 1985 and 1986. Humana adjusted its insurance plans and underwent restructuring. It closed clinics and purchased some health-maintenance organizations. That same year, Medicare ceased its practice of prepayment and started requiring bills before all reimbursements. This meant a significant slowing of cash flow for Humana. It was followed by further government cost-reimbursement strictures that directly affected Humana. Public pressure to contain the cost of health care was growing.

By 1988, Humana had greatly reduced losses caused by its insurance operations and seemed intent on recovery. By 1989, after five years of losses, Humana's health-plan division made $4 million, its first operating profit. Raising premiums up to 25%, reducing its markets from 50 to 17, operating only where it had a strong hospital presence, and insuring that patients are sent to its hospitals, Humana began to rebound by the end of the 1980s. Continuing to move counter to the industry, in 1990, while competitors increased their debt loads through leveraged buyouts, Humana's debt to capital ratio reached an all-time low of 37%.

In October 1990 Humana announced that it had agreed to acquire Chicago-based Michael Reese Health Plan Inc. and Michael Reese Hospital and Medical Center. At the time of the agreement, Michael Reese was one of the largest private academic medical centers in the United States. Michael Reese Health Plan had 240,000 members; Humana had five times as many members.

Humana has remained one of the top three hospital-management chains since the mid-1970s, outlasting the growth explosion and severe restructuring of the health-care industry during that period. It faced the 1990s with a record of firm, centralized management and tough cost controls.

Principal Subsidiaries: Humana Health Plan of Alabama, Inc.; Humana Medical Corporation; Humana Alaska Realty, Inc.; Humana Health Plan of Alaska, Inc.; Humana of Arizona, Inc.; Humana Health Plan of Arkansas, Inc.; Huntington Intercommunity Hospital; Humsoch, Inc.; West Anaheim Community Hospital; West Hills Hospital; Westminster Community Hospital; Health Care Indemnity, Inc.; Humana of Aurora, Inc.; American Medicorp Development Co.; Brentwood Hospital, Inc.; Doctors Hospital of Augusta, Inc.; Edison Homes-Southeast, Inc.; Extendicare Properties, Inc.; Group Health Insurance, Inc.; HAC Inc.; H.H.U.K., Inc.; Healthcare Technology Assessment Corporation; Humana Health Institutes, Inc.; Hospital Alaska, Inc.; Humana Hospital Corporation, Inc.; Humana Mobile Nurses Corps., Inc.; Humdeco, Inc.; Medical Specialties, Inc.; PMM, Inc.; Primary Medical Management, Inc.; Suburban Medical Center at Hoffman Estates, Inc.; Sun Bay Medical Office Building, Inc.; Community Hospital of the Palm Beaches, Inc.; Community Hospitals of Humana Inc.; Humana Health Plan of Florida, Inc.; Humana Health Insurance Company of Florida, Inc.; Humana Medical Plan, Inc.; Humana of Florida, Inc.; Humhosco, Inc.; Gwinnett Community Hospital, Inc.; Humana Health Plan of Georgia, Inc.; Humana of Illinois, Inc.; Humana of Kansas, Inc.; A.C. Medical, Inc.; GSD, Inc.; Humana Broadway Corp.; Humana Care Plan, Inc.; Humana Health Plan, Inc.; Humana International Holdings, Inc.; Humana Medical Plan of Kentucky, Inc.; Southwest Jefferson Community Hospital, Inc.; Humana Health Plan of Louisiana, Inc.; Humana Louisiana, Inc.; WGH, Inc.; Humana Health Plan of Maryland, Inc.; Humana Health Plan of Michigan, Inc.; Humana of Mississippi, Inc.; Humana Insurance Company; Humana Health Insurance of Nevada, Inc.; National Care Services Corp. of Nevada; Sunrise Hospital; Humana Health Plan of North Carolina, Inc.; Humana Health Plan of Ohio, Inc.; Humana Health Plan of Pennsylvania, Inc.; Humana Health Plan of South Carolina, Inc.; Humana of Tennessee, Inc.; Beaumont Hospital, Inc.; Humana Health Plan of Texas, Inc.; Humana Hospital of Baytown, Inc.; Humana of Texas, Inc.; Humana PPO, Inc.; MGH Medical, Inc.; General Hospitals of Humana, Inc.; Humana Health Plan of Utah, Inc.; Chicago Medical School Hospital, Inc.; Humana Virginia Hospital Corporation; Humedicenters, Inc.;

ACH, Inc.; Humana of West Virginia, Inc.; Insurance Resources Company, Ltd. (Bermuda); The Wellington Private Hospital Limited (U.K.); Societe Anonyme de l'Exploitation de l'Hopital de la Tour (Switzerland).

Further Reading: ''History of Humana,'' Humana corporate typescript, 1989.

—Carol I. Keeley

MAXICARE HEALTH PLANS, INC.

5250 West Century Boulevard
Los Angeles, California 90045
(213) 765-2000
Fax: (213) 765-2693

Public Company
Incorporated: 1980
Employees: 600
Sales: $400 million
Stock Exchange: NASDAQ

Maxicare Health Plans helped popularize the concept of national health maintenance for profit in the 1980s. By the end of that decade, however, it epitomized the problems and pitfalls of the new industry. Maxicare began its second decade struggling to emerge whole from bankruptcy, under the protection of the federal courts. Maxicare began an an innovative concept for reshaping the country's health-care-delivery system and rapidly mushroomed into a profitable chain. At one point, Maxicare stock traded at 55 times earnings.

The untried idea of minimizing medical costs and maximizing earnings through group-arranged, prepaid doctor care proved to be fraught with unanticipated difficulties. It was not long before Maxicare collapsed into a legal and financial morass. In 1990, ten years after its inception, a new board of directors and second generation of top management vowed to restructure Maxicare, pay creditors, sell unprofitable assets, and emerge a leaner, more efficient health-maintenance organization.

Maxicare began as Fred W. Wasserman's dream. It was founded by Wasserman and his wife, Pamela K. Anderson. Wasserman saw his opportunity in the 1973 Federal HMO Act, which requires employers who are engaged in interstate commerce to offer workers a choice between conventional insurance coverage or HMO membership. Maxicare originated as a California nonprofit HMO in 1973. In 1980 Wasserman convinced a group of Los Angeles–area physicians to convert the company into a for-profit HMO. Maxicare was supported by the charter participation of Lockheed Corporation and Northrop Corporation. Selling prepaid health-care plans to employers, Wasserman rapidly built Maxicare into a national network by acquiring HMOs across the country.

Maxicare began interstate operations in 1982, by purchasing CNA Health Plans, which had operations in Illinois, Indiana, and Wisconsin. Maxicare's net income ballooned from $5.4 million in 1983 to $20.4 million in 1985. By the end of 1987 Maxicare owned or managed 33 consumer-oriented, high-quality health-maintenance-organization systems in 26 states, with a combined enrollment of 2.3 million members. By the mid-1980s, the husband-and-wife duo had parlayed their initial $37,000 investment into the nation's largest for-profit HMO. As the number of HMOs in the United States nearly doubled, to more than 600, between 1984 and 1986, competition stiffened, and Maxicare found itself paying inflated prices for the local health-maintenance organizations it acquired as part of its growth strategy. Maxicare grew quickly, especially in the Southeast, but some of the local plans Maxicare acquired proved to be poorly managed, with sizably underestimated expenses.

Wasserman's dream began to unravel in 1986, when Maxicare acquired two HMOs, HealthCare USA and HealthAmerica Corporation, for $446 million. The highly leveraged transaction doubled Maxicare's enrollment, to about 2.3 million members, and boosted the company's overall revenues to $1.8 billion, from only $118 million in annual revenues six years earlier. The two new HMO subsidiaries, however, brought hidden costs and considerable debt. Maxicare's undiscriminating growth strategy had emphasized fast expansion, and the company simply bought almost every HMO it could. Maxicare soon became a victim of its own centrally managed, inter-entity borrowing system, which was taxed by a handful of overextended HMO subsidiaries.

Maxicare's long-term debt soared to $464 million in 1987, at a time when competition and health-care costs intensified. Shortly after the acquisitions, the company began experiencing serious financial and operating difficulties, which resulted in Maxicare reporting net losses of $255.9 million in 1987 on $1.8 billion in revenues. In 1988 Maxicare's losses swelled to $611.8 million on revenues of $1.6 billion. The growing reservations of lenders toward the HMO industry made it difficult for Maxicare to obtain the further financing needed to turn the company around.

In the wake of Maxicare's inability to stem losses, the company's senior management—including Chairman Wasserman and President Anderson—and five of its seven directors resigned, in August 1988. Peter J. Ratican, who had been an outside member of Maxicare's board since 1983, was named Maxicare's second chairman, chief executive officer, and president. The senior management team Ratican assembled immediately launched an in-depth review of Maxicare's operatons. Wasserman remained for a time after his resignation as a consultant to Maxicare. Ratican brought more financial, rather than health-care management, experience to the job. He had worked for a time at Price Waterhouse, where Maxicare was among his audit clients. He also had served as a medic in the California National Guard. Prior to joining Maxicare in 1988, Ratican was a member of the office of the president, and chief financial officer of De Laurentiis Entertainment Group.

In mid-1988 New York–based Bankers Trust Company dealt Maxicare a particularly critical blow. Bankers Trust and five other lenders had provided Maxicare with a revolving bank loan. In mid-1988 Maxicare lost its ability to make interest payments on the $175 million loan, Bankers Trust forced a fire sale of some of Maxicare's local HMO plans.

Initially, under pressure from Bankers Trust, Ratican abandoned Wasserman's plan for a national HMO company, focusing instead on California and select midwestern and southern states. Beginning in late 1988 Ratican began selling some of Maxicare's plans, for an estimated total of $120 million. The money was then used to reduce the company's overall debt and to offset ongoing administrative and personnel costs. Ratican also hired McKinsey & Company, New York–based management consultants, to identify ways to improve management, client relations, and claim processing. McKinsey was the first of three management consultants Ratican would hire between August 1988 and March 1989.

Dramatic change was spurred by Ratican's decision to increase Maxicare's premiums by an average 32%—twice the annual hike of its competitors—combined with the company's highly publicized financial problems. The move prompted massive client defections.

After missing principal loan payments in January 1989, Maxicare's new management unsuccessfully attempted to pursue several financial-restructuring alternatives, including exchange offers, new arrangements with trade creditors, new infusions of equity, securing new investors, and selling Maxicare or any of its subsidiaries outright. Discussions with outside parties concerning such alternatives, however, never moved past the preliminary stage.

Ratican's goal simply became to avoid complete liquidation of Maxicare's assets while nursing the ailing company. Increases in health-care costs continued to outpace increases in premiums and overall revenues by nearly two to one. On March 17, 1989—still wrestling with close to $300 million in long-term debt, mounting losses, and unavailable financing—Maxicare and 45 of its direct and indirect subsidiaries filed for protection from creditors under chapter 11 of the federal bankruptcy code. Two additional local Maxicare subsidiaries subsequently filed for chapter 11 protection in April 1989.

Soon after filing, Maxicare found itself inundated with lawsuits filed by participating hospital and doctor groups, alleging delinquency in making payments. Even Maxicare shareholders filed a class-action suit, alleging violation of securities laws. State insurance regulators struggled with the dilemma of how to repay Maxicare's medical constituents. Federal bankruptcy laws shielded Maxicare from state regulators' attempts to seize plan assets in their respective states in order to cover enrollees' unpaid claims. In 1989 a handful of states unsuccessfully appealed to the bankruptcy court to allow their individual insurance regulators to supervise debt repayment to creditors under their authority.

Through the reorganization process, the bankruptcy court consistently dismissed claims by various states, including Illinois, Indiana, Ohio, and California, seeking jurisdiction over Maxicare's local subsidiaries. Perhaps the most difficult and influential group of constituents to appease was the nation's health-care providers, many of whom unabashedly challenged Maxicare in bankruptcy court. Two dozen Philadelphia hospitals and other providers participating in Pennsylvania's Medicaid program, for instance, asked the judge to appoint a trustee to oversee Penn Health, the Maxicare subsidiary that administered the program. Settlement in some of the many disbursement cases involved transferring existing Maxicare plans to other health-maintenance organizations. Many Maxicare providers had to settle for partial payment. The bankruptcy court eventually extended full protection to Maxicare from creditor interference, pressure, or cancellation during the reorganization process.

At the time of its filing, Maxicare was in the midst of an asset-disposition program. At the end of 1987 Maxicare had managed a system of 33 HMOs in 26 states with combined enrollment of about 2.3 million members. By the time it filed for bankruptcy, Maxicare had sold or closed 23 HMOs in 17 states with a combined enrollment of about 837,000 members in order to raise cash and reduce its operating losses. In March 1989, Maxicare was operating HMOs in 13 states with a combined enrollment of about one million members. Between March 1989 and May 1990, Maxicare sold or closed an additional seven HMOs located in six states. Maxicare also sold nearly $5 million in real estate and property, including a California medical building and other clinic facilities located throughout the United States. During the disposition process, in early 1990, Maxicare rejected an unsolicited buyout bid from competitior PacifiCare Health Systems. In acknowledging that the two companies had been unable to reach an accord, Maxicare management reiterated its commitment to an independent reorganization.

Many other HMO companies struggled with similar problems. The concept of providing a full range of medical services for one annual fee appeared to have worked better in theory than it did in practice. Other national HMOs also were unable to hold down costs by keeping patients visits and charges to a minimum.

Wall Street also had its reservations. Maxicare stock plummeted to $2 a share just before the company filed for bankruptcy, from its all-time high of $28 a share. Maxicare's management, however, found itself facing a broader challenge: regaining the confidence of investors, consumers, financial institutions, and the medical community. Based on surveys it conducted in 1988 and 1989, Maxicare reported that at least 80% of its enrollees remained satisfied with the services the company provided, even though many employers had opted not to renew their Maxicare contracts. To curb defections, Maxicare moved quickly to improve its services, instituting new practices such as paying claims within 15 working days after receipt.

By 1990 Maxicare was marketing its services aggressively with the help of an advertising agency, trying to convince the public that as one of the nation's first HMOs, it remained one of the best. Maxicare signaled its revitalization with a new patriotic logo. Decked in red, white, and blue, the logo silhouettes three Maxicare members looking ahead to what was hoped to be a brighter future. The new logo was an inverted, updated version of Maxicare's old logo. Maxicare officials also began commenting publicly about assuming new HMO accounts, but declined to identify them. On July 9, 1990, Ratican told *Managed Care Report* that his personal goal was independently to build Maxicare back to a 500,000-plus-enrollee concern within five years. Refuting suggestions that Maxicare management would sell out after completing the company's financial reorganization, Ratican stated that he and his management team were determined "to stick it out and turn it around because that's what we came to do."

A reorganization plan first filed in January 1990 was adopted by Maxicare and its subsidiaries, creditors, and bondholders in May 1990 and received final approval from the bankruptcy court in July 1990. The plan provides creditors and shareholders of the multistate health-maintenance organization with $129.3 million in cash payments; ten-year 13.5% senior notes with a face amount of $67 million; and common stock and stock warrants that are to be traded publicly. Creditors also are to share in the cash proceeds of a distribution trust established to liquidate Maxicare assets that would not be used in its ongoing businesses and operations.

Maxicare's reorganization calls for creditors and shareholders to receive at least as much as they would have if the company had been completely liquidated. Maxicare has said that about $16 million in enrollee and other priority administrative claims will be paid in full.

The reorganization plan also calls for an estimated $200 million in claims from general unsecured creditors of Maxicare's ongoing operations—mostly physicians and hospitals—to receive $47 million in cash, $35 million in senior notes, and 49% of the reorganized company's common stock. Another $110 million in claims from general unsecured creditors of Maxicare's discontinued or divested operations are to receive $17.8 million in cash and $10 million in face-amount of senior notes. Members of the Bankers Trust–led bank group—who are general unsecured creditors of the parent holding company—represent about $150 million in claims, and are to receive up to $12 million in cash, $22 million in face amount of senior notes, and 15.9% of the common stock of the new Maxicare. The company also has pledged approximately $7 million of notes to the banks as collateral. Holders of four bond issues, representing about $300 million in claims as general unsecured creditors of the parent holding company, are to receive approximately $2 million in cash and 33.1% of the new common stock. Maxicare's public shareholders are to receive 2% of the reorganized company's common stock and stock warrants entitling them to acquire up to an additional 5% of the common stock on a fully diluted basis.

The reorganization plan also provides Maxicare's senior management golden parachutes, including severance and benefits up to annual base compensation if Maxicare is bought out or management control changes. Top management was also assured of $500,000 to $1 million in collective cash bonuses if the firm had at least $60 million cash in hand at the time of the company's effective reorganization date. Top management also has an option to acquire 5% of the company's new common stock at a 20% discount. On the effective date, Maxicare was to be merged into its own subsidiary, HealthCare USA. HealthCare USA, as the surviving entity, was to be renamed Maxicare Health Plans.

On July 16, 1990, the bankruptcy court approved Maxicare's reorganization plan. As part of reorganization, in August 1990, Maxicare appointed three new directors. New directors Leon Clements of Fort Lauderdale, Florida, and Walter J. Filkowski of Oakland, California, are long-time health-care management professionals, and W. Robert Friedman of New York City is an investment banker. In keeping with the court-approved reorganization plan, up to nine new members will be appointed to Maxicare's board of directors. The new board of directors also includes Ratican, who continues as Maxicare's chairman and chief executive officer, and Eugene Froelich, Maxicare's chief financial officer.

At the time the bankruptcy court approved Maxicare's reorganization plan in July 1990, company officials said it had about 305,000 enrollees in seven states—Illinois, Indiana, Wisconsin, California, North Carolina, South Carolina, and Louisiana. The disposition or closing of local HMO subsidiaries resulted in a reduction of Maxicare employees from a one-time high of 8,000 to about 600. Maxicare's annual sales also had declined in 1989, to $400 million from a one-time annual high of $1.84 billion. A vastly streamlined Maxicare also had cut its losses from $611.8 million at the end of 1988 to $22.3 million in the third quarter of 1989, primarily reflecting the expense of its reorganization, Maxicare officials said. Ratican told *Managed Care Report* that he remains optimistic about the company's revamped future. He predicted that by late 1992, Maxicare will have at least 375,000 enrollees, which should increase to an anticipated 420,000 enrollees by the end of 1994.

Principal Subsidiaries: Maxicare (California); Maxicare (Midwest); Maxicare Health Insurance Co. (Wisconsin); Maxicare Louisiana, Inc.; Maxicare North Carolina, Inc.; Maxicare Southeast Health Plans, Inc. (South Carolina); Maxicare Indiana Inc.

Further Reading: Andresky, Jill, "The mess at Maxicare," *Forbes,* June 27, 1988; Cole, Patrick, and Jon Friedmann, "Even Heroic Measures May Not Save Maxicare," *Business Week,* March 27, 1989; "Maxicare Poised to Reorganize," *Managed Care Report,* July 9, 1990.

—Diane C. Mermigas

NATIONAL MEDICAL ENTERPRISES, INC.

2700 Colorado Avenue
Santa Monica, California 90404
U.S.A.
(213) 315-8000
Fax: (213) 315-8329

Public Company
Incorporated: 1968
Employees: 44,000
Sales: $3.93 billion
Stock Exchanges: New York Pacific London

As one of the nation's largest health-care providers, National Medical Enterprises has continually adjusted its own strategies to accommodate a rapidly changing market. National Medical Enterprises (NME) spent its first decade building and acquiring medical facilities and related services. Industry changes during the mid-1980s prompted NME to shift its emphasis from acute-care to specialty hospitals. The company's Specialty Hospital Group, a division consisting of psychiatric, substance-abuse, and rehabilitation services, was NME's major strength in the late 1980s. A previous strength, the long-term care operations acquired in 1980 with The Hillhaven Corporation, was spun off as an independent company in 1990. With this move, NME then concentrated on its specialty and general hospitals and on related services, where it hopes to limit the cost-reimbursement problems and cost-containment regulations plaguing other sectors of the health-care industry.

NME's founder and CEO, Richard K. Eamer, has degrees in accounting and law. Co-founders Leonard Cohen and John Bedrosian are also attorneys. Eamer's interest in the enterprise was piqued by his own work as a financial consultant and hospital attorney. In 1968 he joined forces with Cohen and Bedrosian, although the company is often dated to 1969, when NME acquired its first hospitals in California—four general and three convalescent—and offered public stock. That same year, NME also purchased a medical office building and three potential building sites.

The building, owning, and operating of numerous hospitals allowed NME to develop cost-cutting skills. Attention to both cost management and physician input became trademarks as NME concentrated on building services around community hospitals. Interest in efficiency also led to NME's early diversification into hospital equipment and supplies, a hospital-consulting firm, and even a construction company that specialized in building hospitals. In the early 1970s the focus was on growth. The company launched seven construction projects in 1971, in addition to another hospital purchase, and had tripled in size within a year. In 1973 NME took its first steps outside of California by acquiring a general hospital in Seattle, Washington, and by building another in El Paso, Texas.

By this time, the hospital-management and cost-cutting techniques of NME were already being hired out. There were both domestic and international divisions within NME to oversee management services provided to other hospitals by 1974. Management of non-NME-owned hospitals and health-care-equipment rental were significant income sources during the company's growth years.

Throughout this period, the central concept was to profit from cost-efficient, well-managed hospitals that satisfied both doctors and patients. NME applies standard business practices in its health-care ventures. As Eamer told *Forbes,* "in many ways, running a hospital chain is like operating a hotel or retail chain." The first decade was devoted to building a diversified, multi-facility hospital company with an eye on market needs. These efforts culminated in the 1979 purchases of Medfield Corporation and The Hillhaven Corporation. Medfield added five Florida-based hospitals, including one psychiatric institution, to NME; the Tacoma, Washington–based Hillhaven was the nation's third-largest chain of nursing homes.

By the end of 1979, NME was the nation's fourth-largest publicly owned hospital chain, with the majority of its revenues coming from acute-care hospitals. These two major acquisitions presaged the new decade's changes. Up until this point NME, like the rest of the hospital industry, operated with an eye to the Medicare and Medicaid legislation passed in 1965, which assured reimbursement for medical care of the poor, disabled, or elderly. This assurance spawned enormous growth in the investor-owned hospital industry, a growth which in turn eventuated problems of reimbursement.

NME began to shift focus from acute-care hospitals to alternative facilities such as nursing homes, and to develop its products-and-services segment, which included health-care equipment rental for home use and visiting-nurses agencies before this problem became visible. In addition, management-services contracts were booming. In 1980, NME signed a five-year, $150 million contract with Saudi Arabia to help develop health-care facilities in that country. More international contracts came in 1981, and by the end of that year NME had more than $1 billion in sales.

The health-care business was the second-largest industry in the United States during the early 1980s, second only to food and agriculture. NME acquired National Health Enterprises in 1982, whose 66 additional long-term care facilities made NME the nation's second-largest nursing home owner. In order to better manage its own size, NME subdivided into four operating groups; international (largely consultant work), hospital, nursing homes, and medical products and services. In 1983, NME bought the Psychiatric Institutes of America (PIA), one of the nation's largest mental-health-care providers, based in Washington, D.C.

From 1981 to 1983, corporate revenues doubled. Entry into the private psychiatric industry allowed NME to profit from a sector whose size doubled every two years throughout the 1980s. In 1983, NME further streamlined its specialty interests by forming Recovery Centers of America (RCA), a subsidiary comprised of substance-abuse-recovery operations.

By 1984, the hospital business began a decline, the result of overexpansion and of cost-containment efforts by both government and private health-care interest groups. NME continued to look to what it considered more stable and growth-likely medical-service alternatives. These included its equipment-leasing and home-care services, and even extended to health insurance and a Miami-based health-maintenance organization (HMO) acquired in 1984.

By 1985 NME was the second-largest publicly owned health-care-services company in the nation, but changes within the industry mandated changes and restructuring. The following year, NME sold its recent HMO purchase, as well as a number of unprofitable outpatient clinics and acute-care hospitals. Emphasis was placed on the specialty facilities—especially rehabilitation and substance-abuse centers and psychiatric hospitals—in an effort to bypass the nonpayment problem by shifting away from Medicaid- or Medicare-dependent services. The Rehab Hospital Services Corporation (RHSC) of Pennsylvania had been merged with NME in 1985 for this purpose. The company also began developing academic medical-center-complex strategies.

As the industry, and NME's stock, wobbled in the late 1980s, the company concentrated on internal reorganization instead of expansion. Restructuring produced the new subdivisions of hospitals, specialty hospitals, long-term care, and retail services in 1986. NME also continued divesting the acute-care hospitals hit by the drop in occupancy rates, shorter stays, and other results of the health-care cost-containment squeeze. Within one year, the company had unloaded a quarter of its businesses, including ten acute-care hospitals. Many other hospitals were converted to specialty services. NME's specialty hospitals division—consisting of PIA, RHSC, and RCA—became the company's new core business and growth field. NME's specialty hospitals supplanted the acute-care hospitals, which had accounted for 90% of NME's revenues in 1969, and in 1990 NME spun off its long-term-care facilities and related operations, as The Hillhaven Corporation.

NME retains a 14% equity interest in Hillhaven, and the parent company expects this change to help it avoid the short-term challenges created by current health-care legislation and the recompensation crackdown. Medicaid accounts for 50% of Hillhaven's revenues, but less than 3% of the specialty hospitals division's revenues, and less than 6% of the general hospitals division's revenues.

Because government programs have not kept pace with the rising cost of health care but private insurance rates have, NME has begun to focus on services that are less dependent on Medicare and Medicaid. With this safeguard and the steady growth in specialty-services industries in the late 1980s, NME may have found its niche.

Still one of the nation's largest health-care providers, NME holds fast to its policy of high-quality, cost-effective care. By concentrating on specialty services such as psychiatric, rehabilitative, and substance-abuse recovery and by limiting itself to profitable acute-care hospitals, NME seems bound to ride out the changes in United States health care.

Principal Subsidiaries: NME Hospitals, Inc.; Psychiatric Institutes of America; Recovery Centers of America, Inc.; Rehab Hospital Services Corporation.

Further Reading: Eamer, Richard K., *The History of National Medical Enterprises, Inc. and the Investor-Owned Hospital Industry,* New York, The Newcomen Society in North America, 1989.

—Carol I. Keeley

HOTELS

HILTON HOTELS CORPORATION
HOLIDAY INNS, INC.
HYATT CORPORATION
ITT SHERATON CORPORATION
MARRIOTT CORPORATION
TRUSTHOUSE FORTE PLC

HILTON

HILTON HOTELS CORPORATION

9336 Civic Center Drive
Beverly Hills, California 90209
U.S.A.
(213) 278-4321
Fax: (213) 859-2513

Public Company
Incorporated: 1946
Employees: 38,000
Sales: $998.20 million
Stock Exchanges: New York Pacific

Hilton Hotels Corporation began as a single hotel purchased by Conrad N. Hilton, who was, in fact, shopping for a bank. By the late 1940s, Hilton owned a worldwide chain of premium hotels. In the 1960s, Hilton sold its international operations and concentrated on management contracts and franchising. The company created innovative joint-venture arrangements that are now standard industry practice. It then entered what would become a prime source of revenue for the company: casino-hotels. Hilton expanded into gaming in 1971; by 1989, gaming provided 44% of the company's income. In the late 1980s the company recommitted itself to international expansion under the name Conrad Hotels, and began to expand domestically with the CrestHil line of moderately priced hotels and a suite-only line of hotels.

Conrad Nicholson Hilton was born in San Antonio, New Mexico, the second of eight children. Before he was 18, Conrad had worked as a trader, a clerk, a bellboy, and a pianist. By age 25 he had also worked in politics and banking. In 1919, following the death of his father, Hilton left the army and went to Texas. He had intended to take advantage of the oil boom by buying a small bank. Instead, he found bank prices prohibitive and hotels so overbooked he could not find a place to sleep. When one owner in Cisco, Texas, complained he would like to sell his property in order to take advantage of the oil boom, Hilton struck a deal. Hilton pulled together an investment group and the funds were transferred within a week. The Mobley, in Cisco, became Hilton's first hotel.

The hotel was booked solid, and Conrad and his partner, L.M. Drown, rented their own beds and slept on chairs in the office. They also converted much of the hotel's public space into additional guest quarters. Making use of wasted space became a hallmark of Hilton's. With the Mobley running smoothly, Hilton bought two more Texas properties in 1920; the Melba, in Fort Worth, and the Waldorf in Dallas—named after the prized New York hotel he later added to his chain. In 1925 Conrad Hilton built the first hotel to carry his name, in Dallas.

With expansions well underway, Hilton had consolidated his properties into Hilton Hotels, Incorporated, in 1929, when the stock market crashed. The El Paso Hilton was completed in November 1930 and opened with a fanfare. A year later, Hilton owned eight hotels and was more than half a million dollars in debt when a young bellboy slipped him $300—his life savings—so Hilton could feed himself and his family.

In 1931 the Moodys, a Galveston, Texas, family from whom Hilton had borrowed, took possession of his hotels when he defaulted on his $300,000 loan. The Moodys then hired Hilton to manage their own and his hotels, now known as the National Hotel Company. Nine months later, in 1932, Hilton and the Moodys decided to part. The separation, however, was in no way peaceful. The Moodys and Hilton sued and countersued one another regarding the terms of their agreement for separation, which Hilton claimed allotted him one-third of the hotels and one-third of the stock if the arrangement failed to prove satisfactory. In 1933, while Hilton continued to battle the Moodys in court, the Moodys defaulted on the loan for the El Paso Hilton, and Conrad Hilton managed to raise $30,000 and buy back that hotel. In 1934 Hilton settled with the Moodys, who lent him $95,000 and returned the Lubbock, Dallas, and Plainview hotels. According to Conrad Hilton, while Depression-era hotel owners saved less than one hotel out of five, Hilton emerged with five of his eight hotels, and he met his debts by the summer of 1937.

In 1938, Hilton bought his first hotel outside of Texas, the Sir Francis Drake in San Francisco. He sold it two years later at a $500,000 profit to raise capital to purchase the Stevens in Chicago, then the largest hotel in the world.

Although U.S. entry into World War II spawned caution, Hilton acquired three new properties, one in Los Angeles and two in New York. Thus, in 1942, his name stretched from coast to coast. The New York properties included the Roosevelt and the Plaza. Hilton claimed he was practicing for New York's Waldorf-Astoria, whose picture he had clipped from a magazine when the hotel opened in 1931 and carried with him since.

In 1945, Hilton traveled to Chicago to complete the purchase of the Stevens, which he had initiated in 1940, and ended up acquiring the Palmer House as well. In May 1946, Hilton Hotels Corporation was formed. It made history the next year as the first hotel company to have its stock listed on the New York Stock Exchange. Conrad N. Hilton was president and the largest stockholder.

Despite its reputation, the Waldorf-Astoria was not a profitable hotel. While negotiations to lease that hotel were taking place, Hilton worried his board members with his interest in international hotels in a postwar climate uncertain for international business. Nevertheless, Conrad Hilton pursued the venture that would become the Caribe Hilton in San Juan, Puerto Rico. An agreement was made to form a wholly owned subsidiary—Hilton Hotels International—for which Hilton formed a separate board. In 1949 Conrad Hilton bought the lease on the Waldorf-Astoria. The Waldorf made a $1 million profit in its first year under Hilton management. The first European Hilton was opened in Madrid in 1953.

The largest hotel merger in the industry took place in 1954 when Hilton Hotels purchased the Statler Hotel Company for $111 million. The Statler chain consisted of eight hotels, with two more under construction. Statler was noted for its fine properties and solid reputation. The chain was about to be sold to a New York realty firm when Hilton made a plea to Statler's widow. She agreed to sell to Hilton, in order to keep the hotels in "the hands of hotel people." Earnings per share nearly doubled between 1953 and 1955, largely as a result of this acquisition. In 1955, another overseas Hilton was opened, in Turkey, and the Continental Hilton of Mexico City opened the following year. In 1964 Hilton International was spun off and became a public company with Conrad Hilton as its president. Hilton was made chairman of the board of Hilton Hotels that same year.

The late 1960s saw significant changes, beginning with the 1965 formation of Statler Hilton Inns, a corporate franchising subsidiary, and a change of presidents. In 1966 Hilton's son, William Barron Hilton—known as Barron—assumed the presidency. Barron Hilton's conservative fiscal strategies set a decidedly different course for the company his father had built. The following year, Barron Hilton persuaded his father, as the largest shareholder of Hilton International, to swap his stock for that of Trans World Airlines (TWA). Hilton remained chairman of Hilton International. The expectation had been that TWA stock would rise, but its value halved over the next 18 months. Meanwhile, foreign travel boomed and Hilton lost the rights to his name overseas.

In 1971, Barron Hilton engineered the $112 million purchase that would generate the largest percentage of the company's revenues within a decade: two casino-hotels in Las Vegas, Nevada. The Las Vegas Hilton and the Flamingo Hilton marked the company's entry into gaming. This move paid for itself, particularly during the late 1970s and early 1980s, when the occupancy rate at both hotels remained steady in contrast to industrywide trends. Barron Hilton then concentrated on franchising the Hilton name and managing other hotels. In 1975 Hilton sold a 50% interest in six major hotels to Prudential Life Insurance Company of America for $85 million. Hilton continued to manage the properties in exchange for a percentage of room revenues and gross profits. This was one of the first management leaseback deals in the industry. Joint-venture arrangements later became standard industry practice.

In 1977 the purchase of the Waldorf-Astoria's building and land was finalized for $35 million. The decade closed with the death of Conrad N. Hilton in 1979, at age 91. Barron Hilton became chairman of the board. During the 1980s Hilton continued to make its money primarily though casino gambling, leasing and management, and franchise fees. These were sound measures during recession years: while revenues for owned hotels increased an average of 4% in 1980 and 1981, management contract fees increased by 6% in 1980 and 14% in 1981. Overall earnings for Hilton increased by 6% during these years, and the company grew rich in liquid assets. It put this capital to use in hotel improvements and in 1981, the $34.4 million purchase of another casino-hotel in Nevada, the Sahara Reno. Barron Hilton maintained a no-partnership policy for the company's casino-hotels. Although the hotels suffered from the loss of convention bookings during the recession, an addition to the Las Vegas Hilton in 1982 made it the largest hotel in the world, and further convention facilities were added in 1985. In 1982, a new international subsidiary was founded, Conrad International Hotels. Construction began on a casino-hotel in Australia the following year.

By 1985 gaming was providing 40% of the company's operating income, and earnings had increased 20% annually since Hilton's entry into that industry. In 1985, however, after spending $320 million to build a casino in Atlantic City, New Jersey, Hilton was denied a license to operate. The New Jersey Casino Control Commission's primary objection was Hilton Hotel's long-standing relationship with Chicago labor attorney Sidney Korshak, who had been linked with organized crime figures and who *The New York Times* in 1976 had labeled "a behind-the-scenes fixer." Hilton severed its ties with Korshak, who had acted as a labor consultant for the company, and the gaming commission granted a new hearing. In April 1985, before the rehearing took place, however, the hotel-casino was sold to Donald Trump at cost.

While Hilton focused on the casino-hotels, Marriott and Hyatt were expanding in the luxury-hotels market. To keep pace with its competitors, Hilton pledged $1.4 billion to renovate older properties. Barron Hilton also concentrated on solving the problem of his father's will.

When Conrad Hilton died, he had bequeathed the bulk of his holding—a 27% block of Hilton shares—to the Conrad N. Hilton Foundation. This foundation, incorporated in 1950, gives aid to Catholic nuns. This provision left Barron Hilton with 3.6% of Hilton Hotels, but he claimed to have exercised an option on the foundation's shares immediately, buying their portion at the market rate of $24. Ownership of the stock was contested for the next decade. At issue was the interpretation of an option Conrad Hilton had allotted Barron Hilton in his will: Barron Hilton claimed the will allowed him to buy the entire stock from the foundation at the 1979 price. The estate's executor, who was Conrad's personal attorney, claimed the will intended that Barron Hilton be entitled to no more than 7% of the shares. Meanwhile, Hilton and ex-wife Zsa Zsa Gabor's daughter also contested the will. The attorney general's office of California joined the case, arguing that the foundation was entitled to the shares at market value, or $225 million, in 1985. To complicate the issue further, Golden Nugget casino's chairman Steve Wynn attempted to buy the disputed shares in 1985 at their current market price—$72 a share—in order to launch a takeover of Hilton.

In November 1988 a settlement was reached. Barron Hilton got 4 million of the disputed shares, the foundation kept 3.5 million shares, and 6 million shares went into a trust, with Hilton serving as the executor of the trust. In addition, Hilton was to receive 60% of the trust's share dividends until 2008, after which they revert to the foundation.

Hilton closed the decade enjoying a 70% occupancy rate in its newly rejuvenated domestic hotels, greater international expansion, and properties that are estimated to put Hilton's value between $4 billion and $6 billion. In May 1989, Chairman Barron Hilton solicited bids for the chain. By December 1989, however, the company had not received a satisfactory bid, and Hilton decided not to sell.

For the 1990s, Hilton is concentrating on two areas of development: its growth overseas through Conrad International and the launching of two new hotel concepts, all-suite hotels and CrestHil by Hilton, a line of moderately priced hotels. International properties under construction in 1990 included hotels in Hong Kong, Turkey, and Belgium. In 1990 more than 270 hotels and inns in the United States were operating under the Hilton name.

Principal Subsidiaries: BAC 1-11 Corp; Benco, Inc.; Hapeville Investors; Hilton Hawaii Corp.; Hilton Casinos, Inc.; Hilton Hotels U.S.A.; Hilton Inns, Inc.; Hilton New Jersey Corp.; Hilton Hotel Partners I, Inc.; Hilton Hotel Partners II, Inc.; Hilton Pennsylvania Hotel Corp.; Hilton Products, Inc.; Hilton Quebec, Inc. (Canada); Hilton Washington Corp.; Hilton Tours, Inc.; Hilton Equipment Corp.; Hotel Waldorf-Astoria Corp.; Hotels Statler Co., Inc.; Hilton Systems, Inc.; Palmer House Co.; Hilton Gaming Corp.; Kenner Investors, Inc.; Stevens Hotel Corp.; The Beverly Hilton Corp.; The New York Hotel Corp.; Compass Computer Services, Inc. (50%); Hilton Service Corp. (51%); Main & Hokombe Corp. (40%); Statler Dallas Corp. (49%).

Further Reading: Hilton, Conrad, *Be My Guest,* New York, Prentice Hall Press, 1957; Moore, Thomas, ''Barron Hilton Fights for Hilton Hotels,'' *Fortune,* May 27, 1985.

—Carol I. Keeley

HOLIDAY INNS, INC.

1100 Ashwood Parkway, Suite 200
Atlanta, Georgia 30338
(404) 551-3500
Fax: (404) 551-3551

Wholly Owned Subsidiary of Bass PLC
Incorporated: 1954 as Holiday Inns of America
Employees: 20,000
Sales: £4.04 billion (US$6.52 billion)

Holiday Inn Worldwide, the descriptive trade name for Holiday Inns, Inc. is one of the largest international hotel chains, with approximately 1,600 hotels and 320,000 rooms. The company is credited by industry analysts with advances in standardization of service quality across a global network of independent franchises, guaranteed room rates, and computerized reservations. Holiday Inns is a leader in the U.S. hotel industry in the midprice market, the slowest growing and most competitive market segment. Approximately 85% of the Holiday Inns are operated by franchisees.

The historical importance of the Holiday Inn corporation has not yet been evaluated. Yet its proper place is suggested by cultural historians like Warren I. Belasco, whose book, *Americans on the Road: From Autocamp to Motel, 1910–1945,* about the rise of 20th century tourism in the United States, places the Holiday Inn company alongside Marriott and McDonald's in importance.

Kemmons Wilson founded the company in 1952, following a motor tour where he and his family encountered unpleasant accommodations. Many Holiday Inns had chaplains on call, and the Bible in each room was opened to a new page daily to create a caring and home-away-from-home atmosphere.

According to Belasco, the Holiday Inn style that materialized in the 1950s was "already outlined" by 1930. The popularity of automobiles and touring, the lure of the newly designated wilderness areas, the availability of campgrounds, and the infatuation with being a tourist contributed to the Depression-era roots of the Holiday Inns. Americans continued to take auto vacations in the mid 1930s; rail and Pullman revenues fell in 1933 while expenditures on gas, oil, and other expenses for vacation motor touring remained unchanged. Kemmons Wilson was aware of some early motel industry issues of the 1930s: the negative image of motels, the question of whether to employ women in motels, and the practice of bargaining for room rates in the absence of fixed nightly charges.

In August 1952, when Wilson opened the first Holiday Inn in Memphis, Tennessee, it was a 120-room property that could boast, according to the company, "a private bath, air conditioning and telephone," as well as then-luxury symbols, a swimming pool, free ice, free parking, and dog kennels. Children under 12 stayed free. In 1957, when the company went public, trading its stock on the over-the-counter market, the entire offering sold on the first day. Five years later, Holiday Inn's stock was traded on the New York Stock Exchange.

In the 1960s, Holiday Inn hotels were opened in Canada and throughout Western Europe, while continuing to expand in the U.S. at a rate of what the company called one new property "every two-and-a-half days." By 1970, the chain estimated its gross sales at more than $1.2 billion.

In 1972 the "Holiday Inn University," in operation since 1959, opened special facilities in Olive Branch, Mississippi, a few miles outside Memphis. The Holiday Inn University contributed to the consistency of the company's service by providing for the education and professional advancement of its franchisees and property managers, who were offered the opportunity to study management topics, housekeeping systems, and employee relations in short-term, intensive seminars on a college-like campus, complete with sports facilities.

Even after Kemmons Wilson's retirement in 1979, and well into the mid-1980s, new properties were being constructed at company estimates of "one every 7 days." When Wilson retired, he turned the management over to university graduates with degrees in hotel management, a sign of the evolution of an industry that Wilson had done so much to help develop. As *Nation's Business* for March 1989 pointed out, Kemmons Wilson was a classic American entrepreneur: "being in business means more to him than the kind of business he is in."

Michael Rose served as president from 1979 to 1984, when he became chief executive officer of Holiday Corporation, the holding company for the hotels and gambling casinos. At that time, Kenneth Hamlet, with a B.S. degree from the Cornell University School of Hotel Administration, succeeded Rose as president of the hotel company.

Because properties industrywide became greatly overbuilt during the 1980s—as much as 13% overbuilt in every major U.S. city—the company experienced a downturn in profits of nearly $60 million in 1986 for the first time in its history. In 1986 the company was the first U.S. motel chain to open in the People's Republic of China with the Holiday Inn–Lido Beijing Hotel, a venture which brought less press visibility or profits than anticipated and was in part responsible for the drop in profits.

The decline in profits paved the way for Bass PLC in the United Kingdom to purchase seven European hotels in 1987. The purchase was in keeping with a trend in the 1980s that saw three major hotel chains acquired by British parent companies: Howard Johnson, Rodeway Inns, and Travelodge. Because the U.S. market for hotels was more competitive and more overbuilt than in Europe, two of the three chains, Howard Johnson and Rodeway, were re-sold shortly after takeover.

In 1988 Bass purchased Holiday Inns International, which included all properties outside of North American, plus 13 in the United States. In February 1990 Bass concluded the buyout of Holiday Inns from Holiday Corporation at a total cost of $2.23 billion. That same year, Holiday Corporation had created a separate company, Promus, consisting of the gambling casinos in Nevada and New Jersey, the Hampton Inns chain, and the Embassy Suites and Homewood Suites hotels. Michael Rose, chief executive officer of Holiday Corporation, left that post to become chairman of Promus. Bass acquired Commonwealth Hospitality Ltd., 38 Canadian hotels with 8,700 rooms primarily operating as Holiday Inns. In Great Britain, Bass began developing Holiday Inn Garden Court hotels in addition to the Holiday Inn hotels acquired.

The company's location in Memphis was detrimental to its public visibility. For nearly four decades, according to the summary published in *Public Relations Quarterly* in Summer 1987, the company had operated as if it had no competition with virtually no marketing communications at all until 1975. Its location in Memphis severely hampered its press relations, and marketing communications operations were regionally-focused rather than nationally targeted. Each international region handled its own advertising. The communications staff had little experience in other allied segments of the hospitality, travel, and leisure industries.

The analysis of communications management in the *Public Relations Quarterly* of Summer 1987 pointed out that because of the regionalism of the company, most communications operations were directed to employees, a necessary procedure in a service company where staff came face-to-face with customers. There were no on-going contacts with the trade and industrial press. At the helm there was considerable skepticism about the effectiveness of press relations and their relevance to sales. Most efforts of Holiday Corporation were aimed at improving the local reputation in Memphis of the company as a good citizen, and working to improve the civic climate through philanthropy. At the corporate level, the communications director saw his job as one where his primary responsibility was to "communicate the values of the chief executive to mid-management and subsidiaries." He thought it impractical for top management to attempt to communicate worldwide in any medium. Following the profits downturn in 1986, communications operations were brought into line with industry practice. Under Hamlet's leadership, the company placed its emphasis on technology in the late 1980s, and developed completely refurbished communications and marketing operations staffed by hotel industry experts whose goal was to outmarket the competition.

Bass has been chiefly involved in the production and distribution of beer, soft drinks, and on-premise retailing. Vertical integration between these businesses and Holiday Inns resulted in the use of Bass's existing capabilities in customer service industries, property management, and integrated data base networks. In addition, one of Holiday Inn's achievements has been its computerization of a global reservation system, Holidex, considered innovative when it was introduced in 1965, and in its third generation at the beginning of the 1990s. Another company achievement has been the standardization of service quality and room rates. In 1990, Kenneth Hamlet resigned as president of Holiday Inns, Inc., and was replaced by Bryan Langton, head of the Bass Hotels and Restaurant Division. Langton also serves as chairman and chief executive officer of Holiday Inn Worldwide.

Further Reading: Belasco, Warren James, *Americans on the Road: From Autocamp to Motel, 1910–1945*, Cambridge, Massachusetts, MIT Press, 1979.

—Claire Badaracco

HYATT CORPORATION

200 West Madison Avenue
Chicago, Illinois 60606
U.S.A.
(312) 750-8023
Fax: (312) 750-8550

Private Company
Incorporated: 1957 as Hyatt Hotels Corporation
Employees: 50,000
Sales: $2.40 billion

Owned, operated, and privately held by the Pritzker family of Chicago, the Hyatt hotels are a worldwide chain that has made business travelers and the development of spectacular "fantasy" properties its niche. The two most important historical events associated with the Hyatt Hotel chain are the development of its trademark high-rise atrium lobbies, first pioneered at Peachtree Plaza in Atlanta in 1967, and the collapse of the skywalk at the Kansas City, Missouri, Hyatt in 1981.

The Pritzker family built the company as a result of the "favored customer" rapport between First National Bank of Chicago, which was eager to lend the fledgling company money, and father Abraham Nicholas (A.N.) Pritzker, as well as the teamwork of his sons Jay, Robert, and Donald, according to an in-depth portrait of the deliberately low-profile family in *Fortune* April 25, 1988. Jay graduated from Northwestern University at 18, and completed a law degree at Northwestern while concurrently serving in the navy, based at Glenview Naval Air Station, following his service as a flight instructor during World War II. After serving in Washington, D.C., with the federal agency that ran foreign-owned companies whose assets had been seized during the war, Jay went into business for himself, buying a lumber and plywood operation in Eugene, Oregon.

In 1953 Robert Pritzker, an industrial engineer, took over management of Colson Company, his brother Jay's recently acquired small manufacturing company in Elyria, Ohio, and successfully restructured the ailing company within a short time. Their brother, Donald Pritzker, joined them in their management company Pritzker & Pritzker (P & P) when he finished law school in 1959.

In 1957 Jay Pritzker bought a small airport motel in Los Angeles named "Hyatt House" after its original owner, Hyatt von Dehn. Within four years, Jay expanded the single property into a chain of six hotels and made Donald manager of operations, reporting to Jay. According to *Fortune,* Don "had a captivating smile, an uproarious laugh, and a wit that would show up a stand-up comedian." Don died in 1972 at the age of 39 of a heart attack, and Hugh M. Friend Jr., Jay's brother-in-law, became president.

Hyatt's great success during the years 1957–1967 was attributable to the deal-making skills of Jay, the managerial ability and personality of Don, and to its interest in innovative hotel design. In 1967, a watershed year in Hyatt's history, the company went public and also bought an unfinished hotel in Atlanta with an unusual atrium, designed by the architect John Portman. The Portman atrium was a 21-story interior courtyard, designed so that each hotel room entered off the high-rise open space, set off with a central glass elevator leading to all floors, and hanging green vines growing from each floor's balcony. The overall effect was revolutionary in hotel design, because the Portman interior eliminated the impersonal hallway with rows of doors and brought an open-air congeniality, with the spin-off of greater safety, feeling of security, and warmth to the hotel interior. The Portman lobby became the hotel's signature, and advanced the concept of public space in buildings.

Peachtree Center in Atlanta, where the hotel is located, consists of 15 buildings, more than ten million square feet. John Portman's development had begun with converting an old building into furniture showrooms, which led him to build new, bigger buildings which became the Atlanta Merchandise Mart in 1961. The mart stimulated downtown business activity, created a rebirth of the city's center, and brought new business. Portman then built an office tower, which helped increase demand for hotel rooms. Portman's design failed to convince financial backers. The developers of the large hotel property were in financial trouble when the Pritzkers took over. After the Hyatt Regency opened, its occupancy rate reached 94.6%. In 1977, Hugh Friend left the company, and Jay Pritzker became president, in addition to his responsibilities as chairman and chief executive officer. The family moved Hyatt's headquarters to Chicago, where it could oversee matters more closely. They gradually bought back the public shares of stock, and took the company private in 1979. Thomas Jay Pritzker, Jay's son, became president in 1980.

The National Bureau of Standards called the 1981 collapse of two skywalks at the Kansas City Hyatt Regency Hotel the most devastating structural collapse ever to take place in the United States. Insurance industry experts in *Insurance Review* compared it to the eruption of Mount St. Helen's. Nearly five years after the collapsed skywalk killed 114 people and injured 229, insurance carriers and the judicial system had not settled all outstanding claims. More than 2,000 lawsuits for a total of $120 million were settled between 1981 and 1986. In June 1986, 900 individuals remaining in a federal class action suit against the hotel settled all claims for $1,000 each. In August 1986 the Missouri Court of Appeals ruled on the issue of insurer liability by concluding that all insurance companies with policies on the hotel would participate in payment of damages. Hyatt was managing the hotel for Hallmark Properties, its builder. "Gross negligence and misconduct" were finally attributed to engineers Daniel Duncan, Jack Gillum, and their former company, G.C.E. International

Inc., whose "hurry-up" design system caused them to be pouring concrete on one part of the building while finishing the design on the rest of the building.

Design innovation continues to set Hyatt apart, along with its top-ranked, cohesive family management teams, and the cluster of separate companies that make up the Pritzker family portfolio, all located within its headquarters at 200 West Madison or within the city block; each company has a distinct job. Pritzker & Pritzker, for example, is "actually a small investment bank whose 17 professionals serve one client," according to *Fortune*'s profile. One of the few partners is Penny, Donald's daughter, and a lawyer with Pritzker & Pritzker, who is concentrating on developing retirement housing called Classic Residence by Hyatt Corporation. Another new target for the Hyatt Hotels is the "urban villages" concept, where scaled-down versions of the Regency prototype design will be built in the urban fringe area market. For the Hyatt International subsidiary, the developer Chris Hemmeter has built elaborate "fantasy" properties in Hawaii. Hemmeter's style is to add special effects like crashing waterfalls, grotto bars, and free-roaming peacocks. The $360 million Hyatt Regency Waikokola, which develped the concept of the fantasy resort, will have 1,244 rooms in three towers on 60 acres. The atrium of one tower will have ten small islands covered with trees and tropical birds. A seven-acre lagoon will be stocked with reef fish for snorkelers, and miniature deer will roam free on the grounds.

Hyatt has conducted futures research on business travelers according to Adam Aron, the senior vice president of marketing for Hyatt Hotels, interviewed in *American Demographics* for January 1990, and seeks to apply new technology to guests' complaints on things as small as the irritation of the theft-proof coathanger to a computer-controlled check-in where the guest's credit card will serve as the door key, bypassing the front desk altogether. In research and development Hyatt has become the industry pioneer.

Every indication from the industry suggests that Hyatt hotels will continue to innovate not only in the area of building design and business travelers services such as "mini-camp weekends" where travelers can bring family along for a reduced price, but also in its joint-venture financing. The complexity of joint ventures is made far easier because the company is private. In 1989, the Chicagoans turned Yugoslavian debt into a five-star hotel venture, when First Chicago Bank invested directly in the project, continuing its "good customer" rapport with Hyatt. This first Yugoslavian debt-equity swap was a complicated transaction: Hyatt and the bank received majority ownership in return for $10.2 million in local currency that came from conversion of a three-times restructured debt held by the bank. Yugoslavia bought back its own debt, and the bank and Hyatt reinvested their profits into a new hotel project in Yugoslavia, with the bank completing another $25 million loan to the project. According to dealmakers, the involvement of First Chicago as a principal rather than as a broker for another entity persuaded the Yugoslavian government, which holds 49% interest against Hyatt's 51% in the venture, to participate.

Much of the strength of future joint-venture financing for the so-called "trophy properties" that are the trademark of the Hyatt Hotel chain will come from the Japanese, according to Hyatt's Laurence Geller, interviewed in the *Cornell Hotel Administration Quarterly,* in May 1989; Geller was executive vice president of Hyatt Development Corporation, a separate company from the hotels, and he observed in the interview that "a cadre of lenders follows Hyatt" internationally.

Hyatt Hotels, along with Hyatt International, P&P, the Hyatt Development Corporation, Marmon Group, and the rest of the Pritzker's portfolio will undoubtedly continue to be well-managed by a harmonious family team, all of whom are also lawyers. The impressive business acumen of the Pritzker family is exemplified by the personal asset valuation of $25,000 of A.N. Pritzker's estate when he died at 90 in 1986. It was A.N. himself who estimated that he sheltered more than $200 million in taxes alone by setting up the family trust prior to the 1985 tax laws which negated such advantages. Over nearly four decades the quiet clan has built an estimated wealth that exceeds $3.5 billion according to *Fortune's* estimate. The success of the Pritzkers as managers and their properties undoubtedly will continue to use the Hyatt's historic image as an industry pioneer as a central part of its corporate philosophy and strategy.

Principal Subsidiaries: Hyatt Hotels Corp.; Hyatt International Corp.; Hyatt Development Corp.

Further Reading: Worthy, Ford S., "The Pritzkers: Unveiling a Private Family," *Fortune,* April 25, 1988.

—Claire Badaracco

ITT Sheraton
WORLDWIDE HOTELS, INNS, RESORTS & ALL-SUITES

ITT SHERATON CORPORATION

60 State Street
Boston, Massachusetts 02109
U.S.A.
(617) 367-3600
Fax: (617) 367-5676

Wholly Owned Subsidiary of ITT Corporation
Incorporated: 1941 as Standard Equities Corporation
Employees: 125,000
Sales: $4.38 billion

The world's leading international hotel company and third-largest hotel company in terms of number of rooms, ITT Sheraton Corporation owns, leases, manages, or franchises some 450 hotels, inns, and resorts in 65 countries on five continents. Servicing 22 million guests worldwide each year, ITT Sheraton has been the hotel industry's leader in a number of areas, including the use of new technology for reservations and the penetration of new international markets. After some lapses in quality during its expansion into franchises, the company instituted a rigorous system to ensure consistent worldwide standards in both corporate and franchised properties.

Ernest Henderson and Robert Moore, the hotel chain's co-founders, had not originally intended to enter the hotel business. Harvard classmates in the 1910s, they tried many businesses, from assembling Model-T cars and radios, to importing paper-fiber suits and German shepherd dogs. Shortly after the stock market crash, with stock prices low, they turned to securities. Henderson, Moore, and Henderson's brother George bought an investment company—Beacon Participations—relatively cheaply. From there, they embarked on highly unorthodox financial paths that frightened off some stockholders but led, after the purchase of two more investment companies—Atlantic Securities and Standard Investing Corporation—to what became the Sheraton Corporation of America. The group chose the hotel business because it believed that real estate, and in particular hotels, would recover most quickly after the Depression.

The Henderson brothers and Moore developed a pattern of buying lagging properties and turning them around at a substantial profit—the backbone of Sheraton's early success. Shortly after 1933—a year in which industry-wide hotel occupancy rates dropped to the lowest ever, 51%—they purchased the Continental in Cambridge, Massachusetts. The Continental had first opened its doors the day the stock market crashed; six months of declining business led to foreclosure, and, a few years later, to the closure of the bank that had foreclosed. For a very modest sum, therefore, the Hendersons and Moore started in the hotel business.

After paying off mature bonds, the remaining assets of their third investment company, Standard Investing Corporation, were used to buy the 200-room Stonehaven Hotel in Springfield, Massachusetts. A few years later, they consolidated Standard Investing with International Equities Corporation to form the Standard Equities Corporation. By that time, the Hendersons and Moore had purchased three hotels in Boston, one of which later gave the chain its name because the hotel's electric sign—which bore the words "Sheraton Hotel"—would have been prohibitively costly to replace.

Within a few years, they purchased the Copley Plaza, a world-renown Boston institution. This was, according to Ernest Henderson—president and spokesman for the company—their introduction to the major league. After the Copley, they began to seek out projects that would yield two dollars in value for every dollar expended.

Throughout the 1940s, domestic expansion continued with purchases of hotels stretching from Maine to Florida. Competition lay in the form of the growing Hilton, Statler, Pick, Knott, and Milner hotel companies. The success of Henderson's company, which put it in the running with these other chains, was due to its pulling itself up by its bootstraps and by sheer frugality. Ernest Henderson—his brother had dropped out of the picture by now—was known to go on endlessly about the need to extinguish unused lights.

The company received one substantial infusion of outside capital. In 1946—a booming year for the hotel industry with its highest-ever industrywide occupancy rate of 95%—Standard Equities merged with U.S. Realty and Improvement Company, a holding company, to form the United States Realty–Sheraton Corporation, which was shortly thereafter renamed the Sheraton Corporation of America. As part of this merger, Henderson and Moore acquired several office and apartment buildings in New York City, which were later resold for a profit, in addition to some other nonhotel properties, including the Martin Electric Company of Detroit.

From that time on, Sheraton brought innovations to the hotel industry, particularly with technological advances. In 1948, Sheraton was the first to use the telex system for a reservations network. In 1958, it introduced Reservatron, the industry's earliest automated electronic reservation system, which made Sheraton the first hotel chain to centralize and computerize reservations. In 1967, Sheraton updated that system with Reservatron II, a computer system for personalized reservations. In 1970, Sheraton was the first to institute a toll-free 800-number system, allowing customers direct access to reservations.

Henderson used federal depreciation allowances to reduce Sheraton's taxable income, thus increasing its cash flow and freeing up funds for expansion. The 1950s saw the growth of loosely banded hotel groups and the construction of new properties, particularly motels. Sheraton followed suit by building newer, more expensive hotels in 1957 as well as motor inns, partly in response to the development of interstate highways and increased air travel. At this time, Sheraton chose to build new as opposed to fixing up old because the supply of poorly run existing hotels was exhausted. The company fully utilized its audit potential by mortgaging its hotels and four of its office buildings. In order not to bring down the whole company if a depression were to hit, the hotels were held in subsidiary corporations.

Not content with simple domestic growth, Sheraton's international expansion began with the acquisition in 1949 of two Canadian hotel chains, the Laurentien Hotel Company and the Eppley chain. Ten years later, Sheraton went beyond North America with a flourish that would mark its future: four Hawaiian properties were purchased and the stage was set for Sheraton's eventual dominance of the Hawaiian hotel market, with 12 luxury hotels. Sheraton followed with a 1961 Middle East project in Tel Aviv, then hotels in Puerto Rico and Jamaica, and in 1963 with its first South American hotel, the Macuto Sheraton in Venezuela.

In the United States during the 1960s, as family vacations by car became increasingly popular, the dominant chains were taking root. Despite the increase in hotel business from family car trips, some industry analysts considered the lodging industry overbuilt and predicted doom for many hotels. Increased air travel, although it cut the number of stopovers, led to an increase in hotel business. Sheraton had started the decade strong. With the highest cash flow in the hotel industry in 1958, Sheraton sold approximately 30 to 40 hotels between 1945 and 1960, most of them at substantial profits. Times were lean, however, with the glut, and a few years later, Sheraton was forced to sell more hotels to reduce the company's debt.

Up until this time, the most importance difference between Sheraton and Hilton, the top U.S. chains, was that while Hilton was the largest operator of hotels in the world, largely because of its network of leases, Sheraton was the largest owner of hotels. Even though other hotels had been hit by bankruptcy and many were in the red because of overcapacity, Sheraton was still making money in real estate. In fact, Sheraton was in the red quite a bit of the time—but only on the surface. Ernest Henderson's clever accounting kept profits low even though assets were substantial.

In the early 1960s, the Sheraton style began to change. In order to spread its name without tying up funds, the company managed hotels owned and built by others. In 1962, recognizing the merits of franchising and the prospective demand of other hotels to use Sheraton's well-known name along with its advanced reservation system, Sheraton followed the industry trend by forming a franchise division. Henderson seemed to be looking forward to the fall-out from the 1960s glut, that is, the opportunity to buy bargain-priced hotels, in the same way that he was able to buy hotels and survive the fall-out of the 1930s.

Henderson died in 1967 and the chain passed to his son, Ernest III, who had become president and treasurer in 1963. With the elder Henderson's death, Sheraton was up for sale. International Telephone and Telegraph Corporation (ITT)—long the international equivalent of AT&T and in the 1960s a leader in the conglomerate merger wave—acquired Sheraton as a wholly owned subsidiary in 1968. Harold Geneen, then president of ITT, wanted companies that were capable of a minimum of 10% annual growth rate, and those that would bring to ITT a greater degree of public recognition. Geneen's policy was to attach the ITT name to all its subsidiaries. Sheraton fit well into ITT's line of consumer services, particularly as ITT already owned a rental car company and an airport parking company; the trend toward package travel service had begun.

Given this new ITT affiliation, Sheraton began to depend increasingly on consumer and market research when making development decisions. Just after the acquisition, Claude Feninger, former product manager for hotel operations of ITT—ITT had previously had 16 Holiday Inn francishes in the U.S.—was named president of Sheraton-International, the overseas properties division. Ambitious plans were laid to fashion a global network of business and convention hotels, luxury hotels and resorts, as well as inns.

Howard "Bud" James, who became ITT Sheraton president and CEO in 1970, moving the younger Henderson into the chairman slot, is often cited as the reason that Sheraton moved so far ahead, particularly because he saw the value of decentralized management, domestically and globally. Sheraton's U.S. division, therefore, has regional managers who are responsible not only for their "own" hotels but six or seven other properties as well. Internationally, Sheraton's properties are divided into four geographic divisions, along with a franchise division, for management purposes.

After the early 1970s, Sheraton underwent a change in its development philosophy. Prior to that time, as was Henderson's way, Sheraton operated almost all of its hotel properties. Under the guidance of ITT, Sheraton evolved from a real estate company with heavy equity involvement into a hotel management company with low equity involvement. It did so by relying more heavily on franchises and management contracts. For Sheraton and the other prominent hotel chains, such as Holiday Inn, Hilton, Marriott, and Ramada, franchising and managing, rather than owning and operating, certainly had their virtues: financial risk was greatly reduced, and because of the elimination of depreciation, Sheraton was able to maintain steady earnings flow from its old properties. Such arrangements do not guarantee high earnings. If demand for rooms fall, Sheraton's revenue decreases because that revenue is simply a percentage of operating profits.

By the mid-1970s, Sheraton was the industry leader in selling franchises and management contracts, which had by this time become widespread among the big national chains. In 1976, Sheraton's gross sales from owned, leased, managed, and franchised properties topped $1 billion. Despite the excitement produced by international expansion—Sheraton's operations expanded from 4 to 55 foreign countries in just over ten years—in 1985, Sheraton owned only 14 of its 482 hotels, barely 3%. At that time, a flaw in Sheraton's franchising system began to appear: loss of control over service quality. In the rush to expand with franchises, Sheraton had not devised a system for compliance with the high service-standards that the Sheraton name had originally implied. This problem, which had not fully surfaced until the mid-1980s, was addressed with a sweeping reorganization.

Through marketing campaigns and incentives, Sheraton targeted groups to increase sales. One concept to differentiate Sheraton in a crowded, competitive market, was the Sheraton Towers, the first of which opened in Boston in 1970. The Towers, designed for the business traveler, were essentially hotels within hotels, with fancier rooms, and unusual amenities such as concierge service. With Sheraton Club International, a frequent traveler program launched in 1987, Sheraton was highly successful in retaining repeat customers, particularly those in business. Such travelers along with the convention market, which is sometimes booked as much as ten years ahead of time, are an important part of Sheraton's business. To take advantage of an aging U.S. population, Sheraton, in 1977, began offering a 25% discount to members of several senior citizens' organizations. Weekend deals and family plans had been used since Sheraton's early days to fill empty rooms on the weekend, after the bulk of hotel guests—business travelers—left.

As was the case in the 1930s and the 1960s, some analysts in the 1980s contended that the hotel industry was overbuilt, particularly the luxury segment, in which Sheraton has most of its properties. Because any night a room is empty can never be sold again, a glut in the hotel business can prove disastrous. Sheraton, however, denied the existence of such a glut, globally or even nationally, even though it admitted that pockets of excess capacity existed in certain cities, such as in Boston in the mid-1980s. Sheraton continued to respond to the competition with target marketing because it already had diversification ranging from the more utilitarian business hotels from its earlier days to the more luxurious hotels and resorts. Because of Sheraton's worldwide spread of hotels and commitment to the long-term view, it was in a good position to ride out temporary difficulties that affected other hotels.

In 1983, the new Sheraton chairman, president, and CEO, John Kapioltas, former president of Sheraton's Europe, Africa, Middle East, and South Asia division, who was promoted in part because of his development success, presided over an effort to bring to North America the same standards he had applied to five-star properties around the world

After expanding its domestic-resort network with new properties in California, Colorado, and Hawaii, Sheraton continued to lead the way with more industry initiatives. In 1985, it signed an agreement to operate the Great Wall Sheraton Hotel, Beijing, the first hotel in China to bear the name of an international hotel company. Five years later, Sheraton had four hotels in China bearing its name. Sheraton became the first U.S. hotel company to operate in Eastern Europe, with the 1986 opening of a Sheraton hotel in Sofia, Bulgaria. In 1989, it announced the first U.S.-Soviet joint venture to own and operate two hotels in Moscow, the first of which was scheduled to open in 1992.

Throughout the 1980s, Sheraton's net income fluctuated widely. It and an ITT development in Florida had a combined net loss of $6 million on revenues of $626 million in 1984 compared to a net profit of $19 million on revenues of $540 million in 1983. This substantial reversal may have led to ITT's 1985 announcement that it would welcome minority shareholders for Sheraton. Despite ITT's scaling back across the board in the late 1980s, it was not likely to sell Sheraton outright, given the great visibility Sheraton afforded and the fact that in 1985 ITT outlined an $80 million plan to upgrade Sheraton technology.

In 1986, a five-year internal reorganization of Sheraton began with the removal of the distinction between corporately owned and franchised hotels. In the company's early years, Ernest Henderson had stressed the importance of good reputation. By the mid-1980s that reputation was suffering: wherever customers saw the name they expected the same outstanding service—although, according to Sheraton surveys, they did not always seem to be getting it..

Over a period of five years, Sheraton sold and/or canceled the franchises for approximately 60% of its franchised properties that could not or would not meet its standards. To set itself apart from the competition, Sheraton launched a new ad campaign, "At Sheraton, Little Things Mean A Lot," in addition to the Sheraton Guest Satisfaction System (SGSS), a concept designed to increase guest-service standards and monitor how employees work to achieve that goal. Standard requirements were upgraded as of 1989, including not only the new service standards and SGSS, but a new inspection program, life-safety standards, training, the upgrading of existing properties, and opportunities for future growth.

Despite the increasingly complex and competitive market in which mergers and acquisitions have become common, Sheraton continued to move with its program of selective growth. By 1990, Sheraton had 161 corporately owned and-operated properties and 293 franchised properties. Considerable sums were spent for existing property improvements, including major restoration projects of Sheraton's U.S. landmark properties, such as the historic Carlton in Washington, D.C., and the luxurious Moana Surfrider in Waikiki Beach in Hawaii, both of which reopened in 1989. Money had also gone toward building new properties.

In 1990 ITT Sheraton had ambitions plans for the next decade. It intended to extend its world presence to at least 75 countries, with a greater emphasis on quality and uniformity. Internationally, Sheraton had in 1990 more than 50 projects under development, including plans for countries new to the system, as well as further developments in Europe, the Middle East, and South America. At the same time Sheraton was well-positioned for "The Pacific Century" with four new Sheratons under construction in Australia, and management contracts lined up for 23 Indonesian hotels. Domestically, ITT Sheraton had plans for several markets, including more convention hotels and all-suite hotels. As of 1990, more than 20 corporately-managed and franchised hotels were scheduled to join the Sheraton network in North America.

Sheraton continued to be in keen competition with Holiday Inn and the upscale Marriott Hotel chain, which had just edged Sheraton out of the number-two spot in number of rooms worldwide, for customers. A flexible attitude in joint ventures and other arrangements with a variety of institutions, dating back to the early days of Ernest Henderson's unorthodox paths, continued to hold new options for Sheraton in the future.

With the help of ITT, Sheraton's business was restructured and its service made uniform. That same company, just past its 50th anniversary was poised for the next century—with a policy of selective growth, high service standards, and rigorous checking procedures to ensure the strength of the ITT Sheraton name.

Principal Subsidiaries: The Hotel Source; Unifood.

Further Reading: ''Daring Financial Paths Lead Sheraton to Growth,'' *Business Week,* September 12, 1959; Henderson, Ernest, *''The Sheraton Story,''* New York, Newcomen Society in North America, 1959; Henderson, Ernest, *The World of ''Mr. Sheraton,''* New York, D. McKay Company, 1960; *Sheraton World Fiftieth Anniversary Issue,* Boston, ITT Sheraton Corporation, 1987.

—Aileen C. Hefferren

MARRIOTT CORPORATION

Marriott Drive
Washington, D.C. 20058
U.S.A.
(301) 380-9000

Public Company
Incorporated: 1929 as Hot Shoppes Inc.
Employees: 229,900
Sales: $7.54 billion
Stock Exchanges: New York Midwest Pacific Philadelphia Tokyo

Marriott is a giant corporation that operates 4,000 hotel rooms and each year develops more than $1 billion of real estate. Marriott has been a public company since 1953, but it has always been led by a Marriott—first the founder, J. Willard Marriott, and since 1964, his son J.W. Marriott Jr. Although the company is concerned primarily with lodging, it began just before the Depression as a food business, and food and drink continue to be a mainstay of the operation, contributing 70% of the company's revenues.

J. Willard (Bill) and Alice S. Marriott were newlyweds, recently transplanted from Utah, when they opened an A & W root beer stand in Washington, D.C., in May 1927. The Marriotts quickly noticed that soft drinks sold well during Washington's long, hot summer, but that business needed a boost during the cooler months. Tacos and tamales, the first Mexican food in the area, were added to their winter menu. The Marriotts called their restaurant The Hot Shoppe, and offered medium-priced food in a family environment. In 1928, the Marriotts opened their third restaurant, which offered curbside service. Business was strong and in 1929 the restaurant was incorporated as Hot Shoppes, Inc.

As Hot Shoppes evolved into a chain of restaurants, the Marriotts maintained close family supervision of all facets of the business; for many years Alice served as company bookkeeper while Bill ran the business with "benevolent and paternalistic labor relations and a flair for promotion" as *Forbes* reported in 1971.

Hot Shoppes remained popular in the Washington area through the Depression. In 1937, Marriott branched out from the restaurant business for the first time, pioneering in-flight catering with boxed lunches for Eastern, American, and Capital Airlines flights from Washington's old Hoover Airport.

In 1939, Marriott's food service–management business won an account at the U.S. Treasury building. In 1940 Marriott opened five new restaurants. In 1955 Marriott entered the hospital food service market at the Children's Hospital in Washington, and in 1957, another business segment made its debut when Marriott's first hotel, the Twin Bridges Marriott Motor Hotel, opened in Arlington, Virginia. Over the next few years, the company continued to open hotels as well as Hot Shoppes restaurants.

In 1964 Marriott handed the presidency to his son, Bill Marriott Jr. At the time, the company owned 45 Hot Shoppes and four hotels, as well as its its other businesses, and that year the company's name was changed to Marriott–Hot Shoppes, Inc. Bill Marriott Jr. wanted to accelerate the pace of growth. The new president first concentrated on the lodging segment of the business. Over the next six years, Marriott almost quadrupled in size, surpassing Howard Johnson and Hilton Hotels in both revenues and profits. The company grew both by acquisition and by starting up new businesses. Marriott became international when it acquired an airline catering kitchen in Caracas, Venezuela, in 1966. In 1967 the 22-unit Big Boy restaurant chain was acquired, and in 1968 the company started a fast-food chain, Roy Rogers. Also in 1967, shareholders approved a corporate name change to Marriott Corporation; and in 1968 the company's stock was first listed on the New York Stock Exchange.

By 1971 Marriott was "the most highly diversified company in the away-from-home market," Bill Marriott Jr. told *Forbes*. Marriott brought in new management techniques to help the company grow in an organized and controlled manner. He divided the company into three basic groups: food operations, in-flight services to airlines, and hotels and specialty restaurants. Each group was headed by a president who reported directly to Marriott. With the three groups further divided into 16 divisions, the company was never dependent on one segment for profits. Another management change came in the planning-and-research area, which became the most intense one in the industry.

Along with tight family control and cost control, Bill Marriott Jr., who succeeded his father as CEO in 1972, also agreed with his father that labor unions helped neither the worker nor the company. Marriott works hard to keep unions out of all phases of the corporation because its executives believe that the company is much more flexible without union rules and that they can offer better benefits to their employees. Backing this belief is a generous profit-sharing plan and a system of incentive bonuses.

During the 1970s, casinos became a popular investment in the leisure market, but Marriott avoided that segment of the business and concentrated on hotels. Marriott's hotels generally catered to upscale travelers and concentrated on businessmen willing to pay extra for quality. Marriott hotels continued to rise in both cities and suburbs. Because of their business orientation, most facilities had meeting rooms and banquet facilities. Convention hotels were built in growing convention cities such as Boston, New York, and Anaheim, California. As airline travel grew, Marriott also began to locate new hotels near airports. Over the decade, Marriott spent more than $3 billion on hotels, increasing its hotel rooms by an average of 17% a year.

Marriott planned carefully and came out ahead in the shaky economic atmosphere of the late 1970s and early 1980s. The company bought back a third of its stock, and in 1982 purchased the Gino's restaurant chain as well as Host International, an airport-terminal food, beverage, and merchandising company, making Marriott the largest operator in that business. During this time Marriott also kept building hotels, even as others pulled back.

By the early 1980s, Bill Marriott realized that the hotel division would not be able to maintain its growth rate by operating only in the upscale market. Finding that customers were least satisfied with middle-priced hotels, Marriott sent researchers out to discover exactly what customers were willing to give up in exchange for less expensive rates.

In 1983, after three years of research and planning, Courtyard by Marriott emerged. The first opened that year near Atlanta, Georgia. The 150-room, two-story Courtyards do not offer bellmen, room service, or large meeting and banquet facilities, but do offer the high-quality rooms the chain is known for. Costs were also kept down by building the hotels in groups of 10 to 12 and hiring one management team for each cluster.

Marriott's research team also indicated that several other segments of the residence market could be popular. One of these was timesharing, which Marriott decided to enter by placing timesharing units near its resorts. The venture began with the purchase of American Resorts Group in 1984. By 1989 the company owned four timesharing resorts in Hilton Head, South Carolina, and Orlando, Florida, and was in the process of developing several more.

Bill Marriott also realized that the company could grow faster if Marriott did not own most of its hotels. The company then tended to build hotels for later sale, but retained control through management contracts. Marriott believes that this system provides more rapid profit growth and limits risk while allowing more uniform service than franchising.

During the mid-1980s Marriott made several changes. In November 1985 the company bought the Howard Johnson Company. At the time of the purchase, it sold the Howard Johnson hotels to Prime Motor Inns but kept 350 restaurants and 68 turnpike units. Marriott's services group grew in 1985 with the purchase of Gladieux Corporation, and then Service Systems. The 1986 acquisition of Saga Corporation, a diversified food-service management company, made Marriott the largest food-service management company in the country.

A major disappointment in the restaurant segment occurred in 1987, when the company made an unsuccessful bid for Denny's, a chain of 1,200 restaurants. Had the bid succeeded, it would have made Marriott the largest operator of family restaurants in the country. Later that year Marriott sold franchise rights for the Big Boy system to Elias Brothers Restaurants.

To complement the Courtyards, Marriott decided to enter the luxury all-suite market, targeting extended-stay travelers. The new units, called Marriott Suites, were planned for suburbs and medium-sized cities. The first one opened in Atlanta, Georgia, in March 1987. Later in the year the company purchased the Residence Inn Company, an all-suites hotel chain. At the other end of the spectrum, the first Fairfield Inn economy lodges were tested in the same year after three years of development.

In 1988 the company began to test market a new restaurant, called Allie's after Alice Marriott. First, 13 former Big Boys were converted to Allie's. After a successful test in San Diego, California, the company planned to roll out the restaurant nationwide by opening more than 600 units, both new and converted, by 1993. These family-style restaurants concentrate on all-you-can-eat food bars with items like Mexican food and barbeque.

Also in 1988, the 100th Courtyard opened, in Chicago; 12 Fairfield Inns were in operation and 24 more Marriott Suites were added, for a total of 130. With Marriott Hotels and Resorts, Courtyard By Marriott, Fairfield Inn, and Residence Inns by Marriott, the company's business included more than 470 hotels by the end of 1988. In the crowded, competitive lodging market, Marriott's occupancy rates are about 12% over the industry average.

A relatively new market segment for Marriott is its "lifecare community" residences, which incorporate retirement living with long-term nursing care when needed. After almost six years of research, Marriott felt ready to enter this market, long dominated by nonprofit organizations, in 1988. By the end of 1988 Marriott operated nine facilities—eight under contracts gained in the acquisition of Basic American Retirement Communities. During 1989, the company announced plans to build 150 "senior living communities" by the mid-1990s.

In 1990 Marriott undertook a major restructuring, which included the sale of the company's airline catering division for $570 million and planned to sell its restaurant business and to buy back ten million shares of stock. The company's three core businesses became lodging; food and services management; and food, beverage, and merchandise operations at airports and on turnpikes. The company also hoped to continue to expand its senior services business. Marriott is the largest lodging operator in the United States and the second-largest caterer, after McDonald's.

Further Reading: O'Brien, Robert, *Marriott: The J. Willard Marriott Story*, Salt Lake City, Utah, 1977; "A Most Remarkable Man," Washington, D.C., Marriott Corporation, [1985]. "The Marriott Story," *Forbes*, February 1, 1987.

—Vera A. Emmons

TRUSTHOUSE FORTE PLC

166 High Holborn
London WC1V 6TT
United Kingdom
(071) 836-7744
Fax: (071) 240-6860

Public Company
Incorporated: 1970
Employees: 93,000
Sales: £2.47 billion (US$3.99 billion)
Stock Exchange: London

Trusthouse Forte (THF) owns and operates a wide range of hotels and eating establishments around the world. Its portfolio includes a number of the most prestigious European hotels as well as more modest franchise operations like TraveLodge and Kentucky Fried Chicken (England). The company's rapid growth has made it one of the world's hotel leaders: with 75,000 rooms in 800 hotels, THF ranks eighth in the world in number of rooms but first in terms of profitability, a reflection of its crisp management style and great strength in the highly profitable luxury market. Besides approximately 1,000 restaurants, the company also runs the largest contract catering business in the United Kingdom, serving meals to North Sea oil workers, athletes competing in the Commonwealth Games, and Chase Manhattan executives in New York.

Trusthouse Forte's somewhat unusual name refers not to a history in the fields of insurance and weaponry, but to the 1970 merger of two unlikely partners, Trust Houses Group and Forte's Holdings Ltd. The former was the creation of some of England's most aristocratic and civic-minded families, while the latter represented the lifework of an aggressive and talented immigrant named Carmine Monforte, who after many years and many successful acquisitions became Lord Charles Forte, Knight of the Realm. The merger of these disparate companies is an example of the dramatic changes in 20th-century England.

Trust Houses, the older of the two companies, was formed in 1904 by the fourth Earl Grey in response to two related problems of the English countryside. Because the farming industry had suffered a long recession and because the advent of the railroads had meant the end of England's extensive coach lines, country inns across rural England were falling to ruin rapidly by the end of the 19th century. Not only were the inns decaying physically, but their owners had tried to recoup lost revenue by encouraging more alcohol consumption, a pastime whose appeal is strong in a time of depression. In an attempt to curb the growth of public drunkenness as well as to save the many splendid country inns from further decline, Earl Grey asked each county in England to form a Public Home Trust Company to pool local funds to buy and rehabilitate the inns and install new managers with strong economic incentives to sell more food and lodging and less alcohol. Most of the original equity was put up by eminent families in each county, and under a special legal agreement this 1% nucleus remained in charge of corporate administration, able to outvote the other 99% of the shareholders. Profits were to be kept low or even donated to charities.

The first ''Trust House'' was acquired in Hertfordshire in 1904. It was an immediate success, hailed as nothing less than the rebirth of the traditional English country inn. By the end of World War I, the company operated some 100 hotels around the country well known for their cleanliness, service, and good food. After weathering the postwar recession, the company expanded considerably in the 1920s and 1930s, reaching a peak of 222 hotels just before World War II. Dividends were still kept low so that the company could use its resources to maintain high standards and expand further. Along the way, Trust Houses acquired many of England's oldest and most famous hotels, including Brown's, The Cavendish, the Hyde Park Hotel, and the Grosvenor House. During World War II nearly all Trust Houses's holdings were requisitioned for military use, and a certain number of these were never returned. The company nevertheless was operating 181 hotels in 1971, with a total of 10,300 rooms and an enviable reputation for quality and British tradition, several of the inns dating back to the 16th century. Trust Houses also had modified somewhat its profit policy, and had even begun a program of modest diversification that would prove important in the company's later history.

Over the years, Trust Houses had acquired a strong position in the contract catering business through the purchase of Lockhart Catering and its subsidiary, the Merchant Company. In 1966, riding 20 years of the postwar hotel boom, Trust Houses bought and merged with John Gardner Catering, one of Britain's largest catering concerns. Gardner had been a successful butcher in Victorian London who expanded into ships' chandlery—provisioning outward bound vessels with food. By the 1920s, Gardner was supplying meals to factories and offices, a role which became critically important when the government required wartime factories to feed their workers. With the enormous surge in industrial capacity during the war, Gardner found business increasing proportionately. Thus fortified, the caterer continued growing after World War II, eventually attracting the attention of the newly profit-oriented Trust Houses. When the two companies merged in 1966, its catering arm was called Gardner Merchant, and may well have been the magnet between Trust Houses and an otherwise very different corporate concern, Forte's Holdings Ltd. Five years later, Lord Charles Forte had completed their unlikely alliance and emerged as the most powerful member of the combined board of directors.

Carmine Monforte was born in Monforte, Italy, in 1908. His father was a small landowner who went first to the United States to work and later, in 1911, joined relatives living near Edinburgh. The elder Monforte's great-uncle, Pacifico, had come to Scotland 25 years before and discovered that the Scots knew little about the making of fine ice cream. He set up a business to rectify that failure and was thus in a position to help his grandnephew when he arrived as well as young Carmine, who joined his father shortly thereafter. In the town of Alloa, the Monfortes opened an Italian-style café called the Savoy, which quickly became one of the city's most fashionable watering holes. The original café grew into several, and by the time Carmine Monforte returned from schooling in Italy his father was running a chain of successful cafés and ice cream shops. Carmine Monforte, or Charles Forte as he became known, was dispatched to England to develop and operate a similar chain of ice cream shops in a number of provincial cities. In 1935, Forte moved to the capital and with £2,000 borrowed from his father opened England's second milk bar, on Regent Street. Forte's Holdings had been launched.

Successful and ambitious, Forte had acquired a total of nine restaurants in London by the onset of World War II. At that point, despite Monfortes's obvious anglophilia, he was interned on the Isle of Wight as an Italian national and potential wartime threat—an unusual background for a man later knighted. His restaurants continued to thrive, however, and by 1949 he was able to make his first major purchase, the famous Criterion Brasserie in Picadilly Circus. Two years later, Forte's reputation as an able restauranteur won for him a contract to supply the 1951 Festival of Britain. His career in catering received its first real impetus from the 1954 acquisition of the Café Royal restaurant and banqueting rooms, located in the exclusive Mayfair section of London. The Royal had long been famous as a favorite spot of English writers and artists, but Forte was equally interested in its 20 banquet rooms with a seating capacity of 2,500. Thus firmly started in the catering business, Forte went on to claim the first contract for food service at Heathrow Airport in 1955, a year which saw his company's pretax profits reach £21,000. By the end of the 1950s, Forte had expanded his catering interests to include many of the roadside service areas springing up along the country's new system of freeways. These were christened Little Chef and were patterned closely on the U.S. fast-food concept.

A new era for Forte began in 1958 with his purchase of the Waldorf Hotel in central London. The shift from catering to hotels mirrored that made by Trust Houses from hotels to catering—in each case, an easy sidestep into a closely allied service industry—and set the stage for the subsequent merger of the two companies. Forte aggressively expanded in the hotel business, making use of catering profits to broaden his base in both fields. In the mid-1960s, he startled the hotel world by announcing the simultaneous purchase of three of the finest hotels in Paris, the George V, Plaza Athenee, and Hotel de la Tremoille. These five-star hotels were famous for their sumptious decors and attentive service, and when their staffs learned that the new owner was not only a foreigner but also a man who sold hot dogs at Heathrow and hawked burgers along highways, they took the unusual step of protesting publicly the sale to express their concern for the future of the hotels. They misjudged Forte's acumen, and his sense of history; he proceeded with the purchase and then left the hotels essentially unchanged. They remain three of the very select group of European five-star hotels. Indeed, the Paris hotels were only the first in what would become the world's largest collection of exclusive inns.

At approximately the same time, Forte made his only purchase outside the hotel and catering industries when he acquired Lillywhites Limited, the famed London sporting-goods store and exporter of sporting wear. By 1970, Forte's Holdings had amassed a total of 43 hotels with 12,500 beds, was the largest caterer in Britain, and made a pretax profit of £5.6 million. Forte became Lord Charles Forte of Ripley when Queen Elizabeth II knighted him in that year for contributions to charitable and cultural events. It was also the year in which he merged Forte's Holdings with Trust Houses to form the present company.

Trust Houses over the years had come to resemble a modern diversified corporation more and an aristocratic gift to the nation less, and as a final concession to the contemporary world it agreed that by merging with Forte it would be able to compete in the increasingly complex and international hotel business better. The merger was not without its share of maneuvering and bitterness. Shortly after the combined company was formed, it became the target of a takeover attempt by Allied Breweries Limited, an English brewing conglomerate. Most of the THF board members from the Trust Houses side favored the merger, while Forte and his bloc fought vehemently to maintain the company's independence. Forte eventually won the prolonged battles against both Allied and the opposing board members. The latter promptly resigned *en masse*, leaving Forte as chief executive of the new hotel and catering giant. With his son, Rocco, Forte set out to expand the base of 26,000 hotel rooms already owned by the company.

Not long before the merger, Trust Houses had acquired a small stake in TraveLodge, the U.S.-based economy hotelier. Forte and son pursued this opening, and by 1973 had upped their share of TraveLodge to 95.5%, since brought to full ownership, adding to THF a substantial share of the vast budget motel market in North America. A TraveLodge motel typically has fewer than 100 rooms and lacks restaurant and conference facilities, instead offering its customers low prices and roadside convenience. Taking a more direct role in the company's management since 1980, THF has revamped many of the motels, while increasing their number to about 400 for a total of 38,000 rooms, including a small number with newly added restaurant and bar accommodations. In addition to TraveLodge, THF also operates 15 three- and four-star Viscount hotels in the United States, as well as 5 in the most luxurious five-star class, including the Palace in Philadelphia and the Plaza of the Americas in Dallas. Because of the preponderence in its U.S. holdings of the low profit-margin TraveLodge motels, overall profitability for THF hotels remains a remarkable fourfold higher in Great Britain than in the United States, a disparity the company hoped to reduce.

In Britain, THF continued its hotel expansion with the 1976 purchase of the Lyons hotel group, a substantial—5,600 beds—assortment of first-rate hotels in London and other cities, and with a more recent acquisition of the 54 Kennedy Brookes and Hanson hotels. THF has largely resisted the temptation to mold its many diverse hotels into one or more "brand" concepts, preferring to let each of its properties retain the individual flavor that made it popular in the first place. Management, accounting, and training are all standardized, but the company has by and large retained the personality and charm of the hotels themselves. By 1990, however, there were signs that this policy might soon change as THF had introduced the ''Forte'' brand of four-star hotels, offering business travelers in the United States, Britain, and elsewhere what it hoped would become a recognized symbol of quality and comfort. By the late 1980s the company was also operating 30 Post House three-star hotels and had introduced the TraveLodge brand in Britain, chiefly along the system of arterial highways where they could be added to existing THF restaurants. In 1990 Trusthouse added the 43-unit Crest chain of hotels to its British portfolio, giving the firm a total of approximately 300 hotels in the United Kingdom and 30 in Europe, as well as the 400 TraveLodge units in the United States. A handful of inns in the Middle East and Caribbean round out the hotel picture.

On the catering side, THF has been invested heavily in the fast-food end of the market. As chief executive since 1983, Rocco Forte has been instrumental in this restaurant expansion, which, unlike THF's hotel business, is clearly oriented toward the branded, lower end of the spectrum. From its initial contract for motorway service areas in 1959, THF has built a stable of 26 such areas under the general name of Welcome Break, each of which typically includes a Little Chef restaurant, a TraveLodge, and retail shops along with the necessary petrol station. The Little Chef brand is THF's largest restaurant chain, with some 315 units. Another 100 Happy Eater restaurants serve much the same market, while the addition of Harvester steak houses gives the company a sizable presence in the mid-price sector as well. Probably the most significant development in the public catering division, however, was the 1987 agreement with Pepsico to operate Pepsi's Kentucky Fried Chicken restaurants in the United Kingdom on a 50-50 joint-venture basis. Under this agreement, THF is now part owner or franchiser of about 310 such restaurants, with plans for more.

Trusthouse Forte has built an empire of hotels and food-service establishments to serve every aspect of both industries. From the most luxurious hotels and restaurants to the most economical roadside chains, THF makes its presence felt throughout Europe and North America. This diversity is not, however, reflected in its profit ratios: although the catering division exceeds the hotel sector in sales, the latter accounts for approximately 68% of total profits, with five-sixths derived from the U.K. hotels alone. These generally upper-end hotels thus form the nucleus of the entire THF group, giving the company an imbalance it will try to redress in the 1990s, probably through further proliferation of its fast-food franchises and the continual expansion of TraveLodge in the United States, where the company hopes to raise profit levels. With Charles Forte, in his 80s in 1990, and son Rocco still firmly in charge of the company, the original Monforte ice cream business should continue its history of confident growth.

Principal Subsidiaries: Trusthouse Forte Hotels Ltd.; Kelvin Catering Ltd.; Trusthouse Forte (UK) Ltd.; Puritan Maid Ltd.; Trusthouse Forte Catering Ltd.; Gardner Merchant Ltd.; Trusthouse Forte Inc. (U.S.A.); Airport Catering Services Ltd.; Leased Hotels Ltd. (50%); Forte & Company Ltd.; Forte Holdings Ltd.; Trusthouse Forte Airport Services Ltd.; Trusthouse Forte Bermuda Ltd.; Les Grands Hotels Associes S.A. (France); Lillywhites Ltd.; Little Chef Ltd.; Lockhart Catering Equipment Ltd.; Motorway Services Ltd. (92%); Anchor Hotels Limited; Grosvenor Theatrical Productions Ltd.; Happy Eater Ltd.; Quaglino's PLC (98%); Ring & Brymer Ltd.; The Savoy Hotel Plc (69%); THF International Management Ltd. (Bermuda); THF Oil Ltd.; Trusthouse Forte Ireland Ltd. (Republic of Ireland); Trusthouse Forte International Ltd.; Trusthouse Forte Service Areas Ltd.; Trusthouse Forte Hotels Inc. (U.S.A.); Trusthouse Forte Group; Finance NV (Netherlands); Welcome Break Limited; Forte Hotels International Inc.; Gardner Merchant Keyline Travel Ltd.; Hudson & Hill Ltd.; Jermyn Publications Ltd.; Kentucky Fried Chicken (Great Britain) Ltd. (50%); Lillywhites Cantabrian Ltd.; Stangard (Metal Workers) Ltd.; T. Giusti & Sons Ltd.; Trusthouse Forte California Inc. (U.S.A.); Trusthouse Forte Food Services Inc. (U.S.A.).

Further Reading: Borer, Mary Cathcart, *The British Hotel Through the Ages,* London, Lutterworth Press, 1972; MacKay, Colin Neil, ''How to Be a Knickerbocker Glory Millionaire,'' *Accountancy,* August 1977; Seal, Kathy, ''Trusthouse Forte Began as Humble Catering Business,'' *Hotel & Motel Management,* November 3, 1986; *THF: A World Power in Hospitality,* London, Trusthouse Forte, 1988.

—Jonathan Martin

INFORMATION TECHNOLOGY

AMDAHL CORPORATION
AMSTRAD PLC
APPLE COMPUTER, INC.
AUTOMATIC DATA PROCESSING, INC.
CANON INC.
COMPAGNIE DES MACHINES BULL S.A.
COMPAQ COMPUTER CORPORATION
CONTROL DATA CORPORATION
CRAY RESEARCH, INC.
DIGITAL EQUIPMENT CORPORATION
ELECTRONIC DATA SYSTEMS CORPORATION
FUJITSU LIMITED
HEWLETT-PACKARD COMPANY
ING. C. OLIVETTI & C., S.P.A.
INTERNATIONAL BUSINESS MACHINES CORPORATION
NCR CORPORATION
NIXDORF COMPUTER AG
PITNEY BOWES INC.
RICOH COMPANY, LTD.
STC PLC
UNISYS CORPORATION
WANG LABORATORIES, INC.
XEROX CORPORATION

amdahl

AMDAHL CORPORATION

1250 East Arques Avenue
Sunnyvale, California 94088
U.S.A.
(408) 746-6000
Fax: (408) 746-6468

Public Company
Incorporated: 1970
Employees: 8,700
Sales: $2.10 billion
Stock Exchanges: American London

Amdahl Corporation is a leading manufacturer of large-scale data-processing systems. In addition it produces data-storage subsystems, data-communications products, and software, and has an extensive educational service. Competing with International Business Machines (IBM), the world's leading manufacturer of large-scale computers, Amdahl has carved out its own niche. Although Amdahl's fortunes have changed in this volatile market, it remains strong, competitive, and innovative. Amdahl's customers include private and public corporations, financial institutions, governmental bodies, universities, and research foundations located throughout the world.

Amdahl Corporation was founded on October 19, 1970, in Sunnyvale, California, by Gene M. Amdahl, who was at the time a leading computer designer. Amdahl designed his first computer while doing graduate work at the University of Wisconsin. He had left South Dakota, where he was born in 1922, to pursue his doctorate in theoretical physics. With a knowledge of electronics gained in the navy, and a brief computer-programming course, Amdahl designed and helped construct an early computer known as WISC (Wisconsin Integrally Synchronized Computer).

Joining IBM in 1952, Amdahl became chief designer of the IBM 704 computer, released in 1954. In 1955 Amdahl and other systems designers began conceptualizing a new computer for IBM, which they christened the Datatron. IBM's Stretch, also known as the IBM 7030, was an outgrowth of the Datatron, which utilized the new transistor technology. The name Stretch, not an acronym, stood for "stretching the limits of computer technology development." Although a financial failure for IBM, Stretch was the precursor to the successful IBM System 360. Meanwhile, in 1956, Amdahl, unhappy at IBM after having been removed as head of a project, decided to leave the company. He worked at two other high-technology firms during his absence from IBM. Returning to IBM in 1960, Amdahl became principal architect for the phenomenally successful System 360, introduced in 1964.

Appointed as an IBM fellow, Amdahl was free to pursue his own research projects. In early 1969, while director of IBM's Advanced Computing Systems Laboratory in Menlo Park, California, he began to investigate the company's cost-pricing cycle as it applied to the large computer they were developing. His team concluded that to make this computer pay for itself, IBM would also have to market two scaled-down versions of this advanced technology. After IBM management insisted that Amdahl stay with the original plan to create only one large processor, he recommended they shut down the laboratory, which they did in spring 1969.

Over the next few months, Amdahl reviewed the policies that prevented IBM from aiming at the high end of computer-line development. He presented his analysis to IBM's three top executives. Although they agreed with this analysis, they said it would not be in IBM's best interests to change company policies. Amdahl decided to strike out on his own.

Amdahl submitted his resignation to IBM in September 1970 and founded Amdahl Corporation just a few weeks later. He took no technical personnel from IBM when he left; Amdahl was joined only by young financial specialist Ray Williams and two secretaries. Amdahl and Williams determined they would need between $33 million and $44 million to see a product to completion. In fact, it took $47.5 million. They picked a difficult year for raising money. By 1970 new capital-gains taxes and an advancing recession made venture capital scarce. At first Amdahl and Williams took their business plan to investment bankers, who felt Amdahl Corporation could not effectively challenge IBM. They received $2 million from Heizer Corporation, venture capitalists in Chicago, the day after expending the founders' investment. Amdahl Corporation was on its way.

At the same time, three other young California computer companies—MASCOR—Multiple Access Systems Corporation, started by staff who left IBM after the closing of the Advanced Computing Systems Laboratory—Berkeley Computers, and Gemini Computers—had gone bankrupt. Many of their people went on to Amdahl Corporation to form an impressive technical team.

During Amdahl Corporation's first eight months, it continued the search for more capital. The needed funds came from Fujitsu, a leading Japanese computer manufacturer who suggested a joint development program and licensing under Amdahl's patents. This 1971 agreement was accompanied by the $5 million investment Amdahl needed to complete its second phase of development.

In 1972 Nixdorf Computers, a leading German computer manufacturer, agreed to invest $6 million if Nixdorf could represent Amdahl in Europe. At last, money began to flow in. Fujitsu increased its investment, and some U.S. investors appeared. Amdahl amassed $20 million to build a prototype computer and a production facility.

Amdahl Corporation decided to offer stock publicly in early 1973, but could not find an underwriter, then experienced delays with the Securities and Exchange Commission until 1974, during which time the stock market had declined. At this point, Amdahl returned to the private market.

IBM's announcement in 1972 of the 370—its first computer with virtual memory—forced Amdahl to scrap its initial computer design. Underestimating the demand for a computer with this flexible, advanced memory technology, Amdahl had been developing a computer like the IBM 370, but without virtual memory.

In August 1974 Eugene R. White, a vice president at Fairchild Camera and Instrument Corporation who had 11 years of management experience with General Electric Corporation, was appointed president of Amdahl Corporation. White effected changes that helped save the company. He laid off almost half the employees, and concentrated on marketing and field support services. He was also instrumental in negotiations with Fujitsu and Heizer to get the funding necessary to complete the company's first product.

In June 1975, Amdahl shipped its first computer, the Amdahl 470 V/6, to NASA's Goddard Spaceflight Center in New York. The computer competed directly with IBM's System 370 Model 168. This success was followed by sales to the University of Michigan, Texas A & M University, and the University of Alberta. Massachusetts Mutual Life, Amdahl's first commercial customer, chose Amdahl's 470 V/6 over the IBM 370 when IBM raised its prices and delayed delivery. Other customers followed Massachusetts Mutual Life, among them, AT&T.

Determined to best IBM, Amdahl was the first truly plug-compatible manufacturer. Plug-compatible manufacturers are those who make computers compatible with both IBM hardware and software. As described in September 1977 *Fortune*, the Amdahl equipment provided better performance for less money. IBM's machines were water cooled; Amdahl's were air cooled, which decreased installation costs by $50,000 to $250,000. The use of LSI (large-scale-integration), many integrated circuits on each chip, meant the Amdahl 470 V/6 was one-third the size of IBM's 360/168; the V/6 also performed more than twice as fast and sold for about 10% less. Machine sales remained slow due to concerns over the company's survival. By spring of 1977, however, Amdahl had 50 units in place, seriously challenging IBM in large-scale computer placements. To improve its cash position, Amdahl decided to sell rather than lease its equipment. IBM responded by slashing prices, forcing Amdahl to follow suit.

In 1976 Amdahl successfully went public with its stock. With the new funds, the company converted its debt to equity, had substantial cash reserves, and found itself operating at a profit. Revenues climbed from less than $14 million in 1975 to $321 million in 1977, with a net income of $48.2 million.

In response to the challenge from Amdahl, IBM announced several machine enhancements. Not until the announcement of its 3033 in 1977, however, did IBM come up with a competitor to the price/performance ratio of Amdahl's 470 V/6. Amdahl responded by announcing a new computer: the 470 V/7. About one-and-a-half times faster than IBM's 3033, it would cost only 3% more. A year later Amdahl had installed 100 of the machines.

Even after two years of full operation, Gene Amdahl and Gene White still spent much time in high-level sales. Many customers insisted on meeting Amdahl before closing the deal. The company had been loosely organized even at the top; any mention of a chief executive officer was omitted intentionally from the corporate bylaws.

In 1977 John C. Lewis joined Amdahl as president. He had been president of the business-systems and data-systems divisions of Xerox Corporation and had spent ten years in management at IBM. Gene White became deputy chairman.

In early 1979, IBM introduced a line of medium-sized computers called the 4300 series. This line, coupled with reports that IBM would soon be announcing the H-Series of large computers, prompted many Amdahl customers to lease rather than buy equipment to be able to shift to an IBM product. This development created serious cash-flow problems at Amdahl. Revenues dropped by $21 million in 1979, with a 64% drop in net income.

On September 1, 1979, Gene Amdahl resigned as chairman, a post he had held since 1970. Deputy chairman Eugene R. White became chairman of the board and chief executive officer, a post that had never before been filled. Staying on the board as chairman emeritus, Amdahl led a new technical-excellence committee and participated in planning the company's major strategy. Less than a year later he resigned from the board to form Trilogy Corporation, a computer company which would compete directly with Amdahl and IBM. Recognized as one of the world's leading innovators in computer design, Amdahl again put his creativity to work on a new venture.

Meanwhile, in 1979 Amdahl Corporation failed in an attempted merger with Memorex Corporation, a manufacturer of computer-data-storage equipment. In 1980, Amdahl tried to merge with Storage Technology Corporation, maker of printers and tape and disc storage subsystems. Both attempts failed because Fujitsu, Amdahl's largest shareholder, added modifications to the agreements which the merger partners rejected. The Japanese corporation feared losing its influence in a merger and wanted to keep tight reins on proprietary technology.

In November 1980, IBM announced the 3081 processor, previously labeled the H-Series, which offered twice the performance of IBM's top model, the 3033. The industry waited for Amdahl's response. Six days later Gene White announced the 580 series, with processors twice as powerful as the Amdahl 470 series, while still compatible with it, and more compact and more energy efficient. Amdahl's new product was not slated for shipment until April 1982, however, and did not actually ship until August 1982, causing a drop in net income. IBM planned to release its new product in late 1981. In addition Amdahl's early 580 series processor had significant reliability problems, and did not anticipate some of the features of the new IBM product. After the U.S. Justice Department dismissed a 13-year-old antitrust suit against IBM, the giant computer manufacturer was able to price its products more aggressively and move faster with new technologies.

To expand its market in mid-1980, Amdahl completed the successful acquisition of Tran Telecommunications Corporation, a maker of digital data communication networks. In 1982 Amdahl branched into the realm of storage devices by offering the direct-access storage device supplied by Fujitsu. This expansion enabled Amdahl to broaden its product base and provided a buffer against the vicissitudes of direct competition with IBM's large-scale computers. By 1988 Amdahl's sales of storage devices had grown to about 20% of total sales.To remain competitive in its fierce battle with IBM, Amdahl was spending 13% of total sales on research and development in 1983, while IBM spent only 6.3%.

In 1984 Amdahl developed UTS, its version of UNIX, the operating system developed by AT&T. This step provided Amdahl with new markets. Amdahl claimed that UTS—which is compatible with UNIX—run on the Amdahl 580 operated 25% faster than IBM's comparable operating system and for a lower licensing fee. The developers of the operating system ensured its complete compatibility with IBM's control programs.

Amdahl introduced multiple domain feature (MDF) in late 1984. MDF enabled a computer to run two or more different operating systems concurrently, while also performing multiple tasks. In just over two years, 30% of the Amdahl 580 series sites used this feature, cutting costs on software, hardware, and personnel.

In 1984 Heizer decided to liquidate its Amdahl stock. Fujitsu bought the offering, expanding its holdings to about 49%. The Japanese firm was prohibited by mutual agreement from owning more than 49.5% of the shares, and in 1990 held about 43% of the company's stock.

Over the years Fujitsu provided important components and subassemblies for Amdahl processors, including LSI logic chips and very-large-scale-integration emitter-coupled logic chips, which are essential to Amdahl products. Fujitsu also played an important role in the design and manufacture of peripheral products. The two companies worked closely in supporting each other in their respective technological developments.

In May 1985 a former IBM executive, E. Joseph Zemke, joined Amdahl as chief operating officer, sharing the office of the president with president and CEO John C. Lewis. Zemke had most recently been president and CEO of Auto-Trol Technology of Denver, Colorado, and had been corporate director of marketing at IBM.

Amdahl's model 5890, introduced in October 1985 to compete directly with IBM's Sierra-class CPU, stood up against its IBM counterpart in reliability and technology, and offered multiprocessor capabilities that enhanced the performance range of Amdahl processors. In late 1986, Amdahl began shipping its new model. The computers performed even better than advertised and final quarter sales boosted revenues to nearly $1 billion. The success of the model 5890 was reflected in Amdahl's increased customer base. Between 1980 and 1985 its customer sites in the United States grew from 450 to 1,350, and globally from 14 to 19 countries. The company also increased sales of its large-scale disc-storage products made by Fujitsu.

Continued shipment of its successful product lines during 1987 catapulted Amdahl's revenues to $1.5 billion, an increase of almost 56% over the previous year, and earnings jumped nearly 250%. The company upgraded its successful 5890 to keep abreast of improvements in IBM's 3090 computer. Its further commitment to UTS enhanced its strength.

John C. Lewis was elected chairman of Amdahl in May 1987, retaining the title of CEO. E. Joseph Zemke became president, but continued his duties as chief operating officer. Gene White, formerly chairman, again became vice chairman. At this point Amdahl Corporation appeared successful in a fiercely competititve market.

For most of its existence, Amdahl had played catch-up to IBM's product announcements, but in May 1988, it took the initiative and announced a new product line, the 5990 processor. New customers poured in. IBM reacted quickly to defend its 69% of the U.S. large-scale-computer market share, but the new processor—acknowledged as the fastest in the industry—not only out performed IBM by almost 50% but was more compact and cost less. By the end of 1988 Amdahl had shipped over 40 of its new mainframes.

The price and performance features of Amdahl's products raised sales nearly 17% to $2.1 billion. IBM responded by discounting its systems. Amdahl announced its own discounts, but this decreased profit margin caused earnings to fall by 30% in 1989.

Against formidable odds, Amdahl has survived as a significant competitor in a mainframe market dominated by IBM. Its consistent ability to produce computers with a superior price/performance ratio has helped keep Amdahl competitive. Staying on the leading edge of technology and catering to its customers's needs launched Amdahl over $2 billion in revenues in 1989. Amdahl is expanding globally, with one-third of its revenues coming from Europe and 8% from the Asia and Pacific region.

Principal Subsidiaries: Amdahl Canada Limited; Amdahl International Management Services Limited (U.K.); Amdahl Pacific Services Pty, Ltd. (Australia); Amdahl Australia Pty. Ltd.

Further Reading: Uttal, Bro, "Gene Amdahl Takes Aim At I.B.M.," *Fortune,* September 1977; Amdahl, Gene M., "The Early Chapters of the PCM Story," *Datamation,* February 1979; Schmedel, Scott, "Taking on the industry giant," *Harvard Business Review,* March-April 1980.

—Ann T. Russell

AMSTRAD PLC

Brentwood House
169 King's Road
Brentwood, Essex CM14 4EF
United Kingdom
(0277) 228-888
Fax: (0277) 211-350

Public Company
Incorporated: 1968 as AMS Trading Company
Employees: 1,200
Sales: £577.32 million (US$931.91 million)
Stock Exchange: London

Amstrad plc, the consumer-electronics and computers manufacturer, has, since 1980, achieved a name for turning electronic products—television, video cassette recorders, word processors, personal computers, camcorders, and satellite dishes—into affordable goods found in homes and businesses throughout Europe, North America, and Australasia.

For many people, Amstrad is synonymous with Alan Sugar, the founder and marketing genius behind the company. In 1965, aged 17 years, Sugar began selling reconditioned television sets from his home in Hackney, north London. After working as a salesman for several local electrical shops, Sugar, the son of a London East End garment maker, started his own company in 1968. AMS Trading Company, later abbreviated to Amstrad, began business as a buyer and seller of electrical goods. Originally, these goods were not manufactured by Sugar's company. Its first products included cigarette lighters and home intercoms. In the next few years, Amstrad broadened its product range to include hi-fi amplifiers, tuners, car radios, aerials, and transistor radios.

In 1969, Sugar opened Global Audio, his first retail venture. By 1970 he already had tired of mere retailing, and sought a new avenue of expansion. He decided to manufacture plastic turntable covers at £2.95 each. He found a way to reduce radically the cost of production, as a result achieving high sales volumes and margins, along with low retail prices.

A year later, in 1971, Sugar expanded his manufacturing capacity by appointing four Far Eastern contractors for his electrical components. By 1974, most of Amstrad's products were being manufactured in the Far East.

As a measure of its early growth, Amstrad's sales reached a total of £207,534 in 1971 with profits of £24,242. In 1972, sales and profits tripled. By 1973, profits rose to £194,063 on sales of £1.32 million.

In 1978, Sugar declined Audiotronic Holdings's offer to purchase a 78% stake in Amstrad for £2 million. He chose instead to list his company on the stock market. By then, sales of his products were soaring. Volume sales of car radio-cassette players, for example, were 276,000 in 1976, rising to 418,000 a year later, and reaching 588,000 units in 1978.

Sales touched one million units in 1979. Finally in 1980, when a host of U.K. consumer-electronics manufacturers were going to the wall in the face of persistent competition from U.S. and Far Eastern manufacturers, Sugar brought Amstrad to the London Stock Exchange. At the time the company's 1980 turnover was £8.8 million, and profits stood at £1.4 million.

Amstrad's fortunes grew steadily during the early 1980s. Between 1980 and 1983, compound profit growth for the company averaged 56%. Hong Kong eventually became Amstrad's manufacturing base when a subsidiary, Amstrad International (Hong Kong), was established there in 1982. Sugar chose as a top executive in the Far East a Hong Kong woman, Callen So. She became marketing and sales director in 1982, having joined the group in 1971 as a secretary at the age of 19 years. So's appointment was evidence that Alan Sugar never insisted on formal qualifications when hiring his senior managerial staff.

Sugar was responsible for Amstrad's renowned agility in product development and marketing, allowing the company to jump in and out of markets at will. At the height of the 1982 recession, for example, Sugar took Amstrad out of the depressed car-radio cassette-player market. This move was not difficult to achieve because the manufacture of these products had always been placed with subcontractors in South Korea. Sugar had no directly employed workers to lay off as he left one market and leaped into another.

More importantly, Sugar displayed no emotional or technical commitment to retaining products whose markets have fallen away. In 1984, Amstrad dropped out of selling video cassette recorders not long after entering the market, again owing to a depression in that particular area. However, the company just as quickly returned to the same market a year later, having changed its supplier in Japan to help improve margins.

Amstrad doubled in size each year during the early 1980s. By 1983, Sugar had identified the potential for large profits to be made from the expanding personal computer (PC) market. In 1984, Amstrad launched a new home computer, the CPC464, known as Arnold. The 64k-memory personal computer was introduced as a direct competitor of the 64k computer put on the market by Commodore Computers. Having had the CPC464 assembled in South Korea, Amstrad used popular retail outlets such as Comet, Dixons, and Rumbelows to sell its units. The machines, operating on cassette programs, were aimed at the beginner computer market.

Also in 1984, Amstrad augmented its U.K. manufacturing capacity by building a new 160,000-square-foot factory at Shoeburyness, at a cost of £2.5 million. The new factory began manufacturing consumer products, such as medium-sized color television sets and VHS video recorders. It also produced audio equipment, including remote-control hi-fi units. Indeed, after Amstrad achieved in two years a 40% share of the U.K. audio market on the strength of its Tower music systems, Sugar, at the age of 37, won the Guardian Young Businessman of the Year Award in 1984.

Part of Sugar's success has come from Amstrad's no-frills policy in developing new product lines. Sugar believes strongly in giving customers what they want, and nothing more. As he told his 1985 annual general meeting: "We produce what the mass market customer wants and not a boffin's ego trip."

Later that year, Amstrad eclipsed its early success in the personal computer market when it introduced the PCW8256 word processor, pitched at those looking for a sophisticated typewriter and incorporating the latest in word-processing software. The PCW8256 was typical of Amstrad products in that its market included people who had never yet bought a word processing unit because of the high price. By paying close attention to component costs, quality control, and packaging, Amstrad succeeded with the PCW8256, as with its other products, in delivering a particular product to a particular market at just the price the mass-market customer could afford.

The one problem with the PCW8256 was its incompatibility with IBM software. Amstrad remedied this difficulty in 1986 by introducing its new PC1512 computer line. The IBM-compatible personal computer took on IBM on the U.S. computer giant's home ground. Here was a personal computer with word-processing software, complete with a monitor, disc drive, and printer, that was both relatively inexpensive and simple to use.

Amstrad's expansionist phase included paying $7.7 million, in 1986, for the name and right to market the products of Sinclair Research Ltd., the troubled computer company founded by U.K. inventor Sir Clive Sinclair. Backed by Malcolm Miller, Amstrad's marketing and sales director, the Sinclair acquisition gave the company access to a significant slice of the leisure end of the U.K. computer market.

Continuing from strength to strength, in 1987 Amstrad was listed on the FTSE-100 in London, the market index of the United Kingdom's top 100 companies, a mere seven years after the company first came onto the market. Building on the success of the PC1512 computer line, Amstrad brought to the market its upgraded PC1640 model. The PC1512, with its powerful color system, appeared a perfect fit for the home-computer market. The PC1640, on the other hand, with its enhanced graphics facility, was ideal for the expanding business-computer market.

By now, Sugar and his marketing team had perfected their product-development formula: catch sight of a rising product, study it, copy it, amend it to include a few user-friendly gadgets, and then farm out its production to a Far Eastern or Scottish manufacturer. Then, after fixing a retail price with two nines in it and lower than anyone else's, Amstrad would introduce the consumer product to those who previously had been unable to afford such an item. Finally, Amstrad would bombard its market with blanket advertising.

In late 1987, Amstrad launched the successor to its successful PCW8256 word processor, the PCW9512. The enhanced word processor, fitted with a letter-quality, daisy-wheel printer, put yet another nail in the coffin of the office and home typewriter, much as Alan Sugar had intended.

As a measure of Sugar's success, his own share stake in Amstrad grew in value at one point in 1988 to £590 million. However, problems began for the company in 1988. In that year, Funai-Amstrad, of which Amstrad was a 49% stake holder and a top customer, began production of video cassette recorders (VCRs) in the United Kingdom. Shifting the VCR manufacturing base from the Far East to the United Kingdom was intended to help Amstrad escape the effect of a rising yen and anticipated sanctions from the European Commission on electronic goods manufactured overseas.

As Amstrad grew, flexibility suffered as Sugar struggled to maintain direct control of his company. In 1988, he spent much of the year establishing further subsidiaries in Italy, West Germany, the Netherlands, and Belgium. The company work force doubled to 1,600 people. Sugar reacted to this expansion by delegating more and more responsibility to his lieutenants in the field, while previously he had been able to bark orders across his headquarters' open-plan offices, so near was his senior management team.

After 20 years of solid growth, Amstrad revealed a profit slump from £160 million a year earlier to £76 million in 1989, on static turnover. City analysts were both stunned and satisfied that the skepticism many had long exhibited towards the company had proved warranted. With his customary candor, Sugar acknowledged that 1989 had been a disastrous year for Amstrad.

The consensus is that during the late 1980s Sugar's management team had extended itself too far as the company grew too rapidly. Sugar had not been able to keep his eye on his company when it mattered most. As one rival told a national newspaper in 1989, "Amstrad has always been a company that Alan could put his arms round. And now it's growing too big for that." Technical and managerial difficulties at Amstrad appeared to be the causes of Sugar's troubles in 1989. When he ought to have supported his management team, Sugar did not. Instead, he displayed his long-standing distaste for bureaucracy. Amstrad has never had more than four layers of management, and Sugar could always reach any one layer with speed.

A management stretched to the limit of its capabilities was going to make mistakes, and Amstrad's did. In 1988, a sophisticated component used in the new PC2000 computer was found to be faulty, delaying the launch of the line. The fault was not detected at an early stage, but was found after the computers had been manufactured and distributed, requiring them to be recalled. The screening and repair of other products in Amstrad's PC2000 line, including the PC2286 and PC2386, forced a slow-down in supply to the company's distributors. A £325 million build-up in inventory followed, which Sugar swore at the time would not be cleared by resort to fire sales. Instead, he promised an orderly reduction in inventory through an aggressive marketing campaign.

Worse was to follow. A decision by Amstrad to take personal responsibility for the PC2000's distribution in West Germany led its former distributor, the Schneider Company, to depress demand for the new products by dumping its existing stock at bargain prices. Elsewhere, a labor shortage in Taiwan led one audio subcontractor to delay delivery of its order. In the United Kingdom Funai-Amstrad failed to meet VCR production targets. This delay led to lower than anticipated VCR sales in the United Kingdom during the Christmas season in late 1988.

Then a global shortage of computer microchips led to soaring prices for the components and higher production costs for the PC2000 line. To secure a steady supply of microchips, Amstrad bought into, but lost out on, a stake in a U.S. microchip supplier, Micron Technology. The value of the holding fell from £45 million to £30 million before the supply of memory chips improved, and was reflected in Amstrad's poor 1989 profits.

The launch of the television satellite Sky heralded a major new market for Amstrad, the supply of Astra satellite dishes and receiving equipment. In the financial year ended June 30, Amstrad sold £107 million worth of Sky equipment in the United Kingdom, the Netherlands, and Germany, and now sees satellite as being an important part of the group's product range. The subsequent merger between Sky and BSB (British Satellite Broadcasting), resulting in Astra's becoming the preferred system, further enhances Amstrad's already dominant position in this market.

In 1989, Sugar brought Callen So from Hong Kong to his Brentwood headquarters to play a role in components sourcing. From her new base she supported efforts to relocate Amstrad's manufacturing base in Europe, in part because the cost advantage of using Far East suppliers had been reduced, but also to avoid anti-dumping measures against Amstrad threatened by the European Commission in Brussels after 1992. Sugar also recruited a team of managerial experts. Prominent among the new recruits was Peter Thoms from Gillette, who became the new finance director, freeing Ken Ashcroft to deal with inventory control and City relationships, and John Benjamin from Mars Inc., who became the new manufacturing director.

During a troubled 1989, Sugar saw his personal stake in Amstrad fall sharply by £1 million a day to settle, at one point, at £118 million. This still left Alan Sugar the 70th-wealthiest man in the United Kingdom, according to the *Sunday Times*. During this period, Amstrad fell to third place in the league table of U.K. business microcomputer suppliers, behind Compaq with a 13.3% market share, and IBM, leading with a 26.1% share. Amstrad's own 11.3% share kept it ahead of Apple, the U.S. computer maker, which trailed with a 5.8% share.

In late 1989, Sugar announced that his company was abandoning the audio and music-systems market. Long adept at pinpointing the needs of the audio market, Amstrad had decided that the margins available from the market no longer warranted the effort. As Sugar told *Financial Weekly* on November 10, 1989, "Our success is at the bottom and calls for a disproportionate amount of management effort when compared with sales and net margins generated."

The abandonment of the audio market was significant because it signaled a marked change in the company's strategy. Until 1989, Sugar had maintained that he was interested in products that sold a minimum 100,000 units a year, but now the criterion for participation was colored by talk of profit contribution rather than volume.

Sugar was suggesting unwittingly that Amstrad was reaching maturity. He continued: "Until recently, most of our products have been relatively low-ticket items, requiring mass sales to provide budgeted profits." As products increased in price, particularly for the business market, the profit margin had allowed Amstrad to sell fewer units while maintaining the company's overall targets. In other words, volume was no longer to be considered the sole source of the company's profits.

In 1990, Alan Sugar insisted that Amstrad's problems of recent years were behind it. The company's share price began to climb from a five-year low reached in 1989, after Sugar threatened to privatize Amstrad once again if City investors did not look upon it more favorably.

Defying its critics, who insisted that Amstrad's problems would prove fatal, in April 1990 the company unveiled plans for a combined telephone, facsimile, and answering machine in a bid to return to financial health. Sugar announced at the time that his company would introduce one product every month. Reporting the year's results in October 1990, Sugar was able to confirm that inventory had been reduced from a peak of £325 million to a manageable £180 million, and that the company was once again cash-positive.

Recognizing the potential for growth in laptop computers, Amstrad launched its new and highly regarded ALT range in early 1990, followed by a totally redesigned range of desk to PCs, the Generation-3 range.

Alan Sugar faces a test of his management skills in future years. The question is whether he can allow Amstrad to grow still further, and continue to prosper. He will have to relinquish direct control and give more power to his lieutenants to allow Amstrad to reach its full potential. Four appointments of 1990 key managers as main board directors-designate suggest that he can.

Principal Subsidiaries: Amstrad International (France); Amstrad Inc. (U.S.A.); Amstrad España (Spain); Amstrad GmbH (Germany); Amstrad BV (Netherlands); Amstrad NV (Belgium); Amstrad Pty Ltd. (Australia); Amstrad Italia (Italy); Amstrad Benelux BV (Netherlands).

Further Reading: Skapinker, Michael, "The London street trader who would like to be as big as Sony," *International Management*, September 1986; Lloyd, Tom, "A One Man Band? If It Is, It's a Big One," *Financial Weekly*, October 7, 1987; Vlessing, Etan, "Amstrad's Sugar Goes Back to School," *Financial Weekly*, November 10, 1989; Thomas, David, *Alan Sugar: The Amstrad Story*, Random, Century, 1990.

—Etan Vlessing

Courtesy of Apple Computer, Inc.

APPLE COMPUTER, INC.

20525 Mariani Avenue
Cupertino, California 95014
(408) 996-1010
Fax: (408) 974-5192

Public Company
Incorporated: 1980
Employees: 14,517
Sales: $5.28 billion
Stock Exchange: New York

Apple Computer company was started with almost no capital in a garage in 1976. Within ten years it was a leader in the personal computer industry with a reputation for innovation and risk-taking.

Apple was founded in April 1976 by Steve Wozniak, 26 years old, and Steve Jobs, 21, both college drop-outs. Their partnership began several years earlier when Wozniak, a talented, self-taught electronics engineer, began building boxes that allowed him to make long-distance phone calls free. The pair sold several hundred such boxes.

In 1976 Wozniak was working on another box, the Apple I computer, without keyboard or power supply, for a computer hobbyist club. Jobs and Wozniak sold their most valuable possessions, a van and two calculators, raising $1,300 with which to start a company. A local retailer ordered 50 of the computers, built in Jobs's garage. They eventually sold 200 to computer hobbyists in the San Francisco Bay area, for $666 each. Later that summer, Wozniak began work on the Apple II, designed to appeal to a greater market than computer hobbyists. Jobs hired local computer enthusiasts, many of them still in high school, who assembled circuit boards or designed software.

Jobs wanted to create a large company and brought in Mike Markkula, a retired electronics engineer who had managed marketing for Intel Corporation and Fairchild Semiconductor. Chairman Markkula bought one-third of the company for $250,000, helped Jobs with the business plan, and in 1977 hired Mike Scott, as president. Wozniak worked for Apple full-time in his engineering capacity. Jobs recruited Regis McKenna, owner of one of the most successful advertising and public relations firms in Silicon Valley. McKenna designed the Apple logo and began advertising personal computers in consumer magazines. Early microcomputers usually had been housed in metal boxes. Jobs housed the Apple II in a more attractive modular beige plastic container. Apple's professional marketing team placed the Apple II in retail stores, and by June 1977, annual sales reached $1 million. It was the first microcomputer to use color graphics, with a television set as the screen. The Apple II expansion slot made it more versatile than competing computers.

The earliest Apple IIs read and stored information on cassette tapes, which were unreliable and slow. By 1978 Wozniak had invented the Apple Disk II, at the time the fastest and cheapest disk drive offered by any computer manufacturer. The Disk II made possible the development of software for the Apple II. The introduction of Apple II, with a user manual, at a consumer electronics show signaled that Apple was expanding beyond the hobbyist market to make its computers consumer items. By the end of 1978, Apple was one of the fastest growing companies in the United States, with its products carried by over 300 dealers.

In 1979 Apple introduced the Apple II+, with far more memory than the Apple II and an easier startup system, and the Silentype, the company's first printer. VisiCalc, the first spreadsheet for microcomputers, was also released that year. Its popularity sold many Apple IIs. By the end of the year sales were up 400% from 1978, at over 35,000 computers. Apple Fortran, introduced in March 1980, led to the further development of software, particularly technical and educational applications.

In December 1980, Apple went public. Its offering of 4.6 million shares at $22 each sold out within minutes. A second offering of 2.6 million shares quickly sold out in May 1981.

Meanwhile Apple was working on the Apple II's successor. It was to have expanded memory and graphics capabilities, and be able to run the software already designed for the Apple II. The company, fearful that the Apple II would soon be outdated, put time pressures on the designers of the Apple III, despite the fact that sales of the Apple II more than doubled to 78,000 in 1980. The Apple III was well received when it was released in September 1980 at $3,495, and many predicted it would achieve its goal of breaking into the IBM-dominated office market. However, many Apple IIIs proved to be defective; Apple had released it without adequate testing. Production was halted and the problems were fixed, but the Apple III never sold as well as the Apple II. It was discontinued in April 1984.

The problems with the Apple III caused Mike Scott to reduce the number of employees in February 1981, a move with which Jobs disagreed. As a result, Mike Markkula became president and Jobs chairman. Scott was named vice chairman and soon left the firm.

Despite the Apple III, the company forged ahead, tripling its 1981 research-and-development budget to $21 million, releasing 40 new software programs, opening European offices, and putting out its first hard disc. By January 1982, 650,000 Apple computers had been sold worldwide. In December 1982, Apple became the first personal computer company to reach $1 billion in annual sales.

In 1983 Apple lost its position as chief supplier of personal computers in Europe to International Business Machines (IBM), and tried to challenge IBM in the business market with the Lisa computer. Lisa introduced the mouse, a hand-controlled pointer, and displayed pictures on the computer screen that substituted for keyboard commands. These innovations come out of Job's determination to design a non-intimidating computer that anyone could use.

Unfortunately, the Lisa did not sell as well as Apple had hoped. Apple was having difficultly designing the elaborate software to link together a number of Lisas, and was finding it hard to break IBM's hold on the business market. Apple's earnings went down and its stock plummeted to $35, half of its sale price a year earlier. Mike Markkula had viewed this presidency as a temporary position, and in April 1983, Jobs brought in John Sculley, formerly president of Pepsi-Cola, as the new president of Apple. Jobs felt the company needed Sculley's marketing expertise.

The production division for Lisa had been vying with Jobs's Macintosh division. Macintosh offered Lisa's innovations at a fraction of the price. Jobs saw the Macintosh as the "people's computer," for people who did not understand computers. With the failure of the Lisa, the Macintosh was seen as the future of the company. It was launched with a television commercial in January 1984. The Macintosh itself was unveiled soon after, with a price tag of $2,495 and a new 3½- inch disc drive that was faster than the 5¼-inch drives used everywhere else, including the Apple II. Apple sold 70,000 Macintoshes in the first 100 days. In September a new Macintosh was released with more memory and two disc drives. Jobs was convinced that anyone who tried the Macintosh would buy it. A national advertisement offered people the chance to take a Macintosh home for 24 hours and over 200,000 people did so. At the same time Apple sold its two millionth Apple II. In the next six months Apple released numerous products for the Macintosh, including a laser printer and a hard drive.

Despite these successes, Macintosh sales temporarily fell off after its promising start. The company was troubled by internal problems. Infighting between divisions continued, and poor inventory-tracking led to over-production. Jobs and Scully had initially been inseparable, but Jobs decided to oust Sculley. Jobs lost the ensuing show-down. Sculley reorganized Apple along functional lines in June 1985 to end the infighting caused by the product-line divisions, and Jobs left Apple in September with several other Apple executives. They founded a new computer company, Next Incorporated, which would later emerge as a rival to Apple in the business computer market.

The Macintosh computer finally moved Apple into the business office. Corporations saw its ease of use as a distinct advantage. It was far cheaper than the Lisa, and had the necessary software to link office computers. In 1986 and 1987 Apple produced three new Macintoshes with improved memory and power. Apple and the Microsoft Corporation produced sophisticated software. By 1988, over one million Macintoshes had been sold, with 70% of sales to corporations. Software was created that allowed Macintoshes to be connected to IBM-based systems. Apple grew rapidly; income for 1988 topped $400 million on sales of $4.07 billion, up from income of $217 million on sales of $1.9 billion in 1986. Apple had 5,500 employees in 1986 and over 11,700 by the beginning of 1989.

In 1988, Apple management expected a worldwide shortage of memory chips to continue. They bought millions when prices were high, only to have the shortage end and prices fall soon after. Apple ordered sharp price increases for the Macintosh line just before the Christmas buying season, and consumers bought the less expensive Apple line or other brands. In early 1989, Apple released significantly enhanced versions of the two upper-end Macintoshes, the SE and the Macintosh II, primarily to compete for the office market. At the same time IBM marketed a new operating system that mimicked the Macintosh's ease of use. In May 1989 Apple announced plans for its new operating system, System 7.0, which would allow Macintoshes to run tasks on more than one program simultaneously. System 7.0 was to be available to users in 1990.

Apple was reorganized in August 1988 into four operating divisions: Apple USA, Apple Europe, Apple Pacific, and Apple Products. Dissatisfied with the changes, many longtime Apple executives left. In July 1990, Robert Puette, former head of Hewlett-Packard's personal computer business, became head of the Apple USA division. Sculley saw the reorganization as an attempt to create fewer layers of management between the bottom and top of Apple, thus encouraging innovation. Analysts credit Sculley with expanding Apple from a consumer and education computer company to a business computer company, one of the biggest and fastest-growing corporations in the United States.

Competition in the industry of information technology has involved Apple in a number of lawsuits. In December 1989, Xerox Corporation, in a $150 million lawsuit, charged Apple with unlawfully using Xerox technology for the Macintosh software. Apple did not deny borrowing from Xerox technology, but explained that the company had spent millions to refine that technology, and had used other sources as well. In 1990 the court found in favor of Apple in the Xerox case. In March 1988, Apple had brought suits against Microsoft and Hewlett-Packard, charging copyright infringement. These cases were still in process in 1991.

Principal Subsidiary: Claris Corporation

Further Reading: Frieberger, Paul, and Michael Swaine, *Fire in the Valley, The Making of the Personal Computer,* Berkeley, California, Osborne-McGraw-Hill, 1984; Hogan, Thom, "Apple: The First Ten Years," *A+: The #1 Apple II Magazine,* September 1987; Rose, Frank, *West of Eden,* New York, Penguin Books, 1989.

—Scott Lewis

AUTOMATIC DATA PROCESSING, INC.

One ADP Boulevard
Roseland, New Jersey 07068
U.S.A.
(201) 994-5000
Fax: (201) 994-5495

Public Company
Incorporated: 1949 as Automatic Payrolls, Inc.
Employees: 19,000
Sales: $1.70 billion
Stock Exchanges: New York Midwest Pacific

Automatic Data Processing (ADP), from its very modest beginning has evolved into one of the leading computer services companies in the United States. Since becoming a public company in 1961, ADP has, without fail, increased its earnings every quarter. This enviable record can be largely attributed to the business sense and work ethic of its founders.

In 1949, Henry Taub, a recently graduated accountant, borrowed $2,000 and started a company processing payrolls for small businesses in his New Jersey hometown. He gave the company the modern-sounding name "Automatic Payrolls, Inc.," although the equipment he used—aged calculators, a mechanical bookkeeping machine, and an addressograph—was old fashioned even for then.

A few years later, a young insurance salesman named Frank Lautenberg met Taub and saw great promise in his company. "I sold Henry some insurance, and he sold me on his company," said Lautenberg. Like Taub, Lautenberg was the son of a silk mill worker. When he was ten, his father took him to the factory to experience the frightening clatter of the machines and breathe the fiber-filled air. "Get an education so you never have to work like this," Lautenberg's father said, and the boy did so.

Lautenberg, who recognized a good idea that needed marketing, persuaded Taub to let him print cards at his own expense, and in his spare time, began selling the services of the young payroll processing company. He succeeded in gaining several accounts for the company, and in 1952, took a pay cut to become the company's first full time salesman. By 1957, the company's accounts numbered 100.

Taub, his brother Joe, and Lautenberg devoted themselves to making the business succeed. Taub told *Forbes,* April 23, 1984, "We were young, none of us was married. . . . We wanted to prove ourselves, and we had an opportunity to incubate. The concept of farming out payroll was not widely acceptable so we had the chance to develop slowly." He added, "It was a labor intensive business with low capital requirements. We didn't have to raise a million dollars in the stock market and then turn somersaults the next morning to please the stockholders."

In 1957, the company encountered modern technology when they invested in an IBM tab machine. Yet theirs was a company that was market driven, not technology driven. Lautenberg explained to Katherine Davis Fishman in her *The Computer Establishment,* "Our customers were not concerned with the means we used to provide a solution to their payroll problems. We were never asked whether we were using the newest accounting machine or a dated version, whether delivery would be made by bus, truck, or car—or whether our staff was full-time or part-time, where we saw the future, or how fancy our offices were. . . . The customers' only care, as it is today, was about our ability to deliver the promised service. The methods we chose . . . were selected based on the *minimum* needed to get the job done properly."

The company was able to move smoothly into large-scale automation when the time and the technology were right. ADP invested in an IBM data-processing system in 1961. It developed its own elementary software, and the investment paid off in increased capacity and greatly reduced turnaround time. That same year the company changed its name to Automatic Data Processing, and made its first public offering.

In 1962 ADP opened an office on Wall Street to provide brokerage firms with payroll and basic accounting services. Opening this office was a well-calculated move, based on several successful client relationships in that market, and a clear demand for ADP's dependable recordkeeping services. Its success with this particular industry enabled ADP to build its reputation as a company that could package and deliver industry-based standard services and databases.

Between 1963 and 1968, the company's sales grew from $1 million to $15 million. The growth was due primarily to ADP's acquisition of payroll and accounting service-bureaus in large cities. Many service bureaus, although relatively successful, were struggling to custom-tailor their offerings for too few clients in specialty markets. ADP, however, operating from a marketing perspective, not a technology perspective, was determined to keep programing costs down. They ignored the lure of exotic software packages for small, low-margin markets and concentrated primarily on delivering basic payroll and general ledger accounting services to a broad market. "We are suspicious of anything that won't return 20% before taxes," Lautenberg told *Business Week,* May 24, 1969.

In each newly acquired operation, ADP installed its widely useful software packages, and if possible, retained local management, supporting it with sophisticated marketing methods. This strategy proved enormously successful. Josh Weston, then ADP's president, told the author of *The Computer Establishment,* "When we bought the Miami service bureau, it had revenues of less than $20,000. The principal stayed on, and now sits on a business three times the size of the whole company at the time we bought him out."

In 1968 a sharp increase in Wall Street trading volume buried the brokerage firms' back offices in paperwork, and trading hours at the exchange had to be curtailed. Part of the reason was the inability of many brokers' new electronic data processing systems to handle the sudden major increase in volume. ADP's shirtsleeve approach to doing business proved especially valuable to its Wall Street clients, and throughout the crunch, none of its clients was put on restriction by the exchanges because of paperwork problems. Around this time, the company moved its headquarters from its founders' hometown of Paterson, New Jersey, to Clifton, New Jersey.

Although 1969 was, as *The New York Times* on November 29, 1970, termed it, "a grim year" for Wall Street, it was ADP's best year in the brokerage service business, having added 15 new clients. ADP's characteristic dependability, coupled with careful product development, was paying off. The head of operations at Bear, Stearns estimated that installation of ADP's new management system to control and route securities had cut the error rate in the security tracking area to one-tenth of the former rate.

Growth continued. In 1970, ADP was the first computer services company to reach the Big Board at the New York Stock Exchange. It was servicing more than 10,000 payroll accounts through 16 data centers around the country and was doing the back office chores for 55 brokerage firms, more than all competitors combined. One of its most significant purchases during this period was of a main competitor in brokerage services, the RCA Systems Center, in 1971. The purchase added 10 clients. In 1973 sales reached $90 million and pretax earnings amounted to $16.7 million.

The days when customers handed their data over to computer service companies to be batch-processed, with the paper load delivered back the next day, were changing. Technology gave customers more choices. One of the choices available was interactive computer services, in which the user rented a terminal and access to a vendor's computer and software, and did its own processing. Another choice was time-sharing, in which the customer took advantage of the economies of scale, and sent data into a shared system for processing.

Many time-sharing companies started up quickly, and died the same way. ADP changed with the times, albeit, slowly and carefully. The company batch-processed the majority of its payroll work, and used its fleet of more than 100 vehicles for delivery. With the acquisition of the time-sharing giant Cyphernetics Corporation in 1975, however, ADP acquired telephone lines covering the United States, and satellite transmission to six European countries. As it had in the past, ADP developed and applied its new capabilities in response to customer need, but it did not rashly abandon its older methods just for the sake of the new.

ADP continued its steady growth and continued to develop its strong market position. By 1978, it had acquired more than 60 companies, it had 50 service bureaus around the United States and 4 overseas, and its yearly return on shareholder's equity was 30% higher than IBM, Digital Equipment Corporation, or Control Data Corporation.

The recession of the early 1980s caused many of the 80,000 companies using ADP's payroll processing services to reduce their staffs, resulting in some business loss for ADP. This development, coupled with the growing number of companies buying their own computers and processing payroll in-house, had ADP looking at additional, related lines of business.

The company turned the computer revolution to its advantage by becoming a hardware supplier. It offered customers "value added" services such as systems configuration, communications networks, training for particular software, and constant updating. "Most of the customers we deal with have more important things on their minds than to muck around with what we can do better," Weston said in *The Computer Establishment*.

Another new, related line of business for ADP was electronic banking. The market was hardly penetrated when ADP licensed this program from its creator, and began selling automatic teller machines to banks all around the country.

In early 1983, Frank Lautenberg left the company to serve as U.S. Senator for New Jersey, and ADP President Josh Weston assumed the additional title of chief executive officer. Soon after, the company brought on William J. Turner, a group president whose computer expertise and managerial vision quickly began to change the company.

Turner first oversaw a major reorganization, in which the company went from product-based and geographical divisions to industry divisions. Integrating the company's services effectively combined and segregated all the company's left hands, and all the right hands, and made it easier to determine what each of the hands was doing.

Payroll and commercial services accounted for 55% of ADP's total revenues in 1984. The company was becoming more diversified, but ADP did not hesitate to divest itself of unprofitable ventures, such as one sold in 1985 which let customers pay bills by phone. "When you get to be over $1 billion big, it won't help to come up with $1 million ideas," Weston told *Business Week*, December 9, 1985.

Several ventures that offered the numbers Weston liked were collision-repair estimating for the insurance industry, as well as related information services for auto dealers and repair shops. ADP was selling tailor-made service packages not only for a type of client, but for several related industries. The company stepped into a virtually untapped market, with service packages that yielded healthy returns. By 1984, ADP dominated this market and was enjoying an annual growth rate of 30%.

ADP's Turner-led internal reorganization, along with its strong penetration in information-rich industries laid the foundation for a significant shift in the company's direction. Long the dependable back-office number cruncher, ADP was moving to provide clients with integrated information services for the front office. The movement to the front-office got its fast start in 1983 when it purchased GTE Telenet Information Services, a stock quote company, and was further aided in 1985 through the purchase of Bunker Ramo Info Systems from Allied Corp.

The company in 1985 began wooing large customers in addition to the moderate-sized companies it had always considered its market. Before long, the company won clients such as Beatrice, Harcourt Brace Jovanovich, and B. F. Goodrich.

As large as ADP itself was growing, however, those in charge remained in touch with the rank and file employees. The company moved its headquarters to Roseland, New Jersey, and in this building, as in the old one, there was no executive dining room and no parking slots reserved for management. All employees are able to buy equity at a discount, and over 50% of the work force own company stock.

Turner, with his technological expertise, effectively led the company out of the past and into the future. Elected president in 1986, he ushered in a huge capital improvement program to bring its brokerage information services up to date, and, at the same time, leave its competition well behind.

The 1980s were a time when information services were becoming more and more sophisticated, a time when clients wanted customized, real-time services that they could control from their own versatile workstations. ADP began developing its FS Partner, a sophisticated market-data quotation and branch-office automation system that also gave brokers the power to study the trading patterns of potential clients and to run elaborate "what-if" scenarios. In 1987, ADP reached agreements with Merrill Lynch and Shearson Lehman Hutton, to further develop and install its FS Partner systems. These two companies had been clients of ADP's biggest competitior, Quotron. As the FS Partner began taking hold in the market, it was rendering the Quotron system obsolete.

The Wall Street fiasco of 1987, and subsequent layoffs and mergers in the business resulted in a 10% reduction in brokerage services revenues at ADP. Many saw ADP's capital-intensive investment in the brokerage information services as risky but acknowledged that risk was the nature of the business. The enormous investment was part of a long-term plan, and although ADP suffered from the cyclic nature of the investment industry, it was also counting on it.

As part of its $100 million investment in brokerage information services, the company moved its brokerage computing centers to a new facility in Jersey City. It doubled the capacity of its Mount Laurel, New Jersey, stock-quote computing center.

Turner's impact on this company goes beyond the nuts and bolts aspect. His technological revival at ADP is supported by a new management strategy he calls "turnaround management." He takes a stint at the head of each of the business units and shakes up management's ingrained assumptions about its business, and, ideally, makes it responsive to the present climate and future direction of this new ADP.

In 1988, the company's smaller ventures such as information services to auto dealers and insurance companies, interactive accounting services, and computer leasing services were flourishing. ADP was processing 10% of the nation's private sector paychecks, and had the lion's share—40%—of the U.S. brokerage information business. That year, Turner left ADP.

As part of ADP's continual pruning of business ventures that fail to yield high returns or that do not fit its long-term strategic objectives, the company sold its automatic teller machine and its banking businesses in 1989. An industry expert commented on ADP's business acumen in the *Wall Street Transcript,* November 13, 1989, "We've seen a dramatic decrease in the revenue growth rate, coupled with continued gains in profitability. It shows that the business is managed well. It shows that ADP has cost control, and that management understands the leverage points within the organization and can screw down costs. It's a rare trait in the computer services business. It's a rare trait in the technology sector in general."

ADP's future success will depend on its ability to keep operating costs low, while producing not only dependable, but state-of-the-art information and data processing services. It has come a long way from the time when it toed a cautious technological line and stayed away from specialty software applications.

Principal Subsidiaries: ADP Atlantic, Inc.; ADP Automotive Claims Services, Inc.; ADP Benelux B.V. (Netherlands); ADP Central, Inc.; ADP Credit Corp.; ADP Dealer Services Ltd. (Canada); ADP Financial Information Services, Inc.; ADP Information Services, Ltd. (U.K.); ADP Network Services International, Inc.; ADP Network Services, Ltd. (U.K.); ADP of New Jersey, Inc.; ADP of North America, Inc.; ADP-WHT Corporation; American Computer Trust Leasing (79%); Automatic Data Processing Limited (U.K.); Automatic Data Processing (H.K.) Ltd. (Hong Kong); Automatic Data Processing Community Urban Redevelopment Corporation; Canadian-Automatic Data Processing Services Ltd. (Canada, 50%).

Further Reading: Fishman, Katherine Davis, *The Computer Establishment,* New York, Harper & Row, 1981; Mayer, Martin, "How to manage a revolution," *Forbes,* April 23, 1984; McClellan, Stephen T., *The Coming Computer Industry Shakeout,* New York, John Wiley & Sons, 1984; Bernstein, Amy L., "Mr. Service," *Information Week,* April 10, 1989.

—Carole Healy

Canon

CANON INC.

7-1, Nishi-shinjuku 2-chome
Shinjuku-ku, Tokyo 163
Japan
(03) 3348-2121
Fax: (03) 3349-8957

Public Company
Incorporated: 1937 as Precision Optical Company
Employees: 44,401
Sales: ¥1.35 trillion (US$9.39 billion)
Stock Exchanges: Tokyo Osaka Nagoya Kyoto Fukuoka Niigata Sapporo Luxembourg Frankfurt

Although it scarcely predates World War II, Canon has already become one of the world's leading manufacturers of optical electronics. Its principal products are 35-millimeter cameras—including the ubiquitous AE-1—and photocopiers, but it also produces calculators, laser printers, facsimile machines, electronic typewriters, and optical equipment for medical applications.

The history of Canon dates back to 1933, when a young gynecologist named Takeshi Mitarai worked with some technician friends to develop cameras. Their first major invention had applications that ranged far beyond the medical field. In 1934 Mitarai and his colleagues developed Japan's first 35-millimeter camera, closely patterned after the German Leica 35-millimeter camera, the industry standard. They named it the Kwanon, after a Buddhist figure representing mercy. In 1937 they incorporated their venture under the name Precision Optical Company.

In 1941 Precision Optical made a significant contribution to Japanese medical imaging technology when it developed the nation's first indirect x-ray camera, which played a major role in preventing spread of tuberculosis in Japan. When Japan went to war with the United States, the Japanese economy was entirely given over to supporting the military.

The company barely survived World War II. It was unable to manufacture its mainstay 35-millimeter cameras for the duration of the war, and only Mitarai's tireless efforts kept it afloat in the economic desolation that followed Japan's surrender in 1945. With raw materials rationed and capital scarce, Mitarai had to scramble just to keep his production lines going and the company's finances in order. He also drilled into his workers the importance of producing high-quality products, but his most important move may have been persuading the Allied occupation forces to stock Precision Optical cameras in their post exchanges and ships' stores. This arrangement laid the groundwork for Canon's later success as an exporter; U.S. servicemen bringing their cameras home with them gave the company its first foothold in the U.S. market. In 1947 Precision Optical changed its name to Canon Camera Company Limited, using a transliteration of the original Kwanon. The company changed its name to its current form in 1969.

Another international breakthrough for Canon occurred in the early 1950s, when news photographers covering the Korean War found that the best Japanese lenses were every bit as good as German lenses, the traditional industry standard. The export market began to open up, and Canon prospered throughout the decade. The company created an American subsidiary, based in New York, in 1955 and two years later it formed a European subsidiary, Canon Europa, headquarterd in Geneva. In 1956 Canon added an 8-millimeter movie camera to its product lines, and in 1959 it became the first company in the world to manufacture an 8-millimeter camera with a built-in zoom lens.

By the early 1960s Canon had become the dominant Japanese producer of middle-priced cameras, leaving the higher end of the market to Nikon. The company continued to grow, more than tripling in size between 1959 and 1963. In 1964 it ventured into business machines when it introduced the Canola 130 electronic calculator, the first in the world to use the now-standard ten-key keypad. In 1970 Canon and Texas Instruments produced the Pocketronic, the first all-electronic hand-held calculator. Canon became an innovator in the field of photocopying when it introduced its first plain-paper copier in 1968. Until that time Xerox had dominated the copier market with its own process, known as xerography.

In spite of these engineering successes, however, Canon was plagued by weaknesses in marketing strategy in the late 1960s and early 1970s. Although it was a part of the spectacular overall penetration of the U.S. market by Japanese calculator makers, the company failed for the most part to distinguish itself from its competitors. It also frittered away its technical advances by failing to exploit their sales potential before rivals could catch up to them. This problem affected its copier lines as well as its calculators. In 1972 it developed the "liquid dry" copying system—so named because it uses plain paper and liquid developer but turns out dry copies—but doubted its own marketing strength and feared that competitors would infringe on its patents. Therefore, instead of selling the system itself, it licensed the technology to other manufacturers, effectively wasting its earnings potential. These mistakes hindered Canon's financial performance, and in 1975 it failed to pay a dividend for the first time since World War II.

Into this leadership void stepped Ryuzaburo Kaku, the company's managing director. He won approval from Mitarai, who was still chairman and president, to change management and sales practices. Under Kaku, Canon began to streamline its operations and chain of command and market its products more aggressively. In 1976 the company introduced its revolutionary AE-1 35-millimeter camera, which used a microprocessor to focus automatically and set the length of exposure, with an advertising blitz led by television commercials featuring tennis star John Newcombe. "It was a big gamble because 35-millimeter cameras had never before been advertised on TV," Mitarai said, but it paid off handsomely. According to *Fortune,* January 12, 1981, by 1981 the AE-1 had become so popular that one industry analyst called it "the Chevrolet of the 35mm market." Kaku's emphasis on faster new-product development led to laser beam printing technology in 1975 and a new retinal camera that made pupil-dilating drugs unnecessary in 1976. In 1977 Kaku was named president of the company, succeeding Mitarai, who remained chairman.

In 1982 Canon introduced the first personal copier, so called because all the essential reproduction components were contained in a cartridge that users could replace themselves. Again, it was accompanied by a massive ad campaign, this time starring actor Jack Klugman. In less than a decade, Canon's salesmanship had undergone a radical change from passive to highly aggressive. When Canon overtook Nikon as Japan's camera sales leader in the early 1980s, former Nikon chairman Kyojiro Iyanaga explained his rival's success by saying "We still make the best cameras. Canon just outmarketed us."

Canon continued to introduce new products in the 1980s to compete effectively in mature markets. Much of its success, however, came in new markets, such as integrated office workstations and desktop publishing systems. Often that meant challenging large companies that were well entrenched in their markets. In 1982 it came out with an electric typewriter, initiating a one-on-one competition with International Business Machines (IBM). Within a year, it captured 11% of that market, while IBM's share shrank from 26% to 17%. In 1983 it took on Xerox with a laser printer that offered similar quality at one-third the price. Canon also engaged Ricoh in a rivalry over facsimile machines in the early 1980s and laid the groundwork for a future duel with IBM in the computer business. It began a research push aimed at developing optical integrated circuits for personal computers of the future, and in 1984 Canon Sales started marketing the Apple Macintosh in Japan. Canon also joined with Apple to develop software for the Japanese market. Later in the decade, the company's optical chip efforts paid off when former Apple chief Steven Jobs chose Canon's chips for his new Next computer. In 1989 Canon acquired a 16.7% interest in Next Incorporated, along with the exclusive right to market the Next in Asia, for $100 million.

Canon has experienced sharp sales and profit growth since its low-water mark in 1975, prospering in a time when, as Ryuzaburo Kaku himself has put it, rival corporations resemble "warring feudal lords" like those who battled to control 16th-century Japan. Between 1975 and 1985, its annual sales grew sevenfold, to $3.3 billion, and its profits showed a twentyfold increase, to $136 million. Although the company's founder named its first product after a pacific figure from Buddhist mythology and preached to his workers that producing quality products contributed to peace and the advancement of civilization, in fact, Canon had to fight for its survival in these difficult years that followed World War II. Mitarai's sermons were actually stump speeches on the importance of workmanship at a time when "Made in Japan" meant shoddiness. Canon has always had to fight for its market share, and its aggressive marketing continues to make it successful.

Principal Subsidiaries: Dai-ichi Seiki Kogyo Co., Ltd.; Canon Virginia Inc., (U.S.A.); Canon Electronics Inc.; Canon Seiko Co., Ltd.; Oita Canon Inc.; Canon Components Inc.; Canon Inc. (Taiwan); Canon Business Machines, Inc. (U.S.A.); Canon Giessen GmbH. (Germany); Canon Bretagne S.A. (France); Copyer Co., Ltd.; Canon Precision Inc.; Canon Chemical Co., Ltd.; Canon Sales Co., Inc.; Canon U.S.A., Inc.; Canon Europa N.V. (Netherlands); Canon (UK) Ltd.; Canon France S.A.; Canon Latin America, Inc. (Panama); Canon Australia Pty. Ltd.; Canon Singapore Pte. Ltd.

Further Reading: The Canon Story 1989/90, Tokyo, Canon Inc., 1989.

—Douglas Sun

COMPAGNIE DES MACHINES BULL S.A.

121, avenue de Malakoff
75116 Paris
France
(1) 45 02 90 90
Fax: (1) 45 02 96 96

State-Owned Company
Incorporated: 1933
Employees: 43,617
Sales: FFr33.72 billion (US$5.84 billion)

French nationalism has insisted that the country maintain a strong presence in the international computer business, and since 1976 Compagnie des Machines Bull—known informally as Groupe Bull—has been the government-owned candidate for that role. In order to survive international competition, many European computer manufacturers have been forced to become international themselves, in order to amass the requisite technical expertise and marketing strength. As a result, Bull has long been allied with various foreign corporations, including General Electric, NEC, Olivetti, and Honeywell, and today stands as the only computer-maker with native roots in both the United States and Europe, and is Europe's largest computer maker. Groupe Bull's two divisions, Bull S.A. in Paris and Bull HN Information Systems in Massachusetts, together produced sales of $5.3 billion in 1988—but made just 1% profit for their efforts, and followed that with a loss in 1989. Poor profits have not been unusual for Bull ever since it locked horns with International Business Machines (IBM) in the late 1950s and emerged the clear loser. It thus remains a question whether Bull, even with government subsidies, will be able to find a profitable niche for itself in the tightening global information business.

The origins of Bull lie in the need of insurance companies to process their voluminous data quickly. In 1919 a young Norwegian engineer named Fredrik Rosing Bull invented a counting and sorting machine for his employer, the Storebrand Insurance Company of Oslo. The machine used punch cards to tabulate figures at a rate which, though slow by modern standards, far exceeded the output of Storebrand's best secretaries. Bull did not live to enjoy the fruits of his ingenuity, dying in 1925 at the age of 43. Several years later the employee of a French bank, Georges Vieillard, was asked to develop a better adding machine. He discovered that the patents to Bull's tabulator were held by a Norwegian cancer clinic. Vieillard bought the patents for about $4,000—though he continued to pay royalties for many years—and subsequently founded a Paris company to develop and market the Bull machines. Vieillard quickly ran out of money and turned for help to his punch card supplier, Papeteries Aussedat. The latter was owned by the Callies family, who promptly formed a joint venture with Vieillard called Compagnie des Machines Bull. By 1935 Bull had launched its first significant line, the 150 series of tabulators, and thus found itself locked in a struggle with the French subsidiary of IBM.

For the remainder of the 1930s Bull grew at a modest rate. Most of its customers were banks, nearly all of them French. The company's real expansion came only after World War II had spurred the French scientific community to develop a rudimentary computing machine. Bull seized on this technology immediately after the war, forming alliances with Olivetti and Exacta in Italy and West Germany to develop the computer's business and military potential. In 1951 the company introduced the world's first germanium-diode computer, the Gamma 3, and its sales began a swift climb from $1.5 million in 1950 to $92 million in 1963. By the mid-1950s Bull had wrested 50% of the French market from IBM. It opened sales centers across Europe and in Latin America and became a source of considerable pride for the French business community. Bull even exported computer parts to the United States under the Remington Rand name, further proof that the company had earned its skyrocketing stock value. At decade's end, with George Vieillard still managing the firm and the Callies family supplying capital strength, Bull's future appeared assured.

In retrospect, however, it is clear that the company made a significant blunder in 1956. Responding to IBM's introduction of new technology, Bull outlined plans for a new, very large, very fast computer to be available by 1960, and called for that reason the Gamma 60. In effect, IBM had raised the ante, and Bull eagerly matched the pot, its confidence high after a run of record-setting profits. Bull, however, had reached the limit of resources—the Gamma 60 was slow in development, late in delivery, and plagued by a series of mechanical flaws.

By 1962, with IBM's surge continuing unabated, Bull began to feel a profit squeeze. Realizing that international competition demanded international cooperation, the company signed long-term research-and-development agreements with Honeywell, NEC, and RCA; but these were no immediate help, and by late 1963 Bull's situation was grave. That year the company lost $25 million and could hope to save itself only by merging with a wealthy suitor. General Electric (GE), which coveted Bull's computer experience and worldwide marketing base, offered to buy into the ailing company.

French President Charles de Gaulle forbade the deal, however, because Bull was crucial to the development of French nuclear weapons and therefore could not be tied to any foreign powers. For a precarious year Gaullist nationalism strove with capitalist reality, but the issue was never really in doubt: to compete with IBM, Bull needed the muscle and know-how that GE could offer. In 1964 GE paid $43 million for its 66% of the partnership, the French government created a separate company for military research, and together GE and Bull—minus the ousted Callies family—set out to battle IBM.

IBM proved to be more than a match for the new partners, and GE's computer venture lasted only a few years. By the end of the 1960s, though Bull-GE was finally showing a profit, the U.S. partner had lost its stomach for the endless struggle with IBM and sold all seven of its computer-manufacturing plants to Honeywell. The purchase changed Bull's name once again, this time to Honeywell Bull (HB). The new marriage lasted a bit longer and was somewhat more successful than the Bull-GE association. Honeywell was the second-largest computer-maker in the United States, and with its technical experience and financial support was able to raise HB's sales to about $500 million in 1974. At that time the company controlled 17.3% of the French computer market, behind IBM but well ahead of relative newcomer Compagnie Internationale de l'Informatique (Cii). The latter had been hastily assembled in 1966 by de Gaulle in response to GE's purchase of Bull, and by the mid-1970s it was apparent that the government wanted to unite France's two native computer companies. In 1976 the merger was effected, with the French state owning 53% of the newly christened Cii-HB, and Honeywell the remaining 47%.

At this juncture, Cii-HB was still predominately a mainframe manufacturer and still had trouble posting profits. In 1980 sales hit $1.3 billion but profit remained a slim $29 million, and in the following year the company lost money. Honeywell was therefore perhaps not greatly disturbed to learn in 1981 that its share of Cii-HB had become the target of President Francois Mitterand's new Socialist government. Mitterand wanted to make Cii-HB a fully nationalized concern, and in 1981 signed a contract calling for a gradual buy-out of Honeywell's stake in the consortium. Honeywell and the again-renamed Compagnie des Machines Bull would continue to share research and development, however, along with their long-standing partner NEC. Bull surprised most observers by announcing that it was committed to a program of worldwide acquisitions designed to strengthen its microcomputer and office-products divisions.

As new chairman Jacques Stern had predicted, Bull climbed out of the red by 1985 and continued its aggressive tactics. With NEC supplying the processors for a new line of mainframes—the DPS9—and the Bull Questar and Micral lines providing office-equipment and microcomputer solutions, the French company soon emerged as a well-rounded international computer maker. Bull still lacked a major opening to the U.S. market, for which reason in 1987 it hooked up with its old partners in a new venture, the Massachusetts-based Honeywell Bull.

Bull acquired 42.5% of Honeywell's $1.85 billion computer business at the same time that NEC bought 15%, and Honeywell kept 42.5% for itself. The deal signaled Honeywell's retreat from the IBM battleground, emphasized the following year when Bull bought up another 22.6% of the joint venture and renamed it Bull HN Information Systems. Groupe Bull Chairman Stern thus found himself with a two-headed corporation. Bull HN operated in the United States, and Bull S.A. operated out of Paris; and in 1989 it further solidified its U.S. base with the $1.4 billion purchase of Zenith's microcomputer interests, Zenith Data Systems. The resulting firm is truly a worldwide consortium.

Profits again dipped and then disappeared in 1989. Francis Lorentz, elected chairman and CEO in 1989, must attempt to bring his company's goals into focus. Even with the government's help—Mitterand fed Bull over US$1 billion in capital between 1983 and 1990—some observers doubt that Bull will be able to continue selling everything from micros to mainframes. The industry as a whole is moving rapidly toward greater specialization, each company scurrying to find a niche in which it can offer value-added products while buying its standard components as needed. Bull has long been a champion of the so-called open-systems approach, whereby all computers and software will eventually be compatible with one another. Such compatibility tends to make much computer equipment interchangeable, encouraging low-priced mass production and forcing most competitors to find a way to sell something more than the typical products.

Bull prides itself on its willingness to get involved with each company's data requirements and tailor a system accordingly. Like most computer firms, Bull no longer simply sells machines, it provides information networks; and by doing so hopes to keep France at the forefront of global developments for many years to come.

Principal Subsidiaries: Bull S.A. (97.5%); OGIC; SOFOM; European Computer Industry Research Centre (Germany, 33.3%); Bull International NV (Netherlands); Bull HN Information Systems Inc. (U.S.A.).

Further Reading: ''Machines Bull's Computer Crisis,'' *Fortune,* July 1964; ''Facts and Figures,'' Paris, Groupe Bull, 1989.

—Jonathan Martin

COMPAQ

COMPAQ COMPUTER CORPORATION

20555 SH 249
Houston, Texas 77070
U.S.A.
(713) 370-0670
Fax: (713) 374-1740

Public Company
Incorporated: 1982
Employees: 10,000
Sales: $2.88 billion
Stock Exchange: New York

Compaq Computer Corporation is a leader in the design, development, manufacture, and marketing of portable, desktop, laptop, and personal computer systems for business and professional users. Since its February 1982 founding in Houston, this company has set many U.S. business records. In its first full year of operation, for example, Compaq reached $111.2 million in revenues, the most successful first year of sales for a U.S. company. In 1986 Compaq was the first company to achieve *Fortune* 500 status in fewer than four years.

When International Business Machines Corporation (IBM) introduced its first personal computer (PC) in 1982, Compaq was among dozens of other companies entering the market with IBM look-alikes—computers which look and perform like IBM PCs, but are less expensive. Compaq set itself apart from other look-alike manufacturers by becoming an innovator itself, producing IBM-compatible PCs that are faster, superior in quality, and offer additional user features. Compaq's management team also set the company apart from others in the PC industry. Made up of seasoned professionals from Texas Instruments (TI) and IBM, their prior experience in the volatile computer industry gave Compaq the tools necessary to survive through a phenomenal growth period in 1983. Compaq's staff also had the technical and business grounding to establish new industry standards on its own—without following IBM.

Compaq's beginning was in the summer of 1981, when Joseph R. "Rod" Canion, James M. Harris, and William H. Murto, three senior managers from TI, decided to start their own company. They had not yet determined what their company would produce and market; managing a Mexican restaurant or manufacturing storage devices for minicomputers or beeping devices for finding misplaced items were among their original ideas. The entrepreneurs eventually decided to build a portable PC that met industry standards set by IBM. With only $1,000 each to invest in their company, Canion, Harris, and Murto approached Ben Rosen, president of Sevin-Rosen Partners, a high-technology venture capital firm in Houston. Rosen, who is Compaq's chairman, offered an initial investment of $2.5 million.

Compaq was established just after an era in which PC entrepreneurs had proliferated. The technological breakthrough of the microprocessor—an extraordinarily powerful semiconductor chip—enabled smaller computers to be built which were also faster, less expensive, and easier to use. Because the much-less-expensive microprocessor miniaturized computers, the demand for PCs increased, and development costs decreased significantly. As a result, many PC companies were established. While these early companies were successful in technological leadership and had a flair for marketing, deficiencies in inventory management and quality control eventually lead many of them to fail. When Compaq arrived on the scene, venture capitalists were beginning to force many entrepreneurs to turn control over their companies to more experienced management professionals. As Rosen—who had lost a $400,000 investment in another PC start-up—explained to *Management Today* in May 1985, "In the early days, it was an area for flamboyant people. . . who transformed their personalities into companies. Now the business requires a very different kind of manager. It has become a very unforgiving industry."

Unlike most new PC companies, Compaq's management had the benefit of the experience of long-time professionals. Prior to joining Compaq, each of its original 20 employees had worked in the computer industry for 15 to 20 years. Their experience in management and engineering at such companies as TI and IBM, two pioneers in the industry, provided Compaq with a solid foundation. Compaq's management style is of the kind that was scorned by early iconoclastic PC entrepreneurs. Compaq makes decisions by a consensus approach to management which allows every division of the company a say in product development. Compaq also instituted some traditional corporate mechanisms, such as tight fiscal controls and a forecasting system.

In 1983, Compaq's consensus management proved valuable. Canion, Compaq's CEO, strongly supported the idea of producing a briefcase-size, or laptop, computer. The marketing research director, however, concluded that the market for such a computer did not exist. Canion relented and Compaq waited while other companies—such as Gavilan Computer Corporation and Data General Corporation—attempted to market such a product and failed. Meanwhile, Compaq shipped its first two products, the Compaq Portable and the Compaq Plus. These computers set the standard for full-function portable PCs. In 1983 Compaq shipped more than 53,000 portable PCs—which were larger than a briefcase—throughout the United States and Canada. That year, Compaq grew from 100 to 600 people, and production increased from 200 machines in January to 9,000 in December.

A key factor in Compaq's growth has been a strong cooperative relationship with its dealers. With nearly 90 PCs on the market aimed at business professionals, shelf space is very competitive. Compaq does not have a direct sales force of its own, and thus does not compete with its authorized dealers. This arrangement gives dealers more incentive to carry Compaq computers. Compaq also motivates its authorized dealers through what is called "Salespaq," whereby Compaq pays a percentage of the dealer's cost of advertising, sales training, or incentives.

Compaq's ability to develop, produce, and market new products in a very short time period is another key ingredient of its success. Once a product has been approved, Compaq undertakes all aspects of its development simultaneously: factories are built, marketing and distribution arrangements are made, and engineers refine the product design. The product cycle in the PC industry is typically 12 to 18 months; Compaq delivers in 6 to 9 months. This fast turnaround in product development enables Compaq to introduce latest technology before its competitors. In 1984, for example, IBM announced a new version of its PC, which experts felt would set back other PC manufacturers. Compaq pulled its resources from every branch of the company, and within six months introduced and shipped its Deskpro line of desktop PCs. Fifteen months later IBM shipped its portable PC, which was two pounds heavier and offered fewer features than Compaq's portable model. From the first quarter of 1983 to the last quarter in 1984, Compaq's production increased from 2,200 computers to 48,000. Despite the 1984 industry shakeout, Compaq reported an increase in sales, to over half a billion dollars. In March 1985, Rosen's original investment of $2.5 million increased in value to $30 million.

Expediency in product development was also an important quality which lead to a turning point in Compaq's history. In 1985 Intel, a leading manufacturer of microprocessors, wanted to market its new powerful microprocessor, the 80386, as soon as possible. Intel felt confident that a Compaq product based on the new microprocessor would see a quick entry into the market. Compaq and Intel worked together to correct defects in the 80386 microprocessor, and Intel redesigned many features of the chip to meet Compaq's standards. Their collaboration resulted in Compaq's 1987 introduction of the Deskpro 386. Based on Intel's new chip, this new PC performed over three times faster than IBM's fastest PC, and nearly twice as fast as Compaq's closest competitor. It took IBM nine months to introduce a comparable machine using Intel's 80386. By then, Compaq was developing a portable version of its new PC.

From 1986 through 1989, Compaq's revenues increased fivefold to $3 billion, while other PC makers—including Apple Computer and Sun Microsystems, the two top contenders—have had setbacks. Much of this growth is due to Compaq's successful marketing efforts in Europe. Led by Eckhard Pfeiffer, former head of TI's European consumer-electronics operation, Compaq began its European campaign in 1984, before most other U.S. vendors. In 1989, Compaq became the number-two supplier of business PCs to the European market, achieving $1.3 billion in international sales. With the PC market in Europe growing a third faster than the U.S. market, Compaq has an edge on other PC manufacturers.

In November 1989, Compaq introduced the Compaq Systempro personal computer and the Compaq DESKPRO 486. These PCs utilize what is known as Extended Industry Standard Architecture (EISA), a hardware design that Compaq developed to challenge IBM's Microchannel hardware design for its PS/2 PCs. These technologies increase the speed of PCs, enabling them to perform more complex operations, such as networking and multitasking. EISA will take Compaq beyond the PC market and attract customers accustomed to using more powerful minicomputers and mainframe computers. By incorporating EISA into its new products, Compaq began to set industry standards. While IBM is producing computers based on the Mirochannel technology, many other manufacturers are using EISA technology. Initial sales of the Systempro were slow but, as CEO Canion told *Business Week*, July 2, 1990, "We realized we were opening up a whole new market. . . . We knew it would take some time."

Compaq's entry into the PC market on the heels of IBM gave it a market in which to grow. Its dedication to innovation within industry standards set by IBM is what enabled Compaq to surpass others in the IBM look-alike industry and meet IBM head-to-head as they both enter the minicomputer and workstation markets. Compaq's unique relationship with its authorized dealers, its experienced management team, and its ability to turn out a new product more quickly than any other vendor in the industry have made this company one of the fastest-growing in the history of U.S. business.

Principal Subsidiaries: Compaq Computer Australia Pty. Limited; Compaq Computer GesmbH (Austria); Compaq Computer N.V./S.A. (Belgium); Compaq Canada Inc.; Compaq Computer A/S (Denmark); Compaq Computer S.A.R.L. (France); Compaq Computer Gmbh (Germany); Compaq Computer Hong Kong Limited; Compaq Computer S.p.A. (Italy); Compaq Computer B.V. (Netherlands); Compaq Computer New Zealand Limited; Compaq Computer Norway A.S.; Compaq Computer Asia Pte Ltd. (Singapore); Compaq Computer S.A. (Spain); Compaq Computer AB (Sweden); Compaq Computer AG (Switzerland); Compaq Computer OY (Finland); Compaq Computer Limited (U.K.).

Further Reading: "Compaq's Compact," *Management Today,* May 1985; Kotkin, Joel, "The Hottest Entrepreneur in America is . . . the 'Smart Team' at Compaq Computer," *Inc.,* February 1986; Uttal, Bro, "Compaq Bids for PC Leadership," *Fortune,* September 29, 1986; Gannes, Stuart, "America's Fastest-Growing Companies," *Fortune,* May 23, 1988; Whiting, Rick, "Compaq stays the course," *Electronic Business,* October 20, 1989; Webber, Alan M., "Consensus, Continuity, and Commonsense: An Interview with Compaq's Rod Canion," *Harvard Business Review,* July–August 1990.

—Lynn Hall

CONTROL DATA

CONTROL DATA CORPORATION

8100 34th Avenue South
Minneapolis, Minnesota
U.S.A.
(612) 853-8100
Fax: (612) 853-5300

Public Company
Incorporated: 1957
Employees: 18,000
Sales: $2.93 billion
Stock Exchanges: New York Midwest Pacific Frankfurt Amsterdam Basel Lausanne Geneva Zürich

The history of Control Data Corporation might be entitled "The Rise and Fall of William C. Norris." Although the company is functioning, and its founder, Norris, continues, in his active retirement, to be at corporate headquarters, Control Data bears little resemblance to the computer giant that Norris and his associates created with such astonishing speed and success. Gone are the heady days of supercomputer breakthroughs, victories over industry Goliath IBM, and a 50% share of the vast market for computer peripherals. Gone too is Norris's unique corporate philosophy, which demanded of business not only profits but a serious commitment to projects for social justice. Although Control Data has not openly repudiated such goals, it is not hard to predict that Norris's many idealistic ventures—usually labeled by the business press as foolhardy drains on profit—will be quietly wound down.

President and CEO Lawrence Perlman oversees a much-sobered, scaled-back Control Data (CD), one trying desperately to overcome recent losses with a strategy based on selling "data solutions" not the high-powered hardware that made the company famous. In each of the firm's eight business divisions, ranging from the media researcher Arbitron to military contracts, CD offers to its customers a combination of hardware, software, and consulting services to design the most advantagious data system possible. In an era of standardized computer components and strong price competition, CD will try to stay alive by marketing its most valuable commodity—30 years of experience as one of the leaders in high-speed data processing.

William Norris was born in 1911 in a small Nebraska town. After a childhood largely divided between farm chores and his love for electrical gadgets, Norris got a degree in electrical engineering from the state university, and joined the navy in 1941. There he was assigned to a group of scientists and technicians charged with code breaking and fast analysis of the information thus gained. Such cryptological work required the processing of large amounts of data, and the navy team was soon evolving early examples of what would later be called the computer. At war's end the navy, anxious to keep together so valuable a group of researchers, helped Norris and a handful of colleagues to form Engineering Research Associates (ERA) in Saint Paul, Minnesota.

ERA was a privately owned company, but nearly all of its work was done for the navy and other branches of the armed forces, and it benefited from access to innovative data research done elsewhere in the military. This unique position made ERA the early leader in computer design. By 1952 the company employed 1,500 people, and had installed about 80% of U.S. computers, as measured in dollars. In that year the company was sold, however, becoming a part of Remington Rand's already growing computer division. Within a few years Norris was named head of all computer operations at the newly created Sperry Rand, from which vantage point he had an excellent overview of the developing computer industry.

Sperry Rand should have remained on top of that industry, given its sizable technological lead and corporate resources, but poor management and a lack of commitment to computers soon allowed IBM to forge past the confused Sperry. Norris, frustrated by these matters, in July 1957 was one of a dozen Sperry engineers who resigned in order to found Control Data Corporation in Minneapolis. The new partners sold stock to raise $600,000, rented space in a warehouse, and set out to beat IBM in the one area of the market they knew best—large, fast computers used by the military and scientific communities. With no customers, equipment, or track record, Norris's venture could hardly have seemed a threat to IBM, which by that time had established its absolute domination of the data-processing world. CD had a secret weapon, however: Seymour Cray, age 31, already acknowledged as the brightest computer designer in the world. It was Cray who one day decided to build the fastest computer in the world, an idea Norris took up as CD's rallying cry.

With typical bravado, Norris in effect sold the new computer before buying a local manufacturing concern, Cedar Engineering, that was to build it. When the first CDC 1604 mainframe computer was delivered to the navy shortly thereafter, Control Data had indeed created the world's fastest and most powerful computer, and won for itself and Seymour Cray a reputation for technical wizardry. Cray was later to leave CD and found his own Cray Research.

From the beginning, CD grew at a remarkable pace. With few salesmen and no marketing program, CD's computers virtually sold themselves. They were the best large computers available at any price, but they were also cheaper than IBM's. Control Data originally sold no software with its machines, as its customers were all sophisticated users best able to design their own programs. In a scant five years the company became the world's fourth-largest computer maker, on its meteoric rise passing a host of failing giants unable to match IBM in the market for general-purpose computers, where CD wisely chose not to compete. Even as sales mounted and the company expanded, Norris recognized that IBM would soon retaliate with its own "supercomputer," and he set about diversifying his business.

Between 1960 and 1979 Norris bought up some 88 other companies in three related fields. The first and most important of these was computer peripherals. Creating a new corporate division in 1961, Norris stocked it with manufacturers of disc drives, controllers, and other components for use with CD's own computers as well as for sale to rival companies. Norris was criticized widely for this move into original-equipment manufacturing, but it proved to be a complete success. The expertise gained in designing peripherals for its own high-performance computers gave CD a crucial technological advantage in what became an increasingly important field, and soon many other computer makers found it easier to buy components from CD than to make their own. In addition, by the late 1960s CD was offering a line of disc drives for IBM and IBM-compatible computers, tapping a vast if somewhat risky market. Peripherals became one of CD's largest and most profitable divisions, in 1983 reaching $1.5 billion in sales and controlling 50% of the overall market.

The second area into which Norris diversified was data services. He recognized that most computer users could neither afford nor make use of a machine as large as the 1604, but they might very well be willing to pay for a few hours of its time. He accordingly began selling timeshares of CD's in-house 1604 in the early 1960s, also offering to substantial customers the programming experience of CD's own engineers. Such timesharing originally involved sending material back and forth from CD headquarters in Minneapolis, but by 1967 telephone lines linked each client with one of a number of computing facilities around the country. While Norris was busy building CYBERNET, as this data service came to be called, he also set in motion a 1968 lawsuit that would result, unexpectedly, in a huge expansion of CD's service capabilities.

In past skirmishes with IBM, Norris believed that his giant opponent had thwarted CD sales by promising customers the imminent arrival of a new IBM machine said to be both better and cheaper that CD's model. This phantom machine never materialized, but the resulting drop in CD sales threatened to exhaust the company's limited resources. To prevent a repetition of this strategy, when CD rolled out its new 7600 supercomputer, Norris filed an antitrust suit against IBM in December 1968, charging that IBM had promoted a non-existent computer solely in the hope of forcing CD out of business. The complex case was resolved five years later, when in settlement of the suit IBM gave to CD its Service Bureau Corporation, a data-services firm similar to CYBERNET with about 20,000 customers worldwide. The lawsuit was vintage Norris—an audacious attack upon the industry's undisputed leader, vigorously pursued to a settlement that amounted to a complete victory for CD. Not only had Norris prevented a second predatory marketing campaign by IBM, he had doubled the size of his data-services division while incidentally demonstrating that IBM was not unbeatable.

The third area of Norris's balanced diversification was the 1968 purchase of Commercial Credit Corporation of Baltimore, Maryland. CD needed extra financial resources to fund the leasing of its equipment, and when Commercial Credit, a well-established financial-services company with about $3.4 billion in assets, became the object of an unwanted takeover bid Norris stepped in and bought it. Analysts doubted the wisdom of the move, noting that the two firms could not have been less alike in corporate philosophy and products; but Commercial Credit performed admirably for Norris, both as CD's leasing company and as a profit center in its own right. It never became the dynamic international powerhouse Norris hoped that it would, but few projects ever met the CD chairman's demanding expectations.

From the late 1960s Norris's expectations included a role for CD in making the United States a better and more equitable nation. CD was an outstanding success from the day it opened its doors, within eight years employing 10,000 people, and reaching $160 million in annual sales. By 1970 CD revenue topped the $1 billion mark, and with 30,000 employees Norris might well have been satisfied with his contribution to U.S. society. The race riots of 1967, however, opened his eyes to deeper problems facing this country, and with his usual confidence Norris set about solving them. He initiated CD's corporate activism with the construction of a new plant in the middle of Minneapolis's northside ghetto in 1967, and soon afterward decreed that all future plants would be similarly located to provide jobs for the chronically unemployed. Control Data purposely sought out one of the most depressed rural areas in the country, Crampton, Kentucky, and built a manufacturing facility there. In Saint Paul, Minnesota, CD provided employment in part-time shifts for working mothers and poor students. It opened a factory in San Antonio, Texas because Norris was concerned about the low percentage of Hispanic employees in the company. In each case, CD provided day-care centers, counseling services, and even bail bonds for its new workers, whom in many instances were hired specifically because they had little education or a poor employment history. In each case the new plants were a success.

Norris dreamed of going much further. Something of an industrial visionary, Norris spent much of the 1960s and 1970s trying to address social problems in a way that would also profit CD. Such a unique formula alienated both the social activists, who depicted CD as profiting from human misery, and Norris's business colleagues, who at best thought him a dreamer with excess cash in his pocket. None of that disparagement discouraged Norris, who pushed ahead with job-training programs, prison education, small-business consulting services, inner-city industrial parks, and financial help for the small farmer. Above all, Norris spent heavily to develop a computer-based educational system called PLATO, which he saw as the answer to America's widespread failure in the schoolroom. In each of these ventures Norris expected to make a profit; he was not interested in philanthropy but in addressing the problems of society with the energy generated by a healthy capitalist economy. The results have been mixed. PLATO has been largely unsuccessful, but inner-city employment has been far more successful, and if CD's efforts have not revolutionized prison education or created a raft of new small businesses, it did set a remarkable example of corporate ethics and determination.

In the early 1980s CD developed grave problems of its own, and many observers thought Norris and his idealistic projects were the cause. The company had continued its prodigious growth throughout the 1970s and reached an earnings peak of $289 million in 1981, at which time nearly 60,000 people around the world worked for CD. Data services, peripherals, mainframes, Commercial Credit Corporation, and military contracts were all doing well—with all cylinders firing, CD appeared poised for another decade of success. Profits slipped in each of the next three years, however, dropping to $140 million in 1984; and then, to the astonishment of the computer industry, CD virtually collapsed. The following year, 1985, ended with a catastrophic loss of $567 million on sales of $3.7 billion, followed by another $265 million deficit in 1986. The following two years showed a slight profit, but in 1989 the company again staggered under a massive loss of $680 million, this time on sales of less than $3 billion. Industry analysts were not suprised by William Norris's long-expected fall, and the Utopian businessman formally retired in 1986 at the age of 75.

In retrospect, it is clear that CD's troubles lay elsewhere. In peripherals, the company's bread-and-butter division, its share of the world market dropped from 50% to 23% between 1980 and 1984. This was due to a number of factors. Stiff Japanese competition and a sudden flurry of technological innovation left CD behind, and when the cost of manufacturing IBM-compatible discs grew prohibitive CD gave up that market entirely, taking a $130 million write-off. In addition, 1984 and 1985 saw a severe recession in the computer industry as a whole; sales of CD peripherals and the profit margin fell together, plunging the division deeply into the red. In other areas, remote data processing and mainframes were also suffering, the former due to the emergence of the microcomputer, the latter hurt by renewed competition from Digital Equipment Corporation, IBM, and Cray Research, the latter a company formed by CD's former illustrious employee. In the sea of red ink only Commercial Credit managed to keep its head above water.

A crisis was reached in the fall of 1985 when CD was unable to pay its short-term bank loans. From that point Norris and Robert Price, his successor, embarked on an emergency program of asset sales and employee cuts that continued for the rest of the decade. CD was forced to toss out its valuables along with excess baggage, resulting in what amounts to a new company. Commercial Credit, remote data processing, the ETA supercomputer division, training and educational programs, and even peripherals were all sold to raise cash to keep the parent company afloat, leaving mainframe and data services as the only survivors of the business Norris had built. Robert Price and new CEO Lawrence Perlman now preside over a company that is determined to avoid the kind of head-to-head commodity competition that nearly destroyed CD in the 1980s.

Thus, although it remains in the mainframe business, CD has developed a complex network of agreements with other manufacturers to incorporate their products into the CD line of computers. Data services is inherently free of straight price competition, as are the media-monitoring work of Arbitron, the on-line wagering systems supplied by Automated Wagering Systems, and the many military contracts handled by the government-systems division. In each of these fields, CD seeks to provide customers with a systemic solution to complex data problems, rather than selling standard products like disc drives, mainframes, or even supercomputers. Such a strategy is now universal among the world's computer leaders.

Principal Subsidiaries: The Service Bureau Corp.; The Arbitron Corp.; AUTOCON Industries; Computer Peripherals, Inc. (80%); Kerotest Manufacturing Corp.; Magnetic Peripherals (67%); Data Services, Far East, Inc.; Communications Solutions, Inc.; United School Services of America; Dataven Inc.; Financial & Human Resources Venture Fund, Inc.; VTC Incorporated.

Further Reading: Worthy, Ford S., "Does Control Data Have a Future?," *Fortune,* December 23, 1985; Gullo, Karen, "The Long View," *Datamation,* July 1, 1986; Worthy, James C., *William C. Norris: Portrait of a Maverick,* Cambridge, Massachusetts, Ballinger Publishing Company, 1987.

—Jonathan Martin

CRAY RESEARCH, INC.

655A Lone Oak Drive
Eagan, Minnesota 55121
U.S.A.
(612) 683-3800
Fax: (612) 683-3899

Public Company
Incorporated: 1972
Employees: 4,700
Sales: $574.67 million
Stock Exchange: New York

Cray Research is the premier producer of supercomputers, providing both the machines and the software programs to operate them. Supercomputers are high-performance computer systems that can handle a large number of calculations in a very brief time. From its beginning, Cray Research has been engaged in all phases of supercomputer production, including design, development, manufacture, and marketing, and has geared its efforts toward the high-priced end of the computer market. It has been the world leader in sales of supercomputer systems, which are now in their third generation of development. A spin-off of part of its research-and-development operation into a separate company, Cray Computer Corporation, was completed in 1989.

Cray Research was formed through the efforts of Seymour Cray, a recognized genius in the design of supercomputers. Cray was born in 1925 in Chippewa Falls, Wisconsin, and spent a boyhood devoted to tinkering with electronic gear. After service in World War II working as a radio operator and then functioning as a specialist in breaking Japanese codes, he attended the University of Minnesota, earning a bachelor of science degree in electrical engineering and another in applied mathematics, both in 1950. He decided to enter the computer industry and took a job with Engineering Research Associates, founded by William C. Norris. Through a series of mergers, Engineering Research Associates was brought under the control of Sperry Rand Corporation. Norris left Engineering Research Associates and established Control Data Corporation in 1957. Cray soon followed him to the new company. Among his early projects at Control Data, Cray developed the 1604, one of the first computers to use transistors in place of vacuum tubes.

Control Data shared in the booming computer industry of the 1960s, experiencing a period of rapid growth. Cray became disenchanted with the bureaucracy that this growth created and insisted that the company build him a separate research facility in his home town of Chippewa Falls. In this new facility, he came up with the CDC 6600, the first commercial computer capable of handling three million program instructions per second. Cray's special talent was in putting the circuits of a computer very close together, reducing the time taken for electric signals to pass between them. This closeness, however, increased the heat generated by the circuits. Cray was able to introduce innovative ways of removing this heat.

Cray's success at Control Data eventually hit a stumbling block. In 1972, top management at the corporation halted his plans for a new computer, telling him he could continue working on it only after another computer project was completed.

Instead of waiting, Cray and a group of followers left Control Data to set up Cray Research. Their purpose in starting the new company was to design the first supercomputer, which they ultimately named the CRAY-1. Cray Research was initially situated in Cray's laboratory in Chippewa Falls. After several years of work on the supercomputer project, in March 1976, the company delivered its first computer to a customer, the National Center for Atmospheric Research. This sale enabled it to earn back its original investment.

The CRAY-1 was the fastest computer then available and used the technique of vector processing. Vector processing employs a system wherein a series of operations are manipulated as opposed to scalar processing, which processes one operation at a time. The CRAY-1 could execute 32 operations simultaneously, making it able to complete ten times the work of some larger systems. While it was delivering its first sale, the company also made its first public offering of stock. The company complemented its supercomputers with software programs, releasing its Cray Operating System (COS) and Cray Fortran Compiler in 1977.

During its early years of operation, Cray Research sold its supercomputers to government laboratories and agencies. The main application of supercomputers is in physical simulation, wherein computer models are used to analyze and forecast the response pattern likely to take place in a system composed of physical variables. Early applications of these models were in gauging the effects of nuclear weapons and in meteorology. Since these types of applications were performed under the aegis of the government, it was felt that the market for supercomputers would be very limited. In 1978, however, Cray Research was given its first order from a commercial organization.

The CRAY-1 system became the CRAY-1/S and the CRAY-1/M systems. As the 1980s began, the company decided to begin development of the next generation of supercomputers. To concentrate his efforts on that development, Seymour Cray resigned as CEO in 1980, and in 1981 he stepped down as chairman. John Rollwagen became CEO in 1980 and chairman in 1981. Cray retained his ties with the company as an independent contractor and as a member of the board of directors. The new project called for the design and development of the CRAY-2, intended to be the first computer on the market that used chips made of gallium arsenide. When the gallium arsenide chips were not available, Cray returned to silicon. The CRAY-2 system was completed in 1985, achieving a performance level ten times that of the CRAY-1.

Because the CRAY-2 project contained an element of risk due to its innovative technology, Rollwagen had the company initiate a second project based on a further upgrade of the CRAY-1 technology. Under the direction of Steve S. Chen, the CRAY X-MP system was devised. This system marked the first use of multiprocessors, where a number of microprocessors are linked together to take on bigger jobs. Introduced in 1982, the CRAY X-MP was originally a dual processor, with a speed three times that of the CRAY-1.

As had been done with the CRAY-1, both the CRAY-2 and the Cray X-MP supercomputers evolved into more sophisticated systems. The CRAY X-MP served as the basis for a series that consisted of 11 models. The more innovative CRAY-2 design had three-dimensional circuit interconnections linking circuit boards within a module. Software enhancements were also made available, with the 1986 introduction of a new operating system, UNICOS, which combined the COS system with the AT&T UNIX System V. This advance was especially important because UNIX was well established as the industry standard, especially in areas of scientific application, where supercomputing has been so useful; meanwhile an advanced Cray Fortran Compiler, named CF77, was also made available.

By the mid-1980s Cray Research began working on another generation of supercomputers, again following several paths. In 1986, Chen began working on a new system of highly innovative design, relying on significant technological advances in five different areas. After spending nearly $50 million on the project, the company decided to discontinue it. Chen left the company in 1987, taking 45 engineers from Cray Research, to form Supercomputer Systems, Inc., with plans to build a supercomputer using as many as 256 microprocessors.

Seymour Cray completed design work on the CRAY-3 supercomputer system in 1987. The CRAY-3 marked another effort to use gallium arsenide chips, a prospect made more feasible by the production of the first of the new type of chips suitable for computer production in the 1980s. While awaiting the CRAY-3, the company developed and introduced the CRAY Y-MP system, which combined the power of eight central processing units to give it 30 times the power of the original CRAY-1.

Cray Research passed two important milestones in 1987. First, it delivered its 200th computer system, especially noteworthy since it had taken from 1976 to 1985 to reach a total of 100 computer shipments. This rapid expansion made possible the second milestone, the inclusion of Cray Research among the nation's largest companies, listed in the *Fortune* 500. This period of rapid expansion was possible because the company was able to market its supercomputer systems to commercial corporations engaged in petroleum exploration, automobile production, and the aerospace industry.

Cray Research underwent a major restructuring in 1989. Delays in the development of the CRAY-3 system were creating very high research costs, and the scheduled date for completing the project was reportedly postponed. In addition, the company had embarked on another project, the C-90, as a new stage in the CRAY Y-MP product line. Rather than discontinue one of the projects, Chairman John Rollwagen decided to create a new company, Cray Computer Corporation, to be headed by Seymour Cray. Located in Colorado Springs, Colorado, Cray Computer would continue the development of the CRAY-3 supercomputer. On November 15, 1989, Cray Research issued shares of Cray Computer to its stockholders, retaining a 10% ownership in the new company. Seymour Cray resigned from the board of directors of Cray Research, severing formal connections with the company he had formed, although he remained a stockholder.

Even after this spin-off Cray Research retained a solid position as the leading company in the production of supercomputers, with about two-thirds of the world market. In 1989, it phased out the CRAY-2 and CRAY X-MP as new models of the CRAY Y-MP were coming on-line. There were continuing plans for development of the C-90 project, which was renamed the CRAY Y-MP/16. The company also began development of enhanced systems for supercomputer networking to facilitate scientists' access to Cray supercomputers from a variety of other types and brands of computers. In addition, there were plans to bring to the market an entry-level supercomputer, which would use the technology of the CRAY Y-MP, but would have a much lower price with reduced installation and operating costs. Cray Research maintains a policy of investing 15% of its revenue in development and engineering.

As the market for supercomputers expanded, Cray Research diversified its sales efforts both in terms of type of customers and geographic region. In 1989 governments remained the largest customers, buying 31% of Cray Research's output; other important purchasers of Cray machines included universities, aerospace, petroleum, and automotive companies, energy producers, and weather and environment analysts. Sales in North America that year were 61% of the total. Approximately 75% of revenue between 1987 and 1989 was derived from sales of computer systems, with remaining income from leased systems and service fees. In addition to its corporate headquarters and software support operations in Eagan, Minnesota, Cray Research has manufacturing and development facilities in Chippewa Falls and Rice Lake, Wisconsin, and support operations in Mendota Heights, Minnesota. It maintains sales offices in 29 cities throughout the United States and has 19 subsidiary operations in other countries.

By the beginning of the 1990s, Cray Research was facing increasing competition from Steve Chen's Supercomputer Systems, backed by IBM. Once the newly formed Cray Computer enters into the production of the CRAY-3, it is expected to be a formidable competitor. Even more important, Japanese companies—Fujitsu, Hitachi Ltd., and NEC Corporation—have entered the supercomputer market. NEC developed the SX-3 which, by linking four processors, is six times as fast as the CRAY Y-MP. Fujitsu planned to introduce the VP-2000. Their capabilities, however, will be surpassed by those of the CRAY-3. Further, speed is not the only measure of supercomputer performance. Capacity measured by the number of parallel processors and software capability must be factored into a machine's performance rating. Given these factors, the standard Cray Research supercomputer is still able to handle large problems much faster than the new competitors from Japan.

The presence of Japanese producers in the market for supercomputers raised concerns that the same process whereby Japanese producers captured the U.S. and world markets in automobiles, personal computers, and consumer electronics might take place in the supercomputer industry. Part of the concern rested on the fact that much of the basic research on supercomputers done by Japanese companies was government sponsored and that the Japanese firms entering the supercomputer market were large computer-manufacturing companies with much greater resources than Cray Research. By early 1990, the office of the U.S. Trade Representative, the agency responsible for monitoring trade disputes and imposing sanctions placed a high priority on investigating claims of Japanese protectionism in its domestic supercomputer market.

Cray Research still has substantial advantages in systems and applications software, and its UNICOS and COS software are now the standards for supercomputers. It has also been able to make itself felt in the Japanese market by installing 20 supercomputers there by 1990. By mid-1990, only three Japanese supercomputers were imported into the United States. In part this low level of imports was the result of a boycott of imported supercomputers. The Department of Defense was prohibited by law from purchasing supercomputers from non-U.S. manufacturers, and most other purchasers voluntarily followed suit.

Cray Research is taking measures to provide for better distribution of its products. It has entered into an arrangement with Control Data to make Cray supercomputers available to Control Data's customers, using Cray products to replace Control Data's line of supercomputers that was discontinued in 1989. Marcelo Gumucio, who directed Cray Research's marketing operation, was named president and chief operating officer in 1988. By placing more emphasis on the marketing of its products, with less attention paid to product development, Cray Research anticipated that it would be better able to meet the challenges of international competition in the supercomputer industry.

In 1990 Rollwagen asked for Gumucio's resignation as president and chief operating officer because of his formal management style. Gumucio had increased the number of reports and procedures required of employees for the purpose of setting specific goals, a strategy to combat the increasing competition the company was facing. Rollwagen resumed operating responsibilities. His management style aimed at freeing design experts to follow their own interests in research. The goal of this strategy was to enable Cray Research to meet competition by continual innovation in the company's products.

Principal Subsidiaries: Cray Asia/Pacific, Inc. (Hong Kong); Cray Computadores do Brasil Ltda. (Brazil); Cray Research (Canada) Inc.; Cray Research France S.A.; Cray Research GmbH (Germany); Cray Research Japan, Ltd.; Cray Research (UK) Ltd.

Further Reading: Schatz, Willie, ''Who's Winning the Supercomputer Race?'' *Datamation,* July 15, 1989; Mitchell, Russell, ''The Genius: Meet Seymour Cray, Father of the Supercomputer,'' *Business Week,* April 30, 1990.

—Donald R. Stabile

digital

DIGITAL EQUIPMENT CORPORATION

146 Main Street
Maynard, Massachusetts 01754
U.S.A.
(508) 493-5111
Fax: (508) 493-8780

Public Company
Incorporated: 1957
Employees: 124,000
Sales: $12.94 billion
Stock Exchanges: Midwest New York Pacific Zürich Geneva Basel Frankfurt Munich Berlin

Digital Equipment Corporation is a leading designer and manufacturer of networked computer products and services. Its products serve a variety of applications, such as scientific research, computation, communications, education, data analysis, industrial control, time-sharing, commercial data processing, graphic arts, word processing, office automation, health care, instrumentation, engineering, and simulation.

Digital is best known for launching the minicomputer industry. Its introduction of the minicomputer sparked a revolution which altered the way people perceived the computer. Digital brought the computer out of the hands of computer programmers by making computers that people could interact with and that were smaller, faster, and less expensive than competitors'. The company's minicomputers set the stage for the development of the personal computer in the mid-1980s. Digital's own entry into the personal computer market, however, in the early 1980s was a failure.

Digital was distinguished by its entrepreneurial style of management. For that reason it was much-watched during the 1970s and early 1980s when it experienced its fastest growth. In 1982 the company's management structure was praised in Thomas J. Peters's and Robert H. Waterman's *In Search of Excellence,* but Digital's success was not without turbulence. After a period of phenomenal growth in the 1970s, Digital began to outgrow its unique entrepreneurial structure which had made it a serious challenger to the industrial computer giants.

In the summer of 1957, Ken Olsen asked American Research & Development (ARD), a venture capital firm in Boston, for $100,000 to establish a company to build computers. Olsen and his partner, Harlan Anderson, were 31 and 28 years old, respectively. They had just come out of Massachusetts Institute of Technology's (MIT) Digital Computer Laboratory. General Georges Doriot, the head of ARD and a professor at the Harvard Business School, advised them to write a business proposal. Doriot encouraged them not to use the word "computer," since large corporations like General Electric and RCA were already failing in the nascent industry. Doriot, who later jointed Digital's board of directors and influenced Olsen's leadership style, was concerned that a proposal from the young, inexperienced engineers would not be readily received.

Heeding Doriot's advice, Olsen and Anderson proposed to produce printed circuit modules instead of computers, and promised to turn a profit in their first year. ARD offered them $70,000, and the two engineers located their company in the small mill town of Maynard, Massachusetts.

In early 1958 Digital shipped its first products, the Digital Laboratory Module and the Digital Systems Module. The company sold $94,000 worth of these modules to research facilities. Despite the recession of the late 1950s, Digital turned a profit at the end of its first year.

The Whirlwind and SAGE computers which Olsen and Anderson had worked on at MIT, influenced Olsen's commitment to producing computers which are interactive and interlinked. The Whirlwind was used to power a cockpit flight simulator for the navy; while other universities were designing computers to calculate complex equations, MIT designed the Whirlwind for immediate interaction with the user. The SAGE (Semi-Automatic Ground Environment Defense System), a U.S. Air Force project during the cold war, was a massive network of computers and radar systems used to detect enemy aircraft in the nation's airspace.

When Olsen and Anderson established Digital, the only computers commercially available were million-dollar mainframes from companies such as IBM, Univac, and Burroughs. The people who worked with these computers were programmers provided or trained by the company. Olsen had observed students waiting in line to use Whirlwind's interactive offspring, the TX-O, an early transistorized system at MIT's Lincoln Laboratory, while an IBM machine was virtually ignored. Seeing the need for more interactive computers, Olsen sought to wean computers away from programmers.

In 1960, the company introduced its first computer, the PDP-1 (Programmed Data Processor). The PDP-1 came with a cathode-ray tube (CRT), a screen which allowed the user to see what was being entered and received from the central processing unit. This novel addition to computers demonstrated Olsen's commitment to making computers accessible to users. Unlike the room-sized mainframe computers of the day, the PDP-1 was no larger than a refrigerator. It cost $120,000, when comparable machines by other manufacturers were selling for $1 million.

In 1963 Gordon Bell, who would become Digital's most eminent engineer, designed the PDP-5. The PDP-5 was the forerunner of Digital's PDP-8, the first minicomputer. That same year, Bell also designed a large-scale computer, the PDP-6. These two computers illustrated the company's ability to build a wide range of computers. In 1964 the price for

Digital's products ranged from $27,000, for the PDP-5, to $300,000, for the PDP-6.

There was virtually no organizational structure during the early stages at Digital. Olsen was committed to creating an environment much like the research labs at MIT. A temporary position as liaison between MIT and IBM in 1959 convinced Olsen that the hierarchy at companies like IBM did not allow for creativity and the flow of ideas. Unlike other computer companies at the time, Digital did not lease its computers. Leasing computers, with a contract for support and services, kept customers dependent on the companies. Since Digital's customers, mostly scientists and engineers, did not require technical support, the company provided virtually none of the software and maintenance services offered by its giant competitors. Digital did not spend its capital on software design and maintenance services, and passed its savings along to customers. Olsen also felt that leasing hindered technical development by creating a reluctance to allow a product to become obsolete.

Digital survived without an organizational structure for seven years. By 1964 various engineering groups were not coordinating with other functions of the company, causing bottlenecks in certain areas of manufacturing and order processing. As a result, product shipments were often delayed. That year, Digital's profits dropped to $900,000 from $1.2 million in 1963.

It was then that Olsen decided to structure the company into a team of product line managers. Under this structure, the product line manager became an entrepreneur within the company competing with other teams for its centralized manufacturing and sales forces. Each manager had complete responsibility for a product line, from conceptualization to sales, and was accountable for its performance. This matrix organization, as it was called, was responsible for an abundance of products developed over the next 15 years. By the mid-1970s, the company developed more than 20 new product lines. While the matrix organization resulted in dynamic growth, it also created uncertainty among some of Digital's employees, and in 1966 Olsen's partner, Anderson, left.

In the fall of 1965 Digital unveiled the PDP-8. This machine triggered the minicomputer industry, and the company grew from a small technical company into a major computer manufacturer. The PDP-8 was small and attracted users who wanted to integrate it into their larger mainframe systems. It sold for $18,000, at that time a very low price for a high-performance general-purpose computer. Digital sold 50,000 PDP-8s over the machine's 15-year life span, and the PDP-8 contributed to growth in revenues and profits of between 25% and 40% per year. Between 1965 and 1967 alone, profits multiplied sixfold to $4.5 million.

Because Digital's computers were versatile and accessible, they inspired a market new to the computer industry known as OEM, or original-equipment manufacturer. Other companies bought Digital's computers and integrated their own hardware and software programs for specific applications, such as scientific instrumentation, and sold the package as their own product. This unique arrangement saved Digital the costly, labor-intensive job of writing software and servicing its machines that decreased overhead costs while revenues poured in. OEMs also opened up new markets to Digital. Because of their adaptable nature, Digital's computers were used for a wide variety of applications, from calculating scientific problems to running electronic scoreboards in sports stadiums.

The business world now began to view computers as a viable industry. Attempts by larger companies to buy Digital were rebuffed; Olsen firmly refused to sell out, and Digital itself has never acquired another company. This position has distinguished Digital from most other computer companies.

As Digital's entrepreneurial style permeated the industry and the availability of investment capital increased, dreams of starting companies abounded among engineers. In 1968 Edson de Castro, an engineer who worked on the design of the PDP-8, left Digital to start his own company. Data General would become Digital's first serious competitor in the minicomputer market.

In January 1970 Digital announced plans to build the PDP-11, to be sold for $10,800. It was the first time that Digital had announced a machine still in the design stage. Data General had already announced a machine in the same class of computers a year earlier and was beginning to encroach upon Digital's customer base. When *Industrial Research* named the PDP-11 one of the most significant technical products introduced in 1970, sales increased. Eventually, 500,000 PDP-11s were sold. By 1972 Digital was back on top of the minicomputer market.

Digital has been a pioneer in human resource activities. To bring growth to otherwise depressed communities, the company established plants in places hard hit by recessions, such as Maynard, and Springfield, Massachusetts. Digital is also known for its no-layoff tradition. During the recession of 1970, while the rest of the industry was laying off hundreds of people, Digital put its employees to work in other areas of the company, from sweeping the parking lot to sales. Digital also funded a study of the reproductive health of women who worked in one of its semiconductor plants. The study found a correlation between high exposure to semiconductor material and miscarriages, and Digital publicized the study despite the potentially negative consequences. Digital's lack of rigid hierarchy is also unique as is the ability of employees to directly influence decision making. Decisions are made by consensus of engineering, marketing, design, and review committees.

Digital's salesmen do not work on commission. Digital believes that commissions are unfair to salespeople and that they stand in the way of customer satisfaction. Olsen's fundamental corporate values became formalized policy in 1974. His basic tenets, were "honesty, integrity, doing the right thing."

Digital entered the personal computer market due to market pressure from the outside and the eagerness of its engineers from the inside. On May 10, 1982, Digital announced three personal computer products, the Rainbow 100, the DECmate II, and the Professional 325 and 350, but internal competition to build a personal computer had drained Digital's resources to develop and market the products effectively. While Digital hesitated and its engineers battled out their varied personal computer products, other companies had already entered the market.

The failure of the personal computer project was one example of the problems beginning to surface as a result of Digital's matrix organization. The consensus required to initiate product lines made it difficult for Digital to respond quickly to market needs. Another problem was the existence of too many independent product domains within the company. While Digital produced many products and established itself in a number of different markets, customer territories became unclear and intense competition between the domains drained Digital's resources. Furthermore, the company's growth and new market areas overwhelmed sales and service forces as they tried to meet the demands of new customers. Further, with nearly 70 minicomputer manufacturers to compete with, DEC's sales force was also busy defending its lead in the minicomputer market.

Other product line teams developed technologies which brought Digital successfully into the new decade. In 1979 the engineering group headed by Gordon Bell developed the VAX line of computers. VAX architecture evolved into a range of computers from small desktop machines to computer clusters, which could compete with mainframes. Interlinked, these machines gave companies complete automation throughout their varied divisions.

Olsen had the foresight to realize that Digital's sales and marketing force was not ready for the potential success of the VAX systems, and the more businesslike customers that it would attract. Thus, Olsen began to transform Digital into a unified marketing organization by redirecting its product lines into a market-oriented scheme. Rather than simply allowing the product line teams to develop and sell any product, Digital identified markets to target, assigning product lines to each area.

By 1984 Olsen had completely reorganized Digital. This change shifted profit and loss responsibility away from product line managers. It took five years to dismantle the matrix organization, which had existed for 19 years and was a symbol of Digital's growth and success. Due to the shift in power, more than 50 managers left to start their own companies or to join others.

The timing of Digital's new direction could not have been better. By the early 1980s the corporate world had become a multivendor environment where machines of different sizes and applications, and sometimes from different manufacturers, could not communicate or share information. Over the next 18 months ten new VAX computers were unveiled. These machines could network not only among themselves, but with other vendors' products as well. Consequently, Digital lured an estimated $2 billion in sales away from IBM. In 1986 Digital's profits rose 38% in an industry which was declining.

By introducing the minicomputer, Digital established a market for itself. It made small, interactive computers when the industry giants were producing large, expensive computers. Digital's growth is a result of its ability to enter, and develop, new markets with quality machines. Through its matrix organization and OEM agreements, Digital achieved very fast growth, steadily increasing its share of different markets, and responding more quickly and more aggressively than others to the demands and specific problems of its customers. As Digital entered the 1990s, it continued its dedication to multivendor networking and to delivering quick solutions to customers.

Digital faces the challenge of maintaining its status as a major computer corporation. The minicomputer market is losing out to smaller and more powerful microcomputers, and critics question Digital's ability to continue its transition into a large corporation under the direction of its founder and president, Ken Olsen. Digital's consistent product philosophy and expert engineering of networking a wide range of computer sizes and applications may make it one of the most successful computer companies in the 21st century.

Principal Subsidiaries: Computer Insurance Company of Rhode Island; Computer Insurance Company Limited (Bermuda); Digital Computer Taiwan Limited; Digital Equipment Aktiebolag (Sweden); Digital Equipment B.V. (Netherlands); Digital Equipment Bertriebliche Altersversorgungsgesellschaft m.b.H. (Germany); Digital Equipment of Canada Limited; Digital Equipment Caribbean, Inc.; Digital Equipment Centre Technique (Europe) S.A.R.L. (France); Digital Equipment China Ltd.; Digital Equipment do Brazil Ltda.; Digital Equipment Co. Limited (U.K.); Digital Equipment Corporation A/S (Norway); Digital Equipment Corporation A/S (Denmark); Digital Equipment Corporation (Australia) Pty. Ltd.; Digital Equipment Corporation (Consultancy) Ltd. (U.K.); Digital Equipment Corporation Espana, S.A. (Spain); Digital Equipment Corporation Finance B.V. (Netherlands); Digital Equipment Corporation Gesellschaft m.b.H. (Austria); Digital Equipment Corporation International; Digital Equipment Corporation International (Europe) (Switzerland); Digital Equipment Ireland Limited; Digital Equipment Corporation OY (Finland); Digital Equipment Corporation de Puerto Rico; Digital Equipment Corporation (New Zealand) Limited; Digital Equipment Corporation S.A./A.G. (Switzerland); Digital Equipment (DEC) Limited (Israel); Digital Equipment (DEC) Technical Center (Israel) Limited; Digital Equipment Filipinas Incorporated (Philippines); Digital Equipment Finance Corporation; Digital Equipment Foreign Sales Corporation B.V. (Netherlands); Digital Equipment France; Digital Equipment GmbH (Germany); Digital Equipment Hellas Ltd. (Greece); Digital Equipment (Holdings) B.V. (Netherlands); Digital Equipment Hong Kong Limited; Digital Equipment International B.V. (Netherlands); Digital Equipment International Betriebliche Altersverorgungsgesellschaft m.b.H. (Germany); Digital Equipment International GmbH (Germany); Digital Equipment International Ltd. (Switzerland); Digital Equipment (Korea) Inc.; Digital Equipment (Malaysia) Sdn. Bhd.; Digital Equipment de Mexico, S.A. de C.V.; Digital Equipment N.V./S.A. (Belgium); Digital Equipment Overseas Finance N.V. (Netherlands Antilles); Digital Equipment Panama, Inc.; Digital Equipment Part Center B.V. (Netherlands); Digital Equipment Portugal; Digital Equipment PRC Limited (Hong Kong); Digital Equipment S.p.A. (Italy); Digital Equipment Scotland Limited; Digital Equipment Services, Inc.; Digital Equipment Singapore (PTE) Limited; Digital Equipment Taiwan Limited; Digital Equipment (Thailand) Ltd.; Digital Growth Inc.; Digital Incorporated; Digital International Sales Corporation; Kam Hon Development Company, Limited (Hong Kong); Nihon Digital Equipment Corporation KK (Japan); Old Colony Insurance Limited (Bermuda).

Further Reading: Olsen, Kenneth H., *Digital Equipment Corporation: The First Twenty-five Years,* New York, The Newcomen Society in North America, 1983; Petre, Peter, "America's Most Successful Entrepreneur," *Fortune,* October 27, 1986; Rifkin, Glenn, and George Harrar, *The Ultimate Entrepreneur,* Chicago, Contemporary Books, 1988.

—Lynn Hall

ELECTRONIC DATA SYSTEMS CORPORATION

7171 Forest Lane
Dallas, Texas 75230
U.S.A.
(214) 604-6000
Fax: (214) 991-8847

Wholly Owned Subsidiary of General Motors Corporation
Incorporated: 1962
Employees: 60,000
Sales: $5.47 billion

Electronic Data Systems Corporation (EDS) is a recognized leader in the management of information technology. The company designs, installs, and operates data processing systems for customers in the automotive, communications, energy, financial, government, health-care, insurance, retail distribution, transportation, utilities, and manufacturing industries. Innovators in facilities management, EDS originated the concept of long-term fixed-price contracts for this industry. It became a wholly owned, independently operated subsidiary of General Motors Corporation (GM) in 1984. EDS owns the largest private digital telecommunications network in the world and conducts business in all 50 states and in 27 countries.

This multi-billion dollar corporation sprang from modest beginnings on June 27, 1962. A frustrated IBM salesman named H. Ross Perot incorporated EDS on his 32nd birthday. Earlier that year in January, Perot had already fulfilled his entire annual sales quota because of a recent change in IBM's commission structure. Not satisfied with the administrative job then offered him by IBM, he recognized an unmet need among IBM's many computer customers. Most companies had few knowledgeable personnel to operate their new computer equipment. Perot wanted to offer skilled electronic data processing management services to these companies. He presented his ideas to IBM executives, but they were not interested.

At the age of 19 Perot received a much desired appointment to the U.S. Naval Academy. Although he valued his time in the military, he found the military too restrictive to make it his career. In 1952, while still in the navy, he was recruited by IBM. Initially he found their business style comfortable, but left ten years later to found EDS.

EDS developed a business concept later termed "facilities management." Companies would concentrate their energies on what they did best, leaving the computing and data processing tasks to EDS, who could do them more efficiently and economically.

Ross Perot spent the first five months of his new business canvassing the east coast and midwest to find a first customer for his computer services company. He had bought wholesale computer time on an IBM 7070 computer installed at Southwestern Life Insurance in Dallas. Once he sold this time at retail, he was in business. Collins Radio in Cedar Rapids, Iowa, became EDS's first customer, and a new industry was born. In November 1962, with money from his first sale, Perot hired IBM salesmen Milledge A. "Mitch" Hart and Thomas Marquez.

As EDS grew, Perot modeled employee behavior on the high standards of IBM. He demanded conservative dress, honesty with customers, and no alcohol consumption during business hours. He expected employees to stay sharply focused and highly disciplined.

Although he ran the company with almost military precision, Perot established a management that listened to employee suggestions and ideas. According to an April 1969 article in the trade journal *Datamation,* Perot's goals were "to create a climate of complete intolerance to company politics, to provide the finest personal and financial advantages for employees, to make EDS an exciting place to work . . . to promote from within. . . . " He believed in loyalty, but held duty at an even higher level. A motto over his office door read, "Every Good and Excellent Thing Stands Moment by Moment on the Razor's Edge of Danger and Must be Fought for." Ross Perot expected employees to fight for their ideas.

In 1963 EDS signed its first long-term commercial facilities management contract with Herman Lay of Frito-Lay. While other services companies offered short-term contracts of 60 or 90 days at hourly rates, EDS wrote five-year fixed-price contracts. EDS set up a customer's data processing system, provided the staff to run it, and once the system was running smoothly, removed some personnel and reassigned them to new projects. Because EDS could cut expenses over the life of the contract by decreasing personnel costs, its profits increased. The customers benefited because they could budget long-term electronic data processing costs. These longer contracts gave EDS stability.

The passage of Medicare legislation in 1965 gave EDS the opportunity to enter another lucrative market. Government agencies involved were about to take on a mountain of paperwork. EDS organized Medicare and Medicaid claims processing systems in many states. By 1968 Medicare and Medicaid contracts provided about 25% of EDS revenues, and by 1977 health care claims processing accounted for nearly 40% of EDS's sales.

In 1963 EDS executed its first insurance company contract with Mercantile Security Life. By 1990 EDS was the largest insurance data processor in the country. In 1968 it signed a Dallas bank as its first financial institution customer and later became the world's largest provider of data processing services to banks and savings and loans. Beginning with eight credit unions in 1974, EDS serviced more than 3,000 in 1990. While in 1978 EDS had only three employees in its

Washington, D.C., office, in 1990 6,000 people worked in EDS's government arena.

In 1968, prompted by an employee's question about the worth of the company's stock, Perot began to investigate the advisability of a public stock offering. He made the initial release small: 325,000 of his own shares and 325,000 new EDS shares—about 7% of the company. The offering met with phenomenal success, opening at $16.50 per share and closing at $22. Perot and EDS each received $5 million dollars. The shares climbed to a high of $160 in 1970; by April of 1971 they had dropped to about $66, and in 1973, with a sharp decline in the stock market, EDS stock plummeted to $15 a share.

Perot served as president from the company's inception in 1962 until he appointed Hart to that position in 1970. Hart was president until his resignation in 1977. Perot stayed on as CEO and chairman of the board and resumed the presidency from 1977 to 1979.

EDS pioneered the concept of distributed processing, by which systems and terminals communicate with each other from remote locations. It developed computer systems set up to serve a specific industry. These systems could then be modified according to each customer's needs. In the 1970s EDS developed Regional Data Centers, where customers could transmit their work to be handled by EDS's data processing equipment and personnel.

The company's revenues doubled almost every year between 1964 and 1970. In the 1970s, revenue increases slowed to 22% in 1971 and 13% in 1977.

In the early 1970s EDS bought Wall Street Leasing, a computer-services subsidiary of Dupont Glore Forgan, Inc., one of the country's leading retail stock brokers. Perot appointed EDS vice president, Morton H. Meyerson, to attempt the rescue of the financially troubled firm. With encouragement from the Nixon administration, which feared a financial disaster on Wall Street, Perot had begun by investing $10 million in Dupont Glore Forgan. By 1973 he had invested further funds in Walston and Company, another retail brokerage house, and had proposed a merger between Dupont and Walston. By early 1974 Perot was defeated by the losses at Dupont and Walston. He left Wall Street some $60 million poorer.

A lawsuit filed in 1976 by F. & M. Schaefer Corporation and F. & M. Schaefer Brewing Company, for whom EDS operated a data processing facility, contributed to the slowdown of revenue growth in the mid-1970s. Schaefer claimed that the EDS data processing system was inaccurate and deficient, resulting in inadequate and misleading information. EDS maintained that Schaefer filed the suit to avoid payment of more than $1.2 million owed to EDS. In the 1978 out-of-court settlement, EDS paid Schaefer Corporation $2.3 million and retained $1.3 million already paid by Schaefer.

In early 1976 EDS entered the international market by signing a contract with King Abdulazziz University in Saudi Arabia. Later that same year EDS signed a three-year $41 million contract with the government of Iran to provide computer services for their social security division and training for Iranian personnel. In December of 1978 EDS suspended all operations because Iran was six months behind in payments. The scope of the Khomeini revolution grew in Iran, and after the jailing of Iranian officials with whom EDS worked, Perot ordered home EDS employees and their families. A few employees remained, hoping the chaos would be resolved. The situation worsened with the arrest of EDS executives Bill Gaylord and Paul Chiapparone, with bail set at $12 million. Since diplomatic channels seemed closed, Perot took direct action. In early 1979 he organized a rescue team headed by Green Beret Colonel Arthur D. "Bull" Simons, whom Perot had previously hired to make private forays into Vietnam looking for servicemen missing in action. Although Gaylord and Chiapparone actually walked out of prison on their own when a mob released all prisoners, they needed the EDS team to get them out of the country.

In the mid-1970s EDS began a shift away from facilities management, since many companies were becoming interested in running their own data processing systems. In 1979, Morton H. Meyerson became president while Perot continued as chairman of the company. Under Meyerson, EDS diversified its business interests through acquisitions of turnkey systems—sale of systems to be installed—for hospitals, small banks, and the small-business field. With the purchase of Potomac Leasing in 1979, EDS moved into federal government contract work. The bulk of EDS business still remained in facilities management, with processing of health care claims a large percentage of the business through the 1970s and into the 1980s.

Always moving with the times, EDs became a systems integrator, sending in teams of experts to connect and coordinate a company's entire computer systems, software, and telecommunications. In 1982, as the result of its experience in systems integration, EDS won a $656 million ten-year contract for Project Viable, to streamline and update the U.S. Army's computerized administrative facilities and to build a network connecting 47 bases across the United States.

On June 27, 1984, although the company never had a contract with an automobile manufacturer, EDS became a wholly owned subsidiary of General Motors Corporation (GM). The $2.5 billion purchase price was the largest ever paid for a computer services business. GM agreed to maintain EDS as a separate entity, keep key personnel, and issue a special class of common stock, called class E, which would be tied to EDS's performance, not GM's. Perot would retain managerial control of EDS and serve on GM's board of directors.

GM needed EDS to coordinate and manage its huge, unwieldy data-processing system and to cut its $6 billion annual data-processing costs. Roger B. Smith, GM's chairman of the board, thought Perot's management style would be an asset to his giant corporation.

Problems surfaced within a year when the differences in management style between Ross Perot and Roger B. Smith became evident. The August 1984 issue of *Ward's Auto World* suggested "Mr. Perot is a self-made man and iconoclast used to calling his own shots. . . . Roger B. Smith [is] a product of the GM consensus-by-committee school of management, never an entrepreneur."

EDS saw revenue increases as the result of the General Motors business. In 1985, the first full year after the acquisition, EDS revenues tripled to $3.4 billion. By 1986 personnel had almost tripled to 44,000 from 1984 levels. EDS also branched out into telecommunications and factory automation. Although EDS revenues increased substantially, profit margins fell to 5.5% in 1985. GM preferred contracts which stipulated a fixed percentage for profit; EDS, on the other hand, wanted to continue the fixed-price contracts it had been using since inception. Additional problems arose as the result of the differing company cultures.

In 1986 GM management bought Perot's Class E shares for more than $700 million. For the first time in the 24 years since he started the company, Ross Perot was no longer in charge of EDS. Morton Meyerson also resigned.

At that time, Lester M. Alberthal became president and CEO. He had joined EDS as a systems engineer trainee in 1968. In June 1989 he was named chairman of the board of EDS. Under Alberthal's leadership, EDS broadened its customer base and reduced its dependence on GM-generated revenues from 70% in 1986 to 55% in 1989. Revenues climbed to new highs.

Under Alberthal, the company diversified, moving into energy, transportation, communications, manufacturing, and other new areas of business. Diversification included further expansion of international business. Administration of the company was reorganized through a leadership council, to spread responsibility and authority for daily operations to lower levels of the EDS hierarchy and allow the top executives to focus attention on development of long-range strategy.

Within the GM alliance, EDS developed the world's largest digital private telecommunications network: EDSNET. Consolidating the networks of both GM and EDS took three years, a staff of 2,000 people, and a cost of over $1 billion. In 1989 EDS opened its Information Management Center in Plano, Texas. The 153,000 square-foot facility serves as the heart of EDS's extensive worldwide communications network and information processing centers where voice, data, and video transmissions travel to their destinations via state-of-the art media. This center is the hub of operations for 15 North American and 6 international Information Processing Centers located all over the world. EDS can respond immediately to the needs of its more than 7,200 customers, who are able to take advantage of the leading edge of information technology.

Throughout the years, EDS contributed to the community and the nation as part of its company policy. In May of 1989 and again in 1990, EDS supported Project JASON, which enabled 225,000 children around the country to witness live the undersea exploration of the Mediterranean Sea. Dr. Robert D. Ballard, the scientist who discovered the wreck of the Titanic in 1985, led this excursion. EDS provided satellite links and solved technological problems to ensure the success of this undertaking. EDS created an Education Outreach Program for the communities where the company is located. EDS "adopted" several public schools and worked with teachers to help improve the quality of education.

EDS emphasizes employee training, spending over $100 million per year on the Systems Engineer Development program, to give customers the best service available. The firm has the technology and skills to continue global expansion of its information technology services.

Principal Subsidiaries: E.D.S. Federal Corporation; EDS Financial Corporation; EDS Technical Products Corporation; National Heritage Insurance Company; VideoStar Connections, Inc.

Further Reading: Louis, Arthur M., "The Fastest Richest Texan Ever," *Fortune,* November 1968; Burlingham, Bo, and Curtis Hartman, "Cowboy Capitalist," *Inc.,* January 1989; Levin, Doron P., *Irreconcilable Differences: Ross Perot versus General Motors,* Boston, Little, Brown and Company, 1989; Mason, Todd, *Perot: An Unauthorized Biography,* Homewood, Illinois, Dow Jones-Irwin, 1990.

—Ann T. Russell

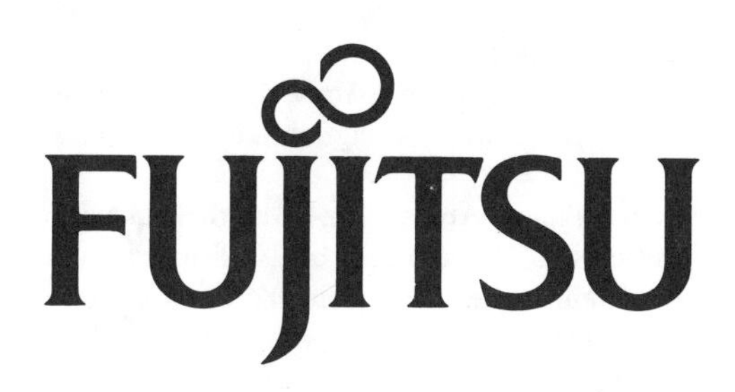

FUJITSU LIMITED

6-1, Marunouchi 1-chome
Chiyoda-ku, Tokyo 100
Japan
(03) 3216-3211
Fax: (03) 3216-9365

Public Company
Incorporated: 1935
Employees: 114,010
Sales: ¥2.55 trillion (US$17.74 billion)
Stock Exchanges: Tokyo Osaka Nagoya London Zürich Basel Geneva Frankfurt

Perhaps the most dramatic example of Japan's ability to overcome long odds in a short space of time has been the growth of its computer industry, and the undisputed leader among Japanese computer makers is Fujitsu Limited. Ranked second in the world behind IBM, Fujitsu is very much a product of Japan's willingness to tackle large-scale industrial projects with a combination of private ambition and governmental funding. Since 1950 Fujitsu has become the Japanese government's primary weapon in its struggle to develop an indigenous computer industry in the face of IBM's superior might, and the company offers a range of mainframes, minicomputers, and microcomputers, which not only are substantially cheaper but which some users also find superior to their U.S. counterparts.

Fujitsu is also a world leader in supercomputers—offering a model that runs at four gigaflops, for those keeping track—and maintains lesser positions in such varied lines as workstations, automated-teller machines, and retail automation. Alongside its computer products, Fujitsu continues its original role as one of Japan's leading makers of telecommunications equipment, working closely with Nippon Telephone and Telegraph on a vast array of technological innovations. Fujitsu has also become a power in the semiconductor industry, where it both supplies its own needs and offers customers a choice of up-to-date integrated circuits, gate arrays, and the world's first 64-megabyte dynamic random access memory cell. As Japan moves toward the so-called fifth generation of ''thinking'' computers and the eventual adoption of an entirely new form of operating system, Fujitsu will almost certainly remain at the forefront of the advancing world computer revolution. Whether it will ever have the strength to battle IBM on the latter's home turf is another question, but given Fujitsu's startling growth in the postwar era and Japan's now-famous competitiveness, few would rule out the possibility entirely.

Fujitsu was created on June 20, 1935 as the manufacturing subsidiary of Fuji Electric Limited and charged with continuing the parent company's production of telephones and automatic exchange equipment. Fuji Electric, itself a joint venture of Japan's Furukawa Electric and the German industrial conglomerate Siemens, was part of Japan's attempt to overcome its late start in modern telecommunications. Spurred by Japan's expanding military economy, Fujitsu quickly branched off into the production of carrier transmission equipment in 1937 and radio communication two years later. Yet the country's telephone system remained archaic and incomplete, with German and British systems in use that were not fully compatible. World War II ruined a large part of this primitive system, destroying some 500,000 connections out of a total of 1.1 million, and leaving the country in a state of what might be called communication chaos. At the insistence of the occupying U.S. forces, Japan's Ministry of Communications was reorganized and nearly became a privately owned corporation that would have simply adopted existing U.S. technology to rebuild the country's telephone grid. However, a coalition led by Eisaku Sato convinced the government instead to form a new public utility, Nippon Telephone and Telegraph (NTT). Created in 1952, NTT soon became a leading sponsor and purchaser of advanced electronic research, and it remains one of Fujitsu's key customers.

The link with NTT may well have been Fujitsu's greatest asset, but Fujitsu was only one of a series of increasingly determined government partners for the country's young computer industry. Fujitsu first became interested in computers in the early 1950s, when Western governments and large corporations began making extensive use of them for time-consuming calculations. After a number of years of experimentation Fujitsu succeeded in marketing Japan's first commercial computer, the FACOM 100. This was a start, but the Japanese computer business was still in its infancy when IBM brought out the first transistorized computer in 1959. So great was the shock of this quantum leap in design that the Japanese government realized it would have to play a far more vigorous role if the country was not to fall permanently behind the United States. The government formulated a comprehensive plan that included restrictions on the number and kind of foreign computers imported, low-cost loans and other subsidies to native manufacturers, and the overall management of national production to avoid needless competition while encouraging technological innovation. Of equal importance, in 1961 the Japanese government negotiated with IBM for the right to license critical patents, in exchange allowing the U.S. giant to form IBM Japan and begin local production.

Patents in hand, seven Japanese companies entered the computer race. All of them except Fujitsu quickly formed alliances with U.S. companies to further their research—Fujitsu, refused by IBM in a similar offer, remained the only ''pure,'' or *junketsu*, Japanese computer firm, committed to the development of its own technological expertise. The other Japanese companies were all much larger than Fujitsu and devoted only a fraction of their energy to computers, while Fujitsu soon devoted itself to communications and computers. Able to build on its already substantial electronics experience

Fujitsu was directed by the government to concentrate on the development of mainframes and integrated circuitry, and in late 1962 it was given the specific goal of developing a competitor to IBM's new 1401 transistorized computer. The government stalled IBM's plans for local production and enlisted Hitachi, NEC, and Fujitsu in what it called project FONTAC, the first in what would become a series of government-industry drives. From the perspective of the marketplace, FONTAC was a complete failure—before it got off the ground IBM had launched its revolutionary 360 series, pushing the Japanese further behind than when they started—but as a first try at a coordinated national computer program, FONTAC proved to be extremely important. Fujitsu and the other Japanese manufacturers could afford poor initial performance, knowing that funds were available for further research and development. In particular, the Japanese government had by this time formed the Japanese Electronic Computer Company (JECC), a quasi-private corporation owned by the seven computer makers but given unlimited low-interest government loans with which to buy and then rent out newly produced computers. In effect, this allowed Fujitsu and the others to receive full payment for their wares immediately, thus greatly increasing corporate cash flow and making possible the huge outlays for research and development.

The result of JECC's largesse was immediate: in the space of a single year—1961 to 1962—Japanese computer sales increased by 203%. In 1965 Fujitsu, relying largely on technology developed as part of the FONTAC project, brought out the most advanced domestic computer yet built, the FACOM 230. The company had quickly become JECC's leading manufacturer, supplying approximately 25% of all computers purchased by the firm during the 1960s. In addition, Fujitsu had continued its substantial work for NTT, with over half of its telecommunication products going to the phone company by the end of the decade. NTT remained a critically important governmental agency for Fujitsu and the computer industry, routinely shouldering research-and-development costs and paying high prices to ensure that its suppliers remained profitable. NTT also sponsored a super-high-performance computer project in 1968, similar in design and scope to one begun the previous year by the Ministry for Trade and Industry (MITI), to develop a new computer for its complex telecommunications needs. Both of these ambitious programs, were paid for by rival government ministries.

Despite this concerted effort, however, by 1970 the Japanese were suffering from IBM's recent introduction of its 370 line. Worse yet, under international pressure the Japanese government had agreed to liberalize its import policy by 1975, giving the local computer industry a scant five years in which to become truly competitive. MITI responded by making computer prowess a national goal, greatly increasing subsidies, and reorganizing the six remaining companies into three groups of cooperative pairs. Fujitsu, as the leading mainframe maker, was paired with its archrival Hitachi and given the task of matching IBM's 370 line with a quartet of its own heavy duty computers, to be called the M series.

The need to build IBM-compatible machines led Fujitsu to an important decision. In 1972 the company invested a small but vital sum of money in a new venture started by Gene Amdahl, a former IBM engineer who had been largely responsible for the design of its 360 series computers. Amdahl Corporation had been formed with the express intent of building a cheaper, more efficient version of IBM's 370 line, which made a joint venture with Fujitsu highly advantageous for both partners. With its strong government support, Fujitsu had access to the capital Amdahl badly needed, while the U.S. engineer was a valuable source of information about IBM operating systems. Fujitsu and Amdahl persevered in what became a most profitable sharing of technology and capital.

A key factor in the Fujitsu-Amdahl deal was the Japanese company's confidence that it could rely on NTT to pay top dollar for whatever computer evolved from the new venture. In this, as in many other situations, NTT served as a kind of guaranteed market for Fujitsu, which in turn was well on its way to becoming a world leader in telecommunication technology and hence a more valuable supplier to NTT. The Fujitsu-Hitachi M series of high-speed computers emerged in the late 1970s. With the M series, which remains the basis of Fujitsu's production line, the Japanese had achieved a rough parity with the IBM systems. Fujitsu had become one of IBM's very few real competitors in the area of general-purpose mainframe computers; and sometime in 1980 Fujitsu became the only company in the world to outsell IBM in its native country, taking a narrow lead in Japanese computer sales that it has maintained.

Since the watershed events of the 1970s, Fujitsu has pushed ahead with an impressive array of projects in each of its three main marketing areas. In computers, which remain the source of 60% to 70% of overall corporate revenue, Fujitsu has continued the success of its M series while branching out into minicomputers, workstations, and personal computers. The company spent much of the 1980s in a legal dispute with IBM over the latter's charge that it had improperly copied IBM's software. An arbitrator decided in 1988 that, after $833 million in payments to IBM, Fujitsu could continue to buy access to IBM software at a cost of at least $25 million a year. The agreement was meant as a spur to further mainframe competition. Since 1982 Fujitsu also has become a leading manufacturer of supercomputers, with some 80 such units installed as of the end of the decade. Though easily the leading mainframe maker in Japan, Fujitsu has had little success exporting its products—with only 22% of corporate sales made overseas, Fujitsu remains overly dependent on its Japanese business. In particular, the company has been unable to break into the U.S. market, where, in addition to the obvious presence of IBM, its mainframe bias is seen as somewhat outdated. The recent tendency in large computer systems has been toward greater distribution of processing power, aided by individually tailored software applications—two areas in which Fujitsu is notably weak.

Fujitsu remains strong in telecommunications, however, where it continues its close relationship with NTT as well as with the newly emerging New Common Carriers. In light of its origin in the telecommunication field, it is not surprising that Fujitsu has become a world leader in the development of Integrated Services Digital Network (ISDN), the inevitable convergence of data processing and telecommunications. ISDN will eventually carry voice, image, data, and text all on one system, and Fujitsu has been intimately involved in NTT's development of the new service, which seems significantly more advanced in Japan than in the United States.

Fujitsu is also active in other improvements in telecommunications such as COINS (corporate information network systems), PBXs (private branch exchanges), and digital switching systems. The company also provided important terminal and branching equipment for the recently completed Trans-Pacific Cable #3, the Pacific Ocean's first optical submarine cable. Fujitsu maintains a strong presence in its third product area as well, electronic devices. In 1987 the firm was prevented by the United States government from acquiring Fairchild Camera, a leading U.S. manufacturer of memory chips, but it still manages to sell about $2.5 billion worth of chips annually. The very fact that Fujitsu was barred from purchasing Fairchild is a testament to the company's strength in semiconductors as well as computers. In conjunction with the Japanese government and other Japanese computer firms, Fujitsu continues to refine its chip technology in anticipation of the imminent arrival of the fifth generation of computers, machines that will be able to write their own software and in some meaningful sense "think."

In July 1990 Fujitsu, continuing its tradition of cooperation with non-Japanese companies, announced that it would buy an 80% stake in ICL, Britain's largest and most important mainframe maker. Fujitsu and ICL—which had become a subsidiary of STC in 1984—had collaborated on several projects, beginning in 1981. Fujitsu paid £700 million for its ICL holdings.

Fujitsu has become one of a select group of companies able to compete with IBM in the mainframe arena. Its great task will be to export its computers more successfully. It is one thing to sell Fujitsu mainframes to Sony, and quite another to place them overseas. IBM remains the undisputed mainframe leader around the world, but Fujitsu and the Japanese have demonstrated more than once their ability to surprise everyone but themselves. Information processing, which in the long run means IBM, remains the one manufacturing area in which Japan has not yet been able to dominate the field; if that should change anytime in the near future Fujitsu may be carrying the flag.

Principal Subsidiaries: Fujitsu Laboratories Ltd.; Shinko Electric Industries Co., Ltd.; Fuji Electrochemical Co., Ltd.; Fujitsu Denso Ltd.; Fujitsu Kiden Ltd.; PFU Limited; Fujitsu TEN Limited; Hasegawa Electric Co., Ltd.; Fujitsu Yamanashi Electronics Limited; Kyushu Fujitsu Electronics Ltd.; Fujitsu Isotec Limited; Fujitsu Kasei Ltd.; Fujitsu System Integration Laboratories Ltd.; Fujitsu Automation Limited; Fujitsu VLSI Limited; Yamagata Fujitsu Limited; Fujitsu Tohoku Electronics Ltd.; Fujitsu Miyagi Electronics Ltd.; Shinano Fujitsu Ltd.; Fujitsu Sinter Limited; Fujitsu Peripherals Limited; Fujitsu Buhin Limited; Nihon Dengyo Limited; Fujitsu FACOM Information Processing Corporation; Fujitsu Dai-ichi System Engineering Limited; Fujitsu Social Science Laboratory Limited; Fujitsu Basic Software Corporation; Fujitsu Distribution Systems Engineering Limited; Fujitsu Kansai System Engineering Limited; Fujitsu Tokai Systems Engineering Limited; Fujitsu Financial Systems Engineering Limited; Fujitsu Tohoku Systems Engineering Limited; Fujitsu Financial Information Systems Limited; Fujitsu Social Systems Engineering Limited; Fujitsu Dai-ichi Communication Software Limited; Fujitsu Technosystems Limited; Ishikawa Fujitsu Software Limited; Fujitsu Oita Software Laboratories Limited; Fujitsu Kyushu System Engineering Limited; Gunma Fujitsu Limited; Okinawa Fujitsu Systems Engineering Ltd.; Fujitsu Minami-Kyushu Systems Engineering Limited; Fujitsu Shizuoka Engineering Limited; Fujitsu Program Laboratories Limited; Fujitsu Kansai Communication Systems Limited; Fujitsu Kyushu Communication Systems Limited; Fujitsu Nagano Systems Engineering Limited; Fujitsu Aichi Engineering Limited; Fujitsu Keihin Systems Engineering Limited; Fujitsu Shikoku Infortec Limited; Fujitsu Business Systems Ltd.; Fujitsu Logistics Limited; Fujitsu Office Machines Limited; Fujitsu Trading Ltd.; Fujitsu Supplies Limited; Fujitsu Microcomputer Systems Limited; Fujitsu OA Limited; Fujitsu Network Engineering Limited; Fujitsu Microdevices Ltd.; Fujitsu Documents Service Limited; Totalizator Engineering Limited; Fujitsu Digital Technology Limited; Fujitsu Advanced Printing & Publishing Co., Ltd.; Fujitsu Fudosan Ltd.; Iwaki Densi Ltd.; Ten Onkyo Ltd.; Fujitsu Kosan Limited; Fujitsu America, Inc. (U.S.A.); Fujitsu Business Communication Systems, Inc. (U.S.A.); Fujitsu Systems of America, Inc. (U.S.A.); Fujitsu Microsystems of America, Inc. (U.S.A.); Fujitsu Canada, Inc.; Fujitsu Customer Service of America, Inc. (U.S.A.); Fujitsu Imaging Systems of America, Inc. (U.S.A.); Intellistor, Inc. (U.S.A.); Fujitsu Microelectronics, Inc. (U.S.A.); Fujitsu Component of America, Inc. (U.S.A.); Fujitsu Network Switching of America, Inc. (U.S.A.); Fujitsu Australia Ltd.; Fujitsu Australia Wholesale Pty. Ltd.; Fujitsu New Zealand Holdings Ltd.; Fujitsu New Zealand Ltd.; Fujitsu Microelectronics Asia Pte. Ltd. (Singapore); Fujitsu (Singapore) Pte. Ltd.; Fujitsu Korea Ltd.; Fujitsu Microelectronics Pacific Asia Ltd. (Hong Kong); Fujitsu Electronics (Singapore) Pte. Ltd.; Fujitsu Component (Malaysia) Sdn. Bhd.; Fujitsu Microelectronics (Malaysia) Sdn. Bhd.; Fujitsu España, S.A. (Spain); Fujitsu Mikroelektronik GmbH (Germany); Fujitsu Microelectronics Ltd. (U.K.); Fujitsu Microelectronics Italia S.r.l. (Italy); Fujitsu Microelectronics Ireland Ltd.; Fujitsu Europe Ltd. (U.K.); Fujitsu Deutschland GmbH (Germany); Fujitsu Nordic AB (Sweden); Fujitsu Italia S.p.A. (Italy).

Further Reading: Hills, Jill, *Deregulating Telecoms,* Westport, Connecticut, Quorum Books, 1986; Anchordoguy, Marie, *Computers Inc.: Japan's Challenge to IBM,* Cambridge, Harvard University Press, 1989; "Company History," Fujitsu corporate typescript, 1989; *Creative Partners in Technology,* Santa Clara, California, Amdahl Corporation, 1989.

—Jonathan Martin

HEWLETT-PACKARD COMPANY

3000 Hanover Street
Palo Alto, California 94304
U.S.A.
(415) 857-1501
Fax: (415) 857-5518

Public Company
Incorporated: 1947
Employees: 95,000
Sales: $11.90 billion
Stock Exchanges: New York London Paris Tokyo Frankfurt Stuttgart Zürich Basel Geneva Lausanne Pacific

Hewlett-Packard Company produces electronic products and systems for computation and measurement. Hewlett-Packard (HP) sells nearly all of its products to businesses, research institutes, and educational and health-care institutions, and is one of the United States's 15 largest exporters. Its products can measure power, radiation, and radio frequencies; can count trace particles in air and water; and can analyze breakdowns in computers and other electrical systems.

Hewlett-Packard was founded in 1938 by William Hewlett and David Packard, both recent graduates of Stanford University's electrical engineering program. Encouraged by Professor Frederick Terman, who urged graduates to start their own businesses in California, the two men rented a cottage behind Packard's house in Palo Alto, California, and, with $538, began part-time work on a resistance-capacity audio oscillator, for testing sound equipment, that Hewlett had developed for his master's thesis. After assembling several models—baking paint onto the instrument panel in Packard's kitchen oven—they won their first big order, for eight oscillators, from Walt Disney Studios, which used them to develop and test a new sound system for *Fantasia*.

On January 1, 1939, Hewlett and Packard formalized their venture as a partnership, tossing a coin to decide the order of their names—Hewlett won. In 1940, with a product line of eight items, the two men moved their company and its three employees to a building in downtown Palo Alto.

During World War II Terman, who was then in charge of antiradar projects at Harvard, contracted his former students to manufacture microwave signal generators for his research. When the war ended, HP took full advantage of the growth in the electronics sector, particularly for defense and industrial projects. Also at this time the founders decided upon their roles in the company: Hewlett led technological development, and Packard took charge of managing the business. Hewlett-Packard was incorporated in 1947. By 1950 the company had 70 products, 143 employees, and revenues of $2 million.

HP introduced a revolutionary high-speed frequency counter, the HP-524A, in 1951. This device, which reduced the time required to measure radio frequencies from ten minutes to about two seconds, was used by radio stations to maintain accurate broadcast frequencies, particularly on the then-new FM band.

The company maintained stable and impressive growth through the end of the decade. In November 1957 Hewlett-Packard offered shares to the public for the first time. It also moved into a larger complex in the Stanford Research Park.

In 1958, with revenues of $51 million, HP made its first corporate acquisition: the F.L. Moseley Company of Pasadena, California, a manufacturer of graphic recorders. The company's expansion continued, internationally, in 1959 with the establishment of a marketing office in Geneva, and a manufacturing facility in Boeblingen, West Germany. After adding another factory in Loveland, Colorado, in 1960, Hewlett-Packard purchased the Sanborn Company, a medical-instruments manufacturer based in Waltham, Massachusetts.

The company gained wider public recognition when it was listed on the Pacific and New York stock exchanges in 1961, and then made the *Fortune* 500 a year later. In 1964 Hewlett-Packard developed a cesium-beam "flying clock," accurate to within one-millionth of a second. To promote the device, called HP-5060A, company engineers embarked on a 35-day, 35,000-mile world tour to coordinate standard times.

In 1963 Hewlett-Packard expanded its presence in Japan through the creation of a joint venture with Yokogawa Electric Works, and in 1965 it acquired the F & M Scientific Corporation, another analytical-instruments manufacturer, based in Avondale, Pennsylvania. Also that year, the company opened its central research laboratory, one of the world's leading electronic research centers.

Though primarily a manufacturer of instruments for analysis and measurement, Hewlett-Packard developed a computer in 1966. The HP-2116A was developed specifically for HP's own production control; the company had no plans to enter the computer market. Two years later, however, HP introduced the HP-9100A, the first desktop calculator capable of performing scientific functions. In 1969 David Packard was appointed deputy secretary of defense in President Richard Nixon's administration. In 1971 Packard left the government and returned to his company as a director.

HP, meanwhile, developed a hand-held scientific calculator called the HP-35. The device, known as the "electronic slide rule," was designed partially by Bill Hewlett. It was introduced in 1972 and soon made up 13% of the company's sales. When Texas Instruments entered the market in 1973, Hewlett-Packard's device, which retailed at $395, was forced into the high end of the market.

Hewlett-Packard made its first decisive move into business computing with the HP-3000. This signaled a major change in company strategy: diversification into computers, a field dominated by IBM and Digital. In the spring of 1974 Hewlett and Packard decided that the company was growing too fast;

the company was falling behind, despite record earnings. The founders refocused on product leadership. They established a new, highly decentralized research-and-development structure, letting each of the company's 23 divisions conduct its own research and development.

Bill Hewlett relinquished the presidency in 1977 to John Young, a career HP man determined to make the company successful in the computer market. Although he was chosen by Hewlett and Packard, Young was virtually unknown to the company's customers and 37,000 employees. Nonetheless, a year later he replaced Hewlett as CEO, also.

Hewlett-Packard introduced its first personal computer, the HP-85, in 1980. The market's initial reaction was cool, leading Young and other managers to investigate new, IBM-compatible designs, which were introduced in the mid-1980s. HP's broad move into computers proved to be a good one, as the company quickly established itself as a leading computer vendor. Like other vendors, however, HP had designed each of its major computer lines for a specific use, making each model incompatible with the others. This resulted in redundant research and development and product-support costs and limited expansion possibilities for customers. In response to these problems, HP began a six-year program to develop architecture and software that would be compatible with existing programs, for all its subsequent computers. In the meantime, HP introduced a number of other products, including the HP-9000 technical workstation, the HP-150 touchscreen PC, the ThinkJet printer, and the LaserJet printer—the single most successful product in Hewlett-Packard's history.

In 1986 the company introduced its new family of Spectrum computer systems, developed at a cost of $500 million. The project was based on the newly developed universal design, Precision Architecture. This architecture used a new concept called RISC—Reduced Instruction Set Computing. RISC enables computers to run through programs at double or triple conventional speed by eliminating many routine instructions. Critics claim, however, that the stripped-down set of instructions makes the program less flexible and over-specialized.

Despite these criticisms, market projections were good, and the system itself was state of the art. HP initially failed to capitalize on its technology. The company had adopted a new sales strategy as early as 1984, focusing on markets rather than product lines. Sales efforts were redoubled on every level. The company even began joint marketing with telecommunications and peripherals companies previously regarded as competitors.

John Young's leadership of Hewlett-Packard is highly regarded. The Precision Architecture line gained much wider acceptance after its problematic introduction, and came to be viewed as a bold gamble. By 1988, Young had restored the company's momentum, with profits rising 27% during that year. Hewlett and Packard, as directors, are no longer involved in the company's day-to-day business. In 1987, their sons, Walter B. Hewlett and David Woodley Packard, were elected to the board.

In April 1989 Hewlett-Packard paid $500 million for the ailing Apollo Computer, a pioneer in the design, manufacture, and sale of engineering workstations. The purchase doubled HP's share of the networked-workstation market and boosted it from the fourth-largest to the largest producer in that fast-growing segment.

In buying Apollo, Hewlett-Packard did more than increase its workstation market share to 30%. It also won original-equipment manufacturer business with companies like Mentor Graphics Corporation, the leading designer of computer-aided engineering software. Mentor and companies like it buy workstations, equip them with their own software, and resell the machines for special uses, such as computer-aided engineering.

Apollo was not HP's only new partner during the late 1980s. In 1988 and 1989 the company entered trade agreements with several companies. Hewlett-Packard cooperates with Hitachi, for microchips; Canon, for printers; Yokogawa, for logic systems; Northern Telecom, for microprocessor development systems; Sony, for digital audio tapes; Arthur Anderson, for computer-integrated-manufacturing management consulting; Samsung, for workstation development; and 3Com, for marketing and research. It also bought Eon Systems, a manufacturer of equipment that monitors computer networks and purchased a 25% stake in Hilco Technologies, a maker of factory software and a 10% share of Octel Communications, a voice-mail system supplier which also has a European distribution deal with Hewlett-Packard.

The company expects that its collaborative efforts are the key to its future. It is well-positioned for the post-1992 unified European economy, and has an enviable balance of foreign and domestic sales.

Principal Subsidiaries: Hewlett-Packard Inter-America; Hewlett-Packard Delaware, Inc.; Hewlett-Packard Pipeline Company; Hewlett-Packard Puerto Rico; Hewlett-Packard Hellas; Hewlett-Packard Finance Company; Hewlett-Packard Atlantic, Inc.; Hewlett-Packard Delaware Trading, Inc.; Fleet Systems Inc.; Hewlett-Packard Delaware Holding, Inc.; Hewlett-Packard Delaware Investment, Inc.; Hewlett-Packard European Distribution Operations Netherlands, Inc.; The Tall Tree Insurance Company; EON Systems, Inc.; Apollo Computer, Inc.; Hewlett-Packard Laboratories Japan, Inc.; Hewlett-Packard Delaware Funding, Inc.; Hewlett-Packard (Canada) Ltd.; Grupo Hewlett-Packard S.A. de C.V. (Mexico); Hewlett-Packard S.A. (Switzerland); Hewlett-Packard Australia Ltd.; Hewlett-Packard Sales (Malaysia) Sdn. Bhd.; Yokogawa Hewlett-Packard Ltd. (Japan); Hewlett-Packard Hong Kong Ltd.; Hewlett-Packard GmbH (Germany); Hewlett-Packard Penang Sdn. Bhd. (Malaysia); Hewlett-Packard Asia Limited (Hong Kong); Hewlett-Packard France; Hewlett-Packard Ireland Ltd.; Hewlett-Packard Singapore (Sales) Pte. Ltd.; Hewlett-Packard Taiwan; China Hewlett-Packard, Ltd.; Samsung Hewlett-Packard Ltd. (Korea); Hewlett-Packard FPG (Taiwan); Hewlett-Packard Italiana S.p.A. (Italy).

Further Reading: "Highlights of Hewlett-Packard Company History," Hewlett-Packard corporate typescript, 1988; "Hewlett-Packard: In Brief," Palo Alto, California, Hewlett-Packard Company, [n.d.].

—John Simley

olivetti

ING. C. OLIVETTI & C., S.P.A.

Via Jervis 77
10015 Ivrea (TO)
Italy
(125) 525
Fax: (125) 52 2524

Public Company
Incorporated: 1908
Employees: 56,937
Sales: L9.03 trillion (US$7.13 billion)
Stock Exchanges: Milan Brussels Frankfurt Paris Vienna Zürich

Long a world leader in the manufacture and sale of typewriters, in the 1980s Olivetti plunged into the information-technology market, where it has become a top European maker of computers and computer systems. Olivetti's transformation from a sleepy producer of office equipment into a multi-dimensional designer of information networks is due largely to the ambition and international perspective of the company's chairman, Carlo De Benedetti. De Benedetti and his brother Franco gained effective control of the nearly bankrupt Olivetti in 1978, and, realizing that the computer was about to alter the office-products market, began building a company that would be able to survive in the increasingly competitive international information business.

The results of their efforts have been mixed. Streamlined into four autonomous operating companies, Olivetti is probably the European computer maker best prepared to weather the post-1992 open market; but it remains a question whether any of the European information companies will be able to withstand the continued invasion of Europe by U.S. and Asian competitors.

Olivetti was founded in 1908 in the small northern Italian town of Ivrea, not far from Milan. Camillo Olivetti had been much impressed, on his various trips to the United States, with the typewriter, already well established in U.S. offices but still largely unknown in his native Italy. Olivetti pulled together a modest capital fund of L350,000 and opened his own typewriter-manufacturing plant in Ivrea, employing 20 workers.

In 1911 he exhibited the first Italian typewriter, the Olivetti M1, at the Turin Universal Exposition. The M1 was not significantly more advanced than the U.S. machines on which it was modeled but, as Olivetti commented at the time, "the aesthetic side of the machine has been carefully studied." The M1's "elegant and serious" design were typical of Olivetti. As the company grew, this preoccupation with design developed into a comprehensive corporate philosophy, which embraced everything from the shape of a space bar to the color scheme for an advertising poster. Many years later the Museum of Modern Art in New York City recognized Olivetti's enduring commitment to design by mounting an exhibition of its products and honoring the company as the West's leading design firm.

During Olivetti's first 20 years, Italy suffered the effects of World War I, uncontrolled inflation, political instability, and finally the crash and Depression of 1929. Olivetti itself, however, enjoyed remarkable and lasting success in the relatively immature Italian industrial economy. The little plant in Ivrea expanded rapidly, adding both floor space and employees as fast as they could be assimilated; yearly machine production shot up tenfold between 1914 and 1929—from 1,300 to 13,000 typewriters. As the company added new models to its line—the M20 in 1920 and M40 ten years later—it opened sales offices in six foreign countries, originating Olivetti's consistently international approach to business. In 1928 Camillo Olivetti's son Adriano had opened the company's first advertising office, which soon employed some of Europe's leading artists to communicate Olivetti's commitment to aesthetics as well as efficiency. Adriano Olivetti, born in 1901, gradually took on more of the company's management, becoming general manager and effectively head of the firm in 1933.

The Olivettis also took an interest in the living conditions of their workers. The company began building housing for its workers in 1926, and made an effort to create a corporate environment designed to foster its employees. As Adriano Olivetti gradually gained control of the family business during the 1930s, he embarked on an ambitious plan for the entire town of Ivrea, building schools, housing, roads, and recreation facilities in addition to regularly expanding the Olivetti plant itself. Olivetti founded a magazine and later a publishing house to further his social ideals, and remained a leading force in European industrial philosophy until his death.

Providing the wherewithal to support such philanthropy was Olivetti's continuing success in the marketplace. The company increased typewriter production threefold between 1929 and 1937, at which later date some 40% of its machines were of the new, portable variety introduced in 1933. Other new products were added during these years as well—office furniture, adding machines, and teleprinters—presaging the company's eventual emergence as a diversified office-products manufacturer. Olivetti went public in 1932, initially capitalized at L13 million and managed to maintain its profitability through the worst years of the Depression. Within ten years, corporate capital had tripled, employees numbered 4,700, and Olivetti machines were being exported to over 22 countries.

As World War II dragged on, however, the position of the Olivetti family, which was Jewish, became untenable. Adriano Olivetti was forced to flee the country shortly after his father's death in 1943; but when he returned at war's end, he was able to pick up the pieces quickly and join the postwar economic boom.

Olivetti enjoyed unprecedented growth in the years following the war. The company expanded its export business to include the entire industrialized world. It also acquired Underwood, the American typewriter manufacturer, and built new plants in southern Italy, Spain, Brazil, Argentina, Mexico, and the United States. Its growing collection of office products all exhibited the aesthetic sensitivity that had made Olivetti famous in the world of design, and Adriano Olivetti pursued his vision of an industrial giant responsive to the needs of both consumer and worker.

In 1959, in addition to its line of typewriters, adding machines, teleprinters, and office furniture, Olivetti unveiled the Elea 9003, Italy's first computer. This room-sized machine was built with an eye toward eventual competition with IBM and the other early computer developers, but within a few years Olivetti realized that it could not match strides with the more advanced U.S. products and abandoned the mainframe market.

Adriano Olivetti's death in 1960 brought to an end the Olivetti family's direct management of the corporation. The company employed some 40,000 people, less than half of whom worked in Italy, in 1960, and its capital had reached L40 billion. Despite an impressive list of awards and international acclaim, the company entered a period of falling profit and gradual insolvency. Olivetti found itself in need of outside capital and management, and in 1964 it was rescued by a consortium of Italian banks and industrial concerns. Bruno Visentini was made president.

When Olivetti left the mainframe market during the early 1960s, it did not ignore the electronic revolution then just beginning. In addition to converting its adding machines to what we now call calculators, the firm began manufacturing electronic typewriters, banking terminals, and telecommunications equipment. Olivetti also entered two new markets, offering the Copia 2000 line of copiers and an increasing array of industrial-automation systems, including robots and precision machine tools. Most significantly, the company continued to produce smaller computers, and by 1965 was selling both minicomputers and an early version of the desktop micro. Olivetti thus survived a period of technological change and international competition that proved to be too much for many other long-established machine manufacturers.

Olivetti survived the Asian challenge, but it did not prosper. By the end of the 1970s the firm employed a peak of 62,000 individuals, and had L1.55 trillion in sales in 1978; but with corporate debt at an alarming level, Olivetti turned once again to the financial markets for help. Carlo and Franco De Benedetti, a pair of young entrepreneurs acquired 14% of the company for a bargain price of $17 million. Carlo De Benedetti brought to Olivetti more than an infusion of capital; he pushed the company to drop its traditional corporate style. Despite the recent electronic overhaul, the company had remained relaxed and rather friendly. For years Olivetti had supported various artistic and philanthropic projects, building day-care centers for its employees as well as beautiful typewriters for its customers, but it had not been especially concerned with efficiency and profit. De Benedetti realized that such a business would not survive the challenge posed by Asian international competitiors.

Olivetti continued its expansion in the information-technology market, but with new vigor, efficiency, and aggressiveness. Olivetti accordingly added new products, like cash registers, automated teller machines (ATM), and advanced copiers, to its line of electronics systems and made a major commitment to its micro- and mini-computer divisions. Its 1982 personal computer, the M20, was widely recognized as a solid machine, but it was not IBM compatible. The following year Olivetti pushed into production the M24, which was not only IBM compatible but an attractive enough product to bring De Benedetti the international trading partner he had hoped to find. AT&T offered to sell Olivetti micros under its own name in the United States, while Olivetti would sell AT&T minis outside the United States. In addition, AT&T agreed to buy 22% of Olivetti, retaining an option on a further 18%.

The deal was signed in December 1983 and was an immediate success. AT&T sold the Olivetti machines as fast as it could get them, distributing some 200,000 units in 1986 alone, while Olivetti produced more modest but acceptable sales figures with the AT&T minis. De Benedetti made the cover of *Time* as Olivetti sales reached L7.3 trillion and profits hit L565.5 billion. Olivetti, however, was late on several key innovations in 1987. As a result, AT&T's sales fell off drastically, bringing with them Olivetti profits, and the two partners nearly ended relations in April 1988. Amid mutual recriminations, De Benedetti reaffirmed his faith in Olivetti by upping his share in the company to 20%, which also made a takeover by AT&T less likely. Profits continued to fall nevertheless, from a 1986 high to a 1988 low of L356 billion, as Olivetti's stock price and market share both took a beating in the tightening computer race.

De Benedetti took decisive action in the beginning of 1989. He and Vittorio Cassoni, the new managing director of Olivetti, completely revamped the firm's lines of command, creating four new and separate companies under the ownership of Olivetti. In order of decreasing sales, these companies are: Olivetti Systems and Networks, which handles the production and marketing of all professional level personal computers and minicomputers; Olivetti Office—which manages the bulk of the company's traditional business in fields like typewriters and calculators, as well as personal computers, photocopiers, and facsimile machines for home and office; Olivetti Information Services—which offers a wide variety of information services, including software, large-scale integration projects, and custom-tailored information networks for large users; and the Olivetti Technologies Group, a collection of 24 smaller companies engaged in the ancillary computer hardware field and the development and management of large-scale industrial projects. De Benedetti and Cassoni hope that the new organization will provide a more efficient format for Olivetti's extremely wide variety of products and technologies.

Olivetti's leadership is well regarded and bold, as demonstrated by Olivetti's ascent to the number-two position in the American ATM business, and its purchases of Acorn Computer in Great Britain and Triumph-Adler in Germany. De Benedetti is clearly commited to making Olivetti a leader in value-added information services, steering clear of head-to-head hardware battles with companies like IBM. Olivetti has apparently patched up its differences with AT&T, which remains a potentially valuable partner, but in an industry which undergoes technological revolutions every 18 months, it is hard to say who will remain a viable manufacturer of world-class computers and who will finally be remembered only as a maker of antique typewriters.

Principal Subsidiaries: Baltea S.p.A.; Olivetti-Canon Industriale S.p.A.; Ibimaint S.p.A.; Olivetti Information Services S.p.A.; Olivetti Office S.r.l.; Olivetti Systems & Networks S.r.l.; Olivetti Sanyo Industriale S.p.A.; Olteco S.p.A.; Tecnost S.p.A.; Teknecomp S.p.A.; Olivetti-Logabax S.A. (France); Scanvest Olivetti A/S (Norway); TA Triumph Adler AG (Germany); ISC-Bunker Ramo Corp. (U.S.A.); S.I.A.B. S.A. (France); Acorn Computers Ltd. (U.K.); Olivetti-Hermes S.A. (Switzerland); Pegasus Inc. (Japan); Decision Systems International; Olivetti Management of America, Inc. (U.S.A.).

Further Reading: Design Process: Olivetti 1908–1983, Ivrea, Italy, Ing. C. Olivetti & C., S.p.A., 1983; *Olivetti News,* October 1988.

—Jonathan Martin

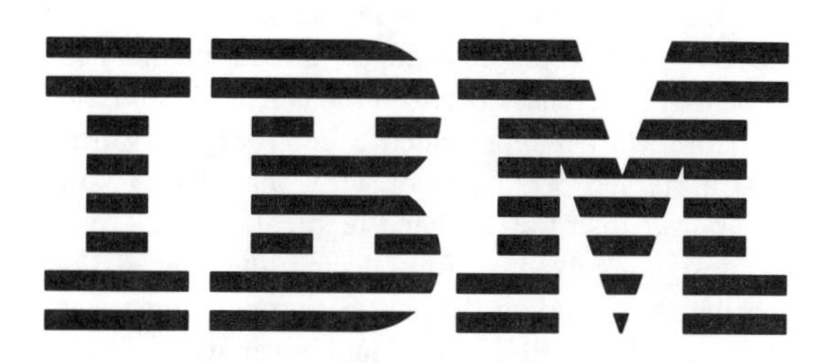

INTERNATIONAL BUSINESS MACHINES CORPORATION

Armonk, New York 10504
U.S.A.
(914) 765-1900
Fax: (914) 765-4190

Public Company
Incorporated: 1910 as Computing-Tabulating-Recording Company
Employees: 383,200
Sales: $62.71 billion
Stock Exchanges: New York Midwest Pacific Philadelphia Cincinnati Boston Paris Frankfurt Vienna Tokyo Zürich Geneva Basel Montreal Toronto Brussels London Amsterdam Lausanne

International Business Machines (IBM) may truly be said to have attained a place of mythic importance in contemporary culture. Because of its enormous size, power, and success, and because it sells that most modern of tools, the computer, IBM has come to symbolize modern life itself for many. The company's nickname—Big Blue—is a phrase that may have been originally suggested by IBM's army of uniformly dressed salesmen, whose dark suits and white shirts were required by the firm's leader, Thomas Watson Sr. Watson transformed a company called Calculating-Tabulating-Recording into a world leader in information technology known as IBM.

Calculating-Tabulating-Recording (CTR) was formed in 1910 by Charles Ranlett Flint. The so-called "father of trusts" merged two of his earlier creations, International Time Recording Company and Computing Scale Company of America, with a third, unrelated entity known as Tabulating Machine Company. The latter had been founded some years before by Herman Hollerith, an engineer who invented a machine that would sort and count cards based on the pattern of holes punched in each.

Hollerith had supplied the U.S. Census Bureau with these machines for use in the 1890 and 1900 census, and the device was quickly adopted by other organizations in need of rapid computation. As perfected, the tabulator operated in a simple three-step manner. Small cards were punched in a variety of patterns, each one representing a different category of the subject under survey; the assembled cards were run through a sorting machine, set to distribute them according to relevant categories; at the same time an accounting machine kept track of the results, and, in the later, more sophisticated models, performed any number of calculations based on those results.

Such a machine found increasing use in a society evolving rapidly into a largely urban, commercial matrix, where the ability to monitor and analyze large sums was critical to business profitability. Flint was less interested in Tabulating Machine Company than in the other two members of his new creation, which in any case got off to a slow start and threatened to stay that way.

In 1914 Flint hired a new general manager for CTR. Thomas Watson was already a well known, if not notorious, figure in U.S. business. Watson had gone to work for John Patterson at National Cash Register (NCR) in 1895 and quickly proven himself a quintessential "NCR man": bright, aggressive, and loyal, he rose to the position of general sales manager for the entire company in 1910. At Patterson's order, Watson then set up a company whose supposed purpose was to compete with NCR. The company's real purpose, however was to eliminate NCR's competitors. In 1912, along with John Patterson, his former employer at NCR, Watson was convicted of violating the Sherman Antitrust Act on behalf of the company. Shortly after Watson and Patterson were convicted, Patterson fired Watson. Watson was then hired by Charles Flint. Watson never admitted any wrongdoing, and in 1915 the government dropped its case against NCR after the company became famous for its help during a catastrophic flood in its hometown of Dayton, Ohio. The threat of a jail sentence now past, Watson was made president of CTR.

Watson understood immediately that his company's future lay in its tabulating division, and it was there that he committed most of his energy and resources. Scales and clocks were useful items, but the United States would soon be a nation of office workers in need of basic office tools like the tabulator. Watson hired many ex-NCR men and patterned his own well-disciplined sales force along NCR lines—intense competition was combined with equally intense corporate loyalty; salespeople were courteous, spotlessly dressed, and, above all, understood that CTR sold not a product but a service. A completed sale was just the beginning of the salesman's job; in effect, he had to become a partner in the customer's business, and together they designed a tabulating system for that particular organization.

As was the case at NCR, Watson's sales force became a key factor in his company's success. In a pattern that still holds today, many customers remained loyal because they trusted and to an extent relied upon the CTR salesman's knowledge of their business. Numerous, well-trained, devoted, and well-paid, the CTR sales staff actually dominated the company, ensuring that new technology followed upon the needs of customers and not the reverse. Throughout IBM's history—the company's name was changed to International Business Machines Corporation in 1924—it has been not technological leadership but massive and talented sales energy that has kept the company ahead of competitors.

Watson pushed hard in the late 1910s to make CTR the industry leader in tabulating design. He gradually turned back all boardroom challenges to his plans, and by 1925 was both chief executive officer and chief operating officer. In the ten years since Watson's arrival, CTR sales had shot up from

$4.2 million to a temporary peak of $13 million in 1919, weathered a minor crises in the early 1920s, and now stood poised to ride the booming U.S. economy. The newly named IBM faced some formidable competitors—Remington Rand, Burroughs, and NCR, among others—but from the beginning Watson steered clear of mass-produced, low-priced office products like typewriters and simple adding machines, concentrating instead on the design of large tabulating systems for governmental and private customers. With superior products and a more dedicated salesforce, by 1928 IBM was the clear leader in its specialized field and a force in office technology as a whole.

The company was remarkably profitable. In 1928, for example, its profit of $5.3 million was nearly as great as that of giant Remington Rand, though the latter more than tripled IBM's sales of $19.7 million. In 1939, IBM's profit of $9.1 million exceeded that of the next four companies combined, and was an impressive 23% of sales.

IBM's business was particularly profitable for several reasons: the company focused on large-scale, custom-built systems, an inherently less competitive segment of the business; IBM's policy of leasing, rather than selling, its machines to customers was very profitable; IBM maintained cross-licensing agreements dating back to the mid-1910s with its chief competitor, Remington Rand, preventing the two leaders from falling into competitive squabbles. The company required its customers to buy IBM cards for their IBM tabulators. The cards could not be read by any other machine. This last condition made it almost impossible for IBM customers to try other products. With literally millions of such cards already punched, IBM's clients tended to stay put.

The U.S. government filed a suit in 1932 alleging that the IBM–Remington Rand cross-licensing agreement and IBM's exclusive punch card design were anticompetitive. In 1936, after learning that IBM sold nearly 85% of all keypunch, tabulating, and accounting equipment in the United States, the Supreme Court ordered IBM to release its customers from all such card restrictions. The Court's decision had little impact on the company's growth, however. Even the Great Depression did not check IBM's progress, as most cash-pressed companies needed more numerical information not less. In addition President Franklin D. Roosevelt's New Deal created a vast federal bureaucracy in need of heavy-duty calculators made by IBM. In 1935, at the same time the Justice Department was pursuing its case against IBM, the newly formed Social Security Administration placed an order with the company for over 400 accounting machines and 1,200 keypunchers. The pattern was clear; modern society rested on massive organizations, which required machines capable of massive calculations, which were made by IBM. By the end of the 1930s Thomas Watson was enjoying praise for his enlightened employee relations as well as for his "thinking machines."

During World War II both private and governmental demand for IBM tabulators increased. The machines were needed to monitor the manufacture and movement of vast resources. Sales boomed, more than tripling to $141.7 million in five years. The war offered IBM another opportunity, less immediately exciting but in the long run of far greater importance. The armed forces needed high-speed calculators to solve a number of military problems relating to ballistics and, later, the development of the atomic bomb. Partly as a result, IBM helped build what might be called the world's first computer, the Mark I. This machine was similar to the first electromechanical calculators built a few years earlier, which used IBM punch cards to work out long arithmetic sums; the Mark I was also capable of retaining a set of rules which could be applied to any later input. Such a memory is one of the essential differences between the calculator and the computer, and the Mark I represented a great step forward. With 765,000 parts and 500 miles of wire, the Mark I still delivered less power than today's hand-held calculator.

Computer design evolved rapidly during the war. IBM joined the partnership building the new Electronic Numerical Integrator and Calculator (ENIAC) at the University of Pennsylvania. ENIAC was useful to the military and gave IBM the experience it needed to proceed with its own electronic machine. When the war ended in 1945, interest in ultra-high-speed calculators died down quickly; few outside the army needed a room-sized machine designed to analyze howitzer trajectories. Only a handful of scientists continued refining the advances won by ENIAC, eventually creating a more salable machine called UNIVAC around 1948. When IBM's old rival, Remington Rand, began to market UNIVAC in 1951, it took a significant lead in the new computer business. IBM continued its typically cautious approach. IBM waited until the new product proved its lasting appeal before leaping into the fray. Since it controlled 85% of the market for which computers were targeted, and because even electronic computers then still used IBM punch cards, Watson was not especially alarmed by Rand's success.

Thomas Watson Jr., his father's heir apparent, strongly favored an all-out push into the computer market. By the time Watson Jr. became president in 1952 he had won the struggle with his father and led IBM into an immense research program designed to surpass Rand. The new president staked his reputation, as well as a significant portion of IBM's assets, on the computer campaign and by 1955 IBM's new 705 general purpose business computer was a success. By the following year Remington Rand had already lost its lead. It was no surprise that IBM came to dominate in computers so quickly, since at that time the computer business was only a small segment of the office-products market, which IBM continued to control. The 85% of offices using IBM tabulating equipment simply switched over to IBM computers.

In 1949 Thomas Watson's younger brother, Dick Watson, was also brought into the business. The 30-year-old Dick Watson was named president of IBM World Trade Corporation, the parent company's new subsidiary for international sales. In 1949 World Trade had sales of only $6.3 million but operated in 58 countries. In the more important of these countries World Trade set up a subsidiary to market IBM products and even do additional research and development. Thus, as the world's industrial powers awoke to the computer age, they found themselves greeted by IBM. It was not unusual for local IBM units to achieve market domination comparable to that of the parent company in the United States. Only in Japan and the United Kingdom were local competitors able to match IBM's presence, forcing the latter to settle for around 33% of the market. Barely on the sales map in 1949, World Trade eventually surpassed IBM domestic in total revenue.

Meanwhile, the U.S. computer business filled up with potential rivals. Some of these, like RCA, General Electric, and the newly merged Sperry Rand, were as large as or larger than IBM and should have been able to mount a serious challenge. In every case, however, competitors either lacked an adequate sales organization or were not fully committed to the commercial computer business. RCA, for example, made important contributions to computer technology, but mainly with an eye toward possible applications in its growing television business. Sperry Rand, on the other hand, still controlled the successful UNIVAC machine but was hopelessly behind IBM in sales experience and customer loyalty.

In 1952 the government filed a second, more ambitious antitrust suit against IBM. In 1956 IBM entered into a consent decree which ordered it to divest many of its card-production facilities, sell its machines as well as lease them, submit to certain cross-licensing agreements, and create a subsidiary to compete with itself in the service end of the business. None of these injunctions limited IBM's success, but the 1957 appearance of a small company called Control Data did.

Control Data Corporation (CDC) was a pioneer in niche specialization in the computer world. This tactic seemed to be the only way to compete successfully with IBM. The newcomer made very large, very fast computers for scientific and governmental users in need of maximum crunching power, and after a brief battle, IBM largely ceded the field to CDC. IBM's bread and butter remained the medium to large business computer.

In 1958 Sperry Rand and Control Data brought out the first second-generation computers, which used transistors instead of vacuum tubes. No sooner had IBM met this challenge with its own line of transistorized machines, than it faced the arrival of the industry's third generation—integrated circuitry. Once again IBM lagged in technological change as Honeywell and CDC brought out the first integrated circuit units in the early 1960s, but this time Big Blue's response necessitated a companywide revolution. Integrated circuitry was clearly destined to become the industry standard, and IBM decided to bring out a complete line of such computers. After an unprecedented capital-spending program involving six new plants and many thousands of new workers, the company introduced its 360 line in April 1965. Small, fast, and accompanied by a new set of exclusive software, the 360s were an immediate and lasting success, remaining the worldwide computer leader for more than a decade.

Sperry Rand, GE, Burroughs, RCA, Honeywell, NCR, and Control Data were unable to close the gap between themselves and IBM, which now delivered 65% of all U.S. computers. Control Data filed yet another antitrust suit in 1968, charging that IBM had sold "phantom" computers to its customers to keep them from placing orders for superior CDC products. The government filed its own suit the following year, supporting CDC's claims and alleging other monopolistic practices. Encouraged by these efforts, IBM's competitors, big and small, filed 22 similar lawsuits in the next few years. IBM beat back every one of them, however, with one exception. The Justice Department continued its battle for 13 years, until President Ronald Reagan's administration dropped the suit shortly before a ruling was expected.

Niche specialization was clearly the only way to survive in the face of IBM's power. In 1960 Digital Equipment Corporation (DEC) brought out a relatively small, inexpensive computer designed for researchers, effectively creating the micro-computer business. Micros were only a further step in the evolution of the computer, but IBM chose not to enter the market. DEC was soon joined by a host of other micro manufacturers offering a wide range of computers for ever smaller tasks, culminating years later in Apple's marketing of the personal computer for home use. IBM failed to join this race until 1980, at which late date it was unable to dominate the market, as it does mainframes and minicomputers.

In 1971 Tom Watson retired from IBM after suffering a heart attack. His successor, Frank Cary, remained in charge until 1981, at which time John Opel was named CEO. Under these men and IBM's present Chairman, John Akers, the 360 line of computers grew into the 370. Sales continued to climb and corporate profit hit $3 billion by 1980. Yet many observers felt that IBM was drifting, and, in 1985, for the first time in 20 years the company's earnings actually declined a bit.

The mid-1980s brought more steady but unspectacular growth. IBM began to lose sight of customer preferences, and the computer industry became increasingly competitive. In addition, the decade's biggest opportunity seemed to fizzle before it got started: Integrated services data networks—or the merging of telecommunications and information technology—may result in intense competition between IBM and AT&T. IBM thus took a 16% stake in MCI, one of AT&T's chief competitors, and in 1985 bought the California-based PBX-maker Rolm for $1.5 billion. Rolm's PBX, or private branch exchange systems allow very large operations to process hundreds of calls at one time. Three years later, however, it had sold the MCI stock, bartered away much of its Rolm interests, and seemed to be withdrawing from integrated services. Results for the last five years of the 1980s were not encouraging: the firm reported disappointing earnings and cut 37,000 jobs.

IBM remains supreme in larger computers; its 370 mainframe holds about 70% of that market. Critics, however, note that the mainframe market is shrinking relative to other computer businesses, which will leave IBM vulnerable. New companies continue to chip away at Big Blue's customers. Computers seem to be getting smaller, and are being tailored to customer needs, as more companies explore the advantages of distributed data networks. Furthermore, IBM's business may be affected by the continued incursion of Japanese manufacturers.

Principal Subsidiaries: IBM Credit Corporation; Satellite Transponder Leasing Corporation; IBM World Trade Corporation.

Further Reading: Sobel, Robert, *IBM: Colossus in Transition,* New York, Times Books, 1981; DeLamarter, Richard Thomas, *Big Blue: IBM's Use and Abuse of Power,* New York, Dodd, Mead & Company, 1986.

—Jonathan Martin

NCR CORPORATION

1700 South Patterson Boulevard
Dayton, Ohio 45479
U.S.A.
(513) 445-5000
Fax: (513) 445-1418

Public Company
Incorporated: 1900 as National Cash Register Company
Employees: 56,000
Sales: $5.96 billion
Stock Exchanges: New York London Zürich Basel Geneva

When National Cash Register Company was formed during the 19th century, it had one product—cash registers. Today NCR, as it is now known, develops and markets a wide range of computer and terminal systems; office-automation products; automated teller, data processing, and tele-communications services; semiconductor components; soft-ware; and business forms and supplies.

NCR's first years were shaped largely by John Henry Patterson, who was president from 1884 to 1921. Patterson's early emphasis on sales, his initiation of business practices which became standards for other companies and industries, and his pioneering efforts in industrial welfare made NCR a role model for other companies during the late 1800s and early 1900s.

While running a dry-goods operation in Ohio during the early 1880s, Patterson found he was losing money because not all sales were being reported by his clerks. When Patterson learned of a device called a cash register, he ordered two from James and John Ritty, who had recently established a Dayton, Ohio–based company called National Cash Register. In 1882 the Rittys sold part of their company and renamed it the National Manufacturing Company.

Patterson, meanwhile, was reaping such financial rewards from the use of his cash registers that he bought stock in the Ritty's company. He eventually joined the board of directors and suggested that the company use nationwide marketing techniques to sell its cash registers. Patterson's ideas met with opposition, and in 1884 he bought additional stock and took control of the company. Once president, Patterson again named the company National Cash Register Company.

Patterson moved quickly to change NCR's emphasis from manufacturing to sales. His interest in sales led to the concept of quotas and guaranteed sales territories for agents. Patterson also provided his agents with sales seminars, training brochures, and scripted sales pitches, and required them to wear white shirts and dark suits. All of these practices were new at the time but soon became widespread at other-companies.

Cash register sales responded almost immediately to Patterson's techniques. Sales more than doubled to 1,000 machines a year by 1886, while by 1888 the number of NCR employees had grown from about 12 to over 100. About this time Patterson also began to produce various forms of printed advertising. Beginning in the late 1880s, prospective customers were inundated with weekly or monthly advertising circulars and direct-mail letters describing products. Employees' publications were introduced to bolster communication and enthusiasm about meeting sales quotas. *Output*—the first employee newspaper—listed sales, discussed the benefits of cash registers, and printed encouraging words from satisfied customers. During his first decade, Patterson also established an international division.

Poor economic conditions in the 1890s affected NCR like many other companies in the United States. Between 1892 and 1897 the company's production was reduced and employees worked scaled-down weeks. The company also looked more closely at the manufacturing side of business. A system of interchangeable parts for cash register models was introduced, streamlining production and trimming overhead.

In 1894 the company constructed a new and larger ''safety-conscious'' facility in Dayton with the aid of bank loans. The following year Patterson hired Thomas J. Watson, who rose quickly through the sales ranks to become a sales manager in New York and later became part of an inner circle of Dayton executives. It was Watson who led the campaign to reduce competition, including a massive advertising blitz as well as an adamant defense of patents. By 1897, NCR's competition had been reduced to three companies, down from over 80 a decade before.

In 1900 NCR reported the sale of its 200,000th cash register, and employed 2,269 people. That same year the company was chartered as a New Jersey corporation for the purpose of selling stock. Construction of a ten-building facility began in 1906, and overseas operations were growing as well. In a company publication that year, NCR boasted that its sales force extended from Norway and Alaska to New Zealand and China, with nearly 1,000 agents in more than 270 offices.

That same year a young inventor named Charles F. Kettering gave the company its first electric cash register. Kettering, who had been hired just two years earlier, also developed NCR's Class 1000 machine, a low-cost redesigned register which remained in production for nearly 40 years with only minor changes. Kettering left the company in 1909 and joined the automotive industry.

Spurred by the success of Kettering's cash register and the Class 1000 machine, sales continued to climb throughout the early 1900s. By 1911 the one millionth machine had been sold. NCR's aggressive battle to secure patent rights and fend off competition led the American Cash Register Company to file an antitrust complaint based on the recently approved Sherman Act. In 1912 the government brought NCR to trial and presented 32 cases of alleged trade interference. The following year Patterson, Watson, and 20 other officers were found guilty of trade restraint and unlawful monopoly in three of those cases. Two years later the decision was reversed by a higher court.

The Dayton Flood of 1913 brought another kind of prominence to NCR. Under Patterson's leadership, the company responded to the flood by suspending all operations and providing relief shelter in company facilities. In 1913 Watson left the company after a falling out with Patterson.

During the early stages of the World War I, NCR continued to make cash registers while involved in wartime production contracts with the government. By 1919 the company was operating almost solely on a wartime production basis.

John Henry Patterson passed the reins of the company presidency in 1921 to his son Frederick Beck Patterson. In 1922 Frederick Patterson also assumed the duties of the chairman of the board after his father's death. The 1920s marked NCR's gradual entrance into its accounting-machine era. NCR already had proved its dominance in the cash register field, having controlled over 95% of that market prior to the outbreak of the war. In 1921 NCR announced its class 2000 itemizer, which provided 30 totals and embodied what the company believed were the best features of all previous registers.

Frederick Patterson exercised voting control over NCR after the death of his father, while Comptroller Stanley C. Allyn and director John H. Barringer led the company's first major diversification drive. The company's profits rose from $2.8 million in 1921 to $7.8 million in 1925. Because of its success, the company went public with stock sales for the first time.

The 1920s were good years for office-equipment firms. After 1925, competitors made inroads into the cash register market, while NCR failed to introduce new products. Sales flattened for NCR, and by 1928 Remington Rand topped the list of business-machine companies, taking in $59 million to second-running NCR's $49 million. Young IBM was fourth at the time with $19 million reported in sales.

In attempts to hasten the diversification drive, NCR purchased the Ellis Adding-Typewriter Company in January 1929. That same year the company announced the class 3000, NCR's first hybrid machine, which represented a step up in the area of payroll, billing, and accounting operations. The promise of the new machine was dampened by the Depression later that year. Sales and earnings plunged while the company began a four-year process of cutting the number of its employees in half. With the company nearly bankrupt by 1931, New York bankers Dillon, Read and Company, who had set up the 1925 stock sales, were ready to invade the company.

Quick action was needed. NCR's board of directors sought out Edward Deeds to take control of the company, and Frederick Patterson agreed to step down as chairman in 1931. Patterson remained as president until Deeds assumed that additional post in 1936, and it was Deeds who turned things around. Joining NCR at the beginning of the century, Deeds had been put in charge of engineering and construction for a new factory. By 1910 he had become vice president. Deeds left NCR for Delco in 1915, and later helped found the Wright Airplane Company with Orville Wright, Charles Kettering and H.E. Talbott. Deeds's success by 1931 was evident, as he sat on the corporate boards of 28 companies.

Shortly after Deeds took control, the company purchased the Remington Cash Register Company, whose assets strengthened NCR's position. In 1934 the company moved back into the black. Despite broad price fluctuations, by mid-decade sales were stabilizing and overseas operations were expanding in Great Britain, Europe, Central America, South America, and the Middle East and Far East. By the end of the decade NCR was third in the business-machine field behind Remington and fast-climbing IBM. NCR in 1939 earned $12 million less than it did the year prior to the Depression. In 1940 Stanley Allyn assumed the post of president, while Deeds continued to serve as chairman and chief executive.

World War II had a significant impact on NCR, as well as on other data-processing and business-machine companies, spurring the conversion from office tabulating equipment to data processing. By the time the United States entered the war in 1941, NCR's expansion into Central America and South America in the 1930s had become important, and helped to offset the wartime reduction or elimination of operations in Japan, Germany, and Australia. For the next few years the sale of rebuilt machines was the only business NCR continued in countries directly involved in the war. By 1942, the U.S. War Production Board halted the manufacturing of all cash registers in order to conserve metal.

Wartime contracts for such items as bomb fuses and rocket motors covered the overhead during the war, while reconditioning of machines provided modest profits. An in-house research program in the electronics field developed prior to the war paid dividends when the navy asked NCR to build a computer-like device to calculate bombing navigational data. NCR worked on a secret operation for the navy to help break the German ENIGMA communication cipher. The company produced the Bombe, a high-speed electromechanical decrypting machine, building 120 Bombes during the course of the war. This project remained secret until its declassification in the 1980s.

By the war's end a pent-up market for cash registers and accounting machines resulted in a hiring surge for the company in Dayton. Business boomed after the war. Between 1946 and 1949 NCR reestablished itself in war-torn areas of the United Kingdom, West Germany, and Japan. Improvements and expansion continued into the early 1950s, with a rebuilt plant in Australia, a new factory in Toronto, and new office buildings in Hawaii and Mexico.

NCR continued its electronics work begun during the war years and in 1952 secured a defense contract for a bombing navigational computer. That same year NCR entered into a stock-purchase agreement with Computer Research Corporation, which became NCR's electronics division the following year. Development of a computer geared toward scientific work had limited impact, and the company's role in the computer industry remained conservative in the mid-1950s. The 1956 introduction of the Post-Tronic, an electronic posting machine for banking, was successful. Sales of the Post-Tronic eventually passed the $100 million mark before the machine passed out of use near the end of the 1960s.

With NCR on the edge of new era, the aging Deeds retired as chairman in 1957 and was succeeded by Allyn. Robert S. Oelman, who had been instrumental in procuring wartime contracts as a company vice president, became president. Later that year NCR announced the 304, a general-purpose computer based on solid-state technology. NCR's first ''small'' computer debuted in 1960. This computer, the 390, was manufactured by Control Data Corporation (CDC) for NCR.

In the early 1960s NCR increased its development of computers, as well as peripheral devices and software. In 1962 Oelman became chairman of the board and R. Stanley Laing was named president two years later. Mid-decade saw NCR continue to operate under a split strategy of selling products to its old customer line as well as to new customers in the data-processing market. NCR's computer-related products were successful, but its innovations still remained conservative and the company's marketplace continued to revolve around banking and retailing.

In the 1960s NCR formed its business forms and supply division. In the late 1960s, NCR became known as one of the ''Seven Dwarfs,'' because of its relative position of inferiority to IBM. Joining NCR in these ranks were General Electric (GE), RCA, Burroughs, UNIVAC, CDC, and Honeywell. With GE and RCA bowing out of the computer field in the early 1970s, the five remaining became known as the BUNCH, an acronym made up of the first letter of each name.

NCR announced its third generation of computers in 1968 with the introduction of the Century Series. The series included a variety of business applications and allowed NCR to market its wares to a broader customer base. NCR's failure to take advantage of new conditions calling for terminals and software cost it some market share and resulted in a trend of declining profits from 1969 to 1972.

The first half of the 1970s marked the greatest transition period in the history of NCR, as it attempted to move full-force into the computer market. The period was marred by a number of setbacks that were worsened by an inflationary economy and poor business climate. Labor costs to produce older technology products were enormous, and the company also had marketing problems. Layoffs followed declining earnings and the company was hit by a three-month strike at its Dayton plant in late 1971. The strike idled 8,500 production and maintenance employees, sharply reduced equipment deliveries, and cost the company millions of dollars in lost orders.

In 1971 NCR entered into a cooperative agreement with CDC to establish a computer peripherals company. The following year NCR established its microelectronics division. Declining profits continued through 1972, and NCR posted its first net loss since 1933.

With revenues on shaky ground, William S. Anderson was named president in 1972 and chairman of the board in 1974. Anderson, who had been successful in heading up NCR's Far East operations and NCR Japan, was the first president to come from outside the parent company. His success in Japan was due in part to revamping the company's marketing organization there, and as president, Anderson quickly moved to modify NCR's marketing structure through a similar ''vocationalizing'' system. The branch-manager system, in which a branch manager was responsible for sales from a number of different industries, was replaced by a system where a district manager oversaw one major marketing area, and marketing personnel were trained to specialize in a single vocational area. Areas of specialization included retail, finance, commercial business, industrial, medical, educational, governmental, and media. In 1974, NCR reported its computer business was finally out of the red. That same year the company's name was changed from National Cash Register to NCR Corporation.

NCR began making great strides in the computer field after naming Charles E. Exley Jr. president in 1976. A 22-year veteran of Burroughs Corporation, Exley oversaw the introduction of a new series of computers and related equipment during the later part of the decade. NCR's 1976 announcement of the 8000 series was well received, and improvements were made throughout the remainder of the decade.

NCR's push into computers resulted in strong earnings, while the company began a series of smaller company acquisitions that boosted expertise in factory data systems, microcards, and IBM-compatible data systems. In fewer than five years NCR revamped its entire product line. During this time the company withdrew from the mainframe computer arena and moved closer to its traditional core industries such as banking and retailing. In 1979 the company passed the $3 billion revenue mark.

NCR came into the 1980s strong, posting its first double-digit increase in revenue in 1980, but strong growth stalled in 1981, and earnings dropped. Product lines besieged by bugs in the late 1970s resulted in user lawsuits being filed against NCR in the early 1980s. In 1980 a lawsuit was filed by the small Oakland, California, drycleaning firm Glovatorium. Glovatorium, a first-time computer user, had purchased an NCR Spirit/8200 system to do routine accounting, but the system failed to work. NCR defended its case on the grounds that contracts with Glovatorium had contained limitations of liability and disclaimers. The California judge ruling in the case in 1981 said NCR had targeted first-time computer users and was under a special obligation to be fair in dealing with the user. Punitive damages totaling $2 million were awarded along with compensatory damages for breach of warranty and intentional misrepresentation. The following year NCR agreed to a $2.6 million settlement with Glovatorium. The Tower family of microcomputers was introduced in 1982, and became one of the keys to NCR's success in the mid-1980s.

In 1983 Exley was named chief executive officer and in the following year board chairman. Under Exley, NCR underwent a corporate restructuring process, made a push back into personal computers, began reemphasizing fiscal control, and started a long-term plan of repurchasing its own stock. By 1986 NCR was again posting double-digit increases, while most of the computer industry was suffering from a market recession.

NCR's revenue had grown to $6 billion by 1988, as the company developed customized products that generated significant indirect sales. Meanwhile NCR's microelectronic division became a leading producer of semiconductors, and the company surpassed IBM as the largest worldwide supplier of automatic teller machines (ATMs). Personal computers and the Tower microcomputers also saw significant sales gains in the emphasis switch from mainframes to distribution processing.

In 1988 Gilbert P. Williamson was promoted from executive vice president to president, while Exley remained chairman and CEO. The following year overall sales began to dip, although foreign sales were rising. The company closed out the decade as the last thriving member of the BUNCH that had avoided a merger or sellout of interests.

NCR expected to keep its products on par with the computer industry's powerhouses. In late 1989 it announced it was jumping into the market for microcomputers that were based on a powerful new microchip. The announcement helped NCR land an agreement with Businessland Inc. to begin selling the new line in 1990.

According to Exley, NCR entered the 1990s with a goal to "reach all markets." The company had operations in nine countries with products sold in more than 120 countries. NCR expected continued success in the ATM and semiconductor markets and expanded sales in transaction- and information-processing markets. The company also expected indirect sales to increase, with a number of NCR-manufactured products being sold bearing other companies' labels.

NCR looked for benefits from the implementation of "concurrent engineering," to keep its operations on par with Japanese competitors through a more-timely and less-costly manufacture of products. Concurrent engineering eliminated a number of independent steps of production, some which had been contracted out, and replaced that system with one where design engineers and manufacturing personnel collaborated in a closer working environment, thereby reducing the time needed to correct glitches. NCR had introduced concurrent engineering in 1987 in its new Atlanta, Georgia, plant and by the 1990s the concept was implemented to some degree in all of NCR's manufacturing facilities.

Principal Subsidiaries: NCR Nederland N.V. (Netherlands); NCR Australia Pty. Ltd.; NCR Canada Ltd.; NCR France, S.A.; NCR GmbH (Germany); NCR Japan Ltd.; NCR Espana, S.A. (Spain); NCR (Switzerland); NCR Ltd. (U.K.); Applied Digital Data Systems, Inc.; NCR Danmark A/S (Denmark); NCR Argentina SAIC; NCR de Mexico, S.A. de C.V.

Further Reading: Crowther, Samuel, *John H. Patterson, Pioneer in Industrial Welfare,* New York, Doubleday, Page & Company, 1923; Allyn, Stanley C., *My Half Century with NCR,* New York, McGraw-Hill, 1967; McClellan, Stephen T., *The Coming Computer Industry Shakeout,* New York, John Wiley & Sons, 1984; *Celebrating the Future, 1884-1984,* Dayton, Ohio, NCR Corporation, 1984; Bernstein, Mark, "John Patterson rang up success with the Incorruptible Cashier," *Smithsonian,* June 1989.

—Roger W. Rouland

NIXDORF COMPUTER AG

Fürstenalle 7
D-4790 Paderborn
Federal Republic of Germany
(05251) 150
Fax: (05251) 15-1105

Wholly Owned Subsidiary of Siemens AG
Incorporated: 1952 as Labor für Impulstechnik
Employees: 28,000
Sales: DM5.26 billion (US$3.11 billion)

For much of the postwar era Nixdorf Computer epitomized the *Wirtschaftswunder,* Germany's extraordinary recovery from the devastation of war. From its headquarters in the provincial town of Paderborn, Nixdorf built a worldwide reputation for quality and innovation in the field of small- and medium-sized computers, becoming a source of considerable pride in a country still suffering from the war's physical and psychological wounds. In the year following the death of Heinz Nixdorf, the charismatic founder and owner of the corporation, Nixdorf was honored as 1987's "most admired German company." After a decade of more than 20% annual sales growth, profit in that year reached an all-time high of DM264 million and there was talk of Nixdorf eventually challenging the world's computer leaders.

All the more shocking, therefore, were the events of the following 18 months, during which short time Nixdorf profits dwindled and then disappeared in a sea of red ink. By late 1989 the erstwhile pride of Germany was headed for bankruptcy, a victim of one of the sudden storms that periodically lash the international computer industry. Nixdorf family members and their powerful allies at Deutsche Bank insisted that the corporation remain in German hands, and in early 1990 the industrial giant Siemens gathered up the remains of Nixdorf for about $350 million. Heinz Nixdorf's miraculous creation remained Nixdorf in name alone, but Germany as a whole maintained control of one of its symbols of economic strength.

Heinz Nixdorf was born in Paderborn in 1925, the son of a railway clerk. After service in the Luftwaffe at the end of World War II, he enrolled at Frankfurt University to study physics and business but left before taking a degree. With a small amount of borrowed capital, Nixdorf founded his own company, the Labor für Impulstechnik, in a basement workshop in Essen in 1952. He devised and built a calculator using radio tubes and sold it to West Germany's largest electrical utility, the Rheinische Westfalische Elektrizitatswerke. Word spread of Nixdorf's innovative machines, and Impulstechnik began supplying some of Europe's leading electrical manufacturers with products they later sold under their own names. Chief among these customers were Groupe Bull of France and Wanderer Werke in West Germany.

When the former was bought out by General Electric in 1964 the resulting drop in Nixdorf sales taught its founder an important lesson. Henceforth his company would not rely on such unpredictable relationships with industrial giants; it would manufacture and sell its own equipment. Nixdorf developed a line of calculators and billing machines superior to those it supplied to Wanderer and quickly proceeded to outsell its own best customer. Nixdorf soon simplified matters by buying out Wanderer—considered a remarkable coup for a 15-year-old company. Nixdorf thus acquired extensive production facilities and a widespread sales force, with which it set about revolutionizing the use of computers in small businesses and banking.

In the mid-1960s few people yet envisaged any but IBM's theory of computer utilization, in which ever-larger central processing units handled a growing amount of corporate data from a single location. Heinz Nixdorf recognized that most companies did not need more computational muscle; they needed to put such tools to work efficiently. To do so, they required two elements IBM was not particularly interested in supplying—small, versatile computers and a sales force willing to tailor such machines to the specific needs of each customer. This strategy was not only generally sound but also addressed the realities of the West German economy, whose companies tended to be smaller, family-owned concerns not capable of IBM-style investments but still in need of computing efficiency. For these users Nixdorf brought out its 820 general-purpose minicomputer in 1968, adding both the sales force and software needed to adapt such a machine to the daily needs of each small-business client. As a result of this campaign, Nixdorf sales rose from DM28 million in 1966 to DM263 million four years later, beginning the pattern of explosive growth that did not end until the debacle of 1989.

During the 1970s Nixdorf continued to defy conventional wisdom by exploiting the niche it had uncovered. The company's first international sale provided the Swedish banking industry with 1,000 terminals for its various branch locations, and by 1972 Nixdorf had opened sales and manufacturing centers in 21 other countries as well. The most important foreign target was the United States, but Nixdorf met with only limited success in the U.S. market. In 1969 it bought the electronic division of Victor Comptometer, a U.S. manufacturer of office equipment, and in 1977 it added the Massachusetts-based Entrex, Inc., but at no time was Nixdorf able to gain more than 1% of the U.S. market. It was not that the company seemed in need of additional sales. By 1978 Nixdorf had passed the DM1 billion mark and employed some 10,000 people around the world.

Heinz Nixdorf and his family still owned 100% of the company stock, which some observers felt gave Nixdorf a decided advantage over its main German competitor, Siemens, a multi-billion-mark conglomerate unable to keep up with the rapidly changing computer world. While such a concentration of ownership offered more flexibility and the ability to move quickly, it also limited the company's capital base, however, and in 1978 Nixdorf dallied with a number of suitors eager to buy up large chunks of the corporation. But the entrepreneur refused to relinquish control, instead making a conditional sale of 25% of his stock to long-time ally Deutsche Bank in 1979.

In addition to its traditional strength in small businesses and banking, Nixdorf expanded in 1974 to provide information services for the retail sector. Nixdorf's retail involvement primarily involved point-of-sale equipment, an area in which the company became one of the European leaders. The fourth leg of Nixdorf's marketing platform was in place by 1982, when its new telecommunications division created Germany's first digital telephone switching system. Heinz Nixdorf predicted that telecommunications would provide 50% of corporate revenue by the century's end, as the gradual convergence of telecommunication and computer systems opened a vast new field known as integrated service digital networks.

To pursue such goals Nixdorf needed yet more capital, and in 1984 the company made its first public offering of stock, first in West Germany and then also on the Swiss markets. Response was outstanding, as expected for a company whose 1984 sales had reached DM3.27 billion and continued to climb at about 21% per year. Heinz Nixdorf had become something of a legend in his native land; the employer of 20,000 skilled German workers was a symbol of that country's unflagging determination to remain a world leader in the crucial computer industry.

When the founder died unexpectedly of a heart attack while dancing at a company party in March 1986 his employees were stunned, but none doubted that under new chairman Klaus Luft the Nixdorf ascent would continue. At that time the company offered both a full line of IBM-compatible minicomputers, workstations, and terminals, and a new series of TARGON machines using the UNIX "open" operating system—the only real competitor to that of IBM.

Nixdorf was Europe's largest seller of software and had built perhaps the world's most dedicated, knowledgeable sales force to help its many smaller customers make intelligent use of the machines and programs they purchased. The company always worked from the customer to the machine, not vice versa, in that way earning the kind of loyalty that ensures repeat sales. For all of these reasons, therefore, the financial community was puzzled when it became apparent that 1988 profits were not going to be as spectacular as Nixdorf had expected. As the months went by, a rather embarrassed Klaus Luft admitted that profits would indeed not be spectacular at all, except in a wholly negative sense: profits for the year were DM26 million, down 90% from the previous year's record DM264 million.

The year 1989 proved to be an unprecedented nightmare for Nixdorf. A first half loss of DM297 million snowballed into a second half nearly twice as bad. Since Deutsche Bank and the Nixdorf family—who still controlled 100% of the voting stock—were determined to keep the company in German hands, the Siemens buyout was the most advantageous solution.

Nixdorf was overcome by an unfortunate combination of factors largely outside its control. The company suffered a triple blow from the economy at large. The price of computer chips skyrocketed; the Nixdorf mix of sales shifted rapidly from high-margin bank installations to low-margin office and retail work; and, most importantly, increased world competition and standardization of products severely depressed hardware prices. The international movement toward so-called open systems means that an increasing percentage of equipment is interchangeable, which drives standard part prices down and forces competitors to "add value" to their own products in order to justify a higher final price. Nixdorf thus found itself paying more for the computer chips with which it assembled machines that sold only at lower prices. The element the company could have better managed was the excessive growth of its highly paid personnel, most of them software designers and engineers.

Despite such difficulties, Siemens was happy to pay US$350 million—a good price—for its smaller cousin. The acquisition gave Siemens a strong position in the midrange computer market, where it was previously weak, and made the parent company the seventh-largest computer maker in the world. For the Nixdorf family, the deal brought to an abrupt end one of Germany's most successful postwar economic creations, as another maverick entrepreneur was swallowed up by a larger competitor whom only a few years before it had consistently outperformed in the marketplace.

Principal Subsidiaries: Nixdorf Computer Leasing GmbH; Nixdorf Computer GmbH & Co. Verwaltung; Nixdorf Computer Datenverarbeitungssysteme GmbH; Nixdorf Computer Miete GmbH; Nixdorf Entwicklungsgesellschaft fur Kommunikationstechnik mbH; Nixdorf Microprocessor Engineering GmbH; Nixdorf Software Engineering GmbH; Nixdorf Computer Pty. Ltd. (Australia); Nixdorf Computer Ges. m.b.H. (Austria); Nixdorf Computer SA (Belgium); Nixdorf Computer Canada Ltd.; Nixdorf Computer China Ltd. (Hong Kong); Nixdorf Computer A/S (Denmark); OY Nixdorf Computer AB (Finland); Nixdorf Computer France SA; Nixdorf Computer SA (France); Nixdorf Computer Lyon SA (France); Nixdorf Computer Distribution SA (France); Nixdorf Computer Ltd. (U.K.); Nixdorf Computer AE (Greece); Nixdorf Computer Ltd. (Hong Kong); Nixdorf International Financial Services Ltd. (Republic of Ireland); Nixdorf Computer International Ltd. (Republic of Ireland); Nixdorf Computer Ltd. (Republic of Ireland); Nixdorf Computer S.p.A. (Italy); Nixdorf Computer Japan K.K.; Nixdorf Computer SA (Luxembourg); Nixdorf Computer SA (Morocco); Nixdorf Computer B.V. (Netherlands); Nixdorf International Finance B.V. (Netherlands); Nixdorf Computer Ltd. (New Zealand); Nixdorf Computer A/S (Norway); Nixdorf Computer (Singapore) Pte. Ltd.; Nixdorf Computer International Singapore Pte. Ltd.; Nixdorf Regional Headquarters Pte. Ltd. (Singapore); Nixdorf Computer (Pty) Ltd. (South Africa); Nixdorf Computer SA (Spain); Nixdorf Computer AB (Sweden); Nixdorf Computer AG (Switzerland); Nixdorf Computer Ticaret A.Ş. (Turkey, 51%); Nixdorf Computer Corporation (U.S.A.); Nixdorf Computer Engineering Corporation (U.S.A.); Nixdorf Computer C.A. (Venezuela).

Further Reading: "Nixdorf 1952–1988: History of a Company," Nixdorf corporate typescript, [1988].

—Jonathan Martin

Pitney Bowes

PITNEY BOWES INC.

One Elmcroft Road
Stamford, Connecticut 06926
(203) 356-5000
Fax: (203) 351-6303

Public Company
Incorporated: 1920 as Pitney-Bowes Postage Meter Company
Employees: 31,404
Sales: $2.88 billion
Stock Exchanges: New York Midwest Philadelphia Boston

Pitney Bowes (PB) is the world's largest supplier of postage meters. It has regular operations in 16 countries and markets in over 120. PB's operations are focused in three areas: business equipment, including mailing, copying, facsimile, and voice-processing systems; business supplies, such as price-marking and merchandise-identification equipment; and financial services, primarily lease financing. Pitney Bowes built its reputation on its postage meter. The company remains the world's leading maker and lessor of the machines—the postal service does not allow their sale, for fear of tampering—that were its primary products in the early years.

Arthur Pitney patented his postage-stamping machine in 1902 and spent the next 12 years fine-tuning it and attempting to enlist both the postal service's acceptance and financial backing. To the U.S. Post Office, confronted with the impracticality of the adhesive postage stamp in the face of the increasing volume of mail, Pitney's machine offered a solution. It would stamp the mail at its source and keep track of the amount of postage used, saving labor and decreasing costs for both businesses and the postal service. Tested with impressive results by the post office in Pitney's hometown of Chicago in 1914, ultimate approval of the machine did not come until after World War I.

Meanwhile, in New York, Walter Bowes's Universal Stamping Machine Company was doing brisk business with the U.S. Postal Service, providing stamp-cancelling machines on a rental basis. Bowes also had some foreign success, selling his machines in Germany, England, and Canada. In 1917 Bowes moved his operations to Stamford, Connecticut, now the headquarters of Pitney Bowes. Although Bowes's machine was profitable, he worried that Pitney's similar invention would render it obsolete. Thus, in April, 1920, the two men decided to pool their resources.

The merger of Pitney's American Postage Meter Company and Bowes's Universal Stamping Machine Company created the Pitney-Bowes Postage Meter Company. The day after the merger officially took effect, Pitney and Bowes succeeded in pushing legislation through Congress to allow all classes of mail to be posted by meters instead of stamps, and the Pitney-Bowes postage meter was licensed for use throughout the postal system.

By 1922 PB had branch offices in 12 cities and 404 postage meters in operation. In the same year, Bowes's previous international experience paid off and PB's postage meter was approved for use in England and Canada. PB experienced early growing pains, however. As the meter gained exposure in the early 1920s, demand for the machines began to outstrip PB's ability to manufacture, distribute, and service them. Also, it was felt in many quarters that PB enjoyed a government-created monopoly. Thus, in its first decade of existence, PB's scope of operations was limited by government regulation—lobbied for by PB's competition—restricting PB from reaping the advantages of its technologically superior product.

In 1924 Arthur Pitney retired from the company after a dispute with Bowes and started a company of his own, manufacturing postage-permit machines to compete with PB's meters. Uncertainty reigned at PB, and Walter Wheeler II, Bowes's stepson, was promoted from New York branch manager to general manager in Stamford in an attempt to find new leadership and new direction.

PB's share of the market was still uncertain because of the postal service's equivocation on postal regulations. Permit mail required counting to assess fees while metered mail did not; but the postal service, wary of establishing a monopoly for PB, required all mail to be counted. Although PB's future hung by a thread for most of the 1920s, by 1927 the company had 2,849 meters in operation and branches in 20 cities.

Finally, after a congressional hearing at which Arthur Pitney testified by letter against preferential treatment for the system he invented, a bill to impose uniform regulations on permit and metered mail was killed in the Senate. The postal service was free to exercise its preference for the more efficient, reliable, and safe postage meter. Henceforth first-class mail was posted only by meter or adhesive stamp.

Pitney-Bowes began to grow and diversify, producing machines for stamping, counting, cancelling, and metering mail. PB's 1929 profit of $300,000 represented a 100% increase over that of the previous year. PB expanded abroad as well, establishing cross-licensing and patent-sharing agreements with similar firms in Great Britain and Germany. Throughout the 1930s, government restrictions on the metered-mail business eroded and Pitney-Bowes's field of operations grew wider. By the end of 1930 there were 6,838 postage meters in service. By the end of 1933 there were 9,620.

The Depression meant retrenchment at Pitney-Bowes, as it did in most sectors of the economy. PB was fortunate to be in a growth industry and did not face critical financial difficulties, but its profits shrunk considerably during these years. The company was forced to cut wages by 10% and also suspended stockholder dividends. The union movement received a boost during the Depression, but PB, under the leadership of Walter Wheeler, had provided benefits to its employees for years, so the union movement found little support at Pitney-

Bowes. PB emerged from the Depression earlier and healthier than most firms, partly due to the nature of its product, and partly due to Wheeler's leadership.

Pitney-Bowes's success in the industry and the further relaxation of postal service restrictions on metered mail stimulated competition in the production of postage meters. Many small firms sought a share of the market, as did some heavy hitters like IBM and NCR. PB consistently kept ahead of its competition. Its development of the omni-denomination meter in 1940 was a breakthrough in the industry. Not only was PB prospering, with 27,000 meters in service in 1939, but the U.S. Postal Service had a $2 million dollar budget surplus in fiscal 1939, largely due to the efficiency of the metered-mail system.

Like most other large manufacturers, PB converted its plant to defense production during World War II. Pitney-Bowes's wartime priorities, as established by Walter Wheeler, who became president in 1938, were maximum production of war goods, maintenance of meters in operation to handle American mail, and planning for postwar manufacture of new products. The production of postage meters was completely halted during the war. Instead, PB manufactured replacement parts for guns, aircraft, and radios, and was a four-time recipient of the army-navy "E" Award, given for excellence in wartime production.

In 1945, anticipating the broadening of its product base, PB shortened its name to Pitney-Bowes Inc. By the end of 1947 the number of PB postage meters in service had grown to over 60,000, from 40,000 during the war years. PB expanded and modernized its plant and office space in Stamford to accommodate projected growth. In 1949 PB introduced a desktop postage meter, which brought small business customers within its reach.

PB's postwar diversification began with the acquisition of the Tickometer Company, whose namesake product counted paper items such as labels and tickets. Pitney-Bowes simplified the Tickometer Machine's design and promoted its use for many new purposes. For the most part, PB limited its diversification to fields relating to those functions performed in mail rooms.

Throughout the 1940s and 1950s Wheeler worked hard to maintain good labor-management relations and progressive incentive, benefit, and profit-sharing plans. This was reflected in a high rate of productivity at PB and in the decision of the majority of workers not to seek union representation. The wisdom of this strategy was demonstrated by PB's continual outperformance of its competition in these years.

By 1957, however, due to the virtual disappearance of domestic competition, PB was faced with government antitrust action. PB cooperated fully with investigators. Wheeler even went so far as to prepare a 12-volume history of Pitney Bowes and submit it to the Department of Justice. Wheeler maintained, as he always had, that it was PB's productivity, efficiency, and personnel relations that made it difficult for other companies to compete, not anticompetitive practices. Pitney-Bowes eventually agreed to sign a consent decree that required the company to license its patents to any manufacturer who wished to compete, at no charge.

In 1960, when Walter H. Wheeler retired as president and chief operating officer, PB had 281,100 postage meters in service and metered mail accounted for 43% of U.S. postage. PB's gross income was over $57 million. Products other than postage meters accounted for 20% of gross income, a result of PB's growing diversification.

Diversification has been an important facet of Pitney-Bowes's strategy since the 1960s. Because PB no longer had a monopoly in the postage-meter market, diversification was necessary for growth. In 1967 PB established a copier-product division whose first product was a tabletop office copier. Although PB was a latecomer to the market dominated by Xerox, its copiers had two advantages: they were reasonably priced and included excellent service packages. Service had long been a hallmark of PB's operations because the post office never allowed PB to sell its meters, only lease them. PB was responsible for the day-to-day operations of every meter it leased, so a large service fleet was already in place. This service team made expansion into other markets much more manageable for PB.

In 1968 PB acquired Monarch Marking Systems, which has since grown into the largest U.S. supplier of price-marking, merchandise-identification, and inventory-control equipment and supplies. At the end of 1968, PB's sales of postage meters, while still growing, accounted for only 53% of total sales.

In 1973 PB was forced to write off its 64% investment in a joint venture with Alpex Computer Corporation to manufacture point-of-sale terminal systems, at a loss of $42 million. More modest losses from this venture continued to mount for several years, stemming both from disputes with the Internal Revenue Service over allowable write-offs and from an $11 million lawsuit filed by Alpex.

PB established leasing companies in the United States and the United Kingdom in 1977 to support marketing efforts for its business products. This was a record year for Pitney Bowes—the company dropped the hyphen from its name in 1970—with postage meters and price-marking systems both posting record sales.

In 1979 PB made a major acquisition, adding the Dictaphone Corporation and its subsidiaries Data Documents and Grayarc to the company, for $124 million. The purchase made PB the worldwide leader in sales of voice-processing and dictation equipment, and PB still controlled over 90% of the postage-meter market.

PB filled a gap in its copier line in 1981 by arranging a marketing agreement with the Ricoh Company of Japan to make its tabletop model available in the United States. This brought the number of copier models marketed by PB to eight. PB also received a $111 million contract from the post office to help further automate the handling of mail by developing computers to "read" envelopes and parcels.

PB entered the facsimile-machine market in 1982 and soon became the leader in new placements of facsimile equipment. The company became one of the top suppliers of fax machines to large and medium-sized businesses in the United States and began seeking new international markets by the late 1980s.

It is PB's policy to compete only in markets in which it is guaranteed a prominent share, whenever possible. In 1987 about 80% of the company's sales were in industries that PB led. In line with this strategy, PB sold Data Documents in 1988.

In 1990 Chairman George Harvey reaffirmed Pitney Bowes's commitment to growth through expansion of research-and-development programs and aggressive pursuit of further international markets in all three operating segments. During the 1980s the company had begun developing machines that communicate with other machines by using integrational software. By 1992 the company expected almost all of its products to have that capacity.

Pitney Bowes laid off 1,500 workers and underwent a costly retooling in 1989, and the company began to push more sophisticated mailing systems—like its Star system, which picks the most efficient carrier for each package. PB also got a boost from the post office, which has been pushing big mailers to use bar-code envelopes. PB's secure market positions should provide a solid base for further expansion and diversification.

Principal Subsidiaries: Pitney Bowes Real Estate Financing Corp.; Dictaphone Corp.; Monarch Marking Systems, Inc.; Pitney Bowes Credit Corp.; Wheeler Group Inc.; Adrema Leasing Corp. (Germany); Colonial Pacific Leasing Corp.; Pitney Bowes of Canada Ltd.; Baldwin Cooke Inc.; Baldwin Cooke Co. Ltd. (Canada); Dictaphone Canada, Ltd.; Dictaphone Co. Ltd. (U.K.); Dictaphone International A.G. (Switzerland); Dodwell Pitney Bowes K.K. (Japan); Monarch Marking (S.E.A.) Pte. Ltd. (Singapore); Monarch Marking Systems Australia Pty. Ltd.; Monarch Marking Systems Ltd. (Canada); Monarch Marking Systems de Mexico, S.A. de C.V.; PB Leasing Ltd. (U.K.); Pitney Bowes France S.A.; Pitney Bowes Ges.m.b.H. (Austria); Pitney Bowes Deutschland GmbH (Germany); Pitney Bowes Marking Systems Ltd. (U.K.); Pitney Bowes Oy (Finland); Pitney Bowes (Ireland) Limited; Pitney Bowes Svenska (Sweden); Pitney Bowes A.G. (Switzerland); Pitney Bowes plc (U.K.); Data Documents Systems, Inc..

Further Reading: Cahn, William, *The Pitney-Bowes Story*, New York, Harper and Brothers, 1961.

—Robin Carre

RICOH

RICOH COMPANY, LTD.

15-5, Minami-aoyama 1-chome
Minato-ku, Tokyo 107
Japan
(03) 3479-3111
Fax: (03) 3403-1578

Public Company
Incorporated: 1936 as Riken Kankoshi Company Limited
Employees: 37,000
Sales: ¥835.46 billion (US$5.81 billion)
Stock Exchanges: Tokyo Osaka Nagoya Fukuoka Sapporo Hiroshima Niigata Kyoto Amsterdam Frankfurt Paris

A diversified manufacturer of automated office equipment and electronic and consumer products, Ricoh Company has facilities throughout Asia, Europe, and North America. The firm's goals are to achieve globalization by boosting overseas production—particularly in the United States and Europe—and to become a leader in the office-automation market.

Although the company's initial efforts lay in another area of image technology—photography—its ability to win market share was evident as far back as 1936, when Riken Kankoshi Company was formed to produce positive sensitive paper, used to develop film. Under the leadership of Kiyoshi Ichimura the firm instantly took the lead in the Japanese sensitized-paper market. In 1938, after deciding to produce cameras as well, Ichimura changed the company's name to Riken Optical Company and introduced the Olympic 4.

The flash bulb and color film invented during the 1930s, and other developments such as new chemicals for film developing and computer-designed lenses originated during World War II, were marketed to the public after the war. In 1950 Riken introduced another camera, the Ricohflex III.

Five years later the company entered the copier market when it developed its first diazo copier, the Ricopy 101. This was followed by the Ricoh Synchrofax in 1959, two micro enlargement copiers in 1960 and 1962, and two duplicators, also introduced in 1960 and 1962.

In 1962, with a handful of employees and $100,000, the company established its first overseas subsidiary, Ricoh Industries USA. The subsidiary initially imported cameras, but it soon began marketing copiers when it realized the sales potential in the United States.

In 1963, following the establishment of its successful subsidiary, the Japanese parent company changed its name to Ricoh Company and continued its success in both copier and photographic equipment.

In 1965 Ricoh entered the budding field of office computers with the debut of the Ricoh Typer Standard, a data-processing system. It also introduced the Ricopy BS-1, and electrostatic coated-paper copier.

The 1970s marked a decade of growth and change for Ricoh and its U.S. subsidiary. During the 1970s Ricoh began to sell cameras and other electronic goods on the U.S. market. Ricoh Industries USA, whose annual sales had climbed to $1.3 million by 1970, was renamed Ricoh of America. In 1973 Ricoh established its second U.S. subsidiary, Ricoh Electronics, in Irvine, California. Created to assemble copier supplies and parts, the subsidiary made Ricoh the first Japanese company to produce copiers in the United States.

During the mid-1970s Ricoh made advances in three important markets. The Rifax 600S, the world's first high-speed digital facsimile machine, made its debut in 1974 along with the Rinac 1000 System, an information-retrieval system. This was followed by the Ricopy DT1200, the company's first plain-paper copier, in 1975. Also in 1975, Ricoh was honored with Japan's highest award for quality control, the Deming Prize.

In 1976 Ricoh introduced the Ricoh Printer 40, an impact (daisy-wheel) printer, followed by the Ricoh WP-1, a word processor. By this time the company's products covered the field of office automation.

In 1978 Ricoh established Rapicom, formed to develop and market stand-alone, high-speed digital facsimile products, as well as satellite facsimile equipment. Ricoh of America opened a research-and-development facility in Santa Clara, California, in 1977. In 1979, however, the company assigned U.S. research-and-development functions to a new entity, Ricoh Systems.

Despite the fact that it now operated four United States–based companies, Ricoh did not have much U.S. visibility, due in part to the company's agreement to sell copy machines in the United States under the labels of Savin and Pitney Bowes, two U.S. manufacturers. Early in the 1980s Ricoh announced its intention to market copiers under its own name and to become a major player in the worldwide office-automation market. Takeshi Ouye, president of Ricoh, planned to move carefully into the office-automation market, predicting in June 1980 in *Modern Office Procedures* "We will be in a position to market a total automation system within ten years." Ricoh already held the leading position in the international plain-paper copier market, and its additional office products—offset duplicating equipment and systems, diazo copiers, and facsimile, microfilm, word-processing, document, and storage-retrieval equipment—gave the company a boost in its quest for a leading rank in office automation.

In 1981, Ricoh of America began to market Ricoh copiers in the United States. By 1984 the company had achieved a 7% share of the U.S. market. The firm then decided to venture into more advanced copying machines, moving from the $5,000-and-under price range to the $6,000-to-$13,000 range. This step put Ricoh in direct competition with Xerox.

Ricoh's four-year-old Rapicom subsidiary landed a major account for Telepress, Ricoh's satellite facsimile product, when it agreed in 1982 to supply the product to Gannett

Company, publisher of *USA Today.* Telepress eliminated the practice of physically transporting the newspaper for printing and then again for distribution.

In 1983 Ricoh introduced an ultra-compact hand-held business computer, the Ricoh SP25, in addition to a new personal computer, the Ricoh SP200, and its first laser printer, the Ricoh LP4120. The company also added two more printers to its line the following year: the Ricoh JP5320, an ink-jet model, and the Ricoh TP3220, a thermal printer.

Longtime Ricoh President Takeshi Ouye was elected chairman in 1983, while Hiroshi Hamada became president. Under their leadership, the company continued to globalize. Previously, much of the company's new-product research was done overseas, particularly in the United States, and then transferred to Japan, where the products were manufactured. Hamada felt that Ricoh should develop more products domestically and boost production capacity by manufacturing the products both at home and overseas. In the United States, for example, the company made its operation more independent and more responsive to the U.S. economy, merging its U.S. research-and-development operation, Ricoh Systems, with Ricoh Electronics, the production facility, both of which had reported separately to Ricoh in Japan. In addition, the company established Ricoh UK Products Limited in the United Kingdom in 1983, while Ricoh Nederlands opened offices in France and Italy in 1984, as well as a Belgian office in 1985.

In the mid-1980s the company continued aggressive marketing and product-development efforts with the introduction of the RINNET System, a local area network; a color copier; an electronic filing system; an electronic whiteboard; and two minicomputers developed in cooperation with AT&T. As a result, sales grew 20% annually from 1982 to 1985. Ricoh's alliance with AT&T began with a three-year original-equipment-manufacturing (OEM) contract, in which Ricoh agreed to equip its facsimile machines with AT&T telephones. This was followed, in 1984, by an agreement allowing Ricoh to market AT&T's minicomputers in Japan. In 1985, the two firms created AT&T Ricoh Company, a joint venture to produce and market modified versions of AT&T's compact telephone systems. Ricoh lent its Japanese marketing-and-service network to AT&T, and AT&T helped Ricoh enter the telecommunications field.

In 1984 the company's Atsugi, Japan, plant established a production-technology research center and received the *Nihon Keizai Shimbun* Award for factory automation. Ricoh also established the Ricoh Research Institute of General Electronics Company, and Ricoh Finance. In addition, the company added a thermal-paper and toner–production facility to its Fukui plant, while Sindo Ricoh Company began producing zoom plain-paper copiers and toner.

In the United States, Ricoh Electronics opened a fully automated thermal-paper-manufacturing plant in Irvine, California. In addition, Ricoh began construction of Ricoh Research and Development Center.

In 1985 Ricoh Corporation (Canada)—formerly Rapifax of Canada—opened a new facility in NePean, Ontario. Ricoh also established two marketing companies in 1986: Ricoh Espana, a joint venture with a Spanish distributor of Ricoh products, and Ricoh France, a wholly owned subsidiary. When Ricoh UK Products began production in May, Ricoh became the first Japanese company to manufacture copiers in the United Kingdom. By 1988 the firm had also added facsimile equipment and supplies to its production capabilities.

Under the guidance of President Hiroshi Hamada, Ricoh established its second European manufacturing subsidiary, Ricoh Industrie France, which produced plain-paper copiers and other office-automation equipment and supplies at a new plant in Alsace.

The firm also strengthened its position in the semiconductor arena with the purchase of Panatech Research & Development Corporation's semiconductor division in 1987. In May 1987 Ricoh opened a semiconductor-design center in San Jose, California. The center expanded research-and-development efforts for Ricoh's semiconductor products, which so far included CMOS, a large-scale integrated device that is incorporated in its copiers, facsimiles, and cameras.

In Japan Ricoh introduced Imagio, a new line of office-automation equipment that utilizes a digital system which processes images, produces 20 copies a minute, and functions as an input/output station for electronic filing systems. In addition, the introduction of several new copiers, including a high-speed, multi-functional desktop model, enabled Ricoh to maintain its position as Japan's leading plain-paper-copier company.

In April 1987 Ricoh reorganized and consolidated its U.S. subsidiaries. The move, calculated to create a "separate Ricoh in North America," was another move toward globalization for Ricoh. According to Hamada, in the company's annual report for 1988, the new unit was to "gradually assume greater independence in virtually all aspects of its operations." Hamada also revealed plans to create another independent Ricoh in Europe, a plan which would begin by increasing production capacity.

In 1988 the company released a lightweight, compact eight-millimeter camcorder in the United States and Japan. The company also opened Ricoh Software Research in Santa Clara, California, to develop custom software for three-dimensional computer-aided design and database markets. The software products are designed for existing and future original-equipment-manufacture clients. Also that year, Ricoh's overseas sales exceeded domestic sales for the first time. Ricoh's product line included facsimile machines, data-processing equipment, cameras, and copying machines and supplies. It was one of only a few companies making four different types of copying machines: the diazo, the electrofax, the plain-paper copier, and the duplicator.

While many Japanese companies suffered decreases in their export businesses during the mid- to late 1980s because of the high value of the yen, Ricoh's overseas sales grew. Its success was attributed to substantial gains in sales of facsimile machines and laser printers. In addition, Ricoh's two main office products, copiers and facsimile machines, have earned a major share of the U.S. market. In 1987 Ricoh's share of the laser-printer and scanner market was about 24%. Ricoh's goal is to double that share by employing more aggressive marketing efforts through an expanded sales force and its American network of dealers, distributors, and OEM arrangements.

Despite the aggressive sales strategy, Ricoh suffered profit declines in 1986 and 1987, due partly to slimmer profit margins caused by appreciation of the yen. To cope with the high yen, the company planned to continue increasing overseas production. In the late 1980s, it began making copiers at its third U.S. manufacturing plant. This, and a fourth plant, will double Ricoh's U.S. production. According to the company, about 20% of the products made at the existing facilities, which include copiers, facsimiles, sorters, automatic document feeders, and supplies, are exported to Japan and Europe.

The increase in overseas production puts the firm well on its way to reaching its goal of globalizing and becoming a leader in the office-automation market. In addition, by positioning itself as a supplier of comprehensive automated systems for the office, Ricoh will also be in a prime position when Japanese companies begin to automate their own offices.

Principal Subsidiaries: Ricoh Corporation (U.S.A.); Ricoh Finance Corporation; Ricoh Corporation (Canada), Ltd.; Ricoh Electronics, Inc.; Ricoh Thermal Systems, Inc.; Ricoh Development of California, Inc. (U.S.A.); Ricoh Europe B.V. (Netherlands); Ricoh Office Systems Nederland B.V. (Netherlands); Ricoh Deutschland GmbH (Germany); Ricoh UK Ltd.; Ricoh UK Products Ltd.; Taiwan-Ricoh Co., Ltd.; Ricoh France S.A.; Ricoh Industrie France S.A.; Ricoh Optical Industries Co., Ltd.; Tohoku Ricoh Co., Ltd.; Hasama Ricoh Co., Ltd.; Ricoh Tokki Co., Ltd.; Ricoh Denshi Co., Ltd.; Ricoh Keiki Co., Ltd.; Ricoh Research Institute of General Electronics Co., Ltd.; Ricoh Microelectronics Co., Ltd.; Ricoh Educational Equipment Co., Ltd.; Ricoh Information System Co., Ltd.; Nihon Business Supply Co., Ltd.; Hokkaido Ricoh Co., Ltd.; Miyagi Ricoh Co., Ltd.; Saitama Ricoh Co., Ltd.; Tokyo Ricoh Co., Ltd.; Kanagawa Ricoh Co., Ltd.; Aichi Ricoh Co., Ltd.; Osaka Ricoh Co., Ltd.; Hyogo Ricoh Co., Ltd.; Fukuoka Ricoh Co., Ltd.; Ricoh Tecnonet Co., Ltd.

—Kim M. Magon

STC PLC

1B Portland Place
London W1N 3AA
United Kingdom
(071) 323-1000
Fax: (081) 565-2381

Public Company
Incorporated: 1910 as Western Electric Company Limited
Employees: 36,393
Sales: £2.61 billion (US$4.21 billion)
Stock Exchange: London

STC, formerly Standard Telephones and Cables, is Britain's second-largest electronics group, a major manufacturer of computers, telecommunications equipment, and transmission cables, both wire and fiber optic. STC has been a world leader in underwater cable, laying several intercontinental lines. It is working with U.S. and European telecommunications companies on cellular telephones and other advanced technologies. It also has worked on defense projects from World War II to the present.

The company began in 1883 as a tiny branch office of Western Electric, a subsidiary of the U.S. AT&T, set up to market in Britain the recently invented telephone. Telephone use grew rapidly in Britain, as did Western Electric, London, which sold cable, telephones, and switchboards to the companies that were stringing telephone lines throughout Britain. By the mid-1890s, Western's biggest British customer, National Telephone Company, was considering building its own factories, particularly since Western imported most of its material from factories on the Continent, and National preferred buying from a British factory. In 1898, Western bought the Fowler-Waring Cables Company, near London, which already had a huge order for cable from National. That purchase and U.S. technical expertise kept Western's orders flowing, although its switchboards were still made in Europe or the United States, and the development of the telephone infrastructure in Britain lagged behind that of the United States, Canada, and New Zealand.

By 1908 the company was producing two kinds of switchboards, one for National and one for the Post Office, the entity that operated the telephone system. By 1909 Western employed about 1,000 people in the United Kingdom. It also made power cables for the London underground system. A great deal of British business went to larger companies, but Western Electric partially made up for this loss with foreign sales, opening offices in Sidney, Johannesburg, and Buenos Aires.

In 1909 J.E. Kingsbury, an Englishman who had run the company since 1883, was removed by U.S. headquarters, and a U.S. manager, G.E. Pingree, was installed in his place. In 1910 the company was incorporated as Western Electric Company Limited, which was firmly controlled by its parent firm in the United States.

World War I was a stimulus to Western sales. Communication with headquarters in the United States was difficult and the company adapted to wartime production on its own. Western developed a 12-line portable switchboard for field use as well as various types of listening devices. Working conditions in its factories were poor and the hours long. In 1918 the company came under the management of the International Western Electric Company and joined the Engineering Employers' Federation, resulting in a reduction of the workweek from 57 hours to 47 hours.

Western expanded in the postwar years. It fought for several years with its unions over wages, finally locking out Amalgamated Engineering Union members for three months in 1922. Western broke the union and reduced wages. Western won huge contracts from the Post Office to supply cable, and to dig the ducts and manholes through which the cable would go. Telephone technology was developing rapidly, mainly through the efforts of Western Electric's New York laboratories. The technology was transferred to Britain by bright young engineers sent to the United States to study and work.

Western moved into broadcast technology with the manufacture of inexpensive consumer radios in 1923. Because of the growth of telephone and radio, Western had cash on hand when many other companies were barely hanging on, and was able to acquire new factories relatively cheaply. Partly because of its advanced U.S. technology, the company won contracts in Sweden, France, and Italy. It also increased its influence in Europe by organizing an international committee to increase the European telephone infrastructure.

Western's parent company concentrated on the U.S. market, where telephones were far more prevalent than in Europe, and had always viewed its overseas operations as too consuming of management's time. International Telephone and Telegraph Corporation (ITT) bought International Western in 1925 for US$29.3 million, renaming the company Standard Telephone and Cables, Ltd. (STC). Standard was a bigger component in ITT than it had been in Western, and it now worked harder at creating its own technology. It obtained telephone contracts in Egypt and China, and helped build the British end of the first transatlantic two-way radio service. The company won radio contracts throughout the world. Aware of how important it was to remain technologically competitive, the corporation set up two laboratories, one in Britain, one in Paris.

By 1930, the money from U.S. investors that had fueled much of the expansion had dried up, and the company was forced to close the laboratories, fire thousands, and slash the wages of many others. Profits tumbled from £576,224 in 1930 to £36,163 in 1931. During the 1930s technological advances made telephone technology cheaper. As a result of lower rates, the number of telephones in Britain grew from 2 million in 1930 to 3.3 million in 1939. STC also made advances in radio that allowed more distant and clearer transmission and telephone contact with boats at sea. By the late 1930s STC was able to rehire some of the workers laid off in the early 1930s.

The onset of World War II cut off STC from its contacts in New York and associates on the Continent. New factories were built outside of London, where they would have less chance of being bombed. The company grew with extreme rapidity, manufacturing miles of new types of cable, thousands of switchboards, parts for Spitfire and Hurricane airplanes, mine detectors, and gyroscopic gun-sights. Radio and telephone both came of age during the war, and STC built much of the equipment necessary for rapid expansion. STC manufactured many types of communications equipment, including radar, radio, and x-ray guidance. These developments would leave STC in an excellent position for radio-use expansion in the postwar world, led by civil aviation. World War II also enabled STC to develop business contacts throughout the world. The company went from 12,000 employees in 1939 to a peak of 25,000 in 1943, and 16,000 in 1945.

During the first few years after the war, with material restrictions and government controls, STC had little opportunity to take advantage of its wartime advances. Its first major opportunity came at the coronation of Queen Elizabeth II in 1953, which was televised, giving television and STC a huge amount of publicity. Sales in the mid-1950s increased in several areas: the telephone was being purchased as a consumer item, microwave transmission was becoming an important technology, and civil aviation was developing rapidly. At the same time STC was missing opportunities to advance in television and was developing transistorized switchboards only slowly. As the British Empire diminished, STC built overseas factories to keep profits coming in from those markets. STC laid undersea cables between the United Kingdom and Belgium, the United Kingdom and Sweden, and Newfoundland and Novia Scotia in Canada.

However, the company's net income fell badly in 1956, and the British government reduced spending in 1957, further hurting STC because so much of its income came from sales to the Post Office. The recession of 1958 hurt the company. STC often failed to turn its technological superiority into contracts; the pursuit of profit was not considered gentlemanly by many in the top management. Production managers were looked down upon while engineering managers were exalted. The company did little advertising and wrote few press releases.

In 1959 Harold S. Geneen took over ITT. One of his first moves was to have all of STC's top management interviewed by psychiatrists and the company's structure analyzed by outside consultants. A U.S. manager, Rex B. Grey, was brought in to increase profits. Unprofitable branches were sold off, and the company began to plan in five-year units. By the early 1960s, demand for telephones was so great that the Post Office began buying again, providing STC with large contracts. An electro-mechanical division was formed, and STC opened a distribution center. It also opened a new branch in Northern Ireland.

Research and development started to bring positive results. STC provided advanced equipment to the British Broadcasting Corporation and to airplane manufacturers. Because of advances in undersea telephone cable, STC cable and repeaters were used for all of one transatlantic cable and half of another. It once again won contracts all over the world, in radio, microwave transmission, and coaxial cable. The company began to grow again through acquisition, moving into the areas of heating and air conditioning and car rentals, among others, but the economic turndown at the end of the 1960s halted STC's growth.

Kenneth Corfield took over as managing director in 1970, immediately focusing STC's energies on the areas in which it had been successful, such as undersea cable. Huge undersea-cable orders rolled in during the 1970s and 1980s, making STC Britain's leading exporter of telecommunications equipment. STC manufactured nearly 500 types of cable during this period, including fiber-optic cables. In 1976 the company laid one of the world's first fiber-optic lines, setting itself up for the 1980s when fiber-optic technology would become an important growth area in telecommunications and STC would install many of the first undersea fiber-optic cables.

Corfield eliminated production in microwave, aviation, and other smaller areas in which STC was losing money. STC's telephone exchanges, another major money maker, steamed ahead technologically, moving toward fully electronic exchanges, bringing in profits and prestige, and winning marketshare from its rivals.

As part of Corfield's restructuring, parts of the company were reorganized during the 1970s, leading to plant closures and difficult labor relations within some parts of STC. Radio operations were closed. More operations were automated, further clouding the labor-relations picture as some employees lost their jobs to robots and computers. Simultaneously, Corfield began a dialogue between various levels of management and workers, trying to boost morale. Information on contracts won or lost was given to employees as soon as management had it, and company positions on relocations and retraining were spelled out in detail. Working conditions improved because of increased pressure from below and a greater willingness to spend money from above.

With the continuing economic integration of Europe and huge U.S. companies like Western Electric looking for world markets, British companies increased cooperation in designing telecommunications equipment. In July 1979, STC and ITT decided to offer 15% of STC's ownership to the British public to more firmly establish its identity as a British company. The offering sold out immediately, and share prices climbed rapidly. STC pulled further from its parent company's orbit in 1981 when the management of ITT's British Business System Group was transferred to STC. STC became part of a three-company consortium that designed a new digital telephone switching system for the British Post Office. The system, with the new information services it made possible, was introduced just as Britain was shifting from a manufacturing-based to a service-based economy, and proved extremely popular. Partly as a result of this shift, departments were set up within STC to identify new markets and develop new products for them. STC began manufacture of information terminals for retail and banking use, pocket radio-pagers, and electronic security products. STC was working in extremely competitive markets, and speeded up its product-development process.

The company was quick to realize that the profitability of these products would grow far more rapidly than the profitability of installing telephone cable. Thus, STC changed its market. Instead of slowly producing huge, capital-intensive products for large customers like the Post Office, it became more of a consumer-electronics manufacturer, quickly creating products that required light assembly rather than the massive retooling of factories.

ITT sold an additional 10% of its ownership in March 1982, and another 40% that October, making the company predominantly British-owned for the first time in its history, and completely removing a perceived ambiguity over STC's loyalties that its British competitors had long exploited. It expanded further into the rapidly emerging information industry in 1984 by buying International Computers Ltd. (ICL), Britain's largest computer company. STC became Britain's second-largest electronics group, while ITT's share of the company dropped to 24%. In October 1987 Northern Telecom Ltd., the Canadian telecommunications giant, acquired the remaining ITT stock. STC then bought Northern Telecom's U.K. telecommunications operations.

STC increased its cooperation with foreign telephone transmission companies in the late 1980s, including a 1989 deal with Société Anonyme Telecommunications, which controls 30% of the French market, to work jointly on research and development and marketing.

In the late 1980s STC continued its expansion into the rapidly growing information field, acquiring 50% of Regnecentralen AS, a Danish computer supplier that it folded into ICL. In 1989 STC bought Computer Consoles Inc., based in Waltham, Massachusetts, for $168 million, and Datachecker Systems, another U.S. company, for $90 million. STC also had stakes in Spanish and Indian computer companies. Nevertheless, 70% of STC's sales were in Britain in 1988. The company's yearly profits varied widely in the closing years of the 1980s, partly because of acquisition costs and fluctuations in segments of the computer industry as a whole. STC lost £54 million in 1985 because of its dash for growth through acquisition. It soon recovered, however, under the leadership of Lord Keith of Castleacre, who led a coup against Corfield in 1985. STC reported profits of £230 million by 1988. Lord Keith was replaced by Arthur Walsh in May 1989.

In July 1990, STC sold 80% of ICL to Fujitsu, of Japan, for £750 million. STC used the money to pay debts and to invest in the growing communications-systems market.

Principal Subsidiaries: STC Ltd.; STC Distributors Ltd.; STC Holdings Inc. (U.S.A.); STC Investments Ltd.; STC Properties Ltd.; STC Technology Ltd.

Further Reading: Young, Peter, *Power of Speech, A History of Standard Telephones and Cables*, London, George Allen & Unwin, 1983; Dodsworth, Terry, and David Thomas, "Telecom Strategy Takes Shape," *Financial Times*, February. 17, 1988; Dodsworth, Terry, "STC: Now a Dash for Growth," *Financial Times*, March 2, 1988; Russell-Walling, Edward, "Telecomms on Right Wavelength," *Financial Weekly*, July 21, 1988.

—Scott Lewis

UNISYS

UNISYS CORPORATION

Post Office Box 500
Blue Bell, Pennsylvania 19424
U.S.A.
(215) 986-4011
Fax: (215) 986-2312

Public Company
Incorporated: 1886 as American Arithmometer Company
Employees: 80,000
Sales: $10.10 billion
Stock Exchanges: New York Midwest Pacific Cincinnati Amsterdam Antwerp Basel Brussels Geneva Lausanne London Zürich

Unisys Corporation, which was known as Burroughs Corporation until it merged with Sperry Corporation in 1986, is the second-largest computer company in the United States. Mainframe computers constitute the core of its product line, and in recent years it has begun to make smaller computers as well. Unisys is also the nation's 15th-largest defense contractor, running a sizable military-electronics business. The company has all but phased out the accounting machines which were its mainstay until the computer age.

Unisys can trace its origin to 1885, when William Seward Burroughs invented the first recording adding machine. Burroughs called his device an arithmometer, and the next year he and three partners founded the American Arithmometer Company in Saint Louis, Missouri, to market it. Creating a commercially viable version proved difficult, and it was not until 1892 that Burroughs was able to patent a salable model. Once on the market, the adding machine became a success, and in 1897 Burroughs was awarded the Franklin Institute's John Scott Medal in honor of his invention. He died of tuberculosis the next year, before realizing much profit from his invention.

The company was renamed the Burroughs Adding Machine Company in his memory in 1905 and moved its headquarters to Detroit, Michigan. During the early years of the new century, Burroughs consolidated its position in the adding machine business. It acquired Universal Adding Machine and Pike Adding Machine in 1908 and Moon-Hopkins Billing Machine in 1921. By 1914 the company offered 90 different types of data-processing machines which, with the help of interchangeable parts, could be modified into 600 different configurations. The core of its customer base was accountants, and in 1917 Burroughs stepped up its courtship of those customers with the debut of a magazine devoted to accountancy called *Burroughs Clearing House*.

By the 1920s Burroughs had established itself as a mainstay of the office-machine industry. It remained so for the next three decades, with adding machines still at the heart of its product line. All of that changed as a result of J. Presper Eckert and John W. Mauchly's invention of ENIAC, the first electronic computer in 1946. At first the market for computers appeared to be limited to a handful of government agencies that used them for large-scale number crunching. The only companies to commit themselves to computer research and development were large electronics and office-machine firms, for whom the computer was a natural extension. When the Defense Department awarded the design contract for its new SAGE early-warning computer system in 1952, it had Burroughs, IBM, RCA, Remington Rand, and Sylvania to choose from. It picked IBM, giving that company an advantage that its competitors have yet to overcome.

Burroughs did not plunge wholeheartedly into computer technology at first, although it, with Sperry Rand's UNIVAC unit, NCR, Control Data, and Honeywell strove to keep up with IBM during the 1950s. At the end of the decade its reputation was still, in the words of a *Time* magazine correspondant, that of "a stodgy old-line adding machine maker." Even so, in 1952 it developed an add-on memory for Eckert and Mauchly's ENIAC. In 1953 the company shortened its name to Burroughs Corporation, in recognition of its diversification. In 1956 Burroughs introduced its first commercial electronic computer and acquired ElectroData Corporation, a leading maker of high-speed computers. It also entered the field of automated office machines, introducing its Sensitronic electronic bank bookkeeping machine in 1958.

Burroughs entered the computer field during the tenure of President John Coleman, whose last major act as president was to negotiate a partnership agreement between his company's computer operations and those of RCA, which was also looking for a way to catch up to IBM through a pooling of financial resources. RCA approved the agreement in 1959, but Coleman died before he could sway Burroughs's board of directors, and the plan was never realized. Business historian Robert Sobel has written that the Burroughs-RCA partnership might have produced "the best possible challenger for IBM."

Coleman was succeeded by Executive Vice President Ray Eppert. Under Eppert, Burroughs expanded its place in the rapidly growing bank-automation market in 1960 when it began selling magnetic inks and automatic check-sorting equipment. In 1961 the company introduced its B5000 computer, which it said was less expensive and simpler to operate than other commercial mainframes. Expansion and diversification during early years of the computer age led to a fourfold increase in sales between 1948 and 1960, from $94 million to $389 million. At the same time, however, increased research-and-development costs cut profit margins, a problem the company struggled with until the late 1960s.

Despite this surge in earnings, Burroughs remained among the smallest of IBM's main competitors in the early 1960s. Despite the fact that the B5000 had won a following with its distinctive design, Burroughs's computer product line remained narrow and the company was still too dependent on accounting machines. Research-and-development costs still hacked away at profit margins, and the company's future was clouded.

In 1964 Ray Macdonald became executive vice president and began to oversee the company's day-to-day operations. With the help of several like-minded executives, he took control of Burroughs from Eppert and committed it to a course of steady profit growth through cost cutting. Macdonald succeeded Eppert as CEO in 1967. Burroughs's financial performance continued to improve and the company became a Wall Street favorite before the decade was out.

Burroughs scored a major coup in 1967 when the Defense Department awarded it the contract to build the Illiac IV supercomputer, which had been designed by a team at the University of Illinois. The Illiac IV was 10 to 20 times faster than any existing supercomputer and was delivered to NASA's Ames Research Center in California in 1972. The sudden lag in research and development created by Macdonald's policy of cutting costs also contributed to two significant technical failures at about this time. The B8500 mainframe, which had been scheduled for delivery in 1967, had to be scrapped altogether in 1968 after Burroughs engineers realized they could not produce reliable components at a reasonable price. The B6500 was plagued by breakdowns because the development team, in order to bring the project in on time and under budget, had cut corners in designing its high-speed circuits and had not tested the completed machines properly before delivery.

An interesting aspect of Macdonald's stewardship was his re-emphasis of accounting machines as an integral part of Burroughs's product line. Foremost among his talents was a genius for salesmanship, and the company's efforts to market its high-speed accounting machines won a considerable chunk of the market from rival NCR. In 1974 Burroughs entered the facsimile-equipment business when it acquired Graphic Services for $30 million. The next year the company paid $8.8 million for Redactron, a maker of automatic typewriters and computer-related equipment.

Ray Macdonald retired in 1977 and was replaced by Paul Mirabito, his hand-picked successor. It was during Mirabito's brief tenure that the consequences of Macdonald's fiscal policies began to manifest themselves in earnest. In 1979 IBM announced a powerful new generation of computer systems. Burroughs countered by announcing its own new series of systems. Unfortunately, although its design ideas were good, the company did not have the development or manufacturing resources to translate them into actual computers. Its inability to deliver finished products resulted in an embarrassing stream of canceled orders. Years of salary cuts and other forms of budget-tightening had also engendered low morale among field engineers and a reputation for poor service. Customer complaints came to a head in 1981, when 129 Burroughs users sued the company over product unreliability and difficulty in getting their machines fixed.

Mirabito retired in 1979 and was replaced by W. Michael Blumenthal, the former chairman of Bendix and treasury secretary in the Carter administration. The move came as a surprise to industry observers. Blumenthal took over a company that was deceptively profitable, chalking up record sales of $2.8 billion in 1979. He immediately set about shaking up Burroughs's corporate culture, firing veteran executives and replacing them with his own appointees, phasing out the adding machine and calculator businesses, implementing a plan to improve repair service, and discontinuing accounting practices that tended to inflate earnings. Blumenthal's reforms did not come without cost, however; in July 1980 the company reported its first drop in quarterly profits in 17 years.

Blumenthal concentrated on Burroughs's computer business in an effort to secure the position of the largest of IBM's U.S. competitors. In 1981 the company covered one of its weak spots when it acquired System Development Corporation, a software-development firm, for $9.6 million. Burroughs also acquired Memorex, a maker of disc drives and other data-storage equipment, that year for $85.2 million, despite Memorex's shaky financial condition. These moves added $1 billion to the company's annual sales.

Blumenthal eventually decided that economies of scale were necessary to compete with IBM. In 1985 Burroughs launched a $65-per-share takeover bid, worth $3.7 billion, for Sperry. Sperry had been a takeover candidate since holding unsuccessful merger talks with ITT in March 1984. Its board of directors and investors, from whom Burroughs hoped to acquire shares, balked at the offer and the deal fell through. Burroughs came back with a $70-per-share bid, worth $4.1 billion, in May 1986, and a four-week battle ensued. Sperry executives, anxious to preserve the company's independence, argued against selling out and the board put up a defense that included an $80-per-share stock buyback offer and casting about for a white knight. Sperry eventually agreed to a $76.50-per-share deal worth $4.8 billion. It was by far the largest merger in the history of the computer industry and one of the largest in U.S. corporate history. Combined, the new company was the second-largest computer firm in the nation, leapfrogging over Digital Equipment Corporation.

Sperry, which was founded in 1933, originally made aircraft instruments. In 1955 it jumped into the computer business when it merged with Remington Rand, which had in its turn acquired Eckert-Mauchly Corporation, the company founded by the developers of the ENIAC and the UNIVAC, in 1950. Sperry Rand quickly became one of the industry's leading companies due to its technical prowess. By the 1960s it had acquired a reputation for wonderful products but dreadful management and marketing, a legacy it inherited from Remington Rand. At the time of its acquisition by Burroughs, Sperry had profitable defense-electronics operations but a struggling computer business.

Six months after the acquisition, the combined company announced that it would adopt the name Unisys. It was selected from suggestions submitted by Burroughs and Sperry employees, and was conceived as a condensation of the words "United Information Systems." But the work of rationalizing the two companies still remained. Over the next two years Unisys cut its work force by 20%, shedding 24,000 of its 121,000 employees, and sold unwanted and redundant businesses to generate cash. In December 1986 it sold Sperry Aerospace to Honeywell, and it later sold off Memorex's marketing arm.

At the same time, Unisys diversified its product line. In 1987 it acquired Timeplex, a high-tech communications-equipment company, for $300 million and Convergent Technologies, a maker of office workstations, for $351 million. By 1989 the company had begun to move into the small-and-mid-sized computer market and had adopted AT&T's popular Unix operating system as the standard configuration for its machines. In 1989 Unisys began manufacturing its own personal computers for the first time in its history.

In the late 1980s Unisys was not entirely successful, however. Despite strong earnings growth from the time of the Sperry deal through 1988, the company posted a loss of nearly $100 million in the first quarter of 1989. Management shake-ups in 1987 had resulted in the departure of two key executives—Vice Chairman Joseph Kroger, the former president of Sperry who commanded intense loyalty from former Sperry employees, and Paul G. Stern, a physicist whom Blumenthal had brought into the company from IBM and made president and chief operating officer in 1982. Sluggish sales, manufacturing cost overruns, and fierce price competition among the many companies using the Unix system all cut into revenues.

Unisys also found itself caught up in the Pentagon procurement scandal of 1989 when federal prosecutors charged former Vice President Charles Gaines, who headed the Washington, D.C., office of one of the company's defense units, and other executives with fraud, bribing Defense Department officials into giving them classified procurement documents, and making illegal campaign contributions to members of Congress. Unisys had already begun its own internal investigation when the government made its accusations public. The company spent the next 12 months working with prosecutors to hammer out an agreement under which it pleaded guilty and paid a fine.

Excessive inventory and slow responses to changes in the defense and information technology industries caused Unisys to lose money in 1989. When President James A. Unruh became CEO in April 1990, he stated that Unisys's products and strategy would not change, but that its "execution" would.

Principal Subsidiaries: Unisys Canada Inc.; Convergent, Inc.; Timeplex, Inc.; Unisys International Company; Unisys Finance Corporation; Unisys Australia Limited; Unisys Espana S.A. (Spain); Unisys (Schweiz); A.G. (Switzerland); Unisys Belgium; Unisys Deutschland G.m.b.H. (Germany); Unisys Eletronica Ltda. (Brazil); Unisys France; Unisys Italia S.p.A. (Italy); Unisys Limited (U.K.); Unisys Nederland N.V. (Netherlands).

Further Reading: Uttal, Bro, "How Ray Macdonald's Growth Theory Created I.B.M.'s Toughest Competitor," *Fortune,* January 1977; *Unisys Profile,* Blue Bell, Pennsylvania, Unisys Corporation, 1989.

—Douglas Sun

WANG LABORATORIES, INC.

One Industrial Avenue
Lowell, Massachusetts 01851
U.S.A.
(508) 459-5000
Fax: (508) 452-0896

Public Company
Incorporated: 1955
Employees: 26,796
Sales: $2.87 billion
Stock Exchanges: New York Zürich Basel Geneva Lausanne

Wang Laboratories was started in the early 1950s as a one-man unincorporated research-and-development company providing services in the areas of specialized electronics and digital equipment. From this beginning Wang evolved into a pioneer in the calculator market as well as in niche markets of word processing and small business computers. Today Wang markets, designs, and manufactures computers and peripheral equipment, specializing in office automation.

Founded in 1955 by An Wang, Wang Laboratories originally had no plans to develop and build computers. Wang had left his native China in 1945 to study applied physics at Harvard, where he earned his doctorate in 1948. After graduation Wang performed postdoctoral work at Harvard's Computational Laboratory, where he invented the magnetic pulse memory core which was to become a standard component of computers for the next 20 years.

Wang left the Harvard laboratory in 1951 after the institution announced it was suspending computer research and founded his own company later that year. The company focused on the development of specialized electronic and digital equipment which would utilize Wang's magnetic core. When Wang began his business he had no contracts and no orders, only a $70-a-month office in Boston and $600.

Wang Laboratories initially sold magnetic cores and provided contractual services to perform research and development. Wang was his own salesman, and frequently attended electronic trade shows attempting to drum up business. In 1952 Wang secured the first of many consulting contracts to custom design digital equipment when the company was hired to develop a synchronizer and counting device for a Cambridge, Massachusetts, company called Laboratory for Electronics.

Wang's first encounter with International Business Machines Corporation (IBM) came long before Wang's entrance into the computer market. In 1951 An Wang had offered IBM a license on his pending patent of the magnetic memory core. This began four years of negotiations on a patent sale. Meanwhile, Wang had been contracted by IBM to devise a method for using magnetic cores to perform memory functions for IBM's electronic calculating machine. Wang was awarded a patent on the core just weeks after it was sold to IBM in 1956. Years later, An Wang suggested that IBM had encouraged a challenge to the patent claim in order to hasten a sale.

When Wang Laboratories incorporated in 1955, An Wang was registered as president and treasurer. Following the patent sale to IBM, the company's focus gradually began to shift from consulting to development and sales of its own products. The transition ultimately proved fruitful, but the mid-1950s were also a time that An Wang later admitted was fraught with business mistakes.

In the late 1950s Wang was busy with a number of government contracts, an arena Wang Laboratories still serves despite the company's transition to computers. As a result of one such contract with the United States Air Force, the company developed an angular encoder to measure cloud cover. This technological breakthrough in the application of transistors spurred the advance of Wang's encoders and also aided in the development of automated control systems for companies producing and using machine tool makers.

By the late 1950s Wang Laboratories was marketing various types of control units sold under the brand name Weditrol (Wang Electronic Digital Control Units). In the last two years of the decade the fledgling company produced 60 to 80 of those units annually, and sold them for about $700 each.

With funds needed for expansion, Wang entered an agreement in 1959 with Warner & Swasey Company, a Cleveland, Ohio–based machine tools company which was buying Wang's control systems. An Wang forfeited 25% of the company's holdings to Warner & Swasey in return for $50,000 worth of an equity investment and another $100,000 to be made available for short-term loans. "I regretted the alliance almost at once," Wang later wrote, noting he had given up too much control for too small a price.

During this period Wang also lost the exclusive right to manufacture a semi-automated hyphenating phototypesetting machine it had developed. In the late 1950s Wang agreed to design and build the machine for Compugraphic. The product was cheaper than competing fully automated systems on the market. At the time the only phototypesetters able to justify text were extremely expensive, costing upwards of $1 million. Wang's hyphenating process could greatly increase the productivity of newspapers, such as those served by Compugraphic's equipment. The finished product was dubbed Linasec, and Wang Laboratories received about $30,000 for each machine Compugraphic sold. Even though Wang retained the patent on the Linasec, Compugraphic retained the right to manufacture the machines while immune to royalty payments. Wang closed out the decade with about 20 employees.

In the early 1960s Wang embarked on a new direction and developed its own sales organization to sell products directly to users. The company was growing, and to accommodate the growth it moved twice during this time—to Natick, and then

Tewksbury, Massachusetts. The first big year for Linasec was 1963, when the company recorded $300,000 in sales. Linasec revenues more than doubled in the next two years, allowing Wang to exceed $1 million in sales for the first time, in fiscal 1964.

Wang's greatest success of the decade evolved around the creation of its landmark LOCI and 300 series programmable calculators. The LOCI debuted in 1965 and was the company's first electronic scientific calculator. It also spurred the creation of the desk calculator market, where Wang held almost sole proprietorship for much of the late 1960s.

While Wang dominated the new desktop-calculator market, the company again found itself in need of capital for further expansion and repayment of short-term loans. In 1967 Wang went public and sold 210,000 shares of common stock through the New York Stock Exchange. The company was, by then, a well-known leader in the electronic desktop-calculator field.

The stock offering shared top billing with President Lyndon Johnson's proposed tax increase in July 1967. Shares were originally offered at $12.50, but when the Wang shares were finally sold in August, the stock received a sizzling reception. The stock opened the day with a bid of 36 and closed better than four points higher. Wang established its presence overseas in 1967. The company ultimately located sales, service, and administrative offices in Europe and Asia, as well as the United States and Canada.

Foreseeing competition in the calculator market, in 1967 Wang made its first attempt to build a computer. The computer was inadequate though, largely a result of Wang's minimal programming experience. The following year Wang acquired that experience when it purchased Phillip Hawkins, of Arlington, Massachusetts, then the state's largest supplier of data-processing services.

While some of Phillip Hawkins's staff left the company shortly after the $7.4 million purchase, the deal did bring Wang the programming experience needed to build computers. In 1970 the company announced it would enter the computer market with the 3300 model. This model, too, had drawbacks, and it was not until the introduction of the 2200—Wang's fourth computer—that the company successfully penetrated the minicomputer market.

An Wang still held control of the company he founded, and despite internal disagreements, the company decided to gradually begin withdrawing some of its less-developed and lower-priced calculators from the market in order to prepare for an eventual total withdrawal from the calculator market.

Meanwhile, Wang's success in the desk-calculator market continued while the company developed its first computers. In 1969 Wang posted a 40% sales increase over the previous year and had more than 1,000 employees. In 1970, the huge success of calculators helped the company record its first year of $25 million in sales.

The period between 1970 and 1975 was a time of word-processing and computer-product introductions, but it was also a period of unstable earnings. The computer industry chuckled at Wang's debut into the word-processing market, the 1200 BASIC, which was an electronically controlled dual-cassette typing system dependent on an IBM typewriter's internal workings to serve as a terminal. Performance problems with the 1200 arose during its first year on the market, and Wang saw its first-ever quarter of declining revenues in 1973.

This situation worsened with the oil crisis which struck in 1973. The year before, various auto-dealer packages had accounted for 70% of Wang's business. When the bottom dropped out of the automotive-sales market, Wang also suffered greater losses. In 1975 the company turned to periodical bank loans, reduced salaries, and—for the first time—was forced to lay off workers.

The following year, though, the company made an impressive turnaround, with growth stimulated by sales of Wang's new computer systems. Then, in 1976, the introduction of a cathode-ray-tube (CRT)–based word-processing minicomputer finally gave Wang a significant corporate presence and propelled Wang into the office-computer market.

Wang strengthened its marketing efforts during this time, including a three-month television advertising campaign in 1978 which portrayed Wang as David and IBM as Goliath. Wang, then the 32nd-largest computer maker, was only the second, after IBM, to use television advertising.

By the end of 1978, Wang boasted that it was the largest worldwide supplier of CRT-based word-processing systems and the largest supplier of small business computers in North America. Beginning in 1978, Wang also began increasing its assets through a number of acquisitions, including a partial purchase of InteCom, in 1984. That acquisition was complete by 1986. Other Wang acquisitions included the 1978 purchase of Graphic Systems and the 1988 purchase of Informatics Legal Systems. Minority-interest purchases included U.S. Satellite Systems, in 1982, and Telenova, in 1985.

Between 1976 and 1984 Wang's revenues skyrocketed 61% annually. Meanwhile, the company made a further commitment to development of word-processing and data-processing products, increasing its research-and-development budget from $3 million in 1976 to $160 million in 1984. During this growth surge, Wang also broke into the *Fortune* 500 market: by 1983, nearly half of company revenues were generated by *Fortune* 500 customers.

This eight-year period—the longest running period of consistent financial growth for Wang in company history—was also marked by continual developments in improved product lines. Later products took direct aim at IBM's large portion of computer-market revenues. Wang's VS (virtual storage) computers were introduced in 1977, its Office Information Systems series was introduced in 1979, and its Integrated Information Systems line was introduced in 1980.

Wang continued to move to cut into IBM's market share in the 1980s. In 1980 a word processor, designed to compete with an IBM model, was introduced. The battle was enhanced by a price reduction in 1981. That same year Wang introduced office machines that transmit voice as well as data. The following year a Wang personal computer debuted, taking aim at IBM's dominance in that market. By 1984 Wang had acknowledged that IBM had set the standards, and the company responded by marketing other products that allowed its computers to use IBM software and communicate with IBM PC (personal computer) models.

Ten years after Wang had left calculators for computers, a computer-market recession hit, sending profit margins into a nose dive. After reaching $1 billion in sales in 1982, and $2 billion in sales in 1984, sales plummeted in the third quarter of 1985, with Wang posting its first decline in ten years. Wang responded to a net income falloff of 66% by announcing a layoff of 1,600 or 5% of its workers, and pay cuts for executives.

In the 1980s Wang began to attempt to penetrate IBM's market, which often meant costly setbacks when its attempts went awry. Critics suggested that Wang had been too slow to respond to the growth of personal computers, clinging to its once-heralded minicomputers of the late 1970s, which in the late 1980s were being pushed aside by the smaller and sometimes more powerful personal computers. The company also had a poorly regarded service division, which failed to keep pace with Wang's sales and development. Wang had also made initial, unsuccessful attempts to build a better PC, than IBM, before committing to build computers that were compatible with IBM machines.

During the later half of the 1980s the company underwent a number of organizational changes which brought on resignations of top-level management. John F. Cunningham was named company president in 1983, with An Wang retaining his board chairmanship and position as CEO. Cunningham had been at Wang since 1967, and made his mark promoting office automation. In July 1985, amid news of sharply declining revenues, Cunningham resigned. Following Cunningham out the door less than two months later was Executive Vice President Jon A. Kropper.

An Wang resumed his position as president until he named his son Fred to the position in 1986. That same year the company celebrated its 35th anniversary, with the best news coming early in the year when the company was awarded a $480 million, five-year agreement with the air force mini-computer multi-user program.

After resuming the position of president, An Wang quickly increased his visibility throughout the company and initiated changes which saw marketing executives reporting directly too him. Only a week after reorganizing the marketing division in the spring of 1986, the company's top marketing executive, J. Carl Masi Jr., resigned. Masi, Kropper, and Cunningham, all went on to head smaller computer firms.

Later that year Fred Wang, who was then serving as treasurer, was named president. Under Fred Wang, profits varied, with the company earning modest profits in 1986, then losing $70 million his first full year. Wang reported a $92 million profit in 1988 only to lose $424 million in 1989. While the company continued to upgrade its systems, Wang's U.S. revenues shrunk and the company stayed afloat through overseas sales. By 1989, An Wang was in more control of the company's sales divisions in the wake of a $67 million third quarter loss. The company announced further layoffs and executive pay cuts.

In August 1989 An Wang announced that Fred Wang would resign as president, and later that month Richard W. Miller, a former General Electric executive, was appointed to succeed him. Just a week before the resignation the company announced it had hired an investment-banking firm to raise capital and renegotiate its revolving credit agreements to prevent Wang's creditors from calling in its loans.

During the 1990s Wang began to market information systems to manage all of an organization's business information. The Freestyle system has integrated the computer, handwriting, and use of telephone and facsimile machines into a single system designed to meet all data-processing and communication needs for office workers.

By late 1989 Wang was supporting almost $1 billion of debt, having lost an additional $500 million in 1989. Miller announced plans to overhaul the company, selling off noncore operations, real estate, and leasing operations, and cutting an additional 2,500 jobs.

The Wang family now owns less than 35% of company holdings, although it has retained control of operations through special stock classes. How long Wang Laboratories will be run by a Wang, how Wang will fare in the future, and whether Freestyle will create another new marketing opening, remain uncertain.

Principal Subsidiaries: Wang Credit Corp.; Wang International; Financial Limited (Republic of Ireland); Wang Informatis Legal and Professional Systems, Inc.; InteCom Inc.; Wang Information Services Corp.; Wang Financial Information Services Corp.; Wang Australia Pty. Ltd.; Wang Gesellschaft m.b.H. (Austria); Wang Europe, S.A./N.V. (Belgium); Wang Canada Ltd.; Wang Industrial Co. Ltd. (China); Wang Computer China Limited; Wang (UK) Ltd.; Wang France S.A.; Wang Pacific Ltd. (Hong Kong); Wang Nederland B.V. (Netherlands); Wang Svenska AB (Sweden); Wang Computer Ltd. (Japan); Wang New Zealand Ltd.; Wang de Panama, S.A.; Wang Computers (Pte.) Ltd. (Singapore); Wang (Schweiz) A.G. (Switzerland); Wang Computadoras, Inc. (Puerto Rico); Wang Deutschland GmbH (Germany); Wang Italia S.p.A. (Italy); Wang de Mexico S.A. de C.V.; Wang Europe S.A./N.V. (Luxembourg); Wang Computer Korea, Ltd. (South Korea); Wang Espana, S.A. (Spain); Wang Ireland Ltd.; Wang Latin America, S.A. (Venezuela).

Further Reading: McClellan, Stephen T., *The Coming Computer Industry Shakeout: Winners, Losers and Survivors,* New York, John Wiley & Sons, 1984; Wang, An, and Eugene Linden, *Lessons, An Autobiography,* Reading, Massachusetts, Addison-Wesley Publishing Company, 1986; *Wang Laboratories: A Corporate Overview,* Lowell, Massachusetts, Wang Laboratories, Inc. 1987.

—Roger W. Rouland

XEROX

XEROX CORPORATION

800 Long Ridge Road
Stamford, Connecticut 06904
U.S.A.
(203) 968-3000
Fax: (203) 968-4312

Public Company
Incorporated: 1961
Employees: 111,400
Sales: $17.64 billion
Stock Exchanges: New York Midwest Boston Cincinnati Pacific Philadelphia London Paris Basel Berne Geneva Lausanne Zürich Amsterdam Düsseldorf Frankfurt

Xerox has become virtually synonymous with photocopying. Xerox was a small company in 1960 when its first practical copier was introduced, but the company zoomed into the *Fortune* 500 during the next few years. About 1,800 people worked there in 1959, and 55,000 in 1969.

The company began in 1906 as a photography-paper business named the Haloid Company, in Rochester, New York. Its neighbor, Kodak, ignored the company, and Haloid managed to build a business on the fringe of the the photography market. In 1912 control of the company was sold to Rochester businessman Gilbert E. Mosher for $50,000. Mosher became president but left the day-to-day running of the company to its founders. Mosher kept Haloid profitable and opened sales offices in Chicago, Boston, and New York City. To broaden the company's market share, Haloid's board decided to develop a better paper. It took several years, but when Haloid Record finally came out in 1933 it was so successful that it saved the company from the worst of the Great Depression. By 1934 Haloid's sales were approaching $1 million. In 1935 Joseph R. Wilson, the son of one of the founders, decided Haloid should buy the Rectigraph Company, a photocopying-machine manufacturer that used Haloid's paper. Haloid went public to raise the money, and selling Rectigraphs became an important part of Haloid's business.

In 1936 Haloid's 120 employees struck for benefits and higher wages. Mosher proved intransigent, and Wilson stepped in and offered concessions. Tension and resentment between labor and management persisted until World War II. During the war the armed forces needed high-quality photographic paper for reconnaissance, and business boomed. When the war ended Haloid faced stiff competition from new paper manufacturers.

Haloid needed to come up with new products, particularly after a showdown between Mosher—who wanted to sell Haloid to another company—and Wilson—who did not. Wilson won, and in 1947 Haloid entered into an agreement with Battelle Memorial Institute, a nonprofit research organization in Columbus, Ohio, to produce a machine based on a new process called xerography.

Xerography, a word derived from the Greek words for "dry" and "writing," was the invention of Chester Carlson. Carlson was born in Seattle, Washington, in 1906, and was a patent lawyer employed by a New York electronics firm. Frustrated by the difficulty and expense of copying documents, in 1938 Carlson invented a method of transferring images from one piece of paper to another using static electricity. In 1944 Battelle signed a royalty-sharing agreement with Carlson and began to develop commercial applications for xerography.

In 1949, two years after Haloid signed its agreement with Battelle, Haloid introduced the XeroX Copier, spelled with a capital "X". The machine required much of the processing to be done manually. The XeroX was difficult and messy to use and made errors frequently. Many in the financial community thought that Haloid's large investment in xerography was a big mistake, but Battelle engineers discovered that the XeroX made excellent masters for offset printing, an unforeseen quality that sold many machines. Haloid invested earnings from these sales in research on a second-generation xerographic copier.

In 1950 Battelle made Haloid the sole licensing agency for all patents based on xerography, but Battelle owned the basic patents until 1955. Haloid licensed the patents liberally to spread the usage of xerography to corporations like RCA, IBM, and General Electric. In 1950 Haloid sold its first commercial contract for a xerographic copier to the state of Michigan. Meanwhile, Haloid's other products were again highly profitable, with paper sales increasing and several successful new office photocopying machines selling well.

In 1953 Carlson received the Edward Longstreth Medal of Merit from the Franklin Institute, for the invention of xerography. In 1955 Haloid revamped its 18 regional offices to make them showrooms for its Xerox machines instead of photo-paper warehouses, hired 200 sales and service people, began building the first Xerox factory in Webster, New York, and introduced three new types of photography paper. Haloid also introduced the Copyflo, Haloid's semi-automatic copying machine. In 1956 Haloid president Joe Wilson, Joseph R. Wilson's son, formed an overseas affiliate called Rank Xerox with The Rank Organisation, a British film company seeking to diversify. This arrangement paved the way for Xerox factories in Great Britain and a sales and distribution system that brought Xerox machines to the European market. In 1958 Haloid changed its name to Haloid Xerox, reflecting its belief that the company's future lay with xerography, although photography products were still more profitable. That balance quickly changed with the success of the Xerox 914 copier, introduced in 1960. It was the first automatic Xerox copier, and the first marketable plain-paper copier. The company could not afford a blanket advertising campaign, and placed ads in magazines and on television programs where it hoped businesspeople would see them. The company also offered the machines for monthly lease to make xerography affordable for smaller businesses.

Demand for the 650-pound 914 exceeded Haloid-Xerox's most optimistic projections, despite its large size. *Fortune* later called it "the most successful product ever marketed in America." Sales and rental of xerographic products doubled in 1961, and kept growing. In 1961 the company was listed on the New York Stock Exchange and changed its name to the Xerox Corporation; photography operations became the Haloid photo division. In 1962 Xerox formed Fuji Xerox in Japan with Fuji Photo Film Company. Also during the 1960s Xerox opened subsidiaries in Australia, Mexico, and continental Europe. The company had sunk $12.5 million into developing the 914, more than Haloid's total earnings from 1950 to 1959, but the 914 led the company to more than $1 billion in sales by 1968. In 1963 Xerox introduced a desktop version of the 914. Although this machine sold well, it was not very profitable, and Xerox has depended on its larger machines ever since.

With its suddenly large profits, Xerox began a string of acquisitions, purchasing University Microfilms in 1962 and Electro-Optical Systems in 1963. The market for copiers continued to expand at such a rate that they remained Xerox's chief source of revenue. The 1960s were a tremendously successful time for Xerox, which became one of the 100 largest corporations in the United States, and, in 1969, moved to Stamford, Connecticut.

In the late 1960s Xerox began to focus less on copiers and more on designing an electronic office that would not use paper. With this end in mind the corporation bought a computer company, Scientific Data Systems, in 1969, for nearly $1 billion in stock, only to have it fail and close down in 1975. Xerox also formed Xerox Computer Services in 1970, bought several small computer firms in the next few years, and opened the Xerox Palo Alto Research Center (PARC) in California.

Scientists at PARC invented what may have the world's first personal computer. So innovative was the work of the PARC scientists that many features they invented later appeared on Apple Macintosh computers. In December 1989 Xerox sued Apple Computer for $150 million, alleging that Apple had stolen the technology that helped make its computers so successful. Apple co-founder Steven Jobs, who later hired some researchers from PARC, claimed that his company had refined Xerox's work, and thus made it original.

PARC's innovations were overlooked by Xerox; the computer division and the copier division competed for resources and failed to communicate. Products were released by the office products division in Dallas, Texas, that PARC had never seen before. Disagreements broke out at Xerox headquarters at the suggestion of change, further stifling innovation.

In April 1970 IBM introduced an office copying machine, giving Xerox its first real competition. IBM's machine was not as fast or as sophisticated as the Xerox copiers, but it was well built and was backed by IBM's reputation. Xerox responded with a suit charging IBM with patent infringement. The dispute was settled in 1978 when IBM paid Xerox $25 million. Meanwhile, Xerox itself became the defendant repeatedly for antitrust violations, including a suit by the Federal Trade Commission.

Distracted from its market by these legal battles, Xerox lost its lead in the industry when Kodak came out with a copier that was more sophisticated than Xerox's. IBM and Kodak followed a strategy similar to that of Xerox, leasing their machines and attracting many large accounts on which Xerox depended.

Xerox had become inefficient as its executives concentrated on growth during the 1960s. Xerox had spent hundreds of millions of dollars on product development but introduced few new products. Engineers and designers were divided into small groups that fought over details as they missed deadlines. While the company sought to perfect the copying machine it failed to challenge the new products on the market, and Xerox's market share dropped.

By 1985 Xerox's worldwide plain-paper copier share had dropped to 40%, from 85% in 1974. Yet Xerox's revenues grew from 1.6 billion in 1970 to $8 billion in 1980, partially because Xerox began to sell the machines it had been renting, depleting its lease base.

Beginning in the mid-1970s, Japanese products emerged as an even more dangerous threat. Xerox machines were big and complex and averaged three breakdowns a month. Ricoh introduced a less expensive, smaller machine that broke down less often. The Japanese strategy was to capture the low end of the market and move up. By 1980 another Japanese competitor, Canon, was challenging Xerox's market share in higher-end machines.

In the late 1970s Xerox began reorganizing, making market share its goal, and learning some lessons about quality control and low-end copiers from its Japanese subsidiary. The company also cut manufacturing costs drastically. Xerox regained copier market share, but intense price competition kept copier revenue around $8 billion for most of the 1980s.

In 1981 Xerox finally began releasing new products, beginning with the Memorywriter typewriter. This typewriter soon outsold IBM's and captured over 20% of the electric typewriter market. By January 1983 Xerox had unveiled a Memorywriter that could store large amounts of data internally. In 1982 the 10-series copiers, the first truly new line since the 1960s, was introduced. These machines used microprocessors to regulate internal functions and were able to perform a variety of complicated tasks on different types of paper. They were also smaller and far less likely to break down than earlier Xerox copiers. The 10-series machines used technology developed at PARC, which was becoming more integrated with the company.

Xerox began gaining market share for the first time in years, and morale improved. It also released computer workstations and software and built a $1 billion business in laser printers. The workstations proved to be an expensive flop, and by 1989 the company planned to close its workstation-hardware business. Xerox also moved to protect its 50% share of the high-end market in the United States with machines that make 70 or more copies a minute. The major high-end competition was Kodak, but the Japanese—led by Ricoh—were again launching a drive for this market.

During the 1970s Xerox had also diversified into financial services. In 1983 it bought Crum and Forster, a property-casualty insurer, and in 1984 it formed Xerox Financial Services (XFS), which bought two investment-banking firms in the next few years. By 1988 XFS supplied nearly 50% of Xerox's income—$315 million of the $632 million total. XFS performed well, able to raise funds at a low cost because it was backed by the Xerox "A" credit rating.

Xerox spent more than $3 billion on research and development in the 1980s, looking for new technologies, such as those for digital and color copying, to promote growth. Xerox was a leader in developing technologies, but often had trouble creating and marketing products based on them, particularly computers.

In 1988 Xerox underwent a $275 million restructuring, cutting 2,000 jobs, shrinking its electronic typewriter output, dropping its medical systems business, and creating a new marketing organization, Integrated Systems Operations, to get new technologies into the marketplace more effectively. Xerox's comeback was so impressive that in 1989 its Business Products & Systems unit won Congress's Malcolm Baldridge National Quality Award for regaining its lead in copier quality. Xerox demonstrated its ability to change in the late 1970s when it responded to the first wave of Japanese competition. Many analysts believe that Paul A. Allaire, a career Xerox man named CEO in 1990, must repeat that performance if Xerox is to survive as an independent corporation.

Principal Subsidiaries: Rank Xerox (U.K., 51%); Xerox Financial Services, Inc.; Crum and Forster, Inc.; Xerox Credit Corporation; Van Kampen Merritt Inc.; Furman Selz; Xerox Life; Fuji Xerox (Japan, 51%).

Further Reading: Dessauer, John H., *My Years with Xerox,* Garden City, New York, Doubleday & Company, Inc., 1971; *The Story of Xerography,* Stamford, Connecticut, Xerox Corporation, 1978; Jacobson, Gary, and John Hillkirk, *Xerox: American Samurai,* New York, Macmillan Publishing Company, 1986; Alexander, Robert C., and Douglas K. Smith, *Fumbling the Future,* New York, William Morrow and Company, Inc., 1988; *1988 Fact Book,* Stamford, Connecticut, Xerox Corporation, 1988.

—Scott M. Lewis

INSURANCE

AEGON N.V.
AETNA LIFE AND CASUALTY COMPANY
ALLIANZ AG HOLDING
AMERICAN FAMILY CORPORATION
AMERICAN FINANCIAL CORPORATION
AMERICAN GENERAL CORPORATION
AMERICAN INTERNATIONAL GROUP, INC.
N.V. AMEV
AON CORPORATION
ASSICURAZIONI GENERALI SPA
AXA
BERKSHIRE HATHAWAY INC.
CAPITAL HOLDING CORPORATION
THE CHUBB CORPORATION
CIGNA CORPORATION
CNA FINANCIAL CORPORATION
COMMERCIAL UNION PLC
CONNECTICUT MUTUAL LIFE INSURANCE COMPANY
THE CONTINENTAL CORPORATION
EMPIRE BLUE CROSS AND BLUE SHIELD
THE EQUITABLE LIFE ASSURANCE SOCIETY OF THE UNITED STATES
FIREMAN'S FUND INSURANCE COMPANY
FIRST EXECUTIVE CORPORATION
GENERAL ACCIDENT PLC
GENERAL RE CORPORATION
GREAT-WEST LIFECO INC.
THE HOME INSURANCE COMPANY
JOHN HANCOCK MUTUAL LIFE INSURANCE COMPANY
KEMPER CORPORATION
LEGAL & GENERAL GROUP PLC
LINCOLN NATIONAL CORPORATION
LLOYD'S OF LONDON
MARSH & MCLENNAN COMPANIES, INC.
MASSACHUSETTS MUTUAL LIFE INSURANCE COMPANY
THE MEIJI MUTUAL LIFE INSURANCE COMPANY
METROPOLITAN LIFE INSURANCE COMPANY
MITSUI MARINE AND FIRE INSURANCE COMPANY, LIMITED
MITSUI MUTUAL LIFE INSURANCE COMPANY
MUNICH RE (MÜNCHENER RÜCKVERSICHERUNGS-GESELLSCHAFT)
THE MUTUAL BENEFIT LIFE INSURANCE COMPANY
THE MUTUAL LIFE INSURANCE COMPANY OF NEW YORK
NATIONALE-NEDERLANDEN N.V.
NEW ENGLAND MUTUAL LIFE INSURANCE COMPANY
NEW YORK LIFE INSURANCE COMPANY
NIPPON LIFE INSURANCE COMPANY
NORTHWESTERN MUTUAL LIFE INSURANCE COMPANY
PENNSYLVANIA BLUE SHIELD
PRINCIPAL MUTUAL LIFE INSURANCE COMPANY
PROVIDENT LIFE AND ACCIDENT INSURANCE COMPANY OF AMERICA
PRUDENTIAL CORPORATION PLC
THE PRUDENTIAL INSURANCE COMPANY OF AMERICA
RELIANCE GROUP HOLDINGS, INC.
RIUNIONE ADRIATICA DI SICURTÀ SPA
ROYAL INSURANCE HOLDINGS PLC
SAFECO CORPORATON
THE ST. PAUL COMPANIES, INC.
THE STANDARD LIFE ASSURANCE COMPANY
STATE FARM MUTUAL AUTOMOBILE INSURANCE COMPANY
SUMITOMO LIFE INSURANCE COMPANY
THE SUMITOMO MARINE AND FIRE INSURANCE COMPANY, LIMITED
SUN ALLIANCE GROUP PLC
SWISS REINSURANCE COMPANY (SCHWEIZERISCHE RÜCKVERSICHERUNGS-GESELLSCHAFT)
TEACHERS INSURANCE AND ANNUITY ASSOCIATION
THE TOKIO MARINE AND FIRE INSURANCE CO., LTD.
THE TRAVELERS CORPORATION
UNION DES ASSURANCES DE PARIS
USF&G CORPORATION
VICTORIA HOLDING AG
"WINTERTHUR" SCHWEIZERISCHE VERSICHERUNGS-GESELLSCHAFT
THE YASUDA FIRE AND MARINE INSURANCE COMPANY, LIMITED
THE YASUDA MUTUAL LIFE INSURANCE COMPANY, LIMITED
"ZÜRICH" VERSICHERUNGS-GESELLSCHAFT

AEGON N.V.

Mariahoeveplein 50
Post Office Box 202
2501 CE The Hague
The Netherlands
(70) 344 32 10
Fax: (70) 347 52 38

Public Company
Incorporated: 1983
Employees: 9,409
Assets: Dfl 56.42 billion (US$29.57 billion)
Stock Exchanges: Amsterdam NASDAQ London Basel Geneva Zürich Tokyo

AEGON is a prime example of the move toward larger units in the insurance industry. The company was formed by the merger of two insurance firms, AGO and Ennia, in 1983. These two companies were themselves the result of merger—they were formed in the late 1960s when Algemeene Friesche, Groot-Noordhollandsche, and Olveh became AGO, and Eerste Nederlandsche, Nieuwe Eerste Nederlandsche, and Nillmij merged into Ennia. The history of these firms is the story of combining still smaller companies into larger and more competitive organizations. The second-largest Dutch insurance company, AEGON's name, made up of the initials of its major predecessors, reflects its roots, while its structure is designed to help the company compete successfully in a mature, internationalized market.

The company's earliest predecessors were burial funds such as the Broederlijke Liefdebeurs (the Fraternal Fund of Love), which was established in Haarlem in 1759. Burial funds were set up to serve a locality or industry and offered some protection from a city-provided pauper's funeral. The funds became increasingly common in the 19th century. The burial funds had a number of distinctive characteristics. Statute limited them to operating in only one Dutch province. Low premiums that appealed to working people were collected weekly at the insured's home, and fixed premiums did not always mean a fixed death payment. Burial funds also traditionally insured young children free.

One such fund was started when J. Oosterhoff, a civil servant and former burial-fund agent, decided to go into business for himself in 1844. He and another civil servant founded Algemeene Friesche in Friesland. After several years of growth, Oosterhoff wanted to expand nationwide. In 1860, the company passed a government examination of its actuarial practices and became a full-fledged mutual insurance company, and all the people it insured gained equal rights. Ordinary life insurance companies could become national concerns and offer a broader range of insurance products, including annuities, term policies, whole life policies, endowment policies, and group life insurance. When Algemeene Friesche's organizational form changed, it continued to offer basically the same product but in a broader market.

Groot-Noordhollandsche also began as a burial fund. This fund was established by a local vicar in the western Netherlands in 1845, a year after Oosterhoff set up Algemeene Friesche. Groot-Noordhollandsche also became an ordinary life insurance company, in 1918.

Another burial fund that grew into a life insurance company was the Dordrecht. The Dordrecht's main competitor in the 1880s was an ordinary insurance company, so the burial fund's managers reorganized to remain competitive. In 1883 the Dordrecht became an industrial life insurer, underwriting low-cost policies aimed at working men, basically the same market it had served as a burial fund.

Other life insurance predecessors of AEGON, however, did not come out of the burial fund tradition. Vennootschap Nederland was set up to offer a complete line of life insurance products, the first firm to be able to make that claim.

Vennootschap Nederland was established by Count A. Langrand-Dumonceau in 1858. Langrand-Dumonceau was a colorful European financier who had begun his career selling pencils, paper, and wallets as a youngster. As soon as possible, he left his native Belgium to join the French Foreign Legion, but his career there was short lived—Langrand-Dumonceau was one of the few legionaires ever to have his legion contract annulled. Back home in Belgium, he founded a number of life insurance companies, the most important of which was the Royal Belge. In 1858 he established Vennootschap Nederland, and that same year became one of the founding directors of Der Anker in Vienna. At age 32 he headed four insurance companies and was a self-made millionaire.

Langrand-Dumonceau's companies sold a very popular tontine, a policy in which the capital of group savings was divided among the survivors after a specified period. The right to claim the surrender value of a policy or to borrow on the policy made the product attractive to small savers with few options. About 1860, however, the millionaire began to expand into mortgage banking throughout Western Europe. When an economic crisis hit in the late 1860s his empire crumbled. While his insurance companies survived because they had been more carefully managed, they were no longer as sound as they had been before Langrand-Dumonceau's entry into banking. In 1913 Vennootschap Nederland merged with Eerste Nederlandsche, an almost unheard-of step in an industry that generated growth from within.

Another insurance firm, the Olveh, began as a self-help organization for civil servants in 1877. The Olveh was patterned after a similar Austrian union, which had been very successful in promoting the interests of its members. The group's goal was to reduce the cost of living and provide some security for members by setting up consumer cooperatives, a savings plan, and a life insurance program. In 1878 the life insurance end of the Olveh became a separate company, and in 1879 it began to offer the same coverage for members and nonmembers of its parent organization. By 1909 all ties with the original self-help organization had been cut, but it retained the association form.

Another of AEGON's predecessors was the Nillmij. The Nillmij was established in the Dutch East Indies in 1859 by C.F.W. Wiggers van Kerchem, one of the colony's foremost financiers who had set up the first general bank in the Indies. The Nillmij was successful because of its unique relationship with the colonial government. Van Kerchem used his influence to win the active support of authorities. Some premiums were collected by government tax collectors and military paymasters; the governor and commanders of the colonial army and navy recommended the Nillmij as a way for civil servants and military personnel to save outside of their pension systems. The Nillmij's monopoly continued until the 1880s. In 1883 the government stopped helping the company collect premiums, and competition from the Dordrecht, the Olveh, Eerste Nederlandsche, and others gained a foothold in the colony.

While the Nillmij's special relationship with the government initially made it successful, government regulation of the life insurance industry at home made operation more difficult for domestic companies. State regulation of life insurance dated to special decrees issued by Napoleon Bonaparte in 1809. Royal decrees of 1830 and 1833 strengthened these controls. Under them, the government controlled entry into the field and defined what constituted life insurance. In 1860 the government formulated the mortality table to be used and the interest rate to be charged. Foreign life insurance companies operating in the country were exempt from these rules, which often meant that they could charge lower rates.

In 1880 the Dutch Supreme Court ruled that the royal decrees were not binding, and government regulation ended. Although the regulated system had been criticized, life insurers were concerned that the public would lose faith in an unregulated industry. It was not until 1922—a year after the bankruptcy of the largest Dutch life insurance company, the Algemeene Maatschappij van Levensverzekering en Lijfrente (the General Company for Life Insurance and Superannuation)—that new regulations of the industry were passed, with input from life insurance companies.

Despite the problems of life insurance regulation, Dutch life insurers generally did not offer any other type of insurance product, just as other insurers did not offer life insurance. Another of AEGON's predecessors, Eerste Nederlandsche, had pioneered non-life coverage, specifically accident and health insurance.

Eerste Nederlandsche introduced accident insurance in the Netherlands about 1880. The company's founder brought the concept to the Netherlands after a visit to England, where he became familiar with the Railway Passengers Assurance Company. Eerste Nederlandsche filled another niche as well, offering collective accident insurance for factory and construction workers. Since health and accident insurance was still new, however, the new company's directors decided to also provide life insurance for security.

Although Eerste Nederlandsche was involved in administering payments when the Workmen's Compensation Act was passed in 1901, government social insurance was the impetus for a reorganization of the company. The accident and health department became a separate company, the Nieuwe Eerste Nederlandsche, whose shares were held by the parent firm. The company also decided to diversify at this time, becoming one of the first to offer insurance against liability and burglary. It also began to insure bicycles, and in 1911 wrote its first motor vehicle policy.

By 1913 AEGON's predecessors, Algemeene Friesche, Eerste Nederlandsche, Groot-Noordhollandsche, Olveh, and Nillmij were strong competitors in the life insurance field, while Nieuwe Eerste Nederlandsche was successfully staking out new areas of insurance. Algemeene was by far the largest Dutch insurer, the Dordrecht was second, and Eerste Nederlandsche, Nillmij, and Olveh all had places in the top ten. All of these companies except the Dordrecht were primarily domestic firms. The Dordrecht had successfully established a presence in Hungary, Italy, and northern France. Other companies' attempts to sell insurance abroad, especially Venootschap Nederland's efforts in Prussia and New York, were not as successful.

During World War I, Dordrecht's foreign interests meant that it was more seriously hurt than companies with primarily domestic operations. Even in neutral Holland, war led to interruptions in premium collection and mobilization of part of the staff.

The postwar years meant growth for the larger insurance companies. An increased emphasis on security and sharing risks increased profits for these companies. Acquisitions became a more acceptable way to put profits to work. Algemeene Friesche and Groot-Noordhollandsche especially grew through acquisitions between the wars, and Eerste Nederlandsche took over the Dordrecht in 1919. When Algemeene Maatschappij van Levensverzekering en Lijfrente failed in 1921 Algemeene Friesche took over its Dutch business, and the Nillmij acquired its business in the East Indies.

Expansion and profitability came to an abrupt end with the Depression and then World War II. The German Army occupied the Netherlands on May 10, 1940. Communications abroad were cut off, as eventually were communications within the country as well. Nearly all men were sent to work in Germany or went underground to avoid being transported to work camps. Potential customers concentrated on survival in a time of chronic food shortages. Eerste Nederlandsche's headquarters was among the many buildings destroyed when Germans bombed the Hague in March 1945.

The German occupying force also required that Jewish employees be dismissed and that all Jewish policies be surrendered. While the Insurance Board unofficially asked for inconspicuous noncooperation and the Dutch government in exile declared the measures null and void, companies did not always avoid compliance.

The war reached the Dutch East Indies in 1942, with even more devastating results. The European population there was interned, and the companies that operated there simply vanished.

Postwar rebuilding offered new opportunities for insurance companies, while testing their flexibility. Premium income expanded rapidly between 1945 and 1950, by approximately 13% overall. Increases in group insurance and insurance-based pension plans contributed to this growth. Government involvement in social programs increased in the aftermath of World War II, and the impact was mixed. The state's social security program, enacted in 1957, promoted financial planning with social insurance as one basis and supplementary private insurance as another. Compulsory car insurance offered new opportunities in 1961. The Disability Law of 1967, however, ended group disability insurance, a concept the Nieuwe Eerste Nederlandsche had pioneered.

In this new environment, the division between general and life insurance became less pronounced. Large life insurance companies such as Algemeene Friesche and Groot-Noordhollandsche gained experience in general insurance by acquiring smaller firms. Insurance companies also began to diversify into noninsurance areas, especially mortgage banking.

The insurance companies that operated in the Dutch East Indies, however, faced more difficult postwar problems. Operations had to be rebuilt from scratch. Currency restrictions and inflation drastically cut profits. Finally, the colony became independent in 1949 and Dutch concerns were nationalized by the Indonesian government in 1957. The Nillmij, which had originated in the Dutch East Indies, had to change dramatically to continue to operate. Its subsidiary in the Netherlands was made the parent company, and the assets of the former parent in Indonesia were nationalized.

The movement toward combining accelerated during the 1960s. Postwar emphasis on European cooperation culminated in the establishment of the European Economic Community in 1957. The movement toward a single European market gave larger companies a competitive edge. Inflation and rising operation costs—especially the cost of computerizing operations—also made bigger companies more profitable.

Mergers in the United States, Great Britain, and Canada were followed by the merger of the largest and second-largest Dutch insurance companies, the Netherlands Insurance Company and the Nationale Levensverzekering-Bank, in 1963. Algemeene Friesche, Groot-Noordhollandsche, and the Olveh merged in 1968 to form AGO; and Eerste Nederlandsche, Nieuwe Eerste Nederlandsche, and the Nillmij merged in 1969 to form Ennia.

Both mergers involved major organizational changes, but the AGO merger proved especially difficult because the firms involved had different structures. Algemeene Friesche and the Olveh were mutuals while Groot-Noordhallandsche had retained its *vereniging*, or association, structure. In a series of steps, the new company became a holding company with subsidiaries concentrating on different aspects of the insurance market. AGO Life Insurance Company and AGO General Insurance Company operated as limited companies, while AGO Holding Company retained the *vereniging* structure and was not owned by shareholders.

The mergers were completed as the Dutch insurance market was contracting. Pension-linked insurance business dropped, and the collapse of the housing market undermined mortgage operations. High interest rates also had an adverse impact. In this domestic climate, worldwide insurance expansion was attractive. Attempts to establish foreign branches or subsidiaries during the 1950s and 1960s had not been very successful. Europe and the United States, the largest single insurance market in the world, offered potential for expansion as domestic opportunities diminished.

In 1979 AGO acquired a majority interest in Life Investors in Cedar Rapids, Iowa. Ennia began its foreign acquisitions in earnest when it established operations in Spain in 1980. In 1981 Ennia purchased National Old Line Insurance Company of Little Rock, Arkansas. In 1982, the year before AEGON was formed, 50% of AGO's life insurance income came form foreign sources as did 46% of its general insurance income. For Ennia, 55% of general insurance premiums were foreign, although its foreign life insurance business remained small.

The mergers that formed AGO and Ennia had made both companies more effective competitors both at home and abroad. By 1983, however, both managements were exploring other opportunities. Merger again looked advantageous, and for the same reasons: cost reduction, the economies of combining computer networks, and a better basis for foreign expansion. With European integration looming in 1992, those advantages were even more important.

AEGON was formed in November 1983, becoming the second-largest Dutch insurance firm behind Nationale-Nederlanden. The new company continued to pursue a strategy of expansion at home and abroad. In 1986 it purchased the troubled mortgage bank Friesch-Groningsche Hypotheekbank and improved earnings there by the end of the decade. That same year it increased its presence in Spain, buying Union Levantina de Seguros. AEGON's chairman, J. F. M. Peters, said Spain's entry into the European common market and the country's economic development made it an attractive market. Citing opportunities for growth in the United States, Peters announced the purchase of Monumental Corporation of Baltimore, Maryland, the same year.

By the end of the 1980s, management reorganization and cost controls had led to rising profits. European deregulation with its increasing competition had some short-term impact on profits. AEGON's selective expansion in profitable markets and its cost-reduction measures promise to help the company meet those new challenges as its components have adapted over their long history to meet the challenges of change in the past.

Principal Subsidiaries: AEGON International B.V.; AEGON Nederland N.V.; AEGON NEVAK Holding B.V.; AEGON Onderlinge Ziektekostenverzekering U.A.; AEGON Reinsurance N.V.; Algemene Friese Onderlinge.

Further Reading: Working for Security, The Hague, AEGON, [1983].

—Ginger G. Rodriguez

AETNA LIFE AND CASUALTY COMPANY

151 Farmington Avenue
Hartford, Connecticut 06156
U.S.A.
(203) 273-0123
Fax: (203) 273-0079

Public Company
Incorporated: 1853 as Aetna Life Insurance Company
Employees: 45,500
Assets: $87.10 billion
Stock Exchanges: New York Pacific Basel Geneva Zürich

Aetna Life and Casualty Company markets a diverse array of insurance lines and financial services to individuals, public and private institutions, and corporations. Aetna is investor-owned—owned by its stockholders—rather than a mutual company—owned by its policyholders. It is the largest investor-owned insurance and financial-services company in the nation and, based on assets, is classed among the 15 largest U.S. corporations.

Aetna was founded in 1853 as the Aetna Life Insurance Company. In the mid-19th century, fire and then life insurance grew to fill the vacuum left by the reduced need for marine insurance as the shipping industry declined. Aetna Life was originally formed as an affiliate of the older Aetna Fire Insurance Company and profited from its association with Aetna Fire's reputation for reliability and quickness in paying claims. However, a new state insurance regulation passed in New York in 1849 and strengthened in 1853 prohibited the same company from providing both fire and life insurance. In 1853, the Connecticut legislature granted a petition for the separate incorporation of the Aetna Life Insurance Company.

Aetna Life's founding president, Eliphalet Bulkeley, originally divided his time between practicing law and developing the fledgling life insurance firm. He was also active in the formation of the Republican Party in Connecticut, starting a long tradition of political activism by Aetna leaders. Bulkeley guided Aetna through its difficult first years, when new insurance laws in some states required capital deposits beyond the stockholders' resources, hindering Aetna from doing business in those states. The depression of 1857 further threatened the firm's financial stability, but Aetna survived in the face of multiple bank closings. During this period the company regained its financial footing partly by hiring its first midwestern agent, a Connecticut man, who opened an office in Wisconsin to serve the burgeoning market in those states.

The year 1861 was significant for two reasons: the Civil War began and Aetna modified its form of ownership. Both events profitably affected Aetna's growth. Seeking security during the uncertain war years, many people bought life insurance policies for the first time. In addition, Aetna modified its form of investor ownership to permit policyholders to control their own funds in a separate mutual department that operated within the overall management structure. Originally, Bulkeley had resisted the mutual plan that placed ownership in the hands of policyholders; he disliked the speculative nature of dividend payment and could not countenance an approach to management that divided responsibility among all policyholders. Pressure from the public and from competing insurance companies helped change Bulkeley's mind. The result was the creation of a mutual department whose accounting system was separate from that of management; within this department, policyholders controlled their own funds and received dividends, but did not vote for the management of their interests in the company. The firm as a whole continued as an investor-owned company with all the efficiency of management Bulkeley believed was inherent in that arrangement. Partly due to this revision of the ownership structure, in just five years, from 1861 to 1866, Aetna jumped from 15th among 40 life insurance companies nationwide to 5th among 80.

Bulkeley died in 1872 and was succeeded by Thomas O. Enders, first clerk and later secretary of the firm. Bulkeley had presided over Aetna during the speculative postwar years, and had maintained careful control over the risks the company assumed. The 1870s were a period of national economic crisis, and Enders was hard-pressed to keep the firm alive, despite its earlier successes. Not only did Enders have to contend with a nationwide depression that began in 1873, but he also oversaw the disastrous results of a major change in premium payment made toward the end of Bulkeley's presidency. Until then, Aetna and most other insurance companies had accepted interest-bearing notes as half payment for premiums. In the wake of questions from the state insurance commissioner about the booking of these notes as assets—and the negative press elicited by the commissioner's report—Aetna management decided to start requiring full cash payment for premiums. Although Aetna was innovative in this change and most other insurance companies soon began to follow the new practice, the firm's policyholders were outraged. Many canceled their policies, and new policyholders were not forthcoming. In desperate straits following the policy change and weakened by the financial crisis of the 1870s, Aetna steadily declined. Enders resigned in 1879.

Aetna passed back into family hands when Morgan G. Bulkeley, Eliphalet Bulkeley's son, took over the firm and remained in that position for the next 43 years. Although Morgan Bulkeley had been a director on the Aetna board since his father's death, he had chosen to apprentice as a dry goods merchant rather than rise through his father's firm. His primary interest was in politics. He was active in the state Republican Party his father had helped form. By 1879, he had been a councilman and alderman and was successfully running for mayor of Hartford. He subsequently became governor of Connecticut and then a U.S. senator. Bulkeley maintained firm control over both his government office and his corporate office. While governor, Bulkeley loaned the state of Connecticut $300,000 from Aetna's funds during a period of financial need. In 1911, Bulkeley lost his senate seat and returned full-time to his position with Aetna.

Aetna did very well under the second Bulkeley. Its total assets increased from $25.6 million in 1879 to $207 million in 1922, while premium income increased more than twentyfold during the same period. The number of employees grew from 29 to 2,000. Aetna's success was in large part due to innovations in forms of insurance. The first years of Bulkeley's presidency were spent getting the ailing company back on its feet, but in the 1890s Aetna made its first move to diversify, initiating a period of rapid expansion. In 1891, under its existing charter, Aetna began to write accident insurance, and in 1899 added health insurance. In 1893 its charter was expanded, allowing Aetna to pioneer in the development of liability insurance. In 1902 it opened a separate accident and liability department to handle employers' liability and workmen's collective insurance. Eager to profit from the rapidly growing market for automobile insurance, in 1907 Aetna management transformed the liability department into Aetna Life's first affiliate, the Aetna Accident and Liability Company.

For a few years, this new company issued all the new forms of insurance Aetna offered, but soon further diversification was necessary. In 1912 Aetna offered the first comprehensive auto policy, providing all kinds of auto insurance in one contract, and in 1913 a second Aetna affiliate was formed, the Automobile Insurance Company. The charter of this second affiliate also allowed it to handle other insurance lines: loss of use, explosion, tornado and windstorm, leasehold, rent. In 1916 Aetna Auto began to offer marine insurance, a line that was greatly broadened during World War I. Meanwhile, the Aetna Accident and Liability Company was expanding its business in fidelity and surety bonds, and in 1917 changed its name to the Aetna Casualty and Surety Company.

When Bulkeley died in 1922, Morgan Bulkeley Brainard, grandson of the original Bulkeley, succeeded his uncle as president. Unlike his uncle, Brainard was a company man. Following college, law school, and two years in a law firm, he joined Aetna as assistant treasurer, later becoming treasurer and then vice president. According to Richard Hooker's *Aetna Life Insurance Company: Its First Hundred Years, A History,* Brainard described his uncle as having "built up an unusually strong organization by the sheer force of his personality." Brainard intended to initiate a new style of leadership. "Where Governor Bulkeley could bring men around him and have them work for him by the inspiration of his presence, I cannot. I have got to surround myself with as able a group of men as I possibly can." Accordingly, Brainard focused on efficiency of administration, concentrating particularly on relations and communications with agents in the field. He streamlined procedures, regularized paperwork, and reduced the costs of doing business. The new approach worked. In 1922 life insurance in force was $1.3 billion. By 1929 assets amounted to $411 million and life insurance in force to $3.79 billion. In 1924, Aetna had also acquired a third affiliate, the Standard Fire Insurance Company, which further strengthened its position.

Such expansion, however, did not come without costs. The Automobile Insurance Company, one of Aetna Life's affiliated companies, had contributed to the spectacular increases of the 1920s. In 1922 its premium income reached $11 million; in 1923, $19 million; and in 1924, premium income reached $30 million, but its success was not grounded in a solid financial base. In March 1926, Brainard discovered that Aetna Auto had understated its liabilities and taken on more business than it could handle. The marine division of the affiliate had expanded swiftly during the war years, but had exercised poor judgment in selection of risks, especially following World War I, when solicitation of marine business should have been curtailed. The Automobile Insurance Company had also gained new business by assuming risks from other companies. As his forebears had done in times of financial crisis, Brainard rapidly retrenched. He cut business drastically, resulting in premium income of just $7.9 million by 1927 for the auto affiliate. Reserves were increased to cover liabilities and future underwriting losses.

This crisis during the mid-1920s helped prepare Aetna for the economic shock of the Great Depression. Brainard had, in effect, stemmed the tide of speculation within Aetna while the rest of the country continued to speculate up to the stock market crash of 1929. As a result, during the worst years of the Depression, Aetna's income dropped by only a little more than 10%. Cautious management kept the company solvent. Dividends were not paid between 1932 and 1934, but no Aetna employees were dismissed. In 1929 only 11.7% of Aetna's assets were in common stock, and almost half of that in the stock of Aetna affiliates, another condition that helped Aetna survive during the 1930s. Although the company did suffer because it had assumed growing numbers of farm mortgages which defaulted during the Depression, Brainard's careful business practices kept the losses to a minimum.

World War II finally helped pull Aetna and the nation out of the Depression. The war gave Aetna several opportunities to develop new types of insurance coverage. In cooperation with other insurers, Aetna issued a bonding contract for $312 million that insured the construction of seven aircraft carriers. Aetna was also involved in insuring the production of the atom bomb under the Manhattan Project, a uniquely challenging actuarial task since much of the information was classified. In addition, Aetna was centrally occupied with developing its lines of employee group insurance during these years. Ordinary life insurance premiums remained almost steady during World War II, but group insurance increased dramatically during the war years, increasing overall premium income by almost 65%. Group insurance premiums declined quickly after the war with the switch to a peacetime economy, but Aetna's prewar experience with group insurance helped it rally with relative ease.

In the postwar years, Aetna continued to diversify cautiously. It explored the possibilities of insurance coverage for air travel, became involved in several large bonding issues, and pioneered in the area of driver's education. In 1955, two years after Aetna's centennial, Brainard resigned. Vice president Henry Beers succeeded him as Aetna's fifth president. Brainard's association with Aetna did not end, however, with his resignation; at that time, he became Aetna's first chairman.

With Beers's inauguration, the long history of family control ended and a new era of shorter presidencies began. In 1962 Beers became chairman and J. A. Hill took over as president. One year later Olcott D. Smith succeeded Beers as chairman. In 1972 John H. Filer succeeded Smith as chairman, and Donald M. Johnson was named president in 1970. In 1976, William O. Bailey succeeded Johnson. Through these years of fairly rapid changes in management, the position of chairman and chief executive officer gained ascendancy over that of president and chief operating officer.

In 1960, Aetna entered the international market with the purchase of Excelsior Life Insurance Company of Toronto. To facilitate flexible management of these expanding operations and allow diversification into noninsurance fields, Aetna Life and Casualty Company, a holding company, was created in 1967 with subsidiaries: Aetna Life Insurance Company, Aetna Casualty and Surety, Standard Fire Insurance, and the Automobile Insurance Company. Later that same year Aetna purchased the Participating Annuity Life Insurance Company, becoming the first major insurance firm to enter the variable-annuity market. In 1968 Aetna was first listed on the New York Stock Exchange.

In the late 1960s, Aetna experienced sharp drops in earnings, a trend that reflected an industrywide increase in claims. The decline was reversed in the early 1970s, partly due to nationwide decreases in losses and increases in premiums and partly due to Aetna's move to control costs and concentrate on the most profitable lines of insurance. However, rapid diversification into noninsurance fields later in the same decade seemed to undermine earlier gains. Particularly ill-fated acquisitions were Geosource Inc., an oil-field-services concern, and Satellite Business Systems, a communications firm.

In 1972 Chairman Smith initiated a management change that echoed Brainerd's initiation of his new leadership style 50 years before. In place of administration by one man, Smith introduced the "corporate office" approach, a consensual relationship of the four top managers—chairman, president, and two vice presidents—with the chairman still slightly dominant. Corporate structure was also reorganized.

In 1981 the company reorganized its operations into the current five insurance divisions. The employees benefits division offered group insurance, health-care services, and pension and related financial products to business, government units, associations, and welfare trusts. The personal-financial-security division provided automobile and homeowner insurance, life and health insurance, and retirement funding and annuity products to individuals, small businesses, and employer-sponsored groups. The commercial insurance division marketed property-casualty insurance and bonds for businesses, government units, and associations, including workers' compensation. The American Re-Insurance Company reinsured commercial property and liability risks in domestic and international markets. The international insurance division handled insurance and investment products in non-U.S. markets. The activities of these five insurance sectors were supported by the operations of a financial division that managed all of the firm's investment portfolios.

Income declined in the early 1980s. In 1981, hoping to lead industrywide price increases, Aetna raised commercial insurance prices, a mistimed move that cost it as much as 10% of its business. In addition, the company was forced to lower its 1982 statement of earnings by 39%, in response to a ruling by the Securities and Exchange Commission that disallowed Aetna's practice of booking future tax credits as current earnings.

In 1984, James T. Lynn became chairman and chief executive officer. Like his predecessors in the Bulkeley family, Lynn was active in Republican politics when he accepted the post with Aetna. Trained as a lawyer, he served as secretary of housing and urban development from 1973 to 1975, and as director of the Office of Management and Budget from 1975 to 1977. He implemented a policy of prudent retrenchment, selling subsidiaries that were not performing well and emphasizing Aetna's long-standing priority on insurance. As it had in the past, this policy again proved profitable for Aetna: earnings more than doubled from 1984 to 1985, with record increases in 1986 and 1987.

Ronald E. Compton became president in 1988. Earnings declined by 23% from the previous year, a downturn reflecting increased competition in commercial property-casualty business, rising loss costs in auto and homeowners insurance lines, and losses in international operations. In 1989 the decline continued at the rate of 5% from the previous year, with commercial property-casualty insurances lines affected by two natural disasters, Hurricane Hugo and the San Francisco Bay–area earthquake.

During its first century of existence, control of the company remained largely in the hands of the family of its founding president, Eliphalet A. Bulkeley. Known as a pioneer in new types of insurance, Aetna effectively managed innovations with prudent corporate management and rapid financial retrenchment in periods of decline. In more recent years, its leadership structure has changed and its business diversified into noninsurance fields, not always to the advantage of the company. Under Chairman James T. Lynn, Aetna had benefited from a renewed priority on insurance.

Principal Subsidiaries; Aetna Life Insurance Company; Aetna Life Insurance & Annuity Company; Aetna Casualty & Surety Company; American Re-Insurance Company; Aetna International, Inc.

Further Reading: Hooker, Richard, *Aetna Life Insurance Company: Its First Hundred Years, A History,* Hartford, Connecticut, Aetna Life Insurance Company, 1956.

—Lynn M. Voskuil

ALLIANZ AG HOLDING

Königinstrasse 28
D-8000 Munich 44
Federal Republic of Germany
(89) 38 00 0
Fax: (89) 34 99 41

Public Company
Incorporated: 1890 as Allianz Versicherungs-Aktien-Gesellschaft
Employees: 152,000
Assets: DM133.27 billion (US$78.88 billion)
Stock Exchanges: Berlin Bremen Düsseldorf Frankfurt Hamburg Hanover Munich Stuttgart London Zürich Geneva Basel

Allianz AG Holding is the parent company of the largest insurance group in Europe, with the strongest world network. It was founded as Allianz Versicherungs-Aktien-Gesellschaft in 1890 by Carl Thieme, director of the Munich Reinsurance Company, and the private banker Wilhelm Finck, at the time when the German economy had got back into its stride after a long depression and was entering the second phase of its industrial revolution.

Taking advantage of the rapid spread of mechanization in the workplace and the steeply rising number of industrial and traffic accidents, Thieme and Finck began by concentrating on accident and liability insurance. However, from the 1890s until World War I, Allianz grew and prospered mainly through freight insurance, which with reinsurance has been fundamental to the Allianz story from its beginning. In the view of leading experts of the time, the freight insurance market was very overcrowded, but Paul von der Nahmer, Allianz's second company chairman who led the firm from 1894 with Carl Thieme and from 1904 alone, spotted the great possibilities offered by the rapid expansion in the volume of German trade. In 1913, when Allianz had already become by far the largest German freight insurer, this division produced almost 45% of the firm's premium income.

Before World War I, Allianz had already begun to extend its scope, although it was still far from offering a full composite range. In 1900 it received the first German license to sell plant insurance, and in 1911 it was also licensed to insure against mechanical breakdowns, a service available exclusively from Allianz until 1924. For three decades the role played in the firm's business by these two classes of insurance did not increase, but Allianz's expertise in this area due to its early involvement is one reason for the firm's present undisputed position as market leader in the field of engineering—that is, mechanical, plant, and equipment—insurance. In 1905 Allianz included direct fire insurance in its list of benefits.

Allianz's advance from medium size to the rank of largest insurance group in Germany took place within a few years, between the end of World War I and the mid-1920s. Before the war the Berlin-based firm had drawn only about 20% of its premium income from abroad. Afterward, like all German insurers, it was cut off from international markets almost completely but later, in a rise unparalleled in the history of German insurance, it came to dominate the whole industry. The foundation for this achievement had been laid by Paul von der Nahmer with his sound and far-sighted financial strategy. As one of the few people to assess accurately the effects that war would have on the future of Germany's currency and its insurance industry, he had taken early steps to provide Allianz with substantial foreign currency reserves that helped it to achieve an almost proverbial stability amidst the chaos of inflation. After his death in 1921 his successor, Dr. Kurt Schmitt, used these financial reserves to enable Allianz to achieve the highest turnover of all German insurers.

In 1917, at the age of 31, Schmitt was made executive managing director. His innovations were to lead the company to the top of the German insurance industry and to a major global presence. He attempted to establish a foothold in all markets, to expand into all classes of insurance, and to extend the company's international activities. The conditions of the Treaty of Versailles had stood in the way of the former aim, but his efforts to make the firm active in all classes of insurance were therefore all the more successful. In 1918 he established the motor insurance company Kraft-Versicherungs-AG (Motor Insurance AG), the first large company in Germany to specialize in motor vehicle risks. Immediately after the war ended he also sought collaboration with large life insurance companies. When these negotiations unexpectedly broke down early in 1922, Schmitt, by now chairman of the board of Allianz, founded within the space of ten days the Allianz Lebensversicherungsbank-AG (Allianz Life-Assurance Bank AG), which by 1927 had grown into the largest life insurance company in Europe.

During the hyperinflation of 1922–1923, numerous mergers speeded the firm on its way to the top. Specialist insurance companies were finding it particularly hard to survive, and the German insurance market was hit by a wave of mergers. Allianz concentrated on absorbing only those companies that would fill existing gaps in its own range, both of services and of regions served.

In the years of rapid currency depreciation, Allianz's merger policy differed markedly from that of other companies. It succeeded because it was directed towards maximum rationalization. Whereas in other groups mergers tended to result in little more than a hodgepodge of individual companies, the Berlin group immediately welded all its member companies into an organic whole, created a new overall structure, and finally undertook radical rationalization at home and abroad. The latter task was achieved principally by Hans Hess, who had joined Allianz in 1918.

Until the early 1920s Allianz, in common with all other German insurance companies, employed outdated administration and organization techniques. The Allianz board was the first to realize that combating the effects of inflation and employee rationalization would have to be top priorities. Hess succeeded in introducing the basic principles of scientific management into the insurance business. By means of an assortment of technical and, even more importantly, organizational impovements, he managed a significant increase in productivity and a reduction in costs. He spread a network of branch offices across Germany and ensured that the latest equipment was installed. He replaced the old, strongly independent insurance agents, each working for several companies covering the most varied types of insurance, with agents trained in composite insurance and working solely for Allianz. He also set up a system of incentive schemes for employees, run with an element of sporting competition. Alongside this initiative came the extension of the social installations and services provided for staff. These measures gave the firm great stability in periods of crisis. Even during the world depression Allianz was able to maintain its volume of premiums and considerably increase the number of personnel.

Whereas during the inflation period the firm had concentrated on broadening its scope, after the stabilization of the currency in 1923–1924 it set its sights on growth in volume. It was engaged in a major expansion of its capacities when in the mid 1920s a new wave of amalgamation policies hit German industry, and large groups formed for chemicals manufacture, electrical engineering, and heavy industry gave rise to a significant increase in risk potential.

In 1927 the group surprised the public by announcing a merger with the famous Stuttgarter Verein Versicherungs-AG, the market leader in accident and liability insurance. It was the largest merger to date in the history of German insurance. When in the summer of 1929 the Frankfurter Allgemeine Versicherungs-AG, the second-largest insurance group in Germany, collapsed as the result of illegal, loss-making noninsurance deals, Allianz decided within 24 hours to meet all of the Frankfurter's obligations to its clients. With Münchener Rückversicherungs-AG, Allianz immediately founded the Neue Frankfurter Allgemeine Versicherungs-AG to assume the Frankfurter's liabilities. This dramatic rescue operation saved the whole insurance industry from a serious loss of public confidence and from state intervention in its affairs.

The industry could not, however, escape government interference after Adolf Hitler came to power in 1933 and enlisted savers and insurance policy holders in his secret financial preparations for war. From 1935 onwards the regime obliged insurance companies to increase their subscriptions to government loans; from the summer of 1942 three-quarters of their investment capital was affected in this way.

It was in an attempt to protect the industry from this sort of encroachment that in 1933, after much hesitation, Kurt Schmitt agreed to become trade minister in Hitler's second cabinet. He was convinced he would be able to restrain National Socialism and lead it in the direction he wished it to go. A few weeks were enough to make him regret his action; he gave up the attempt, and after a year took the first opportunity to withdraw from politics. In 1935 he became chairman of the supervisory board of Allianz Lebensversicherungs-AG and in 1938 he was made chairman of the board of directors of Münchener Rück. In 1933 he had been succeeded as chairman of Allianz Versicherungs-AG by his former deputy, Hans Hess, who during the whole of the Third Reich made no secret—even in public—of his profound dislike of Nazism and took part in the resistance movement against Hitler.

During the 1920s and 1930s Allianz expanded its range, venturing into completely new areas of insurance. Its innovations in the field of engineering insurance were particularly forward-looking. It was the first in Germany to offer installation and guarantee insurance, in 1923, and construction and civil engineering insurance, in 1934. While other insurers still saw their role purely and simply in terms of providing financial compensation for loss, Allianz built up an independent technical-advice and loss-prevention service. In 1920, using special engineers, it carried out the first regular inspection of powerplants. From 1924 it also published *Der Maschinen-Schaden* (Mechanical Breakdown), a periodical that today continues to combine the utmost practicality with high scientific standards. In 1932 Allianz set up its first materials- and equipment-testing installation, which swiftly became a highly-reputed center for loss research. The firm completed its activities in this area in 1938 with the introduction of a fire damage prevention service. However, political conditions in the inter-war years meant that it could only scratch the surface of its international aspirations.

World War II hit Allianz hard. The head office in Berlin was completely demolished, and since it was situated in the eastern part of the city there could be no question of rebuilding it. The partition of Germany also meant the loss of a large part of its marketing area, together with several of its most successful branch offices. At the end of the war the various specialized sections of the company were scattered all over Germany in numerous different locations. There were no longer any headquarters. With the difficulty of communications between the western zone of Germany and West Berlin, particularly after the Berlin blockade of 1948, it became clear that in the interest of the company as a whole, Berlin must now be ruled out as a future base. The seat of the central management was therefore moved to Munich, and that of Allianz Lebensversicherungs-AG to Stuttgart.

In October 1948 Hess relinquished the chairmanship of the board of management. He was succeeded by Hans Goudefroy, who made it his business to preserve the assets of the Allianz group and its internal stability even after the currency reform of 1948. In the mid-1950s, under his leadership, Allianz completed its second phase of rationalization. The adoption of electronic data processing—in 1956 the board of directors started using one of Europe's earliest computers—is a striking example of the many innovations embraced since then by Allianz. At the same time, by a rapid expansion of its foreign business network, the group regained its leading position in the German insurance market. Such dramatic growth was without precedent in Europe. Outstripping all other insurers, Allianz acquired a presence in every part of the Federal Republic of Germany, and owing to its new slogan, " . . . höffentlich Allianz versichert!" (I hope you're insured with Allianz!), created in the mid-1950s, it became known to virtually everybody.

During the 1950s and 1960s Allianz concentrated almost exclusively on the home market, with the emphasis on private insurance, though it did make some advances in the large-risk industrial sector, particularly in the area of engineering insurance.

In February 1962, following the premature death of Goudefroy at the end of the preceding year, the chairmanship of the board of management was taken over by Alfred Haase, previously organization manager of the Allianz group. In a smooth transition, Haase carried on the work of his predecessor, further expanding the network of agents, developing the domestic private insurance business, and continuing internal rationalization. During his term of office the Allianz Allgemeine Rechtsschutzversicherungs-AG (Allianz General Patent Insurance A.G.) was founded; it commenced trading in 1970. Haase also presided over further developments in loss prevention. In 1969 the old testing installation was renamed the Allianz Center for Technology and in 1971 it was enlarged by the creation of the Institute of Motor Vehicle Technology.

At the turn of the 1970s the German insurance industry was faced with new problems, most notably a cost explosion due to steep wage rises throughout the whole economy. In addition a sharp increase in the accident rate had taken the motor insurance sector into the red. Competition throughout the industry was becoming much fiercer, too. Although Allianz's turnover continued to climb, net yield began to fall. Into this very difficult situation stepped Wolfgang Schieren, who in 1971 came to the group as managing director. As had happened half a century before under Kurt Schmitt, there began a new phase in the firm's history. Schieren began by ordering a halt to staff recruitment and instigating a radical cost reduction program. While competitors' staff numbers continued to rise, the Munich group was already economizing in order to invest for the future.

A second consequence of Schieren's appointment was that Allianz ceased concentrating its acquisition activities primarily on private insurance and gave equal consideration to large-risk industrial and commercial business. Within a few years the firm became the foremost German concern in this increasingly important sector, in certain areas of which, such as engineering insurance, it is a world leader. Restructuring of the organization of industrial insurance formed part of this new orientation. In 1987 an operation began that was to extend over several years, aimed at simplifying the hitherto complicated classifications of large-risk industrial insurance.

Finally, under Wolfgang Schieren, Allianz evolved from a domestically-focused business to an internationally oriented insurer. In 1970 the group's premium income was DM4 billion, only 3.2% derived from abroad; in 1989, out of a total income of DM31.8 billion, 40% came from foreign premiums. Allianz reacted promptly to the increasing internationalism of German industry as West Germany developed, from the beginning of the 1970s, from being a mere exporter to being a foreign investor. As Allianz expanded its services to industry, it wanted to offer its clients insurance cover for their foreign investments too. It was realized early on at Allianz's Munich headquarters that dramatic changes were taking place in industry and that an insurer who was active only at a national level could no longer meet the needs of increasingly multinational enterprises.

During the first phase of these foreign activities Allianz tried to gain a footing in foreign markets mainly by setting up new companies. The Allianz International Insurance Company Ltd. began trading in London in 1975, and similar companies were established in Spain and the Netherlands. In France the Paris board of directors was enlarged. In 1977 the firm ventured into the U.S. market for the first time, setting up the Allianz Insurance Company to deal in property insurance in Los Angeles. This development ended the first phase of Allianz's foreign expansion.

In 1974, constrained by the legal upper limit set for foreign investors, Allianz had bought a 30% share in a Brazilian insurance company which from then on traded under the name of Allianz Ultramar. In 1977 the group acquired from Commercial Union of London the Anglo-Elementar-Versicherungs-AG with headquarters in Vienna, and two years later, in the United States, the North American Life and Casualty Company, based in Minneapolis, Minnesota, as well as the Fidelity Union Life Insurance Company of Dallas. In the same period Allianz established a foothold in Australia, and in 1981 it moved into Chile.

The creation of this world network went almost unnoticed by the public until the beginning of the 1980s when Allianz, in a dramatic takeover attempt, tried to obtain a majority holding in the British Eagle Star Insurance Company. By June 1981 the German group had acquired almost 30% of Eagle Star's shares. At the end of 1983 there was a battle between Allianz and the conglomerate BAT Industries for the remaining shares. BAT emerged the victor, though Allianz made a profit of £156.5 million by selling off the Eagle Star shares bought in 1981.

In 1986 Allianz did succeed in establishing itself in the United Kingdom, however, when it acquired from BTR plc the Cornhill Insurance Company, founded in 1905. Cornhill's foreign interests afforded, among other advantages, an entry into the developing east Asian market. In 1984 Allianz had already taken a further step towards internationalism with the acquisition of a majority holding in the Riunione Adriatica di Sicurtá (RAS), the second-largest insurance company in Italy. Through RAS's wide foreign network Allianz gained entry into several countries in which it previously had had little or no representation.

Interests were acquired in Argentina, Spain, and Greece, and a new company was formed in Indonesia. In collaboration with local banks, life-insurance companies were set up in Spain and Greece. In 1985 Allianz reorganized as Allianz AG Holding, to reflect its size and diversity. In September 1989, in the fight for control of the French insurance group VIA/Rhin et Moselle, Allianz acquired—within the space of a few days—first 50%, then 65% of the shares as the previous owner, the conglomerate Compagnie de Navigation Mixte with the help of Allianz managed to fend off a takeover attempt by the state insurance company AGF and the bank Paribas. Another sensational acquisition, this time in Budapest at the end of 1989, was that of a 49% interest in Hungary's former state insurance company Hungária Biztositó, which had come into being three years earlier when the state monopoly company was split into two parts. Allianz thus demonstrated its interest in any east European market willing to adapt to the free market economy. Finally, Allianz made a considerable stir at home by buying a 51% interest in the

Deutschen Versicherungs-AG, which was founded on July 1, 1990, to take over the business of the former East German state insurance service. The crowning achievement among all these foreign activities was undoubtedly the acquisition of the Firemen's Fund Insurance Company of Novato, California, a U.S. insurance group which in 1989 received $3.4 billion in premiums. By this one move the Allianz group almost quadrupled its premium income in the United States. No other insurer is as active internationally as Allianz.

This unprecedented expansion would not have been possible without group restructuring. The dual functioning of Allianz Versicherungs-AG as a primary insurance company operating in the home market as well as a holding company, proved a hindrance to the expansion of international activities and increased industrial involvement as well as to the marked growth of its inter-group company reinsurance. In June 1985 the direct German property insurance business was transferred to a fully owned subsidiary under the name Allianz Versicherungs-AG (Allianz Insurance AG). The interest in Allianz Lebensversicherungs-AG (Allianz Life Assurance AG) and the foreign subsidiaries remained under the holding company now trading as Allianz AG, which has also taken over the reinsurance business passed on by the Allianz companies. In spite of all the group's business successes and new acquisitions, this reorganization must be seen as the most significant event in Allianz's history since World War II.

With its superior structure and management, technical equipment, and international presence, as well as the wide range of services it offers, Allianz has set world standards. In technical insurance in particular it is always the first to advise on occasions when even the largest construction projects, such as the Eurotunnel that is to link the United Kingdom and the Continent, are in need of support. The Allianz Center for Technology is undoubtedly the foremost institution in the European insurance industry for loss-research and prevention. It constitutes an essential basis for the full risk services offered by the enterprise.

In the recent past these many successes have boosted dramatically the price of Allianz shares, which doubled in value between 1975 and 1982, and increased tenfold by the end of 1989. In 1990 Allianz had the highest stock market capitalization of any German enterprise.

Principal Subsidiaries: Alico-Beteiligungsgesellschaft mbH; Allianz Allgemeine Rechtsschutzversicherungs-AG (50%); Allianz Beteiligungsgesellschaft mbH (89.2%); Allianz Grundstücks-AG; Allianz Kapitalanlagegesellschaft mbH; Allianz Unternehmensbeteiligungsgesellschaft AG; Allianz Vermögensverwaltungsgesellschaft mbH; Allianz Versicherungs AG; Allianz Verwaltungsgesellschaft mhH; Allianz Zentrum Für Technik GmbH; Aquila Beteiligungsgesellschaft mbH; Assecuranz-Compagnie Mercur AG (50%); Beta-Vermögensverwaltungsgesellschaft mbH; Frankfurter Versicherungs-AG (49.9%); Globus Versicherungs-AG (98.8%); Interunfall Allgemeine Versicherungs-AG; Komet Automobil-Beteiligungsgesellschaft mbH; Kraft Versicherungs-AG (49.8%); Münchener Lebensversicherung AG (75%); Nona-Vermögensverwaltungsgesellschaft mbH; Oktava-Vermögensverwaltungsgesellschaft mbH; Prima-Vermögensverwaltungsgesellschaft mbH (69.4%); Quarta-Vermögensverwaltungsgesellschaft mbH (57.2%); Quinta-Vermögensverwaltungsgesellschaft mbH; Septima-Vermögensverwaltungsgesellschaft mbH; Sexta-Vermögensverwaltungsgesellschaft mbH; Firemen's Fund Insurance Company (U.S.A.); Deutschen Versicherungs-AG (51%); Akquila, Incorporated; Allianz Arab-German Insurance Company S.A. (Luxemborg); Allianz Compañia de Seguros S.A. (Chile); Allianz-Ercos S.A. de Seguros y Reaseguros (Spain, 51%); Allianz Europe Ltd. (Netherlands); Allianz Finance B.V. (Netherlands); Allianz France Société Anonyme d'Assurances sur la Vie (France, 98.6%); Allianz Industrial Compañia de Seguros y Reaseguros, S.A. (Spain): Allianz Insurance Company (U.S.A.); Allianz Insurance (Singapore) Pte. Ltd.; Allianz Nederland N.V. (Netherlands); Allianz of America, Inc. (U.S.A., 52%); Allianz of South Africa (Proprietary) Ltd.; Allianz Pace Assicurazioni e Riassicurazioni S.p.A. (Italy, 50%); Allianz RAS Holding France (96.2%); Allanz RAS Tutela Giudiziaria S.p.A. (Italy); Allianz S.A. (Spain); Allianz (UK) Ltd.; Allianz Underwriters Insurance Company (U.S.A.); Allianz Versicherung (Schweiz) AG (Switzerland); Anglo-Elementar Versicherungs-AG (Austria, 91.7%); Cornhill Insurance PLC (U.K., 99.7%); Fidelity Union Life Insurance Company (U.S.A.); North American Life and Casualty Company (U.S.A.); Via Assurances I.A.R.D. Société Anonyme d'Assurances et de Réassurances à Primes Fixes (France, 64.7%).

Further Reading: Arps, Ludwig, *Wechselvolle Zeiten: 75 Jahre Allianz Versicherung 1890–1965,* Munich, Allianz-Versicherungs-AG, 1975; Borscheid, Peter, *100 Jahre Allianz 1890–1990,* Munich, Allianz Aktiengesellschaft Holding, 1990.

—Peter Borscheid
Translated from the German by Olive Classe

AMERICAN FAMILY CORPORATION

American Family Center
1932 Wynnton Road
Columbus, Georgia 31999
U.S.A.
(404) 323-3431
Fax: (404) 323-1448

Public Company
Incorporated: 1973
Employees: 3,005
Assets: $6.52 billion
Stock Exchanges: New York Pacific Tokyo

Established in April 1973 as the holding company for a specialized insurance subsidiary, the American Family Corporation now operates more than 25 insurance and broadcasting units throughout the world, with the bulk of its business in the United States and Japan. The company's chief operating units, the American Family Life Assurance Company of Columbus, Georgia, (AFLAC) and AFLAC Japan, have developed a number of unique marketing techniques to sell a product which they introduced more than 30 years ago—supplementary cancer expense insurance. The company has been one of the fastest-growing companies in the health insurance industry. AFLAC, American Family's chief operating company, was founded in 1955 with about $300,000 in capital. American Family now has assets in excess of $6 billion.

In 1955, a young lawyer named John B. Amos returned to his hometown of Columbus, Georgia, and with his two brothers, Bill and Paul, and father Shelby, founded the American Family Life Assurance Company of Columbus, Georgia. After struggling for three years, selling life, health, and accident insurance door-to-door in Georgia and Alabama, Amos decided that AFLAC would do better if it could find a specific market niche. In 1958 he developed a cancer insurance policy based on the polio policies of previous decades, and AFLAC's 150 licensed agents sold 5,810 cancer care policies in the first year.

AFLAC's cancer-care policy was intended to cover the expenses not covered by comprehensive health insurance. John Amos's research reckoned that most comprehensive policies covered only about 70% of the costs of cancer treatment. The early policies were designed to cover up to 50% of the average cost of cancer treatment, with the extra coverage to help protect against such expenses as travel and loss of income. The increase of cancer incidence and the high cost of its treatment made the policies popular. By the end of 1959 AFLAC was writing $900,000 in premiums and had begun to operate in Florida.

The company continually looked for new ways to market its policies. In 1964 it began making presentations to groups rather than to individuals and developed the "cluster-selling" technique, which was very successful. Agents first approached a company or organization for permission to make a presentation to its employees or members. The agent made a group sales pitch with the implicit endorsement of the company. This method allowed agents to reach more prospects at a given time, and the cooperation of the organization was a selling point. In addition, many companies implemented a payroll deduction plan for the premiums, reducing AFLAC's processing costs. Cluster-selling boosted the company's premiums to $7 million by 1967.

Cluster-selling proved a very effective way to sell cancer insurance. American Family built up an aggressive, well-paid sales force that would typically sell to 5% of a group's members immediately. The salesman would return later, and usually sign up the rest. Years later John Amos explained the technique's success: "Sooner or later, there's going to be a cancer in the group. If he's insured, he's satisfied, and the word gets around to the rest of them. And if he's not insured, he's sorry, and we get the rest of them."

During the late 1960s AFLAC greatly increased the number of states in which it did business. An agreement with the Globe Life Insurance Company, of Chicago, which was licensed to sell insurance throughout the country, resulted in AFLAC's policies being sold nationwide; Globe sold the policies and AFLAC reinsured them, so that when AFLAC wanted to be licensed itself, it could show state insurance commissioners that its policies were already available in their state and that the company was already making good on claims. Between 1969 and 1971 AFLAC increased the number of states in which it operated from 11 to 42.

In 1973 the American Family Corporation was formed as a holding company for AFLAC. A year later the company's headquarters moved from a modest collection of houses into the new 18-story American Family Center. In June 1974, American Family's shares were listed on the New York Stock Exchange.

During the 1970s a number of companies, seeing American Family's success, introduced cancer policies of their own. By the end of the decade there were about 300 insurers selling cancer coverage. American Family, however, handily controlled the market, having sold about 60% of all cancer policies. The company, in fact, claimed to be the world's fastest-growing insurance company. Between 1972 and 1977 annual premium income rose 294% to $205 million, while earnings jumped to $25 million—a 181% increase.

Much of American Family's success in the mid-1970s was the result of its entry into the rapidly expanding Japanese market. When Chairman John Amos visited Japan in 1970, he was convinced that it would be an excellent market for his cancer-care policies. The Japanese industry, however, was well entrenched, and foreign companies found it virtually impossible to get licensing. Amos was not deterred, and quickly formulated a plan to gain acceptance for his company's product in Japan.

When AFLAC was licensed by Japan's Ministry of Finance to sell insurance, in 1974, it was only the second U.S. company to be allowed to do so in more than two decades. Part of AFLAC's success came from the fact that it offered a product that was not yet available from Japanese insurers, at a time when cancer awareness was expanding. Another factor was AFLAC's decision to employ retired workers as its agents, a move that impressed both former co-workers—potential policyholders—and the Ministry of Finance. Also, Amos's choice of company officers was truly inspired: it included many luminaries of the Japanese insurance industry. Furthermore, these executives enlisted the support of the medical community even before AFLAC applied for its license.

Once AFLAC received permission to sell its product, it further moved to insure its own success by signing up large Japanese industrial and financial groups as agents—a variation on the cluster-selling theme. AFLAC paid commissions to the companies, which made the presentations themselves. Huge conglomerates like the Mitsui and Mitsubishi groups, and the Dai-Ichi Kangyo and Sanwa banks tapped thousands of their own employees before having to search for customers. The plan was an unprecedented success. Japanese consumers had the money to buy coverage, meticulously paid their premiums, and had a very high rate of policy renewal. By 1987 the Japanese market accounted for two-thirds of American Family's total revenues, and 70% of aftertax earnings.

Just as American Family's cancer insurance began taking off in Japan, the cancer insurance industry came under close scrutiny from a number of consumer groups in the United States. Two congressional committees investigated the product. The major complaints were that cancer insurance had limited value because it did not cover the entire cost of the disease and that the companies selling it, including American Family, used hard-sell tactics that exploited fear of cancer, particularly in elderly people.

John Amos was characteristically aggressive in defense of his company and its product. In 1979 American Family sued the American Broadcasting Company for alleged damages that resulted from a segment on insurance fraud on the network's "World News Tonight" program. A similar lawsuit was filed against *Changing Times* magazine several months later.

In June 1980 John Amos appeared before the Senate Subcommittee on Antitrust and Monopoly. A Senate aide described the scene to *Barron's*, July 28, 1980: "Amos sat with an attorney on each side of him and four corporate vice presidents behind. There were public relations people handing out press kits by the door. They brought their own easels to display a bunch of charts. The hearing room was packed with sales agents and satisfied policyholders from every state. There were four senators there—Hatch, Laxalt, Leahy, and Thurmond—to introduce their satisfied constituents. There was applause and cheers from the audience at every statement Amos made, and groans every time [Senator] Metzenbaum spoke."

The Metzenbaum committee's report, a study from the Federal Trade Commission, another from the Massachusetts Department of Insurance, along with several independent reports all suggested that cancer insurance was not a good buy because it covered only about a third of the actual costs of the disease, left a policyholder uncovered if struck by any other disease, and had a high premium relative to benefits.

American Family pointed out that in spite of all the controversy millions of informed customers wanted the coverage and continued to buy it. On the subject of fear being used to make sales, John Amos commented, "All insurance is sold on fear." By the time the controversy began to die down, in 1982, Missouri, New York, New Jersey, and Connecticut had all placed restrictions on the sale of dread-disease policies.

American Family had, meanwhile been building a chain of television and radio stations in the southern United States. In 1978, as the company passed the $1 billion mark in assets, American Family acquired WYEA-TV in Columbus, Georgia, and an NBC affiliate in Huntsville, Alabama. In 1979 two CBS affiliates were acquired, in Cape Girardeau, Missouri, and Savannah, Georgia. A year later, the Black Hawk Broadcasting Group, which consisted of two Iowa NBC affiliates, was purchased for $34.2 million.

Throughout the 1980s American Family continued to deal in media-oriented companies. In 1981 the group sold WYEA-TV to remain flexible within FCC regulations at a gain of about $1 million. Communicorp, an advertising and print media subsidiary, was also formed that year. In 1982 the cable franchises acquired in the Black Hawk Broadcasting deal were sold to CBS for a profit. In 1984 the Howard Printing Company was purchased for 56,952 shares and merged into Communicorp. Several more television stations were acquired in the latter half of the decade: WITN-TV in Washington–New Bern, North Carolina, for $25 million, in 1985; a Baton Rouge, Louisiana, CBS station for $59 million, in 1988; and an ABC station in Columbus, Georgia, in 1989, for $45 million. By the end of the 1980s, the broadcasting group was contributing about 5% of American Family's total revenues.

In 1983 several executive changes took place at American Family. Paul Amos, John Amos's brother, was moved up from president—a position he had held since his brother Bill's retirement in 1978—to vice chairman. Sal Diaz-Verson became president of the holding company, and Daniel P. Amos was elected president of AFLAC. Daniel Amos, John Amos' nephew, became deputy CEO in 1988, in preparation for his eventual promotion to CEO.

American Family's business in Japan became more significant throughout the 1980s. By 1986 AFLAC Japan's policies increased to 5.4 million, compared to 731,000 a decade earlier. In 1981 cancer became the leading cause of death in Japan, and while cancer insurance was criticized in the United States, it was welcomed by the Japanese, whose general health insurance picture was very different. Health insurance was written under the country's nationalized medicine program,and certain diseases were not covered. A co-payment of at least 10% was also a standard feature. Supplemental dread-disease policies, therefore, became extremely popular, particularly with cancer, where many costs are non-medical. Cancer insurance was widely accepted, and AFLAC Japan controlled 88% of the market by 1988.

While American Family's success in Japan has been stunning, there are certain pitfalls. Japanese regulations prevent the repatriation of Japanese earnings to the United States. The company earns 70% of its revenues in Japan, and cannot invest that money outside the country. Also, with such a large percentage of its income earned in yen, fluctuation in the value of the foreign currency is a threat to American Family's bottom line.

While the overwhelming majority of American Family's revenues have been, and continue to be, generated by cancer insurance, the company has introduced a number of other products over the years. In 1970 intensive-care coverage was introduced. Supplemental senility policies were introduced in Japan in 1984, providing coverage for Alzheimer's disease and three other forms of senility. In 1985 a universal life insurance policy was introduced, followed by a Medicare supplemental policy a year later. In 1988 two new lines were introduced: accident insurance and advance life insurance, which allowed a policyholder to receive 25% of death benefits upon diagnosis of heart attack, internal cancer, or stroke, leaving 75% for beneficiaries.

During the late 1980s founder John Amos himself, suffered from cancer. Amos died in 1990 and was succeeded as chairman by his brother, Paul S. Amos. Paul Amos's son, Daniel P. Amos, added the duties of CEO and chief operating officer of American Family Corporation, while remaining president of AFLAC. John Amos had built a huge financial corporation out of a small market niche. With assets of over $6 billion, the company's future looks secure, and the company's new management team looks for new ways to expand.

Principal Subsidiaries: American Family Life Assurance Company of Columbus; AFLAC Japan.

Further Reading: McMennamin, Breeze, " 'A Heck Of A Sales Force,' " *Forbes*, March 1, 1977; "American Family: Big Profits from Cancer Insurance," *Dun's Review*, March 1978; Englade, Kenneth F., "The First American Family of Japan," *Across the Board*, March 1987.

—Thomas M. Tucker

AMERICAN FINANCIAL CORPORATION

One East Fourth Street
Cincinnati, Ohio 45202
U.S.A.
(513) 579-2121
Fax: (513) 579-2580

Public Company With Privately Held Common Stock
Incorporated: 1955 as Henthy Realty Company
Employees: 53,000
Assets: $11.97 billion
Stock Exchanges: Cincinnati Pacific

American Financial Corporation is a diversified holding company with 53% of its assets in property and casualty insurance, life insurance, and tax sheltered annuity programs. Other subsidiaries include a savings and loan association, food products, television and radio operations, film/video production, petroleum marketing and crude oil production, and portfolio investment, as well as two theme parks and a sports center located in Cincinnati, Ohio.

American Financial Corporation's principal founders were chairman and president, Carl H. Lindner, and his younger brothers, Robert D. and Richard E. The Lindner family, born and raised in Ohio, started in business without benefit of a formal education, family connection, or family money. Carl Henry Lindner, born April 22, 1919, and his brothers left high school before graduating to help with the family's small dairy business. The business finally succeeded in the 1940s under Carl Lindner's leadership, with an entrepreneurial concept credited to their father. The Lindners' United Dairy Farmers outlets, stores where purchasers could save on the cost of milk by direct purchase instead of home delivery, were spread through the Cincinnati area. While United Dairy is still in operation under the direction of Robert Lindner, primary owner and manager, the success spurred the Lindner brothers into further business ventures.

On November 15, 1955, Henthy Realty Company was incorporated in Ohio by the Lindners. By 1959, the company owned three small savings and loan associations in Ohio and recorded assets of $17.7 million.

In September 1960, the company adopted its present name, American Financial Corporation (AFC). Through its subsidiaries, this financial holding company owned office buildings in Cincinnati, Norwood, and Loveland, Ohio; leased motor vehicles; and developed commercial properties.

In 1962 American Financial Corporation obtained property and casualty insurance business with the acquisition of Dempsey & Siders Agency. In 1963 AFC undertook life insurance business by acquiring United Liberty Life. The same year AFC acquired 98% of the outstanding shares of Athens National Bank in Ohio. The stock purchase totaled $2.3 million in cash and assumption of seller debt.

During the 1960s, American Financial Corporation acquired large stock positions in a number of companies, including the Insurance Company of North America, Chubb & Son, and Ohio Casualty. From 1968 to 1972, AFC pursued several companies, acquiring or gaining control of 16 concerns and their subsidiaries, 7 of which were insurance related.

AFC remained active in the financial arena, and in 1966 sold its interest in Athens National Bank before acquiring a 92% share of The Provident Bank in Ohio. According to *Barron's*, July 4, 1988, the management of Provident Bank resisted the takeover bid. AFC triumphed and its assets increased to nearly $350 million.

In February 1971, AFC pursued a new venture—*The Cincinnati Enquirer.* AFC acquired 95.5% of the daily newspaper, beating out such competitors as the Knight-Ridder chain and Omaha investor Warren Buffett. At the close of 1971, AFC's stockholders numbered more than 14,000, and its assets stood at over $538 million.

By late 1973 AFC had amassed approximately 96% of common stock and 85% of the warrants and had gained financial control of a West Coast conglomerate, National General Corporation. The merger was completed in March 1974.

National General Corporation, incorporated in Delaware in 1952 as National Theatres, Inc., was involved in the operation of motion picture theatres in the United States and abroad, motion picture production and distribution, and cable and closed-circuit television, but 70% of National General Corporation's (NGC) assets were in insurance and publishing.

NGC's holdings included the publishers Grosset & Dunlap, Inc., and Bantam Books, Inc.; the Great American Life Insurance Company of East Orange, New Jersey, procured in 1968; and its parent sponsor, the Great American Insurance Company.

Great American Life Insurance Company (GALIC) was originally domiciled in East Orange, New Jersey. The company was sponsored by Great American Insurance Company, and initial resources were generated by the purchase of 100,000 shares of common stock. GALIC was incorporated and licensed in 1959. In 1962, GALIC sold an additional 100,000 shares of common stock to its sponsor for nearly $1.3 million. At that time, GALIC, licensed in all states except Kansas and New York, wrote nonparticipating life insurance, accident, and health insurance.

The Great American Insurance Company (GAIC) was incorporated in New York on March 6, 1872, and began business in New York City the following day with $1 million in authorized capital. The company remained at this status until 1903, when it received additional capital of $500,000 and was paid surplus funds of over $913,000. Eight years later, in

May 1911, The Rochester German Insurance Company, located in Rochester, New York, merged with GAIC.

Starting in 1918, Great American Insurance Company began steadily to increase its capital from the $2 million gained in 1911 from the merger. GAIC created a holding company in 1929, which was dissolved in 1953. The increases in capital were facilitated by the trading of shares in a number of other insurance companies, including the Detroit Fire & Marine Insurance Company, the American Alliance Company, Great American Indemnity Company, and the Rochester American Insurance Company.

In May 1948, GAIC's corporate structure was simplified. Its wholly owned subsidiary, County Fire Insurance Company, in Philadelphia, was dissolved, the outstanding capital stock cancelled, and its assets and liabilities transferred to GAIC. In 1953 the group was simplified further by dissolution of the affiliate, Great American Corporation, and a merger with the affiliate, American Alliance Insurance Company.

First Insurance Company of Hawaii was acquired by GAIC in 1963. Another acquisition, that of Constellation Insurance Company, renamed in 1975 Constellation Reinsurance Company, was completed two years later. By 1966, GAIC's assets had grown to $15.6 million.

In 1967 control of Great American Insurance Company was taken by the newly formed Great American Holding Corporation. The following year this holding company became a subsidiary of National General Corporation and then was merged with that organization less than four months later. The administrative offices of Great American Insurance Company were moved to the National General Corporation's headquarters in Los Angeles, California, in 1970.

The offices were again moved after the merger of National General Corporation and American Financial Corporation, this time to Cincinnati, Ohio, AFC's headquarters. AFC had already gained control of GAIC in December 1971. AFC's 1974 merger with National General Corporation gave AFC direct ownership and all outstanding capital stock in GAIC, whose assets totaled $566 million. According to *Barron's*, July 4, 1988, "What attracted [Carl] Lindner to the company [National General Corporation] was its giant property and casualty operation, Great American Insurance Co. . . . "

With the NGC merger and the acquisition of Great American Insurance Company and GALIC, AFC's assets escalated to over $2 billion. The merger also launched American Financial Corporation as one of the country's major international insurance concerns.

Great American Insurance Company and its subsidiaries were licensed to write and were writing practically all forms of insurance in every state and territory, as well as in Canada and in other countries. There were approximately 5,600 agents and brokers representing the company worldwide, with regional offices in 18 U.S. cities.

While Carl Lindner remained in active control as chairman, GAIC administration was directed by Stanley R. Zax, president since December 1973. GALIC was led by Jovite LaBonte, who had been appointed president and director in 1972.

Under LaBonte's direction, GALIC stopped writing group life coverage and individual and group accident and health policies in 1974. The company's business—produced through managing general agents, agents, and brokers—included nonparticipating ordinary life and term contracts. In 1975, GALIC introduced a new product line—tax sheltered and single-premium annuity contracts. By 1980 these contracts produced 97% of all premium income.

Although the property and casualty insurance industry experienced some difficulty at the time of NGC's merger, AFC had now moved decisively into the insurance industry. *The National Underwriter,* October 24, 1975, reported that, according to Charles Keating, who was AFC's executive vice-president from 1973 to 1977, " . . . the management of AF[C] has been intentionally evolving toward the insurance business ever since it was formed. . . . " An estimated 60% of AFC's revenues in 1975 were being generated from property and casualty insurance, mostly from Great American Insurance Company.

The stock market collapse in 1973–1974 lessened the values AFC was able to realize from the sale of Bantam Books, Grosset & Dunlap, and the various theatre units gained from the NGC merger. Inflation caused insurance claims and expenses to soar above premium income. Housing starts plummeted during the 1974–1975 recession. The merger was costly—more than $500 million in cash, security, and debt assumption.

By early 1975, American Financial Corporation was facing a serious crisis—the maturity of an $85 million debt issue without cash or bank lines for payment. This situation existed in spite of the fact that, at the close of 1974, GAIC's new premiums written exceeded $387 million and consolidated policyholders' surplus funds totaled $112 million. To cover the debt, AFC sold several small insurance operations. American Empire Insurance Company and Constellation Reinsurance Company were sold to and absorbed by Great American Insurance Company. AFC also sold *The Cincinnati Enquirer*, the price in excess of $50 million providing a $10.6 million profit for AFC. In addition, GAIC increased premiums for commercial lines and shortened auto policies to six months. AFC was soon back on solid ground.

AFC's insurance divisions underwent considerable structural change in 1976. AFC sold its 68% interest in United Liberty Life Insurance Company to GAIC for consolidation purposes. Great American Insurance Company in Cincinnati was incorporated as the result of the merger of Great American Insurance Company in New York with American Continental Insurance Company of Ohio. The latter had been incorporated in October 1942, as Manufacturers & Merchants Indemnity Company, and had undergone several name changes: to Selective Insurance Company in 1956, to American Financial Insurance Company, and then American Continental Insurance Company in 1972. In October 1976, all AFC's insurance operations were consolidated under Great American Insurance Company.

At the close of 1976, GAIC had 4,320 employees and had written $578 million in net premiums. Its subsidiaries included Agricultural Insurance Company, American National Fire Insurance Company, Great American Life Insurance Company, Republic Indemnity Company of America, American Alliance Insurance Company, Fidelity National Life Insurance Company, American Insurance Agency, American-

Financial Insurance Group, and the Constellation Reinsurance Company. In 1977, the latter was reorganized and sold.

From 1977 to 1979 AFC and GAIC pursued a number of stock and acquisition interests. In 1977 AFC purchased the Stonewall Insurance Company, which included two property-casualty insurance and two life-health subsidiary companies. GAIC purchased the outstanding stock in these enterprises, but later sold the two life insurance divisions.

In 1978 GAIC acquired K.C.C. Holding Company and purchased all outstanding stock in American Continental Insurance Company and its two affiliate insurance companies. In late 1979, the outstanding capital stock was acquired in Transport Management Company in Dallas.

Ronald F. Walker, GAIC's executive vice president since 1972, took over its presidency in 1980. During Walker's first year in office, Great American Insurance Company sold two of its life insurance subsidiaries to Great American Life Insurance Company: United Liberty Life Insurance Company and FN Life Insurance Company. The latter was absorbed by GALIC, now located in Ohio, by a merger in 1982. Carl Lindner continued to serve actively as chairman and CEO.

In 1981, Lindner made the company private. He and his immediate family owned nearly 90% of AFC and the majority of its subsidiaries, including Great American Insurance Company and Great American Life Insurance Company.

Lindner had long established a reputation for insurance company acquisitions. During the 1980s AFC made major stock purchases in Mission Insurance Company (MIC), a property-casualty insurance concern in California, which concentrated on workers' compensation insurance. The insurance industry was beginning to emerge from the past decade's recession years, and by early 1984 Lindner had acquired a 49.9% interest in the MIC group.

Mission Insurance Company's financial troubles soon came to light—a situation blamed on poor underwriting and the company's reinsurance business. Final reports in 1983 showed a loss of $37.3 million. Stock plunged from 41 to 6⅜; a loss of $198 million was recorded in 1984, leaving a net worth of $43 million to support the $400 million of premiums in force.

In March 1985, AFC initiated a recapitalization program for MIC. Shares of the Transport Indemnity Company, a trucking insurance company acquired by GAIC in 1981 that had been losing money, were added to MIC's capital and surplus.

AFC's efforts did not solve the failing concern's problem. In October 1985, the California Insurance Commissioner declared MIC insolvent and placed it under conservatorship. For the first nine months of the year, AFC was $31 million in the red. According to *Barron's,* July 4, 1988, "Lindner's American Financial took a loss of $162 million, writing off the entire value of its stock interest and Mission loans."

During AFC's harried involvement with MIC, Great American Insurance Company, then ranked number 24 among casualty insurers, was operating as the company's core insurance operation and generating enormous cash revenues. In mid-1984, about the same time MIC's flaws had surfaced, GAIC implemented significant price increases.

By 1986, the property and casualty insurance industry had rebounded from its crisis era. AFC added several new product lines including life. Great American Life Insurance Company's activity had by then become focused predominantly on individual tax-sheltered annuities, which accounted for almost all premium income in 1986.

American Financial Corporation's annual report for 1987 showed that property and casualty insurance represented 27% of its revenues, with life insurance and annuities at 8%. While ranked as the second-largest contributor of revenues, property and casualty insurance was AFC's highest source of assets, with life insurance and annuities second at 26% and 21%, respectively. That year, Great American Insurance Company showed net earnings of $200 million. The years 1988 and 1989 saw slightly smaller net earnings of $188 and $102 million, respectively.

Nearly all of the 1987 premiums of AFC's annuity and life insurance business were related to annuities, sold primarily to teachers. These annuity premiums increased 26% from 1985 to 1986, and decreased by 11% from 1986 to 1987. The decline was attributed to a reduced demand for IRAs due to new tax regulations.

Since 1959, American Financial Corporation, with Carl Lindner always at the helm, has grown from a small company with $17.7 million in assets and 50 employees, to a conglomerate with 53,000 employees and $12 billion in assets. American Financial's primary insurance business in 1990 was in multi-line property and casualty insurance, headed by its wholly owned subsidiary, Great American Insurance Company. Continually evolving to capture long-term success, in 1989 the company introduced a new group of specialty product lines, including animal mortality and a broad range of individually tailored insurance programs. In January 1989, GALIC stopped writing additional life insurance policies. Great American Life Insurance Company's business remains almost exclusively in tax-sheltered annuities.

Principal Subsidiaries: Great American Insurance Company; Great American Life Insurance Company; Hunter Savings Association; Chiquita Brands International, Inc. (81%); Great American Communications Company (65%); Hanna-Barbera Productions, Inc.; The Charter Company (51%); American Money Management Corporation; Kings Island Company; The Penn Central Corporation (34%); Sprague Technologies, Inc. (32%); Spelling Entertainment Inc. (45%); The Circle K Corporation (15%).

Further Reading: "Carl Lindner Wields His Clout in the Boardroom," *Business Week,* July 2, 1984; Norris, Floyd, "Rescue Mission: Saving Carl Lindner's Ailing Insurer Won't Be Easy," *Barron's,* October 14, 1985.

—Janie Pritchett

AMERICAN GENERAL CORPORATION

2929 Allen Parkway
Houston, Texas 77019
U.S.A.
(713) 522-1111
Fax: (713) 831-1980

Public Company
Incorporated: 1926 as American General Insurance Company
Employees: 13,205
Assets: $32.06 billion
Stock Exchanges: New York Pacific London Zürich Basel Geneva Lausanne

Founded in 1926 as a fire and casualty insurance business, American General Corporation is one of the nation's largest insurance and financial-services organizations. Divided into three business segments—home service insurance, special markets insurance, and finance and real estate—more than half its earnings still come from traditional door-to-door insurance sales. During the 1980s, American General (AG) developed a reputation for buying other insurance companies—a practice unprecedented in the industry—and assimilating them profitably. This strategy of growth through acquisition has become a trademark. Since 1980, AG's size has tripled.

Gus Sessions Wortham, a native of Houston, Texas, first worked in the insurance firm he and his father had founded, John L. Wortham & Son Agency. Gus Wortham was managing the agency when his father died in 1924, and the next year Wortham formed his own business after the Commission of Appeals of Texas ruled that single insurance companies could combine lines of business, allowing multi-line underwriting of both fire and casualty insurance. Thus, with the backing of several business associates and the John L. Wortham & Son Agency, Gus Wortham formed one of the nation's first multi-line insurance companies on May 8, 1926: the American General Insurance Company. Operations began on June 7, 1926.

With the help of Gus Wortham's experience and business instincts, AG earned an underwriting profit in its first year in operation. It paid its first dividend on common stock in its third year, shortly before the stock market crash of 1929. Dividends have been paid every year since, without reduction or interruption.

AG, like the city of Houston itself, saw tremendous growth through the 1930s. The company's capital and surplus exceeded the $1 million mark by 1936; three years later, AG was licensed to operate in nine states, including Texas, and had assets of nearly $2.2 million. In the same year, 1939, AG's first subsidiary was established, The American General Investment Corporation. This was the company's first foray beyond fire and casualty insurance. The American General Investment Corporation eventually expanded its original offerings—financing for automobiles and real estate projects—to become a main link in AG's mortgage and real estate business segment.

In 1945 AG made its first acquisition, implementing a growth strategy for which it would later become unique in the industry. The acquired company, Seaboard Life Insurance Company, was a successful Houston-based life and health insurer that predated AG by one year.

In 1953, a healthy and thriving AG hired Benjamin N. Woodson away from the National Association of Life Underwriters, where he was managing director. AG hired Woodson, an industry leader who came with extensive contacts, specifically with an eye toward expanding into the national market. Those contacts were quickly put to use finding and acquiring other companies. Known as "Woody," AG's future president oversaw enormous expansion from the time of his hiring to his retirement as chairman and CEO in 1978.

In the decade that followed the addition of Woodson to the AG team, the company's emphasis was on expanding its life and health insurance segment. Toward that end, AG purchased life insurance companies in Nebraska, Hawaii, Oklahoma, Pennsylvania, and Houston, as well as a fire and casualty company in Marshall, Texas.

A milestone was reached in 1964 when AG purchased the Maryland Casualty Company, a Baltimore, Maryland–based property and liability company dating to 1898. In one move, AG doubled its size and became a major property and casualty insurer. This single purchase, long a goal of Gus Wortham's, made AG a presence in every state, as well as in Canada. Thus, AG became a major player in the national property and liability markets very quickly.

In the meantime, a new 24-story home was being built for AG one mile west of downtown Houston, on the banks of Buffalo Bayou. The corporation moved in 1965, and this location expanded to 36 acres and 5 office buildings by 1990.

The New York life insurance market became AG's next territory, with the acquisition of Patriot Life Insurance Company in 1966. In 1967, the Variable Annuity Life Insurance Company (VALIC) attracted AG's interest. VALIC was noted for innovations in sales of tax-deferred annuities to the employees of nonprofit organizations. AG acquired majority stock in VALIC by 1975, and it later became a wholly owned subsidiary. At the end of 1968, AG surpassed $1 billion in assets when it acquired a 65-year-old regional insurer, the Life and Casualty Insurance Company of Tennessee. That same year, AG bought one-third of California–Western States Life Insurance Company (Cal-West). Cal-West was large but ailing. In 1970 Cal-West hired a new, dynamic 38-year-old president and CEO, with hopes of achieving a turnaround. By 1973 AG owned 63% of Cal-West, but was showing yet more interest in the man who was engineering that company's rebound: Harold Swanson Hook.

When Hook was hired by Cal-West, he had already served as president of two life insurance companies and had developed two very successful management programs. Hook had been raised on his family's dairy farm outside of Kansas City, Missouri, and was hired immediately after graduating from the University of Missouri, as an assistant to the president of National Fidelity of Kansas. Within five years, Hook made industry history as the youngest insurance company president in the nation. He was then 31. Later, Hook became president of the U.S. Life Insurance, a subsidiary of USLIFE, in New York. Still climbing, Hook moved to Cal-West in Sacramento, California, where he stopped losses and built earnings back up. By 1975, Hook had joined AG and set about the task of managing what Woodson had purchased.

Harold Hook was elected the third president of AG in 1975. He became chairman and CEO when Woodson retired in 1978. Hook philosophized that size equals survival in the insurance industry, stating that acquisition is the only efficient way to grow. As he told *Business Week,* May 9, 1983, "our competitive advantage is our ability to acquire, integrate and control complex operations." To achieve this, Hook has applied his theories of management in a system he devised. Hook's management theories are taught to more than 80% of AG's employees, usually by graduates of Hook's Sacramento, California, school, Main Event Management Corporation. Hook contends that this implementation of a uniform philosophy and language accounts for AG's remarkable record with regard to assimilation and management. To date, it has successfully integrated more than 20 companies.

Since Hook became president, the corporation has tripled its size. Cal-West was acquired in 1975; VALIC in 1977. AG concentrated on acquisition-expansion in the state of New York and developed a long-term business strategy that has helped it to focus its energies and shed companies outside its business interests. In 1980, American General Insurance Company became American General Corporation. With the name change, it became a general business corporation.

Between 1982 and 1984, the corporation doubled its size. In 1982, AG attracted attention when it launched what AG itself called "the most aggressive acquisition program" in insurance-industry history—a strategy that has since become its trademark. In 1982, under this program, AG made the largest single life insurance company acquisition in history, with the purchase of NLT Corporation.

NLT was the parent company of the National Life and Accident Insurance Company of Nashville, Tennessee. AG needed the state of Tennessee's approval to pass the 10% stock maximum and was declined. The company then offered a stock swap, which NLT refused. NLT in turn made a bid for AG. AG rejected the bid and filed suit to stop the takeover proceeding, then announced what was dubbed the "godfather offer:" a $46-a-share merger proposal. This $1.5 billion, two-step merger was completed in late 1982. There were initial concerns about debt, but Hook shaved NLT staff by one-third and divested overlapping and irrelevant subsidiaries, increasing cash flow more than $50 million. It was reported that NLT was 70% absorbed within six months of the purchase.

That same year, AG acquired Credithrift Financial of Indiana and thus stepped into the consumer-credit business, later expanded further by the addition of General Finance Corporation. AG then ran a close second to its own life insurance acquisition record when it purchased, for $1.2 billion, Gulf United Corporation's insurance properties.

In 1988, AG's consumer-finance operations were doubled by the acquisition of the consumer-finance division of Manufacturers Hanover. In order to rid the firm of its most cyclical units, concentrating then on the faster-growing operations, AG shed its property-liability insurance business, as well as its group life and health insurance operations. On May 26, 1989, AG sold its property liability segment to "Zürich" Insurance Company—a multi-line, Swiss-based insurer—for $740 million. An agreement for the sale of AG's group insurance operations to Associated Insurance Companies for total consideration of up to $195 million, including $175 million in cash, was announced on September 21, 1989.

AG itself was the subject of a takeover bid in April 1990, when the much-smaller Torchmark Corporation offered $6.3 billion to acquire AG. The bid was withdrawn within days, after receiving a chilly reception. Torchmark then undertook a proxy battle to win five seats on AG's 15-member board.

Once again, AG rebuffed Torchmark, but its slim 60% victory persuaded the American General board to take action. At the May 2, 1990, annual meeting Hook announced that American General was putting itself up for sale, and that he expected the company to fetch more than $7 billion. The board's decision to put AG on the block was made, according to Hook, because "we recognized that . . . we were in play. We wanted to be in control of the process." Hook also said that if an acceptable offer was not received in several months, the company was prepared to dismantle and sell its subsidiaries.

Principal Subsidiaries: American General Life and Accident Insurance Co.; Gulf Life Insurance Co.; The Variable Annuity Life Insurance Co.; American General Life Insurance Co.; American General Life Insurance Company of New York; American-Amicable Life Insurance Company of Texas; Financial Life Assurance Company of Canada; American General Finance, Inc.; American General Investment Corp.

Further Reading: American General Corporation: History 1926–1986, Houston, American General Corporation, [1986].

—Carol I. Keeley

AMERICAN INTERNATIONAL GROUP, INC.

70 Pine Street
New York, New York 10270
U.S.A.
(212) 770-7000
Fax: (212) 770-7821

Public Company
Incorporated: 1967
Employees: 33,000
Assets: $46.14 billion
Stock Exchanges: New York London Tokyo Paris Zürich Basel Geneva Lausanne

American International Group (AIG) is a holding company for a network of subsidiaries primarily engaged in insurance and insurance-related activities. AIG operates in over 130 countries and jurisdictions, and its combined revenues make it the largest United States–based international insurance organization. The corporation, whose earliest roots were in Asia, has had an active history of mergers, acquisitions, and consolidations, which ultimately resulted in the formation of American International Group.

In 1919 a 27-year-old U.S. businessman, Cornelius Vander Starr, opened a two-room, two-clerk insurance agency in Shanghai and named it American Asiatic Underwriters (AAU). AAU, which later became part of American International Underwriters (AIU), initially served as an underwriter for insurance companies that had established branches in Shanghai. During a trip to New York in 1921 Starr added representation of other U.S. companies to his operations, including the Globe & Rutgers Company. Later that decade Starr brought representation of the Pittsburgh, Pennsylvania company, National Union Fire Insurance into his fold.

Starr's next quest was to gain general life insurance agency powers, but he found no U.S. companies willing to assume the risk because there were no life-expectancy statistics available for the Chinese population. In 1921 Starr overcame this obstacle by forming his own company, Asia Life Insurance Company (ALICO). ALICO's most popular product was a 20-year endowment policy, with rates established on the basis of Starr's personal observation that in general Chinese enjoyed longer life expectancies than their Western counterparts.

In 1926 Starr opened a New York office under the name American International Underwriters to serve as an insurance writer on U.S.-owned risks outside of North America. Like its Chinese counterpart, AIU also served as a general agent for U.S. insurers. By the end of the decade Starr's Chinese operations were seeing modest profits, and branch offices for both general and life insurance had been established throughout the Shanghai region. In 1931 Starr joined British and Chinese businessmen in a partnership and established the International Assurance Company (INTASCO).

AIU established a foundation for Latin American business in 1932 when George Moszkowski, who ran the company's New York office, negotiated the purchase of the Central American and Caribbean portfolios of an American insurer withdrawing from foreign operations. AIU's operations in Central America remained modest throughout the decade.

Before, during, and after World War II, AIU was able to capitalize on world economic and political situations. With much of the world on the brink of war, in 1939 Starr moved his headquarters to New York, temporarily closing the Shanghai office. After hostilities broke out operations of dominant Italian, German, and British agencies were reduced, and AIU expanded in Central America. In 1940 AIU established a regional headquarters in Cuba, and a half dozen offices in South America soon followed. AIU's Central American business grew with the local economies of these neutral countries during the war years.

At the end of World War II, the Shanghai office was reopened under the guidance of K.K. Tse. Several profitable years followed until the late 1940s, when the future of foreign activities in Shanghai grew dim. In 1949 key employees and documents were airlifted out of Shanghai and the regional headquarters moved to Hong Kong. In late 1950 operations in China were closed.

Meanwhile, many surrounding countries were recovering from war. With economic improvement underway, AIU entered Japan and West Germany by selling insurance to occupying U.S. troops. AIU's prewar operations in Europe had been limited to small agencies in France, Belgium, and the Netherlands, but postwar conditions, resulting in tight financing for local insurers, placed AIU in a position to expand its European business. At the same time, expansion of American business abroad created opportunities for AIU's "home-foreign" business.

In 1947 Starr began a reorganization designed to revive war-torn operations and lay the groundwork for future growth. Starr's first move was to announce the incorporation of a Philippine arm of the American Life Insurance Company, the Philippine American Life Insurance Company (Philam Life), in 1947. U.S. businessman Earl Carroll was named to head up the new company, which grew quickly, largely through the sale of endowment policies. These policies provided farmers and small merchants with the means to build their savings in a country with few banks. Sales revenue was frequently reinvested in the local economy.

INTASCO, which until this time had maintained a relatively small life insurance business, was reorganized in 1948 when Starr took control of the business, which had been started as a partnership. He added "American" to the company's name, changed the company's abbreviated name to

AIA, and assigned it the Southeast Asian territories of Malaysia, Singapore, and Thailand and the home-base front of Hong Kong.

That same year Starr began uniting his somewhat-fragmented network of insurance companies, beginning with the creation of two Bermuda-based entities. The first, American International Underwriters Overseas, Ltd. (AIUO), became the parent of all established AIU agency companies overseas. The second, American International Reinsurance Company, Inc. (AIRCO), was designed to hold companies dealing primarily in life insurance. AIRCO also took control of company investment programs and served as a reinsurer for these subsidiaries. The last in Starr's trio of new organizations was American International Underwriters Association (AIUA), established in 1949 to serve as a partnership of American insurance companies that were represented by AIU. AIUA provided for pooled business in stipulated percentages and shared assets that were kept overseas to meet local regulations.

Perhaps the most dramatic reorganization occurred within Starr's oldest life insurance company, ALICO. After lying dormant for a decade, the company was renamed American Life Insurance Company and assigned the Caribbean, Middle East, and some growing African nations. ALICO marketed life insurance to populations previously not attractive to insurers.

The 1950s were a period of rapid expansion for AIU. Branches were established in Western Europe, the Middle East, north Africa, and Australia. By the end of the decade AIU was operating in 75 countries. The 1950s also marked the emergence of Starr's companies in domestic markets.

In 1952 AIRCO acquired a majority interest in the Globe & Rutgers Insurance Company, a medium-sized American fire insurance company once represented by AIU. A Globe & Rutgers subsidiary, the Insurance Company of the State of Pennsylvania, came with the purchase. Founded in 1794, the Pennsylvania subsidiary was the second-oldest stock insurance company in the United States. American Home Assurance Company, which was founded in 1853, was also included in the package. Globe & Rutgers was later merged with American Home and took its name.

Starr and his colleagues joined the American Home board but left the company largely under old management. Earnings at the new subsidiary fluctuated greatly for several years. A net loss of $1.4 million was reported in 1957, followed by a net profit of better than $950,000 the following year. In an effort to stabilize earnings, AIRCO sold American Home's agency business to another insurer in 1962. That same year Starr named Maurice R. Greenberg as American Home president, and the company formed the American International Life Assurance Company of New York to specialize in term and group insurance. Greenberg had begun his insurance career ten years earlier with Continental Casualty Company. In 1960 he joined American International and was assigned the task of developing an overseas accident and health business.

In leading American Home, Greenberg focused on broker sales, allowing the company to issue its own policies and maintain underwriting control. The company concentrated on commercial and industrial risks, which involved negotiated rather than state-controlled rates. American Home also developed substantial reinsurance facilities in order to cover large shares of major risks and control insurance ratings. Greenberg initiated new products and services such as personal accident insurance, which emphasized deductibles. Meanwhile, American Home avoided medical insurance. The new sales system caught on, offering brokers the high deductibles that traditional insurers avoided but that some large corporations sought in order to cut costs.

During the late 1960s American International's corporate structure began to resemble its present form as it became an important commercial and industrial property and casualty insurer. While a new company organization was being forged through further acquisitions and reorganization, the insurance group began capitalizing on its innovative products and entrance into new markets.

Acquisitions during this period included controlling interests in the National Union Fire Insurance Company of Pittsburgh, Pennsylvania, which had been represented by AIU since 1927, and the New Hampshire Insurance Company. The former, which was threatened by high underwriting losses, was transformed much like American Home, and then linked with it in a pooling agreement. Commerce and Industry Insurance Company, a small property insurer specializing in highly protected risks, and Transatlantic Reinsurance Company were also acquired during this period.

The wholly owned American International Group was formed by AIRCO in 1967. AIG represented the beginning of a major corporate reorganization, with the company formed to hold shares of other domestic companies, including American Home and New Hampshire. ALICO was soon added to AIG's holdings. Greenberg was elected president and CEO of AIG in 1967. The following year Starr died, having seen only the beginning of a new era for the insurance empire he had created.

In 1969, after going public, AIG acquired majority interests in National Union, New Hampshire, and American Home, paying for its increased stake in the three companies with AIG stock. In 1970 AIU and its agencies and subsidiaries became wholly owned subsidiaries of AIG.

Throughout the 1960s AIU's overseas business grew, despite the loss of its large Cuban business following Fidel Castro's takeover of that country. Since it had entered most major markets a decade earlier, expansion during this time was limited to growth within areas with established territories. In an effort to strengthen AIG's overseas position, an 18-month program was initiated in 1972 which created a regional system of benefits managers for Europe, Africa, Central America, South America, the Middle East, the Far East, and United States. That same year the AIG subsidiary ALICO became the first foreign-owned company granted a license to sell insurance to Japanese nationals in Japan.

During the early 1970s AIG increased its specialization, by forming a number of new groups. Subsidiaries created by AIG during this time included A.I. Credit Corporation to finance general insurance premiums written through both affiliate and non-affiliate insurers; North American Managers, Inc., to sell insurance in the United States for foreign companies; AIG Oil Rig, Inc., to initiate and manage insurance for off-shore oil- and gas-drilling rigs; AIG Risk Management, Inc., to provide worldwide risk-management services; AIG Data Center, Inc.; and American International Insurance Company of Ireland, Ltd. During this period AIG also acquired all remaining shares of the New Hampshire and National Union companies.

AIG's profits took off in the 1970s, at a compounded growth rate of roughly 20%, with AIG's net income surpassing $50 million by 1975. High premiums in the new market areas of oil rigs and pension-fund management as well as the use of limited-partnership insurance for high risks contributed to the growth.

Consolidation and reorganization continued in 1976, when AIU stopped writing policies for insurance companies it did not own. That same year the company was organized into four broad categories: the foreign general insurance division, the brokerage division of domestic general insurance, the agency division of domestic general insurance, and a life insurance division. The following year the subsidiary Transatlantic Reinsurance was reorganized as a major reinsurer, with shares sold to seven other companies. AIG absorbed its parent company, AIRCO, in 1978, completing a nine-year consolidation plan to simplify corporate structure.

In 1979 AIG entered Eastern Europe and initiated joint ventures with state-owned insurers in Hungary, Poland, and Romania. In succeeding years similar operations were started in China and Yugoslavia. At the end of the 1970s AIG had 20% annual growth in revenues and had increased its size nearly tenfold. In 1979 AIG reported over $250 million in net income.

During the 1980s AIG ventured into health-care services, and acquired a variety of financial and investment sources as well as real estate holdings. Acquisitions included United Guaranty Corporation, a residential-mortgage insurance company; the Swiss bank Uberseebank A.G.; Ticino Societa d'Assicurazioni Sulla Vita, a Swiss-based life insurer; Southeastern Aviation Underwriters—later renamed AIG Aviation, Inc.—an airlines, aviation, and space-program insurer; and Jurgovan & Blair, a health-maintenance-organization consulting business. In 1981 AIG, in combination with Presidio Oil Company, purchased a majority interest in 109 natural gas wells.

In 1984 the company reported its first decline in profits, largely due to underwriting losses including those resulting from a major hurricane. Some of AIG's specialty companies, such as AIG Oil Rig, AIG Energy, AIG Entertainment, and AIG Political Risk, which were created during the preceding 15 years, were consolidated in 1984 under the name AIG Specialty Agencies, Inc. That same year AIG special services division was introduced to underwrite risks such as extortion, kidnapping, and ransom demand.

In 1985 AIG's profit margin rebounded, with the company exceeding 1983 earnings and posting a net income of $420 million. In 1987 AIG surpassed $1 billion in net income. That same year AIG was authorized by the South Korean government to begin life insurance operations, ending a 15-year struggle to break into the Korean market. AIG became the second foreign insurance company in South Korea, with its largest international competitor, CIGNA Corporation, given approval earlier in the year.

Two important AIG executives, National Union President Joseph P. DeAlessandro and American Home President Dennis Busti, left AIG in 1987 for other companies. Maurice Greenberg's son, Jeffrey W. Greenberg, was moved over from the presidency of AIU's North American division and named new president of National Union, while Joseph R. Wiedemann was named American Home president. Wiedemann had been president of AIG's Boston-based subsidiary Lexington Insurance Company.

AIG broadened its trading markets in 1987 when it became the first foreign insurance organization on the Tokyo Stock Exchange. The following year AIG was listed on the London International Stock Exchange. Additional listings include Paris and Switzerland, added in 1990.

AIG continued diversification moves in 1988, forming a Hong Kong–based venture to introduce American fast-food franchises into the Asian market. The venture marked the first time an American institutional investor—AIG's Financial Investment Corporation of Asia—moved into an overseas franchise market.

That same year AIG also experienced some difficulty. It was involved in what is believed to be one of the largest insurance-related arbitration awards in history. Enron Corporation was awarded a $162 million claim from insurers for Peruvian properties which had been expropriated, and AIG was forced to pay nearly two-thirds of the judgement.

Throughout the 1980s AIG operated as one of two major sources of environmental-impairment-liability (EIL) insurance. Early in 1989 Greenberg proposed the creation of a hazardous-waste-cleanup tax funded through a 2% premium fee assessed on all commercial and casualty and property policies, with insurers matching that amount. Greenberg suggested the tax could help fund cleanup of Environmental Protection Agency Superfund sites and ultimately bring more insurers into EIL writing, but critics charged the plan was self-serving.

The late 1980s saw continued consolidation for AIG. The financial-service-group was formed in 1987 to consolidate specialized financial operations. UNAT, AIG's general insurance company on the European continent, was formed later that year to consolidate operations in Europe and prepare for the elimination of trade barriers among European nations in 1992. Headquartered in Paris, UNAT's expanding territory includes France, Belgium, the Netherlands, Sweden, Norway, and Denmark.

In 1989 AIGlobal was formed to provide a single source of comprehensive property and casualty, life, and group insurance, and facilitate corporate financial services for multinational companies. That same year International Healthcare and Jurgovan & Blair were merged to form American International Healthcare, Inc., an international consulting and management company for health-care services.

The major portion of AIG's business today involves large commercial and industrial risks marketed through brokers, while about one-half of the company's operating income comes from foreign sources. The emphasis AIG places on overseas operations can be seen in the corporation's advisory board and board of directors. In 1987 Henry Kissinger, former U.S. secretary of state, was named chairman of AIG's advisory board, which also includes former ambassadors to the United States from France and Japan. From 1987 through 1990 AIG continued diversification into financial services. In 1987 a joint venture, AIG Financial Products Corporation, was established to structure complex financial transactions, including interest-rate and currency swaps. In 1988 AIG acquired ownership of 30% of A.B. Asesores Bursatiles, a

Spanish brokerage, and invested in certain investment-management and venture-capital operations in the United Kingdom and Hong Kong.

AIG Trading Corporation, a joint venture engaging in commodity transactions, was established in early 1990, and later that year AIG acquired International Lease Finance Corporation, which is engaged primarily in the acquistion of new and used commercial jet aircraft and the leasing of such aircraft to domestic and foreign airlines.

During 1990 Transatlantic Holdings, Inc., a holding company formed to hold Transatlantic Reinsurance Company and another reinsurer, Putnam Reinsurance Company, went public in a secondary offering. AIG continued to hold approximately 41% of Transatlantic Holdings after the public offering.

In June 1990, acording to *Business Week*, July 2, 1990, AIG agreed to buy Fischbach Corporation for $43 million. Fischbach, a Florida-based contractor, was an AIG performance-bond customer that had begun to experience financial difficulties. If Fischbach had failed, AIG could have been forced to pay hundreds of millions of dollars to companies with which Fischbach had contracted, acording to *Business Week*. After the purchase, AIG sold 51% of Fischbach to contractor Peter Kiewit Sons'.

AIG moved into the 1990s planning further consolidation of European operations under UNAT. Accelerated growth is projected for overseas operations with Asian business leading the way. Increased domestic competition in the property and casualty industry is also expected. The keys to AIG's success in the past—a vast geographical range, diverse and innovative products and services, anticipation of political change, and the ability to move quickly into new markets—should continue to bolster its firm position as an international presence operating in a myriad of insurance-related markets.

Principal Subsidiaries: American Home Assurance Company; American International Assurance Company, Limited (Hong Kong); American International Reinsurance Company Limited (Bermuda); American International Underwriters Overseas, Limited (Bermuda); American Life Insurance Company; International Lease Finance Corporation; Lexington Insurance Company; National Union Fire Insurance Company of Pittsburgh, Pa.; New Hampshire Insurance Company; United Guaranty Residential Insurance Company.

Further Reading: History of AIG, New York, American International Group, Inc., 1985.

—Roger W. Rouland

N.V. AMEV

Archimedeslaan 10
3584 BA Utrecht
The Netherlands
(30) 57 91 11
Fax: (30) 52 23 94

Public Company
Incorporated: 1883 as N.V. Levensverzekering Maatschappij Utrecht
Employees: 11,586
Assets: Dfl 30.22 billion (US$15.84 billion)
Stock Exchange: Amsterdam

AMEV has long been one of the three largest groups in the Dutch insurance industry. It became the sole shareholder in the largest savings bank in the Netherlands in 1990, and is also the country's largest private landowner. In addition to playing a leading role in the Dutch economy, it is a major multinational group in the field of financial services. Its subsidiaries operate in 11 countries on four continents, and in 1989, before its merger with VSB Groep, only 37% of the group's income came from the Netherlands, compared with 42% from the United States, 17% from the rest of the European Community, and 4% from Australia and Southeast Asia. Yet the company's headquarters are still in Utrecht, where the burial fund from which it has grown was founded, and from where the group controls its four main divisions, AMEV Nederland, VSB Groep, AMEV International, and Brabant, which, respectively, control its Dutch insurance business, its Dutch banking concerns, its foreign financial subsidiaries, and its non-insurance activities.

The burial fund Let op Uw Einde was set up by W.P. Ingenegeren and D. Stolwerk in 1847 to collect and manage weekly payments from poorer households wishing to avoid the consignment of family members to paupers' graves. It was one among 1,200 such funds that spread throughout the Netherlands in the 19th century, and by 1871, with branches in Amsterdam, Rotterdam, and Den Bosch—as well as Antwerp—it had become the largest fund, with nearly 150,000 members. In the same year, in order to clarify the question of whether the fund belonged to its directors or to its members, the fund bought the directors' shares from them, and now appeared to be on a secure legal and financial footing. In 1880, however, the Dutch Supreme Court declared government regulation of life insurance unconstitutional and thus prompted fierce competition among the burial funds, the existing life insurance companies, and a number of newly founded enterprises. The directors of the Let op Uw Einde fund, which by this time had over 260,000 members, had to decide whether to try to go on operating as a mutual fund with no actuarial reserves, or become a life insurance company which, by offering a range of premiums based on mortality tables, could offer premiums lower than any burial fund's, and which would have a more secure legal status as a company with limited liability. In 1883 Let op Uw Einde's directors, W.P. Ingenegeren—the founder's grandson—and P.J. Bol, set up N.V. Levensverzekering Maatschappij Utrecht, or Utrecht Life Insurance Company, which gradually took over the issuing of new policies. The burial fund took care of investments until 1893, when Utrecht took it over. In this way Utrecht acquired trained and experienced office and sales staff, and by paying back the fund's original investors on the basis of a 3.5% rate of return when the actual rate was about 4%, it started out with a very useful amount of free capital.

W.P. Ingenegeren's policy toward his staff was an unusually liberal one. For example, he introduced the eight-hour working day for all the company's employees in 1897, 40 years before Dutch law compelled employers to do so. The company was ahead of its time in other ways. Its multinational presence was established very early. The burial fund had established a Belgian office in Antwerp, and then branches of Utrecht were established in that country in 1883, in France in 1889, and in Denmark in 1899. The foreign branches became autonomous subsidiaries in the early 1980s. The company also had agents in Alsace, Luxembourg, Italy, Switzerland, and Russia. Utrecht's association with land development started in 1898, with the purchase of some uncultivated heathland in the province of Brabant, an apparently reckless move that surprised most observers in the insurance world at that time, but that eventually proved a wise investment. The company handed the land over to the new Nederlandsche Heide Maatschappij, a company specializing in reclaiming heathland for development, and by the 1930s it supported a flourishing settlement.

Utrecht's first two decades of success culminated in the 1902 opening of a new head office building, designed by a prominent Rotterdam architect and featuring electric lighting throughout, and in the issuing of its one millionth life policy, in 1906. Three years later it arranged its first group policy, for the personnel of Nederlandsche Heide Maatschappij.

World War I caused such serious losses to the company's investment portfolio—especially where the shares were denominated in rubles, marks, or Austrian crowns—that the directors had to create extra reserves and suspend the distribution of profits. The company weathered the economic crisis of 1921–1924 by drawing on these reserves, and it did not resume profit distribution until 1926. In these years its rate of expansion actually accelerated, and in 1929 total policies issued reached three million. In 1920 the company had taken on the financial structure it retains today, when N.V. Algemeene Maatschappij tot Exploitatie van Verzekeringsmaatschappijen (General Company for the Management of Insurance Companies) was created to hold the majority of shares in the Utrecht Life Insurance Company, its foreign branches, and any further acquisitions. The abbreviation "AMEV" became the company's official name in 1968.

Another economic crisis, in 1934–1935, found the company better prepared, though many life insurance policies were terminated. The company then had to struggle through the German occupation, during which the economy collapsed, and the company head office was destroyed in 1944 by a British bombing raid.

By 1958 the Dutch economy, and the insurance industry in particular, had returned to prewar levels of activity and Utrecht, while celebrating its 75th anniversary, entered the age of computers with the acquisition of an IBM machine, which began operating in 1960. 1963–1964 saw a wave of mergers throughout the Dutch financial-services industry, and the creation of the Nationale-Nederlanden, Amro Bank, and Algemene Bank Nederland (ABN), which are still dominant today. From 1963 onward AMEV also became an insurance group, extending its holdings beyond the Utrecht company to take in the non-life insurance company Holland van 1859 of Dordrecht—with which it had had cross-shareholdings and cross-directorships since 1958—together with the Nieuwe HAV-Bank of Schiedam, taken over in 1963; the life insurers VVM and the non-life company AVS, taken over in 1966; and De Groote Bossche van 1838, taken over in 1968.

Around 1972 there was an influx of British capital into the real estate business, followed by a dramatic drop in share prices in 1973, large-scale bankruptcies from the end of 1975, and finally, a significant drop in house prices in the early 1980s. It is not surprising that the late 1970s and early 1980s saw all the leading Dutch insurance groups investing abroad, in order to break out of a relatively small home market in which 61 life and 828 non-life insurance companies were offering services to 14 million people in a mature market.

One way into the wider market for insurance was through restricted joint activities with other companies. The most successful example of this has been the AREA Benefits Network, which was formed in 1978 in response to the needs of multinational corporations by AMEV, La Royale Belge, Eagle Star of the United Kingdom, and Allianz Leben of Germany. The network is based in Brussels and covers 41 countries. By 1987 half of all new group policies in the Netherlands were coming to AMEV through the AREA system rather than through its own agents. AREA's joint activities with American International Group have extended coverage to more than 90 countries.

The other way into the wider market, and the method preferred by the major insurance groups, has been through mergers and acquisitions. AMEV has concentrated its efforts on four areas, the European Economic Community, the United States, Australasia, and Southeast Asia.

Having had a presence in France, Belgium, and Denmark for many years, AMEV was now looking to expand into other European markets. In 1979 it acquired the U.K. company Gresham Life Assurance, which had been founded in 1848, and merged it with its own U.K. subsidiary, AMEV Life Assurance. It has since set up Gresham companies offering unit trusts and mortgages. Its holding in the Bilbao Insurance Group of Spain rose from an initial 25% in 1982 to 53% by the end of 1984. An Irish subsidiary, AMEV General Insurance, was created in 1982. In 1985 AMEV acquired Bishopsgate Insurance, based in Southampton, United Kingdom, from its French owners, and also bought two Belgian insurance companies, De Ster and Eurobel, from their U.K. owners. At the same time it entered by way of its French subsidiaries into a joint venture with its AREA partner La Royale Belge. In 1988 AMEV's two Belgian non-life companies, "Utrecht" Allerlei Risico's and De Ster 1905 NV, were merged under the name of the latter company, but since the beginning of 1990 the life and non-life businesses in Belgium have operated as AMEV Levensverzekeringen and AMEV Verzekeringen, respectively, in line with the policy of using the AMEV name and logo wherever possible.

AMEV had begun a program of acquisitions in the United States, which constitutes about half of the world market for insurance, by setting up a subsidiary, AMEV Inc., in 1970 as a holding company for various investments. The overwhelming importance of its U.S. holdings dates from 1978, however, when it acquired the Time Insurance Company of Milwaukee, Wisconsin. Time's main product is health insurance, and its fortunes have risen and fallen in line with this sector of the U.S. market. While several companies left the field in the 1980s, others, including Time, benefited from the rise in expenditure both on medical operations and on doctors' protection against liability suits. Time Insurance is the tenth-largest player in the personal health insurance market. By 1988, spending on health care had reached 11.3% of the U.S. gross national product, and this sector alone provided nearly half of AMEV's income from the United States in 1989.

AMEV's acquisition of Interfinancial of Atlanta, Georgia, in 1980 was its largest U.S. venture thus far, costing US$134 million, a figure representing over one-third of its stock market capitalization at that time, which is an indication of how important the acquisitions program seemed to AMEV's directors. The next major U.S. acquisition was a set of four companies—two life insurance firms and two mutual fund companies—from The St. Paul Companies of Minnesota, for which AMEV paid US$137.5 million in 1984. AMEV's U.S. operations also include several non-insurance firms, including AMEV Venture Management, founded in 1979; the AMEV Financial Group, dealing in mutual funds, and founded in 1988; and the General Furniture Leasing Company.

AMEV's ventures in Australia, New Zealand, and Southeast Asia have been on a much smaller scale, and somewhat less successful. AMEV's first major foreign venture of the postwar era had been the establishment of AMEV Australia, in Melbourne, in 1967, as a holding company for shares in motor and life insurance firms. In 1980 it added to its portfolio 80% of the shares in the Australian subsidiary of the U.K. firm United Dominion Corporation, which it renamed AMEV Finance. Legal changes in 1985 and 1986 allowed AMEV Australia to achieve outright ownership of its three Australian companies. Four years later the group sold off AMEV Finance, as well as the relatively unprofitable agency portfolio of AMEV Life. The group also pulled out of New Zealand in response to changes in the taxation of life insurance which it regarded as unfavorable. Finally, AMEV South East Asia was set up in 1984 after the acquisition of Ka Wah AMEV

Insurance in Hong Kong. In 1986 AMEV South East Asia bought 40% of Malayan Motor and General Underwriters, a non-life insurance firm based in Singapore.

These and other acquisitions transformed AMEV from an insurer deriving only 14% of its premium income from abroad in 1976 to an international group deriving more than 40% of premiums from abroad only four years later; this rose to 56% in 1984 and 63% in 1989. Nationale-Nederlanden and AEGON, AMEV's rivals at the top of the Dutch industry, also depend on foreign operations for most of their premium income. AMEV International had been set up in 1983 to coordinate all of the group's insurance and financial-services subsidiaries outside the Netherlands. In practice this meant concentrating on activities in the rest of the European community, since the U.S. subsidiaries are organized under AMEV Holdings in New York, the group's largest single source of income.

Meanwhile, there were changes in the Dutch companies of the AMEV group. In 1984–1985 all of its financial-services subsidiaries were integrated into a single organization under the name AMEV, in order to simplify the non-life business and make it more accessible to agents and customers. The change in image was accompanied by a change in marketing strategy. While the life and non-life sectors continue to be separate inside the company, and are known respectively as AMEV Levensverzekering and AMEV Schadeverzekering, they share marketing services for the five sectors identified by AMEV Nederland—average-income families, higher-income families, small- and medium-sized businesses, large businesses, and professionals. The investment activities of AMEV Levensverzekering are handled mainly by a subsidiary formed in 1988, AMBA (AMEV Maatschappij voor belegging in aandelen NV). AMEV Levensverzekering has investments of Dfl 10.8 billion, of which about a quarter is in mortgages, nearly half in debenture loans, about a tenth in shares, and nearly a sixth in real estate. An indication of the sheer size of AMEV's investments is the fact that its position as the largest private landowner in the Netherlands has been achieved on the basis of just 3% of the capital invested, not by N.V. AMEV as a whole, but by this life insurance arm of AMEV Nederland. As for the non-life side of the business, the main source of revenues for AMEV Schadeverzekering, as for other Dutch non-life insurers, is accident and sickness insurance, since the state system covers only 70% to 80% of most workers' lost earnings, and excludes people who are higher-paid.

The smallest of AMEV's four divisions, Brabant, was established in 1969. Having disposed of all its interests in textiles and most of its interests in jewelry, it was then chiefly involved in property development in the Netherlands, France, and Belgium, and in providing venture capital for industry. Its holdings, most of which are below the 50% level, include shares in the Dutch currency exchange company De Grenswisselkantoren NV and in the children's clothing manufacturers, the Harvest International group. Brabant also serves to test out markets which AMEV International has not yet entered.

In preparation for the European Single Market targeted for 1992, several corporations in the financial-services field have been seeking to set up *allfinanz* arrangements, allowing them to cover both banking and insurance and thus be ready for the competition which seems likely to develop in the 1990s. The cooperation agreements between the Allianz insurance group and the Dresdner Bank in Germany, or between the Banque Nationale de Paris and the Union des Assurances de Paris in France, were early examples of this trend, but both took place in countries whose laws already had been revised to allow for them. In the Netherlands, however, where the two sectors were kept strictly separate, AMEV began a new chapter in its history in March 1989, when it announced that it was to swap shareholdings of 15% with the Verenigde Spaarbank Groep (VSB Groep), with a view to a full merger once Dutch law was revised to permit it. VSB's holdings included the largest savings bank in the Netherlands, the finance house FMN, and the Dutch segment of the Visa credit card network, but at about one-third of AMEV's size, it seemed unlikely that the eventual merger could be anything but a takeover, as it has proved to be. In 1990, after the necessary legal changes had been made, AMEV became the sole shareholder in the VSB Groep and VSB in turn disposed of its holding in AMEV. The two groups were well matched, both being well-established market leaders for services to individuals and families and both, more recently, developing their provision for commercial and upper-income customers.

Since by 1990 the European Community's central agencies had not finished work on all the directives required for unifying the market, and since the member states varied in their ability and political willingness to implement those that were ready, there were likely to be variations between member countries in tax treatment of insurance and in systems for distributing policies for some years to come. Differences in social customs and economic development also persisted, and led, for instance, to a 1986 situation in which, the average West German citizen was spending over 20 times as much on insurance annually as his Greek counterpart. Those states such as France, which have public welfare provision sufficient to make private non-life insurance more important than life insurance clearly will require a different kind of strategy from those in which every kind of insurance is underdeveloped.

These national variations suggest that cross-border mergers with partners well versed in local practice might be more successful than trying to push into unknown markets from a single country base, however strong. Thus AMEV has not stopped at merging with VSB, but announced in April 1990 that an agreement had been reached on a merger with the largest insurance company in Belgium, Groupe AG of Brussels, the origins of which go back to 1824, when Belgium and the Netherlands were a single kingdom. The merger was to be effected through holding companies owned equally by both groups, rather than through mutual shareholdings, to avoid integration expenses, some tax liabilities, problems of different accounting systems in the two countries, and the possibility of intervention by the European Commission which, in 1990, forbade the creation of a single company out of corporations from different member-states. Groupe AG was to pay AMEV Dfl 575 million plus interest over ten years to compensate for AG's smaller size. The aim was to establish the European community's 12th-largest insurance group by 1991.

AMEV's directors also have ensured that there can be no takeover of the group without their consent, by bringing the holdings of preference shares by the Münchener Rückversicherungs-Gesellschaft of Munich and the Stichting Continuiteit AMEV (AMEV Continuity Foundation) up to the equivalent of 50% each of the value of ordinary shares. The Continuity Foundation is controlled by N.V. AMEV's management.

Assessing the potential of a group like AMEV involves considering the internal conditions of the insurance industry, the economic framework of the Netherlands, and the international situation. First, above a certain level of economic development it becomes very nearly impossible for insurance companies not to do well, since, in the European Economic Community countries, the growth in total premium value is consistently greater than the growth of gross national product. This is to be expected in countries with aging populations and fitful, uneven rises in general prosperity. AMEV's declared intention of developing services to higher income groups is telling in this regard. On the other hand, any insurance company that deals in both the life and non-life fields, and offers personal loans, pensions, and other investment services as well, is likely to find that the price of diversification is exposure to a wider range of influences on its activities. The ups and downs of house building and sales will affect its mortgage business and fluctuations in interest rates can help or hinder the growth of lending in particular and investments in general, while fluctuations in exchange rates can put on, or take off, several percentage points in profits or losses, as, for instance, in 1984, when 3.8% of AMEV's net profits were due entirely to successful foreign-exchange transactions.

Secondly, state regulation of insurance in the Netherlands has been relatively light. There are no rules for contract or premium rates and there is a high degree of self-regulation. Theoretically this should mean greater competition in the insurance field, as the barriers to market entry are lower in the Netherlands than in, for instance, Germany or France. In practice, as in most developed markets, the ideal of free competition long ago gave way to oligopoly, and the insurance industry, with its dependence on long-term contracts, is characterized by very stable market shares in most countries. In the Netherlands, the ten largest insurers in 1989 accounted for over 80% of the market. As in other oligopolies, this dominance gives the market leaders the ability to dictate terms to rivals, intermediaries, and customers alike; to bar entry to the market, especially to firms that do not already have links with insurance; and to keep premiums higher than they would otherwise be. This also explains wny AMEV and its rivals have always preferred to acquire existing foreign firms rather than try to start up wholly new companies: insurance is an oligopoly in AMEV's other markets. A study of the Dutch insurance industry undertaken for the European Commission and published in 1985 suggested that for several years there had been a tacit agreement among the companies to avoid price competition.

Thirdly, AMEV's merger activity in the 1990s, unlike that of the 1980s, is intended to cut across both national borders and boundaries between sectors of the financial-services industry—though the latter is still not possible in the United States. This in itself is evidence enough that AMEV expects competition to be fiercer, and profitability less easily achieved in the European Single Market, the success of which depends on the full implementation of the European community's plans for 1992 and beyond. The record of implementation so far suggests that the unifying process will take much longer than was originally expected. However long it takes, AMEV—working together with Groupe AG—will probably be a major player in Europe, and will be able to use the profits from its large U.S. holdings to try to compensate for any setbacks.

Principal Subsidiaries: AMEV Australia Ltd.; AMEV General Insurance Co. Ltd. (Ireland); AMEV Holdings Inc. (U.S.A.); AMEV International N.V.; AMEV Nederland N.V.; AMEV South East Asia Ltd. (Hong Kong); AMEV (UK) Ltd.; Brabant N.V.; VSB Groep N.V.

Further Reading: De Utrecht 75 Jaar, Utrecht, N.V. AMEV, 1958; Bollerman, J.B.J., and J.N.J. Broenink, *The Burial Fund: Mind Your End 1847–1893,* Utrecht, N.V. AMEV, 1983; Aaronovitch, Sam, and Peter Samson, *The Insurance Industry in the Countries of the EEC,* Brussels, Office for Official Publications of the European Communities, 1985.

—Patrick Heenan

AON CORPORATION

123 North Wacker Drive
Chicago, Illinois 60606
U.S.A.
(312) 701-3000
Fax: (312) 701-3100

Public Company
Incorporated: 1980 as Combined International Corporation
Employees: 17,294
Assets: $9.16 billion
Stock Exchanges: New York Midwest London Toronto

Aon is a Gaelic word meaning "unity." When the former Combined International Corporation adopted Aon as its name, in 1987, the word was chosen to represent one of the most diversified groups of insurance companies in the United States. Through its subsidiaries the Aon Corporation underwrites a broad line of accident and health insurance, life insurance, and specialty property and casualty insurance, and offers brokerage, reinsurance, employee benefits consulting, and insurance-premium finance services. The holding company grew rapidly through acquisition during the 1980s.

The corporate structure of Aon originated in 1980, when the Combined International Corporation was set up as a holding company for the acquisition-hungry Combined Insurance Company of America. The latter company had been formed in 1947 through the merger of the Combined Mutual Casualty Company of Chicago and Combined Insurance Company of America of Pennsylvania. Both companies belonged to self-made millionaire and self-help proponent W. Clement Stone. Stone controlled a number of insurance companies operating in various states at the time. He had begun his insurance career at the age of 16.

W. Clement Stone was born on Chicago's south side in 1902. His father died when he was two years old, and by age six, Stone was earning money as a paperboy to help his dressmaker mother. At age 13 the entrepreneurial Stone had his own newsstand. At 16 he embarked on an insurance career, selling policies for an agency his mother had started in Detroit, Michigan.

In 1922, at the age of 20, W. Clement Stone set up a Chicago-based insurance agency with a $100 investment. During the 1920s the Combined Registry Company, which acted as agent for about six insurers, grew rapidly, employing 1,000 agents nationwide by 1930. The Depression hit the company hard, however, and Stone was forced to reduce the number of agents to 135. In 1939 Stone acquired his first insurance company, the American Casualty Company of Dallas, later known as the Combined American Insurance Company of Dallas. That same year he organized the Combined Mutual Casualty Company of Chicago, followed by the Combined Casualty Company of Philadelphia, renaming it the Combined Insurance Company of America, and paving the way for the 1947 merger.

When the Combined Insurance Company of America got its start just after World War II, the company wrote accident and health insurance, hospitalization, and non-cancellable accident and health insurance. An army of door-to-door salesmen carried Combined's policies direct to homes and businesses. At the end of 1947 Combined had assets of $2.2 million.

In December 1949 the company acquired the Boston Casualty Company, an accident and health insurer, and renamed it Hearthstone Insurance Company of Massachusetts. In 1954 Combined acquired the First National Casualty Company of Fond du Lac, Wisconsin. During the 1950s, Combined and its subsidiaries grew substantially. Between 1949 and 1959, premiums increased an average of 17% annually while assets jumped from $2.9 million to $20.3 million. The company relied on direct sales of low-cost accident and health policies, which were a good risk for Combined.

W. Clement Stone's personal philosophy—the "positive mental attitude," or PMA—was the cornerstone of the company's day-to-day operations. Stone, wearing a flamboyant bow-tie, was known to enter the boardroom shouting, "is everybody happy?" Salespersons lived by slogans like "what the mind can conceive and believe, the mind can achieve" and "when you have nothing to lose and everything to gain by trying, by all means try." Employees were encouraged to greet each day with the upbeat maxim "I feel healthy. I feel happy. I feel terrific."

Sales pitches were memorized and repeated by the company's door-to-door representatives. W. Clement Stone remarked years later: "it's impossible to fail when you follow this step-by-step set-up." Indeed, Combined Insurance Company's sales continued to expand throughout the 1960s. By 1969 Combined's written premiums totaled $187 million, up from $27 million a decade earlier; assets were $225 million, up from $20.3 million.

In 1965 Combined began selling low-cost, low-benefit life insurance, which gradually became a significant segment of the company's business. In 1968 the company acquired the Commerce and Industry Insurance Company of New York, a fire and property insurer that sold to preferred commercial, institutional, and industrial clients. The Commerce and Industry shares were exchanged for 50,000 shares of the American Home Assurance Company of New York six months later.

In January 1970 Matthew T. Walsh, former executive vice president and international sales manager, became president of Combined Insurance when the 67-year-old W. Clement Stone assumed the new offices of chairman and CEO. Walsh had been with the company since 1946. At the same time,

Clement Stone, the 41-year-old son of the founder, became president of Combined's European operations. Although W. Clement Stone stepped down from the day-to-day running of the company, his influence directed the company.

Throughout the next decade, Combined pushed overseas. Having already penetrated English-speaking markets like Canada, Great Britain, Australia, and New Zealand in the 1960s, Combined entered West Germany in 1977, France in 1979, and Japan in 1980. Combined tailored its policies to fit conditions in these countries: in New Zealand, for example, where socialized medical programs cover virtually the entire cost of hospitalization and doctors' bills, Combined sold supplemental policies that protect against loss of income in case of illness or accident. By 1980 17% of the company's revenues came from outside the United States.

In December 1971, just two years after assuming the presidency of Combined Insurance, Matthew T. Walsh resigned. Walsh said he was leaving because his years at Combined had given him ''sufficient means to do all the things I've always wanted to do while still young enough to enjoy them.'' W. Clement Stone resumed the president's chair until a replacement could be found. Clement Stone took the reins as president and chief operating officer in 1972, and CEO in 1973.

The recession of 1973 sent stock prices plummeting. Between 1970 and 1977 Combined's price dropped about 66%. Nevertheless, growth continued at an impressive rate during the decade. Because Combined focused on the low end of the insurance market, the company did not suffer from problems that faced other insurers during the late 1970s. While those companies struggled with skyrocketing health costs and accident settlements, Combined prospered. Between 1969 and 1979 assets grew to $1.57 billion—about 16% annually.

By the end of the 1970s, Combined Insurance Company was looking for acquisitions. In 1980 the company formed the publicly owned Combined International Corporation to act as a holding company, in order to avoid state-by-state regulation. The holding company was monitored by the Securities and Exchange Commission and was not subject to scrutiny by each state's insurance commission.

In 1981 the new Combined International Corporation made its first acquisition when it bought the Union Fidelity Corporation along with its Nashaming Valley Information Processing unit, for $105.5 million. Union Fidelity was an accident and health insurer, which excelled at direct-response marketing and sold 75% of its policies through direct-mail and newspaper campaigns. The unit was expected to give Combined's door-to-door marketers a needed boost. Combined suffered from the rising costs of recruiting and maintaining a large battalion of field representatives, and the company's domestic sales had been flat for the two years prior to the acquisition.

In March 1982 Clement Stone abruptly resigned as president and CEO of Combined, citing personal reasons. His father once again resumed control of the company. After his resignation, Clement Stone received a $3.4 million consulting contract.

At age 79, W. Clement Stone was once again caretaker of the company he had founded. At the same time, the company was troubled by stagnation in domestic premiums. Although the slump in growth was offset in the short-term by excellent investment results, a plan to deal with rapidly changing markets was needed.

Combined solved its leadership problems with the acquisiton of the Ryan Insurance Company in August 1982. Combined spent $133 million for the 18-year-old specialty insurer and brokerage, which had been a pioneer in credit life insurance for auto dealerships and extended mechanical warranty insurance agreements. Founder Patrick G. Ryan then became president and CEO of Combined. Stone remained chairman. Although W. Clement Stone had called an unexpected adjournment which lasted for five hours at the special shareholders meeting which had been called for the purpose of approving the acquisition, Stone finally approved the deal, and Combined at last had a new leader.

Pat Ryan's management style differed considerably from W. Clement Stone's. Ryan, while himself a good motivator, was generally described as less flamboyant and more diplomatic. The new CEO of Combined demonstrated his approach by announcing a major acquisition just two months after taking charge of the company's operations. Combined purchased the Chicago-based insurance brokerage Rollins Burdick Hunter Company for $109 million. Rollins Burdick, which was well known for its large corporate clients, absorbed Combined's other brokerage operations, making it the eighth-largest insurance broker in the United States. The acquisition provided Combined with a source of fee income that was not readily susceptible to decline because of the less competitive nature of corporate insurance.

In 1982, although revenue rose 27%, net earnings dropped 19%. Ryan began to cut costs and integrate Combined's greatly diversified operations. In 1983 revenues grew 18% and operating earnings jumped 47%. The Ryan Insurance subsidiary stretched its extended warranty insurance to appliances, and Union Fidelity took advantage of the growing need for supplemental health insurance.

In April 1986 Combined bought the Life Insurance Company of Virginia for $557 million. The acquisition further widened Combined's product line, notably adding an array of interest-sensitive universal life products for upscale markets.

In January 1987 the Rollins Burdick Hunter unit bought five regional operations: Allen, Hart, Franz and Zehnder of Los Angeles; Schroeter, White and Johnson of Oakland, California; Pilot Insurance Agency of Winston-Salem, North Carolina; Todorovich Agency of St. Louis, Missouri; and the agency operations of Springhouse Financial Corporation of Philadelphia, Pennsylvania.

In March 1987 Combined International Corporation's shareholders voted to change the name of the company to Aon Corporation. Patrick Ryan said the name change was necessary to eliminate confusion between the holding company and its subsidiary, Combined Insurance Company of America.

Continuing its diversification, Aon bought the employee-benefits consulting firm Miller, Mason and Dickenson for $12 million in the summer of 1988, and in September bought the nation's ninth-largest reinsurance agent, Reinsurance Agency.

In January 1989 Aon restructured its subsidiary Rollins Burdick Hunter Company, setting up a holding company to oversee four units: Rollins Burdick Hunter Company, the brokerage; Rollins Specialty Group, a newly created unit concentrating on brokerage services for financial institutions, associations, and affinity groups; Miller, Mason and Dickenson, the newly acquired employee-benefits consultant; and Aon Risk Services—a reinsurance brokerage operating through Aon Reinsurance Agency, formerly Reinsurance Agency.

As Aon entered the 1990s the company planned to continue to grow through the acquisition of carefully selected companies, and continued to rely on its existing lines of insurance. Since its founding in 1947 the group has grown from a modest accident and health insurer into one of the most diverse insurance groups in the United States. Aon's management is highly regarded, and its marketing of unique insurance products can be expected to continue in the future.

Principal Subsidiaries: Combined Insurance Company of America; The Life Insurance Company of Virginia; Rollins Burdick Hunter Group, Inc.; Ryan Insurance Group, Inc.; Union Fidelity Life Insurance Company.

Further Reading: Garino, David, "Clem Stone Discovers that Positive Thinking Sells Insurance Policies," *The Wall Street Journal,* February 27, 1969; "Healthy Policy: Combined Insurance Thrives at Low End of Market," *Barron's,* February 4, 1980.

—Thomas M. Tucker

ASSICURAZIONI GENERALI S.P.A.

Piazza Duca degli Abruzzi 2
34132 Trieste
Italy
(040) 6711
Fax: (040) 671600

Public Company
Incorporated: 1831 as Assicurazioni Generali Austro-Italiche
Employees: 6,563
Assets: L16.99 trillion (US$13.42 billion)
Stock Exchanges: Milan Rome Turin Trieste Florence Genoa Bologna Tokyo New York Frankfurt Paris London

Assicurazioni Generali, a joint-stock insurance company with worldwide operations, was founded in Trieste in 1831. It is the largest insurance company in Italy and ranks third among Italy's largest corporations, after the state industrial group IRI and Fiat.

Trieste's position on the Adriatic and its role as chief port of the Austro-Hungarian Empire made it a center of shipping and commerce, when the first ventures in maritime insurance were established in the mid-1700s after the Hapsburg King Charles VI had declared it a free port. Following the upheavals of revolution and the Napoleonic Wars, Trieste experienced an economic boom. In 1825, some 20 insurance companies were active, chiefly in maritime insurance.

Generali was founded by Giuseppe Lazzano Morpurgo, a businessman from a leading family in Gorizia, who brought together a group of Trieste financiers and merchants in November 1831 to found the Ausilio Generale di Sicurezza. Their intention was to establish a company with sufficient capitalization to expand beyond the geographical territory reached by other Trieste houses. Like its chief competitor at the time, the Adriatico Banco d'Assicurazione—today known as Riunione Adriatica di Sicurtà or RAS—the Ausilio Generale founding members were drawn from Trieste's multiethnic business community, which included Austrians, Slavs, Italians, Germans, and Greeks.

At the first shareholders' assembly, conflicts among the partners over statutes led to the dissolution of Ausilio Generale. A month later the remaining partners formed the Assicurazioni Generali Austro-Italiche, with an initial capitalization of 2 million florins, divided into 2,000 shares of 1,000 florins each. Statutes were approved on December 26, 1831. Almost immediately, founding member Giuseppe Morpurgo left Trieste to establish the company's Venice headquarters, which was placed under the direction of Samuel della Vida from Ferrara.

Other Generali founders included Marco Parente, a businessman with ties to the Vienna Rothschild family, and Vidal Benjamin Cusin, grandfather of two future secretary-generals of Generali, Marco Besso and Giuseppe Besso. The company's other members included Giovanni Cristoforo Ritter de Zahony, a Frankfurt native with a Hungarian title; the shipbuilder Michele Vucetich; Alessio Paris, who in 1826 had been a founder of the competitor Adriatico Banco, and Giambattista Rosmini, an Italian lawyer who managed the new company in his role as legal advisor.

The adjective "Generali" was intended to convey the fact that the company's activities were not limited to maritime and flood insurance but, as Article 2 of the first charter indicated, "insurance of land [i.e., fire and shipping insurance] . . . security of the life of man in all its ramifications, pensions and whatever other area of insurance permitted by law." The first agencies were opened rapidly, amounting to some 25 in the principal cities of the Hapsburg Empire in the first two years. Branches, agencies, and affiliates were established in France in 1832, and in 1835 to the east in Switzerland and Germany, in Transylvania, and Galizia. Administration of the company was divided between the Trieste and Venice headquarters, with Venice in charge of operations in Italy and west Europe while the central management in Trieste handled operations elsewhere in Austria-Hungary and east Europe. In 1837, the Venice office began to operate in the field of credit insurance, while limiting its transport insurance solely to goods being shipped from Venice.

In 1835, a struggle for power developed between the president, Zahony, and legal administrator Giambattista Rosmini, with Morpurgo supporting the president. The board of directors sided with Rosmini, who succeeded in forcing Zahony and Morpurgo out of the company. At this time, the charter was rewritten and the position of president was abolished, to be reinstated in 1909. The dispute had a deleterious effect on business; four other board members left with Zahony and Morpurgo, and the directors compelled Rosmini to share power with Masino Levi, former agent in the Padua office, who was named general secretary.

The following 40 years under Levi's direction saw unprecedented growth for Generali. Expansion was effected according to the company's geographical division, with activity on the Italian peninsula overseen by the Venice office, while Trieste was responsible for other European operations. Generali was especially active in east and central Europe, where offices opened in Saxony, Prussia, and Silesia in 1837, expanding further in 1838 to Corfu, Bavaria, Russian Poland, Serbia, and Valacchia. The company's Hamburg operations center was run for many years by the mathematical prodigy Wilhelm Lazarus, who compiled the first mortality tables for Germany.

However, while growth was surging on the continent, expansion on the Italian peninsula was slower. Prior to the unification of Italy, protectionist laws in effect in the separate Italian states greatly restricted activity by foreign insurance companies. For example, until 1850 Generali representatives in the Bourbon kingdom of Naples frequently had to make appeal to the throne to avoid suspension of their activity. In the Papal States, business was possible only in the Romagna region. In the kingdom of Piedmont, the Società Reale Mutua held a legal monopoly in fire insurance, and heavy legal hindrances existed in other fields until 1853. At Parma and Piacenza, Generali was only able to begin activity in 1837, when the Milan agency succeeded in winning monopoly rights in the region from the Bourbon duchess Maria-Luigia.

Expansion throughout Europe was carried out by means of a tiered system. Territories were grouped around a central general agency responsible for gradually increasing growth in new expansion zones. Where Generali was unable to establish an autonomous agency, an affiliate was authorized. From its lucrative Pest agency in Hungary, Generali extended operations to Bucharest in 1847 and to Belgrade in 1856. In the following decade, operations started in Bosnia and the remaining area of Turkish domination, enlarging Generali's territory to include the whole of the Middle East, especially in the branch of fire insurance. The first fire insurance policies in Alexandria were issued by Generali in 1851, limited to the city's European quarter.

Later in the 19th century, Generali's attention turned to eastern and other non-European countries. Between 1879 and 1882 Generali opened agencies or representative offices in the main ports of the Near East and the Far East, along the sea routes of the Lloyd Austriaco line which had its terminal in Trieste: Generali's territory was thus extended throughout Greece, to Beirut, Tunis, Bombay, Colombo, Shanghai, and Hong Kong. Across the Pacific Ocean, agencies were opened in San Francisco, California, and in Valparaiso, Chile. New kinds of insurance were initiated; in 1877, Generali began extending coverage to plate glass, in 1881 to injury, and by the end of the century to theft.

In 1878, Marco Besso replaced Masino Levi as secretary general, inaugurating a period of modernization and diversification. Besso had come to Generali in 1863 as the company's representative to Rome, where he successfully negotiated the acquisition of the Vatican's failing Pontificia insurance house. Taking over the company at the age of 35, Besso established Generali's life insurance activities and initiated a policy of real estate investment. During his period of tenure the company acquired the Procuratie Vecchie, one of the Renaissance palaces on Venice's Piazza San Marco, and built its imposing Rome headquarters in Piazza Venezia.

Also during this period Generali laid the groundwork for its future as a major European group with the constitution of its first wholly owned subsidiaries. It established Cassa Generale Ungherese di Risparmio (General Savings Bank of Hungary) in 1881, followed by Unfall (Austrian General Accident Insurance) in 1882, which today operates under the name Erste Allgemeine.

Marco Besso was replaced by his brother Giuseppe Besso in 1885, who served as secretary general until 1894. However, Marco Besso continued to guide Generali, acting as president from 1909, when the position was reinstated, until his death in 1920. During the years 1894 to 1909, he acted as consulting director while the post of secretary general was filled by Edmondo Richetti, who had joined the company ten years earlier as director of the Austrian Unfall branch.

During these years Besso formed what was to prove a fruitful long-term relationship with Italy's principal merchant bank, the Banca Commerciale Italiana (COMIT), which exsists today. Less than two years after COMIT was founded in 1894, Besso was installed on the board of directors where he remained for life. Except for a ten-year period coinciding with World War II, Generali and COMIT traditionally have held reciprocal seats on each other's boards.

During this period, Franz Kafka was hired by the company's general agency in Prague as an office worker. However the aspiring novelist left after nine months, suffering from nervous ailments.

In 1914, on the eve of World War I, Generali was enjoying a position of tremendous strength. Its assets totaled 12,600,000 crowns (L13,323,000). While the war brought unprecedented destruction to the very areas of Europe in which Generali was most active, the company suffered more from political pressures than from financial loss. At the outbreak of hostilities, Generali's two most important offices found themselves in opposing camps of warring nations. The Venice headquarters made every effort to be regarded as Italian, whereas Generali's Trieste office reaffirmed its loyalty to the Hapsburgs. The governments of France and England regarded Generali as a part of the Austro-Hungarian empire, and the company's activities were curtailed in both countries until 1916.

Generali however, was viewed with equal suspicion in Vienna. The Trieste headquarters was relocated to the Austro-Hungarian capital, where activities were supervised by a substitute managing director, Emanuel Ehrentheil. Generali, like much of Trieste, had always divided its loyalties between Italy and the Hapsburgs. Since much of Generali's personnel transferred to Italy at the outbreak of fighting, the authorities placed most of Generali's officers on a list of suspected Italian nationalists. Claiming suspicion of foreign espionage, the Military Command investigated the directors and searched their homes. In 1916 the company's assets temporarily were sequestered under a decree to prevent the flight of foreign capital. Despite this, on May 31, 1918, a Generali life policy was written for the last Hapsburg emperor, Charles I.

In 1918, with the armistice, Trieste was united with the Italian republic and Generali assumed as its insignia the Lion of St. Mark, symbol of Venetian power and justice. After the collapse of the Hapsburg monarchy in central Europe, new nationalist states replaced the politically united territories that Generali had cultivated for nearly a century. In addition to the damage inflicted by the fighting, the new order resulted in complex monetary, legal, and economic problems in the insurance industry. Authorized to continue its activity in all the former Austro-Hungarian territories, Generali initially restricted itself to handling life insurance in Czechoslovakia and Yugoslavia.

Adjusting for the devaluation of the lire from its 1913 rates, the company estimated that its assets had fallen by 17% since the outbreak of war, but two years later Generali was on the road to an impressive recovery, and under the direction of Edgardo Morpurgo, from 1920, the company marked its 100th anniversary in extraordinarily good health.

Despite the economic crisis of 1929, Generali's capital rose from L13 million to L60 million in ten years, and gross premiums in life insurance rose from L1 billion to L6 billion. The company boasted 3,150 representatives in Italy and

5,765 in foreign countries. It had 30 subsidiaries and associated companies—6 in Italy and 24 abroad. Real estate holdings were valued at L292 million, which then included urban and agricultural property in 17 different countries. Faced with the effects of the Depression in the United States and the need to have strong liquid assets readily available, the company established a new department at its central headquarters, solely in charge of financing.

Notable events in the 1930s included the acquisition of Alleanza & Unione Mediterranea in 1933, which was merged with Securitas Esperia, already controlled by Generali, to form Alleanza-Securitas-Esperia (Allsecures), no longer a part of the Generali group. Life insurance activities absorbed from this group formed the basis for the Alleanza Assicurazioni company, which is the largest private life insurance company in Italy, second only to the state-run giant, INA. Significant growth occurred, meanwhile, in Generali's French holding La Concorde, and the Austrian Erste Allgemeine. Benito Mussolini's alliance with Nazi Germany ensured that Italian interests in Austria were not lost after Adolf Hitler's *anschluss* in 1934.

However, the extension of Germany's anti-Semitic laws to Italy had a devastating effect on the Generali group. With the rise of fascism in Italy, Morpurgo, who was Jewish, had struggled to maintain control, enrolling in the Fascist Party and appointing a staunch supporter of Mussolini as managing director. Gino Baroncini—who came to Generali from the Milan-based subsidiary Anonima Grandine, an insurer covering crop damage by hailstorms formed by Generali in 1890—was to determine the company's structure and course for much of the next 30 years. In 1938, however, Morpurgo was forced to leave the company, eventually fleeing to Argentina. He was replaced by Count Giuseppe Volpi di Misurata, who served until the fall of the Fascist government in 1943.

The company also lost 66 Jewish employees, including 20 directors. With Trieste under a German high command, Generali's central headquarters were moved to Rome, and its status as an Italian company was formalized by an official decree. Antonio Cosulich, a Trieste shipbuilder and member of the board, was named as chairman and served until 1948, with Baroncini continuing as managing director.

The end of the war renewed prospects for a return to normal operating conditions in Western Europe, but in Eastern Europe all rights, property, and interests pertaining to Italy or Italian citizens were seized. Generali's agencies and affiliates in Hungary, Czechoslovakia, Poland, and Romania suffered the worst losses while those in Yugoslavia, Bulgaria, Albania, and east Germany fared slightly better. In all, the Generali group lost 14 subsidiaries as well as substantial real estate holdings in Eastern Europe. Efforts by Baroncini to recover some of the losses in Eastern Europe were only partly successful: L13 billion were eventually restored to the company in payments from various countries, about one-tenth of what was lost. There were further losses in the former Italian colonies, such as Libya and Ethiopia.

But in 1945 tensions did not immediately ease in Trieste, where a bloody campaign of terror was waged by Yugoslavia at the end of the war, when Yugoslavian nationalists tried to win control of the city. After the declaration of the Free Territory of Trieste, the city led a tense existence from 1947 to 1954, until a hard-won international compromise resulted in the city's being awarded to Italy.

Generali's solid asset base made the work of reconstruction possible, and already by 1948 the company's Western European operations were on the way to recovery. Spurred by the loss of Eastern and Central European markets, attention turned to Latin America, where a majority ownership was acquired in the Argentinian company Providencia. At the beginning of the 1950s, operations resumed in Greece and the Middle East and in Brazil, Guatemala, Venezuela, Ecuador, and Colombia. In South Africa, Generali acquired a controlling interest in the new Standard General Insurance, then in a phase of considerable expansion.

From 1948 to 1953, Senator Mario Abbate succeeded Cosulich as president of the company. Formerly he had been chairman of the Milan subsidiary Anonima Grandine. Already elderly and in ill health, Abbate's was largely a titular presidency. Chief executive responsibility was shared by Baroncini and Michele Sulfina, a Generali manager who had served with Edgardo Morpurgo in the 1920s and 1930s. In 1950, during Abbate's tenure, direct operations resumed in the United States after Generali had obtained the necessary authorization to offer shipping and fire insurance as well as reinsurance. At this time, and as Italy entered its postwar economic boom, the company dedicated itself to reorganizing and restructuring its Italian assets. Thus in 1955 the two old Milan firms constituted to handle injury and hailstorm insurance in the 19th century, Anonima Infortuni and Anonima Grandine, were merged to form the Milan head office.

Mario Tripcovich, who succeeded the aging Senator Abbate as president in 1953, came from the Trieste shipbuilding concern founded in 1895 by his father, Diodato Tripcovich, himself a member of Generali's executive council for 20 years. The younger Tripcovich had spearheaded efforts to improve Generali's position in the United States, insisting on buying the Buffalo Insurance Company in 1950.

Tripcovich was succeeded in 1956 by Camillo Giussani, who acted for a period as simultaneous chairman of Generali and the Banca Commerciale Italiana. The strengthening of bonds between the two companies was to continue in the decades that followed. As the Italian economy surged ahead, so did Generali, achieving first place among foreign insurers operating in Austria and France, thanks to its considerable presence in both countries, through La Concorde in France and Erste Allgemeine in Austria. The company was active in 60 different countries, and was diversifying into previously unheard-of areas. When television came to Italy, Generali initiated policies covering equipment and antennae, fire, theft, and destruction of cathode tubes.

The decade was also characterized by the entrance of powerful shareholders into the elite group of Trieste financiers and industrialists who had traditionally occupied seats on Generali's executive council. In 1956 Mediobanca, Italy's largest semi-private bank, acquired a 3.5% share. Guiding this move was Enrico Cuccia, president of the bank since 1949, who was to have a hand in Generali's course in decades to come.

Baroncini, the engineer of Generali's postwar recovery, was named chairman in 1960 and served until 1968 when he was succeeded by another former official of the COMIT bank, Cesare Merzagore. In 1966 an international cooperation agreement was reached with a leading U.S. insurer, Aetna Life and Casualty, under which each company provided reciprocal services to the other's clients while abroad.

In the 1970s Generali rationalized its foreign activities, aiming at a greater local integration. Companies such as Generali France, Generali Belgium and, in West Germany, Generali Lebensversicherung were created as domestic companies governed by local laws, and often were strengthened by mergers with local companies. Reinsurance activity was increased. The Europ Assistance Service companies were also established, providing tourist assistance in the European market.

Enrico Randone became Generali's chairman in 1979, taking over from Merzagore, who remained as honorary chairman. By this time the company had assumed its present name. Two years later a robust Generali celebrated its 150th anniversary. Total premiums amounted to L1.395 trillion, real property was valued at L581 billion, and equity investments at L1.09 trillion. This marked the beginning of a significant decade for the company. The prospect of a unified European market in 1992 prompted an increase in mergers and acquisitions in the major European markets, as Europe's large insurers prepared for tough competition.

Generali had distinguished itself in the postwar decades as a slow-moving giant, too dignified for U.S.-style hostile takeover bids. In 1988, however, the Italian company tried to acquire Compagnie du Midi, one of the larger French insurance groups. This bid was ultimately unsuccessful, as the threat of takeover drove Midi to seek protection in a merger with its largest competitor in France, the AXA group. The widely publicized adventure ended in a boardroom battle between the two French managers. Midi's president Bernard Pagezy was driven out by his younger partner Claude Bébéar, while Generali won no more than a joint partnership with AXA-Midi, in accordance with French regulations on foreign investment.

During this period, the large shareholders controlling nearly 23% of Generali stock proved to be influential in determining company strategy. Mediobanca heads this list, controlling 5.6%. Another 4.8% is held by the Euralux investment group whose members include Italy's powerful Agnelli family. The Banca d'Italia owns a similar portion of shares.

Generali closed the decade with the constitution of AB Generali Budapest, the first mixed-ownership insurance company in eastern Europe, 40% of the joint venture being owned by Generali and 60% by Allami Biztosito, a Hungarian state-owned insurer. In 1990, Generali made its first real entrance into the U.S. business world, buying the Kansas City, Missouri–based Business Men's Assurance Company of America from its parent BMA Corporation for about US$285 million, or less than L360 billion. Another significant achievement was Generali's link-up with Taisho Marine and Fire Insurance Company (now Mitsui Marine and Fire Insurance Company), the third-largest insurer in Japan, whereby Generali was able to open a liaison office and general agency through Taisho Marine and Fire in Tokyo, and Taisho was able to operate in Italy through the offices of Generali subsidiary la Navale.

Several important changes, both for the company and the industry will have an impact on the long-term direction taken by Generali. The group will be challenged by the continuing trend toward expansion by all the largest European companies, seeking to ward off foreign competition, particularly from the United States and Japan. Generali is one of the five largest insurance groups in Europe, and has the broadest foreign presence of any European company.

In 1991, the 80-year-old chairman Enrico Randone retired, with several other senior officers who have guided Generali's policy for the past few decades. The company has staked its success on long-term planning and careful management—Generali is the only company of its size in Europe to have three managing directors. The group should continue to play a leading role in the European insurance scene, without threat of takeover from Italian or European competitors, but competition will become tougher in the next decade as European companies continue to decline in number.

Principal Subsidiaries: Agricoltura Assicurazioni—Soc. Mutua (51%); Alleanza Assicurazioni S.p.A. (63.67%); Unione Mediterranea di Sicurtà S.p.A. (68.01%); Navale Assicurazioni S.p.A. (98.56%); Gefina; Genagricola; Genedil; La Concorde S.A. (France, 61.66%); Generali France (99.91%); La Federation Continentale (France, 52.49%); La Lutece (France, 49.50%); Compagnie Dakar Saint-Louis (France, 56.54%); Generali Lebensversicherung (Germany, 80%); Deutscher Lloyd Lebensversicherung (Germany); Deutscher Lloyd Versicherung (Germany); Erste Allgemeine Versicherung (Austria, 81.19%); Union Suisse (Switzerland, 53.68%); Graafschap Holland (Netherlands); Caja de Prevision y Socorro (Spain); Transocean Holding Corp. (U.S.A.); Transocean do Brasil (Brazil); Standard General Insurance (South Africa, 89.48%).

Further Reading: Sancin, Luciano Giulio, "Storia dell'assicurazione—Sui primordi e su alcuni sviluppi dell'assicurazione in Italia," *Quaderni dell'instituto per gli studi assicurativi*, No. 2, 1945; Palladini, Giovanni, "Le Compagnie di assicurazioni di Trieste," *Trieste Economica*, December 1966; *Le Assicurazioni Generali: Cenni Storici*, Trieste, Assicurazioni Generali, 1966; *An Introduction to Generali*, Trieste, Generali Group, 1988; *The Insurer Without Frontiers—a World Directory*, Trieste, Generali Group, 1989; Lindner, Claudio, and Giancarlo Mazzuca, *Il leone di Trieste: il romanzo delle Assicurazioni Generali dalle origini austroungariche all'era Cuccia*, Milan, Sperling & Kupfer, 1990.

—Paul Conrad

AXA

23, avenue Matignon
75008 Paris
France
(1) 40 75 57 06
Fax: (1) 40 75 57 50

Mutual Company
Incorporated: 1817 as Compagnie d'assurances Mutuelles contre l'incendie dans les départements de la Seine Inférieure et de l'Eure
Employees: 16,000
Assets: FFr4.014 billion (US$695 million)

AXA, an insurance group with mutual companies at the head of its financial structure, is the second-largest insurance group in France and the 30th largest in the world. Although it has only been operating under its present name since 1984 and is located in Paris, AXA's roots are in 19th-century Normandy. After a rather uneventful history before the 1950s, it recently experienced spectacular growth as well as extensive internationalization. Under the influence of one man, Claude Bébéar, AXA successively bought and absorbed several companies, some of which were twice its size. In 1990 AXA once again faced a phase of restructuring and merging.

The first company in the history of AXA was created in 1817. This company was responsible for the two main characteristics of the group before the 1970s: its location in Normandy and its legal status as a mutual company. Jacques-Théodore le Carpentier, with 17 other property owners, established the Compagnie d'assurances Mutuelles contre l'incendie dans les départements de la Seine et de l'Eure, a fire insurance company situated at Rouen. In the company's legal documents it was stated that every shareholder was to be both insurer and insured party for five years, this being the basic principle of mutuality, where the insured parties own the company. On the properties insured was a plaque bearing the letters P.A.C.L. (propriété assurée contre l'incendie), indicating that they were insured against fire loss. The first damage for which the company had to pay occurred in 1819, amounting to FFr7.5. Realizing the impossibility of sharing this cost among 1,264 shareholders, the company invented the reserve fund. Soon afterwards in 1822, the famous fire of Rouen Cathedral required shareholders to pay for a more important claim, an event not easily forgotten.

Great changes following the industrial revolution, as well as increasing competition from companies such as La Providence or La Paternelle, created in 1838 and 1843, respectively, required the company to expand and diversify its activities. Adolphe Lanne, manager since 1832, decided to create two companies. The first one, Mutualité Immobilière, replaced the original company; the second, Mutualité Mobilière, was to insure movables risks. The people of Rouen called the former Ancienne Mutuelle to distinguish it from the latter, which went into business in 1847. In 1852 a major quarrel occurred between insurance companies and the French government. Concerned about the dangers associated with the recent invention of the match, insurers tried for more than 20 years to have its production restricted or even forbidden. The government held on, and eventually established a state monopoly for the making and selling of matches. In the meantime the board made two decisions. They would extend activities to cover the whole of France, and the Mutualité Mobilière would now also cover real estate risks. In 1881, Mutualité Immobilière and Mutualité Mobilière merged under the name of Ancienne Mutuelle, which it retained until 1977. At this time the new chairman, M. Masselin, decided to offer life insurance. In this way Mutuelle Vie life insurance company was born.

The beginning of the 20th century and World War I did not bring any great change for Ancienne Mutuelle (AM). After moving offices in Rouen in 1902, the first important step was undertaken just after the war when in 1922 Anciennes Mutuelles Accidents, an automobile insurance branch was established. It developed quickly and was to make a major contribution to the company's profits.

In World War II, the company did not escape so lightly. In April 1944 its new offices were bombed by U.S. forces; this loss was followed by the death of Gaston de Payenneville, chairman since 1913. AM emerged from the war in poor shape generally, although the accident and life divisions were less severely afflicted. Soon the necessity of a tighter group structure became apparent. This change was accomplished in 1946 with the constitution of the Groupe Ancienne Mutuelle under the leadership of André Sahut d'Izarn. In 1948 the Groupe was thriving once more, proving the validity of its motto: "E cinere suo re divide"—"rising again from its ashes." From the mid-1940s until the 1970s the Groupe experienced steady though unspectacular growth achieved by a succession of mergers with other insurance mutual companies. The first, in 1946, was with the Ancienne Mutuelle du Calvados, created in 1819 and a long time collaborator of AM. Then in 1950 the Mutuelle d'Orléans asked to join the Groupe, via the Mutuelle Vie, since it was a life insurance company. Next came the Mutualité Générale life insurance company, also known for insuring the French *communes*—cities, or parts of cities, with individual legal status. Finally in 1954 La Participation, created in 1899 as a non-life insurance company, entered the AM.

In 1955, before the Groupe began to expand abroad, André Sahut d'Izarn could count within his company eight mutuals and further nonmutual companies which were 100% subsidiaries. Among the latter was the Ancienne Mutuelle Transport de Bétail, created in 1939 in order to insure rail transport of livestock. It soon became a public company, after which it was acquired by AM. In 1977 it became the AMRE, the reinsurance company of AM.

In 1955, AM went into business in Canada, focusing particularly on Quebec. This step, together with the arrival at AM of a young graduate, Claude Bébéar, the son of a schoolteacher, marked the beginning of a great phase of expansion at AM. In the midst of the political events of May 1968 in Paris, André Sahut d'Izarn celebrated in fitting style the 150th anniversary of the Groupe. The party in Belbeuf, Normandy, is said to have been particularly lavish and welcomed a very special guest: a computer, recently acquired.

After this phase of development, AM experienced a crisis. The death of chairman André Sahut d'Izarn in June 1972 may have been a contributing factor. In April 1974, the longest strike known in insurance history began. It lasted for more than two months and totally paralyzed the AM Groupe. Eventually it ended in June with the nomination of Claude Bébéar as chairman and the establishment of an innovative social policy.

From this point, the history of AXA, at that stage Groupe Ancienne Mutuelle, cannot be separated from the story of Claude Bébéar's ambition and rise to power. In the French insurance world, Bébéar was known as the cowboy of insurance, also described by *le Nouvel Economiste,* October 21, 1988, as the "avant-garde insurer" and elected by his peers in 1988 as Manager of the Year. He started by changing the name of the group, with its old-fashioned connotations, replacing the adjective *ancienne* with *unies*, or "united." By 1978, Mutuelles Unies had already taken control of the Compagnie Parisienne de Garantie and the Mutuelle de l'Quest, specializing in legal protection, also joined the group. Two years later, Mutuelles Unies and its subsidiaries achieved a total turnover of FFr2.4 million with 2,300 employees around the world and more than 700 sole agents working for the group.

The first major opportunity for Bébéar to expand through acquisition occurred in 1982 with the spectacular purchase of the Drouot Group. Established in 1948 as a public company quoted on the Paris stock exchange, the Drouot Group only began operating under this name from 1977, although its history went back to the 19th century. At the time of its purchase, the results of its automobile insurance division were poor and its financial policy was not very sound. Nevertheless the takeover battle turned out to be fierce and highly publicized; Bébéar was trying to absorb a company at least as big as his own. This takeover bid is also said to have been quite traumatic for the Drouot employees. According to the *Expansion,* May 31, 1990, other companies began to fear what they called "other drouotisations." Trying to justify himself, Bébéar explained in the same paper: "We may be upsetting people but we are also cutting out the dead wood." Not only did he achieve the latter, but he soon took further significant steps, transforming Mutuelles Unies into AXA in 1984. He chose this name because it had no meaning whatsoever, was internationally pronounceable, and was an easily-remembered palindrome.

The next stage occurred in 1986, with Drouot as the vehicle. Drouot made a takeover bid for La Providence, an old company owned by an ancient line of the French aristocracy. At this very moment La Providence was merging with Le Secours, another insurance company established in 1880. When AXA—via Drouot—took control of La Providence at the end of a long takeover battle, Bébéar killed two birds with one stone and acquired both La Providence and Le Secours, merged under the name of Présence. These were important life and non-life insurance companies with a large network of domestic and international branches, especially in Europe. They had also had, until the 1960s, considerable presence in the French colonies, La Providence in Algeria and Le Secours in Indochina.

Although the purchases of Drouot and Présence were crucial points in AXA's development, AXA's last coup remained its most famous. It began in 1988 when Bernard Pagezy, chairman of the holding company la Compagnie du Midi, including the AGP (Assurances du Groupe de Paris), came to see Claude Bébéar. Threatened with absorption by the Italian insurers Generali, Pagezy asked AXA for protection. He proposed to give Bébéar Midi's insurance interests in exchange for participation and protection. This happy marriage did not last very long, and the collaboration soon turned into a fight as AXA began to think seriously about buying le Midi. It was through the proceedings of February 1989's general meeting that Bébéar, assisted by Generali, the very same company that Midi feared, eventually managed to take 100% control of la Compagnie du Midi. After a short period as AXA-Midi, the company's name reverted to AXA.

By acquiring Midi, not only had AXA taken over a major holding company but now as a result controlled Midi's enormous international network. The Compagnie du Midi had had a significant presence abroad, especially in the United Kingdom. In 1982 it had taken possession of London & Hull, an airline, marine, and industrial insurance company. Five years later, it bought life insurers Equity & Law. Its U.K. interests alone achieved a turnover in 1988 of FFr5.5 million.

In February 1989 AXA could boast 42 companies around the world, 4,000 general agents, 16,000 employees, and a turnover of FFr45 million. Only nine years earlier, Mutuelles Unies had had 2,300 employees, 700 agents, and a turnover of FFr2.4 million. Claude Bébéar had definitely proved his business acumen. The structure of AXA, with mutual companies heading the group, protects the company—according to French legislation—from any kind of takeover bid.

The most recent challenge undertaken by AXA was a total restructuring of the group, which is still in progress and the outcome of which is still uncertain. The restructuring began in 1986 when Bébéar, for the first time in French insurance history, began the complete transformation of AXA's distribution network. Instead of a traditional system, whereby each company had its own general agents, insurance brokers, and other sales organizations, Bébéar chose to reorganize horizontally. He merged all group companies into three main units, each of them corresponding to a single channel of distribution. As a result, AXA consists of three entities, each specializing in one channel of distribution. Axa Assurances includes the company's general agents, Uni Europe the insurance brokers, and Franklin Assurances deals with the remaining sales organizations. This structure is only valid for France; foreign distribution has not been affected. Bébéar is convinced of his system's efficiency and of its relevance to the market. Whether he is right or not remains to be seen.

Principal Subsidiaries: AXA Belgium; AXA Canada; Equity & Law (U.K.); London & Hull (U.K.).

Further Reading: Gallix, Lucien, *Il était une fois . . . l'assurance,* Paris, l'Argus, 1985; *L'Argus se souvient 1877–1987,* Paris, la Sécuritas Editeur, 1987; Antoni, Marie-Louise, "Claude Bébéar, un assureur d'avant-garde," *Le Nouvel Economiste,* November 21, 1988; Alexandre, Roger, "Tu fusionneras dans la douleur," *L'Expansion,* May 31, 1990; Allard, Laurence, and Georges Quioc, "Axa-Midi: Bilan d'une Stratégie de Mouvement," *Le Figaro,* June 5, 1990.

—Sonia Kronlund

BERKSHIRE HATHAWAY INC.

BERKSHIRE HATHAWAY INC.

1440 Kiewit Plaza
Omaha, Nebraska 68131
U.S.A.
(402) 346-1400
Fax: (402) 346-3375

Public Company
Incorporated: 1889 as Berkshire Cotton Manufacturing Company
Employees: 20,000
Assets: $9.46 billion
Stock Exchange: New York

Berkshire Hathaway and its subsidiaries are involved in several different businesses, the most significant of which is property and casualty insurance and reinsurance. It conducts this business nationwide through 12 subsidiaries, headed by National Indemnity Company of Omaha. Other businesses of Berkshire Hathaway include newspaper and encyclopedia publishing; manufacturing of candy, uniforms, home cleaning systems, and other products; retailing of furniture and jewelry; and operation of a savings and loan. Through the investment portfolios of its insurance subsidiaries, Berkshire Hathaway often buys significant shares of other publicly traded companies; its chairman, Warren Buffett, has become renowned for his stock-picking expertise.

Berkshire Hathaway began as a textile company. Berkshire Cotton Manufacturing Company was incorporated in Massachusetts in 1889. In 1929 several other New England textile manufacturers with much common ownership—Valley Falls Company, Coventry Company, Greylock Mills, and Fort Dummer Mills—merged into the company, which was then renamed Berkshire Fine Spinning Associates. This operation accounted for about 25% of the fine-cotton-textile production in the United States.

The glory years of the New England textile industry were numbered. The Great Depression of the 1930s contributed to its decline, as did competition from the South and overseas. Wages were lower in the South, and southern workers had fewer alternatives than New Englanders to working in the textile mills. Also, market factors favored the coarser types of goods produced in the South. Wage differentials also were a factor in foreign competition.

The New England textile business recovered somewhat during World War II, thanks to military demand for its products, and had a similar brief recovery during the Korean conflict. Still, the industry declined again after each of these upswings.

In 1955 Berkshire Fine Spinning merged with Hathaway Manufacturing Company, a New Bedford, Massachusetts, textile maker dating back to 1888. The resulting company, Berkshire Hathaway Inc., had more than 10,000 employees and nearly six million square feet of plant space, but its financial performance was dismal. Berkshire Hathaway closed its extensive operations in Adams, Massachusetts, in 1958, and the same year sold its curtain plant in Warren, Rhode Island, to Pilgrim Curtain Company. The company recovered a bit the following year; a contract negotiated between Berkshire Hathaway and its unionized employees in 1959 marked the first wage increase for New England textile workers since 1956. By late 1959 and into 1960, the company was operating profitably and had a backlog of unfilled orders. Depressed conditions returned quickly, however, and in 1961 Berkshire Hathaway cut its work week to four days at several plants and showed a loss for the year. In 1962 the company closed three plants in Rhode Island and showed even greater losses, due to depressed prices for its products.

The financial hemorrhaging continued into the mid-1960s, despite cuts in Berkshire Hathaway's work force and an extensive plant modernization. In 1965 came a major change in the company's management. A partnership—Buffett Partnership, Ltd.—led by investor Warren Buffett had purchased enough stock to control the company, and—in a resulting dispute—Seabury Stanton, a 50-year Berkshire Hathaway employee, resigned as president. Kenneth V. Chace, a vice president who had been with the company 18 years, replaced Stanton. Between this time and 1984 the company's operations were gradually moved from New Bedford to Omaha, Nebraska, where Buffett was based.

Berkshire Hathaway was profitable in 1965 and 1966, but profits fell sharply as it began its 1967 fiscal year. The company was shopping actively for acquisitions to help it diversify, and in 1967 it entered the insurance business, buying National Indemnity Company and National Fire & Marine Insurance Company for a total of $8.5 million. Acquisition of the two Omaha-based companies, which were handling automobile insurance primarily, was expected to help Berkshire Hathaway overcome the cyclical nature of the textile business.

In 1968 the company made another significant acquisition, of Sun Newspapers, a group of Omaha-area weeklies. In 1969 it bought Illinois National Bank & Trust Company of Rockford. Buffett, who became Berkshire Hathaway's chairman in 1969, tended to acquire companies whose management and products he liked, rather than buying companies with the intention to make major changes. His reputation as an expert investor grew during the 1970s.

Berkshire Hathaway's expansion and diversification continued at a steady pace. During 1969 and 1970 it bought a controlling interest in Blue Chip Stamps, which in turn owned See's Candies—a chocolate maker and retailer—and Wesco Financial Corporation, a savings and loan operator. The Berkshire Hathaway insurance operations grew with the formation of Cornhusker Casualty Company as part of the National Indemnity group in 1970 and Lakeland Fire and Casualty Company—now National Indemnity Company of

Minnesota—also as part of that group, in 1971. Also in 1971, Berkshire Hathaway acquired Home & Automobile Insurance Company—now National Liability and Fire Insurance Company. In 1972 Berkshire Hathaway formed Texas United Insurance Company, which it later merged into National Indemnity; in 1976 the National Fire & Marine subsidiary acquired its only wholly owned subsidiary, Redwood Fire & Casualty Insurance Company.

In 1977 Berkshire Hathaway acquired Cypress Insurance Company and formed Kansas Fire & Casualty Company. The same year, it made another move into the newspaper business by purchasing, through Blue Chip Stamps, the *Buffalo Evening News.*

The *News* was a six-day paper, published in the afternoon, competing against a morning paper with a Sunday edition, at a time when morning papers were outstripping evening papers in popularity. After the acquisition by Berkshire Hathaway, the *News* began publishing a Sunday edition and competed intensely with its rival, the *Courier-Express*, which shut down in 1982, leaving the *News* with a monopoly.

Berkshire Hathaway formed another insurance company, Continental Divide Insurance Company, in 1978. Through a merger with a company called Diversified Retailing Company, Berkshire Hathaway acquired two more insurers, Columbia Insurance Company and Southern Casualty Insurance Company, in 1978; Southern Casualty was later merged into National Indemnity Company. Even with Warren Buffett's growing reputation, not every company was eager to become part of Berkshire Hathaway; CSE Corporation, the holding company for Civil Service Employees Insurance Company, turned down an informal takeover offer in 1979. Because Berkshire Hathaway does not execute hostile takeovers, the acquisition was not pursued.

In 1980 Berkshire Hathaway spun off Illinois National Bank & Trust, a move required by the Bank Holding Company Act of 1969. A year later, the company sold Sun Newspapers to a Chicago publisher, Bruce Sagan.

In 1981 Berkshire Hathaway instituted an unusual corporate philanthropy program that won praise from shareholders. Buffett announced that shareholders would be able to direct a portion of the company's charitable contributions. With this policy, he hoped to foster an "owner mentality" among shareholders, he said at the time. Shareholders responded enthusiastically, with more than 95% of eligible shares participating in every year since the program's inception. The amount they were allowed to direct to charities of their choice was $2 a share in 1981; that figure had risen to $6 a share by 1989. Buffett's own favorite causes are population control and nuclear disarmament.

During the early 1980s the textile business continued to languish, and the insurance industry was hit by poor sales and price cutting. Berkshire Hathaway's performance, however, was buoyed by the performance of its investment portfolio. Buying noncontrolling but significant blocks of stock in such companies as The Washington Post Company, Media General, and GEICO Corporation, Berkshire Hathaway's stock holdings grew in value by 21% in 1981—a year in which the Dow Jones Industrial Average declined by 9.2%. Berkshire Hathaway's per-share earnings grew 23%.

In 1983 Blue Chip Stamps merged with Berkshire Hathaway; Blue Chip had been 60% owned by Berkshire. That year, Berkshire Hathaway also acquired 90% of the Nebraska Furniture Mart, a high-volume Omaha discount retailer—and the largest U.S. home furnishings store—that had been founded by a Russian immigrant, Rose Blumkin. The Blumkin family retained management and the remaining ownership of the store, although Rose Blumkin left the business in 1989 as a result of an argument with her children. Buffett has been known to promote the store during annual shareholder meetings, running buses to the store after the meeting, and many out-of-town shareholders have ended up buying furniture there. Also in 1983, another insurance company, National Indemnity Company of Florida, was formed and added to the National Indemnity group.

Early in 1985, Berkshire Hathaway participated in Capital Cities Communications's acquisition of American Broadcasting Companies. Buffett agreed to put up $517.5 million in financing for the deal and came out with an 18% share of the merged company, Capital Cities/ABC. The investment community saw the move as unusual for Buffett, who had tended to hunt for undervalued companies and stay away from high-priced deals. Buffett, however, said he saw the investment climate changing, with good prospects for companies like television networks, which have intangible assets rather than heavy investments in plants and equipment.

Also in 1985, Berkshire Hathaway decided to leave the textile business. The company had sought, but not found, a buyer for the money-losing business, and ended up liquidating the business. Buffett lauded the efforts of Kenneth Chace—who remains a Berkshire Hathaway director—and of Garry Morrison, who recently had succeeded him as president of the textile business. Buffett also had kind words for the unionized textile workers, who had made only reasonable demands in view of the company's financial position. In the end, however, Berkshire Hathaway could not compete with low-cost foreign textile producers.

Late in 1985, Berkshire Hathaway agreed to acquire Scott & Fetzer Company, a Cleveland, Ohio–based, diversified manufacturing and marketing company, for about $320 million. Scott & Fetzer's products include *World Book* and *Childcraft* encyclopedias and Kirby vacuum cleaners. The sale was completed shortly after the beginning of 1986.

Berkshire Hathaway's insurance business underwent several changes in 1985. In a tight market for insurance, many commercial insurance buyers needed a financially stable company to underwrite large risks, so National Indemnity, Berkshire Hathaway's largest insurance company, advertised, in an insurance trade publication, its willingness to write property and casualty policies with a premium of $1 million or more. The advertisement produced an explosion in large-premium business for Berkshire Hathaway; the company wrote $184.5 million in net premiums for large accounts from August 1985 through December 1986, compared with virtually no such business previously. Also during 1985, Berkshire Hathaway reached an agreement with Fireman's Fund Insurance Company which allowed it a 7% participation in Fireman's Fund's business. John J. Byrne, an executive of GEICO—an insurer partly owned by Berkshire Hathaway—had left GEICO to become chairman of Fireman's Fund earlier in the year, and had arranged the deal. Another insurance move during the year was the establishment of Wesco-Financial Insurance Company by Berkshire Hathaway's Wesco Financial Corporation subsidiary.

In 1986 Berkshire Hathaway acquired 84% of Fechheimer Bros. Company, a uniform manufacturer and distributor based in Cincinnati, Ohio. Fechheimer's management had responded to the solicitation for acquisitions that appears in Berkshire Hathaway's annual report.

During 1987, the stock market was continuing an upward rise that had begun early in the decade. Buffett's policy of buying, for Berkshire Hathaway's investment portfolio, undervalued stocks and holding them long-term, paid off well. In August 1987 *The Wall Street Journal* reported that in the five years since the market's surge began, Berkshire Hathaway's stock portfolio had grown in value by 748%, far surpassing the Dow Jones average, which increased 233.6%, and another market barometer, the Standard & Poor's (S.&P.) 500 stock index, which gained 215.4%. When the stock market crashed in October 1987, wiping out the year's gains, Berkshire Hathaway's portfolio weathered the storm, it was up 2.8% for the period of January through November 1987, while the S.&P. 500 declined 2.5%.

Just before the crash, Berkshire Hathaway had bought $700 million worth of preferred stock, convertible to a 12% common stake, in Salomon Inc., a Wall Street investment firm whose fortunes were closely tied to the market. Even after the crash, however, Buffett expressed confidence in Salomon's management and his conviction that the investment would prove valuable.

Another major event of 1988 was the listing of Berkshire Hathaway's stock on the New York Stock Exchange. The stock had traded in the over-the-counter market previously. The move was designed to reduce transaction costs for shareholders. Berkshire Hathaway became the highest-priced stock on the exchange, at about $4,300 a share, up from $12 a share when Buffett bought the company. The price later ran up to more than $8,000 a share; a stock split could reduce the price, but would also encourage more frequent trading—something that Buffett would rather not encourage, preferring shareholders to be in for the long haul. Buffett himself owns 45% of the company's shares, with a net worth of about $4 billion.

Buffett and Berkshire Hathaway have themselves proven to be long-term shareholders in other companies, leading some to see Buffett as a protector against hostile takeovers. During 1989, his company bought significant shares of The Gillette Company, USAir Group, and Champion International Corporation, with all the purchases widely interpreted as defenses against takeovers. Another major purchase was 6.3% of Coca-Cola Company, making Berkshire Hathaway Coke's second-largest shareholder.

In 1989 Berkshire Hathaway bought an 80% interest in Borsheim's, an Omaha jewelry store run by the Friedman family, relatives of the Nebraska Furniture Mart's Blumkins. The store has since joined Nebraska Furniture Mart as a stop for attendees of Berkshire Hathaway's annual meetings.

Buffett has been an outspoken investor and business operator. In 1989 the Wesco Financial–owned Mutual Savings & Loan Association of Pasadena, California, pulled out of the U.S. League of Savings Institutions, which was lobbying for more lenient provisions in the federal bailout of the savings and loan industry. Buffett likened the bailout to a "mugging" of taxpayers. Buffett has also spoken out on the need to tie executive compensation to performance.

Principal Subsidiaries: National Indemnity Co.; Continental Divide Insurance Co.; Cornhusker Casualty Co.; Kansas Fire & Casualty Co.; National Indemnity Co. of Florida; National Indemnity Co. of Minnesota; National Fire & Marine Insurance Co.; Redwood Fire & Casualty Co.; Columbia Insurance Co.; Cypress Insurance Co.; National Liability & Fire Insurance Co.; Wesco Financial Corp. (80%); Borsheim's (80%); The Buffalo News; Fechheimer Bros. Co. (84%); Kirby; Scott Fetzer Manufacturing Group; See's Candies; World Book.

Further Reading: Laing, Jonathan R., "The Collector: Investor Who Piled Up $100 Million in the '60s Piles Up Firms Today," *The Wall Street Journal,* March 31, 1977; Loomis, Carol J., "The Inside Story of Warren Buffett," *Fortune,* April 11, 1988.

—Trudy Ring

CapitalHolding

CAPITAL HOLDING CORPORATION

680 Fourth Avenue
Louisville, Kentucky 40232
U.S.A.
(502) 560-2000
Fax: (502) 581-0632

Public Company
Incorporated: 1904 as Commonwealth Life Insurance Company
Employees: 7,900
Assets: $14.97 billion
Stock Exchanges: New York Pacific

Capital Holding Corporation is a major provider of insurance and other financial services in the United States, Europe, and the Far East. The firm's predecessor and now its largest subsidiary, Commonwealth Life Insurance Company, traces its heritage back to the turn of the century, when the company sold its first life insurance policy to one of its own employees. It was restructured under the present name in 1969 in order to make it easier for the firm to grow through the acquisition of other companies. The company offers health, life, property, and casualty insurance through a combination of personal sales and direct marketing and also provides consumer banking and investment services. The company is one of the ten largest stockholder-owned life insurance companies in the United States.

When founded in 1904, Commonwealth was intended to serve as a catalyst to economic development in Kentucky and as a means to keep both business and capital within state borders. To emphasize this connection, the firm was named after the Commonwealth of Kentucky. It also adopted the state's motto, "United We Stand, Divided We Fall," and its seal. Two of the company's founders figured prominently in its early years. Colonel Joshua D. Powers, the firm's first president, was a lawyer, a state legislator, and founder of several corporations. Darwin W. Johnson joined the company as secretary-treasurer after working for several years in the tobacco business.

Initially, Commonwealth sold insurance only in Kentucky, specializing in ordinary life insurance and also inexpensive coverage for low-income workers. This latter type of insurance policy was called industrial, or weekly premium debit, insurance because the insurance agent collected the premiums in person, every week. Although these premiums were often paid in the form of chickens, eggs, or produce, the company's fortunes grew rapidly, leading to expansion into other states, including Alabama. Because of the concentration of blue-collar workers, urban areas offered the most lucrative marketing opportunities.

Over the next 20 years, Commonwealth's business experienced both peaks and valleys. Between 1914 and 1918, its life insurance sales increased, although death losses from World War I and an influenza epidemic depressed overall financial results. The postwar recession of 1921 did not affect the company's growing prosperity, which continued during the rest of the decade. The company sustained major losses due to the Great Depression, but rebounded by 1935 as a result of the intensified efforts of its field sales force.

During this period, the company was led by Darwin Johnson, who had succeeded an ailing Joshua Powers as president in 1922. Johnson's death in 1936 touched off a power struggle on the board of directors that ended in the election of Homer Ward Batson as the company's next president. When Batson took over, the company was experiencing serious financial problems. Although it appeared on the surface that the company was doing well, many of its loans were not guaranteed with sufficient collateral and others had little chance of ever being repaid. In addition, the company's practice of paying liberal dividends to shareholders, even during the Depression years, resulted in a critical shortage of funds. Batson immediately implemented a series of measures intended to increase the company's capital and place it on stronger financial footing. All officers were required to take a salary reduction; unnecessary lights were to be turned off, and clerks were expected to use pencils until they were too short to be held comfortably. The consolidation of several field offices, elimination of problem policies, and suspension of dividend payments for 1938 contributed to the company's economic recovery.

Not all of Batson's initiatives proceeded as smoothly. In 1936, he sent form letters to the recipients of several small loans to request full payment. One of these borrowers was James E. Dunne, the publisher of *Dunne's Insurance Reports*. In response, Dunne proceeded to circulate a scathing assessment of Commonwealth's financial condition among the subscribers of *Dunne's Insurance Reports*. He subsequently attempted to oust Batson as president and ruin the company. Commonwealth's management eventually ran a series of advertisements in local newspapers to restore public confidence in the company.

Dunne's allegations of mismanagement and insolvency later were brought before a Jefferson County grand jury, but the company successfully defended itself against the charges. However, to provide stronger control over Commonwealth's future financial operations, the state's insurance commissioner required the company to submit all loan applications for over $20,000 to both the insurance commission of Kentucky and that of the state in which the loan was to be made.

With this incident behind it, Commonwealth turned its attention to the marketplace. It found that its existing industrial insurance benefits were no longer competitive and the methods by which premiums had been calculated were out of date. A revitalized product line introduced in 1941 boosted sales force morale and increased insurance sales.

That same year, the board of directors elected Morton Boyd as president and Batson became honorary chairman. Boyd focused on expanding Commonwealth's insurance business through the agency sales force.

The onset of World War II restricted the availability of many goods and provided few alternatives for consumer spending. High employment levels increased the demand for life insurance, spending considered helpful to the war effort because of its anti-inflationary effects. With customer demand higher than ever, Commonwealth's sales force had difficulty covering the market because it competed with the military for manpower and supplies such as gasoline. The war also affected the nature of the company's insurance policies. New issues written by Commonwealth and other insurers excluded members of the military from receiving death benefits. Policyholders who had purchased insurance prior to entering the military were allowed to retain their coverage. This procedure cost the company a significant amount of money in wartime mortality claims. When the war ended, the company concentrated on improving sales efficiency and quality through better recruitment and training of agents. Blue collar unemployment drove the weekly premium insurance business down, but sales of ordinary insurance picked up the slack.

The company continued to grow during the rest of the 1940s. The insurance business was becoming increasingly competitive, with many firms using the success of a particular product in one state as a springboard to marketing in another location. Commonwealth watched with more than a casual interest as one of its competitors in Alabama, Liberty National Life Insurance Company, successfully marketed burial insurance policies that also provided for the funeral service to be handled by a funeral home owned by the company. In order to counteract a likely expansion of this program into Kentucky, Commonwealth designed a similar product based on a standard weekly premium policy. The Kentucky Funeral Directors' Association was contracted to handle the funeral arrangements so that Commonwealth did not have to directly enter the funeral business. The product was an instant success, with some agents writing as many as 100 policies in the first week.

Growth continued in the 1950s with only a minor disruption caused by the Korean War. Commonwealth embarked upon a program of aggressive expansion beyond Kentucky. In 1952, it developed a new concept in life insurance that enabled policyholders to pay their premiums through regular automatic withdrawals from their checking accounts. Although the company met with some initial resistance from bankers, other insurers become enamored with the simplicity of the concept. Their decisions to introduce similar versions of Commonwealth's Bank-O-Matic program eventually persuaded reluctant bank executives to lend their support.

By 1954, the Korean War had given way to a recession that forced Commonwealth to curtail its ambitious expansion plans and focus instead on maintaining its field sales force. When agent turnover started to increase in response to a drop in sales, the company invested heavily in recruitment and training of new sales personnel. As the economy recovered, competition in the life insurance market intensified and Commonwealth introduced a new family coverage policy.

In 1958, Boyd became chairman and was succeeded as president and chief executive by William H. Abell, who had previously served the company as general counsel and a member of the board. Under his leadership, the branch-agency system was restructured into a more efficient and unified organization, improvements were made in agents' retirement benefits, and several product innovations were launched.

As Commonwealth entered the 1960s, it became evident that weekly premium insurance was no longer a viable product. Social Security and increased wages for middle-class workers decreased need for the burial insurance benefits that had made the weekly premium concept so popular. The gradual loss of business in this area compelled Commonwealth to investigate new avenues of growth. In addition, competing life insurance companies that offered health and accident coverage were able to offer customers a more complete selection of insurance products, enabling them to attract sales personnel. Commonwealth initially considered entering the health and accident field, but, when it appeared that the federal government would be heavily guiding the nation's health-care system, the company shifted its focus to automobile, fire, and casualty insurance.

The company originally intended to enter this market via acquisition, but ultimately developed the business internally as a subsidiary. By mid-1962, a pilot operation based in Louisville, Kentucky, began selling residential fire and homeowners insurance and individual automobile policies. Problems arose, ranging from computer billing errors to underwriting mistakes, and the new operation barely broke even. However, Commonwealth gradually expanded its new-products market beyond Kentucky.

Aggressive expansion into other states proved to be more difficult than originally anticipated because the company's contacts, particularly among local bankers, were not as strong as in its home state. It was at this time, however, that Commonwealth was offered the opportunity to acquire the Indiana-based Empire Life and Accident Insurance Company. Empire's chairman sought the merger to resolve an ongoing conflict between two of its executives who were also his sons-in-law. The companies joined forces on October 31, 1963, under the Commonwealth banner. This development gave Commonwealth a stronger position in Indiana, and added a significant number of black customers to its rolls. Since its early years, when advertising stressed that Commonwealth wrote ''white lives only,'' Commonwealth had served only the white market. Kentucky funeral parlors were still segregated at this time, so with the Empire merger, the company was forced to begin handling black burial business in Kentucky, resulting in the formation of the Kentucky Bonded Funeral Company.

The state of Florida was identified as the company's next site for expansion. Commonwealth management believed that by targeting a southern state, the company would meet with less sales resistance than it had faced in Indiana. Florida was also especially attractive due to its projected growth in population and economy.

Commonwealth continued to experience problems in hiring additional general agents due to a lack of attractive sales incentives and a narrow product line. By the late 1960s, the Vietnam War had made this situation even worse. Despite a healthy economy, which enhanced the market potential for insurance, the lack of available staff to cover sales territories placed the company's expansion strategy on indefinite hold. This situation became more critical as the war intensified and the costs of developing the Florida market increased. Attempts to acquire other companies proved fruitless, since most candidates were reluctant to be part of Commonwealth.

After much consideration, the company embarked upon a plan to form a holding company. At first, this holding company would consist of the existing Commonwealth organization but, in time, would serve as an umbrella for acquired subsidiaries that would be permitted to operate autonomously. The new organization was incorporated in Delaware in 1969 as Capital Holding Corporation, a name which was felt to be appropriate regardless of the type of business the company purchased. William Abell, Commonwealth's president since 1958, assumed the same position in the holding company and became chairman after the 1969 acquisitions of National Trust Life Insurance Company and Peoples Life Insurance Company. The following year, Capital purchased First National Life Insurance Company. The operations and sales force of this New Orleans, Louisiana–based organization were later integrated with those of Commonwealth, paving the way for the company's entry into the Louisiana market.

Capital's gradual growth through acquisition created opportunities and provided the necessary resources to expand its product line and improve its competitive standing. It also benefited from such socioeconomic factors as the baby boom of the 1970s, a growing young adult market, and the increasing availability of disposable income. However, the company suffered from weak management and a conservative board of directors that remained fixated on the outmoded method of selling life insurance door-to-door. By the latter half of the decade, Commonwealth instituted a training program to help its agents increase their return on collection calls by converting these customers into buyers of new insurance products.

Several new products were also introduced. One of these policies, the Capitalizer, represented a major departure from the company's traditional philosophy. Until this point, Commonwealth had sold policies with set premiums and had assumed the risk of changing interest and mortality rates and expenses. In contrast, the Capitalizer offered an adjustable premium that would vary according to future profits or losses in the company's investments or changes in its mortality experience. This feature enhanced the company's ability to compete with mutual funds, which had recently become popular.

Thomas C. Simons, who was hired away from another insurance company to become the company's chief executive officer in 1978, set out to make major changes in Commonwealth's marketing strategy. He believed that the company's strength was its ability to sell products to the middle-income bracket of the market. His goal was to find new ways to reach this market before larger insurers did.

In 1981, Capital acquired National Liberty Corporation, a holding company that sold health insurance to middle-class consumers by direct mail, telephone solicitation, and television commercials. In addition to providing Capital with a business that fit its existing operations, National Liberty offered an efficient marketing system with the capability to improve both sales productivity and customer service.

One year later, Capital began selling insurance and other financial products at service centers within Kroger's retail food stores, capitalizing on a growing consumer trend toward one-stop shopping, and setting the stage for similar future strategies.

In 1984, Capital purchased First Deposit Corporation from Parker Pen Corporation. This acquisition gave Capital the capability to market banking services through direct mail and also made it the owner of a small New Hampshire bank and a California-based thrift organization. That same year, Bank of America agreed to allow Capital to sell automobile, homeowners, and life insurance from specific bank branches in return for an office rental fee. However, by 1986, this venture still had not shown a profit and Capital terminated the project. Despite this setback, 1986 ended on a high note with the successful acquisition of Worldwide Underwriters Insurance Company, a direct-response marketer of automobile and homeowners insurance. In 1987, as it strengthened its hold on the moderate-income segment of the marketplace, the company sold its Georgia International Life Insurance Company subsidiary, which focused primarily on higher-income households.

Capital joined with four other insurance companies in 1988 to settle previous complaints lodged by Delaware's insurance commissioner. The companies were accused of collecting higher life insurance premiums from blacks, reflecting differences in life expectancy between the black and white populations. Although the insurers claimed that they had not sold such policies in over 20 years and were unaware that race-based premiums were still being paid, they agreed to increase the death benefits for black beneficiaries who had overpaid on their policies.

Simons died in August 1988 and was succeeded as chairman and chief executive officer of Capital Holding by Irving W. Bailey II. He had been with the company for ten years and had most recently served as president and chief operating officer. Bailey continued his predecessor's strategy of developing niche businesses, which, unlike life insurance, face little price competition. Under Simons, the company had introduced such products as burial policies for people with annual incomes under $15,000, life insurance policies for people making between $15,000 and $25,000, and insurance policies specifically developed for veterans.

Soon after Bailey took over, Capital Holding launched a new "living payout" policy that supplemented other life insurance plans. Capital would pay insured people with terminal illnesses one-half of the total face value of their primary policies while they were still living. Upon their deaths, Capital Holding would recoup this amount from the primary insurance company. In 1989, Capital purchased Southlife Holding Company, a Nashville, Tennessee–based insurer, to increase its market share in the home-service field.

By 1990, Capital Holding consisted of four major operating groups. The agency group markets life and health insurance to the company's home-service customers in the eastern and southeastern United States through three regional subsidiaries: Commonwealth Life Insurance Company, Peoples Security Insurance Company, and Public Savings Insurance Company. The direct response group, consisting of National Liberty Corporation and Worldwide Insurance Group, markets life and health insurance through television and newspaper advertising, direct mail, and telephone sales. Investment services are handled through the company's accumulation and investment group, and the banking unit operates a credit-card-based loan business through First Deposit Corporation and the First Deposit National Bank. The door-to-door method of selling insurance on which the company was built had given way to the use of more sophisticated marketing and sales techniques. Capital Holding Corporation faces the future with a connection to its past that provides the company with the direction it needs to remain competitive in the financial-services industry.

Principal Subsidiaries: ACI Financial Corporation; Capital Assignment Corporation; Capital Broadway Corporation; Capital Enterprise Insurance Company; Capital General Development Corporation; Capital Initiatives Corporation; Capital Landmark Insurance Company; Capital Real Estate Development Corporation; Commonwealth Life Insurance Company; C.U. Members Insurance Services, Incorporated; First Deposit Corporation; First Deposit Life Insurance Company; First Deposit National Bank; First Deposit Savings Bank; Insurance America Sales Agency; Kentucky Bonded Funeral Insurance Company; National Home Life Assurance Company; National Home Life Assurance Company of New York; National Liberty Corporation; National Liberty Life Insurance Company; National Liberty Marketing, Incorporated; National Standard Life Insurance Company; Peoples Security Life Insurance Company; Redding Financial Corporation; The Financial Group, Incorporated; Veterans Life Insurance Company; Worldwide Underwriters Insurance Company.

Further Reading: Gerard, Victor B., *Commonwealth Life Insurance Company: A History of the Development Years,* Louisville, Kentucky, Commonwealth Life Insurance Company, 1984; Drummond, James, "Sharp Marketing," *Forbes,* February 5, 1990.

—Sandy Schusteff

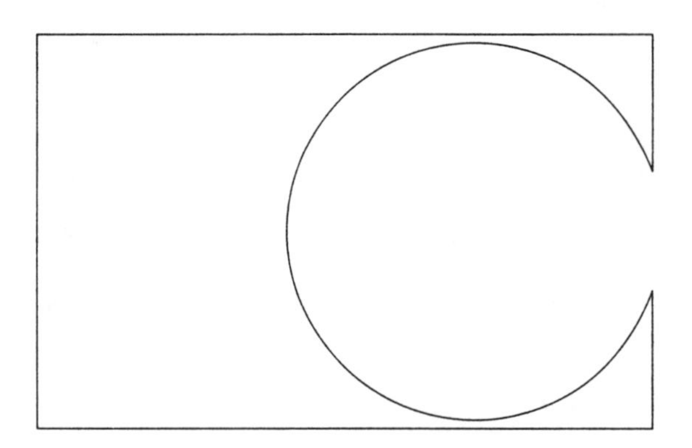

THE CHUBB CORPORATION

15 Mountain View Road
Warren, New Jersey 07061
U.S.A.
(201) 580-2000
Fax: (201) 580-3544

Public Company
Incorporated: 1882 as Chubb & Son
Employees: 9,800
Assets: $11.18 billion
Stock Exchange: New York

The Chubb Corporation operates as a holding company and, through subsidiaries around the world, is engaged in property and casualty insurance. The company's other business ventures include life and health insurance, real estate development, financing, and education. Chubb is able to offer various types of specialized coverage at higher prices than its competition because of its diverse experience and fine reputation. Chubb has continuously reported profit gains while maintaining very high reserves.

Chubb traces its roots to the partnership of Chubb & Son, a New York underwriter of cargo and ship insurance formed by Thomas Chubb and his son, Percy Chubb, in 1882. Soon after its formation, Chubb & Son was one of the 100 founders of the New York Marine Underwriters (NYMU). Chubb first operated as a representative of NYMU and Sea Insurance Company Limited of England. In 1901 NYMU, Chubb's principal property and casualty affiliate, was reorganized as Federal Insurance Company.

During its first 40 years of business, Chubb & Son grew quickly, acting as an agent for several insurers. The company established itself as a respected underwriter of insurance for ships and cargo. During the 1920s the company explored new areas. In 1921 Chubb & Son began to represent U.S. Guarantee Company. Through that company, Chubb began to underwrite fidelity, surety, and casualty insurance. In 1923 Chubb opened its first branch, in Chicago. In March 1929 Chubb and another transportation insurance agent, the Marine Office of America, organized Associated Aviation Underwriters, the largest aviation insurance–underwriting group in the United States. Seven companies represented by Chubb and eight insurers represented by the Marine Office joined to form the association. During the Depression Chubb's growth slowed as the insurance industry suffered. Nevertheless, in April 1930 Chubb & Son bought a 9,000-square-foot plot in Manhattan to house its companies and allow room for expansion. In 1939 Chubb founded Vigilant Insurance Company, a wholly owned fire and marine subsidiary. During World War II the economy recovered and Chubb & Son's business began to grow more quickly.

In December 1941 Chubb gave employees with more than six months of service their first Christmas bonuses. The workers each received half of their bonus in cash, and half in war bonds. Also in December 1941, Chairman Charles A. Seibert, a 55-year veteran of the company, announced his retirement.

Chubb's growth continued apace. The company acquired The Colonial Life Insurance Company of America in 1957, and in 1959 Chubb & Son reincorporated under the laws of New York. In 1967 the company's management formed The Chubb Corporation to act as a holding company. Chubb & Son became a wholly owned subsidiary of The Chubb Corporation, as did Chubb & Son's subsidiaries. The property and casualty companies within the Chubb group of insurance companies are managed by Chubb & Son, which handles domestic property and casualty insurance companies and U.S. branches of foreign insurers.

The primary property and casualty insurance company managed by Chubb & Son remains Federal Insurance Company. The Chubb Corporation saw many changes in the late 1960s. In July 1967 Chubb acquired Pacific Indemnity Corporation of Los Angeles. In November 1967 Pacific Indemnity president and chief executive officer Carl Fisher was elected senior vice president and director of Chubb.

In January 1969 First National City Corporation—now Citicorp—agreed to acquire The Chubb Corporation. In April 1969, however, the two corporations confirmed that the Department of Justice was examining the antitrust implications of the merger. Later that month, the two companies agreed to postpone the merger until the summer of 1969 in order to allow the Department of Justice to complete its study of the transaction. On June 13, 1969, the Department of Justice announced its intention to bring suit to bar the acquisition. Three hours later First National City Corporation canceled the planned merger.

In September 1969 William M. Rees, then president of The Chubb Corporation, was elected chief executive officer, and became responsible for all operations excluding investment. Investment responsibilities and general corporate policy and development remained with Chairman Percy Chubb II.

In 1970 Chubb acquired Bellemead Development Corporation, a Delaware real estate company with land holdings primarily in New Jersey and Florida. This acquisition was Chubb's first major move into the real estate field. Chubb confirmed that its real estate consultants placed a value of more than $25 million on Bellemead's properties, if sold individually on the open market.

In 1971 Chubb acquired United Life & Accident Insurance Company and founded Chubb Custom Market. Chubb Custom Market became involved heavily in the entertainment industry. The subsidiary specializes in insurance for the film industry, and insured *E.T., The Extra-Terrestrial; Tootsie; The Verdict;* and *Missing* in 1983. When Dustin Hoffman developed laryngitis and was unable to perform for three days during the filming of *Tootsie,* Chubb covered the additional expense. In addition to insuring films, Chubb Custom Market provides entertainment coverage for television productions, special entertainment events, and Broadway shows. In 1983 Chubb insured 75% of Broadway productions. Chubb's coverage was popular because of its comprehensive nature, which included theft, injuries, and equipment failure.

On June 9, 1971, American Financial Corporation, a Cincinnati, Ohio–based financial holding company, sold 875,000 shares of Chubb stock to Salomon Brothers in a transaction valued at more than $54 million. American Financial had begun to acquire the stock in 1969, and had planned to attempt a buyout of Chubb. Salomon Brothers resold the shares, which represent a 14% stake in Chubb, to the public later in the day. In 1973 Chubb, through the international division of Chubb & Son, joined First National City Corporation's subsidiary, FNC Comercio, in buying a majority interest in Companhia de Seguros Argos Fluminense, a Brazilian multiple-line insurance company.

The Chubb Corportion formed Chubb Life Insurance Company of America in 1978 to serve as an intermediate holding company for life insurance subsidiaries. In 1981 the company began to consolidate the activities of The Colonial Life Insurance Company of America and United Life & Accident Insurance Company at Chubb Life's headquarters in Concord, New Hampshire. This consolidation was completed in 1984.

In 1983 The Chubb Corporation completed and relocated to a new head office on 185 acres in Warren, New Jersey. In 1984, Chubb focused its efforts on growth in its international division. The company sought to increase international property and casualty insurance business and to expand its worldwide coverage for U.S. multinationals. Chubb—which in 1984 considered itself the country's fourth-largest insurer of U.S.-based multinationals—did not offer universal contracts or preformulated programs; instead the company created policies tailored to meet the needs of its clients. Chubb hoped to maintain 20% annual growth of its international business. Also in 1984, Chubb acquired Volunteer State Life Insurance Company of Chattanooga, Tennessee, and Chubb discontinued its money-losing medical-malpractice insurance policies.

During the summer of 1987 a nine-person delegation from the People's Republic of China spent two days at the company's New Jersey headquarters. The company's relations with China date back to before World War II, when Chubb owned and operated the Cathay Insurance Company. The delegation, consisting of representatives from the People's Insurance Company of China and government officials, studied Chubb's safety and loss control problems. That year, Chubb acquired Sovereign Corporation, a life insurance holding company. Significantly higher catastrophe losses due to the Chicago rainstorms, Edmonton tornados, and a hurricane in Bermuda, lowered profits for 1987.

In May 1988 Chubb, through a New York firm called Good Weather International Incorporated, began advertising rain insurance in ten states. Drought insurance was also offered to midwestern farmers by the Chubb subsidiary, Federal Insurance. Chubb usually approves each policy that its independent agents sell, but in this case Good Weather was given the authority to approve Chubb policies. Because rain insurance is a small part of Chubb's business—Chubb issued $5 million of coverage to approximately 200 farmers in 1987—the company set a total limit of $30 million of coverage.

Response was moderate until early June, when lack of rain threatened farmers with the most serious drought in over 50 years. On June 14 and June 15, 1988, Good Weather received over 6,600 applications seeking $275 million worth of coverage, and applications kept coming after the deadline. While farmers worried about the drought, Good Weather and Chubb worried about the flood of applications. The figures were not totaled until the end of June; in the confusion, agents had signed up at least $350 million of coverage for nearly 9,000 farmers. The drought continued, and on July 15, Chubb notified 7,616 farmers that they had been denied coverage. In a goodwill effort, Chubb offered to return double the original premiums to farmers who had applied on June 14 or 15. The effort was unsuccessful, and in 1991 there remained many lawsuits. Chubb decided to discontinue drought insurance.

In July 1988, Dean R. O'Hare, chairman and chief executive officer of The Chubb Corporation and Federal Insurance Company since May, was elected chairman and chief executive officer of Chubb & Son. In August 1988 Chubb agreed to let American National General Agencies Incorporated (ANGA) take over its entertainment insurance underwriting responsibilities on the East Coast. Headquartered in Los Angeles as a wholesale entertainment insurance broker, ANGA branched into New York to assume the underwriting function for production risks through Chubb Custom Market.

In 1989 Chubb took great strides in reestablishing goodwill. This time, its efforts were successful, and 1989 was a good year for the company overall. Chubb Life Insurance of America joined The Geese Theatre Company in April 1989 in establishing a theater residency program in Concord, New Hampshire. The Geese Company is a nonprofit touring theater company that works exclusively in prisons. Chubb generated more goodwill later that year when it won the Insurance Marketing Communications Association Special Award from Members. The competition recognizes and awards superior marketing communications work in the property and casualty industry.

In late 1989 Chubb reported increases in net income for the first nine months of 1989 compared to the previous year. The company's net income for the nine months ending September 30, 1989, was $313.7 million compared to $275.7 million in 1988. Catastrophe losses in the third and fourth quarter, however, counterbalanced these increases in net income. Hurricane Hugo and the California earthquake had a significant impact on Chubb's 1989 earnings. In 1989 revenues from international operations approached $500 million. Chubb worked to continue increasing its international activities. The company wanted international business to provide 25% of its business by the year 2000.

The drop in the property and casualty industry has affected Chubb less than some of its competitors. The company's focus on specialty products has helped The Chubb Corporation overcome industry trends. Chubb showed great improvement in life and health insurance during 1989, and anticipated continued earnings increased as group health operating conditions improved. In 1991 modest but steady earnings advances were expected, with emphasis on product development and new-agent recruitment.

Principal Subsidiaries: Chubb & Son Inc.; Bellemead Development Corporation; Chubb Life Insurance Company of New Hampshire; Chubb Insurance Company of Canada; Chubb Insurance Company of Europe, S.A. (Belgium).

Further Reading: [no title], Warren, New Jersey, The Chubb Corporation, 1988.

—Leslie C. Halpern

CIGNA CORPORATION

One Liberty Place
Box 7716
Philadelphia, Pennsylvania 19192
U.S.A.
(215) 761-1000

Public Company
Incorporated: 1981
Employees: 47,677
Assets: $57.78 billion
Stock Exchanges: New York Pacific Philadelphia

CIGNA Corporation was formed in 1982, when INA Corporation, with its strong position in property and casualty insurance, and Connecticut General Corporation, with its strength in group employee benefits, combined. The resulting corporation immediately became one of the largest international, publicly owned insurance and financial-services companies based in the United States. CIGNA is a major provider of insurance, health care, employee-benefit products and services, pension and investment management, and related financial services.

CIGNA gained its preeminent position by combining some of the oldest and most important companies in the insurance marketplace. Its oldest subsidiary is Insurance Company of North America (INA), a company rich with tradition. INA was formed by a group of prominent Philadelphians in November 1792, in Pennsylvania's State House, where the Declaration of Independence had been signed just 16 years earlier. Connecticut General Life Insurance Company was incorporated in 1865. That company began to expand from its focus on life insurance and employee benefits almost a century later, when it acquired another company with a long history of its own, Aetna Insurance Company, in 1962. Another major component of CIGNA was put in place in 1984, when the company acquired the American Foreign Insurance Association (AFIA) to expand its international operations.

Insurance Company of North America was organized in Philadelphia, then the financial center of the United States and its busiest port, when the country was just beginning to develop economically. With only 32 corporations and few native manufacturing concerns in the country, all marine insurance was written in London or in the United States by private individuals or partnerships that could afford to underwrite coverage.

In November and December 1792 a group of businessmen—including a carpenter, a cobbler, and a stationer, as well as bankers, lawyers, and merchants—met to set up a general insurance company. These businessmen had their own concerns at heart: they felt that their businesses could not grow unless reliable insurance was made available close to home. Only two small fire insurance companies had been formed in the new nation so far, and Philadelphia businessmen sought greater protection.

Insurance Company of North America wrote several policies on December 19, 1792, its first day in business. John M. Nesbitt, a Philadelphia merchant, was elected president of the company and Ebenezer Hazard, secretary. Hazard, a businessman, scholar, and historian, was responsible for the daily conduct of business, and, remaining in Philadelphia during the yellow fever epidemic of 1793, kept the office open. The Insurance Company of North America was incorporated by the Pennsylvania state legislature in 1794 and authorized to write marine, fire, and life insurance.

The company initially insured only ship hulls and cargoes in local and international commerce. In late 1794, however, INA's directors and officers agreed to insure buildings and their contents against fire, becoming the first U.S. company to offer insurance on personal possessions and on business inventories.

In the early 19th century, INA followed the pioneers west. In 1807 INA set up its first agency, in Lexington, Kentucky, establishing the American agency system. The company appointed independent agents as far as the frontiers of Pennsylvania, Kentucky, Ohio, and Tennessee. Banking on westward expansion, INA invested in toll bridges and toll roads and bought bonds of the just-purchased Louisiana Territory.

INA'S westward expansion helped the company stay afloat when its marine insurance business lost money. Problems began in 1799 when Great Britain began to seize U.S. ships at sea. The maritime embargo of 1808, the War of 1812, and the depression of 1813 all had detrimental effects on the company's marine profits.

After the War of 1812 ended in 1815, the insurance environment became more competitive. As rates fell, INA faced a different kind of threat. John Inskeep, who became INA president in 1806, had the company invest profits instead of paying dividends. This conservative investment and reserve policy, coupled with its expanding fire insurance business, kept the company profitable.

In the mid–19th century, INA played a major role in forming the Philadelphia Board of Marine Underwriters, an organization that standardized premium rates and policy formats, gathered statistics, reported on insurance fraud, and kept up with commercial regulations and maritime law. A committee of the board reported on the seaworthiness of all vessels that entered the Port of Philadelphia. The board helped reduce operating expenses for the companies involved.

Formation of the Philadelphia Board of Marine Underwriters coincided with the high point for marine insurance in the 19th century. Between 1840 and 1861 U.S. foreign-trade tonnage quadrupled. The increase was due partially to the new clipper ships. Clipper ships were well built and had excellent safety records; in short, they were good insurance risks.

By 1859 INA had entered another lucrative area: it insured gold shipments from the California gold fields discovered a decade earlier. Its agent in California, Joshua P. Havens, sent premiums to INA's Philadelphia office in gold dust, which the secretary exchanged for currency.

From 1861 to 1865, when the Civil War disrupted many of INA's traditional markets, the company compensated by placing even more emphasis on the potential in the West. In 1861, as secession spread, the directors stopped accepting business or renewing policies in the South. In 1863 they organized offices in the West into a separate department. From 40 appointed local agents in the territory in 1860, the western-business department grew to 1,300 agents by 1876. In 1875, a decade after the Civil War, a southern department was also added.

Expansion in the West increased business, but also posed a new risk. Rapidly growing cities were not well-built cities, and INA suffered losses in a series of major fires: 700 buildings burned in New York City in 1835; 1,000 buildings were lost in Pittsburgh, Pennsylvania, in 1845; most of Saint Louis, Missouri was lost in 1851; and Portland, Maine, was destroyed almost totally by fire in 1866.

The Great Chicago Fire, which started on October 8, 1871, burned about 17,450 buildings valued at $200 million. Claims for that fire left many insurance companies bankrupt. Eighty-three other companies could settle their claims only in part. INA was one of 51 companies that did pay in full, settling legitimate claims totaling $650,000. Its reliability brought in new business.

INA, however, faced an even heavier loss a year later. The Boston Fire of November 9, 1872 gutted 600 buildings at a cost of $75 million, causing the collapse of 25 more insurance companies. INA faced the heaviest claim total—$988,530—but again paid in full.

On April 18, 1906, a 48-second earthquake shook San Francisco, California. Earthquake damage was slight, but the resulting fires were uncontrollable because water mains had ruptured. INA sent special agent Sheldon Catlin to the city to settle claims. Catlin found that most of the damage to property came from the fires, which had burned out of control for three days, not from the earthquake itself. Since INA was liable for fire damage but not earthquake damage, his determination was not a popular one within INA. Under pressure from other insurance companies, the home office decided to settle all claims at two-thirds value. On Catlin's recommendation, however, INA reversed its own decision, and agreed to pay all claims in full. That amounted to a liability of $3.7 million, plus $1.3 million in claims due from INA's affiliate, Alliance Insurance Company. INA was one of 27 companies to pay claims from the San Francisco Earthquake and Fire in full.

As the company was expanding its fire insurance coverage, it also expanded its marine coverage inland. In 1890 INA established a lake-marine department in Chicago to cover risks during transit on rivers, lakes, and canals. The company originally refused to insure steamboats, an important part of the movement to settle the Mississippi River Valley, because steamboat captains were considered too reckless. At the end of the century George W. Neare & Company, a steamboat operator, persuaded INA President Charles Platt that insurance coverage was necessary to revitalize river transport. The company selected its risks carefully, and eventually prospered in the field.

INA faced losses in its regular marine division in the last decade of the 19th century because such risks were hard to classify. During the mid 1890s Benjamin Rush, a conservative, old-line Philadelphian who came to work at INA as assistant to President Platt in 1894, worked nights and weekends with two young clerks to compile profit-and-loss statements for 198 route and cargo categories over a five-year period. His statistical analysis allowed the company to select risks more carefully. In 1900 INA posted the first profit in its marine line for many years, and the line remained profitable until World War I. Rush's work earned him the title "father of modern marine underwriting."

Expanding industry before World War I meant growth in fire insurance business. John O. Platt, a nephew of Charles Platt and head of INA's fire branch, set up the improved-risk-engineering department to devise ways to make industry safer and lower insurance risks. The department eventually offered three services: property valuation, fire prevention, and rate analysis.

Rush succeeded Eugene Ellison as president in 1916, in time to face claims due to attacks by German U-boats—INA paid $21,740 as its share of the coverage for the *Luisitania*, for example—and fires caused by sabotage in U.S. munitions plants. Nevertheless, World War I did not seriously threaten profits.

Despite a generally conservative outlook, INA often insured unusual risks. Hence, in 1905, the company began to insure automobiles against fire and theft, and added collision coverage in 1907. By the end of World War I, demand for this type of coverage had grown so much that INA organized a casualty affiliate, Indemnity Insurance Company, in 1920. The Great Depression hit Indemnity hard, but in 1932 INA brought in John A. Diemand, who had extensive experience in casualty insurance, to improve the company's performance.

With the approach of World War II, INA faced new problems. Male employees enlisted and the company was not fully staffed. Cities were unable to replace outdated fire-fighting equipment, increasing risks. Auto insurance fell off due to gas rationing, and the lack of new-home construction affected property insurance lines. Ships unused to taking wartime security measures were lost to the Germans.

INA again found new and unusual risks to insure. The company wrote policies covering the accidental death of war correspondents and photographers, expanded its aviation coverage, covered test pilots, and insured 30 scientists working on the Manhattan Project, which developed the atomic bomb. "We were pulling rates out of the air," Edwin H. Marshall, underwriter for these unusual coverages, told William H.A. Carr, in *Perils: Named and Unnamed.*

In the postwar years INA boomed along with the economy. During the 1940s Diemand, by now president of the company, tackled a long-standing issue. INA had organized a casualty affiliate in 1920 because INA itself was forbidden by law to offer a full line of insurance. Diemand's advocacy of multiple-line underwriting authority, earlier promoted by Rush, now became a crusade. "Every company should have the privilege of meeting the requirements of any policyholder at any time as long as there is no law or ruling of an insurance department to prevent it," Diemand said in his address on INA's 150th anniversary. Diemand felt that multiple-line underwriting would provide broader and more convenient coverage for policyholders, who would have access to insurance packages from one agent, and at the same time would enable companies to cut processing and marketing costs.

Diemand's major opposition came from insurance cartels and conservative insurance associations that regulated insurance sales. In 1945 Public Law 15 left regulation of the insurance industry to the states, and slowly states extended the right to sell multiple-line insurance. By 1955 the right had been granted in all states. This victory allowed Diemand to pioneer the comprehensive homeowners policy, offering fire, theft, personal liability, medical payment, and extended coverages.

In 1964 Bradford Smith Jr. succeeded Diemand as chairman of the board and chief executive officer. Smith automated operations, reorganized the company along functional lines, and emphasized participative management, which he defined as taking individual responsibility and cooperating with all company branches.

Changes in the U.S. business environment as well as changes within the company prompted another reorganization in 1968. Insurance Company of North America became the major subsidiary of INA Corporation, which added diversified services through other subsidiaries and extended its regional and international network of offices. As part of its expansion, INA Corporation organized or acquired several life insurance subsidiaries, which remained relatively small compared to its major interests in property and casualty insurance. In the 1970s the company diversified into a related area when it began acquiring hospital management companies and health-maintenance organizations (HMO).

All of these moves reflected INA's desire to become a major financial organization offering a broad range of services. In 1981 the company saw a business combination with Connecticut General Corporation (CG) as a way to achieve that goal. CG offered a major presence in employee benefits and life insurance to complement INA's activities in property and casualty insurance, and a combination was a way to operate more efficiently through economies of scale.

Connecticut General dates back to 1865, when Guy R. Phelps, one of the founders of Connecticut Mutual Company, saw a need for "substandard" insurance, or life insurance for poor risks. Originally the new firm was to be called Connecticut Invalid, but because of concern that the word "invalid" could be read in two ways, it became Connecticut General Life Insurance Company and began to insure healthy lives along with substandard risks. Two years later the company withdrew completely from insuring higher risks, and through conservative management survived a period when many other life insurance companies failed.

Under Secretary, then President Thomas W. Russell, the company prospered from post–Civil War growth in life insurance sales. Within a few years, CG had agents in over 25 states, but increasing competition, rate cutting, and poor public perception of a company that had insured the disabled caused the sales force to shrink as quickly as it had grown. By the 1870s CG concentrated on New England and a few surrounding states.

The company's early policies, handwritten by clerks who had to demonstrate good penmanship to get the job, reflected the society it served. Death from drinking, hanging, or dueling canceled a policy. Travel was also restricted: a policyholder could not travel south of Virginia or Kentucky from June to November because of additional risk of illness due to heat. Late premium payments led to the automatic cancellation of the policy in question, with no grace period. Policies had no cash value, and benefits were paid only in a lump sum 90 days after proof of death, signed by five witnesses, was received.

Under Thomas Russell, CG weathered the depression following the panic of 1873 and a takeover attempt by Continental Life Insurance Company of Hartford, Connecticut. By 1880 the firm was again stable and began to grow.

Russell died in 1901 and was succeeded by Robert W. Huntington, who had joined the company as a clerk 11 years before. CG had only 12 home-office employees and was licensed to do business in four New England states, New York, Pennsylvania, and Ohio. Huntington emphasized good investments, especially in farm mortgages, railroads, and utilities. He also cut operating expenses, and used the savings to enter new areas.

In 1912 CG created an accident department. The next year CG began to offer group insurance when it insured the 100 employees of the *Hartford Courant*. Group insurance developed slowly for CG until 1917, when changes in corporate taxes made it a deductible expense. CG established its group department in 1918, and got its first big contract—covering the 5,400 employees of Gulf Oil—that year. Business picked up again in 1919, when contributory plans were developed. Previously, employers had paid the total cost of coverage.

World War I meant a growing economy and more group insurance coverage, but when an influenza epidemic struck in the autumn of 1918, CG was hit particularly hard because it had a high proportion of very young policyholders. Although claims were high, the epidemic eventually encouraged more life insurance business.

During the 1920s Frazar Bullard Wilde, head of the Accident Division, brought CG into another new area of insurance, aviation insurance. Wilde had served in the field artillery in France during World War I, where the use of airplanes caught his imagination. In 1926, when other insurance companies were not yet convinced of the validity of insuring flight, Wilde began writing policies that covered aircraft passengers. In 1930 the company wrote a group life insurance policy for Western Air Express, which included 46 pilots, and in 1932 CG insured 1,000 employees of United Airlines as well.

When the stock market crashed in 1929, CG's diversified investments kept the company going, but within two years new business had decreased sharply and business cancellations mounted. In addition, the company's heavy investment in farm mortgages meant that—with increasing foreclosures and the inability to lease farms—CG became a farm owner. In most cases, the company retained the former owners as managers and encouraged them to save their pay to buy back the property.

In 1936 Wilde succeeded Huntington as president. Wilde emphasized high-quality products and a good sales force. Ten years later he supported a new approach to marketing life insurance that would have a major impact on the company:

estate planning. Stuart Smith, who had joined the company during the Depression, brought the estate-planning concept to CG. Smith emphasized the sale of life insurance as part of complete estate planning. When he was promoted to the home office in 1946, CG made estate planning its only approach to selling insurance. Smith taught the technique to Connecticut General agents, which enabled them to plan insurance coverage by taking into consideration a client's total assets, family circumstances, and plans for the future. Smith emphasized planning services for CG policyholders.

Another area of emphasis after the war was developing group hospital and surgical benefits to compete with the Blue Cross and Blue Shield plans that had just been developed. Just as CG had supported emerging technology after World War I by insuring airline pilots and passengers, after World War II the company began insuring atomic energy workers, covering employees of the Brookhaven and Argonne laboratories.

CG established a group pension service in 1929 to serve its group insurance policyholders. The Revenue Act of 1942 provided some tax incentives for employers to establish pension programs; and the Social Security Act, passed in 1935, stimulated private savings for pensions to supplement the government program, and thus benefited CG. After 1960 changes in Connecticut state law led to significant growth in CG's pension business.

Also in the postwar years, CG pioneered financing of shopping centers, in addition to financing commercial agricultural enterprises and providing loans on residential and business properties in the cities. Company investment became a major factor in the development of the modern suburban shopping mall.

In 1962 CG purchased Aetna Insurance Company (Aetna), a major firm in fire and casualty insurance, in order to broaden its position in insurance. Aetna brought a history even longer than its new parent's to the acquisition. The company was established in 1819, and two years later it became the first U.S. company to sell insurance in Canada. In 1851 the company began to sell life insurance too, but just two years later this part of its operations was spun off into a separate company, now known as Aetna Life and Casualty Company. Aetna faced the same marine insurance risks as did INA, and was also hit by massive claims due to urban fires in the late nineteenth century. Aetna's directors acted on a policy they voiced frequently after the Chicago Fire in 1871: "Every dollar must be paid," and pay they did. The company paid $3.78 million after the Chicago Fire, $1.6 million a year later in Boston, and almost another $3 million following the San Francisco Earthquake and Fire. Aetna's ability to cover all its losses in full enhanced its reputation as a major fire insurance company.

By the 1960s the acquisition of Aetna, with its sound fiscal management and preeminent position in fire and casualty insurance, was attractive to CG, which aimed to gain market position in property and casualty insurance, where it had virtually no operations at all. The acquisition was part of a trend in the industry toward larger companies that could offer full lines of insurance.

After acquiring Aetna as its property and casualty arm, CG began dramatic expansion of employee benefits programs, such as group health insurance and pensions. CG was most successful in life, health, and pensions, and its property and casualty operations remained small. By 1981 group life and health benefits accounted for 33% of its operating income; individual life, health, and annuities accounted for 28%; and property and casualty business for only 18%—down from almost 35% a decade earlier.

As the trend toward larger multiline insurers continued, in 1981 INA and CG announced that they would bring their complementary interests together by forming CIGNA Corporation. INA was most successful in the property and casualty fields where it had operated the longest, and group insurance had remained a relatively small part of its operations. INA also had a strong international presence, while CG had focused primarily on U.S. markets. By March 31, 1982, all necessary approvals had been secured and CIGNA was formed. Robert D. Kilpatrick of Connecticut General and Ralph Saul of INA became co-CEOs, and the board of directors was drawn equally from both predecessor organizations.

The new company got off to a difficult start because of a declining economy in the early 1980s, but the anticipated economies of scale did materialize, and the company continued to expand. In 1984 CIGNA acquired AFIA, formerly the American Foreign Insurance Association, to strengthen its position abroad. AFIA had been formed in 1918 by a group of insurance executives to offer insurance written by its members overseas. After exploring conditions for insurance sales in Australia, New Zealand, Japan, Hong Kong, India, and Singapore, the board of AFIA established agencies in South America, Asia, and the Far East. AFIA weathered the Depression, but World War II, which engulfed many of the areas where it was most profitable, slowed growth and cut profits. By 1949, however, AFIA was back on its feet and ready to expand along with the booming postwar economy. In 1984 the company had contacts in over 100 countries and offered CIGNA a good way to expand its international market. Merged into CIGNA's own substantial international operations, AFIA "Worldwide" became part of CIGNA International, which was renamed CIGNA WorldWide.

By 1990 CIGNA was operating effectively in an insurance marketplace noteworthy for ever-larger competitors, and it continued the trend when it acquired EQUICOR-Equitable HCA Corporation, a large group insurance and managed-health-care company. The acquisition accelerated the growth of CIGNA's managed medical-care programs.

CIGNA is still subject to the perils of insurance. Fire and natural disasters in 1989 that included Hurricane Hugo and a California earthquake resulted in losses and led CIGNA to raise rates. CIGNA's growth and acquisitions, however, have made the company strong in a broad line of insurance products and financial services, both at home and abroad. This foundation has positioned it to perform well against growing competition.

Principal Subsidiaries: Connecticut General Life Insurance Company; Insurance Company of North America; CIGNA Property and Casualty Insurance Company.

Further Reading: James, Marquis, *Biography of a Business: 1792–1942*, Indianapolis, Indiana, The Bobbs-Merrill Company, 1942; *Connecticut General Life Insurance Company, 1865–1965,* Hartford, Connecticut, Connecticut General Life Insurance Company, 1965; Carr, William H.A., *Perils: Named and Unnamed,* New York, McGraw-Hill, 1967.

—Ginger G. Rodriguez

CNA FINANCIAL CORPORATION

CNA Plaza
333 South Wabash Avenue
Chicago, Illinois 60685
U.S.A.
(312) 822-5000
Fax: (312) 822-6419

Public Company
Incorporated: 1897 as Continental Assurance Company of North America
Employees: 16,700
Assets: $31.86 billion
Stock Exchanges: New York Midwest Pacific

As the unified holding company for a diverse group of insurance entities that date back to the post–Civil War era, CNA Financial Corporation was conceived in 1967 but was not born until 1975. Six decades after its founding as an innovative provider of personal accident and health insurance, Chicago-based CNA was among several large insurers that formed holding companies in the late 1960s to overcome state insurance regulations against diversification. CNA's foray into non-insurance ventures proved disastrous, however, and the firm was close to insolvency in 1974 when Loews Corporation acquired control late that year. The New York–based conglomerate quickly installed new management and launched a sweeping reorganization that restored CNA's financial base and set the stage for solid growth. CNA provides underwriting, marketing, and servicing for its various companies, chief among which are the Continental Casualty Company and Continental Assurance Company. It offers broad coverages, including life insurance, in its many forms; property and casualty; health, hospital, and disability; general and specific liability; and workers' compensation. CNA in 1990 was one of the largest and strongest insurance companies in the United States.

The origins of CNA Financial trace back to the late 1800s, even before the incorporation in 1897 of what is now known as Continental Casualty Company, CNA's principal property and casualty insurance subsidiary. After the Civil War, a hospital benefit organization called the National Benefit Company was formed to provide health insurance for workers involved in construction of the Northern Pacific Railroad. Cyrus W. Field, a prominent financier who built the first transatlantic telegraph cable in 1866, was the principal investor.

In the early 1890s, National Benefit merged with its biggest competitor, the Northwest Benefit Association based in Duluth, Minnesota, and as the only provider of health insurance at the time, the newly merged company grew rapidly until the Illinois Department of Insurance ruled that it needed nearly $100,000 in additional capital. New investors were found, and it was reorganized in Milwaukee, Wisconsin, as the National Benefit and Casualty Company. With the refinancing, a large group of agent representatives in the field, and franchises to do business with nearly every railroad, the future looked bright. The firm, however, ran short of capital again and was put out of business by the Wisconsin superintendent of insurance.

Two years after that failure, a new insurance company was organized by some of National Benefit's investors. This was the founding, on November 29, 1897, of the firm that is the "C" in CNA: Continental Assurance Company of North America. Incorporated in Hammond, Indiana, but headquartered in Chicago, the new firm was licensed to operate in Illinois, Indiana, Michigan, and Ohio, with $100,000 in initial capital and a surplus of $60,000. The first president was C.B. Hubbard, and its general manager was B.A. Scott, who had been an executive with National Benefit.

Continental Assurance got off to a fast start by offering the same popular accident and health coverage, called disability insurance today, that had propelled National Benefit's growth, attracting many of the agents and franchises of the old company. By February 1, 1898, agencies had been set up in all four states, and gross assets had grown to $228,000, leaving surplus and capital of $205,733 after insurance reserves. At the end of 1898, assets had reached $294,527 and capital and surplus stood at $252,618.

In 1900 Gerald Bunker was elected president and the firm changed its name to Continental Casualty Company. By the end of the year, it merged with three other insurers: Metropolitan Accident Company of Chicago, the Northwestern Benevolent Society of Duluth, and the Railway Officials and Employees Accident Association of Indianapolis, Indiana. During the next year the company survived the stock market panic which was brought on by an attempt to corner the market in Northern Pacific Railroad shares. The fledgling firm successfully pursued expansion during the two-year depression that followed.

In 1902 Continental introduced the first type of accident and health policy with a monthly premium, affordable for those who could not pay quarterly or annual premiums. By 1904 the firm was doing business in 41 states and territories, and in one month nearly 15,000 policies were issued. Within a year, Continental had branch offices in nine states and territories, from New York City to Honolulu, Hawaii.

Aside from a boost to its railroad-oriented business, the merger with the Railway Officials and Employees Accident Association brought a key manager into Continental, a London-born insurance executive named Herbert George Barlow Alexander. He had been a successful New York agent for the Indianapolis-based firm and was its agency superintendent at the time of the merger. H.G.B. Alexander, as he was known, joined Continental as a vice president, soon became general manager, and was elected president in 1906, a position he held until his death in 1928.

In 1911 Continental Casualty ventured into life insurance with the organization of Continental Assurance Company. Although management of the two firms was the same, a separate, wholly owned subsidiary was required because Continental Casualty could not sell life insurance under its charter. The new firm was licensed in 11 states and the District of Columbia, with $100,000 in capital and surplus of $60,000.

Despite four business recessions between 1903 and 1912, Continental was growing rapidly, and by 1914 it had moved three times to satisfy its need for more office space. In 1915, as the prewar economy was recovering, Continental ventured into miscellaneous casualty lines, starting with workers' compensation. In the next few years, Continental sold coverage for liability, burglary, plate glass, and steam boilers, among other risks.

In 1917 Continental Casualty participated in what was the largest group insurance contract at the time. With Equitable Life providing the life insurance, Continental wrote an accident and health policy covering 35,000 employees of the Union Pacific Railroad and its affiliates. The premium for Continental's share of the business alone was $800,000 a year. The policy, however, was in danger of cancellation after the outbreak of war, with the federal government's takeover of the railroads. Unable to continue the premiums, the Union Pacific issued a termination notice effective December 31, 1918. Officials of Continental and Equitable fought hard to convince William G. McAdoo, U.S. secretary of the treasury and director general of the railroads, that cancellation would cause an uproar among Union Pacific workers. Although he was concerned about charges of favoritism, as the Union Pacific was the only railroad that provided group insurance for its employees, McAdoo agreed on December 16, 1918, to renew the contract and to assume its obligations. This action is thought to be the U.S. government's first involvement with group insurance. In 1990 CNA claimed to be the second-largest provider of federal health insurance programs.

By 1919 the combined assets of Continental Casualty and Continental Assurance had reached $5.8 million, with capital and surplus of nearly $1.4 million. By 1928, however, the year of H.G.B. Alexander's death, assets had soared to nearly $33.4 million, while capital and surplus stood at almost $10.9 million, making "the Continental Companies in point of financial security by far the strongest in the entire West," according to the firm.

During the 1920s, the Continental Companies introduced several new products and marketing strategies that contributed to their growth. In 1921 Continental Assurance established the Bank Plan, which in cooperation with local banks allowed customers to obtain a combination of savings and life insurance, by encouraging them to save a certain amount each month. Within ten years, the Bank Plan was credited with putting $35 million of life insurance on Continental's books. Following on the success of its Bank Plan, Continental Assurance introduced in 1926 a salary-investment plan, which was a payroll-deduction program for obtaining insurance through one's employer.

Continental Casualty wrote a group insurance contract for the Cleveland Teachers Association in 1923, which CNA claims to be the first association group policy written by any insurer. At about the same time, the casualty company also established surety facilities, providing bonds required in business activities such as construction and court proceedings. By 1923 Continental was operating in every U.S. state and territory of the United States, as well as every province of Canada.

After the death of H.G.B. Alexander, who brought the firm from a small but innovative provider of accident and health coverage to a multi-line property, casualty, and life insurance company during his tenure as president, Continental's structure changed less dramatically, but the firm posted substantial growth while pursuing a number of insurance-industry innovations. Continental, for instance, was the first to offer polio insurance on a national basis, as well as group dental insurance and health insurance for senior citizens.

The Continental Companies more than doubled in size under the leadership of Alexander's successor, Herman A. Behrens, an experienced insurance executive who started with Continental as a vice president in 1912 and became general manager in 1923. He served as president of Continental Assurance from 1928 until his death in 1945, and served as president of Continental Casualty until 1937, when he became chairman. Assets of Continental Casualty increased from nearly $20.4 million in 1927 to more than $53.3 million in 1943, while the amount of premiums increased from $14.6 million to $31.7 million. By 1928 the Continental Companies had more than 800 employees in Chicago, and the firm paid more than 150,000 claims that year.

In 1929 the firm offered every kind of life and casualty insurance except marine and fire, which was available through an affiliation with the National Fire Insurance Company of Hartford, Connecticut, whose president, F. D. Layton, was a director of Continental Assurance. During the 1930s this relationship grew as Continental Casualty and National Fire teamed up to provide coverage for the growing number of automobile owners. At that time, insurance laws did not permit multiple-peril policies, but they did allow companies such as Continental and National Fire to combine on a joint contract. National Fire's policy covered physical damage to a customer's automobile while Continental provided liability coverage, allowing "one-policy convenience" for agents and insureds alike.

In 1938 Continental Casualty created a new subsidiary, Transportation Insurance Company, to provide personal-property and inland marine insurance. Accident and health carriers were not allowed to provide that kind of coverage, but it was legal to set up a subsidiary to do so. Continental also started offering hospitalization insurance that year, with a range of benefits costing from 2¢ to 15¢ per day.

In 1941 Continental established a division to provide accident, health, and hospitalization insurance for people in high-risk occupations and older age groups, and it started offering hospital and surgical benefits on a group basis at wholesale rates in 1944. In the same year, Continental became the first insurer to write all-risks aviation insurance on a worldwide basis. The firm's personal accident policies were selected by the U.S. government to insure aviators during and after World War II.

Leadership passed in 1945 to Roy Tuchbreiter, who became president of the Continental Companies after the death of Behrens, the firm's chairman since 1937. Martin P. Cornelius, the son of Continental's first cashier and a lifelong Continental executive, had served as president of Continental Casualty from 1937 until he was named general counsel in 1944. By 1952 Continental had leaped to $2 billion worth of life insurance in force, up from $420 million in 1942, according to *Business Week* of October 11, 1952, which cited Continental's growth as "only an exaggerated example of what has taken place in life insurance as a whole during the past generation."

After ten years of study, Continental Casualty established a special-risks division in 1953, and within a few years the firm's willingness to insure test pilots, participants in the Indianapolis 500, and other persons requiring unusual coverages earned it the nickname "Lloyd's of Chicago," according to a *Newsweek* article of October 20, 1958. Patterned after the well-known London insurance exchange, the new unit was bringing in 7% of the casualty company's $240 million in premiums by 1957.

In 1956 Continental acquired 67% of National Fire in an exchange of stock, forming what was then known as the Continental-National Group. In 1956 the group's combined net premiums of $414.9 million made it one of the three largest insurers in the United States offering insurance for casualty, life, and fire and allied lines, according to Continental's annual report of 1956. Despite the diversification, accident and health coverage still accounted for more than half of the premiums and most of the profits at Continental Casualty. In 1956 also, Tuchbreiter became chairman, a title he held until 1964.

With all its growth, diversifications, and acquisitions, Continental Casualty was still relying on its original business of accident and health insurance for more than 54% of its net premiums in 1956, with automobile coverage a distant second at 19%. In life insurance, Continental pioneered the concept of a quantity discount that year, in which the premiums decreased with increasing amounts of insurance.

By the early 1960s Continental Assurance had caught the attention of investors as one of the fastest-growing publicly owned stock life companies, as opposed to mutual life insurers, which are owned by their policyholders. Continental was the sixth-largest stock life company by then. It had by far the highest price-earnings ratio, selling at $192 or 51.8 times earnings per share.

Continental's last major insurance-company acquisition, the one that put the "A" in CNA, took place in 1963 when American Casualty Company of Reading, Pennsylvania, was acquired in a $40 million stock transaction. That put 529,532 shares of Continental Casualty stock into the hands of Accident and Casualty Insurance Company of Winterthur, Switzerland, a holding that became significant when CNA became embroiled in a takeover battle more than a decade later.

The firm, then known as the Continental National American Group (CNA Group), also acquired American's subsidiaries, Valley Forge Insurance Company and Valley Forge Life Insurance Company, in the deal. American Casualty, originally founded in 1884 as the American Protective Mutual Insurance Company Against Burglary of Reading, Pennsylvania, was the first U.S. company to offer burglary insurance. In 1902 it reorganized as a publicly owned casualty and surety company and was renamed American Casualty. An affiliate formed in 1944 to write fire and property coverage, American Aviation and General Insurance Company, later became Valley Forge Insurance. In the late 1940s both American and its subsidiary expanded into property, casualty, and surety coverage when laws restricting the writing of multiple lines of insurance were lifted. Between 1945 and 1955 the firm's annual premiums increased from $11 million to $74 million, and in 1956 it formed the Valley Forge Life subsidiary. By 1963 American's premium volume had reached $165 million, making the insurance company group the third-largest fire and casualty stock company in the United States, in terms of combined premium volume. It totalled $546.8 million.

In 1964 Continental Assurance's assets reached $1 billion. In 1965 Howard C. Reeder became the CNA Group's chairman. In the mid-1960s the CNA Group was not immune to the tough times that hit the insurance industry, caused by "skyrocketing inflation, which causes premium increases to lag behind cost increases; astronomical settlements awarded by juries; spiraling medical costs; more heavily concentrated business risks; and laws in many states prohibiting insurers from revising rates quickly and effectively," according to an article by Jacque W. Sammet, president of Continental Casualty, in the February 1972 issue of *Nation's Business.* Between 1955 and 1970 stock liability companies suffered $1.5 billion in underwriting losses, he noted, and the 14 largest firms alone suffered $609 million in losses during the 1960s.

In 1963 Continental Casualty's underwriting losses stood at $14.6 million, and the red ink would continue to flow for the rest of the decade. The losses were more than offset by investment income, but CNA executives were still alarmed. In 1965 Continental Casualty's top echelon held a strategy session at which it pored over a huge underwriting loss of $34 million, according to Sammet, and the idea of scrapping the casualty business was discussed and rejected. The plan adopted was: more emphasis on commercial accounts and a range of cost-cutting moves. Within three years, CNA was at least breaking even on insurance underwriting.

In 1966 the CNA Group briefly flirted with a merger with the Continental Insurance Companies of New York, called Continental Corporation today. Despite the similarity in names, the insurers have always been totally unrelated. The merger of the two firms, each with about $2 billion in assets, would have made sense. Besides consolidating their overhead, the New York insurer was strong in fire and casualty business, weak in accident and health, and had no life insurance operation—the opposite of the Chicago Continental. Three weeks after acknowledging that merger "studies" were underway, the idea was dropped abruptly.

Reeder soon steered the company in another direction, converting the CNA Group into a holding company called CNA Financial Corporation, on December 31, 1967. At the time, many large insurance companies were doing the same thing to get around state regulations against investing in non-insurance ventures. Reeder then took CNA on an acquisition binge. By the end of 1969 he had acquired one of the country's best-known mutual funds as well as two personal-finance operations, a major West Coast homebuilding company, a nuclear-core leasing company, insurance companies in Canada and California, and a 29% stake in a nursing-home operator. CNA also established new subsidiaries in real estate development, hotel development, and investment services.

The move that drew the most attention on Wall Street was the payment of about $20 million in stock for New York's Tsai Management & Research Corporation, a mutual fund founded by Gerald Tsai Jr., one of the hottest stock pickers of the mid-1960s, who became CNA's executive vice president in charge of acquisitions and CNA's huge investment portfolio. Tsai Management ran five mutual funds, including the Manhattan Fund introduced at the bull market's peak in 1966. The Manhattan Fund reached a value of about $500 million in 1968 but slid to $380.9 by the end of its first year under CNA's ownership. CNA widely was considered to have overpaid for the mutual fund operation, but Reeder wanted to enhance CNA's image.

At first, CNA's diversification strategy caught the fancy of investors. The stock doubled between 1968 and 1969, the year it started trading on the New York Stock Exchange. The company's profitability, however, was eroding. Several of the new acquisitions were losing money, and insurance underwriting results were still a problem, although income from the investment of premiums made up for that. Kane Financial Corporation, one of the consumer-credit subsidiaries, lost $16.5 million in 1970 and 1971. CNA Nuclear Leasing was barely profitable, but it tied up $200 million in credit. The Manhattan Fund, the country's worst-performing mutual fund in 1970, lost $1.5 million, and CNA Realty had heavy losses from, among other things, developing hotels in the overbuilt Honolulu, Hawaii, market.

Breaking precedent, a divided board of directors reached outside of the company for new leadership when Reeder reached mandatory retirement age in 1971. With the six inside directors abstaining from the vote, CNA's seven outside directors picked Elmer L. "Nick" Nicholson, president of Fidelity Mutual Insurance Company in Philadelphia, Pennsylvania, as the new chairman. Nicholson moved quickly to dismantle Kane Financial and CNA Realty. He tried to sell CNA Nuclear Leasing but did not succeed until 1974. He also reorganized the holding company into four groups: insurance, asset management, real estate, and financial services. He started a long-range strategic planning effort and established new management-performance incentives.

The losses at non-insurance subsidiaries were trimmed to $1.1 million in 1972 from $6.5 million in the prior year, but CNA's worst problems were only beginning at Continental Casualty and Larwin Group, a West Coast homebuilding firm that CNA had acquired for $200 million in stock in 1969. Larwin was growing fast because housing was on an upswing, and between 1970 and 1972 the firm went into nine new markets, including New York, Chicago, and Washington, D.C. At the same time, Larwin ventured beyond its expertise in single family homes and got involved in apartment buildings and recreational properties. In 1973 the housing market turned sour. Eventually, Larwin was written off at a loss of more than $124 million.

Meanwhile, profits were tumbling at Continental Casualty, which was forced by unexpected underwriting losses to put $17 million into reserves in the third quarter, producing the first quarterly net loss in the company's history. CNA assured Wall Street that there would be no more earnings surprises, but the company then was forced to put another $15 million into reserves in the fourth quarter, plus yet another $29.7 million in early 1974. At the holding company level, pretax operating income went from $127 million in 1972 to $24.9 million in 1973, and then to a loss of $188.2 million in 1974.

In October 1973 CNA again tried to merge its way out of its problems by agreeing to be acquired by Gulf Oil Corporation in a proposed $850 million stock-and-debt deal. For Gulf, the non-energy diversification would have reduced its dependence on crude oil profits endangered by tension in the Middle East. CNA needed a partner with deep pockets: its surplus, the financial "cushion" left after deducting legally required insurance reserves from assets, was eroded to $482.4 million and would plummet to $125.8 million in the following year. Less than a month after the deal was announced, however, Gulf called it off. No reason was given. The aborted deal left CNA vulnerable to a takeover. Its stock had dropped from about $20 in early 1973 to less than $8 a year later.

In March Loews Corporation, a New York conglomerate headed by Laurence A. Tisch, announced that it owned more than 5% of CNA's stock, and in May it sought approval from Illinois insurance authorities to seek control. Accident and Casualty Company of Switzerland, which had a 7% stake in CNA stemming from the sale of its American Casualty holdings to CNA, was also interested in a takeover.

CNA fought bitterly for the next five months, but in October the board accepted Loews's offer to buy 20 million common shares at $6 each, which would give it 56% of the stock. That same day, the company revealed that losses would total $135 million in the third quarter, including another $40 million required to increase the insurance reserves. CNA disclosed it still had need for $122 million in additional capital on top of its existing reserves of $736 million. With $85 million in stock market losses in the third quarter alone, surplus had dropped to $100 million from $277 million at the beginning of the year, and Continental Casualty was "uncomfortably close to insolvency," according to a November 9, 1974, article in *Business Week*. As a result, Loews withdrew its CNA bid while it studied the insurer's financial disclosures. Within a few days, Loews cut its offer to $5 a share, which the board immediately accepted, noting that Loews planned to inject new capital into the company.

By December, Nicholson resigned and Tisch was named chairman. Loews had acquired 83% of a company with $4.5 billion in assets for about $206 million. When the new team from Loews moved in, what it found "was a bloated management mess," said a November 1, 1976, article in *Business Week*. CNA's two-year-old headquarters building in Chicago had the top three floors reserved for lavish executive offices. Belt-tightening was the first move for Loews, a $2.7 billion conglomerate of theater, tobacco, and hotel interests whose own headquarters staff then numbered less than 20 people. The three levels of executive suites were closed down, and about 1,400 people were dismissed. Within less than a year, only 5 of CNA's original headquarters staff of 400 would remain.

Loews then hired a seasoned insurance-industry executive to head the operation. Edward J. Noha, former executive vice president at Allstate Insurance, took over as chairman of the insurance operations in February 1975. First he obtained a $50 million cash infusion from Loews to shore up CNA's surplus position, then he launched a massive reorganization. By June 1975, all of the insurance operations were combined under six departments reporting directly to Noha, with two of the most important—marketing and administrative services—filled by former Allstate executives. The objective was to improve sales by getting agents to sell all of CNA's insurance products at the same time. In addition, Noha's new team reviewed CNA's insurance lines and eliminated the unprofitable ones.

Noha also reversed the strategy of relying on investment income to cover underwriting losses. Noha made clear that CNA was in the insurance business, and that underwriting income produced profit. To do so meant raising rates, which is what he did. Within the first half of 1975, the Continental Casualty unit posted pretax profits of $7 million, compared to a $23 million loss in the first six months of the prior year.

Laurence Tisch and his staff took over the non-insurance operations and moved quickly to cut costs. Tisch sold 55 nursing homes CNA owned and cut the staff of its home-building subsidiary to 96 from 600 people. By the end of the first year under new management, CNA as a whole posted a $107 million profit versus a $207 million loss in 1974. By 1983, when it sold General Finance Corporation for $193 million, CNA had divested, discontinued, or written off nearly all of its non-insurance operations.

CNA continued to improve its financial stability during the 1980s, a period when the insurance industry generally was racked by underwriting losses due to severe rate competition, and poor results on investments. In 1984, the sixth year of a decline in insurance rates, the property and casualty industry experienced an underwriting loss of about $21 billion, producing the industry's first net loss since 1906. CNA, however, did not weaken its surplus by extensive price-cutting, as many insurers did. Thus, CNA had the financial capacity to increase its volume once the soft market had turned around. As a result, in 1989 CNA was the eighth-largest insurer in the United States, as measured by premium income. In 1975 it had been 17th largest.

Under Noha CNA also moved to strengthen its business relationships with the independent agents who sell its products. Independent agents, who represent several insurers, had steadily lost market share to direct-writing agents, who sell for one company only. CNA introduced the High Performance Agency program, that permitted its agents to retain independence while enjoying many of the benefits of company personnel. Participants in this program account for one-quarter of CNA's casualty sales force while generating more than half of CNA's property and casualty premium. At year end 1989, surplus had reached $3.1 billion on the casualty side and $786.4 million for life insurance, up from a consolidated surplus of $125.8 million in 1974. Assets stood at $31.9 billion as of September 1990, up from $4.8 billion in 1974.

Principal Subsidiaries: Continental Casualty Company; Continental Assurance Company; National Fire Insurance Company of Hartford; American Casualty Company of Reading, Pa.; Valley Forge Life Insurance Company; Columbia Casualty Company; Transcontinental Insurance Company; Transportation Insurance Company; CNA Management Company Ltd. (U.K.)

Further Reading: "The Second Fifty," Chicago, The Continental Companies, 1947; "How Loews' Lean Management Fattened the Profits at CNA," *Business Week,* November 1, 1976.

—Paul R. Merrion

COMMERCIAL UNION PLC

St. Helen's
1 Undershaft
London EC3P 3DQ
United Kingdom
(071) 283-7500
Fax: (071) 283-7500

Public Company
Incorporated: 1861 as Commercial Union Fire Insurance Company Ltd.
Employees: 20,900
Assets: £15.75 billion (US$25.42 billion)
Stock Exchanges: London Paris

Commercial Union (CU) has been one of the leading names in insurance for more than one hundred years. In terms of premium income it is among the top three British composite—life and non-life—insurance companies. Its subsidiaries provide all types of insurance—fire, motor, accident, marine, aviation, and life, and from its earliest days CU has operated on an international scale. In 1989, just under 40% of its non-life business came from the United Kingdom, a similar amount from North America, and the rest from other countries around the world. Its life business is concentrated mainly in the United Kingdom and the Netherlands.

The company owes its origin to the Great Tooley Street Fire of London in 1861. This was the worst fire in London since 1666. It raged for two days through the warehouses that crowded the south bank of the Thames. The destruction was so great that the affected insurance companies reacted by more than doubling their rates for warehouses. Some of the leading merchants refused to pay the new rates and called a protest meeting. The merchants resolved that if the existing insurers would not moderate their rates, they would form a new insurance company that would fix its rates on a more precise evaluation of the risks. Since the other insurers would not negotiate, a prospectus was issued and capital raised, and within three months of the fire the Commercial Union Fire Insurance Company was born.

The other companies must have regretted their panic reaction to the 1861 Fire, because the Commercial Union made rapid headway at their expense. Its shareholders included some of London's most enterprising businessmen. The company's first chairman was Henry Peek, later a member of Parliament but at this time the young head of a firm of tea and coffee wholesalers. Another of the original directors was Jeremiah Colman, who was building a large export trade in Colman's mustard. These commercial shareholders placed their fire insurance with the new company, and with its more equitable rates it soon attracted a large volume of business. Within two years the older insurance companies were forced to adopt the principle of classification of risks that CU had pioneered.

Thereafter, CU did not compete with the other companies on rates, but it continued to expand rapidly. The 1860s were a boom period for business in the United Kingdom, and CU's directors applied the same energy to building up their new company as to their own businesses. They recruited able managers from other companies, opened branches in major provincial cities, and appointed agents throughout the country, all within a very few years. At the same time CU moved into life and marine insurance. Its first life policies were issued in 1862, and its first marine underwriter was appointed in 1863. In the company's early days, profits from life and marine business helped keep it going when fire claims were high.

It was the fire business, however, which offered the greatest opportunities for growth at this time. Britain's cities and industries were growing fast, with large increases in the amount of property to be insured each year. CU was one of many new companies to respond to the growth in demand. Not content with a buoyant home market, the more enterprising British companies saw that the same opportunities existed abroad and set about exploiting them.

The directors of CU were particularly alert to overseas opportunities, because they already had good trading connections abroad through their import and export businesses. In their first year they appointed an agent in Hamburg, and by the end of the 1860s had agencies in many of the foreign ports used by British merchants.

The United States was an early target. CU began by appointing agents in San Francisco and New York, and was doing business in Chicago and Boston in 1871–1872 when both cities suffered disastrous fires. CU, unlike some local companies, met the resulting claims in full, and gained the reputation as a company that could be relied upon. By the 1880s its U.S. business was nationwide and was providing more than one-third of the company's fire premium income.

In the same period CU was expanding rapidly in Europe, Canada, and Australia. In the 1890s India and Southeast Asia also became important, helped by Britain's imperial presence. By the end of the century, CU was drawing three-quarters of its premium income from abroad, and in total worldwide fire income ranked second only to the British company, Royal Insurance. In 40 years it had overtaken all but one of its immediate competitors, in a market which itself had been growing at an unprecedented rate.

Up to this point CU's growth had been almost entirely self-generated, and each department—fire, life, and marine—had worked largely on its own, although under the supervision of committees of directors. In the next phase of the company's history, between 1900 and 1914, it began to pursue growth through acquisition, and to act in a more cooordinated way.

CU had taken over several small companies in the 1890s to improve its geographical representation both at home and abroad, but its first strategic takeover was that of the

Palatine Insurance Company of Manchester in 1900. Palatine not only had a useful fire business but had also achieved success in the relatively new field of accident insurance. By buying this company, CU gained a foothold in another fast-growing area of insurance, and became the first British company to handle all four classes of insurance—fire, life, marine, and accident.

Shortly after the takeover of Palatine, CU took another important step by appointing its first general manager, Evan Roger Owen, a Welshman who had headed CU's fire department with great success since 1885. By 1900 his reputation was such that the Phoenix Fire Office offered him its top job, and the CU board had to decide whether to lose him to a rival or promote him. It chose the latter course. Owen was general manager from 1900 to 1920, and played a leading part in enlarging and reshaping the company in those years.

During this period, the whole insurance industry was concentrated into fewer and larger composite companies, with CU one of the leaders of this trend. Within a few years it acquired half a dozen major companies. In the United Kingdom, these included the largest of the specialist accident companies, Ocean; another composite, Union Assurance; and the oldest of all the British companies, the Hand in Hand. Abroad, it purchased two U.S. companies, the American of Philadelphia, Pennsylvania, and the California Insurance Company. Two of these acquisitions were a result of the 1906 San Francisco fire; CU was strong enough to withstand severe losses but other companies were not, and both Union Assurance and the American of Philadelphia were rescued by CU.

By these acquisitions and its own vigorous expansion, CU's business grew rapidly throughout the world. By 1914 it was the largest of the British composite companies, with a premium income of £7.5 million—almost four times what it had been in 1901. CU's business continued to grow throughout World War I, despite disruption in Europe and the Atlantic, but it lost its number-one position in the British insurance industry in 1919, when two of its major rivals, Royal, and Liverpool & London & Globe, merged.

After the hectic growth of the previous two decades, the next two were relatively uneventful. Now that CU was one of the giants of the industry it was more dependent on industry trends, and economic conditions were becoming less favorable. In 1921 the postwar depression caused the first drop in CU's income since 1908. Later in the 1920s there was a recovery, but in 1929 the Great Depression brought a more lasting setback. Nevertheless, CU continued to grow as the market for insurance was steadily widening. In particular, the growth of motoring between the wars created a huge new market for accident insurers, and CU was well placed to benefit from this demand both in the United Kingdom and in the United States.

CU continued to make acquisitions in the 1920s. It took over another small composite, British General, in 1926. In the tougher conditions of the 1930s, the emphasis switched from expansion to cost-cutting. As was usual in those days, most of the companies acquired by CU continued to do business under their old names and through their own sales organizations, although under central control. Consequently, there was much scope for economies. Full integration was still a long way off, but in the 1930s a start was made on combining administrative systems. When World War II began, this process was accelerated in the United Kingdom by shortages of staff and space.

World War II and its long aftermath of austerity in Britain halted CU's expansion in Europe for most of a decade. It took time to rebuild business connections in Europe. It was only in the 1950s that living standards in Europe began to rise again, to create more demand for insurance. The use of cars in the United Kingdom, for example, was severely limited by gas rationing until 1950, but increased rapidly after that.

CU was fortunate at this time that so much of its business lay outside Europe, in places where expansion could continue uninterrupted. In the 1950s, however, just as business in the United Kingdom was reviving, conditions in the United States became more difficult. Fiercer competition was driving rates down at a time when claims were rising and government regulations were imposing new burdens on insurers. As a result, all companies were finding it more difficult to make profits in this market. This situation brought about the next great change in CU's history.

This development was the takeover of North British and Mercantile Insurance Company, a company with assets totalling £127 million compared with CU's £192 million, and with a still larger proportion of its business in the United States. In 1957 this company had a very bad year in the United States and, after efforts to restore the situation on its own, decided that it could only improve matters as part of a larger group. It therefore entered into a friendly merger with CU in 1959.

North British and Mercantile was the product of an old merger. The North British Insurance Company was founded in Edinburgh in 1809. It gradually extended its business from Scotland to northern England, and from fire to life, before merging with Mercantile Fire Insurance of London in 1862. Mercantile had been founded only the year before, like CU because of the increase in fire rates. Why it chose to merge with another company so early in its life is not clear, but whatever the reasons the combination of London and Scottish enterprise proved a fruitful one. The new company built up a large overseas business and by 1901 was the fourth-largest British fire insurer. It then became a composite, and was still one of the leading companies in 1959.

The addition of so large a company to the CU group, and the urgent need to pool its U.S. business and cut costs, made drastic reorganization necessary. CU had recently appointed a new general manager, Sir Francis Sandilands, and during the 1960s he carried through the most fundamental changes in the company's structure since Owen's time.

The process of integrating CU's older subsidiaries was still far from complete, but was hurried to a conclusion and combined with the absorption of North British. The group's U.K. staff was reduced from 11,500 at the time of the merger to 8,000, largely by early retirement and natural wastage, seven years later, and proportionate savings were made in the United States and other territories. By the end of the decade, CU had a single management structure. Its new unity was symbolized by an impressive new head office—a starkly modern tower block, clad in blue tinted glass, close to Lloyds of London and the Bank of England.

CU's takeover of North British in 1959 was the largest insurance merger in the United Kingdom in more than 30 years, and was followed by a series of mergers among the other leading companies. Size had become a critical factor in the U.S. market, and universally mergers were seen as the way to reduce costs and achieve a more balanced spread of risks. CU had already begun to profit from this strategy and in 1968 it determined to do so again.

Its new partner was Northern and Employers Assurance, which ranked fourth among the U.K. composites. The company had existed in this form for only eight years, having been created by a 1960 merger similar to CU's. Formerly, Northern had been a Scottish-based composite, with a broad mix of businesses, mainly in the U.K. and Commonwealth countries. It had joined forces with Employers' Liability Assurance (Employers'), the company which pioneered employers' liability insurance in the United Kingdom in the 1880s. Employers' had then broadened out into other fields and developed a large business in the United States, which by 1960 was causing problems. Together, Northern and Employers had a substantial life business, which complemented CU's comparative weakness in this area.

This important acquisition, its second in ten years, restored CU for a time to the position of top U.K. composite. Northern and Employers was quickly integrated into the group, and again there were large savings of manpower. The U.K. staff, after rising to 11,800 in 1968, dropped to 8,400 in 1972, while premium income continued to grow. As a result, profits rose rapidly in the early 1970s. In 1975, however, the company suffered its first loss for many years, mainly due to underwriting losses in the United States. Conditions there were proving difficult for all insurers, partly because of increasing state control of premium rates, but CU's results were exceptionally bad. Profitability was restored in the following few years by reducing the company's less successful business in the United States.

Meanwhile, the United Kingdom had entered the European Economic Community, and CU saw that it must strengthen its position in that market. To this end, it made two important acquisitions in the early 1970s: a Belgian company, Les Provinces Réunies; and a Dutch one, Delta Lloyd. The latter was the second-largest composite in the Netherlands and was particularly strong in life business, adding significantly to the group's stake in that sector.

In the 1980s CU further reduced its U.S. business, following bad results in 1984–1985, and made more acquisitions in Europe, with the result that continental Europe accounted for 30% of CU's worldwide premium income. The company's profits reached a new peak of £202 million in 1988, but fell back to £150 million in 1989.

In 1990, the new holding company, Commercial Union plc, was formed under a scheme of arrangement to facilitate expansion into a variety of financial-service activities which complement the core businesses of life and general insurance. Operations comprise a comprehensive range of such services, including unit trusts and investment management, stockbroking, and personal equity plans.

Principal Subsidiaries: Commercial Union Assurance Company plc; The British & European Reinsurance Company Ltd.; Commercial Union Life Assurance Company Ltd.; Commercial Union Properties Ltd.; The Northern Assurance Company Ltd.; Commercial Union of Canada Holdings Ltd.; Commercial Union France SA; Delta Lloyd Verzekeringsgroep NV (Netherlands); Les Provinces Réunies SA (Belgium); Commercial Union Corporation (U.S.A.).

Further Reading: Liveing, Edward, *A Century of Insurance: The Commercial Union Group of Companies, 1861–1961*, London, Commercial Union, 1961.

—John Swan

Connecticut Mutual

CONNECTICUT MUTUAL LIFE INSURANCE COMPANY

140 Garden Street
Hartford, Connecticut 06154
U.S.A.
(203) 727-6500
Fax: (203) 727-6644

Mutual Company
Incorporated: 1846
Employees: 21,000
Assets: $11.66 billion

The Connecticut Mutual Life Insurance Company (CM), in its second century of operation, is the 12th-largest life insurance company in the United States, with more than $70 billion of life insurance in force for its more than one million policyholders. Its staff of more than 2,900 full-time agents is based in all 50 states, the District of Columbia, Guam, and Puerto Rico, and writes a complete portfolio of participating permanent and term life insurance, universal life insurance, and other interest sensitive products.

By the mid-1840s the city of Hartford, Connecticut, with a population of nearly 13,000, was a leader in the burgeoning U.S. insurance industry. Even though the city was located some 40 miles from the sea, it became a center for first marine and then fire insurance. The concept of life insurance, however, which was firmly rooted in Europe, was not as well accepted in the United States. Many Americans believed that life insurance was nothing more than a lottery, and in 1846 there were fewer than 15,000 lives insured in the entire country. Those life insurance policies came from British underwriters who controlled the five life insurance companies that had been doing business in the colonies since 1787.

Guy Rowland Phelps, a graduate of the Yale medical school and a practicing physician, and his attorney friend Elisha Pratt felt that there was a future for life insurance in the United States. They decided to found a company in Connecticut, a state where no such enterprise existed. On May 6, 1846, a petition for a life insurance company was introduced in the state legislature and on June 12, Governor Isaac Toucey signed the charter creating the first life insurance company in Connecticut and the sixth oldest in the United States.

The company's first board of directors was elected on July 29, 1846, and in August of that year, Eliphalet Bulkeley was elected Connecticut Mutual's first president. Phelps became the company's first secretary and Elisha Pratt its first vice president. The board created a "guarantee fund" of $50,000 to protect CM from any heavy initial losses. By the end of the year more than $100,000 in new applications had been received.

Each application was screened by the entire Connecticut Mutual board, using the Carlisle Table of Mortality, a table based on the lives of 45,000 people in England. By using what was then considered scientific methods of risk evaluation, the average life span of any person could be calculated by considering the individual's lifestyle and general health. This conservative approach limited the number of people who were eligible for coverage. Coverage was generally limited to the United States, and death was not covered if the policyholder traveled south of Virginia and Kentucky from June to November because of the risk of yellow fever. For an extra 3% premium, policies permitted travel to and from any major seaport in the world, providing the traveler chose "first class vessels." The company also charged extra premiums to permit travel to Central America, Europe, the Mediterranean, and the coast of Africa.

Many insurance companies at the time covered slaves. One company had a special "Negro life insurance policy" that was not valid if the slave was either kidnapped or chose to run away. Planters usually insured only those slaves who worked in dangerous planting jobs or on the accident-prone loading docks at seaports serving the cotton trade. Phelps had strong views against writing this type of insurance. Whether his position was inspired by an abolitionist point of view or that of a shrewd underwriter is not known.

The California gold rush created an increased demand for special coverage from those who wanted to cash in on opportunities in the West. Connecticut Mutual's board, as always, took a very conservative stand when reviewing these requests, but between 1848 and 1853 the company issued more than 2,200 of these special policies.

Phelps never forgot that the company was a mutually held concern and worried that it might become careless in its approach to risk taking; but conservatism also restricted many of CM's opportunities for growth, and the board's frugality caused a serious rift with its field staff. Agents complained about low pay and that the board did not spend enough on advertising. At the same time, Elisha Pratt, who was running the company's agency in Boston, advocated increasing agents commissions to attract more professional salespeople. CM had traditionally sought men of high social and business standing to sell its policies because their good reputations and lofty status in the community would make them more credible; but reputation alone did not assure sales, and CM's agents' records were inconsistent.

These grievances led Pratt to challenge control of the company at Connecticut Mutual's second annual meeting in January 1848. Pratt arrived from Boston with proxies in hand and took the board members by surprise. When the smoke cleared, CM's president Bulkeley had been defeated by Hartford financier James Goodwin. The battle resulted in the resignations or retirement of several board members. Elisha Pratt himself resigned as vice president on September 18 of the same year. He went on to help found the Union Mutual Life Insurance Company in Boston.

James Goodwin, CM's new president, was a member of the influential Morgan family by marriage. His relationship with what became the most powerful banking firm in the nation ended up having very practical uses for CM. The company became the first commercial account of what would eventually become J.P. Morgan and Company. Goodwin used those financial resources to invest in urban and farm mortgages and initiated a program of investing in the "West," which at the time meant as far as Chicago and Saint Louis.

In the spring of 1861, 16 of the major life insurance companies, including CM, met in New York to consider the impact of the Civil War on life policies in force at the time. They decided to offer those insured the option to either pay an additional war-risk premium or renew their policies once they were discharged from military service. By the time the war ended, CM had paid in excess of $110,000 to the beneficiaries of 64 policyholders who had lost their lives as a result of the war.

The end of the Civil War brought an explosive growth in the life insurance business. Limits on policies were increased to $25,000. During the years following the war, the number of CM life policies issued increased from 1,200 in 1859 to more than 8,000 in 1864. As a result of this boom, many new life insurance companies were formed, causing increased competition in the life insurance business for both buyers and sellers of life insurance. The growth in the number of companies doing business created a drain on CM's existing employee pool. Many former employees, including both board members and agents, resigned and participated in forming new companies. Not all these new companies were sound risks. During the post-Civil War years, over 50 new insurance companies failed, causing a credibility problem with the buying public. To make matters worse, Phelps, after taking ill at a board meeting, died on March 18, 1869.

Like every insurance company in the United States, CM was forced to take a hard look at investments in the West after the Great Chicago Fire. Under Goodwin's leadership the company had made considerable investments in what were considered frontier communities. After the smoke in Chicago had cleared, Goodwin toured the smoldering ruins and returned to Hartford to confer with his associates. The board decided to reinvest in the city, granting a $1.7 million loan, the largest in company history, to industrialist Potter Palmer to help rebuild many structures, including Chicago's famed Palmer House Hotel. In the three years following the Chicago Fire, CM invested over $3.7 million in rebuilding the city.

CM managed to weather the financial storm created by the depression of 1873, which followed the downfall of the nation's most influential banking house, Jay Cooke and Company, and a ten-day closing of the New York Stock Exchange. During the depression, CM showed its optimism for the future in the face of mass unemployment and bank and business failures by building a new home office in Hartford.

On March 15, 1878 Goodwin died. He was succeeded by Jacob L. Greene, an attorney and agent who had been with CM for eight years. Greene continued Goodwin's policy of western investment and was responsible for introducing post-maturity settlements, which offered the options of receiving policy proceeds over a specific period of time or a life income for the beneficiary.

Greene was also chiefly responsible for an industrywide change in the way premiums were calculated. Life insurance premiums were based on a formula that took three factors into account: the mortality tables, a fair estimate of the ongoing cost of doing business, and an anticipated return on investment of reserve funds of 4%. Greene anticipated that interest rates might drop below 4%, but calculating premiums using a lower rate of return created an increase in premium rates, which shocked the board and agents alike. William Cahn in *A Matter of Life and Death*, reported that Greene responded, "No life insurance is safe which is not more than safe," and stuck to his controversial policy of using a lower interest rate in the formula. Within 25 years a majority of U.S. life insurance companies followed suit.

Greene also faced the controversial tontine system during his tenure. Introduced by the Equitable Life Assurance Society to increase sales of life coverage, tontine policies revived an insurance concept developed in the late 1700s to raise money for French nobility. The idea was also embraced by other companies under names such as "percentage dividends," "life rate endowments," and "deferred dividends." A tontine policy not only provided security for a policyholder's family after his death, but also the possibility of making a fortune on the policy if he lived. Under the tontine plan, money earned on the policyholder's premiums was withheld by the company for a specific period of time. If the insured died during that period, the face value of the policy was paid to his family. If the insured lived for the agreed-upon period of time and continued to pay his premiums, he shared in the added profits his money had earned and in money earned by those who had forfeited their own funds because they could not keep up the premiums.

The possibility of becoming wealthy as a result of buying life insurance created more business, but many people bought policies they could not afford to maintain. Accumulated funds were put into "tontine reserves," and opponents of the concept claimed that companies were making fortunes off the lapsed policies of those unfortunate enough to be unable to keep making payments.

For 30 years the CM board and Greene were the most vocal critics of the tontine system. Their refusal to offer a tontine plan caused a decrease in sales, again creating problems in hiring and keeping agents in the field. Four months after Greene's death in March 1905, the Senate Assembly of the New York legislature launched an investigation into the business affairs of insurance companies. Along with other restrictions imposed on the industry, the tontine system was outlawed.

John M. Taylor, CM's fifth president, faced damage control as a result of the tontine investigations. In addition, congressional hearings into corporate abuses and the passage of the Sherman antitrust provisions had produced a general distrust of large corporations. Sales and growth lagged, and in the 30 years preceding the turn of the century CM slipped from the second- to the eleventh-largest life insurer in the nation.

Taylor attacked the problem on several fronts. He began to redevelop a strong agency system. CM's conservative reputation made finding suitable representatives a major challenge.

In an attempt to strengthen the agency system, Taylor appointed Robert H. Kellogg, a veteran CM agent, to the post of regional superintendent of agencies. Kellogg in turn named

Griffin M. Lovelace as his assistant. Kellogg instituted a program to recruit quality agents to represent CM's product line, and Lovelace was responsible for training them. He believed that insurance should be sold on the basis of the specific needs of the buyer. This required a more educated agent, so Lovelace held a series of agent meetings that evolved into an agent training program. Professional agent organizations, the National Association of Life Underwriters and the American College of Life Underwriters, were created, the latter to help provide professional training for underwriters.

Taylor also introduced new products. The company began selling business insurance, which covered the loss of key personnel. CM introduced industrial insurance and disability insurance, liberalized the terms for payment of premiums, provided an opportunity to reinstate policies after they had lapsed, and relaxed its policies on insuring women.

In 1913 the Connecticut legislature, as a result of a petition by CM, passed a statute permitting life insurance companies to execute trusts. CM gained the authority to hold the proceeds of any life policy and pay beneficiaries under terms previously agreed upon by the purchaser of the policy. The statute permitted the new policy to be extended to those who already had policies in force.

Henry S. Robinson succeeded John Taylor as CM's sixth president. His term in office began with a nationwide influenza epidemic. CM paid out over $1.6 million in claims. In 1926 the company moved into a new home office located in the Lord's Hill section of Hartford, and later that year Robinson died, leaving his duties as president to James Lee Loomis.

Despite business growth, Loomis was concerned about the nation's economy, and he was proved right by the collapse of the New York Stock Exchange in 1929. The disaster took several years to affect CM. As interest rates and dividends to policyholders dropped, Loomis oversaw the transfer of CM investments into more secure U.S. government securities. The company survived the Depression without major losses, and in 1930 the board appointed one of CM's most successful agency managers, Peter M. Fraser, as new vice president.

Loomis prepared Fraser for the company presidency, emphasizing the investment end of the business. Fraser began investing in new areas. One was Florida real estate. Fraser saw Florida as the nation's next great recreation area due to increased leisure time and a trend toward winter vacations. The company also began to invest heavily in hospitals and churches and initiated a policy of making mortgage loans in the midwestern corn belt.

When Fraser became president in 1945, the company began a period of growth. Total CM assets passed the $1 billion mark and CM's urban portfolio grew from $17.3 million to over $204 million.

Fraser's successor, George F.B. Smith, became CM's tenth president but was forced to retire due to ill health less than one year from his election to the post. The search for a replacement concluded with the election of Charles J. Zimmerman, who left his post as managing director of the Life Insurance Agency Management Association to assume the CM presidency. A former agent with CM's New York City agency and general agent in Chicago, Zimmerman had substantial sales experience and was aware of the circumstances in which field agents worked. He was surprised by CM's poor agent support. Recognizing the role of an agent as an insurance counselor, he made educating his sales team a priority. By 1970 eight of every ten CM agents had attended college, and the trend toward a better-educated sales force had a firm foothold.

Throughout the 1960s and 1970s CM looked for more ways to broaden the financial services it offered the public. The company's new breed of agents became qualified practitioners in fields such as business preservation, employee benefits, estate management, and all phases of business insurance. Zimmerman's successor, Edward B. Bates, was just such an agent.

Under Bates, CM moved into the electronic age, forging a tight technical relationship between the agent in the field and the home office. Bates also promoted community involvement. CM joined with other insurance companies to invest over a billion dollars in cities throughout the country for on-the-job-training, tutorial programs for underprivileged children, and other community projects.

Bates was succeeded by Denis F. Mullane, who reassumed the presidency when his successor, S. Caesar Raboy, retired in 1989. Mullane spearheaded a drive to bring the company fully into the computer age by streamlining information processing and installing more sophisticated computer systems capable of handling electronic mail. CM also developed a program to further improve agents' knowledge and skills in 1983. The program included training agents to use a software package as a sales tool.

With a portfolio of competitive disability-income and whole-life insurance, and attention to clients, Connecticut Mutual Life Insurance Company should remain an industry leader.

Principal Subsidiaries: CM Life Insurance Company; Diversified Insurance Services of America; GroupAmerica Insurance Company.

Further Reading: Cahn, William, *A Matter of Life and Death,* New York, Random House, 1970; Yalanis, Despina, "A History of Connecticut Mutual Life Insurance Company," Hartford, Connecticut, Connecticut Mutual Life Insurance Company, 1990.

—William R. Grossman

THE CONTINENTAL CORPORATION

180 Maiden Lane
New York, New York 10038
(212) 440-3000
Fax: (212) 440-7130

Public Company
Incorporated: 1968
Employees: 16,000
Assets: $13.00 billion
Stock Exchanges: New York Midwest Pacific

The Continental Corporation is a holding company for a group of insurance companies. Continental operates a number of other financial service companies in areas such as risk-management consulting, and credit, but its mainstay is commercial and personal property and casualty insurance. Incorporated in 1968 to manage a growing group of insurance companies, Continental's roots go back to 1853. Started as a single fire insurance company with capital of half a million dollars, Continental has assets of more than $13 billion.

On October 2, 1852, a group of 12 prominent New York businessmen met at the Metropolitan Bank to set up a new fire insurance company. Presiding was Henry C. Bowen, a dry goods merchant who, having found it difficult to get adequate fire protection from existing local companies, decided to organize a large company himself. With the help of his associate, Hiram Barney of the law firm Barney, Humphrey and Butler, Bowen rounded up enough investors to subscribe the $500,000 capital to start the new company. The men christened their new company the Metropolitan Insurance Company. When the group filed for a charter, however, they discovered that a similar name was already being used by another new fire insurer, so a new name was selected—the Continental Insurance Company.

Although Henry Bowen was an energetic and capable businessman, he recognized his lack of experience in the insurance field. He also had many other obligations that prevented him from assuming direct leadership of the company. At the board of directors meeting in December, Bowen nominated the former mayor of New York City, William V. Brady, as president of the company. Brady had the political ties and the business acumen to get the fledgling company off the ground, but he also lacked direct experience in the insurance business. For that reason, George T. Hope, former secretary of the Jefferson Fire Insurance Company and himself a volunteer fire fighter, became Continental's second in command.

Throughout the first half of the 19th century, large cities had no professional fire fighters. Volunteer fire brigades rushed to the scene of the fire as much out of sport—the first to arrive at the scene of a fire was customarily awarded a cash prize by the building's insurer—as out of concern. Fire-fighting equipment was primitive, usually consisting of hand-pump engines drawn by hand not horse. Fire codes were virtually nonexistent, and fire represented a constant threat to businesses and homes.

On January 7, 1853, the Continental Insurance Company issued its first policy. President Brady, Secretary Hope, and two clerks, A. Ransom and J. Vanderlip, worked in the company's first office in the basement of 6 Wall Street. Before long, a messenger and a full-time surveyor, P. Flender, were added to the payroll. Clients came to the office to apply for a policy, and their property was inspected before the company agreed to issue it. Coverage for $10,000 was considered sizable, and $20,000 was the largest line allowed. In April 1853, Continental expanded its business outside of New York City by appointing agents in other locations. The first agency was established in Cleveland, Ohio. By 1855 Continental was insuring property against fire in Boston; Chicago; Cincinnati, Ohio; Louisville, Kentucky; Baltimore, Maryland; and San Francisco, California.

On May 1, 1857, William V. Brady retired as president of the company and was replaced by George T. Hope. Hiram H. Lamport became secretary. George Hope's extensive experience in the insurance trade was a great asset to Continental. Even before becoming president, Hope had taken steps to ensure the company's success. In July 1856, Continental began issuing participating policies, which not only granted policyholders a part of the company's profits, but also made them liable to the same extent for any losses. After stockholders received their dividends, a share of the profits was paid to each participating policyholder according to their premiums, in the form of interest-bearing scrip that could be redeemed for cash at a specified date. Meanwhile, the cash was held as a special catastrophic reserve fund by the company. If the company's losses went beyond the usual reserve allotment, as they did after the Chicago fire of 1871, the scrip fund would be tapped to cover them. Despite its success, the scrip program was discontinued before the turn of the century.

In 1860 the Continental Insurance Company moved its offices from Wall Street to Broadway, and soon many other insurance companies did the same. Continental's new office operated under the austere conditions typical of the day. Hope's desk was elevated so he could oversee each worker's activities and deter any loafing. The president also had an electric switchboard with which he could summon any employee by ringing a bell on his desk.

In 1861 war broke out between the states. The Continental Insurance Company came out strongly in favor of the Union. Founders Bowen and Barney had supported Abraham Lincoln in the presidential election just a year before, and their anti-slavery views were widely known. During the war, Continental supported the cause by granting leaves of absence with full pay to three employees who volunteered for the Union Army. The company also donated $500 for the establishment of a local guard for the city's financial institutions while the militia was away fighting; that guard was called out in July 1863, when 50,000 demonstrators took to the streets to protest unfair draft laws. The ensuing riots resulted in 1,000 deaths and fire damage to 50 buildings.

Throughout the war, Continental continued to operate profitably and pay its dividend. In December 1864, Continental contributed $500 for the establishment of a full-time professional fire department in New York City. The department began to operate a steam fire engine company in 1865.

In 1868 Continental established an office in Brooklyn, and a year later Continental followed the newly complete railroads west to Chicago, where it set up its western department. R. J. Taylor headed the Chicago office and implemented several new procedures there, including acceptance of notes for premium payments at 10% interest and an installment plan, which covered property for five years with the total premium paid in five annual installments.

On October 8, 1871, the Great Chicago Fire erupted. Fanned by fierce winds, the blaze lasted for two days and wiped out 7,450 buildings on 2,000 acres. The total damage amounted to more than $200 million. Continental sent Special Agent Barrett to the scorched city to survey the damage. The home office in New York received a telegram from the western department's secretary, Jonas Oakley, with bad news: "Barrett's estimate—twelve hundred thousand" and the location of the company's new office, "Address Nine South Halsted St."

The company's losses from the Chicago Fire eventually totaled $1.7 million. Continental's $800,000 scrip fund was liquidated to cover the catastrophic losses, and the shareholders' surplus was wiped out as well. In response to the grave circumstances, director Abiel A. Low recommended an increase in the capital of the company from $500,000 to $1 million. Low, an importer of goods from Asia, spoke so enthusiastically at the October meeting of Continental's board that the whole amount of the capital increase was subscribed before the directors adjourned. While dozens of fire insurance companies went bankrupt as a result of the Chicago Fire, Continental remained in business.

Just a little over a year later, disaster struck again. Fire broke out in Boston's shopping district and 776 buildings were destroyed. Continental's losses were $700,000. Abiel Low again clamored to preserve the company, this time suggesting a 40% assessment on the $1 million capital. The action was approved by shareholders. About 30 fire insurers were bankrupted by the Boston fire. Continental's survival promoted its credibility with the public, and by the end of 1878 cash assets were $3.33 million, up almost $1 million from before the Chicago fire in 1871.

During the 1880s, Continental began issuing new kinds of insurance. In January 1882, the company began issuing marine insurance, and six months later it issued tornado insurance. In 1885 the company issued hail insurance on crops, but found the business to be unprofitable and dropped it two years later. In 1892, however, the coverage was reintroduced on a more limited basis when a number of Continental agents began offering competitors' hail insurance to its farm clients. At times the company had to subsidize unprofitable lines to maintain its market share in other areas.

On July 28, 1885, Continental's president, George T. Hope, died at the age of 67. During his 28 years as president, the company's assets grew from less than $1 million to more than $5 million. The company's vice president, Hiram H. Lamport, replaced Hope as president and served until 1889 when he was replaced by Francis C. Moore.

Moore set out to make risk assessment more reliable. He devised a system, the Universal Mercantile Schedule, to determine fire danger in any building. Moore constantly compiled statistics, and his book *Guide to Agents,* sold over 30,000 copies. In 1902 Moore retired, having boosted the company's assets to $13 million.

Moore's successor was his stepson, Henry Evans. Even before becoming president, Evans had made a mark on the company. In 1885, when President George T. Hope's death led to conflict over the succession, Evans devised his own reorganization plan and presented it to the board of directors. Among other things, Evans's plan called for Hiram H. Lamport's resignation. The board was impressed by the young Evans's boldness, and he was given more and more responsibilities, including reorganizing the company's operations in San Francisco. After a five-month stay in San Francisco, Evans returned to the home office and was put in charge of the entire agency department after only ten years with the company. Shortly thereafter Evans was elevated to second vice president, then to vice president, and in 1902 he assumed the presidency.

Two of Continental's greatest disasters occurred just a short time after the 42-year-old Evans took the helm. In February 1904, a fire destroyed 2,500 structures in Baltimore. Continental's losses totaled $925,000. Two years later the San Francisco earthquake and ensuing fire razed the city. The fire took a heavy toll: Continental paid $1.75 million in claims and lost the records of its Pacific Coast business, and 20 other companies went bankrupt.

Despite the huge losses experienced by Continental after the Baltimore and San Francisco fires, the company remained solvent. Evans hoped, in fact, to expand by operating a multitude of insurance companies under the Continental umbrella. Just two months after the San Francisco fire, Continental's board authorized $500,000 of the company's funds to capitalize a new company, The Fidelity Fire Insurance Company. In 1910 Evans merged Fidelity with the ailing Phenix Insurance Company of Brooklyn, creating the Fidelity-Phenix Fire Insurance Company of New York.

In 1911, Continental began issuing automobile insurance. Early policies insured against "loss by fire, explosion, self-ignition or lightning; also against loss or damage by collision, burning or derailment; or by stranding and sinking, including average salvage charges while the automobile is being transported in any conveyance by land or water; and against theft, robbery, or pilferage by any persons other than those in the employ of its owner; if the amount is $25 or more for any one occasion." In June 1914, Continental began offering coverage specifically designed to cover collision.

In 1915 Evans organized a third insurance company, the American Eagle Fire Insurance Company. Before World War I, foreign companies controlled about two-thirds of U.S. insurance business. Playing upon patriotic sentiment, Evans used the slogan "America Fore" in advertising the three companies—Continental, Fidelity-Phenix, and American Eagle. In 1918, the group adopted the slogan as its official name. The America Fore Group was the forerunner of today's Continental Corporation.

As the United States prepared to enter World War I, insurance companies were criticized for not insuring necessary high risks such as munitions plants. In 1915 Evans organized a meeting with the heads of several other insurance companies to discuss providing insurance for such operations, among them the Hercules Powder Company. Evans convinced the group to insure that company, which was later completely destroyed in an explosion. When it was discovered that Continental had no liability itself, Evans was criticized. His reply that his contribution had been getting the other insurers together showed that the president held to the same questionable ethical standards as other capitalists of his day.

During World War I Continental, for the most part, conducted business as usual. The company did, however, offer some new lines such as full war coverage insurance against possible damages from bombardment, explosion, and riots. A year after the war ended, the America Fore Group participated with seven other companies in the formation of a marine insurance company called the Marine Office of America (MOA). The MOA grew substantially through acquisition in the succeeding decades.

In 1920 Evans announced a reorganization of the America Fore Group and became chairman of the board of the whole organization. An Alabamian, Joseph E. Lopez, became the president of Continental and served for just 11 months. He was succeeded by Norman T. Robertson, who had previously headed the American Eagle Fire Insurance Company. Robertson resigned in 1924 after Henry Evans's death and joined a New York brokerage.

Continental shared in the country's good fortune in the 1920s. Chairman Ernest Sturm and President Paul Haid, both taking office in late 1924, led the company through the period of prosperity. Aviation and automobile insurance provided new sources of revenue, and the value of Continental's equity investments skyrocketed.

In 1929 the stock market crash wiped out millions of investors, seriously affecting Continental. The company's stock price plummeted from 104½ to 46½ between September and November 1929. Continental's losses on investments were so severe in the early depression that the company decreased its authorized capital from $20 million to $5 million. In many cases Continental, like other insurance companies in the Depression, offered financially troubled corporations very lenient terms for paying premiums, and thus it helped some companies stay in business. Despite the dismal economic outlook, Continental continued to pay its dividend throughout the Depression without interruption.

In 1932 Paul Haid resigned from Continental's presidency to head a new trade organization called the Insurance Executives Association. Haid had decided to move on because of disagreements with chairman Ernest Sturm. Bernard Culver, who came to the group with its 1927 acquisition of the Niagara Fire Insurance Company, became the new president and replaced Ernest Sturm as CEO in 1936. When the office of chairman was reinstated in 1946, Culver was elected by the board to that position, which he filled until poor health forced his retirement in 1950.

As the country emerged from the Depression, new hazards arose. By 1939 Europe was once again at war. Ships carrying cargoes through the war zones were at great risk, and by September 1939, Continental was once again offering full war coverage. Shortages of products, particularly those related to the automobile industry, disrupted Continental's business. Demand for automobile coverage declined as the war consumed rubber, steel, and gasoline, keeping consumer car production low.

In 1944, the United States Supreme Court ruled against price fixing in the insurance industry in *U.S.* v. *Southeastern Underwriters Association*. The insurance industry was upset with the ruling because most companies were too small to rely solely on their own experience in setting premiums. As a result of the industry's protests the federal government passed the McCarran-Ferguson Act, which exempted insurance rate fixing from the jurisdiction of the Sherman Antitrust Act and gave the power of insurance regulation to the states.

By the end of the war, Continental had recovered entirely from its pre-Depression losses. In February 1945, the company increased its outstanding capital to $20 million by transferring $15 million from the surplus. After the war, general prosperity accelerated Continental's growth, but a number of catastrophes, including a severe rain and wind storm that ripped through 11 northeastern states in November 1950, caused extensive damage. The "Big Blow," as it was called, resulted in claims of $13 million for the America Fore Group.

In 1951 Frank A. Christensen, president of the group since 1946, became chairman and CEO. One year later he proposed establishing a subsidiary that would finance premiums for businesses. The subsidiary, named AFCO, although it was not limited to financing premiums written by America Fore companies, got off to a slow start. Nonetheless, within three years a similar premium finance subsidiary was set up in Canada—CAFO.

In 1955 the America Fore Group spent $13 million to modernize its headquarters, which it had occupied since 1912. The upgrading was intended in part to boost employee morale, and consequently productivity.

In 1956 Continental participated in the Nuclear Energy Property Insurance Association, which was formed to deal with the extraordinary risks involved in building nuclear power facilities. The association could offer $50 million worth of coverage on each plant.

In 1957 J. Victor Herd, after a year as president of the group, replaced Frank Christensen as the company's chairman and CEO. Herd had begun his insurance career at the age of 15 as a map clerk and examiner for the American Central Insurance Company. He first came to the America Fore Group in 1929 with its acquisition of the Niagara Fire Insurance Company, but left a year later to join the Fire Association Group. In 1942, he returned to America Fore as a corporate secretary. He rose to vice president in 1944 and then executive vice president in 1951. In 1959 Nicholas Dekker took over as president, while Herd remained in the top job.

Under Herd, one of the company's most energetic leaders, the group made a number of important acquisitions in the late 1950s. They included the Firemen's Insurance Company of Newark, the companies of the Loyalty Group in 1957, and The Yorkshire Insurance Company of New York in 1958. In 1959 the Continental Insurance Company and Fidelity-Phenix merged through a stock conversion. A year later, Continental's stock, listed on the New York Exchange since 1916, was introduced on the Midwest and Pacific exchanges as well.

In 1960 the America Fore Loyalty Group, as it was then called, began a corporate restructuring to simplify its management. The group consisted of a dozen companies from three insurance families: the Continental Insurance Company, Niagara Fire Insurance Company, the Fidelity-Phenix Insurance Company, The Fidelity and Casualty Company of New York, and the Niagara Insurance Company (Bermuda) Limited on the America Fore side; Firemen's Insurance Company of Newark, Milwaukee Insurance Company of Milwaukee, Commercial Insurance Company of Newark, National-Ben Franklin Insurance Company of Pittsburgh, and Royal General Insurance Company of Canada on the Loyalty side; and The Yorkshire Insurance Company of New York and Seaboard Fire and Marine Insurance Company on the Yorkshire side. Under the new structure, President Nicholas Dekker took the newly created office of vice chairman, while Nathan H. Wentworth became president. The early years of the 1960s produced excellent earnings, based in part on exceptional performance of the group's equities and debt investment.

In 1962 Chairman J. Victor Herd proposed changing the name of America Fore Loyalty Group to the Continental Insurance Companies. Herd said, "The Continental Insurance Company . . . has an eminent 110-year history of its own, and a well-known service mark, the Continental soldier." The group then launched a sizable advertising campaign to promote its new name.

Continental's acquisitions continued in the 1960s both at home and overseas. In December 1962, Continental took over the American business of the Norwich Union Fire Insurance Society, Ltd., of Norwich, England. In January 1965, Continental bought the Buckeye Union Casualty Company along with its subsidiaries. At the same time, the company also acquired a major marine insurer, Appleton & Cox. In 1966 it bought the Boston Marine Insurance Company and became involved in the life insurance trade with the purchase of a substantial share of Franklin Life Insurance Company of Springfield, Illinois. In 1967 Continental acquired American Title Insurance, and in June 1968, the outstanding shares of the Glens Falls Insurance Company and its subsidiaries. Overseas, Continental bought a major interest in the Phoenix Assurance Company of London. Later the company set up a Belgian affiliate with the British company called Phoenix Continental S.A.

Continental also acquired several noninsurance businesses in the 1960s. In 1966 it purchased the Underwriters Adjusting Company, an independent property adjuster, and a 20% interest in Diners Club, the charge card concern; in 1966, Capital Financial Services of Columbus, Ohio, a consumer credit company. Continental also established its own data processing services company, INSCO, in 1968.

On September 9, 1965, Hurricane Betsy devastated New Orleans, Louisiana. More than 50 people were killed and estimated property and crop damage was about $1 billion. Continental's claims amounted to $9.5 million.

Civil unrest in the late 1960s led to increased damage claims. Riots spurred by racial tension in locations such as Detroit, Los Angeles, and Newark, New Jersey, resulted in millions of dollars worth of claims and a reluctance on the part of insurers to cover urban properties. Some insurance companies looked for federal guarantees on their risks in riot-affected areas, but Continental opposed such measures.

On August 5, 1968, a new holding company, The Continental Corporation, was established to oversee the increasingly diverse companies in the group. Advertisements in *The New York Times* and *The Wall Street Journal* featured a beleaguered stork carrying a jumbo sack and read, "The Continental Insurance Company is proud to announce the birth of its parent." J. Victor Herd assumed the roles of chairman and president of the new holding company in addition to his responsibilities at the Continental Insurance Company. He remained chairman and CEO until his retirement in 1970, after 53 years in the insurance business. Nathan Wentworth succeeded Herd, and Milton Mays became Continental president in 1971.

Chairman Wentworth's first task was to organize Continental's sprawling businesses. Two marine insurance subsidiaries, MOA and Appleton & Cox, were merged into the Marine Office-Appleton Cox—later renamed the Marine Office of America Corporation (MOAC), and in 1972 Operation Sacred Cow was initiated to streamline the company's operations. The program operated on the premise that no business practice, no matter how entrenched, was immune to change if it interfered with the company's goal of higher profits. The SUCCESS program, which was to determine the most efficient uses of staff, was also started in 1972. Continental hoped to save $7 million annually simply by achieving greater efficiency with its current staff.

In 1971 Continental introduced the first no-fault automobile coverage in 43 states. No-fault coverage was an improvement over ordinary liability insurance because it allowed accident victims to collect no matter who was at fault and eliminated the settlement delays that resulted from litigation.

Continental had introduced coverage called the Comprehensive Business Policy in 1963. In 1973 Wentworth adapted the plan to cover the needs of individuals. Called Personal Comprehensive Protection (PCP), the new line covered all of the basic family insurance needs in one policy. Continental marketed the coverage nationwide. In March 1975, Continental introduced what it called the Insurance Store, an ad campaign that sold the concept of the independent insurance agent, rather than individual lines of insurance. Both the PCP and the Insurance Store campaign were designed to simplify insurance and make it more appealing to the average consumer.

On April 3, 1974, a series of more than 100 tornadoes blasted through the area from Georgia to Michigan. Hundreds were killed in what the National Weather Service called the most severe tornado disaster since 1925. Xenia, Ohio, where the tornado cut a swath 100 yards wide and stretching the length of the town, was the hardest hit. Continental paid claims of $22 million in Xenia alone.

Continental's network of companies continued to grow during the 1970s. In 1973, Continental became the major shareholder in the Puerto Rican-American Insurance Company and purchased a 10% interest in the French multiple line insurer La Preservatrice. In 1974, Continental acquired the First Insurance Company of Hawaii, set up an Iranian joint venture—the Hafez Insurance Company—with the British Royal Insurance Company, Limited, and acquired 10% of and entered into an operating agreement with the West German Alte Leipziger group. In 1975 the company bought heavily in

Latin American countries, including a controlling interest of the Guatemalan insurer, Commercial Aseguradora Suizo Americana, S.A., and minority interests in several companies in Brazil, Colombia, Guatemala, Argentina, and Venezuela. In 1976 Continental bought the Unionamerica Insurance Group, an insurer of specialized risks, and reorganized the companies into the Swett and Crawford Groups.

In 1976 Nathan H. Wentworth retired as chairman and was replaced by John B. Ricker Jr. as chairman and CEO. Ricker quickly announced a major reorganization of the company. The group's approximately 40 subsidiaries were divided into four primary operating units: property and casualty insurance, international insurance and reinsurance, life and health insurance, and financial services. Five support units were also set up: systems and procedures, investment and finance, human resources, corporate affairs, and administrative services. Ricker's reorganization of Continental reduced the number of executives reporting to the chairman from 25 to 7.

Chairman Ricker, a former navy man who had come up through Continental's marine insurance side, intended to cut back on the group's underwriting. He told *Nation's Business,* February 1978, "I felt we were writing too much insurance. . . . Besides, we were writing types of insurance that are the worst to make profits on—workers' compensation, general liability, and auto liability."

During 1974–1975 the property and casualty industry as a whole had suffered severe losses. Competition in the property and casualty areas, higher liability awards, and static premiums caused further damage to the already declining industry. Since Continental's property and casualty business accounted for about 80% of premiums written, losses in that area were a serious blow.

In 1977 property and casualty business rebounded somewhat and Continental's performance improved considerably after two consecutive losing years. A year later, earnings hit $5.66 per share, but the improvement was short-lived. When high interest rates brought increased return on equity and debt investments in 1979, property and casualty insurers lowered their premiums to gain market share, since the difference could be made up through investment gains. When the investment returns dropped in the early 1980s, the entire industry was hurt. Continental's combined loss and expense ratio was exceptionally bad compared to its competition. To make matters worse, stiff competition had eroded Continental's national market share from 3.5% to 2.5% between 1975 and 1981. With a number of subsidiaries, in the red, analysts blamed Continental's management for failing to move aggressively in the changing insurance environment. Yet despite the turmoil Continental continued to pay its dividend.

In the early 1980s the property and casualty industry continued to face unfavorable conditions. Continental took steps to streamline its operations and devise a clear strategy for the future. In 1981 Diners Club was sold to Citibank at a loss. Although Continental expressed a desire to remain in the life insurance business, it sold Franklin Life; Chairman Ricker told *National Underwriter*, June 5, 1981, that Continental would continue looking for a life insurance company that "complements and supplements our marketing strategy."

In 1981 Continental launched Continental Risk Services, a subsidiary intended to help companies manage risks. The new company marketed its services to companies that no longer accepted the need to spend a certain amount on liability losses. The aim was to minimize expenditures both before and after occurrence of losses.

In December 1982, John P. Mascotte replaced the retiring John Ricker as chairman and CEO of the Continental Corporation. Mascotte had been with the company only 19 months, having been lured from the Mutual Benefit Life Insurance Company. Although he had limited experience in Continental's primary business—property and casualty insurance—Mascotte brought keen marketing expertise to the job. At age 43 one of the youngest CEOs of a major financial corporation, Mascotte slashed overhead by 25%, eliminating Continental agents who did not come up to the company's new profitability standards. More than 1,700 of Continental's agents were either let go or induced to resign, and within two years Continental's profits began to improve considerably. Mascotte was pleased with the results of the measures, but acknowledged the unseen costs when he told *Forbes* magazine, December 31, 1984, "If there's one thing I had to do over, I wouldn't have called it shooting the stragglers," referring to a phrase he once used to describe the cost-cutting measures.

When Mascotte took over at Continental he intended to expand the company's life and health insurance operations. By the late 1980s, he had abandoned this plan. "Staying in the business as a marginal player made little sense; gearing up to be a market leader would have consumed too much capital," he said in the company's 1988 annual report. That year Continental sold National Life Insurance Company of Canada, Commercial Life, and Loyalty Life. In 1989 the company left life insurance entirely with the sale of the William Penn Companies.

Throughout the 1980s, Continental concentrated on establishing its overseas businesses. By 1986, 20% of the group's revenues were generated outside of the United States. The company's international strategy changed from holding minority interests in many companies to gaining control of a fewer number of companies. According to *Business Insurance,* November 24, 1986, Continental divested minority interests in 10 to 15 foreign affiliates between 1983 and 1986. The company planned to either own foreign subsidiaries outright or "have minority shareholdings in a few companies that offer reciprocal business to Continental."

Continental still suffered because of the poor insurance market in the late 1980s, but its performance relative to the industry as a whole showed marked improvement. Chairman Mascotte called 1988 a "very frustrating" year because of weak earnings, but he pointed out stronger loss reserves and improved managerial and financial controls as reasons for optimism. Hurricane Hugo and the California earthquake of 1989, however, brought extremely heavy losses and prompted Continental to raise premiums. Whether or not the increased premiums would improve the company's situation remained to be seen, as earlier attempts at rate increases had resulted in a loss of market share. Nevertheless, as the Continental Corporation entered the 1990s it was a fundamentally sounder company than it had been ten years earlier.

Principal Subsidiaries: AFCO Acceptance Corp.; AFCO Credit Corp.; American Loyalty Insurance Co.; Bayside Reinsurance Co., Ltd. (Bermuda); Boston Old Colony Insurance Co.; The Buckeye Union Insurance Co.; CAFO Inc. (Canada); Casualty Insurance Co.; CIC Acceptance Corp.; CIC Asset Management Corp.; Commercial Afianzadora, S.A. (Guatemala); Commercial Aseguradora Suizo Americana, S.A. (CASA) (Guatemala); Commercial Insurance Co. of Newark, N.J.; Commercial Life Insurance Co.; Continental Center Assoc.; Continental Equities Corp. of America; Continental Guaranty & Credit Corp.; The Continental Insurance Co.; The Continental Insurance Co. of Canada; The Continental Insurance Co. (Europe) Limited (U.K.); The Continental Insurance Co. of New Jersey; The Continental Insurance Co. (U.K.) Limited; Continental International Life Insurance Co.; Continental Life Insurance Public Limited Co. (U.K.); Continental Life (International) Limited (U.K.); Continental Life Unit Trust Management Limited (U.K.); Continental National Life Insurance Co.; Continental Pensions PLC (U.K.); Continental P.H.I. Limited (U.K.); Continental Re Management Inc.; Continental Reinsurance Corp.; Continental Reinsurance Corp. Intl. (Bermuda) Limited; Continental Reinsurance Corp. (U.K.) Limited; Continental Reinsurance Management Co. Ltd. (U.K.); Continental Reinsurance Management Holding Co. Limited (U.K.); Continental Risk Services (Barbados), Ltd.; Continental Risk Services (Bermuda) Ltd.; The CPI Group Inc.; CPI Pension Services Inc.; CRB Management, Inc.; Ctek, Inc.; Deutsche Continental Reinsurance, A.G. (Germany); The Dominion Insurance Corp. (Canada); East River Group, Ltd. (Bermuda); East River Insurance Co. (Barbados) Ltd.; East River Insurance Co. (Bermuda) Ltd.; The Fidelity and Casualty Co. of New York; Firemen's Insurance Co. of Newark, New Jersey; First Benefit Insurance Producers, Inc.; First Benefit Services, Inc.; First Commercial Life Insurance Co.; First Fire & Casualty Insurance of Hawaii, Inc.; First Indemnity Insurance of Hawaii, Inc.; First Insurance Co. of Hawaii, Ltd. (60%); The Glens Falls Insurance Co.; Global Marine Services, Ltd. (Canada); Groupe Barthelemy, S.A. (France); Harbor Insurance Co.; Hull and Cargo Surveyors, Inc.; Insurnet, Inc.; Inter-Continental Seguradora S.A. (Brazil); International Central Bank & Trust Corp.; International Trust Corp. of Illinois; The Ivanhoe Reinsurance Co. Ltd. (Bermuda); The Ivanhoe Reinsurance Co. Ltd. (U.K.); Kansas City Fire and Marine Insurance Co.; Lombard Continental Insurance Co. PLC (U.K.); Lombard Group, Inc. (Hong Kong); Lombart Insurance Co., Ltd. (Hong Kong); Loyalty Life Insurance Co.; The Maiden Lane Syndicate Inc.; MOAC (Australasia) Limited; Marine Office of America Corp.; Marine Office of America Corp., Ltd. (Canada); Marine Office of America Corp. Italia, SpA; Marine Office of America Corp. (U.K.) Limited; Marine Office of America (Deutschland) GmbH (Germany); Marine Office of Asia Ltd. (Hong Kong); The Mayflower Insurance Co., Ltd.; National-Ben Franklin Insurance Co. of Illinois; The National Life Assurance Co. of Canada; Niagara Fire Insurance Co.; Pacific Insurance Co.; Promotora Continental S.A. (Guatemala); Puerto Rican-American Insurance Co.; Security National Life Insurance Co. (Puerto Rico); Servicios y Comisiones Continental, S.A. de C.V. (Mexico); Settlement Options, Inc.; The South Place Syndicate Inc.; Underwriters Adjusting Co.; Unionamerica Insurance Co., Ltd. (U.K.); Unionamerica Management Co., Ltd. (U.K.); Unionamerica Management Co. Ltd. (U.K.); United States P&I Agency, Inc.; Workers Compensation and Indemnity Co. of California.

Further Reading: Kelchburg, Ann M., and Ronald G. Mullins, *A History of the Continental Insurance Company,* New York, The Continental Corporation, 1979.

—Thomas M. Tucker

EMPIRE BLUE CROSS AND BLUE SHIELD

622 Third Avenue
New York, New York 10017
U.S.A.
(212) 476-1000
Fax: (212) 490-1322

Nonprofit Company
Incorporated: 1934 as Associated Hospital Service of New York
Employees: 9,618
Assets: $2.20 billion

Empire Blue Cross and Blue Shield (Empire) is the largest private not-for-profit health insurer in the country. It provides both hospital and physician coverage for approximately ten million customers in the 28 counties of eastern New York State, including the greater New York City area. Empire was created by the 1985 merger of Blue Cross and Blue Shield of Greater New York with Blue Cross of Northeastern New York, both of which were early products of nationwide innovations in nonprofit insurance made necessary by the Great Depression. After years of spectacular growth, Empire and its fellow nonprofit insurers are struggling with inflation, as the cost of medical care in the United States continues to rise.

Blue Cross and Blue Shield of Greater New York was the older and larger of the two companies that eventually formed Empire and was itself the result of a 1974 merger of two Depression-era health insurance firms. The Great Depression took an especially heavy toll on "voluntary" hospitals, those not-for-profit institutions relying for their fiscal well-being on charitable contributions, endowments, and limited patient payments. All three sources of income declined steeply in the early years of the Depression, forcing administrators of voluntary and government hospitals to revise their financial strategies. One suggested way to increase the amount of money contributed by patients was to provide them with an insurance policy requiring affordable monthly payments while protecting them from the burden of sudden, exorbitant hospital bills. Such a plan was first used at Baylor University's hospital in 1929 and proved to be both popular and economically feasible. The concept was discussed at the 1932 national convention of the American Hospital Association, an umbrella organization for some 6,000 voluntary and government hospitals, and it was soon adopted by many groups around the country. An association in Saint Paul, Minnesota, was the first to use the Blue Cross name, and this too soon caught on.

In New York City, the United Hospital Fund (UHF) served as administrator for the area's many voluntary hospitals. UHF and the other concerned parties agreed in 1932 to create a separate nonprofit membership corporation to institute a health insurance plan for its affiliated hospitals. After necessary legislation was passed by the state of New York, the Associated Hospital Service of New York (AHS) was incorporated on October 9, 1934, with the help of $30,000 in seed money from The Commonwealth Fund and The Josiah Macy Junior Foundation. From the outset AHS was a creation of the hospitals themselves, which meant that both the agent and the eventual recipient of its insurance funds were one and the same. This apparent conflict of interest was at the root of much criticism later leveled at the Blue Cross and Blue Shield organizations, although by stature no such conflict exists in the current operation of Empire Blue Cross and Blue Shield.

From its inception, the AHS plan was a success. In 1935 individual rates were as low as 80¢ a month. The "three cents a day plan" was advertised as "No more than the cost of your daily paper," and the AHS Blue Cross plan enrolled more than 40,000 subscribers within a year. Its coverage included most basic hospital services for a period of 21 days, after which a percentage of costs would be covered. In 1936 the program was extended to cover the employee's spouse and unmarried children under age 19 as well, at a cost of 7¢ a day. In the years that followed, coverage was extended to include most of the recent developments in medical technology, and in 1947 an Inter-Plan Bank made it possible for members of one Blue Cross plan to receive treatment at other participating Blue Cross hospitals around the country. By 1945, a scant ten years after its founding, AHS subscribers numbered 2.2 million, a large percentage of them participants in group plans sponsored by unions and employers.

At the same time AHS was starting, a similar concept was gaining popularity among doctors. In 1939 the first Blue Shield plan was adopted by a physicians' organization in California to pay for doctors' fees through the same type of nonprofit insurance coverage as Blue Cross provided for hospitals. New York's Dr. Frederic Elliott, a radiologist, was instrumental in prodding the state legislature to draft legislation necessary before such an organization could be formed in New York, and in November 1940 the Medical Expense Fund was incorporated in New York City. The infant fund was no sooner in operation than it found itself competing with a similar plan created by AHS, Community Medical Care, Inc. The inevitable merger of the two concerns took place in June 1944, when the United Medical Service, Inc., (UMS) was born. At its inception UMS had about 80,000 subscribers on its rolls.

UMS offered its clients, initially large corporations such as J.P. Morgan & Company and Time, Inc., a choice of three benefit plans and premium schedules: Surgical benefits, surgical-medical benefits, and a general medical plan that covered home and office visits. As with AHS's hospital coverage, public awareness of rising medical costs helped to make UMS remarkably successful in a short period of time.

Four years after its founding, the company could boast of 1.5 million subscribers and 16,000 participating physicians. Also in 1949 UMS adopted the Blue Shield name and logo and became a member of the national Blue Shield Association which was founded in 1946.

The decades following saw a growing U.S. economy and a corresponding rise in the cost of technologically more advanced health care. The rising expense of doctor and hospital services became an increasingly difficult problem for elderly citizens, upon whom the brunt of such costs fell. In 1966 the federal government created a national health insurance fund called Medicare for citizens 65 years and older. To administer so massive a distribution of tax dollars the government asked the Blue Cross and Blue Shield companies around the country to manage, respectively, the hospital and physician portions of Medicare coverage. Blue Cross and Blue Shield plans were chosen for this task because of their size and because, as nonprofit institutions, they enjoyed widespread respect and trust from the public.

The addition of the Medicare business meant a substantial increase in subscribers, claims, and cash flow at both AHS and UMS, and it meant increased staff and more overtime work. It also subjected all Blue Cross and Blue Shield organizations to increased government scrutiny and a flurry of concerns about potential conflicts of interest, particularly on the part of Blue Shield plans. With medical costs escalating every year, some observers felt that the Blue Shield plans, most of whose governing boards were dominated by doctors, had little incentive to contest the fees charged. Prodded by such critics, Secretary of Health, Education and Welfare Joseph Califano decreed in 1978 that any organization serving as a Medicare or Medicaid intermediary must be directed by a board the majority of whose members are consumers and public representatives. UMS had to comply.

As a courtesy to its smaller sister company, AHS for many years had handled the marketing and billing functions of UMS. As a result, many consumers had come to think of the two companies as one, and in 1974 their loose alignment was formalized by a merger. The two companies became Blue Cross and Blue Shield of Greater New York and were able to offer insurance coverage for both hospital and physician bills to New York area residents, while gaining economies of scale created by the unification of two such large companies.

Shortly before the merger, AHS had formed its first health-maintenance organization (HMO) to compete with the rapidly growing number of such firms in the New York area. Blue Cross and Blue Shield of Greater New York (BC/BS) added a second HMO in 1978 and two more in the next few years. The continuing acceleration in health care costs has prompted BC/BS to initiate a number of cost containment measures aside from HMOs, including extensive advisory services to help its subscribers avoid unnecessary hospital stays, and a more critical approach to the bills submitted by hospitals and doctors. Cost containment clearly remains the top priority at all Blue Cross/Blue Shield plans.

In 1985 BC/BS merged with a second leading New York state nonprofit insurer, Blue Cross of Northeastern New York. The latter's origins were very similar to those of AHS and UMS: responding to the depression-era distress of local voluntary hospitals, the Associated Hospital Service Capital District (AHSCD) was founded in July 1936 in Albany. Closely modeled on the New York City AHS, the Capital District association was the fifth Blue Cross organization in the state of New York and the 21st in the nation. The new company's first customer was William Barnet and Son, Inc., of Rennselaer, for whom it provided coverage similar to what the earlier AHS offered in Manhattan. By the end of its first year of operation, the firm had paid out 33 claims.

AHSCD early formed a relationship with a local medical care insurance association that covered doctors' fees called Northeastern New York Medical Service, Inc., which eventually became a Blue Shield affiliate. Although the two companies had a working relationship, unlike many other pairs of Blue Cross and Blue Shield organizations, the two were never merged. After AHSCD was merged with BC/BS the latter discontinued all relations with the Albany Blue Shield, which later suffered financial reverses and was taken over by a fellow Blue Shield plan.

In 1956 AHSCD began to provide coverage for the relatives of U.S. servicemen through an organization called CHAMPUS, and in 1957 AHSCD made use of its proximity to the state legislature in Albany to win the contract to provide the first health plan for the state's 77,000 employees. Three years later it began to provide coverage for federal employees as well. AHSCD did not adopt the Blue Cross name until 1965, one year before it joined the other Blue Cross members in administrating the new Medicare system for the federal government.

The 1985 merger of Blue Cross of Northeastern New York with BC/BS created the largest private not-for-profit health insurance firm in the country. The company originally kept its Albany and New York divisions quite separate, with a strict segregation of duties and a president headquartered at each location. This scheme was subsequently abandoned and the two partners more fully integrated under the direction of chief executive Albert A. Cardone and his 13 divisional vice presidents.

Having processed some 48 million claims in 1989 alone, Empire Blue Cross and Blue Shield obviously finds itself at the center of today's crisis in health care. Empire provides coverage for giant organizations such as IBM, AT&T, and the City of New York, but also prides itself on its programs for individual subscribers of all income levels. As the middleman caught between ten million customers increasingly fed up with soaring medical costs and a legion of health care professionals ethically committed to providing the best medical care possible, Empire must do its best to negotiate a compromise level of care that is both affordable and adequate.

Further Reading: Breed, William C., *History of Associated Hospital Service of New York,* New York, [n.p.], 1959; Karp, Richard, "Physician, Heal Thyself," *Barron's,* September 11, 1978; Robertson, Beverly, *History of Blue Cross of Northeastern New York,* New York, Empire Blue Cross and Blue Shield, 1987.

—Jonathan Martin

THE EQUITABLE LIFE ASSURANCE SOCIETY OF THE UNITED STATES

787 Seventh Avenue
New York, New York 10019
U.S.A.
(212) 554-1234
Fax: (212) 554-2275

Mutual Company
Incorporated: 1859
Employees: 16,000
Assets: $61.77 billion

Known for decades as one of the largest life insurance companies in the nation, The Equitable Life Assurance Society of the United States can describe itself today as a diversified financial services company. Besides its traditional insurance operations, Equitable also is involved heavily in real estate development and, thanks to its 1985 acquisition of Donaldson, Lufkin & Jenrette, in securities brokerage.

Equitable was started in Manhattan in 1859 when Henry Baldwin Hyde, an ambitious young cashier for the giant Mutual Life Insurance Company of New York, left that firm to found his own. Life insurance ran in Hyde's family; his father was one of Mutual's top salesmen and would sell many policies for Equitable. Hyde organized his new firm as a joint-stock company, enlisting his friends to help sell shares. William Alexander, a lawyer and minor politician whom Hyde knew through their mutual association with the First Presbyterian Church of New York, was chosen as the firm's first president, with Hyde running its day-to-day affairs through the office of vice-president.

Equitable got off to a good start, selling 769 policies worth a total of more than $2.6 million in its first year. Business boomed during the Civil War, as the ravages of armed conflict impressed upon many the wisdom of insuring their lives. In 1865, the last year of the war, the firm had $27.6 million worth of coverage in force. Equitable had begun selling policies overseas almost immediately after its founding. It had an agent in Southeast Asia as early as 1860, and over the next two decades it established its presence elsewhere in the Far East, in Europe, the Middle East, South America, and Canada.

William Alexander died in 1874 and was succeeded by Henry Baldwin Hyde. Business continued to skyrocket during Hyde's active stewardship, and in 1886 Equitable surpassed Mutual to become the largest life insurance company in the world. That year, it sold $111.5 million worth of policies, giving it a total of $411.8 million of coverage in force. During those boom year, the firm could boast of having among its directors Ulysses S. Grant and financier John Jacob Astor.

Henry Hyde retired in 1898 and died the next year. He was succeeded by his close friend James Alexander, nephew of William Alexander; Hyde's son James Hazen Hyde became vice president. Besides sharing their family affiliations with Equitable, both were men of culture and devoted Europhiles. They both spent much of their time in Paris, and, not coincidentally, the firm intensified its French operations in the first few years of the new century. Both men, however, also set into motion events that presented Equitable with its first major crisis.

It started in January 1905, when James Hyde threw a lavish coming-out party for his niece. It was covered heavily in the society pages and rumors circulated through the press that it had been paid for with company funds. The resulting controversy, aggravated by a power struggle between Hyde and Alexander over the role of Alexander's son in the firm, led the directors to commission an internal review of its management practices. The report, presented in May, found sloppy management and financial irregularities on the part of Equitable officers and lax oversight by its directors, and recommended immediate and radical reorganization. Given these findings, Hyde had little choice but to sell his substantial holdings in the firm. He found a buyer in financier Thomas Ryan, who persuaded the directors to elect his associate Paul Morton, who had been secretary of the navy under Theodore Roosevelt, as chairman. Ryan then got George Westinghouse, former President Grover Cleveland, and New York Appeals Court Judge Morgan O'Brien to act as trustees and administer Ryan's share of the firm.

Paul Morton's first acts as chairman of Equitable were to secure the resignations of all of its officers, including Alexander and Hyde, and appoint himself president. His presence helped restore public confidence in Equitable, but his reign lasted only five years; he died suddenly in 1911 and was succeeded by retired judge William Day. During Day's tenure, Equitable amended its charter and became a mutual company—that is, one in which the policyholders and not the shareholders have the right to elect its directors. Proposals for mutualization had surfaced as part of the fallout from the scandals of 1905; the idea was later taken up by J. P. Morgan, who bought Thomas Ryan's shares in 1909, and it was finally pressed home by industrialist Coleman DuPont, who bought the shares in turn from Morgan's estate in 1915.

World War I did not affect Equitable very much, except to inspire it to invest heavily in war bonds. The influenza epidemic of 1918, however, cost the firm about $8 million in death claims. After the war, the economic disruption in Europe, combined with generally higher mortality rates abroad and laws and tax rates that the firm considered to be onerous, inspired Equitable to discontinue all foreign operations. The process was a drawn-out one, but by 1925 the firm was selling only a few policies outside the United States.

The 1920s were boom years for Equitable, as they were for the nation as a whole. In 1929 the firm booked more than $1 billion worth of new policies and had $6.8 billion worth of coverage in force. William Day retired in 1927, citing ill health, and was succeeded by Thomas Parkinson, who would see Equitable through the Great Depression and World War II. During the Depression, the firm suffered a steady decline in business. It also filled its investment portfolio with government bonds, since other kinds of securities were hard to find and risky when they could be found. Because of its investments in mortgages, Equitable also came into possession of a number of farms during this time as borrowers defaulted. It sold most of these properties during World War II, once food and land prices began to turn up again.

World War II had little effect on Equitable. As it had during World War I, the firm authorized a policy rider that restricted coverage against death in war or aviation mishaps. The sudden splurge in government borrowing that sustained the U.S. war effort and the consequent low yields to be had from government bonds did prompt a change in Equitable's investment policy. In 1942 the firm took its first plunge into large-scale housing development, building a series of apartment complexes in Brooklyn. It followed this in 1946 with another series of apartment buildings in the Bronx.

Parkinson stepped down as president and chief executive officer in 1953 and was succeeded by Ray Murphy, who also became chairman in 1956. The next year, he relinquished the CEO's job to James Oates Jr. a lawyer and one-time utilities executive. In 1959 Equitable marked its centennial with a gala celebration at New York's Madison Square Garden. At the end of its first hundred years, the firm had nearly $10 billion worth of assets and $34.4 billion of insurance in force, making it one of the largest insurance companies of any kind in the nation. Ironically, that year also saw the death of James Hazen Hyde, who had been living in Paris in self-imposed exile since selling his share of the firm.

Under Oates's stewardship, Equitable became known during the 1960s as an insurance company with a social conscience Beginning in 1962, the firm began a job-training program for school dropouts in New York in an attempt to address the problem of hardcore minority unemployment. The idea originated with Oates, who was serving on President Kennedy's Committee on Youth Employment at the time. In 1968 Equitable pledged $60 million to an industry-wide drive to finance the rehabilitation of housing units in urban slums. The firm also invested in Columbia, Maryland, a city developed during the late 1960s on the "new town" model, an urban planning concept intended to create self-sufficient communities of manageable size.

Oates retired in 1969 and was succeeded by J. Henry Smith, who had first given thought to entering the insurance business during his senior year in college, after chatting with an Equitable salesman who had sold a policy to his father. Equitable began to diversify during Smith's tenure. In 1973 it acquired Informatics, a California-based computer systems company. The next year, it entered the field of property and casualty insurance when it acquired Houston General Insurance, Traders & General Insurance, and Associated Employers General Agency from an insurance holding company, W.R. Berkeley. Smith retired in 1975 and was succeeded by Coy Eklund, and the trend toward diversification continued. In 1976 Equitable joined with Newmont Mining Company, The Williams Companies, Fluor Corporation, and Bechtel to form a consortium that bought Peabody Coal Company from Kennecott Copper. That same year, the firm joined an industrywide move toward investing heavily in real estate, when it acquired 17 buildings as part of the self-liquidation of Tishman Realty and Construction. In 1977 it acquired six hotels from Marriott, bringing the total worth of its real estate holdings to more than $1.3 billion.

Equitable was gradually metamorphosing into a fully diversified financial services company. Two developments that occured later in the decade, however, threatened to block that progress. A minor controversy swirled around the firm in 1975 when the Department of Justice filed a conflict-of-interest suit against Eklund over his directorship of Chase Manhattan Bank, out of concern that he might be tempted to give Chase Manhattan preferential treatment in investing Equitable premiums. Eklund finally resolved the dispute in 1978 when he announced that he would not seek re-election to his bank post. In 1979 the firm was forced to lay off 550 employees because of sharply rising labor costs and increased competition from young, up-and-coming competitors. The move, which came despite a record earnings year in 1978, was a radical departure from the firm's long tradition of loyalty to its employees and dealt a serious blow to staff morale. Lower productivity, unionization, and discrimination suits all loomed.

To deal with these threats to its financial performance while maintaining its position as the nation's third-largest life insurance company, Equitable pursued an apparently paradoxical course of divestiture on the one hand and expansion and diversification on the other. In 1980 it sold Houston General Insurance to Japanese giant Tokio Marine and Fire; it also sold its Toronto-based subsidiary Heritage Life Assurance to Unicorp Financial, a Canadian insurance holding company. In 1981 it sold Equitable General Insurance to GEICO Corporation.

On the other hand, Equitable continued its push into real estate. In 1982 it bought Equitable Life Mortgage Realty Trust, the real estate investment trust (REIT) that it managed. Buying REITs was widely considered to be a cheap way of acquiring large pools of property. The firm also announced plans to build a new headquarters skyscraper in Manhattan despite softening demand for office space. Equitable's real estate development activity was given additional impetus by a 1983 change in New York state insurance law allowing insurance companies to engage in almost any financial service other than banking. That year, it acquired Kravco, a Pennsylvania-based shopping center developer, and 50% of Continental Companies, a Miami-based hotel developer. In 1984 it bought 19 shopping centers from Iowa-based General Growth Properties. This last move gave the firm more than 100 shopping center properties and brought the total worth of its real estate assets to $21 billion.

Equitable took fullest advantage of the more liberal laws under which it could operate; in 1985, it acquired an 89% interest in the prominent Wall Street securities firm Donaldson, Lufkin & Jenrette (DLJ). Under the terms of the merger, DLJ founder, chairman, and CEO Richard Jenrette became vice chairman of Equitable. Two years later, he became chairman upon the retirement of Robert F. Froehlke. Jenrette's rapid promotion reflected the increasing importance of investment and other non-insurance operations to Equitable and to insurance companies in general at a time when people were buying life insurance for investment purposes at least as much as for protection.

Equitable also continued to divest in the late 1980s. In 1987 the firm sold Equitable Life Leasing to mortgage banker Lomas & Nettleton. In 1988 it sold National Integrity Life Insurance and Integrity Life Insurance to Australia-based National Mutual Life Assurance of Australasia. Equitable had not yet done a sufficient job of cutting costs and improving financial performance to suit the firm's directors. John Carter, who succeeded Coy Eklund as CEO in 1984, retired in 1990 amidst this displeasure at the relatively young age of 55, and was replaced by Richard Jenrette. Chief financial officer Glen Gettier also resigned and was replaced by Thomas Kirwan, previously chief financial officer of the firm's insurance operations.

In December 1990, Equitable announced its intention to proceed with the development of a plan to demutualize. Equitable would be the first major life insurance company to explore the use of New York State's new demutualization law, which took effect in 1988, as a means of increasing its capital base. The formal demutualization plan must first be approved by Equitable's board and requires the approval of the New York State Insurance Department and certain classes of policyholders. It is a lengthy and complex process that requires a year to 18 months to be implemented.

In making the announcement, Jenrette stated that the decision to seek new capital is part of a three-step program to strengthen Equitable. The first step was a reduction in Equitable's annual operating expenses by more than $150 million, a program carried out earlier in the year. The second step was to strengthen management, most notably through the addition of Joseph Melone as president. Equitable hoped that Melone's background as head of Prudential's field operations would complement Jenrette's financial background.

Principal Subsidiaries: Equitable Variable Life Insurance Company; The Equitable of Colorado, Inc.; Equico Securities, Inc.; Equitable Seimei Hoken (Japan); Traditional Equinet Business Corporation of New York; Pension Financial Management Group; Equitable Alliance Capital Management Corporation; Donaldson, Lufkin & Jenrette, Inc.; Equico Capital Corporation; Equitable Capital Management Corporation; Equitable Real Estate Investment Management, Inc.; Equitable Agri-Business, Inc.

Further Reading: Burley, R. Carlyle, *The Equitable Life Assurance Society of the United States: 1859–1964*, New York, Appleton-Century-Crofts, 1964; "Why Equitable Life Looks Good But Feels Bad," *Business Week,* March 26, 1979.

—Douglas Sun

FIREMAN'S FUND INSURANCE COMPANY

777 San Marin Drive
Novato, California 94998
U.S.A.
(415) 899-2000
Fax: (415) 899-3600

Wholly Owned Subsidiary of Allianz AG Holding
Incorporated: 1863
Employees: 10,146
Assets: $11.72 billion

Fireman's Fund Insurance Company offers a wide range of property and casualty insurance nationwide. In addition to fire insurance, Fireman's offers homeowner policies, automobile insurance, entertainment-industry coverage, inland marine, marine, workers' compensation, and a variety of commercial insurance products through some 6,000 independent agents. In 1991 Fireman's Fund became the U.S. arm of Allianz AG Holding, a German insurer.

Originally a goldrush town, by the 1860s San Francisco, California, boasted an economy whose growth was hampered by the frequent fires that swept through its wooden buildings. Volunteer firefighters worked at will, with no remuneration for their risks. Both these factors made well-established insurance companies wary of offering coverage to San Francisco–based businesses. In 1863 a ship's captain named William Holdredge conceived and created Fireman's Fund Insurance Company to insure San Franciscans against fire. Holdredge knew the success of his company would depend on his ability to reassure customers that their property could survive a fire. Thus, in order to motivate San Francisco's firefighters, Holdredge established a retirement fund for the firemen and financed it with 10% of his company's annual net profit. Holdredge underscored his business philosophy by calling his new firm the Fireman's Fund Insurance Company.

The young company grew apace and soon began to look for growth opportunities. In 1866 a state regulation allowing fire insurance companies to include marine underwriting was passed. Fireman's participated in this new activity eagerly. When in the autumn of 1871, 32 New England whaleships lingered too long in the inhospitable Arctic Ocean and were crushed by the ice, Fireman's Fund made its move. Bankruptcy followed for several whaling concerns, and many Atlantic coast insurance companies refused further coverage for this industry. Fireman's Fund agreed to cover the whalers, simply stipulating that all whaling ships leave the Arctic area by September 15. This requirement assured the marine division a healthy profit from grateful whalers desperate for insurance.

Also in 1871 the Great Chicago Fire resulted in over half a million dollars in claims, which wiped out Fireman's Fund's capital. A $250,000 assessment was leveled on company stockholders, and the company paid all claims within 60 days. This was the first of three devastating fires. At the end of 1872 a massive fire ravaged Boston, causing $189,589 in losses to Fireman's Fund. The ashes blew away 32 less-stable insurance companies, but Fireman's survived by reorganizing and reducing its capital. Yet another test came in 1875, when the entire mining town of Virginia City, Nevada, burned to the ground and Fireman's was left with more claims to pay.

Despite these liabilities, insurance remained a profitable business. By 1882, the company had gross assets of $1.32 million and had paid $4 million in claims. It also had a fine reputation, which helped it to absorb 11 competitors more seriously damaged by the catastrophic losses of this period, between 1889 and 1900. This growth also led the company to open offices in New York, Georgia, Hong Kong, Shanghai, and the Philippines. By the end of 1905, Fireman's Fund had 6,000 independent agents, and by January 1906 it was offering the country's first nationwide auto insurance.

In April 1906, San Francisco was hit by an earthquake that took hundreds of lives and leveled thousands of acres. Fireman's headquarters and records were destroyed. Estimates completed a week after the disaster put client claims at $11.2 million; the company had assets of approximately $7 million.

The shortfall was covered by assessing stockholders $300 per share. Because all records were destroyed, Fireman's Fund simply took each claimant's word as evidence of coverage. The company settled 8,600 claims without litigation by paying half in cash and half in new stock.

As part of the plan, after all earthquake claims had been paid, Fireman's Fund Insurance Company distributed its remaining assets to stockholders and went out of business. It was succeeded immediately by Fireman's Corporation, a newly formed company whose leadership was identical to that of Fireman's Fund Insurance Company. The corporation, whose debt-free status allowed it to handle all business not connected with the earthquake, took over all of its predecessor's ongoing business and its agency network.

The new Fireman's Fund prospered, taking on many patriotic activities during World War I. Company executives worked actively with government officials, giving fire-prevention advice for possible enemy targets such as bridges, factories, railways, and warehouses. The firm took all the war-risk business available, receiving appropriately high premiums for the high-risk business. As a result, company assets more than doubled between 1914 and 1919.

The postwar years saw many new developments. Among them was a burgeoning movie industry that brought opportunity fairly pounding at the insurance industry's door. The company began to underwrite film productions, whose paper, wood, and fabric sets made fire a real danger. As the movie industry became more sophisticated, the escalating costs of delays, contract disputes, and possible injuries to personnel made insurance indispensable. Props became more elaborate, with a corresponding rise in their replacement value. Some, like a full-size replica of the H.M.S. *Bounty*, sailed through movies unscathed, but the insurance company paid dearly for others, like the Los Angeles–born polar bear that ambled from the edge of an ice floe and vanished during filming in Alaska.

In addition to fire and entertainment-industry insurance, the company issued marine, tornado, war-risk, explosion, earthquake, automobile, luggage, sprinkler-leakage, and use and occupancy coverage during the 1920s. Fireman's also underwrote more unusual ventures, like the 1927 construction of Charles Lindbergh's *Spirit of St. Louis.*

Corporate expansion was also a feature of the late 1920s, when Fireman's Fund formed three new subsidiaries. The Occidental Indemnity Company was organized in 1927, to provide workers' compensation for longshoremen. Next came the Occidental Insurance Company, and in 1930, the Fireman's Fund Indemnity Company.

In 1929 the company increased its capital by the issue of 100,000 shares, to be sold at $50 per share. This issue added $2.5 million, bringing net capital to $7.5 million.

Despite the stock market crash in October, Fireman's Fund's California income for 1929 was $4 million. Although the years between 1930 and 1934 were lean ones, total assets by the end of 1936 were $3.7 million, and the company had 1,500 employees and 10,000 agents. Between 1933 and 1937 Fireman's Fund insured part of the Golden Gate Bridge construction, against the advice of critics, who predicted imminent collapse.

World War II did not disrupt Fireman's Fund's progress. Fireman's Fund President James Crafts led the company into the 1950s capably, and in 1954 the company showed a net profit of $18 million before taxes. A year later things began to change; in 1956 the industry as a whole had a total underwriting loss of $4.8 billion.

Partly at fault were stock market changes that affected insurance company portfolios. Spiraling inflation also played its part. The major factor, however, was a series of unforeseen disasters: several tornadoes and hurricanes; a marine collision off Nantucket, Massachusetts, involving the ships *Andrea Doria* and *Stockholm;* and an air collision in which two aircraft went down over the Grand Canyon in Arizona. Each of these tragedies brought heavy underwriting losses in its wake.

During the 1950s an increasing number of vehicles appeared on the roads, with a concomitant rise in the number of accidents. This situation had spurred the states of Massachusetts and New York to make auto insurance compulsory. Almost 30 other states were considering the same law. At the same time, new direct-writing auto insurance companies, profiting through both the rise in auto ownership and new antitrust legislation, were offering less expensive coverage by eliminating agents, who acted as middlemen. The amount of agent-handled auto insurance business was cut by almost a quarter during the mid-1950s.

To meet inflation and decreasing business, insurers raised rates. Customers of the company's 128 district offices around the country were cautioned that the value of their property had risen, and that premiums must rise accordingly. In 1957 Fireman's Fund moved to a new headquarters, which soon housed a new data processing system designed to streamline operations.

Buttressed by a cautious investment strategy, these measures helped the company get back on track. By the end of 1962 the number of premiums written in all divisions came to a total of $306 million. The company also made several profitable additions to its business during the early 1960s, including the Fireman's Fund Insurance Company of Texas, incorporated in 1962, and the American Insurance Company plus its two subsidiaries, American Automobile Insurance Company and The Associated Indemnity Company, acquired in 1963.

President James F. Crafts became chairman of the board in 1962, handing the presidency to Fred H. Merrill. By this time, Fireman's Fund's coverage included disability; individual, group, and franchises; accident and health programs; and hospital, surgical, and other benfits. More unusual ventures included insuring Michelangelo's *Pieta* during its journey from Rome to the New York World's Fair and the *Apollo XI* command module used in the first moon landing, on its tour of all 50 state capitals.

In 1966 Fireman's Fund Insurance Company became a holding company called Fund American Companies, passing its former name on to a California subsidiary of Fund American. In November 1968 Fund American Companies and its subsidiaries were acquired by American Express Company through an exchange of stock valued at about $500 million. The Fund American Companies was dissolved and Fund American president Merrill and chairman Crafts were elected directors of American Express; Merrill also served as chairman of its executive committee.

Known as Fireman's Fund American Insurance Companies after the merger, and eventually as Fireman's Fund again, the American Express subsidiary allowed customers to pay for their insurance with their American Express cards. In 1975 Fireman's Fund became a 7% partner in a lucrative new Saudi Arabian insurance company, the Red Sea Insurance Company. Two years later Fireman's insurance premiums reached $2 billion.

In 1977 the company became the subject of a sex-bias suit filed by ten present and past women employees. The class-action suit affected 20,000 women workers. Settlement, reached in 1979, ordered the company to pay legal fees and $19,500 to each of seven original claimants. The court's decree also specified that certain percentages of graded job vacancies were to be filled by qualified women for five years.

The late 1970s were so lucrative for the insurance industry that many new competitors appeared, and Fireman's Fund was forced to cut premium prices in order to keep its market share. The result was an industry underwriting loss of $34 billion between 1979 and 1983. Fireman's Fund suffered along with the rest. A 1982 decision to strengthen market share by cutting prices proved to be a costly mistake; profits plunged from $244 million in 1982 to $30 million in 1983. In 1983, American Express removed Fireman's Fund's two top executives, replacing them with William M. McCormick and American Express president Sanford I. Weill. McCormick and Weill laid off 1,600 employees and sold unprofitable businesses in Canada and Singapore.

The ABC television network chose Fireman's Fund to insure its participation in the 1984 Olympics. The cost of

ABC's $200 million worth of protection against political boycotts was not disclosed.

The price-cutting debacle and subsequent losses led American Express to contribute $230 million to Fireman's Fund's reserves in December 1983, but this was not enough; a capital contribution of $200 million the following November did not remedy the situation either. By the end of 1984 the company had sold seven real estate properties to a European investment group. The $145 million sale, which included the company's headquarters building in Novato, California, specified ten-year lease-back agreements in all cases, with options for further 15-year leases.

These measures were not enough to keep the merger between Fireman's Fund and American Express afloat. In 1985 Fireman's Fund had a net loss of $87 million on revenue, and American Express—whose own earnings were being siphoned off by Fireman's Fund—decided to offer Fireman's Fund's shares to the public. American Express replaced the retiring Weill—who had been chairman and CEO of Fireman's Fund Company's holding company, Fireman's Fund Corporation—with GEICO Corporation Chairman John J. Byrne in 1985. McCormick remained at Fireman's Fund as chairman and CEO. In the 1985 transactions, Fireman's Fund Corporation, with its subsidiaries Fireman's Fund Insurance Companies was spun off as an independent company.

In September 1985, American Express offered 49% of its Fireman's Fund shares, after selling Fireman's Fund's life, accident, and health lines to American Express Travel Related Services for $330 million. A further 6% of its holdings was to go to a newly formed Fireman's Fund employee stock-ownership company, and the remaining 45% was to be held by American Express for a year, giving Fireman's Fund a chance to buy them back. These shares, however, were actually held until 1989, when Fireman's Fund exchanged a new issue of preferred stock, valued at $342 million, for 9.5 million common shares held by American Express.

In 1986 Fireman's Fund bought the third-largest U.S. mortgage banker, Manufacturers Hanover Mortgage Corporation. To provide additional taxable income for any loss by underwriting activities, Fireman's bought the Michigan-based company for $260 million, renaming it the Fireman's Fund Mortgage Corporation.

Also a product of the mid-1980s was a decision to leave the state of Massachusetts, in 1987. The company's auto insurance operation in that state had been only marginally profitable since the 1950s. Terms of the agreement included a payment to the state's auto pool for hard-to-insure motorists of $45 million for the year, plus another similar payment for 1988. In 1987, McCormick left the company, and Byrne became CEO of both the parent and Fireman's Fund Insurance Companies.

In 1989 Hurricane Hugo, an earthquake in California, and an oil refinery fire in Texas all proved expensive for the insurance industry. Fireman's annual financial summary reflected these heavy drains: $2.7 billion in earned premiums, showing a downturn from almost $3 billion only a year earlier.

At the end of 1989, company interests in investments and in commercial insurance led to a name change. The holding company once again became Fund American Companies, Inc., a title last used in 1966. The insurance subsidiary kept the name Fireman's Fund Insurance Companies.

In 1990 sale of the company to Europe's largest insurer, Allianz AG Holding, of Germany, for $3.3 billion, was announced. The sale was completed on January 2, 1991. The price, which analysts called about 175% of Fireman's Fund's book value, allowed Allianz large-scale entry into the lucrative U.S. insurance market. Terms of the transaction included Allianz's acquisition of all Fireman's Fund Insurance stock, plus its portfolio of bonds and short-term investments. Fireman's common stock portfolio was repurchased by Fund American for $2.2 billion. In 1991, stockholders approved the dissolution of Fund American over the next three to five years.

Principal Subsidiaries: Fireman's Fund Corporation; Fireman's Fund Insurance Company; The American Insurance Company; American Automobile Insurance Company; Associated Indemnity Corporation; Fireman's Fund Insurance Company of Georgia; Fireman's Fund Insurance Company of Hawaii; Fireman's Fund Insurance Company of Iowa; Fireman's Fund Insurance Company of Louisiana; Fireman's Fund Insurance Company of Ohio; Fireman's Fund Insurance Company of Wisconsin; Interstate National Corporation; Interstate Fire and Casualty Company; Chicago Insurance Company; Interstate Indemnity Company; Fireman's Fund Insurance Company of Texas; National Surety Corporation; Fireman's Fund Indemnity Corporation; Fireman's Fund Insurance Company of New Jersey; Warner Insurance Company; San Francisco Reinsurance Company; San Francisco Insurance Company (UK) Limited; Southern Fund Insurance Corporation; Standard General Agency, Incorporated; Fireman's Fund Mutual Insurance Company; American Standard Lloyd's Insurance Company.

Further Reading: Todd, Frank Morton, *A Romance of Insurance: Being a History of the Fireman's Fund Insurance Company of San Francisco,* San Francisco, Fireman's Fund Insurance Company, 1929; Crafts, James F., "A Romance of Insurance," New York, Newcomen Society in North America, 1951; Bronson, William, *Still Flying and Nailed to the Mast: The First Hundred Years of the Fireman's Fund Insurance Company,* Garden City, New York, Doubleday & Company, 1963.

—Gillian Wolf

FIRST EXECUTIVE CORPORATION

11444 West Olympic Boulevard
Los Angeles, California 90064
U.S.A.
(213) 312-1000
Fax: (213) 477-3279

Public Company
Incorporated: 1964
Employees: 1,050
Assets: $19.26 billion
Stock Exchange: NASDAQ

Incorporated in 1969, First Executive Corporation (FE) is a holding company engaged in the life insurance industry through its two principal subsidiaries—the California-based Executive Life Insurance Company (EL) and the Executive Life Insurance Company of New York (EL-NY). Insurance products include immediate and deferred annuities, individual term and whole life, group permanent life, and guaranteed investment contracts.

On the verge of folding in 1974, the company gained notice for innovations that made it into one of the fastest-growing insurers in the industry in the 1980s. First Executive became a top buyer of bonds from Michael Milken, head of the California operation of Drexel Burnham Lambert. This association cost the company much scrutiny as Milken came under federal indictment in 1989, and Drexel went bankrupt in 1990. The loss of public and agent confidence combined with a rocky junk bond market to result in the announcement of an $835.7 million fourth-quarter loss in spring 1990. The consequent subject of Securities and Exchange Commission (SEC) probes, lawsuits, and bad publicity, FE was required to develop a new strategy to fuel growth and win back confidence.

First Executive Corporation is the successor to a corporation formed in 1964. The company acquired 90% of Executive Life Insurance Company, of California, in 1967 and then, in 1968, acquired ICOA Life Insurance, of Salem, Oregon. ICOA then was merged into Executive Life. Later that year the parent company acquired 74% of Executive Life Insurance Company of New York.

In 1969 the company was reorganized as First Executive Corporation. Over the next five years, the company struggled to grow. By 1974, it had an insignificant investment portfolio and was behind on its interest payments, still losing money, and about to default on a $15 million loan. Fred Carr, then a much-publicized mutual fund manager, left his own consulting business to take over the reins of FE. Carr invested some of his own money in the company, renegotiated the loan, and was soon in the CEO seat. Within nine years, FE became one of the fastest-growing insurance firms in the United States.

Born to parents who ran a vegetable stand in Watts, California, and with his college education ended when he was drafted, Carr had worked at jobs that ranged from pumping gas to selling door-to-door by the age of 32, but always was interested in stocks. This interest was confirmed by his rise to prominence on Wall Street in the 1960s.

At FE, in 1974, Carr had room for innovation. FE's insurance business was small, with growth possibilities for new policies, clients, and products, and the small investment portfolio was not committed to low-yielding long-term investments. In the mid-1970s, the life insurance industry was changing. Until then, the best-selling products were whole life, a combined insurance and savings plan with modest interest rates, and term insurance, which provides coverage in the event of death. As interest rates increased in the 1970s, small insurers offered new products with higher returns than whole life. This business made them competitive with large insurers, who could not offer such products without running the risk of having customers cash in old policies.

In 1975 FE offered single premium deferred annuities (SPDAs), a product best suited for a company short of capital. What began as a defensive strategy became the company's fortune; sales of SPDAs went from $11.6 million in 1976 to $1.1 billion by 1981. The policy required just one payment, which earned tax-deferred interest for the duration of the annuity. Policyholders could withdraw money at any time and were guaranteed high first-year yields, with rates above a stated minimum thereafter. The policies were irresistible to investors—especially in 1981 and 1982 when rates on the annuities reached 15%. FE kept its staff small by working with independent agents. Company revenues bloomed from $727 million in 1977 to $1.6 billion by 1982.

With the earnings from SPDA sales, First Executive was able to build its investment portfolio. In 1979 FE introduced another product—irreplaceable life. A variation on the whole life policies, irreplaceable policies have lower premiums and higher cash-accumulation yields. Less flexible than universal life policies, they targeted upper-income buyers for whom the appeal was investment more than insurance. The lower premiums and higher yields were afforded by FE's portfolio, then generating higher yields than the major insurers. By the time SPDA sales slowed in 1983—in part because of lower interest rates and the 1982 Tax Equity and Fiscal Responsibility Act, which affected the penalties and tax-interest conditions of the SPDAs—FE's irreplaceable life policies were top sellers.

At the same time, FE's invested assets were profiting from innovation; its growth rate more than doubled between 1976 and 1982. A good portion of these were short-term investments and an unusually large amount was also high-risk. By the end of 1982, more than 15% of FE's portfolio was invested in the B- and BB-rated bonds known as junk bonds. Most of these bonds were issued by little-known companies.

This investment allowed FE to offer higher yields on policies, soon to become a costly controversy. FE was one of Drexel Burnham Lambert's largest customers. Carr had close ties to the firm's high-yield-bond department head, Michael Milken, and Drexel subleased office space from FE. Both Drexel and Milken later would be involved in an extensive criminal investigation.

In 1982 Charter Corporation, the largest seller of SPDAs, abandoned the annuities after a rush by worried policyholders; the second-largest seller, Baldwin-United, went bankrupt, leaving FE in the lead in sales. That year, FE acquired Bay Colony Life Insurance Company of Delaware, which was renamed First Delaware Life Insurance Company. SPDA sales slowed, but the company's life insurance sales increased tenfold between 1981 and 1983. Clients were reassured by the 12.6% yield that FE's portfolio averaged during the first half of 1983, compared with an industry average of 9.9%. Policy surrenders remained at a minimum. First Executive was writing more new policies than industry notables Aetna and Connecticut Mutual, but Carr's unconventional investment practices attracted the attention of insurance regulators.

FE further expanded in 1984 by the purchase of Lincoln Liberty Life Insurance Company in Nebraska. In the same year, the New York State Insurance Department fined FE's New York subsidiary $100,000 for not cooperating with examiners. In 1987, FE paid a $250,000 fine when EL-NY pleaded guilty to violating eight sections of insurance law. It was the biggest fine ever imposed by the state on an insurance company. In addition, FE gave the subsidiary a $151.5 million cash infusion.

The fines and infusion primarily were related to problems with the company's surplus relief reinsurance arrangements. Reinsurance treaties are a standard part of the insurance industry; they essentially reduce risk by sharing it. A company reduces its liabilities by transferring future claims obligations to another insurer in return for a fee. This action also increases the company's surplus by reducing the amount of reserves required against future claims on issued policies. Treaties are subject to regulations as the resultant accounting of capital is integral to a company's ability to pay claims and support the issuance of new contracts. Because of EL's risky investments, regulations called for it to have a higher reserve than most. In the 1987 probe, the New York regulatory agency rejected nearly all of EL-NY's surplus relief from reinsurance contracts because of a circular arrangement made with companies that had connections to FE and letters of credit backed by the company's own assets. Additionally, the company failed to receive regulatory approvals, and file certain forms; it took credit for some treaties that never were executed. The industry regulators contended that the company had been undercapitalized for three years.

The New York inquiries sparked similar investigations into EL in California, FE's biggest unit. Within a week of the New York unit's fine, California insurance regulators were contesting $188 million worth of EL's reinsurance contracts, charging that the company was not complying with a 1985 order. The setback to FE was considerable; it relied heavily on reinsurance to support expansion by freeing up capital. In addition to the bad press of the regulatory investigations affecting sales, reinsurers began to command higher fees among other assurances.

Other problems were gaining momentum. The junk bond market was falling apart, and in 1987 junk bonds accounted for more than 40% of FE's assets. First Executive was still one of Drexel's largest customers, and Milken held stock in two companies in which FE was a major shareholder. The October stock plunge shook things up further; by December 1987, FE's $13 billion bond portfolio had $675 million worth of paper losses and its stock portfolio had $74 million in paper losses. FE put its New York unit up for sale.

FE's total assets, which had grown 65% in 1986, grew only 14% in 1987. Its annuity sales fell 42%. Although sales dropped, FE's policy renewal rates were still among the industry's best. In addition to the shadow of its association with Drexel and Milken and flagging sales and market uncertainty, FE was confronted with stiffer insurance regulations in 1988. The revision of tax laws by Congress eliminated many of the advantages of deferred annuities. Insurance regulators in California and New York tighted rules governing surplus relief reinsurance treaties. In 1987, FE was only able to buy half of the surplus relief reinsurance it was seeking. Accordingly, First Executive had to de-emphasize the sale of capital-intensive SPDAs, once its mainstay. It also had to reduce its enticing interest rate promises and rely less on high-yield, low-rated bonds. New York state regulators now limited the percentage of junk bond investments allowed in an insurance company's portfolio to 20%. In 1988, FE injected $345 million of new capital into EL. It later was charged that the California unit was insolvent on a statutory basis at the end of 1987.

In 1989 the Drexel specter expanded. Milken faced a 98-count federal indictment for securities crimes, and the SEC probe extended to Drexel's customers. At the same time, Congress was examining FE's role in the 1985 takeover of Pacific Lumber Company by a Houston, Texas, investor, who used Pacific's pension plan surplus to pay for the takeover. The pension plan then was terminated and replaced by an FE annuity. FE bought $70 million worth of bonds floated in the takeover and at issue was the $37 million contract for annuities to cover Pacific employees that was alleged to have been improperly won.

Carr contended that his enterprise was still healthy; debt was low and expenses were at a minimum. Cutbacks of capital-intensive annuities left more profit in the coffers, and FE pointed out that while revenues dropped $500 million from 1987 to 1988, earnings increased by about $28 million.

In July 1989 Executive Life and Drexel agreed to pay $30 million to settle a class-action lawsuit. The suit involved 4,200 investors who charged that they had been cheated in a tax-shelter scheme. The transaction involved notes purchased by Drexel, later sold to EL, on interests originally purchased by Hollywood, California, businessman Gerald Schulman, in a series of fraudulent transactions, at 80% below their value.

In December 1989 a transaction came to light that had taken place a year earlier involving six newly formed firms through which FE substantially reduced its stated junk bond holdings. The six companies were all incorporated on the same day, with the same address, and with the same CEO—a former consultant to EL. To each company, FE gave a cache of junk bonds and some cash, and received co-issued bonds in return. The six individual investments each were below the disclosure threshold. The arrangement allowed FE to alchemize $700 million in junk bonds into $800 million worth of securities. With a lessened reserve obligation, FE's balance sheet appeared sounder than it was. This transaction was later reversed by the California Insurance Department.

In January 1990, FE disclosed plans to take a $515 million charge against fourth-quarter earnings because of write-offs in its junk bond portfolio. It later came to light that, even after the write-offs, the bonds were worth $1.4 billion less than the company paid for them.

Earlier in the month, the impending $460 million sale of the New York unit collapsed. The buyer was unable to arrange junk bond financing. Then, in February 1990, Drexel declared bankruptcy amid the growing turmoil of the junk bond market. About 45% of FE's assets were in junk bonds at that moment; junk bonds were trading at about 60% to 80% of their face value. Customers began cashing in policies, creating more cash-reserve worry, and the SEC began to investigate FE's financial condition to see whether it had mislead its investors. The value of the company's stock dropped by almost 70%.

California's department of insurance installed two full-time examiners at EL to monitor the unit during a rush of policy redemptions and public worry in the wake of the junk bond market plunge. In April 1990 FE posted an $835.7 million fourth-quarter loss. Policy surrenders in the first two months of 1990 totalled $559 million. The company also confirmed that the SEC had opened formal investigations of possible violations of security laws since 1988. A number of civil lawsuits and state actions were filed alleging securities violations related to rights of offering. Other investigations were ongoing by the Pension Benefit Guaranty Corporation and the Labor Department regarding FE's pension terminations. In 1991 FE was involved in a number of federal and state stockholder lawsuits, charging entrenchment, mismanagement, material misstatements, and excessive involvement with Drexel, among other things. In May the company's New York unit was fined $25,000 and reprimanded for "sloppy" record keeping during the 1980s that prevented any accurate determination of company reserves.

Clearly, First Executive faced monumental challenges. The company needed a new growth strategy to fund the capital reserve necessary to rebuild its insurance business. First Executive Corporation faced an unstable bond market in 1990, and public investors were apprehensive.

Principal Subsidiaries: Executive Life Insurance Company; Executive Life Insurance Company of New York; First Delaware Life Insurance Company; First Stratford Life Insurance Company; Lincoln Liberty Life Insurance Company.

Further Reading: "Fred Carr's second hurrah," *Financial World,* March 15, 1983; Hector, Gary, "A Go-Go Insurer Adds Zest to Life," *Fortune,* March 5, 1984; Weberman, Ben, "Fred Carr is Back," *Forbes,* September 24, 1984; Hilder, David, B. "Carr Suffers Slings, Arrows of First Executive's Fortune," *The Wall Street Journal,* March 13, 1987; Gilbert, Nick, "A Closer Look at First Executive," *Financial World,* May 5, 1987; Rose, Frederick, "First Executive Posts a 4th-Quarter Loss of $835.7 Million; SEC Probe Disclosed," *The Wall Street Journal,* April 3, 1990.

—Carol I. Keeley

General Accident

GENERAL ACCIDENT PLC

Pitheavlis
Perth
United Kingdom PH2 ONH
(0738) 21202
Fax: (0738) 21843

Public Company
Incorporated: 1885 as General Accident & Employers Liability Assurance Association Ltd.
Employees: 30,000
Assets: £8.12 billion (US$13.11 billion)
Stock Exchange: London

General Accident is the holding company for General Accident Fire and Life Assurance Corporation, which is the third-largest composite insurance group in the United Kingdom. The company was founded in Perth, Scotland, in 1885 at the height of the Industrial Revolution, when Great Britain had become known as the "workshop of the world."

British preeminence as an industrial power had been purchased at a high price. Unsafe factory machines and hazardous working conditions led to the death and maiming of thousands of British workers. In response to trade union pressure, the British government introduced the Employers' Liability Act of 1880. This act made employers liable to workmen involved in certain on-the-job accidents.

In 1885, a group of Perth entrepreneurs saw the insurance potential of this new legislation. In return for an annual premium, the group would safeguard employers against any liability arising from employee accidents. The importance of employers' liability insurance to the new company was reflected in the company's original name, General Accident & Employers Liability Assurance Association. The first board of directors of General Accident (GA) came from diverse backgrounds. Chairman George Kyd was an agricultural auctioneer and land owner. Among the directors was a farmer, a doctor, a bank manager, and a brewer.

Premium income from the first 13 months amounted to only £2,833 with claims of £335 and expenses of £1,942. Yet this modest beginning did not inhibit expansion. Beyond the Perth office, GA assigned representatives to London and to Aberdeen and Edinburgh, Scotland. In 1887, 27-year-old Francis Norie-Miller became the chief executive of the company as a result of his appointment as secretary. An insurance innovator with enormous energy, he dominated the management of GA for many years and remained highly influential until retiring as chairman in 1944.

With the appointment of Norie-Miller, 1887 became a landmark year in the company's fortunes. That year the company entered into an arrangement with Malcolm's Diary & Time-Table of Glasgow to insure for £100 passengers killed in railway accidents, on the condition the victim possessed a copy of a Malcolm's time-table or diary. Malcolm's paid a 1¢ premium to GA for every 25 items sold. This GA insurance innovation was the beginning of a lucrative coupon insurance scheme.

Because of diversification into new insurance markets, the company was renamed General Accident Fire and Life Assurance Corporation in 1906. In 1896, GA produced its first prospectus for motor coverage. In 1899, Scottish General Fire Assurance Corporation was incorporated into GA, which now provided both fire and accident coverage. Norie-Miller also established a U.S. office in 1899.

In the first decade of the 20th century GA established overseas branches in Australia, Canada, South Africa, Belgium, France, and Holland. Norie-Miller instituted the home bonus in 1908, whereby five years without a claim earned the insured party a free premium in the sixth year of insurance. From its inception, the motor department made steady progress, including a notable first, the issuance of a policy for the Prince of Wales in 1908.

The steady growth of General Accident was interrupted by the outbreak of World War I in 1914. Many of GA's young employees served in the trenches, and two floors of the London head office were converted for the use of war-refugee services. These refugees included some Belgian employees of the GA office in Antwerp.

The postwar period saw an improvement in the living standards of most Britons and motor-car ownership was no longer a preserve of the rich. In 1924 Norie-Miller introduced a scheme which boosted GA's motor-insurance performance dramatically. In collaboration with Morris Motors, GA arranged that each car sold by that company would have free insurance coverage for one year; the premium to be paid by Morris. This plan had a high claims cost because premiums were not tied to individual risks, but it introduced GA to a large section of the motoring community, and many motorists retained GA, for auto and other types of insurance. The resulting business served GA well in the years which followed, especially after the introduction of the Road Traffic Act in 1930, which made third-party motor insurance compulsory for all drivers. By 1937, General Accident had already issued one million motor policies in Britain.

Following the introduction of the Road Traffic Act, the motor market became attractive not merely for its own sake but also because of the access it offered to growth in other fields of insurance. The structure of the British insurance industry was highly monopolistic. The Fire Offices Committee (FOC), representing the older insurance companies, dominated the fire insurance market. The FOC restricted entry to the market through the manipulation of rates and limits on reinsurance facilities. Denial of entry to one market curbed access to all others. Despite GA's powerful position in the motor market, the company had been excluded from tariff membership and its share of the fire market was correspondingly limited. Observing that the motor market had proven far more difficult for the tariff offices to control than other markets, GA used its motor insurance to expand into areas from which it had been excluded by the FOC.

Throughout the 1930s GA expanded in the United States as well as in Britain. Having issued its first U.S. auto insurance policy in 1911, GA enjoyed a period of prolonged prosperity in the U.S. auto market even during the Depression. The Potomac Insurance Company of Washington, D.C., GA's U.S. subsidiary, increased the firm's involvement in fire insurance. Meanwhile, Francis Norie-Miller, the architect of this U.S. expansion, became chairman of the board of GA in 1933.

With the outbreak of World War II, in 1939, General Accident again curtailed its insurance activities while many of the company's employees served their respective countries. GA's head office in Great Britain lost contact with many of its overseas branches as a result of the German occupation of Europe and the war with Japan in the Pacific. In 1944 Norie-Miller relinquished the chairmanship of GA. Norie-Miller's son, Stanley Norie-Miller, served as chairman from 1951 until 1968.

GA continued to grow during the postwar period, acquiring several new subsidiaries. In the United States GA formed Pennsylvania General Fire Insurance Association in 1963. In Britain GA took over The Yorkshire Insurance Company in 1967. Yorkshire shareholders chose to sell a majority holding to GA despite a higher bid by Phoenix Assurance because of GA's strong standing among insurance investors.

A prolonged period of steady growth enabled GA's assets to reach £1 billion in 1975. By the early 1980s assets were over £3 billion and total premium income was more than £1.5 billion. U.S. operations continued to generate one-third of premium income.

During the 1980s, deregulation of the financial-services industry led to a blurring of the historically rigid boundaries between insurance brokers and insurance companies in the complex British insurance market. These measures and the proposed integration of the European Economic Community in 1992 created an opportunity for enormous growth, but competition among insurers intensified.

In response to this competition, General Accident decided, in 1986, to modify its corporate identity. GA launched an advertising campaign which presented a new image, attempting to combine both professionalism and humanity.

GA also committed itself to an increasingly acquisitive strategy. By the end of the 1980s, GA had acquired over 500 estate agencies. With this policy GA enlarged its housing insurance business and created new channels for the distribution of other insurance products, especially lucrative life policies. The move into the estate-agency business was not initially successful: the depressed British mortgage market during the late 1980s and into 1990 subjected GA to considerable losses.

GA also assumed a heavy financial burden when it bought out NZI Corporation, a New Zealand–based insurance and banking firm, in July 1988. NZI was to be the platform from which GA launched an expansion into the Pacific market, especially the relatively untapped markets of Korea and Taiwan. But the poor state of NZI's banking arm resulted in substantial and embarrassing losses for GA. In the first six months of 1989 alone, NZI lost £29.3 million. During the late 1980s, the once-profitable U.S. insurance market also developed problems. Large awards against drivers as well as punitive regulation of premium rates by many state governments let to severe losses in the motor market. GA's pretax losses in Massachusetts grew from $4.5 million in 1984 to $13 million in 1986. In 1988 these losses prompted GA to withdraw entirely from Massachusetts.

Worldwide, weather conditions caused massive losses through damage claims in the late 1980s. The October 1987 hurricane that swept southern Britian and the North American Hurricanes Gilbert and Hugo in 1988 and 1989 were followed, in early 1990, by a severe storm in Great Britain. The storm cost GA an estimated £48 million in claims. Life assurance premiums have also risen due to the scare caused by acquired immune deficiency syndrome (AIDS).

In July 1990 General Accident plc was formed to acquire the assets of General Accident Fire and Life Assurance Corporation. The holding company remains in a position of strength. Nelson Robertson, appointed chief general manager in January 1990, has predicted average growth will continue for the remainder of the decade.

Principal Subsidiaries: General Accident Fire and Life Assurance Corporation plc; General Accident Life Assurance Ltd.; General Accident Reinsurance Co. Ltd.; The Guarantee Society Ltd.; The Road Transport & General Insurance Co. Ltd.; Scottish Boiler & General Insurance Co. Ltd.; Scottish General Insurance Co. Ltd.; Scottish Insurance Corporation Ltd.; The Yorkshire Insurance Co. Ltd; The New Zealand Insurance PLC; General Accident Financial Services Ltd.; Grampian Properties Ltd.; Multiple Credit Services Ltd.; General Accident Insurance Company of America (U.S.A., 99.9%); NZI Insurance Australia Ltd.; La Brabanconne SA Belge d'Assurances (Belgium, 92.2%); Yorkshire-Corcovado Companhia de Seguros (Brazil, 86.4%); The General Accident Assurance Company of Canada (99.9%); Pilot Insurance Company (Canada); The Hong Kong Reinsurance Company Ltd.; General Accident Insurance Company Kenya Ltd. (57%); NZI Corporation Ltd. (New Zealand); General Accident Insurance Company; Puerto Rico Ltd. (80%); General Accident Insurance Company South Africa Ltd. (51%); General Accident Insurance Company (Zimbabwe) Ltd. (91.4%)

Further Reading: Romance of a Business: Forty Years Work 1885–1924, Perth, General Accident, 1924; Gray, Irvine, *A Business Epic 1835–1935: General Accident, Fire & Life Assurance Co. Ltd,* Perth, General Accident, 1935; Knight, Alice W., *The Yorkshire Story*, York, [n.p.], 1975; "The First Hundred Years," Perth, General Accident, 1985.

—Michael Doorley

GENERAL RE CORPORATION

Financial Centre
695 East Main Street
Stamford, Connecticut 06904
U.S.A.
(203) 328-5000
Fax: (203) 328-6423

Public Company
Incorporated: 1921 as General Casualty and Surety Reinsurance Corporation
Employees: 2,300
Assets: $10.39 billion
Stock Exchange: New York

General Re Corporation is the parent company of the largest reinsurer in the United States and third-largest in the world, a position it has maintained since its reformation at the end of World War II. Reinsurance is a means by which an insurance company is able to dilute its total liability by ceding a percentage of its policies to another insurer, who is therefore said to provide "reinsurance." Such a practice was frowned upon in the early history of insurance as little more than gambling, but with the growth of insurance coverage in the 20th century reinsurance has become a widespread, profitable, and even prestigious business. General Re handles roughly 10,000 active claims every year, many of them routine disbursements made in conjunction with its primary insuring partners, others in response to extraordinary disasters like the 1989 San Francisco earthquake.

General Casualty and Surety Reinsurance Corporation was formed by the 1921 merger of Norwegian Globe and Norwegian Assurance, two insurance companies under the direction of Robert Iberstein. The new company, with Iberstein as president, began operations in New York with a capital fund of $800,000. As reinsurance was not yet widely practiced in the United States, General Casualty and Surety had few domestic competitors, and even overseas only a handful of European firms were actively pursuing reinsurance clients. In 1923 Iberstein and his board of directors resigned and James White, an engineer of some renown and a business consultant, took over the company's leadership. White than renamed the company General Reinsurance Corporation.

An excellent national economy allowed General Reinsuranc to expand rapidly until the Great Depression struck in 1929. President White assembled a board of directors that included Edgar H. Boles, a lawyer formerly associated with the Lehigh Railroad. In 1930 Boles became president of General Reinsurance. The company had assets of approximately $12.3 million at the time. As the Depression lengthened, General Reinsurance not only struggled with the generally poor economic conditions but also sustained a number of heavy losses as an insurer. The experience and sagacity of Edgar Boles is widely credited with saving the company.

During these early years, General Reinsurance concentrated primarily on fire and casualty reinsurance, forming treaties with its primary insurance customers that called for General Reinsurance to assume a fixed proportion of the primary insurer's total liability. An alternative type of reinsurance, known as facultative and often used for large, well-defined risks, requires that the two insurers negotiate a separate premium for each new policy written. Because it was nearly alone in the domestic U.S. reinsurance market, General Reinsurance early discovered that it could charge a healthy fee for its services without losing significant amounts of business. Its assets rose steadily, and despite the setbacks of the 1930s, General Reinsurance built a reputation as a solid, "blue chip" firm.

Increased international competition during and immediately after World War II forced General Reinsurance to seek additional sources of capital. In 1945 the company found a suitable partner in Mellon Indemnity Corporation, a somewhat smaller insurance company owned by the Mellon family of Pittsburgh, Pennsylvania. Mellon Indemnity actually wrote little insurance, serving mainly as an investment vehicle for the Mellons, but its strong balance sheet was attractive to General Reinsurance. In November of 1945 a stock swap merged the two companies, which together boasted $38 million in assets and wrote $18 million worth of premiums in the following year. Edgar Boles remained as president of the new company, 40% of which was owned by the Mellon family.

In 1946, Edgar Boles retired after 16 years as the head of General Reinsurance. His replacement, Edward Lowry, served from 1950 to 1960, and played an important role in formulating General Reinsurance's business philosophy for the coming decades. Under Lowry the board decided that General Reinsurance could best make use of its leadership position and strong assets by adopting a conservative posture. General Reinsurance would accept only those policies that met its standards for safety and premium level, thereby assuring itself of a net profit from its underwriting business alone. In addition, General Reinsurance decided to make only the most prudent of investments, chiefly in bonds, to maintain unusually large reserves against the threat of multiple catastrophes, and to pay out a dividend smaller than the industry norm. Bolstered by the Mellons's financial security and golden name, General Reinsurance set out to become not only the largest and most profitable of U.S. reinsurers but also the industry's most distinguished aristocrat.

This policy succeeded in every respect. Under the leadership of James Cathcart and Robert Braddock, two members of the management team put together by Edward Lowry, General Reinsurance enjoyed several decades of remarkable health. The firm stuck to its high-priced premiums, demanding and getting the kind of fees that allowed it to earn a consistent profit on its underwriting business. A standard measure of underwriting success is the so-called combined ratio, which matches operating losses and expenses against annual underwriting income. If those figure come out about even—or, as it is expressed, 100%—the company's underwriting division is at least not running at a loss, and the firm can anticipate earning good money on its extensive investments; but at General Reinsurance, the combined ratio hovered around 97% during the 30 years following its 1946 merger with Mellon—an apparently slight advantage, but a good indication that General Reinsurance was not only highly profitable but also building unusually large reserves against potential future losses.

In the form of assets, these reserves increased over the years. From the $38 million recorded in 1946, General Reinsurance's assets rose to approximately $175 million in 1960 and four times that amount a decade later. Part of these riches were used to open branches in Canada and Brazil as well as an additional half-dozen locations in the United States; but most of General Reinsurance's growing wealth was simply reinvested in secure, low-tax bonds. This expanding portfolio supplied the lion's share of General Reinsurance's profit, which showed an enviable 16% annual compounded growth rate from 1959 to 1969. Such sustained profitability, in turn, allowed the company to further strengthen its asset base and continue its tough premium pricing.

As profit growth increased even faster in the early 1970s, General Reinsurance's extraordinary record began to attract attention. Reinsurance looked more appealing when it was accompanied by a 22% annual increase in profit, as General Reinsurance's was during the decade of the 1970s, and the once-exclusive club of reinsurers was soon crowded with new competitors. Prudential and Sears's Allstate formed reinsurance divisions, followed by newcomers to the entire insurance field like Ford, Armco, and Gulf Oil. The many large companies that had recently formed "captive" insurance units to handle their own risk management were also soon chasing the apparently easy money in reinsurance.

General Reinsurance responded to the suddenly difficult market conditions by doing nothing. It chose not to compete at the depressed premium level and issued a number of dark warnings about the danger of doing business with reinsurance firms lacking the experience and capital reserves sufficient to meet the next nationwide catastrophe. True to its philosophy, General Reinsurance accepted only those policies for which it could charge top dollar, and as a result its underwriting premiums dropped in 1979 for the first time in corporate history. Chairman Harold Hudson Jr. was also faced with the departure of a number of key executives and a growing perception in the industry that General Reinsurance's patrician style of reinsurance was out of date. In response, Hudson initiated a few changes, most notably the 1980 organization of General Re Corporation, which acquired General Reinsurance Corporation and its subsidiaries. The formation of the holding company followed General Reinsurance's acquisition of its first primary insurance subsidiary, and both moves signaled a new conpetitiveness at General Re, although the company reiterated its conviction that reinsurance was no place for fast-moving profit hounds and that survival was the real measure of success in a business that in a sense depends on disaster.

It appears that Hudson and his conservative colleagues at General Re were correct—or at least they have not been proven wrong. After enduring a few nervous years as a probable takeover target and a brief mid-1980s profit dip, General Re turned around its underwriting slump and continued its traditionally steady growth. Despite the onslaught of competitors, General Re remains the dominant factor in U.S. reinsurance, writing some 10% of all U.S. polices, while its field of challengers thinned after only a few years. As the company has always maintained, reinsurance is a business for those with deep pockets, and General Re's current portfolio of $8.8 billion in invested assets in 1989 amply meets even its conservative definition of adequate reserves. Furthermore, by 1990 the industry shake-out was not yet finished, as the years immediately following a major disaster have usually been hard on the reinsurance business; 1989 was a very bad year for disasters in the United States, and that should be very good for General Re.

Principal Subsidiaries: General Reinsurance Corporation; North Star Reinsurance Corporation; General Star Management Company; General Star National Insurance Company; General Star Indemnity Company; United States Aviation Underwriters, Inc.; Herbert Clough, Inc.; General Re Services Corporation; Genesis Underwriting Management Company; Genesis Indemnity Insurance Company; Genesis Insurance Company; General Re Financial Products Corporation; General Reinsurance Limited (U.K.); General Reinsurance Corporation (Europe) (Switzerland); Reinsurance Company of Australasia Limited (Australia); General Re Correduria de Reaseguros, S.A. (Spain); General Re Compania de Reaseguros, S.A. (Argentina); General Reinsurance Corporation (Japan).

Further Reading: Rumely, Paul, *The History of General Re: 65 Years in Reinsurance.* Stamford, Connecticut, General Re Corporation, 1986.

—Jonathan Martin

Great-West Lifeco Inc.

GREAT-WEST LIFECO INC.

100 Osborne Street North
Winnipeg, Manitoba R3C 3A5
Canada
(204) 946-7705
Fax: (204) 946-7838

Public Company
Incorporated: 1891 as The Great-West Life Assurance Company
Employees: 7,500
Assets: C$18.89 billion (US$16.31 billion)
Stock Exchanges: Winnipeg Toronto Montreal

Great-West Lifeco is the holding company for The Great-West Life Assurance Company, a company begun during a major recession in a small Canadian western prairie town almost a century ago. Great-West Lifeco is, in turn, 86.2% owned by Power Financial Corporation. The Great-West Life Assurance Company meets the insurance, retirement, and investment needs of more than six million people across North America. A combination of conservative investment strategies, adaptation to the changing business environment, and innovation in both products and policy have brought Great-West into its second century of business.

In the early 1890s, Winnipeg was a frontier town of lumbermen and plains traders. As a stop on the slowly growing Canadian Pacific Railway, it was a promising growth point in the western province of Manitoba. The difficulty of transportation combined with drought created hard economic times for the region during the decade, however. An optimistic local businessman, Jeffry Hall Brock, recognized that capital was needed to invest in local farm and retail development. His vision was to collect western Canadians' savings via insurance sales, thereby offering them security and protection while financing development. At this time, only 9 of the 40 insurance companies in Canada were Canadian. Not one of these companies was based in western Canada.

The Great-West Life Assurance Company was incorporated in 1891 with a name that reflected the company's regional pride; the hyphen was a typesetter's error. In the first year, 834 policies were sold, representing more than $2 million worth of protection, by a sales force of three that included Brock. The bold enterprise attracted the involvement of the area's outstanding businessmen, and early shareholders included bakers, farmers, a harnessmaker, and the sheriff. Support came from bustling Toronto as from well as many local rural communities. The mayor of Winnipeg, Alexander Macdonald, became Great-West's first president in 1892. Brock was made managing director.

The company issued its premier manual in 1892, offering six insurance plans. The first claim was received that same year. By the end of 1893, Great-West—competing with 5- to 50-year-old companies across Canada—had the eighth highest returns. At this point, the self-confident young company made the remarkable decision to enter the eastern Canadian markets. Its well-established competitors were situated in the East, as were the country's banking, financial, and manufacturing institutions. The West had essentially one industry: agriculture. In Great-West's first three years, it had achieved the financial backing and business volume that had taken other companies up to 15 years to reach.

Great-West's prosperity continued during the next two decades. By the turn of the century, the company was represented in every province and was the country's fastest growing life insurer. As the economy improved when the region's depression lifted, the service industry benefited. In 1896 Great-West gained the largest percentage of new business written, out of 21 Canadian life insurance companies, to make it only $80,000 behind the industry leader in aggregate gain of business in force. The first shareholder dividends were paid in 1901, and dividends have been paid every year since.

In 1906 the company crossed the border and established U.S. operations in North Dakota. The next year, Great-West topped all Canadian companies in paid-for business. From 50 applications a month in 1893, the company received an average of 375 applications a month by 1909. However the growth proved a strain on the founder's health. Brock essentially left the company in 1912 for health reasons, and he died in 1915. C.C. Ferguson succeeded Brock as CEO in 1915, one year after the onset of World War I.

With the war came a boost to the area's economy, which had declined as the wheat boom receded and freight rates climbed, but the war presented the life insurance industry with the problem of wartime policies. Most firms charged extra premiums for those in the service, but Great-West kept its extra charges at a minimum as part of its war effort. Throughout the war, the company managed to keep up its record, maintained since 1906, for writing more ordinary business in Canada annually than any other company. Nevertheless, the war's impact was felt: claims for wartime deaths totaled $1.5 million. Almost as catastrophic was the flu epidemic that flared up at the war's end from 1918 to 1919, which cost Great-West more than $1 million in death claims.

Canada, like other countries, then contended with conditions following the war: high rates of inflation and unemployment, labor unrest, slowed agricultural output. Though economic conditions worsened through the 1920s, Great-West showed a steady increase in business. In 1920, U.S. operations were extended into Michigan and Minnesota. That same year, Great-West became one of the first companies to offer group insurance. The concept took many years to catch on. In 1940 group insurance was still only 9% of the company's total business. In later years it comprised more than half. In 1926 Macdonald retired as president, succeeded by G.W. Allan, who had been company director for 22 years.

Great-West, which had initially concentrated its investments in farm mortgages, had diversified since the war into government bonds and city mortgages. Because of its diversified investments and the fact that stock holdings were a very small part of the company's portfolio, Great-West was well insulated when the market crash of 1929 occurred. In fact, that year was the best to date in the company's history.

The Great Depression years of the next decade provided a new challenge. Business declined between 1932 and 1937, but Great-West managed a gradual increase in assets during the period. By the company's 45th anniversary in 1936, it provided coverage for nearly one million people in North America, issuing an average of 60 policies per business day. New insurance plans were introduced during the Depression, including a policy for the professional woman and a family protection policy. By summer of 1939, Great-West was again enjoying record-breaking figures in applied business.

The decade of depression was ended by the outbreak of World War II, which stimulated employment and industrial activity. The life insurance industry was dramatically revived, and between 1939 and 1945 Great-West enjoyed a tremendous growth in the business, as well as expansion into Indiana, Missouri, Ohio, Kansas, California, and Pennsylvania. Group insurance and group pension plans steadily increased. Also during the war years, Great-West entered into the individual accident and health insurance fields. The company changed presidents in 1940, when M.F. Christie took the job, and again in 1943, when W.P. Riley assumed the position.

During the postwar boom, the company's business boomed too. In 1946 Great-West's business-in-force reached the $1 billion mark. It would reach its second billion only six years later and its third three years after that. The company continued its expansion in the United States entering seven more states between 1946 and 1952. In 1958 it started doing business in five more states and the District of Columbia. Also in 1958 Great-West began technological expansion; it purchased the first computer in western Canada.

Growth continued throughout the prosperous 1960s. In 1968 Great-West became the first Canadian company authorized to sell a variable annuity in the United States. More than $1 billion of new business was placed in that year.

Business in the United States grew rapidly. By 1973 Great-West was licensed in 28 states and the District of Columbia, and opened a marketing office in Denver, Colorado, in 1973. The company separated its Canadian and U.S. operations, except for investment and corporate operations, in 1979. It also opened the company's U.S. headquarters in Denver that year. By then Great-West Life was operating in 45 states. From 1979 to 1983 U.S. business nearly doubled.

During the next decade, Great-West concentrated on product development, asset management, and developing the two regional operations. The Canadian and U.S. markets developed different needs during the 1980s. One of the company's new products was a universal life policy, first introduced in 1982—the first of its kind designed for the Canadian market. A similar policy was introduced in the United States the following year.

Another Great-West innovation was a system it introduced in Canada that paid agents levelized commissions and offered loan arrangements for agents needing additional income. It was the first insurance company in North America to adopt such a system. This arrangement allowed the sales force to experiment with the sale of new products with less fear of financial repercussion. As a result, universal life business increased from 30% in 1983 to almost 60% in 1985. Over those three years, career agents enjoyed a 65% compound growth in average earnings.

In the mid-1980s, the company's structure changed. Great-West had been a joint shareholder-policyholder–owned company from its inception 1891 to 1969 when the Investors Group acquired controlling interest in the company's common shares. Investors Group was acquired by Power Corporation, a Montreal-based holding company with interests in publishing, pulp and paper, and financial services, in 1969. In 1984 Power Corporation formed a subsidiary to hold Great-West and its other financial-service companies. This corporation, called Power Financial, in turn created a holding company in 1986: Great-West Lifeco now holds 99.4% of Great-West Life Assurance Company's stock.

Another first came in 1988 when Great-West entered into a joint venture with New England Life Insurance Company of Boston. The arrangement allowed Great-West to provide New England Life with a range of services including group life and health products, with both companies sharing in the risks and profits. This innovation allowed New England to benefit from Great-West's product line while Great-West gained from New England's sales force and established markets. In 1989 Great-West Life acquired Crown Life's group life and health business in the United States.

Over the course of the 1980s, the company's U.S. operations went from generating 40% of the total business to 60%. In the United States, the primary sales are in business insurance and executive planning markets, while in Canada, Great-West is a major insurance carrier of life and health insurance and retirement products in all markets.

As Great-West approached its centennial, it was determined to continue its focus of providing benefits and services through employer-sponsored programs. The company's ability to adapt to the changing business environment, its care in fund management, and its willingness to innovate are the strengths that Great-West brings to its second century.

Principal Subsidiaries: Great-West Life & Annuity Insurance Co.; G.W.L. Properties Ltd.; Gold Circle Insurance Co.; GWL Properties Inc.; Great-West Realty Investments, Inc.; Great-West Life Financial Corp.

Further Reading: "United States Operations Span 75 Years," *Key News*, January 1981; Fleming, James, *Merchants of Fear*, New York, Viking Press, 1986; *Across the Company*, November-December 1989; "Historical Review of the Great-West Life Assurance Company," Great-West Life corporate typescript, [n.d.]; "The History of Great-West Life," Great-West Life corporate typescript, [n.d.].

—Carol I. Keeley

THE HOME INSURANCE COMPANY

59 Maiden Lane
New York, New York 10038
U.S.A.
(212) 530-6800
Fax: (212) 530-7056

Wholly Owned Subsidiary of TVH Acquisition Corporation
Incorporated: 1853
Employees: 5,073
Assets: $6.69 billion

The Home Insurance Company is the 23rd-largest property and casualty company in the United States. Home provides virtually all lines of insurance, with the bulk of its business being industrial property insurance and liability for large accounts. The company has undergone numerous changes over the course of its history, and has contributed significantly to the face of modern property and casualty insurance.

When Home was founded in 1853 insurance was very different from what it is today. Property owners purchased insurance to hedge the risk of loss. Claims were not expected to cover more than the value of the lost property, and sometimes covered less. Only a few types of insurance were available, and insurance companies were generally limited in the types of coverage they could offer. Indeed, many merchants had trouble getting enough protection for their property. To help solve this problem, a group of New York City merchants established The Home Insurance Company. Paid-in capital was $500,000, large for an insurance company in those days.

Simeon Loomis was Home's first president. Loomis brought some insurance experience with him when he came to New York from Hartford, Connecticut. After two years, Loomis left Home over matters of policy, and was replaced by secretary Charles J. Martin. Martin led Home Insurance for the next 33 years.

One of Home's most significant contributions to the insurance industry was its popularization of the insurance agency system. Insurance companies were warned by state commissioners not to expand too widely. The comptroller of the state of New York cautioned mutual companies against selling insurance outside of their own counties. The promoters of Home, however, named 18 agencies in the first month of operations, and 128 throughout the United States and Canada by the end of the year. Only one other company in New York used independent agents to sell its insurance in 1853, and the concept caught on quickly. Thirty years later, in 1883, Home's president, Charles Martin, reported that 37 of the city's 57 insurers sold through agencies.

Another innovation in property insurance instituted during Home's early years was the concept of safety engineering and risk management. A position for a surveyor was included in the company's original bylaws. Among the surveyor's duties was attending "to the interests of the company in surveying buildings and watching risks which the company may be insured."

About one-third of Home's premiums were written in the South, and when the Civil War started in 1861, the loss of this income slowed the company's growth. Home honored all policies, Union and Confederate. In 1864, another $1 million was added to Home's capital base, through subscription. With total paid-in capital of $2 million, Home was the largest fire insurer in the country.

Nineteenth-century fire-control techniques were not adequate to protect U.S. cities, which had grown rapidly. New York City, for example, did not have a full-time fire department until 1865. Several major conflagrations in the latter half of the century resulted in the payment of hundreds of thousands of dollars to claimants. In 1866 big fires in Portland, Maine; Glens Falls, New York; and Vicksburg, Mississippi, put a strain on insurance companies' resources, but the biggest blow came in 1871, in Chicago.

The Great Chicago Fire destroyed $200 million worth of property and bankrupted 68 insurance companies. Home paid $2.5 million in claims. The company's stockholders injected another $1.5 million in capital to keep Home going. A year later a fire in Boston forced 30 more insurance companies into insolvency. The Home Insurance Company paid claims of $750,000, and in the late 19th century insurers began to promote the development of better fire protection and risk management.

Home's business expanded with the westward expansion of the United States. Home commissioned architect William Le Baron Jenney to design an office building for its Chicago-based operations. The Home Insurance Building was completed in 1885 and, at ten stories, was the world's first skyscraper—its weight was supported by a steel skeleton rather than by walls.

In 1903, as Home celebrated its 50th anniversary, it had premiums totaling $147 million. A year later a major fire in Baltimore, Maryland, cost Home $600,000 in claims but brought about changes in fire protection. Equipment sent to Baltimore from New York and other cities proved useless because hose fittings were not standardized. Insurance companies lobbied for national uniformity in fire-fighting equipment, and Home, which had been the leading insurer in Baltimore, led the movement. In 1906, the San Francisco Earthquake and Fire resulted in property losses of $250 million. Home paid $2.2 million in claims. Great fires became rare in the 20th century because of more effective building codes and improved fire-fighting technology.

In the early 1900s automobile insurance was a growing field. Home's automobile division became the foundation of its casualty insurance business. In 1930 a subsidiary, The Home Indemnity Company, took over Home's casualty lines.

Home's assets grew 50% during World War I. In 1918, after the war, Home was one of the founders of the American Foreign Insurers Association, which offered coverage to European industries. After a brief dip in the postwar economy, Home grew steadily through the 1920s as well. The Depression, which followed the stock market crash of 1929, caused a downturn in Home's premium income. By 1935 the economy had improved considerably, and World War II brought full economic revival.

In 1944 the United States Supreme Court ruled against the industrywide practice of cooperating to set premium prices in *United States v. Southeastern Underwriters Association.* Insurers argued that most companies were too small to rely solely on their own experience in setting premiums. As a result of these protests the McCarran-Ferguson Act was passed by Congress in 1945, exempting insurance-rate fixing from the Sherman Antitrust Act, and placing responsibility for industry regulation in the hands of state governments.

After the war Home's automobile insurance business began to grow quickly. Along with the larger number of cars, however, came a larger number of accidents. Home decreased its automobile underwriting as a result.

During the 1950s new laws allowed underwriters to sell a wider variety of insurance, and Home began selling insurance packages, which included several types of coverage for a monthly premium. Homeowners' and industrial packages were marketed, as record numbers of Americans bought homes in the 1950s and 1960s.

In the 1960s insurance company stocks were priced low at a time when most stocks were doing well. Home's stock portfolio soared in value while the company's market value remained low. As a result, in 1968 Northwestern Industries, a diversified railroad holding company, announced it would attempt to take over the insurance company. Home's president, Kenneth E. Black, turned to City Investing Company, a diversified holding company. City Investing's chairman, Robert Dowling, had long been a director of Home, and Home Insurance became a subsidiary of City Investing in 1968.

Civil unrest in the late 1960s resulted in a large number of damage claims in urban areas. Government-imposed FAIR (Fair Access to Insurance Requirements) plans, and assigned risk plans spread the risk of undesirable underwritings among a number of insurance carriers. This system gave protection to customers who would otherwise have had trouble getting insurance.

John H. Washburn, great grandson of an earlier Home president of the same name, was elected president in 1968, CEO a year later, and chairman in 1973. Robert H. Tullis, became president in 1973.

In 1974 a severe recession, characterized by high inflation and descending stock prices, reduced the value of Home's surplus and investments. At the same time, average claim settlements were rising rapidly. Home experienced record losses from underwriting, particularly as a result of writing high-risk casualty policies and failing to reserve adequately. The situation was so severe that some analysts speculated that Home was on the verge of bankruptcy, but the period of record losses was followed by a period of record gains for Home. The cyclical property and casualty markets rebounded in the latter half of the 1970s.

In 1975 Cityhome Corporation, a subsidiary of City Investing, was incorporated to parent The Home Insurance Company and its affiliates. In 1978 Cityhome became known as The Home Group. City Investing also decided that The Home Group was overdue for restructuring. Home's reputation had begun to suffer, and the head of City Investing's financial division, Peter C.A. Huang, undertook the task of cleaning up Home.

Huang, the son of a former Chinese minister of finance, is a brilliant financier, but had little patience with Home's existing management, and fired 434 employees—mostly senior staff—while assuming the duties of chairman and later president himself. Huang instituted major changes in the company's top management, its corporate structure, and its accounting system. Management was decentralized by region, and the memo-writing approach to strategic policymaking was abolished. New financial accounts included detailed breakdowns of all business areas. Huang's purge left Home without a core of experienced insurance managers, but, as Huang told *Institutional Investor* in 1981, Home Insurance was "the only non-inbred insurance company, the only one run by non-insurance people."

In 1982 the Home Reinsurance Company began operations, reinsuring risks domestically and internationally. By 1988 its assets totaled more than $485 million. Home Insurance and its subsidiaries recorded devastating underwriting losses in 1984 and 1985. Combined operating losses for the two years totaled $396.9 million.

In May 1984 a group of investors headed by Merrill Lynch Capital Markets, and including City Investing chairman George Scharffenberger, bid to take Home Insurance Company's parent private. A week later a second group, headed by Miami investor Victor Posner, offered City an even more favorable deal. The Posner group's bid allowed for equity participation by City's current management, and was given a favorable recommendation by the City board. By summer, however, neither group had successfully raised the necessary funds to complete the transaction. In September, the Merrill Lynch group, assisted by leveraged buyout specialists Kohlberg Kravis Roberts & Company, offered to buy just three of City Investing's major manufacturing units. The price was right and the deal was accepted. The rest of City was split up; some assets being sold outright, and others, including Home Insurance, being temporarily spun off to shareholders until a buyer could be found.

Scharffenberger hired his attorney, Marshall Manley, to head City Investing during the transition. Manley was then asked to stay on as president of the Home Group. Under Manley, two life insurance subsidiaries, PHF Life and Federal Home Life, were sold in 1985 for $130 million. In 1986 James J. Meenaghan, formerly president and CEO of Fireman's Fund, became president and CEO of Home. He focused company strategy and sought to strengthen senior management. In August 1987, a brokerage house, Gruntal and Company, was purchased for $148 million. In 1988 Carteret Savings Bank was acquired by Home Group for $266 million. Home incurred significant debt to make these purchases, and its preferred stock was downgraded. Home's debt increased from $94 million in 1985 to $479 million in 1989. The company's shares dropped from a high of $31½ in 1986 to $7 in 1990.

In 1989 Hurricane Hugo battered the southern Atlantic coast and territories of the United States, and the second great earthquake in a century rocked San Francisco. Home's losses for the year were $50 million, relatively low compare to other carriers, some of which had claims totaling ten times that amount.

In May 1989 The Home Group changed its name to AmBase Corporation. The company organized its subsidiaries into three groups: insurance, consisting of The Home Insurance Company and its subsidiaries, Commonwealth Insurance Company—Home's Canadian affiliate—and U.S. International Reinsurance; banking, made up of Carteret Bancorp, Imperial Premium Finance, and Carteret Mortgage; and investment services, built around Gruntal Financial Corporation and Home Capital Services. A fourth unit of AmBase was its Sterling Forest Corporation, a real estate development near New York City valued at over $35 million.

In 1989, AmBase Chairman George T. Scharffenberger announced that the company planned to sell its insurance operation. Proceeds were earmarked to reduce the holding company's debt. AmBase would continue to operate its banking and investment-service units, while the Home Insurance Companies and affiliates, around which the firm had grown, would continue to conduct their business as either a subsidiary of another company or independently.

In February 1991 Home Insurance was purchased by TVH Acquisiton Corporation, an investor group whose principal partners include Trugg-Hansa Holding AB—Sweden's second-largest insurer—and Industrial Mutual Insurance—Finland's second-largest insurer.

Few insurance companies have survived as long as The Home Insurance Company. Home has weathered the great storms; despite the financial turmoil of the 1980s Home is in sound financial condition and appears ready to face the challenges of the future.

Principal Subsidiaries: City Insurance Company; Cityvest International, Limited; The Home Indemnity Corporation; The Home Insurance Company of Illinois; The Home Insurance Company of Indiana; Home Lloyd's Insurance Company of Texas; U.S. International Reinsurance Company; Commonwealth Insurance Company (Canada).

Further Reading: ''Home Observes Its 125th Anniversary,'' *National Underwriter (Prop/Cas)*, April 14, 1978; Tullis, Robert H., *The Home Insurance Company: Men of Vision During 125 Years*, New York, The Newcomen Society in North America, 1978.

—Thomas M. Tucker

JOHN HANCOCK MUTUAL LIFE INSURANCE COMPANY

John Hancock Place
Boston, Massachusetts 02117
U.S.A.
(617) 572-6000
Fax: (617) 572-6451

Mutual Company
Incorporated: 1862
Employees: 20,000
Assets: $32.34 billion

John Hancock Mutual Life Insurance Company is the nation's ninth-largest life insurer, with $198 billion of life insurance in force covering 17 million lives in 1990. John Hancock Mutual Life is the dominant member of the John Hancock Financial Services group, which includes mutual funds, a securities brokerage, a consumer bank, and real estate and venture-capital companies.

John Hancock Mutual Life Insurance Company was founded in 1862. It alone survives, of six life insurance companies founded that year in the United States. Twenty-eight such companies were founded between 1860 and 1865; only seven survived to the 1950s. In the two years following the Civil War, 24 more were started. It was a boom time for life insurance, and hard selling by the new companies reaped a rich harvest. Life insurance in force rose to an estimated $2 billion in the 1860s.

Hancock was chartered on April 21, 1862, in Massachusetts, where a Department of Insurance had been established in 1855, the first of its kind in the new world. It was the first company to be formed under two recently signed laws that helped to regularize a previously uncertain and at times dishonest business. As if to emphasize the point, the new company took for its namesake the Massachusetts native—first to sign the Declaration of Independence and later governor—whose signature became synonymous with a pledge of fidelity.

The more important of the two laws dealt with nonforfeiture. The practice in the industry had been to confiscate policies after one payment was missed. Nonforfeiture, paying surrender value of a life policy after the fifth year, became the U.S. norm after passage of this 1861 law in Massachusetts. The other law, passed in 1858, required each insurance company to demonstrate its worth yearly.

Hancock's first president was George P. Sanger. Forty-three years old, Sanger was district attorney for Suffolk County, in which Boston is located, and a former judge. Indeed, he continued as district attorney for seven years. Only then, in 1869, did he quit public office to be a full-time insurance executive.

By November 1863 Hancock had 176 policies in force, for $332,700 total value. In the next two months, the company wrote 111 more policies. Matters continued prosperous, and in 1869 the company moved from a small office, where the company medical examiner examined applicants in a crowded corner, to roomier quarters in the Sears Building. In 1872 the company redeemed its guarantee capital and became strictly mutual.

Sanger returned to public life as U.S. attorney for Massachusetts in 1874; his successor was George Thornton. During the economic depression of that time, Hancock suffered financially, but it remained solvent and honored its obligations.

Prudential Insurance Company had at the same time introduced industrial life insurance for the less affluent. Premiums were paid weekly rather than annually or semiannually. Its premiums and benefits were lower than those of ordinary life insurance. Policies were started for as little as 5¢. For many years it was the only insurance available on the lives of children—a feature that was to bathe it in controversy. Industrial life was new, and no one knew how closely U.S. mortality would mirror English mortality rates, on which this insurance was based. In addition U.S. companies had to keep fixed reserves, while the English did not.

Industrial agents' work was part social work. The agent was expected to know everyone on his route, often including several people crowded into one or two rooms. His territory required up to 1,000 calls a week for collection of premiums. If the total collections for which the agent was responsible held steady, he was rewarded; if they fell, he was penalized. Agents were to make calls three or four days a week, and solicit new business on the other days. He was welcome to sell other kinds of insurance as well. Perhaps the most striking thing about industrial insurance was its educational aspect: people grew used to having insurance and dealing with an agent.

Prudential had the field to itself for four years. Then, in March 1879, Hancock got a new president, no less a figure than the Massachusetts insurance commissioner, Stephen H. Rhodes, who by midsummer was selling industrial insurance in Boston. By year end, Hancock had 9,327 industrial policies totaling $951,000, after only six months of selling the coverage. It was a welcome addition to the line. Metropolitan Life Insurance Company entered the industrial field the same year. These three—Prudential, Metropolitan, and Hancock—were to dominate that business, with Boston-based Hancock trailing a distant third behind the other two, both based around New York.

By 1881 Hancock had 36,012 industrial policies in force, and by 1889 it had issued 256,000 industrial policies worth $30 million; total worth of Hancock's policies was $39 million. Hancock's burgeoning prosperity was demonstrated partly by its move in February 1891 to its own richly ornamented home-office building in Boston, with "monumental figures in colored mosaic" in the staircase hall, against a background of "nearly thirty thousand cubes or 'tessera' of enamel overlaid with gold and covered with a thin film of glass . . . made by a process known alone to the Venetians,'' as described by R. Carlyle Buley in *The American Life Convention, 1906–1952: A Study in the History of Life Insurance.* Such grandeur was and for some time remained typical of insurance companies, whose home offices and other downtown buildings have provided almost as much commentary for architects as their policies have for insurance writers.

During 1891 Hancock's insurance in force reached $54.5 million, up from $17.8 million in 1886. Hancock had managed to find its way in the uncharted waters of the early industrial insurance years.

Prudential and Metropolitan still were the leaders by far. Other companies had dropped from the race. Industrial insurance had a high lapse rate, with most lapses occurring in the first six months of the policy. In this period lapses were costly to the companies, who tried hard to prevent them.

The problems of insuring children came to a head in 1895, when Massachusetts considered the prohibition against insuring children under ten. The practice was denounced for five days in a Boston hearing room as encouraging cruelty and even murder. The tide turned when Haley Fiske, the Metropolitan vice president and lobbyist, testified, and the bill was soundly defeated. Other states considered such a bill, but only Colorado passed one; it lasted into 1921.

In 1902 Hancock's industrial agents were urged to push ordinary life insurance. The name of the company newsletter for agents, ''Our Industrial Field,'' was changed to ''The John Hancock Field.'' Hancock was diversifying. It also was growing. By 1905 it had 1.5 million policies, up from not quite 900,000 in 1897. Its insurance in force came to $245 million, up from $115 million. This was small compared to Metropolitan and Prudential, who with Hancock together held some 15.5 million industrial policies, of the total of 16.8 million such policies in the United States, worth $2.3 billion.

In 1905 the Armstrong Committee's investigation of the New York State insurance industry achieved a general overhaul of the life insurance industry, and it led to needed reforms. At Hancock, however, 1905 was remembered for its exposure of ''the mistakes and misdeeds of a few individuals prominent in the business, followed by an investigation of Draconian severity,'' according to *Historical Sketch of the John Hancock Mutual Life Insurance Company of Boston, Massachusetts: A Half Century Completed, 1862–1912.*

The investigation produced ''tremendous shock'' but did ''not for a second impair or suspend'' operations and ''furnished moreover an example of the inherent soundness. . . of the old line insurance plan,'' said *The Satchel,* the company magazine, in 1907.

In 1906 Stephen Rhodes died at 83, after more than 30 years at the Hancock helm. He was succeeded by Roland O. Lamb, 58, who had been with the company since 1872. Lamb was no sooner installed than another home-office building was completed. It was fire-resistant with an exterior of pink granite; its interior displayed several kinds of marble. Modern for its day, it boasted eight elevators and a drinking fountain offering refrigerated water on each floor.

In 1924 Hancock helped launch the group insurance business in the United States by offering such insurance to employers. By 1990 the company would have 1,000 group clients. Group policies, with life and industrial policies, were to form the core of business through Hancock's first 100 years.

The Great Depression shook up the world but not Hancock's labor whose business rose 7.3% in 1930, the Depression's first full calendar year. New business declined, however, in 1932, and Hancock cut its dividend.

Guy W. Cox became Hancock president in 1936. In 1937, its agents picketed the company's New York office on Christmas Eve. Six months later, the National Labor Relations Board considered filing a complaint against Hancock in connection with the petition for union election by the United Office and Professional Workers of America. In November of that year, Hancock's industrial agents sought a union election among Hancock employees.

The company purchased an aircraft carrier, the *Hancock,* in 1944, for use by the U.S. Navy in World War II. It was the result of a joint financing effort by agents, other employees, and policyholders. Agents carried patriotism a step further with their pledge to bring the appeal for a wastepaper-salvage drive to homes they visited in the course of business.

In 1944 Guy Cox became chairman, and Paul F. Clark, a former agent, became president at age 51. Clark would become chairman three years later. In the spirit of postwar recovery, Hancock began on-the-job training for returning veterans in 1946. In the same year, the company advertised on radio for the first time, sponsoring Boston Symphony Orchestra performances.

In 1948, in an investment market where even 5% was an unheard-of return, Hancock had assets of more than $2 billion. New investments in 1947 had topped $300 million. At that time, Hancock was earning 3%, down from 5% in the prior years. With a surplus of $166 million, its portfolio was unspectacular; fewer than $15 million were in common stocks, though by law it was allowed to carry ten times that amount. In addition, Hancock was lending on real estate to only 50% to 55% of market value rather than the 66.7% allowed. Yet Hancock, the largest life insurance company in the United States outside the New York metropolitan area, had the third-highest growth rate at that time of all insurance companies. The company's finance committee, by Massachusetts law, made final decisions in investments. Guy Cox chaired the committee, and caution ruled its deliberations. Before investing in the stock of a paper company, analysts were sent to view the whole paper industry. Hancock was willing to take three months to decide on a given issue.

Over 30% of Hancock investments lay in U.S. government bonds, and almost as much in public-utility bonds and notes. Average net interest for 1947 was 2.91%, but the new investments averaged 3.14%. Things were looking up, after more than a decade of having to buy low-interest-bearing securities.

Hancock was experimenting with financing of rental housing. Two ''Hancock villages'' went up, one in Boston, another in Dearborn, Michigan. The latter encountered labor and other problems. Meanwhile, in Boston a new home office was raised—26 stories, making it the highest building in town. It also had the longest escalator in the United States. As high as the new building was, it was ''dwarfed by the life insurance idea,'' said President Clark at its opening. It replaced a ten-story building which in 1922 had won the Boston Society of Architects award for its designer, J. Harleston Parker.

The 1940s wrought a marked change in the life insurance industry. Government investment rose sharply during the war, to an all-time high of 46% of the total. By 1951 it had dropped to 17%. The nation looked to the industry for capital, with its net yearly rise in assets of $4 billion to $5 billion. The industry responded. By December 1951 it was looking into natural gas in the southwestern United States and iron ore in Labrador. It was looking beyond the bond market to private, or individual, placement between corporate need and the investor.

The 1950s were a time of political nervousness. Senator Joseph McCarthy of Wisconsin held the stage on Capitol Hill, and the cold war was a fact of life. Hancock succumbed at least temporarily, refusing a lease renewal in 1953 to the Community Church of Boston, which had rented its home-office auditorium for 30 years for its liberal lecturers.

What to do with the money was the main life insurance issue, however. By 1954 Hancock ranked fifth among U.S. insurance companies, with $3.8 billion in assets, and was investing as much as $4.6 million a week. Investments had earned 3.07% in 1953, up from the all-time low of 2.9% in 1947. Hancock moved to higher yields, looking increasingly to mortgage loans, which had risen to 20% of its portfolio, from not quite 12% in 1949. High return, however, had to be joined with safety, which made the task difficult.

By the mid-1960s another story was unfolding. Hancock was showing a new aggressiveness. According to *Business Week* of January 15, 1966, it was "second to none of the old-line mutuals in selling itself," as it did in building its skyscraping monument in Chicago, the John Hancock Center, then second in height only to the Empire State Building. Hancock had just elected its youngest-ever chief executive officer, 49-year-old Robert E. Slater, an actuary and a firm believer in the use of the computer. Slater was busy reshaping the company, looking ahead to a time in which baby boomers, born in the post-World War II decade, would be buying much of the country's life insurance.

In the 1960s ordinary life insurance was the company's biggest moneymaker, followed by group accident and health, group annuities, and group life. The old industrial insurance was no longer a consideration.

Byron K. Elliott, 67 and a Hancock employee since 1933—had been a judge in Indiana before that—remained as chairman and ran the $7.8 billion investment portfolio. The rest of the executive suite was considerably younger. Gerhard D. Bleicken, the new executive vice president, was 52. A team averaging age 52 was running insurance operations. Self-renewal was the theme. Still, with 32% of its portfolio in mortgages—compared to 42% for Prudential—63% in bonds, and only 5% in stocks, Hancock was unquestionably a conservative investor. Changes were coming, however. Hancock formed a real estate subsidiary in 1968 and entered the mutual fund business the next year. An international group program was begun. It was the start of broad diversification.

Hancock entered the Canadian market in 1969, and in 1971 entered the property and casualty insurance markets. Its 1972 income topped $2 billion for the first time. The company was in the securities business by then, with its John Hancock Income Securities Group. Slater resigned in December 1969 and was replaced by Gerhard Bleicken as chairman and CEO. In May 1972 the first black director, who was also the first woman director, Mary Ella Robertson, was elected.

Hancock was again making architectural history with the John Hancock Tower, its new home-office building in Boston. The Chicago John Hancock Center, a $95-million investment, had been hailed as innovative and workable. The Hancock Tower, built five years later, was another story. In 1974, the tower's windows began to blow out and fall to the ground, 60 stories at the farthest. The cause was a flaw in the design of the windows. The double-pane windows were replaced for $47 million, and the cost of the whole structure rose from an original $52 million to $144 million. The initial construction of the building had created other problems, including a weakening of the foundation of nearby Trinity Church, which sued Hancock for $4 million. Hancock in turn sued the architects, I.M. Pei & Associates; the general contractor; and the window-glass manufacturer, who in turn countersued Hancock.

The late 1970s were bringing what Hancock called winds of change into the life insurance industry. Rising inflation and interest rates and deregulation offered circumstances in which policyholders borrowed on life polices at 5% or 6% to reinvest in money-market securities paying twice that. The prime rate shot up, and in 1980 many life insurance companies found themselves faced with a negative cash flow, for the first time in memory. The prime rate dropped later in the year, from an astronomical 20%, and the crisis eased. Insurers knew things would never be the same, however. From this realization came substantial changes in the company that would outdo any changes of the 1970s.

One of the first things to change was the investment strategy. There would be no more fixed-interest, long-term loans. The company would build a liquidity reserve of short-term securities. The fixed-income portfolio would be examined constantly by means of thorough computerized programs.

During the 1980s, Hancock entered most segments of the financial-services industry and become a vocal proponent, alone among life insurance companies, of deregulation. The "level playing field" became a byword: all financial institutions—banks, brokerages, insurers—should have equal access to all financial services. By 1985 Hancock was in money management, stock brokerage, venture-capital management, equipment leasing, and real estate syndication. Hancock wanted to be a financial supermarket, but it was an old conservative company in a yet-more-conservative industry. As a mutual company, it had no shareholders and had never been run with profit in mind. It was the sixth-largest insurer, down from fifth, with assets of $25 billion. Its old ways had sent it into sharp decline. Its policyholder base had shrunk 30% in the previous ten years, to $7 million. New business bookings had peaked in 1981, as consumers moved from whole-life policies to cheaper term coverage.

Hancock had to change. To stay with traditional life insurance would have meant to "shrink the company," said chairman and CEO John G. McElwee. Instead it would offer banking, investment, and insurance products. It already had gone into credit cards and a half-dozen other non-insurance products and had bought a regional brokerage house and banks in Ohio and New Hampshire. There was, however, question whether its predominantly middle- and lower-income policyholders would buy such services.

McElwee was succeeded by E. James Morton in March 1986. Stephen L. Brown became president and chief operating officer. In 1986 Hancock helped found the Financial Services Council, a coalition of 18 manufacturers, retailers, and financial firms who lobby for "pro-competitive" reform of laws affecting financial services. Normally rivals, these firms coauthored a draft bill for reform that was unveiled in October 1987.

The United States lagged behind England and Canada in rallying government, business, and consumers around the idea of integration of financial services. Hancock was prevented from buying a savings-and-loan institution, for example, because the savings and loan owned a brokerage that underwrote corporate equities and debt. Instead, Hancock bought a consumer bank, First Signature Bank and Trust Company, in New Hampshire, a limited-purpose bank with a 7% growth cap as required by the 1987 banking law. It was the most Hancock could do. Forbidden to become a holding company because mutually held, it was unable to demutualize for lack of enabling legislation in Massachusetts.

President Brown offered a goal of "reciprocal access" to financial services, whether for banks or insurance companies, and a vision of financial services as one competitive industry that is controlled by appropriate legislation. By 1986 Hancock had slipped to number eight among life insurance companies, with assets of over $27.3 billion. Manufacturers, retailers, and foreign competitors already had entered the insurance and other financial markets, while bank holding companies and mutual life insurers operated under restraint.

John Hancock Mutual Life Insurance Company remained in 1990 a life industry giant, though somewhat diminished. It is a historic company, whatever its stature, founded as it was during the Civil War in one of the nation's most historic cities, Boston. Throughout its existence, Hancock has taken what steps were necessary to survive and grow, whether by entering the infant industrial life business in the 1880s or by entering many non-insurance areas in the 1980s. The company aimed to be a major competitor in financial services in the 1990s and beyond.

Principal Subsidiary: John Hancock Variable Life Insurance Company.

Further Reading: Schwab, Emil, ed., *Historical Sketch of the John Hancock Mutual Life Insurance Company of Boston, Massachusetts: A Half Century Completed, 1862–1912,* Boston, John Hancock Printing Shop, 1912; O'Donnell, Terence, *History of Life Insurance in Its Formative Years,* Chicago, American Conservation Company, 1936; James, Marquis, *The Metropolitan Life: A Study in Business Growth,* New York, Viking Press, 1947; Buley, R. Carlyle, *The American Life Convention, 1906–1952: A Study in the History of Life Insurance,* New York, Appleton-Century-Crofts, 1953; Keller, Morton, *The Life Insurance Enterprise, 1885–1910: A Study in the Limits of Corporate Power,* Cambridge, Massachusetts, Belknap Press, 1963; Grun, Bernard, *The Timetables of History: A Horizontal Linkage of People and Events,* New York, Simon & Schuster, 1979.

—Jim Bowman

KEMPER CORPORATION

Long Grove, Illinois 60049
U.S.A.
(708) 540-2000
Fax: (708) 540-4279

Public Company
Incorporated: 1967
Employees: 10,000
Assets: $12.70 billion
Stock Exchange: New York

Kemper Corporation is the non-operating holding company of the Kemper Organization. The firm is divided into two major concerns, insurance services and investment services. The insurance services group includes five independent life, reinsurance, and property and casualty insurance firms that generate about 60% of the company's gross annual revenues and 55% of its annual profits. The investment services division, Kemper Financial Companies, since 1986 is 88% owned by Kemper Corporation and 12% owned by the division's employees. This arm consists of ten regional brokerage firms and investment operations that contribute 39% of the parent firm's annual revenues and 15% of its annual net income.

Kemper Corporation's origins are tied directly to the general business climate of the early 20th century. In 1912, a new Illinois state law requiring compensation for industrial accidents, which were common for the industry at the time, was passed.

Sensing opportunity, a 25-year-old insurance salesman named James S. Kemper proposed to a group of Chicago lumber-industry leaders that they take control of the situation by organizing their own mutual insurance firm. Kemper pointed out that the group could also contain rising premium costs by making workshops safer.

Kemper was rewarded for his plan by being named manager of the new Lumbermens Mutual Casualty Company, incorporated in Illinois on November 18, 1912. Still one of the larger mutual casualty carriers in the United States, Lumbermens owns 40% of today's Kemper Corporation. Lumbermens issued its first policy, to the Rittenhouse and Embree lumberyard, seven days after the firm was incorporated.

In 1913 James Kemper founded National Underwriters insurance exchange to provide supplementary fire insurance for lumbermen. Slow growth continued through World War I. In 1919 Lumbermens opened offices in Philadelphia; Boston; and Syracuse, New York. By this time the company was providing auto insurance as well as workers' compensation and liability insurance. The company's product line has continued to grow steadily.

By 1923 Lumbermens had organized or acquired two subsidiaries and had begun operating in Canada. Around this time, Lumbermens and National Underwriters informally adopted the name Kemper Insurance to refer collectively to the interests James Kemper had organized. Although the two companies were independent, they shared office space. According to company lore, a receptionist coined the name in order to shorten her phone salutation to callers.

James Kemper incorporated American Motorists Insurance Company (AMICO) in 1926. Organized as a stock company, AMICO became part of the Kemper Insurance group but had no financial relationship to Lumbermens. During the Depression, Glen Cove Mutual Insurance Company, a New York mutual company, joined Kemper Insurance and, after a reorganization, reemerged as American Manufacturers Mutual Insurance Company.

During World War II Lumbermens continued to grow. The company placed patriotic advertisements and employed more women, as men went off to fight. In the years after the war, Lumbermens continued to organize subsidiaries, and—in 1948—the company moved to a larger building on Chicago's Wacker Drive.

In 1954 James Kemper became U.S. ambassador to Brazil, but his group of companies continued to grow. The Fidelity Life Association was organized in 1954. Kemper Insurance's first move into life insurance, Fidelity Life, was a mutual company that, again, had no financial ties to Lumbermens. Also in 1954, the Kemper companies invested in an automatic billing machine that helped cut office expenses. This system got a boost in 1957, when the group installed computers to process the vast amounts of data Kemper Insurance collected.

As the company grew, Kemper management, which as of 1959 included James S. Kemper Jr., decided to establish a non-operating holding company in order to give the group greater diversification flexibility. In October 1967, Kemperco Inc. was incorporated in Delaware as a holding company for the property and casualty and life insurance operations of Kemper Insurance. Kemperco was owned primarily by Lumbermens, but its stock was also publicly traded. The holding company began operations in June 1968, with 11 operating subsidiaries. Management established objectives for the new company, including annual average earnings growth of no less than 15% and continuation of diversification into related businesses.

Kemperco's internal development included the organization of National Loss Control Service Corporation in July 1968. The division, known as NATLSCO, offered consulting services in the areas of fire protection, safety, industrial hygiene, air pollution, and boiler and mechanical inspection services. Diversification through external integration included the acquisition of a 40% stake in Extel Corporation, a maker of telecommunications devices, including printers and stock-quotation equipment.

In 1969 Kemperco added a reinsurance division, Kemper Reinsurance Company, and in 1970 Kemperco purchased

Supervised Investors Services, now known as Kemper Financial Services, to manage the firm's investment portfolio. The company's assets also included Bank of Chicago, which owned a local commercial banking operation. In 1972, the company acquired Kemper Investors Life Insurance Company, National Automobile and Casualty Insurance Company, and Sequoia Insurance.

The Kemper organization had outgrown the three buildings it then occupied in Chicago, and in 1971 it had moved to a 1,000-acre campus in Long Grove, Illinois, northwest of Chicago. In 1971 assets managed by the financial-services reached more than $2 billion, and investment income totaled $14 million—more than double the investment income four years earlier. In 1972 the firm reported a 13% volume increase compared to 1971, to $329 million. Much of this growth resulted from acquisitions.

When the 1973 Arab oil embargo sparked runaway inflation in the United States, Kemper suffered. Net income for the fiscal year plunged more than 19%, to $18.9 million, as a slump in Kemper's automobile, worker's compensation, and general liability insurance units offset the steady growth posted in the first three quarters of the year by the other divisions.

Kemper launched a corporate-identity program, and established one-year and five-year internal performance objectives in order to maintain the goal of 15% annual earnings growth set in 1968. As part of its corporate-identity program, Kemperco changed its name to Kemper Corporation, on January 15, 1974. Companywide, profits continued to plunge nearly 37% from the disappointing showing in 1973, with net income dipping to $12.6 million.

This two-year slump prompted Kemper management to reevaluate its operations. In 1974, insurance-premium income contributed about 90% of the company's gross revenues, while investment income contributed about 6.5%. Despite modest diversification, Kemper was still dependent on the maturing insurance industry for the lion's share of its income. Kemper Corporation suffered its worst performance ever in 1975, when net income slid 26% from 1974, to $9.3 million. Repositioning proved to be a wise tactic. In mid-1975 Kemper Corporation launched a new market-sensitive approach, and in 1986 the holding company enjoyed the highest earnings in its nine-year history. Net income soared more than 238%, to $31.4 million, while total assets topped $1 billion for the first time. In 1977 Kemper Corporation posted profits of more than $57 million on sales of $808 million. The company's assets by 1977 topped $1.3 billion.

James S. Kemper Jr. announced his intention to resign as chief executive officer on April 1, 1979. Around this time, the company hit another round of financial bumps after three years of steady growth in revenues and profits. Joseph E. Luecke, Kemper Corporation's new chief executive officer, blamed an annual inflation rate of 13.3% for hurting the company's auto and commercial property insurance rates. Also during 1979, Kemper Corporation adopted the umbrella designation Kemper Group to refer to what had been called the Kemper Insurance and Financial Companies.

In 1979 Kemper's catastrophe losses passed $1 billion for the first time in the history of the insurance industry. Kemper's share of these losses amounted to about $25 million. A catastrophic loss is defined by the Insurance Services Offices as a total insured loss to the industry of $1 million or more. A record 50 such losses were recorded in 1979.

In 1980 Kemper once again reevaluated its dependence on property and casualty operations. Continued diversification into reinsurance and financial services lowered the contribution of insurance operations to earnings by nearly 18% between 1970 and 1980. Kemper management, led by chairman and chief executive officer Joseph E. Luecke, responded by launching an expansion that would carry the firm far beyond property and casualty insurance. One aspect of the diversification program was the purchase of a 24.9% stake in Gibraltar Financial Corporation of California, a savings and loan holding company. Kemper sold some of its other assets, such as its LaBow, Haynes Company insurance brokerage in Seattle, Washington, and its 95% stake in the Bank of Chicago. Combined with the sale of Kemper's 33% stake in Extel Corporation, a manufacturer of communications equipment, Kemper realized a capital gain of about $12 million.

In 1981, Kemper reported a slide in property and casualty insurance business as a result of high interest rates, and while sales climbed 40% over the previous year, operating income suffered. The high interest rates that had helped the investment operations post significant gains in the fiscal year also caused inadequate pricing throughout the insurance industry, resulting in a decline in underwriting results. The diversification program launched in the previous year was expected to cover losses as uncertainty about interest rates continued.

James S. Kemper, founder of Lumbermens, died September 17, 1981. Late in 1981, Kemper announced its intention to acquire Loewi Financial Companies, widening the company's involvement in the financial-services industry. The Milwaukee, Wisconsin–based company owned Blunt Ellis & Loewi, a regional brokerage firm with offices in six midwestern states. Loewi had been a distributor of Kemper Financial Services financial products for several years before the purchase, which was completed in 1982 at a cost of $64 million in cash and stock. It was the first of several acquisitions that expanded Kemper's financial-services division over the next three years.

The timing of the brokerage acquisitions coincided with the decline of the performance of Kemper's investment in Gibraltar Financial savings and loan operation in California. Kemper had lost almost $10 million in 1980 and almost $30 million in 1981 as a result of its investment in Gibralter. The long-term diversification program was meant to help soften the blow that Kemper's property and casualty insurance business would see in 1982 and beyond.

During 1981, Kemper's property and casualty insurance units contributed just 49% of the firm's operating income, compared to 60% in 1980. Rate competition and inflation were blamed for sharp declines in the industry, and Kemper responded by committing $20 million for expansion of its life insurance business, which continued to grow, along with Kemper's annuity products.

In 1982 operating earnings for Kemper's property-casualty operations fell more than 51% compared to the previous year, although life insurance, reinsurance, investment services, and other operations rose by nearly 38%. The expansion of the financial-services business continued with the purchase of Bateman Eichler Hill Richards of Los Angeles for $50 million. Kemper acquired its third brokerage firm in two years with the purchase of an 80% equity stake in Cleveland-based Prescott Ball & Turben in a deal valued at $64 million. The acquisitions made Kemper the 11th-largest brokerage operator in the nation.

The slump in Kemper's property and casualty division continued in 1983, although the firm remained optimistic about long-range prospects. Operating earnings fell 11.7% compared to the previous year, although Kemper's life insurance division posted a 6.1% gain in earnings. In the boardroom, James W. Harding retired as president of the corporation and chief financial officer of the Kemper Group. Kemper Corporation chairman and chief executive Luecke assumed the additional post of president.

Early in 1984, the investment-services division again broadened its operations with the acquisition of Burton J. Vincent, Chesley & Company, a Chicago-based regional securities firm. Kemper's life insurance unit, which saw earnings improve by 43%, continued to offset disappointing showings by the property and casualty business for the fourth straight year. CEO Luecke labeled 1984 the worst year in Kemper Corporation's relatively short history.

In 1985 operating earnings in the property and casualty division rebounded significantly. The company also instituted cost-cutting programs that contributed to improved results. The financial division continued its expansion when Kemper acquired an 80% stake in Boettcher & Company, a Denver, Colorado–based regional brokerage firm, for $16 million. Also in 1985, Kemper began selling its stake in Gibralter Financial. The savings and loan had been losing money consistently since 1980. The sale of its Gibralter stock was completed in May 1986.

James S. Kemper Jr. announced his retirement as chairman of Kemper Corporation in the spring of 1986. Having joined the Kemper organization in 1959, the son of the founder was instrumental in the decision to form Kemper Corporation in 1967.

Improving market conditions helped Kemper's property and casualty operations continue to recover in 1986. Organizational changes and further cost-cutting measures also helped improve bottom-line results, although operating results at the firm's life insurance segment declined by 32%. In an effort to maximize earnings, the company placed its financial-services business in an independent holding company, Kemper Financial Companies in December of 1986. Kemper Corporation then sold 12% of the unit to 1,100 employees in a deal worth about $88 million and retained the remaining 88%.

The stock market crash in October 1987 caused a shakeout in the financial services industry and also at Kemper Financial Companies, especially at the company's securities brokerage units. Overall, the financial-services arm ended 1987 relatively unscathed by the stock market crash, posting earnings 25% higher than those in 1986.

Kemper's property and casualty insurance operations continued to improve as the firm launched a reorganization of the business. Kemper sold most of its accident and health business and established separate profit centers for its national personal and commercial insurance lines.

By 1988, the company was finally beginning to see the fruit of the ongoing diversification program, that had been launched nearly ten years earlier. Net income reached $220 million on revenues of $2.4 billion as the firm's life insurance, reinsurance, and investment-services operations all posted significant gains. Kemper also sought to further control expenses by establishing Kemper Clearing Corporation, a joint operation that clears securities trades for all of the company's securities brokerage operations. Kemper's property and casualty business suffered a decline in earnings, despite improved underwriting results. The division also exited the troubled Massachusetts auto insurance market, a move that cost the firm $21 million.

As the 1980s came to a close, Kemper Corporation plotted yet another major restructuring, that would take the company further away from its sister company, Lumbermens, in an effort to spur profits. The first step was the reduction of Lumbermens Mutual Casualty Company's ownership of Kemper stock to 38.3% from 48.8%, effective April 1, 1989. This was accomplished through the sale of Kemper's American Motorists Insurance Company unit to Lumbermens in exchange for 9.6 million Kemper shares. The move boosted earnings per share by reducing the number of shares outstanding by nearly 15%.

In late 1989 Banco Santander, Spain's fourth-largest bank, acquired a 3% stake in Kemper Corporation for $60 million. The companies teamed up to offer investment and management services to clients in the United States, Europe, and South America and also began offering insurance services to customers in Chile.

In March 1990 the three members of the Kemper Group that were not also members of Kemper Corporation—Lumbermens Mutual Casualty Company, American Motorists Insurance Company, and American Manufacturers Mutual Insurance Company—became known as the Kemper National Insurance Companies, and the Kemper organizations ceased to be referred to as the Kemper Group. Luecke remained chairman of the boards of Kemper Corporation and of the three Kemper National Insurance Companies and David B. Mathis, a Kemper Corporation vice president, became president and chief operating officer of Kemper Corporation. Gerald L. Maatman became president and CEO of the Kemper National Insurance Companies.

Kemper Corporation management takes pride in the fact that return on investment remained at about 16%, on average, since the holding company began operations in 1968. It has weathered fluctuations in its property casualty business, losses stemming from natural and manmade disasters that could have crippled smaller firms, and proceeded with a diversification program that helped the company survive when its core businesses languished.

Principal Subsidiaries: Federal Kemper Life Assurance Company; Kemper Financial Companies Inc. (88.3%); Kemper Reinsurance Company; Economy Fire & Casualty Company; Federal Kemper Insurance Company; National Loss Control Service Corporation.

—Christopher A. Scott

LEGAL & GENERAL GROUP PLC

Temple Court
11 Queen Victoria Street
London EC4N 4TP
United Kingdom
(071) 248-9678
Fax: (071) 528-6222

Public Company
Incorporated: 1920 as The Legal & General Assurance Society
Employees: 6,839
Assets: £17.46 billion (US$28.19 billion)
Stock Exchange: London

Legal & General Group is one of Great Britain's largest insurance concerns. Although it also writes marine, fire, and accident policies and offers investment-management services, life insurance has always stood at the core of its operations. In fact, it sold nothing but life insurance until after World War I, and its reputation today is that of a safe, solid, old-fashioned firm.

The Legal & General Life Assurance Society was founded in 1836, when British life insurance was just beginning to thrive. At that time, rapid population increase in Great Britain and a surge in real personal income were creating favorable conditions for the life insurance industry. Between 1834 and 1836, 310 joint-stock life insurance companies were created, of which Legal & General has turned out to be one of the most durable. Its founders were six London lawyers—Sergeant John Adams, Basil Montagu, W.C.L. Keene, Kenyon S. Parker, J.H.R. Chichester, and George L. Baker—who convened their first board meeting in a legal office at 18 Lincoln's Inn Fields in June 1836. At that meeting, Adams was elected as chairman and the company's initial capitalization was set at £1 million, a goal it reached through sale of stock in 1839. The first board of directors was set at 24 members, raised to 30 at the next meeting, and shares were limited to members of the legal profession.

In October 1836, Legal & General accepted its first policy, for the solicitor Thomas Smith. Although the society carefully screened each applicant for insurance, Smith proved not to be a good risk—he died four years later and his policy of £1,000 was paid after the society had received only about £177 in premiums. That fall, the firm appointed six provincial agents, including one in Edinburgh, and within its first year of business it accepted more than 100 policies.

Legal & General began to loan money to both corporate and individual customers soon after its founding. In 1841 it loaned £20,000 to the Stockton and Hartlepool Railway, and in 1852 it authorized £60,000 worth of credit to the Regent Canal Company. A request from the Great Western Railway in 1846 for a loan of £65,000 was, however, turned down. A substantial number of London aristocrats also took out loans from the firm at this time, more likely than not to cover gambling debts.

Legal & General expanded throughout the rest of the 19th century. In the 1850s it entered the real estate business, investing heavily in the development of Birkenhead, near London, and the transformation of Belvedere Estate into a residential area in 1860. To serve its growing core life insurance business, Legal & General established its first office outside London, in Manchester, in 1889. At the turn of the century, the firm's total assets exceeded £2 million and it was the second-largest insurance company, in terms of capitalization, in Great Britain doing only ordinary life business.

Legal & General emerged from World War I intact, despite four years of paying an unusually high number of claims because of war casualties and the influenza epidemic of 1918. In 1920 the society incorporated and dropped the word "Life" from its name. The company began writing fire and accident policies, a business that immediately proved successful; the new popularity of automobile and airplane travel created a huge demand for accident insurance. In 1929 the restriction of society membership to those in the legal profession was lifted. The Great Depression's effect on the world economy in the 1930s was scarcely felt by the British insurance industry. In fact, historian G. Clayton points out, in his *British Insurance*, that, if anything, widespread pessimism in bad times tends to increase the demand for insurance.

Legal & General expanded overseas and by acquiring other companies. In 1931 it opened a life insurance office in Johannesburg. In 1933 it strengthened its pensions operations when it acquired the London office of New York–based Metropolitan Life Insurance after restrictions placed on U.S. insurance companies in the wake of the 1929 stock market crash made it unprofitable for Met Life to continue its British business. The next year Legal & General further strengthened its position both at home and abroad by acquiring Gresham Life Assurance and Gresham Fire and Accident. The Gresham mergers were particularly important for the firms' long histories of doing business overseas. Gresham's fire insurance business in Australia provided a base from which Legal & General would begin to penetrate the Australian market in 1948.

World War II put a tight squeeze on the British insurance industry. Men and money fueled the war effort, so firms were asked to contribute the former by releasing employees devoted to generating new business and the latter by buying up low-interest government bonds, often selling securities paying higher yields in order to do so. Fire insurance claims skyrocketed as German bombs fell on England. Legal & General was among the many firms forced to relocate their offices outside London for the duration because of the bombing. After several temporary relocations, the company ended up at a former school at Kingswood in Surrey. Its head office remained in Kingswood after the return of peace, and later its central computer was located there as well.

Once the war ended, the firm picked up where it had left off in 1939. In 1947 it began writing fire and accident policies in South Africa, as well as life insurance. In 1956 it added life insurance to its non-life business in Australia. Back home, the firm added marine insurance in 1949, using Andrew Weir & Company as its agent. In 1960 it acquired Andrew Weir's marine subsidiary, British Commonwealth Insurance.

From just after World War II through the late 1960s, Legal & General ranked behind Prudential as Great Britain's second-largest life insurance company when measured by total sums insured, maintaining about 10% of the market. It grew substantially early in the decade, and total assets reached the £1 billion mark by 1970. The 1960s, however, were not without contention for the firm: in 1966 angry shareholders complained when Legal & General failed to raise its dividend and the firm's directors did not adequately explain why. Rumors circulated in the financial press over the next year that Legal & General would "go mutual," with the shareholders selling out to the policyholders, but at its 1967 annual meeting the firm declared that the firm would not change hands.

After a reorganization of the executive office in 1970, increasing internationalization of operations marked the decade for Legal & General. In 1972 it entered into cooperation agreements with three European insurance companies: Colonia of West Germany, La Paix of France, and Reale Mutuale of Italy. In 1973 it joined with the West German firm Cologne Reinsurance Company to purchase Victory Insurance, Britain's second-largest reinsurance company. Legal & General took the majority interest and subsequently bought Cologne's minority stake. In the same year, it sold off Gresham Life Assurance but retained most of its overseas businesses. Between 1974 and 1976, it signed cooperation agreements with AGO Holding—now part of AEGON of the Netherlands, Assubel of Belgium, Ireland's Life of Eire, Vadoise Vie of Switzerland, and Nippon Life. In 1976 Legal & General merged its South African general insurance business with that of Norwich Union under the name Aegis Insurance Company. The company also took some domestic actions during the 1970s. In 1971 it introduced a pensions-management subsidiary and set up the Tyndall Fund–Unit Assurance Company to gain a foothold in the unit-trust field. In 1973 Legal & General acquired the real estate developer Cavendish Land.

At the end of the decade, Legal & General underwent a major reorganization. It separated its British insurance operations, its international operations, and its investment-management activities into the three separate subsidiaries. The new parent company, still called Legal & General Group, became a non-insurance company. The move was made to give Legal & General greater financial flexibility and to differentiate its activities more clearly.

After this reorganization, Legal & General ventured into the U.S. market in 1981 when it acquired Government Employees Life Insurance Company for $140 million. It changed the Washington, D.C.–based company's name to Banner Life the next year. In 1984 it acquired Unilife Netherlands, the Dutch subsidiary of the Unilife Assurance Group, and added it to Legal & General Netherlands. At the same time, however, not all of Legal & General's overseas ventures were working out. The firm decided to terminate its general insurance businesses in France and Australia in 1981. In 1987 Legal & General sold its 45% stake in Aegis Insurance, joining the trend among British companies toward divesting South African holdings because of declining profitability, shareholder pressure, and worries over political instability in that country.

The late 1980s were marked by Legal & General's attempt to bolster its U.S. operations amid some difficulty at home. Throughout much of the decade, the performance of Legal & General's pension fund asset management was embarrassingly poor. In 1987 the amount of assets managed by its investment arm shrank from £12.5 billion to £11 billion after the U.S. stock market crash. To remedy the situation, the firm lured David Prosser from his position as chief of the Coal Board's pension fund in January 1988 to head up its investment-management operations. In Prosser's first year, the investment division's asset pool increased to over £14 billion, and in March 1989 Legal & General strengthened its position in the U.S. market when it acquired William Penn Life Insurance from Continental Corporation, a U.S. insurance concern, for $80 million.

Legal & General also expanded in another direction when it reached a cooperative agreement with Kyoei Mutual Fire and Marine Insurance Company of Tokyo in 1989. The agreement gave the company greater access to the Japanese market. At the same time, it provided more business from Kyoei's industrial clients moving into the unified European market. Legal & General may have a reputation for being old-fashioned, but it seems to have made the proper moves to position itself for the future. Internationalization and diversification have been the watchwords in the financial-service industries, and Legal & General has done well expanding into the United States and Europe. Recognizing that its investment-management operations are important enough to justify their own division was also wise. The firm has grown considerably from the cozy joint venture between six lawyers, and there seems to be no reason why it should not keep growing in times to come.

Principal Subsidiaries: Legal and General Assurance Society Limited; Legal & General Independent Intermediaries Limited; Legal & General Investment Management (Holdings) Limited; Legal & General Mortgage Services Limited; Legal & General Finance PLC; Legal & General Finance Inc. (U.S.A.).

Further Reading: Leigh-Bennett, E.P., *On This Evidence,* London, Baynard Press, 1936; Clayton, G., *British Insurance,* London, Elek Books, 1971.

—Douglas Sun

LINCOLN NATIONAL CORPORATION

1300 South Clinton Street
Fort Wayne, Indiana 46801
U.S.A.
(219) 455-2000
Fax: (219) 455-2733

Public Company
Incorporated: 1905 as Lincoln National Life Insurance Company
Employees: 16,465
Assets: $25.07 billion
Stock Exchanges: New York Midwest Pacific London Tokyo

Lincoln National Corporation is a multi-line insurance company, specializing in reinsurance, which continues to maintain its headquarters in the midwestern city of its origin. Its founders selected the name "Lincoln" as a symbol of integrity in an era when insurance companies were often suspect, and Robert Todd Lincoln quickly authorized the use of his father's image. Through the years the company grew both by internal expansion and by acquisitions, always maintaining stable leadership and highly conservative accounting and investment principles.

Lincoln National Life Insurance Company was preceded by a troubled firm in Fort Wayne, Indiana, called the Fraternal Assurance Society of America, which seems to have been a purely commercial operation. Its founder was Wilbur Wynant, who organized a number of supposedly nonprofit fraternal insurance companies which promised to pay benefits by leveling assessments on surviving policyholders. Wynant, who was new to Fort Wayne in 1902, persuaded a number of respected business and professional men to join him in the company, but within two years Wynant had skipped town, and his local associates were left to pick up the pieces or fold the company. The local businessmen reorganized as a legal reserve company to be capitalized at $200,000 but prepared to open for business when $100,000 in stock was sold.

Lincoln National Life Insurance Company was incorporated in Fort Wayne on May 15, 1905. A few months later the New York state investigation of the insurance industry known as the Armstrong Committee exposed widespread abuses and led to much more effective state regulation of the industry. Lincoln National was fully prepared for the more stringent regulations, and used the Lincoln name and image to good effect in promoting the new company amid widespread public suspicion of all insurance companies. Arthur Fletcher Hall, formerly an agent for Equitable Life Assurance Society of the United States, was brought from Indianapolis, Indiana, to serve as secretary and manager, and for practical purposes he was the chief executive officer from the beginning, although a local businessman held the unsalaried office of president. When the company began to write policies in September of 1905 it had three agents, including Hall. By 1911 the company had 106 agents and was in sound financial condition.

Arthur F. Hall was the dominant figure at Lincoln National Life Insurance for the company's first 37 years, and he did not hesitate to employ able and determined associates. In 1911 Hall hired Franklin B. Mead, the firm's first full-time actuary. Mead was much more than a numbers man. He devised careful plans for underwriting life insurance policies and for writing reinsurance policies for other companies, and he was a skilled manager. Mead provided statistical support for the company's medical director, Calvin English, and Lincoln National soon achieved a reputation for writing profitable insurance on carefully screened substandard—or undesirable—risks. While the typical insurance company rejected about 11% of those who applied for coverage, Lincoln National turned down only about 4%.

In 1916 the company adopted the policy of securing additional insurance in force by taking over other companies. Michigan State Life Insurance Company, acquired in 1916, was even younger than Lincoln Life, but it had grown more quickly. Michigan State Life had been a tool of Frederick L. Apps, who had involved Michigan State Life in a complex fraud. When Lincoln National purchased Michigan State Life, a web of companies set up by Apps to support the insurance company collapsed. Michigan State Life itself was a sound purchase. The merger was so successful that Hall took over another successful midwestern firm in 1917, the Pioneer Life Insurance Company of Fargo, North Dakota. Beyond the additional insurance acquired, these mergers also greatly increased the number of experienced agents selling Lincoln National policies throughout the Midwest.

During World War I the company grew quickly. Between 1913 and 1914 Lincoln National's reinsurance more than doubled, to $2 million. By 1917 reinsurance was bringing in $9.6 million. Lincoln National did not hesitate to pick up business from large German reinsurers at this time. In 1917 the company took over the Pittsburgh Life, with its $2.5 million reinsurance business; but the great influenza epidemic of 1918–1919 had a far greater effect on the company. Death claims almost equaled those the company had paid out over the preceding decade, and extraordinary measures were required to pay benefits. Stockholders went without dividends and the members of the executive committee personally loaned $300,000 to the company, but Mead rightly predicted that deaths attributable to the war or the epidemic would raise demand for life insurance importance.

Lincoln National was highly successful throughout the 1920s. The firm built its own office building on the southern edge of downtown Fort Wayne in 1921, part of the site it still occupies, in order to accommodate the growing number of home-office employees. Hall became president in 1923, the year the headquarters building was occupied. Hall was a paternalistic chief executive and encouraged athletic and cultural activities for employees. As was typical in the 1920s, women employees were required to resign when they married, but Hall did sponsor tennis and basketball programs for single women. There was also a nine-hole putting course atop the new building, open to clerical employees as well as to management.

In 1928 Hall employed Louis A. Warren, who was establishing his reputation as a Lincoln scholar, to direct the Lincoln Historical Research Foundation. Hall had only a vague idea of doing something in line with the company's name, but Warren soon persuaded him that the company should sponsor and finance a major research library devoted entirely to the life of Abraham Lincoln. When Warren finally retired 28 years later, the company's library had grown into a national center for Lincoln scholars, and it is called the Louis A. Warren Lincoln Library and Museum, funded entirely by the company.

Under Hall's conservative management Lincoln National avoided the extravagant financial schemes of the late 1920s, although he arranged another successful merger—with Merchants Life Insurance Company of Des Moines, Iowa—in 1928. Hall fought off efforts to sell control of the company to interests based in New York or Chicago and announced his determination to keep Lincoln National in Fort Wayne. Its business was still entrenched in the Midwest and most of its policyholders lived on farms or in small towns. Throughout the 1920s the company had acquired a considerable amount of farm property as a result of defaults on mortgages it held as investments, but Hall worked diligently to make the farms pay, and the company reluctantly found itself raising livestock and distilling mint. The company shifted investment emphasis from mortgages to corporate bonds before the stock market crash of 1929, and began to sell off its farm properties in 1928, even at a loss rather than try to farm the land itself.

The Depression brought unprecedented problems for Lincoln Life and the entire insurance industry. Failed investments were more numerous than ever before, but the company began to be troubled by suicides among policyholders, often disguised as accidents. There was also an expensive problem resulting from policies written by agents desperate for business on persons who were high risks or simply unable to pay for the insurance. The company's rejection rate increased by 75% between 1928 and 1931. Its basic business remained sound and profitable, despite the Depression, and its reinsurance business for some 300 insurance companies was particularly successful.

In 1932 the company unveiled a monumental statue of "Abraham Lincoln, The Hoosier Youth" by sculptor Paul Manship, who received $75,000 for the work. The Lincoln image was a vital theme in the company's advertising during the 1930s. Home-office employment remained stable throughout the Depression, but the proportion of men increased significantly as the company protected the jobs of family men at the expense of unmarried women. There was not always sufficient work for all of the employees, but the company avoided layoffs and prepared for busier and more prosperous times to come. The Depression also meant opportunities for healthy companies to acquire less successful firms, and Lincoln National took over three smaller life insurance companies between 1932 and 1933: Northern States Life Insurance Company of Hammond, Indiana; Old Line Life Insurance Company of Lincoln, Nebraska; and Royal Union Life Insurance Company of Des Moines, Iowa. The company's business was still primarily midwestern, but Lincoln National reached $1 billion of insurance in force in 1939, a goal which Hall had hoped to reach by 1930.

Franklin Mead had long been the second-ranking executive at Lincoln National, and was Arthur Hall's likely successor until Mead's own death in 1933. Mead's successor as chief actuary and prospective president was Alva McAndless, always known as "Mac," who had joined the company in 1919. Hall, in failing health, became chairman of the board early in 1939, and McAndless became president and chief executive officer. His primary concern was not in writing insurance policies—that part of the business flourished—but the low yield on the company's investments. Indiana insurance law had been changed to permit greater investment in corporate bonds, but McAndless disliked the high-yielding 30-year obligations of utilities and railroads, while few new mortgages were available on farm property, and interest on government bonds slipped as low as 1.9% in 1940. The company turned increasingly to mortgages on urban property, particularly homes.

During World War II the company contended with higher federal taxes and a greatly altered investment climate. Labor costs were also a concern. In 1941 the company increased starting salaries for the first time since the onset of the Depression. The tight labor market also persuaded the company to relax its ban on the employment of married women. During the war there was a reduction in automobile accidents, as driving declined as a result of gasoline rationing. Life insurance companies had long escaped most federal income taxes, but wartime demand for revenue led to some changes in the laws in 1942, and the company began to pay a modest level of corporate income tax from 1943 onward.

McAndless also planned for postwar expansion. He particularly hoped to develop Lincoln National's agency force and prod agents to sell more life insurance. By 1945 the company's profits depended more upon its extensive reinsurance business. McAndless also kept dividends moderate and built up extensive cash reserves, both to provide against emergencies—like the Depression—and to take advantage of attractive opportunities. The company had been unable to finance an attractive acquisition during the Depression, and its leadership did not wish to be caught short again. In 1951 Lincoln National purchased the Reliance Life Insurance Company of Pittsburgh from the Mellon National Bank for $27.5 million cash. Reliance was an exceedingly conservative firm with a strong agency force. Mellon had been forced to sell the operation in order to meet the requirements of the Bank Holding Act. It was a very large merger for the early 1950s, and Lincoln National made the most of it. It retained Reliance employees, as promised; reduced expenses; and greatly improved investment results. Reliance agents were particularly strong in the South, a region in which Lincoln National was very weak.

McAndless was very much a detail man. He was always tight with the company's money and held a close rein on the company. Under McAndless Lincoln National's leadership became increasingly shallow as strong managers left for positions of greater authority. His management style was not well-suited for the much larger company which resulted from the Reliance merger, but before any plans were made for a change in leadership, McAndless died of a heart attack early in 1954. McAndless was succeeded by another actuary, Walter O. Menge, who had worked for Lincoln National since 1937. Menge was a systematic chief executive who understood how to manage a large and complex business and could delegate authority. He planned carefully and made effective use of Lincoln National's large capital base while recognizing its problems. Lincoln National faced lagging sales of ordinary life insurance and a decreasing market share in a highly competitive market. He increased efforts in group insurance and continued to seek attractive acquisitions. In 1957 Lincoln National made its first move beyond the United States, acquiring the Dominion Life Assurance Company of Waterloo, Ontario.

New York state had long been known for the rigor of its insurance regulation, and only in 1960 did Lincoln National begin to write insurance there, through a new subsidiary. The effort eventually proved unsuccessful and the company no longer offers life insurance in the New York market. Two years later it acquired American States Insurance Company of Indianapolis in an effort to broaden its business beyond life insurance. This was also a defensive acquisition, to help protect Lincoln National's position as the largest reinsurer of life insurance policies in the country. General Reinsurance Corporation, a large non-life reinsurance company had recently entered the life reinsurance market, and Menge believed that his firm should offer a full line of coverage in both the insurance and reinsurance markets in order to remain fully competitive. A year later Lincoln National made its first direct move into the European reinsurance market, although it had long written reinsurance for European firms. The company established a new subsidiary in Paris, the Compagnie de Reassurance Nord-Atlantique, and soon extended its business into Asian and African markets. Lincoln National agents sometimes complained that the firm's extensive reinsurance business only encouraged new competitors in the life insurance field, but reinsurance was a large and very profitable part of Lincoln National's business, more successful in many ways than its agency business.

As Lincoln National grew larger and more complex, becoming a major competitor in the international reinsurance market, Walter Menge and his associates began to plan a reorganization. There was no thought of leaving Fort Wayne, but there were plans for a holding-company structure. Before this could be achieved Menge moved up to chairman in 1964, and was succeeded as president by actuary Henry F. Rood. Rood pushed forward with plans to adopt the holding-company structure and dreamed of Lincoln National becoming a financial department store. He established subsidiaries in the Philippines and Great Britain. The Lincoln Philippine Life Insurance Company was established for legal reasons in a nation where the company already did business, but the British market was vastly different, and Lincoln National's methods were resented widely.

Henry Rood served as president of Lincoln National for only four years before he became chairman, although he remained chief executive officer for a further three years. Thomas A. Watson assumed the office of president in 1968. A marketing expert in group insurance, he had joined the firm in 1945. Rood carried through the 1968 creation of the Lincoln National Corporation as the holding company for all of the firm's operating companies, but Watson had the responsibility for implementing the reorganization.

In 1969 Lincoln National Corporation was listed for trading on the New York Stock Exchange, an appropriate symbol of the new holding company's wider outlook. So too was its acquisition of Chicago Title and Trust Company in 1969, but this purchase brought unexpected problems. Title insurance was a new line of business for Lincoln National, but far more troublesome was Chicago Title's bond-brokerage subsidiary, Halsey, Stuart & Company. The bond business was unfamiliar to Lincoln National, and Halsey Stuart's investment-banking salaries were far higher than those paid in the insurance industry. Thus Halsey, Stuart was sold in 1973. That same year the holding company also divested its British subsidiary, which had never met expectations. Selling insurance in Great Britain was a business which the Fort Wayne executives admitted they did not fully understand. Watson also withdrew from other overseas operations, for business reasons in France, and to avoid local political trouble in the Philippines. At home Watson sharply increased investment in sales agencies in an effort to improve the basic life insurance business.

Thomas Watson moved relatively early to open Lincoln National's offices and agencies to women and blacks. In 1973 it established Lincoln Life Improved Housing, to rehabilitate abandoned dwellings near its Fort Wayne headquarters, a program which continues.

Watson planned carefully for an early retirement and in 1977 passed the presidency to Ian M. Rolland, a Fort Wayne native who had joined Lincoln National in 1956. Like most of his predecessors, Rolland was an actuary, although he had a wide range of experience within the company.

As chief executive officer Ian Rolland stressed systematic organization and sophisticated planning as essential for a large and complex corporation. He continued Lincoln National's policy of acquisitions, most notably Security Connecticut Life Insurance Company in 1979. Security Connecticut had no agents of its own and sold its life insurance policies entirely through independent agents and brokers. The combination of company-employed and independent agents has been successful for Lincoln National, despite the potential for conflict between agents. In 1981 Lincoln National acquired First Penn–Pacific Life Insurance Company, an Illinois firm. First Penn–Pacific brought with it growing sales in universal life policies, which quickly became a major part of Lincoln National's life insurance business. By 1983 Lincoln National, through its various subsidiaries, had $100 billion of life insurance in force, and it continued to expand by acquiring both life and property and casualty insurance companies. The larger but less visible reinsurance business grew more by internal expansion, but the firm did acquire National Reinsurance Corporation in 1984, which brought important additions in property and casualty reinsurance. Lincoln National also cautiously reentered the British market in 1984, this time by purchasing an established British company, Cannon Assurance Limited. The following year it sold both its Canadian life insurance subsidiary and Chicago Title and Trust, withdrawing entirely from the title insurance business.

From the mid-1980s Lincoln National had greatly increased its activity in group health insurance and had established its own health-maintenance organizations in Indiana and Florida. Lincoln National organizes its business in five major lines: property and casualty, group life and health, individual life, life and health reinsurance, and pensions and annuities. It ranks as the nation's seventh-largest publicly held insurance company.

The individual life business is steady but highly competitive, and Lincoln National has accepted a lower market share in order to avoid low-profit policies. The company sold National Reinsurance in May 1990 and withdrew from most of its property and casualty reinsurance business, but it continues to emphasize its traditional strength in life reinsurance and is expanding its role in the health reinsurance market. During the 1980s the company developed a variety of investment programs, particularly individual annuities and corporate pensions. Despite early problems, the health-maintenance organizations are now profitable and are growing in size and in geographical scope, expanding into Texas and California.

Lincoln National had not advertised its individual life insurance since the mid-1980s and it is much better known within the insurance industry than to the public at large.

As a financially sound company which pursues a long-term plan rather than immediate profit, Lincoln National has been concerned that it might become a takeover target. In 1986 the company adopted a poison-pill provision to restrict any partial takeover effort, and in July of 1990 it announced the sale of $312 million in new convertible preferred stock to Dai-Ichi Mutual Life Insurance Company. The Japanese firm plans to work closely with Lincoln National and to form several joint ventures, but is committed to a long-term holding and has pledged not to acquire more than 9.8% of the voting shares or to cooperate with any group accumulating shares. The alliance with Dai-Ichi places Lincoln National in an exceptionally strong financial position, but the precise relationship between the two firms remains to be determined.

Principal Subsidiaries: American States Insurance Companies; American States Life Insurance Company; American Union Reinsurance Company; Cannon Lincoln PLC (U.K.); Corporate Benefit Systems Services Corporation; Employers Health Insurance Company; First Penn-Pacific Life Insurance Company; Healthwin Insurance Company; K&K Insurance Group, Inc.; Lincoln European Reinsurance Company (Belgium); Lincoln National Life Insurance Company; Lincoln National Investment Management Company; Lincoln Security Life Insurance Company; Lynch & Mayer, Inc.; Modern Portfolio Theory Associates, Inc.; Preferred Financial Corporation; The Richard Leahy Corporation; Security-Connecticut Life Insurance Company; Western Security Life Insurance Company; W.W. Vincent & Company.

Further Reading: Neely, Mark E. Jr., *Easy to Remember: A Brief History of the Lincoln National Life Insurance Company,* Fort Wayne, Indiana, Lincoln National Corporation, 1980.

—Patrick J. Furlong

LLOYD'S OF LONDON

1 Lime Street
London EC3M 7HA
United Kingdom
(071) 623-7100
Fax: (071) 626-2389

Wholly Owned Society of Corporation of Lloyd's
Incorporated: 1871 as Society of Lloyd's
Employees: 7,716
Assets: £19.24 billion (US$31.06 billion)

Lloyd's is not an insurance company but a society of individuals who personally accept unlimited liability for claims under insurances accepted on their behalf "each for his part and not one for another." The Corporation of Lloyd's supplies the marketplace and regulates the conduct of the market without dictating what risks shall be insured or what premiums shall be charged. Lloyd's is a unique institution, a survival from the age, 300 years ago, before insurance companies existed.

In today's Lloyd's, business can be placed only by approved insurance brokers, known as Lloyd's brokers. There are nearly 29,000 individual underwriting members, called Names, grouped in some 400 underwriting syndicates. One person, the active underwriter, is empowered to accept insurances on behalf of the syndicate members. A syndicate is not a partnership: each member is liable only for a personal fraction of any insurance. Each syndicate has a managing agency which appoints the active underwriter. The membership of a syndicate varies from year to year. Each member's affairs at Lloyd's are managed by a member's agent. What began simply as a meeting place for persons interested in marine insurance has evolved into a regulated market for general insurance all over the world.

In the 1680s Edward Lloyd opened a coffeehouse in Tower Street, London, near the docks. He sought to attract a clientele of persons connected with shipping and in particular marine underwriters, those willing to transact marine insurance. By 1689 he was well established. In 1691 his coffeehouse moved to Lombard Street. Lloyd provided shipping intelligence. After his death in 1713 the business was carried on by a succession of masters. From 1734 the business published *Lloyd's List,* a newspaper featuring shipping news. The paper still appears daily.

In the early 18th century Lloyd's became the main, though not the only, place where marine underwriters congregated. The Bubble Act of 1720 gave two newly formed corporations, The London Assurance and The Royal Exchange Assurance, the exclusive right to transact marine insurance as corporations, but expressly allowed individual private underwriters to continue operating. The two corporations exercised the utmost caution and took only a fraction of the growing market, leaving scope for private underwriters. Some of these were also willing to effect gambling insurances, where the policyholder did not stand to lose financially if the event insured against occurred, that is, he had no insurable interest. Such insurances on ships and cargoes were forbidden by an Act of 1745 but persisted on lives and specific events.

In 1769 some underwriters who disapproved of gambling insurances broke away. They persuaded a Lloyd's waiter, Thomas Fielding, to open a New Lloyd's Coffee House which, in five years, drove the old one out of business. The new Lloyd's became cramped. In 1771 nine merchants, underwriters, and brokers formed a committee which took over the premises and appointed two masters to run them. Lloyd's moved into the Royal Exchange in 1773. By the Life Assurance Act, 1774, Parliament prohibited gambling insurance on lives, thus vindicating the stand of those who had reorganized Lloyd's.

In 1779 Lloyd's had only 179 subscribers. These enjoyed the sole right of entry to the underwriting room at Lloyd's. The wars with France from 1792 to 1815 brought great prosperity for marine insurers, among them John Julius Angerstein, an underwriter and broker who served as chairman in 1786, from 1790 to 1796, and again in 1806. At the height of the wars the number of subscribers rose to over 2,000.

British entrepreneurs chafed at the law against new marine insurance companies. In 1824 the Bubble Act was at last repealed, but peace had signaled a decline in marine insurance. The number of subscribers fell from 2,150 in 1814 to 953 in 1843. In 1846, to raise money, a higher subscription was imposed on those subscribers who underwrote insurances and only 189 paid. In 1844, the committee of Lloyd's abolished the office of the masters and assumed full responsibility, through its secretary, for administering the market.

In 1848 Captain G.A. Halsted of the Royal Navy was appointed secretary, a post he held for 20 years. From 1850 Lloyd's began to appoint politically prestigious persons from outside its own community to the chairmanship. The most notable was G.J. Goschen, a young liberal member of Parliament who later became chancellor of the exchequer. He was chairman from 1869 to 1886 and again from 1893 to 1901. After 1901 Lloyd's reverted to having chairmen who worked in the market.

During the first half of the 19th century the committee was largely concerned with intelligence-gathering for the benefit of Lloyd's members. Beginning in 1811 it appointed firms and persons in ports throughout the world to provide shipping information. By 1829 there were over 350 Lloyd's Agents, as they were called. Lloyd's Agents receive no remuneration except for services rendered to underwriters such as surveying damaged property. They could, however, hope for some commercial advantage from their association with Lloyd's.

Marine underwriters have always felt the need for information about ship construction. As early as 1760 they formed a registration society which published a book of details of ships for the use of subscribers only. In 1798 shipowners began publishing a similar book. In 1834 the two publications were merged to form Lloyd's Register of Shipping, administered by a committee representing shipowners, merchants, and marine underwriters. The register operates as a corporation separate from Lloyd's.

The provision of intelligence loomed large in the work of Henry Hozier, who was secretary from 1874 to 1906. In addition to strengthening Lloyd's central staff, he saw the desirability of getting information promptly, and set up coastal telegraph stations for that purpose. By 1884 Lloyd's had 17 stations at home and 6 abroad. They worked in cooperation with the Admiralty. Hozier was knighted. He was a pioneer of wireless telegraphy which Lloyd's used early in the 20th century.

For much of the 19th century the committee exercised little power over its underwriting members. Lloyd's remained a loosely run club. Not until 1851 did a general meeting resolve that any member becoming bankrupt should forfeit his membership. Legislation was sought to strengthen the committee's powers. The Lloyd's Act, 1871, made Lloyd's a corporation, the Society of Lloyd's. The objectives of the society were stated as the carrying on of marine insurance by members and the collection and publication of intelligence. At that time Lloyd's participation in non-marine insurance was negligible and the Act made no reference to it or, indeed, to insurance brokers.

Between 1849 and 1870 the underwriting membership of Lloyd's had doubled. The committee became increasingly concerned to see that applicants for membership had the necessary means to support their underwriting. From 1856, in a few cases, guarantees or deposits were required, but it was not until 1882 that they became mandatory. Even then they related only to marine insurance.

After 1871 the volume of non-marine insurance became significant. Its growth was largely due to the efforts of C.E. Heath, an underwriter who began his own business in 1881. Besides transacting fire insurance he pioneered new forms such as all risks insurance on property on land, and on household burglary. C.E. Heath underwrote on behalf of a syndicate which in 1887 comprised 15 Names.

In 1908, at Heath's prompting, Lloyd's took steps towards tightening security under Lloyd's policies. A general meeting agreed that all underwriters should provide certificates of solvency from approved auditors and that premiums be held in trust accounts for the payment of claims. This had beneficial effects in the following year. The Assurance Companies Act, passed in 1909, which for the first time imposed a measure of regulation on companies transacting the main classes of general insurance, left to the Corporation of Lloyd's the primary responsibility for regulating Lloyd's underwriters, as did subsequent regulatory Acts.

The years 1875–1900 saw the accelerating development of Lloyd's in two respects. Thanks to the activities of Lloyd's brokers, much business began to reach Lloyd's from the United States and other overseas sources. Reinsurance, that is, the acceptance of liabilities assumed by direct insurers under their own policies, came to be transacted at Lloyd's, which pioneered novel forms of reinsurance contracts.

World War I affected Lloyd's favorably, creating a large demand for war-risk coverage at high premiums. The state took 80% of the war risk on ships, leaving 20% to private underwriters. The state also insured cargoes at sea at fixed rates, leaving underwriters free to offer lower rates for any business they wanted. They made large profits on the desirable cargo business while the state was losing money on the residue. Insurance of war risk on property on land was left to private enterprise for three years. Lloyd's took the lead in providing coverage where most insurance companies were unwilling to do so. The business proved profitable.

At Lloyd's, all policies were prepared by brokers who then had to take them to the underwriting room for signature on behalf of all the syndicates concerned, a tedious process. In 1916, to save clerical labor, the committee sanctioned an optional system whereby policies could be signed on behalf of all the underwriters concerned in a new bureau, Lloyd's Policy Signing Bureau. In 1924 use of the bureau, renamed Lloyd's Policy Signing Office, became mandatory.

The first quarter of the 20th century saw the development of three new classes of insurance—motor, aviation, and credit. Credit insurance involved a guarantee that moneys due would be paid. In 1923, one syndicate transacting this business failed through reckless underwriting. The committee of Lloyd's banned future direct insurance by way of financial guarantees but allowed reinsurance of such business to continue.

The reputation of Lloyd's depends on claims being met by underwriters. Some underwriting syndicates may fail through dishonesty or poor underwriting. In 1927 Lloyd's set up a central fund, financed by a continuing small levy on premiums. This fund is held in trust for the benefit of policyholders whose claims are not met.

In World War II Lloyd's again prospered although war risks were undertaken by the government. Special arrangements had to be made to protect Lloyd's U.S. business. Lloyd's established a U.S. trust fund into which all premiums in U.S. dollars had to be paid and held for the benefit of policyholders.

The first half of the 20th century was a profitable time for Lloyd's. Its underwriters proved themselves more flexible than insurance companies. They identified risks overcharged by company cartel rates and, by selective underwriting, skimmed the cream of the business. Large insurances had to be shared among many individual underwriters. The increasing size of insurances led to a growth in the size of syndicates. In 1890 a syndicate with ten Names was exceptional. By 1952 there were 16 syndicates with 100 Names or more. The largest had more than 300 Names. Large syndicates developed for motor insurance, of which Lloyd's had no more than 5% of the £100 million market in 1950.

The growth of Lloyd's had three consequences. Firstly, the need for further underwriting capacity started a hunt for new Names to provide the capital required. Brokers were well placed to find people. They also organized underwriting syndicates. A number called underwriting agents acted as both members' agents and managing agents. Secondly, the various interests at Lloyd's formed market associations to deal collectively with the problems they encountered. Marine underwriters formed their own association within Lloyd's in 1909. An association for fire and accident—non-marine—underwriters was formed in 1910 and Lloyd's Insurance Brokers' Association was founded. Lloyd's Motor Underwriters' Association dates from 1931, and Lloyd's Aviation Underwriters' Association from 1935. Thirdly, pressure on space at the Royal Exchange became acute. In 1928 Lloyd's moved out to specially built premises in Leadenhall Street.

The years since 1950 saw the most spectacular growth at Lloyd's. In 1957 a further building had to be opened on an adjoining site across Lime Street. In 1983 the old Leadenhall Street building was demolished and Lloyd's commissioned a new structure, designed by Richard Rogers, for the site. This was opened in 1986, the Lime Street building being retained. Meanwhile much work had been transferred to out-stations at Chatham and Colchester.

Between 1952 and 1968 the membership of Lloyd's nearly doubled, from 3,157 to 6,052. In considering how to increase underwriting capacity, Lloyd's appointed a working party under the chairmanship of the Earl of Cromer. Meanwhile, in 1969, membership, hitherto confined to the commonwealth, was opened to nationals of all countries. Eligibility was extended to British women in 1970. It was not until 1972 that women were admitted to the underwriting room.

The Cromer working party issued its report in 1970. It favored the admission of corporations as members, but this recommendation was not adopted. However, thanks to the profitability of Lloyd's, membership again rose steeply, reaching 20,145 in 1982 and 33,532 in 1988, although by 1990 it had fallen to 28,770.

One growth area since 1950 has been U.K. motor insurance. Lloyd's holds one-sixth of the market, thanks partly to a modification of Lloyd's normal procedure which required all business to be transacted in the underwriting room. Since 1965, Lloyd's has allowed motor syndicates to deal directly with non-Lloyd's intermediaries if they are sponsored by a Lloyd's broker. Motor syndicates therefore can operate as if they were insurance companies.

About half of Lloyd's business is derived from the United States. U.S. insurance brokers have cast envious eyes on Lloyd's brokers who alone have access to Lloyd's and therefore receive commissions on all business placed there. The big Lloyd's brokers found themselves exposed to takeover overtures from their U.S. counterparts. In 1979 Marsh & McLennan, the largest U.S. broker, acquired C.T. Bowring. In 1982 Alexander & Alexander acquired Alexander Howden. Since 1982 two Lloyd's brokers have acquired two large U.S. brokers: Sedgwick took over Fred S. James and Willis Faber merged with Corroon & Black.

In a market such as Lloyd's, where hundreds of enterprises competed from time to time, unsatisfactory situations arise. One such event was the affair of the Sasse syndicate in 1976. Its active underwriter authorized an underwriting firm in New York to write business on his syndicate's behalf. The firm transacted a large volume of bad business which led to heavy losses. The Sasse syndicate exceeded the premium income it was authorized to write. Some members of the syndicate, faced with heavy calls, sued Lloyd's, alleging that losses arose from a failure to supervise. It became apparent that the machinery of Lloyd's was not working properly. In 1979 the committee appointed a working party under the chairmanship of Sir Henry Fisher to examine self-regulation at Lloyd's. The working party reported in 1980. It made 79 recommendations for improvements. Apart from a general tightening up, the working party recommended a new governing body with wider powers. It drew attention to the growing influence of the big brokers. In 1978 the six largest brokerage groups had placed more than half of Lloyd's business and the proportion was growing.

Lloyd's accepted the main recommendations and sought legislative powers to bring them into effect. The result was the Lloyd's Act of 1982. This act put a new body, the Council of Lloyd's, over the committee, which had consisted of 16 persons, mainly underwriters, active in the Lloyd's market. The council was to include, in addition to the 16 committee members, 8 representatives of the Names not working in the market—external members—and 3 nominated persons not members of Lloyd's. At the prompting of the governor of the Bank of England, a prominent accountant, Ian Hay Davison, was appointed chief executive and became a nominated person and one of three deputy chairmen of Lloyd's. The Act also provided for the separation of brokers and managing agents. They were to divest themselves of financial interests in each other. The separation was achieved by 1987.

At about the time of the Act, scandals erupted involving two leading broker groups. Large amounts of premiums had been siphoned off from some profitable syndicates by means of reinsurance with companies in which the chairmen and other directors of the groups had a financial interest. The reverberations of these events continued for some years with expulsions and suspensions, but none involved any loss to policyholders as distinct from Names. Lloyd's premium income did not suffer. The council made determined efforts to stamp out internal abuses.

Lloyd's business has been consistently profitable as a whole, except in 1965 to 1967, although in any year some individual syndicates may make serious losses involving large cash calls on their members who are personally liable, without limit of amount, for their share of the insurances written for their account. Among risks that have turned out badly are computer leasing insurances and liability insurance in the United States, where retrospective liability has arisen for disability caused by asbestosis and for pollution damage.

In 1986 the government appointed the Neill Committee to consider whether those who participated at Lloyd's as Names had protection comparable to that provided for investors under the Financial Services Act of 1986. The committee reported in 1987. It detected a number of shortcomings and made 70 recommendations for remedy. They included an amendment to the constitution of the council by which it would consist of 12 working members of Lloyd's, 8 representatives of external members, and 8 nominated members from outside Lloyd's, including the chief executive, so that the working members would be in the minority. The council accepted the recommendations beginning with the change to its membership. In three years most of the other changes were implemented.

Lloyd's remains what it has been since the 1770s—a market place for insurance granted by relatively wealthy members. Business is still placed by personal contact between broker and underwriter despite the increasing use of electronics in the service of the market. The council of Lloyd's provides more and more central services such as a central accounting system and training. It exercises a closer control over all units in the market without encroaching on the freedom of underwriters. The means test imposed on new members has been raised from £100,000 to £250,000. Since 1988 membership has fallen somewhat but members have increased their commitments. At the start of the 1990s, the premium capacity of Lloyd's stood at £11 billion, which comfortably exceeds the amount of business available. The business available in 1989 was approximately £6 billion.

Principal Subsidiaries: Additional Securities Ltd.; Lloyd's of London Press Ltd.

Further Reading: Wright, Charles, and C.E. Fayle, *A History of Lloyd's from the Founding of Lloyd's Coffee House to the Present Day,* London, Macmillan, 1928; Gibb, D.E.W., *Lloyd's of London: a Study in Individualism,* London, Macmillan, 1957; *Self Regulation at Lloyd's: Report of the Fisher Working Party,* London, Lloyd's of London, 1980; Flower, Raymond, and Michael Wynn Jones, *Lloyd's of London: an Illustrated History*, Colchester, Lloyd's of London Press, 1981; Cockerell, Hugh, *Lloyd's of London, a Portrait,* Cambridge, Woodhead-Faulkner, 1984; Hodgson, Godfrey, *Lloyd's of London: A Reputation at Risk,* London, Penguin Books, 1986; Brown, Antony, *Hazard Unlimited,* Colchester, Lloyd's of London Press, 1987; Davison, Ian Hay, *A View of the Room: Lloyd's Change and Disclosure*, London, Weidenfeld and Nicolson, 1987; *Regulatory Arrangements at Lloyd's: Report of the Committee of Enquiry (Neill Report),* London, HMSO, 1987.

—Hugh Cockerell

MARSH & McLENNAN COMPANIES

MARSH & MCLENNAN COMPANIES, INC.

1166 Avenue of the Americas
New York, New York 10036
U.S.A.
(212) 345-6000
Fax: (212) 345-4810

Public Company
Incorporated: 1923 as Marsh & McLennan, Incorporated
Employees: 24,000
Assets: $2.04 billion
Stock Exchanges: New York Midwest Pacific London

Marsh & McLennan Companies is a leading worldwide provider of services on insurance brokerage, reinsurance brokerage, consulting, and investment management.

In 1885 an ambitious young Henry Marsh left Harvard College without graduating and joined R.A. Waller & Company, a Chicago-based insurance agency founded in 1871, the year of the Great Chicago Fire. Marsh's lack of a degree proved no disadvantage in this period of U.S. history. The 1880s and 1890s were a period of political corruption and gross materialism in the United States, yet the age was also one of tremendous industrial expansion and urban growth. In 1889, following the death of Robert A. Waller, Henry Marsh and another employee, Herbert J. Ulmann, bought a controlling interest in the firm, which they renamed Marsh, Ulmann and Company.

In this age of big business, Marsh was convinced that huge profits could be made by managing the insurance affairs of large corporations in return for appropriate commissions. As Marsh himself declared, "What's the use of shooting hummingbirds when elephants are so much easier to hit." Marsh realized that very large companies could set aside sufficient funds to cover themselves against potential losses without placing the risk with insurance companies. In 1901 Henry Marsh talked Charles Schwab, president of the United States Steel Corporation, into adopting such a scheme, with Marsh's company managing an appropriate fund to estimate potential risks to U.S. Steel. In this way Henry Marsh pioneered the modern-day concepts of self insurance and risk management.

Henry Marsh met his future partner and associate, Donald McLennan, in the course of his attempts to secure railroad contracts for his growing insurance agency. McLennan had begun an insurance agency in partnership with L.B. Manley in Duluth, Minnesota, in 1900. Duluth's position on the Great Lakes had made it a major transfer point for the products—mostly agricultural—of the Great Plains. Goods arrived by rail and were loaded onto steamers to be shipped east. When the lakes froze during winter, such products were stored in warehouses owned by the railroads.

McLennan had recognized the enormous insurance potential in these activities. He quickly became an expert on railroad insurance, constantly traveling the Midwest and meeting with company executives. During one round of sales negotiations, McLennan was reported to have spent 30 consecutive nights in a railroad car.

As it transpired, Henry Marsh, Daniel Burrows, and Donald McLennan all had been promised the insurance account of the Chicago Burlington and Quincy Railroad by different directors. Rather than argue over the account, the three men joined forces. All realized the advantages of combining their skills and resources into one company with a view to securing still more insurance contracts.

On December 22, 1904, the *Chicago Record-Herald* reported the launching of the "New agency of Burrows, Marsh & McLennan" with annual premiums of $3 million. Soon other railroad contracts were secured, including The Great Northern and Northern Pacific. In 1906, following the retirement of Daniel Burrows, the new firm became known as Marsh & McLennan (M&M).

In the newly reorganized firm, Marsh concentrated on securing more contracts, while McLennan supervised the railroad account. Marsh's sales tactics sometimes surprised the more staid McLennan—Marsh would stop at nothing to obtain new contracts. He often sailed to England, and even went so far as to rearrange the deck chairs in order to "accidently" meet potential new clients. On one such trip in 1910, Marsh met Theodore Vail, the president of the American Telephone and Telegraph Company (AT&T) and secured that company's business.

By 1917, the year the United States entered World War I, M&M had established offices throughout the country. During the war, McLennan became responsible for the allocation and regulation of building materials for purposes other than those directly related to the war effort. For the duration of the war, no U.S. company could build an industrial plant without McLennan's approval. In this way McLennan acquired many business contacts throughout the United States, enhancing M&M's reputation in the postwar period.

During the economic boom of the 1920s, M&M continued to prosper. In 1923 the legal structure of the company was changed from a partnership to a corporation, Marsh & McLennan, Incorporated. The stock was now held under a voting trust agreement by Marsh, McLennan, and four other people. Marsh became chairman, while McLennan increasingly assumed responsibility for the firm's management. The same year, the reinsurance brokerage firm, Guy Carpenter & Company, became a separately managed business of Marsh & McLennan.

The Great Depression of the 1930s had an adverse effect on the insurance industry. Many institutions and individuals simply could not afford to pay insurance premiums. Although premiums from most types of insurance declined, the life insurance business actually increased, as people craved financial security. The passage of the Social Security Act of 1937 further sparked interest in life and accident insurance as people became more concerned with financial security. Many firms adopted retirement programs to supplement Social Security benefits, and employed M&M to operate such funds. The American Can Company employed M&M to devise a pension plan for its employees, and also asked it to organize the fee-billing service.

After the entry of the United States into World War II, the conservative McLennan was invited to meet with New Deal President Franklin Roosevelt, who asked his advice on the management of the U.S. war industry. McLennan later spoke of his meeting with the famous president: "When I left the White House, I went to my room at the hotel, took a cold shower and then walked around the block several times. It took me at least 48 hours to rekindle my dislike of the President. Never in my life have I met a more charming individual."

Neither Marsh nor McLennan lived to see the end of World War II, however. Henry Marsh died on April 13, 1943, and McLennan on October 9, 1944. Charles Ward Seabury became chairman of the board and Laurence S. Kennedy its new president. The company survived the loss of its two founders and continued to prosper. In 1947 Ford Motor Company selected M&M to handle all its insurance. The postwar boom in consumer spending, much of it on credit, also provided an opportunity for innovation: M&M developed consumer credit insurance which it sold to eight of the nine major New York banks.

Following Seabury's retirement and Kennedy's death in 1955, Hermon Smith became the CEO and chairman. In 1957 Cosgrove & Company, the West Coast's largest regional broker, was merged into Marsh & McLennan. Between 1958 and 1962, 14 other agents and brokers were acquired. By 1962 M&M had become an international company with offices in the world's major financial centers, yet the structure of the company had not changed since 1923. In 1955 shareholders had numbered only 21, up from the original 6 shareholders in 1923. While technically a corporation, it nevertheless operated as a partnership. There were no stockholder meetings and stockholders' identities and the number of shares they held were kept secret. Beginning in 1957, when a stockholder died, retired, or turned 70 years old, his stock had to be sold back to the company.

Given the growing complexity of the insurance business and his desire for company growth, in 1958 Smith began to explore the idea of going public. In March 1962, 673,215 shares of M&M stock were offered to the public. This decision marked a transition in the company's ability to grow.

The 1960s signaled the beginning of a period of unparalleled expansion as M&M embarked on a series of acquisitions of smaller insurance agencies. In 1968, M&M acquired Edwards George and Company of Pittsburgh, Pennsylvania, and R.H. Squire of New York City. Revenues also increased dramatically throughout the 1960s. The company's first annual report, in 1962, recorded revenues of $52 million; by 1968 revenues had jumped to $106 million. In 1969, to administer its services more efficiently, Marsh & McLennan reorganized, and became known as MarLennan Corporation. Henceforth the company would provide a variety of its professional and financial services under the banners of separately managed companies. The first of these, the Putnam Management Company, became part of M&M in 1970. In 1975, M&M's employee-benefit-consulting business was consolidated in William M. Mercer Inc.

The 1970s marked a new phase in international development. John Regan, who became chief executive in 1973, was determined to transform the company into a global insurance force, and embarked on a policy of buying foreign brokerage firms in the world's major financial cities. In 1973 Marlennan acquired a 33.3% interest in the French insurance brokerage Faugere et Jutheau. In 1975 the company acquired a 15% interest in the German firm Gradmann & Holler, and a 29.5% interest in Henijean & Cie in Belgium. That year its name changed again, to Marsh & McLennan Companies.

Not all acquisitions proceeded smoothly, however. In 1980 Regan set his sights on C.T. Bowring, a large London brokerage firm. The acquisition of such a firm would allow M&M direct access to the profitable Lloyd's of London insurance market, open only to British firms. Many executives of Bowring, an old, traditional English firm, resented the takeover by the U.S. brokerage. In long, and often acrimonious, discussions, Bowring executives—despite their dependence on M&M business—continued to reject Regan's terms. Undaunted, Regan went directly to the shareholders, a tactic that outraged Bowring's management. Bowring chairman Peter Bowring appealed to the British Insurance Brokers Association and the British government for help in preventing the incursion. Questions were raised in the House of Commons about the need to protect the British insurance industry. The French, it was reported, would never have allowed this to happen. Despite much rhetoric, little was done to help Bowring. With shares priced far above their market value, British shareholders could not resist the temptation to sell. In the end, Regan paid $580 million for Bowring, more than twice its book value.

Many executives resigned from the British firm. This development stunned Regan, who worried that such a loss of talent would severely hamper the effectiveness of his new acquisition. Regan claimed that he would have abandoned the takeover if he had known it would cause such a personnel exodus. Nevertheless, C.T. Bowring continued to function.

The Bowring purchase was a crucial move in M&M's transformation into a global company. Six months after the takeover, M&M revenues had jumped 28%, while net income increased 22%, to more than $100 million.

M&M's strategy in the 1980s was to diversify beyond insurance into consulting and money management. In 1982 insurance-program management separated from the consulting activities of Mercer to become a separate company, later called Seabury & Smith. M&M's consulting capabilities expanded in the 1980s to include National Economic Research Associates; Temple, Barker & Sloan/Strategic Planning Associates; and Lippincott & Margulies.

In 1990 Marsh & McLennan again refocused on globalization. In January 1990 Marsh & McLennan completed its purchase of a majority stake in Gradmann & Holler, Germany's largest insurance broker. Frank J. Tasco, who took over as chairman in 1986, upheld the policy of innovation that characterized M&M management since the days of Henry Marsh and Donald McLennan.

Principal Subsidiaries: Marsh & McLennan Incorporated; William M. Mercer Companies, Inc.; Temple, Barker & Sloan/Strategic Planning Associates, Inc.; The Putnam Companies, Inc.; Seabury & Smith Planning Associates, Inc.; Guy Carpenter & Company, Inc.; C.T. Bowring Reinsurance Ltd. (U.K.); Clayton Environmental Consultants, Inc.; National Economic Research Associates, Inc.; Lippincott & Margulies, Inc.

Further Reading: Osborn, Neil, ''The American Invasion of Lloyd's,'' *Institutional Investor,* October 1979; Osborn, Neil, ''The Bloody Battle for Bowring,'' *Insurance,* August 1980; Thomas, John D., ''Tales of Marsh & McLennan,'' *M: The Employee Magazine of Marsh & McLennan Companies,* Volume 14, Number 2, 1987.

—Michael Doorley

MassMutual

MASSACHUSETTS MUTUAL LIFE INSURANCE COMPANY

1295 State Street
Springfield, Massachusetts 01111
U.S.A.
(413) 788-8411
Fax: (413) 730-6003

Mutual Company
Incorporated: 1851
Employees: 11,000
Assets: $25.06 billion

Massachusetts Mutual Life Insurance Company has changed slowly over a long period of time, and by doing so has undergone a complete metamorphosis: from personal insurer to financial giant. Today MassMutual insures individuals, businesses, and groups. The firm has also expanded into other fields, and is now a major pension manager, investor, and lender. It is the 11th-largest life insurer in the United States, and though the 1980s were a time of ferment for both the insurance industry and MassMutual, the company continues to grow and prosper on an even keel.

MassMutual opened in 1851 in Springfield, Massachusetts, in a room with three chairs, a table, and a city map on the wall. George W. Rice, a young insurance agent who was selling policies for Connecticut Mutual Life in Hartford, Connecticut, had wanted to open a business in neighboring Massachusetts. Like Connecticut Mutual, the new agency was a mutual company—a company owned by its policyholders.

Rice's Massachusetts Mutual was one of about a dozen mutual companies that had sprung into existence between 1843 and 1851. Mutual companies became attractive vehicles in the nascent insurance industry because they required little working capital, but a Massachusetts state law required an initial stock subscription of $100,000 for insurance companies, so Rice encouraged 31 investors to purchase stock in the new venture. In 1867 MassMutual retired the stock and became the mutual company it was intended to be.

Caleb Rice, a relative of George W. Rice, was the company's first president. He steered the company's growth for its first 22 years—making him the longest-serving president in company history. Rice wore many hats. A former lawyer, state legislator, and county sheriff before coming to MassMutual, Rice was elected the first mayor of Springfield in 1852. MassMutual sold its first policy on August 2, 1851, to Harvey Danks, a MassMutual agent. Soon after, roaming agents like Danks sold policies to many other individuals, but not just to New England homeowners and workers. At higher premiums, MassMutual insured railway and steamship workers, gold-rush adventurers, and people traveling south of the Mason-Dixon Line.

For the next several decades, MassMutual's expansion mirrored that of the United States. In the 1850s, the country was expanding westward. The company followed suit. By 1855 agencies were functioning in New York City, Cleveland, Chicago, and Detroit. In 1868, MassMutual reached the West Coast—before the transcontinental railroad was completed—and established an office in San Francisco.

Between 1850 and 1900 the volume of life insurance in force in the United States rose from $96 million to nearly $7.6 billion. Expansion and aggressive marketing were largely responsible for the growth. The late 19th century, however, was an age of great technological advancement and ushered in a new era for life insurance companies. In 1885, MassMutual bought its first typewriter. Soon after, telephones were installed, which facilitated better communication between agents and the home office.

In 1886 Colonel Martin Van Buren Edgerly was named president. Edgerly had joined MassMutual in 1859 and spent his entire career with the company. He was the first of many career men to take the helm of MassMutual, which tends to look inward for leadership. This reliance on inside talent underscores the company's larger dependence on agents.

Edgerly oversaw a decade of carefully regulated growth, and was replaced in 1895 by John Hall. Hall steered the company through the late 19th century, including the Spanish-American War of 1898—during which the company took minimal losses—and through the numerous business scandals of the early 20th century.

In these years of the robber barons, many insurance companies played fast and loose with laws governing their conduct. To encourage agents to sell more, firms paid excessive commissions. Dishonest executives used sizable assets of companies to control other corporations and for private purposes. MassMutual, under Hall's stewardship, kept clean and continued its regulated growth: the home-office staff grew from 16 in 1884 to 100 in 1907. MassMutual also continued, without change, its practice of selling only life insurance policies payable in a lump sum at death or maturity. The company's first innovation came in 1901, when it began offering policies under which proceeds would be paid over a fixed period or for life.

The company was not a target of the 1906 Armstrong Committee investigation, which uncovered many abuses by New York life insurance companies. The commission had been appointed by the New York state legislature, and its findings affected life insurers throughout the United States. Henceforth, companies were required to distribute dividends annually, and to restrict the size of commissions, and regulate the nature of their investments. The investigation constituted a purge of sorts and signified the industry's maturation.

In the wake of the Armstrong investigation, insurance companies offered more services and products to attract customers who had been disenchanted by the exposed corruption. In 1914, MassMutual instituted a premium waiver in the event of disability, and in 1918, MassMutual designed policies with clauses that provided income in the event of disability. Few significant losses were posted during World War I, although the influenza epidemic of 1918 hit the company hard. By 1924 there were 400 home-office employees, and the amount of insurance in force passed $1 billion.

The stock market crash of 1929 and the ensuing Great Depression hit MassMutual hard. Death claims and policy lapses increased greatly, due to an unusual number of suicides and general economic hardship. So pervasive were policy terminations that the company's insurance in force on July 1, 1932 was less than it had been at the beginning of the year. MassMutual, aside from being an insurer, became a last resort for desperate people seeking financial help. The company doled out millions of dollars in low-interest policy and premium loans. In 1932 alone, the company made $26 million in new policy loans, and from 1929 to 1937 the company made $129 million in policy loans and another $63 million in premium loans. The Depression also saw the introduction of new products. In 1930, MassMutual introduced its first family-income policy. Seven years later, the firm issued its first substandard risk product, and in 1938, the first pension trust policy was issued. Under the leadership of President William H. Sargeant and Bertrand Perry, who succeeded Sargeant in 1936, MassMutual stumbled, but emerged from the Depression and World War II virtually unscathed.

When Alexander MacLean assumed the presidency in 1945, he became the first actuary to take the reins of the company. Consequently, many new products and services were introduced during his tenure. As unions and collective-bargaining units grew in strength, the atmosphere became more conducive to the development of group coverage. In 1946, MassMutual first entered the growing group business, offering group policies and managing group pensions. MassMutual's first group product was a combination pension and insurance policy for Brown-Forman Distillers, the Louisville, Kentucky–based company that produced Jack Daniels whiskey. By 1950 the group department had grown exponentially, employing 200 people in the home office and in the field.

As the postwar economy boomed, MassMutual continued its steady growth. By 1951, assets totaled $1.4 billion and the company had more than $3 billion of insurance in force. The home-office staff numbered 1,350, serving a client base of more than 700,000. There were 87 general agencies and 110 district agencies in 44 states. This decentralization was a key to the company's success. The company hired general agents who in turn hired and trained local groups of agents. Successful general agents were often promoted to the Springfield home office. To further develop the strength of field agents, MassMutual instituted a training program for field representatives and encouraged its workers to complete the American College's Chartered Life Underwriter designation. The system worked. Between 1948 and 1957, the total life insurance in force doubled, from $2.7 billion to $5.4 billion.

In the increasingly complex postwar world, investing became a thorny problem. Bonds and mortgages were traditionally the investments of choice, because they were low-risk, high-security outlets, but in the 1950s, when insurance companies began to purchase more lucrative, riskier stocks, MassMutual followed suit. Still, the firm's original purpose—selling whole-life policies—remained constant.

During the late 1960s James Martin, who was named president in 1968, involved the company in several public-oriented initiatives: investing $75 million in a Springfield office, retail, and hotel complex, and supporting downtown mortgage-financing pools to rejuvenate urban development in medium-sized cities like Springfield. In 1969, assets topped $4 billion.

MassMutual surged ahead during the economic downturn of the early 1970s, installing new computer technology, and liberalizing the work place. In 1974 MassMutual became the first major life insurance company to institute flextime. Soon after came the installation of a new database linking the home office with general agencies, allowing field agents to obtain information on policies more quickly.

During the late 1970s inflation and the ensuing recession caused interest rates to soar. Individual investors began investing in high-yield money market accounts. Many life insurers, MassMutual included, experienced a rash of policy loans and had to borrow money at expensive rates to cover the loans since the bulk of their assets were tied up in long-term, low-yield securities. In this environment, many insurance companies turned toward the design and sale of new financial products for relief. MassMutual largely resisted the temptation, sticking to life and health insurance and pension-related products.

It became apparent that changes were in order when MassMutual began to lag behind other, more innovative insurance companies. In 1981, when insurance in force grew by an average of 16% for the top 50 insurance firms, MassMutual's insurance in force rose only 9.9%. William Clark, who had taken over as president in 1980, saw that it was time to shift gears, and in the next seven years MassMutual introduced several new products and changed investment policies. Clark also reorganized the company.

In 1981 MassMutual introduced universal life policies—two years after they first appeared on the insurance scene. The policies offered flexibility in paying premiums and allowed money collected from premiums to go into an account that could be invested in high-yield money market funds. Universal life, along with other new products, proved a big seller.

To discourage policy loans, MassMutual introduced a program, through which 750,000 whole life holders accepted a much higher schedule of dividends in return for an adjustable rate of interest on future policy loans. In 1985 a large dividend-scale increase was implemented for life and health policies: $440 million in dividends were distributed that year.

The firm was reorganized in 1983 into four divisions: individual products, group life and health, group pensions, and investments. Each was accountable for its own business. At roughly the same time, a new subsidiary was created—MML Investors Services—that served as an outlet selling noninsurance financial products. Its chief product is a line of mutual funds.

During the 1980s, group pensions became increasingly important. In anticipation of this, the unit was upgraded to a division in 1981. By 1984 the group-pension division's assets had reached $5 billion, making MassMutual one of the biggest managers in the country. In 1989 pension sales reached

$1.5 billion. The division offers a variety of products, ranging from interest-guarantee contracts to annuity contracts.

As assets grew, due in part to the growth of pensions, MassMutual devised new strategies for its investment-management group. In 1985 assets stood at $15.7 billion. By 1989 they had risen to $25.1 billion. Traditionally, MassMutual had specialized in long-term investments, but after the reorganization, the firm diversified its holdings. With more assets behind it, MassMutual became increasingly involved in mortgage lending. In 1985, for example, the investment-management group issued $693 million in commercial mortgage pass-through certificates—the largest commercial loan issue ever. The amount of invested assets under investment management's control grew from $12.4 billion in 1985 to $21.8 billion in 1989. Individual life insurance in force was $81.5 billion in 1989, up from $54.1 billion in 1985; and new sales have tripled since 1985 for life and health benefits.

Despite the sea changes of the last dozen or so decades, MassMutual has weathered the storm. MassMutual resisted the industry trend toward centralization of client services but is a top-quality, highly solvent insurer.

Massachusetts Mutual's methods and products have changed greatly since 1851. Its philosophy—pragmatic and agent oriented—has not. While the firm has come to rely on products other than life insurance, it still views serving policyholders and employee-benefit clients as its primary reason for being. Despite the huge growth of the group pension and financial products divisions, MassMutual is still essentially an insurance company.

Principal Subsidiary: MML Investors Service.

Further Reading: Massachusetts Mutual Life Insurance Company: A Commitment to Service, 1851–1987, Springfield, Massachusetts, Massachusetts Mutual Life Insurance Company, 1987.

—Daniel Gross

THE MEIJI MUTUAL LIFE INSURANCE COMPANY

1-1, Marunouchi 2-chome
Chiyoda-ku, Tokyo 100
Japan
(03) 3283-9084
Fax: (03) 3215-8123

Mutual Company
Incorporated: 1881
Employees: 49,778
Assets: ¥10.09 trillion (US$70.16 billion)

The Meiji Mutual Life Insurance Company, Japan's oldest life insurer, is a world leader in the industry, with ¥138 trillion worth of life insurance in force, and premium income of ¥2.5 trillion in 1990. With almost 42,000 agents and 322 group representatives, Meiji Mutual is one of the world's largest life insurance companies. In Japan, from headquarters in Tokyo, stretches a network of about 100 regional offices, 9 group marketing offices, and almost 1,500 agency offices. In 1990 Meiji subsidiaries and affiliates were in 16 cities around the world.

In 1858 Japan's feudal, shogunate leadership was bankrupt and its peasants bowed by debt and taxation. The cry within Japan was for *isshin,* or restoration. The cry was to restore the emperor and expel the barbarians. The emperor, a 16-year-old boy who was given the name Meiji, meaning "enlightened rule," was restored, and was to rule for 44 years, before his death in 1912.

Another slogan of the day was *bummei kaika*, or civilization and enlightenment, and insurance was one of the businesses expected to contribute to this goal. Insurance was to provide economic security that would work to prevent retaliatory or immoral behavior in times of disaster.

Abe Taizo was one of the hundreds of Japanese businessmen who visited the West at Japanese government expense during the 1870s and 1880s, primarily to discover how to succeed in business. Taizo and his fellow students abroad returned to Japan and promptly went into business. Taizo founded, in July 1881, Japan's first life insurance company, which he named Meiji, after the emperor. Three other insurance companies were formed about this time, Tokyo Maritime Insurance Company and the Imperial and Nippon life companies. The fortunes of these companies were to run parallel and even converge in the decades to come.

In the 1880s the national fascination with things British led to basing premiums on British actuarial findings. British mortality, however, was steady until age 40, when it took a sharp rise; Japanese mortality took two sharp rises, at 20 and at 40. This discrepancy cost Japanese insurance firms.

Meanwhile, the Meiji-era rulers—essentially managers trained under the shoguns—set the rules. They planned, built, and financed industries they thought the country needed. These were sold to the top families, such as Mitsui and Mitsubishi. Thus industries were established with a fair degree of efficiency.

By 1902 Japan had 37 life insurance companies, including three of foreign origin, which were sharply restricted by law. The early 1900s in Japan had a variety of economic ups and downs, but life insurance endured. Slightly over half of the coverage was offered by private, non-government-operated companies, of which there were 40 in 1929, compared to 50 fire insurance companies, 35 marine, and 29 transport. These private life insurance companies had issued 4.9 million policies by 1929.

By 1929 there were ¥1.2 billion worth of new life policies a year in Japan, up from ¥278 million in 1914. The value of policies had jumped tenfold in ten years, though growth had waned in the last four. The number of insured per 1,000 population had risen from 29 in 1919 to 198 in 1929. In 1931, as the world reeled from the shock of depressed stock prices, 22 major life insurance companies in Japan, Meiji among them, formed an investment company, Life Insurance Securities, Ltd., to buy and hold reliable stocks for joint investment.

At the end of the 1930s, Meiji Mutual, now an affiliate of the Mitsubishi *zaibatsu*, or conglomerate, was one of the country's top four life insurance companies. Meiji and its three largest competitors all announced huge profits for 1939. Meiji's profit rate was only 120%, compared to Mitsui Life's 862% and Yasuda Life's 453%; Sumitomo Life earned 121%. Such profits were possible because life insurance companies were exempt from Japan's anti-profiteering law.

It is unclear precisely how Meiji Mutual fared during World War II, although the large *zaibatsu* did very well. In all likelihood, Meiji Mutual participated in financing the war, while insurance in force continued to grow. Meiji Mutual was not a part of a *zaibatsu*, despite its connection to Mitsubishi, which was a *zaibatsu*. In post–World War II Japan, Meiji Mutual was not, therefore, a target of U.S. occupation forces engaged in dissolving the *zaibatsu*. In that postwar era life insurance had fallen on particularly hard times. Life insurance companies such as Meiji Mutual suffered from loss of investment in demolished factories and from inflation. Not until the mid-1950s did Meiji and others reach a level of prosperity comparable to that of before the war. Life insurance recovered, however, before some enterprises, many of which remained somewhat depressed.

In following years the figures told a happier story. The number of policies had risen from 365 billion in 1948 to 1.78 trillion in 1954. The rise had been steady, at more than 30% a year, except for 1950, when it was 15%. In the next ten years life insurance continued to grow. Premium income rose sevenfold; insurance in force and assets grew ninefold. By August 1966 more than 50 million policies were in force, worth some ¥24 trillion, more than Japan's national income for 1965. Seven of ten Japanese households had some kind of life insurance, 53% from private companies such as Meiji Mutual, the rest from postal (government) life insurance and farm-cooperative aid societies. Japan was fourth in the world in the value of insurance in force, following the United States, Great Britain, and Canada. Per capita value of policies, however, was considerably behind these countries.

The 1970s brought a new union of sorts between Meiji Mutual and the onetime *zaibatsu* Mitsubishi, when Meiji Mutual joined a combine of interlocking but separate companies, all financial-service institutions, including Mitsubishi Trust & Banking Corporation and The Mitsubishi Bank. The fourth member of this high-powered group was Tokio Marine and Fire Insurance Company. The four pooled resources to form, in essence, a multi-service financial institution serving common clients. Remaining separate, they were immune from regulations forbidding involvement in each others' businesses.

In the 1970s Meiji Mutual began moving overseas. In 1971 it offered group benefit plans to Japanese companies operating outside Japan. Eventually it serviced these plans in cooperation with U.S., European, Asian, and Australian insurers. By the late 1980s Meiji was a major participant in two worldwide insurance networks, Swiss Life and AREA Benefits Network. Meiji Mutual expanded into Latin America in 1973, operating through a Brazilian company, the America Latina Companhia de Seguros, in São Paulo, of which it was a 10% owner, and through Tokio Marine and Fire Insurance.

In 1976 Meiji Mutual bought a majority interest in Hawaii-based Pacific Guardian Life Insurance Company, which had been established in 1961. In 1985 Meiji Mutual became Pacific Guardian's sole owner, the first Japanese company to own a U.S. life insurance company outright. By March 1990 Pacific Guardian was licensed to operate in 19 western states of the United States and on the islands of Guam and Saipan.

The 1980s were a time of considerable overseas expansion by Meiji Mutual. By 1990 its overseas investments—securities, loans, and real estate—amounted to ¥2.6 trillion, more than a quarter of its total assets. In 1989 alone overseas investments grew by ¥401 billion.

Meiji Mutual had continued to operate with the Mitsubishi Group, which listed Meiji Mutual as one of its insurance and credit affiliates, along with The Mitsubishi Bank, The Mitsubishi Trust & Banking Corporation, and Tokio Marine and Fire Insurance. Meiji Mutual computerized its operations in the late 1980s. Nationwide networks put its sales force in instant touch with corporate headquarters in Tokyo. In 1989 Meiji Mutual's new Meijiseimei Toyocho Building opened in Tokyo, housing its computer operations.

Meiji Mutual opened offices in New York City in 1987, the Meijiseimei Insurance Agency of New York; in Los Angeles in 1988, Meijiseimei Insurance Services of California; and later in San Francisco and Honolulu; and in Hong Kong in 1989, Meijiseimei International Hong Kong. In 1989 and 1990 Meiji Mutual also opened offices in Australia, the United Kingdom, and Canada. In August 1989, Meiji Mutual was one of seven Japanese investors in an 18.25% share of the investment bank CS First Boston. In March 1990, it acquired a 1% interest in The Hongkong and Shanghai Banking Corporation.

Meiji Mutual continued to pursue extensive cooperative ventures abroad, in 1988 with a British firm developing financial software; in 1989 with the Equitable Life Assurance Society on a number of fronts, including management of Meiji Mutual's international investments; and in 1990 with Dresdner Bank, with which Meiji was to share research.

On April 1, 1990, Meiji Mutual had a sudden movement of top officers. Hiroshi Yamanaka resigned as chairman of the board to become an advisor to the board; Terumichi Tsuchida moved to chairman from president; Kenjiro Hata became president. The apparent orderliness of the sudden moves bespeaks the apparent orderliness of Meiji Mutual's long existence.

Principal Subsidiaries: Pacific Guardian Life Insurance Company, Ltd.; The Meiji Life Insurance Agency, Ltd.; The Meisei Credit Guaranty Co., Ltd.; The Meisei Real Estate Management Co., Ltd.; The Meisei System Service Co., Ltd.

Further Reading: Benedict, Ruth, *The Chrysanthemum and the Sword: Patterns of Japanese Culture*, Boston, Houghton Mifflin, 1946; Kawai, Kazuo, *Japan's American Interlude*, Chicago, University of Chicago Press, 1960; Hirschmeier, Johannes, and Tsunehiko Yui, *The Development of Japanese Business 1600–1973*, Cambridge, Harvard University Press, 1975.

—Jim Bowman

METROPOLITAN LIFE INSURANCE COMPANY

1 Madison Avenue
New York, New York 10010
U.S.A.
(212) 578-2211
Fax: (212) 578-7298

Mutual Company
Incorporated: 1866 as National Travelers' Insurance Company
Employees: 65,000
Assets: $98.74 billion

Metropolitan Life Insurance Company is the second-largest life insurer in the United States. The company has been a leader in the field since shortly after it was established. Metropolitan grew by providing insurance for the worker—small policies with premiums collected each week. The company dominated the field for most of the 20th century.

Metropolitan's origins can be traced to the National Union Life and Limb Insurance Company, a firm originally chartered in 1863 to underwrite the lives and limbs of Union soldiers during the Civil War. The company had trouble getting started. Simeon Draper, the company's chief promoter, found it difficult to raise the necessary $100,000 capital. A company insuring only servicemen during the bloodiest war in U.S. history did not seem to be a very promising business proposal. Frustrated, Draper stepped down and a group of businessmen from Brooklyn petitioned the New York legislature to revise the company's charter to allow life insurance for civilians as well. National Union Life and Limb's president, Major General Daniel E. Sickles, a war hero, resigned shortly before the company actually began writing policies. Sickles was replaced by Orison Blount, a respected member of the business community. Blount, though multi-talented, had no experience in the insurance business, and the company struggled to gain a foothold.

In 1865 the company changed its name to National Life and Travelers' Insurance Company, and underwent two reorganizations within a period of two years, in 1866 splitting its life and casualty lines into separate companies, National Life Insurance Company and National Travelers' Insurance Company. The latter company initially offered only casualty lines, selling its first policy in 1867, and adding life insurance to its casualty lines later that year. National ultimately evolved into one of the premiere life insurance companies in the United States, Metropolitan.

On March 24, 1868, National Travelers' Insurance Company was reorganized as Metropolitan Life Insurance Company. The company's president, James R. Dow, had led the National Travelers' Insurance Company for several years. Originally, Dow had applied for the position of medical examiner for the casualty insurer, but because of his pleasant disposition, and a $15,000 investment, he was appointed a director and elected president. Dow and another director of the company, Joseph F. Knapp, had lobbied for the reorganization—in order to head the company in a single direction. When the company changed its name to Metropolitan Life Insurance Company it also dropped its casualty insurance business.

Metropolitan's early years saw the rapid growth of the life insurance industry. The Industrial Revolution had introduced more hazards to everyday life, creating a widespread demand for insurance of all kinds. The Civil War had been a particular boom for the life insurance trade, and the industry grew at a frenzied pace in the war's wake. Whole life insurance was the preferred type of policy. Endowments were somewhat popular, term insurance was less common, and annuities were rare. In 1869, $614 million worth of life insurance had been written in the United States, of which Metropolitan had written 2,930 policies valued at $4.86 million.

The industry's growth was somewhat reckless in these early years. Many companies had trouble attracting agents without paying outrageous commissions. To get business, many agents insured questionable risks. Although Metropolitan had a successful first year, it was still small compared to other life insurers. It had just $594,000 in assets, compared with the $30 million of Mutual Life of New York—the largest life insurance company at that time.

A significant portion of Metropolitan's business in the early years came from New York City's population of German immigrants. The company had two outstanding German-speaking agents, Abraham Kaufmann and Moritz Reno. A German division was soon set up, headed by Kaufmann. In 1869 Kaufmann initiated a relationship with a German fraternal society called the Hildise Bund. Metropolitan sold small life insurance policies to members of the society, with the bund collecting the premiums on a weekly basis. The organization required life insurance—with Metropolitan—as a condition of membership from each of its applicants. As German settlers migrated west, so too did the bund's relationship with the company. The cheapest policy was for $500 coverage, and the cost was 35¢ per week. The premiums collected were turned over to Metropolitan quarterly. Metropolitan's agreement with the Hildise Bund was the company's first excursion into the field that would turn it into a giant—workingman's, or industrial, life insurance.

In 1871 Dow died, and was succeeded as president by Joseph F. Knapp. In 1873 a severe depression gripped the nation. Metropolitan's business dropped from 8,280 new policies in 1874 to 510 in 1879. Many life insurance companies were unable to meet their obligations and failed. As a result, popular confidence in life insurance hit an all-time low.

In 1879 Knapp traveled to London to observe the success of the Prudential Assurance Company of London, a company that had become successful writing industrial insurance. Knapp's interest in insurance for the masses was longstanding. He returned to New York more determined than ever to push Metropolitan into industrial insurance.

Knapp imported hundreds of British insurance agents familiar with industrial insurance to spearhead Metropolitan's efforts. These recruits trained local agents in the art of writing life insurance for small amounts, collecting the premiums weekly, and accounting to the home office. Metropolitan's success was stunning: $9 million in industrial insurance was written the first year; $18 million the second; and by 1886, just six years after the policy was officially introduced, Metropolitan had over $100 million of industrial life insurance in force. The company expanded its agency force rapidly during the 1880s. Hundreds of new agents ventured west and south to sell insurance to the country's working class. The cost of this expansion was great, and Knapp risked at least $650,000 of his own money to keep Metropolitan going during difficult years. By the time of Knapp's death in 1891, Metropolitan had established itself as the leader in industrial insurance, with more policies in force than Prudential and John Hancock combined.

In October 1891, following the death of Knapp, vice president John Rogers Hegeman became president, but it was the company's new vice president, Haley Fiske, who was in charge of the company's day-to-day operations and policy-making. While Metropolitan was a leader in industrial insurance, its ordinary life business had dwindled. Fiske initiated an effort to recover it.

For the most part, life insurance companies were offering so-called tontine insurance. Named after its Neapolitan inventor, Lorenzo Tonti, these policies paid dividends to their subscribers. Tontine policies were basically annuities, but their values increased based on one's longevity. As subscribers died, their portion of the fund was ceded to surviving policyholders. The last survivor took all. Although Metropolitan had written such policies in its early days, in the 1890s it was critical of them. The company's rate book of 1892 stated, "The Metropolitan believes the time has come when the plain common sense men who make up the bulk of life insurance policyholders are looking for a plain business contract . . . which leave nothing to the imagination; which borrow nothing from hope; require definite conditions and make definite promises in dollars and sense," as quoted in Marquis James's *The Metropolitan Life: A Study in Business Growth*. Metropolitan began to make inroads into the ordinary life business, writing no-frills non-participating policies like whole life, term life, single-premium life, limited-payment life, and endowments.

The late 1890s and early 1900s were a time of journalistic muckraking, and insurance companies, like big business in general, became targets for the pens of journalistic zealots. Particularly unpleasant for Metropolitan were accusations that industrial insurance, which covered even a family's youngest children, encouraged infanticide for the collection of benefits. Metropolitan spearheaded the defense of industrial insurance, and after several years the controversy died down. Life insurance companies, however, were not out of the investigative woods. In a few years the most comprehensive probe yet would bring about reform in the industry.

In 1905 a New York State legislative committee headed by Senator William W. Armstrong launched an investigation of the major life insurance companies, hoping to do away with any abusive practices. The chief counsel for the investigation was Charles Evans Hughes, later governor of New York and chief justice of the Supreme Court. Hughes called top executives of all the major life insurance companies to testify before the committee, including several officers—Hegeman among them—of Metropolitan, the fourth-largest life insurer at the time.

Although acknowledging that there were certain deficiencies in industrial insurance, the committee made no recommendations for change to the life insurance market. Tontine insurance, which Metropolitan had decided years before not to write, was outlawed altogether. Limits were placed on the amount of ordinary insurance that companies could write each year. Huge companies such as New York Life Insurance Company and Equitable were forced to change drastically their business practices, but Metropolitan was given merely what amounted to a slap on the wrist—abuses were cited but no remedies proposed nor penalties imposed. It gave the company a degree of public confidence not enjoyed by other companies, which helped its sales surge past its competitors' in the next few years. By 1909 Metropolitan had more life insurance in force than any other company.

The Armstrong Committee hearings did bring to light some questionable practices conducted by Metropolitan, however, and resulted in charges of third-degree forgery and perjury being brought against Hegeman. The actual impropriety of certain transactions was questionable, and in time all of the charges were dismissed.

While this controversy shook the halls of justice, Metropolitan agents continued the business of writing life insurance. The company had grown considerably over the years. As 1905 dawned the company had $1.47 billion of insurance in force. In 1909 the headquarters at 1 Madison Avenue was expanded. The company commissioned the architectural firm Le Brun and Sons, the same firm that had created its original edifice at the same address in 1893, to design a new building. The well-known Metropolitan Tower was the result. The 50-story tower was the world's tallest building until 1913 and was considered one of the wonders of the modern world.

In 1913 Metropolitan was authorized to write accident and health insurance. In 1914 it wrote its first group accident and health policy on its own employees. A year later annual medical and dental check-ups were given to employees. In 1909 the company instituted a revolutionary program, paying nurses to administer bedside care to sick policyholders. The company also pioneered in publicizing health and safety practices. Beginning in 1898 Metropolitan published informative booklets on safety and health. "Health Hints for the Home" was later distributed under the title "A Friend in Need is a Friend Indeed." The company later used radio, motion pictures, and other media to carry its messages of safety and health.

In January 1915 Metropolitan transformed from a stock company to a mutual company, in effect becoming owned by its policyholders. The change was intended to thwart future attempts by unscrupulous stockowners to manipulate the insurance company's millions for personal gain. From this point on, the company's profits were redistributed to its policyholders in the form of dividends.

U.S. participation in World War I resulted in about 18,000 claims by the survivors of U.S. servicemen on life insurance policies at Metropolitan and 7,500 claims from Canadian servicemen. By the end of the war $8.25 million was paid in death benefits. After the war, a worldwide flu outbreak took a far greater toll, claiming 83,000 Metropolitan policyholders by June 30, 1919. Met paid $27.6 million as a result of that epidemic.

In April 1919 president John R. Hegeman died, after 28 years at the Metropolitan helm. He had spent a total of 49 years as an officer of the company, having seen its assets increase by a factor of 55, and insurance in force by a factor of 17. His close associate over those years, Haley Fiske assumed the presidency.

For the next ten years, Fiske continued to introduce new forms of coverage and improve old forms. In 1921 industrial policies were liberalized to pay full benefits beginning with the date of issue rather than half benefits for the first six months. In 1928 a double-indemnity clause provided for the payment of double the face value of an industrial insurance policy in the case of accidental death. These improvements were made without additional premiums.

During the prosperous early 1920s, all forms of life insurance sold extremely well. Group policies added considerably to Metropolitan's success during the decade. Assets topped $2 billion in 1926. The company's group life insurance in force grew from $60 million in 1919 to $2.25 billion a decade later. In 1928 the company wrote the largest group policy to date, for the General Motors Corporation for $400 million.

In March 1929 Frederick H. Ecker became president of Metropolitan upon Haley Fiske's death. Several months later the stock market crashed and the Great Depression started. Metropolitan's conservative investment policies helped it to weather the hard times. The company had stayed out of the speculative equities markets and had focused instead on real estate and bonds. The stock market crash initially had a positive impact on life insurance sales. Investors who had lost heavily tried to supplement the losses to their estates by increasing their life insurance. Ordinary insurance sold at record volume in 1930 and 1931. As the Great Depression deepened, however, and unemployment reached massive proportions, new policies stagnated and many policyholders were forced to discontinue their premium payments and allow their policies to lapse. In addition, many borrowed money against their policies or surrendered them for the cash value. Metropolitan was in sound financial condition and had no trouble meeting its obligations. Adjustments in the company's investment portfolio were necessary as rents fell and farm commodity prices dropped; Metropolitan reduced its investments in city mortgage and farm lending.

The Great Depression of the 1930s and the New Deal philosophy that accompanied it focused a great deal of attention on the nation's financial industries. In the late 1930s U.S. President Franklin D. Roosevelt urged Congress to look into malpractice of big business. The lawmakers responded by establishing the Temporary National Economic Committee for the Investigation of Concentration of Economic Power. The TNEC, as the committee became known, spent a year, beginning in 1939, interviewing officers of life insurance companies. The first witness called was Metropolitan's Frederick Ecker, chairman of Metropolitan's board of directors since 1936, when Leroy A. Lincoln had become president. After much testimony, the TNEC issued its report in 1941. Government officials were hoping for federal regulation of ordinary life insurance, and the addition of industrial insurance to the new Social Security program. The TNEC, however, in a mere three pages, suggested only that the states beef up their existing regulatory mechanisms. The committee's most forceful recommendation affected a large segment of Metropolitan Life's business, asking for a change in the operation of the industrial insurance business, and stating that in the alternative the elimination of such coverage might be required. Without proposing any new means of federal regulation, however, the life insurance industry was, for the most part, left to police itself.

World War II resulted in a number of policy changes for Metropolitan customers. While existing policies were continued under the same terms, new policies were written as war risks with special premiums and stipulated conditions. For the most part, the business of life insurance remained the same, except for the extraordinary numbers of claims due to combat. By March 1946 Metropolitan paid out $42.1 million on 51,956 lives lost as a direct result of the war.

After the war, Metropolitan continued to grow rapidly and its investment dollars went into real estate projects all over the country, including landmark middle-income complexes in the Stuyvesant Town and Riverton districts in New York City. The rents on these properties were kept low in exchange for tax breaks from the city.

In 1951 Leroy A. Lincoln became chairman of the board at Metropolitan. Charles G. Taylor took over the duties of president but soon was replaced by Frederick W. Ecker, whose father had held the office years before and was now elevated to honorary chairman. Throughout the 1950s, Metropolitan was the leading life insurer in the United States, having enjoyed that position steadily since 1909. Metropolitan held to a conservative investment posture, and continued to offer low-cost insurance. In 1954, the company was the first in life insurance to install a major computer system. Metropolitan continued to support health and safety practices. In 1956 the company was behind a push to set up poison control centers.

In 1957 Frederick W. Ecker became CEO of Metropolitan and in 1959, chairman of the board. The younger Ecker's leadership stressed conservatism. Metropolitan was the largest private capital pool in the country, and the company managed it so tightly that some thought the company old-fashioned. Equities investments were avoided in the 1960s as they were in the 1920s. Other insurance companies implemented more aggressive investment and marketing strategies.

In 1963 Gilbert Fitzhugh became president of Metropolitan. In 1966 he moved up to chairman of the board and the presidency was filled by Charles A. Siegfried. In 1966 Metropolitan was replaced by Prudential as the number-one life insurer in terms of assets. Prudential surpassed it in number of policies in force in 1974.

In 1968, a year after race riots rocked U.S. cities, the life insurance companies made a commitment to invest in inner cities. Metropolitan Life invested $322 million for rebuilding or new building of housing. Chairman Fitzhugh recognized the need of the company to respond to recent changes in the business, and Metropolitan, for the first time, purchased common stocks for its portfolio. Equities investments reached $1 billion in 1972. In addition to loosening up the company's investment strategy, Fitzhugh looked for new areas of insurance to market. Metropolitan began offering aviation reinsurance after 1971, and formed a subsidiary, Metropolitan Property and Liability Insurance, in 1972.

Metropolitan also made changes in its life insurance business. New products were offered, including individual variable annuities, in 1969, and after 1972 the company abandoned the debit insurance business upon which it had been built. Agents would no longer collect premiums weekly or monthly on low-cost policies.

Beginning in 1970, Metropolitan began to decentralize its operations by setting up a number of regional service centers across the country. By the end of the decade, Metropolitan had head offices at Tampa, Florida; Tulsa, Oklahoma; Providence, Rhode Island; Dayton, Ohio; Pittsburgh, Pennsylvania; Aurora, Illinois; and New York City. Regional computing centers for record keeping were set up at Greenville, South Carolina; Wichita, Kansas; and Scranton, Pennsylvania.

In October 1973 Richard R. Shinn became chairman of Metropolitan Life. Like his predecessor, Shinn had spent his entire career at Metropolitan, becoming president in 1969. Shinn continued Metropolitan's course of diversification. In 1975 the company began writing individual retirement annuities. In 1976 a subsidiary to reinsure health insurance, Metropolitan Insurance and Annuity Company, was established. In 1978 a subsidiary to reinsure property and casualty business, Metropolitan Reinsurance, began operations.

Metropolitan focused also on group policy coverage. In 1974 its group life broke an industry record with $118.68 billion in force. In 1976 Metropolitan introduced Multiple Employer Trust group policies, which provided insurance under employee benefit programs. In 1978 group plans covering 50 to 200 employees were introduced. By 1979 Metropolitan had more than $200 billion of group insurance in force. Total life insurance in force topped $300 billion.

By the end of the decade, the flaws of Metropolitan's decentralization program, begun in 1970, became apparent. Spreading out the company's bureaucracy had caused frustration among employees, and the sales staff was defecting at a rate of 40% per year—high turnover for Metropolitan. While agents were encouraged to solicit middle- and upper-income customers, few big policies were written. The corporate initiative to push bigger policies was simply being ignored. One frustrated Met salesman commented, as reported in *Business Week* of November 21, 1977, ''This metamorphosis has not been thought out as thoroughly as executives at the top might lead you to believe. Just go out and try to sell a policy over $10,000. You'll find the underwriters in the home office using a fine-tooth comb. They think anybody who wants a big policy is trying to cheat the company. It takes seven to eight weeks to get the big cases through.''

Revitalizing the company's personal insurance sales mechanism became a priority in 1979. The number of managers between the chief marketing officer and the sales representative was reduced from six to three over the next five years. An open-door policy was instituted in order to eliminate the memo-writing mentality at Met. Executive vice president Pierre Maurer, in charge of the reorganization, told employees in 1983, ''Always wage war against paper—it's the greatest waster of management time and energy,'' as reported by *Best's Review* of July 1984. By the mid-1980s, Metropolitan was a leaner company, having eliminated 60% of its redundant middle management.

In 1980 Metropolitan purchased the Pan Am Building in New York City for $400 million. The sale was the largest single building purchase in history. The company also established a joint venture with Metropolitan Structures of Chicago, resulting in one of the largest commercial real estate development companies, with a net worth of $500 million. In the whirlwind financial climate of the 1980s, Metropolitan entered risky investment areas. It dabbled in leveraged buyouts, and in venture-capital investments for high-technology research and development.

Deregulation of financial services throughout the 1980s gave impetus to a number of new subsidiaries. In 1982 Metropolitan Tower Life was formed to write specialty lines. In 1983 MetLife Marketing Corporation was set up to supplement the agency distribution system; MetLife General Insurance Agency was formed to sell products, through agents, that Metropolitan Life Insurance Company did not offer; and MetLife Capital Corporation was established as an equipment-leasing company. In 1984 the company began using the name Metropolitan Life and Affiliated Companies, better to reflect its diverse nature. Also in 1984, a highly successful advertising campaign featuring the well-known *Peanuts* comic characters kicked off with the slogan, ''Get Met. It Pays.''

A new management team, with John J. Creedon as CEO and president and Robert Schwartz as chairman, took over in 1983. Both were career Metropolitan men. Metropolitan continued to expand its product mix in an effort to regain lost ground from its rival, Prudential. In 1984 Metropolitan's ''whole life plus'' policy, offering up to one-third more coverage with no increase in premium, introduced just three years prior, became the company's best-selling policy.

In 1985 Metropolitan acquired Charter Security Life Insurance Companies and in so doing took over its line of Single Premium Deferred Annuities. A number of other acquisitions were completed that year: the Century 21 Real Estate franchise organization; the fifth-largest full-service mortgage banker in the United States—Crossland Capital Corporation, which was renamed MetMor Financial, Inc.; Albany Assurance Company, Ltd., of the United Kingdom, a major marketer of variable life insurance and pension products; and Litton Industries Credit Corporation, a leasing company, renamed MetLife Capital Credit Corporation.

While looking for new markets for its products overseas, Metropolitan found some untapped markets in the United States. The company discovered that recent immigrants make good insurance customers. In 1983 Metropolitan began a marketing program geared to selling insurance to the 15 million Spanish-speaking people permanently residing in the United States. By 1985 Met was number-one in the seven top Hispanic markets nationwide. In 1986 the company began to develop an Asian-American marketing strategy.

In 1986 Metropolitan introduced two new individual life insurance products, single premium life and universal variable life. It continued to add new companies to enhance its mix of financial services in the later 1980s. In 1987 the assets of insolvent annuity-writer Baldwin-United Corporation and the Texas Life Insurance Company were acquired. In 1989 the group life and health business of the Allstate Insurance Company was purchased.

The trend in the late 1980s was toward globalization of financial markets. In keeping with the trend, Metropolitan initiated operations in Tokyo in January 1987. Six months later, the company entered into an agreement with Spain's Banco Santander to sell insurance and pension products in that country. Metropolitan began selling insurance in Taiwan in 1989.

MetLife HealthCare Management Corporation was established in 1988 to set up health-maintenance organizations. During the 1980s, health insurers were faced with rising health-care costs. Metropolitan, long in the business of promoting healthful habits, in 1987 sponsored a two-hour television program as part of its assault on the fastest growing problem for health insurers—acquired immune deficiency syndrome (AIDS). By 1989 it had committed $6.5 million for AIDS education.

In 1989 Robert G. Schwartz took over the duties of president and CEO upon John J. Creedon's retirement. Schwartz stated that the company's first priority for the future was to "build upon the inherent strength in our traditional lines of business—personal insurance, group insurance, and investments." Schwartz also identified the goals of increased productivity, development of the company's people, accurate assessment of demographic changes, and strengthening Metropolitan's ability to respond to market changes.

Metropolitan Life Insurance Company's sheer size and long tradition make it something of an institution in itself. While the company was for a time the victim of its own success—content to follow market changes rather than anticipate them—the Metropolitan that emerged from the 1980s was positioned for success in the years ahead.

Principal Subsidiaries: MetLife Security Insurance Companies; Metropolitan Insurance and Annuity Company; Metropolitan Property and Casualty Insurance Company; Metropolitan Reinsurance Company; Metropolitan Tower Life Insurance Company; Texas Life Insurance Company; MetLife Capital Corporation; MetLife Capital Credit Corporation; MetLife Funding, Inc.; MetLife Securities, Inc.; MetLife-State Street Investment Services, Inc.; State Street Research & Management Company; Century 21 Real Estate Corporation; Cross and Brown Company; Farmers National Company; MetMor Financial, Inc.; Corporate Health Strategies, Inc.; MetLife HealthCare Management Corporation; MetHotels, Inc.; Metropolitan Life Holdings Limited (Canada); Metropolitan Life Insurance of Canada; Metropolitan General Insurance Company (Canada); Metropolitan Insurance Company (Canada); Metropolitan Trust of Canada; Morguard Investments, Limited (Canada); MetLife (UK) Limited; Albany Life Assurance Company, Limited (U.K.); Metropolitan Reinsurance Company (UK) Limited; ACFC Corporate Finance Limited (U.K.); Albany Home Loans Limited (U.K.); Century 21 Real Estate Agency Limited (U.K.); Santander Met, S.A. (Spain, 50%); Seguros Genesis (Spain); Metropolitan Insurance and Annuity Company (Taiwan); Kolon-Met Life Insurance Company, Ltd. (South Korea, 50%).

Further Reading: Dublin, Louis I., *A Family of Thirty Million: The Story of the Metropolitan Life Insurance Company*, New York, Metropolitan Life Insurance Company, 1943; James, Marquis, *The Metropolitan Life: A Study in Business Growth*, New York, Viking Press, 1947; "Metropolitan Life: Citadel of Safety," *Forbes*, September 1, 1962; Van Aartrijk, Peter Jr., "Meet the New Metropolitan Life," *Best's Review*, July 1984.

—Thomas M. Tucker

MITSUI MARINE AND FIRE INSURANCE COMPANY, LIMITED

3-9, Kanda-surugadai
Chiyoda-ku, Tokyo 101-11
Japan
(03) 3259-3111
Fax: (03) 3291-5466

Public Company
Incorporated: 1918 as Taisho Marine and Fire Insurance Company, Limited
Employees: 7,643
Assets: ¥3.67 trillion (US$25.53 billion)
Stock Exchanges: Tokyo Osaka Nagoya Luxembourg Paris

Mitsui Marine and Fire Insurance Company is the third-largest non-life insurance company in Japan. With about 46,000 agencies in operation, Mitsui offers domestic customers a full range of auto, fire, personal accident, and liability insurance. Mitsui's roots lie in the shipping business of its former parent, Mitsui Bussan. The company has developed an extensive network of overseas subsidiaries and liaison offices on all six inhabited continents, and, with the 1988 creation of its first U.S. subsidiary, Mitsui has set its sights on a bigger piece of the vast but highly competitive U.S. market.

Mitsui was founded as Taisho Marine and Fire Insurance Company in October 1918 by the powerful Mitsui *zaibatsu,* or trading group. World War I had prompted an enormous increase in Japanese shipping and shipbuilding, as Japan hurried to fill orders previously handled by the war-depleted Western powers. As one of Japan's leading shipowners, and a force in nearly every sector of Japanese trade, Mitsui Bussan rapidly expanded its cargo business under the favorable market conditions—by war's end controlling about 40% of Japan's three-million-ton merchant fleet. It also opened its first shipyard, in Okayama Prefecture, a forerunner of the Mitsui Shipbuilding and Engineering Company. To protect its growing fleet of ships—and the cargo it carried—Mitsui used a part of its large war revenues to establish its own insurance company, Taisho Marine and Fire Insurance Company. The new venture was in operation by the end of 1918, processing orders from Mitsui's numerous sales representatives around the world.

Although chartered as an independent company, Taisho remained very firmly in the Mitsui family of concerns. It insured Mitsui ships, land, and property at favorable rates and, by competing with Mitsubishi's Tokio Marine and Fire Insurance Company, provided its parent with an additional weapon in the continuing struggle against its chief rival. In addition, as the new venture gained capital, it would be expected to serve as a source of investment funds for future Mitsui expansion, thus joining the Mitsui Bank in forming the financial backbone of Mitsui's extremely complex commercial empire.

Before this plan was well under way, however, a nationwide disaster nearly brought Taisho to an early end. On September 1, 1923, a devastating earthquake struck Tokyo and Yokahama, destroying thousands of delicately built Japanese homes and buildings, setting fire to many square miles of city property, and creating local tidal waves that washed away coastal villages. As one of Japan's few property and casualty insurers, Taisho faced claims many times greater than its total assets. It was estimated that over 100,000 people died and half a million homes were destroyed by the earthquake, prompting the Japanese government to absolve the insurance companies of all but 10% of their liabilities. Even so, the government was forced to loan Taisho and the other insurers sufficient funds to cover the payments, saddling the new company with a debt so large it remained on the books until 1949.

Having survived a great challenge, Taisho—not yet five years old—steadied itself, and was soon prospering in the 1920s. By 1924, the company had already opened its first overseas office, in London, as Mitsui's extensive international interests made foreign expansion all but inevitable for Taisho. The 1920s were rich years for the Mitsui group, which by decade's end had acquired a controlling interest in no fewer than 130 companies. As the *zaibatsu's* chief insurer, Taisho enjoyed a similar surge, until the Great Depression brought the business world to a temporary standstill.

The 1930s were a period of difficult progress for Taisho. Its underwriting business continued to expand along with the Mitsui interests, but Mitsui and its affiliates increasingly suffered from the hostility and open violence of Japan's right-wing, ultranationalist groups. With the 1932 assassination of Takuma Dan—Mitsui's *obanto,* or top manager—the rightists assumed a position of growing power and led Japan ever closer to war with China. As armament became increasingly important to the Japanese economy, Taisho's property and casualty policies became a matter of grave concern. As the 1923 earthquake had made clear, a national calamity such as war was could destroy the Japanese insurance industry.

Even Taisho's great concern proved to be a gross underestimation of the war's effect. By 1945 the combined efforts of Allied submarines and bombers had devastated essentially all of Japan's merchant fleet and a great proportion of its industrial base. In the universal chaos, insurance claims had little meaning—the nation as a whole would have to be rebuilt, insurers and insured alike. Taisho and the Mitsui *zaibatsu* had no sooner begun this process, however, than General Douglas MacArthur and the Allied occupation forces took steps to dismantle Mitsui and the other *zaibatsu,* which were perceived as inherently anticompetitive. The Mitsui empire was split into hundreds of small companies, and Taisho was forced to survive in a far more competitive economy.

By the early 1950s the postwar Japanese economy had already made remarkable progress, and nowhere more so than in shipping and shipbuilding. Always a key industry for insular Japan, shipping rebounded with astonishing speed, and by 1956 Japan had become the number-one shipbuilder in the world. Such success meant a similar boom for Taisho's hull and cargo insurance division, which in turn solidified the company's asset base and helped secure its fire and casualty business. An additional factor in Taisho's postwar recovery was the growing number of automobiles in Japan. With every year of continued prosperity, the number of Japanese who owned automobiles increased dramatically, helping auto insurance eventually to become Taisho's leading division.

In 1955 Taisho resumed its overseas expansion with the opening of a liaison office in New York, followed rapidly by offices in Hong Kong, San Francisco, and Bangkok. In the meantime, Mitsui Bussan, the *zaibatsu's* trading company, had slowly regrouped, and in 1959 was officially reborn as the New Mitsui Bussan. As in the prewar era, Taisho once again closely allied itself with the resurgent Mitsui group, buying the third-largest number of shares in New Bussan and becoming an important member of the group's recently resurrected monthly meetings. The new Mitsui group was not as tightly integrated as the *zaibatsu* had been, with less-extensive cross-holdings of stock and, in particular, no single, family-owned holding company in charge of the various affiliates; yet Taisho's role in the group remained substantially as it had always been, providing both insurance and financing for the other group members when they embarked on new ventures.

In the 1960s Japan emerged as a world economic power. For Taisho, the combination of shipping supremacy and a growing domestic population of automobile owners led to continued profitability and expansion. Overseas, the firm pushed particularly hard in the South Pacific, where new offices in Australia, New Zealand, Malaysia, and Indonesia solidified its already strong presence. In 1970 Taisho's three main divisions—auto, fire and comprehensive, and marine and aviation insurance—produced premium revenues of ¥43.6 billion; a decided increase over the ¥27.1 billion registered by Taisho a mere two years previous, and another indication of the Japanese economy's fervid growth.

Taisho and the Japanese shipping business suffered a permanent setback in 1974 and 1975, when the Organization of Petroleum Exporting Countries (OPEC) oil embargo brought to a close the great age of Japan's shipbuilding industry. The enormous oil tankers manufactured and insured by the Japanese were no longer needed as the world cut down on oil imports; as a result, the share of Taisho's revenue generated by shipping began to decrease steadily. As high as 25% in 1970, the proportion stood at less than 9% in 1989. Taisho more than compensated for the difference, increasing every other aspect of its business—especially automobiles, which are now subject to compulsory liability coverage in Japan. By 1978, premium income totaled nearly ¥280 billion, a sevenfold increase over the figure for 1970.

In 1989 Taisho's premiums nosed over ¥400 billion, and the company had spread its affiliated offices over much of the globe. As a world power in the insurance industry, Taisho formed many international joint ventures, including a 1981 deal with Aetna Life and Casualty Company and Italy's Assicurazioni Generale; a United Kingdom deal with the Sun Alliance Group; and a Saudi Arabian initiative called the Arab Japanese Insurance Company.

In June 1990 Taisho president Ko Matsudata announced that, effective April 1, 1991, Taisho Marine and Fire Insurance Company would change its name to Mitsui Marine and Fire Insurance Company. This move illustrated the general resurgence the former *zaibatsu*—now known as the less-formally aligned *kieretsu*—enjoyed during the 1980s and into the 1990s. Having survived the catastrophe of war and the lesser problem of Japan's declining shipping revenue, Mitsui remains a consistently profitable concern.

Principal Subsidiaries: Taisho Marine & Fire Insurance Co. Ltd.; P. T. Assuransi Insindo Taisho (Indonesia); Metro-Taisho Insurance Corp. (Philippines); Taisho Marine and Fire Insurance (Malaysia) Sdn. Bhd.; Taisho Monarch Insurance Co., Ltd. (Kenya); Hong Kong and Orient General Insurance Co. Ltd. (Hong Kong); Arab Japanese Insurance Co., Ltd. E.C. (Bahrain); Fire, Equity & General Insurance Co., Ltd. (Nigeria); Taisho Investment (Luxembourg) S.A.; Taisho Realty Corp (U.S.A.); Taisho Investment (Bahamas) Ltd.; Taisho Marine & Fire Insurance Co. (U.S.A.); Taisho Finance International Ltd. (U.K.); Taisho Investment (Jersey) Ltd. (U.K.); Taisho Claims Service Corp. (U.S.A.)

Further Reading: Roberts, John G., *Mitsui: Three Centuries of Japanese Business,* New York, Weatherhill, 1973; "Mitsui Bussan K. K.," in *International Directory of Company Histories,* Volume I, edited by Thomas Derdak, Chicago, St. James Press, 1988.

—Jonathan Martin

MITSUI MUTUAL LIFE INSURANCE COMPANY

2-3, Ohtemachi 1-chome
Chiyoda-ku, Tokyo 100
Japan
(03) 3211-6111
Fax: (03) 3213-0274

Mutual Company
Incorporated: 1927
Employees: 32,191
Assets: ¥6.30 trillion (US$43.83 billion)

Among the top ten life insurers in the world, Mitsui Mutual Life Insurance Company for years also has ranked sixth among its Japanese competitors in premium income, contracts in force, and assets. Along with The Mitsui Trust & Banking Company and Mitsui Marine and Fire Insurance Company, Mitsui Mutual functions in the banking and finance sector of the Mitsui Group, one of Japan's largest and most powerful corporate combinations. Mitsui Mutual maintains close relationships with other members of the Mitsui Group and with its Japanese competitors. Mitsui Mutual's ties to other Japanese insurers are so close that they have sometimes been referred to as a cartel.

Launching a company in Japan usually requires some degree of acceptance by the companies already in that field. A new company seeks a niche—a business specialty that it can develop within a group of competitors. Mitsui Mutual, has focused on customer service–oriented products from the start, but the company began to change its traditional approach in the 1970s. During the 1970s and 1980s Mitsui Mutual initiated product and investment changes that expanded its business, notably pioneering international group life insurance. Despite some retrenchment in overseas investment to cope with worldwide and domestic market fluctuations, the indications are that the next decade will see Mitsui Mutual expand further, especially in the European and Southeast Asian markets.

Mitsui Mutual is a relative newcomer among the companies in the Mitsui Group, which dates back to the rise of the merchant class in Japan in the last half of the 17th century. Like other *samurai* warriors, head of the family Sokubei Mitsui had become a *chonin*, a merchant, when times changed. He established a soy and sake brewery, which he passed on to his son Takatoshi. Takatoshi Mitsui expanded the business to include a dry-goods store named Echigoya in honor of an ancestor, a pawnshop, and a currency exchange that later became a bank. The Mitsui corporate symbol, a circle (the heavens) surrounding a well-frame (the earth), which contains the *mitsu* (mankind), is said to have been suggested by a dream Takatoshi Mitsui's mother had. The symbol may have seemed grandiose when applied to Echigoya in 1676, but time seems to have borne out this largeness of vision. With the opening of Japan to Western trade, cultural, and business influences in the late 19th century, the Mitsui Group was already firmly established in manufacturing, finance, and other types of enterprises. The Mitsui Bank was a major commercial bank when the Banking Act of 1882 formalized a niche system for the banking industry, creating banks for specific types of business. Major banks, such as the Mitsui Bank, became cores of financial combines known as *zaibatsu*.

The Mitsui Group had become a powerful springboard for launching new businesses by 1927, when Mitsui Mutual Life came into being. The group's long tradition of successful enterprise was a substantial advantage for a company hoping to win public trust. The tradition of private savings is strong in Japan. By the same token, insurance has been a popular form of savings since the 1890s, when the first modern forms were introduced into Japanese commerce.

Recovery from a post–World War I recession and from the Great Kanto Earthquake of 1923 were well under way in 1927, but the feeling of personal and financial vulnerability remained even as business and industry gained momentum between wars. The market for life insurance grew with the influx of industrial workers into factory towns and retail and other business employees into the cities. It grew even faster as preparations for war progressed in the 1930s.

The niche that Mitsui Mutual realized it could fill was the need for an increased emphasis on individualized types of insurance and customer service. Strict government regulations imposed the same system of premium rates and rates of return on all insurance products. A prospective insurance customer would base a choice not on the prospect of direct financial returns but on such factors as the company's stability, length of service, investment policies, and attention to personal needs.

Although Mitsui Mutual's positioning proved effective in promoting growth, the company, like other Japanese companies, suffered with Japan's defeat in World War II. The prewar Mitsui *zaibatsu* had been the oldest and largest industrial group in Japan. Its holding company had been owned by 11 households of the Mitsui family, controlling 294 major companies, but not even the powerful Mitsui companies could retain their overseas holdings through war and defeat—and by the war's end their domestic markets were in shambles.

Business began anew after World War II. The *zaibatsu* were no longer operative; the occupation authorities replaced them with a new, antimonopolistic philosophy that encouraged competition in the market.

The former *zaibatsu*, however, began efforts to reunite their companies, not as *zaibatsu*, but as *keiretsu*—a network of closely associated companies with noncontrolling financial interests in one another. Mitsubishi and Sumitomo were among the first former *zaibatsu* to develop *keiretsu*—and the advantage this gave them is evident in their leading positions today. Mitsui lagged behind, partly because of an affinity for the new concept of opportunity for individual companies to compete and partly because of the reluctance of some of its larger companies to rejoin. Toshiba, for example, formerly a member company, decided to form its own *keiretsu*.

During the 1950s and 1960s, as the nation's domestic economy resurged, Mitsui succeeded in reuniting a number of its former member companies and added new groups of companies, expanding not only in numbers but in the range of types of its business concerns. While the Mitsui Group has never regained the topmost leadership position, the conglomerate has remained a leader. Mitsui Mutual continued to play a large role in insuring other members of the Mitsui Group.

With the economy's recovery, the market for insurance responded positively to Mitsui Mutual's individualized, "self-designed" insurance product approach. Individual and group life insurance products proliferated during the decades of rapid economic growth after the war.

The investment policies pursued by Mitsui Mutual up to the 1970s had always been conservative and closely tied to the fortunes of the domestic economy. The company was a major institutional investor. In 1972 Mitsui Mutual was ready to strike out in a new direction: overseas investment. By 1988 Mitsui Mutual's investments in overseas securities reached close to $6 billion. The company concentrated its investments mainly in Europe and North America, with some activity in Southeast Asia. Mitsui Mutual also struck out in another direction in the 1970s, broadening its financial services. The company's conservative lending policies have provided Mitsui Mutual with a solid base for expansion. In 1978 the company began an international lending program, the success of which has contributed to a shift in the emphasis of Mitsui Mutual activity to the international scene. The company also added consumer lending through special policyholder cards that expedite loans for individuals, and subsidiaries offer investment advice and mortgage securities. As a pioneer in international group insurance in the 1970s, Mitsui Mutual established a network of agreements with more than 200 insurance companies in 40 countries around the world. Among its business partners are Aetna Life and Casualty Company in the United States and Assicurazioni Generali in Italy. The company also has agreements with three leading European reinsurance companies.

Mitsui Mutual's success has brought some problems, however. In the 1980s, when Japan's economy reached the height of prosperity, insurance-company income began to overflow the capacity of domestic opportunities for profitable investment. Even though the government had liberalized its strict control of the insurance business, Japanese insurers with excess cash to invest followed Mitsui Mutual's example in placing their investment money in overseas real estate developments and other types of long-term overseas investment prospects.

Other surprises were in store as the decade came to a close. The stock market crashed in 1987, monetary-value fluctuations ensued, and by the fall of 1990 the Japanese market showed about a 15% loss overall. Mitsui Mutual Life Insurance Company, like other insurers, was quick to put a hold on immediate investment programs and, for the moment, retrench.

For the long haul, however, company president Koshiro Sakata intended to expand overseas operations, adding to the staff in international administration while carefully monitoring the risks. A tool that was expected to contribute to expansion abroad was the investment index model developed by the company in 1986 that has helped the company maintain one of the highest yield levels in the industry since it was put into use to manage funds for variable life insurance policies.

Principal Subsidiaries: Mitsui Seimei America Corporation (U.S.A.); Mitsui Life Investment Luxembourg S.A.; Mitsui Life Investment Bahamas Company, Ltd.; Mitsui Life Asset Management America Corporation (U.S.A.); Mitsui Seimei Investment Jersey Ltd. (U.K.); Mitsui Life International London Ltd. (U.K.).

Further Reading: Reischauer, Edwin O., *Japan, the Story of a Nation*, Tokyo, Charles E. Tuttle Co., 1971; Prindl, Andreas R., *Japanese Finance: A Guide to Banking in Japan*, New York, John Wiley & Sons, 1981.

—Betty T. Moore

MUNICH RE (Münchener Rückversicherungs-Gesellschaft)

Königinstrasse 107
Postfach 40 13 20
D-8000 Munich 40
Federal Republic of Germany
(89) 38 91 0
Fax: (89) 39 90 56 7

Public Company
Incorporated: 1880
Employees: 1,850
Assets: DM20.11 billion (US$11.90 billion)
Stock Exchanges: Frankfurt Berlin

Munich Re—known as Münchener Rückversicherungs-Gesellschaft in German-speaking countries—is the world's largest reinsurance company, in terms of net premium income more than twice the size of its nearest rival, Swiss Reinsurance Company. Munich Re has a well deserved reputation in the insurance world for consistently profitable performance and considerable financial muscle. It rarely boasts of this achievement—quiet strength has long been one of Munich Re's hallmarks.

The modern reinsurance industry is dominated by central European, particularly German, companies. This is due to the fact that the German insurance industry of the 19th century had few of the inhibitions about reinsurance which characterized the then-leading insurance industry, that of the United Kingdom. Munich Re was not the first reinsurance company to be established—the Cologne Re preceded it by 34 years—but it was the first to be totally independent of a primary insurance operation.

Its founder, Carl Thieme, a native of Erfurt in Thuringia, had reached the sound but—in the 1870s—unfashionable conclusion that dependence on a primary insurer meant reinsurance operations had to take on a narrow range of often poor quality risks with frequently disastrous financial results. Instead Thieme sought to set up an independent reinsurance company which could choose its risks according to their quality and spread the risks by operating in all extant classes of insurance.

Thieme, already an experienced and successful insurance agent in Munich, had developed good connections with the leading figures of the Bavarian financial world of the time. Chief among these was Theodor Cramer-Klett, who had been instrumental in developing in Bavaria a modern banking system capable of servicing the rapid industrialization that was going on in Germany under the protectionist policies of Otto von Bismarck.

Undeterred by the perilous state of the German insurance industry in the 1870s—Bismarck had even considered nationalizing it—Thieme and Cramer-Klett, along with four others, decided to set up a joint-stock operation with a capital of the then-large sum of three million marks. The share capital, partly paid, was subscribed by eight shareholders, most of whom were the cofounders of the new company. On April 19, 1880, Munich Re was formed. Thieme also favored the conclusion of mutually binding treaties between insurer and reinsurer instead of the hitherto traditional individual placement of risks. He regarded treaties as both more efficient and more secure from the point of view of both insurance and reinsurance companies. The new company's first treaty was with the Thuringia Insurance Company, whose Bavarian agent Thieme was and remained until 1886.

By the end of the first year's trading, gross premium income had passed one million marks. In 1888 Munich Re shares were offered for the first time on the Munich stock exchange by the bankers Merck, Finck & Company, themselves founded by the ubiquitous Cramer-Klett, and competition for shares was intense. The firm's capital base was expanded several times in the closing years of the century and by 1914 stood as some 20 million marks. In that year Munich Re was able to offer its shareholders a 40% dividend on profits from a turnover which had grown to nearly 177 million marks—a powerful statement of the company's financial soundness. At its founding in 1880 Thieme had employed just five employees. By 1914 the staff numbered 450.

Thieme had been anxious from the start to see Munich Re establish itself not only in other parts of Germany but also in foreign countries. Thus the establishment of offices in Hamburg and Vienna in the year of founding was matched by Munich Re's first reinsurance treaty with a foreign insurance company, the Danish Almindelinge Brand-Assurance-Compagni of Copenhagen. During the 1880s the company used an office in St. Petersburg.

Thieme, however, realized that the greatest reinsurance opportunities lay in Britain and, increasingly, in North America. To exploit these markets a London branch office was set up in 1890. London was regarded as a notoriously difficult insurance market for foreign firms to penetrate, but Munich Re managed to do this under the able and energetic leadership of the London manager, Carl Schreiner. In 1892 Schreiner founded Munich Re's first U.S. operation by putting up the required security of US$500,000.

Thieme was astute enough to realize that if new classes of insurance could be created then Munich Re would be well placed to secure the resulting reinsurance treaties. As Thieme wished Munich Re to retain its status as a reinsurer—a policy maintained to this day—he chose to help set up new insurance operations rather than risk the wrath of his clients by attempting to take Munich Re into the field of primary insurance.

In 1890 Thieme's efforts to introduce personal accident insurance into Germany led to the founding of Allianz, and his interest in export credit insurance resulted in the creation of

Hermes in 1917, a large proportion of whose initial share capital was provided by Munich Re. At the turn of the century, Munich Re was one of several insurers introducing machinery and luggage insurance. Munich Re pioneered machinery insurance in association with Allianz and at about the same time introduced luggage insurance into central Europe.

The risks as well as the potential profits of an international spread of business became apparent in the first two decades of the next century. The Baltimore fire of 1904 and the San Francisco earthquake and fire in 1906, the latter costing Munich Re 11 million marks, demonstrated the size of losses which the reinsurance industry could now face. The promptness of Munich Re's settlement of its primary insurers' claims contributed much to the establishment of reinsurance as an industry on an equal footing with primary insurance.

The outbreak of World War I in Europe in 1914 again proved the double-edged nature of international coverage. Munich Re, with its comparatively large commitments in the United Kingdom and North America, found its business in the United Kingdom suspended, a blow compounded by the growing anti-German feeling in the United States and the eventual total loss of its U.S. business in 1917 when the United States entered the war on the Allied side.

Hard on the heels of Germany's military defeat in 1918 came occupation, reparation payments, and, most damaging of all, the ruinous hyper-inflation of 1923 when the German mark plummeted out of control. In 1924–1925, after the stabilization of the mark, Munich Re's turnover amounted to only 127 million marks, less than two thirds of its 1914 turnover in real terms.

In 1917, Munich Re had helped found the Hermes Kreditversicherungsbank by providing share capital and accepting the reinsurance of risks. Hermes was an export-credit-insurance operation designed to offer wartime protection to German exporters, but in the postwar period it was used to help stimulate German export trade back to recovery. Gains made in this sector, however, were offset almost immediately by the onset of the Depression in 1929. Munich Re was forced to cut both salary and staffing levels in the early 1930s—in 1932 staff numbers sank to 342 against a 1920 total of more than 600. Munich Re also found it necessary to assist a number of ailing primary insurance companies—a far-sighted move at a time of great financial difficulty.

During the difficult interwar years, control of Munich Re was largely in the hands of Wilhelm Kisskalt, who succeeded Thieme as chief executive in 1922. He in turn was succeeded by Kurt Schmitt in 1938, another former employee who had transferred to the Allianz in 1914 and had become general manager there in 1921.

In 1933 Schmitt became minister of economic affairs in the new National Socialist government of Adolf Hitler. According to Munich Re, Kisskalt and Schmitt hoped that Schmitt's acceptance of the post would enable him to exercise a moderating influence on the extremist policies of the new Nazi government, and when this hope proved illusory, Schmitt resigned of his own accord in 1934. This episode did not appear to harm the fortunes of Munich Re—in the mid-1930s its turnover exceeded prewar levels for the first time.

During World War II, as in World War I, Munich Re lost its position in the huge insurance markets of the Allied nations. Although this had a considerable impact on its growth, Munich Re's turnover still reached 230 million marks by the end of the conflict in 1945. In spite of the briefness of Schmitt's official association with the former German leadership, Munich Re found it expedient to appoint a new chief executive that year, at the start of the Allied occupation. The new chief executive was an Austrian, Eberhard von Reininghaus. Although he may have been regarded with more favor than his predecessor, this did not prevent the Allies from occupying Munich Re's headquarters in Munich's Königinstrasse until 1951. More seriously, Munich Re found itself banned from operating abroad in common with all other German companies. This compounded the damage already caused by the massive economic dislocation in Germany in the immediate postwar period. Munich Re was once again forced to cut its staff—by 1950 only 302 were left—and turnover for the 1949–1950 fiscal year amounted to only half that of 1945.

Munich Re adopted a policy of concentrating on whatever gaps remained in the home insurance market. The impact of the Marshall Plan and the reorganization of the German currency began that process of economic recovery now known as the German "economic miracle" of the 1950s and 1960s. Insurance and reinsurance benefited from the economic upturn and by the middle of the 1950s Munich Re's turnover had surpassed all previous levels at nearly a third of a billion Deutsche marks. Eberhard von Reininghaus died in 1950 and his place was taken by Alois Alzheimer, who had joined Munich Re in 1929. Alzheimer, general manager for the next 18 years, oversaw the restoration of the company's fortunes and its reestablishment as a leading player in the world's reinsurance industry. At the time of his retirement in 1969, Munich Re's annual turnover exceeded DM2 billion.

General manager Horst K. Jannott is the second-longest serving chief executive of Munich Re after Thieme. A lawyer by training, he joined Munich Re in 1954, made his name in balance sheet mathematics, and progressed rapidly to the top of the corporate ladder. During his stewardship Munich Re's gross premium income has increased nearly sixfold to stand at DM12.4 billion in 1989.

The mid-1970s marked a significant shift in the balance of the company's profits away from reinsurance toward what the company calls its "general business," primarily investment income. Reinsurance profitability began to decline rapidly in the early years of the decade and recorded a loss for the first time in 1977 of about DM15 million. By 1981 this figure had increased to DM116 million and by 1989 had reached DM381 million. Munich Re's increasingly large losses in this part of its business have been spectacularly offset by the growth of profits in its general business. In 1977 this brought in about DM49 million, and in 1989, DM900 million.

Consequently, Munich Re has been able to turn in consistently strong and rising net profits. The decline in reinsurance underwriting results has been caused largely by overcapacity in the reinsurance industry and consequent severe rate competition, plus the growing tendency of primary insurers to organize their own reinsurance cover, ceding to the established reinsurance companies a growing proportion of the more volatile risks. Against this background, Munich Re's ability to offer regular dividends of 18% to 20% is quite an achievement.

Also apparent over the last two decades has been the increasing proportion of foreign business written by Munich Re, despite the effects of a strong Deutsche mark in the same period. At the end of the 1970s about 40% of its business originated outside West Germany and foreign business was outperforming domestic business. Half of these foreign earnings came from other European countries, the remainder from the rest of the world. The early 1980s registered a slowdown in the growth of foreign premium income, partly due to an appreciating Deutsche mark and partly due to setbacks in the transport and life insurance sectors. Disasters such as the 1985 Mexico earthquake and Hurricane Gilbert—the latter cost Munich Re between DM100 million and DM120 million—and the increasingly high cost of U.S. liability claims further cut into foreign profits. At the end of the decade, the foreign sector picked up as the Deutsche mark began to depreciate against both dollar and sterling. By 1989 about half of Munich Re's earnings came from abroad.

This upturn was not solely the result of external factors such as the Deutsche mark rate of exchange. Munich Re's wisdom in declining to provide coverage on war risks was proved during the 1980–1988 Gulf War between Iran and Iraq, which cost other underwriters heavily.

Munich Re, in accordance with German regulations, consistently undervalues the worth of its assets. In 1987 its two principal holdings—25% in Allianz and 46% in Allianz Lebens—were valued by the market at DM10 billion, yet the recorded book value for all Munich Re's holdings at the time amounted to only DM2.4 billion. Munich Re defends this extremely conservative accounting policy on the grounds that it needs substantial hidden reserves as a cushion against unexpected losses. As a result, Munich Re is widely considered to be one of the most undervalued insurance operations in the world.

The diversity as well as the size of Munich Re's holdings is an important part of its strength. Munich Re has holdings, often cross-holdings, in a number of other insurance operations, but also in non-insurance companies—for example, it has a 7.5% holding in Heidelburger Drueck, Europe's largest maker of printing equipment, and a 6.3% stake in MAN, a vehicle manufacturer. This means it is in a comparatively better position than many of its rivals to weather downturns in the insurance and reinsurance industries.

In contrast to Europe's primary insurance industry, which is still characterized by a network of national trade restrictions, the reinsurance industry has been relatively open since the mid-1960s. Many analysts think that deregulation in the primary insurance industry in 1992 will lead to a smaller number of larger insurance groups with a reduced requirement for direct reinsurance coverage. They predict nonproportional reinsurance coverage, for example, the increasingly important catastrophe coverage and liability coverage, as the future growth areas in the industry.

Munich Re believes the company is well positioned to survive the expected contraction in traditional reinsurance and to exploit the new growth areas because of its size, acknowledged expertise, and network of cross-holdings. Instead of using its assets to pay for diversification into direct insurance—here it differs from Swiss Re, its nearest competitor, which is in the process of doing this—Munich Re remains committed to its traditional core business of reinsurance and related activities. Munich Re is adamant that this concentration will leave it in an unassailable position.

Principal Subsidiaries: Munich Reinsurance Company of Australia; Munichre Service Limited Hong Kong; Munich Reinsurance Company of Canada; Muenchener de Mexico, S.A.; Munichre New Zealand Service Limited; Munchener Correduria de Reaseguros (Spain); Munich Reinsurance Company of South Africa; Munich American Reinsurance Company (U.S.A.).

Further Reading: 1880–1980, 100 years of Munich Re, Munich, Munich Re, 1980.

—D.H. O'Leary

THE MUTUAL BENEFIT LIFE INSURANCE COMPANY

520 Broad Street
Newark, New Jersey 07102
U.S.A.
(201) 481-8000
Fax: (201) 268-4316

Mutual Company
Incorporated: 1845
Employees: 3,100
Assets: $11.60 billion

The Mutual Benefit Life Insurance Company focuses on providing individual life insurance. The company has responded to changing lifestyles and needs by expanding its product lines to include group life and health insurance, pensions, corporate-owned life insurance, and asset-management services. Throughout its history, Mutual Benefit Life has maintained its commitment to its policyholders, who are also its shareholders. The company has withstood pressure to issue forms of insurance that were not favorable for policyholders, and it has implemented several innovative insurance practices which later became standard in the insurance industry. As a mutual company, Mutual Benefit Life is controlled by its policyholders. It is also one of only a handful of insurance companies licensed in all 50 states and the District of Columbia.

When Mutual Benefit Life was founded in 1845, few people had heard of life insurance. Only about 5,000 Americans owned life insurance policies. Robert Livingston Patterson, however, understood that life insurance was necessary to help families who lost a wage earner. A New York–based importer and exporter, Patterson went to England to gather more knowledge about insurance. Back in the United States, he persuaded a group of men to join him in the development of a new company. They chose the name Mutual Benefit because it aptly depicted their primary purpose.

The founders met their first complication when they approached the New York state legislature, which had just granted a charter to another insurance company and was unwilling to grant an additional charter to Mutual Benefit Life. Undaunted, Patterson and his 11 associates received their charter in New Jersey on January 31, 1845, becoming the first life insurance company in New Jersey and the fourth in the United States.

According to some accounts, the fledgling company first operated out of a founder's grocery store. The first official company address, however, was 295 Broad Street in Newark, New Jersey, with another office on Wall Street in New York City. The company's first prospectus stated that all funds, or capital, would derive from premiums paid by policyholders, and all policyholders would become shareholders of Mutual Benefit Life. The company also promised to pay all claims within three months after proof of death and to buy back policies from owners who wished to sell for any reason. These pledges were innovative concepts at the time, but later became common throughout the insurance industry.

In July 1845 the first Mutual Benefit Life field agent, in Norwich, Connecticut, was appointed to extend the company's reach. Soon after, agents were appointed in Ohio, the District of Columbia, Massachusetts, and as far south as Georgia. The company launched an aggressive promotional campaign and held public meetings to educate people about the value of life insurance.

In December 1845 Mutual Benefit Life paid its first claim. By the end of the first year of operation, the company had issued 936 policies, with total premiums of more than $88,000. The company had issued 13 policies that insure slaves as a form of property insurance for the slave owners. Policies insuring women numbered 39 and carried an additional $15 premium, which was later dropped. At that time, insurance for women was unusual because, as childbearers, women were bad risks. In 1845 the company had developed its first group life insurance policy, insuring four key officers of a whaling firm.

In 1847 Walt Whitman became a Mutual Benefit Life policyholder, for only one year. The company insured many other notables, including U.S. presidents Grover S. Cleveland, William McKinley, William Howard Taft, and Warren G. Harding. President Grover Cleveland had been named after the grandfather of Lewis C. Grover, one of Mutual Benefit Life's founders and its second president.

By 1848 the company had 138 agents in 21 states and the District of Columbia. Also in 1848, the company's original 20-year charter was extended indefinitely by the New Jersey legislature, and the Newark staff, consisting of president Patterson, secretary Benjamin C. Miller, and three other employees, moved to Newark's Market Street.

The company enjoyed brisk business during its first decade, but during its second ten years experienced a significant decline in the number of new policies. Energetic promotion reversed the trend; in fact, the company's assets tripled in the 1850s, and the 1860 annual report boasted that Mutual Benefit Life had a higher asset to liability ratio than any other insurance company in the nation.

In 1862 Lewis C. Grover became Mutual Benefit Life's president and the company moved into a new building on Clinton and Broad Streets in Newark. During the Civil War, many policyholders were unable to deliver their premium payments to the company. Company mathematician Amzi Dodd spearheaded an effort to help families recover policies which otherwise would have been canceled. Because Dodd had worked in Virginia and had a great affinity for southerners, he was appointed to handle the southern policies and to arrange payment of claims, even on policies which had lapsed due to non-payment. Dodd also traveled to the

South to seek out owners of lapsed policies and offer reinstatement in appropriate cases. The Civil War had boosted sales of life insurance policies, but also wiped out many southern agencies.

In 1871 and 1872, typhoid pneumonia swept across the country, increasing mortality and the company's losses. In 1873 a financial depression and widespread mistrust of life insurance—fueled by the many fly-by-night operations that had sprung up in the under-regulated industry—brought down many life insurance firms. Mutual Benefit Life, however, prevailed and emerged from the 1870s as the nation's third-largest life insurance company.

During the last two decades of the 19th century, the company maintained its strong position under the leadership of Amzi Dodd, elected president in 1882. Dodd often sat at his desk in stockinged feet, and wrote personal notes of condolence to most beneficiaries of deceased policyholders. Under his guidance, business increased annually, and by 1890 the company's assets totaled more than $69 million.

In 1902 Dodd turned over the company's leadership to Frederick Frelinghuysen who saw Mutual Benefit Life through the strenuous Armstrong Committee investigation of 1905. During a period of scandals within the insurance industry, the New York state legislature probed into the financial and business aspects of insurance companies during a series of 57 hearings. The investigation ended with new insurance legislation, whose requirements Mutual Benefit Life already met. Later in 1905 the company moved to a new seven-story building on Broad Street in Newark. In 1909 the company instituted a policy to encourage the hiring of women. The first woman employee had been hired in 1862, but the new policy opened the door for many others. The company had separate dining rooms for women, men clerks, and men officers.

In 1912 eight Mutual Benefit Life policyholders died aboard the *Titanic;* two years later two more policyholders were killed when the *Lusitania* sank after being torpedoed by a German submarine. During World War I, 556 Mutual Benefit Life policyholders were killed. The influenza epidemic of 1918 also took a great toll, resulting in 1,489 death claims, totaling almost $5 million. Despite losses, the company was able to pay its scheduled dividends.

In 1924 John R. Hardin, a company director since 1905, was elected president. Three years later Mutual Benefit Life moved to Newark's Broadway and Second Avenue.

Vice president Edward E. Rhodes developed the company's first disability insurance plan in 1929. A few months later, when the stock market plummeted, Mutual Benefit Life faced multiple policy surrenders, and claims due to suicides. Sales increased the following year, but fluctuated for more than a decade after the crash. To spur sales, the company implemented a retirement income bond and also a policy that combined life insurance with a guaranteed annuity income. In addition, the company took the opportunity to stress the value of life insurance as a source of immediate funds during times of great need.

By 1933, when several banks were in serious trouble, many policyholders could not pay their premiums because fund transfers were interrupted. After a New Jersey banking holiday on March 3, 1933, Mutual Benefit Life and other insurance companies were placed under special emergency restrictions set by the state legislature. According to the restrictions, applicants had to show hardship or extreme need before a loan against a policy or policy surrender valued at more than $100 could be approved. The restrictions ended within a year, and Mutual Benefit Life emerged with a new, low-cost life insurance contract called the Ordinary Life Increasing Premium policy—a forerunner of the company's OLIP plan and one of the forces behind an increase in business in 1933. The OLIP policies offer lower premiums to younger insureds.

During the Depression, Mutual Benefit Life reduced employees' salaries but did not lay off any workers. The company also encouraged policyholders who had borrowed up to half of their original policies' cash surrender value to surrender their policies and start again with new policies. In 1934 Mutual Benefit Life had more than 500,000 policies in force and elected its first woman officer, agency field secretary Mildred F. Stone.

The following year the company implemented a monthly budget plan whereby businesses deducted employee's monthly life insurance premiums from their salaries. In 1938 revisions to the social security law significantly increased new life insurance.

In 1941, when the United States entered World War II, the company paid benefits on 98 war-related deaths; another 25 policyholders were listed as missing in action. The company's total war-related loss was a relatively insignificant 1,332 claims totaling $4.8 million. In 1943 the National Association of Insurance Commissioners recommended that all insurance companies limit the coverage of armed forces personnel. Under this recommendation, servicemen's deaths outside the United States or Canada would not be covered while the policyholder was in active service, regardless of the circumstances. If a serviceman was fatally injured while on leave in France, for example, he would not be covered. Mutual Benefit Life adopted the recommendations but continued coverage outside the designated area when the death was not war-related.

Sales were slow throughout World War II, and Mutual Benefit Life began to exploit opportunities in the growing business market, initiating pension trusts and employee benefit plans. In 1945, its centennial year, the company surpassed $1 billion in assets.

In 1946 W. Paul Stillman was elected the first chairman of the board of directors, and John S. Thompson was elected president. Under this new leadership, the company entered a very active period that saw new investment policies, sales methods, and products for the company. One of those products was special-class underwriting, which provided life insurance to many who were otherwise uninsurable.

In 1951 the company helped finance the New Jersey Turnpike. Two years later, Thompson became the board's vice chairman, making way for 44-year-old H. Bruce Palmer to become the youngest president in the company's history. In 1953 the company added a double-indemnity rider for deaths resulting from accidental bodily injury and began a monthly premium-payment plan for individual policyholders. In 1957 Mutual Benefit Life moved into its present home office at 520 Broad Street in Newark, and group life and health insurance coverage were added to the company's product line.

Mutual Benefit Life maintained its strong and steady, but unspectacular, growth throughout the 1960s, 1970s, and

1980s. Robert V. Van Fossan was elected chairman and chief executive officer in 1972. Three years later, the company's western home office and group insurance headquarters opened in Kansas City, Missouri. Frank E. Sullivan was elected president in 1978. In 1981 the company established Mutual Benefit Financial Service Company, which designs and manages annuities and tax-advantaged investments, and Mutual Benefit Life soon established itself as a leading insurance company in investment-product sales. Five years later, Mutual Benefit Life acquired Help-U-Sell, Inc., a national real estate franchise company.

In 1987 Sullivan became vice chairman and Henry E. Kates assumed the presidency at age 48, after serving as Mutual Benefit Life's executive vice president of individual insurance. In 1989 Kates was named president and chief executive officer, following the death of Van Fossan.

Kates has led the way in extending Mutual Benefit Life's reach beyond the United States. In 1989 the company entered into a joint venture with the Tong Yang Group, one of the largest industrial complexes in South Korea. The joint venture made Mutual Benefit Life one of the first U.S. insurance company to move into the South Korean market, and it was the first step forward in the company's plans for marketing on a global scale. The joint venture company, called Tong Yang Benefit Life, has grown rapidly in a short time, selling Mutual Benefit Life's insurance and financial services.

As Mutual Benefit Life poised for the 1990s, it began exploring other foreign opportunities, particularly in Europe. Anticipating a slower economy but a growing interdependency with other countries, the company continues to emphasize steady growth, skilled management, sound diversification, and continued responsiveness to the needs of policyholders.

Principal Subsidiaries: Mutual Benefit Financial Service Company; MBL Life Assurance Corporation; MBL Holding Corporation; Muben Realty Company.

Further Reading: Stone, Mildred, *Since 1845: A History of the Mutual Benefit Life Insurance Company,* Newark, New Jersey, The Mutual Benefit Life Insurance Company, 1957.

—Kathleen Poole

MONY

THE MUTUAL LIFE INSURANCE COMPANY OF NEW YORK

1740 Broadway Street
New York, New York 10019
U.S.A.
(212) 708-2000
Fax: (212) 708-2056

Mutual Company
Incorporated: 1842
Employees: 9,000
Assets: $19.01 billion

The Mutual Life Insurance Company of New York (MONY) has been successful for most of its history. It played a key role in the development of the U.S. life insurance industry. Although it has been selling conventional whole life policies for more than a century, MONY has accounted for several industry innovations. Despite its conservative heritage, MONY diversified in the rough and tumble 1980s, branching off in several directions and acquiring new companies. Now the 11th-largest insurance firm in the United States, MONY is heading into the 1990s on solid footing.

MONY is the oldest continuous writer of insurance policies in the United States. It was chartered in 1892, and began business on February 1, 1843, at the beginning of an eight-year boom that saw the founding of other insurance giants like Aetna, Massachusetts Mutual, and New York Life. MONY's founders—Alfred Pell, who had worked for the Mutual Safety Insurance Company, and Morris Robinson, a businessman—decided in 1841 to form a life insurance company. They received a charter from the state of New York on April 12, 1842, and opened the doors of the Mutual Life Insurance Company of New York for business less than a year later.

From its inception, MONY was a mutual company, owned by its policyholders and run by a board of trustees elected by policyowners. Offering whole life and term insurance, MONY was an industry pioneer, helping to develop mortality tables, actuarial techniques, and premium computations—all essential tools of the insurance trade.

At first, MONY concentrated its organization and sales in large eastern cities. As the company expanded, however, full-time MONY agents established themselves in far-flung cities and contracted with the firm to sell insurance in their territories. MONY institutionalized this system in 1858, when the first general agent was appointed. Reflecting the hazards of 19th century U.S. life, MONY was cautious about whom it insured. At first standard rates were given only to those living in northern states and in the settled parts of the northwest territories, areas with comparatively lower death rates. MONY also tried to avoid issuing standard policies to people traveling to China or around the Cape of Good Hope, or to seamen engaged in whaling. In 1886 the company policy handbook precluded "gamblers, barkeepers . . . saloon keepers, keepers of billiard parlors," among others, from receiving the comfort of MONY insurance.

By the outbreak of the Civil War in 1861, MONY had business all over the country. Because no policies provided for insurance in the case of war, MONY called together 16 leading companies to determine a common policy for insuring soldiers. Surprisingly the company did not suffer any losses on war risks, even though every southern policy was considered surrendered. All operations below the Mason-Dixon Line stopped during the Civil War.

In its early years, MONY followed a conservative investment policy, investing heavily in government securities, New York state bonds, and real estate mortgages. Sound fiscal management, under the leadership of Frederick Winston, who served as president from 1853 to 1865, helped MONY's assets multiply from $1.3 million in 1851 to $44 million in 1870.

In 1866 MONY began paying dividends annually, to stave off competition from companies like The Equitable and New York Life. Together with the latter two, MONY constituted the Big Three, for whom the period 1870 to 1906 was a boom time. In these years, MONY's insurance in force increased more than fivefold. In 1885 MONY introduced deferred dividend policies, which paid dividends at the end of a specified interval, usually longer than one year. They proved immensely popular. Within three years after their introduction, less than 1% of the company's new business consisted of the old annual dividend policies.

In 1885 Richard McCurdy, a company vice president assumed control. Determined to make MONY the biggest of the Big Three, he dispatched agents throughout the West and Southwest, pursued an ambitious investment policy, and took steps to extend MONY's coverage not only throughout the United States but overseas. He succeeded. In the first three years of McCurdy's stewardship, new insurance doubled. By 1904 it would quadruple. In 1889 MONY surpassed New York Life in new business, and four years later, in 1893, it overtook The Equitable.

In 1886 alone MONY established foreign agencies in Mexico City, Hamburg, Berlin, Sydney, and London, and in Puerto Rico. Over the next 20 years, 19 other foreign agencies were established. They ultimately proved to be more trouble than they were worth. Prussia, for example, prohibited the company from doing business there in 1900, and Germany followed suit in 1904. Other countries required investment in local government bonds, which effectively forced MONY out of those countries. By 1914 all foreign agencies were closed.

In the 1880s MONY also acquired an entrepreneurial bent—building large office buildings and renting out excess space, and buying debentures of other banks. MONY's high-ranking status and go-go spirit made it a chief target of the Armstrong Committee investigation of 1905, which agency looked into charges of fraud and abuse in the New York insurance industry. McCurdy and other MONY executives testified before the committee, which recommended new restrictions on insurance companies operating within the state. The New York legislature responded by placing prohibitions on the holding of common stock, limiting the amount of new insurance any company could issue in a given year, and banning deferred-dividend policies—a MONY mainstay. In the wake of the investigation, MONY switched to more conservative investing and marketing policies. McCurdy cut his salary in half and then resigned in late 1905. More importantly, the company underwent structural renovations, switching from a general agency system to a managerial agency system. Under the managerial system, general agents working on commission became salaried branch-office managers.

McCurdy was succeeded by Charles Peabody, a former lawyer who sat at the helm until 1927. He was succeeded by David Houston, who ran MONY until 1940. The two guided MONY with conservative hands, presiding over uninterrupted growth. During that 35-year period, MONY extended coverage to the middle and lower classes, began training its agents more extensively, and offered more specific kinds of coverage. In 1913 MONY introduced disability benefits. In 1925 a payroll deduction plan was implemented for the payment of premiums of group coverage. Assets and insurance in force grew continuously. Between 1903 and 1930 insurance in force tripled, from $1.5 billion to nearly $4.5 billion; assets in the same period grew from $401 million to $1.05 billion.

The only period in which MONY did not experience continuous growth was the Great Depression, which, as it did to every other sector of the U.S. economy, hit MONY hard. Voluntary terminations, service contractions, policy lapses, and general economic morass caused a temporary dip in assets and a long decline of insurance in force. In 1931 the issuance of disability income benefits in connection with life insurance policies was discontinued. The company continued, however, to introduce new products during the 1930s. In 1934 a family protection policy was offered, and a family income plan was offered in 1940. Even with the economic recovery of the late 1930s, MONY did not immediately regain its prior vitality. In 1942 the amount of insurance in force—about $3.6 billion—was only 80% of the 1930 total.

In 1940 Lewis Douglas was elected president; he led the company's postwar comeback. Under Douglas MONY changed its investment policies. Insurance companies had traditionally put most of their money into low-interest, low-risk bonds. In 1944, for example, 83% of the assets was tied up in bonds, with less than 1% in stocks; 13% was in mortgages. In the 1950s insurance companies moved to more lucrative stocks and to diversify into lending. By 1959 bonds accounted for less than half of admitted assets, while stocks constituted 6%; mortgages made up 32%.

During the 1950s MONY was carried along by the strong tide of the postwar boom, which caused almost every financial institution to prosper. Aside from shifting investment gears in the 1950s, MONY expanded again, reentering Alaska in 1949 and Texas soon after. In 1952 the first personal sickness and health policies were made available. As unions and collective bargaining units grew in strength, the atmosphere became more conducive to the development of group coverage. In 1953 MONY developed its first group plan for small businesses, providing pension, life insurance, disability, hospital, surgical, and polio benefits. In 1954 MONY made its initial foray into the general group field. By 1959 assets had grown to $2.7 billion and insurance in force topped $7 billion.

In 1961 Roger Hull took over MONY's reins, and during the next several years, he oversaw further expansion and the development of new coverages. In 1963 the first substandard-risk accident and health policy was written, and in 1965 MONY became the first New York firm to enter the group variable-annuity field. Assets and insurance in force grew steadily every year, so that in 1971 assets edged toward $4 billion, and insurance in force was nearly $17 billion.

Up until the 1970s growth took place within MONY's basic structure; new products and services were generated from within. Then MONY began acquiring other companies and developing new ones. In rapid succession, a number of services were added. In 1970 MONY established an investment fund—MONY Fund; in 1971 it gained control of North American Life and Casualty Company. Two years later, MONY formed two more companies: MONY Life of Canada, to serve insurance needs of Canadians, and MONYCo, a holding company that would manage several other newly acquired and newly created subsidiaries. In 1975 under the leadership of Richard Fricke, who had taken over in 1972, MONY entered the property-and-liability reinsurance business.

The 1970s had its problems: the oil squeeze of the early part of the decade and the rampant inflation of the latter part. Under the leadership of Fricke and James Devitt, who succeeded Fricke in 1979, however, MONY experienced tremendous, nonstop growth. Through most of the 1970s, MONY remained the 11th-largest insurance company in the United States, as ranked by assets. Between 1970 and 1979, insurance in force doubled, from nearly $16 billion in 1970 to $33.9 billion in 1979.

Some of MONY's growth can be attributed to its unique and pioneering advertising efforts. In 1971 MONY switched the lion's share of its advertising from print to television, becoming the first major insurance company to rely almost exclusively on the spoken rather than the written word for promotions. In 1975 MONY aired the first advertisement in which death and the need for life insurance were explicitly discussed. A young, unknown actor—John Travolta—was featured in that first commercial; he played a son who was forced to work as a busboy after the death of his inadequately insured father.

James Attwood took the helm of MONY in 1983 after James Devitt's retirement. Attwood, who had previously worked at The Equitable, was the first MONY chief to come from outside the company. Prior to 1983 MONY had 7 subsidiaries; four years later, in 1987, the number had grown to 33. In 1985 MONY acquired Evaluation Associates, Inc., an investment consultant group. Two years later it bought Kelly & Associates, a third-party administrator for group and pension benefit programs. In 1986 MONY added Financial Services Corporation, a broker-dealer. The same year, MONY purchased Unified Management Corporation, an investment management company that offered a variety of mutual funds and was, at the time, the tenth-largest mortgage company in the United States.

To help manage all these new units, Attwood substantially restructured the company in 1985, reorganizing several operations, separating its design and sales units, and dividing the primary businesses into five units. Technology also helped spur growth. In 1983 MONY added TOPS, the total on-line policyowner service, a huge database that streamlined operations and made MONY more responsive to customers.

The 1980s also brought the introduction of new services and products. In 1985 MONY was the first insurance company to offer additional life insurance protection for policyholders who died as a result of an automobile accident while wearing a seat belt. More importantly, financial services were expanded in the 1980s. MONY had started a modest pension division in 1981. Through aggressive marketing, MONY grew to manage $5.2 billion in pension funds by 1987, and assets under management have continued to grow—to $7.9 billion in 1988 and $8.7 billion in 1989. Subsidiaries of the parent company also ventured into other areas of the financial sector. In 1987, for example, a MONY unit issued a ten-year, $150 million Eurodollar bond issue.

In 1989 MONY had nearly $22 billion in assets, and insurance in force was $84 billion, up from $51 billion in 1983. Despite all this growth, MONY had slipped a little. In 1987 MONY was the nation's 14th-largest insurer in terms of assets, 20th in terms of new policies issued, and 24th in terms of total life insurance in force.

MONY entered the 1990s a more diverse and diffuse company than ever before, the economic downturns of the 1980s having caused some retrenchment. In 1989 for example, MONY unloaded Financial Services Corporation, which it had acquired just three years prior. The same year, James Farley, who took over as CEO in 1988, initiated a multimillion dollar cost cutting program. Simultaneously feeding off its deep, strong roots in the insurance industry and drawing sustenance from newly initiated services, MONY is looking to ascend to the top of the industry again.

Principal Subsidiaries: MONY Life Insurance Company of America; MONY Legacy Life Insurance Company; MONYCO, Inc.

Further Reading: Clough, Shepard B., *A Century of American Life Insurance: A History of the Mutual Life Insurance Company of New York, 1843–1943,* Westport, Connecticut, Greenwood Press, 1970.

—Daniel Gross

NATIONALE-NEDERLANDEN N.V.

Johan de Wittlaan 3
2517 JR The Hague
The Netherlands
(70) 358 15 81
Fax: (70) 358 12 80

Public Company
Incorporated: 1963
Employees: 25,161
Assets: Dfl 92.89 billion (US$48.68 billion)
Stock Exchanges: Amsterdam Paris Geneva

In 1963, The Netherlands Insurance Company, the largest insurance company in the country, merged with its archrival, the second-largest insurance company in the country, the Nationale Life Insurance Bank. The merger made the company more competitive in the increasingly international market and spread out the necessary costs of computerizing operations.

Since the merger, Nationale-Nederlanden has agressively pursued acquisitions throughout the world and started up new operations in Asia, Spain, and Greece. The company offers life and non-life insurance, reinsurance, investments, and related financial services in 21 countries. It remains the largest insurance group in the Netherlands despite similar mergers among its competitors, and is the third-largest enterprise in the country in terms of market capitalization. Nationale-Nederlanden emphasizes growth through further international expansion and optimization of its existing operations in the mature home market.

The Netherlands Insurance Company was the first of the partners to be established. In the early years of the 19th century, the Dutch insurance market was served primarily by small regional companies. One exception was the Netherlands Fire Insurance Company of Tiel, which established agencies throughout the country. The company's agent in Zutphen was Gerrit Jan Dercksen, who was assisted by his cousin, Christiaan Marianus Henny. The two men appointed subagents in the Zutphen area to expand their business.

In 1844, however, the Tiel company changed the rules under which its agents operated: subagents became full agents themselves. This move limited Dercksen and Henny to Zutphen, while their former subagents gained the territory outside the city. The two men lost a substantial portion of their income because of the change.

Within the year, Dercksen and Henny had established their own company, Insurance Company against Fire Damage, soon renamed The Netherlands Insurance Company in 1845. The new company did not only operate in the Zutphen area; the partners appointed underwriting agents in Amsterdam and Rotterdam almost immediately.

Dercksen and Henny failed to see a profit for a number of years. The two were inexperienced in assigning premiums for different risks and their mistakes hurt the new company. A fire in a sugar refinery in 1849, for example, cost them Dfl 12,000, one-quarter of the shareholders' paid-up capital. The company was also forced frequently to pay claims for arson, and it did not initially have much success in taking these cases to court.

Dercksen and Henny aggressively tried to decrease their risk. They imported special fire engines from England for the Zutphen district volunteer fire brigade. They gave farmers a discount for planting Lombardy poplars, which are natural lightning conductors, to protect their property. They hired inspectors to visit insured properties regularly, and they took out reinsurance policies. It was said that Dercksen and Henny even went up to their office's attic during thunderstorms to watch the farms they insured through a telescope; if lightning struck one of those properties, they could call the fire brigade immediately and limit their losses.

Soon after it was founded, The Netherlands Insurance Company began to expand abroad. In 1856 the partners appointed an agent in Batavia, the capital of the Dutch East Indies. The Dutch merchants they served there paid high premiums and the claims burden was low. The company was able to use its base in the Dutch East Indies to expand into other Asian ports, including Singapore, Hong Kong, the Philippines, Japan, and China. At the same time, The Netherlands Insurance Company followed Dutch merchants to other areas, including South Africa and the Caribbean. Before 1900, The Netherlands Insurance Company had 139 foreign agents.

By the time The Netherlands Insurance Company became a profitable international concern, the original partners were gone. Henny, the sole manager after Dercksen's death, retired in 1894. He was succeeded by his son, Carel Henny, who had worked for insurance companies in Denmark and England, as well as for his father's firm, to prepare to take over the company.

The young Henny moved the firm's headquarters from the provincial Zutphen to the country's administrative capital, The Hague, in 1896. In 1903 he made another move, adding a life insurance department to The Netherlands's traditional sphere of fire insurance. Within a short time, he added the accident-insurance company Fatum and the industrial life insurance company Victoria to become an all-lines insurance company.

Carel Henny's impact on the company was felt in other areas as well. He was among the first to improve the working conditions of employees. He introduced a pension plan, limited working hours, and granted holiday leave. Lower-paid employees could spend their free time at company holiday homes.

World War I limited The Netherlands's operation in some of its European agencies, especially those in Belgium and France, but the economic crisis that followed the war had a greater impact. The worldwide Depression stopped the company's growth and destroyed its profitability for the first time since C. M. Henny's death.

In the middle of the economic crisis The Netherlands Insurance Company joined the Nationale for the first time in a joint venture, insuring employee pension plans. These contracts were guaranteed by the new Bureau for Group Insurance.

The economic collapse, however, was followed by the devastation of World War II. The German army occupied the Netherlands on May 10, 1940. The Netherlands Insurance Company's head office in The Hague was in the path of the German army's Atlantic Wall, its defense against an Allied invasion, and in 1943 part of the office within the artillery range of one of the German bunkers had to be destroyed.

Since communication abroad was cut off by the German invasion, the government transferred the seat of the company to the Netherlands East Indies. The company's headquarters had to be moved once again when the East Indies were occupied by Japan in 1942, this time to the Netherlands Antilles. Overnight, J. van der Velden, head of the Curaçao branch office, became head of The Netherlands Insurance Company in the free world.

Eventually the war made it almost impossible for The Netherlands to operate domestically. The German occupying force insisted that Dutch companies dismiss all Jewish employees. Jewish possessions, including insurance policies and securities, were confiscated. The Netherlands Insurance Company lost almost all of its men employees, who were sent to work in Germany or went underground to avoid being transported there. Severe food shortages meant that people in the western part of the country were concerned solely with food procurement. In the last year of the war, communication with the rest of the country was cut off.

After the war, The Netherlands and other insurance companies played a large role in reconstruction by financing home building and the rebuilding of industry. When foreign communications were reestablished after the war, The Netherlands Insurance Company management found that non-Dutch operations had been continued and even expanded during the war years. Expansion continued during the postwar years as the company began acquiring local firms that had established reputations, instead of setting up its own branches. The company had acquired its first foreign subsidiary, the Belgian De Vaderlandsche, in 1939. After the war, Dutch emigrants in Canada and Australia offered a new opportunity. In 1954 The Netherlands set up Associated National Insurance of Australia; in 1956 it bought Canada's oldest insurance company, The Halifax, and in 1959 Commercial Life Assurance Company of Canada was acquired.

In the 1950s, more than a century of operations in the East Indies came to an end after the Dutch colony there became independent as the republic of Indonesia. President Sukarno nationalized all Dutch companies. It was not until 1972 that Nationale-Nederlanden re-established itself in that country.

Postwar government-sponsored social security programs initially seemed like another kind of threat to the company. Insurance companies were able to promote the idea that social security was simply a base of financial security that had to be built upon through supplementary private insurance. By promoting the idea of security, the Netherlands Insurance Company shared in the prosperity of the 1950s.

The Nationale Life Insurance Bank also prospered during the postwar years. The Nationale Life Insurance Bank was founded in 1863 by Rotterdam lawyer William Siewertsz van Reesema and insurance agent Simon van der Heldt. The two men felt that they could profitably challenge the numerous burial societies for the premiums of middle-class working men. They offered low premiums for life insurance coverage averaging about Dfl 300. That sum could provide a funeral for a man and a small sum for his family. Soon van der Heldt and van Reesema also offered old-age insurance and "trousseau insurances," which provided money for young people setting out on their own.

The Nationale found itself turning a profit sooner than The Netherlands Insurance Company had, but it also faced some problems. Strict government supervision of the life insurance industry, including a requirement that Dutch companies use outdated mortality tables, meant that foreign insurance companies could charge lower premiums. Epidemics that hit less-affluent members of Dutch society, among which the Nationale found most of its clientele, also hurt the company: a cholera epidemic in 1868 and a smallpox epidemic in 1872 led to a larger-than-expected number of claims.

Around the turn of the century, the Nationale made some efforts to set up offices in Denmark and Belgium, but it was not long before the board of directors decided that the risks involved in expanding outside the country were too great and ended those experiments. The board decided that it was more important to increase public trust within the country. In 1886, the company introduced the Nationale Maid of Holland on its promotional material. The maid continued to advertise the Nationale, representing respectability and reliability, until 1970. In addition to the new advertising symbol, the Nationale provided an extended account of its operations in its annual report to increase public confidence.

In 1880 government control of life insurance companies ended. While the Nationale no longer had to contend with obsolete mortality tables, the company was concerned that the public would lose faith in an unregulated industry. Managing director J. W. Niemeijer advocated legislation to provide reasonable government control. It was not until 1922—a year after the bankruptcy of the largest Dutch life insurance company, the General Company for Life Insurance and Superannuation—that legislation was actually enacted. Niemeijer chaired the committee that wrote legislation establishing the Insurance Control Board to supervise the industry.

Like The Netherlands Insurance Company, the Nationale felt the effects of depression and war. The Nationale's head office on the banks of the Maas River in Rotterdam was involved in World War II from the time that German troops crossed the Dutch border. German airborne troops took over the building for its strategic location opposite the two most important bridges over the Maas. The head office building sustained severe damage due to the fighting, and Rotterdam itself was damaged heavily during a German bombing raid on May 14, 1940, which destroyed the city center and killed 2,000 residents.

The Nationale was also instrumental in postwar reconstruction and shared in postwar prosperity. In 1956 the company expanded its non-life portfolio when it acquired the Tiel

Utrecht Fire Insurance Company, a group of nine non-life insurance companies. The Netherlands Fire Insurance Company of Tiel, whose agency policies had led to the formation of The Netherlands Insurance Company more than 100 years previously, was one of this group of companies. The acquisition made the Nationale, long the largest life insurer in the country, the second-largest non-life insurer as well. The Nationale had become The Netherlands Insurance Company's biggest competitor.

The 1960s brought new challenges to the prosperous competitors. One by-product of the war was the move toward European cooperation, which peaked when the European Economic Community was established in 1957. A country's membership in the new organization meant that the nation's larger companies had a better chance of remaining competitive in the European market.

Another trend developing as the 1950s turned into the 1960s was increasing automation. Particularly in the insurance industry, computers could keep records and do basic calculations more efficiently than could clerks, but the cost of computerizing a large company was a deterrent.

These trends led to consolidation among insurance concerns, especially in the United States, Great Britain, and Canada. In April 1963, just months after the Nationale celebrated its 100th anniversary, the Nationale and The Netherlands Insurance Company merged, in an effort to remain competitive under changing circumstances.

The two companies had some experiences working together through the Bureau for Group Life and Pensions, established in 1932. They approached integration slowly. Their first joint project was to establish a new administration center for processing information. Both companies used punch cards to keep track of data, but the amount of information was growing so quickly that punch cards were no longer sufficient. In 1966 the new administration center was completed and new computers were delivered to process much of the administrative workload. The cost of automation was considerably lower than it would have been if the two firms had approached it separately.

Following the merger international expansion was vigorously promoted through the international division. The British company Orion became the first foreign acquisition of Nationale-Nederlanden in 1963, followed by the Agder Assuranceselskab in Norway in 1964 and the Life Association of Scotland in 1968.

Nationale-Nederlanden continues its foreign acquisition policy because it is the most promising growth field, given the small, mature domestic market. In 1979 the company took a major plunge into the U.S. insurance market when it acquired Life Insurance of Georgia after a lengthy struggle. The new company has been the basis for additional U.S. acquisitions. Nationale-Nederlanden also continued to grow in Canada, where it acquired Calgary's Western Union Insurance Company in 1987. Two years later a general management office for North America was set up in Washington, D.C., to coordinate activities in that part of the world.

At the same time, Nationale-Nederlanden moved into Australia, where it acquired Mercantile Mutual in 1981, indicating the company's intention to focus more attention on the Pacific. Nationale-Nederlanden became the first European insurer to establish operations in Japan in 1985, reinstating ties The Netherlands Insurance Company had had until World War II. It moved into Taiwan in 1988 when its affiliate, the Life Insurance Company of Georgia, was granted one of two licenses given to U.S. insurance firms each year. The following year Life Insurance Company of Georgia was granted a license to operate in South Korea.

Nationale-Nederlanden also expanded within Europe. The company established operations in Greece and Spain in the 1980s to take advantage of these countries' growing economies. At home the company began to offer new kinds of health insurance to meet the increased need for private health care created by a downsizing of the Dutch National Health Service, and increasing affluence.

In 1983 Nationale-Nederlanden consolidated its premier position in the Dutch insurance industry—despite the merger of the second- and third-largest firms, Ennia and AGO—when it took over Amfas, the number-four company. Amfas was in serious financial trouble at the time because of problems in its marine-insurance division and poor performance in its real estate division. Nationale-Nederlanden also added a credit company and a mortgage bank to its domestic operations to strengthen its presence in the country's financial-services sector.

Despite the difficulty in meshing acquired companies into operations and sluggish earnings growth among acquisitions, Jaap van Rijn, who became chairman of Nationale-Nederlanden in January 1989, says the company remains on the lookout for other appropriate acquistions. He explained that the company will continue to emphasize local autonomy and open communication in managing its international network.

Van Rijn also said Nationale-Nederlanden will need to continue to develop innovative products and use technology more efficiently to keep growing in the saturated insurance market. Like his long-ago predecessor, Carel Henny, Van Rijn said the company must continue its commitment to employee benefits and community improvement.

Principal Subsidiaries: Nationale-Nederlanden Life Insurance Company N.V.; Nationale-Nederlanden General Insurance Company N.V.; RVS Life Insurance N.V.; RVS General Insurance N.V.; Tiel Utrecht Insurances; N.V. Life Insurance Company Victoria-Vesta; N.V. General Insurance Company Victoria-Vesta; RVS Insurances N.V. (Belgium); De Vaderlandsche N.V. (Belgium); Victoria-Vesta N.V. (Belgium); Hibernian Life Association Limited (Ireland, 50%); The Life Association of Scotland Limited; The Orion Insurance Company PLC (U.K.); The London & Overseas Insurance Company PLC (U.K.); Proodos General Insurances S.A. (Greece); Le Groupe Commerce Compagnie d'Assurances (Canada); La Compagnie d'Assurances Belair (Canada); The Halifax Insurance Company (Canada); Western Union Insurance Company (Canada); NN Financial (Canada); Midwestern United Life Insurance Company (U.S.A.); Security Life of Denver Insurance Company (U.S.A.); Wisconsin National Life Insurance Company (U.S.A.); Life Insurance Company of Georgia (U.S.A.); Southland Life Insurance Company (U.S.A.); Associated Doctors Health & Life Insurance Company (U.S.A.); Peerless Insurance Company (U.S.A.); The Netherlands Insurance Company (U.S.A.); Excelsior Insurance Company (U.S.A.); Indiana Insurance Companies (U.S.A.); First of Georgia Insurance Company (U.S.A.); FATUM General Insurance N.V. (Surinam); P.T. Maskapai Asuransi Nasuha (Indonesia, 49%); The Netherlands Insurance (Malaysia) Sdn. Bhd. (49%); Mercantile Mutual Insurance (Australia) Limited; Mercantile Mutual Life Insurance Company Limited (Australia); Mercantile Mutual Casualty Insurance Limited (Australia); Nationale-Nederlanden Reinsurance Company N.V.; Netherlands Reinsurance Group N.V. (51%); 'Transatlantica' Reinsurance Company N.V.; B.V. Finance Company 'VOLA'; Westland/Utrecht Mortgage Bank N.V.; Georgia US Data Services, Inc. (U.S.A.); The Investment Centre, Inc. (U.S.A.); Blue Cross Medical Consultancy (Singapore) Pte. Ltd.; Mercantile Mutual Finance Corporation Limited (Australia); Mercantile Mutual Funds Management Limited (Australia); Mercantile Mutual Investment Mangement Limited (Australia); Alcredima (Belgium); Fiducre (Belgium); LAS Investment Assurance (U.K.): LAS Pensions Management (U.K.).

Further Reading: Dankers, Joost, and Jaap Verheul, *Secure in a Changing World: Nationale-Nederlanden 1963–1988,* Maarssenbroek, the Netherlands, Nationale-Nederlanden N.V., 1988; "Nationale-Nederlanden," The Hague, Nationale-Nederlanden N.V., 1989.

—Ginger G. Rodriguez

NEW ENGLAND MUTUAL LIFE INSURANCE COMPANY

501 Boylston Street
Boston, Massachusetts 02117
U.S.A.
(617) 578-2000
Fax: (617) 578-3776

Mutual Company
Incorporated: 1835
Employees: 3,178
Assets: $16.75 billion

New England Mutual Life Insurance Company is a broad-based corporation offering insurance, personal financial services, and institutional investment. Its subsidiaries offer diverse services, including commodity trading advice; estate equity management; private financing to small and midsized companies; financial, educational, and planning services; brokerage of mutual funds; investment partnerships; individual retirement accounts (IRAs); and marketing and sales support to other New England subsidiaries.

In April 1835 Willard Phillips, a Massachusetts lawyer, chartered and founded New England Mutual Life Insurance Company. The New England issued its first life insurance policy in February 1844.

Phillips was influenced strongly throughout his life by his New England heritage. A writer on law, insurance, and economics, Phillips was involved in politics, his law practice, and scholarship sufficiently to see a need to form a life insurance company. In 1835 interest in life insurance was increasing. William Lloyd Garrison had begun to speak out against slavery; public education was a concern to Horace Mann; and Willard Phillips saw the need for the ordinary man to accumulate capital through frugality and savings. His company, with mutual ownership at its core, would give dividends back to the policyholders, the dividends being the return of excess premiums collected to cover safely the worst possible contingencies.

The charter for the New England Mutual Life (NEL) contained a clause providing that each year the Massachusetts General Hospital would be paid one third of NEL profits. All insurance companies chartered by the Massachusetts legislature were subject to the same provision. Eventually amended to provide the hospital with one third of profits over 6%, the legal rate of interest, this provision cut down on the early profitability of NEL. Among the original subscribers were prominent Bostonians like Josiah Quincy, John Lowell, Charles Curtis, Charles Francis Adams, Samuel Eliot, and Copley Greene.

Agents soon were selling policies and were paid 5% commission on the first year's premium and 2.5% commission on following years. Married women who had policies written before marriage were allowed to have their policies continue intact, payable separately from their husbands' estates. Willard Phillips petitioned the legislature for this change, which was an early victory for women's rights.

The first dividends—20% of the policy premium—were paid by NEL in 1848. Dividends could be paid in cash, used to reduce future premiums, or used to buy additional insurance, as the insured preferred.

Elizur Wright joined NEL in 1844. In 1858 he became one of two insurance commissioners in Massachusetts. Wright, who was shocked by abuses in the British insurance industry, introduced progressive ideas at NEL such as lower rates to non-drinkers and extended coverage to the elderly. He also devised a method of calculating early reserve valuation tables, which was eventually legislated for use and adopted by all insurance companies.

Benjamin F. Stevens became president of NEL in 1865. He was to remain as president until 1908. In 1865 he chaired the Chamber of Life Insurance, the first insurance trade association. Stevens had worked for Willard Phillips and NEL as secretary of the company. He was a member of the crew on the U.S.S. *Constitution* on its around-the-world tour in 1844. The *Constitution* would, in 1956, be used as the NEL logo.

During Stevens's term as president, the agency commission of NEL rose to 15% of the first year's premium and 7.5% of following years. Stevens had NEL pay "fair compensation" to the agents and was not swayed by competition from other companies.

After the Civil War, NEL had general agents in New York City; Buffalo, New York; Cleveland, Ohio; Detroit; Indianapolis, Indiana; Chicago; and Saint Paul, Minnesota.

In 1868 NEL opened an office in London, but it closed in 1872. Differing political, social, and economic conditions in England and other countries showed NEL that mutual life insurance was not yet salable outside the United States.

Despite the economic fluctuations of 1869 and 1873, NEL prospered. In 1885, NEL's 50th-anniversary, total insurance in effect was $65 million. The company had expanded to other states, such as Maine and Alabama, despite the poor economy.

In November 1872, the Great Boston Fire destroyed 65 acres of Boston real estate. NEL was then located at 39 State Street, near the area burned. Securities and other valuables were removed from the office by company officer Dwight Foster. The NEL building, however, escaped the fire. When Boston was rebuilt, the NEL State Street property was taken by eminent domain, and NEL built another headquarters at 87 Milk Street, where it remained from 1873 to 1941.

During World War I, NEL, as it had done during the Civil War, issued new insurance policies to servicemen with an extra war-risk premium of $37.50 per $1,000. One-third of the premiums paid was refunded after the war. The influenza epidemic of 1918 caused NEL to pay claims that were 50% greater than those paid during the war.

As early as 1908, NEL began to use independent auditors to review the company books. Many companies simply relied on state examiners.

Alfred Foster served as president of NEL from 1908 to 1921 and Daniel F. Appel, vice president, became president in 1921. Appel had been with NEL for 28 years. He had been superintendent of agencies and secretary of the company in 1905. When Appel became president, George W. Smith became vice president. Smith started with NEL as an actuarial clerk and had been a vice president of the agency and underwriting divisions.

In 1932, during the Great Depression, life insurance company security values were based on 1931 quotations; otherwise many companies would have appeared insolvent. It was not until 1940 that security values, bonds, and mortgages were again carried at amortized rates. At NEL, George Smith wisely purchased short-term treasury bills to keep the company liquid. Despite the economy, NEL paid its claims.

In 1933 the Securities and Exchange Act was passed. Although NEL and other insurance companies did not issue securities directly, they did buy them through investment bankers and securities dealers. To avoid the strict rules of SEC registration, investment bankers and securities dealers then began to "privately place" unregistered securities on behalf of insurance companies.

In the 1930s, insurance companies began to sell an increasing number of group insurance policies, along with corporate pensions. Aetna, Travelers, Metropolitan, and Prudential had high rates of success in the group insurance market. NEL saw group insurance as highly competitive, but began to sell individual group policies to a selected clientele comprised of small pension trusts, partnerships, and people with estate problems. NEL became a leader in this area.

George Smith served as president from 1928 to 1951. He built a new headquarters on Boylston Street for $2.5 million. The old headquarters on Milk Street was eventually torn down, and the land was sold to the city of Boston.

During World War II NEL and other companies placed war clauses in policies for servicemen that provided only for a return of premiums as a death benefit. This was in contrast to policies for servicemen in World War I and the Civil War, when coverage was provided at extra cost. NEL had 250 home office and field associates in the U.S. services locations.

O. Kelley Anderson, who had started with NEL as a director in 1947, was elected president of NEL in 1951 and served until 1966. During those years the company grew steadily. Individual sales, stock values, and investment earnings grew. Overall costs to policyholders dropped.

Anderson, who was in the investment-trust industry before joining NEL, now directed the company into the group life market, as well as group health. Walter Tebbets was hired to spark this effort. In 1952 and 1953 the approach to the group life market proved successful, and the NEL board approved the entry into the disability and hospital insurance markets. By 1964 group life covered 226,000 employees, and $1 billion of insurance was in effect. Group life was 16% of new insurance sold. Group health in 1966 was $12.9 million and group annuity was $10.9 million.

In 1957 NEL purchased a UNIVAC II computer, and in 24 months all punch card records were transferred to the computer. NEL reassigned with no reduction in pay any employee affected by the computerization of the records. No NEL employee lost a job because of it. In 1962 NEL built a $7.5 million addition to its building.

The Anderson years showed a shift in the distribution of assets at NEL. Decreases were made in federal and state bonds, public utilities, and railroads. Increases were made in industrial bonds, common stocks, and mortgage loans. Anderson resigned from NEL as chairman and director in 1971.

Abram T. Collier became president of NEL in 1966. A lawyer and general counsel at John Hancock before coming to NEL, Collier was a director of New England Merchants Bank. He quickly developed new equity products. Collier attempted to get employees to work together in solving problems and started a progress sharing plan as an incentive for employee savings. A deferred compensation plan was started for agents, and financial seminars with advice from attorneys, trust officers, and accountants were offered.

Collier involved NEL in the equity investments market to develop new capital for both the company and policy holders. A then-recent change in Massachusetts law enabled life insurance companies to purchase a majority of shares in corporations the business of which was supplementary or complementary to life insurance. NEL purchased Loomis, Sayles & Company, an investment counseling firm, with $2 billion in assets. The purchase was of 75% of Loomis stock, with 25% retained by Loomis. By 1983, after 15 years, assets of Loomis had grown to $12 billion. In 1990 Loomis had $21 billion under management.

During the Vietnam War NEL and other insurance companies participated in the Urban Investment Program making $1 billion available in loans to finance black business, housing, and other inner city needs. An additional $1 billion was subsequently advanced.

In the 1970s NEL entered the real estate investment trust (REIT) market, as real estate market prices and stocks continued to appreciate. In 1990 NEL's subsidiary, Copley Real Estate Advisors, had $11 billion in assets under management, including the company's new headquarters on Boylston Street in Boston. NEL occupied 25% of the building and Copley Real Estate rented out the additional 520,000 square feet. The revenues are split by NEL and Copley.

In order to manage the REIT program in the 1970s, NEL set up its own mortgage investment pool. It borrowed $50 million at 7.75% and reinvested it at 9.25% during the 1974–1975 recession. In order to curb inflation in the real estate investment program, NEL issued loans with the reserved right to call them after 10 years, even if the loans were initially written for 20 or 30 years.

In late 1960s and early 1970s NEL changed computers from UNIVAC to IBM. All individual policies and dividend valuations, as well as accounting, investment, group, and other procedures, were added to the new computer, which brought the agencies into closer contact with the home office.

In 1969 Ted Phillips, to become NEL president in 1974, joined the company in charge of home-office administration. A lawyer with John Hancock, Phillips was also a fellow in 1965 with Brookings Institute in Washington, D.C., where he worked on legislation concerning the federal Department of Health, Education and Welfare.

In 1969 the Massachusetts legislature increased premium taxes for out-of-state as well as domestic insurance companies. In addition, Massachusetts insurance companies were taxed 1% on gross investment income. This put NEL and other Massachusetts insurance companies at a disadvantage with their out-of-state insurance competitors. In 1978 premium taxes levied on Massachusetts companies were replaced with a stipulation that insurance companies invest $100 million over five years into the Massachusetts economy through the Massachusetts Capital Resources Corporation.

John A. Fibiger was hired in 1973 to boost group insurance sales, and the long term group disability and group variable annuity markets were explored.

In 1969–1970 and 1974–1975, a large number of policy loans were made by astute investors who could reinvest the proceeds at higher interest rates. NEL attempted to influence the Federal Reserve Board for higher and more flexible policy loan rates. Attempts were not unsuccessful.

In the 1970s the agency structure was strengthened. Agents were permitted to sell products other than life insurance. From 1974 to 1976 several new projects were undertaken and completed: new policy lines were written, computer conversion was completed, new group-annuity products were developed, the real estate mutual fund and investment counseling businesses were developed further.

NEL showed its first loss in 1985, an $11.8 million operating loss. In 1986, however, a $6.5 million operating gain, made possible by a $38 million tax break, appeared as a hefty $177 million gain. The explanation for this circumstance is that the National Association of Insurance Commissioners allowed realized investment gains to be moved up into the bottom line for overall operations.

In 1981 Ted Phillips became chief executive and chairman. John Fibiger became president. Phillips and Fibiger began a detailed analysis of the company and its potential. A new mission statement was set forth. Phillips and Fibiger saw the company as a broad-based financial institution with growth as a goal, supplying first-quality services in a multitude of different markets. NEL purchased Covenant Life Insurance, in 1981, in order to have a stock subsidiary available in planning for the future. It was renamed Connecticut Life Insurance Company.

In positioning the company for the 1980s and beyond, the company took several steps away from the traditional. Individual policies were revised to project very low net costs. The Vanguard series of new policies treated non-smokers as preferred risks, increased interest rates on policy loans to 8%, and allowed dividends to reflect federal tax deductions. Other Vanguard series provided for lower dividends in early policy years with higher dividends in later years. NEL in 1981 introduced universal life policies with flexible premiums. In 1983 variable life was introduced, with investment options in stocks, long-term bonds, or money-market instruments.

In 1982 NEL mutual funds had substantial assets. One of them, NEL Cash Management Fund, had assets of $847 million. The NEL Equity Services Company offered instruments that provided investment with tax advantages. Discount brokerage was offered in 1983. NEL agents could now compete better with banks, security firms, and others.

By 1985, 55% of NEL professional and managerial positions were filled by women. Equal opportunity and affirmative action policy at the company were programs sponsored by presidents Abram Collier and Ted Phillips.

The company in 1989 had total assets of $16.75 billion with $77.4 billion of insurance in force. It expected to continue in the 1990s as a leader in life and health insurance coverage and to offer many other diversified financial products.

Principal Subsidiaries: New England General Life Insurance Company; New England Variable Life Insurance Company; New England Financial Advisors; New England Investment Companies, Inc.; New England Institutional Marketing.

Further Reading: Clark, Sydney A., *The First Hundred Years of the New England Mutual Life Insurance Company: 1835–1935*, Boston, New England Mutual Life Insurance Company, 1935; Collier, Abram T., *A Capital Ship, New England Life: A History of America's First Chartered Mutual Life Insurance Company 1835–1985*, Boston, New England Mutual Life Insurance Company, 1985; Suskind, Ron, "Matters of Life and Death," *Boston Business,* June 1, 1988.

—John D. Cathcart

NEW YORK LIFE INSURANCE COMPANY

51 Madison Avenue
New York, New York 10010
U.S.A.
(212) 576-7000
Fax: (212) 576-6794

Mutual Company
Incorporated: 1841 as Nautilus Insurance Company
Employees: 8,181
Assets: $46.65 billion

New York Life Insurance Company is one of the five largest mutual insurance companies in the United States. It has provided its policyholders with financial security and investment opportunities since 1841. As a mutual company, New York Life is owned solely by its policyholders, to whom it pays annual dividends and provides long-term coverage on a wide range of insurance products. The company prospered during its first 100 years of operations, as the growth of the nation's population and economy created an expanding market for life insurance. Since World War II New York Life has maintained its competitive edge by diversifying into group insurance, health care, annuities, and mutual funds. Its policies represent over $300 billion in insurance coverage.

Life insurance was an infant industry when New York Life's predecessor, Nautilus Insurance Company, began operations in the 1840s. Marine and fire insurance were important, but people hesitated to assign a cash value to human life, and often associated life insurance with gambling.

As the economy became more industrial and the population more mobile, society recognized the need to secure a family's welfare against the loss of a breadwinner. In 1840 New York State passed a law allowing a married woman to insure her husband's life with immunity from having the benefits seized by his creditors. Such legislation recognized the use of life insurance in a developing industrial economy and widened its potential market beyond wealthy speculators.

New York Life has its origins in a charter granted by the New York state legislature to Nautilus Insurance Company in 1841, for the sale of fire and marine insurance. The company began issuing policies in April 1845 and soon decided to jettison its fire and marine business in order to concentrate on life insurance. By 1849 the company was so securely established in this new business that it petitioned the state legislature and had its name changed to New-York Life Insurance Company. In 1917 or 1918 the company dropped the hyphen in its name.The company's early operations coincided with the development of U.S. life insurance. Policies issued by the company were usually limited to short periods of time and placed a variety of restrictions on their owners. Policyholders in the 1840s could not travel south of Virginia and Kentucky during the summer because the company considered the southern climate a health risk. Southerners applying for policies faced higher premiums and restrictions on their travel as well. Before 1850 the company considered overland travel to California too dangerous for policyholders to undertake without paying an extra premium. Epidemic diseases were of great concern to the company in its early years. Outbreaks of cholera and yellow fever often threatened the company's security, and temporarily forced it to restrict new business to Manhattan and Brooklyn in 1849.

Despite such natural threats, the company grew quickly and established an adequate reserve for paying out dividends and benefits to policyholders. This success was largely due to the company's most innovative contribution to the young industry, the use of agents to sell policies. Previously, insurance sales had centered on a home office that served local merchants and elites wealthy enough to protect their property and lives. New-York Life's use of agents to seek out new business greatly expanded the market, and the company soon established agencies in New England, the southern states, and as far west as California.

The Civil War presented the company with its first major crisis, since it had developed a sizable southern business. President Abraham Lincoln's prohibition of commerce with the Confederate states during the war cut off communication between the home office and its southern policyholders, creating a host of problems, including lapsed payments and unpaid claims. The company compensated for these losses, however, by issuing policies to soldiers and civilians involved in combat. One of the few companies to take on such war risks, New-York Life managed continued growth despite its southern losses. In fact, the company sold over half of the 6,500 new life insurance policies issued in New York City in 1862.

After the war, New-York Life expanded quickly with the nation's booming economy. The company recovered its southern business by paying benefits on death claims left unsettled during the war and by allowing former customers to renew their lapsed policies. As the nation pushed westward, so too did the company, establishing agencies in Utah, Montana, and Nevada in 1869 and in San Francisco in 1870. New-York Life also became an international name during this era, opening offices in Canada in 1868, Great Britain in 1870, Paris in 1884, Berlin 1885, Vienna in 1887, Amsterdam in 1891, and Budapest in 1894.

Intense competition marked the insurance industry in the last two decades of the 19th century, and it was during this time that the company emerged as one of the largest mutual insurance companies in the nation. Competition was fueled in part by the introduction of tontine policies, a type of life insurance in which a number of policyholders would forego their annual dividends and award the money to the last survivor of the group. The winner enjoyed a considerable payoff for his or her longevity. New-York Life began selling tontine policies in 1871, and by 1900 its growth in sales made it one of the nation's three biggest mutual insurance companies, along with Mutual Life Insurance Company and Equitable Life Assurance Society.

Reorganization of the company's agency system also promoted its growth. In 1892 President John A. McCall implemented the branch office system, the structure by which the company now operates. The home office opened branch offices throughout the United States to act as liaisons between the company's New York operations and its agents in the field. Improved communications allowed for more effective administration of the agency force through sales incentives and professional training.

The boom of the 1880s and the 1890s did not go unchecked. New-York Life entered the 20th century at odds with progressive reformers, who accused the rapidly growing insurance companies of mismanagement and malfeasance. In 1905 the New York state legislature convened an investigative committee under the leadership of William W. Armstrong to examine the state's insurance companies and make recommendations for regulatory reform. With the legal assistance of future U.S. Supreme Court Chief Justice Charles Evans Hughes, The Armstrong Committee heard testimony from the industry's most powerful executives, including John A. McCall.

The Armstrong Committee found New-York Life free from many of the abuses common in other companies, but it also recommended curbing the practices that had pushed the industry's expansion since the Civil War. In 1906 New York outlawed the sale of tontine policies, prohibited excessive commission for agents, and limited the amount of new business a company could do each year. The company officers actively lobbied for revision of these laws. Under the vocal leadership of Darwin Kingsley, who had become president in 1907, the company achieved some success in having its new business ceiling increased and agent incentives reinstated later in the decade.

New-York Life prepared early for World War I, selling securities and borrowing in order to increase cash reserves and meet wartime obligations. During the war the company also issued war-risk policies. The war's greatest challenges came in its aftershocks. The worldwide influenza epidemic of 1918 and 1919 hit the United States with unexpected ferocity: death claims resulted in a $10 million loss for the company, almost twice the cost of benefits paid during the war.

During the Russian Revolution of 1917 the company's assets in Moscow were seized. Soon after, New York Life began its withdrawal from Europe, a reaction to unfriendly regulation and a volatile world economy.

The company's assets were not involved in the stock market crash in October 1929 because state regulation and conservative planning had kept New York Life investments out of common stocks and in more secure government bonds and real estate. In 1929 New York Life moved into its current corporate headquarters on Madison Avenue in New York City. The move represented the company's entry into a modern era of closer ties to the nation's economy and diversification into new financial markets. The company weathered the Great Depression and became an important source of capital in the cash-short economy. Its greatest losses during the Depression were in the form of lapsed payments and canceled policies, a trend finally reversed by the booming wartime economy of the 1940s.

Wartime production and the postwar baby boom revived the insurance industry, and New York Life tailored its products and investments to take advantage of these economic and demographic changes. With the development of group insurance in the first half of the 20th century and the passage of the federal Social Security Act in 1935, people began to buy insurance less for its one-time benefit to surviving family members and more for its lifelong investment security. New York Life introduced its first group insurance policies in 1951 and expanded its coverage in group and personal policies to include accidents and sickness as well as death. Two years later it offered the employee protection plan, a combination of individual life and group sickness coverage designed for small businesses. The success of its group plans has sustained New York Life's remarkable growth since World War II. In 1974 it created a pension department and began selling employee protection insurance, another policy plan popular with small businesses. In the 1970s alone, New York Life's group insurance sales increased by 152%.

Recognizing the need for housing in the postwar nation, New York Life began moving its assets out of wartime government securities and into real estate development in the late 1940s. The company established a mortgage-loan program for veterans in 1946 and also invested in residential housing developments in Queens and Manhattan and in Chicago and Princeton, New Jersey, during the 1940s and 1950s. In 1969 it established the Nautilus Realty Corporation to handle its commercial and residential real estate operations, which proved to be of increasing importance as inflation in the 1970s and 1980s made other investments less desirable.

In the 1960s New York Life introduced the family insurance plan, a policy of comprehensive family coverage. When economic recession and inflation caused the lapse rate on new policies to increase in the early 1970s, the company created an insurance conservation office to study ways of better serving—and thus keeping—customers. The introduction of its Series 78 policies in 1978 made conversion between short-term and life policies more flexible for investment purposes and reduced premiums for women, who were buying an increasing percentage of the company's personal policies. Further innovations have included a widening variety of annuities, cost-of-living adjustments in benefits, and the sale of mutual funds. In 1986 the company introduced NYLIFE as a new brand name for its financial products, differentiating this growing business from its traditional life insurance policies.

Inflation and high interest rates in the early 1980s hurt New York Life's new business sales and reduced its reserves, as policyholders borrowed against their policies for cheap credit. The company quickly adapted to these circumstances by taking advantage of deregulation in the financial-services industry. In early 1984 it acquired MacKay-Shields Financial Corporation and two years later the company began marketing its own MainStay mutual funds through this new subsidiary. The company also expanded its annuity business through its subsidiary, New York Life Insurance and Annuity Corporation.

Another major growth area for New York Life during the 1980s was health care. The spiraling cost of medical care in the 1970s and 1980s strengthened the appeal of insurance as a security against long-term illness. In 1987 New York Life purchased controlling interest in Sanus Corporation Health Systems, one of the largest health-care companies in the nation. New York Life's greatest concern in the health-care field is AIDS. In the late 1980s New York Life became one of the most visible promoters of AIDS awareness in New York City as well as a generous supporter of the American Foundation for AIDS Research. The company has opposed antitesting laws introduced in various states, arguing that testing for the AIDS virus is a necessary step in assessing the risks involved in new policies.

Diversifications into real estate development, mutual funds, partnership investments, annuities and pensions, and health care have preserved New York Life's market position, and it entered the 1990s ready to take advantage of expanding demand for these new products.

Principal Subsidiaries: New York Life and Health Insurance Company; New York Life Insurance and Annuity Corporation; NYLIFE Insurance Company of Arizona; New York Life Insurance Company of Canada.

Further Reading: Hudnut, James M., *Semi-Centennial History of the New-York Life Insurance Company*, New York, New-York Life Insurance Company, 1895; Abbott, Lawrence F., *The Story of NYLIC*, New York, New York Life Insurance Company, 1930.

—Timothy J. Shannon

NIPPON LIFE INSURANCE COMPANY

5-12, Imabashi 3-chome
Chuo-ku, Osaka 541-01
Japan
(06) 209-4500
Fax: (06) 222-0852

Mutual Company
Incorporated: 1889
Employees: 95,223
Assets: ¥21.38 trillion (US$148.74 billion)

Nippon Life Insurance Company is the world's largest life insurance company in terms of insurance-in-force, premium income, and total assets, and one of Japan's most influential financial institutions. Nippon Life is the biggest shareholder on the Tokyo Stock Exchange, owning approximately 3% of the market's total shares. With rare exceptions, Nippon Life is a conservative investor, with a diversified portfolio that demonstrates preference for steady, long-term returns over high-risk, high-yield instruments. The company has grown to gigantic proportions, and it continues to grow despite periods of instability in the domestic and international economies and some dramatic losses during the 1980s. Although not an innovative company, Nippon Life has a remarkable number of firsts to its credit, beginning in 1889, when the company originated the policies that helped make it the first major life insurance company in Japan.

In 1947 Nippon Life also became the first of Japan's life insurance companies to reorganize itself as a mutual life insurance company. In 1959 the company originated made-to-order insurance, combining payment on maturity and payment on the death of the policyholder—a product innovation that dominated the market for more than a decade. The 1970s saw a flurry of Nippon Life product innovations. The company had pursued a vigorous program of overseas investment since about 1915, but in 1981 it achieved another first when it established the industry's first overseas real estate subsidiary. That same year, Nippon Life became the first Japanese life insurance company to acquire real estate in the United States—a 50% interest in a New York City office building.

Although as an industry front-runner Nippon Life far outdistances its competition, the company also places a high priority on its close relationships with other companies, both in Japan and overseas. As an underwriter and purveyor of financial services as well as an investor, Nippon Life is committed to globalization. Despite some necessary retrenchment of foreign investment to cope with market conditions, President Josei Itoh has emphasized globalization.

Close relationships among influential financial institutions in the busy mercantile center of Osaka in the late 1880s created the opportunity for Sukesaburo Hirose to found Nippon Life. In the three decades that had passed since Japan's dramatic opening to Western commerce and culture, the centers of trade had begun to reflect a new receptivity on the part of consumers to concepts that were well established overseas. The idea of providing personal financial protection for future exigencies was not entirely foreign, but for centuries it had taken the form of mutual-aid societies centered within religious communities.

Hirose, a banker from Shiga Prefecture, sensed that a secular form of financial protection would be readily accepted in a busy urban center such as the Kansai region. He consulted bank executives in Osaka about starting a company. The ten biggest banks there had formed a powerful bankers' association, which, with the new Meiji government's help and encouragement, eventually controlled the supply of money in Osaka. These bankers helped Hirose cope with such problems as opposition from rival business factions, and on July 4, 1889, Nippon Life began operations in Osaka as a limited company.

Public acceptance came quickly. As residents of an island nation with limited resources, the Japanese felt personally vulnerable, and opportunities to gain protection from future adversities have generally been welcomed—for example, Japan has usually had one of the highest ratios of savings to income. This factor—along with a need to trust one another as members of close-knit, interdependent communities—has conditioned Japanese consumers to buy a large amount of insurance.

By April 1890 Hirose opened Nippon Life's first branch office—a storefront in Tokyo. Three years later, visitors to the World Columbian Exposition in Chicago could witness Hirose's rapid outreach to the overseas market: Nippon Life's collection of annual reports and bilingual versions of its prospectus. The company was neither tapping overseas markets nor investing in them yet, but it did gain visibility as a basis for future outreach to foreign markets.

The next branch office to be opened—in Kyushu in 1895—reflected the company's growing prosperity. It was a spacious, free-standing building. Before the turn of the century, Nippon Life was Japan's top purveyor of life insurance based on insurance-in-force figures. The company became an important lender to local merchants. Rapid growth continued through the first decade of the 20th century, and accelerated as Japan entered the political arena of world powers as a World War I Allied power. By 1916 Nippon Life was investing in British, French, and Russian bond issues.

In the early 1920s growth slowed with the pace of the post–World War I economy and as a result of the widespread destruction of the Great Kanto Earthquake in 1923. The following year, the company established the Nippon Life Lifesaving Society, described in company's literature as "a major step forward" because it directly supported health-care services.

Intensive direct marketing helped turn Nippon Life's growth curve upward by the end of the decade, and the company regained its leadership position in contracts issued. Team spirit among personnel was cultivated formally through sales training and informally through company-sponsored athletics. At one such session in 1933, management made the prophetic announcement: "Nippon Life aims to be number one in the world."

As preparations for war went forward in the 1930s, Nippon Life developed one of its innovations: a new type of insurance based on the contribution method, allocation of profits that has since become the basis of most Japanese-issued insurance. The new insurance went on the market in 1940, and Nippon Life insurance-in-force contract values soared to approximately 20% of the nation's total.

Destruction and defeat in World War II brought Nippon Life's progress to a standstill. In 1947, under General Douglas MacArthur's forces Nippon Life took its first steps toward recovery when the company reorganized itself as a mutual life insurance company. Again under strict control by a government encouraging its growth, the company began to cope with problems such as forfeiture of overseas holdings and inflation that not only devalued insurance contracts but also slowed development of new business. By 1949, however, Nippon Life had recovered sufficiently to start a new community service: a "mobile angels clinic"—a van carrying medical services to underserved areas. By 1950 some businesses were already beginning to prosper and income was on the rise.

The company introduced another product in the 1950s that immediately became popular: monthly-installment-based insurance. At the same time, women began to figure prominently among the company's representatives, who fanned out on door-to-door sales sweeps each morning after a brief pep rally. In 1953 women sales representatives numbered 2,000. By 1990 there were more than 80,000—constituting some 95% of Nippon Life's workforce.

Nippon Life introduced the first made-to-order insurance with a term rider, combining payment on maturity and payment on the policyholder's death, in 1959. It became a leading product throughout the following decade and well into the 1970s. The company introduced a large-scale IBM computer system in 1962 to automate its burgeoning sales and investment records.

The 1960s were marked by further expansion into many areas of business and community service—corporate welfare and pension plans, for example. With the increased variety of company activity came increased emphasis on training, and in 1961 the company built a special training facility at Nakanoshima. In 1963 the company opened its Nissay Musical Theatre in Tokyo. As the nation's economy boomed, raising profits and personal incomes, the traditions of saving and investing in insurance and other financial products remained strong, supporting further company growth.

In the 1970s some government restrictions were lifted, which made it possible for Nippon Life to develop and introduce a new range of insurance-related products. Individual term insurance and annuity plans and life insurance related to asset formation are products that continue to be popular. The company also diversified its investment portfolio, adding consumer loans, real estate, bonds, and other equities. As deregulation spread from the Western economies, Nippon Life had new opportunities for risk-taking.

With the first purchase of real estate interests in the United States in 1981, Nippon Life acquired more of the type of investment the company has traditionally favored: long-term income properties. Not all these investments have been successful from the start, however. For example, among the large office towers the company purchased in major U.S. cities is a $200 million building in Dallas, Texas, that has been slow to lease.

The stock market crash in the late 1980s provided some sobering experiences. Nippon Life's strong asset base, however, made such events affordable as learning experiences. For example, seven months after paying $508 million for 13% share in Shearson Lehman Brothers in 1987, the value of Nippon Life's stake in the company had dwindled to about $225 million. Shearson's majority owner, American Express, began to offer American Express cards through Nippon Life's salespeople. Knowing how to benefit from close ties with other businesses continues to be a key factor in Nippon Life's success.

Despite some liberalization, the life insurance business in Japan is still under strict, but favorable, government control. Nippon Life dwarfs its competitors in sheer asset size, as well as in the number and value of contracts. Among the company's greatest assets may be a good sense of timing and the patience to get to know a market thoroughly before entering it. Because Nippon Life does not rush into a market without thorough research, the company does not plan to compete for life insurance sales in the United States. Although the company's investment capital overflowed domestic opportunities as the 1990s began, market reverses triggered a quick hold on investment in the United States, Europe, and Southeast Asia during the late 1980s, until signals of a stable recovery could be detected. Nippon Life's management has made it clear that prompt expansion will come when the conditions are right—notably into the European Economic Community and Southeast Asia.

Principal Subsidiaries: Nissay Computer Co., Ltd.; Nippon Insurance Service Co., Ltd.; Osaka Agency of Nippon Life Insurance Co., Ltd.; Tokyo Agency of Nippon Life Insurance Co., Ltd.; NLI Insurance Agency Inc. (U.S.A.); Nissay Investment Co., Ltd.; Nissay Mortgage Co., Ltd.; Nissay BOT Capital Management Corporation; Nissay Card Service Co., Ltd; Nissay Leasing Co., Ltd.; Seiwa Credit Co., Ltd.; Nissay Trading Co., Ltd.; Daiichi Mutual Fire & Marine Insurance Co., Ltd.; Akita Atorion Building Co., Ltd.; Shinjuku NS Building Co., Ltd.; Tsudanuma Building Maintenance Service Co., Ltd.; Ohmiyua Sonic City Co., Ltd.; Nissay Okinawa Kogyo Co., Ltd.; Seiwa Kaikan Co., Ltd.; Nangoku Nissay Building Co., Ltd.; NLI International Investment Luxembourg S.A.; NLI Asset Management Corporation (U.S.A.); NLI International Inc. (U.S.A.); NLI International Limited (U.K.); NLI International Canada Inc.; NLI International Singapore Pte. Ltd.; PanAgora Asset Management Ltd. (U.K.); NLI International Australia Limited; Nissay Business Service Co., Ltd.; Nippon Life Lifesaving Society; Nippon

Life Health Consultant; Nissay Athletics Co., Ltd.; NLI Properties, Inc. (U.S.A.); NLI Properties Canada Inc.; NLI Properties UK Limited; Seiwa Real Estate Co., Ltd.; Nishiyamato Development Co., Ltd.; Seiko Building Maintenance Service Co., Ltd.; Taisei Building Maintenance Service Co., Ltd.; Nissay Stadium Co., Ltd.

Further Reading: Reischauer, Edwin O., *Japan: the Story of a Nation*, Tokyo, Charles E. Tuttle Co., Inc., 1971; Prindl, Andreas R., *Japanese Finance: A Guide to Banking in Japan*, New York, John Wiley & Sons, 1981.

—Betty T. Moore

Northwestern Mutual Life

NORTHWESTERN MUTUAL LIFE INSURANCE COMPANY

720 East Wisconsin Avenue
Milwaukee, Wisconsin 53202
U.S.A.
(414) 271-1444
Fax: (414) 299-7049

Mutual Company
Incorporated: 1857 as Mutual Life Insurance Company of the State of Wisconsin
Employees: 3,012
Assets: $28.52 billion

Northwestern Mutual Life Insurance Company (NML), the tenth-largest U.S. company in 1989 ranked by assets, offers life and disability insurance as well as a variety of annuities. NML is the only one of the ten largest U.S. insurance companies to have been chartered west of Philadelphia. It remained a specialty company, issuing only individual life insurance policies, until the 1980s, when the introduction of strategic planning caused the company to change its orientation from a product- to a market-driven company. The resulting diversification added group life and disability insurance to the company's product mix, but its emphasis has remained largely on its traditional individual life policies. ''The Quiet Company,'' NML's corporate slogan, emphasizes that it puts the policyholder first, and it ranked first in dividend performance more often between 1940 and 1990 than any other company. A conservative approach to risk management in both investment and underwriting has been a characteristic of the company since its founding.

NML began as the entrepreneurial vision of ''General'' John C. Johnston, of Catskill, New York, who earned his rank as head of the local state militia. In 1850, at age 68, Johnston and his son moved to New York City, where they became agents in the employ of the Mutual Life Insurance Company of New York. Within three years of their arrival, the Johnstons were operating the company's most successful agency.

In 1854, at age 72, General Johnston sold his interest in the company and moved with his grandson, John H. Johnston, to a 3,000-acre farm near Janesville, Wisconsin. He soon determined that the area would benefit from low-cost, mutual life insurance. Consequently, with a petition signed by 36 of the area's leading citizens as the first board of trustees, the state legislature chartered the Mutual Life Insurance Company of the State of Wisconsin on March 2, 1857. Explicitly modeled on the New York company, it was to be headquartered in Janesville and to limit its investments to mortgages on Wisconsin real estate and government bonds. Its first policy contracts were issued on November 25, 1858. Johnston never served as president but was a general agent.

When many of the original trustees left the company, their places were taken by men from Milwaukee, Wisconsin, anxious to obtain control of the company. Following the legislature's revocation of the provision requiring a Janesville headquarters, the trustees voted on March 7, 1859, to move the company to Milwaukee. Johnston had lost control of the company and terminated his association as an agent on March 11, 1859.

The Milwaukee group elected as president Samuel S. Daggett, formerly of the Milwaukee Mutual Fire Insurance Company. The company's only full-time employee was the secretary, Amherst W. Kellogg. Since trustees met quarterly and the officers were part-time, the trustees established an executive committee of five trustees in June 1859, including the president and vice president as ex officio members. This step marked the beginning of the committee system which, despite some recent modifications, became the most conspicuous feature of the company's managerial organization.

Like any fledgling insurance company, there was a need to increase sales, and a sales force was established under a general agency system. Beginning in 1859, when the first out-of-state contract was made in Minnesota's Saint Paul–Minneapolis area, the company began to expand beyond Wisconsin. In 1860, the first-out-of-state local agency was appointed, in Iowa. By 1867, the company had expanded its mortgage holdings beyond Wisconsin, although its primary holdings were still Wisconsin, primarily Milwaukee, real estate. To reflect the fact that the company was becoming a regional institution, it changed its name in 1865 to the Northwestern Mutual Life Insurance Company. At that time, ''Northwest'' described the states now in the Midwest. When Samuel Daggett died in 1868, the company he helped nurture had passed through its formative years.

The search for a successor to Daggett led to the most serious power struggle in NML's history. The pivotal figure was Heber Smith, the superintendent of agents. By collecting proxies from the policyholders, Smith helped elect Lester Sexton as the new president in 1869. When Sexton died after two months in office, John H. Van Dyke, a young lawyer, was elected to replace him. Smith, who was elected vice president, believed that individuals seeking loans had to purchase policies. The issue was trusteeship, whether funds should be invested on a criterion other than that of obtaining the highest yield consistent with safety. After the Panic of 1873, the board of trustees wanted to exercise its judgment over loans, and in 1874, Henry L. Palmer, a lawyer and one of the original group of Milwaukee investors, was elected president. Palmer would remain president for 34 years.

The agents were not left voiceless. An association of agents had been created in 1868, but was inactive for several years. It was revived in 1877 and continues to serve as a forum unique to the life insurance industry at which field agents discuss problems of mutual interest and maintain communication with the home office. A year later the company hired salaried loan agents, effectively separating the selling of insurance from the lending of funds. In 1887 the finance committee was established to focus exclusively on financial and investment questions. It was created to ease the burden on the executive committee, but its membership duplicated most of the important personnel.

In 1881 NML created the insurance and agency committee with general responsibility for all phases of the insurance program. From that point until the turn of the 20th century, the life insurance industry was one of the fastest growing industries in the United States. Many new types of contracts were innovated by companies aggressively competing for sales. NML approached most of these new developments with its traditional conservatism. NML established an inquiry department in 1878 to cope with a problem inherent in insurance sales, "moral hazard," namely, that persons most likely to submit claims would be those most likely to demand policies. Health examinations and character check were required for each applicant. The company restricted itself only to the "healthiest" regions of the country, those that did not have high mortality rates. By 1907, the company's sales agencies were closely integrated with Northwestern's overall management policies. Management also attempted to be more responsive to the policyholders by establishing a policyholders examining committee in 1907 which annually evaluated everything from the company's accounting practices to managerial performance.

The growth of sales and development of new types of policies led to abuses in the industry. The 1905 Armstrong Committee investigation in New York, aimed at the three largest companies in that state, provoked a similar investigation by the Wisconsin legislature aimed at NML. While the Armstrong hearings discovered considerable concentration of control at the top, NML was found to have a relatively large group of self-perpetuating managers.

The rivalries that existed between the heads of the New York companies led to such practices as twisting—use of misrepresentation to have someone end one life insurance policy and buy another—and rebating—return of part of a premium payment—in the attempt to increase sales. Even though NML condemned and canceled agents found guilty of these practices, the legislature found examples. Similarly, the Armstrong investigation strongly criticized deferred dividend policies. NML dropped these policies before that investigation was under way, but the Wisconsin legislature echoed the New York findings.

Lastly, the Armstrong investigation was concerned that the sales of the New York companies were too large to be absorbed by the mortgage market. On the other hand, the Wisconsin legislature found NML's conservative financial policies to be excellent. What was disappointing to the legislature was the relatively small portion of the company's portfolio invested in its home state. The largest state for investment was Illinois, where the growing Chicago real estate market absorbed over a third of the company's loans until 1907, and a quarter of the loans thereafter.

The Wisconsin investigation led to an attempt to legislate the principle of trusteeship that NML tried to follow. Many of the unworkable laws were repealed or amended in 1915. NML came through this difficult period relatively unscathed because of the three principles its president, Henry Palmer, instilled into the corporate character: conservative underwriting standards, simplicity of operation, and conservative investments.

When Palmer stepped down in 1908, he had established a managerial succession that made George C. Markham the obvious choice. In the wake of the Armstrong investigation, insurance markets began to change. Group insurance and disability and double indemnity clauses were started at this time, but NML's management refused to adopt any of these innovations. Markham's administration was not market-oriented; it was preoccupied with investment problems. Many disability clauses were later proved unsound. In 1909, the company took the lead in the new field of business life insurance for partners and for key personnel. Nevertheless, agent dissatisfaction developed because the company would not enter new areas such as disability and group insurance. NML found itself developing into a specialty company by limiting its policies to individual life insurance.

When NML moved to Milwaukee, it occupied offices near the corner of Broadway and Wisconsin. It had outgrown several offices since then, but its new ones were never more than a block away. In 1910, it purchased a city block at the east end of Wisconsin, four blocks away. True to its conservatism, NML built a "Roman temple" in an age of skyscrapers. When the new building was occupied in 1914, the company became more compartmentalized. The sense of personalism that had characterized the days when executive and clerk worked side-by-side were gone. The fact that the new cafeteria offered free lunch on a daily basis was little compensation.

During World War I, NML followed the practice of the insurance industry in adding a "war-risk" clause to policies, resulting in increased premium costs for service men. At the same time, the federal government provided life insurance policies to men in service.

William D. Van Dyke whose father had been president in the 1870s, replaced Markham in 1919. Van Dyke, a lawyer, was an investment specialist, an important talent during the 13 years he served as president. By 1919, NML was the sixth-largest life insurance company and the leading farm mortgage lender among life companies. Since farm conditions were poor in the 1920s, the company began to explore other possibilities. NML led the field in the move toward larger loans, and, after 1925, increased its urban loans. In spite of a decline in the value of its large holdings of railroad securities and its hesitancy to invest in the expanding utility field, NML's rate of earnings was superior to that of other life companies.

During the 1920s the companies with the greatest sales growth were those with two or more lines of contracts, such as group and ordinary life or life and health insurance. NML made only modest changes in policy contracts and investment plans, and continued to grow. Its expanding operations required the construction of an addition to the home office in 1932.

The absence of diversification led to agent unhappiness. While the sales department was in the vanguard of the industry in preparing agents to sell to the needs of prospects, there was little effective coordination between the underwriting and sales departments. Michael Cleary, vice president since 1919, moved to improve the company's relations with agents.

With the Great Depression in 1929, the problems facing the company's investment and operations policies became as grave as those facing the underwriting and marketing programs. Shortly after the stock market crash, NML acquired a large amount of real estate due to foreclosures on farms and railroads.

As the Depression worsened, policyholders began to demand cash. In response to the outflow of funds, NML made several changes to make its products more marketable. In 1933, women were accepted as risks for the first time in 58 years, but they were limited to half the insurance a man could purchase. Age limits were generally lowered, and a new family-income plan was adopted.

Van Dyke died in 1932, and the company was without a president for four months until Michael Cleary was selected. Cleary's good relations with those in the field soon expanded to include those in the home office. He helped maintain morale during a difficult time for the life insurance industry. The need for additional personnel to help with these tasks meant that the agency force increased between 1929 and 1933.

In 1938 the federal government began another investigation of the insurance industry. The Temporary National Economic Committee called many executives to Washington, then echoed many of the complaints of the Armstrong Committee. NML emerged with an enhanced reputation for corporate ethics, service to its policyholders, and honesty in its policies and practices.

With the advent of World War II, the war-risk clause was added to policies sold after October 1940. The clause went into effect two weeks after the bombing of Pearl Harbor on December 7, 1941.

Michael Cleary suffered a fatal heart attack in 1947 and was replaced by Edmund Fitzgerald, who had first joined NML in 1932 as a part-time employee. Fitzgerald's name would later be borne by one of the company's largest and most famous investments, the Great Lakes freighter that sank in 1975.

Home office expenses rose to double premium income between 1946 and 1954. Under Fitzgerald, an administrative restructuring with additional specialized service and research functions was completed by 1955. NML began to computerize its operations in the late 1950s, cutting costs, improving service, and delaying the need for a new building. Fitzgerald needed to increase the yield on NML's portfolio. In 1933 NML had the second-largest mortgage account among the major firms; it was the second-lowest by 1947. NML had the smallest stocks and bounds portfolio in 1933, and the third largest by 1947. By 1955, the company ranked fifth in mortgage holdings, and its holdings of private securities had increased relative to the public bonds it purchased during World War II.

By not diversifying, NML had not kept up with its rivals, and its relative position within the industry was falling. The decision to remain an individual, select-risk insurer, however, was made to maximize safety. NML attempted to meet the market conditions of the postwar era with the same methods which had proved successful in the past. The agency system was improved. A "short course" for agents had been introduced in 1935, and sophisticated agent training was introduced following the war. More advanced training was left to various Chartered Life Underwriter (CLU) programs, and NML had the highest proportion of CLUs on its staff of all the major companies. The designation, Chartered Life Underwriter, was granted by the American College of Life Underwriters to individuals who had successfully completed the college's battery of courses on economics and insurance. Recruitment was difficult in the postwar years. Although agent income was high due to postwar prosperity, alternative employments outside the life insurance industry provided a great deal of competition.

Fitzgerald led the company into a greater involvement with national organizations and national issues, ending the company's historical isolation. NML became more involved in its home city, Milwaukee. When Fitzgerald retired in 1958, his successors, Donald Slichter, who became president that year, and Robert Dineen, who followed him in 1965, continued on the path of stable growth and selective change.

Competition forced NML to introduce products which it had resisted for years. In 1956 it took on some substandard risks; these risks occurred in a population less healthy than those included in the actuarial calculations for insurance premiums. Since substandard risks were excluded from the calculations for normal premiums, persons in the less-healthy group had to pay an additional premium. The company's version of double indemnity was introduced in 1959. Another area pursued was the pension trust business. Initiated by agents in 1938, these trusts involved large numbers of individual policies for employees of corporations. Such trusts were costly to service, cumbersome to administer, difficult to protect from the competition, and similar to group insurance. Eventually, this business was lost because of the company's refusal to rewrite them as a single group policy. On the other hand, the insurance service account introduced to the industry in 1962 was a particularly effective innovation. Customers with multiple policies could remit a monthly payment covering all policies rather than receive an annual bill for each policy.

In 1967, Francis Ferguson was elected president of "the sleeping giant," as the company was described in the industry, "the most stubbornly traditional of the top ten" companies, according to John Gunda's *The Quiet Company.* A corporate reorganization from vertical to horizontal was accomplished by 1968, with departments realigned by groups. Ferguson introduced the concept of strategic planning, which, in the 1980s, turned NML from a product- to a market-driven company. He introduced extra ordinary life in 1968, which replaced whole life as the company's most popular product within a year, because it helped counter the negative effect of inflation on whole life policies. As the Depression-era employees began to give way to those from the baby-boom generation, a desire to grow and to innovate was felt within the company. Growth bonuses were introduced as an incentive to agency growth, and, finally, NML decided to market its products more aggressively. It purchased a share of the commercial time on the broadcasts of the 1972 Olympic games and introduced its corporate slogan, "The Quiet Company." The giant had awakened.

The company's investments also became more visible, particularly the *Edmund Fitzgerald.* Other notable investments included major real estate ventures and energy exploration. An addition to the home office, Northwestern Mutual Place, was completed in 1981.

In 1980, Ferguson became chairman of the board, and Donald Schuenke was elected president. Together they presided over a transformation of NML. The company, shifting from its historic specialist role, began to diversify. All previous product innovations had been risk-based on individual lives. In 1982, NML made its initial move in the direction of group and health insurance by acquiring the Standard of America Life Insurance Company. That same year, non-annuity investment products and fee-based services were added when NML acquired Robert W. Baird & Company, Wisconsin's largest investment-banking organization.

In 1989, NML was owned by its more than two million policyholders. Its $28.5 billion in assets ranked it as the nation's tenth-largest life insurance company, with over $200 billion insurance in force, 7,000 agents associated with over 100 general agencies, and almost 300 district agencies representing the company in every state of the union. Investment operations were conducted out of the home office and 13 real estate investment field offices located throughout the country. Donald Schuenke became chairman, and James Ericson was elected NML's 15th president.

While the 1980s brought significant change, there was still much that remained familiar, in addition to the lunch served free in the company's cafeteria, as it had been since 1915. Most significantly, there was the belief in the equal treatment of all policyholders, fiscal conservatism, an insistence on efficiency, and the adherence to excellence.

Principal Subsidiaries: Robert W. Baird & Company, Inc.; Mortgage Guaranty Insurance Corporation; MGIC Investment Corporation; MGIC Mortgage Insurance Corporation; Mortgage Guaranty Reinsurance Corporation; NML Corporation.

Further Reading: Tyrrell, Henry F., *Semi-Centennial History of the Northwestern Mutual Life Insurance Company,* Milwaukee, Wisconsin, Northwestern Mutual Life, 1908; Jones, Laflin C., *To Have Seen a Century,* Milwaukee, Wisconsin Northwestern Mutual Life, 1957; Williamson, Harold F., and Orange A. Smalley, *Northwestern Mutual Life: A Century of Trusteeship,* Evanston, Illinois, Northwestern University Press, 1957; Gurda, John, *The Quiet Company: A Modern History of Northwestern Mutual Life,* Milwaukee, Wisconsin, Northwestern Mutual Life, 1983.

—Louis P. Cain

PENNSYLVANIA BLUE SHIELD

1800 Center Street
Camp Hill, Pennsylvania 17089
U.S.A.
(717) 763-3151
Fax: (717) 763-3544

Nonprofit Company
Incorporated: 1939 as Medical Service Association of Pennsylvania
Employees: 6,000
Assets: $848.27 million

Pennsylvania Blue Shield is the nation's largest Blue Shield association. Including its vast Medicare accounts, Pennsylvania Blue Shield processed more than 79 million claims in 1989, paying out $5.3 billion in benefits to eight million people. Blue Shield associations provide non-profit insurance coverage for most physicians' bills, and as such they find themselves at the center of national dissatisfaction with the rising cost of health care. As the nation's largest Blue Shield group, Pennsylvania Blue Shield now devotes an increasing amount of its energy to cost containment—a simple phrase masking the enormous complexity involved in bringing the cost of medical care under control.

The first Blue Shield organizations were patterned after the successful Blue Cross plans introduced during the Great Depression. Blue Cross provides non-profit insurance for hospitalization, as opposed to physician, costs. Prior to that time most of the country's voluntary, that is non-profit, hospitals had managed to survive on a combination of charitable contributions, private endowments, and limited patient payments. With the catastrophic downturn of the 1930s, however, all three sources of income were cut back and voluntary hospitals faced potential bankruptcy. In 1929, the first non-profit hospital insurance plan was introduced in Texas, and its success was soon imitated by hospital groups around the country. By providing an increasing number of lower income individuals with affordable monthly payments, these Blue Cross associations helped member hospitals stabilize their finances, while making health care more widely available at a time of near poverty for many.

Plagued by similar problems, physicians sought a plan for an insurance association of their own. Three factors seem to have played a part in their growing support for an insurance program. First, many of their patients could no longer afford decent medical services, a circumstance that was increasingly criticized by many as scandalous. Such widespread impoverishment meant a decrease in doctors' revenue as well, a trend that was understandably viewed with alarm by the physicians, and provided a second impetus toward insurance. Last, under President Franklin Roosevelt, the United States government showed a willingness to involve itself more deeply than ever before in the workings of the U.S. economy. It had been often proposed that the government should in particular take over health-care services. The combined pressure of these three considerations induced physicians to create the first pre-paid medical insurance plan, in California, in the early 1930s. As had the Blue Cross plans, the new Blue Shield concept soon caught on around the country during the pre–World War II years.

In October 1938 the Pennsylvania Medical Society's governing body debated the adoption of such a plan. As presented by Chauncey Palmer, the plan called for a voluntary organization of medical professionals to provide services for low income subscribers, who would in turn pay a fixed monthly fee while remaining free to use the participating doctor of their choice. As the financial intermediary between doctors and patients, the Medical Service Association of Pennsylvania, MSAP, as the new insurance company would be called, was to receive the monthly subscriber payments and disburse checks to the proper physicians as services were rendered. The new association would be run by a board of directors dominated by doctors, but its policies and fees would be subject to the jurisdiction of the state insurance commissioner and department of health.

The necessary legislation was finalized by the summer of 1939 and MSAP was incorporated in that same year, with headquarters in Harrisburg, Pennsylvania, and initial capital of $25,000 borrowed from the Pennsylvania Medical Society. Palmer was named its first president and Lester Perry, one of the association's earliest and strongest supporters, its secretary and executive director. Initial premiums were set at 35¢ a month for an individual, $1.05 for two persons, and $1.75 for a family, with services largely restricted to surgical and obstetrical procedures. To help the new association get off the ground and to reduce overhead costs, an agreement for unified recruiting and marketing was reached with Hospital Service Association of Pittsburgh, which later became a Blue Cross organization. At the end of MSAP's first year, subscribers numbered 7,163 and from gross income of $32,000 the association realized a net income of $7,000.

The onset of World War II forced the relocation of subscribers, and MSAP enrollment dropped slightly during the war's first few years. The association soon regained momentum, and by war's end had upped membership to 27,000 subscribers and 3,300 physicians. In 1945 the Pennsylvania Medical Society substantially increased its loan to MSAP as a sign of its long term commitment and to secure more firmly the association's reserve funds. Under new president J. Arthur Daugherty, who would remain the head of MSAP until 1968, the association quickly proved its strength in the booming postwar economy. In 1946 the number of new subscribers increased substantially, and MSAP began its pursuit of large corporate and union accounts—starting with the United Mine Workers and the Congress of Industrial Organizations (CIO). In the same year MSAP first received permission to use the Blue Shield name and logo, although the corporate name was not changed until 1964.

The years immediately following the war witnessed phenomenal growth at MSAP. The 1945 subscription total of 27,000 rose tenfold by 1948, and from there skyrocketed to 1.6 million only three years later, making MSAP the nation's third-largest Blue Shield organization. The association's coverage was considerably expanded as doctors and customers alike became more confident about what was still a relatively new concept in U.S. health care. Along with its expanded coverage MSAP pursued ever larger accounts, in 1951 landing the 150,000 employees of United States Steel and soon coordinating national coverage for multi-state corporate clients. This rapid growth in all phases of its business forced MSAP early on to join the computer age, and in 1956 the company installed an advanced IBM 650 computer featuring a memory bank with the then-remarkable capacity of 1,000 words.

During the 1950s, Americans not only developed a taste for increasing numbers of consumer goods, they also began to expect much more comprehensive and technologically advanced medical services. A pattern was beginning—patients naturally wanted the best care money could buy, and doctors for both financial and ethical reasons were more than happy to supply such care. With the persuasive arguments of technology urging them on, neither side of the exchange had any incentive to refuse new and more costly techniques, and the overall national health bill started climbing. As the "bank" for millions of Pennsylvania subscribers, MSAP found its physician payments rising uncontrollably, and in 1960 it was forced for the first time to ask state regulators for a premium increase.

Insurance Commissioner Francis Smith granted an increase equal to about 75% of MSAP's request, but at the same time he cautioned the association to remember the "public purpose of Blue Shield" and take whatever steps were necessary to control its costs. The latter goal, of course, has proven beyond the reach of anyone in U.S. medicine, but MSAP did inaugurate a series of overview committees to monitor rising costs and created a Subscriber Advisory Council to give its subscribers a greater voice in management of the association. Despite these measures, Pennsylvania Blue Shield—the name was taken in 1964—has since that time endured a steady stream of criticism for its role in the general inflation of medical expenses.

In 1965 the U.S. government took steps to cushion the older segment of the U.S. population from inflation by creating Medicare, a national health-care plan for persons 65 and over. Pennsylvania Blue Shield was chosen in February 1966 to administer Part B of the Medicare program, that part providing insurance for physicians' bills. Pennsylvania Blue Shield was forced to double the number of its employees in order to handle the enormous increase in new Medicare business, and soon became the leading Blue Shield Medicare provider in the country. The association also introduced Blue Shield 65-Special in 1966 to cover the 20% of medical expenses not paid by Medicare. The rapid rise in customers and claims threatened to overwhelm Pennsylvania Blue Shield's data-processing capability, and from 1968 to 1975 it contracted with Electronic Data Systems of Texas to handle its information flow.

By 1970 the rising cost of physician care had outstripped Pennsylvania Blue Shield's premium income and the company suffered the first of a string of annual losses. It was again forced to petition the state for a rate increase, as it has every year since; but this time the public mood was less receptive. Perhaps because Pennsylvania Blue Shield was now receiving large amounts of federal dollars as a result of its Medicare work, or simply because in 1970 the country was highly suspicious of all manifestations of "big business," the association came under widespread and prolonged attack for its rate request. Insurance Commissioner Herbert Denenberg for three years refused to grant a premium increase, instead demanding that Pennsylvania Blue Shield take further measures to cut costs and balance its board of directors between laymen and physicians. To make matters worse, in 1976 the Federal Trade Commission embarked on a nationwide investigation of Blue Shield plans to determine if the conflict of interest inherent in their role had tended to keep medical costs needlessly high. As Blue Shield associations were founded and run by doctors to help pay doctors' bills, it was evident that Blue Shield had little incentive to contest or deny the payment of such bills, which therefore continued on their inflationary spiral. The FTC eventually dropped its investigation, and Blue Shield organizations like Pennsylvania Blue Shield moved to balance their boards' composition. The charge of conflict of interest has remained a thorn in the collective side of Blue Shield.

In response to this controversy, Pennsylvania Blue Shield stepped up its internal policing, in many cases forcing its providers of both Medicare and regular Blue Shield coverage to refund unjustified payments. In a host of other areas the company attempted to put a cap on rising expenses. It cut back coverage for certain surgical procedures, instituted a second surgery-opinion program, and provided a stiff review board for its new dental coverage; but by the early 1980s, Pennsylvania Blue Shield and other traditional health insurance firms were losing considerable ground to the new health-maintenance organizations (HMOs) springing up around the country. HMOs, which charge a flat monthly fee for unlimited access to a reduced number of services, were able in many cases to undercut the premium schedules of typical Blue Shield providers such as Pennsylvania Blue Shield. Fighting back, Pennsylvania Blue Shield formed the first of its three Keystone HMOs in 1981, gaining a foothold in what appears to be a growing trend among corporate and private subscribers alike.

Along with its new HMOs, Pennsylvania Blue Shield has added a number of other subsidiaries in related medical fields, including a marketer of medical office automation systems, a pre-certification center for the detection of unnecessary procedures, and even a small learning center for preschool and kindergarten children. The balance of its time and energy, however, is still devoted to defining and implementing a program of health insurance acceptable to both consumers and providers. In 1989, for example, although Pennsylvania Blue Shield showed a healthy net increase in reserves of $80 million, on premium income of $2.3 billion, the company's annual report featured a 23-page roundtable discussion of the crisis in health care expenditures. The nation's largest Blue Shield and Medicare B provider is clearly feeling pressure from all sides of the health-care marketplace;

less clear is whether it or anyone else will be able to resolve a workable compromise among the many competing forces.

Principal Subsidiaries: Camp Hill Insurance Company; Keystone Health Plan Central; Keystone Health Plan East; Keystone Health Plan West; KHP Services; Keystone Technologies, Inc.; Health Benefits Management Inc.; Carefree Learning Center for Children; Omni Med Consultants.

Further Reading: Angelos, William M., *A Legacy of Value,* Camp Hill, Pennsylvania, Pennsylvania Blue Shield, 1989.

—Jonathan Martin

PRINCIPAL MUTUAL LIFE INSURANCE COMPANY

711 High Street
Des Moines, Iowa 50392
U.S.A.
(515) 247-5111
Fax: (515) 247-5930

Mutual Company
Incorporated: 1879 as The Bankers Life Association
Employees: 11,101
Assets: $23.31 billion

Principal Mutual Life Insurance is the primary member of The Principal Financial Group. The Principal Financial Group encompasses 20 insurance and financial-services companies, most of which are subsidiaries of Principal Mutual Life Insurance Company, which is among the ten-largest mutual life insurance companies in the United States. Other companies in the group are involved in stock brokerage, financial planning, investment management, and health, homeowners, and automobile insurance.

The U.S. Civil War, of 1861 to 1865, had increased interest in life insurance, which previously had been primarily an investment for the wealthy. By 1869, 110 companies in the United States were selling life insurance, but many of them sold policies that could be canceled easily, so the companies could collect premiums without ever having to pay benefits. The Principal Mutual Life Insurance Company began in 1879 as The Bankers Life Association. Edward A. Temple, a banker in Chariton, Iowa, was seeking a way to provide low-cost life insurance for fellow bankers and their employees. In addition to the plentitude of disreputable insurers, most life insurers were based in the East, and Temple was suspicious of eastern companies. He also believed that even reputable local companies charged excessive premiums.

Upon hearing of a life insurance plan set up by a group of ministers, under which each member of the group helped pay benefits when one of the members died, Temple set out to develop a similar system for bankers and bank employees. Under his plan, each participant would pay a deposit of $1 multiplied by his age upon joining, plus an initiation fee of half that much, for an insurance certificate with a face value of $2,000. The number of certificates a person could buy depended on his age. Once in the association, members would be assessed quarterly for funds to pay for the death losses that had occurred within the period, with the total annual assessment not to exceed 1% of the insurance in force.

The concept caught on quickly among Temple's fellow bankers, and in June 1879 they incorporated The Bankers Life Association. On July 1, the association's directors elected Temple president. They also voted to extend membership beyond bankers and bank employees to anyone recommended for membership by a bank the association used as a depository, who could meet the association's strict standards, which were designed to keep mortality rates low. The association screened out people in occupations or geographic areas perceived to be hazardous or with intemperate lifestyles. Women were also excluded, because childbearing was deemed too risky.

Bankers Life grew quickly; by the turn of the century it was open for membership in 21 states. With its selective standards and frugal operation—it had no paid staff until 1893, relying instead on volunteer labor—it was able to keep assessments low, and agents' sales pitches emphasized the low cost. By 1900 the association had $143 million worth of insurance in force; it surpassed the $200 million mark by its silver anniversary in 1904.

As the century turned, however, many assessment insurance companies were going out of business because of increasing assessments. Bills were introduced in many state legislatures to outlaw assessment companies. Bankers Life lobbied successfully against such measures, but at the same time there was a push within the association to convert it to a mutual legal reserve company, charging level premium rates and maintaining a required surplus fund. Temple strongly opposed such a change, so there was no action on it until after his death in 1909. His successor as president, Ernest E. Clark, was more sympathetic to the idea, and the conversion was effected in 1911, with the association becoming The Bankers Life Company.

The conversion was not an immediate hit; within the following three years, 195,000 of the 245,000 assessment certificates that had been in force in 1911 remained so. Of the other 50,000, one-third had been converted to level premium policies, but the rest had been allowed to lapse. By 1915, the amount of insurance in force had dropped to $398 million, a loss of $100 million since 1911. This loss came despite the fact that in the year after conversion of the company, it had for the first time made insurance available to men as young as 15—the previous minimum age had been 21—and, finally, to women.

George Kuhns, who was elected president in 1916 after Clark resigned because of ill health, set out aggressively to make Bankers Life Company grow once again. He embarked on a strenuous, but not initially successful, drive to get more certificate holders to convert to level premium policies; again, the number of outstanding certificates declined because of more lapses than conversions. The company also dropped many of the occupational, travel, and residency restrictions on policyholders. Growth of insurance in force returned in the first six months of Kuhns's presidency, with a rise to $415 million, and it continued to grow.

Growth did slow during World War I, partly because of a shortage of salespeople and partly because the federal government offered free insurance to armed forces members on active duty. The war did not create a major drain of the company's reserves, but the influenza epidemic toward the war's end did. Both the war and the epidemic, however, whetted the public's appetite for life insurance, and sales boomed after the war. By 1925 insurance in force grew to $844 million.

In order to help postwar sales grow, Bankers Life Company stepped up its advertising in the expanding market for insurance; it was a pioneer in the use of direct mail. Another means of promoting the company was the Des Moines radio station WHO, which Bankers Life Company acquired in 1925. The company became identified with the station, which featured several Bankers Life employees as performers and had a clear-channel signal that carried it throughout the Midwest. WHO became a National Broadcasting Company affiliate in 1927, but the next year lost its clear-channel status and had to share the frequency with station WOC of Davenport, Iowa. Both stations protested to the Federal Radio Commission, to no avail, and WHO was sold to WOC in 1930.

Gerard Nollen had become president of Bankers Life Company after Kuhns's death in 1926. In the first year of his presidency, the company launched yet another campaign to persuade holders of the old assessment certificates to convert to level premium policies. The drive ended with about 40,000 of the certificates still in force, and in 1927 Bankers Life Company had to drastically raise quarterly assessments for the certificate holders, as the emergency reserve fund that had been used to supplement them was depleted. This increase led to a class-action lawsuit by the certificate holders, in which they argued that the company should not have raised the assessments because it had sufficient reserve funds from the regular insurance policyholders, if not from the certificate holders. A district court in Iowa ruled in favor of Bankers Life Company, a decision later upheld by the Iowa Supreme Court and the U.S. Supreme Court.

Overall, the late 1920s were good years for Bankers Life Company; direct-mail advertising and a productive sales force helped insurance in force rise to $925 million in 1929, the company's 50th anniversary. The October 1929 stock market crash and the ensuing Great Depression, however, kept the company from reaching the billion-dollar mark, although insurance in force rose modestly, to $941 million, in 1930. For the next few years many people were unable to pay their premiums and let their policies lapse; still others borrowed against their policies. In 1934 Bankers Life Company had more money going out in loans than coming in through premium payments. Insurance in force dipped to $723 million.

During the Depression Bankers Life Company and other insurance companies strictly limited the amount of insurance a person could buy because lucrative policies were considered a temptation to suicide or murder. Bankers Life Company also tightened the provisions of its policies' disability riders and reduced payments made under these riders because many policyholders were claiming disability. To help boost sales during the Depression, the company introduced a new and popular policy called the Family Protection Plan, which paid larger benefits in the early years, when more protection for dependent children was required; hired its first educational training director to improve training for sales representatives; and increased the quantity and quality of its advertising.

In 1938, with the worst of the Depression over—insurance in force was up to $752 million and premium income showed its first increase since 1930—Bankers Life Company broke ground for a home-office building. The company had rented space before, and its own building was completed in 1940.

In 1941 Bankers Life Company entered the group insurance field when its board authorized the company to issue life, health, accident, annuity, and hospital insurance on a group basis. Group insurance was dominated by a few large companies—Metropolitan, Equitable of New York, Travelers, Aetna, and Prudential. Bankers Life focused its first group insurance marketing efforts on small midwestern companies that did not attract the industry leaders' attention.

The United States's entry into World War II was a boon to the group insurance business. Wartime economic restrictions limited wage increases, so unions demanded—and companies provided—improved benefits.

While this development helped the group insurance industry in general, Bankers Life Company in particular made a name for itself by creating group permanent life insurance. Before this, group life insurance terminated when a worker's employment did; at that time, the worker could convert the group policy to an individual one at his own initiative and expense under most state laws. Bankers Life Company developed group life that could be offered on a permanent basis, after an inquiry from Sperry Rand Corporation. Sperry Rand did not end up buying the insurance, but the retailer Marshall Field & Company did, early in 1943. Other clients followed, including Outboard Marine Corporation, Carrier Air Conditioning Corporation, and the Chicago Tribune.

Group permanent life insurance fell out of favor in the inflationary postwar economy, but it had established Bankers Life as a force in group insurance. Another factor that built the company's group business was its decision to offer group coverage to small companies through employer's associations.

During the booming postwar years, Bankers Life Company entered new fields and offered new products. It began selling individual accident and health insurance in 1952. In 1957 it began offering holders of ordinary life insurance policies the option to buy extra coverage for a small extra premium without taking a medical examination—an innovation that soon caught on with other insurance companies. In 1962 it started marketing a life insurance policy that, like other mutual insurers' policies, paid dividends, but that had the lower premium rates offered by stock companies, which did not pay dividends to policyholders. Presiding over these changes were several company veterans: Edmund McConney, who had succeeded Nollen in 1946, with Nollen moving up to the newly created position of chairman of the board; Dennis Warters, who became president in 1956; and Earl Bucknell, elected president in 1961.

In 1968, as Bucknell was moving up to chairman and chief executive officer and Harold G. Allen was succeeding him as president, Bankers Life Company went into the mutual fund business. It formed Bankers Life Equity Services Corporation—now Princor Financial Services Corporation—as a broker-dealer to market the funds, and Bankers Life Equity Management Company—now Principal Management—as investment adviser to the funds. In 1990 the 11 funds totalled $751 million. Also in 1968, Bankers Life Company adopted the corporate identity "The Bankers Life" in an effort to distinguish itself and its affiliates from other companies using "bankers" in their titles.

Further diversifying, Bankers Life Company formed the BLC Insurance Company—now known as Principal Casualty Insurance Company—to offer automobile and homeowners insurance policies. Unlike others in the field, the company offered these policies not directly to individuals, but through employers, such as the city of Des Moines, Iowa.

In 1977 Bankers Life Company went to market with an adjustable life insurance policy, in which holders could adjust premium costs and coverages. In 1981 it formed BLC National Insurance Company—now Principal National Life Insurance Company—which offers individual annuities and universal life insurance policies, with flexible premiums and benefits.

Throughout the 1970s and 1980s a flurry of government regulations made employee benefits—and, as a result, the insurance business—far more complex. Among the most important new regulations was the Employee Retirement Income Security Act of 1974, which set standards for funding and investment of pension plans.

Enhancing the expertise of its group pension department, Bankers Life Company increased its share of the pension-investment market during the 1970s. Principal Financial Group and a subsidiary, Invista Capital Management—which was formed in 1985 as Value Investors—manage more than $18 billion for pension funds and other tax exempt fund sponsors.

Bankers Life Company also reflected the growing internationalization of business in the 1980s, becoming the U.S. affiliate of the Group Insurance International Network, formed in 1984. Through such international networks, multinational employers are able to obtain employee benefits coverage for two or more of its foreign-based subsidiaries through one master contract. The insurer is also affiliated with another network, Insurope.

In 1985 The Bankers Life group adopted the name The Principal Financial Group as the trademark identity for all its companies because the name The Bankers Life no longer suited the company; its clientele had grown far beyond the bankers and bank employees it originally was intended to serve. In 1986 The Principal Financial Group's largest member company, Bankers Life Company, changed its name to Principal Mutual Life Insurance Company when its policyowners voted to do so.

The company's diversification continued into the late 1980s. In 1986, it acquired Eppler, Guerin & Turner, the largest independent stock brokerage firm in the Southwest, along with Delaware Charter Guarantee & Trust Company, which administers individual and group retirement plans for stock-brokerage-firm clients and mutual fund distributors. In 1987 it formed Principal Health Care, which operates health-maintenance organizations and preferred-provider organizations—two types of health-care plans that gained popularity in the 1980s.

Also in 1987, Principal Mutual Life Insurance Company opened an office in Washington, D.C., and hired Stuart J. Brahs, a veteran employee-benefits-industry representative, as its vice president of federal government relations, feeling that with increased regulation of employee benefits, the industry needed a louder voice in Washington.

In 1987 G. David Hurd was named president of Principal Mutual Life Insurance; he had been with the company since 1954, and his appointment continued the practice of promoting from within. He succeeded John R. Taylor, who in 1989 also turned the titles of chairman and chief executive officer over to Hurd. Taylor had been company president since 1984, succeeding Robert N. Houser, who has assumed the post from Allen in 1973. At the end of 1989 the company reported $100 billion worth of insurance in force and $26 billion in assets.

Principal Subsidiaries: Principal National Life Insurance Company; Principal Financial Services Corporation; Invista Capital Management, Inc.; Delaware Charter Guarantee & Trust Company; Principal Residential Advisors, Inc.; Principal Portfolio Services, Inc.; Principal Marketing Services, Inc.; Principal Casualty Insurance Company; Principal Health Care, Inc.; The Principal/Eppler, Guerin & Turner, Inc.; Healthcare Preferred Inc.; HMO IOWA, Inc.; Principal International, Inc.

Further Reading: Wall, Joseph Frazier, *Policies and People, The First Hundred Years of The Bankers Life, Des Moines, Iowa,* Englewood Cliffs, New Jersey, Prentice-Hall, 1979.

—Trudy Ring

PROVIDENT LIFE AND ACCIDENT INSURANCE COMPANY

PROVIDENT LIFE AND ACCIDENT INSURANCE COMPANY OF AMERICA

1 Fountain Square
Chattanooga, Tennessee 37402
U.S.A.
(615) 755-1011
Fax: (615) 755-1883

Public Company
Incorporated: 1887 as Mutual Medical Aid and Accident Insurance Company
Employees: 5,700
Assets: $11.85 billion
Stock Exchange: NASDAQ

Provident Life and Accident Insurance Company of America is one of the leading multi-line insurers in the United States. Established in 1887 during the southern industrial boom, Provident has weathered two world wars, the Great Depression and, more recently, health-care-cost inflation and increasing industry regulation. The company was a pioneer in first covering "uninsurable" workers, such as those at coal mines, blast furnaces, coke ovens, and certain railroad occupations. Provident later pioneered group medical and hospital coverages. Despite its name, Provident did not sell its first life insurance policy until 1917. Provident maintains a reputation for prompt claim payment and conservative investment. Its primary business segments are employee benefits, group pension, individual disability income, and individual life.

Provident's forerunner, the Mutual Medical Aid and Accident Insurance Company, was founded in Chattanooga, Tennessee, in May 1887. Founders included lawyers, an architect, and a real estate salesman, none of whom had any real knowledge of insurance. Chattanooga was enjoying a boom at this time, as mineral hunters had discovered coal and iron ore nearby in the 1870s. There was an industrial explosion in the South in the 1880s. Chattanooga's future seemed limitless in 1887, as steel went into production south of the Mason-Dixon Line for the first time, and the mineral wealth ignited development. The insurance industry was dominated by the eastern old-line companies who would not cover high-risk workers. Mutual Medical chose these "uninsurables" for its market niche. The employing company would withhold 2.5¢ a day from laborer's wages in return for $7.50 coverage a week for lost time, and compensation for death or lost limbs. For workers whose only other recourse had been passing the hat, the policies were attractive.

The founders were forced to reverse their medical-aid policies almost immediately, after realizing that a single yellow fever epidemic—like the one in 1878—could wipe out the company. They bought back some 100 medical policies and resolved to sell only accident insurance. The company changed its name and incorporated with its current name in December 1887. When local iron ores proved unsuitable for steelmaking, Chattanooga's development stalled. Companies withdrew, businesses defaulted, and seven banks collapsed. In five years of business, Provident had moved five times. It had 850 accident policies and no life policies. By 1892 Provident had also moved through 15 directors, and two Scotsmen offered to pay $1,000 for a one-half interest in the directionless company. Thomas Maclellan and John McMaster bought out the other owners by 1895.

In those days the insurance industry was regarded with deep suspicion, as many unsound insurance companies had soured public confidence. Maclellan and McMaster applied themselves foremost to reversing this mistrust, even choosing to go without salaries when necessary in order to pay claims promptly. By 1893 the number of policyholders had doubled. The following year saw premiums coming in from out of state. As full owners in 1895, McMaster became president and Maclellan secretary and treasurer. Their partnership ended in 1900 due to differences, and, by prior agreement, the company went to the higher bidder. Maclellan then took over the company and became its president.

Maclellan added two lines to Provident's coverage: sickness insurance and industrial insurance. Sales—which had been McMaster's strength—suffered with McMaster's departure. In 1905, the Armstrong Committee's investigation of New York State's insurance industry sparked more public mistrust, and state legislatures moved to enact reforms, including requirements of larger reserves. In 1909 Provident was forced to withdraw from Alabama and West Virginia after legislative reforms. It remained, however, in Tennessee, Kentucky, and Virginia, collecting premiums of $108,000 in those three states in 1909. While its field of operations was shrinking, Provident was hit with increased competition when insurance companies flocked to the South, where regulatory laws were less severe than elsewhere. Maclellan reorganized the company in 1910 with added capital, changing it from a mutual to a stock company. In 1911 Provident's previously shrunken territory doubled when it entered North Carolina, Georgia, and Alabama.

When World War I started in 1914, domestic fears affected financial markets, and Provident's policy lapses were more than 20%. To combat this, the company slashed operating expenses and entered new sales regions. At the end of 1915, Provident had increased its premium income by $100,000 over the previous year. The war-revived economy combined with the coal boom of 1916, and Provident prospered also. By the end of 1916, the company had a more than 65% increase in premium income. The year 1916 saw the sudden death of Thomas Maclellan, who was then succeeded by his son, Robert J. Maclellan, as president. Two new departments, railroad and life, were formed. After 30 years of operation Provident Life and Accident Insurance Company finally sold its first life insurance policy—to its new president, Robert J. Maclellan.

Provident was hard hit by the influenza epidemic in 1918–1919 that killed nearly ten times the number of Americans lost in World War I. The disaster proved a good advertisement for insurance, however, and Provident's premium income increased as a consequence in 1919 by more than 50%, exceeding $1 million.

Provident thrived along with the U.S. economy in the 1920s. It moved into a new 12-story building in 1924. That same year, the company wrote its first group plan, for the Tennessee Electric Power Company. Because the company maintained a policy of fair, prompt payment, only three of the 48,000 claims Provident processed in 1926 ended up in court. Most of its 100,000 policyholders were still working in the mines, lumber camps, steel mills, and railroad yards. An automobile liability department was formed as that industry blossomed in the 1920s, but losses closed the department in 1924. In 1925, the company's operations were still concentrated in the Southeast, but they spread north and west in 1926, with the purchase of the Standard Accident Company of Detroit. Within two years, Provident had extended to 34 of the then-48 states. With the Standard purchase came $500,000 annually in premiums. The 1929 acquisition of the Meridian Insurance Company, of West Virginia, added another $300,000 in premiums.

After the stock market crash of 1929, Provident's premium income declined. In 1931 Provident purchased the accident insurance business of the Southern Surety Company. The Des Moines, Iowa-based company's accident premiums totaled $1 million annually. The acquisition of Southern also provided an experienced staff. Provident managed not to borrow during the difficult years of the early 1930s, and by 1934, sales were picking up slightly. By its 50th anniversary, in 1937, Provident's assets were nearly $10 million, and it had an annual premium income of $7.5 million.

More industry changes came at the close of World War II as labor unions gained power and group insurance policies came into focus as an ordinary, and thus deductible, employer business expense. In 1946 Provident's accident and health income had grown by 25% over the year before. This growth rate was more than double the national average for the industry. The company's first subsidiary was formed in 1951, the Provident Life and Casualty Insurance Company. The subsidiary sold no casualty insurance; it was formed to allow Provident to do business in New York according to its state insurance laws, without subjecting the rest of the company to those same regulations. New York was the last frontier left for the company, as it had entered Canada in 1948. In 1952 R.L. Maclellan succeeded his father, Robert J. Maclellan, as president. The company moved into yet larger quarters. In 1955 it wrote the largest single group hospital and surgical policy in history, with premiums exceeding $5 million annually. Of 250 companies writing group life in 1954, Provident ranked 11th. Meanwhile, Provident's insurance pension business had grown in just six years to a $2 million operation in 1954. The following year it was $5 million. Robert J. Maclellan died in 1956, not long after celebrating his 50th year with the company.

In 1960 Provident made another move into larger quarters. Growth also was reflected in its premium income, which nearly doubled between 1959 and 1965. Asset growth was fueled largely by increasing individual life products sales. In 1964 Provident reported $5 billion worth of life insurance in force. It closed the decade with triple the assets and premium income of 1959.

The accident department signed one of its largest accounts in 1970, with the American Medical Association. R.L. Maclellan died in 1971, and Hugh Maclellan, another grandson of the company's first Maclellan, assumed the presidency. Two subsidiaries were formed in 1974 to stimulate the company's flexibility: the Provident General Insurance Company, which sold automobile and homeowners' insurance; and the Provident National Assurance Company, which sold variable annuities. This last grew out of the purchase of the American Republic Assurance Company. Especially strong was Provident's group department, whose premium income in the 1970s placed it among the top ten writers of group health insurance—ahead of established giants such as John Hancock and New York Life. Self-insurance flourished after the Employee Retirement Income Security Act was passed by Congress, sending ripples throughout the industry by the mid-1970s. In 1976 *Forbes* ranked Provident first in sales growth and in earnings per share among the top investor-owned life insurance companies. In 1977 Hugh Maclellan left the presidency to chair the finance committee, and H. Carey Hanlin took his place.

The 1980s dealt Provident and the insurance industry a series of hard blows. By 1980 Provident ranked seventh among the nation's stockholder-owned life insurers for insurance in force. Its primary business was group life, group accident, and health insurance, with the group business concentrated among groups of 500 or more. Between 1969 and 1979, sales of individual life insurance increased 73%, with the emphasis on tax-favored insurance plans. Then the mid-1980s brought a rash of regulations for the taxation of life insurance companies, starting with the stop-gap Tax Equity and Fiscal Responsibility Act (TEFRA) in 1982. While TEFRA reduced company taxes, the 1984 Deficit Reduction Act increased them considerably. Then the 1986 Tax Reform Act, by redefining the nature of life insurance policies, restricted certain promising Provident tax-favored products, such as corporate-owned life insurance.

While adjusting to these changes, Provident was also contending with health-care cost inflation that rocketed in 1986 and 1987, with claims costs rising by 20% to 25% a year. The company suffered low earnings during these years. To right itself, Provident responded with large-loss-case management, preferred-provider organizations (PPO), and flexible benefit plans. Unlike most of its competitors, Provident decided not to invest in company-owned health-maintenance organizations (HMO). This decision proved sage when other companies with massive capital investments in HMOs were hit doubly hard by that industry's problems. The combination of health-care-cost inflation; government regulation; AIDS; new high-tech, high-cost medical treatments; and stock market volatility proved significant hurdles for Provident and others in the industry. As the company celebrated its centennial in 1987, it also reached the trough in its downcycle, when declining earnings and the purchase of the group business of Transamerica Occidental further reduced company profits.

Provident continued low earnings in 1988 but rebounded to close 1989 with record earnings, after addressing inadequate pricing and focusing on core business.

In 1988, the Department of Health and Human Services began an investigation into Provident and others, to determine whether Medicare had paid for services that should have been covered by the insuror. Suits were pending in 1989, with Provident cooperating in the investigation. In 1988, the presidency passed from Hanlin to Winston W. Walker.

The company's post-tax net income increased 65% in 1989 over 1988, with an especially strong recovery in the employee benefits portion of its business. Despite considerable challenges, particularly in the 1980s, Provident proved to be a survivor.

Principal Subsidiaries: Provident Life Capital Corporation; Provident Life and Accident Insurance Company; Provident Life and Casualty Insurance Company; Provident National Assurance Company; Provident Marketing Corporation; Health Point Corporation.

Further Reading: "Reducing Risk: Provident Life's Managed Benefits are Surging," *Barron's*, October 27, 1980; Longworth, John, *Provident: A Centennial History*, Chattanooga, Tennessee, Provident Life and Accident Insurance Company, 1986.

—Carol I. Keeley

PRUDENTIAL CORPORATION PLC

1 Stephen Street
London W1P 2AP
United Kingdom
(071) 405-9222
Fax: (071) 548-3725

Public Company
Incorporated: 1848 as Prudential Mutual Assurance, Investment, and Loan Association
Employees: 40,000
Assets: £39.11 billion (US$63.13 billion)
Stock Exchanges: New York London Hong Kong Paris Frankfurt

The Prudential Corporation (the Pru) is a dominant force in financial services in the United Kingdom. The corporation's pretax trading profit in 1989 totaled £385.5 million. The company is the third-largest property owner in Britain, after the Crown and the Church of England. Its holdings of 3.5% of the stock quoted in London makes the Pru the largest investor in British stock markets. The corporation also operates the largest life assurance, pension, and reinsurance companies in the United Kingdom. The corporation's other ventures include an estate agency and a unit trust operation. Sir Brian Corby, the chairman, had declared bluntly in a 1986 announcement of corporate changes that "our ultimate aim is that everyone in Britain considering an important financial decision should look to the Prudential . . . first."

In 1848 political rebellion surged across Europe, while England contended with Chartist unrest. For a group of investors who gathered in London in May of 1848, however, revolution promised financial opportunity. Secure in the knowledge that crises create a desire for security, they pledged to raise £100,000 to organize the Prudential Investment, Loan, and Assurance Association which was in the end registered as the Prudential Mutual Assurance, Investment, and Loan Association. The company soon was renamed Prudential Assurance Company Limited. The founders, led by Chairman George Harrison, included a doctor of divinity, a naval officer, a leather merchant, a surveyor, a surgeon, and an auctioneer. In this competitive industry mere survival was an achievement. Between 1844 and 1883 1,186 insurance promotions were launched; 612 companies actually were formed, but only 93 survived in 1883. During some parts of that time period, insurance companies failed at the rate of 100 per year.

Most of those companies echoed the Prudential's early determination to serve an established middle-class clientele. The Prudential hoped for a patronage from clergymen, barristers, and successful tradesmen, seeking what was perceived as a profitable market segment. The poor had unhealthy occupations and inadequate housing and suffered most from the frequent epidemics of the period. Conventional wisdom in the insurance field also emphasized the inconvenience of managing a myriad of small policies. The anticipated high overhead of any collection system convinced most professionals to avoid this segment of the market. Following such conventional wisdom brought the Prudential to the edge of bankruptcy. In its first 18 months, the company generated a mere £1,500 in premium income. In 1851, the amount was still under £2,000. By 1852, the prospects for the company's survival were bleak.

New conditions in the insurance industry in the 1850s provided the Prudential with the opportunity to thrive. As late as 1845, insurance remained a prerogative of the upper classes of British society. Of a population of 25 million people, fewer than 100,000 held life assurance. This distribution changed with the emergence of industrial life assurance companies selling policies to members of the working class. H.A.L. Cockerell declared in *The British Insurance Business* that these companies "revolutionized the social distribution of life assurance." Such a company offered policies worth £20 or less and established a regular collection system outside the registered office, its legally designated location for official correspondence.

Two events in 1852 encouraged the Prudential to consider a change in policy. A select committee of the House of Commons called for an expansion of insurance to all classes of society. Perhaps more important, the operatives of the Prudential had become restive with the existing approach. A deputation called on the secretary of the Prudential and urged entrance into the industrial field. The agents wished to follow the example of friendly societies, a form of benevolent association, which provided benefits to their members. These associations offered an example of close personal contact between agent and member. The directors offered a lukewarm response. Only a few industrial policies were issued in 1854, but they proved to be the seed of future greatness.

Henry Harben, who succeeded Henry Charles Barfoot as secretary in 1856, recognized the possibilities of industrial assurance. The *Century of Service* recalled his shrewd observation that "it is far more prudent to take the pick of the small policies than to have the crumbs which fall from the rich man's table." Careful management and cautious expansion produced a more stable company. In 1864, Harben turned a potential disaster into a tremendous success for the company. Gladstone, then chancellor of the exchequer, criticized the operations of insurance companies, including the Prudential. Harben counterattacked vigorously. Not content with a war of words in the press, he called in independent actuaries who confirmed his claim that the company was sound and well managed. As a result of those actions, the Prudential experienced a dramatic rise in business and began to establish its reputation for reliability.

Gladstone's attack inadvertently aided the Prudential in another way. Gladstone's attack made many small companies vulnerable. Many went out of business. In 1860, the Prudential had acquired its first firm, British Industry, changing the corporate name to the British Prudential Assurance Company. That action had spurred growth in industrial policies. The Prudential acquired an additional five companies in the 1860s.

By 1880, the Prudential had become the leading company in industrial policies. By that time no other industrial-insurance companies extant in 1854 still existed. The following decades witnessed steady growth for the company. By 1905, the Prudential had issued 25 million policies in a population of 43 million. As Barry Supple acknowledged in *The Royal Exchange Assurance,* a history of a rival company, the Prudential had become "virtually a universal habit."

Leadership of the company remained in the hands of its founders into the 20th century. Edgar Horne, a founding director, served as chairman between 1877 and 1905, when Henry Harben succeeded him. Two years later, Harben, 84 years of age, passed the chairmanship to his son, Henry Andrade Harben. When H.A. Harben died in 1910, Thomas Dewey—with the company for 53 years—became chairman. Founder Horne's son, William Edgar Horne, was chairman between 1929 and 1941.

The Prudential succeeded because of a single-minded determination to meet the needs of its customers. Around the turn of the century, a post office official selling government insurance policies summed up the difficulties of competing with the Prudential. The commemorative volume, *Century of Service,* recalled with pride the competitor's complaint that the Pru "made a point of smoothing over difficulties, of waiving objections and carrying through the business very promptly." Good customer relations became the touchstone for evaluating policy. Maintaining contact between company and customer became the first priority in times of economic difficulty. The company worked to keep on the books customers who had fallen in arrears. The company also initiated a policy of bonuses for industrial policyholders. Between 1905 and 1948 over £78 million had been paid. The block system of collections, established by the 1920s, became the hallmark of the company's operations. Each agent had an area on the map defined as his territory. He would make a set number of calls per week. The efficiency of the system allowed management to reduce staff and cut costs. By 1948 representatives visited five million homes. The "man from the Pru" had become a national institution, celebrated in popular culture.

Never was the stature of the Prudential more evident than in its participation in the two world wars. Warfare poses a true crisis for insurance companies since no actuary can calculate the likely number of casualties. Certainly no actuary could have predicted the carnage of the Western front in World War I. The Courts (Emergency Powers) Act of 1914 had protected many customers against forfeiture of coverage due to nonpayment of premiums. The Prudential volunteered to honor the policies of those who died as a result of the war, providing that the policy had been initiated before the war. The Pru's most dramatic contribution came in 1915. The country badly needed U.S. dollars. The Prudential placed its total dollar securities, valued at £8.75 million, at the government's disposal.

During the World War II, the Prudential invested £242 million, over 50% of corporate assets, in government and government-guaranteed securities. The Prudential paid £5.5 million in war claims. The company could have denied half of those claims, since the policies in question had restricted liability to a return of premiums already paid. The directors, however, chose to suspend that provision. The traditions of customer service and national service became indistinguishable in such actions.

The giant company had become a national institution. In the decades following World War II the Prudential did not undertake initiatives in a changing economy, but remained a dominant force in life assurance, emphasizing its traditional strengths. By the 1970s some financial observers began to believe that the Pru owed its dominance to sheer inertia, as the company failed to create new service and delivery systems. Senior managers began to realize, in the words of Brian Corby, the lifelong Prudential employee who became CEO in 1982, that "the Pru has no God-given right to stay the biggest." This simple realization, which Corby expressed to the *Investors Chronicle* in March 1986, laid the foundations for the most significant change since the decision to sell industrial policies.

Searching for methods that would make it more responsive to market forces, the company chose a policy of decentralization. In 1978, the corporate holdings were reorganized. Prudential Corporation was established as a holding company. Prudential Assurance became a subsidiary. In 1984 a more thorough reorganization created seven operating divisions: U.K. individual, U.K. group pensions, international, Mercantile and General Reinsurance, Prudential Portfolio Managers, Prudential Property Services, and Prudential Holborn. A number of ancillary services remained outside this divisional structure. By 1986, the reorganization began to show signs of success. As the *Financial Times* of May 4, 1986 noted: "The City finally woke up to the fact that a series of apparently unrelated corporate moves were in fact part of a strategy to bring the bulk of the iceberg out of the water."

The new approach emphasized foreign expansion and acquisitions. Fiammetta Rocco in the August 1989 *Institutional Investor,* pointed out that the Pru had been unique among the great 19th-century insurance companies because it thrived as an English rather than an imperial institution. After World War I, the Prudential had expanded into general insurance, and the new general branch had engaged in modest overseas enterprises. In 1921, the Pru had begun to sell fire and accident insurance in the Netherlands and France. Other operations in Europe, the Commonwealth, and South America followed. However, these enterprises did not alter the character of the company. The attitude toward acquisitions began to alter slowly. Between 1968 and 1973, the Pru acquired the Mercantile and General Reinsurance Company from Swiss Reinsurance Company. This purchase established the Prudential's preeminence in the reinsurance field. Other major additions included the purchase of the Belgian firm L'Escaut in 1972—sold in 1990—the Canadian firm Constellation in 1978, and the Insurance Corporation of Ireland (Life), now Prudential Life of Ireland, in 1985.

Most important was the acquisition of the U.S. Jackson National Life Company in 1986. Approximately 2,000 companies were selling insurance in the United States at the time. Jackson National Life ranked 18th in new ordinary insurance sold, 60th in premium income, and 91st in assets. Purchase of one of the fastest-growing U.S. insurance companies did more than give the Pru an important share of the U.S. market. The purchase price of US$608 million brought an innovative and technologically advanced firm into the Pru family. Jackson National Life had been a leader in developing term life and universal life policies. Its operations were computerized and more efficient than the Prudential's administration. Jackson National Life would become an in-house resource for the modernization of Prudential's management. This acquisition indicated the Prudential's determination to recast itself at the end of the 20th century.

The determination to reshape the company did not require abandoning the company's established principles. The company had thrived because of its care for customer needs, willingness to deal with small customers, and determination to judge success on the basis of long-term profitability. These principles guided new ventures such as entrance into estate agency. The Prudential sought access to the younger generation of consumers, a group not concerned with life insurance, but interested in acquiring housing.

In 1985, the Prudential purchased an East Anglian real estate agency as an experiment. Success in the local operation inspired a national effort. Because most estate agencies were small and local, Prudential Property Services became a major force almost overnight. By 1989, the company had over 800 local offices. Due to the expense of this rapid expansion and the downturn in the property market, the company expected to lose as much as £35 million in 1989. The Prudential's plan, however, anticipated that this enterprise would encourage young adults to become customers for other Prudential products.

Circumstances forced some changes on the Prudential Corporation. The company's reorganization coincided with revolutionary changes in financial services in Great Britain. Prior to that decade, insurance companies, banks, and building societies had offered discrete services. New government policies under Prime Minister Margaret Thatcher spurred innovation. In 1984 the government abolished life assurance premium relief, a tax advantage which had attracted many customers. The move shocked insurance companies, who were forced to adjust to the new situation. As Brian Corby informed the *Financial Times*, reported March 4, 1984, "we must recognize we are in competition for the savings pound with every one else."

Seeking opportunities to expand its services, the Prudential Corporation established Prudential Holborn as its unit trust investment branch in 1985. The move appeared natural. No company seemed better suited to deal with small, cautious investors. The venture did not meet with immediate success. Prudential Holborn was founded just in time to feel the effects of the stock market crash. The unit trust business remained depressed for the rest of the decade. Prudential Holborn lost £105 million in 1988, and made a profit of £1.7 million in 1989. Prudential Corporation, though, remained content that the company was well positioned for an inevitable rise in the market.

This rapid expansion into a number of new services created a novel problem for the Pru: lack of consumer recognition. The corporate name was famous but the general population could not keep pace with the rate of corporate change. In 1986 a company survey discovered that only 20% of those who knew the Pru realized that the company had recently entered the mortgage business. Clearly, the other 80% were not thinking of the Pru first for every financial need. The diversified Pru required a higher profile and more advertising. When the Thatcher government deregulated the State Earnings–related Pension Scheme in 1988, the Pru launched a massive campaign for new pension business. Ten million people were covered by the state plan. Those who chose to leave would receive a rebate which could be invested in a new plan. The Prudential spent £7 million on advertising. In the opening stages of deregulation, the company issued 220,000 new contracts worth £110 million.

After a decade of reorganization, the Prudential Corporation presented a blend of traditional practice and innovation. The famed sales force remained 12,000 strong, still visiting five million homes for pension contributions and life assurance premiums. In an age of computers, this labor-intensive approach appeared anachronistic, but the system produced £1.3 billion in premium income in 1988. Prudential needed to convert this sales force into specialists able to market an integrated package of financial services, and 4,000 had been retrained by the end of 1989.

The leadership of the Prudential Corporation provided the best indicator of future development. Sir Brian Corby, who directed much of the reorganization, had been trained as an actuary. His successor, Michael Newmarch, who became CEO in April 1990, also was a lifelong Prudential employee. However, Newmarch had served as an investment manager not as an actuary. The new portfolio manager in 1989, Hugh Jenkins, had no previous experience with the Prudential Corporation. This highly regarded manager oversaw a portfolio valued at £35 billion. Asked to comment on the appointment of Newmarch, Jenkins observed discreetly that, "the investment function has come to the top." This phrase may sum up the future of the company as well.

Principal Subsidiaries: Prudential Assurance Company Limited; Prudential Holborn; Prudential Property Services; Prudential Corporate Pensions; Mercantile and General Reinsurance; Prudential Portfolio Managers; Jackson National Life (U.S.A.).

Further Reading: A Century of Service: The Story of the Prudential 1848–1948, London, Prudential Life Assurance Company, 1948; *Briefing Notes on Prudential Corporation,* Prudential corporate typescript, 1988; Purves, Libby, "Safe not Sorry," *Assets,* Spring 1989; Rocco, Fiammetta, "Remodeling Britain's Pru," *Institutional Investor,* August 1989.

—Joseph Bator

THE PRUDENTIAL INSURANCE COMPANY OF AMERICA

751 Broad Street
Prudential Plaza
Newark, New Jersey 07102
U.S.A.
(201) 802-6000
Fax: (201) 802-3128

Mutual Company
Incorporated: 1875 as Widows and Orphans Friendly Society
Employees: 105,000
Assets: $163.97 billion

The Prudential Insurance Company of America is the largest insurance company in North America and one of the largest financial institutions in the world. Along with its primary business, insurance, it also operates in securities, investments, residential real estate, employee benefits, home mortgages, and the corporate relocation industry. Prudential provides a broad array of diversified financial services for individuals, groups, and institutions: life, health and disability insurance, annuities and IRAs, estate or financial planning services, mutual funds, security and commodity services, liability insurance, home equity and mortgage services, real estate brokerage, deposit and personal management accounts, and credit card services.

Prudential started business as the Widows and Orphans Friendly Society in 1873 and in two years changed the name to The Prudential Friendly Society. Two years later the name became The Prudential Insurance Company of America. John F. Dryden, the founder of Prudential, studied the activities of the British Prudential Assurance Company, which was offering industrial insurance to workers. Several key elements marked this major innovation in life insurance; one, it only cost pennies a week; two, it protected against lapses in the account by having agents visit the customers at home each week to pick up the premium; three, it was tailored not to the wealthy or middle class but to the workers in industry and commerce. It was not easy to start such an innovative venture in 1875. The severe 1873 depression and the labor disorders of the period made investors wary of new ventures. Unable to find backers in his native New England or in New York, Dryden crossed the Hudson to Newark, New Jersey, and convinced several Newark citizens to purchase $30,000 of capital stock.

The first prospective of the company succinctly set its aims: relief in sickness and accident for people of meager means, pensions for old age, an adult burial fund, and an infant burial fund. The diverse ethnic groups coming to the United States shared a desire to provide a respectful, dignified burial for their loved ones. Dryden's goal met the immigrants' cultural need.

In the earliest years of the company the directors failed to recognize Dryden's vision or organizational talents. As a result he was passed over for president, and Allen L. Bassett was installed. However, Bassett, a real estate broker in Newark, soon had a falling out with the directors. Noah Blanchard, a tanner in Newark, took over as president. As the depression of the 1870s lengthened, Metropolitan Life Insurance (Met), the industry leader, suffered as many customers cancelled their ordinary life policies. In a defensive reaction, in 1879, the Met offered industrial insurance and pirated the Prudential's best agents. In reaction The Prudential (Pru) opened offices to sell industrial policies in New York. Decades of fierce competition followed. In 1881 Noah Blanchard died, and finally the directors elected John Dryden president by one vote. He served in that position for 30 years. During those years he led Prudential to several major innovations and established a corporate culture that marked Prudential for generations in the future.

Under Dryden's leadership Prudential enjoyed explosive growth. In 1885 it reported 422,671 policies in force, by 1905 it had 6.49 million. Assets grew from $1.03 million in 1885 to $102.38 million in 1905. Prudential expanded to neighboring states, and in 1909 opened its first international branch in Toronto, Canada.

In 1896 the advertising department created one of the United States most memorable and durable logos. The Rock of Gibraltar plus the slogan, "The Prudential has the strength of Gibraltar," became familiar to millions of Americans across the generations.

In 1905 a New York state legislative committee under Senator William W. Armstrong opened investigations into the insurance industry with Charles Evans Hughes as chief investigator. The major companies of that day were targets of the investigation into violation of customer interests. The Prudential emerged relatively unscathed.

When Dryden died in 1911, his son Forrest Dryden succeeded to the presidency. Under Forrest's leadership the company continued its rapid growth. In 1911 insurance in force totaled $2 billion. In 1921, when he resigned, it exceeded $5.6 billion. Corporate assets rose from $259 million to $830 million in 1922.

Control of the company became a problem during Forrest Dryden's term. With such huge resources and a conservative investment philosophy in a day of wild financial dealing, Prudential assets looked appealing to potential purchasers. Tired of fending off corporate suitors and raiders, the board took the first steps to make the company mutual and to sell the company to its policyholders.

Later in Forrest's tenure the company suffered several setbacks. World War I drained the company with heavy claims. Then, as a result of the 1918–1919 influenza pandemic,

Prudential paid out over $20 million for flu-related deaths. Shortly afterward Forrest Dryden brought scandal to the firm. During a legislative investigation into the insurance industry Forrest appeared ignorant about the most basic operations of the firm and did not satisfactorily explain a conflict of interest he had with certain stocks he held. In 1921 he resigned from Prudential, and Edward D. Duffield became president.

During Duffield's term Prudential experienced little growth. While it innovated by offering group insurance coverage to home office staff in 1924 and started group health in 1925, the Great Depression strangled most growth. Mortgages valued at $1.5 billion in 1931 bottomed at $787 million in 1935, even though the value of policies in force grew $1.5 billion between 1930 and 1935. In 1938, when Duffield died suddenly, he left a company still tremendously successful but no longer an exciting leader in the industry.

Franklin D'Olier succeeded Duffield as president. He concluded that deadwood littered the managerial ranks of the Pru. Privately he told his family that he would no longer urge young, ambitious men to join the Prudential family; seniority so dominated corporate policy that creativity and efficiency suffered.

While D'Olier recognized the problems Prudential faced with its conservative managerial corps he could never attend to them. A larger crisis commanded his tour of duty at the Pru. Hitler's actions in Europe and the U.S. commitment to World War II drew more and more of D'Olier's attention. The government repeatedly called on D'Olier to help with the war efforts. He helped organize the New York regional civil defense and later served on the Strategic Bombing Survey Commission.

Two major lights illuminated Prudential during the war. First, in 1942 the Pru finally converted to a mutual company, a process started in 1915. Second, Prudential benefited from the talents of Edmund Whittaker, who had joined the company in 1928, when D'Olier feared the Prudential was about to run out of actuaries. Whittaker moved rapidly through the ranks and, as head of group sales, helped Prudential seize the forefront in developing group sales. He led Prudential into major medical coverage, group credit insurance, and group insurance in multiple employer collective bargaining units. He typified the young executives who shortly would remake Prudential and the industry. When Whittaker characterized actuaries as the "engineers of insurance," he explained his own successes. In a speech to Prudential agents, reported in William Carr's *For Three Cents a Week,* Whittaker told them to look beyond the next premium. "We who are trying to compete with the ideas of nationalized programs are required to be social engineers. So far we have been good salesmen and good managers. We have not measured up too well as social engineers. If we don't do better, our system of private enterprise will pass by default to social planning."

In 1946 Prudential entered a new era. Carroll M. Shanks took office as Prudential's seventh chief executive officer. He did more to energize and remake the company than all the men since Dryden. At 40 years of age, he was the youngest president since Dryden, the man he most resembled. Shanks had joined Prudential in 1932 and was known for his unorthodox methods. During his 15 years as president he remade the company. He led the company into a bold decentralization that stunned the industry. He developed a parade of new products. He adopted innovative investment strategies that won a significant advantage for Prudential and its customers, and set up a personnel system that became the talent bank of the industry.

Shanks knew how stultifying the seniority system was and believed that only massive pruning would save the company. Within months of his taking office, resignations or early retirements were announced down to the level of middle management. Orville Beal, a future president of Prudential and one of the first to be promoted by Shanks, recalled those days in Carr's *From Three Cents a Week.* "The change was electric. Prudential held great possibilities, great potential, which was not yet realized. . . . We didn't blaze many trails in the insurance industry before Shanks took over. . . . He shook up the organization. . . . He got us going again."

In mid-1945 he drastically reorganized the Pru with massive decentralization. Shanks opened regional home offices across the nation. Each new regional home office would have its own senior vice president in charge and with total responsibility for the region. He would operate as president of a small company. He would handle most areas—sales, investments, general management, and all issues from policy to claims. Newark would retain the corporate senior officers, actuaries, and evaluation and staff departments. The reorganization dealt with many of the problems in Newark. It attacked the excessive specialization that separated workers and produced indecision; it cut the many levels between the president and operating employees; it eliminated layers of red tape and provided new opportunities for energetic and creative managers.

Each regional home office occupied a striking modern office building that dominated its city and told the region that the Pru had arrived in style and strength. Quickly the regional home offices, the first opened in Los Angeles in 1948, helped Prudential establish a new national presence. Policy called for the regional office to invest its dollars in the local community. With the advent of each of the eight home regional offices, Prudential sales jumped and investment income also rose sharply. In the first year regional sales in Los Angeles went up 20%.

The regional home offices enabled Shanks to freeze out inert executives. As the new leaders trained in the regional home offices spread out across the land, they created a multitude of new products, often tailor-made to the particular markets of their region. Quickly Shanks moved them to the national scene. The Prudential earned more on its investments. In 1962 the life insurance industry averaged a return of 4.29% on all invested assets, while the Prudential averaged 4.65%, producing an additional $60 million for the Prudential.

The creative spurt that Shanks excited extended to almost all products. Group pensions sold $44 million in 1945 and by 1955 exceeded $194 million; group life sales exceeded $589 million in 1949, a record for both Pru and the industry. The Prudential set up employee security programs that combined group life and health insurance. The Pru changed major medical insurance in the 1950s when it revised the method for computing the deductible. In 1951 the Pru's district agents voted to go on strike, the first formal job action by a white collar union in the nation. The American Federation of Labor led the workers for three months as they negotiated for improvements and succeeded in obtaining recognition of the union as their bargaining agent.

Under Shanks Prudential revised its investment strategies. After 1958 the Pru ceased to buy bonds on the market and instead negotiated separate loans with corporations for higher rates, while the corporations received more rapid, less costly, and more flexible financing. In 1956 Shanks created a commercial and industrial loan department to seek out small business loans.

Shanks consistently looked for niches where the Prudential could risk a small amount yet increase its average return significantly above its competitors. For instance, in 1950 Prudential began buying common stocks after permissive legislation opened up this opportunity. In 1964 Prudential had 3% of its assets in common stock and realized $75 million in capital gains.

When Shanks retired in 1960 the Prudential board named Louis R. Menagh Jr. as chief executive officer. At 68 he was one of the oldest to win the post but also the first to work to the top after starting as the lowest clerk. Menagh retired in October 1962, and the board named Orville E. Beal president. Beal exemplified the personnel advantages of decentralization. During the years he headed the regional home office in Minneapolis, Minnesota, he dealt with the diverse issues that he then faced in Newark. As a result, he was willing and able to pursue Shanks's bold vision.

In 1964 Prudential sold its first group variable annuity policy. Those annuities were invested entirely in common stocks and were seen as a much more attractive hedge against inflation than prior annuities, usually based on bonds, mortgages, and similar investments. In 1967 Beal announced that Prudential had finally surpassed the Metropolitan as the world's largest insurance company. The Met announced total assets of $23.51 billion while the Prudential announced $23.6 billion.

One of the great strengths of Prudential, from the earliest Dryden days, was its service to customers across the broadest possible economic range. The company sold industrial insurance to blue collar workers and offered ordinary life policies to white collar workers. With increases in worker income it was no longer necessary to market industrial policies featuring weekly premiums. In 1968 Beal abandoned the Pru's last pay-by-the-week policies, closing an important chapter in the company's history.

In 1968 Prudential established PIC Realty Corporation as a wholly owned subsidiary that would own or lease commercial real estate through joint ventures with established real estate developers. The Prudential would share profits directly as a principal in real estate development.

Beal stepped down in 1968. He turned the keys over to Donald MacNaughton, who led the company through some of its most expansive innovations. He particularly addressed issues of corporate social responsibility. In July 1967 Newark suffered terribly after one of the worst urban riots in U.S. history. Prudential was especially vulnerable, located in downtown Newark. Employees were afraid to go to work; middle managers resisted moving to the region. MacNaughton pledged to use Prudential's resources to help with problems of the urban centers. One of his first acts as president was to pledge $50 million to Newark. He helped the insurance industry pledge $1 billion to help U.S. cities, later increased to $2 billion. In his nine years as CEO, MacNaughton developed an array of new products for the company and plunged it into the international marketplace ahead of most of its competition. In 1969 Prudential celebrated total assets of over $25 billion; when MacNaughton retired in 1978 reported assets were $35.8 billion.

The New Jersey legislative revision of insurance laws in 1967 broadened the operations of life insurance companies. Henceforth they would be permitted to offer fire and casualty coverage, individual variable annuity plans, direct investment in real estate, investment management services, mortgage investing, and owning or leasing business or communication equipment. The Prudential took advantage of these new opportunities. MacNaughton knew that several trend lines boded ill for the life insurance industry; with inflation corroding the pay checks of U.S. workers, each year fewer customers saw great value in policies that pledged fixed payments. Life insurance assets grew 87% between 1950 and 1960 but between 1970 and 1980 grew only 70%. MacNaughton knew that one of Prudential's greatest asset was its corps of agents, who needed new products to sell. His vision was to provide the new middle class consumer with all insurance needs at one stop.

In 1970 Prudential entered the property and casualty insurance business. Unable to secure all the necessary state licenses and without a sufficiently large body of trained and certified agents, Prudential contracted with Kemper Insurance. Kemper provided "shell" companies that enabled Prudential to set up business in 26 states. Analysts at the time saw the arrangement as an astute move for the Pru. Homeowners insurance policies were often written for three to five years, and corporate profits suffered from inflation. Prudential wrote all its policies at current rates. The Pru carefully selected the geographic regions it would enter to minimize losses. However, the retraining costs to certify 30,000 agents were great. By 1972 Prudential dropped its contract with Kemper and continued in the casualty and fire field through its holding company subsidiary, Prudential Property and Casualty Insurance Company.

MacNaughton continued the search for higher returns in a period of inflation and stagflation. In 1973 the Pru formed Prudential Reinsurance Company (PRURE), insuring other insurance companies against extraordinary losses. In 1974 Prudential purchased CNA Nuclear Leasing, renaming it Prudential Lease. In its first year contracts grew by 88% and it returned 16% on equity. PRURE gave the Prudential its first entrance into the international market. The global commercial reinsurance business was virtually unregulated, and PRURE could be run easily with minimal administrative costs. MacNaughton felt strongly about the Prudential's need to go multinational. Quoted in *Business Week*, February 9, 1976, he stated, "This organization cannot continue to be a successful domestic company if it doesn't know a hell of a lot more about what's going on abroad than it does now. If we get so that we don't understand multinational business, then multinational business will eventually find someone else who does."

In 1976 Prudential acquired Hanbro Life Assurance Ltd. of Britain. It was Prudential's vehicle to enter the European Common Market, since the Pru expected that all member state insurance companies would soon be permitted to operate in all member states. MacNaughton developed many more product lines between 1973 and 1978. PIC Realty Canada, Ltd. owned and developed property in Canada. Prudential Health Care Plan operated health maintenance organizations. Pru Capital Management provided administration and management services to Prulease. Le Rocher, Compagnie de Reassurance wrote reinsurance in Europe. Pru Funding offered long term loans and operation leases for Prulease. Pru Supply contracted to supply fossil fuels or other inventories. Prudential General Insurance Company provided group casualty and property protection, and Pru Service Participacos, a wholly owned Brazilian subsidiary, provided services to another Brazilian property and casualty company.

MacNaughton retired in 1978 and was succeeded as CEO by Robert Beck. Beck joined Prudential in 1951 as an agent. During Beck's tenure the lapse rate on life policies continue to grow. The Pru had always relied on the assets accumulated from whole life sales to fuel the growth of assets. Beck needed to find new sources to replace those lost to the decline in whole life policies. Beck attacked the problem by entering new markets. The company formed Dryden and Company and Gibraltar Casualty Company to sell to the surplus lines market the coverage of unusual and difficult insurance risks. Pru also formed additional subsidiaries to market group and commercial property and casualty insurance. In 1979 Prudential signed with Sony Corporation to form Sony-Prudential to sell life insurance in the Japanese market. Beck also led Prudential in another investment opportunity; PRUCO formed a subsidiary, P.G. Realty, to purchase, sell, and operate farmlands in Nebraska. Later other subsidiaries were formed to operate farm lands in Florida.

Beck's most controversial acquisition came when he purchased the Bache investment and brokerage house in 1981. Bache was to be a troubled acquisition in a specialized industry new to the company. The Prudential now could sell money market funds, mutuals, tax shelters, real estate partnership, as well as stocks and bonds, all hedges against inflation. With Merrill Lynch selling life insurance, Citibank selling group life insurance through its credit cards, and American Express owning its own insurance companies, Prudential felt obliged to respond. Yet customers saw each of the various functions differently and ultimately did not trust the wisdom of a single adviser, seeing conflicts of interest.

Prudential continued to search for ways to maximize income from investments. In 1981 the company formed Property Investment Separate Account, a vehicle to enable pensions funds to invest in real estate. Pru developed successful investment initiatives: SMALLCO invested in firms under $200 million, and MIDCO in firms between $75 and $460 million capital.

Under Beck the Prudential continued to diversity, opening health maintenance offices in Oklahoma; Atlanta, Georgia; and Nashville, Tennessee. New life insurance subsidiaries were formed in Texas, Arizona, and Illinois. These new insurance companies did not need to rely upon whole life policies to accumulate capital. The company formed the Mircali Asset Management firm to manage global investments for other institutions.

In September 1986 Robert Beck retired. His successor as CEO and chairman of the board, 54-year-old Robert C. Winters, had joined Prudential in 1953. Winters took over after several decades of unprecedented growth in the company. Prudential's assets had more than doubled since 1978. After many years of spinning off a seemingly endless line of subsidiaries and holding companies, Winters saw his tenure as a time to digest and rationalize the gains of the earlier years. A new corporate strategy needed to be articulated that made sense out of the recent spate of expansion, one that gave form to future plans.

In 1987 the company reorganized its Prudential Realty Group into four new firms: Prudential Property Company, Prudential Acquisition and Sales Group, Prudential Mortgage Capital Company, and the Investment Service Group. Prudential offered its customers virtually every variety of insurance known, both for individuals and groups; it offered property and casualty insurance as well as residential mortgages. Under Winters it acquired Merrill Lynch Realty and Merrill Lynch Relocation Management and offered customers a nationwide system of real estate brokers. Pru sold its shares in Sony-Prudential to Sony. It formed a Prudential Life Insurance Company Ltd. in Japan, which offered a full range of individual life policies. Other subsidiaries were formed or acquired to sell policies in Spain, Italy, South Korea, and Taiwan.

The October 1987 panic on the market cost Prudential $1 billion in paper value, but it also marked the end to runaway leveraged buy-outs (LBOs) and massive mergers and acquisitions. The managers at the Pru made millions for the company in the heady days of LBOs. From one financial package put together to help sell a company, the Pru earned $200 million on an investment of $650 million.

There was, however, a negative side to the boom years of the market. Many of the sophisticated financial packages the Prudential and others crafted were tax havens for the customers. When the 1986 tax reform act eliminated the rationale for the many tax shelters, they were quickly abandoned by customers. Also, the packages designed by the financiers were often so sophisticated that neither the customers nor the agents marketing the devices could understand them. Many of the innovations tried by Prudential and others continued to falter. The Prudential pumped $2.4 billion into Bache with continual losses. In 1989, a difficult year for the Pru, Bache lost $48 million.

When Prudential started in business in 1870s, it faced fierce competition with the Metropolitan and other insurance companies. As it approaches the 21st century it faces a new kind of competition and a very difficult competitive world. Under President Joseph Melone, as it sets its strategy to enter the financial services industry, it not only enters competition against U.S. giants such as American Express, Sears, General Electric Credit Corporation, PrimeAmerica, and Merrill Lynch, but also faces fierce competition from overseas financial-service titans.

In 1990 Ronald D. Barbero was elected president to replace Joseph Melone, who left after six years in that office. The Pru sees its future focused around products that are tailored to the needs of newly sophisticated financial consumers. It has made a great success out of its guaranteed income contract that remakes the way the middle-class consumer looks at income investments. It is building a new service industry around its acquisition of Merrill Lynch's real estate business. Its agents will have ready access to consumers as they execute the largest purchase of their lives. Pru will not only offer mortgages, appraisal services, title insurance services, home equity loans, loans to furnish new homes, and homeowner's life and casualty insurance, but will also offer industrial relocation services.

Principal Subsidiaries: Gifford Fong Associates, Inc.; Merrill Lynch Mortgage Corporation; PIC Realty Canada, Ltd,; PRUCO, Inc.; PRICOA International Bank, S.A. (Luxembourg): The Prudential Life Insurance Company, Ltd. (Japan); AMODA, Sdn. Bhd. (Malaysia, 40%); HSG Health Systems Group Limited (Canada); Jennison Associates Capital Corp.; PRICOA Vita S.p.A. (Italy); PRUCO, Inc.; PRUCO Life Insurance Company; Premisys Real Estates Services, Inc.; PRUCO Life Insurance Company of Illinois; Prudential Fund Management Canada Ltd.; Prudential of America General Insurance Company (Canada); Prudential Overseas Funding Corporation N.V. (Netherlands Antilles); U.S. High Yield Management Company; Prudential Realty Securities II, Inc.; Prudential Special Equity Fund (Luxembourg, 47%); PruServicos Participacoes, S.A. (Brazil); Tesseract Corporation; The Prudential Insurance Company of Korea, Ltd.; The Prudential Insurance Company of New Jersey; The Prudential Investment Corporation; The Prudential Life Insurance Company of Arizona; The Prudential Real Estate Affiliates, Inc.; Prudential Mutual Fund Management, Inc.

Further Reading: Fifty Years the Prudential: The History of a Business, Charged with Public Interest, Newark, New Jersey, The Prudential Insurance Company of America, 1927; Sheehan, Robert, "That Mighty Pump, Prudential," *Fortune,* January 1964; Carr, William H.A., *From Three Cents a Week . . . The Story of The Prudential Insurance Company of America,* Englewood Cliffs, New Jersey, Prentice Hall, Inc., 1975.

—Thomas J. Heed

RELIANCE GROUP HOLDINGS, INC.

Park Avenue Plaza
55 East 52nd Street
New York, New York 10055
U.S.A.
(212) 909-1100
Fax: (212) 909-1864

Public Company
Incorporated: 1961 as Leasco Data Processing Equipment Corporation
Employees: 9,500
Assets: $10.40 billion
Stock Exchange: New York

Reliance Group Holdings has grown from a small office data-processing equipment firm in 1961 into a major insurance and financial-services group in one generation under one chief. The holding company is best known for its insurance group, which includes separate subsidiaries for property and casualty insurance, life insurance, and title and mortgage insurance. Reliance's insurance operations constitute the nation's 27th-largest property and casualty operation. The parent company also includes a development subsidiary in commercial real estate. Reliance's international consulting group contains several subsidiaries in energy, environment, and natural resources consulting. A financial arm invests in other businesses, primarily television stations.

By the time he received a bachelor of science degree in economics from the University of Pennsylvania's Wharton School of Finance in 1959, Saul Steinberg was already in the business of leasing computers, then a new concept. In 1961, at age 22, Steinberg founded the Leasco Data Processing Equipment Corporation. The company grew rapidly, expanded its capabilities, and in 1965 went public.

By 1968, Leasco sought to diversify its fields of business. Among its major purchases in the last two years of the 1960s was Reliance Insurance Companies of Philadelphia, which included Reliance Insurance Company and its subsidiaries. Leasco bought 91% of Reliance in September 1968, and the balance in winter 1981. Reliance insurance had been writing insurance since 1817, officially incorporating in 1820, and became the company's largest subsidiary.

Reliance Insurance started as the Fire Association of Philadelphia in 1817, organized by 5 hose and 11 engine fire companies. It became the nation's first association of volunteer fire departments. Its office was the front room of Caleb Carmalt, one of the founders. The association first met in his house on September 17, 1817. Michael Fox, president of Diligent Engine Company, was elected chairman. The new group took the place of several previous associations that had never succeeded because of internal squabbles among members.

The association started with no money, and trustees pledged their property as security. The founders agreed not to pay dividends until the company accumulated $15,000 in capital. The original 13 trustees agreed that dividends should go to the unpaid firemen. As a benefit, members received a 5% discount on their own property fire insurance. In addition to underwriting fire insurance, the association served as mediator between its member engine and hose companies; as rivals to get to a fire first to collect the commission, fire companies often damaged each other's equipment and assaulted each other.

The association adopted a fire mark with a fireplug attached to a hose and the initials F.A. on both sides for homeowners to place on their facades to let firefighters—and potential arsonists—know the houses were insured. Samuel Bleight, a storeowner with a weaving business in his basement, bought the first policy for his three-story building. The company took ten risks its first year.

The first time the association applied to the state legislature for a charter, it failed after the representative from Philadelphia stated that "the petitioners were men unworthy of public confidence and destitute alike of public spirit and mental worth." Association members immediately launched a successful campaign to defeat the representative in his next bid for reelection. Existing insurance companies also fought the charter. They "may have feared the Fire Association's influence on their own business, though they gave as their real cause of opposition . . . the fact that the new organization was without cash capital," according to *The Fire Association of Philadelphia,* a corporate history published in 1917 to celebrate its first century. On March 27, 1820, the governor of Pennsylvania signed a charter for The Trustees of the Fire Association of Philadelphia.

The company wrote 29 risks the first year of its charter. Business grew steadily, and by 1832, it wrote 583 policies. Although the first companies joined the association without charge, it subsequently imposed an entrance fee. By November 1829, 44 companies were members. By 1850, the association amassed a surplus of $100,000.

That year, the Great Fire of Philadelphia started at a store and spread to a warehouse where it caused an explosion and created panic. The fire spread so fast that it could be seen across the Delaware River in Trenton, New Jersey, and tremors were felt in Wilmington, Delaware. The largest fire in Philadelphia history up to that time, it destroyed 367 buildings, killed between 17 and 33 people, some drowning after jumping into the river. More than 100 people were reported injured, and losses were valued at $1.5 million, of which the association owed about $100,000, enough to wipe out the surplus it had accumulated. The trustees, however, promptly secured a loan based on their own personal liability, and paid all claims. This step created so much goodwill that its business expanded rapidly in the next few years.

During the Civil War, association members operated ambulances to transport the wounded to hospitals when they arrived in Philadelphia. In 1871, the city of Philadelphia organized its own fire department. The trustees voted to continue the association as a stock company under an amended charter. The state legislature approved the new charter on May 5, 1871. Four of the previous trustees and nine other stockholders were elected to the board of directors. At that time, the association became solely an insurance company and started writing policies outside Philadelphia. Its assets at the time totaled $1.71 million.

Business got a boost as a result of the Great Chicago Fire of 1871. The association soon developed a field of agents to write policies across the country. For the first two years, shareholders received dividends twice a year of $5 a share, which increased gradually to $10 in 1876.

As the company history reported, the association was able to pay large claims promptly when they came due. These included $309,000 after the great Baltimore Fire in 1904 and $1.84 million following the 1906 San Francisco Earthquake and Fire. By 1917, the association reported business of $4 million a year. It had expanded its coverage to include marine, tourist baggage, registered mail, explosion, sprinkler leakage, tornado, earthquake, and automobile insurance.

In 1919, the association started a subsidiary, Victory Fire Insurance Company, which had the same officers as the parent company. In the 1920s, it founded another subsidiary, Reliance Insurance Company and added riot and civil commotion insurance to its offerings. The year of the 1929 stock market crash, the association made $93,605 in underwriting profit, but this sum was more than offset by its $410,000 losses in investments.

World War II took its toll on the insurance business, including the association, which lost money between 1942 and 1946. By 1947, it broke even, and 1949 "was by far the banner year in the company's long history," *Best's Insurance Reports,* 1950–1951 edition, stated. In 1950, the association merged its subsidiaries into the parent company. The Fire Association of Philadelphia changed its name to Reliance Insurance Company in 1958.

From then on, the insurance company grew both through acquisition and establishment of subsidiaries. In the property and casualty field, it bought General Casualty Company of Wisconsin in 1956—sold in 1990 to Winterthur Swiss Insurance Company for $630 million—and United Pacific Insurance Company in 1967.

Reliance also started Eureka Insurance Company in Wisconsin in 1959, which changed its name to Planet Insurance Company in 1963. Since 1973, Planet has written Reliance's commercial mass-marketing business. In 1976, Planet took over Reliance's standard business in Texas. Another subsidiary, Regent Insurance Company, also started in 1963 in Wisconsin, writes auto, fire, inland marine, workers' compensation, and other insurance. Reliance started General Casualty Company of Illinois, sold in 1990, and Reliance Insurance Company of Illinois. The property and casualty operations evolved so that Reliance Insurance Company handled most eastern operations; General Casualty was responsible for most midwestern business until its sale; and United Pacific took care of the West.

The company's strategy was expansion in selected specialty lines. In 1971, the parent company formed Reliance Financial Services Corporation, an intermediate holding company for its insurance branches. The insurance operations are governed by a complicated structure, in which Reliance Group Holdings owns Reliance Group, Inc., which in turn owns Reliance Financial Services Corporation, which in turn owns Reliance Insurance Company and its subsidiaries.

In 1972, the Reliance insurance group divided its pool so that Reliance Insurance Company and its subsidiaries handled most standard lines, while United Pacific Insurance Company handled the nonstandard and other operations. Other property and casualty subsidiaries included Reliance Insurance Company of New York, founded in 1978, and Reliance Lloyds, founded in 1980.

In December 1973 Leasco Corporation changed its name to Reliance Group, Inc. The move represented corporate strategy to move away from computer-related services and into financial ones in the early 1970s, and recognition that insurance constituted the biggest part of the group. Three years later, Reliance Group founded Commonwealth Land Title Insurance Company, which would become the lead company in the group for mortgage and title insurance.

In 1981, Steinberg, still chairman of the board and chief executive officer decided to make the company private. He founded Reliance Group Holdings, Inc., a holding company for his and his family's stock that acquired all outstanding shares of Reliance Group, Inc., through cash purchase, debentures, or preferred shares of Reliance Group Holdings.

In 1982, Reliance insurance group expanded its life insurance business, as United Pacific Life Insurance Company marketed annuities for savings and retirements. The same year, the company incorporated Reliance Life Insurance Company of Rhode Island. The next year, it founded United Pacific Reliance Life Insurance Company of New York.

In 1986 the company went public again. Reliance Group Holdings, Inc. sold slightly more than 20% of its stock with a 15 million-share offering. Steinberg, his family and their trust retained the rest.

To find specialty markets suitable for Reliance's selective growth strategy, the group founded Reliance National Insurance Company late in 1987. It entered insurance markets of professional liability, construction, transit, health, technical property, and risk management. The value of Reliance's investments took a nose dive with the stock market crash of 1987. The company's net income per share decreased from $1.68 in 1987 to 32¢ in 1988 and to 29¢ in 1989. Like the insurance market in general, Reliance's underwriting market worsened in the late 1980s, as a result of disaster payments from hurricanes and the 1989 San Francisco earthquake.

In 1989, the insurance group included these divisions: property and casualty, life, and title and mortgage. Property and casualty wrote $1.79 million in premiums in 1989, using more than 3,000 independent agents. Reliance Insurance Company remained the biggest part of the group, which also included specialized risk and surety companies such as Reliance National Insurance Company, bought by the company in 1988 to write specialty lines. It was originally known as Hanseco Reinsurance Company, then John Hancock Reinsurance Company until Reliance changed the name in 1989 to make it sound like part of the family. Also writing specialty property and casualty coverage were Reliance Reinsurance

Corporation and Cananwill, a premium finance company. Reliance aimed to be a sole source for its agents by giving them all of the lines they needed through one subsidiary or another.

Expansion continued in 1989. The life insurance group founded United Pacific Financial Services, which offered securities and insurance to financial institutions through its broker-dealer, Reliance Life Distributors, and its insurance agency, Reliance Marketing Management. That year the life insurance group's assets totaled $5.77 billion.

In 1989 the California Department of Insurance (CDI) accused United Pacific Life Insurance of earning an annual rate of return about $10 million in excess of what it determined to be "fair and reasonable." However, CDI deferred the case while it reexamined its method of determining fair rates of return.

The title and mortgage-insurance branch grew with the purchase of Transamerica Title Insurance Company from Transamerica Corporation in 1990. The move boosted the size of the operation by almost 50%. In previous years the business of this segment had contracted; pretax income fell from $27.5 million in 1987 to $25.3 million in 1988 to $20.5 million in 1989. Reliance's 1989 annual report attributed the decline to "a decrease in commercial and residential real estate activity and increased price competition in commercial title insurance." Additionally in the mid-1980s Commonwealth Mortgage Assurance Company, the mortgage insurance arm, had experienced losses because of declines in the real estate market.

At the same time that the insurance business was growing, Reliance Group Holdings and its predecessors were developing other areas of business. The company bought Container Transport International in the 1960s, and turned it into the world's largest container transport company before selling it in 1979. Leasco purchased several specialized management consulting firms, which became the Reliance Consulting Group. The group provided three types of consulting: energy, environment, and natural resources; professional personnel services; and commercial productivity. The branches included RCG International, Inc., which, like Reliance Insurance, grew through acquisition of select specialized companies. Two more divisions, Herbert W. Davis & Company and Werner International, provided quality and cost-control consulting to manufacturers. The consulting group grew steadily, netting $67 million in revenues and $3 million in pretax profits in 1989.

In 1977, the company moved into real estate, forming Continental Cities Corporation, which became Reliance Development Group, Inc. This division handled all real estate operations of the parent company and other subsidiaries. The subsidiary additionally designed, developed, and managed commercial buildings. Projects the firm was developing in 1989 included office complexes in Tucson, Arizona, and Fort Worth, Texas. The group was working on residential and retail facilities, including ten shopping centers in the United States. Additional projects included the Oriental Warehouse in San Francisco's financial district, involving renovation of a historic brick structure combined with new construction of 420 apartments and commercial space, and mixed-use development for a tract of more than 500 acres in the Dulles International Airport corridor near Washington, D.C.

Reliance Capital Group, L.P. constituted the investment branch of the Reliance conglomerate. Its major holding consisted of Telemundo Group, Inc., a 36-station Spanish television network headquartered in New York, including the largest television station in Puerto Rico. In December 1989, Reliance Capital sold its investment, Days Corporation, parent company of Days Inn of America, the world's third-largest hotel chain; it had been purchased in 1984. The company nearly tripled the value of its investment in the sale, netting a $20 million pretax profit.

The company planned to continue its long-time strategy of growth through selective acquisitions and expansion. Under this strategy, it developed from a young man's computer leasing company into a major conglomerate.

Principal Subsidiaries: Reliance Insurance Company; Reliance National Insurance Company; General Casualty Companies; Reliance Surety Company; Reliance Reinsurance Corporation; Cananwill; United Pacific Life Insurance Company; United Pacific Reliance Life Insurance Company of New York; United Pacific Financial Services; Commonwealth Land Title Insurance Company; Transamerica Title Insurance Company; Commonwealth Mortgage Assurance Company; Commonwealth Relocation Services, Inc.; Reliance Development Group, Inc.; RCG International, Inc.; RCG/Hagler Bailly; RCG/Moody-Tottrup; RCG/Personnel Sciences; RCG/Vectron; Herbert W. Davis & Company; Werner International, Inc.; Telemundo Group, Inc.

Further Reading: The Fire Association of Philadelphia, Boston, Walton Advertising & Printing Co., 1917.

—Charles Pekow

RIUNIONE ADRIATICA DI SICURTÀ SPA

Corso Italia 23
20122 Milan
Italy
(02) 72161
Fax: (02) 8900740

Public Company
Incorporated: 1838
Employees: 3,621
Assets: L8.38 trillion (US$6.62 billion)
Stock Exchanges: Milan Rome Florence Genoa Turin Trieste

Riunione Adriatica di Sicurtà (RAS), the second-largest insurance company in Italy, was founded on May 9, 1838, in Trieste when its parent company, Adriatico Banco d'Assicurazione, decided that expansion could no longer be delayed.

Trieste was then part of the Austro-Hungarian Empire, and, profiting in part from the commercial decline of Venice, was undergoing a period of unprecedented economic and financial strength. The population, which was to keep climbing, had risen to 53,000. As a major seaport, Trieste quickly became a major center for the budding European insurance industry. The city's first insurance company, the Compagnia di Assicurazioni, dates back to 1766. In 1826, when the Adriatico Banco was set up, more than 20 insurance companies were already in operation.

The Adriatico Banco was set up to deal in maritime insurance. Its directors and board members included Ambrogio Ralli, the descendant of an illustrious Greek family from Chios; Danilo Dutilh, a trader and sugar producer who was of Dutch origin; Alessio Paris, a fabrics trader and friend of the poet George Byron, who was active in the Panhellenic movement; and Angelo Giannichesi (Angelos Giannikesis), a Greek from the island of Xanthi, who was to become a major financial backer of the Greek revolution. In 1829 the company adopted a new charter, and diversified into both river-transportation insurance and credit insurance. The latter innovation, largely a response to the needs of the rapidly expanding commercial sector, made the Banco the first company in Italy, and one of the first in continental Europe, to provide this kind of insurance on a regular basis.

Less than a decade later, further innovation was called for. Some board members already had pushed unsuccessfully for operations to be extended to other cities and had warned of the threat of competition from abroad. The response, when it finally came, was Riunione Adriatica di Sicurtà (RAS). Established to specialize in fire insurance and cargo-transport insurance, the new company, with registered capital set at an impressive one and a half million florins, was designed specifically to satisfy the desire for internationalization. The introduction to the new company's charter stated that: "While fire insurance has been a haven for many, it has not exactly been unprofitable for those originating the policies and we may observe that in all those countries where such systems operate, insurance companies have always made considerable profits in spite of a great number of accidents of huge proportions. This double advantage has given the Adriatico Banco, which has been operating in Trieste for twelve years and specializing in maritime and credit insurance, pause for thought. It has thus been decided to set up a new company with its own sizeable and independent capital, to deal in fire insurance as well as insurance for goods in transit. In this way it is able to extend to the whole of the Austrian kingdom, and elsewhere, the services that it has always been proud to offer in Trieste."

Almost immediately branch agencies or representative offices were opened in Athens; Budapest; Graz, Austria; Leghorn, Lugano, and Milan, Italy; Berlin; Kotor, Yugoslavia; Lvov, Russia; and Prague. In 1840, operations were expanded to include reinsurance, and in 1846, livestock coverage. By 1844, further agencies had been opened in Cologne; Gdansk, Poland; Florence; Hamburg; Nuremberg; Szczecin, Poland; and Warsaw. At this time the company initiated a long-standing policy of basing expansion on the establishment of autonomously run agencies headed by socially and financially prominent individuals who would then be flanked by company insurance experts or secretaries. Thus, as early as 1838, a Venice agency was established that was designed to function as a center of expansion into the territory of the Lombard-Venetian Kingdom.

The list of RAS founders includes Giannichesi, who was to be managing director for more than 20 years; the German Baron Herman Lutteroth; Stamaty Zizinia, a Greek noble; Trieste merchant Vita Salem, and Gustavo Adolfo Ulrich of Saxony. Whereas the heads of the Adriatico Banco were predominantly of Greek Orthodox backgrounds, RAS's shareholders and board of directors consisted of Middle-Europeans: Slavs, Germans, and Austro-Hungarians. Nevertheless, Greek influence remained strong and there is little doubt that the support of Giannichesi and other RAS shareholders during the Greek independence movement was to be instrumental in the Greek government's 1842 decision to grant RAS a ten-year monopoly on fire insurance in the new kingdom. This was to have negative financial repercussions, however, since at the time of the disastrous 1917 fire in Thessaloniki, RAS policies amounted to several million gold francs.

The new company's charter included safeguards against possible takeovers. Capital had been distributed in 1,500 shares of 1,000 florins each. Share trading needed the approval of the directorate. Each director-administrator was required to own 30 shares, and only shareholders could become agents.

Political events disrupted RAS operations. The revolutions of 1848 interfered with trade and manufacturing. However, as soon as peace was restored to the continent, innovation continued. In 1853, RAS introduced insurance against hailstorms in Bohemia and later extended it to the Lombard-Venetian Kingdom. A general agency for transport insurance was set up in Marseilles. After RAS was granted permission by Victor Emmanuel II of Sardinia—later to become king of a united Italy—to extend its operations to his realm, which included Sardinia, Piedmont, and Genoa, an agency was opened for the first time in Genoa.

The following year the company opened its first life insurance department. Affected by the world economic crisis, business was slow. Between 1854 and 1857, 508 policies had been issued, compared with 12,550 between 1857 and 1860. In 1856, to cover its life insurance annuities, the company made its first real estate acquisition, the Hotel de la Ville in Milan, which it still owns. Because of the world recession of 1857, in 1858 no dividends were distributed. However, business was to improve. A publication distributed during the Vienna World Exposition in 1873 showed that of 33 insurance companies operating on Austro-Hungarian soil, RAS came second in terms of insured values, premiums collected, and damages paid.

In 1863, Angelo Giannichesi died and was succeeded by Alessandro de Daninos, a well-respected member of the community of Leghorn who since 1838 had held the post of secretary-general. Greater changes were to follow. After the second war of independence against Austria in 1859, the kingdom of Sardinia began to expand gradually and RAS followed suit. In 1862 an act of incorporation led to the takeover of the Adriatico Banco by RAS. Headquarters were moved to Florence when the national capital for the new kingdom of Italy was established there in 1865. Three years later authorization was obtained from the pope for RAS to operate in the Papal States. In 1871, one year after the fall of Rome and the completion of Italian unification, the company's head office for the kingdom of Italy was moved to Rome.

In July 1878, when RAS celebrated its 40th anniversary, the situation was extremely favorable. Premiums, which had reached 120,000 florins in the first year of existence, had soared to over 9 million florins. The company's network consisted of 12 general agencies, 176 principal agencies, and 4,061 sub-agencies. There were also three agencies, based in Brussels, London, and St. Petersburg, that specialized in reinsurance. The company employed 296 people. The degree of activity outside Italy is illustrated by the fact that in 1881 RAS's general agency in Budapest celebrated the issue of its one-millionth fire policy on Hungarian territory.

Operations in Italy were also expanding, and when in 1898 it became compulsory for many industries to hold accident insurance, RAS, which was already handling this type of insurance through a specialized Austrian affiliate—Interunfall—set up a new Italian company, L'Assicuratrice Italiana, to deal in accident and public liabiliity insurance. A similar Paris-based company, La Protectrice, was to be established in 1911.

One of the new subsidiary's first clients was Luigi Amadeo of Savoy, Duke of the Abruzzi, who in 1899 took out accident insurance for his expedition to the North Pole with Captain Umberto Cagni. Towards the end of the century, RAS began selling plate glass and, in 1900, theft insurance.

Starting in 1872, operations in Italy had been organized into three separate geographical areas: Milan, Venice, and Rome. In 1908, however, a central directorate for Italy was set up in Milan, and a new price schedule for life insurance policies was devised. A few years later, work began on the company's new headquarters in Trieste, opened in 1914, in what today is called Piazza della Repubblica. It was also decided to expand operations into the Iberian peninsula, with Barcelona chosen as a site for the head office. Four agencies were opened in the newly created state of Albania.

World War I left Europe in the midst of incalculable destruction, and RAS, which was active in almost all the combatant countries, found itself facing hard times. Communications between headquarters and many branch offices had been interrupted, and insurance operations were frequently disrupted by military occupation, currency devaluation, and personnel shortages. Irredentist movements in the Trieste area created other tensions, and after the Austrian police described the general directorate as "a nest of irredentists," headquarters were forcibly transferred to Vienna. Still incorporated under Austrian law—Trieste became Italian in 1918 at the close of World War I—in 1916 the Italian branches of RAS briefly risked sequestration under an Italian decree calling for the confiscation of firms belonging to enemy nations. This decree was revoked in 1917. Although the world conflict was still raging, RAS took the first steps to reestablish the Italian reinsurance market, setting up La Riassicuratrice, a subsidiary which was to be merged later with L'Assicuratrice Italiana. At the close of the war, the company rewrote its charter and converted its registered capital into Italian lire. The new charter created the office of president. The first person to hold this position was Scipione de Sandrinelli, the former mayor of Trieste. Upon his death in 1922 he was succeeded by Eugenio Brunner, who was to occupy the post until 1933.

RAS's foreign expansion continued. In 1928, representative offices were opened in China, India, and Morocco. In 1928, the kingdom of Romania, which after the war had absorbed territories such as Transylvania and Banat where RAS had long-standing operations, passed an official decree authorizing RAS activity. The following year, the company crossed the Atlantic Ocean for the first time, setting up a directorate in Brazil.

A new breakthrough in the insurance field came when the company issued its tourist's policy in 1934, possibly the first global insurance ever promoted on the Italian market. It insured the policyholder against all risks—accident, loss of tickets, loss or theft of baggage—involved in traveling to and residing at a holiday destination. It also insured against damages to the insured's home in his absence.

The darkening of the European political scene in the late 1930s had a direct effect on RAS; its president, Arnoldo Frigessi, who was of Jewish descent, was forced to resign because of the racial laws adopted by the Fascist regime. He was replaced by Fulvio de Suvich, a company director who had served as under secretary of state at the Foreign Ministry but who was at odds with dictator Benito Mussolini over relations with Nazi Germany. Frigessi, like his father, had spent his entire working life at RAS, and was credited with much of the impetus behind the company's continuing international expansion. By the time the war broke out, RAS was operating directly, or through affiliates, in 26 other countries.

The company was at the head of a group consisting of 16 subsidiaries, 10 of which were based outside Italy. There were 16 directorates, 74 general agencies, and 459 principal agencies in Italy and abroad. In 1938, total premiums from all branches amounted to L538 million.

Frigessi went into hiding but refused to leave Italy. When Rome was liberated in 1944 he returned to RAS, coordinating operations in central and southern Italy. In 1946 he returned to Trieste, first as managing director and then, in 1947, as president. Until his death in 1950, Frigessi's efforts were directed largely at expansion in North America and South America to make up for the vast loss of business in eastern Europe.

At the close of World War II, Italy was in a state of near collapse. The economy was in tatters and, not surprisingly, insurance activity had ground to a virtual halt. The value of premiums had plunged, and because of Italy's enemy status many of the company's overseas assets had been seized and its operating licenses revoked. The 1947 Peace Treaty, for example, called for the surrender of all Italian property in Hungary, Romania, and Bulgaria to the Soviet Union as a form of war compensation. Not long after, the insurance market was nationalized in Czechoslovakia, RAS's second-largest market. The company was also forced to abandon operations in Albania, Poland, and Yugoslavia. The withdrawal from eastern Europe cost the company almost a third of its total business. At the same time, the establishment of the free territory of Trieste—which was returned to Italy in 1954—led to the relocation of company headquarters to Milan.

Reestablishing the insurance business in the postwar period was to prove a slow and painstaking process. Deteriorating political conditions in various countries—Egypt, Libya, South Africa—were to curtail more of RAS's international activities. At home, there was a compelling need to deal with runaway inflation and widespread unemployment. There were changes in management and ownership. Enrico Marchesano, a highly respected Banca Commerciale official who joined RAS in 1934, and, with the exception of a two-year period in which he served as head of the Institute for Industrial Reconstructon, remained with RAS for the rest of his career, became president and managing director. In 1948, Piero Sacerdoti, who had spent most of his career first with L'Assicuratrice and then with La Protectrice, was made director-general of RAS. Sacerdoti, who is credited with successful attempts to revitalize the company, initiated studies on public liability regarding damages caused by nuclear energy. Between 1949 and 1971, under the leadership of Mario Pontremoli, the RAS subsidiary L'Assicuratrice Italiana increased premiums to L90 billion, equaling those of the parent company. The establishment of subsidiaries abroad continued, with the birth of Consolidated Insurances of Australia in 1960 marking RAS's extension to that continent.

In Italy during this period, innovations in the insurance industry included that of linking insurance to financial investment and planning. In 1954 RAS joined COFINA—over which it was to acquire total control in 1972—a company which sought to encourage stock purchases by issuing insurance policies that would pay off remaining stock-purchase installments in the event of a policyholder's death. In the same year, the company inaugurated the Pluvius policy, offering protection against rainy weather to vacationers. Group policies were launched in 1958. In 1960, RAS was the first to offer a banking insurance plan by offering depositors at CARIPLO, the large Milan bank, policies providing for a doubled bank account in the event of death. In 1963 it was the first Italian insurance company to sell policies by mail. Three years later, Compagnia di Genova, another RAS subsidiary, launched a nautical policy for leisure craft, the first in Italy.

By now prosperity had returned to Italy and the insurance market was expanding. The administration of President Ettore Lolli, from 1967 to 1983, oversaw the creation of DIVAL, a financial-services company that began by trading shares in Three R, a Luxembourg-based unit trust set up by RAS together with the IRIS Holding Company owned by the N.M. Rothschild bank and the Rockefeller family. In 1974 a new RAS subsidiary, Continentale Allgemeine, was set up in Zürich. In 1980 RAS incorporated L'Assicuratrice Italiana, and in 1983, two days after the publication of the law legalizing Italian unit trusts, RAS launched the first such Italian fund, GESTIRAS.

After World War II there had been changes in the company's shareholding structure. During the interwar period, RAS shareholdings had been characterized by a broadly diffused structure, but some 20 families with long-standing RAS connections—such as the Brunner, Economo, Frigessi, Ralli, Ravano, Pavia, and Ottolenghi families—for the most part of Triestino, Venetian, or Lombard origins, enjoyed particular influence. After the war, several new shareholders—including, during the 1950s, the Holy See—appeared on the scene. After 1952, Italmobiliare, the holding company of industrialist Carlo Pesenti, gradually became the principal stockholder.

Pesenti died in September 1984, and soon after it was announced that Allianz, the Munich-based European insurance group, would be buying Pesenti's 38% share along with other holdings purchased from Toro Assicurazioni and Saes, a subsidiary of IFI, the Agnelli family's holding company. As agreed, in 1987 Allianz's share rose to 51.51%. The other major stockholders were Imigest Fondo Imicapital with 2.01%, the Banca d'Italia with 1.09%, Fonditalia Management with 0.6%, and Credito Italiano with 0.49%. The remainder of the stock was mostly on the market.

Under the direction of Umberto Zanni, appointed president in 1986, the company has flourished, although there have been problems. The 1989 balance sheet, the 151st in the company's history, showed RAS's gross premiums amounting to L2.52 trillion—about US$2 billion—while total premiums for the entire insurance group, which includes 11 Italian and 18 foreign companies, amounted to over L5.43 trillion. RAS also holds a controlling interest in an additional 37 companies, 18 in the field of financial management or investment and 19 agriculture, real estate, or services. In the trust division, assets managed by the group amounted to almost L7 trillion.

Although profits were boosted by real estate sales, 1989 was a difficult year. Like most Italian insurance companies, RAS has been faced with mounting accident claims—largely automobile—which in 1989 rose 20% to 779,541. Substantial underwriting deficits exist in many divisions. In particular, there were significant losses in the automobile division which Chairman Zanni says were structural and likely to increase unless third-party motor insurance rates, which are set by the government, are allowed to rise. Much of the company's future prosperity will also depend on developments in the financial sector. Although the situation is expected to improve, redemptions of investment funds in 1989 still exceeded subscriptions. Confusion regarding rules and regulations in the life insurance sector had led to a fall-off in new business.

The link-up with Allianz has been of enormous importance to RAS and is likely to be increasingly significant. In autumn 1990, the first branch of a new bank, RASBANK, in which RAS has a 65% stake, Allianz a 25% holding, and Hypobaruk, Munich, a 10% stake, opened. In spring 1990, RAS participated—with a 6% share—in Allianz's 64.5% takeover of Navigation Mixte, one of France's top five insurance companies, a move which gives the group control over four French insurance companies with premiums equal to about FFr10 billion. Important joint ventures are also under way in Spain, where RAS and Allianz joined Banco Popolar in forming Europensiones and Eurovida. From Allianz's point of view, the link-up has also been a success. In an interview that appeared in *Corriere della Sera* on June 20, 1990, Allianz's chairman, Wolfgang Schieren, said that Allianz's position in Italy is now stronger than in any country other than Germany. "We have a market share of 10%; almost 35% of Allianz's foreign activity . . . and 14% of worldwide premiums come from Italy."

RAS is now convinced that the main challenge for the future will come from the completion of the single European market. Company directors, however, have been outspoken in urging the Italian government to develop a clear policy regarding the insurance industry that would permit it to prepare properly for the tough competition that is expected to come from its more developed European rivals.

Principal Subsidiaries: Lavoro & Sicurtà; L'Italica (94.83%); Società Finanziaria Assicurativa; Unione Subalpine di Assicurazioni (69.22%); Ras International N.V. (Netherlands, 99%); Allianz-Ras España S.A. (Spain, 75%); Interunfall/Ras, (Austria, 76.08%); Continentale Allgemeine (Switzerland); Canadian Home Assurance Co. (Canada, 99.69%); Companhia Adriatica de Seguros (Brazil, 80%); Allianz-Ras Holding (France, 38.15%); Sark Sigorta (Turkey, 33.59%).

Further Reading: Sanzin, Luciano Giulio, "Storia dell Assicurazione—Sui Primordi e su Alcuni Sviluppi dell'Assicurazione in Italia," *Quaderni dell "Istituto per gli studi assicurativi,"* number 2, 1945; Palladini, Giovanni, "Le Compagnie di Assicurazione di Trieste," *Trieste Economica,* December 1966; Irneri, Giorgio, *"Passato e Avvenire delle Assicurazioni nella Regione Friuli-Venezia Giulia,"* Trieste, [n.p.], 1967; Tedeschi, Erminio, *Historical Notes. RAS: 1938–1988,* Milan, Riunione Adriatica di Sicurtà, 1989; Di Martino, Anna, "L'erede può Aspettare," *Il Mondo,* February 12/19, 1990; Panzeri, Emilio, "RAS rimandata in tecnica ma promossa in Finanza," *Assicurazioni,* February 1990; De Feo, Marika, "La Ras? Dovrebbe guadagnare di piú," *Corriere della Sera,* June 20, 1990.

—Sari Gilbert

ROYAL INSURANCE HOLDINGS PLC

1 Cornhill
London EC3V 3QR
United Kingdom
(071) 283-4300
Fax: (071) 623-5282

Public Company
Incorporated: 1988 as Trushelfco Plc
Employees: 20,000
Assets: £9.99 billion (US$16.13 billion)
Stock Exchange: London

The Royal Insurance Company—now Royal Insurance plc—was formed in the United Kingdom in 1845. With six principal operating companies, it is one of the world's largest general and life insurance companies. The parent company of the group is Royal Insurance Holdings, which was formed in 1988 and controls 264 subsidiary and 27 associated companies. The operating companies, Royal UK, Royal USA, Royal International, Royal Canada, Royal Re, and Royal Life Holdings, have a major presence in the United Kingdom, United States, Canada, the Netherlands and elsewhere in Europe, Central America, South America, Africa, the Middle East, and the Pacific Rim. The Royal writes almost all classes of insurance, on everything from personal belongings to industrial complexes. At the end of 1989 the group's capital and reserves had increased to £2.66 billion, and total premium income for the year had risen 19% to £4.74 billion.

In 1989 the most important of the operating companies in terms of net premium income were Royal USA and Royal UK. Royal USA has a wide presence in the United States and writes most types of property and casualty insurance. The commercial market provides the largest share of premium income. Royal UK is one of Britain's leading general insurance companies in terms of premium income, with domestic insurance providing over one-third of all premium income. Royal Life Holdings was established in 1979. It is the specialist life and financial services arm of the group and has also expanded into estate agency, or real estate, and unit trust management. Royal International is responsible for the development of the group's direct, non-life business throughout the world, other than in North America and the United Kingdom. In the late 1980s it decided to concentrate on pursuing opportunities in the Pacific Rim.

Royal Canada is based in Toronto and operates in all provinces via a network of local offices and independent insurance brokers. It specializes in personal motor insurance.

Royal Re, based in London, is owned partially by the German insurer Aachen & Munich. It is one of the largest professional reinsurance companies in the U.K., writing business in over 80 countries. It concentrates on reinsurance of property.

The Royal Insurance Company was established in the major commercial center of Liverpool on May 31, 1845, to provide insurance coverage " . . . against the risk of loss or damage by fire or by storm or by other casualty . . . " on all types of property, and to provide life insurance and annuities. The capital of the company was £2 million, divided into 100,000 shares of £20. Under the leadership of Percy Dove, the first manager and actuary, who had joined the company from the Royal Exchange Assurance, the company immediatley embarked on a policy of expansion, taking advantage at home of the fact that from 1853 life insurance premiums became permissible deductions from tax liabilities at all income levels. Overseas widespread industrialization brought with it an increase in the value of property worth insuring and in the income available to insure it.

In the United Kingdom, in marked contrast to its older rivals, the Royal undertook a deliberate policy of aggressive advertising, spending from £20,000 to £30,000 annually to place advertisements in magazines, reviews, railway stations, and public places. By way of contrast, the Pelican Insurance Company was at the same time spending £375 annually on 1,500 railway posters.

Expansion overseas began immediately, and by 1850 agencies had been established in Australia, Canada, Singapore, and South America. The company's operations in the United States, which have had a major effect on its financial position, began in 1851 when the first agency was opened in New York. Baltimore, Maryland; Philadelphia, Pennsylvania; Savannah, Georgia; and Charleston, South Carolina, each had an agency by the end of the year. By the time the company arrived in San Francisco in April 1853, agencies had been established in a total of ten U.S. cities. The U.S. insurance market expanded rapidly as new forms of insurance were devised to meet widening demands, particularly those of businesses. Employers' liability insurance was first introduced in 1885 and automobile liability in 1898. By 1915, blanket bonds of many kinds were being offered to provide comprehensive protection for business and financial institutions. By 1901, the Royal was the leading British company in the U.S. insurance market.

Although beaten to the West Coast of the United States by the Liverpool and London Fire and Life Insurance Company, the Royal was far more adventurous in its policy of overseas expansion than most of its rivals. In the 1850s, it was one of three British companies to establish agencies in Melbourne, Australia. Ten years later, the number of British offices in Australia had risen to ten. By 1863, the Royal and the Sun Fire Office were the only companies offering insurance in the commercial center of Smyrna, Turkey. By the early 1880s, 16 British and six foreign offices were represented there. Not all overseas expansion prospered, however. The company incurred heavy losses from fierce competition in Italy in the 1870s and political instability forced it to withdraw altogether from Spain in 1877. Despite these difficulties, by the end of the 19th century, the Royal was one of Britain's greatest exporters of insurance.

An enduring characteristic of the Royal has been its growth through mergers and acquisitions. In 1891 the company absorbed the Queen Insurance Company by exchange of shares. The chairman of the Queen told shareholders that they were to be admitted into partnership with a company second to none in the world, which possessed a magnificent, safe, and progressive business. Ten years later, the Kent Fire, the United Kent Fire, and the Lancashire (fire and life) insurance companies had all been acquired. When the British and Foreign Marine and the British Engine companies were added a few years later, the Royal was in a position to write all classes of nonlife insurance and life insurance. The only exception to this was industrial life business, whereby premiums are collected by a representative of the insurance company, on a weekly, fortnightly, or monthly basis. In 1919, the biggest merger in British insurance history took place when the Royal acquired the enormously successful Liverpool and London and Globe Insurance Company. The latter was established in Liverpool in 1836 as the Liverpool Fire and Life Insurance Company and had risen to an eminent position principally through acquisition. In 1847 it purchased the business of the London, Edinburgh and Dublin Insurance Company and in 1864 it merged with the long-established Globe Insurance Company. The Royal and the Liverpool and London and Globe were the major provincial insurance companies of the late 19th century. The Liverpool had a greater share of the British and colonial markets than the Royal.

The merger of the Royal and the Liverpool was part of a wider trend that gathered pace in the early 20th century, toward the establishment of large composite insurance companies. A major impetus for this trend was provided by the Workmen's Compensation Act of 1906, which extended employers' liability to all workers and provided the opportunity for insurance companies to offer a wider range of services.

Throughout the next 40 years, the Royal expanded its operations both at home and overseas. The number of branches increased from 70 in 1920 to 217 in Britain and Ireland in 1960, 175 in the United States, and 94 branches and offices and an extensive network of agencies elsewhere. In 1951 the company celebrated the centenary of its involvement in the United States. Chairman Colonel Alan Todd remarked that the company had every reason to feel proud of the leading position it occupied in that country. Progress was maintained in all the leading insurance markets. Experience in China provided the only exception: in 1950, after over 100 years' presence the Royal decided to withdraw.

A new wave of acquisitions began in 1961, when the Royal took over the London and Lancashire Insurance Company to achieve greater economy and efficiency of operations throughout the world. In Canada, two insurance companies, the Western Assurance Company and the British American Insurance Company, were acquired. By the end of the 1960s the Royal, with the greatest total fire and accident premium income, headed the "Big Four" insurance group, followed by Commercial Union, General Accident, and Guardian Royal Exchange.

The 1970s saw further expansion overseas. In 1975, the Royal became the first foreign company for 25 years to be licensed to write business in Japan, and in 1977 it acquired a 20% stake in the German insurer Aachen & Munich. Pretax profits continued to rise until 1979. The company identified a number of factors contributing to the fall: an abnormally high level of weather losses, particularly in the United Kingdom, the United States, and the Caribbean; rapid inflation; the strength of sterling against most of the world's currencies; and increases in burglary, vandalism, and arson.

The 1980s saw extensive corporate restructuring of the Royal Insurance group. In 1981, two divisions, the general overseas division and the life division, were incorporated as Royal Insurance (Int) Ltd. and Royal Life Insurance Ltd., respectively. Both were to operate as separate companies. The engineering, marine, and aviation businesses were integrated into the appropriate operating companies, and worldwide operations were divided into eight profit centers, all in the form of separately incorporated companies with their own capital and reserves.

Throughout the 1980s, fluctuations in the overseas insurance markets had serious repercussions on the Royal's financial position. In the early 1980s the industry as a whole complained of over-capacity at a time of worldwide economic recession. The Royal cut back its operations in Australia and Canada in 1983 after suffering severe losses, and in 1985 withdrew from workers' compensation in Australia after that business had been nationalized in some states. By 1988 Australia was producing excellent results both in terms of higher insurance profits and premium growth.

Expansion in the United States continued in 1982, when the group acquired the Milbank Insurance Company and a year later the Missouri-based Silvey Corporation and American Overseas Holdings. At this point the United States was the Royal's largest single market, representing 41% of its worldwide general insurance premiums. Soaring underwriting losses in 1984 due to severe competition caused the company to increase rates in the United States to restructure the organization to make it more responsive to the needs of the market place, and to cut back on expenditure by relocating the head office from New York to Charlotte, North Carolina. This remedial action proved successful as the group recorded a steady recovery in U.S. business from 1985 until 1989, when profits were hit by the effects of Hurricane Hugo, the San Francisco earthquake, and strong competition. A loss of £98 million in 1989 prompted a major strategy review by the company. In October 1987 the Royal became the first British insurance company to seek a full listing for its shares on the New York Stock Exchange but this did not materialize. In early 1989, the U.S. Maccabees Life Insurance Company was acquired by the group.

In 1987 the new managing director, Peter Duerden, instigated a new four-year reorganization program for Royal Insurance (UK) called Operation Staying Ahead. Company representatives and a team of management consultants completely overhauled the personal insurance, commercial insurance, organizational and personal resources, and electronic systems of the company, in order to make it more responsive to developments in the market, particularly those caused by the revolution prompted by the 1986 Financial Services Act. Changes involved the replacement of the old system of 60 administrative branches with 12 area branches, each accountable for its own profit figures. Product marketing was henceforth to be fused with product development. Increased training was to be made available to staff, after it had been reassessed. Finally, over £20 million was to be spent on computer systems.

Severe operating difficulties in the U.K. market in the early 1980s caused pretax profits to drop from £132 million in 1979 to £11 million in 1984. In that year the Royal announced a strategy to expand its long-term life and pensions operations, both overseas and in the U.K. To do this effectively the group acquired Lloyds Life Assurance in June 1985. The acquisition of this company, renamed Royal Heritage Life, put the Royal among the top-ten largest life companies in the U.K. Taking advantage of the changes in the market prompted by the 1986 Financial Services Act, the company moved from its core business into estate agencies and related services, and unit trusts. Interests in over 810 U.K. estate agencies were purchased from 1985, and three new unit trusts were set up in 1987, putting the Royal among the top 20 U.K. managers by the size of its funds.

Innovation continued on a different front. In 1987, the Royal announced an agreement to sponsor the Royal Shakespeare Company (RSC) by providing £1.1 million over three years. This would enable the RSC to undertake an annual tour of major U.K. cities. At that time this was the biggest single sum committed by a commercial company to an arts organization in the United Kingdom.

The creation of a single European market in 1992 will provide U.K. insurance companies with a major opportunity and a major challenge. Life insurance in the United Kingdom is substantially cheaper than in other EEC countries—commercial fire and theft insurance in Italy, for example, is 245% more expensive. In 1989 the group set up a small life company in Spain, and also signed an agreement with the Fondiaria Group of Italy to acquire a 90% stake in Lloyd Italico, a company to be formed from a general insurance operating division within the Fondiaria Group, the remaining 10% being retained by Italia, a Fondiaria subsidiary. An agreement was also signed with Assurances Generales de France, the second-largest French insurer, for development of their respective businesses. The immediate challenge for all U.K. insurers is to establish distribution networks to take full advantage of the opportunities in continental Europe.

Principal Subsidiaries: Royal Insurance plc; Royal Life Holdings Ltd.; Royal Reinsurance Co. Ltd. (80%); Royal International Holdings Ltd.; Royal Insurance UK Ltd.

Further Reading: The Business of Risk, Royal Insurance Company 1851–1951: The Hundred Year Background of the Royal Insurance Company Limited and the Royal Liverpool Insurance Group in the United States, New York, Royal Insurance Company, 1951; Cockerell, H.A.L., and Edwin Green, *The British Insurance Business 1547–1970: An Introduction and Guide to Historical Records in the United Kingdom,* London, Heinemann Educational Books, 1976; Cosgrave, John N., *We Hold Thee Safe: A History of Royal Insurance in the United States,* Charlotte, North Carolina, Royal Insurance 1986; *Royal Insurance Profile,* London, Royal Insurance, 1989.

—Serena Kelly

SAFECO CORPORATION

SAFECO Plaza
Seattle, Washington 98185
U.S.A.
(206) 545-5000
Fax: (206) 545-5730

Public Company
Incorporated: 1923 as General Insurance Company of America
Employees: 8,600
Assets: $10.12 billion
Stock Exchange: NASDAQ

SAFECO Corporation is one of the largest diversified financial corporations in the United States. Originally a property-and-casualty insurance company, it also is engaged in health and life insurance, real estate management and development, surety, commercial credit, and investment management. An industry innovator, SAFECO was a stock company that offered participating policies, a concept so new that it required legal battles for the right to be sold. Another innovation was the blanket policy, which combined coverages and later became a standard product. Diversification into real estate and financial services came in the late 1960s. SAFECO's variety of conservative risk policies maintained the company through the recession-plagued 1970s and the natural disasters of the 1980s.

SAFECO dates to the founding of the General Insurance Company of America in 1923. This Seattle, Washington–based company was the project of Hawthorne K. Dent, who was a vice president of Northwestern Mutual Fire Insurance Company when he resigned to launch his own company. During the 1920s, eastern stock companies dominated the insurance industry, though smaller mutual companies had begun to be a presence. Mutual insurance companies were owned and organized by their policyholders, who shared the dividends when the company earned a profit. If the company had insufficient surplus to meet its claims and expenses, the policyholders were assessed to make up the deficit. Most mutuals in the early 1920s were these "assessable mutuals," and they avoided high-risk business. Competition between the two varieties was sometimes fierce, as agents tried to choose between the lower prices of the mutual policies and the established strength of the larger stock companies. Dent's own father had been beaten in such a brawl while a salesman for Northwestern in its early days.

General borrowed ideas from both the mutual and the stock companies; it combined policyholder dividends and careful risk selection with the financial strength of capital paid by stockholders to protect policyholders in case of loss. Dent's plan was for policyholders to benefit from the mutual system's cost-saving devices without the assessment liability. Soliciting $2 million from the community's business leaders to back his vision, Dent's new enterprise was underway in April 1923.

As a stock insurance company committed to giving consumers a low-cost product and financial indemnity, General made an early practice of caution and conservation. This extended to such rules as turning off lights, not accepting collect calls, and watching paper clips.

In General's early days, fire insurance was the principal basis of insurance companies. When the number of automobiles more than doubled between 1919 and 1929, however, auto insurance gained prominence. General's immediate challenge was to woo independent agents away from the closed distribution system created by the established industry giants. One way to do this was by offering new, innovative products. General was the first capital stock company to issue a participating fire insurance policy. Participating policies paid dividends to policyholders at the policy's expiration. Dent also created the American Insurance Agency, a wholly owned subsidiary, as another draw for agents. The agency trained young hirees to sell insurance in Seattle. These direct agents competed with independent agents.

In its first five years, General's annual premium volume increased from less than $500,000 to $6.5 million, in 1928. When automobiles flourished, General formed the General Casualty Corporation, in 1925, to write liability insurance for that industry. In 1928 First National Insurance Company was formed to sell higher-cost policies. That same year, General paid its first stockholder dividends. The company had been formed with a policy of paying no dividends for a five-year period in order to build a surplus.

The year 1929 marked the stock market crash and the onset of the Great Depression. Also in 1929, the parent company's name became General America Corporation. During this period, General continued to innovate and enlarge on its product line. These innovations met with some resistance and the company was often involved in litigation. At one point, General took the insurance commissioner of Oregon to that state's supreme court to force acceptance of the participating policy. The court declared the concept legal and an example of lower-cost insurance in the public interest. As insurance buyers were extremely cost-conscious during these years, General's low rates garnered many new customers. This sparked rate wars. The rate wars caused the insurance commissioner of the state of Washington to call a halt finally, as both companies and policyholders were at risk. General suffered a drop in profits during the price wars, but it had steady growth in sales and was Washington's leading fire insurance company by 1935.

Throughout the 1930s, General expanded across the United States and into Canada, as well as into new market areas. By 1936 the home-office staff had grown to 250 from its starting 14. The company reported its highest net profit in 15 years in

1937. Despite the nation's economic climate during the 1930s, General's premium volume doubled every five years. In 1937 the company launched another innovation: the blanket policy, which combined varieties of coverage. In another five years, blanket policies were accepted widely throughout the industry.

In 1940 the Tacoma Narrows Bridge collapsed, and General suffered its first real underwriting error. The tragedy cost the company $50,000. With the attack on Pearl Harbor in 1941, land war-risk insurance was immediately in demand. Many companies withdrew such coverage in a panic, but General continued its coverage, hoping to prevent the government from entering that sector of the industry. General's war-risk premium income was more than $2 million in 1942, when the government formed the War Damage Corporation to insure land war risks.

Big changes in the insurance industry followed the 1944 Supreme Court ruling that insurance constituted interstate commerce and that insurers were therefore subject to federal antitrust laws. Congress passed the McCarran Act in 1945, shifting regulation back to the states, but changes already had taken place. Competitive innovations thrived, and direct writers became widely accepted. Use of employees to sell insurance—direct writers—was rare prior to World War II.

By 1950 General was an acknowledged industry leader. The company increased its automobile writings by 207% between 1947 and 1952, while industry auto insurance growth averaged 51%. In 1951 General's combined loss-and-expense ratio was lower than any of the nation's 30 largest stock casualty insurance companies. Its carefully selected business was one of General's strengths from the start. In 1953 General organized a new subsidiary, Selective Auto and Fire Insurance Company of America. The subsidiary soon officially changed its name to SAFECO Insurance Company of America. Among other innovations, SAFECO put independent agents back into competition with direct writers. Although there was resistance to some new sales policies—such as taking cash with applications, direct billing, and six-month renewal dates rather than a year—SAFECO brought in more than $6 million in premiums during its first full year of operation.

During the 1950s the company's underwriting units were regrouped, forming commercial lines, personal lines, and surety. When SAFECO was launched in 1953, the company committed to a strong marketing and advertising campaign for the first time. That campaign would go on to include the Pink Panther after 1978, and later, the sponsorship of the "CBS Evening News" with Walter Cronkite. A new subsidiary bearing the company's original name, General Life Insurance Company of America—the forerunner of SAFECO Life Insurance Company— was formed in 1957. Until this time, the company had concentrated on property and casualty insurance. Life insurance seemed a good ballast for the unpredictible expenses of property and casualty coverage. SAFECO was not alone; many insurance companies entered the life insurance business between 1955 and 1965. SAFECO Life showed a profit in 1958, its second year, after writing almost $20 million of business in-force. Within ten years, SAFECO Life reached $1 billion of business in-force. H.K. Dent died in 1958, at the age of 78. Willis Campbell had succeeded Dent as president in 1952.

General had accumulated enough capital by the 1960s to diversify further. Winmar Company, a Seattle-based real estate development and management firm, was purchased in 1967 in order to invest in commercial real estate ventures. In 1968 General Insurance Company of America became SAFECO Corporation. Also that year, SAFECARE Company was formed to design and build convalescent centers and hospitals; it has since become a subsidiary of Winmar. SAFECO Credit Company was formed in 1969 to provide short- and medium-term business financing.

When Willis Campbell had become president of General in 1952, it was a property and casualty insurance company with revenues of more than $77 million. Campbell became chairman of SAFECO 1966, with Gordon Sweany assuming the presidency. By 1966 the company had grown into a diversified financial services institution with revenues of more than $227 million.

The 1970s were an uncertain time for securities values and money management, but SAFECO continued to grow. In 1977 Sweany became chairman of the board while R.M. Trafton took over as president. Both had law degrees and had worked with the company for a cumulative 68 years. Between 1960 and 1980, the company showed an underwriting profit every year except for two. In 1979 SAFECO was the 27th-largest U.S. property and casualty underwriter.

Per-share earnings for the company more than doubled between 1976 and 1980. At the same time, other major property and casualty companies were suffering a decline, largely as a result of the widening gap between inflationary costs and state-regulated restrictions of rate increases. SAFECO profited when others did not because the company did not slash premium costs with the strategy of making up the difference in investment income. The company pulled out of New York and New Jersey when rate commissioners in both states restricted premiums. Pulling out of New York cost SAFECO about 10% of its total premium volume, but the move was reported to increase profitability.

Hurricane Frederic cost SAFECO $5 million in property losses in 1979, but the company still showed a strong profit for the year. In addition to the loss of premium income from the New York and New Jersey business, SAFECO had high cash outlays in 1980, including a $25 million payment to the Internal Revenue Service following a tax audit. At this time, the company's biggest premium category was personal automobile, which outperformed the industry because of SAFECO's conservative risk selection and its concentration in less populated areas. Automobile lines and homeowners insurance line began suffering substantial underwriting losses in the early 1980s, however, as home fires and thefts increased and the cost and frequency of auto claims shot up. Despite record gains in its life and health insurance operations, SAFECO reported a first quarter loss of $41 million in 1985.

Battling with the volatile stock market, increased medical costs, stiff price competition, and fluctuating inflation and interest rates left SAFECO in a weakened position by 1988, when the company was suddenly hit with California's Proposition 103. This proposition cut state property and casualty rates by 20%. The company suffered losses of $5.3 million as a result of Hurricane Hugo's record damages on the southeastern U.S. coast and $4.6 million for the California earthquake's damages. SAFECO, nonetheless, managed a strong return by 1989 year end with the help of healthy investment performance and sharply increased life profits. Despite considerable underwriting losses, property and casualty operations still provided 66% of SAFECO's 1989 pretax earnings.

Early in 1990 insurance regulators in Pennsylvania moved to block SAFECO's decision not to renew its 8,000 auto insurance policies in that state. The nonrenewal decision followed premium rollback legislation passed in February. The 1990s decade thus began with further struggles between the industry and its regulators.

Principal Subsidiaries: First National Insurance of America; General America Corp.; General Insurance Company of America; PNMR Securities, Inc.; SAFECO Administrative Services, Inc.; SAFECO Life Insurance Company; SAFECO National Insurance Company; SAFECO Properties, Inc.; SAFECO Services Corporation; SAFECO Credit Company, Inc.; SAFECO Insurance Company of America; SAFECO Insurance Company of Illinois; SAFECO Asset Management Company; SAFECO Assigned Benefits Services Company; SAFECO Securities, Inc.; Agena, Inc. (20%).

Further Reading: Saunders, Dero, "The Muddy Trackers," *Forbes,* July 7, 1980; Saunders, Dero, "Portrait of a Bottom Fisherman," *Forbes,* May 25, 1981; Copeland, Sid, *The SAFECO Story,* Seattle, SAFECO Corporation, 1981.

—Carol I. Keeley

THE ST. PAUL COMPANIES, INC.

385 Washington Street
Saint Paul, Minnesota 55102
U.S.A.
(612) 221-7911
Fax: (612) 221-8294

Public Company
Incorporated: 1853 as Saint Paul Fire and Marine Insurance Company
Employees: 14,000
Assets: $11.03 billion
Stock Exchange: NASDAQ

The St. Paul Companies is Minnesota's oldest business corporation and one of the oldest insurance companies in the United States. The St. Paul is a worldwide insurance organization whose members provide insurance underwriting and brokerage, and investment-banking services. The company's subsidiaries provide commercial and personal insurance services. The St. Paul is the largest medical-liability insurer in the United States.

In the years preceding the founding of The St. Paul people living in the Minnesota Territory were insured primarily by agents representing eastern insurance companies. Most wintertime claims and claim payments had to wait for spring, when travel and communication resumed.

In 1853 Alexander Wilkin, the secretary of the territory, and The St. Paul's first and youngest president, approached his neighbors, George and John Farrington, with the idea of starting a Saint Paul, Minnesota–based insurance company. The need for local fire insurance was particularly great, and George Farrington, a local banker, saw the opportunity to stem the flow of cash out of the territory. Farrington introduced a bill of incorporation in the territorial legislature that same year, and Saint Paul Fire and Marine Insurance Company was incorporated.

The St. Paul was to operate as a mutual company, but it also sold traditional, or stock, policies. Mutual policyholders were to share in both the profits and losses of the company; stock policyholders would not. The company's charter permitted it "to make insurance on all descriptions of property against loss or damage by fire," and "to make insurance on all descriptions of boats and vessels, the cargoes and freights thereof. . . . "

The company needed to sell $100,000 of insurance in order to raise the capital to begin business. To accomplish this end, the company's ten founders each applied for $10,000 policies on their own property. Shortly thereafter it was discovered that none of the founders possessed property worth $10,000. The members of the board rejected their own applications and rewrote them for $5,000 each. In February 1854 the company issued its first policy, a mutual policy for $800. It insured the home and furnishings of Robert A. Smith, the territory's librarian and private secretary to Governor Willis A. Gorman, who in turn purchased the company's first stock policy.

The St. Paul sustained its first fire loss in April 1855 when a row of offices and a bakery burned to the ground, resulting in $3,000 in claims. This loss was followed by a much greater problem, the panic of 1857, in which many New York companies folded. In Saint Paul all but three of the local banks were forced to close. The St. Paul and other insurance companies were forced to accept "notes of indebtedness" as premium payments. These notes could not be converted into cash to cover day-to-day operating expenses, and as a result 47 fledgling insurance companies closed. The St. Paul, faced with severe cash flow problems, elected to not issue any new policies for a time, and was forced to sell its office furniture to maintain operations.

A period of stagnation occurred starting in 1861, during the Civil War. The St. Paul's president, Alexander Wilkin, died on a Mississippi battlefield. He was succeeded by James C. Burbank, the company's first full-time president, in April 1865. Also in 1865, The St. Paul reorganized as a stock company. One of Burbank's first duties was to oversee The St. Paul's expansion into the Canadian market. By 1866 the company was writing business in Manitoba. A shareholder-elected board voted to pay semi-annual dividends, and in July 1867 the company issued its first stock dividend, of $1.50 per share. Following the Civil War, The St. Paul grew. It constructed a new corporate headquarters. A model for fire-resistant structures of the future, the building was built of metal and stone.

In 1871 the Great Chicago Fire strained the company's resources. The fire left 275 people dead, 100,000 people homeless, and destroyed over 17,000 buildings. Over 200 insurance companies experienced fire-related losses, and many were financially ruined: about one-quarter of the 200 companies went out of business, and most that survived paid as little as 4¢ on the dollar to settle their claims. At a meeting of The St. Paul's board, it was agreed that all claims would be paid full. President Burbank predicted that this decision would ultimately bring a return as word got out that the company was covering its losses. In that year claims submitted by policyholders exceeded by 165% the amount the company collected in premiums. The St. Paul paid a total of $140,000 to cover losses. The St. Paul's assets were greatly reduced, and it paid no dividends that year. The company's sales did improve as a result of the decision to pay all claims, however, and The St. Paul recouped its losses.

Burbank died in 1876, and the company's secretary, Charles H. Bigelow, was elected president. Shortly thereafter The St. Paul was faced with the insurance price war of 1877. The insurance market was becoming more competitive as the country grew and prospered. The result was too many insurance companies offering lower prices in order to compete. Under Bigelow's leadership the company dropped unprofitable agencies, introduced new products such as cyclone insurance and crop hail coverage, and instituted more stringent guidelines in accepting new customers. The St. Paul rode out the price war intact, without lowering its rates. Insurance buyers were not only affected by the price; product and service diversity were also important to a successful business plan.

During the late 19th century, the company expanded into new types of insurance coverage. However, the San Francisco Earthquake and Fire of 1906 took a heavy toll on The St. Paul's new-product-development plans. Claims in excess of $1.2 million were paid, in full, and the company's reputation grew. In 1911 Charles Bigelow died, and his son, Frederic Bigelow, succeeded him as president. In the years following Frederic Bigelow's appointment, the United States prepared for World War I. The St. Paul adjusted its charter to include losses incurred resulting from acts of war. In 1917 The St. Paul covered the loss of 260 vessels, totaling over $4 million, most of which was repaid by Germany over 50 years. During the war The St. Paul began overseas expansion in a modest fashion, when it began to issue policies in Great Britain to cover losses incurred as a result of bomb damage, but in a relatively short period of time the British government cut the rates charged by U.S. companies by about 50%, but The St. Paul continued to insure against bomb damage in England for the duration of the war. The St. Paul also added automobile insurance to its product line during this period.

As a result of massive losses incurred during World War I, most European insurance companies were all but paralyzed. The St. Paul became a charter member of the American Foreign Insurance Association (AFIA), a group of companies that pooled its resources, and with combined capital of $135 million, began to market insurance abroad. The company was soon doing business in 25 foreign markets, and another period of diversification and new-product development began.

Throughout the 1920s The St. Paul introduced all-risk coverage for the jewelry trade and for other "priceless objects" of artistic and historical significance. The policy insured items in transit from almost every known risk, except theft, because fire and marine insurance companies were prohibited from writing liability coverage. The St. Paul's leadership decided, therefore, that a liability company was needed, and in 1926 a subsidiary, St. Paul Mercury Indemnity Company, was formed. The St. Paul also added aircraft insurance and surety bonds to its product line in 1929.

After serving as The St. Paul's president for 27 years, Frederic Bigelow became chairman in 1938, and Charles F. Codere became The St. Paul's fifth president. Shortly thereafter, the United States entered into World War II. At the onset of the war, U.S. insurance companies wrote marine insurance through a specially formed syndicate, but as losses grew, the U.S. government assumed the burden of covering the staggering war losses. The War Damage Corporation, a company financed by the federal government and run by private insurance companies, wrote over nine million policies and collected close to $250 million in premiums by the war's end.

In 1948, Charles Codere became chairman, and A.B. Jackson was elected The St. Paul's new president. Codere and Jackson worked well together, and the company greatly expanded its product lines and services. Liability insurance was offered to real estate brokers, insurance agents, and hospitals. The St. Paul refined its package policy program, allowing its agents to offer more and diverse coverage in one policy. Package policies had been introduced during World War II to provide the military with an insurance package to cover liability, shipping, and fire insurance. This method of issuing coverage continued after the war, with The St. Paul offering packages for a variety of commercial risks. Jackson also was instrumental in the organization of two new associations to insure nuclear reactors.

In 1957, with the acquisition of the Western Life Insurance Company of Helena, Montana, The St. Paul broke into the life insurance market. By 1964 Western Life sales had more than doubled. The St. Paul's agents were now able to sell all forms of insurance, sales volume continued to increase, and The St. Paul acquired several general agencies—which sold the insurance products of many different companies—to work with its independent agents more effectively. Management training programs were also initiated in 1958, computers were installed in 1956 to speed up the handling and processing of information, and in 1961 The St. Paul rebuilt and enlarged its offices.

When Charles Codere retired in 1963, A.B. Jackson succeeded him and Ronald M. Hubbs became The St. Paul's next president. During the 1960s the emphasis was on customer service. Hubbs was instrumental in the development of over 40 property and liability service centers nationwide. Each center was self-contained; it had its own underwriters, risk management staff, marketing, claims and policy services, and office support personnel. The company believed decentralization would bring it closer to its customers.

In 1968 The St. Paul reorganized. Saint Paul Fire and Marine Insurance Company became The St. Paul Companies. The name St. Paul Fire and Marine Insurance Company was retained for the property-liability insurance subsidiary. In the years following the reorganization, The St. Paul Companies diversified its insurance-related business and branched into other areas of consumer and business services.

In 1970 St. Paul Guardian Insurance Company was formed to market personal lines of insurance. Two years later St. Paul Investment Management Company, an investment-management firm, was started, and in 1973, St. Paul Life Insurance Company, whose purpose was to market life insurance through independent agents representing St. Paul Fire and Marine, was formed.

In 1973 A.B. Jackson retired as chairman. He was succeeded by Ronald Hubbs, and Carl B. Drake became the eighth president of The St. Paul Companies. Less than one year later, The St. Paul acquired John Nuveen & Co., a firm that trades, markets, underwrites, and distributes securities. Nuveen was founded in Chicago in 1898, and had been a pioneer in tax-exempt bonds for individual investors, which it introduced in 1961. The corporation also added St. Paul Risk Services Inc., which provided consulting services to self-insure institutions and firms, and St. Paul Surplus Lines, which again broadened the coverage offered by St. Paul Fire and Marine.

In the midst of this growth the public was becoming more concerned about the quality of the products and services it was receiving. This concern, combined with changes in the medical field—particularly new drugs, transplants, the growth of large group medical practices and group medical plans, and less personal doctor-patient relationships—contributed to an increased number of medical liability claims. Insurance companies selling malpractice coverage began to suffer massive losses. Medical cases often take years to settle, and court awards continued to grow.

The St. Paul, the largest carrier of medical liability insurance, stopped accepting new policies for a short time. When the company began to write new business again, it based premiums on the practitioners' past record. This "claims made" standard had been used in other types of liability for many years. It led to more accurate pricing and seemed to stabilize the market. The company also raised its malpractice premiums. The company later created a medical services division, which brought together The St. Paul's underwriting, marketing, and administrative expertise in health-care-related fields. The company introduced simplified-language policies, starting with its personal liability catastrophe coverage, with the hope that it would reduce claims.

In 1980 Chairman Drake refocused on insurance-related businesses. The company began to divest all non-insurance subsidiaries, and resumed expansion of its insurance-related interests. Under a new president, Robert J. Haugh, these divestitures were completed by 1984, when The St. Paul's net loss was $210 million. The company then undertook a new series of acquisitions. Among these purchases were Seaboard Surety Company, a provider of fidelity and surety bonds and Swett & Crawford Group, a Los Angeles–based wholesale broker in excess and surplus lines. Atwater McMillian—renamed St. Paul Specialty Underwriting in 1988—a company that handles specialty risk accounts and surplus lines was formed in 1981.

During the 1980s more demanding consumers, an evolving marketplace, and government deregulation resulted in another price war that hurt The St. Paul's liability business. During the same years The St. Paul also expanded its involvement in European markets. The company acquired the London-based Minet Holdings PLC in 1988, making The St. Paul the seventh-largest insurance-brokerage firm in the world. Shortly after the Minet acquisition, The St. Paul established St. Paul (U.K.) Limited.

On May 1, 1990, Robert J. Haugh retired and was replaced by The St. Paul's new chairman and CEO, Douglas W. Leatherdale, who has continued the company's strategy for an increasing presence in the European market. The St. Paul also formed Minet Europe Holdings Limited as part of the Minet group. This new company will manage the expansion of The St. Paul's European market.

Principal Subsidiaries: St. Paul Fire and Marine Insurance Co.; Minet Holdings PLC (U.K.); Seaboard Surety Co.; John Nuveen & Co.; St. Paul Re; St. Paul (U.K.), Ltd.; St. Paul Specialty Underwriting, Inc.

Further Reading: "A History of the St. Paul," Saint Paul, Minnesota, The St. Paul Companies, 1988.

—William R. Grossman

Standard Life

THE STANDARD LIFE ASSURANCE COMPANY

3 George Street
Edinburgh EH2 2XZ
United Kingdom
(031) 225-2552
Fax: (031) 245-6168

Mutual Company
Incorporated: 1825 as The Life Insurance Company of Scotland
Employees: 5,099
Assets: £19.29 billion (US$31.14 billion)

The Standard Life Assurance Company (the Standard), is the largest mutual life office in the European Economic Community (EEC). Although it once transacted business worldwide, it now restricts itself to the United Kingdom, the Republic of Ireland, and Canada. The bulk of Standard Life's business is obtained through agents and brokers.

The Standard has its origins in the Insurance Company of Scotland, a fire office established in Edinburgh in May 1821. At a meeting of the company's partners on March 23, 1825, it was decided that a new company, to be called The Life Insurance Company of Scotland, should be set up. One reason given was that while Scotland had only four native offices dealing in life insurance, there were 20 such agencies for English companies. The new life office was to conduct its business from the premises of its parent company—at 200 High Street, Edinburgh—and the same company was to provide the necessary staff. Business capital was set at £3 million divided into 60,000 shares of £50 each. In fact, only £500,000 were issued. One of the main attractions for partners in the new enterprise was that at the end of the first year of trading they would receive a capital gain as well as a proportion of the business profits.

The company's first policy—now on display in Standard Life's training center—was issued to Alexander H. Simpson, a Paisley merchant aged 38, whose assured sum of £1,500 with profits was provided for by a single payment of £670 12s. 6d. When the claim arose in 1866 the aggregate of bonus and sum assured came to £3,982 10s.—which illustrates the company's somewhat generous and even wayward terms in its early transactions. In these years of development, the company based its premium rates on those already offered by existing life offices. Difficult actuarial problems were referred to one of the leading directors, the calculating prodigy William Wallace. Born in 1768, Wallace had been a bookbinder, but gave up this trade for the life of a mathematics teacher and in 1819 was appointed professor of mathematics at Edinburgh University. So highly were his services valued by the company that it took legal advice in an effort to retain him on the board when, in 1829, in accordance with the terms of the deed of copartnery—or copartnership—it became his turn to retire for a year. The legal decision was adverse, but there was no animosity and on his return to the company Wallace was awarded 60 guineas by his colleagues for his work over the years. He retired in 1838. Eventually the inconvenient rule that directors should retire in rotation without the right to be reelected was abolished by the Standard Life Assurance Company's Act of 1883.

If the company's premium rates were too generous to some policyholders, the additional premium rates charged for foreign travel and residence were unnecessarily high and discouraged new business. For instance, for a journey to Siberia an extra premium of £10 was charged, and an extra eight guineas for residence in Trinidad. To the company's great credit, however, is the fact that it led the way later in abolishing these irksome restrictions. Nevertheless further business would have been lost in 1831 if the company had gone ahead with its plans to exclude the risk of death from cholera as a condition of a life policy. This restriction, had it been introduced, might have spelled the end for the company after only six years as the Standard stood to lose far more in terms of potential business than in paying out on policies. Luckily, the directors shelved the proposal in favor of a donation to the Board of Health towards the cost of combating the epidemic.

In April 1831 the company decided to separate completely from the fire office, and accordingly new premises were found at 21 South St. Andrews Street. An accountant, James A. Cheyne, was appointed manager, with a former cashier of the Scottish Union Company as secretary. In December of the same year a committee was formed to draw up plans to launch a new company by act of Parliament. Early in 1832 it was agreed that this company should be called The Standard Life Assurance Company. A bill was drafted and duly given the royal assent. The act establishing Standard Life in 1832 reproduced in the main the conditions of the original deed of copartnery. The staff of Standard Life in 1832 consisted of 15 directors, a manager, a secretary, a clerk, and an apprentice. As figureheads the company elected the Duke of Buccleuch as governor and the Marquis of Lothian as his deputy. The former was succeeded in 1884 by the sixth duke, who had been deputy governor from 1866. The two titular offices went into abeyance in 1917 but were revived after 1925.

From 1832 the company continued to progress and to expand its operations. Efforts were made to increase the number of agencies in Scottish towns, and local boards of directors were appointed. Negotiations were opened for agencies in the large towns of the north of England and the Midlands. In Ireland Dublin, Belfast, and Limerick all had representatives, and the company's chief agent for Canada was consulted with a view to establishing a local directorate in Quebec. Much of the credit for these initiatives, and for the subsequent success that led to the Standard's position in the front rank of life offices, was due to the industry and acumen of one man, William Thomas Thomson. Trained as an accountant in Edinburgh—he was later instrumental in forming the Institute of Actuaries—Thomson arrived at the Standard in 1834 as secretary and three years later was promoted to manager and actuary. In 1835 he presided over the company's first division of profits ten years after its inauguration; as manager he was involved in negotiations for a move from St. Andrews Street to more spacious premises at 3 George Street at the end of 1837. Having acquired the new property for £2,400, Standard Life spent over £3,000 on extensive alterations over 18 months, with John Steell as sculptor; his facade motif of the biblical Ten Virgins was later adopted by the company as a logo. In June 1839 the new head office was ready for occupation. Subsequently, the premises were extended by the acquisition of numbers 1 and 5 George Street. Within two years after the move an independent investigation of the company's affairs revealed that apart from its satisfactory financial position the Standard had the edge over its competitors in at least two important respects. Its bonus results were far better than, for instance, those of the Equitable Society; and unlike the latter, as well as other life offices, the Standard did not charge entry money, which was an extra premium demanded of new policyholders for the privilege of joining a flourishing institution. The generally favorable view of the company's affairs was echoed by George Gray of Perth, an agent and policyholder at the Standard's AGM in 1840. He predicted that with this independent seal of approval the company could now go on to do more business than it had ever imagined possible.

Indeed it did. A historian of the company, J. H. Treble, maintained that "during the years 1825–1832 internal organisational problems and the lack of a dynamic management had led to a succession of profoundly disappointing results." Under the dynamic leadership of Thomson and a reforming board of directors this trend was dramatically reversed. Between 1845 and 1860 the Standard transacted "a larger amount of Business . . . than any other Office." During the final ten years of Thomson's management even this considerable achievement was to be eclipsed, for between 1864 and 1875 the company never failed to obtain a total of less than £1 million of new life contracts in any of its financial years. One of Thomson's most significant decisions as manager was to solve the problem of restrictions on foreign travel by policyholders. In 1846 he established the Colonial Life Assurance Company (the Colonial), which was specifically designed to handle business in the British Colonies and India, and could offer attractive terms based on the Colonial's more accurate assessment of mortality risk in the countries concerned. Within a year the company had set up local boards of directors in the principal cities of Canada and the main West Indian islands, as well as opening negotiations with interested parties in India, Ceylon, Cape Town, and Sydney. Within six months of opening for business the demand for Colonial's stock was greater than the new company could supply. In time Thomson could boast that the Colonial prospectus "has been the groundwork on which the foreign rates of many home institutions have been based: it is the textbook of British Offices in settling the terms on which they permit British assurers to go abroad." The Colonial went from strength to strength. By 1859, despite the recent depredations of the Crimean campaign and the Indian Mutiny, its funds had reached £342,354. By 1864 the total assurances issued exceeded £5 million and the company, which, after all, owed its existence to the Standard, had become a serious competitor in the home market. A fusion of the two companies presented no problems as the concerns shared a manager in Thomson and some directors. The merger took place early in 1866. The Colonial did not lose its identity as a result of the amalgamation. The two departments were kept separate at head office for 25 years afterwards; each had its own secretary and staff. Having swallowed the Colonial, the Standard, already a leading name at home, was now the best-known life assurance company in the British colonies.

Besides the Colonial, the Standard absorbed eight other insurance companies between 1844 and 1878. These were the York & London, in 1844; Commercial Assurance, in 1846; Colonial & General, in 1847; the Experience, in 1850; the East of Scotland, in 1852; the Minerva, in 1864; the Victoria & Legal & General in 1865; and the India Life Assurance Company, in 1878. Before the takeover of the York & London the Standard had no chief office in London although it did employ an agent, Peter Ewart, from 1840. When it moved into the York & London's old premises at 82 King William Street, the Standard arranged that its London board should consist largely of former York & London directors; Ewart the agent became a full-time resident secretary. Acquisition of the Commercial and the Experience, Scottish life offices of fairly recent foundation, increased the Standard's business in its home nation, although, as Treble pointed out, the company's record in Scotland in the years 1850 to 1865 is disappointing. By acquiring the Minerva in 1864 the Standard gained funds of nearly half a million pounds for an outlay of a fifth of this sum—a considerably larger volume of business than had been acquired by any previous absorption. The company also benefited by acquiring the Victoria & Legal & General.

If, despite Thomson's flair, the Standard's Scottish premium income remained static in mid-century, the company's income from England and Ireland over the same period increased threefold. One important factor in this growth was the company's progressive relaxation of restrictions on its insurance contracts, beginning in 1851, although at the time the company's inspector of agencies, William Bentham, attributed the Standard's success largely to the attractive bonus and the distinguished ability and increasing energy of the management. Indeed it was Bentham himself, in his ten years as inspector, 1853–1863, who, by a ruthless weeding-out of inefficient English agents, contributed much to the company's prosperity. However by 1870 it was recognized in a report that this prosperity was under threat from the continued use of the tontine system of bonus calculation, a scheme that benefited long-surviving policyholders, discouraged new entrants, and acted as a drain on profits. In 1865 an alternative scheme had been floated, and in time this proved so popular that in 1875 the tontine system was closed to new entrants. Another important development was the introduction of the endowment policy in 1870. Throughout these years of startling growth, Thomson ensured that the Standard's funds were being invested shrewdly. He bought government annuities with guaranteed good yields. When the price of gold was about to plummet he acquired land in Fife and invested heavily in government bonds. Through its foreign branches, the company also took up land holdings abroad, notably in

Canada, where a permanent office had been established in Montreal in 1846.

Following the establishment of the Montreal office, agencies were set up in all the major cities and towns from the Canadian Atlantic coast westward as far as Toronto. By 1847 the West Indies were well served by agencies. In the late 1880s the company's central office was located in Barbados, where it remained until 1924 when it was moved to Trinidad. The Standard's association with India had begun with the founding of the Colonial in 1846. Following the merger of the two companies, all Standard business in the East came under the control of the Calcutta office. China had been represented by agents for many years before an office was set up at Shanghai in 1900. As in India, only European lives were insured at first. By 1925 the branch office in Shanghai had been declared redundant and the Standard's representation reverted to agents. South Africa was well covered by agents from 1854 until a branch office was opened at Port Elizabeth in 1895. In 1900 this was moved to Cape Town, and shortly after the end of the Boer War, Johannesburg became the centre of operations. The Standard also did business in Egypt from 1898 and its Cairo headquarters, built in 1904, became one of the city's landmarks. From 1889 the Colonial expanded its presence in Uruguay and Argentina, though with some initial difficulty due to local indifference to the benefits of life assurance. In time the problems were overcome. The Uruguay branch flourished, but in Argentina a punitive tax on foreign companies forced the Standard to withdraw from the country in 1923. The company did not extend its business into Europe until 1890, when a branch in Brussels immediately proved successful. At about the same time branches were opened in Copenhagen, Stockholm, and Christiana. A Spanish office was opened in Barcelona in 1904. Having opened a Budapest branch in 1898, with Charles Szilagyi as secretary/agent, the Standard built an opulent headquarters in 1901 on a prime site, from which it conducted an extensive business until the outbreak of World War I. In an enemy country conditions for the company were arduous, although Szilagyi coped admirably, sending telegraph messages back to head office from the U.S. embassy via The Hague, before being dismissed from his post by the Communist state regime. By 1919 the branch was being run by a workers' committee of three clerks, one of whom doubled staff salaries. In 1921 the company withdrew from Hungary, however, and policyholders received their full sums assured. Belgian business never recovered from the effects of German occupation. Although business already on the books was still carried on in the years immediately after the war, no new risks were accepted by the Brussels, Barcelona, and Stockholm branches.

William Thomson retired from the Standard in 1874 and was succeeded as manager by his son Spencer. By this time, the company was already the U.K.'s leading life office and Spencer Thomson presided over a major investment program. Private Acts of Parliament of 1883 and 1891 broadened the Standard's powers of investment, and from the 1890s the work of the board's Stock Exchange Committee and the use of U.K. and U.S. brokers were signs of an increasing interest in the equity market. Low land prices at home tempted the Standard to invest considerably in overseas property, particularly in territories covered by its overseas branches. Canada, the West Indies, Denmark, and Argentina were favorite targets, and Canada was consistently favored for mortgage transactions over four decades. The Scottish financier James Ivory, a director of the Standard from 1906, was for many years a major consultant on investment policy. He worked at first with Thomson's successor, Leonard Dickson, who was appointed manager in 1904. Dickson himself had been appointed directly from the board—an unorthodox procedure—and his premature death in 1919, from injuries sustained while trying to halt a runaway horse, deprived the company of a shrewd business mind just at the point when the Standard's fortunes were beginning to revive following World War I.

Dickson's successor, Stuart McNaghten, proved to be nearly as influential a figure in the history of the Standard as William Thomson. Having arrived at the company as actuary in 1911, he was able to put his considerable experience in rival life offices to good use. As manager he was responsible for a number of significant innovations. His multi-option Acme policy of 1921–1922 proved attractive and was copied by other life offices. He also pioneered life insurance for women, establishing a special women's department in the early 1920s at the company's West End branch in London. In 1925 the Standard's centenary was marked by the most important event since its inception—its mutualization. Through this scheme, Standard Life became a mutual company owned and controlled by its policyholders, company profits being distributed to its policyholders in the form of bonuses. Although some U.S. corporations had already adopted this course it was, according to the *Daily Telegraph,* the first instance of a British proprietary company being mutualized. In 1928 the Standard was one of the first offices to introduce occupational pension schemes. By the following year it was the fourth-largest U.K. life office. Remarkably, despite its change of status, there was little change of personnel at the company's helm during these interwar years. Half of the premutualization board were still directors in 1937–1938. The period of McNaghten's managership saw a close interrelationship with the Bank of Scotland and with investment trusts, such as British Investment, Edinburgh Investment, and Scottish American Mortgage. McNaghten also presided over a drastic reduction in the Standard's overseas operations. A withdrawal from Europe in the early 1920s was followed by a departure from Egypt, India, and China in the 1930s, and a phased withdrawal from South Africa.

McNaghten retired in 1938 after 19 years as manager and was succeeded by Albert E. King, who left in 1939. A. J. Mascall steered the company through the first three years of World War II, from which it emerged, thanks partly to its severance from Europe, relatively unscathed. The postwar years saw the Standard go from strength to strength. Under manager Andrew Davidson and then Alex Reid, funds increased in the ten years from 1946 by over £100 million to £157 million, and the company eclipsed its Scottish competitors to become one of the five largest U.K. life offices. Since mutualization, the company's attractive bonus record had been a major ingredient in its success, and in 1955 the present two-tier system was introduced, to be followed in 1963 by the introduction of the special claims bonus. In 1964 Reid was succeeded by J. B. Dow, who in 1966 helped set up the Insurope consortium, consisting of the Standard and six European life and pension offices brought together to provide international employers with a pool of expertise on pension schemes. The original group was later enlarged to include offices operating worldwide.

By the time Dow retired in 1970, Standard Life had become the largest mutual company in the United Kingdom, with one of the lowest expense ratios. New manager D.W.A. Donald, who had joined the Standard at the age of 17 in 1932 and was a respected writer on insurance matters, brought his company into a still closer connection with the three Scottish banking groups and the British investment trusts, and in his time the Standard became a major shareholder in oil exploration companies. By the mid-1970s, Standard Life was the fourth-largest life office in Britain and was among the Scottish companies with the most multiple directors, a remarkable continuity from its position of 20 years before. Donald's successor George Gwilt, who like his predecessor had spent his entire working life with the Standard, was a pensions expert. It was largely due to him that this side of the company grew to the extent that, by the early 1980s, group pensions business accounted for half the Standard's premium income. Since then, Standard Life continued to expand, under the leadership of A. Scott Bell, who took over from Gwilt in 1988, and who was instrumental in negotiating a joint venture with the Halifax Building Society to market unit trust contracts.

Principal Subsidiaries: The Heritable Securities and Mortgage Investment Association Limited; Standard Life Pension Funds Limited; Standard Life Investment Funds Limited; Standard Life Trustee Company Limited; Standard Life Trust Management Limited; Cutlers Gardens Estates Limited; Standard Life Property Company Limited; Standard Life Investment Management Services Limited; Whiteleys of Bayswater Limited; Standard Life Portfolio Management Limited; Bonaventure Trust Incorporated; The Standard Life Assurance Company of Canada; Halifax Standard Life (Holdings) Limited (50%); Halifax Standard Trust Management Limited (50%).

Further Reading: Walford Papers, Chartered Insurance Institute, London; Schooling, Sir William, *The Standard Life Assurance Company, 1825–1925,* Edinburgh, William Blackwood and Sons, 1925; Norman, G.A.S., *The Overseas History of the Standard Life Assurance Company,* The Standard Life Assurance Company corporate typescript, 1958; Clayton, G., *British Insurance,* London, Elek Books, 1971; "A Century and a Half for Standard Life," *Post Magazine and Insurance Monitor,* October 16, 1975; Scott, John, and Michael Hughes, *The Anatomy of Scottish Capital,* London, Croom Helm, 1980; Treble, J.H., "The Pattern of Investment of the Standard Life Assurance Company, 1875–1914," *Business History,* volume 22, number 2, 1980; Butt, John, "Life Assurance in War and Depression: the Standard Life Assurance Company and Its Environment, 1914–39," in *The Historian and the Business of Insurance,* edited by O.M. Westall, Manchester, The University Press, 1984; Treble, J.H., "The Record of the Standard Life Assurance Company in the Life Assurance Market of the United Kingdom, 1850–64," in *The Historian and the Business of Insurance,* edited by O.M. Westall, Manchester, The University Press, 1984; Trebilcock, Clive, *Phoenix Assurance and the Development of British Insurance,* Volume I, Cambridge, The University Press, 1985.

—R.M. Healey

STATE FARM MUTUAL AUTOMOBILE INSURANCE COMPANY

One State Farm Plaza
Bloomington, Illinois 61710
U.S.A.
(309) 766-2311
Fax: (309) 766-6169

Mutual Company
Incorporated: 1922
Employees: 52,236
Assets: $35.49 billion

State Farm Mutual Automobile Insurance Company has been the number-one automobile insurer in the United States since 1942. The company has a long-standing reputation for offering vehicle insurance at low rates, while maintaining a standard of superior service. It is no accident that State Farm, with its 20% share of the U.S. market, is well in the lead of its competitors. From its inception State Farm instigated several revolutionary practices, and while its maverick business practices far from endeared the company to its rivals, it gained the reputation of industry pacesetter. As an article in *The Wall Street Journal,* June 14, 1976 stated, ''State Farm's whole history is one of turning the insurance industry upside down and coming out on top.''

State Farm began in 1922 as one man's plan to offer low-cost automobile insurance to the farmers of Illinois: thus the name, State Farm Mutual Automobile Insurance Company. State Farm's early success and strong standing in a volatile marketplace is surely due to the vision of the company's founder, George Mecherle. Mercherle's beginnings are as modest as the company's success is extraordinary. He was a farmer until he was 40, when his wife's failing health forced them to leave their farm and Mecherle started selling insurance with a Bloomington, Illinois, company. Running his own farm had shaped Mecherle into a man who was constantly looking to innovate and improve conditions. When, in his characteristic outspoken, straightforward manner, he told his boss at the insurance company some of his ideas for improving the business, the boss said, ''Well George, if you don't like the way we run things, go start your own company.''

Mecherle did just that. He brought to the auto insurance business a fresh perspective, and with the help of a few choice people, began instituting his own ideas, which began with establishing a mutual automobile insurance company. Unlike a capital stock company, which distributes dividends, a mutual company adjusts premium costs and will refund a portion of the company's surplus to policyholders during periods when claims are lower, and income higher. At the time, the insurance industry set its own rates, and did not distinguish between groups of drivers based on location, driving record, or any other risk criteria. Mecherle decided it was possible to form a mutual insurance company that catered to rural and small town drivers who, as a group, had fewer accidents and cost insurers less in claim payments. Because claim costs for this group tended to be lower, premiums could be lower, and State Farm undercut its competitor's rates significantly.

This innovation of tying insurance rates to risk level established State Farm's legacy as a smart insurer that passed savings on to the customer. *The Wall Street Journal* observed that, ''Until the late 1950s, the company's competitors were clinging to their traditional insurance rates while State Farm was boasting in ads of savings of 'up to 40%' on its auto insurance.''

State Farm was also a pioneer in the practice of charging its customers an initial lifetime membership fee to cover the cost of processing new policyholders and the agent's commission. This one-time, nonrefundable fee allowed State Farm to keep the policy premium low, and it generated essential income which fueled the company's early growth.

Aside from its independent approach to rates, another key element in State Farm's success was its unique agent force. Normally, insurance agents represented a number of different companies, took large commissions, and shouldered a great deal of the paperwork involved in writing and maintaining policies. Mecherle simply tapped into the network of farmer's mutual insurance companies formed to protect members against fire or lightning damage, as well as farm bureaus and other local institutions established throughout various regions. His first agents were men who were well placed in the community, such as the officials from the local farm bureau, or sometimes an area's school principal. These agents worked part-time for State Farm and received less commission than their counterparts selling insurance full-time for other insurance companies. Selling a sound, affordable insurance package to a population that needed it, however, State Farm agents were able to make their money on sales volume. Furthermore, State Farm's central office in Bloomington handled most of the paperwork, which freed up its agents to spend the bulk of their time selling.

The strategy worked so well that State Farm outgrew its offices three times in the first seven years. The home-office staff grew from five people in 1925 to 183 in 1927. The company reached a point in the early 1940s where its operations had become so scattered, some employees wore roller skates to speed delivery of interoffice mail.

The beauty of many of State Farm's policies was that they benefited both company and customer. For instance, State Farm followed other companies in offering semiannual—and later monthly—policy payments, which customers found easier to pay, and, at the same time, led to accounting advantages for State Farm. State Farm also streamlined operations from the start, simply collecting premiums for a renewed policy on a vehicle, whereas most automobile insurers rewrote the policy each year.

Before long, the company was turning away unsolicited applications for insurance that were coming from prospective customers in urban areas. In 1926 a subsidiary, the City and Village Automobile Insurance Company, was formed, but because it lacked economy of scale, was soon absorbed by State Farm Mutual, which rewrote its bylaws to allow for the extension of services to those urban customers not originally eligible for State Farm insurance.

In 1928, just six years after the company's founder told a banker in Bloomington, "I've never had an account here . . . I've never cashed a check here, as far as I know. I've never tried to borrow your money. But I'm going to start a little business in this town and, by golly, you're going to lend me the money I need to get started," the company opened its first branch office, in Berkeley, California, and annual income surpassed $1 million. In 1929, the company moved into its own eight-story building, to which it added five floors in 1934. In 1939, State Farm built another eight-story building next door, to which it also added five floors in 1948. In the early 1970s the company built its present headquarters at a site on the eastern edge of Bloomington.

The company's growth was not just a matter of volume; State Farm continually expanded the services it offered. In January 1929 the company formed a subsidiary, State Farm Life Insurance Company, which, like its parent company, has flourished.

During the banking holiday that brought in the New Deal era, State Farm Mutual operated at a loss, but it continued to operate at a time when many insurance companies folded. The National Recovery Act eliminated discounts on auto parts, and increased wages under this act sent repair costs higher. State Farm tightened in its belt, dropped coverage in its highest risk areas, and continued to attract and satisfy customers.

In 1935 it diversified again with the formation of the subsidiary State Farm Fire Insurance Company, which in 1950 merged with State Farm Casualty Insurance Company to form State Farm Fire and Casualty Company, which quickly became the largest insurer of homes and pleasure boats in the nation. In 1937 George Mecherle became chairman of the board of directors. Ramond Mecherle, who had been with the company for 13 years, was elected president, and G. Ermond Mecherle, who had been acting as director of personnel, was elected secretary.

Under G. Ermond Mecherle's direction, State Farm established a progressive program that addressed employee welfare on several levels, including financial, physical, and educational. He also worked to improve morale. Posture chairs made their appearance as early as 1935.

In 1939 State Farm launched a campaign to reach one million automobile insurance policyholders. The "One million or more by '44" effort relied heavily on advertising, and the company's advertising budget, which amounted to only $16.25 in 1923, swelled to an astonishing $202,000 in 1941.

With the advent of World War II in 1941, car production for civilian use came to a standstill, gasoline was rationed, and rubber for new tires became largely unavailable. State Farm wrote only 607 fewer policies than the year before—which had been a record-breaking year of growth for the industry in general, and State Farm in particular. State Farm kept growing, pulling further ahead of its competitors, both mutual and stock. In March of 1944, in spite of the war, State Farm had one million auto insurance policies in effect. This represented a 110% increase in five-and-a-half years.

The postwar years were chaotic and fraught with serious problems for the auto insurance industry. There was a shortage of dependable, well-educated personnel, as well as a severe lack of sufficient office equipment and office space. This was at a time when Americans were rediscovering their automobiles, driving them farther, and driving them faster. Claims were flooding into insurance companies, their numbers rising 41% in 1945, and 57% in 1946. The total underwriting loss for the industry during 1945 and 1946 was estimated at $300 million, and for a few months in 1946, State Farm was losing money at a rate of $1 million a month.

It took State Farm several years to regroup and effectively meet the demands of its customers. During this period, State Farm established stricter criteria for accepting new policyholders, setting an age limit on cars and not accepting those policyholders who were very young or very old. State Farm also worked to educate the public in a national automobile-safety campaign. As part of a restructuring plan, branch offices were established in 1947, the first of which opened in Saint Paul, Minnesota, and a committee was appointed to organize the overcrowded and disorganized Bloomington home office.

George Mecherle exhibited his characteristic leadership during this difficult time. According to Karl Schriftgiesser, author of the *The Farmer From Merna,* Mecherle told the organizational committee, "Let us assume . . . that we are about to start all over, *build a new company*. . . . Remember there is nothing sacred here, nothing that can't be done away with. Be as rough as you want. The only thing I insist upon is that you do not depart from the basic principles on which State Farm has been built—the membership plan, the continuous policy, 6-months premium, and the happiness of our agency force."

The committee restructured the company headquarters along geographical lines—with each department representing a region of the country and functioning independently on a day-to-day basis—which scaled down and refined operations significantly. When George Mecherle died in 1951, State Farm had over two million auto insurance policies in effect.

Due to special requirements in state laws, State Farm Life Insurance was unable to do business in New York, Connecticut, and Wisconsin, so to serve these states the subsidiary State Farm Life and Accident Assurance Company was incorporated in 1961. The next year, State Farm General Insurance Company was established to protect low-value property.

In 1962, State Farm offered auto insurance for 20% savings to students who were doing well in school, based on the hope that if they were home studying for their good grades, they would be less likely to be out driving cars. In 1963 the company instituted monthly premium payments, and agents were authorized to make on-the-spot auto claim payments of up to $250, which improved customer service considerably. In 1965 State Farm began offering limited health insurance. The policy offered $15 for every day a policyholder spent in the hospital. This payment was touted as a possible supplement to other health insurance a person may have, perhaps to help pay for a babysitter or a housekeeper while a mother was away from home.

In 1966, an advanced computer system was installed, linking regional offices to headquarters in Bloomington. This investment, and the attention State Farm was paying to customer service earned State Farm praise from consumer groups in 1970.

There were periods when State Farm experienced large underwriting losses, that is, when payments on claims were much higher than income provided by premiums. Through smart investing and the ability to mobilize to cut costs during loss years, however, State Farm has stayed on top. A classic example is underwriting in 1971, in which State Farm's profit was $263 million, compared to $38 million in 1970. State Farm made headlines with its $30 million refund to policyholders as a result of high earnings in 1971.

The company has taken independent stands on controversial issues: company executives feel that the insurance industry should not be exempt from Federal antitrust laws, as it has been for decades. State Farm also supports federal no-fault-insurance legislation. There has been criticism that the company discriminates against minorities. It divides urban areas up into different risk zones, and charging higher rates to those in higher risk zones, which tend to be in the inner city. The company had also been challenged in a number of court cases in the late 1970s and in the 1980s alleging sex and racial discrimination in its hiring of agents. To criticism that State Farm has long been ''creaming off'' the best drivers, Vice President Thomas C. Morrill once responded, ''every underwriter tries to screen risks, but this isn't to say we go only after the cream. We just try to exclude the dregs.''

During the 1980s, the property and casualty insurance industry was rocked by a number of problems. The industry suffered sharp increases in claims costs, especially natural-disaster claims and environmental-cleanup costs in the commercial arena. The rising costs of car parts, labor, medical treatment, and litigation is also impacting the cost of insurance, and customers are complaining.

In 1988, in reaction to the rising cost of insurance, California voters approved Proposition 103, legislation calling for an overhaul of the state's insurance system, resulting in major rate reductions for auto, homeowners', and business insurance, and a regulatory panel to approve rate increases, replacing the long-standing system in which insurers set their own rates. State Farm is one of the insurers that appealed this ruling and, along with other insurers, was required to justify its rate levels.

In 1989, a policyholder lawsuit was brought against State Farm. The suit alleges that State Farm is holding as its reserve twice as much as the industry standard, and seeks a court order requiring State Farm to distribute $6.87 billion in refunds to policyholders. State Farm claims its conservatism is practical and necessary; CEO Edward B. Rust Jr. told *Business Week*, August 21, 1989, ''When it comes to claim time, customers don't want an IOU.''

In 1989 disaster-claim payments were more than twice as large as in any other year on record. Between Hurricane Hugo in South Carolina and earthquake damage in California, State Farm paid out nearly $35 million to cover damage to vehicles, and $570 million for property damage.

Despite these problems for the property and casualty insurance industries, State Farm continues its strong position relative to its competitors in all of its insurance lines. State Farm's earned premiums on health insurance places the company third among health insurers. In addition, the outlook for the life insurance industry is one of growth, and State Farm Life affiliates, ranked eighth among life insurers, are in position to capitalize on this growth. As the numbers of persons with AIDS rises, and more AIDS-related deaths occur, life insurers fear the related financial burden will reach unprecedented proportions later in the decade—and a controversy has arisen over life insurers' right to screen applicants for AIDS.

Throughout the years, State Farm has built a record on its ability to deliver automobile, other property and casualty, health, and life insurance at competitive prices. This has been achieved through innovative marketing strategies, financially sound business practices, lobbying in the political arena, and large-scale public relations campaigns. In this competitive industry, State Farm's ability to keep its customers well-serviced, and its own smart business practices will continue to be the key to its future success.

Principal Subsidiaries: State Farm Life Insurance Company; State Farm Life and Accident Assurance; State Farm Fire and Casualty; State Farm General Insurance; State Farm Lloyds.

Further Reading: Schriftgiesser, Karl, *The Farmer From Merna*, New York, Random House, 1955; Cole, Robert J., ''Unorthodox Insurer,'' *The New York Times*, October 28, 1973; Starr, Mark, ''State Farm's Policies Make It Number One But Irk Competitors,'' *The Wall Street Journal*, June 14, 1976.

—Carole Healy

SUMITOMO LIFE

SUMITOMO LIFE INSURANCE COMPANY

2-5, Nakanoshima 2-chome
Kita-ku, Osaka 530
Japan
(06) 231-8401
Fax: (03) 3231-9724

Mutual Company
Incorporated: 1907 as The Hinode Life Insurance Company, Ltd.
Employees: 11,356
Assets: ¥14.86 trillion (US$10.34 billion)

Sumitomo Life Insurance Company is Japan's third-largest life insurer, and also offers financial services. Sumitomo Life administers its individual, group, and business policies through a branch-office network. The Sumitomo Group, of which Sumitomo Life is a part, is Japan's third-largest *keiretsu*, or business group, and can trace its history to the early 17th century.

The Hinode Life Insurance Company was founded in 1907 and, from the start, established close business ties with the Sumitomo *zaibatsu*, or conglomerate. By 1925 these ties had become such that the Sumitomo *zaibatsu* took over the management of Hinode. Because Hinode was a mutual company, however, the company was not owned outright by the Sumitomo *zaibatsu*, but rather by its policyholders. Hinode was certainly a member of the conglomerate, and since much of its business involved other branches of the *zaibatsu*, those branches, in effect, owned a large part of Hinode.

In 1926, to signify this close relationship, Hinode became The Sumitomo Life Insurance Company. Sumitomo Life continued to expand its business until after World War II, when the Supreme Commander for the Allied Powers ordered Sumitomo and all other *zaibatsu* to disband.

Like other former *zaibatsu*, however, the Sumitomo companies—each now operating independently—began to come together again, even before the end of the occupation of Japan in 1952. Japanese law still prohibits the huge *zaibatsu*, and the postwar *keiretsu* are held together by a looser arrangement than were the *zaibatsu*.

The companies are connected partly by relationships between executives who grew up in the *zaibatsu* tradition, but financial links between the companies and cross-ownership of stocks are often more important, and are becoming stronger. Sumitomo Corporation, leader of the *keiretsu*, "has fostered trade among companies within the group, expanded the financial interrelationships, and strengthened formal management ties among companies at the core of the group," states *Business Week*, March 31, 1990.

Beginning in the 1950s, the life insurance business in Japan has grown and expanded along with both the Japanese economy and the increase in assets of individuals. As the Japanese economy underwent a tremendous expansion in the 1970s and 1980s, so, too, the life insurance business went through a transformation of products and markets in the same period. Sumitomo Life's portfolio was continuously adjusted to take advantage of opportunities, such as those presented by changing regulations, which determined what type of products could be offered.

In the 1980s most life insurance companies fundamentally changed their investment strategies, which meant a decrease in loans to large corporations and an increase in stock purchases. Prior to the 1980s, 20% of asset increases were invested in securities and real estate with the remaining new money used for long-term loans. In the 1980s the loan market changed and Sumitomo Life had favorable results making loans to small and medium-sized companies. The market had then become more competitive, and with changes in laws, the majority of funds were reallocated to overseas investments.

The factors affecting the Japanese life insurance business in the late 1980s that would guide the operations for the 1990s are deregulation of Japan's financial industry that created competition from banks and securities firms; an aging Japanese society in which 13.8 million people in 1990 were 65 or older, with the percentage increasing steadily; globalization of markets in which Sumitomo Life could offer a variety of services worldwide; unification of the European Economic Community in 1992 and the strength of the yen; all along with rising interest rates, fluctuations in the stock market, and changing lifestyles and values of the Japanese.

Sumitomo Life had responded by providing timely new products and services, by strengthening its internal operations to improve sales and efficiency, and by strengthening its presence and visibility in communities in which it did business. A three-year "New Challenge" plan, instituted in 1989, was aimed at increasing profitability, competitiveness, and efficiency.

A subsidiary, Sumitomo Life Insurance Agency America, was established in 1986 with offices in New York and Los Angeles to provide employee benefit assistance and to act as an insurance advisor concerning overseas employee benefit schemes for Japanese companies around the world. Reinsurance agreements were signed with 17 major life insurance companies in 13 countries. One example is a 1989 agreement with a Mutual of Omaha affiliate, United of Omaha, to market group life, health, dental, and long-term disability contracts to Japanese-owned businesses in the United States, and to share in the profit and losses of such a venture. While still new, the program was expected to be highly profitable.

A goal of Sumitomo is to be a total life insurance planner and financial advisor to individuals at various stages of their lives. The new products developed in response to a changing society are directed toward two broad categories of the life insurance market: death-benefit policies and survivor-benefit policies. Japan's aging society and large rise in personal assets have called for increased single-premium endowment policies, savings policies, and individual pension policies. Sumitomo Life saw a growing need for medical insurance and group pensions for the aging population, to supplement the public pension system. In 1990 individual pension policies made up one of the fastest growing areas in the Japanese life insurance industry. Other trends include variable insurance, first introduced in 1986, group life insurance for small companies through their unions and cooperatives, and welfare plans and supplementary packages for medium-sized companies. Since 1988 life insurance companies had been allowed to sell government bonds over the counter, and Sumitomo Life was offering new products that combine life insurance with government bonds.

One of the most important ways for a life insurance company to invest its assets is through loans to corporations, government agencies, homeowners, and consumers. In addition, assets can be allocated to capital market activities, like investments in securities and real estate. Sumitomo Life had been strengthening its foreign operations and global investments, and diversifying its assets to remain profitable and competitive in the 1990s. It had learned about employee benefit and social security systems in other countries and had formed relationships with insurance organizations around the world. Sumitomo Life had 13 subsidiaries licensed to invest in securities. Ties with international financial institutions were strengthened with a 1990 agreement forming a new investment advisory firm with Security Pacific Corporation, a California bank, called Sumisei Secpac Investment Advisors. The company also established ties with the Sedgewick Group PLC, the third largest insurance broker in the world, in which Sumitomo Life will introduce Japanese firms to the Sedgwick Group, which will then advise on insurance matters. In 1982 Sumitomo Life Realty in New York was established to invest in real estate in major U.S. cities. It recently bolstered its overseas real estate efforts with offices in London and Australia; an office in France was planned for 1990. The realty operations had in 1990 assets of $1.5 billion in office buildings, hotels, and shopping centers. For the coming years the company planned to direct real estate investments into public works and urban development projects.

Sumitomo Life has contributed to corporate good-citizenship by financing, along with Yamaha Corporation, a musical center in Poland in memory of Polish composer Frederic Chopin, and Izumi Hall, a concert hall at Osaka Business Park, designed for classical concerts, among other such efforts.

A significant move for the 1990s to increase profitability and reduce risk in rapidly changing financial markets is the development of a computer system to set forth the difference in the fund management techniques used by life insurance companies compared to those of other financial ventures. Users are expected to be able to evaluate Sumitomo Life's overall risk level, giving the company a new level of expertise in the industry. Introduction of this pioneer project was planned for 1993.

Principal Subsidiaries: Sumitomo Life International (UK) Limited; Sumitomo Life Realty (N.Y.), Inc. (U.S.A.); Sumitomo Life Luxembourg S.A.; Sumitomo Life America, Inc. (U.S.A.); Sumitomo Life Insurance Agency America, Inc. (U.S.A.); Sumitomo Life Investment Singapore Limited; Sumitomo Life Canada, Inc.; Sumitomo Life Asset Management (HK) Limited (Hong Kong); Sumitomo Life Hong Kong Limited; Sumitomo Life Deutschland GmbH (Germany); Sumitomo Life Australia Limited; Sumitomo Life France S.A.; Sumitomo Life Bahamas Limited; Sumitomo Life Cayman Limited; Sumitomo Life Realty (U.K.) Limited; Sumitomo Life Jersey Limited; Sumitomo Life Realty (Australia) Limited; Sumitomo Life Realty (France) S.A.

—Paula Cohen

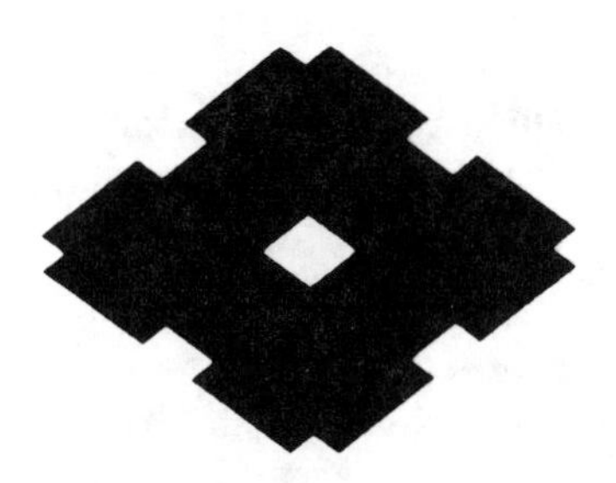

THE SUMITOMO MARINE AND FIRE INSURANCE COMPANY, LIMITED

27-2, Shinkawa 2-chome
Chuo-ku, Tokyo 104
Japan
(03) 3297-1111
Fax: (03) 3297-6879

Public Company
Incorporated: 1944 as The Osaka Sumitomo Marine and Fire Insurance Company, Limited
Employees: 6,115
Assets: ¥1.59 trillion (US$11.10 billion)
Stock Exchanges: Tokyo Osaka Nagoya

The Sumitomo Marine and Fire Insurance Company has existed in its present form only since 1954, but its roots stretch far into the history of Japanese insurance. Ranking fourth among Japanese non-life insurance firms in 1990, with a 7% share of the Japanese market, Sumitomo specializes in fire and automobile insurance. It is a conservative company but is a pioneer in women's long-term accident insurance.

Sumitomo traces its origins to two insurance companies—the Osaka Marine and Fire Insurance Company, founded in 1893, and The Sumitomo Marine and Fire Insurance Company, founded in 1917 as Fuso Marine Insurance Company. The Osaka was among the Japanese insurance industry's pioneers.

Japanese insurance companies initially operated unfettered by regulations, but the lack of regulation resulted in fierce competition, questionable business practices, and several bankruptcies. In 1900 the Japanese government laid down a set of principles to govern the industry: non-life issuers had to be licensed by the government and had to be either stock or mutual companies. The law further prohibited companies from selling both life and non-life insurance policies, and from conducting other businesses.

It was in this regulatory environment that Fuso Marine Insurance Company was founded in 1917. One of Fuso's financial backers was Kichizaemon Sumitomo, a member of the powerful Sumitomo family. One of the chief interests of the Sumitomo *zaibatsu*, or conglomerate, was shipping. Japanese shipping and shipbuilding had expanded greatly during World War I, creating a greater demand for maritime insurance.

A year after its founding, Fuso began writing fire and transit insurance, and later added personal accident, automobile, and aviation insurance. In 1920 a branch office was opened in New York City. During the Depression, the Sumitomo group increased its holdings in Fuso. Sumitomo eventually held over 40% of the firm's 200,000 shares, and in 1940, Fuso became a Sumitomo subsidiary and changed its name to The Sumitomo Marine and Fire Insurance Company.

In the meantime The Osaka grew extensively, spreading its operations throughout the world. In 1942 it merged with the Settsu Marine and Fire Insurance Company. Two years later it merged with Sumitomo, to become The Osaka Sumitomo Marine and Fire Insurance Company, based in Osaka.

The Osaka Sumitomo merger was part of a larger consolidation of the industry during the 1940s. World War II was a lean time for the Japanese insurance industry. All policies written in foreign countries were lost, and after the outbreak of war, the industry was placed under strict wartime control. To meet wartime emergencies many companies were forced to merge. In 1940 there were 43 Japanese insurance companies; in August 1945 there were only 16. During the war, Osaka Sumitomo was forced to withdraw from Europe and the United States and concentrate its business in Asia.

With Japan's defeat, Osaka Sumitomo faced huge losses. Its overseas assets and connections were obliterated and, with the cessation of trade and the destruction of ships, marine underwriting ground to a halt. The end of the war brought other serious problems. High inflation was rampant, and the insurance industry was near collapse because the destruction of houses, stores, factories, and ships created losses insurers could not cover.

Osaka Sumitomo shifted its attention to fire insurance, reorganized its management structure, and started the arduous process of rebuilding. As Japan's economic rehabilitation proceeded, so did the company's. When overseas trade began to grow, marine insurance picked up as well.

At war's end, the Sumitomo *honsha*, or holding company, held about 17% of Osaka Sumitomo's shares. When the Allied occupation government forced the break-up of the *zaibatsu*, the Sumitomo group had to divest itself of some of its shares. Thousands of shares in Osaka Sumitomo were put up for sale.

Since World War II the company has grown with little uninterruption. In 1950 Osaka Sumitomo reappointed the two London brokers who acted as its agents before the war. The same year Osaka Sumitomo resumed transactions with underwriters in France, West Germany, Canada, and Italy. During the boom decade of the 1950s the firm also reopened relations with firms in the United States, Switzerland, and India, and acted as the Japanese agent for the Insurance Company of North America. In 1954 its recovery well under way, the company changed its name to The Sumitomo Marine and Fire Insurance Company and moved its head office to Tokyo. That year, paid-in capital stood at ¥600 million. The company had 1,661 employees in its head office and 14 Japanese branches.

As the Japanese economy grew throughout the 1950s and 1960s, so did Sumitomo. The company continued to write fire, shipping, personal accident, and automobile policies, but the new conditions created by increased trade required Japanese insurance companies to take on new risks. Sumitomo and other insurers began to insure supertankers, airplanes, and industrial complexes. In 1957 Sumitomo established offices in New York and Hong Kong. Growth continued, and by 1964 paid-in capital stood at ¥5.4 billion. By 1969 that total had reached ¥6 billion.

In 1971 Sumitomo made a new foray into the U.S. market, signing a reciprocal agreement with Chubb & Son, and receiving a license to write marine insurance in New York State. That year, assets reached ¥100 billion and paid-in capital stood at ¥9.3 billion. Sumitomo continued to grow during the 1970s. By 1974 assets had doubled to ¥200 billion. Two years later, a subsidiary, The Sumitomo Marine and Fire Insurance Company (Europe) Ltd., was established in London. By 1979 total assets had doubled again, to ¥400 billion.

The 1980s saw a period of continued growth, expansion into foreign markets, and the development of new technologies, products, and services. In 1980 Sumitomo began participating in the New York Insurance Exchange, and a Singapore branch was established to serve Southeast Asia. In 1981 Sumitomo established its second major overseas subsidiary—The Sumitomo Property & Casualty Insurance Company—in Hong Kong.

In 1982 Sumitomo established an office in Beijing, furthering its work with the People's Insurance Company of China, begun in 1972. During the recession of the early 1980s, Sumitomo's expansion slowed but did not stop. Although insurance in force, premiums written, and assets continued to rise, Sumitomo experienced a 5% decline in profits in 1982. In 1983 Sumitomo claimed ¥586.5 billion in assets, 40% of which consisted of bonds and stocks. Loans accounted for about 20% of corporate assets.

While other insurance companies diversified their asset holdings during the turbulent 1980s, Sumitomo maintained a conservative portfolio. In 1989, for example, loans constituted 23% of assets, while stocks and bonds rose to make up nearly half of the company's holdings.

In 1984 Sumitomo installed an on-line computer system to deal with rising numbers of auto claims. It also brought out new products. In 1983 Sumitomo began to offer family personal accident insurance, a special automobile policy, and an insurance gift certificate—a Japanese first. In 1985 Sumitomo offered a new long-term family traffic personal accident assurance, and women's long-term accident insurance which incorporated a savings plan into the insurance.

Overseas expansion continued unabated. In 1985 Sumitomo received a license to conduct non-life insurance business in France. Sumitomo opened an office in Madrid in 1988, giving it representation in 20 countries.

Sumitomo outgrew its old building and, in 1985, started construction of a new 21-story headquarters building in central Tokyo. This physical growth corresponded to immense growth in assets. Between 1985 and 1989 assets doubled—from ¥742 billion to ¥1.59 trillion.

In 1988, under the leadership of President Sumao Tokumasu, Sumitomo inaugurated a five-year plan, to coincide with the corporation's 100th anniversary in 1993. Under the plan, Sumitomo hoped to upgrade products, improve profitability, and increase efficiency. In 1988 Sumitomo introduced the New Age Intelligent System, a computer-assisted driver evaluation system. In 1989 it integrated data processing for all branches of insurance. By 1990, Sumitomo was a licensed insurer in 16 countries, represented by 27 overseas offices and 59 branch offices in Japan.

Principal Subsidiaries: The Sumitomo Marine & Fire Insurance Company (Europe) Ltd. (U.K.); The Sumitomo Property & Casualty Insurance Company (H.K.) Ltd. (Hong Kong); Sumitomo Marine Staff Services Co., Ltd.; Sumikai Computer Center, Ltd.; Sumitomo Marine Automobile Claims Survey Co., Ltd.; Sumikai Buildings' Services Co., Ltd.; Sumikai Marine Services Co., Ltd.; Sumitomo Marine Agencies Services Co., Ltd.; Sumitomo Marine Claims Services Co., Ltd.; Sumikai Head Office Maintenance Services Co., Ltd.; Nishiki Shoji Co., Ltd.; Sumikai Loan Management Services Co., Ltd.; Sumitomo Marine Investment Management Co., Ltd.

Further Reading: "The Sumitomo Marine and Fire Insurance Company, Limited," Tokyo, The Sumitomo Marine and Fire Insurance Company, Limited, [1954]; Uemura, Mitsuo, "Spiritual Guideline and Strategy for Management," *Sumitomo Quarterly*, September 1982.

—Daniel Gross

SUN ALLIANCE GROUP PLC

1 Bartholomew Lane
London EC2N 2AB
United Kingdom
(071) 588-2345
Fax: (071) 826-1159

Public Company
Incorporated: 1989
Employees: 15,076
Assets: £15.09 billion (US$24.36 billion)
Stock Exchange: London

The Sun Alliance Group represents the amalgamation of four separate British insurance operations, three of them companies and one a chartered corporation. All of them were prominent in the development of the British insurance industry. The most senior of the four, the Sun Insurance Office, retained its separate identity for almost 250 years until its 1959 merger with the most junior, the Alliance Assurance Company, founded in 1824. The other two members of the combination, the London Assurance Corporation and the Phoenix Assurance Company, date from 1720 and 1782, respectively.

Sun Alliance Group, the holding company which replaced Sun Alliance and London Insurance in January 1989, is not an insurance company and the group is therefore no longer bound in law to observe those restrictions which prevent insurance companies from conducting non-insurance business.

SUN INSURANCE OFFICE

The Sun Fire Office, as it was originally known, was founded in 1710. Its founder was the eccentric Charles Povey, whose interest in astronomy may have influenced his choice of name. Financial considerations caused Povey to sell his interests in the concern to the 24 members of the Company of London Insurers in 1710. Thereafter Povey exercised no official control over the infant Sun Fire Office.

The Sun's first decade gave little intimation of its future size and significance. A disparate and shifting body of managers, in the main lacking significant City connections, coupled with a limited number of staff and types of transaction, held back development. From about 1720, however, there occurred a series of events that were to help set the Sun firmly in the forefront of London's fire offices: a complete reorganization of the firm's capital structure; the appointment of the first of a series of able and honest men to the two principal positions of treasurer and secretary—Colonel Robert Dalzell and Thomas Watts; and a restructuring of the Sun's management.

Control of the Sun's affairs had originally been confined to two bodies—the general meeting of managers and, of more practical importance, the Committee of Management appointed from among them. From about 1720, the latter body took the important step of appointing subcommittees to conduct and report on particular aspects of the office's business. By about 1730 there were four of these, each controlled by a manager and staffed by clerks. These subcommittees were the ancestors of the Sun's modern departmental system.

The Sun's managers were powerful, as shareholders exercized no control over their activities and were not permitted to see accounts, a state of affairs then typical of most British insurance companies and not remedied until the end of the 19th century.

The managers themselves underwent transformation during the decades after 1720. From this date we find them to be men of education, real ability, and social distinction, linked with Parliament, the City, the landed aristocracy, and, later in the century, with those entrepreneurs and magnates who engineered the world's first industrial revolution. One such Sun official, William Hamilton—manager from 1809 to 1859, treasurer from 1846 to 1852—recovered the Rosetta Stone from the French in 1801, and in the next year saved the Elgin Marbles from shipwreck.

The period 1720 to 1790 was one of rapid expansion. By 1786 the Sun had a private firefighting force and over 120 agents in the provinces. By 1790 it could claim a dominant position among the nation's insurance companies, with a gross premium income of over £100,000, much larger than that of its rivals, the Phoenix and Royal Exchange. The four decades which followed, however, were a time of stagnation. By the 1780s, risks had grown extremely complex, actual rates of loss had soared, and established ofices, like the Sun and the London, considered it necessary to raise premium levels again and again, especially on the extremely high-risk mills and distilleries that lined the River Thames in London and had begun to spring up across the land.

This situation was exploited fully by the numerous new insurance ventures that had been founded in response to the country's growing need for insurance services and that now began to offer discounted rates. This led to a destructive rate war, which put many offices out of business altogether and depressed the industry until the 1830s. One such new company, the Phoenix Assurance, set up in 1782 and soon to become an important rival, was acquired by the Sun in 1984.

The Sun survived by entering new types of business and expanding into new geographical areas. Thus 1810 saw the establishment of Sun Life Assurance and 1836 the creation of a special foreign department to handle foreign business.

The Sun's first foreign ventures were into Europe, initially the Baltic seaboard cities of Germany, later into France and Spain. The experiment met with mixed results—hostility from local insurance companies and the obstructive actions of governmental bureaucracies proved almost as damaging as the disastrous Hamburg fire of 1842 that cost the Sun

£117,000 and almost succeeded in driving it from the Continent entirely.

The Sun turned instead to the more promising territories of the British Empire, and over the next 60 years set up agencies in virtually every British colony or dominion. The massive U.S. market was successfully penetrated when the Sun acquired the Watertown Insurance Company of New Jersey in 1882. The Chicago and Boston fires of 1871 and 1872, but more especially the San Francisco disaster of 1906—which cost the Sun £333,000—enabled the Sun to display its solidity and trustworthiness to an admiring American public.

Perhaps because of the cautious nature of its management the Sun had lagged behind its rivals, notably the Phoenix, in establishing foreign operations. It led the way, however, in organizing the major British fire offices in the 1840s into the Association of Tariff Offices, whose function was to prevent a repetition of the rate wars of previous decades.

One perhaps unintended result of the Sun's foreign exposure was its recognition of the need for formal statutes and publicly accessible accounts. These were achieved, in 1891, by the passing of the Sun Insurance Office Act, by which name the Sun Fire Office became known until its merger with the Alliance Assurance Company in 1959.

In 1907 the Sun set up an accident department, reflecting the growth of this type of insurance in the dawning age of mass transport and machines. The department grew rapidly in size, particularly after 1945 when a far greater general level of affluence significantly increased the number of vehicles on British roads. In the inter-war years the Sun also pioneered many new types of accident insurance, for example a golfer's policy in 1921 and caravan cover in 1938.

The outbreak of World War I in 1914 had comparatively little direct influence on the financial position of the Sun since it, in common with most other British insurers, excepted war risks from its cover. This did not mean it escaped the war years unscathed—naturally a large number of its staff served in the nation's armed services, and a fire at Salonika, Greece, in 1917 caused losses amounting to nearly £300,000. The straitened years of the Depression caused the Sun—and the British insurance industry in general—a reduction in the growth of premium income and an increase in the rate of default on policies, indicating the financial difficulties facing both private individuals and commercial enterprises.

The Sun had entered the field of marine insurance in 1921 and sought, both by its 1931 acquisition of the Elder's Insurance Company of Liverpool and its 1938 agreement with the Royal Exchange to operate a joint marine underwriting account, to establish itself in a field still dominated by the London.

The coming of World War II in 1939 posed no serious financial threat to the Sun, although once again the company lost a large number of its staff to the armed services. However the exigencies of total war demanded, as they had not in World War I, the temporary removal of the Sun's operations from London to the greater safety of the countryside.

In the 1920s, the Sun had several times reorganized its U.S. operations and this process continued in the 1950s, finally resulting in 1958 in the setting-up of a common management structure in the United States for its own operations and for those of the Royal Exchange Assurance and the Atlas Assurance Company.

LONDON ASSURANCE CORPORATION

The expansion of British trade in the first decades of the 18th century revealed inherent weaknesses in the extant system of maritime insurance in London. In 1719 a wealthy City merchant Sir James Lambert, the goldsmith and banker Stephen Ram, and the broker Philip Helbut, floated the idea of a new marine insurance operation.

A subscription was opened for what was initially known as Ram's Insurance and under the patronage of Lord Chetwynd a petition was presented to King George I arguing that Case Billingsley's concurrent petition for an exclusive charter for maritime business represented an unfair attempt to monopolize marine insurance. Case Billingsley, a solicitor, had been instrumental in the founding of Lord Onslow's Insurance in 1718, subsequently to become the Royal Exchange Assurance Corporation.

At the same time Lambert and Ram—Helbut by this time having dropped out—persuaded James Colebrook, who had also established a subscription for an insurance company, to unite with them, and all three repetitioned the king. The attorney general decided that neither petition should be rewarded with a charter, and there matters might have rested had not the government made known its requirement for £600,000 for the Civil List—a public fund to support the royal household—whereupon Lambert and Ram each offered £300,000 for a charter. In June 1720 Lord Chetwynd's Insurance was incorporated under the name of the London Assurance Corporation. The transaction of marine insurance was made exclusive to it and to its slightly senior rival, the Royal Exchange Assurance Corporation.

Business began in a City coffee house under a governor, two deputies, and a court of directors. The London became associated in the public mind with those numerous ludicrous or fraudulent enterprises that together constituted the notorious South Sea Bubble of 1720, the collapse of which in the autumn of that year ruined thousands of speculators.

The London, distancing itself as best it could from official suspicion, realized that in the chaotic circumstances following the crash it could not keep to the original schedule of payments for its charter, and boldly—and successfully—sought 50% remission of the sum. Thus the London survived the perilous days of its infancy. By the end of that tumultuous year marine underwriting was in full swing.

Until the acts of 1806 and 1811 prohibiting the insurance of slave ships and their cargoes, it was a matter of course for those operating in the notorious triangle trade between Britain, West Africa, and the Americas to insure their vessels with City insurers, and the London became heavily involved in this business. As well as covering against shipwreck and "insurrection of negroes," the London also offered insurance against loss due to piracy. Claims for the latter were frequent in the 18th century because of Britain's almost continuous state of war with one or other of the European powers. Between 1744 and 1746 the London hosted the Commission for the Distribution of Reprizals, a body which sought to reimburse shipowners who had genuinely suffered loss at the hands of French or Spanish warships. Despite such circumstances, the London also insured large numbers of foreign vessels, principally Spanish and Portuguese.

The fortunes of the London were not exclusively anchored

to the success of maritime business. From the beginning, Lord Chetwynd and the directors had envisaged the London's engagement in the fire insurance business, no doubt stimulated by the example of the Sun Fire Office, set up barely ten years before. Consequently the directors sought and secured another charter in 1721, which empowered the London to underwrite fire business. Almost immediately agents were appointed in all parts of the kingdom. The London followed the Sun in setting up its own corps of firefighters. Curiously, the London set up no agencies for marine business in the major ports until 1829 when its Liverpool agent was instructed to handle this business too.

Like the Sun, the London arrived relatively late in the appointment of foreign representation, partly because business in the core area of marine insurance tended to gravitate towards the City. Not until 1853 were overseas agents appointed, but in that year alone, ten appeared in the Far East, India, and at the Cape of Good Hope. In the next three decades representation spread to South America, Japan, and Australasia. The first U.S. agency for fire businsess was set up in 1872, followed by a marine operation four years later. By 1881, the London had reached San Francisco and six years later Chicago. This process of foreign expansion had been initiated by J.C. Powell during his governorship, between 1822 and 1846. Powell also carried out a reform of the corporation's internal structure in the 1830s. Powell had a distinguished predecessor in Alexander Aubert, governor from 1787 to 1805, a fellow of the Royal Society and a noted astronomer.

One of the earliest major losses involving the London was the destruction of its own premises in Cornhill Street in 1748. Losses exceeded premium income threefold and the years to the end of the century were ones of slow recovery. A steady rise in premiums during the 19th century was once again offset by the San Francisco disaster of 1906, which cost the London the then-huge sum of £966,750.

The London was also notable during the late 18th and early 19th centuries for the size and frequency of donations it considered patriotic. It voted £200 towards the cost of suppressing the 1797 mutiny in the fleet and £500 towards the relief of dependents of British casualties of the 1815 Waterloo campaign.

In 1824, the Alliance Assurance Company succeeded in having the act of 1720, limiting the transaction of marine insurance to the London and Royal Exchange, repealed despite very considerable opposition from the two corporations. The next ten years were a period of declining profitability for the London. One of its responses was to consolidate its position by a series of mergers and acquisitions, beginning with the Commercial & General Life Assurance Company in 1853 and followed by the Asylum Life Assurance Company four years later. The year 1853 also saw the amalgamation of the Ship and Fire charters by special act of Parliament.

Life insurance for the London, although it had begun as far back as 1721, remained quiescent until the early decades of the 19th century, in contrast to the energetic efforts being made at the Pelican Life Assurance. One reason for this was the London's tardiness in applying the principles of actuarial science to its operations. Consequently, it was not until after 1945 that life premiums exceeded £1 million.

The opening decade of the 20th century was one of slow growth for the London but World War I stimulated its marine business enormously, with premium income reaching a peak in 1917. The extremely conservative nature of the corporation was modified during the war by its having to employ women on the staff for the first time. The fast rate of expansion in the interwar period—characterized especially by the acquisition or establishment of several large operations in Australasia and the United States—produced a general restructuring of the London's management system that split responsibility for home and foreign business and resulted in 1932 in the appointment of the corporation's first general manager.

The Depression, which had begun three years earlier, naturally reduced the rate of growth of premium income and this remained at a comparatively low level until the outbreak of World War II in 1939. The London's directors appear to have regarded the Munich crisis of 1938 as clear warning of the imminence of war and they decided to evacuate the majority of the corporation's staff from London to the greater safety of Somerset and Buckinghamshire, where they remained for the duration of the war and indeed for two years afterward. Once again, under the stimulus of wartime conditions, the London saw its marine business grow rapidly, reaching a high in 1942 at over £2.5 million in premium income, although by this time its fire business had outstripped marine business in size. Although damaged during the blitz of 1940, the London's City headquarters remained structurally intact, so the corporation faced few of the housing difficulties experienced by other less fortunate firms.

Despite an 1891 act of Parliament granting the London the right to conduct accident insurance, it did not, like the other major insurance companies, seriously consider the subject until the passing of the Workmens' Compensation Law in 1905. This stimulated the London, as it did the others, to enter the field in 1907. In the next 50 years accident business grew rapidly, outstripping life in premium income by the 1950s, to rank third behind marine and fire.

PHOENIX ASSURANCE COMPANY

The punishing premiums levied by the Sun, the London, and the Royal Exchange on the mills and distilleries in the last decades of the 18th century caused a group of "sugar-bakers," or distillers, led by the forceful and influential Nathaniel Jarman, to set up its own fire office in 1782, simply and appropriately called the New Fire Office until 1813, when it became the Phoenix Assurance Company.

The New Fire Office provided the first serious competition in the fire business for the veteran offices. Significantly the Sun, most affected by the arrival of this new competitor, early on decided on a policy of limited cooperation with the Phoenix, an unusual measure testifying to the success of the Phoenix's policy of offering discounted premiums if the insured also took out further insurances with the company.

The Phoenix's survival and growth depended at least as much upon the energy and intelligence of its senior management. Notable in this respect were George Griffin Stonestreet, secretary from 1786 to 1802, and his successor Jenkin Jones, secretary from 1802 to 1837. Under their guidance the Phoenix weathered the depression in the insurance industry in the late 18th century and early decades of the 19th century. By 1815 the Phoenix had overtaken the Sun in premium income.

This period also saw the Phoenix establish the Pelican Life Assurance in 1797, acquire several large provincial operations, set up agencies across Britain, and, perhaps most importantly, penetrate the European market from the Baltic Sea to the Iberian Peninsula. Simultaneously the Phoenix established itself in Canada—in Montreal in 1804—although the War of 1812 and the burning of Washington, D.C., by British troops put an end to its first operation in the United States.

These early foreign ventures are indicative of the Phoenix's foremost place in the overseas expansion of British insurance companies. The middle decades of the 19th century were costly for the Phoenix. In the Hamburg fire of 1842 it lost £250,000, more than twice as much as its rival, the Sun, a loss which hit it nearly as hard as did the disastrous 1807 fire at St. Thomas in the Virgin Islands.

The directors of the Phoenix, viewing their widely spread foreign risks, might have used such disasters as good reason for contracting or closing down some of their numerous foreign liabilities. Instead, largely through the far-sighted advocacy of Jenkin Jones, they chose to reaffirm their commitment to their foreign enterprises. The wisdom of retaining foreign risks became apparent two generations later when, by the early years of the 20th century, foreign business began to outstrip home earnings.

These decades and the three that followed saw the establishment of agencies in the Far East, the Cape of Good Hope, Australasia, Eastern Europe, and the eastern Mediterranean. In 1879 a New York operation was once again set up, replacing the reinsurance work that the Phoenix had undertaken for other British offices up to that point. The San Francisco disaster of 1906 affected the Phoenix particularly badly—initially, there were doubts about its capacity to survive its liabilities—but, like the other Sun Group companies, the Phoenix settled with an alacrity and generosity which impressed the Americans. Although business in the last two decades of the 19th century was relatively stagnant, legally the era was one of significance for the Phoenix. The 1895 Phoenix Assurance Company Act enabled the Phoenix to add life and accident business to its operations—a provision it chose not to exploit until 1907—and placed the company on a modern footing by requiring it to publish its accounts. In 1901 the Phoenix became a limited liability company.

Until 1907 the Phoenix dealt soley with fire insurance, although it enlarged itself periodically by the acquisition of smaller fire insurance companies. In that year the Phoenix reabsorbed its own offspring, Pelican Life Assurance, at that time known as the Pelican and British Empire Life Office, and thus began its career as a composite insurer. Life business further expanded with the 1909 aquisition of the highly respected Law Life Assurance Society. In 1910 the Phoenix entered marine insurance with the purchase of the Union Marine.

Although the 1905 Workmens' Compensation Law had persuaded the Phoenix to move tentatively into accident insurance, it was not until the 1922 acquisition of the important London Guarantee and Accident Company, with its U.S. interests, that the Phoenix fully established itself in this type of business.

World War I proved financially costly for the company. The Treaty of Versailles failed to provide for the return of the Phoenix's German interests confiscated at the outbreak of hostilities. At a stroke, the Phoenix lost about 7% of its total fire premiums. Compounding this loss was the abrupt disappearance of its Russian business as the newly created U.S.S.R. canceled all foreign undertakings in the former Russian Empire. Similarly, the aftereffects of the collapse of the Ottoman Empire and the destruction wrought by the Greco-Turkish War of 1922 destroyed the Phoenix's position in Turkey. The Phoenix's entry into the expanding aviation insurance market in 1931 helped to offset the effects of the Depression although it was not until the arrival of jet airliners in the 1950s that the Phoenix appointed its first full-time aviation underwriter. The interwar years were also characterized by the setting-up of branch offices to replace the numerous agencies established during the previous century. E.B. Fergusson, managing director from 1939 to 1957, used the years of World War II as an opportunity to make a series of worldwide journeys, setting up new operations in territories hitherto unexplored by the Phoenix, for example in Ethiopia, Persia—now Iran—and Palestine. The two decades after 1945 were sometimes frustrating for the Phoenix, as newly independent countries either nationalized the Phoenix's operations or, by bureaucratic obfuscation and corruption, rendered them unprofitable. However, in the home market, in North America, and in Australasia the Phoenix recorded high levels of growth in this period, particularly through the successful marketing of new multiperil property insurance policies that began to replace the straight fire policies common until then.

In 1959 a major rearrangement of the company's capital base took place, increasing authorized capital to £5 million. Nine years later the Continental Insurance Company of New York, the second-largest insurance company in the United States, bought one and a half million Phoenix shares, and the two companies pooled senior management and U.S. operations. By this move, the Phoenix sought to increase its capital yet again for expansion into other areas of insurance. Continental benefited from the Phoenix's long-established representation in the Commonwealth and the Far East.

The next decade and a half were years of comparative hardships for Britain and for the Phoenix. By the early 1980s senior management had become disillusioned with the performance of the Continental pool, and in 1984 the Phoenix disposed of its 6.25% share. Continental simultaneously sold its 24.3% shareholding in the Phoenix to the Sun Alliance.

ALLIANCE ASSURANCE COMPANY

Despite the depressed conditions in the British insurance industry in the first 30 years of the 19th century, in 1824 two prominent City financiers, Sir Moses Montefiore and Nathan Mayer Rothschild, decided to set up a new insurance company distinguished by a larger share capital and a more influential board than any existing operation. They invited three other men eminent in the spheres of commerce and finance to become co-presidents—Samuel Guerney, member of Parliament John Irving, and Francis Baring of the powerful Baring banking family. The subscribed capital was huge by the standards of the time—£5 million divided into 50,000 shares—a measure of the reputation of the founders. The new company was endowed from its inception with a range of contacts and influence in financial and political affairs as well as a capitalization that made it the equal of the already veteran Sun, the London, and the Royal Exchange.

Its name seems to have arisen from its combination of fire and life business in the one office and also because of stipulation in its prospectus that made it a condition that shareholders had to invest in the Alliance by taking out insurance with it equal to the sum held as shares. The Alliance's first actuary was Benjamin Gompertz, a fellow of the Royal Society, writer of important works on statistical analysis, and a founder of the Institute of Actuaries.

Without delay, the directors proceeded to the appointment of provincial and foreign agents and by 1825 the Alliance had representation in New York, Quebec, Montreal, and the Indian subcontinent. The Alliance's North American ventures proved unsuccessful. It closed its U.S. operation in 1826 and, after a series of fires in Quebec and Montreal, withdrew from Canada in 1850. Not until the final decades of the century did the Alliance re-establish itself in North America.

The checkered history of the Alliance's North American operations was shared by the majority of British insurance companies that tried to enter that lucrative but risky market. However, the Alliance was unusual in the speed and ruthlessness with which it shut down agencies. After the San Francisco earthquake and fire, which cost it £690,000, the Alliance decided to withdraw from the Pacific coast altogether. This readiness to close, open, and close again was explained by the Alliance's directors as a policy of concentration on quality rather than on quantity of representation.

The Alliance is principally notable for its expansion through the acquisition of established London, provincial, and dominion insurance companies. This process of acquisition began in the 1840s and continued unabated into the first decades of the 20th century, chiefly under the capable leadership of Robert Lewis, managing director from 1912 to 1917, who had begun his insurance career with the Provincial Insurance Company in 1853. The Provincial Insurance Company soon afterward was acquired by the Alliance. Until its 1959 merger with the Sun Insurance Office, the most significant acquisitions were those of the Imperial Fire and Imperial Life companies in 1902.

Already a composite insurance company in that it offered both fire and life insurance from its founding, the Alliance nevertheless had great trouble entering the field of marine insurance. In 1824, on behalf of the Alliance, member of Parliament William Huskisson—a former Sun manager—proposed a bill for the repeal of the 1720 Act which restricted the underwriting of marine business to the Royal Exchange and the London. Huskisson, who later achieved the melancholy distinction of being the first person ever killed by a railway engine, pushed the bill successfully through Parliament but an Alliance shareholder countered by obtaining an injunction restraining the Alliance from taking on marine business. The Alliance's way out of this impasse was to set up a separate new company, the Alliance Marine, whose shares it finally managed to acquire in 1905.

In common with the other Sun Alliance companies, the Alliance entered the accident business in 1907. It managed to do this, unusually, without needing to acquire an already established accident operation.

The conjunction of these four insurance bodies into the Sun Alliance Insurance Ltd. and the London Insurance Company, predecessor to the current Sun Alliance Group, was essentially a result of the post–World War II trend towards the formation of ever-larger units in industry and commerce. The Alliance was the first to merge with the Sun Insurance Office, in 1959. The new holding company, called the Sun Alliance Insurance, acquired all the shares in the two operations.

A larger merger, with the London, followed six years later, creating a new group called the Sun Alliance and London Insurance. In January 1989 the Sun Alliance and London Insurance plc changed its name to the Sun Alliance Group. The years immediately following the London merger were dominated by the process of integrating the diverse operations of the new group, and by the formation of a central head office administration. The introduction of new types of fire and life cover and the elimination of unprofitable businesses helped offset the losses that inflation, gathering pace in Britain in the 1970s, the stock market crash of 1974, and the severe drought of 1976, inflicted on the group.

Sun Alliance entered the 1980s with a comfortable asset base, a very high solvency margin—125% in 1984—and the ambition to become one of the strongest composite insurance companies in the United Kingdom. All this seemed to point to the Sun Alliance's expansion through a major acquisition. Still, the announcement in July 1984 of its £400 million bid for the remaining equity of the Phoenix Assurance—a price that many analysts considered low, perhaps reflecting the Phoenix's troubled financial state in the preceding years—took the British insurance industry by surprise.

Other analysts saw the move as an attempt to make the Sun Alliance safe from foreign predators, expressing suprise that it had not gone for a major U.S. acquisition, to build up its presence in the world's largest insurance market and to forestall any aggressive moves by a U.S. company.

Sun Alliance's initial equity holding in Phoenix had been 24.3%, bought from Continental as the price of Phoenix's withdrawal from Continental's pool. This deal marked the first step in a process of disengagement from Continental that ended in 1988 with the selling of Phoenix's Canadian subsidiaries to Continental in exchange for a 75% stake in the French Groupe Barthelmey. There followed a period of restructuring as the Sun Alliance digested its huge purchase, especially with regard to the Phoenix's wide foreign representation. A long-running inter-union dispute resulted, since Phoenix staff belonged to a different union from that of Sun Alliance's employees, and Sun Alliance wanted all its staff to belong to one union.

Despite the estimated £155 million that the group lost in the October 1987 hurricane, which devastated parts of southern England—the Sun Alliance had, and still retains, a very high share of the U.K. property insurance market—it has nevertheless pursued a policy of expansion into new areas of insurance by the careful acquisition of operations already successfully established in the field, two such purchases being First Health, a leader in the area of medical expenses insurance, and Bradford Pennine, a specialist motor subsidiary.

In August 1989, Sun Alliance raised its shareholding in its rival Commercial Union to 14.5% at a cost of £256 million. Sun Alliance explained this move as a defensive measure to prevent a large European insurer—rumored by some analysts to be Allianz of Germany—from gaining a major foothold in the U.K. insurance market. Other analysts, however, remembering Sun Alliance's methods during its successful 1984 bid for the Phoenix, chose to interpret this as a first step toward another protective acquisition and the creation of a giant U.K. composite capable of withstanding a hostile takeover attempt by any foreign predator.

Sun Alliance's results for 1989 were impressive, despite a 14% fall in pre-tax profits from the 1988 figure. The *Financial Times* called it the U.K.'s "highest quality financial company," and noted its continuing underlying asset strength and high solvency margin of 119%. This was the result of the Sun Alliance's determined defense of its money-making areas, for example U.K. property insurance, and its portfolio of high quality investments.

The incorporation of a new holding company, Sun Alliance Group plc, in January 1989, enabling the group to move into non-insurance business, is firm evidence of its intention to expand by moving into financial services, in addition to maintaining—and perhaps enlarging—an already dominant position in the British insurance industry.

Principal Subsidiaries: Sun Alliance and London Insurance plc; Sun Alliance and London Assurance Co. Ltd.; Sun Alliance Group Properties Ltd.; Sun Alliance Insurance International Ltd.; Sun Alliance Insurance Overseas Ltd.; Sun Alliance Insurance UK Ltd.; Sun Alliance Investment Management Ltd.; Sun Alliance Management Services Ltd.; Alliance Assurance Co. Ltd.; Bradford Insurance Co. Ltd.; The Century Insurance Co. Ltd.; Guildhall Insurance Co. Ltd.; Hogg Robinson Property Services Ltd.; Legal Protection Group Ltd.; The London Assurance; London Guarantee & Reinsurance Co. Ltd.; National Vulcan Engineering Insurance Group Ltd.; The Pennine Insurance Co. Ltd; Phoenix Assurance plc; Property Growth Assurance Co. Ltd.; The Sea Insurance Co. Ltd.; Sun Alliance Fund Management Ltd.; Sun Alliance Linked Life Insurance Ltd.; Sun Alliance Pensions Life & Investment Services Ltd.; Sun Alliance Pensions Ltd.; Sun Alliance Trust Co. Ltd.; Sun Alliance Unit Trust Management Ltd.; Sun Insurance Office Ltd.; Caribbean Alliance Insurance Co. Ltd. (Antigua, 75%); Sun Alliance Holdings Ltd. (Australia); Sun Alliance Australia Ltd.; Sun Alliance Life Assurance Ltd. (Australia); Sun Alliance Phoenix SA (Belgium); London Seguradora SA (Brazil); Sun Alliance Insurance Company (Canada); Sun Alliance and London Assurance Co. (Canada); Yonge Wellington Property Ltd. (Canada); Sun Alliance International Life Assurance Co. Ltd.; A/S Forsikringsselskabet Codan (Denmark, 67.2%); A/S Forsikringsselskabet Codan Liv (Denmark, 67.2%); Fjerde Søforsikringsselskab A/S (Denmark); Groupe Barthélémy SA (France); Sun Alliance Immobilier SA (France); Securitas Bremer Allgemeine Versicherungs AG (Germany, 98.8%); Securitas Gilde Lebensversicherung AG (Germany, 99.4%); Sun Alliance Insurance (Hellas) SA (Greece); Hollandsche Verzekering Societeit van 1808 NV (Netherlands); Phoenix of East Africa Assurance Co. Ltd. (Kenya, 61.4%); Sun Alliance Insurance (Malaysia) Sdn. Bhd (60%); Sun Alliance Insurance Ltd. (New Zealand); Sun Alliance Life Ltd. (New Zealand); Sun Alliance Insurance Co. of Puerto Rico Inc. (97.1%); Protea Assurance Co. Ltd. (South Africa, 79.7%); Sun Alliance Insurance (Singapore) Ltd.; Sun Alliance SA (Spain, 94.6%); Wm. H. McGee & Co. Inc. (U.S.A.); London Guarantee & Accident Co. of New York (U.S.A.); Phoenix Assurance Co. of New York (U.S.A.); Sun Insurance Co. of New York (U.S.A.); Phoenix Prudential Assurance of Zimbabwe Ltd. (53.2%).

Further Reading: Schooling, Sir W., *The Alliance Assurance Company,* London, Alliance Assurance, 1924; Drew, B., *The London Assurance: A Second Chronicle,* London, London Assurance, 1949; Dickson, P.G.M., *The Sun Insurance Office 1710–1960,* London, Oxford University Press, 1960; Hurren, G., *Phoenix Renascent—a History of the Phoenix Assurance Company,* London, Phoenix Assurance Company, 1973; *A History of the Phoenix Assurance Company,* London, Phoenix Assurance Company, Ltd., 1975.

—D.H. O'Leary

Swiss Re SR

SWISS REINSURANCE COMPANY (Schweizerische Rückversicherungs-Gesellschaft)

Mythenquai 50/60
CH-8022 Zürich
Switzerland
(01) 208 21 21
Fax: (01) 208 29 99

Public Company
Incorporated: 1863
Employees: 21,410
Assets: SFr13.20 billion (US$8.56 billion)
Stock Exchanges: Zürich Basel Geneva

Schweizerische Rückversicherungs-Gesellschaft, known as Swiss Reinsurance Company or Swiss Re in English-speaking countries, is the oldest professional reinsurance firm in Switzerland and the second-largest reinsurance company in the world. It is notable for the range of its international activities, the fine reputation of the services it offers, and its powerful financial base. The premium income of Swiss Re, as it is popularly known, is divided almost equally between reinsurance and direct insurance.

Professional reinsurance began in the 1840s in Cologne, where the first company specializing in this kind of insurance was set up in 1846. Switzerland was the first country outside Germany to take up the idea, which was put into effect when the Swiss Reinsurance Company was founded. The Swiss have contributed to the development of reinsurance by providing it with a theoretical foundation, as well as by taking the first steps towards internationalization and setting an early example of how to survive through times of crisis.

The insurance industry got well under way in Switzerland soon after the middle of the 19th century. The moving spirit was Alfred Escher, statesman and entrepreneur, who laid the foundation of Zürich's development as a financial center with the establishment of the Schweizerische Kreditanstalt. In 1857 it played a decisive part in the creation of the Schweizerische Lebensversicherungs- und Rentenanstalt, the first major life insurance company in Switzerland. The evolution of fire insurance in Switzerland was given impetus by a conflagration in the cantonal capital of Glarus on May 10 and 11, 1861. With victims receiving very little in the way of compensation payment, the disaster exposed the deficiencies of existing insurance arrangements. So on November 7, 1861, here was a general meeting of the Allgemeine Versicherungs-Gesellschaft Helvetia, founded in 1858 at St. Gall. It was the first Swiss company to sell marine insurance and also had provision in its statutes for the supplying of fire insurance. The meeting resulted in a decision to set up the Helvetia Schweizerische Feuerversicherungs-Gesellschaft St Gallen. The purpose of the new company was to provide fire insurance cover for buildings and movables in Switzerland and other countries. M.J. Grossman was appointed managing director of the new venture and remained at the head of both companies until 1910—nearly half a century. The insurance companies that started up in Basel in 1863–1864 also owe their existence directly to the Glarus fire.

This market situation and the possibility of extending into neighboring countries were seen as offering a good basis for the introduction of professional reinsurance into Switzerland. The initiative was taken by M.J. Grossmann, who reckoned that the reinsurance yield alone of the two Helvetia companies justified a separate company, especially as in previous years over 20% of insurance premium was earned by foreign reinsurers. At the beginning of July 1863, Grossmann put his ideas on the subject into a memorandum addressed to the Schweizerische Kreditanstalt in Zürich and proposing the establishment of a reinsurance company in conjunction with the Helvetia. This memorandum is a landmark in the history of insurance, offering the first clear formulation of the fundamental principles underlying professional reinsurance.

Grossman began by mentioning the first independent reinsurance company in Cologne. He suggested that the emergence of modern reinsurance was due to growing competition, which obliged insurers to make constantly increasing efforts to satisfy customers, with ever-larger amounts of money being involved, a considerable portion of it—the excess, in terms of the trade—going into the pockets of reinsurers. Reinsurance arrangements, he continued, could not be made with companies supplying insurance cover to the same clientele, so the best thing would be to have reinsurance supplied by firms that did nothing else, since they had greater experience and more specialized knowledge of that branch of the business, and there would be no danger of their using inside information to poach business. Here was an allusion to a vital element in insurance practice: the safeguarding of trust. The document also stressed the need for internationality. The company should provide cover for Swiss insurance firms, but it also should enter into reinsurance relations with foreign firms.

This memorandum led to the establishment of the Swiss Reinsurance Company. It was hoped from the start that the company would be set up in collaboration with the Schweizerische Kreditanstalt, which would supply the necessary capital and confer special prestige on the new company. It was assumed that as regards organization it was much easier to start a reinsurance company than a direct insurer. On July 10, 1863, the Helvetia board of directors agreed to the plan, and to the memorandum being sent on to the Kreditanstalt, with which negotiations could begin. Under the chairmanship of Alfred Escher, the board of directors of the bank looked at the proposal and on September 18, 1863, set up a committee to examine it more closely.

The Swiss Reinsurance Company was finally established with participation of the Schweizerische Kreditanstalt, the Helvetia, and the Handelsbank of Basel. Swiss Re's share capital was SFr6 million, with a payment of 15% from stockholders. Its purpose, according to its statutes, was to provide reinsurance cover to domestic and foreign insurance companies and private insurers in the fields of marine, fire, and life insurance. As a joint-stock company, the Schweizer Rück (Swiss Re) needed authorization from the Zürich cantonal government. Its charter, dated December 19, 1863, bears the signature of Gottfried Keller, the famous Swiss writer, who drew up the document in his capacity as official clerk to the canton from 1861 to 1876.

The board of directors of the Swiss Re, chaired by M.J. Grossmann and including among its members well-known figures from the Swiss insurance and banking worlds, met on December 26, 1863, to draw up its constitution. It was decided to send a circular letter, written in French and German, to insurance companies considered to be desirable potential customers. Georg Schmidt was asked to become managing director of the new enterprise, with effect from May 1, 1864. He had begun his career with the Aachener und Münchener Feuer-Versicherungs-Gesellschaft. In 1859, as a senior official of the Dresdner Feuer-Versicherungs-Gesellschaft, he had been responsible for setting up its subsidiary, the Oësterreichischer Phönix in Wien.

The early history of professional reinsurance in Switzerland showed some of the structural features peculiar to this security system between insurers. These first years showed the necessity of adequate capital backing and of commitment between partners to a shared purpose, in order to ensure long-term balance of risks. Like the basic principles outlined in Grossmann's memorandum, the importance of these requirements was demonstrated by the new company's practical experience.

Individual classes of insurance were tackled in the order in which they appeared in the statutes. On January 1, 1864, Swiss Re carried out is first contract, taking on part of Helvetia General's direct and indirect marine insurance business, as stipulated when the new company was founded. Next came fire and finally—in 1865—life reinsurance. It seems that the business prospered from the very beginning, with showers of proposals for reinsurance deals, but the first annual report notes that extreme care should be taken in selecting reinsurance customers, on the principle of "better no deal at all than a bad one."

In spite of this cautious policy, the company was soon making considerable losses, and the founders' optimistic expectations about the earning potential of reinsurance were at first unfulfilled. In December 1864, at the end of the first year of trading, realizing that a contract he had concluded on behalf of the firm was going to result in a loss, Georg Schmidt committed suicide.

Fire insurance had produced particularly unsatisfactory results on account of a markedly worsening trend in direct insurance damage claims. Reinsurers also had to cope with heavy commission payments. Remedial measures adopted by the company seemed to bring about a rapid improvement, and a plan to drop fire insurance business was abandoned. At the general meeting of May 14, 1869, a decision was made to cover the losses by reducing the share capital from SFr6 million to SFr4.5 million. The company's faith in the future of reinsurance in Switzerland, in spite of its early difficulties, paid off in the end. Not only were the losses made up, but the firm even managed to achieve profits and was able to pay a dividend.

The four decades from the beginning of the 20th century to the outbreak of World War II saw Swiss Re develop into the leading reinsurer of its time. The period is colored by the influence of Charles Simon, one of the leading entrepreneurial personalities in the history of reinsurance. A native of Alsace, he entered the company in 1895, became deputy director and—until 1919—managing director, and finally served until his death as chairman of the board of directors. He did not confine his activities to the world of insurance. He was an expert mountaineer and a respected art collector, and the University of Zürich gave him an honorary doctorate in recognition of his literary studies. He was succeeded by Erwin Hürlimann, who became a member of the board of management in 1904, took over as managing director in 1919, and was on the board of directors from 1930 to 1966, serving as its chairman from 1942 to 1958. The two men worked together in close collaboration for nearly 40 years, making decisions that shaped the future of Swiss Re.

Improved profits enabled the company to extend its activities into other classes of insurance. Having signed its first accident reinsurance contract in 1881, Swiss Re went on to take on motor-vehicle third-party insurance in 1901 and engineering reinsurance in 1904. It now had over 100 employees. In 1893, a relief fund started in 1885 was turned into an independent scheme to assist white-collar workers; it was further extended in 1913, when the company celebrated its 50th anniversary. In addition, profits were being reinvested to strengthen the firm's reserves. This far-sighted funding strategy proved its worth when Swiss Re's foreign business was severely affected by the 1906 San Francisco Earthquake. The company suffered a gross loss of SFr8.4 million, SFr4.3 million of which it had to bear itself. Half the loss could be met by the additional reserves that had been built up and the rest came out of the profits of other sections of the business; the result was a temporary reduction of the dividend. The company's generous treatment of claims enhanced its world reputation and brought a compensatory increase of business. As well as fire reinsurance, life, accident, and liability reinsurance grew steadily in importance.

On October 25, 1913, after 15 years of operating from various sites, the company moved into prestigious and imposing new head offices on the Mythenquai beside the lake at Zürich. This is still the headquarters of Swiss Re, which over the years has acquired a number of other buildings, old and new.

The 1920s saw a considerable expansion of Swiss Re's foreign activities. Ever since it was founded, the firm had done business abroad. Its presence in the main insurance markets was strengthened by the steady creation of branches and subsidiaries all over the world. Its first overseas base was the U.S. branch of the Swiss Re, opened in New York City in 1910. In 1916 the parent company acquired a majority holding in the English Mercantile & General Insurance Company, founded in 1907.

At the outbreak of World War I, only about 20% of Swiss Reinsurance's premium income was coming from Switzerland. When the war ended, the company was able to press ahead with its policy of foreign expansion, assisted by its strong financial base and the stability of the Swiss currency.

In New York in 1923 it founded the North American Reassurance Company, the first firm in the U.S. market to specialize in life reinsurance. Subsequent expansion was concentrated principally in Europe, where Swiss Re did business in 11 countries with 31 insurance companies, mainly direct insurers and most of them in Germany. Some were well-known long-established companies forced by the economic collapse brought on by inflation to seek a partner with strong capital resources. The explanation of direct insurance's large contribution to Swiss Re's premium income can be traced back to this point.

In 1924, in the course of the development of its foreign reinsurance business, Swiss Re acquired the Bayerische Rückversicherung AG of Munich, founded in 1911, which had gone up for sale after its parent company, the Bayerische Versicherungsbank, was acquired by Allianz. In the years following World War II, this company proved to be extremely valuable, since during the Allied occupation of Germany Swiss firms could not maintain direct links with their German partners. Erich R. Prölss, the long-serving head of Bayerische Rück, is one of the most important names in German insurance law. In 1940, restrictions placed on foreign insurers led to the founding under U.S. law of a company that was to become the North American Reinsurance Corporation and that took over the major part of the business of Swiss Re's U.S. branch.

Thanks to Switzerland's neutrality and the security offered by its currency and laws, Swiss Re's worldwide reinsurance connections survived World War II, and the company used the universal trust it inspired to extend those connections. Its overseas activities were boosted by new branches and subsidiaries set up mainly in the United States, Canada, South Africa, and Australia. In 1968, in the interest of clear market definition, Swiss Re parted company with its U.K. associate, renamed Mercantile & General Reinsurance, and in 1969 set up the Swiss Reinsurance Company (UK) Ltd. in London. Consultancies were opened in Central America, South America, and East Asia.

In Germany, Swiss Re reorganized the direct insurance companies within its sphere of influence. Whereas formerly they had been loosely linked in what was called the Swiss Club, the groups were fitted now into a tighter structure. Since 1938, subsidiaries and associated companies had been owned by the Neue Holding AG, which changed its name in 1970 to Schweizer Rück Holding AG. In 1974, Swiss Re used the Schweizer Rück Holding subsidiary to set up the SR Beteiligungen Aktiengesellschaft, with offices in Munich. On January 1, 1975, Swiss Re transferred to the Munich company its majority holding in the Magdeburger Versicherungsgruppe of Hannover, and its major stake in Vereinte Versicherungen, formerly the Vereinigte Versicherungsgruppe, formed in 1974 from a number of older companies and renamed in 1987. It all amounted to a process of separation of functions and relocation from Switzerland to Germany. At the same time, these measures would extend Swiss Re's direct insurance business, which alongside reinsurance plays its own important part in the activities of the group.

On top of all these other German activities, a start had been made on setting up a financial-service group. In 1987, with this aim in view, a finance holding company, the Schweiz Allgemeine was established in Munich, to which the mh Bausparkasse AG, previously part of the Magdeburg Insurance Group, was incorporated, while in 1988 Swiss Re acquired the Harald Quant Group's 50% holding in the Augsburger Aktienbank. At the same time the Schweiz Allgemeine Direkt Versicherung AG was started in Augsburg for the sale of insurance direct to the client.

Swiss Re has strengthened its direct insurance by acquisitions in other European countries besides Germany. In 1977 it bought a majority interest in the Schweiz Allgemeine Versicherungs-Aktien-Gesellschaft of Zürich, founded in 1869, a major international insurer with foreign subsidiaries of its own, and in 1988 it became the owner of Lloyd Adriatico S.p.A., Trieste, a prominent Italian direct insurer, as well as acquiring the third-largest reinsurance firm in Switzerland, the Union Rückversicherungs-Gesellschaft of Zürich.

With its extensive international activities Swiss Re has made reinsurance an important Swiss export. Over 90% of the company's reinsurance premiums come from abroad, the largest markets being North America and Germany. Most of its direct insurance business comes from Germany, mainly from sickness, motor, and liability insurance. The volume of direct insurance business done by the group is likely to increase further.

Reinsurance being a complex international operation, the company has always been very much concerned with employee training. In 1960 the Swiss Insurance Training Centre was set up in the form of a trust to provide instruction for insurance workers from all over the world, especially from developing countries. Entrepreneurial initiative has led to clients being offered, in addition to actual reinsurance cover, a wide range of services relating to the assessment and avoidance of risks. In this connection, the Swiss Re Group includes consultancy firms that advise on damage assessment and claims adjustment. The company also carries out scientific investigations into general and specific problems of direct insurance and reinsurance; the results, published in its own documentation series, constitute important contributions to the theory and practice of the industry. One publication, *sigma,* which has been appearing regularly since 1968, analyzes trends and structural changes and sets out international comparisons; another, *experiodica,* started in 1973, prints useful excerpts from specialist literature. Thus Swiss Reinsurance Company uses the knowledge and experience gained through its international business to propagate reinsurance expertise and the requisite high degree of professionalism.

Principal Subsidiaries: Schweizer Rück Holding AG; SR Beteiligungen AG (Germany); Europäische Allgemeine Rückversicherungs-Gesellschaft in Zürich; North American Reinsurance Corporation (U.S.A.); Swiss Reinsurance Company (UK) Ltd.; Union Rückversicherungs-Gesellschaft; Lloyd Adriatico S.p.A. (Italy); Magdeburger Versicherung AG (Germany); Schweiz Allgemeine Versicherungs-Aktien-Gesellschaft; Vereinte Versicherung AG (Germany); mh Bausparkasse AG (Germany).

Further Reading: de Mestral, Aymon, *Charles Simon Humaniste et Réassureur 1862–1942*, Zürich, Compagnie Suisse de Rénaissance à Zürich, 1947; *Schweizerische Rückversicherungs-Gesellschaft Rückblick 1863–1963,* Zürich, [n.p.], 1963; "Swiss Reinsurance Company—A Century of Progress: 1863–1963," *Post Magazine,* 1964; Gerathewohl, Klaus, *Reinsurance Principles and Practice,* Volume II, Karlsruhe, [n.p.], 1979; Eisenring, Max E., *Skizzen aus 125 Jahren Geschichte der Schweizerischen Rückversicherungs-Gesellschaft in Zürich,* Zürich, [n.p.], 1989; Koch, Peter, "Über die Anfänge der professionelle Rückversicherung in der Schweiz," *Zeitschrift für Versicherungswesen,* 1990.

—Peter Koch
Translated from the German by Olive Classe

TEACHERS INSURANCE AND ANNUITY ASSOCIATION

730 Third Avenue
New York, New York 10017
U.S.A.
(212) 490-9000

Nonprofit Company
Incorporated: 1918
Employees: 3,504
Assets: $44.37 billion

Teachers Insurance and Annuity Association (TIAA) and College Retirement Equities Fund (CREF) constitute the largest pension fund in the world, based on assets under management. From TIAA's original $1 million endowment provided by the Carnegie Corporation, the nonprofit TIAA-CREF has grown to over $87 billion in combined assets. TIAA-CREF is unique in providing a nationwide portable private pension for 1.4 million employees of some 4,500 nonprofit educational institutions. Innovations allow policy holders to invest their retirement funds in socially conscious stocks such as companies that do not do business with South Africa or that are not in the nuclear-energy business.

The concept of institutionalized pension funds and retirement security only became an issue in industrialized society. In the pre-industrial world older individuals were provided for either by their children or through the local church. Limited pension plans did exist in the United States before the 20th century, but they did not become common until the 1910s. For some in the United States, the concept of pensions threatened the U.S. ideals of personal liberties and accentuated fears of a paternalistic government. In 1861, however, the government did provide pensions to those who served in the Civil War. A few private corporations had annuity plans beginning in 1875. By 1932, however, only 15% of U.S. workers were covered by a retirement plan. Corporate pension systems were not always established out of concern for the workers but rather as a means to reduce employee turnover and to promote loyalty, or to control employees.

In 1890 Andrew Carnegie, as a newly appointed university trustee, became concerned over the lack of compensation received by college teachers. He saw that their small salaries did not permit them to accumulate savings for retirement. Only a few universities and colleges had initiated retirement plans or funds, but they generally assisted only those professors who remained employed with the institution for longer than 15 years. These systems varied, with plans such as that of Columbia University that allowed retirement at one-half salary after both 15 years of service and after attaining the age of 65. Carnegie became convinced of the need to provide pensions for college teachers through discussions with Henry Smith Pritchett, president of Massachusetts Institute of Technology. Pritchett and Carnegie recognized that retirement pensions could strengthen higher education by improving the financial security of college teachers. The result was the founding in 1905 of the Carnegie Foundation, reincorporated under a federal charter as the Carnegie Foundation for the Advancement of Teaching in 1906.

Originally endowed with $10 million from bonds issued on Carnegie's United States Steel Corporation, the Carnegie Foundation became the major provider of pensions to college teachers in private, non-sectarian institutions meeting certain academic and financial requirements. In 1908, Carnegie increased the endowment by $5 million to extend the Carnegie pensions to teachers in state universities, bringing the total gift to $15 million.

The original 52 member institutions included the major private universities in the United States and Canada in 1906. The charter members included Amherst College, Columbia University, Cornell University, Harvard College, John Hopkins University, Massachusetts Institute of Technology, McGill University, Princeton University, Radcliffe College, Vassar College, and Yale University. A few of these initial member institutions already had pension funds but saw the usefulness of a more integrated system.

The post–World War I era saw a rapid increase in both institutional members and in individual participants at those institutions. By 1915 membership had increased to 73 public and private institutions, and the foundation realized it no longer could support additions to this free pension system. In 1916, the foundation proposed a "comprehensive plan of insurance and annuities," based on a philosophy of joint responsibility and cooperation between the college and the teacher.

In its broad outline the proposal followed the recommendations of a recent Massachusetts commission on public-employee pensions, praised in the foundation's 1914 annual report. The Massachusetts commission had recommended contributory pensions, with individual ownership of annuity contributions and equivalent contributions to the annuity by the government as employer. In 1917, the foundation established the Commission on Insurance and Annuities, which included representation from such organizations as the American Association of University Professors, Association of American Universities, National Association of State Universities, and Association of American Colleges, to explore the proposed plan.

The commission defined and unanimously approved the principles of a sound pension system, and recommended establishment of a new Teachers Insurance and Annuity Association. In 1918, TIAA was incorporated as a nonprofit life insurance company under New York state law. The capital stock of TIAA was held by Carnegie Corporation, which provided the $1 million endowment.

The usual method of contribution for TIAA annuities was joint payments divided equally between the individual and the individual's employer. Contributions usually averaged 10% of the salary, 5% each from the employer and the employee. Because of this structure, TIAA employed no agents and paid no commissions. This arrangement helped to keep operating costs low, an advantage for educators.

The new corporation was led by president Henry Smith Pritchett. Pritchett, president of the Carnegie Foundation for its first quarter-century, guided the transformation of the free pension system. Under his leadership the foundation also conducted pension studies and established a separate division for an educational-studies program. He viewed pensions as a means of strengthening higher education and, by enabling older professors to retire with dignity, as a method of enticing and retaining younger faculty. The new board of trustees consisted of individuals from academia, finance, and business. It included people from Columbia University, University of Toronto, McGill University, the Mutual Life Insurance Company of New York, the National City Bank, J.P. Morgan & Company, and, of course, the Carnegie Foundation for the Advancement of Teaching.

The 1920s brought relative security and prosperity to TIAA. The Depression loomed at the end of the 1920s when W.O. Miller, comptroller of the University of Pennsylvania, predicted, "It is only a matter of time when institutions of higher learning will find that their responsibility for the protection of teachers and their dependents against the major hazards of life will be inescapable," as reported in *Educational Review*, November 1927. The Great Depression accentuated the need for security. TIAA retirement funds, growing in popularity, took several forms. In TIAA's early years, colleges and universities often had made participation in the retirement plan voluntary, but this trend reversed in favor of compulsory participation during the 1930s. Voluntary participation may have encouraged non-participation if the university did not provide support services, such as a contact to explain the details. This was especially true during the Depression years of the 1930s, when premiums increased because, as schools experienced financial difficulties, new business fell dramatically. Between 1925 and 1935, however, the number of annuity contracts grew fourfold.

By 1935, 105 of 117 colleges that did require joint contributions participated in TIAA. Henry James, the president of TIAA in 1935, urged institutions to act as guiding forces in providing for the security of their employees. Henry James's observations changed the nature of TIAA, from playing a passive investment role to a more active role in disseminating information and advising. He urged colleges to have an officer or a staff benefit committee for disseminating information about insurance and annuities to employees. James was a man dedicated to academia. Having won a Pulitzer Prize for biography in 1930, he was a trustee in the Rockefeller Institute, Carnegie Corporation, New York Public Library, and a fellow of Harvard University.

The Social Security Act was passed in 1935, providing for the first national old-age pension. Retirement benefits were first paid in 1940. National, compulsory, and contributory, Social Society was designed to soften the effects of the massive unemployment of the Depression, provide long-term security, and remove older employees from the work force. Social Security did have many flaws and has been amended many times since its founding. The act excluded among other groups, individuals working at colleges and universities. Colleges initially had requested the exclusion, concerned about the budgetary implications and wary of government interference in educational affairs. TIAA urged colleges to reconsider their position, noting the importance of Social Security benefits for nonacademic college employees. While professors were provided for under TIAA plans, most of the college or university support staff had no retirement benefits. Beginning in the late 1930s, TIAA encouraged extension of Social Security participation to college and university employees; this finally was achieved in the 1950s. TIAA's position was that Social Security represented a national social movement toward economic security, deserving of colleges' cooperation and participation.

In 1938 TIAA was given corporate independence. For its first two decades, TIAA had received grants form the Carnegie Foundation and then Carnegie Corporation to pay its operating costs. As the volume of TIAA's business increased, TIAA and Carnegie Corporation agreed that long-term philanthropic support of TIAA annuities was no longer necessary or desirable. A separation settlement, a series of payments through 1938, was made and TIAA's stock transferred from Carnegie Corporation to a newly chartered board, Trustees of T.I.A.A. Stock, now known as the Board of Overseers.

The war years of the early 1940s brought little growth to TIAA. The postwar years, however, saw a dramatic increase in college enrollment because of the GI Bill. The demand for college professors increased accordingly, as did TIAA's policyholders, from 39,250 at the end of 1945 to 45,000 in 1946. An increasing number of institutions were willing to provide for nonacademic employees' retirement because of the exclusion of colleges from Social Security coverage. TIAA retirement plans increased by 45 in 1945. An additional 123 were added in 1946 and 1947.

By 1947, in a substantial number of colleges, 15% of the individual's salary was contributed to the pension fund, with the staff member and the college each paying half this amount. By 1950, TIAA had $299.6 million in assets.

In 1950, the Association of American Colleges and the American Association of University Professors (AAUP) polled college administrators and active and retired faculty on retirement issues. Of those surveyed, 54% indicated that their benefits were adequate. A large majority of AAUP chapters, however, argued that benefits were too meager in light of inflation. The report urged some provision for cost-of-living pension increases. Other issues in the study were the lack of fixed age for retirement, and who would fix the age; and the payment of benefits to those who either retired early or left the profession. These issues would surface again in the 1980s.

A partial answer to the problem of inflation was the variable-annuity corporation, College Retirement Equities Fund (CREF), formed by TIAA in 1952. CREF was designed to provide benefits based on the fluctuations of the cost of living as reflected in the movement of the stock market. TIAA may also have been attempting to regain part of the insurance market lost to investment companies that were posting higher rates of return than the fixed TIAA annuities. CREF was the nation's first variable-annuity organization.

CREF was chartered through a special act of the New York state legislature. Like TIAA, CREF was established as a nonprofit organization dedicated to serving the nonprofit educational community.

Membership in CREF was restricted to current TIAA members, of which 20% had elected to join by 1954. Participating TIAA institutions had three options: to stay solely with the fixed-dollar TIAA annuity, to participate in CREF but limit the amount its employees could invest in CREF to a specific percentage of total contributions, or to allow individuals to put up to 50% of their retirement premiums into CREF, with the balance to TIAA. Most institutions joining CREF chose the third option. The structure of CREF was designed to assure the employer that his contributions would be used as an annuity.

In the latter half of the 1950s, TIAA-CREF expanded its insurance operations. In 1956, TIAA received a $5 million grant from the Ford Foundation to develop group total disability and major medical insurance coverages. Such coverages would insure against the expenses associated with long-term disability and major catastrophic illness. These plans were used as a further means of attracting and retaining quality employees.

In 1969, TIAA-CREF briefly sought a federal charter for College Benefit System of America, intended to solve TIAA-CREF's problems at that time with state licensing and taxation of insurance companies outside of New York. TIAA-CREF dropped the federal-charter effort, however, as more states supported tax-free licensing for TIAA-CREF's annuity business.

In 1971 TIAA-CREF, with Ford Foundation grant support, organized The Common Fund for nonprofit organizations, to provide small colleges with expert investment management of their endowment funds. In 1972 TIAA-CREF joined with colleges and other organizations to establish the Investor Responsibility Research Center, for the study of social-responsibility issues and portfolio investments.

In 1978, technical amendments to the Employee Retirement Income Security Act of 1974 (ERISA) opened up other profit-making funds for retirement purposes. IRAs (individual retirement accounts) were an outgrowth of ERISA. Growing dissatisfaction with the lack of investment choices became the major complaint of participants. As early as 1983, CREF's performance was criticized as being 54% poorer than most pension funds, by one analyst, *Pensions & Investment Age*, June 13, 1983, reported. In that same year the National Association of College and University Business Officers (NACUBO) established a committee to study TIAA-CREF. NACUBO issued an unfavorable report, and TIAA-CREF slowly began to consider proposals for changing its pension system.

TIAA-CREF began to study the feasibility of introducing a new CREF money market account to complement the CREF stock account and the traditional TIAA annuity. Concurrently, management began the process of registering CREF with the Securities and Exchange Commission (SEC) in preparation for the introduction of additional CREF investment funds. The SEC's approval was delayed in August 1987 when a number of parties—several colleges, competitors, and an educational association—requested a hearing.

Another controversy during the 1980s was over the issue of transferability and removal of retirement funds. TIAA-CREF would not allow transfer of funds from the CREF portion, earning interest from the performance of the stock market, to the TIAA portion, earning fixed interest. A policyholder could not withdraw funds to invest in another plan or annuity to gain a better interest yield. In 1988 universities such as Johns Hopkins began offering alternatives to TIAA-CREF. While the impetus for these changes was the issue of the transfer or removal of funds, a secondary issue revolved around who would decide the risks the pension fund would take, TIAA-CREF management or the policyholders.

A major step in resolving these issues was the selection in 1987 of Clifton Wharton Jr. as the chairman and chief executive officer. Wharton had served as president of Michigan State University, chancellor of the State University of New York—the nation's largest university system—and held numerous directorships on corporate boards. He also served as a trustee of The Aspen Institute and the Council on Foreign Relations.

Wharton first reorganized the structure into four major divisions: TIAA investments, CREF investments, pension services, and insurance services. Before Wharton, the company had a myriad of departments that reported to seven vice presidents. In 1988 consummation of an agreement with the SEC opened the door for introduction of the new CREF Money Market Account.

In 1989 TIAA opened life insurance eligibility to employeesin public elementary and high schools. This program also increased the variety of TIAA's life insurance services already available to participants. The organization introduced a new retirement-income option, the Interest Payment Retirement Option. This plan pays annuity interest only, while the principal remains intact, giving participants flexibility to postpone their retirement decisions.

In January 1990 TIAA introduced its Teachers LongTerm Care insurance coverage, designed to allow educators and their spouses to retain financial security throughout extended periods of care in nursing homes, adult day-health-care centers, or at home. This coverage became one of the nation's most comprehensive long-term-care insurance programs. As of January 1, 1990, TIAA-CREF phased out its major medical insurance which had been steadily losing business since the mid-1970s.

On March 1, 1990, TIAA-CREF announced the introduction of two additional funds—the CREF Bond Market Account and the CREF Social Choice Account. The latter invests only in companies that meet certain standards of social responsibility. The Social Choice Account, for example, does not invest in companies that have economic ties to South Africa or that produce and market alcoholic beverages or tobacco. Concurrently, TIAA-CREF made new options available to employer retirement plans, permitting CREF accumulations to be transferred or cashed in upon termination of employment, subject to employer approval.

TIAA and CREF are recognized widely as leaders in the pension and insurance industry, and as major institutional investors. TIAA's investment performance long has been above the life insurance industry average. Together TIAA and CREF have increased financial security and asset protection for educational employees. The future looks not only secure; it looks bright for the Teachers Insurance and Annuity Association.

Principal Subsidiary: Southland Financial Corporation.

Further Reading: Davis, L.J., "$60 Billion in the Balance," *New York Times Magazine*, March 27, 1988; Greenough, William C., *It's My Retirement Money Take Good Care of It: The TIAA-CREF Story,* Homewood, Illinois, Richard D. Irwin, 1990.

—Jenny L. Presnell

THE TOKIO MARINE AND FIRE INSURANCE CO., LTD.

2-1, Marunouchi 1-chome
Chiyoda-ku, Tokyo 100
Japan
(03) 3212-6211
Fax: (03) 3214-3944

Public Company
Incorporated: 1879 as Tokio Marine Insurance Company
Employees: 11,874
Assets: ¥7.68 trillion (US$53.43 billion)
Stock Exchanges: Tokyo Osaka Nagoya Sapporo Niigata Kyoto Hiroshima Fukuoka

The Tokio Marine and Fire Insurance Company, the largest and oldest nonlife insurance company in Japan, played an early and important role in the century-long development of Japan's insurance industry. Its presidents and managers set industry precedents while they prudently guided the company through many economic and social upheavals. From its inception, Tokio Marine sought markets in the West, thus contributing to the process of Japanese westernization. Today, this investor-owned company offers insurance in several areas: hull, cargo and transit, fire, voluntary and compulsory automobile, personal accident, and other lines including general liability and workers' compensation. With a well-established domestic network of 47 branches and 434 sub-branches, Tokio Marine is committed to expanding its international presence.

Tokio Marine Insurance Company was founded in 1879. Its beginnings were closely tied to the onset of Japanese westernization in the mid-19th century. In 1639 the Tokugawa government came into power and isolated Japan from the rest of the world for more than two centuries. During this period of seclusion, no Japanese was allowed to travel abroad, and trade with foreign nations was strictly regulated. Even in the absence of contact with the West, primitive types of insurance were developed for internal trade. In 1859, however, the Japanese ports were reopened, and Japan was again in touch with the West. Foreign insurance companies immediately established agencies in these ports to protect the risks of foreign shippers. In 1868 the embattled Tokugawa regime collapsed, and the Meiji restoration government took power. Its first acts were to restore full communication with the West and adopt Western economic structures. Many young industries were financed by the Meiji government, including insurance firms, which were modeled after western companies.

In 1878, representatives of the government, financiers who had been feudal lords, and Eiichi Shibusawa agreed on the need for a marine insurance company. Shibusawa was a leader in the development of modern industries in Japan. On Shibusawa's commission the plan for Tokio Marine was drafted by Katsunori Masuda, one of the few Japanese experts on insurance at that time. Masuda proposed an initial capital investment of ¥500,000 and branch offices or agencies in all the major port cities. On August 1, 1879, the Tokio Marine Insurance Company was born, funded by both the government and private investors.

Tokio Marine received its early impetus from the rapidly expanding insurance needs of the westernizing Japanese economy rather than from a single visionary leader. Mochiaki Hachisuka became the firm's first president. Almost immediately, however, he was called to serve in the Foreign Ministry and was succeeded by Munenari Date. Date led the new company until 1883, when he too resigned to fill a government post. Mochimasa Ikeda, the third president, served until 1896. All three presidents had been feudal lords before the Meiji government took over; they championed the Western example but knew little themselves about the business of insurance. During these early years, the firm was held together by Masuda, who became general manager.

Originally, Tokio Marine insured only cargo. Even with this limited product line, however, its business grew quickly. Mitsubishi and Mitsui both trading companies, not only patronized the new insurance firm but also acted as agents in Japanese cities where Tokio Marine could not yet establish branch offices. Wholesalers around the country also served as agents, and soon an extensive network was established with minimal solicitation on the part of Tokio Marine. By carefully selecting risks among ships with first-class ratings, the firm's early leaders assured its secure beginning.

In the early 1880s, however, the young firm was beset by extensive losses. In 1881 four insured cargoes were sunk, capped in 1882 by the loss of the *Gulf of Panama*, a ship whose cargo was worth ¥86,000. These claims would have exhausted the reserves—funds kept in reserve for the payment of claims and usually not booked as profit—as well as investments of Tokio Marine if the Meiji government had not again offered a grant in 1883. At this time, the government also expanded the firm's charter to permit the writing of hull insurance.

The years leading up to World War I were punctuated by the Sino-Japanese War of 1894 to 1895 and the Russo-Japanese War of 1904 to 1905. After an economic crisis in 1890, both wars briefly stimulated the newly industrialized but unstable Japanese economy, resulting in the inception and growth of many new businesses. In the insurance industry, many new companies were started and failed. Following the Sino-Japanese War, 19 non-life insurances firms were formed, but only 6 survived beyond 1910. In order to regulate the speculation in this field, the government enacted the Insurance Business Law in 1900. The statute tightened methods of accounting and prohibited companies from concurrently writing life and non-life insurance.

Tokio Marine suffered during the 1890s from the too-rapid expansion of its own business as well as increasing competition from new businesses. Building on its newly solidified capital base, the company looked to foreign markets, establishing agencies in Liverpool, London, and Glasgow in 1891, and in San Francisco, California in 1893. The British operations rapidly raised the level of premium income from hull insurance, a line that was not expanding as quickly as expected in Japan. In 1890 domestic hull insurance generated barely ¥11,000. In the first half of 1891, overseas hull insurance brought in ¥82,000, and by the second half of the same year that amount had more than doubled. In the first half of 1892, foreign agencies generated ¥290,000 in hull insurance, leaving cargo-insurance income far behind.

The rapid increase in premiums, however, was followed by a multitude of claims. In 1892 overseas losses were beginning to climb, amounting to ¥226,000; by the second half of 1893, losses had reached ¥667,000, with overseas premiums only ¥775,000 for the same term. At the same time, Tokio Marine was faced with stiffening competition at home. Two new marine companies were formed in 1893: The Nippon Kairiku Insurance Company, and the Imperial Marine Insurance Company. In the early 1990s, Tokio Marine lost the cargo business of rice, grain, and fertilizer wholesalers to Nippon.

Tokio Marine responded to the overseas crisis by closing the San Francisco agency in 1897 and the London office in 1898, and negotiating with brokerage firms to act as its agents. Domestically, the firm took the opposite approach and countered its competition by assuming responsibility for its own promotion rather than relying on agents from other companies. To weather the two financial crises, Tokio Marine was forced to draw on its capital, effecting a reduction of ¥375,000. Accepting responsibility for the company's performance, Mochimasa Ikeda resigned in 1896 and was succeeded by Heigoro Shota. Shota resigned almost immediately to become general manager of the Mitsubishi shipyards, and Michinari Suenobu was appointed to succeed him. Despite corporate and financial upheaval, Tokio Marine opened a branch office in Osaka in 1896.

Tokio Marine benefited greatly from the economic revival during the war with Russia. In 1903, the firm's overall profit was less than ¥100,000; by 1910, it exceeded ¥1 million and reserves were comparable to those of longer-standing British companies. The first decade of the 20th century also saw the consolidation of Japan's commercial enterprises into large family-run financial blocs called *zaibatsu,* a structure that characterized the Japanese economy until after World War II. Fiscal retrenchment inevitably followed the prosperous wartime years; in this environment, the *zaibatsu* were thought to be more secure. Tokio Marine became part of the Mitsubishi *zaibatsu*. In these years of mergers and reaffiliations, the company formed its first subsidiary. In 1907 it cooperated with the Meiji Fire Insurance Company to form Tomei Fire and Marine Insurance Company, a firm that reinsured the preferred risks of both companies. A reinsurer does not write policies directly, but contracts with the primary insurer to share the risk for large or preferred risks, thus backing the insurer's ability to settle claims.

In the years leading to World War I, the nonlife insurance industry expanded both in size and in product lines. Marine insurance grew with the expanded marine business during the war with Russia, while competition in fire insurance markets increased. Many new companies were formed to handle the growing needs. In addition, new types of insurance expanded the scope of the industry.

The performance of Tokio Marine during these years reflected the general industry expansion. The directors had learned from the firm's financial setbacks in the 1890s and, with prudent retrenchment, prospered during the lean years after the war with Russia. In 1912 Tokio Marine reentered the U.S. market, establishing an agency for marine insurance in New York, with sub-agencies soon following in San Francisco and four other U.S. port cities. In 1913 the company applied for permission to add six new lines of insurance: inland transit, fire, personal accident, credit, theft, and automobile. In 1914 approval was granted for transit, fire, and automobile. Tokio Marine thus became the first Japanese firm to offer automobile insurance.

Expansion continued and escalated during World War I. With the outbreak of war, trade and industry grew rapidly. From 1914 to 1918, exports tripled, and industrial production increased fivefold from 1914 to 1919. The need for non-life insurance concomitantly grew as well, and Tokio Marine strengthened its position by acquiring control of several other insurance companies. In 1915 it purchased the Meiji Fire Insurance Company, in 1916 became part-owner of Fukuju Fire, and in 1917 acquired stock in Hokoku Fire. In addition, when Mitsubishi, one of its long-standing customers, moved to create its own insurance company, Tokio Marine became a large shareholder in the new firm. From 1908 to 1918 Tokio Marine's assets increased 12-fold. In 1918 the firm began to write fire insurance in the United States. At the same time it changed its name to The Tokio Marine and Fire Insurance Company Ltd., to reflect its expanded business.

In 1920 Japan's postwar economy slid into a depression that lasted most of the decade and prefigured the global Depression of the 1930s. Shipping and trading were particularly affected, and the non-life insurance business suffered accordingly. Tokio Marine and other major companies weathered the crisis, but many smaller companies could not stay afloat on their own. Tokio Marine spearheaded a move toward consolidation of the insurance market. To protect themselves, the smaller, less secure companies became affiliated with those that were larger and more stable. Reinsurance pools and tariff agreements were also used to regulate the market and to establish consistent conditions for determining premium rates. Tokio Marine was instrumental in organizing one of these pools, the Hull Insurers' Union, in December 1927.

The years of financial crisis were exacerbated in 1923 by the Great Kanto Earthquake, which killed 100,000 people and destroyed property valued at over ¥10 billion. Aggregate net assets of all nonlife firms amounted only to ¥235 million; a serious attempt at payment of all claims would have wiped them out. Prime Minister Gonnohyoe Yamamoto, however, publicly called for settlement of claims, and popular pressure exploded in 1924 in seven mass rallies supporting the prime minister's appeal. Kenkichi Kagami, then a managing director of Tokio Marine, led a coalition of insurance companies into an agreement with the government, in which the government and the nonlife insurance companies shared the financial burden of the earthquake, even though in some cases the companies were not liable. Because most claims were for settlement on fire policies, an area Tokio Marine had only recently entered, its payments were not debilitating.

Although the 1920s continued to be years of economic decline, Tokio Marine operated with a surplus and was able to expand its presence overseas. In 1921 it established the Standard Insurance Company of New York, its first subsidiary in the United States, to handle the growing fire insurance business. The company also began to expand in other parts of the world. In 1926 it concluded an operating agreement with Cornhill Insurance Company, a British firm. According to the terms of this agreement, the two firms shared liability on all policies, with Tokio Marine managing operations in Japan, China, and Southeast Asia, and Cornhill handling them in Europe, Africa, and Australia.

At home, the 1920s were years of corporate consolidation for Tokio Marine. The firm had lost business when Mitsubishi formed its own insurance company, and to forestall further losses the executives of Mitsubishi Marine and Tokio Marine coordinated their operations in 1925. At that time, Michinari Suenobu, chairman of Tokio Marine's board but also an executive at Mitsubishi, resigned and was succeeded by Kenkichi Kagami, Tokio Marine's managing director. Kagami, who had been board chairman at Meiji Fire since 1922, was concurrently made chairman of Mitsubishi's board. Under Kagami, the three firms cooperated and exchanged personnel. In 1933 they began to exchange capital as well. Tokio Marine also purchased numerous smaller subsidiaries during the 1920s.

In 1929, the collapse of the U.S. stock market initiated a global depression. Japan began to recover in 1932, after it went off the gold standard and adopted an inflationary policy. Nonlife insurance firms profited in this inflationary environment and developed smoothly in the early 1930s. In 1937, however, war broke out with China. Japan's relations with Britain and the United States declined when Japan's friendships with Italy and Germany deepened in the turbulent years before World War II.

To prepare for economic withdrawal from much of the Western world and to finance the war with China, the Japanese government instituted strict economic controls of the insurance industry, in 1937. Nonlife insurance firms were required to reinsure domestically, rather than in London, a center for reinsurance. When war broke out in Europe in 1939, the requirement became a need. Two Japanese syndicates were established for domestic reinsurance in 1938 and 1939. To enlarge reinsurance capacity, the Toa Fire & Marine Reinsurance Company was established in 1940, with 42 domestic insurance companies as shareholders. Because Tokio Marine was now required to reinsure with the government-approved companies or syndicates, Tomei Fire's function became meaningless and it merged with Toyo Marine and Fire, another Tokio Marine subsidiary. Tokio Marine suspended or shut down all operations in England in 1941, when the British government froze all Japanese assets.

In 1939 Kenkichi Kagami died. At his death, the three affiliated companies—Mitsubishi Marine, Meiji Fire, and Tokio Marine—decided to elect separate presidents. Sakae Suzuki became president of Tokio Marine. The three companies, however, increased the exchange of officers to maintain coordination. In 1941 the Japanese government decreed the need for mergers of financial institutions in order to raise funds for the war effort. At the government's insistence, the three closely affiliated companies were dissolved as separate entities in 1944, and a single firm under Tokio Marine's name emerged in their place. Suzuki became chairman of the new Tokio Marine, and Shunzo Kameyama, president of the old Mitsubishi Marine, became president.

Although operations abroad ceased during World War II, domestic operations sustained a measure of growth, at least initially. As Japanese occupation of foreign soil expanded, the market for nonlife insurance also grew, particularly in Manchuria. In 1943 attacks on Japan increased, and the need for war-risk insurance climbed. Air raids became more frequent, and underwriters wrote more policies. Payments also escalated. Following the major air raid on Tokyo in March 1945, the numbers of policies and payments reached their peak. Between January 1942 and September 1945, income from war-risk policies issued by Japanese companies reached ¥500 million, and payments amounted to ¥46 billion. In early August 1945 the United States dropped atom bombs on Hiroshima and Nagasaki, and on August 15, Japan surrendered. The Japanese fleet and all major cities had been completely destroyed. With no risks left to insure, Tokio Marine and other nonlife insurance companies simply ceased to function. Chairman Suzuki resigned in 1945, and Kameyama was appointed in his place.

Occupation forces arrived in Japan on August 30, 1945, under General Douglas MacArthur, Supreme Commander for the Allied Power (SCAP). Under the SCAP administration, economic controls were inaugurated that reversed the trend of Japanese business and American-style antitrust legislation was passed. One of SCAP's first directives dissolved the *zaibatsu*. Over the next few years, companies had to divest themselves of stock held in other businesses in their respective *zaibatsu*. Top management personnel who had held their positions during the war were dismissed.

The following years, 1946 and 1947, were the most difficult years in Tokio Marine's history. First its office building then its replacement were requisitioned by SCAP. The company ended up in a suburb of Tokyo until 1950. Under the Restriction of Securities Decree of November 1946, Tokio Marine was forced to divest itself of stock amounting to ¥96 million that represented more than 76% of its total holdings. At Tokio Marine, Kameyama was forced to resign as chairman, Issaku Yatsui as president, as well as other top managers and directors. Tukujiro Tanaka became the new president, but the post of chairman was not filled. By 1948 Tokio Marine had complied with most of SCAP's directives.

Marine business, in general, had declined after the war, and the firm concentrated on fire insurance. It introduced fire-prevention techniques to the Japanese insurance market. By 1947, with government support, the shipping industry began to show signs of recovery and the company's marine business grew substantially between 1949 and 1954. In 1950 the company moved back to central Tokyo. In 1951 it became an early proponent of office automation, and in 1953 purchased IBM automation equipment.

The company gradually reopened communications in foreign markets. In 1950 it signed reinsurance treaties with London companies. In 1953 it resumed overseas training of personnel. In 1956 it renewed direct underwriting operations in England and the United States. These domestic and foreign successes revived Tokio Marine's profitability. In 1949 the firm resumed dividend payments, and by 1956 had almost recovered its prewar position in the industry. In the period from 1949 to 1954 total assets increased more than fivefold and working assets sevenfold. In 1957 the position of chairman of the board was re-established, and President Tanaka was appointed to fill the post. He was succeeded by Mikio Takagi as president.

The 15 years from 1955 to 1970 were years of spectacular growth for both the Japanese economy and for Tokio Marine. From a nation devastated by World War II, Japan rose to become second in gross national product only to the United States by 1968. The 1960s were especially profitable for Tokio Marine. In 1964 its direct premiums totaled ¥39.3 billion, with total assets of ¥86.5 billion. By 1973 direct premiums had climbed to ¥238.5 billion with total assets of ¥491 billion. Although both marine and fire insurance coverage did well, much of the new business came from auto insurance. In 1956 Japan adopted compulsory auto insurance. Although premium income from compulsory insurance could not be counted as profit, supplemental voluntary auto insurance also increased. By 1967 Tokio Marine's combined auto insurance exceeded 50% of the company's total business. In 1966 Tanaka was succeeded by Kenzo Mizusawa as chairman. Genzaemon Yamamoto became president.

Tokio Marine introduced several other lines of insurance during the 1960s. Compulsory auto insurance had given the Japanese public a new awareness of the advantages of personal insurance, and Tokio Marine added new lines of personal coverage to its largely corporate business. Several types of personal accident insurance were offered: householders' and storekeepers' comprehensive, traffic personal accident, long-term comprehensive, and earthquake insurance for individual citizens. Its corporate lines continued to develop as well. The firm added aviation insurance, nuclear-energy liability, movables comprehensive, and employees' housing-loan credit insurance.

Between 1964 and 1975 Tokio Marine increased to 19 the number of foreign countries in which it did business. In the United States, Tokio Marine affiliated with the Continental Insurance Company and directed more of its efforts toward non-marine business. In both European and U.S. markets the company did an increasing amount of reinsurance. Yamamoto became chairman in 1972, and Minori Kikuchi followed him as president.

In the early 1970s, the rapid growth of the previous decade slowed dramatically. The growth in premium income of nonlife insurance companies in Japan dropped from 40% in 1970 to 12.8% in 1971. The economic slump was exacerbated by the oil crisis of 1973. To counteract the domestic downturn, Tokio Marine focused even more intently on overseas expansion and plotted a strategy of internationalization in the mid-1970s. Net overseas premium income increased from ¥14 billion in 1969 to ¥49.7 billion in 1978. In 1978 Kikuchi advanced to the chairmanship, and Fumio Watanabe followed him as president.

The 1980s were years of stable financial growth for Tokio Marine, especially from investment income. In 1980 it purchased three subsidiaries from the Equitable Life Insurance Society of the United States. One year later it became the first Japanese nonlife insurance company to begin operations in Italy. Investment income soared as the firm invested extensively in high-yield foreign securities. Auto-premium income also continued to climb, bolstered by a premium ratehike in 1983. In 1984 President Watanabe became chairman, and Haruo Takeda succeeded him as president. In 1985 Tokio Marine reported a record ¥25 billion net profit. In 1989 the firm purchased a 10% stake in Delaware Management Holdings, the fifth-largest independent money-management firm in the United States, in order to train itself in the management of pension funds. By 1989 Tokio Marine was the world's largest property and casualty insurance company. In 1990 Takeda advanced to the chairmanship, and Shunzi Kono became president.

Principal Subsidiaries: Arab International Co. (Egypt); Tokio Marine Management (Australiasia) Pty. Ltd. (Australia); America Latina Companhia de Seguros (Brazil); P. T. Asuransi Jayasraya (Indonesia); The Koryo Fire & Marine Insurance Co., Ltd. (Korea); United Prime Insurance (Malaysia) Sdn. Bhd.; Jerneh Insurance Corp. Sdn. Bhd. (Malaysia); Tokio Marine Internacional S.A. (Mexico); La Rural del Paraguay S.A.; Pan-Malayan Insurance Corp. (Philippines); The Arab-Eastern Insurance Company Limited EC. (Saudi Arabia); The Tokio Marine & Fire Insurance Co. (Singapore) Pte. Ltd.; Tokio Reinsurance Co. Ltd. (Switzerland); The Sri Muang Insurance Co., Ltd. (Thailand); Tokio Marine South-East Servicing Co., Ltd. (Thailand); Tokio Marine International Fund (Bahama) Co. Ltd.; Tokio Marine International Fund (Luxembourg) S.A.; The Wuphoon Insurance Co. Ltd. (Hong Kong); Tokio Marine Realty Co., Ltd. (U.S.A.); The Tokio (New York) Corp. (U.S.A.); Houston General Insurance Co. (U.S.A.); Trans Pacific Insurance Co. (U.S.A.); TM Claims Service, Inc. (U.S.A.); First Insurance Co. of Hawaii, Ltd. (U.S.A., 40%); Tokio Marine Management, Inc. (U.S.A.); Tokio Marine de Venezuela, C.A.

Further Reading: The Tokio Marine & Fire Insurance: The First Century, 1879–1979, Tokyo, The Tokio Marine & Fire Insurance Co., Ltd., 1980.

—Lynn M. Voskuil

TheTravelers

THE TRAVELERS CORPORATION

One Tower Square
Hartford, Connecticut 06183
U.S.A.
(203) 277-0111
Fax: (203) 277-7979

Public Company
Incorporated: 1863 as The Travelers Insurance Company
Employees: 35,000
Assets: $56.75 billion
Stock Exchanges: New York Pacific London

The Travelers Corporation is a diversified multi-line insurer that has been an insurance-industry leader for more than a century. The company introduced accident insurance to the United States in 1864, wrote its first automobile policy in 1897, and initiated aviation insurance in 1919. Today the company is one of the largest insurers in the world.

On March 24, 1864, James G. Batterson, founder of The Travelers Insurance Company, met local banker James Bolter at the Hartford, Connecticut, post office. Bolter had heard about Batterson's plan to start a company to insure travelers against accidents, and asked Batterson how much it would cost to insure him against an accident on his way home for lunch—a distance of four blocks. "Two cents," replied Batterson, who quickly pocketed Bolter's pennies. James G. Batterson had just written the first accident policy for Travelers Insurance Company, although the company did not officially open for another week. Bolter, incidentally, arrived home safely.

James Batterson was born in 1823, the son of a Bloomfield, Connecticut, stonecutter. At age 15 he was apprenticed to a printer in Ithaca, New York, during which time he spent his evenings studying the books of his friends in college. After three years Batterson was called back to help with his father's stonecutting business, which, under Batterson's leadership, earned a nationwide reputation. Batterson contributed to the design and sculpting of the National Soldiers Monument at Gettysburg, Pennsylvania, as well as other monuments at Antietam, Maryland; San Francisco, California; and Galveston, Texas.

In the 1860s accident insurance was an unknown commodity. Travelers Insurance Company employed extensive advertising to help promote its unique service; early ads incorporated news stories of disasters. A variety of promotional novelties were employed, and Thomas Nast, a popular cartoonist, illustrated a number of the early advertisements.

During the first few years of operation Travelers was constantly mapping new ground. Premium fluctuations and restrictions on policies frustrated agents and customers, but slowly accident policies gained consistency and caught on with the public. The Industrial Revolution had increased the number of occupational hazards, which were publicized by accident insurers. Travelers agents also sold accident policies at railway stations, promoting sales by "being at the right place at the right time."

In 1865 Travelers began selling life insurance, becoming the first insurance company to offer more than one line of insurance. For the rest of the 19th century, most companies focused on a single line of insurance. When other carriers began to diversify at the turn of the century, Travelers already had extensive experience and a substantial lead as a multiline insurer.

An umbrella was seen in Travelers ads as early as 1870. It frequently appeared in corporate advertisements over the next 90 years. In 1960 the company adopted the familiar red umbrella as a symbol of the protection provided by Travelers's policies.

In 1889 Travelers diversified into liability insurance. Employer's liability, a predecessor of workers' compensation, was first sold in the United States by a British company in 1885. When Travelers began to offer employer's liability insurance, it sent inspectors to manufacturing facilities to evaluate risks and recommend safety procedures. Resistance to precautionary methods was gradually overcome when shop owners found that their insurance premiums were lower when they followed basic safety procedures. In 1904 the Travelers's inspection team became a special division, devoted to the elimination of accidents on the job.

In 1897 Travelers wrote its first automobile policy. Early automobile policies were based on the old horse-teams policies. In 1906, however, a new schedule of rates was devised expressly for automobiles based on horsepower.

In 1899 Travelers entered the field of health insurance. The first health policies were not heavily advertised, but were offered to customers who inquired about them. The policies cost $10 a year for an indemnity of $25 per week up to 26 weeks and $2,500 for permanent disability. Initially covering only 15 specified diseases, policies were expanded in the 1920s to include many more ailments, and general health insurance was born.

In 1901 James G. Batterson died, leaving control of the company to Sylvester Dunham. Dunham introduced the branch office system to Travelers. Before 1902 the company's agents were responsible for selling policies, recruiting agents, and for performing administrative chores. With the opening of its first branch office, in New York City, Travelers set up an administrative system to support the agents, allowing them to concentrate on selling insurance. The branch office serviced existing policyholders, oversaw sales operations, and provided inspection and investigation services. Offices were soon set up in Louisville, Kentucky; Philadelphia, Pennsylvania; and Cleveland, Columbus, Cincinnati, and Toledo, Ohio, and have since grown to number in the hundreds.

In 1903 the first class of 12 agents began training at the industry's first vocational school, started by Travelers. In 1957 a building was dedicated to an education center, and a dormitory, Denniston Hall, named for the first instructor housed the students.

In the early part of the 20th century Travelers introduced several more new lines of insurance. In 1906 it opened an indemnity department which insured boilers and machinery; in 1911 modern workers' compensation insurance was added; and in 1915 the indemnity department added burglary insurance. Group insurance, which would later make up a substantial segment of Travelers's business, was introduced in 1913, written for the employees of the Ohio Electric Railway Company.

During World War I Travelers attracted some of the tens of thousands of men entering the military with special war riders. Many extraordinary claims were paid as a consequence of the war. When the cruiseliner *Lusitania* was sunk by a German submarine in 1915, 17 Travelers policyholders were killed. The company demanded $426,000 from the German government, but no payment was made. A year later, when a German U-boat, the *Deutschland,* was picking up supplies in Connecticut, it accidentally rammed an escort tugboat, sending the tugboat's five-man crew to the ocean floor. The crew had been insured by Travelers's workers' compensation insurance, and when the *Deutschland* docked to inspect its own damage, it was met by a Travelers accident adjuster who served an injunction ordering the German commander to file a bond to secure any future litigation. After the *Deutschland* posted $500,000 bond, the submarine was allowed to leave.

Sylvester Dunham died in 1915, and was succeeded by Louis F. Butler. Butler was a native of Hartford, born in 1871. He started his career at Travelers as an office boy for J. G. Batterson, and was soon promoted to actuary, and, in 1907, secretary of the company. He became a vice president in 1912, and served as president until his death in 1929, just one week before the stock market crash.

After World War I, in May 1919, the Travelers introduced a comprehensive aviation insurance program which included life, public liability, workers' compensation, and passenger accident policies. President Woodrow Wilson was among the first group of flyers covered by such insurance. Travelers also published one of the first aviation-safety publications, *Airplanes and Safety,* in 1920.

When the stock market crashed in 1929, many institutional investors were ruined. Travelers, however, had placed its investment portfolio under the care of L. Edmund Zacher. Zacher, who had become president just two days before the crash, had had the foresight to take Travelers's money out of equities and put it in United States government bonds, one of the safest investments available.

The company had escaped financial ruin, but suffered a sharp decline in premiums. A number of life insurance policyholders committed suicide; others threatened to do so if Travelers did not loan them money, which it did not. One such incident occurred in 1933, when a policyholder sent a letter to the company threatening to kill himself unless Travelers agreed to loan him one-third of his policy's face value for three years at 5%. The letter gave instructions to reply in the public notices section of *The New York Times.* President Zacher sent the following reply: "Status: Many men are today in equally trying financial circumstances but are giving a brave fight. Your moral support and affection will add more to the happiness of your family than any monetary consideration. Your family would not approve of your proposal. Keep its Respect. Zelevart." Years later a man in New York City confessed to his agent that he had been inspired by Zacher's reply and carried on.

During World War II Travelers underwrote a number of extraordinary risks, like munitions, bombers, fighter planes, and submarines. Travelers also underwrote the Alcan highway project, between Fairbanks, Alaska, and Dawson Creek, British Columbia, eventually linking up with the Pan American highway extending south to Rio de Janeiro. Travelers insured a wide variety of industrial risks, including oil fields in Iran and construction sites in South America. Perhaps the riskiest underwriting of all was that of the Manhattan Project, which secretly developed the atomic bomb. This experience led Travelers to participate in insuring nuclear power plants after the war.

In 1945 Jesse W. Randall became president of Travelers Insurance Company. Francis W. Cole became chairman of the whole group, which now included Travelers Indemnity Company, a subsidiary.

After World War II, Americans began to move out of the cities, into the suburbs. Expensive new appliances like TVs, refrigerators, and air conditioners promoted the installment loan. Better highways encouraged greater production of automobiles. These new trends affected Travelers. The company offered packaged insurance plans for individuals. The Extended Coverage Plan and the Additional Extended Coverage Plan offered homeowners protection from more hazards than ever. In 1955 all of a homeowner's insurance needs—fire, personal liability, windstorm, medical coverage for outsiders injured on the premises, and living expenses when a home becomes uninhabitable—were included in the Homeowners Policy. In 1957 the Premium Budget Plan allowed homeowners to pay monthly premiums.

The increase in automobile use resulted in a large increase in accidents. In the ten years after the war, accidents increased 30%, and the cost of bodily injury claims rose 86%. Travelers began losing money on its automobile liability lines until 1959, when the company began basing insurance rates on a driver's safety record. Studies had shown a driver with even one accident or traffic violation in the past three years was significantly more likely to have another mishap. With the new rating system, the Travelers was able to make the auto-accident insurance division profitable again.

In 1952 J. Doyle DeWitt became president of Travelers. During DeWitt's term, group insurance came to play a greater role in the company's profits. Group major medical, in particular, showed stunning growth during the 1950s and 1960s. In 1958 Travelers opened its first suburban neighborhood branch office, near Atlanta, Georgia. The new neighborhood offices catered to homeowners and people with small businesses. Also in 1958, with business booming, Travelers installed its first computer to help keep up with the paperwork.

During the 1960s Travelers continued to adjust to societal changes. Crime rates continued to increase, as did traffic accidents. Health-care costs were skyrocketing, and court settlements had higher limits. The new Medicare program took a sizable bite out of the company's health insurance premiums. Travelers lost some ground to other insurance companies. In 1965 Sterling Tooker, the company's new president, announced Travelers's intention to respond to the changes that were slowing the company's growth. Morrison H. Beach was put in charge of developing the company's long-term planning. The company hired Thomas F. Malone from the Massachusetts Institute of Technology to head a new research department in order to spot trends and help the company respond to them.

At the end of 1965 Travelers Insurance Company reorganized its capital structure, becoming The Travelers Corporation. The new corporation held the stock of Travelers Insurance Company and its former subsidiary, Travelers Indemnity Company. The Travelers Corporation also operated as a reinsurance company. In 1966 Travelers added the Phoenix Insurance Company to its holdings. Phoenix was the 29th-largest U.S. property and casualty insurer.

In 1967 The Travelers entered the mutual funds business when it opened the Travelers Equities Fund. The fund was among the top performers. The company's diversification served as a buffer in 1968 when property and casualty underwritings lost $64 million.

In 1969 Sterling Tooker resigned as president and CEO of The Travelers Corporation and was succeeded by Roger C. Wilkins. J. Doyle DeWitt remained chairman. Later in the years, The Travelers insured the *Apollo II* astronauts. By 1970 The Travelers' premiums had doubled from their 1960 level.

In 1971 Morrison H. Beach became The Travelers' president and Roger Wilkins became chairman. The Travelers ranked second among diversified financial company in the United States.

During the early 1970s The Travelers began to mass market insurance and financial services to individuals through their employers. This bulk sales method allowed The Travelers to offer lower rates and reduced The Travelers' processing costs because premiums were often collected through payroll-deduction programs.

In 1974 The Travelers restructured its departments, splitting the property and casualty division along personal and commercial lines. The life, health, and financial-services divisions remained intact. In 1975 the company's earning dropped to $100 million, from $127 million in 1974. The cyclical nature of property and casualty insurance was responsible. Earnings from the property and casualty lines in 1974 were $32.6 million, down from $89.6 million in 1973. Property and casualty earnings bottomed out at $2 million in 1975 before bouncing back in 1976 and 1977, peaking in 1978.

In 1976 Edward H. Budd became president of The Travelers. Budd had joined the company in 1955 as an actuarial assistant. He became senior vice president in charge of the property and casualty business in 1974. Morrison Beach became chairman, and remained CEO until 1981. Budd replaced Beach as chairman in 1982, at a time when the insurance industry was struggling due to record health-care costs and stiff competition between insurers.

The 1980s were a time of intense competition and deregulation for financial companies. In the early 1980s property and casualty insurers were caught in a downward spiral. Unlike its competitors, Aetna and CIGNA, however, The Travelers was able to escape the worst of the cycle, largely because group-insurance and pension-planning operations continued to grow rapidly. The Travelers acquired or formed a number of new companies to the group during the decade, including Keystone Life Insurance Company, in 1980; Travelers Lloyds Insurance Company, in 1981; Provident Travelers Mortgage Securities Corporation, in 1983; Bankers and Shippers Insurance Company of New York, in 1984; Travelers Keystone Fixed Income Advisors, and Travelers Plan Administrators, in 1985; Whitaker Health Services, in 1986; and Health Plan of Virginia, in 1987. Minority interests in a number of financial companies were also acquired.

In 1982 The Travelers expanded its activities in the securities market when it purchased the clearing unit of Moseley, Hallgarten, Estabrook, and Weeden. In 1986 it became a major player in securities with its $157.5 million purchase of Dillon, Reed & Company, one of Wall Street's oldest investment-banking firms. The traditional Dillion, Reed gave The Travelers a significant foothold in the rapidly changing securities market.

In January 1985 Alva O. Way, president of The Travelers Corporation since 1983, resigned unexpectedly. Way had come to The Travelers from the American Express Corporation. Edward H. Budd, chairman and CEO, took over as president following the announcement.

The Travelers relied more on mass marketing of its products and services during the 1980s than it had previously. Health-care costs continued to grow in the 1980s. In 1986 and 1987 the company acquired a substantial health-maintenance organization (HMO) from Whittaker Corporation for $48 million. HMOs grew in popularity because they were expected to keep health-care costs down. In 1989, however, the travelers lost about $18 million on its HMOs, and sold five HMOs for $1 each.

In 1987 Travelers suffered a substantial second-quarter loss of $337 million because of doubtful real estate investments it had made in the Southwest. As a result of these real estate investments the company's securities rating was downgraded. In 1988 Travelers began cost-cutting measures through staff reductions; 465 employees were dismissed, another 420 left voluntarily. A year later 225 more jobs were trimmed.

The Travelers Corporation, always an innovator in the insurance industry, played a crucial role in the widespread acceptance of casualty insurance throughout the United States. The company has also had a hand in developing new forms of coverage, and its progressive posture leads one to believe The Travelers Corporation will continue to adapt successfully to changes in the marketplace.

Principal Subsidiaries: The Travelers Insurance Company; The Travelers Life and Annuity Co.; The Travelers Life Insurance Company; The Travelers Insurance Company of Illinois; Travelers Life Insurance Company; The Travelers Corporation of Bermuda Ltd.; The Travelers Indemnity Company; The Phoenix Insurance Company; The Charter Oak Fire Insurance Company; The Travelers Indemnity Company of Rhode Island; The Travelers Indemnity Company of America; Constitution State Insurance Company; Travelers Reinsurance Company of Bermuda, Ltd.; Travelers Equities Sales, Inc.; Travelers Investment Company; The Massachusetts Company, Inc.; Travelers Keystone Fixed Income Advisors, Inc.; Travelers Mortgage Securities Corporation; The Prospect-Company; Constitution Plaza Inc.; The Travelers Asset Management International Corporation; Panther Valley, Inc.; Plaza Corporation; Derby Advertising Inc.; Constitution State Service Company; Travelers Marine Corporation; Travelers E.B.S. Inc.; The Travelers Corp. (UK) Ltd.; Travelers Lloyds Insurance Company; Center For Corporate Health Inc.; Travelers Plan Administrators, Inc.; Resource Information Management Systems Inc.; Travtech Inc.; Dillon, Reed and Company, Inc.; Travelers Health Network, Inc.

—Thomas M. Tucker

UNION DES ASSURANCES DE PARIS

9 Place Vendôme
75052 Paris Cédex 01
France
(1) 42 86 71 71
Fax: (1) 74 54 30 26

Wholly Owned Subsidiary of Société Centrale Union des Assurances de Paris
Incorporated: 1968
Employees: 29,936
Assets: FFr52.40 billion (US$9.07 billion)

Union des Assurances de Paris (UAP) is 75% owned by the French state, and is France's largest insurer, active in all major branches of insurance: accident, motor, reinsurance, life, and in personal savings and investments. The recent history of UAP has been one of large-scale changes, since the group was formed by the state-decreed merger of three nationalized insurance groups in 1968. The theme of change looks set to continue. Apart from the possibility that ownership of UAP will be transferred increasingly to the private sector, there are challenges to be faced as insurance companies in France redefine their role, expand into new business areas, and prepare for the abolition of trade barriers in the single European market on January 1, 1993.

The three nationalized insurance groups which were merged to form UAP—l'Union, l'Urbaine, and la Séquanaise—were all established in the 19th century. The first group to be founded was l'Union-Incendie, which opened its doors in 1828 to offer insurance against fire risks. L'Union-Incendie—and in 1838 l'Urbaine-Incendie—were among the first insurance companies to be founded in France after the Napoleonic period ended with the restoration of the monarchy in 1815. The new regime lifted the ban on all forms of insurance which had been imposed during the revolutionary period. Maximilian Robespierre's government had denounced insurance as immoral speculation on the pain and suffering of others, and as being against the public interest. This mistrust of insurance was shared by Napoleon Bonaparte, who maintained the ban. Even after insurance companies had been granted the right to do business, companies such as l'Union-Incendie faced a struggle against public mistrust throughout the 19th century. Successive French governments entertained the idea of bringing the insurance industry under state control through nationalization, but insurance remained in the hands of private entrepreneurs until well into the 20th century. In 1889 both l'Urbaine-Vie and l'Urbaine-Accident were exhibitors at the Universal Exposition in Paris, with the aim of demonstrating the benefits to individuals of insuring against risk.

The basis for public mistrust of insurance companies was the fear that economic power and the assets of many policyholders would fall under the control of wealthy individuals—universally decried as speculators—if those people were allowed to take charge of an insurer. To prevent such an eventuality, the FFr10 million share capital of l'Union-Incendie was divided into 2,000 shares with the high face value of FFr5,000. In this way it was thought that the company would be able to keep track of its shareholders.

The company was founded by a combination of bankers, merchants, stockbrokers, public officials, and liberal politicians. Its first director was Myrtil Maas, a young mathematician who earlier had been involved in the founding of the Compagnie d'Assurances Générales, in 1819. These were the very early days of the actuarial profession in France. The following year saw the birth of l'Union-Vie, which offered life insurance contracts for individuals.

An even more distinguished group came together at the foundation of l'Urbaine-Incendie in 1838; including, among others, a former director of the Bank of France, a mayor of Paris, a deputy to the National Assembly, the director-general of the Paris-Orléans railway, and a leading industrialist in the sugar refining trade. During the course of the century, the company was to expand both through internal growth and by absorbing other insurance companies. In 1843, for instance, l'Urbaine-Incendie took over the business of le Dragon, and in 1848 two further companies came under its wing, l'Indemnité and la Bienfaisance. Insurance was a high-risk business; five out of every six companies to be formed failed to survive into the 20th century. Intense competition led to premium-cutting wars. L'Urbaine-Incendie was not immune; in its first 50 years of operation the company suffered eight annual losses. L'Urbaine-Vie, the life insurance company formed by the directors of l'Urbaine-Incendie, had an even more tempestuous history: founded in 1844, it was liquidated in 1851, only to be re-created by l'Urbaine in 1865. An accident insurance company, l'Urbaine-Accidents, was launched under the banner of l'Urbaine in 1880. The following year it merged with la Seine, an accident insurer set up in 1838, to form l'Urbaine et la Seine.

The third constituent part of UAP, la Séquanaise, was formed in Besançon in 1889 as a mutual insurance society—that is, an insurance company owned by its policyholders. Not venturing at first into traditional life insurance, the initial growth of la Séquanaise was based on establishing a dominant position in the personal-savings market. This area, known as capitalization, was to remain the core of the company's business. The first policy issued, which soon became a major success, was the Titre A contract. For a single FFr5 premium, the holder received the right to a maturity value of FFr100 on expiry—99 years in the future. The appeal of the contract was enhanced by the fact that policyholders' names were also entered in monthly lotteries, the winners of which received the FFr100 payout immediately. The success of contracts like this made la Séquanaise the second-largest player in the capitalization market by the end of the century. Around the turn of the century, 99-year Titre A contracts gradually were superseded by policies with shorter terms to maturity, including the variable-term contracts, which were to become the sector's staple product. Other companies were launched by la Séquanaise, operating in different fields of insurance, such as life insurance—la Séquanaise Vie, 1906—and fire and accident insurance—la Séquanaise IARD, 1924.

The early part of the 20th century proved to be a golden age of growth for insurance companies, helped by legislation in the late 19th century that obliged employers to compensate industrial workers for injuries sustained at work. The need to insure against potential liabilities brought huge amounts of new business to the insurance sector, which gained added respectability from being seen to fill a socially useful function. The importance of reliable cover being made available to industrial employers forced governments to take a more active interest in insurance companies. This led both to tighter state control, and a certain degree of state guarantee against failure.

As a result of the legislation in 1898 regarding compensation for industrial accidents, the period before World War I was marked by signs of increasing prosperity and self-confidence among UAP's forebears. In 1899, l'Union-Incendie purchased offices in the Place Vendôme in Paris, which were to become the headquarters of l'Union and later of UAP; in 1904 la Séquanaise also moved, from Besançon to a more prestigious location in Paris; l'Union-Vol, offering insurance against theft, was formed in 1909, with the addition of a personal savings arm, l'Union-Capitalisation, in 1912. From 1914, l'Union tried to make the best of wartime conditions. Instructions went out from l'Union-Vie to its network of distributing agents to press home the need for adequate insurance in such uncertain times. For a surcharge, policies could be tailored to cover risks associated with war, but l'Union-Vie undertook that any profit made on such policies would be redistributed to surviving policyholders after all claims had been met, rather than serving to enrich the company's shareholders.

Personal insurance provided much of the stimulus for growth in the period between the wars. The meager nature of the benefits on offer from the state-sponsored social security system created significant opportunities for growth in volume of life and illness insurance contracts. Life insurance showed the fastest growth in the combined business of l'Union, l'Urbaine, and la Séquanaise in the period from 1913 to 1938: total life insurance premiums of the three groups rose by 142% over the period, while fire and accident premiums grew by 106% and capitalization by 87%, after allowing for inflation. The overall premium total for the three groups grew from FFr167.5 million in 1913 to FFr352.5 million in 1938, adjusted to 1913 values.

The most important change in the history of French insurance came with nationalization in April 1946, when 34 companies—approximately half of the entire insurance sector—were taken into state control, among them l'Union, l'Urbaine, and la Séquanaise. At this stage, the nationalized companies were left to function as separate entities. Further upheaval resulted from legislation later the same year by which the government, committed to the creation of a welfare state, took over management of industrial accident compensation under the wing of the social security system. This closed off a major field of activity for the insurers—l'Urbaine et la Seine, for example, lost around half of its total business from this one change.

Nonetheless, the 20 years from 1947 to 1967 saw a sixfold increase in real terms in the combined income of the various branches of l'Union, l'Urbaine, and la Séquanaise, as French society grew richer, consumed more, and needed more protection. The life insurance branches of all three groups introduced with-profits contracts for the first time after World War II. State legislation added new business opportunities as well as taking them away: from 1958 onwards, French motorists were bound by law to cover themselves against third-party damages claims. Far from being a moneyspinner, motor insurance turned out to be a lossmaker for the insurers, partly because of the state-imposed cap on premiums, abandoned in 1962. Two years later the principle of no-claims bonuses was introduced.

Diversification went beyond insurance-related activities. L'Union became the majority shareholder in SEMICLE, a housebuilding consortium founded in 1954 in partnership with several other public-sector businesses such as Renault and Banque Nationale de Paris (BNP), with the aim of meeting the growing demand for new accommodation in Paris and elsewhere. In the insurance sector itself, expansion into reinsurance continued with the acquisition by l'Union's nonlife insurance branch of a majority stake in les Réassurances. Abroad, the nationalized insurers spread their operations far and wide: in 1961, the life and nonlife branches of l'Union did more than FFr100 million of business in 64 territories outside France. By then political change had already put paid to subsidiaries in some countries: la Séquanaise liquidated its 20-year-old subsidiary in Saigon in 1952, when war broke out in Indochina, and offices in Egypt were lost in 1956 when President Gamal Abdel Nasser nationalized all insurance operations on Egyptian territory. The following year, l'Urbaine-Capitalisation abandoned North Africa altogether, and in 1962 Algerian subsidiaries ceased operation when that country achieved independence.

Despite the growth experienced by l'Union, l'Urbaine, and la Séquanaise in the postwar period, the French insurance industry had not progressed with anything like the speed or vitality of insurers in other countries, such as West Germany and the United Kingdom. In 1968 secret discussions on the future shape of the nationalized insurance sector led to the reorganization of the many state-run companies into four major groups, the largest to be known as UAP, incorporating the previously independent groups of l'Union, l'Urbaine, and la Séquanaise. At that time, l'Urbaine, with four different presidents between its five branches, most typified the inefficiency and duplication that the restructuring was designed to circumvent. La Séquanaise, by contrast, had placed all of its four branches under the authority of a single president and board of directors as early as 1949. As for l'Union, its financial position was healthy but this still left it a long way short of commanding the kind of resources available to its major foreign competitors.

Together, the three constituent parts of UAP accounted for 11% of France's nonlife market in 1967, 20% of life insurance, and 70% of insurance-linked personal savings. Between them, they held investments worth FFr7.5 billion. Overnight, UAP became the second-largest insurer in Europe, after Allianz of West Germany.

The constituent parts of UAP were placed under the direction of a single president—Dominique Leca, formerly president of l'Union—and board of directors, but otherwise retained separate management and separate identities. This was a temporary arrangement: Leca's task was to merge the parts into a unified whole. This was not without problems, since the companies had operated in competition with each other until the enforced merger.

Major restructuring took place in 1969, with the creation of UAP branches for nonlife, life assurance, and savings. The nationwide distribution networks established by the three earlier groups were not, for the time being, forced to integrate. At the same time, UAP came under pressure from the government to decentralize operations, and between 1969 and 1975 the number of staff employed outside Paris rose from 900 to 2,700. Along with rationalization, the application of modern information technology (IT)—introduced by Leca into l'Union in the late 1950s—was pursued throughout UAP. Within a few years, the insurance sector became one of the largest users of IT in France. In 1970, UAP expanded further with the acquisition of two insurers, la Vigilance-Vie and l'Avenir.

Before Leca reached the end of his presidency, the legal status of UAP changed. In 1973, the UAP holding company, Société Centrale, was reincorporated as a limited company with capital of FFr168 million, divided into 1.68 million shares of FFr100 each. The state retained 95% of the capital, with the other 5% being distributed free to UAP's 8,000 staff.

When Leca retired in 1974, his successor as president, René Delestrade, inherited a company whose commercial prospects were hampered by generally worsening economic conditions in France and the rest of the world. Other problems were peculiar to UAP's situation as a state-controlled entity: premiums in some business areas were still subject to state guidance and, having been protected for nearly three decades from the need to be entrepreneurial, UAP found that its costs were measurably higher than those of its private-sector rivals. At this time, the invasion of UAP's traditional businesses by mutual assurance companies, particularly in motor insurance; by banks, in life insurance and savings; and by foreign insurers, in all areas, led to progressively fiercer competition. Meanwhile, industrial relations went through a confrontational period, with unions accusing management of acting against workers' interests, and losses continued to pile up in UAP's motor insurance operations. However, the life insurance and savings divisions continued to thrive.

The drive into new territories and new businesses resumed. Leca had renewed UAP's expansion into French-speaking African states—Cameroon, Morocco, Gabon, Tunisia, and the Ivory Coast—in the early 1970s, and Delestrade's presidency saw significant moves such as the acquisition of 33.4% of New Ireland insurance in 1975—UAP became the majority shareholder in 1987—and the takeover of Commerce Group in Canada in 1977. In the following year, UAP Assistance was launched on the domestic market, offering subscribers emergency medical and technical assistance.

Delestrade's retirement in 1980 initiated the first of four changes of president in eight years at UAP. Delestrade was followed by Pierre Esteva, who served from 1980 to 1983; Yvette Chassagne, who followed in 1983 and stepped down in 1986; Jean Dromer, whose service lasted from 1986 to 1988, and Jean Peyrelevade, who was appointed in 1988. The frequent comings and goings at the top contributed to the problems of management discontinuity and lack of long-term strategy, aggravated by uncertainty over privatization resulting from the 1987 stockmarket crash.

UAP came under attack in the media for its lack of accountability to clients. A campaign begun in 1982 called for a full disclosure of how UAP employed the billions of francs under its supervision, and condemned the tight-lipped discretion which for years had characterized UAP's relationship with the outside world. Yvette Chassagne, the first woman to be made head of a national organization of UAP's size, went on the counterattack with a revolutionary media-based campaign promoting the openness of the company. UAP formed customers' consultative committees to aid communication between employees and clients. Chassagne's priority was publicity; she appeared in person in television advertising, and used sponsorship—for example, of an expedition to the North Pole—to raise the company's profile.

Repeated attempts to change UAP's inherently bureaucratic mentality met with limited success during the 1980s. Despite the efforts of his predecessors, President Jean Peyrelevade had to make efforts to ensure that more responsibility was given to employees, and to end secretive decision-making. Many in the group had hoped that privatization would provide the opportunity for just such a shakeup. In 1986, parliament had approved an opposition motion to push ahead with privatization, but the worldwide stockmarket crash of October 1987 made flotation impractical. The following year, Peyrelevade announced his wish to float 49% of UAP, with the long-term aim of reducing the state's holding to 34%. In 1990, no more than 25% of the group's capital could be floated publicly. In February 1990, however, UAP took advantage of a change in the law allowing foreign investors to own shares in state-controlled companies. As part of a rights issue that increased UAP's capital by FFr10.5 billion, FFr2 billion of shares was offered to investors outside France, and was received enthusiastically.

A further change in UAP's ownership took place with the exchange of 10% share stakes with BNP. The share swap was accompanied by agreements on commercial cooperation, including an arrangement to distribute UAP nonlife policies through BNP branches, which would provide UAP with an extensive addition to its sales network. The cross-shareholding was made possible by a change in the law allowing banks to become shareholders in insurance companies.

Having gained a significant presence in the banking sector with its 1984 acquisition of Banque Worms, UAP stepped into personal banking in 1988 by becoming the first insurance company to launch a credit card. This did not herald substantial diversification beyond the core activity of insurance, according to Jean Peyrelevade, who commented on the occasion of the 1990 share issue: "We do not by any means have the intention of becoming a financial conglomerate. We want to be a universal insurer, present in all segments of the insurance business and present internationally, especially in

Europe.'' UAP's operations abroad, reorganized since 1984 into UAP International, provide over 40% of the group's total income, and make it the second-largest insurer in Europe, with a 1.5% market share. Peyrelevade's stated aim is to double this share.

Significant minority stakes have been built up in other large European insurers, including 31.9% of Royale Belge, number two in Belgium; 25% of the United Kingdom's Sun Life; and, in France, 34% of Groupe Victoire, which is controlled by Compagnie Financière de Suez, but which gives UAP a notable interest in major German insurer Colonia.

UAP's reinsurance business was merged in 1989 with Scor SA, in which UAP holds a stake of 40%. Scor is the world's fifth-largest reinsurer, and in the late 1980s made significant acquisitions of its own in Italy and Germany. UAP's personal life and medical insurance business should thrive on the opportunities for growth presented by the French state's gradual retreat from health-care and pension provision.

The history of UAP and its predecessors has been shaped by government policy; UAP's future success will depend far more on its ability to perform as a market-driven, quasi-independent company. Large-scale expansion is likely to take the form of equity participation in other providers of financial services. Deals like the share swap with BNP, and a smaller exchange in 1990 with Banco Central in Spain, will open up new avenues of business, give UAP experience of new markets, and forge links with new partners.

Principal Subsidiaries: UAP Vie; UAP Incendie Accidents; UAP Assistance; UAP International; Navigation et Transports (64%); Banque Worms; Compagnie Financière de Rombas (80%).

Further Reading: Ruffat, Michele, Edouard-Vincent Caloni, and Bernard Laguerre, *L'UAP et l' Histoire de l'Assurance*, Paris, UAP, 1990.

—A. Bowden

USF&G® INSURANCE

USF&G CORPORATION

100 Light Street
Baltimore, Maryland 21202
U.S.A.
(301) 547-3000
Fax: (301) 547-3700

Public Company
Incorporated: 1896 as United States Fidelity and Guaranty Company
Employees: 12,600
Assets: $13.60 billion
Stock Exchanges: New York Pacific London Basel Geneva Zürich

USF&G Corporation is a large U.S. property and casualty insurer that markets its insurance solely through independent brokers and agents. An early leader in the casualty-surety field, the company's emphasis in this area has changed little since the early 20th century and still includes automobile, workers' compensation, other liability, homeowners, and commercial multi-peril insurance lines, as well as surety bonds. USF&G's operations were expanded in 1959 to include life insurance, and again in 1985 through the formation of a financial-services subsidiary.

While the company has suffered major loses in each of the last three decades, during that same span it has consistently ranked among the top 15 writers of property and casualty policies in the United States. With life insurance business on the rise and a major acquisitions phase for its financial-services segment completed, the company entered the 1990s expecting to offset profit declines associated with the cyclical casualty business.

USF&G Corporation was organized as a holding company in 1981, but its roots lie in the formation of what is now its lead subsidiary, the United States Fidelity and Guaranty Company (USF&G Company). The USF&G Company was founded in 1896 by John Randolph Bland, a former secretary for the Baltimore Merchants and Manufacturer's Association.

Bland's duties with the merchant's association had included handling credit and collection inquiries, and the observations he made inspired him to start USF&G Company. He noticed that attorneys who served as collectors often had difficulty recovering debt payments. In response to this problem, Bland devised a plan for a company that would serve a dual function, as both collection agency and surety company.

The backbone of Bland's plan was to establish a nationwide listing of attorneys who would serve as collection agents. Attorneys would be sought in each county and major city in the country. They would pay to have their name listed, and also be required to take out a surety bond from the company, guaranteeing prompt remittance of collections.

Bland was able to raise slightly more than $250,000 in subscribed capital, with Baltimore, Maryland, businessmen making up the bulk of contributors. During the early months of 1896 Bland's plan took shape, and in March the company was incorporated. USF&G's first board of directors included businessmen as well as politicians, and included former seven-time Baltimore Mayor Ferdinand C. Latrobe, and former Maryland Governor Frank Brown, who became the company's first president. Less than a year into operations Brown resigned.

Bland, initially first vice president and general manager, was named Brown's successor. As president for the next 26 years, he guided company expansion under a growth-with-profit philosophy. Bland based his philosophy—which called for widespread operations—on the theory that as risks are spread they grow smaller and more predictable.

USF&G's original charter was limited to issuing surety bonds and insuring the fidelity of attorneys and other persons of trust. At the outset, Bland expected the bulk of business to come from personal suretyship; but the number of commercial attorneys listed soon came to double the number guaranteed for personal collections, and almost immediately corporate suretyship became the dominant business.

That business, during the waning years of the 19th century, consisted largely of fidelity bonds issued for bank employees, fiduciaries, and public officials, as well as contract performance bonds after 1898. By 1899 the company was operating in every state and territory in the country.

USF&G marked the new decade by amending its charter to include burglary insurance. Business mushroomed, and during the early 1900s USF&G became known as one of Baltimore's Big Four bonding and insurance companies. Encouraged by success at home, the company established operations in Europe in 1901 and in Canada two years later. While Bland and other surety pioneers had convinced Americans of the need for corporate suretyship, the act of indemnifying employees did not catch on in Europe, and overseas operations were closed in 1903, as Canadian efforts were beginning.

USF&G became embroiled in fierce domestic competition during the early 1900s, characterized by rate wars and agent raiding. Chief among USF&G's early competitors was the National Surety Company of New York. A 20-year rivalry between the two companies began in 1902, after a National Surety agent named William B. Joyce promised to deliver business to Bland's company following a sellout of the New York firm. However, at the last minute, National Surety was reorganized and Joyce named a vice president of the company.

In 1904 the Great Baltimore Fire claimed the USF&G headquarters building, but company records were saved. During the next two years USF&G used a church as its headquarters, before moving into a new office on the site of its former headquarters.

Having established itself as a national powerhouse in the surety field, USF&G entered the casualty business in 1910. The growing use of automobiles and the passage of workers' compensation laws in a number of states made entrance into the field timely and profitable. Aside from automobile and workers' compensation, the company's initial casualty lines included coverage of plate-glass windows, steam boilers, and flywheels. Health insurance lines and a forgery bond were also introduced in 1910.

Casualty business, led by automobile and workers' compensation insurance, grew quickly during the next several years. USF&G's contract bond business also blossomed as a result of increased road construction.

When the United States entered World War I in 1917, USF&G began writing casualty insurance for army supply bases under construction. Meanwhile, increased premium sales led to the wartime development of a separate automobile department, four subsections in the company's liability department, and expansion of the company's branch system. By 1919 casualty insurance premiums more than doubled total proceeds from all bonding lines.

In 1921 USF&G celebrated its 25th anniversary, and Bland announced that the "largest surety-casualty corporation in the world" would add a seven-story annex to its headquarters. Six years later that annex was increased in size to 12 stories. In 1922 USF&G formed the affiliate Fidelity Insurance of Canada.

Bland and Joyce, who had risen to president of National Surety, reconciled their 20-year-old differences in 1922, just a year before the USF&G founder died. Bland's son, R. Howard Bland, was named president, moving up from the position of vice president and secretary, which he had held for seven years.

During the prosperous mid-1920s USF&G undertook several new ventures, which included the guaranteeing of real estate mortgages. No new mortgages were covered after 1928, but the brief endeavor came back to haunt the company during the Depression. Manufacturers and wholesalers credit insurance was also introduced during the mid-1920s, but the company soon abandoned this field as well, believing it required too many specialists.

Other endeavors had more promising results. In 1927 the company reinsured and then absorbed the Atlantic Surety Company of Raleigh, North Carolina. The following year the affiliate Fidelity and Guaranty Fire Corporation was organized to write fire and allied insurance coverages, that were not written by USF&G Company. Aviation-risk coverage was added to USF&G lines in 1928.

With the decade drawing to a close, USF&G was in its best financial shape ever. The October 1929 stock market crash and ensuing Depression brought significant loses to the company, and severely taxed surplus funds. USF&G took its biggest loses from mortgage guarantees, but no line escaped problems. Premium volume plunged, and the company's investment portfolio lost much of its value. The company continued to meet its liability obligations, but by 1931, its surplus had dropped to $4.7 million, down from a solid $17 million just three years earlier.

Dividend payments were suspended in 1931, and the following year E. Asbury Davis became president. Davis had been a director since 1923 and chairman of the board since late 1931. Bland traded positions with Davis, and became chairman. Market values continued to depreciate, and in June 1932 the company reduced the par value of its one million shares of common stock from $10 to $2, transferring $8 million from its capital account to its depleted surplus fund.

Shortly after the stock market crash USF&G had established reinsurance operations in Europe, but, prompted by rumors of war, USF&G once again withdrew from Europe in 1934. At the same time, the U.S. economy was improving, and a new advertising campaign was introduced to boost the company's image. During the next several years USF&G used the slogan "consult your insurance agent or broker as you would your doctor or lawyer." The company recorded its first postcrash profit in 1935, and revenues continued to increase throughout the remainder of the decade. In 1940 USF&G resumed dividend payments.

After the United States entered World War II in 1941, USF&G once again began covering government projects, and was commissioned by the United States to serve as a fiduciary agent in writing war-damage insurance. This led to USF&G's involvement in government undertakings which included the construction of the Pentagon Building outside Washington, D.C., and the atomic bomb project at Oak Ridge, Tennessee. Nearly 500 USF&G employees participated in the war effort, and some agencies closed while others were maintained by wives, sisters, and daughters.

USF&G celebrated its 50th anniversary in 1946. Postwar prosperity contributed to a record-high $105 million in assets logged for the year, making USF&G the largest insurance and surety company in Maryland and the fourth largest in the country.

In 1947 USF&G's charter was amended to include fire and allied lines, which had been written through the company's affiliate, Fidelity and Guaranty Fire Corporation, since 1928. Anticipating future corporate reorganization, the subsidiary Fidelity and Guaranty Insurance Underwriters was formed in 1951. Established in Ohio, the new wholly owned subsidiary gave the company power to write fire and allied lines in states where multi-line laws had not been approved. In 1952 USF&G and Fidelity and Guaranty Fire Corporation merged, after a majority of states had legalized multiple-line companies.

In 1955 Davis retired as president, leaving the company in its strongest financial position to date. Charles L. Phillips, a 35-year USF&G veteran, succeeded Davis as president and chairman. In 1959 William E. Pullen was named president, and the following year he replaced the 70-year-old Phillips as chairman.

Before the decade drew to a close, USF&G completed its move to becoming a full multiple-line insurer with the December 1959 formation of the wholly owned subsidiary Fidelity and Guaranty Life Insurance Company.

In 1962 USF&G began steps to acquire the New York—based Merchants Fire Assurance Corporation and the Merchants Indemnity Corporation. Later that year, Walter J. Jeffrey, was named president. Jeffrey, a former senior vice president and chief administrative officer, assumed the additional duties of chairman after Pullen's retirement in 1965.

The company sustained losses in 1964 and 1965 resulting

from a high number of severe storms accompanied by heavy losses in its automobile and fire lines. Despite the setbacks, sales were on the rise, and in 1965 the company announced that its five-year-old life insurance subsidiary had passed the $500 million premium mark.

Merchants Fire Assurance and Merchants Indemnity were purchased in 1965 and the following year merged into USF&G, adding both capital and business to USF&G operations. In 1969 a second life insurance subsidiary was added with the acquisition of Thomas Jefferson Life Insurance Company, which carried a license to do business in New York, the only state where Fidelity and Guaranty Life was not operating.

USF&G entered the 1970s with new leadership and plans for a new corporate headquarters. In 1970 Williford Gragg was named president, and also became chairman two years later. In 1971 the company broke ground for a 40-story headquarters in Baltimore.

Just as the company was settling into its new building, the insurance industry began to sag. By the time the relocation was completed in late 1974, several insurance companies were on the verge of bankruptcy. The industry recession hit USF&G hard, and the company posted record loses of $1 million a month between January 1973 and October 1974.

By 1975 the company was back in the black. Two years later the subsidiary Fidelity and Guaranty Insurance Company was incorporated in Iowa. The new company was chartered for all lines of property-casualty insurance except medical malpractice and international, but emphasized homeowners and automobile coverage.

Underwriting profits grew throughout the late 1970s, and in 1978 Gragg reported that USF&G had the highest underwriting profit of any stock insurance company in the country. Later that year, Jack Moseley became president. Moseley also assumed the additional duties of chairman two years later.

In October 1981 the USF&G Corporation was formed as a holding company to organize the group's 13 subsidiaries. Company officials at the time said the reorganization would "give management greater flexibility in planning and executing business."

Two months later the company agreed to a $3.5 million settlement with as many as 20,000 employees, former employees, and job applicants accusing USF&G of sex and race discrimination in hiring practices. The company agreed to set goals for the hiring of women and minorities, but did not admit to discriminatory practices.

During the early 1980s premium volume fell, and the company responded by cutting prices to meet competition and increasing reserve funds to accommodate growing claims. Earnings were hurt, but profits were maintained through investment earnings and the use of tax credits.

In 1982 the company established the Light Street Income Fund, which operated during the next four years. The fund's goal was to generate investment income by purchasing high-yield stocks in time to get dividends and then selling those stocks to investors at a predetermined price. Two years later USF&G became one of the first insurance companies to offer tax-exempt bonds. The $170 million offering included 50 different sets of bonds, mostly with maturities after the year 2000.

In 1984 an industry recession and investment losses caught up with USF&G. The recession, precipitated by low premium prices, rising costs, and a number of expensive natural disasters, resulted in a $64 million net loss for USF&G. In 1985 that deficit grew to $108 million.

Despite the losses, the company continued to expand and diversify. Three wholly owned subsidiaries were formed to operate as offshore reinsurers. F&G International Insurance was formed in 1984, in Bermuda; St. George Reinsurance was formed in 1985, in the British West Indies; and St. Andrews Insurance was formed in 1986 in Barbados.

In 1985 the wholly owned subsidiary USF&G Financial Services Corporation (FSC) was formed. A five-year acquisitions phase for FSC followed, resulting in the acquisition or formation of more than 20 subsidiaries, which now operate as independent companies in more than 40 countries. Today FSC operations include four divisions: investment management offers pension, employee benefit, and financial consulting services; human asset management provides multinational strategic and operational consulting; marketing management provides a range of administrative and development services; and capital asset management offers domestic and overseas computer sales and leasing services.

In 1986 USF&G erased its deficit and began looking for investment opportunities. The company launched a Swiss franc bond in 1987, and the following year the company introduced its Pacholder Fund to sell high-yield low-rated bonds. Both the Pacholder Fund and the eurobond offering met cool receptions, and the company's investments lost $225 million in 1987 and 1988. In 1988 USF&G purchased Citicorp's investment-management unit for $102.5 million, as part of a five-year plan to spend $200 million enhancing investment yields.

Some of USF&G's more novel income-generating strategies drew fire from the Securities and Exchange Commission (SEC). In 1988 the company reached a resolution with the SEC regarding charges that it violated disclosure and accounting rules. The charges stemmed from the company's handling of Light Street Income dividends between 1984 and 1985. USF&G did not admit to the disclosure violations, but did agreed to follow regulations in the future.

In December 1989 the Fidelity Insurance Company of Canada was sold for $68 million. USF&G closed the decade with a declining profit margin, after posting a record profit of $373 million in 1987. Investment income quadrupled during the 1980s to an unprecedented high of $898 million in 1989, while assets grew to a record-high $13.6 billion.

During the 1980s life insurance sales grew from $9 million to $898 million and came to represent nearly 10% of company revenues and better than 25% of all assets. FSC revenues tripled between 1987 and 1989, rising to $182 million. FSC also closed the decade expecting to reduce its operating costs, having concluded a major acquisition phase which it plans to build on.

USF&G continues to follow John Randolph Bland's growth with profit philosophy. The company aims to continue increases from life insurance and financial-service subsidiaries, in order to offset large property and casualty losses in the future. With over 5,300 independent agents and brokers marketing property and casualty insurance, the flagship USF&G Company started by Bland nearly a century ago is expected to remain firmly entrenched as the corporation's dominant business.

Principal Subsidiaries: United States Fidelity and Guaranty Company; Fidelity and Guaranty Insurance Company; Fidelity and Guaranty Insurance Underwriters, Inc.; Automated Products, Inc.; F&G Re, Inc.; F&G International Insurance, Ltd. (Bermuda); St. George Reinsurance, Ltd. (British West Indies); St. Andrews Insurance, Ltd. (Barbados); Fidelity and Guaranty Life Insurance Company; Thomas Jefferson Life Insurance Company; USF&G Financial Services Corporation.

Further Reading: Fitzpatrick, Clarke J., and Elliott Buse, *Fifty Years of Suretyship and Insurance*, Baltimore, Maryland, Horn Shafer Company, 1946.

—Roger W. Rouland

VICTORIA

VICTORIA HOLDING AG

Victoriaplatz 1
D-4000 Düsseldorf
Federal Republic of Germany
(211) 4770
Fax: (211) 477 2222

Public Company
Incorporated: 1853 as Allgemeine Eisenbahn-Versicherungs-Gesellschaft
Employees: 8,700
Assets: DM22.10 billion (US$13.08 billion)
Stock Exchanges: Berlin Düsseldorf

VICTORIA Holding AG is the fourth-largest insurance group in Germany, offering coverage in all branches of life and non-life insurance. During its history, VICTORIA has been responsible for several innovations in the German insurance industry, despite a generally cautious approach to development. Any major changes have been carried out only after the most careful consideration. VICTORIA has been accused of being slow to adapt, but its conservative policy has helped it to reach its current position in the German insurance world.

VICTORIA is the result of the combination of several insurance companies whose names have changed over more than 135 years. It became a public limited company on September 26, 1853, under the name of the Allgemeine Eisenbahn-Versicherungs-Gesellschaft (the General Railway Insurance Company). Railway insurance was an innovation introduced by Otto Crelinger, a banker and member of the board of the Berlin-Potsdam Railway Company.

In 1843 Otto Crelinger applied for a royal license to found a railway transport insurance company, claiming that "it is a peculiarity of steam transport that it carries risks which in part cannot be anticipated and in part cannot be avoided, even with the greatest of care, and which are certainly of a more diverse and dangerous nature than those involved in any form of land transport up until now." It was Crelinger's idea to include the insurance charge in the fare and thus to insure all passengers automatically for a sum of between £150 and £450 (1,000 to 3,000 taler).

It took ten years for permission to be granted by King Friedrich Wilhelm IV of Prussia. This delay resulted to some extent from initial fears that insurance of this type might encourage railway companies to neglect safety standards. However, Crelinger's request was granted finally, and he became the first managing director of the company that was later to become VICTORIA. His company extended coverage for railway transport to related insurance against death, accidents, or fire on the railways, but it remained primarily a transport insurer. Its transport insurance turned out to be very popular and was extended to apply to land and inland waterway transport in 1858.

In 1861 the company became involved in life insurance, introducing the innovative product of a life insurance policy with premium refunds. This policy proved to be a major success. One year after its introduction, the company's total life insurance premium income exceeded one million taler, which was quite a considerable sum. Ever since then, the company's main strength has been in life insurance.

In 1875 the company took the name of VICTORIA zu Berlin Allgemeine Versicherungs-Actien-Gesellschaft (VICTORIA of Berlin General Insurance PLC), a step that underlined the company's diversification into general insurance. The premium refunds were extended to various other types of insurance, such as accident insurance in 1883.

Under the leadership of Otto Gerstenberg, VICTORIA focused its attention still further upon the general public. Gerstenberg's career with the company started in 1873, when he joined as a mathematician. In 1888 he became general manager and from 1913 to 1931 was president of the board. From 1892 onwards the company offered popular insurance (Volksversicherung) to its customers. This was a type of life insurance new to Germany, a plan that VICTORIA took from the United Kingdom after studying the Prudential's policies in London. Anyone could take out this type of insurance without the need for a doctor's examination. The insurance payments were low and were collected weekly by 2,600 uniformed employees. This type of popular insurance became extremely successful. The company's particular attachment to popular insurance was to last until the 1970s, when, due to a buoyant economy and the provisions of the welfare state, insurance of this kind became obsolete. Under Gerstenberg's management, VICTORIA had become Germany's largest life insurance company by the turn of the century and Europe's largest by 1913.

At the same time VICTORIA branched out further, with the founding of the affiliated VICTORIA Feuer-Versicherung AG (the VICTORIA Fire Insurance Company, VFC) in 1904 being of major significance. VFC's activities included insuring not only against fire, but also against burglary, floods, accident, liability, and all kinds of car insurances. It grew quickly and became VICTORIA's second most important area of business. To this day VFC is VICTORIA's most important subsidiary with several subsidiaries of its own.

Before World War I, VICTORIA had become a multinational enterprise. It extended its activities to all north, east, and west European countries, excluding the United Kingdom, and to the Balkans. World War I was extremely damaging to VICTORIA. The losses from the withdrawal of foreign investments were minor compared with those resulting from all the claims made during the war and, worse still, from the hyperinflation that followed.

Economic historians have characterized the interwar period as a time of relative stagnation. This was certainly VICTORIA's experience. The company had to adapt to new economic conditions. Fearing the negative impact of political events, VICTORIA acted with characteristic caution. In 1923 it founded two subsidiaries in the Rhine, VICTORIA am Rhein Allgemeine Versicherungs-Actien-Gesellschaft, offering life insurance, and VICTORIA am Rhein Feuer- und Transport-Versicherungs AG for fire and transport insurance. In the same year French and Belgian troops occupied the Ruhr district, causing widespread fear that this region would be separated from the rest of Germany. In founding its VICTORIA am Rhein subsidiaries, the company had safeguarded its interests.

All these changes were time-consuming and expensive to implement. Only by 1927 had VICTORIA's assets returned to the level at which they had started at the turn of the century. However, VICTORIA still remained ahead of its competitors. In 1932 it accounted for 80% of all the premiums collected from abroad by German insurance companies. This situation was in line with its prewar status. The tradition of popular insurance continued as well and was strengthened in 1939 by the acquisition of VICTORIA's rival in this field, Vorsorge.

In 1938, after the Treaty of Munich, which brought the Sudetenland in Czechoslovakia under Nazi rule, VICTORIA took over the activities of a Prague company in that region. World War II, however, caused VICTORIA major setbacks. Not only did it have to cope with unfavorable conditions in western Germany, but it also lost its main geographical area of activity, central and eastern Germany, as well as its direct foreign investments. Furthermore, VICTORIA's head offices in Berlin were destroyed.

By its 100th anniversary in 1953, however, VICTORIA had recovered its standing. During the 1950s, it steadily strengthened its position in the insurance market. Once more, its policy was one of cautious growth. By this stage the company chiefly operated from Düsseldorf, Berlin having become an isolated outpost of the free market economy. Although the company retained an office in Berlin, new offices were built in Düsseldorf in 1952. Four years later, the two affiliated companies of VICTORIA am Rhein were merged with the two VICTORIA zu Berlin companies.

The 1960s were years of economic prosperity for West Germany. VICTORIA showed steady and rapid growth. During the decade, its annual premium income tripled and two important steps were taken. VICTORIA bought the Deutscher Automobil Schutz Allgemeine Rechtsschutz-Versicherung AG (DAS), a relatively small company specializing in legal expenses insurance. DAS gradually expanded to become Europe's largest company in its particular area of insurance. The second important step for VICTORIA was a return to overseas expansion. The company made direct investments in the Netherlands, Austria, Portugal, and Spain. Furthermore, VICTORIA took part in the International Group Program, formulated by the U.S. insurance company John Hancock Mutual Life. The program was aimed at multinational enterprises wishing to offer uniform insurance to all their employees worldwide. A similar scheme, the International Network of Insurance, was started in 1979. Through these ventures VICTORIA became the leading German insurer in such international insurance networks.

The 1970s saw a further tripling in VICTORIA's premium income, despite the overall downturn in the world economy. In 1971 VICTORIA branched out into health insurance. It bought 10% of the German Gilde-Versicherung AG from the U.K. Sun Alliance group. Rumors spread that the Sun group would draw VICTORIA into its orbit. These were vigorously denied by VICTORIA's chief executive, Heinz Schmöle, who emphasized his group's determination to remain independent.

Past events were remembered and prompted Shmöle's denials when VICTORIA's shares were subjected to considerable speculation during the winter of 1969–1970. In the 1920s VICTORIA had found itself the object of one of the first German attempts at a hostile takeover bid in Germany. This attempt—by the Michael group—was unsuccessful, but caused anxiety at VICTORIA. Again in 1983 a group led by two large German competitors, tried unsuccessfully to buy a majority shareholding in VICTORIA. Although VICTORIA made a tempting target, chief executive Dr. Jannott stated in 1989 that rumors of takeovers did not worry the company at all. VICTORIA's shareholders are diverse, Münchener Rück being the largest of 8,000 shareholders with its 12% stake.

VICTORIA has made little effort to diversify outside insurance. Its acquisition in 1970 of a 25% stake in the paper company Zellstoff AG was sold off a little later. The only investment it retained outside insurance was in a small shipping company.

VICTORIA has never tended to run large advertising campaigns or give special offer premiums. Instead, it has built its success on a reputation for reliability and efficient service. The group focuses on private customers, from whom more than 70% of group premium income derives. Today VICTORIA, together with DAS, has a network of nearly 200 local branches throughout Germany, dealing with up to 7,000 claims per day. In the field of car insurance, the company prides itself on its ability to settle claims within seven days.

In 1989 VICTORIA underwent major restructuring after a decade of careful planning. It was the first restructuring in over 135 years of the group's history and was intended to increase VICTORIA's competitiveness. Under German law, the Spartentrennungsprinzip prevents life, health, damages, accident, legal, or credit insurance from being offered together by a single company. Insurers wishing to provide cover in these different areas are forced to create a separate company for each, with one company in charge. VICTORIA was unusual among Germany insurance groups in having a life insurance company at its head, because life insurance had dominated VICTORIA's activities, especially in its first 60 years. Other insurance groups in Germany were headed either by damages insurance companies, by reinsurance companies, or by holding companies. There was always a danger that with a life insurance company at the head of the VICTORIA group, it might suffer badly from losses in other group companies dealing with damages insurance or reinsurance, which by their nature carry considerably greater financial risk.

The VICTORIA group therefore created a holding company, VICTORIA Holding AG, bringing itself in line with other German insurance groups and allowing itself greater flexibility. VICTORIA Holding has majority shareholdings in three main enterprises, VICTORIA Life, VICTORIA Insurance,and VICTORIA Health, which in turn hold investments in several insurance companies in Germany and abroad.

The restructuring of the group is only one of the steps by which chief executive officer Jannott has tried to increase VICTORIA's competitiveness. On an international level he has strengthened VICTORIA's relationship with Japan's Dai-Ichi Mutual Life and its investment in the United States in the Munich-American Reinsurance Company (MARC) group, in which VICTORIA has a 10% shareholding. The MARC group's capital has increased 11-fold since 1985. In Europe, VICTORIA has occasionally taken over small private firms such as the Greek company Olympiaki in 1989.

VICTORIA seems committed to slow but sure expansion. Its policy in Europe is to rely not on takeovers, but on building up the number of its customers and encouraging them to take on other insurance policies offered by the group. The main instrument for establishing international contact with customers is DAS, market leader in its field in most European countries.

Within Germany and in preparation for competition in Europe, many financial services companies have joined together to offer customers Allfinanz, or a financial supermarket, where a variety of financial services are made available under one roof, and to which customers can go both for banking and insurance. VICTORIA has denied wanting to become involved in Allfinanz. It has, however, developed close working ties with the Dresdner Bank over several decades, and holds a 25% stake in the building society Heimstatt Bauspar AG. Since January 1990 it has entered into close co-operation with the Bayerische Vereinsbank and Dresdner Bank. Each company arranges for its customers to benefit from services that the other offers. Jannott has stated that there should be no merging of the two companies' roles and that VICTORIA will remain a specialized insurance company.

Principal Subsidiaries: VICTORIA Krankenversicherung AG (75%); VICTORIA Lebensversicherungs AG; VICTORIA Versicherung AG; VICTORIA Rückversicherung AG; VICTORIA Grundstückverwaltungs-Gesellschaft GbR; D.A.S. Deutscher Automobil Schutz Allgemeine Rechtsschutz-Versicherungs-AG (90%); VICTORIA International Aktiengesellschaft fur Beteiligungen; VICTORIA-Volksbanken Versicherungs-AG (Austria, 74.6%); Nieuwe Hollandse Lloyd Verzekerings-Groep N.V. (Netherlands); Landwehr Beheer N.V. (Netherlands).

Further Reading: *VICTORIA Versicherung 1853–1928*, Berlin, VICTORIA, 1928; "80 Jahre VICTORIA-Versicherung," *VICTORIA Zeitung* number 8/9, 1933; *Hundert Jahre VICTORIA Versicherung*, Berlin, VICTORIA, 1953; *Die Hundertjahrfeier der VICTORIA-Versicherung*, Berlin, VICTORIA, 1953; *Im Zug der Zeilen*, Düsseldorf, VICTORIA, 1978.

—Harm G. Schroter

winterthur

"WINTERTHUR" SCHWEIZERISCHE VERSICHERUNGS-GESELLSCHAFT

Post Office Box 357
General Guisan-Strasse 40
CH-8401 Winterthur
Switzerland
(052) 85 11 11
Fax: (052) 23 66 20

Public Company
Incorporated: 1875 as Schweizerische Unfallversicherungs-Actiengesellschaft in Winterthur
Employees: 17,329
Assets: SFr31.99 billion (US$20.75 billion)
Stock Exchanges: Zürich Basel Geneva

"Winterthur" Schweizerische Versicherungs-Gesellschaft ("Winterthur" Swiss Insurance Company) was the first firm in Switzerland founded especially to sell accident and liability insurance. It has the largest share of the Swiss insurance market and has expanded to become an international insurance group. Through its own branches and subsidiaries and in cooperation with other insurers it offers cover worldwide in all classes of the business.

The company takes its name from Winterthur, the industrial town in the Swiss canton of Zürich known not only as an important center of the engineering industry but also as the home of several major art collections. The founders of the company were well-known entrepreneurs and businessmen, responding to a need created by the increased risk of workplace accidents that had accompanied the industrialization process. The pattern for the company had been set principally by the workmen's compensation insurance available in Germany since the early 1870s. The founders were encouraged by the fact that Switzerland was about to introduce regulations, on the German model, governing legal liability for risks to railway and factory workers.

The man who took the initiative was Colonel Heinrich Rieter, member of the Swiss parliament and owner of the Winterthur spinning mill and engineering works Johann Jakob Rieter & Co. This company had pioneered the industrialization of Switzerland, equipping its factory, around 1800, with the first spinning plant in the country. Napoleon's continental blockade of English imports favored domestic Swiss production. Soon the mill acquired its own repair shop, which before long was also producing new machines. In 1832 Johann Jakob Rieter & Co. dispatched a complete set of spinning machinery to Austria. In due course the engineering works would include railway carriages and weaponry among its products.

On February 10, 1875, under the chairmanship of Heinrich Rieter, the heads of Winterthur's leading enterprises met to discuss the possibility of founding a Swiss accident insurance company. They agreed that such a company was needed, and as the result of Rieter's efforts the founding meeting of the Schweizerische Unfallversicherungs-Actiengesellschaft (Swiss Accident Insurance Joint-Stock Company) took place in Winterthur on March 2, 1875. The share capital, fixed at SFr5 million, was subscribed by Swiss—mainly Winterthur—industrialists and businessmen. Three thousand shares were issued first, each with a nominal value of SFr1,000, for a down-payment of 20%; the remaining 2,000 shares were deferred to 1880, with a premium payable by other buyers.

From the outset Heinrich Rieter was the venture's driving force. He had made a close study of the problems of insurance and of Swiss industry's need for Swiss insurance cover. Salomon Volkart and Heinrich Sulzer-Steiner also played leading roles in the founding of the company. In 1851 Salomon Volkart, together with his brother Johann Georg Volkart, had created the Winterthur firm Gebrüder Volkart (Volkart Brothers), producing Indian raw cotton and European manufactured goods. Heinrich Sulzer-Steiner was the true founder of Switzerland's engineering industry. In 1860 he had gone into the Winterthur engineering firm Gebrüder Sulzer (Sulzer Brothers) founded by his father Johann Jakob Sulzer and his uncle Salomon Sulzer. In 1856, with the English engineer Charles Brown, Sulzer-Steiner had developed the valve steam engine, and in 1866 he had introduced steam central heating. Heinrich Rieter was the first president of the "Winterthur" advisory board, with Salomon Volkart as vice president. From 1884 until his death in 1906, Heinrich Sulzer-Steiner headed the body later designated the supervisory board. On many occasions members of the well-known industrialist family of Sulzer, serving on board and committee, have had a decisive influence on "Winterthur's" development.

The company's statutes had to be approved by the cantonal government of Zürich. The charter, dated March 27, 1875, bears the signature of the famous Swiss writer Gottfried Keller, who as clerk to the canton of Zürich drew up official documents. This document authorized the company to begin supplying individual and collective accident insurance. Around the same time, the firm later to be known as the Zürich Insurance Company, which had been founded in 1872 under the name of the Versicherungs-Verein to offer reinsurance and marine insurance, extended its activities to include accident insurance.

"Winterthur's" practical organization and its charges and conditions were taken in their essentials from those current in neighboring Germany. Accordingly the company chose as its first head not someone specializing in insurance, but the Winterthur town notary Friedrich Gysler, a distinguished lawyer and an acquaintance of the founders. He held office for only a year. In 1876 he was succeeded by

C. Widmer-Kappeler of Zürich. The first people to be insured were the employees of the town of Winterthur's large industrial firms. From the beginning, a chain of agencies was built up in the individual Swiss cantons. When the Swiss Factory Act came into force in 1878 the company began selling liability insurance, and it promptly availed itself of the opportunities for foreign business provided by the regulations. This tendency to seek business abroad was shared by the Zürich Insurance Company. Both firms took the idea of accident and liability insurance from Germany, first introducing the two types of cover into Switzerland and then selling them worldwide. In 1875 "Winterthur" set up branches in Germany, Austria-Hungary, Belgium, Holland, Luxembourg, Denmark, and Norway. A year later it opened a general agency in Paris for France and the French colonies; it even established itself in Finland.

The rapid and large-scale spread of the company network in Switzerland and Austria entailed heavy expenses that could not at first be met by the volume of business achieved. In addition, premiums were clearly too low in some countries—tariffs cannot simply be transferred indiscriminately from one state to another—and liability insurance was hit by several exceptionally heavy compensation payments. The annual report for 1891 speaks of a marked disparity between premium income and the total disbursed in settlement of claims. In both the following years the figures were even worse, and in 1883 the managing director, C. Widmer-Kappeler, fled abroad. At the general meeting there was a proposal, later withdrawn, that the company go into liquidation. Under new management, however, the firm made a recovery without having to cut benefits. Premium rates were adjusted to actual costs, types of cover not in demand were withdrawn, and expenses were reduced by the adoption of appropriate economies.

Gradually the firm got back on an even keel. It owes its successful development from the turn of the century onwards chiefly to the personality of Gottfried Bosshard. He came to "Winterthur" from the judiciary in 1898 and served the firm from then until 1940, ending up as delegate to the board of directors. It is largely thanks to Bosshard that the company achieved its fine reputation. In a wider sphere, he played a major part in the evolution of insurance law in Switzerland; the University of Zürich recognized this achievement in 1929 by making him an honorary doctor of law.

At the same time as it was increasing its geographical spread—moving into Spain, for example, in 1910—the company was also anxious to introduce new lines of insurance and types of cover. In the field of accident insurance, provision was now offered against death from acute infectious illness; in liability insurance, cover for material damage was added to that hitherto available only for personal damage. Finally, "Wintherthur" started offering burglary-and-guarantee insurance and, following a decision of the general meeting of 1900, extended its activities to the whole area of material damage insurance. With so much of its business in Switzerland, "Winterthur" suffered considerable losses as a result of the legal transfer, effective from April 1, 1918, of workmen's accident insurance into the Swiss state accident insurance scheme. The company was forced to rechannel its activities into individual accident and liability insurance and foreign business.

The balance was redressed mainly by the introduction of motor insurance. In 1918, when it took over the portfolio of the German firm of Agrippina, "Winterthur" started selling comprehensive motor insurance, which had been initiated by Agrippina in 1901. To this was added motor-vehicle third-party insurance, which had been obligatory in some Swiss cantons since before World War I. In the 1920s "Winterthur" expanded considerably in this area, which today constitutes a basic component of its income.

Under Heinrich Fehlmann, who succeeded Bosshart, first in 1918 as director and then in 1921 as chairman of the board, the firm continued to grow and prosper. Premium income rose from SFr4 million in 1890 to SFr30 million in 1930 and SFr69 million in 1940. When inflation brought about the decline of the German currency, German insurance companies—which at the time occupied an important position in the Swiss market—could no longer meet their commitments in Swiss francs and had to give up business. The resulting gaps in the market made way for the establishment of life insurance companies in Switzerland, notably, in 1923, the "Winterthur" Lebensversicherungs-Gesellschaft ("Winterthur" Life Assurance Company). Like its parent company, "Winterthur" Life soon turned its attention abroad, starting with Belgium, Germany, and France. It is now the second-largest life assurance company in Switzerland.

The growth of the two companies found visible expression in new head office buildings, completed in 1931 and now quite a feature of the Winterthur scene. The most striking effect made by the complex on the townspeople is reflected in its nickname, "Accident Tower."

Immediately after the end of World War II, "Winterthur" set about rebuilding its extensive foreign business. There were branches in most of the countries of Western Europe; to these were added property and life insurance acquisitions, beginning with Europeia—in Portugal in 1958, followed by Union et Prévoyance of Belgium in 1964 and Heimat of Austria in 1966. In 1962 "Winterthur" had succeeded in taking over the Eidgenössische Versicherungs-Aktien- Gesellschaft (Federal Insurance Company Ltd.) of Zürich, founded in 1891 and steeped in Swiss tradition. In the same period "Winterthur" extended its own activities to include many new types of business, particularly in the area of engineering insurance. This process of expansion was taken into account in 1975, the year the company celebrated the centenary of its founding, when it changed its name to "Winterthur" Schweizerische Versicherungs-Gesellschaft ("Winterthur" Swiss Insurance Company). In 1978 the "Winterthur" Rechtsschutz-Versicherungs-Gesellschaft ("Winterthur" Legal Insurance Company) came into being.

During the 1970s and 1980s, under the leadership of Hans Braunschweiler, the Winterthur insurance group kept up and intensified its postwar policy of expansion through the purchase of other companies. In two decades these acquisitions led to an eightfold increase in "Winterthur's" gross premium income, which rose from SFr1.3 billion in 1968 to SFr10.4 billion in 1988. Two-thirds of these premiums came from foreign business, concentrated mainly in Western Europe and North America.

"Winterthur" already had explored the possibility of trading in the United States in the 19th century, but had been put off by the distance involved and the $100,000 security required. After much reflection and investigation, "Winterthur" opened a New York City branch in 1936. In 1950 "Winterthur" bought the American Casualty Company, to which it handed over its own existing U.S. insurance clientèle. After the sale of this company to the present Continental National American, "Winterthur" in the United States was left with only reinsurance. It came back into the U.S. direct insurance business in 1982, when it acquired the important, long-established Republic Insurance group of Dallas, Texas. In 1988 the Southern Guaranty Companies of Montgomery, Alabama, joined "Winterthur," followed in 1990 by the General Casualty Group of Sun Prairie, Wisconsin. "Winterthur" now operates a widely varied organization in the United States. Its Canadian activities began with the acquisition of two companies now doing business under the name of Citadel General, Toronto.

At home in Switzerland, in 1987 "Winterthur" bought a majority holding in the Neuenberger Versicherungs-Gruppe (Neuchatel Insurance Group), founded in 1869. "Winterthur" has always laid emphasis on its trade in Germany, centered largely on insurance for the medical profession. In 1987 "Winterthur" took on a minority holding in the Nordstern insurance group. The Transatlantische Gruppe (Transatlantic), acquired in 1989, confines itself mainly to brokerage and direct marketing of motor insurance. In the United Kingdom, "Winterthur" sells life insurance through Provident Life, founded in 1877. In 1989 the Churchill Insurance Company Ltd., specializing in telephone sales of car insurance, started up. The acquisition of the Intercontinentale insurance group in 1988 tripled "Winterthur's" share of the Italian insurance market and secured its position there.

In addition to these successful exercises in partnership, since the beginning of the 1970s "Winterthur" has been arranging cooperation deals with well-known insurance companies for the purpose of protecting its clients' interests in areas where it has no branches or subsidiaries of its own. It was this kind of cooperation that led in 1976 to the establishment of the Norwich Winterthur Group, in which "Winterthur" and the U.K. firm Norwich Union each hold 48.5%, and the Japanese Chiyoda Fire and Marine, the remaining 3%. The Norwich Winterthur Reinsurance Corporation Ltd., of Norwich, forms part of this cooperative venture. In 1979 Itaú Winterthur Seguradura S.A. (Itaú Winterthur Insurance Company Ltd.) was set up in Sao Paolo, Brazil, as a base from which to cover South America.

With its tight trading network "Winterthur" has a large share of the Swiss insurance market. In the 14 most important countries where it operates, it does so directly through its own branches and subsidiaries. In addition, cooperative ventures are opening up new insurance markets in the Middle East and Far East and in Africa, Australia, and South America. With an eye to the European Common Market, Union et Prévoyance was rechristened Winterthur-Europe Assurance in 1989 and in 1990 provided with branches in four more countries; in addition, Winterthur-Europe Vie (Winterthur-Europe Life Assurance) was set up. These companies allow "Winterthur" to extend its protection right across the frontiers of the European Community.

Principal Subsidiaries: Winterthur Life; The Federal; Winterthur Legal Assistance; Vitodurum Insurance Company; Vitodurum Holding; Neuchatel General (71.6%); Neuchatel Life; Winterthur-Europe Insurance (Belgium, 98%); Winterthur-Europe Life (Belgium); Winterthur Garantie (Germany); Transatlantische (Germany); telcon (Germany); Winterthur (Austria); Winterthur Assicurazioni (Italy); Intercontinentale Assicurazioni (Italy); Veneta Assicurazioni (Italy, 96.4%); Venete Vita (Italy); SAPA (Italy, 99.9%); Winterthur (UK) Holdings; Provident Life (U.K.); United Standard (U.K.); Winterthur Insurance (U.K.); Churchill Insurance (U.K.); Europeia (Portugal, 99.2%); Winterthur U.S. Holdings; Winterthur Reinsurance of America (U.S.A.); Southern Guaranty (U.S.A.); General Casualty (U.S.A.); Republic Financial Services, Inc. (U.S.A.); Commonwealth Insurance (Cayman, 91%); Winterthur International (Bermuda, 71%); Winterthur-Participagões (Brazil); Winterthur Canada Financial; The Citadel Life (Canada); The Citadel General (Canada).

Further Reading: Schweizerische Unfallversicherungs-Gesellschaft in Winterthur, Winterthur, "Winterthur" Lebensversicherungs-Gesellschaft, 1932; *Winterthur Lebensversicherungs-Gesellschaft in Winterthur 1923–1948,* Winterthur, "Winterthur" Schweizerische Versicherungs-Gesellschaft, 1948; *Schweizerische Unfallversicherungs-Gesellschaft in Winterthur 1875–1950,* Winterthur, "Winterthur" Schweizerische Versicherungs-Gesellschaft 1950; Markun, Sylvia, ed., *Facetten Europas—100 Jahre Winterthur-Unfall, 50 Jahre Winterthur-Leben, Mitteillungen* Jubilee Edition, Winterthur, "Winterthur" Schweizerische Versicherungs-Gesellschaft, 1975; *100 Jahre Winterthur Versicherungen,* Winterthur, "Winterthur" Schweizerische Versicherungs-Gesellschaft, 1975; Koch, Peter, "Der schweizerische Beitrag zur Entwicklung des Versicherungswesens," *Schweizerische Versicherungs-Zeitschrift,* 1985; Koch, Peter, "Versicherer aus aller Welt in Deutschland," *Versicherungskaufmann,* July 1987; *Von Winterthur in alle Welt,* Winterthur, "Winterthur" Schweizerische Versicherungs-Gesellschaft, 1990.

—Peter Koch
Translated from the German by Olive Classe

THE YASUDA FIRE & MARINE INSURANCE COMPANY, LIMITED

THE YASUDA FIRE AND MARINE INSURANCE COMPANY, LIMITED

26-1, Nishi-shinjuku 1-chome
Shinjuku-ku, Tokyo 160
Japan
(03) 3349-3111
Fax: (03) 3348-3046

Public Company
Incorporated: 1887 as Tokyo Fire Insurance Company, Ltd.
Employees: 10,830
Assets: ¥2.80 trillion (US$19.48 billion)
Stock Exchanges: Tokyo Osaka Nagoya Kyoto Hiroshima Fukuoka Sapporo Niigata

Japan's oldest fire insurance company, The Yasuda Fire and Marine Insurance Company, Ltd., is a global leader in the non-life insurance industry. As its roots in fire and marine insurance diminished, Yasuda Fire expanded into automobile and personal insurance in the latter half of this century. The company's greatest growth, however, has come from its innovative maturity-refund-type insurance—policies that entitle the policyholder to a percentage of the amount insured upon maturity and offer dividends from the premiums. In addition, Yasuda Fire has developed comprehensive financial services. With these services, the company hopes to sustain its current international presence, as well as its leadership in the non-life insurance industry in Japan.

Tokyo Fire Insurance Company, Ltd. was established in 1887 as Japan's first fire insurance company. A merchant, Seisuke Yanagawa, developed the basic framework for the insurance company, but differences among the founders caused Yanagawa and other to leave the organization within the first year. Yanagawa, who later became a Buddhist priest, is considered to be its founder. Taketsura Yui became the first president. He was replaced in 1889 by Shosuke Orita.

The new company worked to cultivate an awareness of fire insurance, and five branch offices were added within a year. Fires themselves helped to spread awareness, but the Great Yokosuka Fire of 1890, which destroyed 830 homes, nearly toppled the young enterprise. Though Tokyo Fire's commitment to reimbursement generated credibility and more clients, it also resulted in debt. Tomoyuki Hayashi replaced President Orita, who stepped down after accepting responsibility for the consequences of the Yokosuka fire. Hayashi was followed by Norinago Ando, who used his personal assets to help the company when it covered losses from three more large fires in the 1890s, but financial restructuring became necessary.

A leading Japanese entrepreneur, Zenjiro Yasuda, accepted the challenge. Creator of the Yasuda *zaibatsu*, a large financial group, he is considered the founder of present-day Fuji Bank and Yasuda Mutual Life Insurance Company. Between 1893 and World War I, Tokyo Fire grew steadily. In the economic fecundity following the Russo-Japanese War, competition within the fire insurance industry posed a problem. This difficulty was resolved in 1907 when Tokyo Fire joined four other leading companies to form the Fire Insurance Association, whose regulations would help manage competition. This period also marked the company's entry into the Chinese market.

Japan's economic prosperity during World War I extended to the fire insurance industry, generating still more competitors. The postwar depression of 1920 and related industry slump, the death of Zenjiro Yasuda in 1921, and the Great Kanto Earthquake of 1923 left Tokyo Fire in dire condition. Government assistance was required by most insurance companies to meet costs incurred by the earthquake. By 1926, in an ailing world economy, Japan entered a major depression. The lifting of the gold embargo in 1930 caused a decline in property values that decreased premium income. The fire insurance industry saw many company failures or consolidations; in 1927, Daiichi Fire joined the Yasuda group because of business setbacks of their principal shareholders.

Under the leadership of Yasuda's son, Zennosuke, Tokyo Fire had begun hiring university graduates—an innovation at the time—and had expanded its policy-holder base beyond the previous Tokyo concentration. The company also expanded into Asia and Europe. In 1931, Tokyo Fire increased its insurance coverage to include personal accident, credit, burglary, automobile, and glass. In 1936, President Takafusa Shijo was succeeded by Kanji Minami, who was then vice president and an industry leader. Minami would later become chairman of The Joint Fire Insurance Association of Japan, while still president of Tokyo Fire.

The 1930s presented further challenges. A fire destroyed the Shirokiya department store in Tokyo in 1932. Two years later, all fire insurance claims records were broken by a huge fire in the port city of Hakodate. The Sino-Japanese War in 1937 brought an increase in business both in size of policies and in premiums paid. Unchecked competition among insurers continued.

Minami was succeeded by Suehiko Hayashi in 1939. Hayashi was then the vice president of Imperial Marine. As World War II escalated, the non-life insurance industry was stalled. Along with other companies, Tokyo Fire closed offices and halted European operations, moving instead into China, Southeast Asia, and the Pacific. The war also drained the industry of manpower. During World War II, Japan's insurance laws were extensively revised. These changes were implemented by 1940, giving the industry's minister considerable power. Non-life insurance firms, which had numbered 48 in 1940, were reduced to 34 by 1943. There were only 16 by the war's end.

The non-life insurance companies included in the Yasuda group were consolidated into two by 1943—Tokyo Fire and Imperial Marine. The following year, on the government's recommendation for merger, Tokyo Fire, Imperial Marine, and First Engine and Boiler joined to become Yasuda Fire and Marine Insurance Company, Ltd., under President Sotaro Tojura.

Imperial Marine was founded in 1893 by four men, one of whom was Zenjiro Yasuda. The company adopted a policy of low-risk, gradual growth. In 1918, Imperial Marine entered the fire insurance industry. Operations in this field, as well as the origins through Yasuda, brought the company into close contact with Tokyo Fire, including the sharing of a president and other top positions prior to their merger.

Founded in 1908, First Engine and Boiler Insurance Company, Ltd., was Japan's first insurance company to specialize in steam-boiler coverage. Although begun in the recession following the 1904–1905 Russo-Japanese War, the company enjoyed steady growth until steam boiler use was reduced by the spread of electricity in factories in the mid-1930s. First Engine was authorized in 1938 as the government-sanctioned inspector of boilers, which led to an increase in business, but the government advised the company to merge in 1943.

A massive earthquake in 1943, coupled with fear of air raids on the Japanese mainland, prompted regulation that placed the non-life insurance industry under the complete control of the wartime government. The law required war insurance to be added to fire insurance. Profits from the war insurance were given to the government, which covered all war claims.

After World War II ended in 1945, Yasuda Fire faced economic restructuring when the largest *zaibatsu* were broken up by the occupation authorities to end control of the Japanese economy by a relatively few families. This challenge was dwarfed by one other: Japan's devastation by war. Nearly one-fourth of the homes covered by Yasuda Fire had been burned or damaged, and fires continued for up to three years after the bombing had stopped. While claims mounted, the number of policies written declined. The marine insurance sector suffered similar difficulties; low insurance coverage was coupled with increasing repair costs.

During more than six years of Allied occupation, the Japanese non-life insurance industry was further regulated under antitrust laws and laws to encourage the development of labor unions. The industry established a rating association based on a U.S. model.

Yasuda Fire's second president, Bun-ichi Higaki, replaced Sotaro Tokura in 1949. Yasuda Fire's management group was then replaced by employees from within the company, further breaking ties with the Yasuda *zaibatsu*.

The Korean War began in 1950, and the resultant reconfiguration of powers led to the 1951 peace treaty between Japan and 48 countries, as well as the Japan-U.S.A. Security Treaty. The country then regained its independence.

During this time, Yasuda Fire concentrated on recovery along with the rest of the nation. Foreign operations were resumed in 1949. By 1953, company personnel were studying insurance systems abroad. Yasuda Fire also became a pioneer in the application of computer systems to the insurance process.

The country's economy had regained strength by 1955. Soon the automobile industry bloomed. The higher rate of traffic accidents led to compulsory auto liability insurance in 1956. Yasuda Fire, in efforts to hold down risks, did not initially participate in this growth area, although auto insurance would later become a major portion of its sales. Between 1955 and 1960, Yasuda Fire applied itself to real estate acquisitions, internal restructuring, capital building, and overseas operations. In 1959, a Yasuda operation commenced in Brazil, and a New York subsidiary was established in 1962.

Until 1963, when Takeo Miyoshi became president, fire insurance and casualty insurance were the largest source of premium income for Yasuda Fire. Under Miyoshi, the company changed its marketing policy to place prime emphasis on automobile insurance. In just over ten years, Yasuda Fire was at the top of the compulsory auto liability insurance industry.

In 1964 Japan joined the International Monetary Fund and the Organization for Economic Cooperation and Development. As a result, industry restraints were lifted and competition increased in the insurance industry. Yasuda Fire responded with increased marketing efforts and the development of new insurance product lines. A strong earthquake in 1964 prompted the company to develop earthquake coverage, offered two years later. In 1969 Yasuda Fire and other leading nonlife insurance companies introduced the sale of long-term comprehensive insurance based on a maturity-refund policy. The premium income in the first year of sales broke all records.

Yasuda Fire began the industry's first agent training system in 1971. The early 1970s also saw great expansions in the company's presence overseas, including Norway, Belgium, Southeast Asia, and Guam. Foreign premiums reached the ¥67.6 trillion mark by 1975.

President Miyoshi led a strategy he called "expansion and balance" during the 1970s, exemplified by the new company headquarters, completed in 1976, and the establishment that same year of the Yasuda Kasai Fine Art Foundation and the Seiji Togo Memorial Yasuda Kasai Museum of Art. Despite the two oil crises of that decade and related economic slowdown, Yasuda Fire increased its assets, which reached the ¥500 billion mark in 1977, and developed further its presence overseas with the establishment of a European and U.S. department.

Yasuda Fire embarked on the 1980s with fresh strategies and a structural overhaul. Strategies involved the expansion of markets, the balance of performance of insurance lines, and general efficiency. The organizational overhaul included a new legal department and more emphasis on public relations. After leading the company as president for 17 years, Miyoshi became chairman in 1980. Vice president Yasuo Miyatake took over the presidency. Office automation increased and policy innovations continued. By 1982, company assets had reached the ¥1 trillion mark. In 1983, Yasuo Goto assumed the presidency as the global recession induced by the oil crises began to abate. At this time, 30% of Yasuda Fire's assets came from its various maturity-refund insurance policies, making the management of those funds a high priority. Under Goto, the company moved toward financial services, additional forms of personal insurance such as long-term women's insurance, and greater computerization. In 1986, Yasuda Fire began marketing medical insurance.

The next year, the company topped the ¥2 trillion asset mark. Yasuda Fire observed its centennial with several cultural events, including the purchase in 1987 of Vincent van Gogh's masterpiece, *Sunflowers.* This purchase, at $39.9

million, tripled the previous record-high payment for a work of art. Yasuda Fire explained that van Gogh began the first of the seven *Sunflowers* in 1888, when the company started operations; only one painting of the series was destroyed—in the 1945 bombing of Nagasaki. This masterpiece was added to the collection of Yasuda Fire's art museum, which contains more than 600 works of art, including pieces by Pablo Picasso, Pierre Auguste Renoir, Paul Gauguin, and Grandma Moses. In 1988, the museum featured an exhibition of modern French painting on loan from Leningrad's Hermitage museum.

On the eve of its centennial, Yasuda Fire was the 2nd-largest non-life insurance company in Japan and the 15th-largest insurance organization. In 1988 and 1989, the company focused on global expansion and comprehensive financial services. There were overseas offices in 21 countries in 1989, and financing services were focused on small and mid-sized businesses and on individual clients.

Over its history, Yasuda Fire has shifted from insuring property to insuring people. The fire and marine policies on which it built its reputation, maintained through wars and natural disasters, were overtaken in the 1980s by automobile and personal accident insurance. The insurance line of maturity-refund insurance policies especially helped Yasuda Fire to attain its current position as a leader in the industry.

Principal Subsidiaries: Yasuda Building Management Co., Ltd.; Yasuda Kasai Information Technology Co., Ltd.; Yasuda Claims Research Co., Ltd.; Yasuda Agency Association Ltd.; The Yasuda Marine Service Co., Ltd.; Yasuda Business Service Co., Ltd.; The Yasuda Training and Planning Co., Ltd.; Yasuda Loan Service Co., Ltd.; Yasuda System Development Co. Ltd.; Yasuda Credit Card Co., Ltd.; Yasuda Career Bureau Co., Ltd.; The Yasuda International Investment Management Co., Ltd.; Yasuda Research Institute Co., Ltd.; Yasuda General Finance Co., Ltd.; Yasuda Credit Co., Ltd.; Yasuda Kasai International (U.S.A.), Inc.; Yasuda Kasai Realty, Ind. (U.S.A.); Yasuda Fire & Marine Insurance Company of America (U.S.A.); The Yasuda Fire & Marine Company of Europe Ltd. (U.K.); Yasuda Claims Limited (U.K.); PanFinancial Insurance Co., Ltd. (U.K.); The Yasuda Fire Investment (Europe) S.A. (Luxembourg); Companhia de Seguros America do Sul Yasuda (Brazil); The Yasuda Management Service Co. Ltd. (Bermuda); The Yasuda Fire Bahama Ltd.; William S.T. Lee Insurance Co., Ltd. (Hong Kong); The Yasuda Fire Asset Management Co., Ltd. (Hong Kong); The Yasuda Reinsurance Co., Ltd. (Hong Kong); P.T. Asuransi Yasuda Indonesia; People's Trans-East Asia Insurance Corporation (Philippines); Yasuda Management (Singapore) Private Limited; Yasuda International Services Co., Ltd. (Thailand); Yasuda Bahrain Kuwait Insurance Company (E.C.).

Further Reading: The Yasuda Fire and Marine Insurance 1888–1988: A Century of Achievement, Tokyo, The Yasuda Fire and Marine Insurance Company, 1988.

—Carol I. Keeley

YASUDA LIFE

THE YASUDA MUTUAL LIFE INSURANCE COMPANY

9-1, Nishi-shinjuku 1-chome
Shinjuku-ku, Tokyo 169-92
Japan
(03) 3342-7111
Fax: (03) 3348-4495

Mutual Company
Incorporated: 1880
Employees: 24,473
Assets: ¥5.42 trillion (US$37.70 billion)

The Yasuda Mutual Life Insurance Company, Japan's oldest life insurance company, stands on its reputation as a dependable life insurer. In an ever-widening Japanese market, the company is also known as an industry pace-setter, most recently for its insurance lines aimed at Japanese women. Internationally, Yasuda Mutual has formed astute alliances to take advantage of Japan's eminent position in global financial markets while expanding its awareness of alternate investment opportunities and knowledge of new management strategies.

Yasuda Mutual's beginnings and early history are closely tied to the founding of the Yasuda *zaibatsu,* the financial conglomerate owned and managed by the Yasuda family. The group was organized following the collapse of the Tokugawa government in 1868, which had secluded feudal Japan from the rapidly industrializing West since 1639. The victorious Meiji Restoration government reopened communications with the West. It concentrated on modernizing Japan and catching up with the technologically superior Western nations. In this context, already consolidated families, such as Mitsui, quickly took advantage of new capitalist potential and government incentives, diversifying quickly and successfully. Unlike Mitsui, Yasuda had no pre-Mieji existence as a business concern. Its founding and progress were rather the vision of one man, a son of a lower class samurai, Zenjiro Yasuda.

With the rise of the Meiji government, Zenjiro Yasuda became an entrepreneur with almost reckless ambition and imagination. As a member of the board of Nippon Ginko, the Bank of Japan, he was an upstart who diluted the longer established power of the Mitsui family. He quickly began to amass newly available capital, forming the Yasuda Bank, now Fuji Bank, the center of the Yasuda *zaibatsu.* Unlike the other heads of large families—Mitsui, Mitsubishi, and Sumitomo—Yasuda consolidated his empire in banking and finance, specializing in backing small- and medium-sized traders and industrialists.

In 1880, as part of his financial empire, Yasuda founded the Yasuda Mutual Life Insurance Company. Along with the rest of the *zaibatsu* concerns, the company prospered. In 1893, the Yasuda *zaibatsu* absorbed the Tokyo Fire Insurance Company—later renamed the Yasuda Fire and Marine Insurance Company—a young insurance firm unable to survive without Zenjiro Yasuda's aid. He was also one of the largest financiers of the Russo-Japanese War from 1904 to 1905; in the aftermath of the war, the government asked Yasuda to help the troubled Hayaku Zenjiro bank survive. He proposed a government loan of ¥6 million. In 1912 the existing Yasuda Bank was incorporated with capital of ¥10 million. At the same time, the Yasuda *hozensha,* or family holding company, was formed to manage and direct all Yasuda concerns, including Yasuda Mutual. The stock for these companies was all held by family members, however, and the Yasuda group remained private.

In the 1920s, post–World War I Japan declined into severe economic depression. Nationalist radicals, many opposed to the terms of the Portsmouth Treaty that had ended the war with Russia in 1905, divided the country with rioting and political assassinations. In this tense atmosphere, Zenjiro Yasuda was not a respected man. He had been accused of profiteering after the Russo-Japanese War. In 1921, the same year Prime Minister Hara Kei was assassinated by a nationalist fanatic, Zenjiro Yasuda was killed by a disgruntled visionary incensed by the financier's refusal to fund a workers' hotel. Zenjiro's son, Zennosuke Yasuda, assumed leadership of the *zaibatsu.* Under his guidance, the conglomerate's operations were modernized; a university education, for example, became a prerequisite for many Yasuda positions.

The Yasuda *zaibatsu* survived the postwar political upheaval and economic depression to come into its own in the late 1920s. By 1928, the group was ranked behind only the Mitsui and Mitsubishi groups in total capital; in that year, the Yasuda *zaibatsu* encompassed 66 companies and reported total capital of ¥308 million. Yasuda Mutual reflected the successful trend of its parent company. By 1939 the company was reporting profit rates of 453%. In 1940 and 1941, those rates soared even higher, to 1,642% and 3,089%, respectively, surpassing even Mitsui Life. Although the Anti-Profiteering Law had been revised and extended in 1937, it did not apply to the insurance industry, thus allowing the kind of spectacular growth experienced by Yasuda Mutual in the 1930s and early 1940s.

World War II occasioned a change in the Yasuda *zaibatsu* structure. To fund the war effort, the Japanese government began forcing consolidation of major financial institutions. Although Yasuda avoided full consolidation, it did streamline family members' efforts. Hajime Yasuda, primary heir to the Yasuda empire and now head of the conglomerate, announced Yasuda's new structure in January 1942: all Yasuda family members would withdraw from related and subsidiary companies, assuming new leadership positions as board members over all *zaibatsu* concerns.

With Japan's defeat in August 1945, the organization of Yasuda again changed, this time to check the earlier move toward amalgamation. By the end of August, occupation forces had arrived under General Douglas MacArthur, Supreme Commander for the Allied Powers (SCAP). Under the SCAP administration, economic controls reversed the consolidating trend of Japanese business and enforced democratization and deconcentration of the Japanese economy. Early directives from the Allied powers included mandates for the dissolution of the *zaibatsu*, preferably according to proposals from the *zaibatsu* themselves. Responding to what they saw as an inevitable redirection of the Japanese economy, Yasuda executives assumed a leadership role in planning for the dissolution of their own group and ultimately that of other *zaibatsu* as well.

The Yasuda Plan was submitted in October 1945 and stipulated that the Yasuda *zaibatsu* would be dissolved and that Yasuda Bank would cease to control Yasuda subsidiaries. Shares held by family members in the bank, the holding company, and all other subsidiaries, including Yasuda Mutual, would be sold to a government control commission and the proceeds used to purchase ten-year government bonds. In addition, family members and executives appointed by them would resign from all Yasuda companies. The Mitsui and Sumitomo *zaibatsu* reluctantly agreed to the proposal, but Mitsubishi held out longer. The Yasuda Plan, with some revisions, was accepted by the U.S. government in November.

When the occupation ended in 1952, Japanese business reorganized itself once again along the original *zaibatsu* lines. Although the holding companies had been dissolved, the banks had remained intact; Yasuda Bank, renamed Fuji Bank, and the other *zaibatsu* banks now became the nuclei of business groups that were remarkably similar to the prewar *zaibatsu*. The families themselves never quite regained the extent of their prewar power. Mitsui was most acutely affected by the occupation; Yasuda, however, did reclaim some of its former holdings. Hajime Yasuda, the prewar *zaibatsu* chieftain who had announced the reorganization of 1942, became chairman of Yasuda Mutual after the occupation, a post he still held in the early 1990s. He also promoted other businesses that had been Yasuda subsidiaries during the *zaibatsu*'s heyday.

Despite a rapidly expanding postwar economy and the reconsolidation of the *zaibatsu*, the Japanese life insurance industry was slow to recover in comparison to other industries. By 1955, life insurance in force amounted to only 40% of the prewar amount. In the 1960s, the rate of recovery increased, with total life insurance assets doubling in the years from 1962 to 1966. Yet by 1966, life insurance assets amounted to only 5% of total assets of all Japanese financial institutions, compared with 10% before the war. In the tight money market then prevailing, most life insurance funds were loaned to emerging and expanding businesses rather than invested in negotiable securities, as had been the case in prewar Japan.

In 1987 Yasuda purchased an 18% voting stake in PaineWebber for $300 million. The investment gave Yasuda two voting positions on PaineWebber's board, an advisory board position for Yasuda President Norikazu Okamoto, and up to a 25% share in PaineWebber's common stock. The move increased the company's exposure to international money markets.

In 1988 the company established a firmer presence in the United States by forming Yasuda Life America Agency Inc., a subsidiary dedicated to strengthening and expanding insurance coverage for Japanese-affiliated companies in the United States. Internationalization through foreign investment also continued to escalate. In 1989 and early 1990, facing uncertainty in the Japanese economy, Chairman Yasuda and President Okamoto invested in foreign bonds rather than Japanese government bonds, increasing foreign bond assets to ¥821 billion, a 34% climb over the previous year. Such diversifying investments reflect Yasuda Life's strong commitment to becoming a truly international company in a rapidly changing global market. In the early 1990s, as Japan's fifth-largest life insurance company, Yasuda Mutual continued to search for investment opportunities.

Principal Subsidiaries: Yasuda Life International Investment S.A. (Luxembourg); Yasuda Life International Investment (Cayman) Ltd.; Yasuda Life International Investment (B.V.I.) Ltd. (British Virgin Islands); Yasuda Life Global Investment (Jersey) Ltd. (U.K.); Yasuda Life America Capital Management Ltd. (U.S.A.); Yasuda Life International (London) Ltd. (U.K.); Yasuda Life International (Hong Kong) Ltd.; Quaestor Investment Management Ltd. (U.K); Yasuda Life International (Singapore) Ltd.; Yasuda Realty America Corporation (U.S.A.); Yasuda Properties (U.K.) Ltd.; Yasuda Life America Agency Inc. (U.S.A).

Further Reading: "Three of Japan's Zaibatsu," *The Oriental Economist,* December 1945; *The Yasuda Fire and Marine Insurance 1888–1988: A Century of Achievement,* Tokyo, The Yasuda Fire and Marine Insurance Company, 1988; Roberts, John G., *Mitsui: Three Centuries of Japanese Business,* New York, Weatherhill, 1989.

—Lynn M. Voskuil

"ZÜRICH" VERSICHERUNGS-GESELLSCHAFT

Mythenquai 2
CH-8002 Zürich
Switzerland
(01) 205 21 21
Fax: (01) 201 33 97

Public Company
Incorporated: 1872 as Versicherungs-Verein
Employees: 33,250
Assets: SFr50.65 billion (US$32.85 billion)
Stock Exchanges: Zürich Basel Geneva

"Zurich" Versicherungs-Gesellschaft ("Zürich" Insurance Company) is Switzerland's largest insurance company and the parent company of one of the most important insurance groups in the world. It has branches in all major countries and owns numerous subsidiaries. While "Zürich" at first limited its activities to accident insurance and to personal liability insurance, after World War II it extended its business into all classes of insurance.

The insurance business developed relatively late in Switzerland but has gone on to achieve great importance. Initially the basic concepts of the business were taken from neighboring countries and adapted to Swiss conditions. However, Swiss insurance practice, legislation, and expertise reached such a high level that they spread abroad. "Zürich" played a decisive part in the international activities of the Swiss insurance business from the start.

The original phase of growth in the Swiss insurance business took place in the middle of the 19th century. Its development was sustained by the beginning of industrialization, the building of the railway network, the creation of more efficient credit banks, and the enterprising spirit of the time. Switzerland was emerging at that time as a leading financial center and was set to become one of the most important countries in the insurance industry. The statesman and entrepreneur Alfred Escher made a considerable contribution to the insurance business, and with the founding in 1856 of the Schweizerische Kreditanstalt (Swiss Credit Bank) he paved the way for "Zürich's" international influence as a financial center.

Initially insurance business was carried out by specialist companies in the individual insurance classes. Two insurance companies in Basel and in St. Gall were already working in marine insurance. As exports were growing, it was felt by Swiss economists and in the country's financial circles that it was necessary to create another marine insurance company, in Zürich. Seventeen leading manufacturers and traders became members of the founding committee, formed in June 1869 on the initiative of the board of the Swiss Credit Bank. On October 9, 1869, the statutes of the Schweiz Transport-Versicherungs-Gesellschaft (Switzerland Transport Insurance Company) were approved by the ruling council of the canton of Zürich and on January 15, 1870, the company began trading. The first president of the board was John Syz-Landis and the first managing director Wilhelm Berend Witt. It was intended from the outset that the company should be international in its activities.

It soon became apparent to the young company that it required the support of considerable reinsurance, which could not be covered by existing companies. Schweiz therefore took the decision to found its own reinsurance company. The shareholders in Schweiz were invited to take a share in the proposed company through a circular letter, dated October 23, 1872, from a ten-man founding committee under the leadership of John Syz-Landis. The members of the committee already had collaborated in the founding of Schweiz and belonged to the board of the company. The new company was to be run by the firm Versicherungs-Verein and was to take on a part of Schweiz's risks in the manner of a surplus reinsurance. By November 16, 1872, the statutes had already been approved by the ruling council of the canton of Zürich. The licensing document carries the signature of the poet Gottfried Keller, who was first state clerk in Zürich from 1861 to 1876, and in that capacity signed the documents for the ruling council.

Close ties existed between the two companies thanks to the unified personnel in all their divisions, operating from one office. Together with reinsurance, the Versicherungs-Verein from its inception also dealt with direct marine insurance both at home and abroad. Substantial damage claims and fierce competition in the insurance markets caused considerable problems for the young company. The direct marine and reinsurance businesses on their own proved insufficiently profitable to sustain the young company, which consequently looked towards new fields of activity.

On a proposal put forward by the board, it was therefore decided at the Versicherungs-Verein general meeting in April 1874 to extend the company's activities to accident insurance. This class of insurance had grown rapidly in importance as industrialization spread. At first, however, this type of insurance had been limited, covering travel insurance and workers' insurance. Accident insurance first became available in England, where from 1849 the Railway Passengers Assurance Company was the first to provide insurance cover against railway accidents. Later it was to extend cover to other types of transportation. In Germany a law was first passed on June 7, 1871, which took into consideration the greater risks for employees caused by the increasing mechanization of factories. This law forced manufacturers to pay compensation for any personal injury to their workers. The increased liability made it necessary for companies to insure their work force against accidents in the factory and the requirement brought about the creation of collective workers' insurance (*Arbeiterkollektivversicherung*).

In view of the high level of industrialization occurring in the Swiss economy, it was evident that similar developments would take place in the confederation. The board of Versicherungs-Verein recognized the sign of the times and broke new ground in Switzerland with its introduction of accident insurance. The significance of this step was underlined by the change in the company's name to the Transport- und Unfall-Versicherungs-Aktiengesellschaft Zürich (Transport and Accident Insurance plc Zürich). The importance Swiss industry attached to this branch of insurance is shown by the fact that a further accident insurance company was also created in Winterthur in 1875.

"Zürich's" growth as a separate company only began with the introduction of accident insurance. Transport insurance was discontinued "for the forseeable future" at the end of 1880, and the company stopped taking on more reinsurance business. For a while the name of the company stayed as it had been, although from 1886 it added an explanatory sentence to clarify its activities, declaring that "the company deals exclusively in accident insurance." When liability insurance began to be developed in Germany as a new branch of insurance alongside accident insurance, with the two branches becoming independent of one another, "Zürich" also started offering liability insurance. The company was able from then on to offer insurance cover not only against accidents but also against employers' liabilities for assessment of damages. The expansion of business into these areas led to the company's change of name to the "Zürich" Allgemeine Unfall- und Haftpflicht-Versicherungs Aktiengesellschaft ("Zurich" General Accident and Liability Insurance plc) on December 14, 1894. The company kept this name until 1955. These changes finally brought about the complete separation of Zürich from Schweiz, although friendly relations and business contacts have been preserved. "Zürich" now began to develop into a worldwide company.

The company first had to build up its own independent work force. Until 1875 Schweiz's staff had also taken care of "Zürich's" business. The development of accident insurance required a specialized staff, both for internal running of the company and for customer services, since this insurance sector catered to a different clientele and operated within a completely different structure. This was particularly the case for liability insurance, with its complex legal aspects. In 1880 the company had 27 employees. By the turn of the century the number had grown to 140. Business in this branch of insurance was stimulated in Switzerland by laws passed between 1875 and 1881 establishing liability for railway and steamer companies as well as for factories.

Together with its activities in Switzerland, company business was extended to other areas at an early stage. The network it was to build up abroad is still its greatest asset in international competition today. The first step was taken as early as 1875 in Germany, where agencies were opened in Berlin, Hamburg, Stuttgart, and Reutlingen. Further areas of business to be developed were the Rhineland, Westphalia, Saxony, and Alsace-Lorraine, the latter at that time part of the German empire. In the same year representative offices were opened in Austria-Hungary and in Denmark. Dealings in France followed in 1878. The Berlin branch which was opened in 1880 came to take on a particularly important role in the company's further development, since it was from here that business in Denmark, Norway, Sweden, Finland, and Russia was coordinated.

At the end of 1880, with the resignation of W. Witt, "Zürich" was for the first time given its own chief executive, Heinrich Müller. He was devoted to the business and set the company on a firm footing without neglecting the continued development of its activities abroad. His successor, Fritz Meyer, came from the treasury for the town of Zürich and made sure he consolidated the company's technical reserves. During his time in office, from 1900 to 1918, the company erected its own administrative office building on the Mythenquai in Zürich, where the company headquarters are still to be found. Above all, it also developed its workers' accident insurance business in France and considerably expanded its business in offering insurance against liability in Germany, where the introduction of the Civil Code on January 1, 1900, extended the need for such insurance into numerous new areas. The company's premium income in 1900 was SFr15.4 million. Business in Switzerland accounted for SFr3.7 million of this total, while France represented the largest premium income with SFr5.5 million, followed by Germany with SFr5 million.

A decisive move for "Zürich" was the starting up of business in the United States, although "Zürich" already ran its U.S. subsidiary in Chicago in collaboration with a German fire insurance company. Zürich received the authorization to trade in the state of New York in 1912. The New York insurance commissioner had great influence on other states in the union. The U.S. accident and liability insurance company grew unexpectedly strong and brought in considerable premium income, but was also a heavy burden in terms of provisions and costs. To cover reserves, a large amount of capital was invested in U.S. dollars in the United States; after World War I this capital formed the basis for the further expansion of the U.S. company. Since then it has occupied a particularly important central role in the "Zurich" insurance group's activities. At the same time "Zürich" gained a foothold in England, Canada, Italy, and Spain. In 1925 an agreement was made with Ford, the largest car manufacturer of that time, whereby preferential insurance terms were offered on Ford cars.

While establishing branches and founding subsidiaries under its own name in foreign countries according to national law, "Zürich" also acquired domestic insurance companies. This policy, like the starting of activities in the United States and the creation of a life assurance company for the group, dates from the time of August Leonhard Tobler, who first served as vice director of the company and then became the head of Zürich from 1918 to 1927. It was under his leadership that the company developed into an internationally active insurance group, a status that has continued to grow with the acquisition of substantial insurance companies. The continuity in the management of the company has contributed to this achievement.

During the first 50 years of its existence, "Zürich's" activities were limited to damage and accident insurance. As a result of the decline of the German currency due to inflation after World War I, the German life assurance companies which held a strong position in the Swiss insurance markets were no longer able to fulfill their commitments in Swiss francs. They were therefore forced to withdraw from

Switzerland. Swiss companies filled the gaps created in the market, with the result that numerous new life assurance companies were founded there. In the course of these developments the Vita Lebensversicherungs-Gesellschaft was created as a subsidiary of "Zürich." It soon undertook business abroad, where it grew rapidly. It showed pioneering spirit when in 1926 it introduced a health service which offered regular checkups with a doctor and published medical leaflets giving advice on healthy living.

World War II caused the loss for "Zürich" of important areas of business in central and Eastern Europe. The rebuilding of "Zürich" in Germany began in Düsseldorf and Frankfurt. The Frankfurt tower block next to the old opera house became the administrative center for the German "Zürich" network in 1961. A string of further insurance companies is tied to the German branch of the company. The Deutsche Allgemeine Versicherungs-Aktiengesellschaft, founded in 1923, has concentrated particularly on offering motor insurance through direct sales. "Zürich" resumed its policy of international expansion, which had been halted by the war, in numerous other countries. The company opened many new offices as well as its own life assurance companies, in particular in the United States, Canada, the United Kingdom, and Australia.

The period after World War II was marked for "Zürich" by its development into a company dealing in all branches of insurance. Due to the systematic extension of the classes covered by the company, the branch-related balancing-out of risks was put alongside the international one. Until the beginning of the 1950s, the emphasis of activities had lain in the field of accident and liability insurance, whose dominant position was expressed in "Zürich's" slogan "The world's largest purely accident and liability insurer." The company was innovative in its introduction of these branches of insurance in major countries. The company's expansion into further sectors was reflected in its change of name to "Zürich" Versicherungs-Gesellschaft in 1955. In 1970 fire insurance was also offered by the company for the first time in Switzerland.

The acquisition of large insurance companies and groups in various foreign countries was of crucial bearing on the present scope of the company's business and a policy carried out under the management of Fritz Gerber, the chairman and for many years director general of the company. Three important examples illustrate this policy. In 1965 "Zürich" bought the Alpina Versicherungs-Aktiengesellschaft in Switzerland, which had established its own network abroad. In 1969 the Agrippina Versicherungs AG was bought from a private bank. Agrippina had been created in Cologne in 1844 as a marine insurance company and was therefore well established in the German insurance market, with a number of subsidiaries of its own. The acquisition in 1989 of the Maryland Casualty Group, with its headquarters in Baltimore, Maryland, greatly strengthened "Zürich's" business with private customers as well as doubling premium income in the United States.

From 1972, "Zürich's" centenary year, to 1990, the parent company's gross premiums rose from SFr2.3 billion to SFr6.1 billion, and those of the "Zurich" insurance group from SFr4 billion to SFr17.1 billion. "Zürich" does business worldwide in some 80 countries, with a particularly strong presence in its traditional markets in Switzerland, the United States, and Germany. Its successful international development can be attributed largely to the use the company has made of the respected name of the financial center of Zürich together with its historical role in the expansion of accident and of personal liability insurance. With a view to future business in the European Common Market, "Zürich" International companies have been established in Belgium, Germany, the United Kingdom, France, Italy, and the Netherlands and offer special Euro-policies for industrial insurance. This type of insurance will be supported by computer system Zurinet, ensuring international communication of information. With its experience in accident and liability insurance the "Zürich" group should continue with its successful development in the European industrial insurance market.

Principal Subsidiaries: Vita Lebensversicherungs-Gesellschaft; Alpina Versicherungs-Aktiengesellschaft; Agrippina Versicherung Aktiengesellschaft (Germany); Deutsche Allgemeine Versicherungs-Aktiengesellschaft (Germany); Maryland Casualty Company (U.S.A.).

Further Reading: "Zurich" Allgemeine Unfall- und Haftpflicht-Versicherungs-Aktiengesellschaft in Zürich, Die Gesellschaft in den ersten fünfzig Jahren ihres Bestehens 1872–1922, Zürich, Zürich Allgemeine in Zürich, 1923; *75 Jahre "Schweiz" Allgemeine Versicherungs-Aktiengesellschaft 1869–1944,* Zürich, [n.p.], 1945; Zürich Allgemeine Unfall- und Haftpflicht-Versicherungs-Aktiengesellschaft, *75 Jahre "Zürich," Werden und Wachsen der Gesellschaft 1872–1947,* Zürich, Art. Institut Orell Füssli AG, 1948; *25 Jahre "Vita" 1922–1947,* Zürich, "Vita" Lebensversicherungs-Aktiengesellschaft, [1948]; *Hundert Jahre "Schweiz" Allgemeine Versicherungs-Aktien-Gesellschaft Zürich 1869–1969,* Zürich, Art. Institut Orell Füssli Zürich AG, [1969]; *Die "Zürich" Gruppe stellt sich vor, 100 Jahre . . . ,* Zürich, Zürich Versicherungs-Gesellschaft, [1972]; Koch, Peter, "Der schweizerische Beitrag zur Entwicklung des Versicherungswesens," *Versicherungswirtschaft,* 1985; Koch, Peter, "Versicherer aus aller Welt in Deutschland," *Versicherungskaufmann,* July 1987.

—Peter Koch
Translated from the German by Philippe A. Barbour

MANUFACTURING

AISIN SEIKI CO., LTD.
ALFA-LAVAL AB
ARMSTRONG WORLD INDUSTRIES, INC.
ATLAS COPCO AB
BAKER HUGHES INCORPORATED
BALLY MANUFACTURING CORPORATION
BICC PLC
THE BLACK & DECKER CORPORATION
BORG-WARNER CORPORATION
BRUNSWICK CORPORATION
CARL-ZEISS-STIFTUNG
CASIO COMPUTER CO., LTD.
CATERPILLAR INC.
CITIZEN WATCH CO., LTD.
DAEWOO GROUP
DAIKIN INDUSTRIES, LTD.
DEERE & COMPANY
DEUTSCHE BABCOCK AG
DOVER CORPORATION
DRESSER INDUSTRIES, INC.
EASTMAN KODAK COMPANY
ELECTROLUX GROUP
FANUC LTD.
FLEETWOOD ENTERPRISES, INC.
FUJI PHOTO FILM CO., LTD.
THE FURUKAWA ELECTRIC CO., LTD.
GKN PLC
HALLIBURTON COMPANY
HANSON PLC
HASBRO, INC.
HAWKER SIDDELEY GROUP PUBLIC LIMITED COMPANY
THE HENLEY GROUP, INC.
HITACHI ZOSEN CORPORATION
HYUNDAI GROUP
ILLINOIS TOOL WORKS INC.
INCHCAPE PLC
INGERSOLL-RAND COMPANY
INTERCO INCORPORATED
ISHIKAWAJIMA-HARIMA HEAVY INDUSTRIES CO., LTD.
JOHNSON CONTROLS, INC.
KAWASAKI HEAVY INDUSTRIES, LTD.
KHD KONZERN
KOMATSU LTD.
KONICA CORPORATION
KUBOTA CORPORATION
LUCAS INDUSTRIES PLC
MCDERMOTT INTERNATIONAL, INC.
MAN AKTIENGESELLSCHAFT
MANNESMANN AG
MASCO CORPORATION
MAYTAG CORPORATION
MINOLTA CAMERA CO., LTD
MITSUBISHI HEAVY INDUSTRIES, LTD.
NHK SPRING CO., LTD.
NIKON CORPORATION
NINTENDO CO., LTD.
NIPPON SEIKO K.K.
NIPPONDENSO CO., LTD.
NTN CORPORATION
OUTBOARD MARINE CORPORATION
PARKER HANNIFIN CORPORATION
PIONEER ELECTRONIC CORPORATION
POLAROID CORPORATION
PREMARK INTERNTIONAL, INC.
RUBBERMAID INCORPORATED
SCHLUMBERGER LIMITED
SEIKO CORPORATION
AKTIEBOLAGET SKF
THE STANLEY WORKS
SULZER BROTHERS LIMITED (GEBRÜDER SULZER AKTIENGESELLSCHAFT)
SUMITOMO HEAVY INDUSTRIES, LTD.
TOYODA AUTOMATIC LOOM WORKS, LTD.
TRINOVA CORPORATION
TYCO LABORATORIES, INC.
VALMET CORPORATION (VALMET OY)
VARITY CORPORATION
WHIRLPOOL CORPORATION
YAMAHA CORPORATION

AISIN
AISIN SEIKI CO., LTD.

AISIN SEIKI CO., LTD.

1, Asahi-machi 2-chome
Kariya City, Aichi 448
Japan
(0566) 24-8687
Fax: (0566) 24-8894

Public Company
Incorporated: 1943 as Tokai Aircraft Co., Ltd.
Employees: 9,400
Sales: ¥406.13 billion (US$2.82 billion)
Stock Exchanges: Tokyo Osaka Nagoya

Aisin Seiki Co., Ltd. is a leading international manufacturer and supplier of sophisticated automotive components for engines, driving systems, suspensions, and clutches. It also is involved actively in the fields of die-cast parts and home appliances, manufacturing knitting and sewing machines and other apparel machinery, beds, toilet fixtures, and gas heat-pump air conditioners. Although Aisin is working to increase non-automotive sales, only about 6% of 1989 sales were non-automotive.

Aisin Seiki is one of 15 members of the Toyota Group, and is about 22%-owned by Toyota Motor Corporation, to which 70% of Aisin's products are sold. Aisin Seiki's automotive original-equipment manufacturing dominates its sales.

Aisin was founded in 1943 as Tokai Aircraft Company, by Kiichiro Toyoda, the founder of the Toyota Group. Tokai Aircraft was founded to manufacture engine parts for World War II aircraft. In 1945, at the close of the war, Tokai Aircraft switched its production to sewing machines and automotive parts, both products that had been in short supply during the war. In 1949 Tokai Aircraft Company changed its name to Aichi Kogyo Company. This change marked the beginning of Aisin Seiki Company as it exists today.

During the 1950s and 1960s, Aisin's operations were confined to Japan. As part of the Toyota Group, Aisin grew steadily, supplying parts to its parent automotive company and continuing to produce sewing machines. The year 1969 and the 1970s, however, saw aggressive international growth for the company. In 1969 Aisin reached a technical agreement for power-steering gears with Zahnradfabrik Friedrichshafen of West Germany. Aisin-Warner Limited was also established as a joint venture in 1969.

Aisin U.S.A. was formed in 1970, and in 1971 Aisin Europe was established in Belgium. A technical agreement for bumper shock-isolators was concluded with Menasco Manufacturing Company in the United States in 1972. The formation of Aisin (U.K.) Ltd. and Aisin (Australia) Pty. Ltd. also took place in 1972. The Liberty Mexicana subsidiary was formed in Mexico in 1973, and Aisin do Brasil was established in Brazil in 1974. The year 1977 saw the formation of Aisin Asia in Singapore, and in 1978 Aisin Deutschland was established in West Germany. Finally, in 1979, the Elite Sewing Machine Manufacturing Company was established in Taiwan as a joint venture.

Aisin U.S.A. was established to import aftermarket auto parts for imported cars—mostly Toyotas—in the United States and also to import specially prepared aftermarket parts for U.S.-made automobiles. In 1990 Aisin U.S.A. imported twice as many parts for American cars as for imported cars. At the same time, Aisin Seiki Company supplied a wide range of products worldwide through its network of 14 overseas subsidiaries and its branches in North America, Europe, Southeast Asia, and throughout the Pacific. In 1989, only 5% of Aisin's sales had been to export markets.

Since World War II the Japanese economy has been growing steadily. The increase in individual consumption brought about a sharp rise in domestic demand, and business expanded. Aisin answered the increased demand for consumer production and has worked consistently to improve efficiency in its factories, increase sales, and cut costs through rationalization.

Managers of the automotive sector worked during the late 1980s to increase sales of automotive-body products such as seat components, sun-roofs, and electronic control equipment for automatic transmissions. This increase contributed to an almost 10% sales growth in 1989. Automotive-body products are the largest single group of products Aisin Seiki offers, comprising about 25% of sales.

By 1990 Aisin's home and industrial and the new business sectors were still very small in scale but growing rapidly. Through expanded sales of gas heat-pump air conditioners and beds, sales increased 14.2% in 1989. Into the 1990s, intensive research and development has continued in new products such as cryocoolers, Stirling engines, and a supplemental drive unit for artificial human hearts.

During the late 1980s Aisin made efforts to strengthen project development in the United States by separating the manufacturing division from Aisin U.S.A. and creating a new subsidiary, Aisin U.S.A. Manufacturing Company. Aisin America, Inc. was also established to control jointly both the manufacturing and sales divisions.

Aisin develops highly competitive, high-performance products. The company hopes that quality-assurance activities, upgraded production efficiency, and positive sales activities will help strengthen its production system. Aisin expects to continue its economic growth. Factors such as the introduction of the Japanese consumption tax, a rise in petroleum prices, the instability of the foreign-exchange rate, and a deceleration in international business, however, may hurt business.

Principal Subsidiaries: Aisin U.S.A., Inc.; Aisin America, Inc. (U.S.A.); Aisin U.S.A. Mfg., Inc.; Liberty Mexicana

S.A. de C.V. (Mexico); Aisin do Brasil Com. e Ind., Ltda. (Brazil); Aisin Europe, S.A. (Belgium); Aisin Deutschland GmbH (Germany); Aisin (U.K.) Limited; Aisin (Australia) Pty. Ltd.; Aisin Asia Pte., Ltd. (Singapore); Elite Sewing Machine Manufacturing Co., Ltd. (50%, Taiwan); Institut Minoru de Recherche Avancee S.A. (France).

—Joan Harpham

α ALFA-LAVAL

ALFA-LAVAL AB

Post Office Box 12150
Gustavslundsvägen 147
S-102 24 Stockholm
Sweden
(08) 809900
Fax: (08) 256759

Public Company
Incorporated: 1883 as AB Separator
Employees: 20,000
Sales: SKr15.23 billion (US$2.45 billion)
Stock Exchanges: Stockholm London Amsterdam Geneva New York

Alfa-Laval's operations are divided into three divisions: industry, which accounts for approximately half the group's sales; foods 30%; and agricultural equipment 20%. The industry division comprises five business areas: automation, dosing and analyzing equipment, flow equipment, separation, and thermal equipment. The product range includes separators for liquids in food-processing and other industries, heat exchangers, dosing and analyzing, flow-control, and automation equipment. The food division's product range includes complete production lines and individual components for the food-processing industry. These products are used for the manufacture, storage, and pasteurization of dairy products and fruit juices, oils and fats, wine and beer, fish and meat, and other foods. The agricultural division has gradually shifted toward an increasing range of goods and services related to milking equipment. Aftersales services accounted in 1989 for more than half of the agricultural division's sales.

Alfa-Laval (AL) is a highly international company, with 90% of sales coming from abroad. The European Community accounted for 36% of total sales in 1989, North America 21%, Asia 12%, and Scandinavia—including Sweden, Norway, and Finland—17%. AL has subsidiaries in more than 40 countries, and its products are sold in a further 100 countries. Even though the agricultural division accounts for only one-fifth of the group's sales, Alfa-Laval traditionally is connected with agriculture.

In 1877 the Swedish engineer Gustaf de Laval began to develop the first Swedish milk separator. A year later he secured a patent for his design. Gustaf de Laval, after matriculating at Uppsala University, entered the Technological Institute, and passed the final examination in 1866. Times were hard and de Laval was forced to take a position as clerk in the general store at the Falun mines; an engineer with a first-class diploma, he weighed out nails, herring, and salt to miners. In 1867, however, Gustaf de Laval received a grant from the Swedish House of Lords, and finished his studies at Uppsala University in 1872, receiving the degree of doctor of philosophy.

The process of mechanically separating cream and milk through the physical application of centrifugal force was first exploited by the German Wilhelm Lefeldt in 1876 and the Danish L.C. Nielsen in 1878. The latter technology was acquired by Burmeister & Wain of Copenhagen in 1882. Lefeldt's and Nielsen's separators could not work continuously, unlike Gustaf de Laval's superior system. On February 26, 1878, de Laval entered into partnership with Swedish engineer Oscar Lamm. Together they founded the trading company Oscar Lamm Jr. of Stockholm. The partnership was successful, with de Laval in charge of the technical side and Lamm the financial and commercial aspects of the business. Lamm tried to interest influential agents in Europe, among these H.C. Petersen & Company, Copenhagen; Bergedorfer Eisenwerk near Hamburg; Th. Pilter, Paris; the trading firm D. Hald & Company, London; and Boeke & Huidekooper of Groningen in the Netherlands. In the company's first year of business, 1879, overseas sales accounted for 50% of the company's turnover. Foreign demand for cream separators rose sharply, and in 1883 around 80% of sales were from overseas. Almost 97% of exports were sold through foreign distributors in the more industrially advanced countries. The product in question was the energy-intensive power-driven cream separator. Manual cream separators were not introduced until 1887.

The company did not set up a domestic marketing division until four years after it had established its foreign distribution network. Its agents were already specialized in marketing dairy equipment, and cream separators complemented their existing product mix.

Four other European companies also manufactured power-driven cream separators in the late 1870s. They were Nielsen & Petersen—from 1882 owned by Burmeister & Wain—in Denmark, and Lefeldt, Fesca, and Petersen in Germany. The industrial exploitation of this process was protected by patent. The holder of the patent for the separation method secured temporary legal protection against imitation and had the opportunity of gaining an international monopoly. The patent on the application of centrifugal force for separating milk and cream, which had been granted in 1884, expired in the countries in which it had first been granted in 1892—namely in Sweden, Denmark, France, Germany, and the United States—and in countries where these patents had subsequently been registered. The reason no domestic cream separator industry had evolved in more industrially advanced countries like the United Kingdom and France is probably that foreign patent registrations from the late 1870s blocked the establishment of an indigenous industry until the beginning of the 1890s.

The work that Oscar Lamm put in during his travels produced positive results, and overseas sales increased during 1880. The growth of the business demanded another form of collaboration between the two partners and a limited company was the natural solution. On April 5, 1883, the company's statutory meeting was held, with de Laval and Lamm as the major shareholders. Oscar Lamm controlled 48% of the company shares and Gustaf de Laval 47%. The remaining 5% of the company was controlled by four individual members of the new board. Lamm was chairman of the board and managing director. In the same year the company, named AB Separator (ABS), established a subsidiary in the United States. The managing director for this new company, the De Laval Cream Separator Company, was J. H. Reall of New York. He was not an engineer, nor did he own a workshop, but edited and published the *Agriculture Review* and the *Journal of the American Agricultural Association*. The Swedish separators were manufactured by P. Sharples of Westchester, New York. In 1886, Oscar Lamm left the corporation as managing director, and was replaced by John Bernström in 1887. Gustaf de Laval was elected to the Royal Swedish Academy of Science and to the Royal Swedish Academy of Agriculture and Forestry. In the United Kingdom, the Dairy Supply Company, ABS's main customer, became sole agent.

At the same time, Gustaf de Laval constructed a turbine engine, which could be used as a power source for the separator. A very important acquisition was the Alfa patent, bought in 1889 from a German, Clemens von Bechtolsheim.

In the years prior to 1890, the Danish company Burmeister & Wain won an ever-increasing share of the market. Burmeister & Wain was a major competitor both in Denmark, where it almost ousted ABS, and after 1883 in the international market. ABS marketed a product inferior to that of Burmeister & Wain; its cream separator had a lower skimming capability. In the short term, however, ABS managed to increase its sales because of the high demand from small dairies overseas, which Burmeister & Wain could not yet cater to effectively. Burmeister & Wain's dominant market position in Denmark, ABS's decline in that market, and Lefeldt's inferior position in relation to foreign competitors in its home market, Germany, can be taken as evidence of the key importance of product quality to company growth.

When ABS began to find it hard to sell power-driven separators, it fitted them out with a new energy source—the turbine. At the same time, ABS launched its manual cream separators in the hope of reaching new groups of customers. Fourteen years were to pass before another Swedish company established itself in the Swedish and overseas markets. Before this competition had begun to seriously threaten ABS's future, the market was broadened to include more countries.

Further Swedish companies began to establish themselves in the home market when de Laval's patent ran out shortly after 1890. A new wave of patent registrations took place in the international market in the following decade, but these new entrants to the market produced manual cream separators.

In the mid-1890s, ABS diversified further by constructing industrial separators. The principle of centrifugal force was thus applied to a higher level of technology. At the same time, ABS diversified into technically simpler manual cream separators. Lower prices for these products ensured a far wider market than for power-driven separators.

By 1898 there were 35 plants worldwide manufacturing separators. Newcomers gained entry to the market by producing manual cream separators, which were not only less resource-intensive but also had a far larger market than the power-driven variety. Of the companies established after Burmeister & Wain, Lefeldt, and Fesca, the most prominent were Sharples in the United States, Mélotte in Belgium, Josef Meys, of Hennef in Germany, Edmond Garin, of Cambrai in France, and Svenska Centrifug in Sweden.

The most dangerous rival to the Alfa system was the Belgian Mélotte patent. ABS acquired U.S. exploitation rights for this patent, but never made use of those rights, and thus greatly benefited the sales of its own system in the United States. In Europe, however, the Mélotte system was a major competitor.

After 1903 there came a wave of new companies worldwide, which exploited the expired Alfa patent. With only a few exceptions, entry to the market for the new companies was secured via manual cream separators. By 1906 ABS was competing with 50 companies in the German market. By 1912, there were 135 firms operating in the international market, 70 of them in Germany and 16 in Sweden. The most important of these were AB Pumpseparator and AB Baltic in Sweden, ABS's former agents Bergedorfer Eisenwerk—which became a major competitor in 1904, Miele & Cie. and Westfalia in Germany, and A/S Titan in Denmark. These were mostly companies already established in other branches of engineering production, which had moved into separators.

In Stockholm, news had been received of impending bankruptcy at ABS's competitor, Svenska Centrifug AB. ABS's management persuaded several major Centrifug stockholders to exchange their shares at above-par rate for Alfa shares. In 1905, a majority stake was taken in Centrifug, including its subsidiary, Gloria Separator GmbH Berlin. The next competitor to be bought by ABS was one of the most important dairy machine plants in Germany and one of the largest in Europe in the early 1900s, the Bergedorfer Eisenwerk. As in the case of Svenska Centrifug, the financial position of the enterprise was too weak for the owner Carl Bergner to demand better sales terms, least of all to fight a takeover bid.

The last big competitor to be bought before World War I was Burmeister & Wain, in 1910. This firm, at the time equal in reputation to ABS, and financed with capital from its U.S. subsidiary, had been bought for SKr1.8 million so that it could be closed down; it would not have contributed anything new to ABS's existing business.

During the period 1905 to 1910, when ABS began to take over competitors, it had at its disposal sufficient capital to act without endangering its own liquidity. During the 25 years between the foundation of its first overseas subsidiary in the United States in 1883 and the takeover of Bergedorfer Eisenwerk in 1907, more than SKr100 million had flowed into the coffers of the parent company in Stockholm.

The profits of the U.S. subsidiary company, transferred between 1895 and 1914, amounted to about SKr46 million. This sum provided the stockholders' dividend, so that ABS could use the net consolidated profit of the whole company for reinvestment.

Production and organization techniques were also transferred from the U.S. subsidiary to the parent company and its European subsidiaries. In this way, ABS secured advantages of scale in the international separator market. Already in 1892 the U.S. subsidiary, the De Laval Cream Separator Company (Lavalco), was buying out all the U.S. shareholders and had built a new factory at Poughkeepsie, New York. This factory was highly profitable. In 1895 Francis Arend became managing director of Lavalco. The company had branches in Philadelphia, Pennsylvania, and in Chicago, and a subsidiary in San Francisco, California. A branch office opened in Canada in 1899, and became a subsidiary in 1912 under the name of the De Laval Dairy Supply Company. In 1899, the Swedish ABS participated in the formation of the De Laval Steam Turbine Company in the United States, by contributing US$240,000. In 1908, Gustaf de Laval left the ABS board of directors. He died five years later at the age of 67. In 1911, new subsidiaries were formed in Milan and Riga.

By the time World War I began in 1914, ABS had acquired shares in Goldkuhl & Broström, Buenos Aires. This was raised to a majority interest in 1927, when the name was changed to Sociedad Alfa-Laval. In 1960, it became a wholly owned ABS company.

In 1915, ABS's John Bernström resigned as managing director and was replaced by his nephew, Captain Erik Bernström. J. Bernström left his post as chairman of the board in 1916, to be succeeded by Ernst Trygger, and his son Richard Bernström was vice chairman until his death in 1919. The U.S. company Lavalco produced a milking machine in 1918, and four years later the first milking machine based on the Lavalco design was manufactured by ABS in Sweden. In 1922 Axel Wästfelt succeeded Erik Bernström as managing director, and the company Zander & Ingeström became ABS's sales representative for industrial separators in Sweden and Norway. In the United Kingdom the De Laval Chadburn Company was formed in 1923 for sales of milk and industrial separators. In 1925 an ABS subsidiary was formed in Helsinki, and in 1926 British De Laval Chadburn Company changed its name to Alfa-Laval Company, a wholly owned ABS company. In the same year subsidiaries were formed in Sydney, Australia, and Palmerston North, New Zealand. Between 1927 and 1929, subsidiaries were formed in Oslo, Warsaw, Danzig, and Zagreb, Yugoslavia.

In 1928, in cooperation with its Swedish competitor AB Pump-Separator, ABS bought the rival company AB Baltic. Only a few months later, ABS acquired its last major Swedish competitor, AB Pump-Separator itself. Both acquisitions, AB Baltic and AB Pump-Separator, had been more energetic than ABS in seeking ways to take advantage of the upswing in trade at the beginning of World War I, and had expanded their capacity and grown faster than ABS. These two acquisitions were the most important mergers within the Swedish separator industry.

In 1930 Jacob Wallenberg, of the Swedish banking house Stockholms Enskilda Bank, was elected to the board of directors. The U.S. company Lavalco had a bad year and ceased paying dividends until 1935. The German subsidiary Bergedorfer Eisenwerk also operated at a loss until the end of 1933. In 1934, the Alfa-Laval Company (U.K.) moved to facilities in Brentford, near London. A new subsidiary was formed in Melbourne in 1936, and the last important Swedish competitor, Eskilstuna Separator, was acquired in 1939. The outbreak of World War II brought with it an upswing for the U.S. companies. During the war, Lavalco increased the number of personnel from 700 to 2,300 and the U.S.-based Turbinbolaget increased personnel from 1,100 to 2,400. The companies' sales increased by more than five times the prewar figure. More than 50% of the Poughkeepsie factory's capacity was taken up by precision work for defense purposes, but at the German factory in Bergedorf manufacture of munitions was extremely limited. In 1942 Francis Arend, managing director of Lavalco, died and was succeeded by Ralph Stoddard, who three years later was succeeded by his son, George. ABS acquired Arend's 10% share in Lavalco.

In 1939, Alfa-Laval Company at Brentford began producing industrial separators and milking machines, and increased its sales by 70%. During World War II's so-called Skagerack blockade, Sweden and ABS were cut off from many business partners, but this period was to be a watershed between the old and the new periods.

In the United States Lavalco was given the task of constructing an oil separator for the U.S. Navy. Orders started pouring in from marine authorities, shipowners, and shipyards. U.K. Alfa-Laval Company became the European development center for these industrial separators. The research-and-development activities were transferred to Stockholm and several engineers were sent away on study visits, to rubber plantations in Southeast Asia, to olive groves in Italy, and on board whalers in the south Atlantic. Thousands of owners of olive groves and vineyards in Italy and France exchanged their ancient equipment for separators. By 1945, there were hundreds of applications for separators within industry and scientific research.

During the 1950s, the cellulose industry became the major customer group for plate heat exchangers, or PHEs—used in the pasteurizing process and for yeast manufacture. ABS's interest in these developments was taken care of in Germany by Bergedorfer Eisenwerk. PHEs could be used to comparable advantage in breweries and yeast manufacture and, later, distilleries, wine producers, and other foodstuff industries came to appreciate their virtues. One successful Swedish competitor, Rosenblads Patenter, was taken over by ABS in 1962. ABS dominated the market for PHEs in the chemical and marine sectors while the strength of its U.K. competitor, the Aluminium Plant and Vessel Company (APV), lay in the food and beverage sectors. APV is the same size as Alfa-Laval in this sector. ABS's major competitor in Europe was the family-owned company Westfalia AG in Oelde, Germany, and in the U.S. the Sharples Separator Company of Philadelphia. Westfalia and APV combined forces against ABS.

Production of separators began in Nevers, France, in 1947, and the U.K. manufacture of milking machines was moved to Cwmbron in Wales in 1949. A year later, the Italian subsidiary acquired plant and storage facilities in Muggio/Monza near Milan, and a subsidiary was established in Brussels in 1952. ABS formed new subsidiaries in Switzerland in 1960; in Bombay in 1961, and in Sao Paulo and Lima in 1962. In the same year, Turbinbolaget in the United States was sold to Lehrman Brothers. In 1963, ABS (AB Separator) changed its name to Alfa-Laval AB. Further subsidiaries were formed in Santiago de Chile and Mexico City, and in the United States Lavalco acquired G & H Products, Jay-Ro Services, and Hercules Filter. In 1966, the Spanish company Touron y Cia (Tycosa), Madrid, became a wholly owned company. A new Alfa-Laval subsidiary was formed in Amsterdam and took over industrial sales from the agent, Koopman & Company, in 1967. At the same time, a new subsidiary was formed in Zürich after Alfa-Laval's takeover of its agent, Wenger. In 1968,

Bergedorfer Eisenwerk merged with STAL Refrigeration AB of Norrköping, Sweden. The new company was known as Stal-Astra GmbH. In Melbourne, H. Hamilton Pty, Ltd. was acquired and the name changed to Alfa-Laval Separation A/S. Lavalco acquired two new subsidiaries, American Tool & Machinery, and Contherm Corporation. In the same year a subsidiary was formed in Kuala Lumpur, and a minority interest was acquired in the Japanese firm Kurose. In 1970 a subsidiary was formed in Algeria, and new office and storage facilities were built in Dublin and Melbourne. The Spanish subsidiary purchased property near Madrid, and constructed workshops, warehousing, and office facilities there. In 1974, property and buildings were purchased in Lidcombe, near Sydney. Alfa-Laval Engineering was formed in Tokyo and another subsidiary established in Caracas. In Leewarden, the Netherlands, Tebel Maschinefabrieken was acquired for the manufacturing of machines for cheesemaking. In 1975 a subsidiary was formed in Iran in connection with the delivery of two large dairy facilities. In 1976, an office was opened in Moscow, and Lavalco established production facilities in Branchbury, New Jersey, also building workshops and offices for its spray-dryer department. In the same year, Sullivan Systems of the United States, a producer of refining systems for vegetable oil, was acquired. In 1977, a subsidiary was formed in Athens; the West German subsidiary acquired Atmos Lebensmitteltechnik, a manufacturer of machines for the meat industry; STAL Refrigeration formed a subsidiary in the United States; De Laval Company (U.K.) purchased the Ibex Engineering Company, Hastings; and the OTEC project for the utilization of temperature differences in tropical oceans was initiated. In 1979 the U.S. company changed its name to Alfa-Laval Inc. and the Canadian company became Alfa-Laval Lté. In 1980, Alfa-Laval Company (U.K.) bought Dairy Supplies Hereford. A subsidiary was formed in Harare, Zimbabwe. In 1981, the West German company Bran & Lübbe, Norderstedt, a producer of dosing pumps and system and measurement instruments for the food industry, was acquired. This company has subsidiaries in a number of countries. The French Alfa-Laval company bought the firm Jean Pagées et Fils of Lyon, office and service center facilities were built in Singapore, a subsidiary was formed in Nairobi, and the Peruvian subsidiary constructed offices and warehouses. In the same period, Alfa-Laval increased its interest in the Japanese firm of Nagase-Alfa to 70% and Alfa-Laval Service was established in Japan as a wholly owned company for the sale of spare parts to the industrial sector. Alfa-Laval Contracting was formed in the United Kingdom, and in West Germany Alfa-Laval acquired 26% of the shares in G. Riedel Kälte- und Klimatechnik. In 1983 offices were opened in Cairo and Damascus to service the Middle Eastern market.

In early 1985, Alfa-Laval established a subsidiary in Portugal and an office was opened in Peking. In the same year, 100% of the free-floating shares of the Swiss company Chemap and its subsidiaries were acquired. Chemap is one of the world's largest manufacturers of fermenters. Haven Automation International, Hong Kong, along with its subsidiaries, was purchased. The company serves the marine and offshore markets in Southeast Asia. In Australia, Heat Transfer Pty. Ltd., a manufacturer of a specific type of tube heat exchanger, was acquired and a majority holding was taken in Bioter S.A., one of the market leaders in fish feed in Spain. In New Zealand, Alfa-Laval purchased the company Manus Nu-Pulse.

Two companies in Sweden and one in the Netherlands, the Tebel Pneumatiek, were sold during 1985. The total number of Alfa-Laval's employees decreased by 636 to 15,394; 5,239 new employees were appointed in Sweden and 10,155 abroad. In 1986 Alfa-Laval established a finance company, Alfinal, in Belgium. Finance companies were also formed in Denmark and West Germany, and a leasing company was started in Spain.

After a long period at the helm of Alfa-Laval, since 1922, Axel Wästfelt had retired as managing director in 1946 and was replaced by the English-born Harry G. Faulkner. Faulkner had been an auditor in the U.K. subsidiary of accounting company Price Waterhouse & Company and went on in the 1930s to become managing director of Electrolux. During Faulkner's leadership Alfa-Laval grew at a rapid pace in all traditional areas, particularly overseas. He led the company aggressively in industrial marketing, in sharp contrast with the preceding decades. In 1960, the 36-year-old Hans Stahle took over as managing director.

A principal feature of the change lay in the transfers of companies, which were carried out during the merger-happy 1960s, in consultation with Jacob Wallenberg, chairman of the board from 1960 to 1970. The factory manufacturing industrial separators was moved from the Stockholm center to Tumba, 25 kilometers southwest of the city, and in 1964 the head office followed. In 1980 Hans Stahle became chairman and was succeeded as managing director by Harry Faulkner, son of Harry G. Faulkner. During the 1980s, a large number of divisions within manufacturing and administration were formed into affiliates responsible for their own accounting. In 1989 Harry Faulkner was replaced by Lars V. Kylberg, who joined Alfa-Laval in May 1989. In October of the same year, Hans Stahle died while still executive chairman and was succeeded by Peder Bonde.

It was during the directorship of Harry Faulkner that Alfa-Laval bought the Sharples Separator Company, at the end of 1988. Sharples was until 1988 the world's largest manufacturer of decanter centrifuges, with a very strong position in the U.S. domestic market. It was the same company that had already in 1883-1884 cooperated with Alfa-Laval in the U.S. market, and since 1887 had turned out to be one of the Swedish company's most aggressive competitors, particularly in the United States. Harry Faulkner pointed out that of the 20 acquisitions made between 1986 and 1988 by Alfa-Laval, Sharples was the largest. The acquisition of Sharples was of strategic importance since it greatly strengthened the separator business which forms the core of Alfa-Laval's operations. The Sharples group has subsidiaries in some ten countries and production facilities in both the United States and Europe. The group's annual sales are approximately US$100 million. Koppens Machinenfabriek in the Netherlands and Krämer & Grebe in West Germany were also integrated into the Alfa-Laval group in 1989. During the first half of 1990, Alfa-Laval acquired TW Kutter in the United States, an engineering company and food processing equipment distributor. In the heat exchanger sector, Alfa-Laval purchased the Italian company Artec. Furthermore, joint-owned sales companies were formed in Hungary and Poland and negotiations were in progress in 1990 for the establishment of subsidiaries in other former Eastern bloc countries. Between 1985 and 1989, the number of employees in the original Alfa-Laval group was reduced by 4,000 as a result of rationalization, restructuring of production, and the sale of peripheral operations, and a total of 7,500 new employees joined the group as a result of acquisitions. The total number of employees during 1989 increased by 2,561, from 17,156 in 1988 to 19,717 in 1989. In 1989 new managing director Lars V. Kylberg pointed out that "in recent years our sales have doubled in North America. In the booming Pacific Basin, we are firmly rooted in Singapore and the Asian countries. Our overall strategy for the coming years is to grow within our core business."

Principal Subsidiaries: Alfa-Laval SA (Argentina); Alfa-Laval Equipamentos Ltda. (Brazil); Alfa-Laval Ltd. (Canada); Alfa-Laval SA de CV (Mexico); Alfa-Laval, Inc. (U.S.A.); Alfa-Laval (Hong Kong) Ltd.; Alfa-Laval (India) Ltd.; Alfa-Laval KK (Japan); Alfa-Laval South East Asia Pte Ltd. (Singapore); AG Alfa-Laval (Austria); Alfa-Laval Flow Equipment (Belgium); Alfa-Laval Industri A/S (Denmark); Alfa-Laval Industri OY (Finland); Alfa-Laval SA (France); Alfa-Laval Industrie GmbH (Germany); Alfa-Laval SPA (Italy); Alfa-Laval Nederland NV (Netherlands); Alfa-Laval Industri AS (Norway); Alfa-Laval Industriegesellschaft AG (Switzerland); Alfa-Laval Company Ltd. (United Kingdom); Alfa-Laval (Australia) Pty Ltd.; Alfa-Laval (NZ) Ltd. (New Zealand); Alfa-Laval Agrar GmbH (Germany); Bran & Lübbe GmbH (Germany); Alfa-Laval Agri International AB; Alfa-Laval Food Engineering AB; Sattcontrol AB; Alfa-Laval Separation AB; Alfa-Laval Thermal AB.

Further Reading: Wohlert, Claus, *Framväxten av svenska multinationella föreag*, Stockholm, Almpvist & Wiksell International, 1981; Fritz, Martin, *Ett världsföretag växer fram. Alfa-Laval 100 år, Del II: Konsolidering och expansion*, Stockholm, Alfa-Laval AB, 1983; *The Growth of a Global Enterprise: Alfa-Laval 100 Years*, Stockholm, Alfa-Laval AB and Esselte Wezäta, 1983; Wohlert, Claus, "Concentration tendencies in Swedish industry before World War I," in *The Concentration Process in the Entrepreneurial Economy since the Late 19th Century*, edited by Hans Pohl and Wilhelm True, in *Zeitschrift für Unternehmensgeschichte*, 1988.

—Claus Wohlert

ARMSTRONG WORLD INDUSTRIES, INC.

313 West Liberty Street
Lancaster, Pennsylvania 17604
U.S.A.
(717) 397-0611
Fax: (717) 396-2787

Public Company
Incorporated: 1891 as Armstrong, Brother & Company, Inc.
Employees: 26,000
Sales: $2.51 billion
Stock Exchanges: New York Philadelphia Pacific

Armstrong World Industries is a leading international manufacturer and marketer of interior furnishings for homes and other buildings. Its products include resilient floorings such as Solarian no-wax flooring, ceramic tile, ceiling systems, and a broad line of furniture sold under the names Thomasville and Armstrong. To a lesser extent the company also produces specialty products such as gaskets, insulation materials, and coverings for the building, automotive, textile, and other industries.

In 1860 Thomas Morton Armstrong, the 24-year-old son of Scottish-Irish immigrants from Londonderry, Ireland, used $300 of savings from his job as a shipping clerk to buy a small cork-cutting shop in Pittsburgh. The firm was originally named for his partner in the venture, John O. Glass, but Glass's interest was purchased by Armstrong's brother in 1864 and the company's name was changed to Armstrong, Brother & Company.

Armstrong's original business was cutting cork stoppers, first by hand then after 1862 by machine, from the bark of cork trees which grow in Portugal, Spain, and northern Africa. During the Civil War, 1861 to 1865, the company made bottle stoppers for the Union Army and was singled out for official praise for fulfilling its contracts at the agreed prices with top-grade corks. This good publicity enabled Armstrong to land a large contract with a New York drug firm after the war, beginning the move toward national distribution of its products. In 1864 Thomas Armstrong pioneered the concept of brand-name recognition in his industry by stamping "Armstrong" on each cork and offering a written guarantee of quality with each sale.

Originally cork was purchased from American importers, but in 1878 Armstrong made arrangements to purchase, process, and ship corkwood and corks direct from Spain, thus beginning the foreign operations which eventually would make the company the largest cork processor in Spain. By the 1890s Armstrong was the world's largest cork company, employing more than 750 people, most of whom Thomas Armstrong knew by name. In 1891 the company incorporated as Armstrong, Brother & Company and, in 1893, purchased the Lancaster Cork Works, beginning its long involvement with the Pennsylvania Dutch area. During the 1890s Armstrong expanded its cork product line to include insulation, cork-board, gaskets, and flexible coverings for machinery. In addition, foreign markets were expanded with sales offices opening in Montreal and Toronto in 1895. In that year the corporate name was changed to Armstrong Cork Company. Thomas Armstrong died in 1908 and was succeeded as president by his son, Charles Dickey Armstrong.

Searching for new cork-based products, the company decided to add linoleum floor covering to its line and, in 1908, the first Armstrong linoleum was produced in a new plant in Lancaster. Invented in England in 1863 by Frederick Walton, linoleum was basically a mixture of cork flour, mineral fillers, and linseed oil, which was pressed under high temperature onto burlap backing and colored with pigments. The linoleum line was the beginning of the company's involvement with floor products, which in the 1990s, in a variety of modern forms, provided nearly one-half of its sales volume.

Under Charles Armstrong's leadership the firm expanded its product lines with cork insulating board and other insulating materials, packaging closures, and gaskets, as well as linoleum and related flooring materials, becoming in the process a much more consumer-oriented company than before. He also continued his father's policy of responsibility towards his employees by initiating benefits which were rare, if not unprecedented, early in this century. In 1909 he established free dental service for employees. Other pioneering examples of corporate responsibility followed: extra pay for overtime in 1913, shop committees to communicate with management in 1919, paid vacations in 1924, and group life insurance in 1931. Armstrong was one of the first U.S. companies to provide such fringe benefits as pensions and group medical insurance. Thus Charles Armstrong's presidency expressed the company's philosophy that employees should be provided for voluntarily by industry rather than by means of government compulsion.

Charles Armstrong became chairman of the board in 1928 and the next year John J. Evans succeeded him as president. In 1934, the vice president, Henning Webb Prentis Jr., who was to have a great impact on the company's development, became the next president of Armstrong.

Prentis had joined the firm in 1907 when, as a 23-year-old with an M.A. in economics, he took a job with Armstrong's insulation division in Pittsburgh in order to gain some practical experience before beginning a teaching career. It was a significant hiring decision. Prentis became interested in the possibilities of advertising and public relations. He wrote the first promotional literature on cork products to be published by Armstrong, including selling aids for retailers and booklets on home decoration for consumers. In 1911 he became head of the tiny advertising department and persuaded management to support a three-year, $50,000 advertising campaign. In 1917 he arranged for the company's first national advertisement in the mass media, to appear in the September 1917 issue of *The Saturday Evening Post.* He pioneered his industry's recruitment of college graduates as salesmen and, with Charles Armstrong's support, helped develop the strenuous training programs which enormously strengthened company management. He improved distribution practices by initiating price lists with discounts based on quantities purchased, and insisted on the establishment of close, friendly relations with wholesalers and retailers.

Thanks largely to Prentis's marketing innovations, Armstrong grew substantially during the 1920s, reaching nearly $48 million in sales by 1929, when the company moved its headquarters from Pittsburgh to Lancaster, Pennsylvania. When the Depression cut sales in half and produced large losses by 1934, Prentis was appointed president to improve the company's situation. He diversified by purchasing rubber- and asphalt-tile factories, and in 1938 acquired two glass companies, Whitall Tatum and Hart Glass Manufacturing.

The company's personnel policies helped to maintain morale and loyalty during those hard times. One example was the research employee who was laid off because of the Depression but continued to come to work without pay and, eventually rehired, made significant contributions to the development of a new flooring process. With Armstrong's debt-free balance sheet, Prentis's efforts were successful. By 1935 dividends on the common stock were restored and in 1936 Armstrong had its most profitable year to that point, a stunning achievement at a time when the country was still in the grip of the Great Depression. By 1937 the common stock had climbed from a low of $3.25 in 1932 to a price of approximately $65.

In addition to improving Armstrong's profitability, Prentis became much more of a public figure than his predecessors. He spoke frequently on behalf of conservative business philosophies in opposition to the New Deal policies of the Roosevelt administration. He served as director of the United States Chamber of Commerce and as president of the National Association of Manufacturers. When World War II began, Prentis organized Armstrong's conversion to war production, including the establishment of a munitions division. In 1942 and 1943 he served as deputy director of the War Production Board for the Philadelphia region, becoming an employee of the government administration which he had so frequently criticized.

After the war, Armstrong prepared to meet the tremendous demand for building materials for new houses. Two more asphalt-tile plants, a fiberboard plant, and a bottle-closure plant were built. In addition the company expanded its industrial-adhesives business and added the production of glass bottles to its packaging division. By 1950 annual sales had climbed to $163 million, and earnings were at record levels. In that year Prentis became chairman of the board and was succeeded as president by Clifford J. Backstrand.

Backstrand's goal was to use the growth to date to increase profits. He emphasized not only marketing but also research, realizing that product innovation was essential for successful competition in the postwar period. He completed the building industry's biggest research-and-development center. To help sell products in the home-remodeling market, in 1953 Armstrong built in Lancaster an "idea house" filled with Armstrong products, to be used as a showcase for dealers and customers. Creativity within the company was encouraged by giving special recognition and awards to employees who came up with ideas for new products and new processes. During the 1950s cork was largely replaced by chemicals and synthetics as the basis of the company's products. By 1960 building materials accounted for 60% of sales, and industrial specialties and packaging were each 20% of sales. Backstrand improved the company's accounting methods for measuring the profitability of various operations, establishing the concept of return on capital employed as a gauge of achievement. In 1962 Backstrand became chairman and Maurice J. Warnock was appointed president.

By the early 1960s Armstrong had extensive foreign operations, manufacturing textile-mill supplies in India and flooring in plants in Canada, Britain, and West Germany, as well as continuing to process cork in Spain. Warnock attempted to reduce the company's strong dependency on the housing and construction markets by entering the consumer products field with a liquid wax with detergent that cleaned and polished floors at once. Successful at first, this move to enter the supermarket-oriented consumer market eventually failed to justify its invested capital and was discontinued. Otherwise, Warnock's tenure as president was successful with new efficiencies in organization, improvement in flooring products, and continued growth in sales to $460 million in 1967. In 1966 and 1967 Armstrong entered the carpet business with the purchase of Brinton Carpets and E.&B. Carpet Mills. By the end of the 1960s, over one-third of Armstrong's sales came from products developed by the company within the previous decade. Armstrong invariably promoted from within and, in accordance with this policy, Warnock was succeeded in 1968 by a flooring executive who had spent his entire adult life with the company, James H. Binns.

Binns's tenure as president from 1968 to 1978 brought significant changes in the makeup and direction of the company, based on his belief that Armstrong's future lay mainly in the interior-furnishings market, which was entering a boom period. In 1968 Armstrong acquired the furniture manufacturer, Thomasville Furniture Industries, and the furniture wholesaler, Knapp & Tubbs, although the latter company was sold in 1972. In 1969 Binns sold the line of cleansers, waxes, and polishes to Chemway Corporation and the extensive packaging operations to Kerr Glass Manufacturing Company. The insulation-contracting business was sold to its former employees. Altogether Binns sold off businesses with about $125 million in annual sales, about one-fourth of sales volume. By the early 1970s about 90% of sales were concentrated in building products and home furnishings, and about 10% in industrial products such as gaskets and textile-mill supplies. This ratio continued into the 1990s.

In 1978, Binns became chairman of the board, and Harry A. Jensen served as president and CEO until his retirement in 1983. Through the 1970s and much of the 1980s Armstrong continued to grow in the same directions. The production of linoleum was discontinued in 1974, but the company continued to develop new types of resilient flooring, among which Solarian no-wax flooring became a well-known brand name. In 1980 the corporate name was changed to Armstrong World Industries to reflect its growing international base of operations and the fact that it was no longer based on the cork business. Sales generally trended upward with some annual fluctuations due to changes in the building cycle, reaching $1 billion in 1977 and $2 billion in 1987. Earnings followed the same pattern with net income increasing from $66 million in 1979 to $187 million in 1989.

Between 1983 and 1988, Joseph L. Jones served as president and chairman. His successor, William W. Adams, oversaw a series of significant events in the late 1980s. In 1988 Armstrong entered the ceramic-tile business by acquiring American Olean Tile Company, adding about $200 million to 1989 sales. In December 1989 Armstrong completed the sale of its carpet division, abandoning that business which was not producing an adequate return on investment, thus reducing annual sales by about $300 million. In addition, in 1989 the company sold Applied Color Systems, a small digital color-processing-control business.

In July 1989 Armstrong learned that the Belzberg family of Canada had acquired 9.85% of its stock and had announced the intention of gaining control of the company and selling its furniture and industrial-products divisions. The Belzberg's stock ownership increased in 1990 to 11.7%. In April 1990, Senate Bill 1310 of the Pennsylvania legislature, the strongest anti-takeover bill passed by any state, with support from Armstrong, became law. The bill provided for seizure of short-term profits in a failed takeover, limited voting rights of hostile shareholders, and guaranteed severance pay to employees who lost jobs because of a corporate takeover. A few days after passage of the law, the Belzbergs lost a proxy attempt at the company's annual meeting, seating only one of four candidates for directors on the board. At the end of the next month, the Belzbergs sold their Armstrong stock at a loss of about $18 million. In June 1990, Armstrong and the Belzberg affiliates resolved the remaining issues between them by withdrawing lawsuits and counter-suits against each other.

In 1990 the company was still involved in litigation involving personal-injury suits and other claims based on asbestos-containing insulation products, a business which was sold by Armstrong in 1969. The claims are being paid by insurance income under the Wellington Agreement on asbestos-related claims. In 1988, Armstrong and 20 other companies replaced the Wellington Asbestos Claims Facility with the Center for Claims Resolution, which is still in operation. Other cases brought by public school districts, private property owners, and others are still pending, as is a lawsuit filed with the U.S. Supreme Court by 29 states.

Armstrong has come a long way from a one-room cork shop to its present position as a leader in the international home-furnishings industry with an outstanding brand-name reputation. Its success has been characterized by strong, innovative leadership.

Principal Subsidiaries: American Olean Tile Company, Inc.; Armstrong Ventures, Inc.; Charleswater Products, Inc.; Chemline Industries, Inc.; Design Ideas Incorporated; Thomasville Furniture Industries, Inc.; The W.W. Henry Company; Armstrong World Industries (H.K.) Limited (Hong Kong); Armstrong FSC, Ltd. (Bermuda); Armstrong (Japan) K.K.; Armstrong-Nylex Pty. Ltd. (Australia, 51%); Armstrong/Pat Davie (China) Limited (51%); Armstrong (Singapore) Pte. Ltd.; Armstrong World Industries Canada Ltd.; Armstrong World Industries—France, S.A.; Armstrong World Industries, G.m.b.H. (Germany); Armstrong World Industries Italia S.r.l. (Italy); Armstrong World Industries Ltd. (U.K.); Armstrong Europe Services (U.K.); Inarco Limited (India, 40%); Armstrong World Industries Pty. Ltd. (Australia); Armstrong World Industries, S.A. (Spain); Armstrong World Industries (Schweiz) A.G. (Switzerland); Armstrong World Industries (Thailand) Ltd.; ISO Holding, A.G. (Switzerland); Armstrong World Industries—A.C.I.B.V. (Netherlands); Armstrong World Industries—Pontarlier S.A. (France); Armstrong World Industries—Europacoustic (Belgium).

Further Reading: Armstrong: a Historical Summary, Lancaster, Pennsylvania, Armstrong World Industries, Inc., 1985; *The Story of Armstrong,* Lancaster, Pennsylvania, Armstrong World Industries, Inc., 1985.

—Bernard A. Block

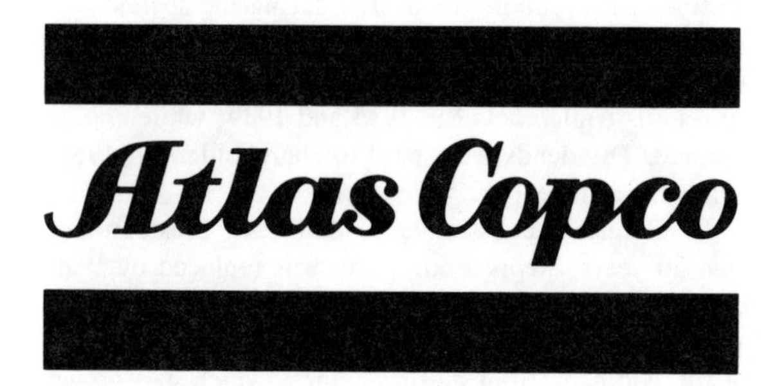

ATLAS COPCO AB

Sickla Industrivägen 3
105 23 Stockholm
Sweden
(08) 743 8000
Fax: (08) 644 9045

Public Company
Incorporated: 1873 as AB Atlas
Employees: 20,638
Sales: SKr15.04 billion (US$2.42 billion)
Stock Exchanges: Stockholm Frankfurt Düsseldorf Hamburg

Atlas Copco AB is one of the world's leading producers of compressors, mining and construction equipment, and automated industrial tools. The company has gone through several transformations since its founding in 1873 as AB Atlas. It was initially a specialized manufacturer of railway equipment, but switched at the beginning of the 20th century to diesel engines and pneumatic products. The production of diesel engines was abandoned after World War II, allowing the company to concentrate on the pneumatic equipment sector and erect an extensive international sales network that has made Atlas Copco into one of Sweden's biggest multinational concerns. Closely connected to the Wallenberg banking dynasty, Atlas Copco had to call on its financial support to weather several severe crises during its existence prior to World War II. In the postwar period, the profitability of Atlas Copco has improved greatly, despite a few temporary setbacks.

AB Atlas was established to supply equipment for the Swedish railways, with two factories located in Stockholm and Södertälje. Atlas was the brainchild of Eduard Fränckel, the chief engineer for Swedish State Railways (SJ), who became the company's first managing director. A second key figure behind Atlas was D. O. Francke, a Gothenburg industrialist and financier who headed the banking enterprise Göteborgs Handelskompani. The biggest shareholder in Atlas was André Oscar Wallenberg, the founder of Sweden's first commercial bank, Stockholms Enskilda Bank. Wallenberg had involved the bank in financing a number of railway construction projects and his interest in Atlas was a natural extension of this activity.

Atlas was soon the largest manufacturing company in Sweden in terms of production capacity. The large size of Atlas's planned operations reflected the optimistic outlook for the country's economy. The industrial revolution was gaining momentum in Sweden in the early 1870s and engineering firms were enjoying their first sustained period of profits. Atlas was entering a crowded field when it came to transportation equipment. Although it was profitable until 1877, Atlas then plunged into a deficit due to falling orders from Swedish state and private railways as the country entered a recession in the late 1870s.

Atlas's losses mounted during the 1880s as economic growth remained weak. Göteborgs Handelskompani, which was suffering financial reverses, gradually reduced its stake in Atlas, while Stockholms Enskilda Bank kept the company afloat through loans and consequently increased its control. A solution to Atlas's financial problems was difficult since the company was saddled with large and costly production facilities and faced fierce competition in the market for railway equipment and other heavy industrial goods at a time of economic slowdown. The company's situation revealed that "the initial investment in Atlas had not only been made at the wrong time but also in the wrong industry," one corporate historian, Professor Torsten Gårdlund, has concluded.

Burdened with excess production capacity, Atlas had to find other business besides making railway carriages. It produced steel and wrought-iron parts for bridges and other structures and made an unsuccessful diversification into marine steam engines and boilers by buying a shipyard in Gävle in a drastic attempt to develop more profitable product lines. When these efforts produced poor results, the Södertälje and Gävle facilities were closed and activity was concentrated in Stockholm. In 1887, the Wallenbergs ousted company president Fränckel, who had been criticized for lax management, and replaced him with Oscar Lamm, a mining engineer.

With Atlas continuing to suffer losses and Stockholms Enskilda Bank having a significant part of its assets tied up in the company, Knut Wallenberg, who had become head of the bank on his father's death in 1886, decided at the end of 1890 to allow Atlas to be liquidated. The shareholders lost their investment and the bank suffered heavy losses as its creditor. A new company named Nya AB Atlas (New Atlas Company) took over its assets, with Stockholms Enskilda Bank subscribing for the major part of the share capital. Under the firm control of the Wallenbergs, Nya AB Atlas became the cornerstone for the family's industrial empire, which now embraces most of Sweden's multinational corporations.

After the financial reorganization, the company developed a new specialty, heating ducts for buildings. It also began production of steam engines, steam locomotives, and machine tools. After the turn of the century it gradually phased out most of these products, including its original business of railway equipment, as it continued to change its product mix. It focused instead on two promising areas, oil-driven engines and air machinery and compressors. Production of compressed air equipment began in 1901 and by the start of World War I, pneumatic products had become the company's dominant business area. Gunnar Jacobsson, who oversaw the development of this division, became the president of Nya Atlas in 1909, succeeding Lamm.

In an attempt to improve the production and sales of oil-driven engines, its other main product area, Nya Atlas merged in 1917 with AB Diesels Motorer, which had been founded by the Wallenbergs in 1898 to acquire the Swedish patent rights for the engine developed by the German engineer Rudolf Diesel. Atlas had cooperated with Diesels Motorer from the beginning in developing the engine for commercial use, while acquiring a minority stake in the engine concern. Diesels Motorer first developed a stationary engine for power generation, later followed by a marine engine. After several difficult years during which large investments were needed to perfect the engine, Diesel Motorer reported its first profit in 1906 and found growing export markets in both the United States and Russia as sales of the marine engine climbed.

The creation of the new company, Atlas Diesel, came at a time when demand for its products was strong due to World War I, producing good prices and profits, as neutral Sweden supplied both sides of the conflict. The merger also meant that Stockholms Enskilda Bank, which owned two-thirds of Nya Atlas and half of Diesels Motorer, could gain a profit from its long-term investment in the two concerns while retaining 40% of the share capital in the new company, which was now valued at two and a half times the worth of the combined figures of its component companies. Nya Atlas President Jacobsson was appointed head of the new company.

Atlas Diesel began life with a healthy order book. The company's exports were dominated by diesel engines, which accounted for four-fifths of total foreign sales. These consisted mainly of marine engines supplied to the Allied nations to power their naval vessels. The end of the war brought with it a weakening in the business cycle. Deflationary policies were adopted in major export markets and deliveries to Russia were disrupted by revolution and civil war. By 1920, profits were practically nonexistent; during the next four years the company ran up heavy losses as the diesel engine business in particular suffered setbacks.

Debts mounted and Stockholm Enskilda Bank had to provide further credit. The company embarked on a cost-cutting program selling its headquarters in Stockholm and reducing its work force from a peak of 1,450 in 1917 to 240 in 1923. With the company considered to be overcapitalized, the share capital was drastically reduced from SKr220 million to Skr10 million in 1923 and Skr5 million in 1925. To reduce the debt burden, most of the old Atlas facilities were then sold and the production of compressors and pneumatic products was moved to the southern Stockholm suburb of Sickla, where Diesel had its factories.

The completion of the financial reorganization and concentration of production at Atlas Diesel occurred as Sweden was emerging from the economic crisis of the early 1920s. Sales improved for both pneumatic products and engines, but interest payments and depreciation charges kept profits low. Moreover, Atlas Diesel was concentrating its resources on the diesel engine business, although sales of pneumatic tools were providing almost all of the profits. Management, dominated by engineers, favored investment in diesel engines because it was the company's most technologically advanced product group and therefore enjoyed great prestige. The company thus was in a poor financial position to withstand the effects of the 1930s Depression, which hit it with devastating effect. Atlas Diesel once again plunged into a deficit, and there were discussions about shutting down the company. Instead, Stockholms Enskilda Bank, the principal owner, decided to recapitalize the company.

The company's operations were modernized and rationalized under the strict supervision of the Wallenbergs, with emphasis placed on expanding the profitable pneumatic side of the business. Profitability recovered during the second half of the 1930s due to an improvement in the business cycle resulting from rearmament programs across Europe. Sales of pneumatic tools tripled between 1935 and 1939, while engine sales doubled. Dividends were paid to shareholders in 1935, for the first time since 1919.

In 1940, Gunnar Jacobsson, who had been president for more than 30 years, stepped down and was replaced by Walter Wehtje, a close friend of Marcus Wallenberg Jr., the board chairman. Wehtje's brief was to continue shifting the focus of the company from diesel engines, which had grown so technologically complex that their sales could not even cover their manufacturing costs, to the compressed air division, which had become the company's sales leader at the beginning of the 1930s and accounted for two-thirds of sales by the end of the decade. Nevertheless, the engine business was expanded during World War II as Atlas Diesel supplied motors for torpedo boats, and hydraulic gears used in other military equipment for the Swedish armed forces.

In the early postwar years, Wehtje decided that the company's manufacturing of diesel engines could not continue, and in 1948 the diesel engine division was sold to Nydqvist & Holm. Simultaneously, Wehtje decided to expand the air compressor division, whose sales had already doubled during World War II, by setting up a network of sales subsidiaries and agents around the world. This network was to be complemented by an expansion of production capacity in Sweden and the acquisition of manufacturing plants abroad. By this time, the company's compressed air tools had reached a high technical standard after years of research. It had pioneered a new technique of rock drilling, called the Swedish method, by combining a lightweight rock drill with a tungsten carbide bit. This product, developed in cooperation with Sandvik, would soon help Atlas Diesel penetrate international markets.

Manufacturing capacity was increased by purchasing several troubled factories in Sweden to ease the production bottleneck at the Sickla facility. Atlas Diesel also acquired its biggest manufacturing site abroad in 1956 when it bought the Belgian compressor company Arpic, in Antwerp.

Although it had disposed of the diesel engine business, the company retained the name Atlas Diesel until 1955 when it changed to the present Atlas Copco. Copco stood for Compagnie Pneumatique Commerciale, the name of a Belgian subsidiary that had been adopted in its abbreviated form by a number of Atlas affiliates in other countries.

By the mid-1950s, Wehtje's strategy of international expansion was paying off with exports accounting for 65% of total sales. In 1957, Wehtje retired at the age of 60, having seen sales increase from SKr20 million to SKr315 million, the number of subsidiaries triple to 24, and the work force expand from 1,500 to 6,000. His successor was Kurt-Allan Belfrage, a former diplomat and deputy managing director.

During the 1960s, the company's annual sales more than tripled from SKr380 million to SKr1.28 billion. As market demand grew, plants were acquired in Denmark, Italy, India, Brazil, Spain, and Mexico in addition to the existing facilities overseas in the United Kingdom, Finland, and Belgium. Popular products included portable compressors and new pneumatic hand tools in addition to rock drilling equipment. More than 80% of Altas Copco's sales were outside Scandinavia. Profits fluctuated during the 1960s due to increased costs, such as sharply rising wages, research and development investment, and marketing activity.

Atlas Copco underwent a reorganization in 1968 in an effort to promote decentralized management, with the company split into three basic groups: Atlas Copco MCT (mining and construction equipment), Atlas Copco Tools (industrial technology), and Atlas Copco Airpower (compressors). When Belfrage retired in 1970, the company's work force had grown to 13,000 with a presence in 34 countries.

Erik Johnsson, the deputy manager for sales, was appointed the new president. He was replaced in 1975 by Tom Wachtmeister, who had held several senior positions in the company, including director of corporate planning. Strong global demand resulted in more than quadrupling sales during the 1970s. Atlas Copco reported a turnover of Skr5.3 billion by the end of the decade.

Atlas Copco was put to the test in the early 1980s when a worldwide recession left the company reeling with a sharp fall in profits in 1982 and 1983. Wachtmeister oversaw a stringent rationalization program that included shutting down one quarter of the company's 46 factories and shedding one fifth of the 20,000-strong work force. He also decided to shift the product emphasis away from mining equipment, which had generated 65% of the turnover in the late 1970s but had suffered a sizable drop in sales during the recession.

Atlas Copco experienced a recovery in profits in 1984 and 1985 due to renewed demand in western Europe as well as the devaluation of the Swedish krona in 1982, an important development for a company with 92% of its sales from outside Sweden. Atlas Copco suffered another setback in profits in 1986 due to unexpected foreign exchange losses.

The company's results have improved sharply since then. Between 1987 and 1989, earnings climbed by 109% to SKr 1.53 billion. The upswing in the company's recent fortunes can be traced to its strategy of concentrating on its core product areas, unlike its more diversified rivals. The strategy reflects Wachtmeister's belief that Atlas Copco should dominate every market segment in which it is active. It also stems from the policy within the Wallenberg sphere that companies belonging to it should not compete with each other. This policy prevented Atlas Copco from expanding into the related area of robotics, which is the preserve of ASEA, another Wallenberg concern.

Since 1987, Atlas Copco has been acquiring other companies to build up its market position. Takeover candidates have included Desoutter in the United Kingdom, Chicago Pneumatics in the United States, Secoroc in Sweden, and Georges Renault in France. Internal reorganization in the sales and administrative divisions, together with reduction of inventory stockpiles, have helped cut costs.

The air compressor division is now the biggest group within the company, generating 58% of the profits in 1989, while accounting for 46% of sales. Atlas Copco is Europe's leading producer of air compressors and dominates the global market for oil-free rotary compressors. It recently established a joint venture with Iwata Air Compressor, giving it a foothold in the Japanese market. It lacks a significant presence in this product area in the United States.

The industrial technology group, which makes automated industrial tools, has also been targeted for expansion. The division, which now accounts for one-fifth of both sales and profits, was augmented by the acquisition of Chicago Pneumatics in 1988 and the United Kingdom's Desoutter in 1989. Atlas Copco claims to be the world's biggest producer of pneumatic tools with a strong market position in both Europe and the United States.

Intense competition and slow markets have hit mining and construction equipment, formerly one of the company's top divisions. While it accounts for 33% of corporate sales, it generates only 22% of profits. In 1988, Atlas Copco acquired Secoroc, a manufacturer of rock-drill bits. The purchase led to a price war with the Swedish concern Sandvik, which formerly cooperated with Atlas Copco in marketing drill bits.

Atlas Copco remains financially strong and able to grow further through more takeovers. The company is optimistic about the 1990s since a host of infrastructure projects, such as improved motor and rail links in Europe, should mean increased sales. The company has warned that it might move its headquarters from Sweden if the country's high production costs are not brought under control. Such a transfer would be relatively easy since 80% of its production is located abroad and its biggest division, Atlas Copco Airpower, is already based in Belgium.

Principal Subsidiaries: Atlas Copco Airpower (Belgium); Atlas Copco Applied Compressor Technique (Belgium); Atlas Copco MCT; Uniroc; Wagner Mining Equipment (U.S.A.); Atlas Copco Industrial Technique; Atlas Copco Tools; Chicago Pneumatic Tool Company (U.S.A.); Atlas Copco Assembly Systems; Monsun-Tison; Ets. G. Renault (France); Desoutter Brothers (U.K.); Roboflow Corp. (U.S.A.).

Further Reading: Gårdlund, Torsten, et al, *Atlas Copco 1873–1973: The Story of a World-wide Compressed Air Company,* Stockholm, Atlas Copco, 1973; Brown, David, "Atlas Copco Changes Sales Tack," *The Financial Times,* September 4, 1985; Burton, John, "Atlas Copco: Investor Faith Regained," *The Financial Times,* July 3, 1990.

—John Burton

BAKER HUGHES INCORPORATED

3900 Essex Lane
Houston, Texas 77027
U.S.A.
(713) 439-8600
Fax: (713) 439-8699

Public Company
Incorporated: 1987
Employees: 20,400
Sales: $1.76 billion
Stock Exchanges: New York Pacific Zürich Basel Geneva Lausanne

Baker Hughes is the product of the 1987 merger of two oil-field-services companies with surprisingly similar histories. As the early Baker Oil Tools and Hughes Tool Company surged and retreated with their inventiveness and the vicissitudes of the global oil market, so will their modern offspring, the world's second-largest supplier of drill bits, oil-rig components, and services that aid the world petroleum industry.

Baker and Hughes followed such similar paths that, despite their difficult combination in the late 1980s, it is not surprising that the two firms make for such a cozy modern fit. Both were founded shortly before World War I by aggressive entrepreneurs who won valuable patents and earned gushing royalties on early oil-extraction devices. Both continued as domestic powerhouses well past the turn of the century, when, at slightly different cues, they embarked on massive worldwide expansion and diversification projects. Baker and Hughes became public companies within ten years of each other as the influence of their founding families diminished. The two rivals experienced the fluctuations of an unpredictable world oil market jarred by political and economic events. Finally, the companies suffered financial slumps in the lean years of the 1980s, leading to their turbulent but successful consolidation.

There were differences, however, between Baker Oil Tools—later Baker International—and Hughes Tool. Hughes became the neglected plaything of Howard Hughes Jr., the founder's famous billionaire son, who used the oil company's constant wellspring of cash to finance financially successful ventures in airplanes, real estate, and motion pictures. Baker, on the other hand, built a reputation, through careful yet ambitious expansion, as one of the industry's best-run firms, largely on the efforts of E.H. Clark, an executive whose tenure spanned 40 years.

The invention of the first rotary drill bit, used to drill oil wells through rock, led to the creation of Sharp-Hughes Tool Company in 1909. Howard Hughes Sr. and Sharp developed and manufactured the rotary drill bit, an invention so important to the fledgling oil industry of 1909 that variations of the same bit are used today. When Sharp died in 1912, Hughes bought Sharp's share of the business. Hughes incorporated the business the following year, and in 1915 dropped Sharp's name from the company. Armed with the exclusive patent to an essential product, Hughes brought his Houston-based company unrivaled market dominance for decades. Even after many key patents expired, during the 1930s and 1940s Hughes Tool was able to dominate the drill-bit business. During World War I Hughes developed a boring machine that could drill into enemy trenches. Explosives then could be dropped into the trenches. Although the secretary of war personally thanked Hughes for his contribution, the machine was never used because of the sudden shift, toward the end of the war, from trench warfare to active warfare.

If the market dominance of Hughes Tool was secured by the elder Howard Hughes before World War I, its tenor as an undiversified, closely held giant was set by the founder's son and namesake. The 19-year-old Howard Hughes Jr. inherited the company in 1924 following the death of his father. Under Hughes Jr., the oil-field-product company became a massive enterprise that he used largely to fund his various avocations. During World War II Hughes operated a gun plant and a strut-making facility for aircraft, in Dickinson, Texas.

Howard Hughes, who himself founded Hughes Aircraft Company, purchased over 78% of TransWorld Airlines's stock, and held a substantial investment in RKO Pictures, remained the sole owner of Hughes Tool until 1972, when he put the company on the market. Hughes Tool became a publicly owned company, in a transaction reportedly valued at $150 million. Although successful, despite a general slump in the drilling industry from 1958 to 1972, Hughes Tool had remained undiversified, primarily because Howard Hughes wanted it that way. ''Mr. Hughes, of course, felt he was personally diversified, so he never really considered diversifying the tool company,'' Raymond Holliday, a former Hughes chairman, told *Business Week*, October 13, 1980. With public stockholders and a booming oil economy, especially after the Organization of Petroleum Exportion Countries (OPEC) oil embargo of the early 1970s, Hughes Tool made up for lost time, bringing on worldwide acquisitions and start-up projects.

Under the leadership of Chairman James Lesch the firm purchased the Byron Jackson oil-field-equipment division of Borg-Warner in 1974, for $46 million. In 1978 Hughes bought Brown Oil Tools, another family-owned business, whose founder had under-utilized his 377 lucrative patents. With its massive expansion and the favorable oil-industry climate, Hughes Tool surged. By 1981—a peak year in the industry—new business activities, which largely meant non-drill-bit products and services, accounted for 55% of the company's sales.

When the bottom fell out of the market in 1982, Hughes found itself a bloated, overextended, and debt-ridden concern. Under the guidance of President William Kistler, an engineer who came up through the core drill-bit division, the company retrenched to its roots, concentrating on bits and shying away from services. For example, the company shut down 30 foreign offices and streamlined 11 divisions into one. In 1983 Hughes hired outside consultants Bain & Company to trim fat, laying off 36% of its work force. The company still had one weapon neither world markets nor competitors could take away: a patented O-ring rock-bit seal. In 1986 Hughes won a $227 million patent-infringement judgement from Smith International, a California concern that had copied Hughes's drill seal too closely. In 1985 Hughes had been awarded $122 million from Dresser Industries for patent violation. One rival that had innovated around Hughes's patent rather than copying it was Baker International.

Hughes Tool floundered through the mid-1980s. For the three years beginning in 1983, Hughes lost $200 million. Often cited as a potential takeover target, the company was faced with an offer it could not refuse when approached for a merger with Baker.

Like Hughes Tool, Baker grew out of a single invention—the Baker Casing Shoe—a device to ensure the uninterrupted flow of oil through a well, developed in 1907 by Californian Reuben C. "Carl" Baker. Baker licensed his patents and incorporated the Baker Casing Shoe Company in 1913, mainly to protect his numerous patents on products that would soon become the industry standard. During World War I Baker was a member of the local draft board, although his company did not devote any of its production to goods to support the war effort. Baker lived off his royalties until the 1920s when he began manufacturing his own tools. In 1928, after successfully manufacturing tools in Huntington Park, California, for several years, Baker called the company Baker Oil Tools, a name it would carry for 40 years.

The Depression hit Baker hard, causing it to lay off numerous workers, but the late 1930s and 1940s were years of solid growth. During this period the company started offices in many states including Texas, Wyoming, Illinois, Missouri, and Louisiana. During World War II Baker retooled to produce gun-recoil mechanisms. Following the war Baker prospered. In the ten years after 1948 it opened 50 new offices in 16 states. In 1956 Carl Baker retired at age 85, leaving the company in the hands of Theodore Sutter, an executive who had joined the company in the early 1920s. Carl Baker died shortly after his retirement. Under Sutter the company began to expand globally, and it went public in 1961.

When E.H. "Hubie" Clark Jr. assumed control of Baker in 1965, the company developed into a global powerhouse. Clark, who had joined the company as a recent mechanical-engineering graduate from the California Institute of Technology in 1947, led Baker, now based in Orange, California, to new heights. Although Baker remained based in California, in 1965 the company's Houston operation was as large as the California operation. Clark acquired some 20 companies, the largest of which was Reed Tool Company, a drill-bit manufacturer acquired in 1975. Clark worked hard to predict trends in oil supply and demand. Baker operations were begun in Peru, Nigeria, Libya, Iran, and Australia, among other countries, and in 1976 the company changed its name to Baker International Corporation.

The company's reputation for quality and Clark's renown as a manager put Baker into the 1980s in solid shape. Even Baker could not avoid the downturn of petroleum-related business after 1981. Clark and Baker President James D. Woods sought to improve efficiency in the slow-growing industry. The eventual answer was to merge with its Houston-based competitor, Hughes Tool. Both companies had been losing money and they hoped to eliminate overproduction by merging.

"This industry is plagued with overcapacity," said one Baker official, as he announced on October 22, 1986, that the two oil-services firms would merge. Wall Street immediately applauded the move, a complex stock swap that favored Baker stockholders by giving them one share of the new company for each share they owned, compared with an eight-tenths-of-a-share deal for Hughes shareholders. Reflecting the greater general strength of Baker, its executives were to be given the top posts: Clark was to be the new chairman and Woods the new president and chief executive officer, while William A. Kistler, Hughes's chairman, would be named the combination's vice chairman. The new company's home would be Houston, where Hughes was based, and where Baker already had extensive operations. Baker's Orange, California, headquarters housed relatively few employees.

Wall Street showed its excitement over the merger by trading up the stock prices of both companies following the merger announcement, but the federal government frowned on the potential antitrust ramifications of combining two such powerful outfits. Indeed, the U.S. Justice Department announced on January 25, 1987, that it would attempt to block the merger, citing reduced competition in markets for some oil-exploration machinery. As top executives worked out a consent agreement with the Justice Department, Hughes executives attempted to pull out of the merger. Baker responded in strong terms: it would sue Hughes for $1 billion if it failed to carry through with the agreement. After several delays Hughes capitulated. On April 3, 1987, Hughes agreed to the terms of the consent decree—which included the divestiture of the domestic operations of Reed Tool Company and some other units—and the merger was completed, creating an oil-services company second in size only to Schlumberger.

The consolidated company has not stopped charging forward since its merger. Baker Hughes outpaced its competition in the late 1980s. Part of its success was in realignment: Woods slashed 6,000 jobs, closed several plants, and took a $1 billion write-off for restructuring expenses. The result was $90 million less in annual costs and impressive sales. As the company headed into the 1990s, it was set to continue a fast pace of new-business exploration through research, acquisitions, sales, and diversification—such as using technology and know-how to address environmental concerns.

Principal Operating Divisions: Baker Hughes Drilling Equipment; Baker Hughes Production Tools; Baker Hughes Process Equipment; BJ Services.

Further Reading: The Baker Story, Houston, Baker International Inc., 1979.

—Adam Lashinsky

BALLY MANUFACTURING CORPORATION

8700 West Bryn Mawr Avenue
Chicago, Illinois 60631
U.S.A.
(312) 399-1300
Fax: (312) 693-2982

Public Company
Incorporated: 1968
Employees: 27,200
Sales: $2.07 billion
Stock Exchanges: New York Boston Philadelphia Cincinnati Midwest Pacific

Bally Manufacturing Corporation, a leader in the recreation industry, owns and operates four casino hotels and 310 health-and-fitness clubs. The company designs, manufactures, sells, and services gaming and coin-operated amusement equipment including slot-machines, video games, instant-ticket lottery games, and German wall-machines, which are wall-mounted slot-machines.

The fun and games began in 1931, during the Great Depression in Chicago, current site of Bally headquarters. Roy Moloney, Joel Linehan, and Charles Weldt invested in Lion Manufacturing, with plans to manufacture games, novelties, and push cards, an early form of a lottery. Led by Moloney, the three men decided to market a hand-controlled machine they had adapted from an older French parlor game similar to pool, called bagatelle.

In 1932 the group introduced the first pinball game, with seven plays for a penny, called Ballyhoo. The name, taken from a humor magazine with a brightly colored cover, was influential in two ways: it inspired the colorful baseboard for pinball that survives today; and it gave the young company a brand name. More than 50,000 Ballyhoo machines were sold within seven months, each for $16.50 plus shipping. The company continued working with small devices such as shavers, ballpoint pens, sewing machines, air conditioners, the first humidifier, and cola dispensing machines. By the end of the 1930s Lion employed 500 people.

The outbreak of World War II caused Lion to alter production. The company developed gun-sights for B-52 bombers, an oxygen regulator for fighter pilots, and detonator fuses. During peak war production, Lion manufactured 6,000 fuses a day, seven days a week. For its contributions Bally received the army-navy "E" Award.

Following the war Lion jumped back into the gaming business, making bumper and six-pocket pool tables as well as childrens' amusement park rides. Lion experimented with the manufacture of televisions and related equipment, including the first remote control for television. The remote project was later abandoned; the device was awkward because it depended on an electrical wire between the set and the control unit. In the late 1950s Lion introduced an advanced cola vending machine, which combined syrup and soda water while dispensing, as well as a coffee machine business that dispensed a freshly brewed cup each time. The vending machine market was hot. Lion sold the coffee machine business to Seeburg, a Chicago-based company, and the United States' largest jukebox manufacturer, in 1960. The pinball public was still playing, however, so Lion concentrated on developing more gaming machines.

The death of Roy Moloney in 1957 rocked the company. After six years of confusion, Lion sales and marketing manager William T. O'Donnell took charge and attracted a group of investors to buy the company in 1963. By the mid-1960s the pinball market declined somewhat. New legislation legalized the production of slot machines, however, spurring new casino openings in Nevada. Because most machines in use were at least 20 years old, Lion saw an untapped market.

The newly revitalized Lion promptly designed a revolutionary slot machine called Money Honey that combined mechanical play with electric pay-out techniques. The sound generated when a player hit the jackpot could overwhelm a casino floor. Such audio devices were not simply marketing gimmicks of the time; they previewed the style of electronic video games to come.

In the mid-1960s Lion designed and developed its Slot Data System (SDS), the first computerized data-controlling system for slot machines. Before SDS, players could cheat machines; the state of Nevada calculated losses up to 10% of an estimated $500 million in slot machine revenue. Because of the success of Money Honey and SDS, Lion became the leading producer of slot machines.

After more than 30 years in business, Lion incorporated as Bally Manufacturing in March 1968. O'Donnell initiated acquisitions, including Midway Manufacturing, a competing amusement game producer, and Lenc-Smith, a tool and die maker. Bally's growth continued into the 1970s. In 1974 Bally acquired all of the shares of American Amusements, Incorporated, a chain of shopping-mall game arcades. Bally renamed the subsidiary the Aladdin's Castle chain.

Moving as fast as the pinball in the game that made its name, Bally acquired Germany's Gunter Wulff Automaten, another large-scale coin-operated gaming producer. With this acquisition, Bally opened a European distributorship.

In 1975 the Bally Distributing Company was purchased for $9.5 million in cash and stock. That year was the beginning of a four-year period during which Bally reached record operating results. In 1977 Chairman O'Donnell initiated Bally's diversification into casino hotels. Plans for Bally's Park Place were launched just in time for the 1978 New Jersey state decision to begin licensing casino operators.

The sailing was not smooth for the Park Place opening. In May 1979 Xcor International's Williams Electronics, a competing producer of slot machines, filed suit against Bally. Williams claimed that Bally's New Jersey casino venture would give Bally a monopoly in slot machine sales, O'Donnell said the case had no merit. Bally had in fact sued Williams in a Chicago court for anticompetitive action in New Jersey.

O'Donnell's plans neared fruition in 1979, when Bally's official license application reached the New Jersey Casino Control Board. In an ironic and abrupt circumstance, William T. O'Donnell's reputation—and position as chairman of the Bally Manufacturing Corporation—was called into question. According to an article in *The Wall Street Journal* of August 13, 1980, New Jersey legislation required that key executives and any persons holding substantial stocks in a casino corporation be "investigated and found qualified to hold a casino license before the company can be licensed."

Bally's Park Place opened under a temporary license, on the condition that O'Donnell resign while the New Jersey Gaming Enforcement Division investigated his alleged former association with crime figures. Richard Gillman, a former investment banker who joined Bally in 1970, was named chairman of Park Place.

Robert Mullane was elected the new chairman of the board of Bally Manufacturing in 1979. Mullane, who had experience in the securities and vending-machine businesses, had joined Bally in 1971.

Bally entered the 1980s with nearly 50 years in the amusement games industry. In this decade all markets became increasingly international in scope, with many U.S. companies merging, dissolving, or initiating leveraged buyouts to survive. Within the decade Bally would divest itself of most of the businesses upon which it was founded.

Bally grew steadily during the 1970s, and in 1980 its computer and video game market boomed. In contrast to the younger pinball market, video games appealed to an older customer with more expendable income. Bally's Aladdin's Castle division thrived, rocketing from 20 arcade centers in 1974 to 221 centers by year-end 1980. Bally's innovative Space Invaders video game drew a revenue of $133.9 million. In 1981 the company introduced Pac-Man, which it assembled and distributed under license from Namco of Japan. Ms. Pac-Man, introduced in 1982, became the most popular coin-operated game ever. Baby Pac-Man, brought out the same year, combined video and pinball playing fields, to attract both markets.

While reaping huge profits from the video game craze, Bally diversified in preparation for both a market drop and increasing competition from Japanese designers, who were beginning to manufacture in the United States. Two major acquisitions of 1982 were Six Flags Corporation, the world's second-largest amusement park operator; and Scientific Games, Incorporated, the inventor and largest supplier of instant-ticket computerized lottery games.

In 1983, Bally's amusement game revenue plunged 60%; but the company did not sink with the falling market demand. Having anticipated long-term growth in leasure-time markets, Bally acquired Health & Tennis Corporation. Within four years it became the world's largest owner and operator of fitness centers. In 1984 Bally purchased Lifecycle, Incorporated, from Augustine Nieto Jr. The subsidiary, renamed Life Fitness Incorporated, produced and marketed fitness equipment including computerized weight-training machines. Within six years Life Fitness became the official fitness equipment supplier to the U.S. National Football League.

Bally's fastest growing division by mid-year 1984 was Scientific Games. Because of the availability of essentially tamper-free electronic lottery machines, 18 states had lottery systems in place, with 20 more states considering the option.

The California State Lottery contract, worth $30 million–$40 million, did not go to Bally unnoticed. In the July 1, 1985, issue of *The New Republic*, it was noted that Bally lawyers were responsible for drafting a law that required potential lottery contractors to reveal income tax returns of all owners, officers, and directors, "an apparently insurmountable obstacle for its competitors." The same article criticized that "this nice bit of . . . work, turn[ed] the appeal of openness and 'full disclosure' into a device for closing off competition."

Bally's next move was the 1985 purchase of MGM Grand Hotels, owner of two casinos in Nevada. Atlantic City casinos now numbered 11. While business slowed as a result of increased competition, Bally's Park Place, catering to the one-day visitor—and smaller spender—continued providing the company a steady cash flow.

In what *Fortune* of December 23, 1985, aptly called the "Atlantic City Reshuffle," high-rolling licensees began to buy one another out. Real estate financier Donald Trump, owner of two Atlantic City casinos, held 9.9% of Bally's stock in the first quarter of 1987. Trump threatened a takeover. In an eye-for-an-eye style punchout, Bally not only bought Trump out but also bought the Golden Nugget casino to increase its casino holdings. In the scuffle, Bally paid heavily.

To finance its four casino properties and growing debt—and to streamline operations—Bally sold its Six Flags Amusement Parks in 1987. The October stock market crash foiled Bally's proposed plan to sell off its profitable health and fitness division for $500 million. The company considered other options.

By mid-year 1988 Bally announced, after 57 years in the big business of games, the sale of its amusement game manufacturing division to its competitor WMS Industries, formerly Williams Electronics. In 1989 the Aladdin's Castle arcade chain was sold. The same year Bally announced the move of its lottery and video poker machine industry from Illinois to Nevada. Adding to its casino holdings, Bally agreed to acquire the London Clermont Club in 1990, and finalized the acquisition of the software company Logistics to its Bally Systems subsidiary.

Bally Manufacturing Corporation entered the 1990s as flexible as it was during the volatile 1980s, with restructuring plans in progress. To Bally's credit, the company maintained its edge as the world's largest full-service gaming company and leading position in the fitness-center industry.

Principal Subsidiaries: Bally's Park Place; Bally's Grand; Bally's Las Vegas; Bally's Reno; Bally's Health & Tennis

Corp.; Bally Gaming, Inc.; Bally Gaming International GmbH (Germany); Bally Wulff Automaten GmbH (Germany); Bally Wulff Vertriebs GmbH (Germany); Life Fitness, Inc.; Life Fitness Europe GmbH (Germany); Scientific Games, Inc.

Further Reading: "The Bally Story," Bally corporate typescript, 1983.

—Frances E. Norton

BICC Group

BICC PLC

Devonshire House
Mayfair Place
London W1X 5FH
United Kingdom
(071) 629-6622
Fax: (071) 409-0070

Public Company
Incorporated: 1945 as British Insulated Callender's Cables Limited
Employees: 46,035
Sales: £3.79 billion (US$6.12 billion)
Stock Exchange: London

The 1945 merger of Great Britain's two largest cable manufacturers, British Insulated Cables and Callender's Cable and Construction Company, created British Insulated Callender's Cables Limited, a company with a muscular portfolio of worldwide subsidiaries. BICC, as the company came to be called, employs people on five continents, utilizing their energies in one of the following five corporate divisions, as ranked by gross sales. Balfour Beatty designs and constructs nearly anything asked of it, from quiet suburban residences to dockyards, dams, highways, and tunnels beneath the English Channel. Metal Manufactures is one of Australia's largest industrial conglomerates, dominating the market in communication cables, plastic piping, and copper tubing, while also playing significant roles in the construction and consumer-electronics businesses. BICC Cables manufactures and sells cables for the transmission of energy and information primarily in western Europe but elsewhere also, including Dubai, Malaysia, Pakistan, and Zimbabwe; it is the largest such company in Britain and one of the largest in the world. Performing much the same function in North America are Cablec Corporation and Phillips Cables, headquartered, respectively, in the United States and Canada, collectively referred to as BICC North America. Finally, BICC Technologies is a much smaller division working in the area of communication and control systems for industrial and commercial concerns. In 1989 the construction division accounted for more than 50% of total sales.

BICC has its origin in the late-19th-century scramble to devise the safest and most economical means to distribute electricity across the length and breadth of the United Kingdom. In 1882, when the Edison Company demonstrated the feasibility of incandescent lighting by illuminating its London offices at Holborn Viaduct, William Ormiston Callender realized that he was in the wrong business. Callender and his five sons ran a profitable construction company, importing for the purpose of road surfacing large amounts of the petroleum compound bitumen. Spurred by the recent developments in electricity, William M. Callender, one of the sons, invented a process for insulating electric wire using vulcanized bitumen, a tar-like, elastic substance that could be used as a coating for copper wire that is flexible, strong, waterproof, and nonconducting. First used in an installation at the Marquis of Salisbury's home, vulcanized bitumen-insulated wire proved to be excellent for the transmission of low voltage and was soon adopted for a wide variety of such applications.

The Callender family built a plant in Kent, and Callender's Cable and Construction Co. Ltd. quickly became a leader in the rapidly proliferating electrical business. Among many other innovations, the Callenders devised a method of laying cable beneath city streets, running the lines through shallow iron troughs that were then filled with more bitumen. Callender's also began making a second type of low-voltage cable using oil-filled jute as insulation, thus acquiring expertise in both of the methods favored for the distribution of low-voltage electricity.

About the time that Callender realized the value of his bitumen supply, James B. Atherton heard a lecture in New York on the remarkable electrical properties of paper—specifically, that it was a poor conductor. Atherton was in the fur business, but he too was caught up in the excitement over electricity. Arming himself with the British rights to certain U.S. patents he returned to London and founded the British Insulated Wire Company (BI) in 1890. Joining him on the board of directors was famed Italian inventor, Sebastian de Ferranti, through whose influence the company was asked to manufacture new high-voltage cables for the main London generators at Deptford. Carrying 11,000 volts, the paper-insulated cables passed every test, proving the viability of paper insulation and giving BI a strong debut in the marketplace. The company refined its manufacturing techniques, eliminating production problems while bettering the flexibility and other properties of its insulation, and by 1903 had joined forces with the Telegraph Manufacturing Company of Helsby and Anchor Cable of Leigh. The new company was British Insulated and Helsby Cables Limited. It quickly became the leading supplier of high-voltage cable in the nation.

Both BI and Callender's were involved in virtually every important cable project in the United Kingdom since 1900, including telegraph, telephone, electrical, and petroleum networks operating below ground, in the air, and across the ocean. In 1904, for example, the two competed for and collaborated on the electrification of the London Underground, together laying about 250 miles of high-voltage wire. Along with a third company W. T. Henley's Telegraph Works, BI and Callender's early established themselves as the dominant power cable manufacturers in the country, vying with one another for business in all sectors of the vast electrical industry. Though the companies tended originally to pursue opposite ends of the high-low-voltage spectrum, by World War II either of them was well equipped for any type of power-distribution assignment.

During the early part of the war, British shipping suffered severe losses caused by German magnetic mines hidden in the Channel and ocean traffic lanes. P.V. Hunter of Callender's designed a magnetized cable strong enough to push through ocean swells yet light enough to float, and Callender's produced about 2,000 such "minesweeps," each one approximately 500 yards long and capable of detonating submerged mines at a safe distance from the sweeper ship. The entire cable industry subsequently worked on practical methods of degaussing, or demagnetizing, the British fleet, eventually manufacturing many thousands of miles of cable for installation in the hulls of seagoing vessels. The combination of sweeping and degaussing succeeded in substantially reducing the damage inflicted by magnetic mines. Later still, BI and Callender's contributed to the construction of a gasoline pipeline across the English Channel to supply the World War II D-Day forces with fuel.

By war's end the two companies, already the largest U.K. cable manufacturers, merged their forces to become British Insulated Callender's Cables (BICC). The company's formidable assets and technical expertise provided sustained growth during the decades following. BICC's experience with cable installation led the company into the allied fields of civil engineering and large-scale construction work. Balfour Beatty, the group's construction subsidiary, pursued a wide variety of such projects throughout the British Commonwealth. Indeed, BICC as a whole was active around the globe, establishing an especially strong Australian presence in both cables and construction and later expanding there into the retail electrical and electronics businesses. At home, the company dominated the U.K. cable market, making the most of its powerful position to win contracts on the nation's most important electrical and civil engineering projects.

BICC carved for itself a secure place in the heavy-construction industry, but the company's profits failed to dazzle the stock market. By the 1960s the firm was generally recognized as a rather stolid blue chip: safe, slowly growing, and modestly profitable. Between 1966 and 1970, for example, sales increased from £300 to £400 million but profit remained around £20 million. Investors were sometimes made uneasy by BICC's heavy dependence on the price of copper, which it needed to make its power cables. Importing some 300,000 tons a year, the company's profitability was directly tied to the fluctuating copper market. In addition, BICC's product mix was not calculated to excite the interest of stock watchers. Contracts for the electrification of a London subway extension or the widening of highways do not provide the cachet of a so-called glamour stock.

With or without the market's enthusiasm, however, BICC continued its steady growth throughout the 1970s. Its Australian division became easily the largest of BICC's many overseas operations, while the U.K. construction arm, Balfour Beatty, remained the company's most reliably profitable subsidiary. In 1979 BICC began diversifying into the rapidly growing electronics field, for a more balanced and, hopefully, recession-proof portfolio. The firm bought Vero, a U.K. manufacturer of printed circuit boards, and the U.S. companies Boschert and Sealectro, makers of switching equipment and high-frequency connectors, respectively. Chairman Sir Raymond Pennock predicted that by 1990 a quarter of BICC's revenue would be generated by electronics. Of equal interest was the 1981 agreement with Corning, the U.S. glass maker, to build a plant in Wales for the purpose of manufacturing fiber optical cables. These hair-thin fibers of glass are capable of transmitting many more telephone and data messages than comparable copper wires and were certain to become the new standard for long-distance trunk lines. The Corning-BICC plant was finished in 1983 at a cost of £17.5 million and was an immediate success.

In 1981 BICC sales hit £1.36 billion and its profit £102 million, both healthy figures, and the company looked forward to the new decade with much confidence. The worldwide recession of the early 1980s soon took its toll, however, with profit levels slipping into a trough from which they did not fully emerge until 1987. Halfway through these doldrums, in 1984, the BICC board of directors named Sir William Barlow as its new chairman. Barlow, the former head of Britain's postal service, soon brought in Robin Biggam as president and CEO, and the two men designed a program of sharp labor cuts and further acquisitions to prod their sleepy giant. Upper-level management was also shaken up, the much-heralded electronics division pared down to a handful of companies in fields directly allied to BICC's main interests, and the Australian division, Metal Manufactures, restructured to provide greater control. Most significantly, BICC closed out the decade with several major purchases of foreign cable companies. Its acquisition of Cablec and BRIntec in the United States made BICC the leading high-power cable maker in North America, with combined sales of around US$750 million.

For the first time, BICC expanded into continental Europe, with the purchase of Ceat Cavi, Italy's second-largest cable concern, and of 20% of GEGC, Spain's cable leader. With the imminent end of all European trade barriers, BICC is thus well positioned to compete for transnational cable contracts.

The combination of stringent staff reductions and international expansion showed excellent results. In 1987 profits finally passed the 1981 level, with the company recording earnings of £128 million on sales of £2.49 billion. The following year showed further gains, as did 1989 over 1988. Earnings in 1989 were £201 million on sales of £3.79 billion. With Balfour Beatty ready to bid on a number of large contracts in the rebuilding of Britain's infrastructure, BICC heads into the 1990s in a strong position. Though still not exactly a stock market celebrity, this quiet industrial powerhouse continues to build on its exceedingly firm foundations.

Principal Subsidiaries: Balfour Beatty Ltd.; BICC Cables Ltd.; BICC Technologies Ltd.; Metal Manufactures Ltd. (Australia, 61.6%); BICC Cables Corporation (U.S.A.).

Further Reading: Byatt, Ian C., *The British Electrical Industry: 1875–1914*, New York, Oxford University Press, 1979; Crisp, Jason, "Tuning in to a wire-less future," *The Financial Times*, April 22, 1981; Garnett, Nick, "Limbering up for the acquisition trail," *The Financial Times*, May 11, 1987; "BICC Plugs into the 1990's," *Management Today*, February 1989; Waller, David, "Radical changes in a quiet revolution," *The Financial Times*, July 6, 1989.

—Jonathan Martin

THE BLACK & DECKER CORPORATION

701 East Joppa Road
Towson, Maryland 21204
U.S.A.
(301) 583-3900
Fax: (301) 583-3318

Public Company
Incorporated: 1910 as The Black & Decker Manufacturing Company
Employees: 38,600
Sales: $3.19 billion
Stock Exchanges: New York Pacific London Frankfurt Zürich Basel

The Black & Decker Corporation principally sells industrial and consumer portable electric tools. More than any other firm, Black & Decker (B&D) created the post–World War II consumer market for power tools. During the 1960s Black & Decker branched into several new endeavors, including garden and lawn equipment, yet it remained a fairly small company with just over $1 billion in sales at the end of the 1970s. At that time it dominated the world market in power tools, but foreign and domestic competitors threatened its position. During the 1980s, however, Black & Decker rationalized its operations and diversified its markets through two major acquisitions. As a result, The Black & Decker Corporation is a producer of a wide line of do-it-yourself and professional hardware and housewares.

Alonzo G. Decker and S. Duncan Black, two industrial tool designers and engineers, formed The Black & Decker Manufacturing Company in September 1910. With $600 from the sale of Black's second-hand car and a loan of $1,200, they set up a machine shop in a rented warehouse in Baltimore, Maryland. Black was the president of the company. In their first years the partners contracted to manufacture industrial products invented and sold by others.

In 1916 Black and Decker began to design and manufacture their own electric-powered tools. The German-made electric tools then available were heavy and difficult to operate, and, as a result, had not been commercially successful. Black and Decker designed a universal motor—the first for electric-tool use—which used either alternating or direct current, and trigger switch modeled after the mechanism in the Colt revolver. The first tool incorporating these innovative elements was a ½-inch portable drill with the innovative "pistol grip and trigger switch" that have remained standard for electric drills ever since. The drill was comparatively light at 21½ pounds, and it was considered inexpensive at $230.

B&D grew consistently during the 1920s, as businesses bought labor-saving devices to deal with rising labor costs. In 1917 the company was awarded patents for its pistol grip and trigger switch and constructed a factory on the outskirts of Towson, Maryland. By 1918 sales surpassed $1 million. Immediately after World War I, more portable electric tools were introduced including a ⅜-inch drill, a grinder, and a screwdriver. To accommodate demand the Towson plant was expanded three times by 1927. A Towson headquarters building was also constructed in 1924.

Black & Decker used aggressive salesmanship and product services to build its client base. The company's first service centers were opened in Boston and New York in 1918. B&D also organized clinics to teach distributors how to use and sell the tools; demonstrators toured the country in two buses. At the end of the 1920s the company even outfitted a monoplane to showcase its tools. In addition, the firm began its first mass-media campaign in the *Saturday Evening Post* in 1921.

With its initial success The Black & Decker Manufacturing Company expanded outside the United States, marking the beginning of its development into a global business. During the last year of World War I, burgeoning overseas sales led the company to establish representatives in Canada, Great Britain, the Soviet Union, Australia, and Japan. Canada was the site of B&D's first foreign subsidiary, started in 1921. Four years later a London sales and service subsidiary was formed. In 1928 the British company began manufacturing operations at a leased facility in Slough, outside London. The British company eventually built its own plant at Harmondsworth, Middlesex, in 1939. In 1929 an Australian subsidiary was established in Sydney. Until the 1950s the British subsidiary remained Black & Decker's only foreign manufacturing operation. It was the most important of B&D's many foreign operations after World War II.

In the latter half of the 1920s Black & Decker expanded its U.S. operations by several acquisitions. In 1926 the Marschke Manufacturing Company of Indianapolis, Indiana, a maker of grinders, was purchased. Two years later the Van Dorn Electric Tool Company of Cleveland, Ohio, was acquired. In 1929 B&D purchased the Fleming Machine Company of Worcester, Massachusetts, and the Domestic Electric Company of Cleveland. Fleming Machine made wire brushes, saws, and grinding stones, and Domestic Electric was a major producer of electric motors. In addition Black & Decker acquired the Loadometer Company, from which it previously had bought the rights to a portable truck-weighing scale.

Like other businesses, The Black & Decker Manufacturing Company experienced great difficulties during the Depression. Despite huge layoffs, including Alonzo Decker's son, the company nearly went bankrupt. Employee loyalty—some workers continued to work although the company could not pay them—and a large influx of capital from outside investors kept Black & Decker afloat. The Marschke Manufacturing Company acquisition did not prove successful, and that company was sold in 1932. Black & Decker continued to develop new products. In 1930 and 1931 the firm marketed a portable circular saw, an adjustable-clutch electric screwdriver, and a new, streamlined housing for its drills. A line of power tools using the new induction motors, the High Cycle line, was introduced in 1935. As the decade ended there was a cascade of new B&D products, including an electric hammer, an industrial vacuum cleaner, a portable metal cutter, a portable trim saw, and the Shorty series of drills.

When the United States entered World War II Black & Decker switched to the production of fuses, shells, and other products to contribute to the war effort. Alonzo Decker and S. Duncan Black were determined to avoid the problems which had followed World War I. They believed that the key would be postwar consumers. Although the company had developed an inexpensive ½-inch drill in 1923, and introduced the Cinderella washing machine in 1930, its forays into the consumer market had not been successful. In 1942 the Black & Decker Post-War Planning Committee was established. This group developed plans for Black & Decker to manufacture power tools for do-it-yourselfers and homeowners. The committee believed B&D could provide cheaper tools using new, less-expensive plastic housings to tap this unexplored market.

In 1946 The Black & Decker Manufacturing Company introduced the world's first power tools for the consumer market, the inexpensive Home Utility line of ¼-inch and ½-inch drills and accessories. In the first five years, one million ¼-inch drills were produced. This success led to the addition of other products to the Home Utility line. A set of circular saws was introduced in 1949, and a finishing sander and jigsaw in 1953. Black & Decker also continued to market new tools for professional users, including an impact socket wrench introduced in 1949 and two heavy-duty routers introduced in 1957. As a result of great demand, the company began construction of a large new plant in Hampstead, Maryland, in 1951; by 1955 this facility had been expanded to more than four times its original size. The old Towson plant ceased production in 1965, although the site remained Black & Decker's headquarters.

In the 1950s and 1960s B&D resumed the overseas expansion begun in the 1920s. Manufacturing operations were organized in Australia in 1956. During the 1960s production facilities were built or acquired in West Germany, France, Italy, Spain, Canada, and Mexico. In addition, sales and service subsidiaries were established in many other countries. The U.K. subsidiary successfully expanded into other European markets, and, as a result, a new plant was built at Maidenhead in 1962. Three years later this factory was expanded, and another plant was opened in Spennymoor, Durham. By 1969 43% of B&D's sales and earnings came from its foreign operations.

Despite personnel changes, The Black & Decker Manufacturing Company remained under the leadership of the Black and Decker families during the 1950s and 1960s. In 1951 president and co-founder S. Duncan Black died at age 67. Black was succeeded as president by his partner, Alonzo G. Decker, who also took on the new post of chairman in 1954. The following year, however, Decker died. Robert D. Black, S. Duncan Black's brother, succeeded Decker. In 1960 Decker's son, Alonzo G. Decker Jr., was named president. The 54-year-old Alonzo Decker Jr. had started B&D as a floor sweeper in the early 1920s. In 1964 he replaced Black as chief executive officer.

Although Black & Decker enjoyed healthy profits, by the late 1950s the company was not increasing beyond its 20% share of the U.S. market. To generate growth the company branched out into other types of labor-saving machinery. The Master Pneumatic Tool Company of Bedford, Ohio, maker of portable pneumatic tools, was acquired in 1959. Production of portable air tools was begun at a new facility in Solon, Ohio, in 1960. The Value line was introduced in 1967 to offer standardized, less-expensive models. The pneumatic tools business remained a minor part of B&D's operations, until that sector was sold in 1986.

In 1960 Black & Decker purchased De Walt of Lancaster, Pennsylvania, makers of radial arm saws and other woodworking equipment. An improved line of radial arm saws was introduced in 1966. To expand the woodworking operations Black & Decker bought the Carbide Router Company of Moonachie, New Jersey, in 1970 and the Wisconsin Knife Works of Beloit, Wisconsin, the following year.

Black & Decker also entered the garden- and lawn-care field in the late 1950s. It introduced electric lawn edgers and hedge trimmers in 1957. The first electric lawn mowers were unveiled in 1966, and a cordless model went into production three years later. In 1973 the business was expanded by the purchase of McCulloch Corporation, a manufacturer of gasoline engines and chain saws. During the mid-1970s production of certain outdoor-tool models was scaled back because of the unpredictable nature of their sales. Sales of outdoor tools depended upon weather conditions and seasonal buying patterns. McCulloch performed very well during the energy crisis of the early 1970s, which spurred the use of woodburning stoves, thus popularizing chain saws, but in the early 1980s the subsidiary began losing money. In 1983 the chainsaw business was sold.

Black & Decker power tools continued to enjoy success during the 1960s and early 1970s, as prices were cut and products improved. The cost of B&D's ¼-inch drill was reduced in increments from $15.98 in 1963 to $7.99 in 1970. A research-and-development task force brought out dozens of new tools each year, maintaining Black & Decker's status as an industry innovator. The Workmate portable worktable and accessories were first marketed in England in 1973, and soon proved very successful around the world. Beginning in 1964 Black & Decker also made extensive use of television advertising. Sales surpassed $100 million in 1964, $200 million in 1969, and $500 million in 1974. To accommodate the new demand the company built two plants in North Carolina, at Fayetteville and Tarboro, in 1966 and 1970, respectively. In 1974 a plant also was constructed in Easton, Maryland.

In 1975 Decker retired as chief executive officer, to be replaced by Francis P. Lucier who had been named president in 1970. Although Decker remained chairman, this marked the end of the founding families' executive control of the company. In 1975 B&D also experienced its first break in postwar growth, and many employees were laid off. The firm's future looked dim in the face of growing competition from Japanese and German toolmakers. Offering lower-priced, high-quality tools, the Japanese firm Makita Electric Works steadily gained on Black & Decker. By the early 1980s Makita had nearly equaled Black & Decker's 20% share of the world market in professional tools. High turnover among the top executives also contributed to Black & Decker's woes.

Promoting a program of globalization, 48-year-old Laurence Farley was promoted to president and chief executive officer in 1983. The new head of B&D was determined to develop a world market for standardized consumer goods, including housewares. He implemented a sweeping reorganization scheme, closing five plants in England, Ireland, and the United States. Two years later more plants were closed in the United States, Brazil, Mexico, and Canada. Farley also integrated the global operations of Black & Decker, in the process firing 25 European managers and closing the European headquarters in Brussels. In 1985, to help bring home the reorganization, The Black & Decker Manufacturing Company revamped its hexagonal trademark and changed its name to The Black & Decker Corporation. The name change was meant to give greater emphasis to the marketing and sales side of the company.

Black & Decker's new path under Farley grew out of the firm's earlier development of cordless technology. In 1961 Black & Decker had introduced the world's first self-contained cordless electric drill. This tool and others that soon followed were powered by nickel-cadmium batteries, that failed to deliver the necessary performance. Nevertheless, the firm developed a cordless minimum-torque-recreation tool and a lunar surface drill, both of which were used by NASA on several space missions.

Using this earlier experience, Black & Decker introduced the Dustbuster cordless vacuum cleaner in 1979. This product was an immediate success, establishing B&D as the leader in the hitherto untapped small-appliance niche market. the Dustbuster was followed by the Spotliter rechargeable light and other cordless appliances. To put Black & Decker squarely in this new business, Farley paid $300 million in 1984 for the small-appliance operations of General Electric (GE). By purchasing the largest U.S. producer of irons, toaster ovens, portable mixers, coffee makers, and hairdryers, Black & Decker was able to gain a large chunk of the market immediately, without risking the loss of Black & Decker hardware shelf space to its housewares. Farley also believed production costs would be lowered by integrating the research and production of power tools and housewares.

During the two years following the 1984 purchase, Black & Decker undertook a $100 million brand-transition program. Meanwhile, the company also developed its own upscale light appliances, such as the Spacemaker series. Black & Decker also introduced more cordless appliances, including a mixer and an electric knife. Farley began marketing the company's small-appliance line overseas. In Britain, where B&D has long enjoyed considerable name recognition, the first Black & Decker appliances were introduced in 1985. Other markets soon followed. In addition, GE's expertise in manufacturing electric motors enabled Black & Decker to design more efficient power tools using a smaller and more powerful 47-millimeter motor.

Yet Black & Decker's sales performance remained unspectacular, and fears that Laurence Farley was not sufficiently committed to product development, contributed to his replacement as president by Nolan D. Archibald. A year later Archibald also was named chief executive officer and chairman of the board of Black & Decker. Archibald came to The Black & Decker Corporation from Beatrice Company, where he headed the consumer durables group. Bringing in his own management team, the new B&D chief cut 3,000 jobs by 1987 and spurred product development. The company's worldwide operations were restructured into product groups. In 1986 the household-products group introduced a number of successful products, including the Cup-at-A-Time coffeemaker. Greater efficiency at Black & Decker led to record sales of $1.9 million and improved profits in 1987.

Once he had returned Black & Decker to efficiency and profitability, Archibald set out to expand the company's operations through acquisition. In January 1988 he attempted to purchase American Standard to obtain its line of plumbing fixtures, but American Standard escaped through a leveraged buyout. Archibald acquired Emhart Corporation in early 1989 for $2.8 billion. With its True Temper lawn and garden tools, Kwikset locks, GardenAmerica sprinkler systems, Price Pfister faucets, and various fastening systems. Emhart's product line complemented Black & Decker's own products. Archibald combined the two companies' distribution and sales networks.

As a result of the acquisition, Black & Decker assumed a $4 billion debt. In order to reduce debt, Black & Decker planned to sell Emhart's non-complementary operations and cut staff.

The Black & Decker Corporation has regained its world dominance in manufacturing inexpensive, quality hardware goods and power tools. B&D's purchases of Emhart Corporation and the General Electric small-appliance division appear to have been successful. The wider range of do-it-yourself products and an attractive line of upscale small appliances add to Black & Decker's potential for future growth. Black & Decker has succeeded because of attention to consumer needs, high production standards, and savvy marketing.

Principal Subsidiaries: Advanced Technology Inc. of Delaware; Black & Decker (U.K.); Black & Decker Canada Inc.; Black & Decker Eletrodomesticos Ltda. (Brazil); Black & Decker G.m.b.H. (Germany); Black & Decker Housewares Ltd. (Singapore); Black & Decker Inc.; Black & Decker (U.S.Pte.) Inc.; Black & Decker Italia S.p.A. (Italy); Black & Decker (Australasia) Pty. Ltd. (Australia); Black & Decker (Belgium) S.A.; Black & Decker, S.A. de C.V. (Mexico); Black & Decker (France) S.A.R.L.; Emhart Corporation; Emhart Deutschland G.m.b.H. (Germany); Emhart Industries, Inc.; Emhart International Ltd. (U.K.); Emhart Scandia AB (Sweden); Planning Research Corporation; PRC Business Information Systems, Inc.

Further Reading: "A.G. Decker of Black & Decker," *Nation's Business,* December 1969; *Highlights of Progress,* Towson, Maryland, The Black & Decker Corporation, 1987.

—Neal R. McCrillis

BORG-WARNER CORPORATION

200 South Michigan Avenue
Chicago, Illinois 60604
U.S.A.
(312) 322-8500
Fax: (312) 322-8398

Private Company
Incorporated: 1928
Employees: 75,000
Sales: $2.22 billion

Borg-Warner Corporation (BWC) was created in 1928 by the merger of four midwestern manufacturing companies: Borg & Beck Company, Warner Gear Company, Marvel-Schebler Carburetor Corporation, and Mechanics Universal Joint Company. These four companies had prospered during the early 20th century by supplying innovative parts to U.S. car manufacturers. Borg-Warner continued to be heavily dependent upon this business. Nevertheless, diversification, especially after 1955, eventually brought BWC to appliances, heating and air conditioning, chemicals, financial services, and protective services. These new operations enabled Borg-Warner to weather the trend toward integration among U.S. carmakers. The steady if unspectacular growth experienced by Borg-Warner was interrupted in 1986 when the company went private through a leveraged buyout. Faced with a large debt load, the corporation sold most of its diversified operations and returned to its core business of automotive parts manufacturing.

During the late 19th century Charles W. Borg, a Swedish immigrant, went into business with Marshall Beck in Moline, Illinois, making machines to turn out wagon poles. Eventually, Borg & Beck took on work for some of the early automobile manufacturers. In 1910 Borg's son, George Borg, and a company engineer invented the single-plate clutch. George Borg was able to sell his clutch to a small automobile company that was desperately seeking a new clutch for its army trucks. By the time Borg & Beck moved to Chicago and George Borg replaced his father as president in 1918, the company had produced 200,000 clutches, making it the leading U.S. manufacturer of clutches.

Also at the turn of the century, Tom and Harry Warner—two brothers in Muncie, Indiana—designed a differential gear for automobile transmissions. The gear allowed a car's two drive wheels to turn at differing speeds when it was cornering. With local industrialist Abbot L. Johnson at its head, Warner Gear Company was established in 1901. Seeing a demonstration of the Warner differential at a 1903 New York automobile show, Ransom E. Olds ordered 4,000 of them for his new line of cars, the Oldsmobile. This marked the beginning of Warner Gear's great success producing drive-train components.

After World War I, Warner Gear suffered as a result of the the increasing self-sufficiency of car manufacturers. The company's new secretary-treasurer, Charles S. Davis, made a daring proposal. In 1904, three years after marrying Abbot Johnson's daughter, Davis had been put in charge of one of his father-in-law's businesses. In 1919 Davis was brought to Warner Gear as the secretary-treasurer. He proposed that the company develop a standard transmission for all makes of cars. If buyers could be sold on the idea, mass production of the component would allow Warner Gear to underprice all competitors. Davis was correct, and the T-64 became one of the most common transmissions in the United States.

Marvel-Schebler Carburetor and Mechanics Universal Joint were also very successful in producing automobile parts. The founders of Marvel Carburetor and of Schebler, B.N. Pierce and Schebler, had been partners in a woodworking business. Around the turn of the century, the men sensed that automotive parts had a more promising future than violin-making. Pierce and Schebler invented two carburetors, and after several more years dissolved the partnership. Each man kept the rights to a carburetor and went into business. Schebler stayed in Indianapolis, Indiana, and Pierce relocated to Flint, Michigan, and started Marvel Carburetor. In 1928 the Schebler firm was acquired by Marvel Carburetor Company. Marvel made carburetors for various major carmakers and had had a contract with Buick since 1911.

Four machinists in Rockford, Illinois, had formed the Mechanics Machine Company in 1890. With the assistance of the banker P.A. Peterson, the company grew, and by 1911 was producing automobile transmissions, axles, and differentials. Universal joints, however, made the company's fortune. Mechanics Machine had an exclusive contract with Chevrolet to supply malleable-iron-housing universal joints. A self-lubricating model developed after World War I, the Oil-Tite, was an even greater success since it ended the burdensome task of greasing the universal every 500 miles. In 1925 the company was renamed the Mechanics Universal Joint Company.

In early 1928 the leaders of Borg & Beck, Warner Gear, Marvel-Schebler Carburetor, and Mechanics Universal Joint began merger negotiations. The negotiators agreed that each company could continue to operate with some autonomy. A merger, however, would give the companies the size and strength to bargain more effectively. Meetings were held through the first half of 1928. Participants, in effect, wanted to create a federation of companies to decrease the risks involved in producing auto components. At any time carmakers could decide to produce their own components or stop purchasing parts from any of the many small contractors.

An agreement was reached in May 1928. A month later the details of the merger were settled and the new firm, Borg-Warner Corporation, acquired Borg & Beck, Warner, Marvel, and Mechanics Universal. Borg-Warner's headquarters was located in Chicago—at 310 South Michigan Avenue, where it remained until 1958 when it was moved a block to 200 South Michigan Avenue. George Borg was named president and Charles Davis was made chairman of the board. Borg soon decided to pursue other interests, and in March 1929 he switched positions with Davis. Davis remained president of BWC until 1950.

As president of Borg-Warner, Davis adopted a policy of loose coordination. His leadership was of great importance in the early years. Taking control of what was initially a holding company for the different firms, Davis provided general supervision and financial support while the presidents and supervisory boards of the divisions retained a great deal of autonomy. Product development, purchasing, labor relations, and sales remained the preserve of each division. Competition between the divisions was encouraged.

In the next few years many companies joined the new corporation. The first of these was the Galesburg Coulter Disc Company of Galesburg, Illinois, acquired in January 1929. Galesburg Coulter Disc had been manufacturing components for Borg & Beck's clutches for many years. Stephen Ingersoll had begun producing coulter discs, cutting discs that are attached to plows, in 1884. In 1904 the business was incorporated; production increased more than ten times during the next decade. In the 1920s Roy Ingersoll, Stephen Ingersoll's son and president from December 1927, invented a patented technique to make heat-treated coulter discs.

During the 1920s there was an unexpected opportunity to produce plates for automotive-component manufacturers such as Borg & Beck; Galesburg Coulter Disc also sold a great number of disc plates to the Long Manufacturing Company of Detroit. Formed in 1903, Long Manufacturing produced automotive clutches and radiators. At the insistence of Roy Ingersoll, Long Manufacturing was brought into BWC in 1929. The third major U.S. producer of clutches, the Rockford Drilling Company of Rockford, Illinois, also was acquired by BWC in 1929.

That same year the Morse Chain Company was acquired by Borg-Warner. Frank and Everett Morse of Trumansburg, New York, had begun making bicycle chains in the 1880s. Frank Morse developed the "Morse Silent Chain," which he later equipped for use as a timing chain for automobiles. Because it vastly improved the engine's performance, it set the industry standard for timing chains in the 1920s.

BWC enjoyed steady growth and made continual improvements in its product line during the 1930s. In 1930 Ford contracted Borg-Warner to construct transmissions for its new standard lever gearshift. A plant was constructed to accommodate this large contract. Warner Gear engineers developed the first overdrive, sold to Chrysler in 1934. A year later Davis implemented a program to develop an automatic transmission, although it came to fruition only after World War II. Still head of Galesburg Coulter Disc Division, Roy Ingersoll developed several new ventures, including a washtub business that captured 40% of the U.S. market. He also produced a successful all-steel furnace at the Kalamazoo, Michigan, plant.

The only radically new course taken by BWC was unplanned. In August 1929 Davis purchased the Detroit Gear and Machine Company in order to gain needed factory space. Detroit Gear had been acquired in 1925 by a new firm called the Norge Company. The head of Norge, Howard K. Blood, was committed to the production of mechanical refrigerators and insisted that Borg-Warner purchase and develop his new Rollator refrigerator. Unlike previous refrigeration systems, the Rollator was a self-contained unit, similar to modern refrigerators.

As head of the new division Howard Blood then purchased the Alaska Company of Muskegon, Michigan, a manufacturer of refrigerator boxes. The Borg-Warner directors reluctantly approved the acquisition, and invested $1 million to renovate and equip the plant. The consumer durables market was remarkably resilient during the Depression. Norge expanded in 1934 with the purchase of the Detroit Vapor Stove Company, a maker of gas stoves. The division already had introduced a line of washing machines, an electric iron, and an air conditioner. By 1936 the Rollator refrigerator was the second-best-selling refrigerator in the United States.

Borg-Warner's plants switched to war production as soon as the United States entered World War II. Components for jeeps, tanks, trucks, ships, and airplanes flowed out of its plants. BWC's most famous wartime project was its amphibious vehicles. In autumn 1941 the navy contracted Borg-Warner to develop an amphibious tank for the marines to use in the Pacific theater of war. Davis put Robert Ingersoll, Roy Ingersoll's son, in charge of the project. Robert Ingersoll was later given the task of building amphibious tractors, and the LVT3, or Beach Buster.

In 1950 Charles Davis stepped down as president, and his friend Roy Ingersoll took over. While in Paris in 1954 Davis died, and Ingersoll became chairman of the board. To accommodate the expansion of Borg-Warner since 1928, Ingersoll established a system of group vice presidents, each responsible for several of the 30 divisions. Ingersoll also constructed a central research facility, which came to be known as the Roy C. Ingersoll Research Center, in Des Plaines, Illinois.

By 1953 more than half of the firm's output was still in automotive parts. After the war this sector flourished. In 1948 Borg-Warner was contracted by Ford to produce half of its automatic transmissions. The corporation expanded production and factory space to meet the demand. Foreign carmakers, including Jaguar, wanted so many of the firm's transmissions that Borg-Warner established a United Kingdom subsidiary. In 1958 Borg-Warner's contract to manufacture Ford-O-Matic transmissions ended. Because of high U.S. labor costs, the firm also lost other customers such as Massey-Ferguson.

Although Roy Ingersoll stepped down as president in 1956, he remained chairman of the board until 1961. His son, Robert Ingersoll, served as president from 1956 to 1968, chief executive officer from 1958 to 1972, and chairman of the board between 1961 and 1972. Both Ingersolls realized that automakers would continue to make more of their own components as they became more fully integrated. Under the Ingersolls, Borg-Warner rushed to diversify, adding 26 new divisions during the 1950s. As a result of several acquisitions between 1955 and 1959, industrial equipment became a major business for the company. Central to this new endeavor was the 1955 purchase of the Byron Jackson Company, a producer of industrial tools and pumps. During the 1940s this firm had built the six massive pumps for the Grand Coulee Dam. Each pump moved 720,000 gallons of water per minute. In addition to its existing international subsidiaries in Canada and England, Borg-Warner expanded into Australia, Brazil, and Mexico.

The most important developments for BWC in the 1950s and 1960s were in air conditioning and chemicals. There was a large, untapped market for air conditioning. Borg-Warner executives decided to purchase the York Corporation of York, Pennsylvania, in 1956. York was the oldest firm in the business and had a reputation for high-quality products. It had scored many firsts, installing the first air conditioning system in a cinema in 1914, and in 1948 it built the first hermetically sealed room air conditioner. York, however, had lacked the capital necessary to handle growing demand. The York Division was given control of all Borg-Warner's heating and air conditioning operations, and a plant idled by the lapse of the Ford-O-Matic contract was reopened by the new division.

Chemicals were not completely new to Borg-Warner in the 1950s. In 1934 BWC had purchased a very small operation named the Marsene Corporation. Borg-Warner executives saw Marsene's small Gary, Indiana, plant as an experimental foray into the chemical business. The scientist in charge, Robert Shattuck, had developed cyclo rubber which, when properly treated, was an excellent insulator for electrical wiring. During World War II Marsene's wire insulation enjoyed a sudden burst of popularity. Unbeknownst to Shattuck and his employees, cyclo-rubber-coated cables were being used for a new device which proved crucial in the Battle of Britain: the radio detecting and ranging device, or radar.

The Marbon Chemical Division, the name given to Marsene in 1954, developed acrylonitrile-butadiene-styrene (ABS) resins, marketed under the name Cycolac. In 1958 the Western Electric Company contracted Marbon to supply Cycolac for its telephones, and other buyers soon followed. A plant was constructed near Parkersburg, West Virginia, to handle the sudden demand. Between 1961 and 1967 Cycolac sales jumped 350%, cornering half the market in ABS resins. By 1967 chemicals accounted for about $100 million of BWC's sales.

James Bere became president of Borg-Warner in 1968 and chairman when Ingersoll resigned after he was named U.S. ambassador to Japan in 1972. Bere had been brought to BWC in 1961 by Robert Ingersoll. Ingersoll promoted the young executive to the presidency over the heads of four company veterans.

From the late 1960s to the early 1980s Borg-Warner recorded a stable if unremarkable performance, surpassing $3 billion in sales by 1984. Its manufacturing groups experienced sporadic growth, prompting BWC to sell certain operations, including the Norge Division, in July 1968; the Ingersoll Products Division, formerly Coulter Disc, in 1980; and the York Division, including the residential air conditioning and heating operations acquired from Westinghouse Electric Corporation in 1981, in 1985. The York diversification had underperformed since its acquisition.

In late 1978 James Bere and Richard Riley, head of Firestone Tire and Rubber Company, arranged a merger which would have put BWC and Bere in charge of a vastly expanded organization at a cost of just $860 million. Firestone had been faced with a recall of 7.5 million radial tires and was experiencing management troubles. After an upswing in the company's fortunes in early 1980, however, Firestone directors balked at the agreed price, and the deal fell through in April 1980.

More typical of James Bere were his moves to develop service operations, aiming for an even mix of services and manufacturing at Borg-Warner. In 1978 Bere purchased Baker Industries, propelling Borg-Warner into the protective-services industry. Further acquisitions were made in the early 1980s to expand this business. Operating under the Wells Fargo and Burns International names, BWC became the largest provider of protective services in the country. This group recorded over $1 billion in sales in 1985.

In 1968 Borg-Warner had retained the financing subsidiary of Norge, the Borg-Warner Acceptance Corporation. By 1979 it was producing 14% of BWC's earnings. In addition Borg-Warner acquired the Chilton Corporation, a credit-reporting network and information service based in Dallas, in 1986.

After a difficult transition period among its top management, the future of Borg-Warner seemed to have been settled with the selection of Clarence Johnson as president in April 1984. He became chief executive officer a year later. After working as a Federal Bureau of Investigation agent, Johnson came to BWC in 1952, working in the firm's automotive-manufacturing operations. The selection of Johnson allowed Bere to set his retirement date for 1987.

Borg-Warner's growth, however, was halted in 1987 when it became the object of a hostile takeover attempt by GAF Corporation, a chemical company based in Wayne, New Jersey. Samuel J. Heyman, the chairman of GAF, was searching for acquisitions to expand his company's chemical business, and Borg-Warner's profitable chemical operations had attracted his attention.

After the BWC directors rejected a management-led buyout in February 1987, Johnson and the retired Bere tried to ward off Heyman by cutting corporate staff, selling the industrial products group, and putting the financial-services operation up for sale. Nevertheless, GAF, with almost 20% of the BWC's shares, offered to purchase Borg-Warner for $3.16 billion at the end of March 1987. Wary of a ''poison pill'' plan adopted by Borg-Warner in early 1986, Heyman claimed his acquisition was a friendly one. Heyman's record, however, suggested he would strip Borg-Warner of its non-chemical businesses. Borg-Warner's diversified character, lack of debt, and low share price made BWC a good prospect for such a breakup.

Borg-Warner's independence was finally preserved by the sudden appearance of a $4.2 billion leveraged buyout offer from Merrill Lynch Capital Partners. Although Merrill Lynch promised to respect the wishes of Borg-Warner executives, the $2.75 billion in debts contracted during the buyout forced drastic action. At Merrill Lynch's insistence Bere was brought back as chief executive in June 1987. This was swiftly followed by wholesale changes in top management, including the departure of Johnson. Bere, one of eight managing partners and a 2.5% shareholder in the now-private firm, arranged the sale of all Borg-Warner operations except the automotive group and the guard and courier businesses. The largest sale involved the chemicals group, which was bought in September 1988 by General Electric for $2.3 billion. In addition, Bere implemented major cuts in the staff and research budgets, closing the Roy C. Ingersoll Research Center at the end of 1988.

Since 1987 Borg-Warner has been revived as a much smaller, more efficient corporation. Its businesses are limited to automotive-parts manufacturing and protective services. The structure of BWC harks back to the firm's early years, when it was a very successful supplier to U.S. car makers. Precipitous diversification into disparate fields after World War II led to mediocre results in the 1960s and 1970s. Only chemicals and plastics, developed by the firm over several decades, were stable and profitable additions to the core business. In the 1990s the streamlined Borg-Warner should be able to count on continued growth in its auto-parts manufacturing, possibly allowing it to develop new operations in keeping with its traditional strengths.

Principal Subsidiaries: Baker Industries, Inc.; Borg & Beck De Venezuela, S.A.; Borg-Warner Automotive; Borg-Warner de Mexico, S.A.; Borg-Warner do Brasil, S.A. (Brazil); Borg-Warner Ltd. (Canada); Burns International Security Services, Inc.; Pyro Chem Inc.; Warner Gear International (U.K.); Wells Fargo Alarm Services; Wells Fargo Armored Service Corporation; Wells Fargo Guard Services.

Further Reading: Oursler, Will, *From Ox Carts to Jets: Roy Ingersoll and the Borg-Warner Story,* Englewood Cliffs, New Jersey, Prentice-Hall, 1959; "Soothing the pains of growing too fast," *Business Week,* February 18, 1967; "Hot for glory," *Business Month,* January 1989.

—Neal R. McCrillis

THE COMPANIES OF
BRUNSWICK

BRUNSWICK CORPORATION

One Brunswick Plaza
Skokie, Illinois 60077
U.S.A.
(708) 470-4700
Fax: (708) 470-4765

Public Company
Incorporated: 1907 as Brunswick-Balke-Collender Company
Employees: 21,000
Sales: $2.83 billion
Stock Exchanges: New York Midwest Pacific London Tokyo

Brunswick Corporation, the oldest and largest manufacturer of recreation and leisure-time products in the United States, has used its commercial successes in billiard and bowling products to become a large and diversified manufacturer of marine, recreational, and defense and aerospace products. Brunswick began as a family firm, merged to become the Brunswick-Balke-Collender Company in 1884, and was renamed the Brunswick Corporation in 1960. During the 1980s the company, which once described itself as the "General Motors of Sports," moved to dominate the marine and powerboat industry.

John Moses Brunswick was born in 1819 in Bremgarten, Switzerland. At 14, Brunswick emigrated to the United States. He landed in New York City and worked briefly as an errand boy for a German butcher but soon emigrated to Philadelphia, Pennsylvania, where he served a four-year apprenticeship in a carriage shop. In 1839 he moved to Harrisburg, Pennsylvania, where he worked as a journeyman carriage maker, and married Louisa Greiner. The Brunswicks moved to Cincinnati in 1840.

Brunswick found work as a journeyman carriage maker for several local firms until 1841, when a major economic downturn severely depressed the market for carriages. During the depression he worked as a steward on an Ohio River steamboat then as commercial trader. Though he prospered financially he became ill, and after spending several months in bed Brunswick used his accumulated commercial profits to open his own carriage shop in 1845.

Brunswick's Cincinnati, Ohio, woodworking shop began by making functional, high-quality carriages. Brunswick was willing to expand his product line and the shop soon began to produce cabinetwork, tables, and chairs. Brunswick boasted that "if it is wood, we can make it, and we can make it better than anyone else."

Brunswick's willingness to diversify was more than a manifestation of the pride that he took in his work; it was also an early attempt to diversify his product line to counteract fluctuations in the business cycle. For many years Brunswick's growth was internal, but in later years the firm acquired outside businesses to expand its product line.

By the mid-1840s the economy had begun to recover and with it came increased manufacturing activity. In this environment Brunswick began to prosper, and he became active in local political, religious, and social circles. Legend has it that in 1845, at a lavish dinner party, John Brunswick was led into another room where his host proudly displayed a fancy billiard table, which had been imported from England. Brunswick saw the opportunity to expand his woodworking business. Thus began Brunswick's long association and ultimate domination of the sporting-goods market.

Billiards long had suffered from a poor reputation. Indeed, sports in general had very limited mass appeal in the United States prior to the 1850s. Sporting equipment was ornate and was designed for sale to men of wealth. Brunswick's first tables were elaborate luxury items, and as such found a limited market.

In 1848 Brunswick expanded his market by sending his half-brothers, David and Emanuel Brunswick, to Chicago to establish a sales office and factory. Other sales offices were opened in New Orleans, Louisiana, and St. Louis, Missouri, while half-brothers Joseph and Hyman Brunswick worked in the firm's Cincinnati offices. In 1858 the business was reorganized as J. M. Brunswick & Brother. In 1866, the company was renamed J. M. Brunswick & Brothers when Emanuel Brunswick joined Joseph and John Brunswick as a principal in the firm.

By the late 1860s the U.S. billiards market was dominated by three firms: Brunswick; Julius Balke's Cincinnati-based Great Western Billiard Manufactory, and a New York–based company named Phelan & Collender, run by Michael Phelan and his son-in-law, H. M. Collender. In 1873 Brunswick merged with Balke to form the J. M. Brunswick & Balke Company. In 1884, following the death of his father-in-law in 1879, Collender merged with Brunswick & Balke, to form the Brunswick-Balke-Collender Company.

During the 1870s Brunswick's half-brothers left the firm to start rival firms and billiard parlors in Chicago and San Francisco, California. It is not entirely clear under what circumstances each of them left but by 1872 Brunswick's son-in-law, Moses Bensinger, and two long-time employees were vice presidents at Brunswick.

During this period of rapid growth John Brunswick remained in Cincinnati while Bensinger, who increasingly directed the company's day-to-day operations, greatly expanded the company's Chicago facilities. In July 1886 John Brunswick died. He was succeeded by H. M. Collender, who served as president until his own death in 1890. Julius Balke, too ill and old to take over as president, stepped aside, and—after buying out another vice president—Bensinger was named president of Brunswick-Balke-Collender.

Bensinger aggressively expanded the firm's product line. Since many billiard tables were being sold to taverns, he expanded the company's line of carved wooden back bars. Back bars covered the wall behind a bar and served a functional and decorative purpose. They were intricate and elaborate status symbols and also greatly enhanced Brunswick's image as craftsmen. Initially the bars were custom built, but their popularity soon had the company's Dubuque, Iowa, factory operating at full capacity. Before long Brunswick bars were installed across the United States and Canada.

In the 1880s Bensinger added another product, bowling pins and bowling balls. Taverns had begun installing lanes, interest seemed to be growing, and Bensinger was determined to be ready for this new market. He actively promoted bowling as a participatory sport and helped to standardize the game. Bensinger also was instrumental in organizing the American Bowling Congress. Although the company continued to expand its markets and product lines, bowling was to become the financial backbone of the firm.

Throughout this growth and expansion, Brunswick remained a family firm. John Brunswick's surviving son, Benedict Brunswick, and Julius Balke Jr. were Brunswick executives, and Bensinger's son, Benjamin Bensinger, worked first as a clerk, then as a salesman, and was rapidly working his way up in the company. In 1904, upon the death of his father, Benjamin Bensinger became the president of Brunswick-Balke-Collender, at age 36. The firm had several sales offices, and manufacturing plants in Chicago, Cincinnati, Dubuque, and New York, and in 1906 Bensinger opened a large manufacturing plant in Muskegon, Michigan. The Muskegon plant, which grew to over one million square feet in the 1940s, became the cornerstone of the firm's manufacturing, producing such products as mineralite (hard rubber) bowling balls.

In the 1910s the temperance movement threatened not only the fixtures and bar business but also billiards and bowling. In 1912, in anticipation of Prohibition—which started in 1920—Brunswick suspended its bar-fixtures operations, which accounted for one-fourth of annual sales, and sought to replace it with automobile tires and the world's first hard-rubber toilet seats. Rubber products best utilized the firm's existing facilities. By 1921 the Muskegon plant was producing 2,000 tires a day. Then the price of rubber tripled in 1922, Brunswick sold its tire line to B. F. Goodrich, who began to manufacture tires under the Brunswick name as the Brunswick Tire Company.

Brunswick also began to manufacture wood piano cases and phonograph cabinets. Edison Phonograph was the principal buyer of Brunswick's cabinets. The demand for phonographs was so strong that Bensinger decided that Brunswick should manufacture its own line of phonographs. By 1916 the Muskegon plant was producing Brunswick phonographs and putting them on the market for $150—40% less than comparable models. In 1922 it also began producing records under its own label. Jazz greats such as Duke Ellington, Cab Calloway, and Benny Goodman and classical artists such as Irene Pavlovska and Leopold Godowsky all recorded on the Brunswick label. In 1925 Brunswick teamed up with General Electric to manufacture an all-electric phonograph called the Panatrope, which came equipped with or without a radio. In 1930 Brunswick sold the Brunswick Panatrope & Radio Corporation to Warner Brothers for $10 million.

The company had gone public in 1924, and in 1930 Benjamin Bensinger was named chairman of the board and his oldest son, Bob Bensinger, became president. Bob Bensinger had worked for the firm since 1919 and with his brother, Ted, guided Brunswick through the Depression. Even with the repeal of Prohibition in 1933 and the popularity of pool halls, the Great Depression was hard on Brunswick. The company marketed a line of table-top refrigerators called the Blue Flash and a successful line of soda fountains to replace its once-thriving bar and fixture business.

During World War II Brunswick found new markets and new products and once again prospered. United Service Organizations (USO) centers and military bases eagerly purchased billiard and bowling equipment. Brunswick also made wartime products, including mortar shells, flares, assault boats, fuel cells, floating mines, aircraft instrument panels, and aluminum litters.

At the end of the war Brunswick became involved in a high-stakes battle with the American Machine and Foundry Company (AMF) over the automatic pinsetter for bowling alleys. AMF produced pinsetters in the late 1940s but these proved unreliable. In 1952 AMF installed an improved version of its machine and called it a pinspotter. Brunswick, which had toyed with the idea of an automatic pinsetter as early as 1911, had to develop a working pinsetter quickly or risk losing its domination of the bowling market. Telling customers that it would be "worth waiting for," Brunswick scrambled to develop its own machine. In 1954 Brunswick formed the Pinsetter Corporation with Murray Corporation of America. By the time the pinsetters were in production in 1955, Brunswick had bought out Murray, and Brunswick aggressively sold its machine to a rapidly expanding market.

Brunswick's policy of selling pinsetters on credit, suburban expansion, and an aggressive advertising campaign all combined to make bowling centers enormously popular in the late 1950s. After the introduction of the pinsetter the company prospered as never before. Sales, which had been $33 million in 1954, jumped to $422 million in 1961. Although Brunswick's earnings did not leap correspondingly—sales were up almost 13-fold, but earnings increased just less than six times—Ted Bensinger, named CEO in 1954, received most of the credit for Brunswick gains. Brunswick acquired 18 new firms to further diversify its markets. Companies like MacGregor Sports Products, Union Hardware, Zebco, and Owens Yacht Company made Brunswick a major force in equipment for golf, roller skating, fishing, and boating. Brunswick's most important purchase proved to be the 1961 acquisition of the Kiekhaefer Corporation, which built Mercury outboard motors.

Brunswick also sought firms outside recreational sports, and in 1959 it purchased A.S. Aloe and entered the medical-supply business. To complement the Aloe purchase Brunswick also acquired Sheridan Catheter & Instrument Corporation in 1960, Roehr Products Company in 1961, and Biological Research in 1961. Brunswick's medical-supply business became known as the Sherwood Medical Group. Brunswick also developed a popular line of school furniture in the 1950s and kept active in its defense-products division.

An unexpected decline in the bowling industry, which represented 60% of sales, in the early 1960s presented Brunswick with serious financial problems. Jack Hanigan was brought in as president in November 1963 to handle Brunswick's financial problems. Ted Bensinger became chairman and he and his brother both remained on the board of directors into the 1970s. Hanigan aggressively sought to reorganize Brunswick and to position the firm for future expansion. In 1965 he formed a technical and new-business division which developed, among other things, Brunsmet, a metal-fiber product. In 1967 Hanigan merged this division and the defense division into the technical-products division. These new divisions, along with further expansion of the company's medical lines, growth of the Kiekhaefer-Mercury products, and the recovery of bowling in the late 1960s, all helped Brunswick to reach record sales of $450 million in 1969.

The 1973-to-1974 oil embargo caused problems at Brunswick, particularly in its profitable marine-engine division, but the company was able to further diversify its products and remained strong. The technical-products division continued to grow, producing, among other things, radomes and metal-fiber camouflage. Hanigan retired as chairman and CEO in 1976 and was replaced by K. Brooks Abernathy.

To promote stability Brunswick had been organized into four business groups: marine, medical, recreational, and technical. Jack Reichert, president of the Marine group, became president of Brunswick in 1977 as sales topped $1 billion for the first time. Not content, Brunswick moved into energy and transportation control systems by acquiring Vapor Corporation for $90 million in 1978, as well as actively expanding its international markets.

Brunswick successfully fought a hostile takeover bid by the Whittaker Corporation in 1982. Whittaker wanted Brunswick's Sherwood Medical Group medical-supply business. Whittaker was forced to withdraw is offer when American Home Products stepped in as a white knight, and Sherwood was sold to American Home Products in March 1982 for $425 million in Brunswick stock. In April 1982 Reichert took over as CEO of Brunswick. Reichert sought to decentralize Brunswick to improve efficiency and stress quality output. The firm's 11 sectors were reduced to 8, corporate staff was cut, and executive perquisites were trimmed, reducing bureaucratic costs. Reichert transferred division staff to production sites in an attempt to enhance product quality. He also moved to include hourly employees as shareholders and increased pension payments to former employees.

During the latter half of the 1980s, Brunswick made a series of significant moves aimed at reasserting itself in the field of recreation. In 1986 Brunswick acquired two pleasure-boat manufacturers, U.S. Marine and Sea Ray, for $773 million. These purchases, along with the acquisitions of MonArk Boat, Marine Group, Fisher Marine, and Starcraft Power Boats in 1988, made Brunswick the world's largest manufacturer of pleasure boats and marine engines. These companies also made Brunswick vulnerable to fluctuations in marine sales.

Brunswick had enjoyed six consecutive years of record earnings from 1982 through 1988. That string of record years ended in 1989, when restructuring charges arising from a downturn in the marine market resulted in a net loss. The company returned to profitability in 1990.

In 1989 and 1990 Brunswick disposed of the business units that had theretofore comprised its technetics and industrial products divisions. With the culmination of these actions, Brunswick emerged as a company whose interests were focused upon a broad range of recreational products and services, and in selected defense and aerospace markets.

Principal Subsidiaries: Brunswick International Ltd.; Marine Power International Ltd.; Mariner International Company; U.S. Marine Corporation; Ray Industries Incorporated; Mercury Marine Ltd. (Canada); Mercury Marine Ltd. (Australia); Brunswick International GmbH (Germany); Vapor Canada Ltd.; Brunswick International Ltd. (Canada); Brunswick GmbH (Germany); Nippon Brunswick Company Ltd. (Japan, 50%).

Further Reading: Kogan, Rick, *Brunswick: The Story of an American Company from 1845 to 1985*, Skokie, Illinois, Brunswick Corporation, 1985.

—Timothy E. Sullivan

CARL-ZEISS-STIFTUNG

D-7920 Heidenheim
Postfach 1380
Carl-Zeiss-Strasse 2-60
D-7082 Oberkochen
Federal Republic of Germany
(7364) 200
Fax: (7364) 20 33 70

Private Company
Incorporated: 1889
Employees: 32,247
Sales: DM4.4 billion (US$2.60 billion)

The Carl-Zeiss-Stiftung, a "juridical person" under German civil law, is the sole owner of two industrial enterprises, Carl Zeiss of Oberkochen and Schott Glaswerke of Mainz. These enterprises develop, produce, and sell high-quality precision-engineered optical glass and electronic products. The Carl-Zeiss-Stiftung enterprises have—as a percentage of sales—one of Germany's highest research and development budgets. The company has no private or state associates, and no shareholders. *Stiftung* is sometimes inaccurately translated as a special type of "foundation," a term suggesting an institution with purely charitable or scientific aims. The Carl-Zeiss-Stiftung, however, is a business organization with specific technological, scientific, economic, and social aims and functions. Usually companies are owned by individuals, banks, or states. The above-mentioned enterprises, however, are owned by the Stiftung and owe much of their character to its 1896 statute provisions.

The origins of the Carl-Zeiss-Stiftung date from 1846, when Carl Zeiss, later awarded the title of university mechanic by the Grand Duke of Sachsen-Weimar, opened an instrument maker's shop in Jena. He soon specialized in the manufacture of microscopes. At the request of Carl Zeiss, the physicist Ernst Abbe developed the theory of the microscope and designed instruments with better resolution power and better color rendition than was hitherto possible. These improved microscopes sold from 1872, and—in particular microscopes with homogenous immersion objectives, introduced in 1877, and those with apochromatic objectives, available in 1886—greatly assisted the bacteriologists' identification of infectious bacteria.

At that time the availability of only a small number of glass types with different optical properties limited progress in microscope image quality. In 1884 the chemist Otto Schott, together with Ernst Abbe, Carl Zeiss, and the latter's son Roderich, established a glass research laboratory, which developed into the Jenaer Glaswerk Schott & Genossen. By 1886, 44 different types of optical glass were in production. In cooperation with Ernst Abbe, Otto Schott carried out systematic research work into the dependence of optical and other glass on chemical composition. Schott's inventions included thermometer glass, chemical- and heat-resistant borosilicate glass. His optical glass contributed to the development of modern optical instruments. For microscopes and later also for telescopes, optical systems with apochromatic correction, that is, considerably reduced color aberrations, were designed.

Abbe's achievements as a social reformer of employment conditions were as significant as his scientific innovations. In 1889 he founded the Carl-Zeiss-Stiftung, which in 1891 he made the sole owner of the Zeiss works and a partner in the Schott works. In 1919 Schott made his own share of the glass works available to the Carl-Zeiss-Stiftung, which thus became the sole owner of both enterprises. In the 1896 statute of the Carl-Zeiss-Stiftung, Ernst Abbe formulated its aims and principles. The guiding principle of the Zeiss and Schott works and their associated enterprises throughout the world was to secure their economic, scientific, and technological future and in this way to improve the job security of their employees. The Stiftung's enterprises were obliged to produce high-quality, precision-engineered instruments, optical glass, and similar products, to fulfil long term social welfare obligations to their employees, to support science and technology outside as well as within the enterprises, and to participate in projects which served the general good. The employment and career of an employee would depend only on his capabilities and performance, not on his origin, religion, or political views. The employees were to elect their own representation on the works council, and they received the right to a fixed minimum income, paid holidays, sickness benefit, profit sharing, disablement and pension benefits, and a nine-hour day, all of which was realized as early as 1896. In 1900 the eight-hour day was introduced.

This scientific and social basis was reinforced economically by product diversification and by a growing export organization. In addition to microscopes Zeiss marketed photo lenses from 1890, measuring instruments from 1893, and terrestrial telescopes from 1894. Astronomical optics followed in 1897, medical instruments in 1898, photogrammetrical instruments in 1901, surveying instruments in 1908, and eye glasses in 1912. Schott solved the cooling problem for large optical components with a diameter of up to 1.4 meters, as early as 1894. In 1913 Schott offered 97 types of optical glass, and by 1923 the number had increased to 114.

International relations were cultivated at an early stage. Zeiss visited the Paris World Fair in 1867, and Schott was repeatedly active as a manager in Spain, establishing a chemical factory in Oviedo, Spain, and a production facility for window glass in Reinosa, Spain. These were not, however, owned by Schott. Abbe exchanged ideas with British microscopists, and from 1878 he published papers in English.

In 1899 about two-thirds of Zeiss instruments were sold abroad. A network of branches and agencies was built up, beginning with Zeiss sales offices in London, in 1901, and Vienna, in 1902. Branch factories were established in Vienna; in Györ, Hungary; Riga; and London in the first years of the 20th century.

In this period the Carl-Zeiss-Stiftung financed a number of projects for the benefit of Jena University and of the community, including a university building in 1908 and the Volkshaus, literally the "People's House," but in reality a palace with a library, museums, lecture halls, and a concert hall. Other projects in which the Stiftung was involved included a school of opticians, a children's hospital, and a public baths.

The Carl-Zeiss-Stiftung's constituent businesses, according to its statute, do not have a president but have several board members instead. This arrangement provides a degree of continuity even if a manager retires or dies. When Abbe retired in 1903 and died in 1905, Otto Schott, Siegfried Czapski, and Rudolf Straubel took over the burden of responsibility. Long-standing leaders of the organization included Erich Schott, who created a glass electric division in the glass works and was a board member from 1927–1968, and Walther Bauersfeld, who was a Zeiss board member from 1908–1959. Bauersfeld received worldwide esteem for his invention of a planetarium, which strikingly demonstrated the real and apparent movements of the sun, moon, fixed stars, and planets by projection on the inside of a dome.

The reputation of the Carl-Zeiss-Stiftung, the excellence of its products, and the commercial success of its enterprises had a far-reaching impact on the industries in which it was involved. Bausch & Lomb of Rochester, New York, acquired licenses from Zeiss, who bought shares in this U.S. company in 1908. World War I put an end to this successful collaboration in 1915. Another well-known microscope manufacturer, Rudolf Winkel of Göttingen, was reorganized after some financial problems with the help of Carl Zeiss in 1911 and integrated into the organization in 1957. Today Zeiss microscopes are made in Göttingen.

From 1910 to 1926 various German camera factories were amalgamated step-by-step into the Zeiss Ikon AG, famous for its Contax brand. In 1910 Zeiss acquired shares and in 1931 the majority of the Prontor-Werk Alfred Gauthier GmbH, now a producer of items for Carl Zeiss instruments. In 1927 the Schott works acquired a majority share in a company now called Schott-Zwiesel-Glaswerke AG that produced consumer glassware. Three years later a majority share was acquired in the company now known as Deutsche Spezialglas AG, a manufacturer of ophthalmic glass and various types of special technical glass. In 1928 Carl Zeiss acquired shares of the M. Hensoldt & Söhne Wetzlar Optische Werke AG, which today produces Carl Zeiss telescopes and riflescopes. Hermann Anschütz-Kaempfe, the inventor of the gyrocompass, was impressed by the ideas of the Carl-Zeiss-Stiftung, to which he offered his majority share of his company Anschütz & Co. GmbH, producers of navigation instruments, shortly before his death in 1931.

Thanks to its solid foundations the Carl-Zeiss-Stiftung survived through times of hardship. During World War I, the work force was considerably enlarged due to the demands of riflescope, distancemeter, and aerial camera production. After the war and the subsequent period of hyper-inflation it became necessary to reduce personnel. In accordance with the statute of the Carl-Zeiss-Stiftung, compensation for dismissal was paid.

In 1933 a National Socialist was appointed to the post of *Stiftungskommissar* (foundation deputy), as the one-man supervising authority of the Carl-Zeiss-Stiftung. The board members and work forces of both enterprises, Carl Zeiss and Schott Glaswerke, offered concerted resistance. The foundation deputy was ousted from his post in 1934, and Abraham Esau, a professor loyal to the Stiftung, took his place. Today the foundation deputy is assisted by advisory boards at the two enterprises. Each advisory board has six appointed and six elected members.

After 1933 production of a wide range of glass materials, glass products, and optical instruments continued. New developments included the phase contrast microscope, the prototype of which was first seen in 1936, and a new instrument for rapid surveying, in 1942. During World War II demand for military optics—range finders, rifle scopes, and periscopes for example—increased again. The additional workforce consisted of both Germans and laborers from occupied countries.

In 1945, after World War II, the Allied government brought the entire management and the leading scientists of the enterprises of the Carl-Zeiss-Stiftung to Heidenheim, which became its new legal base after the two Jena enterprises were expropriated in 1948 by the East German authorities without compensation. Only in West Germany could it continue its existence on the basis of Abbe's statute. The Schott Glaswerke and Carl Zeiss have since regained international renown for their numerous technical innovations.

However, the 126 managers and scientists in West Germany had to overcome enormous difficulties. Having arrived without technical documents, they had to rely on memory. In 1946, in Oberkochen near Heidenheim—in what is today Baden-Württemberg—a new optical plant was established, initially in rented premises. The glass experts continued production in Zwiesel and Landshut, Bavaria, until 1952, when a new factory was opened in Mainz.

Schott also established a number of production and sales subsidiaries at home and abroad; for example, ampule factories in Brazil and France between 1954 and 1974. In 1967 the present Schott Glass Technologies Inc. of Duryea, Pennsylvania, in the United States was founded for the production of optical glass. In Germany the Schott-Ruhrglas GmbH, manufacturing special glass tubing, was established in 1969. Carl Zeiss acquired two spectacles factories—Marwitz & Hauser, in which it had acquired a majority shareholding in 1958, and Titmus Optical Inc., of the United States—in 1974. The contact-lens maker Wöhlk has been a Zeiss subsidiary since 1980, when Carl Zeiss acquired a major stake.

After the postwar reconstruction of the company, the employment rights of the workers became effective once more; they had not been practicable during the state of emergency after World War II. On the occasion of this event the Federal President Theodor Heuss visited Oberkochen on May 1, 1954, and stated: "German destiny is branded on few establishments of world significance as it is on this Zeiss establishment."

The original plants in Jena were dismantled by the Russian authorities in 1946, and more than 300 specialists were forced to work in Russia for some years. The Zeiss and Schott enterprises in Jena were temporarily struck off the trade register. Expropriation and nationalization of its former factories had removed the basis of the existence of the Carl-Zeiss-Stiftung in Jena. Nevertheless, the factories in Jena were restored to working order. From 1954 there were legal disputes in many countries regarding the matter of identity of the Carl-Zeiss-Stiftung and the use of the name Zeiss and its trademarks. In 1971 a compromise contract was finally drawn up in London. Under the contract, the Carl-Zeiss-Stiftung, Heidenheim, could exclusively use its name and trademarks with the component Zeiss in West Germany and some other Western countries, including the United States. The Jena party received corresponding exclusive rights in the Comecon and some other countries. In some countries, such as the United Kingdom, both parties could use the name Zeiss. This contract was replaced by a new version in 1990. As far as the identity of the Carl-Zeiss-Stiftung was concerned, the parties adhered to their differing opinions. For the glass works, a settlement valid worldwide was reached in 1981; the enterprise in Mainz was renamed Schott Glaswerke and the Jena enterprise took the name Jenaer Glaswerk. Under the policies and principles of the statute of the Carl-Zeiss-Stiftung, Schott Glaswerke and Carl Zeiss are prepared to master the challenges of the future in the fields of technology and business.

Principal Subsidiaries: Auer-SOG Glaswerke GmbH; Deutsche Spezialglas AG (84%); Schott-Ruhrglas GmbH (74%); Schott-Zwiesel-Glaswerke AG; Glaswerk Wertheim GmbH; Schott Glass Technologies Inc. (U.S.A.); La Verrerie Médicale (France); Vitrofarma Indústria e Comércio de Vidros S.A. (Brazil, 94%); Anschütz & Co. GmbH; Heinrich Wöhlk Institut für Contact-Linsen GmbH & Co. (75%); Marwitz & Hauser GmbH; M. Hensoldt & Söhne Wetzlar Optische Werke AG; Prontor-Werk Alfred Gauthier GmbH; Titmus Optical Inc. (U.S.A.).

Further Reading: Abbe, Ernst, *Gesammelte Abhandlungen,* Volumes I-IV, Jena, G. Fischer, 1904–1928; Auerbach, Felix, *The Zeissworks,* London, W.&G. Foyle, [1926]; Rohr, Moritz von, *Zur Geschichte der Zeissischen Werkstätte bis zum Tode Ernst Abbes,* Jena, G. Fischer, 1936; Kühnert, Herbert, *Der Briefwechsel zwischen Otto Schott und Ernst Abbe über das optische Glas 1879–1881,* Jena, G. Fischer, 1946; Schomerus, Friedrich, *Geschichte des Jenaer Zeisswerkes 1846–1946,* Stuttgart, Piscator, 1952; Schomerus, Friedrich, *Werden und Wesen der Carl-Zeiss-Stiftung,* Stuttgart, G. Fischer, 1955; Kiaulehn, Walther, *Der Zug der 41 Glasmacher,* Mainz, Schott Glaswerke, 1959; Volkmann, Harald, "Ernst Abbe and his work," *Applied Optics,* November 1966; Willam, Horst Alexander, "Otto Schott und das Zeiss Werk," *Klinische Monatsblätter für Augenheilkunde,* 1966; Schott, Erich, *Von Jena nach Mainz,* Mainz, [n.p.], 1984; *100 Jahre Carl-Zeiss-Stiftung;* Heidenheim, Carl-Zeiss-Stiftung, 1988; Hermann, Armin, *Nur der Name war geblieben—Die abenteuerliche Geschichte der Firma Carl Zeiss,* Stuttgart, DVA, 1989.

—Wolfgang Pfeiffer

CASIO®

CASIO COMPUTER CO., LTD.

6-1, Nishi-shinjuku 2-chome
Shinjuku-ku, Tokyo 163
Japan
(03) 3347-4811
Fax: (03) 3348-3629

Public Company
Incorporated: 1957
Employees: 3,614
Sales: ¥304.83 billion (US$2.12 billion)
Stock Exchanges: Tokyo Osaka Amsterdam Frankfurt

Casio Computer Co., Ltd. manufacturers desktop electronic calculators, digital and analog timepieces, digital notebooks and diaries, electronic musical instruments, audiovisual products, computers, and other consumer and industrial electronic products. Casio has developed a number of electronic products for consumers and businesses based on digital technology and the use of integrated circuits. During the late 1980s, however, the company expanded its technological base to include such things as liquid crystal display, optics, and electro-photography technology.

In 1969 Casio was among the first Japanese manufacturers to fully automate an assembly plant, and this sort of innovation has allowed the firm to remain cost-competitive with other larger electronic manufacturers. Much of Casio's success has been based not only on its technological and assembly innovations but also on its aggressive marketing and sales strategies. As a result of its assertive marketing, the company sells its diverse products in over 140 countries. By 1990 Casio planned to diversify its markets further by expanding its manufacturing facilities and subsidiary operations in Asia, North America, and Europe.

Casio Computer Company was founded in Tokyo in 1946 by the Kashio family. Four Kashio brothers—Toshio, Kazuo, Tadao, and Yukio—and their father founded a company that was to be managed under a "spirit of creation"; the company philosophy remains "creativity and contribution." As of 1989, the Kashio brothers still owned about 10% of all outstanding Casio stock. The Kashio family retains effective financial control of the company. Other major holders of Casio stock are Japanese financial companies, none of which owns more than 4.29%. The four Kashio brothers remain active in the management and operation of the company. Toshio Kashio serves as chairman, Kazuo Kashio is president, Tadao Kashio is a senior advisor, and Yukio Kashio is the senior managing director.

The name Casio is an anglicized version of Kashio, demonstrating that from the beginning the company was acutely aware of the economic significance of international marketing. The Kashios felt that in the post–World War II environment a westernized name would help the company make its consumer and business products more marketable, both domestically and internationally.

Casio was incorporated in 1957, following Toshio Kashio's invention of the first purely electric—as opposed to electromechanical—small calculator. The company capitalized on this invention and became the only Japanese manufacturer to specialize in electric calculators. Over the years Casio has used its calculator sales to foster its continuing research-and-development programs and to finance new product lines.

After the introduction of semiconductors in the mid-1960s, electromechanical technology was replaced with electronic technology, and in 1965 Casio introduced the world's first desktop electronic calculator with a memory. Casio has consistently sought to expand its product line while relying upon calculators as its primary base of operations.

Prior to 1965 electromechanical calculators were large and expensive. Electromechanical calculators were literally desktop size, ranged in price from $400 to $1,000, and could complete only four functions—addition, subtraction, division, and multiplication. These earlier devices, limited in function and speed, were also prone to mechanical failure. The development of semiconductor and integrated-circuit technologies during the 1960s began to reduce the size and cost of electronic calculators dramatically and simultaneously enhanced their reliability. Electronic calculators were also easier to read, despite their smaller size, due to technical breakthroughs in light-emitting diodes (LED) and liquid crystal displays (LCD), and these new technologies required significantly less power to operate. Casio helped to develop LED and LCD technologies, and by the 1980s these technologies played an increasingly important role in the development of Casio's digital-timepiece and LCD-television markets.

In 1964 the first transistorized, programmable, desktop calculators were introduced, and Japanese manufacturers, including Casio, began to assemble electronic calculators. The entire output from all Japanese electronic manufacturers in 1965 was only about 5,000 units. In 1969 Casio's Kofu factory became the first Japanese plant to mass produce electronic calculators. Very few of these early Japanese electronic calculators were destined for the U.S. market. In 1965 the United States imported just 69 electronic calculators from Japan, and in 1966 Japanese calculators accounted for less than 1% of the U.S. market. Casio did not begin to market its own products in the United States until 1970.

In the 1970s Japanese electronic products, particularly consumer electronics, began to capture a larger share of the ever-expanding U.S. market. By the mid-1970s Japanese electronic manufacturers came to dominate the U.S. electronic-calculator market.

By the 1980s Japan had become the world's leading electronics exporter while the United States was the largest consumer of electronic products. While U.S. firms have concentrated on military, industrial, and commercial products, Japanese firms have emphasized consumer products.

Casio is organized into four operating divisions: electronic calculators, electronic timepieces, electronic musical instruments, and electronic office equipment and other sectors. In the Japanese market Casio has 35% of the calculator market, 25% of the timepiece market, and 38% of the office-equipment market. By 1989, desktop electronic calculators accounted for roughly 42% of the company's annual sales. Casio also held the largest market share of the world calculator market. By 1989 exports, primarily to Europe and the United States, accounted for about 62% of Casio's annual sales.

The calculator division grew steadily, manufacturing standard electronic calculators, high-performance scientific calculators, pocket computers, and digital diary systems. Electronic notepads and digital diaries greatly expanded Casio's markets, particularly its domestic sales. The electronic-timepiece division also prospered, making a variety of digital and analog watches, many with built-in memory and storage features.

After years of market expansion during the 1970s and 1980s, however, Casio found that market demand in timepieces became stagnant. As a result of market saturation, Casio introduced a number of new timepieces to maintain market demand during the late 1980s, including such products as watches that measure altitude, depth, and barometric pressure; phone-dialing watches; and watches that can record caloric consumption or serve as a pedometer.

The electronic-musical-instrument division manufactures such products as electronic keyboards and digital synthesizers, guitar synthesizers, digital horns, and other sound generators. Casio introduced electronic keyboards into the U.S. market in 1980, and has since come to dominate that market. Like its electronic-timepiece division, musical products suffer from potential market saturation. After an initial surge in sales, the company began to market enhanced or new lines of products to maintain market demand. During the late 1980s Casio began working to expand its musical markets by appealing to professional musicians and by developing sound products for use in live performances.

The electronic-office-equipment division manufacturers such products as LCD televisions, TV/VCR combination units, office computers, electronic cash registers, point-of-sale scanning systems, and other audiovisual products. Casio hopes to build on its LCD technology to further expand its product lines and ensure future growth and development.

In 1988 Casio introduced a new automated data-processing product line. An integrated business system designed to be used without costly programming, Casio refers to the product as an Active Data Processing System (ADPS). It includes a processing unit which Casio hoped would create a universal business data format and a data-management system. Casio planned full-scale marketing of this new computer in early 1991 and strengthened its sales network. Casio hoped to use ADPS to strengthen and expand its role in business markets.

Since research and development plays a crucial role in the long-term viability of electronic manufacturers, Casio has consistently devoted about 4% of its annual sales revenues to research and development. Among the more promising technologies being pursued by Casio is COF (chip on film) technology. COF technology is a method of mounting information on a computer chip that allows increased functional capabilities in lighter and thinner settings. The company has already adapted COF technology for use in electronic calculators, digital diaries, and printers. Moreover, Casio intends to incorporate this technology in smaller and lighter watches, LCD televisions, computers, and memory cards.

Casio has attempted to expand its markets not only through technical enhancements and new product lines, but it also has moved aggressively to increase the scope of its operations by expanding internationally. Due to market saturation in the United States and in traditional electronic products, Casio appears to be most interested in European and Asian expansion as well as the development of new applications and enhancements of its digital, sensor, LCD, and COF technologies.

Principal Subsidiaries: Aichi Casio Company; Yamagata Casio Company; Roudri Casio Company; Casio Electronics Manufacturing Company; Casio Information Services Company; Casio Micronics Company; Casio System Development Company; Keiji Casio Company; Kofu Casio Company; Kyowa Seiki Company; Osaka Casio Company; The Casio Lease Company; Yamagata Casio Company; Casio Seimitsu Industrial Company; Casio Electronic Devices Company, Ltd.; Casio Computer Company GmbH (Germany); Casio Computer Ltd. (Hong Kong); Casio Electronics Company, Ltd. (U.K.); Casio Electronex S.A. de C.V. (Mexico); Casio Europe B.V. (Netherlands); Casio, Inc. (U.S.A.); Casio Korea Company, Ltd.; Casio Taiwan Ltd.; Casio Manufacturing Corporation (U.S.A.); Casio Electronics Manufacturing Co., Ltd.

—Timothy E. Sullivan

CATERPILLAR®

CATERPILLAR INC.

100 Northeast Adams Street
Peoria, Illinois 61629
U.S.A.
(309) 675-1000
Fax: (309) 675-5815

Public Company
Incorporated: 1925 as Caterpillar Tractor Company
Employees: 60,409
Sales: $11.13 billion
Stock Exchanges: New York Midwest Pacific London Paris Brussels Frankfurt Zürich

Caterpillar specializes in the manufacture of heavy vehicles for construction and agriculture. With 25 major production facilities worldwide, Caterpillar does about half of its business within the United States and half abroad. After suffering losses of almost $1 billion between 1982 and 1984, Caterpillar regained its profitability. The company's plant-modernization program, to be completed in the early 1990s, will enable Caterpillar to produce more high-quality construction vehicles and diesel engines than any other company, and to do so with the speed and efficiency that can be found only in automated factories.

In 1859 Daniel Best left his Iowa home for California. After about ten years of working at various jobs, Best observed that many farmers transported their grain to special cleaning stations to make it suitable for market. Best thought there was a way to clean grain by machine at the same time as it was being harvested to avoid the costly step of transporting to another site. By 1871 Best had patented his first grain cleaner, which he manufactured and sold with great success. By the 1880s Best owned manufacturing centers in Oakland, California, and in Oregon.

Charles Holt arrived in California in 1863, and would found the firm that would put together what is today's Caterpillar. Intending to further the family business of selling hardwood products, Holt founded C.W. Holt & Company with his savings and operated it with his brothers, who came west from New Hampshire. The Holt brothers then set up the Stockton Wheel Company, in 1883, to season woods in a way that would prepare them for use in the arid midlands of California and deserts of the West. The Holts poured $65,000 into their venture, equipping their factory with the best machinery available. The new subsidiary manufactured wooden wheels, and marked the firm's first experience with the vehicular products that would be the company's strength in the years to come.

In the 1880s the combined harvester and thresher, known as the combine, revolutionized the farming industry because of its ability to cut and thresh, and later to clean and sack grain, in vast quantities, using far less time than previously needed for these individual operations. The Holt brothers' Link Belt Combined Harvester, developed in 1886, advanced agricultural technology further by using flexible chain belts rather than gears to transmit power from the ground wheels to the working parts of the machine. This innovation cut down on machine breakage.

Near the end of the 19th century, the major drawback in large-scale agriculture was the need for animal power. The combine had made large farms profitable, but the cost of housing and feeding large horse teams and the men who drove them cut into earnings. Both the Holts and Daniel Best were interested in solving this problem by using steam-driven engines to supply tractive power.

The Holts built a steam-driven tractor that could haul 50 tons of freight at three miles per hour. The Stockton Wheel Company was then incorporated as Holt Manufacturing Company in 1892. Almost concurrently, Daniel Best refined his steam-engine tractor into one of the finest available during this period, and throughout the 1890s steam-powered tractors were used for hauling freight and plowing fields, as well as for harvesting grain.

In the early 1900s the Holt brothers turned their ingenuity to another farming problem. The land around Stockton, California, where the Holt Company was headquartered, was boggy and became impassable when wet. To overcome this limitation the Holts produced the first caterpillar-style tractor, or crawler. It was built on tracks instead of wheels, and the "Cat" could negotiate any terrain short of a swamp. It soon allowed planters to reclaim thousands of acres of land previously thought useless. In 1906 a steam-powered crawler was perfected, and caught on quickly because of its ability to work on ground that all but swallowed other machines.

In 1908 the engineers who were building the 230-mile Los Angeles Aqueduct used a gas-powered crawler to transport materials across the Mojave Desert. The machine worked so well that 25 more tractors were purchased for further work on the aqueduct, thus giving the Holt tractor credibility with the public and a substantial boost to sales.

In 1908 Daniel Best sold out to the Holts, after decades of individual success. Best's son, C.W. Best, was taken on as company superintendent, but after two years, formed his own company and advanced the state of tractor technology even further on his own.

In 1909 Charles Holt, who had been looking for a new manufacturing plant in the eastern half of the United States, bought the abandoned but relatively new plant of a tractor company that had failed. The new Peoria, Illinois, location offered Holt everything he needed in a manufacturing center, and despite the need to pour capital into retooling the plant, it proved so profitable that by 1911 the factory employed 625 people. At that time Holt began to export his tractors to Argentina, Mexico, and Canada.

After the Peoria plant opened, Holt continued to improve his tractor and expand its range of applications. He experimented with several different materials for the body design to achieve a heavy-duty tractor that was not excessively heavy. Holt knew that his tractors could be used for even more rugged chores than agriculture or freighting, and fitted adjustable blades onto his tractors. He then hired them out to grade roads or move soil and rocks at construction sites.

Soon after World War I broke out in 1914, thousands of troops were caught in trench warfare. Observing such repeated attacks, a British lieutenant colonel, Ernest Swinton, sought an armored machine to resist automatic weapons, that also would be able to negotiate the war-scarred terrain of the battlefield. His requirements resulted in the invention in 1916 of an experimental tank, based on the track-laying tractors designed by Holt and others. A year later the tank was used to such telling effect that it is credited with winning the Battle of Cambrai, in France, for the Allies. Some historians point to this battle as the turning point of the war. Germany had investigated the military applications of the track-laying vehicle well before anyone else and concluded that tractors were without military significance.

Holt tractors themselves served the war effort by hauling artillery and supplies. In all, more than 10,000 Holt vehicles served the Allied forces, and the international exposure that the Holt tractor received during the war did much to popularize the tracked vehicle.

In the early 1920s the Holt company faced the problem of going from wartime boom to peacetime bust. Almost overnight the military orders that kept the factories working at capacity seemed to vanish. Holt used this down period to increase efficiency, both mechanical and human; for example, studies were made to determine how to use space and personnel to the best advantage.

In 1925 Holt and C. W. Best's company merged, this time to form the Caterpillar Tractor Company (Cat). Its first problem was to choose the outlets that would represent the new concern from among the many solid dealerships that Best and Holt had established under their respective names. Caterpillar picked only the most successful sites and quickly began to expand by opening dealerships in Australia, the Netherlands, east Africa, and Tunisia. Caterpillar dealerships developed a reputation for keeping their machines running. The firm insisted that the dealers keep a large supply of spare parts available and employ a large service force.

In 1929 Caterpillar's sales were $52 million, and the Peoria plant alone employed more than 4,000 workers. The crash of 1929, however, hit Caterpillar hard, but not as hard as it might have, thanks to an increase in sales to the Soviet Union in the early 1930s. In the aftermath of the financial world's collapse, Caterpillar went from sales of $45 million in 1930 to $13 million in 1932. Salaries were cut, including those of executives, and many factories went on a four-day workweek or were consolidated with other plants. Yet the company stayed profitable and rebounded in the late 1930s, primarily, again, because of Soviet purchases. The Soviets at that time were forming vast collective farms, some of which approached 400,000 acres in size. Caterpillar products helped make such farms manageable, and the Soviets ordered millions of dollars worth of tractors and combines from Caterpillar. In the early 1930s Caterpillar moved its main office to Peoria, for a more geographically central location.

By 1931, the diesel tractor engine, which had been used before but not widely, was finally perfected for common use by Caterpillar. Previously diesels had been too heavy and undependable for commercial use. The Diesel-60 tractor, however, made the diesel the staple engine for heavy-duty vehicles, as it is to this day. In 1933 Caterpillar's diesel production was double that of all other U.S. firms combined. This boon gave Cat the impetus to redesign many of its old models, making them more efficient and economical. Sales began to rise and continued to do so throughout the late 1930s, as Caterpillar benefited from the huge road-building projects of President Franklin D. Roosevelt's public-works programs. Caterpillar's many innovations in rubber-tired tractors and diesel engines for trucks clearly contributed to revitalizing the firm.

Caterpillar's contributions to World War II were many and varied. Of substantial importance was the conversion of a gasoline airplane engine into a dependable diesel engine. In 1942 Caterpillar unveiled the new RD-1820 radial diesel engine, which was used to power the M-4 tank. The company manufactured other engines, as well, and even artillery shells for the war effort. It set up an aluminum foundry in Decatur, Illinois, to help ease the shortage of this vital material. Caterpillar engineers found that they could make a stronger metal with cheaper, more plentiful raw materials if they used high-frequency electrical induction to harden the steel used in tanks and personnel carriers.

Caterpillar tractors worked in battle zones repairing damaged roads, building new ones, bulldozing tank traps and, constructing pillboxes. Because the Cat was usually seen doing such roadwork with a bulldozer blade attached, the term "bulldozer" came to be used for Caterpillar products. Caterpillar tractors and road-building equipment were used to build the Burma Road. The makeshift repair shop that was set up to service the machines working on that road by the 497th Heavy Shop Company was dubbed Little Peoria.

In the postwar period, Caterpillar experienced enormous growth rather than recession, because of the massive rebuilding campaigns begun both in Europe and Japan, with the use of Marshall Plan and other funds. In the United States itself, demand seemed limitless. Caterpillar could not get its products to its customers fast enough. It launched, therefore, an expansion program in 1949 that was the first step toward becoming a truly international firm with major impact on world industry.

The new plant built in 1949 in Joliet, Illinois, was only the beginning of a program to establish manufacturing centers and subsidiaries around the globe. In 1950 Caterpillar announced the formation of its first overseas subsidiary, Caterpillar Tractor Company Ltd. of Great Britain. To further accommodate the postwar need for construction and road-building equipment, Caterpillar opened up subsidiaries in Brazil in 1954, in Australia in 1955, and in Scotland in 1956. In the 1950s, within the United States, Cat built new factories in Davenport, Iowa; York, Pennsylvania; and Milwaukee, Wisconsin; and parts distribution centers in Morton, Illinois, and Denver, Colorado.

In the 1960s the continuing boom in the construction of highways, dams, and mines kept sales increasing rapidly. By 1970 employment at Caterpillar was twice that of ten years prior. Caterpillar increased its exports, gaining a rival in the heavy-construction industry, Komatsu of Japan.

In 1961 Cat suffered the first of many involved labor conflicts with the United Auto Workers (UAW), when 12,600 workers in Peoria walked off their jobs in a wage dispute. An agreement was reached after only eight days, but this strike was the beginning of a series of increasingly bitter and complex battles between labor and management. Recognizing that industry works abroad by rules that differ from those of the United States, in 1962 Caterpillar announced the formation of a jointly owned venture in Japan. Caterpillar and Mitsubishi Heavy Industries built Cat-designed vehicles in a factory just outside of Tokyo.

After the three-year contract extension signed in 1961 was terminated, another strike began in Peoria. Announced as settled as early as February 1964, the strike was off and on until late October. In 1965 Caterpillar exceeded $1 billion in sales for the first time, announced that its stock would be sold on most of the major European stock exchanges, and started Caterpillar Belgium S.A. to build front-loading tractors there.

The year 1966 brought another confrontation with the UAW, this time in the form of a two-month walkout in Decatur. The lawsuit that Cat filed against the union, claiming an illegal strike, was settled out of court, in exchange for an agreement that stipulated that the union would settle all conflicts not relating to contract specifications before going out on strike. During this year Caterpillar of Canada Ltd. announced the construction of a 64,000-square-foot addition to its distribution warehouse.

In March 1968 the Justice Department moved to block a proposed merger between Cat and Chicago Pneumatic Tool Company, and the merger did not take place. In the same year, Caterpillar was the first company located outside of a major city to enlist in a government-sponsored program to hire and train people considered to be unemployable. This program was directed to persons who had been out of work for extended periods. The hirees would work half of the day at entry-level positions and spend the other half of the day learning job skills for better-paying jobs.

A contract with Ford in 1970 to supply small V-8 truck engines convinced Cat that manufacturing smaller diesels could make money, and the firm spent millions of dollars redesigning and retooling existing plants to build the new engines. Profits earned from an increase in state construction programs helped pay the cost of these investments. By 1972 Cat had announced plans to build a 900,000-square-foot plant in Belgium and a 1.25 million-square-foot production facility in Mossville, Illinois. Sales to the Soviet Union increased during this year.

In 1974 Caterpillar embarked on another dramatic expansion program, announcing plans to build a 650,000-square-foot addition to its Aurora, Illinois plant, a 1.3 million-square-foot addition to its diesel engine shop in Mossville, a 720,000-square-foot addition to its Peoria plant, and a new 670,000-square-foot manufacturing center in Brazil. In 1975 Caterpillar allocated more funds than ever before for expansion and product development. The company expanded its foreign market at this time by selling pipe-laying equipment to China, cashing in on the thaw in relations between China and the United States.

By 1978 the Cat expansion program was paying off. Sales approached $6 billion and the new manufacturing plants were able to turn out thousands of vehicles. The product line had expanded to the point where Cat offered more heavy-duty agricultural, construction, and material-hauling machines than any other company. In 1978 plans were revealed to build more new plants in York, Pennsylvania; Lafayette, Indiana; and Pontiac, Illinois.

The longest UAW strike against Caterpillar occurred in 1979. More than 23,000 workers in Illinois walked out of six of the company's major manufacturing plants. More than 3,500 workers were laid off because of the parts shortages that resulted from the strike. After almost three months of negotiations, a new three-year contract was forged, which offered better wages and a profit-sharing concession.

Caterpillar settled an involved lawsuit with Goodyear Tire & Rubber Company in 1981. Three years previously Goodyear had begun selling a radial earthmoving tire that infringed on Caterpillar's beadless-tire technology. The beadless tire lacked the beads, or edges, that attach the tire to wheel rims, and was more durable and economical than previous designs. In the out-of-court settlement Goodyear agreed to pay Caterpillar an amount mutually agreed upon, and become a licensee of Cat, paying the firm royalties for the use of beadless technology in the further manufacture of the tire.

In 1981 the firm won a political battle to be granted the right to sell $90 million in pipe-laying equipment to the Soviet Union, despite stiff opposition from the administration of U.S. President Ronald Reagan. That year the firm sold more machines than ever before, with sales of more than $9 billion for the year.

The recession of 1982 hit Caterpillar especially hard. The economic downturn caused sales to drop to $6.5 billion that year. Caterpillar laid off almost 12,000 employees at this time, and closed its plant in Mentor, Ohio. Trying to cut overhead, Cat proposed pay freezes and a cut in benefits, prompting a seven-month UAW strike, the longest in the firm's history. To add to the company's problems, barely six weeks after the 37,500 UAW workers left their jobs, a jury awarded Kast Metals a $9.2 million settlement for Caterpillar's failure to live up to an oral agreement to buy steel castings from Kast if Kast were to build a new plant to make the castings.

Caterpillar began 1983 by announcing the first annual loss in earnings in half a century. Cat started laying off workers, and closed a plant in Newcastle-On-Tyne, England. Sales slumped to a recent-history low of $5.4 billion. Yet after the new contract was signed with UAW, Caterpillar acquired a new direction and strategy that made things look better. Despite the concession of a profit-sharing plan, the wage freeze that the firm won in the contract dispute helped stem rising costs. The anticipation of the bottled-up demand that would create a larger market after the recession made investors think that Cat stock might be a good buy. By committing itself to less expansion, more creative marketing techniques, and reduced costs, Caterpillar intended in late 1983 to ride out the economic slump and position itself to return to profitability in 1984.

Caterpillar's problems continued, however, in 1984. Despite this being the expected comeback year for the firm, the plant closings and layoffs continued. The Burlington, Iowa, parts plant locked its doors to workers and, despite optimistic projections of recalling around 3,200 workers in 1985, Cat actually laid off about 3,000 other workers during that year. Caterpillar continued to cut back operations at its factories, then eliminated cost-of-living allowances in wages, and delayed the completion of its Morton, Illinois, distribution center. The firm blamed its second straight losing year on high interest rates and stiff price competition from other companies.

In February 1985 George A. Schaefer was named chairman and CEO of Caterpillar; Donald V. Fites was named president. Despite a net loss of almost $430 million the year before, Schaefer confidently predicted that Cat would make a profit during his first year as company head. During this year Caterpillar made two key strategic moves, which, despite their controversial nature, would be credited with making the firm once again profitable. Caterpillar first shifted some of its production and purchasing functions overseas. This meant that jobs that were in Peoria moved to Scotland or Japan. The high dollar made such a change necessary for company survival, management argued. Secondly, Caterpillar embarked on a $600 million factory-modernization program. It would reduce permanently the labor force needed to make tractors by automating as many manufacturing processes as possible. Approximately 2,300 workers were cut from the Caterpillar payroll during 1985. Company executives argued that the firm needed to compete with Komatsu, which had a much greater manufacturing efficiency than Cat because of its highly automated plants.

In 1986 Caterpillar Tractor Company became Caterpillar Inc., and announced that it had made a profit of almost $200 million in the previous year. The firm bounced back from its problems by marketing a new automated lift truck, which had the potential to secure part of a multibillion dollar market for Caterpillar. The firm even directly challenged Komatsu by expanding Cat's partnership with Mitsubishi Heavy Industries to include the production of hydraulic equipment.

Caterpillar faced, however, another strike during this year. Workers in Joliet walked out for four weeks, but were brought back to work under terms much like those previously rejected. Caterpillar again won a wage freeze, but cash bonuses as well as the firm's promise to lay off other workers as long as the strike continued were enough to get the Joliet workers to settle their grievances.

The weakening of the dollar abroad raised production costs and cut into profits for Caterpillar in 1987. Though the firm improved its sales and earnings over 1986, Caterpillar was still forced to close three factories.

In 1988 Caterpillar again made the kind of large profits it had made in the past, reaping $617 million for the year. In early 1989 Caterpillar's stock took a sharp downturn. The modernization campaign had swelled to a cost of more than $1.8 billion and flattened profits for the year. After its long climb back to profitability, this was a major setback, but it was expected that the modernization project would give Caterpillar a competitive edge during the next ten years. Cat's automated production facilities could turn out vehicles more quickly and efficiently, reducing manufacturing costs by 20%.

Caterpillar is looking to the future with more in mind than plant modernization. It is streamlining its corporate structure by combining the functions of its product lines into two new business groups. One of these will deal with the smaller product line and the other will be concerned with agricultural products. In 1990 the new company chairman and chief executive officer, Donald Fites, saw Cat as a company that is in the right place at the right time. With its new, quick, and flexible production system nearly completed and its expanded product line and reduced labor costs, Caterpillar should be able to deal with any challenge that the market or its competitors can offer into the next century.

Principal Subsidiaries: Carter Machinery Company, Inc.; Caterpillar Americas Co.; Caterpillar of Australia Ltd.; Caterpillar Brasil S.A. (Brazil); Caterpillar Capital Co., Inc.; Caterpillar Commercial N.V. (Belgium); Caterpillar Commercial Services Ltd. (Canada); Caterpillar of Delaware, Inc.; Caterpillar Export Ltd. (Virgin Islands); Caterpillar Finance Corp.; Caterpillar Financial Services Corp.; Caterpillar Financial Services N.V. (Netherlands Antilles); Caterpillar Industrial Inc.; Caterpillar Insurance Co., Ltd. (Bermuda); Caterpillar Insurance Services Inc.; Caterpillar Investment Management Ltd.; Caterpillar Logistics Services Inc.; Caterpillar Overseas S.A. (Switzerland); Caterpillar Paving Products, Inc.; Caterpillar Services Ltd.; Caterpillar Venture Capital, Inc.; Caterpillar World Trading Corp.; CATPAC Two, Inc.; CONEK S.A. de C.V. (Mexico); Production Technology Inc.; Solar Turbines Inc.; Tecnologia Modificada S.A. de C.V. (Mexico).

Further Reading: Century of Change: Caterpillar Special World Historical Edition, Peoria, Illinois, Caterpillar Inc., 1984; Bremner, Brian, "Can Caterpillar Inch Its Way Back Into Heftier Profits?," *Business Week,* September 25, 1989.

—Wallace Ross

CITIZEN®

CITIZEN WATCH CO., LTD.

Shinjuku Mitsui Building
1-1, Nishi-shinjuku 2-chome
Shinjuku-ku, Tokyo 163
Japan
(03) 3342-1231
Fax: (03) 3342-1280

Public Company
Incorporated: 1930
Employees: 3,257
Sales: ¥334.41 billion (US$2.33 billion)
Stock Exchanges: Tokyo Osaka

Citizen Watch Co., Ltd., the second-largest watchmaker in Japan, and in the world, has diversified its product lines. It now manufactures and markets computer peripherals, jewelry, eyewear, industrial machine tools, and precision instruments, but making timepieces, remains its primary enterprise.

Citizen began in Tokyo in 1918 as a horological research center, the Shokosha Watch Research Laboratory. In 1924 the laboratory manufactured its first pocket watch. Six years later, the group organized itself as a corporation, Citizen Watch Company, to facilitate marketing of its products, under President Yosaburo Nakajima. The new company owed its name to Tokyo mayor Shinpei Gotoh, who named Shokosha Lab's first timepieces Citizen watches, so that they would, in his words, be "close to the hearts of people everywhere." In addition to watches, Citizen produced precision instruments used in their manufacture. In 1935 the company built the factory in the Tanashi area of Tokyo that remains its main production facility.

In 1936, Citizen began selling watches in Southeast Asia and the South Pacific; China also became a destination for exports. The company's international horizons remained limited to other Asian countries until well after World War II. In fact, Citizen's export business dried up after the outbreak of hostilities with the United States, as the Japanese economy geared itself to meet military needs. In 1941, the company began producing machine tools, a business it has retained.

After Japan's defeat by the Allied powers in 1945, Japanese industry lay in ruins, and Citizen, along with the rest of the nation, faced the task of rebuilding. That year, Shinji Nakajima took over company leadership as president. In March 1946, less than a year later, Eiinchi Yamada assumed the post. In 1949, Citizen established a subsidiary, Citizen Trading Company, to handle domestic marketing. This move allowed the parent company to focus on manufacturing, research, and development. In 1953 Citizen entered into a joint venture with Rhythm Watch, another Japanese timepiece manufacturer, to sell the latter's clocks.

The export market began to revive in the 1950s. In 1958, Citizen resumed exporting watches to China, and, two years later, it started selling its machine tools there. In 1960, the company entered the all-important American market by providing Bulova Watch with parts for watches to be assembled and sold in the United States. In 1962, Citizen resumed exporting watches to Southeast Asia, and, in 1965, opened a sales office in West Germany, in order to export watches to Europe.

The timepiece industry in postwar Japan was all but monopolized by four companies: K. Hattori & Company, which produced the Seiko and Pulsar brands among others; Citizen; Ricoh; and Orient. In 1965, Hattori and Citizen by themselves accounted for more than 80% of Japanese watch production. Citizen also gained prominence in Japan for several technical advancements: developing Japan's first shock-resistant watch in 1956; marketing the nation's first wristwatch with an alarm in 1958; and, in the late 1950s, developing the first Japanese water-resistant watch. Citizen also made a significant public relations gesture in donating 850 synchronized clocks for use in the Olympic Village at the 1964 Summer Olympics in Tokyo.

The Japanese timepiece industry hit a slump in the early 1960s, as increased competition, slack domestic demand, and rising production and personnel costs all squeezed profit margins. Ricoh and Orient gradually lost their status as watchmakers of consequence, leaving Citizen and Hattori in competition with each other. Diversification was one strategy for continued survival. In 1967, Citizen entered the gem and jewelry business, establishing a subsidiary, Citizen Jewelry, for that purpose. Citizen Jewelery later was merged into Citizen Trading Company. Citizen also placed more emphasis on developing its line of business machines.

Another logical solution to the problem of sluggish domestic demand was to expand overseas business. In the 1960s Japanese watchmakers were not the kings of the export trade that they would become 20 years later. In 1967, Switzerland—known for its high-priced luxury watches—ranked first in the world in watch production, the Soviet Union—which produced cheap, generally inferior movements for sale in developing countries—second, and Japan third. It was not until the next year that Citizen established its first overseas subsidiary, a joint venture called Citizen de Mexico, which sold and later manufactured Citizen timepieces in Mexico. This was the first time that a Japanese watchmaker founded a joint venture for making and selling watches in a foreign country. In 1970 the company set up a subsidiary in Hong Kong, Sunciti Manufacturers, to produce cases and dial plates for mechanical watches. This venture was wholly owned by Citizen and its subsidiaries. Also in that year, Citizen and Bulova formed a joint venture, Bulova-Citizen, to produce tuning-fork watches for sale in Japan. Bulova held a majority stake in the new company, making it the first foreign-owned watch manufacturer that the Japanese government had allowed to take root in its own soil.

Citizen continued to diversify and pursue the export trade in the early 1970s. In 1972 the company entered the eyewear business as import and sales agency for Christian Dior frames. The company also entered the leisure-time business that year by converting its Yodobashi factory into a bowling alley and founding another subsidiary, Citizen Kohatsu, to run it. Citizen Kohatsu also became involved in running skating rinks and tennis facilities. In 1973, Citizen founded another foreign subsidiary, Citizen Latinamerica. The next year, Citizen established Citizen Uhrenfabrik to assemble watches in West Germany, and the year after that, Hanmi Citizen Precision Industry to manufacture watch casings in South Korea. By 1978, overseas production accounted for one-fourth of the company's total output of watches.

Nevertheless, Citizen continued second to Hattori in the 1970s, accounting for roughly 30% of Japanese watch production in a two-company industry. The American market was the ripest plum to be picked in the export trade; Citizen could not hope to match, much less surpass, its rival as long as its presence in the United States was only indirect, limited to parts that Bulova assembled and sold under its own name. Hattori's Seiko brand was achieving name recognition in the United States, but Citizen had none. In 1975, the company established a U.S. sales subsidiary, Citizen Watch Company of America, in Los Angeles; its headquarters moved to New York City later. Citizen sharply curtailed its parts shipments to Bulova and began selling in the United States under its own name.

American sales started out small, accounting for only 10% of Citizen's total sales in 1977. The company made significant inroads in the U.S. midpriced market with its quartz analog and multifunction digital watches, positioning itself for a run at overtaking Hattori. Citizen's success was a major part of the overall success of the Japanese timepiece industry; Japan became the world's second-largest watchmaking nation by 1980, boasting a 21% share of the world market and shaving Switzerland's lead to a mere ½%. Swiss watchmakers refused to acknowledge the growing importance of electronic technology and failed to profit from it until late in the game. Citizen seemed to be on its way to carving out a comfortable sinecure within the U.S. market.

The digital watch boom that started in the mid-1970s changed the scene in the next decade. At first, the scenario seemed propitious for Citizen and Hattori. Although American semiconductor companies were the first to develop digital watch technology, they proved less than adept at exploiting it. By 1980, one-third of all watches sold in the U.S. were digital, but Fairchild Camera & Instrument, Intel, Litronix, and Motorola had all been driven out of the watch business. Texas Instruments was reeling from marketing problems. National Semiconductor was consolidating a modest niche, and venerable Timex found itself unable to get the hang of making digitals.

New players were entering the game to take advantage of this implosion. The old guard of the Far East found itself challenged by an energetic young Japanese rival, Casio Computer, and low-cost manufacturers based in Hong Kong and South Korea. All of these companies prospered by concentrating on the low-priced end of the market, producing a stream of simple, inexpensive, digital watches. These cheaper products proved popular enough to erode Citizens's and Hattori's market shares.

Citizen countered by launching its own line of low-priced digitals, called Vega, but ultimately decided to concentrate on taking the midprice market away from Hattori. Leadership of Citizen passed to Rokuya Yamazaki, who became president in 1981. In the 1980s Seiko became the best-selling watch brand in the United States, with Citizen ranked number two; in fact, they ranked first and second, respectively, in the world in timepiece sales and production. Yet the threat to market share from the makers of low-priced watches still had be fended off. The Japanese electronics firm Sharp joined Casio in this business. In an effort to cope with the situation, the traditional rivals joined forces to cut manufacturing costs through economies of scale. In 1985 Citizen and Hattori Seiko—the name K. Hattori & Company had assumed in 1985—entered into an agreement to supply each other with parts. Citizen would provide Seiko with hands and special driving devices and receive, in return, quartz oscillators, button batteries, springs, and other mechanical parts.

Citizen also responded to the threat by further diversification. The company decided that non-timepiece products should eventually account for half of total sales, compared to 32% in 1985. Citizen expanded its information-equipment group, the descendant of its office-machine business; in 1984, it began exporting its printers and disc drives to the United States. In 1986—the year that Citizen supassed Seiko in volume to become the world's largest watchmaker—the company introduced a new color liquid-crystal-display television that would spearhead its increased involvement in consumer electronics. The company also strengthened its machine tool and precision instrument businesses. In 1986, it joined with the American manufacturer Perkin-Elmer to form Perkin-Elmer Citizen, a venture to produce and assemble analyzers and semiconductor processing devices in Japan. In 1987, Citizen established Citizen Systems, a research facility for developing new information equipment technology, in Los Angeles, and Citizen Manufacturing (UK) to manufacture printers in Great Britain. That same year, Michio Nakajima succeeded to the presidency.

Nakajima recognized that growth in the mature timepiece market was limited, and immediately began to pursue diversification, especially in the fast-growing computer and computer-component markets, Citizen quickly became a respected supplier of laptop-computer components and disc drives. "Citizen executives now strongly feel that . . . diversification is the only way for survival," wrote a correspondent for *The Japan Economic Journal,* July 5, 1986. At the same time, the new products on which Citizen has pinned its hopes depend heavily on their reception in overseas markets, particularly the American market. The strength that the yen acquired relative to the U.S. dollar and other currencies in the mid-1980s has made Japanese goods more expensive to buy in the United States, threatening their market shares. It would appear that Citizen's long-term viability has become dependent on exchange-rate fluctuations and the vagaries of international trade, an area in which politicians, rather than market forces, are operating. Making watches brought Citizen success in its first 60 years. Diversification may be the key to success in its future years.

Principal Subsidiaries: Citizen Iwate Co., Ltd.; Kawaguchiko Seimitsu Co., Ltd.; Citizen Precision Machine Co., Ltd.; Citizen Mechatronics Co., Ltd.; Sayama Precision Industries Co., Ltd.; Tama Seimitsu Co., Ltd.; Ageo Seimitsu Mfg.

Co., Ltd.; Japan CBM Corporation; Tokorozawa Seimitsu Co., Ltd.; Citizen Yoshimi Co., Ltd.; Citizen Otec Co., Ltd.; Citizen Kohatsu Co., Ltd.; Premier Precision Ltd. (Hong Kong); Astar Precision Co., Ltd. (Hong Kong); Goodrington Co., Ltd. (Hong Kong); Walop Ltd. (Hong Kong); Miyota Precision Co., Ltd.; Citizen Electronics Co., Ltd.; Fuji Keiki Co., Ltd.; Cimeo Precision Co., Ltd.; Hokkaido Citizen Corporation; Tohoku Citizen Corporation; Chubu Citizen Corporation; Chugoku Citizen Corporation; Sunciti Manufacturers Ltd. (Hong Kong); Citizen Watches (H.K.) Ltd. (Hong Kong); Citizen of Korea Co., Ltd.; Citizen Latinamerica Corporation (Panama); Citizen Watch Company of America, Inc. (U.S.A.); Citizen Watch Europe G.m.b.H. (Germany); Citizen Uhrenfabrik G.m.b.H. (Germany); Citizen America Corporation (U.S.A.); Citizen Europe Ltd. (U.K.); Farbest Industries Ltd. (Hong Kong); Crown Young Industries Ltd. (Hong Kong); Wah Kong Precision (Jiangmen) Ltd. (China); Taiwan Star Precision Ltd.; Shih Chun Precision Co., Ltd. (Taiwan); Shiang Pao Precision Co., Ltd. (Taiwan); Fuji Star Co., Ltd. (Taiwan); Citizen Precision of Korea Co., Ltd.; Citizen de Mexico, S.A. de C.V.; Plasticos Citizen S.A. (Mexico); Citizen Manufactring (U.K.) Ltd.; Royal Time Citi Co., Ltd. (Thailand); Citizen Machinery Europe G.m.b.H. (Germany); Citizen Computer Peripherals G.m.b.H. (Germany); Citizen Systems Inc. (U.S.A.); CBM America Corp. (U.S.A.); Tokyo Citizen Corp.; Kansai Citizen Corp.; Citizen Watch (U.K.) Ltd.; Citizen Watches Australia Pty Ltd.; Citizen Watches New Zealand Ltd.; Citizen Watch Switzerland AG.

Further Reading: ''Timepieces Industry,'' *The Oriental Economist,* April 1965; ''Companies in Footlight: Citizen Watch Co., Ltd.,'' *The Oriental Economist,* February 1978; ''Corporations in the News: Citizen Watch Co.,'' *The Japan Economic Journal,* July 5, 1986; *This is Citizen,* Tokyo, Citizen Watch Co., Ltd., 1989.

—Douglas Sun

DAEWOO GROUP

541, 5-GA, Namdaemunno, Chung-gu
Seoul
Republic of Korea
(02) 759-2114
Fax: (02) 753-9489

Public Company
Incorporated: 1967
Employees: 91,056
Sales: W13.62 trillion (US$20.11 billion)
Stock Exchange: Seoul

The Daewoo Group was founded by Woo Choong Kim in March 1967. Daewoo means "Great Universe," and although the initial share capital of the company was a modest US$18,000, Kim and his colleagues held great hopes for their business.

Daewoo's success is inseparable from South Korea's rapid transformation from an agrarian country, racked by a long history of hostile invasions and lacking essential resources, to a land where the centrally planned "economic miracle" has become a fact of life. South Korea entered the 1960s with a crippling trade-deficit balance and a domestic market too poor to support indigenous industries. When Korea was divided by the Allies after World War II, the territory north of the 38th parallel inherited all of the country's natural resources. With a far stronger military force than its rivals in the South, North Korea waited less than two years after the withdrawal of U.S. peacekeeping troops to invade. Peace was eventually restored in 1953, but the fear of foreign invasion has remained with the South Koreans and, indeed, has acted as a powerful incentive in the search for economic prosperity.

The Daewoo Group is comprised of 25 subsidiary companies which are linked together in a complicated system of cross holdings. The major company in the group is Daewoo Corporation, which was licensed as a general trading company (GTC) by the Korean government in 1975. GTCs were set up to promote exports, and licenseholders were required to establish offices abroad. Daewoo has a network of over 70 branches covering the United States., South America, Australasia, the Indian sub-continent, Europe, and the Arab states. In all, some 3,500 different products are traded in over 130 countries. In exchange for promoting Korean goods abroad, the Daewoo Corporation was able to finance its expansion through preferential loan agreements, reduced foreign exchange requirements, and improved government advice on exporting and marketing abroad.

The second-largest member of the group is Daewoo Heavy Industries, which is involved in construction equipment, industrial vehicles, and aerospace-industry products as well as the defense industry. Daewoo Heavy Industries and Daewoo Corporation are related through cross holdings of stock. Major contributions to the Daewoo Group are also made by Daewoo Motor and Daewoo Electronics. Daewoo Shipbuilding and Heavy Machinery, however, is proving to be a significant drain on the resources of the group. The diverse interests of the group are controlled by the management committee which Kim chairs.

The Daewoo Group is a *chaebol*, a large conglomeration of companies with widespread interests reporting to a powerful head office, Daewoo Corporation. There are more than fifty *chaebols* in South Korea; the Big Four are the Hyundai Group, the Lucky-Goldstar Group, the Samsung Group, and Daewoo. In order to understand Daewoo's meteoric rise it is necessary to appreciate the place of the *chaebols* in the modern Korean economy. Successive governments have used the *chaebols* as their main method of implementing economic strategies. Incentives have been offered in the forms of massive subsidies, apparently unlimited cheap credit, and protection against foreign competition. On the other hand, Daewoo has been forced to take over ailing companies and to enter industry sectors that the company would have preferred to leave to more appropriate competitors.

Beginning in 1962 the South Korean government instigated a series of five-year plans and forced the *chaebols* to aim for a number of basic objectives. In common with their Far East competitors, Hong Kong and Taiwan, South Korea's governments have relied on a strategy that focuses attention on the importance of exports as the method to decrease the country's balance-of-trade gap and to strengthen domestic production.

Daewoo began trading in 1967 at the start of the second five-year plan, and benefited from government-sponsored cheap loans on borrowing for exports. The company chose to concentrate on the labor-intensive clothing and textile industries which would provide relatively high profit margins while utilizing South Korea's major asset, its large workforce. A factory was set up at Pusan, and in 1990, 3.6 million shirts were made there each month. Daewoo further contributed to the increases in South Korea's level of exports, which averaged 38.6% growth per annum during this period, by producing uncomplicated light manufacturing machines the construction of which, again, was labor intensive.

The third and fourth phases of Korea's economic recovery ran from 1973 to 1981. The country's most significant resource, its supply of labor, was then in high demand, and as wages increased, competitors from Malaysia and Thailand began to erode Korea's comparative advantage in labor-intensive production. The government responded by concentrating on mechanical and electrical engineering, shipbuilding, petrochemicals, and construction. This change in emphasis was designed to continue Korea's export-led expansion and to provide domestic industries with parts that previously had to be imported. A home-based defense industry was also a priority as plans were announced for the total withdrawal of the U.S. peacekeeping force.

Daewoo moved into construction, serving the new village program and, in a far-sighted move, the rapidly growing African and Middle Eastern markets. During this period Daewoo achieved its GTC status and received significant investment help from the South Korean government. Subsidized loans and strict import controls aroused the anger of competing nations, but the *chaebols* were in need of protectionist policies if they were to survive this period of world recession, triggered by the oil crisis of 1973.

Government policy forced Daewoo into shipbuilding, an industry to which Hyundai and Samsung were more suited because of their greater expertise in heavy engineering. Kim's reluctance to take over the world's biggest dockyard, at Okpo, in 1980 is well documented, and his comment on the Korean government indicates a growing frustration as his entrepreneurial instinct was being stifled. "They tell you it's your duty and you have to do it even if there's no profit." Displaying characteristic vigor and enthusiasm, however, Kim soon saw Daewoo Shipbuilding and Heavy Machinery earn a reputation for competitively priced ships and oil-rigs that were often delivered ahead of schedule.

The 1980s were a decade of liberalization for South Korea's economy. Small private companies were encouraged, and Daewoo was made to divest two of the textile companies that had contributed to its success. Protectionist import controls were relaxed, and the government no longer practiced positive discrimination towards the shipbuilding industry. These moves were instigated to ensure an efficient allocation of resources in a free market and to force the *chaebols* to be more aggressive in their dealings abroad.

The great change in attitude shown by the Korean government to the *chaebols* is best illustrated by the fate of one of Daewoo's competitors, the Kukje Group, which went into liquidation in 1985. At that time the government saw the *chaebols* as barriers to economic efficiency and refused to supply Kukje with further credit. Small- and medium-sized companies were to be favored to ensure that the wealth in Korea's two industrial centers, Seoul and Pusan, eventually would be spread throughout the whole country. The only large industries to benefit from government support would be those that were internationally competitive and those that could further a more equitable distribution of income.

Daewoo responded to the challenge by establishing a number of joint ventures with U.S. and European companies. Kim's philosophy for the 1980s was that finished products would eventually lose their national identity as countries cooperated in design and manufacturing before exporting the goods to a further country. In 1986 Daewoo Heavy Industries launched a $40 million Eurobond issue in order to expand exports of machine tools, defense products, and aerospace interests. The president of Daewoo Heavy Industries, Kyung Hoon Lee, hoped that the money would enable his company to move away from simply licensing products from abroad and to enter a new phase of complimentary and long-term relationships with foreign companies.

The 50/50 joint venture with Sikorsky Aerospace illustrates the benefits of operating in partnership with a U.S. company. Daewoo started by building S-76 helicopters from parts imported from the United States and gradually began to produce these parts in Korea. As the South Korean government has always regarded the defense industry as being of utmost importance, Daewoo received generous subsidies to establish new factories. By the end of 1988, Daewoo had enough confidence in the skills it had learned in the Sikorsky project to announce that it was to begin work on civilian helicopters and airplanes, which would be considerably cheaper than those produced by their U.S. counterparts.

Daewoo has used other methods to capture foreign markets. It has excellent experience in turning around faltering companies in Korea and is now, increasingly, applying this knowledge abroad. In 1986 Daewoo acquired a controlling interest in the U.S. ZyMOS Corporation as a means of gaining the technical knowledge necessary to expand its interests in semiconductor manufacturing and semiconductor design. Subsidiaries that actually produce goods abroad, rather than acting solely as sales agents, have also been established. Daewoo now has a microwave-oven assembly plant in Lorraine, France, and has set up a video-recorder company in Northern Ireland. Signaling that South Korea's economic recovery is reaching completion, Daewoo is now considering investment in countries such as Bangladesh and Indonesia where textiles can be produced as cheaply as Korea was able to do in the early 1960s. Other link ups include a deal with Caterpillar to export 100,000 forklifts by 1993, a marketing contract to sell IBM-compatible personal computers, and the production of parts for the European Airbus on behalf of British Aerospace.

The mid-1980s saw an increased emphasis on the motor-vehicle industry. Although the government, fearful of arousing protectionist sympathies in its foreign markets, was reticent in announcing its ambitions publicly, it was clear that South Korea was aiming to become one of the world's major car exporters before the end of the decade. In 1986 the Japanese yen appreciated 25% against the dollar, making Daewoo's already cheap exports even more attractive. Daewoo established a 50/50 joint venture with General Motors to produce an internationally competitive small car and components for a number of General Motors's existing vehicles. Daewoo was not deterred by the difficulties inherent in setting up the required high-technology production lines and relied on the experience gained in other parts of the group to set up sophisticated computer systems in a relatively short period of time.

The joint venture with General Motors was, initially, one of Daewoo's most profitable links with a foreign company. In 1987 247,000 Pontiac LeMans were built, and the car, based on a design by the German car giant Opel, was well received in the U.S. market. Demand for the LeMans and the slightly larger Oldsmobile Royale soon faltered, however, and there were rumors of friction between the management of the two companies. The venture has not been as successful as Hyundai's foray into the international car market, and it appears that Daewoo underestimated the sophistication and technical standards required by the U.S. car buyer.

In 1989 heavy losses suffered by Daewoo Shipbuilding and Heavy Machinery made servicing the company's loans increasingly difficult. In an unprecedented demonstration against the traditional work ethic that had helped South Korea to economic prosperity, workers began an increasingly violent protest against years of long hours and low pay. The only solution available to Daewoo's management was to placate the workers with pay raises of more than 20%.

The reliance on shipbuilding as a way of cementing South Korea's export-led recovery looked even more dangerous as the rapidly appreciating won made exports more expensive. Demand for Daewoo's ships remained constant but the company was forced to sell ships at a loss as a way of guaranteeing a steady supply of orders. The situation was exacerbated by the bankruptcy of US Lines in 1986. A bad debt of $570 million marked the start of the crisis at the Okpo shipyard.

The Ministry of Trade and Industry, however, was no longer willing to bail out one of its most reliable *chaebols,* which was suffering as a direct result of the Daewoo Shipbuilding and Heavy Machinery acquisition forced on it by the government. Instead, the government promised a seven-year moratorium on Daewoo's debt to the Korean Development Bank and offered to provide a further W150 billion in exchange for a number of contributions from the company. Daewoo would have to refinance the shipyards by selling off four subsidiaries, including the profitable Korea Steel Company and Daewoo Investment and Finance, as well as selling Daewoo Shipbuilding and Heavy Machinery's headquarters in Seoul. Subsidiaries were forced to raise W85 billion on the Korean stock exchange, and Kim was ordered by the government to sell his W150 billion investment in Daewoo Securities, the country's largest stockbroker. The government also ordered workers to curb their demands for wage increases and asked to see proof of improved management before the deal to help Daewoo was agreed.

Kim's response was typical of his personal style. He had already moved his office to the shipyard so that he could keep direct control of the worsening situation, and began to take tours around the premises by bicycle to ensure that he could implement changes and cut costs where necessary. By 1990 improvements at the shipyard were already visible, and Kim was confident that by 1992, when Daewoo Shipbuilding is to be merged with Daewoo Heavy Industries, the company would contribute to the profits of the group.

Daewoo entered the 1990s facing more problems than the downturn in the fortunes of its shipbuilding subsidiary. The company was highly leveraged, partly due to the ready availability of government loans, and is currently paying interest of W300 million a day—about US$500,000—on its debts. Daewoo has not marketed itself as well as competitors like Hyundai and, as a consequence, suffers from the lack of a strong brand image. Its heavy industries are now operating in stagnant markets and expenditure on research and development has to be increased if internationally competitive new products are to be successfully introduced. Continuing workers' demonstrations and changes in government policy further add to Daewoo's worries.

Daewoo's strengths include a flexible and open-minded approach to new opportunities and experience in establishing joint ventures with foreign companies. The company's wide range of industries means that risks can be taken without fear of causing the collapse of the whole group, and that synergies between different subsidiaries can be exploited to the benefit of the whole of the corporation. The opening up of the Eastern Bloc may well prove to be more lucrative for a company like Daewoo that concentrates on lower-priced, higher-volume goods than for its Western competitors.

Daewoo also benefits from skilled management and is determined to attract the best domestically educated and expatriate young Koreans to guide the firm into the next century. Daewoo spends US$6 million each year sending graduates abroad, usually to the United States, so that they can further their studies and return with the necessary skills to lead effective research and development departments.

Daewoo's major strength could also be its greatest weakness. Daewoo differs from the other *chaebols* in that its leader is not perceived as an autocratic figure whose decision if final. Instead, Woo Choong Kim delegates tasks to well-trained managers and industry task forces. However, if a major problem does occur—as in the Okpo shipbuilding crisis—Kim will devote his attention to that company until a solution is found. In 1975 Kim announced his intention to retire within ten years, but has repeatedly postponed his departure citing business pressures as the reason.

Principal Subsidiaries: Daewoo Corporation; Keangnam Enterprises Ltd.; Kyugnam Metal Co., Ltd.; Daewoo Heavy Industries Ltd.; Daewoo Precision Industries Ltd.; Daewoo Sikorsky Aerospace Ltd.; Daewoo Electronics Co., Ltd.; Orion Electric Co., Ltd.; Daewoo Electronic Components Co., Ltd.; Daewoo Carrier Corp.; Daewoo Electric Motor Industries Ltd.; Orion Electric Components Co., Ltd.; Daewoo Telecom Co., Ltd.; Daewoo Information System Co., Ltd.; Daewoo ZyMOS Technology Ltd.; Daewoo Motor Co., Ltd.; Daewoo Automotive Components Ltd.; Koram Plastics Co., Ltd.; Daewoo Securities Co., Ltd.; Daewoo Research Institute; Daewoo Capital Management Co., Ltd.; Daewoo Development Co.; Daewoo Shipbuilding & Heavy Machinery Ltd.; Shina Shipbuilding Co., Ltd.; Daewoo Engineering Products Ltd.

Further Reading: Cho Dong Sung, "Government Entrepreneurs and Competition," in *Doing Business in Korea*, edited by Arthur Whitehill, Sydney, Croom Helm, 1987; Lowry, Tom, *The South Korean Motor Industry: A Rerun of Japan?*, London, Economist Intelligence Unit, 1987; United Nations Industrial Development Organization, *The Republic of Korea,* London, United Nations, 1987; McDermott, Michael, and Stephen Young, *South Korea's Industry: New Directions in World Markets,* London, Economist Intelligence Unit, 1989.

—Andreas Loizou

DAIKIN INDUSTRIES, LTD.

Umeda Center Building
4-12, Nakazaki-nishi 2-chome
Kita-ku, Osaka 530
Japan
(06) 373-4351
Fax: (06) 373-4388

Public Company
Incorporated: 1934
Employees: 6,462
Sales: ¥325.84 billion (US$2.27 billion)
Stock Exchanges: Tokyo Osaka Nagoya

Daikin Industries is the leading Japanese manufacturer of commercial air conditioning and refrigeration units. With over 25% of those markets under its control, Daikin also has branched into the residential air conditioning business and most recently added production in the areas of oil hydraulics and computer-aided design/manufacturing (CAD/CAM). As a major manufacturer of air conditioners, Daikin has long been deeply involved in the chemistry of coolants, and now faces the difficult task of finding substitutes for environmentally damaging agents such as the chlorofluorocarbon group.

Daikin was founded in 1924 during a period of robust economic activity in Japan. Although Japan had trailed the Western nations in the adoption of most modern technologies, by the 1920s its major industrial groups had taken shape and were able to provide secondary industries such as air conditioning with the raw materials they needed to get started. In 1924, air conditioning was still a very young industry, the necessary refrigerants only recently having been developed in the United States. Daikin, one of the earliest Japanese entrants in the new business, quickly established a solid customer base and the beginnings of an effective marketing group. The 1927 financial crisis that shook all of Japan proved only a temporary obstacle to Daikin's growth, but the ensuing Great Depression of 1929 caused economic hardship for the company. The lean years of the early 1930s were ended by Japan's intensive military buildup, which eventually provided every industrial concern with all the business it could handle. Daikin's sales soared as the general upturn translated into increased orders even for companies not directly involved in weapons production.

World War II ended with the nearly complete destruction of Japan's industrial base. Scanty records do not indicate the extent of Daikin's losses, but, like most of the country's capital-intensive firms, it faced the massive job of retooling and rebuilding. In addition, the Allied administrative command in Japan dissolved the great *zaibatsu*, or industrial conglomerates, which had organized and controlled most of the country's economic activity. Daikin, which had long been associated with the Sumitomo *zaibatsu*, thus not only had to rebuild its shattered assets but also adjust to a new economic order of decreased cooperation and interdependence. On the other hand, the Japanese government quickly evolved a highly supportive economic policy of subsidies and planned growth, which helped Daikin and the rest of Japanese industry get back on its feet.

The postwar decades were an unqualified success for Daikin. As in the United States, Japanese use of air conditioning and refrigerants in general soared in the 1950s. The increasing construction of high-rise office and residential buildings encouraged the use of the large, centralized air conditioning units in which Daikin specialized. A small but growing number of individual consumers also were beginning to demand air conditioning for the home. Japan's booming industrial economy, particularly the electronics firms, required Daikin's heavy-duty air conditioners. As the Japanese gained a reputation for excellence in electronics, the number of factories needing a temperature- and humidity-controlled environment grew rapidly, contributing to Daikin's impressive domestic sales gains. Finally, like so many other Japanese companies, Daikin began a tentative program of overseas expansion, originally restricted to its immediate neighbors along the Pacific Rim. Its success there encouraged Daikin to enter the important European market in 1972, when it formed Daikin Europe N.V. in Belgium to serve as its European headquarters. Daikin was the first Japanese maker of air conditioners to establish a base in Europe and has remained the Japanese leader ever since.

In the meantime, Daikin had developed a number of ancillary businesses. Its experience in the chemistry of coolants helped Daikin to build a highly successful chemical division specializing in the manufacture and sale of fluoropolymers, and of fluorocarbon gases, the basic ingredient in air conditioning coolants. Similarly, from air conditioning Daikin found its way into the production of refrigerating units for use in factories, warehouses, and restaurants. From its knowledge of coolant hydraulics, Daikin evolved a business specializing in the manufacture of pumps and valves used in oil hydraulics. Daikin has played an increasing role as a supplier of explosives and related equipment to Japan's Defense Ministry. Daikin has used its increasingly diverse production mix to cushion the effect of cyclical depressions in the construction industry, with which it does the great majority of its business. However, air conditioning and refrigeration provide the bulk of Daikin's revenue and will continue to do so for the foreseeable future.

With Japan's emergence as one of the world's leading economic powers in the 1970s, Daikin enjoyed its most productive decade yet. Despite the shock of the 1973 OPEC oil embargo, which caused problems for the Japanese economy, Daikin solidified its leading domestic position and expanded its overseas presence. Daikin as yet had no representation in the highly competitive U.S. air-conditioning market, the world's largest, and it spent a number of years planning a strategy aimed at gaining a foothold there. In the meantime Daikin pushed into Hong Kong, Singapore, and Australia and set up Daikin Air Conditioning (Thailand) Company, Ltd. in Thailand. Daikin also won business in Europe, where the highly urban population began to make greater use of air conditioning at home and at work.

The 1980s were a period of mixed results at Daikin. In a thriving Japanese economy, domestic sales continued at record-breaking levels, and Daikin remained the industry's undisputed leader. Yet overseas business suffered from the 1985 appreciation in the yen, which made Daikin products prohibitively expensive and dropped total overseas operations into the red for several years. Daikin entered the U.S. market focusing on the sale of residential window air conditioners. It hoped to build market share on those and on the popular Japanese concept of "split-room" air conditioning, in which individual room-units are connected to a single outside compressor but remain independently controlled, cutting electric bills. From such residential sales Daikin planned to move on to its bread-and-butter commercial business and eventually build local factories to save on freight and tariffs. Nevertheless, by 1990, Daikin failed to claim a significant portion of the U.S. market and temporarily shelved its plans for local production plants, its progress impeded by the expensive yen and the crowded U.S. market.

In 1982, Daikin inaugurated an electronics division to develop tools for the industrial engineering field. By 1983, when Daikin's corporate sales reached $700 million, the company was manufacturing industrial robots as well as assembling parts developed by American Robot Corporation of Pittsburgh. Robotics proved to be less than successful, however, and was gradually phased out of Daikin's product mix. The electronics division nevertheless went on to manufacture a variety of CAD/CAM hardware and software aimed at the upper end of that market.

A distressing setback was the spate of bad publicity generated by a 1988 trade scandal. Daikin was charged with selling a high-density halogenated hydrocarbon called Halon 2402 to the Soviet Union in violation of Allied trade bans on such materials; Halon 2402 can be used in missile guidance systems. Japan was especially sensitive to such criticism because Toshiba Corporation had suffered a similar scandal in 1987; the Ministry of International Trade and Information and Japan's judiciary pursued well-publicized investigations of the incident. Daikin admitted to selling 1,238 metric tons of Halon 2402, but said it did so by mistake, shipping ultra-pure Halon instead of the normal and unrestricted dilute form. The Japanese government fined Daikin the trivial sum of US$14,000 and forbade the company to sell to communist countries for six months. More painful for Daikin was the public exposure of wrongdoing, particularly discomforting in Japan, where honor is as important in business as it is in private life.

It became clear in the 1980s that chlorofluorocarbons (CFCs) were contributing to the destruction of the earth's critical ozone layer. Along with the rest of the air conditioning industry, Daikin began the 1990s searching for substitutes for a crucial ingredient in its most important product, and needing to find it quickly. Daikin had already reduced CFC levels where possible while increasing its research and development budget to find a long-term solution to the problem. By 1990, under Chairman Kiyoshi Sugasawa and President Minoru Yamada, Daikin hoped it had found the solution in a series of hydrochlorofluorocarbons and hydrofluorocarbons, which it planned to begin producing in 1992–1993.

Daikin remains dependent on air conditioning and refrigeration which contributed about 75% of its sales in 1989, almost 90% of which were generated domestically. It continues to dominate Japan's commercial air conditioning business and has made inroads in the residential market as well. With a leading position in Japan, the company's future growth will have to come at least in part from overseas sales. Daikin appears poised for major expansion in Europe, where it is preparing for the 1992 unified market, but it has yet to succeed in the tough U.S. market. The company's business along the Pacific Rim continues to grow.

In 1989 Daikin's chemical division contributed about 13.5% to Daikin's sales and in the future should yield an ever-growing number of new products, such as the synthetic chemicals Daikin developed for use in the semiconductor industry. Aside from its troubled experience with certain fluorochemicals, Daikin produced fluoropolymers used for molding and the coating of wires. Oil hydraulic systems, defense contracts, and electronics each added about 5% to Daikin's 1989 sales, helping the company weather the worst of the construction industry's ups and downs. Daikin boasts an unusual mix of products in the chemical, mechanical engineering, and electronics fields, a combination of diverse technologies.

Principal Subsidiaries: Daikin Plant Co., Ltd.; Tokyo Daikin Airconditioning and Engineering Co., Ltd.; Osaka Daikin Airconditioning and Engineering Co., Ltd.; Kita-Kyushu Daikin Airconditioning and Engineering Co., Ltd.; Chukyo Daikin Airconditioning and Engineering Co., Ltd.; Daikin Europe N.V. (Belgium); Daikin Australia Pty. Ltd.; A.C.E. Daikin (Singapore) Pte., Ltd.

—Jonathan Martin

DEERE & COMPANY

John Deere Road
Moline, Illinois 61265
U.S.A.
(309) 765-8000
Fax: (309) 765-5772

Public Company
Incorporated: 1868
Employees: 39,000
Sales: $6.23 billion
Stock Exchanges: New York Midwest Frankfurt

Deere & Company is the world's largest manufacturer of agricultural equipment and a major U.S. producer of lawncare and industrial equipment. The company has factories throughout the world and distributes its products through independent retail dealers. Deere has been an industry innovator since John Deere introduced the first successful self-cleaning steel plow in 1837. At that time, most Americans lived on farms; now many of Deere's customers belong to the upper 5% of the nation's farmers, who take in 80% of the net farm income—these farmers run big farms that need sophisticated equipment.

Born in 1804 in Vermont, John Deere was a blacksmith renowned for his craftsmanship and inventiveness. After a business depression in the 1830s, Deere, like many young easterners, migrated west. He settled in Grand Detour, Illinois, where his blacksmith business thrived. He soon saw that the cast-iron hand plow that pioneers had brought from the East did not work well in midwestern soil, which clung to the plow's bottom and made it necessary for the farmer to scrape off the soil every few feet. Deere developed a plow with a polished and specially shaped moldboard and share, which scoured itself after lifting the soil.

This first plow was made from a broken sawblade, but the tool quickly became so popular with Deere's customers that he began to make plows before he got orders for them—a revolutionary practice in those days. In 1843, Deere ordered a shipment of rolled steel from England. This move enabled him to expand his business, and three years later he was able to get steel made to his specifications from Pittsburgh, Pennsylvania, mills. In 1847, Deere moved his business to Moline, Illinois, near the Mississippi River, which provided water power and convenient transportation. By 1850 he was producing 1,600 plows a year.

Known to say, "I will never put my name on a plow that does not have in it the best that is in me," Deere continued to improve his plows and to tailor them for different soil conditions. In 1868 the business was incorporated as Deere & Company. In 1869, Deere named his son, Charles Deere, vice president and treasurer of the company. When John Deere died in 1886, Charles succeeded him as president.

Charles Deere focused on the company's distribution system, establishing wholesale branches to market and distribute Deere equipment to the independent dealers who sold it. The product line was also expanded. The Gilpin Sulky Plow, launched in 1874, had the capacity to plow three acres in 12 hours, and in 1898 the new Deere Gang Plow, which used four horses instead of three and could plow six acres in 12 hours, was introduced. In the early 1900s, Deere plows were powered by steam engines. By the time Charles Deere died in 1907, the company was manufacturing a range of cultivators, steel plows, corn and cotton planters, and other tools.

William Butterworth, who was responsible for bringing together under the John Deere name other farm-equipment companies with whom Deere had done business, became the next president, in 1907. As president, Butterworth engineered the 1911 acquisition of the Van Brunt Manufacturing Company of Horicon, Wisconsin, which produced the first working broadcast seeder and grain drill. Also in 1911, Deere & Mansur Works—which had been established in 1877 by the company to make corn planters—was merged with Deere, as was Joseph Dain's hay-making-tool company. In 1918, Deere bought Waterloo Gasoline Engine Company in Waterloo, Iowa, one of the first makers of tractors.

During World War I, the demand for food motivated many more farmers to begin to use tractors, and agriculture gradually lost its dependence on animal power. Deere sold 8,000 Waterloo Boy tractors in 1918. In 1823, Deere introduced its own tractor, called the Model D.

In 1928, Charles Deere Wiman, John Deere's great-grandson, became president of the company. Wiman concentrated on engineering and product development, and the company grew rapidly. In the 1930s, when the John Deere Combination Unit was introduced, the farmer could bed, plant, and fertilize cotton ten times faster than four men with four mules. The four-row tractor corn planter allowed one man to plant and fertilize between 40 and 50 acres a day. In 1937, despite the Great Depression, Deere reached $100 million in gross sales.

During World War II Burton F. Peek was president. Peek served during the two years that Wiman held the post of colonel of ordinance, in Washington, D.C. Peek and Wiman, when he returned to Deere, continued to focus on innovation in product design, and by the end of the war Deere was a leader. In 1952, Deere was the first farm-equipment manufacturer to modify the self-propelled combine for picking and shelling corn. Three years later, Deere was one of the 100 largest manufacturing companies in the United States.

After Wiman died in 1955, his son-in-law, William A. Hewitt, became president and CEO. He led the company into a major growth period. Seeing that Deere's decentralized operations needed to be coordinated, Hewitt accomplished this by increasing communication between different branches of the company. He also promoted Elwood Curtis, Deere's controller, to vice president.

During the mid-1950s, while Deere's competitors were expanding abroad, Hewitt seized the opportunity to manufacture overseas. In 1956, he sent one of Deere's factory leaders, Harry Pence, to look for possible acquisitions overseas. The first was a small German tractor company called Heinrich Lanz, which was in financial trouble and could be bought cheaply. Other acquisitions or plant constructions followed in France, Spain, Argentina, Mexico, and South Africa. For 15 years, overseas operations suffered huge losses due to managerial mistakes and unforeseen problems in startup activities and in foreign exchange, but Hewitt believed the company had to expand internationally, or risk being forced out of the market. Deere continued to expand in Canada, Western Europe, and Latin America.

In 1957, Hewitt hired Finnish architect Eero Saarinen, the designer of the Gateway Arch in Saint Louis, Missouri, to design a new headquarters building that would belie Deere's provincial, rather conservative image. The new building was completed seven years later in the same Moline location, and it became a tourist site, particularly attractive to farmers.

In the late 1950s, Vice President Elwood Curtis convinced Hewitt to diversify into finance. In 1958 Deere donated its capital stock in Moline National Bank to the John Deere Foundation, and, freed of antitrust constraints, the John Deere Credit Company was established to help finance farm-equipment dealerships. Ten years later, Deere acquired Fulton Insurance Company in New York. Insurance and finance were to become important Deere operations when equipment sales slumped.

Hewitt diversified and expanded Deere to help balance the company's farm-equipment operations. Since tractor sales were dependent on the income of farmers, sales fluctuated according to weather, agricultural prices, and government policy. While agricultural machinery still accounted for most of Deere's sales, in the late 1950s, Deere began to make machinery for construction, along with equipment for street and road maintenance and logging. In 1963, the company began to manufacture and market lawncare and garden equipment. This branch of the company grew rapidly. By 1969, there were 3,700 independent John Deere dealers in the United States and Canada. In 1969, through the dealers, Deere began to operate a network of John Deere parts and service centers.

While the 1960s were a decade of growth and diversification for Deere, it was also a turbulent time. Earnings decreased markedly in 1966 and 1967, mainly due to overseas operations. In 1968, the company suffered losses due to unfavorable weather, low crop prices, and a six-week strike. The United Auto Workers (UAW) demanded a contract from Deere similar to the one it had won at Caterpillar Tractor Company, one of Deere's competitors. Deere refused, and the strike finally ended when the UAW proposed an inverse seniority plan, which gave senior workers up to 95% of their pay if they volunteered to be laid off for one year. This allowed older workers, who were closer to retirement, to take time off while collecting UAW supplemental unemployment benefits. The plan went into effect in late 1967, and in three years Deere laid off 1,698 people, about 70% of them with high seniority.

Throughout the 1960s, Deere expanded its lawn-and-garden product line to include snowmobiles, hand tools, portable heaters, lanterns, chain saws, and other products. In 1972, Deere introduced the John Deere bicycle in an effort to take advantage of a rapidly expanding market. This was also the first year Deere made a profit overseas, as the demand for farm machinery increased both within the United States and abroad.

In 1975, overseas plants accounted for $681 million in sales, and the company expected to grow more in foreign operations than domestically. That year, Deere also began a seven-year, $1.8 billion capital program to increase the capacity of its factories and plants by 30%.

During the 1970s, Deere repeatedly had conflicts with the UAW, as the firm began to mechanize further its manufacturing operations, cut back costs, and lay off workers. In 1976 a six-week strike reduced inventory at a time when the demand for equipment remained strong, and Deere lost a significant amount. In October 1979 UAW members went on strike again, demanding more paid time off and cost-of-living wage increases. Deere argued that its workers already had more paid time off than employees at similar companies, and changes would be too costly. Consequently, Deere factories were shut down for three weeks, until a new contract was agreed upon.

In 1978 Hewitt committed $350 million to overseas expansion. Nonetheless, that year overseas operations took serious losses due to foreign-exchange fluctuation and high start-up costs for its new line of German tractors.

In the late 1970s Deere added 20 products to its construction-equipment sector, and doubled the size of its Davenport, Iowa, plant, with the expectation that the construction industry would grow twice as fast as the farm-equipment industry. By 1982, however, due to high interest rates, the construction-equipment business was in a slump.

In 1982 Deere also experienced the first effects of the farm recession. Hewitt retired as head of the company and later became the United States ambassador to Jamaica. Robert Hanson, a longtime Deere employee and Moline native, became president and CEO. He took up the post at a challenging time. The country was in the midst of a recession, and farm-equipment sales were low. The company's dealers were overstocked, and its plants were running at about 50% capacity. In order to help its dealers survive, Deere incurred a large amount of short-term debt. Hanson cut capital spending by 30%, much of it in labor costs, and Deere began its dramatic reduction of salaried employees. Between 1980 and 1983, the company laid off about 40% of its employees.

In 1982, the newly robotized Waterloo tractor plant lost money, only a year after it began production. Although the plant required fewer workers, Deere lost money because the demand for tractors was so low that the plant had to run at a fraction of its capacity, and overhead was high. In fact, manufacturing operations lost money continually until 1986.

In order to recoup some of the losses, Deere continued to develop its financial sector. In 1982 the company acquired Central National Life Insurance Company and expanded its John Deere Credit Company to include leasing operations. During the early and mid-1980s, Deere was active in helping farmers to finance tractor purchases, offering credit incentives. Deere won the loyalty of many farmers this way. This helped sales at a time when many farmers were tightening their budgets. Farmers' net incomes had decreased about 75% in the past decade, basically due to over-production, which, in turn, cost the government a great deal in surplus storage. In 1983, President Ronald Reagan introduced a payment-in-kind program, which paid farmers not to plant a certain number of acres, in order to alleviate the overproduction problem.

Deere's investment in overseas expansion had not paid off, and in 1983 the company still held a small share of the European market. In an effort to strengthen its links with Japan, Deere began to import Hitachi construction equipment.

Despite Deere's financial troubles, the recession hit Deere much less severely than it did its competitors, and Hanson found ways for the company to make money in sectors other than farm implements. In 1984, Deere acquired a rotating-combustion-engine business from the Curtiss-Wright Corporation, and Deere also bought all rights to Farm Plan, an agricultural-financing service.

Sales in farm equipment continued to decrease markedly. The company survived mainly from its sale of lawn tractors, European sales, and its financial operations. In 1985, Deere continued to cut back on labor costs when it simplified the design of its basic engine and reorganized its factory system, laying of 480 workers. "When you're on the way to the gallows, your attention is clearly focused," Hanson told *Financial World*, May 2, 1989.

In 1985 a $100,000 John Deere tractor sold for about $70,000. About 20% of the dealers in the Midwest closed. This attrition helped the stronger dealers to survive. With sales at $4 billion, Deere lost money before taxes. Deere began a health-maintenance organization for small cities and rural communities in 1985, called Heritage National Health Plan.

In 1986, Deere won an $11 million military contract to develop an implement for repairing bomb-damaged runways. Also in 1986, 12,000 UAW members struck four key plants, seeking a new contract that would protect employees against cutbacks and maintain a cost-of-living adjustment. Deere shut down its remaining UAW plants, and the UAW accused the company of a lockout. Deere's dealers had enough inventory to last several months at the rate they were selling them, and the strike allowed Deere to reduce inventory and overhead. Deere said it could not afford the proposed labor contract, and the strike lasted five-and-a-half months before Deere and the UAW could come to an agreement.

In 1987, Deere lost $99 million, mainly due to depressed sales and the effect of the strike. Hanson continued to push Deere into manufacturing parts such as hydraulic cylinders for other companies, and he also expanded credit operations. Although the lawncare business continued to do well, the company still depended on the farm-implements sector for 60% of its business.

In 1987, Hans W. Becherer was named president of Deere, while Hanson remained CEO. In 1988, the farm economy began to recover from its slump, due to the lower dollar and the improvement of the North American agricultural economy. As the main survivor in the industry, Deere had increased its market share during the recession from 45% to 55%. In 1988 sales increased 30% to $5.4 billion, and net income reached a record $315 million, a one-year turnaround of $414 million. Sales of tractors rose 90%, and sales of harvesting machinery tripled. As the recession lifted, many farmers were ready to buy new equipment.

Deere offered its largest selection of new agricultural products ever in 1988 and 1989, spending about $16 million to display its 44 new combines, tractors, and balers in Denver, Colorado; and Palm Springs, Colorado. In 1988 Deere formed a joint venture with Hitachi called Deere-Hitachi Construction Machinery, which would produce and market earth excavators.

In March 1989, Deere settled a court dispute with the Equal Employment Opportunity Commission (EEOC), which was acting on behalf of 116 former employees who were laid off as part of the labor reductions in 1984. The EEOC alleged that age discrimination was involved, and while Deere denied the allegation, it agreed to pay $4.3 million to settle the dispute rather than go through further litigation. In October 1989, a one-month strike slowed production at Deere's Wisconsin lawncare products plant.

Labor problems aside, Deere's future in farm equipment looks good. The agricultural economy has rebounded and Deere continues to lead the market, one of the few as yet untapped by foreign competitors. Deere has consistently spent 5% of its sales on research and development, helping the company to remain a leader in sophisticated farm implements and other equipment. Deere's long-term success also depends on its ability to diversify shrewdly, and President Becherer has stated that he intends to continue to search out the type of diversified investments that have served Deere & Company so well.

Principal Subsidiaries: John Deere Co.; John Deere Credit Co.; John Deere Intercontinental Ltd. (Belgium); John Deere Industrial Equipment Co.; John Deere Ltd. (Canada); John Deere-Lanz Verwaltungs A.G. (Germany, 99.9%); John Deere (France); John Deere Iberica S.A. (Spain); Tahoe Insurance Co.; Rock River Ins. Co.; John Deere Insurance Group Inc.; John Deere Insurance Co.; Compania Hondurena De MaQuinaria S.A. (Honduras); John Deere Foreign Sales Corp. Ltd. (Jamaica); Deere Credit Services, Inc.; Deere-Hitachi Construction Machinery Corporation (50%); Deere Payroll Services, Inc.; Deere Marketing Services, Inc.; Farm Plan Corporation; Funk Manufacturing Company; John Deere Health Care, Inc.; John Deere Technologies International Inc.; Fabrica Nacional De Tractores y Motores (Venezuela); John Deere Intercontinental Ltd. S.A. (Belgium); John Deere Machines Agricoles (France); John Deere (Proprietary) Ltd. (South Africa); John Deere S.A. (Panama); John Deere Ltd. (U.K.); Svenska John Deere A.B. (Sweden); John Deere Industrial (PTE) Ltd. (Singapore); SLC S.A. Industria e Comercio (Brazil); John Deere, S.A. de C.V. (Mexico); Yanmar-John Deere Engineering Yugen Kaisha (Japan, 50%); Chamberlain Holdings Ltd. (Australia); Agro Systems Corp.; John Deere Catalog Co.; Fort Smith Timber & Land Co.

Further Reading: Historical Highlights: 150 Years of John Deere Contributions to Agriculture, Moline, Illinois, Deere & Company, [1987]; *The Story of John Deere,* Moline, Illinois, Deere & Company, [1989].

—René Steinke

DEUTSCHE BABCOCK AKTIENGESELLSCHAFT

DEUTSCHE BABCOCK AG

Duisburger Strasse 375
D-4200 Oberhausen 1
Nordrhein-Westfalen
Federal Republic of Germany
(208) 8330
Fax: (208) 26091

Public Company
Incorporated: 1898 as Deutsche Babcock & Wilcox Dampfkessel-Werke AG
Employees: 23,586
Sales: DM5.38 billion (US$3.18 billion)
Stock Exchange: Frankfurt

Deutsche Babcock is involved in machine engineering and plant construction through its subsidiary groups Deutsche Babcock Energie-und Umwelttechnik, Deutsche Babcock-Borsig, and Deutsche Babcock Handel. Its products include power stations and boilers, oil and gas firing equipment, nuclear-fuel-reprocessing components, air conditioning systems, refrigeration equipment, specialty steels and wire, copper pipes, cast-iron fittings, desulfurization systems, and water-treatment plants. The group's willingness and ability to maintain such a level of diversity says much for the expertise of its research staff, the continuity provided by having just five chief executives in over 90 years, the efficiency and productiveness—which means more than just productivity—of its workers, and the advantages it has gained from its presence, since the turn of the century, in the Ruhr district, at the heart of the German economy.

The company from which Deutsche Babcock originates was founded not in the Ruhr but in Berlin, and by non-Germans. In 1898, Robert Jurenka and Alois Seidl, immigrants from Bohemia in the Austro-Hungarian Empire, signed an agreement with officials of the British boilermaker Babcock & Wilcox to transform its existing Berlin Babcock sales office into a subsidiary of the U.K. Babcock & Wilcox. They purchased a factory in Oberhausen in the Ruhr district in order to manufacture the sectional boiler developed by U.S. engineers George Herman Babcock and Stephen Wilcox—from whom all three Babcock & Wilcox companies, in the United States, Britain, and Germany, take their names, although Deutsche Babcock now has no connection with either of the others. Their boiler was not only the most economical made at the time, but also the safest, since its chambers lacked the rivets or welds which made other models prone to explosion. Robert Jurenka served as president and chief executive of the company until his death in 1942, steering it with evident success through World War I, the social upheavals of 1919 and hyper-inflation, the rise of the Nazis, and the plunge into World War II. Having started with 30 employees, the company had 1,600 by 1927, producing boilers at Oberhausen and steam generators in the Gleiwitz works acquired in 1909. Under an agreement with the other Babcock companies, Deutsche Babcock expanded, not into Western Europe or overseas, but into the East, building a significant presence in Upper Silesia, which was then part of Germany, in Poland, and in the Soviet Union. Under Jurenka's leadership Deutsche Babcock achieved a record of concern for its workers that was good even by German standards, and which many in the United Kingdom and the United States might have envied. Its health insurance fund dates from the company's founding; supplementary pensions were introduced for its retired workers in 1938; it was the first company in Germany to introduce the five-day week, before 1914; and as early as 1930 the working week was 42½ hours for blue collar workers and 40 hours for white collar staff.

In 1945 Robert Jantscha, who had succeeded Jurenka as head of the company three years before, had to deal with the crisis caused by the bombing of much of the Oberhausen plant and the loss of business in Eastern Europe, after the transfer of Upper Silesia to Polish control and the imposition of Stalinism throughout the region. Deutsche Babcock began again by repairing agricultural machinery and, as soon as capital became available, expanding production on a one-million-square-meter site at Friedrichsfeld, which the company had bought in 1921. By 1960 the company, which at that stage had only six subsidiaries, employed 11,000 people in boilermaking and the building of boilerhouses and chimneys, and in the production of firing equipment, valves, and fans. The company produced a total of 150 products at that date, compared with 700 in 1990.

It is difficult to judge to what extent the course of Deutsche Babcock's development depended on the overall rise in prosperity in the Federal Republic of Germany, especially as the causes of the *Wirtschaftwunder,* or economic miracle, are themselves the subject of great and continuing controversy. Discussion, outside Germany, of the country's economic system, which involves both "concerted action" between government bodies and interest groups and *Mitbestimmung*—co-determination—between shareholders and workers, has perhaps tended to exaggerate their impact, especially on a company like Deutsche Babcock. Firstly, since coordination among the federal government, the state governments, and the main economic organizations was not made legally enforceable until 1967, the growth which predated it owed more to informal processes of consultation, under pro-business governments led by the Christian Democrats up to 1966, than to any imposition of a single framework from above. Secondly, co-determination was not legally prescribed outside the coal and steel industries until 1976. Its extension to all large and medium-sized companies meant that Deutsche Babcock had to allow half of the membership of its supervisory board to be chosen to represent its employees—including among the ten board members three full-time officials of I.G. Metall, the main trade union in the group. It seems likely, then, that Deutsche Babcock has benefited at least as much from successful industrial relations, internally generated, as from externally developed formal structures.

The company achieved considerable prestige in 1961, with the launch of Germany's first nuclear-powered vessel, the *Otto Hahn,* which was fitted with a reactor designed and constructed by Deutsche Babcock. This was its first major venture into the nuclear field. In 1963 the company was commissioned by the electricity-supply firm Nordwestdeutsche Kraftwerke to begin work on a power station based on the Advanced Gas-cooled Reactor (AGR) system developed by Deutsche Babcock's British associate. Nearly three decades later, after the decline of the U.S. nuclear-power industry, the Chernobyl disaster and its lingering effects, and the fiasco of the British government's attempt to sell off nuclear power stations which nobody wanted to buy, this departure appears to have been one of Deutsche Babcock's greatest mistakes, on commercial and environmental grounds. Yet at the time it may well have seemed that the power station order was a sign of general confidence both in Deutsche Babcock's technical expertise and in West Germany's ability to keep itself at the leading edge of industrial change.

By the mid-1970s the German nuclear-power industry was the subject of fierce competition between the Kraftwerk Union, formed by AEG and Siemens in 1969, and the consortium created in 1971 between the U.S. Babcock & Wilcox, Deutsche Babcock, and Brown Boveri. The oil crisis of the early 1970s made the industry's future look bright. Deutsche Babcock committed itself to a series of deals with Soviet companies for the supply, not only of nuclear-generating components, but of gas-pipeline equipment, cryogenic equipment, and a gypsum plant. Then, in 1978, the disaster at Three Mile Island, Pennsylvania, became a major embarrassment for the U. S. Babcock & Wilcox, which had built the nuclear power plant. The 1980s saw the ascension of the Green Party and Germany's biggest postwar demonstrations against the industry Deutsche Babcock had entered with high hopes only 20 years before.

The company had by no means put all its capital and research efforts into nuclear power, and the late 1960s and early 1970s were years of expansion and diversification into new fields, though the company still supplied 56% of West Germany's boiler market in 1972. After Robert Jantscha's death in 1967 his successor Hans Ewaldsen undertook a program of acquisitions within Germany and oversaw the increase in the share of foreign business in group turnover from 13% when he became president to over 50% in the 1980s. As of 1980, when the present structure of parent company and operating units was introduced, the group had nearly 80 subsidiaries, half of which were based outside West Germany. In 1975, in the midst of Ewaldsen's expansion program, the U.K. parent Babcock & Wilcox—now called F.K.I. Babcock—decided that profits coming from Germany were inadequate and sold its 25.02% of the company's shares carrying 33.92% of voting rights, to the Iranian government. Less than four years later the shah of Iran was overthrown, but the new regime retained the holding in Deutsche Babcock until 1987, when it was sold to a consortium of German banks.

By then Deutsche Babcock had come through several difficult years. In 1976 Ewaldsen had made public his concern that German makers of power-station boilers were becoming less able to compete on price with foreign corporations. Nevertheless the company continued to win orders for a variety of plant-construction projects from all over the world, including United Arab Emirates in the same year, Libya in 1978, Kuwait in 1980, and Iraq in 1981, demonstrating that the Iran-Iraq War was not at all bad for some European, American, or Japanese businesses. Meanwhile a virtual moratorium on nuclear power station construction in the Federal Republic of Germany, a general decline in power-industry orders, and foreign exchange difficulties over the Kuwait venture combined to force Deutsche Babcock to cut dividends in 1981 and withhold them altogether in 1982. Like other German companies in the mechanical-engineering sector, however, Deutsche Babcock continued to spend heavily on research and development and to seek new markets outside Europe, in competition with Japanese and American firms.

In 1983 Hans Ewaldsen became chairman of the group's supervisory board, and his place as president was taken by Helmut Wiehn. The new president, only the fourth in the group's history, came to office during a general upturn in the economy. This was reinforced, for Deutsche Babcock and its rivals, by the creation of a new market in air-pollution control systems initiated by the worldwide reversion from nuclear power to coal, and by the tightening of environmental controls in West Germany in 1983 and 1984. Between 1983 and 1988 the proportion of the group's sales designated as "environmental engineering" rose from 10% to over 25%. Whether because of social and political pressures or as a canny business venture—probably both—Deutsche Babcock's research-and-development funds now go mainly toward new technologies, not only for reducing emissions from coal-fired power stations, but also for controlling air pollution and improving water and soil quality. Another sign of the times is the making of cooperation agreements with engineering companies in Czechoslovakia and the Soviet Union during 1988, placing Deutsche Babcock alongside many other German firms in the newly opened markets of Eastern Europe, and, indeed, bringing the group back to territories in which it was first involved over half a century ago. Both in its home market and increasingly beyond it, Deutsche Babcock is well-prepared for the economic and social changes of the 1990s.

Principal Subsidiaries: Deutsche Babcock Anlagen AG; Deutsche Babcock Handel GmbH; Deutsche Babcock-Borsig AG; Deutsche Babcock Energie-und Umwelttechnik AG; Balcke-Dürr AG; Babcock-BSH AG; A Friedr. Fleuder AG.

Further Reading: Wiehn, Helmut, *From Boilermaking to Mechanical Engineering and Plant Construction,* Oberhausen, Deutsche Babcock, 1985.

—Patrick Heenan

DOVER CORPORATION

280 Park Avenue
New York, New York 10017
U.S.A.
(212) 922-1640
Fax: (212) 922-1656

Public Company
Incorporated: 1955
Employees: 20,049
Sales: $2.12 billion
Stock Exchanges: New York London

Dover Corporation is a diversified manufacturing holding company composed of about 45 subsidiaries with about 40 lines of industrial products. Dover's management implements a distinctive approach: subsidiaries are allowed to operate with almost complete autonomy. Dover-subsidiary managers operate with great independence and are rewarded on the basis of long-term earnings growth and return on investment of individual businesses. The company is often thought of as a portfolio of companies rather than a conglomerate because of its hands-off organizational structure and philosophy of management. Dover-owned companies manufacture a range of industrial products, supplying the building industry and the electronics, petroleum, industrial, and aerospace markets.

Dover is split into six groups. Five of the groups are independently operating subsidiaries. The sixth group is comprised of companies reporting directly to headquarters and called corporate companies. Dover's five major subsidiaries are Dover Elevator International, Dover Technologies, Dover Resources, Dover Industries, and Dover Diversified. The company is the largest producer of new elevators in the United States. It is also the second-largest in Canada and the third-largest in the United Kingdom. The elevator business provides over one-third of Dover's profit.

Dover Corporation was formed in 1955, when New York stockbroker George Ohrstrom Sr. recruited Fred D. Durham to manage four companies he had bought in the 1930s and 1940s. One of those companies was C. Lee Cook Company, a maker of seals and piston rings for compressors. C. Lee Cook had been built largely by its owner and president, Fred Durham, before being sold to Ohrstrom. Durham was made Dover's first president in 1955.

Dover was originally composed of four companies: Cook; Rotary Lift, a manufacturer of automotive lifts; W.C. Norris, a maker of sucker rods for oil-well pumping; and Peerless, which was sold in 1977. Cook, Rotary Lift, and Norris in 1991 were still part of the company.

Dover's corporate offices, opened in 1955, were in Washington, D.C. In December of that year 930,000 common shares of Dover stock were listed on the New York Stock Exchange. The stock split in a ratio of 3 for 2 in 1965, and has split a number of times since.

Dover's corporate culture was molded by Durham, who felt that "business, like any other human enterprise, thrives best where creativity and initiative are encouraged in an atmosphere of maximum autonomy." Durham set out to give Dover an environment in which executives could work creatively and without the hindrance of bureaucracy. As Durham intended, autonomy, decentralization, and a minimal corporate staff have become Dover's hallmarks. At the end of Dover's first year of operation the corporate staff consisted of three people, including Durham. In 1990 the New York headquarters employed 22 people, including executives.

Each division functions independently with its own president and board of directors. Between 1955 and 1979 Dover bought 14 companies, mostly privately owned or controlled. As part of Dover, the acquired company retains much of its autonomy, and, in most cases, its pre-acquisition management, while benefiting from Dover's financial strength. At first Dover's corporate office assumed the role of central banker, monitoring subsidiaries' fiscal plans and overseeing capital spending in order to insure high return on capital. Divisions were encouraged to keep cash flow heavy, in order to keep debt low and allow Dover to take advantage of acquisition opportunities and give divisions financial help when needed. The corporate office handled all financing.

The 1958 acquisition of the Shepard Warner Elevator Company gave Dover entry into the electric-elevator business. The purchase of Hunter-Hayes Elevator Company and Reddy Elevator Company in 1964 solidified Dover's position in that industry. For years Dover was number three in the U.S. elevator industry, behind Otis and Westinghouse.

In 1961, Dover bought Cincinnati, Ohio–based OPW, the leading U.S. maker of service station nozzles and other hazardous-fluid-handling equipment. When Fred Durham reached age 65 in 1964, OPW president Thomas C. Sutton was elected Dover's third president and chief executive officer. Dover's second president, Otto G. Schwenk, had served from 1961 to 1962. Schwenk was let go when Dover company presidents, united in opposition to his attempts to expand the corporate staff, threatened to resign. Also in 1964, Dover's corporate headquarters were moved to New York.

Under Sutton's leadership Dover experienced tremendous growth. Sales leaped from $68 million in 1964 to $835 million in 1981. Sutton stuck closely to Durham's management philosophy, and eliminated the corporate position of internal auditor. To Dover's nucleus of well-managed companies many others were added, in accordance with a policy that required acquisitions to display such qualities as product excellence, market leadership, strong management, and high return on capital.

Throughout the 1960s Dover's product base was expanded through acquisitions into a wide range of areas. Major purchases include De-sta-Co, a toggle clamps and flapper valves producer bought in 1962; the 1964 acquisition of Blackmer Pump Company, a maker of industrial pumps; Groen Manufacturing, a maker of steam-jacketed kettles and other equipment for the food-service industry, purchased in 1967; and Ronningen-Petter, which produced filter-strainer units, was bought in 1968. Also in 1968, Dover spun off its Dura-Vent subsidiary to employees. The Dura-Vent sale demonstrated another important facet of Dover's corporate strategy: divestiture of non-core businesses. Dover's 1966 acquisition of Turnbull, however, was not executed as seamlessly. The Turnbull acquisition negated corporate growth for two years as Dover's elevator division struggled to digest Turnbull.

During the 1960s the company began to export a broad range of its products through independent distributors and, later, through its own subsidiaries. During the 1960s and 1970s Dover operated primarily in the building industry—mostly elevators—the petroleum-services-equipment industry, and manufactured goods for various industrial uses.

In 1975 Dover acquired Dieterich Standard Corporation, a Denver, Colorado–based manufacturer of liquid-measurement instruments. Dieterich president Gary L. Roubos came to Dover with Dieterich. Roubos, with a background in chemical engineering and business administration, was elected Dover's president and chief operating officer within two years of the Dieterich purchase. In 1981 Roubos was named CEO, and in 1989 he became chairman. Roubos continued his predecessor's winning strategy. Acquisitions were typically small companies, mostly bought in exchange for cash. They were market leaders, or had proprietary lines that meshed with Dover's existing businesses and had good growth prospects. Dover acquisitions, almost without exception, have had higher-than-average returns on invested capital. Beginning in 1963 and into the early 1980s the company averaged one non-elevator takeover a year. In the years Roubos served as president, from 1977 to 1989, sales doubled from $1 billion to a little over $2 billion. Difficulties in assimilating Weaver, an automotive lift company, caused that company to be shut down. Typically divisions that have been sold were not a good fit with Dover's other product lines.

In July 1979 Dover acquired Universal Instruments Corporation of Binghamton, New York. Universal, the world's leading manufacturer of automated assembly equipment for electronic circuitry, moved Dover into the electronics business. By 1989 Dover Technologies, Dover's electronics division, owned 12 companies. By 1980 the electronics market had become the second most important growth area for Dover, following petroleum-production products. During the 1980s, with the industry moving toward electronic-circuit miniaturization and cost reductions and quality enhancement through use of computer-controlled automation, Universal's sales soared.

Although petroleum-production and -marketing equipment was Dover's fastest-growing segment during the 1970s and 1980s, it was sensitive to the volatility of deregulation, environmental regulation, and pricing by the Organization of Petroleum Exporting Countries (OPEC). The Norris division's sucker rods for lifting oil from wells were prey to the cyclical nature of the oil-drilling business and to the deregulation of the gasoline business. By the early 1980s, with the country in the midst of a recession, demand for oil-production equipment, an area that had comprised one-third of pretax profits, was sluggish. For instance, OPW, the leading supplier of gasoline-pump nozzles, had experienced rapid growth during the 1970s, with the installation of new pump nozzles for unleaded gasoline and the conversion of many gas stations to self-serve. Rotary Lift had done very well in the automobile-service industry during the 1970s; a number of mass-merchandisers were entering the automobile-service business and buying machinery from Rotary Lift. Recessionary pressures in the early 1980s, however, deterred purchases in the automotive service and repair industry. The diversity of Dover's product line, and moves into such areas as electronics, aerospace, and other growth areas, have helped cushion the company against such economic swings.

While Dover continued to grow under Gary Roubos's leadership, its size and complexity began to hamper its approach. Thus, in 1985, Dover's management was restructured. The resulting arrangement created five major subsidiaries, each with between five and nine of its own related subsidiaries headed by a chief executive officer. The presidents of the approximately 40 companies that comprised Dover reported to the CEO of one of the five subsidiaries. The five subsidiary chiefs reported to the Dover CEO. Each subsidiary continued to seek to add complimentary acquisitions. The five subsidiaries were divided into four business sectors for reporting purposes. The sectors created in 1985 reflected the principal areas of market activity. They were building industries, comprised wholly of Dover Elevator International; the electronic products segment, representing Dover Technologies; the petroleum industry sector, representing Dover Resources; and industrial and aerospace products, comprised of the Dover Industries and Dover Sargent subsidiaries.

In 1989 Dover again revised its structure, into six sectors, to reflect shifts in market activity. Since the 1985 restructuring, distinctions created among petroleum, industrial, and aerospace companies had become increasingly blurred and decreasingly descriptive. The six sectors created in 1989 were Dover Elevator International, Dover Technologies, Dover Resources, Dover Industries, Dover Diversified, and Corporate Companies. All sectors except Corporate Companies are also subsidiaries in their own right. True to character, each subsidiary office has three to five employees.

Dover bought about 25 companies between 1985 and 1989, for $460 million, but has taken on relatively little debt. In general, Dover's capital expenditures are financed with internally generated resources. The results are impressive, as evidenced by Dover's low debt, excellent long-term growth, and consistently above-average return on equity. In 1989 the company made no acquisitions, for the first time since 1980.

During the late 1980s and into 1990, market conditions in the defense-electronics industry had been highly competitive, and performance of Dover's six defense-electronic companies had been weak. At Universal Instruments 1989 profits declined 36%, and Nurad suffered an $8 million loss in the commercial radio market. Dover had responded to the flat market conditions by making management changes, ending Nurad's involvement in the commercial radio field, and trimming back operations. Beginning in 1988, Nurad was also the subject of a criminal investigation of its activities as a government contractor.

Dover's net earnings declined 1% in 1989 on a sales increase of 9%, while earnings per share increased 3% due to the company's ongoing share repurchase program. Dover management expected ailing sectors to rebound in 1990. Despite the short-term earnings drop, Dover continued to operate smoothly and profitably into the 1990s.

Principal Subsidiaries: Dover Elevator International, Inc.; Dover Industries, Inc.; Dover Technologies; Dover Resources, Inc.; Dover Diversified.

Further Reading: "Early History of Dover Corporation," Dover corporate typescript, [1971].

—Paula Cohen

DRESSER INDUSTRIES, INC.

1600 Pacific Building
Dallas, Texas 75201
U.S.A.
(214) 740-6000
Fax: (214) 740-6584

Public Company
Incorporated: 1905 as S.R. Dresser Manufacturing Company
Employees: 31,400
Sales: $5.31 billion
Stock Exchanges: New York Boston Cincinnati Midwest Pacific Philadelphia

Dresser Industries is a worldwide supplier of equipment and services for gas and petroleum exploration and development, energy processing, engineering, and mining. Five industrial segments divide the operations of the company. The oilfield products and services division provides equipment and services for oil and gas exploration, drilling, and production. Energy processing and conversion equipment, the processing division, furnishes products and services for gas reinjection and the conversion of hydrocarbon raw materials into fuels and lubricants. The engineering services division consists of the M.W. Kellogg Company, a wholly owned subsidiary. Primarily concerned with construction and engineering for the hydrocarbon process, it also focuses on the production and installation of pollution-control equipment, mainly for coal-fired power plants.

A joint venture called Komatsu Dresser is the company's mining and construction equipment division, formed by the combination of Dresser's Western Hemisphere construction-equipment operations and those of Komatsu Heavy Industry in Japan. Dresser's general industry segment concentrates on industrial products like pipe couplings, gas meters, and assembly tools for use in aircraft, automobiles, and electronics.

In 1880 Solomon Dresser opened a small business called S. R. Dresser and Company in Bradford, Pennsylvania. Thirty-eight years old, he was an experienced oilman who had followed the oil boom from West Virginia to Pennsylvania without making a significant strike himself. The business was a pragmatic compromise, for Dresser reasoned that a steady living might be easier to earn if he became a supplier rather than a prospector in the oil industry.

Accordingly, he designed an expanding india-rubber packer to seal off the crude oil from water and other fluids underground. Careful to patent his product first, he then offered it for sale in a little downtown store. Dresser's assessment of the packer's market potential was correct. By 1884 his business had prospered, with offices in Allentown and Clarendon, Pennsylvania, and in Bolivar, New York.

He next tried to solve a problem in the natural gas field. Often found in association with petroleum, gas must be transported in leakproof piping to maintain adequate pressure. The lack of such piping during this period meant that only cities within 100 miles of a gas field could enjoy the new energy source. If the drilling site was far from a town, extra gas was simply wasted by burning it in a stack close to the well. Dresser's answer to this puzzle was a leakproof pipe coupling, which appeared in 1885. Perfected two years later, it was destined to lay the foundation of his future fortune. Finding somewhere to test it was not easy; the location had to be close to an unexplored gas field so that he could run his own line to a town.

On a hunch Dresser moved temporarily to Malta, Ohio, close to where gas had been found many years earlier. He bought land leases and explored the area thoroughly. When his hunch proved correct, he laid a pipeline from the gas field and was able to start supplying Malta customers by October 1891. Within two years, the service was bringing in a monthly gross of $400. Satisfied with the project's progress, Dresser returned to Bradford.

Having been tested in actual service, the coupling now needed some recognition for wide sales. The big break came in 1894 when a Standard Oil superintendent placed an experimental order for nine of Dresser's sleeves, or elongated couplings. Orders for couplings in Ohio and Pennsylvania followed, and the product soon came into its own with orders from many other companies.

The oil industry was booming. The 1901 Spindletop discovered near Beaumont, Texas, yielding 100,000 barrels of oil per day, made Texas a new center for the oil industry, though oil had also been found in 15 other states. Cheap and plentiful, it was now used by most industrial facilities and in all forms of transportation.

Solomon Dresser's business flourished, prompting his decision to incorporate his company. He signed the new charter in December 1905, giving the corporation's name as the S.R. Dresser Manufacturing Company and naming four directors besides himself. Capital stock of $500,000 consisted of 5,000 shares with a par value of $100 apiece. Of these, each director got one, Dresser the other 4,996. The financial statement prepared for this incorporation showed company resources of $550,000, with 14 patents accounting for almost $180,000.

Dresser's next innovation came in 1907 with a new Bradford plant. Producing strain-resistant steel couplings to replace the inferior iron ones previously obtained from outside foundries, the facility was one of Dresser's last triumphs. A frequent stroke victim, he died in January 1911, leaving his son-in-law, Fred A. Miller, at the helm of the company.

Now president of S.R. Dresser Manufacturing Company as well as its general manager, Fred Miller proved an able administrator. Profits climbed steadily, and a surplus of almost $500,000 marked the end of the 1914 financial year.

The upward trend during the years of World War I continued. The 100,000 gallons of oil that the United States shipped to Europe daily constituted 90% of the supply needed to fuel the Allies's military vehicles and aircraft. Since there were shortages at home, the pipelines grew faster and farther; by 1918, upward of two million Dresser couplings had been used on more than 9,000 miles of pipeline all over the United States and Canada.

At the beginning of the 1920s the thirst for oil continued to grow as the number of new automobiles rolling from assembly lines swelled to 2.25 million, from 187,000 just ten years earlier. Dresser's annual sales figures reflected this increase: $1.5 million in 1923, they reached an all-time high of $3.7 million by 1927.

Nevertheless, in 1928 the family decided to sell the business, since there was no one to succeed the aging Fred Miller. The buyer was W.A. Harriman & Company, an investment-banking firm intending to make the Dresser business into a public company with separate ownership and management. Under the terms of the agreement, the number of shares increased from 5,000 to 300,000, of which 100,000 were designated Class A and offered at $48 each. The remainder, designated Class B, were held back until 1931. Miller remained as chairman of the board in a consultative capacity.

The new company president was Henry Neil Mallon. Thirty-three years old, Yale-educated, Mallon had seen the war's end as a major and then had worked as a factory worker at the Continental Can Company in Chicago, where he had advanced rapidly to the position of general manager. Initially ignorant about Dresser's business, he investigated every facet of operations thoroughly. Mallon's attention to detail resulted in a gross profit of $1.29 million for 1929, despite the October stock market crash.

However, profitability did not nullify an immediate need for reorganization and updating. Advances in production brought ever-longer pipes needing fewer joints, and a new practice called "welding," cheaper and faster than couplings, was threatening the company with competitive obsolescence. It was time to expand both the product line and the marketing field.

An unexpected new opportunity came in the form of a Canadian government decision to protect local manufacturers by limiting imports. Mallon gladly complied, importing only certain parts of the couplings from Bradford and buying others from Canadian manufacturers. Couplings were then assembled at Dresser's new Toronto plant, which opened in 1931 as a subsidiary, the Dresser Manufacturing Company, Ltd., enabling Canadian customers to continue to buy the company's products.

The expansion staved off a drop in profits for a year. Then, the Depression's domino effect took its toll. Earnings for 1931 sank to $691,787, a stunning $300,000 less than the year before. The economic clouds darkened in 1932, when the annual profit was only $11,621—the lowest since the company's incorporation in 1905. Still, there was enough money to start a company store offering grocery staples to employees and laid-off workers at wholesale prices.

In 1933 Dresser acquired the common stock of Bryant Heater Company. A victim of the Depression because of the decline in the home-construction business, Bryant cost a mere $65,000. Updating started at once, and by the end of the 1930s there was a completely new line of heating products as well as a broader distribution program for sales.

In 1937 Dresser acquired the Clark Brothers Company of Olean, New York, an engineering firm manufacturing gas engines, compressors, and pumping equipment for the oil and gas industries. Internationally recognized, it brought $2.3 million in assets, plus John O'Connor, Clark Brothers's sales manager, who would achieve a great deal for Dresser in the future. In return, Dresser gave Clark greater financial resources and an expanded product line. Dresser merged with Clark in 1938 to become Dresser Manufacturing Company.

By the end of the 1930s, Dresser Manufacturing boasted a product line of 128 new items. Its employee roll stood at 700, and net sales for 1939 were close to $6 million. Between 1939 and 1942 the company undertook several other ventures. Bovaird Seyfang Manufacturing Company, based in Bradford, cost Dresser $592,135 but gave it a new line of engines, engine parts, and tanks for oilfield use. A discovery that fertilizers, synthetic fibers, and refrigerants could be made from distilled natural gas led to an investment of $125,000 in the new Gulf Plains Corporation. Gulf Plains, with its own distillate recovery plant in Texas, gave Dresser entry to these lucrative products, including manufacture of compressors by Clark Brothers.

In 1940 Dresser acquired a half-interest in the Van der Horst Corporation of America, holders of several patents on processes for lining engine cylinders with a chromium-like substance. Unlike true chromium, Porus-Krome could be lubricated, thus helping to prolong the lives of marine and aircraft engines during the years of World War II.

Like other companies in the vital oil-supply business, Dresser stored parts in case of enemy attack. Its pipeline components were now used to carry oil, gas, and water at military posts around the world. The Clark division also began to manufacture 2,600-horsepower engines for freighters, while aircraft parts such as landing gear, wing flaps, and bomb doors came from the other Dresser divisions. One of the company's most urgent assignments was at the secret Manhattan Project, which was engaged in research to develop the atomic bomb. These defense contracts were lucrative. Sales for 1944 sales totaled just under $55 million.

By the end of the war, expansion had made restructuring necessary. The first matter to receive attention was the company's name, which became Dresser Industries in October 1944. Five months later, the need for larger headquarters with good rail and air connections took operations to Cleveland, Ohio.

International markets were burgeoning, largely through the efforts of executive vice president John O'Connor, known throughout the company as "the world's most travelled executive." Accounting for almost 10% of company business, foreign markets now included Britain, China, and Mexico. One of O'Connor's major achievements was persuading the Soviet Union to build a $6 million natural gas-liquification plant outside Moscow. Slated for completion in 1949, the project fell victim to a Commerce Department trade ban early in 1948 and was unfinished until 1954.

In 1950 the company decided to move its headquarters again, this time to Dallas, Texas, the epicenter of the U.S. oil business. In tandem with the move, company operations were streamlined. Previously, new units had kept their corporate structure and their separate charters. Now, Dresser adopted an arrangement by divisions, although each separate company would retained its own identity. In this way, each subsidiary had the advantages of Dresser's size and capital, since strong management ties were maintained with the parent organization. At the same time, Dresser had the equal advantage of decreased size, thus enjoying the efficiency of a small company's close contact between management and work force.

One business that underwent this transformation was the Roots-Connersville Blower Corporation, a manufacturer of boosters, compressors, and exhausters. Liquidated in 1952, the company became the Roots-Connersville Blower Division. Later, all members of the Dresser lineup acquired divisional status, while still enjoying autonomy.

In the 1940s and 1950s, the company continued expansion, with a shift in product line emphasis from capital goods items to expendable ones needing frequent replacement. This idea had been tested in 1945, when the company had acquired Security Engineering, a maker of drilling bits. Still, the product mix at the beginning of the 1950s showed only a 12% ratio of expendable items.

In November 1949, the Magnet Cove Barium Corporation of Houston, Texas, joined the ever-expanding list of subsidiaries, costing Dresser $2.8 million. A well-run, technologically advanced company, Magnet Cove—later known as Magcobar—was a supplier of drilling mud, a little known although essential ingredient in completing an oil well. The mud, composed of barite and other ingredients, was mixed to suit each well. Drilling mud was needed for several important functions such as lubricating the drill bit, partially supporting the weight of the casing, and preventing fluids under high pressure from entering the well.

Scope for expansion also lay in simplifying the complex international currency regulations that complicated business between foreign oil producers and U.S. companies. Dresser solved the problem in 1952, by setting up a Liechtenstein subsidiary, Dresser Vaduz. Charged with the responsibility of executing and monitoring all foreign license agreements, Dresser Vaduz also funneled profits between the different countries, thus saving the parent company huge U.S. taxes by keeping profits overseas. By 1959, besides the foreign licensees, there were subsidiaries in Canada, Britain, and Mexico, as well as in Peru, Brazil, and Venezuela.

Though company objectives had been achieved by 1957, the bonanza was coming to an end. Net sales, reaching $274.43 million in 1957, were down by $50 million by the end of 1958. One cause was the decline in drilling; while almost 60,000 wells were drilled in 1956, the number in 1958 declined to only 49,000. Some sources attributed this slump to the declining number of independent oilmen, caused by the 1956 natural gas price controls.

In 1962, Mallon retired, leaving a 1961 net sales figure of $235.73 million for his successor, John Lawrence. Dissatisfied with this total, Lawrence began to exercise his firm belief in broad product lines by aiming acquisition offers at companies ancillary to the oil and gas supply business, with two notable mergers resulting.

Harbison-Walker, a maker of heat-resistant bricks and other materials for industrial furnaces, was a $125 million company that cost Dresser approximately $150 million. Though its recent sales had been unspectacular, the imminent development of a durable new fire-resistant brick would help it to play its part in Dresser's 1969 sales figure of $700 million—the highest in company history.

Symington-Wayne, a maker of gas station and railroad equipment, carried a price tag of about $94 million, and added a new dimension to the product line. Its principal product, a gasoline-dispensing pump, fitted Dresser's line of supplies for the oil and gas industries. By early 1970, a hefty backlog of orders had added about $103 million to Dresser's volume, with gasoline pumps and other service station equipment accounting for 45%.

The year 1969 brought disaster. California's Santa Barbara Channel was fouled by an offshore well blowout that spilled 10,000 barrels of oil before it could be controlled. The resulting pollution, regarded as an environmental disaster, affected 200 miles of ocean as well as beaches. Concern for the environment brought strict new pollution-control laws in the following year.

Dresser's response was swift. In 1970 the newly appointed president and chief executive officer, John V. James, ordered pollution-control plans to be submitted by each Dresser division. Agreements for joint action were also negotiated with all offshore drilling partners. In 1972, the company acquired Lodge-Cottrell, a British manufacturer of electrostatic precipitators for pollution removal from the stacks of coal-fired electric utility plants.

President James grappled with this issue as well as with the energy crisis sparked by a 1970 Libyan cutback in oil production. A man whose talents lay in planning, James had gained experience in an army intelligence unit during World War II. Various positions dealing with long- and short-range planning had honed his skills, which he now applied to guarding Dresser's progress during the events following the Libyan incident. The OPEC countries' nationalization of operations, increase in taxes, and 12% price increase between 1970 and 1973 did not affect Dresser's sales figures, topping $1 billion by the end of 1973.

Turning his attention to his capital goods markets, James introduced the concept of "multiproduct" plants—facilities which could change products according to need. One such factory was in the Federal Republic of Germany. Formerly making gasoline pumps, it now met decreased demand with a shift to pneumatic tools.

In 1974 Dresser acquired Jeffrey Galion, bringing to the company worldwide plants that manufactured mining and construction equipment. The price of $120 million and more than 400,000 shares of Dresser common stock brought valuable additions to the product line.

Acquisition of the Waukesha Motor Company brought Dresser a selection of internal combustion engines using natural gas, diesel fuel, and gasoline. The large amounts of power needed for hospital, petroleum-exploration, marine, and construction equipment came from these engines. The broadening of the market potential they gave Dresser were well worth the $20.1 million the merger cost. The 1970s ended on a note of peaceful growth, reflected in the 1979 net sales figure of $3.5 billion. In contrast, the next decade began on a note of change.

When price controls were eliminated in 1981, oil companies expanded their exploration programs, drilling 77,500 wells in that year alone. This increase reduced the need for imported oil, while raising the price of domestic crude oil. Yet, despite this lucrative year, it was not long before an economic recession caused a slump in both energy and construction industries.

Nevertheless, the acquisitions strategy continued. During 1982, James's last year as chairman, selected lines of heavy equipment from International Harvester joined the Dresser fold. The following year, James's successor, John J. Murphy, began to dispose of unprofitable companies, acquiring others to give the company a wider profit selection. A life insurance company, a finance company, and a car leasing operation joined the Dresser lineup before the end of 1983. Other measures included the permanent closing of five of the company's eighteen fire-brick plants, the temporary closing of others, and production cuts in still others. Nevertheless, 1983 sales figures of \$3.47 billion were down from \$4.16 billion in 1982.

Reasoning that cooperation with former rivals would cut competition, Murphy decided to target possible opportunities for joint ventures. In 1986, Dresser and the Halliburton Company, a market leader in the drilling fluids field, joined forces to form the M-I Drilling Fluids Company. The following year there was a 50–50 collaboration with Ingersoll-Rand, suppliers of compressors, turbines, and electric machinery. The new company, Dresser-Rand, was joined by a third joint venture the same year, when Western Atlas International, came into being. Formed by a collaboration between Dresser and Litton Industries, the new company was a combination of Dresser's Atlas wire line operations and the Litton Resources Group of Litton Industries.

Yet another joint venture saw the light of day in September 1988, when Komatsu of Japan and Dresser formed the Komatsu Dresser Company. A maker of heavy construction equipment, Komatsu had lost profits owing to relentless competition by U.S. companies unaffected by the strong yen. Dresser, itself a victim of competition on the home front, gladly accepted a chance to learn about efficient new Japanese manufacturing methods. An unusual feature distinguished this alliance—an agreement to keep both product lines separate to offer consumers wider choices.

Though the restructuring led to a \$50 million loss in 1987, this trend was soon reversed. The oil-drilling industry was once more on the rise, owing to new horizontal drilling technology that significantly increased the reachable amount of oil. Once more supplies of all types were in demand.

Principal Subsidiaries: Dresser Insurance Co.; Property & Casualty Insurance Limited; Dresser Finance Corporation; Direko, Inc.; Swaco Geolograph Company.

Further Reading: Payne, Darwin, *Initiative in Energy,* New York, Simon and Schuster, 1979; Knowles, Ruth Sheldon, *First Pictorial History of the American Oil and Gas Industry 1859–1983,* Athens, Ohio, Ohio University Press, 1983.

—Gillian Wolf

EASTMAN KODAK COMPANY

343 State Street
Rochester, New York 14650
U.S.A.
(716) 724-4000
Fax: (716) 724-0663

Public Company
Incorporated: 1889 as Eastman Company
Employees: 137,750
Sales: $18.40 billion
Stock Exchange: New York

A multinational corporation whose name and film are familiar to photographers around the world, Eastman Kodak Company is a diversified manufacturer of photographic imaging equipment and supplies, chemicals, health-care products, and information systems. It is recognized widely as a tightly managed company with superior international marketing.

The company bears the name of its founder, George Eastman, who became interested in photography during the late 1870s while planning a vacation from his job as a bank clerk in Rochester, New York. Taking a co-worker's suggestion to make a photographic record of his intended trip to Santo Domingo, the 24-year-old Eastman soon discovered that the camera, film, and wet-plate-developing chemicals and equipment he had purchased were far too bulky. Instead of following through with his original vacation plans, Eastman spent the time studying how to make photography more convenient. He discovered a description of a dry-plate process that was being used by British photographers. He tried to replicate this process in his mother's kitchen at night after work.

After three years Eastman produced a dry glass plate with which he was satisfied. He obtained a U.S. patent for the dry plate and for a machine for preparing many plates at one time, and started manufacturing dry plates for sale to photographers. Henry A. Strong, a local businessman impressed by Eastman's work, joined him on January 1, 1881, to form the Eastman Dry Plate Company. Eastman left his position at the bank later that year to give his complete attention to the new company.

The new venture almost collapsed several times during its early years because the quality of the dry plates was inconsistent and Eastman insisted that the defective plates be replaced at no charge to the customer. Despite these setbacks, he was determined to make the camera "as convenient as the pencil."

As his business grew, Eastman experimented to find a lighter and more flexible substitute for the glass plate. In 1883 he introduced a new film system using gelatin-coated paper packed in a roll holder which could be used in almost every plate camera available at that time. The company was recognized the following year as Eastman Dry Plate and Film Company. Strong was president and Eastman treasurer and general manager of the 14-shareholder corporation. The company also opened a sales office in London in 1885 to take advantage of the growing European photography market.

In 1888 Eastman's company introduced its first portable camera. Priced at $5.00, it included enough film for 100 pictures. After shooting the roll of film, the owner sent both the film and the camera to Rochester for processing. For $10.00, the company sent back the developed prints and the camera loaded with a new roll of film. This breakthrough is considered to be the birth of snapshot photography. It was also at this time that Eastman trademarked "Kodak," which he invented by experimenting with words that began and ended with his favorite letter, "K". The company advertised its new camera extensively using the slogan, "You push the button, we do the rest."

The following year, the Eastman Photographic Materials Company was incorporated in the United Kingdom, to distribute Kodak products outside the United States from its headquarters in London. The company built a manufacturing plant in 1891 outside London to accommodate the growing product demand overseas, and set up additional distribution sites in France, Germany, and Italy by 1900.

In 1889, the firm's name was changed to Eastman Company and then again in 1892 to Eastman Kodak Company. Eastman became president of the company upon Strong's death in 1919.

Eastman was committed to bringing photography to the greatest number of people at the lowest possible price. As his company grew and production of both the camera and film increased, manufacturing costs decreased significantly and allowed the firm to introduce a number of new cameras, including the Folding Pocket Kodak Camera in 1897. It also brought out the first of a complete line of Brownie cameras, an easy-to-operate model that sold for $1.00 and used film that sold at 15¢ per roll, in 1900.

Over the next 20 years, the company continued to introduce photographic innovations. In 1902 Kodak brought to market a new developing machine that allowed film processing without a darkroom. The 1913 introduction of Eastman Portrait Film provided professional photographers with a sheet film alternative to glass plates.

In 1912 George Eastman hired Dr. C.E. Kenneth Mees, a British scientist, to head up one of the first U.S. industrial research centers. Based in Rochester, this lab was where various tools and manufacturing processes that provided the company with a continuing stream of new products in the 1920s were invented. These new products, including 16-millimeter Kodacolor motion picture film, the 16-millimeter Cine-Kodak motion picture camera, and the Kodascope projector, were targeted at the mass market and priced appropriately.

Kodak developed other new products to support the country's involvement in World War I. In 1917 the company developed aerial cameras and trained U.S. Signal Corps photographers in their use. It also supplied the U.S. Navy with cellulose acetate, a film product, for coating airplane wings, and produced the unbreakable lenses used on gas masks.

George Eastman had always been civic-minded; even as a struggling bank clerk he donated money to the Mechanics Institute of Rochester. As Eastman Kodak grew, his philanthropy extended to such institutions as the Massachusetts Institute of Technology, the Hampton and Tuskegee institutes, and the University of Rochester. He was instrumental in starting numerous dental clinics around the world, and he enjoyed a reputation as a paternalistic employer for his profit-sharing programs and insurance benefits for workers.

In 1932 George Eastman committed suicide at the age of 77, leaving a note that read, "To my friends. My work is done. Why wait? G.E."

That same year, the company introduced the first eight-millimeter motion picture system for the amateur photographer, consisting of film, cameras, and projectors. Three years later, it made available 16-millimeter Kodachrome film, the first amateur color film to gain commercial success. Similar film products for 35-millimeter slides and 8-millimeter home movies were introduced in 1936.

New photographic products continued to be introduced over the next decade, even as the company devoted part of its manufacturing capability to the production of equipment and film for the military during World War II. Following the war, Kodak focused its total attention once again on amateur photography with the introduction of a low-priced Brownie 8-millimeter movie camera in 1951 and the accompanying projector one year later.

In 1953, the company formed Eastman Chemical Products to market alcohols, plastics, and fibers for industrial use. These substances were manufactured by Tennessee Eastman and Texas Eastman, two subsidiaries that had been formed in 1920 and 1952, respectively. The company had begun to manufacture these items because of its own use of chemicals in film manufacturing and processing.

Until this point, the company had always included the cost of film processing in the cost of film. A consent decree filed in 1954 forced Eastman Kodak to abandon this practice, but it also provided an opportunity for the company to serve a new market, independent photofinishers, with its film-developing products. Beginning in 1986 Kodak acquired several photofinishing laboratories, including Fox Photo and American Photographic Group, to further solidify its relationships with photographic consumers and professionals.

By 1958 the company had made significant advances in 35-millimeter color slide technology and introduced the first completely automatic projector called the Kodak Calvalcade. A line of Kodak Carousel projectors introduced three years later became highly successful.

In 1963, one year after astronaut John Glenn had used Kodak film to record his orbit of the earth, the company introduced the Instamatic camera. Using a film cartridge instead of film roll, the Instamatic revolutionized amateur photography and became a commercial success because it was easy to use. Two years later, Kodak brought out a similar cartridge system for super-8 format Instamatic movie cameras and projectors. In 1972 five different models of a pocket version of the Instamatic camera were launched and became immediately popular.

That same year, the company formed Eastman Technology to develop new produces in areas unrelated to its traditional businesses. Its first acquisition was Spin Physics, a San Diego, California–based producer of magnetic heads used in recording equipment. This purchase was completed in 1973.

In the early 1970s, Eastman Kodak became the defendant in a series of antitrust suits filed by several smaller film, camera, and processing companies. These legal actions alleged that Kodak illegally monopolized the photographic market. The most widely publicized suit, filed by Berkey Photo, charged that Kodak had violated the Sherman Antitrust Act by conspiring with two other companies, Sylvania Companies—a subsidiary of GTE Products Corporation—and General Electric Company, to develop two photographic flash devices. Berkey requested that Eastman Kodak be divided into ten separate companies and asked for $300 million in damages. The case was settled in 1981 for $6.8 million.

In 1975, Kodak introduced the Ektaprint Copier-Duplicator, putting itself into direct competition with two firmly entrenched rivals, Xerox and IBM. Kodak considered this market to be a good fit with its existing microfilm business and already had established a foothold with a similar product, the Verifax machine, which had been introduced in 1953. This copier used a wet process like that used in photography, but it had become obsolete when Xerox introduced a technological advancement called xerography, which was less messy and produced better-quality copies than previous systems. After careful research and planning, the Ektaprint copier was developed to serve businesses with large-scale duplicating needs. Not only could the Ektaprint produce numerous copies at high speed, but it could also collate them while duplicating, a unique feature at the time. Despite its innovative attributes and high-quality image production, however, Ektaprint lost about $150 million over its first five years, due primarily to the company's slow entry into the market.

In 1976 Eastman Kodak took on another well-established firm when it challenged Polaroid Corporation's 30-year lock on instant photography with a new line of instant cameras and film that developed pictures outside the camera within a few minutes. The company had missed an opportunity to get in on the ground floor of this technology in the 1940s when it declined an offer to market an instant camera invented by Polaroid founder Edwin Land. The general feeling among Kodak's management had been that Land's camera was a toy and the quality of its pictures was not up to the company's accepted standards. Eastman Kodak had also gained from Polaroid's success. It had become the exclusive supplier of negatives for Polaroid's instant, pull-apart color film in 1963. In 1969, however, Polaroid elected to take over this part of its film manufacturing itself. At the same time Polaroid cut prices drastically to bring its instant cameras more in line with the Kodak Instamatics. Kodak was convinced that Polaroid's instant photography products posed a threat to the company's market leadership. However, the company's methodical product-development process, which emphasized long-term product quality over quick market entry, as well as Polaroid's ownership of hundreds of related patents, proved to be major obstacles to an immediate competitive response. When Kodak finally introduced its own instant camera four years after the decision was made to develop it, the company was plagued by production problems and a Polaroid lawsuit alleging patent infringement. Although the company captured about 25% of the U.S. instant camera market within its first year, reports of quality flaws with the camera's instant photographs and Polaroid's response with another new instant camera stifled sales. Polaroid successfully exploited the business applications of instant photography—for identity cards, for example—and retained its strong position in the market.

During this period, Eastman Kodak's President and Chief Executive Officer Walter A. Fallon and Chairman Gerald B. Zornow oversaw product development. When Zornow retired in 1977, Fallon assumed the chairmanship and was succeeded as president by Colby H. Chandler. With Eastman Kodak since 1941, Fallon had worked his way up from production to direct the U.S. and Canadian photographic division. He had been responsible for the launch of the pocket Instamatic camera line. Chandler had joined the company in 1951, and as Fallon's successor in the U.S. and Canadian photographic division he was directly responsible for both the instant camera and the Ektaprint copier.

Upon becoming president, Chandler faced a challenge to Eastman Kodak's dominance in the photographic paper market by several Japanese competitors and U.S. suppliers, including Fuji Photo Film Company and 3M Company. These firms undercut Kodak's prices for a paper product of similar quality. Fuji also had the advantage of competing against a strong U.S. dollar, which reduced Eastman Kodak's profits significantly in foreign markets. The company responded with price reductions of its own but suffered lower earnings and a decreasing level of investor confidence. Losing the title of official film of the 1984 Summer Olympics to Fuji added further insult to injury.

As the U.S. economy entered a recession in the late 1970s and sales of the company's consumer photographic products declined, higher sales in other areas, such as chemicals, business systems, and professional photofinishing, set profits back on an upward trend. Several prior years of flat earnings across product areas were attributed largely to a lack of strategic planning. At the end of 1978 company operations were reorganized to consolidate the U.S., Canadian, and international photographic areas into one division. The company's first director of corporate planning was also hired to speed the product-development process and institute the controls needed for new products to become profitable more quickly.

The year 1980 marked the company's 100th anniversary. That year Kodak introduced the Ektachem 400 blood analyzer. This entry into the health sciences field represented a natural application of the company's film-manufacturing technology and reinforced its already strong presence as a supplier of x-ray film to hospitals and other health-care facilities.

During the 1980s the company faced intensifying Japanese competition in photography and a continuing decline in product demand. Rapid technological breakthroughs by other firms threatened to replace Eastman Kodak's core product line with more advanced equipment. The company instituted several measures to improve its performance. These included a stronger emphasis on nonphotographic products with high profit potential, a more aggressive approach to protecting its chemical imaging capabilities, a broader international marketing strategy, and a sharper focus on making acquisitions to bring the company up to speed technologically, particularly in electronics.

In 1982 the company purchased Atex, a major supplier of electronic text-editing systems used by publishers. Formed as an entrepreneurial venture in 1972 and leading its field at the time of the acquisition, Atex later lost ground to fast-changing computer technology as Kodak's traditionally slow-moving product-development process was unable to keep pace with the industry.

Despite its shift in priorities to other areas, Eastman Kodak continued to support its bread-and-butter line of photographic products. In 1982 it introduced a line of small cameras that used film discs instead of cartridges and was considered a replacement for the pocket Instamatic camera.

Since the company's founding, Kodak had maintained a policy of treating its employees fairly and with respect, earning the nickname of the "Great Yellow Father." It was George Eastman's belief that an organization's prosperity was not necessarily due to its technological achievements, but more to its workers' goodwill and loyalty. As a result, company benefits were well above average, morale had always remained high, and employees never felt the need to unionize. This protective culture came to an end in 1983, however, when the company was forced to reduce its workforce by 5% in order to cut costs. Competitive pressures from the Japanese and both domestic and international economic problems had slowed product demand. Even the widely publicized disc camera failed to sustain its initial, "hot" sales rate.

Upon Fallon's retirement in 1983, Colby Chandler took over as chairman and, in an attempt to keep up with the pace of change, pointed Eastman Kodak toward the electronics and video areas in earnest. During the 1970s, the company had brought out products that either lacked quality or important features, or arrived too late on the scene to capitalize on new opportunities. Of all the products introduced during Fallon's tenure, only the Ektaprint copier was considered a success, although it gradually lost its marketing advantage to competitive offerings with greater speed and more features. Neither the instant nor the disc cameras had met original expectations and the Ektachem 400 blood analyzer was unable to match the number of tests performed or the reliability of competing products. Two improved versions of the blood analyzer were subsequently introduced in 1984. The company's x-ray film business also took a beating as hospital admissions dropped and attempts by medical institutions to control costs increased.

The company's new electronics division consisted of its Spin Physics subsidiary, a solid-state research laboratory, and another facility dedicated to the production of integrated circuits. Many of the products later introduced by the division, however, resulted from acquisitions or joint ventures with other companies. For example, in 1984 Kodak launched its first electronic product, a camcorder combining an eight-millimeter video camera and recorder, which was developed jointly with Matsushita Electric Industrial Company of Japan. This represented a major departure for Kodak, which historically had been self-reliant in everything from manufacturing cardboard boxes to maintaining its own fire department. It was not the first time that Eastman Kodak had considered marketing a video product. In the mid-1970s the company had elected not to market a videocassette recorder it had developed internally because it would have been priced much higher than its cameras; Kodak believed that consumers would be resistant to the cost.

Also in 1984 Kodak introduced complete lines of videotape cassettes for all video formats and floppy discs for use in personal computers. It bolstered the latter area in 1985 with the purchase of Verbatim Corporation, a floppy disc manufacturer. After five years of disappointing sales, Verbatim was sold to Mitsubishi Kasei Corporation of Japan.

Kodak underwent another major reorganization at the beginning of 1985 in order to capitalize more quickly on growth opportunities. Seventeen business units and a new Life Sciences Group were formed, the latter division to be involved in developing biomedical technology. Each of the 17 operating units, which had previously existed as a centralized group under the photographic division, were given more autonomy and flexibility to run their businesses as independent profit centers.

The company re-entered the 35-millimeter camera market in 1985 with a product made by Chinon Industries of Japan. Fifteen years earlier, it had withdrawn from the market because it was not convinced of the 35-millimeter camera's mass appeal.

In 1986, ten years after Polaroid filed its patent-infringement suit over Eastman Kodak's instant camera, a federal appeals court upheld a lower court ruling and ordered the company to leave the instant camera business. Eastman Kodak was forced to offer its customers trade-in options for their obsolete cameras. The financial implications of this development and the continuing struggle to boost earnings led the company to institute another work force reduction in 1986, this time by 10%. Although the domestic picture was somewhat grim, the fact that nearly 40% of the company's sales came from overseas helped produce strong bottom-line gains over the previous year. A weakening U.S. dollar blunted the impact of foreign competition and allowed Eastman Kodak to reclaim lost ground in its core businesses while also entering new ones. An employee's suggestion to apply the company's manufacturing capabilities to the production of lithium batteries resulted in the successful introduction of a complete line of alkaline battery products under the Supralife brand.

Kodak also formed the Eastman Pharmaceuticals Division to establish an even stronger presence in health care. Joint-venture agreements and licensing arrangements with existing pharmaceutical companies initially occupied division management's attention. In 1988 Eastman Kodak acquired Sterling Drug, a manufacturer of prescription drugs and such consumer products as Bayer aspirin and Lysol cleaners, to make the company more competitive in the pharmaceutical industry. The acquisition, however, was viewed unfavorably by the company's shareholders because Sterling had a second-rate reputation as a pharmaceutical manufacturer and had no blockbuster drugs in its product line. One year later, this negative perception seemed correct. Intense competition had reduced the sales of Sterling's existing pharmaceuticals while new products under development showed questionable effectiveness during testing.

In 1988 evidence came to light indicating that toxic chemicals from the company's Rochester plant had leached into the area's groundwater, posing a possible health hazard to local residents. In April 1990, the company admitted that it had violated New York's environmental law and was fined $2 million. It also agreed to clean up the site of its Kodak Park manufacturing facility and reduce chemical emissions from the plant by 1992.

Eastman Kodak continues its founder's legacy of providing customers with quality products and services. Chaired by Kay R. Whitmore, who served as president under Colby Chandler until Chandler's retirement in 1990, Eastman Kodak is exploring various ways to integrate electronics with its conventional silver halide imaging technology.

Vulnerable to economic peaks and valleys and fluctuating currency exchange rates, the company's global initiatives will require a stronger presence in European and Asian markets as trade relations between East and West grow closer. Eastman Kodak possesses a solid foundation of innovation, technology, and material science upon which to build.

Principal Subsidiaries: Eastman Kodak Credit Corporation; Eastman Kodak International Finance B.V. (Netherlands); Eastman Kodak International Sales Corporation (U.S. Virgin Islands); Eastman Technology, Inc.; Torrey Pines Realty Company, Inc.; Cyclotomics, Inc.; Datatape Incorporated; Electronic Pre-Press Systems, Inc.; Interactive Systems Corp.; Northfield Pharmaceuticals Limited; Ultra Technologies, Inc.; Verbatim Corporation; Eastman Chemical Products, Inc.; Holston Defense Corporation; Eastman Gelatine Corporation; Mustang Pipeline Company; Pinto Pipeline Company of Texas; Eastman Chemical International Ltd.; Eastman Chemical International, A.G. (Switzerland); Eastmanchem, Inc. (Canada); Eastman Canada, Inc.; Kodak Argentina, Ltd.; Kodak Brasileira C.I.L. (Brazil); Kodak Chilena S.A.F. (Chile); Kodak Colombiana, Ltd.; Kodak Mexicana, Ltd.; Kodak Panama, Ltd.; Kodak Export Limited; Laboratorios Kodak Limitada; Foto Interamericana de Peru, Ltd.; Kodak Caribbean, Limited; Kodak Uruguaya, Ltd. (Uruguay); Kodak Venezuela, S.A.; Kodak (Near East), Inc.; Kodak (Singapore) Pte. Limited; Kodak Phillippines, Ltd.; Kodak Limited (U.K.); Kodak Ireland Limited (U.K.); Kodak Pathe (France); Kodak A.G. (Germany); Eastman Kodak International Capital Company, Inc.; Kodak Ges. m.b.h. (Austria); Kodak Oy (Finland); Kodak Nederland B.V. (Netherlands); Kodak S.p.A. (Italy); Kodak Portuguesa Limited; Kodak S.A. (Spain); Kodak AB (Sweden); Eastman Kodak (Japan) Ltd.; K.K. Kodak Information Systems (Japan); Kodak Japan Ltd.; Kodak Imagica K.K. (Japan); Kodak Far East Purchasing, Inc.; Kodak New Zealand Limited; Kodak (Australasia) Proprietary Limited; Kodak (Kenya) Limited; International Biotechnologies Inc.; Kodak (Egypt) S.A.; Komal S.B. (Malaysia); Kodak (Export Sales) Ltd. (Hong Kong); Kodak Taiwan Limited Inc.; Kodak Korea Ltd.; Sterling Drug Inc.

Further Reading: Chakravarty, Subrata N., and Ruth Simon, "Has the world passed Kodak by?," *Forbes*, November 5, 1984; *Journey Into Imagination: The Kodak Story,* Rochester, New York, Eastman Kodak Company, 1988.

—Sandy Schusteff

Electrolux

ELECTROLUX GROUP

Lilla Essingen
S-105 45 Stockholm
Sweden
(08) 736 6000
Fax: (08) 564478

Public Company
Incorporated: 1910
Employees: 152,900
Sales: SKr84.92 billion (US$13.68 billion)
Stock Exchanges: Stockholm London Geneva Oslo Paris Zürich Basel NASDAQ

To the average consumer, the name Electrolux says two things: vacuum cleaners and refrigerators. Through expansion, diversification and, latterly, a voracious appetite for acquisition, Electrolux Group has become a major multinational. It still supplies its traditional products, claiming top position in the European household-appliance market and is the third-largest producer of household appliances, such as vacuum cleaners and refrigerators, in the United States. These products account for just over half of its 1989 turnover, but Electrolux also supplies a wide range of commercial and industrial products and services. Under the Electrolux umbrella comes a host of other familiar brand names, such as Flymo lawnmowers in Europe and Eureka vacuum cleaners in the United States.

This empire has its origins in the perspicacity and the marketing flair of Axel Wenner-Gren, who spotted the potential of the mobile vacuum cleaner only a few years after its invention by Englishman H. C. Booth in 1901.

In 1910, the young Wenner-Gren bought a part share in the European agent of a U.S. company producing one of the early vacuum cleaners, the clumsy Santo Staubsauger. After a couple of years as a Santo salesman for the German-based agent, Wenner-Gren sold his share of the company and returned to Sweden, where he was to find the building blocks for the future Electrolux: Lux and Elektromekaniska AB.

Sven Carlstedt had formed Elektromekaniska in 1910 to manufacture motors for a vacuum cleaner based on the Santo, which was produced by Swedish engineer Eberhardt Seger. Since its founding in 1901, Lux had manufactured kerosene lamps. Now confronted with a shrinking market owing to the popularity of electric lighting, Lux head C.G. Lindblom proposed to Sven Carlstedt a joint venture for the production and marketing of a new vacuum cleaner.

In 1912 Wenner-Gren became the agent for the Lux vacuum cleaner in Germany, subsequently taking on the United Kingdom and France in addition. Over the next few years, Wenner-Gren's role in the company grew, while the machine gradually became lighter and more ergonomic.

Wenner-Gren foresaw a potential sales bonanza in Europe after the end of World War I. Initially unable to persuade his colleagues to step up production capacity in readiness, he overcame their reluctance by guaranteeing a minimum sales figure through his own sales company, Svenska Elektron.

Lux and Elektromekaniska merged in 1919 as Aktiebolaget Elektrolux. Wenner-Gren was president and major shareholder. In 1921, the Lux V appeared. In many ways it resembled a modern cylindrical vacuum cleaner, but it glided along the floor on ski-like runners instead of wheels. This model was to present serious competition to the upright Hoover machines in the 1920s.

The convenience and attractive styling of its product helped to get the new company off to a promising start, but the salesmanship of its chief probably played an even bigger part. Wenner-Gren was a great believer in the door-to-door sales techniques already espoused by competitors such as Hoover in the United States. Vacuum cleaners were demonstrated to potential customers in their own homes and buyers were allowed to pay for their machines by installments. Wenner-Gren knew how to get the best out of his sales force.

To today's sales managers, sales training, competitions, and slogans like "Every home an Electrolux home" are familiar methods of boosting sales, but when Wenner-Gren introduced them they were revolutionary. He also believed in leading from the front. The story of how he sold a vacuum cleaner to the Vatican is part of the company mythology. Four competitors demonstrated their machines first, each vacuuming their allocated area of carpet. When Wenner-Gren's turn came, instead of vacuuming the fifth area, he went over the first four again. The resultant bagful of dust persuaded the pope to add his palace to the growing number of Electrolux homes.

Advertising, too, was imaginative. Not only did Electrolux make extensive use of the press, but in the late 1920s, citizens of Stockholm, Berlin, and London were liable to encounter bizarre vacuum cleaner–shaped cars in the streets.

Bizarre or not, the sales methods worked and the company grew. Throughout the 1920s, new sales companies sprang up, not only all over Europe but also in the United States in 1924, Australia in 1925, and in South America. Many of these were financed by Wenner-Gren himself rather than by Electrolux in Sweden. Vacuum cleaner-manufacturing plants also started to open overseas, firstly in Berlin in 1926 and a year later in Luton, England, and Courbevoie, France.

By 1928 Electrolux had sales of SKr70 million. It had five manufacturing plants, 350 worldwide offices, and 20 subsidiaries. In spite of all of this it was often short of funds, partly because of the system of payment by installments. To grow further, the company needed to raise capital. It was decided to float the company on the London Stock Exchange and to issue more shares. Prior to flotation in 1928, Electrolux bought out many of the related companies which Wenner-

Gren owned, though he retained his minority shareholding in the American Electrolux Corporation until 1949.

Flotation on the Stockholm stock exchange was postponed until 1930 owing to the stock market crash. When the shares did appear they were greeted with some mistrust, as it was thought that the company was overvalued and that sales would suffer during the anticipated recession. These doubts were to prove unfounded.

The company had already started to diversify. Floor-polishers, a natural progression from vacuum cleaners, came in 1927. However, the main diversification of the 1920s came through the acquisition in 1925 of Arctic, a company manufacturing a novel machine, the absorption refrigerator. This type of refrigerator has no moving parts, though early models required connection to a source of running water. Power can be provided by electricity, gas, or kerosene. The other system of refrigeration is compression, which relies on electric power. Early compressors were noisy and bulky, so Electrolux had several advantages over its competitors, which were producing compression refrigerators.

A new air-cooled version of Electrolux's absorption refrigerators was introduced in 1931, and by 1936 more than one million had been sold. Demand for the machines grew as restrictions were placed on the use of food preservatives by legislation such as the United Kingdom Food Preservative Act of 1927. In the United States, Servel Inc. had acquired a license to manufacture Electrolux's refrigerators.

Electrolux's original vacuum cleaner factory on Lilla Essingen was devastated by fire in 1936. When it was rebuilt the following year, the opportunity was taken to fit it with the latest equipment and install a central research laboratory.

In 1926, Wenner-Gren had become chairman of the board, with Ernst Aurell taking over as president. During the 1930s Wenner-Gren remained chairman but reduced his involvement in the running of the company, prior to resigning from his post in 1939. Harry G. Faulkner, a British accountant who had been instrumental in the company's consolidation prior to the 1928 flotation, was president throughout the 1930s, having succeeded Aurell in 1930.

With intensive marketing and continued investment in research and development, Electrolux rode out the Depression years. By 1939 annual sales stood at SKr80 million.

In 1939 Gustaf Sahlin, former president of the United States Electrolux Corporation, took over from Faulkner. Throughout World War II, despite the non-availability of some plants, Electrolux managed to sustain many of its usual activities, opening operations in Australia, Venezuela, and Colombia. At home in Sweden, it acquired companies in the fields of commercial laundry equipment and outboard motors. Much energy, however, was diverted into the war effort, including the manufacture of munitions and of air cleaners for the Swedish forces.

After the war, Electrolux resumed its normal operations, initially under Elon V. Ekman, who had become president in 1951, and from 1963 to 1967 under his successor Harry Wennberg. The period was not without its setbacks, however. Firstly, many subsidiaries which had been opened in eastern European countries before the war disappeared from view behind the Iron Curtain, and secondly, despite a British government contract to supply 50,000 built-in absorption refrigerators for prefabricated temporary houses, the company began to face problems in the refrigerator market. Compression technology had advanced and was proving more effective for the larger refrigerators which consumers were now demanding. Though it at first concentrated on improving the design of the absorption refrigerator, Electrolux was eventually obliged to adopt compression technology.

Meanwhile diversification continued. During the 1950s Electrolux started making household washing machines and dishwashers, and extended floor-cleaning-equipment production to an increasing number of countries, including Brazil and Norway. When, in 1956, Axel Wenner-Gren sold his remaining shares in Electrolux to the Swedish finance group Wallenberg, annual turnover exceeded SKr500 million. The association with Wallenberg has often stood Electrolux in good stead, for instance in helping to arrange overseas funding and insulating the group from any hostile takeover bids.

In 1962, in an attempt to solve its refrigerator problems, Electrolux bought the Swedish firm of ElektroHelios. Like Electrolux, it dated from 1919 and had a major share of the Scandinavian market in compressor refrigerators and freezers, as well as making stoves. In the following year, a wide range of food-storage equipment was launched by the group, putting it in a strong position to benefit from the demands generated by the flourishing frozen-food industry.

Until the 1960s, Electrolux had continued to operate along the lines conceived by Wenner-Gren in the early years. A new phase began in 1967, when Hans Werthen was recruited from Ericsson, another member of the Wallenberg group of companies. Werthen has remained with Electrolux for over 20 years, first as president, and since 1975 as chairman, with first Gösta Bystedt and then Anders Scharp succeeding him as president. Under this regime, a series of momentous acquisitions was to allow Electrolux to multiply its turnover by a factor of 60 in 20 years.

Werthen found the Electrolux group in the doldrums; it had run into internal and external problems, and its technology was outmoded. Electrolux, an international company, had not been effectively integrated with its acquisition ElektroHelios, which still focused on the Scandinavian market. In many ways the merged companies had continued to behave as if they were still competitors, resulting in a net loss of market share in the refrigerator market. Only the vacuum cleaners were profitable: to use Werthen's own words, "they represented 125% of the profits."

Approaching the problem from outside, Werthen managed to resolve the Electrolux-ElektroHelios conflict and get rid of the organizational overlap. His new head of production, Anders Scharp, set about updating production technology to challenge the much more advanced techniques he had seen in United States appliance factories. Werthen believed that Electrolux's problems could not be overcome simply by operational improvements. It had a more fundamental problem: size.

As Werthen saw it, the group was neither small enough to be a niche player, nor large enough to gain the economies of scale it needed to compete with giants such as Philips and AEG. Growth was the only way forward, and in the overcrowded market place for household goods, this meant acquisition.

The initial focus was on Scandinavia. One smaller competitor after another, many of them struggling for survival, was bought up swiftly. The Norwegian stove manufacturer Elektra and Danish white-goods company Atlas were among the first acquisitions of the late 1960s. Soon Electrolux was shopping for competitors outside Scandinavia. The 1974 acquisition of Eureka, one of the longest-established vacuum cleaner companies in the United States, gave Electrolux a large slice of a valuable market overnight.

At around this time there were glimmerings of hope for the absorption refrigerator. Being quiet-running, they are ideally suited to installation in living spaces, such as caravans and hotel rooms. Electrolux managers soon scented these new opportunities. After taking over competitors Kreft and Siegas in 1972, the group became world leader in this sector.

As well as expanding its share of its existing markets, Electrolux soon started to see acquisition as a way of entering new areas, usually those related to existing products, as with the British lawnmower manufacturer, Flymo, which it bought in 1968. Werthen saw lawnmowing as an activity allied to floor-cleaning. The provision of cleaning services seemed a logical extension to the production of cleaning equipment, and this prompted the purchase of a half share in the Swedish cleaning company ASAB.

Buying up the venerable Swedish firm of Husqvarna in 1978 gave Electrolux not only a new pool of expertise in commercial refrigeration, but also a flourishing chainsaw-manufacturing concern, which complemented its interests in outdoor equipment. Taking over a clutch of other chainsaw manufacturers over the following decade has enabled Electrolux to claim leadership of the worldwide chainsaw market.

There were some more radical departures from existing product lines. In 1973, Electrolux bought Facit, a Swedish office equipment company. Initial doubts about whether Electrolux had the know-how to manage a high-tech company proved unfounded.

The purchase of Swedish metal producer Gränges was greeted with equal scepticism, since again the connection between the new and existing businesses appeared to be rather tenuous. Gränges was seen as a loss-making company, but when Electrolux bought it in 1980, Werthen had already been chairman of its board for three years and had overseen a marked upturn in its fortunes. Gränges became part of Electrolux in 1980, and today Gränges' aluminum products and car seat belts represent a major aspect of Electrolux's business, although other parts of Gränges have been sold off.

Under the presidency of Anders Scharp from 1981, the emphasis was on consolidation and expansion of existing lines. Within this area the takeovers became increasingly ambitious as Electrolux saw within its grasp the title of one of the world leaders in household appliances. Major steps in this direction were the acquisitions of Zanussi in Italy, White Consolidated in the United States, and the white-goods and catering-equipment divisions of the United Kingdom's Thorn EMI, in 1984, 1986, and 1987, respectively.

Electrolux has a reputation for buying only when the price is right and for turning around sick companies, even at the cost of heavy staff cuts and management shakeups. As *The Wall Street Journal* of March 21, 1986, pointed out, discussing the acquisition of White Consolidated, the group balance sheet has looked unhealthy immediately after some of the larger acquisitions, showing an equity-asset ratio as low as 21%.

Electrolux has bounced back confidently, making divestments as well as acquisitions. One of Werthen's earliest acts as president was the sale of AB Electrolux's minority shareholding in the United States Electrolux Corporation to Consolidated Food, which raised SKr300 million. The purchase of the long-established company Eureka a few years later gave the Swedish group a new foothold in the United States vacuum cleaner market, although it found itself in the curious position of competing against its own brand name. Further divestments were made following acquisitions when it was considered that all or part of the new member did not fit in with the group's strategy. Facit, for instance, was sold to Ericsson in 1983, and shortly after the purchase of White Consolidated, its machine-tool division, White Machine Tools, was sold off.

Another method of raising cash is through the sale of assets, although Electrolux acquisitions have not been primarily motivated by a desire to asset-strip. For example, in the case of Husqvarna, the purchase price of SKr120 million was more than covered within six months by the sale of its land and other property.

A third way of recovering the costs of acquisition has been the use of a troubled company's accumulated losses wherever possible to reduce the group's tax liability. This was a major incentive in the acquisition of Gränges.

Not every company is delighted to hear Electrolux knocking on its door. Many a takeover has been resisted by the target company, although Electrolux has also been called in to rescue a troubled company—as happened with Zanussi—or asked to act as a white knight—notably for the United States household appliance company Tappan in 1979.

Experience has helped Electrolux assimilate new companies into the group. Even when its attentions were not originally welcomed, its undeniable success in rapidly reversing the fortunes of sick companies like Husqvarna have won over many doubters.

By dint of sound design, effective marketing, and sheer opportunism, Electrolux has grown in 70 years from a single-product, all-European company into an international group of around 550 companies covering 50 countries. Although it cannot promise to sustain the phenomenal growth of the 1970s and 1980s, Electrolux is optimistic about the future. Already at or near the top of the domestic appliances tree it is now looking to attain the same international status in other product lines, such as lawnmowers, industrial cleaning equipment, and components such as refrigerator compressors. It is also looking for new geographical markets; already doing business in many parts of the Far East, in 1989 Electrolux arranged for Sharp to distribute some of its products in Japan.

Electrolux still invests significantly in improving its traditional products. Vacuum cleaners continue to get lighter and refrigerators quieter and more efficient. A robotic vacuum cleaner for the industrial market is expected by the year 2000. In the interests of the environment, the company plans to eliminate chlorofluorocarbons from Electrolux refrigerators by 1995.

The group's future depends very much on the successful integration of members in different parts of the world. For a consumer-goods manufacturer it is particularly important to remain sensitive to local preferences while exploiting economies of scale to the full. There is, therefore, a delicate balance to be attained between local and central control. The group says it aims to use local managers in its subsidiaries wherever possible.

The Electrolux board has always consisted predominantly of Swedes, though, and according to *The Financial Times* of June 30, 1989, this has led to accusations that the group is not a multinational but "an international company run by Swedes." President Anders Scharp told the *Financial Times* that he, too, felt the company to be too Swedish. His objective, he said, is to internationalize his management team. To this end an internationally oriented executive development program has been introduced.

Principal Subsidiaries: White Consolidated Industries, Inc. (U.S.A.); Gränges Sweden AB; Zanussi (Italy); The Eureka Co. (U.S.A.).

Further Reading: Gordon, Bob, *Early Electrical Appliances,* Princes Risborough, United Kingdom, Shire Publications Ltd., 1984; Sparke, Penny, *Electrical Appliances,* London, Unwin Hyman Ltd., 1987; Lorenz, Christopher, "The Birth of a 'Transnational,' " *The Financial Times,* June 19, 21, 23, 26, 28, and 30, 1989; *Electrolux: Two Epochs that Shaped a Worldwide Group,* Stockholm, Electrolux, 1989.

—Alison Classe

FANUC LTD

FANUC LTD.

Oshino-mura
Yamanashi 401-05
Japan
(0555) 84-5555
Fax: (0555) 84-5512

Public Company
Incorporated: 1972 as Fujitsu Fanuc Ltd.
Employees: 1,882
Sales: ¥178.12 billion (US$1.24 billion)
Stock Exchange: Tokyo

The name of Fanuc is an acronym for Fuji Automatic Numerical Control, and those four words sum up a fair amount of basic information about this company. Headquartered at the base of Japan's Mount Fuji, Fanuc is the world's leading manufacturer of numerical control (NC) equipment for machine tools, devices that put the automation into automated factories. NC devices are the forerunners of industrial robots. Fanuc has been a world leader in robotics since the 1970s.

Fanuc was founded as a wholly owned subsidiary of Fujitsu in 1955, after that electronics giant decided to take the plunge into the factory automation business. Its first employees were a team of 500 engineers, and Fujitsu chose from among them a young executive engineer named Seiuemon Inaba to head the subsidiary. It was a move that would prove beneficial for both the company and the man. Inaba, who received a doctorate in engineering from Tokyo Institute of Technology after joining Fujitsu in 1946, has since remained at the top of Fanuc's chain of command. His name has become virtually synonymous with that of the company.

At first, Fujitsu Fanuc devoted itself solely to research and development. U.S. companies led the way in automation technology at that time; in fact, no Japanese company produced NC machine tools until the mid-1960s. Once the Japanese NC industry entered the field of play, however, Fujitsu Fanuc dominated the game. By 1971, it controlled 80% of the domestic market for NC equipment. In 1972 Fujitsu spun-off its highly successful subsidiary, retaining a substantial minority interest. The remaining shares were put on the open market. In 1975 Seiuemon Inaba became president of the new company.

Fujitsu Fanuc, as it continued to call itself until 1982, began its life as an independent company with the proverbial silver spoon in its mouth. As a major Japanese NC manufacturer, it was well suited to spearhead the Japanese NC industry's entry into the export market. In 1975 it licensed U.S. manufacturer Pratt & Whitney to market its NC drilling machines in North America. In the same year it entered into a licensing agreement with German engineering firm Siemens, which was also a minority shareholder in the company, giving Siemens the exclusive right to market Fujitsu Fanuc products in Europe. In 1985 the European Economic Community would find that the deal violated its rules regarding monopolies and fined the companies $840,000. In 1978 Fujitsu Fanuc took its manufacturing operations abroad, building a plant in South Korea. By 1982, it had captured half of the world NC market.

Its position as an NC manufacturer notwithstanding, it is the company's commitment to the related field of robotics that has brought it the most attention and acclaim. Fujitsu Fanuc started selling robots in 1975, but they accounted for only a tiny percentage of sales at first, Kawasaki and Hitachi being the leading Japanese robotics companies at the time. Inaba sought to change that situation in the 1980s. In January 1981 Fujitsu Fanuc opened a showcase plant in Yamanashi Prefecture, in which robots and NC machine tools made parts for other robots. The factory, which would otherwise require 500 human workers, was run by a staff of 100 people, whose duties consisted of maintaining the robots and assembling the parts into finished products.

This vision of robots manufacturing other robots caught the fancy of the press and, evidently, other robotics companies. A string of joint ventures followed the opening of the new plant. In 1982 it granted Taiwan's Tatung Co. sole import rights for its robots. In 1983 it also joined with the 600 Group, a British machine tool manufacturer, to form 600 Fanuc Robotics, which would sell Fanuc robots in the United Kingdom.

Fanuc's most important move of 1982 was to enter into a joint venture with General Motors (GM), called GMFanuc Robotics, to produce and market robots in the United States. The new company was 50% owned by each partner and was based in Detroit, with GM providing most of the management and Fanuc the products. This was not the first alliance between Japanese and U.S. robotics concerns; Japanese companies on the whole lacked the advanced technology necessary to create sophisticated robots, while the U.S. plants lacked Japanese manufacturing skill. By linking up with its largest single potential customer in the United States, Fanuc all but assured itself of a lucrative share of the U.S. market. In its early years, GMFanuc Robotics made mostly automobile assembly robots and sold them to GM. Although both companies denied it at the time, few industry observers doubted that GM gave preferential treatment to GMFanuc robots when considering bids from suppliers. GMFanuc sales described a steep upward curve, and within six years it became the world's largest supplier of robots.

Inaba's goal of increasing Fanuc's robot sales was not simply a business matter, but a reflection of his personal interest in robots. Known in Japan as the Emperor of Robots, Inaba said in 1981 that it was his dream to develop within four years a robot that would help assemble Fanuc's robot-made robot parts into finished robots. By the middle of the decade, Fanuc had indeed developed assembly robots, which were used to put together parts for motors at its motor factory.

Fanuc's success in robotics has brought Inaba to the attention of the U.S. financial press. There is his passion for the color yellow, for instance, because, as he put it, "In the Orient, yellow is the emperor's color." Fanuc factories, offices, and assembly lines are all painted in such a shade. The workers' jumpsuits are also yellow, head to toe. Inaba is known for his demanding and authoritarian management style—at meetings, his subordinates are not allowed to speak unless spoken to; for his company's commitment to a futuristic industry like robotics; and for the profoundly scenic location of its headquarters.

In the mid-1980s, sales of automation equipment dropped substantially. Manufacturers who pumped large amounts of capital into automation equipment suddenly found themselves with weak cash flows and were unwilling to invest further. GM cut back on its commitment to robotics, GMFanuc sales fell, and Fanuc was further hurt by the relative strength of the yen against the dollar, making its products more expensive in the U.S. Fanuc, nevertheless, managed to maintain a healthy profit margin despite these difficulties, and it kept expanding its activities.

In 1987, it tightened its grip on the U.S. market by entering into a joint venture with another pillar of U.S. industry, General Electric (GE). The two companies formed GE Fanuc Automation to manufacture computerized numerical control (CNC) devices. The deal marked something of a defeat for GE, which had failed in its attempt to become a factory automation powerhouse. GE stopped making its own CNC equipment and turned its Charlottesville, Virginia, plant over to the new company, which geared it up to produce Fanuc CNC devices.

In 1988 Fanuc once again joined forces with General Motors, this time to form GMFanuc Robotics Europa, to market robots in Europe. In 1989 it took advantage of relaxed East-West tensions to increase its presence in the USSR. It joined with Mitsui, a huge Japanese trading company and with Stanko Service, a Soviet machine-tool service organization, to form Stanko Fanuc Service, which would maintain and repair Fanuc products there.

Fanuc's success has always been derived from the circumstances that its products are the most reliable and yet the least expensive on the market, allowing it to brush aside its competition in good times and to maintain its advantage in lean times. In a cutting-edge field like automation, a huge commitment to research and development is required. One-third of Fanuc's nearly 1,800 employees are engaged in such activity, the highest ratio of any Japanese manufacturer. As with every other facet of the company's operations, Fanuc's R & D bears the personal stamp of Seiuemon Inaba. He once gave his Product Development Laboratory a clock that ran ten times faster than normal, as a gentle reminder of the importance of staying ahead of the competition. Inaba has made the German engineering slogan *Weniger Teile*, which means "fewer parts," Fanuc's slogan; machines with fewer parts are cheaper to produce and easier for automatons to assemble.

It may be an unusual captain who paces the bridge at Fanuc, and his methods have worked admirably. A master businessman as well as a master engineer, Seiuemon Inaba has guided his young company along a steep ascent that shows no signs of flattening out. Although factory automation has slumped in the United States, there is no sign of flagging sales in Japan. On July 29, 1989, *The Japan Economic Journal* reported that demand for automation equipment in Japan was so strong that manufacturers like Fanuc were having trouble filling orders on time. Even with its Yamanashi Prefecture plant operating around the clock, the company declared that it would have to increase production capacity to keep its customers happy.

Principal Subsidiaries: Fapt Ltd.; Fanuc Kosan Ltd.; Fanuc Sensor Manufacturing Ltd.; Fanuc Pertronics Ltd.; Fanuc Information Systems Institute; Mold Institute Ltd.; Fanuc Robot Dorf Ltd.; Fanuc USA Corp.; Fanuc Taiwan Limited; Fanuc France S.A.; Fanuc Germany GmbH; Fanuc UK Ltd.; Fanuc Italia S.p.A. (Italy); Fanuc Sweden A.B.; Fanuc Singapore Pte. Ltd.; Fanuc Oceania Pty. Ltd. (Australia); Fanuc Hong Kong Ltd.

Further Reading: "Fanuc edges closer to a robot-run plant," *Business Week*, November 24, 1980; Wiegner, Kathleen K., "The dawn of battle," *Forbes*, October 26, 1981; Bylinsky, Gene, "Japan's Robot King Wins Again," *Fortune*, May 25, 1987; "Fanuc Throws One-third of its Entire Labor Force into the Most Powerful R&D Setup of the Industry," *Business Japan*, April 1989.

—Douglas Sun

FLEETWOOD

FLEETWOOD ENTERPRISES, INC.

3125 Myers Street
Riverside, California 92523
U.S.A.
(714) 351-3500
Fax: (714) 351-3931

Public Company
Incorporated: 1950 as Coach Specialties Company
Employees: 12,000
Sales: $1.55 billion
Stock Exchanges: New York Pacific

Fleetwood Enterprises is the world's largest manufacturer of travel trailers, motor homes, folding trailers, and manufactured housing. The company's travel trailers are currently marketed under the names Avion, Prowler, Terry, and Wilderness. Fleetwood's line of motor homes are sold under the names Jamboree, Bounder, Flair, Pace Arrow, Southwind, Tioga, and Limited. The company's folding trailer division, acquired in December 1989, manufactures products under the Coleman name. Manufactured housing is sold under the corporate name, Fleetwood. All four product lines are marketed through a network of more than 3,600 dealers in the United States and Canada. Fleetwood offers financing to its recreational vehicle dealers and to their customers through Fleetwood Credit Corporation. The company supplies its dealers from 45 production facilities located in 16 states in the United States and Canada.

Fleetwood was founded by the company's current chairman and CEO John C. Crean in a greenhouse in southern California in 1950. Under the name Coach Specialties Company, he and his wife manufactured and sold a new and improved line of window blinds for travel trailers. At the same time, Crean built a travel trailer for his own use. One of his window-blind customers, a trailer dealer, was so impressed by the trailer's construction that a deal was struck for Crean to assemble trailer units with materials supplied to him by the dealer. Production was to be in quantities large enough to make sure the dealer could keep pace with his seasonal orders. As the summer travel-trailer season came to a close, Crean continued his new enterprise but opted to build mobile homes instead of trailers. Mobile homes, currently referred to as manufactured housing, provided a more stable market for growth because of increasing demand for inexpensive housing in southern California. The name Fleetwood was chosen from a line of automobiles. By 1954 the company had outgrown its greenhouse to become a thriving enterprise with three production plants.

The growth of the manufactured home market was caused by the product's moderate price. The cost of a quality manufactured home runs about one-third that of on-site constructed home, in each case excluding land. Off-site production eliminates the use of many different contractors, construction is not affected by weather, and less time is required for construction because every component arrives at the assembly point ready to use. Manufactured homes are trucked in sections to the homesite, where they are assembled in a matter of days, instead of the normal on-site construction times that can stretch into weeks and months.

In 1957 the company changed its name from Coach Specialties Company and reincorporated as Fleetwood Enterprises. During the 1950s the manufactured housing industry had split into two distinct markets. Fleetwood had its feet firmly planted in the mobile home market, and because of its healthy growth had accumulated a large cash surplus. The other market, the recreational vehicle (RV) market, John Crean saw offered good opportunities. In 1964 Fleetwood acquired Terry Coach Industries, Inc., and Terry Coach Manufacturing, Inc. This was a time when an ever-increasing number of U.S. outdoor enthusiasts wanted to travel. The company's line of travel trailers included sleeping, eating, and bathroom facilities. As the size and weight of these units grew, Fleetwood designed and built a line of fifth-wheel travel trailers, a model that is exclusively built to be towed by larger pick-up trucks. As sales grew and the market expanded, the company continued to open new production plants to meet increasing sales. In 1965 Fleetwood became a public company. By 1990 the company operated 12 travel trailer plants in the United States and Canada.

As the RV market boomed, Fleetwood continued to diversify with the acquisition of Pace-Arrow, Inc., a motor home manufacturer. The acquisition was a logical extension of the company's travel trailer business. Motor homes are similar to travel trailers in construction and use. The interior looks the same as a travel trailer except that the motor home provides an area for the driver. The entire unit is constructed on a purchased truck chassis. The product line offers two types, both of which are self-contained. Type A motor homes are full-size units, having sleeping room for four to eight people and are typically equipped with air conditioning, on-board power generators, and stereo systems. In 1990 Type A units typically sold for $50,000 to $80,000. Type C units are smaller, built on cut-away van chassis, and usually accommodate fewer people. In 1990 Type C units sold for $25,000 to $50,000. At a time when inexpensive gasoline and the U.S. public's wanderlust fueled the RV market, Fleetwood was marketing a diverse product line, the prices of which accommodated a wide range of buyers' budgets. The company rounded out its product line with the acquisition, for cash, of Avion Coach Corporation in 1976. Avion augmented the company's line of trailers with its expensive, luxury class models. In 1977, the company incorporated in the state of Delaware keeping the same name.

The 1970s was a period of rapid growth and expansion for Fleetwood. As the decade ended, the revolution in Iran, skyrocketing gasoline costs, and the buying public's fear of a recession, along with rising interest rates created an across-the-board slump in sales. Two-thirds of the Fleetwood's product line were vehicles that were intended for use on U.S. highways. Gasoline shortages, which in some states resulted in day-to-day rationing along with the spiraling costs of fuel shook the RV market to its foundations. Many manufacturers were forced out of business as RV retailers began closing their doors and defaulting on their bank financed inventories. The ensuing recession brought with it escalating interest rates, making mortgages for all types of housing and for financing RVs prohibitive. The company, for the first time since the early 1950s, found itself in a situation calling for drastic cutbacks in production and staffing.

The year 1980 was difficult for Fleetwood. It was forced to close nine of its production plants. The cutbacks closed three travel trailer plants, three motor home facilities, and three manufactured housing plants. Fleetwood had to consider massive worker layoffs.

Fleetwood was forced to take a hard look at its entire structure during these hard times. It developed a tightly focused management policy, employing regionalized management within its housing group, which permitted the company to react more quickly to market trends. Housing design and development has been spread to five areas: west coast, central, southeast, mid-Atlantic, and Florida. Each plant facility began operation as a separate profit center with day-to-day decisions made locally. Fleetwood slowly rode out the recession, and in 1982 Fleetwood's motor home division was projecting sales of 40,000 units in 1983.

The rapid growth and expansion Fleetwood had experienced in the 1980s had not been without legal and regulatory problems. The company is subject to provisions of the Housing and Community Development Act of 1974. These provisions, which are regulated by the U.S. Department of Housing and Urban Development (HUD), resulted in an action by the department against Fleetwood in 1985 claiming potential safety defects in 4,000 mobile homes made by the company during the years 1981 through 1984. Fleetwood was ordered to notify the owners of the mobile homes in question about possible defects in the units' walls, floors, and beams. The problems did prompt HUD to initiate an investigation into engineering techniques used by other mobile home manufacturers.

The four-year-old dispute came to a head in February 1988, resulting in a U.S. Justice Department complaint filed against Fleetwood in Wilmington, Delaware, seeking civil penalties in excess of $20 million. The complaint alleged the existence of certain standards violations in manufactured homes produced by several of Fleetwood's subsidiaries. On February 9, 1989, Fleetwood entered into a settlement agreement with HUD and the Justice Department. The settlement resulted in the dismissal of government charges against Fleetwood in exchange for a settlement payment.

Fleetwood, along with other companies in the manufactured housing industry were the target of a class-action suit filed in Delaware in 1985. The complaint alleged that veterans who had purchased mobile homes had paid excessive prices and finance charges as a result of illegal rebates that were falsely certified to the Veterans Administration by the manufacturers. In 1990, the court certified a class of plaintiffs consisting of certain veterans who purchased mobile homes from Fleetwood dating back as far as April of 1981. Two of the company's subsidiaries pleaded guilty to six counts of filing false certifications in 1987, resulting in approximately $650,000 in fines and civil settlements. In 1990, the company was still vigorously defending itself from further legal actions.

Fleetwood Credit Corporation (FCC) was established in 1986. The finance company's objective was to become the major source of both wholesale and retail financing of Fleetwood's RV products on a nationwide basis. Using $25 million of its own funds, the company hired Robert B. Baker, former head of Nissan Motor Acceptance Corporation to head the project. FCC began operations by servicing just twelve Orange County, California, dealers. In the early 1990s the company had lending operations in southern and northern California, Oregon, Indiana, Massachusetts, Georgia, New Jersey, and Texas. Fleetwood Credit showed a net income of $2.9 million in 1990, a 56% increase over the previous year.

In 1989 Fleetwood acquired the Coleman Company's folding trailer business. The Coleman product line ranged in retail price from $2,000 to $10,000, and in 1989 it accounted for more than 30% of the folding trailer market. With the acquisition of this line, Fleetwood had products for most consumers' budgets. The company has also introduced new lower-priced trailer models in response to changing market conditions. Its eye on the future, the company in 1990 purchased a 75-acre parcel in southern California to develop as a site-built housing tract.

Principal Subsidiaries: Fleetwood Homes of California, Inc.; Fleetwood Homes of Florida, Inc.; Fleetwood Homes of Georgia, Inc.; Fleetwood Homes of Idaho, Inc.; Fleetwood Homes of Indiana, Inc.; Fleetwood Homes of Mississippi, Inc.; Fleetwood Homes of North Carolina, Inc.; Fleetwood Homes of Oregon, Inc.; Fleetwood Homes of Pennsylvania, Inc.; Fleetwood Homes of Tennessee, Inc.; Fleetwood Homes of Texas, Inc.; Fleetwood Homes of Virginia, Inc.; Fleetwood Homes of Washington, Inc.; Westfield Manufactured Homes, Inc.; Fleetwood Travel Trailers of California, Inc.; Fleetwood Travel Trailers of Indiana, Inc.; Fleetwood Travel Trailers of Maryland, Inc.; Fleetwood Travel Trailers of Nebraska, Inc.; Fleetwood Travel Trailers of Ohio, Inc.; Fleetwood Travel Trailers of Oregon, Inc.; Fleetwood Travel Trailers of Texas, Inc.; Fleetwood Travel Trailers of Virginia, Inc.; Fleetwood Motor Homes of California, Inc.; Fleetwood Motor Homes of Indiana, Inc.; Fleetwood Motor Homes of Pennsylvania, Inc.; Fleetwood Folding Trailers, Inc.; Buckingham Development Company; C.V. Aluminum, Inc.; Continental Lumber Products, Inc.; FEI Corp.; Fleetwood Credit Corp.; Fleetwood Foreign Sales Corp. (U.S. Virgin Islands); Fleetwood Holidays, Inc.; Fleetwood Insurance Services, Inc.; Fleetwood International, Inc.; Gibralter Insurance Company, Ltd. (Bermuda); Gold Shield Fiberglass, Inc.; Gold Shield Fiberglass of Indiana, Inc.; GSF Installation Company; Hauser Lake Lumber Operation, Inc.; Housing Supply, Inc.

Further Reading: ''A Glimpse of Fleetwood Enterprises, Inc.'' Fleetwood Enterprises corporate typescript, 1987.

—William R. Grossman

FUJI PHOTO FILM CO., LTD.

26-30, Nishiazabu 2-chome
Minato-ku, Tokyo 106
Japan
(03) 3406-2444
Fax: (03) 3406-2173

Public Company
Incorporated: 1934
Employees: 19,677
Sales: ¥928.54 billion (US$6.46 billion)
Stock Exchanges: Tokyo Osaka Nagoya Fukuoka Niigata Sapporo

Fuji Photo Film originated as a cinematic-film producer and grew by serving the consumer film market through the 1970s. Fuji's traditional products are motion picture and consumer films and magnetic tapes. Research into electronics has allowed the company to branch into other forms of imaging, including relatively new areas combining multi-layer emulsion coating, photochemistry, and photo-engineering. Although electronic systems are somewhat new to Fuji, it is building on its experience in office and medical technology and graphic communications.

In 1934 Dainippon Celluloid, Japan's first cinematic film manufacturer, spun off its troubled photographic division. Named Fuji Photo Film Company, the new company already employed 340 people and named Shuichi Asano as its first president. Its product line included motion picture film, dry plates, and photographic paper. The company struggled for three years, mainly due to the poor quality and high prices of its products relative to imports.

Fuji's first task was to build a reputation in the domestic market. Brand reliability proved critical in the photosensitive-materials industry, since buyers were not willing to risk losing a desired image to inadequate materials, regardless of cost. During its first three years, the company continued to lose sales, increase debt, and struggle to meet research expenses. Fuji could not expand without first addressing quality, so it employed a German specialist to assist in the area of emulsion technology.

The combination of outside consultation and its own research allowed the company to introduce its first film as an independent in 1936, as well as a motion picture negative film. The negative film was much harder to produce, and demonstrated Fuji's new technical competence to Japanese studios.

Fuji built a second factory in Odawara in 1938. Color research began in a new laboratory in 1939, but World War II halted such work. During the war the government set aside all sensitized materials for the military, so consumer-film development had to wait out the war. In 1945 Allied bombing raids partially damaged two Fuji factories, but recovery during the postwar era involved more than infrastructural repair.

The Allied powers allowed civilian trade to resume in 1947, and Fuji immediately began exporting to outlets in South America and Asia. Japanese producers still enjoyed a good reputation in optical products, enabling Fuji to export its cameras and binoculars. In the area of film and other sensitized materials, however, Japanese technology still lagged behind U.S. and European producers.

Although it produced x-ray and cinematic film, Fuji did not produce large amounts of film for the amateur consumer market until the 1950s. In the meantime, it resumed color research and produced its first color film in 1948. In 1949 Indian buyers received a shipment of Fuji motion picture film, the company's first substantial postwar sale.

As the 1940s ended, so did a shortage of raw materials—including silver, paper, and petroleum-based chemicals—that kept Fuji from producing amateur photographic products in large quantities. Licensing agreements between Fuji and Eastman Kodak of the United States allowed Fuji to equal Western producers in terms of black-and-white amateur roll film quality. Fuji, now able to supply its products in large quantities, introduced its first amateur roll film in 1952. By 1958 Fuji had introduced three additional black-and-white roll films.

Fuji enjoyed burgeoning domestic demand for the next 20 years, due in part to tariffs on film imports. During the 1950s Fuji captured the Japanese market for consumer films—a market which would quickly comprise 15% of the world's total film sales.

After setting up an export sales division in 1956, Fuji reached 27 export agreements by 1958 in Asia, North America, and Central America. Fuji first entered North America in 1955, and established its U.S. subsidiary ten years later.

As Fuji's international base grew, it still had to fight a perception of poor quality. In order to make a serious drive abroad, the company first had to develop film and paper compatible with the processing systems most commonly used worldwide. In 1966 Fuji introduced its first amateur slide film compatible with overseas processors. By 1969 all its films, photo paper, and chemicals were fully compatible. Employing the sales network it had established in the 1950s, exports began to flow.

In 1970 Fuji had nine overseas offices, and by the end of the decade it had 14 offices and subsidiaries abroad. These subsidiaries then branched out. Fuji's U.S. subsidiary, for instance, opened six offices between 1971 and 1982.

Recognition in these markets proved more difficult. Eastman Kodak's dominance in consumer films forced all producers to make compatible products in the postwar decades. Fuji learned this after it introduced a cartridge-film eight-millimeter home movie system in 1967. Fuji's product had the support of 14 Japanese and European manufacturers, including AGFA-Gevaert, Europe's largest photographic manufacturer. Kodak introduced its own system shortly after, which quickly gained control of the world market. Fuji had to abandon its system and rushed to develop compatible films. Fuji's overseas growth was slow during the 1970s, adhering to the industry's pace of product development.

In 1970 Kodak held more than 90% of the $400 million U.S. market, but Fuji's color films were already faster than Kodak's—meaning they required less light for adequate exposure. In addition, Fuji films were better on warmer tones, including red, orange, and flesh tones. While Kodak pursued the convenience-based mass market, Fuji targeted professionals and serious amateurs. Although it would take several years before Fuji posed a serious threat to Kodak, its quality created a position of strength.

Relative to its competition, Fuji strengthened itself during the 1970s, partially due to the appreciation of the yen between 1971 and 1980. One factor in the growth of Fuji's non-Western markets was its development of manufacturing facilities. Operations in Brazil, Korea, and Indonesia began with Fuji assistance. The operations began with package assembly, but eventually produced pre-sensitized materials, color processing chemicals, and optical products for export. Such manufacturing bases made the company less vulnerable to currency fluctuation and reduced overhead.

Where Fuji saved on manufacturing it spent heavily on research. Fuji began magnetic research in 1954, introduced products by 1960, and in 1963 produced video tape for domestic television. Magnetic products became the key to Fuji's long-term growth. In 1977 this research led to the introduction of Japan's first eight-inch floppy computer discs.

Fuji also developed products related to the photographic process for other industries. In 1967 for instance, Fuji, Mitsubishi Heavy Industries, and Konan Camera Institute developed a system to photographically trace blueprints onto construction materials. In addition to such new applications for heavy industry, Fuji continued to develop new technology for x-rays and other electronic systems for medical technology.

Fuji's core business continued to be film, however, and it pushed for additional access to lucrative Western markets just as Japanese film sale growth began to slow. Fuji had first entered the U.S. market as a private-label film supplier in 1960, and produced its first color film there in 1970. In 1972, it marketed the first film under its own brand name. Fuji went directly to retailers with its new film and received a 2% share of the American market, which more than doubled during the 1970s. Fuji's marketing well timed, and in 1976 Fuji also caught the attention of professionals and serious amateurs when it beat Kodak with an introduction of faster film, something it accomplished in 1984 as well.

Fuji spent heavily to build its U.S. share but had relatively little success. Kodak's research expenditures were still large by comparison, and when Kodak introduced Kodacolor II film in 1972, Japanese companies had to hurry to put comparable films on the market. The recession during the late 1970s complicated Fuji's international drive. Industrywide production overcapacity and price increases for silver and oil-based chemicals cut into earnings.

While silver was still necessary for photographic imaging, its price jump demonstrated the wisdom of Fuji's research into electronic imaging technologies and its mid-1970s hiring campaign for electronics engineers. While many companies posted declines, Fuji's profits were only stagnant for 1977 and 1978.

Fuji was then the third-largest film maker behind Kodak and AGFA-Gevaert, but the Japanese companies responded to the setbacks more aggressively. Fuji and its domestic competitor, Konishiroku, raised their film prices only 7%—while competitors raised their prices from 10% to 30%—despite silver prices skyrocketing from $6 to $49 an ounce in 1979.

Silver inflation alone had cost Fuji ¥15 billion in 1979, and exchange losses on export sales cost an additional ¥4.6 billion. By 1979 consumer demand for magnetic products like audio and video tape began to climb dramatically, providing Fuji a faster recovery than its competition. Despite continued increases in raw material costs, Fuji's earnings improved quickly due to escalating demand served by the new magnetic-products division.

In 1980 earnings jumped 130%. Silver prices dropped, and sales for magnetic products still grew. Magnetic products, now 9% of sales, pushed exports up to 32%, where they remained for the entire decade. Fuji was well poised for a renewed assault on Western film markets.

In the 1980s the U.S. amateur film market changed rapidly. Consumers preferred higher-quality 35-millimeter over Kodak's disc, cartridge, or instant photography. Although the market changed to the advantage of manufacturers like Fuji, who specialized in 35-millimeter films, consumers still demanded convenience. Autofocus cameras and faster film required more sophistication from manufacturers.

Despite this favorable shift in consumer preferences, the photo industry as a whole had matured. Further, while Fuji hoped to gain ground in the U.S. market, that market was only twice as big as the Japanese market in terms of photo sales. Fuji entered the 1980s resolved not only to increase its portion of film sales worldwide, but also to find growth for its products in imaging and electronics.

Minoru Ohnishi replaced Kusuo Hirata and became Fuji's youngest president ever in 1979. Ohnishi had worked for five years in the late 1980s as head of the U.S. subsidiary. His nontraditional appointment overlooked older officers, but he was able to use his experience in the U.S. market to establish a sales network for new products like magnetic tape, optics, and hybrid electronic systems.

Fuji's growth through the early 1980s had come at the expense of smaller manufacturers like 3M and AGFA-Gevaert. Now the second-largest film manufacturer, it set its sights on Kodak's core. By 1982 Fuji's share of the U.S. market had slowly climbed to 5%, and Ohnishi set a 10% goal.

There were several factors behind Fuji's confidence. First, Kodak's product development in the 1970s was weak. Fuji had kept up with increasingly sophisticated demand by introducing faster and higher resolution films for both cinematic and amateur uses several times. Second, Fuji's research investments had been well placed. Kodak turned from chemical research to electronics late, while Fuji had already recognized the technology's long-term value in processing and imaging. Although Kodak's research expenditures dwarfed Fuji's, Fuji spent a larger share of its earnings on research. In 1979, Kodak applied for 255 patents in the U.S. and Japan, compared to Fuji's 270.

Fuji was the first non-U.S. company to produce videotape. The consumer and trade press praised Fuji tape quality from its introduction. By 1982 magnetic products were already 12% of revenues. With broad distribution, a good reputation, and a skyrocketing market, Fuji made large gains.

Magnetic products, like film, provide high margins. Unlike its position in the consumer film market, Fuji enjoys a prominent role in the magnetic-products marketplace. Between 1978 and 1982 magnetic-division sales increased almost fivefold to $97 million. By 1983 films were only half of Fuji's business.

Newer areas like biotechnology and office automation had been paid for not with debt but with cash generated from film products and stock sales. Such electronic systems, like microfilm records for offices and electronic imaging for x-rays, began to contribute to earnings on their own. In addition, Fuji enjoyed high profit margins in all areas. Pretax operating margins increased one-third to 24.4% from 1976 to 1981. Fuji's film, tape, and computer-disc manufacturing was highly automated, allowing workers to circulate among factories for increased productivity.

The climate for high-technology industries proved intense in the 1980s, due in part to trade friction and yen appreciation. In addition, Fuji was relatively new to electronic systems, and other companies had a large lead in areas like medical technology. In order to remain competitive in these new areas, Fuji had to keep cash available and increase momentum in film sales. Fuji steadily increased its U.S. advertising budget, peaking when it outbid Kodak as sponsor to the 1984 Olympics in Los Angeles. Eventually spending $7 million on the campaign, Fuji entered the event with a 6% share of the U.S. market.

Simultaneously, the company strengthened distribution. In 1979 Fuji sold film in 30% of all film outlets in the United States; by 1984 it sold in 60%, expanding beyond specialty photo outlets. By the end of the Olympic year its share jumped to 8%, allowing Ohnishi to predict not only a 15% share in ten years, but also to carry out a more aggressive approach late in the decade. As Fuji stepped up its efforts to reach the professional market in 1986, its market share approached 10%.

Fuji did not face the same battle abroad that it faced in the United States. It already sold over half of the film and photo paper in Southeast Asia, and the 1984 opening of a Chinese office gave it a lucrative foothold in an untapped and huge market. Brand loyalty was not as significant outside the United States, and in 1982 Fuji enjoyed a 10% share in Europe, Fuji's second-largest market. One year later it captured 15% of that market, prompting the company to construct its first European plant, in the Netherlands, in 1984. Producing selected sensitized materials, the plant paved the way for continued growth on the continent and lessened difficulty with currency fluctuation.

By the mid-1980s the U.S. market had begun to open to Fuji. Despite growth, profits there were still elusive. Videotape prices dropped sharply due to overproduction, and advertising costs continued to climb. While a U.S. market that declined overall was bad for Kodak, it helped Fuji, which was not as reliant on photography. Fuji could still pursue market share while continuing to find growth industries for other forms of imaging.

Fuji's renewed drive in the late 1980s came with more confidence. After a surprisingly successful introduction in Japan, Fuji was first on the U.S. market with a disposable camera. In Japan, a market less receptive to instant-photography items, Fuji sold 1.5 million cameras in six months. While the traditional market declined, Fuji managed to discover a completely new segment of consumer photography.

By 1988 Fuji had achieved its 10% share and the exchange rate was favorable for building in the United States. It built a plant in South Carolina to make presensitized plates. Fuji can expand these facilities, as it has other overseas plants, to serve the consumer market. Such a move would provide faster delivery, immunity from currency exchange losses, and eliminate charges of dumping. Fuji also announced plans to open a U.S. video tape factory in 1991.

With a double-digit market share firmly in place, Fuji sought to increase use of its processing systems, since Kodak's Colorwatch processing network still provided an obstacle, steadily increasing its share of the photofinishing market. Increases in vendor use of a company's processors create demand for its paper and chemicals. Fuji launched its own system, Fujicolor Circle, offering technical support and promotional discounts. For the first time in 15 years of U.S. activity, Fuji put its logo on the back of its paper, no longer fearing consumer preference for Kodak. Fuji's distribution was now strong enough, and it had been successful with its mini photoprocessing labs. Quicker to respond than retailing, processing systems allowed Fuji to capture 16% of the U.S. market for photo paper.

Fuji entered the 1990s with strength and conservative confidence, favoring profitability over mass sales. Despite problems created by the strength of the yen, Fuji has kept earnings stable during its overseas expansion. With a double-digit market share in the United States and Europe, the subsidiaries need to maintain efficient distribution to make further gains. In addition, market share can grow for its electronic systems given the company's record of successful product introductions, broader demand for imaging systems, and its ability to stay competitive in new areas.

Having achieved prominence in consumer film sales—still 49% of its total sales including cameras—Fuji has as much to lose from smaller companies as it does from the market leader. Domestic tariffs were eliminated in 1990, so Fuji's traditional core business of domestic films may erode. Since film manufacturers make large margins on film, price wars that lower earnings are not likely. When competition in electronic systems intensifies, Fuji may need that traditional cash flow.

Fuji's is the world's second-largest film supplier and positioned for further growth in all markets of consumer film sales. Its award-winning cinematic film continues to earn a large share of the purchases made by professional studios. Less reliant on its traditional film business, the company looks for gains in electronic systems involving imaging for medical, office record-keeping, and industrial uses. It faces experienced competition in these new areas and a recession in the early 1990s in industries like printing, but its high-margin cash flow generated from its core business should allow it to overcome difficulties in these costly new areas.

Principal Subsidiaries: Fuji Photo Optical Co., Ltd.; Fujicolor Service Co., Ltd.; Fuji Photo Equipment Co., Ltd.; Fuji Color Trading Co., Ltd.; Fuji Medical Systems Co., Ltd.; Fuji Special Paper Co., Ltd.; Fuji Magnetape Co., Ltd.; Fuji Micrographics Co., Ltd.; Fuji-Hunt Electronics Technology Co., Ltd.; Fuji Magne-Disk Co., Ltd; Fuji Film Battery Co., Ltd.; Fuji Sangyo Co., Ltd.; Fuji Technics Co., Ltd.; Fuji Service Co., Ltd.; Fuji Photo Service Co., Ltd.; Fuji Photo Film U.S.A., Inc.; Fuji Photo Film Hawaii, Inc. (U.S.A.); Fuji Medical Systems U.S.A., Inc.; Fuji Photo Film, Inc. (U.S.A.); Fuji Hunt Photographic Chemicals, Inc. (U.S.A.); Fuji Photo Film Canada, Inc.; Fuji Hunt Photographic Chemicals, Ltd. (Canada); Fuji Photo Film do Brasil Ltda. (Brazil); Fuji Photo Film (Europe) GmbH (Germany); Fuji Magnetics GmbH (Germany); Fuji Photo Film (U.K.) Ltd.; Fuji Photo Film Finance (U.K.) Ltd.; Fuji Photo Film B.V. (Netherlands); Fuji Hunt Photographic Chemicals, N.V. (Belgium); Fuji Hunt Photographic Chemicals (Deutschland) GmbH (Germany); Fuji Hunt Photographic Chemicals (U.K.) Ltd.; Fuji Hunt Photographic Chemicals (France) S.A.; Fuji Hunt Photographic Chemicals (Italia) Srl (Italy); Fuji Hunt Photographic Chemicals (Sverige) A.B. (Sweden); Fuji Film Espana, S.A. (Spain); Fuji Photo Film (Singapore) Pte Ltd.; Fuji Hunt Photographic Chemicals Pte Ltd. (Singapore); Fuji Photo Film (Thailand) Ltd.

Further Reading: ''50 Years of Fuji Photo Film,'' Tokyo, Fuji Photo Film Company, [1984].

—Ray Walsh

THE FURUKAWA ELECTRIC CO., LTD.

6-1, Marunouchi 2-chome
Chiyoda-ku, Tokyo 100
Japan
(03) 3286-3064
Fax: (03) 3286-3747

Public Company
Incorporated: 1920
Employees: 7,600
Sales: ¥713.90 billion (US$4.97 billion)
Stock Exchanges: Tokyo New York

Furukawa Electric Co., Ltd. is the core company of the Furukawa Group, an assemblage of firms concerned with the manufacture and sale of electric wires and cables, nonferrous metals, and related products. Together with Sumitomo Electric Industries, Furukawa leads Asia in the sale of electric cable products. With four major research centers, Furukawa has traditionally been at the head of new developments in its field. Furukawa is expanding into such promising fields as superconductive materials, semiconductors, and shape memory alloys. Furukawa is also internationalizing rapidly, and sells its products in ten major foreign markets.

The origins of Furukawa Electric date back to 1877, when the Furukawa *zaibatsu*, or industrial combine, was formed by Ichebei Furukawa, a leading industrialist in late-19th-century Japan. With the backing of financier Shibusawa Eiichi, Furukawa gained ownership of some copper and silver mines, forming the basis for his *zaibatsu*. In 1884 he succeeded in smelting copper, and opened the Honjo Copper Smeltery, the forerunner of the modern Furukawa.

By 1896, when Yokohama Electric Cable Manufacturing Company was incorporated, the company was producing over one-third of Japan's copper, with over 20 major mines in its possession. Ichebei was among Japan's most prominent business figures, his success due largely to his insistence on using the best mining and transport technology possible.

In 1907, four years after Ichebei's death, Furukawa was involved in an incident that heightened its environmental awareness. Discharge from the company's Ashio mine polluted the surrounding area so badly that several hundred people were poisoned. As a result of the ensuing scandal and costs, the company committed itself to keeping its operations and products as environmentally safe as possible.

The years 1908 to 1920 laid the groundwork for the modern Furukawa Electric. In 1908 Furukawa Kogyo, the dominant force in the Furukawa Group, bought the Yokahama Electric Cable Manufacturing Company. Shortly thereafter this firm was the first in Japan to manufacture lead-sheathed and insulated cables. Furukawa Kogyo then consolidated the Yokahama Electric Cable Manufacturing Company with the Honjo Copper Smeltery, and in 1920 added the Nikko Copper Electrolyzing Refinery to expand the company's potential. The resulting Furukawa Electric Company was capitalized at ¥20 million. Kumakichi Nakajima was the firm's first president.

Furukawa Electric distinguished itself as a technical innovator from the start. In 1922 the company linked the cities of Shanghai and Chee-fu with underwater telephone cables. At the time this was considered an extraordinarily challenging project.

The worldwide Great Depression of the 1930s slowed Furukawa's expansion, but the firm was able to realize a few more technical accomplishments. In 1937 Furukawa again advanced communications systems by laying telephone cable in the Korean Strait, enabling disparate parts of that country to contact one another. Wire and cable were vital to the war effort, and the late 1930s and war years saw a boom in the need for Furukawa products. Uses for wire and cable ranged from weaponry to telecommunications, and government contracts rejuvenated Furukawa.

After the war, the occupation authorities dissolved Furukawa and other *zaibatsu*. Although Furukawa Group companies maintained and strengthened less formal ties, the links between the various Furukawa enterprises are not as strong as many members of the Furukawa *keiretsu* (business group), would like.

In 1952 Furukawa Electric was awarded the Deming Prize for maintaining high standards of quality control. Furukawa continued to grow throughout the 1950s, and formed Furukawa Aluminum Company in 1959. Established with the participation of the Aluminum Company of America, Furukawa Aluminum established a tradition of expansion and innovation in the aluminum-manufacturing field.

In 1966 Furukawa exported two complete factories to Romania for the price of over ¥1.3 billion, in the first of a series of international projects. The deal to manufacture complete power-cable and wire-drawing plants was the largest order the company had then filled.

In 1970 Furukawa launched a three-year campaign to expand industrial capacity by about 20% over previous levels. Spending over ¥30 billion to open new plants, Furukawa reasoned that the increased demand created by government contracts would make greater production levels profitable. To manage the expected boom, Furukawa set up new subsidiaries to manufacture electric insulation materials, copper foils for printed circuits, and rolled wire.

During the early 1970s, however the expected sales increases failed to materialize, due to the worldwide recession and the belief among copper buyers that prices were artificially high and would soon fall, which made investors delay purchase orders. In 1972 the firm had trouble paying its dividend and yielded only a meager profit.

In 1973, however, Furukawa began to recover from this setback, making over ¥1 billion in profits for the year. The firm again began to diversify its product line, and even expanded operations into Poland. Furukawa, along with several other large Japanese firms, developed a large copper mine in Poland. The mine was financed by the Japanese consortium, and the Poles repaid the investors in ore. Furukawa also began to diversify its products again during this year. In anticipation of increased auto sales after the end of the recession, Furukawa started to manufacture pollution-control devices.

In 1974 Furukawa bounced back from the recession, this time due to an increase in copper prices and the company's excess production capacity, the result of its 1970 expansion. Also in 1974, Furukawa introduced the first optical-fiber cables, used for telecommunications, to the world. These cables transmit large amounts of information at great speed, and Furukawa was able to find many additional commercial uses for the cables.

Government actions that curbed consumer spending brought lower sales for the second half of 1975, but Furukawa still managed to spend ¥10 billion retooling equipment. Furukawa also continued to expand internationally, buying a copper smelter in Mexico and developing a copper mine in Peru.

Also in this year, Furukawa was involved with a group of other Japanese companies in the development of a fiber-optic cable that can transmit millions of bits of information a second more reliably than could the previous microwave systems. Furukawa specialized in work involving picture transmission and computer-to-computer information exchange.

In 1978 Furukawa developed an experimental solar heating system that used an improved electrical conductor to transmit energy more efficiently for domestic needs. Another environmentally sensitive development was a special battery that helped make the electric car more viable. The battery features a combination of nickel and zinc, making it more powerful and able to hold a charge longer than conventional batteries.

The firm continued to expand and internationalize during 1978; Furukawa announced that it had agreed to lay a 300-mile voltage line in Iran to connect Teheran with a power station near the Caspian Sea. This news came after the company revealed that it would build a large copper refinery in Mexico and a new aluminum plant in Fukui, Japan. In 1980, in cooperation with Japanese National Railway, Furukawa developed a lightweight aluminum-covered trolley cable to make ski lifts and trolley cars safer and more efficient. The firm also began to produce a very popular solar heat collector in 1980.

By 1980 Furukawa had rebounded so well from its sales slump that Aluminum Company of America doubled its ownership in Furukawa Aluminum for the price of ¥2 billion. In 1981 Furukawa absorbed Furukawa Metal Industry, a wholly owned subsidiary, and increased its percentage of shares in Furukawa Aluminum. These acts gave Furukawa Electric more influence within the Furukawa Group. Also, to boost profits that lagged due to a slowdown in government investment in electrical products, Furukawa was able to land a ¥12 billion contract to build a telephone network in Iraq.

In 1981, through the use of a special high-heat fusion splicing method, Furukawa was able to lead in the development of single-mode fiber-optic connectors. The new connectors lessen resistance and allow for lower power levels. Furukawa also developed a high-power field magnet that increases the usefulness of this portable power source.

A three-year plan to increase profits was announced by Furukawa in 1982. The plan involved expanding fiber-optic cable production by one-half through increasing investment in new factories and opening a new branch in the United States to increase exports. Sales had reached ¥100 billion, and the firm had plenty of empty plant space for new ventures.

In 1983 a drop in demand for rolled-copper products and aluminum, combined with a depreciation in the yen, cut profits about one-fifth. Yet Furukawa continued to be a technological leader within the industry. Furukawa was the first Japanese company to use shape memory alloys for commercial use, adapting them to serve as shutters in electronic dry-boxes. This improved on the old magnetic shutters. Furukawa also developed a new stronger, more heat-resistant fiber-optic cable in 1983 in conjunction with other Japanese firms. The most significant innovation of the year for Furukawa was its continuous transit system by magnet, which was a method of transporting public transit cars by a series of electrically powered conveyor belts. A quarter-mile test track was built at a laboratory outside Tokyo, and two experimental trains of three cars each were successfully operated.

In 1984, together with Oxford Instruments, Furukawa formed a new company to develop a superconductive magnet. Furukawa-Oxford Magnet would attempt to adapt the superconductive magnet for commercial use. Furukawa held 49% of the stock in the new company and 51% of the rights to its technology. The firm also developed a very pure form of bismuth oxide for use in semiconductors.

In 1986 Furukawa increased its profitability even more, due to increased need for electric wires and cables for automobiles and appliances. This increased earning power was reflected in the firm's buyout of most of the other stockholders in Furukawa Aluminum, which is now owned almost exclusively by the Furukawa Group.

Internationally, Furukawa created a new subsidiary, Fitel, to manufacture and sell fiber-optic cable in the United States, as well as a similar subsidiary in China, ShianFu Optical Fiber. To further expand the usefulness of and demand for fiber optics, in 1986 Furukawa developed a fiber scope flexible enough to be used for examining the insides of damaged pipes.

Furukawa reached ¥425 billion in sales in 1987, through increased production of fiber optics and the commercialization of products such as memory disc materials, gallium compounds, and wire for a diverse range of uses—including superconductive magnets and cooking equipment.

The partnership with Oxford Instruments brought dramatic results in 1987. Furukawa unveiled its new jointly developed superconducting magnet in January. Using special wire treated with chemicals which Furukawa helped to develop, the magnet should help adapt superconductive technology for potential consumer use. Later in the year, Furukawa accomplished a related breakthrough when it was the first to successfully magnetize a coil made out of superconductive material.

In 1988 Furukawa continued its research into superconductivity. The company developed a new technique for manufacturing basic superconductors at the rate of two or three a minute. Later in the year Furukawa developed a ring-shaped coil magnet from high-temperature superconductive wire. Still later Furukawa made strides in developing a wire that maintained superconducting properties even at high temperatures. This activity put Furukawa at the forefront of those firms scrambling to develop technology to bring superconducting materials into common use.

Furukawa also made news in the development of shape memory alloys, which it had adapted for use in automobiles. In 1988 Furukawa obtained the patent for a copper shape memory alloy held by Raychem. Furukawa continued to develop more uses for the material since the company holds the commercial rights to the material.

Also in 1988 Furukawa opened a new research institute in Yokohama. During the 1990s Furukawa planned to diversify by broadening its main business line of wire and cable to include new business areas, developing new materials such as semiconductors, and expanding its electronic material sales by manufacturing more printed circuit boards and memory discs. Furukawa also planned to continue its program of internationalization.

Principal Subsidiaries: Furukawa Aluminum Co., Ltd.; Furukawa Industrial S.A. Produtos Elétricos (Brazil); Conduphon Industria, Comercio Representacão e Servicos Ltda. (Brazil); Furukawa Electric Cables (Malaysia) Sdn. Bhd.; Asia Cable Engineering Co., Pte. Ltd. (Singapore); P.T. Tembaga Mulia Semanan (Indonesia); Bangkok Telecom Co., Ltd. (Thailand); Thai Furukawa Unicomm Construction Co., Ltd. (Thailand); ALPHA Industries Sdn. Bhd. (Malaysia); Furukawa Electric America Inc.; Southwire Furukawa Cable Company (U.S.A.); FITEL GENERAL INC. (U.S.A.); United Technologies Furukawa Corp. (U.S.A.); Furukawa Saudi Arabia, Ltd.; Polifoam Plastic Processing Co., Ltd. (Hungary); Shianfu Optical Fiber and Cables Co., Ltd. (China); International Components Technology Corp. (U.S.A.); FE Magnet Wire (Malaysia) Sdn. Bhd,; Furukawa Metal (Thailand) Co., Ltd.; Thai Metal Processing Co., Ltd. (Thailand); FEMCO Magnet Wire Corp.(U.S.A.); Taho Engineering Co., Ltd. (Taiwan); Furukawa Electric Singapore Pte. Ltd.; Furukawa Finance Netherlands B.V.

Further Reading: Link to 21, Tokyo, Furukawa Electric Co., Ltd., [1987].

—Wallace Ross

GKN PLC

Post Office Box 55
Redditch, Worcestershire B98 OTL
United Kingdom
(0527) 517715
Fax: (0527) 517715

Public Company
Incorporated: 1902 as Guest, Keen & Nettlefolds Ltd.
Employees: 36,000
Sales: £2.68 billion (US$4.33 billion)
Stock Exchanges: London Tokyo Frankfurt Düsseldorf Amsterdam Antwerp Brussels

GKN was born out of the mergers of three companies. Since the mergers in 1900 and 1902, it has evolved into an industrial giant centered on three main businesses, automotive, industrial services, and defense.

Although the mergers took place at the beginning of the 20th century, the companies out of which GKN evolved were very much older. The group, however, has changed so much in the intervening years that there is little left of its original elements. They were essentially family companies and typical of the entrepreneurial spirit responsible for the United Kingdom's leading position in the iron and steel industry during much of the 19th century.

One segment of the story begins with John Guest, who in 1767 ran an iron-smelting works at Dowlais in southern Wales. When Guest died his son Thomas succeeded him and he was followed in turn by his son Sir Josiah "John" Guest, an able entrepreneur, who raised Dowlais Iron Company to prominence. Sir John Guest's wife, Lady Charlotte Guest, was one of the most striking characters to emerge in the company's formative years. After her husband's death in 1852 she ran the company for three years. In 1889 the company built a new integrated steel works on the coast at Cardiff, at which iron was produced from 1891 and steel from 1895.

The second strand of the tripartite merger is centered on Arthur Keen, who was responsible for the two mergers which created GKN. Keen went into business with a U.S. businessman who had acquired the British patent rights for an automatic bolt-making machine. In 1864, the business went public as the Patent Nut & Bolt Company. Keen's requirement for steelmaking technology led to the amalgamation with the Dowlais Iron Company and the creation of Guest, Keen & Company in 1900.

The third element in the merger, Nettlefolds, was centered on the manufacture of custom woodscrews, and stemmed from a partnership comprising John Sutton Nettlefold and his brother-in-law Joseph Chamberlain, who in 1854 set up a woodscrew factory at Smethwick. The company flourished to become the leading screwmaker in the United Kingdom. In 1880 it took over the Birmingham Screw Company, and also registered as a public company, Nettlefolds Ltd. Further diversification took place in 1887 when a wire-rods, steel-hoops, bars, and wires plant was set up in Rogerstone, Newport.

In 1902, Guest, Keen & Company and Nettlefolds Ltd. came together, linking companies with diverse activities in a bid to exploit the benefits of horizontal integration. The first chairman of the newly created company was Arthur Keen, under whom the business was consolidated. This consolidation, based upon steel, continued throughout the first half of the 20th century, with Guest, Keen & Nettlefolds moving into areas such as rolling, forging, pressing, stamping, and machining.

Arthur Keen died in 1915, to be succeeded by his son, Arthur T. Keen, who died in 1918. The company emerged from World War I still centered on steelmaking, fasteners, and coal mining, primarily aimed at the railway and construction markets.

In 1919 the Earl of Bessborough took over as chairman, and the company took the lead in the nut and bolt industry with the acquisition of F. W. Cotterill. The group continued on the acquisition trail with the takeover in 1920 of John Lysaght, which had subsidiaries involved in steelmaking and re-rolling in the United Kingdom and Australia. This acquisition was particularly significant. With the Lysaght purchase came Joseph Sankey, which produced steel presswork, including wheels, chassis, and motor body parts, marking the group's entrance into the motor industry.

In 1920 Edward Steer, a member of the Nettlefolds family, became chairman, a position he was to hold until 1927 when H. Seymour Berry took over. After Berry's death following a riding accident in 1928, Sir John Field Beale headed the company. He was to preside over GKN during the Depression and the economic recovery of the 1930s.

In 1929 the steel industry was hit by the Depression, which resulted in a new wave of mergers. Three years later, the government introduced duties on imported steel to make domestic steel more attractive, and these moves, combined with rearmament in the latter part of the decade, provided the impetus for a further round of new investment in the industry.

Against this background, GKN continued to expand. In 1930 the group took over Exors. of James Mills, one of the world's largest manufacturers of bright steel bars, and entered the Swedish market with the acquisition of Aug. Stenman A.B., a Swedish manufacturer of hinges and fasteners. Four years later, it acquired 46.8% of Guest, Keen, Williams Ltd., the steel and engineering group, which is an associate company and one of the largest steel fabricating and engineering companies in India.

Also in 1934, the iron and steel operations of the Dowlais works, which had once stood at the forefront of the iron and steel industry, were transferred within the group to the Cardiff, Margam, and Port Talbot works of Guest Keen Baldwins Iron and Steel Company. This was a newly formed company created to acquire the heavy iron and steel operations of GKN Ltd. and Baldwins Ltd.

The company was expanding steadily under the chairmanship of Sir Samuel Beale, the younger brother of Sir John Field Beale. Sir Samuel Beale led GKN through World War II, and was to remain a director until 1957.

After the war, the Labour government set about economic reconstruction. The industry was asked to draw up a five-year plan for reorganization and modernization, to reverse the deterioration in its competitive position.

GKN expanded its iron-using and steel-using businesses, such as castings and pressings, to support the fast-expanding United Kingdom motor industry. J.H. Jolly took over as chairman in 1947, and in 1948, just three years before the nationalization of the steel industry, the group acquired Brymbo Steel Works in North Wales. In the same year it transferred its trading activities to two new companies. GKN (Midlands) took over the bolt and nut works at Darlaston and the screw works at Smethwick, while GKN (South Wales) Ltd. took over the re-rolling works and wire and nail plants at Cardiff.

Then in 1951 came the much heralded and controversial Iron and Steel Act under which the three steelmaking companies, Brymbo, G.K. Baldwin, and John Lysaght, together with GKN (South Wales), were nationalized. Two years later Sir Kenneth Peacock took over as chairman.

Steel nationalization proved to be relatively short-lived, and with the return of the Conservative government the industry was denationalized in 1955. GKN bought back its four companies and at the same time Guest, Keen, Baldwins, which had been jointly owned with Baldwins and had been the group's largest source of steel supply, became a wholly owned subsidiary, Guest, Keen Iron and Steel Company.

The group was still largely dependent on its original core businesses, but the 1960s were to see a transformation which gathered speed in the ensuing decades. During the 1960s, when the United Kingdom economy proved far less buoyant, it undertook major restructuring and reinforced its links with the growing motor industry, primarily through the acquisition of Birfield Ltd., which supplied components for the Austin-Morris mini. The group entered the defense-equipment market, winning an order for the FV432 armored personnel carrier for the British Army in 1962.

In 1967 the Labour government renationalized the steel businesses. Restructuring, which began in 1961 and was aimed at streamlining the businesses to make them more competitive, resulted in a series of subdivisions. The steel operations were the first to be restructured, with the creation of GKN Steel Company, which was nationalized in 1967.

The shake-up continued with the regrouping of its fastener, forgings, and castings, rolled and bright steel, building supplies and services, and engineering operations. GKN International Trading was created to deal with exports, and the group's overseas interests in Australia, New Zealand, South Africa, and Sweden were also reorganized. The group continued to expand in its traditional areas and to diversify, for example into gas-fired central-heating systems.

In 1963 GKN bought three suppliers of forgings to the motor industry: Ambrose Shardlow, in partnership with United Steel, Smethwick Drop Forgings, and Smith's Stampings. Three years later it took over the diversified Birfield Ltd., which brought with it a 39.5% stake in Uni-Cardan AG, a European automotive-components maker based in West Germany. GKN has since raised its stake in Uni-Cardan to nearly 97%. The Uni-Cardan acquisition proved to be of primary significance to the group's strategy. Among Uni-Cardan's products were constant-velocity joints, which permit the full transmission of torque from a car's engine to the wheels. These joints, originally designed for front-wheel-drive vehicles, were to play a crucial role in the growth of GKN's automotive business both at home and abroad.

In 1969 GKN unveiled a joint venture with Broken Hill Proprietary (BHP) of Australia to build a new steel complex at Westernpoint, Australia. The complex was constructed in two phases, the second of which was completed in 1978. The following year GKN sold its half interest to BHP.

In the 1970s GKN continued to increase its involvement in the automotive business and to build up its presence in distribution at home and abroad and its investment in service businesses. The decade also posed major problems. In the latter part of the 1970s the group's chairman Sir Barrie Heath, who took over from Sir Raymond Brookes in 1975, had to contend with hyperinflation, the oil crisis, and a collapse in demand for steel and automotive parts.

During the chairmanship of Sir Barrie, a management committed under Trevor Holdsworth undertook strategic restructuring to pull the company through moving out of Australia and broadening the manufacturing base in the United States.

During the 1970s, GKN acquired a large number of small distribution companies, largely in the fastener and steel sectors. It later extended this strategy to automotive components, signaling a move into vehicle-parts and accessories distribution on a worldwide scale. The acquisitions continued on the steel and automotive sides, including Kirkstall Forge Engineering, the largest independent manufacturer of heavy-duty axles in the United Kingdom.

In 1974 the Brymbo Steel Works were returned to GKN by the then-government-owned British Steel Corporation (BSC) in exchange for GKN Dowlais, in a deal which, while ending the group's long historical association with the Dowlais plant, gave it an internal source of supply. In the same year GKN took another significant step on the steel side with the purchase of Miles Druce & Company, making GKN the largest steel stockholder in the U.K. private sector. In 1974 GKN invested in the services sector with the formation of the United Kingdom's first national cargo-pallet hire pool, GKN Chep, with Brambles Industries of Australia.

In 1976, GKN stepped up its attack on the United States market with the formation of GKN Automotive Components Inc. to supply constant-velocity—universal—joints for the new generation of front-wheel-drive cars. Within a year the group announced a further United States move, unveiling plans to set up a production plant, costing $50 million, in Sanford, North Carolina. Three years later, GKN announced that a second constant-velocity joint factory was to be built in North Carolina, in Alamance County, costing some $80 million. The two plants were commissioned in 1980 and 1981.

In 1977, the group was still stepping up investment in steelmaking and rerolling with the opening of a new rod mill and steel works in Cardiff, costing £52 million. It announced a £48 million rolling mill for Brymbo Steelworks.

The group's United States involvement was enhanced in 1979 with the acquisition of Parts Industries Corporation of

Memphis, Tennessee, the fourth-largest vehicle parts and accessories distributor in the United States. It raised its European profile in this area with the purchase from Unilever of Unigep Group of France and in the United Kingdom with the purchase of Armstrong Autoparts and Sheepbridge Engineering, both possessing large distribution chains.

The company sold off operations which did not fit into its strategy, which in 1979 included its 50% stake in John Lysaght (Australia) and the divestment of GKN Bolts and Nuts Ltd., one of the pillars of the company when it was formed in 1902. This sector had been suffering heavy financial losses.

1979 also brought its frustrations. GKN had bid for Fitchell and Sachs, the largest supplier of car parts in West Germany, after taking a minority stake in 1976. However, after three years of patient negotiations, the bid was blocked by the West German courts.

At the end of the decade, GKN set about further restructuring which reflected the increasing importance of automotive components and the non-manufacturing businesses. It was preparing for the 1980s, which were to prove another period of rapid change, under the initial chairmanship of Sir Trevor Holdsworth, who retired in 1988, and then of David Lees.

The cold wind of recession hit the group in the early 1980s, and the decade started with a shock. GKN announced a loss of £1 million for 1980, the first since it was incorporated in 1902. Sir Trevor Holdsworth, who was responsible for fundamental changes to group strategy, set about slimming down and reshaping the group. Its work force, for instance, had shrunk from 93,000 in 1980 to 38,000 when he retired. As the new structure evolved, the group moved out of steel, further internationalized through local investments and joint ventures, built up the automotive side, and developed industrial-service businesses from its involvement in distribution.

The decade brought a series of sales and acquisitions, reflecting deep-rooted changes. In 1981 GKN and Brambles of Australia took an 50/50 interest in Redland Purle, the largest private-sector waste-disposal operator in the United Kingdom. The business is now known as Cleanaway Ltd. In the same year there was another major change when GKN and BSC merged their steel re-rolling and associated businesses to create Allied Steel and Wire Ltd. In the following year, when the group became Guest, Keen and Nettlefolds plc, it won a large contract from the British Army for its Saxon armored personnel carrier.

In 1983, another strand of the business took shape with GKN and Costain of the United Kingdom merging their scaffolding and building-services operations to create GKN Kwikform, now a market leader in the United Kingdom. That year the group expanded further in the United States with the acquisition of Meineke Discount Muffler Shops, one of the largest franchized exhaust-system fitters, while in the United Kingdom it set up a facility to produce fiber–glass reinforced road springs for commercial vehicles. Another success in the defense area came in 1984 when the group was awarded a contract for its Warrior tracked armored personnel carrier.

During 1984 and 1985, the group expanded its vehicle-parts-distribution businesses in the United States, and in Australia with the acquisition of Quinton Hazell Automotive. Viscodrive GmbH was created in West Germany to develop viscous drive-control units and a year later, in 1985, Viscodrive Japan and Translite were set up to market the units and composite leaf springs to the Japanese motor industry.

Another name change came in 1986 when the group became GKN plc, reflecting the move away from its original businesses. This change was underlined when in the same year the group sold its steel-stockholding operations and merged its engineering steels and forgings activities with BSC to form United Engineering Steels, with operating assets of about £600 million.

The group's international expansion continued apace. In 1986 and 1987, GKN made further European acquisitions in Spain and Italy, in the driveshaft and powder-metallurgy areas, respectively. During 1987 it became a market leader in vending services following several acquisitions, and sold Allied Steel and Wire, which did not fit in with its strategy.

In 1988, the group hit the headlines by taking a 22.02% stake in Westland, the troubled U.K. helicopter and aerospace group. The deal roughly doubled the group's defense sales which then accounted for about 5% of its £2 billion turnover.

It also forged an alliance with Jaguar cars. The two companies created a joint venture to supply all the major body pressings for the Jaguar/Daimler range of saloon and high-performance sports cars. In the United States GKN made some important changes, selling its imported-vehicle-parts distribution business and expanding the distribution of domestic-vehicle parts through the acquisition of Mid-America Industries.

In 1989 the group reported record pre-tax profits of £214.8 million, a far cry from the beginning of the decade. During that decade the group's emphasis has shifted overseas. Sales of the United Kingdom subsidiaries in 1989 accounted for less than 37% of total sales of £2.7 billion against 68% a decade before.

The automotive side has attained international prominence by developing local supplies. It now accounts for 61% of sales and numbers Ford, Toyota, and Honda among its customers. In 1988 the group sold off the underperforming GKN Autoparts distribution business.

The automotive division has rapidly increased sales to Japanese vehicle manufacturers on a worldwide basis. This link was enhanced in 1989 when GKN was granted a listing on the Tokyo Stock Exchange.

The industrial services sector has become increasingly significant and represents 35% of group sales. It covers an array of businesses including the highly successful Chep pallet and container hire operations, waste management, scaffolding, and vending.

The defense side, which makes Warrior and Saxon military personnel carriers, is the smallest division, responsible for 4% of 1989 sales. It will have to contend with the repercussions of changes in Eastern Europe, but these could provide GKN with a wealth of opportunities in other areas. In 1990 the group also began looking at possible ventures in East European countries.

Principal Subsidiaries: Ayra Durex, SA (Spain, 64.8%); Birfield Extrusions Ltd.; Birfield Trasmissioni SpA (Italy, 96.7%); GKN Automotive, Inc. (U.S.A.); Glaenzer Spicer SA (France, 96.5%); Hardy Spicer Ltd.; Industrias Mecanicas de Galicia, SA (Spain, 66%); Lohr & Bromkamp GmbH (Germany, 91.4%); Uni-Cardan AG (Germany, 96.7%); Viscodrive GmbH (Germany, 96.7); Walterscheid Schmiede und Presswerk GmbH (Germany, 96.7%); GKN Cardantec International GmbH (Germany, 96.7%); Ayra Cardan, SA (Spain, 64.8%); BRD Company Ltd; Birfield Trasmissioni SpA Cardantec Operations (Italy, 96.7%); Gelenkwellenbau GmbH (Germany, 96.7%); Glaenzer Spicer SA Cardantec Operations (France, 96.5%); Nordiska Kardan AB (Sweden, 96.7%); Jean Walterscheid GmbH (Germany, 96.7%); Walterscheid Agmaster, Inc. (Canada, 96.7%); Walterscheid, Inc. (U.S.A., 96.7%); GKN Axles Ltd; GKN Comaxle SpA (Italy); Laycock Engineering Ltd; GKN Bound Brook Ltd; GKN Bound Brook Italia SpA (Italy); GKN Firth Cleveland Ltd.; GKN Saini SpA (Italy); GKN Sheepbridge Ltd.; GKN Composites Ltd.; GKN Tadchurch Ltd.; Translite KK (Japan, 60%); GKN Technology Ltd.; GKN Sheepbridge Stokes Ltd.; GKN Sankey Ltd.; GKN Defence; GKN Kwikform Ltd. (60%); GKN Kwikform BV (Netherlands, 60%); GKN Kwikform Industries Ltd. (Australia); GKN Rentals (Australia); GKN Chep Ltd. (70%); Sankey Vending Ltd.; GKN Vending Services Ltd.; Automatic Catering Supplies Ltd.; ACS Coffee Service Ltd.; GKN Sankey Finance Ltd.; GKN Property Maintenance Ltd.; GKN Occupational Health Ltd.; BKL Extrusions Ltd.; Econopack Ltd; Stenman Holland BV (Netherlands); GKN Chep SA (Pty) Ltd. (South Africa); GKN Parts Industries Corporation (U.S.A.); Meineke Discount Muffler Shops, Inc. (U.S.A.); Sparks Tune-up Centers, Inc. (U.S.A.); GKN Group Management Services Ltd.; GKN Group Services Ltd.

Further Reading: GKN: Brief History of Guest, Keen & Nettlefolds, Redditch, GKN, 1980; Jones, Edgar, *A History of GKN: Volume One: Innovation and Enterprise,* Basingstoke, Macmillan, 1987; ''A Three-Legged Stool,'' *The Financial Times,* May 16, 1990; Barnett, Correlli, *The Audit of War,* London, Macmillan, [n.d.].

—Bob Vincent

HALLIBURTON COMPANY

3600 Lincoln Plaza
500 North Akard Street
Dallas, Texas 75201
(214) 978-2600
Fax: (214) 978-2611

Public Company
Incorporated: 1924 as Halliburton Oil Well Cementing Company
Employees: 65,500
Sales: $5.66 billion
Stock Exchanges: New York London Zürich Geneva Basel Lausanne Toronto

Halliburton Company is a worldwide engineering and oilfield service corporation. Its three main divisions provide insurance, engineering, and construction for the energy and other industries, and service and equipment for oil and gas exploration and development.

One of Halliburton's most important operations is oil well cementing. This process protects oil from contamination by underground water, strengthens the walls of a well, lessens the danger of explosions from high pressure oil and gas, and protects fresh water veins from contamination by oil. It was the first service offered by company founder Erle Palmer Halliburton.

Erle Halliburton learned the cementing technique in California, during a period of employment with the Perkins Oil Well Cementing Company that began and ended in 1916. Fired for suggesting too many method changes, he decided to utilize the engineering and hydraulics he had learned in the U. S. Navy, and go into the cementing business on his own. He borrowed a pump and wagon, pawned his wife's wedding ring to finance his venture, and moved to Burkburnett, Texas, to introduce his services to the oil industry. Halliburton's method met with little interest in Texas.

Undaunted, he transferred his operation to Oklahoma. Here his luck soon changed, bringing the need for additional equipment, a patent for his process, and efficient management. To cope with these needs and increasing demands for his service, in 1920, Halliburton organized the Halliburton Oil Well Cementing Company. One year later, 17 trucks carried his crews and equipment to drilling sites in Louisiana, Arkansas, and other oil-rich areas from a base in Wilson, Oklahoma, as well as from the new company headquarters in Duncan, Oklahoma. Part of this growing reputation came from uncompromisingly reliable service; it was enhanced by new equipment invented by Halliburton to meet the needs of each project. One creation that revolutionized the oil industry was the jet mixer, a mechanized mixer that did away with hand-mixing of the minimum 250 bags of cement and water slurry needed for each well. Because it could control the proportions of cement and water; it eliminated wasted slurry that would harden before it could be poured.

By 1922 the company owned $14,000 worth of equipment, and was paying some of its cementers $300 monthly. Two years later, Halliburton with his wife, Vida, as his partner, set out to expand. To finance this they converted their partnership into a corporation and offered a substantial interest in their business to other oil companies. Their trump card lay in their meticulous patenting of all new processes and devices, which had left the oil companies unable to have oil wells cemented without using Halliburton services. Company patents also covered processes designed for well recementing, a maintenance necessity that gave the Halliburtons relative independence from competitors.

In 1924 the Halliburton Oil Well Cementing Company became a corporation in Delaware. The Halliburtons held 52% of the stock, and the Magnolia, Texas, Gulf, Humble, Sun, Pure, and Atlantic oil companies jointly held 48%. So as to retain equal voting rights with their partners, the Halliburtons placed 4% of their stock in a voting trust.

By the time the company reached its ten-year milestone in 1929, research and development had improved processes and equipment to the point where a mixture made up of 2,500 sacks of cement could be injected into a well in 48 minutes. By 1929 the use of four new company planes made for speedy contract completion. Marking this important anniversary was the Halliburton entry into Canada, as well as offering for sale a wide range of oil well apparatus.

The 1930s saw automobile production soar from 2.3 million vehicles in 1931 to 4.5 million by 1940. Domestic oil heating became more popular, growing from 100,000 homes supplied in 1929 to 2 million by 1940. Both circumstances benefited the oil industry. As the decade ended, oil and gas were supplying 44.5% of the U.S. total energy requirements.

Halliburton's expansion kept pace with demand. In 1932, it opened four new branches, enabling it to send 75 cementing and well-testing crews to sites in seven states. The company introduced bulk cementing to replace hand moving of heavy cement sacks. Eager to participate in the marine oil exploration taking place in the Gulf of Mexico, Halliburton also began to mount equipment on ships and barges.

In 1940 the Halliburtons bought Perkins Cementing Company, extending operations to the West Coast and the Rocky Mountain region. In the same year, the company established its first South American subsidiary, in Venezuela. These two moves were profitable; just one year later, earnings reached $13.5 million, of which $2 million was net profit.

Soon after the Japanese attack on Pearl Harbor, the company began to make gun-mount bearings for the U. S. Navy at its Duncan shops. Other war material manufactured included parts for the B-29 bomber, and jigs, fixtures, and dies for the Boeing airplane plant in Wichita, Kansas. Wartime contracts were lucrative; when World War II ended in 1945, annual earnings reached $25.7 million.

In 1948 Halliburton shares were offered on the New York Stock Exchange for the first time. Having split its shares on a four-to-one basis a year earlier, Halliburton was able to offer 600,000, to which the Atlantic Refining Company added a further 80,000 shares. Of these, 50,000 shares were offered to employees before the balance were offered to the public.

By the end of the 1940s, although well cementing and bulk cement sales accounted for about 70% of company revenues, there were other profitable undertakings, all supported by specially designed equipment. Electrical well services provided information on the types of formations penetrated by a drill; acidizing of geological formations increased oil flow; and specialized equipment deposited various cements and chemicals into wells. Most profitable of all was a new process called Hydrafrac, licensed exclusively to Halliburton for a period of time by its developer, the Stanolind Oil and Gas Company. Designed to increase well productivity, this method used jellied gasoline, which was pumped under pressure into the bottom of a well to split the rock formation. The resulting crack was then propped open with quantities of sand, making penetration of tight rock formations easier. The Hydrafrac process made it possible to rejuvenate many dwindling oil wells, and reduced the number of sites necessary to drain a field. A surge in annual revenues showed Hydrafrac's great success: $57.2 million in 1949, increasing to $69.3 million the following year, and leaping to $92.6 million by 1951.

Between 1950 and 1955 the company expanded in all directions. Drilling activity increased dramatically; the company had 7,000 employees; drills probed to more than 4,000 feet in an average well, as compared to 3,600 feet five years earlier. Offered for rental as well as for sale, equipment then included formation testing tools to obtain fluids and pressure readings from oil-bearing rock, plus other new equipment used in well completion operations. Wall cleaners, depth measuring equipment, and production packers were other lines that drillers could rent or buy. Services provided by the company included electronic logging and sidewall well-coring, and the transporting of cement and fracturing sands to drilling sites from nearby Halliburton storage areas. Oil exploration in the Texas and Louisiana Gulf Coast areas was flourishing; 23 vessels as well as about $10 million worth of other equipment were available for offshore drilling purposes. There were almost 200 operating centers in the United States, as well as 32 service locations in Canada, and subsidiaries in Venezuela and Peru. The company also had operations in Mexico, Saudi Arabia, Sumatra, Italy, Germany, Australia, and Cuba.

Research and development kept the company at the forefront of oil exploration technology. Costing $3 million in 1956 alone, it rewarded the company's efforts with a new composition for cementing deep wells and a method for making the fracturing sand radioactive, among other innovations. All of this was reflected in the annual sales figures, which reached $152.4 million by the end of 1955, and produced net profits of $16.3 million.

Erle Halliburton died in 1957, after 28 years as company president and 10 as chairman. Cited by *The New York Times* as one of the richest people in the United States, he left behind him a fortune estimated at between $75 and $100 million—the days of a pawned wedding ring long gone.

The same year saw acquisition of Welex Jet Services. Originally based in Fort Worth, Texas, Welex broadened the Halliburton line of electronic testing and logging services. In the same year other companies were acquired including Jet Research Center and FreightMaster, a maker of rail car couplings.

The end of the war had brought an increased demand for oil. Due partly to freedom from wartime price controls and partly to the technological advancement that brought plastics, synthetic fibers, fertilizers, and other petrochemical products into the daily life of the U.S., these demands were willingly fed by the oil drillers. Production almost doubled between 1945 and 1954, reaching a level of 2.3 million barrels daily. Such overexpansion came to a head in 1957 when a slump followed, bringing with it a corresponding decrease in the demand for exploration equipment. The company's annual sales figures showed the trend of the time: its net income before taxes, $38 million in 1957, decreased to $27.6 million in 1958, rallied to $33.9 million the following year, only to sink once again to $26.9 million by 1960. Because Halliburton was chiefly a supplier of drilling-related services, however, recovery was relatively swift. These services, plus the equipment required to implement them, were needed both for the deeper wells then being drilled, and for stimulation of existing sites.

Offsetting the oil exploration slump, Halliburton continued with its acquisition program. Otis Engineering Corporation joined the company in 1959. Brown & Root became a Halliburton subsidiary in 1962. A firm internationally known for the construction of military bases, petrochemical plants, and offshore platforms, Brown & Root was a private subsidiary of the Brown Foundation. Other Brown subsidiaries acquired at the same time were Southwestern Pipe, a manufacturer of explosives and thin-walled pipe; Joe B. Hughes, a trucking business; and Highlands Insurance Company, chiefly concerned with casualty insurance. Together, the four new subsidiaries broadened Halliburton's product and service lines, giving the company entry into many overseas markets and providing ways to adapt Halliburton skills to new purposes. Two company staples quickly found new uses: blended cement was now sold for building projects and thin-walled pipes for playground equipment and bicycles.

By 1965 Halliburton's acquisitions program resulted in 16 units that were autonomous but closely coordinated into three main areas. One division was oil-field services and sales; the second was the engineering segment headed by Brown & Root, the focus of which were international construction projects such as bases in Saigon and parts of NASA's Manned Spacecraft Center near Houston. The third division, specialty sales and services to general industry, included power supply units and transformers for the electronics industry, missile cleaning for defense, and, through two subsidiaries, insurance. Earnings reflected the company's steady growth; 1960's total earnings of $181.5 million rose to $525.7 million by 1965.

In the 1960s, offshore oil exploration became a major activity. Successfully undertaken in the Gulf of Mexico since 1938, offshore drilling produced about 12,500 wells by 1970, accounting for approximately 15% of U. S. oil and 10% of its gas. Anticipating its participation in offshore activities, Halliburton equipped Brown & Root well, spending $100 million to ensure competitiveness. The company had developed an automated mixing system for drilling mud, used in offshore operations. Designed to cut costs by monitoring and controlling fluid density, the new system came in tandem with a 50% interest in IMC Drilling Mud, a company with special emphasis on overseas expansion.

In 1968 the company's marine capabilities were broadened further by the acquisition of Jackson Marine Corporation, a Texas company specializing in the construction of vessels for offshore petroleum exploration, and the purchase of an 80% interest in New Orleans-based Taylor Diving and Salvage Company. The latter company proved its worth within a year by developing an underwater chamber that could be lowered to depths of 600 feet, then pumped dry. It was used for the undersea repair of damaged pipes.

Offshore exploration proved lucrative; by 1970 the company's net income reached $46.3 million, up from $33.1 million in 1965. Other profitable ventures were hydraulic cushioning for railroad cars; electronics and explosives for the defense and aerospace industries; plant and road construction; transportation; and pollution control.

Destined for permanent importance, concern for the environment had attracted national attention a year earlier, after a well eruption in California's Santa Barbara channel spilled 10,000 barrels of oil. Outrage over the resulting 200-mile-square oil slick hampered offshore exploration, as well as the construction of oil refineries—and nuclear power plants. As could be expected, oil imports rose.

Halliburton, nevertheless, prospered. Total revenues of $1 billion in 1970 grew to $2.1 billion by 1973, despite the Arab oil embargo that led to huge OPEC price increases in 1974. Acquisitions giving the company new entry into overseas markets encouraged industrial variety. The reconditioning and stimulation of older wells then became more profitable than it had ever been before, especially as the equipment the company used for its own projects was not available on the open market. Lucrative as oil-field services were, however, they were now contributing a smaller proportion to the company's total revenues. A larger part came from construction projects like steel mills, municipal construction, and paper mills.

The Halliburton corporate structure was relatively simple. In the 1970s although the company had 55,000 employees worldwide, the Dallas headquarters housed fewer than 30 people; day-to-day activities were handled by each segment. Operations were still divided into three main segments: oil-field services and products, producing 46% of 1975's total earnings; engineering and construction, contributing a 51% share; and speciality services and products, responsible for the remaining 3%. Each of these three groups had several internal divisions, themselves divided into several hundred profit centers run by field managers. Headquarters kept in touch with these field managers in a monthly reporting system that monitored specified financial goals.

By 1975 there were 40 subsidiaries in all parts of the world, most of which were smoothly fitted into their appropriate company segments. The exception was Ebasco Services, acquired along with Vernon Graphics from Boise Cascade in 1973. Like Brown & Root, Ebasco's main business was the engineering and construction of fossil fuel and nuclear electric power plants. Its merger led to a Justice Department antitrust suit, claiming unfair competition. Ebasco was, therefore, sold in 1976.

By 1977, price controls had drained enthusiasm for domestic oil exploration. Imports now cost a total of $45 million, as against $7.7 billion in 1973. Two years later the situation changed. Instability in Iran and the higher prices imposed by OPEC countries now stimulated domestic production, to alleviate international oil shortages. Beginning in June 1979, price controls were to be phased out over 28 months, although they were replaced with a windfall-profits excise tax to keep prices high, a method of encouraging oil conservation.

All these developments as well as the slowdown of offshore exploration in the North Sea, where most major discoveries had already been made, affected the oil supply business. Halliburton's total income, in 1977, $660.2 million, reached $717.5 in 1978, sinking slightly to $648.2 in 1979.

Joint ventures in construction fields helped to offset the oil-field slowdown. In 1976 Brown & Root and Raymond International, a competitor, teamed up in a $22 million bridge construction project in Louisiana; a similar arrangement the same year paired Brown & Root and Norwegian Petroleum Consultants.

It was the company's old faithful, however, oil well cementing, that formed the basis for post-slump recovery; by 1980 Halliburton was servicing 60% of the market. Its service of stimulation of existing wells to retrieve remaining oil was garnering a 50% share.

In early 1981 all oil price controls were eliminated and well drilling increased proportionately; 77,500 new wells appeared in 1981, as compared to about 48,500 in 1978.

The upward trend brought competition for Halliburton, when Dresser, Schlumberger, and other industry giants began to diversify into the traditional Halliburton strongholds of cementing and stimulation. By keeping service prices at competitive levels, Halliburton's market share remained at its usual high level, however, and company strength in drilling muds and well logging operations continued to be a flexible guard against competition.

By 1980 the company's total revenues reached $8.3 billion. In 1982, an economic recession plus sharply lower oil prices began to affect the oil exploration industry and its suppliers. The slowdown showed in the total income figure for 1983, which was down to $1.2 billion.

Many smaller companies were unable to withstand the hard times. Halliburton merely downsized, slashing its employee roll from 115,000 to 65,000 by 1986, to an eventual 48,600 workers by 1988.

This was not a smooth time for the company. A lawsuit alleging that Brown & Root mismanaged a south Texas nuclear power plant construction project cost a 1985 settlement of $750 million, producing a $340 million loss for the year.

The acquisitions program continued unabated. A 60% share of Geophysical Services, a maker of seismic analysis systems for oil exploration, was bought from Texas Instruments. Gearhart Industries joined the company lineup; within a year its wireline services consolidated with Welex, and its geophysical operations with Geophysical Services.

Research and development became even more active including the development of horizontal drilling techniques. Spearheaded by the Geophysical Services unit, other research focused on continuous three-dimensional control for seismic surveys in offshore exploration.

As the 1980s drew to a close, Halliburton was engaged in about 40 other research and development projects. Streamlining for profitability, it had divested itself of its life insurance subsidiary, plus two other non-oil-industry-related businesses. Its total revenues, showing assets of $4.2 billion, were $5.66 billion.

Principal Subsidiaries: Otis Engineering Corporation; Halliburton Geophysical Services, Inc.; Sierra Geophysics, Inc.; Halliburton Geodata Ltd.; Brown & Root, Inc.; Brown & Root Industrial Services, Inc.; Brown & Root Services Corporation; Halliburton Environmental Technologies, Inc.; Highlands Insurance Company; Health Economics Corporation.

Further Reading: Haley, J. Evetts, *Erle P. Halliburton: Genius with Cement,* Duncan, Oklahoma, [n.p.], 1959; Hudson, Rex, "A Brief History of Halliburton Services (1916–1977)," Halliburton corporate typescript, [1977]; "Erle Palmer Halliburton," Dallas, Texas, Halliburton Company, [n.d.].

—Gillian Wolf

HANSON PLC

1 Grosvenor Place
London SW1X 7JH
United Kingdom
(071) 245-1245
Fax: (071) 235-3455

Public Company
Incorporated: 1964 as Wiles Group Limited
Employees: 90,000
Sales: £7.00 billion (US$11.30 billion)
Stock Exchanges: London New York Zürich Basel Geneva Paris

Hanson PLC (Hanson) is a British-American industrial conglomerate, or, as its founders prefer to describe it, an industrial management company, whose manufacturing subsidiaries are located principally in the United Kingdom and the United States. Sales are divided almost equally between the U.S. and the U.K. companies while the United States employs slightly more than half the total work force. The group's portfolio of operating companies has been built up by acquisition between 1965 and the 1990s and includes in the United Kingdom three broad groups: consumer products such as cigarettes, batteries, and vitamin and mineral supplements; building products such as bricks, and electrical goods and accessories; and industrial products such as gas meters, pumps, gas and electrical heaters, honeycomb and panel products, and prefabricated buildings. Its most recently acquired U.K. subsidiary is ARC Ltd., producers of crushed stone products, formerly part of Consolidated Goldfields PLC bought by Hanson in 1989.

In the United States the group's activities, carried on by some 150 companies, are coordinated by its major subsidiary, Hanson Industries, and again fall into three categories: industrial products, which include chemicals, mobile hydraulic cranes, leather supplies, commercial aircraft fittings, office furniture and supplies distribution, and Gold Fields Mining Corporation; building products, which include Kaiser Cement and a number of companies in the Hanson Lighting Group as well as Jacuzzi, market leader in whirlpool baths and spas; and consumer products such as vacuum cleaners, cookware, plastic housewares, and textiles. The group also has substantial interests in associate companies in the United States and Australia. Market capitalization in September 1989 stood at £11 billion, giving Hanson sixth place in the 1989 ranking of U.K. listed companies. A year before, with capitalization at £7.3 billion, Hanson was fifth in the rankings and thus achieved one of its stated goals, a place in the top ten U.K. companies before 1988.

The origins of Hanson go back to 1964. In March of that year a small City (London financial district) merchant bank, Dawnay Day, floated the Wiles Group on the stock exchange. The group was an animal byproducts, sack hire, and fertilizer business created by George Wiles and based in Hull, Yorkshire. In August 1964 Wiles started to diversify through the acquisition of Oswald Tillotson Ltd., a company operating in the field of commercial vehicle sales and distribution. James Hanson and Gordon White were on the board of Oswald Tillotson Ltd. and held a controlling interest in the company.

James Edward Hanson and Vincent Gordon Lindsay White were both born in Yorkshire and, after war service, started their early careers in their respective family businesses. The Hanson family road-haulage business was 100 years old when it was nationalized in 1948. James Hanson then spent some years in Canada building up a transport business with his brother. In the late 1950s he joined Gordon White—a family friend, whose own family publishing-and-printing business, Welbecson, was acquired by Wiles in 1965—in a venture importing U.S. greeting cards. Thus, the partnership that has underpinned the development of Hanson was already formed when the two men joined first Tillotson and then Wiles.

Between 1965, when James Hanson became chairman of the Wiles Group, and 1969, when the company was renamed the Hanson Trust, further acquisitions were made to develop the group into an industrial holding and management company. Its principal objective was defined by James Hanson as ". . . to expand profitability while achieving careful expansion through acquisitions." The purchase of Scottish Land Development in 1967, for £700,000, took Wiles into the hire and distribution of earth-moving and construction equipment and pumps. In 1968 the group paid £3.2 million for West of England Sack Holdings, which expanded its existing business in that field. In the same year it bought the Butterley Company for £4.7 million, an acquisition that took it into a new field of operations, the manufacture of bricks for house construction.

Hanson was by no means the only company then searching for under-performing and asset-rich companies to target as prospective acquisitions. In 1968 the conglomerate Slater Walker took a large shareholding in the Wiles Group. James Hanson and Gordon White over the years consistently pointed out the difference between the takeovers made for financial reasons—the fast track—and those, like Hanson's, for industrial reasons: "We are the work horses."

Between 1971 and 1973 Hanson expanded its brick-making activities with the acquisition of the National Star Brick & Tile Company for £2.1 million, British Steel Brickworks for £2.7 million, and NCB Brickworks for £2.2 million. It also bought a majority interest in a property development company, City and St. James. The changing scope of its activities led to a restructuring of its operations first in 1970, when it sold the commercial vehicle distribution operation, and then again in 1972, when the expansion of brick manufacturing warranted the creation of a separate division.

In 1973 the Bowater Corporation, eager to diversify out of the low profit-making newsprint and pulp activities and fresh from its merger with Ralli International, master-minded the previous year by Jim Slater, made an agreed bid for Hanson, but when the bid was referred to the government's Monopolies and Mergers Commission, Bowater withdrew. This experience, combined with the prevailing uncertain economic climate in the United Kingdom, led James Hanson and Gordon White to look further afield for development prospects, more particularly because White, "in disgust at socialism," wished to leave Britain. In that year, therefore, White went to the United States. From the 1950s until the mid-1970s, merger activity in the United Kingdom was high and encouraged by governments, particularly the Labour government of Harold Wilson, which established the Industrial Reorganization Corporation specifically to promote mergers such as that of General Electric Company and Associated Electrical Industries Ltd. On the other hand, reference to the Monopolies Commission of mergers which might operate against the public interest sometimes brought a negative response. Even when the commission's verdict was not unfavorable, changing conditions in the period of consideration could lead to the breaking off of the engagement, as happened with Hanson and Bowater. The commission was generally neutral on the matter of industrial conglomerates, although it pointed to the risks of the creation of stock to finance the purchase and to the danger of a failure to increase efficiency after the merger. More damning criticisms of the merger movement and its results in the United States were made by a U.S. congressional report in June 1971.

In the United Kingdom the asset-stripping activities of other companies tarnished the public image of the industrial conglomerate in the later 1970s. Hanson has insisted that it is an industrial management company.

In the United States Hanson Industries was formed as a holding company in 1973, with Gordon White as executive chairman. His first major acquisition came the following year when, at a cost of $32 million, Hanson Industries bought Seacoast Products—which remained part of Hanson until 1986—a Florida-based company manufacturing animal foodstuffs, fish meal, and edible oils.

In the 1970s, against the background of a turbulent world economy, shaken by two large increases in world oil prices, Hanson's growth on both sides of the Atlantic was steady rather than spectacular. In the United States in 1976, Hygrade Foods, the second-largest seller of hot dogs in ballparks, was acquired along with other purchases in the food servicing and vending and textile industries. In the United Kingdom, Hanson acquired Rollalong, which manufactured mobile accommodation units. In addition, Hanson purchased two flour milling and cereal companies, yarn and thread manufacturers, and a builders' merchants.

All these acquisitions fell into what is now recognized as the Hanson pattern. Hanson looks for and buys companies manufacturing basic, low technology products. By introducing a system of centralized and strong financial controls combined with decentralized operating management, Hanson increases profitability both for shareholders and for the holding company, thus building up its resources for further acquisitions. Some acquisitions have required further financing with bank debt, and the Hanson gearing has risen sharply at various times in the 1980s, to be quickly reduced in part by disinvestment. The diversity of Hanson's portfolio spreads the risk with the steady demand for food and other consumer products balancing the upswings and downturns in demand for building-industry supplies. The caution of the two founders is well-documented. James Hanson said, "I've always thought about the down-side risk on a take-over rather than the upside potential—we don't gamble." It was this approach, according to Gordon White, that led to the decision in 1974 not to buy 51% of Avis, the U.S. car hire business. White recalled "I told him it could put us straight in the big league but that if it went wrong it would bust us."

Hanson's purchase, for £25 million, of Lindustries in the United Kingdom in 1979 was its largest to date and presaged a decade of even greater spending and growth, taking Hanson very definitely into the big league. In 1980 Hanson Industries acquired McDonough, with footwear manufacturing and retailing and cement manufacturing interests for an agreed bid of $180 million. In the following year, in what was to become a typical Hanson activity, it recouped $49 million by selling the concrete and cement business. In the United Kingdom there were two major acquisitions in 1982, the Berec Group, manufacturers of Ever Ready batteries, for £95 million and United Gas Industries, makers of gas meters and of gas and electric fires, for £19 million. In the following year Hanson bought United Drapery Stores (UDS) for £250 million and immediately recovered almost three-fifths of the purchase price by selling Richard Shops and some of the other UDS subsidiaries. Allders Stores, a department store chain, and Allders International, which owned and operated duty-free shops at United Kingdom airports and on ferries and cruise ships, remained part of Hanson until 1989 when sold for £210 million.

By 1984, with turnover up to over £2 million, Hanson was increasingly seen on both sides of the Atlantic as a predator, a reputation it enhanced in that year with the acquisition of the London Brick Company for £247 million, making Hanson the world's largest brick manufacturer. At the same time in the United States it paid $535 million for U.S. Industries, stepping in with a brisk offer to replace a management buyout. This acquisition gave Hanson interests in diverse fields ranging from clothes to lighting manufacture, and subsidiaries in office and domestic furniture-making as well as heavy engineering. By doubling the size of the U.S. operation, the USI acquisition put Hanson Industries among the top 150 companies trading in the United States. In the following year in the United Kingdom, the attempt to increase its interests in the engineering industry failed when Powell Duffryn successfully resisted Hanson's takeover bid; in the United States Hanson Industries sold the food service management company Interstate United for more than three times the price it had paid in 1978.

1986 was marked by two major acquisitions. In the United States Hanson Industries won control of and paid $930 million for SCM Corporation, a typewriter, food, and chemical concern described by *Fortune International* as "sluggish." The chemical division, which is the world's second largest producer of titanium dioxide, has a successful sales and profits record under Hanson. In the two years after the acquisition of SCM, disposals of parts of the conglomerate raised more money for Hanson than it had paid for the purchase. On top of that, 52% of the typewriter business Smith Corona was sold, by flotation on the New York Stock Exchange, in 1989.

Similarly much of the purchase price of Hanson's 1986 U.K. acquisition, the Imperial Group, bought for £2.5 billion after United Biscuits had failed to gain control of the group, was covered by divestments. Hanson disposed of the Imperial diversifications—the Courage Brewery and off-license chains, Golden Wonder crisps, the hotels and restaurants, and the food interests where the brand names of Ross Young and Lea & Perrins brought a premium price—while retaining the original Imperial tobacco business.

The increasing importance of and value put upon brand names in a multinational business world was reflected in the purchase in 1987 by Hanson Industries of the U.S. conglomerate Kidde, an acquisition regarded at the time in New York as one for which White had, at US$1.7 billion, grossly overpaid; 18 months later Kidde's return on capital was up by more than 8% and the acquisition had come to be seen as an "excellent purchase." With over 100 different businesses, including such diverse products as kitchenware and Jacuzzi whirlpool baths, the Kidde acquisition took Hanson Industries into the top 60 U.S. companies. The Hanson investment criteria required that an investment must contribute to profits within one year and pay for itself within four years.

By the beginning of 1989 financial journalists and Hanson watchers were openly speculating about when or where the next takeover would come. The previous year had, for the first time in the 1980s, passed without a Hanson acquisition while disposals had enriched its war chest, giving the company disposable cash of £12 billion. The 1980–1981 recession had been a powerful stimulus to corporate slimming. The increasing application of "hansonization"—the combination of tight financial control with subsidiary autonomy on operational management—had played a part in reducing the number of badly managed candidates for acquisition. Within Hanson, expenditure of more than £500 over budget in the United Kingdom, and US$3,000 in the United States required head office authorization.

In August 1989, when Minorco was obliged to admit defeat in its attempt to take over Consolidated Goldfields PLC, Hanson stepped in with a successful bid of £3.5 billion. Following its usual post-acquisition policy, Hanson closed down Goldfields's London head office and sold its South African gold-mining interests and the U.S. aggregates business, Amey Roadstone Corporation, America (ARC).

Since 1964 Lord Hanson, who was knighted in 1976 and made a peer in 1983, and Sir Gordon White—knighted in 1979—have built up a company that is one of the largest in the United Kingdom and the United States. Their partnership, relying on Sir Gordon's creativity and Lord Hanson's administrative ability, by their own accounts is sustained by daily telephone calls and the assistance of small head office staffs of about 120 in the United States and 100 in the United Kingdom and of senior managers, many of whom have been with Hanson for 20 years. Both believe in maximum delegation of responsibility, adhering to a view stated more than 50 years ago by John Crabtree, founder of Crabtree Electricals, since 1982 one of Hanson's subsidiaries: "There are far too many Managing Directors and Presidents of companies who fancy themselves as experts in some minor phase of the business and who drive their subordinates to desperation by riding their personal hobbies." Lord Hanson expressed his business philosophy in Dominic Lawson's article in *The Spectator,* October 7, 1989: "Many companies here are not rewarding their shareholders sufficiently and are more concerned with management stability and welfare than they are with the welfare of shareholders, which is *all* that matters. We don't run this business for ourselves . . . " The company gave second priority to customers, and third importance to employees. This philosophy is reflected in the fact that Hanson operating managers are not offered high basic salaries but are rewarded with performance-related bonuses. Without looking for synergy or economies of scale and without the creation of a Hanson corporate culture or loyalty to the parent company, Hanson has achieved the objectives of its founders.

Principal Subsidiaries: Imperial Tobacco Ltd; British Ever Ready Ltd; Lindustries Ltd.; Hanson Amalgamated Industries; Hanson Engineering; ARC Ltd.; London Brick Company Ltd.; Butterley Brick Ltd.; Hanson Housewares (U.S.A.); Hanson Recreation and Leisure (U.S.A.); SCM Chemicals Inc. (U.S.A.); Hanson Office Products (U.S.A.); Grove Manufacturing Company (U.S.A.); Weber Aircraft Inc. (U.S.A.); Gold Fields Mining Corporation (U.S.A.); Hanson Lighting (U.S.A.); Hanson Building Products (U.S.A.); Kaiser Cement Corporation (U.S.A.).

Further Reading: Campbell-Smith, D., "Much More than a Predator," *The Financial Times,* December 23, 1983; Fay, Stephen, "The Rise and Rise of Hanson and White," *Business,* March 1986; Lawson, Dominic, "The Hard Man from Huddersfield," *The Spectator,* October 7, 1989; Bowen, David, "Secrets of a Big Game Hunter," *The Independent on Sunday,* July 29, 1990.

—Judy Slinn

HASBRO, INC.

1027 Newport Avenue
Pawtucket, Rhode Island 02862
U.S.A.
(401) 431-8697
Fax: (401) 431-8400

Public Company
Incorporated: 1926 as Hassenfeld Brothers Incorporated
Employees: 8,200
Sales: $1.41 billion
Stock Exchanges: American London

Truly successful toy companies do not just make toys; they manufacture popular culture. Hasbro, which is one of the two largest toymakers in the world, certainly fits that description. From America's Action Hero to a plastic anthropomorphized potato to the most famous dog and the largest bird in the world, Hasbro toys are instantly recognized by millions of Americans. Hasbro makes G.I. Joe and Mr. Potato Head and owns licenses for the *Peanuts* and "Sesame Street" characters. Thanks to acquisitions, it also makes Playskool and Romper Room preschool toys, and owns boardgame-maker Milton Bradley.

Hasbro traces its origin to an enterprise founded in Providence, Rhode Island, in 1923 by Henry, Hilal, and Herman Hassenfeld, brothers who had emigrated to the United States from Poland. The Hassenfeld brothers engaged in the textile remnant business—selling cloth leftovers. By the mid-1920s they were using them to make hat liners and pencil-box covers. Soon, with eight employees—all family members—they began making the boxes themselves, after realizing their popularity. In 1926 the company incorporated under the name Hassenfeld Brothers Incorporated.

Hilal Hassenfeld became involved in other textile ventures, and Henry took control of the new company. Although a paternalistic employer, Henry Hassenfeld was also a tough and shrewd businessman. During the Great Depression—with 150 employees in 1929 and 200 employees in 1930—Hassenfeld Brothers commanded annual sales of $500,000 from sales of pencil boxes and cloth zipper pouches filled with school supplies. At that point, however, the company's pencil supplier decided to raise its prices and sell its own boxes at prices lower than the Hassenfeld's. Henry Hassenfeld responded with a vow to enter the pencil business himself, and in 1935 Hassenfeld Brothers began manufacturing pencils. This product line would provide the company with a steady source of revenue for the next 45 years.

During the late 1930s the Hassenfeld Brothers began to manufacture toys, an extension of the company's line of school supplies. Initial offerings included medical sets for junior nurses and doctors and modeling clay. During World War II Henry's younger son, Merrill Hassenfeld, acted on a customer's suggestion to make and market a junior air-raid warden kit, which came complete with flashlights and toy gas masks.

By 1942, as demand for school supplies tapered off, the company had become primarily a toy company, although it continued its large, profitable pencil business. Hilal Hassenfeld died in 1943, at which point Henry Hassenfeld became CEO and his son, Merrill Hassenfeld, became president. Also during World War II, the company ventured into plastics, to support its toy-making, and was forced, due to labor shortages, to reduce employment to 75.

After the war Merrill Hassenfeld began marketing a girls make-up kit after seeing his four year-old daughter play with candy as though it were lipstick and rouge. In 1952, the company introduced its still-classic Mr. Potato Head, the first toy to be advertised on television. In 1954 Hassenfeld became a major licensee for Disney characters. By 1960, revenues hit $12 million, and Hassenfeld Brothers had become one of the largest private toy companies in the nation.

Henry Hassenfeld died in 1960. Merrill Hassenfeld then assumed full control of the parent company, while his older brother Harold Hassenfeld, continued to run the pencil-making operations. Merrill Hassenfeld's succession was logical given his interest and expertise in the toy business, but it also marked the beginning of an intramural rivalry between the two sides of the company; Harold Hassenfeld would come to resent the fact that the pencil business received a lower percentage of capital investment even though it was a steadier performer and accounted for a higher percentage of profits than toys.

In 1961 Hassenfeld Brothers (Canada) Ltd., now Hasbro Canada, was founded. Hassenfeld Brothers seemed to defy the vagaries of the toy business in the early 1960s, when it introduced what would become one of its most famous and successful product lines. According to author Marvin Kaye in *A Toy is Born,* the company conceived G.I. Joe in 1963 when a licensing agent suggested a merchandise tie-in with a television program about the U.S. Marine Corps called "The Lieutenant." The company liked the idea of a military doll, but did not want to pin its fate on a TV show that might prove short lived; so it went ahead and created its own concept, and in 1964 Hassenfeld unleashed G.I. Joe, a foot-high "action figure" with articulated joints. In its first two years, G.I. Joe brought in between $35 and $40 million and accounted for nearly two-thirds of the company's total sales.

The company changed its name to Hasbro Industries in 1968—it had sold its toys under the Hasbro trade name for some time—and went public. Only a small portion of Hasbro stock went on the open market, however; the majority stake remained in the hands of the Hassenfeld family. At the same time, Hasbro decided that it could no longer ignore the public's growing disapproval of war toys, which was fueled by disillusionment with the Vietnam War. In 1969 G.I. Joe, still the company's leading moneymaker, was repackaged in a less militaristic "adventure" motif, with a different range of accessories. Also in 1969, the company acquired Burt Claster Enterprises, the Baltimore, Maryland–based television production company responsible for the popular "Romper Room" show for preschoolers. Burt Claster Enterprises had also begun to manufacture a line of "Romper Room" toys. Nevertheless, a month-long Teamsters strike and troubles with Far Eastern suppliers hurt Hasbro in 1969, and the company posted a $1 million loss for the year.

The 1960s ended on a turbulent note for Hasbro, providing a foretaste of the decade to come. In 1970 Hasbro decided that it had to diversify, and it opened a chain of nursery schools franchised under the "Romper Room" name. The company hoped to take advantage of President Richard M. Nixon's Family Assistance Plan, which subsidized day-care for working mothers. Running the preschools was a very big mistake. Merrill Hassenfeld's son, Alan Hassenfeld, told *The Wall Street Journal,* December 13, 1984, "We'd get phone calls saying, 'We can't find one of the kids.' The whole company would stop." Within five years Hasbro had left the day-care business. Another ill-fated diversification move was Hasbro's line of Galloping Gourmet cookware, which sought to capitalize on a contemporary television cooking show of the same name. That venture literally fell apart when termites ate salad bowls stacked in a warehouse.

In addition, two products from Hasbro's 1970 line turned into public relations disasters: Javelin Darts were declared unsafe by the government, and Hypo-Squirt, a water gun shaped like a hypodermic needle, was dubbed by the press a "junior junkie" kit. Both products were promptly removed from the market. The continuing success of "Romper Room" and its related toy line proved to be a bright spot for Hasbro, although the company came under fire from the citizens' group Action for Children's Television because the program was used as an advertising vehicle for toys.

In 1974 Merrill Hassenfeld became CEO and his son, Stephen D. Hassenfeld became president of Hasbro. Hasbro regained its profitability but floundered once again later in the decade. Poor cash flow accounted for some of the problem, but the company's underlying mistake was casting its net too far and too wide in an effort to compensate for G.I. Joe's declining popularity. Hasbro discontinued G.I. Joe in 1975 because of the rising price of plastic, which was caused by rising crude oil prices. By 1977—the year Hasbro acquired *Peanuts* characters licensing rights—the company suffered $2.5 million in losses and carried a heavy debt. The financial situation became serious enough that Hasbro's bankers forced it to suspend divident payments in early 1979. The toy division's poor performance fueled Harold Hassenfeld's resentment that the Empire Pencil subsidiary continued to receive a smaller proportion of capital spending to profits than did the toy division. The dam threatened to burst in 1979, when Merrill Hassenfeld died at age 61. Stephen Hassenfeld was chairman Harold Hassenfeld's heir apparent, but Harold Hassenfeld refused to recognize Stephen Hassenfeld's authority.

The feud was resolved in 1980, when Hasbro spun off Empire Pencil, which had become the nation's largest pencil maker, and Harold exchanged his Hasbro shares for shares of the new company. At the same time, Stephen Hassenfeld became the toy company's CEO and chairman of the board, dedicated himself to turning Hasbro around. Where it had once been overextended, the company slashed its product line by one-third between 1978 and 1981, and its annual number of new products was cut by one-half. Hasbro also refocused on simpler toys, like Mr. Potato Head—products that were inexpensive to make, could be sold at lower prices, and had longer life cycles. This conservative philosophy prevented Hasbro from entering the hot new field of electronic games, as did the fact that it could not spare the cash to develop such toys. The decision to stay out of the market was vindicated in the early 1980s, when the electronics boom turned bust and shook out many competitors.

Perhaps the most important symbolic event in Hasbro's revival was the 1982 return of G.I. Joe. The U.S. political climate made military toys socially acceptable again, and G.I. Joe was reintroduced as an antiterrorist commando, complete with a cast of comrades and exotic villains, whose personalities were sculpted with the help of Marvel Comics. Two years later, Hasbro introduced its highly successful Transformers line—toy vehicles and guns that can be reconfigured into toy robots. Transformers were tied into a children's animated TV series and proved so popular that *People* asked Stephen Hassenfeld to pose with them for its cover.

In 1983 Hasbro acquired GLENCO Infant Items, a manufacturer of infant products and the world's largest bib producer. Hasbro also sold about 37% of its own stock to Warner Communications in exchange for cash and Warner's struggling Knickerbocker Toy Company subsidiary, which made Raggedy Ann and Raggedy Andy dolls. The new Warner holdings did not threaten the company's autonomy, however; the shares were put into a voting trust controlled by the Hassenfeld brothers and other Hasbro executives. In 1984 Stephen Hassenfeld, remaining CEO and chairman, retired as president and was succeeded by his brother, Alan.

In the early 1980s Hasbro was the nation's sixth-best-selling toymaker, with revenues of $225.4 million and $15.2 million in profit. Flushed with its newfound strength, in 1984 it acquired Milton Bradley, the nation's fifth-best-selling toymaker, and second only to General Mills's Parker Brothers subsidiary in production of boardgames and puzzles. Milton Bradley had been founded by its namesake, a Springfield, Massachusetts, lithographer who set up shop in 1860 and immediately turned out a popular reproduction of a portrait of presidential candidate Abraham Lincoln. Bradley's portrait, however, showed Lincoln clean-shaven, so when Lincoln grew his beard, sales fell off. Looking for a way to stay in business, Bradley invented and produced a boardgame called The Checkered Game of Life, a distant precursor of a popular Milton Bradley game, The Game of Life, which was introduced in 1960. The game's success convinced Bradley to stay in the game business. During the Civil War he produced a lightweight packet of boardgames for the amusement of Union troops. The company had incorporated in 1882.

During the late 19th century, Milton Bradley (MB) relied mostly on favorites like chess and checkers and traditional European games. During the 20th century, however, the company designed and marketed more original games, sometimes with great success. During the Depression, a Milton Bradley financial game called Easy Money became popular. In the 1950s, Milton Bradley pioneered games with tie-ins to television shows—Concentration was an early favorite. In 1968

MB acquired Chicago-based Playskool Manufacturing, which was noted for its preschool toys. Among Milton Bradley's later successes was the "body action" classic Twister, which was published in 1971 and became a popular prop with talk-show hosts for a while after Johnny Carson challenged Eva Gabor to a go-around on "The Tonight Show."

In 1984, however, Milton Bradley had found itself in an uncertain financial position after fending off a hostile take-over from British conglomerate Hanson Trust. In the wake of that failed bid, several unidentified parties bought up large blocks of MB stock, fueling speculation that another takeover attempt was imminent. Finally, in May 1984, MB agreed to be acquired by Hasbro for $360 million. MB's strength in boardgames and puzzles complemented Hasbro's plastic toys and stuffed animals. Milton Bradley's Playskool subsidiary provided a solid preschool line including classics like Lincoln Logs and ABC blocks. The new Hasbro Bradley Incorporated immediately challenged Mattel's position as the nation's leading toymaker. In 1985 Hasbro Bradley became Hasbro, Inc.

If Hasbro's and Milton Bradley's product lines merged well, their chief executives did not. Stephen Hassenfeld remained president and CEO of Hasbro Bradley, with Milton Bradley chief James Shea Jr. becoming chairman. After only a few months, however, Shea resigned. Stephen himself became chairman, with brother Alan Hassenfeld replacing him as president.

Hasbro surpassed Mattel to become the largest toy company in the world in the mid-1980s. Having done so, it then attempted to dethrone Mattel's Barbie, queen of the fashion doll market. In 1986 Hasbro introduced Jem, a record producer who was also, secretly, a purple-haired rock musician. Jem posted strong initial sales, then failed. Hasbro retired Jem the next year. In 1988 the company brought out Maxie, a blonde doll which was made the same size as Barbie so that Barbie accessories could fit it. Maxie lasted twice as long as Jem; it was discontinued in 1990.

In 1989 Hasbro acquired bankrupt rival Coleco Industries for $85 million, just four years after a *Toy and Hobby World* survey declared that Transformers had passed Coleco's Cabbage Patch Kids as the best-selling toy in the United States. In addition to the dolls, which had fallen from their peak of popularity during the 1985 Christmas season, Coleco also owned the rights to the classic boardgames Scrabble and Parchesi. The Coleco acquisition proved to be Stephen Hassenfeld's final triumph, however. In 1989, he died at age 47. Forty-one-year-old Alan Hassenfeld became chairman and CEO.

Alan Hassenfeld has worked for the family business for virtually all of his adult life and had maintained a close working relationship with his brother. While it is Alan's task to keep Hasbro at the top of its industry, it was Stephen who brought it there, converting the relatively modest toy company that their grandfather had founded into a juggernaut.

Principal Subsidiaries: Claster Television, Inc.; Hasbro Promotions and Direct, Inc.; Hasbro Foreign Sales Corp. (U.S. Virgin Islands); Hasbro Managerial Services, Inc.; Milton Bradley Company; Playskool Baby, Inc.

Further Reading: Kaye, Marvin, *A Toy is Born,* New York, Stein and Day, 1973; "Hasbro, Inc.: Company History," Hasbro corporate typescript, 1990.

—Douglas Sun

HAWKER ■ SIDDELEY

HAWKER SIDDELEY GROUP PUBLIC LIMITED COMPANY

18 St. James's Square
London SW1Y 4LJ
United Kingdom
(071) 930-6177
Fax: (071) 627-7767

Public Company
Incorporated: 1935 as Hawker Siddeley Aircraft Co. Ltd.
Employees: 4,500
Sales: £2.14 billion (US$3.45 billion)
Stock Exchange: London

Hawker Siddeley is one of Britain's largest engineering groups, along with British Aerospace and Rolls Royce. It was one of the pioneers of the aviation industry, but diversified over the years to remain competitive, first to electrical and mechanical engineering, and more recently to electronic components.

Hawker Siddeley is still associated with the romance of the early days of aviation. Its founder, Tommy Sopwith, produced the famous Sopwith Camel that shot down Germany's World War I flying ace, the Red Baron. In World War II the company produced the Hawker Hurricane, which played a crucial role in the Battle of Britain in 1940. In 1960 Hawker Siddeley acquired another of the country's pioneers in aircraft development, the de Havilland Aircraft Company.

Yet when Hawker Siddeley's aerospace interests were nationalized in 1977, they were responsible for only one quarter of the company's annual sales. After World War II Hawker Siddeley had slowly diversified from aviation, its focus since it had been formed from the merger of several aviation firms in 1935. With the important acquisition of the Brush Group in 1957 and a number of other long-established firms throughout the 1960s, Hawker Siddeley began to produce a variety of mechanical components and electric motors. By the 1970s, it was a diverse, if somewhat unfocused, heavy industrial producer.

To remain competitive in the 1980s, Hawker Siddeley had to concentrate on its higher profit areas and divest itself of its unrelated concerns. Under chief executive Dr. Alan Watkins, the company is building upon its solid reputation for dependability and financial soundness with the aim of becoming a dominant global player in its best markets.

In 1910, Tommy Sopwith, whose love for high-speed movement had already drawn him to race motorcycles, cars, and motorboats, decided to take the next logical step, to aviation. Sopwith had tried ballooning, but feeling that the future was with airplanes, he used the income from the estate of his father, an affluent engineer, to purchase a monoplane, a single-seat, makeshift vehicle like the other flying machines available at the time. With the help of other enthusiasts, Sopwith taught himself to fly at a race track that was no longer in use.

Sopwith soon earned his pilot's license—the 31st issued in Britain—and traded up to a new biplane. The plane paid for itself. Sopwith won £4,000 for flying from Eastchurch, Kent, to Beaumont, Belgium, at 177 miles the longest flight ever made from Britain to the Continent. In 1911 he began a stunt flying career in the United States. His exploits in Boston, New York, and Chicago helped him discover the potential of this new form of transport as well as earn him a nest egg.

In 1912 Sopwith, then 25, was back in England, where he established a flying school that trained two future marshals of the Royal Air Force. He began to design airplanes, and by the end of the year, decided to invest his earnings in producing the planes. He set up Sopwith Aviation Company in an old roller skating rink outside London. Since money was tight, despite his winnings from competitions, he rented out his new factory each Saturday for roller skating.

Sopwith concentrated on design and hired his long-time mechanic, Fred Sigrist, to construct the machines. He also hired an Australian who had learned to fly at his school, Harry G. Hawker, to test and demonstrate them. By 1913, the company employed six fitters and carpenters along with a new general manager, R.O. Cary. Sopwith-built planes performed well in competitions, and their successes gave the young company a good reputation. By 1914, Sopwith Aviation had about 100 employees.

The future of Sopwith Aviation changed dramatically when World War I began in August 1914. Britain required high-performance military aircraft, and Sopwith was determined to provide them. The company grew to over 2,000 employees by 1918—predominantly women by the end of the war years—who produced 14,000 aircraft of 10 major types.

All of the single-engine Sopwith models—the Sopwith Strutter, a two-seat biplane fighter; the Sopwith Pup, a single-seat scout biplane; and the Sopwith Camel, single-seat fighter—were virtually handmade of fabric over wooden frames. Though it was difficult to learn to fly, the Sopwith Camel was considered the greatest aircraft of the day by skilled aviators. A letter found on a captured German pilot stated that, "Of all the allied aeroplanes, the Sopwith Camel is the most to be feared." It was a Camel that Canadian airman Captain Roy Brown flew when he shot down Germany's most famous flier, the Red Baron (Manfred Von Richthofen).

Sopwith Aviation had proved itself in action, but continuing its success after the war years was difficult. Former war planes flooded the just-emerging civil aviation market, and prices plummeted. At the same time, some potential customers turned to new competitors. The United States had also developed an aviation industry to meet wartime demand, and its innovative production methods meant efficiency.

When Sopwith Aviation was unable to pay the taxes on wartime excess profits, the company was liquidated in September 1920. Two months later Sopwith was back in business with his partner, the Australian test pilot Harry Hawker. The HG Hawker Engineering Co. Ltd. manufactured parts for aircraft that were already in operation, designed and built motorcars and motorcycles, and built aircraft to order.

Only seven months later, on July 12, 1922, Hawker died in an accident while practicing for the annual Aerial Derby, but the company named for him was off to a strong start. By 1925, Sopwith, the chairman of Hawker, had put together perhaps the strongest design team in the business: Fred Sigrist as joint general manager, Sydney Camm as chief designer, F. S. Spriggs as the general manager, and F. I. Bennett as chief engineer. Under their direction, Hawker began to produce all-metal aircraft and began an aggressive marketing campaign. The company supplied the airforces of Yugoslavia, Norway, Sweden, Canada, New Zealand, South Africa, India, Egypt, and Persia, and produced seven types of aircraft for the British government. By 1933, Hawker was one of the largest aircraft construction companies in the country.

In 1934, Sopwith saw that rearmament meant further growth for his company, and he acquired Gloster Aircraft, a company known for strong management but lacking a good design team. In 1935 he made the move that resulted in the modern Hawker Siddeley Group when he purchased the Armstrong-Siddeley Company's aviation interests.

Unlike Sopwith Aviation, John Davenport Siddeley's business began with its roots firmly in the ground. The son of a manufacturing family, Siddeley came to motorcar design through cycling. He designed and raced cycles and worked in cycling-related jobs. He applied what he had learned with cycles to automobiles, becoming an agent for the French Peugeot Company. Shortly after 1900, he set up his own Siddeley Autocar Company, which produced a model that was basically the Peugeot with some of Siddeley's own modifications. In 1909 he formed a partnership, the Siddeley-Deasy Motor Company, with the explorer Major Henry Deasy, to increase production.

As with Sopwith Aviation, World War I got the young firm airborne. Siddeley-Deasy's Parkside works built airframes and the Beardmore-Halford-Pullinger aero-engine. Siddeley himself worked on the engine and developed an improved, water-cooled model, the 240-horsepower, six-cylinder Siddeley Puma engine.

After the war, Siddeley-Deasy was acquired by Armstrong Whitworth Development, a holding company. When Armstrong Whitworth formed an aircraft subsidiary in 1920, Siddeley concentrated on that part of the business, eventually buying the subsidiary in 1926 and renaming it Armstrong-Siddeley. Two years later, Siddeley was ready to expand again, buying the aircraft manufacturer A.V. Roe.

Siddeley had learned his trade in motorcars, and his priorities remained with automobile development. Aero-engines were less important to him, and aircraft took a distant third place. The company lost its preeminent position in air-cooled airplane engines, and Siddeley dismissed his chief aviation designer, John Lloyd, when Lloyd argued that non-Siddeley aero-engines should be used in the company's aircraft.

After Siddeley sold Armstrong-Siddeley to Hawker in 1935, the new company became known as Hawker Siddeley Aircraft Co. Ltd., controlling not only the Hawker and Armstrong-Siddeley aviation interests but also the recent acquisitions, Gloster Aircraft and A.V. Roe. Siddeley, a stubborn man with definite ideas about engineering, remained chairman of Armstrong-Siddeley Development, a separate holding company, until he retired the next year.

Hawker Siddeley was formed just in time for Britain's buildup of armaments prior to World War II. This time the Air Ministry was not as concerned with aircraft design as it was in the World War I when flight was newer. Instead it was more interested in company management and in how well firms could deliver necessary equipment on time.

The Hawker Siddeley aviation companies met the government's requirements. The company provided 40,089 aircraft to the Royal Air Force during the war, 30% of all RAF equipment. The Hawker Hurricane became the best-known plane. A Camm design, the Hurricane went into production in 1936. During the Battle of Britain in 1940 two Hurricanes were in the air for every Spitfire, and they shot down more enemy aircraft than all other defender-aircraft put together. A.V. Roe's Lancaster bomber also played an important role in the war effort and added to Hawker Siddeley's profits and prestige.

The company had to expand to meet wartime demand. At its peak during World War II, Hawker Siddeley employed 100,000 people. During the latter part of the war years, Sopwith removed himself from running day-to-day affairs of the company to concentrate on overall policy as chairman. Frank Spriggs took the title of executive chairman.

Business remained good with the return of a peacetime economy. A.V. Roe developed civil versions of its military planes, and Gloster flew the first aircraft with a Whittle jet engine. The company became particularly strong in Canada, where A.V. Roe Canada was formed in 1945.

In 1948 Sopwith renamed the firm the Hawker Siddeley Group, emphasizing that it would concentrate on two core business areas, industrial and aerospace production. In 1957 he began diversification outside aviation when Hawker Siddeley acquired the Brush Group of companies. Brush, which had been founded by a U.S. engineer, Charles Brush, in 1879, was a leader in electrical engineering. That same year, Hawker Siddeley also purchased the Canadian Dominion Steel and Coal Corporation, a major producer of mining machinery and tunneling equipment, to build upon its successes in Canada.

In 1960 Sopwith showed that he intended Hawker Siddeley to remain strong in aviation by acquiring three other aviation firms, Folland, Blackburn, and de Havilland. His move was a response to government pressure to integrate the aircraft industry into larger units to utilize the economies of scale. The resulting company became one of the top two British aircraft producers and one of the top ten manufacturing engineering companies in the world.

By 1963 Sir Thomas Sopwith, described in the *Dictionary of Business Biography* as one "who had seen aviation move from the string and canvas biplane to the jet liner," decided to step down from an active role in Hawker Siddeley. He took the honorary position of "life founders president" and was succeeded by his former managing director and vice chairman, Roy Dobson.

Dobson followed Sopwith's careful approach to diversification until he was succeeded by Sir Arnold Hall as chairman in 1967. Hall had begun his career in aviation during World War II and had joined Hawker Siddeley in 1955. Since then he had been part of all major British aircraft developments, including the Harrier jump-jet, the 146 short-haul airliner, and the Hawk trainer. Under Hall, Hawker Siddeley became a mechanical and electrical engineering conglomerate. His tenure was marked by slow but steady growth, both in size and profits.

Hall was able to maintain this growth even after nationalization of the company's aviation interests in 1977. Hawker Siddeley was prepared for this move, and after Hall's determined diversification, its aviation-related businesses accounted for only a quarter of sales. The company retained its foreign aircraft interests, such as the Australian company, Hawker de Havilland, Ltd. Hawker de Havilland, which designs and builds aircraft and aerospace components, has been a steady profit maker.

Hall's careful approach, considered admirable in the early 1970s, was seen as dated by the end of the decade. Analyst Roger Cowe said in a *Guardian* article of October 22, 1987, that Halls' diversification efforts ''got rather out of hand,'' making the company '' a mess of engineering and other interests with little rationality.''

When Bob Bensly took over as managing director in March 1984, he and financial director David Bury faced Hall's legacy of slow growth, along with the impact of a sluggish economy. Hawker Siddeley's diesel orders were down, and its other mature industries like electric motors and generators, transformers, and switchgear were also in a slump.

Bensly reviewed the company's operations. He established a better accounting system and reorganized United Kingdom operations, merging some smaller units and functions such as marketing. Bensly stated that the company would remain committed to its traditional core businesses, including diesels and transformers, despite their underperformance, but he looked to the areas in which Hawker Siddeley performed best—controls, instrumentation, and cables—to maximize growth. Bensly added to Hawker Siddeley's electrical interests to build a major world position in the field by acquiring firms, especially in the United States. He disposed of companies with low returns or those outside its core businesses. In 1984, for example, Bensly acquired 40% of Safetran, a U.S. manufacturer of railroad signaling and crossing equipment. By 1987, he was making his 144th U.S. acquisition, Aerospace Avionics in New York. In the first six months of 1988, he purchased von Weise Gear Company, a U.S. maker of fractional horsepower motors and gear reducers that could be integrated into another Hawker Siddeley subsidiary in the United States, Fasco Industries. He sold companies such as Invergordon Distillers.

As the 1980s drew to a close, Hawker Siddeley's heavy industry components had increased sales. Its subsidiaries, Brush Electrical Machines, Westinghouse Brake & Signal, and Mirrlees Blackstone had substantial new contracts to upgrade the British Rail locomotive fleet. Brush also won the lucrative contract to power the new Channel Tunnel shuttle trains. In addition, analysts were claiming that Bensly had given Hawker Siddeley a sharper focus by changing its emphasis from heavy engineering to lighter electrical and electronic components. His approach was low risk. While he made a great number of acquisitions, they were primarily of small companies. Bury warned that the company would soon have to shift to larger acquisition targets.

Another change in company policy, however, was left to a new chief executive. Alan Watkins, former head of the aerospace division of Lucas Industries, took over as managing director and chief executive officer in August 1989, with his eye firmly focused on growth. ''If you don't become a real continental or global player, the fact that you are growing at 5% or 10% a year is neither here nor there,'' he said when he took the job, as reported in the *Sunday Times* of August 13, 1989. Watkins aimed at a growth rate of 20% fueled by substantial acquisitions, especially in Europe, where Watkins wanted to increase Hawker Siddeley's presence.

To achieve that level of growth, Watkins intended to concentrate on six or seven core businesses. He hoped to make Hawker Siddeley the number two or three producer worldwide in at least several of those areas. Acquisitions since Watkins came on board—Standard Aero of Canada and GEC Alsthom Electromotors—indicated his intentions of remaining in aviation maintenance and electric motors. His purchase of a small Japanese instrumentation business indicated his intention of being a global investor.

Watkins identified several other means of reaching his goal of growth. He intended to revamp the company's corporate structure, upgrade its outdated manufacturing plants, and group the company's businesses to work together better. Watkins saw ''pockets of excellence'' in the company; and planned to expand them.

Hawker Siddeley changed from a purely aviation firm, to a diversified electrical and mechanical engineering firm and producer of electrical and electronic components. Founder Tommy Sopwith died in 1989 at age 101, leaving a company with the qualities he identified as being the key to success: ''The courage to think and the capacity to do.''

Principal Subsidiaries: Aerospace Avionics Inc. (U.S.A.); Augier S.A. (France); Brook Crompton Controls Ltd.; Brook Crompton Ltd.; Brook Crompton Betts Pty. Ltd. (Australia, 51%); Brush Electrical Machines Ltd.; Brush Fuses Inc. (U.S.A.); Brush Switchgear Ltd.; Brush Transformers Ltd.; Bunnings Ltd. (Australia, 24.2%); Clarostat Mfg. Co. Inc. (U.S.A.); Crompton Greaves Ltd. (India, 37.5%); Crompton Externacell Ltd. (Singapore); Crompton Lighting Ltd.; Crompton Parkinson Ltd.; Crompton Stud Welding Ltd.; Daytronic Corporation (U.S.A.); Dimetronic SA (Spain, 90%); Electro Corporation (U.S.A.); Electromotors Ltd.; Elmwood Sensors Inc. (U.S.A.); Elmwood Sensors Ltd.; Fasco Controls (U.S.A.); Fasco Consumer Products (U.S.A.); Fasco Motors (U.S.A.); Harowe Servo Controls (U.S.A.); Hawker Energy Products Ltd.; Hawker de Havilland Ltd. (Australia, 70%); Hawker Instruments Inc. (U.S.A.); Hawker Instrumentation Supplies Ltd.; Hawker Noyes Pty. Ltd. (Australia); Hawker Pacific Pty. Ltd. (Australia); Hawker Siddeley Canada Inc. (59.1%); Hawker Siddeley Electric Africa (Pty.) Ltd. (South Africa); Hawker Siddeley Power Engineering Ltd.; Hawker Siddeley Power Plant Ltd.; Hawker Siddeley

Power Transformers Ltd.; Hollybank Engineering Co. Ltd.; HDA Forgings Ltd.; Insumat Ltd.; KW Battery Co. (U.S.A.); Lister-Petter Ltd.; Lister Shearing Equipment Ltd.; Mirrlees Blackstone (Stamford) Ltd.; Mirrlees Blackstone (Stockport) Ltd.; Oldham Crompton Batteries Ltd.; Oldham France SA; OptoSwitch, Inc. (U.S.A.); Power Conversion, Inc. (U.S.A.); Safetran Systems Corporation (U.S.A.); Standard Aero Ltd. (Canada); Saro Products Ltd.; South Wales Electric (Private) Ltd. (Zimbabwe); South Wales Switchgear Ltd.; Torin Ltd.; Tungstone Batteries Ltd.; Uniross Batteries Ltd. (70%); Von Wiese Gear Company (U.S.A.); Westcode Semiconductors Ltd.; Westinghouse Brake & Signal Co. (Australia) Ltd.; Westinghouse Brake & Signal Ltd.; Westinghouse Brake and Signals Holdings Ltd.; Westinghouse Systems Ltd.

Further Reading: Higham, Robin, and David J. Jeremy, ''Sir Thomas Octave Murdoch Sopwith,'' in *Dictionary of Business Biography: A Biographical Dictionary of Business Leaders Active in Britain in the Period, 1860–1980*, Volume V, edited by David Jeremy, London, Butterworths & Co. Ltd., 1986; Higham, Robin, and R.P.T. Davenport-Hines, ''John Davenport Siddeley, 1st Lord Kenilworth,'' in *Dictionary of Business Biography: A Biographical Dictionary of Business Leaders Active in Britain in the Period, 1860–1980* Volume V, edited by David Jeremy, London, Butterworths & Co. Ltd., 1986; ''The Courage to Think; The Capacity to Do,'' *Hawker Siddeley World,* June-August, 1989.

—Ginger G. Rodriguez

THE HENLEY GROUP INC.

THE HENLEY GROUP, INC.

Liberty Lane
Hampton, New Hampshire 03842
U.S.A.
(603) 926-5911
Fax: (603) 926-5661

Public Company
Incorporated: 1986
Employees: 11,400
Sales: $1.57 billion
Stock Exchange: NASDAQ

The Henley Group is a holding company whose operating subsidiaries can—and in most cases will—each operate as an independent company. Many of its executives are managers of Henley's predecessor companies. Their goal is to acquire and develop low-risk, underperforming properties, and, after some time, to divest or trade these subsidiaries at a profit, paying out generous dividends in the process.

The Henley Group was created in 1986, when 35 diverse but unprofitable businesses were spun off by Allied-Signal. Under the leadership of Michael D. Dingman, chairman and chief executive officer, Henley raised $1.2 billion, in a record initial public offering.

The formation of Henley began in November 1985, when the board of directors of Allied-Signal approved reorganization plans. The recently merged Allied Corporation—a chemical giant—and The Signal Companies—an aerospace and engineering company—decided to concentrate on two industries: aerospace and electronics. That left 35 unrelated businesses. Because selling them individually would take years and tie up his managers, Allied-Signal chairman and CEO Edward L. Hennessy Jr. chose to unload them all in one major effort. He bundled them into Henley and gave Allied-Signal stockholders one share of the new company for every four of their Allied-Signal shares.

Henley's original offices were located in New York City because its people were working closely with Allied-Signal, located in New Jersey, immediately following the spin-off. Henley moved to La Jolla, California in 1987 because many of its executives, including Dingman, had been working there since their days with Signal, which was headquartered there. In 1988 Henley opened an office in Hampton, New Hampshire, and Dingman relocated to the East Coast. The company operated dual offices for several years, and in 1990 Henley phased out the La Jolla office, making Hampton its world headquarters.

Former Allied-Signal President Dingman, a rowing enthusiast, named Henley after the English town famous for its regattas. A self-described turnaround man, Dingman said of Henley, "When I saw it, I was intrigued by somebody's lack of insight. . . The success I've had in my business career has been taking other people's junk and making it worth more," according to *Business Week,* June 2, 1980. Dingman had built Wheelabrator-Fry into a $1.5 billion environmental and energy company. He sold Wheelabrator-Frye to The Signal Companies in a 1983 stock swap and, as president of Signal, engineered that company's move into high technology by selling off its low-tech companies.

The first six months after Henley went public were spent streamlining the company's operations into three main businesses. Henley formed Fisher Scientific Group, the Wheelabrator Technologies Group, and a manufacturing group.

The principal businesses of Fisher Scientific Group included the design, manufacture, distribution, sale, and service of medical diagnostic and therapy-management products for use in hospitals and independent clinical laboratories. Fisher Scientific Group also manufactured and distributed infusion systems for the regulation and control of intravenous solutions.

The Wheelabrator Technologies Group is the nation's leading developer and operator of refuse-to-energy systems, which dispose of solid waste and generate electricity. Its operating units are involved worldwide in process-engineering, design, and construction services for such industries as oil and gas processing, pulp and paper, ferrous and nonferrous metals, electric utilities, nitrogen fertilizers, plastics and petrochemicals. Its operating units also design, finance, construct, own, and operate refuse-to-energy systems, cogeneration plants and other small power plants, and provide chemical processing systems.

The manufacturing group includes businesses engaged in the manufacture of seamless copper and copper-alloy tubing and other seamless nonferrous tubing; nonpolluting materials cleaning systems; precision profile wire screens for groundwater and industrial applications; lithographic blankets and plates for the printing industry; precision bearings; parts and components for the semiconductor market; metal stampings and wire products for the automotive market; and components related to the aerospace industry.

In June 1986, Henley acquired IMED Corporation for $163 million. IMED develops and sells systems to control the flow of intravenous solutions for hospital patients. IMED fit in with Henley's Instrumentation Laboratory Inc., a maker of chemical analyzers, and Fisher Scientific Group. These companies were part of Henley's medical-technical group—among Henley's most promising businesses.

Another milestone in Henley's evolution as an independent company was the purchase of the 15% of Henley's stock that Allied-Signal had retained for $466 million in January 1987. Henley also repurchased approximately 39 million shares of its own common and preferred stock, reducing shares outstanding by 30%.

In 1987 Henley created three public companies to increase shareholders' value. By creating separate entities whose activities are concentrated in one industry, investors are offered a ''pure play'' instead of a ''conglomerate play,'' and are willing to pay a premium for the opportunity. Henley therefore distributed approximately 20% of the common stock of its Fisher Scientific Group subsidiary to Henley shareholders, and its Wheelabrator Technologies subsidiary sold 6.9 million shares of its common stock in an initial public offering that raised $119 million. It also distributed approximately 45% of the common stock of its Henley Manufacturing Corporation subsidiary to Henley shareholders.

In 1986, Henley began purchasing Santa Fe Southern Pacific Corporation common stock, and by early 1988 owned 15.7%, or nearly 25 million shares. Henley and Santa Fe Southern Pacific Corporation had discussed a merger, but discussions were terminated in 1988.

In 1987, despite stock market turbulence and sluggish economic forecasts Henley's operating companies continued to post strong performances. In 1988 Henley divided itself into two public companies and distributed its third stock dividend in 21 months. The division of assets—known as a reverse spinoff—enabled Wheelabrator Group and the new Henley Group to be independently valued, resulting in a higher total market value of these businesses. The Wheelabrator Group owned Henley's investment in Wheelabrator Technologies and certain related assets, and the new Henley owned the rest of Henley's previous assets.

That same year Henley traded its Signal Capital operations and its investments in Santa Fe Southern Pacific Corporation, American President Companies, and Oak Industries with Itel Corporation for $827 million in cash and a 40% stake in Itel. It was a $1.2 billion transaction.

Late in 1988, Henley and investment banker Wasserstein Perella & Company formed a partnership to acquire half interest in Pneumo Abex Corporation, an aerospace and industrial company, from IC Industries, in a $1.3 billion transaction. Pneumo Abex participates in most commercial aircraft production programs, and its customers include Boeing, Cessna, McDonnell Douglas, and all major commercial airlines. Also in 1988, Henley's manufacturing subsidiary was acquired by New Hampshire Oak.

At this point Henley owned Signal Landmark Holdings and held approximately 12% of Wheelabrator Group, 81% of Fisher Scientific Group, 82% of Cape Horn Methanol, 50% of Pneumo Abex, and 40% of Itel Corporation. At the end of 1988 Henley had assets of $2.8 billion.

In 1989 Henley stock underperformed the market averages for the first time. This situation strengthened Henley's determination to continue distributing the value of its assets to shareholders by separating Henley's investments and operations from the parent company in the most tax-efficient manner. To accomplish this task, Henley continued to seek to liquidate its investments and exchange its holdings for other assets.

In August 1989, Henley completed a cash tender offer for the 20% of Fisher Scientific Group common stock not previously owned by Henley, making it a wholly owned subsidiary. Fisher Scientific Company, Henley's largest operating unit, is one of the oldest and most respected names in the $17 billion world market. The company distributes more than 100,000 different products, including its new products for environmental testing and research, plasma analysis, and electronic research.

In April 1989, Henley agreed to purchase the 50% interest in Pneumo Abex Corporation the company did not already own. Pneumo Abex had net sales of $901 million in 1989. At year-end in 1989, Henley again divided, into two public companies: Henley Properties and another new Henley Group. This was the fourth time the Henley Group had divided itself since it was created. Operations of Henley consisted of a group of diversified businesses, conducted mainly through three major operating segments: Fisher Group—Fisher Scientific, Instrumentation Laboratory, and IMED; Aerospace Products and Services—Pneumo Abex, Cleveland Pneumatic Company, NWL Control Systems, and Abex Aerospace; and Industrial Products—Abex Friction Products and Jetway Systems.

Henley Properties, with assets of $680 million, has 24 real estate developments and other properties in southern California, Hawaii, Illinois, Michigan, Wisconsin, and New Hampshire. These holdings include one of the last large, undeveloped ocean-front properties in southern California and important housing developments in and near San Diego, California.

Henley's waterfront property in Bolsa Chica, California—the principal portion of its southern California holdings—had languished for 25 years as local groups blocked plans for residential development. Dingman made peace with the anti-growth groups by increasing the amount of area set aside for parks and wildlife and ecological preserves and by agreeing not to build a new harbor. Housing construction was slated to begin by early 1991.

In January 1990 Henley announced that had it ended a prior agreement to sell its IMED unit to Advanced Medical Technologies, due to delays in reaching a final agreement and concerns about the ability to finance the deal. In May 1990, Henley announced plans to spin-off its two largest operating units, Pneumo Abex and Fisher Scientific Group, as separate public companies.

Prior to the spin-off, Henley owned Pneumo Abex and Fisher Scientific Group, as well as 82% of Cape Horn Methanol, 38% of Itel, 7% of Wheelabrator Group, and held an option to buy 15% of Henley Properties. After the spinoff, Henley Group retained 65% of Pneumo Abex, 82% of Cape Horn Methanol, 34% of Itel, 7% of Wheelabrator Group, an option to buy 15% of Fisher Scientific Group, and 15% of Henley Properties.

According to Dingman, next on the company's agenda is to dispose of a substantial portion of its investments, including all or a portion of the Itel shares. These dispositions may take the form of sales, further dividends, or exchanges.

Principal Subsidiaries: Pneumo Abex (65%); Cape Horn Methanol Limited (Cayman, 82%); Itel (34%); Wheelabrator Group (7%).

Further Reading: Baum, Laurie, and John Byrne, ''Wall Street Is Just Wild About Henley,'' *Business Week,* June 2, 1986; Dumaine, Brian, ''Wall Street Likes A Spinoff Known as Dingman's Dogs,'' *Fortune,* June 9, 1986; Lorenz, Christopher, ''Junk With A Lot Of Potential,'' *The Financial Times,* January 23, 1987.

—Lori Oleinick

Hitachi Zosen
HITACHI ZOSEN CORPORATION

HITACHI ZOSEN CORPORATION

3-28, Nishikujo 5-chome
Konohana-ku, Osaka 550
Japan
(06) 466-7500
Fax: (06) 466-7572

Public Company
Incorporated: 1934 as Hitachi Shipbuilding
Employees: 7,473
Sales: ¥343.86 billion (US$2.39 billion)
Stock Exchanges: Tokyo Osaka Nagoya

The Hitachi Zosen Corporation is a global leader in engineering and constructing heavy equipment and ships. Its predecessor, the Osaka Iron Works, was founded by British entrepreneur Edward H. Hunter on April 1, 1881. Hunter had come to Japan in 1865 and had worked in the Onohama Shipyard in Kobe before moving to Osaka. He built a modern shipyard at the junction of the Aji and Nakatsu rivers where his first vessel, the *Hatsumaru,* was completed in 1882. At the time Japan was in the midst of a 50-year transformation from a semi-feudal to an industrial nation initiated by the restored Meiji emperor to catch up with Western technology. The Osaka Iron Works, producing ships and other heavy equipment, was crucial to Japan's modernization. Hunter said the company should ''conceive and construct everything ourselves.'' This philosophy continues to guide the Hitachi Zosen Corporation.

The Osaka Iron Works's first yard, a six-acre facility with a dock 72 meters long and 11.5 meters wide, could construct wooden and iron ships weighing up to 1,000 tons. The company also produced compound engines and boilers, irrigation pumps, bridges, and other equipment for the rapidly developing Japanese industrial sector there.

In 1900, Osaka Iron Works began operating a second yard, the Sakurajima works, at the mouth of the Aji River to build ships weighing over 1,000 tons. A passenger-cargo ship, the 1,568-gross-ton *Taigi Maru,* was the first ship launched from the new yard and the first ship weighing over 1,000 tons built by the company. In 1908, Osaka Iron Works launched the first tanker built in Japan; its 531-gross-ton *Tora Maru* joined the Standard Oil fleet.

Hunter married a Japanese woman and changed his name to Hanta. In 1915, his son and successor Ryutaro Hanta, successfully completed a licensing agreement to use the Isherwood method to build ships. The technique, which originated in Great Britain, significantly reduced both costs and construction time.

As Japan's industrial capacity developed, its shipping needs expanded. The Osaka Iron Works acquired other facilities to meet the demand, including the Innoshima Shipyard in 1911, the Bingo Dockyard in 1919, Harada Shipbuilding Works in 1920, and the Hikojima Dockyard in 1924.

The Osaka Iron Works also produced a number of notable engineering works outside of shipbuilding during the early decades of the 20th century. The company began providing equipment to the hydroelectric industry in 1924, when it received its first order for water gates for a dam. In 1926 the Otabashi Bridge, which is still in use, was built in Gifu Prefecture using a new cable erection method pioneered by the company.

In the 1930s militant nationalists who encouraged aggression in Asia increasingly influenced the government. Japan secretly began augmenting its navy, in violation of treaties it held with Britain and the United States. In 1931 Japan invaded Manchuria, setting up a puppet regime called Manchukuo, and by 1937 Japan was at war with China. In 1941 Japan attacked the United States, precipitating U.S. entry into World War II.

Much of Japan's military success came as a result of its powerful modern navy. A number of old merchant ships built by Osaka Iron Works, known as Hitachi Shipbuilding after 1934, were converted to naval use. While most of the large ships were built by Hitachi's competitors like Mitsubishi, Ishikawajima, Kawasaki, Mitsui, and Harima, the company did produce smaller vessels designed for military use including minesweepers, large landing craft, and *Maru-Yu* series transport submarines. Hitachi also built at least one aircraft transport ship with a flight deck for the army, the *Kumano Maru.* The 465-foot vessel was launched at Innoshima in January 1945.

In 1943, Hitachi opened the Kanagawa works and acquired Mukaishima Shipyard. The company changed its name to Hitachi Shipbuilding and Engineering that year. After the war, the U.S. occupation forces reorganized defense-related industries. Despite serious bomb damage at its shipyards during the war, Hitachi began building fishing and coastal transport ships almost immediately.

While other industries received government assistance to rebuild in the 1950s, the shipbuilding industry was left on its own. Japanese shipbuilders like Hitachi had to be flexible to survive—management sometimes put high-level engineers to work on the assembly line to fill orders on time. The industry developed extremely efficient methods to compete with European shipyards, and Japanese rock-bottom prices and top quality increased foreign orders. By 1955, Japan was the greatest shipbuilding nation in the world, and Hitachi was one of the busiest shipbuilders in Japan. Political uncertainties in the Middle East after the Suez Canal was closed temporarily in 1956 forced oil producers to seek economical means of bypassing the canal. Japanese shipbuilders were ready to meet the demand for larger oil tankers.

Meanwhile, Hitachi Shipbuilding and Engineering also entered other areas. In 1957 the company built the world's largest diesel engine with B&W Diesel of Denmark. In 1964 the company built its first full-scale turnkey plant, a chemical-fertilizer plant for the Gujarat State Fertilizer Company of India, in a record 33 months.

The Japanese shipbuilding boom continued into the 1960s. New technology allowed the construction of bigger ships. By 1966 Hitachi was capable of building ships weighing 250,000 tons, a feat unthinkable only a few years earlier. Technological developments revolutionized the shipbuilder's methods. By the early 1970s Hitachi designed huge 250,000-ton tankers entirely by computer. Ships assembled at the company's Sakai Works used automated machinery to piece together various sections.

Hitachi opened several overseas offices during this period—in New York and London in 1956, Hong Kong in 1960, and Düsseldorf in 1961. With many of its orders for new ships and equipment coming from foreign countries, the Japanese shipbuilding industry was caught by surprise by the 16.9% revaluation of the yen in 1971. Prices for Japanese ships had gone up substantially in recent months, however, and the industry remained optimistic.

Hitachi Shipbuilding and Engineering acquired Maizuru Heavy Industries in 1971, and the Maizuru works became Hitachi's principal naval vessel and equipment production site. A year later, Hitachi opened a branch office in Singapore. In 1973 Hitachi began production at its new Ariake works in Kyushu. The Ariake works had two docks, 630 meters and 360 meters, respectively, and was equipped with state-of-the-art shipbuilding machinery. The facility was capable of producing ships weighing up to 600,000 tons.

The oil crunch of 1973 to 1974 soon crimped Hitachi's growth plans. Reduction in oil shipments eliminated demand for new supertankers and put many ships in mothballs. The glut in shipping capacity precipitated a depression in the industry that would last almost 15 years. Although the new Ariake works had enough large ships on order to keep it active through 1977, new supertanker orders dropped off and Hitachi had to realign its production capabilities. The Ariake works accepted orders to build oil rigs, oil storage tanks, and natural gas storage tanks, and in 1974 the Mukaishima works began specializing in steel structures like bridges, water gates, steel stacks, and pipes.

With about 50% of its turnover continuing to come from shipbuilding, Hitachi was hit hard by declining orders and canceled orders for supertankers as the 1970s went on. Further trouble came when rising material costs reduced the company's profit margin. Hitachi had continued to enter into fixed-price contracts long after European shipbuilders had gone over to flexible contracts. The company recorded a 25% decrease in earnings despite a 28% increase in turnover in 1975. In 1979 the company lost almost ¥11 billion. The industry as a whole addressed declining profits by petitioning the Ministry of Transport (MOT) to subsidize scrapping of redundant facilities. The MOT authorized scrapping 35% of the industry's capacity. In addition, the 39 largest Japanese shipbuilders formed a cartel to voluntarily limit production. Demand hovered under even this limit, and cartel members accepted orders at about 10% below cost in 1980, an improvement over quotes 40% below cost that shipbuilders made to keep the docks from falling idle in preceding years.

Hitachi Shipbuilding and Engineering continued to slim down its work force in the 1980s and to increase nonshipbuilding activities. In 1982 Hitachi's plants and machinery and offshore structures groups accounted for more than half of the company's turnover for the first time. The company changed its name in English to Hitachi Zosen Corporation that year and opened a branch office in Beijing.

In 1986, Hitachi Zosen purchased the Chicago-based Clearing Inc., a company it had licensing agreements with since 1955, for $64 million. Hitachi Clearing produces automotive stamping presses at its facility in Chicago.

Hitachi Zosen undertook a major restructuring in 1986, organizing its units along product lines. At the same time, new pressures on Hitachi Zosen came from the lower prices developing nations offered on heavy equipment and ships. Manufacturers in Korea and Taiwan, paying their workers less, could drastically undercut Hitachi Zosen's bids. The appreciation of the yen against the dollar also hindered growth.

The Japanese Ministry of Transport called for another 20% reduction in excess industry capacity in addition to the 35% cut of 1979, and after reporting a loss of ¥70 billion in 1986, Hitachi Zosen announced plans to eliminate more jobs over the next two years. By 1988 the company employed only 5,596 workers, down from 24,660 ten years earlier. The shipbuilding industry received governmental permission once again to organize a "depression cartel" to set production ceilings and force prices up.

In 1989 the shipbuilding industry finally began to show signs of a real recovery in demand. As a result of increased oil imports to industrialized countries and the gradual aging of the world's oil tankers in general, orders for new ships increased 54% industrywide, and Hitachi Zosen's leaner shipyards were booked solid for two years. The company actually turned some orders away. Even better, analysts expected the demand to remain strong throughout the 1990s.

Historically more marine-dependent than its Japanese competitors, Hitachi Zosen Corporation increased its nonshipbuilding activities in the late 1980s, placing greater emphasis on lines such as steel structures, construction machinery, environmental protection facilities, nuclear power equipment, industrial machinery, prime movers, and plants. This diversity, combined with greater global demand for ships, should provide opportunities for growth to the Hitachi Zosen Corporation.

Principal Subsidiaries: Hitachi Zosen Singapore (Pte.) Ltd.; Hitachi Zosen Engineering Singapore (Pte.) Ltd.; Hitachi Zosen Co. (HK) Ltd. (Hong Kong); Hitachi Zosen Clearing Inc. (U.S.A.); Hitachi Zosen International S.A. (U.K.); Hitachi Zosen U.S.A., Ltd.; P.T. Petrindo Hitachi Zosen (Indonesia); Hitachi Zosen Engineering & Construction Co., Ltd.; Hitachi Zosen Information Systems Co., Ltd.; Ataka Construction & Engineering Co., Ltd.; Toyo Umpanki Co., Ltd.; Hi-System Control Corp.; Naikai Shipbuilding & Engineering Co., Ltd.

Further Reading: "Those Rich, Polluted, Soon-to-be-Automated Japanese," *The Economist*, December 18, 1971; Tanzer, Andrew, "The Japanese Do It Again," *Forbes*, October 16, 1989.

—Thomas M. Tucker

HYUNDAI GROUP

140-142, Chongno-gu
Seoul
Republic of Korea
(02) 746-1114
Fax: (02) 741-2341

Public Company
Incorporated: 1947 as Hyundai Engineering & Construction Company
Employees: 889
Sales: W5.70 trillion (US$8.41 billion)
Stock Exchange: Seoul

Hyundai Corporation is the trading arm of Hyundai Group, one of South Korea's largest *chaebols,* or conglomerates. The corporation integrates the group's sales and marketing strategies, imports natural resources through overseas investment and joint ventures, and provides assistance for overseas operations. The corporation leads the 28 members companies of the group in sales. Since the companies belonging to the Hyundai Business Group are closely linked, the history of Hyundai Corporation must be viewed as part of the story of the group.

Hyundai Business Group has displayed spectacular growth since it was founded in 1947. The group's rapid expansion to a point where its interests include car manufacture, construction, shipbuilding, electronics, and financial services, reflect the achievements attained during South Korea's economic miracle.

The company has grown to a formidable strength in several areas, and its rise to prominence in the construction, shipbuilding, and automotive sectors has taken the world by surprise. The specialized divisions are now run as independent affiliated companies.

Hyundai's growth was linked inextricably to South Korea's reconstruction programs following World War II and the Korean War, and to the state-led capitalism which resulted in a polarization of the country's corporate structure and the domination of the economy by a number of conglomerates. World War II left the country devastated, and the small recovery Korea had been able to make following this conflict was reversed during the Korean War, which lasted from 1950 to 1953.

The *chaebols,* which are similar to Japan's *zaibatsu,* worked with the government in rebuilding the economy, and formed an integral part of Korea's economic strategy and its drive, through a series of development plans, to build up its industrial base.

One man, Ju Jung Chung, has been at the center of Hyundai's progress since 1950. Chung, honorary chairman in 1990, left school at an early age and developed what has been described as an autocratic and unconventional management style. He noted those areas of industry which the government had selected as crucial to economic development and structured the group accordingly. His son, Seyoung Chung, had taken over as chairman, but his father, in the 1990s, still exercised considerable influence.

The foundation of Hyundai was laid before the Korean War, in 1947, when Chung set up Hyundai Engineering & Construction Company. The company was involved in the early stages of the country's recovery following World War II. After the Korean conflict, development intensified, and Hyundai was quick to take on a key role, working on civil and industrial projects, as well as housing programs.

In 1958 it set up Keumkang Company to make construction materials and four years later, when the first of Korea's five-year development plans was launched, Hyundai was well placed to win a range of infrastructure contracts. This plan and its successors aimed to lay the foundations for an independent economy by targeting sectors of industry for expansion.

Against this background Hyundai expanded its construction and engineering operations as the economy's momentum increased. In 1964 it completed the Danyang Cement plant which in 1990 produced well over one million tons of cement. In 1965 the company undertook its first overseas venture with a highway-construction project in Thailand. Hyundai expanded rapidly overseas, developing a market with particular success in the Middle East. Its projects in this region included the US$931 million Jubail industrial harbor project in Saudi Arabia.

In 1967 the group took one of its most significant steps, setting up the Hyundai Motor Company, and thus sowing the seed for what was to become the country's leading domestic car manufacturer. Initially the company assembled Ford Cortina cars and Ford trucks.

Two years later Hyundai took another step abroad with the establishment of Hyundai America, incorporated in Los Angeles, to work on housing complexes and other civil projects. In 1970 it further enhanced its position in the construction sector by setting up Hyundai Cement Company to deal with increased demand at home and overseas.

Towards the end of the 1960s the government had begun to promote the heavy and chemical industries. Oil and steel were both targeted. The planners then turned their attention to the consumption of indigenous steel and focused on shipbuilding, which was then relatively backward, producing only coastal and fishing vessels, and on the automotive industry. The ambitious plans for these industries were to be of great significance both to Hyundai and the nation as a whole, and the 1970s proved to be a period of rapid development.

Hyundai's entry into shipbuilding was to provide the country with a sharp increase in shipbuilding capacity and eventually take Korea's shipbuilding industry to second position in the world, behind Japan. In 1971 Chung decided to begin shipbuilding, and by the following year the company's shipyard had held its ground-breaking ceremony in Mipo Bay, Ulsan, on the southeastern tip of the Korean peninsula. In the following year, the yard was incorporated as Hyundai Shipbuilding and Heavy Industries Company.

The Ulsan yard was still at the planning stage when Hyundai won its first contract, for two oil tankers, from Livanos, a Greek shipowner. The order paved the way to a loan from Barclays Bank of the United Kingdom. Chung had to borrow capital from foreign banks to build the yard which was opened in 1974. In the following year, the Hyundai Mipo Dockyard Company was set up to do conversions and repairs.

This sector developed rapidly throughout the 1970s but the group was hit by the first oil crisis and the consequent decline in demand for large tankers. However Hyundai quickly won four orders for large tankers from the Japanese, its main competitors, and concluded technical cooperation deals with Kawasaki Heavy Industries of Japan and Scott Lithgow of the United Kingdom. Before the market collapsed, 12 large tankers were built at the yards.

This collapse forced Hyundai to turn to the building of medium-sized vessels. It also took steps to remain abreast of technological developments in the industry and to develop spin-offs. In 1975 Hyundai Shipbuilding and Heavy Industries created an industrial-plant and steel-fabrication division and in the following year began to produce marine engines, carrying famous names such as Sulzer and B&W.

A further collaboration was clinched in 1977 with Siemens, of West Germany, which led to the creation of the electrical-engineering division. In the following year, the company changed its name to Hyundai Heavy Industries Company (HHI) to reflect its diverse operations. At the same time it incorporated its engine and electrical engineering divisions into Hyundai Engine and Machinery Company and Hyundai Electrical Engineering Company, respectively.

One of the most significant moves in Hyundai's relatively short history was made in 1975, when the group began constructing an integrated car factory, adjacent to its heavy-industry complex at Ulsan. It was to be the foundation of Korea's largest auto company, one which was to dominate Korea's home and export markets. By the late 1980s UBS Phillips and Drew Global Research Group ranked Hyundai 13th in the world auto industry, with the production of 819,000 vehicles and 1.9% of the world retail market.

The aim of this ambitious project was to move away from car assembly only and to produce, with government backing, a Korean car, a four-seat sedan called the Hyundai Pony. To this end, it called on overseas expertise and finance, a policy used not only by Hyundai but by other Korean industrial groups as well.

George Turnbull, a former managing director of British Leyland, who was then vice president of Hyundai Motors, was in charge of the project. The car was styled by the well-known Italian designer, Giorgetto Giugiaro, was powered by a Mitsubishi Motor engine, and used French and U.K. components. The project was financed largely by U.K., French, and Japanese sources.

The vehicle was launched in 1975. By the following year, Hyundai was producing 30,000 cars, and by 1979 the total had risen to 110,000. Although Hyundai could sell every vehicle it produced in the protected home market, it soon sought to attack export markets by reserving approximately one-fifth of its production for overseas sale.

The company first tested the European market, and its potential for sophisticated markets, by setting up a network of dealers in the Benelux countries, where there were no dominant local manufacturers.

Other areas of the group saw intense activity throughout the 1970s. In 1975 Dongsu Industrial Company, a construction-material manufacturer, was created, followed in the same year by Seohan Development Company, a welding and electrode carbide maker.

Since it was so heavily reliant upon exports and several essential imports, the group in 1976 set up Hyundai Corporation, its trading arm. At the same time it created Hyundai Merchant Marine Company, which concentrated on cargo services, chartering, brokerage, and related services. The trading arm has proved to be an important source of revenue, and has grown into one of the country's top exporters.

In the same year, on the construction side, Hyundai formed Koryeo Industrial Development Company and Hyundai Housing and Industrial Development Company, whose operations included construction design and property development.

Hyundai Precision & Industry Company was created in 1977. Its activities include auto parts, container manufacture, and locomotive parts.

A year later, the group turned its hand to the timber industry with the formation of Hyundai Wood Industries Company, which makes wood products and furniture. In 1978, the group expanded its heavy and chemical industries to include iron and steel manufacture, when it absorbed Incheon Iron & Steel Company and Aluminum of Korea.

The 1980s brought problems for HHI. Two of its key businesses, shipbuilding and overseas construction, the development of which had been actively encouraged by the government in the 1970s, encountered worldwide decline during the decade. Korean shipbuilders saw new export orders in 1985 slump to only US$522 million, compared with US$2.3 billion the year before, while profits plummeted. Overseas construction orders also fell away quickly after reaching a peak of more than US$13 billion in 1981 and 1982.

In both cases, Korean industry had to discard its policy of growth at any price. There were job cuts and a move towards more sophisticated projects such as industrial plant construction, and improved technology, especially to meet the Japaneses challenge. In addition the company had to contend with damaging strikes, which hit its shipyards and other parts of the group, notably the car factories. HHI instituted major productivity improvements at the beginning of the decade and stepped up its diversification with the creation of the Offshore & Steel Structure Division in 1980.

Through this division it launched a major drive into the offshore market, into which it had broken in the late 1970s with orders for the Jubail project in Saudi Arabia. The division initially operated one yard, but, as demand increased, a second was added in 1983.

In 1982 HHI took over three dry docks from Hyundai Mipo Dockyard, which brought the total it operated to seven. Hyundai Mipo, which looked after the company's ship repair and conversion business, was reorganized and moved to a new repair yard two kilometers away from HHI.

A year later, HHI undertook further reorganization by turning its maritime-engineering division into the special and naval shipbuilding division, which now concentrates on building naval craft such as destroyers, frigates, and patrol boats.

The increased emphasis on new technology and innovation was reflected in the setting up of Hyundai Welding Research Institute in 1983, whose work has since been extended to take in factory automation, and the creation of a research-and-development center, the Hyundai Maritime Research Institute, a year later.

Work continued on developing products such as the new generation of very large crude carriers, the world's first semi-submersible drilling rig, delivered in 1987, and a mixed container-passenger vessel for a Norwegian operator in 1988. The company also broke into the gas-carrier market in 1986.

The latter part of the decade was clouded by strikes, which were to tarnish the Korean shipbuilding industry's image. In addition, the company had to contend with higher wage costs that blunted the competitive edge it had over its Japanese rivals. HHI also became embroiled in a legal wrangle with Sir Yue-Kong Pao's World-Wide Shipping Group in 1988. The dispute was over an order for very large crude carriers, which it had agreed to build in 1986 when the market was in a trough.

The strikes that affected the Ulsan yard in the latter part of the 1980s hit production and sales, and in 1988 HHI was to record its first-ever loss, of W29 billion, on sales which declined slightly to W945 billion, after breaking even the previous year. In 1990 the yard was hit by further strikes, although it managed to land a US$600 million order for ten combination vessels from a Norwegian shipping group.

The 1980s were to prove equally eventful for Hyundai Motor Company. After the oil shock of 1979 the government took steps to protect the industry, which had by then made large investments in plant and equipment. It kept a tight grip on the development of this sector and in 1981 divided the market, restricting Hyundai to car and large commercial vehicle manufacture. These regulations were revised in 1986 following the recovery of the market, and Hyundai was able to resume manufacture of light commercial vehicles.

By the middle of the decade, Hyundai had taken Canada by storm. Its Pony sub-compact vehicle became Canada's top-selling car less than two years after entering the market. Hyundai's sales in Canada, where it was also selling the Stellar, shot from none in December 1983 to 57,500 units in the first nine months of 1985, to top those of Honda and Nissan combined. Total production in 1985 had risen to 450,000.

In 1985 the company announced plans to build a car-assembly plant at Bromont, near Montreal, and at the same time decided to enter the U.S. market. The entry into the U.S. market, begun in 1986, proved an immediate success. Its low-priced Excel model was well received, and of the 302,000 cars exported in that year, 168,000 were sold in the United States, where sales were to increase to 263,000 the following year.

Hyundai's initial success in the United States faded before the end of the decade when sales began to flag. Its problems in its key overseas market were attributed to the lack of new models, increasing competition in the weakened U.S. car market, and the severe strikes that hit the company in the latter part of the 1980s and in 1990.

Hyundai decided to move upmarket with the introduction of the Sonata, a four-door sedan, in late 1988, but initial sales proved disappointing. A year later this car was being manufactured at the Bromont plant, following the opening of the factory in 1989. In the same year Hyundai signed a deal with Chrysler to build 30,000 midsize four-door cars for the U.S. company, starting in 1991. Chrysler is linked to Mitsubishi, which in turn is affiliated with Hyundai, in which it holds a 15% stake.

Hyundai planned to increase production at the Canadian plant to 100,000 by the time the Chrysler deal came into effect. Export sales, which were also hit by the appreciation of the won and the depreciation of the yen, have remained sluggish. Increased wage costs also affected the group but had the advantage of boosting domestic sales which, for the industry as a whole, increased 50% to 356,000 units in 1989.

The group became intent on reducing its dependence on the U.S. markets. By 1990 the domestic market was proving increasingly important to the essentially export-oriented group. Both the car and construction markets were enjoying strong demand at the end of the decade. This situation helped Hyundai Engineering & Construction, like the vehicle operations, to take up the slack created by declining markets abroad, particularly in the Middle East. The group had accumulated experience in a broad range of plant construction, including Korea's first nuclear power plant. Meanwhile exports in the shipbuilding sector were showing a marked improvement.

Hyundai also stepped up its presence in the electronics field, following the creation in 1983 of Hyundai Electronics, to produce semiconductors, telecommunication equipment, and industrial electronic systems. The company, which was centered on industrial markets, was seeking to increase its presence in consumer electronics, despite formidable competition from domestic companies such as Samsung and Goldstar.

The group as a whole has shown itself capable of taking diverse markets by storm and is determined to maintain and expand its markets, not the least by stepping up research-and-development spending. However, the country's drive towards democracy has brought new uncertainties. In the changing economic and political environment the group faces a labor force seeking higher wages, a less competitive currency, and increasing competition in the all-important overseas markets.

Principal Subsidiaries: Hyundai Heavy Industries Co. Ltd; Hyundai Motor Company; Hyundai Engineering and Construction Co. Ltd; Hyundai Corporation; Hyundai Petrochemical Co. Ltd; Inchon Iron and Steel Co. Ltd.

Further Reading: Woronoff, Jon, *Asia's "Miracle" Economies,* Seoul, Si-Sa-yong-o-sa Inc., 1986; James, H., *Korea—An Introduction,* London, Kegan Paul International, 1988; *Hyundai,* Seoul, Hyundai Business Group, [1989].

—Bob Vincent

ILLINOIS TOOL WORKS INC.

8501 West Higgins Road
Chicago, Illinois 60631
U.S.A.
(312) 693-3040
Fax: (312) 399-0324

Public Company
Incorporated: 1915
Employees: 15,700
Sales: $2.17 billion
Stock Exchanges: New York Midwest

In 1912, four Smith brothers advertised for experienced manufacturing workers to help them set up a new business producing metal-cutting tools to serve expanding midwestern industry. With the backing of their wealthy and influential father—Byron Laflin Smith, the founder and president of the Northern Trust Company—the brothers formed Illinois Tool Works in Chicago. The company prospered, especially when World War I and World War II increased demand for its automobile and truck components. Under Smith-family management throughout its history—the family still owns about 40%— Illinois Tool Works (ITW) became known as a company with conservative management and innovative products that made big profits on small items.

Today the company is somewhat changed. ITW management emphasizes acquisitions, even if it means going into debt, more than it did previously. The company remains well managed, and its emphasis on research and development puts it in a good position to take advantage of future opportunities.

In 1857, just 20 years after the city of Chicago was incorporated, Byron Laflin Smith's father set up Merchants' Loan & Trust to help fledgling businesses get off the ground, becoming the first Chicago resident to own a Chicago banking institution. The city's population was approximately trebling each decade as railroads and the Great Lakes made it a transportation and manufacturing center. As the city grew, the corresponding real estate boom made rich men richer. The elder Smith took advantage of all these opportunities to make his family one of the wealthiest and most influential in the Midwest.

After graduating from the University of Chicago, Byron Smith went to work for his father at Merchants' Loan & Trust. Working in the family business did not last long, however; when he was 25 Smith struck out on his own, founding the Northern Trust Company in 1879, which was to become one of the city's premier banking institutions.

A successful man in his own right by the early years of the 20th century, Smith saw other opportunities in the growing city. Through his business connections, Smith realized that there was an increasing need for large-scale production of machine tools for the growing transportation and communication industries. These emerging industries needed more parts than small machine shops could provide, and Smith thought he and his sons Solomon, Harold C., Walter, and Bruce were just the men to fill the need.

In 1912 the Smiths placed their advertisement for experienced manufacturing workers. They chose Frank W. England, Paul B. Goddard, Oscar T. Hegg, and Carl G. Olson to help get Illinois Tool Works off the ground, and Harold and Walter Smith managed the new company. Solomon Smith continued to work at Northern Trust—he succeeded his father as president when Byron died two years later—and Bruce went to work in New York.

In 1915, Harold C. Smith became president of Illinois Tool Works, and Walter and Solomon Smith continued to serve on the board of directors—as did Harold Smith on the board of Northern Trust. Harold built on the company's initial success selling tools to manufacturers, and soon expanded the company's product line into truck transmissions, pumps, compressors, and automobile steering assemblies. While investing heavily in modern plants and equipment, Smith insisted on the conservative financial approach that ITW became known for, maintaining cash reserves and eschewing debt. Under Smith, ITW also became known for producing high-quality products. Smith's strategy served the growing company well when World War I broke out; the war years boosted company profits handsomely.

In 1923 ITW engineered a new product that brought it into a different industry niche. The Shakeproof fastener, the first twisted-tooth lock washer, was to lead ITW into the profitable area of industrial fasteners. Shakeproof became a separate operating division offering a full line of related items, including preassembled washers and screws and thread-cutting screws. Each item in the Shakeproof division's product line sold for an average of less than 1¢ a piece, but ITW took the leadership position in the industry, and its sales volume produced strong profits.

Harold C. Smith died in 1936. He had built ITW into an industry leader in metal-cutting tools, manufacturing components, and industrial fasteners. Smith had also been an industry leader as well, serving as director of both the Illinois Manufacturers Association and the National Association of Manufacturers. After Smith's death, his son, Harold Byron Smith, became president of ITW. The oldest of four boys, Harold B. Smith had joined the company in 1931. Harold B. Smith followed his father's successful, conservative management practices, but he introduced some innovations as well. Smith emphasized research and development, encouraging engineers to develop new products, even outside of ITW's traditional product areas. He also decentralized the company, setting up separate divisions to pursue specific markets. This philosophy, followed by Smith's successors, means forming individual operating units that concentrate only on their own product niche.

Under Harold B. Smith, ITW became known as a problem solver. Its salesmen developed new products to answer customer's specific needs—even when customers had not requested a solution. That practice also led to increased sales.

World War II, like World War I, produced a boom for the company, which by this time manufactured components for almost every type of equipment needed for the war effort. Even the wartime labor shortage could not prevent ITW from increasing its cash reserves.

Smith put some of the company's wartime profit into research and development, leading directly to expansion in the 1950s. One new and profitable area was plastic and combination metal-plastic fasteners. The company already had extensive expertise in the fastener industry with its Shakeproof division. Successful plastics manufacture and marketing led to the formation of another new operating unit, Fastex, in 1955.

Another area of expansion after the war, based in part on ITW's experience with plastics, was into the production of electrical controls and instruments. ITW's Licon division was formed in 1959 to produce electric switches and electromechanical products. ITW became a leader in miniaturizing these components. Its solid-state switches and preassembled switch panels brought the company into the computer and defense industries in addition to increasing sales in its traditional industrial base.

It was clear by this time that Illinois Tool Works was outgrowing its name; it no longer manufactured just tools. Smith set up a separate Illinois Tools division during the 1950s to concentrate on the original cutting-tool business and the company's initials, ITW, became the more frequently used, but unofficial, name for the business as a whole.

ITW's special expertise in gears led to two other developments during the 1950s. The company set up the Illinois Tools Division Gear School in 1958 to train engineers—especially those of customer firms—in the intricacies of gearing. ITW's development of the Spiroid right-angle gear led Smith to found the Spiroid operating unit in 1959 to produce specialty gearing for defense and general industries.

A new opportunity emerged from ITW research and development in the early 1960s. Company engineers had been looking for less bulky, lower-cost packaging for six-packs of beverages than the traditional cardboard boxing. Metal holders cut both the fingers of the customers and, occasionally, the cans they were meant to hold. ITW's increasing familiarity with plastics led to the invention of a flexible plastic collar to hold the cans. This simple patented invention generated substantial savings for beverage makers, from 40% to 60%, according to ITW estimates. It led to the formation of another new operating unit, Hi-Cone, in 1962. In the decades since, plastic drink packaging has virtually replaced cardboard packaging for six-packs. The company's development of a 12-pack holder with a carrying handle promises to be as successful. The six-pack holder has become one of ITW's most important moneymakers, and earnings from the Hi-Cone division offset fluctuations in profits from the company's products that serve heavy industry.

In 1970 Harold B. Smith stepped down from the chairmanship of ITW. By this time ITW was an internationally recognized name. The Smith family's emphasis on decentralized operation meant that many of the company's production facilities were near large overseas customers, often under the control of local subsidiaries in the country where they were located. ITW components supplied heavy industries, the food and beverage industries, and the packaging industries in West Germany, Belgium, Australia, Spain, Italy, France, Great Britain, and New Zealand. The company's performance, however, mirrored the economy and suffered from inflation during decade.

With Smith's retirement, the first non-Smith took the top spot at ITW. Silas S. Cathcart became chairman. Smith's son, Harold B. Smith Jr., was president and chief operating officer from 1972 through 1981, and Smiths continued to serve on the board of directors. Under this leadership, the 1970s saw some new developments despite the sluggish economy. Most notable was ITW's entry into the adhesives industry with the purchase of Devcon Corporation. Devcon was a leader in specialty chemicals and manufactured adhesives and sealants.

When John D. Nichols took over as CEO in 1982, he was determined to keep ITW growing by investing more excess cash in developing new product lines and in making acquisitions, while cutting costs elsewhere to maintain profitability. He kept production costs low, for example, by developing what he termed ''focus factories,'' where a single product is produced in a highly automated setting.

Nichols expanded ITW's industrial tools and systems businesses by purchasing Heartland Components, which makes customized replacement industrial parts, in 1982; Southern Gage, which makes industrial gages and N.A. Woodworth, which makes tool-holding equipment, in 1984; and Magnaflux, which makes nondestructive testing equipment and supplies, in 1985. Nichols formed a separate operating unit for automotive controls in 1983, and a division for producing equipment for offshore geophysical exploration, Linac, in 1984.

In 1986 Nichols made another significant acquisition when he purchased Signode Industries for $524 million. The Glenview, Illinois, company makes plastic and steel strapping for bundling items, as well as sketch film, industrial tape, and other related items. The company fit in well with ITW's own plastics line. Nichols followed tradition by breaking the company down into smaller units, and within a year and a half over 20 new products had been developed as a result of the merger. The Signode acquisition nearly doubled ITW's revenues.

Nichols acquired 27 companies in related product lines for ITW in the 1980s. Only three firms had been purchased before Nichols's tenure. His acquisitions mean that company debt has reached higher levels than in the past. Nevertheless, ITW's earnings have also grown, and analysts expect them to continue to grow.

Principal Subsidiaries: Astermann Pty. Ltd. (Australia); B&L Plastics Inc.; B-Flute Co., Ltd. (Japan); Better Formed Metals Corporation; Cumberland Leasing Co.; Delta Strepping Industries Inc.; Devcon Limited (Ireland); Devcon de Mexico, S.A.; Fixlock A.B. (Sweden); ITW Belgium S.A.; ITW Canada Inc.; ITW Limited (U.K.); ITW-Ateco G.m.b.H. (Germany); ITW de France S.A.; ITW Enterprises Corp.; ITW Fastex Italia S.p.A. (Italy); ITW New Zealand; ITW

Asia (Pte.) Limited (Singapore); ITW International Inc.; ITW Espana S.A. (Spain); ITW Overseas Holdings Inc.; ITW Overseas Investments Corp.; ITW Hi-Cone Holdings (Ireland); ITW Hi-Cone (Ireland); ITW Real Estate II Corp.; ITW SPIT S.p.A. (Italy); ITW Switches Asia Ltd. (Taiwan); Lakeville Corp.; Meritex Plastic Industries; Meritex (PENANG) Sdn. Bhd. (Malaysia); Mima, Inc.; Minigrip, Inc.; N.A. Woodworth Co.; Plastiglide Mfg. Corp.; Paslode GmbH (Germany); Paslode Corp.; Societe de Prospection et D'Invention Techniques (France); Spezial-Produkte Fur Industrie Und TechMik Haandels GmbH (Germany); ITW do Brasil Participacoes Ltda. (Brazil); Ramset Japan; Scanilec B.V. (Netherlands); Shippers Paper Products Co.; Signode B.V. (Netherlands); Signode Bernpak GmbH (Germany); Signode Canada Inc.; Signode Corporation; Signode do Brasil Commercio e Servicos Ltda. (Brazil); Signode Europa G.m.b.H. (Germany); Signode Fasteners Inc. (Canada); Signode Foreign Sales Corp. (Virgin Islands); Signode Hong Kong Ltd.; Signode International Corporation; Signode International Trading Corporation; Signode K.K. (Japan); Signode Overseas Inc. of Illinois; Signode System GmbH (Germany); W.A. Deutsher Pty. Ltd. (Australia); Waterbury Burkle Co.; Waterbury Tag Co.; Industra Products (UK), Ltd.; Micro-Poise Holdings U.S., Inc.; Milhab Road Facility, Inc.; Rans Service, Inc.; Rans Service Ltd. (Japan, 66.5%); Ransburg-Gema Pty. Limited (Australia); Ransburg Automation Limited (Japan); Ransburg Canada Limited; Ransburg Electropainters (Hong Kong) Limited; Ransburg Equipamentos Industriais Ltda. (Brazil, 50%); Ransburg-Gema, Inc.; Ransburg-Gema Limited; Ransburg-Gema AG (Switzerland); Ransburg-Gema GmbH (Germany); Ransburg-Gema KK (Japan, 66.5%); Ransburg-Gema SA (Spain); Ransburg-Gema SA (France); Ransburg-Gema s.r.l. (Italy); Ransburg-Gema Pumpen GmbH (Germany); Ransburg-Gema UK Limited; Ransburg Industrial (Hong Kong) Limited; Ransburg International Corporation; Ransburg Leasing Corporation; Ransburg Manufacturing Corp.; The Simco Company, Inc.; Simco (Europe) B.V. (Netherlands); Simco Japan, Inc. (50%); Simco Nederland BV (Netherlands); Wabash Comercial Ltda (Brazil).

Further Reading: Boorstin, Daniel J., *The Americans: The National Experience,* New York, Vintage Books, 1965; "ITW History," Illinois Tool Works corporate typescript, [1981].

—Ginger G. Rodriguez

Inchcape plc

THE INTERNATIONAL SERVICES AND MARKETING GROUP

INCHCAPE PLC

St. James's House
23 King Street
London SW1Y 6QY
United Kingdom
(071) 321-0110
Fax: (071) 321-0604

Public Company
Incorporated: 1958 as Inchcape & Co. Ltd.
Employees: 46,000
Sales: £2.95 billion (US$4.76 billion)
Stock Exchange: London

Inchcape, which describes itself as an international services and marketing group, was launched as an overseas trading company in 1958, yet the origins of its constituent companies date back to the late 18th and early 19th centuries. With ten core business streams in three key areas, the group operates in 60 countries. During the late 1980s Inchcape consolidated its already strong reputation for expert local marketing on behalf of prestigious principals around the world. The most valuable of these principals is the Toyota Motor Corporation of Japan, for whom Inchcape is the sole distributor for passenger cars in ten countries, including the United Kingdom, Belgium, Greece, Hong Kong, Singapore, Guam, and Brunei. This accounts for some 8% of Toyota's exports worldwide. In April 1990, Toyota paid £110 million cash to Inchcape for a half stake in Toyota (GB), Inchcape's United Kingdom–based distributing business. With this acquisition, Toyota also acquired a holding of nearly 5% in Inchcape itself.

The creation of Inchcape dates back to the early expansion of commerce with India by a group of Scottish merchants. In 1847 a meeting took place in Calcutta between William Mackinnon and Robert Mackenzie, two merchants from Campbeltown, which led to the formation of their general merchanting partnership, Mackinnon Mackenzie & Company. Realizing the benefits of combining trading with ocean transport, especially with the gold rush to Australia in 1851, the business expanded and diversified. In 1856, Mackinnon—aged 34—founded the Calcutta & Burmah Steam Navigation Company, secured from the East India Company the contract for carrying the mails between Calcutta and Rangoon, and incorporated the company in London with a capital of £35,000, of which Mackinnon Mackenzie & Company invested £7,000, becoming agents for the new shipping line. As a result of their success in carrying troops from Ceylon—now Sri Lanka—to India during the Indian Mutiny of 1857 to 1859, and through Mackinnon's contacts with the influential civil servant Sir Henry Bartle Frere, the partners obtained further contracts to support a fleet of coastal steamers carrying mails around the Indian coast with extensions to the Persian Gulf and Singapore. In 1862, C&B raised sufficient additional capital—a total of £400,000—to float the company under the new name of the British India Steam Navigation Company (BI). Mackinnon Mackenzie & Company continued to act as agents for the BI for nearly 100 years.

Sir William Mackinnon also promoted steamer traffic to the Dutch East Indies, establishing a Dutch-registered shipping line around Java, and forming the Netherlands India Steam Navigation Company in 1868. With the opening of the Suez Canal in 1869, BI ships entered the Mediterranean Sea, establishing a trunk line between London and India via the Suez Canal in 1876. In the process, Mackinnon Mackenzie & Company became one of the greatest Eastern agency houses, and the BI posed a mighty challenge to all other shipping lines operating between the United Kingdom and the East, including the giant Peninsular & Oriental Steam Navigation Company (P&O).

These events were the backdrop to the formative years of James Lyle Mackay, created Lord Inchcape in 1911. Born in 1852, the son of an Arbroath shipmaster, Mackay left Scotland at the age of 20 and worked in the customs department of Gellatly, Hankey and Sewell. Mackay, who joined Mackinnon Mackenzie & Company's Calcutta office in 1874, was to become the heir to the Mackinnon businesses after the death of Mackinnon in 1893. Mackay first became a partner after saving the BI's Bombay office from bankruptcy, and was to become president of the prestigious Bengal Chamber of Commerce a record three times between 1890 and 1893. A member of the Viceregal Council and a close friend and confidant of Lord Lansdowne, Viceroy of India, Mackay gained a knighthood for his contribution to the solution of India's currency problems and the ultimate adoption of the gold standard in India. Mackay returned to the United Kingdom in 1894 as a director of the BI, replacing William Mackinnon's nephew, Duncan Mackinnon, as chairman in 1913. Continuing his work on the Council of India, Mackay's growing reputation as an outstanding public servant led to his being offered the viceroyalty of India in 1909. Prime Minister Herbert Asquith opposed Mackay's nomination, however, on the grounds of his commercial interests in the subcontinent, and Mackay was offered a peerage in 1911 by way of compensation. He chose the name of Baron Inchcape of Strathnaver, commemorating the Inchcape Rock, located 12 miles from Arbroath, and expressing his loyalty to the clan Mackay, whose home is in Strathnaver. Between 1913 and 1932, Lord Inchcape personified Britain's shipping industry as chairman of the BI and the P&O, after effecting a merger between the two lines in 1914.

Less well known than Lord Inchcape's shipping activities is his consolidation of an extensive group of commercial interests in India and beyond. These began with his accumulation of shares in Mackinnon Mackenzie & Company. Sir William Mackinnon had no son, his nephew Duncan died in 1914, and his great-nephews were killed in World War I, so

Inchcape became the sole surviving senior partner of the Mackinnon enterprise, and by 1950 the Inchcape family held a controlling interest. Inchcape's chairmanship of the BI and P&O resulted in a very close connection between Mackinnon Mackenzie & Company and the shipping line, to the extent that many observers came to believe that they were one company.

Mackinnon Mackenzie & Company spawned a variety of other enterprises to serve the BI routes. The BI originally employed small private firms in local ports of call as agents, but eventually replaced them with firms within the Mackinnon complex. These all came under the control of the senior partners and ultimately under Lord Inchcape himself. To separate the trading businesses from the shipping line, the Macneill & Barry partnership was developed to take over the extensive tea and merchanting operations that Lord Inchcape had acquired in 1915. Amalgamated in 1949, Macneill & Barry Ltd. comprised three merchant partnerships formed in the second half of the 19th century: Barry & Company, Macneill & Company, and Kilburn & Company, involved in tea, coal, jute, river steamers, and various trading enterprises. Their principals included the Assam Company, the oldest tea company in India; the River Steam Navigation Company; and the India General Steam Navigation and Railway Company. Between 1951 and 1956, Macneill & Barry took over Kilburn & Company, and the three groups set up Pakistan-based companies. In 1965 the two river steamer businesses were sold to the government of India.

In 1906, Mackay made a successful strategic acquisition, of Binny's, a south-India-based textile business. Founded in 1799, Binny's originally carried out banking and general merchanting, diversifying in the 1840s into agriculture and textiles. Indian production of textiles boomed in the 1860s, when the U.S. Civil War interrupted cotton supplies, and by the late 19th century Binny's mills managed 70,000 spindles with over 1,500 looms. Yet in 1906, with the crash of the great Arbuthnot & Company banking house with whom it was closely involved, Binny's faced bankruptcy. Its greatly undervalued assets were acquired by Mackay and a consortium of Mackinnon partners for £53,000. Binny & Company Ltd., as it had become in 1906, made record profits in World War I with the production of khaki cloth, and by 1917 was supplying over a million yards per month. Binny & Company was subsequently restructured, setting up an engineering department, and rose to greater prominence during World War II, producing one billion yards of cloth a year by 1942.

Owing to the need to supply shipping-agency services to the BI, Mackinnon group enterprises were established in east Africa, the Persian Gulf, Australia, and London. In east Africa, as Sir William Mackinnon began to open up the region to British influence, the BI operated a steam shipping service. In 1872, an agency was established by Archibald Smith, a member of the staff of William Mackinnon & Company, in Glasgow, together with a Mackenzie man from Calcutta, operating as BI agents and general traders. In 1887, Sir William won from the sultan of Zanzibar the right to administer a coastal strip of land in return for customs revenue, which led to the founding of the Imperial British East Africa Company (IBEA), partly in response to the build-up of German interests in this area. Smith Mackenzie took a stake in IBEA and acted as its agents, until the charter was surrendered in 1897. Smith Mackenzie & Company and the agency for Shell in east Africa became joint coaling agents to the admiralty during World War I and in the 1930s gained the agencies for British American Tobacco, Imperial Chemical Industries, and British Overseas Airways Corporation.

In 1862, when a contract was won to carry mails eight times a year up and down the Persian Gulf, the merchant partnership which became Gray Mackenzie & Company was formed, helping to develop navigation on the Euphrates and Tigris rivers, and establishing a diversified trading business in an area that was also facing German expansionism. In World War II, Gray Mackenzie & Company acted as agents for the British government in unloading military cargoes; the growth of its business was helped by the spectacular development of the oil industry and the rapidly growing need to service the expanding ports of the Middle East.

The Mackinnon complex also branched into Australia, with BI services at first managed by the British India and Queensland Agency Company Ltd. The Mackinnon partners invested in the formation of a major Australian shipping conglomerate in 1887, the Australasian United Steam Navigation Company (AUSN), formed with a capital of £600,000. In 1894 Mackay was appointed to the Board of the AUSN and, in 1900, spent several months in Australia successfully restructuring the business. In 1915, he created a new merchant partnership, Macdonald Hamilton & Company, formed by two trusted Mackinnon appointees, B. W. Macdonald and David Hamilton. The AUSN, which had once owned 42 steamers, declined in the face of increasing competition from railways in the 1920s, and Macdonald Hamilton & Company diversified its activities into mining, pastoral management, and operating the P&O agencies in Australia. The P&O acquired Macdonald Hamilton's P&O-related activities in 1959 and 1960.

The London partnership of Gray Dawes & Company was set up to serve the BI as a shipping and broking agency, and eventually became a bank and a travel agency. It represented the interests of Smith Mackenzie & Company and Binny & Company in London, and set up a secretarial department to administer the estate of James Mackay, the first earl of Inchcape, after his death in 1932.

These diverse Mackinnon group interests were consolidated and reorganized during the 1950s, coming together as Inchcape & Company Ltd. in 1958 at the initiative of the third Earl of Inchcape. Tax considerations necessitated the conversion of these companies into private limited companies—whose former partners became the principal shareholders—controlled through London-based subsidiaries. Also in 1958, Inchcape & Company became a public company through a public offering of 25% of its equity, and since 1958 has embarked on a program of growth and diversification, principally through acquisitions. The group today reflects the merger and acquisition activities of the last quarter century far more than it represents the original companies which came together in 1958.

The original Inchcape companies—Gray Dawes, Binny & Company, Gray Mackenzie, Smith Mackenzie, Duncan Macneill, Macneill & Barry, the AUSN, and Mackinnon Mackenzie itself—have now been eclipsed in importance by the development of the companies since acquired. In India, the remaining Inchcape businesses have been consolidated into the Assam Company Limited, now one of the largest tea groups in the subcontinent, and 74%-owned by Inchcape. In 1989, the Indian businesses contributed £24 million of group turnover and 3.2% of group profits. The East African businesses of the group have been sold due to declining profitability and political problems, but in the Middle East, Gray Mackenzie contributed £4.3 million towards group turnover in 1989 and 2.6% of group profits. Macdonald Hamilton & Company in Australia has been sold, but Inchcape's new businesses in Australasia contribute £8.1 million to group turnover, and 0.9% to group profit. Gray Dawes has also left the group. Gray Dawes Bank was sold in the early 1980s, and Gray Dawes Travel was acquired by its management in the late 1980s.

During the 1960s and 1970s, under the leadership of the third Earl of Inchcape, the company expanded to over 150 times its previous capitalization, due principally to a series of successful acquisitions, especially those of the Borneo Company in 1967, Gilman & Company in 1969, Dodwell & Company in 1972, Mann Egerton & Company in 1973, Anglo-Thai Corporation in 1975, A.W. Bain Holdings in 1976, and Pride & Clarke, which held the Toyota agency for the United Kingdom, in 1978. In this period, through several capitalization issues, 64 original shares costing £80 in total in 1958 were worth nearly £2,000 by 1975.

The merger with the Borneo Company almost doubled the size of Inchcape overnight, bringing in new interests in Canada, the Caribbean, Hong Kong, Malaysia, Singapore, Brunei, and Thailand. The Borneo Company operated jointly with Inchcape in the United Kingdom and Australia, but introduced two new activities into the group's portfolio, motor vehicle distribution and timber and construction business. This merger, in which Inchcape entered new geographical regions in familiar businesses and entered new businesses in regions which it knew well—allowing considerable local autonomy to existing local staff—established a pattern for subsequent acquisitions, and Inchcape gained a reputation in the City for being a fair and honorable operator.

Through Peter Heath, originally a director of the Borneo Company, Inchcape acquired Gilman & Company, one of the great trading groups of Hong Kong. Gilman & Company was seeking an acquirer but did not wish to be taken over by an existing Hong Kong business. The acquisition of Dodwell & Company gave the group further interests in this region, which it maintained as quasi-independent companies, rather than forming one large entity. Dodwell & Company was founded in Shanghai in 1858, and by the 1970s had established extensive businesses in shipping, motors, and business-machine trading in Hong Kong, Japan, and many other Far Eastern ports and cities.

Mann Egerton, acquired in 1973, laid the foundations for Inchcape's now extensive motor-distribution business. Founded at the end of the 19th century in Norwich by an electrical engineer and an early motoring pioneer, Mann Egerton sold cars manufactured by de Dion, Renault, and Daimler for between £200 and £300 per car, at the turn of the century initially from branches in the eastern counties of England. By the 1970s, Mann Egerton distributed British Leyland cars, as well as an extensive range of luxury cars, but faced a possible takeover bid from an unwanted source, and felt increasingly vulnerable as a result of a wave of oil shocks.

The acquisition of Anglo-Thai Corporation involved the issue of nearly nine million Inchcape £1 ordinary shares, three times the number issued before, increasing Inchcape's market value by about 90%, and adding to group assets in the Far East and Southeast Asia. In one of the group's few predatory bids, valuable businesses such as Caldbeck Macgregor & Company, a well-known importer and distributor of wines and spirits, were included. In 1976, with A. W. Bain Holdings, Inchcape developed an important insurance business through a share issue second only to that involved in acquisition of the Anglo-Thai Corporation. With Pride & Clarke, the group gained the valuable concession of exclusive Toyota distribution in the United Kingdom after an issue of £1 millions in £1 ordinary shares and £6.9 million in cash, in what some observers called the biggest bargain of the century. In 1989, motors contributed two-thirds of group turnover and 53.6% of group profits, the greater part contributed by Toyota.

Inchcape—reincorporated as Inchcape PLC in 1981—under the chairmanship of Sir George Turnbull, is reinforcing concentration on its core businesses. Inchcape's key businesses lie in three main areas: services, marketing and distribution, and resources. The service businesses consist of buying, insurance, inspection and testing, and shipping. The marketing and distribution businesses cover business machines, consumer and industrial services, and motors. The resource-based businesses cover tea and timber. Fiscal 1989 results saw an increase of profits before tax of 19%—from £148 million to £176 million; earnings per share were up 17%, and dividends per share were up 19%. Turnbull announced in *The Daily Telegraph* that "we have continued to grow in our main business activities, and we have maintained our programme of capital investment in our business streams and the main thrust of that investment is to ensure that we are building up a company that will continue to grow in the long term." Inchcape was considered to have produced good results in spite of political uncertainty in Hong Kong and despite increasingly difficult conditions in the U.K. car market.

Inchcape earns more than half its profits in the Far East and Southeast Asia and from the motor business. Analysts, commenting on Inchcape's outlook for the future, consider that its deal with Toyota will prove highly advantageous in the later 1990s, and might offset uncertainties in Hong Kong. This preoccupation with the Far East and with motors is a far cry from Inchcape's position in 1958, when most of its assets lay in India and the Middle East. Inchcape has transformed effectively from a series of colonial trading partnerships to a modern services and marketing organization, yet it relies heavily on its long-established roots in distant markets for its strong reputation for specialist expertise and local market knowledge.

Principal Subsidiaries: The Motor & Engineering Company of Ethiopia Ltd. (94%); Williamson Balfour SA (Chile); Caldbeck MacGregor (Australia) Limited; Inchcape Pacific Limited (Hong Kong); Dodwell & Company (Japan); Atkins Kroll Inc. (Guam); The Assam Company Limited (India, 74%); Gray Mackenzie & Company; Inchcape Berhad (Singapore, 63%); The Borneo Company Private Limited (Singapore, 63%); Borneo Motors Singapore Private Limited (65%);

The Borneo Company (Thailand); International Motor Company SA (Belgium); Toyota Hellas SA (Greece); Bain Clarkson Limited; Gellatly Hankey & Co. Limited; Mann Egerton and Company Limited; Toyota (GB) Limited; Inchcape Inspection and Testing Services Limited.

Further Reading: Griffiths, P.J., *A History of the Inchcape Group,* London, Inchcape & Company Ltd., 1977; Jones, Stephanie, *Two Centuries of Overseas Trading: The Origins and Growth of the Inchcape Group,* London, Macmillan, 1986; Jones, Stephanie, *Trade and Shipping: Lord Inchcape 1852–1952,* Manchester, Manchester University Press, 1989; *Inchcape Company Pamphlet,* London, Inchcape Corporate Affairs Department, 1990; Griffiths, P.J., *A History of the Joint Steamer Companies,* London, Inchcape & Co. Ltd. [n.d.].

—Stephanie Jones

INGERSOLL-RAND COMPANY

200 Chestnut Ridge Road
Woodcliff Lake, New Jersey 07675
U.S.A.
(201) 573-0123
Fax: (201) 573-3319

Public Company
Incorporated: 1905
Employees: 31,623
Sales: $3.45 billion
Stock Exchanges: New York London Amsterdam

Ingersoll-Rand Company grew out of the efforts of four late-19th-century inventors. Simon Ingersoll, a farmer and inventor, patented a rock drill in 1871, then sold the rights to his patent; Henry Clark Sergeant improved upon Ingersoll's drill and convinced businessman Jose F. de Navarro to invest in the idea; William Lawrence Saunders developed many diversified forms of the rock drill; and Addison Crittenden Rand also improved rock drills. Rand also was successful in persuading mining companies to substitute the new technology for the traditional hammer and chisel.

In 1870 inventor Simon Ingersoll, who worked at truck farming to support his family, accepted a contractor's commission to develop a drill that would work on rock. Ingersoll worked on the invention in a New York machine shop owned by entrepreneur Jose F. de Navarro. He received a patent on the rock drill in 1871, but the new tool did not stand up to New York's rocky streets.

Henry Clark Sergeant, one of the partners in the machine shop, made an important change in the drill design. He separated the front head from the cylinder, since a drill in two pieces could better resist breakage. Sergeant then persuaded de Navarro to buy Ingersoll's patent, and de Navarro organized the Ingersoll Rock Drill Company in 1874, with Sergeant as its first president. Ingersoll, who was forced to sell most of his patents and work halfheartedly at farming to feed his family, died nearly destitute in 1894.

Henry Clark Sergeant, however, was able to turn ideas into profitable businesses. Sergeant had been inventing since he was a teenager, and had secured his first patent when he was 20. In 1868, at the age of 34, he had arrived in New York City where he started a machine shop that specialized in developing the ideas of other inventors. As the business grew, he took a partner and moved into de Navarro's shop. After de Navarro formed the Ingersoll Rock Drill Company, Sergeant worked for several years to improve Ingersoll's drill by using compressed air rather than steam to operate it.

In 1885 Sergeant developed a completely different rock drill and formed the Sergeant Drill Company to manufacture it. In 1888 he merged the two companies, becoming president of the Ingersoll-Sergeant Rock Drill Company. After several years he became a director and devoted himself to inventing.

At the same time Ingersoll was patenting his rock drill in 1871, Addison Crittenden Rand moved to New York City from Massachusetts. Rand's brother, Alfred T. Rand, had been instrumental in founding the Laflin & Rand Powder Company, a mining firm. Addison Rand had formed the Rand Drill Company to develop a rock drill and air-compressing machinery for his brother's company. Rand's firm developed the Little Giant tappet drill and the Rand Slugger drill and marketed them effectively, convincing mining companies to switch from hammer and chisel to rock drills with air compressors.

Rand was known for his paternalistic approach to business. He carefully selected his employees and trained them for skilled positions. Rand avoided unions, and was personally affronted when employees at his Tarrytown, New York, plant struck in 1886. The plant was shut down for a year before Rand would agree to a settlement.

In 1905 Michael P. Grace—a brother of William R. Grace, who founded W. R. Grace & Company—brought Ingersoll-Sergeant Drill Company and the Rand Drill Company together. The two companies had specialized in slightly different segments of the drill market—Ingersoll-Sergeant specialized in construction work while Rand focused on underground mining—and their interests were complementary. The new company was incorporated as the Ingersoll-Rand Company (I-R) in June 1905 and billed itself as "the largest builder of air power machinery in the world." The Grace family owned the largest single block of stock, and a Grace has served on the I-R board ever since.

William Lawrence Saunders became the first president of the company. Saunders, an engineer, had developed a compressed-air drilling apparatus for subaqueous use while in his 20s. The widely used invention made development of Russia's Baku oil fields possible. Saunders had inspected an underwater rock drilling and blasting project himself, diving down to it so he could design a subaqueous drill appropriate for the job. He was active in engineering societies, and established an award given by the American Institute of Mining and Metallurgical Engineers to recognize achievements in mining methods. He also established *Compressed Air*, the company's industrial trade journal, in 1896 and served as its editor. In addition, Saunders was a two-time mayor of North Plainfield, New Jersey.

As president of Ingersoll-Rand, Saunders expanded upon the company's original line of rock drills and air compressors. He promoted development of diverse types of these machines. He also led Ingersoll-Rand into related areas of the tool business. I-R expanded into pneumatic tools in 1907 by acquiring the Imperial Pneumatic Tool Company of Athens, Pennsylvania. In 1909 the company bought the A.S. Cameron Steam Pump Works and entered the industrial pump business. In 1913 he added centrifugal pumps to I-R's product list. Under Saunders I-R also acquired the J. George Leyner

Engineering Works Company. This firm had developed a small, hammer-type drill that could be operated by one man. I-R began to began to produce the jackhammer in 1913, and it quickly became a popular item.

Saunders moved to the board of directors in 1913 and was replaced as president by George Doubleday. Doubleday was determined to make Ingersoll-Rand the leader in its product areas—drills, air compressors, jackhammers, pneumatic tools, and industrial pumps. Doubleday led Ingersoll-Rand for 42 years.

Doubleday carefully adhered to the principles that Saunders had used to guide the company, using Ingersoll-Rand's four major plants in Phillipsburg, New Jersey; Easton and Athens, Pennsylvania; and Painted Post, New York, to handle increasing business. In these locations, I-R was the major employer. Community life centered on the firm: many workers lived in company-owned houses, and community and school events were held in company buildings. Doubleday hired boys off the farm and trained them to become skilled machinists through a seven-year apprenticeship. These artisans accepted the company's credo of pride in personal work, and only a handful of quality-control specialists were needed. Doubleday charged a premium price for the high-quality machinery this system produced.

Little is known about the company itself under Doubleday or about Doubleday's personal life—he refused even release a photograph of himself to the press—and he provided a bare minimum of information about Ingersoll-Rand. Under Doubleday the company never released a quarterly report and its annual report was a single folded sheet of paper containing only the figures the New York Stock Exchange required.

Advances were made in the firm's products during the Doubleday years, however. In 1933 I-R introduced a new portable-compressor line, which was improved during the 1950s with the introduction of the revolutionary sliding-vane rotary portable unit. Ingersoll-Rand began to compete in the "big drill" field in 1947, when it introduced the Quarrymaster, which was used in quarrying, open-pit mining, and excavation. A self-propelled jumbo drill, the Drillmaster, was introduced in 1953, followed by the Downhole drill in 1955. Doubleday also purchased General Electric's centrifugal-compressor business in 1933, to become the leader in that sector of the business. In 1948 the company designed the first natural gas transmission centrifugal compressors.

When Doubleday retired in 1955 Ingersoll-Rand was indeed on sound financial footing. The company had over $100 million in cash and no debt. With an operating profit margin of 37% and a net profit margin of 19%, it had paid a dividend every year since 1910, and return on stockholders' equity was 23%.

Doubleday had reached those impressive numbers, however, by abandoning the marketing orientation that he had originally brought to the job. By the end of his tenure he was 89 years old, and had become too conservative. The company's capital was the result of Doubleday's unwillingness to upgrade the company's plants to keep manufacturing costs low; to promote research and development to retain I-R's technological edge; or to maintain sufficient foreign parts inventory to keep equipment running overseas. He also eschewed diversification outside of I-R's basic product lines.

Doubleday died in 1955, and an interim management team followed his policies for another four years. Robert H. Johnson was named chairman of the company in 1959. At 58, Johnson had spent 35 years with the company he had joined as a salesman.

Johnson cut the company's premium prices to remain competitive. He also spent $25 million to increase parts inventories abroad, and thereby doubled sales overseas in five years; invested in research to promote a return to technological leadership; and increased spending for plant and equipment from an approximate average of $2 million a year to $15 million in 1965. Johnson put the company's excess cash—over 65% of I-R's total assets in 1966—to work through a policy of careful acquisitions. He invested, for example, in Lawrence Manufacturing Company, which specialized in producing mechanical moles for urban underground utility tunneling.

Johnson's successor as CEO, 52-year-old William L. Wearly, gave those policies new momentum. Wearly, who took the top position in 1967, was the first leader at Ingersoll-Rand who had not grown up with the company, another sign that it was leaving its conservative past behind. Wearly came to I-R as a consultant in 1962 after leaving the presidency at Joy Manufacturing. With Wearly came a new generation of managers: President D. Wayne Hallstein was 49, while the four newest vice presidents were under 44. The youth of the new management team was no accident; Johnson had decided that managers who were over 55 had been too thoroughly indoctrinated in the Doubleday method of doing business and bypassed them completely.

Wearly reaped the advantages of Johnson's investment in plant and equipment, which allowed Ingersoll-Rand to increase sales—especially abroad—because of increased manufacturing capacity. Wearly also increased capacity through overseas acquisitions in England, Italy, Canada, South Africa, and Australia.

Wearly then took Ingersoll-Rand into new, diversified areas to help offset the cyclical nature of the capital-goods market. The acquisition of The Torrington Company in 1968, which brought needle and roller bearings, knitting needles, metal-forming machines, universal joints, and roller clutches to the company catalog, was especially important. So was Wearly's 1974 acquisition of the Schlage Lock Company, which produces locks, door hardware, and home and business security devices. Both acquisitons have been consistent moneymakers for I-R.

Wearly had clearly moved away from the company's tradition of operating paternalistic plants in small towns. By the early 1960s Ingersoll-Rand operated 36 plants in the United States and 17 abroad. One of them, its Roanoke, Virginia, plant, became the first factory in the country to use computerized direct numerical control of a production line. The plant used a computer to run machine tools and to automatically move parts from one tool to another on conveyer belts without human assistance. The new Roanoke facility took over much of the capacity of the old Athens, Pennsylvania, plant, which had been crippled by strikes and rising labor costs. In 1959 the company had threatened to leave Athens if the union did not make significant concessions on work methods, and Ingersoll-Rand had won the new five-year contract it wanted. A decade later those union concessions were not forthcoming, and the Athens plant was substantially bypassed—by a mechanized system instead of by other workers.

Wearly's policies seemed destined to pay off in the early 1970s, when factors like the search for new energy sources, Mideastern oil money, growing East-West trade, and Third World industrialization led to increased demand for almost all Ingersoll-Rand products. Five years later, the boom turned into a bust. Capital spending had slowed after the energy crisis of 1973. Coal and railroad strikes hurt the company because it was still a major supplier of coal-mining machinery. Wearly said that President Jimmy Carter's human rights emphasis hurt business in the Soviet Union and Brazil. All of these factors left Ingersoll-Rand with too much capacity and too much inventory.

Wearly retired in 1980 and Thomas Holmes, a 30-year employee, took over as CEO. Holmes convinced Clyde Folley, a member of Price Waterhouse's governing board who had worked on the Ingersoll-Rand account, to become chief financial officer. The two executives faced the global recession and resulting fall in earnings and sales, especially of oil-drilling and construction equipment.

The company closed 30 production plants and cut staff by one-third. The company's tight cash supply was spent only in the areas where returns were highest—bearings, locks, and tools—not on the traditional focus of the company—engineered equipment, coal-mining equipment, and air compressors. Holmes and Folley tied management compensation to return on assets instead of sales to promote more efficient asset use, and centralized inventory controls.

Holmes, Folley, and Theodore Black then initiated joint ventures with competitors. One of the most important of these ventures is Dresser-Rand, a 50-50 partnership formed in 1986 with Dresser Industries, another major mining- and oil-equipment company. In 1987 I-R formed another joint venture in mining with B.R. Simmons. Folley said the joint ventures allowed the company to cut staff and losses while competing more effectively with Japanese and West German companies. Pooling talent also helps the firms stay current technologically. By the end of the 1980s Dresser-Rand was turning a profit.

Ingersoll-Rand had once again weathered recession by the time Holmes stepped down in 1988. His successor, Theodore Black, was able to focus on significant positive aspects of the company. Ingersoll-Rand continued to emphasize new-product development, introducing improved home air compressors, new papermaking technology, and a new type of camshaft in 1988. Ingersoll-Rand also continued to make appropriate acquisitions, including a Swedish company that designs waterjet cutting systems, a Canadian manufacturer of paving equipment, and a German maker of special-purpose hydraulic rock drills, in 1988. In 1990, the company purchased The Aro Corporation, one of its larger recent acquisitions. Ingersoll-Rand continued to utilize state-of-the-art computerized production and design techniques. New techniques that utilize manufacturing cells to produce a product from start to finish with much less labor than a production line can produce more, higher-quality goods.

Ingersoll-Rand has changed since its early days when it emphasized staying on top of a few product lines in a centralized, paternalistic working environment. It appears that this strong company, which operates across industries and around the world, will continue to withstand international economic fluctuations to provide what the world needs to grow and develop.

Principal Subsidiaries: Beebe International, Inc.; California Pellet Mill Co.; Ingersoll-Rand International Sales, Inc.; Ingersoll-Rand International Holding Corporation; Ingersoll-Rand S.A. (Switzerland); Woodcliff Insurance, Ltd. (Bermuda); Schlage Lock Company; Von Duprin, Inc.; Simmons-Rand Company (85%); The Torrington Company; Kilian Manufacturing Corporation; Torrington France, S.A.R.L.; Torrington G.m.b.H. (Germany); Ingersoll-Rand G.m.b.H. (Germany); Western Land Roller Company; Ingersoll-Rand (Australia) Ltd.; Ingersoll-Rand S.E. Asia (Private) Ltd. (Singapore); Ingersoll-Rand Benelux (Belgium); Ingersoll-Rand Canada, Inc.; Torrington, Inc. (Canada); Torrington Industria e Comercio Ltda (Brazil); Ingersoll-Rand World Trade, Ltd. (Bermuda); Compagnie Ingersoll-Rand (France); Ingersoll-Rand Sales Company, Ltd.; Ingersoll-Rand Holdings Limited (U.K.); Ingersoll-Rand Company Limited (U.K.); The Torrington Company Limited (U.K.); Ingersoll-Rand Italiana S.p.A. (Italy); Newco, S.p.A. (Italy); Ingersoll-Rand Japan Ltd.; Tokyo Ryuki Seizo Kabushiki Kaisha (Japan); Compania Ingersoll-Rand S.A. (Spain); Ingersoll-Rand Company South Africa (Proprietary) Ltd.; Ingersoll-Rand Aktiebolag (Sweden); Ingersoll-Rand Services & Engineering Company (Switzerland); Ingersoll Rand Acceptance Company S.A. (Switzerland); Ingersoll-Rand China Limited; Silver Engineering Works, Inc.; The Aro Corporation; N.V. Aro S.A. (Belgium); Aro Canada, Inc.; The Aro Corporation (U.K.) Limited; Ingersoll-Rand Philippines, Inc.; Ingersoll-Rand Investment Company, S.A.; Ing. G. Klemm Bohrtechnik GmbH (Germany); Samiia International (France); Ingersoll-Rand (India) Limited (74%).

Further Reading: Johnson, James P., *New Jersey: A History of Ingenuity and Industry*, Northridge, California, Windsor Publications, 1987.

—Ginger G. Rodriguez

INTERCO INCORPORATED

101 South Hanley Road
Saint Louis, Missouri 63105
(314) 863-1100
Fax: (314) 863-5306

Public Company
Incorporated: 1911 as International Shoe Company
Employees: 28,800
Sales: $1.77 billion
Stock Exchanges: New York Midwest

INTERCO is a major manufacturer of furniture and home furnishings and a manufacturer, distributor, and retailer of men's footwear and athletic footwear. The corporate name was changed from International Shoe Company in 1966. In 1990 the corporation consisted of four core companies in two operating groups: Broyhill and Lane in furniture and home furnishings, and Florsheim and Converse in footwear manufacturing and retailing.

The corporation was organized in 1911 as the International Shoe Company (ISC) by the consolidation of Roberts, Johnson & Rand Shoe Company and the Peters Shoe Company, both of Saint Louis, Missouri. The company built a reputation for manufacturing quality footwear in basic styles in the low-to-medium price range.

The early years of ISC were under the direction of the Johnson brothers, Jackson and Oscar, and their cousin, Frank C. Rand, son of Henry O. Rand, one of the two financial backers of the firm. John C. Roberts was the other backer. The Johnsons and the Rands, from Mississippi, had moved to Memphis, Tennessee, in 1892 to organize the Johnson, Carruthers & Rand Shoe Company. They sold out in 1898 and moved to Saint Louis to organize a new shoe concern. Jackson Johnson served as president of the newly formed company, then as president of ISC until 1915, and finally as chairman until his death in 1929. It was his vision and entrepreneurial drive that led to the formation of the International Shoe Company. He was succeeded briefly as president of ISC by his younger brother, Oscar Johnson, who died suddenly in 1916. Frank C. Rand guided the company as president from 1916 to 1930, and as chairman from 1930 to 1949. He joined the firm as a stock clerk after graduating from Vanderbilt University in 1898, and rose to vice president ten years later. Rand was the guiding force behind the tremendous growth of the corporation during the 1920s, and in the survival of the company during the difficult years of the Great Depression.

The corporation benefited from production demands that came with the outbreak of war in Europe. In 1916 orders came from the War Department as the United States prepared for its involvement in the war. Military orders placed with the shoe industry in general were huge. The importance of shoes as war material was demonstrated when, in 1917, the War Department was forced to takeover the Hamilton Brown Shoe Company of Saint Louis when it was idled by a strike.

In 1921 ISC was restructured and chartered in Delaware. At that time it had 32 shoe factories in Missouri, Illinois, and Kentucky, and had recently acquired the three tanneries of Kistler, Lesh & Co. as part of the long-range goal to achieve full vertical integration. In May 1921 ISC acquired W.H. McElwain Company of Boston, with ten shoe factories, two tanneries, and four shoe-material factories, all in New Hampshire. It was a profitable manufacturer that was experiencing serious labor problems. The company had approximately 5,000 workers and in the previous year had raised wages by 10% and reduced the workweek to 48 hours. McElwain's factories had been organized by the United Shoe Workers. The company experienced some difficulties in the recession of 1920–1921 and proposed a wage reduction of 22%, which was unacceptable to the union. A strike of all McElwain plants was called in January 1921. The sale of the company to non-unionized International Shoe in the spring of 1921 was, in part, a means of resolving this labor dispute.

The merger of ISC and McElwain was challenged by the Federal Trade Commission as a violation of the Clayton Antitrust Act. The commission argued that the combined companies would lessen competition and create a monopoly in shoe manufacturing. The company's position was that no substantial competition had existed between the two companies, and that the McElwain Company was in such financial straits that sale or liquidation were the only options. The commission's order that ISC divest itself of its McElwain holding was, in 1930, reversed by the Supreme Court. The newly merged companies had combined annual sales of $130 million and could produce 120,000 pairs of shoes daily.

During the 1920s, with minor exceptions, sales and profits increased regularly. In 1927 the corporation increased its authorized common stock in order to provide its stockholders with a four-for-one split. A dividend of $2.00 was declared on the new stock, and by January 1928 the corporation was reporting a net income of $4.55 per share.

Profitability was achieved in part at the cost of good labor relations. ISC was not unionized. It tended to control production by means of layoffs of workers. The company also attempted to reduce wages periodically, proposed by management as a means of lowering shoe prices and thereby gaining steady employment for its workers. Although unorganized, workers in the factories did resist this strategy but with limited success.

The year 1929 was ISC's best to that date. Sales and profits reached new highs, and dividends were increased by 50% to $3.00 per share. That year it produced 54.73 million pairs of shoes, the largest output ever by a single firm. ISC had not missed a dividend payment from its founding 17 years earlier, and by 1929 it had made millionaires of 38 members of the firm. The economic collapse that came at the end of the

1920s would affect the business, but ISC was a well-managed firm, and it was to remain profitable through most of the Depression years. During those difficult years ISC did as most others; it periodically laid off workers and cut wages and salaries when necessary. It also cut the price of its product line, and kept most of its factories operating, although at a reduced level. In 1932 the corporation reported a 9.72% rate of return on investment, as compared to 19.29% in 1929. The rate of return rose to 13.53% by 1935. On occasion the corporation found it necessary to increase production, as it did in mid-1931. Some of the New Hampshire plants were placed on an overtime schedule. The spurt in demand was attributed to lower priced footwear, and the relative absence of labor problems was the reason for increasing production at the New Hampshire factories.

The most difficult times for ISC came in the late years of the Depression. In 1937 ISC raised worker's wages twice for a total of 10%, only to be forced to rescind the increase the following April, of 1938, when the economy again declined. In July of that year ISC reported six-month earnings of 19¢ per share—the lowest earnings of the Depression era. Nonetheless, it had survived the worst of the Great Depression and had emerged as a strong company and a major force in the shoe industry. ISC did well enough in 1939 to divide $600,000 in bonus money among workers earnings less than $50 per week. In the final report for fiscal 1939, ISC reported that sales in dollars were the highest since 1930, and that production and shipments surpassed any year since 1929.

Management of ISC remained rather stable throughout these years. In 1939 William H. Moulton, who had assumed the office in 1930, retired as president of ISC and was succeeded by Byron A. Gray. Both had joined the corporation in the days of the Roberts, Johnson & Rand Shoe Company, Moulton in 1908 and Gray in 1909. Frank Rand continued as chairman and remained the dominant force in management.

Production by ISC for World War II began in the first half of 1940 as preparedness gained momentum. In July 1940 the U.S. Army let out for bid a contract for 452,028 pairs of service shoes. Of the 13 companies that bid, only ISC had the production capacity to bid on the entire order and came in with a low bid of $2.48 per pair. By the end of 1940 ISC had approximately 30,000 employees, primarily in the Midwest and New England. Contracts throughout the war kept the company's plants operating at close to full capacity. In 1943 the Boston Quartermaster Depot awarded contracts for 7.2 million pairs of service shoes—the largest single order—1.34 million pairs to be manufactured by ISC. From early 1940 to January 1945, ISC supplied the government with 33 million pairs of shoes.

Government contracts were awarded to ISC despite opposition from organized labor. The company was not highly regarded among labor organizers or sympathizers, dating back to 1913, when it was accused by the Illinois Vice Commission of encouraging vice among its women employees because of ISC's unwillingness to pay decent wages. Until the labor legislation of the New Deal era made such practices illegal, ISC used a variety of strategies to prevent its workers from organizing unions. By 1940 a number of ISC's plants had been organized, but the company was involved in litigation with the National Labor Relations Board over its noncompliance with an order to allow workers in the Hannibal, Missouri, plant to organize. In late 1940 labor representatives objected to ISC receiving a War Department contract for 620,000 pairs of shoes. The issue was resolved politically, but it did encourage ISC to work out its labor problems.

The capacity of the corporation had grown enormously during the 1940s and was not limited to war production. Consumer demand for shoes increased with the improving economy during the war years, and the production of shoes was limited only by the supply of raw materials. In 1944 government business constituted 36% of ISC's dollar volume, and 27% of its production. That year ISC manufactured 53.92 million pairs of shoes—surpassing for the first time the production level of 1929. By the end of World War II, International Shoe had approximately 32,000 employees in 67 shoe factories, subsidiary plants, and tanneries located in Missouri, Illinois, Kentucky, New Hampshire, Arkansas, West Virginia, North Carolina, and Pennsylvania. Plant capacity was well over 200,000 pairs of shoes daily. By 1950 ISC had added an additional 3,000 employees and increased capacity to 70 million pairs annually. Its tanneries could process 3.5 million hides annually, and, in addition, the company manufactured rubber heels, cements, containers, and 10 million yards of textiles for shoe linings.

The death of Frank C. Rand in 1949 marked a significant turning point for ISC. His presence had been felt for 31 years as president. It was primarily at his direction that ISC grew through vertical integration, expansion, and the acquisition of other shoe-manufacturing firms. Two of his sons would assume the presidency of the firm, Edgar E. Rand in 1950 and Henry H. Rand in 1955. Although the Rands would continue to have a significant role in the firm, non-family management would determine the future of ISC, and growth would take on different characteristics. The acquisitions in 1952 of the Florsheim Shoe Company, a manufacturer of better-quality men's shoes founded in 1892, and in 1954 of Savage Shoes, Ltd., the largest shoe manufacturer in Canada, were the last sizable acquisitions of shoe manufacturers until the mid-1980s. In 1958, however, ISC acquired its first offshore manufacturer, the Caribe Shoe Corporation of Puerto Rico. The firm was small, with a daily capacity of 3,500 pairs of juvenile shoes, but it foretold of the future. Six months later ISC closed permanently a plant in Chester, Illinois, that had been operating since 1916 and manufacturing approximately 5,000 pairs of juvenile shoes daily.

Additions for the rest of the decade were in shoe retailing operations, and in 1959 ISC formed a new division, International Retail Sales. As a result of this expansion, by 1960 ISC had controlling interest in approximately 800 retail outlets, as compared to 275 in 1955. This was a response to the implications of low-priced imports. ISC moved quickly to ensure the continued profitability of the firm by expanding its retail operations and by diversifying into other product areas. The drive to diversify was guided by Maurice R. Chambers, who had joined ISC in 1949 as a divisional sales manager and who was elected president of the firm in 1962. He was the first person to reach this position who was neither with the original Roberts, Johnson & Rand Shoe Company nor a member of the Rand family. Under his direction, ISC moved aggressively to expand operations outside the continental United States and to acquire companies in areas other than shoe manufacturing or retailing. Chambers's strategy was to seek out well-managed and profitable companies with strong brand identification and, once acquired, to leave the management team intact. Between 1964 and 1978 ISC acquired 21 separate companies, and with the exception of Central Hardware in 1966, all were apparel manufacturers or retailers. The acquired companies were given operating freedom, and some of these units went on to acquire additional firms in related areas of business, adding to the overall growth of ISC. The company was markedly successful in acquiring thriving firms with good product lines, and became a role model for other firms seeking to ensure profitability through acquisitions. In 1966 in keeping with its broader base as a diversified apparel maker, footwear manufacturer, retailer and department store operator, the International Shoe Company adopted the corporate name INTERCO.

During the 1960s there were significant changes in INTERCO's core business. Within a year of Chambers taking office, the company permanently closed six manufacturing facilities—more closings were to come—and set up a special division to import a full line of footwear from Italy. The plant closings reduced overall production capacity approximately 12% and were part of a major effort to streamline and upgrade facilities to meet the surge of import competition. This strategy, coupled with diversification, kept INTERCO profitable despite the fact that by the mid-1970s imports had taken more than 44% of the domestic shoe market. By the early 1970s INTERCO's apparel and general-merchandise subsidiaries were generating approximately 56% of sales and 47% of profit. By 1974 INTERCO had become a billion dollar corporation with ten consecutive years of record sales and earnings.

The expansion and diversification of the late 1960s and the 1970s had created a firm with three major operating divisions. The apparel manufacturing group consisted of 11 apparel companies, with 62 manufacturing plants and 13 distribution centers. The general retail merchandising group operated 856—owned or leased—retail locations in 29 states. The footwear manufacturing and retailing group operated 874 shoe stores and leased shoe departments in 43 states and in Mexico, Canada, and Australia; and it managed 24 factories and 10 distribution centers. A major addition to the footwear group was made with the acquisition in 1986 of Converse, a Massachusetts-based manufacturer of athletic footwear founded in 1908.

A new direction was begun in 1979 when INTERCO agreed to the acquisition of Ethan Allen Inc. for cash and stock totaling $130 million. Ethan Allen, begun in 1932 as a home-furnishings jobber, was a fully integrated manufacturer and retailer of furniture and accessories. With the acquisition in January 1980, Ethan Allen's 24 factories and more than 300 retail showcase galleries became the core of INTERCO's fourth operating group in furniture and home furnishings. That same year, in August, INTERCO, agreed to the acquisition of Broyhill Furniture Industries for cash and notes totaling $151.5 million. At the time of the acquisition, Broyhill, located in western North Carolina, was the largest privately owned furniture manufacturer in the world. The acquisition added 20 manufacturing facilities to the furniture and home-furnishings group.

The largest acquisition in furniture and home furnishings came in 1987 when INTERCO gained control of the Lane Company at a cost approaching $500 million. Lane, based in Altavista, Virginia, was founded in 1912 as a maker of cedar chests, and through growth and acquisition expanded into a full-line manufacturer of furniture in the medium-to-upper price ranges. With the addition of Lane's 16 plants, sales of the furniture and home-furnishings group approached 33% of INTERCO's total sales.

The primary architect of the merger-and-acquisition drive, Maurice R. Chambers, relinquished day-to-day control of the company in 1976, but continued as a major force as a director and as chairman of the executive committee until his retirement in 1981. His successor as CEO, William L. Edwards Jr., continued Chambers's policies. In early 1981 and in anticipation of Chambers's retirement, INTERCO restructured as part of a plan to develop younger managerial talent within the company. John K. Riedy was moved up to the vacant position of vice chairman and was succeeded as president and chief operating officer by Harvey Saligman. Then 42 years old, Saligman had been president of Queen Casuals, an apparel manufacturer founded by his grandfather and acquired by INTERCO in 1976. The move was propitious in that Riedy and Saligman were in place when Edwards died unexpectedly in June 1981. Riedy was elected chairman and CEO, positions he would hold until his retirement in June 1985. His successor in these offices, Saligman, would lead INTERCO into the most tumultuous period of the company's existence.

The acquisitions of Converse in 1986 and Lane in 1987 were an integral part of the reorganization of INTERCO devised by Harvey Saligman. Of the four operating groups in the company, footwear manufacturing and retailing and furniture and home furnishings were the two most profitable and appeared to offer the most promise for the future. Beginning in 1985, Saligman's long-term strategy was to emphasize footwear and furniture and to divest the company of less-profitable operations in apparel manufacturing and retailing. INTERCO's overall performance and stock price in the mid-1980s did not meet expectations and showed no sign of an immediate turnaround. Saligman's restructuring strategy came at a time when heavily leveraged hostile takeovers of undervalued companies were rampant. INTERCO was a prime candidate. Because the company owned well-known brand names, INTERCO was regarded by takeover specialists as worth more broken up than as a conglomerate.

At the annual meeting in June 1985, while reporting a first quarter net income decline of 42%, INTERCO amended its bylaws to create obstacles in the event of a hostile takeover bid. Additional similar action was taken at a board meeting several months later and again the following spring. At the same time INTERCO was proceeding with the divestment or closing of apparel manufacturing firms, including Saligman's family firm, Queen Casuals, and unprofitable retail operations. The acquisitions of Converse and Lane were negotiated at this time. It appears that these acquisitions contributed to a liquidity problem and a lowering of the value of the company's stock, which may have made the company more vulnerable to takeover.

Anticipating a takeover bid, Saligman and INTERCO retained the services of an investment banker, Wasserstein Perella & Company, in July 1988. However, the firm's advice and handling of a takeover challenge brought INTERCO to the edge of bankruptcy. The bid came later that same month from a group of investors led by Steven M. Rales and his brother Mitchell Rales, of Washington, D.C. The initial bid of $2.26 billion, approximately $64 per share, was followed within days by an increased offer of $2.47 billion, or approximately $70 per share. INTERCO's stock had increased by $8.375 to $67.75 a share in response to the first bid, and to $72.50 with the second bid.

INTERCO rejected both bids and took defensive measures to retain its independence. The Rales group had acquired 8.7% of INTERCO's stock before making the bid. It had the resources to pursue the takeover battle, and indicated that its intent was to sell off all INTERCO assets with the exception of the furniture-manufacturing group, which would be retained. Financing and direction of the hostile bid was being provided by Drexel Burnham Lambert. With INTERCO shares trading above the hostile offer, management was encouraged to pursue defensive measures. Wasserstein Perella was authorized to provide confidential financial data to potential friendly merger partners, and Goldman, Sachs & Co. was employed to seek purchasers for the planned divestment of the apparel manufacturing group.

In mid-September the Rales group extended and increased its offer to INTERCO shareholders, but the bid appeared to be in serious trouble. Drexel Burnham Lambert, was charged by the Securities and Exchange Commission (SEC) with insider trading, a charge that eventually would lead to the downfall of that company. Drexel, unable to raise sufficient funds from outside investors, was obliged to provide over $600 million of its own money to support the bid. To counter the Rales bid, INTERCO's board approved a $2.8 billion restructuring and special dividend plan that was valued at $76 a share in cash and debentures. The plan would be financed by the sale of assets, including the possible sale of Ethan Allen, the core of the furniture group. In October INTERCO declared a dividend of $25 per share, and declared its intent to sell securities in the open market with the proceeds to go to stockholders. In effect, INTERCO was taking on an enormous amount of debt to make the company less attractive to a hostile raider. The Rales group increased its bid to $74 a share and indicated the possibility of an additional increase if it was able to gain access to INTERCO's confidential financial data. By early November approximately 93% of INTERCO shares had been tendered to the Rales group, but it was prohibited from purchasing the stock because of legal proceedings instituted by INTERCO in the Delaware courts. The Rales group brought matters to head by establishing a firm deadline for negotiations with INTERCO's board. At the deadline it cancelled the offer to purchase shares. Within weeks Rales sold its stake in the company and took a profit of $60 million on its three million shares.

The withdrawal of the bid did not release INTERCO from its obligation to restructure the firm, and it proceeded with its plans to pay special dividends of cash and securities to shareholders. INTERCO went ahead with the sale of assets, disposing of major units in apparel manufacturing, retailing operations, and Ethan Allen in the furniture group. This was being done in the midst of a declining bond market, which affected the value of the restructured company. The expectation was that the recapitalized firm would give shareholders a total value of $76 a share. By July 1989 the total value was estimated to be $61 and the stock of the restructured firm, which had been expected to trade at approximately $10, was trading for less than $3 per share. The sale of assets never reached the projected level, falling far short of the amount needed to service the company's obligations. By the early months of 1990, INTERCO stock was trading at less than 50¢ per share, and company bonds were trading in the range of 3% to 25% of face value.

In March 1989 Richard B. Loynd was named president and chief operating officer. Loynd had led a leveraged buy-out of Converse and was chairman of that firm when it was acquired by INTERCO. In August, Harvey Saligman, who had initiated the restructuring of the firm and who uncompromisingly resisted the hostile takeover, stepped down and Loynd became chief executive officer of the firm. Saligman noted that INTERCO was entering a new phase of development and that Loynd's experience in leading a company in a highly leveraged environment would be beneficial.

The company that Loynd was to lead into the 1990s was far different from the INTERCO of a few years earlier. The company that had grown in relatively small increments over an extended period of time, and had done so with a minimum of debt, began the 1990s with a negative net worth of almost $1 billion. It had narrowed itself down to the two operating groups, footwear manufacturing and retailing and furniture and home furnishings, with some peripheral assets slated for divestment.

This is the profile of the firm Saligman had projected some years earlier but without the debt generated by the takeover battle. The future of INTERCO was thus clouded. By the summer of 1990 INTERCO was unable to meet interest payments due and was obliged to seek a restructuring of its debt. The cooperation of bond holders and banks allowed INTERCO to survive, but the firm would face a major financial crisis in 1994 when interest on its subordinated bonds was to be paid. If the overall economy remains generally healthy, then INTERCO may be able to generate sufficient operating revenues to service its debt.

Principal Subsidiaries: Broyhill Furniture Industries, Inc.; The Lane Company, Incorporated; The Florsheim Shoe Company; Converse Inc.

Further Reading: Leonard, John W., ed., *The Book of St. Louisans: A Biographical Dictionary of Leading Living Men of the City of St. Louis,* Saint Louis, Missouri, The St. Louis Republic, 1906; Nunn, Henry Lightfoot, *The Whole Man Goes to Work: The Life Story of a Businessman,* New York, Harper, 1953; Nunn, Henry Lightfoot, *Partners in Production: A New Role for Management and Labor,* Englewood Cliffs, New Jersey, Prentice Hall, 1961; *INTERCO: A Review,* Saint Louis, Missouri, INTERCO Incorporated, [1981]; Feurer, Rosemary, "Shoe City, Factory Towns: St. Louis Shoe Companies and the Turbulent Drive for Cheap Rural Labor, 1900–1940," *Gateway Heritage,* Fall 1988.

—George P. Antone

ISHIKAWAJIMA-HARIMA HEAVY INDUSTRIES CO., LTD.

Shin Ohtemachi Building
2-1 Ohtemachi 2-chome
Chiyoda-ku, Tokyo 100
Japan
(03) 3244-5111
Fax: (03) 3244-5131

Public Company
Incorporated: 1889 as Ishikawajima Shipyard Company, Limited
Employees: 15,500
Sales: ¥632.81 billion (US$4.40 billion)
Stock Exchanges: Tokyo Osaka Nagoya Kyoto Hiroshima Fukuoka Niigata Sapporo.

World-renowned for generations as a shipbuilder, Ishikawajima-Harima Heavy Industries Co., Ltd. (IHI) is second in Japan only to Mitsubishi Heavy Industries. IHI is involved in such high-tech industries as aerospace, energy, and material distribution. It is a pioneer in advanced technologies including nuclear fusion, superconductivity, lasers, and advanced compound and ceramic materials. With the decline of the shipbuilding industry, IHI used diversification as well as research and development to foster growth. IHI's desalination plants, for example, have won acclaim in a number of countries—particularly in the Middle East. A major shift in production and marketing emphasis during the 1980s made heavy industry and plant technology the source of close to 70% of the company's income. Also strong is the company's aerospace division, which produces jet engines, and leads the industry in developing space rockets and experimental devices.

In 1853 Lord Nariaki Tokugawa of Mito was appointed by the ruling Tokugawa Shogunate to build a shipyard on Ishikawajima. This island at the mouth of the Sumida River, which flows into Tokyo Bay was strategic for the coastal defense of Japan.

The year 1853 was a particularly propitious time to start a shipbuilding company in Japan. As the number of U.S., British, German, and other interests in the Pacific area increased, new pressures were being brought to bear to lift Japan's centuries-old barriers to trade with foreign nations. Shoguns, powerful clans that were outgrowths of the feudal system, ruled the country, with an emperor as a figurehead. In the mid-19th century, the Tokugawa shogunate in power realized that trade would soon be reopened—by force if not by consent. Even though trade was reopened peacefully after Commodore Matthew Perry had sailed a U.S. fleet into Japanese waters in 1854, the fear of a possible attack spurred the Japanese government to begin production of modern western-style ships.

With the lifting of trade barriers and exposure to new cultural and economic influences, a rapid process of industrialization was soon underway. Feudalism and the shogun system were abolished and power was transferred to an imperial government whose announced intention was to modernize the nation. Coming to the throne in 1868, Emperor Meiji conscripted an army, and, at the same time, set plans in motion to adopt some of the technology and work methods developed abroad.

The new government's plans to become active in the worldwide industrial revolution called for encouragement of private enterprise. Accordingly, the government sold the Ishikawajima shipyard in 1876 to Tomiji Hirano, a civilian. As Ishikawajima Hirano Shipyard, the company became Japan's first private shipyard and, within a year, produced *Tsuun Maru,* the first steamship built by a Japanese shipbuilder.

Diversification began in 1883, with production of the nation's first steel bridge. The Miyako Bridge spanned the Ooka River in Yokohama. Four years later, the company constructed the largest steel bridge yet built in Japan, across Tokyo's Sumida River.

Incorporated in 1889, the company was renamed Ishikawajima Shipyard Company, Limited. In 1892, the company built the nation's first 80-horsepower air compressor and first high-speed power-generating boiler.

Another name change was made in 1893 when Tokyo Ishikawajima Shipyard Co., Ltd. became a joint-stock company. Three years later the company constructed Japan's first thermal power plant facilities. Ishikawajima began manufacturing steel structures for Tokyo's National Sports Hall in 1909, and for Tokyo Central Station in 1911. Ishikawajima constructed Japan's first four-ton open-hearth-furnace charging crane in 1916, and first ingot crane in 1917; both were built for state-run steel-production companies.

After World War I, and despite a severe earthquake in 1923, the company continued its research and development, innovation, and expansion into new product lines. In 1924, the Ishikawajima Airplane Manufacturing Company began operation, and by 1929 the Ishikawajima Automobile Manufacturing Company was established.

The second Sino-Japanese War and the start of World War II increased demand for Ishikawajima's established products and resulted in new product developments such as the 350-ton hammer-head crane in 1935 and the nation's first jet engines ten years later—both for the Japanese Navy. A subsidiary, Ishikawajima Shibaura Turbine Company, began operations in 1936.

Japanese industries achieved a relatively quick recovery following the nation's defeat in World War II. The company, renamed Ishikawajima Heavy Industry Co., Ltd. in 1945, began to renew its reputation as innovator by 1956 when it manufactured the world's largest spherical gas-storage tank. In 1958 Ishikawajima completed Japan's first mobile offshore drilling platform and in 1959 built its largest blast furnace to date. That same year, the company established its first foreign subsidiary, in Brazil.

A new era for Ishikawajima—and the change to its current name—began in 1960 as the company merged with the 53-year-old Harima Shipbuilding & Engineering Company, Ltd. A major shipyard known for its construction of large vessels, Harima had three subsidiaries of its own.

In 1961, IHI developed a variety of steel known as IN, which maintains high toughness at low temperatures. The merged companies combined transport-producing facilities to create additional innovations such as the world's first mammoth tankers, a series of standardized multipurpose dry cargo carriers produced in the 1960s, the world's first barge-mounted polyethylene plant, and a series of high-powered jet engines. A cement calcinating process was developed in the early 1970s.

International operations proliferated from the early 1970s onward, as IHI acquired contracts with overseas companies or formed joint ventures with them. Services the company rendered to developing countries ranged from project planning through design, engineering, construction supervision, plant maintenance, and training of personnel.

As Japan's top manufacturer of jet engines, IHI was part of a five-country consortium, including the United States, United Kingdom, West Germany, and Italy, to develop a V2500 turbofan engine to power 150-passenger commercial jetliners. Under development since 1983, the engine was certified by the U.S. Federal Aviation Administration in 1988 and went into production.

A joint venture in 1988, with Sumitomo Heavy Industries, established Diesel United Company, which rapidly gained 20% of the domestic market in industrial machinery. ICA Technologies, Ltd., another 1986 IHI joint venture—with ATEQ Corporation of Oregon, and Canon Sales Company of Tokyo—was formed to enter the semiconductor-related market. It also established the IHI Granitech Corporation, to advance stone processing for building construction; Ishikawajima Systems Technology Company, a systems engineering company for production of electronics and computers; and Joy Planning Company, in the area of fitness clubs and sports facilities. In addition, IHI entered real estate development of prime idle lands in the Tokyo Bay area. IHI has survived partially because of success in technology and partially because of the company's proactive responses to market conditioning. The company's policy has been almost continual diversification into new and profitable enterprises.

IHI, which maintained close ties with the Toshiba Corporation, has placed its stamp on products and projects around the globe. Examples include large-scale bridges in several countries, a floating pulp plant in Brazil, desalination plants in the Middle East, a rolling mill in Shanghai, container ships in Singapore, an iron ore carrier in Australia, ethylene plant compressors in China, a blast furnace in Korea, laser processing systems in Europe, and cement plants in Indonesia, India, and Saudi Arabia.

Shipbuilding orders declined in the late 1980s. Plant export businesses lost profitability because of the strong yen. IHI, however, continued to show an overall profit in 1989 by scaling down affected operations and concentrating on the expanding air- and space-related divisions. Focus has shifted to domestic markets and the development of electronic products.

IHI's mass-produced machinery remained a strong sector. The 1988 sales for this division were up 20% from 1987. Its products included compressors, dishwashers, precision machining, and turbochargers. IHI was ranked as the top manufacturer of integrated turbochargers for marine diesel engines and automobiles. IHI is also participating in NASA's manned space station project by developing an experimental module.

Principal Subsidiaries: Ishikawajima Construction Machinery Company, Ltd.; Ishikawajima Inspection Company, Ltd.; Ishikawajima Construction Materials Company, Ltd.; Ishikawajima Shibaura Machinery Company, Ltd.; Ishikawajima Packaged Boiler Company, Ltd.; Ishikawajima Noise Control Company, Ltd.

Further Reading: This is IHI, Tokyo, Ishikawajima-Harima Heavy Industries Co., Ltd., [n.d.]

—Betty T. Moore

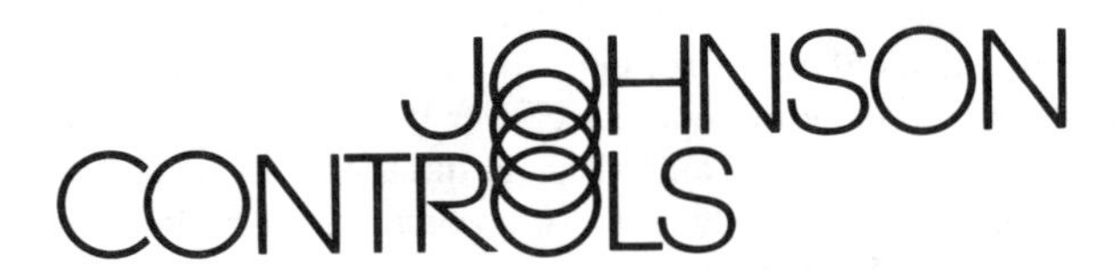

JOHNSON CONTROLS, INC.

5757 North Green Bay Avenue
Milwaukee, Wisconsin 53201
U.S.A.
(414) 228-1200
Fax: (414) 228-2302

Public Company
Incorporated: 1885 as Johnson Electric Service Company
Employees: 43,500
Sales: $3.68 billion
Stock Exchange: New York

Johnson Controls is a diversified company made up of four main businesses: building management and control systems, automotive seating, automobile batteries, and plastic containers. Johnson is a leader in all of these industries, claiming about a one-third share of each market except automotive seating, where it controls approximately a 14% market share. The company's building-controls business is at the forefront of controls technology, and its automotive seating and parts business is rapidly expanding. The largest manufacturer of batteries for the country's automotive replacement market, Johnson Controls is also the largest independent producer of batteries for the original-equipment market. The company's plastics business is expanding as plastic replaces glass in the container industry. In each of its major businesses, Johnson's research-and-development spending has increased over the last several years, and the company introduces new products on a regular basis. Although long the subject of takeover rumors, Johnson Controls has managed to maintain its independence through carefully targeted acquisitions and sound fiscal management.

Warren Seymour Johnson was born in Rutland County, Vermont. When he was two, his family moved to Wisconsin. Johnson worked as a printer, surveyor, school teacher, and school superintendent before he was appointed a professor at the State Normal School in Whitewater, Wisconsin, in 1876. He was known as a highly original teacher. Whatever the job, Johnson's main interest was his laboratory, where he experimented in electrochemistry. In 1883 he produced the first Johnson System of Temperature Regulation, an electric thermostat system which he installed at the State Normal School.

When Johnson received a patent for the electric telethermoscope, he persuaded Milwaukee, Wisconsin, hotelier and heir to the Plankinton Packing Company, William Plankinton, to become his financial backer in producing the device. Their partnership, the Milwaukee Electric Manufacturing Company, allowed Johnson to resign his professorship so he could devote all his time to his inventions. Although retired from teaching, he would always be called "the Professor."

On May 1, 1885, the company was reorganized as the Johnson Electric Service Company, a Wisconsin corporation, in Milwaukee. Plankinton became president and Johnson, vice president and treasurer.

The Professor continued to invent additional control devices, but he also designed products such as chandeliers, springless door locks, puncture-proof tires, thermometers, and a hose coupling for providing steam heat to passenger railcars. The creations for which the young company received the most recognition were the Professor's impressive tower clocks. He developed a system powered by air pressure that increased the reliability of such clocks. The company built its first big clock in 1895 for the Minneapolis courthouse and a year later built the clock for the Milwaukee City Hall tower. Johnson's largest tower clock was installed in the Philadelphia City Hall. A large-scale floral clock for the Saint Louis World's Fair in 1904 received international acclaim and enhanced the growing reputation of the company. The clocks' success helped prove the usefulness of the pneumatic operations the company was utilizing in its control applications.

At the Paris World's Fair of 1900, Johnson's wireless-communication exhibit won second prize. In the same competition Guglielmo Marconi, developer of the wireless telegraph, placed third. The Professor, his sons, and inventor Charles Fortier began to test a variety of alloys in wireless sets. The men built a 115-foot tower several miles south of Milwaukee, but many attempts to transmit messages to the company's downtown factory were unsuccessful. Lee DeForest, whose audion tube would later provide the breakthrough for radio, also worked on the project.

Company directors elected Johnson president of the company in 1901, and a year later the firm's name was changed to Johnson Service Company. Even as president, Johnson was not able to convince the board to provide financial backing for his interest in establishing a national automobile company. Johnson saw the automobile as a way to insure that the company was not completely dependent on temperature-regulating equipment. In 1907 he introduced a gasoline-powered engine. Johnson was the first to receive a U.S. contract to deliver mail with a horseless carriage. At the outset, according to an often-told story, the wary postmaster agreed to pay Johnson an amount equal to his horses' feed bills for the mail service. The company's failure to expand those automobile interests was a source of frustration to Johnson until his death in 1911. He had assigned more than 50 patents, most of them concerned with harnessing power generated by fluid, air, or steam pressure, to Johnson Service Company.

Harry W. Ellis was elected president in 1912. Ellis, who had been manager of the Chicago branch office, decided to concentrate on opportunities for growth in the controls field. He sold all of the company's other businesses, improved the efficiency of factory operations in Milwaukee, and introduced a modern accounting system.

In 1885, the year the company was incorporated, it had sold the rights to sell, install, and service its temperature-control-regulation systems to two firms. The firms did not perform up to expectations, but the situation was not changed for years. By 1912 Johnson had regained the rights to do business directly throughout the country and had established 18 U.S. branch offices, six Canadian offices, and direct agencies in Copenhagen, Berlin, Saint Petersburg, Manchester, and Warsaw.

The Professor had insisted that only trained Johnson mechanics could install his company's devices and Ellis reinforced this policy. He insisted that the company was to serve not just as a producer of regulation equipment but as a single source for design, installation, and service. Johnson's temperature-control business expanded in tandem with the country's building boom. Skyscrapers became popular as structural steel replaced iron and other building systems were refined. During World War I, the company's temperature-control business was classified by the War Industry Board as nonessential to the war effort, since it was seen as a means of providing comfort. Johnson contracts dropped off as civilian construction was sharply reduced. The firm looked to the government buildings for business and began seeking contracts to retrofit old buildings with new temperature-control systems.

In 1919 the company's new contracts exceeded $1 million. Although a business depression meant that few new office buildings were being constructed, movie theaters, department stores, and restaurants were introducing air-cooled interiors. By 1928 the company's new contracts passed the $4 million mark.

The Great Depression dealt a serious blow to the construction industry, and most new building-control installations in the 1930s aimed for economy. Projects in schools and government buildings that were assigned by the Public Works Administration also had fuel savings as a goal. Johnson's new Dual Thermostat, which allowed a building to save fuel by automatically lowering temperatures at times when the building was unoccupied, was in demand.

Joseph A. Cutler was elected president of the company in 1938. A former engineering professor at the University of Wisconsin, his presidency, like that of Ellis, would last almost 25 years.

After the United Stated entered World War II, Johnson was classified as part of an essential industry, evidence of the change in the way the public perceived building controls. Johnson's contributions to the war effort included installing temperature-and-humidity control systems in defense facilities and the engineering of special military products. The company also made leak detectors that were used to test barrage balloons used over military installations, ships, and landing barges; developed the radiosonde to help combat pilots encountering unknown flying conditions to gather weather data; and manufactured echo boxes, devices that tested radar sets.

After World War II ended, civilian construction boomed and with it, the company's new contracts. Along with this boom came a renewed interest in air conditioning. By 1949 the company's sales were $10 million.

In 1956 Johnson began to build and install pneumatic control centers that allowed a single building engineer to monitor panels displaying room temperatures, ventilating conditions, water temperatures, and the outdoor temperature. To assure a steady and reliable source of customized control panels for these centers, Johnson purchased a panel-fabrication company in Oklahoma in 1960. Operations at company headquarters in Milwaukee were also expanding, so the company bought and eventually expanded an additional building there for its brass foundry, metal fabrications, assembly operations, and machining work.

Richard J. Murphy was elected company president in 1960, the year the company celebrated its 75th anniversary. Murphy had started with the company as a timekeeper in 1918 and had moved up through the ranks. Although his presidency lasted only six years, he was responsible for many innovations. Murphy established an international division, with subsidiaries in England, France, Australia, Belgium, Italy, and Switzerland. Each international office was managed as a virtually independent business, as were operations in the United States and Canada. In 1964 construction of the first foreign manufacturing plant began in Italy.

Since World War II, Johnson had enjoyed an excellent reputation for its work in atomic-research plants and other installations requiring exceptional levels of reliability. In 1961 the Systems Engineering & Construction Division was established. It provided equipment for all 57 air force Titan II launch complexes and most other major missile programs. The National Aeronautics and Space Administration contracted with Johnson throughout the 1960s for mission-control instrumentation for the Apollo-Saturn program.

In 1962 Johnson, along with its main competitors Honeywell and Powers Regulator, were charged in a federal antitrust suit with price-fixing in the sale of pneumatic temperature-control systems. The suit's resolution in a consent decree, coupled with new competitors entering the controls market, meant increasingly competitive bidding. Johnson occasionally won contracts on which it ended up making little or no profit.

By the early 1960s it became apparent to Johnson management that electronics technology could be used to control all aspects of maintaining a building. To improve its in-house electronics capability, the company purchased the electronics division of Fischbach & Moore in 1963. Because of its increasing involvement in projects requiring exacting quality standards and high-quality components, Johnson acquired Associated Piping & Engineering Corporation and Western Piping and Engineering Company in 1966. The companies fabricated expansion joints and piping for nuclear and fossil fuel generating plants and many other industrial applications.

Fred L. Brengel became the sixth Johnson president in 1967. He had joined the company as a sales engineer in 1948 and served as manager of the Boston branch office and sales manager of the New England and Midwest regions before becoming vice president and general sales manager in 1963.

The same year Brengel was elected president, Johnson introduced the T-6000, a solid-state, digital data logger that used ''management by exception''—the system announced when its variables were outside specified limits so an engineer's attention was only called for when needed. The T-6000 not only performed heating, ventilating, and air conditioning functions, but also monitored fire and smoke detection, security, and emergency lighting systems.

Just a year after Brengel assumed the presidency, Johnson acquired Penn Controls, a 50-year-old company that manufactured controls for original-equipment manufacturers, distributors, and wholesalers. With its Penn acquisition, Johnson improved its competitive edge by having its own supply of electrical products for installation projects. Penn also had manufacturing plants and subsidiaries in Canada, the Netherlands, Argentina, and Japan, which helped Johnson expand its international markets. The year it acquired Penn, the company's sales rose about 20%, to $155 million.

Johnson introduced the JC/80, the industry's first minicomputer system that managed building controls, in 1972. One of the many advantages of the JC/80 was that operators of the system needed only a minimal amount of technical training. The JC/80, which could cut fuel requirements by as much as 30%, was introduced at the ideal time, just a year before international embargoes on oil would change the way people viewed energy consumption. Virtually overnight, people became interested in reducing energy costs.

The company adopted its present name, Johnson Controls, in 1974. By 1977 it had captured approximately 35% of the estimated $600 million market for commercial-building control systems. It had 114 branch offices in the United States and Canada and more than 300 service centers, staffed by 10,000 engineers, architects, designers, and service technicians. In spite of a worldwide recession, the company's sales rose to almost $500 million that year.

Although Johnson fared well in the boom market for energy-conservation products, new companies were beginning to crowd the building-controls field. To diversify, the company merged with Globe-Union, the country's largest manufacturer of automotive batteries, in 1978.

Founded in Milwaukee in 1911, Globe Electric Company's original aim had been to serve the battery needs of streetcars, rural light plants, and switchboards. In 1925 Globe's treasurer, Chester O. Wanvig, entered an agreement with Sears, Roebuck and Company President General Robert Wood to produce automobile replacement batteries for the company. Globe shareholders declined the opportunity and Wanvig organized the Union Battery Company to serve Sears. In 1929 Globe Electric and Union Battery consolidated, with Wanvig as president. By the late 1930s Globe-Union had ten manufacturing plants across the United States.

In the late 1950s Globe-Union invented the thin-wall polypropylene battery container, a major technological breakthrough that won the company a leadership position in the industry. The thickness of the battery walls was reduced and the container was lighter and stronger than hard-rubber cases. In 1967 Sears used this technology in its DieHard battery, made by Globe-Union. By 1971 Globe-Union had become the largest U.S. manufacturer of automotive replacement batteries, with its sales climbing past $100 million that year. The company turned to nonautomotive battery applications in 1972 when it formed an industrial-products unit. One of its best-known creations was the Gel/Cell, a line of sealed, portable lead acid units for the standby power needs of security and telecommunications applications.

Johnson's merger with Globe-Union doubled its sales, broadened its financial base, and gave it leadership in a new field. Three years after the merger, sales surpassed $1 billion. In the early 1980s Johnson took the lead in developing controls for ''intelligent buildings,'' which featured state-of-the-art technology to manage energy, comfort, and protection needs. Despite the entrance of many new companies into this sector, Johnson remains a leader in the field. In the latter part of 1989, Johnson announced a joint venture with Yokogawa Electric Corporation to manufacture control instrumentation and to integrate and service industrial automation systems for the North American market.

Johnson greatly expanded its automotive business in 1985 when it acquired Hoover Industrial, a major supplier of seating and plastic parts for automobiles and a new entrant in the plastic-container industry. Although company officials denied it, industry analysts speculated that the acquisition may have at least in part been an attempt to thwart a possible takeover attempt by Miami financier Victor Posner. One of Posner's companies owned almost 20% of Johnson in 1985.

At the time of its purchase, Hoover was changing its emphasis from supplying seating components to building completely assembled automotive seating. The company had an excellent reputation for its just-in-time delivery system, which meant the company supplied its automotive customers with needed parts and components precisely when they needed them, neither before nor after, to avoid customer storage charges.

The same year it purchased Hoover, Johnson also acquired Ferro Manufacturing Corporation, a supplier of automotive seating components and mechanisms. Hoover and Ferro units unrelated to Johnson's major businesses were sold shortly after the acquisitions were completed.

With its new components in place, Johnson became known as a supplier that consistently meets automakers' demands for parts suppliers that can design, engineer, assemble, and deliver modular systems to their plants ''just-in-time.'' In addition to supplying components to the major domestic carmakers, Johnson also supplies several of the Japanese auto manufacturers' U.S. operations, including Toyota, Honda, and Nissan and a Toyota–General Motors joint venture.

James H. Keyes was elected chief executive officer in 1988, after serving as president since 1986. A certified public accountant, he joined Johnson as an analyst in 1966 and held several key executive positions, including treasurer and chief operating officer.

Johnson expanded its plastics business in 1988 by acquiring Apple Container Corporation and the soft drink bottle operations of American National Can Company. In mid-1989 the company purchased Pan Am World Services, a leading provider of high-tech and other facility-management services for military bases, airports, and space centers. This acquisition was intended to bolster Johnson's recent entry into the business of providing engineering and protection services for commercial buildings.

Johnson's controls business has had an international presence, concentrated in Europe and the Far East, since the 1960s. During the mid-1980s Johnson began to expand its plastic-container and seating businesses into Europe. This aggressive expansion was facilitated primarily through acquistions. By 1990 Johnson claimed to hold leadership positions in both markets.

In 1989 Johnson's battery group acquired Varta, the largest automotive-battery maker in Canada. By mid-1990, however, Johnson sought to sell part of that business.

Although there have been repeated rumors about possible takeovers of Johnson, the company's management is committed to rebuffing all such attempts. President Keyes told

Forbes in March 1989, "It depends on whether you take a short-term view and want to improve returns immediately, or you take a long-term view and seek to maintain market leadership. We've chosen the latter approach."

The company expects its automotive and plastics businesses to represent larger portions of its total sales in coming years because of the higher growth likely in those two industries. Its other two businesses are also expected to achieve steady growth. Johnson is expanding its building-controls business by focusing more on the needs of smaller buildings and by beginning to tap the large-building controls-service market. In 1989 the battery division unveiled the EverStart, a new automotive battery that carries its own emergency back-up power system. It was called the first real breakthrough in battery technology in decades.

President Keyes insists that Johnson can only maintain its competitive momentum if it strives to exceed customer expectations. Remaining responsive to market changes, spending on research and development, and maintaining its stable management should continue to promote Johnson's long-term growth.

Principal Subsidiaries: Johnson Controls International Inc.; Hoover Universal Inc.

Further Reading: Right for the Times: Johnson Controls 100th Anniversary, Milwaukee, Wisconsin, Johnson Controls, Inc., 1985.

—Mary Sue Mohnke

KAWASAKI HEAVY INDUSTRIES, LTD.

1-18, Nakamachi-dori 2-chome
Chuo-ku, Kobe 650-91
Japan
(078) 371-9530
Fax: (078) 371-9568

Public Company
Incorporated: 1896 as Kawasaki Dockyard Co., Ltd.
Employees: 16,600
Sales: ¥767.07 billion (US$5.34 billion)
Stock Exchanges: Tokyo Osaka Nagaya

Kawasaki Heavy Industries, which for much of the 20th century was one of the world's leading shipbuilders, today sells more motorcycles and lawn mower engines than it does ships. Long a diversified company, Kawasaki was able to survive the drastic and apparently permanent slump which overtook the shipbuilding industry after the 1973 oil embargo by continuing its evolution into a multi-faceted manufacturer of rolling stock, aircraft, and industrial plants.

Kawasaki was one of the handful of firms that helped propel Japan into the modern industrial world, with early efforts in the automobile, aircraft, power-plant, and heavy-machinery industries as well as in shipbuilding. From its 19 worldwide plants, Kawasaki participates in a wide array of large-scale construction and engineering projects, with shipbuilding reduced to 8% of overall sales and continuing to dwindle in importance.

Shipbuilding gave Kawasaki its start in the world of heavy industry. When Japan emerged from two centuries of isolation in the mid-1800s, its first need as an island nation was to develop a modern shipbuilding industry. The Meiji government at first attempted to run its own shipping lines, but when that effort failed, the government offered considerable subsidies and favorable leasing terms to anyone who cared to try to imitate the sleek Western steamship designs. Shozo Kawasaki was only too eager to accept the challenge. Born in 1836, Kawasaki had survived two maritime disasters as a young man. He attributed his survival to the technical superiority of Western ships in which he had been sailing, and decided to devote his life to bringing such innovations to Japanese shipping. In April 1878, he accordingly borrowed ¥30,000 and leased harbor land in Tokyo from the Japanese government to begin his own shipbuilding company. Kawasaki hired a bright young engineer and opened for business, but he soon discovered that Japanese shipping lines were reluctant to abandon their ancient sailing vessels and traditional style of doing business. After a long wait the new firm finally received its first order, for the 80-ton *Hokkai Maru,* and Kawasaki invited thousands of business and government leaders to view its christening. This early venture succeeded in announcing the company's arrival in the burgeoning Japanese industrial sector.

Before long Kawasaki had as much work as he could handle. When the Meiji government began divesting major shipbuilding facilities, it offered one to Kawasaki, who happily moved his operations from Tokyo to Hyogo in 1886 and named the company Kawasaki Dockyard. With the Sino-Japanese War of 1894 spurring demand for ships, Kawasaki went public in 1896 as Kawasaki Dockyard Co., Ltd. Its first president was 31-year-old Kojiro Matsukata, and Kawasaki himself remained with the company only as an advisor. Matsukata immediately ordered the construction of a new, vastly larger dry dock which, upon completion in 1902, solidified Kawasaki's position as one of Japan's leading shipbuilders. At the same time, Matsukata bought up adjacent land and began a series of larger construction slips, increasing the company's building capacity from 6,000 to 31,000 gross tons. Both moves enabled Kawasaki to take advantage of various state subsidies with which the Japanese government encouraged industrial growth, but in a country lacking an industrial economy, it remained difficult for Kawasaki to get materials and parts. In most cases company engineers had to manufacture whatever they needed themselves, an inefficient but educational method of building modern steamships.

In 1906 Kawasaki opened a new factory to produce a variety of rolling stock—railroad cars, locomotives, and related parts. This was only the first of a series of such diversifications. The firm was soon not only building ships and railroad cars but also supplying its own steel plates and castings, as well as taking orders for large civil-engineering projects such as bridges. By the end of World War I, Kawasaki had, in addition, established itself as a maker of airplanes and automobiles, as it sought to keep pace with its heavy-industry rival, Mitsubishi. Kawasaki turned the relative backwardness of the Japanese economy to its advantage: it used the government's enforced education in the industrial arts to expand into new technologies as they found their way to Japan. This process accounts for the breadth of Kawasaki's current interests, and is similar to the development of other Japanese heavy-industry giants.

In the meantime, Kawasaki's shipbuilding business flourished. In 1907 the company introduced its first marine turbine engine, and shortly thereafter adopted German diesel technology. A chunk of the company's business involved naval contracts, like the 1905 construction of Japan's first submarine and the 1910 delivery of a 5,000-ton cruiser. These projects solidified Kawasaki's relationship with the Japanese navy, and in particular its role as a leading builder of submarines and anti-submarine aircraft. After weathering a brief recession, Kawasaki and Japanese shipbuilding a whole enjoyed a boom during World War I, when the Allies turned with increasing frequency to the Japanese for their shipping requirements. The jump in orders raised production to 12 times the prewar high, with Kawasaki finishing 35 ships in

1918 alone and creating an entirely new class of standardized freighters weighing between 6,000 and 9,000 tons each. These stock boats were highly successful.

The postwar recession in shipbuilding proved to be unusually harsh. In addition to the natural decline in orders, an Allied-sponsored arms-limitation agreement of 1921 forced the cancellation of several large warships still in Kawasaki docks. Perhaps worst of all was the company's failure to cut production of stock boats quickly enough. The excess boats were unsold, and despite rapidly expanding business in its steel, aircraft, and civil-engineering divisions Kawasaki was soon in serious financial trouble. A 1927 bank run left the company without working capital and forced a major restructuring: the rolling stock division was spun off as a separate entity; about 20% of the company's 16,000 employees were permanently laid off, and longtime-president Matsukata retired to be replaced by Fusanosuke Kojima. These decisions had no sooner been reached than the Depression struck in 1929, necessitating a second round of bank negotiations and corporate reductions.

War pulled Japan out of the Depression in 1931, when that country invaded Manchuria. Along with plentiful government subsidies, the growing need for warships quickly reinvigorated Kawasaki. Between 1937, when China was invaded, and the 1945 Japanese surrender, Kawasaki's employees produced 109 warships, including four aircraft carriers and 35 submarines. Midway through the war the Japanese government essentially took control of the shipbuilding industry, establishing a set of six standard warships to be built under their direction as needed. It was a period of intense productivity at Kawasaki, which also supplied the war effort with aircraft from the newly founded Kawasaki Aircraft Company. Merchant shipping picked up as well. Japan's need for oil spurred the introduction of what would later grow into the supertanker. Kawasaki had built 21 of these by the end of the war in August 1945.

Losses suffered by Kawasaki at war's end amounted to more than ¥1.7 billion, and the company once again required a major restructuring. It shed its steel division—which, as Kawasaki Steel Corporation, remains one of the country's foremost steel producers—and wrote off much of its debt. At this juncture Kawasaki was composed only of the shipbuilding, engine, and electrical-machinery divisions of the original entity, with rolling stock, aircraft, and steel all operating as separate companies.

Employment at Kawasaki had immediately dropped to less than 25% of its wartime peak, and the company was saddled with unpaid-for ships. The Kawasaki docks were still largely in one piece and functioning, however, and the company achieved prodigious postwar growth. For the first few years little was built, but with the growing perception of Communist China as a threat, the Allies encouraged Japan to rebuild its economy.

In August 1947 the Japanese government adopted the Programmed Shipbuilding Scheme, by which it directed the construction of new ships as needed while providing funds to the shipping lines to help them cover the purchase price. The scheme, which remains in effect, gave the shipbuilding industry the capital needed to restore productivity.

Thus fortified, Kawasaki resumed operations at all of its plants. Japan's shattered infrastructure promised work for a company with Kawasaki's construction capabilities, and its machinery, steel, and engine divisions were soon operating at full throttle. In particular, the Kawasaki steel division opened three new works and took the lead in Japanese sheet-steel production. The shipbuilding business was flooded with more orders than it could handle.

Beginning with the Korean war in 1950 and continuing through to the oil embargo of 1973, Kawasaki and the rest of Japan's shipbuilders enjoyed nearly unbroken success. By the mid-1950s Japan had become the world's leading shipbuilder—a remarkable achievement for a country broken by war only ten years earlier—and as the national economy surged toward eventual world leadership, Kawasaki flexed its muscle in several fields. Growing oil dependence of industrialized countries created a lucrative market for supertankers, and Kawasaki was soon expert in building these largest of all ships. At the same time, Kawasaki was also filling construction orders for everything from a cement plant in Malaysia to a baseball stadium in Koshien, Japan, while improving its technical expertise in engine and machinery design. Many of the latter improvements were the results of working agreements with leading European and U.S. firms, as Kawasaki pursued its policy of international cooperation. The company early formed alliances with Escher Wyss of Switzerland and IMO Ltd. of Sweden, and later worked with aeronautical giants Lockheed, Boeing, Hughes, and Messerschmidt on a wide variety of civil and military projects.

In 1969 the present Kawasaki Aircraft Heavy Industries was created by the reintegration of Kawasaki Aircraft and Kawasaki Rolling Stock with the original parent, Kawasaki Dockyard. The newly formed conglomerate suffered a blow in 1973 when the Arab oil embargo brought supertanker orders to an abrupt halt. Since that date the Japanese have steadily withdrawn from the shipbuilding field, and Kawasaki and the other big makers have turned their energy to more promising, and less competitive, endeavors. The diversity of Kawasaki's current portfolio is one result of this massive shift. Shipping now accounts for less than 10% of the company's revenue, less even than sales of leisure products like motorcycles and jet skis. Its shipbuilding business now tends to involve military and more exotic varieties of commercial vessels, as Kawasaki seeks to avoid direct competition with Korea, the new price leader in merchant shipping.

In contrast, Kawasaki's machinery and construction division has grown into the company's largest. Here Kawasaki builds everything from factory robots to an ethylene plant in Bulgaria, and also offers bridges, tunnel-boring machines, and breeder-reactor research. Almost as large is the aircraft division, doing a significant amount of work for the Japanese Defense Agency and the national space program. In rolling stock, Kawasaki supplied the New York subway system with a set of stainless steel, graffiti-proof cars, and has continued to deliver some of Japan's fastest railroad trains. Add to these three divisions the company's old standby and its newest addition—ships and leisure products—and one has a corporation capable of supplying modern civilization with most of its industrial needs.

Principal Subsidiaries: Kawasaki Heavy Industries (U.S.A.) Inc.; Kawasaki Rail Car, Inc. (U.S.A.); Kawasaki Loaders

Manufacturing Corp. (U.S.A.); Kawasaki Motors Corp. (U.S.A.); Kawasaki Motors Manufacturing Corp. (U.S.A.); Canadian Kawasaki Motors Inc. (Canada); Kawasaki do Brazil Industria e Comercio Ltda.; Kawasaki Motors (UK) Ltd.; Kawasaki Heavy Industries (Europe) B.V. (Netherlands); Kawasaki Motors N.V. (Netherlands); Kawasaki Jet Ski Europe N.V. (Netherlands); Kawasaki Motoren G.m.b.H. (Germany); Kawasaki Heavy Industries (H.K.) Ltd. (Hong Kong); Kawasaki Motors Pty. Ltd. (Australia).

Further Reading: Chida, Tomohei, and Peter N. Davies, *The Japanese Shipping and Shipbuilding Industries*, London, The Athlone Press, 1990.

—Jonathan Martin

KHD KONZERN

Deutz-Mülheimer Strasse 111
Postfach 80 05 09
5000 Cologne 80
Federal Republic of Germany
(221) 8220
Fax: (221) 822 3525

Public Company
Incorporated: 1864 as N.A. Otto & Cie.
Employees: 16,425
Sales: DM4.06 billion (US$2.40 billion)
Stock Exchanges: Frankfurt Düsseldorf Brussels Antwerp Paris

Klöckner-Humboldt-Deutz AG (KHD) and KHD Konzern (known in English as the KHD group), of which KHD is the parent company, are active in three main areas of business: engine manufacturing, agricultural technology, and the building of industrial plants. In 1989, engine manufacturing and related technology came first in the KHD group's activities, representing 62% of the group's world turnover, followed by agricultural technology (27%) and industrial plant construction (11%). More than two-thirds of turnover was achieved abroad. KHD is the world leader in the production of air cooled diesel engines.

The company's early history can be effectively retraced by following the letters of the firm's initials in reverse order. The "D" stands for Deutz, a suburb of Cologne, on the right bank of the Rhine, the original location of what was to become the vast KHD group. The Cologne businessman Nikolaus August Otto had been working on engine construction since 1860. As he did not have the financial means to cover his research costs, he went into partnership with the Cologne entrepreneur Eugen Langen, leading to the founding of the firm N.A. Otto & Cie. on March 31, 1864, and of the first engine factory in the world. After the atmospheric-pressure gas engine developed by Otto won a gold medal at the 1867 Universal Exhibition in Paris, and after the first orders had been received and a further investor—the Hamburg businessman Ludwig August Roosen-Runge—found, the company was able to leave its cramped workshop in the center of Cologne and to build a factory between Deutz and Mülheim on the right bank of the Rhine. As early as 1869, 87 engines were built here by the 40 employees. After Roosen-Runge had retired from the company, the petrol engine manufacturing factory Deutz AG was founded on January 5, 1872. Known by the abbreviation GFD, it was to provide a model for the German engine-building industry for the next half century. The same year saw the arrival of two figures who would play a major part in the company: Gottlieb Daimler, who joined as technical director, and Wilhelm Mayback, director of the construction department.

1876, when Otto and his employees brought the four-stroke engine into production, was an historic year in engine construction. It was known as the Otto engine, and paved the way for the motorization of industry and transport. New engines were developed in the following years: in 1884 the petrol engine with electric ignition, in 1898 a non-crosshead diesel engine, and in 1912 an unsupercharged diesel engine. At the same time output grew steadily, as did the plant and the work force. By 1913 the company was making 90,000 engines, the factory had grown 15 times in size since 1869, and there were 4,100 employees.

The years immediately after World War I were marked by the founding of syndicates. The first, in 1921, was with the engine manufacturer Oberursel AG, which had grown rapidly during the war through the construction of aeroplane engines, but which found itself in difficulty after 1918. The establishment of the syndicate put an end to competition between the two companies and their manufacturing programs were merged. In line with these changes, the firm's name was altered to the Motorenfabrik Deutz AG.

From 1906 the development of the company was closely influenced by Peter Klöckner, an entrepreneur from Duisburg who joined the GFD board in that year. In 1924, after acquiring a majority shareholding, he became chairman. Since 1915 he had been chairman of the engine manufacturers Humboldt AG, which had moved to Kalk, the neighboring suburb to Deutz. This company had sprung from the Maschinenfabrik für den Bergbau von Sievers & Co. (The Engine Plant for von Sievers & Co. Mining), which had become an *Aktiengesellschaft* (public limited company) under the title of Maschinenbauanstalt Humboldt AG in 1871 and which had continued to operate under its new name from 1884, after going into liquidation and undergoing restructuring. At first, production had been geared towards the mining industry, but by the end of the 19th century steam turbines and locomotives were also important products for the company. Before World War I the company employed around 5,000 employees.

The end of the war led to a major crisis for the Maschinenbauanstalt Humboldt AG as well as for the Motorenfabrik Oberursel. In his efforts to find a solution for the work force and the management of the two companies, Klöckner, as chairman of both, formed a syndicate between the Motorenfabrik Deutz and the Maschinenbauanstalt Humboldt in 1924, which eventually led to the merging of the two in 1930 together with the Motorenfabrik Oberursel, under the company name of Humboldt-Deutzmotoren AG. The "H" of KHD's initials stems from this event.

1936 saw the takeover of the heavy goods vehicle and bus manufacturer C.D. Magirus AG of Ulm, which had been severely affected by the Depression. This fusion with a manufacturer of commercial vehicles completed the company's product range. Above all, the takeover gave Humboldt-Deutzmotoren AG an additional secure market for its high-speed diesel engines, the output of which had been increasing since the 1920s.

The "K" entered the company name in 1938. After Peter Klöckner had secured approximately 78% of the capital of Humboldt Deutzmotoren, together with his stake in Klöckner Werke AG, an agreement was drawn up binding the company still more firmly to the Klöckner empire as a subsidiary. The company's present name, Klöckner-Humboldt-Deutz AG, was introduced with this agreement.

Humboldt-Deutzmotoren AG overcame relatively quickly the far-reaching repercussions of the Depression, which struck the company particularly hard due to the dependence of its product range on a buoyant economy. After the low of winter 1932 had passed—the company's work force had almost halved between 1929 and January 1933 to stand at roughly 4,400—a boom followed in the German production goods industry, aided in no small part by the National Socialist policy of building up armaments, in which KHD participated. In addition, rationalization measures carried out earlier now brought results. Production, measured in horsepower, rose some 750% from 1932–1933 to 1937–1938 to over one million horsepower, while the time for manufacturing one horsepower was more than halved from over 24 hours to a little over 12 hours. In the business year 1938–1939, the last before World War II, KHD achieved a turnover of 234 million reichsmarks with 19,300 employees, and the Cologne works alone achieved a turnover of almost 140 million reichsmarks with over 12,000 employees. In the crisis of 1932–1933, the turnover, although not including the Ulm Magirus factory at that time, had been only around 32 million reichsmarks.

KHD was not at that time a major supplier to the German army and therefore was not purely an armaments firm. The boom in 1938–1939 was based primarily on growing demand from the civilian sector. However, from 1939–1940 at the latest, the company began taking genuine orders for armaments.

When sales of a newly-developed tank engine fell through, with KHD's failure to break a competitor's monopoly, and when the order for the development of an airplane motor turned out to be a very lengthy affair, KHD turned its attention to the construction of submarine engines in the period that followed. In the Cologne-Poll factory a tank repair plant was also established. From 1941 most orders for KHD products came from the armed forces, since orders from abroad and from the private sector dwindled steadily owing to political developments and economic restrictions under the Nazi regime. The company was officially recognized as an armaments company in 1942 and was, furthermore, awarded the Golden Flag as a National Socialist Model Company and as a Model War Company, after numerous unsuccessful attempts to gain these titles.

In the years that followed, the consequences of the war began to be felt more and more severely in all divisions of the KHD works. There was a final economic upturn in 1940–1941, but from then onwards production and turnover proceeded to decline steadily. This situation was partly due to the increasing number of Allied air attacks on Cologne, which destroyed large sections of the production installations. This Allied action escalated in the summer of 1943, forcing the transfer of the production works to districts outside Cologne. In late summer of 1944, production in Cologne came to a complete halt. By the end of the war, KHD production had been relocated to 120 different places.

The conscription of large sections of the work force also created problems, with 4,345 employees from the Cologne plant already called up for military service by August 1943. These losses had to be covered through the intensified recruitment of women, pensioners, and young people, and, from 1942 onwards, as was the case in practically all German manufacturing companies, increasingly through the use of foreign workers, forced labor, and prisoners of war. The number of civilian foreigners working in the Cologne KHD plant had reached almost 2,000 by mid-1943, and constituted 25% of all the employees involved in production. These were supplemented by further prisoners of war and by around 400 Italian military internees.

When the U.S. Army took the right bank of Cologne in the middle of April 1945, the KHD plants were at a standstill. Only an emergency service of 40 people had been retained. An initial survey estimated that 45% of the buildings had been totally destroyed and 31% partly destroyed. Only 25% were still considered usable. The company's machines were in far better shape; 82% of the machinery was found to be ready for use once it had been brought out of storage. The first months after the war were spent clearing up and repairing the damage, but production resumed in some areas once a permit was issued by the U.S. military command on June 19, 1945 for the manufacturing of materials for the Allied forces. After a few setbacks caused by the economy measures of the British military command responsible for Cologne from July 1945, permission was granted on April 15, 1946, and June 1, 1946, for the production of the 11-horsepower farm tractor that had been extraordinarily successful before the war, and of small engines, respectively. This production allowed KHD to return to its traditional activities.

The German monetary reform of June 1948 marked a very important turning point for the company. Although production had resumed relatively early at KHD, production volume remained relatively low until this event. German monetary reform brought about a sharp increase in output and by the financial year 1950–1951 the company's highest prewar results had been easily surpassed, with a turnover of DM292 million from 15,700 employees. One particular development alongside the production of tractors made a significant contribution to this success—the air-cooled diesel engine. It had been in production from 1936 and led to initial military successes in the war. These air-cooled, high-speed engines were mass-produced from 1948 and were installed in heavy duty vehicles and tractors. KHD became the world leader in the production of these engines.

The restructuring of the German economy brought about the break-up of the Klöckner group on July 1, 1953, and with it the dissolution of its agreement with the Klöckner Werke AG. Klöckner AG's shareholding in KHD had to be dissolved with the result that the head company, Klöckner & Company, consolidated its shareholdings in KHD and became the main shareholder, represented primarily by the Henle family of Duisburg. In the same year KHD formed a syndicate with the Vereinigten Westdeutsche Waggonfabriken AG (VWW) whose two factories had been established in Mainz and in KHD's immediate neighborhood in Cologne-Deutz. It was possible for the two to cooperate, since the production capacity of the carriage factories was not being put to full use even after German monetary reform, allowing KHD to pass on production orders to VWW. In 1959 VWW was finally taken over by KHD.

As KHD celebrated its centenary in 1964 the company was able to look back with pride on its development since the war. Turnover for the business year 1963–1964 stood at DM1.6 billion, with a third of this figure derived from exports. By this time the group had around 250 representative agencies worldwide. In the mid 1960s, however, the German economy reached a postwar high and KHD saw a halt in its growth, for the first time since the war. This brought home to the company the difficulty of operating in sectors that were particularly dependent on a strong economy, such as farming, construction, and shipbuilding.

Important steps were taken by KHD in the production of commercial vehicles. By the end of 1971 KHD had entered a joint venture with three other European companies, the DAF group in the Netherlands, Saviem in France, and the Volvo group in Sweden, to buy materials for the development and production of middle-weight commercial vehicles. At the beginning of 1975 the company entered into close partnership with the Fiat group. Both partners divided up their commercial vehicles divisions and created new companies in this sector in Germany, France, and Italy, whose subsidiaries were brought together under the holding company Industrial Vehicles Corporation B.V. (IVECO), with headquarters in Amsterdam. KHD's share in this company, however, was only 20%.

Despite these measures, many observers criticized the company for its apparent lack of convincing entrepreuneurial direction, claiming that the company was developing along the wrong lines, and that its position in international markets was insignificant. The chairman was accused in particular of not concentrating the KHD group's efforts.

At this time KHD had a change of chairman. Heinrich Jakopp, who had held the position for 32 years, was succeeded by Karl-Heinz Sonne, who had previously been chairman of the Bayerische-Motoren-Werke (BMW) in Munich. His aim was to restructure and reorganize KHD so that "the ship that had run aground should be made to float again" within six to eight years. In this reorganization, the company made cutbacks in certain areas of production that did not seem to have a promising future, namely railway carriage and locomotive construction, bridge building and steelworks, and building machinery. However, Sonne placed increased emphasis on the production of tractors and agricultural machinery as well as plant construction. In spring 1968 and at the end of 1969 respectively, KHD acquired majority shareholdings in the agricultural machinery companies Fahr AG in Gottmadingen and Ködel & Böhn GmbH in Lauingen. The plant construction division was extended in spring 1969 through the acquisition of a majority holding in Westfalia Dinnendahl Gröppel AG (Wedag) of Bochum, previously a competitor of Humboldt. Wedag and Humboldt finally merged to become KHD Industrieanlagen AG in 1972.

In the middle of 1975 Bodo Liebe took over as chairman of KHD. Without making any fundamental changes to Sonne's strategy, he was initially successful in improving the company's position. Although no dividends had been paid out to shareholders in 1973, KHD shares had increased 200% in value within five years. The complete withdrawal from the commercial vehicles business represented an important step for the company. On January 1, 1980, KHD made use of its right to withdraw from IVECO and to sell its 20% shareholding to Fiat. One motive for this move was to strengthen the company's position as an independent engine supplier. The proceeds from this transaction, estimated at between DM600 million and DM1 billion were placed tax-free in a Dutch subsidiary, KHD Nederland, to finance future expansion schemes. Through this sale KHD's former "grocery shop," as Liebe called it, reduced its operations to three key areas: motors—engines and turbines—representing roughly 50% of activities; agricultural machinery—tractors and harvesters—representing more than 30% of business; and industrial plants, representing around 20% of total turnover.

Liebe's success did not continue unabated. In his attempt to establish at least one of KHD's three production areas as world leader in its field, costly misjudgments and bad investments were made. Liebe had not expected that a stagnation and even a drop in sales would result from his policy of concentrating on the company's three basic requirements of energy, maintenance, and the acquiring of raw materials. He set much store by the maxim of survival through growth, growth which was to be financed by the money from the profits set aside from the IVECO share sell-off. The KHD board also considered it essential to establish a firmer footing in the North American market. This ambition, coupled with the unfavorable economic climate and Liebe's characteristic optimism, led the KHD group into deep crisis.

KHD's management saw the large increase in petrol prices towards the end of the 1970s as offering a good opportunity to break into the North American market with its air-cooled diesel engine. Its first step in this direction was the acquisition in autumn 1979 of a former engine plant in Richmond, Indiana, belonging to the American Motors Corporation, which was converted to adapt KHD engines for the U.S. market. The plant was originally intended to have the capacity to produce 20,000 engines a year. However, production fell well short of this target. In 1981 and 1982 it was only with difficulty that a mere 7,000 engines were produced and sold. In 1983 the plant was shut down. In autumn 1981 a large engine factory was projected for Canada, in Boucherville near Montreal, that was intended to produce 10,000 engines on its completion in 1983. Production would eventually be increased to between 30,000 and 70,000 units. Furthermore, a new engine was specifically designed for the U.S. market which, it was initially thought, could be built into U.S. Army jeeps. KHD lost out to U.S. competition, however, so that the Canadian factory had to be shelved even before production had begun or a single order taken. Up to this point the Canadian episode had cost KHD approximately DM80 million.

Yet KHD committed itself once again to the U.S. market. As Liebe's strategy included the strengthening of the company's range of end products, specifically tractors and agricultural machinery, to support the company's all-important engine manufacturing division, KHD bought the greater part of the agricultural machinery company Allis-Chalmers Corporation of Milwaukee, Wisconsin, in May 1985 for US$107 million. Together with the production of combine harvesters, the existing stock of components, and the production rights for tractors, engines, and components, the takeover included

Allis-Chalmers's entire sales division, with a network of 1,100 agricultural machinery dealerships. However, instead of yielding the expected turnover of US$500 million for 1987, with KHD's German factories operating at full capacity, the acquisition proved misjudged. It was not the bargain it had seemed, owing to miscalculations. Since 1979 the volume of trade in the U.S. agricultural machinery market had diminished by 75%, overcapacity and old stock were squeezing prices, and the fall of the dollar made the proposition of exporting from Germany more expensive than had been envisaged. What Liebe had seen as a step into a new era led KHD to the verge of financial collapse.

A further West German venture similarly failed to bring positive results. After its unsuccessful attempt to gain a foothold in North American with air-cooled diesel engines, KHD took over the Motoren-Werke Mannheim AG (MWM) at the end of 1984 for around DM80 million. MWM's water-cooled diesel engines seemed a sensible addition to KHD's product range. However, KHD's management had clearly underestimated the need to restructure MWM. In the first two years of business under KHD, losses of around DM100 million were recorded.

The year 1987 was decisive for KHD. Operating losses and structural changes swallowed up around DM725 million in that year, drying up almost all of the "war provision" or "piggy-bank savings," as the proceeds from the IVECO sale were described. At the same time, turnover for KHD AG and the KHD group had fallen from DM4.6 billion and DM5.7 billion, respectively, in 1984 to DM3.15 billion and DM4.43 billion.

By this time the in-house maxim "Könner halten durch" (Experts cope through thick and thin) no longer rang true. At the height of the crisis in January 1988 Bodo Liebe was succeeded as chairman by Karl-Josef Neukirchen who, in view of the problems he had to face and the policies to which he adhered, was soon seen as Germany's equivalent to Lee Iacocca, the man who saved Chrysler.

Neukirchen tackled the radical restructuring of the KHD group that involved a large reduction in the work force. From 1987 to 1989 the number of employees was reduced by 32% to 16,425. Worldwide, 6,300 KHD employees lost their jobs. The savings achieved amounted to an annual figure of around DM300 million and were, in Neukirchen's opinion, absolutely essential for the group's survival. The cuts affected many areas of the work force, giving rise to a new interpretation of the company's abbreviation KHD—"Keiner hilft dir" (No one will help you). Management was also pared down in Neukirchen's structuring measures. Together with Liebe, three other board members had to step down in January 1988.

In addition the group's structure was tightened considerably. After KHD had got rid of 15 subsidiaries in 1988 that together represented losses of DM200 million, the Deutz-Fahr-Werk in Gottmandingen was also sold. The group finally managed to dispose of its "black hole" in the United States, Deutz-Allis, in December 1989, at a further or one-time loss of DM282 million. The restructuring of the company begun in 1987 was completed with the sale of the KHD Luftfahrttechnik GmbH of Oberursel in May 1990. In 1989 the group was able to show a profit for the first time since 1985.

In addition to these measures, the KHD group was split into strategic business units that were made fully responsible for their business performance, while KHD AG was to operate as the managing holding company.

The KHD group's aims for the future are clearly defined: concentration on its key businesses and considerable commitment to research-and-development spending. Particular emphasis has been laid on the production division with which the company started in 1864. Neukirchen wishes to extend the high-speed diesel engine division to make it competitive in world markets. The second part of KHD's redevelopment is also due to begin. Following the three-year program to save the group by divestments and cut-backs, the company then intended to return to the offensive. A completely new production program for air-cooled diesel engines and plans for two new engine factories in Cologne and Mannheim were in preparation. The agricultural machinery division would concentrate increasingly on the European and North African markets and would follow the trend for more powerful engines. Finally, the company aimed to pay more attention to the environmental aspects of new industrial development projects. Furthermore, KHD was hoping for a recovery of business in all its divisions through the liberalization of Eastern European markets.

Principal Subsidiaries: Motoren-Werke Mannheim AG; MWM Diesel und Gastechnik GmbH; INDUMONT Industrie-Montage GmbH; HUMBOLDT-LOTZ Elektrotechnik GmbH; Ad. Strüver KG (GmbH & Co.); W. Schmidt-Bretten GmbH; Deutz MAG S.A. (France); DEUTZ DITER S.A. (Spain).

Further Reading: Goldbeck, Gustav, *Kraft für die Welt, 1864–1964,* Düsseldorf, Klöckner-Humboldt-Deutz AG, 1964; Reuss, Hans-Jürgen, "Die Vorläuferfirmen der Klöckner-Humboldt-Deutz AG von 1864–1930," *Rechtsrheinisches Köln,* Number 2, 1976; Reuss, Hans-Jürgen, "Die Entwicklung der Klöckner-Humboldt-Deutz AG von 1930–1964," *Rechtsrheinisches Köln,* Number 3, 1977; Rüther, Martin, "Zur Sozialpolitik bei Klöckner-Humboldt-Deutz während des Nationalsozialismus," *Zeitschrift für Unternehmensgeschichte,* Number 33, 1988; Aders, G., "Die Firma Klöckner-Humboldt-Deutz AG im Zweiten Weltkrieg," *Rechtsrheinisches Köln,* Number 14, 1988 and Number 15, 1989.

—Martin Rüther

KOMATSU LTD.

KOMATSU LTD.

3-6, Akasaka 2-chome
Minato-ku, Tokyo 107
Japan
(03) 3561-2616
Fax: (03) 3587-2003

Public Company
Incorporated: 1921
Employees: 15,398
Sales: ¥792.81 trillion (US$5.52 billion)
Stock Exchanges: Tokyo Osaka Nagoya Luxembourg Frankfurt

A large Japanese multinational firm, Komatsu is the second-largest manufacturer of construction tractors and earth movers in the United States, after Caterpillar. Products include forklift trucks, dump trucks, bulldozers, hydraulic excavators, road surface survey vehicles, and rough-terrain cranes.

In 1988 Komatsu sharpened its competitive edge in the U.S. market by forming a joint venture with Dresser Industries, Komatsu Dresser Company. This combination of a major U.S. producer with a major Japanese global player, Komatsu, added considerable research-and-development resources to the U.S. firm. Furthermore, the combination has enabled Komatsu to move assembly of its construction equipment to the United States, using Dresser plants that were running at 50% capacity while Komatsu was unable to fill all of its orders.

Komatsu divisions produce a wide variety of products, including plastics injection molding machinery, electronic parts, optical tablets, laser machines, armored cars for the military, small-diameter pipe jacking systems, machine tools, diesel engines, and hydraulic presses. In addition, the company has business in real estate, trading, computer software, and printing and publishing.

While its main manufacturing operations are in Japan, Komatsu owns production plants as well as sales and services units in other countries, mainly in the United States, Canada, the United Kingdom, Mexico, and Indonesia. Other operations with foreign partners are located in India, New Zealand, Malaysia, China, Republic of Korea, Turkey, Germany, and Italy. Sales and support offices are found in Belgium, the Soviet Union, China, Spain, France, Singapore, Australia, Cuba, Austria, Kenya, Algeria, South Africa, Ivory Coast, Egypt, Iran, Pakistan, and India.

The firm has shown a quick response to the 1992 integration of Europe by the European Common Market. British operations included purchase agreements with the British firm of Perkins Engines Ltd. for diesel engines to power Komatsu excavators. The U.K. plant in Birtley is the main production facility for European construction equipment. Other parts come from Spain, France, Belgium, and Germany. An additional agreement with the Italian firm of FAI to manufacturer under license mini-hydraulic excavators adds to a strong European presence.

Komatsu had its origins in 1894 when the Takeuchi Mining Company was founded. A major expansion occurred in 1917, during World War I, when the Komatsu ironworks was established to manufacture mining equipment and machine tools to expand the mining operations. The name Komatsu came into existence in 1921 when the ironworks separated from the mining company to become Komatsu. Tashiro Shiraishi, an engineer, was the founder and first president, serving until 1925. In the 1920s and 1930s the firm grew as a major manufacturer of machine tools and pumps, including development of a metal press in 1924 and the firm's first farm tractor in 1931. Production of steel materials began in 1935.

By 1929 the number of employees had risen to 742, from its original 1921 work force of 121 employees. During the height of the Great Depression in 1933 it dropped to 505 workers. The firm soon increased production and by 1936 increased its staff to 601. Mitsugi Nakemura served as president during the Depression and war years, from 1934 to 1946.

During World War II the firm expanded by supplying the navy with antiaircraft artillery shells and bulldozers. Bulldozer production gave the company its major product after the war, a redesigned bulldozer, which came off the assembly line in 1947. One year later diesel engines were produced. From 1947 to 1964 President Yoshinari Kawai provided key leadership in rebuilding the company and making it a global multinational corporation.

The Korean War gave the Japanese economy an economic boost with orders from the U.S. to supply its troops in Korea. At that time the firm had plants in Awazu, Osaka, Kaweasaki, Himi, and Komatsu, Japan. Production of forklift trucks, dump trucks, armored cars, and shell mold castings were added to the line. By 1959, defense production included armored personnel carriers and self-propelled cannons.

International activities increased in 1955 when both construction equipment and presses were shipped outside the country. In 1958, operations started in India with an agreement between the firm and the Indian government to manufacture tractors. Another license agreement was signed with a U.S. manufacturer, Cummins Engine Company, to make and sell diesel engines.

By the early 1960s the firm had grown to the point where a new headquarters was needed, and the present headquarters, Komatsu Building, was constructed in Tokyo. In 1964, the firm received the Deming Prize for implementation of quality control. William Edwards Deming was the father of quality control in the United States. Until the late 1970s, he was almost totally ignored by his fellow Americans, while his lectures and writings on quality control between 1950 and 1952 became the bible of Japanese manufacturing.

Ryoichi Kawai became president in 1964. The 1960s meant an economic build-up for Japan as a result of the Viet Nam

War. Komatsu's expansion continued at a rapid pace. The latter part of the decade saw a new engine plant starting production in Japan, as well as a radio-controlled bulldozer and the establishment of a technical research center.

In 1970, the firm began its first direct investment operations in the United States, with the establishment of Komatsu America Corporation. Other foreign operations soon followed, in Singapore in 1971, and Australia in 1979. Mexico, Brazil, and China, became sites for Komatsu's bulldozer plants during the 1970s.

In 1981, Komatsu was awarded the Japan Quality Control Prize, to honor the company's outstanding production quality. The following year Shoji Nogawa became president. The 1980s brought the flowering of global operations. In 1985, after a number of incentives from the state of Tennessee, Komatsu purchased a 55-acre empty plant in Chattanooga. This purchase reflected a decision by the firm to challenge its number-one world competitor, Caterpillar, in its home market. U.S. and Canadian operations expanded, including the joint venture with Dresser Industries. Two plants were built in the Canadian provinces of Quebec and Ontario. European operations included an interest in the West German construction firm of Hamomag AG, a licensing agreement with FAI of Italy, and a plant in the United Kingdom.

The year 1987 marked expansion in other areas such as the establishment of two financial subsidiaries in Europe, the marketing of plastics injection molding machinery, and the development of a telephone with a data terminal. From 1985 to 1987 construction equipment sales dropped each year. As a result the company president, Shoji Nogawa, was dismissed by Chairman Ryoichi Kawai and succeeded by CEO Masao Tataka.

Participation in the global market became essential for all large firms, and a reorganization of Komatsu reflected this necessity. In 1988 an international-business division was set up in the Tokyo headquarters. The division had three regional groups which were the main focus of the firm's international business operations: the Americas, Europe, and Japan. The goals of the division included development of joint ventures around the world and overseas purchase of parts.

Another organizational change in 1988 was the establishment of a new subsidiary, Komatsu Trading International, to increase imports to Japan. This development was a response to the Japanese government commitment to reduce its trade surplus by importing more foreign products. As a result logging machinery from Canada, backhoe loaders from Italy, and high-powered motor boats from Norway were brought into Japan for sale in the domestic market under importer agreements between Komatsu and companies in the respective countries.

In 1988 Komatsu made an agreement with the Robbins Company of Seattle, Washington, which purchased Komatsu's technology on softground tunnel-boring machinery to be used in constructing the tunnel under the English Channel.

In 1989 Tetsuya Katada became CEO. Extensive use of robots and continued modernization of Komatsu plants around the world were means of insuring global competitiveness.

Principal Subsidiaries: Komatsu Dresser Company (U.S.A., 50%); Komatsu UK Ltd.; Dina Komatsu Nacional S.A. de C.V. (Mexico, 68.4%); P.T. Komatsu Indonesia (55%); Komatsu Dresser Brazil (50%); Komatsu America Industries (U.S.A.); N.V. Komatsu Europe S.A. (Belgium); Komatsu Baumaschinen Deutschland (Germany); Komatsu Industries Europe G.m.b.H. (Germany); Komatsu Singapore Pte.; Komatsu Australia Pty.; Komatsu Overseas Finance PLC (U.K.); Komatsu Finance (Netherlands) B.V.

Further Reading: Fact Book '89: Komatsu, Tokyo, Komatsu Ltd., 1989.

—Joseph A. LeMay

Konica

KONICA CORPORATION

26-2, Nishi-shinjuku 1-chome
Shinjuku-ku, Tokyo 163
Japan
(03) 3349-5251
Fax: (03) 3349-5250

Public Company
Incorporated: 1936 as Konishiroku Honten Co., Ltd.
Employees: 5,091
Sales: ¥509.11 billion (US$3.54 billion)
Stock Exchanges: Tokyo Osaka Nagoya Niigata Luxembourg Frankfurt Düsseldorf Paris

Konica Corporation produces a wide range of products in four categories: cameras and optical products, photographic materials and photo-related industrial equipment, business machines, and magnetic products. The products that accounted for the largest share of the company's sales in early 1990 are film, 26%, and business machines, 32%. Even though it is Japan's second-largest producer of photographic materials, Konica is often called "Japan's Kodak" due to its long history and reputation for producing medium-grade cameras. Although it is not the leader in any one industry, Konica remains highly competitive in several.

The company was founded in 1873, during the first decade of Japan's industrial revolution, by Rokusaburo Sugiura, who suggested that his employer, the Konishiya apothecary in Kojimachi, Tokyo, begin to sell the new cameras and photographic materials that were being imported from Europe and the United States. The apothecary owners consented and gave Sugiura permission to use the Konishiya name. This was seven years before Kodak was founded.

In 1876 Sugiura changed his name to Rokuemon Sugiura VI to continue the succession of his father's name, moved the business to Nihonbashi, Tokyo, and renamed it Konishi Honten. In about 1880, Rokuosha, a subsidiary company, became a subcontractor for Konishi, producing cameras for commercial applications. By 1882 Konishi had established three factories for manufacturing lithographic materials and equipment, and matte paper for picture mounting and had begun to produce box cameras. By 1890, Konishi expanded camera production from an on-order basis to planned production, and four years later, was producing a variety of studio, field, and folding cameras.

In 1902 a Rokuosha factory was established to manufacture photographic paper and dry plates in what is now Shinjuku, Tokyo. A year later, the company began to market the box-shaped Cherry hand camera, the country's first name-brand camera. Also in 1903, Konishi introduced the Sakura—or cherry blossom, the Japanese national flower—brand name on Japan's first domestically produced photographic paper.

During the next five years, the Sakura brand name was to be found on many new Konishi cameras, including the Sakura Honor Portable, a box camera, and the Reflex Prano, the first Japanese large format single-lens-reflex (SLR) camera. In 1909, Konishi introduced three new name-brand camera models: Pearl, Lily, and Idea, all known for their quality construction.

World War I, which began in 1914, stimulated the Japanese economy and forced many industries to become less dependent on foreign goods. The importation from Germany, for example, of barium compound–coated paper and paper base was barred during the war, and Konishi's Rokuosha developed a method of producing photographic base paper in cooperation with Mitsubishi Paper Company. At the close of the war in 1919, Japan's total industrial production had almost quadrupled that of the 1914 level, and in the same period, the size of the industrial work force had more than doubled.

A 1916 Konishi catalog reported that the company was exporting the Lily Number 2 camera to Great Britain. This was considered a matter of considerable pride because Great Britain was regarded as the birthplace of photography. During the next ten years, the company developed a variety of new camera models, photographic papers, and processes.

Konishi Honten was renamed Konishiroku in 1921 and reorganized as a limited partnership. On September 1, 1923, the company's headquarters was completely destroyed in the Great Kanto Earthquake. The structure was rebuilt very quickly, and Konishiroku was back in business by the next month.

In 1925 Konishiroku received orders for gun cameras from the Japanese Imperial Navy Command. Rokuosha developed the first domestically produced photographic lens for the navy's gun cameras that year. Known as the Hexar F/4.5—Hexar was taken from the lineage of Rokuemon Sugiura: *roku* means six, or hexa—it was a copy of a lens produced by Thornton, a British company. Although Japanese cameras had included imported photographic lenses up to this time, the Japanese Navy was determined to achieve self-sufficiency in defense matters and had urged the production of such a lens.

In the same year, the company introduced the Pearlette, the first of a well-received line of cameras that would be produced for many years. It was the first metal-bodied camera produced by Konishiroku and was considered innovative, even though it was modeled after Kodak's vest-pocket camera. To publicize the camera and promote photography, Konishiroku formed the Pearlette League, a club for those whose first camera was a Pearlette. The club offered publications, contests, and a variety of other activities.

During the next ten years, Konishiroku introduced a variety of new products. In 1929 it began to market Sakura brand film, one of the first films produced in Japan. The company introduced its first movie projector in 1931 and its first movie camera in 1935.

In 1936 the company was registered as a publicly owned corporation with the name Konishiroku Honten Company. In 1938, as the liklihood of war increased, the Japanese government placed restrictions on cameras produced for consumers, and Konishiroku directed its major efforts to military products. It developed two types of ultra-compact aerial cameras for the Japanese Army in 1939 and 1940. In 1940, five years after Kodak introduced its Kodachrome color film, Konishiroku unveiled its Sakura natural color, Japan's first color film.

Rokuemon Sugiura VIII, grandson of the company's founder, became president of Konishiroku in 1941. Two years later, the company changed its name to Konishiroku Photo Industry Company, and established a research center. In 1944, under an industrial readjustment order, Konishiroku amalgamated with Showa Photo Industry.

In 1945, the company's Yodobashi factory, warehouse, and research center were damaged by U.S. air raids. At the end of the war, in September, all factories that had been taken over for military production reverted back to the manufacture of consumer goods. Despite a severe shortage of parts, Konishiroku resumed production of several cameras.

Before the war, Konishiroku had developed and built a prototype of the Rubikon, a general use camera using 35-millimeter film. The camera had not yet been put into production. When war broke out and the company's plants were directed entirely to the manufacture of cameras and optical instruments for military applications, the Rubikon was converted into a camera for taking x-ray pictures and was used for medical applications. After the war, Konishiroku returned the Rubikon to its original design but decided to change its name, as the old name was too much like the Rubicon, the river Caesar crossed on his march to seize Rome. As the name was considered unsuitable in a time so recently removed from war, the name of the camera was changed to Konica—from ''Konishiroku'' and ''camera''. Thus was the company's first 35-millimeter camera introduced in 1947.

In 1947 Konishiroku was listed as one of Japan's five leading photographic-lens makers and one of three camera-shutter producers. Konishiroku produced approximately half of all Japanese cameras. Materials such as goat skin for camera bellows, sheet steel for shutters, and piano cord for shutter control were all in short supply, but camera companies were finding substitutes for these materials.

In 1948 *The Dream,* the first Japanese color motion picture, won an award from the Japanese Motion Picture Technology Institute. The film had used Sakura color film.

The following year, Japan experienced a deep economic depression. Many small- and medium-sized businesses failed and unemployment was high. Only the Korean War, beginning in June 1950, rescued the economy, with large special procurement orders that stimulated many industries, including those making cameras and optical instruments.

For Konishiroku, the 1950s were a time of growth and continued product refinement. In an effort to increase its U.S. exports, the company established Koniphoto Corporation in Philadelphia, Pennsylvania, in 1956, to market its cameras and photographic materials. That same year, the company won the Deming Prize for Industrial Efficiency for the excellence of its quality-control activities in upgrading productivity. W.E. Deming, a U.S. specialist in statistical quality control, had spurred the development of quality control in Japan in a series of visits to Japan that began in the early 1950s.

In 1962 the company moved Koniphoto from Philadelphia to New York City and opened Konica European Center in Hamburg as a marketing outpost. The following year, it closed its Yodobashi factory and built a large, state-of-the-art factory in Hachioji, a Tokyo suburb. The first Japanese company to produce x-ray film, Konishiroku had begun its manufacture in 1933 under the Sakura name and produced its first x-ray processor in 1963. The following year, it unveiled Sakura color negative film, the industry's fastest color negative film. In December 1965, after overcoming a variety of technical challenges, Konishiroku introduced the Konica Autoreflex, the industry's first automatic-exposure 35-millimeter SLR.

In 1967, Konishiroku suffered heavy losses caused by the production of defective color film and its inability to increase its market share. Up to this time, members of the company's top management had been selected from the controlling family; but in 1968, a new management team was put in place to turn the company around, and Ryousuke Nishimura became the new president. The new team was successful in slowly diversifying the company into fields that made use of technologies related to cameras and optical instruments and in making the company's products more competitive. Planning for new products became market oriented, with management collecting appropriate market information before undertaking development of a new product. The new management team also improved employee training and personnel selection, as well as employee-evaluation methods.

The 1970s were a period of rapid expansion for Konishiroku. In 1971 the company introduced the U-Bix 480, its first photostatic plain-paper copier. By 1978, plain-paper copiers would account for 23% of the company's total sales. Many of Japan's camera companies had begun to produce small copiers. Their expertise in optics and their existing distribution networks aided this diversification.

Konishiroku celebrated its 100th anniversary in 1973 and began to use the Konica name on more of the products it sold in the European and North American markets. In the same year, the company established a subsidiary called Konishiroku Photo Industry (Europe) in Hamburg to market photographic products. The year 1973 also saw the installation of a new company president, Hiroshi Tomioka.

In 1975, a year of growth and change for Konishiroku, the company introduced the Konica C35 EF, the first of a new generation of compact cameras with a built-in electronic flash. U-Bix copiers were well received, with sales reaching the 50,000-unit mark by 1975. That same year, the company exported its first photographic-paper-making plant to the Soviet Union.

Konishiroku introduced the Konica C35 AF, a camera featuring an automatic focusing system, in 1977. Although more than a dozen camera manufacturers had signed agreements with Honeywell to use its automatic-focus technology, Konica's autofocus camera was the first to reach the market. Coupled with the introduction two years earlier of the Konica C35 EF with its built-in flash, Konica was regaining its reputation as an innovator.

In 1978 Konishiroku moved its headquarters to Tokyo's Shinjuku ward and opened a branch office in Great Britain to market cameras and photographic materials. That same year, the company was one of four Tokyo-based companies accused by Minnesota Mining and Manufacturing Company of dumping color photographic paper in the United States at prices considerably below what they charged in their home markets. In June 1979, toward the end of his tenure as president, Hiroshi Tomioka told *Focus Japan* that because his company "had bought very little equipment during its business slump in the late 1960s, it now has little to lose from carrying out a radical scrap-and-build operation to utilize advanced technologies."

In 1979 Konishiroku established a photo-products-marketing subsidiary, Konica Corporation (USA), the first foreign operation to sport the popular Konica name. The company also introduced the Konica FS-1, the camera industry's first motorized, auto-loading, and auto-winding compact SLR camera. Nobuhiko Kawanto became the company's new president that year.

Konishiroku's most notable activity in 1979 was the purchase of its first shares in the U.S.–based Fotomat chain of photofinishing stores, which had experienced a drop in profits the previous year. In an attempt to gain an established channel to the U.S. markets for film and photographic-paper, Konishiroku purchased 8% of Fotomat. In return, the photofinisher agreed to sell Konishiroku film under the Fotomat name and to purchase its photographic printing paper from the Japanese company. The company increased its stake in Fotomat to 20% in 1982, to about 62% in 1985, and completed its acquisition in 1986. Fotomat had begun to lose money by 1982, suffering from shortsighted business decisions, overexpansion, and increased competition from mass merchandisers who set up their own photo laboratories and from minilabs, which provide customers with prints in an hour. By 1988, Fotomat had dwindled from a peak of 3,850 kiosks and stores to 1,700 outlets and was reorganized. It also somewhat belatedly recognized the importance of minilabs and began converting many of its kiosks and stores to while-you-wait developing centers.

The price of silver, an essential ingredient in films, skyrocketed in 1980, and Konica, like other film producers worldwide, was forced to repeatedly raise its film prices. Early that year, both Konica and its principle domestic competitor, Fuji Photo Film Company, were investigated by Japan's Fair Trade Commission for conspiring to fix x-ray-film prices. That same year, Konishiroku announced it would go into the audio- and video-magnetic-tape business with Ampex Corporation.

In the early 1980s, Konica obtained exclusive rights to sell Polaroid products in the Japanese market. It also established subsidiaries in both Australia and Canada to market cameras, photographic materials, and magnetic products.

Megumi Ide was named company president in 1983, the same year that Konishiroku introduced the Konica AF3 camera, with the company's own infrared autofocus system replacing the Honeywell autofocus system. The company introduced its first video camera that year, the Konica Color CV, which was touted as the world's smallest and lightest video camera for home use.

Konica's business-machines division picked up steam in the 1980s. The company acquired a 30% interest in Royal Business Machines in 1984 and agreed to sell its plain-paper copiers under Royal's name. The following year, it agreed to start supplying Olivetti with copiers that would be marketed throughout Europe under the Olivetti name. In effect, Konica would end up competing with itself in the European copier market. The company also agreed to export a copier plant to China that year.

The year 1986 saw much activity for Konishiroku. It purchased the balance of Royal Business Machines's stock, and it changed that company's name to Konica Business Machines U.S.A. It entered into an agreement with IBM to sell that company's high-speed copiers under the Konica name worldwide. Konishiroku introduced a dramatic improvement over conventional floppy discs, the super-high-density 5.25-inch floppy disc and drive system with a ten-megabyte memory capacity, which it had developed and would produce and market in cooperation with Omron Tateisi Electronics Company and Citizen Watch Company. It introduced the Konica Color 7 copier, a reasonably priced, full-color copier that produced copies said to be difficult to distinguish from color photographs.

The company also established two new business-division production plants: one in Lüneberg, West Germany, in 1987, for manufacturing plain-paper copiers and the other in Maryland, in 1990, for manufacturing copier supplies. Between 1984 and 1989, the company acquired business-machine sales agencies in several new locations, including the United States, Australia, Italy, and Belgium.

Japan's leadership in facsimile terminals can be attributed to its strength in copier technology. Konica entered this market a bit late, offering its first facsimile terminals in 1988. It is interesting to note how the Japanese government aided the early demand for facsimile machines. Japan was one of the first countries to allow facsimile machines to be connected to regular phone lines, and the Japanese Ministry of Justice approved facsimile copiers as legal documents when the machine's technology was still in its nascent stage.

Konishiroku introduced a high-quality aspherical plastic pick-up lens for use in compact disc players in 1984, the same year it established Konica Technology, in Sunnyvale, California, a research, development, and marketing subsidiary for high-technology products. It also introduced its first minilab system that year, the Nice Print System–1, the world's first washless print-processing minilab. The revolutionary system required no water hookup and needed only to be plugged in to an electrical outlet to operate. Competitors soon rushed to market similar systems.

In the 1980s Konishiroku's problems with Fotomat, its inability to capitalize on its washless minilab system, and an increasingly competitive copier market all contributed to Konishiroku's financial difficulties. Between 1982 and 1985, Konishiroku's sales rose 24% but its net income for the same period fell by 17%. To aggravate the situation, beginning in 1986 the rising yen began to play havoc with Konica's profits. Fluctuating exchange rates have narrowed the profit margin of the company's exports.

In 1985 Konica began construction of the Kobe plant, a totally automatic production facility for the design and production of computer peripheral equipment and printers. Konica began to market its first laser printers in 1990.

In fall of 1987, Konishiroku changed its name to Konica Corporation. Although the company had been unifying its product and brand names in European and North American markets since 1973, many people, even in Japan, did not know that Konishiroku produced U-Bix copiers and Sakura film. By unifying its corporate and product names, the company raised its corporate profile worldwide. It also increased its advertising budget, and sponsored athletic teams, such as the U.S. rhythmic gymnastics team, and began to fly a blimp bearing the Konica name in Japan, as do competitors Fuji and Kodak. The company also funded the Konica Gallery, a Japanese gallery in the British Museum that opened in 1990. As Konica claims just 20% of the Japanese film market, such efforts are needed at home as well as internationally.

Konica introduced two important new products in 1987: its first still video system, which records images on a magnetic disc for immediate viewing on a television set, and the world's fastest color negative film, the Konica SR-V3200, which doubled the light sensitivity of any film on the market of that time. That same year, the company announced it would become the first Japanese producer of photosensitive materials to set up a manufacturing plant in the United States. In 1989 Konica Manufacturing U.S.A. opened in Whitsett, North Carolina; it produces color photographic paper.

In 1987 Konica's medical-products division began to sell a desktop system for analyzing blood, at the rate of 80 patients an hour; an x-ray–developing system that cut developing time to 45 seconds, half the time taken by other techniques; and the Konica Direct Digitizer, which enables the digitization of radiographic images.

Konica was one of seven Japanese companies accused of dumping by the European Community Commission in 1988. The companies were accused of making photocopiers in Europe using mainly Japanese parts in an attempt to avoid an anti-dumping duty. Konica responded that 40% of its copier parts were manufactured locally.

Konica introduced two new cameras in 1989. The Kanpai—Japanese for "toast" or "cheers"—with a voice-activated shutter, is intended for use at parties and other social events and has received a favorable market reception. The Konica A4, the world's smallest and lightest fully automatic compact camera, won the European Compact Camera of the Year Award for 1989–1990. That year, Konica also introduced the SR-G series of film, a new series of color negative films offering a high level of image quality and speed.

Konica's increasing emphasis on research and development has paid off. Between 1985 and 1989, the company's research-and-development expenditures rose from ¥13.3 billion to ¥19.6 billion. In the test-marketing stage in Japan, in 1990, was a customer-operated minilab that would allow users to have film developed any time of the day. Plans called for the possible appearance in the United States of the minilab in the 1990s. Although it is still attempting to get a foothold on the U.S. film market, Konica's prospects for success are poor, as Kodak and Japanese rival Fuji Photo Film dominate the market heavily, with Konica holding just a 1.7% market share in the United States. Konica also sells film to other companies, bringing its total share of the color negative film market to about 6%.

Each of the industries in which Konica is engaged is highly competitive, from technological, production, and marketing standpoints. Its diversification and increased emphasis on research and development should help it weather industry downturns. The company's outlook hinges on the high value of the yen, trade imbalances, and protectionist trade policies. These are problems that all Japanese manufacturers who export their products must face.

Principal Subsidiaries: Konica Trading Corporation; Konica Sales Corporation; Konica Medical Inc.; Konica Color Kizai Co., Ltd.; Konica Business Machines Japan Co., Ltd.; Konica Magnetix Corporation; Nihon ID System Co., Ltd.; Konica Distribution Center Co., Ltd.: Konica Physical Distribution Service Co., Ltd.; Yamanashi Konica Co., Ltd.; Kofu Konica Co., Ltd.; Konica Gelatin Corporation; Konica Packaging Corporation; Konica Fine Chemicals Co., Ltd.; Konica Nikko Chemical Corporation; Konica Magnetic Products Inc.; Konica Supplies Manufacturing Corporation; Konica Denshi Co., Ltd.; Konica U.S.A., Inc.; Konica Medical Corporation (U.S.A.); Konica Photo Service U.S.A., Inc.; Konica Capital Corporation I (U.S.A.); Fotomat Corporation (U.S.A.); Konica Quality Photo (West) Inc. (U.S.A.); Konica Quality Photo (East) Inc. (U.S.A.); Konica Imaging U.S.A., Inc.; Konica Canada Inc.; Konica Europe GmbH (Germany); Konica UK Ltd.; Konica France S.A.; Konica Business Machines U.S.A., Inc.; Konica Business Machines (Canada) Ltd.; Konica Business Machines International GmbH (Germany); Konica Bureautique S.A. (France); Konica Business Machines (U.K.) Ltd.; Konica Mercian Business Machines Ltd. (U.K.); Konica Vickers Business Machines Ltd. (U.K.); Konica Peter Llewellyn Business Machines Ltd. (U.K.); Konica Business Machines Australia Pty. Ltd.; A.B.E. Rentals Pty. Ltd. (Australia); K.B.A. Properties Pty. Ltd. (Australia); Apeco of Australia Pty. Ltd.

Further Reading: *Konica's History: The History of Japanese Photography*, Tokyo, Konica Corporation, 1987; *Konica Corporation*, Tokyo, Konica Corporation, 1989.

—Mary Sue Mohnke

Kubota

KUBOTA CORPORATION

2-47, Shikitsuhigashi 1-chome
Naniwa-ku, Osaka 556-91
Japan
(06) 648-2111
Fax: (06) 648-3862

Public Company
Incorporated: 1930 as Kubota Limited
Employees: 15,500
Sales: ¥662.87 billion (US$4.61 billion)
Stock Exchanges: Tokyo Osaka New York Paris Frankfurt Luxembourg

Kubota Corporation prides itself on being flexible and adjusting as necessary to compete under changing economic conditions. Kubota, originally a small manufacturer of iron castings, took advantage of the emphasis on industrialization that Japan's aggressive foreign policies required. The company came up with novel techniques to produce cast-iron pipes at the turn of the century to serve developing municipal water systems. When the market for piping peaked, around 1912, Kubota began to manufacture machine tools in time to take advantage of the demand for heavy industry that World War I prompted. Depression between the wars led to more innovative production techniques and more diversification. Overcoming the devastation of World War II, the company has taken advantage of major trends, rapid reindustrialization, and the partnership between government and business in the same way: by innovating and diversifying.

Today Kubota Corporation produces farm and industrial machinery, pipe and fitting equipment, housing materials, and electronic components in plants in Japan, Brazil, Indonesia, Thailand, Spain, Germany, and the United States. The company is determined to stay on top of its markets through its established methods and has committed more resources to research and development so it can continue its role as an innovator in heavy industry.

Gonshiro Oode was the fourth and last child of a very poor Inno Island farmer who supplemented his family's income by working as a coppersmith. In 1885, when he was only 14 years old, Oode left home to try to get a job in Osaka. This was a difficult task because the boy had no relatives or friends in the city to help him during an era when one's contacts determined where one worked and lived. Eventually, however, Oode was accepted as an apprentice at the Kuro Casting Shop. His apprenticeship was indeed the bottom of the ladder; it initially consisted of babysitting and running errands. But Oode was diligent, and he was soon promoted to a position in which he could learn metal-casting processes.

Three years later, Oode joined Shiomi Casting, which produced metal domestic items. The job change enabled him to learn more about metal-casting techniques. By saving every penny possible, Oode was able to accumulate ¥100 in a year and a half.

With the capital he had saved, Oode founded his own company, Oode Casting, in 1890. His timing was propitious. In 1868 the restored Meiji Emperor had abandoned Japanese isolation and opened contact with the outside world. That was the beginning of the industrialization of Japan's economy which spurred the development of the iron and steel industries. By 1890 metal for manufacturing was in great demand, and Oode Casting was successful from the beginning. Oode moved his business to larger quarters three times in the company's first five years.

Although the company has never been a "war plant," except during World War II, part of Oode Casting's success was due to Japan's aggressive foreign policies. Japan invaded Korea on the Asian mainland in 1894, setting off the Sino-Japanese War. The Japanese army needed modern equipment, and Oode Casting could provide it. Oode expanded by hiring more than ten employees, and he changed the company's name to Oode Casting Iron Works.

After Japan's modern forces won the Sino-Japanese War Oode continued to expand his company. He increased his product line, adding castings for domestic items and for cutting machines.

In 1897 a customer, Toshiro Kubota, took a typically Japanese step to promote Oode's success. Kubota asked if he could adopt Oode as his son. The move meant that he would officially sponsor the younger man and that Oode would be able to inherit from him. Both his natural parents were dead by then, and Oode agreed to the plan. He took the Kubota family name and changed his company's name to Kubota Iron Works to reflect his new relationship.

With Toshiro Kubota's patronage, Gonshiro Kubota was able to devote more time to developing new techniques. His invention of a new method of producing cast-iron pipe in 1900 established his company's reputation. Gonshiro Kubota had long grappled with how to produce pipe domestically for a modern national water system, which had become a national priority about 20 years before. Importing the necessary iron pipes was delaying the project. He invented a jointless-type cylindrical outer mold to produce jointless cast pipes by the vertical round-melt casting method and set up mass production in 1901. In 1904 Gonshiro Kubota invented another method, vertical rotary-type casting. His new processes made domestic cast-iron pipe production possible.

In 1904 war once again meant a boost for Japanese heavy industry and Kubota. Czar Nicholas II began the Russo-Japanese War when he backed the claims of Russian lumber exploiters along the Yalu River, which was in Japan's sphere of influence on the Chinese mainland. Japan easily defeated Russian forces. While the war was brief and one-sided, it promoted what has been called "a second industrial revolution" because Japanese leaders committed the country to modernization. Building the country's infrastructure called for more pipes and more cast iron. Kubota thrived.

Kubota had already committed himself to manufacturing machine tools when World War I broke out. In order to meet the needs of developing heavy industry, Kubota turned to manufacturing steam engines and iron-making machines. The company's main Osaka factory concentrated almost exclusively on producing machinery, and new factories were opened in Amagasaki and Okajima to produce the traditional lines of iron pipes and castings.

Some of that production was sold abroad for the first time: in 1917 Kubota exported 2,000 tons of iron pipe to Java, beginning the company's entry into Southeast Asian markets. Shortly afterward, in 1918 and 1919, Kubota opened regional offices in Tokyo, Kyushu, and Kure to improve his sales network. By 1919 the company had 1,500 employees.

Kubota emphasized innovation and use of state-of-the-art technology to remain competitive during the recession that followed World War I. The company invented heat-resistant castings and automatic carbon feeders. Kubota himself made trips abroad in 1919 and 1927 to learn new methods of producing high-grade cast pipes. His trips led to practical applications of a revolutionary centrifugal casting method. In 1937 the company opened the Sakai Engine Plant, the largest plant to that point in Asia. Sakai was noteworthy for using the conveyer belt to automate production. Kubota also entered new product lines in the years between the wars, including agricultural and industrial motors.

Demand for cast-iron pipes once again increased after World War I as domestic infrastructure projects were readdressed. Kubota took over the Sumida Iron Works in Tokyo as a subsidiary in 1927 and thereby gained a major share of the pipe market.

The acquisition made it easier to meet new foreign demands for Kubota's high-quality cast-iron pipes. The company expanded its presence in Southeast Asia in 1929, when it began to export pipes to Dutch territorial Indochina. In 1932 it began to establish a name in Europe as well when it filled an order from Groningen, Holland, for 2,400 tons of 30-inch cast-iron pipes for a city waterworks project. Kubota became an effective competitor abroad because of its reputation for quality, a highly motivated sales force, and an emphasis on after-sales service.

In 1930 the company underwent a reorganization to insure that it would continue to be successful when its self-made founder was no longer managing. Kubota was incorporated that year. It was not long after the company's incorporation that the threat of war loomed once again. The 1930s were a decade of Japanese expansion. The country was dominated by military and industrial groups who looked abroad to compensate for overpopulation and a shortage of raw materials. In November 1936 the increasingly authoritarian Japanese government signed the Anti-Comintern pact with Germany, becoming part of a coalition of European and Asian powers. In September 1940 Japan joined Germany and Italy in the Tripartite Pact, which divided Asia and Africa into spheres of influence. Under the pact, Japan was to get Southeast Asia. With Germany's initial defeat of the European imperial powers, it appeared to Japanese expansionists that Southeast Asia was available for the taking, and they moved in to stake their claim. Japan's attack on Pearl Harbor, Hawaii, on December 7, 1941, signaled its intentions.

War was once again good for heavy-industrial producers such as Kubota. Now producing engines as well as pipes and machine tools, the company benefited handsomely from the war effort.

The war ultimately devastated the country, however, and led to the postwar rule of the Allied victors. One advantage of General Douglas MacArthur's tenure was his determination to put the country back on its feet. Kubota's agricultural-equipment division and cast-iron pipes for restoring the country's basic services brought the company back to prosperity.

Shortly after the war ended, Kubota's power tiller, the K-2, won a prestigious prize in the Okayama Agricultural Power Equipment Competition. The prize confirmed Kubota's preeminent position in the agricultural-machine industry. Kubota went on to develop machinery especially suited for Japanese agriculture, culminating in the production of the first domestically produced tractor and a special tractor for rice cultivation in 1960. Kubota also developed a wide range of rice transplanters. By the end of the 1960s, the company could offer a fully integrated mechanized system for rice production: earth-moving, rice-planting, harvesting, and threshing machines.

Kubota also continued to innovate in its traditional product areas. In 1954 the company expanded its pipe manufacturing operations by adding asbestos cement pipe and vinyl pipe to its product list. In 1959 Kubota became the first Japanese company to develop a spiral-welded steel pipe.

In 1952 the company entered the plant-construction business when it designed and constructed a cement-mixing plant for the Yoyokawa Agricultural Water Utilization Office of the Ministry of Agriculture and Forestry. This successful venture established Kubota's reputation for building new, technologically modern facilities, and the company built up-to-date plants for a variety of clients.

In 1960 Kubota advanced into a new related area when it developed Colorbest, a roofing and external-wall material that is lightweight and nonflammable. Within 30 years the new material had captured 75% of its market. Other building materials, including home siding, aluminum-cast fences and gates, and interior home products such as enameled cast-iron bathtubs have been added to Kubota's housing-materials and equipment division, making the company a major producer of building products. Kubota management recognized the postwar development of the company by adopting a new slogan, "Everything from Nation Building to Rice Growing."

By the 1960s, Japan had made a remarkable recovery. Its industry was advancing at an unparalleled rate, and Japanese exports increased almost fourfold over the decade. The massive postwar investment in heavy machinery and a rebuilding effort that involved developing state-of-the-art factories were partly behind the industrial resurgence.

Also important in Japan's recovery was the relationship that Japanese businesses had with government and with banks. Norihiku Shimizu, a Japanese economist, called the collaboration "Japan, Inc., the biggest company in the world." What Japan, Inc. meant for Kubota was the opportunity to establish policies with government and business leaders, favorable national policies, and a higher rate of debt than in other industrialized countries. The average Japanese company has a debt to equity ratio of 80 to 20, just the opposite of those of U.S. companies.

Like other major Japanese industrial producers, Kubota took advantage of this economic climate by expanding overseas. The company established subsidiaries in Brazil in 1957, Taiwan in 1961, the United States in 1972 and 1973, Iran in 1973, France in 1974, and Thailand in 1977. The company opened overseas offices in Taipei, Los Angeles, Bangkok, New York, Athens, Jakarta, London, and Singapore. A casting plant using the latest techniques and computer technology was constructed in East Germany in 1985.

Just as the company had made Japanese rice cultivation more efficient in the 1950s, the agricultural-machinery division looked at conditions in foreign countries to provide custom-made solutions to indigenous agricultural conditions wherever it competed. It also adapted its pipe technology and water-control systems to flood control in Third World countries.

Japan's success in competing in world markets, however, provoked a backlash. By the end of the 1960s, other nations where Kubota was doing business were condemning Japan for taking advantage of the relatively free foreign markets while restricting foreign access to its own expanding economy. The international outcry—and the U.S. 10% import surcharge—along with a severe recession due to the shock of 1973 when the cost of the oil imports that Japanese industry relied on rose dramatically, meant that changes had to take place in the Japanese way of doing business.

At Kubota, more resources were devoted to research and development. The office of business planning and development was established in 1982 to promote innovation, and a research and development headquarters was established in 1984. By the end of the 1980s 1,500 employees were working on new-product and technical development. The advances developed by the research team have been especially pronounced in the electronics area, where Kubota has become a major producer of industrial sensors, scales using microcomputer technology, optical-fiber technology used in steel mills, computer equipment, and other electronic equipment.

In 1989 Kubota expanded its computer interests when its Ardent Computer Corporation merged with Stellar Computer to form Stardent, which produces graphics supercomputers. Kubota promoted a different image for its centennial in 1990 by replacing the name Kubota Limited with Kubota Corporation. Kubota has a long tradition of successful adaptation. The company has taken advantage of the government's modernization programs and foreign expansionism to grow into numerous areas of heavy industry and high-tech production. Diversification and innovation, which have served Kubota well historically, promise to keep the company successful.

Principal Subsidiaries: Kubota House Co., Ltd.; Kubota Construction Co., Ltd.; Kubota Computer Inc.

Further Reading: Introducing Kubota, Ltd., Osaka, Kubota, Ltd, 1989; "Gonshiro Kubota: The Founder of Kubota, Ltd. Profile and Achievements," *Kubota Times,* First Quarter 1990.

—Ginger G. Rodriguez

LUCAS INDUSTRIES PLC

Brueton House
New Road
Solihull B91 3TX
United Kingdom
(021) 627-6000
Fax: (021) 627-6171

Public Company
Incorporated: 1897 as Joseph Lucas & Son
Employees: 56,000
Sales: £2.19 billion (US$3.53 billion)
Stock Exchanges: London New York

Lucas Industries's automotive division, the basis of the company's activities since before 1910, accounts for nearly two-thirds of the company's turnover, and makes Lucas one of the ten largest suppliers of automotive components in Europe. In the 1990s, as in the 1900s, the key to Lucas's success is diversification—both through acquisitions, mostly overseas in recent times, and through developing new products. As recently as 1980 the company's chief products were batteries, lamps, and other electrical components for British motor cars. By 1990, its automotive division had survived the collapse of the British motor industry by moving into producing high-tech engine-management systems and braking systems for car companies all over the world, while its aerospace and industrial divisions are in the forefront of product innovation and cross-border joint ventures.

This enormous and diverse company has its origins in Birmingham, home of Joseph Lucas, one of the minor industrialists, or "little masters," whose enterprise characterized the city in the mid-19th century. His first business ventures were far removed from the sophistication and range of the Lucas Industries of today. Lucas began the 1860s as a dealer in hollowware such as buckets, shovels, and chamber pots, as well as paraffin. In 1875 Lucas founded the Tom Bowling Lamp Works, named after the ship's lamp which was its main product, and Joseph Lucas's business began to prosper. From about 1880 the management of the company passed increasingly into the hands of Joseph's son, Harry, and in that year Joseph Lucas received a patent for The King of the Road bicycle lamp that made the company's name and fortune. The partnership of Joseph Lucas & Son, set up in 1882, was vigorous in defending the patent against the numerous copies that appeared, and in expanding the range of goods offered in its catalogs, with the aim of supplying everything that cycle repairers and manufacturers might need. By 1897, when Joseph Lucas & Son was incorporated as a public company, it had achieved a leading position in this area and was ready to move into what Harry Lucas called "motoralities."

In its growth from a small family firm into a household name, Lucas resembled other West Midlands enterprises of the day, such as Cadbury Brothers, GKN, and Austin Motor Company. Lucas also benefited from being in the right place at the right time. As the 20th century began, motor manufacturers found that companies already established in the Midlands were well able to supply the components they needed, so, unlike elsewhere, there was no development toward vertical integration. Lucas made itself indispensible to the British motor industry from its creation, and from this early stage continued to benefit from economies of scale.

Joseph Lucas died in 1902, just as investment in research on motor vehicle components was causing the company's profits to fall. The company showed its commitment to its new interests by opening a showroom in London soon after Joseph Lucas's death, and from 1904 to 1907 sales and profits rose steadily, stimulated by the legislation of 1903 that had made cars more attractive to potential customers by raising the speed limit, and had also made the components industry much busier by making lights compulsory at night. In 1914 Lucas's catalog offered six kinds of complete dynamo lighting systems for cars. In the same year the company acquired Thomson-Bennett, which specialized in magnetos, and so extended its product range to include ignition equipment. The timing was excellent. World War I saw an unprecedented rise in the demand for magnetos, for airplanes as well as for cars and motorcycles. Yet it may have seemed that the government was giving to Lucas with one hand and taking away with the other, for the introduction of British Summer Time—daylight savings—in 1916 led to a permanent fall in the sales of cycle lamps. It was this change, and the impact of the slump immediately after the war, that induced Lucas to shift the balance of its business by introducing much cheaper versions of its cycle lamps and by negotiating with the motorcycle manufacturers to take Lucas's combined magneto-dynamos rather than those made by the company's German rival Bosch. Thomson-Bennett (Magnetos) was renamed the Lucas Electrical Company in 1919, probably in order to maximize the benefits of the parent company's reputation.

In 1923 Harry Lucas went into semi-retirement as a consultant director. He died in 1939. The company came under the control of his son, Oliver Lucas, and of Peter Bennett, formerly of Thomson-Bennett, as joint managing directors, and expanded rapidly is size and range. The company used its market position to enforce restrictive agreements with its potential rivals in the same fields. Although at first William Morris of Cowley, Oxford, was by far the biggest customer for Lucas's starting and lighting equipment, management knew that, like other leaders in light engineering, Lucas's strength depended on responding flexibly to changes in the market, and were careful to maintain close relations with Morris's rivals as well. The company continued the policy of investing vigorously in acquisition, rather than in research and development. The biggest acquisitions of the interwar years took place in 1925, when Lucas bought out two rivals in the motor accessories business, CAV—which dominated the supply of components for commercial vehicles—and Rotax. This gave Lucas a virtual monopoly of lighting, starting, and ignition equipment until after World War II when Ford and General Motors both set up in-house components plants. After some initial suspicion the major motor manufacturers of the day appear to have accepted this situation, since Lucas was able to pass on to them the benefits of the economies of scale which these acquisitions permitted.

In other cases Lucas mixed acquisition with restrictive agreements, for example in 1930, when S. Smith & Sons sold its lighting, starting, and ignition operations to Lucas, and the two companies then drew up lists of products each could manufacture only with the other's consent. Again, in 1931, Lucas and its former rival Bosch of Germany set up a joint venture, CAV-Bosch, to develop diesel engines, and made an agreement to stay out of each other's markets for motor components. CAV-Bosch passed entirely to Lucas in 1937, when the German company, probably under pressure from the Nazi government, sold its interest. Lucas was faced with the first strike by any of its workers in 1932, when 140 objected to plans to introduce bonuses based on time and motion studies. The plans were withdrawn, only to be implemented two years later as the "Lucas Point Plan System," with the result that the workers did one-and-a-half times as much work as before for one-and-a-third times as much pay.

Another agreement with a foreign company, this time with the Bendix Corporation, provided the basis for what is now Lucas Aerospace. Rotax and CAV had made Bendix starter drives for cars since before Lucas took them over. In 1932, Bendix, which was leaving the motor industry in order to expand its aviation business, sold two-thirds of the shares of its British brake-manufacturing subsidiary to Lucas, along with licenses for Rotax to make aviation equipment, such as the inertia starter then being introduced for larger airplanes. Once again, Lucas benefited from the research spending of others, including, in this case, the U.S. government, and as Rotax grew it continued to rely on licenses from Bendix far more than on internal research.

Meanwhile Lucas protected its near-monopoly in the British motor-components industry through an agreement with Autolite, the leading firm in the U.S. market. From 1937 to 1940 Lucas paid Autolite $50,000 a year to stay out of Britain, promised to stay out of the U.S. market in return, and arranged to exchange technical information and licences. A company that had made itself the country's main supplier of motor components, and was fast becoming crucial to the aviation industry too, was bound to benefit from the rearmament of the late 1930s and the war production which followed. Even after the sale of new cars was banned and the production of commercial vehicles was restricted, orders for equipment for motor vehicles, especially the Bedford truck favored by the army, as well as equipment for boats, airplanes, and motorcycles, made Lucas's output higher than it had ever been in peacetime. Oliver Lucas served on the government's supply council, and directed design and development at the Tank Board, but it is not clear whether his involvement in the development of the jet engine during the war began as an official or as a commercial matter. In the end, it was CAV's experience in fuel injection and Lucas Electrical's skills in sheet metal working that ensured that Lucas took full advantage of the opportunity and engaged in research on combustion, development of the fuel system, and manufacture of the relevant equipment for the jet.

The withdrawal of government contracts at the end of the war left Lucas a more prosperous and diverse company than it had been six years earlier. Its traditional expertise in components was now taken up with orders for spare parts and repair work, and complemented by the company's involvements in the jet project and the growing market for diesel engines both in Britain and abroad. Even the resources committed by its Rotax subsidiary to work on the expensive and unsuccessful Brabazon airliner, in the late 1950s, was not wasted, since the technical knowledge gained from the project was applied to work on V-bombers, starting with the Vickers Valiant in 1948.

In 1951 Lucas set up a series of divisions each based on the respective subsidiary company, with central control limited to matters of personnel and finance, under a renamed holding company, Joseph Lucas (Industries) Ltd. Its chairman was Bertram Waring, who had been joint managing director with Peter Bennett from 1948, when Oliver Lucas died. There followed a decade of growth for CAV, based on the development of the first mass-produced distributor pump and of more sophisticated electrical equipment for commercial vehicles; for Rotax, working on the V-bomber series and on electrical-generating equipment for tanks; and for the components division, as mechanical windshield wipers, reversing lights, and long-range driving lights appeared and became standard. Thus the Lucas group continued to play its strongest cards, building upon its reputation and near-monopoly in the components field, and on its past record for government contracts in aviation and electricals. At the same time, the cycle-accessories business from which all these modern activities had developed was in decline, and Joseph Lucas (Cycle Accessories) was closed in 1962.

In 1963 a Monopolies and Mergers Commission revealed that up to 1956 Lucas and its nearest rival, Smiths Industries had operated under a restrictive agreement which divided up the market between them. This explained why the most important division, Joseph Lucas (Electrical), concentrated on electrical components other than instruments. The report concluded that the domination by Lucas and a few other companies of the motor components industry, whether sustained by restrictive agreements or not, was justified in order that the motor industry should continue to have reliable supplies of cheap but good-quality components.

Nevertheless, Lucas was soon exposed to an unfamiliar degree of competition as the strikes that hit the components industry in the late 1960s encouraged motor manufacturers to abandon old loyalties and switch to multi-sourcing for their components needs. The impact that a strike, at any stage of the car production process, could have was demonstrated spectacularly in August 1977, when a strike by Lucas toolmakers closed down the entire U.K. car industry. Even so, Lucas and its rivals within the British components industry were able to stay ahead of overseas competitors as long as the British motor industry itself was in the forefront of development. The British Motor Corporation was the first company in the world to introduce front-wheel drive, for example, and Lucas and the other component firms retained their leading position on the basis of their familiarity with this new technology. Meanwhile CAV, already the world leader in making fuel injection equipment swallowed up a rival, Simms, in 1968, which gave it 90% of the British fuel-pump industry.

Between 1967 and 1970 the group's aerospace division spent more than £20 million, £3 million of which was lent by the government's Industrial Reorganization Corporation, on making acquisitions that increased its size by 50%, but that also meant that it came to depend to a large extent on supplying Rolls Royce's airplane-engine business. Following the financial collapse of Rolls Royce in 1971 Rotax, renamed Lucas Aerospace, laid off one-sixth of its workforce, but then picked up new orders from the Ministry of Defence, becoming one of its leading contractors, with the result that nearly half of Lucas Aerospace's business is military. In 1976 a combined committee of the company's shop stewards made several suggestions for diversifying away from military production into a variety of other fields, which became famous as The Lucas Plan, but these suggestions were rejected by the management. The only loss-making part of the aerospace division's business proved to be Thomson-Lucas, a joint venture—with the French company Thomson-CSF—which was dissolved in 1988. Lucas Aerospace remains Europe's largest designer and maker of aircraft equipment, and the only company in the world to manufacture every component system used in aircraft, both military and civil, apart from navigation, radio, and flying controls. In 1973 the non-aerospace elements of the former Rotax subsidiary were spun off to a new company, Lucas Defence Systems.

Lucas began the 1970s as the 54th-largest British company. Kenneth Corley was appointed group chairman in 1970, to be succeeded after only three years by Bernard Scott, at which time Bertram Waring retired, after 47 years at Lucas, a period which had taken the company from national dominance in cycle and motor accessories through to participation in worldwide changes in the motor and aerospace industries. In 1970, the group was five times the size it had been only 20 years before. The renaming of the group in 1974, as Lucas Industries, was accompanied by the introduction of a uniform corporate identity for all its subsidiaries. The name Lucas was added to each subsidiary's name, and Lucas Industries became the first group—as opposed to individual company—to advertise on British television. To offset falling orders from the home market Lucas, along with GKN, led the way in expanding into continental Europe, beginning with investments in France, West Germany, and Italy, including taking full control of Rotodiesel, the leading firm in the French diesel market, in 1974. The next move was into the United States, and the manufacture of the diesel-powered vehicle which the oil crisis of the mid-1970s had suddenly made attractive. The group is involved in markets all over the world, through its existing subsidiaries and its program of acquisitions. By 1975, for example, one-third of all cars made had brakes manufactured by the Lucas subsidiary Girling or its licencees. Nevertheless, it was the Lucas Battery Company which had the highest level of overseas manufacturing of all the Lucas companies.

Expansion through acquisition abroad has been accompanied by stabilization through restructuring at home, under the successive chairmanships of Godfrey Messervy and, since 1987, Tony Gill. Just as Lucas had benefited from the growth of the British car-assembly industry in the 1960s, so it suffered as the industry contracted in volume production and fell behind in product development, and in 1981 Lucas showed an overall loss for the first time in its history. The group was back in profit by 1983, thanks to its nonautomotive divisions, and from then on the group's activities moved largely out of the United Kingdom into overseas markets. Between 1979 and 1988, the proportion of U.K. sales to total group turnover fell from 51% to 38%, and from 1989 onwards the non-U.K. subsidiaries accounted for a greater proportion of group sales than did the British subsidiaries. This change in markets was accompanied by major cuts in the U.K. production base; between 1985 and 1989 the group as a whole disposed of 14 units, closed 25 production sites, and cut its work force by 35,000.

The restructuring of the components side of the group culminated in 1988 with the creation of Lucas Automotive as the largest of the group's three divisions, bringing together the subsidiaries remaining after Lucas had withdrawn from automotive lighting, starter motors, and alternators, and concentrating on producing engine-management and braking systems. The new division followed the trend in the components industry toward supplying complete systems rather than separate parts, designed in much closer collaboration with the car makers than had been customary. There has been an increasing degree of partnership with Japanese corporations, such as with Sumitomo on car-body systems, or Yuasa Battery Company on car batteries, in response to the growing likelihood that Japanese components firms will make inroads into the European market as deeply as they already have in the United States. Lucas Automotive's success in 1989 in attracting orders from BMW and Saab-Scania for fuel injection systems was an indication of its ability to compete directly in Europe.

In the motor industry, on which Lucas still depends for more than half of its business, the trends towards globalized production and demand, high technology, and greater expectations of high-quality production seem likely to go on challenging Lucas Automotive and its rivals in the components industry. The involvement of Lucas Aerospace in work on the A330 and A340 airbuses, and on the EJ200 engine for the forthcoming European fighter aircraft, suggest that this division will depend less on national orders and more on multinational projects. Lucas Applied Technology, the smallest of the group's three divisions, includes specialist subsidiaries likely to grow in response to the increasing demand for high technology, such as Lucas Industrial Systems, which produces electronic measurement and control equipment for a variety of industrial processes, or Lucas Instruments, the world's major designer of acoustic and vibration measurement equipment.

Throughout its history Lucas has proven to be flexible in making the most of social change and political decisions. This flexibility allowed it to grow from a small family firm specializing in cycle accessories in the second half of the 19th century to a company involved in automotive components and aerospace from the earliest days of each of these industries, and finally into a multinational giant with interests and commitments far beyond its Birmingham origins. In the past, this flexibility has been Lucas's major strength, while its weakness has been a recurrent tendency to become too dependent on its monopoly position and its tradition of close contact with the British government. The future of Lucas Industries needs to be seen within the context of the single European market, where Lucas will be competing against powerful rivals, in Europe and in the world, both for private business and for government contracts.

Principal Subsidiaries: Lucas Aerospace Ltd.; Lucas Automotive Ltd.; Lucas CAV Ltd.; Lucas Electronics Ltd.; Lucas Industries Inc. (U.S.A.); Lucas Industrial Systems Ltd.; Lucas Engineering & Systems Ltd.

Further Reading: Nockolds, Harold, *Lucas: The First Hundred Years,* Volumes I–II, Newton Abbot, David & Charles, 1976–1978.

—Patrick Heenan

MCDERMOTT INTERNATIONAL, INC.

1010 Common Street
New Orleans, Louisiana 70112
U.S.A.
(504) 587-5400
Fax: (504) 587-6433

Public Company
Incorporated: 1946 as J. Ray McDermott & Company
Employees: 30,000
Sales: $2.64 billion
Stock Exchange: New York

McDermott International, one of the world's leading energy-services companies, is the only marine construction firm with a global operation. What began as an oil-field-services enterprise has evolved into a dual-unit operation that handles not only marine construction services, but also power-generation systems and equipment, serving both domestic and international markets. McDermott International experienced financial problems in the late 1980s, but began to rebound.

McDermott operates in two business segments, providing marine construction services to the global oil and gas industry for offshore development, drilling, and for production and transportation of oil and gas; and making power-generation systems and equipment, principally for the utility industry and the U.S. government. McDermott has operations in more than 30 countries. McDermott's operations focus on five core businesses: marine construction, project management, fossil power generation, commercial nuclear power, and U.S. government operations. The company's business is about 75% domestic, and 25% international.

McDermott began on a much smaller scale. What is now known as McDermott International originated in 1923, when 24-year-old R. Thomas McDermott received a contract to build 50 wooden rigs to drill for oil. The contract came from an east Texas wildcatter, or oil prospector. McDermott asked his father, J. Ray McDermott, to supervise construction of the rigs, and named the business after the elder McDermott.

Over the next two decades the firm expanded, establishing itself in Texas and then moving to south Louisiana when exploration headed in that direction. In 1923 J. Ray McDermott & Company moved its headquarters from Eastland, Texas, to Luling, Texas, after a boom in oil exploration in that area. McDermott continued to grow during the Depression. In the early 1930s the Houston area enjoyed an oil boom, and in 1932 J. Ray McDermott & Company moved to Houston. McDermott first opened a New Orleans, Louisiana, area office in 1937—across the Mississippi River from McDermott's present headquarters. Some years later, McDermott moved its headquarters to Louisiana.

McDermott became associated with the J.G. McMullen Dredging Company in 1938, and bought that company in 1939, branching into dredging. The Olsen Dredging Company was established in 1939 as a result of this purchase. The company remained a small, regional concern during World War II. In April 1946 J. Ray McDermott & Company was reorganized and incorporated in Delaware. By this time, the company was supplying services to support oil and natural gas production in the marshlands.

In the late 1940s oil and gas companies became interested in exploiting fields beneath the Gulf of Mexico. McDermott, with its floating equipment for marshland work, formed joint ventures and made acquisitions which enabled it to pioneer the construction and installation of platforms and pipelines to support drilling and development near shore. In August 1947, McDermott set the world's first steel template platform in 20 feet of water in the Gulf of Mexico, for the Superior Oil Company. Prior to this, the few offshore platforms in existence had rested on wooden pilings. Steel was stronger and more durable than wood, and the template design of these new platforms distributed weight better. Soon after, a second platform was installed in 50 feet of water, and the offshore marine construction business was launched. McDermott formed its contracting division—the major operating segment during its early years—in 1947.

With the 1948 purchase of all of the assets of the Harry F. Allsman Company, its joint venture partner for several contracting jobs in the Gulf of Mexico, McDermott boosted its efforts in the offshore construction area. This acquisition included equipment assets that helped McDermott meet the new demand for offshore construction.

In 1949 McDermott commissioned the world's first derrick barge, which was built specifically for offshore work. The barge significantly increased the kind of work that could be performed offshore. By 1953 McDermott had built another derrick barge, with a lifting capacity of 250 tons.

In 1950, to handle numerous customer requests for pipeline construction, J. Ray McDermott & Company established a pipeline department. That same year, McDermott constructed the first Gulf of Mexico pipeline. Also in 1950, the company added an oil division.

In 1953 DeLong-McDermott—a joint venture formed that year by McDermott and the DeLong Engineering Company—built the first mobile air-jack rig using a jacking, or elevating, device patented by L.B. DeLong. Later in 1953, DeLong-McDermott merged with Southern Natural Gas Company to form The Offshore Company, a drilling contracting firm. McDermott held a one-third interest in The Offshore Company. The Offshore Company became a major competitor of McDermott in the deep-water drilling business, and McDermott gradually sold its interest in Offshore, completing the divestiture in 1971.

J. Ray McDermott & Company went public in 1954. It was listed on the New York Stock Exchange in January 1958. In 1956 Bayou Boeuf Fabricators became McDermott's fourth division, and the world's largest offshore-structure-fabrication yard. The division's name was changed to McDermott Fabricators in May 1958.

In 1957 McDermott established a subsidiary, J. Ray McDermott (Venezuela), C.A., to fabricate the world's first aluminum platforms for the highly corrosive waters of Venezuela's Lake Maracaibo. In 1958 McDermott acquired Associated Pipeline Contractors, to supplement its domestic pipeline business and provide international expansion opportunities. Associated Pipeline Contractors was involved in the laying of large-diameter, cross-country oil and natural gas transmission lines. In 1959 McDermott sold Associated Pipeline to Reading and Bates in exchange for common stock.

In 1959 McDermott acquired Dupont Fabricators, to supplement the light-fabrication capabilities of McDermott Fabricators. Dupont eventually became part of McDermott Fabricators. That same year, McDermott Fabricators created a marine department primarily for the repair of the company's heavy construction equipment. The marine department repaired McDermott's own equipment and that of other companies. In 1962 the department became a separate operating division, McDermott Shipyard division.

McDermott continued to move into the international sphere, establishing an office in Beirut in 1960. In 1962 McDermott installed the first platform placed in Cook Inlet, Alaska. In 1963 McDermott Overseas, McDermott Far East, McDermott Enterprises France, and Oceanic Contractors were established as subsidiaries of the company. In March 1964, McDermott had eight direct subsidiaries that operated under five divisions: contracting, oil, McDermott Fabricators, Harvey Lumber and Supply Company, and McDermott Shipyard.

In 1965 the first 500-ton derrick barge was introduced. By 1967, however, increasingly large jackets—the skeletal outer structure that supports the deck of the platform—required new methods of installation. Prior to 1967, derricks on barges lifted the jacket from a cargo barge and set it in position. In the summer of 1967 McDermott first executed what is now the common method of launching large jackets. At that time a jacket that McDermott was to install in 340 feet of water was too heavy for the derrick to raise. Therefore, the jacket was fabricated on its side and slid onto a barge. At the installation site, it was slipped off the cargo barge and into the water. As it floated horizontally in the water, the jacket was gradually ballasted until it turned upright and then it was guided into place.

In 1968 the oil and natural gas exploration and production operations handled by the oil division of McDermott were transferred to a newly formed company, TransOcean Oil. In 1969 McDermott acquired the stock and subsidiaries of Hudson Engineering Corporation. Hudson had a background in petrochemical process engineering and in offshore engineering facilities. Another key acquisition during this period was the purchase in November 1971 of Ingram Corporation's foreign marine construction equipment business. This purchase expanded McDermott's operations into three new areas: Australia, Trinidad, and Brazil.

R. Thomas McDermott died in 1970, after serving as chairman for nearly 25 years. Edward J. Hudson succeeded McDermott as chairman, serving from July 1970 until August 1974.

McDermott changed significantly from 1969 to 1979. McDermott's growth and expansion continued with major acquisitions—including The Babcock & Wilcox Company, purchased in 1978. The addition of the established power-generation company was McDermott's first diversification outside the marine construction business.

James Cunningham, chief executive officer and chairman from 1979 until 1988, was instrumental in the 1978 acquisition of Babcock & Wilcox, for which McDermott paid a total of approximately $748 million. The acquisition was meant to provide balance against the cyclical marine construction business. The two engineering firms shared some common ground. Both were in the energy business and both worked in steel formation. The similarity in basic technologies and engineering and the fact that both firms served the same markets paved the way for the Babcock & Wilcox acquisition. Babcock & Wilcox had interests in the manufacture of equipment such as process controls, boiler-cleaning products, and metal tubing. In the 1950s the firm became a leader in the development of nuclear power and had become a key part of the United States Navy's nuclear program. By the time it was acquired by McDermott in 1978, Babcock & Wilcox was a major supplier of products and services to the electrical-power and other industries throughout the world.

In acquiring Babcock & Wilcox, McDermott became a much larger, diversified company. To reflect its growth, J. Ray McDermott & Company became McDermott Inc. in 1980. In 1983, with McDermott's international business growing in stature, the company was reorganized again. McDermott International, McDermott's wholly owned Panamanian subsidiary since 1959, became the parent company of McDermott Inc. and its subsidiaries. McDermott International had been established as the international subsidiary of J. Ray McDermott & Company. McDermott's reorganization as a Panamanian company allowed it to avoid paying income tax on most of its operations.

In the 1970s new technologies in marine construction permitted offshore structures to grow quickly in size. In 1978, McDermott installed Shell Oil's Cognac structure in 1,025 feet of water in the Gulf of Mexico. Cognac was the first jacket installed in more than 1,000 feet of water.

In 1978 a federal grand jury returned indictments which alleged conspiracy among some officers of McDermott and of its competitor Brown & Root to restrain or eliminate competition in marine construction. McDermott and Brown & Root each pleaded no contest to the antitrust charges and were fined $1 million each.

Dependent on the oil economy, McDermott's problems were compounded when the bottom fell out of the energy business during the early 1980s. As profits dropped, oil companies cut back on capital spending, and marine construction also took a beating. Starting in the early 1980s, there was less demand for boilers, as a result of power-generating overcapacity, and the generating market shrank as well. McDermott did not make a profit in 1988 or in the following two years.

In 1979 James E. Cunningham became chairman. Cunningham, a chemical engineer and 30-year McDermott employee, was credited with keeping the firm afloat when the marine market shrank from more than $2 billion in 1982 to $500 million in 1989. Cunningham implemented a financial restructuring which streamlined the company.

McDermott shrank by 57% between 1979 and 1988. Most of the employee reductions were made at Babcock & Wilcox. A number of plants were closed or sold.

Robert Howson took over as chairman of the board and CEO in August 1988. McDermott had grown since Howson, a civil engineer, came to the company in 1957. Although the 1980s were difficult for McDermott, Babcock & Wilcox was a bright spot on the McDermott balance sheet. Babcock & Wilcox, which offers services such as design, construction, and maintenance of steam-generating equipment, has not had a losing year since its sale to McDermott and has, in effect, carried the parent company since the early 1980s. For the fiscal year ending March 31, 1990, McDermott's business overall consisted of about 75% power-generation work and 25% marine construction, compared to about 65% and 35%, respectively, ten years before.

The oil business began to improve in 1988, and by mid-1988 McDermott's business had begun to improve. Chairman Howson has consolidated operations, focusing on McDermott's five core businesses and reduced the company's debt. Revenues for fiscal 1990 were $2.64 billion, up from $2.16 billion in 1989. Babcock & Wilcox generated $1.7 billion in revenues for fiscal 1990.

McDermott still lost $10.2 million in fiscal 1990, up from net loss of $91.7 million in 1989, and $261.7 million in fiscal 1988. The improvement from 1989 to 1990 was mainly the result of gains from the sale of McDermott's Bailey Controls operations for $295 million and half of its commercial nuclear services operations for $51 million to form a new commercial nuclear service joint venture. Funds from these sales helped McDermott reduce short-term debt. McDermott's marine backlog—the number of orders received—grew two and a half times, from $650 million to $1.6 billion in fiscal 1990.

McDermott still performs all facets of marine construction. It takes about a year to fabricate a large—at least 400-feet high—fixed offshore platform. While McDermott has competitors in each segment—design, engineering, and fabrication—it is the only worldwide contractor that can handle all phases of the process from beginning to end. McDermott has constructed most of the world's drilling platforms.

McDermott's real strength in marine construction lies in its fleet of very powerful offshore equipment, which allows more work to be completed onshore. With 200 vessels, McDermott has the largest fleet of marine equipment used in major offshore construction. Technological advances have paved the way for diversification in marine construction for McDermott, which has long constructed high-horsepowered tugboats, pushboats, and offshore supply vessels. It has branched into the construction of ships for the U.S. Navy, including prototype small waterplane area twin hull ships and torpedo test craft.

McDermott would like to grow in core-related areas, but it must further reduce debt. The company would like additional work in government markets. About one-fifth of McDermott's business in fiscal 1989 was government related. During the early 1990s a continued shortage of equipment propelled an expected surge in power equipment sales. McDermott expected its boiler business to expand significantly between 1990 and 2000. Babcock & Wilcox is the top boilermaker in terms of the number of boilers it has built in the United States.

McDermott also hopes to expand its overseas operations, including those in the Pacific Rim, where McDermott began doing business in the mid-1960s. McDermott is building boilers in China as part of a joint venture and is involved in offshore marine construction work there.

Principal Subsidiaries: McDermott International Investments Co., Inc. (Panama); Hydro Marine Services, Inc. (Panama); McDermott Incorporated (92%); The Babcock & Wilcox Company; McDermott Scotland Limited (U.K., 75%).

Further Reading: Deepwater: Marine Construction's Frontier Technology, New Orleans, Louisiana, McDermott International, 1985; *McDermott,* Spring 1990; *The Story of Oil and Gas Offshore,* New Orleans, Louisiana, McDermott International, [n.d.].

—Gwen M. LaCosse

MAN AKTIENGESELLSCHAFT

Ungererstrasse 69
D-8000 Munich 40
Federal Republic of Germany
(89) 3 60 98 0
Fax: (89) 3 60 98 250

Public Company
Incorporated: 1873 as Gutehoffnungshütte Aktienverein AG
Employees: 63,707
Sales: DM17.05 billion (US$10.09 billion)
Stock Exchanges: Munich Berlin Düsseldorf Frankfurt Hamburg Bremen Hanover Stuttgart Basel Geneva Zürich

MAN has taken a complicated path to become one of Europe's largest engineering and heavy-vehicle manufacturers. Operating as a subsidiary for much of its history, the corporation is today comprised of several midsize companies. Decentralized management has always typified the organization, but during the 1980s management decided to distance itself even more from the production process. MAN's challenge is to remain an effective competitor in the European markets it built steadily during the booms and recessions between 1960 and 1990 and to capitalize on its research investments as interest in mass transit and alternative fuels grows worldwide.

Segments of MAN originated centuries ago, but the core of what is today the MAN Group began in 1844 when Carl Buz and Carl August Reichenbach leased Ludwig Sander's four-year-old engineering plant in Augsburg. The partners purchased it outright in 1855. Each pursued his own markets, and their respective divisions are still among MAN's largest.

Reichenbach's uncle, Friedrich König, had invented the first flatbed press, in 1811, which allowed printers to keep pace with the industrial age. Reichenbach developed his uncle's invention and produced the company's first flatbed letterpress in 1845 under the name of C. Reichenbach'sche Maschinenfabrik.

Considered the company's oldest division, Reichenbach's branch grew with the industry. In 1873 the company introduced Germany's first rotary press, which increased printing output exponentially—eventually to 8,000 eight-page newspapers each hour. Six years later Reichenbach expanded into producing presses for commercial printing. By the turn of the century the company's presses printed in six colors, and by the 1920s the company offered offset printing and rotogravure. The company automated manufacture of printing plates, called stereotyping, which hence became much faster.

Although 19th century printing developments were dramatic, engine technology like that produced by Reichenbach's partner moved even faster. Buz used the same facilities simultaneously to develop steam engines and driving systems. He called his business Maschinenfabrik Augsburg. Heinrich Buz, Carl's son, ran both divisions from 1864 to 1913. When he took over, the company already produced heavy-engineering products like water turbines and pumps in addition to the engines and presses.

It was Heinrich Buz's emphasis on engine research that by the turn of the century positioned the company for decades of growth as a vehicle producer. Anticipating the transition from steam to combustion engines, Buz provided facilities for Rudolf Diesel and helped fund his engine development from 1893 to 1897. At first used in stationary factory automation, diesel engines were increasingly used in water vessels and, by 1918, in submarines. The company raced the industry to expand applications to land-based moving vehicles.

Buz expanded internationally through a tactic still used at MAN. Rather than pay heavy start-up costs, Buz licensed partners worldwide. In an era of escalating industrialization, finding such partners was not difficult due to the sound reputation of the company's steam engines and printing presses.

The company renamed itself M.A.N. (Maschinenfabrik Augsburg-Nürnberg) in 1898 when Maschinenfabrik merged with Maschinenbau AG Nürnberg. The latter company provided additional mechanical and engineering expertise, with which M.A.N. developed more efficient fuel pumps that could be used in larger moving vehicles.

M.A.N.'s solid-fuel injection methods made engine construction simpler and less expensive. In 1923 the company introduced the first diesel engine with direct injection, which greatly improved fuel efficiency. It made land-based commercial vehicles with diesel engines possible and provided M.A.N. an early lead in a dominant industry of the 20th century.

The costly race to improve engines led to additional consolidation of research efforts. Gutehoffnungshütte Aktienverein AG (GHH) bought an interest in M.A.N. in 1920 and acquired a majority interest the following year. GHH—literally the Iron Works of Good Hope—had been the basis of heavy industry in Oberhausen on the Ruhr River since 1758, when the first of three foundries that merged in 1873 to form the company was established. GHH and M.A.N. shared information but pursued separate strategies and markets for 65 years. GHH's interest in M.A.N. continued to grow, reaching 75% by the early 1980s. M.A.N. had become larger than its parent after World War II, when Allied law forced GHH out of coal mining and steel manufacture. From that point until the companies merged, in 1986, M.A.N.'s earnings determined those of GHH.

Between the world wars, M.A.N.'s engine research and development led to higher-output engines for small spaces as well as for large-scale power stations. The German government used M.A.N.'s 11-cylinder, double-acting two-stroke diesel engine in its fast marine craft in 1935. During World War II U-boats used M.A.N.'s turbocharged engines with increased fuel-consumption efficiency. This wartime production led to advances that would one day be used in commercial vehicles, and it also aided M.A.N.'s large-scale engineering works like shipbuilding and plant construction.

Wartime industrialization affected the printing division too. After World War II the sheet-fed press superseded the letterpress. M.A.N. introduced its large-format Ultraman press, which could use up to seven colors. Yet the leading position in the company that the engine and mechanical works gained during the war continued to improve after the war. In 1989 printing sales were DM1.8 billion, which is only 10% of the corporation's total.

In 1955 when the commercial-vehicle division moved its headquarters to Munich, it was the corporation's most prominent division. Postwar growth had solidified M.A.N.'s position as one of Europe's largest engineering companies. M.A.N. opened a Hamburg plant in 1955 to make and repair diesel engines, ship boilers, steam turbines, and mechanical and engineering devices for more general applications. By 1990 these areas represented about 19% of sales. In 1969 M.A.N. purchased what would become its plant-construction division. Sensitive to international business cycles, it also represented 19% of sales by 1989.

Hans Moll became group chief executive in 1973. He had risen through the commercial-vehicles division, where he more than doubled sales from 1968 to 1973. Moll's postwar predecessors had placed great value on M.A.N.'s nonvehicular divisions. As a result, during the 1970s sales and research had been evenly split between commercial vehicles and engineering products. Under Moll, however, engineering products, diesel engines, and printing equipment shared a marketing department while commercial vehicles had one of its own. Although vehicle contracts could be more lucrative, M.A.N. would be stung by this new emphasis in upcoming recessions.

Sales skyrocketed in 1976 even as overseas orders began to drop. The recession of the late 1970s hurt most Western capital-goods manufacturers, but M.A.N. fared somewhat better because few of its divisions suffered from business cycles simultaneously. In response to rising labor costs, M.A.N. rationalized by automating. Starting in commercial vehicles, management reduced the entire work force 3% to 39,000 employees. While sales decreased 60%, the labor cuts kept earnings stable around DM35 million for 1976 and 1977.

Despite these measures, M.A.N. could not stave off declines in the late 1970s. In 1977 orders fell off 12%. While printing-equipment, commercial-vehicles, and stationary-diesel-engine markets were steady and growing, marine-equipment and power-station-equipment divisions operated well below capacity. Foreseeing trouble, Moll decided to market components to supplement company earnings when there were few finished vehicle contracts. This strategy, however, was not pursued effectively for another ten years, when it was not timely enough to help.

M.A.N.'s most significant competition in the late 1970s came from Third World engineering companies, which threatened its traditional markets. In response M.A.N. pursued markets for its sophisticated technology more aggressively. The ten-year-old research division began to introduce production techniques and produce experimental vehicles for the long-term alternative-fuels market by 1978. By developing more advanced technology, M.A.N. hoped to remain immune to fledgling competition for several decades.

While the company researched alternative energy sources, more efficient transit systems, and uranium enrichment for nuclear power, however, it also created more bureaucracy. These new bureaucrats changed the way the company, used to active managerial participation in production, worked. Communication became more formal, and attempts to coordinate traditional information networks with expert specialists increased segmentation. Like its biggest competitor, Daimler-Benz, M.A.N. built up its foreign presence through regional manufacture and assembly. Short-term returns from foreign expansion proved slim because of M.A.N.'s reliance on large, finished-vehicle contracts in these markets.

M.A.N.'s overseas expansion normally proceeded conservatively. In a typical venture, M.A.N. held a one-third share of a Turkish plant, allowing the company to keep the largest share of the Turkish market for trucks and buses and to supply lucrative contracts in the Middle East. Eventually, M.A.N. helped establish an engine plant there, of which it also held 30%.

Almost half M.A.N.'s sales came from abroad as the 1980s began, when a European recession led the company to increase attention to Asia, North America, and OPEC nations. The increasing value of the Deutsche mark made M.A.N. products less attractive to foreign buyers, however. In addition, the currency difference led to competitive imports, eroding the once-solid domestic share.

The company's sales efforts in the Middle East paid off in 1981, when it signed contracts worth DM270 million with buyers in Iraq and Jordan. While demand for heavy trucks continued to drop internationally, M.A.N. continually increased its market share by relying more heavily on its African and Middle East business.

In the United States, domestic manufacturers shied away from renewed demand, giving European manufacturers of commercial vehicles an entry. M.A.N. set up a plant in North Carolina to build articulated buses in 1980, spending DM20 million in start-up costs.The company hoped the return on its overseas investment would make up for the expiration of long-term military contracts. Instead, lagging vehicle sales caught up with M.A.N. despite specialized management, new products, and new markets.

The first in a series of setbacks occurred in the United States, where the federal government cut subsidies to urban transit programs in the early 1980s. The most detrimental blow came when Iraq canceled its nearly completed contract for 1,000 trucks. It took M.A.N. several years to recover since these vehicles did not meet European standards. At the same time, an especially long recession in shipbuilding left cargo space unused, put 10% of the global fleet in storage, and shifted the production center to East Asia. As Taiwan and South Korea became the dominant regions for shipbuilding, the secondary market for European engines and parts also declined. M.A.N. had to close one of its two marine diesel engine plants in the Federal Republic of Germany. The company was also hurt by currency fluctuations and buyers' needs for long-term financing during a period of high interest. Its divisions' down cycles finally coincided.

For the two years ending 1984, M.A.N.'s losses totaled DM477 million and half of that figure came from the commercial-vehicles division, where sales fell nearly 27%. The division cut 1,700 of its 59,000 employees in 1983. The heavy-vehicle and diesel-engine divisions also suffered. Truck production fell one-third to 16,000 and M.A.N. operated at only 20%–25% capacity. Although reduced demand from developing countries caught other European truck manufacturers as well, M.A.N. was especially dependent on exports. In 1981 M.A.N. sold 25% of its trucks in the Middle East. In 1983 the region purchased fewer than 50 trucks. The general engineering operations also suffered from dependence on exports. Unable to handle payment programs, developing countries cut industrial installations.

The failure of an Argentine engine venture and problems with other overseas affiliates led GHH to reassess M.A.N.'s ability to adjust to market fluctuations. While GHH held more than 75% of M.A.N., the relationship was financial, not managerial, and the parent found it difficult to implement change in its powerful subsidiary. The GHH response at first was to replace its own personnel. Feeling chief executive Manfred Lennings did not respond quickly enough, GHH replaced him with Klaus Götte. Like Moll at M.A.N., Götte had worked in several firms before coming to GHH, contrary to the traditional West German career path within one organization.

Even as Lennings departed, M.A.N. was showing signs of revival. Job cuts, 25% of M.A.N.'s overall work force, alleviated some of the losses from the continuing export recession. A renewed domestic market reduced exports to one-third of sales from a high of 50% in the late 1970s. European demand for trucks was improving, and the formation of the European Economic Community allowed the company to pursue those markets more competitively. Since these countries were more reliable customers and were easier to serve than those overseas, M.A.N. began to categorize them as domestic. As the 1980s waned, M.A.N. reduced its overseas expansion. In the United States, even though M.A.N. was the market leader in articulated buses, its plant operated well below capacity. M.A.N. held on to it, however, eventually hoping that it would prove to be a fruitful toehold in U.S. markets.

In 1985 M.A.N. made its first dividend payout in three years. It turned in a marginal operating profit of DM32.5 million, but gained DM375 million from selling its holdings of Motoren und Turbinen Union to Daimler-Benz. The sale helped M.A.N. avoid acquisition by General Motors, which would have captured M.A.N.'s 10% share of the West German heavy-truck market and its extensive service network, giving it a significant entry into European Economic Community markets.

Daimler-Benz was not the only West German interest prompted into action by this near-deal. A competitor's unusually favorable offer prompted GHH to take stronger action. In 1985 GHH announced plans to merge with M.A.N., regroup their divisions, and move headquarters to Munich. Although the Middle East, China, and U.S. affiliates were still viewed as potentially strong contributors, the consolidated group hoped to sell 80% of production in Europe.

The merger was executed in 1986 and the resulting company became MAN Aktiengesellschaft. Otto Voisard, Moll's successor as M.A.N. chief executive, stepped down, and the two companies reorganized into five new ones: MAN Nutzfahrzeuge (heavy vehicles), MAN Roland (printing equipment), MAN Gutehoffnungshütte (plant and engineering equipment), MAN B&W Diesel, and MAN Technologie (research and development). Each supplied a representative to the company board, headed by Götte.

The costs of the merger kept profits flat for three years, and the company cut its work force by another 15,000—to the lowest level in 12 years. MAN emerged more profitable with a lower break-even point in commercial vehicles. Under Moll, 25,000 units had to sell to meet costs. By 1989 the company not only sold more but also required only 20,000 units to be sold each year to cover costs.

In order to keep its share of the new crucial European market for heavy trucks, MAN began to invest DM130 million, or 2%–4% of sales, in research annually. Still hesitant to expand sales extensively outside Europe, the new commercial-vehicles division sold 94.3% of its vehicles in Western Europe in 1987, up from 88.1% the year before. The change reflected MAN's new European emphasis, but was also partially due to continued decreases in overseas demand, where two foreign operations posted losses totaling DM60 million. The overseas growth MAN once saw was a thing of the past.

In the late 1980s MAN emerged from a 15-year period of cutting its workforce and assuming overseas losses, while simultaneously becoming stronger in Europe. To capitalize on the recovery, the MAN companies will become more independent in the future. For instance, MAN Nutzfahrzeuge, now a nearly independent midsize entity, will pursue more joint ventures producing components and finished vehicles, rather than its own large-scale contracts where the risk is larger. With a reorganization to reflect its more narrowed focus and increased strength in markets close to home, MAN has become one of Europe's largest and most efficient engineering companies.

Principal Subsidiaries: MAN Nutzfahrzeuge GmbH; Ferrostaal AG; MAN Gutehoffnungshütte GmbH; MAN Roland; MAN B&W Diesel GmbH; MAN Technologie GmbH; RENK Aktiengesellschaft; Deggendorfer Werft; SMS Schloemann-Siemag AG; Battenfeld GmbH; SMS Hasenclever; Kabel-und Metallwerke; Kabelmetal Messing GmbH; Schaltbau GmbH; Schwäbische Hüttenwerke GmbH.

Further Reading: "How MAN Manages," *Management Today,* July 1978; *MAN Museum Augsburg: History—Facts, Figures, Exhibits*, Munich, MAN, [n.d.].

—Ray Walsh

mannesmann *technologie* 

MANNESMANN AG

Mannesmannufer 2-4
Postfach 55 01
D-4000 Düsseldorf 1
Federal Republic of Germany
(211) 820 2249
Fax: (211) 820 2554

Public Company
Incorporated: 1890 as Deutsch-Österreichische Mannesmannröhren-Werke Aktiengesellschaft
Employees: 125,785
Sales: DM22.33 billion (US$13.22 billion)
Stock Exchanges: Düsseldorf Frankfurt Geneva Zürich Basel Vienna Paris

Mannesmann, which celebrated its hundredth anniversary in 1990, has, in the course of its history, developed from a steel-tube manufacturer into a highly diversified group with a worldwide presence. It is involved in machinery and plant construction, industrial drive and control systems, electrical and electronic engineering, automotive technology, and its traditional area, steel-tube production.

The history of Mannesmann began five years before the company's founding with a major technical achievement. In 1885, the brothers Reinhard and Max Mannesmann invented a rolling process for the manufacture of thick-walled seamless steel tubes, the so-called cross-rolling process, at their father's file factory in Remscheid. Introducing the invention, they founded tube mills between 1887 and 1889 with several different business partners, in Bous on the Saar; in the Bohemian Komotau; in Landore, Wales; and at home in Remscheid. The machine building industry was unable to supply the necessary plant for the application of the rolling process, and the iron and steel industry was not able to provide the necessary supplies of high quality semi-finished products. As a result, numerous other inventions had to be made and long years of experiments passed before the initial difficulties in the industrial exploitation of the new process were overcome.

In 1890, a technical breakthrough was achieved with the brothers' invention of the pilger rolling process. The name was taken from the analogous Luxembourg Echternach pilgrims' procession as during the rolling process the pre-pierced thick-walled steel ingot is moved forward and backward and turned at the same time in order to be stretched into a thin-walled tube. The combination of the pilger and the cross rolling processes became known as the Mannesmann process. On July 16, 1890, the tube and pipe mills existing on the Continent were brought into Deutsch-Österreichische Mannesmannröhren-Werke Aktiengesellschaft which had its headquarters in Berlin. Reinhard and Max Mannesmann formed the first board of management but left it in 1893. In that year the company headquarters was moved from Berlin to Düsseldorf, at that time the center of the tube and pipe industry.

From about this time, seamless medium-sized steel tubes were successfully produced and sold worldwide at a profit, by far surpassing rival products in quality. It was thus possible to reduce the loss of more than 20 million marks, that had accumulated during the company's first years of business, and eventually to pay the first dividend in 1906.

The success of Mannesmann's tubes alarmed competitors grouped in associations and syndicates. Feeling their very existence threatened, they stopped supplies of large and small tube sizes, for which seamless production was not yet possible, to dealers selling Mannesmann tubes. In order to be able to supply a complete range of products, Mannesmann built a factory for the production of longitudinally welded tubes in the second half of the 1890s; the company also acquired shares in companies involved in tube and rolled steel trading and pipeline construction.

Mannesmann's position in the export business, which was important from the beginning of the company, was consolidated and expanded by the acquisition of the British Mannesmann tube mill in Landore, Wales, which had been founded by the Mannesmann and Siemens families but had never overcome its start-up problems, and by the founding of a Mannesmann tube mill with its own electrical steelworks in Dalmine, Italy. Since the turn of the century, branch offices undertaking storage and direct-sales business, sometimes with tube processing workshops and pipeline construction capacities, were set up in cooperation with well established companies all over the world, especially in South America, Asia, and South Africa.

Except for the works in Dalmine and Bous, which operated their own small steelworks, Mannesmann continued to be dependent on supplies of semi-finished products from third parties; even Bous had to buy scrap and pig iron. With the tendency towards horizontal integration by means of increasing cartelization and vertical integration in the formation of vertically structured coal and steel groups that mined their own ore and coal, produced pig iron and crude steels, and converted them to finished products, this dependence on suppliers began to endanger Mannesmann's existence. Accordingly the company's foremost strategic goal became to achieve self-sufficiency in semi-finished products and thus to enable the company to determine price, quality, and the actual delivery period. In the process, iron ore and pit—or hard—coal mines, a lime works, a factory for the production of refractory materials, and finally, in 1914, a plate rolling mill with an open-hearth steelworks at Huckingen on the Rhine were acquired. Plans for the expansion of the steelworks and the construction of blast furnaces were thwarted by the outbreak of World War I.

In the period that followed, the company was forced to employ emergency labor, to cope with changes in its range of products, and to make up for the loss of export business, which had formerly accounted for 60% of sales. The British Mannesmann Tube Company, with its works in Landore and Newport, was lost. The Italian subsidiary in Dalmine had to be sold under duress. The loss of the works on the Saar and in Bohemia could only be avoided by allowing French and Czechoslovakian companies to participate.

This was not a time to shape and realize long-term corporate strategies. In the decade from 1914, day-to-day problems required full attention. At the end of the war, plants had to be replaced completely or were, upon instant transfer to peacetime production, no longer usable.

Export contacts were reestablished, and machinery in the remaining works was replaced and expanded to compensate for the loss of production capacity. Although Mannesmann's major steelworks had not yet been built, this construction plan was by no means abandoned. Measures were carried out that efficiently supplemented the existing installations. The mining division was strengthened by the acquisition of another pit coal mine and of a coal trading company with its own inland fleet. The works harbor at Huckingen was expanded to accommodate seagoing vessels, and the works area was enlarged by the purchase of further land.

In November 1925, Mannesmann turned down the offer to take part in the formation of what was at the time the largest German coal and steel group, Vereinigte Stahlwerke AG, and decided to maintain its independence even in those difficult times. This decision resulted in the creation of a company-owned semi-finished product manufacturing unit. In 1927, Mannesmann began to build a blast furnace, the Thomas steelworks, and auxiliary plants and shops. Despite a few strikes, a general lockout, and delays caused by harsh winter weather, expansion proceeded so quickly that as early as May 1929 two blast furnaces, each producing 800 tons a day, the sinter plant, and the Thomas steelworks with four converters holding 30 tons each, went into operation. The steelworks already had numerous facilities which, not only in terms of technology but also in terms of safety standards and regard for the environment in general, were ahead of their time. With the blast furnace and the Thomas steelworks, the company integrated the ore and pit coal mines on one side with the steel and rolling mills on the other, and completed its development into a fully vertically structured coal and steel group, typical—until the 1970s—of the Ruhr industry. Mannesmann thus became independent of outside suppliers of semi-finished products and was able to make full use of the advantages offered by the combination of mining and steelmaking.

To promote sales, the domestic marketing organization was made more efficient by the establishment of warehousing companies. Shareholdings in trading, production, and assembly businesses in many European and overseas countries were acquired. The Landore works lost during the war was recovered. Holdings in a company for the construction of power supply plants in Berlin and in a pipeline construction firm in Leipzig were acquired, to promote Mannesmann's tube sales. The latter two participations marked the beginning of new activity for Mannesmann that has since developed into a group of companies operated by Mannesmann Anlagenbau AG. The participation in the family-owned Maschinenfabrik Gebr. Meer in Mönchengladbach, founded in 1872, which had for many years successfully constructed rolling mills for the manufacture of seamless tubes and tube processing machines, did not represent an attempt to diversify, but resulted from the fact that the company could no longer design and build its own rolling mills as it had done since 1886. Since the task was now assigned to others, Mannesmann intended to make sure that new designs were not made accessible to competitors.

Technical developments in the period before the outbreak of World War II were characterized by the successful solution of problems in the manufacture of tubes of high-alloy stainless steel and the successful application of the extrusion process and the introduction of a new rolling mill for the manufacture of thick-walled seamless steel tubes. At the same time, the semi-finished and heavy plate product lines were extended, with the contribution of newly acquired companies. The Depression and the ensuing economic boom, further invigorated by government job-creating schemes, both affected the company. The production and sale of all Mannesmann products were governed by national, European, and international cartels, from the mid 1920s until the end of World War II.

The outbreak of World War II hit the company during a phase of plant replacement. The Bous works and its staff were moved to Düsseldorf. Production remained essentially unchanged, but to a far greater extent than in World War I, the works replaced their conscripted work force with unskilled workers, women, civilian foreign workers, and prisoners of war.

All works were bombed several times and suffered varying degrees of damage. With the Allies approaching, the plants were vacated and—as far as possible—protected against plunder by emergency crews. By order of the Allies, Mannesmann was liquidated and in 1952 divided into three independent groups of companies, one of them Mannesmann AG. By 1955, Mannesmann AG had absorbed the other two and more or less reestablished its former unity. Mannesmann was the first group in the coal and steel industry to be split up into independent smaller groups, convene a general meeting of shareholders, pay a dividend, have its shares quoted at the stock exchange, increase its share capital, issue a loan, and regain its former structure.

The Czechoslovakian works were lost, and the Bous works, reintegrated in the 1930s, were confiscated again and later brought into a French company in which Mannesmann's stake rose from 40% to 51% in 1959, and finally to 100% in 1985. The British Mannesmann company had already been sold in the 1930s.

Even before the company's future was definitely settled, it again began to build up extensive activities abroad. Between 1952 and 1955, Mannesmann founded its own steel and tube mills in Brazil, Canada, and Turkey, establishing its presence in several important markets. While the Canadian joint venture was divested in the early 1970s, the Turkish joint venture, small at the start, has been repeatedly enlarged. Companhia Siderúrgica Mannesmann S.A. in Belo Horizonte developed into the Brazilian group of companies that supplies Mannesmann products and services, in particular to the South American markets. Its range of products and services includes rolled and drawn high-grade and special steel products, steel wires and welding rods, steel tubes, steelworks and rolling mill machinery and equipment, compressors, excavators, plastics injection molding machines, hoists, hydraulic systems, and components for industrial drive and control systems. The group runs its own ore mines, and has eucalyptus plantations for charcoal production. Its marketing is carried out by an independent trading company, Mannesmann Comercial S.A., of São Paolo.

Other participations—for example, in companies producing irrigation systems, forage silos, agricultural tractors and engines, and plastics tubes and pipes, turned out to be less successful. Their future prospects looked unpromising and they were eventually given up. The traditional coal and steel companies, on the other hand, were—since the 1960s—exposed to growing international competition. In many countries, new large, low-cost plants were constructed that aimed at the world market. International competition, frequently government-supported, threatened to eliminate European producers.

With investment expenses rising steeply, it was doubtful whether Mannesmann would in the future be able to compete worldwide in tubes, rolled steel, and tube processing. The existing excess production capacity for steel tubes, rolled steel products, and pit coal left very little hope for continuing with satisfactory profits. As a traditional coal and steel group, Mannesmann's outlook was not promising.

By the end of the 1960s, Mannesmann had already broken away from tradition and was looking for new ways to secure its future. Domestic ore mining came to a complete halt and coal mining interests were brought together in a unified company, the Ruhrkohle AG.

The gradual acquisition of G.L. Rexroth GmbH between 1968 and 1975 reflected the new trend of development. From modest beginnings, the company was expanded and internationalized to become the world leader in hydraulics. In addition to hydraulic components and systems, the company's range of products and services comprised pneumatics and linear motion technology, electric servo drives, gears, and couplings. Rexroth marked the beginning of the restructuring of the Mannesmann group. This first step was successful and pointed the way forward for the company.

In 1970, Mannesmann and Thyssen agreed on a division of labor; Mannesmann took over tube production and tube laying from Thyssen and transferred its own rolled-steel production and sheet processing activities in Germany to Thyssen. The new Mannesmannröhren-Werke became the world's largest producer of tubes. Despite capacity reduction and concentration on the most efficient plants, further drastic restructuring became necessary as market conditions turned out to be worse than even the most pessimistic forecasts had anticipated. When losses reached almost DM1 billion in 1986–87, the situation became temporarily very grave. By 1988, the worst problems had been overcome. However, structural adjustment which, at the semi-finished products level, led to cooperation with other long-established steelworks, was not yet completed. Cross-border cooperation between the European tubemakers was one way to preserve the European tube industry. Two forward-looking strategies at Mannesmannröhren-Werke were participation in a company for the production of hydride stores for the storage and transportation of hydrogen and development of purest gases, and in a company producing automotive components with manufacturing facilities in a converted former steelworks.

With the acquisition of Demag AG, a well-established group with a rich and eventful history, Mannesmann strengthened its activities in machinery and plant construction during the first half of the 1970s. By the middle of the decade, about 30% of the company's external sales was already coming from these divisions.

At the beginning of the 1980s, Mannesmann gained access to the growing electronics markets by acquiring Hartmann & Braun in 1981 and Kienzle Apparate GmbH in 1981–1982. Hartmann & Braun is an international company in the field of measurement, control, and automation engineering. It has subsidiaries in Germany, in other European countries, and overseas. The change of emphasis in Mannesmann's range of products towards the processing industry, with its higher growth potential, proved successful. Mannesmann's second acquisition in this field, Kienzle, operates in data processing and supplies electronic systems for motor vehicles. Mannesmann had previously entered data processing both as a user and through its successful development of printers. Kienzle enabled Mannesmann to operate in the center of data processing. Originally Kienzle supplied only the German market; later it became international and established sales operations in other countries, some with local partners.

The acquisition of a majority holding in Fichtel & Sachs AG in 1987 and in Krauss-Maffei AG in 1989 enabled Mannesmann to consolidate its leading position in the machinery and plant-construction sectors. A key motive for the acquisition of Krauss-Maffei was the possibility of expanding Demag's plastics machinery activities and thus ensuring—according to the standard set by Mannesmann—lasting success in world markets. Most of Krauss-Maffei's other divisions—process engineering technology, transport technology, foundry technology, automation technology, surface treatment technology, and defense technology—offered good growth potential.

Following the Fichtel & Sachs investment, the group's total activities have comprised in addition to the highly cyclical plant business, a less cyclical mass-market products business with closer proximity to consumers. In the latter business, foreign sales have been gaining an increasing importance. In most of their fields of activity, the Mannesmann companies are of a size that enabled them to carry out the necessary development work, produce at competitive cost, and maintain extensive sales and service organizations.

In 1990, Mannesmann again broke new ground. Believing that in a highly developed economy the service sector would grow at an above-average rate and that telecommunications would be a particularly promising service, a consortium headed by Mannesmann tendered for the license to construct and operate the private D2 cellular telephone network. The acceptance of the bid submitted by Mannesmann Mobilfunk GmbH was of major importance to Mannesmann. It provided the company with an opportunity to enter the service sector.

The change in Mannesmann's corporate structure was clearly reflected in the sales breakdown. In 1968, coal, steel, and tubes accounted for half of external sales, and machinery and plant construction for 16%. 20 years later, the situation was very different: in 1989, machinery and plant construction and electrical and electronic engineering together accounted for 53% of external sales, and tube mills only 22%. At the same time sales quintupled, rising from DM4.4 billion in

1968 to DM22.3 billion in 1989. In 1990, the 100th year of its corporate history, Mannesmann was a broadly diversified capital goods producer occupying a leading position in most of its fields of activity.

Principal Subsidiaries: Mannesmann Demag AG; Mannesmann Rexroth GmbH; Krauss-Maffei AG; Mannesmann Anlagenbau AG; Fichtel & Sachs AG; Hartmann & Braun AG; Mannesmann Kienzle GmbH; Mannesmann Mobilfunk GmbH; Mannesmannröhren-Werke AG; Mannesmann Handel AG; Mannesmann SA (Brazil).

Further Reading: Wessel, Horst A., *Kontinuität im Wandel—100 Jahre Mannesmann 1890–1990*, Gütersloh, Mannesman AG, 1990.

—Horst A. Wessel

MASCO CORPORATION

21001 Van Born Road
Taylor, Michigan 48180
U.S.A.
(313) 274-7400
Fax: (313) 563-5975

Public Company
Incorporated: 1929 as Masco Screw Products Company
Employees: 42,000
Sales: $3.15 billion
Stock Exchange: New York

Masco Corporation is the world's largest faucet manufacturer as well as the leading U.S. cabinet and furniture manufacturer. The company manufactures hundreds of household items, from ventilators to locks. Masco Corporation's best-known product is the single-handled Delta faucet, developed and promoted in the 1950s by the company's founder, Alex Manoogian. Masco Industries, a public company created and partially owned by Masco, is a major producer of metal and plastic products, primarily for the transportation, construction, and petroleum industries.

In 1920, Alex Manoogian, at the age of 19, immigrated to the United States from Smyrna, Turkey, fleeing political turbulence and danger that threatened him as a Christian Armenian in Moslem Turkey, in the light of the government's systematic genocide of the Armenians. After holding several odd jobs in Bridgeport, Connecticut, including brief employment in a screw machine business, Manoogian came in 1924 to Detroit, Michigan, where he worked in a screw machine business and learned about metalworking for automobile components. In 1929, six weeks after the stock market crash, he founded Masco Screw Products Company with two partners, Harry Adjemian and Charles Saunders, who left during the first year. They began with a few thousand dollars, several used screw machines, and a truck, less than $33,000 in assets. "Masco" was derived from the first letters of the partners' last names plus "co" for company.

The automobile industry was still young and largely untested, and Masco's initial years were difficult. Hudson Motor Car Company was the first customer, with a $7,000 contract, but Masco could not yet afford to pay salaries. Manoogian was sales manager, estimator, foreman, press operator, and repairman.

The first plant was located on the fifth floor of an old building, with a furniture manufacturer on the floor below. Soon after business began, oil from the Masco machines leaked through the floor, ruining newly upholstered furniture. Manoogian was able to remain in business by arranging extended payments for the furniture damage.

During the 1930s, Masco worked mainly with Chrysler, and had contacts with Ford, Graham Page, Spicer Manufacturing, and Budd Wheel. Since Masco produced parts to the specifications of these firms, the company did not distinguish itself through product design and instead focused on providing excellent service.

In 1931, Manoogian brought his family to the United States, and married Marie Tatian. In 1934, his brother Charles joined the company, followed a few years later by another brother, George. By 1936, all sales were to the automotive industry and had increased almost fourfold since the first year, to $234,000. In 1937, Masco went public, its shares selling for $1 on the Detroit Stock Exchange.

Later in 1937, the plant caught fire. Fortunately, snow that had accumulated on the roof of the building melted and poured over the heavy machinery, reducing the fire's damage. Although Masco was in business again three months later, this was the one year in its history when the company lost money.

Like most U.S. metalworking companies during World War II, Masco worked exclusively for the defense industry. In 1942, its sales reached $1 million and continued to increase for two years. When the war ended in 1945, sales declined as Masco returned to manufacturing for the automotive industry.

In 1948, Masco offered more stock to the public. The sale of 13,000 shares generated the capital to buy the Ford Road Plant in Dearborn, Michigan, which then became the company headquarters.

In 1950, just after the Korean War began, Masco resumed production for the defense industry. Although sales increased, profits remained flat, due to the payment of wartime excess-profits taxes. Masco began work on a new kind of artillery-shell timing mechanism, a precision-made part that demonstrated the company's expertise in metalworking. Chrysler asked Masco to bid on a contract that required a new metalworking technique called cold extrusion, one unfamiliar to Masco engineers. Soon the company was producing satisfactory parts by cold extrusion. In 1953, when wartime contracts ended, Masco could not afford to continue developing the new technology, and did not resume using cold extrusion until 1967.

The year 1954 was a turning point for the company when Alex Manoogian won a small contract to manufacture parts for a new type of faucet being produced in California. At the time, Masco was still an automotive-parts manufacturer with little experience in plumbing fixtures. The unusual design of this faucet was its single handle, which controlled both cold and hot water. Unfortunately, the faucet, nicknamed by plumbers "the one-armed bandit," did not operate properly, and orders for it ceased. Because of his metalworking expertise, Manoogian detected the deficiencies in the faucet and redesigned it. He paid the original owners for licensing rights to produce and market his own version. At first, he formed a separate company to protect Masco if the new faucet did not sell. He tried to interest plumbing manufacturers in marketing the faucet, but they claimed there was no market for it. Eventually, Manoogian transferred the rights to Masco, which produced and marketed the Delta faucet. Sales increased rapidly, topping $1 million by 1958. In 1959, Masco bought a separate plant in Greensburg, Indiana, for faucet manufacturing. That year also, Manoogian's son, Richard, graduated from Yale University and helped start the new faucet operation.

From the beginning of his career, Richard Manoogian led the company toward expansion. He engineered Masco's first major acquisition in 1961, Peerless Industries, a manufacturer of plumbing products, to widen Masco's production capabilities. In the same year, Masco closed its Dearborn plant and moved automotive-parts production to Ypsilanti, Michigan. The faucet sector, which continued with steady success, offset the cyclical nature of the automotive industry. By 1962, Delta faucet sales reached $7 million and accounted for over half of Masco's sales. By then, Masco Screw Products Company was an inappropriate name for a supplier to both the automotive and construction industries, and the name was changed to Masco Corporation. In 1962, Masco acquired Mascon Toy Company, a manufacturer of toy telephones and play furniture, but Mascon was sold in the late 1960s, because of its low profit margins and its incompatibility with Masco's other interests.

Later in 1962, Masco was placed on the American Stock Exchange, and Smith Barney, the investment-banking firm, accepted Masco as a client, opening new sources of financing. Masco began an aggressive plan of acquisition and diversification spearheaded by Richard Manoogian.

In 1962, Masco acquired Steel Stamping Company, and in 1964, Nile Faucet Corporation, broadening its capabilities in the automotive and plumbing parts sectors. Over the next few years, as the construction industry flourished, the company began to expand its product line, acquiring Auto-Flo Company and Auto-Flo Corporation, which produced airhandlers, such as ventilators, and furnaces, and Gibbs Automatic Molding Company, a plastics firm.

Masco headquarters moved in 1967 to new facilities in Taylor, Michigan. The company began using the technique of cold extrusion, a process that resulted in greater structural strength and improved energy efficiency. In 1968, Masco acquired the Burns Companies, which manufactured components by cold forging and by automatic screw machines, followed by a series of acquisitions in the metalworking industry throughing 1970, including Punchcraft, Inc.; Molloy Manufacturing Company; Century Tool Company; Keo Cutters, Inc.; and Commonwealth Industries.

In 1968, Richard Manoogian was made president of Masco, while Alex Manoogian became chairman of the board. Masco had become a major manufacturer of plumbing products for the kitchen and bathroom, with sales of $5.5 million. In 1969, Masco was listed on the New York Stock Exchange.

During the 1970s, Masco's two main markets, the automobile industry and the construction industry, fared badly in the country's recession. American automobile companies faced increasing foreign competition. Inflation and high interest rates caused a 34% decline in the number of new homes by 1974.

Nevertheless, Masco earnings continued to grow at an average of 20% per year. Masco had become the leading supplier of many household items, and it continued to diversify. Plumbing products for do-it-yourself home improvement continued to do especially well, and renovation and replacement accounted for more than half of Masco's faucet sales by 1975. In 1972, Masco began to market a new faucet design, a double-handled faucet, called the Delex, based on the same rotating-ball principle as the Delta. Masco continued to introduce new models in the next few years, and by 1975 had increased its market share to 22%.

In 1971, Masco entered the communications business when it acquired Electra Corporation, which manufactured the scanning monitor radios. That year Masco began to manufacture parts for trailers and other recreational vehicles with its purchase of Fulton Company in 1971 and Reese Products in 1973. In 1972, Masco bought several small manufacturing companies for its automobile sector, and in 1973 bought American Metals Corporation.

In 1973, Masco made its first foreign acquisition with Holzer and Company, a West German manufacturer of airhandlers. That same year, Masco entered the petroleum equipment sector, acquiring 47% of Emco, a Canadian manufacturer of oil pipes and plumbing hardware. Foreign sales in 1973 accounted for 4% of the company's total, increasing one year later to 7%.

Between 1973 and 1974, when the automobile and construction industries hit their worst slump of the decade, Masco's stock value plummeted from 46 times earnings to a multiple of 20, although sales were up 23% and earnings were up 22%.

In 1975, Manoogian took advantage of the growing market for citizens band (CB) radios and acquired Royce Electronics. CB sales continued to soar at the beginning of 1976, but by the end of the year, the supply of CBs exceeded demand. When the federal government expanded the available channels from 23 to 40, the 23-channel radios became virtually obsolete. Royce's sales plummeted from $53 million to $17 million, and the company suffered $1 million in losses. Masco sold 51% of Royce in 1976 and its remaining shares in 1977.

Nevertheless the company remained in the communications sector. Electra continued to make scanning monitor radios and other electronic products. In 1976, Masco sued RCA Corporation, Teaberry Electronics Corporation, and Sanyo Electric Company, for infringing on Electra's patents for scanning radio receivers. Sanyo produced the radios in Japan for the other two companies, but Masco required that firms sign a licensing agreement to sell the scanners. The case was settled in court when Sanyo agreed to pay Electra royalties under a new licensing agreement.

Masco continued to penetrate the petroleum equipment market in 1976, acquiring A-Z International Companies and Grant Oil Tool Company, both manufacturers of drilling tools, as well as Dansk Metal and Armaturindistri of Denmark. Masco also created Forming Technology Company, a firm with technologically advanced equipment that produced larger metal components swiftly and economically. In 1977, Masco acquired Walker McDonald Manufacturing Company and R & B Manufacturing Company, producers of petroleum equipment, and, in 1978, Rieke Corporation, which made closures for oil drums and other large containers. In 1979, Masco purchased Jung-Pumpen, a West German maker of sump pumps, and Arrow Specialty Company, a maker of engines and engine repair parts.

During the late 1970s, Masco began to advertise its faucets on network television. In a March 16, 1981, interview with *Forbes,* Richard Manoogian stated, "Everybody thought we were crazy. . . . They told us that the only time you buy a faucet is when your old one leaks." Masco realized that there was a steady consumer demand for the product and continued to expand its line of faucets. By 1980, Masco had increased its market share to 28%.

In 1980, while automobile production slowed 24%, Masco worked with car manufacturers on design, to create additional car parts. In 1981, while the housing industry was in its worst state since the mid-1970s, Masco's sales in that sector continued to grow. Masco's products in the home-improvement area were not subject to extreme economic swings, and the home-improvement sector was growing faster than the industrial one.

Masco continued to expand in 1980, acquiring Alup-Kompressoren Pressorun, a West German maker of air-compressors; Lamons Metal Gasket Company; and Arrow Oil Tools, a manufacturer for the petroleum industry. In 1981, Masco introduced a nonceramic toilet, which used much less water and was insulated to muffle the sound of flushing.

Diversification continued in 1982. Masco acquired two small companies that made valves and related products for the oil industry, as well as Evans-Aristocrat Industries, which made steel measuring tapes; Baldwin Hardware Manufacturing Company, which made hardware for builders; and Marvel Metal Products, which made steel work stations for the office.

The year 1982 was the first since 1956 that earnings for operations did not increase, due to the effects of the recession. Masco's sales in the cold-extrusion industry declined 17%, primarily because of the depressed automobile and construction industries.

In 1983, Masco acquired Brass Craft Manufacturing Company, a maker of plumbing supplies. Building and home improvement product sales were up over 50% to $500 million, due to profitable acquisitions and steady faucet sales. At the same time, decline in oil prices spurred a drop in petroleum-equipment sales.

For many years, the cyclical industrial sectors—petroleum and construction equipment and automobile parts—had lowered Masco's overall yearly results, even though total annual sales had continued to grow. In 1984 Richard Manoogian spun off Masco's industrial businesses into a separate, publicly held company, Masco Industries (MI). This change gave Masco Corporation a firmer identity as a home-improvement and building-products company, enabling it to focus on that sector. While the move allowed both companies to expand more quickly, it also gave Masco Corporation continued access to MI's metalworking technology. Richard Manoogian became CEO of the new company, and its headquarters remained in Taylor, Michigan, with Masco Corporation. Masco Corporation distributed 50% of MI stock to shareholders as a dividend and retained the other half, worth about $50 million. A year later, Masco ownership of MI decreased to 44%.

In the restructuring, the two companies formed Nimas Corporation as a vehicle to facilitate Masco's leveraged buy-out of NI Industries, a large diversified company. NI Industries manufactured many building products, including Thermador cooking equipment, Weiser locks, Waste King appliances, Artistic Brass faucets, and Bowers electrical outlet boxes, Masco's first entry into the electrical-equipment business. NI also produced several automobile and defense products. Masco paid $483 million for the company; using Nimas allowed Masco Corporation and MI to make an expensive acquisition without placing the debt on either company's balance sheet.

During the next few years, MI focused on developing its manufacturing technology and expanding through acquisitions, investing more than $1 billion. As a result, yearly earnings suffered, although sales increased from $545 million in 1984 to $1.7 billion in 1989.

Erwin H. Billig became president of Masco Industries in 1986. Between 1986 and 1989, MI diversified into architectural products, acquiring manufacturers of steel doors, door frames, metal office panels, security grills, sectional and rolling doors, and similar items. By 1989, it had become one of the largest U.S. producers of steel door products. MI also entered a new sector of automotive parts in 1986, acquiring several manufacturers of components such as windshield wiper blades, roof racks, brake hardware repair kits, and front-wheel-drive components. MI focused on establishing its own niches in the market, which continued to expand as the need for replacement parts for longer lasting automobiles increased. MI production of customized goods for the defense industry, including cartridge casings, projectiles, and casings for rocket motors and missiles, declined in the late 1980s, as the U.S. government began to decrease defense spending.

After the creation of MI, Masco Corporation continued its expansion, acquiring, in 1984, Trayco and Aqua Glass, both kitchen-and-bathroom-products manufacturers with sales of about $70 million. At the same time, Masco phased out its Electra personal-communications products, a market no longer suited to the company's criteria for growth.

In 1985, Masco acquired Merillat Industries, a manufacturer of cabinets, and Flint and Walling Water Systems, which made water pumps. Masco also introduced the largest faucet selection in the history of the plumbing industry. Wayne B. Lyon became president of Masco in 1985, while Richard Manoogian served as chairman and CEO of both Masco Corporation and Masco Industries.

In the early 1980s, Richard Manoogian saw a great potential for growth abroad and acquired the Berglen group of companies, which distributed faucets in the U.K., and 25% of Hans Grohe, the top European hand-shower manufacturer. Due to disadvantageous foreign currency rates, sales in dollars in Europe had remained stagnant for several years, but European sales in domestic currencies were thriving.

In 1986, Masco filed lawsuits against several plumbing suppliers —Waxman Industries, Keystone Franklin, and Radiator Specialty Company—for infringement on the Delta faucet trademark. In 1987, Masco's competitors agreed to mark packages more clearly, following the trademark specifications. It was the first of several trademark infringement cases involving the Delta name.

Masco moved into the furniture industry in 1986, acquiring Henredon Furniture Industries and Drexel Heritage Furniture, and one year later, Lexington Furniture Industries. The three companies represented about $700 million in sales. Masco also acquired Walkins Manufacturing Corporation, a producer of spas, and Fieldstone Cabinetry.

In 1987, Masco purchased Marbro Lamp Company and Hueppe Duscha, a West German maker of shower equipment. Masco also issued 1.2 million shares in order to finance its acquisition of La Barge Mirrors; two new furniture companies, Hickorycraft and Alsons Corporation; and Marge Carson, Inc., a manufacturer of plumbing products. By 1988 furniture sales accounted for about 25% of the company's $2.9 billion sales, and Masco continued to expand, acquiring American Textile Company and the Robert Allen Companies.

In 1988, MI transferred nine of its smaller businesses to TriMas Corporation, a spin-off, primarily a manufacturer of industrial fasteners. Two years later, Masco Corporation sold TriMas its recreational vehicle–accessories and its insulation-products businesses.

In 1989, earnings declined, and Masco Corporation's stock sold at discounted rates, due to investor uncertainty about the future of the home-improvement sector. Consequently, the company repurchased four million of its common shares in 1989, and in 1990, the board voted to repurchase up to ten million additional common shares.

Expansion continued in 1989, as Masco bought Universal Furniture of Hong Kong, its largest overseas acquisition. Foreign sales, mainly in Canada and Europe, accounted for about 13% of Masco's total revenues.

Demographically, the outlook is promising. The targeted market of middle-aged homeowners for home-improvement products and furniture will continue to increase. MI's position as the sister company of Masco, along with its unique design and manufacturing capabilities, puts it in a favorable stance for following and advancing the latest technologies. The two companies should benefit from their shared experience and versatility in the global marketplace of the 1990s.

Principal Subsidiaries: Baldwin Hardware Manufacturing Corporation; Brass-Craft Manufacturing Corporation; Drexel Heritage Furnishings, Inc.; Fieldstone Cabinetry, Inc.; Hickorycraft, Inc.; Masco Building Products Corporation; Masco Corporation of Indiana; Delta Faucet Company; Weiser Ltd.; Robert Allen Fabrics, Inc.

Further Reading: Masco 50: the first fifty years 1929-79, Taylor, Michigan, Masco Corporation, [1979].

—René Steinke

MAYTAG CORPORATION

403 West Fourth Street North
Newton, Iowa 50208
U.S.A.
(515) 792-8000
Fax: (515) 791-8115

Public Company
Incorporated: 1925 as Maytag Company
Employees: 26,019
Sales: $3.09 billion
Stock Exchange: New York

Maytag Corporation's reputation rests on the dependability of its machines, and this dependability has enabled the company to charge premium prices. As acquisitions were made during the 1980s, and multiple lines of a product sold in different price ranges, it has taken sophisticated marketing to maintain separate images for brands made in the same factories. While Maytag traditionally sold in the upper quarter of the appliance market, its acquisitions expanded its sales to all but the lowest fifth of the appliance market. Maytag maintains quality through tight control over production. It makes almost all of its own parts, coats its own screws, and tests all machines coming off of the assembly line.

Maytag Company was started by Frederick Louis Maytag and three partners in 1893 to produce threshing-machine band cutters and self-feeder attachments. The company soon began to produce other pieces of farm machinery, not all of it top quality: its corn husker, called the Success, caused the partners many problems because of its poor quality, and farmers often called Maytag out to their fields to fix the Success.

When Maytag bought out his partners in 1907, he had learned his lesson; a Maytag product would always be dependable. Today, each Maytag appliance is tested before it comes off the assembly line, and the company has documented proof to back up its claim of fewer washer repairs.

Maytag built his first washer in 1907, to bring his agricultural-equipment company through the slow-selling season as well as to fill a need for home-use washing machines. Home washing machines were already on the market, but Maytag wanted to make them more efficient. His first washer, called the Pastime, revolutionized washing. It had a cypress tub with a hand crank that forced the clothes through the water and against corrugated sides. The washer was a hit, and Maytag continued to improve on it. In 1911 he brought out the first electric washing machine, and in 1914 he introduced the gas-engine Multi-Motor for customers without access to electricity. The first aluminum washer tub was brought out in 1919, and the Gyrofoam, the first washer to clean with only water action, rather than friction, entered the marketplace in 1922. This revolutionary washer was the first with an agitator at the bottom of the tub instead of the top. This change allowed for the elimination of friction. Sales of this machine pushed Maytag, previously the 38th-largest U.S. washing machine company, into first place.

At this juncture, the farm-implement portion of the business was discontinued. L.B. Maytag, son of the founder, became president of the company in 1920. Under his direction the company began to market nationally. In 1925 Maytag incorporated and was listed on the New York Stock Exchange. In 1926 another Maytag son, E.H. Maytag, assumed the presidency and held the position until his death in 1940. Over the next years, several interesting attachments were offered on washers. A butter churn and a meat grinder were two options offered to buyers. By 1927 Maytag had produced one million washers.

During the Great Depression, Maytag held its own; the company even made money. At his father's death in 1940, Fred Maytag II, grandson of the founder, took over the presidency. During World War II, the company made only special components for military equipment. In 1946 production of washers started up again, and in 1949 the first automatic washers were produced in a new plant built for that purpose. In 1946 Maytag began marketing a line of ranges and refrigerators made by other companies under the Maytag name. During the Korean War the company again produced parts for military equipment, although washer production continued.

During the 1950s the appliance industry grew rapidly. Maytag first entered the commercial laundry field at this time, manufacturing washers and dryers for commercial self-service laundries and commercial operators. During these years full-line appliance producers began targeting Maytag's market. Full-line operators like General Electric, Whirlpool, and Frigidaire provided washers and dryers, refrigerators, stoves, and other appliances. Maytag was much smaller than the full-line producers. It limited itself to the manufacture of washers and dryers, which it marketed with ranges and refrigerators built by other companies, and established its reputation as a premium brand.

The ranges and refrigerators Maytag had been marketing with its washers and dryers were dropped in 1955 and 1960, respectively, but the company soon re-entered the field with its own portable dishwasher and a line of food-waste disposers in 1968. When Fred Maytag II, the last family member involved in the company's management, died in 1962, E.G. Higdon was named president and George M. Umbreit became chairman and CEO.

By the late 1970s over 70% of U.S. households were equipped with washers and dryers. Laundry-equipment sales had peaked in 1973 and the lifetime of such equipment was 10 to 12 years—often longer for Maytag. To help boost sales, prices became more competitive. Chairman Daniel J. Krumm, who had been elected president in 1972, set the company in a new direction in 1980 when he made the decision to make Maytag into a full-line producer, eventually selling a wide range of major appliances rather than just washers, dryers, and dishwashers.

The expansion was effected by acquisition. The first purchase was Hardwick Stove Company in 1981, followed in 1982 by Jenn Air Corporation, the leading manufacturer of indoor electric grills with stove-top vent systems. These products added a full line of gas and electric cooking appliances to the Maytag line and were sold under the Maytag umbrella. Maytag Company meant this diversification to increase its sales in both the new-home market as well as the replacement market; companies make bids to developers based on kitchen packages, not individual components. The larger replacement market had also changed: large chains selling several brands side by side dominated the market. Chairman Krumm felt the diversification was necessary despite the cyclical nature of the building industry.

The new strategy paid off. Consumers began to buy again, and Maytag's sales increased in all areas in 1983. In 1986 the move toward becoming a full-line producer continued with the purchase of Magic Chef in May. Magic Chef's Admiral brand gave Maytag a presence in the refrigerator and freezer sector. Besides Admiral refrigerators, Magic Chef also produces other home appliances under the names Toastmaster, Magic Chef, and Norge. The merger gave Maytag the fourth-largest share of the U.S. market.

The Magic Chef purchase also helped protect Maytag from the threat of takeover. As the industry consolidated and other companies began to sell higher-priced appliances—Maytag's traditional forte—Krumm responded by moving into the medium-priced market. Magic Chef was Maytag's first step into that market.

The merger of Maytag and Magic Chef doubled Maytag's size and necessitated a restructuring. Maytag Company's name was changed to Maytag Corporation and three major appliance groups were formed: the Maytag appliance division, Magic Chef, and the Admiral appliance division. Hardwick Stoves and Jenn Air were included in the Maytag division. The president of Magic Chef remained as head of that division, which included Toastmaster—sold in 1987—Dixie-Narco, and Magic Chef air conditioning operations. The Admiral division included Norge and Warwick product lines, part of the old Magic Chef. Each division was given a great deal of autonomy. Other mergers within the industry during 1986 resulted in four companies—Whirlpool, General Electric, White Consolidated Industries, and Maytag—controlling 80% of the industry.

By the middle 1980s Krumm was ready to move Maytag into foreign markets. With the aim of being a European competitor before the unification of the European Economic Community in 1992, Maytag bought Chicago Pacific in early 1989. The primary reason for this purchase was Chicago Pacific's Hoover division. Hoover produces and sells high-quality washers, dryers, refrigerators, dishwashers, and other products primarily in Great Britain and Australia, but also in continental Europe. It also sells vacuum cleaners in the United States, a new product for Maytag. The European market will not be an easy one for Maytag to enter, however; brand loyalty is high in Europe, and people are used to machines constructed in a certain way.

Another reason for the Chicago Pacific purchase was to further ward off takeover. The $500 million debt the company assumed with the acquisition helped make the company less attractive to raiders.

During the late 1980s, Daniel Krumm spent at least $2 billion in cash and stock to expand Maytag. Sales tripled, but the acquisition of Chicago Pacific was a long-term commitment, not expected to pay off immediately. Maytag continues to use quality as a marketing tool in the fiercely competitive world of appliance selling. Even Maytags need repairs sometimes. When the company stopped making wringer washing machines in 1983, it ran off enough replacement parts to last for 25 years.

Principal Subsidiaries: Admiral Company; Dixie-Narco, Inc.; Hoover North America; Hoover PLC (U.K.); Hoover Trading; Hoover Australia; Jenn-Air Company; Magic Chef Company; Maytag Company; Domicor, Inc.; Maycor Appliance Parts & Service Company; Maytag Financial Services Corp.

Further Reading: Hillinger, Charles, "Washdays, Birthdays: Maytag Notes 80 years," *Los Angeles Times,* May 8, 1987.

—Vera A. Emmons

MINOLTA CAMERA CO., LTD.

3-13, Azuchi-machi 2-chome
Chuo-ku, Osaka 541
Japan
(06) 271-2251
Fax: (06) 266-1010

Public Company
Incorporated: 1937 as Chiyoda Kogaku Seiko Kabushiki Kaisha
Employees: 6,680
Sales: ¥306 billion ($2.13 billion)
Stock Exchanges: Tokyo Osaka Nagoya Frankfurt Düsseldorf

Since Kazuo Tashima began using German technology to produce one camera a day in 1928, Minolta Camera Company has gone on to become one of Japan's Big Five camera makers. Although Minolta initially did so by copying German technology, it then developed new products on its own, and marketed them successfully in Europe and the United States. As the market for camera equipment matured in Japan, Europe, and the United States, the firm diversified into a number of related areas. Minolta is a major producer of cameras, business equipment, radiometric instruments, and planetariums, with production facilities in Japan, the United States, Germany, Malaysia, and Brazil, and a worldwide marketing network.

Minolta began modestly in 1928 when 28-year-old Kazuo Tashima agreed to represent his father's import-export company, Tashima Shoten, on a government-backed trade mission to Paris to promote Japanese silk. In Paris Tashima toured a factory that specialized in high-grade optics, and decided he could produce similar equipment in Japan profitably. Japanese businessmen, including Tashima's father, opposed the idea of producing optical equipment domestically. Unable to start his new venture as a part of Tashima Shoten, Tashima borrowed money from his father's chief clerk and went into business on his own.

Tashima opened shop on November 11, 1928, calling his venture Nichi-Doku Shashinki Shoten (Japan-German Camera Company). The name reflected the company's reliance on German technology and expertise. Partners Willy Heilemann, an importer of German items in Kobe, and Billy Neumann, a German engineer with a background in optical instruments, brought state-of-the-art German technology to the new firm. By March 1929 the staff of about 30 was producing each day one bellows camera, called the Nifcalette—with imported lens and shutter. Within three months, production had grown to 100 cameras a month.

A year later the Great Depression hit Japan hard, bringing labor strife and strikes. Tashima later referred to his company as "a small boat which set sail right into the storm." Nevertheless, Tashima promoted development of new camera models as the depression intensified, and introduced several models in 1930 and 1931.

A new model introduced in 1933 first carried the Minolta brand name, which Tashima created. The name sounds like the Japanese word, *minoru-ta*, which means ripening rice field. The term reminded Tashima of a proverb his mother frequently used, "The ripest ears of rice bow their heads lowest," meaning that the more successful one becomes, the more humble one must be. The name, however, also has a Western meaning, as an abbreviation for Machinery and Instruments Optical by Tashima.

In 1934 the company began to sell the Minolta Vest, the product that made its reputation. Like other camera companies, Minolta used sheepskin to make a flexible camera bellows. When a shortage of imported sheepskin threatened production, the company developed the first rigid bellows of synthetic resin for the Minolta Vest. The innovation made the Vest easier to focus and less expensive. For the first time, a Minolta product was successful outside of Japan.

The Vest's success made expansion possible. Tashima built new production facilities, including a factory devoted to lens production at Sakai. His emphasis on innovation led to the development of the first twin-lens reflex camera in Japan, the Minoltaflex, in 1937. That same year, Tashima reorganized and incorporated the company and renamed it Chiyoda Kogaku Seiko Kabushiki Kaisha (Chiyoda Optics and Fine Engineering Limited) to reflect its broader focus.

In September 1940 Japan joined Germany and Italy in the Tripartite Pact, which divided Asia and Africa into spheres of influence. Japan's was to be Southeast Asia. As it became clear that war was ahead, Japanese military planners determined to develop precision optical equipment for range-finding, navigation, and bombing aids.

During World War II, when the U.S. military used electronics to track enemy ships and aircraft, the Japanese chose optics. Chiyoda Kogaku Seiko produced high-powered binoculars and other optical instruments with wartime uses. Demand was so high that it opened the Itami plant in 1942 solely to manufacture optical glass.

Japan ultimately was devastated by the war. One of the primary goals of the Allied occupation forces was the restoration of Japan's economy. That helped Tashima, who was just as determined to put Minolta back on its feet. Employees dug through the company's bombed-out factories to salvage parts. In 1946 the company produced Japan's first postwar camera, the Semi III.

Since the Japanese camera industry's major prewar competitors, the Germans, had been ruined during wartime bombing—while the Japanese developed their own optical industry—worldwide markets first opened to the Japanese in the postwar years. The Minolta Semi III was the first camera to be exported after the war, with a shipment of 170 cameras in 1947.

Also that year, Chiyoda Kogaku Seiko became the first company to produce coated lenses in Japan, and in 1948 it began to design and produce a camera to compete with the industry standard, the Leica 35 millimeter. Chiyoda Kogaku Seiko designed a new sand-cast body in which lenses could be changed, with a hinged back cover to make film loading easier. The new Minolta 35 included a faster f2.8 lens and more-dependable flash photography.

The company still had to contend with its poor image in overseas markets. Japan had copied German lens technology, and the made-in-Japan label still implied goods of inferior quality. Other Japanese camera firms changed that perception. Takeshi Mitarai of Canon—then known as Precision Optical—persuaded U.S. occupation forces to stock his cameras in military stores. U.S. servicemen stationed in the East took their cameras home, and Japanese-made cameras soon came to stand for high-quality lenses. That new reputation was reinforced industrywide when U.S. photographers assigned to the Korean War began to use Nikon cameras; they claimed that their Nikon lenses were superior to the Leicas they were accustomed to using. Chiyoda Kogaku Seiko began exporting to the United States in 1955. The company introduced another breakthrough, the achromatic double-coated lens, in 1956, giving the company entry into the European market.

In 1958 Chiyoda Kogaku Seiko put its optical experience to a new use by building its first planetarium. The timing was propitious—the Soviet Union had launched Sputnik I, the first earth-orbiting artificial satellite, the year before, sparking new interest in space.

Also in 1958, Chiyoda Kogaku Seiko introduced its first single-lens reflex (SLR) camera. The SLR allowed a photographer to see exactly what was being shot through the camera lens by using an angled mirror that reflected the image to the viewer. Previous cameras—called rangefinder cameras—used two lenses, one to take the photo and one for the photographer to look through. When interchangeable lenses came into use in the early 1950s, the rangefinder posed problems: the photographer saw the same image no matter what lens was used, instead of seeing what the camera would actually photograph. The difference between the two images could be substantial. By the mid-1950s the major Japanese camera companies were developing the more convenient SLRs, and Chiyoda Kogaku Seiko introduced its version, the SR-2, in 1958. Its major competitor was Nikon's SLR, also introduced in 1958, which was recognized as the best of the SLRs at the high end of the market.

Chiyoda Kogaku Seiko opened its first overseas subsidiary, Minolta Corporation, in New York City in 1959. The company chose to name the subsidiary Minolta because of the popularity of its Minolta brand name. Shortly thereafter, Chiyoda Kogaku Seiko changed its own name to Minolta Camera Company. In the 1960s the company continued improving its camera line. It introduced the Uniomat, with a programmed shutter, in 1960, which led to fully programmed autoexposure in the Hi-Matic. In 1962 John Glenn chose the Hi-Matic to take the first photos of earth from space. In 1966 Minolta introduced its longest-running camera line, the SR-T series, which was produced continuously until 1981. These cameras featured through-the-lens light metering, using a patented light compensator to improve exposure in backlit photos. These new products made Minolta more competitive in Europe, so Minolta opened a European subsidiary, Minolta Camera Handelsgesellschaft, in Hamburg in 1965.

More importantly Minolta diversified. In 1960 the company entered the office copying market—an area that would prove as successful as cameras—when it produced the Copymaster. In 1962 it expanded into the data-retrieval field with the Minolta 401S microfilm reader-printer; and in 1965 the company opened its Mikawa plant, which produced the Minoltafax 41, the first copier that could reduce document size.

Minolta continued to develop its links with the U.S. space program, developing the Minolta Space Meter, a state-of-the-art technology for measuring exposures, for the first manned orbit of the moon, in 1968. The meter was used on nine more Apollo missions, including the mission that landed a man on the moon in 1969.

Minolta developed digital watches, video recorders, and pocket calculators in the 1970s, although not all the company's innovations were successful. In 1975 a Minolta-developed office copier that used a complex, high-resolution technology just as plain-paper copiers took over the industry. The company introduced a single-lens reflex camera using cartridge film in 1976, but despite a $2 million U.S. advertising campaign the product was unsuccessful.

Other camera developments were more successful. In 1977 Minolta produced one of the first "smart" cameras. Its XD Series cameras had the first system to override user aperture settings in poor lighting.

Minolta also advanced in other areas. Its MS-18 Planetarium, built in Tokyo, contained the first fully automated planetarium system, and its new photocopiers produced higher-quality images and included both enlarging and reducing capabilities. Those successes were particularly important because the camera market was saturated in Japan, Europe, and the United States.

Minolta responded by redefining itself. It adopted a new logo in 1981 to reflect its broader purpose, and redefined its mission as processing light and images in all types of environments.

In 1983 Tashima, who had run the company since he founded it, left active management. Tashima relinquished the presidency to his son, Hideo Tashima, and became chairman of the board, the position he held when he died in 1985.

In the 1980s Minolta made advances in office-automation products, including copiers and a new word processor, but new camera technology brought the company the most attention. In 1985 Minolta unveiled its Maxxum, a SLR 35-millimeter camera with an autofocusing system. The Maxxum became a successful competitor to the less-expensive non-SLR cameras, such as Canon's Snappy and AE-1. A U.S. advertising campaign costing over $15 million and technological advances that made the Maxxum the European Camera of the Year for 1985 aided its success. The Maxxum challenged Canon's preeminence in the 35-millimeter market, but it was not long before Minolta's Japanese competitors struck back with autofocus cameras of their own. Canon improved on the Maxxum by building the focusing system into the lens itself instead of housing it in the camera body with a mechanical link to the lens, as Minolta had done. Canon's advance made focusing faster, but its camera was more expensive than the Maxxum.

The camera wars were not over, but Minolta's presence in areas like office automation equipment and planetariums promised to smooth out the ups and downs in the photographic market.

Principal Subsidiaries: Minolta Camera Sales Co., Ltd.; Minolta Business Equipment Trading Co., Ltd.; Tokyo Minolta Business Equipment Co., Ltd.; Kanagawa Minolta Business Equipment Co., Ltd.; Yamanashi Minolta Business Equipment Co., Ltd.; Aichi Minolta Business Equipment Co., Ltd.; Kyoto Minolta Business Equipment Co., Ltd.; Osaka Minolta Business Equipment Co., Ltd.; Kobe Minolta Business Equipment Co., Ltd.; Ehime Minolta Business Equipment Co., Ltd.; Fukuoka Minolta Business Equipment Co., Ltd.; Minolta Corporation (U.S.A.); Minolta Business Systems, Inc. (U.S.A.); Minolta Copier Corporation of New York (U.S.A.); Minolta Office Systems, Inc. (U.S.A.); Mohawk Marketing Corporation (U.S.A.); Minolta Business Equipment (Canada), Ltd.; Minolta Canada Inc.; Minolta G.m.b.H. (Germany); Minolta (UK) Limited; Minolta France S.A.; Minolta (Schweiz) AG (Switzerland); Minolta Business Equipment (Belgium) N.V.; Minolta Hong Kong Limited.

Further Reading: ''Minolta Through Six Decades,'' *Minolta Messenger*, Number 7, 1988.

—Ginger G. Rodriguez

MITSUBISHI HEAVY INDUSTRIES, LTD.

5-1, Marunouchi 2-chome
Chiyoda-ku, Tokyo 100
Japan
(03) 3212-3111
Fax: (03) 3201-6258

Public Company
Incorporated: 1964
Employees: 44,392
Sales: ¥1.89 trillion (US$13.15 billion)
Stock Exchanges: Tokyo Osaka Nagoya Kyoto Hiroshima Fukuoka Niigata Sapporo

Since the 1880s the diversified collection of industrial manufacturers now known as Mitsubishi Heavy Industries (MHI) has constituted the heart of the vast Mitsubishi group. Essentially all of Mitsubishi's many industrial offspring were developed as adjuncts to its shipbuilding business, begun in 1884. After suffering several dissolutions in the 20th century, MHI reemerged in 1964 as the world's leading shipbuilder and a powerful competitor in half a dozen related engineering fields. Since the disastrous mid-1970s slump in shipping, caused principally by the OPEC oil crisis, MHI has accelerated its investment in other fields and reduced shipbuilding to a comparatively minor 11% of sales. Its heavy-machinery, power-plant, and construction-equipment divisions are all larger than the original shipbuilding business. With the addition of aircraft production, rocket design, and countless other engineering projects, MHI ranks as one of the world's foremost heavy industrial manufacturers.

The Mitsubishi interest in shipping and shipbuilding extends back to the group's founding in 19th-century Japan. Yataro Iwasaki, born in 1834 to a rural *samurai* family, early in his life became an official with the *Kaiseken*, the agency responsible for regulating trade in his native Tosa domain, on the island of Shikoku. By adroitly straddling the roles of public official and private entrepreneur, Iwasaki was able to start a small shipping company in the late 1860s. In 1875 the Japanese government gave Iwasaki the 13 steamships which he had operated on its behalf during a brief military engagement with Formosa, making his newly named Mitsubishi Shokai—or Three-Diamond Company, the source of the firm's logo—the dominant shipping agent in Japan.

With extensive mining interests and a talent for currency speculation, Iwasaki became so successful that the government created a rival shipping firm, the KUK, to foster competitive pricing. After a short fare war that threatened the ruin of both firms, Mitsubishi's shipping assets were merged with those of the KUK, in 1885, to form a single, state-sponsored company. Mitsubishi retained a small amount of stock and exercised some control in the new firm, but its interest shifted to land-based industries, in particular mining and shipbuilding. In 1884, unable to make a go of shipbuilding, the Japanese government had loaned and then transferred outright its two leading shipyards to the private sector. Mitsubishi took control of the best of these, which was located in Nagasaki, becoming Japan's premier builder of ships and the only one capable to competing in the international marketplace.

Japan's shipbuilding industry was still relatively primitive, however, and remained so until the 1896 Shipbuilding Promotion Law combined with the Sino-Japanese War to spur domestic demand. Mitsubishi, by this time known as Mitsubishi Goshi Kaisha, became the favorite supplier of large ocean-going vessels to the state shipping company NYK, building 43% of all ships ordered between 1896 and World War I. Despite the close ties between the two companies, it appears that Mitsubishi did not receive preferential treatment. Indeed, although Mitsubishi gained fame in 1898 as the supplier of Japan's first ocean-going steamship—the 6,000-ton *Hitachi Maru*—its delivery was so tardy that the NYK awarded a second, similar contract to a British firm.

From 1896 through 1904, the eight years between Japan's wars with China and Russia, Mitsubishi's shipbuilding business increased by nearly 300%. In 1905 it acquired a second dockyard, in Kobe, and by 1911 employed some 11,000 workers at Nagasaki alone. Mitsubishi's shipbuilding division was not yet especially profitable—a disproportionate amount of the parent company's profit still came from mining and stock dividends—but it soon gave rise to a panoply of subordinate industries which supplied the yards with raw materials and parts. For example, in 1905 the Kobe yard spawned what would eventually become Mitsubishi Electric Company, a leading manufacturer of generators and electric appliances. Other shipbuilding divisions grew into power plants and independent producers of airplanes, automobiles, and heavy equipment. Bolstered by its highly profitable mining interests, Mitsubishi could afford the vast sums of money and years of work required to transform its subsidiaries into world leaders.

When World War I began in 1914, Japanese shipping lines were unable to procure enough foreign ships to maintain their booming business, and so turned to local manufacturers like Mitsubishi. Overall Japanese production increased more than tenfold between 1914 and 1919, with Mitsubishi leading the field. So great was the surge in business that the Iwasaki family, still in control of Mitsubishi Goshi Kaisha—the group's holding company—decided to spin off a number of its leading divisions into separate, publicly held companies, thereby gaining access to outside capital without substantially weakening the company's dominant position. In 1917 the Mitsubishi Shipbuilding Company (MSC) was created, along with Mitsubishi Bank; Mitsubishi Iron Works; and a trading company for the entire group, now called Mitsubishi Corporation. The major components of the Mitsubishi *zaibatsu*, or conglomerate, were thus in place by 1920, although the ensuing years would bring many modifications to its structure.

As is generally the case, the wartime build-up in ship orders was followed by a severe depression. As business declined below prewar levels many shipbuilders were bankrupted and all were forced to make drastic lay-offs. The slump continued throughout the 1920s, merging into the Great Depression; Mitsubishi's lack of shipbuilding contracts continued until the beginning of World War II. In the meantime, however, MSC was actively pursuing a number of other technological developments, most notably the airplane and the automobile. Having made its first airplane in 1916 and first auto in the following year, MSC grouped these products under Mitsubishi Internal Combustion Engine Manufacturing Company, in 1920. This offshoot went through several changes before taking the name of Mitsubishi Aircraft Company, in 1928, at which time it was already one of Japan's leading manufacturers of military aircraft. After six years of independence, however, the aircraft and automobile facilities were once again united with MSC to form Mitsubishi Heavy Industries, in 1934. It is not clear why this strategy was adopted, but the imminent prospect of war with China may have suggested the need for a more unified industrial force.

To stimulate the moribund shipping industry, the Japanese government, in 1932, instituted the Scrap and Build Scheme. This policy called for shipowners, aided by government subsidies, to replace their older, smaller vessels with fewer new, more efficient ships. In this way Japan's excess capacity could be reduced while simultaneously modernizing its fleet and promoting new shipbuilding technology. As the leading Japanese builder, Mitsubishi Heavy Industries (MHI) greatly benefited from this program, and even more so from the program's successor, the 1937 Superior Shipbuilding Promotion Scheme. This campaign was clearly prompted by Japan's preparations for war, as it subsidized the construction of very-large cargo ships with an eye to their eventual use for the transportation of troops and supplies. In the years following, government intervention in shipbuilding escalated to outright control, as the Imperial Navy placed all dockyard facilities under its direct command in 1942. The MHI yards at Nagasaki and Kobe produced a wide range of government warships, including the world's largest battleship, the *Musashi*. In addition, MHI used its aircraft experience to build 4,000 bombers and some 14,000 of the famous *Zero* fighters, widely recognized as the finest flying machine in the Pacific during the war's early years. The *Zero* provided an early example of the cost efficiency and quality that marked Japanese industrial design. A lightweight machine, the *Zero* could be produced quickly and economically, yet it boasted superior aerobatic abilities and heavy firing power. The *Zero* made Mitsubishi infamous in the West, discouraging postwar marketers of other Mitsubishi products from highlighting the company name in advertising.

At the end of the war, in 1945, an estimated 80% of Japan's shipyards were still in usable condition. Mitsubishi's main yard at Nagasaki, however, did not escape the effects of the world's second atomic explosion. At war's end the occupying Allied forces halted all shipbuilding activity, restricting the heart of Japan's industrial economy. During the two years in which this ban remained in effect, MHI kept busy by repairing damaged vessels and even using its massive plants for the manufacture of furniture and kitchen utensils.

With the growing realization that Japan could be a strategic asset in the postwar battle against Asian communism, the Allies relaxed the more stringent limitations, and many Japanese companies resumed production. For MHI, occupation forces waited until 1950 to chop its mighty assets into three distinct and geographically separated firms: West Japan Heavy Industries, Central Japan Heavy Industries, and East Japan Heavy Industries. Part of an effort to destroy the Mitsubishi *zaibatsu* as a recognizable entity, the division of MHI was intended to force the three companies to compete against each other for contracts, and hinder their growth.

The rest of the Mitsubishi group was similarly fragmented, and although it gradually reassumed its former shape, the Iwasaki family no longer controlled the various subsidiaries by means of a single holding company. Instead, each of the major Mitsubishi companies acquired stock in its fellow companies, and a triumvirate composed of the former MHI companies, Mitsubishi Bank, and the group's trading company became the unofficial head of what remained a voluntary economic entity. It is remarkable that this loosely connected portfolio of war-ravaged corporations should then have proceeded to outperform its global competitors over the next few decades. The three heavy-industries companies, in particular, faced an almost impossible situation. Forced to compete with one another, forbidden from pursuing the military contracts which had formerly provided a huge portion of its business, and confronted by international competitors whose technological progress had not been interrupted by the war, the new MHI trio appeared destined for failure.

Several factors combined to help MHI get past this critical period. The 1947 Programmed Shipbuilding Scheme provided low-interest government loans to the shipping companies which needed but could not afford new vessels. In effect, the government decided which ships should be built and helped pay for them, injecting the capital needed to restart a business cycle that nearly had ground to a halt. Secondly, the three companies were able to use some of their idle aircraft facilities in the manufacture of motor scooters and automobiles. Under the direction of head designer of the *Zero*, Kubo Tomyo, the rejuvenated auto division sold about 500,000 scooters before the government asked it to resume making small autos in 1959. Thirdly, Japan's shipbuilders realized that the Japanese economy depended on ships and their manufacture, and that if Japanese ship producers could not compete in the postwar international market the entire nation would suffer.

Driven by such a threat to its existence, the former MHI companies hired an increasing number of highly competent engineering graduates from Japan's leading universities and set them to work emulating the advanced technology of the United States and Western European countries. Able to rely on trade unions which were loyal and flexible in the extreme, they were soon producing ocean-going vessels equal in quality to but less expensive than anything made in the West. The Korean War of 1951 to 1953 provided a huge increase in orders, and after surviving the short depression following the Korean War, the companies were able to exploit the rapidly developing worldwide demand for oil tankers. The tanker market was in turn given a tremendous jolt by the Suez Canal crisis of 1956, since the canal closing sparked a surge of orders for larger, more efficient ships able to complete the long journey around Africa. Between 1954 and 1956, total orders at Japanese builders more than tripled to 2.9 million gross tons, of which at least two-thirds were placed by foreign shipping companies.

The post-Suez depression in shipbuilding was severe enough to prompt fresh diversification at MHI. Increased research financing was devoted to civil engineering, plant construction, and automobiles, all of which MHI's years of experience in heavy industry had well prepared it to undertake. In 1958, in cooperation with 23 other Mitsubishi Group corporations, Mitsubishi Heavy Industries created Mitsubishi Atomic Power Industries. MHI continues to dominate contemporary Japanese production of atomic power. Automobile production rose steadily, if not as quickly as at rivals Toyota and Nissan, and by 1964 the Nagoya plants were manufacturing 4,000 cars per month. Even aircraft production had been resumed by the early 1960s.

With the world increasingly dependent on imported oil, and Japan's construction skills honed to perfection, Mitsubishi was hit by an avalanche of orders for tankers during the 1960s and early 1970s. To accommodate this extraordinary boom, the three parts of MHI were once again united, resulting in the 1964 rebirth of Mitsubishi Heavy Industries. This giant's 77,000 employees and $700 million in sales were spread among a handful of the most important heavy industries, but shipbuilding utilized the bulk of MHI's resources. A new dock with 300,000-gross-ton capacity was built at Nagasaki in 1965, followed by the 1972 completion of a mammoth 1-million-gross-ton supertanker facility at the same yard. This ultra-efficient dock enjoyed only a short life, however—the oil crisis of 1973 and 1974 soon brought tanker orders to a near standstill, permanently crippling the entire Japanese shipbuilding industry.

The downturn was devastating. By 1975, the last of the peak tanker years, 40% of MHI sales and one-third of its workers were involved in shipbuilding. By 1985 those numbers were 15% and 17%, respectively, and they have since continued to decline. Once again, the Japanese were confronted with a catastrophic loss of business, but MHI managed to shift its assets fast enough to survive. Having already spun off its automobile division to form Mitsubishi Motors Corporation in 1970, MHI aggressively pursued clients in the power-plant and factory-design fields. It also resumed its position as the top supplier of military hardware to Japan's growing defense force. MHI has streamlined its production facilities by shifting employees from older industries like shipbuilding to newer ones such as machinery and power-plant production, at the same time allowing natural attrition to shrink its overall labor bill.

The result is a more diversified MHI than ever before. The company's sales are generated by a continually increasing number of activities, with the power-plant and machinery division responsible for 71% of the corporate total. Mitsubishi Motors is no longer a consolidated subsidiary of its parent. In 1990 MHI owned less than 26% of the automaker's stock. Given MHI's traditionally poor marketing and consumer sales skills this separation will likely prove a boon for each company. In 1989 shipbuilding accounted for only 11.4% of total sales, a figure which highlights MHI's remarkably adaptive postwar history. Not only did the company rise from the rubble of postwar Japan to become the world's leading shipbuilder, it even more miraculously survived the sudden and near-total destruction of that market in the 1970s.

Principal Subsidiaries: Mitsubishi Heavy Industries America, Inc. (U.S.A.); MHI Corrugating Machinery Company (U.S.A.); Mitsubishi Engine North America, Inc. (U.S.A.); MHI Forklift America, Inc. (U.S.A.); Bocar-MHI S.A. de C.V. (Mexico); Mitsubishi Brasileira de Industria Pesada Ltda. (Brazil); CBC Indústrias Pesadas S.A. (Brazil); ATA Combustão Técnica S.A. (Brazil); Mitsubishi Heavy Industries Europe, Ltd. (U.K.); MHI Equipment Europe B.V. (Netherlands); Saudi Factory for Electrical Appliances Company, Ltd. (Saudi Arabia); Bohai & MHI Platform Engineering Co., Ltd. (China); Mitsubishi Heavy Industries (Hong Kong) Ltd.; MHI-Mahajak Air-Conditioners Co., Ltd. (Thailand); Thai Compressor Manufacturing Co., Ltd. (Thailand); Highway Toll Systems Sdn. Bhd. (Malaysia); MHI South East Asia Pte. Ltd. (Singapore).

Further Reading: Lubar, Robert, "The Japanese Giant That Wouldn't Stay Dead," *Fortune,* November 1964; Tindall, Robert E., "Mitsubishi Group: World's Largest Multinational Enterprise?," *MSU Business Topics,* Spring 1974; "Mitsubishi: A Japanese giant's plans for growth in the U.S.," *Business Week,* July 20, 1981; Wray, William D., *Mitsubishi and the N.Y.K., 1870–1914: Business Strategy in the Japanese Shipping Industry,* Cambridge, Harvard University Press, 1984; Chida, Tomohei, and Peter N. Davies, *The Japanese Shipping and Shipbuilding Industries: A History of Their Modern Growth,* London, The Athlone Press, 1990.

—Jonathan Martin

NHKニッパツ

NHK SPRING CO., LTD.

1, Shin-isogo-cho
Isogo-ku, Yokohama 235
Japan
(045) 751-1261
Fax: (045) 753-5881

Public Company
Incorporated: 1939
Employees: 4,161
Sales: ¥186.57 billion (US$1.30 billion)
Stock Exchanges: Tokyo Osaka Nagoya

NHK Spring Co., Ltd. the world's largest maker of springs and related products, is made up of four main divisions: suspension springs, seating, precision springs and components, and industrial machinery and equipment. The latter group includes services and products related to power stations and petrochemical and natural gas plants, electronics, and chemical products. The company's performance is closely tied to the automotive industry, with 80% of its total sales represented by the many spring and seating products it supplies to carmakers. The remaining 20% is devoted to such products as parts for office and communications equipment, pipe supports, chemical products, machinery devices, and household furniture and space-saving multistory car parking structures for residential and commercial use. Known for its fierce independence, the company is proud that it is not tied to any one automaker or brand name. It has long acknowledged its vulnerability due to its close ties to the automotive industry and has sought to expand and gain greater stability through diversification. Like many other Japanese vehicle manufacturers and their parts suppliers, NHK has stepped up efforts to establish foreign subsidiaries, licensing agreements, and joint ventures, in an attempt to diversify and blunt the effects of the high value of the yen and protectionist trade policies.

The company was founded in 1939, two years after Japan began its invasion of China. Little information about the company's early decades is available. In 1940 NHK opened a manufacturing plant and established its headquarters in Yokohama. Three years later the company—whose initials stand for Nippon Hatsujo Kabushikikaisha—opened a plant in Ina.

Although information about the company's activities during World War II is not available, it is reasonable to infer that NHK was involved in military production, since most Japanese companies were expected to contribute to the war effort. By 1940 Japan's military expenditures were double those of just three years earlier.

Beginning in 1942, Yokohama, site of NHK's original plant and home office, was hit hard by U.S. air strikes. By mid-1945, Yokohama's port, which was Japan's largest, was closed because of damage caused by Allied air and sea attacks. By the end of the war, approximately 50% of Yokohama had been destroyed by U.S. air raids. It is unlikely that NHK emerged unscathed.

In 1958 NHK merged with Daido Spring Company, which had a manufacturing facility in Kawasaki. Three years later, the company constructed a plant in Toyota City to manufacture auto seating parts.

In 1961 NHK opened a liaison office in the United States to bolster its North American marketing efforts. It became the first Japanese spring maker to open an overseas operation when it formed a joint venture in 1963 with a Thai company to manufacture suspension springs, an operation that later branched out into seat and gasket production. This was the first of many joint ventures and licensing agreements that the company would establish.

NHK opened spring-production plants in Hiroshima in 1964, in Ohta in 1969, and in Atsugi in 1970. In 1969 the company established a joint venture known as Union & NHK Auto Parts in Taiwan to produce suspension springs and later added seat production. It obtained a technical license in 1970 from Donald Arthur Girard, a U.S. company, to manufacture pipe clamps, and the following year, NHK granted a technical license to Delta Motors in the Philippines to manufacture automotive seating.

Beginning in the latter part of the 1960s, the automobile industry emerged as one of the major forces in the Japanese economy. The Japanese auto-parts industry, in which NHK has long been a major player, had a 1965 output of ¥640 billion. By 1985 this figure grew to ¥13 trillion.

In 1973 NHK constructed its Shiga plant, for the manufacture of springs, torsion bars, and stabilizers and also established the joint venture NHK Gasket (Thailand) Company. The following year NHK granted a technical license to a Philippine company, UE Automotive Manufacturing, for suspension springs, and obtained a technical license from P.L. Porter Company, a U.S. company, for a mechanical lock.

In 1975 and 1976 NHK established two joint ventures in Brazil, NHK-Cimebra Industria de Molas and NHK-Fastener do Brasil Industrial e Comercio, to manufacture springs and fasteners. Also in 1976 the company established its first U.S. subsidiary, NHK International Corporation, in Schaumburg, Illinois, to market its products throughout North American.

Three years later, NHK obtained a technical license from Wickes Manufacturing Company in the United States to manufacture automotive seating, and it also established the joint venture NHK Gasket Singapore Company.

By the late 1970s the United States began to pressure Japan to open its markets to U.S. manufacturers and to take additional steps to narrow a serious trade imbalance. In 1981 Japan's Ministry of International Trade and Industry imposed a voluntary restraint agreement that limited the number of passenger cars that Japan could export to the United States.

Before 1980 there were only 18 Japanese automobile parts manufacturers doing business in the United States, but beginning in 1981, that figure began to increase rapidly. In 1987 alone, 46 new operations were established, and about 74 tooled up in 1988. By 1989 the U.S. Commerce Department reported that 232 Japanese auto-parts suppliers were producing or would soon be producing parts in the United States. Much of this increased presence can be attributed to the growing presence of Japanese auto and truck assembly plants in the United States, Canada, and Mexico. By 1990 most of the major Japanese vehicle manufacturers had at least one assembly plant in North America, with a combined U.S. production capability of just over two million units a year. By establishing manufacturing plants in North America, Japanese parts suppliers have been able to continue the relationship they had with Japanese vehicle producers and to respond to a growing demand that vehicles produced in the United States contain a certain percentage of locally produced parts.

On October 6, 1980, NHK chairman Kiyotoshi Fujioka told *Asian Wall Street Journal Weekly*, "We are no longer living in an age when we can just keep on exporting products. The thing to do now is go overseas and start production." That year NHK established a joint venture, EGUZKIA-NHK in Spain and signed a three-year agreement with Australia's Henderson's Industries to provide it with technical assistance to produce leaf, helical, and torsion bar springs and stabilizer bars. The company also constructed a plant in Komaki, to manufacture industrial machinery and electronics.

In 1981 NHK announced a new five-year plan known as Vision 80 that was designed to promote diversification and to move the company away from its heavy reliance on the volatile automobile market. The new strategy detailed plans to develop and market products to serve the nuclear power, construction, civil engineering, and electronic industries.

NHK constructed a plant in Komagane in 1981 to produce control cables, chemical products, and electronic components. The plant features a completely integrated production system, in which all aspects of production from research and development to completed products are handled at one location. Since 1962, when polyurethane resins were first developed, NHK had been developing and marketing products made of hard and soft urethane, which are among the chemical products it manufactures at the Komagane plant. The urethane parts are used in a wide range of products such as automobiles, consumer electronics, air conditioning pipeline, low-temperature pipe support systems, and housing for electrical equipment. Also in 1981 the company granted technical licenses to the Far East Machinery Company in Taiwan to manufacture pipe supports and to Compagnie Tunisienne de Ressorts a Lames in Tunisia for suspension springs.

In 1982 NHK granted a technical license to P.T. Muaratewe Spring in Indonesia to manufacture suspension springs. The company built a second plant in Ina to manufacture wire springs in 1983. The same year it granted a technical license to Auto Coil Springs in Malaysia for suspension springs and to the Bombay Company for precision springs. Also in 1983, NHK obtained a technical license from Gebrueder Ahle GmbH to produce suspension springs.

The company established the NHK Group Central Research Institute in 1983 for basic research and to produce engineering improvements that could be applied to NHK products worldwide. The institute was established to complement the efforts of NHK's product-development division, which researches and develops both automotive and nonautomotive products. That same year, NHK was recognized for its development of an automatic, micro-computerized machine that produces several different types of coiled springs.

In 1984 the company granted technical licenses to Jamna Auto Industries Pvt. Ltd. in India to produce suspension springs, to Dae Won Kang Up Company in Korea for stabilizers, and to Lear Siegler in the United States for automotive seating. Also that year it obtained licenses from Rota Bolt Limited in Great Britain to produce load-monitored fasteners and from JASCO Products in the United States for air support systems.

In 1985 NHK and General Motors (GM) announced they would set up a joint venture company known as NHK Inland Corporation in Japan to produce lightweight auto suspension springs made of fiber-reinforced plastic, which is half the weight of steel. GM agreed to provide the design and technology to NHK. The venture, which began operation in a plant near Yokohama in the fall of 1986, planned to sell its parts to vehicle manufacturers in Japan and other Asian countries.

The same year, NHK also granted a technical license to China National Automotive Industry Import and Export Corporation to produce suspension springs at the Liaoyang Automotive Spring Factory.

The company agreed in 1986 to form a joint venture with Suzuki Motor Company to manufacture seats for most of Suzuki's cars and motorcycles. Suzuki was reported to have asked NHK for help because its regular seating-components suppliers were lagging in new-product development and had proved unable to cut costs sufficiently to meet the rising value of the yen. At that time, NHK was already supplying auto seats to Fuji Heavy Industries and Isuzu Motors and producing seats in a joint arrangement with Toyota Motor Corporation.

Also that year NHK granted a technical license to Recticel S.A. in Belgium to produce its Super Seal products, foamed elastic sealing materials with a fixed shape. The company also announced it had agreed to provide technical assistance in suspension spring production to Rassini Rheem, part of the Sidermex Mexican steel complex and a leading producer of car springs through Sidermex, its parent firm.

The year 1987 was one of growth for NHK. The company established a joint production subsidiary for coil springs with Associated Spring, a division of Barnes Group, one of the leading U.S. spring companies. The new company was known as NHK-Associated Spring Suspension Components. NHK also formed two joint ventures with Lear Siegler Seating Corporation to make automotive seating in Canada and the United States. By 1989 the joint ventures had constructed manufacturing plants in Woodstock, Ontario, and Frankfort, Indiana, to supply car seats and related components to CAMI Automotive, a GM/Suzuki joint venture, and Subaru-Isuzu Automotive.

The company also announced the development of two important new products in 1987: a silicon nitride ceramic coil spring which maintains its elasticity at extraordinarily high temperatures, is corrosion-proof, and is four times more elastic than other ceramic springs; and a new air adjustable car seat. The seat can be reshaped by regulating the air inside it and can be adjusted for maximum safety and comfort at various travel speeds. NHK also began that year to manufacture seat cushions utilizing its newly introduced Neo-Curl, an extremely light and porous seat cushion material made of hardened, short-staple polyester fiber with a urethane binder.

NHK also granted technical licenses to two Taiwanese firms in 1987, to Champion Engineering Company to produce its multistory parking system and to Tsuang Hine Company for seat production.

The company purchased the stabilizer manufacturing operations of Mather Metals in 1987, and the following year, it established New Mather Metals in Toledo, Ohio. Also in 1988 NHK obtained a technical license for a seat reclining device from P.A. Rentrop-Hubbert & Wagner Fahrzeugausstattungen GmbH, and granted a technical license for suspension leaf springs to JAI Parabolic Spring Ltd. in India.

In 1989 NHK acquired a plot of land in Yokohama to relocate its office and existing Yokohama plant, which was forced to make way for a highway scheduled to open in 1994. The company's 1989 profits were adversely affected because it encountered larger than expected startup costs as it transferred its production facilities to the new headquarters plant.

NHK continued to diversify slowly. Despite the ambitious five-year diversification program it announced in 1981, the company entered the 1990s with the same 80% of its total sales devoted to the automotive industry as it had posted at the onset of the previous decade. This is due in part to the company's demonstrated ability to change and grow with the automotive industry and its growing presence on the international automotive scene. NHK has announced its plans to branch out into allied industries and introduce new products more aggressively than it has in the past. No doubt this will mean continued establishment of joint ventures and technical pacts and an expanded commitment to developing new products both in the automotive and nonautomotive segments of its business. Sales and profits in the coming years will continue to be affected by exchange rate fluctuations, protectionist trade policies, and inflation, both on the home and international fronts.

Principal Subsidiaries: NHK Sales Co., Ltd. (53%); Yokohama Kiko Co., Ltd. (60.3%); NHK Precision Co., Ltd. (74.1%); Nippon Reclining Seat Co., Ltd. (60%); NHK Transport Co., Ltd. (80%); NHK Spring (Thailand) Co., Ltd. (70%).

Further Reading: NHK Spring, Yokohama, NHK Spring Co., Ltd., 1989.

—Mary Sue Mohnke

NIKON CORPORATION

Fuji Building
2-3, Marunouchi 3-chome
Chiyoda-ku, Tokyo 100
Japan
(03) 3214-5311
Fax: (03) 3201-5856

Public Company
Incorporated: 1917 as Nippon Kogaku K.K.
Employees: 6,770
Sales: ¥284.41 billion (US$1.98 billion)
Stock Exchanges: Tokyo Osaka Kyoto Hiroshima Fukuoka Niigata Sapporo

Nikon Corporation is the grandaddy of Japan's Big Five photographic firms. Its cameras have been the standard for professional photographers and advanced amateurs since the 1950s. When those markets became saturated in the 1980s, the company expanded its product line to remain competitive. A member of the Mitsubishi *keiretsu*, or business group, Nikon manufactures photography equipment and electronic imaging equipment, semiconductor-manufacturing equipment, surveying and measuring instruments, microscopes, binoculars, telescopes, and ophthalmic and medical products.

In 1917 three of Japan's foremost makers of optical equipment merged, in order to offer a full line of optical products. The German optical-glass industry was by far the most advanced at the time. The company was called Nippon Kogaku (Japan Optics) and began producing optical glass in 1918. The new company had negotiated for technical assistance with the German engineering firm Carl Zeiss, but the negotiations fell through. Nippon Kogaku then, in 1919, employed eight leading, independent German engineers.

World War I had little effect on the new company, but postwar government policies that promoted the importation of foreign technology to develop domestic industry helped Nippon Kogaku. In the 1920s the company used German technical advice to develop a line of ultra-small prism binoculars and the precise JOICO microscope. By 1932 Nippon Kogaku designed its own camera lenses, the Nikkon brand. Nippon Kogaku was listed on the Tokyo Stock Exchange in 1939.

Nippon Kogaku expanded during the 1920s and 1930s. Military leaders saw expansion as the best way to attack the domestic problems of overpopulation and shortages of raw materials. The country looked to Southeast Asia as its natural extension, and in September 1940 Japan joined Germany and Italy in the Tripartite Pact to secure its interests in this area. As the threat of a major war increased, Japanese government planners chose to concentrate on improving precision optics for navigation and bombing equipment rather than radar and sonar, chosen by the U.S. government. The decision meant new business for Nippon Kogaku and its competitor Minolta, both of which were primarily optical-equipment producers at the time. It also increased German technical aid to Japanese firms that were involved in the war effort, and Nikon gained expertise through Japan's German ally.

After World War II, Nippon Kogaku continued to prosper, shifting from optics with military applications to optics with consumer applications. The company produced microscopes, binoculars, eyeglasses, and surveying instruments—for which there was great demand as Japan rebuilt its shattered infrastructure.

The company also entered the area for which it would become best known, introducing its first camera in 1946. Other Japanese firms already had begun selling cameras. Minolta had produced cameras since it was founded in 1928; and Canon produced Japan's first 35-millimeter camera in 1934. However, the standard remained the German Leica 35-millimeter camera, accepted by professional photographers as the top of the line since its introduction in 1925.

The war temporarily took German cameras out of the market place. Although Nippon Kogaku had the advantage of German lens technology and the support of U.S. occupation forces that wanted to rebuild Japanese industry as soon as possible, the company did not immediately take advantage of the lack of competition in international markets. Company management insisted on producing cameras for the Japanese market.

It was not long before Japanese cameras became better-known internationally. U.S. occupation forces found Japanese 35-millimeter cameras in post exchanges and took them back to the United States. The simple sand-cast bodies, uncomplicated iris shutters, and high-quality lenses soon earned Japanese cameras an excellent reputation, despite the poor reputation other Japanese-made goods suffered.

Nippon Kogaku's Nikon-brand cameras earned special attention for their high quality. Demand increased further when U.S. combat photographers covering the Korean War favored Nikon lenses, and photojournalists began asking Nippon Kogaku to make special lenses to fit their Leicas. The company's reputation spread by word of mouth among professional photographers. By the mid-1960s photographers for *Life*, *National Geographic*, and *Stern*—Germany's largest-selling picture magazine—used Nikon 35-millimeter cameras. The Nikon had been accepted as the professional standard, and advanced amateurs followed the example, helping Nikon cameras to make inroads into that market as well.

One reason for Nippon Kogaku's success was its development of a completely new type of camera, the single-lens reflex (SLR) camera. The SLR lets a photographer see exactly what the camera will record, using an angled mirror to reflect images from the camera lens to a viewing screen. The rangefinder camera produced by Leitz, maker of the Leica, used two lenses, one for the film and a separate one for the viewer. That method worked until interchangeable lenses were developed in the 1950s. If a photographer used a wide-angle or telephoto lens, the Leica's viewer lens still showed a standard image. There could be a considerable difference between what the eye saw and what the film recorded.

Nippon Kogaku brought the Nikon F SLR to market in 1959 and improved it when other Japanese companies offered competing models. Leitz did not introduce its SLR until 1964. Leitz's SLR was judged by the professional community to be an amateur model, not advanced enough for professional use. By then, the Nikon camera had become the high-end 35-millimeter standard. Even so, it was cheaper than the competing Leicaflex; in 1965, the Nikon F with a coupled light meter and standard f2 lens sold for $413, while a similarly equipped Leicaflex sold for $549.

Another reason for Nippon Kogaku's success in the international market was its ties to the Mitsubishi *keiretsu*, its transfer agent. After World War II, the United States had broken up the *zaibatsu*, powerful Japanese business conglomerates, such as Mitsubishi; but the trading companies, banks, and industrial concerns that had composed the *zaibatsu* continued to cooperate. For Nippon Kogaku, its ties to Mitsubishi meant ready credit and exporting advantages.

Nippon Koguku also marketed its photographic equipment by promoting what it called "photography culture," sponsoring photo contests and photo exhibits and establishing clubs that gave amateurs photographic advice.

Nikon cameras were best-sellers, and Nippon Kogaku was profitable by the mid-1960s. When other major Japanese camera companies, such as Canon and Minolta, entered the office-equipment field by introducing copiers, calculators, and related equipment, Nippon Kogaku continued to emphasize cameras. The company introduced new SLR cameras and an eight-millimeter movie camera during the 1960s and 1970s, as well as a new all-weather camera. The U.S. National Aeronautics and Space Administration chose Nikon SLR cameras for use in the space shuttle program.

Changing economic conditions in the 1980s forced Nippon Kogaku to reevaluate its reliance on cameras. By 1982, 80% of Japanese households owned at least one 35-millimeter camera with all the attachments. Markets in Europe and the United States also were saturated. At the same time, new production techniques—such as use of computers to design lenses—and new materials—such as lightweight, tough plastics for camera bodies—took some of the skill and much of the profit out of making cameras. Since Nippon Kogaku, unlike other Japanese camera makers, was not heavily involved in office equipment or the new video technology, two-thirds of its revenues still came from the mature camera market in 1982.

At the same time, other Japanese companies mounted a new threat to the 35-millimeter camera market. In 1976 Canon introduced a new camera, the impact of which rivaled the introduction of the SLR camera in the 1950s. Canon's AE-1 used a semiconductor chip to change automatically some of the settings the photographer would change on traditional 35-millimeter SLRs. Casual photographers often were intimidated by the need to set shutter speed, lens aperture, and focus, so when Canon pushed the AE-1's ease of use in an advertising campaign its sales took off. Encouraged by that success, Canon next brought non-SLR 35-millimeter cameras back into the picture with its simple Snappy. That camera was a threat to the "snapshooter" market firmly held by U.S. camera makers Kodak and Polaroid, not Nippon Kogaku's high end of the market. Nippon Kogaku introduced the FG 35-millimeter SLR, a programmed, automatic model, in mid-1982 and promoted it with a major ad campaign aimed at men who tended to buy SLRs. Nevertheless, Canon was slipping ahead of Nippon Kogaku in overall camera sales. Nippon Kogaku still held its reputation for building better cameras, but its conservative business approach was causing it to lose ground, just as Leitz's had caused it to lose out to Nippon Kogaku 30 years earlier. To survive, Nippon Kogaku not only had to continue camera development but also to diversify.

In the camera field, the company moved into the simpler end of the market with its successful One-Touch camera in 1983. The next year the Nikon FA received the Camera Grand Prix, a Japanese award. The company followed the One-Touch with the Nikon F-501, a new autofocus SLR camera, which received the 1986 European Camera of the Year Award. In 1989 another new autofocus SLR, the Nikon F-801, received both the Camera Grand Prix in Japan and the European Camera of the Year Award. By the beginning of the 1990s, Nikon Corporation—the name Nippon Kogaku had adopted officially in 1988—could claim to have a complete lineup of cameras ranging from the professional top-of-the-line models to compact autofocus models for less serious photographers.

Nippon Kogaku had also diversified into areas in which it already had a foothold, including ophthalmic technology. It produced sunglasses, plastic eyeglass lenses, and eyeglass frames, and in 1979, marketed its automatic eye refractive index measuring machine. In 1980, the company moved in a new direction, developing a dental root implant using bioactive glass, which bonds with living bone tissue.

In 1972, Nippon Kogaku entered an important new area, marketing its laser interferometric X-Y measuring system, a measuring instrument for integrated circuits. In the 1980s, the company put more effort into developing semiconductor-production machinery, and Nikon has become a world leader in that area. Nippon Kogaku continued to develop microscopes, telescopes, and binoculars as well as more advanced equipment for surveying and measuring instruments.

It also made its first forays into new types of electronic imaging equipment: a color film scanner, used for computer input of photos and a color printer for computer graphic production. The Still Video Camera System needs no film at all—it records images electronically on floppy discs, allowing images to be reproduced immediately or transmitted over telephone lines. Nikon lenses are being used in new high-definition television.

Nippon Kogaku's 1988 name change to Nikon recognized that optical equipment was no longer the company's focus in the electronics-oriented environment. The company known for its advanced optical glass has parlayed its reputation as a leading camera maker into success in other fields. While its conservatism has sometimes meant that Nikon Corporation has been slow in responding to new competitors, it has also meant maintaining a reputation for high quality.

Principal Subsidiaries: Tochigi Nikon K.K.; Mito Nikon K.K.; Sendai Nikon K.K.; Nikon Photo Products Inc.; Nikon

Tec Corporation; Nikon Inc. (U.S.A.); Nikon Precision Inc. (U.S.A.); Nikon Europe B.V. (Netherlands); Nikon AG (Switzerland); Nikon GmbH (Germany); Nikon Precision Europe GmbH (Germany); Nikon U.K. Limited; Nikon France S.A.

Further Reading: Focusing on the Future: 1989, Tokyo, Nikon Corporation, [1989].

—Ginger G. Rodriguez

NINTENDO CO., LTD.

60, Fukuine Kamitakamatsu-cho
Higashiyama-ku, Kyoto 605
Japan
(075) 541-6111
Fax: (075) 551-2722

Public Company
Incorporated: 1889 as Marufuku Company, Ltd.
Employees: 689
Sales: ¥291.20 billion (US$2.03 billion)
Stock Exchanges: Tokyo Osaka Kyoto

Nintendo is a toy and home-entertainment concern that is famous worldwide for its popular home video games. Nintendo's products moved in the mid-1980s from the relative obscurity of the amusement arcade to change the concept of home entertainment in both Japan and the United States. Nintendo's main United States product, the Nintendo Entertainment System (NES), and its Japanese counterpart, the Family Computer (Famicom), were embraced by the consumers of both nations with an enthusiasm normally granted to short-term fads. In Japan, one in three households bought a Famicom, and sales trends in the United States pointed toward a similarly spectacular distribution rate for the NES. Nintendo's success proved to be no mere fad. What kept Nintendo Mania, as it was known in the United States, from going the way of other toy booms was Nintendo's ability to maintain customer interest in its arcade-quality home video games over a long period of time. Nintendo's products and its marketing methods—which featured restraint, an obsessive interest in quality control, and an effective public relations scheme—gave it, according to a Nintendo executive quoted in *Business Week*, November 9, 1987, "a boom with no bust."

Nintendo was founded as the Marufuku Company, Ltd., in Kyoto, Japan, in 1889 by Fusajiro Yamauchi, the great-grandfather of the current president of Nintendo. Marufuku made playing cards for the Japanese game of Hanafuda, which is said to have had its origin in Tarot cards. In 1907, Marufuku introduced the first Western-style playing cards in Japan. Marufuku first made the Western-style cards for Russian prisoners of war during the Russo-Japanese War of 1904–1905, after the soldiers wore out the decks they had brought from Russia.

Between 1907 and World War II Marufuku solidified its status in the playing-card business. World War I, in which Japan fought on the side of the Allies, did not affect business in any remarkable way. In 1925, however, Marufuku began exporting Hanafuda cards to Japanese emigré communities in South America, Korea, and Australia. The years 1925 to 1928 also saw Marufuku developing a new, more effective marketing strategy which placed its products in tobacco shops. These marketing moves were complemented by Marufuku's aggressive advertising, as Japan's business practices became more Westernized.

World War II devastated the Japanese economy, and delivered a hard blow even to the previously modest but stable home amusement market. However, the playing card industry and Marufuku fared far better than most. In the austere postwar climate, when entertainment had to be cheap and simple, the demand for playing cards only decreased slightly. Marufuku, whose physical plant had not been damaged much in the war, thrived in the years following the war.

Hiroshi Yamauchi became Marufuku's president in 1949, embarking on a wide-ranging program to modernize and rationalize the way his family's company was run. In 1952, Marufuku consolidated its factories, which had been scattered throughout Kyoto. In 1951, Yamauchi changed the company name to one more appropriate to the leisure industry; he called it the Nintendo Playing Card Company, Ltd. In Japanese, the word "Nintendo" has a proverbial meaning that loosely translates as "you work hard but, in the end, it's in heaven's hands."

Business boomed in the postwar era. In 1953 Yamauchi responded to a shortage in playing-card-quality paper by challenging his company to develop plastic playing cards. After initial difficulties in printing and coating the plastic cards, Nintendo started mass-production. In 1959, Nintendo first showed its sharp eye for the children's market when it released playing cards in Japan that were printed with Walt Disney cartoon characters. By 1962, business was so good that Nintendo decided to go public, listing stock on the Osaka and Kyoto stock exchanges.

A year later, Nintendo began the drive towards diversification and innovation that eventually led it to the late-1980s boom that made its name a household word. First, in 1963, Nintendo augmented its product line by marketing board games as well as playing cards. By 1969, the game department was so successful that a new game-production plant was built in Uji city, a suburb of Kyoto. The year 1970 saw Nintendo introducing electronic technology for the first time in Japan with its Beam Gun Series. An especially popular example of this technology was the laser clay-pigeon shooting system, introduced in 1973, in which arcade players aimed beams of light instead of birdshot at targets projected on a small movie screen. By 1974, Nintendo was exporting this and other projection-based games to the United States and Europe.

In the next few years, arcade-game technology made remarkable strides, with Nintendo in the vanguard. In 1975, in cooperation with Mitsubishi Electric, Nintendo first developed a video game system using a video player—a technology made more complex the next year when a microprocessor was added to the system. By 1977, this technology was being marketed as part of the first, relatively unsophisticated generation of home video games.

In the amusement arcade, Nintendo's games were beginning to feature higher and higher levels of technology. In 1978, Nintendo developed and started selling coin-operated video games using microcomputers. This innovation, which in 1981 resulted in such arcade hits as Donkey Kong, gave to arcade video games the complex graphics and stereo sound that Nintendo would later market for home use.

As the 1980s began, Nintendo started selling the Game and Watch product line—a hand-held series of electronic games, such as football, with liquid crystals and digital quartz micro-hardware. By this time, Nintendo found that its export business required a firmer foothold in the United States and established Nintendo of America, Inc., a wholly owned subsidiary, in New York City. In 1982, the U.S. office was moved to Redmond, Washington, and established there with an operating capital of US$600,000.

In the 1980s the company focused on the development and marketing of home video technology. A new plant was built in 1983 in Uji city to meet the production requirements of Nintendo's new flagship product, the Family Computer. Famicom, which allowed arcade-quality video games to be played at home came to be placed in more than 35% of Japan's households.

With Famicom swiftly selling in Japan, Nintendo began exporting it to the United States. In 1985, however, when Nintendo was ready to go into U.S. homes, the home video market there seemed all but tapped out. The United States had experienced a dramatic home video boom in the late 1970s and early 1980s, but by mid-decade this boom had ended, leaving the U.S. industry with hundreds of millions of dollars in losses. The sales of the U.S. home video industry had plummeted from a $3 billion peak in 1983 to a $100 million trough in 1985. These figures did not daunt Nintendo. Nintendo quietly testmarketed its games during the darkest depths of the U.S. slump. The U.S. response was quite enthusiastic. Nintendo concluded that the problems in the U.S. home video market were caused by an excess of uninspiring, low-quality games with which an undisciplined industry had flooded the market, losing the trust and patience of its customers as it went after quick profits.

Nintendo came to the United States in full force in 1985 with its American version of the Famicom, renamed the Nintendo Entertainment System. First year profits were astounding, and the skilfully-managed demand of the U.S. market showed few signs of softening from its introduction to the end of the decade.

According to Yamauchi, Nintendo owed its success to its ability to control the quality and amount of game software being sold for its NES systems. The NES hardware was similar to its Japanese precursor, the Famicom, consisting of a Nintendo control deck, hand controls, and the game cartridges themselves. The VCR-like control deck sported an eight-bit computer that generated stereo sound and images in 52 colors. It hooked up with the purchaser's television set to allow the viewer to play a complex video game—which could take up to 70 hours to complete—by manipulating a joy stick that controlled movement in two dimensions.

The NES control deck was sold at close to cost, about US$100, to place it in as many homes as possible. Nintendo then made a profit by selling its own game cartridges at US$25 to US$45 apiece, and by arranging lucrative licensing agreements with the numerous computer software manufacturers who were eager to get a piece of Nintendo's pie by creating software for Nintendo's games.

From the very beginning of its U.S. home video foray, Nintendo gained customer loyalty and enthusiasm by producing or licensing sophisticated, challenging, and surprising software for its NES. By 1989, this practice had translated into a 75% to 80% share of a US$3.4 billion home videogame market.

The business strategies that brought Nintendo to its position of dominance soon came under intense scrutiny. Stymied competitors, the U.S. government, and Nintendo's own licensees—who found that Nintendo's mode of granting licenses for game software could soak up as much as 50% of their profits—all came to regard Nintendo's trade practices with a suspicion that led to widely publicized litigation.

Nintendo and most industry analysts maintained that a lack of quality control killed the first home video craze in the early 1980s. To avoid making the same mistake, Nintendo erected a demanding series of market controls. Each of its licensees, was limited to developing only six new game titles a year. Nintendo manufactured its own patented game cartridges and required would-be software programmers to buy the cartridges in batches of 10,000 and then to assume full responsibility for re-selling the game cartridges after they had been programmed by the licensee. To make certain that hardware competitors and software licensees would not try to circumvent Nintendo's control, Nintendo included a microchip in each game cartridge. Games programmed on cartridges lacking this microchip appeared scrambled when one tried to play them. Nintendo reserved the right to modify games or to forbid a licensee's attempts to market a game that had been deemed unsatisfactory in evaluations conducted by the company. When a licensee's game gained approval, the developer had to wait two years before selling a version of its game to Nintendo's competitors. Because of these safeguards, the quality of Nintendo-compatible software remained high. Yet dissatisfaction developed in the U.S. industry with Nintendo's control.

In December 1988, Tengen Incorporated, a subsidiary of Nintendo's arch-rival Atari and a Nintendo software licensee, filed an antitrust suit. Tengen wished to make games that would run on Nintendo's NES without having to go through Nintendo's series of quality-control measures. Having cracked the code programmed into the microchip in Nintendo's cartridges, Tengen released a game without Nintendo's approval. Nintendo filed a countersuit in February 1989 claiming patent infringement. By then Tengen's parent company Atari had jumped into the fray, filing a separate US$100 million antitrust suit against Nintendo. As the litigation piled up, it became apparent that cultural differences in business practices were near the heart of the conflict.

The 1980s were otherwise a successful decade for Nintendo. It concentrated on popularizing its existing products and developing new ones. In Japan, Nintendo developed and started to sell a Family Computer Disk Drive System, which hit the mature Japanese market in 1986. The way this new product expanded communications capabilities of the Famicom was dramatically showcased in 1987, when Nintendo in Japan organized a nationwide Family Computer Golf Tournament. Players throughout Japan used modems, public telephone lines and disc facsimile technology to compete against each other from their own living rooms in Nintendo's home videogame version of golf. The network, which Nintendo soon hoped to duplicate in the United States, allowed people throughout Japan not only to play Nintendo games against each other; it also enabled people to download information from stock companies and trade in stocks, shop, or make ticket reservations.

In 1989, Nintendo announced a deal with Fidelity Investment Services, Boston, to bring this technology to the United States. For about US$200, American owners of Nintendo's NES could buy a modem, a controller-joystick, and a Fidelity-designed software cartridge that would allow the use of their home-entertainment hardware for a more serious purpose: managing stock portfolios. A US$3 million grant in 1990 to MIT's Media Lab was earmarked for researching the possibility of making videogames more educational.

Despite such serious uses of its equipment, Nintendo remained synonymous with high-technology home fun, largely due to its expert marketing techniques and customer support. In 1988, Nintendo began publishing *Nintendo Power* magazine for its U.S. customers. This magazine, aimed at adolescents, was filled with game-playing tips and announcements concerning recently developed games and hardware. For those times when *Nintendo Power* could not help a frustrated game-player, Nintendo introduced a 24-hour telephone bank with advice from 100 game counselors.

Further public-relations efforts included a deal with Ralston Purina Company in May 1989 to market a citrus-flavored Nintendo Cereal System, featuring edible versions of the heroes from Nintendo's video games. In 1989 Nintendo also teamed up with PepsiCo and the nationwide toy retailer Toys 'R' Us for special joint promotions and in-store displays. Nintendo spent $60 million on U.S. advertising that year.

In 1989, Nintendo also returned to the handheld electronic game market it had created a decade earlier. The battery-operated Game Boy, about the size of a paperback book, featured interchangeable game cartridges, stereo sound, and complex dot-matrix graphics. In Japan, Nintendo unveiled a new 16-bit advanced version of the Famicom, dubbed the Super Family Computer. Its more complex electronics meant more challenging games, more interesting graphics, and more realistic sound. Nintendo waited to release the U.S. version of the 16-bit machine until it felt the American market was ready.

Nintendo hopes eventually to raise its U.S. household penetration rate from 17% to the 35% it has achieved in Japan. Once Nintendo gets the hardware in place, Yamauchi wants to mirror in the United States the profit-producing ten-to-one software-to-hardware ratio that Nintendo has achieved in Japan.

Principal Subsidiaries: Nintendo of America, Inc. (U.S.A.); Nintendo of Canada, Ltd.

Further Reading: McGill, Douglas C., ''Nintendo Scores Big,'' *The New York Times*, December 4, 1988.

—René Steinke

NIPPON SEIKO K.K.

Nissei Building
6-3, Ohsaki 1-chome
Shinagawa-ku, Tokyo 141
Japan
(03) 3779-7120
Fax: (03) 3779-7433

Public Company
Incorporated: 1914 as Nippon Seiko Goshi Gaisha
Employees: 9,025
Sales: ¥275.83 billion (US$1.92 billion)
Stock Exchanges: Tokyo Osaka Nagoya

Nippon Seiko is one of the world's largest producers of ball bearings. Founded in the Osaki section of Tokyo in the early 20th century, Nippon Seiko grew steadily as Japan industrialized, and soon became that country's largest bearing manufacturer. After considerable expansion within Japan, the company entered overseas markets in the 1950s and 1960s. It has since established production facilities in the United States, Great Britain, Brazil, and South Korea. During the 1970s Nippon Seiko began to diversify into automobile components and other high-precision mechanical equipment. While international trade friction began to threaten export sales during the 1980s, Nippon Seiko's new-product development and extensive overseas operations have secured its place in global high-technology markets.

Nippon Seiko had its beginnings in 1895 when its founder, Takehiko Yamaguchi, traveled to Europe. Yamaguchi went to Europe to learn about nail manufacturing and was surprised to discover how much Japan's technology lagged behind Europe's. In 1906 Yamaguchi began his own manufacturing business in Osaki, producing precision metalworking machinery. He chose Osaki, then a rural community, because of the low price of real estate. Eight years later Yamaguchi incorporated Nippon Seiko Goshi Gaisha, a private company that produced precision nuts and bolts. Also in 1914, Nippon Seiko began to produce the first ball bearings in Japan. Until this time, ball bearings had been imported from Sweden, but as Japan began to militarize, the need for a domestic source of bearings increased. In 1916 Yamaguchi reorganized this business, changing its name to Nippon Seiko K.K. and incorporating it as a joint-stock company.

As Japan's first producer of ball bearings, Nippon Seiko faced constantly increasing demand for this basic machinery component. Japanese business prospered during World War I, and Nippon Seiko increased its production to meet the demand of Japan's rapidly growing industries. Nippon Seiko continued to grow during the Depression as the company supplied industrialists who were providing the Japanese government with armaments. The build-up of the Japanese Navy during the early 20th century also powered the company's expansion, and in 1925 it began to manufacture bearings exclusively. Nippon Seiko increased its productive capacity twice in the 1930s, building a steel-ball plant in Tamagawa in 1934 and another plant in Fujisawa in 1937. The Fujisawa plant has since grown into Nippon Seiko's largest, while the Tamagawa plant remains its oldest operating facility. During World War II Nippon Seiko continued to supply bearings to military suppliers and Japanese industrialists. After World War II Nippon Seiko continued its domestic expansion—serving comercial, rather than military, producers—opening a plant in Ohtsu in 1953 and one in Ishibe in 1959. The Ohtsu plant is the world's leading ball bearing factory, and the Ishibe plant now specializes in automotive bearing-production.

Nippon Seiko first began to look for export markets in the late 1950s. In 1958 it signed a 15-year export and technical-assistance agreement with Hoover Ball and Bearing Company of Ann Arbor, Michigan, a leading producer of ball bearings for the U.S. auto industry. These two companies established JAMCO (Japan-American-Company) in 1962 to import Nippon Seiko's bearings to the United States, and they constructed its first plant in Hackensack, New Jersey, to handle light assembly operations. A year later Nippon Seiko founded NSK-Torrington, its second joint venture in the United States, with the Torrington Company of Bennington, Vermont.

The development of other interests worldwide quickly followed this initial expansion, and by 1965 Nippon Seiko was doing business on five continents. Deutsche Nippon Seiko, the predecessor to the company's current German subsidiary NSK Kugellager, was founded in West Germany in 1963. Two years later the company established operations in Australia and Brazil. Nippon Seiko exported ball bearing plants to Czechoslovakia in 1967, Pakistan in 1968, Poland in 1970, and Bulgaria in 1972.

Having gained entry to international markets through export sales, Nippon Seiko then turned its attention to developing overseas production facilities. In 1970 it opened its first overseas factory, in Sao Paulo, under the direction of its subsidiary NSK do Brasil Industria e Comercio de Rolamentos. A year later the company announced plans to build a $5 million factory in the United States. Hoover-NSK Bearings, an autonomous joint venture between Nippon Seiko and Hoover Ball and Bearing Company, opened its first plant in Ann Arbor, Michigan, in 1973. In 1975 Nippon Seiko became the sole owner of the company, buying out Hoover Ball and Bearing's interest for $10.6 million. Nippon Seiko reorganized the company in 1985 and renamed it NSK Corporation. For its Western European markets, Nippon Seiko established NSK Bearings Europe in London in 1974, and opened a plant in Peterlee, Great Britain, two years later. Nippon Seiko's development of overseas production during the 1970s has helped the company to circumvent trade barriers by relying less on export sales and more on domestic facilities to serve non-domestic customers.

Since 1980 Nippon Seiko has pursued product diversification in the mechatronics field. Mechatronics, a combination of electronics and mechanics, encompasses a vast array of modern technologies that integrate computer and mechanical systems. During the 1980s, the company adopted the slogan "Motion & Control Technology" to reflect its commitment to this field, and has since applied mechatronics to three primary areas of new-product development: robotics, automobile components, and high-precision machine parts.

The company's first venture into mechatronics involved direct-drive motors developed by Motornetic Corporation of Santa Rosa, California. Direct-drive motors are commonly found in audio players, since they produce less noise than conventional belt- or gear-driven motors. Nippon Seiko was interested in applying this technology to factory automation, and through an agreement with Motornetic it began supplying Japanese industrial robotics companies with these units in 1983. Three years later Nippon Seiko bought out Motornetic for $3 million and acquired its well-known brand name, Megatorque Motor, for its direct-drive motors. The company's domestic plants in Maebashi and Soja produce mechatronic products, including robot modules and direct-drive motors used in factory automation. Nippon Seiko also maintains a general research center in Fujisawa, where a staff of 500 researchers develops new mechatronic products and applications. Nippon Seiko plans to expand its line of robotic products and compete aggressively in markets for factory-automated equipment.

As modern technology has revolutionized the automobile industry, Nippon Seiko's interest in it has expanded beyond simple bearing production. Building upon its earlier association with the Torrington Company, Nippon Seiko established the joint venture NASTECH (North American Steering Technologies) in 1987 to manufacture and sell automotive steering gears. NASTECH was also the company's first overseas non-bearing-production venture. In 1988 Nippon Seiko began marketing wheel-hub units, its latest advance in automotive bearings, through an agreement with New Departure Hyatt, the bearing division of General Motors. Wheel-hub units are designed to replace the traditional bearing sets used in wheel axles, since they are lighter, easier to install, and do not need relubrication. As the company entered the 1990s, much of its research and development remained concentrated in automotive products, including electronic four-wheel steering systems, constant-velocity joints, airbags, and automatic seatbelts. This production is concentrated in the Soja plant, which produces constant-velocity joints and steering gears, and the Kirihara plant, which produces seatbelts and other automotive safety products.

The third area of Nippon Seiko's mechatronic product development is high-precision machine parts. Modern technology demands greater precision and endurance from industrial tools, as well as sophisticated electronic systems to run them. Nippon Seiko has expanded upon its bearing line to supply needs as advanced as jet engines and nuclear power plants. In 1984 the company opened a plant in Fukushima, its most advanced facility for producing precision miniature bearings. Through the use of new materials and production processes, it has increased the durability and precision of its bearings to within 0.01 of a micrometer. The company also produces ball screws and linear guides that control linear motion in manufacturing equipment. One of Nippon Seiko's most important product innovations in recent years has been precision X-Y tables. X-Y tables are high-precision positioning devices used in automated manufacturing and assembly. They allow for greater speed and higher accuracy in such processes and are often used in factory robotics.

Nippon Seiko's vigorous overseas expansion has not gone unnoticed, and it has encountered increasing resistance in some markets. In the late 1980s U.S. bearing manufacturers complained of losing domestic markets to foreign importers who, they claimed, competed unfairly. An investigation by the Commerce Department concluded that nine foreign countries were dumping bearings in the United States, selling them at prices below fair market value. Nippon Seiko was assigned a percentage penalty that required it to raise export prices by 56%, in order to reflect the true costs of its products in U.S. markets. In addition, the Department of Defense instituted a five-year buy-American policy for the purchase of all bearings used in U.S. weapon systems. Nippon Seiko continues to face trade barriers produced by nervous domestic producers and the appreciated yen.

Despite such international friction, Nippon Seiko's global position remains strong. Through product diversification and overseas production it has been able to overcome many of the difficulties facing Japanese companies in world markets. From 1985 to 1990, non-bearing product sales increased from ¥75 billion to ¥103.5 billion, and now represent over 37% of total sales. Overseas production has expanded to seven factories in four nations and now accounts for 11.1% of the company's total output. The company is represented by either subsidiaries or sales offices in 14 foreign countries. At home, Nippon Seiko opened a new head office building in 1987 at the company's birthplace in Osaki, and it hopes to continue capitalizing on Japan's healthy economy and expanding domestic demand. It also plans to counter slowing export demand by further integrating worldwide production. With the opening of a new plant in South Korea in 1987, Nippon Seiko will continue to play a prominent role in the expanding economics of Asia's Pacific Rim, and it looks forward to entering markets opened by the 1992 integration of the European Economic Community.

Principal Subsidiaries: NSK-Atago & Co., Ltd.; NSK Corporation (U.S.A.); NSK Bearing Canada, Ltd.; NSK do Brasil Industria e Comercio de Rolamentos Ltda. (Brazil); NSK Bearings Europe Ltd. (U.K.); NSK Kugellager G.m.b.H. (Germany).

Further Reading: "A Brief History of Nippon Seiko K.K.," *NSK News Letter*, July 1990; "History of NSK," Nippon Seiko corporate typescript, [n.d.]; "Motion & Control Technology," Tokyo, Nippon Seiko K.K., [n.d.].

—Timothy J. Shannon

ND DENSO

NIPPONDENSO CO., LTD.

1-1, Showa-cho
Kariya City, Aichi 448
Japan
(0566) 25-5511

Public Company
Incorporated: 1949
Employees: 39,252
Sales: ¥1.30 trillion (US$9.06 billion)
Stock Exchanges: Tokyo Osaka Nagoya

Nippondenso Company is Japan's leading producer of automobile components and one of the larger international components manufacturers, recognized primarily for its compact and lightweight electronic and electrical parts of innovative design. As the second-largest member of the Toyota Group, more than half of Nippondenso's products go to Toyota Motor Corporation (TMC), which owns better than 20% of Nippondenso stock. Nippondenso also supplies nearly all other major Japanese automakers except Nissan; numerous U.S. manufacturers including the Big Three, Ford, General Motors, and Chrysler; and major European auto manufacturers such as Volvo, BMW, and Fiat.

Nippondenso produces more than 3,000 component parts in eight separate product areas, including car heaters and air conditioners, electrical automotive equipment, fuel management and control products, radiators, meters, diesel injection systems, filters, and other automotive and nonautomotive products. The company's emphasis on quality control and improved manufacturing efficiency throughout its history, its aggressive international expansion program, and its well-funded research-and-development activities since the 1960s have produced steady sales growth and allowed Nippondenso to capture dominant positions in many of its world markets.

Nippondenso rose to its international presence from TMC's in-house electrical and radiator operations, which began after Toyoda Automatic Loom Works formed an automobile division in 1933. In 1936 the Japanese government passed legislation to promote domestic production of automobiles. Loom Works separated its automobile division from the rest of the company, and the motor division developed an in-house electrical-parts factory.

The inability of Loom Works to fund adequately automobile production on its own and the fact that legislation had made automobile production potentially profitable led to the 1937 establishment of Toyota Motor Corporation. Soon afterwards, the Toyota Group was reorganized around TMC rather than Loom Works. The limited number of Japanese independent parts manufacturers in the late 1930s, especially those that produced electrical parts, led to the development of parts makers with close ties to automobile manufacturers.

Shortly after Toyota Motor Corporation was formed, it built a factory in Kariya to produce starters and coils. In 1943 a radiator plant was added, and the two factories eventually became the basis for Nippondenso.

Japan's involvement in World War II contributed heavily to the development of Toyota and its affiliates through wartime contracts. After Japan surrendered to the Allies in 1945, the automobile industry was reshaped by the Supreme Command for the Allied Powers, and TMC was compelled to spin off Nippondenso as an independent company.

Nippondenso Company was incorporated on December 16, 1949, as an automotive electrical-equipment maker with ¥15 million in capital and 1,445 employees. Torao Hayashi was named president. Nippondenso's first products as an independent company included starters, ignition coils, distributors, voltage regulators, radiators, meters, oil coolers and cleaners, horns, dynamos, windshield wipers, and car heaters.

In March 1950 Nippondenso announced it would cut personnel in response to recession. A two-month strike resulted and was resolved after Toyota president Kiichiro Toyoda and the company's managing director and executive vice president resigned. Shortly thereafter, 1,760 employees retired voluntarily.

In the 1950s Nippondenso used standardization and quality control to rise to the top of its field. Hayashi and other top executives initially viewed quality control as a means to standardize and to procure U.S. military contracts. Nippondenso also looked to foreign cooperative agreements during the decade as a way of improving standardization techniques, gaining technological knowledge, and expanding product lines.

Following the recommendations of U.S. and Japanese quality-control experts, Nippondenso established a program that combined design, processing, and cost controls. In 1950 Nippondenso formed an inspection department that learned statistical quality-control methods. The following year use of control charts was initiated, and in 1952 random sampling and other testing methods were adopted. In 1954 the company embarked on a five-year quality control program, which included compiling an inhouse training manual for employees and subcontractors. The program initially targeted improvements in standardization and inspections. In 1956 Nippondenso established a quality-control staff office and an independent committee to oversee quality-control programs.

Beginning in 1953 Nippondenso entered a three-year technical agreement with Robert Bosch of West Germany for the production of electronic parts, fuel injection pumps, and spark plugs. As a result of the Bosch tie-up, Nippondenso's product line was expanded in the latter part of the decade to include car air conditioners, engine regulating equipment, fuel injection systems, and diesel engines.

In 1957 and 1958 Nippondenso deemphasized finished product inspection and focused quality-control efforts on improved process-control methods. At the same time, it extended quality-control techniques into design and prototype-manufacturing areas. In 1958 Nippondenso purchased precision measuring equipment and automatic inspection devices to help workers control quality themselves. By the end of the decade sales had grown 23 times from 1950 levels and surpassed ¥10 billion.

In 1960 Nippondenso began working with integrated-circuit (IC) technology and developed an electromagnetic fuel pump fitted with a diode transistor. Two years later the company created an IC device that dims headlights automatically.

In 1961 Nippondenso implemented a second five-year quality control plan that was designed to strengthen the company's management. Later that year, long-range planning efforts of the Quality Control Committee, established in 1956, along with supervisors for planning, development, and production-line activity, were recognized when Nippondenso received the prestigious Deming quality-control award.

Beginning in the latter half of the 1960s Nippondenso expanded in a number of areas; in 1965 new domestic plants were established in Hiroshima and Ikeda to manufacture radiators, radiator-fan motors, and oil coolers. Two years later Nippondenso's fourth plant, a starter and alternator production facility, was opened in Anjo.

Between 1965 and 1966 three new domestic manufacturing and sales subsidiaries were formed: Nippon Wiper Blade Co., Ltd. in Saitama Prefecture, GAC Corporation in Nagano Prefecture, and Asahi Manufacturing in Aichi Prefecture. These companies produce windshield-wiper parts, small motors for automobiles, bus air conditioners, lead wires for automobile components, and central air conditioning systems. In the following year Nippondenso also began exporting automotive components in order to supply the growing number of Japanese automakers assembling automobiles in East and Southwest Asian countries.

Nippondenso's interest in marketing supplies to major U.S. automakers and an increase in Japanese-made cars exported to the United States led to the 1966 establishment of the company's first overseas facilities, which were branch offices in Chicago and Los Angeles. About the same time, liaison offices were opened in New York and Montreal. New products featuring increased automation were also introduced by Nippondenso during the mid-1960s. These included power seat and power window motors, automatic door locks, and a mechanical cruise-control system.

In 1967 Hayashi became the company's first chairman of the board. Tatsuo Iwatsuki, a former vice president and managing director who had been with the company since its incorporation, became president.

The company made a commitment to integrated-circuit technology in 1968 with the opening of its IC Research Center, the first of its type in the automotive industry. That same year it set up the Electronics Product Division to assemble printed circuit boards. The rapid growth of Nippondenso, especially in the latter half of the 1960s, resulted in eightfold sales increase from 1960 to 1969. By the end of the decade the company recorded annual sales in excess of ¥90 billion.

In the 1970s Nippondenso stepped up the pace of its international expansion, research, and product development. In 1970 Nippondenso established Nippon Soken near the Nishio plant for basic automotive-component research. Also in that year the new Nishio plant in Japan began manufacturing a number of the company's principal products, including car heaters and air conditioners, radiators, radiator-fan motors, fuel injection pumps, and electronic fuel injection components. Four years later another domestic plant opened in Takatana to produce meters, oil filters, machinery, and tools.

Between 1971 and 1976 the company bolstered its worldwide presence by establishing nine overseas subsidiaries. In 1971 Nippondenso formed its first overseas subsidiary, Nippondenso of Los Angeles, to assemble and sell air conditioners and import and sell rebuilt electrical automotive equipment and spark plugs. From 1972 onward, Nippondenso formed subsidiaries in Australia and Asian nations in response to more stringent domestic content regulations.

As business with U.S. automakers expanded in the early 1970s, Nippondenso established additional import and sales subsidiaries in North America. In 1972 Nippondenso Canada was established in Toronto. Three years later, Nippondenso Sales, Inc. was set up in Detroit. In 1973 Nippondenso's first European subsidiary, Nippondenso (Europe) B.V., was established in Amsterdam to import and sell air conditioners and air conditioner compressors. Also in 1973, Iwatsuki was named chairman of the board. Takaaki Shirai, another former vice president and managing director, was named president.

Nippondenso responded quickly to changing market needs in the 1970s. After the 1973 oil crisis struck and fuel economy became an international issue, Nippondenso refocused its research-and-development programs and produced an engine control system; and after air pollution became a growing concern later in that decade, Nippondenso produced an electronic fuel injection system that regulated exhaust emissions. The two developments enhanced the company's reputation and boosted sales. So did the push toward smaller, fuel-conserving cars, which increased demand for the compact Nippondenso-made components.

Other Nippondenso innovations during the decade included an electronically controlled automatic transmission developed in conjunction with Toyota in 1970. More electronically controlled systems followed, including a spark advance system, knock control system, and idle speed control system. IC-based technology produced an electronic fuel injection system, new igniters, regulators, and speed sensors. The decade's innovations also included an antiskid device, electronic cruise control, a power trunk opening computer, and such nonautomotive applied electronics products as industrial manufacturing robots, an automatic fire extinguisher, and a portable refrigerator. The 1975 introduction of a new spark plug with a patented U-groove electrode, marketed by Nippondenso of Los Angeles, boosted U.S. sales and contributed to Nippondenso's firm establishment in the spark plug market.

Also in 1977, Takaaki Shirai became chairman of the board, and was succeeded as president by Fubito Hirano. Hirano, like other presidents before him, had climbed the corporate ladder via the offices of managing director and vice president. By the end of the decade 8.4% of net sales were coming from overseas operations. Sales over the previous ten years had grown by 500%, to better than ¥500 billion. The sale of automobile air conditioners and heaters continued to pace earnings, followed by growing sales of electrical components.

Sales continued to climb throughout the 1980s, although earnings slipped mid-decade due to the high value of the yen. During the decade, the company focused on product diversification, international expansion, and construction and automation of factories.

In 1980 Nippondenso formed its first South American subsidiary, in Brazil. That same year, the company entered Malaysia with the formation of Nippondenso (Malaysia) SDN./BHD. Three years later a second Malaysian subsidiary was established. Products of the three new sales and manufacturing subsidiaries included air conditioners, air conditioner compressors, windshield washers, alternators, starters, and radiators.

In 1982 Hirano was named chairman of the board and Kengo Toda, a former vice president and managing director, was named president. That same year Nippondenso opened a domestic plant in Daian to produce distributors, spark plugs, magnetos, sensors, and actuators.

Nippondenso bolstered its European presence in 1984 with the formation of Nippondenso (Deutschland) GmbH, an import and sales subsidiary established for air conditioners, air conditioning compressors, sensors, emission devices, and actuators. Another import and sales subsidiary, Nippondenso (U.K.) Ltd., was formed in 1984 to handle windshield washers, emission control products, and air conditioner parts.

Nippondenso's new products during the first half of the 1980s focused on automobile components emphasizing comfort, safety, and improved driving capabilities. Comfort-related items included a knee warmer, a seat heater, and a mosquito killer. Expanded electronics technology produced an electronically controlled diesel injection system, an electronic suspension control system, and a traction-control system. Nippondenso, which had a history of producing a majority of its specialized manufacturing equipment itself, also entered the automation business during the early 1980s, with the introduction of a magnetic stripe card reader recognition system and a bar-code scanner.

In 1985 Nippondenso posted its fifth consecutive year of increased sales and earnings, reaching all-time highs of ¥954 billion and ¥42.8 billion, respectively. Company officials attributed financial gains largely to increases in overseas production and domestic sales. Nippondenso's strongest push in overseas expansion during the decade was in the United States. In 1984 the marketing and service joint venture A-B Nippondenso was formed when Nippondenso and Allen-Bradley Company of the United States agreed to cooperate on factory automation. The agreement called for cooperation in the development and sales and service of electronics products, and was designed to help Nippondenso advance in factory automation and to help Allen-Bradley, a major manufacturer of control devices and factory automation systems, to enter the Japanese market.

In 1984 the wholly owned subsidiary Nippondenso Manufacturing U.S.A. was formed in Battle Creek, Michigan, for the manufacture and sale of radiators, car heaters, refrigerators, cooling units, condensers, and windshield washers. The $18 million Nippondenso Technical Center U.S.A., in Southfield, Michigan, was also established in 1985. The center's goal was to provide engineering services for U.S. customers, test product designs, and perform other research-and-development activities. That same year Nippondenso developed its second comprehensive domestic testing facility at its corporate headquarters. The new Kariya facility was equipped with laboratories to simulate weather for visibility evaluation, and to simulate driving.

Net sales continued to grow in 1986 and 1987 and passed ¥1 trillion, but net profits declined as a result of the rapidly appreciating value of the yen. Net earnings fell better than ¥10.4 billion in 1986 and ¥1 billion the following year. In 1987 Toda was promoted to chairman, and Taro Tanaka assumed the duties of president. Two domestic plants in Toyohashi and Kota were also opened in 1987.

In the late 1980s rapid expansion continued, accompanied by increased net earnings. Between 1987 and 1989 five major U.S. subsidiaries were formed, including three joint ventures. In January 1989 Michigan Automotive Compressor, Inc. was formed as a joint venture between Nippondenso and Toyoda Automatic Loom Works, for the manufacture and sale of air conditioning compressors and magnetic clutches. In September of that year, Nippondenso established Purodenso Company in Jackson, Tennessee, as a 50–50 joint venture with Purolator Products Company of Tulsa, Oklahoma, to produce and sell air cleaners and oil filters for Toyota, Saturn Corporation, and others. Two months later Nippondenso and Robert Bosch GmbH founded Associated Fuel Pump Systems Corporation as a 50–50 joint venture to produce fuel pumps for Big Three and Japanese automakers operating in the United States.

Nippondenso also continued expansion outside of North America in the late 1980s. In 1987 manufacturing and sales subsidiaries were established in Taiwan and Thailand. Nippondenso Tool and Die (Thailand) Co., Ltd. was Nippondenso's first offshore producer of dies, and Nippondenso Taiwan Company was set up to produce electrical automotive equipment, radiators, and automotive heaters and air conditioners for TMC's subsidiaries in Taiwan.

In the first broad-based cooperation agreement among Japanese auto-parts makers belonging to different groups, Nippondenso agreed in 1987 to help an Isuzu Motors affiliate with radiator production techniques. Nippondenso Finance (Holland) B.V. was also established in 1987. This subsidiary was to carry out group finance and fund-raising activities in the European market. In 1988 Nippondenso struck a deal with Champion Spark Plugs to produce 20 million spark plugs annually under the Nippondenso brand name.

In 1989 Nippondenso and Japan's Shinwa Tsushinki Company agreed to cooperate on the development of mobile communications. That same year, Nippondenso and Valeo, the largest French automotive components manufacturer, together established VND in Spain, to produce and sell distributorless ignition coils.

In 1989 Nippondenso also acquired IMI Radiators of the United Kingdom. The new subsidiary, which specializes in production of oil coolers, intercoolers, and radiators for European automakers, was renamed ND Marston. Nippondenso also formed Australian Automotive Air, Pty. Ltd. in 1989 to manufacture condensors, cooling units, and electric fans for car air conditioners.

Nippondenso's growing interest in the home, office, and factory automation markets resulted in a number of new products in the latter half of the 1980s, including a programmable controller for manufacturing equipment, marketed through A-B Nippondenso. Nippondenso also introduced new factory automation products, including a compact bar-code handy scanner, marketed as the world's smallest and lightest, and a bar-code handy terminal, which combines scanning, storing, and transmission functions. Security systems that make use of finger print–reading devices and a hands-free automobile telephone, and an automobile facsimile transceiver, a combined transmitter and receiver, were also introduced. Other new automobile components included a navigation system and a traction-control system.

After a profit decline in 1986 and 1987, Nippondenso closed the decade with a rebound in earnings, which climbed to a high of ¥48.3 billion in 1989, while net sales reached ¥1.3 trillion. Sales continued to be paced by car air conditioners and heaters, which accounted for about 36% of revenues, and electrical automotive equipment, which represented about 20% of sales.

Nippondenso entered the 1990s by breaking into the Italian market with the January 1990 formation of Nippondenso (Italia), for the import and sale of starters and alternators. In February 1990, Nippondenso's tenth domestic plant began operations in Agui, producing machinery and tools.

Nippondenso's plans for the future are represented in the company's motto "to be pioneering, innovative and creative." Further international expansion is planned with the goal of establishing a comprehensive global presence and a leading share in at least 15 of its major product markets, concentrating on improvement of electronic components; communications systems; ceramics actuators and heaters; factory-automation systems; information devices; environmental cooling control systems for factories, offices, and trains; and refrigeration systems for perishable-food delivery trucks.

Principal Subsidiaries: Asmo Company Ltd. (73.4%); Anjo Electric Company Ltd. (99.8%); Hamanakodenso Company Ltd. (75.8%); Nippondenso America, Inc. (U.S.A.); Nippondenso (Europe) B.V. (Netherlands).

Further Reading: Kamiya, Shotaro, *My Life With Toyota,* Toyota City, Toyota Motor Sales Company, 1976; Cusumano, Michael A., *The Japanese Automobile Industry: Technology and Management at Nissan and Toyota,* Cambridge, The Council on East Asian Studies, Harvard University, 1985; Toyoda, Eiji, *Toyota: Fifty Years In Motion,* Tokyo, Toyota Motor Company, 1987; *Toyota: A History of the First 50 Years,* Toyota City, Toyota Motor Corporation, 1988.

—Roger W. Rouland

NTN CORPORATION

3–17, Kyomachibori 1-chome
Nishi-ku, Osaka 550
Japan
(06) 443-5001
Fax: (06) 445-8588

Public Company
Incorporated: 1927 as NTN Manufacturing Company, Ltd.
Employees: 6,953
Sales: ¥329.19 billion (US$2.29 billion)
Stock Exchanges: Tokyo Osaka Nagoya

NTN Corporation is one of Japan's largest manufacturers of bearings, second in domestic market share only to long-time rival Nippon Seiko, and one of the largest exporters of friction-reducing products in the world. As a natural extension of its bearing business, it is also Japan's principal manufacturer of constant-velocity joints, which are used in automobile transmissions, railway cars, construction machinery, and steel-manufacturing equipment.

NTN traces its lineage back to Nishizono Ironworks, a factory located in the city of Uchibori in Mie Prefecture, which began developing and manufacturing ball bearings in 1918. The Japanese bearings industry was then in its infancy; Nippon Seiko had become the nation's first producer of ball bearings no more than several years earlier. In 1923 Nishizono Ironworks merged with Osaka-based Tomoe Trading Company to manufacture and sell bearings under the brand name NTN. Four years later, however, the partnership broke up and the Nishizono side of the operation, retaining the NTN name, set up a privately owned company called NTN Manufacturing Company, with an initial capitalization of ¥50,000. It reorganized as a joint-stock company in 1934, and three years later it changed its name to Toyo Bearing Manufacturing and offered shares to the public for the first time.

Also in 1937 Japan invaded Manchuria, beginning eight years of war in the Far East. What little export trade Japanese bearing makers had conducted to this point ended by 1941; but as war increased the demand for bearings, and companies made rapid advances in manufacturing techniques, production increased 22-fold between 1937 and 1944, and producers prospered. In 1938 Toyo Bearing established a domestic subsidiary, Showa Bearing Manufacturing Company, in Mukogun, Hyogo Prefecture. The next year Toyo Bearing absorbed Showa Bearing, which became its Mukogawa plant, and merged its operations with those of its newly constructed plant at nearby Kuwana.

By the end of World War II, however, U.S. bombing raids and shortages of steel and other raw materials had brought Japanese bearing makers to a near-standstill. The industry began to revive in the late 1940s, as the shattered nation rebuilt, and domestic demand for its products, as well as demand from other Asian nations, increased. In 1950 Toyo established a separate marketing arm, NTN Sales. The company emerged from these years as one of Japan's five largest bearing makers, along with Nippon Seiko, Koyo Seiko, Fujikoshi Kozai, and Asahi Seiko. Together, these firms accounted for 80% of the nation's bearing output in 1951. In 1954 NTN was awarded the first Deming Prize, for statistical quality control.

Toyo began to diversify its product lines during the 1950s and continued to do so into the next decade, although all its products related to its mainstay, bearings. In 1956 it began manufacturing expansion compensating bearings. In 1961 it entered into a licensing agreement with the West German bearing company INA Wälzlager Schaeffler, under which Toyo produced needle bearings using Wälzlager Schaeffler's technology. The two set up a joint venture, NTN Wälzlager Europa, to market the needle bearings in Europe. In 1963 Toyo secured a similar licensing pact with the British firm Hardy Spicer to produce Birfield-type constant-velocity universal joints. The next year it obtained a license from another British company, GKN Transmission, to manufacture its constant-velocity joints in Japan and formed NTN Bearings–GKN to do so; and in 1965 it began producing pipe fittings and oil-impregnated sintered bearings.

Such growth and diversification as Toyo underwent in the 1960s might be expected to create unwieldy corporate management, but the company avoided this problem by creating subsidiaries to handle new products, thus distributing the decision-making load through a decentralized command structure. In 1961 Toyo created Kongo Bearing Company to handle the production of pillow blocks. The next year, it founded Senyo Kosakuki Kenkyujo, which made ball bearing equipment. This trend continued into the 1970s; in 1971 it created Toyo Bearing Okayama Company to manufacture roller bearings and automotive tapered bearings, and the next year it founded Shohin Kaihatsu Kenkyusho to manufacture other automotive equipment. The company also changed its name to NTN Toyo Bearing Company in 1972.

After riding out the effects of sluggish demand at home, especially in automotive industry, Toyo began pursuing the export market in earnest in the 1960s. In 1963 it established its first sales subsidiary outside Japan—NTN Bearing Corporation of America, followed in 1964 by NTN France. In 1968 it established a sales subsidiary in Canada, NTN Bearing Corporation of Canada. A manufacturing subsidiary, NTN Manufacturing Canada, followed in 1973. In 1971 it founded American NTN Bearing Manufacturing Corporation and opened a plant in Schiller Park, Illinois, its first manufacturing operation in North America. It also established a sales subsidiary in Hong Kong, NTN Trading–Hong Kong, and a West German manufacturing subsidiary, NTN Kugellagerfabrik.

Like its compatriots, NTN made its mark in the high-volume sector of the European and U.S. markets, exporting ball and roller bearings used in automobile parts and electrical equipment. The Japanese bearing exporters became successful enough and their products pervasive enough to produce resentment among their competitors, especially in Great Britain. In 1972 the British government, acting on complaints from its own bearing industry that the Japanese had captured almost one-fifth of the domestic market for standard ball bearings and over two-thirds of the market for bearings for small electric motors, pressed Japanese companies to restrict their exports for two years; but European bearing makers could not avoid the fact that these bearings were of superior quality—a far cry from the 1950s, when Japanese bearing companies were plagued by a scarcity of high-grade steel. In fact, many European companies were buying Japanese bearings, including those made by NTN Kugellagerfabrik, for their own use. NTN Toyo's overseas expansion continued unabated in the mid-1970s. In 1975 it established two sales subsidiaries in Latin America, NTN de Mexico and Panama-based NTN Suramericana. It also opened another factory in Illinois, this time in Elgin.

In fiscal 1977, however, NTN Toyo posted an operating loss of nearly ¥1 billion, as a strong yen made exports prohibitively expensive. Most of its bearings sold in foreign countries were still made in Japan, not by overseas subsidiaries, making them vulnerable to exchange-rate fluctuations. In addition NTN Toyo and other Japanese bearing makers were fined by the European Economic Community for dumping, the practice of gaining an unfair advantage by selling one's products at less than fair value. In 1978 the company was forced to suspend dividend payments for the first time in 12 years.

The strong yen soon weakened, and NTN Toyo's exports surged once again. Strong domestic demand from automobile manufacturers, themselves experiencing an export boom because of the weak yen, also served to boost sales. In fiscal 1979 the company posted a profit of ¥3.4 billion with strong increases in sales and all of its overseas plants reported to be running at full capacity.

With its financial health restored, NTN Toyo targeted its constant-velocity-joint business and its operations in the United States for expansion in the 1980s. In 1982 it added a facility for producing the automotive joints to its Okayama plant. It also entered into a joint venture with the Korean automaker Hyundai Motors, under which Hyundai would manufacture the joints on a license from NTN Toyo. In 1983 NTN Toyo licensed its constant-velocity-joint technology to two more foreign companies, Lepco Company of Australia and Taiway of Taiwan.

The company focused on producing tapered roller bearings in the United States over the next two years. It expanded its Elgin plant in 1984 to increase its capacity to produce the tapered bearings. The next year, it entered into a joint venture with Detroit-based Federal-Mogul Corporation—one of NTN's many U.S. distributors—to manufacture tapered bearings and cylindrical roller bearings. The new company was called NTN-Bower Corporation, with the second name coming from a division of Federal-Mogul, and was given two Federal-Mogul plants and a related research facility. NTN Toyo controlled 60% of the joint venture. In 1987 NTN Toyo exercised its option to buy the remaining 40% of NTN-Bower and became sole owner.

In 1985 NTN opened its Nagano works, specializing in precision miniature bearings. The following year, the company built its Kuwana plant, Japan's first plant dedicated to bearings for use in aerospace products.

By increasing its manufacturing capacity in the United States, NTN Toyo reduced its reliance on bearings exported from Japan for its presence in the U.S. market. It could not cut that reliance entirely, and its bearing exports caused some friction. In 1987 the U.S. bearing manufacturer Timken brought a suit before the U.S. Department of Commerce charging that NTN Toyo, Koyo Seiko, and other Japanese bearing makers were dumping their goods. The Commerce Department found the Japanese companies guilty and ordered NTN Toyo to pay a fine of 47% of the price of the products it had exported to the United States.

In 1988 the company established a technical center in Ann Arbor, Michigan, and once again expanded its U.S. manufacturing operations, adding a bearing-hub production facility to its Elgin plant. It also entered into a joint venture to manufacture constant-velocity joints in Australia with Borg-Warner Australia and GKN Transmission. The new company was called Unidrive, and was 50% owned by Borg-Warner Australia, with 30% going to GKN and 20% to NTN Toyo.

In 1989 NTN Toyo shortened it name to NTN Corporation. The company also established NTN Driveshaft in Columbus, Indiana, to manufacture constant-velocity joints and opened a new research-and-development center.

NTN has achieved substantial success by doing one thing very well and sticking to it. While other large corporations have seen far-flung diversification as the key to success, NTN continues to make nothing but bearings and bearing-related products. Since becoming a major exporter in the late 1960s, its presence in foreign markets had caused occasional controversy, which was not unexpected. What counts is that NTN has found its bearings and is sticking to them.

Principal Subsidiaries: NTN Bearing Corp. of America (U.S.A.); NTN Bearing Corp. of Canada Ltd.; NTN Wälzlager (Europa) G.m.b.H. (Germany); NTN Bearings Ltd. (U.K.); NTN France S.A.; NTN-CBC (Australia) Pty. Ltd.; NTN Bearings (N.Z.) Ltd. (New Zealand); NTN Trading–Hong Kong Ltd.; NTN Bearing–Thailand Co. Ltd.; NTN Bearing–Singapore (Pte.) Ltd.; NTN Bearing–Malaysia Sdn. Bhd.; P.T. NTN Bearing–Indonesia; NTN de Mexico S.A.; NTN Sudamericana S.A. (Panama); Toyoda NTN (Argentina) S.A.; NTN Danmark A/S (Denmark).

Further Reading: NTN Company Profile, Osaka, NTN Corporation, 1990.

—Douglas Sun

OMC

OUTBOARD MARINE CORPORATION

100 Sea-Horse Drive
Waukegan, Illinois 60085
U.S.A.
(708) 689-6200
Fax: (708) 689-7247

Public Company
Incorporated: 1936 as Outboard Marine & Manufacturing Company
Employees: 13,418
Sales: $1.46 billion
Stock Exchanges: New York Boston Midwest Pacific Philadelphia

Outboard Marine Corporation is a worldwide manufacturer and supplier of outboard motors and powerboats. Other products include runabouts, cruisers, performance boats, and craft for offshore fishing. Outboard Marine also markets clothing for boating, and resort wear.

Motorized transport was just becoming an everyday part of life in 1907, when Ole Evinrude invented the first practical outboard engine for boats. Evinrude placed an advertisement in a motor magazine to introduce his motor, drawing so many inquiries from U.S. and overseas readers that he decided to try large-scale production. Needing financial help with this undertaking, he found a backer and established the Evinrude Motor Company in 1910.

The business was an instant success—its market not only recreational boaters but also the Scandinavian fishing fleets operating in the North Sea. Friction between the partners forced Evinrude to sell his share to his backer in 1914 and depart, after signing a guarantee restricting him from the outboard motor industry for five years. The company continued without him, becoming a subsidiary of the gasoline-engine manufacturer, Briggs & Stratton Corporation, in 1926.

By 1921 Evinrude was back in business, in a venture he called the ELTO Outboard Motor Company. His new offering was the Evinrude Light Twin Outboard, a motor partly made of aluminum, reducing its weight by a third. Popular with the fishing fleets, this revolutionary engine outstripped sales of Evinrude's original outboard motor within three years. It also attracted the attention of a competitor, Johnson Motor Company, which brought out its rival lightweight engine in 1922. Johnson gained market share, snatching the lead four years later with an updated model weighing a trim 100 pounds, costing a thrifty $190, and able to drive a boat at a zippy 16 miles per hour. Neither the Evinrude Company nor ELTO could match this. Now far ahead, Johnson produced a net profit of $433,000 in 1927, far outpacing Evinrude's $25,000 and ELTO's $30,000.

A new engine in 1928 restored the ELTO Company, whose annual net profit rose to $300,000. Evinrude merged ELTO with Briggs & Stratton the following year, becoming president of the brand-new Outboard Motors Corporation.

Outboard scarcely had time to find its feet before the stock market crash of 1929 tested its staying power. Already responsible for $500,000 in bank loans as a result of the merger, the company had to increase its debt to $600,000 between 1930 and 1932, when operating deficits totaled $550,000. To keep the business afloat, the entire inventory was sold at bargain prices, and Evinrude sacrificed his salary until his death in 1934.

Johnson's fate was worse. A too-costly advertising campaign, as well as an ill-timed offering of matched motors and hulls, drained all cash reserves by 1930, when control of the company passed to its bankers. Next came an attempt to lessen its reliance on seasonal sales by entry into the refrigerator-compressor market. This last-ditch effort did not revive the business, and shortly thereafter, Johnson was for sale.

In 1935, the Outboard Motors Corporation bought the Johnson Motor Company. Its $800,000 price tag brought Outboard a well-known line of outboards and plant and equipment worth $1.5 million. It also brought Outboard established overseas markets in China, Burma, Iran, and Albania, to broaden Evinrude's array of dealers in Europe, Australia, and New Zealand. Another plus was Johnson's niche in the refrigeration market; Outboard established the Gale Products Division at Galesburg, Illinois, to manufacture this new line.

Expansion brought changes. No longer devoted to purely marine interests, the company changed its name in 1936, to the Outboard Marine & Manufacturing Company. Stephen F. Briggs resigned his Outboard chairmanship temporarily—he had held this position since 1929—to take the Johnson helm. He instituted a rigorous cost-cutting regime, and by 1937 the Johnson division's gross sales were $4.3 million, as compared with Evinrude-ELTO's $2.5 million.

By now, Outboard Motors accounted for about 60% of U.S. outboard motor production. There were three engine lines, suiting most needs: the ELTO line for the buyer seeking thrift; Evinrude, the prestige line; and Johnson, offering special features. Though there was cooperation, operations were largely independent. This left each division to award contracts to outside bidders as well as those sharing a place under the Outboard umbrella. Even export sales operations were handled differently; although they were all routed through the Waukegan headquarters, Johnson tended to sell directly to its dealers, while most Evinrude sales were passed through distributors and then to the dealers.

In addition to the engines, selling mostly in seasonal markets, there were other items broadening the product lines. The Lawn-Boy lawnmower had been an Evinrude staple since 1932, along with pumps for drainage, firefighting, and lawn spraying. Offerings from Johnson included small generators, a gasoline engine for washing machines, and refrigerators. In combination with the motors, all these produced net sales of $6.8 million by 1937, generating profits of $945,000.

In the early 1940s, Outboard's facilities were all converted to the production of war materials. Bomb fuses, aircraft engines, and firefighting apparatus flowed from the Outboard factories, along with landing-boat motors for the Navy. Evinrude four-cylinder engines carried troops across the Rhine. Net sales for 1945 reached $1.8 million, topping $2.5 million the following year.

The personnel who steered the company through the hectic war years were Outboard oldtimers. In addition to Briggs, there was Joseph G. Rayniak, in 1990 director of manufacturing research, whose career dated back to the Johnson brothers' two-horsepower Light Twin, unveiled in 1922. There was Finn T. Irgens, holder of 92 patents, who had risen to be director of engineering from a start with Ole Evinrude, in 1929. There was Ralph Evinrude, who had succeeded to the company presidency after his father's death in 1934.

These longtime staff members were all on hand with the return of peacetime, when the company converted its facilities back to the production of Johnson and Evinrude outboard motors. Spending $8 million on plant expansion and improvement by 1952, Outboard then offered models ranging from one-cylinder, 3-horsepower engines to two-cylinder, 25-horsepower models.

Several acquisitions broadened the Outboard product line during the 1950s. The first, in 1952, was RPM Manufacturing Company of Missouri, whose speciality was a rotary power mower that Outboard planned to sell under its familiar Lawn-Boy tradename. Featuring a detachable engine useful as an outboard, the mower was already a best-selling unbranded item in both the Sears and the Spiegel catalogs. Outboard coped with the huge volume of existing orders by completing entire units in one factory, rather than using the more time-consuming method of piecemeal assembly in several locations.

In 1956, the company changed its name to Outboard Marine Corporation (OMC) in 1956. The same year, OMC purchased Industrial Engineering, Canada's largest chain-saw manufacturer, for C$2.55 million plus 40,000 shares. OMC moved this new subsidiary to Peterborough, Ontario, and changed its name to Pioneer Saws Ltd.

Cushman Motor Works of Nebraska joined the company subsidiary list in 1957. Well known in the utility vehicle field, Cushman had manufactured the Airborne, a motor scooter dropped by parachute for ground transport of paratroopers. Later the company's lightweight vehicles became popular for agricultural, industrial, and recreational use. Costing 114,000 shares at 30¢ par, the new acquisition added three-wheel mail carriers, golf carts, and motor scooters to the OMC product line. Besides the Johnson and Evinrude motors then being sold by about 7,000 retail dealers, the swelling list of OMC offerings included Gale Buccaneer motors sold through hardware jobbers, as well as a number of unbranded models sold for retailers.

The company's most innovative engine appeared in 1958. The first mass-produced die-cast aluminum engine, it was a four-cylinder, 50-horsepower outboard, completely manufactured by OMC, its V-blocks came from Johnson, its steel parts from Evinrude, while the Gale division contributed its carburetors and ignition systems.

Export sales of all items surged ahead during the 1950s. Seeing a 215% gain in exports between 1949 and 1956, OMC expanded its export department in 1956, gaining a new subsidiary called Outboard Marine International S.A. By 1960, taking the next logical step of overseas production, the company was manufacturing and assembling motors in Brugge, Belgium. All these developments showed in the annual net sales, which soared from $27 million in 1950 to $171.5 million by 1959.

During the 1950s, OMC's main objective had been acquisition to broaden basic product lines. In the 1960s, the company's aim was to improve all these products and find growing markets for them. Ensuring its industry leadership by constant innovation and improvement to existing products, OMC allocated more than $7 million annually to research and development.

As the 1960s began, the United States was in the trough of a recession. First-time buyers as well as those seeking bigger and better leisure-time equipment put their purchases on hold. Because its principal markets were tied to leisure-time activities mostly practiced on a seasonal basis, OMC sales sank to a 1961 low of $132.3 million.

The economic turndown did not, however, prevent the company from starting a five-year philanthropic program in 1961. In response to a request to benefit the United Nations Food and Agriculture Organization's freedom-from-hunger campaign, OMC contributed several hundred outboard engines each year to be used in fishing, part of a program to increase food production in underdeveloped countries. Also in 1961, the company established the OMC Boats Division to produce and market 16- to 19-foot boats featuring both outboard and the newer stern-drive engines. Production began the following year, helping to raise sales to $151.9 million by 1962.

The stern-drive, or inboard-outboard motors, were available both as separate units for boat-builders, or as components of boats produced by OMC. Built to give the fuel economy and dependability of inboard engines, they were nevertheless as versatile as outboards. By 1965 the company was selling only about 20,000 stern drives a year, however, and sales of the outboards were still outpacing them tenfold. The problem stemmed from the engine's state-of-the-art technology; many dealers did not know how to repair these motors, and owners were often ignorant of maintenance needs. OMC met this challenge by developing computerized week-long repair and maintenance classes for dealer training. Four schools, two permanently stationed in San Francisco, California, and Waukegan, Illinois, and two mobile units familiarized customers with the new engines.

During the 1960s, public interest in novel sports offered new market potential. Alert to novel trends, OMC entered the snowmobile industry with enthusiasm, introducing the Evinrude Skeeter and the Johnson Skee-Horse in 1964, each sure to thrill riders with speeds of more than 30 miles per hour. Another innovation was the Evinrude Aquanaut for skin diving, also sold under the Johnson tradename Air-Buoy. Consisting of a floating gasoline-powered compressor, the unit supplied air to two masked divers at the same time. Another breakthrough was the loop-charged outboard, devised after the company went back to powerboat racing for the first time since World War II.

By October 1967, OMC's fiscal year-end sales had reached $233.4 million. Of this amount, 10% came from power mowers, with golf carts and utility vehicles sharing second place at 7%, and with snowmobiles, the fastest-growing segment of the business, also at 7%. Chain saw sales accounted for 4% of the final figure, while a full 70% came from marine products. The only failure of the decade was the boat-building enterprise; initially small operating losses grew each year, until the line was sold to Chris-Craft in 1970. Otherwise, the 1960s had been lucrative, as the 1969 net sales figures of $327.1 million showed.

The 1970s began with a dip to $304.5 million in the annual net sales figures. This was partly due to the unprofitable boat line, and partly to a line of tent campers that had never fulfilled expectations after the 1967 acquisition of their manufacturer, Trade Winds Campers. The company discontinued the line in 1971, and immediately saw the improvement in their net sales figures, which soared to $394 million by 1972.

There were other disappointments. Golf cart sales sank to 2% of sales by 1974, and were discontinued in 1975. Chainsaw sales totaled $19.1 million in 1976; resulting in losses for the company and reflecting a flattening of future market potential. OMC discontinued them the following year. Snowmobiles, constituting about 4% of sales volume in 1972, were offered in 1973 with an optional Wankel engine costing about $235 more than the conventional motor. Though this was the United States first introduction to the revolutionary rotary engine, OMC's hopes of success were dashed by heavy competition from other snowmobile brands, as well as by two winters of sparse snow. Snowmobile production came to an end in 1976, after a fiscal 1974 operating loss of $13.9 million.

Fuel shortages were another downside. Coming to an OPEC-inspired zenith in 1973, they brought fears of a buying slowdown in the peak spring quarter. An OMC environmental executive warned of possible gasoline rationing by the petroleum industry, and outlined steps for fuel conservation among boaters.

In the same year, OMC purchased a five-acre site in Hong Kong. Intended as a first step towards larger outboard motor markets in Asia, the move was also encouraged by a Hong Kong government program designed to attract specific, technologically advanced industries. Assembly operations began in the plant in 1975, with the manufacture of electronic outboard motor components following two years later.

In 1974 Charles D. Strang succeeded W. C. Scott as president. Strang's interest in powerboats, beginning in boyhood, had lasted through college and a post as a research associate at Massachusetts Institute of Technology. During a later period of employment with the makers of Mercury outboard motors, interest had deepened into vocation. In 1966 his experience in the powerboat industry had brought him to OMC. Eight years later he rose to the presidency.

An environmental question was one of his first challenges. It began in 1976, when OMC was cited by both the U.S. and Illinois environmental protection agencies for polluting a drainage ditch and Waukegan harbor with polychlorinated biphenyls (PCBs). The company filed suit against both agencies after lengthy negotiations, charging that the federal government had dragged its feet in spending funds authorized for pollution-control use. Company attorneys also stated that the PCB-contaminated pipes had been replaced in 1976, but the agencies likewise filed suit, asking that the company be ordered to remove the contaminants from the harbor, and to pay a maximum penalty of about $20 million, reflecting a $10,000 fine for each day the PCB sources had been in place. This suit was to dog OMC's footsteps throughout the 1980s.

Reorganizing his domestic operations was another Strang priority, with bringing together the Evinrude and Johnson divisions at the top of the list. Complete separation of the two since the company's beginnings had fostered an intense rivalry between them, along with disregard for competition by manufacturers outside the company. To unite the company against outside competitors, in 1978 Strang centralized all domestic manufacturing operations at the corporate headquarters in Waukegan, Illinois, charging vice president James C. Chapman with responsibility for their coordination, as well as for manufacturing policy.

Next came long-range plans for dealing with the competitors themselves. Chief among these were the Japanese firm, Yamaha, eating into OMC's European market, and Brunswick Corporation, makers of premium-priced Mercury outboards. A joint venture between Yamaha and Brunswick had produced a low-cost engine called Mariner; thus Brunswick then had an engine at both high and low ends of the market, leaving OMC sandwiched in the middle. With his newly united company behind him, Strang cleared this hurdle by slashing prices by 25% and also by making sure that all products offered by competitors were available in the OMC lineup. In another move, he bought out independent distributors overseas, thus gaining greater control over foreign marketing operations.

Threatening OMC's competitiveness was a 1980 Department of Energy proposal that boating be banned on weekends. As a result of this suggestion, public concern about gasoline shortages caused OMC net sales to plummet to $687.4 million in 1980, from $741.2 million just one year earlier. It was not easy to maintain the company's competitive edge against the Japanese at this time, but Strang slashed budgets, reducing his work force by one-third, to save an annual pretax amount of $47 million. The reward for this effort showed at the end of fiscal 1982, when net sales reached $778 million.

OMC was now in a position to spend $100 million on the construction and tooling of nine new plants. Contrary to previous practice, each plant was designed to specialize in one manufacturing function. In addition, overseas plants were refined to reduce operations costs and provide more efficient handling and storage.

Streamlining made product innovation easier. Power steering, variable-ratio oiling—delivering exact mixtures of gasoline and oil to the engine—and saltwater protection were new features appreciated by powerboat buyers. Starting in 1983, OMC began to prepare the way for a new stern-drive engine, to supersede previous models. After reviewing the stern-drive market, the company sent interviewers to dealers and service department personnel, gathering information for the ideal stern-drive engine. The result was the OMC Cobra, introduced in 1985. Designed for both boat builders and consumers, its 7.5 liter engine delivered 340 horsepower.

In 1984, James Chapman stepped into the presidency of the company, succeeding Robert F. Wallace, whose short tenure had lasted from January 1982. Like his predecessors, Chapman grappled with the Waukegan Harbor question. This issue was finally laid to rest in April 1989, when the U.S. Department of Justice ordered OMC to fund a trust to remove the pollutants from Lake Michigan.

Changes made by Chapman included the sale of the Cushman and Lawn-Boy operations, for greater concentration on marine activities. Cushman, sold to Ransomes America Corporation in October 1989, brought $150 million. Scarcely one month later, Lawn-Boy was bought by the Toro Company for $85 million.

Chapman's marine acquisitions included the purchase of Four Winns, Sunbird, Bramco, and Stratos Boat Company, Ltd., in a deal costing OMC $120 million. Other acquisitions included Donzi Marine Corporation, in December 1988, and Chris-Craft, a 1989 addition costing $58 million. Net sales, reaching almost $1.1 billion in 1987, soared to $1.5 billion by the end of the 1980s.

Principal Subsidiaries: Outboard Marine Asia, Ltd. (Hong Kong); Outboard Marine Australia Pty. Ltd.; OMC Europe (Belgium); Outboard Marine Corporation of Canada, Ltd.; Outboard Marine de Mexico, S.A. de C.V.; Bramco, Inc.; OMCCC Inc.; Ryds Batindustri AB (Sweden); Donzi Marine Corporation; Sea Nymph, Incorporated; Sunbird Boat Company, Incorporated; Adventurent, Inc.; Hydra-Sports, Inc.; Carl A. Lowe Industries, Inc.

Further Reading: "The Put-Put," *Fortune*, August 1938; Rudolph, Barbara, "Why putt-putt isn't sputter-sputter," *Forbes*, June 7, 1982; *Golden Jubilee: Outboard Marine Corporation, 1936–1986,* Waukegan, Illinois, Outboard Marine Corporation, [1986].

—Gillian Wolf

PARKER HANNIFIN CORPORATION

17325 Euclid Avenue
Cleveland, Ohio 44112
U.S.A.
(216) 531-3000
Fax: (216) 383-9414

Public Company
Incorporated: 1938 as Parker Appliance Company
Employees: 30,000
Sales: $2.38 billion
Stock Exchanges: New York Boston Midwest Pacific Philadelphia

Motion control through the use of air, liquid, and gas is the principal concern of Parker Hannifin Corporation. Operating internationally through numerous subsidiaries, the company manufactures fluid power systems and components for use in industrial machinery, military equipment, air, sea, and space craft, and automobiles.

Because Parker Hannifin serves more than 800 different industries, the company splits its operations into two main segments, supplying both original components and aftermarket maintenance parts. The industrial segment provides motion-control systems and parts for manufacturers in the agricultural, packaging, processing, and military-equipment fields, as well as those concerned with heating, refrigeration, and air conditioning, plus automotive markets. Products manufactured by this segment include hydraulic and pneumatic cylinders, pumps, motors, fluid filters, hose fittings, and tubing.

The company's aerospace segment produces parts and systems for both military and commercial aircraft as well as for space and marine craft. Systems for in-flight fueling, nose-wheel steering, temperature-control, and cryogenics come from this section of the company.

Parker Hannifin started as an automobile-brake company. The automotive market has been a lucrative one since its turn-of-the-century infancy. Thought of at first as a rich man's toy, private transportation was within the reach of the middle class well before 1911, when Henry Ford sold 78,000 Tin Lizzies. By 1918, the first year of the Parker Appliance Company's existence, there were more than one million cars a year coming out of factories in Detroit, Michigan; Cleveland, Ohio; and other centers.

Engineer-inventor Art Parker entered this profitable field modestly, with a pneumatic brake booster designed to make stopping easier for trucks and buses. This initial effort was doomed; the company's first promotional tour came to an abrupt end when an ice patch on a Pennsylvania hill sent Parker's only truck careening over a cliff. This catastrophe sank his bank balance but did not douse his dream of heading a motion-control-manufacturing business.

In 1924 he tried again, offering new flared-tube fitting components to expand his one-product line. Useful for many purposes, these attracted a wide variety of industrial manufacturers. The successful new start encouraged Parker to broaden his horizons. Noting opportunities in the fledgling aviation industry, he made lifelong customers of such pioneers as Donald Douglas of Douglas Aircraft Company and Robert Gross of Lockheed, who soon learned to rely on him as much for his knowledge of hydraulics as for dependable parts. Parker accepted their challenges willingly, helping them to design a hydraulic successor for the heavy gear-and-chain-driven parts then being used to move all airplane control surfaces. This cooperation was so valuable that neither Parker nor the flight industry suffered during the Depression. Instead, all parties flourished, aided by the growing military importance and commercial potential of their products.

Like the aviation section, the automotive division of the Parker Appliance Company grew during the Great Depression years. Though there was a drop of almost 500,000 in privately owned vehicles between 1930 and 1935, this decline did not affect Parker's profits. Travelers without their own cars simply used buses, which always need parts for maintenance and repair.

Now indispensable to two transport industries, the company achieved $2 million in sales in 1934. Other businesses were not so lucky: although almost four million cars rolled off assembly lines in 1935, many smaller factories had to close their doors. A victim of the Depression, the bankrupt Hupp Motor Car Corporation sold its Cleveland building to Parker, which is still headquartered there.

By 1938 the company was ready to look for international markets for its aircraft components. Technologically advanced in both the automotive and the aviation fields, Germany seemed to be a good prospect. Parker and his wife, Helen, changed their minds after a three-month tour of German aircraft factories, because the activity they saw there convinced them that Adolf Hitler was arming for war.

Once back in Cleveland, Art Parker took immediate action. First, he licensed several patents for military-aircraft parts that would broaden his previously patented product lines. His next step was to concentrate his energies on the aircraft market, shifting his focus from the automotive side of the business. Then, he placed an order for lathes—the largest that his manufacturer had ever filled.

Equipping his business for the demands of war took huge amounts of money. No longer able to channel capital from his recently abandoned commercial and industrial base, Parker insured himself against a cash-flow shortage by selling 10,000 shares of stock. During the final days of 1938, Art Parker saw his business become a public company.

By the time President Franklin Roosevelt declared war on Japan and its allies in December 1941, patents held by the Parker Appliance Company were setting standards for such components of military aircraft as hydraulic-tube couplings, fuel-system valves, and pumps. Two years later, there were 5,000 employees working three shifts seven days a week to produce these parts.

Though urgent at the time, this focus on purely military equipment to the exclusion of other business proved costly after the war. Art Parker, who died eight months before hostilities ended, however, was spared the sight of idle factory floors and the employment roll that had shrunk to 200 people as soon as the company's lone customer, the U.S. government, turned its attention back to peacetime pursuits. Although the prospect of bankruptcy now faced Helen Parker, she chose to keep the business running and to recruit new management.

With the help of the company's banker, Charles Sigmier, S. Blackwell Taylor was persuaded to assume the presidency of Parker and to bring his business associate Robert Cornell with him. The two men set to work immediately, selling off surplus inventory and machinery before they did anything else.

Setting long-term goals to provide direction was their second task. The strategic operations plan they formulated, quickly dubbed the Corporate Creed, emphatically stated that the company was not for sale. It also stressed that management would now strive to reduce the percentage of government business, while still increasing sales to government customers; a wise precaution that would stand the company in good stead during the Korean War. Other proposals declared that growth would henceforth take place both internally, through research and development, and externally, through friendly acquisitions. Parker, however, had to be the dominant party in all acquisitions, which would be undertaken to expand the company's product lines and keep it on the cutting edge in the field of fluid power. Targets would be profitable family-owned businesses wherever possible, and each new subsidiary would enjoy considerable autonomy. Along with these decisions came the resolve to supply only top-quality products and service.

The postwar era also brought increasing interest in automation, much of which relied on fluid power to control motion through pneumatics and hydraulics. Making every effort to meet these needs by developing the range of their products, Parker also began to experiment with synthetic rubber to be used for more effective seals. The demand for these seals soon became so universal that the company became a leader in the worldwide standards that were benefiting original-equipment industries as well as many other engineering concerns. Another innovation was the decision to emphasize the production of replacement parts for those components whose constant motion caused them to wear out.

In 1957, a year that showed sales totaling $28.5 million, the Parker Appliance Company acquired the Hannifin Corporation of Des Plaines, Illinois. A manufacturer of hydraulic and air-power cylinders and of presses and other essential products used in liquid, gas, or air pressure systems, Hannifin was not a small company itself. Its $7.5 million price brought Parker two Illinois plants and one in Ohio, plus an employee roll of 600. It also brought a name change, for the Parker Appliance Company now became the Parker Hannifin Corporation. In line with company policy, the former Hannifin customers now became customers of the entire corporation. Also in line with company policy, the new acquisition was assured that there would be no competition for the original equipment manufactured by clients; none of the Parker Hannifin divisions has ever competed with its customers by producing identical parts.

In 1960 Parker Hannifin organized an international division to market its products worldwide. Situated in Amsterdam, it was followed in June 1962 by Parker Hannifin NMF GmbH in Cologne, West Germany, a subsidiary gained by the purchase of Niehler Maschinenfabriek, a manufacturer of hydraulic components. These two new channels brought the company a stronger market for valves, pumps, hoses, air filters, and regulators, as well as for the industrial products of its other ten semi-autonomous subsidiaries.

Also burgeoning at this time was the aircraft division, which had entered the specialized field of cryogenics. Joining the product line of tube fittings, missiles, space vehicles, and systems for the control of wingflaps and landing gear was a ball valve handling liquid oxygen for the *Saturn* space booster. Other components for both commercial and military use included hydraulic torpedo parts and ground support equipment. Important for military action, these items played a significant strategic role when the U.S. entered the Vietnam War in 1965. Later this division would produce another important device; a special assembly for the main flight control of the Sikorsky Black Hawk helicopter. Consisting of only five pounds of bulletproof steel, it continues to function if damaged.

Keeping ahead of the competition in these ways had taken a great deal of prior planning. Mindful of the need for ultramodern manufacturing plants, in 1961 the company had made a heavy investment in equipment to increase capacity and improve operating efficiency. This paid off handsomely the following year, with year-end sales of more than $61 million.

This modernizing, plus the strategic acquisition of profitable foreign companies that continued throughout the 1960s, added a line of refrigeration components and expanded the range of other Parker Hannifin products now being made in Canada, Italy, France, and South Africa. Like domestic plants, overseas plants manufactured standardized components that were easily replaceable. The wisdom of this practice was reflected in 1967 sales, which totaled more than $152 million.

In 1968, outgoing President Robert Cornell was succeeded by the founder's son, Patrick Parker. Parker had spent three years running the seals division after gaining experience in various departments in Cleveland. Parker introduced new training for machine operators to ensure skilled technical labor for affiliates and subsidiaries. Next came two 1973 courses for distributors and customers. Designed to explain the increasingly complex range of Parker Hannifin products, the first course covered basic industrial hydraulic technology; the second, advanced circuit analysis.

To reduce Parker Hannifin's vulnerability to the cyclical swings of the capital-goods field, the new CEO focused on the lucrative automotive aftermarket. Reasoning that wear on cars always makes replacement parts necessary, he set his sights on the Plews Manufacturing Company, a maker of quick-disconnect couplings, acquiring this concern in 1968. A 1971 newcomer was the Ideal Corporation, which manufactured hose clamps and turn indicators. Following shortly afterwards were the Roberk Company, which made windshield wipers and rear view mirrors, and in 1978, EIS Automotive Corporation manufacturers of hydraulic replacement parts for drum- and disc-brake systems.

The automotive section was not the only business segment receiving company attention at this time. The aerospace division, although offering a profit potential of 14%—compared to 12% apiece from the other two units—was not growing fast enough. In 1978 Parker Hannifin remedied this situation by broadening both its customer base and its product line. Parker Hannifin acquired two new subsidiaries: Vansickle Industries, a maker of replacement wheels and brakes for lightweight private aircraft, and Bertea Corporation, providing electro-hydraulic flight controls for commercial airliners. Both companies had previously been leaders in their fields, Bertea showing a 12-month backlog of orders as well as a $19 million contract on primary flight-control actuators for new Boeing 767 airliners.

Internal efforts were also needed to pull the company successfully through business cycle troughs. A recession in 1971, causing profits to tumble, prompted a new strategic plan called cycle forecasting. The brainchild of Tommy McCuiston, vice president of corporate planning, the forecasting plan is based on the premise that each industry follows its own cyclical rhythm for a period normally lasting three to four years. Six phases are apparent during this time span: growth, prosperity, warning, recession, depression, and recovery. Each phase demands planning providing for the next. During the growth phase, the company anticipates prosperity by expanding the work force and speeding up its training programs. In line with its acquisition philosophy, it also looks for new manufacturing sources. The prosperity phase finds Parker Hannifin executives planning for the months of warning ahead. Expansion is curbed and superfluous companies are sold at this period of peak earning power. The kingpin of the strategy is strict inventory control, allowing for heavy manufacturing activity during depression periods, before growth-phase demand makes production expensive because of overtime wages.

Proof of the strategy's success came with the year-end sales figures for 1980, which passed $1 billion for the first time. Another benefit of the planning came to the fore in the research field, allowing the company to move actively into the field of biomedical engineering. Here, long-used principles of hydraulics were applied to the development of life-enhancing equipment like the implantable insulin dispenser for diabetics, made by the aerospace division.

In 1984, Paul Schloemer succeeded Patrick Parker as CEO and president. Adding 14 acquisitions to Parker's previous 50, Schloemer guided the corporation into the untapped areas of industrial filters and pneumatics, with the addition of Schrader Bellows, in 1984; and electromagnetic motion control, with the acquisition of Compumotor in 1986.

The 1980s brought other significant changes. A weaker dollar against the Japanese yen and the West German mark lost a considerable amount of value between 1984 and 1987. This brought down the price of U.S. technology and products to a level competitive with those of Japan and Europe, making it cheaper to produce components for foreign machinery in the United States than to import them for later assembly.

The automotive market scored heavily here. Quoted in a 1987 article in *Fortune*, investment strategist John Connolly noted that between 1986 and 1987, Honda had scaled down from one-half to one-quarter the number of parts it planned to import for cars assembled in the United States. This trend, plus joint product ventures like the Mazda/Ford Probe alliance assured a market for automotive components that helped the company achieve more than $2 billion in sales in 1988, its 70th anniversary.

Other promising trends for growth came from the aerospace division. Several air disasters and near misses brought commercial airlines and air-safety associations to the conclusion that tighter maintenance procedures and more frequent replacement of aircraft are necessary. This means a greater need for complete hydraulic systems and parts for aircraft in frequent service.

In November 1989 Parker Hannifin sold its three automotive aftermarket components divisions to an investor group headed by the president of the Parker automotive group. The company received about $80 million in exchange for its automotive-parts business, and continued to manufacture original equipment for the automotive market. Parker Hannifin also divested its small biomedical group in January 1990. The biomedical group had 1989 sales of about $4 million. These sectors were sold to allow Parker Hannifin to concentrate on its core motion-control markets—both industrial and aerospace—which the company expects to continue to grow. Anticipatory strategic planning, state-of-the-art research, inventory control allowing for efficient filling of backlog and new orders, and many company subsidiaries should help the Parker Hannifin Corporation maintain stability through the 1990s.

Principal Subsidiaries: Bertea Corp.; Brownsville Rubber Co., Inc. (Mexico); Crossroads Realty, Inc.; Parker-Hannifin Disc Co.; Parker-Hannifin International Corp.; Parker-Hannifin (Canada) Limited; Parker-Hannifin N.V. (Netherlands); Parker-Hannifin SpA (Italy); Parker-Hannifin RAK SA (France); Fernand Grando SA (France, 80%); Parker-Hannifin (Espana) SA (Spain); Parker-Hannifin (U.K.) Ltd.; Parker-Hannifin (Africa) Pty. Ltd. (South Africa); Parker-Hannifin Argentina SAIC; Parker-Hannifin (Australia) Pty. Ltd.; Parker-Hannifin do Brasil Industria e Comm. Limitada (Brazil); Parker-Hannifin Sweden AB; Parker-Hannifin Japan Ltd.; Parker-Hannifin Singapore Ltd.; VSI de Puerto Rico, Inc.; Airborne Mfg. Co.; Clark-Feather Manufacturing Co.; Ermeto Armaturen GmbH (Germany); Jackes-Evans of Mississippi, Inc.; Airborne Electrosystems, Inc.; Airborne International, Inc.; Airborne Support Systems, Inc.; JB Systems, Inc.

Further Reading: Parker, Patrick, *Parker Hannifin Corporation,* New York, The Newcomen Society in North America, 1980.

—Gillian Wolf

PIONEER ELECTRONIC CORPORATION

4-1, Meguro 1-chome
Meguro-ku, Tokyo 153
Japan
(03) 3494-1111
Fax: (03) 3495-4428

Public Company
Incorporated: 1947 as Fukuin Electric Works, Ltd.
Employees: 7,250
Sales: ¥511.70 billion (US$3.56 billion)
Stock Exchanges: Tokyo Osaka Amsterdam Luxembourg New York

Pioneer Electronic Corporation has played a significant role in the development and popularization of consumer audio equipment in the post–World War II era. Pioneer concentrates on three areas of the entertainment market—home audio, car stereo, and video products. Home audio was the company's original arena and remains the source of 38% of its sales, while car-stereo revenues have gradually declined to 30% of the corporate total. The variable in Pioneer's future remains its effort to market a home video player using laser discs in place of the more popular tapes. Video-disc technology is at the heart of Pioneer's video division, which accounts for 28% of company sales. Relying on its solid position in home and car audio systems, Pioneer has devoted its resources to bringing its disc concept to the brink of mass-market acceptance; the warmth of that reception will largely determine Pioneer's future growth.

Pioneer is largely a creation of the Matsumoto family. Nozomu Matsumoto was born in Kobe in 1906, the son of a Christian missionary. He inherited his parents' religious faith, which may have played a role in his early desire to bring "technological innovation based on deep emotions" to the Japanese people. Specifically, when Matsumoto heard a new, Western-built phonograph speaker in 1932, he was so struck by its superior tone that he immediately resolved to make such products available in Japan.

In 1936 Matsumoto founded a tiny company called Fukuin Shokai Denki Seisakusho, or Gospel Electric Works. From its workshop in Osaka, Matsumoto and a colleague struggled to devise a "dynamic" speaker like the Philco model he had listened to, and after a year of experimentation the A-8 was brought to market in 1937. In recognition of its groundbreaking role Matsumoto christened the speaker Pioneer, and graced it with the corporate logo still in use today: the Greek letter omega—symbol of electrical resistance—and a tuning fork.

Matsumoto soon grew dissatisfied with his Osaka location, and in 1938 moved the company to Tokyo. In a factory above which his growing family lived, Matsumoto built and repaired radios and speakers and began to build a modest reputation as a reliable local craftsman. The founder's sons, Seiya and Kanya Matsumoto, helped run the production lines while their father was out making deliveries and sales. Matsumoto's wife Chiyo served as company chef, maintenance staff, and accountant. Before Matsumoto's sons were old enough to take a hand in running the company, war swept over Japan. The Matsumoto family survived intact, as did Nozomu Matsumoto's commitment to bringing audio enjoyment to the Japanese. In 1947, as the national economy slowly regrouped under Allied supervision, Matsumoto incorporated Fukuin Electric and resumed his quest.

Soon after graduating from Chuo University with a business degree, Seiya Matsumoto joined his father's company as head of marketing and sales. Seiya Matsumoto was a natural salesman, remaining in charge of the company's sales division from that time until he was made president in 1982. His brother's talents were more mechanical, like his father's, and when Kanya Matsumoto was finally coaxed into joining the firm, he oversaw the technical and manufacturing aspects of the business.

Fukuin made great strides in the postwar boom economy, with sales and profits climbing at a steady pace while the company continued to build its reputation as a maker of audio components, especially speakers. The Japanese electric industry as a whole enjoyed similar success, and by the mid-1950s Fukuin was selling a significant number of components to its bigger competitors. This was a profitable business, but not likely to build the kind of mass brand-name recognition that would make the company a true audio giant. Achieving such recognition would require the production and effective marketing of complete stereo sets, and in the early 1960s Matsumoto and his sons set out to achieve that goal.

The company first changed its name, from Fukuin (Gospel) Electric to the less denominational Pioneer. It next brought out, in 1962, the first stereo system with detachable speakers, a variation on the usual one-piece console design. This experiment, known as the PSC-5A, was extremely successful and became the stereo industry's standard format. Pioneer also committed itself to the production of full stereo component sets, hoping to share in the blossoming overseas trade with a full range of audio products.

Having thus raised the stakes by positioning Pioneer as a competitor with Japan's leading audio manufacturers, founder Matsumoto realized that his company would need executive experience on a scale greater than he or his sons could provide, and in 1963 Yozo Ishizuka was brought in from Toshiba as managing director. Ishizuka is generally credited with smoothing Pioneer's transition from family business to multinational, something that Nozomu Matsumoto made possible by his graceful withdrawal from the executive suite. Over a period of years Matsumoto gradually relinquished control, eventually naming Ishizuka president in 1971, while he himself remained a rather distant chairman of the board.

In 1964 Pioneer brought out its S-71X modular stereo set, a runaway success that solidified acceptance of separable stereo equipment and put Pioneer on the audio map. The S-71X, introduced at a time when Japanese electronic goods were fast becoming the standard around the world, was instrumental in Pioneer's explosive growth in the 1960s. Under the careful guidance of Ishizuka, Pioneer expanded its range of products, opened the first of its overseas sales offices, and pared its debt burden to virtually nothing. Perhaps of greater significance was the company's decision to enter the nascent car-stereo business. With Japan well on its way to becoming one of the world's leading automobile manufacturers, Pioneer was able to popularize the concept of quality stereo systems in even the most modestly priced cars. Car stereo quickly became an important part of Pioneer's overall sales, and remains so.

Along with a number of other Japanese companies, Pioneer began research into the possibility of home video equipment as early as 1972. Within a few years, however, President Ishizuka and Chairman Matsumoto agreed that their company had fallen too far behind to continue competing in the development of video systems based on magnetic tape, and instead focused on the idea of optical discs that reproduce images by means of a laser beam. As the race for video technology continued, it became clear that Pioneer's technically superior disc equipment would succeed or fail in isolation—none of the competing companies followed Pioneer into laser disc manufacturing, choosing either tape or discs played with a needle similar to that used on a phonograph. Each year Pioneer's risk increased. If it was able to build a cheap, reliable laser disc machine the market would be won, but it seemed more likely to most observers that the company was digging its own grave.

As befit its name, however, Pioneer persevered with its disc research, in 1978 announcing that it had perfected the first laser optical video-disc player, and in 1981 introducing a similar machine for home use. Even if laser disc had immediately taken off, Pioneer would still have been years behind its chief rivals. Victor Company of Japan (JVC) had watched revenue from video cassette recorder sales climb from $36 million in 1976 to $1.4 billion in 1981, when Pioneer finally entered the market. As it turned out, disc sales did not take off at all. Pioneer's machine had several drawbacks. The laser disc player was far more expensive than its VCR counterpart; the discs themselves were to be sold, not rented, making them costly; and the discs could not be "rewritten," or recorded on at home.

Despite these formidable problems, Pioneer remained committed to the disc concept, making it its mission to "never let the LaserDisc be a failure," as stated in *The Spirit of Pioneer.* The company poured an enormous amount of money and effort into the disc program in the early 1980s, only to be greeted with a worldwide recession in audio sales compounded by the falling value of the U.S. dollar, in which Pioneer received a substantial percentage of its revenue. As a result, in 1982 the company lost money for the first time in its 44-year history.

In April of 1982 President Ishizuka died suddenly, leaving Pioneer without direction at a critical juncture in its history. Since Nozomu Matsumoto felt that he was too advanced in years to reassume control, Seiya Matsumoto stepped in as the new president while Kanya Matsumoto became his second in command. The brothers faced a difficult situation. Given a lingering recession and consumers' continued indifference to disc technology, neither Pioneer's immediate prospects not its long term health was secure.

During the early 1980s the company added to its product line answering machines, dictating machines, cable TV equipment, and, in 1982, its successful first compact-disc (CD) player. In 1983 Pioneer introduced a Laser-Karaoke device, which in effect allows consumers to make their own home music videos; and in the following year, Pioneer began marketing the first CD players for automobiles. The combination of these innovations and Seiya Matsumoto's leadership was enough to restore Pioneer to profitability in 1983 and 1984, but 1985 ended in another deficit, emphasizing once again the critical role of laser-disc sales in the company's future. Pioneer had bet on laser, and after ten years of research, production, and marketing it had little to show for its daring.

During the late 1980s and early 1990s the laser-disc market began to show improvement, as the cost of players decreased and a greater number of movies found their way onto disc format. The Pioneer CLD-100, introduced in 1989, was modestly priced and can play both video discs and CDs, which means that the CD revolution will likely carry Pioneer's video concept along with it. Sales were up substantially, to almost 120,000 players in 1989, and if the industry finally manages to design discs that are rewriteable, the future will belong to laser technology, and to Pioneer. The company also posted annual profits for the remainder of the decade.

Pioneer remains as committed as ever to the laser concept, recently spending $200 million to buy DiscoVision Associates of California, a leading optical-disc research firm. Optical discs will eventually be used for many kinds of information storage, including computer information, and it is possible that Pioneer's long years of persistence in laser technology will yield unforeseen dividends in such potentially vast markets, although it will have to contend with Sony, Hitachi, and other giants now crowding the field.

Principal Subsidiaries: Pioneer LDC, Inc.; Pioneer Communications Corporation; Tohoku Pioneer Electronic Corporation; Pioneer Video Corporation; Pioneer Precision Machinery Corporation; Hiwada Electronic Corporation; TECHNO Corporation; Pioneer North America, Inc. (U.S.A.); Pioneer Electronics (USA) Inc.; Pioneer Communications of America, Inc.; Pioneer LDCA, Inc. (U.S.A.); Pioneer Laser Entertainment, Inc. (U.S.A.); Pioneer Electronics Technology, Inc. (U.S.A.); Pioneer Industrial Components, Inc. (U.S.A.); Pioneer Video Manufacturing Inc. (U.S.A.); Pioneer Electronics of Canada, Inc.; Pioneer Electronic (Europe) N.V. (Belgium); Pioneer Electronics Manufacturing N.V. (Belgium); Pioneer Electronics Deutschland GmbH (Germany); Pioneer Electronics Denmark A/S; Pioneer High

Fidelity (G.B.) Ltd. (U.K.); Pioneer Electronics B.V. (Netherlands); Pioneer Electronics B.V. (Netherlands); Pioneer Electronics France S.A.; Pioneer Electronics (Italia) S.p.A. (Italy); Pioneer Electronics Espana S.A. (Spain); Pioneer Electronics Australia Pty. Ltd.

Further Reading: ''Pioneer Electronic: Still committed to videodiscs after a wobbly start,'' *Business Week,* January 24, 1983; *The Spirit of Pioneer,* Tokyo, Pioneer Electronic Corporation, 1989.

—Jonathan Martin

Polaroid

POLAROID CORPORATION

549 Technology Square
Cambridge, Massachusetts 02139
U.S.A.
(617) 577-2000
Fax: (617) 494-0249

Public Company
Incorporated: 1933 as Land-Wheelwright Laboratories
Employees: 11,441
Sales: $1.90 billion
Stock Exchanges: New York Pacific

Polaroid was founded on Edwin H. Land's belief that consumer markets should be created around inventions generated by scientific research. His philosophy often resulted in products that were scientifically innovative but not commercially viable. Instant photography products, introduced in 1947, saved Land's company from financial disaster and continue to be Polaroid's principal source of income. Polaroid stock plummeted in the 1970s. With Land's retirement in 1982, the succeeding team of managers, many of whom had built careers at Polaroid, began to reformulate Polaroid's corporate culture. While the company continues to be a scientific innovator, it also has cultivated an aggressive marketing department, which bases product development on market research.

In 1926 Edwin Land's desire to create a commercial monopoly based on scientific invention prompted him to pursue independent research on polarization rather than to return to Harvard after his freshman year. After creating a prototype synthetic polarizer in New York, Land returned to Harvard, in 1929. A polarizing material selectively screens light waves. It could, for example, block waves of light that create glare while allowing other waves through. With the help of George Wheelwright III, a young Harvard physics instructor, Land obtained access to a laboratory and began producing small sheets of polarizing material. Land applied to patent this process in 1929, and a patent was granted in 1934. In June of 1932, eager to explore the invention's practical applications, Land and Wheelwright abandoned their academic careers and founded Land-Wheelwright Laboratories, backed with Wheelwright's capital.

In 1933, the men incorporated their laboratory. Land-Wheelwright's staff—Land, Wheelwright, their wives, and a handful of other researchers—concentrated on developing polarizing material for no-glare car headlights and windshields. Enthusiasm for their work ran high, but commercial success eluded the Land-Wheelwright crew. Rebuffed by carmakers in Detroit, the company had no customers during the height of the Great Depression.

Photography giant Eastman Kodak provided the company's first financial break when it made a $10,000 order for photographic polarizing filters, later dubbed Polafilters. These plates, which consisted of a sheet of polarizing material sealed between two glass discs, increased contrast and decreased glare in photographs taken in bright light. Despite the fact that it had no machinery to mass produce such filters, Land-Wheelwright accepted the order, developed and built machines necessary to produce polarizing sheets and bond it to glass discs, and delivered the order to Kodak on schedule. By this time, a friend had christened the material ''Polaroid,'' and the name was adopted. In 1935 Land convinced American Optical Company to produce polarized sunglasses. Such glasses could screen out glare rather than simply darken the landscape, and Land-Wheelwright contracted to begin production of Polaroid Day Glasses, a long-time source of revenue for Polaroid.

Land formed Polaroid Corporation in 1937 to acquire Land-Wheelwright Laboratories. Eight original shareholders fronted $375,000 to back Land and his projects. They invested in Land and his ideas, allotting him a voting trust of stock that gave him control of the company for the next decade. Wheelwright left the company in 1940 to become a navy lieutenant, and never rejoined the firm. Researchers had devised a number of commercial applications for Polaroid—such as lamps, windows, stage lights, and three-dimensional photographs called Vectographs—but most of these products never became significantly profitable.

Polaroid continued to court the major automakers, attempting to induce one of them to demonstrate its headlight system at the 1939 New York World's Fair. The carmakers all refused the project, but Chrysler agreed to run a Polaroid three-dimensional (3-D) movie at its display. Audiences dodged water that seemed to spray out of a garden hose into the crowd and gawked through chunky Polaroid-made glasses of oppositely polarized lenses as an automobile appeared to dance itself together in the air above them. The public loved 3-D, but filmmakers were content with the magic of color and sound, and passed over the new technology.

In another unsuccessful marketing project, variable-density windows were installed on the observation car of the *City of Los Angeles.* Two polarized discs were mounted in the train wall; by means of a knob, passengers could turn the inner disk so that the window gradually became grayer until it was completely dark. As with 3-D film, the novelty of polarized windows was not commercially viable.

In 1939, Day Glasses were the source of most of Polaroid's $35,000 profit. Although sales rose to $1 million in 1941, the company's 1940 losses had reached $100,000, and it was only World War II military contracts that saved Land and his 240 employees. By 1942, the wartime economy had tripled Polaroid's size. A $7 million navy contract to work on the Dove heat-seeking missile project was the largest contract Polaroid had ever had, although the bomb was not used during World War II. Polaroid produced a number of other products for the armed forces, including a device that determined an aircraft's elevation above the horizon, an infrared night viewing device, goggles, lenses, and color filters for periscopes, and rangefinders.

Also during the war, the 3-D technology forsaken by moviemakers was employed in a machine-gunner training unit. Polaroid designed a trainer in which the student operated a life-size anti-aircraft gun against the 3-D simulation of an attacking plane. Reconnaissance planes were equipped to take 3-D Vectographs, which provided relief maps of enemy territory. When viewed with polarized glasses, the 3-D pictures exposed contours of guns, planes, and buildings that camouflague obscured in conventional photographs. Vectographs were used in planning almost all Allied invasions, including that of Normandy.

By the end of the war, in 1945, Polaroid's sales had reached $16 million, but as military contracts declined, so did staff, and Polaroid was down to about 500 employees, from a war-time high of 1,250. Sales fell to just $4 million in 1946 and were less than $2 million in early 1947.

By 1946 Land had realized that Polaroid Corporation was in deep trouble. Land had also come to believe that instant photography was Polaroid's only research line with potential to save the company. The research, however, was far from complete. In desperation Land announced in early 1946 that the instant camera system would be demonstrated at the February 21, 1947, winter meeting of the Optical Society of America. Working around the clock, Polaroid scientists developed a working model of the system, which allowed Land to take an instant picture of himself at the Optical Society meeting. The photograph developed itself within a minute. The image of Land peeling back the negative paper from an instantly produced picture of himself made front page news in *The New York Times*, was given a full page in *Life*, and was splashed across the international press.

Land had first considered developing instant-photography technology in 1943, when, on Christmas day, his three-year-old daughter asked to see the photographs her parents had taken earlier that day. Prompted by his daughter's query, Land conceived, in a flash, an instant, self-developing film and a camera that would process it.

It was an additional nine months before the camera was offered to the public via Jordan Marsh, Boston's oldest department store. The original camera, which weighed five pounds when loaded, sold for $89.75; film cost $1.75 for eight sepia-toned exposures. On the first day the camera was offered, demonstrators sold all 56 of the available units, and the cameras kept selling as fast as the factory could produce them. First-year photographic sales exceeded $5 million. By 1950 more than four thousand dealers sold Polaroid cameras, when only a year earlier Kodak had virtually monopolized the U.S. photography market.

The 1950s were a decade of rapid expansion. Sales mounted, spurred on by an aggressive television advertising campaign. Instant photography could be demonstrated graphically on television. Black-and-white film was introduced in 1950 to an enthusiastic public. Enthusiasm quickly turned to ire, however, as the black-and-white images began to fade and disappear. Unable to develop a non-fading black-and-white film, Polaroid provided sponge-tipped tubes of a liquid polymer, which the consumers hand-applied to each picture to set the image. This awkward process was not eliminated until 1963.

Despite the inconvenience, demand for instant photography held. To accomodate growing sales, Polaroid built a plant in Waltham, Massachusetts. The company's common stock was listed on the New York Stock Exchange in 1957. Polaroid formed its first international subsidiaries in 1959, in Frankfurt and Toronto. In 1960 it established Nippon Polaroid Kabushiki Kaisha in Japan, and licensed a Japanese firm to produce two cameras for overseas sale.

During the 1960s Polaroid continued to offer improvements and variations on the original instant film and camera, although other products were also introduced. Polaroid's first color film was introduced in 1963, along with a non-fading black-and-white film. In 1965 the inexpensive Swinger was pitched to teens. Selling for less than $20, the camera took only black-and-white pictures, sustaining the market for Polaroid black-and-white film. In 1966 the ID-2 Land Identification system was introduced. It produced full-color, laminated identification cards in two minutes. In 1967 Polaroid began construction on several new factories, to boost production of cameras, film, color negatives, and chemicals. The company's stock split two for one in 1968. During the late 1960s Polaroid was outpacing other top stock market performers. In 1970 sales reached $500 million.

In October 1970 two prominent black workers at Polaroid called on other black employees to leave their jobs until Polaroid ceased all business in South Africa. Polaroid had no subsidiaries or investments in the country, but its products were distributed through Frank & Hirsch. Some items were sold directly to the government, which used them in creating passbooks, part of the identification system that contributes to apartheid. South African commerce accounted for less than 0.1% of the company's annual profits.

Polaroid sent two black and two white employees to South Africa to assess the situation. In 1971 based on sentiments expressed by black South Africans, the company decided to maintain its business in South Africa, but stopped selling its products to the government. In addition, black workers at Frank & Hirsch would receive equal pay for equal work and be educated for promotion. Polaroid established a foundation to subsidize black education in South Africa, and made $25,000 in contributions to black cultural associations. These efforts were not popular with many Americans, who favored total boycott of the South African economy until apartheid was ended. Polaroid continued its association with Frank & Hirsch until 1977, when the distributor was found to be selling products to the government once again, and Polaroid terminated the relationship.

The October 1972 cover of *Life* featured a cluster of children grasping after a photograph whizzing out of the new SX-70 wielded by inventor Land. The public eagerly purchased the camera, yet Polaroid stock price began to decline shortly after the introduction of the SX-70, mostly due to a general stock market decline. Despite the fact that sales in the early 1970s continued to grow at a rate of 20% per year, the tremendous expense of research, manufacturing, and marketing for the SX-70 caused earnings to fall. Financial analysts, who had always received Polaroid stock coolly, began to question Polaroid's stability. In a 1974 conference Polaroid executives admitted that it did not expect to make more than $3 a share that year. In actuality, earnings were only 86¢ per share. Polaroid stock plummeted. By July 1974, just 26 months after the SX-70 was introduced, the stock had fallen from 149½ to 14⅛.

In 1975 Land turned the presidency of Polaroid over to Bill McCune, a senior vice president who had been with the company since 1939 and had worked closely with Land on the development of the first instant camera and film. Manufacture of the SX-70 remained very costly, and numerous design features required modification. Yet Land was satisfied with the camera and wished to pursue research on Polavision, an instant motion picture system. McCune and others, however, favored improving the SX-70. Highly skeptical of Polavision, McCune wanted to base new product lines on market research, rather than following Land's method of creating a consumer demand for Polaroid's latest invention. Land introduced Polavision at the 1977 annual meeting and a limited introduction followed. Although a scientific marvel, the instant films lasted only two and half minutes and were silent. Videotaping was just hitting the market, and so Polavision was never a consumer success.

Land received his 500th patent and was inducted to the National Inventors Hall of Fame in 1977. Polaroid's corporate culture began to shift when McCune was voted chief executive officer in 1980. While Land's entrepreneurial drive had created the company, a more diversified, market-oriented management was needed to continue to propel it. In 1982 Land retired fully, devoting his attention to research at the Rowland Institute for Science, which he had established in 1965.

In 1976 Polaroid entered a costly and lengthy patent-infringement battle with Eastman Kodak Company. Kodak had been producing the negative component of Polaroid's black-and-white film since 1944, and its color negative since 1957. Shortly after viewing the SX-70 film prototype in 1968, however, Kodak terminated its partnership with Polaroid, and began its own instant-photography research. In 1976 Kodak introduced the EK-4 and EK-6 instant cameras and PR-10 instant film. Polaroid filed suit within a week, charging 12 patent infringements in camera film and design.

Legal preparations dragged on for five years, until the trial began in October 1981. Ten of the twelve original counts were pressed. After 75 days of testimony and three years of deliberation, U.S. District Court Judge Rya Zobel ruled that seven of the ten Polaroid patents were valid and had been infringed upon. As a result, Kodak's line of instant-photography products was terminated in 1986. When settlement talks began, Polaroid claimed about $6.1 billion in damages, lost sales, and interest.

In August 1988, Shamrock Holdings offered to buy Polaroid at $40 a share plus 40% of the award from the Kodak settlement. Polaroid refused the offer and soon after sold 14% of its outstanding shares to an employee stock ownership program (ESOP). Shamrock charged that the ESOP was a form of management entrenchment, and sued. Delaware courts upheld Polaroid's position, and Shamrock raised its offer to $45 a share. Polaroid again refused, and subsequently announced a $1.1 billion common-stock buy-back. Shamrock again sued Polaroid in February 1989, for management entrenchment, but Polaroid's tactics were again upheld.

The fight against Shamrock was lead by Chairman McCune and I. MacAllister Booth, who had become president in 1983 and CEO in 1986. The pair pruned Polaroid staff in the early 1980s and reorganized the company into three divisions: consumer, industrial, and magnetic products.

The first success reaped from this new marketing strategy was the Spectra, introduced in 1986. The up-scale Spectra came out of market research indicating that instant-camera users wanted better picture quality. Again responding to this desire, Polaroid introduced Hybrid IV, an instant film of near 35-milimeter quality, during the early 1990s. Polaroid also introduced a line of conventional film and videotapes.

Marketing strategies also continued to become more sophisticated. In 1990 a $60 million advertising campaign emphasized new uses for instant cameras. Suggested uses include recording household items for insurance purposes or keeping a visual record of properties when house-hunting. In addition, the company is cultivating its commercial markets, which contribute at least 40% of photographic sales.

While Polaroid's product lines may be more fully guided by market demand, Polaroid continues to be a research-and-development-driven company. In 1990 research focused on an electric camera, which stores images on magnetic disc rather than film; an area in which the company may profit from joint ventures. Other promising projects include Helios, a new medical imaging system that the company thinks could be very profitable; Joshua, a mini-camera that produces credit-card size pictures; and a printer that coverts television images to hard copy. It is Booth's hope that market research will generate stable, profit-making ventures, as Polaroid carries Land's creative scientific spirit into the 1990s.

Principal Subsidiaries: Inner City, Inc.; Mag Media, Ltd.; Media Duplication Services, Ltd.; Polaroid Caribbean; Polaroid Foundation; Polaroid Ges.m.b.H. (Austria); Polaroid S.A. (Belgium); Polaroid AS (Denmark); Polaroid U.K. Ltd.; Polaroid S.A. (France); Polaroid GmbH (Germany); Polaroid S.p.A. (Italy); Polaroid Nederland B.V. (Netherlands); Polaroid AB (Sweden); Polaroid AG (Switzerland); Polaroid Australia Pty. Ltd.; Polaroid Far East Ltd. (Hong Kong); Nippon Polaroid K.K. (Japan); Polaroid do Brasil Ltda. (Brazil); Polaroid Canada Inc.; Polaroid de Mexico, S.A. de C.V.

Further Reading: Polaroid Corporation: A Chronology, Cambridge, Massachusetts, Polaroid Corporation, 1983; Dumaine, Brian, "How Polaroid Flashed Back," *Fortune*, February 16, 1987; Wensberg, Peter C., *Land's Polaroid*, Boston, Houghton Mifflin, 1987; ; Hammonds, Keith H., "Why Polaroid Must Remake Itself—Instantly," *Business Week*, September 19, 1988.

—Elaine Belsito

PREMARK INTERNATIONAL

PREMARK INTERNATIONAL, INC.

1717 Deerfield Road
Deerfield, Illinois 60015
U.S.A.
(708) 405-6000
Fax: (708) 405-6013

Public Company
Incorporated: 1986
Employees: 24,700
Sales: $2.59 billion
Stock Exchanges: New York Pacific London

Premark International is divided into three groups. The consumer and decorative products group produces Wilsonart laminates for building and furniture construction, West Bend small appliances, and Precor physical fitness equipment. The food-equipment group produces commercial food mixers, weighing and wrapping equipment, ovens, and refrigeration units. Premark's third division, Tupperware, manufactures high-quality plastic food and serving containers, educational toys, and home products.

Premark International was formed in 1986, with the breakup of the six-year-old Dart & Kraft merger. Originally a food concern, Kraft returned almost completely to food. The Dart side of the merger, consisting of the Tupperware, Ralph Wilson Plastics, and West Bend operations, became Premark. Hobart, which was acquired by Dart & Kraft, became part of Premark. Kraft felt its earnings were held back by these companies, whose combined 1985 sales of $1.8 billion lagged behind Kraft's sales of $7.06 billion.

Premark opened its doors on October 31, 1986. Its first year was rough, ending with a $98.3 million loss, partly due to a $46 million charge for plant consolidations and inventory adjustments. Tupperware wrote off $98 million in assets at two plants. Tupperware's foreign operations provided 60% of the division's revenue. Restructuring of overseas plants plus taxes on their earnings cost $17.1 million. The plant write-downs plus the taxes added up to a $57.9 million loss for Tupperware.

Before the changing lifestyles of the 1980s started Tupperware's slide, the line of plastic storage containers enjoyed a secure market niche. Created in 1942 by New Hampshire inventor Earl Tupper, the containers found fervent champions in the company's first distributors, who sold them at home parties. This direct sales method had advantages over the attempts Tupper made to sell his wares to retail outlets—it eliminated competition, produced a relaxed shopping mood, and allowed for demonstration of the airtight seal that was added in 1947. By 1949 Tupper had distributors in Miami and the Northeast, with weekly sales between $1,000 and $1,500. Noting the success of the home party sales method, Tupper stopped selling his food savers through stores in 1951 and founded Tupperware Home Parties.

In September 1958, Tupper sold his business to the Rexall Drug & Chemical Company for $16 million. The company's new status as a Rexall subsidiary brought it access to markets in Hawaii and Canada. Rexall was subsequently renamed Dart Industries. By 1969 there were 14 plants throughout the world manufacturing Tupperware. The line was popular in Australia, Japan, the Philippines, and Malaysia. This international popularity showed in sales, which reached $509 million in 1976, with the help of new subsidiaries in Argentina and Chile.

In the 1980s, Tupperware updated and modernized plants and equipment. It completed construction of a new hydroelectric generating station providing partial power for its Rhode Island plant, with the goal of saving 21,000 barrels of oil annually. The first U.S. plant of its kind to receive a license under federal energy regulations, it was designed to help reduce dependence on foreign oil. Other new plants started production in Portugal, Brazil, and Mexico.

In 1982 more than 50% of company sales came from overseas markets. Tupperware manufactured 225 products. Tupperware's $890 million in sales were 9% of the Dart & Kraft total, providing 26% of its profits.

Two years later, sales sank to $777 million, and the bonanza was over. More women entered the work force every year, which affected both the market and the dealer force. Women who might have sold Tupperware opted for other careers. Full time working women also had little time to host and attend Tupperware parties. Instead, they picked up cheaper plastic food containers and disposables in retail stores.

The company responded to the change on several fronts. First, they made William Jackson, president of the profitable Duracell battery division, chairman of Tupperware. The party plan was revised, to accommodate the needs of working women—in addition to the traditional home parties, short, 20-minute parties were added at work sites and other locations outside the home. A preview catalog was introduced to allow party guests to settle on possible purchases before attending a party. The company improved promotional programs to attract independent dealers, and the company rolled out its entry into the cookware market—Ultra 21 plastic food containers for the freezer, microwave, or oven.

Ultra 21 had been on the drawing board since 1981, when Dart & Kraft bought the patent from Carborundum Company. In 1984, the company built a $140 million resin plant in Georgia to supply the necessary raw material, and spent millions advertising the new product line. Between July and December 1985, Ultra 21 captured 30% of all nonmetal cookware sales, attracting many purchasers to Tupperware parties. However, raw materials and production expenses were high, eroding the profit margin. Sales restructuring and advertising had not yet affected the bottom line, and 1985 profits declined by 10%. Sales shrunk to $762 million.

Ohio-based Hobart Corporation, core of Premark's food-equipment group, also was well known in 1986. Founded in 1897 as an electric-engine manufacturer, it was sold in 1904 to four investors. The same year, Hobart produced its first kitchen appliance—an electric coffee grinder. The company's product line expanded rapidly to include KitchenAid dishwashers, food mixers, and commercial food equipment.

David A. Meeker, a young engineer who joined Hobart in 1925, married the daughter of one of the investors, and became president and chief operating officer in 1945. He invented several Hobart products, obtaining about 80 patents. Meeker remained president until 1963, and chief operating officer until 1970. His son, David B. Meeker, became president and chief executive officer in 1970. By the 1970s Hubart was a leading food-equipment manufacturer, with sales exceeding $350 million.

In 1981, Hobart had become the focus of a takeover bid by Canadian Pacific Enterprises, the U.S. unit of a $8.5 billion Montreal corporation with interests in oil, steel, forest products, and agribusiness. Attracted by Hobart's 25 U.S. plants, 12 overseas facilities, and its sales and service organization which supported marketing operations in 100 countries, Canadian Pacific offered $32.50 per share—an estimated $300 million. Hobart did not accept the offer, preferring to remain independent. Hobart appealed to the Senate Judiciary Committee to hold hearings opposing the takeover bid. Two congressmen wrote to Treasury Secretary Donald T. Regan, urging that the offer be blocked on grounds of national security. Realizing it might not be able to fight off future takeovers, Hobart instead accepted Dart & Kraft's $460 million offer.

Dart & Kraft immediately streamlined Hobart's operations. It closed plants, four of them European, cut the work force by 16%, and slashed more than $65 million from inventories. To improve marketing and product strategies, Hobart and its subsidiaries introduced new products.

By 1986 products were available under the Hobart, Vulcan, Stero, Foster, and Wolf trademarks. More than 25% of Hobart's $681.9 million in sales came from exports to over 100 countries. In 1986 the food-equipment group provided $24.7 million in profits, although restructuring and plant consolidation cost Premark $21.5 million.

Premark's consumer-products group also required reorganization after the spin-off. Facing stiff pricing competition from other small-appliance manufacturers, the West Bend division consolidated production capacity, targeted new product categories in housewares, and expanded its domestic and Japanese distribution efforts for Premiere cookware. Precor, supplying physical-fitness equipment, expanded its product line. Ralph Wilson Plastics, producing Wilsonart brand decorative plastic laminates, benefited from the increasing popularity of easy-care laminates for furniture surfaces and for building remodeling and updating. Group sales for 1986 reached $455.1 million, with profits of $23.6 million.

In 1987 Tupperware made a determined effort to reach buyers without access to parties. Consumers could call toll-free to get the preview catalog, creating new avenues for parties and demonstrations. Television commercials boosted consumer awareness of new products as did new party formats, and national print advertising in women's service magazines like *Ladies Home Journal*.

Tupperware's delivery system also was in need of reorganization. Independent dealers took weekly orders to local distributors, often located in other cities. Orders were filled from distributors' inventories and delivered by the dealer to the party host. Payment was collected at the time of delivery. This system did not reach all potential customers, since dealers avoided parties in downtown areas with expensive, limited parking. Dealers also were leery of rural locations, because of the great driving distances.

The company's answer to this problem was a four-year, $60 million outlay for new warehouses and a major distribution center in Hemingway, South Carolina, and Halls, Tennessee. Tupperware also tested a new factory-to-customer delivery system called Tupperware Express. Scheduled for nationwide use by 1990, it ran into problems—dealers needed training to adapt from payment-on-delivery to payment-with-order. Sales declined in test areas, although final sales for 1988 increased 8% to $967.2 million.

In 1988, Premark sold its Georgia-based Dartco plant to Amoco Performance Products, with another plant in Neshanic, New Jersey, for $25 million. The Georgia plant, producing liquid-crystal compounds called Xydar, the raw material for the Ultra 21 line. Ultra 21, however, was successful only in the United States and Japan, losing $15 million in 1987. Premark found it more profitable to let Amoco provide the raw materials for Ultra 21. The line has since been replaced by the Tupperware cookware system.

The lifestyle changes affecting Tupperware also affected the other Premark divisions. The food-equipment group found new markets in changing fast-food menus that required new equipment. One chain of chicken restaurants ordered 5,000 catalytic fryers during 1987, and a Mexican fast-food outlet bought 1,000 grooved griddles to be used for fajitas.

The trend toward take-home food also improved sales for the food-equipment group. Grocery stores were experimenting with in-store bakeries, building about 2,500 bakeries in 1987 alone. Each cost about $130,000 to equip, though some went as high as $300,000. Pizza gained popularity in England, while Japanese consumers turned increasingly to Western-style food. These trends helped food-equipment group sales reach $874 million in 1988, contributing $57.8 million to the company's profits.

Consumer and decorative products group sales reached $555.8 million in 1988, increasing 14% over 1987 despite heavy competition. In December 1988, Premark acquired the Tibbals Flooring Company for $94 million. Precor, the physical fitness company, introduced a stair-climbing machine, an advanced treadmill, and an exercise bicycle offering computer programming to let cyclists compete on a display screen. These new products accounted for 37% of Precor's 1988 sales.

In 1989, Premark's sales reached $2.6 billion. The company cited unfavorable foreign exchange rates, high promotional expenses, and substantial capital outlays, especially for Tupperware Express for lowering profits. Tupperware profits also were hurt by lower sales in Latin America, Japan, and the United States, while the food-equipment group suffered because of reduced profit margins and lower domestic production volume. Even so, Premark bought Sikes Corporation for $201 million in 1990. The decorative ceramic-tile company took Premark more deeply into the decorative building-products industry.

Principal Subsidiaries: Ralph Wilson Plastics Company; The West Bend Company; Tibbals Flooring Company; Tupperware; Florida Tile; PMI Food Equipment Group.

Further Reading: Fishman, Charles, "Is the Party Over?," *The Orlando Sentinel,* March 15, 1987.

—Gillian Wolf

RUBBERMAID INCORPORATED

1147 Akron Road
Wooster, Ohio 44691
U.S.A.
(216) 264-6464
Fax: (216) 264-5206

Public Company
Incorporated: 1920 as The Wooster Rubber Company
Employees: 8,400
Sales: $1.34 billion
Stock Exchange: New York

Rubbermaid is a leading U.S. manufacturer of housewares and other goods, with an emphasis on innovation, a record of steady growth throughout its history, and a sterling brand name. Started in a kitchen, the company—whose products are now primarily plastic rather than rubber—has been a household name in household products for most of the 20th century.

The Wooster Rubber Company got its start in May 1920, when five Wooster, Ohio, investors formed a company to manufacture toy balloons, sold under the Sunshine brand name. The Wooster Rubber Company, contained in one building, was sold to Horatio B. Ebert and Errett M. Grable, two Aluminum Company of America executives, in the mid-1920s. Grable and Ebert retained the firm's management. By the late 1920s, a new factory and office building had been constructed to house the prosperous business, but the fortunes of The Wooster Rubber Company fell during the Depression. In 1934 Ebert spotted Rubbermaid products in a New England department store, and worked out a merger between the two firms.

Rubbermaid got its start in 1933, when a New England man named James Caldwell, who had first entered the rubber business as an employee of the Seamless Rubber Company in New Haven, Connecticut, looked around his kitchen during the depths of the Great Depression to see what he could improve. Caldwell and his wife conceived 29 products, among them a red rubber dustpan. Although the rubber dustpan, designed and manufactured by Caldwell and his wife, cost $1.00—much more than the 39¢ metal pans then available in stores—Caldwell "rang ten doorbells and sold nine dustpans," as he recalled in an interview published in *The New York Times* on May 19, 1974. Convinced there was a market for his products, Caldwell gave his enterprise a name—Rubbermaid—and expanded his line to include a soap dish, a sink plug, and a drainboard mat, selling these products in department stores throughout New England.

In July 1934 Caldwell's fledgling merged with The Wooster Rubber Company, located in a small town 50 miles from Cleveland, Ohio. Still called The Wooster Rubber Company, the new group began to produce rubber household goods under the Rubbermaid brand name. With the merger, under Caldwell's leadership, The Wooster Rubber Company had a happy reversal in fortunes, and sales rose from $80,000 in 1935 to $450,000 in 1941. Of the 29 new products Caldwell and his wife had thought up in their kitchen in 1933, the company had marketed 27 of them by 1941.

In 1942, however, U.S. involvement in World War II caused the government to cut back civilian use of rubber, so that raw materials would be available for products necessary to the war effort. This eliminated Rubbermaid's housewares business, but the company was able to convert to military manufacturing. Beginning with rubber parts for a self-sealing fuel tank for warplanes, and moving on to other products such as life jackets and rubber tourniquets, the company manufactured military goods through the end of the war, in 1945. In 1944 Wooster Rubber introduced an employee profit-sharing plan.

Following the advent of peace, The Wooster Rubber Company picked up its prewar activities where it had left off, and resumed production of rubber housewares. Because wartime shortages had not yet been completely redressed, however, no coloring agents were available, and all Rubbermaid products were manufactured in black for several months. In 1947 the company introduced a line of rubber automotive accessories, including rubber floormats and cup-holders.

The company's first international operations commenced in 1950, when The Wooster Rubber Company began producing vinyl-coated wire goods at a plant in Ontario, Canada. By 1956 the plant was producing a complete line of Rubbermaid products.

In 1955 The Wooster Rubber Company went public, offering stock on the over-the-counter market. This capital infusion allowed the company to branch into plastic products, which make up more than 80% of the company's sales, and in 1956, a plastic dishpan was introduced. This switch required significant retooling from the manufacture of exclusively rubber goods.

In 1957 The Wooster Rubber Company changed its name to Rubbermaid Incorporated to increase its association with its well-known brand name. The following year, the company began its first expansion beyond its traditional focus on household goods by broadening its targeted market to include restaurants, hotels, and other institutions. Rubbermaid initially produced bathtub mats and door mats for these customers. By 1974 industrial and commercial products provided 25% of the company's sales.

After James Caldwell's retirement, the company presidency was taken over by Donald E. Noble, in 1959. During that same year, Rubbermaid stock was sold for the first time on the New York Stock Exchange. The following year, Rubbermaid's management set a goal of doubling the company's earnings every six years, a goal which was consistently met throughout Noble's tenure.

In 1965 Rubbermaid made its first move outside North America, purchasing Dupol, a West German manufacturer of plastic housewares, whose products and operations were very similar to Rubbermaid's U.S. operations. "Our plan is to grow from within except when an acquisition can lead us into a market we already have an interest in," Noble told *The Wall Street Journal* on August 2, 1965, explaining the company's policy towards its steady growth during this period.

In 1969 Rubbermaid added the sales party to its traditional marketing efforts, a sales technique first popularized by Tupperware. The party division had its own line of slightly more elaborate merchandise, accounting for around 10% of Rubbermaid's sales within five years. Nevertheless, the party plan was not profitable until 1976.

In the early 1970s Rubbermaid marketed a line of recreational goods such as motorboats and snow sleds, but the company lacked the necessary distribution to support the products and abandoned the effort. "We bombed," the company's vice president of marketing told a *Wall Street Journal* reporter on June 9, 1982.

Rubbermaid continued to grow in the early 1970s, but the combination of government controls on prices and the shortage of petrochemical raw materials caused by the energy crisis of the early 1970s kept a lid on earnings. In 1971 Rubbermaid began to market its products through direct supermarket retail distribution. Although initially profitable, this practice resulted in the company running afoul of the Federal Trade Commission (FTC) in 1973. The FTC challenged the company's pricing policies in connection with its role as distributor, charging Rubbermaid with illegal price-fixing and violations of antitrust laws. The complaint alleged that Rubbermaid engaged in price-fixing between wholesalers because it sold its products directly to some retailers—acting as its own wholesaler—and also allowed other wholesalers to sell its products, while stipulating the price for the products. Rubbermaid discontinued its minimum price agreements with wholesalers and retailers in 1975, citing pending legislation and negative public opinion. In 1976 the FTC ruled unanimously that Rubbermaid had violated antitrust laws and issued a cease-and-desist order to prevent the company from renewing these practices.

As part of its continued growth, Rubbermaid opened a new plant in La Grange, Georgia, in 1974, to relieve demand on its main Ohio plant and to supply the automotive-products division. Despite rising earnings since 1968, a sharp increase in the price of raw materials, combined with a change in accounting practices, caused a large drop in Rubbermaid profits in 1974. By this time, Rubbermaid was selling 240 different items, of which about one-tenth were products introduced that year. The company continued to place strong emphasis on innovation and the introduction of new products, generated by a research-and-development staff of designers, engineers, and craftsmen. This staff built prototypes to be used and critiqued by thousands of consumers, resulting in an eight-month process from drawingboard to store.

The company experienced labor unrest in 1976, when 1,100 members of the United Rubber Workers called a strike at Rubbermaid's only unionized plant, in Wooster, Ohio, after rejecting a proposed contract. Although the strike eventually was settled amicably, traditionally, the company has sought to minimize union activity by building plants outside union strongholds, in places such as Arizona, where it began construction of a plant near Phoenix in 1987 to serve its western markets. In 1985 the company successfully negotiated a contract with its Ohio workers, providing a three-year wage freeze in return for guarantees against massive lay-offs.

Noble retired in 1980, and Stanley C. Gault, a former General Electric (GE) executive who had grown up in Wooster and worked his way through college in a Rubbermaid plant, took over as chairman. Despite the company's record of steady growth throughout the 1970s, caused in part by Rubbermaid's expansion from old-line department stores into discount and grocery stores, Gault felt that the company had become somewhat stodgy and complacent. In 1980 he set out to quadruple its sales—about $350 million in 1981—and earnings—about $25.6 million, in 1982—by 1990. Anticipating a recession, Gault streamlined operations and introduced racy new products, such as the "Fun Functional" line of brightly colored containers. Gault's stress on growth through the introduction of new products was exemplified by the company's campaign to reap 30% of each years' sales from products introduced during the last five years.

By 1983 Gault had eliminated four of Rubbermaid's eight divisions: the unstable party-plan business and the automotive division were each sold at a loss and the European industrial operations centered in the Netherlands, and the manufacture of containers for large-scale garbage hauling were also eliminated.

The remaining divisions were combined into two areas: home products—accounting for about 70% of the company's sales—and commercial products. The home-products division was further restructured into seven product groups: bathware, food preparation and "gadgets," containers, organizers, sinkware, shelf coverings, and bird feeders and home horticulture. Rubbermaid continued to advertise heavily in both magazines and on television, emphasizing consumer promotions to get customers into the store and offering rebates and coupons for its products for the first time.

In tandem with the product reorganization, about half of Rubbermaid's middle management was eliminated, and 11% of the company's management was fired. Many top spots were filled by former GE employees.

In 1981 Rubbermaid had made its first outright acquisition, buying privately held Carlan, owner of the Con-Tact plastic coverings brand name. In the 1980s Rubbermaid was able to move successfully beyond housewares and institutional customers, entering new industries through the strategic purchase of other companies. The company entered the toy industry in 1984 by buying the Little Tikes Company; went into the booming computer field in 1986, with MicroComputer Accessories; into floor-care products with SECO Industries in the same year; and into the brush industry with a Canadian company, Viking Brush, in 1987.

Rubbermaid formed a joint venture with a French company, Allibert, to manufacture plastic outdoor furniture in North Carolina in 1989. In addition, the company expanded its capacity in plastic and rubber products in 1985 with its purchase of the Gott Corporation, which makes insulated coolers and beverage holders. Rubbermaid formed a second joint venture—with the Curver Group, owned by Dutch chemical maker DSM—in 1990 to make and sell housewares and resin furniture in European, Middle Eastern, and north

African markets through Curver-Rubbermaid. Rubbermaid expanded its existing product lines into the office supplies market as well during this time. This diversification resulted in continued growth throughout the 1980s, despite the rising price of petrochemical resins, the raw materials for plastics.

The company had set a goal of $2 billion in sales by 1992, looking to international markets such as Europe for its next arena of growth. Throughout its history, Rubbermaid had successfully relied on constant innovation and strong management to grow steadily. Rubbermaid faced challenges in tailoring its familiar U.S. formula to foreign markets, and in lessening its reliance for raw materials on volatile petrochemical supplies, but given the company's past record, Rubbermaid's future appears bright.

Principal Subsidiaries: Rubbermaid-Allibert Inc. (France, 50%); Curver-Rubbermaid (Netherlands, 40%); Rubbermaid Commercial Products Inc.; The Little Tikes Company; Micro-Computer Accessories, Inc.

Further Reading: Christensen, Jean, "How Rubbermaid Invites Profits," *The New York Times*, May 19, 1974; Campanella, Frank W., "Wide and Growing Line Spurs Rubbermaid Gains," *Barron's*, October 3, 1977; Neiman, Janet, "New Structure Poured for Rubbermaid Push," *Advertising Age*, November 9, 1981; Yao, Margaret, "Rubbermaid Reaches for Greater Glamour in World Beyond Dustpans and Drainers," *The Wall Street Journal*, June 9, 1982; Taylor, Alex III, "Why the Bounce at Rubbermaid?" *Fortune*, April 13, 1987.

—Elizabeth Rourke

Schlumberger

SCHLUMBERGER LIMITED

277 Park Avenue
New York, New York 10172
U.S.A.
(212) 350-9400
Fax: (212) 350-9654

Public Company
Incorporated: 1956
Employees: 46,000
Sales: $4.84 billion
Stock Exchanges: New York Paris London Amsterdam Frankfurt Basel Geneva Lausannne Zürich

With a French and American board of directors and employees at work in over a hundred different nations, Schlumberger Limited is the definitive multinational corporation. Schlumberger built its reputation in the business of oil-field services, where it still does the bulk of its work.

As oil is found all around the world, so is Schlumberger, providing a range of services that includes the pinpointing of oil reserves, both on- and off-shore; the drilling of boreholes; precise determination of the depth and extent of oil and gas pockets; the pumping and monitoring of oil flow; and the rehabilitation of old or discontinued wells. In addition to its near monopoly of such services, Schlumberger's Measurement & Systems Division is the world's largest manufacturer of meters for gas, water, and electric utilities; supplies computer-aided design and manufacturing systems; and builds a number of advanced devices for the nuclear and military markets.

Though somewhat diversified, Schlumberger has always depended on the oil industry for profit, which means that the 1980s were not kind to the company. With steadily falling oil prices and a concomitant drop in drilling activity, Schlumberger has had to struggle to remain what investment banker Felix Rohatyn described in 1981 as the "best business in the world." After a few anxious years, the company seems to have come through the slump in remarkably good shape. If and when the oil business regains momentum, Schlumberger will no doubt resume its tradition of geometrical expansion in both sales and profit.

Schlumberger is the creation of two brothers of that name, Conrad, born 1878, and Marcel, younger by six years. Rooted in the Alsace region of France, the Schlumberger family had made its mark in both politics and business; the Schlumberger brothers' great-grandfather served as prime minister under Louis Philippe and their father, Paul Schlumberger, later amassed a fortune in the textile industry. Conrad Schlumberger early displayed a genius for science, and by 1907 had become a professor of physics at the École des Mines, while his brother Marcel pursued mechanical engineering and business. Conrad became interested in the electrical resistance generated by different types of rock formation, and was soon testing his results on the family's summer estate in Normandy. In 1914 Conrad successfully completed the first commercial application of this technique, locating a body of copper ore for a client in Serbia. World War I brought all experimentation to a halt, but in 1919 Conrad and Marcel Schlumberger set up a modest business in Paris to pursue the further evolution of electrical prospecting, as it was called.

At this point the brothers received crucial financial backing from their father, who made it clear that he considered their work a type of scientific inquiry, and only secondarily a means to monetary rewards. This scientific bias has remained strong at Schlumberger, which has always depended on its technological superiority. Bolstered by this aid, which eventually reached Ffr500,000, Conrad resigned from his teaching position in 1923 to devote his energy to the new company, Société de Prospection Électrique. In that same year the brothers received their first order from an oil company, resulting in the successful mapping of an oil-rich salt dome in Romania.

A few years later the Pechelbronn Oil Company of France asked the Schlumbergers to make such measurements not from ground level, but from the interior of an already drilled borehole. Conrad asked Henri Doll, his son-in-law and longtime technical supervisor, to design the necessary equipment, and in September 1927 the men compiled the first "wireline log" by lowering an electrical recording device down a Pechelbronn oil well and measuring the resistance every few feet. The results were accurate, meaning that oil deposits could now be located and measured without resorting to expensive and time-consuming mechanical coring.

The world did not immediately beat a path to the Schlumberger door, however. By the time logging teams had been sent to Venezuela, the United States, and the Soviet Union, the Great Depression had taken hold, and drilling activity had come to a virtual halt. The Venezuelan tests went so well that Royal Dutch Shell became interested and ordered additional work to be done in Romania, Sumatra, and Trinidad. Furthermore, the Soviet Union proceeded with its drilling in the Baku oil fields regardless of the Depression, and there the Schlumbergers landed sufficient orders to get them through the first lean years. An ardent socialist, Conrad Schlumberger was pleased to do business in Soviet Russia.

The young company's biggest break came with its introduction to the U.S. market in 1932, when Shell asked it to run logs in California and on the Texas gulf coast. These again proved successful and Schlumberger was soon picking up business among the many wildcatters in Texas and Oklahoma. In 1934 the brothers founded Schlumberger Well Surveying Corporation in Houston, Texas, to meet the growing demand for their services, and this U.S. division soon became the largest and most profitable of the parent company's worldwide business.

Once underway, Schlumberger expanded rapidly, despite

the Depression. The brothers had a long technological lead on any would-be competitors, an advantage the company has maintained to this day by consistently hiring top engineering talent and spending liberally on research and development. In addition, Schlumberger remained very much a family organization, with the resulting high degree of trust and unity helping to keep employees motivated and loyal. This became of greater importance after the death, in 1936, of Conrad Schlumberger. Marcel Schlumberger assumed control of a burgeoning business, which was already doing more than 1,000 logs a month in North America alone, but he soon had help from other members of the extended family.

As world Depression gave way to World War II and France was overcome by Germany, Marcel Schlumberger worked with Jean de Menil to move the corporation from Paris to Trinidad. De Menil, the husband of Conrad Schlumberger's daughter Dominique, was a banker who became head of Schlumberger's financial affairs in 1939. De Menil is generally credited with managing the move to Trinidad. De Ménil remained overseas and eventually became head of Schlumberger's South American and Middle Eastern businesses, operating out of the Houston office.

Although information is sparse, it is clear that the war was not good for Schlumberger's business. It was necessary to retreat before the Nazi advance, and the war effectively scattered key members of the Schlumberger family. Doll, the company's top technician, fled to Connecticut, where he formed a company called Electro-Mechanical Research that went on to do important work for the Allied war effort. Schlumberger eventually bought out Electro-Mechanical, and Doll emerged as the head of all technical research for Schlumberger worldwide. On the other side of the Atlantic Ocean, Marcel's son-in-law René Seydoux spent two years as a German prisoner of war before assuming control of all European operations. In Houston Pierre Schlumberger—Marcel's son, and the only male heir of either of the founders—began to rebuild the U.S. business in 1946 and guided it back to a position of leadership.

Thus fragmented by war, the Schlumberger family was held together largely by Marcel, whose devotion to the business became legendary. In 1940, when it was clear that France would soon fall and many thought that the Schlumbergers would be ruined, Marcel Schlumberger was offered $10 million for his business by the head of rival Halliburton Oil. It is said that Marcel did not even respond to the suggestion, but instead showed his guest to the door.

When Marcel Schlumberger died in 1953, the remaining Schlumbergers were unable to decide on a successor. The firm was left divided, roughly between Doll, who controlled technical research; de Menil, who controlled the business in South America and the Middle East; Seydoux, who controlled the company's European business; and Pierre Schlumberger, who ran the company's U.S. operations.

Pierre Schlumberger, the natural candidate to follow his father as president, strongly favored incorporating the company and selling stock to raise capital needed to take advantage of the booming postwar economy. Other family members resisted the idea, fearing a loss of both control and quality, but in 1956 Schlumberger Limited was formed in Curaçao, Netherlands Antilles. That location was chosen for tax purposes, and Pierre became president and Henri Doll chairman.

The new corporation was headquarted in Houston. It remained under family control, as it does to this day, but it began to sell stock, and the fresh capital allowed Schlumberger to expand rapidly at a time when postwar U.S. oil drilling was at its peak. As the undisputed technical leader in the field, Schlumberger charged what it pleased, and when the initial financial statements were made public in 1958 they showed a first year profit of $12.2 million.

The next 25 years may someday be thought of as the company's golden age. By carefully managing the high profits earned by its wireline business, Schlumberger diversified slowly into a number of related fields, giving each acquisition the time and resources needed to make it healthy. Aside from a pair of French electronics firms, the company's first significant purchase was the 1959 acquisition of Forages et Exploitations Pétrolières (Forex), a French oil drilling company. A complementary deal was the 1960 formation of Dowell Schlumberger, a joint venture with Dow Chemical to provide oil-well completion services such as cementing and flow stimulation. Schlumberger was now a complete oil-services company, able to set up drilling operations anywhere in the world.

As oil drilling gradually fell from its 1957 peak, Pierre Schlumberger and his advisors thought it prudent to expand further into the electronics field. This was a natural extension, as Schlumberger had always used sophisticated electrical monitoring devices and was at home in the electronics field. Accordingly, the firm made a major acquisition in 1961 when it swapped stock with Daystrom, a manufacturer of various electronic instruments primarily for military use. With $90 million in sales, Daystrom was nearly as large as Schlumberger ($130 million), but did not turn a profit for several years after. The parent company pursued many other electronics concerns, eventually absorbing 11 French companies and several in England and the United States. Most of the newcomers required years of work before paying dividends; in 1966, for example, 42% of Schlumberger's $343 million in sales was generated by the electronics division, whose operating deficit held down overall corporate profit to $28 million.

After a few wobbly years in the early 1960s, the Schlumberger board of directors decided that Pierre Schlumberger should step down as president. Promoted to his place was Jean Riboud, a longtime friend of the Schlumbergers, particularly Marcel. Riboud guided Schlumberger for the next 20 years, during which time the company's net income and worldwide reputation rose with equal regularity.

Riboud immediately moved corporate headquarters from Houston to New York City and reorganized the now diffuse company on the basis of product lines rather than geography. In 1970 Riboud further diversified the Schlumberger portfolio with the $79 million purchase of Compagnie de Compteurs, an aging French manufacturer of utility meters, which also took a few years to become profitable. By 1980 it had made Schlumberger the largest meter manufacturer in the world and formed the heart of one of the company's four divisions.

The 1973 OPEC oil embargo spurred a massive worldwide increase in oil exploration and drilling, with Schlumberger positioned to benefit from every new well. Its wireline services helped to find new oil, Forex-Neptune drilled the wells, and Dowell Schlumberger kept them pumping. In the space of five years Schlumberger sales jumped from 1972's $812 million to a robust $2.2 billion in 1977, with profit exceeding

$400 million in 1977. Schlumberger earned spectacular profits by delivering a superior and much-needed product.

The boom years at Schlumberger reached their peak in 1982. At that time the company had sales of $6.3 billion and profits of $1.35 billion, a staggering 21% ratio that made Schlumberger the most profitable of the world's 1,000 largest corporations. The firm's hold on the wireline logging business rivaled that of IBM's in computers, with seven out of every ten logs in the world taken by Schlumberger. Its drilling operation was the world's largest, and it produced more utility meters than anyone else.

As 1982 drew to an end, however, a close observer would have noticed that Schlumberger's quarterly profits were slipping, and they continued to do so as a world recession and greater oil conservation combined to put the brakes on oil exploration. In addition, Chairman Riboud had made a tactical mistake, and was about to make a second. In 1979 Riboud paid $425 million to buy the leading American semiconductor manufacturer, Fairchild Camera and Instrument Corporation. Schlumberger hoped that Fairchild's technical expertise would help keep it ahead of the pack in its various fields, but the move was a failure from the beginning. Fairchild lost money and drained valuable research-and-development dollars from the rest of Schlumberger, and the parent company was forced to write off much of Fairchild's assets and sell the rest to National Semiconductor in 1987, at a loss of $220 million.

Schlumberger's second mistake came in 1985, when it paid $1 billion for SEDCO, another enormous drilling company. Riboud apparently assumed that the oil glut would soon turn around—it did not, and Schlumberger struggled through a number of years with underutilized assets and poor earnings. Write-offs and retrenchment pared corporate sales to $4.7 billion in 1989, but with profit again hovering just under 10%, Schlumberger seems to have weathered the worst of the oil depression without serious damage. Given the additions of SEDCO and GECO, one of the world's top seismic data companies, Schlumberger is poised to benefit from a long-awaited recovery in oil. Its wireline testing services remain the industry's unchallenged leader, and its growing stable of electronic subsidiaries should help keep the company at the forefront of technical innovation. As long as oil remains one of the primary sources of energy it is likely that oilmen will turn for advice to Schlumberger.

Principal Subsidiaries: Schlumberger B.V. (Netherlands); Nepfor Limited (Netherlands Antilles); Schlumberger Offshore Services N.V. (Netherlands Antilles); Triton Industries, Inc. (Panama); Kintore Investments Limited (Bermuda); Schlumberger Holdings Limited (British Virgin Islands); SEDCO Forex International, Inc. (Panama); Anadrill International, S.A. (Panama); BVI Holdings Limited (British Virgin Islands); MC&C Holdings Limited (British Virgin Islands); Schlumberger Technology Corporation: GECO A.S. (Norway).

Further Reading: Brown, Stanley H., ''It's a 'Slumber-jay' and It's a Money Gusher,'' *Fortune,* September 1973; *Schlumberger: The First Years,* New York, Schlumberger, 1979; Auletta, Ken, *The Art of Corporate Success: The Story of Schlumberger,* New York, Penguin Books, 1984; ''This Is Schlumberger,'' New York, Schlumberger, 1988.

—Jonathan Martin

株式会社 服部セイコー
SEIKO CORPORATION

SEIKO CORPORATION

6-21, Kyobashi 2-chome
Chuo-ku, Tokyo 104
Japan
(03) 3563-2111
Fax: (03) 3535-3594

Public Company
Incorporated: 1881 as K. Hattori & Co., Ltd.
Employees: 1,546
Sales: ¥421.78 billion (US$2.93 billion)
Stock Exchange: Tokyo

The watches of the Seiko Corporation are marketed with a multi-brand strategy that includes Seiko, Lassale, Jean Lassale, Pulsar, Alba, and Lorus. From the jeweled Jean Lassale styles to the models that incorporate miniature televisions or computers, they are intended to serve a wide variety of needs. Seiko Corporation is the nucleus of the Seiko group. It is one of the world's largest clock and watch manufacturers. In the 1989 fiscal year, Seiko produced about 109 million watches and 32 million clocks. Seiko Corporation, formerly Hattori Seiko, is the only public company of the group. Its function is to market watches, clocks, eyeglasses, and other products made by the manufacturing components of the group: Seikosha Co. Ltd.; Seiko Instruments Inc., and Seiko Epson Corporation.

In 1881, in Uneme-cho, Kyobashi, part of Tokyo's Ginza district, Kintaro Hattori, a jeweler, established K. Hattori & Co., Ltd. Although 21 years old, Hattori was already an eight-year veteran of the business world. According to the company typescript, "A Brief History of Hattori Seiko Co. Ltd.," it was enough experience to lead him to observe, "On a rainy day, every retail shop will have less customers. However, jewelers can make good use of these slack days by repairing timepieces and thus not waste precious time."

Near the end of the 19th century, increasing railroad traffic produced growing demand for accurate timepieces. In 1884 the adoption of the worldwide 24 time-zone system, with its reference meridian at Greenwich near London, produced a standardization of time that further increased that demand. In 1892 Hattori established the Seikosha clock-manufacturing plant in Ishiwara-cho, Tokyo. Initially employing ten workers, the firm made primarily wall clocks, at that time, the most popular type of timepiece. In October 1893 the plant was moved to its present site in Taihei-cho, Tokyo. Two years later, the main office was moved to new facilities at Ginza that included a clock tower which stood over 50-feet high. As tall buildings were a rare sight in Tokyo at the time, the tower garnered much attention.

The firm added pocket watches to its product line in 1895. Alarm clocks were added in 1899 and table clocks in 1902. As the market expanded, the company began exporting clocks to China, and by 1912 China received 70% of Japan's total export of timepieces. In 1913, Hattori opened its first overseas branch, in Shanghai.

To partially satisfy the growing demand for pocket watches Hattori introduced its first line of wristwatches, which were sold under the Laurel brand name. The wristwatch gained in popularity worldwide, and by the end of the World War I, had replaced the pocket watch as the standard portable timepiece.

In 1917, K. Hattori & Co., Ltd. became a public company. In September 1923, an earthquake hit Tokyo, destroying the Seikosha plant. Hattori tried to compensate hundreds of customers, who had lost a total of 1,500 timepieces left for repair, with replacement clocks and watches. In 1924, annual production was less than 10% of the 1922 output. In 1924, also, the Seikosha plant introduced the first Seiko brand wristwatch.

In 1927, Kintaro Hattori, at age 69, was honored as the imperial nominee to the House of Peers, and Hattori launched its first ladies' wristwatch, the smallest ever produced in Japan.

Using the micro-engineering expertise acquired in its clock and watch production, the Seikosha plant began producing camera shutters in 1930. Eventually, Hattori became one of the world's largest suppliers of camera products, although its brand names do not appear on the products.

In 1934, Kintaro Hattori died, and his eldest son, Genzo Hattori, became president. Genzo Hattori chose to satisfy market needs by adopting a unique corporate structure. It allowed private plants to develop products to be marketed by K. Hattori. In 1936 K. Hattori & Co., Ltd. marketed a total of 2.06 million clocks and watches, the highest figure since the opening of the Seikosha plant, while Japan's total watch and clock production came to 3.54 million. In 1939 the company started marketing Braille pocket watches.

As Japan entered World War II, K. Hattori's normal marketing activities were hindered, as reflected in the Seiko group's 1945 production figures. Only 6,260 clocks and 13,318 watches were produced by K. Hattori's affiliates for marketing by K. Hattori. Production was slowed in part because members of the Seiko group, like many other Japanese companies, were ordered to produce military items, such as time fuses and ammunition.

By 1953, however, K. Hattori & Co., Ltd. had recovered to its prewar sales level. In that year, the company purchased a total of 2.46 million watches and clocks from group plants, representing 54.3% of Japan's total production, and exported 101,000 watches and clocks. By the late 1950s, the firm's watches were gaining international attention, and Hattori had begun marketing watches in the United States and other countries. The company marketed its first self-winding wristwatch in 1955. Utilizing conveyor-belt production technology, by 1959, production of watches then reached three million per year.

In 1964, Chairman Genzo Hattori died. Shoji Hattori, president since 1946, recognized the need for the company to strengthen its global marketing after a visit to Europe in 1962, during which he was asked if there was a watch industry in Japan. Seiko, with the reputation earned by its quartz clock, became the official timer of the Olympic Games in Tokyo, an honor previously held by the Swiss. The company supplied the games with 1,278 stopwatches, made up of 36 different styles plus the world's first portable quartz chronometers. The sponsorship of various events, including tennis, golf, soccer, track, and other sports, resulted in increased international recognition. Its quartz technology allowed production of a full range of precision timing equipment, designed to meet the needs of sports competitions under varied conditions. This expertise has since helped the firm to become the sponsor or official timer of more than 150 international sports events annually.

Like other Japanese companies, K. Hattori employed a global marketing strategy, and looked to overseas expansion. With advertising of new styles and substantially lower prices, it successfully challenged the Swiss in Asian markets, in Hong Kong, Bangkok, and Singapore. Hattori (Hong Kong) Ltd., a new subsidiary, was established in 1968. Marketing was then directed to Britain, West Germany, France, Spain, Italy, and Greece. In the mid-1960s the United States, initially a difficult market for the Japanese to penetrate, presented an additional challenge. Rather than competing with cheap American brands or with high-priced Swiss watches, K. Hattori entered the mid-range of the market, offering jewel-lever watches with an average price tag of $50.

In 1969 K. Hattori began marketing the world's first quartz watch, under the Seiko name. The watch resulted from a "technology contest" between Suwa Seikosha and Daina Seikosha—two K. Hattori affiliates. The new watch, Seiko Astron 35SQ, was encased in 18 karat gold and featured an accuracy within five seconds per month. Developed and manufactured at the Suwa Seikosha plant, it was launched to the Japanese market with a retail price of ¥450.000.

By the early 1970s—a few years after the introduction of the world's first quartz wristwatch—the Seiko brand soared in popularity, and Seiko adopted the slogan, "Someday all watches will be made this way." In 1972, Hattori marketed the world's first ladies' quartz watch, also made at Suwa Seikosha. A year later, it introduced the first Seiko liquid-crystal display (LCD) digital quartz watch. Also manufactured at Suwa Seikosha, the product included built-in illumination and six-digit numerical readout that displayed the time in hours, minutes, and seconds.

In 1970, the firm established Seiko Service Centre (Australia) Pty. Ltd., and Seiko Time Corporation in the United States, the latter adding a Canadian office in the following year. In 1971, the firm expanded into the United Kingdom with Seiko Time (U.K.) Ltd. Seiko Time GmbH was established in West Germany in 1972. Global expansion of the sales effort continued with the opening of Seiko Time Ltda., Brazil, in 1974; Seiko Time (Panama) S.A. in 1977; Seiko Time S.A., Switzerland, in 1978; Seiko Time AB, Sweden, in 1979; and Hattori Overseas (Hong Kong) Ltd. in 1979.

In 1975 the company introduced its plastic ophthalmic lenses. Initially, in 1977 the lenses were exported to a U.S. supplier but since 1986 have been marketed in the United States under the Seiko name. Also in 1975, the firm began marketing digital quartz chronographs.

In 1974, Shoji Hattori died, and Kentaro Hattori, Shoji's nephew and Genzo's oldest son, took over as president. The year 1977 saw record earnings and new products for Hattori Seiko, many of which appeared under brand names other than Seiko. The firm developed Lorus clocks for the export market in 1977. The clock line, which included a pendulum wall clock, a battery transistor wall clock, and alarm clocks, was first sold to countries in Southeast Asia. In the same year, the firm began marketing the digital quartz calculator, a digital quartz world timer, digital quartz alarm chronograph, quartz watches with 100-meter-depth water resistance, and quartz watches with five-year batteries.

In 1978, Seiko introduced twin quartz watches, with two crystals, which offered accuracy within five seconds per year, and quartz divers' watches with 600-meter-depth water resistance, followed in 1979 by the ultra-thin quartz watch with 0.9 millimeter movement, along with the analog alarm quartz watch. In addition, K. Hattori introduced the Alba brand in Japan, which included digital quartz, and began exporting the Alba analog and digital quartz to Southeast Asia. On the other side of the globe, it began marketing the Pulsar brand watches in the United States. The United States also saw the first Lorus quartz watches in 1983.

Despite the busy production years of the 1970s, success came to a sudden halt in the 1980s. During the decade's first few years, profits were far less than those of the late 1970s. "In a boom that has sent prices of many high-technology companies to record levels, Hattori's shares have fallen to the mid-700-yen range (about US$3.50), barely half their top price in 1978," reported *Business Week,* June 15, 1981.

The firm acquired Jean Lassale, a Swiss subsidiary, and developed a product that combined Seiko's quartz movements with a very-thin Swiss-style case. By seeking higher profit margins from luxury products, the company expected to make up for declining profit margins on its less expensive products. The Jean Lassale purchase was part of a pricing strategy to offer a more expensive line to complement lower- and medium-priced watches and appeal to a wider range of customers.

As the yen began to rise in the mid-1980s, competition tightened and the company faced difficult times. New competitors entered watchmaking, from fashion designers to companies who bought watch parts from other watchmakers. With marketing and manufacturing handled by separate companies, trying to compete was difficult.

In 1983, the company changed its name from K. Hattori & Co. Ltd. to Hattori Seiko Co., Ltd., partly to further promote the Seiko name. Watches that featured a black-and-white liquid crystal display TV screen entered the market in 1982. The intention, according to Ichiro Hattori, was not to fill a niche for a frivolous product but to promote the company's name and image. The success of the Seiko TV watches proved that some people liked their watches to do more than tell time. Consequently, in 1984, Hattori Seiko introduced the world's first computer wrist watches, manufactured at Seiko Instruments & Electronics Company. At the same time, Hattori Seiko launched the world's first LCD battery-operated, pocket color-television.

Reijiro Hattori, Kentaro's brother, became president of Hattori Seiko in 1983. Kentaro remained as chairman. Four years later, Reijiro stepped up to chairman when Kentaro died. Ichiro Hattori, president of Seiko affiliates Seiko Instruments Inc., and Seiko Epson Corporation, also died that year. Hattori Seiko then appointed for the first time a non-Hattori-family person to the top. Shiro Yoshimura became president. In 1989 Hattori Seiko introduced a new subsidiary, Hattori (Thailand) Ltd. In an effort to prepare for a new global economy, the Seiko name was brought into heavy use throughout the world. In June 1990, the parent firm changed its name from Hattori Seiko Co., Ltd. to Seiko Corporation. As of 1990, watches accounted for 57% of Seiko Corporation's sales; and clocks were 12.5%; jewelery was 7.3%, and opthalmalic products, personal-care-products, and other products were 23% of sales. Seiko Corporation has a market share that covers more than 100 countries, including 30% of the medium- and high-quality watch market in the United States alone.

Principal Subsidiaries: Seiko do Brasil Ltda. (Brazil); Seiko Canada Inc.; Atlantic Time, S.A. (Panama); Seiko Corporation of America (U.S.A.); Seiko Optical Products, Inc. (U.S.A.); Compagnie Générale Horlogère S.A. (France); Seiko Deutschland GmbH (Germany); Seiko Nederland B.V. (Netherlands); Seiko Sweden AB; Jean Lassale S.A. (Switzerland); Seiko U.K. Limited; Seiko Hong Kong Ltd.; Hattori Overseas Hong Kong Ltd.; Alba Time (Hong Kong) Ltd.; Seiko (Thailand) Ltd.; Seiko Australia Pty. Ltd.

Further Reading: Minard, Lawrence, and Jack Willoughby, ''Japan's Dark Horse Computer Company,'' *Forbes,* October 22, 1984; Boyer, Edward, ''A Family Rift Roils Seiko,'' *Fortune,* November 12, 1984.

—Kim M. Magon

AKTIEBOLAGET SKF

S-415 50 Göteborg
Sweden
(31) 371000
Fax: (31) 372832

Public Company
Incorporated: 1907
Employees: 46,667
Sales: SKr25.06 billion (US$4.04 billion)
Stock Exchanges: Stockholm London Paris Geneva Basel Zürich New York

Aktiebolaget SKF is the acknowledged leader of the world's rolling bearing industry and in a number of other precision engineering products. SKF controls about 20% of the world market in bearings, more than double the market share of its nearest competitors. Despite a period of low profitability in the early and mid 1980s caused by overcapacity in the world's bearing industry and the impact of Japanese imports on its principal European market, SKF seems unlikely to relinquish this leading position in the near future.

SKF was established in 1907 in Göteborg, Sweden, by the textile company Gamlestadens Fabriker. Its founder was Sven Wingquist, a maintenance engineer at the Gamlestadens factory who had become increasingly disillusioned with the poor performance and high cost of the imported bearings used in the factory's overhead shafts. These latter also tended to misalignment, causing additional functional difficulties in the bearings.

Granted facilities for research by an unusually far-sighted management, Winquist developed a superior single row deep groove ball bearing. Gamlestadens decided to set up a new company named Svenska Kullagerfabriken (SKF) to sell the new product. Initially SKF production took place in Wingquist's own workshop, but soon a separate factory was built in Göteborg.

Wingquist went on to develop a bearing capable of diminishing the effects of misalignment between shaft and housing. This, the double row self-aligning ball bearing, established SKF's fortunes and helped propel it to the forefront of the industry.

Wingquist's talents, however, extended beyond pure engineering. From an early stage, he appears to have recognized that Sweden's domestic market was far too small to underwrite the expansion in sales which alone could generate sufficient profits to keep SKF in business and capable of competing with its major European, particularly German, rivals. Wingquist therefore undertook a series of sales trips across Europe and subsequently set up sales offices and appointed agents. Subsidiary companies were established in France and the U.K. and factories were built.

From the start, SKF's fortunes were closely bound up with those of the automotive industry, which in the first decades of the 20th century had a growing requirement for SKF's quality bearings. SKF therefore chose to locate its plants close to major established motor plants—for example, in the United Kingdom at Luton, near the large Vauxhall/Bedford plants. In the years immediately preceding World War I, automotive manufacturers were enjoying a boom period, and by 1912 SKF found itself unable to meet demand for its bearings due to supply problems with the foreign balls used in its bearing products. SKF therefore decided to produce its own balls in Göteborg. In 1913 the company could literally afford to strengthen its position in the crucial German market by the acquisition of a half share in the Norma Compagnie at Canstatt. SKF, in common with most Swedish businesses, derived considerable advantage from Sweden's declaration of neutrality in 1914, trading with both the Allied and Central powers and successfully increasing its market share, particularly outside Europe, at the expense of its German, British, and French competitors whose countries were at war.

1916 was a significant year for the company. A steel works at Hofors Bruk in central southern Sweden was bought to provide SKF's bearings plants with a dedicated supply of high quality steel. The size of SKF's research laboratory at Göteborg was doubled, testifying to the company's recognition of the importance of innovative technology in maintaining market share. SKF also acquired one of the few remaining independent Swedish producers of ball bearings and converted its factory to the production of axle boxes and bearings housings. Finally, in order to avoid the hazards and high insurance costs of wartime transatlantic shipment, SKF established a plant at Hartford, Connecticut, for the supply of bearings to a U.S. motor and armaments industry rapidly expanding under the stimulus of the wartime requirements of the Allied powers in Europe. Next year a second French factory was opened on the outskirts of Paris.

Nevertheless, there were occasional setbacks. The Russian installation, set up in 1914 and expanded during the next three years, was nationalized without compensation in the wake of the 1917 Revolution. However, the second decade of the century was in general a period of continuous expansion for SKF. By 1919 it had twelve plants in full operation, a world-wide sales network, and a staff of almost 12,000.

Profits in the first years of the 1920s were blighted by the onset of economic depression. This onset was SKF's first experience of an economic pattern which to a large extent determined its fortunes ever since—the level of consumer spending influencing the level of purchase of consumer durables, in its turn determining the level of capital investment by manufacturers in new machinery.

Nonetheless, the early and mid years of the decade saw SKF enhance its reputation for innovation with the introduction of spherical and taper roller bearings. By 1925, steel production at the Hofors mill had reached 24,000 tons and in the next year it doubled in response to improving economic conditions in Western Europe. In 1926 SKF decided that its Volvo subsidiary should enter the car and truck manufacturing industry. SKF used Volvo as a practical testing ground for its bearings until 1935 when Volvo became an independent company. SKF has retained close links with its former subsidiary. In 1927, SKF again displayed its eminence in the field of technological innovation when an employee patented a series of bearing measuring devices and established a set of measuring standards for use in the industry at large.

The Depression which began in 1929 enabled SKF to buy a number of rival German bearings companies, giving the company a leading position in the important German market. These separate operations were concentrated at Schweinfurt and Canstatt. In that year, SKF was quoted for the first time on the international stock exchange, and acquired the Swedish engineering firm Lidköpings Mekaniska Verkstad AB, thus incorporating machine tools in its product range.

As in the early 1920s, so in the opening years of the 1930s, SKF's profits suffered during the worst years of the Depression. Special emphasis was placed on the development of new types of bearing, leading in 1932 to the patenting of the "narrow type" spherical roller bearing and the self-aligning spherical roller bearing. The premium on efficiency in the production process caused SKF to introduce automation at about this time.

By 1935 the effects of the Depression had begun to recede in Europe and the United States. The ensuing rise in capital expenditure on new plant and machinery and the increasing pace of rearmament in Europe made the next five-year period up to the outbreak of World War II one of great prosperity for SKF.

Although Sweden once again chose neutrality in 1939, conditions for its export-dependent industries were not as generally favorable as they had been during World War I. During this time, SKF factories were taken over and headed by local governments. Swedish companies took advantage of their nation's neutral position to trade actively with both Allied and Axis powers, but the Nazi occupation of Denmark and Norway, Germany's unrestricted submarine warfare, and British naval blockades deprived SKF and other companies of their traditional sea-routes out of Scandinavia. From 1942 large-scale British and American bombing raids over France and Germany sought to achieve the wholesale destruction of Nazi Germany's industrial base and thus Germany's capacity to continue the war. Realizing how crucial efficient and large-scale bearings production was to the Axis war effort, Allied bombers paid particular attention to bearings plants, in particular those at Schweinfurt and Canstatt. By the end of hostilities in 1945, the SKF plants lay in ruins. As in the previous conflict and the Depression of the early 1930s, SKF used the war years to good effect for the development of new products. In 1943 the company introduced its revolutionary OK oil-injection shaft coupling, enabling rolling bearings to function efficiently in marine propeller shafts.

Postwar reconstruction of the German and French plants was paralleled by new building of factories in countries formerly outside SKF's traditional manufacturing area—for example in Spain, Canada, and Holland. In Sweden itself, new facilities for the continuous annealing and tube-rolling of steel were added to the Hofors mill. In answer to the requirement for steel in a postwar Europe rebuilding its shattered industries, SKF increased its production capacity by acquiring Hellefors Jernverk, and in 1957 a new ball and roller factory was completed on the original Göteborg site. A notable feature of the immediate postwar decades was the rate of increase of automation in SKF's bearings production, facilitating the introduction in 1953 of SKF's first high precision bearings.

SKF expanded beyond Europe and the United States to two newly industrializing countries of the Third World, Brazil and India, both engaged in the rapid expansion of their automotive and textile industries and therefore requiring large quantities of bearings. SKF started activities in these countries at the latters' request. These two countries represented vast potential markets for SKF products and offered in addition the important advantage of labor costs cheap by European and U.S. standards.

Meanwhile in Europe the creation of the European Economic Community (EEC) and the growing penetration of the European bearings market by cheap Japanese imports presented SKF with new opportunities and difficulties. Sweden had successfully negotiated with the EEC in 1972 for the free entry of its industrial products into the community, but of more importance to SKF, with its particularly high level of plant investment in EEC member states, was its management's growing awareness that the new trading conditions created by the establishment of the EEC trading block could be turned to the group's advantage in helping it fight its Japanese competitors—NTN, NSK, and Koyo Seiko.

SKF's plan involved concentrating production of particular products in specific plants, treating Europe as if it were a single nation in economic terms rather than a collection of six—and later nine—separate states. This would prevent wasteful duplication of production, allowing economies of scale by permitting longer runs of fewer types of bearings or tools at each individual factory. Finished products could then be transported across Community boundaries progressively being freed from import duties and quotas.

SKF restructured itself in the early 1970s. SKF's bearings and related products were formed into three new divisions—a European bearings division, an overseas bearings division and SKF Industries Inc. The overseas bearings section became responsible for the group's non-European production and sales companies outside North and Central America while SKF Industries handled the U.S., Canadian, and Mexican operations. Also created were cutting tools, steel, and engineering products divisions. Lidköping—manufacturing grinding machines—was preserved as a separate profit center.

Pursuing its niche strategy—establishing a dominant position in particular segments of the bearings and precision tools industries—SKF in the late 1960s and early 1970s took steps to become the leading supplier of bearings to Europe's, particularly France's, newly revitalized aerospace industry. It acquired Les Applications du Roulement (ADR) for the manufacture of airframe bearings and in 1975 bought a 60% shareholding in SARMA, a French aerospace engineering research company. During this period it became increasingly apparent that the highest rates of growth were being recorded in some of the group's non-bearing activities—for example, cutting and machine tools—although these still accounted for only a small proportion of the value of total group sales.

Consequently SKF chose to strengthen its position in these areas by acquiring some leading manufacturers, including the Swedish engineering firm Malcus Industri in 1969 and the large British cutting-tool manufacturer, the Sheffield Twist Drill & Steel Company, in 1975. This strategy of buying into positions of dominance in particular sectors of the bearings and precision engineering industries is characteristic of SKF.

The mature nature of the European bearings market in the 1970s and its penetration by the Japanese—especially worrying in the large volume markets such as the motor industry—placed a premium on retaining existing customer loyalty and on emphasizing the quality of SKF products over those of its rivals.

In order to make full use of the opportunities created by the new EEC trading conditions, SKF instituted a global forecasting and supply system (GFSS) in 1974 to improve coordination of the type and quantity of bearings produced at its five major European plants. GFSS became an integral part of SKF's strategy of refusing to cede any product to its Japanese competitors.

SKF's decision not to surrender any part of its home European market to the Japanese led to a period of further cost-cutting and rationalization in the late 1970s and early 1980s and served to reduce the groups's overall profit levels during this time. SKF also redefined itself, its goals, and the best means to achieve them.

In essence SKF saw the need to transform itself from a primarily manufacturing-oriented business into a group of companies much more responsive to its customers' changing requirements. In 1968 SKF had centralized control of its activities by setting up its group headquarters in Göteborg. Hand in hand with this change went renewed emphasis on closer collaboration between its research and development and its marketing staff. This arrangement, combined with continuing technical innovation and improvement, made possible by the establishment of the SKF Engineering & Research Center (ERC), enabled SKF to stay ahead of its Japanese competitors despite their lower production costs and greater production efficiency.

Such restructurings and shifts of emphasis could not alleviate the effects of the recession which afflicted the bearings industry in the early 1980s, largely caused by overcapacity. By 1983, overall employment in the industry had fallen by about 15% and several manufacturers had gone out of business altogether. Demand was especially depressed in Europe, a factor which affected SKF severely because of its heavy dependence on European sales. SKF was compelled to reduce the size of its work force at several plants with sometimes divisive results. The prospect of 600 redundancies at SKF's Luton plant in the United Kingdom caused the 1,700-strong work force to walk out on strike in early 1983, and lowered both morale and productivity. The closure of the Ivry plant near Paris in the same year triggered a lengthy protest occupation by Confédération Générale du Travail militants, resulting in a series of violent confrontations with the police.

Although the group had to resort to a policy of severe cost-cutting, redundancy, and plant closure, it is significant that SKF did not waver in its commitment to the research and development of new technology. One object of research at this time was the so-called ''plasma'' steel-making process, a method of recovering the base metal from metal wastes by means of an ionized superheated gas stream. The economic rationale for plasma technology was its potential for reducing the cost of producing special steels. By the mid 1980s, SKF had invested SKr200 million in the commissioning of plasma plants at Landskrona and Malmo—all this at a time of recession in the metals and metals recovery industries. During the early 1980s, SARMA had expanded production on the basis of a substantial involvement in the European Airbus program, but cuts in the program in 1983, combined with a state of general depression in the aerospace industry, forced the closure of SARMA's Champigny plant in 1984. It is, however, worth noting the use of SARMA's special carbon-fiber rods in the European Space Agency's satellite launcher Ariane 4.

In the middle of the decade, SKF benefited from a general economic upturn in Europe, but its overall profit level was dented by a sharp deterioration in the performance of its U.S. operation, SKF Industries Inc. Sales of bearings dropped almost 15% in volume, mainly due to the penetration of Japanese imports. Additionally losses at SKF Steel amounted to some SKr65 million, caused by overcapacity in the world's steel industry and the unexpectedly high cost of the two new plasma plants. Nonetheless SKF made important acquisitions in 1985: SKF Española, which became a fully owned subsidiary after SKF bought 99% of its shares, and Waldes Truarc Inc., a U.S. maker of fasteners, evidence of SKF's desire to strengthen its presence both in this field and, as the 1986 acquisition of aerospace bearings manufacturer MRC showed, in the U.S. market generally. Also important was the formation of SKF Miniature Bearings, reflecting the group's keenness to penetrate this high growth area of the bearings business.

In Europe too SKF had increased its strength in fastening systems and linear motion products. The German SKF subsidiary Seeger-Orbis had bought the British company Anderton in 1983 for £1.4 million, thereby placing SKF in a leading position in the European market and providing the group with another valuable bridgehead into the United States. Between 1983 and 1985, the group's components business registered a near 40% growth in sales. SKF's steel division was not so successful. SKF decided to pull out of this loss-making area of its business, and from October 1986 steel operations ceased to be part of its activities. Instead, SKF merged its steel subsidiary with the Finnish steel manufacturer Ovako Oy, forming a new steel company named Ovako Steel—in which SKF has a 50% shareholding—to concentrate on the production of special steel. Significantly, Ovako Steel did not take on SKF's plasma projects.

In that year SKF announced the formation of a 50-50 joint venture with the Japanese bearings producer Koyo Seiko, the first foreign bearings company to gain a foothold in the Japanese home market. SKF was attracted by the 20% stake held in Koyo by Toyota, and Koyo by the prospect of access to SKF's advanced technology. Recognizing in Southeast Asia the fastest growing market for bearings in the world, SKF began to increase productive capacity in the region, culminating in the decision four years later to build a new plant in Malaysia.

In 1987 the bearings operations were once again restructured, this time around product types and functions, forming SKF Bearing Industries, SKF Bearing Services, and SKF Specialty Bearings. The tools and component systems divisions—engineering products—remained unaltered. Each of the new bearings groupings assumed worldwide total responsibility for its own products and services.

Simultaneously SKF decided to withdraw from its involvement in plasma technology. A West German industrial waste company, Berzelius Umwelt-Service, was allowed to acquire a 25% holding in ScanDust, SKF's wholly owned subsidiary at Landskrona, while in January 1990 SKF and the other owners of SwedeChrome, based in Malmo, decided to close down the company after a slump in the price of ferrochrome proved the plant's inability to operate at a profit. This step may have led SKF to regret its decision in the early 1980s not to build smaller and more efficient plants. With the acquisition in 1988 of the Austrian bearings manufacturer Steyr Walzlager and the British aerospace engineering firm AMPEP, the group increased its presence in the European bearings market and in bearings for aerospace purposes. However, SKF's dependence on free trading conditions was illustrated in that year by an anti-dumping investigation in the United States in which SKF and other European and Asian manufacturers were accused of unfair price-cutting. In May 1989 the U.S. Commerce Department began imposing import duties as high as 50% and demanding a security deposit against every import shipment. This requirement, combined with a rise in U.S. demand, led SKF to strip out production lines in Europe and ship them to the United States. There was a certain irony in the accusation of an unfair pricing policy, since SKF and other European bearings manufacturers had themselves called for an EEC investigation of Japanese pricing in the European market.

Fortunately the overcapacity which had dogged the world's bearing industry for almost a decade had begun to recede in 1988, and by 1989 the better balance between supply and demand had begun to show in SKF's profits. SKF, so often the predator, found itself under threat from the Swedish industrial group Trelleborg when the latter acquired a 10.1% equity holding in the group in 1988. Trelleborg claimed the stake was for investment purposes only, but some industry analysts believed the move could herald a full bid for SKF in the future. The stake was sold by Trelleborg in 1989. SKF started its own tender of $107 million for the U.S. bearings manufacturer McGill Manufacturing. This move clearly demonstrated SKF's wish to build up its U.S. manufacturing base and thereby avoid burdensome import duties. McGill, however, was acquired by Emerson.

SKF's principal tasks for the 1990s will be to coax more profitability out of its mainstream bearings operations and to lessen the group's dependence on its West European sales by significantly increasing its market share in Eastern Europe, North America, and the Far East, particularly Japan. SKF's long tradition of technical innovation—instanced in the recent opening of an SKF College of Engineering—and its recognition of the importance of high-quality customer service should go far in helping it attain these goals. In Europe, still the most important area for SKF, the group's new structure should enable it to take the fullest possible advantage of the EEC trade deregulation scheduled for 1992.

Principal Subsidiaries: SKF Bearing Industries Argentina (99.9%); SKF Steyr Ges.m.b.H. (Austria, 75%); SKF do Brasil Limitada (Brazil); SKF France (99.9%); SKF Bearings India Limited (51%); SKF Industrie S.p.A. (Italy); SKF South Africa (Pty) Ltd.; SKF Sverige AB; SKF Mekanprodukter AB; SKF (U.K.) Limited; SKF Bearing Industries Co. (U.S.A.); SKF GmbH (Germany, 99.9%); SKF Roulements Specialisés s.n.c. (ADR) (France); SKF Avio (Italy); MRC Bearings (U.S.A.); SKF Tools AB; SKF & Dormer Tools (Sheffield) Limited (U.K.); Prototyp-Werke GmbH (Germany); SARMA (France); RFT S.p.A. (Italy); Anderton International Limited (U.K.); Seeger-Orbis GmbH (Germany); SKF Textilmaschinen-Komponenten GmbH (Germany); Lidköping Machine Tools AB; Ovako Steel AB (50%).

Further Reading: SKF, *The Story of SKF*, Göteborg, SKF, 1982; SKF, *The World of SKF*, Göteborg, SKF, 1988.

—D.H. O'Leary

THE STANLEY WORKS

1000 Stanley Drive
New Britain, Connecticut 06050
U.S.A.
(203) 225-5111
Fax: (203) 827-3895

Public Company
Incorporated: 1852
Employees: 18,464
Sales: $1.97 billion
Stock Exchanges: New York Pacific

The Stanley Works is a manufacturer of a broad range of tools and hardware both for home use and for industrial and professional applications. Stanley is a global manufacturer, with production facilities in 11 countries. Stanley is an old and successful company in a hidebound industry—metal-working—that has proven extremely vulnerable to foreign competition since the 1960s.

The company was founded in 1843 by Frederick T. Stanley, a 41-year-old merchant and manufacturer whose previous work experience included stints as a clerk on a Connecticut River steamboat and as an itinerant peddler in the South. In 1831, Stanley, in partnership with his younger brother William Stanley, had opened a small facility in New Britain, Connecticut, for the manufacture of house trimmings and door locks. Though the business failed to survive the Panic of 1837, it seemed to have served as the prototype for a second manufacturing venture in New Britain—Stanley's Bolt Manufactory—which Frederick Stanley, again in concert with his brother, established in 1843.

The establishment of this "manufactory" marks the official beginning of the Stanley story. The company's present name was adopted in 1852, when the Stanley brothers—along with five neighbors—were granted a charter of incorporation by the state of Connecticut for a newly organized firm, The Stanley Works. This corporation, initially capitalized at $30,000, was to be directed by Frederick T. Stanley, who was named its first president.

During its early years Stanley was one of hundreds of similar companies in antebellum America producing hardware and builders' goods. Frederick Stanley was not unique in perceiving an entrepreneurial opening for such goods in a nation growing and industrializing as rapidly as the United States. There were scores of shops similar to his in Connecticut alone.

If Frederick Stanley had an early competitive advantage, at least locally, it may have been in his manufactory's power source, a single-cylinder high-pressure steam engine, which he had purchased from the firm of William Burdon of Brooklyn. This relatively sophisticated engine enabled Stanley's Bolt Manufactory and, later, The Stanley Works, to produce goods—whether bolts, T-hinges or wrought-iron straps—in a more capital-intensive and efficient way than was the case in less automated shops in the area.

Nevertheless, the firm's early growth was not exceptionally rapid. Total sales were $7,328 in 1853 and $21,371 in 1854, and rose to about $53,000 in 1860, on the eve of the Civil War. Only after that conflict ended would the dramatic rise of The Stanley Works begin.

To say that the firm's rise postdated the Civil War is not to imply that the war itself was directly or fundamentally responsible. More significant than any war-induced demand for Stanley's products were deep-seated economic forces related to industrialization and increased market size and integration. Productivity gains made possible through mechanization and the creation, via the railroad, of an embryonic national market transformed the U.S. business environment in the late 19th century, presenting new opportunities to—and posing new problems for—most U.S. manufacturers. Alfred D. Chandler describes this transformation in his *The Visible Hand: The Managerial Revolution in American Business.*

In order to exploit new production and marketing possibilities and to overcome problems arising from oversupply and greater competition, Stanley developed new business strategies and structures. In so doing, it integrated and expanded its operations, and employed new productivity-enhancing and competition-dampening methods of production, marketing, and organization.

Such policies resulted in the dramatic growth of The Stanley Works. Frederick T. Stanley seems to have had little to do with the company's rapid postwar ascent; from the 1860s to the time of his death in 1883, he increasingly withdrew from active business operations, devoting more of his time to politics and civic affairs in New Britain. The animating spirit behind Stanley's rise was William H. Hart, whose career with the firm stretched from 1854 to 1918.

Prior to joining Stanley in 1854 at the age of 19, Hart, like number of 19th-century industrialists, had worked in the railroad industry—as a freight agent and assistant station manager. Hart rose quickly at Stanley, assuming the position of secretary-treasurer a few months after joining the firm and in 1856, before he had reached the age of 21, winning election to the board of directors. From there, he gradually took on more direct managerial responsibility, eventually rising to the position of president, a post he held from May of 1884 to February of 1915.

Under Hart's leadership, the firm pursued a number of successful strategies that enabled Stanley to thrive even in the fiercely competitive business environment of the day. Hart expanded hardware production facilities in New Britain in 1866, for example, and in 1909 opened new facilities in Niles, Ohio—strategically located in the steel belt of northeastern Ohio—and in Canada in 1914. He helped to reduce

Stanley's production costs by mechanizing operations to a greater degree and by repositioning equipment in his factories. Manufacturing technology improved dramatically under his helm—Stanley was particularly important in the development of a process for the cold rolling of wrought-iron strip—and the firm came to hold several significant manufacturing patents, including one issued in 1889 for the development of the first hinge to use ball bearings.

At Hart's urging, the firm made several small but noteworthy innovations in the marketing of hardware, packing installation screws along with the firm's hinges and shipping hardware in labeled boxes. In 1870, when Stanley opened a sales office in New York City, the firm began to devote attention to developing export markets for its products, a precocious strategy for the time.

Hart also tried to diversify the company and to develop a fuller product line. By moving into the production of steel strapping at the turn of the century, for example, Stanley was able not only to diversify its operations but to vertically integrate to a degree. The move into steel strapping was to prove of major consequence to the company; Stanley was one of the nation's leading manufacturers of this product before moving out of the industry in 1987.

Stanley had an impressive record of expansion in the period between the beginning of the Civil War and the end of World War I. The company's net sales by 1872 had already reached $480,000, a ninefold increase over the figure for 1860. By 1919, the year after Hart stepped down as chairman of the board, net sales were over $11 million. Nor was Stanley's a case of growth at any cost; in 1877 the firm began an unbroken streak of yearly dividends. During World War I Stanley produced belt buckles, gas mask components, and ammunition tubes.

Although William H. Hart was the central figure in the rise of The Stanley Works—the company's trademark was heart-shaped for a time—Stanley survived his departure. By the time Hart retired as chairman in 1918, he had created a corporate culture and strategy conducive to continued growth.

Stanley's efforts to reduce costs, often through external integration, and to diversify did not abate with Hart's retirement. After years of trying, for example, the firm was able to cut energy costs by purchasing—and later rebuilding—a hydroelectric power plant on the Farmington River near New Britain. Even more important, however, was the firm's 1920 merger with its crosstown neighbor in that city, The Stanley Rule & Level Company, an old-line manufacturer of measuring devices and hand tools, which had been founded in 1857 by a cousin of Frederick Stanley. The acquisition of Stanley Rule & Level—at the time one of the largest and most respected companies in its field—allowed The Stanley Works to increase its labor force by some 1,200 workers, its capitalization by 50%, and its net sales by $6 million. In addition, it brought Stanley the benefits of diversification, without distancing the company from its historical roots or its areas of experience and expertise: hardware, hand tools and measuring devices, were naturally complementary.

Stanley Rule & Level had long been active in the merger and acquisition business itself. As early as 1863 the firm had acquired a competitor, the Brattleboro, Vermont, rule factory of E.A. Stearns & Company. Two later acquisitions, that of the Atha Tool Company of Newark, New Jersey, in 1913 and that of the Eagle Square Manufacturing Company—a maker of carpenters' steel squares, based in Shaftsbury, Vermont—in 1916 contributed significantly both to the company's growth and to its appeal.

Although similar strategies were being employed elsewhere as well, the consolidation of Stanley Rule & Level into The Stanley Works—and the success of this consolidation—clearly spurred the development of one of Stanley's principal growth strategies in the post-1920 period, the aggressive pursuit of competing or related companies through merger or acquisition. Other, less dramatic, growth strategies were also employed. During the interwar period, the company continued to expand operations into new geographical areas, both at home and abroad. Stanley opened a woodworking plant in 1923, for example, in Pulaski, Tennessee, near timberlands which the company had acquired previously. By 1926 Stanley was producing hardware in Germany, and in 1937 the firm opened a factory in Sheffield, England, for the manufacture of hand tools.

Technological innovations also continued under Hart's immediate successors, at times furthering the company's efforts to develop a fuller product line and to diversify. Perhaps the most impressive individual innovation during the interwar years was Stanley's introduction in 1931 of the first automated entranceway in the United States, a technology the company patented under the name Magic Eye. The Magic Eye, which opened doors through the activation of a photoelectric cell, and other devices based on similar technology are mainstays of Stanley's product line. A number of other products were also introduced during the period, most notably a line of electric tools, which were produced under a new division established in 1929.

If Stanley's culture and strategy were still conducive to profits and growth, they were not enough to assure either. Between roughly 1930 and 1945, economic and political conditions were at work that minimized the difference corporate culture and strategy—good or bad—could make. Stanley's fortunes declined sharply during the Great Depression, which hit manufacturing and construction—and thus the tool and hardware industries—extremely hard. The company's net income was negative in 1932, for example, and, after paying out dividends, Stanley ran a deficit on its income account in 1934 as well.

Stanley's performance in the 15 years after 1930 was neither fundamentally shaped nor adversely affected by corporate decisionmaking. The four men who successively followed William Hart as president—his son, George P. Hart, who served from 1915 to 1918; E. Allen Moore, whose term began in 1918 and ended in 1923; Clarence F. Bennett, who was president from 1923 until 1941; and Richard E. Pritchard, who served between 1941 and 1950—each performed ably, but to little effect.

With the advent of World War II Stanley, of necessity, had been forced to retool, transforming itself for the most part into a manufacturer of military hardware. Annual sales rose significantly as a result, reaching $44 million in 1943. Yet wartime sales were just that; Stanley sold 460 million belt links for machine gun bullets and 36 million cartridge clips during World War II, but this contribution did not boost its postwar performance.

The same management strategy that had helped the firm to succeed earlier limited the company's performance in the decades after the war. In emphasizing manufacturing matters, key decisionmakers tended to neglect the marketing and financial dimensions of Stanley's operations. This situation was particularly true between 1945 and the early 1960s.

Despite the fact that Stanley—like many traditional New England manufacturers—continued to produce high-quality products during this period, the company's expansion was slow and its earnings erratic. For example, Stanley's annual net sales, already over $90 million in 1951, had grown only to $95.4 million by 1960; moreover, the company's earnings for 1948—$5.25 million—were surpassed only twice between that year and 1965.

Stanley's sluggish performance in this period was shaped in part by structural factors. Much of America's basic manufacturing sector—the principal market for Stanley's products—was not mature, which dampened opportunities for rapid growth. Even when opportunities did present themselves in basic manufacturing—some segments of the metalworking industry did, in fact, grow rapidly during this period—Stanley, entrenched in its traditional lines, could not always move quickly. Indeed, were it not for the postwar baby boom, which boosted the U.S. construction industry and thus the demand for builders' tools, Stanley's record might have been worse.

While Stanley's management neglected certain key business functions, they were not totally inert and their policies were not ineffectual. Under the leadership of John C. Cairns, chief executive officer from 1950 to 1966, the company made several important acquisitions and continued efforts to expand to modernize existing operations. During the 1950s Stanley acquired the Humason Manufacturing Company of Forestville, Connecticut, a maker of springs and screw machine parts; the H. L. Judd Company of Wallingford, Connecticut, a large producer of drapery hardware; and the Florida-based Denison Corporation, a manufacturer of aluminum window frames and doors. In addition, in 1957 Stanley opened a 115,000-square-foot, state-of-the-art steel-strapping plant in New Britain, which nearly doubled the firm's manufacturing capacity for this product.

Nonetheless, as Stanley entered the decade of the 1960s, its management's recent performance had been disappointing. Fortunately for Stanley, a bright and energetic young executive, Donald W. Davis—the most important figure in the company's history since William H. Hart—was coming to the fore.

Born in Springfield, Massachusetts in 1921, Davis joined The Stanley Works in 1948. He rose rapidly at Stanley and in 1962 was promoted from his position as general manager of the steel-strapping division to executive vice president of the firm. With this promotion Davis took *de facto* control of the company, functioning as Stanley's chief operating officer between 1962 and 1966, when he was named president and chief executive officer.

In the quarter century between 1962, when Davis assumed control, and 1987, when he turned over day-to-day managerial responsibilities to Richard H. Ayers, Davis was able not merely to rouse Stanley from its long postwar slumber, but to transform the company into an aggressive leader in the globally competitive tool and hardware industry.

Stanley's rejuvenation program under Davis can be broken down into several distinct parts. Each part of the program was shaped by his recognition that if Stanley was to remain a central player in the industry, the company would have to become more competitive and would have to assume a more aggressive, growth-oriented posture. Davis believed that as world markets became more integrated, Stanley—as well as The Black & Decker Corporation, Snap-On Tools Corporation, and other U.S. tool and hardware companies—would have to face the harsh reality of global competition for the first time.

Davis called for increased competitiveness and faster growth at The Stanley Works. Under his leadership the company rationalized production and modernized plant facilities; aggressively pursued mergers and acquisitions, while at the same time divesting itself of poorly performing or non-strategic divisions and product lines; identified new markets and penetrated such markets once identified; devoted much more attention to marketing and advertising; and exploited more fully international manufacturing and marketing opportunities.

In order to see these policies through, Davis, along with Garth W. Edwards, vice president for finance, overturned company policy in the mid-1960s by taking Stanley into long-term debt. This gambit proved extraordinarily successful; over time, borrowed funds helped to accomplish Davis's goals without compromising Stanley's financial integrity through excessive leveraging.

Davis used retained earnings, equity capital, and borrowed funds to build a number of new plants—the hand-tool plant that Stanley opened in New Britain in 1964 was the largest in the world at the time—and to upgrade existing facilities. Between 1979 and 1983 the company spent about $55 million yearly on upgrades alone. In part as a result of such efforts, Stanley was able over time to improve substantially both its capital-labor ratio and its overall manufacturing productivity.

During Davis's tenure Stanley made more than 25 major acquisitions, including Berry Industries, Volkert Stampings, Mac Tools, Taylor Rental Corporation, Proto Industrial Tools, and Textron's Bostich Division. During the 1980s Davis streamlined the company by selling off its garden-tool and electric-tool businesses, its drapery-hardware business, and its steel and steel-strapping divisions. In 1986 Stanley sold its South African interests to local management.

Stanley's modernization, acquisition, and rationalization strategies under Davis were impressive. More impressive still were the company's efforts during the same period to identify and penetrate new markets. In particular, Stanley's early and aggressive push during the early 1970s into the so-called do-it-yourself (DIY), or consumer, hand-tool market has paid handsome returns. This market—propelled by such factors as inflationary building and repair costs, a shortage of skilled tradesmen, and the movement of upscale baby boomers into older homes—has become one of Stanley's largest and most profitable markets and one of its most important in strategic terms. Because the DIY market, unlike Stanley's others, is counter-cyclical, the chances that a general economic downturn would spell disaster to the firm were now significantly reduced.

In order to establish itself in the DIY market, and for other strategic reasons as well, Stanley, formerly a production-driven company, committed itself under Davis to developing its marketing capabilities. By working more closely with wholesalers and retailers of its products, increasing its market research, and, perhaps most importantly, making a sizable investment in TV advertising, the company over time has done just that. The phrase "Stanley helps you do things right"—coined by Davis—is familiar in different languages around the world.

Stanley became a much more international company under Davis. Not only did the firm increase its commitment to exporting but it also expanded foreign production by acquiring facilities in Latin America, Canada, France, and West Germany. Perhaps most significant of all, given geopolitical trends, was Stanley's 1986 move into the Pacific Rim with its acquisition of Taiwan-based Chiro Tool Manufacturing Corporation.

By the time Davis stepped down at Stanley—Richard H. Ayers succeeded him as president and chief executive officer in 1987 and as board chairman in 1989—the company bore little resemblance to the one he had taken over in the early 1960s. Stanley had not merely survived, but had flourished under his helm, with net income and earnings at all-time highs in 1989.

Moreover, Davis seems to have left the company in good hands under Ayers, the youthful new CEO. Ayers had considerable experience in manufacturing even before joining Stanley in 1972. Strong management under Davis and Ayers has enabled Stanley to remain vital. Strong management, of course, meant that tough decisions often had to be made, decisions to stand up to labor—most notably during an 18-week strike against Stanley by the International Association of Machinists in 1968—to sell off divisions, reduce the size of the work force, and move production offshore.

Since taking control of the firm, Ayers has continued many of the successful policy initiatives begun under his predecessor and is, if anything, more globally oriented in his strategic thinking than was Davis. The prospects for each of Stanley's three main product groups—consumer products, builders' products, and industrial products—seem positive.

Principal Subsidiaries: The Farmington River Power Co.; Mac Tools, Inc.; Mechanics Tools, Inc.; Chiro Tool Manufacturing Corporation; Stanley-Vidmar, Inc.; Stanley-Vidmar Systems, Inc.; Stanley Germany Inc.; Stanley International Sales, Inc.; Stanley Inter-America Distribution Center, Inc.; Stanley Foreign Sales Corporation; Stanley Works Financial Inc.; Stanley Door Systems Inc.; Stanley Structures, Inc.; Stanley Magic-Door, Inc.; Stanley Home Automation, Inc.; Acme Holding Corporation; Taylor Rental Corporation; Stanley-Bostitch, Inc.; The Parker Group, Inc.; Halstead Enterprises, Inc.; Stanley Canada Inc.; Stanley Tools (N.Z.) Ltd. (New Zealand); Ferramentas Stanley Ltda. (Brazil); Herramientas Stanley S.A. de C.V. (Mexico); Herramientas Stanley S.A. (Colombia); Stanley-Bostitch, S.A. de C.V. (Mexico); Stanley Tools SpA (Italy); Stanley-Mabo S.A. (France); SICFO S.A. (France); Stanley Atlantic, Inc.; The Stanley Works Pty. Ltd. (Australia); Stanley Works Asia Pacific Pte. Ltd. (Singapore); The Stanley Works (Hong Kong) Ltd.; The Stanley Works Sales (Philippines), Inc.; Stanley Works Asia Pacific Ltd. (Taiwan); The Stanley Works (Bermuda) Ltd.; The Stanley Works Japan K.K.; Stanley Tools Thailand Ltd.

Further Reading: Leavitt, Robert Keith, *Foundation for the Future: History of The Stanley Works,* New Britain, Connecticut, The Stanley Works, 1951; "Stanley Tries the Faster Track," *Business Week,* November 5, 1966; Davis, Donald W., *The Stanley Works: A 125 Year Beginning,* New York, The Newcomen Society in North America, 1969; Uchitelle, Louis, "The Stanley Works Goes Global," *The New York Times,* July 23, 1989; Uchitelle, Louis, "Only the Bosses are American, *The New York Times,* July 24, 1989.

—Peter A. Coclanis

SULZER

SULZER BROTHERS LIMITED (Gebrüder Sulzer Aktiengesellschaft)

CH-8401 Winterthur
Switzerland
(52) 81 11 22
Fax: (52) 23 42 83

Public Company
Incorporated: 1914
Employees: 33,967
Sales: SFr6.38 billion (US$4.14 billion)
Stock Exchange: Zürich

The Swiss technology multinational Gerbrüder Sulzer (known as Sulzer Brothers in English-speaking nations) is perhaps best known for its diesel engines and industrial looms. However, it has even larger interests in the provision of plant and services for the construction industry, as well as a significant involvement in medical technology and several other diverse areas. It owes its growth and profitability to the ingenuity and energy of its founders and their successors, who had the vision to forge links abroad as a means of overcoming the constraints of Switzerland's small domestic market and limited natural resources. From the earliest days, ideas, expertise, and materials were imported, and Sulzer not only exported its finished products but also quickly established the beginnings of a manufacturing base outside Switzerland. While remaining loyal to its Swiss origins and character, Sulzer has a presence in six continents.

The beginnings of Gebrüder Sulzer must rate among the most picturesque of any multinational company. The story began in a little shed in the dried-up town moat of Winterthur, near Zürich, in northeast Switzerland. The grandfather of the company's two official founders had been born in Winterthur in 1751. Salomon Sulzer was the son of the landlord of a coaching inn. Legend has it that Salomon Sulzer had studied theology, and was serving as pastor to a parish by the shores of Lake Zürich, when he developed an interest in the growing trade of brass foundry, and that he eventually abandoned his ministry in order to take up an apprenticeship as a brass founder in Schaffhausen. Documentary evidence is not so specific about his early career, but gives the impression that he was gifted, unorthodox, and adventurous, qualities which were to characterize the careers of his descendants and the development of the Sulzer enterprise.

At the age of 23, Sulzer returned to his home town of Winterthur. Realizing the economic potential, in those early days of Europe's industrial revolution, of a cheaper substitute for copper machinery and tools, he planned to set up his own brass foundry. This intention was opposed by the town council, ostensibly on the grounds that the foundry would constitute a fire hazard, but perhaps, in reality, out of a desire to protect the local coppersmiths from competition.

Eventually, Sulzer was permitted to set up his foundry in the disused moat beyond the town walls. Its early products included fire engines and presses. In the town itself Sulzer opened a turner's workshop for producing articles made of wood, horn, iron, and brass. A house called the Fig Tree accommodated this shop and, above the shop, a flat in which Sulzer and his family lived. The Fig Tree was located in the town's disused moat. At first business was good, and in due course Salomon Sulzer's only son, Johann Jakob Sulzer, born in 1782, began to learn both the foundry and turnery trades. Salomon Sulzer formed social and business contacts with his neighbors, through whom he acquired contacts in the fitting trade and the mining and salt-production industries. He predicted accurately that the future lay in cast iron, which would in its turn be a much cheaper substitute for brass. For the time being, however, the technology for casting iron was not available in Switzerland.

Despite its auspicious start, by the turn of the century Salomon Sulzer's enterprise was beginning to suffer seriously from the effects of the Napoleonic Wars. From 1798 to 1799 Switzerland had been the scene of the struggle of the Russian and Austrian armies against the French. Troops were billeted in Winterthur and trade was next to impossible. Sulzer was forced to accept work at the Dieuze salt works in Lorraine, a job which he found through the good offices of a neighbor. Johann Jakob Sulzer-Neuffert—it was customary in Switzerland for a man to append his wife's surname to his own on marriage—took over the management of the family business, such as it was, in 1806. The following year, his father, Salomon Sulzer, died in Lorraine.

Under the management of Johann Jakob Sulzer, the fortunes of the business began to improve. Fire engines for neighboring villages, saucepans, and bells were the staple products. Salt works abroad were also beginning to buy Sulzer pumps. The foundry moved from the moat to a more prestigious site by the Holdertor, one of the town gates.

Katherina Neuffert, Sulzer's wife, set the tone of the enterprise's treatment of its employees. She wrote that, if her vision of the company's future came true, "the workers will be looked after better here than anywhere else." The Sulzers had two sons, Johann Jakob, born in 1806 and named after his father, and Salomon, born in 1809 and named after his grandfather.

Johann Jakob Sulzer-Neuffert agreed with his father's views about the importance of cast iron. The industrial revolution brought an ever-increasing demand for iron, especially in the form of machinery for cotton mills and the associated machine tools. Already iron foundries had sprung up in France, Germany, and—in particular—England; obviously these were not over-keen to share their expertise with possible competitors, but the Sulzer family connections opened doors.

After the two Sulzer-Neuffert sons had served their apprenticeships in the family firm, they set off, one after the other, to complete their engineering training with a period of travel abroad. Their travels were designed to give them the opportunity to discover all they could about iron, and also about mechanical engineering. Johann Jakob Sulzer Jr. spent several semesters at the Paris Ecole des Arts et Métiers (School of Applied Arts and Crafts), as well as working at the important English-run iron foundry at Chaillot, France. Salomon Sulzer worked in a foundry in Munich.

In the meantime, Johann Jakob Sulzer made his own experiments with iron foundry. He was keen to be among the first Swiss manufacturers of cast iron. In Zürich, a competitor, Escher Wyss, had already stolen a march on him. When the two sons returned, the family felt confident enough to embark on the construction of an iron foundry. Overcoming the difficulties of finding investors prepared to risk their capital in a new type of venture, they opened their iron foundry on a new site in the Zürichstrasse in 1834. That is regarded as the year of the founding of the company, known thereafter as Gebrüder Sulzer (Sulzer Brothers) after young Johann Jakob and Salomon Sulzer.

The sons knew that to make a success of cast-iron manufacture they needed a new type of furnace, the so-called cupola. Their father was reluctant to make the additional investment, so the sons ordered it without his knowledge. After initial disapproval, the older man was forced to recognize the value of the acquisition in terms of both quality and productivity. Subsequent expansions followed a similar pattern, with the elder Johann Jakob being carried along in the wake of his more adventurous sons.

Also at this time there began a tradition of staff training which has persisted at Sulzer. The first workers were foreigners, mostly from Bavaria, but the Sulzer brothers realized that it would be more effective as well as more patriotic to use Swiss engineers. Accordingly, from 1834 onwards Sulzer provided training courses for young apprentices. The system was later formalized, and in 1870, by which time there were as many as 95 apprentices, a works training college was founded. This institution continued to operate under Sulzer management until 1989, when it was handed over for management by the canton, though Sulzer still maintains a supervisory interest.

In 1836, the firm was expanding. In its first two years of trading it had acquired 12 skilled journeymen, all of whom lodged with the young Johann Jakob Sulzer-Hirzel and were provided with meals by his wife, Marie Louise Hirzel, in the forerunner of the works canteen which soon followed. The mortgage on the foundry site had already been repaid. In 1839 a new, larger foundry was built, and the original 1834 building, still in use to this day, became a workshop. The brothers continued to supervise the work in person and the company gained a reputation for quality cast-iron goods. Output grew from 400,000 pounds in 1837 to over 1.6 million pounds after the new foundry began production, to 5 million pounds in 1884.

Johann Jakob Sulzer-Hirzel was always searching for new products, and during this period the company began to make boilers and stoves. A boiler made in 1841 for heating the Winterthur grammar school enhanced the company's reputation for quality and reliability; it remained in service for a century. Sulzer-Hirzel also tried to use the latest production techniques, and in at least one case a novel piece of equipment suggested a new product line. In 1839 the foundry acquired its first steam engine, four horsepower, to replace the two horses that formerly turned the capstan working the bellows. A steam engine was then such a novelty that the citizens of Winterthur paid to come and look at it. Soon it was to become one of Sulzer's main products.

Ten years later, Sulzer-Hirzel went on a trip to England where the manufacture of steam engines was at a more advanced stage. He brought back with him, together with his notebooks of research findings, a British steam engineer by the name of Charles Brown, who, as chief engineer, became the first Sulzer employee to hold a managerial position. Sulzer Brothers, now recognizably an industrial concern rather than a group of craftsmen, began to manufacture its own steam engines, most of them destined to power ships. Soon the engines became the mainstay of the enterprise, and Sulzer also went on to build some of the ships themselves. Steam railways were an obvious progression, and in 1871 Charles Brown went on to found the Swiss Locomotive and Machine Works (SLM) as a parallel enterprise. Among its products was the steam railway on Mount Snowdon in Wales, completed in 1894 and still running. In years to come SLM was to become part of Sulzer, which would also have dealings with Brown Boveri, a company which Brown's son founded in Baden.

As the original brothers withdrew from the day-to-day running of Sulzer, retiring in 1860 and 1872, their sons Albert, Heinrich, and Edward Sulzer took over. They demonstrated the same spirit of innovation. In 1872 the company put on show a new steam engine, the first to incorporate valves, at the Vienna World Fair. After a slow start, due to the economic difficulties that beset Switzerland during the 1870s, this valve-based steam engine led to a period of dramatic growth for Sulzer. Between 1880 and 1895 the number of employees rose from 1,240 to 3,200. Despite the success of the latest engine, the quest for new products did not cease. In 1876 a patent was obtained for a rock-drilling device. From 1877 metal piping and tanks went into production, together with refrigeration equipment.

The first plant outside Winterthur was opened in 1885, at Ludwigshafen, Rhineland-Palatinate, Germany. The chief motivation for this new departure was the desire to circumvent import duties, but it was to be only the first of many foreign installations for Sulzer. The year after its opening, a new heating and ventilation division was added to the German works.

The company continued to flourish through the early years of the 20th century. In 1909, the 75th anniversary of the company's founding, Winterthur and Ludwigshafen between them could boast a work force of 5,500. A new plant had been built at Upper Winterthur. Output of heating systems had increased by a factor of six over the preceding quarter century. Overseas expansion was beginning in earnest; by 1914, sales offices had opened in Milan, Paris, London, Cairo, Moscow, Bucharest, and Kobe, Japan.

New products continued to appear. The company had been working for some years to realize the ideas of Rudolf Diesel, who had taken out patents in 1892 and 1893. Although Sulzer was not the first to build a diesel engine, it had spotted the marine applications of this form of propulsion before any one else. The first diesel-powered oceangoing ship had been launched as far back as 1900, and the first diesel locomotive was to make its maiden run out of Winterthur in 1913; both had Sulzer engines. Sulzer also put the world's first reversible two-cycle marine diesel engine on the market in 1906.

Despite these technical triumphs, some challenging business problems faced the original brothers' grandchildren, who had assumed control during the first decade of the 20th century. Sales of the large steam engine, hitherto the firm's best-selling product, were suffering from the advent of the steam turbine and the electric motor. This threat to the company was mitigated by using the spare capacity arising from the dwindling demand for steam engines to step up output of the profitable new diesel engines.

Sulzer's management, however, felt that considerable capital investment was needed before the company's newer products could become as commercially viable as the old ones had been. In any case, the company was outgrowing its original structure—there were now eight partners. Consequently, on the eve of World War I Gebrüder Sulzer was incorporated and became a limited company, able to raise share capital. Its name appeared on the public register of companies for the first time in June 1914.

During World War I, demand for diesel engines soared. Diesels became the chosen power source for submarines, because of their fuel efficiency and the comparative safety of diesel fuel in storage. Sulzer supplied diesel engines for the submarines of the U.S. Navy, and in 1917 the company granted a license to the Japanese Navy allowing it to upgrade its diesels in accordance with design improvements developed at Winterthur.

All this time, the policy of staff care and training that went back to the days of Katherina Neuffert was sustained, in spite of the fact that employees now numbered over 6,000. Canteens and recreational facilities were provided, and in 1918 a hostel for invalid employees was opened in the mountains. The following year saw Sulzer launch Switzerland's first regular house newspaper.

Some of Sulzer's research and development at this time was aimed at improving compression technology, essential to the diesel but also relevant to industrial evaporation processes. Sulzer installed the world's first thermo-compression plant for industrial evaporation in 1917. Innovations between the wars related not only to diesels and compressors but also to such diverse fields as turbines, funicular railways, and ship propellers.

The company was hit badly by the worldwide Depression of the 1930s. Sulzer's management implemented rigorous cost-saving measures and managed to reduce spending by around 22.5% in the three years from 1936. Staff numbers dropped back to 4,000. In spite of the cost-cutting measures, some assets also had to be sold. The Ludwigshafen works was sold off in 1940, though Sulzer was able to retain its heating and ventilation divisions.

Despite the Depression technical innovations and improvements continued. Industrial weaving machines and gas turbines were among the new products added to the range during this period. The firm also strengthened its overseas capacity, adding manufacturing plants in France and England, and a marketing operation in Argentina. The war years saw further overseas expansion, with the opening of offices in New York and Madrid.

The company's perseverance in the face of the adversity of the Depression and war stood it in good stead during the postwar boom. Subsidiaries were created in Brazil, Johannesburg, Vienna and Norway, during the 1940s and 1950s. During the 1950s, the work force, already back to pre-Depression levels, grew from 6,200 to 10,400. In 1959 Sulzer celebrated its 125th anniversary with the opening of a new foundry at Winterthur, where its site now occupied an area of 330 kilometres square, three times as much as it had 25 years before.

The jubilee year of 1959 also saw the death of Hans Sulzer, who had been a cabinet minister, like his brother Carl Sulzer and uncle Edward Sulzer, as well as the chairman of Gebrüder Sulzer. He was succeeded by a new generation: Hans's son Georg Sulzer became chairman, and Hans's nephew Henry Sulzer also joined the board, along with Herbert Wolfer and Alfred Schaffner. Their aggressive approach to marketing and product development was rewarded in 1963, when Sulzer became worldwide market leader for the low-speed marine diesel engine. By 1966 Sulzer was providing one-third of engine capacity for newly launched oceangoing vessels, representing almost 2.5 million horsepower in total.

The 1960s saw Sulzer strengthening its competitive position through the acquisition of other Swiss firms operating in the same or similar markets. Notable examples included the acquisition in 1961 of the Swiss Locomotive and Machine Works of Winterthur, founded by Charles Brown 90 years previously, and—following the purchase three years earlier of a 50% share—the takeover in 1969 of the Zürich-based engineering firm of Escher Wyss. A temporary joint venture with Brown Boveri of Baden for the manufacture of turbo engines during the 1960s and 1970s ended when the two parent companies divided up the enterprise, with Sulzer retaining the capacity to manufacture the smaller turbines. By 1968 Sulzer had 32,500 workers and a turnover of SFr1.68 billion. The large corporation known today was taking shape.

Although the company was hit by the 1973 oil crisis, its vigorous worldwide growth continued into the 1980s. Weaving machine plants were built in Japan and in the United States, while domestic output of these machines also grew. Also in Japan, a fruitful and enduring joint venture with Toyoda Automatic Loom Works was established in the 1970s. Plants for pump manufacture in the Netherlands, West Germany, Brazil, and South Africa enabled Sulzer to meet local requirements better.

The Sulzer family had been quick to realize the importance of computerization and was building the foundations for its current electronics division as early as 1962. In 1969 it acquired an interest in ELMA Electronic, now a wholly owned subsidiary of Sulzer. Industrial automation was the focus of its early work, although it now makes electronic components as well as robotic systems, both for its own use and for sale to customers. A corporate computer center opened to serve the company's administrative functions in 1972.

Both in its product lines and in its production methods, Sulzer has continued to innovate—its research-and-development budget was SFr228 million in 1989. The company claims to have the most advanced foundry in Europe. Today the forge is robotically controlled and casting too is computerized. The machine shop boasts the world's largest longitudinal milling machine.

In 1988 Sulzer undertook a radical review of its business situation and strategy. Despite its valuable asset base the company recognized the need to improve profitability. Three options were considered: reorganization, further diversification, or focusing on the strongest areas of the business. This third option was adopted, as the one with the greatest long-term potential.

Accordingly, Sulzer began a period of reshaping, during which it began developing what it calls its pillar businesses, those in which profitability and market share are outstanding and where the company is highly regarded by its business partners. These pillar businesses consist of construction services, such as air conditioning and refrigeration—represented by the building and construction service group with 1989 turnover of SFr1.5 billion; weaving machines—led by the Sulzer Rüti Group, whose 1989 turnover was SFr1.1 billion; and medical engineering—Sulzermedica, with SFr600 million in 1989 turnover. The area of medical engineering, with products such as pacemakers, defibrillators, and artificial heart valves and hip joints, is being expanded through acquisition; 1989 saw three important purchases in this field—Intermedics in the United States, and in Switzerland Allo Pro and a majority shareholding in Protek. Apart from the three existing pillar businesses, Sulzer planned to nurture certain promising divisions, largely through internal growth, during the 1990s. These potential pillar businesses include chemical engineering, paper machinery, and surface technology.

Less profitable areas are under scrutiny and will be sold off if they cannot be made profitable within a time limit. Gas turbines, knitting machines, and the historic diesel engines are among the areas in which disinvestment has taken place. The pumps, refrigeration, and turbo compressor divisions have begun to show signs of improving profitability, however.

This focus on profitable business areas is only one of five key objectives in Sulzer's strategy for the 1990s, as summarized by Fritz Fahrni—since 1988 president of corporate executive management. Other objectives are: improvement of the quality of the end product; a motivated work force, both technical and managerial; satisfied shareholders, a corollary of a profitable portfolio; and a dynamic response to the requirements of a changing marketplace.

Sulzer believes that its key objectives will be best achieved through a decentralized company structure, which will encourage a spirit of entrepreneurship. Business units will be strategically independent, but will receive support from the central organization in terms of the management of human and financial resources, research-and-development services, and international marketing.

Georg Sulzer retired as chairman in 1981; since the retirement of Peter Sulzer in 1989 there have been no Sulzers on the board. Although no longer family run, Gebrüder Sulzer continues to bear the hallmark of the Sulzer family, maintaining its position not only by research to ensure that it is at the leading edge of technology, but also by shrewdly assessing and quickly adapting to the changing marketplace, entering into alliances with other firms when necessary.

A demonstration of this policy came in July 1990 when Sulzer, as the world's second-largest diesel manufacturer, announced the formation of New Sulzer Diesel, a cooperative venture with other companies from West and East Europe to safeguard the European diesel industry against competition from the Far East. The chairman of the board and executive president of this company is Peter Sulzer. By maintaining its traditions of nurturing and developing staff, and ensuring that its products measure up to the Swiss reputation for quality workmanship, Sulzer should ensure that it enters the 21st century in good shape.

Prinicpal Subsidiaries: Swiss Locomotive and Machine Works (99.6%); Sulzer-Escher Wyss Ltd. (99.9%); Bell Engineering Works Ltd. (78.9%); Sulzer-Burckhardt Engineering Works Ltd.; Plasma-Tecknik AG; Gebrüder Sulzer Holding GmbH (Germany); Compagnie de Construction Mécanique Sulzer (France, 99.9%); Chauffage et Climatisation Sulzer S.A. (France, 99.9%); De Pretto-Escher Wyss s.r.l. (Italy); Sulzer Italia S.p.A. (Italy); Sulzer (UK) Holdings Ltd.; Sulzer España, S.A. (Spain); Sulzer Bros. Inc. (U.S.A.); Sulzer do Brasil S.A. (Brazil); Sulzer Bombas e Compressores S.A. (Brazil); Toyoda-Sulzer Sales Ltd. (Japan, 51%); Toyoda-Sulzer Manufacturing Ltd. (Japan, 49%).

Further Reading: *Das Jubiläumsiahr 1984 im Rückblick,* Winterthur, Sulzer, 1984; Labhart, Walter, *Schweizer Pioniere der Wirtschaft und Technik,* Zürich, Verein für wirtschaftshistorische Studien, 1984; *Die Berufsschule Sulzer im Rahmen der Lehrlingsausbildung 1870–1989,* Winterthur, Sulzer, 1989; ''Ein Technologiekonzern auf dem Weg in die 90er Jahre,'' *zfo* Number 2, 1990; Knobel, Bruno, *A World-Wide Company is Born,* Winterthur, Sulzer, [n.d.].

—Alison Classe and Olive Classe

SUMITOMO HEAVY INDUSTRIES, LTD.

Shin-Ohtemachi Building
2-1, Ohtemachi 2-chome
Chiyoda-ku, Tokyo 100
Japan
(03) 3245-4321
Fax: (03) 3245-4337

Public Company
Incorporated: 1934 as Sumitomo Machine Manufacturing Co., Ltd.
Employees: 6,000
Sales: ¥369.37 billion (US$2.57 billion)
Stock Exchanges: Tokyo Osaka Nagoya Frankfurt

Sumitomo Heavy Industries, one of the major companies affiliated with the Sumitomo Group of Japan, manufactures industrial machinery and equipment, and is one of Japan's foremost shipbuilders. It is also the leading maker of mass-production machinery, including injection molding machines and actuators.

The Sumitomo Group traces its origins to the 17th century when Masatomo Sumitomo opened a medicine and book shop in Kyoto and laid the foundation for the family's business involvement over future generations. Upon Sumitomo's death in 1652, his brother-in-law, Riemon Soga, became head of the Sumitomo family. Soga's earlier experience as an apprentice in a copper refinery influenced the company to shift toward that industry. In 1590 Soga had opened his own shop in Kyoto called the Izumiya and adopted the *igeta*, or well frame, symbol as Izumiya's logo. The *igeta* was registered as the trademark for the Sumitomo Group in 1885 and later adopted by Sumitomo Heavy Industries and most of the other affiliates.

By 1888, the company's mining operations had expanded sufficiently to warrant the opening of a machinery production and repair shop at Sumitomo's Besshi copper mine. In 1897 Sumitomo established the Uraga Dock Company for shipbuilding. In 1934 the Besshi machine shop was merged with Uraga Dock to form Sumitomo Machine Manufacturing Company, which functioned as a subsidiary of the Sumitomo *zaibatsu*, or conglomerate.

Over the next 11 years, the company's name was changed several times, from Sumitomo Machine Manufacturing Company to Sumitomo Machinery Company, in 1940, and to Shikoku Machinery Company, in 1945. As one of Japan's leading industrial concerns, the Sumitomo *zaibatsu* was disrupted significantly by military action during World War II. After 1945, the *zaibatsu* was broken up into independent companies, in compliance with the orders of the Supreme Commander of Allied Powers (SCAP). These orders gradually were relaxed over the next decade, allowing the Sumitomo affiliates to reestablish ties with each other and coordinate planning activities.

In 1952, Shikoku Machinery Company again became Sumitomo Machinery Company. In 1957, Sumitomo Machinery opened its first overseas office, in New York City. In 1959, it established its Nagoya manufacturing plant and also incorporated Shin Nippon Machine Manufacturing to produce turbines, pumps, fasteners, blowers, and heat exchangers.

Sumitomo Machinery opened Japan Air Filter Company, Ltd. in 1960 to produce air purifying equipment and dust collectors. In 1962, the company formed the Hiratsuka Research Laboratory to develop cryogenic technology. Overseas expansion continued over the next several years, with the opening of a London office in 1964 and the establishment of Sumitomo Machinery Corporation of America in 1966, including a production plant for power-transmission equipment in New Jersey. The plant was transferred to a larger facility in Virginia in 1988. In 1969 Sumitomo Machinery Company merged with Uraga Heavy Industries to form Sumitomo Heavy Industries.

The 1970s were a period of consistent growth and development for Sumitomo. It incorporated Sumitomo Jukikai Environment in 1971 to build water-treatment plants and manufacture industrial waste-disposal equipment. After completing the world's largest forging press in 1971, the company inaugurated the Oppama Shipyard and Toyo Works in 1972 and incorporated Lightwell Company in 1973 to design and produce data-processing equipment and software. Sumitomo established its Systems Research Laboratory in 1975.

Internationally, Sumitomo acquired an interest in Cyclo Getriebebau Lorenz Braren GmbH in West Germany and established Sumitomo Maquinas Pesadas do Brasil in 1974. It opened an office in Singapore in 1979. New products included the first cyclotron medical diagnosis system in 1972. Sumitomo also launched Japan's first supertanker in 1975.

In 1980 Sumitomo launched Japan's first gas turbine naval escort ship, and in 1982 completed the *Kinokawa Maru*, the world's first voice-controlled ship. The company also received an order for the *Nippon Maru*, Japan's first original-design schooner, for training merchant mariners. The *Nippon Maru* was launched in 1984.

These developments were bittersweet, however. Stagnation and excessive capacity in the shipbuilding industry forced Sumitomo to deliver its ships at a loss throughout most of the decade, a disappointment when compared to the profits of the previous ten years. Only the continued growth of Sumitomo's machinery divisions, the construction boom in Japan, and internal cost reductions enabled the company to improve profits.

The company focused on technology and software engineering during the 1980s. It entered the business of electron beam accelerators in 1986 by buying Radiation Dynamics. The following year Sumitomo began developing the world's smallest syncotron for making computer chips. This operation brought together the cryogenic, vacuum, superconducting, and accelerating technologies in which Sumitomo had gained expertise since the establishment of the Hiratsuka Research Laboratory. In 1987, Osaka University ordered a large cyclotron from Sumitomo. In 1989 Sumitomo entered a joint agreement with CGR-MeV, of France, to work on high-energy linear accelerators.

The firm incorporated Sumitomo Heavy Industries Forging in 1980 to manufacture casting and forging equipment and Sumitomo (S.H.I.) Construction Machinery Company in 1986 to manufacture construction equipment. Several acquisitions during the 1980s strengthened the company's base of operations. These include Nittoku Metal Industries, Ltd., in 1984, which led to the establishment of the precision-products group; Radiation Dynamics in 1986, Lumonics Inc. of Canada, the largest laser equipment manufacturer in the world, in 1988; and RPC Industries of San Francisco, California, a manufacturer of low-energy machines, in 1989. Sumitomo also entered the real estate business in 1988 to redevelop idle facilities into more profitable endeavors. The company incorporated SHI Resort Development Company the following year, to turn its old Kawama works site into a seaside resort area.

In 1989 Shigeru Gohda was named company chairman and Masataka Kubo was named president. Sumitomo Heavy Industries continues to focus on its main manufacturing areas, producing iron and steel production systems, presses, loading and unloading systems, physical distribution systems, printing machines, precision dies, aircraft components, heavy steel structures, and other products. Future strategies for growth center on expanding the company's involvement in advanced fields such as semiconductor-manufacturing systems, accelerator science and technology, cryogenics and superconductivity technology, biotechnology, nuclear engineering, and mechatronics. Sumitomo plans to expand its international presence through export sales, joint ventures, and technology transfer.

Principal Subsidiaries: Shin Nippon Machine Mfg., Ltd.; Sumitomo Heavy Industries Forging, Ltd.; Sumitomo Jukikai Environment, Inc.; Japan Air Filter Co., Ltd.; Sumitomo (S.H.I.) Construction Machinery Co., Ltd.; Lightwell Co., Ltd.

Further Reading: A Brief History of Sumitomo, Tokyo, Sumitomo Corporation, 1990; *The Sumitomo Group*, Tokyo, Sumitomo Corporation, [n.d.].

—Sandy Schusteff

TOYODA AUTOMATIC LOOM WORKS, LTD.

2-1, Toyoda-cho
Kariya-City, Aichi 448
Japan
(0566) 22-2511
Fax: (0566) 23-3255

Public Company
Incorporated: 1926
Employees: 6,837
Sales: ¥437.44 billion (US$3.04 billion)
Stock Exchanges: Tokyo Osaka Nagoya

Toyoda Automatic Loom Works (Loom Works) is the originator of the Toyota Group of companies and is recognized as a diversified corporation whose central activities include automobile assembly and the manufacture of automobile components, industrial vehicles, and textile machinery. Founded in the 1920s to produce and sell automatic looms, the company is one of Japan's larger integrated manufacturers of textile machinery, producing both weaving and spinning machines, and the largest domestic manufacturer of forklift trucks. The company manufactures engines for Toyota Motor Corporation passenger cars in addition to diesel engines for the industrial vehicles it produces, which are marketed under the Toyota name.

Since World War II, Loom Works's focus has shifted gradually from textile machinery to automobiles, with a growing percentage of its activities involving consignment work for Toyota, which owns better than 20% of Loom Works's stock. In the past two decades Loom Works has established joint ventures in the United States with other Toyota Group members for the local production of two of its principal products, air conditioner compressors and industrial vehicles. It also has attracted compressor-production work from major U.S. automobile manufacturers. Additions to its U.S. production facilities exemplify Loom Works's future plans, which call for increased manufacturing and sales activities in the U.S. market.

Toyoda Automatic Loom Works owes its original emphasis to Sakichi Toyoda, a well-known Japanese inventor and entrepreneur who perfected Japan's first power-driven loom in 1897. During the next three decades Toyoda went on to acquire 84 patents while developing 35 loom models.

Prior to World War I, Toyoda was involved in the formation of a number of small thread-producing and textile-machinery factories and companies, but it was the war that helped firmly establish the beginning of the Toyoda empire by fueling an economic boom for spinning mills. Based on a factory he had built a few years earlier, Toyoda established Toyoda Spinning and Weaving, in 1918 to produce high-quality thread for the automatic loom he was developing. Three years later Toyoda established Toyoda Spinning and Weaving Works, in Shanghai.

In 1925 Toyoda perfected an automatic loom designed for mass production, and installed 320 automatic looms in a pilot plant in Nagoya. In 1926 he separated the loom-production department of Toyoda Spinning and Weaving and established Toyoda Automatic Loom Works in Kariya, Japan, to concentrate on the production of automatic looms.

Capitalized at ¥1 million, the new company soon became the main firm of the Toyoda family's enterprises. Toyoda's eldest son by adoption, Risaburo Toyoda, was named president, and Kiichiro Toyoda, Sakichi Toyoda's oldest natural son, was named managing director in charge of loom production. Sakichi Toyoda had been unable to make his natural son, Kiichiro, president of Loom Works and heir to the family's fortune because of Sakichi's adoption in 1915 of Risaburo, the husband of his oldest daughter and younger brother of Kazuo Kodama, who was head of the Mitsui Trading branch in Nagoya. Sakichi Toyoda had become indebted to Kazuo Kodama when Mistui Trading financed his 1914 move into cotton spinning.

In 1927 construction of a foundry, iron works, and woodwork shop near the Loom Works's headquarters was completed, and the company began production and sales of the Toyoda G-Type Automatic Loom. The new looms were sold for ¥630, or about three times the cost of conventional looms because one worker could operate 25 of the Toyoda looms at a time. Sales quickly took off as textile producers automated their operations in order to cut production costs.

Sakichi Toyoda had acquired both domestic and overseas patent rights for his automatic loom, and in 1929 he agreed to sell all of those rights excluding those for Japan, China, and the United States. The Platt Brothers of Great Britain, the world's largest manufacturer of spinning and weaving machinery, purchased the patents for £100,000, worth about ¥1 million in Japan. Sakichi Toyoda then gave the entire sum to his son Kiichiro to invest in automobile research. Sakichi Toyoda died a year after he sold his automatic loom patents, leaving his goal of producing automobiles in the hands of Kiichiro Toyoda.

Kiichiro Toyoda, a mechanical engineer who had studied at the University of Tokyo, handled most of the initial engineering work on the study of automobiles. In 1930, he set aside a corner of the Loom Works plant for his research and began working on the development of a small gasoline engine. Kiichiro Toyoda was also instrumental in the development of several new products that Loom Works began manufacturing that year, including high-draft spinning frames, a carding machine, and other machines used in raw textile spinning processes.

In 1931 Loom Works began buying and testing engine components made by foreign producers, while seeking domestic firms that could copy parts. Risaburo Toyoda initially viewed the investment in automobile research as risky, but Kiichiro Toyoda maintained enough power in the company to establish a Loom Works automobile division in 1933. Kiichiro Toyoda began recruiting Japanese automobile experts, and later that year the automobile division purchased a new Chevrolet car and began disassembling it to analyze the vehicle's components. By the end of 1933, Kiichiro Toyoda's staff completed a prototype motorcycle engine.

In 1934 Kiichiro Toyoda convinced stockholders to raise the capitalization of the company to ¥3 million and add automobile and steel manufacturing to the businesses included in Loom Works articles of incorporation. Soon afterwards, the company began construction of a pilot automobile plant and steel mill within the Loom Works's compound.

With increased funding, automobile research and production activities were stepped up in 1934. The company's engine-casting specialist, Suda Takatoshi, was dispatched to the United States to study automobile factories, materials, and the manufacturing of components. By the end of the year, Loom Works had developed the Model A-1 engine, its first prototype automobile engine.

In May 1935 Loom Works completed its first prototype passenger car, the Model A1, comprised of a Chrysler body and many parts from Ford and Chevrolet automobiles. About the same time, the Japanese government began to firm up particulars of the pending Bill Concerning the Manufacture of Motor Vehicles, which was being designed to promote domestic production of automobiles. Kiichiro Toyoda learned that the bill would place an emphasis on the production of trucks, and Loom Works quickly began trial development of trucks. Full-scale production of motor vehicles was initiated in July 1935, and the following month stockholders agreed to double the company's capitalization to ¥6 million to help fund increased automobile activities. In September the prototype Model G1 truck was completed. Loom Works established an automobile sales department in 1935, and hired Shotaro Kamiya, a former executive at General Motors's Japan subsidiary, to head up the sales efforts.

In 1936 the Bill Concerning the Manufacture of Motor Vehicles became law, and Loom Works was licensed as one of two automobile-production companies in Japan. Construction of a new automobile-assembly plant on land near the Loom Works's facilities was completed in May 1936 and included an electronics department, which later became Nippondenso Company. That same year officials changed the name of its automobile from Toyoda to Toyota, believing the new name was easier to pronounce and would generate greater advertising appeal.

By the end of 1936 Loom Works's automobile products included the Model AA passenger car; and open-top version of the Model AA called the AB Phaeton; the Model GA truck, which was an improved version of the G1; and the Model DA bus chassis.

Once the 1936 automobile industry law was approved, Risaburo Toyoda threw his support behind the company's automobile operations, believing the venture could be profitable. Construction of an automobile plant in Koromo followed, but working capital was short. In March 1937 Loom Works's stockholders agreed to separate the automobile division and form the Toyota Motor Corporation, (TMC) in a move to attract additional investors. Risaburo Toyoda was named TMC president, and Kiichiro Toyoda was named executive vice president.

After Japan entered World War II in 1938, Loom Works manufactured parts for TMC for a brief period. Later that year, Loom Works, as other Japanese industries, came under government control, and it began performing ordnance work for the military. In 1939 Loom Works expanded its steel works plant and then began construction of a new steel mill. The following year the steel division was separated from Loom Works, and Toyoda Steel Works, now Aichi Steel Works, was established. Loom Works transferred all its steel equipment and facilities to the new company as an investment.

In 1941 Risaburo Toyoda became chairman of TMC, and Kiichiro Toyoda was named president. By that time TMC had become the nucleus of the Toyota Group, and Kiichiro Toyoda set up a planning council to serve as a liaison group between TMC, Toyoda Steel Works, and Toyoda Machine Works—a machinery-producing factory developed by Toyota in 1937 and spun off as an independent company earlier in 1941. In 1944 Loom Works established a plant in Obu to manufacture castings for automotive parts, including compressor cylinders, cylinder blocks, and crankshafts.

Following World War II Loom Works began taking parts orders from TMC to fill the gap left by ordnance work. Loom Works's textile business began picking up after a 1947 restoration policy put a rush on cotton-spinning-machinery orders, and about this same time the company abandoned its parts work for TMC.

Risaburo Toyoda became Loom Works's first chairman in 1948, and Taizo Ishida was named president. Ishida had served Loom Works as a managing director and the company's first representative on the TMC planning council. In 1949 Loom Works went public and listed its stock on the Tokyo, Nogoya, and Osaka stock exchanges.

While business blossomed for Loom Works in the early postwar years, a cut-off of Reconstruction Finance Bank loans in 1949 and growing recessionary conditions in the automobile industry had edged TMC ever-closer to the brink of bankruptcy during the same span. In 1950 TMC announced it would reduce personnel by a third, and a two-month strike ensued. The labor dispute was resolved after Kiichiro Toyoda and other top executives agreed to take responsibility for the automaker's financial plight, and voluntary resignations from laborers followed.

Taizo Ishida agreed to replace Kiichiro Toyoda as TMC president, while maintaining similar duties at Loom Works. While Ishida knew little about automobile production at the time, he realized that Loom Works's future was closely tied to that of TMC, while Toyota Group members recognized that Ishida had been successful in rebuilding Loom Works after World War II.

Ishida initially agreed to serve as TMC president only temporarily, with Kiichiro Toyoda expected to resume his former post once the automaker's financial position had improved; but in 1952 Kiichiro Toyoda died, and Ishida agreed to remain as chief executive of TMC to carry out Kiichiro Toyoda's program of small-car development. That same year Risaburo Toyoda died, leaving Loom Works without a chairman for the next 17 years.

In 1952 Loom Works began manufacturing engines and stamping dies for Toyota automobiles. In 1953, the company established a new plant in Kyowa to manufacture engines and assemble vehicles for Toyota. That same year, on the recommendation of TMC Managing Director Eiji Toyoda, Loom Works initiated the development of forklift vehicles.

In 1955 Loom Works completed its first prototype forklift, a one-ton machine powered by a Type-S engine. The following year the company began manufacturing forklifts, and Toyota Motor Sales Company, formed in 1950 as a sales affiliate for TMC, announced it would market the new forklift and sell the product under the brand name Toyota Forklift.

In 1960 Loom Works began manufacturing automobile air conditioner compressors. That same year, the company established a forklift assembly line at its Kyowa plant and expanded its product line there to include 11 types of forklifts, as well as towing tractors and shovel loaders. Toyota Motor Sales (TMS) began appointing Toyota forklift dealers exclusively to handle industrial vehicles in 1961. By the end of the year Loom Works had climbed to number one in the domestic forklift market. In 1966 Loom Works secured its first major overseas forklift contract, a 188-machine order from the Singapore Port Authority.

Loom Works opened a plant in Nagakusa for the assembly of small commercial vehicles in 1967. In the same year the company began looking outside the Toyota Group for technical collaborations that could improve its fiber machinery and looms; it entered into an agreement with Rieter Machine Works, of Switzerland, for the production of manmade-fiber machinery. The following year Loom Works produced its first open-end spinning machine. In 1968 the Loom Works agreed to a technical tie-in for loom development with Ruti Machinery Works, of Switzerland. In 1969 Ishida was named chairman, a post that had been vacant since the death of Risaburo Toyoda, and Keiji Gonda was named president.

In 1970 Loom Works opened its 84-acre Takahama plant. With a capacity to produce 30,000 units a year, it was the largest factory in the world exclusively devoted to the production of industrial vehicles. In 1971 Loom Works and Sulzer Brothers, of Switzerland, formed the joint venture Toyoda-Sulzer Company, to produce shuttleless projectile looms. That same year, Loom Works joined with George Fischer, Ltd., in a technical tie-in for the production of foundry equipment.

The management of Loom Works returned to the Toyoda family in 1973, when Yoshitoshi Toyoda, nephew of Sakichi Toyoda, replaced Gonda as president. Increased Toyota Group involvement with Loom Works activities followed, and that same year TMS established an overseas industrial-vehicle department, further strengthening marketing efforts of Loom Works–produced industrial vehicles. TMC and Loom Works established the joint venture Toyoda Industrial Trucks U.S.A., in 1974, to manufacture and sell industrial trucks in the United States

By 1975 Loom Works's cumulative production of industrial vehicles had reached 200,000 and the cumulative production of commercial vehicles had reached 500,000. Loom Works began manufacturing compressors for Chrysler and Ford in 1977, and within a year cumulative production of compressors had topped five million units.

In 1978 Loom Works began manufacturing shuttleless rapier looms and also began making the Starlet passenger car for TMC. Sales of open-end spinning machines also got a boost in 1979 when the Chinese government agreed to purchase 10,000 machines in a contract worth about ¥1.6 billion. Between 1977 and 1980, overseas production and marketing activities, as well as increased consignments from TMC, helped push Loom Works's net sales from ¥140.5 billion to ¥208.4 billion while net profits rose from ¥5.6 billion to ¥9.8 billion.

In 1980 Loom Works began manufacturing quieter air-jet looms, known as JA models, in a new facility built on the premises of its main Kariya plant. That same year the company established its first U.S. subsidiary, Toyoda Textile Machinery. Based in Charlotte, North Carolina, the subsidiary was formed to promote sales of the new air-jet looms in the U.S. market.

In a 1980 move to strengthen the sales system of industrial vehicles, Loom Works and TMC each purchased 20% of Tomen Transportgerate, a German company involved in import and sale of Toyota industrial vehicles. Following the 1982 merger of TMC and TMS, Toyota engineers began working in product development at Loom Works, where sales of industrial vehicles had been sluggish since the oil crises of the 1970s. In 1982 Loom Works opened its Hekinan plant and began manufacturing a new diesel engine, which was developed with the assistance of TMC earlier that year.

While sales continued to rise, Loom Works's profits slipped in 1982 and were sluggish in 1983, due in part to increased fixed costs and a decrease in Toyota automobile consignments. In 1984 Toyota Industrial Trucks, U.S.A. merged with TMS, strengthening the joint venture's sales capacity by adding new staff and managerial resources. The product line was further diversified to include such construction vehicles as a skid steer loader.

Increased sales of industrial vehicles and a continuous rise in compressor exports, including 750,000 compressors per year going to Ford, helped Loom Works's profit rise above ¥10 billion in 1985. In 1985 Loom Works founded an electronics division at its Kyowa plant, for long-term research-and-development activities beyond the scope of other divisions. That same year the company developed an automatic guided vehicle (AGV) equipped with a microcomputer, and then installed the AGV, along with industrial robots, at its forklift-producing Takahama plant as part of a new, flexible manufacturing system. In recognition of its efforts to improve quality on a company- wide basis, a year later Loom Works received the prestigious Deming Award for quality control.

In 1986 Loom Works's profits leaped by nearly ¥2 billion. The following year, Loom Works was one of seven Japanese forklift manufacturers to be fined a dumping penalty by the U.S. Commerce Department. In 1987, profits dipped because of rapid appreciation of the yen, and remained sluggish the following year. In response to that appreciation, and to avoid further dumping penalties, Loom Works and TMC in 1988 chose Columbus, Indiana, as a site to establish their joint venture, Toyota Industrial Equipment Manufacturing. Loom Works received 80% ownership in the forklift manufacturing corporation.

In 1988 Loom Works's cumulative production of compressors topped 40 million units, with three-quarters of those units manufactured the six previous years. After securing compressor business with General Motors, in 1989 Loom Works and Nippondenso Company, another Toyota Group member, established the 50-50 joint venture, Michigan Automotive Compressor, Inc. The new company was set up in Jackson, Michigan, for the manufacture of compressors and magnetic clutches. That same year Gentaro Tsuji was named chairman, filling a position that had been vacant for 15 years.

Beefed-up production of textile machinery, industrial vehicles, and compressors helped profits rebound in 1989 to a new high of ¥12.9 billion. Loom Works closed the decade with vehicle assembly representing 42% of sales, while the manufacture of industrial vehicles and compressors each accounted for nearly one-quarter of all sales. The manufacture of engines accounted for 15% of all revenues, and textile machinery contributed nearly 10% of revenues.

Loom Works's goals call for increased overseas production and sales efforts, including local production of compressors and industrial vehicles in the United States. In 1990 both Michigan Automotive Compressor and Toyota Industrial Equipment Manufacturing began production in accordance with those goals. The company planned research-and-development activities in electronics, in a move to improve factory efficiency and existing products.

Principal Subsidiaries: Michigan Automotive Compressor, Inc. (U.S.A., 50%); Toyoda Industrial Equipment Manufacturing, Inc. (U.S.A., 80%); Toyoda Textile Machinery, Inc. (U.S.A.); Tomen Transportgerate GmbH (Germany, 20%).

Further Reading: Kamiya, Shotaro, *My Life With Toyota,* Toyota City, Toyota Motor Sales Company Ltd., 1976; Cusumano, Michael A., *The Japanese Automobile Industry: Technology and Management at Nissan and Toyota,* Cambridge, The Council on East Asian Studies, Harvard University, 1985; Toyoda, Eiji, *Toyota: Fifty Years In Motion,* Tokyo, Toyota Motor Company, 1987; *Toyota: A History of the First 50 Years,* Toyota City, Toyota Motor Corporation, 1988.

—Roger W. Rouland

TRINOVA®

TRINOVA CORPORATION

3000 Strayer
Maumee, Ohio 43537
U.S.A.
(419) 867-2200
Fax: (419) 867-2390

Public Company
Incorporated: 1916 as Libbey-Owens Sheet Glass Company
Employees: 21,597
Sales: $1.94 billion
Stock Exchanges: New York Midwest Pacific London Frankfurt

Until 1986 TRINOVA Corporation was known as Libbey-Owens-Ford, a firm with deep roots in the history of U.S. glassmaking and for many years the sole supplier to General Motors of windshields and other glass products. In 1986, however, Libbey-Owens-Ford completed its metamorphosis from glassmaker to diversified component manufacturer by selling off its glass facilities and adopting a name suggested by the tripartite structure of its remaining operating subsidiaries: Aeroquip Corporation, Vickers Incorporated, and Sterling Engineered Products. These have since been reduced to two, Vickers and Aeroquip which between them fabricate a wide variety of power- and motion-control components for military, aerospace, and general industrial uses. Aeroquip has made a big business out of fluid-conveying-system parts; it manufactures such things as flexible hose, V-band couplings, refrigeration components, and fittings and assemblies. Vickers supplies a wide range of pumps, motors and cylinders, valves, and diagnostic monitoring devices. The power- and motion-control business produces about 80% of TRINOVA's sales. The remainder is generated by a plastics division—formerly Sterling Engineered Products—under the direction of Aeroquip. Plastics sales are mostly to the auto industry. The absence of glass manufacturing in TRINOVA's profile is remarkable—few companies have so successfully managed to shift out of the industry in which they were founded and into a unrelated field while continuing to grow and prosper.

TRINOVA's history is the story of three separate entities: Libbey-Owens-Ford, Aeroquip, and Vickers. The oldest of this trio is Libbey-Owens-Ford, which was itself created by the 1930 merger of two much older firms, Libbey-Owens Sheet Glass and the Edward Ford Plate Glass Company. Libbey-Owens was built by two men who shared a fascination with the manufacture of glass.

Edward D. Libbey was born in 1854 to a family already involved in a glass business, the New England Glass Company. When Libbey was 20 he joined the family firm, gradually taking on increasing responsibilities until he assumed control of the company in 1883. In order to find more economical sources of raw material, and perhaps out of a desire to set up his own shop, in 1888 Libbey moved west and founded the Libbey Glass Company in Toledo, Ohio. Libbey Glass soon made its mark in the manufacture of expensive cut-glass tableware, which achieved a certain cachet in the early 1890s.

Fashionable glassware did not prove especially profitable, however, and by 1893 Libbey Glass was in financial trouble. In that year Edward Libbey took advantage of the Chicago World's Fair. In a desperate effort to attract a wider market, he mounted an enormously expensive exhibit at the fair; the advertising worked. The exhibit impressed enough buyers to rejuvenate sales and pull Libbey out of its crisis, solidifying the company's reputation as a maker of elegant tableware.

In the meantime, Edward Libbey had hired a young plant manager who soon demonstrated a remarkable knack for invention. Michael J. Owens learned glassmaking from the ground up—at age ten he was already working in a glass plant in Wheeling, West Virginia, and was still a young man when he began work for Libbey in 1888. Owens was a man of great mechanical aptitude, and before long Libbey had assigned him a number of projects designed to automate the glassmaking process. Two of these became particularly important—a machine that automatically formed glass tumblers, and another that shaped glass bottles with equal speed and precision. In an age of widespread bottle usage, the latter invention had a great impact on manufacturing standards in the glass industry.

Aided by these production breakthroughs, Libbey Glass prospered through the early years of the 20th century. It was not until 1912, however, that Libbey and Owens latched onto the technique that launched the company's rapid growth. In that year the two men began working with Irwin Colburn on that man's design for a method to produce window glass in a single, continuous sheet. Colburn had already spent years developing his process, and Libbey and Owens struggled for an additional four years before the technique was ready for use. By 1916, however, the three men had succeeded in drawing a continuous, flat sheet of uniform glass from a vat of molten materials. The sheet could later be polished and cut to fit any window frame. To capitalize on their unique achievement Libbey formed a new company, this time called Libbey-Owens Sheet Glass. A new plant for sheet glass production was built in Charleston, West Virginia, and Libbey salesmen were soon trumpeting the breakthrough to their customers. Owens went on to help found Owens Illinois Corporation.

Libbey-Owens enjoyed unusually vigorous expansion during the following decade, its competitive advantage combining with a robust U.S. economy to push sales far beyond expectations. The 1929 stock market crash brought all such rosy reports to an immediate end, however, and was perhaps responsible for Libbey-Owens's decision to join forces in 1930 with another important glass manufacturer, the Edward Ford Plate Glass Company of nearby Rossford, Ohio.

The Ford family already had a place in American glass-industry history. Edward Ford's father, John B. Ford, organized the first plate-glass manufacturing company in the United States in 1867. Their New Albany, Indiana plant was soon joined by others in Louisville, Kentucky and Jeffersonville, Indiana, but the competition of more experienced European glassmakers proved to be too much for Ford, which eventually went bankrupt. Edward Ford and his sons moved to Creighton, Pennsylvania, where in 1880 they founded a second glass company, the forerunner of PPG Industries (Pittsburgh Plate Glass Company). After managing that company for ten years, Ford moved to Ohio. In 1898 Ford bought 173 acres of land along the Maumee River outside Toledo, Ohio and built the largest single-structure plate glass plant in the country. Like many other early industrialists, Ford added a town to his factory, naming it Rossford after his wife and himself.

When the Great Depression hit, Ford and Libbey-Owens managers felt that a merger would help the companies survive, and in 1930 the companies combined. Libbey-Owens-Ford Glass Company (LOF) soon took its place as one of the top manufacturers of flat glass in the country, but of greater long-term significance was the company's growing intimacy with General Motors (GM) and the automotive business.

With headquarters only 100 miles from Detroit, LOF was attracted by the enormous glass requirements of the big automakers, and had soon landed its first orders with GM. GM made LOF its sole supplier of windshields and incidental glass accessories, a relationship which was maintained for the next 30 years. During that time, LOF went from being a diversified maker of glass products sold across the country to a specialized supplier to one vast customer.

Through this relationship LOF grew to be a giant itself. Indeed, with the automaker supplying about half of total sales, LOF expanded right along with GM during the boom decade of the 1950s, when the automobile became ubiquitous throughout the United States. By 1959 sales had topped $300 million and, barring a calamity at GM, the future appeared secure. Glassmaking had become a mature industry, however, with profit margins pared to the bone and an increasing number of effective competitors. Many of LOF's competitors were Japanese, and they exerted a strong downward pressure on industry price levels. In addition, in 1961 GM finally decided that having a single glass supplier was not wise and began to farm out a small but growing portion of its orders to LOF's rival, Pittsburgh Plate Glass.

The combination of these factors made the 1960s difficult for LOF. From 1959's peak of $307 million, sales had dropped to $222 million by 1961 and remained well below expectations until 1967. The slump awoke LOF management to the danger inherent in the company's relationship with GM, and they decided to begin a serious diversification program. In 1965 LOF made its first purchase outside the glass field, buying Modern Patterns and Plastics, a maker of precision tools and jigs. The company's first substantial acquisition was the 1968 purchase of Aeroquip Corporation of nearby Jackson, Michigan. At the time of its sale, Aeroquip boasted 25 plants and some 4,480 employees, sales of $123 million, and a reputation as a leader in its field— fluid conveying components.

Aeroquip was founded in 1940 by Peter F. Hurst, a Bavarian mechanical engineer. Hurst had been forced to leave his home in Berlin during World War II, and he immigrated to the United States. There he founded Aeroquip in April 1940 with the help of a group of Jackson investors led by Don T. McKone Sr. Aeroquip's products at first numbered only two—the reusable hose-fitting and the self-sealing coupler Hurst had developed in Germany for Focke Wulf, a large aircraft manufacturer. Relying primarily on aeronautic sales, the new company already had 100 employees by the time the United States entered the war in 1941.

Hurst was barred by the U.S. government from entering his own plant for much of the war because of his German citizenship: Aeroquip hose fittings had become the standard on U.S. military aircraft. With McKone running the company and military orders increasing daily, Aeroquip sprouted up almost overnight, and sales reached a peak of $6.2 million in 1944. Peter Hurst was allowed to return to the company in 1944, but the end of the war brought a calamitous drop in business for the rest of the decade. Aeroquip retrenched and began to build a more reliable customer base, mixing commercial business with its military orders and, after surviving a prolonged and violent strike in 1948, the company resumed its steady growth.

In 1948 Aeroquip also made its first acquisition, the California-based Aero-Coupling Corporation, which was followed by a series of similar purchases in the related fields of power fluid conveying components. The company opened its first European subsidiaries in 1959, building a pair of plants in West Germany. Sales reached $52.3 million in 1960, split about 60% to 40% between the industrial and military sectors. Sales increased rapidly following the 1963 purchase of Republic Rubber of Youngstown, Ohio. Republic gave Aeroquip the ability to fabricate its own rubber hose as well as couplings, strengthening the parent company by extending its product line and making it less dependent on outside sources of raw materials.

In 1967 Aeroquip began looking for a wealthier partner to supply the capital it needed for further expansion. After negotiations with Westinghouse Electric broke down, Aeroquip agreed to join Libbey-Owens-Ford in 1968, boosting LOF's total sales to $420 million and furthering its progress toward independence from GM. In addition to acquisitions like Aeroquip and the 1970 purchases of Woodall Industries—a Detroit plastics maker—and Dominion Ornamental, a Virginia plastics maker, LOF had tried to counter the mid-1960s slump in glass profits by streamlining its operating methods. Chief among these improvements was the licensing of a revolutionary float glass production process from Great Britain's Pilkington Brothers. This technique—which permanently altered the nature of flat glass manufacturing—allows the production of a continuous, uniform sheet of glass that does not need grinding or polishing; the technique is so efficient that it tripled glass production per man-hour, but LOF had to spend many years and about $100 million revamping its ten plants to accommodate the new technique.

With Aeroquip and a growing stable of plastics companies under its control, LOF was able to reduce its dependence on GM substantially, but the automaker remained critical to both sales and profitability: LOF was still supplying 73% of GM's glass requirements. Thus, when an oil crisis cut GM sales severely in 1974, LOF sales followed suit, dropping 5% to

$655 million; but as GM picked up steam in 1975, LOF sales again pushed close to the $700 million mark. Aeroquip continued to rack up growth and high earnings, which accounted for nearly 40% of corporate profit in 1975. In 1975 LOF consolidated all of its plastics operations into a new subsidiary, LOF Plastics.

When LOF's glass operations slipped into the red in 1980, Chairman Don T. McKone Jr. actively began to seek a further acquisition that could match Aeroquip's highly profitable $455 million in sales. He found it in 1984 with the purchase of Vickers from Sperry Corporation for $265 million. Vickers was founded by Harry F. Vickers, who founded the company in 1921 in Los Angeles, moved it to Detroit in 1929 to better serve the auto industry, and sold it to Sperry in 1937. By that time Vickers had become a diversified maker of hydraulic pumps, transmissions, valves, and controls. In 1954 Vickers had become president of Sperry, and when Sperry merged with Remington Rand in 1955, Vickers served as CEO of the new Sperry Rand Corporation until 1967 and chairman from 1965 to 1967. Sperry Rand had shortened its name to Sperry Corporation in 1979. Vickers was an international power in hydraulic components. When the recession of the early 1980s led Sperry to put the company up for sale, LOF jumped at the chance to add an established name to its non-glass division.

In 1985 LOF Plastics purchased Sterling Plastics for $26.5 million. Sterling was a major custom injector molder, with headquarters in Sterling Heights, Michigan.

Darryl F. Allen, Aeroquip's former chief financial officer, was named president and CEO of the parent company in 1984. Allen completed LOF's liberation from GM. In 1986 he sold all of LOF's glassmaking facilities, its name, and even its logo to Great Britain's glass giant, Pilkington Brothers, receiving in exchange a 30% block of LOF's own stock that Pilkington had bought up a few years earlier. That 30% block had been purchased in 1982 from Gulf + Western Industries, which had bought the shares on the open market. LOF gave up $690 million in annual sales and a 100-year tradition in glassmaking, and changed its name to TRINOVA Corporation. In August 1986, the day after LOF became TRINOVA, LOF Plastics adopted a new name: Sterling Engineered Products. The renamed TRINOVA did not miss a beat, with both sales and profits from its three remaining divisions—Vickers, Aeroquip, and Sterling Engineered Products—remaining on a constant upward trend. On January 1, 1989, Sterling Engineered Products was merged into Aeroquip Corporation, under whose control Sterling now operates.

Allen has set TRINOVA's goals very high—a 16% annual return on equity and sales of $10 billion by 2000. If nothing else, TRINOVA has the satisfaction of knowing that its performance in hydraulic parts and plastics will depend on no one but itself; the years of easy living in the GM empire are gone for good.

Principal Subsidiaries: Aeroquip Corporation; Aeroquip International Inc.; Sterer Engineering & Mfg. Co.; Vickers Incorporated; Vickers International Inc.; Aeroquip A.G. (Switzerland); Aeroquip (Canada) Inc.; Aeroquip GmbH (Germany); Aeroquip Iberica S.A. (Spain); Aeroquip Limited (U.K.); Aeroquip Vickers do Brasil, S/A (Brazil, 99.5%); Double A Hydraulics Limited (U.K.); Polymotor S.p.a. (Italy); EL.GE S.r.l. (Italy); Sterling Engineered Products Inc.; Sterling GmbH (Germany); TRINOVA Export Trading Company (Virgin Islands); TRINOVA Holdings Limited (U.K.); TRINOVA S.A. (France); TRINOVA S.p.a. (Italy); Vickers Systems Inc. (Canada); Vickers Systems GmbH (Germany); Vickers Systems Limited (U.K.); Vickers Systems Limited (Hong Kong); Vickers Systems Pty. Ltd. (Australia); Vickers Systems S.A. (Spain); Vickers Systems OY (Finland).

Further Reading: Our Industrial Heritage, Maumee, Ohio, Vickers, 1988; *The Flying A: 50th Anniversary Issue,* Maumee, Ohio, Aeroquip Corporation, 1990.

—Jonathan Martin

TYCO LABORATORIES, INC.

One Tyco Park
Exeter, New Hampshire 03833
U.S.A.
(603) 778-9700
Fax: (603) 778-7700

Public Company
Incorporated: 1962
Employees: 15,000
Sales: $1.97 billion
Stock Exchange: New York

Tyco Laboratories is a diversified manufacturer of fire-protection and flow-control equipment, packaging materials, and electrical and electronic components—primarily printed circuit boards and underwater cable products. Over the years Tyco has acquired a number of long-established firms whose product lines have evolved from the technological developments of the 20th century. Tyco itself has been transformed from a small technology company to a diversified design and manufacturing corporation.

In 1960, with a science Ph.D. from Harvard, Arthur J. Rosenberg, opened a research laboratory in Waltham, Massachusetts, and did experimental work for the government. Two years later Rosenberg incorporated Tyco Laboratories and branched into the commercial sector. He assembled a team of top researchers and Tyco developed high-tech products for the marketplace.

Tyco's early technological breakthroughs included a silicon carbide laser. This laser was the first blue-light laser and the first to fire a non-stop beam, all at room temperature. Other successful research projects led to the marketing of the Dynalux battery charger, a device which would never overcharge a battery. It had many industrial applications. Other advances came in fluid controls, microcircuitry, and fuel cell catalysts.

Rosenberg established an ambitious growth schedule for his company. To fill the gaps in its development and distribution network, Tyco began to acquire other companies. In 1965, Tyco began a spree of acquisitions which drastically changed the make-up of the company. In 1966, the company bought Industrionics Control, Inc., adding to other recent purchases of Mule Battery Manufacturing Company and Custom Metal Products, Inc. The next year, Tyco acquired the North American Printed Circuit Corporation, General Nucleonics Corporation, and Bytrex, Inc. In 1968, Electralab Electronics Corporation; Air Spec, Inc.; Explosive Fabricators Corporation; Dynaco Inc.; Coating Products, Inc.; and Digital Devices, Inc. were acquired. Accurate Forming Company, CBM Realty Corporation, Linear Corporation, Micro-Power Corporation, and Custom Products Inc. were added to the group in 1969. Tyco's sales increased from less than $1 million in 1963 to more than $41 million for all of its companies by 1969.

This dazzling growth, however, did not occur without complications. By the end of the 1960s, Tyco Laboratories needed a major reorganization to put its new units in order. The price of company stock had dropped dramatically from its peak in the mid-1960s, as Wall Street became disillusioned with high-tech companies. Tyco divested a number of unprofitable units in 1969, and assessed its corporate direction.

In 1970, the Tyco board quietly eased out founder Arthur J. Rosenberg, replacing him temporarily with Joshua M. Berman, a partner in the law firm Goodwin, Proctor, and Hoar, and a director of Tyco Laboratories. In September 1971, Ralph W. Detra took over as president, while Berman remained chairman and CEO. Detra resigned one year later, and Tyco was without a president until April 1973, when the Tyco board appointed Joseph P. Gaziano chairman, president, and CEO.

Gaziano, a graduate of the Massachusetts Institute of Technology, had held a number of positions at the Raytheon Company before leaving in 1967 to run Prelude Corporation, a lobster-fishing concern. Gaziano launched a new era for Tyco Laboratories. During his tenure the company became much larger and more diverse, making acquisitions on a much grander scale than earlier. In January 1974, the stock of Tyco Laboratories was listed on the New York Stock Exchange, and four months later Gaziano completed Tyco's most ambitious acquisition thus far—the $22 million cash purchase of the Simplex Wire and Cable Company.

Simplex specialized in undersea cable, and had its beginnings when Charles A. Morss began manufacturing wire bird cages and fire screens at his firm, Morss and White, in the 1880s. As the revolution in electricity created new uses for wire products, the company adjusted its product lines to include insulated wire. In 1890, the firm changed its name to the Simplex Electrical Company, and it was incorporated five years later, focusing solely on the production of electrical cable. In 1900, Simplex laid the longest underwater telephone cable in the country, across the five-mile strait between Mackinaw City and St. Ingnace, Michigan. The cable lasted 31 years beneath the frigid Great Lakes waters.

In the 1920s, a pair of Simplex scientists discovered that the proteins present in natural rubber were the cause of water absorption, and in 1926 patented a process to remove the proteins. The resulting Anhydrex cables were successfully marketed—lightweight, moisture resistant cables.

During World War II, Simplex began producing submarine cable for the U.S. Navy and U.S. Coast Guard. By the end of the war cable production had increased three-and-one-half times. The company continued to do research for the military even after the war, and a location with greater security was acquired for the submarine-cable division. Located on the banks of the Piscataqua River in New Hampshire, the submarine-cable division became Simplex's flagship operation.

Throughout the 1950s and 1960s, Simplex grew due to technological developments in cable production. New products like flexible pipeline and sodium conductor cables were introduced. In 1966, Simplex began offering installation of undersea cables for the first time.

While Simplex competed with manufacturing giants like Western Union and Anaconda Wire and Cable in the conventional wire and cable markets, it had a lead in the underwater cable market. This specialization was one of the factors that made it attractive to Tyco Laboratories.

In September 1975, shortly after the Simplex acquisition, Tyco purchased the Grinnell subsidiary of International Telephone and Telegraph, (ITT). Grinnell was the market leader in automatic sprinklers. ITT had been ordered by federal courts to divest the fire-protection-equipment and piping manufacturer on antitrust grounds. Tyco president Joseph Gaziano took the opportunity to purchase a well-established company at a reasonable price.

Originally founded in Providence, Rhode Island, in 1850 as the Steam and Gas Pipe Company, Grinnell operated with a member of the Grinnell family high in the corporate hierarchy until the late 1940s. The company began business installing Providence's original gas mains, then operated as a plumbing supplier. Before long its major product became the automatic sprinkling system, a product with which it has led the market ever since.

In 1892, the company was incorporated as the General Fire Extinguisher Company and grew steadily, manufacturing hydrant piping, steam and water heating equipment, iron fittings, brass products, and sundry mill supplies. In 1923, the company was reincorporated, while retaining the same name.

By 1929, humidifying equipment had been added to its product lines. On the eve of the Depression the company employed 4,000 people and had assets of almost $18 million. Over the next few years, however, the number of employees dropped to 2,650, and assets dropped to $12 million at the end of fiscal 1934. General Fire Extinguisher's stock traded at $7 per share in 1934, compared to $45 in 1930.

During World War II, the majority of the company's resources were applied to war production. In April 1944, General Fire Extinguisher changed its name to the Grinnell Corporation. War production had a rejuvenating effect on the company. By the end of 1944, Grinnell employed 6,000 workers and assets were up to $20 million.

In the 1950s, Grinnell diversified into the central station alarm business, which monitors burglar and fire alarms in subscribers' buildings 24 hours a day. In 1949, Grinnell bought a controlling interest in the Automatic Fire Alarm Company, an overseer of automatic fire-protection systems in New York City, Boston, and Philadelphia. In 1950, Holmes Electric Protective Company, which supplies burglar alarm services primarily to banks in New York City, Philadelphia, and Pittsburgh was acquired. Three years later, Grinnell purchased a majority holding in the American District Telegraph Company, the largest central station alarm company in the United States.

In 1961, the Justice Department filed an antitrust suit against Grinnell and three subsidiaries, charging that the four companies had conspired to monopolize the central alarm business, and seeking to force the divestiture of the three subsidiaries—Holmes Electric Protective Company, Automatic Fire Alarm Company, and American District Telegraph. As a result of the trial in 1964, federal judge Charles E. Wyzanski ruled against Grinnell, and ordered that the company "cease and desist" from violating the Sherman Antitrust Act, divest all of its stock in the three central alarm companies, and banned Grinnell's president, James D. Fleming, from corporate leadership. Grinnell appealed, charging that the judge both failed to comprehend the case, and was biased.

The controversial case found its way to the Supreme Court, where the ruling was upheld in 1966. In January 1968, Grinnell divested itself of the three subsidiaries, whose shares were spun off to Grinnell stockholders. Since the subsidiaries' earnings were never consolidated with Grinnell's, the company's balance sheet was not seriously affected. Indeed, Grinnell's own fire-protection and piping business had grown significantly in the 1960s.

In August 1969, Grinnell shareholders voted in favor of a merger with International Telephone and Telegraph despite antitrust suits filed by the United States Justice Department to prevent the acquisition. The merger, however, was doomed. In 1971, federal courts, citing antitrust violations, gave ITT two years to divest itself of Grinnell. The deadline passed without a suitable bid, and ITT put the company under the stewardship of a court trustee in September 1973. After two losing years, Grinnell began to operate at a profit again, and was purchased by Tyco Laboratories.

Tyco paid $14 million and agreed to pay ITT 40% of Grinnell's net earnings for the next ten years, with a minimum payment of $28.5 million. At the time of the acquisition, Tyco's total sales were $58 million, overshadowed by its new subsidiary, Grinnell, whose turnover was $107 million.

Tyco began its third major acquisition in November 1976 when it bought 13% of the Philadelphia-based process-control designer and manufacturer, Leeds & Northrup Company. Through a press release Tyco announced its intention to buy more of Leeds & Northrup's stock. Leeds & Northrup filed suit in federal court, claiming that Tyco's press release was in effect an illegal tender offer and that Tyco had not filed the necessary documents with the Securities and Exchange Commission. Tyco agreed to halt its purchase of the stock temporarily, but over the next two years president and CEO Gaziano waged one of the most convoluted hostile takeover battles in corporate history.

Tyco's agreement to stop buying Leeds & Northrup stock was dependent on the latter company's continued independence. Leeds & Northrup president, David Kimball, began issuing new shares, and arranged for the Milwaukee-based Cutler-Hammer Inc. to buy 9% of Leeds & Northrup stock as a hedge against further encroachment from Tyco. Gaziano protested, but could do little; Tyco was prevented by a court-approved agreement from gaining more than 19% of Leeds & Northrup until March 1978. In January 1978, Tyco gave up its attempt to acquire Leeds & Northrup, and sold its 19% interest to Cutler-Hammer for a $9.2 million profit.

Two months later Tyco bought 8.5% of Cutler-Hammer Inc., which now controlled 33.5% of Leeds & Northrup. By June, Tyco had 28.4% of the Cutler-Hammer shares. Gaziano then raised $25 million through debentures in the Eurodollar market, and increased Tyco's holding in Cutler-Hammer to

32%. Meanwhile, the Koppers Company, a chemical and engineering firm, accumulated 21% of the stock, erecting a formidable roadblock to Tyco's gaining a majority interest in Cutler-Hammer.

Joseph Gaziano responded by selling Tyco's 32% holding in Cutler-Hammer at a profit to the Eaton Corporation, a heavy-equipment manufacturer that planned to merge with Cutler-Hammer, stipulating that Eaton would spin off the Leeds & Northrup shares to Tyco.

Eaton quickly made a tender offer of $261 million for the remaining Cutler-Hammer shares, a bid its board could not refuse, but at the last minute Cutler-Hammer sold the coveted 33.5% holding in Leeds & Northrup to General Signal Corporation. General Signal immediately announced its plan to merge with Leeds & Northrup. After a 20-month effort Gaziano failed to acquire Leeds & Northrup. "It just wasn't meant to be," he told *Forbes* magazine in 1978. Nevertheless, Tyco netted $12.9 million from the transactions.

Gaziano continued to pursue his goal of making Tyco a $1 billion company by 1985. In September 1979, Tyco bought the Armin Corporation for $27 million. Armin was a leader in the production of polyethylene films, products used primarily in packaging.

Armin was incorporated as the Armin Poly Film Corporation in 1967 by Armin Kaufman, a Hungarian immigrant who had come penniless to the United Stated in 1955. The plastic-film maker grew quickly and in 1969, Armin acquired Poly Version, Inc. and the E. Gluck Trading Company through stock exchanges. The Gluck acquisition represented a departure for the company from its main product line. Gluck made watches that sold in retail markets in the $10 to $50 price range under the Sutton, Chateau, Precision, Adventura, and Andre Rivalle labels. In 1975, digital watches with price tags ranging from $100-$150 were introduced under the Armitron and Quasar label. These electronic watches were Armin's first attempt at manufacturing the timekeeping parts of watches itself.

In the mid-1970s, over half of Armin's sales and about 70% of profits came from plastic films. New products like film for sealing tapes, urethane foam sheet-molding compounds, and shrink wrap added to profits in the mid-1970s. Armin's Thermodynamics Corporation subsidiary, acquired in 1973, introduced a new Roto Extrusion process for its main product line—plastic pellets—promising better quality and lower costs.

Armin Corporation proved a profitable acquisition for Tyco Laboratories and Gaziano increased the company's share of the lucrative packaging market through the acquisition—in 1981—of the Ludlow Corporation, a manufacturer of packaging and other materials.

Ludlow dated back to 1868. The company was engaged in the import of jute from India for the manufacture of twines, carpet yarns, furniture webbing, cords, and other textile products at its Ludlow, Massachusetts, plant. In 1916, Malcolm B. Stone became president of Ludlow, and remained head of the corporation until 1957. Stone greatly expanded the operations of the company, buying a jute processing mill near Calcutta in 1920, giving Ludlow first choice of that country's jute crop.

In 1957, Austin B. Mason succeeded Stone. Mason, seeing that Ludlow's products were dependent on one commodity, jute, initiated a broad diversification program. Ludlow began producing paper specialties, including printed chart paper for scientific and military electronic equipment, coated papers, pressure sensitive papers, and gummed packaging paper products. Rubber and vinyl products for the automotive, shoe, and carpet industries also became a major part of Ludlow's product mix. By 1966, jute production, which had accounted for 90% of Ludlow's product lines ten years earlier, made up just 20% of sales.

In 1969, Ludlow entered the profitable mobile home market, a growing segment of the housing market at that time. Carpeting and home furnishings were added, and by 1971, made up more than half of Ludlow's sales. Ludlow's carpets, marketed under the Ludlow and Walters label, were priced at the high end of the market. Ludlow's Forest Products subsidiary, based in Tennessee, produced a variety of non-upholstered furnishings. The company grew throughout the 1970s on the strengths of its diverse operations.

When Tyco Laboratories purchased Ludlow in 1981 for $97 million, Ludlow needed some streamlining. The company sold unprofitable units producing furniture, jute backing, textiles, and bags. Its specialty paper units enjoyed strong markets in medical applications and other technologically advancing fields.

In 1982, Joe Gaziano died suddenly at the age of 47. Tyco Laboratories entered a new period under the leadership of John F. Fort. Fort had risen through the ranks of the Simplex Wire and Cable Company, and was president of that firm at the time of the Tyco takeover. His style differed markedly from Gaziano's.

Fort disposed of Tyco's corporate jets and apartments, and trimmed the corporate staff to 35. He concentrated on making Tyco's existing businesses more profitable. He instituted a compensation program under which employees were rewarded in proportion to the profits their units generated. Fort organized Tyco's subsidiaries into three main units: the fire-protection and plumbing division, which consisted of Grinnell Corporation; the electronics division, made up of Simplex Wire and Cable and the Tyco Printed Circuits Group; and the packaging division, made up of Armin and Ludlow.

Tyco made smaller acquisitions in the mid-1980s, including Micro-Circuit, Inc.; Hersey Products, Inc.; a water meter manufacturer, Atcor, Inc.; a pipe manufacturer; and 48 ITT production and distribution facilities worth $220 million.

In 1987, Tyco's sales passed the $1 billion mark. Tyco's Grinnell subsidiary paid $350 million in 1988 for the Mueller Company, a 132-year-old water and gas pipe manufacturer. The acquisition was expected to make a significant contribution to the fire-protection and flow-controls division.

In 1989, *Fortune* magazine ranked Tyco Laboratories ninth in "total return to shareholders over the last 10 years." Tyco's three main areas of business were producing solid returns and appeared to have excellent growth potential. Pending legislation requiring better fire protection in publicly used buildings promised an expanded market for Grinnell, already contributing 63% of Tyco's sales by the end of the 1980s. Simplex Wire and Cable was the world's leading producer of undersea cables. The Printed Circuit Group focused on the high end of the market, delivering circuit boards in smaller batches with higher prices. Tyco Laboratories, completing its own third decade, has centuries of accumulated experience behind its well-established subsidiaries.

Principal Subsidiaries: Armin Corporation; Ludlow Corporation; Grinnell Corporation; Hersey Products, Inc.; Simplex Wire and Cable Company; Tyco Engineered Systems, Inc.; Tyco Holdings Corporation; Atcor, Inc.

Further Reading: Green, Leslie, and J. Richard Elliot Jr., "Cause for Alarm: The Story of the Anti-Trust Suit Against Grinnell Corp.," *Barron's,* May 30, 1966.

—Thomas M. Tucker

VALMET CORPORATION (Valmet Oy)

Punanotkonkatu 2
Post Office Box 155
00131 Helsinki
Finland
(90) 13291
Fax: (90) 179677

Public Company
Incorporated: 1950
Employees: 19,203
Sales: Fmk10.03 billion (US$2.48 billion)
Stock Exchange: Helsinki

Valmet Oy, known as Valmet Corporation in English-speaking countries, is an industrial corporation, manufacturing heavy machinery and electronic control apparatus. The company is a multidivisional group, with many subsidiary companies. Its main products are paper-making machinery, in which it is a world leader; transport machinery, mainly equipment for handling containers in harbors; control systems for industrial processes with the emphasis on the paper industry; and agricultural and forest tractors and related equipment. The corporation is also active in airplane manufacturing, although on a modest scale.

After World War I, the Finnish government found it feasible to open industrial plants to make arms for the national defense forces. These factories—an airplane factory, a rifle factory, and a factory for manufacturing artillery guns—were run by separate boards of directors, each responsible to the Ministry of Defense. The factories' output was dependent on the national budget, and all orders for production came from the Ministry of Defense within the framework of the budget, decided by the national diet.

When the war between Finland and the Soviet Union ended in September 1944, the Finnish army had to be demobilized and all orders for arms from the arms factories were canceled. The defense factories found themselves in difficulties, as they were ordered to maintain their levels of employment and find new products to manufacture. The first solution to this almost impossible situation came from the articles of armistice which demanded that Finland deliver goods to the Soviet Union as war reparations. Finnish industries were obliged to fulfil this obligation, as were the government-owned arms factories. These factories were consequently transferred from the Ministry of Defense to the Ministry of Trade and Industry. At the same time, two small navy repair yards were transferred. It was apparent that the organization of the factories had to change. A law was passed, giving special status to the corporation about to be formed, as a compromise between a limited company and a state office. The new organization was named the State Metal Works (in Finnish shortened to VMT). Its governing bodies consisted of a large supervisory board, composed mainly of politicians, and a board of directors, consisting of executives from within the corporation. Lieutenant General Leonard Grandell, formerly an experienced officer in the General Staff, was temporarily nominated chairman of the board and chief executive officer. The final choice of chief executive officer was Yrjö Vesa, then deputy managing director of one of Finland's major enterprises in the shipbuilding and machinery industry, the Wartsila group. On February 15, 1947, he was appointed chairman and chief executive officer of VMT.

VMT was assigned a large part of the war reparation program, mainly machinery that could not be supplied by existing private industries. The airplane factory had a particularly large engineering staff, as it had been producing airplanes of its own design. This engineering talent was utilized for the design of many of the items demanded by the Soviets. However, very few of the items included in the reparations program were suited for the commercial market.

Experience soon showed that the form under which VMT operated was not flexible enough for commercial transactions. The Finnish government had to present to the parliament a bill requesting that the group be made a joint stock limited company. The articles of association were approved on November 15, 1950. The name Valmet Oy (Valmet Corporation) was given to the new company. The shares were held by the state, represented by the Ministry of Trade and Industry. The share capital was Fmk 1 billion.

Much of the structure of the old defense works was retained in the organization of the new corporation. The army and navy officers who had been in charge of the different factories remained and were nominated managing directors of divisions within the group.

The most important task was to find products suitable for the different divisions and with good sales potential. After experimenting with many different products, Rautpohja Works, the former artillery gun factory, developed skills in paper-making-machinery production and dropped most of its other activities. Those which were maintained included heavy plate work, such as sluice gates for hydroelectric power plants and overhead cranes. Tourula Factory, the former rifle factory, had problems in finding suitable items for its existing machinery. After trying out many kind of consumer goods, which were later abandoned, Tourula finally switched to agricultural-tractor production. Jyskä Factory, the former artillery ignition fuse factory, specialized in making tools, bolts, and nuts on its automatic lathes, previously used for ignition fuses. The manufacturing of kilowatt-hour meters was also introduced. The airplane factories continued on a decreased scale to manufacture training aircraft for the Finnish Air Force, but diversified into the production of diesel locomotives. The straddle carriers demanded by the Soviet Union as war reparation continued to be produced, initially for sale to the Soviet Union, which seemed to have a huge demand for this kind of carriers, used in sawmills. The company's aeronautical expertise turned out to have other applications, and a department was created to supply equipment for industrial and office air conditioning. The instrument department of the airplane factory developed gradually into a versatile production unit for industrial control equipment.

The shipyards had more problems because they were equipped only for small ships, as included in the war reparation program. Gradually, standard ships for the maritime market were included in the program, but the size of the building beds was a limiting factor. The Soviet Union remained by far the biggest market for the yards.

In 1953, financial problems started to haunt the newly founded company. To find solutions, the advisory board nominated a committee to study the situation, later to be followed by a state committee, nominated by parliament. The recommendations of this committee included a total reconstruction of the company and a change of top management. It was found that the company was under pressure from heavy debts, coming from overvaluing on their books the material inherited from the former defense factories, from selling ships at a loss to the Soviet Union, and from the excessive overhead costs of the organization. As a result of the need to strengthen the financial base of the company, the Bank of Finland and the National Pension Fund joined the company as minority shareholders.

In the spring of 1954, the chief executive, Yrjö Vesa, was released from his position as were the divisional managing directors. All industrial divisions were to report directly to the new chief executive officer. In July of the same year an elderly industrialist, Baron G.W. Wrede, was nominated chief executive officer of Valmet. Even though his time with Valmet was short—he died on February 17, 1958—he and his staff managed to change the company into a commercially viable enterprise. During this time, the main operational divisions were established at the various factories.

After the death of Baron Wrede his deputy managing director, Aarne Härkönen, was nominated chief executive officer. The operation of Valmet continued along the lines already established. The paper-making-machinery division strengthened its position by extending its sales to China, Italy, Poland, and the Soviet Union in addition to the home market. Important features of the early days of the Valmet machines were the differential drives and pick-up presses, the first of their kind in Europe. The first agricultural tractors, developed in the early 1950s, were small machines of only 20 horsepower. In 1956 Valmet launched a standard size 33 horsepower diesel-powered tractor, which was well received in the domestic market. The airplane factory developed into a supplier of diesel locomotives for the Finnish railroads, and also maintained departments for industrial trucks, air conditioning, and instrumentation. The shipyards, mainly supplying the Soviet market, had problems. The crisis of the 1950s had made Valmet careful not to accept orders at loss prices, and although the Soviet orders were large, there were long discussions over pricing. The latter part of the 1950s left Valmet's Helsinki yard without orders, simply because of disagreements on price. Fortunately for Valmet, the sudden boom in shipbuilding, caused by the Suez crisis in 1956, came to its rescue and the yards were kept open.

At the end of the 1950s, Valmet's management decided that the company had to strengthen its main divisions in order to survive when free trade seemed to be the environment of the future. The Valmet paper machines had a good share of many markets, but U.S. manufacturers still seemed to have the upper hand. They sold their machines the world over, even to Finland, while Valmet had not yet managed to export to the United States. To penetrate the North American market, Valmet and Tampella, another Finnish company in the field of paper-making machines, combined their efforts. The contracts for joint deliveries to two big companies, Boise Cascade in Louisiana and Eurocan in British Colombia, were the starting points.

After years of intensive marketing, Valmet became a worldwide market leader in paper-making machines. Many companies in the industry in other countries were assimilated into the Valmet group during this process. Another reason for the success was Valmet's research-and-development activity within this division. The company managed to invent new and superior products, such as new headbox and former designs. Its superior manufacturing techniques, which had already advanced in the artillery gun factory before Valmet was formed, also contributed to its success. Valmet developed a new material for suction rolls as well as a revolutionary machine for drilling the many holes required for these rolls.

Agricultural tractor production caused problems for Valmet as the market only consisted of the Finnish farming industry, and even there competition from major international competitors was fierce. Valmet had to find export markets or other means of increasing the weight of the division. As Valmet had experienced some success in exporting tractors to Brazil, the company found it advisable to enter that country as a locally based manufacturer to reinforce its position there. Thus Valmet do Brasil was established in 1960. Soon it developed into the second largest tractor factory in Latin America. Valmet was inspired by this success to try its luck in other markets. The most important step came in the 1970s when Valmet reached an agreement with the Swedish company Volvo to combine the efforts of the two companies in manufacturing agricultural tractors, leading eventually to Valmet's becoming the sole manufacturer of tractors in Scandinavia.

The airplane factory in Tampere, which had gradually developed into a diesel locomotive factory, was continuing to change shape. After the electrification of the Finnish state railroads had begun, locomotive manufacturing decreased. The making of equipment for increasing international container traffic became more important. By skilful development of harbor transport and loading equipment, based on the old straddle carriers for sawn timber developed for the Soviet war reparations, Valmet became world leader in the modern business of large-container moving machinery. Only Japanese companies in the Far East have been able to challenge Valmet in this field.

The airplane factory in Tampere never ceased completely its original business of building airplanes, but it changed its mode of operation. In 1958 the decision to equip the Finnish air forces with French jet trainers of the Fouga Magister type led to a long period of employment for Valmet's skilled workmen, building the planes under French license. Most of the airplane production was transferred to the Kuorevesi Factory. The little factory, established during World War II and hidden among dense Finnish forests, far from any city, thrived again. When the Fouga planes were built, the activity continued as Swedish Draken fighters and later English Hawk fighter trainers were assembled. The name of the Kuorevesi Factory was consequently changed to the Valmet Airplane Factory, and the old airplane factory in Tampere was renamed Valmet Tampere Works.

The instrument department of the Tampere Airplane Factory had been developed gradually into a versatile unit manufacturing control equipment for process industries. In 1973, the division received a new factory building in the vicinity of the Tampere Works and was renamed Valmet Instrument Factory, having an independent status equal to other divisions within the Valmet group. The factory had a prominent position as designer and supplier of pneumatic process control equipment. Its main customers were paper and pulp mills and power plants but other types of industry were also served. When electronics replaced the pneumatic control systems, Valmet gradually adapted its systems accordingly.

The shipyards had already been a major cause of financial problems for Valmet. In the early 1960s, Valmet's top management found that new problems were looming around the corner. The orders for the Soviet Union were unprofitable, and Härkönen, then president and chief executive officer, presented to the supervisory board a plan to cut down on Valmet's shipbuilding activities. It was based on the fact that Helsinki was a harbor, providing considerable ship repair work for a yard. However, maintaining a yard for repair without new building was not feasible. Repair work was not a steady flow, and new work evened out the flow of work. Therefore it was decided to concentrate all Valmet's shipbuilding activities in Helsinki and devote the Pansio Yard in Turku to other activities. Meanwhile, the Tampere Works had a problem in not having sufficient space available for its air conditioning activities. These were now transferred to Pansio. The former yard was thus divided into two units: a factory, fully specialized in industrial as well as office-building air conditioning, and a heavy steel manufacturing unit, making steel building frames and bridges as well as assisting the shipbuilding division. The structural change was intended to stop losses in Valmet's shipbuilding division and allow possibilities for growth in other, more promising lines of activity.

Aarne Härkönen, president and chief executive officer of Valmet, died on October 19, 1964. Olavi J. Mattila, then secretary of state for trade policy in the Ministry of Foreign Affairs, was nominated chief executive officer. His term was to start at the beginning of 1965. Under his leadership, the structural changes at Valmet continued. The group was to consist of the following independently led divisions, which eventually became separate subsidiary companies: Valmet Paper Machinery; Valmet Tractors; Valmet do Brasil; Valmet Transportation Equipment; Valmet Instruments; Valmet Defence Equipment, later renamed Valmet Aviation Industries after other defense articles, such as assault rifles, were transferred to another company, in which Valmet did not have a majority holding; and Valmet Shipbuilding.

Valmet Shipbuilding was re-established with the construction of a large modern shipyard unit in Vuosaari, east of Helsinki. The new management did not accept the decision of its predecessors to cut down on shipbuilding and thus reversed the strategy. However, the large new Vuosaari shipyard, completed in 1974, was only temporary. In 1986, under new management, Valmet and the Finnish engineering company Wartsila, the largest shipbuilder in Finland, agreed to form two new companies: Valmet Paper Machinery Inc., in which Wartsila became a minority shareholder by transferring its paper manufacturing units to the new company, and Wartsila Marine Industries Inc., a shipbuilding company into which Valmet came as a minority shareholder, transferring its yards to the new company. Soon after the takeover, Wartsila Marine closed the Vuosaari yard, ending Valmet's direct involvement in shipbuilding.

Valmet experienced another financial crisis in 1981. Mattila retired as chief executive officer and was replaced by Matti Kankaanpää, formerly managing director of Valmet Paper Machinery and, since 1980, of Valmet, under the leadership of Mattila as chairman. The crisis was solved by changes in structure and dropping of unprofitable divisions. The company concentrated on its main lines of activity, with emphasis on becoming leaders or at least prominent players in each of these fields of activity. This policy led to many acquisitions and in some cases to divestments.

To improve the public image of the company and erase the image of state-owned enterprise, Kankaanpää decided to make Valmet a public company by floating it on the Helsinki Stock Exchange. In late 1988 Valmet acquired nearly 10,000 new shareholders, many of them employees of Valmet.

Valmet's history is an example of how a group of government utilities can be changed into a commercially viable public company. It also shows that such a transformation can bring many problems, and that these can be solved only by employing the best expertise available, both technical and administrative. During its transformation, the group underwent a complete change of market; from having been a supplier to the Finnish government, it became a producer of machinery for the Soviet Union and domestic Finnish industries, from which position it has now become truly international.

Principal Subsidiaries: Valmet Paper Machinery Inc.; Valmet Automation AB; Valmet Logging Equipment Company Ltd. (Sweden); Valmet do Brasil S.A. (Brazil).

Further Reading: Björklund, Nils, *Valmet*, Jyväskylä, Gummerus, 1990.

—Nils G. Björklund

VARITY CORPORATION

595 Bay Street
Toronto, Ontario M5G 2C3
Canada
(416) 593-3811
Fax: (416) 593-3820

Public Company
Incorporated: 1891 as Massey-Harris Company, Ltd.
Employees: 20,375
Sales: US$2.38 billion
Stock Exchanges: Toronto Montreal New York London

Varity Corporation is one of the world's largest producers of farm and industrial machinery. Often recognized by its former name of Massey-Ferguson, Varity is also a leading manufacturer of diesel engines and, since 1986, components for motor vehicles. From its incorporation in 1891 as the Massey-Harris Company, Varity has developed a worldwide operation. In the 1950s tractor- and diesel-engine manufacturing was added to Massey-Harris's operation by three important acquisitions. With this array of manufacturing concerns, the renamed Massey-Ferguson proved very successful until the late 1970s. In the 1980s Massey-Ferguson and its new chairman and chief executive officer, Victor Rice, fought off collapse while the firm underwent three restructurings between 1981 and 1986. Renamed Varity Corporation in 1986, the company has since directed its efforts toward the manufacture of motor-vehicle components, punctuated by the purchase of Dayton Walther in 1986 and Kelsey-Hayes in 1989, and the closure of Massey Combines Corporation in 1988. Since 1985 the corporation has become a profitable concern once again. Varity is a highly internationalized company; so much so, in fact, that although it is a Canadian company, its financial information is recorded in U.S. dollars.

As Canada was opened to settlers by the railroads in the 1850s, demand for farm machinery in the sparsely populated country grew. Daniel Massey, the son of a New Englander, and his partner R.F. Vaughn founded the Massey Company in 1847 in Bond Head, Ontario. Two years later the company was moved to a new foundry in Newcastle, Ontario. In 1857 Alanson Harris, the son of an American Baptist minister, bought a small factory in Beamsville, Ontario, where he also began producing farm implements.

Massey and Harris were among dozens of small nonspecialized manufacturers seeking to exploit the growing need for farm machinery in the 1850s. Because of their American backgrounds, however, they were able to keep abreast of developments in U.S. farm machinery. Massey's son, Hart Massey, made several trips south to bring back new innovations. Two particularly notable ones were the Ketchum grass mower and the Manny Combined Hand Rake Reaper Mower, brought back to Newcastle in 1851 and 1855, respectively. Through a connection with the D.M. Osborne Company of Auburn, New York, the Harris Company was also able to introduce a steady stream of products into the Canadian market, especially the successful Kirby mower and reaper. In addition Massey and Harris used advertising, easy credit, and promotional devices to boost sales.

Low manufacturing costs facilitated the rapid growth of these two firms, which were able to produce American-type machines for the Canadian market more cheaply than U.S. companies. Canadian tariffs implemented in 1847 and the U.S. Civil War further assisted the Massey and Harris companies by undermining U.S. competition. This was a prosperous period for both Massey and Harris. In 1870 the Massey Manufacturing Company was incorporated, and nine years later it moved into a modern plant outside Toronto. Harris had relocated to new facilities in Brantford, Ontario, in 1872.

In the 1880s the Massey and Harris companies each initiated an export drive. Canadian tariffs on farm machinery reached 35% by 1883, but Massey and Harris both anticipated that they would fall. This encouraged manufacturers to seek new markets other than western Canada where transport costs gave U.S. manufacturers an advantage. Goods could be shipped to Europe, South America, and Australasia at a competitive price, and rising labor costs in Europe spurred demand for farm machinery. The Indian and Colonial Exhibition in London in 1886 introduced Hart Massey and his products to the world's buyers, enabling him to establish London and Adelaide offices. By 1888 both companies had begun developing systems of foreign outlets.

A crucial point in the development of Massey and Harris was reached in 1891. Harris had had great success with a new machine, the open-end binder. It allowed farmers to harvest straw, a very valuable commodity in Europe, from cereal crops. The result was a quickening of the ongoing competition between the Massey and Harris companies in the harvester market. Since they dominated this field, however, the two companies stood to gain considerably by ending this unprofitable competition. In May 1891 the two companies were merged to form the Massey-Harris Company. Hart Massey became president and the three executive positions were taken by men from the Harris Company. This merger was quickly followed by the addition of several smaller companies, providing Massey-Harris with a fuller range of agricultural implements.

The creation of International Harvester Company (IHC)—made up of five smaller companies—in 1902 was followed a year later by the establishment of an IHC subsidiary in Canada. This event, and the possibility of trade reciprocity between the U.S. and Canada, led Massey-Harris to purchase its first foreign manufacturing concern, the Johnston Harvester Company of Batavia, New York, in 1910. This acquisition was the beginning of the company's development into the present multinational organization. The death of Hart

Massey in 1896, after four decades of leadership, marked this evolution away from the pioneer roots.

As trade between the United States and Canada opened up after 1914, Massey-Harris's position worsened, partly because the company did not produce a good tractor at a time when farmers were shifting to powered farming. Finally, in 1928, the company was able to purchase the J.I. Case Plow Works Company of Racine, Wisconsin, which produced the Wallis tractor. In the process the Massey family was bought out, ending their 75-year connection to the company.

At the close of World War I Massey-Harris committed itself to building up foreign sales, but the interwar period was a time of agricultural depression when quotas, protection, and bilateral trade agreements were introduced. To circumvent these trade barriers the company began manufacturing in other countries, at its own plants or in cooperation with local manufacturers. In 1926 a factory was built in Marquette, France. Similar operations were initiated elsewhere. When Australia closed its doors to imports, Massey-Harris sold its operations there to H.V. McKay Proprietary, Australia's largest producer of farm machinery, and then purchased a 26% stake in H.V. McKay.

By 1930 nearly three-quarters of the company's sales were outside Canada. As a result the company was hit hard by the collapse of the international economy after 1929. Despite drastic retrenchment, general manager B.W. Burtsell was unable to stop continuing losses, and in 1935 he counseled the Massey-Harris board of directors to abandon all U.S. operations. James S. Duncan, a second-generation European manager, believed that this would be a fatal mistake. By 1935 Massey-Harris had only a 20% market share in Canada and Duncan felt that the company's survival depended upon international sales. The board agreed, and Duncan succeeded Burtsell as general manager, leading Massey-Harris further into the world market in the 1940s.

During World War II Massey-Harris filled Allied orders, especially at its Racine, Wisconsin, plant, which began to build tanks in 1942. In 1945 the company was ready with a peacetime expansion plan. It had developed a new harvesting machine, the self-propelled reaper-thresher, or combine harvester. In 1922 Massey-Harris had produced the first truly successful combine, the Number 5 Reaper-Thresher, which still depended upon horses or a tractor for tractive power. In 1936 Duncan approved plans for a self-propelled combine, and in 1941 the Massey-Harris Number 21 self-propelled combine was put into production.

Massey-Harris quite naturally wanted to capitalize on its technological lead, hoping to capture the U.S. market for combines. Due to wartime demand, however, steel was in short supply and the company could not launch production on a massive scale. In 1944 Joe Tucker, sales manager of the company's U.S. subsidiary, convinced the U.S. and Canadian governments to release more steel for the Massey-Harris combines in order to demonstrate that the machines used the metal more efficiently than other harvesting equipment. Tucker launched the "Massey-Harris Harvest Brigade:" 500 self-propelled combines were built and sold to operators who each guaranteed to cross the United States, harvesting a minimum of 2,000 acres per machine. The brigade started in the southern United States in April and fanned out, crossing the country by September. Massey-Harris achieved its harvesting goal and established itself to farmers as the leader in self-propelled combines.

In the years immediately following World War II Massey-Harris gained half of the U.S. market for self-propelled combines. The company began to approach the size of the two U.S. farm machinery giants, John Deere and IHC. Nevertheless, this success was undermined by problems, particularly the company's continued weakness in tractors. As a result, in 1953 President James Duncan began discussions with Harry Ferguson, the first individual to utilize the potential of mechanized plowing with his patented system of tractors and implements.

Although possessing only a limited formal education, the energetic Ulsterman had designed and built a motorcycle and an airplane by the time he was 25. After supervising the use of tractors on Irish farms for the British government during World War I, Ferguson had begun to develop his own tractor. In 1945 he established the Harry Ferguson Company to engineer and distribute these tractors. The crucial element in the Ferguson machine was the "three-point linkage" which attached the plow to the tractor. Hydraulic controls provided manual adjustment of the plow. More importantly, the linkage facilitated the use of smaller tractors and better plowing as the implement automatically adjusted itself to differing soils, thereby protecting the machinery from damage and ensuring the driver's safety. In the development of mechanized farming the Ferguson system proved to be as important as Massey-Harris's self-propelled harvester.

Ferguson's company faced many problems with labor, management, and distribution, in addition to an acrimonious lawsuit against the Ford Company. Ferguson apparently decided that his company could not continue alone and in August 1953 he agreed to merge his company with Massey-Harris. Unable to agree with Massey-Harris executives on the book value of his company—Ferguson had argued that his company was worth $17 million while Massey-Harris Executive Board Chairman W. E. Phillips claimed its value was $16 million—Ferguson suggested a coin toss. He lost and the value was set at $16 million. Harry Ferguson soon sold his stock in the new company which was dominated by Massey-Harris. With this acquisition the renamed Massey-Harris-Ferguson became the second-largest farm-machinery company in the world behind IHC.

The company had clearly outgrown its old organization by the mid-1950s and its regular U.S. operations were not profitable. In July 1956 the ailing James S. Duncan was forced to retire as chairman, president, and director after 21 years at the helm. As the directing force behind this move, W. E. Phillips became chairman and chief executive officer. He had been Duncan's friend and neighbor when he was brought into Massey-Harris during the 1942 reorganization. An overhaul of the firm to suit Massey-Harris-Ferguson's global operations soon followed.

In 1959 the again-renamed Massey-Ferguson purchased the tractor operations of Standard Motor Company of Coventry, England and the diesel manufacturer F. Perkins of Peterborough, England. Standard's large factory boosted Massey-Ferguson's tractor production capacity by 100,000 units a year; yet over the years the Perkins acquisition has proven more important. F. Perkins was established in 1932 and by the late 1930s it was producing the successful six-cylinder

Perkins P6 engine. As large manufacturers sought to establish their own diesel production instead of subcontracting with Perkins, the company began to experience difficulties. To survive, a 1957 Perkins memorandum admitted, the firm needed to merge with a complementary company with surplus capital. Perkins proved very important to Massey-Ferguson because it was a successful diesel manufacturer at a time when farm machinery was switching from gasoline engines to the new, lighter diesel engines. Massey-Ferguson also gained an international network which complemented its own. As a separate operation under Massey-Ferguson, Perkins's output tripled by 1963.

The two decades that followed these late 1950s acquisitions were Massey-Ferguson's best years. It held 20% of the agricultural-machinery market and had the world's best-selling tractors and second-best-selling combines. This position was based upon strong sales in every geographical market. The largest number of employees were located in Great Britain, but the company had major operations in France, Italy, Canada, the United States, Australia, and South Africa. The company's stock was also increasingly owned by non-Canadians, particularly Americans. The only significant departure for Massey-Ferguson in this period was its entry into the construction-machinery market in the late 1960s. In 1969 it built a factory near Liverpool, England, to manufacture these products. The buoyancy of the farm-machinery business provided Massey-Ferguson with rising profits, peaking in 1976.

When the agricultural-machinery market collapsed in 1979, Massey-Ferguson was caught unaware and was nearly destroyed by rising interest rates on an accumulated debt of $1.6 billion. That year the company recorded a loss of $262 million. In 1980 Victor A. Rice, president since 1978, was made chairman and CEO to handle what *The Wall Street Journal* described as "one of Canada's worst corporate financial disasters." Born in 1941, the son of a chimney sweep, Rice quit school at 16 to start work, beginning as a mail boy at Ford of Europe. After five years as a comptroller at Perkins Engines, he was moved to Toronto in 1975 as Massey-Ferguson's comptroller.

In 1980, Rice's first job was to conduct a worldwide search for financial assistance—from bankers and the British and Canadian governments—to save the company from sinking under its debt. With President Vince Laurenzo, Rice then implemented a retrenchment policy, cutting costs and closing or selling many plants over the next several years. The British construction-machinery plant and a combine plant in Scotland were closed in 1980. Massive redundancies at the Coventry tractor plant and at Perkins were cut, as was nearly all North American farm-machinery production. The effect was dramatic. Employment was cut 75% from its 1979 level, factory space was cut by two-thirds, and long-term debt was reduced to under $400 million by 1988, down 400% from 1979. In addition, Rice allowed units within the company to operate autonomously in order to quicken decision-making within units.

In 1984 Massey-Ferguson purchased Rolls-Royce Diesels International from Vickers PLC. This year also marked the return of profitability for the first time since 1979. Two years later the company acquired Ohio-based motor-vehicle-components manufacturer Dayton Walther Corporation. In 1985 Massey-Ferguson had placed troubled combine production under newly created Massey Combines Limited, which later went into receivership.

In 1986 Rice further distanced the company from its recent history by adapting a new name, Varity Corporation, a reference to the talented Englishman, William Verity, whose plow company was purchased by Massey-Harris in 1892. Varity Corporation made its largest purchase in November 1989 when it bought Kelsey-Hayes Corporation for $577 million from Fruehauf Corporation. Kelsey-Hayes is the pioneer and world leader in the burgeoning fields of antilock braking systems and aluminum wheels.

With the changes brought in the 1980s, Varity Corporation stood ready to take advantage of its improved position. After cutbacks and modernization, the farm-machinery operations, limited to Britain, Italy, and France, are in much better condition. No longer primarily a farm-machinery manufacturer, 40% to 50% of Varity's business was generated by automotive components, the remainder split between farm machinery and diesel engines, in 1990. The company remained geographically diversified, although Europe now accounts for over half of all sales. No farm-machinery production occurs in Canada, and about 80% of Varity stock is traded in New York. Management has discussed moving headquarters to the United States.

The automotive operations of Perkins and Kelsey-Hayes hold great promise because of their technological excellence in expanding markets. Perkins scored a triumph in 1989 when it unveiled the world's first direct-injection diesel engine for passenger cars. Varity's extensive European contacts should benefit the company as the European Economic Community moves toward a single market and capitalism revives in Eastern Europe.

Principal Subsidiaries: Agricredit Acceptance Corporation (U.S.A.); Dayton Walther Corporation (U.S.A.); Kelsey-Hayes Corporation (U.S.A.); Massey-Ferguson Credit Corporation (U.S.A.); Massey-Ferguson Finance Company of Canada Ltd.; Massey-Ferguson Inc. (U.S.A.); Massey-Ferguson Industries Ltd.; Massey-Ferguson Industrial Ltd. (U.K.); Massey-Ferguson Manufacturing Ltd. (U.K.); Massey-Ferguson Perkins Finance Co. Ltd. (U.K.); Massey-Ferguson SA (France); Massey-Ferguson SpA (Italy); Massey-Ferguson (United Kingdom) Ltd.; Perkins Engines Group Ltd. (U.K.); Perkins Engines Ltd. (U.K.); Varity Inc. (U.S.A.); Varity GmbH (Germany); Varity Nederland NV (Netherlands).

Further Reading: Denison, Merrill, *Harvest Triumphant,* New York, Dodd, Mead & Co., 1949; Phillips, W.G., *The Agricultural Implement Industry in Canada,* Toronto, University of Toronto Press, 1956; Neufeld, E.P., *A Global Corporation,* Toronto, University of Toronto Press, 1969; Byrne, Harlan S., "They Almost Bought the Farm," *Barron's,* May 2, 1988; Davies, Charles, "Rice Harvest," *Canadian Business,* May 1989.

—Neal R. McCrillis

WHIRLPOOL CORPORATION

Benton Harbor, Michigan 49022
U.S.A.
(616) 926-5000
Fax: (616) 926-5486

Public Company
Incorporated: 1929 as Nineteen Hundred Corporation
Employees: 39,411
Sales: $6.29 billion
Stock Exchanges: New York Midwest London

From its beginning as a manufacturer of electrically powered clothes washers, Whirlpool Corporation has become a leading producer of a complete line of household appliances. The number-one source of home laundry equipment in the United States, the company also markets appliances such as dishwashers, refrigerators, ovens, ranges, and air conditioners worldwide under the Whirlpool, KitchenAid, and Roper brand names.

The company that preceded Whirlpool was founded in 1911 by Lou Upton and his uncle Emory Upton, who lent their family name to the machine shop they opened in Saint Joseph, Michigan. Lou Upton, a life insurance salesman, had recently lost his investment in a small appliance dealership that had failed. In an attempt to compensate Upton for his loss, the dealer gave him the patent for a manually operated clothes washer. Emory Upton was able to outfit the machine with an electric motor, and—with a $5,000 stake from L.C. Bassford, a Chicago retailing executive—the Upton Machine Company began producing electric wringer washers. The company soon snared its first customer, the Federal Electric division of Chicago-based Commonwealth Edison.

The relationship lasted three years, until Federal Electric began manufacturing its own washers. Although losing this customer was a major blow, the company stayed afloat by manufacturing toys, camping equipment, and automobile accessories until it rebounded in 1916 with an agreement to produce two types of wringer washers for Sears, Roebuck and Company, which at that time operated exclusively through mail order. Sales of Upton's washers through the Sears catalog grew rapidly during and after World War I. In order to avoid total dependence on the Sears account, however, Upton also launched a washer under its own brand name in the early 1920s.

During the 1920s, Sears's expansion into retailing and its selection of Upton as its sole supplier of washing machines forced the company to find a way to increase its manufacturing capacity and distribution efficiency. This was accomplished through a merger, in 1929, with the Nineteen Hundred Washer Company of Binghamton, New York. The postmerger company, known as the Nineteen Hundred Corporation, survived the Great Depression without any lasting damage and even expanded and modernized its production facilities during this time to handle increasing sales volume.

During World War II the company manufactured weapons parts and related products needed for the war effort. The company also focused on the development of an automatic, spinner-type washer during the 1940s. This machine, nicknamed the "Jeep," was introduced by Sears in 1947 under that company's Kenmore brand name, and then under Nineteen Hundred's own newly introduced Whirlpool brand one year later.

In 1949 Elisha "Bud" Gray II succeeded retiring Lou Upton as president and led the company through the postwar period, which was characterized by heavy consumer demand for convenience products. The Nineteen Hundred Corporation aggressively launched a complete line of Whirlpool home laundry appliances, including wringer and automatic clothes washers, electric and automatic clothes dryers, and irons. In 1950 the company changed its name to Whirlpool Corporation.

Although sales continued to climb, it became clear by the mid-1950s that the company's emphasis on laundry equipment made it vulnerable to increasing competition from more diversified manufacturers. In 1955 Whirlpool merged with the Seeger Refrigerator Company and added a line of refrigerators. The company also began to make air conditioners and cooking-range products in 1955. The two lines had formerly been produced by Radio Corporation of America (RCA), and were marketed under the RCA-Whirlpool name. The company itself operated under the name of Whirlpool-Seeger Corporation until 1957. Between 1955 and 1957 the company introduced its first full line of home appliances under the RCA-Whirlpool brand. The line consisted of 12 types of machines and 150 models. The 1957 merger with Chicago's Birtman Electric Company brought a vacuum cleaner line under Whirlpool's expanding product umbrella.

As its product line grew, Whirlpool's network of independent dealers and distributors, outside of the Sears chain, assumed an increasingly important role in the company's marketing and sales efforts. A subsidiary called Appliance Buyers Credit Corporation was formed in 1957 to provide financing to these distributors and to help strengthen Whirlpool's position as an industry leader. Also in 1957, the company broadened its reach beyond the United States by initiating the first of several acquisitions of major Brazilian appliance manufacturers.

Intensifying consumerism in the 1960s created growing pressure on appliance manufacturers to offer better quality and service. As a result, Whirlpool launched new support services, as well as a continuing stream of new products, such as the home trash compactor. Its toll-free Cool-Line service enabled Whirlpool appliance owners to obtain immediate information on subjects like installation and repair. At the same time, however, price reductions caused by the softening demand for appliances and growing competition led the company to institute a series of measures designed to streamline production and decrease manufacturing costs. Since the Whirlpool name itself had gained wide acceptance, the company also reached a friendly agreement with RCA during the mid-1960s to drop RCA's brand name from the company's products.

Further attempts to diversify yielded mixed results. The company's purchase of Heil-Quaker Corporation in 1964 enlarged Whirlpool's scope beyond consumer appliances to central heating and cooling equipment. This subsidiary was sold to Inter-City Gas Corporation of Canada in 1986 as Whirlpool refocused its attention on home appliances. Its 1966 entry into the consumer-electronics market with the acquisition of Warwick Electronics ended in failure ten years later, at which time the business was sold to Sanyo Electric Company. To close out the decade, the company penetrated the Canadian market for the first time with its 1969 purchase of Inglis, a home appliance manufacturer. Inglis has continued to serve its market as Whirlpool's Canadian arm.

Continued emphasis on consumerism combined with the 1973 energy crisis, a slump in the housing industry, and an economic recession increased pressure on the appliance industry to produce more energy-efficient products and to improve manufacturing efficiency.

During this period, faced with sluggish retail sales, Whirlpool dealers and Sears, still the company's largest customer, liquidated their inventories, a move which forced Whirlpool to lay off over one-third of its workforce. A 1974 strike at its Evansville, Indiana, plant, which produced refrigeration and air conditioning equipment, further tested the company's ability to weather the downturn in the appliance market. Although the strike ended after four months, the plant's compressor facilities closed permanently in 1983 as part of a companywide initiative to reduce manufacturing costs. These developments stood in marked contrast to the period between 1967 and 1973, when manufacturers had built, delivered, and sold one appliance every 3.2 seconds.

By 1977 the market cycled upward, and Whirlpool and its competitors were again experiencing strong demand for labor-saving devices from first-time buyers of the postwar generation, from households replacing existing appliances, and from the military post exchanges with which the company had established a buying arrangement in 1967. As Whirlpool grew, however, traditional appliance retailers struggled against the increasing sales strength of mass merchandisers.

Whirlpool's progress during the 1970s was guided by Chairman John H. Platts, who had started his career with the company in 1941 on the assembly line and was hand-picked to succeed Elisha Gray II in 1971. Improvement of products for residential use remained an important priority for Whirlpool during this period. In 1977 it introduced the first automatic clothes washer with solid-state electronic controls and a line of microwave ovens. The company had originally entered the microwave market in the late 1950s and quickly withdrew due to limited potential.

A move toward vertical integration was also initiated in 1977, when the company started producing its own appliance motors to reduce its dependence on outside suppliers. One of Whirlpool's few failures during the decade involved the launch of a commercial ice-making system for use in hotels and motels and by food purveyors. The product never met sales goals and the business was sold in 1982.

In 1980 Whirlpool was found guilty of discrimination in a suit brought by the Department of Labor, alleging that Whirlpool had taken inappropriate disciplinary action against two employees who had refused to perform what they considered to be hazardous work in the company's Marion, Ohio, plant. After several years of litigation, the Supreme Court ruled in the employees' favor, stating that the act of placing letters of reprimand in their personnel files was discriminatory.

Upon Platts's retirement in November 1982, vice chairman Jack D. Sparks became chairman and CEO, broadening the company's focus. Sparks's sales and marketing experience was felt important as Whirlpool faced an environment of increasing foreign competition in the United States, industry consolidation, and changing consumer preferences. Under Sparks's leadership, Whirlpool embarked upon a major capital spending program to increase manufacturing productivity and instituted a five-year plan to address industry trends.

One result of this planning process was the expansion of the company's product line beyond appliances and into related consumer durable goods. In 1985 Whirlpool entered the lucrative kitchen-cabinet market by acquiring Mastercraft Industries Corporation, followed by the purchase of another cabinet manufacturer, St. Charles Manufacturing Company, the next year. The cabinet business did not produce the hoped for results—Whirlpool was unable to capture a satisfactory share of the residential-construction market—and the cabinet operation was sold in 1989.

Sparks also oversaw the acquisition of the KitchenAid division of Hobart Corporation, which added a popular line of higher-priced dishwashers, ovens, and other kitchen appliances to the Whirlpool product line. Initiated in 1985, the transaction's completion was delayed for a year as White Consolidated Industries alleged antitrust violations. White's suit eventually proved unsuccessful and the acquisition was finalized in 1986.

Sparks also emphasized growth in the company's international markets and formed Whirlpool Trading Company in 1984, to explore overseas opportunities. Two years later the company attempted to forge a joint venture with Dutch N. V. Philips to manufacture and market household appliances overseas. The project fell through due to unstable currency and market conditions.

In 1987 David R. Whitwam, succeeding Jack Sparks as president and CEO, took over the direction and implementation of the company's five-year global strategy. The company continued to focus on increasing manufacturing productivity and reducing costs, while applying new technology to appliance production. Whirlpool contracted with McDonnell Douglas Astronautics Company to develop prototypes of appliances for use in U.S. space stations.

Until 1988 the company operated under a centralized structure, with decision-making concentrated at the senior management level. In 1988 Whirlpool reorganized its activities into seven units in order to maximize efficiency and market responsiveness. These units are: the Kenmore, KitchenAid, and Whirlpool appliance groups; Whirlpool International; Inglis Limited; Whirlpool Finance Corporation; and the company's export group.

Shortly thereafter, the company attempted to acquire Roper Corporation, another major manufacturer and supplier of appliances to Sears. This move would have strengthened Whirlpool's cooking-appliance product line with electric and gas ranges and would also have opened new opportunities in the outdoor-equipment market Roper served with its lawn mowers and garden tractors. The Roper purchase was stymied, however, by General Electric Company (GE), which alleged that Roper had not solicited competitive bids upon receiving the Whirlpool offer as it was required to do so by the Securities and Exchange Commission. As the controversy intensified, Whirlpool withdrew its tender offer and reached a settlement with GE in which GE would acquire Roper's manufacturing facilities while Whirlpool would obtain the rights to the Roper name. The rivals also forged a two-year agreement in which GE would supply Whirlpool with appliance motors and gas and electric ranges.

In 1988 the company successfully revived its proposed joint venture with N. V. Philips. This effort was spurred primarily by Whirlpool's desire to participate in the post-1992 European market for home appliances. The ensuing agreement cleared the way for Whirlpool to market a full line of major home appliances in Europe. Philips's appliances were more appropriately designed for European customers than Whirlpool's models. The following year, the Whirlpool name was added to the Philips product line to strengthen recognition in the European market. This operation, with Whirlpool's businesses in Brazil, Canada, Italy, and Mexico, is the cornerstone of its global strategy.

Whirlpool is positioned to capitalize on growth opportunities in the global marketplace with a comprehensive line of home appliances. Led by chairman, president, and CEO Whitwam, the company faces flattening U.S. demand for its products due to a decreasing number of family households. It has responded by growing on the international front, where greater opportunities exist for expansion. The company must further develop and strengthen its presence while also preserving the profit margins essential for its overseas operation to remain viable.

Principal Subsidiaries: Aspera S.r.l. (Italy); Inglis Limited (Canada); KitchenAid, Inc.; Whirlpool Financial Corporation; Whirlpool International B.V. (Netherlands).

Further Reading: Whirlpool Corporation 1911-1986: Progressing Toward the 21st Century, Benton Harbor, Michigan, Whirlpool Corporation, 1986.

—Sandy Schusteff

YAMAHA CORPORATION

10-1, Nakazawa-che
Hamamatsu, Shizuoka 430
Japan
(0534) 60-2141
Fax: (0534) 64-8554

Public Company
Incorporated: 1897 as Nippon Gakki Co., Ltd.
Employees: 12,423
Sales: ¥384.69 billion (US $2.68 billion)
Stock Exchanges: Tokyo Osaka Nagoya

Yamaha Corporation, one of Japan's most diversified companies, is the world's largest maker of musical instruments. Since 1950 the company has also become a major producer of electronics, audio products, furniture, household products, and sporting goods, and it derives significant earnings from its resorts. Although largely a producer of luxury consumer items, the company has historically performed satisfactorily in recessionary periods.

Yamaha founder Torakusu Yamaha's venture reflected turn-of-the-century Japan's enthusiasm for new technologies and the ability of its middle-class entrepreneurs to develop products based on them. Raised in what is now the Wakayama Prefecture, Yamaha received an unusual education for the time from his samurai father, a surveyor with broad interests in astronomy and mechanics and a remarkable library. The Meiji Restoration, a government-subsidized effort to hasten technological development in the late 19th century, put educated people like Yamaha in a position to capitalize on the new growth.

At age 20 Yamaha studied watch repair in Nagasaki under a British engineer. He formed his own watchmaking company, but he was unable to stay in business due to lack of money. He then took a job repairing medical equipment in Osaka after completing an apprenticeship at Japan's first school of Western medicine in Nagasaki.

As part of his job, Yamaha repaired surgical equipment in Hamamatsu, a small Pacific coastal fishing town. Because of their area's isolation, a township school there asked him in 1887 to repair their prized U.S.-made Mason & Hamlin reed organ. Seeing the instrument's commercial potential in Japan, Yamaha produced his own functional version of the organ within a year and then set up a new business in Hamamatsu to manufacture organs for Japanese primary schools. In 1889 he established the Yamaha Organ Manufacturing Company, Japan's first maker of Western musical instruments. At the same time, the government granted Hamamatsu township status, which provided it with rail service and made it a regional commerce center.

Western musical traditions interested the Japanese government, which fostered and catered to growing enthusiasm for Western ideas. While Yamaha's technical education enabled him to manufacture a product, government investment in infrastructure made it possible for him to create a business. Yamaha Organ used modern mass-production methods, and by 1889 it employed 100 people and produced 250 organs annually.

During the 1890s the more inexpensive upright piano surpassed the reed organ in popularity in U.S. homes. Yamaha saw the potential of this market. In 1897 he renamed his company Nippon Gakki Co., Ltd., which literally means Japan musical instruments. He opened a new plant and headquarters in the Itaya-cho district of Hamamatsu.

In 1899 one of Yamaha's initial investors convinced other investors to pull out of Yamaha in favor of a competitor, a new organ maker that was near failure. Yamaha managed to borrow the money necessary to remain solvent and buy out his partners.

Japan's government not only supported industrialization through heavy manufacturing, but also encouraged upstart businesses to contact overseas markets directly. Expansion into pianos required more research, so the Japanese Ministry of Education sponsored a Yamaha tour of the United States in 1899. He was to study piano making and to establish suppliers for the materials needed to produce pianos in Japan. In one year Nippon Gakki produced its first piano. Governmental and institutional orders were the first filled, including some for the Ministry of Education. In 1902, with U.S. materials and German technology, Nippon Gakki introduced its first grand piano. In 1903 the company produced 21 pianos.

Nippon Gakki demonstrated its new pianos in select international exhibitions. Between 1902 and 1920, the company received awards for its pianos and organs that had never before gone to a Japanese manufacturer, for example a Grand Prix at the Saint Louis World Exposition in 1904.

World War I curtailed sales by a German harmonica marker in Japan, so Nippon Gakki took the opportunity to broaden its product base and begin making and exporting harmonicas. Producing new products that share raw materials and manufacturing skills became a major operating principle for Nippon Gakki.

Yamaha died suddenly during the war. He had succeeded in introducing Western instruments and assembly techniques, but despite his assembly lines, piano making was still a craftsman's industry at his death. Vice president Chiyomaru Amano assumed the presidency in 1917. His political contacts had helped the company expand. He saw the company through repeated labor strife for ten years before being replaced.

World War I produced tremendous growth in Japanese industry, and Nippon Gakki grew with it, supplying Asian markets cut off from traditional sources of supply. By 1920 it employed 1,000 workers and produced 10,000 organs and 1,200 pianos a year. The sales records set during the war continued afterward, despite recession. These gains were largely due to piano sales which doubled to ¥2 million between 1919 and 1921.

The next five years nearly put the company in bankruptcy. Appreciation of the yen, which made Nippon Gakki products less competitive overseas, was part of the problem. In 1922, fire destroyed a new plant in Nakazawa and the main Itayacho plant in Hamamatsu. The next year the Great Kanto earthquake destroyed the Tokyo office and again damaged company plants. Before the company recovered, labor unions went on strike after Amano refused to negotiate. Amano gave in to the union's demands 105 days later, after the company's reserves were depleted.

Board member Kaichi Kawakami, by request of the other directors, took the presidency in 1927. A director of Sumitomo Wire Company, Kawakami made an unexpectedly nontraditional choice in accepting the position at the troubled company. Kawakami cut production costs and reorganized the company. Half of all debts were paid within 18 months of Kawakami taking over.

Between the world wars, Western imports still dominated the Japanese sales of Western instruments. Since Nippon Gakki's advantage was in price alone, Kawakami opened an acoustics lab and research center in 1930 to improve quality. He also hired advisors from C. Bechstein of Germany to improve the quality of the Yamaha piano.

The growth of the public school system of the 1930s expanded the market for Western instruments, and Nippon Gakki introduced lower-priced accordions and guitars to capitalize on the expansion.

When World War II began, Nippon Gakki plants produced propellers for Zero fighter planes, fuel tanks, and wing parts. As with expansion during World War I, these items laid the groundwork for broader diversification in the postwar years. In the meantime, Nippon Gakki had to stop making musical instruments altogether in 1945.

Only one Nippon Gakki factory survived the wartime U.S. bombing raids. Postwar financial assistance from the United States made possible the production of harmonicas and xylophones just two months after receipt of the funds. Within six months it produced organs, accordions, tube horns, and guitars. After the Allied powers approved civilian trade in 1947, Nippon Gakki began once again to export harmonicas.

Nippon Gakki already had experience with wooden aircraft parts dating back to 1920, but wartime activity exposed the company to new technologies. By 1947 Nippon Gakki could cast its own metal piano frames and produced its first pianos in three years. The company also produced its first audio component—a phonograph—in 1947.

Postwar growth was rapid. The Japanese government had fostered the growth of Western music in Japan since 1879, but Nippon Gakki received its biggest boost to date in 1948. That year the Education Ministry mandated musical education for Japanese children—only encouraged before the war— and greatly expanded business.

Kaichi Kawakami's son, Gen'ichi Kawakami, became the company's fourth president in 1950. During his tenure the Japanese rebuilt their economy, and consumer buying power increased. Nippon Gakki became less reliant on institutional purchases. President for 27 years, Kawakami made more progress in popularizing Western music in Japan by beginning the Yamaha music schools in 1954 to train young musicians. With the help of the Ministry of Education, Nippon Gakki founded the nonprofit Yamaha Music Foundation in 1966 to sponsor festivals and concerts and run the music schools.

Kawakami's biggest accomplishments were in production, diversification, and the creation of foreign markets, all of which built the framework for the modern Yamaha Corporation. Kawakami toured the United States and Europe in 1953, a trip that inspired diversification into many areas unrelated to the music industry. Like Yamaha's tour of the United States in 1899, G. Kawakami's tour affected the company's product line and reputation for decades to come.

His return sparked research into new uses for materials since capital was scarce. The company researched uses for fiberglass reinforced plastics (FRP). In 1960 the company produced its first sailboat made of FRP. Later it expanded to produce yachts, patrol boats for Japan's Maritime Safety Agency, and oceangoing fishing vessels. Primarily serving the Asian market, it eventually became Japan's largest FRP boat producer. FRP capability led to introduction of other products, such as archery bows, skis, and bathtubs. Through metals research Nippon Gakki developed sophisticated alloys for electronics as well as less complex alloys for structural purposes. Nippon Gakki soon became a major producer of equipment for the household construction industry, such as boilers and central heating systems.

In its traditional line of pianos, Nippon Gakki expanded production, raised its quality standards, and cut production costs, already lower than the industry average, even further. Through a conveyer belt system and an innovative kiln drying technique that facilitated the rapid drying of wood used in pianos, Nippon Gakki decreased the amount of time required to produce a piano from two years to three months.

The first large-scale marketing drive toward the United States was not related to music at all. In 1954 the government returned the company's World War II-era metal working factory, which had been among confiscated assets. Nippon Gakki produced its first motorcycle in 1955 and established the Yamaha Motor Company Ltd., of which it was partial owner. Later it produced smaller motorized vehicles like snowmobiles, outboard engines, and golf carts. For the next 20 years, however, it was motorcycles for which the West would recognize the Yamaha brand. Following Honda's lead, Yamaha introduced its first motorcycles in the United States in the early 1960s. Along with Suzuki, the three companies made smaller and lower-priced motorcycles and greatly expanded the U.S. market, which had been limited to large cycles for serious enthusiasts. Yamaha also marketed its motorcycles successfully in Asia.

Nippon Gakki began an ambitious drive into electronics in 1959, when it introduced the world's first all-transistor organ to replace electronic organs using vacuum tubes. Nippon Gakki's first electronic instrument represented the company's new competence in product development.

With its new variety of products Nippon Gakki began its first serious export push, establishing its first overseas subsidiary, in Mexico in 1958. In 1959 the company made a few pianos with a U.S. retailer's name on them, and in 1960 it created its own sales subsidiary in Los Angeles. Within a year Yamaha won a conspicuous contract to supply the Los

Angeles Board of Education with 53 grand pianos. For the next seven years, the board annually purchased Yamaha pianos for schools in its jurisdiction. Since Nippon Gakki priced its pianos considerably lower than Western competition, this boost to its reputation for quality allowed it to bid with more success on U.S. institutional contracts.

Having worked well in Japan, Nippon Gakki sponsored overseas musical events and education beginning in 1964, when it opened the first Yamaha school in the United States. Like its Japanese counterpart, it was designed to teach music appreciation to students at an early age and create a long-term market. Financially independent of Yamaha, these non-profit schools operate throughout Europe and the United States and have taught more than one million students.

These educational efforts were just beginning to pay off in Japan. During the 1960s Nippon Gakki's domestic market grew tremendously. Annual piano output increased from 24,000 in 1960 to 100,000 in 1966, making the company the world's largest piano maker.

In the mid-1960s, Nippon Gakki began to produce wind instruments on a large scale. In 1968 Nippon Gakki started exporting trumpets, trombones, and xylophones. Five years in development, the company produced is first concert grand piano in 1967.

U.S. instrument makers did not welcome Yamaha's growth. In 1969 U.S. piano manufacturers sought a 30% tariff on imported pianos, but the U.S. Tariff Commission ruled in Yamaha's favor. Nonetheless, the hearings delayed for three years a tariff reduction that had already been scheduled and established a hostile precedent for Nippon Gakki expansion in North America. In 1973 Yamaha bought its first U.S. manufacturing facility, but a strike there further delayed Yamaha's U.S. drive.

Just as transistors had once replaced tubes in electronics, integrated circuits (ICs) replaced transistors in the 1970s. Because no manufacturer would develop an IC for Nippon Gakki's relatively limited demand, the company built a plant in 1971 to make its own. By developing the technology early, Nippon Gakki established itself as a serious electronics firm, better able to serve the accelerating demand for electronic keyboards and audio components.

Large-scale integrated circuits (LSIs) allowed the company to digitalize its keyboards. Nippon Gakki built an LSI plant in 1976 so it could convert all of its electronic products from analog to digital formats. LSIs also made possible Yamaha's growth as an electronics supplier and the manufacture of advanced electronic systems such as industrial robots. In the early 1990s, 75% of Yamaha's chips were sold to other companies.

Nippon Gakki developed electronic components more quickly than other types of components. In its traditional line of pianos and organs, by contrast, Nippon Gakki still depended on overseas suppliers for components in the 1970s.

While Nippon Gakki's sales in 1979 remained steady, a favorable exchange rate boosted earnings to a record ¥15 billion. The same exchange rate, however, hurt motorcycle sales. Unlike Western companies, however, Yamaha did not pare down to a core business during the 1980s.

Nippon Gakki electronics research paid off well with increasing music synthesizer sales in the 1980s. Yamaha keyboards were among the best selling digital synthesizers in the world during the decade.

Growing sophistication in new technologies and experience in older methods continue to provide Yamaha with new areas in which to grow. The development of LSIs allowed Nippon Gakki to produce its first professional sound systems and to keep pace with the consumer audio industry during the early 1980s. In 1983 the company put its LSIs themselves on the market.

In the early 1980s, Nippon Gakki divided its research facilities to reflect its electronics emphasis. Research was then carried out by four sections: one on semiconductors and LSIs, a second for research applications to audiovisual equipment, a third on hall and theater acoustic design, and the fourth for products design.

While expanding its product line, Nippon Gakki also initiated a program to spread its manufacturing base overseas, adding to its network of marketing subsidiaries. Hiroshi Kawashima, former president of the U.S. subsidiary, spearheaded the U.S. drive. In 1980 Nippon Gakki opened an electronic keyboard plant in Georgia in the hope that basing this new venture in the United States would ease trade tension.

In 1981 second-place motorcycle manufacturer Yamaha Motor tried to gain market share in the United States against first-place Honda. Yamaha introduced new models and increased production. When Honda and other motorcycle manufacturers did the same, the industry faced overproduction. As a result Yamaha Motor posted two consecutive losses totaling $126.1 million. A relatively small motor manufacturer, Yamaha Motor was left with an inventory of one million motorcycles and debts that approached $1 billion. In addition, the price competition among Japanese motorcycle makers caused U.S. manufacturer Harley Davidson to request tariffs in imports, straining Yamaha's U.S. business, since it did not have any U.S. factories. Nippon Gakki remained profitable since it only owns 39.1% of Yamaha Motor, but the period damaged the company's reputation and position at home.

In 1983 the third generation of Kawakamis, Hiroshi, became the company's seventh president. Formerly an employee of Sony, his contributions include strengthening Yamaha's audio business and overseeing overseas production.

By 1984 the company had become so diversified that one of Kawakami's first actions was to decentralize even further. Earnings during the reorganization period posted three straight declines from 1985 to 1987. In 1987 Kawakami changed the corporate name to Yamaha, the name still carried on all its products.

Yamaha is an enigmatic company loosely focused around music. Its products include acoustic and electronic instruments and audio systems, and also include music hall design and resort management. While Yamaha has progressed in establishing an overseas manufacturing network, much of its work is still carried out in Japan. The company no longer enjoys fantastic growth in its domestic market, and the absence of continuing government assistance will make expansion tougher.

Yamaha's product development is ambitious, and it conducts its research economically on materials that can be employed in as many items as possible. Its brand name has a sound reputation, even if limited to luxury items, and as long as the Japanese economy grows, Yamaha stands to improve sales. Making the most of its growth, however, eluded the company during the boom years of the 1980s.

Principal Subsidiaries: Yamaha Plans Co., Ltd.; Yamaha Credit Co., Ltd.; Yamaha Recreation Co., Ltd. (99.5%); Yamaha Kagoshima Semi-Conductor Inc.; Yamaha Corporation of America (U.S.A.); Yamaha Europa G.m.b.H. (Germany); Yamaha Canada Music, Ltd.; Yamaha-Kemble Music (U.K.) Ltd. (87.5%); Yamaha Motor Company, Ltd. (32.1%).

Further Reading: Yamaha's First Century," *Music Trades,* August 1987; *Yamaha: A Century of Excellence: 1887–1987*, Hamamatsu, Japan, Yamaha Corporation 1987.

—Ray Walsh

MATERIALS

AMERICAN STANDARD INC.
ASAHI GLASS COMPANY, LIMITED
BLUE CIRCLE INDUSTRIES PLC
BORAL LIMITED
COMPAGNIE DE SAINT-GOBAIN S.A.
COOKSON GROUP PLC
CORNING INCORPORATED
CSR LIMITED
ECC GROUP PLC
FELDMÜHLE NOBEL AG
HARRISONS & CROSFIELD PLC
"HOLDERBANK" FINANCIÈRE GLARIS LTD.
LAFARGE COPPÉE S.A.
MANVILLE CORPORATION
MATSUSHITA ELECTRIC WORKS, LTD.
MITSUBISHI MATERIALS CORPORATION
NIPPON SHEET GLASS COMPANY, LIMITED
ONODA CEMENT CO., LTD.
OWENS-CORNING FIBERGLAS CORPORATION
PILKINGTON PLC
PIONEER INTERNATIONAL LIMITED
PPG INDUSTRIES, INC.
REDLAND PLC
RMC GROUP P.L.C.
SEKISUI CHEMICAL CO., LTD.
THE SHERWIN-WILLIAMS COMPANY
SSANGYONG CEMENT INDUSTRIAL CO., LTD.
TARMAC PLC
TOTO, LTD.
TOYO SASH CO., LTD.
UBE INDUSTRIES, LTD.
USG CORPORATION
WALTER INDUSTRIES, INC.

AMERICAN STANDARD INC.

1114 Avenue of the Americas
New York, New York 10036
U.S.A.
(212) 703-5100
Fax: (212) 703-5290

Wholly Owned Subsidiary of AST Holding Corporation
Incorporated: 1929 as American Radiator & Standard Sanitary Corporation
Employees: 33,300
Sales: $3.33 billion

In its first 100 years, American Standard evolved from a leading manufacturer of plumbing and heating products to a leading manufacturer of plumbing and air-cooling products. American Standard became the world leader in such staple items as toilets and radiators, diversified into a number of unrelated fields, and then gradually returned to its bread-and-butter industries. Today, American Standard remains the world leader in plumbing products. No longer a factor in heating, the company secured a strong position in commercial air conditioning with its 1983 acquisition of Trane Company. The remainder of American Standard's ambitious purchases have been sold off, most to reduce debt after the parent company was taken private in a $2.5 billion leveraged buyout by Kelso & Company, a relatively small investment banking firm.

The early history of American Standard is bound closely to the figure of Clarence Mott Woolley, born in 1863 to a wealthy Detroit iron manufacturer. Forced to begin working at the age of 15 after the panic of 1873 wiped out his father's fortune, by 1886, Woolley had become a successful salesman of wholesale crockery and built personal savings of around $5,000, not an insignificant amount of money at that time. After investigating a number of promising businesses, in 1886 Woolley became a partner in the newly formed Michigan Radiator & Iron Company of Detroit, makers of cast-iron radiators for residential and commercial heating systems. The cast-iron radiator could be made far more cheaply than its steel predecessor, and Woolley correctly predicted that its advent would mark the beginning of the age of radiant heat.

In 1891, Michigan Radiator merged with the two other leading manufacturers of cast iron radiators, Detroit Radiator Company and the Pierce Steam Heating Company of Buffalo, New York. The merger was an early example of business consolidation, and created a firm with yearly net income of $300,000 and a capital base of $8 million. As secretary and head of sales for the new American Radiator, Clarence Woolley, then only 28, soon proved himself an invaluable and tireless promoter of the company's patented advances in radiant heat. An economic downturn, however, nearly snuffed out the new business in the 1890s. As the depression of the mid-1890s deepened, Woolley recommended pursuing sales contacts he had made with foreign buyers at the 1893 Chicago World's Fair. In 1894, he took the highly unusual step of traveling to Europe to peddle American Radiator products, and, much to the surprise of his skeptical fellow officers, came home with a suitcase full of orders. Thirty train carloads of American Radiator heaters were installed in the new Swiss capital building, and other major orders soon followed. The injection of fresh business kept American alive through the depression's worst years and helped create the company's strong European presence. Over the next 30 years, American added production facilities in many of the major European markets, and by the 1920s about 40% of its revenue was generated overseas.

In 1902, at age 39, Clarence Woolley was named president of American Radiator. From that date until Woolley's retirement in 1938, American Radiator dominated the world heating market by carefully exploiting four basic strengths, as *Fortune* reported in April 1935. The first was the company's sizable technological lead in cast-iron equipment. Although its originally exclusive patents at length expired, American's head start and great size made it a fearsome competitor. In addition, Woolley saw to it that American spent lavishly on research and development—the second of the firm's strengths. With far more capital than its nearest pursuers, American could afford to maintain its technical advantages even without the benefit of exclusive patents.

The company's two other valuable resources were both vested in Woolley himself. By all accounts, Woolley was a consummate industrial salesman, able to drink with plumbers and sweet-talk corporate executives over dinner. American's sales depended on the support of the master plumbers and builders, who both bought and installed heating systems across the country, and Woolley's sales force knew the concerns and complaints of these men inside out. American's fourth great strength was its president's ability to forecast economic conditions, especially recessions. In 1907, for example, Woolley correctly deduced from soaring raw-material prices the imminent arrival of another panic, and kept American's inventories at near-zero levels to avoid having bulging warehouses in a dead economy. In 1915 he laid in an enormous stock of pig iron just before World War I drove up iron prices. It is estimated that this maneuver alone netted American some $2.5 million in savings.

The postwar boom economy pushed American's income to around $10 million annually. Flushed with success, Woolley built a spectacular new Manhattan headquarters for American; its black brick and gold roof quickly distinguished it as an architectural landmark. Just before the Depression, Woolley planned a merger for American, one that would have been a colossal achievement even in that merger-mad era. His plan was to unite four of the largest building-products corporations in the country—H.W. Johns-Manville, Otis Elevator, Standard Sanitary, and American Radiator—into a single immense powerhouse, its unified sales force able to offer the contracting customer nearly everything needed. Woolley however, was able to come to terms only with the Pittsburgh-based Standard Sanitary, the nation's leading supplier of plumbing products. By mid-1929, the merger was concluded; American Radiator & Standard Sanitary Corporation (ARSS) finished that year with income of over $20 million on sales of $187 million, as well as strong cash reserves with which to face the suddenly grim economic scene.

The Great Depression brought new construction to a dead stop, ruining Woolley's plans for a new conglomerate. The anticipated big profits became big losses. In 1932 ARSS lost $6 million—easily the worst year in the company's history. Although the firm had begun to break even by 1935, it was clear that all was not right in the black and gold tower. The 20-odd companies brought together by the 1929 merger had never been properly consolidated, and antagonism between the American and the Standard affiliates was growing. Friction became such that when one American outfit decided to build a warehouse next to a Standard facility, the latter promptly erected a fence around its property and forced American to put in a separate driveway for its own use.

The hostility was aggravated by American's failure to hold up its end of the sales and profit agreement. American's radiator sales were being seriously challenged by the new forced-air-furnace technique, and what little profit the company managed to make was largely generated by its numerous European subsidiaries. The company's overall lack of coordination eventually culminated in a confrontation between Woolley and Standard President Henry M. Reed, who pressed the 75-year-old Woolley to step down as chairman of the combined companies. Finally, in 1938, Woolley agreed, and Henry Reed became the new chief executive.

Reed wasted no time in simplifying ARSS's tangled structure. He cut its 25 operating subsidiaries to 12. Top management underwent a similarly drastic winnowing. With a newly unified sales force, American's performance was on the upswing until the outbreak of World War II in Europe, an event that presented a new set of problems. American had always relied on its strong and highly profitable European division for a disproportionate amount of its net income, but with Europe at war, the fate of American's 16 overseas plants was suddenly in doubt. In addition, American's domestic operations were suffering as a result of the growing popularity of "direct-to-you" stores, which bought plumbing and heating products in bulk and resold them directly to the consumer. Although direct retailing is now a standard practice, in the late 1930s the practice caused bitter controversy for those tradesmen and manufacturers who had a vested interest in the older system, in which all equipment was bought and installed by craftsmen. As the nation's largest such manufacturer, ARSS was naturally concerned about this potentially momentous change in its customer mix.

As events unfolded, however, neither World War II nor the direct-to-you stores slowed American's subsequent growth. The company suffered keenly from several years of lost European sales, but, at war's end, the European affiliates were able to reassume their former dominance quickly. As for the direct stores, American generally stuck by its network of plumber-contractors, who did not fare as poorly as some had predicted. American also began to manufacture forced-air heating systems. Over many years, the company wound down its radiator-based business while adding additional forced-air capacity—and its natural counterpart, air conditioning.

The postwar U.S. economy carried building-products companies along with it. With the suburbs burgeoning and mortgages easily obtainable, the U.S. construction industry threw up record numbers of new homes across the country, each in need of plumbing and heating fixtures, supplied by ARSS. By the mid-1950s, ARSS was pushing $400 million in worldwide sales and continuing to score steady, if modest, profits. Around 1957 however, American entered a ten-year period of disappointing performance. Affected by rising raw material prices and a strongly unionized labor force, American's earnings per share and dividends drifted downward. From 1955 to 1960 domestic sales at ARSS earned a thin 2% on the dollar. The bulk of corporate profits again were being provided by the company's 20 European plants, which faced a less competitive market than U.S. operations.

Around 1963 ARSS began a program of diversification that would occupy it for the next 15 years. By 1963, in addition to its traditional heating and plumbing lines, the company had branched into industrial controls, plastics, heat-transfer equipment, and nuclear-reactor construction. This flurry of activity produced modest results, however; in 1965, sales of $553 million were only marginally higher than they had been in the late 1950s, and profit remained unacceptably low at 3%. As a result two potential merger partners backed off after concluding that ARSS was too weak to purchase. The most serious of these suitors was Boise Cascade. One of that company's executive vice presidents, William D. Eberle, joined ARSS as its new president in 1966 and proceeded to turn the company around. In three years, Eberle more than doubled sales while decreasing the company's dependence on the housing market by means of several major acquisitions. American bought Mosler Safe, a maker of security devices for the banking industry; Westinghouse Air Brake Company, a diversified manufacturer of equipment for the railroad, construction, and mining businesses; and William Lyon Homes, a California home builder. Eberle also changed the company's name to American Standard to indicate its movement away from the heating and plumbing niche.

By 1971 American Standard's sales reached $1.4 billion, its employees numbered some 70,000, and industry analysts judged Eberle's work a mess. By quickly expanding, Eberle had indeed reduced American's dependence on the housing business, but at the cost of massive new debts, a confusing overlay of unrelated businesses, and plummeting earnings. In 1971 Eberle was shuffled out, and his successor, William Marquard, set aside $100 million on the balance sheet to defray the expected cost of undoing Eberle's work. Marquard shut down inefficient plants, reduced employment by 20%, and sold off a number of the more extraneous divisions, using the proceeds to reduce debt and raise earnings. Marquard went further, however, easing American out of its original heating business while developing its railroad, truck brake, and mining-equipment operations. By keeping only those companies that were efficient and profitable, Marquard built a far sturdier, more lucrative business. Although total sales remained steady at $1.6 billion for much of the decade, earnings per share skyrocketed from 1971's 11¢ to $5.25 in 1977.

American was not yet finished with its housecleaning. During the 1980s the company completed its long retreat from Eberle's diversified conglomerate to position itself as a relatively simple manufacturer of plumbing and air conditioning products. Under chairman and CEO William Boyd, American Standard sold the Mosler security business and the various transportation companies. Though generally profitable, these outfits did not mesh well with American's core businesses. American Standard's only major acquisition during the 1980s did mesh, however. In 1983 American Standard purchased the Trane Company, the largest commercial air conditioning products company in the U.S. With $833 million in sales, Trane made up some of the volume American Standard had lost to reorganization. By 1988 the once-heterogeneous mix of companies at American Standard had been boiled down to three basic businesses: plumbing, air conditioning, and railway brake systems, together producing sales of about $3.4 billion. In January 1988 The Black & Decker Corporation, the Maryland-based maker of hand tools and appliances, began a prolonged attempt to buy American Standard. In a complex round of legal and financial maneuvers, American Standard sought to protect its independence while Black & Decker pressed the attack, eventually raising its bid to $2.5 billion, or $77 per share, up from $34 per share before the takeover bid. Finally, in July 1988 after six months of fighting, American Standard found a white knight in the investment-banking firm of Kelso & Company, which took American Standard private in a $2.5 billion leveraged buyout. To reduce the large debts thus incurred, Kelso subsequently sold American's remaining railway-brake business for around $250 million. ASI Holding Corporation, formed by Kelso in 1988, owns the shares of American Standard.

As a private concern, American Standard is not required to publish financial data and its current health is not easily gauged. Judging by its successful 1987 results and the further concentration afforded by the sale of its last extraneous subsidiary, however, American Standard is no doubt moving much as it has in the past. Although not highly profitable, American Standard holds number-one positions in domestic markets for plumbing and commercial air conditioning, with about half its sales to foreign customers.

Further Reading: ''Heating Man,'' *Fortune*, April 1935; ''American Radiator & Standard Sanitary Corp.,'' *Fortune*, March 1940; ''Radiator maker starts to swing,'' *Business Week*, May 3, 1969; ''How American Standard cured its conglomeritis,'' *Business Week*, September 28, 1974; Clifford, Mark, ''Back to basics,'' *Forbes*, June 30, 1986.

—Jonathan Martin

ASAHI GLASS COMPANY, LIMITED

1-2, Marunouchi 2-chome
Chiyoda-ku, Tokyo 100
Japan
(03) 3218-5555
Fax: (03) 3287-0772

Public Company
Incorporated: 1907
Employees: 9,200
Sales: ¥925.93 billion (US$6.44 billion)
Stock Exchanges: Tokyo Osaka Nagoya Kyoto Hiroshima Fukuoka Sapporo Niigata Luxembourg

Asahi Glass Company is a leading producer of glass, chemicals, and electronics in Japan and the Far East. Its products touch almost every aspect of daily life. Even a partial product list includes mirrored skyscraper windows coated with a heat-reflective substance, super-durable paints, glass-reinforced concrete for building, 50% of the cathode-ray tubes in the world, fluorocarbon cooling units for air conditioners, heat-resistant glass doors for microwave ovens, liquid crystal display (LCD) numerals for alarm clocks, and the glass magnetic heads that make video-cassette recorders run.

While all these Asahi products are available only in Japan and the Far East, Asahi Glass is fast expanding its overseas production and sales organizations. With 29 affiliates in 11 foreign countries employing some 16,000 workers, Asahi has become a truly international power, and most observers agree that sometime in the early 1990s the company will emerge as the world's largest diversified glassmaker. Asahi's founder, Toshiya Iwasaki, was born into Japan's most formidable industrial family in 1881, and he decided early in life to build his country's first successful glass company. A nephew of Mitsubishi founder Yataro Iwasaki, Iwasaki studied applied chemistry at the University of London before returning to fight in the Russo-Japanese War of 1904 to 1905. As a member of the Imperial Cavalry, he realized the importance of increasing Japan's native industrial base. Drawing upon his chemical studies, Iwasaki decided to make glass his area of specialization.

Japan had been unable to support even a single glassmaking facility up to that point, although the Meiji government had tried to establish sheet glass manufacturing. The country had just emerged from 200 years of isolation, and in the last half of the 19th century Japanese businessmen scrambled to compress centuries of technological progress into a few decades of growth. They had succeeded in most areas by the turn of the century, but the glassmaking field remained open until Iwasaki founded Asahi Glass in 1907 with a factory in Kansai. Iwasaki was able to draw upon his family's powerful banking and political allies, and from the beginning he planned to build a world-class organization. Instead of merely importing technology from Belgium, then the world leader in flat glass production, he brought over Belgian glassblowers to get his company started properly. By 1909 these craftsmen had succeeded in producing Japan's first flat glass, giving Asahi a national lead it has never relinquished.

Because the Japanese industrial economy remained primitive, Asahi was forced to engineer its own equipment and to produce its own raw materials. This situation led to the 1916 construction of an addition to the Kansai factory, where the company began making its own fire bricks for use in its glass furnaces, and in 1917 to the production of soda ash, required in glass manufacture, at a separate facility in Kita-Kyushu. Asahi thus got its start not only in glass but also in ceramics and in alkali-chlorine-based chemistry, which have remained the firm's three basic divisions. With a concerted marketing effort and the economic boom afforded by World War I, Asahi was soon profitable and grew rapidly. The company faced a temporary setback in the early 1920s, when large quantities of natural soda ash were imported from Kenya and dumped on the Japanese market at artificially depressed prices, undercutting Asahi's position as the country's leading supplier of that commodity. In the ensuing political battle Japan adopted its first anti-dumping legislation, and Asahi recovered by 1924.

Along with the rest of Japanese industry, Asahi found excellent markets and a convenient labor pool in neighboring China. As the two countries edged toward war in the 1930s, Asahi shifted a good part of its growing glass and chemical business from Japan to 17 small Chinese plants. At the outbreak of World War II Asahi found itself with four times as many overseas as domestic plants. The company was caught up in Japan's mammoth war effort, and in 1944 the government merged Asahi with another chemical firm to form Mitsubishi Chemical Industries Limited. The new name was an indication of Asahi's close ties with the Mitsubishi group, which today remains among Asahi's largest stockholders. This belated effort at rationalizing Japan's chemical industry was little help, however, and by the following year Japan was totally defeated. Asahi lost its 17 Chinese factories.

The postwar years were grim. Allied occupation forces took control of the Japanese economy and directed its every move, initially in the hopes of dismantling the great trading companies, or *zaibatsu.* As Mitsubishi was one of the most important *zaibatsu,* the recently formed Mitsubishi Chemical Industries was again broken into its constituent pieces, and a new Asahi Glass was incorporated in 1950. The reborn Asahi faced formidable problems, but equally vast were the opportunities for growth. The company's four domestic plants had survived the war in relatively good condition, and the rebuilding of Japan would require unlimited numbers of new glass products. So too would two inventions still largely unknown in Japan but soon to play a dominant role in its development into economic maturity—the automobile and television. As Japan's young auto industry got off the ground in the 1950s, it sparked a huge increase in the demand for windshield glass, which Asahi met with the 1956 creation of Asahi Processed Glass. Similarly, after the 1953 inauguration of Japanese television broadcasts, Asahi established Asahi Special Glass for the manufacture of cathode-ray tubes. As the subsequent history of Japanese industry made clear, Asahi had established strongholds in what became two of Japan's most important industries, ensuring the company's rapid growth into an international power.

Postwar domestic demand for glass kept Asahi busy for the next two decades, when corporate profits averaged three times those of the rest of Japanese industry. At the same time, Asahi's chemical business continued its evolution from a producer of strictly inorganic substances to a diversified supplier of both organic and inorganic compounds. To its traditional strength in caustic soda and soda ash, Asahi added production facilities for chloromethane, propylene glycol, and eventually fluorine compounds so important today.

Perhaps of greater significance in the long run was Asahi's decision to renew its foreign operations in both glass and chemicals. Beginning with the 1956 construction of Indo-Asahi Glass in Calcutta, India, Asahi committed itself to a program of overseas expansion unusual for a Japanese materials-manufacturing concern. The focus of this expansion has been Southeast Asia, where Asahi has established dominant positions in Thailand, Indonesia, and the Philippines and maintains a significant presence in many other countries. European and U.S. operations, on the other hand, had to wait until the 1980s. Asahi entered the European market in a major way with its 1981 acquisition of Belgium's Glaverbel and the Dutch company, MaasGlas, giving Asahi approximately 10% of the European flat glass market. U.S. investments, which were more recent, have been largely restricted to the automobile industry: Asahi supplies window glass to the U.S. plants of Honda and Toyota from its own factories in Ohio and Kentucky. Finally, to round out its foreign operations, Asahi also manufactured television tubes from plants in Taiwan and Singapore, and Corning-Asahi Video products as part of a 1988 U.S. joint venture with Corning Glass.

Such overseas expansion became especially important after the 1965 worldwide introduction of the float process method of flat glass production. Developed in England but soon licensed around the world, the float process has made it possible for anyone to produce excellent flat glass at low cost and without extensive technological experience. It thus became necessary for Asahi, which for years had exported flat glass throughout Asia, to enter into cooperative ventures with local manufacturing concerns in its various national markets or suffer a sharp reduction in its overall sales. With domestic Japanese demand leveling off after the boom years of 1950 to 1970, Asahi was forced to rely more heavily on foreign joint ventures.

As the 1980s began, the fundamental problem of shrinking domestic demand and increasingly standardized production techniques remained a real threat to Asahi's continued growth. In response, the company at first favored a program of diversification outside the glass industry by expanding its already substantial chemical business. Asahi entered into joint ventures with Olin, PPG Industries, and Britain's ICI to produce a wider variety of compounds, including fluorochemicals and plastics, and pioneered the new ion-exchange membrane technique for its manufacture of caustic soda. A company plan developed in the early 1980s called for reducing glass sales to less than 40% of total Asahi revenue by the year 2000.

That thinking changed in the late 1980s under the leadership of Jiro Furumoto, president and chief executive officer since 1987. Technological developments opened up a range of innovative glass products for Asahi, promoting Furumoto to design what he called "AGC Vision 21." This corporate forecast calls for Asahi sales in the year 2000 of ¥2.4 trillion split evenly between glass and nonglass operations. The key point of Furomoto's plan is to reach ¥800 billion annually in new products, including "new glass," the various applications for glass made possible by recent technological changes. New-glass uses include reflective building glass and glass-reinforced concrete, large, flat television screens for high-definition television, and glass hard discs for personal computers. Far more exotic glass applications are still expected.

Asahi thus plans to maintain and expand its position in the suddenly growing field of glass manufacturing. It will employ its highly automated domestic plants for high-tech, value-added production, while farming out to its foreign subsidiaries the production of standard flat and automobile glass. The other half of Asahi sales will come from chemical products, including old standbys like soda ash and new environmentally safe replacements.The company continues a small business in refractory products—3% of sales—and will pursue its growing segment of the electronics industry—now 4% of sales. If all goes as planned, Furumoto will preside over the world's largest glass-manufacturing concern, a company that is determinedly international in character, well balanced in product mix, and consistently profitable.

Principal Subsidiaries: Asahi Fiber Glass Co., Ltd.; Asahi-ICI-Fluoropolymers Co., Ltd.; Asahi Glass Building Materials Co., Ltd.; Asahi Glass Engineering Co., Ltd.; Asahi Komag Co., Ltd.; Asahi Olin Ltd.; Asahi-Penn Chemical Co., Ltd.; Asahi Glass Coat & Resin Co., Ltd.; Catalysts & Chemical Industries Co., Ltd.; Dainihon Glass Industrial Co., Ltd.; Dokai Chemical Industrial Co., Ltd.; ELNA Co., Ltd.; Hanno Optical Glass Co., Ltd.; Hinode Commercial Co., Ltd.; Hokkaido Soda Co., Ltd.; Ise Chemical Industries Co., Ltd.; Ito Industries Co., Ltd.; Iwaki Glass Co., Ltd.; Japan Siperex Inc.; Japan Sodium Silicate Glass Co., Ltd.; Kashima Chemical Co., Ltd.; Nippon Builder Co., Ltd.; Nippon Drychemical Co., Ltd.; Optrex Corp.; Seimi Chemical Co., Ltd.; Tokai Industries Co., Ltd.; AMA Glass Corporation (U.S.A.); AA Glass Corporation (U.S.A.); AP Technoglass Company (U.S.A.); Belletech Corporation (U.S.A.); D&A Technology, Inc. (U.S.A.); AP Tenntech Corporation (U.S.A.); Corning Asahi Video Products Company (U.S.A.);

Woodward Iodine Corporation (U.S.A.); Asahi Glass America, Inc. (U.S.A.); Glaverbel S.A. (Belgium); N.V. Euro Safety Glass S.A. (Belgium); MaasGlas B.V. (Netherlands); Asahi Glass Europe B.V. (Netherlands); Thai-Asahi Glass Co., Ltd. (Thailand); Thai Safety Glass Co., Ltd. (Thailand); Siam Asahi Technoglass Co., Ltd. (Thailand); THASCO Chemical Co., Ltd. (Thailand); P.T. Asahimas Flat Glass Co., Ltd. (Indonesia); P.T. Asahimas Jaya Safety Glass Co., Ltd. (Indonesia); P.T. Asahimas Subentra Chemical (Indonesia); Asahi TV-Glass Pte., Ltd. (Singapore); Asahi Techno Vision (Singapore) Pte., Ltd.; AG Investment (Singapore) Pte., Ltd.; MCIS Safety Glass SDN. BHD. (Malaysia); Republic-Asahi Glass Corporation (Philippines); Pacific Glass Corporation (Taiwan); Lim Shang Hang Temper-Safe Factory Co., Ltd. (Taiwan); Asahi Glass Hong Kong, Ltd.; The Indo-Asahi Glass Co., Ltd. (India).

Further Reading: Wray, William D., *Mitsubishi and the N.Y.K., 1870–1914: Business Strategy in the Japanese Shipping Industry,* Cambridge, Harvard University Press, 1984; Mushakoji, Kinhisa, "The Process of Internationalization: Asahi Glass Company, Ltd.," Tokyo Institute of Comparative Culture Business Series #99, 1985; "Company History," Asahi Glass corporate typescript, [n.d.]

—Jonathan Martin

Blue Circle Industries PLC

BLUE CIRCLE INDUSTRIES PLC

84 Eccleston Square
London SW1V 1PX
United Kingdom
(071) 828-3456
Fax: (071) 245-8169

Public Company
Incorporated: 1900 as Associated Portland Cement Manufacturers (1900) Ltd.
Employees: 20,818
Sales: £1.28 billion (US$2.01 billion)
Stock Exchange: London

The U.K. cement industry has its roots in the early 1800s. In 1824, Joseph Aspdin, a Leeds bricklayer, patented Portland cement, although others lay claim to its invention. The early years of the U.K. cement industry were characterized by the operating of many small producers in small, regionally competitive markets. Exports represented a fair proportion of earnings for such firms, many of whom operated along the River Thames and River Medway, and shipped cement to Europe in barges. It was a tough industry in these early years, characterized by long hours and a payment-by-results system for its work force.

During the last decade of the 19th century, with U.K. cement manufacturers having enjoyed a lengthy period of little or no foreign competition, they finally began to lose their export markets to domestic production both in Europe and the United States. This situation encouraged a spate of mergers within the industry, notably that between Brooks, Shoobridge and Company and Hilton, Anderson and Company, forming Hilton, Anderson, Brooks and Company.

The formation of Associated Portland Cement Manufacturers (APCM) in 1900 was due largely to the endeavors of Henry Osborne O'Hagan, a financier whose business interests were wide and varied and who principally was involved in share issues and dealings. In this task he was aided by two others, John Bazley White, a cement manufacturer, and his solicitor, H. S. Leonard, whose goal had been to bring about the amalgamation of all the cement manufacturers in the country.

Their task was a difficult one, as the competitive nature of most manufacturers prevented them from divulging necessary information to others in the industry. By July 1900, however, contracts had been drawn up for the amalgamation of 27 cement producers. All of the 27 companies bar 3 were located in the Thames-Medway area. The others were I.C. Johnson and Company of Gateshead; C. Francis, Son and Company of the Isle of Wight; and the Arlesey Lime and Portland Cement Company of Hitchin. Four other producers who refused to join the amalgamation had reached working agreements with the group, and between these 31 producers, over 80% of the country's production was accounted for.

The flotation involved an agreement between London's main cement merchants, ensuring that all their requirements were supplied by APCM—this was the first attempt by APCM to exert market influence from its dominant position—and the purchase of 3,697 acres of freehold land, and 1,058 acres of leasehold land in areas with raw material deposits and suitable dock and wharf facilities. Also involved was the purchase of railways and rolling stock, plant, and river barges.

The new company, Associated Portland Cement Manufacturers (1900) Ltd., had a nominal capital of £8 million, and its board of directors was comprised of one member from each company, with the two largest companies able to nominate the chairman and vice chairman. However the share issue, intended to raise £7.3 million, did not go smoothly, falling £2 million short. O'Hagan, who had failed to get the issue underwritten, had to return to the vendors, who finally agreed to find another £1.1 million, as did O'Hagan. Further trouble arose when three of the vendor firms broke away from the association, apparently unhappy with the lack of public support for the issue.

APCM attempted to impose a higher level of prices in the market, but the builders' merchants, led by George Wragge, reacted by increasing imports until prices assumed their previous levels. These were difficult times for Frederick White, the first chairman, and his 25-strong board of directors. By 1907, in the face of increasing competition in the domestic market, APCM's share of U.K. output had fallen to three-fifths of its 1900 level, and it was struggling to maintain market share in London.

The association sought a price agreement in its early years, with O'Hagan once again playing a major role, although many agreements were made and broken as competition and the rapid use of new technology caused prices to fall. It was clearly beneficial to APCM to secure such an agreement to enable it to set output levels among its constituent manufacturers and ensure a steady production rate in the medium to long term.

Over this period, 1906 to 1910, there were changes on the board of directors. Lord St. Davids was offered the post of chairman when it came to light that three-quarters of the ordinary shares were owned by a syndicate headed by this prominent financier and industrialist. It was agreed between O'Hagan and Lord St. Davids that a further £2 million would be found to try to secure a complete amalgamation of the cement industry.

This undertaking led to a spate of mergers over the next few years, starting with the takeover of Trechmann, Weekes and Company, and—most notably—G. and T. Earle, a high-quality cement producer operating in Lancashire and Yorkshire.

By December 1911, British Portland Cement Manufacturers was formed as a subsidiary of APCM, with capital of

£3.5 million. BPCM contained 33 firms which had been taken over by APCM, and together they controlled around 75% of the industry. A.C. Davis of the Saxon and Norman Cement Company was appointed managing director in control of production. Although he was initially opposed to the amalgamation, his experience and knowledge of cement manufacture was unrivalled, and of great value to the newly formed subsidiary.

During World War I, APCM played a small, but significant role, placing its labor and transport resources at the disposal of the Admiralty, and promising all its workers their jobs back after the war. At the end of the war, the boards of both APCM and BPCM amalgamated, and thereafter both companies shared a board of directors.

An important development in 1918 was the formation of the Cement Makers Federation (CMF), intended to negotiate on behalf of the industry and promote greater cooperation within it. The CMF's members constituted 90% of the industry and it set local prices throughout the United Kingdom. The first two CMFs failed, but the third achieved a small degree of success under an independent chairman, Viscount Woolmer.

After World War I came the slump of the early 1920s, but by the middle of the decade output rose. Over this period, a financial group had been acquiring ordinary shares until APCM was forced to admit Sir Philip Nash of Metropolitan Vickers, and General Critchley, both representatives of the Associated Anglo-Atlantic Corporation, to its board. A young financier by the name of Henry Horne was the head of this corporation; it appears his intent was to gain overall control, although he was bankrupted in the attempt.

In the aftermath, General Critchley pushed for a reduction in the number of executive directors, as APCM was top-heavy, and used the £100,000 annual salaries APCM saved to pay dividends on the ordinary shares. Despite a frosty response this was carried out, leaving only five executive directors, namely Sir Malcolm Stewart as chairman, Alfred Stevens as finance director, Harold Anderson as sales director, and A.C. Davis in charge of works. General Critchley stayed on in charge of publicity, transport, and personnel.

A common-price agreement was reached in 1934, covering price and production arrangements, and by December of that year was in operation in the form of a price and quota scheme. This agreement, although shaky at first, in fact lasted until 1987, and helped APCM determine investment levels, production, and sales.

World War II led to a dramatic increase in production as the United Kingdom prepared its coastal defenses beginning in 1940. However, most government contracts had been completed by 1944, leading to a general decline in sales and a shortage of orders. During the war, two of APCM's most influential figures retired, Alfred Stevens and Charles Davis. Alfred Stevens had been the first secretary of the association, and a managing director since 1906. He had played a vital role in the formation of BPCM.

The first postwar annual meeting, on July 16, 1946, was notable for the retirement of Sir Malcolm Stewart as chairman. He then became president, while the chairmanship went to George Earle, previously of G. and T. Earle. These were difficult times for APCM, which was under threat of nationalization, and also faced problems with the Town and Country Planning Act, which made it more difficult to develop industrial sites on new land.

The threat of nationalization receded in the 1950s. This was a period of rapid expansion in the cement industry, with large-scale public-sector projects in hand. By January 1957, when the new chairman John Reiss was appointed, record figures for both domestic production and exports were announced.

Throughout the early years of the next decade, the company was still pursuing the course of expansion through acquisition, the most notable acquisitions being the Midland Gravel Company and Hilton Gravel, both major quarrying firms. These formed the basis of Blue Circle's sand and gravel division.

Throughout the 1950s and 1960s, APCM faced problems in developing new sites as it sought to expand its production facilities. Most of these problems were caused by the Town and Country Planning Act, and a shift in public opinion toward conservation. However, despite many hold-ups, APCM managed to develop works at Westbury, Wiltshire; a mineral works on the Humber; and cement works at Shoreham in Kent, Dunstable in Bedfordshire, Hope, Cauldon in Staffordshire, and Dunbar in Scotland.

In 1965 John Reiss commissioned the management consultants McKinsey & Company, to analyze APCM's management structure and methods and present a report detailing its findings, conclusions, and recommendations. This report was completed by October 1966; it suggested that the existing management structure was inadequate for the future development of the company. The report concluded that there was no visible cohesion between the finance department, the works department, and the sales department, and that this was having an adverse effect on the profitability of the company.

However, few of McKinsey's recommendations were acted upon in the late 1960s. There was a general feeling that the existing structure had proved itself, and that the proposals for change were too radical. It took a new chairman, Anthony Binny, to recall McKinsey in 1976, and implement these changes in 1977.

In 1978 APCM became Blue Circle Industries. By now the group had four operating groups, namely Blue Circle Cement UK, the largest, and run by John Duthie; Blue Circle Enterprises, responsible for the sale and manufacture of non-cement products, run by Tom Chesterfield; Blue Circle Technical, responsible for research and development, run by David Stirling; and Blue Circle International, responsible for overseas investments and international consultancy activities. The head of this division, responsible for around half of the group's total profits, was Dr. Gordon Marshall.

The most important event in the company's activities toward the end of the 1960s was the construction of the Northfleet works, the largest cement works of its type in the world, which finally came on stream in the early 1970s. This new plant provided Blue Circle with the opportunity to shut down some of its older and less economical factories while still gaining from a net increase in capacity.

The oil crisis and high inflation of 1973 were unfavorable for the company, but a coal strike added a new dimension to its troubles, with the three-day week and cuts in electricity consumption reducing production levels, and creating two million tons of excess capacity by 1975, as exports fell and firms closed down. Sir John Reiss, chairman for 18 years, retired in 1975 and was replaced by Norman Mullins. Sir John Reiss had joined APCM in 1934, succeeded Sir George Earle as chairman in 1957, and was best remembered for his foresight in developing Blue Circle's overseas interests. His replacement, Norman Mullins, died a year after taking over as chairman, leaving Anthony Binny as chairman.

During the last years of the decade and the first years of the 1980s, Blue Circle, began expanding once again, through a series of acquisitions both at home and abroad. The most notable investments were an 82% stake in the Chilean cement company Fabrica de Cemento El Melan, later raised to 96% at a cost of £23 million, and the purchase of Armitage Shanks, a bathroom-fittings manufacturer, in 1980. The purchase of Armitage Shanks showed the extent to which Blue Circle had diversified, and was evidence of its desire to enter the lucrative North American market. Soon Blue Circle had acquired a Texan company, Kilgore Ceramics, expanded its interests in Malaysia and South Africa, and taken over Aberthaw Cement in south Wales.

In the 1980s, Blue Circle's overseas profits dipped dramatically as Chile and Mexico experienced debt problems, affecting sterling values of overseas profits. However, this was offset by continued expansion in the U.S. market. Blue Circle's special products division was absorbed into Blue Circle Enterprises after it continually failed to produce a significant contribution to group profits.

U.S. expansion continued with the purchase of three cement plants from Martin Marietta, based in Oklahoma, Alabama, and Georgia, at a cost of $100 million. This was followed in 1985 by the purchase of the Atlantic Cement Company in New York State for $145 million. Blue Circle now had around 6% of the U.S. market, a considerable achievement in a short time.

Throughout this period of expansion and acquisition, Blue Circle has continually upgraded its existing plants. It has not been afraid to dispose of parts of the group that fail to realize the required level of profits as was the case with Blue Circle Aggregates, sold in 1981, and two builders' merchants, Macnaughton Blair and Johnson and Patan of Scotland.

The year 1989 saw U.K. cement profits rise by nearly 50%, reflecting an increased level of construction activity in the United Kingdom, and the acquisition of Myson, a producer of plumbing and heating equipment. The group also sold its interests in Mexico for £250 million.

Blue Circle's investment in the modernization of existing plants is likely to continue into the next century, with particular expansion in the U.S. market across all its product ranges.

Principal Subsidiaries: Associated International Cement Ltd.; Blue Circle Property Holdings Ltd.; Blue Circle Dartford Estates Ltd.; Crossways 25 Ltd. (50%); Saxon Developments Ltd.; The Ockley Brick Company Ltd.; Ockley Building Products Ltd.; Armitage Shanks Group Ltd.; Birmid Qualcast PLC; Atco Ltd.; New World Domestic Appliances Ltd.; Potterton International Ltd.; Qualcast Garden Products Ltd.; Qualcast Bathrooms Ltd.; Myson Group PLC; Cemento Melon SA (Chile, 98%); Malayan Cement Berhad (59%); Armitage Shanks (South Africa) (Pty) Ltd.; Blue Circle Holdings Inc. (U.S.A.); Blue Circle Inc. (U.S.A.); Blue Circle Atlantic Inc. (U.S.A.); Blue Circle Raia Inc. (U.S.A.); Blue Circle Aggregates Inc. (U.S.A.); Circle Cement Ltd. (Zimbabwe, 76%); Wright Rain Africa (Private) Ltd. (Zimbabwe).

Further Reading: Great Britain Monopolies and Mergers Commission, *Blue Circle Industries Ltd. and Armitage Shanks Group, A Report on the Proposed Merger,* London, HMSO, 1980; Bianchi, P., *Public and Private Control In Mass Product Industries: The Cement Industry Cases,* The Hague, Martinus Nijhoff, 1982; Pugh, Peter, *The History of Blue Circle,* Cambridge, United Kingdom, Cambridge Business Publishing, 1988; Great Britain Monopolies and Mergers Commission, *Blue Circle Industries Plc. and Myson Group Plc.,* London, HMSO, 1989; Bowley, Marian, *The British Building Industry,* Cambridge, University Press, [n.d.]; Francis, A.J., *The Cement Industry 1796–1914: a History,* Devon, David and Charles, [n.d.].

—Marc Cowling

BORAL LIMITED

Level 20
Norwich House
6-10 O'Connell Street
Sydney, New South Wales 2000
Australia
(02) 232-8800
Fax: (02) 233-6605

Public Company
Incorporated: 1946 as Bitumen & Oil Refineries (Australia) Limited
Employees: 25,000
Sales: A$3.62 billion (US$2.86 billion)
Stock Exchanges: Sydney Wellington

Founded as an oil-refining company shortly after the conclusion of World War II, Boral later divorced itself from its initial interests, diversified into a wide range of resource and material fields, and is today one of Australia's largest manufacturers of construction materials. During the 1980s and into the 1990s Boral expanded operations in the United States, the United Kingdom, and continental Europe. The company has a large network of subsidiaries, which in turn own dozens of companies whose interests include: quarrying, bricks, cement, concrete, clay, plaster, road surfacing, scaffolding, steel reinforcement, tire retreading, engineering, elevators, energy, and timber.

Boral, originally known as Bitumen & Oil Refineries (Australia) Limited, was incorporated in 1946. The new company was assisted financially by California Texas Oil Company, whose Australian subsidiary, Caltex, purchased 40% of the initial stock. Caltex also agreed to provide the new company with a 25-year supply of crude oil and technical assistance for three years. In return, Bitumen & Oil guaranteed Caltex a supply of refinery by-products.

An entrepreneurial promoter named David Craig became the company's first chairman, and Elton Griffin was named chief executive. Griffin was an accountant by trade and maintained board positions with several other Australian companies, including the City Mutual Life Assurance Society and Email Limited.

T. G. Murray, another founding director, succeeded Craig as chairman in 1947. Murray also served as board chairman for the City Mutual Life Assurance Society, where Griffin was a director, and was a board member of other major Australian companies.

Bitumen & Oil stock, issued in early 1946, represented the 60% of the company that Caltex did not own. Initially the stock did well on the market as a result of widespread interest in the new corporation. The stock soon fell victim to nose-diving prices, before leveling off once production began in late 1948.

When production finally began, it was on Botany Bay, New South Wales, at a new plant on land in Matraville, leased from the Australian government. Despite difficulties in obtaining permission to construct the facility on the Botany Bay parcel, near Sydney, construction schedules stayed on course.

By 1949 Bitumen & Oil's prospects were good. Chairman Murray told stockholders that year that increased government-sanctioned roadwork should benefit the company, though the cost of interstate transport and the limited supply of steel for drums could limit profits. The company closed out its first full year of production with a net profit of A$40,747.

Bitumen & Oil steadily increased production through the mid-1950s. In 1954 the company embarked on its first major expansion, and Queensland Oil Refineries—now known as Boral Resources (Queensland)—was founded. Activities of the new operation included processing semi-refined oil received from Matraville into heavy fuel oil and bitumen.

The company entered the field of petroleum tars that same year, with the purchase of a minority interest in Petroleum and Chemical Corporation, which provided an outlet for refinery by-products. The acquisition of a smaller company, W. B. Constructions, during this same time gave Bitumen & Oil a base for the manufacture and distribution of emulsion and tars in the states of New South Wales and Victoria.

Bitumen & Oil made a number of acquisitions during the early 1960s, which set the way for expansion in some areas and capital gains in others through the sale of new assets. In 1961 a controlling interest was purchased in Petroleum and Chemical Corporation. That same year Bitumen & Oil targeted Huddart Parker, a shipping group, for its first major takeover. Bitumen & Oil sold some of Huddart Parker's assets shortly after the successful acquisition, but picked up bargaining power within the oil industry, having secured markets to store heavy fuel and diesel oil.

During this time the company also expanded bituminous operations in Victoria, with the formation of Reid Brothers & Carr Proprietary, an asphalt-manufacturing company owned jointly by Reids Quarries and Bitumen & Oil. Fowler Road Construction Proprietary was also purchased and has since become the spray division of Boral Resources (Victoria). Bituminous surfacing operations were then extended into South Australia through the purchase of an interest in Bitumax Proprietary, which later became a wholly owned subsidiary.

In 1963 Bitumen & Oil acquired Mt. Lyell Investments, primarily because of its large interest in the fertilizer industry. Mt. Lyell soon was sold, after plans to manufacture fertilizer from refinery by-products fell through due to unforeseen high costs.

Early in 1964 the Gas Supply Company was acquired, which included gas-manufacturing plants in Victoria, New South Wales, and Queensland. The Victorian operations were later sold. The Norman J. Hurll Group was acquired later that year, and went on to form an integral part of the Bitumen & Oil subsidiary Gas Group. During this same time the company also purchased a majority interest in Mt. Lyell Mining and Railway, a tin-manufacturing company. Company officials later decided to abandon the tin field for the time, and the mining company was sold for capital gain.

A 1964 decision to diversify into construction resources was the highlight of the period marked by major acquisitions. This diversification marked the beginning of a shift in corporate focus. Two large quarry groups were purchased in 1964, paving the way for restructuring and ultimately representing two major building blocks in the formation of Boral as it is known today.

The two groups purchased—Albion and Reid—were consolidated under the name Albion Reid Proprietary, which later became the subsidiary Boral Resources (Victoria) Proprietary. Activities of smaller quarrying companies—including Carr Fowler, Reid Brothers & Carr, and Dammann Asphalt—were then incorporated into the interests of Albion Reid.

On November 19, 1963, the company adopted the name Boral Limited, which was an acronym for Bitumen & Oil Refineries (Australia) Limited. The new name signified the company's move away from its original core business, oil refining. With the formation of the Albion Reid group, Boral had entered the premixed-concrete industry in South Australia. Operations were later expanded to included quarrying, and the subsidiary became known as Boral Resources (South Australia) Proprietary. In 1966 Boral acquired its third major quarry company, Bayview, rounding out the group that was then Boral's foundation.

Boral's acquisitions were put on hold for the next three years while company operations were consolidated. In April 1967 John O'Neill was named a company director and later that year was appointed chairman, following the retirement of T. G. Murray. O'Neill, a director of the City Mutual Life Assurance Society, brought a background to Boral that included the law, banking, oil exploration, and insurance.

Boral merged its oil interests with the French-based Total in 1969. Boral's ultimate goals—to provide larger coverage of the retail petroleum market and acquire an assured crude oil supply—were not completely successful. In a major reorganization spanning the next two years, Boral sold its remaining oil interests to Total, and completely separated itself from its original field.

With oil refining behind it, Boral became increasingly committed to expansion in the building and construction industries. Early acquisitions spurred by this new direction included Warringah Brick in New South Wales, Brittains Bricks in Queensland, and Steel Mills Limited—now Boral Steel Limited—operating in New South Wales and Queensland.

Boral continued expansion into the brick field in the early 1970s, with the purchase of Glen Iris Bricks, now Boral Bricks (Victoria). Meanwhile, the company acquired a trio of concrete-masonry-block companies, including Besser Vibrapac of Queensland, Jaywoth Industries in New South Wales, and Hollostone, operating in Victoria and South Australia.

Boral also expanded into the field of gas and asphalt early in the decade with the acquisition of Brisbane Gas Company, which became Gas Corporation of Queensland, and asphalt operations from Esso.

In 1973 Elton Griffin retired as CEO and was succeeded by Eric J. Neal. Neal, a ten-year veteran of the company, had served in various managerial roles before replacing Griffin. The new CEO was quick to direct other diversification moves, and in 1975 Boral purchased Cyclone Company of Australia, which became Boral Cyclone. The acquisition, brought Boral into the fields of fencing, materials-handling equipment, prefabricated buildings, aluminum window frames and shower screens, wire screen cloth, and hand tools.

Peter Finley was named Boral's fourth chairman in 1976. Finley, a chartered accountant, was, in 1990, vice chairman of the National Australia Bank and chairman of Email Limited, a company of which Elton Griffin had once been a board member.

In 1978 Boral Cyclone purchased the Melwire Group, whose operations include woven-wire conveyor belts, wire screens for heavy industry, and other woven-wire products. Melwire later acquired Mounts Wire Industries, a New Zealand company operating in the same fields. That same year Boral took over its first mining interest and a major Australian gypsum producer, Australian Gypsum Industries. The subsidiary Boral Bricks Proprietary also acquired Albury Brickworks and Pacific Brick Proprietary about the same time. Meanwhile, Boral was also establishing its presence in the United States, with the 1978 purchase of a partial interest in California Tile, a concrete-tile-manufacturing company based near Los Angeles.

Boral entered the 1980s joining a growing number of major Australian industrial suppliers diversifying into energy. Under an agreement with Esso Exploration and Production Australia, Boral began oil and gas exploration in Queensland's Galiee Basin in 1980. A few years later Boral acquired a 37% stake in the Oil Company of Australia (OCA), a Queensland-based gas-exploration company. Subsequent purchase of additional interest in the oil company made OCA an 85%-owned subsidiary.

In 1982, the takeover of BMI Limited of Australia was completed, giving Boral full control over a major construction materials group. BMI's interests were complimentary to those of Boral, and included operations in concrete, asphalt, and bricks, as well as timber, a new area for the company.

Expansion and diversification led to increasing sales, and by 1983 the company passed A$1 billion in sales for the first time. The acquisition of the Augusta, Georgia–based Merry Group, the third-largest manufacturer of clay bricks in the United States, made Boral the fourth-largest brick manufacturer in the world. Once under Boral's wing, the Merry Group went on to acquire brickworks in Maryland, Oklahoma, Texas, Virginia, and South Carolina.

In 1985 Boral purchased Johns Perry, an Australian company involved in heavy engineering, ropes and strappings, and lifts and escalators. The following year the Edenhall Group of the United Kingdom was acquired.

In order to safeguard its cement supply, Boral bought Blue Circle Southern Cement Limited, in 1987. The A$630 million acquisition was Boral's costliest takeover ever. Blue Circle, Australia's largest cement manufacturer, also has interests in coal and limestone. The purchase of Blue Circle and certain U.S. interests helped push Boral's sales over A$2 billion in 1987: the company posted A$2.37 billion in sales, more than double 1983 sales.

Also in 1987, Eric Neal retired as CEO. Neal had played a key role in Boral's expansion in the Pacific, the United States, and the United Kingdom. Neal was succeeded by Bruce R. Kean. Kean, who had joined Boral in 1968, had served as general manager of the company's energy group and later headed up a number of building-products, manufacturing, and overseas operations. Kean picked up where Neal left off, continuing expansion drives in the United States and Australia. The new CEO also led Boral into continental Europe. Acquisitions there included two clay-brick and tile operations and a limestone and gravel processing plant in West Germany, as well as two Dutch brick manufacturers.

During the late 1980s a handful of Australian companies agreed to be bought out by Boral, which led to further expansion into the tool-manufacturing field. These acquisitions included the Bell quarrying concrete, asphalt, and tire business, based in Western Australia; Patience & Nicholson, a cutting-tool company; Trojan, a shovel and hand tool maker; the concrete-masonry-manufacturing company, Calsil Limited; and a window-manufacturing company, Dowell Australia Limited.

Acquisition activity also picked up in the United States in the late 1980s, where Boral acquired Fontana Asphalt, a major southern California asphalt supplier and quarry operator. Other U.S. acquisitions in the late 1980s included Blair Paving and Vernon Paving; another southern California asphalt manufacturer; and U.S. Tile Company, a clay-roofing-tile manufacturer.

Further expansion and acquisitions in Boral's wide range of fields should continue through the 1990s. In an attempt to avoid large revenue fluctuations in the United States, the company planned to diversify away from its predominantly housing-related operations in southeastern and sunbelt states. The expanded U.K. operations—which are similar to Australian operations in housing and non-housing construction—were expected to remain at the mercy of high acquisition prices. In the Asia Pacific region, Boral continued to look for growth from its energy division, while at home revenues from Boral's construction materials division were expected to continue to pace the company.

Boral entered the 1990s on a wave of rising revenues, having posted annual profit increases for 19 consecutive years. While better than 80% of its activities remain in its home country, Boral plans to work to increase profits from operations outside of Australia.

Principal Subsidiaries: Boral Resources Limited; Blue Circle Southern Cement Limited; Cyclone Scaffolding Pty Limited; Boral Concrete Products Pty Limited; Boral Australian Gypsum Limited; Boral Cyclone Limited; Boral Bricks Pty Limited; Boral Johns Perry Limited; Boral Gas Limited.

Further Reading: Brief History of Boral Limited, Sydney, Boral Limited, 1989.

—Roger W. Rouland

SAINT-GOBAIN

COMPAGNIE DE SAINT-GOBAIN S.A.

Les Miroirs
18, avenue D'Alsace
Cedex 27 F-92096
Paris–La Défense
France
(1) 47 62 30 00
Fax: (1) 47 78 45 03

Public Company
Incorporated: 1665 as Compagnie des Glaces
Employees: 87,000
Sales: FFr66.00 billion (US$11.43 billion)
Stock Exchange: Paris

Saint-Gobain began life more than three hundred years ago, in 1665, as the royal glassmakers to Louis XIV, the Sun King of France. Today it is a multinational group of 113 companies, 66 of them outside France, in 21 countries worldwide, but still retains a strong French identity, having survived both nationalization and re-privatization in the 1980s virtually unscathed.

Saint-Gobain is one of the leading 10 French industrial groups and in the world's top 100 in sales. In addition to its 113 consolidated companies, the group includes more than 300 others, mostly subsidiaries.

From its original base of flat glass manufacture in the 17th century using traditional methods, the company rapidly began to organize production on an industrial basis, establishing a strong European presence during the 19th century. It diversified into the chemical sector as well as other glass-based products. It has operated in Brazil since the 1930s, and in the United States since 1974. Following an attempted take-over bid by a much smaller French glass concern in 1969, Saint-Gobain merged with Pont-à-Mousson—founded in 1854—which makes products for the construction industry, and is famous for its cast-iron pipes. The group then took its present form.

In addition to flat—including automotive—glass, a large range of glass products, including bottles and containers, glass fibers, and wool, now account for about half of group sales. The merger with Pont-à-Mousson made Saint-Gobain the world's leading manufacturer of ductile cast-iron piping for water supply systems. The group also produces a wide range of other construction materials, as well as paper, paper-wood products—including cardboard and chipboard; and industrial ceramics.

Saint-Gobain is the only survivor of a group of private manufacturers founded in 1665 as part of the economic revival of France planned by Jean Baptiste Colbert, chief minister of Louis XIV. The letters patent which created the Compagnie des Glaces granted the company a monopoly on production and sale of glass in France. The original name of the company was Dunoyer, after the individual to whom these privileges were accorded. A group of Venetian glassworkers was persuaded to come to Paris, and production began in the Faubourg Saint-Antoine. However, disputes and difficulties arose with the Venetian authorities and workers, and they returned to Venice after two years. The company then formed an association with Richard Lucas de Nehou, proprietor of a glassworks at Tourlaville, near Cherbourg. Glass produced here was sent to Paris for the finishing process of grinding and polishing. In around 1680, Richard's nephew Louis was responsible for the invention that transformed the manufacture of glass, and that remained in use until 1920; it could now be rolled out on a flat surface, allowing much larger sheets to be produced. After Colbert's death in 1683, his successor Louvois allowed the establishment of rival companies, and restricted the original company to the production of blown glass. This led to the establishment in 1692 of a new factory at the village of Saint-Gobain, which lay nearer Paris and was designed for the new process.

Following the death of Louvois, the newly-created companies were united with Dunoyer under the name of Plastrier, but problems continued, and by 1702 Plastrier was declared bankrupt. Rescue came in the surprising form of the Geneva bank of Antoine Saladin. After complex negotiations, Saladin purchased the company, now to be called Dagincourt. The influence of the Swiss bank was to be felt throughout the 18th century.

The company now possessed a more entrepreneurial spirit, and was able to exploit the new technique of rolled glass, benefiting from 18th-century prosperity and the numerous new uses for glass, especially mirrors. Technical expertise was brought in from 1740, to supplement the aristocratic element always prevalent in the company. Various rationalizations and reforms took place during 1755–1760, in response to the expansion of the market.

The company ceased glass-blowing in 1763, and the ovens were improved. At the village of Saint-Gobain itself, a separate workers' enclave was established in 1775, partly as a solution to rivalry between the workers and other villagers.

The French Revolution of 1789 and its aftermath caused serious disruption, and it took 40 years to restore sales to the level of the best years of the Ancien Régime. In 1806 the first attempts at diversification took place, with the implementation of the Leblanc process for producing soda ash, an important ingredient for glass and later for many other industrial materials. This activity was tranferred to new works at Chauny in 1822. The Tourlaville glass works closed in 1824, and production was concentrated at Saint-Gobain. In 1830 the company was incorporated as a société anonyme. The revolution had ended its monopoly, and there was a threat of competition from English glassworks—Ravenhead had been started by ex-Saint-Gobain workers—and several new French glass factories established during the 1820s, notably Saint-Quirin. The distribution of shares in the new company still reflected an aristocratic bias not suited to the world of 19th-century industry. Nevertheless, rationalization was taking place during this period, led by directors recruited from among technical university graduates. The process of mechanization had begun at the turn of the century.

With the boom in public building, the middle of the 19th century was a turning point for Saint-Gobain, heralding a golden age under the long presidency of the Duc de Broglie from 1866 to 1901.

Foreign ventures began with the lease of a factory at Stolberg in Germany in 1857, and in the following year a merger with its principal French rival Saint-Quirin gave Saint-Gobain a second presence in Germany—the glassworks built in 1853 at Mannheim, which was also to be the site of a French workers' city. Two other younger French rivals, Commentry and Prémontré, had been acquired jointly before the merger. These moves were prompted by the growing threat of competition from Belgium, as well as the expanding English glassworks. Broglie's predecessor as president, Antoine-Pierre Hély D'Oissel, recruited Hector Biver, an Englishman who had also worked in Belgium. Following its 1858 merger, the company became the Société Anonyme de la Manufactures des Glaces et Produits Chimiques de Saint-Gobain, Chauny et Cirey. On the chemical side, the company benefited from the presence of the famous chemist Joseph Louis Gay-Lussac, who had been president from 1844 to 1850, and who perfected his method of sulfuric acid production at Chauny. Considerable effort was devoted to improving the social and educational conditions of the workers, with the provision of schools, chapels, orphanages, savings and pension schemes, and even philharmonic and shooting societies. The image of aristocratic incompetence was largely dispelled during the second half of the 19th century.

After two hundred years, a fundamental shift occurred as a result of the merger with the firm of Perret-Olivier in 1874. The company consequently comprised nine chemical works compared with eleven, including three overseas, for glass: the turnover was almost equal in both sectors. Continuing strong Belgian and U.K. competitors in the glass industry were now joined by the United States and Germany, reducing Saint-Gobain's share of an expanding market. Pittsburgh Plate Glass, founded in 1883, attained the size of Saint-Gobain in only six years. The company responded by improving production methods and constructing further production sites in Europe: at Pisa, Italy, in 1889, and at Franière, Belgium, between 1898 and 1900. Subsidiaries were acquired in Holland, Spain, and Germany. Turnover increased from FFr18 million in 1890 to FFr47 million in 1913. Saint-Gobain was now Europe's leading glass producer, with 26.8% of the market, followed by Belgium with 23.3% and Pilkington with 22%. Engineers played a growing role in a centralized administration in this period, but provisions continued to be made for the workers: at Pisa there was a children's home, dispensary, and school, and training in housework was provided.

The early 1900s also saw the introduction of highly significant technical developments in glassmaking, including the Bicheroux and Fourcault processes, which allowed continuous sheets to be produced. A joint venture undertaken with Pilkington to exploit the American Window Glass process, although not a technical success, helped in the forging of a commercial treaty between the glassmakers of Belgium, France, and the United Kingdom, which lasted until World War II. The end of the 19th century also saw a radical change in the chemical division, where new processes resulted in the conversion of plants to superphosphate fertilizer production, for which Saint-Gobain was to remain famous in France until the abandonment of all its chemical interests in 1970.

The presence of French aristocrats and Genevan families still exerted considerable influence on the company, but with the quotation on the French Bourse in 1907 came greater dispersion of capital. From 1893, a new administrator, the archeologist and diplomat Melchior de Vogüé, accelerated administrative reform, giving more power to the divisions and creating the new posts of secretary-general and inspector of finances. He was president from 1901 to 1916. New headquarters were constructed in Paris between 1899 and 1902. Moves were made towards a more open management, with the consensus of shareholders, but capital ventures continued to be financed on an internal basis.

At the beginning of the 20th century, key factors in the company's development were the growth of U.S. competition, further technical developments in glassmaking, and extensions of its use. In addition to new types of continuous processes and improved furnaces, there were innovations in grinding and polishing techniques and, perhaps most significant, the discovery of tempering to produce security glass and allow its shaping. This discovery opened the way for expansion into the automobile market as well as the structural and artistic markets. Security glass was developed and patented by Saint-Gobain, and manufacturing on a production line for Citroën began in 1929. A new factory had been opened in 1920 at Chantereine to exploit the new processes.

International relations were important in the late 1920s; various accords led to stabilization of the industry between manufacturers in the United States, United Kingdom, and France. Saint-Gobain chose the Pittsburgh process for window glass as technically superior to its competitors. Surprisingly, glass bottles and flagons were still being manufactured at this time by the traditional glassblowing method, usually by small family enterprises scattered throughout France, Spain, and Italy. Saint-Gobain gradually absorbed these firms, as the increasing pace of mechanization rendered them uncompetitive. The 1930s witnessed perhaps the most important strategic move in the recent history of the company: diversification into glass fiber. Known by 18th-century English nobles, whose wigs had to be fireproof because of candles, it was also said to have been used in the Empress Josephine's coronation dress. Saint-Gobain, convinced by its U.S. contacts of the potential market for this product, obtained the necessary licenses, formed a new company, Isover, and acquired Balzaretti-Modigliani in Italy. However, production did not begin on an industrial scale until after World War II. Considerable research into improvements followed, which led to the intervention of the TEL and SUPERTEL processes for insulating materials, licensed by Saint-Gobain throughout the world.

Meanwhile the chemical side of the business had continued to decline, partly because of unsucccessful diversifications in this area. Of various diversifications attempted, including petroleum refining, one proved to be a long-term success: cellulose production. This began in 1920 and is the only process surviving from this period. An association with Papeteries Navarre in 1924 led to the formation of Cellulose du Pin, and construction of a works at Facture in the Landes in 1928. It was planned at first to produce fibers for paper-based artificial textiles, but their decline after the war led to a switch to Kraft paper and bags.

The rest of the chemical side continued to be dangerously exposed. Saint-Gobain had refused an offer from Solvay for a merger in 1927 and 1928, which would have created a Franco-Belgian group on a par with ICI or I.G. Farben. Another proposal, from Kuhlmann for a French chemical union, was also turned down. These negative responses may have sprung from the desire by management to cling to the old regime. Management reforms in the 1920s and 1930s had been only tentative, and it was not until the presidency of Pierre Hély D'Oissel from 1936 to 1953 that fundamental changes in management and structure were initiated, heralding the new models of management of the 1950s and 1960s.

The period from 1950 which led up to the merger of the two very dissimilar firms of Saint-Gobain and Pont-à-Mousson in 1970 was characterized by the growing power of the state in the French economy, begun during World War II under the Vichy regime. Senior officials of government were closely involved in the management of a planned economy, and saw much of French industry as archaic and fragmented. The glass industry continued to flourish, and Saint-Gobain acquired a stake in its famous Belgian rival, Glaceries de Saint-Roch. Overseas expansion in glass fiber was dramatic, and the development of a presence in Brazil from 1960 supplemented solid bases in Belgium, Germany, Italy, Switzerland, and Spain. The TEL process was proving successful in the United States, and led to the acquisition of interests in the CertainTeed Corporation and the conversion of three old factories, which gave the company 10% to 15% of the U.S. market. However, another U.S. venture went wrong. A new subsidiary, American Saint-Gobain, founded in 1959, having already acquired four glassworks, then designed a new one in Greenland, Tennessee, intended to exploit the latest techniques in grinding and polishing. Disastrously, this factory did not open until 1962, after the invention of float glass by Pilkington. This revolutionary technique obviated the need for lengthy finishing processes. To compound the problem, the United States reacted strongly to the French invasion by an increase in tariffs of 30%.

Although the invention of float glass effectively killed off American Saint-Gobain, the parent company did not take the new process seriously until 1965, when it had to be acquired on much less favorable terms than were available just after the invention in the 1950s. Saint-Gobain however, made up for lost time by rapidly modernizing all of its factories, starting with those overseas, thus helping amortize the old installations.

The 1960s also witnessed unsatisfactory alliances during the company's last attempts to revive its chemical operations, notably the creation of Péchiney-Saint-Gobain to develop organic chemicals, in particular the new plastics materials. Due to the instability of this sector, a government commission recommended a fundamental regrouping. However, before these recommendations could be acted upon, Rhône-Poulenc preempted them by acquiring Péchiney-Saint-Gobain. Péchiney itself did not want the chemical interests, and Saint-Gobain could not afford to buy them.

During this period the company raised capital to fund various ill-fated ventures. The increasing deficit caused further recourse to the banks, much against the Saint-Gobain tradition. At the end of 1968 came a major turning point: the dramatic offensive by Boussois Souchon Neuvesel (BSN) with a public offer for exchange to acquire 30% of Saint-Gobain, following tentative negotiations, which Saint-Gobain had rebuffed. BSN, a small but ambitious glass producer with an annual turnover of just under FFr600 million, had set its sights on a company with consolidated funds of more than FFr5 billion. BSN had chosen the moment when Saint-Gobain was suffering from the effects of the chemical restructuring as well as internal management struggles; these difficulties were reflected in the low price of the shares at the time. The offensive was a technical failure, securing only 7% of Saint-Gobain's capital, 1 million shares out of the minimum 3.4 million required. A vigorous rescue bid had to be mounted by a consortium of banks led by the Compagnie de Suez, and 40% of the shares changed hands during the battle. This shift left the company badly shaken and with diminished funds. As a direct consequence of this affair, the bankers took the initiative in arranging the merger with Pont-à-Mousson, which they saw as a means of securing Saint-Gobain against further attacks of this nature. Arnaud de Vogüé, president since 1952, was initially reluctant, but eventually recognized the end of the grand liberal regime of Saint-Gobain and the beginning of a new era.

One-third of the size of Saint-Gobain, Pont-à-Mousson, founded in the 1850s, had begun to detach itself from its coal and metallurgical interests during the 1960s. Originally founded by local coal merchants in the Lorraine after the discovery of new iron-ore deposits, the little town of Pont-à-Mousson between Metz and Nancy was chosen as the site of the first blast furnace in 1860. The company began to pursue a strategy of vertical integration, with the control of mines, ironworks, and end products, a policy continued right up until the 1960s. In 1866 it made the key decision to specialize in the production of cast-iron pipes. The invention in Brazil in 1915 of an improved technique of casting pipes using centrifugal force led to the company's establishing production in Brazil in 1937. After World War II, a new importance was given to cast-iron by the ductile iron process, discovered by researchers at International Nickel in Canada during the 1940s. Pont-à-Mousson quickly obtained a license from a U.K. subsidiary of International Nickel, and began production in 1950. Even so, the old type of cast iron pipe remained in production until the end of the 1960s.

In contrast to Saint-Gobain, the dominant personalities in the history of Pont-à-Mousson were engineers, notably Camille Cavallier, sole administrator from 1900 to 1917 and president from 1917 to 1926. In 1970, following the merger, a provisional organizational structure was adopted, based on the Pont-à-Mousson model, and it was Pont-à-Mousson's director, Roger Martin, who succeeded Arnaud de Vogüé at the head of the new group. A gradual process of rationalization then took place, involving decentralization, the establishment of a management structure, and the creation of product-based departments. In 1978, following a convention of all 41 directors, more fundamental reorganization of the new group led to the replacement of the six market departments by ten production-oriented branches. The 1970s also witnessed the jettisoning of the remaining chemical and petroleum investments, as well as the iron and steel interests inherited with Pont-à-Mousson. A brief flirtation with the products for nuclear reactors in 1972 was abandoned for political reasons. In glass fiber, the U.S. presence was reinforced by control of CertainTeed, and in France a new factory for insulation products was built at Orange. The energy crisis helped here: between 1973 and 1975 Saint-Gobain doubled its European production of glass fiber. Significant investments were also made in float glass, with Saint-Gobain building 10 out of the 17 new plants constructed in Europe during 1976.

The new strength of the combined companies was illustrated by their ability to weather the crises of this period, including heavy losses in brassware and machinery during 1977 and 1978, and a sudden downturn in the insulation market in 1981, resulting in massive overproduction.

After the 1978 reorganization, a search for further diversification led to the decision to enter the information technology sector. A joint subsidiary, Eurotechnique, was set up with National Semiconductor to produce electronic components, a partnership established with Cii-HB, and 30% of the capital of Olivetti acquired. However, before this venture could get off the ground, Saint-Gobain was nationalized by the new government of 1981, and forced to liquidate these holdings between 1982 and 1983. Yet Saint-Gobain was the only nationalized company to retain its top management, who continued to pursue their vigorous investment strategy and maintain a high level of industrial activity. The result was increased debt, countered by austerity measures such as plant rationalization. The group had to be slimmed down further with approaching reprivatization in 1986. The effect of these policies was spectacular; global profits increased by a factor of seven in six years.

Saint-Gobain is a French group with a predominantly European base but a growing international involvement. Recent moves include the development of industrial operations in Southeast Asia, which began in 1989 in South Korea. The political and economic changes in Eastern Europe will lead to challenges and opportunities for the group. Acquisition in the United States in 1990 of the Norton Company, which manufactures industrial abrasives, and the purchase of majority holdings in glass, cardboard, and refractory products companies in Italy during 1989 illustrate the dynamic development policy of the group in both its core activities and its continuing efforts to strengthen its international presence.

Principal Subsidiaries: Saint-Gobain Vitrage France; Saint-Gobain Emballage; Saint-Gobain Desjonquères; Pont-à-Mousson SA (99%); Everite; Isover; La Cellulose du Pin (76%); Socar; Société Européenne des Produits Réfractaires; Vetrotex Saint Gobain; Glaceries de Saint-Roch (Belgium, 98%); Barbará (Brazil, 60%); Brasilit (Brazil, 86%); Scan-Gobain Glass (Denmark, 81%); Vegla GmbH (Germany, 99%); Halbergerhütte GmbH (Germany, 99%); Fabrica Pisana (Italy); Balzaretti (Italy, 84%); Vetri (Italy, 73%); Cristaleria Española (Spain, 73%); Gullfiber (Sweden, 99%); Trempex (Sweden, 99%); Stanton PLC (U.K., 99%); TSL Group (U.K., 99%); CertainTeed Corporation (U.S.A.); Norton Company (U.S.A.).

Further Reading: Hamon, Maurice, *Saint-Gobain (1665-1990). The Making of a French Multinational,* [n.p.], Editions Jean-Claude Lattès, 1990.

—Peter W. Miller

Cookson

COOKSON GROUP PLC

130 Wood Street
London, EC2V 6EQ
United Kingdom
(071) 606-4400
Fax: (071) 606-2851

Public Company
Incorporated: 1924 as Associated Lead Manufacturers Ltd.
Employees: 14,500
Sales: £1.98 billion (US$3.20 billion)
Stock Exchange: London

Cookson is an international group which specializes in the refining, casting, and fabricating of non-ferrous and precious metals and the manufacture of ceramics, chemicals, plastics, and printing and refractory products.

The family was established in Tyneside, England, in 1704 when Isaac Cookson, the son of a brazier from Penrith, Cumberland, moved to Newcastle upon Tyne to seek his fortune. He began operations near South Shields, where the company has had a continuous presence to the present day. The family developed major industrial links in coal mining and the manufacture of iron, salt, and glass, but its direct involvement with a company which came to be part of the present group did not occur until it entered lead manufacturing in the middle of the 19th century.

The earliest direct link with the present group also came in lead manufacture, when in 1778 a Rotherham-based family of ironmasters, the Walkers, began to diversify, and set up its first white lead works at Elswick, Newcastle, a site which is still in the ownership of Cookson Industrial Materials. White lead—basic lead carbonate—was then the base for virtually all decorative paints and, as the population grew rapidly and the Industrial Revolution gathered pace, the market for white lead and other lead products expanded. Lead, although a long way behind iron, was the second most heavily utilized metal and was to remain so throughout the 19th century, with British firms processing around a quarter of a million tons a year by 1900.

This initial diversification into lead had been made at a propitious time and the Walkers's network of lead works became larger than its original base in iron. By the end of the Napoleonic Wars, the Walkers's partnership was employing a total capital of approximately £500,000 in lead manufacture, with works in London (Islington, Lambeth, and Southwark), Chester, Derby, Liverpool, and Newcastle under Lyme, as well as the original Elswick works. While some of the smaller works were closed during the 19th century, large smelting and manufacturing sites were purchased at Bagillt and Dee Bank, in north Wales, to work local lead ores, and the Scottish market was supplied by a works in Glasgow.

While white lead remained important, the output of other lead chemicals—especially red lead, used as the base for protective paints for the increasing output of iron and steel in the country—was developed. The Walkers's partnerships were the first to adopt a new process for the manufacture of lead shot, and built several shot towers at the turn of the 18th century—including one at the Chester works which is the only early tower still in operation in the United Kingdom. The Walkers's works processed a large amount of blue lead, especially rolled sheet lead and extruded pipe. These products were in great demand as a result of the large increase in both public and private building in the Victorian years, with sheet being used for roofing, and pipe to convey the newly developed water supplies. As a result of these developments, the partnerships—each works was run by a managing partner, and interlocking partnerships between various works provided some overall control—were the largest single force in the British lead manufacturing industry throughout the 19th century.

Despite its large size and considerable potential, the Walkers's partnership lacked initiative and did not dominate the industry in the second half of the 19th century as it might have done. By then the third and fourth generations of partners from the family were managing the firm, and there is evidence that it was suffering the classic symptoms of hardening of the arteries of commercial instinct. Capital employed grew very little over the 19th century; profitability was never high; the innovation of new techniques was left to competitors, and several of the partners became more interested in their country houses and small landed estates than in the fortunes of the firm. A dispute between the partners with regard to profitability led the partnership into the chancery court with the eventual outcome in 1889 that the assets were sold to a newly formed public company, Walkers Parker and Company. The new company experienced even less financial success, with a number of losses in the highly competitive years up to 1914.

In the second half of the 19th century, innovation in the lead-manufacturing industry came largely from newly established firms which were subsequently drawn into what is now the Cookson Group. It was in 1851 that the Cookson family became involved in lead manufacture. In that year, two of the sons of Isaac Cookson III purchased land at Hayhole on the River Tyne in Northumberland, where they built a white lead works. In the mid 1840s their father and his partner had sold the family's glass-manufacturing companies, because of increasing competition in this area, and the sons needed to find an outlet for their considerable talents. William Isaac Cookson was a very capable scientist and businessman. At the age of 20 he had spent a year in Michael Faraday's laboratory, and he was later to take out several patents for improvements to metal-smelting and chemical processes.

Under William Isaac and later his son Norman, Cookson rapidly became a significant force in the British lead-manufacturing industry. In 1854, the partners bought from the Hawthorn engineering family a second lead works at Howdon on Tyne, close to the Hayhole works. Since lead smelting and refining and the manufacture of red lead were already in operation at Howdon, the Cooksons had developed the capacity for fully integrated production within less than a decade. Over the next 50 years, the works were expanded and were regularly modernized with the introduction of new processes, the major instance being the first successful British introduction of an alternative to the centuries-old stack process for the manufacture of white lead. In the late 1890s Norman Cookson, like his father an amateur scientist of some distinction with several patents to his name, introduced a German-developed chamber process at Hayhole, which doubled Cookson's output of white lead to some 10,000 tons per annum in the early 1900s, around 20% of U.K. output. Cookson's growth brought considerable profitability and, increasingly, leadership of the industry.

By the turn of the 19th century lead manufacturing, like many British industries, was experiencing severe competition, not only from the development of new firms at home but also from imports from continental producers. Most British firms were small family-run companies which were ill-prepared to cope with the competition, although the example of Walkers Parker suggests that the adoption of limited-liability status alone was not a satisfactory solution. For most of the companies, salvation was seen in cooperation, common pricing policies, and the formation of cartels. By 1914 there were British conventions of the red, white, and blue lead manufacturers; each of these conventions in its turn negotiating market shares within international, largely European, conventions.

While the formation of cartels remained important internationally in the years between World War I and World War II, British manufacturers saw amalgamation as the best way to maintain profitability in the face of increasing competition. The earliest proposals date from World War I but in 1924, under the leadership of Cookson and with Clive Cookson as the first chairman, Associated Lead Manufacturers (ALM) was formed. Two years before Imperial Chemical Industries Ltd. was to perform the same function for the British chemical industry, lead manufacturing had a central focus. The initial merger, with a capital of just under £2 million, was of Cookson, and the firm of Locke, Lancaster and W.W.&R. Johnson & Sons, the latter being an earlier amalgamation of several London producers which was now by far the dominant London firm.

ALM thus began its existence with the two major firms in two of the three most significant production areas in the United Kingdom. However, it lacked a presence in the remaining geographical area of significance, the Northwest, and still faced the regionally diversified competition of Walkers Parker. The first of these deficiencies was overcome rather surprisingly by the purchase, in January 1925, of Rowe Bros. & Company, traditionally a builders' merchant and thereby involved in the supply of lead products. Although this purchase would have given ALM an outlet for some of its sheet and pipe production, its true function was to nullify the potential threat of Rowe's growing involvement in lead manufacture. Before World War II, Rowe, in conjunction with Cookson, had purchased the patent rights to a newly invented process for the manufacture of red lead and, perhaps more importantly, had acquired the Runcorn White Lead Company, which brought with it the plant required for a new "quick" process. Even using Cookson's new chamber process the corrosion period for the production of white lead was almost two months, which involved considerable additional costs as compared with the potential, of the as yet little-used quick process, where corrosion took only a few days.

ALM continued to act in the predatory way in which it had begun its existence. Within five years of its inception, the company had purchased all the major lead manufacturers in the country with the exception of the Mersey White Lead Company, which was eventually taken over by ALM in 1972. While there were significant numbers of small, regional producers of lead pipe—and to a lesser extent of lead sheet—in which scale economies were not essential to the producers' survival, ALM dominated the production of lead chemicals. In 1925, ALM took over the Brimsdown Lead Company, another company with a new white lead process, which had been financed by Ludwig Mond and supported by a research laboratory with a number of impressive young scientists, including Stephen Miall, who was to write what was for a long time the standard history of the chemical industry. This acquisition was followed in the years 1926–1928 by the mopping up of several of the smaller Tyneside and London manufacturers and, in 1929, after negotiation had failed, by the aggressive purchase of Walkers Parker shares which eventually led to an agreed merger.

Achieving a dominant position in lead manufacturing was not to be the end of ALM's aims. Not only was there no growth in market size—as a result of the Depression during the interwar years together with increased foreign competition—there were also new substitutes for lead products. Copper was beginning to make inroads into the market for lead pipe but, more significantly, white lead no longer had the virtual monopoly of the paint market. Titanium-based paints and the entry into the market of Imperial Chemical Industries (ICI) with its Dulux brand were to cause ALM increasing problems, although, largely as a result of the former Brimsdown chemists' work on titanium, the group had a small share in a company set up in the 1930s to produce titanium dioxide. That company, now Tioxide Group PLC, was jointly owned by Cookson Group and ICI until December 1990 up until which time, as the world's second-largest titanium dioxide producer, it made a significant contribution to the Group. In 1930, before the impact of these new paints had become serious, however, ALM purchased Goodlass, Wall & Company (GW) of Liverpool, a large paint manufacturer with retail outlets. Although this might have been a useful diversification, particularly since GW owned the Valspar patents with considerable potential for expansion in the market for varnishes, the merger caused problems. The price paid for GW proved too high in the light of subsequent profits, ALM's capital had to be written down, and GW was never integrated, being run as a separate organization until its sale in 1984.

One long-lasting advantage accrued from this merger. The ALM board had become distinctly unwieldy in the late 1920s as a result of the appointment of additional directors following the takeover of various family-owned firms. In 1930 Clive Cookson set up Goodlass Wall & Lead Industries (GWLI) as a holding company, and the power of the ALM board withered. The original GW directors were soon pruned from the board of GWLI, and the power of Clive Cookson and his supporters was complete. It is surprising that rationalization was not taken further in the 1930s. A number of lead works were closed in London and on Tyneside and production geographically concentrated in order to obtain scale economies. The constituent companies essentially remained independent, however, certainly in name—even in the late 1940s at Elswick the switchboard operator had to answer different lines with different company names—and to a considerable extent competing with each other in the market.

World War II enforced further rationalization. Imports of lead were reduced and controlled by the government, while demand fell, largely as a result of the almost complete cessation of private building work. The group had to expand several existing businesses, one being the production of solder, as it gradually became clear that diversification away from lead was necessary. After the war, for a number of lead products, there was only limited recovery of demand. White lead was the major casualty, as it was replaced by other bases for paints, and although a new market was found in stabilizers for the plastics industry, the tonnage needed was small. Most of the white lead plant had to be closed. Owing to the motor industry's growing demand for lead in petrol and batteries, total U.K. demand for lead products continued to expand, reaching a peak in the mid 1960s. In this area and in the supply of lead for cables, GWLI faced competition and found the basic lead-products business less profitable than its traditional business.

As early as 1943, GWLI had begun to diversify into what Clive Cookson called "some allied field of industry." Fry's Metal Foundries of Merton, Surrey, was purchased for £500,000, overlapping with Cookson's existing business in the production of solder but otherwise concentrating on printers' metals and non-ferrous alloys. In 1954 another acquisition in this field, Fry's Diecastings, was made. As with the lead side, where a number of plants had been set up overseas during the interwar years in order to avoid import duties, the purchase of the Fry's companies brought an expansion in foreign holdings. A further area of expansion was at Howdon, where Roland Cookson—nephew of Clive, later to become chairman of the group from 1963 to 1972—added zircon in 1950 to the production of antimony, in which the Cooksons had been involved since the mid-19th century. As with stabilizers for plastics, where GWLI had negotiated for existing U.S. technology through its links with the National Lead Company of the United States, Cookson negotiated a U.K. license to produce zirconium products with TAM Ceramics. These highly refractory materials were beginning to make inroads into the group's existing markets in the ceramics industry and therefore offered a sensible diversification, which was to be considerably reinforced in the 1960s with the purchase of two Staffordshire companies—Harrison & Sons (Hanley) Ltd. and E.W.T. Mayer Ltd.—involved in the production of ceramic glazes.

Although diversification had not taken the group far outside its original activities it had resulted in a lack of focus. In 1949 the lead business, which included antimony and subsequently zircon, had been reorganized into a single company, ALM, with regionally structured management, but this offered little opportunity to concentrate its resources on those products which were most profitable. This problem was exacerbated by the accretion of additional companies and the growing tendency towards inter-company trading below market prices. Gradually, beginning in 1977 with the creation of the antimony and zircon operation Anzon Limited, the group—which had changed its name in 1966 to Lead Industries Group Ltd. (LIG)—began to adopt a divisional structure. Two years later, ALM was divided into three product divisions: chemicals, metals, and paints.

By this time, it was clear that the lead business was in permanent decline. U.K. consumption had declined by more than 25% in the previous ten years, and this had necessitated the closure of several works. Although to some extent offset by the development of new products such as lead-clad steel for buildings, and by overseas expansion in Europe and in the United States, where the lead interests of NL Industries were purchased for $40 million in 1979, making LIG the world's leading producer of lead products, the future of the group clearly lay elsewhere. Already, by the early 1970s ALM accounted for only one-third of group turnover and its contribution to total profits was declining. Further diversification was required.

Fortunately for the group, leadership had moved in the 1970s toward a new set of directors who had only limited links, if any, with the company's traditional lead business and who increasingly recognized the need to reduce those links, not only because of the declining financial returns from lead but also because of its unattractive public image. Leading the new developments were I.G. Butler, group chairman from 1976, and M.J.G. Henderson, his successor in 1990. They recognized that the group was actually less than the sum of its parts, because many of the 100 or so operating subsidiaries, in various parts of the world, did not associate themselves with the name of the group and were directing resources for individual rather than corporate benefit. Since 1983, the change of name from Lead Industries Group to Cookson has provided the focus for a new and much more high-profile corporate image for all the subsidiaries worldwide. A second step was the creation of a clearer divisional structure and the appointment of a chief executive for each division who is responsible for isolating and developing those of its products with major growth potential. The third step was to make further major overseas acquisitions, in recognition of the fact that the U.K. market was not large enough to offer significant opportunity for expansion and profit growth. Among the acquisitions, all by agreed takeover, were A.J. Oster Company in 1978, an American producer of non-ferrous metals, whose chairman is now chief executive of Cookson America Division and, in 1987, Vesuvius Crucible Company of Pittsburgh, a U.S. supplier of ceramics to the steel industry, which was subsequently set up as the Vesuvius Group, with headquarters in Brussels. As a result, the 1980s have seen growth in group turnover from £400 million to £2 billion and in pre-tax profit from £16 million to £183 million. Over the decade, earnings per ordinary share have risen from 6.7 to 31.2 pence.

Cookson proved one of the fastest growing British industrial groups during the 1980s. It has established a reputation as supplier of a wide range of specialist products to industry, including non-ferrous and precious metals, ceramics and refractories, chemicals, and plastics. The group sees itself as "the name behind many big names of industry." Claiming that its products are almost ubiquitous in daily life—they are incorporated in most things from washing machines to motor cars, flame retardants in children's toys to filaments in light bulbs, and printing on drinks cans to household paint—the group has become almost worldwide in its diffusion, with manufacturing plants in more than 40 countries, and 70% of its turnover plus 80% of profit coming from abroad.

Principal Subsidiaries: Cookson Industrial Materials Ltd.; Cookson Ceramics Ltd.; Cookson Metals Ltd.; Cookson Minerals Ltd.; Cookson Plibrico International Ltd.; Cookson Precision Castings Ltd.; Fry's Metals Ltd.; Vesuvius International Corporation (Belgium); Alpha Metals Inc. (U.S.A.); CaMac Corporation (U.S.A.); Cookson America, Inc. (U.S.A.); Polyclad Laminates Inc. (U.S.A.); Stern Metals Inc. (U.S.A.).

Further Reading: Minutes Relating to the Proceedings of the Foundry Co. begun by S. and A. Walker, 1741, and of the Lead Company, begun by Samuel Walker, 1778, Chester, [n.p.], 1879; John, A.H., ed., *The Walker Family: Iron Founders and Lead Manufacturers 1741–1893,* London, Council for the Preservation of Business Archives, 1951; Hedley, W.P., and C.R. Hudleston, *Cookson of Penrith, Cumberland and Newcastle upon Tyne,* Kendal, Cookson, [1966]; Rowe, D.J., *Lead Manufacturing in Britain: a History,* London, Croom Helm, 1983.

—D.J. Rowe

CORNING

CORNING INCORPORATED

Houghton Park
Corning, New York 14831
U.S.A.
(607) 974-9000
Fax: (607) 974-8551

Public Company
Incorporated: 1875 as Corning Glass Works Incorporated
Employees: 26,000
Sales: $2.44 billion
Stock Exchanges: New York Zürich

Corning Incorporated, Corning Glass Works until 1989, began as a producer of specialty glass. The firm specializes in glass, glass fibers, ceramics, and laboratory services. During the 1980s Corning moved from slow-growing markets to development of products in new technologies, such as fiber optics. The company has joint ventures throughout the United States and the world.

Corning traces its beginnings to 1851 when Amory Houghton purchased an interest in Bay State Glass Company of Cambridge, Massachusetts. Three years later he founded Union Glass Company of Somerville, Massachusetts. After selling Union Glass he and his sons bought the Brooklyn Flint Glass Company of Brooklyn, New York, in 1864. Four years later they moved operations to Corning, New York, renaming the enterprise Corning Flint Glass Company. They chose this western New York location because of its favorable location for transportation as well as for acquisition of coal and wood, then necessary for glassmaking.

Amory Houghton Jr. became president in 1875, the year in which Corning Glass Works was incorporated, and remained in the post until 1911. It was during these years that the firm began to exhibit the technological prowess for which it is known today. The company first called upon scientists at Cornell University in 1877 for help in improving the optical quality of its lenses. In 1880 Thomas Edison asked Corning Glass to make bulbs for his electric lights.

An important milestone during Amory Houghton Jr.'s years as president was the establishment of a research laboratory in 1908. It was the fourth such facility in the United States. The laboratory developed a heat-resistant glass, borosilicate, capable of withstanding sudden changes in temperature. One resulting 1912 product was a shatterproof lantern for railway signalmen. Another important borosilicate product, Pyrex, dated from 1915. It found immediate use as laboratory equipment, but it was some years before the company realized its consumer-market potential.

Corning continued to be managed by members of the Houghton family. Alanson B. Houghton succeeded Amory Houghton Jr., and served until 1919, when he was followed by Arthur A. Houghton, president until 1920.

During World War I, when Corning was able to make glass that others could not produce, the company prospered as a supplier to defense contractors. In the postwar years, demand for Corning products led to the invention of a ribbon machine in 1926 which produced blanks for incandescent lamps at the rate of 2,000 bulbs per minute.

Steuben Glass, a division of Corning, originated in Corning, New York, but did not become part of Corning Glass until 1918. It specializes in fine optical glass as well as fine cut glass. Steuben began producing the crystal for which it became famous in 1933, when Arthur A. Houghton Jr., great-grandson of the founder, became president of the subsidiary. He decided that the company was to sell only quality products of the highest design, and he and a vice president smashed over $1 million worth of lesser glass in the company warehouse.

Two presidents served in the decade of the 1920s. Alexander D. Falck was in office until 1928, and Eugene C. Sullivan until 1930. The years of the Great Depression were an era of great expansion for Corning. Under the leadership of Amory Houghton Sr., president from 1930 to 1941, technological innovations continued. Corning built the 200-inch mirror for the Mount Palomar telescope in 1934. It was the largest piece of cast glass up to that time, and was the second version of the mirror. The first, which was miscast, is on display at the glass museum in Corning, New York. Corning developed such products as silicones in the early 1930s, electrical sealing in 1938, and 96%-silica glass in 1939.

During this period Corning began a policy of joint ventures with other companies. Owens-Corning Fiberglas was organized in 1938, a year after Pittsburgh Corning Corporation began producing glass blocks. Dow Corning was established in 1943 to produce silicones.

The early 1940s brought improvements in optical glassmaking. During World War II cathode-ray tubes were mass produced for radar detection systems beginning in 1942. Corning also manufactured a strengthened form of glass tableware for the U.S. Navy. Later advancements in the decade included improved thermometer tubing; ribbon glass as thin as newsprint and used in electronic components; photosensitive glass; and centrifugal casting used primarily for television tubes, which were first automatically produced in 1947.

Glen W. Cole was president during World War II, and was followed by William C. Decker, who served from 1946 until 1961. Amory Houghton Sr. continued to lead as the first chairman of the board, an office created in 1945.

Corning developed electricity-conducting coated glass in 1950 and fused silica in 1952. Color television tubes were introduced in 1953. The process for producing Pyroceram, or glass ceramics, developed in 1957, led to the marketing of Corning Ware cookware the following year.

Amory Houghton Jr. served as president between 1961 and 1964, and then became chairman of the board until his election to the House of Representatives in 1983. During Houghton's tenure as chairman, the presidency was held by R. Lee Waterman until 1971, followed by Thomas C. MacAvoy up to 1983.

Corning made the ceramic heat-resisting reentry shields and the glass windshields for the 1960s Apollo moon program. Cellular-ceramic structures—thin-walled structures used in gaseous heat exchangers—were introduced in 1961 and became key components of automobile catalytic converters beginning in the 1970s. Other developments in the 1960s included chemically strengthened glass in 1964; photochromic glass, which darkens when exposed to light, and fusion sheet glass in mid-decade; and in the late 1960s, hub machines, for cutting hot glass into various sizes and shapes, and optical fibers.

During the 1960s Corning Glass was the undisputed industry leader in glass technology. Sales of bulbs, globes, and panels, Corning Ware, and television-tube blanks grew especially fast in the early 1960s and led to record earnings of $9.28 per share in 1966. Company stock sold at 48 times earnings.

In 1970 Corning's innovations included machinable glass-ceramics and immobilized enzymes. The latter permanently bonds active catalytic materials, such as enzymes, to inorganic substrates, or carriers, leading to the development of radio-immunoassay products for diagnostic testing in 1974. An all-electric melter in 1972, polychromatic glass in 1978, transparent glass-ceramic cookware in 1981, diesel particulate filters in 1986, and dental restorations in 1987 were other breakthroughs.

Despite these innovations, Corning experienced a decline in earnings in the 1970s. Although over one-third of its products were new, the bulk of its sales came from mature products such as bulbs and television blanks for picture glass, which it sold to other companies. Competition was strong and Corning experienced a decline in market share of these products. Japanese imports of television sets, for example, curtailed the demand for Corning television glass.

Another problem involved Signetics, a semiconductor manufacturer, purchased in 1962. In 1970 Signetics lost $6 million on $35 million in sales. Corning had never developed an expertise in electronics and in 1975 sold Signetics, absorbing a pretax loss of $9.5 million. In 1972 Hurricane Agnes caused a severe flood which cut corporate headquarters off from the outside world for a time and cost the company $20 million. Earnings collapsed to $1.76 per share in 1975. In response to these difficulties, Corning closed five plants and eliminated production of domestic black-and-white TV tubes, Christmas ornaments, and acid-waste drain lines. Employment was cut in the 1970s from 46,000 worldwide to 29,000, with an increase in productivity from an industry average of 3% per year to 6%. Research and development continued, with expenditures of about 5% of sales, above the U.S. national average of 2%.

Sales volumes fell in 1982 for some consumer products, such as Corning Ware, Pyrex, and Corelle dinnerware. In 1983 Corning halted production of light bulbs. That year leadership changed from president to joint management by group presidents and Chairman of the board, James Houghton.

Corelle products designs had not changed in more than a decade, and Corning had not advertised, until 1985, that its products had always been suitable for the microwave oven. The company did not begin market research until 1984. As a result Corning modernized designs of older products and introduced Visions cookware, combining the transparency of glass with the heat-resistant qualities of ceramics.

Corning's experience with fiber optics illustrates the problems and the benefits of a company based on research and technology. As a result of Corning's work, glass-fibers, or fiber optics, have replaced copper wire in traditional telephone lines. A hair-thin glass fiber can carry as many telephone calls as a four-inch copper wire, using pulses of light to transfer sound. The difficulty is that light may lose its intensity as it moves through the cable. When Corning began working on fiber optics in the middle 1960s, researchers decided that a 99% loss over a kilometer was economically viable because it could be boosted at that point. After four years of work, and numerous failed experiments the research team developed a working product. Physicist Donald Keck recorded the event in his laboratory notebook with the notation "Eureka."

At the time there was no apparent demand for the product. Telephone companies said that they would produce their own fiber when demand made such a step imperative. Although lacking sales, Corning continued improving the product, making the original product obsolete even before it was sold. By 1972 the fiber wire could be extended 20 kilometers without a repeater, five times longer than standard copper wire. Eventually the distance grew to 100 kilometers. These continued improvements resulted in price declines from several dollars to less than 12¢ a meter in the late 1980s.

Corning reacted to the lack of early demand by entering into several joint ventures with European cable companies, believing that local partners would eventually lead to sales to the state-owned telephone monopolies. At the same time Corning built its own factory in the United States. This move proved successful when deregulation of the telephone industry in the United States led MCI Communications Corporation to order 100,000 kilometers of cable in 1982. Two years later the company spent $87 million on new fiber plant facilities, the largest single Corning investment ever.

By the 1970s, U.S. communication companies were developing and using optical fiber. In July 1976, Corning filed suit against ITT Corporation and its customer, the United States government, charging patent infringements. Five years later, after countersuit by ITT and much legal conflict, ITT settled, agreeing to pay penalties for patent infringement; a short time later, the government settled with payment of $650,000 for having purchased the fiber. During the next few years, Corning filed similar suits against Valtec Industries and Sumitomo Electric Industries in Japan. These suits too were settled in Corning's favor, in 1984 and 1987 respectively.

Corning's work on laboratory glass instruments led it into laboratory-related services, through the acquisition of other firms. MetPath, one of the leading clinical testing services in the United States, was purchased in 1982. Hazelton Laboratories, purchased in 1987, became one of the world's leading independent suppliers of services for biological and chemical research. Enseco, acquired in 1989, specializes in environmental testing.

Corning has entered into more joint ventures—over two-thirds with foreign firms—than most other U.S.-based firms.

More than half of its 1987 profits came from joint ventures. Dow Corning, with $1.5 billion in revenues, is as large as all of Corning's other joint ventures. The international alliances covered the globe, and included more than 15 joint ventures with companies in Europe, Asia, and Australia, producing such products as optical fiber, specialty glass, ceramics, and cookware.

Acquisition of joint-venture partners continued in 1989 and 1990. IBM invested in PCO, an optoelectronics company controlled by Corning. Mitsubishi Heavy Industries, Mitsubishi Petrochemical, and Corning became partners in Cormetech, a pollution-control company. In June 1990 Corning joined with a company in India to form Samcor Glass. Corning entered such relationships to provide instant market penetration and to bring new technologies to the company. In 1989, Corning acknowledged the diversification of its products by changing the company name to Corning Incorporated.

Corning may serve as a prototypical "knowledge" firm. While it has always depended on research for new products, it has moved even more actively into new products, quality of production, and training since the 1970s. For example, Corning's Total Quality program cut irregularities on a new coating process in fiber optics from 800 parts-per-million in 1986 to none in 1988. By 1991 the company planned to have workers spend 5% of their time in paid training. While many U.S. firms have floundered due to Asian competition, Corning has transformed itself into one of the world's leading technology companies, while successfully maintaining its strength in manufacturing.

Principal Subsidiaries: Corning Engineering; Corning Enterprises Inc.; Corning Europe Inc. (U.K.); Corning International Corporation; Crown Corning USA Incorporated; Dow Corning Corporation (50%); Hazleton Laboratories Corporation; MetPath, Inc.; PCO, Inc.; Pittsburg Corning Corp. (50%); Siccor Corp. (50%); Steuben Glass; U.S. Precision Lens, Inc.

Further Reading: Magaziner, Ira C., and Mark Patinkin, *The Silent War: Inside the Global Business Battles Shaping America's Future,* New York, Random House, 1989.

—Robert E. Ankli

CSR™

CSR LIMITED

Level 35
Grosvener Place
225 George Street
Sydney, New South Wales
Australia
(02) 235-8333
Fax: (02) 235-8555

Public Company
Incorporated: 1887 as The Colonial Sugar Refining Company
Employees: 22,350
Sales: A$4.89 billion (US$3.86 billion)
Stock Exchanges: Sydney Auckland London Frankfurt

CSR is one of Australia's largest building and construction materials companies, and operates additionally in New Zealand and the United States. The company is also Australia's largest manufacturer of raw and refined sugar products. While CSR was established in 1855 to refine sugar and soon after diversified into raw sugar milling, its sugar activities represent only about one-quarter of CSR's annual sales. In an effort to change its image from that of solely a sugar producer, CSR has been promoting its increasingly strong position in the building and construction materials industry. The company has substantial operations in quarrying, concrete, cement products, bricks and tiles, plasterboard, insulation, and timber products, as well as investments in aluminum.

The Colonial Sugar Refining Company (CSR) was formed as a partnership in January 1855 under the chairmanship of Edward Knox, an ambitious 35-year-old entrepreneur. Having acquired some of the assets of the defunct Australasian Sugar Company, the partnership bought the Brisbane House sugar refinery in Sydney. Two years later, in 1857, a new holding company—the Victoria Sugar Company—was formed jointly by CSR shareholders and Victorian business interests, and a sugar refinery and molasses distillery were set up at Port Melbourne. Later that year, Knox sold his house and some of his shares in the company and left for Europe by ship. Before he reached Europe, he was bombarded with letters telling him the company was ruined. Knox returned to Australia immediately.

The company underwent serious financial difficulties following the depression in the world sugar trade from 1857 to 1858. CSR countered the potentially disastrous effects of the depression by diversifying into sugar milling. By 1869 the company had built a number of new mills in northern New South Wales. With the construction of the Chatsworth, Southgate, and Darkwater mills CSR entered the sugar-milling industry. Darkwater Mill has since been renamed Harwood Mill and is the oldest continually working sugar mill in Australia. Knox's second son, Edward William, was put in charge of the project.

The 1870's saw further diversification within the sugar industry. CSR had by now established a network of mills and refineries on the Queensland coast and the purchase of a small freight ship—SS *Keera*—in 1873 gave the company an entry into the costal shipping business. In 1874, the Victoria Sugar Company's refinery in Melbourne was destroyed by fire and was replaced by the newly built Joshua Brothers' refinery.

CSR continued its program of expansion throughout the next decade. On his retirement, Knox handed over management of the company to his son, writing to a friend, "I can only expect to leave a kind of smeary, sugary track behind me." Edward William Knox was an impetuous and autocratic manager, and anxious to emulate his father's success. The milling operations were extended to Queensland, where new mills had been constructed in the early 1880s. In 1882 CSR embarked on its first overseas project, building a mill in Nausori, Fiji. The following year, CSR formed the New Zealand Sugar Company to refine sugar in New Zealand, as an equal partnership with the Victoria Sugar Company and business interests in New Zealand. In the mid-1880s, CSR's research team conducted the first sugar cane–fertilizer trials.

On July 1, 1887, CSR was amalgamated with the Victoria Sugar Company and was incorporated as a public company, the Colonial Sugar Refining Company Limited. The new company merged the following year with the New Zealand Sugar Company, and CSR was established as a leader in the Australian sugar industry. As the 19th century drew to a close, CSR continued to acquire mills along the Queensland coast and set up a new refinery in Brisbane. Administrative changes, designed to make management of the spreading company more efficient, were introduced in the early 1890s: sugar cane estates in Queensland were divided into small farms for leasing—with the rights of purchase—to cane growers. In 1899, the company's investment in research and development allowed it for the first time to buy cane on the basis of its analyzed sugar content. Other sugar companies were less advanced in the research and application of chemical analysis, and CSR's commitment to research undoubtedly assisted its domination of the domestic sugar industry. In 1904 the company bred Australia's first successful commercial variety of sugar cane, which it christened Clark's Seedling.

Further expansion took place in the early part of the 20th century. An expedition in 1908 to New Guinea to collect samples of sugar cane, to improve breeding of new cane varieties for commercial use, gave rise to better cane and sugar yields. Two years earlier several Fijian plantations had been sold to a group of company officers who wanted to work for themselves. As World War I approached, CSR continued to consolidate its refining and milling businesses, and sent another cane-gathering party to New Guinea. Trade in Australia benefited from the increase in the British government's demand for sugar and resources after World War I. In 1923 the commonwealth government transferred control of the sugar industry to the Queensland government, and CSR made its first annual refining and marketing agreement with the government. The world Depression of the 1930s was threatening, however, and a downturn in demand was anticipated. In 1933 Edward William Knox retired, four months before his death. His son, Edward Ritchie Knox, took over as general manager.

The onset of World War II precipitated CSR's second major diversification. A pilot plant set up in 1936 to assess the feasibility of making wallboard from the residue fiber of crushed sugar cane provided CSR with what transpired to be a commercial method of disposing of its sugar millery byproducts. In 1939 CSR acquired shares in a chemicals plant in Sydney and opened a wallboard factory nearby, where the new product Cane-ite was produced. To meet the needs of the Australian war effort, CSR reduced its sugar-based production activities from 1939 onwards in order to manufacture war-related materials. A new plaster mill was introduced in Sydney in 1942. Two years later, CSR began mining asbestos when it acquired Australian Blue Asbestos's mine in Wittenoom, Western Australia.

While CSR was known mainly as a sugar producer, the postwar program of diversification changed the corporate profile considerably. The last year of the war marked CSR's first substantial entry into building materials and construction when the company bought an interest in Fletcher Holdings, a large construction and timber company based in New Zealand. During the late 1940s, CSR introduced new building products—plasterboard and floor tiles—and expanded its factory stock in Sydney. The wave of expansion culminated in the formation of a new wholly owned subsidiary, CSR Chemicals, in 1948.

Over the next ten years, under the directorship of Edward Ritchie Knox, CSR continued to expand. The company's sugar operations were extended and facilities for bulk-loading raw sugar were introduced at two of the original Queensland mills, and later extended to cover all twelve mills. In 1955, CSR was appointed coordinator for the Australian sugar industry's conversion to bulk handling. From the mid-1950s on, the company increased its involvement in the building-materials industry. The acquisition in 1959 of the Bradford Insulation Group gave CSR a major share of the insulation-products market throughout Australia. In the same year the CSR Chemicals subsidiary spawned two new subsidiaries, and a new product—particleboard—was introduced. Developments at this time included the takeover of Masonite Holdings, which manufactured hardboard.

The company opened new research centers in Brisbane in 1962, and in Sydney in 1963. The following year it joined American Metal Climax in a project to develop the Mount Newman iron-ore deposits in Western Australia. From the mid-1960s until the early 1980s CSR increased its involvement in resources, including bauxite and alumina, tin, copper, coal, oil and gas, gold, aluminum, and minerals exploration. At the same time as CSR was increasing its investment in resources, it also entered the concrete market for the first time. In 1965 it acquired a 50% share—with Blue Metal Industries—in Ready Mixed Concrete (RMC).

The 1969 takeover of Wunderlich Ltd., a large manufacturer of roof tiles, asbestos cement products, and architectural metal products, gave CSR its first significant entry into the Australian roof-tile industry. The business was subsequently sold in 1983 to Monier. In 1972 the Fijian government bought CSR's Fijian sugar-mills, ending the company's 90-year involvement in the Fijian sugar industry.

The resource ventures begun in the 1960s, during Australia's mineral boom, continued throughout the 1970s. The company began to invest in alumina and bauxite; various gold, tin, and copper ventures; and later, coal, oil, and gas. Extensive investments in a number of established coal mines made in the 1970s proved unsuccessful. The prices of coal and oil dropped almost immediately after the acquisitions had been made, near the peak of the energy cycle. A large proportion of loans made for the acquisition of coal and oil assets were in US dollars. The repayments of these loans increased significantly with the fall in the Australian dollar exchange rate in 1983-1984, coupled with falling energy prices.

To reflect recent diversification, and in an effort to modernize corporate identity, the company dropped "Colonial Sugar Refining Company" from its original name and in 1973 it became CSR Limited. In the following year, CSR entered the cement industry through the joint acquisition, with Pioneer International, of Australian and Kandos Cement. The managerial difficulties CSR was experiencing with such diverse business interests forced a strategic reorganization. The sugar division was formed in 1974 and the mineral division and the building- and construction-materials division were formed the following year.

Further diversification took place in 1977, when CSR bought AAR Ltd., an exploration company with natural gas, oil, and drilling contracts. Thiess, a large coal company, was acquired in 1979. When the resources boom of the 1970s and early 1980s petered out, CSR was left with a debt and interest burden that made the company vulnerable to takeover bids. Investors had lost faith in the company and CSR share prices plummeted. The company was surviving largely on the activities of the sugar and building materials divisions, but the drop in world sugar prices in the early- to mid-1980s made the situation worse. Until the extensive management and corporate restructuring which began in 1985, CSR was a struggling company. Bryan Kelman became general manager in 1983.

In 1981 the company significantly increased its investment in the oil industry when it bought an Australian-based, U.S.-owned oil and petroleum producer, Delhi International Oil Corporation. The major investments in coal, and particularly oil, were badly timed. The Delhi acquisition was hit with falling oil prices, lack of new oil discoveries, and a falling Australian dollar, while carrying extensive debt in U.S. dollars. As a result, the company began a process of repaying much of its debt through the sale of iron ore and some coal assets. This was followed in 1987 with the sale of Delhi for US$985 million, resulting in a loss of over US$600 million.

In 1985, sugar profits fell dramatically. Growing public concern about the health risks associated with sugar consumption and a slump in world prices hit CSR badly. In 1985 sugar was at its lowest price in 200 years. Many cane farmers were living below the poverty line and accused CSR of mismanaging the industry in which it played a dominant role.

In 1987 CSR began the process of changing the company from a diversified resources and industrial group to a diversified manufacturing company in building and construction materials and sugar—core activities in which the company had long years of experience, since 1855 in sugar and since 1939 in building materials. Between 1987 and 1989 the company sold over US$2 billion of low-yielding and lossmaking assets in resources and reinvested these funds in building and construction materials and sugar operations, including large investments in the United States. By the end of the 1980s, CSR had sold all its interests in tin, gold, and mineral exploration, its coal mines, and its oil and gas interests. The head office in Sydney, where the company had been based for 106 years, was also sold to compensate for falling profits. A more steamlined management structure was also introduced. Ian Burgess took over as chief executive of CSR in 1987, and his ruthless approach to restructuring the flagging conglomerate is generally accepted as having saved CSR from takeover or collapse. Burgess had joined the company straight from school in 1950, and was anxious to change the antiquated management style. "It was a very conservative place," he told *The Wall Street Journal* on May 14, 1987, "you even had to get your wife approved. You had to go to your boss and say 'Please sir, can I get married?' " Under Burgess's guidance, each of CSR's divisions was transformed. The building materials division, for example, had employed 157 senior managers. After Burgess's reorganization, there were three. Burgess also dispensed with the CSR annual cricket match, a 94-year-old company tradition. By the end of 1989 the reorganization was complete.

The acquisition of the U.S. Rinker Materials Corporation in 1988 gave CSR a large proportion of the Florida concrete and quarry products market. In 1990 CSR acquired ARC America, a large quarry and concrete products operator with interests in 20 states including Ohio, Indiana, Michigan, Washington, California, Nevada, Texas, and Florida. By the end of 1990 the building and construction division made up 64% of total sales. CSR is one of the largest quarrying and concrete operators in the United States, and has more quarries there than in Australia. The same year, CSR announced record profits. Against a background of high inflation rates and a weak Australian dollar in the mid 1980s, CSR's divestment policy appeared to have paid off. Further expansion in timber, when CSR bought Softwood Holdings in 1988, meant a quadrupling of profits for the timber-products division. Despite slow growth in the construction industry, but with profits increasing by 65% in 1989, CSR began to focus on Europe and the United States for expansion. In 1987, the company bought a 49% share in Redland Plasterboard, a large British construction company with assets throughout Europe. Increasing competition in the U.K. and European plasterboard industry caused CSR to sell out its interest in 1990.

In 1989 controversy concerning the company's alleged negligence in its management of the Wittenoom asbestos mine, which it had sold in 1966, was settled. CSR paid out an estimated A$30 million in damages to over 300 workers suffering from asbestos-related lung diseases. Australian newspapers referred to the event as "Australia's Bhopal."

A commercial development affecting CSR in the 1990s was the deregulation of the domestic refined sugar industry, which began in 1989. CSR is currently reassessing its refining capacity and locations in the face of greater competition, both from domestic sources and eventually from imports. While profits as a commercial refiner are better than those earned as a toll refiner on behalf of the Queensland government, CSR has lost about 20% of its market share within Australia—it now stands at about 75%.

The company has removed itself from the more volatile resources markets, but still has to cope with the cyclical nature of the building and construction industry and the instability of the sugar market.

Because CSR operates in a mature market within the basic end of the Australian building and construction materials sector, major opportunities for growth within Australia are limited. As a result, CSR has focused on the United States as an area for future growth, particularly in quarry and concrete products. CSR already has about 30% of its assets based in the United States. This growth is likely to continue.

Principal Subsidiaries: CSR Finance Ltd.; CSR Investments Pty Ltd.; Farrer Properties Ltd.; Monier PGH Ltd. (51%); Bradford Enercon Inc. (Canada, 70%); Synkoloid Holdings Inc. (Canada); Beadex Holding Inc. (U.S.A.); CSR Hebel Australia Pty Ltd. (82.5%); CSR America Inc. (U.S.A.); Rinker Materials Corp. (U.S.A.); American Aggregates Corp. (U.S.A.); Associated Sand and Gravel Co. Inc. (U.S.A.); ARC Materials Corp. (U.S.A.); Hydro Conduit Corp. (U.S.A.); Southern Aggregates Co. (U.S.A.); Softwood Holdings Ltd.; Hardboards Australia Ltd.; New Zealand Sugar Co. Ltd.; Pioneer Sugar Mills Ltd.; The Haughton Sugar Co. Pty Ltd.; Gove Aluminium Ltd. (70%); Gove Aluminium Finance Ltd. (70%).

Further Reading: Lowndes A.G., ed., *South Pacific Enterprise,* Sydney, Angus & Robertson, 1956; *CSR Limited—130 years,* Sydney, CSR, 1986; Brooks, Geraldine, "Australia's CSR Boosts Its Sagging Fortunes," *The Wall Street Journal,* May 14, 1987; Sherwell, Chris, "CSR Works To A Sweeter Future, " *The Financial Times,* June 11, 1987; Sherwell, Chris, "Shifts in Australian Mining Row," *The Financial Times,* August 24, 1988; Sherwell, Chris, "CSR Sheds Its Unloved Reputation," *The Financial Times,* December 2, 1988; *CSR: Building In Quality; Fact Book,* Sydney, CSR, January 1990.

—Juliette Bright

ECC GROUP PLC

John Keay House
St. Austell, Cornwall PL25 4DJ
United Kingdom
(0726) 74482
Fax: (0726) 623019

Public Company
Incorporated: 1919 as English China Clays Ltd.
Employees: 13,770
Sales: £982.2 million (US$1.59 billion)
Stock Exchanges: London NASDAQ

ECC Group produces and sells industrial minerals all over the world and construction materials in the United Kingdom and the United States. It also builds houses in the United Kingdom. It is the world's largest producer of kaolin, more familiarly known as china clay. More than half of the group's turnover derives from its overseas operations. Group activities are carried on by its subsidiary companies organized in four divisions.

ECC International (ECCI) is concerned predominantly with the production and sale of china clay, a raw material used by a number of industries. Some 80% of china clay output is now used by the paper industry, 12% by the ceramic industry, and 8% by miscellaneous industries, mainly in the manufacture of paint, rubber, and plastics. ECCI also produces and sells calcium carbonate, as well as other industrial minerals. In 1989 the division's sales of industrial minerals exceeded six million tons for the first time. It also has plant hire and transport operations and a small waste-disposal business. Production facilities are in the United Kingdom in Devon and Cornwall, in the United States, Brazil, and Australia. In 1989 ECCI's sales contributed 56% of the group's total turnover of £981.2 million.

The operations of the ECC Construction Materials (ECCCM) division include the production and sale of quarry material, macadam, concrete products, and industrial sand in the United Kingdom and the United States, and a U.K. waste-disposal business. ECCCM contributed 34% of group turnover in 1989. Two smaller divisions are responsible for ECC's other activities; ECC Construction (ECCC), whose operations represented 4% of group turnover in 1989, is concerned with the construction, development, and refurbishment of private housing and, trading as SNW Homes and Bradley Homes, is responsible for building houses in the United Kingdom. IDF International operates worldwide, supplying drilling fluids to the oil and gas exploration industry, operations which accounted for 6% of group turnover in 1989.

Kaolin takes its name from the mountain in China from which European manufacturers of ceramics originally obtained their supplies of the raw material. The increasing demand for ceramics in Europe stimulated a search for raw materials nearer home, and by the early 18th century, china clay deposits had been located in Bohemia, Thuringia, Saxony, and near Limoges in France. In the United Kingdom china clay deposits that were found to be of a finer quality than elsewhere in Europe were discovered in Cornwall in the middle of the 18th century; their exploitation created the United Kingdom's china clay industry. Its development in the 19th century was economically most important to Cornwall, since its growth took place at a time when the industry upon which Cornwall had previously depended for employment and wealth creation, tin mining, was being forced into decline by foreign competition. Changes in the papermaking industry and its expansion in the second half of the 19th century created a new and growing market for china clay.

The processes of extracting, refining, and drying china clay remain in essence the same as they were in the 19th century, although the application of technology has transferred to machines much of the work done by manual labor in the early days, improved the purity of the final product, and made it possible to extract other minerals that formerly went to waste. Even so, waste remains a formidable problem for the group; despite the use of sand and the application of much research, the production of one ton of clay still creates seven tons of waste. The first process is the pit operation, which involves exposing china clay deposits by removing the overburden. Some deposits may be as close to the surface as three feet while others may be hundreds of feet below ground. Hydraulic mining, by firing water jets from a cannon at the clay deposits, frees the deposits and creates a slurry which also contains sand and mica. The slurry is then pumped out and the coarser sand removed before the refining process takes place. This process takes out unwanted minerals such as quartz, mica, and feldspar. Geologically, china clay is formed in granite rocks by the decomposition of feldspar. At this stage chemical bleaching to remove the stains in the clay caused by mineral salts, particularly iron oxide, can add value to the final product, a technological advance not available until after World War II. ECCI operates six refining plants in Devon and Cornwall that take clay from a number of pits and mix it in the quantities required for finished products of varying characteristics. The final drying process, which today usually takes place in natural gas-fired driers, was originally done in coal-fired kilns and even, at some pits, wind and sun dried.

In the first half of the 19th century, production of china clay was in the hands of many small proprietors, some of whom owned the land on which the mine lay and some of whom leased it. Although some consolidation took place later in the century, in 1914 there were still some 70 individual producers. At that time the industry was characterized by low wages, overproduction, and price-cutting. These problems were exacerbated by the outbreak of World War I, particularly for an industry that depended on exporting, to the extent, in 1914, of 70% of its output. During the war, shipping capacity for goods such as china clay, which had little or no military purpose, was severely limited. By 1917 many china clay producers were making losses and few, if any, were making profits. A trade association, Associated China Clays, was established in that year, and in its seven year existence—it terminated in 1924—had some success in stabilizing the industry by setting prices and sales quotas. In 1919, the three largest producers in Cornwall, Martin Brothers Ltd., established 1837; the West of England and Great Beam Company, established 1849; and the North Cornwall China Clay Company, established 1908, merged to form English China Clays Ltd.

Reginald Martin of Martin Brothers was chairman of the new company but the most influential figure, until his early death in 1931, was T. Medland Stocker of the West of England Company. A qualified mining engineer, anxious to see technical improvements and investment in an industry whose development was inhibited by fragmentation and a lack of capital, Stocker's company had before 1919 absorbed a number of smaller china clay companies. Stocker was very much the architect of the 1919 merger. Two more acquisitions, the Melbur China Clay Company and John Nicholls & Company, made shortly after the incorporation of English China Clays (ECC), gave English China Clays 21 pits to operate. With an annual output three times the tonnage of its nearest competitor, Lovering China Clays, ECC was the largest company in the industry. It was not, however, the only company involved in restructuring in the industry; in 1919 H.D. Pochin & Company acquired one of Cornwall's oldest china clay companies, J. W. Higman & Company, and their combined output made Pochin the third-largest producer.

Through the 1920s ECC faced the difficulties caused by the slump that followed the immediate postwar boom. Excess capacity in the china clay industry internationally, as world demand remained below prewar levels, engendered fierce price-cutting competition which became even worse after the failure of the trade association in 1924. The success of a new association, formed in 1927, was short-lived—it lasted only until 1929—although it was reflected in ECC's improved profits in 1929. Over the decade ECC increased its dominance of the industry by further acquisitions. Four companies were acquired in 1927, the North Goonbarrow, the Great Halviggan, the Imperial Goonbarrow, and the Rosevear, and in 1928 the Hallivet China Clay Company was purchased. There were four more smaller acquisitions in 1929, Burthy China Clays, New Halwyn China Clays, the Carbis China Clay & Brick Company, and the Trethowal China Clay Company, and, more importantly because of its consistent refusal to join any trade association, William Varcoe & Sons was acquired in two stages by ECC in 1929 and 1930.

During the depression, the china clay industry was severely affected. Production fell in the United Kingdom by 34% between 1929 and 1931, and remained below the 1929 level throughout the 1930s. Although the effect of the Great Depression was not as severe in the United Kingdom as it was in the United States, it was enough to provide a powerful stimulus to consolidation and amalgamation among the china clay producers, as in many other industries. In the interwar years rationalization, largely taken to mean the merger of small-scale manufacturing units in order to gain the benefit of economies of scale, became as widely practiced as diversification was to become in the 1950s and 1960s.

In these circumstances the merger of English China Clays with its two major, though smaller, competitors, Lovering China Clays and H. D. Pochin & Company, in 1932 was the next logical step towards rationalizing the industry. ECC became a holding company, owning 63% of its new operating subsidiary, English Clays Lovering Pochin & Company (ECLP). The remaining shares were held by members of the Pochin and Lovering families. The first chairman of ECLP was the Honorable Henry D. McLaren, who in 1935 succeeded his father as Lord Aberconway. Reginald Martin, who remained chairman of ECC until 1948, when he was over 70, was managing director of ECLP in 1932 to 1937. Martin's assistant managing director in 1932, who was to succeed him in 1937 and to exercise a major influence over the company until 1963, was John Keay—Sir John Keay from 1950, when he was knighted. An accountant by profession, Keay had joined ECC in 1929 and was responsible, with Reginald Martin, for the success of the negotiations leading to the 1932 merger.

The integration of so many diverse companies—another 12 china clay producers were acquired during the 1930s—would not have been easy at the best of times. In the 1930s when falling demand, surplus capacity, and low prices meant there was little spare cash for investment, it was even more difficult. However, some progress was made in modernizing, mechanizing, and making the industry more efficient. The engineering facilities at the company's 42 pits were reorganized and with the acquisition in 1935 of the Charlestown Foundry, despite its poor condition, the company had a nucleus for engineering. Electrification was extended to more of the company's pits and processes, and in 1936 a new central power station was commissioned at Drinnick, to supply all the company's operations. The company developed brickmaking using the high-temperature-resistant substance molochite, and looked for other uses for this material. A research department was established, initially to work on fractionating clay particles to produce the more highly refined selected particle size (SPS) clay required by paper manufacturers, especially in the United States.

World War II offered ECLP little hope of improving trading conditions. With home demand expected to fall and no hope of maintaining the export trade that, through the 1930s, had taken up nearly 65% of output, a 50% reduction of capacity was enforced by the Board of Trade under its wartime powers. For ECLP, the only bright spot was the Charlestown Foundry, which was able to undertake armaments contracts and, re-equipped with machinery and tools that were to prove of immense benefit to the company in the immediate postwar years, worked to full capacity throughout the war.

When the war ended, it soon became clear that the demand for china clay would expand rapidly. Although ECLP had formulated plans for postwar development, shortages of men, building materials, and fuel precluded any immediate expansion, nor was it an easy task to reopen pits that had been closed for the duration of the war. After representations had been made to the government, a Board of Trade working committee was appointed to look for ways of increasing production. Its report, published in March 1946, recommended short-term measures to alleviate the labor, materials, and fuel problems and suggested a wider ranging enquiry. A Board of Trade committee was therefore appointed, with John Keay from ECLP as its vice chairman. Its report, delivered two years later, condemned the industry, but not ECLP, for among other things, its failure to innovate, poor research, and lack of welfare facilities for its workers. In 1950 an advisory council, on which sat representatives of all parts of the industry, was established. For ECLP, the immediate postwar years meant steady growth and recovery. One innovation for which it was responsible in those years made a major contribution to the U.K.'s postwar housing shortage. Cornish Unit houses, jointly designed and developed by ECC's subsidiaries Selleck Nicholls and John Williams, were bungalows built from concrete using china clay sand. In the ten years immediately after the war, 40,000 were built. ECC's building subsidiaries went on to extend the range of prefabricated building components for both housing and industrial use.

It was not until the early 1950s that restructuring and reorganization paved the way for the emergence of the ECC group as it is today. In 1951 and 1954 ECC was able to buy the shares in ECLP previously held by the Lovering and Pochin families and, with a financial reorganization in 1956, ECLP became a wholly owned subsidiary. The activities of the group's subsidiaries were then reorganized into four trading divisions, each one covering one of ECC's main operations: china clay, building, quarrying, and transport. The changing nature of the business since 1956 later resulted in transport being moved to the ECCI division, and the new IDF division being created.

The 1950s and 1960s saw considerable growth for ECC and real profitability. However, the company continued to be run by those who had been brought up in hard times, and in the 1960s popular opinion within the company held that ECC stood for "every copper counts." Notwithstanding, large amounts of capital were invested in the 1950s and 1960s in modernizing all parts of the china clay production process, and as research and technological developments offered scope for further improvements, the process continued in the 1970s and 1980s. Oil-fired driers replaced the coal-fired kilns in the 1960s to be replaced, in turn, with natural gas-fired driers in the 1980s. From the 1960s onward increasing quantities of china clay were transported as slurry.

ECC continued to acquire steadily the remaining independent china clay producers as well as allied quarrying, stone, building and building materials, and concrete companies, and extended its transport interests. In the last two decades it expanded its activities overseas. A sales presence in the United States that dated back to 1920 became, with the addition of clay manufacturing facilities in Georgia acquired in 1942, the Anglo-American Clays Corporation in 1956. The plant at Sandersville, Georgia, was extended in the 1980s and now specializes in the production of high-brightness hydrous clays and calcined clays. Southern Clay Products in Texas produces ball clay products, and in 1986 ECC acquired the Sylacauga Calcium Products Division of Moretti-Harrah Marble Company, which produces high-quality ground marble. In 1987 the construction aggregate producer J.L. Shiely was acquired in the United States.

In the 1980s ECC, like other United Kingdom companies, started to look at the Pacific region and the Far East as possible areas for development. In 1986, Fuji Kaolin Company, in which ECC had already a 50% interest, became a wholly owned subsidiary of the group, as in the same year did the Kaolin Australia Pty Ltd.

In 1965 a new head office, John Keay House, was opened at St. Austell, Cornwall, which, extended and adapted, remains a quarter of a century later the center of the group's worldwide operations. Despite its size and the increasingly international scope of its activities, the ECC Group has so far maintained a very low profile. How far this profile will continue at a time when public concern for the environment is increasing remains to be seen.

Principal Subsidiaries: ECC International Ltd.; ECC International (Sales) Ltd.; ECC America Inc. (U.S.A.); ECCA Calcium Products Inc. (U.S.A.); Anglo-American Clays Corporation (U.S.A.); ECC Construction Materials Ltd.; Associated Asphalt Company Ltd.; ECC Quarries America, Inc. (U.S.A.); J.L. Shiely Company (U.S.A.); ECC Construction Ltd.; E.H. Bradley Estates Ltd.; ECC Overseas Investments Ltd.; English China Clays, Inc. (U.S.A.).

Further Reading: Hudson, Kenneth, *The History of English China Clays,* Cornwall, ECC Ltd., 1969; *ECC in Focus,* Cornwall, ECC Group, 1989; *There is more to ECC than China Clay,* Cornwall, ECC Group, 1989.

—Judy Slinn

FELDMÜHLE NOBEL AG

Postfach 3209
Mönchenwerther Strasse 15
4000 Düsseldorf 11
Federal Republic of Germany
(0211) 58000
Fax: (0211) 58 02 49

Public Company
Incorporated: 1985
Employees: 35,375
Sales: DM9.51 billion (US$5.63 billion)
Stock Exchanges: Düsseldorf Frankfurt Hanover Berlin Hamburg Stuttgart Bremen Munich

The conglomerate Feldmühle Nobel (Feno) has existed only since 1986. Feno is the legal successor to Friedrich Flick Industrieverwaltung KGaA, which became an *Aktiengesellschaft* (public limited company) and was acquired by Deutsche Bank from the Flick group on December 31, 1985. Dr. Friedrich Karl Flick, the owner, dissolved the Flick group by selling his shares. Feno, founded after this, represents the surviving industrial core of the earlier group. The new group provides an umbrella for the operations of three independent *Aktiengesellschaften*—Feldmühle AG, Dynamit Nobel AG, and Buderus AG—each with its own management and supervisory boards and all with very different products. Feldmühle AG in Düsseldorf produces paper and technical ceramics, Dynamit Nobel AG in Troisdorf manufactures explosives and plastics, and Buderus AG in Wetzlar, which manufactures specialty steel and foundry products, is one of the leading manufacturers in the heating-technology and machine-tool engineering sectors. Each of the three Feno subsidiaries has a long tradition of independent industrial production.

FELDMÜHLE AG

In 1885 the 25-year-old L. Gottstein, a scientist who had just completed his doctorate, purchased the Feldmühle, an old mill at Liebau in Silesia, on the Bober River. He planned to establish a cellulose factory there. The mill, which is first mentioned in 1285, belonged originally to the Cistercian monks of Kloster Grüssau near Liebau. In August 1885, Gottstein, along with other partners, founded the Feldmühle Silesian Sulphite and Cellulose Factory. Gottstein was appointed director of the company. After the necessary construction work had been completed, the factory went into production in October 1886, with two boilers for cellulose production. By the following year, an increase in capitalization had already been approved. During the next three years, despite a general decline in cellulose prices, the company was able to increase the return on sales of Feldmühle cellulose due to its high quality.

In 1891, because of unstable water levels on the Bober, the supervisory board agreed to build a new cellulose factory at Cosel on the Oder River. Cosel's location at the intersection of the navigable Oder and the railway was equally favorable for the delivery of wood and coal and for the dispatch of the end product. The company's name was changed to Feldmühle Cellulose Factory. Because of good trading conditions, diversification was planned. Instead of merely producing unfinished materials for use by paper factories, as had previously been the case, it was decided in 1895 that the company itself should undertake paper production. Subsequently a paper factory was established at Cosel and the works at Liebau were also converted for this purpose. In 1899 a second paper factory went into production at Cosel. Because of the company's increasing size, its headquarters was transferred to Breslau in 1895.

In spite of initial trading difficulties and falling prices in the paper market at the beginning of the 20th century, Feldmühle expanded its production capacity, a move which was to bear fruit during the next phase of economic growth. In 1910 the company's name was changed to Feldmühle Paper and Cellulose Works AG, and in the same year work began on a new plant at Odermünde near Stettin. Construction was complicated at the unfavorable location, the marshy meadows of the Oder valley; 85,890 meters of concrete posts were needed to support the building.

In 1911 Feldmühle continued to diversify, with the production of newsprint at the Odermünde factory. Two years later, countercurrent to the rest of the German economy, the production rate of the paper-manufacturing industry entered a phase of decline. At the beginning of World War I, most outstanding orders were immediately canceled and no new orders were given. The prices of raw materials rose. Feldmühle began to produce materials for the war effort. Cellulose had replaced cotton in the production of gun powder; furthermore, cellulose and paper were soon used as substitute materials in the production of other goods needed for the war. The gasoline shortage was offset partly by the effluent of cellulose factories, the sugar content of which was converted into alcohol. Spirit could be extracted from wood by-products, which had hitherto been discarded. In the factory at Oberlangenbielau, founded in 1917, paper textile products such as soldiers' uniforms, coats, and flags were manufactured from cellulose.

After the end of the war it took some time to accomplish the transition from wartime to civilian production. The factories at Cosel and Obermünde were closed temporarily due to lack of raw materials. In 1919 Feldmühle disposed of the factories at Cosel, and founder L. Gottstein resigned from his post as director to join the supervisory board. The introduction of the rentenmark in Germany in 1923 brought an end to runaway inflation, and meant that Feldmühle's year-end net profits amounted to only 999.19 rentenmarks instead of 999.19 billion marks. In 1925 the company acquired the Pommersche Papierfabrik Hohenkrug, a specialist manufacturer of high-quality writing papers with a history reaching back to 1528. Four years later Dr. Kurt Gottstein became a full member of the management board. In 1928 the company merged with the paper manufacturer Reisholz AG, which owned four factories—at Reisholz, Flensburg, Uetersen, and Arnsberg.

In 1930, the year of global economic crisis, Feldmühle cut back production and employment. Nonetheless, with the help of loans and capital-raising, the company was able to acquire the large German factories owned by Koholyt AG, itself controlled by the U.K. firm Inveresk Paper Company, which had acquired Koholyt from the estate of German industrialist Hugo Stinnes. The Koholyt factories consisted of cellulose works at Sackheim and Cosse, paper factories at Hillegossen and Oberlahnstein, an electronics factory at Lülsdorf, and a grinding tools factory at Wesseling. The devaluation of the British pound and customs restrictions imposed by other countries posed serious threats to exports. In the wake of the economic upturn after 1933, production was increased again and new jobs were created. In 1937 Feldmühle achieved record production levels for the pre–World War II era, manufacturing 272,000 tons of paper and board. Feldmühle continued to supply cellulose products and other goods to the German government during World War II. There is little specific information about the company's wartime activities and Feldmühle refuses to discuss its activities during this period. After World War II, with the division of Germany, the company lost its entire cellulose production base and over 50% of its paper and board capacity. Six factories were lost to Eastern Europe, and the provisional administrative headquarters were transferred to Hillegossen near Bielefeld. In the years immediately after World War II there was a severe shortage of paper. Since 1951 the company's administrative base has been located at Düsseldorf. Also in 1951, a rubber and plastics factory was established at Plochingen in Württemberg. With the introduction of polyethylene film production at the Rhineland factory at Lülsdorf in 1954, Feldmühle became one of the first manufacturers of these packaging films in the Federal Republic of Germany. In 1956 the American Feldmühle Corporation, now Kyocera Feldmühle, was founded in New York. The prewar production record set in 1937 was surpassed in 1957, when the company achieved a production volume of 279,000 tons of paper and board. In 1960 Feldmühle acquired a majority shareholding in Dynamit Nobel AG of Troisdorf.

In 1962 Feldmühle became a 100% subsidiary of the Flick group and the company's name was changed to Feldmühle AG. In the mid-1960s, due to the increase in German paper exports, foreign distribution companies were established; in 1985 Feldmühle owned six such companies. In 1968, licenses to use Feldmühle patents were given to the International Paper Company, the largest paper manufacturer in the United States. In July 1970, with the sale of the electrochemical factory at Lülsdorf to Dynamit Nobel AG, the group's chemical interests were focused on Dynamit Nobel. Kyocera Europa Elektronische Bauelemente GmbH at Plochingen was founded as a joint venture with the Kyocera Corporation of Kyoto, Japan. At the same time the company acquired interests in the Netherlands and in Sweden, and Feldmühle founded a German sales organization for newsprint in cooperation with Stora Kopparbergs Bergslags AB of Falun.

At the end of 1974, Feldmühle's shareholding in Dynamit Nobel was taken over by the parent organization, the Flick group. At the end of the 1970s an extensive rationalization and expansion program was carried out. It was planned that each product should be assigned to the most cost-efficient production source. By 1984 Feldmühle was producing 1.2 million tons of paper and board, 13% of the total paper and board production of the Federal Republic of Germany.

DYNAMIT NOBEL AG

Alfred Bernhard Nobel, a Swede who later became sponsor of the Nobel prize, founded this company in 1865. As a result of his technochemical studies of nitroglycerine he invented "Nobel's patent detonator"—a first step in the development of dynamite—in 1863. Because of transportation problems due to the impact sensitivity of explosive material, Nobel had to locate production sites as near as possible to the place where it was to be used, or close to ports of dispatch. Alfred Nobel & Company was entered in the trade register of Hamburg in 1865. For 14,000 Prussian thalers, Nobel purchased a disused tannery at Geesthacht to the southeast of Hamburg. The nitroglycerine and percussion-cap factory began production on June 1, 1866.

After some initial difficulties, deliveries were soon being made to Belgium, England, Austria, South America, and Australia. After the end of the U.S. Civil War, demand soared in North America and Nobel founded companies to produce his explosive in New York and San Francisco. After numerous fatal accidents had taken place, greater precautionary measures were taken in handling the dangerous product. Nobel's invention of the safe dynamite, named after the Greek for "power," was the result of his efforts to make nitroglycerine safer, and was the most significant event in this field since the introduction of black gunpowder to Europe from China. The company received many contracts, including one for the St. Gotthard tunnel in Switzerland and the Corinth Canal in Greece. Nobel subsidiaries operating dynamite factories were founded in many countries, and production rose from 11 tons in 1867 to 5,000 tons in 1876. In 1876, in the wake of this industrialization, the company was converted into an *Aktiengesellschaft,* with a share capital of 3.5 million marks. Alfred Nobel managed the company until 1879, when he became chairman of the supervisory board, a position he held until his death in 1896.

In 1885, Nobel succeeded in uniting three of his largest competitors in the explosives market with Dynamit AG to form the Deutsche Union. Dr. Gustav Aufschläger became chairman of the management board in 1889. As a result of Nobel's invention of ballastite, the smokeless nitroglycerine powder, gunpowder companies considered the possibility of producing nitroglycerine, which in turn prompted nitroglycerine producers to make plans for manufacturing smokeless gunpowder. To prevent such competition, a general monopoly agreement between the companies of the dynamite group and the gunpowder group was made in 1889 to prevent them from entering each others' markets.

In the years before the outbreak of World War I, Dynamit AG made several significant discoveries and improvements, such as Nobelit, involving the addition of effervescent materials to the explosive for which a patent was applied in 1903.

By 1914, Dynamit AG had become a company of considerable size. International cross-shareholdings in the explosives.

and gunpowder industry produced an unusual situation when war broke out, where both German and British companies were supplying their respective enemies. A share exchange of the companies involved was therefore carried out on neutral territory, in the Netherlands, in 1915. Dynamit AG acquired the shares of the three other companies in the Deutsche Union. When war ended in 1918 the company had to adapt from wartime requirements to civilian production. Job losses were inevitable.

In the 1920s a new era began—the age of plastics. Explosive gelatine and celluloid originate from a common source material, nitrocellulose. Large-scale manufacture of celluloid began in the Troisdorf factory of the Rheinisch-Westfälischer Sprengstoff AG (RWS) of Cologne in 1905. As time passed, a variety of plastics were developed in the Troisdorf factory. Closures and dismantling during the years after World War I made it necessary for Dynamit AG to establish a cooperation agreement with the powerful I.G. Farbenindustrie AG (I.G. Farben). In 1931 Dynamit AG merged with RWS. Through the acquisition of several companies, Dynamit AG was able to present a healthy set of results in 1938, with turnover amounting to 210 million reichsmarks and a work force totaling 36,400. However, in 1945 the assets in all four occupied zones were seized, and many factories were dismantled. Decartelization measures resulted first of all in the dissociation of Dynamit AG from I.G. Farben and from interests held jointly with Wasag-Chemie AG.

In December 1953 the company was released from Allied control. Dynamit AG focused on its former explosives and plastics divisions and also became active in the chemicals sector. In subsequent years, the losses sustained during the war were made good by new acquisitions. Faced with acute shortages of natural fatty acids, an essential raw material, the company increased its involvement in the production of chemical base products.

Since 1959, after becoming a part of the Flick group, the company has been called Dynamit Nobel AG. Dynamit Nobel operates in selected markets of chemistry and technology. Explosive chemistry continues to be one of the firm's main fields of activity. In the field of special chemistry, Dynamit Nobel has applied its experience in treating hazardous chemical reactions to the development and production of added-value organic intermediates. With its years of tradition and quality, Dynamit Nobel is one of the world's top manufacturers in the market of ammunition for hunting, sports, and industrial use. Systems engineering and defense technology constitute a further division, including production of precision moldings for many industries—mainly automobile manufacturing. Dynamit Nobel has ten production plants in Germany. The principal foreign subsidiaries are in Spain, where plastic moldings are produced; Switzerland, where specialty chemicals are produced; and in Austria, France, Nigeria, the United Kingdom, and the United States, where distribution companies have been formed.

BUDERUS AG

In the Middle Ages, German feudal lords reserved for themselves the right to mine for iron ore. In 1707, a member of this class, Count Friedrich Ernst of Solms-Laubach, founded the Friedrichshütte (Friedrich Iron Works) at Laubach. Johann Wilhelm Buderus I, who had been administrator of the works, took over the lease in March 1731. This is considered the founding date of the Buderus company. Buderus's second wife carried on his work after his death in 1753. The company grew rapidly during the next 45 years under their son, Johann Wilhelm Buderus II. In 1807, the latter's three sons joined together, with equal shares, to form the company J.W. Buderus and Sons. After the sudden deaths of his two brothers, Georg Buderus managed the company until 1840. This period saw another phase of expansion through new lease or purchase agreements with other foundries. After the death of Georg Buderus in 1840, his three nephews took over the running of the business. In 1856 an administrative council was formed, whose headquarters were transferred to Wetzlar in mid-1862 after the closure of the Asslar works. 1861 was a year of particular significance in the company's history: the Deutz-Giessen railway was completed, connecting the ore-rich area around Wetzlar with the coal-rich Ruhr area. In the following years, coke-fueled extraction of pig iron came to the fore and charcoal blast furnaces became less important.

Irreconcilable differences of opinion within the family about future strategy led to the dissolution of the partnership in 1870. After a new company had been formed, Georg Buderus II and his son Georg Buderus III began production on the site of today's works at Wetzlar. Georg Buderus III took control of the works in 1873 after his father's death. In 1884, because of the company's continuing expansion and perpetual family disagreements, the company was changed into an *Aktiengesellschaft,* Buderus'sche Eisenwerke. The Buderus family still formed the management and supervisory boards. In 1895, after the death of Georg Buderus III and his brother Hugo's departure from the firm, Eduard Kaiser took over the management of the company, which was in some financial difficulty. This brought to an end the Buderus family's control of the company.

In the following years, Kaiser restored the company's financial health by broadening its product base. This primarily involved the exploitation of products and by-products of the foundry operations. Alfred Groebler succeeded Eduard Kaiser after his death in 1911. During World War I, after many employees had been enlisted, women and prisoners of war were employed to maintain production, which was now focused on the supply of war materials, namely steel. The company's report of 1918 reveals that the adaptation from wartime to civilian production after the end of the war was not difficult for Buderus, as "the company had strayed no more than absolutely necessary from the basis of peace-time production." The policy that had been introduced around 1900 was continued after the war, with the addition of foundries to make use of the pig iron produced. In 1920 the Stahlwerke Röchling AG were founded in cooperation with the Röchling steelworks in Völklingen. Two works were brought to a standstill in 1923 when the French and Belgians occupied the Ruhr district. From 1936 onwards Buderus was controlled to an ever greater extent by Nazi economic policies, limiting its production to war materials. In September 1944, bombing destroyed pig iron production at the Wetzlar works. At the beginning of 1945 Buderus had 8,000 employees, of whom around 45% were foreigners. About 70% of production was intended for military use. In 1946, with permission from the military government, operation of the steel furnaces at Wetzlar resumed. In 1952, those sectors of the Buderus'sche Eisenwerke that had been transferred to public ownership by a vote in 1946, and that had until then been administered by a trust, were combined to form the Hessische Berg- und Hüttenwerke AG. With compensation received for the assets transferred to this *Aktiengesellschaft,* the company purchased a majority shareholding in arms manufacturer Krauss-Maffei AG in Munich in 1955. In 1956 Friedrich Flick acquired the majority of the company's widely held share capital. At the beginning of 1965 Buderus acquired the Röchling group's share of the Stahlwerke Röchling-Buderus AG. From then onwards the company was known as Edelstahlwerke Buderus AG. The shares owned by the state of Hessen in the Hessische Berg- und Hüttenwerke AG were also acquired by Buderus. By the end of the 1960s the company had completed the expansion that had begun after the 1948 currency reform. In the 1950s the technical development of the works had been the key to expansion; after this, growth came chiefly through acquisition.

In 1974, under the executive chairmanship of Hans Werner Kolb, a restructuring of the company was undertaken. Loss-making production sites were closed. Three years later, shareholders voted to change the company's name to Buderus AG, and in 1978 they agreed upon an investment program without parallel in the company's history, expanding facilities and increasing its work force.

In May 1985 negotiations began between the Flick group, with its subsidiaries Feldmühle Nobel AG, Dynamit Nobel, and Buderus, and the Deutsche Bank AG. The group's owner, Friedrich Karl Flick, wanted to retire from business life for a variety of reasons and sold his businesses to the Deutsche Bank in December 1985. After the disposal of the Flick stakes in the U.S. conglomerate W.R. Grace, in the auto company Daimler-Benz, and in the insurance group Gerling of Cologne, the remaining core of the Flick group, Feldmühle, Dynamit Nobel, and Buderus, was brought together to form Feldmühle Nobel AG. Heribert Blaschke was named as chairman of the board. His three colleagues on Feno's board are also chairmen of the group's subsidiaries: Hartwig Geginat of Feldmühle, Ernst Grosch of Dynamit Nobel, and Dr. Wolfgang Laaf of Buderus. All three subsidiaries are legally independent *Aktiengesellschaften.*

As a protection against hostile takeovers, the group's shareholders agreed in 1988 to limit each individual shareholder's voting rights to a maximum of 5% of the share capital. Indeed, Flick's two nephews Gert-Rudolf and Friedrich Christian Flick had planned to acquire a majority stake in Feno during 1988, but their intentions became known and the attempt failed. In June 1989, Veba AG of Düsseldorf acquired a 40% stake in Feno from a group of buyers associated with Friedrich-Christian Flick. Veba already owned 6% of Feno's shares. During the following months this stake was built up to over 50%. Because of the voting restrictions, however, the capital majority did not bring any increase in influence. It was for this reason, among others, that Veba in 1990 sold its stake in Feno for DM4 billion to Stora Kopparbergs Bergslags AB of Falun, Sweden's largest paper manufacturer, itself controlled by the influential Wallenberg group. Through further purchases, Stora now owns about 98% of Feno's shares. As Stora is principally interested in cooperation in the paper sector with Feno's largest and most important subsidiary, Feldmühle, the fate of the other two subsidiaries remains uncertain.

Principal Subsidiaries: Buderus AG (98.72%): Buderus Heiztechnik GmbH; Sieger Heizkesselwerke GmbH; Buderus Bau- und Abwassertechnik GmbH; Ritterhaus & Blecher GmbH; Baustoff-Union GmbH; Ferrum GmbH; Buderus Kuhdenguss GmbH; Buderus Küchentechnik GmbH; Roeder-Grossküchentechnik GmbH; Buderus Sell GmbH; Edelstahlwerke Buderus Aktiengesellschaft; Buderus Handel GmbH; Logana-Speditionsgesellschaft mbH; TBG Mittelhessische Lieferbeton GmbH & Co KG; Senkingwerk GmbH; Wetzlarer Bauverein GmbH; Buderus Corporation (U.S.A.); Buderus Austria AG Heiateduik GmbH; Edelstahlwerke Buderus Nederland B.V. (Netherlands); Dynamit Nobel Aktiengesellschaft; Sprengstoff-Handels-Gesellschaft mbH; Sprengstoff-Verwartungs-Gesellschaft mbH; Vereinigte Jute Spinnereien und Weboreien GmbH; EURODYN Sprengmittel-Gesellschaft mbH; Sprengmittelvertrieb in Beyern GmbH; Menzolit GmbH; Dynamit Nobel RWS Inc. (U.S.A.); Leslie Hewett Ltd, (U.K.); BEDEC Chasse S.A. (France); Dynamit Nobel Iberica S.A. (Spain); Gustav Genschow ''Nobel'' Ges.m.b.-H. (Austria); Rohner AG (Switzerland); FFV Norma AB (Sweden); Feldmühle AG; Altpapierverwertung Wattenscheid GmbH; Conti Bau und Immobilien GmbH; Continentale Versicherungs-Vermittlung GmbH; Conti Marketing-Service GmbH; Feldmühle-Hylte GmbH; Forschungs- und Entwicklungsgesellschaft für Faserstoffe Aktiengesellschaft; Nord-Ostsee Schiffahrtund Transport-Gesellschaft mbH; Papierfabrik, Baienfurth GmbH; Sortiermaschinen-Gesellschaft mbH; Feldmühle Kyocera Europa Elektronische Bauelemente GmbH (52.5%); N.V. Papierfabrik Gennep (Netherlands); S.A. Page (France); Page Verkoopmaatschappij Nederlande B.V. (Netherlands); Page Celstofcrepe A.P.S. Denmark; N.V. Page (Belgium); Feldmühle Wien Gesellschaft mbH (Austria); Comtrade Handelsgesellschaft mbH (Austria); Feldmühle Schweden; Feldmühle Zellstoff AB (Sweden); Feldmuehle Ltd. (U.K.); Gerald Judd Sales Ltd. (U.K.); Feldmühle IMEC S.R.L. (Italy); Papierfabriek Langerbrugge N.V. (Belgium); Feldmühle Vermögungsverwaltung Aktiengesellschaft; Gesellschaft für Fahrzeugund Maschinenwerte GmbH; Mittelstahl-Handelsgesellschaft mbH; Linke-Hofmann-Werke GmbH; Waggonund Maschinenfabrik GmbH; Brandenburger Eisenwerke GmbH; Eisenund Stückblech-Handelsgesellschaft mbH; Gesellschaft für Luftfahrtzubehör mbH Orion; Sächsische Gussstahl-Werke Döhlen GmbH (99.99%); Menzolit GmbH (95%); Magal Indústria e Comércio Ltda. (Brazil); Menzolit S.A.R.L. (France).

Further Reading: *Dynamit Actien-Gesellschaft 1865–1925*, Troisdorf, Dynamit Nobel AG, 1925; *225 Jahre Buderus: Sonderausgabe der Buderus-Werksnachrichten*, Wetzlar, Buderus AG, 1956; *Die Feldmühle. Blick in ein Deutsches Grossunternehmen*, Düsseldorf, Feldmühle AG, 1958; *1885–1960: 75 Jahre Feldmühle*, Düsseldorf, Feldmühle AG, 1959; *Werkzeitschrift 1965*, Troisdorf, Dynamit Nobel AG, 1965; *Chemie und Technik*, Troisdorf, Dynamit Nobel AG, 1987.

—Sebastian Fries
Translated from the German by Susan Mackervoy

HARRISONS & CROSFIELD PLC

20 St. Dunstan's Hill
London EC3R 8LQ
United Kingdom
(071) 626-4333
Fax: (071) 782-0112

Public Company
Incorporated: 1908 as Harrisons & Crosfield Ltd.
Employees: 29,000
Sales: £1.86 billion (US$3.00 billion)
Stock Exchange: London

Since its beginnings in 1844, Harrisons & Crosfield (H&C) has grown from a small partnership based in Liverpool to a public limited company that derives its income from diverse operations in Europe, Asia, Australia, and North America. Its fortunes have been closely linked to Britain's position in the international marketplace, and its history has been molded by a succession of strong personalities.

The partnership between Daniel Harrison, Smith Harrison, and Joseph Crosfield was formed on January 1, 1844. The Harrison brothers, the eldest and youngest sons in a family of 17 children, already were working as tea merchants in Liverpool. Joseph Crosfield was too young to have established himself in business, but at only 23 he was already recognized as an ambitious man and was reluctant to lose his independence by committing himself to a formal partnership.

Nevertheless, Joseph Crosfield's parents persuaded their son to accept the favorable agreement offered by the Harrison brothers. In return for contributing one-quarter of the initial capital of £8,000, Joseph Crosfield was to receive three-tenths of the partnership's profits. With Daniel Harrison as chairman, Smith Harrison as the firm's representative at tea sales, and Joseph Crosfield in charge of the office, the partnership began its long history of trading.

For over 200 years the trade in tea had been controlled by the East India Company, which had obtained a monopoly when granted a royal charter in 1600. The Charter Act of 1813 canceled the East India Company's monopoly and opened both India and China to wider enterprise. The removal of tariffs and shipping restrictions, increasing demand for tea in Britain, and the building of canals and roads in India further encouraged new trading ventures but, because of the prohibitive expense of setting up plantations, the new firms that entered the market had to begin as agency houses rather than as primary producers.

In its first year of trading H&C made a modest profit of £3,000 on a turnover mostly derived from tea but with a small element of coffee trading. It expanded rapidly and in 1854 moved from Liverpool to Great Tower Street in London, where it was based until 1989. The partners' benevolent attitude toward their staff was shown in their provision of free accommodation for unmarried employees and of free lunches for all workers. The firm now concentrated solely on the tea trade and benefited from its proximity to the tea markets of Mincing Lane. In just ten years the small provincial firm had become an established national organization with international aspirations.

During the middle of the 19th century, Britain's trade with its colonies exceeded that of France, Germany, Italy, and America put together. The year 1869 marked a crucial point in the history of the tea trade. The opening of the Suez Canal made transportation quicker and cheaper while the building of all-steel ships made wooden-composite ships such as the *Cutty Sark*—launched in 1869—something of an anachronism. Furthermore, a plague of coffee leaf disease devastated the 1869 coffee crop, forcing planters to focus their attention on producing tea, an obvious substitute that could be grown successfully on the old coffee plantations. H&C benefited from all of these changes and in 1882 its annual sales of tea exceeded 100,000 chests for the first time.

Daniel Harrison's son Joseph was admitted to the partnership in 1855, where he was to remain until his death in 1915. His father retired in 1863 to be replaced by Smith Harrison, who remained chairman of the firm for the next 20 years. By 1883, however, all of the original partners were dead, and despite the continued involvement of members from both families, the future of the firm was beginning to look less secure than during the first decades of rapid growth. Change came in 1894 when two salaried partners joined, representing the new management that was to initiate another period of expansion.

Charles Heath Clark was an expert tea-blender who quickly grasped the commercial possibilities of expanding the range of products offered by the main office in London. H&C began to package tea for provincial merchants and it was a short step for the firm to produce its own brand for retail sale. The demand and supply of tea were both good and H&C benefited from a high margin on sales of Nectar, its proprietary brand. Heath Clark initially launched the brand in South Africa as he was unwilling to antagonize H&C's customers in Britain by appearing to establish a competing brand. Indeed, when Nectar was launched in the United Kingdom in 1904, the cost of advertising the product was greater than any increase in income, and the loss of customer goodwill led H&C to sell the brand to Twinings.

The dynamic Arthur Lampard, a risk-taking entrepreneur, was to lead H&C into the 20th century. His strategy was to turn H&C into a firm with truly international interests, not only as tea agents but also as plantation owners. Lampard visited Russia in 1895 to set up a trade route from Ceylon to Moscow via Odessa in order to cut handling costs for H&C's increasing number of Russian customers. In the same year Lampard visited Colombo, Ceylon, and set up Crosfield, Lampard & Co. to buy tea directly from plantation owners in

Ceylon. Despite an unexpected fall in the market price of tea in 1904, Lampard continued his policy of overseas expansion, and by 1907 branch offices had been opened in New York, Montreal, and Kuala Lumpur.

H&C's reliance on the tea market was soon to be reduced by its entry into the rubber market. In 1900 over two-thirds of the world's annual supply of 40,000 tons of rubber was produced in Brazil, with the remainder coming from equatorial Africa. In 1903 Herbert Brett and W. S. Bennett, two names synonymous with the British rubber trade, enlisted Lampard's help to issue a prospectus for the Pataling Rubber Estates Syndicate, a venture based on an old coffee plantation in Malaysia which had been converted to rubber growing.

H&C was appointed as agent and secretary to the company and Lampard persuaded his more cautious board members to make an investment of £1,000. Lampard was prepared to go without profit for the plantation's first years, for he had forecast that a recent invention, the motor car, was likely to survive as rather more than a fashionable plaything for the rich. In 1905 Lampard and Brett, the latter by now an employee of H&C, purchased several small estates in Malaysia for £50,000 and amalgamated them into the Golden Hope Rubber Estate. Whereas the Pataling Syndicate had been undersubscribed, shares in Golden Hope were sold at a substantial premium. The following year Lampard visited the east coast of Sumatra and set up a plantation with a Swiss planter, Victor Ris, who shared Lampard's vision of large plantations organized in the same efficient manner as Sumatra's huge tobacco plantations.

These ventures in Malaysia and Sumatra carried more risk than those in Ceylon, which was perceived as a maturing economy run by professional and experienced planters. By supporting Malaysian and Sumatran plantation owners—for example, by underwriting new crops, providing fertilizers and harvesting equipment, and acting as sales agents—H&C ensured the success of the plantation and, as an obvious consequence, its investment. The company took responsibility for bookkeeping and the raising of finance and sent powerful visiting agents to inspect the plantations. In this way the fledgling plantations benefitted from high-quality advice on both the financial and agricultural aspects of the business.

Lampard had forecast astutely that his plantation rubber would be of a superior quality to that harvested in wild conditions in Brazil and Africa and his move into rubber growing was followed swiftly by Michelin, Dunlop, and Firestone. Britain's previously unenthusiastic financial sector, which had curtailed investment overseas because of the Boer War of 1899 to 1902, was now impressed by the prominent Lampard who worked ceaselessly to establish the industry worldwide. When the price of rubber rose from around 4 shillings per pound in 1902 to 12 shillings in 1905, Lampard's willingness to take risks was justified totally.

The next important step taken by the partners of H&C was to turn the firm into a limited-liability company. For several years it had been felt that a partnership, with its reliance on capital that could be withdrawn on the death or retirement of a partner, was too restrictive for an organization with ambitious expansion plans. Obtaining limited liability would make extensive capital expenditure possible—and most importantly for a business that was still run largely by the scions of two families—the shareholders of the company could vote against nepotistic elections to positions of responsibility.

A prospectus was issued by the brokers Foster and Braithwaite in May 1908 and the issue was fully subscribed. Existing partners exchanged their partnership capital for £150,000 of ordinary share capital and the first new directors took up 150,000 management shares of one shilling each. Friends, employees, and customers took up large blocks of shares and only £50,000 out of a total issued share capital of £307,500 was bought by private and institutional investors who had no direct link with the company. Years of steady profits and a stated aim of building up reserves rather than recklessly distributing profits ensured the success of the issue.

The worldwide increase in rubber planting was bound to lead to oversupply when crops were harvested four or five years after the first seeds were sown. The price dropped to between three or four shillings per pound in 1906, and reached a low of less than three shillings following the U.S. bank crisis of 1907. H&C weathered several difficult years until 1910, when the internal combustion engine became available, making the mass-production of cars economically viable. The demand for tires led to an annual demand for rubber of 100,000 tons in 1911, and H&C made excellent profits as rubber soared to 12 shillings per pound. The rubber boom forced H&C into building new accommodation to deal with increased paperwork flowing through the London office.

Charles Heath Clark became chairman of H&C in 1911, replacing James Crosfield, who had served the company for 46 years. He took over during a period of rapidly falling rubber prices and slow growth in tea sales. The seaman's strike of 1911 led to riots at Liverpool Docks and a one-month embargo on unloading ships. The London Dock Dispute of the following year further damaged H&C when 100,000 men were called out over a very minor dispute. Nevertheless, an issue in 1912 of £150,000 worth of £1 ordinary shares at a premium of 10 shillings was oversubscribed.

The outbreak of World War I hit H&C badly. Britain diverted its resources to the manufacture of heavy engineering goods to support the war effort and communication with the plantations became increasingly difficult. Shipping restrictions and a low level of demand for tea caused a decline in international trade and many of the staff were called up to serve in the army. To compound the company's misfortune Arthur Lampard died in 1916, and no adequate successor could be found to take over the leadership of the plantation companies until the war was over.

Henry Welch was an important addition to the board in 1917. A solicitor who had built up an extensive practice in the City of London, Welch had experience as a director of several public companies and was responsible for the founding of the National Institute of Industrial Psychology in 1921. His main task was the reorganization of the company's balance sheet as soon as the war was over, when he restructured the share capital of the company to reflect the massive changes that H&C had experienced in the ten years since its incorporation.

Despite the war the directors of H&C did not ignore the possibility of new ventures abroad. Chinese green-leaf tea remained popular in Russia, America, and North Africa and H&C set up a joint venture with an established Chinese company to form Harrisons, King and Irwin in 1917. Based in

Shanghai, with branch offices in Hankow and Foochow, the office was to be one of the casualties of the Japanese invasion during World War II.

Heath Clark, exhausted by his efforts in leading H&C through the war years, resigned from his position as chairman at the end of 1918. George Croll, who had worked for H&C in the Far East, was elected as his successor, but the young man whose energy had made a great impact on the company's plantations was to be dogged continually by ill-health. Two successful issues of £150,000 in ordinary shares at a premium of 7 shillings 65 pence were made in January and July 1919, and the board was strengthened to include a complement of nine full-time members.

However, an issue of £400,000 ordinary shares made in December of the same year was undersubscribed, and for the first time in the company's history a substantial portion of the issue had to be taken up by the underwriters. It was a time of national and international economic gloom and prices for tea and—in particular—rubber plummeted. Plantations were operating at a loss; and Heath Clark became a prime mover in the Rubber Growers' Association, which voluntarily agreed to cut production in India, Ceylon, and the Dutch East Indies. Immediate profits were sacrificed, but future production in a more stable market was guaranteed by withdrawing 25% of possible output in 1921. Heath Clark formally reassumed his old position of chairman on the death of George Croll in 1922.

A significant new venture was begun in 1920 when H&C and the Chartered Company of British New Guinea acquired the assets and goodwill of the China Borneo Company. H&C was given exclusive rights to cut and develop timber and received Borneo government backing to develop the timber industry in Borneo. Production rose from 1.1 million cubic feet in 1919 to 6 million cubic feet in 1940. The timber-supplies division of H&C grew to include ventures in Australia and the United States and now has a particularly strong brand image in its Harcros chain of builders' merchants which was started in 1935.

In 1921 H&C's relatively minor interests in tobacco plantations were sold to Dutch companies. H&C felt that it lacked the experience necessary to turn the growing of tobacco, always a delicate crop to harvest, into a regular source of profits. Profits from tea enjoyed a renaissance in the late 1920s but the boom contained the seeds of its own destruction as increased plantings were to lead to an excess of supply in the early 1930s. However, expenditure on research and development gave a boost to the company when Linatex was invented by Bernard Wilkinson, an assistant on a Malaysian rubber plantation. The Linatex process, which treats rubber to allow its use as an abrasion-resistant lining, gives the twin advantages over mild steel of increased strength and lower cost and continues to be a valuable source of income for the firm.

H&C also diversified into growing coconut palms in the Philippines, Ceylon, and on the Malabar Coast. Once the kernel of the coconut is dried it turns into copra, which is then crushed to produce coconut oil. H&C initially sold this as a raw material for the production of soap and candles but the postwar shortage of butter led to demand for substitute products. Margarine, which is composed largely of coconut oil, became increasingly popular, and production of copra reached one million tons per annum during the 1930s. The depression suffered by the company's rubber interests was partially offset by this boom, and to this day palm oil and copra are important commodities to H&C.

Eric Miller, a director of H&C since 1911, had been largely responsible for the Stevenson Report, which attempted to control the build-up of rubber stocks after the end of World War I. Miller had many close links with the heads of banks and rubber-growing companies and was a born diplomat. He convinced Winston Churchill that sales of British rubber at a good price to the United States would do much to pay off Britain's war debt to that country. As with previous similar agreements, the plan was to restrict production in India, Ceylon, and the Dutch East Indies as a method of stabilizing world prices.

The Wall Street crash of 1929 precipitated the Depression. This was to be a severe test for Eric Miller, who was now chairman of H&C. The company's profits for 1932 fell to £183,000, less than half the amount recorded in 1929. The world withdrew from international trade, putting up tariffs and imposing quotas on imports. Exchange rates fluctuated wildly and companies were reluctant to grant any form of credit as insolvencies became commonplace. H&C was forced again into a voluntary reduction of one of its commodities as the Tea Regulation Scheme limited exports from India, Ceylon, and the Dutch East Indies. Despite these measures, the company was forced to close several of its plantations.

The situation for rubber was even worse. The International Rubber Regulation Committee, to which Eric Miller was appointed by the government of British Malaya, signed an agreement in May 1934 which allocated each rubber trading company a strict production quota. With only a very few exceptions, new plantings of rubber were prohibited.

The outbreak of World War II was a further immense blow to the company as shipping lines closed and trade slumped. The entry of the Japanese into the war in October 1941 led to the invasion and subsequent loss of many of the Far Eastern plantations.

The end of the war saw more years of difficult trading for H&C. Demand for commodities was dampened by economic recession in the United Kingdom and transportation was difficult because of disruption to shipping lines. As in World War I, H&C lost many employees to the armed forces, and the Nazi bombardment of the City and the docks of east London further hampered international traders. Many plantations in the East had been destroyed by the invading Japanese, and when H&C attempted to reestablish operations abroad it was dismayed to see the effects of years of neglect.

The early 1950s saw a deterioration in the relationship between countries in the Far East and those countries which had controlled the majority of their trade. It was a time when war-damaged Britain was losing its old empire and the former colonies were no longer content to accept their traditional role of primary producer to foreign profit-takers. Governments imposed stringent restrictions on the transference of profits from their country to foreign agents and began to seek control over commodity prices. When H&C sought to renew its plantation leases in Indonesia it was forced to surrender one-third of its land to the Indonesian government. The outbreak of civil war in 1958 and increasing unrest in Malaysia and Sumatra left H&C unable to meet the commodity requirements of many of its customers.

H&C reacted to these problems by becoming increasingly involved in new technologies. A process to manufacture cyclized rubber was developed at the Rubber Research Institute of Malaysia and in the mid-1950s H&C began large-scale production. This rubber, which is used in printing inks and paints, was distributed by Durham Raw Materials Ltd., a joint-venture company half owned by H&C. The development of crumb rubber, and the introduction of standard grades for Malaysian rubber from 1965 onwards, did much to stabilize the rubber industry and, as a consequence, to make H&C's profits from this sector more consistent.

H&C also decided to take over the full ownership of the British Borneo Timber Company as part of a strategy to increase the importance of this sector. Throughout the 1970s the company, through its Harcros subsidiary, began to buy up small timber yards throughout the United Kingdom. The acquisition of larger timber merchants, such as the Sabah Timber Company, gave H&C a powerful distribution network from which to pursue further expansion. It was a logical step to use these existing sites to establish a chain of builders' merchants, still under the Harcros name, that supplied a full range of materials to the construction industry.

Eric Miller was knighted in 1958 after being replaced as chairman by Sir Leonard Paton in 1957. Although Paton only served as chairman for five years, he can be considered responsible for beginning the transformation of H&C, arguing long and hard to guarantee an adequate supply of timber from the Borneo plantations. Paton was replaced in 1962 by Finlay Gilchrist, who devised a complex system of defensive crossholdings between the H&C holding company, its subsidiaries, and its associates. By deliberately forging an intricate structure, Gilchrist was able to protect all of the group's interests from predators looking to take over a small, but nonetheless valuable, subsidiary.

Tom Prentice became chairman in 1973 during a turbulent time for the company and needed to rely on all of the skills he had learned in the timber industry in the East. The nationalization of plantations in Sri Lanka—formerly Ceylon—was soon followed by changes in Malaysia which required foreign companies to relinquish 70% of their interests by 1990. The group, supported by Baring Brothers merchant bank, undertook a further complicated restructuring designed to unite the group's interests in order to protect the value of shareholders' investments. Throughout the 1970s this complicated structure withstood the efforts of corporate raiders—most noticeably the Rothschild Investment Trust—and Prentice was able to lead H&C away from its dependence on plantations to encompass fully the opportunities offered by chemicals, building supplies, and agriculture.

Recent years have shown the effects of this diversification away from a reliance on commodities that have proved too cyclical to guarantee consistent profits. In 1982 three large plantation groups—Golden Hope, Pataling, and London Asiatic—were sold to Malaysian concerns for £146 million. In 1984 H&C sold a large portion of its Malaysian investments to Permodalan, the state-controlled investment company. The remaining 30% was sold in 1989 for £145 million, but the plantations in Sumatra still remain in H&C's ownership. H&C was floated on the London Stock Exchange in 1982 and since then has been active in reshaping its activities with a series of purchases and disposals.

In 1985 H&C made a significant acquisition with the purchase of Pauls Plc, a manufacturer of malt and animal feeds. Profits from this company form the backbone of H&C's food and agriculture division, which was strengthened by the acquisition of Edward Baker, a specialist pet-food company, in 1989. George Paul, the chief executive officer of Pauls, was elected to the board of H&C and, along with Thomas Prentice, became joint chief executive officer of the company.

By 1986 H&C intensified its aim of moving away from tropical soft commodities. Palm oil prices had dropped by nearly 50% during the year, and profits from the rubber market were depressed by expenditure on research into disease control. George Paul identified the company's problems as over-diversification, a reliance on primary agricultural products, and weak management in certain sectors. Paul instigated a rationalization plan and hinted that non-core companies would be sold off even if they were of historical importance to the company. As an example, Durham Chemicals Distributors Ltd. was sold in 1987, leaving H&C to concentrate on chemical manufacture rather than distribution.

Paul also took steps to improve H&C's image in the City. Perceived as a steady but rather dull holding company, the board took on the former head of M and G Fund Management, David Hopkinson, to convince the City of the group's intrinsic worth. After frequent allegations of insider dealing, fund managers began to see well-established conglomerates such as H&C as perfect vehicles for regular, long-term growth. Dependence on the plantations was reduced rapidly and by 1986 they accounted for less than one-quarter of the group's profits. The City, which had always preferred to deal directly with the commodity market rather than through holding companies with interests in commodities, was becoming increasingly enamoured with H&C.

In November 1988 H&C announced the reorganization of its chemical interests under the new name of the Harcros Chemical Group. Its component parts include British Chrome and American Chrome, world leaders in manufacturing chromium chemicals, and Troyfel Ltd. and Hardman Inc. which specialize in iron oxide technology and adhesives. At the time of the reorganization George Paul stated that the company's intention was to double the size of this group, through organic growth and selective acquisitions, within the next five years.

The Crossley chain of builders' merchants was bought for £113 million in May 1990 and then amalgamated into Harcros, the flagship of the group's timber and building supplies division. Under George Paul's leadership the company is looking stronger than it has for many years. His success at reorganization has led to the company's being regarded as an innovative major player in its main areas of interest. With a balanced and complementary set of core activities, strong leadership, and a prudently geared balance sheet, the future of Harrisons & Crosfield appears to be secure.

Principal Subsidiaries: Harcos Investment Trust Ltd.; H&C Securities Ltd.; H&C Timber and Building Supplies Ltd.; Linatex Ltd.; Pauls plc.

Further Reading: Ensor, Sir Robert, *England 1870–1914,* Oxford, Oxford University Press, 1936; *One Hundred Years as East India Merchants,* London, Harrisons & Crosfield, 1943; Donnithorne, Audrey, *British Rubber Manufacturing,* London, Jill Duckworth & Co., 1958; Drabble, J. H., *Rubber in Malaya 1876–1922,* London, Oxford University Press, 1973; Coates, Austin, *The Commerce in Rubber,* Oxford, Oxford University Press 1987; Pugh, Peter, *Great Enterprise, A History of Harrisons & Crosfield,* London, Harrisons & Crosfield, 1990.

—Andreas Loizou

"HOLDERBANK"

"HOLDERBANK" FINANCIÈRE GLARIS LTD.

CH-8750 Glaris
Switzerland
(058) 61 34 94
Fax: (055) 27 83 19

Public Company
Incorporated: 1912 as Aargauische Portlandcement-Fabrik Holderbank-Wildegg
Employees: 25,000
Sales: SFr4.97 billion (US$3.22 billion)
Stock Exchanges: Zürich Basel Geneva

Switzerland's "Holderbank" Financière Glaris (Holderbank), with its motto "cement, and all that goes with it," is the world's largest producer of cement products and services. Based in Glaris, near Zürich, Holderbank remains firmly in the hands of Thomas Schmidheiny, although it is a public company.

Since 1912, when the elder Ernst Schmidheiny founded the Aargauische Portlandcement-Fabrik Holderbank-Wildegg, his family has controlled the diversified Holderbank empire, with a presence on five continents. The business was originally named after the town in the Swiss canton of Aargau where the first cement plant was founded.

Gradually taking up the work his father began, the younger Ernst Schmidheiny made sufficient profits early on from the cement products business to stabilize and then expand the group beyond Swiss borders, beginning in the 1920s. In 1923, Holderbank made its first overseas acquisition, the Dutch cement company Nederlandse Cement Industrie, based in Maastricht, near Belgium. In 1926 the Swiss group acquired the Ciments d'Obourg in Belgium.

In 1927 the elder Ernst Schmidheiny oversaw the construction of his 50%-owned cement factory near Cairo, Egypt, completed under the watchful eye of King Fouad I. Expansion abroad in that year also included the building of the Ciments de Chalkis Portland Artificiels plant in Greece. This recognition by Holderbank of the need to find international markets in the interwar years came decades ahead of most other European cement producers, who did not expand overseas to any great degree until after 1945. To control its growing international empire, Holderbank regrouped its interests in 1930 under an umbrella company, "Holderbank" Financière Glaris Ltd.

The founder, the elder Ernst Schmidheiny, did not neglect Holderbank's development at home in Switzerland. In 1914, increased production capacity and earnings enabled his group to acquire rival cement maker Rheintalische Zementfabrik of Ruthi.

Taking over from his father, the younger Ernst was accompanied at the Holderbank helm by his younger brother Max. In 1987, aged 81, Max Schmidheiny led the 75th-anniversary celebrations of his family's industrial empire. Thomas, of the third generation of the Schmidheiny family, has controlled the Holderbank empire since Max Schmidheiny began handing over the businesses in piecemeal fashion toward the end of the 1970s.

Holderbank had been keen during the 1960s to take advantage of a consistently rising curve in world cement production. The first oil shocks in 1973 and 1979, each followed by an economic slowdown, slightly dented production levels. However, worldwide cement production doubled between 1967 and 1986, a period of rapid global expansion for Holderbank.

Growth for the Swiss group was particularly strong after the acquisition in 1970 of specific properties from a rival contractor, the Swiss Cement-Industrie-Gesellschaft (SCI). The deal struck by the two Swiss concerns enabled Holderbank to acquire SCI interests in Mexico, Costa Rica, Lebanon, South Africa, and West Germany—Breitenburger Cementfabrik—in exchange for its own interests, among others, in the asbestos cement sector.

This transaction greatly tightened the Schmidheiny family's hold on Holderbank. To strengthen the decentralized management structure which controls the worldwide Holderbank group, Holderbank in 1991 employed more than 200 specialists in Switzerland, with another 200 on assignment throughout the world. The duties of the specialists range from consultancy work to constructing complex technical and financial projects. Holderbank received its Zürich stock exchange listing in 1958, but to this day remains protected against takeover bids due to the control of the majority of voting shares by the Schmidheiny empire.

Much of the success that Holderbank has known in its 78-year history can be attributed to its search for the best production technology and the lowest production costs. As Thomas Schmidheiny told *International Management* in September 1987: "The grey powder from my friends at Heidelberg [a major German competitor] is the same grey powder that we produce. So we compete essentially on price, and to do that we recognized long ago that we had to have the best production technology and be a low-cost producer."

In 1986 Holderbank made a final break with SCI, with whom it had earlier swapped properties to increase its presence in South America, among other world markets. This deal gave Holderbank control of the Ostschweizer Zementwerke in Unterterzen, Switzerland, in exchange for giving SCI a number of interests in the United States, Belgium, Chile, and Ecuador.

At the same time Holderbank became the leading cement producer in the all-important U.S. market after acquiring in late 1986 the Denver, Colorado–based Ideal Basic Industries for around US$110 million. The acquisition gave Holderbank a commanding 14% market share in the United States, ahead of rival cement concerns Blue Circle Industries of the United Kingdom and Lafarge Coppée of France.

European cement makers, led by Holderbank, employed superior, highly cost-efficient production techniques to gain an advantage in the U.S. market over rival U.S. cement makers. For example, the Swiss group's takeover of Ideal Basic Industries was followed by a vast expenditure to renovate the U.S. group's obsolete production facilities. Holderbank absorbed an extra US$5.7 million increase in interest charges in 1989 to renovate Ideal's Fort Collins plant in Colorado, when the Ideal group as a whole continued its poor record of results by posting a US$24.1 million loss on sales of US$245 million in the same year. Holderbank's other major North American interests include Canada's St. Lawrence Cement, acquired in 1953, and the Dundee Cement Company of Michigan, obtained in 1955.

Recognizing the dependence of the world cement industry on both business cycles and interest rate-sensitive construction industries, Holderbank became aware of the threat of a worldwide economic downturn at the end of the 1980s and began consolidating its global activities in that year.

Starting with its European interests, in 1989 Holderbank sold its small Ciments de l'Adour plant in France and exchanged its interests in the Spanish Rezola plant for an added 8% stake in Ciments de Champagnole, raising its holding in this French operation to 50%. Because of this strengthened French presence, in direct competition with Paris-based Lafarge Coppée, Holderbank gained key contracts such as supplying cement products to the Channel Tunnel project, the extension of France's TGV speed-rail system, and the Euro-Disneyland theme park development near Paris.

In 1990 Holderbank restructured its North American interests ahead of the downturn in construction business on that continent. In March of that year, the Dundee Cement Company, Ideal Basic Industries, and Northwestern States Portland Cement Company, acquired in 1988, were merged with Holnam Inc., Holderbank's U.S. holding company.

This regrouping of U.S. interests, soon after Holderbank's 75th anniversary in 1987, enabled the Swiss group to become the world's leading producer of cement products with a market share of almost 3.5%. Either through direct ownership or a series of minority or majority holdings, Holderbank operates over 30 cement companies in 22 countries worldwide, which together produce well over 43 million tons of cement products annually.

The stakes acquired by Holderbank in early 1990 in three Hungarian cement companies—a 50% stake in the Labatlan cement works and a 33% stake in the twin Jejoscaba works—point to the group's pursuit of opportunities in new Central European markets. Taken together, the three Hungarian cement plants produce about 1.6 million tons of cement products annually.

Besides recruiting its German interests in its push into Eastern Europe, Holderbank has also employed the expertise of its German business, Alsen-Breitenbury, to expand in the European environmental-protection and waste-management business. The particular services offered by Holderbank in these areas include treatment of polluted soil on industrial sites, developing chalk powder for use in flue gas desulfurization plants, and sewage and sludge treatment.

With an expanding foothold in East Europe, and having regrouped its North American interests amid an economic slowdown on that continent, Holderbank looks well placed to consolidate its strength in the 1990s as the world's largest cement products producer.

Principal Subsidiaries: "Holderbank" Management and Consulting Ltd.; Cementfabrik "Holderbank"; Portlandcementwerk AG Olten; SCB Société des Ciments et Bétons; "Holderbank" Concreta AG; Stamm Holding AG; "Holderbank" Chemicals Ltd.; Alsen-Breitenburg Zement- und Kalkwerke GmbH (Germany); Nordcement AG (Germany); Breisgauer Portland-Cementfabrik Kleinkems GmbH (Germany); ENCI-N.V., Eerste Nederlandse Cement Industrie (Netherlands); S.A. Ciments d'Obourg (Belgium); Ciments d'Origny S.A. (France); Hornos Ibéricos Alba S.A. (Spain); Unión Marítima Internacional S.A. (Spain); St. Lawrence Cement Inc. (Canada); Dundee Cement Company (U.S.A.); Ideal Basic Industries, Inc. (U.S.A.); Apasco S.A. de C.V. (Mexico); Industria Nacional de Cemento S.A. (Costa Rica); Productos de Concreto S.A. (Costa Rica); Cementos Boyacá S.A. (Colombia); La Cemento Nacional C.A. (Ecuador); Cementos Caribe C.A. (Venezuela); CIMINAS—Cimento Nacional de Minas S.A. (Brazil); Cia. de Cimento Ipanema (Brazil); Cemento Polpaico S.A. (Chile); The Cyprus Cement Company Ltd.; Société des Ciments Libanais (Lebanon); Anglo-Alpha Ltd. (South Africa); Iligan Cement Corporation (Philippines); Queensland Cement Ltd. (Australia); Milburn New Zealand Ltd.

Further Reading: Boesch, J., Dr. Hans Rudolf Schmid, and Dr. Benedikt Fehr, *Schweizer Pioniere der Wirtschaft und Technik—Drei Schmidheiny,* Zürich, Verein für wirtschaftshistorische Studien, 1979; Arbose, Jules, "The Mysterious Schmidheiny Brothers Flex Their Financial Muscle," *International Management*, September 1987; Bamberger, H.G., "Holderbank—Ein Weltreich aus Zement," *Budget*, September 1988.

—Etan Vlessing

LAFARGE COPPÉE S.A.

28, rue Emile-Menier
75116 Paris
France
(1) 47 04 11 11
Fax: (1) 47 27 54 57

Public Company
Incorporated: 1919 as Chaux et Ciments de Lafarge et du Teil
Employees: 31,000
Sales: FFr22.68 billion (US$3.93 billion)
Stock Exchanges: Paris New York Toronto

Lafarge Coppée (Lafarge) is the world's leading producer of building-materials, with an enormous network of production facilities in more than 30 countries. The French group's founder was Auguste Pavin de Lafarge, a French noble who in 1831 established a small lime kiln along the Rhone River in the Ardèche region of France.

The lime from Lafarge's Le Teil quarry was not unique: it had been used in bridges spanning the Rhone River for centuries. The novelty lay in the expanding range of industrial uses for which the Lafarge family found markets in the mid-19th century. By 1833, Auguste Pavin de Lafarge had already handed over responsibility for the lime quarry to his eldest son, Léon, who later brought his younger brother Edouard into the business.

Lafarge's markets were so geographically spread in the 1840s—the business was by now selling lime in such far-flung regions as the Mediterranean basin—that in 1843 Edouard invited the Marseilles firm of Gueyraud et Fils Cadet, headed by Felix Gueyraud, to help manage Lafarge. Gueyraud, a graduate of the Ecole Centrale des Arts et Manufactures at Paris, brought a much-needed scientific grounding to Lafarge. In 1853, the business began to pay regular dividends to shareholders.

Lafarge was put on the map when in 1864 it won a contract to supply 110,000 tons of hydraulic lime for concrete blocks to form the jetties of the Suez Canal. Suddenly, a medium-sized company was thrust into the big league of cement production with markets now reaching into North Africa.

In the 19th century Lafarge proved its ability to grow by acquisition, transforming itself into a group of companies headed by a single authority. By the turn of the century this organization enabled the group to supply markets in, among other world centers, New York City, Rio de Janeiro, and Saigon.

By the outbreak of World War I, Lafarge had raised its sales of cement products to 800,000 tons annually, making it the world's largest lime producer. The war, however, brought business to a standstill. Lafarge could supply cement for shelters and bunkers, but much of French industry had turned to arms production, leaving the lime producer well behind. Emerging from the war, in 1919 Lafarge moved from a limited partnership to a full business corporation under the name of Chaux et Ciments de Lafarge et du Teil. The group's stock was first listed on the Paris Bourse in 1923.

While the group retained Joseph Lafarge as its chairman and Edouard II, son of Raphaël Lafarge, and Charles Daher, son of Paul Lafarge, as two of the three managing directors, a former banker, Jean de Waubert de Genlis, became increasingly influential on the Lafarge board during the inter-war years.

Jean de Waubert, upon becoming managing director of Lafarge in 1928, made two key changes. First, he moved the group's headquarters from the Ardeche region to Paris, the center of France's industrial and banking structures. He then created a management structure on four levels that has become standard today: general management, technical operations, sales, and finance. Jean de Waubert effectively transformed the group from a fledgling 19th-century company, controlled by a patriarchal family, into a modern, innovative heavy-industrial concern.

Lafarge's expansion in the early part of the 20th century depended heavily on its technical expertise in developing new cement products. The development of Portland cement, for example, made the application of hydraulic lime virtually obsolete. To capitalize on this new product, Lafarge in 1923 set up a Portland cement company in Algeria called Société Nord Africaine des Ciments Lafarge.

Among Lafarge's many acquisitions in this period was the purchase in 1928 of Chaux et Ciments du Maroc in Casablanca, which established a second operational base outside France in North Africa.

The stock market crash in 1929 impacted Lafarge's fortunes greatly. One-third of all manpower in the French cement trade was laid off before 1936. A period of consolidation set in, and Lafarge swallowed up its fair share of failing competitors.

This consolidation enabled Lafarge to complete its transition from lime to cement in the years leading up to World War II. During the war the group's French subsidiaries were divided under the German occupation, until 1945. Lafarge's North African operations continued to operate at full capacity and produce good profits.

After Jean de Waubert's death in 1948, the Lafarge family turned over the company's management to Alfred François, a graduate of the Ecole Polytechnique, and Marcel Demonque, who was trained as an engineer. Lafarge's balance sheets were in the red, its plants required massive upkeep, and the morale of the work force was low.

The group's management turned its attention to organic growth, streamlining existing facilities and building new, more efficient cement plants. The Le Teil quarry, which employed more than 1000 workers, was at long last mechanized. Other investments included a 100,000-ton oven in Fives-Lille, built in 1951. By 1959, Lafarge had emerged from its post-war doldrums to regain the lead role in the French cement industry with 3.2 million tons of cement produced annually.

In 1959, the Lafarge board, headed by group chairman, Alfred François, managed to persuade the Lafarge family to withdraw from day-to-day control of the business. As its support from shareholders grew, Lafarge was able to take on more long-term debt, enabling stronger growth.

Also in this period, Lafarge put down its first business roots in Canada. In 1956 Marcel Demonque proposed building a 200,000-ton-capacity plant in Vancouver, on the west coast of Canada. The subsidiary in which the Paris-based group held a majority stake was named Lafarge Cement of North America.

The Vancouver plant was started up in 1958, not without delays. The ribbon-cutting ceremony in May of that year was interrupted twice by a break-down of the main oven, but initial troubles with the Vancouver subsidiary did not deter Lafarge from doubling its Canadian operations. Two ready-mix cement operations, Anglo-Canadian and Deeks McBride, were bought in 1960. Then, in 1967, Lafarge built a plant in Quebec, under the direction of Ciments Lafarge Quebec. It aimed at capitalizing on contracts from the 1967 Montreal World's Fair.

Lafarge's main rival in Canada during the 1960s was Canada Cement, first established in 1909 by Max Aitken, later Lord Beaverbrook, the British newspaper magnate. By the 1950s, Canada Cement boasted nearly 13,000 shareholders, 97% of whom were Canadian. In 1956, it held a 75% market share in the Canadian cement industry. Canada Cement also perfected the shift from cement production based on teams of workers mixing cement, sand, and gravel with water to create concrete, toward ready-mix concrete mixed at a central site and then transported to delivery points by bulk carriers.

A series of battles in the Canada Cement boardroom and with trade unions convinced the group to consider a merger with Lafarge. The French group, operating in British Columbia and Quebec but not in Ontario, felt—when approached by Canada Cement—that just such a merger would help it extend its network into the country's largest province.

In 1969, Marcel Demonque and Jean-Charles Lofficier, acting for Lafarge, met in Montreal with Peter McEntyre and Taylor Kennedy, who represented Canada Cement. A merger was announced in September of that year. In February 1970, however, the offices of Lafarge Canada and Canada Cement were visited by officers of the Canadian Mounted Police and the merger plans, beset by an antitrust inquiry into the 50% market share the new company would command, were put in jeopardy.

The merger was eventually cleared, and a formal merger between Lafarge Canada and Canada Cement was completed in March 1970. Peter McEntyre became chairman of the combined group, Canada Cement Lafarge, and Olivier Lecerf became its executive vice president. With the new group, Ciments Lafarge France, the Paris-based parent company for the worldwide cement group, had at long last completed its expansion on both side of the Atlantic Ocean.

The other acquisition which catapulted Lafarge into the forefront of the North American cement industry was that of General Portland. Based in Dallas, Texas, General Portland originally grew out of the Cowham system of cement producers, established in 1901. Peninsular Portland Cement, the brainchild of W. F. Cowham, grew throughout the early part of the century through acquisitions of cement plants in Georgia, Kansas, and Iowa, among other regions. Each acquisition proved larger than the last, many boasting of production capacities exceeding 250,000 tons annually.

Cowham did not restrict his business activities to cement production. Investments in the U.S. oil industry, principally in Oklahoma and Kansas, led to his stationing his headquarters in Dallas.

In 1912, Cowham suffered a stroke, opening the way for John Lawson Senior to succeed him as head of what became Cowham Engineering. In 1926, Senior formed Consolidated Cement Corporation, incorporating the Peninsular operations with a series of earlier midwestern acquisitions.

Although the Great Depression hit Consolidated Cement hard, the group emerged from a bout of consolidation in the U.S. cement industry during the 1930s to become a principal supplier of cement to the war effort in the 1940s.

In 1946, John Senior died, having led the cement group for 33 years, a period spanning two world wars and the Depression. The group restructured in Senior's absence, splitting into two companies. The first was Consolidated Cement and the second General Portland, which incorporated plants in the southern states. The twin companies struggled without Senior's direction. General Portland's first year of business in 1959 produced an impressive $12 million in profit, on a turnover of $67 million, but earnings fell off sharply in succeeding years. The original Peninsular cement plant in Cement City, Michigan, was shut down in 1962.

Robert Pflaumer became president of General Portland in 1962 and was succeeded in 1966 by L. James Wade, but neither could stem the fall in earnings of the embattled cement producer as the 1960s drew to a close. By 1970, Canada Cement and Lafarge Canada had completed their own merger. General Portland was benefiting from buoyant growth in the U.S. economy, but this came to an end with the 1973 recession and a slump in house construction, brought on by the oil crisis in that year.

In 1975, with Jim Lendrum serving as General Portland president and chief executive, the board set out to decentralize its operations to recoup profitability. The two key motives were cash conservation and improved productivity per employee—in short, hands-on control of the company.

By 1977, the prospects for General Portland were looking up. Sales for the group reached $200 million annually, with net earnings standing at $8 million. Sales picked up even further in 1979 to stand at the year-end at $277 million, on earnings of $26.7 million.

In 1980, however, General Portland's success was to be eclipsed as Lafarge Coppée, acting through Canada Cement Lafarge, prepared for a takeover bid of all of the group's shares. Also in 1980, Lafarge sold Emballage, its packaging side, to Cellulose du Pin, a part of the rival Saint-Gobain-Pont-à-Mousson group. The French group identified a new growth area in biochemicals, specifically the manufacturing of amino acids in animal feedstuffs. The leading maker of amino acids in Europe at the time was Evence Coppée, with plants in the French towns of Nesle and Amiens. An acquisitive Lafarge set its eye on Coppée's operations. A merger was completed in 1981.

At the same time, across the Atlantic Ocean, Lafarge was eyeing General Portland as a possible U.S. acquisition. In 1980, John Redfern, president of Canada Cement Lafarge, made an initial approach to Jim Lendrum. The General Portland boss refused Lafarge's overture, but not unequivocally.

A period of cooperation between the U.S. and French cement producers ensued. This came to an end in 1981 when Lafarge, elated by the election in France of a pro-business Socialist president, offered to buy up all of General Portland's shares at $45 each. This put the value of the U.S. cement maker at over $310 million. Lafarge Coppée succeeded in acquiring 96% of the unwilling General Portland's shares in August 1981, at a total cost of $349 million.

The acquisition led to a merger between Canada Cement Lafarge and General Portland, giving birth to a holding company, Lafarge Corporation. Lafarge holds 58.8% of Lafarge Corporation's shares. The remaining shares were offered on the New York Stock Exchange in 1982. The merger gave Lafarge Coppée headquarters on both sides of the Atlantic Ocean, in Paris and Dallas.

Meanwhile, Evence IV Coppée, chairman of the Coppée group, was offered a place on the Lafarge board to seal the merger of the two groups. To Coppée, Lafarge represented the same French-speaking culture, and both groups throughout their long histories had been controlled by a family dynasty. Coppée's roots date back to a coke oven patented in 1853 by Evence Dieudonné Coppée. Lafarge could now help Coppée expand its biochemicals and engineering operations.

The early 1980s were difficult for Lafarge Coppée as the group worked to integrate its Coppée and General Portland acquisitions. In 1983, the number of workers in the French group had fallen to 25,500, from over 30,000 two years before. In the same year, Olivier Lecerf had taken a year off as chairman of Lafarge Coppée, enabling Jean Bailly, a close colleague, to spend his last year in the group as board chairman.

Following his trip around the world in 1983, Olivier Lecerf, having returned to the position of chairman, emphasized the importance of his groups moving into the far eastern market, in particular Japan. Breaking into the Japanese cement market has been difficult owing to its heavy restrictions. In 1985 Lafarge Coppée concluded a joint venture with Ajinomoto Company, the Japanese food processor and biochemicals manufacturer. In hope of further Japanese cooperation in the future, Lafarge Coppée's international advisory board includes Yutaka Aso, the chairman of Aso Cement of Japan, and Jack Tang, chairman of South Sea Textile, the Hong Kong–based biochemicals manufacturer.

Since the mid-1980s, the U.S. cement industry has undergone a period of retrenchment. Following Lafarge Coppée's acquisition of General Portland, European companies have taken a 50% market share in the United States. In 1987, senior management at Lafarge was rejuvenated with the arrival of Bertrand Collomb, chief executive of Lafarge Corporation, Bernard Kasriel, in charge of construction materials in Europe, and Jacques Lefevre, who formerly headed Lafarge's finances and international operations.

In August 1989, Olivier Lecerf left Lafarge Coppée after 33 years with the group, and was replaced by Bertrand Collomb as chairman and chief executive. In 1989, Lafarge Coppée acquired as new subsidiaries Cementia of Switzerland and Asland of Spain, thus becoming the world's second-largest cement producer.

Principal Subsidiaries: Ciments Lafarge (99.9%); Portland Zementwerk Wössingen GmbH (Germany, 83%); Lafarge Corporation (U.S.A., 58.8%); Companhia Nacional de Cimento Portland CNCP (Brazil, 50%); GIE Lafarge Coppée Asie (51%); Les Matériaux du Gabon (69.5%); Société des Ciments Antillais (51.5%); Lafarge Coppée (Pte) Ltd. (Singapore); Lafarge Australia Pty Ltd; Lafarge Coopération International (99.8%); Lafarge Fondu International (99.9%); Compagnie du Platre (99.9%); Lafarge Nouveaux Matériaux (50.2%); Allia (75%); Compagnie de Participations Biochimiques (66%).

Further Reading: Dubois, Leon, *Lafarge Coppée: 150 Ans D'Industrie,* Paris, Pierre Belfond, 1987.

—Etan Vlessing

MANVILLE CORPORATION

Post Office Box 5108
Denver, Colorado 80217
U.S.A.
(303) 978-2000
Fax: (303) 978-2041

Public Company
Incorporated: 1901 as H.W. Johns–Manville Corporation
Employees: 17,000
Sales: $2.19 billion
Stock Exchange: New York

Manville Corporation is an international manufacturing and natural-resources supplier operating in three areas: forest products such as paper, cartons, and plywood; fiberglass products such as home insulation; and specialty products that include lighting fixtures and industrial filters. Until the mid-1980s, Manville mined and sold asbestos for use in insulation, building, aerospace, automotive, and other industries. Manville's history is inextricably intertwined with asbestos. The company has divested itself of its interests in all asbestos-related businesses, and is enmeshed in substantial litigation brought by asbestos workers with claims on the effects of working with the material. While operations continue, Manville's future hinges on the decisions issued by the courts in these cases.

In 1858, at the age of 21, Henry Ward Johns founded the H.W. Johns Manufacturing Company in New York City, makers of asbestos textiles, roofing, and insulation materials. Over the next 40 years, until his death in 1898 of "dust phthisis pneumonitis," believed to be asbestosis, Johns discovered some of the applications of asbestos from which it became known as the "mineral of a thousand uses." In 1886, Charles B. Manville founded the Manville Covering Company in Milwaukee, Wisconsin. Manville managed the company until 1900. In 1901, H.W. Johns and Manville merged to create H.W. Johns–Manville (J-M), a corporation engaged primarily in the mining, manufacturing, and supply of asbestos fibers and products to industry and the government.

The management of J-M has been relatively stable over the years. The Manville family remained active in the management of the company through most of the 20th century. From 1921 to 1923, Thomas F. Manville headed the company as president, treasurer, and a member of the board. In 1924, he became chairman; H.E. Manville was elected president, and T.F. Manville Jr. joined the board of directors. By 1928, H.E. Manville and Thomas Manville Jr. sat on the board, while T.F. Merseles was president of J-M. In 1930, H. E. Manville was named chairman of the executive committee and L.H. Brown became president. This hierarchy continued until 1939.

In 1927, J-M became a publicly held corporation. During the 1920s and 1930s, J-M acquired mining and manufacturing operations in the United States and Canada, including, in 1928, the Celite Company of California, miners and processors of diatomaceous earth—diatomite is a filtering agent—and, in 1930, the Stevens Sound Proofing Company of Chicago, owners of patents for sound insulation.

As early as 1929, J-M was defending itself against lawsuits for asbestos-related deaths. Asbestosis is a non-malignant scarring of the lungs caused solely by exposure to asbestos. The incidence of the disease seems to be related to the duration and intensity of exposure. It may take decades for evidence of the disease to appear. Mesothelioma is a form of cancer associated with asbestos that affects the linings of the chest or abdominal cavities and that usually kills its victims within a year of its appearance. The legal issues in asbestos cases centered on two questions. When did the health hazards of working with asbestos become foreseeable? When warnings were issued, did they communicate adequately the danger? From the beginning, J-M claimed that employees were contributorily negligent, because they knew or should have known the dangers associated with asbestos and taken precautions. Manville used this defense, often successfully, in cases filed during the next four decades. Into the 1980s, Manville continued to argue also that there was no known reason to warn insulation workers until 1964 of the dangers of working with asbestos. Plaintiffs countered that warning labels should have been in use as early as the 1950s.

In 1930, Dr. A.J. Lanza, of the Metropolitan Life Insurance Company, began a four-year study, "Effects of Inhalation of Asbestos Dust upon the Lungs of Asbestos Workers." Based on his findings, in late 1933 Lanza recommended that J-M perform dust counts at its plants. Vandiver Brown, Manville vice president, corporate secretary, and chief attorney, wrote Lanza, requesting changes in his report, requesting specifically that he downplay the negative implications of asbestos exposure. In his book, *Outrageous Misconduct: The Asbestos Industry on Trial*, Paul Brodeur described a memo Brown wrote in 1935 to company colleagues in which he noted a speaker who said, " 'the strongest bulwark against future disaster for the industry is the enactment of properly drawn occupational-disease legislation,' which would 'eliminate the jury' as well as 'eliminate the shyster lawyer and the quack doctor since fees would be strictly limited by the law.' " Later that year, Brown wrote that the company's best interests would be served by having asbestosis receive minimal publicity. Brown's correspondence would be entered as evidence in trials almost a half century later, by plaintiffs who, in efforts to win punitive as well as compensatory damages against the company, contended that J-M deliberately downplayed the effects of exposure.

British studies concurrent with Lanza's encouraged Parliament to pass legislation to protect asbestos workers in 1931.

In the United States, three years passed before asbestosis was considered for classification as a disease under workmen's compensation laws.

Beginning in 1936, J-M and nine other asbestos companies funded a study of the effects of asbestos on animals. Dr. LeRoy U. Gardner reported significant changes in the lungs of guinea pigs within a year after exposure to asbestos dust. Gardner died in 1946, before formally reporting his findings.

In 1939, L.H. Brown became president of J-M, a position he held until 1948, and H.E. Manville stepped down as chairman. The year 1940 was significant as the only year in which the name Manville did not appear in the list of company officers. In 1941, H.E. Manville Jr. joined the board of directors, a post he held into the 1960s.

At the start of World War II, J-M was among the world's leading suppliers of asbestos, and 1939 through 1945 were strong years for J-M financially. During those years, tens of thousands of workers in U.S. government shipyards and other installations used thousands of tons of asbestos in building ships and airplanes. In 1943, the Navy Department and the U.S. Maritime Commission published a study that outlined the risks to insulation workers of high asbestos dust levels. In "Minimum Requirements for Safety and Industrial Health in Contract Shipyards," the study reported that asbestosis could arise from breathing asbestos in any job that created dust. Many of the workers and seaman exposed to asbestos during this period would bring suit against J-M years later.

In 1947, J-M signed the first in a series of policies with the Travelers Insurance Company, the company's insurers for the next 30 years. The extent of the insurers' liability in the asbestos suits would be debated and litigated into the 1990s.

In 1948, L.H. Brown became chairman of the board. R.W. Lea was named president. Three years later, L.M. Cassidy, formerly vice president of sales, became chairman; a second vice president, A.R. Fisher, became president and a third, C.F. Rassweiler, was named vice chairman. These men controlled the company until 1957.

From 1950 through 1970, J-M's sales grew at an average annual rate of 4%. While sales of asbestos and other raw materials represented only 13% of J-M's volume, they contributed between 30% and 40% of earnings.

In 1951, John A. McKinney joined the company as a patent lawyer; he was to become president 25 years later. By 1952, the staff included Fred L. Pundsack, Chester E. Shepperly, Monroe Harris, and Chester J. Sulewski, all of whom, along with McKinney, figured prominently in the bankruptcy court protection program some 30 years later. In 1958, J-M acquired L-O-F Glass Fibers Company, which then became and operates today as the Manville Sales Corporation. Francis H. May Jr., of Libbey-Owens-Ford Glass Company, joined Manville and became executive vice president for finance and administration. Fisher was named chairman, as well as president.

During the 1950s, J-M workers who came into contact with insulation on job sites began filing workmen's compensation claims against the company. The company's first-hand knowledge of the dangers of asbestos would become a factor in future suits in which it would be a defendant.

In 1960, Clinton Brown Burnett became president of J-M, a post he held for a decade. Burnett headed the company during a period of rising production costs and price declines. In response, he trimmed operations by closing plants and assembly lines. He led the company through cautious diversification into fiberglass, carpeting, and gypsum; opened a building materials research and development center in New Jersey; and expanded vigorously overseas.

During the 1960s, asbestos received increasing attention from the medical community. In 1963, Dr. I.J. Selikoff, of Mount Sinai Medical Center in New York, reported to the American Medical Association the findings of his study of the effects of asbestos on workers. Selikoff estimated that 100,000 U.S. workers and their family members would die of diseases associated with asbestos in the 20th century. That study, along with the news coverage that followed, brought the problem to the public's attention. In 1964, for the first time, J-M agreed to place warning labels on its products. The labels read, "Inhalation of asbestos in excessive quantities over long periods of time may be harmful."

By 1969, Burnett, now 62, and the board of directors were looking for solutions to two problems: J-M's slow growth over the preceding ten years, and the lack of an heir apparent to succeed the president when he retired. William C. Stolk, a director since 1951, recommended W. Richard Goodwin, a 45-year-old management consultant with a doctorate in experimental psychology, for help with the first problem and, potentially, the second. Goodwin began counseling J-M in June 1968. He joined the company as vice president for corporate planning in April 1969, and was named president in December 1970. Burnett became chairman of the board, only to retire in about a month. He left Goodwin with a solid company, having $145 million in working capital, no long-term debt, and a leading position in environmental control, building materials, and asbestos.

Goodwin immediately implemented the changes he had recommended during his consultancy. He formed a three-man management team, composed of himself and J-M veterans Francis May and John B. Jobe, executive vice president for operations. May and Jobe ran the company while Goodwin concentrated on growth. He led the company into real estate development, recreation, irrigation systems, and construction. Sales rose 91% from 1970 to 1975; profits rose 115% between 1970 and 1974, and earnings in 1976 set a company record. In 1974, J-M's international division, with 22 plants and 4 mines in 12 countries and sales offices worldwide, generated 32% of corporate net profit on 14% of gross sales.

In 1973, Manville and its co-defendants lost their final appeal in *Clarence Borel* v. *Fibreboard Paper Products Company, et al.* The case would be a turning point in asbestos litigation, for the jury found the defendants guilty of contributory negligence. It also awarded the plaintiff damages based on the contention that the companies knew of the dangers inherent in working with the product. In upholding the verdict, the U.S. Appeals Court wrote what was described in *Strategic Management* as a scorching indictment of the defendants.

One of Goodwin's major contributions to J-M was his decision to move the company from Madison Avenue in New York. Goodwin selected the Ken-Caryl cattle ranch, 15 miles from downtown Denver, Colorado, as the site for the new headquarters. When completed, the new building was described in the October 31, 1977 issue of *Business Week* as "ultramodern . . . [the building] juts out like a landlocked ocean liner in a mountain canyon." The building was a tangible reminder that J-M's style had changed drastically.

Goodwin never worked at the new location. Just two weeks prior to its completion, he was summoned to New York to meet with the board of directors. On September 1, 1976, Goodwin, Francis May, and other aides flew in and were met by John A. McKinney, a senior vice president and the company's top legal officer. The next evening, William F. May, John P. Schroeder, and Charles J. Zwick, members of the board of directors, met with Goodwin. Schroeder explained that they represented the nine outside directors on J-M's twelve-member board, and that they all wanted his resignation. Goodwin was surprised but acquiesced. The terms of his separation agreement prevented him from ever discussing his departure or the reasons for it. Industry observers speculated that Goodwin's management style was too casual or flamboyant for the conservative board, and that once he got the company moving in the right direction, the directors replaced him. The next morning, John A. McKinney, who did not know in advance that the board sought to remove Goodwin, was appointed the new president of J-M. The October 1976, *Fortune* quoted McKinney as saying, "It happened so fast, I almost missed it."

Under Goodwin, J-M had stressed growth. Under McKinney, J-M stressed profits. During his first year as president, McKinney eliminated unprofitable diversification and expanded asbestos and fiberglass capacity. One of his early acts as president was to elevate Fred L. Pundsack, a 24-year J-M veteran, to executive vice president of operations, on equal footing with Francis May. Pundsack's directive was to maximize profits.

McKinney quickly earned a reputation as a tough negotiator. In 1977, Quebec threatened to nationalize the company's Jeffrey mine, the world's largest asbestos mine. McKinney put J-M's $77 million expansion plan on hold, and took a hard line with Premier René Levésque. Levésque withdrew his proposal, and J-M resumed its expansion plans. Later in the year, J-M's fiberglass production suffered from a 102-day strike at its Defiance, Ohio, plant. The strike cost the company $7.5 million in lost revenues. McKinney stood his ground, and in October, workers accepted the same offer they had rejected in September, by a two-to-one margin. In May 1977, McKinney was named chairman of the board and chief executive officer. Pundsack became president and chief operating officer.

In 1977, J-M estimated that the $16 million available through primary coverage to settle outstanding asbestos suits would be depleted within two years. New case filings rose from 159 in 1976 to 792 in 1978. Cases were being settled at a faster pace as well, with an average cost to the company of $21,000, of which $15,400 was awarded to the plaintiff, the balance for legal fees. As Travelers was unable to predict the scope and number of future suits, it refused to renew its policy for the 1977 fiscal year. J-M was forced to insure itself.

By 1979, McKinney was spending half of his time on the asbestos problem. He continued to be a tough negotiator. In May 1979, *Fortune* stated, "Asbestos litigation is almost a separate business at J-M." The company was a co-defendant in about 1,500 lawsuits brought by insulation workers who handled J-M's products while working for other companies in construction or in the shipyards. At McKinney's insistence, J-M sued the government to force it to indemnify the company against the suits from shipyard workers, because many of the claimants worked with asbestos insulation during World War II and the Korean War.

In January 1979, J-M completed its acquisition of Olinkraft Inc., a $447 million forest-products company, for about $600 million. W. Thomas Stephens, who was to have a lead role in J-M's later bankruptcy reorganization, moved to J-M from Olinkraft. Olinkraft, now operating as Manville Forest Products Corporation, owned 600,000 acres of timberlands in Louisiana, Arkansas, and Texas. It owned or leased another 100,000 acres in Brazil. Unexpectedly high start-up costs for Olinkraft, combined with a currency devaluation and tax increases in Brazil, caused J-M's net income to fall 20% in the fourth quarter of 1979. Although its stock price fell 40%, Manville surpassed the $2 billion mark in sales for the first time.

1980 revenues were on a par with 1979, with earnings dropping sharply in a weak construction market. The company remained involved heavily with asbestos. McKinney noted that asbestos and Manville were virtually synonymous, telling *Forbes* in May 1980, "The day asbestos isn't good business for us, we'll get out of it." At the same time, he felt that Olinkraft, once past its initial problems, would shape the future of J-M. In 1980 McKinney reported that the company remained optimistic in the face of mounting lawsuits, having won 19 of 28 cases that had proceeded to trial. Of the preceding 24 cases, Manville had won 18.

Effective October 30, 1981, J-M's shareholders approved a reorganized corporate structure consisting of a new parent company, Manville Corporation, and five wholly separate operating subsidiaries: Manville Building Materials Corporation, Manville Forest Products Corporation, Manville International Corporation, Manville Products Corporation, and Johns-Manville Corporation. Johns-Manville shareholders retained their stock, which was converted to Manville Corporation stock on a share-for-share basis.

As of December 31,1981, Manville was a defendant or codefendant in approximately 9,300 asbestos suits brought by 12,800 individuals. Juries were making large awards in punitive damages, which were not covered by insurance. By 1982, settlements approximated $40,000 per case, including legal fees. Manville's consultants estimated that over the next 20 years, the company could be liable for 32,000 cases in addition to the 16,500 that had already been filed, and litigation could cost the company $2 billion, twice the company's assets at the time. By 1985, 19,750 claims had been filed against the company. In addition, Manville was alleged to be liable for asbestos-removal property-damage claims. Manville repeatedly filed appeals to postpone payments in suits it had lost. McKinney continued to assert that the government must pay a portion of the claims arising from exposure in the shipyards and other government jobs.

In 1982, in light of the asbestos litigation, and following losses in the first and second quarters of the year, Manville filed for protection under Chapter 11 of the U.S. Bankruptcy Code, on August 26. While under bankruptcy court protection, Manville's earnings for the first nine months from continuing operations improved from $10 million to $59 million.

Legal expenses, however, increased apace: in one year, 1982–1983, legal costs rose from $1 million for a period of nine months, to $11 million for the same period a year later.

After a dozen court-granted postponements, Manville proposed its reorganization plan on November 21, 1983. The plan was unilateral, since attempts at a negotiated settlement with asbestos victims' representatives had failed. At that time, Manville proposed to split itself into two companies: the first would handle the business, and the second would possess few assets yet all of the liability for the asbestos claims. Manville would be insulated from any and all claims. All cash, after operating expenses, would be funnelled to the second company. Suits would be settle by the company out of court. Concurrently, Manville left the asbestos business, selling its last plant in 1985.

Leon Silverman, court-appointed attorney for unknown future asbestos claimants, helped orchestrate the final reorganization plan, filed on February 14, 1986. This plan resembled the earlier proposal with these amendments: the second company became two trusts, for personal injury—the health fund—and for property-damage claims. The trusts would be funded through cash, future earnings, stock, bonds, and insurance payments worth at least $2.5 billion. Initially, the health-fund trust was to receive $1 billion. Beginning in 1992, Manville would have to pay the health fund $75 million a year. The property-damage trust was to be funded initially with $125 million, with additional funds available. In addition, plaintiffs retained the right to a jury trial if they disagreed with the determination made by the trusts. The plan seemed to satisfy the claimants, but at considerable expense to Manville common stock owners, who saw their investment becoming virtually worthless under the plan. On neither side was there agreement that the trusts were viable solutions. Michael L. Goldberg, attorney for 700 asbestos claimants, estimated in 1988 that the trusts would be almost $200 million short by 1992.

In 1986, McKinney resigned and Josh T. Hulce, who had been president since 1984, abruptly quit. George Dillon, a Manville director for 17 years, became chairman and W. Thomas Stephens was tapped to become president and chief executive officer. Stephens, formerly an industrial engineer with Olinkraft and Manville's chief financial officer during the preceding three years, was credited with playing a pivotal role in bringing Manville out of bankruptcy. One of Stephens's first moves as president was to establish small meetings with Manville employees, who, like the public and the stockholders, had lost faith in the company. Stephens reassured them that Manville would continue to operate much as it had in the past. He intended to concentrate on its core businesses and generate enough cash flow over the next years to fund the trust. Profits doubled in 1987 to a record $164 million.

In 1988, Manville emerged from bankruptcy. After three full years of trimming operations, Manville was again a healthy company with new product lines. It moved out of its headquarters into smaller spaces in Denver, and reinvested the concomitant savings in plant upgrading. In the November 1988, *Business Month*, Stephens stated "Two back-to-back years of record performance should send out a signal pretty loud and clear that we're stronger than ever."

By 1990, almost 130,000 claims had been filed and the Manville Personal Injury Settlement Trust ran out of funds. The dearth of cash was due to the rapid pace of claims settlement, many of which were delayed during Manville's bankruptcy. Manville proposed buying stock from the trusts in an effort to help ease the situation, but the negotiations broke off when it became clear that it was impossible to satisfy both Manville's stockholders and the claimants. Although the company accelerated a $50 million payment to the trust, it was revealed that the claims that had been settled would not be paid for almost 20 years, long after many of the claimants had died. In July 1990, the court imposed a payments freeze while the company tried to determine how to handle the situation. In September 1990, Manville agreed to add up to $520 million to the asbestos fund during the next seven years. The future of the company included resolution of the asbestos issue.

Principal Subsidiaries: European Overseas Corporation; Glaswerk Schuller G.m.b.H. (Germany); International Manville Corporation; Johns-Manville Corporation; Johns-Manville India Limited; Ken-Caryl Ranch Corporation; Manville Canada Inc.; Manville Sales Corporation; Rocky Mountain International Insurance Ltd.; Manville de France S.A.; Manville Deutschland G.m.b.H. (Germany); Manville do Brasil Isolantes Termicos Ltda. (Brazil); Manville Espanola S.A. (Spain); Manville Europe Corporation; Manville Forest Products Corporation; Arkansas & Louisiana Missouri Railway Co.; Pine Pipeline Inc.; Manville (Great Britain) Inc.; Manville h.f. (Iceland); Manville Investment Corporation; Manville International B.V. (Netherlands); Manville Italiana S.p.A. (Italy); Manville Japan Ltd.; Manville Mexicana S.A. de C.V. (Mexico); Manville Produtos Florestais Ltd. (Brazil); Lages Reflorestamento Ltda. (Brazil); Igaras-Servicos Agro-Florestais Ltd. (Brazil); Manville Remedtech, Inc.; New Materials Inc.; New Materials, Ltd. (U.K.).

Further Reading: Solomon, Stephen, "The Asbestos Fallout at Johns-Manville," *Fortune*, May 7, 1979; Brodeur, Paul, *Outrageous Misconduct: The Asbestos Industry on Trial*, New York, Pantheon Books, 1985; Pearce, John A., II, and Richard B. Robinson Jr., "Case 18: Manville Corporation (1987)," *Strategic Management: Strategy Formulation and Implementation*, Homewood, Illinois, Irwin, 1988.

—Lynn M. Kalanik

MATSUSHITA ELECTRIC WORKS, LTD.

1048, Kadoma
Osaka 571
Japan
(06) 908-1131
Fax: (06) 909-7053

Public Company
Incorporated: 1935 as Matsushita Electric Industrial
Employees: 15,000
Sales: ¥891.78 billion (US$6.20 billion)
Stock Exchange: Osaka

Matsushita Electric Works, (MEW) is the industrial counterpart of the better-known Matsushita Electric Industrial Company (MEI), makers of consumer electronic products under brand names including Panasonic and National. MEW's six operating divisions manufacture a wide variety of electrical, lighting, and building products in relative anonymity, most observers assuming incorrectly that MEW is a subsidiary of MEI. While MEI retains 28% of MEW's stock, the latter operates independently, and its mix of products is probably closer to the original interests of Konosuke Matsushita, the charismatic founder and builder of the Matsushita business group.

Konosuke Matsushita was born in 1894 to a farming family. When his father was ruined by commodities speculation, Matsushita went to work in a bicycle shop, at the age of nine. Matsushita became interested in the growing number of uses for electricity in the Japanese economy, and worked for several years in an Osaka light bulb factory. In 1918, at the age of 23, he founded his own company in Osaka to manufacture electric plugs, with both his wife and son-in-law playing active roles in the new venture.

Matsushita's company survived its difficult first years and soon was benefiting from the robust economy of the 1920s. He added bicycle lights and electric heaters to his product line and aggressively cultivated clients in Japan's complex network of retailers, usually unwilling to do business with smaller, independent suppliers. Despite the onset of the Depression in 1929, Matsushita continued to add products to his catalog—radio sets and dry batteries in 1931 and electric motors four years later. Matsushita delivered his products more cheaply than other suppliers, using volume and efficiency to keep his costs low. He also built a reputation as a generous and fair employer, able to inspire loyalty and hard work among employees. His popularity continued right up to his death in 1989 at the age of 94.

On December 15, 1935, Matsushita incorporated his growing business as Matsushita Denki Sangyo—or Matsushita Electric Industrial—the name later applied solely to the consumer products group. The company prospered during World War II, when the Japanese economy required both innovative technology and maximum production from all manufacturers.

Matsushita and other Japanese industrialists eventually watched their factories destroyed and the Japanese economy reorganized according to the plans of General Douglas MacArthur and his occupying officials. Like many other business leaders, Konosuke Matsushita was marked for early retirement by the Allies for his support of the Japanese war effort, but a threatened strike on the part of loyal trade unions convinced the occupation authorities otherwise: Matsushita remained as chairman.

It was at this point, when many of the country's largest conglomerates were broken into smaller pieces by the authorities, that Matsushita was forced to spin off Matsushita Electric Works, to produce industrial complements to MEI's consumer products. In 1947 Masaharu Niwa was named president of the new company, which concentrated on wiring devices for both residential and commercial structures. Given Japan's massive demand for new construction, MEW needed only to survive the first few chaotic postwar years in order to win a virtually unlimited market for its basic products. With Konosuke Matsushita backing MEW by means of his substantial equity holdings, the young company was soon prospering.

In 1951 MEW was listed on the Osaka Stock Exchange, an indication of its need for fresh capital to fund further growth. The following year the company introduced a line of fluorescent lighting fixtures, the beginning of its extensive involvement in lighting systems of all kinds. As the Japanese economy picked up steam during the mid-1950s, MEW continued to add a variety of products to its collection, most of them related to the construction industry but some aimed at the growing consumer markets usually handled by its sister company. In 1953, for example, MEW introduced electric hair dryers and shavers, creating an appliance division which contributes just less than 10% of the company's $6 billion in sales. More typical was its 1958 offering of plastic gutters for the residential housing market, a market for which MEW would eventually develop scores of products ranging from kitchen and bath fixtures to exterior siding.

In the 1960s the Japanese economy came into its own as a global industrial leader. Both of Konosuke Matsushita's creations grew at a prodigious pace, and MEW further strengthened its position in industrial electricial components. Not as dependent on international sales as its parent, MEW waited until the 1970s before making substantial overseas investments. In 1974 it established MS-Relais in West Germany to manufacture electric relays locally for European sales; Europe became an important market for MEW and remains so today. Also in 1974, MEW for the first time ventured into the U.S. market with the establishment of Aromat Corporation, in California. Since then, MEW has increasingly emphasized local production rather than export, adding other plants in Taiwan and Thailand as well as sales corporations in seven countries. To support these growing international facilities, MEW created a Dutch finance company, Matsushita Electric Works Netherlands.

In 1977 Masaharu Niwa was elected chairman of MEW after serving 30 years as its president, with Zenichi Kozaki becoming president and the 82-year-old Konosuke Matsushita remaining a very active director and executive advisor. Konosuke Matsushita had by this time become something of a prophet of Japanese business methods, authoring nearly 50 books promoting "the peace and happiness of society through business." MEW became active in the growing high-technology electronics field when it added an electronics and plastic materials group. Along with another addition, the automation controls group, this electronics initiative has given MEW a foothold in a segment of industry certain to benefit from Japan's always-advancing technological expertise.

The company's bread and butter, however, remains basic lighting, wiring, and building-material products, which together account for approximately 75% of corporate revenue. With the death of Konosuke Matsushita in 1989, MEW in a sense launched into a new era, though the venerable Masaharu Niwa remains as honorary chairman. Still 28% owned by its sister company, MEW remains firmly in the Matsushita group, yet has demonstrated its ability to develop and market an increasingly wide array of high-tech and consumer goods on its own. That combination should enable MEW to maintain its position as one of Japan's top suppliers of electrical and building products.

Principal Subsidiaries: National Wood Products Co., Ltd.; Meiji National Co., Ltd.; Matsushita Gaiso Kenzai Co., Ltd.; Kitakyushu Matsushita Electric Works, Ltd.; Tatsuno Matsushita Electric Works, Ltd.; Obihiro Matsushita Electric Works, Ltd.; Mohka Matsushita Electric Works, Ltd.; NTP Co., Ltd.; Oki Denki Bohsai Co., Ltd.; National Electric Clock Co., Ltd.; Owari Matsushita Electric Works, Ltd.; Aromat Corporation (U.S.A.); Aromat Canada Inc.; SDS-Relais AG (Germany); SDS-Relais (Schweiz) AG (Switzerland); SDS-Relais Austria Ges.mbH; SDS-Relais Limited (U.K.); SDS-Relais Italia S.R.L. (Italy); SDS-Relais France SARL; MS-Relais GmbH (Germany); Matsushita Electric Works (Thailand) Ltd.; NPL Taiwan Co., Ltd.

Further Reading: "History of Matsushita Electric Works, Ltd.," Osaka, Matsushita Electric Works, Ltd., 1989; "Matsushita Electric Industrial Co., Ltd.," in *International Directory of Company Histories,* Volume II, edited by Lisa Mirabile, Chicago, St. James Press, 1990.

—Jonathan Martin

MITSUBISHI MATERIALS CORPORATION

5-1, Shin-Marunouchi 1-chome
Chiyoda-ku, Tokyo 100
Japan
(03) 3211-7412
Fax: (03) 3284-1480

Public Company
Incorporated: 1990
Employees: 9,000
Sales: ¥843.91 billion (US$5.87 billion)
Stock Exchanges: Tokyo Osaka Nagasaki

Mitsubishi Materials Corporation is composed of two companies that have long been integral to the Mitsubishi business group. The mining of coal, mineral ores, and precious metals provided much of the capital needed by Mitsubishi in its infancy, making possible the group's later expansion into heavy industries and trading. Long after the end of the great age of coal, Mitsubishi Mining & Cement (MMC) continued to make its living primarily from the sale of cement and construction aggregates, such as gravel and sand, and from various petroleum products. Having survived the slow decrease in the demand for coal, however, MMC was faced with a similar stagnation in its cement business, which suffered a steady production drop throughout the 1980s. Partially in response to this poor performance, MMC announced a merger, as of December 1, 1990, with its former subsidiary, Mitsubishi Metal, reuniting into a single company what the Allied occupation forces carefully split apart in 1950.

The founder of the Mitsubishi Group, Yataro Iwasaki, was a government official in charge of business affairs in the Tosa domain of Japan. By adroitly playing the roles of both private entrepreneur and public administrator, in 1870 Iwasaki was able to found a highly successful shipping concern called Tsukumo Shokai. Within a year, Tsukumo had ventured into the mining business as well, signing 15 leases on two coal mines in the Shingu domain of Kii Province. These agreements, which could be considered the origin of Mitsubishi Mining & Cement and Mitsubishi Mining Corporation, provide an excellent example of the advantages Iwasaki enjoyed in his dual capacity as capitalist and bureaucrat: the necessary documents were signed by its director, Iwasaki, on behalf of the Tsukumo Shokai and, as legally required, by the local domain official in charge of such matters—Iwasaki.

When the Shingu domain was subsequently unable to pay for a ship Iwasaki had sold to it, the two mines were rendered up as partial restitution in 1874. The year before, Iwasaki had made a second move into mining with the ¥10,000 purchase of the Yoshioka copper mine, whose unusually high profits were made possible by its use of prison laborers. At this point the newly named Mitsubishi remained largely a shipping concern, enjoying a near-monopoly in the Japanese markets, and Iwasaki viewed mining as a useful but minor support for his growing shipping lines. His feelings may have begun to change as early as the mid-1870s, when the first of a series of bitter rivalries developed between Mitsubishi and foreign shippers, in this case the British-owned Peninsula & Oriental lines. With shipping profits dwindling as a result of price competition, Mitsubishi relied increasingly on its extremely lucrative mining interests to keep its house in order.

In 1881, Mitsubishi bought the largest coal mine in Japan, the Takashima mine on the island of Kyushu. Takashima became the showpiece among Mitsubishi's growing collection of mines during the 1880s. It too was worked in part by prison laborers, gaining for Mitsubishi an inordinately high rate of return as well as a reputation in Japan for ruthless treatment of mine workers. The Takashima mine provided coal for Mitsubishi's steamships and also for export to markets along the Pacific Rim.

By 1883 Mitsubishi was locked in a life-and-death struggle with a new shipping rival, the KUK lines sponsored by the Mitsui conglomerate and the Japanese government. So fierce was the price competition that Mitsubishi's shipping division was reduced to a breakeven posture for the next three years, while the Takashima mine continued to show outstanding gains in profits and sales. As a result, by 1885 fully 92% of Mitusbishi's overall earnings were generated by the Takashima mine, with the remainder coming from the Yoshioka copper mine and the new Nagasaki shipyard. This revolution in the Mitsubishi profit structure caused Iwasaki to revise his earlier dream of building a great international shipping line; the shipping business was too volatile to suit his taste, and it was clearly easier to make money in mining and shipbuilding. Iwasaki, therefore, called a halt to the shipping price war, agreeing to form a joint venture, to be called the NYK, with his antagonists. He promptly sold most of his stock in the latter to raise money for new investments in mining and ship construction.

Mitsubishi first acquired a number of metal mines, and then went after the vast Miike coal mines. In the ensuing bidding war with Mitsui, Mitsubishi's top offer of ¥4.59 million fell ¥2,000 short of the best offer, and the mine went to Mitsui. By the mid-1890s, however, Mitsubishi had amassed some 15 other coal mines in Kyushu, as well as an additional 30 metal mines, and in 1896 it paid ¥1.73 million for the rich gold and silver mines of Sado and Ikuno. Together these various mining interests contributed about half of Mitsubishi's profit during the 1890s, supplying the great sums of capital the firm would need in its transition to a full-fledged *zaibatsu*, or conglomerate.

After the Russo-Japanese War of 1904–1905, the Japanese shipbuilding industry grew at a rapid rate, spurred by the need for both military and commercial self-sufficiency at sea. It was not until 1912, however, that Mitsubishi's expanding dockyards were able to show a consistent profit, and as late as 1914 the mining division supported the rest of Mitsubishi's interests. World War I decisively changed this situation. The tenfold increase in shipbuilding orders at Mitsubishi launched the *zaibatsu* on its way to becoming the largest industrial conglomerate in Japan; the mines would never again play so large a role in the corporate profile. In effect, the mines had finished their task of jump-starting the great Mitsubishi industrial machine, and henceforth took their place among the group's myriad secondary components.

After the war's end, the greatly enriched Mitsubishi embarked on a plan of yet further expansion. To pay for this program a number of new corporations were formed and their stock sold to the public in amounts that did not threaten the overall control of Mitsubishi's holding company, Mitsubishi Goshi Kaisha. Among these new companies was Mitsubishi Mining Company (MM), incorporated in 1918, its assets including all of the coal and metal mines yet amassed by the parent company. Allowing for the normal ups and downs of the business cycle, the next 20 years at MM were relatively uneventful. The metal operations became larger and more profitable than the coal mines, which on the whole did not prove to be extensive and were quickly tapped out. The more sagacious among MM's leaders realized that, full or empty, the Mitsubishi coal mines were not the assets they had once been—the age of oil was rapidly overtaking the industrial world.

As Japan's shipping and rail industries gradually converted to oil-based fuels, MM's position in coal became less and less attractive, and the company began withdrawing from the coal-mining business. This was a long process, however; it was not until 1989 that MM closed its last domestic coal mine. The company still operates a few foreign mines to supplyits own coal requirements and for resale on the open market.

In the late 1930s, the frenzied Japanese war economy increasingly dominated all of the Mitsubishi interests. The war placed maximum pressure on all of the Mitsubishi mines, as lead was needed for bullets, minerals for steel, and—especially toward the end of the war—coal was in great demand as a source of synthetic oil. Korean and Chinese war prisoners were used in large numbers throughout the Japanese mining industry, with predictably high mortality rates. It is difficult to estimate wartime profitability at Mitsubishi—orders were immense and a great deal of money changed hands. Given that the war eventually resulted in the total physical destruction of the Mitsubishi *zaibatsu*, along with most of Japan, it would be perverse to say that the war proved to be good business for Mitsubishi. At the least, MM's assets, most of which were buried far underground, probably came through the devastation in better shape than those of the other Mitsubishi members.

As one of the four great *zaibatsu*, Mitsubishi was ordered dismantled by the occupying Allied forces under the direction of General Douglas MacArthur. In 1950, MM was forced to spin off all noncoal operations, and a new Mitsubishi Metal Corporation was formed to handle that business. This segregation of assets presented MM with an obvious problem, as its remaining mines offered a product of decreasing value in a world fueled by oil. If it were to survive, MM would need a rapid overhaul and diversification into more promising industries, and toward that end the company formed a wholly owned subsidiary in 1954 to produce cement. In addition, MM soon developed smaller but healthy divisions for the marketing and distribution of petroleum products—fuel oil and gasoline imported from overseas—and the aggregates used for its cement mixing—sand, gravel, and stone. Relying mainly on its cement business and a dwindling measure of coal sales, MM managed to sustain the company through the 1960s and 1970s.

In 1973, to further strengthen its then-prosperous cement business, MM merged with Mitsubishi Cement Company and the latter's longtime subsidiary, Hokoku Cement, to form MMC. Since that time the company has continued to increase its cement-producing capacity to its present level of 12 million tons per year, while moving cautiously back into metal mining in the form of several South American iron mines. The 1980s saw a steady decline in MMC cement sales, however, as a flood of imported cement and the strong yen combined to depress both demand and price in the domestic market.

Meanwhile, since 1950, Mitsubishi Mining Corporation had also grown apace. Mitsubishi Metals had continued to mine and smelt nonferrous metals profitably through the 1970s. During the late 1970s, however, the company began to diversify into high-technology items, such as super-hard tools, silicon production, and powder metallurgy. In 1989 Mitsubishi Metals closed its last remaining domestic mine, which had produced gold. In 1990, before the merger, mining and trade of gold and silver accounted for about 34% of Mitsubishi Metal Corporation's revenue, while copper accounted for about 20%. Mitsubishi Metal's line of high-tech products brought in 21% of revenues.

In a search for further diversification, Mitsubishi Mining & Cement had, during the 1980s, turned to the application of so-called "advanced ceramics," and begun to manufacture a number of parts for the electronics industry, including ceramic capacitors, ring varistors, alumina film, and also bioceramic products, such as artifical bones for implant surgery. Such technical innovations, while perhaps promising for the future, could not replace the substantial loss of sales in cement. For the second time in its history, MMC found itself locked into a market that at best could be called sluggish, and in 1990 management sought relief in the time-honored traditions of *zaibatsu* fraternity, by merging with its former subsidiary, Mitsubishi Metal Corporation. After the merger, however, Mitsubishi Metal became the dominant influence in-the re-formed group, as its former president, Takeshi Nagaro, became chairman of Mitsubishi Materials, and former Mitsubishi Mining & Cement president Masaya Fujimura became president of of Mitsubishi Materials.

The stated intention of the new venture was to pursue further high-tech applications of the companies' expertise in metals and ceramics, as yet another Japanese industry moves away from the production of raw materials and into the more skilled fields of value-added technology. Mitsubishi Materials Corporation planned to move into real estate and to concentrate more on the opportunities in silicon chips, metallurgy, and advance ceramics.

Further Reading: Wray, William D., ***Mitsubishi and the N.Y.K., 1870–1914: Business Strategy in the Japanese Shipping Industry***, Cambridge, Harvard University Press, 1984; *MMCC: Today and Tomorrow*, Tokyo, Mitsubishi Mining & Cement Co., Ltd., 1987.

—Jonathan Martin

NIPPON SHEET GLASS COMPANY, LIMITED

5-11 Doshomachi 3-chome
Chuo-ku, Osaka
Japan
(06) 222-7511
Fax: (06) 222-3319

Public Company
Incorporated: 1918 as America Japan Sheet Glass Company
Employees: 3,500
Sales: ¥240.57 billion (US$1.67 billion)
Stock Exchanges: Tokyo Osaka Nagoya Luxembourg

Nippon Sheet Glass Company (NSG) is one of the largest glass-manufacturing companies in Japan, with a wide range of products, used mainly in the automotive and construction industries. In 1980s NSG developed high-technology products, including components for computers, communication systems, and electronic devices. The company has operations throughout Japan and overseas offices in Brussels and Somerset, New Jersey.

NSG was founded in 1918, when the Sumitomo Group, a large Japanese conglomerate, in partnership with Libbey-Owens-Ford Company (LOF), a U.S. automotive glass manufacturer, formed a flat-glass subsidiary, America Japan Sheet Glass. LOF provided the technology for making the flat glass. In 1920 America Japan Sheet Glass built Japan's first sheet-glass factory, in Wakamatsu, Japan.

The company struggled in its early years. Not only was it difficult to locate materials, but the company had not yet perfected its manufacturing technique, and the product was of low quality. The company, nonetheless, gradually grew and began to diversify.

In 1927 America Japan Sheet Glass formed a subsidiary, Isolite Insulating Products Company, to manufacture and sell thermal insulation and related products, such as combustion equipment and furnaces. In 1931, because its ties to the Sumitomo Group had become exclusive, America Japan Sheet Glass changed its name to Nippon Sheet Glass Company, Nippon being a common company name within the Sumitomo Group.

During the 1930s, a militarist regime assumed power in Japan. The regime strove to make Japan the supreme economic power in Asia, with the aims of redistributing wealth and nationalizing conglomerates like the Sumitomo group. NSG's management, consequently, faced severe difficulties, and at the same time the demand for sheet glass slid considerably. The company diversified of necessity.

In 1934, following the introduction to Japan of the mechanical means to manufacture hollow glassware, NSG formed Kagami Crystal Works, to produce and sell crystal glassware and glass handicrafts. The new technology greatly reduced cost, and it consequently expanded the market. In 1937 NSG formed another subsidiary, Nippon Glass Fiber Company, to produce and sell glass-fiber products, with uses in textiles, plastics, and insulation. In 1939, NSG founded Tsutsunaka Plastic Industry Company for the production and sale of resin plates, used mainly to fortify glass and plastics, and the production and sales of polycarbonates, used in making molded products.

When Japan went to war with China in 1937, the export of glass products declined considerably. Production of glass products similarly declined. By 1940 the glass industry was severely affected by World War II. Because of the shortages of iron, steel, and other raw materials during the war, restrictions were placed on the construction of new buildings, reducing the demand for window and plate glass. The industry concentrated on producing glass wool for insulating material and photographic plates, both of which had military applications. Overall the industry's production decreased substantially during the war; NSG's decreased 50%.

By 1945, much of Japan's industrial capacity had been destroyed. Many flat-glass manufacturers suffered damage to expensive, large-scale equipment. The Allied occupation authorities saw the glass industry as an important means for economic rehabilitation for Japan, because Japanese glass companies had the necessary technology and raw materials for successful peacetime production. NSG's relationship to the Sumitomo Group, however, was severed, as the Allies instituted an anti-monopoly law that required large *zaibatsu*, or conglomerates, to disband into separate, smaller companies. NSG was forced to loosen its ties to other Sumitomo companies and to function more autonomously. Fumio Nakamura became the first president of NSG in 1945. He led the company not only into its economic recovery but also into its significant growth over the next two decades.

In 1950 NSG established a new subsidiary, Nippon Funtai Kogyo Company, to produce and sell elements used in the manufacture of glass products. Two years later, a new factory was built in Maizuru.

In later postwar years, commercial restrictions on industries were gradually relaxed, and by 1952, Nippon was able to resume less formal relations with other Sumitomo companies. While NSG retained its independent status, Sumitomo companies again were allowed to invest in one another's stock.

As Japan's economy strengthened, NSG's business grew. By 1962 NSG had become the second-largest sheet glass company in Japan. That year Isuro Watanabe became president. In 1964, NSG built another factory, in Chiba, and in 1965 NSG became the first producer of float glass in Japan. Watanabe imported the float glass production technique—involving the pouring of molten glass onto flat metal and allowing the glass to cool slowly—from Pilkington of England. Unlike other forms of sheet glass, float glass does not need to be ground mechanically. The result is a clear, uniform surface without distortions.

In 1966, Seihachiro Takimoto became president of the company. Takimoto brought NSG into a major period of diversification. In 1967, NSG formed Nippon Silica Kogyo Company, to produce and sell silica, an important material used in glassmaking. One year later, NSG organized its central research laboratory, a significant move, as much of NSG's growth came to depend on research and development. In 1968, NSG and NEC Corporation jointly developed the first glass fiber that provided accurate transmission of optical signals and images. SELFOC, one such optical fiber product, became especially important for devices that combined optics and electronics, such as copiers, and medical endoscopes. In the same year NSG formed Hi-Mirror Company, to manufacture and sell mirrors. During the 1960s NSG focused on exporting products, and in 1969 the company established a U.S. subsidiary, Orient Glass, in Los Angeles, to act as a distributor of NSG products in the United States.

The 1970s were a decade of increased internationalization and diversification. In 1970 NSG acquired Nippon Safety Glass, a manufacturer of tempered and laminated glass for automobiles. NSG also, in 1970, formed Nippon Pelnox Corporation to produce and sell synthetic-resin products for a variety of uses in the construction and automotive industries.

In 1971 Jiro Kawase became president of NSG. NSG, in the same year, joined with several Malaysian investors to establish Malaysian Sheet Glass, the only plate glass manufacturer in Malaysia. The company began producing sheet glass and figured glass two years later.

In 1972 NSG established Nissho Kosan Company to handle its real estate and insurance interests. In 1973 NSG established NSG Foreign Trade, to handle the export of plate glass, and NSG Materials Service Company to handle the sale of construction materials, machinery, and tools. In 1973 NSG began research on glass-fiber-reinforced cement, a form of cement thinner and lighter in weight than ordinary cement, that was later to be used in building houses and as part of soundproofing panels.

When the oil crisis hit Japan in 1974, the economy slowed substantially. Kawase faced many problems, since NSG's production capabilities were crippled. NSG continued, however, to move into foreign markets. In a 1975 joint venture with Libbey-Owens-Ford, NSG formed L-N Safety Glass in Mexico. The company was to supply automotive safety glass for Japanese cars.

In 1976 Toshihiko Tsuganuma took over as president of NSG. He improved the financial condition of the company by introducing crucial energy saving techniques. In 1979, NSG established NSG Materials Engineering Promotion Foundation to promote and assist research on inorganic materials that are used for such things as aircraft, computers and medical services.

In 1982 Nobuo Sasuga became president of NSG. Sasuga helped expand NSG's presence in foreign markets. He was also instrumental in expanding the range of NSG products. In 1983 NSG America, Inc., was established in Somerset, New Jersey, for the manufacture and sales of SELFOC optical fiber products. In 1985 NSG, LOF, and Hankuk Glass Industry Company of South Korea signed an agreement to begin producing automotive glass in Korea and established Hankuk Safety Glass Company. Also in 1985, Japan's Transport Ministry introduced a law that forced automakers to use laminates on windshields for safety reasons. NSG doubled its laminates capacity, and sales skyrocketed. In 1986 NSG, Hoya Corporation, and Japan Key Technology Center formed a consortium controlled by the Ministry of International Trade and Industry to promote advanced technology, focusing on the use of glass as memory material for computers and computer-related uses. A year later, NSG established NSG Information System Company for the development and sales of business-related software, and in 1987 NSG established another branch of the subsidiary for the development of information systems and communication networks.

In the late 1980s NSG strengthened its presence abroad, especially in the United States. In 1986, along with Ishizaki Honten, another automotive-supply firm, NSG formed Penstone, Inc., in Michigan, a manufacturer of hardware for the assembly of automotive glass. In 1987 NSG established an automotive-glass distribution center in Brussels. Also that year, in a joint venture with LOF, NSG formed L-N Glass Company in Kentucky. L-N Glass was to act as a supplier of safety glass to U.S. subsidiaries of Japanese automakers, and it soon became the major supplier to Toyota. In 1988 NSG entered into a joint venture with Pilkington, the parent corporation of Taiwan Auto Glass. In 1989 NSG cemented its connection to LOF, acquiring 20% of LOF capital stock from Pilkington, which had acquired LOF in 1986. The $235 million investment furthered NSG's expansion into the U.S. flat glass market.

In 1988 Tatsuji Nakajima became president of NSG. He was the first president who was an engineer by training, and he helped the company to focus on its advanced technology sector. In the same year NSG began to market its Angle 21 glass, developed by the Sumitomo Chemical Company and NSG. A polymer film applied to glass controls light transmission, making the glass transparent or opaque, depending on the angle from which it was viewed.

In 1989, in a joint venture with SDC Coatings, in California, NSG formed Nippon ARC Company in Tokyo. The new company was to combine the parent companies' abrasion-resistant coatings technologies and to market products under the Crystal Coat name, for use in such applications as eyeglass lenses, window glazing, and automotive trim. NSG also acquired a minority interest in Areal Technologies, in California, and acquired the rights to market Areal's disc drives in the Far East.

Following NSG's 1986 agreement with Taliq Corporation of the United States concerning rights to Taliq's light-control film, and NSG's subsequent use of the film with glass, NSG and Taliq began a joint-venture company in 1989 called NSG-Taliq. The company was organized to produce and market N-Kap film in Japan and Southeast Asia.

While NSG was expanding its advanced technology businesses in 1988 and 1989, the demand for sheet glass in the construction industry also increased, with an incentive being the rise in housing investment. In addition, increased sales in the automotive industry aided NSG automotive parts sales.

In 1990 NSG planned to increase its efforts in the development of solar-energy-related products and optic-fiber-related products. Although the globalization of the glass industry is expected to increase competition, the market for glass products is expected to grow considerably, as glass is important in many advanced-technology industries.

Prinicpal Subsidiaries: Tsutsunaka Plastic Industry Company, Ltd.; Isolite Insulating Products Company, Ltd.; Nippon Glass Fiber Company, Ltd.; Hi-Mirror Company, Ltd.; Libbey-Owens-Ford Company (U.S.A., 20%).

Further Reading: *Company Profile*, Osaka, Nippon Sheet Glass Company, 1989.

—René Steinke

ONODA CEMENT CO., LTD.

6276, Onoda
Onoda City, Yamaguchi 756
Japan
(08368) 3-3331
Fax: (08368) 3-2011

Public Company
Incorporated: 1881
Employees: 1,357
Sales: ¥420.68 billion (US$2.93 billion)
Stock Exchanges: Tokyo Osaka Nagoya

Onoda Cement Company is the oldest and one of the largest cement companies in Japan, the country with the largest cement industry in the free world. The company's motto is "Quality and Technology," which emphasizes the traditional areas in which it distinguishes itself from its competitors.

The history of the Onoda Cement Company begins during Japan's Meiji era, from 1867 to 1912. During this era, the Japanese social structure changed from feudal to Western forms through government-sponsored industrial expansion. One of the first steps taken by the Meiji government to modernize was the construction of port and harbor facilities. The first cement in Japan, imported from France in 1870, was used in the construction of piers in the port of Yokosuka. As the demand for infrastructure increased, so did the demand for cement and other imported goods. In an effort to reduce the outflow of gold and silver due to increased imports, the Meiji government began a domestic industrial development program.

Except in military industries and strategic communications systems, private concerns carried out this industrial development program. In certain industries, however, the Meiji government sponsored and constructed pilot plants. One of these industries was cement. The construction bureau of the Ministry of Finance built Japan's first cement plant at Fukagawa, Tokyo, in 1873. Portland cement was manufactured there two years later, in 1875, the same year cement production began in the United States.

One of the crucial features of the Meiji era, the disbanding of the samurai warrior class in 1869, helped provide the financial basis for Onoda Cement Company. After their dismissal from government service, the samurai received pensions from the government that amounted to a percentage of their original salary and varied in value. After about seven years, the pensions became too expensive and were replaced with interest-bearing, nonconvertible bonds. The samurais' incomes fell to a fraction of their original levels, and only a few of them had enough commercial experience to go to work to replace their lost incomes. At the same time, inflation due to weakened paper currency and increased government expenditures reduced the real value of their fixed holdings. Inflation later became a principal reason for the government's decision to sell its various pilot plants.

In May 1881 at Onoda-Mura, Yamaguchi Prefecture, Junpachi Kasai founded Onoda Cement, the first privately owned cement company in Japan. A year later, in 1882, Onoda Cement purchased the government's pilot plant at Onoda. Kasai, himself an ex-samurai warrior, led a group of samurai who pooled their pensions to capitalize the company. Kasai became one of Japan's leading industrialists and part of a group of business leaders who helped reinforce Japan's national integrity. Through their industrial successes, these businesspeople resisted the expansion of Western interests into Japan during a period of global colonization. During the presidency of Kasai's son, Shinzo Kasai, between 1900 and 1930, Onoda became the largest cement firm in Japan.

Transportation is crucial to profitability in the cement industry because cement is a high-bulk, low-value good. Manufacturers maximize revenues by placing plants near either the final market or a water transportation facility, since water transport is the cheapest mode of bulk carriage. Prior to World War II, Onoda solely produced cement; it did not have its own sales and distribution network. Mitsui Bussan, a large *zaibatsu*, or conglomerate, was Onoda's sales and distribution agent in both foreign and domestic markets. The relationship did not compromise Onoda's independence. Onoda was not a subsidiary of Mitsui Bussan but rather a client of its trading services. From its founding Onoda has been proud of maintaining its corporate independence.

The firm expanded extensively before World War II, especially into China and the Japanese colony of Korea, the closest areas for increasing market size. By the beginning of the war over 60% of the firm's assets, roughly 19 plants, were in Korea and China.

In 1924 the cement federation, Rengokai, a cartel organization, was formed to control output. The cartel set uniform curtailment rates that required cement manufacturers to limit production to 60% of capacity. Uniform production curtailment rates favored established firms over newer firms. Established firms retained older equipment, normally scrapped in a competitive environment, simply for the purpose of counting it as production capacity. Older firms could curtail production to 60% of capacity by using 100% of their new equipment and none of their older equipment. Newer firms with a higher percentage of newer equipment found that the 60% cap cut into the machinery they could use in a competitive market, putting them at a disadvantage.

The cement federation agreements covered Japan proper, the colonies, Manchukuo, and the South Seas Mandatory territories. Tensions within the cartel, intensified by the Great Depression, prompted the formation of sales associations to fix exclusive sales territories with sales quotas and standard prices. In 1932 Onoda's Dairen factory seceded from the cartel over a dispute about Manchurian quotas. In December

1933 the cartel responded to this challenge by setting up a mechanism by which to divide markets, the Cement Exporters' Association.

In 1934 Onoda and the Oita Company withdrew from the cartel on the grounds that the industry's leader, the Asano Group, gained an unfair advantage from the uniform curtailment rates because it had predominantly older equipment. When the cartel lost its control it appealed to the government for intervention. In December 1934 the Minister of Commerce and Industry enforced Article 2 of Japan's Major Industries Control Law, for the first time ever, on the cement industry. The government's intervention forced the "outsiders" to comply with the cartel's curtailment rates but actually did very little to control competition since the law only applied to production in Japan proper.

To get around this constraint Onoda built plants in Korea, Kwantung, and Manchukuo and supplied the home market from these sources. This move was easy to accomplish because Onoda and the other "outsiders" operated mainly in western Honshu, Kyushu, and Korea. The national and municipal governments became some of Onoda's biggest customers, since the company now could undercut cartel prices. The cartel responded to these Onoda successes by having the Asano, Mitsubishi, and Yasuda *zaibatsu* set up their own colonial companies. It also secured the 1936 revision of the Major Industries Control Law, which extended the government's control into the colonies as well. The government's solution to the conflict was to have agents of the Rengokai and Onoda meet every three months to set prices and production limits. This arrangement lasted until the eve of World War II, at which time Onoda operated 27 plants with an annual production of 3.5 million tons.

As a result of World War II, Onoda lost 60% of its assets, or a total of 19 plants, including its foreign holdings in China and all of its then-domestic holdings in Korea. The plants left to Onoda after World War II included Ofunato, Fujiwara, Tahara, Hikone, Atetsu, Onoda, Yahata, Tsunemi, and Oita. Together with the loss of plants, Onoda lost its distribution arrangement with Mitsui Bussan when that *zaibatsu* was broken up by the occupation government. The new arrangement called for Onoda to operate its own domestic sales and distribution network while employing Mitsui as its foreign sales and distribution agent.

After the war Onoda president Toyoroku Ando rebuilt the business to re-emerge as the industry's leader in Japan. Ando was a 1921 graduate of Tokyo University and a lifelong employee of Onoda. He spent his first 25 years with the company in Korea, where he rose to manage the Pyongyang factory in 1944. Ando became president in 1945 and improved the efficiency of Onoda's production, distribution, and transportation systems. Under his direction the company began extensive diversification plans. Onoda produces or conducts research into specialized types of Portland cement, ceramics, electronics, ionics, biotechnologies, fluorochemicals, and computer systems.

Onoda began to expand outside Japan in the 1960s with a joint venture with two partners, Mitsui Bussan and Hong Leong Corporation. This joint venture, Singapore Cement, is a bulk importer of Onoda's "Dragon Brand" cement. In 1974 Onoda set up P. T. Semen Nusantara in Indonesia to operate a cement plant at Cilacap, in central Java. Later Onoda expanded into several markets including Hong Kong, Australia, Hawaii, Malaysia, and throughout the Pacific Rim. In the late 1980s Onoda began to expand into both the Chinese and U.S. markets.

Onoda's entry into the United States began with a joint venture with Lone Star Industries of Greenwich, Connecticut, in 1988. The $60 million operation, Lone Star Northwest, conducts business in three states, Washington, Oregon, and Alaska. The venture imports cement and manufactures concrete and aggregates—crushed stones used in making cement and in highway construction.

Onoda's second entry into the U.S. market that year was the purchase of the CalMat Company's cement division, California Portland Cement Company, for $310 million. CalMat is a Los Angeles–area firm dealing in sand, gravel, asphalt, concrete, and land development. The purchase included 13 ready-mix concrete plants, three cement plants, and a cement-importing terminal, and it made Onoda the largest cement producer in California. In 1989 Onoda invested in China in a joint venture with Mitsui Bussan and two Chinese firms, Huaneng Raw Material Corporation and Dalian Cement Factory. This venture, Dalian Huaneng-Onoda Cement Company, planned to construct a $150 million plant at the port of Dalian, Liaoning Province. The plant will be capable of producing 1.4 million tons of high-quality cement for export.

The company's principal innovations include the reinforced suspension preheater (RSP), an advanced cement-manufacturing process developed in 1964 that substantially reduces the amount of energy used in the manufacture of cement. The RSP system is used in more than 20 countries and is recognized as an industry standard. The O-sepa separator is an air separation system sold worldwide. The system, developed in the late 1970s, saves electric energy and improves particle-size distribution. A third product, Bristar, is an efficient, nonexplosive demolition agent used in urban areas to minimize the traditional side effects of explosives: flying debris, noise, vibration, gas, and dust. Another innovation is Chemicolime, developed in the late 1960s. This quicklime technology, used to stabilize wet soils, was used by the U.S. military in Vietnam to strengthen jungle and marshland roads. Its contemporary uses involve construction projects near coastal regions.

Onoda operates three Japanese plants, in Ofunato, Fujiwara, and Tsukumi, and has 104 subsidiaries, all in Japan, except Onoda U.S.A., Inc. and Onoda California, Inc. The company has five product divisions. The cement-products division is the largest and accounts for about one-third of net sales. The building-materials division produces materials that complement concrete construction. The limestone and related-products division produces limestone, gypsum, slag, and specialized sands. The civil and architectural engineering division helps construct cement plants in other nations and develops applications of soil stabilizers and concrete reconditioners. The final division, the "others" division, deals in chemicals, electronics, and land management.

The history of Onoda Cement shows its industrial concentration in Japan and expansion overseas. Before World War II this industrial pattern served Japanese markets, but today it is aimed at both domestic and foreign markets. One aspect of this contemporary trend is Onoda's expansion into the United States.

Principal Subsidiaries: Azuma Shipping Co., Ltd. (79%); Oriental Concrete Co., Ltd. (51.8%); Onoda Chemical Industry Co., Ltd. (99.6%); Onoda Corporation; Onoda Chemico Co., Ltd. (85%); Onoda A.L.C. Co., Ltd.; Abe-Kawa Kaihatsu Co., Ltd. (99.9%); Japan Kanigen Co., Ltd. (70.2%); Nippon Gypsum Board Co., Ltd.; Onoda Engineering and Consulting Co., Ltd.; OACS Co., Ltd.; Onoda Finance Co., Ltd.; Onoda U.S.A., Inc..

Further Reading: Schumpeter, E.B., *The Industrialization of Japan and Manchukuo*, New York, Macmillan, 1940; ''The Cement Industry of Japan,'' *Far Eastern Economic Review*, August 8, 1957; Masson, R.H.P., *A History of Japan*, New York, The Free Press, 1972.

—John C. Bishop

OWENS-CORNING FIBERGLAS CORPORATION

Fiberglas Tower
Toledo, Ohio 43659
U.S.A.
(419) 248-8000
Fax: (419) 248-5337

Public Company
Incorporated: 1949
Employees: 18,300
Sales: $3.00 billion
Stock Exchange: New York

Owens-Corning Fiberglas Corporation (OCF) is the undisputed world leader in fiberglass products for industry and insulation for homes, and one of the world's major producers of polyester resins. The company has sought to enter a number of technical and consumer-oriented markets and—through a combination of marketing techniques and technological leadership—to dominate those markets completely. OCF enjoys 50% of the domestic market for home and industrial insulation; 50% of the domestic market for reinforced plastics, with applications such as automobiles, pleasure boats, and aerospace; and 25% of the domestic market for residential and commercial roofing.

The genesis of OCF, and of the production of modern fiberglass products, dates back to the Great Depression. Owens-Illinois (O-I), then a leader in the development and marketing of new glass products, transformed one of its idle bottle plants into a research facility to study the potential uses of fiberglass. O-I vice president Harold Boeschenstein named engineer Games Slayter to oversee the research and development effort. The project bore fruit quickly with the development of cheap, high-efficiency dust filters for home furnaces, manufactured from glass wool. These filters replaced the much more expensive, traditional steel filters. The truly dramatic breakthrough for O-I and for glass fibers came during a 1932 experiment at the small O-I laboratory in Columbus, Ohio. Dale Kleist was working on ways to melt glass rods. If his experiment worked, the molten glass would seal glass blocks together. The experiment produced, however, a very fine fiber—not what Kleist had in mind. As Kleist mused over how the experiment had backfired, his colleague John Thomas, according to legend, realized that Kleist had stumbled onto a new way to make glass fiber.

Slayter and Thomas predicted that very fine glass fibers would have myriad uses and urged the formation of a joint venture between Owens-Illinois and Corning Glass Works, the country's premier manufacturer of glass products, in 1935. Harold Boeschenstein agreed, and the joint venture began developing new products and technologies immediately, including the first continuous filament fibers in 1937.

In October 1938, a new company was formed from the joint venture. It was called Owens-Corning Fiberglas and its mission was to manufacture glass-fiber products, market them to homes and industry, and develop new related technologies. Some of the technologies were implemented during World War II, when OCF manufactured insulation and fireproof materials for ships and aircraft. Harold Boeschenstein, OCF's director, served on President Franklin D. Roosevelt's War Production Board. The most important use of glass fiber was, of course, in fiberglass, a glass-fiber-reinforced resin product.

After the war business boomed. The company built two new plants and rehabilitated or converted four more from a war footing. Construction products—together with a technological leading edge that no other competitor could match—became a mainstay of its overall strategy. The company expanded into many aspects of new home construction with its distribution of Kaylo fiberglass pipes, and it developed a new process for manufacturing building insulation. Its "Comfort Conditioned Home" was a major national marketing effort in 1957, which promoted fiberglass insulation in homes. OCF led the way with its involvement in the first glass-fiber-reinforced automobile body, Chevrolet's Corvette in 1953. The company also produced many new components for industry, including a wide array of acoustical materials and industrial and automotive insulation.

OCF was so successful that in 1949 Owens-Illinois and Corning Glass works were accused of illegally monopolizing the fiberglass industry through their joint control of the company. Under a court-mandated consent decree in 1949, OCF was required to license its patents to competitors, and both parent companies were forced to relinquish control of what had been their subsidiary for 14 years. As a separate entity, OCF went public in 1952 when it put one-third of its shares on the New York Stock Exchange.

In the 1960s, OCF expanded even more, building plants in Texas, at Waxahachie and Conroe; Indiana; and Georgia, as well as embarking on new construction for its subsidiary company in Bogota, Colombia. The company at this time was moving ahead in three broad areas: new products, new technology, and remarkably efficient marketing techniques.

Among the new products in the 1960s was a new glass-fiber yarn, called Beta, with superior flexing and handling characteristics, and the development of the glass-fiber-reinforced-plastic (FRP) underground storage tank. The development and marketing of this tank underscored the success of OCF in developing new products and in getting them accepted in the market place. Indeed, OCF has created markets for many of its innovative products. Until the late 1960s, steel underground storage tanks—such as those used by the oil industry—were the standard. OCF developed the first FRP tank, which was lighter and stronger than steel, but they were also more expensive. The tank's noncorrosive properties would be the key selling point, long before government-mandated codes for such tanks, which today are utilized not only for petroleum storage, but for toxic chemicals and a wide variety of industrial and agricultural uses. By 1970, 10,000 FRP tanks were in use in the United States, and in the 1980s the company developed the first double-walled storage tanks. By 1985, OCF had sold 100,000 fiberglass underground fuel storage tanks.

The company had pioneered the use of fiberglass in the recreation industry. By the late 1950s, more than 90% of all fishing rods in the United States were made of glass-fiber-reinforced materials, and by the late 1960s, FRP components were common in new cars. The company was also heavily involved in producing components for fiberglass pleasure-boat hulls.

In the 1970s and 1980s, the company enjoyed its market dominance and continued its diversification. It expanded into Europe, Asia, and South America, furthering its technological and marketing lead. New plants were opened in Bakersfield, California, and New York State, as well as in Texas, Pennsylvania, and Florida. The market, research, and product diversification was reflected in OCF's complex organization. By the mid 1980s, the company was split into 11 different divisions, employing some 29,000 persons.

One of OCF's hallmarks has been its intent to dominate any new market that it enters. To this end it uses innovative products, superb communications with retailers, and an overwhelming marketing presence. When successful, the company enjoys tremendous vertical integration in those areas in which it chooses to compete. Two examples illustrate this successful OCF strategy in the 1970s and 1980s. As with FRP storage tanks, fiberglass roofing shingles were met initially with skepticism. Contractors, used to cheaper organically-composed shingles, were reluctant to use the unfamiliar fiberglass products. An aggressive marketing campaign, however, stressed the much greater strength and longevity of the product. This campaign, together with the company's purchase of Lloyd A. Fry Roofing and its subsidiary, Trumball Asphalt in 1977, gave OCF a commanding position in both new home roofing and re-roofing of older homes. In 1980, only 20% of the domestic home roofing consisted of fiberglass shingles, but by 1986, the figure stood at 77%. The downside of this tremendous change was, as one analyst with Salomon Brothers pointed out, a resultant glut in the roof shingle market; because fiberglass shingles are easier and speedier to produce than felt shingles there was a consequent shut-down of many manufacturing facilities nationwide.

The second major example of its marketing genius was the four-to-one brand preference among consumers for Owens-Corning fiberglass blanket insulation over the nearest competitor. OCF's 50% market share of domestic home insulation eclipsed its major competitors such as CertainTeed, Manville, Knauf, and Guardian. This brand preference, for an often-more-expensive product, was furthered in the 1986 by a U.S. Court of Appeals ruling that granted OCF a trademark on a color—pink—for its exclusive use in fiberglass insulation and advertising. The court ruling paralleled OCF's exclusive rights to United Artists's Pink Panther cartoon character for its advertising and promotions. The word "Fiberglas" is also a company trademark. Through a sophisticated computer network, "Pink Link," it can keep track of inventory, and communicate with its retail dealers nationwide, thus diminishing the need for outlets to store large inventories of Fiberglas insulation. OCF's sales force is conceded to be among the best in the business. The company further enhanced its name recognition in 1981 by underwriting the TV program "This Old House."

The 1970s and 1980s saw not only the proliferation of OCF products and an aggressive marketing strategy, but also heavy investment in research and development, forays into new and sometimes unproven technologies, and acquisition of subsidiaries. These activities emphasized the long-term, and saw the company develop expertise in a number of fields that had little resemblance to its core areas of construction products and industrial materials. Primary among these acquisitions was the aerospace and strategic-materials group from Armco, in 1985. The intent was primarily to take control of Armco's high-technology and composites subsidiary, Hitco. Hitco was responsible for research into visionary carbon-based composite materials used in such applications as missile nose cones and light-weight armored plating for army vehicles. OCF was now on the cutting edge of future technologies and product applications that could not be foreseen. The consumer housing market was leveling off; the company was looking ahead to new areas for expansion. Just as in the early 1930s, when Owens-Illinois and Corning Glass delved into a highly speculative joint venture, OCF was again placing its bets increasingly on long term, costly research.

The year 1986 brought the most significant—and traumatic—changes for OCF in the company's history. In early August, Wickes Companies, a Santa Monica, California–based building materials retailer, announced a tender offer to buy up OCF's public stock at $74 a share. Wickes chairman Sanford Sigoloff had already bought almost 10% of OCF's shares earlier and now was out to capture the company to expand Wickes's operations into roofing and insulation. Wickes was on the rebound from bankruptcy proceedings and looking for acquisitions. At a tense meeting in OCF's New York offices, chairman William Boeschenstein, son of the former chairman, rejected Sigoloff's offer and, according to affidavits filed later by Wickes, countered by threatening to "make a substantial financial investment in Wickes," which Wickes labeled the "Pac-man defense."

OCF urged its shareholders not to accept the takeover bid of $74 a share, more than twice the New York Stock Exchange value prior to the bid, while it studied its options for survival. The company was also hoping for a buy-out from a friendly suitor, but this was not forthcoming.

The company chose as its most viable strategy for survival as an independent company a leveraged buy-out, borrowing huge sums of money to recapitalize. After borrowing $2.5 billion from Drexel Burnham Lambert and others, it was able to offer its shareholders a package including $52 a share on its stock plus a junior subordinated debenture, with a face value of $35, but which was valued at issue at half that amount, and one share of newly issued stock. Wickes was forced to withdraw its offer, and walked away with over $30 million in profit by selling its OCF stock. Other shareholders were happy with the windfall. The company that emerged, however, was laden with debt and was almost unrecognizable in terms of organizational structure and goals.

In 1990, OCF bore little resemblance to its former self. Its goal could be put succinctly: retire the debt. The company set about doing that in two ways. It had economized and instituted massive layoffs, early retirement, and mothballed or closed plants in several locations. From a mid-1986 employee roll of 29,000 the company in 1987 had only 17,000. The second strategy was to sell the company's many subsidiaries that were not immediate profit generators. OCF thus sold ten companies in very short order, including Hitco and the entire aerospace and strategic-materials group, Olympic Fastening Systems, the glass-fiber-reinforced-plastic-components division, and Performance Contracting, Inc., which was the largest specialty contracting firm in the United States. Four entire divisions, out of 11, were sold off, accounting for roughly $1 billion in annual sales.

There were enormous cutbacks in long-term research and development. Virtually overnight, OCF transformed itself from a company known for its long-range research-and-development work—fiberglass itself had been 20 years in development before market applications bore fruit—to a "cash machine," spitting out profit to pay its creditors. In its research-and-development division, the company laid off nearly 50% of its work force or lost them through divestiture of assets. In 1986, before the takeover bid, OCF spent $63 million on research and development. In 1987, this figure had been slashed to $29 million.

Long-term research projects with little hope of short-term profit or even markets are difficult to justify in publicly held corporations. OCF had, for instance, been developing liquid crystal polymers, for which no application could be foreseen at the time. The cost and lead-time for such a project require a large research investment, patience, and creative vision, three areas in which the "new" OCF cannot afford to indulge. The project was sold to an Italian company after the recapitalization.

The company did a solid job of retiring the debt. By early 1990, total indebtedness had been reduced to less than $1.5 billion, and the company was generating profit beyond all expectations. Indeed, in the wake of several leveraged cash-outs in the late 1980s, the OCF example had become a textbook example of how to survive. Earnings were solid enough in 1989 to allow it to buy up the 50% share of Fiberglas Canada that had been owned by PPG Industries, a major competitor. Costs were down and profits were generally up, but the company still had a negative book value, that is, its debt outweighed its assets.

After the restructuring, the company emerged as a leaner, more centralized concern with a profit and structural emphasis on its leading cash generators. OCF had organized its remaining divisions into three major units: Construction-products division, industrial-materials division, and international division, which consists of overseas operations exclusive of Europe. The industrial materials division might soon account for the lion's share of OCF's net sales—in 1989 it was more profitable than the construction products division, $183 million as compared to $277 million.

The cyclicality of the housing market and the overall slowdown in housing starts affected the company's profitability in 1989–1990, although the industrial materials division accounted for more and more of OCF's earnings. The "soft" nature of the housing market had affected sales and profitability in the wake of the restructuring, although re-roofing, not affected by housing starts, accounted for 75% of the demand for shingles. Net income and operating profit were both down in 1989 compared with the previous year. Profit in 1988 was $477 million, with 1989 at $430 million. Net income in 1988 was $189 million and $172 million in 1989. The economic slowdown in 1989 and 1990 especially had cut into the company's construction products, automotive, and pleasure boat components.

The former European divisions had been absorbed into the construction-products and industrial materials divisions, primarily due to the similar consumer and industrial purchasing patterns. The emphasis in the international division was on the smaller but growing markets in the developing world. The Asia-Pacific area was the fastest growing, with automotive manufacturing and electronic equipment providing the largest markets. OCF had affiliates—less than 50% ownership—or subsidiaries—more than 50% ownership—in Japan, South Korea, and Taiwan. Latin America was another area of expansion, with OCF manufacturing auto component parts in Brazil, for example. Brazil's unstable fiscal condition, however, was eroding the viability of OCF investments there.

By 1990 OCF's future concerns included asbestos litigation and world petroleum prices. The threat of class-action litigation stemmed from large suits brought against manufacturers and distributors of asbestos products in the 1970s and 1980s. Prior to October 1988, all claims against various asbestos manufacturers were handled through a joint claims facility, set up by 55 corporations that contributed funds to its accounts. The funds were used to pay meritorious claims. On August 6, 1987, OCF notified the joint Asbestos Claim Facility's trustees that it intended to withdraw from the organization. Most of the outstanding claims had been brought by litigants who had been employed by the tire and rubber industry and who worked with asbestos brake linings. The company maintained that it had little involvement in these industries, and would not contribute to the payment plan in the future. In 1990, OCF had roughly 84,500 asbestos-related lawsuits pending against it, but it looked to its liability insurance to handle those matters.

As the end of the 20th century approached, OCF was the dominant manufacturer of fiberglass products in the world. It was exerting tighter control over its foreign affiliates and subsidiaries, such as controlling 100% of Fiberglass Canada, and concentrating on retiring its still considerable debt. The company showed in the 1990s every indication that it would emerge debt-free and refocused on a profit-generating business. William Boeschenstein, chairman and CEO, stepped down in 1990, ending the family dynasty, which guided OCF to its preeminent position in home and industrial fiberglass and polyester resins. OCF President Max O. Weber became chairman and CEO. While cutting back its long-term research, the company could continue in its role as an innovator in products in its chief areas of competition. Few companies are recession-proof, however, and a rise in oil prices combined with a severe cutback in new housing starts might slow growth for OCF and hurt its profitability.

Principal Subsidiaries: American Borate Corporation; Barbcorp, Inc.; Eric Company; Fiberglas Canada Inc.; Karlcorp; Matcorp, Inc.; N.V. Owens-Corning S.A. (Belgium); OCFIBRAS Limitada (Brazil); O/C/FIRST CORPORATION;

OCFOGO, Inc.; OCFSC, Inc. (U.S. Virgin Islands); O/C/SECOND CORPORATION; O/C/ Tanks Corporation; Owens-Corning Cayman Limited; Owens-Corning Fiberglas España, S.A. (Spain); Owens-Corning Fiberglas France, S.A.; Owens-Corning Fiberglas (Italy) S.r.l.; Owens-Corning Fiberglas Netherlands B.V.; Owens-Corning Fiberglas (U.K.), Ltd.; Owens-Corning Real Estate Corporation; Palmetto Products, Inc.; Roscorp, Inc.; Scandinavian Glasfiber AB (Sweden) Veroc Technology A/S (Norway); Willcorp, Inc.

Further Reading: Focus, Toledo, Ohio, Owens-Corning Fiberglas Corporation, October 1988.

—Karl F. Rahder

PILKINGTON PLC

Prescot Road
St. Helens WA10 3TT
United Kingdom
(0744) 28882
Fax: (0744) 692660

Public Company
Incorporated: 1894 as Pilkington Brothers Ltd.
Employees: 60,500
Sales: £2.91 billion (US$4.70 billion)
Stock Exchanges: London Frankfurt Düsseldorf

Pilkington, with over 80% of its turnover outside the United Kingdom and factories in the United States, Germany, Scandinavia, South America, China, South Africa, Australia, and elsewhere, is the main supplier of flat and safety glass to the world's building and automotive industries, and is also a leading manufacturer of eye-care products. This rise to international pre-eminence occurred during the mid- to late 20th century.

The St. Helens Crown Glass Company—to give Pilkington its original name—was formed in 1826 at St. Helens, then a small town at the heart of a coal-mining area of about 10,000 people. Cheap coal had already attracted a number of furnace industries, including glass. Of the six local men who became partners in the new crown—or window—glass business, two already owned a glassworks in the district. One of the others, the son of a leading coal owner in the area, became the new company's bookkeeper and was joined by the local solicitor. The other two, originally brought in only for their capital, were William Pilkington, son of a local doctor who had done well in distilling, and his brother-in-law Peter Greenall, who was in charge of the local brewery. When the two technical men had to withdraw from the glassmaking venture because of an attempt to evade paying excise duty on their flint glass, William Pilkington—who had been apprenticed to a Liverpool distiller, ran the family distillery, and was already considered an astute business man—was called in to take charge. William's elder brother, Richard Pilkington, was brought in when it was discovered that the bookkeeping partner was not keeping the books properly. The local solicitor chose this critical moment to withdraw from the venture. Thus, almost by accident, the Pilkington brothers found themselves landed with a tiny, struggling glassworks, much less profitable than the family distillery.

Skilled glass blowers, drawn mainly from Dumbarton, Scotland, where a glass manufacturer had gone bankrupt, provided the necessary technical expertise, and Peter Greenall—a partner in Parr's Bank at Warrington—saw to it that the struggling young business received an overdraft far larger than its size warranted. William Pilkington, as salesman, traveled through the United Kingdom of Great Britain and Ireland seeking orders while his brother stayed at home and looked after the works and office. Business grew with the increasing demand for glass for the many new houses being built. A second furnace was built in 1834 and a third in 1835. Peter Greenall, who became a member of Parliament in 1841, remained an important, but sleeping, partner in the business, until his death in 1845, when the firm became Pilkington Brothers (PB).

Once the company was in operation, progress was determined partly by a willingness to accept technical change and partly by the initiative and drive of the new generations. The founders each had six sons, and two from each side became partners.

The taxation system for glass manufacturers favored crown glass against its more efficiently produced rival, sheet glass. PB's willingness to venture into sheet glass in the early 1840s stood it in good stead a few years later when the duties on glass were removed. Cheaper sheet glass from continental Europe, and especially from Belgium, drove out of business those U.K. manufacturers who had clung to crown glass. By the 1850s there were only three U.K. survivors: Chance Brothers of Smethwick near Birmingham; James Hartley & Son of Sunderland in the northeast, which had previously been the center of the industry in the United Kingdom; and PB, which thrived in this more competitive climate. Between 1849 and 1854 PB's labor force rose sharply from 450 to 1,350.

The second generation, whose influence began to make itself felt from the later 1860s as the founders retired, embarked upon a vigorous export drive. In the early 1870s, PB stole a great march upon its two remaining U.K. rivals by replacing pot furnaces—which necessitated 24-hour intervals between week-long glassmaking campaigns while the pots were recharged and reheated—with Siemens's glassmaking tanks, which allowed continuous round-the-clock production and much more cost effective eight-hour shifts. PB also chose the very profitable years of the early 1870s to build a new factory for the manufacture of polished plate glass, used in larger windows and mirrors. Intensive foreign competition soon drove the other longer-established U.K. plate glass manufacturers out of business, but PB survived, because it alone had another profitable product to sustain it. In 1903 it emerged as the sole U.K. producer of plate glass. By then Hartley & Son had gone out of business and Chance Brothers, which had failed in its attempt to enter plate glass manufacturing and had delayed in introducing tank furnaces for sheet, was very much a runner-up. PB had emerged as the undisputed leader in flat glass manufacture in the United Kingdom, though it was still subject to continued fierce competition from European producers. Between 1874 and 1894 the firm's capital had grown more than ninefold, from £150,000 to £1.4 million. In 1894, the business was then made a private limited company, Pilkington Brothers Ltd., with £800,000 in ordinary shares and £600,000 in 5%

debentures. There were then ten family shareholders, three of the four senior partners having each brought in two of their sons.

Even during the hard years between 1874 and 1896, PB managed to flourish. Despite reinvestment of £1.25 million, £725,000 were distributed among the family. Between 1894 and 1914, the company did even better: nearly £3 million were reinvested and approximately £2.3 million distributed. The four Pilkingtons of the second generation reaped the financial rewards of their success on a scale far greater than did their fathers.

The third generation, which took over in the Edwardian period, did not match its predecessors' impressive performance. This may have been due to unexpected family losses. One son was killed in the Boer War. Another died of tuberculosis, and his twin brother, Austin Pilkington, who was himself an able manager, fell ill with tuberculosis in 1907 and, in a last attempt to save his life, was sent from the smoke and chemical fumes of St. Helens to live in the dry, thin air of Colorado, where he recovered. Another son, who became company chairman in 1914, died in 1921 at the age of 50, and at about the same time another decided to retire, mainly on grounds of ill health, at the age of 42. In the 1920s the main responsibility for the running of the company and the earning of profits upon which the growing number of non-executive family members depended, fell to the fully recovered Austin Pilkington, together with his younger brother Cecil, a natural sciences graduate from Oxford who became the firm's technical director. They were joined by Edward Cozens-Hardy (Lord Cozens-Hardy after his elder brother's death in 1924), formerly a partner in the London electrical engineering consultancy of O'Gorman and Cozens-Hardy, whose sister, Hope, had married Austin Pilkington. Cozens-Hardy had moved north and taken Austin Pilkington's place at PB in 1908, but had stayed on after his brother-in-law's return.

Just before World War I, this weakened third generation made two decisions which were to lead to much subsequent trouble. Having moved into the continuous melting of sheet glass in the 1870s, it made the mistake of opting for drawn cylinder machinery. This machinery replaced glass blowers but not the flatteners who had to reheat the cylinders and slit them open in order to produce the panes of glass. The large cylinders blown by machine could only be made one at a time. Instead the company should have opted for either the Libbey-Owens-Ford (LOF) or the Fourcault process which drew the sheet of glass direct from the tank. Although these flat drawn processes were still being developed, preference for the compromise deprived PB of what was soon to prove the better alternative and nearly caused it to abandon sheet glass manufacture altogether during the 1920s. The decision also involved PB in a disastrous sheet glass venture in Canada in order to protect its drawn cylinder process rights. Secondly, having sensibly acquired, as a defense against European competitors, an interest in a small plate glassworks at Maubeuge in northern France in the 1890s, it unwisely decided to put down a second plate glassworks in the United Kingdom near the east coast, fearing that European competitors might establish their own factories on British soil if it did not do so. This factory, decided upon just before World War I, was built near Doncaster at great cost during the post-war boom. It swallowed up not only many of the vast reserves accumulated before and during that war but also £1 million of new capital, which had to be raised from the family in 1920.

PB saved itself by taking a world lead in plate glass manufacture at St. Helens. In the early 1920s, in collaboration with the Ford Motor Company of Detroit, it developed a new process which enabled a roughly cast ribbon to be cast continuously by pouring the molten glass out of the tank, instead of having to be ladled from pots to form a single plate of glass at a time, each side of which had to be ground separately and polished separately. Associated with the continuous flowing of the glass ribbon was a long series of grinding and polishing heads under which the ribbon was passed to produce the high-quality glass with more perfect parallel surfaces than had previously been possible. It was this extraordinarily costly process which float glass was to replace, but, being to a large degree continuous—a twin grinder was developed which ground both sides of the ribbon simultaneously, but not a twin polisher—it was less costly than the intermittent processes it replaced. Such high-quality polished plate glass, being thicker than the sheet glass then made, and more lustrous, commanded high prices which would not only cover the costs but also bring in good rates of profit. Sheet had saved plate at Pilkington in the later 19th century. Now the situation was reversed.

Having managed to save its sheet glass production during the 1920s, thanks to plate glass profits, PB then had a stroke of good fortune. The U.S. plate glass manufacturer Pittsburgh Plate Glass (PPG) developed its own method of drawing sheet glass directly from a tank which was superior to that of LOF or Fourcault. PB secured a license for this process in 1929. PPG machines, installed at St. Helens in the early 1930s and subsequently improved there, enabled the company to regain some of its market. The flat glass industry fared better in the United Kingdom because it supplied two markets, the building and motor trades, which survived the depressed years of the 1930s better than most others. There was also money to be made out of raw glass, particularly plate glass, when it was processed into safety glass. PB acquired a majority share in a factory built just outside St. Helens by Triplex (Northern) Limited, which came into production in 1930. Soon afterward it also became involved in safety glass processing plants in Canada, South Africa, and Australia. In 1936, an agreement was reached with Chance Brothers whereby PB would buy its old rival over a number of years. By 1939 it had already acquired nearly half of Chance's shares. It completed the takeover in 1952.

Austin and Cecil Pilkington retired from day-to-day management of the company at a critical moment in 1931, when PB recorded its first loss. Control passed to an executive committee which Cozens-Hardy set up with himself as chairman. His right-hand man was Ronald Weeks, who had been recruited from Cambridge in 1912 and had played a notable part in the management of the plate glass factory, subsequently marrying into the Pilkington family. Ronald Weeks was to gain a national reputation during World War II as General Weeks, deputy chief of the Imperial General Staff and afterward as chairman of Vickers and director of other companies. He became Lord Weeks in 1956. It was under this regime during the early 1930s that the fourth generation of the family began to play a greater part. Geoffrey Langton Pilkington, who was much older than his cousins, had been a director since 1919 and served as company chairman from 1932 to 1949. The others, some of whom had entered the business from university in 1927, served a rigorous probation, being reported upon by departmental managers as they progressed. One of them did not make the grade. Harry Pilkington and Douglas Phelps, the son of a Pilkington daughter, reached the executive committee in 1934; Roger Percival, the son of another Pilkington daughter, followed in 1936, and Peter Cozens-Hardy in 1937. By then Lawrence Pilkington—Harry Pilkington's brother—and Arthur Pilkington, after five years as a regular officer in the Coldstream Guards, had entered the company and joined the executive committee in the 1940s, followed by a much younger member, David Pilkington, born in 1925. This team was to succeed more spectacularly than any of its predecessors.

When PB closed its Maubeuge factory in 1935, as part of the general rationalization of the European plate glass industry which followed an agreement between the European and U.S. manufacturers reached the previous year, it ceased to manufacture any glass outside the United Kingdom. It was soon, however, the major participant in the establishment of a window glass factory built at Llavallol outside Buenos Aires, a joint European venture to safeguard the Europeans' Argentine market. This factory had hardly come into production when World War II broke out and the Pilkington management there had to struggle hard to maintain and extend it during the war years, when communication between Llavallol and St. Helens was difficult and technical assistance from the parent company was unobtainable.

Lord Cozens-Hardy retired in 1939 and Sir Ronald Weeks did not return to the company after the war. With Douglas Phelps as chairman of the executive committee from 1947, succeeded by Arthur Pilkington in 1965, and Harry Pilkington, the future Lord Pilkington, as company chairman from 1949, the fourth Pilkington generation saw the company's assets grow from £12.5 million in 1949 to £206 million in 1973, when Lord Pilkington retired from the chairmanship. This growth was due to the outstanding success of the float glass process and also to diversification into what were, for PB, new branches of the glass industry.

In some respects, change was forced on the company rather than welcomed by it. Manufacture of sheet glass in South Africa in 1951, for instance, came about because the South African government, determined to develop a manufacturing industry in that country, proposed to allow a rival to build a sheet glass factory if PB did not do so. PB's interests would have been best served by exporting as much U.K. glass as possible and thus keeping its machines at home working at full capacity. For similar reasons, PB sheet glass manufacture had to be started in Canada in the same year and in India, with local as well as Pilkington capital, in 1954. In Australia, where Australian Window Glass (AWG) had a financial stake in Pilkington's safety glass processing plants, PB took a share in AWG when PB helped to modernize AWG's obsolete sheet glass factory in 1960. A few years later, PB and AWG took over an aspiring local manufacturer in New Zealand who had attempted to make sheet glass but soon had failed. PB's window glass operations in Argentina, started just before World War II, were developed and led in due course to the acquisition of a sheet glass works in Brazil. Although PB sacrificed sheet glass exports to these factories, it never lost those of plate glass: maintaining a plate glass factory in these countries would have been far too costly. Manufacture of higher-quality glass overseas had to await the development of the less costly float glass process, which tipped the scales further in the direction of manufacture abroad rather than at home.

The float glass process was invented by Alastair Pilkington early in the 1950s. In this process, molten glass was poured onto one end of a bath of molten tin at about 1,000°C and formed into a ribbon which floated, frictionless and in a controlled atmosphere, down the bath through a temperature gradient falling to about 600°C at the other end. At this temperature the ribbon, fire finished, was cool enough to be taken off on rollers without marking the surface. This revolutionary new method of glassmaking produced much more cheaply high-quality glass of polished plate glass standard by removing the large fixed capital investment in grinding and polishing machinery and by cutting working costs. To obtain perfectly parallel, distortion-free surfaces, the polished plate glass process required 20% of the original rough-cast glass to be ground off by many grinding and polishing machines, with vast expenditure of electrical energy. Having experimented with the new process and developed it on a full-scale production plant during the 1950s, PB began to sell its own float glass before the decade was out and licensed the process to other glass manufacturers from 1962. Plate glass could no longer compete at the quality end of the market nor, from the early 1970s, when float technology had progressed further, could the cheaper sheet glass. Pilkington built more float lines at St. Helens, and manufacturers elsewhere in the world sought Pilkington licenses and expertise. Its growing industrial muscle and rising license income led to Pilkington building its own float plant in Sweden in the mid-1970s. Others came on stream in overseas markets which it already dominated: Australia in 1973, and a second in 1988; South Africa in 1977; and Argentina in 1989. Its factories in Brazil were operated jointly with Saint-Gobain and in China with the People's Republic. It also acquired a majority, in Flachglas, the leading German producer, in 1980, followed by the purchase of the glassmaking interests of LOF, second in this field in the United States.

Alastair Pilkington, who invented the float glass process, was unrelated to the St. Helens glassmaking family and was a mechanical sciences graduate from Cambridge University. Although not a member of the Pilkington family, he came to St. Helens as a family trainee in 1947. By the time the float process was being developed, he was already on the board pleading its case. He became a Fellow of the Royal Society in 1969 and was knighted the following year. Between 1973 and 1980 he was chairman of the company.

PB was brought into glass fibers and optical glass as a result of its acquisition of Chance Brothers in the years after 1936. The latter had acquired the U.K. and British Empire rights to glass fiber manufacture from 1930 and had long specialized in optical glass. Glass Fibres Ltd. was formed jointly by PB and Chance Brothers in 1938. A glass fiber factory was built at St. Helens after the war, and others followed at home and abroad to make glass silk for weaving and fibers for insulation and reinforcement. Pilkington Reinforcements Limited is the world's leading supplier of special reinforced belting for engines and machinery, that is, for power transmission.

Chance Brothers's interest in optical glass went back to the 19th century and its world-renowned lighthouse department. During World War II Chance Brothers and Pilkington operated a shadow plant—a duplicate located away from the original factory as a precaution against bombing— at St. Helens and continued to undertake defense contracts afterwards. Since 1957, on the initiative of Lawrence Pilkington, the technical director, optical and ophthalmic glass has been made at a specially built works at St. Asaph in north Wales which soon became the largest producer of unpolished spectacle discs in Europe. In 1966 PB and Perkin-Elmer, a subsidiary of the U.S. multinational Perkin-Elmer Corporation, joined forces at St. Asaph to make optical and electro-optical systems. The joint venture became Pilkington P.E. in 1973, when Pilkington acquired the U.S. company's stake in the business. This side of the business was strengthened greatly by later acquisitions, notably the purchase of Barr and Stroud, the Scottish optical and precision engineers, in 1977; Sola Holdings of Australia in 1979; Syntax Ophthalmic Inc. in 1985; and Revlon's Barnes-Hind and Coburn Vision Care companies in 1987. The business is now divided into Pilkington Visioncare, its ophthalmic side, which is growing throughout the world, including China and Japan, and Pilkington Optronics, the electro-optical side, which supplies the U.K. defense industry, primarily through Barr & Stroud and Pilkington P.E.

The fourth Pilkington generation oversaw this vast expansion overseas and diversification at home as well as the development of float glass and many other activities. They were served loyally by senior managers who acted like proconsuls on their behalf abroad and by others at home who accepted greater responsibility as the business grew and its committee system was expanded. From the mid-1960s, when Arthur Pilkington became chairman of the executive committee, much business which it had previously handled was devolved to the five divisional boards. One or two outstanding managers had joined the executive committee from the 1930s. Now a few more followed Alastair Pilkington to the top.

Harry Pilkington, the company's chairman, was an outstanding businessman with a remarkable head for figures, a clear, analytical brain, limitless energy, and a great devotion to work. He managed to fit in the presidency of the Federation of British Industries in London or the chairmanship of a royal commission with company responsibilities which would by themselves have been more than enough for most chairmen.

The Pilkington family influence persisted for some years after the company went public in 1970. Lord Pilkington, created honorary life president when he retired in 1973, used to come into the office regularly until shortly before his death in 1983, and the fourth generation was represented on the board until 1985 when the youngest, David Pilkington, retired. In 1985 Pilkington Brothers Ltd, became Pilkington Brothers plc, and in 1987 the company dropped "Brothers" to become Pilkington plc. Pilkington became a holding company for a number of major subsidiaries, of which there were 45 in 1990. Economy and efficiency became the watchwords, especially in the difficult years of the early 1980s, when nearly £100 million were spent in redundancy payments in the U.K. alone. While this changed the atmosphere at St. Helens, it revived the company's fortunes and enabled it to ward off a takeover bid from the London-based conglomerate BTR in 1986. Only one Pilkington remains on the board—the chairman, Sir Antony Pilkington, son of Arthur Pilkington, knighted for his service to U.K. business in 1990.

Principal Subsidiaries: Pilkington Glass Ltd.; Flachglas AG (Germany, 93%); Pilkington Floatglas AB (Sweden); Lamino OY (Finland); OY Lahden Lasitehdas (Finland, 71%); Libbey-Owens-Ford Co. (U.S.A., 80%); Pilkington (Australia) Ltd.; Vidrieria Argentina SA (60%); Pilkington Vidros Limitada (Brazil, 96%); Pilkington (New Zealand) Ltd.; Pilkington Insulation Ltd.; Pilkington Visioncare, Inc. (U.S.A.); Barr & Stroud Ltd.

Further Reading: Barker, T.C., *Pilkington Brothers and the Glass Industry,* London, Allen & Unwin, 1960; Barker, T.C., *The Glassmakers,* London, Weidenfeld & Nicolson, 1976.

—T.C. Barker

PIONEER INTERNATIONAL LIMITED

Level 20
Coopers & Lybrand Tower
580 George Street
Sydney, New South Wales
Australia
(02) 364-4000
Fax: (02) 364-4009

Public Company
Incorporated: 1956 as Pioneer Concrete Services Limited
Employees: 11,000
Sales: A$4.91 billion (US$3.88 billion)
Stock Exchange: Sydney

Pioneer International was formed during the period of industrial growth in Australia that followed World War II. Originally founded to supply a limited range of concrete materials to the domestic construction industry, Pioneer has extensive investments in building materials, petroleum refining and marketing, and oil and gas exploration and production. Diversification into mineral mining in the late 1970s proved unprofitable, and the company began to sell its mineral assets in 1989. In the 40 years since Pioneer Concrete Services was founded, the company has grown into a major international operation, with subsidiaries throughout Australia and in 11 other countries. Under the leadership of Sir Tristan Antico, the company has grown to become one of Australia's most productive corporations.

Pioneer Concrete Services was established in 1949 as a partnership between two young Australian entrepreneurs—Tristan Antico and Kelvin Conley—providing concrete placing and formwork to the Australian construction industry. The postwar economic environment in Australia was extremely favorable to the building industry. While the country's infrastructure had escaped damage during World War II, the following years saw an influx of immigrants, which, with the baby boom of the early 1950s, created the need for increased house-building in Australia. The growth of the Australian economy after World War II was relatively slow, but Pioneer benefited from increased government investment in housing in the 1950s.

Pioneer grew slowly during the early 1950s, expanding its businesses with minor acquisitions in New South Wales. The company formed a new subsidiary—Pioneer Readymixed Concrete and Mortar Proprietary Ltd.—in 1954, following the acquisition of a Canberra-based concrete producer which owned one concrete plant. In October 1956 Pioneer was incorporated as Pioneer Concrete Services Limited. Three years later, in 1959, it was listed on the Sydney Stock Market as a public company, and the name was changed to Pioneer Concrete Services Ltd. Following its flotation, Pioneer embarked upon a period of rapid expansion in the pre-mixed concrete and quarrying markets in Australia. Much of the growth came from new acquisitions, but diversification into new building-materials products was also undertaken.

Despite the economic recession in Australia from 1961 to 1962, and the marked decline in government assistance to the construction industry, Pioneer had developed an effective expansion strategy based on conservative spending and consolidation. This allowed the company to prosper while more ambitious construction companies failed. Tristan Antico's guiding policy, from the inception of Pioneer to his retirement as chief executive in 1988, was based on the belief that long-term stability and growth is best maintained by cushioning the company from economic recessions while taking advantage of periods of sustained economic growth elsewhere. Accordingly, the company reacted to the fluctuations in the Australian economy during the late 1950s and early 1960s by embarking on a period of geographical expansion. Having established its first successful foreign venture, a pre-mix concrete plant, in Hong Kong in 1961, Pioneer began to look to the European markets for the first time. Construction and building materials operations were established in the United Kingdom in 1962, where, in the same year, the worst winter in a century hit the industry badly. Pioneer survived its second overseas venture and then had about 140 construction and quarrying operations in the United Kingdom. In the following year, the company established operations in Israel and, in 1964, in Italy. At the same time, Pioneer was expanding throughout the Australian states, and by the middle of the decade had established a wide network of lucrative operations in its home market.

In 1965 a new subsidiary, Pioneer Asphalts Pty. Ltd., was formed, jointly owned by Shell Australia Ltd. This marked Pioneer's first entry into asphalt manufacture and supply. In the same year, the company diversified into aggregate quarrying in Hong Kong. Two years later, Pioneer acquired F. W. Williams Holdings, a large and diverse Australian company with plastic manufacturing operations, and tea and coffee plantations in Papua New Guinea. The program of vigorous expansion and development at home and abroad continued until the end of the 1960s, although profits did not increase proportionately with spending. The company's policy after the 1960s was to consolidate the businesses it had acquired over the last ten years, and to make no further major investment or diversification.

However, expansion continued in the 1970s, although not at the rate of the previous decade. In 1970, Pioneer acquired pre-mix and quarrying companies in Spain and by the middle of the decade the company's interests had spread to Asia, Africa, and most of Europe. In 1973, together with CSR Limited, one of Australia's largest cement manufacturers, Pioneer acquired Australian and Kandos Cement (Holdings) Ltd. The takeover gave Pioneer substantial cement production facilities in Victoria and New South Wales. Antico was knighted in 1973 in recognition of his services to industry.

A significant commercial development took place in 1975, when Pioneer began to invest heavily in resources. Pioneer's first venture into the mineral-exploration field was a joint project with Pennzoil of Australia in 1975. While many companies had suffered losses as a result of making incautious mineral investments during the resources boom of the mid-1970s, Pioneer had considerable experience in the quarrying industry and it was thought logical to invest in other resources. From 1975, profits from Pioneer's building materials division were used to expand the minerals operations in Australia. The drive to exploit mineral mining and marketing continued until 1988, when mineral sales represented only 5% of Pioneer's total revenue.

In the United Kingdom in 1977, the company's subsidiary, Pioneer Concrete UK, was among a number of companies being investigated by the Office of Fair Trading for alleged contract fixing. Pioneer Concrete U.K. was one of 21 companies eventually put on the Register of Restrictive Practices, although senior managers insisted that they knew nothing about local deals, ''many of which were agreed over a drink in the evening,'' according to one newspaper report. With the Australian economy stagnating in the mid 1970s, and with continuing industrial disputes, Pioneer was increasingly dependent on its overseas construction activities. Political unrest in Italy was adversely affecting Pioneer's Italian operations, and in Spain and West Germany, profits were falling. Antico's policy of geographical diversification to insure against isolated economic downturns seemed to be effective; despite recession in most European building markets, and restrictive government construction policies at home, Pioneer announced a 46% increase in earnings for 1976–1977.

In 1978, Pioneer became involved in a major coal coking and steaming development. Set in the Hunter Valley area of New South Wales, the project operated in conjunction with the Electricity Commission of New South Wales and Ampol Petroleum Limited. Initial research indicated that there was enough coal in Hunter Valley to provide mining opportunities for 100 years. The following year, Pioneer acquired a 20% stake in Ampol Petroleum, which was increased to a controlling stake of 65% in 1980. The investment in Ampol marked a crucial commercial turning point for Pioneer; Ampol Petroleum Limited and its associate company, Ampol Exploration Limited, were giant oil exploration, production, and refining companies in Australia. The Ampol companies provide the Pioneer group with 50% of its profits and represent 50% of assets. Pioneer's mineral operations expanded considerably in 1979, notably in uranium and beach-sands mining. Ampol and Pioneer formed a new, jointly owned company to control new mineral acquisitions: the Nabarlek uranium mine and Queensland Mines Ltd., another major uranium producer. When Queensland Mines and Kathleen Investment (Australia) Ltd., a major beach-sands mining company, became wholly owned subsidiaries of Pioneer in 1981, the company's profits rose by 30% in one year.

Widely varying world economic conditions in the early 1980s reversed the dependency Pioneer had had on overseas operations in the previous decade. By the mid-1980s, the company was increasingly reliant on the Australian construction and resource markets. In 1982, Pioneer attempted to take over Mixconcrete (Holdings), a large British building materials producer with widespread concrete plants and aggregate reserves in the United Kingdom. The takeover was completed in 1983, and Pioneer's building materials division became the third-largest readymix concrete producer in the United Kingdom. In Australia at this time, Pioneer was experiencing several commercial problems. A fall in demand for domestic building materials, a sharp decline in concrete and quarrying activities, and the state governments' interference in the pricing of petroleum products threatened the stability of the Pioneer group.

In 1984, Pioneer began a series of investments in the United States, to capitalize on its earlier American successes in concrete production. The US$23 million acquisition of Lone Star Industries's sand, gravel, and quarrying operations in 1985 gave Pioneer the opportunity to cash in on the impending construction boom in the United States. The following year Pioneer was the subject of a hostile takeover bid. F.A.I. Insurances, Australia's largest general insurer, offered A$1 billion for the company, and pursued Pioneer for a year before retreating. Its vulnerability to predators forced Pioneer to make fundamental changes in its strategy. The company had a history of refusing to sell unprofitable assets. However, in 1986 the building materials divisions in Italy, Portugal, and South Africa were sold in an attempt to consolidate Pioneer's more lucrative assets and to strengthen the company's stock rating. In 1987, the year of the stock market crash, Pioneer began an important period of growth and restructuring. The company gained control of Giant Resources, a group with mineral and gold assets in Australia, New Zealand, Canada, and Guyana. Later that year, the Bell Group, a failing investment company, sold its shares in the former Ampol Petroleum—which, had been renamed Ampol Ltd. in 1982—to Pioneer, giving Pioneer the opportunity for full ownership of Ampol.

The acquisition of Giant and the potential for 100% ownership of Ampol, which it achieved in 1988, provided Pioneer with the means of streamlining its increasingly diverse management structure. However, Pioneer's regrouping strategy, in which mineral assets were to be amalgamated under Giant Resources, and petroleum exploration and production controlled by Ampol Exploration was thwarted by the A$32.5 million loss made by Giant in 1988. Sir Tristan Antico retired as chief executive that year but stayed on as group chairman. His deputy, Des Quirk, who had been with Pioneer for 31 years, and who had been responsible for the company's expansion in Europe, took over the leadership. The company changed its name to Pioneer International Limited at the end of 1988.

Ill health forced Quirk into early retirement, and in April 1989 Rodney Price was appointed managing director. Price began to refocus Poineer on its core activities following the disposal of most of the company's mining assets. Taking advantage of the domestic construction boom in order to extricate the company from costly mineral activities is generally considered to have secured Pioneer's future stability. Under Price's leadership there has been a review of all aspects of the company, with the goal of rebuilding Pioneer's traditional concentration on building- and construction-materials and oil refining and exploration.

Principal Subsidiaries: Ampol Exploration Pty Ltd.; Ampol Ltd.; Solo Oil Ltd.; Brick & Pipe Industries Ltd.; Pioneer International Finance Ltd.; Besser (Qld) Ltd.; Pioneer Concrete & Quarries (NSW) Pty Ltd.; Pioneer Plasterboard Pty. Ltd.; Pioneer Roof Tiles Pty Ltd.; Pioneer International Investments BV (Netherlands).

Further Reading: Hutton, John, *Building and Construction in Australia,* Cheshire, Institute of Applied Economic Research, 1970.

—Juliette Bright

PPG INDUSTRIES, INC.

One PPG Place
Pittsburgh, Pennsylvania 15272
U.S.A.
(412) 434-3131

Public Company
Incorporated: 1883 as Pittsburgh Plate Glass Company
Employees: 35,500
Sales: $5.73 billion
Stock Exchanges: New York Pacific Philadelphia Tokyo

PPG Industries is a global producer of flat glass, fiber glass, coatings and resins, chemicals, and medical electronics. It is the world's third-largest manufacturer of flat glass, the second-largest maker of continuous-strand fiber glass, and the world's largest producer of automotive and industrial coatings. It operates about 60 production facilities in the United States, supports 11 research-and-development facilities, and has more than 100 operations worldwide.

PPG is a leading supplier of products for manufacturing, building, processing, and numerous other industries. Its major markets are chemical processing and petroleum refining, commercial and residential construction, and transportation—both original equipment and replacement equipment. PPG is also a major North American producer of chlorine. It sells nearly two-thirds of its yearly output to other industrial processors for use in the manufacture of paper and textiles. PPG has grown from the dream of two men into a global corporation.

Captain John B. Ford and John Pitcairn created the Pittsburgh Plate Glass Company (PPG) in 1883. The first financially successful U.S. plate glass manufacturer was located in Creighton, Pennsylvania, northeast of Pittsburgh. It moved its headquarters to Pittsburgh in 1895. Prior to the 1880s over a dozen plate glass makers had tried unsuccessfully to compete with their European counterparts. Despite U.S. technical ability, plate glass for America's growing cities continued to be imported from Belgium, England, France, and Germany.

Manufacturing profits on glass were inconsistent partly due to the independents who controlled glass distribution. In 1896 Pitcairn established a commercial department and PPG became its own warehouser and distributor. Due to disagreements with Pitcairn regarding distribution, John Ford's sons sold their PPG interests and the Edward Ford Plate Glass Company then was founded near Toledo, Ohio. During the Depression Ford merged with Libbey-Owens Sheet Glass to form Libbey-Owens-Ford Glass Company, now known as TRINOVA Corporation.

Pitcairn became president of PPG, and in 1899 he built the Columbia Chemical Company at Barbeton, Ohio. This independent company produced soda ash, a major raw material used in making glass. This plant was a forerunner of PPG's Chemical Group. By the following year PPG was selling 13 million square feet of plate glass a year and had become the nation's most successful plate glass maker.

Pitcairn continued to expand PPG's product line. Because paints and brushes were distributed through the same channels as glass, they were a logical addition to the company. By the end of 1900 PPG had acquired a major interest in Milwaukee, Wisconsin–based Patton Paint Company, the precursor to PPG's current coatings and resins group.

In the early years PPG had manufactured only plate glass. It marketed but did not produce window glass, or sheet glass. In 1907, however, the first window-glass factory was added to company operations, in Mount Vernon, Ohio. In 1915 a second plant was opened in Clarksburg, West Virginia. Pitcairn's strong interest in innovation and diversification led to the opening of the company's first research-and-development facility in 1910.

The first stage of PPG's development came to an end in 1916 with Pitcairn's death. In 33 years he had led the company through economic panics, foreign competition, and restrictive distribution channels to become the nation's largest plate glass manufacturer. He was also the force behind diversification of the company's product line as well as the development of raw material sources and expansion of marketing outlets for its many products.

In 1919 subsidiaries yielded more than 50% of net return for the year. In November 1920 PPG stockholders voted unanimously to fold the company's subsidiaries into the parent company, making them divisions.

The 1920s were prosperous for PPG. As steel-cage and concrete-reinforced construction became the standard for building, architects were able to design structures with larger window units, and glass consumption reached record levels in the United States. During this decade, the automobile industry also began consuming more glass. The switch from the open touring car to the sedan caused an expanded need for glass, and PPG met the demand.

PPG also made several technological innovations during the 1920s. In 1924 the company switched from the batch method of making plate glass to the ribbon method. Molten glass from a constantly replenished melting furnace flowed through water-cooled shaping rollers. The glass was then cooled and cut into large plates.

In 1928 PPG first mass-produced sheet glass, using the Pittsburgh Process, which improved quality and sped production. For the first time PPG was a major supplier of window glass. The Pittsburgh Process, invented by PPG, involves drawing a continuous sheet of molten glass from a tank vertically up a four-story forming-and-cooling line. In 1928 the Creighton Process was developed. An economical process for laminating glass for automobile windshields, PPG introduced Duplate laminated safety glass through a glass-plastic unit.

In 1924 PPG produced its first auto lacquer. PPG marketed auto lacquers in a number of conservative colors. By 1929

PPG supplied "no less than 500 harmonious hues" to 40 automakers. The company had also begun using a long-lasting, fast-drying finish that Ditzler Color Company, acquired in 1928, had developed

Always seeking to diversify, in 1923 PPG began to use limestone screening, a waste product of soda ash, to manufacture Portland cement. During the Depression, PPG developed new paint and glass products. In the 1930s the company developed titanium dioxide pigments, which greatly increased the opacity of light colors. It also created fast-drying Wallhide flat paint, which made it possible to apply two coats of paint in one day. In 1934 PPG introduced Solex heat-absorbing glass. Also in 1934, it perfected a glass-bending technique which made the production of car windshields easier. In 1938 PPG introduced Herculite tempered glass. Herculite glass was several times stronger and more shatter resistant than ordinary plate glass.

Diversification paid off again during World War II for PPG. In 1940, the year before Japan attacked Pearl Harbor, the glass division had developed Flexseal laminated aircraft glass. During the war, production of automobiles was temporarily halted and building was curtailed, and PPG converted much of its production into materials for military use. Due to the shortage of raw materials during the war, PPG worked hard to develop synthetic resins, which inspired the development of plastics and high-performance paints and industrial coatings.

During the 1950s car production and construction of new homes and glass-and-steel buildings exploded. PPG stepped up production to meet demand, and continued to diversify. Fiber glass had been a laboratory novelty until the 1930s. By 1950, however, it was being used in decorative fabrics and for insulation. In 1952 PPG opened its fiber glass business, making both textiles and reinforcements.

Also during the 1950s, PPG developed lead-free house paints. In 1951, it created the first latex-based interior paint. Three years later it brought a latex exterior house paint to the market. PPG was also one of the first companies to produce a no-wax car finish, and its chemical division introduced several new products, including a swimming pool purifier.

In 1955 PPG's sales topped $500 million. It employed 33,000 people in seven glass plants, three glass-fabricating plants, two speciality plants, two fiber glass plants, 17 coating and resins plants, and five chemical plants. In the early 1960s PPG produced materials for the building, transportation, appliance, container, boating, textile, paper, television, and chemicals industries. In 1963 it became the first U.S. company to manufacture float glass, used in place of plate glass by architects.

During the early part of the 1960s a heavy capital-investment program moved the company toward $1 billion in sales, a goal it reached in 1968. In 1968 the company also changed its name to PPG Industries, to reflect its size, diversification, and global presence. In 1963 PPG introduced Herculite K, glass three to five times more shatter resistant than ordinary window glass. Herculite K became popular for residential storm- and sliding-door units because of its low cost.

During the mid-1960s the company developed a coating process called electrodeposition. Electrodeposition involves submerging positively charged metal parts in a tank containing negatively charged paint particles suspended in water. The opposite charges attract each other, and the metal is coated more uniformly than if it had been sprayed or dipped. In 1969 the Chemicals Group won the Kirkpatrick Chemical Engineering Achievement Award for developing a process for the simultaneous production of perchloroethylene, widely used in dry-cleaning, and trichloroethylene, a degreaser.

The oil embargo; the increased price of oil, natural gas, and electricity; and the dwindling production of fuels in the United States revived interest in solar energy in the 1970s. PPG was the first major corporation to develop a flat-plate solar collector, a unit first marketed in 1975. PPG has also continued to work on high-luster, long-life automotive finishes. It improved its acrylic lacquers and developed acrylic dispersion topcoat finishes with lower solvent emissions during baking, which are less harmful to the environment. In the early 1970s more Americans began to repair and refinish automobiles in order to extend a car's lifespan. PPG's Ditzler refinishes group developed easy-to-apply primers and topcoats that matched factory-applied coatings in performance and apperance.

During the 1970s tinted, insulated, and reflective plate and float glasses came to be known as "performance" glass, or "environmental" glass, and glass became the preferred material for curtain walls because it was more energy efficient and more attractive. In 1973 the last plate glass production line was phased out and was replaced by the float glass production method. Also in 1973, Wallhide Microflo consumer paints were introduced. The Microflo process created air pockets in paint films that helped reflect light more efficiently; it also produced easy-to-apply paint with a smooth, washable surface. In 1975 PPG continued to broaden its color line by introducing a new custom-tinting system for consumer paints called the DesignaColor System.

In 1975 PPG established a fifth division, plastic fabricating, and closed several outmoded plants. The corporation also restructured its marketing organization—disbanding the merchandising division established by John Pitcairn in 1896—and continued to develop high-performance glasses, coatings, and fiber glass products. In 1976 PPG reached $2 billion dollars in sales.

PPG's biomedical systems division was established in 1986 and 1987 with the acquisition of medical-electronics operations from Honeywell, Litton Industries, and Allegheny International. The group produced computer-assisted cardiac recording equipment, patient-monitoring systems, electrocardiogram instruments, defibrillators, and related products for the health-care industry.

The drop in the U.S. auto and construction markets during the late 1980s hurt PPG's sales. Auto makers are PPG's largest customers, and fluctuations in that market reduced the company's profits. In 1989 the company's earnings dropped 1%, interrupting a six-year upward trend. Nevertheless, Vincent A. Sarni, chairman and chief executive officer of PPG Industries, felt PPG was making progress toward goals set for the ten years 1985 to 1994. On February 26, 1990, *Barron's*, reported that "The company has stayed consistently ahead of a goal to show an average annual return on equity of 18%." Sarni believed that by 1994 PPG would reach targeted annual sales of $8 billion even without acquisitions.

In 1989 PPG acquired Olympic stains and paints and Lucite paints to expand significantly its standing as a leading producer of architectural finishes. In 1990 the company acquired its partners' interests in Silenka, a Dutch fiber glass producer. PPG has planned for sustained growth. The company had placed a continuing emphasis on the development of high-technology products and processes, investment in manufacturing facilities, and global expansion.

Principal Subsidiaries: Chemfill Corp.; PPG Biomedical Systems, Inc.; PPG Industries (UK) Ltd.; Silenka B.V. (Netherlands); PPG Industries (France) S.A.; PPG Vermante Pennitalia, S.p.A. (Italy); PPG Industries (Deutschland) GmbH (Germany); Transistions Optical, Inc. (51%); PPG Industries (Europe), Inc.; PPG Industries International, Inc.; PPG Canada, Inc.; Ampaspace S.R.L. (Italy, 80%); Boussois S.A. (France); Industrie Vernici Italiane S.p.A. (Italy, 65.6%); PPG Glass Fibres Ltd. (U.K.); PPG Hellige GmbH (Germany); PPG Iberica S.A. (Spain, 60%); PPG Industries Asia Pacific Ltd. (Japan); PPG Industries Taiwan Ltd. (55%); Taiwan Chlorine Industries Ltd. (60%).

Further Reading: A Concern for the Future: A History of PPG Industries, Inc., Pittsburgh, PPG Industries, [1976].

—Virginia L. Smiley

REDLAND PLC

Redland House
Reigate, Surrey RH2 0SJ
United Kingdom
(0737) 242488
Fax: (0737) 221938

Public Company
Incorporated: 1914 as the Burlesdon Brick Company
Employees: 18,025
Sales: £1.55 billion (US$2.50 billion)
Stock Exchanges: London New York

Redland is a building-materials company whose principal activities are concrete roof tiles, aggregates, stone quarrying, road surfacing materials, concrete products, and clay bricks. Concrete roof tiles, upon which Redland built its business, accounted in 1989 for 42% of its profits; Redland is the world's largest manufacturer of concrete roof tiles. Redland is the fourth-largest aggregates producer in the United Kingdom, and took 37% of its profit from these materials. Bricks made up another 12% of the profits. While Redland has made forays into related areas, including road-marking, concrete pipes, fuel distribution, waste disposal, and most recently plasterboard, the most concentrated growth has been in these three main areas. As chairman Colin Corness explained in 1979, two years after his appointment to chairmanship, "I don't think we want to have an indefinite number of new products, because I'm a great believer in restricting one's product areas, not trying to go into everything simultaneously. One wants to be the best of one's kind in a limited range." Redland is one of four leading building-materials companies in the United Kingdom, along with Tarmac, Ready-Mix Concrete (RMC), and British Plasterboard (BPB).

Redland's success lies in part in its activity outside of both the housing industry and the United Kingdom. The aggregate market, for instance, remains a steady source of income, underpinned by government-funded road-improvement programs. Moreover, the vagaries of the U.K. housing market, so vulnerable to inflation and high interest rates, do not have such a devastating effect on Redland, since over 60% of its profits come from outside of the United Kingdom.

Redland originated as Redhill Tile Company, a small company in Reigate, Surrey, where Redland's headquarters is still located. Redhill manufactured its first concrete roof tile in November 1919 and was registered as a company in January 1920. Although concrete tiles had been introduced to England from Germany around 1895, at the time of Redhill's inception a firm market for concrete roof tiles had not yet developed; slate or clay tiles were traditionally used. However, slate quarries had been going into decline around the time of World War I, and after the war the depleted work force made it difficult for the quarries to keep up with demand for roofing material. Moreover, in 1926 the General Strike kept coal from reaching clay-tile makers so that the tiles could not be cured. The strike also cut off any clay-tile supply from outside the United Kingdom, and concrete tiles broke into the market.

With the gradual acceptance in the 1930s of concrete tiles as viable roofing material, Redhill established new works outside of Surrey, in Leicestershire, Yorkshire, and Northern Ireland. However, with the outbreak of World War II the plants were either shut down or, in the case of the Surrey plant, converted by the government to manufacture munitions. After the war Redhill purchased the government machinery to make the Surrey plant the focus of the company's engineering works. In 1946 Redhill acquired two other tile companies and changed its name to Redland Tiles.

Redland began expanding overseas in 1949, when it acquired a holding in Vereeniging Tiles, a concrete-roof-tile company in South Africa. It also bought a roof-tile factory in Australia in the same year, but was forced to sell it in 1956 when the venture proved difficult to manage so far away from the home base. Redland's first significant overseas expansion, and one that continues to prosper, was its acquistion in 1954 of a majority shareholding in Braas, a concrete tile factory in Heusenstamm, West Germany. Braas had gone on to claim a major share of the tile market in West Germany, as well as to provide a stepping stone for Redland into Western European countries and eventually Eastern Europe, including East Germany, Hungary, and the Soviet Union.

Meanwhile Redland began a program of diversification, merging with or acquiring companies in activities other than tiles in the United Kingdom. In 1955 it amalgamated with Burlesdon Brick Company, formed Redland Holdings, and offered its shares to the public for the first time. In 1962 it extended its new share of the brick market by buying a controlling interest in Eastwoods, the brick manufacturers, for £6.95 million. Between 1955 and 1961 Redland bought up several concrete and stoneware pipe companies, leading to the formation of Redland Pipes. This company developed a number of innovative products, including pipes made of both concrete and glass-reinforced plastic—a combination that makes them both strong and lightweight, and that provides corrosion resistance—but Redland abandoned the manufacture of concrete pipes in 1982 and of glass-reinforced plastic pipes in 1985, because these activities were not sufficiently profitable due to overcapacity in pipe production in the United Kingdom. In 1959 Redland branched into aggregates, taking over Mountsorrel Granite Company in Leicestershire, whose quarries produced granite, and stone for road building. When, in 1966, Redland bought Inns and Company—producer of stone, sand, gravel, asphalt, and ready-mixed concrete—and consolidated its aggregates companies to form Redland Aggregates, it became one of the largest suppliers of sand and gravel in the United Kingdom. In a related field it bought two road-marking materials and equipment companies, Universal Highways in the United Kingdom in 1968 and Prismo Safety Corporation in the United States in 1969, its first toehold in the United States, and formed Prismo Universal. Prismo Universal developed a sprayplastic system of road marking, and a spraygrip process for the safety surfacing of roads but was sold by Redland to a subsidiary of Shell in 1985.

In 1969, Redland made a major move into Australia when it bought a holding in Concrete Industries (Monier) Ltd. Monier's interests were similar to Redland's, covering a broad range of concrete products including precast and prestressed concrete products, as well as tiles and pipes. In July 1987 Monier Roof Tile, in response to a threatened takeover by Equity Corporation Tasman, became briefly a majority-owned subsidiary of Redland, and in December 1987 Redland accepted the Equity Corporation Tasman offer for its shares but purchased Monier's concrete roof tile businesses for A$298 million. This base allowed Redland, in 1974, to begin developing interests in the Far East. It developed majority holdings in concrete-roof-tile companies in Indonesia and Japan, and a minority interest in companies in Malaysia, Singapore, and Thailand.

At the same time Redland set up ready-mix concrete, road surfacing, and industrial cleaning operations in the Middle East. Its first entry into industrial cleaning took place in 1971, when Redland bought Purle Brothers, a U.K. waste treatment and disposal company with industrial cleaning interests. The subsequent history of the company, renamed Redland Purle, was not a happy one; in 1981, Corness admitted that "our venture into waste disposal. . . was prone to mishap and uncertainty and tended, however unfairly, to detract from Redland's enviable reputation." After a controversial incident in 1975, when a lorry driver dumping toxic waste at Pitsea, Esssex, dumped his load out of sequence and was asphyxiated by the resulting poisionous gas when his load combined with a previously dumped load, Redland Purle was taken to court by Essex Council for engaging in activities hazardous to the environment. Redland sold the subsidiary in 1980.

The problems with Redland Purle had more to do with image than with finance, and did not affect Redland's overall financial performance in the 1970s. Indeed, Redland's growing interests outside the United Kingdom cushioned it from domestic problems such as the recession and the three-day working week in the winter of 1973–1974. Along with its newly established overseas markets in the Middle East and Far East, Redland was guaranteed steady growth in Europe, where Redland's business was reorganized in 1972, from both Braas, which kept an eye on Redland's interests in Italy, Switzerland, and Austria, and Redland-Braas-Bredero Europa, a Dutch company responsible for business in the Benelux countries and, at that time, Spain, France, and Scandinavia as well.

Redland began the 1980s with an investigation by the Monopolies and Mergers Commission into the almost four-fifths control of the U.K. concrete-roof-tile market by Redland and Marley Tile. The commission concluded that the two companies should be monitored and must inform the Director-General of Fair Trading if either planned to buy other U.K. concrete-roofing companies. This attention from the Commission may have affected Redland's acquisition strategy in the United Kingdom for some time. For instance, in 1983 it withdrew a £35 million takeover bid for the brickmakers Ibstock Johnsen because of concern that the Commission might not give approval. It did, however, acquire Cawoods Holdings in 1982 and entered a new field—fuel distribution. Cawoods handled primarily coal and oil, with a sideline in aggregates. It was affected by the 1984 miners' strike, suffering a loss of over £1 million. Cawoods's fuel distribution operation were subsumed by British Fuels, a company formed in 1987 with Redland as the majority holder, but Redland sold out entirely in 1988.

Instead of expansion in the United Kingdom, Redland concentrated on large-scale growth in the United States. In 1978 it bought Automated Building Components (ABC) in Miami for US$27 million. ABC manufactured prefabricated timber roof trusses using Gang Nail connector plates—hence the change of name to Gang-Nail Systems. At the same time Redland bought the custom-built storm windows and double-glazing company Season-all Industries for about US$30 million. This venture was unsuccessful and Redland sold it at a loss for US$15.5 million in 1985.

Then, in 1982, Redland increased its U.S. presence when it bought a major interest in limestone quarries in San Antonio, Texas. This Texas quarry group, Boston Industries Corporation, became Redland Worth at the price of US$70.4 million and is now named Redland Stone Products. Other U.S. acquisitions have included two aggregates companies in 1986: Genstar Stone Products in Hunt Valley, Maryland, for US$317.5 million, and MPM in Colorado for US$35 million, partly funded by a one-for-four rights issue. The latter was a joint venture with the U.S. construction materials company Koppers. In June 1988 Redland bought out Koppers's share of Western-Mobile—the company's new name. With this move, Redland became one of the five largest aggregates producers in the United States.

Redland's increased activity in the United States was reflected in the rapid redistribution of its profits. For instance, in the financial year of 1982–1983 the U.K. market accounted for 58% of Redland's operating profits, with virtually none coming from the United States; by 1986–1987, however, the U.S. presence accounted for a full 30% of operating profits, with the U.K market down to 40%. Admittedly this distribution has leveled off more recently; in 1989 operating profit was distributed as follows: United Kingdom 42%, Continental Europe 31%, United States 18%, and Australasia and the Far East 9%.

In 1988 Redland formed a joint venture with the Australian company CSR. The venture acquired PGH Bricks and Pipes, the leading brickmakers in Australia, for which Redland paid A$280 million for a 49% interest. The joint venture also includes the former Monier concrete roof tile businesses in Australia and New Zealand.

In the late 1980s Redland launched a persistent campaign to establish itself in the plasterboard market. Plasterboard is used for building, and is ideal for interior walls, being lightweight and a good form of insulation. Plasterboard sales were estabished at £200 million a year in the United Kingdom, and in the previous ten years the market expanded by about 10% a year. Amid scepticism from the financial world Redland and CSR spent £100 million in a joint venture to break into this growing and potentially lucrative industry, which until now has been dominated by BPB. In September 1989 a new plasterboard factory near Bristol began operating. Since then a three-way price war has been waged between Redland Plasterboard, BPB, and Knauf, a German plasterboard manufacturer also trying to muscle in on the market. In 1990 CSR left the joint venture and Lafarge took an 80% shareholding, leaving Redland with a 20% interest in an enlarged business which includes Lafarge's major plasterboard business in France.

Having established a major presence in the concrete-roof-tile market in Germany, Australia, and the United States—the market in the latter is particularly strong as the construction industry is looking for non-flammable alternatives to timber shingles in areas like California and Florida where fire risk is high—Redland is now making the most of political developments in its search for a new market. Following the thawing of the Cold War, the destruction of the Berlin Wall, and the democratization of Poland, Redland—with the help of Braas—has set up a deal to upgrade existing and build new roof-tile factories in the Soviet Union, Hungary, and Poland. Although Redland has only a 40% interest in these ventures, there is great growth potential given the poor condition of buildings in these countries.

Redland has a reputation for being a safe company, with slow but steady growth and few financial setbacks. The combination of careful expansion into a few related activities and the establishment of strong markets overseas so that it is not dependent on the performance of any one economy has proved a successful strategy. Redland's unexpected move into plasterboard and into the new Eastern European market adds a surprising but welcome spice to its softly softly approach to the building-materials business.

Principal Subsidiaries: Redland Aggregates Limited; Redland Bricks Limited; Redland Engineering Limited; Redland of Northern Ireland Limited; Redland Plasterboard Limited (20%); Redland Properties Limited; Redland Readymix Limited; Redland Roof Tiles Limited; Redland Technology Limited; Ready Mixed Concrete (Eastern Countries) Limited (50%); Bramac Dachstein Ges.mbH (Austria, 24.4%); RBB NV (Belgium, 50%); B&C Danmark A/S (Denmark, 16.9%); Redland Granulats GIE (France); Lafarge Europlâtre SA (France, 20%); Coverland SA (France, 42.7%); VÁÉV-Bramac Kft (Hungary, 12.7%); Braas Italia S.p.A. (Italy, 50.8%); Zanda A/S (Norway, 49%); Lusoceram-Empreendimentos Cerâmicos SA (Portugal, 47%); Redland Ibérica SA (Spain, 47%); Industrias Transformadoras del Cemento Eternit SA (Spain, 47%); Öbrebro Kartongbruk AB (Sweden, 20%); Braas & Co. GmbH (Germany, 50.8%); Genstar Stone Products Company (U.S.A.); Monier Roof Tile Inc. (U.S.A.); Redland Stone Products (U.S.A.); Western-Mobile Inc. (U.S.A.); Monier PGH Limited (Australia, 49%); P.T. Monier Indonesia (60%); Nippon Monier KK (Japan, 60%); C.I. Holdings Berhad (Malaysia, 29.3%); Delmon Ready Mixed Concrete and Products Co. WLL (Bahrain, 49%); Kuwaiti British Readymix Company (Kuwait, 40%); Readymix Maroc SA (Morocco, 49%); Readymix Muscat LLC and Premix LLC (Oman, 40%); Readymix Qatar Limited (Qatar, 49%); Readymix Gulf Limited (United Arab Emirates, 40%); CPCA-Monier (Thailand, 20%); Zanda AB (Sweden, 49%); Teewen BV (Netherlands); RBB Dakpannen BV (Netherlands).

Further Reading: "Redland PLC; A Survey of the Company and Its Activities from 1919–1969," *Redland Record,* Number 26 [1969]; Roberts, John, "Colin Corness is the man 'with too much power,' " *Financial Weekly,* September 21, 1979; Lynn, Matthew, "Plasterboard Set-to," *Business,* March 1990.

—Tracy Chevalier

RMC GROUP P.L.C.

RMC House
Coldharbour Lane
Thorpe, Egham, Surrey TW20 8TD
United Kingdom
(0932) 568833
Fax: (0932) 568933

Public Company
Incorporated: 1930 as Ready Mixed Concrete
Employees: 25,709
Sales: £2.57 billion (US$4.15 billion)
Stock Exchange: London

RMC Group is the largest supplier of ready-mixed concrete in the world. Based in Great Britain, the corporation has subsidiaries in ten countries around the world. In the United Kingdom, RMC is the leading supplier of sand and gravel for the construction industry. The company has also diversified into the retail builders' market, leisure, roadstone, and concrete products.

Before World War II builders doubted that ready-mixed concrete could be successfully delivered to construction sites, although ready-mixed is more convenient than mixing on the spot. Their skepticism stemmed partly from the failure of ready-mix ventures in the United States—in the days before self-agitating cement trucks the concrete was often rock hard by the time it arrived at the site. When a truck mixer that inhibited crystallization was invented in the United States in 1926, Danish engineer Kjeld Ammentorp invested in the new industry in England.

Ammentorp built his first plant at Bedfont, in a pit on land owned by the builders' suppliers Hall and Company. With money from friends in Denmark, Ammentorp incorporated his business, Ready Mixed Concrete, in July 1930. The Bedfont location was ideal not only because it was close to London, where new construction was booming, but also because supplies of aggregates, the raw materials needed for mixing concrete, were abundant in the area. By building the plant directly in the pit, Ammentorp eliminated the need to haul materials.

Building the plant took more time than expected. Permission to build was slow in coming, and the first concrete to pave the yard and the loading bay was not poured until February 1931. Further delays occurred when parts had to be imported from Scandinavia. The completed structure was primitive. Gravel had to be hauled by chain-and-bucket elevators that broke down often. Early workers recalled working through the night with only the warmth of whiskey and rum to spur them on. The production process itself was crude—as one employee recalled in *The Readymixers,* weighing and measuring sand, ballast, and cement and adding water was a hit-or-miss process.

Demand for the new product was not high since the public was not yet convinced the ready-mix method worked. Government road-improvement projects set up to ease the unemployment caused by the stock market crash and ensuing Depression gave Ready Mixed Concrete some work. As profits slowly increased, Ammentorp increased the size of his truck fleet by buying agitators from Denmark.

World War II brought RMC's growth almost to a halt. Although there were a few new contracts for air-raid shelters and emergency construction work, general construction declined. When Ammentorp and other members of the staff were called up for military duty, operations nearly ceased until the end of the war.

The war's devastation of Europe offered many opportunities for the construction industry and those businesses that serviced it. Before taking advantage of the situation, however, Ammentorp had to deal with three challenges: replacing worn-out equipment, overcoming the increasing number of competitors, and building up the supplies of cement that had been depleted by wartime rationing. Ammentorp's salesmanship produced a pretax profit of £9,000 by 1950, when work began on a new Bedfont plant. A year later, Ready Mixed Concrete increased its output by 50% and its profit by 100%.

About the time that Ammentorp was leaving his business to become a soldier, an Australian accountant named Sam Stirling met Bill Freeman, a lawyer from Sidney, on a plane ride in New Guinea. The two men eventually became partners in a venture to supply and deliver ready-mixed concrete in Australia. The company was registered as Ready Mixed Concrete of Australia, and Stirling designed the bright orange diamond-shaped logo that is still in use today.

Like its counterpart in Great Britain, Ready Mixed of Australia suffered a series of losses until 1946. Then Stirling began to think about expanding overseas, in Europe. Stirling was a charismatic man who favored a seat-of-the-pants management style. He appreciated the same traits in other people as well. Bryan Kelman, a young British engineer who had worked with Ready Mixed of Australia on a project in Canberra, came upon Stirling adjusting some of the company's equipment one day when he was visiting the office. Not knowing that Stirling was the owner, Kelman demanded that he leave the equipment alone and leave the premises. Even when Stirling assured Kelman that he did indeed belong there, Kelman held his ground. Impressed, Stirling convinced Kelman to work for him at twice his current pay and sent him to Great Britain to assess the ready-mix market.

After arriving in England in April 1951, Kelman opened a company bank account and met with John Gauntlett, a corporate lawyer in the firm of Linklaters and Paines, to draw up the papers for the formation of Stirling Readymix Concrete. Gauntlett became an important link between the new company and the London business community and eventually became deputy chairman. When Kelman could not find investors for the new company, Stirling came to London himself. But even his charisma and business acumen couldn't convince British financiers that ready-mixed concrete could be a viable industry. Stirling had to get funds from the Australian business community.

With the new funding, Kelman purchased a plant in Liverpool and moved it to Poplar, where operations began in April 1952. Stirling assigned Kelman to convince Ammentorp to sell the now-prosperous Ready Mixed Concrete to the Australian company. Early in 1952, Ammentorp sold his company to Stirling for £92,500, and Stirling Readymix Concrete became Ready Mixed Concrete, based in Great Britain. Ammentorp stayed on as a board member for six years and then left England and the company he had founded.

Kelman returned to Australia, and Stirling sent for Norman Davis, Frank Nugent, and Alf Smith from the Australian operation to sell ready-mixed concrete to still-skeptical customers in England. Ammentorp had not always been prompt in his deliveries and Stirling wanted to change public perception as soon as possible. An opportunity to do so came when the engineering department of a local council hired RMC to fill miles of scrapped tram lines. This new account provided daily work for the company for four years, and the orange trucks became a familiar sight running from the plant to the tram lines.

While Alf Smith remained in London as the chief executive and Davis was put in charge of the Poplar plant, Nugent was busy in the Midlands, setting up the company's first production plant at Queslett, about five miles from Birmingham. While there, he hired a civil engineering graduate named John Camden. When Nugent was sent to Rio de Janiero to supervise international expansion there, Camden was left in charge of the Queslett operation.

Building licenses and controls in the United Kingdom were lifted in 1954, and the postwar reconstruction intensified. RMC grew, often purchasing the plants and equipment of failed competitors. Jim Owen, a Welsh site engineer, and Norman Grant, a technical engineer, joined the company during this time. Both would become RMC executives in the future.

Also in the early 1950s, RMC expanded to continental Europe, although the move was not planned. A deal had been struck with Kellogg, an American contracting firm, for RMC-Australia to pour concrete in Tasmania. While the RMC engineers were waiting for specially ordered equipment to be delivered, Kellogg backed out of the deal. Since the equipment was in transit in West Germany, RMC management in Sydney decided to set up shop there. John Camden established a plant in Düsseldorf. Although postwar Germany was a natural market for the construction industry, exceedingly harsh winters meant little work for RMC. It was four years before the company was ready to build another German plant, this one north of Düsseldorf.

In 1955, Alf Smith returned to Australia and Bryan Kelman was named chairman and chief executive of RMC. A strong proponent of expansion, Kelman aggressively sought mergers with other companies. For part of 1959, RMC opened one new plant in the United Kingdom every ten days. The company expanded just as dramatically in West Germany, where each new plant that opened was formed into a separate company, and also moved into Jamaica and Austria.

In 1961, a lawyer named Hermann Warmke joined the company to handle contracts, personnel, and insurance. Amazed at the lack of organization, Warmke set up regular working hours and a holiday schedule.

A move into Italy was RMC's first unsuccessful expansion. The company closed a production plant in Milan when operating problems mounted, and when a construction job was repeatedly stalled because contractors hit buried Roman ruins, RMC sold or closed its other Italian interests too.

Another less than satisfactory venture was RMC's partnership with two German firms, Rheinisch Kalksteinwerke Wulfrath (RKW), a ready-mix producer, and Dyckerhoff, a major supplier of cement, an important component of concrete. Under the name Beton Union, the three companies built 30 plants, set up so as not to compete with each other. Eventually, this arrangement cut into everyone's profit, and in 1964 RMC pulled out of the union over strategy disagreements. RKW followed suit in 1968. Dyckerhoff then entered the ready-mix market, forcing RMC to invest in the cement business to protect its own supplies. Cement has not been a profitable part of the corporation, however; stiff competition and stringent pollution-control regulations have kept Readymix Zementwerke from producing at capacity.

During the 1960s, ready-mix technology improved. RMC engineer Norman Grant developed the Cusum production method that allowed concrete to be tested within 24 hours rather than days. The company also developed and patented a hydraulic driving device for truck mixers. To ensure its future growth, RMC began to explore sea dredging as an alternate source of gravel as resources were depleted.

In May 1962 the rising cost of operations forced RMC to become a public company. The following winter was a difficult one: below-freezing weather curtailed production and a fire destroyed the Vienna plant. In addition, Sam Stirling's health was failing rapidly. Nevertheless, RMC expanded into Israel, a move that eventually added £11 million annually to company profit. By the end of 1962, RMC had 19 subsidiary companies and 80 plants in the United Kingdom that were supplying a quarter of the country's ready-mixed concrete. The company payroll listed over 800 employees, approximately 300 of whom were owner-drivers. When their self-employed status was challenged, England's High Court decided in RMC's favor and the drivers are still independent.

By 1963 tension between the Australian and British factions of the company peaked. The Australian directors believed that management in Great Britain had become too independent, and set about making plans to sell their shares to another company. In a boisterous board meeting, Kelman offered to top the Australians's asking price by selling 2.8 million shares to institutions and investors instead of to a single buyer. The shares brought £7.5 million.

Under Kelman's chairmanship, the newly independent Ready Mixed Concrete continued to expand. Plants were opened in Northern Ireland and Wales in the early 1960s. During 1963, RMC completed eight corporate acquisitions and formed a partnership with SOPEAL, a small company in Paris, to gain a foothold in France. The company even made an unsuccessful bid for the original Australian company. As the decade wore on, however, the British Labour Party's opposition to firms taking business outside the country made foreign expansion difficult.

In 1965 Bryan Kelman decided to accept an offer to work for the Australian firm that had acquired Ready Mixed Concrete of Australia. After extensive discussions, the board of directors brought John Camden back from Europe and appointed him chief executive. Bob Northcott took Kelman's place as chairman of the board.

As the top executive, Camden's style was very different from Bryan Kelman's; he conducted business more formally. Camden's first objective was to move the company away from its centralized management and give more responsibility to the regional managers. Under Camden's plan, the United Kingdom was divided into regions, and each company was run by general and departmental managers. The result was that local operating companies kept their own identities, and the central office became less involved in their daily operations. The reorganization was unpopular with some senior officers, who resigned.

In 1966 RMC moved into the Republic of Ireland with a ready-mixed concrete plant at Palmerston, to the northwest of Dublin. Despite continuing strife in the country, RMC's business interests thrived and the company acquired other Irish businesses. In Great Britain, RMC acquired a 50% stake in St. Alban's Sand and Gravel. The company also moved into Berlin, where it eventually bought out the city's largest producer of ready-mix concrete.

In 1968 an explosion in a high-rise apartment building that had been built by RMC's joint-venture subsidiary, Taylor Woodrow–Anglian, killed several people. RMC's industrial work ceased until new design criteria for such buildings were approved by the British Ministry of Housing. Litigation stemming from the accident lasted well into the 1980s, and in 1985 RMC sold its shares to Taylor Woodrow. Founder Sam Stirling died in 1968 and was buried in his native Australia.

Early in the same year, RMC entered a takeover fight for Hall and Ham River, a builders' merchant and the biggest supplier of aggregates in southeastern Great Britain. Redland, a major building materials group, made numerous offers to purchase Hall and Ham. RMC executives watched from the sidelines until Redland eventually gave up. The weakened Hall and Ham accepted an offer from RMC, which made the company the leading producer of concrete aggregates in the United Kingdom. Although the purchase was worthwhile because of the aggregates it brought to RMC, management spent many hours cleaning up the disarray in Hall and Ham's operations.

As part of the Hall and Ham deal, RMC acquired a large home called "the Grange at Thorpe" in Surrey. In 1969, the Grange was turned into a technical and training center with Joe Dewar as its first director. The first class included 1,000 Hall and Ham employees who were retrained in RMC methods. The Grange was eventually expanded to include a group training center and a laboratory complex.

Toward the end of the decade, RMC formed a consortium with several other concrete aggregate companies to speed up the excavation of the Queen Mary Reservoir in Sunbury. For the first time, management acknowledged public concern about the industry's effects on the environment. At a shareholders' meeting, Chairman of the Board Bob Northcott warned that RMC would have to start restoring excavation areas even though it would be time-consuming and expensive. Acquisitions during this time included an aggregate business and a ready-mix company in Germany that were then combined to form Ready Mix Kies.

By the 1970s, RMC was the world's largest producer of ready-mix concrete, and highly profitable. The construction industry had accepted not only ready-mixed concrete, but also higher prices for it, and no expensive new plant-building projects were planned.

One of the people who had come to RMC with the Hall and Ham River merger, Tim Hartwright, took Northcott's concerns about the restoration of gravel pits seriously. Hartwright suggested building a safari and water park at one of the worked-out pits. After he and several others visited theme parks in the United States, the company constructed Thorpe Park near the Grange. RMC's financial director, Alan Endsor, was especially pleased with the new venture since he had been recommending that the company begin to diversify its interests. Although RMC encountered some public resistance to the idea at first and a period of low sales in ready-mixed concrete kept the cash flow down, Thorpe Park finally opened in 1979 and went on to become one of Great Britain's top-ten tourist attractions.

In 1972, RMC commissioned a new ten-story corporate office on London Road in Staines and opened a plant in Hong Kong. Bob Northcott retired in 1973 and John Camden became chairman of the board while retaining his position as chief executive. Soon afterward, the economic recession fueled by the oil shortage hit the construction industry. At the same time, the British government placed restraints on business in an attempt to curb inflation. In 1973 Anthony Barber, the Conservative chancellor, introduced an emergency budget designed to slow what he is quoted in *The Readymixers* as calling the building industry's "obscene gains." A miners' strike and the imposition of a three-day work week exacerbated RMC's financial problems. West German operations were also hard-hit by the recession. Industrywide, ready-mix production slumped by 12%. Competition became so fierce that some suppliers were selling concrete at prices below cost. To reduce some of its short-term loan commitments, RMC decided to sell the recently completed corporate office in Staines for £9 million.

By 1976 RMC's finances had improved slightly, and the company began to look for other markets and products that were not as dependent on the construction industry. At the same time, the company explored the possibilities of expansion to the American ready-mix market. Peter Young, RMC's director for corporate planning, was directed to spend five years appraising available growth options. Young looked at three options: first, RMC could continue to use its current business plan; second, the company could expand its conventional businesses; or third, the company could move into new geographical areas and new product markets. Young concluded that RMC would be best advised to expand its traditional business into new geographical areas and expand into new products at home. RMC had already experimented with some diversification. One of its subsidiaries, Hall Containers, disposed of dry and liquid industrial waste. Depleted gravel pits at Kingsmead had been turned into a fishing project, and the theme park at another site, at Thorpe had proven to be successful.

Young's recommendations were put into action immediately. RMC moved into the United States with the purchase of Piedmont Concrete in North Carolina in 1979, and eight months later RMC bought Ewell Industries in Lakeland, Florida. The company entered another new market in March 1979 when it bought the Katelise Group, a do-it-yourself home-improvement business that operated 14 Great Mills Superstores in the southern and southwestern sections of England. By the end of 1979, RMC had also bought the Regent Warehouses chain. RMC entered the service industry when it purchased a 51% share in C. Rowbotham & Sons, an insurance brokerage, that same year. RMC acquired the remainder of the company in 1983. In December 1979, RMC purchased Lander Alarm Company, an electronic security and alarm business in Scotland. The company also joined an oil- exploration consortium led by Arpet Petroleum, a subsid-iary of Atlantic Richfield Company.

Diversification on a large scale came when RMC's ready-mix business was under fire by the government. During the early years of the recession, RMC and other ready-mix companies had made secret agreements to share business in order to keep themselves afloat. When this practice was discovered in an Office of Fair Trading investigation, the companies were brought before the Restrictive Practices Court. The businesses involved were reprimanded and future agreements were banned. A few years later, a Monopolies and Mergers Commission investigation caused more concern. At the time, RMC controlled one-third of the market and company executives were prepared for the worst. However, the commission concluded that while RMC's business did constitute a monopoly, it was not harmful to public interest.

Although effects of the recession were still being felt during the early 1980s, RMC continued to acquire new businesses. The company moved into Spain through a merger with Asland SA that produced Readymix Asland. Acquisitions in Florida also continued. In February 1981, RMC's management was restructured into four sectors: concrete and aggregates, trading and environmental, services and financial, and general industries. That same year, the company changed its name from Ready Mix Concrete to RMC Group.

By 1982 RMC's profits reached £55 million despite some problems. Expansion of the do-it-yourself chain was slower than expected, and business in West Germany and Austria slumped. Government restraints caused a construction lag in France, and RMC plants in Ireland registered their first losses. Although the British and European construction industries remained slow throughout the decade, RMC increased its profits through the aggregate business and its U.S. plants. The insurance subsidiary and some other new acquisitions were also profitable. Efforts to restore its gravel pits led RMC to new profit-making ventures, including growing grapes for wine and evening primroses in a joint venture with Germplasm Resource Management, for their oil.

At the end of 1982, RMC acquired Peakstone, a limestone producer in Derbyshire. The following year proved to be the company's best in a long time as the West German businesses finally started to prosper. A road-building program in the United Kingdom resulted in lucrative contracts for RMC, and the company's security and alarm subsidiaries in Scotland continued to thrive. In 1984 a modern ready-mix concrete plant was built in Birmingham, and the old plants in Bordesley and Queslett were closed. In the United States, RMC took over Metromont Materials in South Carolina and moved into Atlanta, Georgia, in 1985. In 1986, Jim Owen replaced John Camden as group managing director. Camden remains chairman of the board.

In the latter 1980s several events put RMC in an unfavorable light. In the summer of 1989, at least 60 people were killed when an RMC dredger rammed a pleasure boat on the Thames River. In February of the same year, Anthony Hulett, an area manager, and Tony Lewis, a plant manager, were indicted by the Office of Fair Trading for violating the bans on unlawful agreements. Plans for RMC to excavate the Test Valley in Hampshire has brought an outcry by prominent environmentalists.

Protecting the environment seems to be the greatest challenge that RMC, which expanded since it was founded and then diversified to meet the challenge of growth in a mature market, faces in the future.

Principal Subsidiaries: Lieferbeton Ges. mbH (Austria); N.V. Readymix-Belgium SA; RMC France SA; Readymix Asland SA (Spain, 50%); RMC Industries Corporation (U.S.A.); Atlas Aggregates Limited; Butterley Aggregates Limited; Hall Aggregates (Eastern Counties) Limited; Northern Aggregates Limited; St Albans Sand & Gravel Company Limited; Scottish Aggregates Limited; South Coast Shipping Company Limited; Western Aggregates Limited; Quickmix Concrete Company Limited; Readicrete Limited; Ready Mixed Concrete (Eastern Counties) Limited (50%); Ready Mixed Concrete (East Midlands) Limited; Ready Mixed Concrete (Lincolnshire) Limited; Ready Mixed Concrete (London) Limited; Ready Mixed Concrete (Northern) Limited; Ready Mixed Concrete (North West) Limited; Ready Mixed Concrete (Scotland) Limited; Ready Mixed Concrete (South-Coast) Limited; Ready Mixed Concrete (South East) Limited; Ready Mixed Concrete (South-West) Limited (51%); Ready Mixed Concrete (Thames Valley) Limited; Ready Mixed Concrete (Transite) Limited; Ready Mixed Concrete (Wales) Limited; Ready Mixed Concrete (Western) Limited; Ready Mix Concrete (West Midlands) Limited; Ready Mixed Concrete (Yorkshire) Limited; Clugston Asphalt Limited; Dimensional Store Limited; General Asphalt Surfacing Limited; Lincs. Surfacing Contractors Limited; McLaren Limited; North West Aggregates Limited; North West Surfacing Limited; RMC Concrete Products Limited; RMC Industrial Minerals Limited; RMC Mortars Limited; RMC Roadstone Limited; RMC Roadstone Products Limited; RMC Surfacing Limited; Roadstone Surfacing Limited; Shap Concrete Products Limited; Springett Coated Stone Limited; Thos. W. Ward Roadstone Limited; Western Roadstone Limited; Wotton Concrete Products Limited; Wotton Roadstone Limited; Rombus Materials Limited; RMC Engineering & Transport Limited; RMC Technical Services Limited; Great Mills (Retail) Limited; Great Mills (Central) Limited; Great Mills (East) Limited; Great Mills (North) Limited; Great Mills (South) Limited; Durox Building Products Limited; RMC Panel Products Limited; Readymix Drypack Limited; Leisure Sport Limited; Hales Waste Control Limited; RMC Group Services Limited; RMC Finance Limited; Rombus Insurance Brokers Limited.

Further Reading: Cassell, Michael, *The Readymixers,* London, Pencorp Books, 1986.

—Mary F. Sworsky

SEKISUI

SEKISUI CHEMICAL CO., LTD.

4-4, Nishitenma 2-chome
Kita-ku, Osaka 530
Japan
(06) 365-4122
Fax: (06) 365-4385

Public Company
Incorporated: 1947 as Sekisui Sangyo
Employees: 9,316
Sales: ¥504.22 billion (US$3.51 billion)
Stock Exchanges: Tokyo Osaka Nagoya Kyoto Hiroshima Fukuoka Sapporo Niigata Frankfurt Amsterdam

A member of the Sanwa Group, Sekisui Chemical is the largest synthetic resin processing company in Japan. The company manufactures chemicals and plastic products, including polyvinyl chloride (PVC) and various resins for film, joints, pipes, and plates, and for construction and home products. Although it has entered the medical and electronics fields, its mainstay comes from products for the home and what the company refers to as "extensions of the home"—offices and automobiles. The Sekisui portion of the Sanwa Group includes Sekisui Chemical and several subsidiaries, among them Sekisui House, the largest prefabricated home builder in Japan.

A glimpse at post–World War II Japan revealed only devastation. The war left millions homeless and many others, including six million soldiers, looking for jobs. Reconstruction efforts in the economic, industrial, and political sectors, however, were effective. The reform program, led by General Douglas MacArthur through the Allied occupation of Japan, transformed the country's economy; broke up the largest *zaibatsu*, or conglomerates; provided a new sense of freedom for workers; and increased the number of business owners and managers. Recovery took hold. In this era, Sekisui Chemical Company was established as Sekisui Sangyo in Osaka, in 1947.

The company's initial products were chemicals and plastic products for home and industry. In 1948 it set up plants in Nara and Osaka. The company became the first to install an automatic plastic injection molding machine in the Nara plant.

In 1950 Japan's economy began to decline, but the Korean War soon improved things. The nation embarked on a steady path of growth. To keep up with production demands, Sekisui established a new plant in Kyoto in 1952. This was followed by two additional facilities, in Amagasaki and Tokyo in 1953. That same year, the company became listed on the Tokyo stock exchange.

In the 1960s, the plastics industry was experiencing substantial growth. International expansion was its next logical direction. In 1962 a new subsidiary, Sekisui Chemical GmbH, in Düsseldorf, was formed. In New Jersey Sekisui Products, Inc., was established in 1963. That same year, the firm also opened Sekisui Malaysia Company. Eventually, the name of this subsidiary would be changed to Sekisui Singapore (Private) Ltd.

As the company continued to develop products for the housing, industrial, and construction arenas, a new market developed: prefabricated housing. Prefabricated houses allowed components to be made in a factory before being assembled at the home site. By the close of the 1950s, the practice had caught on in Japan. Prefab housing offered a new approach to the traditional Japanese method of tediously cutting wood for a home, piece by piece, according to a carpenter's specifications; in prefab units standard lumber sizes were used.

In the early 1960s, a Sekisui engineer visited Disneyland in California, in part to see the plastic "house of the future," designed by Monsanto Company. He returned to Japan with hopes of creating a similar home, although his efforts were not successful. Like many of the first prefab houses, the new model lacked the style and comfort of conventional homes. Explained a company spokesperson in *Fortune*, of October 17, 1983, "The houses were cheap looking, and people weren't interested."

After improving initial designs to include fiberboard and aluminum panels set in steel frames, Sekisui's prefab homes were better received. In 1960 the firm set up Sekisui House Industry as an independent company. It would be active primarily in building steel-frame houses. In 1961 Sekisui House opened a plant in Shiga and began marketing its Type B, one-story prefab home. In 1962 Sekisui then introduced a new model, the two-story Type 2B. The following year, the firm changed its name to Sekisui House. The remainder of the decade saw a flurry of activity from the young company, including several new models. Among them were the Sekisui House Type E, a one-story home developed in 1965; Type F, a two-story home, also developed in 1965; Type G, a five-story house designed in 1968; and Type H, a two-story model designed in 1969.

By the early 1970s, the "unit house" entered the market as a new form of prefab housing. It differed from previous wood-frame prefabs in that it was enclosed in a steel frame; it utilized concrete and metal in its walls and ceilings. In addition, the home could be built on an assembly line in room-size segments. In 1971 Sekisui erected 260 such homes, which were termed Sekisui Heim. Each could be built in a matter of hours. While the majority of Japanese homes continued to be built by conventional methods, prefab houses have gained a good market share. In 1972 the total housing market in Japan reached a record high: two million new homes. By 1973 the company's Musashi and Nara plants were each producing 2,000 unit homes per month.

In 1970 Sekisui House built a new plant, in Kanto. The following year, the firm was listed on the Osaka and Tokyo stock exchanges. It unveiled the Terrace House and Type K House, which featured a hip roof. The firm's success in the Japanese market sparked ambitious hopes of exporting its prefab homes. In 1973 Sekisui invested in a West German plant, with plans to build 500 homes there annually. Because the houses cost more than expected, however, actual sales were closer to 120. Masaru Tanabe, president of Sekisui House, told *Fortune*, of October 17, 1983, that expectations were not met because "the Germans didn't work hard enough, so our productivity went down." After investing $7 million in the German facility, Sekisui finally gave up in 1982, and the plant was closed.

While the unsuccessful venture in West Germany may have left the company apprehensive about exporting its housing products, it did manage to build a hotel and group of college classrooms and dormitories in Nigeria in the early 1980s. It continued to make capital investments in major rural construction, setting up specialized firms along the way. The company engaged in other real estate activities, including developing and selling housing lots.

In 1972 Sekisui House listed its stock on the Amsterdam and Nagoya stock exchanges. The following year, it built a new plant in Yamaguchi. In 1977 its stock was also listed on the Frankfurt exchange. For its quality-control efforts, Sekisui Chemical was awarded Japan's prestigious Deming Prize in 1979.

In the 1980s the use of computer-aided design helped Sekisui offer more customized homes. Seated before a computer terminal with a Sekisui sales representative, customers could then view a standard model and add extra rooms, or increase the size of present rooms, all with the touch of a few buttons. After sending the order to a regional factory, the finished components could be assembled in a few hours, thanks to the company's highly automated factories. Similar to automobile factories, the plants featured assembly lines that move housing modules into an assembly area. Robots help to collect various components that are to be shipped to a building site. At the site, the structure is assembled in less than a day, although plumbing and electrical work may require another one or two weeks.

With a population of 119 million people living in a comparatively small area, about the size of California, prefab housing continued to be a viable solution for the nation's housing problem. For Sekisui, the homes' success seemed undaunted by the slowing real estate market of the 1980s. By 1982 total housing construction dropped to 1.2 million homes, yet prefab sales continued upward. Overall prefabs dominated 12% of the housing market, surpassing industry expectations. The five manufacturing plants of Sekisui House, by then the largest housing firm in Japan, built more than 40,000 houses in 1983.

At Sekisui Chemical, the recession of the early 1980s sparked a move toward diversification. Chemical companies throughout the world looked to higher-priced specialty products for their profits. Sekisui Chemical, whose sales dropped from $1,338 million in 1981 to $1,294 million in 1982, was no exception. By the end of the decade, its diverse product line would include not only home products and housing materials but agricultural and fishing products, packaging products, and automotive products. By 1984 Japanese plastic and chemical companies saw a return to higher production and profit levels; annual sales at Sekisui climbed to $1.43 billion. An agreement in 1986 with Meisei Electric helped the firm expand its home product line to include home security equipment. Throughout the mid-1980s, chemical companies that had diversified, rather than relying on basic petrochemicals, earned higher profits. Despite the declining yen, the company saw increased sales because of higher domestic demand. By 1987 sales amounted to $3.01 billion—more than double the figures of five years earlier.

Sekisui continued its diversification efforts in 1989, when it formed a joint venture with Union Carbide Chemicals & Plastics Company. The venture, Hexatec Polymers, was developed to make resins for toners used in copying machines and laser printers. The venture relied on Sekisui's technology, as well as the marketing expertise of both firms, to make the new start-up successful.

Automotive products, including parts, anticorrosive materials, and foam products, also held new promise for Sekisui. In 1989 Voltek, a division of Sekisui America Corporation, developed an extrusion coating process for use as an automotive headliner. The new method, which combined polyolefin foam and thermoplastic elastomer, was developed as an alternative to PVC material to resist cracking, heat, and fading. It was first installed on 1990 Toyota Camry and Nissan Sentra models. In addition, the company's polyvinyl butyral film, used in automotive safety glass, had gained more than half of market share.

By the end of the 1980s, Sekisui's new ventures were clearly paying off. The company began producing medical instruments and electronic equipment, such as photoelectromagnetic discs. To prepare for the coming unification of the European Economic Community, it added a new subsidiary, Sekisui International Finance, in 1989. In addition to supplying data on Europe's financial markets, the new venture was developed to handle such financial activities as loans, foreign exchanges, mergers and acquisitions, and technology transfer agreements.

Sekisui House expanded its product line to include wooden and concrete houses, as well as apartments. The firm also began work on a research institute in Kyoto in the late 1980s.

Sekisui Chemical entered the 1990s with a product line that encompassed flooring and furniture for office automation; pipes, gutters, and other construction products; industrial and automotive products; packaging materials; medical and electronic equipment; and agricultural and fishing products. Products for the home ranged from furniture to household chemicals.

Principal Subsidiaries: Sekisui Seikei Ltd.; Sekisui Machinery Co., Ltd. (80.5%); Tokyo Sekisui Shoji Co., Ltd.; Kinki Sekisui Shoji Co., Ltd.; Chubu Sekisui Shoji Co., Ltd.; Sekisui Esudain Co., Ltd.; Sekisui Kobunshi Hanbai Co., Ltd.; Kansai Sekisui Jusetsu Co., Ltd.; Tokuyama Sekisui Co., Ltd. (70%); Hokkaido Sekisui Industry Co., Ltd. (95%); Toto Sekisui Co., Ltd.; Okayama Sekisui Co., Ltd.; Kyushu Sekisui Co., Ltd. (64.6%); Sekisui Hozai Co., Ltd. (57.7%); Sekisui Hoso Co., Ltd. (60%); Hokkaido Sekisui Co., Ltd.; Sekisui Leasing Co., Ltd. (70%); Sekisui Finance

Co., Ltd.; Chushikoku Sekisui Shoji Co., Ltd.; Sekisui Nohan Co., Ltd. (60.4%); Hokkaido Sekisui Heim Co., Ltd.; Kitanihon Sekisui Heim Co., Ltd.; Tohoku Sekisui Heim Co., Ltd.; Fokushima Sekisui Heim Co., Ltd. (52.8%); Gunma Sekisui Heim Co., Ltd.; Hokuriku Sekisui Heim Co., Ltd.; Aiki Sekisui Heim Co., Ltd.; Mie Sekisui Heim Co., Ltd.; Wakayama Sekisui Heim Co., Ltd.; Chugoku Sekisui Heim Co., Ltd.; Hiroshima Sekisui Heim Co., Ltd.; Yamaguchi Sekisui Heim Co., Ltd. (75%); Ehime Sekisui Heim Co., Ltd.; Fukuoka Sekisui Heim Co., Ltd.; Nagasaki Sekisui Heim Co., Ltd.; Kyuseki Sekisui Heim Co., Ltd.; Kumamoto Sekisui Heim Co., Ltd.; Tohoku Sekisui To-You-Home Co., Ltd.; Tokyo Sekisui To-You-Home Co., Ltd.; Nagoya Sekisui To-You-Home Co., Ltd.; Osaka Sekisui To-You-Home Co., Ltd.; Sekisui America Corporation (U.S.A.).

Further Reading: Smith, Lee, ''Now Japan Moves Ahead in Prefabs,'' *Fortune*, October 17, 1983; Onosko, Tim, ''Digitized Dream Dwelling,'' *Omni*, June 1985; Ushio, Shota, and Paula Block, ''Japanese Specialty Chemicals: The Coming Wave,'' *Chemical Week*, July 9, 1986; Levy, Emanual, ''P/A Technics Industrialized Housing,'' *Progressive Architecture*, February 1987.

—Kim M. Magon

THE SHERWIN-WILLIAMS COMPANY

101 Prospect Avenue, Northwest
Cleveland, Ohio 44115
U.S.A.
(216) 566-2000
Fax: (216) 566-3310

Public Company
Incorporated: 1884
Employees: 16,726
Sales: $2.12 billion
Stock Exchange: New York

The Sherwin-Williams Company is a producer and distributor of paints, coatings, paint sundries, various home decorative items, adhesives, labels, and color cards. It also produces motor vehicle finishes and refinish products, as well as industrial finishes for original equipment manufacturers of metal, plastic, and wood products. Its products are sold through 1,865 company-operated stores.

The story of The Sherwin-Williams Company began in 1866, when Henry Sherwin used his life savings of $2,000 to buy a partnership in the Truman Dunham Company of Ohio. The firm was a distributor of pigments, painting supplies, oils, and glass. In four years, this original partnership was dissolved, and Sherwin organized a paint business with new partners, Edward P. Williams and A. T. Osborn. The new business was called Sherwin-Williams & Company.

In 1873 the company purchased its first factory, on the Cuyahoga River, in Cleveland, Ohio. The factory manufactured paste paints, oil colors, and putty. The company's first manufactured product, Guaranteed Strictly Pure Raw Umber in Oil, came off the line in that year.

The paint industry in the 1870s was radically different from what it is today. Painters had to buy the ingredients and mix their own paint each day. At this time prepared paints—paints that were ready-mixed—were concocted and sold by individual dealers who mixed a few popular colors. These premixed paints were available only during the busy spring painting season.

In those days, oil and pigment had to be ground together into a paste. The paste was then thinned with more oil, thinners, and driers. Customers brought their own containers to stores and filled them as needed. Paints had to be stirred continuously to prevent the pigment from sinking to the bottom of the container. In addition, the paint had to be used quickly or it dried out. For these reasons, paints were seldom shipped far from where they were made. The first patent for ready-mixed paint was taken out in 1867 by D.R. Averill of Newburg, Ohio; it made improvements to the existing mixing processes.

In 1877, the company developed the first patented reclosable paint can. This revolutionized the way paint could be used, and more importantly, used over a period of time.

During the 1880s the company continued to develop new products for the paint industry. At the beginning of the decade it improved its liquid paint formula. After two years of test marketing under the Osborn label, it introduced SWP—Sherwin-Williams Paint—the first mixed paint to receive considerable public acceptance.

In 1884 the partnership was dissolved and Sherwin and Williams incorporated as The Sherwin-Williams Company. In the same year, Inside Floor Paint was introduced. This new product encouraged the notion that specific paints should be used for specific purposes. During 1884, Percy Neyman was hired by Sherwin-Williams as the first paint chemist in the industry. Neyman contributed greatly to Sherwin-Williams research and development of new products for the paint industry.

Sherwin-Williams had always been committed to finding and developing new markets for paint products. In 1888, the company saw the possibility of marketing paints and coatings to the railroad industry. It opened a manufacturing facility in Chicago to serve the Pullman Company, and to better serve the farm-implement and carriage industries. In those days, Pullman required as many as 20 coats of high-quality finishes for the elaborate interiors of the Pullman cars. Sherwin hired George A. Martin, an ambitious young man to run the new facility. Martin later served as the third president of the company.

Marketing and advertising quickly became critical to the growing company. Seeing the need to make people aware of its products, in 1890 the company formed a department devoted exclusively to advertising and to publicizing Sherwin-Williams and its products. George Ford was hired to head the department. A year later, a sales agency was opened in Worcester, Massachusetts, which was the model for the company's successful concept of the "company store." In 1905, the "Cover the Earth" trademark was first introduced.

Walter H. Cottingham became the second president of the company in 1909. Sherwin then became chairman of the board of directors. Cottingham strove throughout his career to inspire his workers to attain their maximum potential. Cottingham was adept at launching successful sales campaigns. He was also known as a writer and orator and wrote a collection of "inspirational" editorials and papers on a variety of subjects.

In the early part of the 20th century Sherwin-Williams began acquiring other companies to meet the increasing demand for a variety of different paints and related products. In 1917, under Cottingham's guidance, the company bought the Martin-Senour Company, of Chicago. Three years later, in 1920, the company went public, selling $15 million in preferred stock. Proceeds from the sale were used to purchase the Acme Quality Paint Company, of Detroit; a new plant in Oakland, California; and to expand various existing facilities.

When Cottingham retired in 1922, Martin—who had become vice president and general manager in 1920—took over the leadership of the company. During Martin's tenure as president, Sherwin-Williams developed nitrocellulose lacquer and synthetic enamel. These products made possible the brilliant finishes that covered cars during the 1920s. Such products also reduced from 21 days to a few hours the drying time of newly painted cars.

George A. Martin, like Cottingham, believed in strong advertising for his company and its products. He sponsored the "Metropolitan Opera Auditions of the Air," a successful radio program that ran for years.

Also during Martin's presidency, Sherwin-Williams bought several other high-quality, nationally known companies. Among them were The Lowe Brothers Company, of Dayton, Ohio, and The John Lucas Company, of Philadelphia, Pennsylvania. Both were innovative companies.

Martin's vision focused on finding ways to expand the company and increase its profits. He believed that Latin Americans would respond favorably to high-quality paint products. In 1929 Sherwin-Williams bought the Bredell Paint Company of Havana and enlarged it. Martin expanded the company's manufacturing facilities and established plants in Buenos Aires and Sao Paulo.

For Sherwin-Williams, the early 1940s brought an opportunity to participate heavily in America's World War II effort. Sherwin-Williams, along with other paint companies, supplied camouflage paints for the armed forces. It was said that the invasion of North Africa was delayed while waiting for the delivery of camouflage paints with which to provide proper field cover. The company also received a commission to load shells, anti-tank mines, and aerial bombs. To meet this demand, the company constructed and managed a plant in Carbondale, Illinois.

In 1940, Arthur W. Steudel, a Cleveland native, succeeded George A. Martin as president. Steudel worked his way up in the company through the dye, chemical, and color division. He had many visionary ideas about paint retailing and merchandising. The company's profits increased under Steudel. He served as president until 1961, at which time he became chairman and chief executive officer.

During the 1940s, Sherwin-Williams introduced several new products to the consumer. Kem-Tone, the first emulsion-based, fast-drying paint for the do-it-yourself market was introduced in 1941 and met with remarkable success. Kem-Tone helped deal with the raw material shortage that the nation faced after the war. That same year, the company introduced the Roller-Koater, the first applicator that was not a brush. It was later developed and refined into the paint roller commonly used today.

Soon thereafter, the company introduced Kem-Glo, a porcelain-like enamel and Super Kem-Tone, a high-quality interior paint that had a synthetic rubber content. The prefix "Kem" indicated that the paints were "chemically involved materials." The development of these products was crucial to the expansion and success of the company.

During the 1950s and 1960s the company continued to grow and prosper. E. Colin Baldwin served as president from 1961 to 1969. In 1964 the Sherwin-Williams Company was listed on the New York Stock Exchange. In 1966, Sprayon Products was acquired.

In the 1970s, the company suffered substantial losses. In 1977, on revenues of $1 billion, it had a loss of $8.2 million, and dividends were suspended. Sherwin-Williams's borrowings increased dramatically. Without any debt in 1967, by 1977 Sherwin-Williams had long-term debt of $196.6 million. The following year the debt increased to $242 million. In addition, by 1978 Gulf + Western Industries held 13.47% of Sherwin-Williams's outstanding stock. Walter O. Spencer, CEO since 1971, resigned in 1978. Spencer was replaced, on an interim basis, by William C. Fine. Sherwin-Williams found a new permanent leader in January 1979, when John G. Breen became president and CEO. Breen was a former executive vice president for Gould Inc., a Minneapolis, Minnesota battery manufacturer. In a short time, Breen managed to bring the company back to financial stability and avert the threatened Gulf + Western takeover. Breen first persuaded Gulf + Western Chairman Charles Bludhorn to sell Gulf + Western's Sherwin-Williams shares. Breen convinced Bludhorn that Gulf + Western's Sherwin-Williams holdings were a liability to Gulf + Western and that Sherwin-Williams would be unable to recover financially while the threat of takeover loomed. Bludhorn was, likely, swayed to a greater extent by the fact that his Sherwin-Williams shares were no longer a sound investment. Next, Breen reshuffled Sherwin-Williams management, replacing several vice presidents. He decentralized responsibility and discontinued about 1,000 slow-selling products. Breen also cut the company's long-term debt. In the first half of 1980, Breen's policies yielded a 57% improvement in earnings over the same period in 1979.

In 1979, sales were $1.19 billion and by 1985 were $2.17 billion. Net income rose from 6¢ to $1.60 per share between 1978 and 1985. Breen served as president until 1986, when he became chairman, retaining the office of CEO. Thomas A. Commes became president.

In 1971 Sherwin-Williams introduced POLANE, a coating designed to efficiently cover metal surfaces but found to work exceedingly well on plastics as well. In 1980, Dutch Boy was acquired by the company, substantially increasing its sales. Sherwin-Williams bought the Gray Drug Stores chain in 1981, and then sold that group in 1987.

To reach markets outside the continental United States, the company formed in 1984, BAPCO, an equal partnership, with C-I-L, Inc. of Canada, a subsidiary of Imperial Chemical Industries PLC of England. That same year, Sherwin-William acquired the assets of Dupil-Color, Inc. During 1985 Sherwin Williams chemical operations were sold to PMC Specialties Group. In 1987 the company acquired the Lyons Group. In 1986 Thomas A. Commes was elected president and John G. Breen became chairman. In 1988 the company sold its interest in the BAPCO partnership to C-I-L, Inc.

During the 1980s sales of house paints decreased, notably because of the use of alternative surface finishes such as prefinished aluminum and plastic surfaces. Sherwin-Williams responded to this by substantially increasing its advertising budget from $4 million in 1989 to $15 million in 1990. Sherwin-Williams in 1990 had 20% of the home market. Time will tell if its quality products and quality service will allow it to maintain or even better that position.

Principal Subsidiaries: Sherwin-Williams Canada, Inc. (96.8%); Sherwin-Williams Automotive Finishes, Inc. (Canada); 147926 Canada Inc.; Lyon's Technological Products Ltd. (U.K.); The Sherwin-Williams Co. Resources Limited (Jamaica); Sherwin-Williams (Caribbean) N.V. (Curaçao);

Sherwin-Williams (West Indies) Ltd. (Jamaica); Sherwin-Williams Foreign Sales Corporation Limited (Virgin Islands); Sherwin-Williams Development Corp.; SWDC (Virginia), Inc.; Contract Transportation Systems Co.; Dupli-Color Products Company; Lyons Transportation Lines, Inc.; Certified Distribution Services, Inc.; Sherwin-Williams International Company.

Further Reading: Schlenberg, Fred, "Cleveland, Part I: 'Not just great, but the greatest,' " *American Paint & Coatings Journal*, January 5, 1987; Schulenberg, Fred, "Cleveland, Part II: Sherwin, Williams . . . and Fenn," *American Paint & Coatings Journal*, January 19, 1987; Schulenberg, Fred, "Cleveland, Part III: Era of the empire builders," *American Paint & Coatings Journal*, February 2, 1987; *The Sherwin-Williams Company 1988 Fact Book*, Cleveland, Ohio, The Sherwin-Williams Company, 1988; "Sherwin-Williams History," Sherwin-Williams corporate typescript, 1989.

—Virginia L. Smiley

SSANGYONG CEMENT INDUSTRIAL CO., LTD.

Ssangyong Building
24-1, Jeo-dong 2-ka
Chung-gu, Seoul
Republic of Korea
(02) 266-5151
Fax: (02) 275-7040

Public Company
Incorporated: 1939 as Samkong Fat Limited Co.
Employees: 5,221
Sales: W609.20 billion (US$899.32 million)
Stock Exchange: Seoul

Ssangyong Cement Industrial Co., Ltd. (SCIC) is the parent company of one of South Korea's largest *chaebol,* or family-owned conglomerates. Although the group's activities extend into financial services and cars, non-consumer-oriented industries such as cement, oil, and heavy machinery remain its core businesses. SCIC is the third-largest cement company in the world, yet accounts for less than 20% of the Ssangyong group's total turnover. It retains a controlling share in most of its subsidiaries and the founding family itself has retained a 30% stake in SCIC. Apart from cement, Ssangyong shares most of its industries with the other large *chaebols,* handpicked after the 1960s by the South Korean government to engineer its economic and national reconstruction policies, financed by preferential loan agreements, and long protected against foreign competition. Unlike most *chaebols,* however, it has come a long way in severing political connections and reducing crippling debt ratios.

In 1989, on the 50th anniversary of its founding, the Ssangyong group adapted its corporate logo to symbolize the twin strengths of reliability and innovation—Ssangyong means "twin dragons." The group's greatest strengths lie in knowing when to take second place—stressing after-sales service before advertising—in order to establish itself on a sound commercial basis, and in unstinting research-and-development investment to enhance quality and innovation.

The story of Ssangyong dates back to 1939, when the group's founder Kim Sung Kon, along with a few friends, established Samkong Fat Limited, a soap-manufacturing company. In the years of great scarcity following the liberation of Korea from 35 years of Japanese administration, this soap became the leading brand. A political idealist, Kim Sung Kon joined Yo Woon-Hyong's National Reconstruction party as top financial officer, at 33, thus embarking on one of the most remarkable careers in the modern history of a country known for its uniquely successful mix of government initiative and socially motivated private enterprise.

In 1947 Kim Sung Kon helped found the Koryo Fire and Marine Insurance Co., which he himself would take over in 1959 and which has since developed into a respected subsidiary with assets of US$180.3 million. It has close ties with such well-known insurance brokers and reinsurance companies as Munich Re in Germany and Willis Faber in the United Kingdom, and 150 domestic branches. In 1948 Kim set up the Kumsung Textile Co. with the aim of providing Korea's poverty-ridden people with cotton clothing. The company was successful, despite the scarcity of raw materials and treasury-induced inflation, and Kim rebuilt the factory in 1954, after it had been burnt down in the Korean War, with the help of the UN Korean Reconstruction Agency and turned it—with 30,000 looms and 250 weaving machines—into the largest textile firm in the country.

Kim's political career, always secondary to his business interests, took off with the military revolution of May 16, 1961, which led to his becoming chairman of the Financial Committee in the assembly under the Democratic Republican Party. His relationship with the military junta under president Park Chung Hee was not servile, since he opposed the latter's scheme to restrict the freedom of the press, in which he had interests, and was later fired for his part in the October 2 Revolt in which members of the cabinet sided with the opposition in order to oust the Home Affairs minister. However, he was ideally placed to implement certain aspects of President Park's first five-year plan to establish the national economy on a sounder basis and increase growth from 1.9% in 1953 and 1960 to 7.1%.

In 1962 Kim sold Kumsung Textiles in order to finance a venture into cement, starting with the construction of the world's largest single-unit cement plant at Donghae. Kim did this with the knowledge that two priorities of the five-year plan were production of oil, steel, and cement, in order to build up Korea's independence in strategic industries, and to launch the export drive which has characterized the Korean economy and which was directed actively by successive governments until the 1980s. During the 1980s the trade deficit was turned around, trade barriers and protectionism were dismantled slowly at the insistence of the United States, and new democratic structures were experimented with successfully in government.

Although the plant at Yongwol was dedicated in 1964, it is Donghae, first dedicated in 1968 with 1.7 million tons of production capacity and expanded from 1974 with another 5.6 million tons, which has become the mainstay and pride of SCIC, and of Ssangyong as a whole. Situated on limestone reserves calculated to last 200 years and serviced by the port of Pukyong nine miles away, Donghae has contributed significantly to the total profits of the group. Donghae's after-tax profits in 1988 of US $54.5 million placed it seventh among Korea's leading companies.

Bolstered by Korea's growing infrastructure and its part in the first and second five-year plans representing a strategic industry, the company grew fast enough for Kim Sung Kon to expand into areas congenial to SCIC. In 1967 he took over the Samwha Paper Co.—renamed Ssangyong Paper Co. in 1975—to produce the paper needed to pack cement. He also established the Kumsung Shipping Co.—renamed Ssangyong Shipping Co. Ltd. in 1972—to transport his cement along the Korean coast. Kim's Kumsung Industry Co. Ltd., which he had founded in 1954 after the Korean War to export his cottons, did not fare so well in the 1960s. Renamed Ssangyong Trading Co. Ltd. in 1967 and a forerunner of the present Ssangyong Corporation, licensed as a general trading company in 1975, it only started trading in earnest in goods unrelated to cement in the 1970s, during the "Miracle of the Han River," as Korea's period of rapid growth was termed.

Following the oil crisis of 1973, Kim established a joint venture with the shah of Iran to set up an oil refinery which would help in fueling Kim's cement plants. He planned a major increase in production capacity for Donghae, took over Taehan Cement in 1975, and made moves to enter heavy industry by constructing diesel engines for vessels, generators, and rolling stock. In founding Ssangyong Cement (Singapore) in Singapore in 1973 as a joint venture with a local company, he anticipated later Korean government policy requiring *chaebols* to be more competitive abroad: it was not only the first overseas capital investment by a private Korean firm at a time when foreign exchange was scarce, but it helped to reduce somewhat the reliance on domestic demand and shipments to the Middle East, both of which hit a low from 1980 to 1982. SCIC has since captured a part of the competitive and cartelized Japanese market as its leading foreign supplier as well as expanding its distribution network there.

Having spent a year with his daughter in the United States after the collapse of his political career, Kim returned to Korea following President Park's "October revitalisation reform" in 1973, a kind of amnesty, taking back the chair of SCIC and assuming the presidency of the Korea Chamber of Commerce and Industry. He died of a stroke in 1975, at age 62.

The resulting confusion caused widespread concern, not least to President Park Chung Hee, who declared that the business ought "to be kept well maintained." Shin Hyon Hwack, then president of SCIC, held a meeting with presidents of the group's other concerns and followed the wishes of Kim's wife when they appointed her eldest son, at that time not yet 30, as chairman.

The two men were entirely opposed in management style, yet Kim Suk Won has proved the equal—if not the better—of his father in expanding the group's fortunes. Total turnover increased 26 times between 1975 and 1987, from US$164 million to US$4.2 billion.

Educated at Brandeis University, Kim Suk Won first became auditor for SCIC and managing director at Ssangyong Shipping, but after a year of routine desk work, which he disliked, he told his father: "Please let me do anything I like; I want to learn by myself how the world goes. I assure you that I will return home when I reach 35."

He traveled throughout Korea, observing his countrymen's attempts to break away from poverty and low-tech industries. He then built the country's first ski slope at Yongpyeong, convinced that one day the middle classes would want to use it. They did, and still do.

Kim Suk Won's first major task on assuming the chairmanship was to complete the two projects his father had left unfinished: oil and cement expansion. The former was an uphill battle. During the 1970s, construction of the refinery proceeded at Onsan, although the National Iranian Oil Co. withdrew from the partnership in 1976, leaving a serious shortage of funds. Then, during the second oil crisis in the early 1980s when cement was also piling up in the depots, Kim's patience was rewarded when the Iranians supplied his crude at almost $3 per barrel below the OPEC price. Then equipped with the nation's largest crude-unloading facilities at Onsan, Ssangyong Oil Refining Co. Ltd. had become a major money-earner for the group, with a US$824 million turnover in 1986. It is one of the country's largest oil refiners and is expanding further into petrochemicals, despite increasingly heavy competition and the problem of oversupply which faces all the *chaebols* as they ignore government warnings to specialize rather than diversify further.

During the 1970s Kim's own strategy was to lead the group away from cement, though never ceasing investment in cement. He has expanded the cement business considerably since taking over. Aware of the value of research and technology he opened the Ssangyong Research Center in Taedok Science Town in 1975, initially to develop new types of cement and cement-related products, but also branching into ferrite magnet equipment. Most promising has been its research into ceramics used in high-precision instruments and engines. It is illustrative of the way in which SCIC stands apart from many other Korean companies, which often are plagued with the problem of production and sales outstripping technology and quality. Though production costs for ceramics are high while demand is low, Kim's refusal to hurry beyond capacity coupled with innovative research into new materials means that with ceramics SCIC is well prepared before the new market has even taken off.

Another example of Kim's ability to buck the trend is his long-standing independence of political connections, though with increasing deregulation and domestic unpopularity the loosening of political connections has become inevitable for most *chaebols*. Despite great pressure and the offer of heavy state subsidies, Kim refused to join the lucrative munitions industry in 1976 and 1977. Even when, as a *chaebol*, Ssangyong was pushed into concentrating on heavy industry in the same year, when Ssangyong Heavy Industries Co. (SHIC) was established after the takeover of a bankrupt firm to manufacture diesel engines and other machinery, Kim managed—after 11 years of loss-making—to promote this branch as the center of the machine industry, providing some of the expertise needed in the construction of internal combustion engines. The latter was central to his dream of entering the car industry.

SHIC set up Ssangyong Engine Research Institute in May 1989 to develop a new model engine. Its engines have been approved by the Classification Society and it is poised to take on the international competition. Other car parts and heavy-duty presses are manufactured by Ssangyong Precision Industry Co., which is equipped with the most advanced technology in Korea. Kim also took over Sunglee Machinery Works Ltd. in 1977 to support further his automobile plans, making it manufacture wheel discs over and above its speciality, weaving machines. He established Sunglee Electronics

Co. Ltd. in the same year to produce radio and audio equipment. Kim never attached as much importance to the audio and radio industry as did other *chaebols*.

In 1980 Kim completed his father's projects and it marked the end of his own five-year plan: 5.6 million tons of capacity were added to the plant at Donghae and the oil refinery started operating. He went on to expand the paper industry, producing tissue and sanitary paper in conjunction with Scott Paper Co. of the United States in 1979 and sanitary napkins in an agreement with Uni-Charm of Japan, so that today Ssangyong Paper is the best-known paper company in Korea. He also incorporated Ssangyong Construction Co. Ltd. separately in 1977, rather than firing many trained employees who had worked as an inhouse construction team—at Donghae and Onsan, for instance—as well as in constructing postwar rehabilitation projects. From there, the company went on to win contracts in Southeast Asia and the Middle East, including work on a record-breaking project in 1986: the tallest hotel in Singapore, a contract it would not have obtained without SCIC Singapore's reputation for reliability. Working closely with Ssangyong Engineering Co. Ltd.—established in 1978—and with the expertise of Namkwang Engineering & Construction Co. Ltd.—established in 1947 and taken over in 1986—Ssangyong Construction Co. continued to expand its interests overseas, notably in a joint venture with the Ralph M. Parsons Group of the United States in 1987 into high-tech construction fields, including nuclear waste plants.

Following his streamlining of SCIC operations by emphasising planning and the use of computers, Kim established in 1981—against the advice of his colleagues—the Ssangyong Software & Data Co., renamed Ssangyong Computer Systems Corporation in 1988, which proved its mettle in designing the management system for the Korea Olympics of 1988. Kim said he did not want to be left behind in this field.

His most obvious and profitable success story was agreeing in 1983 to buy the ailing securities firm of the Hyosung Group at a time when Korean financial services were relatively undeveloped and the Korean stockmarket rather thin. When the economy boomed in 1986 and the stockmarket was actively promoted by the economic technocrats in government, Ssangyong Investment & Securities Co. was in the right position to reap the reward: a net profit of US$6.9 million in 1986. Since then, under Koh Byung Woo, a former assistant minister of finance, it has become a co-manager of the Asian Development Equity Fund and an underwriter of Thai and Brazilian funds, establishing offices in New York, London, and Zürich. With the lifting of restrictions on direct foreign investment in 1992, the company, as one of the big five in Korea, foresaw little difficulty in consolidating its position further. It already operates a highly esteemed investment-research institute.

The 1980s were a golden age for the Korean economy, bringing three blessings: cheap dollars, cheap oil, and cheap loans. There were three successive years of 12% economic growth, starting in 1986 when wages were still low, the exchange rate was favorable, and demand was strong. Once the trade deficit had been turned to surplus, overseas investment became imperative, not least because of rising Korean labor costs and the need to get closer to overseas markets. However, between 1987 and 1990 this trend reversed: Korean exports fell because of high domestic costs and the 25% appreciation of the Korean won relative to the Japanese yen. Although the *chaebols* were once more in favor with the government as a means of boosting the slowing economy, credit controls having been eased, the gap between price and quality of products remained a problem.

Kim was aware that the only solution lay in improved efficiency, in which his record was good—per capita sales among employees rose eight times from 1975 to 1986—in better technology, a longstanding aim of his, and in more capital intensive production, something which comes naturally in his line of business. Unlike Samsung or Daewoo, in the labor-intensive electronics and textiles businesses, respectively, Ssangyong has no great need to find a cheaper source of labor in Thailand or China. At the same time, the overseas networks for most subsidiaries are already well established.

Kim's pursuit of "harmony" between "reliability" and "innovation" is perhaps the key reason for the group's steady growth. Not only does he embody a successful move towards second-generation control away from the authoritarian grip of his father, something with which other *chaebols* still have to struggle, but the group has an outstanding record in the labor disputes which have riven Korean society most damagingly since 1987. Taking his cue from his stay in the United States, he delegates authority to company presidents, does not rely on elites and encourages participation of all employees while respecting the authority of juniors, recruits employees from all regions, emphasises the public and social duties of the company, and does not favor nepotism. Only Lee Sung Won, a brother-in-law, and Kim Suk Joon, his youngest brother, are employed by the company, the former as president of Ssangyong Oil Refining Co., Ltd. and the latter of Ssangyong Construction. Kim has made it clear that he will hand over the reins to whoever is most competent.

Kim also likes to work to five-year plans, believing that without long-term planning one can only go downhill, a view borne out by recent analyses of *chaebols* less inclined to take the long-term view. In 1976 the group was the first in Korea to introduce a management information system, which resulted immediately in the stabilization of the quality of its cement. This was followed by the Corporate-Identity Program in 1978 and the Corporate-Culture System in 1988 following two years' research by the planning and development office. These were designed to turn Kim's systematic approach and liberal management into part of a corporate culture unique to Ssangyong. The shift in focus towards heavy machinery and high-tech industries was not made without a carefully directed change in the corporate climate to back it.

While Ssangyong continues to produce cement and oil, Kim has invested massively in car production since 1986 and intends to promote it as the key business of the 1990s in line with government plans to turn Korea into a net car exporter. He took over Dong-A Motor in 1986, an ailing car manufacturing firm with a deficit of US$5.5 million. In order to produce his X-car, a four-wheel-drive wagon-style jeep, he had to start from scratch, knowing the company would be in the red for at least three years. When the initial X-car prototype was completed, Kim rejected it because its balance was faulty. The purchase of 80% equity in the U.K. company

Panther has provided the necessary technical expertise to perfect the model, and also provides an opening into Europe, the intended market for the model. Through Panther, a successful high-class sports car, the Solo II, has been built and marketed selectively in various countries. Furthermore, with help from Mercedes Benz and Nissan and its own diesel technology, Ssangyong Motor Company was doing well with special-purpose vehicles like dump trucks. It had no plans to enter the extremely competitive passenger-car market as Korea's fourth car producer until 1991, when the step-by-step approach will have produced the necessary consolidation of expertise, for Kim is well aware that one wrong move can spell trouble for the entire concern. Kim does not believe in grafting foreign technology nor in selling below cost to boost production and sales—illustrated by the fact that although the Ssangyong group ranks sixth in sales it is in fourth place in terms of profits. Is Kim being too optimistic in predicting an increase in domestic car registration to ten million in the near future? Though his more experienced competitors were recently saved by a surge of domestic demand, the problem of oversupply remains acute. On the other hand, reliability and innovation, backed by the might of SCIC, may yet save the day.

Principal Subsidiaries: Ssangyong Corporation; Ssangyong Oil Refining Co. Ltd; Ssangyong Construction Co. Ltd; Ssangyong Investment & Securities Co. Ltd.; Ssangyong Motor Company.

Further Reading: Ssangyong News, February 1988; *South Korea: Financial Times Supplement*, May 16, 1990; *Ssangyong Business Group,* Seoul, Ssangyong, 1990.

—Marc Du Ry

TARMAC PLC

Hilton Hall
Essington, Wolverhampton WV11 2BQ
United Kingdom
(0902) 307407
Fax: (0902) 307408

Public Company
Incorporated: 1903 as TarMacadam (Purnell Hooley's Patent) Syndicate Limited
Employees: 32,000
Sales: £3.53 billion (US$5.69 billion)
Stock Exchange: London

Tarmac is the United Kingdom's largest representative of the construction and building materials industries. In a sector exposed more than most to fluctuations in economic cycles, the company is reliant to a large degree upon government expenditure. Tarmac has achieved its success more through assiduous management strategy than through rapid volume growth. Each of the company's seven divisions is a separate profit center. The company has developed and maintained a somewhat conservative corporate image, despite dramatic diversification and expansion, particularly toward the end of the 20th century. With divisions leading the British markets in quarrying, construction, housing, and building materials, Tarmac has been transformed into a widespread and growing company.

In 1901, the county surveyor of Nottingham, E. Purnell Hooley, noticed a dustless, unrutted patch of road as he was leaving an iron works. Inquiries revealed that a barrel of tar had burst and the spillage had been covered with slag. Immediately grasping its potential, Hooley began to experiment. A British patent for the process of mixing tar with slag was obtained in 1903, and by the middle of the year a length had been laid in an area where traffic was particularly heavy. In the following year, a local newspaper, the *Newark Advertiser,* reported that the area was "as good today as when new." The new material was christened "tarmac."

In conjunction with John Parker, Hooley incorporated Tar-Macadam (Purnell Hooley's Patent) Syndicate Limited in June 1903, and became its chairman. Despite the support of the natural roadstone industry, for whom Hooley's invention was simply a profitable way of selling aggregate, the syndicate began to fail. An agreement with Alfred Hickman Ltd., a large iron works, forced Parker and Hooley to relinquish a large part of their holding in exchange for an injection of capital by Hickman. In 1905, Hickman took control and changed the syndicate's name to Tarmac Limited. Parker resigned, but Hooley was retained as a consultant on a large fee.

With increased use of automobiles at the beginning of the century the road-covering industry boomed. Unlike all its competitors, Tarmac Ltd. confined itself to one product: tarmac. When D. G. Comyn was made secretary in 1908, Tarmac was well established within the road-building and slag industries. To raise capital for the expansion of its transport stock, the company was liquidated and the assets transferred to a new company. Tarmac Ltd. was reregistered under the same name in 1913.

Tarmac's profits fell by 25% during World War I, as a result of cuts in government road expenditure. Comyn's friendship with the head of the government's road board led to Tarmac's being given contracts to supply the crushed slag needed to build roads through French battlefields. Newly erected works in Yorkshire were handed over for military use, the acute labor shortage being compensated for by several hundred German prisoners of war.

By 1918, Tarmac was drawing up plans for large-scale expansion. The intention to build crushed-slag depots and adjacent tarmac plants on the south coast, owing to a fear of over-production of slag in the Northeast, was thwarted by the high cost of sea freight. Comyn was, however, generally optimistic about postwar demand, having determined government plans to increase road expenditure. In 1919 the company bought existing slag tips in the Midlands and erected new coating plants nearby. Tarmac's first natural-stone quarry, Ffrith in North Wales, was acquired in 1919 but was never developed and was sold in 1951. In 1919 the company also began diversification within the construction industry. The acquisition of the patent on Vinculum, a process for binding the raw materials of concrete using waste slag dust, led to a contract to build houses in Wolverhampton and Birmingham, and the Vinculum division was established.

The 1920s began with extensive geographical and production capacity expansion. This heavy spending on acquisitions and expansion of railroad stock created a need for more capital. At the same time, prices of tarmac were falling despite a sharp increase in the cost of tar largely caused by the occupation of the Ruhr which was a major source of this substance. Comyn refused to raise the price of tarmac, believing that the company and his business connections were sufficiently established to survive a period of poor sales, while Tarmac's smaller competitors would fail. Comyn retired in 1926, due to ill health, in the only year that Tarmac has made a loss.

Comyn's successor, Cecil Martin, reacted to the decline in sales by halving directors' salaries and reducing head office staff numbers by 20%. The company was reorganized and in 1929 a civil engineering division was established. It engaged in road construction and the building of military airfields. An experiment in shipping pre-coated tarmac from northeast plants to Gravesend was unsuccessful, and it was decided to revert to Comyn's plans to build coating plants on the south coast. Preemption by Tarmac's largest rival, Crow Catchpole, which it later acquired, left Tarmac owning only three seaboard plants and with too much slag to dispose of. A series of convoluted deals with rival companies averted potentially crippling losses.

The early 1930s proved to be a stable period for Tarmac. A new product, Settite (bitumen macadam), believed to be superior to slag-based tarmac for road covering, was introduced in 1932. Diversifications into gravel and asphalt production were not successful, but were compensated for by the new spirit of camaraderie among mutually dependent industries. An important feature of this period was the price cooperation among blacktop producers. Where Comyn had sought to outwit his competitors, Martin favored a more amicable approach and was respected in the industry as a man of integrity. His efforts to help create a federation of slag producers in 1934 were eventually rewarded by a price agreement that guaranteed profits on the northeast slag plants. This brought new and lucrative contracts to the company.

By 1935, Tarmac's three divisions—roadstone, civil engineering and Vinculum—were well established, although the company image was still predominantly that of a slag business. Where World War I had been difficult for Tarmac, World War II infused new life into the company. The occupation of France presaged the need for more airports in the United Kingdom, and Tarmac gained contracts from the U.S. Army and Airforce. Since military demand for tarmac was greater than for asphalt, the company's profits rose by over 30% in the first year of the war, and by 43% in the second. By this time, the company had plants in northern England, north Wales, and Scotland, as well as a large transport stock. The increased mechanization of its plants compensated for the labor shortage. The civil engineering division won government contracts of £6 million and produced 5 million tons of road and runway material during the war. The Vinculum division also benefited from government demand for concrete blocks to build air raid shelters.

Despite steadily declining orders after August 1944, Tarmac anticipated an upsurge in demand as a result of the government's rearmament program. Tarmac consequently embarked on a £2 million program of reinvestment and development. New plants were commissioned in Yorkshire in 1949, existing plants were reconstructed and mechanized, and the transport stock was entirely replaced.

In 1954 the company pursued considerable and risky expansion. A new iron foundry was being built in the northeast, and Tarmac proposed to build a massive works, including a wharf for ships of up to 3,000 tons, to deal with the slag produced. In the same year, the company stepped up its transport conversion program, replacing railwagons with trucks. With the promise of a contract in 1956 to build Britain's first, eight-mile stretch of motorway, Tarmac was in need of capital. A rights issue raised £1 million to pay for this growth.

Cecil Martin decided to retire on his 65th birthday in 1957. No chairman was appointed during the period of reorganization which followed Martin's retirement, although his son, Robin, was made managing director of the roadstone division. It was decided to make Tarmac into a holding company with three main subsidiaries: Tarmac Roadstone, Tarmac Civil Engineering, and Tarmac Vinculum. Most of the group's profits came from Tarmac Roadstone. Robin Martin, who managed the subsidiary, had inherited a sound business, albeit one with geographical gaps and no natural stone resources.

A proposed merger of Tarmac and its largest rivals, Amalgamated Roadstone Corporation and Crow Catchpole—a large London-based tar distiller—broke down in 1958, but Tarmac bought Crow Catchpole the following year. With a toe-hold in London and the Southeast, Tarmac entered another phase of growth. The acquisition of Tarslag, a major Midlands-based road materials company, marked Tarmac's first major quarrying venture, and the company rapidly became one of the three largest quarry owners in the Midlands. The consequent boost to Tarmac's construction activities led to the formation in 1960 of an industrial division. Further expansion was restricted during this period to allow the company to focus on internal restructuring, and the formation of a series of localized construction teams.

Robin Martin became group managing director in 1963, when the worst winter weather in 100 years threatened to slow considerably the output of all Tarmac's divisions. Strains on finance and problems with integration of Tarmac's divided structure, coupled with government cuts in roadwork expenditure, dampened the optimism of the early 1960s. In anticipation of a decline in the availability of slag, Tarmac sought to strengthen its quarrying resources. The group's over-dependence on slag sales was relieved by the acquisition, in 1966, of three large granite quarries in the North. Having secured the market for natural stone. Tarmac concentrated on procuring supplies of bitumen, its other main raw material. The opening in conjunction with Phillips Petroleum of Oklahoma of a refinery in Cheshire secured Tarmac's supply of bitumen. In 1968, the company merged with Derbyshire Stone and William Briggs, a large bitumen and building materials supplier and contractor in Scotland. Over the decade, group profits increased sixfold.

With Tarmac's 1971 takeover of Limmer and Trinidad Limited, a London-based quarry-products business with an asphalt lake in Trinidad, it became the largest road-surfacing contractor and blacktop producer in the United Kingdom. The acquisition of Limmer marked the beginning of another period of diversification, particularly in Tarmac's quest to develop strength in the brick and concrete production markets. A growing need for a wider range of aggregates, including sand and gravel, and the acquisitions of several large hybrid companies, precipitated another company reorganization. The existing roadstone and bitumen divisions were renamed Quarry products and building products, to reflect more accurately their activities. Two new divisions were formed from the construction division, and by the middle of the 1970s, Tarmac was operating in five divisions: quarry products, building products, construction, properties and housing, and international. The regrouping reflected not only a new administrative strategy, but also an attempt to change Tarmac's image. Known traditionally as a road-surfacing contractor and producer of blacktop, the company was keen to reaffirm its position as a broad-based construction and building materials producer.

The company's activities during the 1970s are difficult to evaluate. It was a period of dramatic expansion against a background of economic instability in Britain. The housing and properties division was established in 1974, following the acquisition of John McLean and Sons Limited, a leading housebuilder, the previous year. Within a few years, and without any major acquisitions, Tarmac became the third-largest housebuilder in Britain. Eric Pountain, chairman of the Tarmac group, joined the company as chief executive of McLeans and became chief executive of the housing division. Under his leadership and with a policy of slow expansion and rigid financial controls, the housing division thrived. By the end of the decade, one-third of Tarmac's profits came from house building. The division became the management model for the rest of the company and set the precedent for the decentralization program at the end of the decade. The housing division prospered despite adverse economic conditions. The construction division continued its program of rapid expansion and diversification throughout the 1970s.

On the other hand, with the potential for growth in the United Kingdom restricted by the threat of recession, Tarmac began bidding for companies with established assets overseas. Having developed specialist construction skills in marine, soft, and rock tunneling with the takeovers of Mitchell Construction and Kinear Moodie in 1971, Tarmac seemed well placed to expand abroad. The new international division was set up to oversee the group's foreign projects. Few of the construction division's efforts on this front were successful, and it was not until the mid-1980s that the division began to recover from the ill-effects of entering too many high-risk ventures abroad. The acquisition of the Holland Hannen and Cubitts construction company in 1976 was a cautionary event in Tarmac's history of foreign investment; Cubitts Nigeria, a failing African asset which had been overlooked at the time of acquisition, had to be be sold off. It cost Tarmac £16 million.

Despite a successful joint venture with the Egyptian company Arab Contractors in 1977 to build a tunnel under the Suez Canal, and participation in a long-term international consortium on an irrigation scheme in Peru, Tarmac withdrew from most of its overseas projects having incurred several significant losses. By the end of the decade, the performance of the construction division was threatening the stability of the Tarmac group. The company's growing dependence on its housing and quarry products divisions at a time when the almost static British economy was adversely affecting the construction industry precipitated a dramatic fall in share price in 1977.

On balance, the events of the 1970s, although potentially disastrous for Tarmac, prompted the reorganization which has made the company the largest in its field in the United Kingdom. After a purge of top management in 1979, Eric Pountain was appointed chief executive of the Tarmac group. He had distinguished himself as director of the housing division and it was generally accepted that the growth of this division, despite an unfavorable economy, was almost entirely attributable to Pountain's management style and commitment to decentralization. He was the only director with previous experience as chief executive of a public company. He had joined Tarmac, he said, to make a big business work like a small business. Pountain's was an attitude strongly endorsed by Prime Minister Margaret Thatcher's government when it came to power in 1979, and Pountain was knighted in 1985, in recognition of his determination that Tarmac succeed despite the precarious economy of the early 1980s.

The most significant change at Tarmac under Pountain's leadership was the implementation of the decentralization program. Convinced that the company's difficulties in the previous decade were the result of poor management. Pountain implemented the strategy which made the housing division Britain's largest housebuilder in the ten years since its inception. Believing that divisional managers were better placed to assess prospective acquisitions than a board of directors, responsibility for growth and diversification was handed down to individual divisions. Decentralized organization clearly benefited the company, with profits increasing tenfold over the decade.

Reluctant to depend on domestic markets alone, and in view of the slow growth potential for the construction and quarrying industries in the United Kingdom, Tarmac in 1980 embarked on an expensive and ambitious program of acquisitions and development in the United States. The acquisition of the Hoveringham Group in 1981 marked the company's entry into the brick, tile, building-block, and concrete markets. Hoveringham owned quarries in the United States and its takeover gave Tarmac a firm quarrying base in the United States. The £150 million acquisition of Lone Star Industries' ready-mix and concrete-block plants in Florida in 1984, and the takeover of a large underwater limestone quarry at Pennsuco, gave Tarmac control of 10% of Florida's total aggregate, or natural-stone, output. With a source of stone assured, the company began buying ready-mix concrete and brick-building plants throughout the southern states. In 1986 Tarmac paid £263 million for a 60% share in Lone Star Industries, and the following year Tarmac America was established. Several smaller plant and quarry acquisitions followed, giving Tarmac a significant standing in the U.S. aggregates and concrete industries. However, falling oil prices in Texas and severe weather conditions in Virginia in the late 1980s disrupted Tarmac America's activities and by the end of the decade, the division represented only one-fifth of the group's total turnover.

Over the same period, the housing division increased its output from 4,000 homes in 1980 to 11,000 in 1987, contributing with the quarry products division over three-quarters of the group's turnover. Diversification within the building-products division led to the creation of the industrial products division with roofing, construction, and oil interests in both the United Kingdom and the United States.

By the beginning of the 1990s, Tarmac's diversification strategy of the last 20 years had given the company a leading presence in many industrial sectors. Despite what is generally regarded as a cautious approach to expansion and a poor track record overseas, Tarmac has grown dramatically. The company's involvement in the English Channel tunnel project, due for completion in 1995, seems certain to improve Tarmac's standing as an international concern. Tarmac's growth in Europe is likely to expand after the creation of the single European market in 1992 by necessity, if not design.

As one analyst wrote in the *Financial Weekly,* "Tarmac has shown with repeated small acquisitions . . . that it is a group that likes to do more of what it knows, even when markets are static."

Principal Subsidiaries: Tarmac Quarry Products Limited; John McLean & Sons Limited; Tarmac Industrial Products Limited; Tarmac Construction Limited; Tarmac Properties Limited; Tarmac Building Materials Limited; Tarmac America, Inc. (U.S.A.).

Further Reading: Earle, J.B.F., *A Century of Road Materials,* Oxford, United Kingdom, Tarmac Ltd., 1971; Earle, J.B.F., *Black Top,* Oxford, United Kingdom, Asphalt & Coated Macadam Association, 1974.

—Juliette Bright

TOTO

TOTO, LTD.

1-1, Nakashima 2-chome
Kokurakita-ku, Kitakyushu 802
Japan
(093) 951-2371
Fax: (093) 922-6789

Public Company
Incorporated: 1917 as Toyo Toki Company, Ltd.
Employees: 8,570
Sales: ¥293.10 billion (US$2.04 billion)
Stock Exchanges: Tokyo Osaka Nagoya Fukuoka

Toto is Japan's largest manufacturer of sanitary earthenware and metal fittings. The company's line of products includes vitreous china sanitaryware, plumbing fittings, prefabricated bathrooms, water storage tanks, modular kitchens, water heaters, precision ceramics, and other household-oriented products. Though traditionally a business that specialized in water-related household products, Toto has further expanded its product line into non-household projects such as those for hotels and offices. In 1990 it was concentrating much of its research and development on new ceramics.

The company was incorporated in 1917 in Kokura, Japan, with assets of ¥1 million. The company's birth took place during the Taisho era, a time of great social and economic change. As the economy grew and expanded, the number of well-educated urban dwellers increased, and in 1920 Toto constructed Japan's first tunnel kiln—a long narrow kiln with goods carried on conveyors— to produce goods to meet the demand for new, modern urban housing. Throughout the company's first half-century, Toto's growth and development paralleled the growth and activity of the Japanese economy as a whole.

Its growth was stifled in 1927 due to a serious economic depression that struck Japan as a result of overextended capital investment and production. It was the beginning of extremely difficult times for Toto. A financial panic followed the recession and Toto, along with most Japanese businesses, was forced to curtail production in the face of declining demand. The worldwide Great Depression, devaluation of the yen on world markets, and the removal of Japan from the gold standard all contributed to economic chaos. In that same year a huge earthquake caused an even greater strain on Japan's economy, but prompt, massive government expenditures on reconstruction helped Toto survive extremely perilous times. In an effort to stimulate the economy, military expenditures were increased, reconstruction was accelerated again, and a period of military expansionism began, which did not stop until the end of World War II.

During the war years of the 1930s, despite the government's redirection of most Japanese industry to war production, Toto continued to grow, and in 1937 finished construction of a second sanitaryware manufacturing facility in Chigasaki.

The collapse of the Japanese economy brought with it the end of the war. The Allied naval blockade had created extreme shortages in all raw materials, including coal, a basic ingredient needed by Toto to fire its kilns. In August 1945, the company as well as the entire city of Kokura, was spared total annihilation. Kokura had been slated as the target of the second U.S. nuclear bomb. Because of extremely heavy cloud cover, and after three passes by the B-29 bomber carrying the bomb, the plane proceeded to its secondary target, Nagasaki.

At the end of the war, industrial production stood at about one-third that of prewar Japan. By 1965, manufacturing had risen to nearly four times that of the mid 1930s. The average family consumed 75% more goods and services than before the war, and during the 1950s and 1960s, Toto began manufacturing bath fittings as part of the growth experienced in the post-war economy. The company kept pace with increased demand for its products by opening four more plants in the Kokura area, a plant in Shiga, and another located near the Chigasaki plant, which had been built before the war.

In 1970, the year the company began manufacturing enamel baths, it changed its name from Toyo Toki to Toto, Ltd. Along with the new name came the development of new ceramics. Traditional ceramics had several drawbacks. They were inferior in weldability and workability, but these problems were eliminated with the addition of silicon carbide, silicon nitride, and boron nitride into their composition. New ceramics are divided into two classifications. The first is electroceramics, which can function among other things as insulators or semiconductors. The second is engineering ceramics, which offer the important properties of thermal resistance, wear resistance, and corrosion resistance.

During the years preceding the war, Japanese products had the reputation of being inferior in workmanship and materials. As the scope of Toto's markets and sales efforts expanded, an emphasis on total quality control became a priority. The development of an integrated quality-control system brought Toto into a period of rapid growth and diversification of its product line. Sales grew as the company used the just-in-time method in both the ordering and delivery of raw materials it needed for production and in its sales program, by offering the same quick and timely response to the companies it supplied with products.

Most Japanese manufacturing had its roots in job-lot production, that is, producing a narrow range of products well and in great numbers. In its first 60 years of existence Toto concentrated on the production of a limited line of sanitary earthenware products. With mastery of the new and more efficient manufacturing techniques, sanitaryware in 1990 represented less than 20% of the company's total sales and production.

In the 1980s, under the leadership of Hiroshi Shirakawa and then Yoshine Koga, Toto took giant strides in expanding both its product line and sales organization. The company developed and maintained a network of retail sales locations that served the general public as well as designers, along with its traditional distribution to the home construction industry. New products, such as modular kitchens, vanity units, high-quality ceramic tile, water heaters, whirlpool bathtubs, high-tech toilets, "washlets" used in conjunction with computer clean rooms, precision measuring tools, optical connectors, and magnetic discs, contributed to explosive growth in sales in the 1980s. The increase in sales was met with the construction of almost completely automated production plants using both robotics and worker-free automated production lines.

To further increase its line of new products, Toto completed construction of a new research and development laboratory in the Chigasaki plant and was in the 1990s in the planning stages of the construction of a new experimental plant to be used for research and development in biotechnology and membrane filtration technology, using new ceramics.

Along with the growth of its product line and with its research and development commitment, the company had begun overseas expansion of both its sales and manufacturing functions. In 1986 Toto established the Cera Trading Company, the function of which was to import and market other manufacturers' plumbing products in an effort to expand Toto's total market share. Beginning with the company's first joint venture with Kawasaki in 1986, resulting in the formation of the Nihron Yupro Corporation, Toto was in 1990 doing business in France, Germany, Indonesia, Korea, Thailand, Hong Kong, Taiwan, and the People's Republic of China. The company had 12 affiliates doing business in 7 different countries, along with sales offices and agents throughout Asia, Europe, and the United States. In 1990 Toto was expanding its overseas production facilities and entered into technological cooperation agreements with companies in Thailand and with the People's Republic of China. It was attempting further to increase its markets and ultimately to become a worldwide industry leader.

Principal Subsidiaries: Toto Real Estate Co., Ltd.; Aichi Toto Co., Ltd.; Toto Plastics Co., Ltd.; Fukuoka Toto Co., Ltd.; Toto Service Co., Ltd.; Buzen Toto Co., Ltd.; Cera Trading Co., Ltd.; Chiba Toto Co., Ltd.

Further Reading: Hane, Mikiso, *Japan: A Historical Survey,* New York, Charles Scribner's Sons, 1972; Forbis, William H., *Japan Today: People, Places, Power,* New York, Harper & Row, 1975; Schonberger, Richard J., *Japanese Manufacturing Techniques: Nine Hidden Lessons in Simplicity,* New York, The Free Press, 1982.

—William R. Grossman

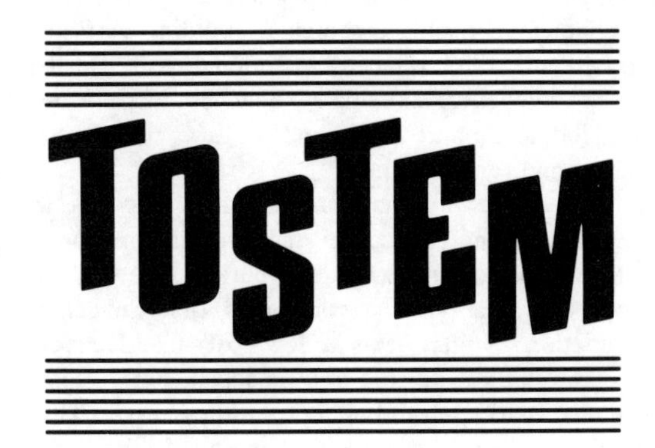

TOYO SASH CO., LTD.

1-1, Ojima 2-chome
Koto-ku, Tokyo 136
Japan
(03) 3638-8111
Fax: (03) 3638-8254

Public Company
Incorporated: 1949 as Myokenya Home Fixtures Wholesaling Co., Ltd.
Employees: 9,571
Sales: ¥412.03 billion (US$2.87 billion)
Stock Exchanges: Tokyo Osaka

Toyo Sash Co., Ltd. is Japan's leading manufacturer and supplier of aluminum building materials, with more than 30% of the domestic market. The company serves the needs of both the housing and the commercial building industries. To the housing industry it contributes window-related products, interior products such as kitchen and bathroom units, wooden floors and doors, and exterior products such as balconies, carports, and ceramic siding. Toyo Sash's products for the commercial building industry range from skylights to steel doors, and during the late 1980s expanded to non-metal materials such as wood and stone. The company's four operating divisions are housing sash, commercial building sash, housing materials, and fabricated home products.

In 1923 Myokenya, a retail fixture dealership, was formed. The company grew modestly until 1947, when it also began to sell wooden fixtures—such as window sashes—wholesale. The company profited from the post–World War II building boom in Japan. Myokenya—and later Toyo Sash—grew very quickly as Japan's wood-frame houses were replaced by more modern structures. In 1949 the business was incorporated as Myokenya Home Fixtures Wholesaling Co., Ltd. In 1953 the company completed its first plant in Katsushika, for the production of standard wooden fixtures.

This steady growth became characteristic of the company. In 1964 Myokenya began preparing to produce aluminum sashes. Also in 1964, the company opened its second plant, in Oyama. Unlike many countries, Japan's aluminum-sash producers are not small independent operations; they are an integral part of the competitive building materials industry. The company entered the aluminum-building-materials market in 1966, with the introduction of a home-window-sash product.

In the fall of 1967 a production subsidiary called Toyo Sash was formed, as was Toyo Sash Sales Company. That same year, the Nanakodai plant was completed. In 1968 Myokenya changed its name to Toyo Sash Housing Company, and Toyo Juko Company—later Tostem Cera Company—was established as a subsidiary. Myokenya's Naruto plant was finished that same year. In 1969 the Nakasato (now Noda) plant—the first plant to be equipped with an integrated production line—opened. A sixth plant was built in 1970, while the company continued to conceive new products. Among these were light storm shutters and the new Taiyo home sash, with two-tier lower-edge design, introduced in 1971.

In October 1971 Toyo Housing Company and its associated companies were merged to form Toyo Sash Company. In 1973 three new plants were completed in Kanuma, Shimotsuma, and Fujihana. August of that year marked the opening of the first Toyo Sash franchise chain outlet.

In the mid-1970s, with confidence inspired by steady growth, the company branched into the housing-exterior industry. In 1975 Toyo Sash began to manufacture storefronts. By 1977, four distribution centers were opened to offer the expanding line of Toyo Sash products to the public—including aluminum bay windows and standardized aluminum balconies. Four more plants were completed during that span. In addition, 1977 saw the creation of four new subsidiaries: Viva Home Company, Toyo Building Sash Company, Taiyo Metal Manufacturing Company, and Royal Sash Manufacturing Company. Viva signaled the company's entry into the home-improvement business. Toyo Building Sash established the start of commercial-buildings sash production; a new series of building sashes was introduced in 1978. Royal Sash marked production of high-quality aluminum doors. The decade closed with the construction of two more plants, and the establishment of Toyo Distribution Service Company, the overseer of the company's entire distribution system.

Toyo Sash devised a new sales system in 1980, creating 45 sales subsidiaries throughout Japan. Having its own sales force has allowed Toyo Sash to undercut its competitors with prices kept low by the absence of middlemen, and customers kept happy by fast, efficient delivery. In what was also to become a key company strategy, Toyo Sash acquired the Nihol Repol Corporation in 1980. It became a stated company policy to acquire only companies that would enhance Toyo Sash's product line, increase technological expertise, or strengthen marketing channels.

A new plant and a new distribution center were opened in 1981, and the company's first electronic data-processing system was installed. Called TRAIN—for Toyo Sash Real Time Advanced Information Network—this system permits wholesalers, distribution centers, plants, and offices to access centralized information on all products, thus assuring fast, efficient service and delivery. With the establishment of Clean Window Remodelings Company in 1982, Toyo Sash entered another market—building-sash remodeling. That same year, a production and a sales company merged with Toyo Sash. At this point, the company's reputation was such that Toyo Sash was awarded the Japanese sash industry's first order from the People's Republic of China.

In 1983, the company's Noda plant received an award for product quality and standardization. Toyo Sash adopted the nickname Tostem in 1984. The company's Shinjuku, Tokyo showroom was opened in 1984; it is the largest showroom in the building materials industry. That same year, Kowa Metal Manufacturing Company was acquired and a new production plant completed.

The following year was distinguished by a flurry of acquisitions, in the midst of which Toyo Sash was first listed on the Tokyo Stock Exchange. Mitsui Light Metal Processing Company and Dai-Ichi Mokko Company were acquired in the first half of 1985. Meiwa Manufacturing Company, Meiwa Company, Nihon Lumber Land Company, Nittetsu Curtainwall Corporation, and Nittetsu Sash Sales Corporation were acquired, later in the year. During this time, Tostem paused in its introduction of new products to concentrate on assimilating these new entities. In November of that busy year, the company opened its first overseas representative office in Hong Kong.

Products introduced in 1986 included a new terrace series and an electrical storm shutter called Al-ease. Al-ease enjoyed such success in the housing industry that the company later developed an electric window shutter for the commercial building industry. These shutters feature soundproofing, remote control, and excellent ventilation. Also inaugurated in 1986 was TOPICS—Toyo Sash Prosperous Information for Customers System. This data-processing system provides current inventory data and price quotes to dealers. Tostem changed its sales structure that year to its present system of subsidiaries. There were also three more acquisitions: Eyeful Home Company, Comalco Fabricators (Hong Kong) Ltd., and Sanyo Chemical Manufacturing Company. Toyo Sash's Ariake plant received the Agency of Industrial Science and Technology Award at the close of 1986.

In 1987 Tostem Thai Company and Kyodo Dieworks Thailand Company were established. The construction of a Toyo Sash plant was begun in Hong Kong, while the Teine and Ichinoseki plants were completed and an Osaka showroom opened. By year's end, Tostem's plants had received two more awards, including another Agency of Industrial Science and Technology Award.

Toyo Sash's growth strategies paid off in 1988, when the company outsold all Japanese competitors during the country's housing boom. That boom was the result of lower interest rates on housing loans and a change in government regulations that allowed larger wooden homes to be built on more sites. At the same time, a commercial redevelopment boom was taking place, boosting Toyo Sash's commercial-building-materials market. At this point, Tostem was clearly the industry's leader; with 35% of the housing sash market, it was setting prices and producing 80 meters of aluminum bars per minute per machine—almost double its competitors' rates. The company's reputation was such that architects were designing around Toyo Sash's casements, avoiding custom-made orders. In all, 1988 was an exceptional year, financially, for the company, and many new products were introduced, including ceramic siding and windows with built-in thermometers and rain sensors.

Most of Toyo Sash's international activities have been geared toward developing production and materials procurement capabilities, and toward expanding markets.

The Tostem Thai plant is the company's first full-scale overseas production facility. It is a low-cost manufacturer whose products initially were sold only in Japan, but Tostem projected eventual marketing throughout Southeast Asia. The company's Hong Kong facilities have taken advantage of the high-rise construction boom taking place there. Part ownership of two U.S. facilities of Alumax Company acquired in 1988 is intended to assure a low-cost supply of aluminum ingots.

Japan Try Company was merged into Tostem in 1989. The company had expected a slow-down in the home-building boom, to be offset by an increase in home renovation. Toward this end, it developed a line of high-value items such as wooden products, prefabricated kitchen and bathroom units, and metal and ceramic sidings. Tostem continued record gains during 1989 as the Japanese economy remained strong. Anticipating the home-renovation and urban-redevelopment market needs has paid off for Toyo Sash.

For fiscal 1990, the housing-sash division represented 68% of the company's total sales, a slight dip from the previous year. The building-sash and fabricated-home-products divisions saw a slight increase, while housing materials stayed roughly the same. Given the company's solid base in the industry, its award-winning product quality and innovation, and its market sensitivity, Toyo Sash Company is equipped for continued success.

Principal Subsidiaries: Tostem Cera Co., Ltd.; Toyo Sash Building Materials Co., Ltd.; Tostem Thai Co., Ltd. (Thailand); Okinawa Toyo Sash Co., Ltd.; ATMOS (U.S.A.) Inc.; Tostem Fudosan Corporation; Kyodo Veneer and Plywood Co., Ltd. (95%).

Further Reading: Group Guide '90, Tokyo, Toyo Sash Co., Ltd., 1990.

—Carol I. Keeley

UBE INDUSTRIES, LTD.

12-32, Nishi-honmachi 1-chome
Ube, Yamaguchi 755
Japan
(0836) 31-1122
Fax: (0836) 22-1271

Public Company
Incorporated: 1942
Employees: 7,177
Sales: ¥426.19 billion (US$2.96 billion)
Stock Exchanges: Tokyo Osaka Nagoya

Ube Industries is one of the largest chemical companies in Japan. Once devoted primarily to the mining and industrial applications of coal, Ube converted itself into a diversified chemical concern in the 1960s, as coal's importance as a raw material declined. The company manufactures cement, petrochemicals, industrial machinery, ceramics, and pharmaceuticals and owns its own transportation operations. Ube is also part of the *zaibatsu*, or financial family, centered around Sanwa Bank, which is Ube's most prominent stockholder, with 4.5% of its shares.

Ube Industries was formed in 1942 when four companies located in and around Ube City in Yamaguchi Prefecture decided to merge. The oldest of these was the Okinoyama Coal Mine, which was founded in 1897 by Yusaku Watanabe. Watanabe was noteworthy for his belief, particularly far sighted at the time, that coal was not just a fuel but a potential source of industrial raw materials. He also believe that the health of his company was inextricably linked to the overall development of the Ube area, a philosophy that the company continues to espouse.

The second of the four companies to be founded was the Ube Shinkawa Iron Works, which was established in 1914 and manufactured coal-mining machinery. Ube Cement Company, which used as its primary raw material limestone found near the Okinoyama mine, was founded in 1921. Lastly, Ube Nitrogen Industrial Company was established in 1933, when the Japanese nitrogen fixation industry was still in its infancy. The company started out synthesizing ammonia and sulfuric acid from coal, and in 1936 it began producing nitric acid and distilling gasoline from the low-temperature carbonization of coal.

The four companies were clearly interdependant. In 1944 Ube Industries added to its position as one of Japan's leading coal-mining concerns by acquiring Nippon Kogyo's anthracite mine at Sanyo. The branch of the company's operations to be most affected by World War II was the nitrogen fixation plant. Ammonia, a major ingredient in both fertilizers and explosives, was a strategically important chemical, and the Ube plant was the nation's fourth-largest producer. Demand for its products ran high during the course of the war, and its importance made it a likely target for U.S. bombers. Just after midnight on July 2, 1945, 100 B-29s from the 20th Air Force destroyed the Ube nitrogen plant almost completely; it was not rebuilt until after the war.

Rebuilding after Japan's defeat was not the only challenge that faced Ube Industries in the postwar years. The coal-mining industry began dying a slow death as crude oil gradually replaced coal as the nation's principal source of energy and the chemical industry's main raw material. For Ube, still heavily reliant on its coal operations, it meant diversification or dying along with the coal trade. In 1955 the company bolstered its cement production capacity by opening the Isa Cement Factory at Mine City, just outside Ube City. It also branched into producing urea and caprolactam, raw materials from which nylon is made, at a new plant in Ube City.

In 1958 coal still accounted for 30% of the company's sales. In 1960, however, Ube began in earnest a 15-year process of phasing coal out of its operations, when it started using oil as its main source of raw materials. From there, it entered the burgeoning field of petrochemicals, beginning with plastics. In 1964 the company began producing low-density polyethylene at a new plant in Chiba Prefecture. It also added to its cement business by opening a factory at Kanda in Fukuoka Prefecture. Over the next ten years, it would invest roughly ¥200 billion in weaning itself from its traditional reliance on coal. Roughly half of this sum would go into chemical and petrochemical production, and one-third into cement production.

This process of diversification and divestiture came to a head in the late 1960s and early 1970s. In 1967 Ube marked the 70th birthday of the Okinoyama mine by closing it down, cutting its oldest link with its corporate past. It also built a new chemical plant at Sakai in Osaka Prefecture. The next year, it added a polypropylene plant to the Sakai facility. In 1970 the company shut down its last remaining major source of coal, the Sanyo anthracite mine. In 1971 it added a synthetic-rubber factory to its plant at Chiba. Ube's sales composition figures for 1972 show that coal had disappeared entirely as a source of revenue; cement accounted for 46% of sales, fertilizers and caprolactam for 29.9%, machinery for 12.1%, and petrochemical products for 12%. The company had become Japan's fourth-largest chemical concern, and its caprolactam output accounted for 10% of the world's supply.

Ube reshaped itself into a fully diversified chemical concern during these years, and it did so organically, suggesting that it had not forgotten the interdependence that had made the merger between its four original companies so logical. Not only did it own the means of manufacture; it controlled the raw materials and the means of transportation and distribution as well. For instance, its cement plant at Isa took limestone mined from a nearby quarry, processed it, and sent the clinkers to Ube City, where they were turned into cement using kilns made by Ube's machinery subsidiary. The finished product was then distributed using Ube's own cement carriers, which were constructed by other Ube subsidiaries, Kasado Dockyard and Ube Dockyard, the carriers using engines made by Ube Machinery Works. Similar interrelationships marked the company's other manufacturing operations as well. In 1974 Ube built a 30-kilometer industrial highway between Mine City and Ube City. The company added a 1,020-meter bridge spanning Ube City's harbor to the highway in 1982. The Ube-Mine Industrial Highway cost ¥15 billion, but increased the efficiency of Ube's transportation operations.

Whatever pride Ube took in its busy journey from coal mine to conglomerate must have been short lived, however. The oil price shocks of the 1970s plunged the Japanese chemical industry into a severe depression. Its primary raw material, once cheap and plentiful, now became scarce and prohibitively expensive. Ube fared no better than its competitors; sales fell off and profits dropped by nearly half just between 1974 and 1975. Coal once again became a viable raw material for Japanese chemical companies, and Ube was at least fortunate in that it had not disposed of all of its coal storage and processing facilities. It did not reopen the Okinoyama and Sanyo mines, however. Instead, it began importing coal from Australia and, later, the United States.

A slump in business naturally resulted in an industrywide excess in production capacity. Despite general overcapacity in cement production, Ube acquired a 46% interest, later expanding it to a majority stake, in Okinawa-based Ryukyu Cement from Kaiser Cement and Gypsum, a subsidiary of U.S. conglomerate Kaiser Industries, for $7 million in 1976. In 1979 the Ministry of International Trade and Industry ordered Ube to shut down its urea plant at Ube City because of industrywide overcapacity for that chemical.

Business from overseas helped fill the breach caused by difficulties at home. In 1978 Ube established a sales subsidiary in the United States, Ube America. It also received an order to build an ammonia plant in China, which it filled as a partner in a joint venture with the chemical company Marubeni. The plant used a heavy residual gasification process invented by Texaco. In 1982, Ube received a contract to build a cement plant in the United Arab Emirates for a local company, Ajman Cement.

The 1990s were marked by a number of joint ventures for Ube, many of them with foreign companies and involving some kind of technical cooperation—technological innovation is an area in which the Japanese chemical industry had traditionally been weak. Its alliances with domestic rivals were often formed for the sake of diversification, a useful strategy in an industry just pulling out of a severe slump. In 1984 Ube joined with Marubeni and Massachussetts-based Wormser and formed Ube Wormser to produce and market Wormser fluidized-bed combusters in Japan. It also formed UM Technopolymer with Mitsubishi Petroleum, and Chiba Riverment and Cement with Kawasaki Steel. Ube entered the pharmaceutical field that year when it joined with Takeda Chemical to produce and market vitamin supplements.

In 1986 Ube and Marubeni tried to tap into the U.S. automotive plastics market when they set up ATC, a joint venture to produce polypropylene compounds for bumpers and dashboards. ATC was 60%-owned by Ube, and based in Nashville, Tennessee, near the proposed site for General Motors's Saturn subcompact car plant. Ube made a significant move toward future diversification that year when it built a new research facility in Ube City, to develop new biotechnical, electronic-material, pharmaceutical, agricultural-chemical, biochemical, and ceramics technologies.

More joint ventures marked the end of the decade, as well. In 1989 Ube and Finnish chemical company Kemira formed Kemira-Ube to manufacture hydrogen peroxide at an Ube plant in Ube City using a process developed by Kemira. Ube was to use half of the hydrogen peroxide to be produced to manufacture nylon and other products, and the other half was targeted for sale on the Japanese market. Ube also entered into a joint venture with the Japanese drug company Sankyo, in which drugs developed by Ube would be taken to clinical trials, produced, and then marketed by Sankyo. In 1990 Ube and Swiss chemical company Ems-Chemi formed UBE-EMS Yugen Kaisha to manufacture lactam, a base material used in certain kinds of plastics. Ube also entered into a joint venture with Rexene, a Dallas-based chemical company, to manufacture amorphous poly-alpha-olefin—a substance used in adhesives—in Japan using Rexene technology, and market it in the Far East and Pacific Rim.

The chemical business has never been Japanese industry's strongest suit. Unlike automobiles and consumer electronics, there have been no wails and moans in the United States about how Japanese caprolactam and polymers are taking over the market; in fact, the chemical industry was considered enough of a hothouse flower so that the Japanese government banned foreign investment in it until only recently. Although it is one of Japan's largest chemical makers, Ube—or Mitsubishi Chemical or Asahi Chemical, for that matter—is rarely, if ever, spoken of in the same breath as Dow or Union Carbide in terms of size and industrywide prominence. What makes Ube interesting is its vertical integration and its long-standing commitment to a cluster of small cities on the southern tip of Honshu, which give it a distinctly provincial air. True to Yusaku Watanabe's vision of the inseparable relationship between company and the community that surrounds it, Ube Industries has embarked on a long-term development project for the Ube area that includes building new schools, hospitals, high-tech research facilities, and expanding Yamaguchi-Ube Airport to accommodate direct flights to major domestic and international destinations. Ube subsidiaries already operate golf courses, hotels, and a television station in the area. Whatever its future, Ube Industries has already proved itself to be more than a run-of-the-mill manufacturer.

Principal Subsidiaries: Ube Industries (America), Inc. (U.S.A.); Ube Europe GmbH (Germany); Ube Chemical Industries, Ltd.; Ube Cycon. Ltd.; Ube-Nitto Kasei Co., Ltd.; Chiba Butadiene Industry Co., Ltd; Ube Synthetic Rubber, Ltd.; Ube Compound Chem. Fertilizer Mfg. Co., Ltd.; Meiwa Plastic Industries, Ltd.; Ube Ammonia Industry Co., Ltd.; Kanto Ube Concrete Co., Ltd.; Osaka Ube Concrete Co., Ltd.; Sakai Ube Concrete Co., Ltd.; Sakai Ube Concrete Co., Ltd.; Hiroshima Ube Concrete Co., Ltd.; Fukuoka Ube Concrete Co., Ltd.; Hokkaido Ube Concrete Co., Ltd. Shizuoka Ube Concrete Co., Ltd.; Nissho Ube Concrete Co., Ltd.; Sawara Ube Concrete Co., Ltd.; Ube Atsugi Concrete Co., Ltd.; Kasado Ube Concrete Co., Ltd.; Toho Concrete

Co., Ltd.; Hagimori Kosan Co., Ltd.; Hokuriku Ube Concrete Co., Ltd.; Hokushin Ube Concrete Co., Ltd.; Senpoku Ube Concrete Co., Ltd.; Niigata Ube Concrete Co., Ltd. Kyoto Ube Ready-mixed Concrete Co., Ltd.; Kushiro Ube Concrete Co., Ltd.; Kashima Ube Concrete Co., Ltd.; Inoue Ube Ready-mixed Concrete Co., Ltd.; Shikoku Ube Concrete Co., Ltd.; Nitto Ube Concrete Co., Ltd.; Kyokuko Ube Concrete Co., Ltd.; Ube Slate Mfg. Co., Ltd.; Ube Pile Co., Ltd.; Nippon Lime, Ltd.; Ube Nisshin Lime, Ltd.; Ube Electric Chemical Co., Ltd.; Shin Taito Steamship Co., Ltd.; Ube Dockyard Co., Ltd.; Shinko Ready-mixed Concrete Transport Co., Ltd.; Shinko Transport & Warehouse Co., Ltd.; Uedagumi Transport Co., Ltd.; Sakai Ube Ready-mixed Concrete Transport Co., Ltd.; Hokkaido Ube Transport Co., Ltd.; Niigata Ube Ready-mixed Concrete Transport Co., Ltd.; Fuji Car Mfg. Co.,Ltd.; Kasado Dockyard Co., Ltd.; Taimei Coal Mine Co., Ltd.; Ube Saiseki Co., Ltd.; Ube Ryokuchi Co., Ltd.; Ube Kosan Inryo Co., Ltd.; Doei Maritime Shipping Co., Ltd.; Ube Trucking Co., Ltd.; Ube Trading Co., Ltd.; Nikko Oil Co., Ltd.; Ube Bussan Co., Ltd.; Bocho Commercial Co., Ltd.; Ube Golf Co., Ltd.; Ube Real Estate Co., Ltd.; Mi-ne Machinery Works Co., Ltd.; Fukushima Ltd.; Richman U.F. Co., Ltd.; Ube Steel Co., Ltd.; UBE-C&A Co., Ltd.; Yuben Shipping Co., (PTE) Ltd.; Ryukyu Cement Co., Ltd.

Further Reading: ''Company of the Month: Ube Industries, Ltd.,'' *The Oriental Economist,* September 1973; ''Company of the Month: Ube Industries, Ltd.,'' *The Oriental Economist*, November 1974; ''Ube Industries, Ltd.,'' *The Oriental Economist*, September 1982; *Ube Industries, Ltd.: Company Profile*, Ube City, Ube Industries, Ltd., 1988.

—Douglas Sun

USG CORPORATION

101 South Wacker Drive
Chicago, Illinois 60606
U.S.A.
(312) 606-4000
Fax: (312) 606-4093

Public Company
Incorporated: 1901 as U.S.G. Company
Employees: 14,200
Sales: $2.19 billion
Stock Exchanges: New York Midwest Zürich Geneva Basel

Gypsum products are the principal goods manufactured by the USG Corporation. The manufacture of gypsum is a highly competitive and price-sensitive undertaking, with easy entry and exit from the field. As a result of these conditions USG Corporation—or the U.S.G. Company, as it was originally incorporated—has exerted substantial influence in the building-supplies field because of its market size.

Understanding gypsum production methods is essential to an understanding of USG's corporate character. Gypsum, or hydrous calcium sulphate, is, in pure form, a white mineral commonly called alabaster. Large quantities of gypsum exist throughout North America. One of the first uses for gypsum was as a fertilizer. Gypsum is made suitable for commercial use by a process called calcination, which involves heating the mineral to remove approximately three-quarters of its water. Calcined gypsum, or plaster of Paris, can recrystallize into any shape with the simple addition of water. In the 1890s gypsum manufacturers perfected a method of strengthening plaster by adding a retarder, which controlled the setting time, thus creating a viable competitor to traditional lime plaster. Because gypsum was plentiful, and available at a relatively low price, and because the manufacturing process was so simple, new firms flooded the market and placed constant downward pressure on prices.

In the early years of the 20th century, several key businesses emerged as gypsum-product leaders. The English family of Nebraska; C.G. Root, Emil Durr, S.Q. Fulton, and Charles Pullen of Wisconsin; Waldo Avery and B.W. McCausland of Michigan; and, lastly, the largest manufacturer in the United States, J. B. King of New York, were all important gypsum processors. By 1901 several attempts to organize some of the industry's producers into a corporate combination had failed. That year 35 gypsum companies consolidated into the U.S.G. Company. The participating firms traded their assets for securities and acquired a $200,000 loan. Directors of the new company, which controlled about 50% of U.S. gypsum output, chose B.W. McCausland as its first president. The company was based in Chicago.

Between 1901 and 1905 each director remained largely concerned with the success of his own plants. This polarization ended in 1905, when McCausland was replaced as president by Sewell Avery, his partner's son. Avery's tenure as president would extend 35 years, until November 12, 1936. Avery then served as chairman, between 1937 and 1951. He and his brother, Waldo Avery, were the company's largest stockholders, controlling about 3.6% of the company's stock. During Sewell Avery's presidency, his character permeated the company's culture. Avery was a conservative businessman who had the last word in virtually all matters. In 1931, when Montgomery Ward and Company was on the verge of financial collapse, Avery became chairman of the board of that company, a position which he held until 1955.

Avery had managed his father's firm, the Alabaster Company, since 1894. When U.S.G. absorbed Alabaster, he became a U.S.G. director and its Buffalo, New York, sales manager. Avery built a strong research division after his promotion to president from his post as Cleveland sales manager. Staffed by engineers and chemists, the new division sought to find new uses for gypsum. The U.S.G. Company, reincorporated in 1920 as the United States Gypsum Company (US Gypsum), has maintained a market share ranging between 50% in 1901 and 34% in 1989. In 1909 Avery set out to diversify the company with one of his first acquisitions, the Sackett Plasterboard Company of New York. Augustine Sackett had invented gypsum wallboard and the specialized machinery to make it. This basic wallboard quickly became one of US Gypsum's major products. Wallboard, a layer of gypsum plaster sandwiched between two pieces of paper, is a convenient building material with strong fire-proofing and insulating qualities.

US Gypsum improved on Sackett's concept and patented a wallboard that had paper folded over its edges to seal in plaster residue, which often escaped during the wallboard's installation. In 1927 CertainTeed Products Corporation introduced its own wallboard, which did not have enclosed edges, and challenged US Gypsum for market share. CertainTeed's managers believed that their less expensive version had a good chance of success. The result was a price contest between the two companies, beginning in 1927 and ending in 1929. US Gypsum had a much larger market than CertainTeed. It, therefore, was able to sell wallboard at a loss only in those markets that CertainTeed also served. In all other markets US Gypsum kept prices up. CertainTeed, however, was forced to sell its product at a loss in all its markets. By 1929 CertainTeed was beaten. The smaller company was licensed to produce US Gypsum's patented wallboard and was forced to sell the product at the price set by US Gypsum. This incident marked the start of US Gypsum's unrivaled leadership in gypsum materials.

In 1928 Avery successfully predicted a recession which eventually became the Great Depression. Avery's instinct for predicting business cycles helped US Gypsum get through the Depression without a single year of losses; this situation was quite unusual for a business involved in the cyclical building industry. Avery moved to protect the company, partly by ordering the construction of new plants closer to East Coast metropolitan centers. Since gypsum is a high-bulk, relatively low-value commodity, transportation costs have a large effect on pricing.

US Gypsum's greatest advantage was size. The company was able to use its size to keep manufacturing and transportation costs down and to compete more effectively. Three specific policies, set by Avery, helped US Gypsum to counter the Depression and maintain its number-one position in the industry. According to *Fortune,* February 1936, diffusion of production facilities allowed US Gypsum to keep transportation costs, and thus total costs down. US Gypsum was also vertically integrated, from mine floor to retailer, and employed highly mechanized techniques when possible. The third element in US Gypsum's success, according to *Fortune,* was a devotion to product diversification. US Gypsum marketed a broad cross section of building materials. Broken down into individual units these products would have been prohibitively expensive to transport. Combined, however, transportation costs were much more reasonable.

Avery took advantage of the company's strong cash position at the beginning of the Depression to purchase nearly a dozen building-material firms weakened by the economic downturn. In 1930 US Gypsum bought into the insulation-board business with the purchase of the Greenville Insulating Board Corporation of Greenville, Mississippi. Also in 1930, it bought into the metal-lath business with the purchase of the Youngstown Pressed Steel Company of Warren, Ohio and the metal-lath division of Northwestern Expanded Metal Company. Avery also made US Gypsum, which had already been in the lime business for 15 years, a leading lime producer in 1930 with the acquisition of lime-producing firms such as the Farnam Cheshire Lime Company. Producers of mineral wool and asphalt roofing acquired in 1933, and asbestos-cement siding acquired in 1937, rounded out the Depression-era acquisitions. The company countered the downturn in new construction by exploiting the remodeling and industrial markets. During the Depression, 15% of sales were to industrial users. Glass-makers used gypsum as a packing material. Cement producers used it to retard setting, and moviemakers used flaked gypsum as snow.

In 1940, a new problem confronted the company's management when the U.S. Justice Department filed suit against US Gypsum and six other wallboard manufacturers, charging them with price-fixing. The claim stemmed from US Gypsum's 1929 cross-licensing of its patented wallboard. The agreement set prices at which the wallboard must be sold. In 1950 the Supreme Court forced US Gypsum and its six licensees—who produced all of the wallboard sold east of the Rocky Mountains—to cease setting prices, and US Gypsum was enjoined from exercising its patent-licensing privilege.

Between 1946 and 1949 US Gypsum invested over $51 million in expansion under the direction of William L. Keady, who had become president in 1942. In 1949, however, Chairman Avery predicted another depression—incorrectly—and began to rein in expansion. Keady resigned as a result of Avery's intervention. Although there was a slight recession in 1949, the company did not step up capital spending again until 1954. In May 1951, when Sewell Avery resigned as US Gypsum's chairman and CEO, his replacement, Clarence H. Shaver, inherited a company which had a capitalized value of $61 million and produced more than 75 commodities in 47 mines or factories. Avery's imprint was an extreme conservatism marked by strong centralized control, rigid cost-cutting practices, and few benefits for employees.

Toward the end of the 1950s US Gypsum extended its expansion internationally. One of its principal discoveries during the decade was the gypsum deposit in Mexico's San Luis Potosi State. This find, one of the world's largest was conservatively estimated to contain at least 300 million tons of commercial deposits.

In the 1960s US Gypsum became the first major U.S. corporation to undertake privately funded housing renovation on a large scale. The highly publicized project began in 1964, when US Gypsum purchased six adjoining tenements in the East Harlem Section of New York City. US Gypsum paid $9,125 to renovate each unit; the cost of constructing new units averaged $22,500. US Gypsum's president, Graham J. Morgan, saw these projects as an opportunity to get in on the ground floor of a potential $20 billion market. Morgan felt the renovation would open up because of the Federal Housing Administration's willingness to provide financing for such projects. By 1969 the company had remodeled completely 32 buildings in New York, Cleveland, Chicago, and Detroit.

In 1973 US Gypsum settled a class-action civil antitrust suit brought against it by wallboard users and buyers. Settlement of those cases, which alleged price fixing, cost US Gypsum $28 million. This case led to a criminal indictment of US Gypsum and three competitors in 1973. The criminal trial eventually found its way to the Supreme Court, which ordered a new trial, and in 1980 US Gypsum settled the case, agreeing to pay $2.6 million in taxes on deductions from earlier civil antitrust judgements.

On January 1, 1985, the holding company, USG Corporation (USG), was created, and US Gypsum became the largest of the holding company's nine operating subsidiaries. Chairman and CEO Edward W. Duffy formed the holding company to protect the bulk of company operations from asbestos litigation against US Gypsum. Asbestos had been a standard additive in wallboard manufacture for decades. US Gypsum had already begun to face property damage suits in 1984 with a $675,000 award to a South Carolina school district. The reorganization of the company was effective January 1, 1985.

In November 1986, the Belzberg brothers of Canada attempted a hostile takeover of USG. USG immediately instituted a plan to buy back 20% of its common stock in an effort to fend off the takeover. By December 1986, however, USG had purchased Samuel, William, and Hyman Belzberg's 4.9% stake, for $139.6 million dollars. The Belzberg family's profits on the transaction were in excess of $25 million dollars.

In October 1987 a partnership led by Texans Cyril Wagner Jr. and Jack E. Brown's Desert Partners attempted to gain control of the company. Wagner and Brown's main business venture was a Midland, Texas, oil and gas partnership with secondary real estate operations. They purchased their 9.83% stake in USG as USG tried to recover financially from the Belzberg takeover attempt. In April 1988 a federal court refused to block USG's poison-pill antitakeover plan. In May 1988 USG announced a restructuring and recapitalization plan designed to block further the takeover attempt, and by

June the plan had succeeded. The plan was expensive, however, and in October 1988 USG sold its Masonite Corporation subsidiary, purchased in 1984. International Paper Corporation paid $400 million for Masonite.

USG's United States Gypsum Company subsidiary remains the largest gypsum producer in the world. The company is divided into four divisions. The gypsum-products division produces goods ranging from wallboard to agricultural and industrial gypsum, cements, and fillers. The interior-systems section produces tile and partition goods. The building-products-distribution section transports a variety of gypsum products and construction accessories throughout the United States, primarily through its L&W Supply Corporation subsidiary. The other-products division markets goods ranging from mineral-wood products to engineering-consulting services. The future of USG Corporation will be affected by the debt it has incurred during restructuring. The firm has an outstanding debt of $2.4 billion and has been forced to abandon Avery's habit of maintaining large cash reserves.

Principal Subsidiaries: United States Gypsum Company; USG Interiors, Inc.; L&W Supply Corporation.; DAP Inc.; CGC Inc. (76%).

Further Reading: ''Gyp,'' *Fortune,* February 1936; ''U.S. Gypsum: No Nonsense,'' *Fortune,* September 1955.

—John C. Bishop

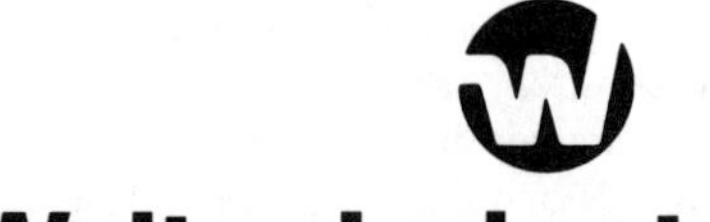

WALTER INDUSTRIES, INC.

1500 North Dale Mabry Highway
Tampa, Florida 33607
U.S.A.
(813) 871-4811
Fax: (813) 871-4430

Wholly Owned Subsidiary of Hillsborough Holdings Corporation
Incorporated: 1955 as Jim Walter Corporation
Employees: 8,200
Sales: $1.4 billion

Walter Industries and its parent company, the Hillsborough Holdings Corporation (HHC), were organized in August and incorporated in September of 1987 by a group of investors led by Kohlberg Kravis Roberts & Company (KKR) to acquire Jim Walter Corporation. Jim Walter Corporation was a Florida-based corporation primarily engaged in residential and non-residential construction, renovation, and remodeling; water and waste-water transmission; industrial and consumer markets; and natural-resources development. When approached by KKR in 1987, Jim Walter Corporation was the nation's fourth-largest home builder, a vigorous public corporation under stable leadership, well known throughout the southern United States for its affordable homes. By 1990, Walter Industries and Hillsborough Holdings stood at the center of controversial asbestos-related litigation and were operating under Chapter 11 bankruptcy court protection.

In 1946, James W. Walter borrowed $400 from his father, a citrus grower, and purchased a "shell," or unfinished home, for $895 from Tampa, Florida, builder, O. L. Davenport. When, just three days later, the 23-year-old, newly married Walter sold the home to a passerby for a profit, he saw a way out of his $50-a-week truck-driving job and $50-a-month apartment. Walter convinced Davenport, also in his 20s, to take him on as a partner. As Walter remembered in *Nation's Business* in 1970, "we made out all right, but I thought we could move faster." Walter encouraged Davenport to run bigger advertisements featuring photographs of the homes; they sold more houses. Walter was enthusiastic about building the business even faster. Davenport was reluctant. After two years, they dissolved the partnership of Davenport & Walter. The men decided to divide the business: one of them would take the assets of about $50,000, the other the business. Since Davenport was the founder, he first opted to take the business. A day after he made his decision, he told his partner he had changed his mind and chose the assets instead. Davenport took his share and bought a motel and small construction firm in Troy, Alabama. Jim Walter continued the business, now called the Walter Construction Company.

In the post-World War II era, housing was scarce. Jim Walter sold unfinished, traditionally constructed homes as affordable, alternative housing. The wood homes were built on concrete foundations or wood pilings. Each home was completely finished on the outside with an unfinished interior. Buyers installed plumbing, electrical systems, insulation, walls, and doors themselves. Homes were sold directly to owners prior to construction, through one of Jim Walter Homes Division sales offices.

In 1955, Jim Walter incorporated the Walter Construction Company as the Jim Walter Corporation. Three men who would be pivotal to the company's success through the coming decades had already joined the firm. James O. Alston came to the company in 1947 and was instrumental in its early growth. Alston was president of the corporation from 1963 to 1970, chairman of the homebuilding operation, and vice chairman of the corporation by 1970. Arnold F. Saraw, a partner in Walter Construction, was secretary-treasurer of the corporation from 1955 to 1970. In 1970, he was promoted to senior vice president, heading the corporate mortgage division. The third man, Joe B. Cordell, an accountant who joined the company in 1958 was vice president and chief financial officer, became president in 1974 and chief executive officer in 1983.

During the 1950s, the company expanded and entered the mortgage business. Initially financing was difficult. The turning point for the fledgling company came in 1956 when Chicago creditors Walter E. Heller & Company approved a $1 million line of credit. Jim Walter's mortgages, like his homes, were attractive to buyers who found more conventional sources too costly. Jim Walter Corporation's innovative financing plan was outlined in the May 19, 1987 edition of *Financial World:* " . . . most of the houses . . . are financed on the basis of ten percent fixed mortgages or installment notes maturing in up to 20 years. Unlike a conventional mortgage, . . . Jim Walter's buyers spread the interest and principal payments evenly across the term to lessen its risk of defaults. Such mortgages were possible because the company required the purchaser to own the land on which the house was to be built. The equity in the land substituted for the traditional cash down payment. The company's mortgage portfolio was traditionally one of its strongest assets. The mortgage finance division maintained more than $1 billion in installment notes in the 1970s. By 1987, Jim Walter's $1.6 billion mortgage portfolio was larger than those of most Florida savings and loans. An evaluation performed in 1988 by Financial Security Assurance, in a maneuver designed to help KKR and Walter Industries refinance $1.2 billion in bank debt, put the value of Walter's mortgage portfolio at $1.75 billion.

Sales of Walter homes historically ran counter to other builders' sales, due to the availability of low-cost financing. Low, fixed interest rates combined with an affordable product ensured that when housing starts were generally down and money was tight, buyers looked for alternatives like those offered by Jim Walter. During 1982, Jim Walter built 10,000 of the 300,000 homes constructed that year. In 1986, Walter homes accounted for just 6,500 of the half-million homes built. The company tallied some of it best years during recessions in the housing industry.

From 1955 to 1962, Jim Walter Corporation was primarily involved in the building industry. Walter's only notable acquisition during the 1950s was the First National Bank in St. Petersburg, Florida, later sold. This foray was the start of a policy of diversification.

During the 1960s and 1970s, the company made a large number of acquisitions and mergers. Walter acquired no less than 15 different subsidiaries in the 1960s, ranging from building-materials and industrial-products manufacturers to a California savings and loan. The Celotex Corporation merger was initiated in 1962 and completed in 1964. A pioneer in sound insulation and a leading manufacturer of building products, Celotex also made a spray-on asbestos insulation. The company also acquired a sugar firm and an oil exploration company. Two paper companies acquired in 1968, Marquette Paper Corporation and Knight Paper Company, rounded out Jim Walter's early acquisitions.

On March 9, 1964, Jim Walter Corporation was first listed on the New York Stock Exchange. Shares initially sold for 50¢. From 1969 until 1979, stockholders enjoyed positive results: dividends increased from 40¢ to $1.80 per share; book value increased from $6.46 to $34 per share. By 1970, the shares had twice split three ways. In 1986, Walter's board of directors approved a five-for-four common stock split, in the form of a 25% stock dividend. In 1987, the KKR group brought the company for $60 a share, with bidding at one point reaching the heady number of $67 per share.

Throughout the 1960s, over 200 competitors tried to emulate the company's success in the production of shell homes. By the end of the 1970s, Jim Walter, the originator of the concept, was the only one left and his "rags-to-riches" saga had become a part of Florida folklore. A Tampa cab driver, who did not recognize his passenger, regaled Jim Walter with the story of Jim's life. In 1968, on the 20th anniversary of the founding of the company, Jim Walter, commemorated his beginnings by buying back the original shell house he had first owned for just three days in 1946.

In 1969, the company bought United States Pipe and Foundry Company of Birmingham, Alabama, for $135 million in stock and cash. By 1979, U.S. Pipe had increased profits five times over. In the July 13, 1979 issue of *Forbes,* Walter called it "the quickest deal I ever made."

At the time of the purchase, U.S. Pipe's modest coke operation and unmined coal reserves attracted little attention. By 1973, however, the Arab oil embargo made coal mining a potential bonanza. In 1976, the company created the subsidiary, Jim Walter Resources, to direct the company's mine-development program. Since Jim Walter knew home building, but not mining, he hired experienced people to guide the mining division. The magnitude of the task that faced a company with no experience in difficult longwall mining, required due to the depth of the coal, was daunting. The company's robust cash flow was able to absorb the crush of hefty capital expenditures during the nearly ten years it took to make the mines operational.

During the 1970s, Jim Walter continued the pattern of diversifying the company, adding another dozen subsidiaries. By the end of the decade, Jim Walter was involved in coal mining; marble, limestone, and granite quarrying; oil and gas production; gypsum and asbestos mining; a savings and loan association; an insurance company; a paper-marketing firm; water and waste-water pipe manufacturing; and retail jewelry. While the various mergers and acquisitions broadened Jim Walter's base of operations, the bulk of its revenues remained in the building industry, with more than 200,000 shell homes completed by 1979. Sales in 1979 exceeded $2 billion a year.

In 1972, Panacon Corporation, the third-largest Canadian producer of asbestos, was merged into Celotex Corporation. As the link between asbestos and cancer became clear, lawsuits from workers began to accumulate. Jim Walter's 1986 10-K form reported that two subsidiaries, Celotex and Carey Canada Inc., were co-defendants with a number of other miners, manufacturers, and distributors of asbestos products in a "substantial number" of lawsuits alleging work-related injuries. Many of the suits requested punitive as well as compensatory damages. According to the company, "the aggregate damages sought in these cases is substantial." What followed was a series of convoluted machinations, suits, and counter suits, on behalf of both defendants and plaintiffs, with mixed results. The company thought its insurance carriers would handle the claims, but coverage after 1977 disallowed asbestos-related claims. In 1985, the subsidiaries and co-defendants entered into an agreement to resolve the claims. All claims filed after June 19, 1985, were to be referred to the Asbestos Claim Facility, set up by the agreement, with the cost of litigation or mediation to be shared by all the defendants according to a formula based on their asbestos litigation experiences.

The home-building division continued to produce strong results through the 1980s. In 1986, Walter maintained 103 sales offices scattered through 29 states, most of them in the South. The homes were constructed by local construction firms who were subcontracted to do the work. Shell homes accounted for 28% of units sold and the 90% completed homes totaled nearly 60%. In the same year, homebuilding and related financing accounted for 14% of total sales and revenues for the company, contributing $108.4 million.

At the same time, Celotex found itself staggering under an ever-mounting litigation load. In 1984, approximately 21,100 lawsuits representing 25,600 persons were pending against one or more of the subscribers of the Asbestos Claim Facility, including Celotex. In 1985, 28,800 lawsuits representing 34,900 persons were pending. As of August 31, 1986, there were approximately 43,900 bodily injury claims pending. By the time Kohlberg Kravis Roberts moved to acquire the company in 1987, pending lawsuits exceeded 50,000. By January 1988, they numbered 58,000.

The actions taken by the subsidiaries allowed KKR to proclaim the company's litigation risk "manageable." Under corporate law, the parent company could not be held liable for claims against its subsidiaries. KKR proceeded with its purchase of Jim Walter Corporation for $2.4 billion in August 1987. The company was a perfect takeover target; healthy profits, strong cash flow, and a raft of subsidiaries that could be sold to reduce debt. At KKR's request, Jim Walter joined the group of investors who bought the company. He became a chairman of HHC and Walter Industries, retaining the existing management team.

The company was split into two holding companies following the sale. Jim Walter Corporation retained ownership of Celotex, and Hillsborough Holdings Corporation kept the other subsidiaries. Jim Walter Corporation was sold to Jasper Corporation. Walter Industries merged into HHC, all under the name of Walter Industries.

In 1989, Houston attorney Stephen D. Sussman, of Sussman Godfrey, filed a suit on behalf of asbestos victims in Beaumont, Texas, an industrial area where many of them lived. The new lawsuit named KKR, Hillsborough Holdings, and Walter Industries as principal defendants. The suit brought about the demise of KKR's plan to restructure Hillsborough Holdings Corporation's debt. Asset sales were blocked, and the price of HHC's junk bonds plummeted. HHC was unable to meet the obligations imposed by the sales of junk bonds that funded the buyout. On December 27, 1989, Hillsborough Holdings Corporation and 31 of its subsidiaries each filed bankruptcy under Chapter 11 in Tampa. Only two subsidiaries, Cardem Insurance Co. and Jefferson Warrior Railroad Company, did not file petitions for court-protected reorganization.

In April 1990 Judge Alexander L. Paskay, Chief Bankruptcy Judge for the U.S. Bankruptcy Court in the Middle District of Florida, recommended that the asbestos suit filed in Texas be heard in his court. In July the U.S. District Court for the same district adopted his recommendation, and the case was moved to the Tampa federal bankruptcy court. In 1990, the company that Jim Walter had built into an empire on the strength of a simple idea like the shell home faced an uncertain future.

Principal Subsidiaries: Best Insurors, Inc.; Best Insurors of Mississippi, Inc.; Cardem Insurance Company, Ltd.; Coast to Coast Advertising, Inc.; Computer Holdings Corporation; Dixie Building Supplies, Inc.; Hamer Holdings Corporation; Hamer Properties, Inc.; Homes Holdings Corporation; Jefferson Warrior Railroad Company; Jim Walter Computer Services, Inc.; Jim Walter Homes, Inc.; Jim Walter Insurance Services, Inc.; Jim Walter Resources, Inc.; Jim Walter Window Component, Inc.; JW Aluminum Company; JW Resources Holdings Corporation; J.W.I. Holdings Corporation; J.W. Walter, Inc.; JW Window Components, Inc.; Land Holdings Corporation; Mid-State Homes, Inc.; Mid-State Holdings Corporation; Railroad Holdings Corporation; Sloss Industries Corporation; Southern Precision Corporation; United Land Corporation; United States Pipe and Foundry Company; U.S. Pipe Realty, Inc.; Vestal Manufacturing Company; Walter Home Improvement, Inc.; Walter Land Company.

Further Reading: Sachar, Laura, "Building the Blue-Collar Dreams," *Financial World,* May 19, 1987.

—Lynn M. Kalanik

INDEX TO COMPANIES AND PERSONS

Listings are arranged in alphabetical order under the company name; thus Eli Lilly & Company will be found under the letter E. Definite articles (The) and forms of incorporation that precede the name (A.B. and N.V.) are ignored for alphabetical purposes. Company names appearing in **bold** type have historical essays on the page numbers appearing in **bold**. The index is cumulative, with volume numbers printed in **bold** type.

ANKLI, Robert E. Professor, Department of Economics, University of Guelph, Ontario. Author of "The Influence of American Manufacturers on the Canadian Automobile Industry," *Business and Economic History*, 1981, and "Missed Opportunities: The Early Canadian and Machine Tool Industry," *American Review of Canadian Studies*, 1989.

ANTONE, George P. Chairman and Professor, Department of History, Appalachian State University, Boone, North Carolina.

BADARACCO, Claire. Assistant Professor, College of Communication, Marquette University, Milwaukee, Wisconsin. Author of annotated edition of *The Cuba Journal 1833–35 of Sophia Peabody Hawthorne*, 1984, and *R.R. Donnelley's "Four American Books Campaign" at The Lakeside Press 1926–1930*, 1990. Guest editor for "Publicity and American Culture" issue of *Public Relations Review*, 1990.

BARBOUR, Philippe A. Assistant Editor, St. James Press, London. Editor of *Wine '89*, 1989, and co-author of *Wine Buyers Guide: Saint Emilion*, forthcoming.

BARKER, T.C. Professor Emeritus of Economic History, University of London; President, International Historical Congress, 1990–1995. Author of *A Merseyside Town in the Industrial Revolution*, 1954, *A History of the Worshipful Company of Carpenters*, 1968, *A History of British Pewter*, 1974, *The Economic and Social Effects of the Spread of Motor Vehicles*, 1987, *Moving Millions*, 1990, and other works in business history.

BATOR, Joseph. Doctoral candidate in History, Northwestern University, Evanston, Illinois; communications consultant and writer, Division of Continuing Education, Northwestern University. Lecturer, Northwestern University, and visiting instructor, Knox College, Galesburg, Illinois, and North Central College, Naperville, Illinois, 1987–89. Author of "The Immigrants' Protective League in the Aftermath of the Restriction of Immigration, 1921–1929," *Transactions of the Illinois State Historical Society: Selected Papers of the Seventh Symposium and Eighth Symposium*, Springfield, 1989, received the Robert P. Howard Award, Illinois State Historical Society.

BELSITO, Elaine. Free-lance writer and editor. Assistant Managing Editor, *Archives of Physical Medicine and Rehabilitation*, 1988-90.

BISHOP, John C. Doctoral candidate in History, Auburn University, Alabama. Author of "Delivering the Goods by Air: The United States Air Cargo Industry, 1945–1955," *Essays in Economic and Business History*, 1990, and "The Flying Tiger Line," "Seaboard World Airlines," "Earl Slick," and "Robert Prescott" in *Encyclopedia of American Business History and Biography*, 1991.

BJÖRKLUND, Nils G. Free-lance writer retired from industrial management. Executive Vice President, Valmet, Tampella, G.A. Serlaohius Oy, 1957–82. Author of industrial memoirs, *Kakkosmies* (The Second Man), 1983, and the history of Valmet Corporation, *Valmet Oy*, 1990.

BLOCK, Bernard A. Documents Librarian and Assistant Professor, Ohio State University Libraries, Columbus, Ohio. Author of "Romance and High Purpose: The National Geographic," *Wilson Library Bulletin*, 1984, and "A Magazinist's View of the Encyclopedia of Associations," *The Reference Librarian*, 1990.

BORSCHEID, Peter. Professor of Social and Economic History, University of Marburg; co-editor of the series *Studien zur Geschichte des Alltags.* Author of *Geschichte des Alters: 16.–18. Jahrhundert*, 1987, and *Mit Sicherheit leben: Die Geschichte der deutschen Lebensversicherungswirtschaft*, 1989.

BOWDEN, A. Researcher and writer in the City of London.

BOWMAN, Jim. Corporate history writer, writing teacher, Columbia College, Chicago, Illinois. Reporter, *Chicago Daily News*, 1968–78; columnist, *Chicago Tribune*, 1982–85. Author of *Good Medicine: The First 150 Years of Rush-Presbyterian-St.Luke's Medical Center*, 1987, and *"Waste Not...": The Safety-Kleen Story*, 1989.

BRIGHT, Juliette. Journalist.

BRÜNINGHAUS, Beate. Manager of the Society for Business History, Cologne; member of editorial staff of the *Zeitschrift fur Unternehmensgeschichte* (*ZUG*) since 1983 and the *German Yearbook on Business History*, 1984–1989. Co-author of "Die Daimler-Benz AG in den Jahren 1933 bis 1945," *ZUG*, 1987.

BURTON, John. Stockholm correspondent, *The Financial Times*. Has written articles for the *International Herald Tribune*, *USA Today*, *Business Magazine*, *International Management*, and other publications.

CAIN, Louis P. Professor of Economics, Loyola University of Chicago; Visiting Professor of Economics, Northwestern University; member of editorial boards of *Journal of Economic History* and *Business History Review*. Author of *Sanitation Strategy for a Lakefront Metropolis: The Case of Chicago*, 1978, and "From Mud to Metropolis: Chicago before the Fire," *Research in Economic History*, 1986.

CARRE, Robin. Teaching Assistant in History, University of Illinois at Chicago.

CATHCART, John D. Archivist, Bentley College, Waltham, Massachusetts. Co-author of "Harry Clark Bentley 1877–1967" in *Biographies of Notable Accountants*, 1989.

CHANDLER, Alfred D., Jr. Straus Professor of Business History, Emeritus, Graduate School of Business Administration, Hàrvard University, Cambridge, Massachusetts. Author of *Strategy and Structure: Chapters in* *the History of the American Industrial Enterprise*, 1962, *The Visible Hand: The Managerial Revolution in American Business*, 1977, winner of the Pulitzer Prize for History, 1978, *Managerial Hierarchies*, 1980, *The Coming of Managerial Capitalism*, 1985, *Scale and Scope: The Dynamics of Industrial Capitalism*, 1990, and other works in business history.

CHEVALIER, Tracy. Literary Editor, St. James Press, London. Editor of *20th Century Children's Writers*, 3rd edition, 1989, and *Contemporary Poets*, 1991.

CLASSE, Alison. Free-lance writer and computer consultant. Contributor to *Computing*, *Accountancy*, *Banking Systems International*, and to *Annual Obituary*, 1989.

CLASSE, Olive. Free-lance writer and translator. Formerly Senior Lecturer in French, University of Glasgow, retired 1990. Author of "*En quelle situation?* Some notes on Racine's *Phedre*," *Newsletter of the Society for Seventeenth Century French Studies*, 1982, and critical notes in J. Pradon's *Phedre et Hippolyte*, Textes litteraires LXII, University of Exeter, 1987.

COCKERELL, Hugh. Visiting Professor in Insurance Studies, The City University Business School, London. Secretary, Chartered Insurance Institute, London, 1945–71. Co-author of *The British Insurance Business 1547–1970*, 1976, and author of *Lloyd's of London—A Portrait*, 1984.

COCLANIS, Peter A. Associate Professor of History, University of North Carolina at Chapel Hill. Author of *The Shadow of a Dream: Economic Life and Death in the South Carolina Low Country, 1670–1920*, 1989, and co-author of "Capital Formation and Southern Industry, 1880–1905: The Case of the Carolina Piedmont," *Journal of Economic History*, 1989.

COHEN, Paula. Consultant in Corporate Archives and History. Author of *Shaping a System of Higher Education: The History of the Cleveland Commission on Higher Education*, 1987, and *A Global Perspective*, 1990.

CONRAD, Paul. Assistant Editor of *Italy Italy* magazine, Rome. Managing Editor of *Sentinel Magazine*, Chicago, Illinois, 1985–89.

COWLING, Marc. Economic Research Consultant, Cowling Associates Economic Consultancy.

DOORLEY, Michael. Doctoral candidate in History and Teaching Assistant, University of Illinois at Chicago.

DU RY, Marc. Training Psychoanalyst; editor of journal of the Centre for Freudian Analysis and Research, London.

EMMONS, Vera A. Assistant Editor of *Business Information Alert*, Chicago, Illinois.

FRIES, Sebastian. Researcher at Gesellschaft für Unternehmensgeschichte, Cologne.

FURLONG, Patrick J. Professor of History, Indiana University at South Bend. Co-author of *Studebaker: Less Than They Promised*, 1984, and author of *Indiana: An Illustrated History*, 1985.

GILBERT, Sari. Free-lance writer. Correspondent in Italy for the *Washington Post*, 1975–85. Author of "Italy's Embattled Deficit Buster," *Institutional Investor*, 1989, and "Deal-making Italian Style," *Institutional Investor*, 1990.

GRIFFIN, Jessica. Assistant Editor, St. James Press, London. Japanese Investment Manager, Thornton Group, London, 1987–89.

GROSS, Daniel. Graduate student in History, Harvard University, Cambridge, Massachusetts. Reporter for *The New Republic*, 1989–90.

GROSSMAN, William R. Free-lance writer. Author of *The Dating Maze*, 1989.

HALL, Lynn. Research specialist in the history of computers and computer technology, Jortberg Associates, Peabody, Massachusetts. Collections Manager, Computer Museum, Boston, 1987–88. Co-author of "Out of the Past...into the Future: Documenting the Evolution of the Computer Industry," *The Business History Bulletin*, 1989.

HALPERN, Leslie C. Senior Technical Editor, Martin Marietta Orlando Aerospace, Orlando, Florida. Author of "Florida's Hot Spots: Prime Locations for Shooting," *The Hollywood Reporter*, 1989, and "APECS: Aerospace Planning Execution and Control System," *The Eagle*, 1990.

HARPHAM, Joan. Free-lance writer; columnist in *Export Magazine*.

HEALEY, R.M. Free-lance writer and historian. Research Assistant at London University (History of Parliament Trust) and for M.P. Patrick Cormack, 1987–90. Editor of *Hertfordshire Society Yearbook*, 1986. Author of *Hertfordshire—A Shell Guide*, 1982, and *The Diary of George Mushet, 1805–1814*, 1982; contributor to *Biographical Dictionary of Modern British Radicals*, 1984, *Dictionary of Literary Biography*, 1991, and *Romanticism—an Encyclopedia*, 1991.

HEALY, Carole. Free-lance writer. Contributing Editor, *Global Press*, 1986–87. Has written business and feature articles for *The Washington Post*, *The Chicago Tribune*, and the *Daily Yomiuri* in Tokyo.

HEED, Thomas J. Associate Dean and Director, School of American/International Studies, Ramapo College of New Jersey, Mahwah. Author of "The Birthing of a Progressive Reformer: Harry S. Truman as Presiding Judge" in *Harry S.*

Truman: The Man from Independence, 1986, and "Business Ventures" in *The Harry S. Truman Encyclopedia*, 1990.

HEENAN, Patrick. Research student at the University of London, free-lance writer. Editor, Books Department of Euromoney Publications, 1989–90. Editor of *1992*, 1990.

HEFFERREN, Aileen C. Assistant Managing Editor of *The National Interest* magazine.

JONES, Stephanie. Free-lance journalist and author; Managing Director, International Business Writing Ltd.; international correspondent, *Executive Search Review*. Archivist, Inchcape Group, 1981–85, and teacher in Economic History, London School of Economics, School of Oriental and African Studies, 1985–88. Author of *Two Centuries of Overseas Trading*, 1986, and *The Headhunting Business*, 1989.

KALANIK, Lynn M. Advertising Copywriter, Richard D. Irwin Inc., Homewood, Illinois. Creative consultant and project director, The Waterkotte Co. Inc., Pittsburgh, Pennsylvania, 1987–88.

KEELEY, Carol I. Free-lance writer and researcher; columnist in *Neon*; researcher for *Ford Times* and *Discovery*. Author of *Oxford Poetry*, 1987, and *Voices International*, 1989.

KELLY, Serena. Deputy Archivist, Baring Brothers & Co. Ltd. Formerly Secretary General, Business Archives Council. Contributor to *Men of Property, the Norwich Enrolled Deeds 1285–1311*, Centre of East Anglian Studies, 1983, and *Business Archives Administration*, 1990; co-author of "Giving Directions to the Town, the Early Town Directories," *Urban History Yearbook*, 1984.

KOCH, Peter. Professor, Aachen Technical University. Formerly Chairman of the Board of Management, Aachen Re, retired 1983. Author of *Bilder zur Versicherungsgeschichte*, 1978, *Versicherungsplätze in Deutschland*, 1986, and *Versicherungswirtschaft—Ein einführender Überblick*, 1989. Co-editor, *Handwörterbuch der Versicherung*, 1988.

KRONLUND, Sonia. Free-lance journalist; contributor to *Les Cahiers du Cinema* and *Liberation*. Honorary Lecturer in French, University College, London, 1989-90.

LACOSSE, Gwen M. Free-lance writer. Reporter, United Press International, 1978–81, and *Rocky Mountain News*, 1981–82.

LASHINSKY, Adam. East Coast Reporter, *Plastics News*, Crain Communications Inc. Author of articles in *Advertising Age*, *Crain's Chicago Business*.

LEMAY, Joseph A. Professor of Political Science, Ramapo College of New Jersey, Mahwah. Editor of newsletter, *Canadian Focus*, 1984–1989. Author of *Environmental Land Use Problems*, 1974, *Quebec and the American Business Community*, 1981, *Public Policy in Canada: American Business Experiences in Quebec*, 1984, and *The International Operations of a New Jersey Multinational Corporation: Ingersoll-Rand*, 1989.

LEWIS, Scott M. Free-lance editor and writer; contributing editor, *Option*. Staff editor, *Security, Distributing and Marketing*, 1989–90.

LOIZOU, Andreas. Business analyst, City of London.

MACKERVOY, Susan. Lecturer in German, Reading University.

MAGON, Kim M. Consultant, KGM Communications; free-lance editor, *World Facts & Maps*. Associate Editor, Technical Reporting Corp., Chicago, 1985–88.

MARTIN, Jonathan. Free-lance writer; doctoral candidate in English, University of Chicago. Screenplay, *A Life of Her Own*, in production.

McCRILLIS, Neal R. Doctoral candidate in history and teaching assistant, University of Illinois at Chicago.

MERMIGAS, Diane C. Senior Business Reporter, Crain Communications; contributor to *Electronic Media* and *Advertising Age*.

MERRION, Paul R. Washington Editor, *Crain's Chicago Business* and Washington Bureau Chief, Crain Communications Inc.

MILLER, Peter W. Information Consultant. Contributing editor to the *Construction Industry Thesaurus*, 1975–80; Research Fellow in Information Studies at Polytechnic of North London,1981–85; and Information Technology Officer at U.K. Library Association, 1985–88. Author of *Computers and the Construction Industry*, 1979, and *Production and Bibliographic Control of Non-Book Materials*, 1985.

MOHNKE, Mary Sue. Free-lance writer. News Bureau Manager and Instructor, Northeastern Illinois University, Chicago, 1979–86; Coordinator of Public Information, Chicago Architecture Foundation, 1976–79; and Publications Editor, Roosevelt National Investment and Life Insurance Company, Springfield, Illinois, 1974-75. Author of "Partners Against Crime," *Illinois Quarterly*, 1990, and "Invisible Neighbors," *North Shore*, 1991.

MOORE, Betty T. Senior Editor, Joint Commission on Accreditation of Healthcare Organizations, Oakbrook Terrace, Illinois. Author of *How to Manage Financial Systems*, 1981, *Housing for the Elderly*, 1984, and *Quality Assurance in Ambulatory Care*, 1990.

NORTON, Frances E. Free-lance writer. Contributor to *Evanston Arts Review* and *Helicon*.

O'LEARY, D.H. Corporate lawyer. Formerly worked in commerce in Japan and in London.

OLEINICK, Lori. Feature Writer for Lerner newspapers. Work has appeared in *Restaurant & Institutions*, *Crain's Chicago Business*, *Chicago Tribune*, *Detroit Free Press* and *Detroit News*.

PEKOW, Charles. Free-lance writer; editor of *Day Care USA*. Author of articles in the *Washington Post* and in the *Washington City Paper*.

PFEIFFER, Wolfgang. Head of Department of Technical and Scientific Information, Carl Zeiss, Oberkochen, and of the Optical Museum, Oberkochen; Chief Editor of *Zeiss Information*. Author of "Spezialgebiete der medizinischen Photographie," *Chemische Rundschau*, 1975, and "Das Mikroskop und seine Geschichte," *Jahrbuch für Optik und Feinmechanik*, 1985.

POOLE, Kathleen. Corporate writer; President, Kathleen Poole & Associates, Inc. Author of *Wildlife at the John F. Kennedy Space Center*, 1989.

POTISK, Karin. Free-lance translator.

PRESNELL, Jenny L. Humanities and Social Sciences Librarian, Miami University, Oxford, Ohio. Reference Librarian, Xavier University, Cincinnati, Ohio, 1984–88. Author of "Angelina Grimke" and "Edward Hyde, 1st Earl of Clarendon," in *Read More about It*, 1989.

PRITCHETT, Janie. Free-lance writer. Co-author of *The Central Florida Career Guide*, 1987.

RAHDER, Karl F. Lecturer in Political Science, Lake Forest College and North Park College, Chicago, Illinois. Author of "The Tibetan Claim to Statehood," *Chicago Review of International Affairs*, 1990.

RIAL, William Y. Director, Provider Relations, Blue Cross and Blue Shield Association, Chicago, Illinois; member of Editorial Advisory Board, *Family Practice News*. Past President, American Medical Association. Co-author of "Emergency Medicine" in *Textbook of Family Practice*, 1990.

RING, Trudy. Reporter, *Pensions & Investments*.

RODRIGUEZ, Ginger G. Free-lance writer and editor; compiles history projects for East Chicago Public Library system. Author of "Drafting Language into the Law" and "A Degree of Opportunity," *Righting Words*, 1988.

ROSS, Wallace. Lecturer and writing consultant.

ROULAND, Roger W. Free-lance writer for *Chicago Tribune, Chicago Sun-Times*, and other newspapers. Author of "One bank era ends, another begins," *The Genoa-Kingston-Kirkland News*, 1987, received First Place Award in business news, Northern Illinois Newspaper Association.

ROURKE, Elizabeth. Free-lance writer and graduate student in History at the University of Chicago.

ROWE, D.J. Senior Lecturer and Senior Tutor in Economics, University of Newcastle upon Tyne. Editor of *Northern Business Histories: a Bibliography*, 1979, and author of "The north-east" in *The Cambridge Social History of Britain 1750–1950*, Volume 1, 1990.

RUSSELL, Ann T. Research specialist in the history of computers and computer technology, Jortberg Associates, Peabody, Massachusetts. Co-author of "Out of the Past...into the Future: Documenting the Evolution of the Computer Industry," *The Business History Bulletin*, 1989.

RÜTHER, Martin. Academic Researcher at the National Socialist Archives Center, Cologne. Author of *Arbeiterschaft in Köln 1928–1945*, 1990, and *Zwischen Zusammenbruch und Wirtschaftswunder. Betriebsratstätigkeit und Arbeiterverhalten in Köln 1945–1952*, 1990.

SACHSE, Wieland. Assistant at the Institute for Economic and Social History, Göttingen University; Scientific Advisor at Wella AG, Darmstadt. Co-author of *Joachim Friedrich Martens (1806–1877) und die Deutsche Arbeiterbewegung*, 1984, and author of *Göttingen im 18. und 19. Jahrhundert. Zur Bevölkerungs- und Sozialstruktur einer deutschen Universitätsstadt*, 1987.

SCHROTER, Harm G. Assistant Professor, University of Berlin. Author of *Aussenpolitik und Wirtschaftsinteresse, Skandinavien im aussenwirtschaftlichen Kalkül Deutschlands und Grossbritanniens 1918–1939*, 1983, and "Risk and Control in Multinational Enterprise: German Business in Scandinavia," *Business History Review*, 1988; co-editor of *Politik, Wirtschaft und internationale Beziehungen*, 1990.

SCHUSTEFF, Sandy. Marketing and communications consultant; Adjunct Professor, Lake Forest Graduate School of Management, Lake Forest, Illinois.

SCOTT, Christopher A. Associate Editor, *Crain's Chicago Business*. Editor, United Press International, 1985–87.

SHANNON, Timothy J. Doctoral candidate in History, Northwestern University, Evanston, Illinois. Author of "The Ohio Company and the Meaning of Opportunity in the American West, 1786-1795," *New England Quarterly*, 1991.

SIMLEY, John. Issues Analyst, Illinois Bell Telephone Co., Chicago, Illinois. Associate Editor, *International Directory of Company Histories*, Volume I, 1988.

SLINN, Judy. Free-lance business historian; Associate, Business History Unit, London School of Economics. Author of *A History of May & Baker 1834–1984*, 1984, and *Linklaters & Paines: The First 150 Years*, 1987.

SMILEY, Virginia L. Free-lance writer.

STABILE, Donald R. Professor of Economics, St. Mary's College of Maryland, St. Mary's City. Author of *Prophets of Order: The Rise of the New Class, Technocracy and Socialism in America*, 1984, and "The DuPont Experiments with Scientific Management: Efficiency and Safety, 1911–1919," *Business History Review*, 1987.

STEINKE, René. Composition instructor, University of Wisconsin—Milwaukee. Author of "The Great Unspoken in Three New Books of Poetry," *The Cresset*, 1989.

SULLIVAN, Timothy E. Assistant Professor of Economics, Towson State University, Baltimore, Maryland. Author of "Industrial Transformation and Market Integration along the American Manufacturing Frontier: the Midwest from 1850 to 1880," *Business and Economic History*, 1988.

SUN, Douglas. Doctoral candidate in English, University of Chicago. Author of book reviews in *Los Angeles Times*, 1988–89.

SWAN, John. Free-lance writer and researcher.

SWORSKY, Mary F. Editor, American Association of Law Libraries, Chicago, Illinois; free-lance writer.

TUCKER, Thomas M. Free-lance writer.

VINCENT, Bob. International Companies News Editor, *The Financial Times*, London. Contributor to *Finance for Growth*, 1989.

VLESSING, Etan. Senior Features Writer, *Chartered Surveyor Weekly*. Financial journalist, *Financial Weekly*, 1989–90. Author of "Muslims in Britain," *Contemporary Review*, 1987.

VOSKUIL, Lynn M. Doctoral candidate in English, University of Chicago. Director, Office of Research Administration, Illinois Institute of Technology, Chicago, 1985–89.

WALDEN, David M. Historian, Timpanogos Research Associates, Salt Lake City, Utah. Author of *Protestant and Catholic Churches of Provo*, 1986, and "The Limits of Medical Dominance: Pre-World War II Chiropractic in Utah." *Chiropractic History*, 1988.

WALSH, Ray. Free-lance writer and broadcaster. Author of "Cracking the Genetic Code," *In These Times*, 1989, and "Stalemate in Hormone-Raised Beef Dispute," *North American Farmer*, 1989.

WESSEL, Horst A. Manager, Mannesmann Archives. Manager, the German Society for Business History, and member of the editorial staff of the *Zeitschrift für Unternehmensgeschichte* and the *German Yearbook on Business History,* 1976–83. Author of "Die Entwicklung des elektrischen Nachrichtenwesens in Deutschland und die rheinische Industrie. Von den Anfängen bis zum Ausbruch des Ersten Weltkrieges," *Zeitschrift für Unternehmensgeschichte*, 1983, and *Kontinuität im Wandel. 100 Jahre Mannesmann*, 1990.

WOHLERT, Claus. Senior Lecturer and Member of the Faculty of Social Science at Uppsala University. Author of "Concentration Tendencies in Swedish Industry before World War I" in *The Concentration Process in the Entrepreneurial Economy since the Late 19th Century*, 1988.

WOLF, Gillian. Free-lance writer. Author of "The Ultimate Slingshot," *Jewish Affairs*, 1989, and "Akh, Odessa!" *Jewish Affairs*, 1990.

ZARACH, Stephanie. Business Development Manager of Book Production Consultants. Research Director of Debrett Business History Research Ltd., 1984–88. Editor of *Debrett's Bibliography of Business History*, 1987.